SCRABBLE®

BRAND Crossword Game

TOURNAMENT & CLUB
WORD LIST

D1340617

Collins

HarperCollins Publishers
Westerhill Road
Bishopbriggs
Glasgow
G64 2QT

First Edition 2007

Reprint 10 9 8 7 6 5 4 3 2 1 0

© HarperCollins Publishers 2007

ISBN-13 978-0-00-725884-0
ISBN-10 0-00-725884-4

Collins® is a registered trademark of
HarperCollins Publishers Limited

SCRABBLE® is a registered trademark of
J.W. Spear and Sons Ltd., a subsidiary of
Mattel, Inc., © 2007 Mattel, Inc. All rights
reserved.

www.collins.co.uk

A catalogue record for this book is
available from the British Library

About the type.
This book is set in Collins Fedra, a
typeface specially created for Collins
dictionaries by Peter Bil'ak, the type
designer.

Computing Support
Thomas Callan

Collins Corpus Programmer
Nigel Rochford

Typesetting
Wordcraft

Printed and bound by
Clays Ltd, St Ives plc

Acknowledgements
We would like to thank those authors
and publishers who kindly gave
permission for copyright material to be
used in the Collins Word Web. We would
also like to thank Times Newspapers Ltd
for providing valuable data.

Editorial Staff

Morven Dooner
Elaine Higgleton
Elspeth Summers

Introduction

Collins **SCRABBLE® Tournament and Club Word List** is the most complete **SCRABBLE®** word list in existence. As such, it is an invaluable tool for any competitive or club player, as well as the ultimate authority for settling disputes between those who play with their friends and family.

More than a staggering 267,000 words are listed in Collins **SCRABBLE® Tournament and Club Word List** – representing an exhaustive list of every valid play in **SCRABBLE®**. The book is divided into two sections: Section One contains every word of between two and nine letters, while Section Two contains words of ten to fifteen letters. In any **SCRABBLE®** game, most words will be between two and nine letters, with longer words being formed only very rarely.

Words not listed include those spelt with an initial capital letter, abbreviations, prefixes and suffixes, and words requiring apostrophes and hyphens, none of which are allowed in Scrabble.

You can find definitions for all the words of between two and nine letters in length in Collins Official **SCRABBLE®** Dictionary.

Accents
As English-language Scrabble tiles are not accented, no accents are shown in *Collins Scrabble Tournament and Club Word List*.

Word Order
Collins Scrabble Tournament and Club Word List is an alphabetical word list, therefore any inflected forms of a base word are given in alphabetical order, and not after the base form, as in many dictionaries.

Offensive Terms
There may be words in *Collins Scrabble Tournament and Club Word List* that most or some players might consider taboo or offensive. We strongly recommend that players check meanings and suitability for general use in *Collins English Dictionary*.

Collins would like to give warm thanks to Darryl Francis and Allan Simmons for their enormous contribution to this word list. They worked tirelessly with the editorial team to get this right. Any errors are the responsibility of the publisher.

COLLINS SCRABBLE
TOURNAMENT AND CLUB
WORD LIST

2-9 LETTER WORDS

A

AA	ABASE	ABBEYS	ABERRANT
AAH	ABASED	ABBOT	ABERRANTS
AAHED	ABASEDLY	ABBOTCIES	ABERRATE
AAHING	ABASEMENT	ABBOTCY	ABERRATED
AAHS	ABASER	ABBOTS	ABERRATES
AAL	ABASERS	ABBOTSHIP	ABESSIVE
AALII	ABASES	ABBS	ABESSIVES
AALIIS	ABASH	ABCEE	ABET
AALS	ABASHED	ABCEES	ABETMENT
AARDVARK	ABASHEDLY	ABCOULOMB	ABETMENTS
AARDVARKS	ABASHES	ABDABS	ABETS
AARDWOLF	ABASHING	ABDICABLE	ABETTAL
AARGH	ABASHLESS	ABDICANT	ABETTALS
AARRGH	ABASHMENT	ABDICATE	ABETTED
AARRGHH	ABASIA	ABDICATED	ABETTER
AARTI	ABASIAS	ABDICATES	ABETTERS
AARTIS	ABASING	ABDICATOR	ABETTING
AAS	ABASK	ABDOMEN	ABETTOR
AASVOGEL	ABATABLE	ABDOMENS	ABETTORS
AASVOGELS	ABATE	ABDOMINA	ABEYANCE
AB	ABATED	ABDOMINAL	ABEYANCES
ABA	ABATEMENT	ABDUCE	ABEYANCY
ABAC	ABATER	ABDUCED	ABEYANT
ABACA	ABATERS	ABDUCENS	ABFARAD
ABACAS	ABATES	ABDUCENT	ABFARADS
ABACI	ABATING	ABDUCES	ABHENRIES
ABACK	ABATIS	ABDUCING	ABHENRY
ABACS	ABATISES	ABDUCT	ABHENRYS
ABACTINAL	ABATOR	ABDUCTED	ABHOR
ABACTOR	ABATORS	ABDUCTEE	ABHORRED
ABACTORS	ABATTIS	ABDUCTEES	ABHORRENT
ABACUS	ABATTISES	ABDUCTING	ABHORRER
ABACUSES	ABATTOIR	ABDUCTION	ABHORRERS
ABAFT	ABATTOIRS	ABDUCTOR	ABHORRING
ABAKA	ABATTU	ABDUCTORS	ABHORS
ABAKAS	ABATURE	ABDUCTS	ABID
ABALONE	ABATURES	ABEAM	ABIDANCE
ABALONES	ABAXIAL	ABEAR	ABIDANCES
ABAMP	ABAXILE	ABEARING	ABIDDEN
ABAMPERE	ABAYA	ABEARS	ABIDE
ABAMPERES	ABAYAS	ABED	ABIDED
ABAMPS	ABB	ABEGGING	ABIDER
ABAND	ABBA	ABEIGH	ABIDERS
ABANDED	ABBACIES	ABELE	ABIDES
ABANDING	ABBACY	ABELES	ABIDING
ABANDON	ABBAS	ABELIA	ABIDINGLY
ABANDONED	ABBATIAL	ABELIAN	ABIDINGS
ABANDONEE	ABBE	ABELIAS	ABIES
ABANDONER	ABBED	ABELMOSK	ABIETIC
ABANDONS	ABBES	ABELMOSKS	ABIGAIL
ABANDS	ABBESS	ABERNETHY	ABIGAILS
ABAPICAL	ABBESSES	ABERRANCE	ABILITIES
ABAS	ABBEY	ABERRANCY	ABILITY

ABIOGENIC	ABMHO	ABORT	ABREACTED
ABIOSES	ABMHOS	ABORTED	ABREACTS
ABIOSIS	ABNEGATE	ABORTEE	ABREAST
ABIOTIC	ABNEGATED	ABORTEES	ABREGE
ABJECT	ABNEGATES	ABORTER	ABREGES
ABJECTED	ABNEGATOR	ABORTERS	ABRI
ABJECTING	ABNORMAL	ABORTING	ABRICOCK
ABJECTION	ABNORMALS	ABORTION	ABRICOCKS
ABJECTLY	ABNORMITY	ABORTIONS	ABRIDGE
ABJECTS	ABNORMOUS	ABORTIVE	ABRIDGED
ABJOINT	ABO	ABORTS	ABRIDGER
ABJOINTED	ABOARD	ABORTUARY	ABRIDGERS
ABJOINTS	ABODE	ABORTUS	ABRIDGES
ABJURE	ABODED	ABORTUSES	ABRIDGING
ABJURED	ABODEMENT	ABOS	ABRIM
ABJURER	ABODES	ABOUGHT	ABRIN
ABJURERS	ABODING	ABOULIA	ABRINS
ABJURES	ABOHM	ABOULIAS	ABRIS
ABJURING	ABOHMS	ABOULIC	ABROACH
ABLATE	ABOIDEAU	ABOUND	ABROAD
ABLATED	ABOIDEAUS	ABOUNDED	ABROADS
ABLATES	ABOIDEAUX	ABOUNDING	ABROGABLE
ABLATING	ABOIL	ABOUNDS	ABROGATE
ABLATION	ABOITEAU	ABOUT	ABROGATED
ABLATIONS	ABOITEAUS	ABOUTS	ABROGATES
ABLATIVAL	ABOITEAUX	ABOVE	ABROGATOR
ABLATIVE	ABOLISH	ABOVES	ABROOKE
ABLATIVES	ABOLISHED	ABRACHIA	ABROOKED
ABLATOR	ABOLISHER	ABRACHIAS	ABROOKES
ABLATORS	ABOLISHES	ABRADABLE	ABROOKING
ABLAUT	ABOLITION	ABRADANT	ABROSIA
ABLAUTS	ABOLLA	ABRADANTS	ABROSIAS
ABLAZE	ABOLLAE	ABRADE	ABRUPT
ABLE	ABOLLAS	ABRADED	ABRUPTER
ABLED	ABOMA	ABRADER	ABRUPTEST
ABLEGATE	ABOMAS	ABRADERS	ABRUPTION
ABLEGATES	ABOMASA	ABRADES	ABRUPTLY
ABLEISM	ABOMASAL	ABRADING	ABRUPTS
ABLEISMS	ABOMASI	ABRAID	ABS
ABLEIST	ABOMASUM	ABRAIDED	ABSCESS
ABLEISTS	ABOMASUS	ABRAIDING	ABSCESSED
ABLER	ABOMINATE	ABRAIDS	ABSCESSES
ABLES	ABONDANCE	ABRAM	ABSCIND
ABLEST	ABOON	ABRASAX	ABSCINDED
ABLET	ABORAL	ABRASAXES	ABSCINDS
ABLETS	ABORALLY	ABRASION	ABSCISE
ABLING	ABORD	ABRASIONS	ABSCISED
ABLINGS	ABORDED	ABRASIVE	ABSCISES
ABLINS	ABORDING	ABRASIVES	ABSCISIN
ABLOOM	ABORDS	ABRAXAS	ABSCISING
ABLOW	ABORE	ABRAXASES	ABSCISINS
ABLUENT	ABORIGEN	ABRAY	ABSCISS
ABLUENTS	ABORIGENS	ABRAYED	ABSCISSA
ABLUSH	ABORIGIN	ABRAYING	ABSCISSAE
ABLUTED	ABORIGINE	ABRAYS	ABSCISSAS
ABLUTION	ABORIGINS	ABRAZO	ABSCISSE
ABLUTIONS	ABORNE	ABRAZOS	ABSCISSES
ABLY	ABORNING	ABREACT	ABSCISSIN

ACCESSION

ABSCOND	ABSTRICTS	ABYES	ACARIDIAN
ABSCONDED	ABSTRUSE	ABYING	ACARIDS
ABSCONDER	ABSTRUSER	ABYS	ACARINE
ABSCONDS	ABSURD	ABYSM	ACARINES
ABSEIL	ABSURDER	ABYSMAL	ACAROID
ABSEILED	ABSURDEST	ABYSMALLY	ACAROLOGY
ABSEILING	ABSURDISM	ABYSMS	ACARPOUS
ABSEILS	ABSURDIST	ABYSS	ACARUS
ABSENCE	ABSURDITY	ABYSSAL	ACATER
ABSENCES	ABSURDLY	ABYSSES	ACATERS
ABSENT	ABSURDS	ACACIA	ACATES
ABSENTED	ABTHANE	ACACIAS	ACATOUR
ABSENTEE	ABTHANES	ACADEME	ACATOURS
ABSENTEES	ABUBBLE	ACADEMES	ACAUDAL
ABSENTER	ABUILDING	ACADEMIA	ACAUDATE
ABSENTERS	ABULIA	ACADEMIAS	ACAULINE
ABSENTING	ABULIAS	ACADEMIC	ACAULOSE
ABSENTLY	ABULIC	ACADEMICS	ACAULOUS
ABSENTS	ABUNA	ACADEMIES	ACCA
ABSEY	ABUNAS	ACADEMISM	ACCABLE
ABSEYS	ABUNDANCE	ACADEMIST	ACCAS
ABSINTH	ABUNDANCY	ACADEMY	ACCEDE
ABSINTHE	ABUNDANT	ACAI	ACCEDED
ABSINTHES	ABUNE	ACAIS	ACCEDENCE
ABSINTHS	ABURST	ACAJOU	ACCEDER
ABSIT	ABUSABLE	ACAJOUS	ACCEDERS
ABSITS	ABUSAGE	ACALCULIA	ACCEDES
ABSOLUTE	ABUSAGES	ACALEPH	ACCEDING
ABSOLUTER	ABUSE	ACALEPHAE	ACCEND
ABSOLUTES	ABUSED	ACALEPHAN	ACCENDED
ABSOLVE	ABUSER	ACALEPHE	ACCENDING
ABSOLVED	ABUSERS	ACALEPHES	ACCENDS
ABSOLVENT	ABUSES	ACALEPHS	ACCENSION
ABSOLVER	ABUSING	ACANTH	ACCENT
ABSOLVERS	ABUSION	ACANTHA	ACCENTED
ABSOLVES	ABUSIONS	ACANTHAE	ACCENTING
ABSOLVING	ABUSIVE	ACANTHAS	ACCENTOR
ABSONANT	ABUSIVELY	ACANTHI	ACCENTORS
ABSORB	ABUT	ACANTHIN	ACCENTS
ABSORBANT	ABUTILON	ACANTHINE	ACCENTUAL
ABSORBATE	ABUTILONS	ACANTHINS	ACCEPT
ABSORBED	ABUTMENT	ACANTHOID	ACCEPTANT
ABSORBENT	ABUTMENTS	ACANTHOUS	ACCEPTED
ABSORBER	ABUTS	ACANTHS	ACCEPTEE
ABSORBERS	ABUTTAL	ACANTHUS	ACCEPTEES
ABSORBING	ABUTTALS	ACAPNIA	ACCEPTER
ABSORBS	ABUTTED	ACAPNIAS	ACCEPTERS
ABSTAIN	ABUTTER	ACARBOSE	ACCEPTING
ABSTAINED	ABUTTERS	ACARBOSES	ACCEPTIVE
ABSTAINER	ABUTTING	ACARI	ACCEPTOR
ABSTAINS	ABUZZ	ACARIAN	ACCEPTORS
ABSTERGE	ABVOLT	ACARIASES	ACCEPTS
ABSTERGED	ABVOLTS	ACARIASIS	ACCESS
ABSTERGES	ABWATT	ACARICIDE	ACCESSARY
ABSTINENT	ABWATTS	ACARID	ACCESSED
ABSTRACT	ABY	ACARIDAN	ACCESSES
ABSTRACTS	ABYE	ACARIDANS	ACCESSING
ABSTRICT	ABYEING	ACARIDEAN	ACCESSION

3

ACCESSORY
ACCIDENCE
ACCIDENT
ACCIDENTS
ACCIDIA
ACCIDIAS
ACCIDIE
ACCIDIES
ACCINGE
ACCINGED
ACCINGES
ACCINGING
ACCIPITER
ACCITE
ACCITED
ACCITES
ACCITING
ACCLAIM
ACCLAIMED
ACCLAIMER
ACCLAIMS
ACCLIMATE
ACCLIVITY
ACCLIVOUS
ACCLOY
ACCLOYED
ACCLOYING
ACCLOYS
ACCOAST
ACCOASTED
ACCOASTS
ACCOIED
ACCOIL
ACCOILS
ACCOLADE
ACCOLADED
ACCOLADES
ACCOMPANY
ACCOMPT
ACCOMPTED
ACCOMPTS
ACCORAGE
ACCORAGED
ACCORAGES
ACCORD
ACCORDANT
ACCORDED
ACCORDER
ACCORDERS
ACCORDING
ACCORDION
ACCORDS
ACCOST
ACCOSTED
ACCOSTING
ACCOSTS
ACCOUNT
ACCOUNTED

ACCOUNTS
ACCOURAGE
ACCOURT
ACCOURTED
ACCOURTS
ACCOUTER
ACCOUTERS
ACCOUTRE
ACCOUTRED
ACCOUTRES
ACCOY
ACCOYED
ACCOYING
ACCOYLD
ACCOYS
ACCREDIT
ACCREDITS
ACCRETE
ACCRETED
ACCRETES
ACCRETING
ACCRETION
ACCRETIVE
ACCREW
ACCREWED
ACCREWING
ACCREWS
ACCROIDES
ACCRUABLE
ACCRUAL
ACCRUALS
ACCRUE
ACCRUED
ACCRUES
ACCRUING
ACCUMBENT
ACCURACY
ACCURATE
ACCURSE
ACCURSED
ACCURSES
ACCURSING
ACCURST
ACCUSABLE
ACCUSABLY
ACCUSAL
ACCUSALS
ACCUSANT
ACCUSANTS
ACCUSE
ACCUSED
ACCUSER
ACCUSERS
ACCUSES
ACCUSING
ACCUSTOM
ACCUSTOMS
ACE

ACED
ACEDIA
ACEDIAS
ACELDAMA
ACELDAMAS
ACELLULAR
ACENTRIC
ACEPHALIC
ACEQUIA
ACEQUIAS
ACER
ACERATE
ACERATED
ACERB
ACERBATE
ACERBATED
ACERBATES
ACERBER
ACERBEST
ACERBIC
ACERBITY
ACEROLA
ACEROLAS
ACEROSE
ACEROUS
ACERS
ACERVATE
ACERVULI
ACERVULUS
ACES
ACESCENCE
ACESCENCY
ACESCENT
ACESCENTS
ACETA
ACETABULA
ACETAL
ACETALS
ACETAMID
ACETAMIDE
ACETAMIDS
ACETATE
ACETATED
ACETATES
ACETIC
ACETIFIED
ACETIFIER
ACETIFIES
ACETIFY
ACETIN
ACETINS
ACETONE
ACETONES
ACETONIC
ACETOSE
ACETOUS
ACETOXYL
ACETOXYLS

ACETUM
ACETYL
ACETYLATE
ACETYLENE
ACETYLIC
ACETYLIDE
ACETYLS
ACH
ACHAENIA
ACHAENIUM
ACHAGE
ACHAGES
ACHALASIA
ACHARNE
ACHARYA
ACHARYAS
ACHATES
ACHE
ACHED
ACHENE
ACHENES
ACHENIA
ACHENIAL
ACHENIUM
ACHENIUMS
ACHES
ACHIER
ACHIEST
ACHIEVE
ACHIEVED
ACHIEVER
ACHIEVERS
ACHIEVES
ACHIEVING
ACHILLEA
ACHILLEAS
ACHIMENES
ACHINESS
ACHING
ACHINGLY
ACHINGS
ACHIOTE
ACHIOTES
ACHIRAL
ACHKAN
ACHKANS
ACHOLIA
ACHOLIAS
ACHOO
ACHROMAT
ACHROMATS
ACHROMIC
ACHROMOUS
ACHY
ACICULA
ACICULAE
ACICULAR
ACICULAS

ACICULATE	ACMATIC	ACQUISTS	ACROPHOBE
ACICULUM	ACME	ACQUIT	ACROPHONY
ACICULUMS	ACMES	ACQUITE	ACROPOLIS
ACID	ACMIC	ACQUITES	ACROSOMAL
ACIDEMIA	ACMITE	ACQUITING	ACROSOME
ACIDEMIAS	ACMITES	ACQUITS	ACROSOMES
ACIDER	ACNE	ACQUITTAL	ACROSPIRE
ACIDEST	ACNED	ACQUITTED	ACROSS
ACIDFREAK	ACNES	ACQUITTER	ACROSTIC
ACIDHEAD	ACNODAL	ACRASIA	ACROSTICS
ACIDHEADS	ACNODE	ACRASIAS	ACROTER
ACIDIC	ACNODES	ACRASIN	ACROTERIA
ACIDIER	ACOCK	ACRASINS	ACROTERS
ACIDIEST	ACOELOUS	ACRATIC	ACROTIC
ACIDIFIED	ACOEMETI	ACRAWL	ACROTISM
ACIDIFIER	ACOLD	ACRE	ACROTISMS
ACIDIFIES	ACOLUTHIC	ACREAGE	ACRYLATE
ACIDIFY	ACOLYTE	ACREAGES	ACRYLATES
ACIDITIES	ACOLYTES	ACRED	ACRYLIC
ACIDITY	ACOLYTH	ACRES	ACRYLICS
ACIDLY	ACOLYTHS	ACRID	ACRYLYL
ACIDNESS	ACONITE	ACRIDER	ACRYLYLS
ACIDOPHIL	ACONITES	ACRIDEST	ACT
ACIDOSES	ACONITIC	ACRIDIN	ACTA
ACIDOSIS	ACONITINE	ACRIDINE	ACTABLE
ACIDOTIC	ACONITUM	ACRIDINES	ACTANT
ACIDS	ACONITUMS	ACRIDINS	ACTANTS
ACIDULATE	ACORN	ACRIDITY	ACTED
ACIDULENT	ACORNED	ACRIDLY	ACTIN
ACIDULOUS	ACORNS	ACRIDNESS	ACTINAL
ACIDURIA	ACOSMISM	ACRIMONY	ACTINALLY
ACIDURIAS	ACOSMISMS	ACRITARCH	ACTING
ACIDY	ACOSMIST	ACRITICAL	ACTINGS
ACIERAGE	ACOSMISTS	ACROBAT	ACTINIA
ACIERAGES	ACOUCHI	ACROBATIC	ACTINIAE
ACIERATE	ACOUCHIES	ACROBATS	ACTINIAN
ACIERATED	ACOUCHIS	ACRODONT	ACTINIANS
ACIERATES	ACOUCHY	ACRODONTS	ACTINIAS
ACIFORM	ACOUSTIC	ACRODROME	ACTINIC
ACINAR	ACOUSTICS	ACROGEN	ACTINIDE
ACING	ACQUAINT	ACROGENIC	ACTINIDES
ACINI	ACQUAINTS	ACROGENS	ACTINISM
ACINIC	ACQUEST	ACROLECT	ACTINISMS
ACINIFORM	ACQUESTS	ACROLECTS	ACTINIUM
ACINOSE	ACQUIESCE	ACROLEIN	ACTINIUMS
ACINOUS	ACQUIGHT	ACROLEINS	ACTINOID
ACINUS	ACQUIGHTS	ACROLITH	ACTINOIDS
ACKEE	ACQUIRAL	ACROLITHS	ACTINON
ACKEES	ACQUIRALS	ACROMIA	ACTINONS
ACKER	ACQUIRE	ACROMIAL	ACTINOPOD
ACKERS	ACQUIRED	ACROMION	ACTINS
ACKNEW	ACQUIREE	ACRONIC	ACTION
ACKNOW	ACQUIREES	ACRONICAL	ACTIONED
ACKNOWING	ACQUIRER	ACRONYCAL	ACTIONER
ACKNOWN	ACQUIRERS	ACRONYM	ACTIONERS
ACKNOWNE	ACQUIRES	ACRONYMIC	ACTIONING
ACKNOWS	ACQUIRING	ACRONYMS	ACTIONIST
ACLINIC	ACQUIST	ACROPETAL	ACTIONS

ACTIVATE

ACTIVATE	ACUMINOUS	ADDABLE	ADDUCIBLE
ACTIVATED	ACUPOINT	ADDAX	ADDUCING
ACTIVATES	ACUPOINTS	ADDAXES	ADDUCT
ACTIVATOR	ACUSHLA	ADDEBTED	ADDUCTED
ACTIVE	ACUSHLAS	ADDED	ADDUCTING
ACTIVELY	ACUTANCE	ADDEDLY	ADDUCTION
ACTIVES	ACUTANCES	ADDEEM	ADDUCTIVE
ACTIVISE	ACUTE	ADDEEMED	ADDUCTOR
ACTIVISED	ACUTELY	ADDEEMING	ADDUCTORS
ACTIVISES	ACUTENESS	ADDEEMS	ADDUCTS
ACTIVISM	ACUTER	ADDEND	ADDY
ACTIVISMS	ACUTES	ADDENDA	ADEEM
ACTIVIST	ACUTEST	ADDENDS	ADEEMED
ACTIVISTS	ACYCLIC	ADDENDUM	ADEEMING
ACTIVITY	ACYCLOVIR	ADDENDUMS	ADEEMS
ACTIVIZE	ACYL	ADDER	ADEMPTION
ACTIVIZED	ACYLATE	ADDERS	ADENINE
ACTIVIZES	ACYLATED	ADDERWORT	ADENINES
ACTON	ACYLATES	ADDIBLE	ADENITIS
ACTONS	ACYLATING	ADDICT	ADENOID
ACTOR	ACYLATION	ADDICTED	ADENOIDAL
ACTORISH	ACYLOIN	ADDICTING	ADENOIDS
ACTORLY	ACYLOINS	ADDICTION	ADENOMA
ACTORS	ACYLS	ADDICTIVE	ADENOMAS
ACTRESS	AD	ADDICTS	ADENOMATA
ACTRESSES	ADAGE	ADDIES	ADENOSES
ACTRESSY	ADAGES	ADDING	ADENOSINE
ACTS	ADAGIAL	ADDIO	ADENOSIS
ACTUAL	ADAGIO	ADDIOS	ADENYL
ACTUALISE	ADAGIOS	ADDITION	ADENYLIC
ACTUALIST	ADAMANCE	ADDITIONS	ADENYLS
ACTUALITE	ADAMANCES	ADDITIVE	ADEPT
ACTUALITY	ADAMANCY	ADDITIVES	ADEPTER
ACTUALIZE	ADAMANT	ADDITORY	ADEPTEST
ACTUALLY	ADAMANTLY	ADDLE	ADEPTLY
ACTUALS	ADAMANTS	ADDLED	ADEPTNESS
ACTUARIAL	ADAMSITE	ADDLEMENT	ADEPTS
ACTUARIES	ADAMSITES	ADDLES	ADEQUACY
ACTUARY	ADAPT	ADDLING	ADEQUATE
ACTUATE	ADAPTABLE	ADDOOM	ADERMIN
ACTUATED	ADAPTED	ADDOOMED	ADERMINS
ACTUATES	ADAPTER	ADDOOMING	ADESPOTA
ACTUATING	ADAPTERS	ADDOOMS	ADESSIVE
ACTUATION	ADAPTING	ADDORSED	ADESSIVES
ACTUATOR	ADAPTION	ADDRESS	ADHAN
ACTUATORS	ADAPTIONS	ADDRESSED	ADHANS
ACTURE	ADAPTIVE	ADDRESSEE	ADHARMA
ACTURES	ADAPTOGEN	ADDRESSER	ADHARMAS
ACUATE	ADAPTOR	ADDRESSES	ADHERABLE
ACUITIES	ADAPTORS	ADDRESSOR	ADHERE
ACUITY	ADAPTS	ADDREST	ADHERED
ACULEATE	ADAW	ADDS	ADHERENCE
ACULEATED	ADAWED	ADDUCE	ADHEREND
ACULEI	ADAWING	ADDUCED	ADHERENDS
ACULEUS	ADAWS	ADDUCENT	ADHERENT
ACUMEN	ADAXIAL	ADDUCER	ADHERENTS
ACUMENS	ADAYS	ADDUCERS	ADHERER
ACUMINATE	ADD	ADDUCES	ADHERERS

ADHERES
ADHERING
ADHESION
ADHESIONS
ADHESIVE
ADHESIVES
ADHIBIT
ADHIBITED
ADHIBITS
ADHOCRACY
ADIABATIC
ADIAPHORA
ADIEU
ADIEUS
ADIEUX
ADIOS
ADIPIC
ADIPOCERE
ADIPOCYTE
ADIPOSE
ADIPOSES
ADIPOSIS
ADIPOSITY
ADIPOUS
ADIPSIA
ADIPSIAS
ADIT
ADITS
ADJACENCE
ADJACENCY
ADJACENT
ADJACENTS
ADJECTIVE
ADJIGO
ADJIGOS
ADJOIN
ADJOINED
ADJOINING
ADJOINS
ADJOINT
ADJOINTS
ADJOURN
ADJOURNED
ADJOURNS
ADJUDGE
ADJUDGED
ADJUDGES
ADJUDGING
ADJUNCT
ADJUNCTLY
ADJUNCTS
ADJURE
ADJURED
ADJURER
ADJURERS
ADJURES
ADJURING
ADJUROR

ADJURORS
ADJUST
ADJUSTED
ADJUSTER
ADJUSTERS
ADJUSTING
ADJUSTIVE
ADJUSTOR
ADJUSTORS
ADJUSTS
ADJUTAGE
ADJUTAGES
ADJUTANCY
ADJUTANT
ADJUTANTS
ADJUVANCY
ADJUVANT
ADJUVANTS
ADLAND
ADLANDS
ADMAN
ADMASS
ADMASSES
ADMEASURE
ADMEN
ADMIN
ADMINICLE
ADMINS
ADMIRABLE
ADMIRABLY
ADMIRAL
ADMIRALS
ADMIRALTY
ADMIRANCE
ADMIRE
ADMIRED
ADMIRER
ADMIRERS
ADMIRES
ADMIRING
ADMISSION
ADMISSIVE
ADMIT
ADMITS
ADMITTED
ADMITTEE
ADMITTEES
ADMITTER
ADMITTERS
ADMITTING
ADMIX
ADMIXED
ADMIXES
ADMIXING
ADMIXT
ADMIXTURE
ADMONISH
ADMONITOR

ADNASCENT
ADNATE
ADNATION
ADNATIONS
ADNEXA
ADNEXAL
ADNOMINAL
ADNOUN
ADNOUNS
ADO
ADOBE
ADOBELIKE
ADOBES
ADOBO
ADOBOS
ADONIS
ADONISE
ADONISED
ADONISES
ADONISING
ADONIZE
ADONIZED
ADONIZES
ADONIZING
ADOORS
ADOPT
ADOPTABLE
ADOPTED
ADOPTEE
ADOPTEES
ADOPTER
ADOPTERS
ADOPTING
ADOPTION
ADOPTIONS
ADOPTIOUS
ADOPTIVE
ADOPTS
ADORABLE
ADORABLY
ADORATION
ADORE
ADORED
ADORER
ADORERS
ADORES
ADORING
ADORINGLY
ADORN
ADORNED
ADORNER
ADORNERS
ADORNING
ADORNMENT
ADORNS
ADOS
ADOWN
ADOZE

ADPRESS
ADPRESSED
ADPRESSES
ADRAD
ADREAD
ADREADED
ADREADING
ADREADS
ADRED
ADRENAL
ADRENALIN
ADRENALLY
ADRENALS
ADRIFT
ADROIT
ADROITER
ADROITEST
ADROITLY
ADRY
ADS
ADSCRIPT
ADSCRIPTS
ADSORB
ADSORBATE
ADSORBED
ADSORBENT
ADSORBER
ADSORBERS
ADSORBING
ADSORBS
ADSUKI
ADSUKIS
ADSUM
ADUKI
ADUKIS
ADULARIA
ADULARIAS
ADULATE
ADULATED
ADULATES
ADULATING
ADULATION
ADULATOR
ADULATORS
ADULATORY
ADULT
ADULTERER
ADULTERY
ADULTHOOD
ADULTLIKE
ADULTLY
ADULTNESS
ADULTRESS
ADULTS
ADUMBRAL
ADUMBRATE
ADUNC
ADUNCATE

ADUNCATED	ADVISER	AEGIS	AEROBOMBS
ADUNCITY	ADVISERS	AEGISES	AEROBRAKE
ADUNCOUS	ADVISES	AEGLOGUE	AEROBUS
ADUST	ADVISING	AEGLOGUES	AEROBUSES
ADUSTED	ADVISINGS	AEGROTAT	AERODART
ADUSTING	ADVISOR	AEGROTATS	AERODARTS
ADUSTS	ADVISORS	AEMULE	AERODROME
ADVANCE	ADVISORY	AEMULED	AERODUCT
ADVANCED	ADVOCAAT	AEMULES	AERODUCTS
ADVANCER	ADVOCAATS	AEMULING	AERODYNE
ADVANCERS	ADVOCACY	AENEOUS	AERODYNES
ADVANCES	ADVOCATE	AENEUS	AEROFOIL
ADVANCING	ADVOCATED	AEOLIAN	AEROFOILS
ADVANTAGE	ADVOCATES	AEOLIPILE	AEROGEL
ADVECT	ADVOCATOR	AEOLIPYLE	AEROGELS
ADVECTED	ADVOUTRER	AEON	AEROGRAM
ADVECTING	ADVOUTRY	AEONIAN	AEROGRAMS
ADVECTION	ADVOWSON	AEONIC	AEROGRAPH
ADVECTIVE	ADVOWSONS	AEONS	AEROLITE
ADVECTS	ADWARD	AEPYORNIS	AEROLITES
ADVENE	ADWARDED	AEQUORIN	AEROLITH
ADVENED	ADWARDING	AEQUORINS	AEROLITHS
ADVENES	ADWARDS	AERATE	AEROLITIC
ADVENING	ADWARE	AERATED	AEROLOGIC
ADVENT	ADWARES	AERATES	AEROLOGY
ADVENTIVE	ADWOMAN	AERATING	AEROMANCY
ADVENTS	ADWOMEN	AERATION	AEROMETER
ADVENTURE	ADYNAMIA	AERATIONS	AEROMETRY
ADVERB	ADYNAMIAS	AERATOR	AEROMOTOR
ADVERBIAL	ADYNAMIC	AERATORS	AERONAUT
ADVERBS	ADYTA	AERIAL	AERONAUTS
ADVERSARY	ADYTUM	AERIALIST	AERONOMER
ADVERSE	ADZ	AERIALITY	AERONOMIC
ADVERSELY	ADZE	AERIALLY	AERONOMY
ADVERSER	ADZED	AERIALS	AEROPAUSE
ADVERSEST	ADZES	AERIE	AEROPHAGY
ADVERSITY	ADZING	AERIED	AEROPHOBE
ADVERT	ADZUKI	AERIER	AEROPHONE
ADVERTED	ADZUKIS	AERIES	AEROPHORE
ADVERTENT	AE	AERIEST	AEROPHYTE
ADVERTING	AECIA	AERIFIED	AEROPLANE
ADVERTISE	AECIAL	AERIFIES	AEROPULSE
ADVERTIZE	AECIDIA	AERIFORM	AEROS
ADVERTS	AECIDIAL	AERIFY	AEROSAT
ADVEW	AECIDIUM	AERIFYING	AEROSATS
ADVEWED	AECIUM	AERILY	AEROSCOPE
ADVEWING	AEDES	AERO	AEROSHELL
ADVEWS	AEDICULE	AEROBAT	AEROSOL
ADVICE	AEDICULES	AEROBATIC	AEROSOLS
ADVICEFUL	AEDILE	AEROBATS	AEROSPACE
ADVICES	AEDILES	AEROBE	AEROSTAT
ADVISABLE	AEDINE	AEROBES	AEROSTATS
ADVISABLY	AEFALD	AEROBIA	AEROTAXES
ADVISE	AEFAULD	AEROBIC	AEROTAXIS
ADVISED	AEGIRINE	AEROBICS	AEROTONE
ADVISEDLY	AEGIRINES	AEROBIONT	AEROTONES
ADVISEE	AEGIRITE	AEROBIUM	AEROTRAIN
ADVISEES	AEGIRITES	AEROBOMB	AERUGO

AERUGOS
AERY
AESC
AESCES
AESCULIN
AESCULINS
AESIR
AESTHESES
AESTHESIA
AESTHESIS
AESTHETE
AESTHETES
AESTHETIC
AESTIVAL
AESTIVATE
AETHER
AETHEREAL
AETHERIC
AETHERS
AETIOLOGY
AFALD
AFAR
AFARA
AFARAS
AFARS
AFAWLD
AFEAR
AFEARD
AFEARED
AFEARING
AFEARS
AFEBRILE
AFF
AFFABLE
AFFABLY
AFFAIR
AFFAIRE
AFFAIRES
AFFAIRS
AFFEAR
AFFEARD
AFFEARE
AFFEARED
AFFEARES
AFFEARING
AFFEARS
AFFECT
AFFECTED
AFFECTER
AFFECTERS
AFFECTING
AFFECTION
AFFECTIVE
AFFECTS
AFFEER
AFFEERED
AFFEERING
AFFEERS

AFFERENT
AFFERENTS
AFFIANCE
AFFIANCED
AFFIANCES
AFFIANT
AFFIANTS
AFFICHE
AFFICHES
AFFIDAVIT
AFFIED
AFFIES
AFFILIATE
AFFINAL
AFFINE
AFFINED
AFFINELY
AFFINES
AFFINITY
AFFIRM
AFFIRMANT
AFFIRMED
AFFIRMER
AFFIRMERS
AFFIRMING
AFFIRMS
AFFIX
AFFIXABLE
AFFIXAL
AFFIXED
AFFIXER
AFFIXERS
AFFIXES
AFFIXIAL
AFFIXING
AFFIXMENT
AFFIXTURE
AFFLATED
AFFLATION
AFFLATUS
AFFLICT
AFFLICTED
AFFLICTER
AFFLICTS
AFFLUENCE
AFFLUENCY
AFFLUENT
AFFLUENTS
AFFLUENZA
AFFLUX
AFFLUXES
AFFLUXION
AFFOORD
AFFOORDED
AFFOORDS
AFFORCE
AFFORCED
AFFORCES

AFFORCING
AFFORD
AFFORDED
AFFORDING
AFFORDS
AFFOREST
AFFORESTS
AFFRAP
AFFRAPPED
AFFRAPS
AFFRAY
AFFRAYED
AFFRAYER
AFFRAYERS
AFFRAYING
AFFRAYS
AFFRENDED
AFFRET
AFFRETS
AFFRICATE
AFFRIGHT
AFFRIGHTS
AFFRONT
AFFRONTE
AFFRONTED
AFFRONTEE
AFFRONTS
AFFUSION
AFFUSIONS
AFFY
AFFYDE
AFFYING
AFGHAN
AFGHANI
AFGHANIS
AFGHANS
AFIELD
AFIRE
AFLAJ
AFLAME
AFLATOXIN
AFLOAT
AFLUTTER
AFOOT
AFORE
AFOREHAND
AFORESAID
AFORETIME
AFOUL
AFRAID
AFREET
AFREETS
AFRESH
AFRIT
AFRITS
AFRO
AFRONT
AFROS

AFT
AFTER
AFTERBODY
AFTERCARE
AFTERCLAP
AFTERDAMP
AFTERDECK
AFTEREYE
AFTEREYED
AFTEREYES
AFTERGAME
AFTERGLOW
AFTERHEAT
AFTERINGS
AFTERLIFE
AFTERMATH
AFTERMOST
AFTERNOON
AFTERPAIN
AFTERPEAK
AFTERS
AFTERSHOW
AFTERSUN
AFTERSUNS
AFTERTAX
AFTERTIME
AFTERWARD
AFTERWORD
AFTMOST
AFTOSA
AFTOSAS
AG
AGA
AGACANT
AGACANTE
AGACERIE
AGACERIES
AGAIN
AGAINST
AGALACTIA
AGALLOCH
AGALLOCHS
AGALWOOD
AGALWOODS
AGAMA
AGAMAS
AGAMETE
AGAMETES
AGAMI
AGAMIC
AGAMID
AGAMIDS
AGAMIS
AGAMOGONY
AGAMOID
AGAMOIDS
AGAMONT
AGAMONTS

AGAMOUS

AGAMOUS	AGENESES	AGGRESSES	AGLARE
AGAPAE	AGENESIA	AGGRESSOR	AGLEAM
AGAPAI	AGENESIAS	AGGRI	AGLEE
AGAPE	AGENESIS	AGGRIEVE	AGLET
AGAPEIC	AGENETIC	AGGRIEVED	AGLETS
AGAPES	AGENISE	AGGRIEVES	AGLEY
AGAR	AGENISED	AGGRO	AGLIMMER
AGARIC	AGENISES	AGGROS	AGLITTER
AGARICS	AGENISING	AGGRY	AGLOO
AGAROSE	AGENIZE	AGHA	AGLOOS
AGAROSES	AGENIZED	AGHAS	AGLOSSAL
AGARS	AGENIZES	AGHAST	AGLOSSATE
AGAS	AGENIZING	AGILA	AGLOSSIA
AGAST	AGENT	AGILAS	AGLOSSIAS
AGATE	AGENTED	AGILE	AGLOW
AGATES	AGENTIAL	AGILELY	AGLU
AGATEWARE	AGENTING	AGILENESS	AGLUS
AGATISE	AGENTINGS	AGILER	AGLY
AGATISED	AGENTIVAL	AGILEST	AGLYCON
AGATISES	AGENTIVE	AGILITIES	AGLYCONE
AGATISING	AGENTIVES	AGILITY	AGLYCONES
AGATIZE	AGENTRIES	AGIN	AGLYCONS
AGATIZED	AGENTRY	AGING	AGMA
AGATIZES	AGENTS	AGINGS	AGMAS
AGATIZING	AGER	AGINNER	AGMINATE
AGATOID	AGERATUM	AGINNERS	AGNAIL
AGAVE	AGERATUMS	AGIO	AGNAILS
AGAVES	AGERS	AGIOS	AGNAME
AGAZE	AGES	AGIOTAGE	AGNAMED
AGAZED	AGEUSIA	AGIOTAGES	AGNAMES
AGE	AGEUSIAS	AGISM	AGNATE
AGED	AGGADA	AGISMS	AGNATES
AGEDLY	AGGADAH	AGIST	AGNATHAN
AGEDNESS	AGGADAHS	AGISTED	AGNATHANS
AGEE	AGGADAS	AGISTER	AGNATHOUS
AGEING	AGGADIC	AGISTERS	AGNATIC
AGEINGS	AGGADOT	AGISTING	AGNATICAL
AGEISM	AGGADOTH	AGISTMENT	AGNATION
AGEISMS	AGGER	AGISTOR	AGNATIONS
AGEIST	AGGERS	AGISTORS	AGNISE
AGEISTS	AGGIE	AGISTS	AGNISED
AGELAST	AGGIES	AGITA	AGNISES
AGELASTIC	AGGRACE	AGITABLE	AGNISING
AGELASTS	AGGRACED	AGITANS	AGNIZE
AGELESS	AGGRACES	AGITAS	AGNIZED
AGELESSLY	AGGRACING	AGITATE	AGNIZES
AGELONG	AGGRADE	AGITATED	AGNIZING
AGEMATE	AGGRADED	AGITATES	AGNOMEN
AGEMATES	AGGRADES	AGITATING	AGNOMENS
AGEN	AGGRADING	AGITATION	AGNOMINA
AGENCIES	AGGRATE	AGITATIVE	AGNOMINAL
AGENCY	AGGRATED	AGITATO	AGNOSIA
AGENDA	AGGRATES	AGITATOR	AGNOSIAS
AGENDAS	AGGRATING	AGITATORS	AGNOSIC
AGENDUM	AGGRAVATE	AGITPOP	AGNOSTIC
AGENDUMS	AGGREGATE	AGITPOPS	AGNOSTICS
AGENE	AGGRESS	AGITPROP	AGO
AGENES	AGGRESSED	AGITPROPS	AGOG

AGOGE	AGREGES	AHEAP	AIKIDO
AGOGES	AGREMENS	AHED	AIKIDOS
AGOGIC	AGREMENT	AHEIGHT	AIKONA
AGOGICS	AGREMENTS	AHEM	AIL
AGOING	AGRESTAL	AHEMERAL	AILANTHIC
AGON	AGRESTIAL	AHENT	AILANTHUS
AGONAL	AGRESTIC	AHI	AILANTO
AGONE	AGRIA	AHIGH	AILANTOS
AGONES	AGRIAS	AHIMSA	AILED
AGONIC	AGRIMONY	AHIMSAS	AILERON
AGONIES	AGRIN	AHIND	AILERONS
AGONISE	AGRIOLOGY	AHING	AILETTE
AGONISED	AGRISE	AHINT	AILETTES
AGONISES	AGRISED	AHIS	AILING
AGONISING	AGRISES	AHISTORIC	AILMENT
AGONIST	AGRISING	AHOLD	AILMENTS
AGONISTES	AGRIZE	AHOLDS	AILS
AGONISTIC	AGRIZED	AHORSE	AIM
AGONISTS	AGRIZES	AHOY	AIMED
AGONIZE	AGRIZING	AHS	AIMER
AGONIZED	AGRODOLCE	AHULL	AIMERS
AGONIZES	AGROLOGIC	AHUNGERED	AIMFUL
AGONIZING	AGROLOGY	AHUNGRY	AIMFULLY
AGONS	AGRONOMIC	AHURU	AIMING
AGONY	AGRONOMY	AHURUHURU	AIMLESS
AGOOD	AGROUND	AI	AIMLESSLY
AGORA	AGRYPNIA	AIA	AIMS
AGORAE	AGRYPNIAS	AIAS	AIN
AGORAS	AGRYZE	AIBLINS	AINE
AGOROT	AGRYZED	AID	AINEE
AGOROTH	AGRYZES	AIDANCE	AINGA
AGOUTA	AGRYZING	AIDANCES	AINGAS
AGOUTAS	AGS	AIDANT	AINS
AGOUTI	AGTERSKOT	AIDE	AINSELL
AGOUTIES	AGUACATE	AIDED	AINSELLS
AGOUTIS	AGUACATES	AIDER	AIOLI
AGOUTY	AGUE	AIDERS	AIOLIS
AGRAFE	AGUED	AIDES	AIR
AGRAFES	AGUELIKE	AIDFUL	AIRBAG
AGRAFFE	AGUES	AIDING	AIRBAGS
AGRAFFES	AGUEWEED	AIDLESS	AIRBASE
AGRAPHA	AGUEWEEDS	AIDMAN	AIRBASES
AGRAPHIA	AGUISE	AIDMEN	AIRBOAT
AGRAPHIAS	AGUISED	AIDOI	AIRBOATS
AGRAPHIC	AGUISES	AIDOS	AIRBORNE
AGRAPHON	AGUISH	AIDS	AIRBOUND
AGRARIAN	AGUISHLY	AIERIES	AIRBRICK
AGRARIANS	AGUISING	AIERY	AIRBRICKS
AGRASTE	AGUIZE	AIGA	AIRBRUSH
AGRAVIC	AGUIZED	AIGAS	AIRBURST
AGREE	AGUIZES	AIGLET	AIRBURSTS
AGREEABLE	AGUIZING	AIGLETS	AIRBUS
AGREEABLY	AGUTI	AIGRET	AIRBUSES
AGREED	AGUTIS	AIGRETS	AIRBUSSES
AGREEING	AH	AIGRETTE	AIRCHECK
AGREEMENT	AHA	AIGRETTES	AIRCHECKS
AGREES	AHCHOO	AIGUILLE	AIRCOACH
AGREGE	AHEAD	AIGUILLES	AIRCRAFT

AIRCREW

AIRCREW
AIRCREWS
AIRDATE
AIRDATES
AIRDRAWN
AIRDROME
AIRDROMES
AIRDROP
AIRDROPS
AIRED
AIRER
AIRERS
AIREST
AIRFARE
AIRFARES
AIRFIELD
AIRFIELDS
AIRFLOW
AIRFLOWS
AIRFOIL
AIRFOILS
AIRFRAME
AIRFRAMES
AIRGAP
AIRGAPS
AIRGLOW
AIRGLOWS
AIRGRAPH
AIRGRAPHS
AIRHEAD
AIRHEADED
AIRHEADS
AIRHOLE
AIRHOLES
AIRIER
AIRIEST
AIRILY
AIRINESS
AIRING
AIRINGS
AIRLESS
AIRLIFT
AIRLIFTED
AIRLIFTS
AIRLIKE
AIRLINE
AIRLINER
AIRLINERS
AIRLINES
AIRLOCK
AIRLOCKS
AIRMAIL
AIRMAILED
AIRMAILS
AIRMAN
AIRMEN
AIRMOBILE
AIRN

AIRNED
AIRNING
AIRNS
AIRPARK
AIRPARKS
AIRPLANE
AIRPLANES
AIRPLAY
AIRPLAYS
AIRPORT
AIRPORTS
AIRPOST
AIRPOSTS
AIRPOWER
AIRPOWERS
AIRPROOF
AIRPROOFS
AIRS
AIRSCAPE
AIRSCAPES
AIRSCREW
AIRSCREWS
AIRSHAFT
AIRSHAFTS
AIRSHED
AIRSHEDS
AIRSHIP
AIRSHIPS
AIRSHOT
AIRSHOTS
AIRSHOW
AIRSHOWS
AIRSICK
AIRSIDE
AIRSIDES
AIRSPACE
AIRSPACES
AIRSPEED
AIRSPEEDS
AIRSTOP
AIRSTOPS
AIRSTREAM
AIRSTRIKE
AIRSTRIP
AIRSTRIPS
AIRT
AIRTED
AIRTH
AIRTHED
AIRTHING
AIRTHS
AIRTIGHT
AIRTIME
AIRTIMES
AIRTING
AIRTS
AIRWARD
AIRWARDS

AIRWAVE
AIRWAVES
AIRWAY
AIRWAYS
AIRWISE
AIRWOMAN
AIRWOMEN
AIRWORTHY
AIRY
AIS
AISLE
AISLED
AISLELESS
AISLES
AISLEWAY
AISLEWAYS
AISLING
AISLINGS
AIT
AITCH
AITCHBONE
AITCHES
AITS
AITU
AITUS
AIVER
AIVERS
AIZLE
AIZLES
AJAR
AJEE
AJIVA
AJIVAS
AJOWAN
AJOWANS
AJUGA
AJUGAS
AJUTAGE
AJUTAGES
AJWAN
AJWANS
AKA
AKARYOTE
AKARYOTES
AKARYOTIC
AKATEA
AKATHISIA
AKE
AKEAKE
AKEAKES
AKED
AKEDAH
AKEDAHS
AKEE
AKEES
AKELA
AKELAS
AKENE

AKENES
AKENIAL
AKES
AKHARA
AKHARAS
AKIMBO
AKIN
AKINESES
AKINESIA
AKINESIAS
AKINESIS
AKINETIC
AKING
AKIRAHO
AKITA
AKITAS
AKKAS
AKOLUTHOS
AKRASIA
AKRASIAS
AKRATIC
AKVAVIT
AKVAVITS
AL
ALA
ALAAP
ALAAPS
ALABAMINE
ALABASTER
ALACHLOR
ALACHLORS
ALACK
ALACKADAY
ALACRITY
ALAE
ALAIMENT
ALAIMENTS
ALALAGMOI
ALALAGMOS
ALALIA
ALALIAS
ALAMEDA
ALAMEDAS
ALAMO
ALAMODE
ALAMODES
ALAMORT
ALAMOS
ALAN
ALAND
ALANDS
ALANE
ALANG
ALANGS
ALANIN
ALANINE
ALANINES
ALANINS

ALANNAH	ALBEIT	ALCALDE	ALDRIN
ALANNAHS	ALBERGHI	ALCALDES	ALDRINS
ALANS	ALBERGO	ALCARRAZA	ALE
ALANT	ALBERT	ALCATRAS	ALEATORIC
ALANTS	ALBERTITE	ALCAYDE	ALEATORY
ALANYL	ALBERTS	ALCAYDES	ALEBENCH
ALANYLS	ALBESCENT	ALCAZAR	ALEC
ALAP	ALBESPINE	ALCAZARS	ALECITHAL
ALAPA	ALBESPYNE	ALCHEMIC	ALECK
ALAPAS	ALBICORE	ALCHEMIES	ALECKS
ALAPS	ALBICORES	ALCHEMISE	ALECOST
ALAR	ALBINAL	ALCHEMIST	ALECOSTS
ALARM	ALBINESS	ALCHEMIZE	ALECS
ALARMABLE	ALBINIC	ALCHEMY	ALECTRYON
ALARMED	ALBINISM	ALCHERA	ALEE
ALARMEDLY	ALBINISMS	ALCHERAS	ALEF
ALARMING	ALBINO	ALCHYMIES	ALEFS
ALARMISM	ALBINOISM	ALCHYMY	ALEFT
ALARMISMS	ALBINOS	ALCID	ALEGAR
ALARMIST	ALBINOTIC	ALCIDINE	ALEGARS
ALARMISTS	ALBITE	ALCIDS	ALEGGE
ALARMS	ALBITES	ALCO	ALEGGED
ALARUM	ALBITIC	ALCOHOL	ALEGGES
ALARUMED	ALBITICAL	ALCOHOLIC	ALEGGING
ALARUMING	ALBITISE	ALCOHOLS	ALEHOUSE
ALARUMS	ALBITISED	ALCOLOCK	ALEHOUSES
ALARY	ALBITISES	ALCOLOCKS	ALEMBIC
ALAS	ALBITIZE	ALCOOL	ALEMBICS
ALASKA	ALBITIZED	ALCOOLS	ALEMBROTH
ALASKAS	ALBITIZES	ALCOPOP	ALENCON
ALASTOR	ALBIZIA	ALCOPOPS	ALENCONS
ALASTORS	ALBIZIAS	ALCORZA	ALENGTH
ALASTRIM	ALBIZZIA	ALCORZAS	ALEPH
ALASTRIMS	ALBIZZIAS	ALCOS	ALEPHS
ALATE	ALBRICIAS	ALCOVE	ALEPINE
ALATED	ALBS	ALCOVED	ALEPINES
ALATES	ALBUGO	ALCOVES	ALERCE
ALATION	ALBUGOS	ALDEA	ALERCES
ALATIONS	ALBUM	ALDEAS	ALERION
ALAY	ALBUMEN	ALDEHYDE	ALERIONS
ALAYED	ALBUMENS	ALDEHYDES	ALERT
ALAYING	ALBUMIN	ALDEHYDIC	ALERTED
ALAYS	ALBUMINS	ALDER	ALERTER
ALB	ALBUMOSE	ALDERFLY	ALERTEST
ALBA	ALBUMOSES	ALDERMAN	ALERTING
ALBACORE	ALBUMS	ALDERMEN	ALERTLY
ALBACORES	ALBURNOUS	ALDERN	ALERTNESS
ALBARELLI	ALBURNUM	ALDERS	ALERTS
ALBARELLO	ALBURNUMS	ALDICARB	ALES
ALBAS	ALBUTEROL	ALDICARBS	ALETHIC
ALBATA	ALCADE	ALDOL	ALEURON
ALBATAS	ALCADES	ALDOLASE	ALEURONE
ALBATROSS	ALCAHEST	ALDOLASES	ALEURONES
ALBE	ALCAHESTS	ALDOLS	ALEURONIC
ALBEDO	ALCAIC	ALDOSE	ALEURONS
ALBEDOES	ALCAICS	ALDOSES	ALEVIN
ALBEDOS	ALCAIDE	ALDOXIME	ALEVINS
ALBEE	ALCAIDES	ALDOXIMES	ALEW

13

ALEWASHED	ALGETIC	ALIENISM	ALIYA
ALEWIFE	ALGICIDAL	ALIENISMS	ALIYAH
ALEWIVES	ALGICIDE	ALIENIST	ALIYAHS
ALEWS	ALGICIDES	ALIENISTS	ALIYAS
ALEXANDER	ALGID	ALIENLY	ALIYOS
ALEXIA	ALGIDITY	ALIENNESS	ALIYOT
ALEXIAS	ALGIDNESS	ALIENOR	ALIYOTH
ALEXIC	ALGIN	ALIENORS	ALIZARI
ALEXIN	ALGINATE	ALIENS	ALIZARIN
ALEXINE	ALGINATES	ALIF	ALIZARINE
ALEXINES	ALGINIC	ALIFORM	ALIZARINS
ALEXINIC	ALGINS	ALIFS	ALIZARIS
ALEXINS	ALGOID	ALIGARTA	ALKAHEST
ALEYE	ALGOLOGY	ALIGARTAS	ALKAHESTS
ALEYED	ALGOMETER	ALIGHT	ALKALI
ALEYES	ALGOMETRY	ALIGHTED	ALKALIC
ALEYING	ALGOR	ALIGHTING	ALKALIES
ALF	ALGORISM	ALIGHTS	ALKALIFY
ALFA	ALGORISMS	ALIGN	ALKALIN
ALFAKI	ALGORITHM	ALIGNED	ALKALINE
ALFAKIS	ALGORS	ALIGNER	ALKALIS
ALFALFA	ALGUACIL	ALIGNERS	ALKALISE
ALFALFAS	ALGUACILS	ALIGNING	ALKALISED
ALFAQUI	ALGUAZIL	ALIGNMENT	ALKALISER
ALFAQUIN	ALGUAZILS	ALIGNS	ALKALISES
ALFAQUINS	ALGUM	ALIKE	ALKALIZE
ALFAQUIS	ALGUMS	ALIKENESS	ALKALIZED
ALFAS	ALIAS	ALIMENT	ALKALIZER
ALFERECES	ALIASES	ALIMENTAL	ALKALIZES
ALFEREZ	ALIASING	ALIMENTED	ALKALOID
ALFILARIA	ALIASINGS	ALIMENTS	ALKALOIDS
ALFILERIA	ALIBI	ALIMONIED	ALKALOSES
ALFORJA	ALIBIED	ALIMONIES	ALKALOSIS
ALFORJAS	ALIBIES	ALIMONY	ALKALOTIC
ALFREDO	ALIBIING	ALINE	ALKANE
ALFRESCO	ALIBIS	ALINED	ALKANES
ALFS	ALIBLE	ALINEMENT	ALKANET
ALGA	ALICANT	ALINER	ALKANETS
ALGAE	ALICANTS	ALINERS	ALKANNIN
ALGAECIDE	ALICYCLIC	ALINES	ALKANNINS
ALGAL	ALIDAD	ALINING	ALKENE
ALGAROBA	ALIDADE	ALIPED	ALKENES
ALGAROBAS	ALIDADES	ALIPEDS	ALKIE
ALGARROBA	ALIDADS	ALIPHATIC	ALKIES
ALGARROBO	ALIEN	ALIQUANT	ALKINE
ALGAS	ALIENABLE	ALIQUOT	ALKINES
ALGATE	ALIENAGE	ALIQUOTS	ALKO
ALGATES	ALIENAGES	ALISMA	ALKOS
ALGEBRA	ALIENATE	ALISMAS	ALKOXIDE
ALGEBRAIC	ALIENATED	ALISON	ALKOXIDES
ALGEBRAS	ALIENATES	ALISONS	ALKOXY
ALGERINE	ALIENATOR	ALIST	ALKY
ALGERINES	ALIENED	ALIT	ALKYD
ALGESES	ALIENEE	ALITERACY	ALKYDS
ALGESIA	ALIENEES	ALITERATE	ALKYL
ALGESIAS	ALIENER	ALIUNDE	ALKYLATE
ALGESIC	ALIENERS	ALIVE	ALKYLATED
ALGESIS	ALIENING	ALIVENESS	ALKYLATES

ALKYLIC	ALLERGIC	ALLOGENIC	ALLSEED
ALKYLS	ALLERGICS	ALLOGRAFT	ALLSEEDS
ALKYNE	ALLERGIES	ALLOGRAPH	ALLSORTS
ALKYNES	ALLERGIN	ALLOMERIC	ALLSPICE
ALL	ALLERGINS	ALLOMETRY	ALLSPICES
ALLANITE	ALLERGIST	ALLOMONE	ALLUDE
ALLANITES	ALLERGY	ALLOMONES	ALLUDED
ALLANTOIC	ALLERION	ALLOMORPH	ALLUDES
ALLANTOID	ALLERIONS	ALLONGE	ALLUDING
ALLANTOIN	ALLETHRIN	ALLONGES	ALLURE
ALLANTOIS	ALLEVIANT	ALLONS	ALLURED
ALLATIVE	ALLEVIATE	ALLONYM	ALLURER
ALLATIVES	ALLEY	ALLONYMS	ALLURERS
ALLAY	ALLEYCAT	ALLOPATH	ALLURES
ALLAYED	ALLEYCATS	ALLOPATHS	ALLURING
ALLAYER	ALLEYED	ALLOPATHY	ALLUSION
ALLAYERS	ALLEYS	ALLOPATRY	ALLUSIONS
ALLAYING	ALLEYWAY	ALLOPHANE	ALLUSIVE
ALLAYINGS	ALLEYWAYS	ALLOPHONE	ALLUVIA
ALLAYMENT	ALLHEAL	ALLOPLASM	ALLUVIAL
ALLAYS	ALLHEALS	ALLOSAUR	ALLUVIALS
ALLCOMERS	ALLIABLE	ALLOSAURS	ALLUVION
ALLEDGE	ALLIANCE	ALLOSTERY	ALLUVIONS
ALLEDGED	ALLIANCES	ALLOT	ALLUVIUM
ALLEDGES	ALLICE	ALLOTMENT	ALLUVIUMS
ALLEDGING	ALLICES	ALLOTROPE	ALLY
ALLEE	ALLICHOLY	ALLOTROPY	ALLYING
ALLEES	ALLICIN	ALLOTS	ALLYL
ALLEGE	ALLICINS	ALLOTTED	ALLYLIC
ALLEGED	ALLIED	ALLOTTEE	ALLYLS
ALLEGEDLY	ALLIES	ALLOTTEES	ALLYOU
ALLEGER	ALLIGARTA	ALLOTTER	ALMA
ALLEGERS	ALLIGATE	ALLOTTERS	ALMAGEST
ALLEGES	ALLIGATED	ALLOTTERY	ALMAGESTS
ALLEGGE	ALLIGATES	ALLOTTING	ALMAH
ALLEGGED	ALLIGATOR	ALLOTYPE	ALMAHS
ALLEGGES	ALLIS	ALLOTYPES	ALMAIN
ALLEGGING	ALLISES	ALLOTYPIC	ALMAINS
ALLEGIANT	ALLIUM	ALLOTYPY	ALMANAC
ALLEGING	ALLIUMS	ALLOVER	ALMANACK
ALLEGORIC	ALLNESS	ALLOVERS	ALMANACKS
ALLEGORY	ALLNESSES	ALLOW	ALMANACS
ALLEGRO	ALLNIGHT	ALLOWABLE	ALMANDINE
ALLEGROS	ALLOBAR	ALLOWABLY	ALMANDITE
ALLEL	ALLOBARS	ALLOWANCE	ALMAS
ALLELE	ALLOCABLE	ALLOWED	ALME
ALLELES	ALLOCARPY	ALLOWEDLY	ALMEH
ALLELIC	ALLOCATE	ALLOWING	ALMEHS
ALLELISM	ALLOCATED	ALLOWS	ALMEMAR
ALLELISMS	ALLOCATES	ALLOXAN	ALMEMARS
ALLELS	ALLOCATOR	ALLOXANS	ALMERIES
ALLELUIA	ALLOD	ALLOY	ALMERY
ALLELUIAH	ALLODIA	ALLOYED	ALMES
ALLELUIAS	ALLODIAL	ALLOYING	ALMIGHTY
ALLEMANDE	ALLODIUM	ALLOYS	ALMIRAH
ALLENARLY	ALLODIUMS	ALLOZYME	ALMIRAHS
ALLERGEN	ALLODS	ALLOZYMES	ALMNER
ALLERGENS	ALLOGAMY	ALLS	ALMNERS

ALMOND
ALMONDS
ALMONDY
ALMONER
ALMONERS
ALMONRIES
ALMONRY
ALMOST
ALMOUS
ALMS
ALMSGIVER
ALMSHOUSE
ALMSMAN
ALMSMEN
ALMSWOMAN
ALMSWOMEN
ALMUCE
ALMUCES
ALMUD
ALMUDE
ALMUDES
ALMUDS
ALMUG
ALMUGS
ALNAGE
ALNAGER
ALNAGERS
ALNAGES
ALNICO
ALNICOS
ALOCASIA
ALOCASIAS
ALOD
ALODIA
ALODIAL
ALODIUM
ALODIUMS
ALODS
ALOE
ALOED
ALOES
ALOETIC
ALOETICS
ALOFT
ALOGIA
ALOGIAS
ALOGICAL
ALOHA
ALOHAS
ALOIN
ALOINS
ALONE
ALONELY
ALONENESS
ALONG
ALONGSIDE
ALONGST
ALOOF

ALOOFLY
ALOOFNESS
ALOPECIA
ALOPECIAS
ALOPECIC
ALOPECOID
ALOUD
ALOW
ALOWE
ALP
ALPACA
ALPACAS
ALPACCA
ALPACCAS
ALPARGATA
ALPEEN
ALPEENS
ALPENGLOW
ALPENHORN
ALPHA
ALPHABET
ALPHABETS
ALPHAS
ALPHASORT
ALPHORN
ALPHORNS
ALPHOSIS
ALPHYL
ALPHYLS
ALPINE
ALPINELY
ALPINES
ALPINISM
ALPINISMS
ALPINIST
ALPINISTS
ALPS
ALREADY
ALRIGHT
ALS
ALSIKE
ALSIKES
ALSO
ALSOON
ALSOONE
ALT
ALTAR
ALTARAGE
ALTARAGES
ALTARS
ALTARWISE
ALTER
ALTERABLE
ALTERABLY
ALTERANT
ALTERANTS
ALTERCATE
ALTERED

ALTERER
ALTERERS
ALTERING
ALTERITY
ALTERN
ALTERNANT
ALTERNAT
ALTERNATE
ALTERNATS
ALTERNE
ALTERNES
ALTERS
ALTESSE
ALTESSES
ALTEZA
ALTEZAS
ALTEZZA
ALTEZZAS
ALTHAEA
ALTHAEAS
ALTHEA
ALTHEAS
ALTHO
ALTHORN
ALTHORNS
ALTHOUGH
ALTIGRAPH
ALTIMETER
ALTIMETRY
ALTIPLANO
ALTISSIMO
ALTITUDE
ALTITUDES
ALTO
ALTOIST
ALTOISTS
ALTOS
ALTRICES
ALTRICIAL
ALTRUISM
ALTRUISMS
ALTRUIST
ALTRUISTS
ALTS
ALUDEL
ALUDELS
ALULA
ALULAE
ALULAR
ALUM
ALUMIN
ALUMINA
ALUMINAS
ALUMINATE
ALUMINE
ALUMINES
ALUMINIC
ALUMINISE

ALUMINIUM
ALUMINIZE
ALUMINOUS
ALUMINS
ALUMINUM
ALUMINUMS
ALUMISH
ALUMIUM
ALUMIUMS
ALUMNA
ALUMNAE
ALUMNI
ALUMNUS
ALUMROOT
ALUMROOTS
ALUMS
ALUMSTONE
ALUNITE
ALUNITES
ALURE
ALURES
ALVEARIES
ALVEARY
ALVEATED
ALVEOLAR
ALVEOLARS
ALVEOLATE
ALVEOLE
ALVEOLES
ALVEOLI
ALVEOLUS
ALVINE
ALWAY
ALWAYS
ALYSSUM
ALYSSUMS
AM
AMA
AMABILE
AMADAVAT
AMADAVATS
AMADODA
AMADOU
AMADOUS
AMAH
AMAHS
AMAIN
AMALGAM
AMALGAMS
AMANDINE
AMANDINES
AMANDLA
AMANDLAS
AMANITA
AMANITAS
AMANITIN
AMANITINS
AMARACUS

AMARANT
AMARANTH
AMARANTHS
AMARANTIN
AMARANTS
AMARELLE
AMARELLES
AMARETTI
AMARETTO
AMARETTOS
AMARNA
AMARONE
AMARONES
AMARYLLID
AMARYLLIS
AMAS
AMASS
AMASSABLE
AMASSED
AMASSER
AMASSERS
AMASSES
AMASSING
AMASSMENT
AMATE
AMATED
AMATES
AMATEUR
AMATEURS
AMATING
AMATION
AMATIONS
AMATIVE
AMATIVELY
AMATOL
AMATOLS
AMATORIAL
AMATORIAN
AMATORY
AMAUROSES
AMAUROSIS
AMAUROTIC
AMAUT
AMAUTS
AMAZE
AMAZED
AMAZEDLY
AMAZEMENT
AMAZES
AMAZING
AMAZINGLY
AMAZON
AMAZONIAN
AMAZONITE
AMAZONS
AMBACH
AMBACHES
AMBAGE

AMBAGES
AMBAGIOUS
AMBAN
AMBANS
AMBARI
AMBARIES
AMBARIS
AMBARY
AMBASSAGE
AMBASSIES
AMBASSY
AMBATCH
AMBATCHES
AMBEER
AMBEERS
AMBER
AMBERED
AMBERGRIS
AMBERIES
AMBERINA
AMBERINAS
AMBERITE
AMBERITES
AMBERJACK
AMBEROID
AMBEROIDS
AMBEROUS
AMBERS
AMBERY
AMBIANCE
AMBIANCES
AMBIENCE
AMBIENCES
AMBIENT
AMBIENTS
AMBIGUITY
AMBIGUOUS
AMBIPOLAR
AMBIT
AMBITION
AMBITIONS
AMBITIOUS
AMBITS
AMBITTY
AMBIVERT
AMBIVERTS
AMBLE
AMBLED
AMBLER
AMBLERS
AMBLES
AMBLING
AMBLINGS
AMBLYOPIA
AMBLYOPIC
AMBO
AMBOINA
AMBOINAS

AMBONES
AMBOS
AMBOYNA
AMBOYNAS
AMBRIES
AMBROID
AMBROIDS
AMBROSIA
AMBROSIAL
AMBROSIAN
AMBROSIAS
AMBROTYPE
AMBRY
AMBSACE
AMBSACES
AMBULACRA
AMBULANCE
AMBULANT
AMBULANTS
AMBULATE
AMBULATED
AMBULATES
AMBULATOR
AMBULETTE
AMBUSCADE
AMBUSCADO
AMBUSH
AMBUSHED
AMBUSHER
AMBUSHERS
AMBUSHES
AMBUSHING
AMEARST
AMEBA
AMEBAE
AMEBAN
AMEBAS
AMEBEAN
AMEBIASES
AMEBIASIS
AMEBIC
AMEBOCYTE
AMEBOID
AMEER
AMEERATE
AMEERATES
AMEERS
AMEIOSES
AMEIOSIS
AMELCORN
AMELCORNS
AMELIA
AMELIAS
AMEN
AMENABLE
AMENABLY
AMENAGE
AMENAGED

AMENAGES
AMENAGING
AMENAUNCE
AMEND
AMENDABLE
AMENDE
AMENDED
AMENDER
AMENDERS
AMENDES
AMENDING
AMENDMENT
AMENDS
AMENE
AMENED
AMENING
AMENITIES
AMENITY
AMENS
AMENT
AMENTA
AMENTAL
AMENTIA
AMENTIAS
AMENTS
AMENTUM
AMERCE
AMERCED
AMERCER
AMERCERS
AMERCES
AMERCING
AMERICIUM
AMESACE
AMESACES
AMETHYST
AMETHYSTS
AMETROPIA
AMETROPIC
AMI
AMIA
AMIABLE
AMIABLY
AMIANTHUS
AMIANTUS
AMIAS
AMICABLE
AMICABLY
AMICE
AMICES
AMICI
AMICUS
AMID
AMIDASE
AMIDASES
AMIDE
AMIDES
AMIDIC

AMIDIN	AMMIRAL	AMOK	AMOUNTING
AMIDINE	AMMIRALS	AMOKS	AMOUNTS
AMIDINES	AMMO	AMOKURA	AMOUR
AMIDINS	AMMOCETE	AMOLE	AMOURETTE
AMIDMOST	AMMOCETES	AMOLES	AMOURS
AMIDO	AMMOCOETE	AMOMUM	AMOVE
AMIDOGEN	AMMON	AMOMUMS	AMOVED
AMIDOGENS	AMMONAL	AMONG	AMOVES
AMIDOL	AMMONALS	AMONGST	AMOVING
AMIDOLS	AMMONATE	AMOOVE	AMOWT
AMIDONE	AMMONATES	AMOOVED	AMOWTS
AMIDONES	AMMONIA	AMOOVES	AMP
AMIDS	AMMONIAC	AMOOVING	AMPASSIES
AMIDSHIP	AMMONIACS	AMORAL	AMPASSY
AMIDSHIPS	AMMONIAS	AMORALISM	AMPED
AMIDST	AMMONIATE	AMORALIST	AMPERAGE
AMIE	AMMONIC	AMORALITY	AMPERAGES
AMIES	AMMONICAL	AMORALLY	AMPERE
AMIGA	AMMONIFY	AMORANCE	AMPERES
AMIGAS	AMMONITE	AMORANCES	AMPERSAND
AMIGO	AMMONITES	AMORANT	AMPERZAND
AMIGOS	AMMONITIC	AMORCE	AMPHIBIA
AMILDAR	AMMONIUM	AMORCES	AMPHIBIAN
AMILDARS	AMMONIUMS	AMORET	AMPHIBOLE
AMIN	AMMONO	AMORETS	AMPHIBOLY
AMINE	AMMONOID	AMORETTI	AMPHIGORY
AMINES	AMMONOIDS	AMORETTO	AMPHIOXI
AMINIC	AMMONS	AMORETTOS	AMPHIOXUS
AMINITIES	AMMOS	AMORINI	AMPHIPATH
AMINITY	AMNESIA	AMORINO	AMPHIPOD
AMINO	AMNESIAC	AMORISM	AMPHIPODS
AMINS	AMNESIACS	AMORISMS	AMPHOLYTE
AMIR	AMNESIAS	AMORIST	AMPHORA
AMIRATE	AMNESIC	AMORISTIC	AMPHORAE
AMIRATES	AMNESICS	AMORISTS	AMPHORAL
AMIRS	AMNESTIC	AMORNINGS	AMPHORAS
AMIS	AMNESTIED	AMOROSA	AMPHORIC
AMISES	AMNESTIES	AMOROSAS	AMPING
AMISS	AMNESTY	AMOROSITY	AMPLE
AMISSES	AMNIA	AMOROSO	AMPLENESS
AMISSIBLE	AMNIC	AMOROSOS	AMPLER
AMISSING	AMNIO	AMOROUS	AMPLEST
AMITIES	AMNION	AMOROUSLY	AMPLEXUS
AMITOSES	AMNIONIC	AMORPHISM	AMPLIDYNE
AMITOSIS	AMNIONS	AMORPHOUS	AMPLIFIED
AMITOTIC	AMNIOS	AMORT	AMPLIFIER
AMITROLE	AMNIOTE	AMORTISE	AMPLIFIES
AMITROLES	AMNIOTES	AMORTISED	AMPLIFY
AMITY	AMNIOTIC	AMORTISES	AMPLITUDE
AMLA	AMNIOTOMY	AMORTIZE	AMPLOSOME
AMLAS	AMOEBA	AMORTIZED	AMPLY
AMMAN	AMOEBAE	AMORTIZES	AMPOULE
AMMANS	AMOEBAEAN	AMOSITE	AMPOULES
AMMETER	AMOEBAN	AMOSITES	AMPS
AMMETERS	AMOEBAS	AMOTION	AMPUL
AMMINE	AMOEBEAN	AMOTIONS	AMPULE
AMMINES	AMOEBIC	AMOUNT	AMPULES
AMMINO	AMOEBOID	AMOUNTED	AMPULLA

AMPULLAE	AMYLASES	ANAGOGIC	ANALYZES
AMPULLAR	AMYLENE	ANAGOGIES	ANALYZING
AMPULLARY	AMYLENES	ANAGOGY	ANAMNESES
AMPULS	AMYLIC	ANAGRAM	ANAMNESIS
AMPUTATE	AMYLOGEN	ANAGRAMS	ANAMNIOTE
AMPUTATED	AMYLOGENS	ANAL	ANAN
AMPUTATES	AMYLOID	ANALCIME	ANANA
AMPUTATOR	AMYLOIDAL	ANALCIMES	ANANAS
AMPUTEE	AMYLOIDS	ANALCIMIC	ANANASES
AMPUTEES	AMYLOPSIN	ANALCITE	ANANDROUS
AMREETA	AMYLOSE	ANALCITES	ANANKE
AMREETAS	AMYLOSES	ANALECTA	ANANKES
AMRIT	AMYLS	ANALECTIC	ANANTHOUS
AMRITA	AMYLUM	ANALECTS	ANAPAEST
AMRITAS	AMYLUMS	ANALEMMA	ANAPAESTS
AMRITS	AMYOTONIA	ANALEMMAS	ANAPEST
AMSINCKIA	AMYTAL	ANALEPTIC	ANAPESTIC
AMTMAN	AMYTALS	ANALGESIA	ANAPESTS
AMTMANS	AN	ANALGESIC	ANAPHASE
AMTRAC	ANA	ANALGETIC	ANAPHASES
AMTRACK	ANABAENA	ANALGIA	ANAPHASIC
AMTRACKS	ANABAENAS	ANALGIAS	ANAPHOR
AMTRACS	ANABANTID	ANALITIES	ANAPHORA
AMU	ANABAS	ANALITY	ANAPHORAL
AMUCK	ANABASES	ANALLY	ANAPHORAS
AMUCKS	ANABASIS	ANALOG	ANAPHORIC
AMULET	ANABATIC	ANALOGA	ANAPHORS
AMULETIC	ANABIOSES	ANALOGIC	ANAPLASIA
AMULETS	ANABIOSIS	ANALOGIES	ANAPLASTY
AMUS	ANABIOTIC	ANALOGISE	ANAPTYXES
AMUSABLE	ANABLEPS	ANALOGISM	ANAPTYXIS
AMUSE	ANABOLIC	ANALOGIST	ANARCH
AMUSEABLE	ANABOLISM	ANALOGIZE	ANARCHAL
AMUSED	ANABOLITE	ANALOGON	ANARCHIAL
AMUSEDLY	ANABRANCH	ANALOGONS	ANARCHIC
AMUSEMENT	ANACHARIS	ANALOGOUS	ANARCHIES
AMUSER	ANACLINAL	ANALOGS	ANARCHISE
AMUSERS	ANACLISES	ANALOGUE	ANARCHISM
AMUSES	ANACLISIS	ANALOGUES	ANARCHIST
AMUSETTE	ANACLITIC	ANALOGY	ANARCHIZE
AMUSETTES	ANACONDA	ANALYSAND	ANARCHS
AMUSIA	ANACONDAS	ANALYSE	ANARCHY
AMUSIAS	ANACRUSES	ANALYSED	ANARTHRIA
AMUSING	ANACRUSIS	ANALYSER	ANARTHRIC
AMUSINGLY	ANADEM	ANALYSERS	ANAS
AMUSIVE	ANADEMS	ANALYSES	ANASARCA
AMYGDAL	ANAEMIA	ANALYSING	ANASARCAS
AMYGDALA	ANAEMIAS	ANALYSIS	ANASTASES
AMYGDALAE	ANAEMIC	ANALYST	ANASTASIS
AMYGDALAS	ANAEROBE	ANALYSTS	ANASTATIC
AMYGDALE	ANAEROBES	ANALYTE	ANATA
AMYGDALES	ANAEROBIA	ANALYTES	ANATAS
AMYGDALIN	ANAEROBIC	ANALYTIC	ANATASE
AMYGDALS	ANAGLYPH	ANALYTICS	ANATASES
AMYGDULE	ANAGLYPHS	ANALYZE	ANATHEMA
AMYGDULES	ANAGLYPHY	ANALYZED	ANATHEMAS
AMYL	ANAGOGE	ANALYZER	ANATMAN
AMYLASE	ANAGOGES	ANALYZERS	ANATMANS

ANATOMIC	ANCON	ANELES	ANGELICA
ANATOMIES	ANCONAL	ANELING	ANGELICAL
ANATOMISE	ANCONE	ANEMIA	ANGELICAS
ANATOMIST	ANCONEAL	ANEMIAS	ANGELING
ANATOMIZE	ANCONES	ANEMIC	ANGELS
ANATOMY	ANCONOID	ANEMOGRAM	ANGELUS
ANATOXIN	ANCORA	ANEMOLOGY	ANGELUSES
ANATOXINS	ANCRESS	ANEMONE	ANGER
ANATROPY	ANCRESSES	ANEMONES	ANGERED
ANATTA	AND	ANEMOSES	ANGERING
ANATTAS	ANDANTE	ANEMOSIS	ANGERLESS
ANATTO	ANDANTES	ANENST	ANGERLY
ANATTOS	ANDANTINI	ANENT	ANGERS
ANAXIAL	ANDANTINO	ANERGIA	ANGICO
ANBURIES	ANDESINE	ANERGIAS	ANGICOS
ANBURY	ANDESINES	ANERGIC	ANGINA
ANCE	ANDESITE	ANERGIES	ANGINAL
ANCESTOR	ANDESITES	ANERGY	ANGINAS
ANCESTORS	ANDESITIC	ANERLY	ANGINOSE
ANCESTRAL	ANDESYTE	ANEROID	ANGINOUS
ANCESTRY	ANDESYTES	ANEROIDS	ANGIOGRAM
ANCHO	ANDIRON	ANES	ANGIOLOGY
ANCHOR	ANDIRONS	ANESTRA	ANGIOMA
ANCHORAGE	ANDOUILLE	ANESTRI	ANGIOMAS
ANCHORED	ANDRADITE	ANESTROUS	ANGIOMATA
ANCHORESS	ANDRO	ANESTRUM	ANGKLUNG
ANCHORET	ANDROECIA	ANESTRUS	ANGKLUNGS
ANCHORETS	ANDROGEN	ANETHOL	ANGLE
ANCHORING	ANDROGENS	ANETHOLE	ANGLED
ANCHORITE	ANDROGYNE	ANETHOLES	ANGLEDUG
ANCHORMAN	ANDROGYNY	ANETHOLS	ANGLEDUGS
ANCHORMEN	ANDROID	ANETIC	ANGLEPOD
ANCHORS	ANDROIDS	ANEUPLOID	ANGLEPODS
ANCHOS	ANDROLOGY	ANEURIN	ANGLER
ANCHOVETA	ANDROMEDA	ANEURINS	ANGLERS
ANCHOVIES	ANDROS	ANEURISM	ANGLES
ANCHOVY	ANDS	ANEURISMS	ANGLESITE
ANCHUSA	ANDVILE	ANEURYSM	ANGLEWISE
ANCHUSAS	ANDVILES	ANEURYSMS	ANGLEWORM
ANCHUSIN	ANE	ANEW	ANGLICE
ANCHUSINS	ANEAR	ANGA	ANGLICISE
ANCHYLOSE	ANEARED	ANGAKOK	ANGLICISM
ANCIENT	ANEARING	ANGAKOKS	ANGLICIST
ANCIENTER	ANEARS	ANGARIA	ANGLICIZE
ANCIENTLY	ANEATH	ANGARIAS	ANGLIFIED
ANCIENTRY	ANECDOTA	ANGARIES	ANGLIFIES
ANCIENTS	ANECDOTAL	ANGARY	ANGLIFY
ANCILE	ANECDOTE	ANGAS	ANGLING
ANCILIA	ANECDOTES	ANGASHORE	ANGLINGS
ANCILLA	ANECDOTIC	ANGEKKOK	ANGLIST
ANCILLAE	ANECDYSES	ANGEKKOKS	ANGLISTS
ANCILLARY	ANECDYSIS	ANGEKOK	ANGLO
ANCILLAS	ANECHOIC	ANGEKOKS	ANGLOPHIL
ANCIPITAL	ANELACE	ANGEL	ANGLOS
ANCLE	ANELACES	ANGELED	ANGOLA
ANCLES	ANELASTIC	ANGELFISH	ANGOPHORA
ANCOME	ANELE	ANGELHOOD	ANGORA
ANCOMES	ANELED	ANGELIC	ANGORAS

ANGOSTURA	ANILITY	ANKER	ANNEALS
ANGRIER	ANILS	ANKERITE	ANNECTENT
ANGRIES	ANIMA	ANKERITES	ANNELID
ANGRIEST	ANIMACIES	ANKERS	ANNELIDAN
ANGRILY	ANIMACY	ANKH	ANNELIDS
ANGRINESS	ANIMAL	ANKHS	ANNEX
ANGRY	ANIMALIAN	ANKLE	ANNEXABLE
ANGST	ANIMALIC	ANKLEBONE	ANNEXE
ANGSTIER	ANIMALIER	ANKLED	ANNEXED
ANGSTIEST	ANIMALISE	ANKLES	ANNEXES
ANGSTROM	ANIMALISM	ANKLET	ANNEXING
ANGSTROMS	ANIMALIST	ANKLETS	ANNEXION
ANGSTS	ANIMALITY	ANKLING	ANNEXIONS
ANGSTY	ANIMALIZE	ANKLONG	ANNEXMENT
ANGUIFORM	ANIMALLY	ANKLONGS	ANNEXURE
ANGUINE	ANIMALS	ANKLUNG	ANNEXURES
ANGUIPED	ANIMAS	ANKLUNGS	ANNICUT
ANGUIPEDE	ANIMATE	ANKUS	ANNICUTS
ANGUISH	ANIMATED	ANKUSES	ANNO
ANGUISHED	ANIMATELY	ANKUSH	ANNONA
ANGUISHES	ANIMATER	ANKUSHES	ANNONAS
ANGULAR	ANIMATERS	ANKYLOSE	ANNOTATE
ANGULARLY	ANIMATES	ANKYLOSED	ANNOTATED
ANGULATE	ANIMATIC	ANKYLOSES	ANNOTATES
ANGULATED	ANIMATICS	ANKYLOSIS	ANNOTATOR
ANGULATES	ANIMATING	ANKYLOTIC	ANNOUNCE
ANGULOSE	ANIMATION	ANLACE	ANNOUNCED
ANGULOUS	ANIMATISM	ANLACES	ANNOUNCER
ANHEDONIA	ANIMATIST	ANLAGE	ANNOUNCES
ANHEDONIC	ANIMATO	ANLAGEN	ANNOY
ANHEDRAL	ANIMATOR	ANLAGES	ANNOYANCE
ANHINGA	ANIMATORS	ANLAS	ANNOYED
ANHINGAS	ANIME	ANLASES	ANNOYER
ANHUNGRED	ANIMES	ANN	ANNOYERS
ANHYDRASE	ANIMI	ANNA	ANNOYING
ANHYDRIDE	ANIMIS	ANNAL	ANNOYS
ANHYDRITE	ANIMISM	ANNALISE	ANNS
ANHYDROUS	ANIMISMS	ANNALISED	ANNUAL
ANI	ANIMIST	ANNALISES	ANNUALISE
ANICCA	ANIMISTIC	ANNALIST	ANNUALIZE
ANICCAS	ANIMISTS	ANNALISTS	ANNUALLY
ANICONIC	ANIMOSITY	ANNALIZE	ANNUALS
ANICONISM	ANIMUS	ANNALIZED	ANNUITANT
ANICONIST	ANIMUSES	ANNALIZES	ANNUITIES
ANICUT	ANION	ANNALS	ANNUITY
ANICUTS	ANIONIC	ANNAS	ANNUL
ANIDROSES	ANIONS	ANNAT	ANNULAR
ANIDROSIS	ANIS	ANNATES	ANNULARLY
ANIGH	ANISE	ANNATS	ANNULARS
ANIGHT	ANISEED	ANNATTA	ANNULATE
ANIL	ANISEEDS	ANNATTAS	ANNULATED
ANILE	ANISES	ANNATTO	ANNULATES
ANILIN	ANISETTE	ANNATTOS	ANNULET
ANILINE	ANISETTES	ANNEAL	ANNULETS
ANILINES	ANISIC	ANNEALED	ANNULI
ANILINGUS	ANISOGAMY	ANNEALER	ANNULLED
ANILINS	ANISOLE	ANNEALERS	ANNULLING
ANILITIES	ANISOLES	ANNEALING	ANNULMENT

21

ANNULOSE
ANNULS
ANNULUS
ANNULUSES
ANOA
ANOAS
ANOBIID
ANOBIIDS
ANODAL
ANODALLY
ANODE
ANODES
ANODIC
ANODISE
ANODISED
ANODISES
ANODISING
ANODIZE
ANODIZED
ANODIZES
ANODIZING
ANODONTIA
ANODYNE
ANODYNES
ANODYNIC
ANOESES
ANOESIS
ANOESTRA
ANOESTRI
ANOESTRUM
ANOESTRUS
ANOETIC
ANOINT
ANOINTED
ANOINTER
ANOINTERS
ANOINTING
ANOINTS
ANOLE
ANOLES
ANOLYTE
ANOLYTES
ANOMALIES
ANOMALOUS
ANOMALY
ANOMIC
ANOMIE
ANOMIES
ANOMY
ANON
ANONYM
ANONYMA
ANONYMAS
ANONYMISE
ANONYMITY
ANONYMIZE
ANONYMOUS
ANONYMS

ANOOPSIA
ANOOPSIAS
ANOPHELES
ANOPIA
ANOPIAS
ANOPSIA
ANOPSIAS
ANORAK
ANORAKS
ANORECTAL
ANORECTIC
ANORETIC
ANORETICS
ANOREXIA
ANOREXIAS
ANOREXIC
ANOREXICS
ANOREXIES
ANOREXY
ANORTHIC
ANORTHITE
ANOSMATIC
ANOSMIA
ANOSMIAS
ANOSMIC
ANOTHER
ANOUGH
ANOUROUS
ANOVULANT
ANOVULAR
ANOW
ANOXAEMIA
ANOXAEMIC
ANOXEMIA
ANOXEMIAS
ANOXEMIC
ANOXIA
ANOXIAS
ANOXIC
ANSA
ANSAE
ANSATE
ANSATED
ANSERINE
ANSERINES
ANSEROUS
ANSWER
ANSWERED
ANSWERER
ANSWERERS
ANSWERING
ANSWERS
ANT
ANTA
ANTACID
ANTACIDS
ANTAE
ANTALGIC

ANTALGICS
ANTALKALI
ANTAR
ANTARA
ANTARAS
ANTARCTIC
ANTARS
ANTAS
ANTBEAR
ANTBEARS
ANTBIRD
ANTBIRDS
ANTE
ANTEATER
ANTEATERS
ANTECEDE
ANTECEDED
ANTECEDES
ANTECHOIR
ANTED
ANTEDATE
ANTEDATED
ANTEDATES
ANTEED
ANTEFIX
ANTEFIXA
ANTEFIXAE
ANTEFIXAL
ANTEFIXES
ANTEING
ANTELOPE
ANTELOPES
ANTELUCAN
ANTENATAL
ANTENATI
ANTENNA
ANTENNAE
ANTENNAL
ANTENNARY
ANTENNAS
ANTENNULE
ANTEPAST
ANTEPASTS
ANTERIOR
ANTEROOM
ANTEROOMS
ANTES
ANTETYPE
ANTETYPES
ANTEVERT
ANTEVERTS
ANTHELIA
ANTHELION
ANTHELIX
ANTHEM
ANTHEMED
ANTHEMIA
ANTHEMIC

ANTHEMING
ANTHEMION
ANTHEMS
ANTHER
ANTHERAL
ANTHERID
ANTHERIDS
ANTHERS
ANTHESES
ANTHESIS
ANTHILL
ANTHILLS
ANTHOCARP
ANTHOCYAN
ANTHODIA
ANTHODIUM
ANTHOID
ANTHOLOGY
ANTHOTAXY
ANTHOZOAN
ANTHOZOIC
ANTHRACES
ANTHRACIC
ANTHRAX
ANTHRAXES
ANTHROPIC
ANTHURIUM
ANTI
ANTIABUSE
ANTIACNE
ANTIAGING
ANTIAIR
ANTIALIEN
ANTIAR
ANTIARIN
ANTIARINS
ANTIARMOR
ANTIARS
ANTIATOM
ANTIATOMS
ANTIAUXIN
ANTIBIAS
ANTIBLACK
ANTIBODY
ANTIBOSS
ANTIBUG
ANTIBUSER
ANTIC
ANTICAL
ANTICALLY
ANTICAR
ANTICHLOR
ANTICISE
ANTICISED
ANTICISES
ANTICITY
ANTICIVIC
ANTICIZE

ANTICIZED	ANTILOCK	ANTIQUATE	ANTITYPE
ANTICIZES	ANTILOG	ANTIQUE	ANTITYPES
ANTICK	ANTILOGS	ANTIQUED	ANTITYPIC
ANTICKE	ANTILOGY	ANTIQUELY	ANTIULCER
ANTICKED	ANTIMACHO	ANTIQUER	ANTIUNION
ANTICKING	ANTIMALE	ANTIQUERS	ANTIURBAN
ANTICKS	ANTIMAN	ANTIQUES	ANTIVENIN
ANTICLINE	ANTIMASK	ANTIQUEY	ANTIVENOM
ANTICLING	ANTIMASKS	ANTIQUING	ANTIVIRAL
ANTICLY	ANTIMERE	ANTIQUITY	ANTIVIRUS
ANTICODON	ANTIMERES	ANTIRADAR	ANTIWAR
ANTICOLD	ANTIMERIC	ANTIRAPE	ANTIWEAR
ANTICOUS	ANTIMINE	ANTIRED	ANTIWEED
ANTICRACK	ANTIMONIC	ANTIRIOT	ANTIWHITE
ANTICRIME	ANTIMONY	ANTIROCK	ANTIWOMAN
ANTICS	ANTIMONYL	ANTIROLL	ANTIWORLD
ANTICULT	ANTIMUON	ANTIROYAL	ANTLER
ANTICULTS	ANTIMUONS	ANTIRUST	ANTLERED
ANTIDORA	ANTIMUSIC	ANTIRUSTS	ANTLERS
ANTIDOTAL	ANTIMYCIN	ANTIS	ANTLIA
ANTIDOTE	ANTING	ANTISAG	ANTLIAE
ANTIDOTED	ANTINGS	ANTISCIAN	ANTLIATE
ANTIDOTES	ANTINODAL	ANTISENSE	ANTLIKE
ANTIDRAFT	ANTINODE	ANTISERA	ANTLION
ANTIDRUG	ANTINODES	ANTISERUM	ANTLIONS
ANTIDUNE	ANTINOISE	ANTISEX	ANTONYM
ANTIDUNES	ANTINOME	ANTISHARK	ANTONYMIC
ANTIELITE	ANTINOMES	ANTISHIP	ANTONYMS
ANTIENT	ANTINOMIC	ANTISHOCK	ANTONYMY
ANTIENTS	ANTINOMY	ANTISKID	ANTRA
ANTIFAT	ANTINOVEL	ANTISLEEP	ANTRAL
ANTIFLU	ANTINUKE	ANTISLIP	ANTRE
ANTIFOAM	ANTINUKER	ANTISMOG	ANTRES
ANTIFOG	ANTINUKES	ANTISMOKE	ANTRORSE
ANTIFRAUD	ANTIPAPAL	ANTISMUT	ANTRUM
ANTIFUR	ANTIPARTY	ANTISNOB	ANTRUMS
ANTIGANG	ANTIPASTI	ANTISNOBS	ANTS
ANTIGAY	ANTIPASTO	ANTISOLAR	ANTSIER
ANTIGEN	ANTIPATHY	ANTISPAM	ANTSIEST
ANTIGENE	ANTIPHON	ANTISPAST	ANTSINESS
ANTIGENES	ANTIPHONS	ANTISTAT	ANTSY
ANTIGENIC	ANTIPHONY	ANTISTATE	ANTWACKIE
ANTIGENS	ANTIPILL	ANTISTATS	ANUCLEATE
ANTIGLARE	ANTIPODAL	ANTISTICK	ANURAL
ANTIGRAFT	ANTIPODE	ANTISTORY	ANURAN
ANTIGUN	ANTIPODES	ANTISTYLE	ANURANS
ANTIHELIX	ANTIPOLAR	ANTITANK	ANURESES
ANTIHERO	ANTIPOLE	ANTITAX	ANURESIS
ANTIHUMAN	ANTIPOLES	ANTITHEFT	ANURETIC
ANTIJAM	ANTIPOPE	ANTITHET	ANURIA
ANTIKING	ANTIPOPES	ANTITHETS	ANURIAS
ANTIKINGS	ANTIPORN	ANTITOXIC	ANURIC
ANTIKNOCK	ANTIPOT	ANTITOXIN	ANUROUS
ANTILABOR	ANTIPRESS	ANTITRADE	ANUS
ANTILEAK	ANTIPYIC	ANTITRAGI	ANUSES
ANTILEFT	ANTIPYICS	ANTITRUST	ANVIL
ANTILIFE	ANTIQUARK	ANTITUMOR	ANVILED
ANTILIFER	ANTIQUARY	ANTITYPAL	ANVILING

ANVILLED

ANVILLED	APARTMENT	APHANITE	APHTHAE
ANVILLING	APARTNESS	APHANITES	APHTHOUS
ANVILS	APATETIC	APHANITIC	APHYLLIES
ANVILTOP	APATHATON	APHASIA	APHYLLOUS
ANVILTOPS	APATHETIC	APHASIAC	APHYLLY
ANXIETIES	APATHIES	APHASIACS	APIACEOUS
ANXIETY	APATHY	APHASIAS	APIAN
ANXIOUS	APATITE	APHASIC	APIARIAN
ANXIOUSLY	APATITES	APHASICS	APIARIANS
ANY	APATOSAUR	APHELIA	APIARIES
ANYBODIES	APAY	APHELIAN	APIARIST
ANYBODY	APAYD	APHELION	APIARISTS
ANYHOW	APAYING	APHELIONS	APIARY
ANYMORE	APAYS	APHERESES	APICAL
ANYON	APE	APHERESIS	APICALLY
ANYONE	APEAK	APHERETIC	APICALS
ANYONES	APED	APHESES	APICES
ANYONS	APEDOM	APHESIS	APICIAN
ANYPLACE	APEDOMS	APHETIC	APICULATE
ANYROAD	APEEK	APHETISE	APICULI
ANYTHING	APEHOOD	APHETISED	APICULUS
ANYTHINGS	APEHOODS	APHETISES	APIECE
ANYTIME	APELIKE	APHETIZE	APIMANIA
ANYWAY	APEMAN	APHETIZED	APIMANIAS
ANYWAYS	APEMEN	APHETIZES	APING
ANYWHEN	APEPSIA	APHICIDE	APIOL
ANYWHERE	APEPSIAS	APHICIDES	APIOLOGY
ANYWHERES	APEPSIES	APHID	APIOLS
ANYWISE	APEPSY	APHIDES	APISH
ANZIANI	APER	APHIDIAN	APISHLY
AORIST	APERCU	APHIDIANS	APISHNESS
AORISTIC	APERCUS	APHIDIOUS	APISM
AORISTS	APERIENT	APHIDS	APISMS
AORTA	APERIENTS	APHIS	APIVOROUS
AORTAE	APERIES	APHOLATE	APLANAT
AORTAL	APERIODIC	APHOLATES	APLANATIC
AORTAS	APERITIF	APHONIA	APLANATS
AORTIC	APERITIFS	APHONIAS	APLANETIC
AORTITIS	APERITIVE	APHONIC	APLASIA
AOUDAD	APERS	APHONICS	APLASIAS
AOUDADS	APERT	APHONIES	APLASTIC
APACE	APERTNESS	APHONOUS	APLENTY
APACHE	APERTURAL	APHONY	APLITE
APACHES	APERTURE	APHORISE	APLITES
APADANA	APERTURED	APHORISED	APLITIC
APADANAS	APERTURES	APHORISER	APLOMB
APAGE	APERY	APHORISES	APLOMBS
APAGOGE	APES	APHORISM	APLUSTRE
APAGOGES	APETALIES	APHORISMS	APLUSTRES
APAGOGIC	APETALOUS	APHORIST	APNEA
APAID	APETALY	APHORISTS	APNEAL
APANAGE	APEX	APHORIZE	APNEAS
APANAGED	APEXES	APHORIZED	APNEIC
APANAGES	APGAR	APHORIZER	APNEUSES
APAREJO	APHAGIA	APHORIZES	APNEUSIS
APAREJOS	APHAGIAS	APHOTIC	APNEUSTIC
APART	APHAKIA	APHRODITE	APNOEA
APARTHEID	APHAKIAS	APHTHA	APNOEAL

APNOEAS	APOOP	APPALLS	APPENDS
APNOEIC	APOPHASES	APPALOOSA	APPERIL
APO	APOPHASIS	APPALS	APPERILL
APOAPSES	APOPHATIC	APPALTI	APPERILLS
APOAPSIS	APOPHONY	APPALTO	APPERILS
APOCARP	APOPHYGE	APPANAGE	APPERTAIN
APOCARPS	APOPHYGES	APPANAGED	APPESTAT
APOCARPY	APOPHYSES	APPANAGES	APPESTATS
APOCOPATE	APOPHYSIS	APPARAT	APPETENCE
APOCOPE	APOPLAST	APPARATS	APPETENCY
APOCOPES	APOPLASTS	APPARATUS	APPETENT
APOCOPIC	APOPLEX	APPAREL	APPETIBLE
APOCRINE	APOPLEXED	APPARELED	APPETISE
APOCRYPHA	APOPLEXES	APPARELS	APPETISED
APOD	APOPLEXY	APPARENCY	APPETISER
APODAL	APOPTOSES	APPARENT	APPETISES
APODE	APOPTOSIS	APPARENTS	APPETITE
APODES	APOPTOTIC	APPARITOR	APPETITES
APODICTIC	APORETIC	APPAY	APPETIZE
APODOSES	APORIA	APPAYD	APPETIZED
APODOSIS	APORIAS	APPAYING	APPETIZER
APODOUS	APORT	APPAYS	APPETIZES
APODS	APOS	APPEACH	APPLAUD
APOENZYME	APOSITIA	APPEACHED	APPLAUDED
APOGAEIC	APOSITIAS	APPEACHES	APPLAUDER
APOGAMIC	APOSITIC	APPEAL	APPLAUDS
APOGAMIES	APOSPORIC	APPEALED	APPLAUSE
APOGAMOUS	APOSPORY	APPEALER	APPLAUSES
APOGAMY	APOSTACY	APPEALERS	APPLE
APOGEAL	APOSTASY	APPEALING	APPLECART
APOGEAN	APOSTATE	APPEALS	APPLEJACK
APOGEE	APOSTATES	APPEAR	APPLES
APOGEES	APOSTATIC	APPEARED	APPLET
APOGEIC	APOSTIL	APPEARER	APPLETS
APOGRAPH	APOSTILLE	APPEARERS	APPLEY
APOGRAPHS	APOSTILS	APPEARING	APPLIABLE
APOLLO	APOSTLE	APPEARS	APPLIANCE
APOLLOS	APOSTLES	APPEASE	APPLICANT
APOLOG	APOSTOLIC	APPEASED	APPLICATE
APOLOGAL	APOTHECE	APPEASER	APPLIED
APOLOGIA	APOTHECES	APPEASERS	APPLIER
APOLOGIAE	APOTHECIA	APPEASES	APPLIERS
APOLOGIAS	APOTHEGM	APPEASING	APPLIES
APOLOGIES	APOTHEGMS	APPEL	APPLIQUE
APOLOGISE	APOTHEM	APPELLANT	APPLIQUED
APOLOGIST	APOTHEMS	APPELLATE	APPLIQUES
APOLOGIZE	APOZEM	APPELLEE	APPLY
APOLOGS	APOZEMS	APPELLEES	APPLYING
APOLOGUE	APP	APPELLOR	APPOINT
APOLOGUES	APPAID	APPELLORS	APPOINTED
APOLOGY	APPAIR	APPELS	APPOINTEE
APOLUNE	APPAIRED	APPEND	APPOINTER
APOLUNES	APPAIRING	APPENDAGE	APPOINTOR
APOMICT	APPAIRS	APPENDANT	APPOINTS
APOMICTIC	APPAL	APPENDED	APPORT
APOMICTS	APPALL	APPENDENT	APPORTION
APOMIXES	APPALLED	APPENDING	APPORTS
APOMIXIS	APPALLING	APPENDIX	APPOSABLE

APPOSE	APRES	AQUABATIC	ARABESQUE
APPOSED	APRICATE	AQUABOARD	ARABIC
APPOSER	APRICATED	AQUACADE	ARABICA
APPOSERS	APRICATES	AQUACADES	ARABICAS
APPOSES	APRICOCK	AQUADROME	ARABICISE
APPOSING	APRICOCKS	AQUAE	ARABICIZE
APPOSITE	APRICOT	AQUAFARM	ARABILITY
APPRAISAL	APRICOTS	AQUAFARMS	ARABIN
APPRAISE	APRIORISM	AQUAFER	ARABINOSE
APPRAISED	APRIORIST	AQUAFERS	ARABINS
APPRAISEE	APRIORITY	AQUALUNG	ARABIS
APPRAISER	APRON	AQUALUNGS	ARABISE
APPRAISES	APRONED	AQUANAUT	ARABISED
APPREHEND	APRONFUL	AQUANAUTS	ARABISES
APPRESS	APRONFULS	AQUAPHOBE	ARABISING
APPRESSED	APRONING	AQUAPLANE	ARABIZE
APPRESSES	APRONLIKE	AQUAPORIN	ARABIZED
APPRISE	APRONS	AQUARELLE	ARABIZES
APPRISED	APROPOS	AQUARIA	ARABIZING
APPRISER	APROTIC	AQUARIAL	ARABLE
APPRISERS	APSARAS	AQUARIAN	ARABLES
APPRISES	APSARASES	AQUARIANS	ARACEOUS
APPRISING	APSE	AQUARIIST	ARACHIS
APPRIZE	APSES	AQUARIST	ARACHISES
APPRIZED	APSIDAL	AQUARISTS	ARACHNID
APPRIZER	APSIDES	AQUARIUM	ARACHNIDS
APPRIZERS	APSIDIOLE	AQUARIUMS	ARACHNOID
APPRIZES	APSIS	AQUAROBIC	ARAGONITE
APPRIZING	APSO	AQUAS	ARAISE
APPRO	APSOS	AQUASHOW	ARAISED
APPROACH	APT	AQUASHOWS	ARAISES
APPROBATE	APTED	AQUATIC	ARAISING
APPROOF	APTER	AQUATICS	ARAK
APPROOFS	APTERAL	AQUATINT	ARAKS
APPROS	APTERIA	AQUATINTA	ARALIA
APPROVAL	APTERISM	AQUATINTS	ARALIAS
APPROVALS	APTERISMS	AQUATONE	ARAME
APPROVE	APTERIUM	AQUATONES	ARAMES
APPROVED	APTEROUS	AQUAVIT	ARAMID
APPROVER	APTERYX	AQUAVITS	ARAMIDS
APPROVERS	APTERYXES	AQUEDUCT	ARANEID
APPROVES	APTEST	AQUEDUCTS	ARANEIDAN
APPROVING	APTING	AQUEOUS	ARANEIDS
APPS	APTITUDE	AQUEOUSLY	ARANEOUS
APPUI	APTITUDES	AQUIFER	ARAPAIMA
APPUIED	APTLY	AQUIFERS	ARAPAIMAS
APPUIS	APTNESS	AQUILEGIA	ARAPONGA
APPULSE	APTNESSES	AQUILINE	ARAPONGAS
APPULSES	APTOTE	AQUILON	ARAPUNGA
APPULSIVE	APTOTES	AQUILONS	ARAPUNGAS
APPUY	APTOTIC	AQUIVER	ARAR
APPUYED	APTS	AR	ARAROBA
APPUYING	APYRASE	ARAARA	ARAROBAS
APPUYS	APYRASES	ARAARAS	ARARS
APRACTIC	APYRETIC	ARABA	ARAUCARIA
APRAXIA	APYREXIA	ARABAS	ARAYSE
APRAXIAS	APYREXIAS	ARABESK	ARAYSED
APRAXIC	AQUA	ARABESKS	ARAYSES

ARAYSING	ARCADIA	ARCHETYPE	ARCTANS
ARB	ARCADIAN	ARCHEUS	ARCTIC
ARBA	ARCADIANS	ARCHFIEND	ARCTICS
ARBALEST	ARCADIAS	ARCHFOE	ARCTIID
ARBALESTS	ARCADING	ARCHFOES	ARCTIIDS
ARBALIST	ARCADINGS	ARCHICARP	ARCTOID
ARBALISTS	ARCANA	ARCHIL	ARCTOPHIL
ARBAS	ARCANAS	ARCHILOWE	ARCUATE
ARBELEST	ARCANE	ARCHILS	ARCUATED
ARBELESTS	ARCANELY	ARCHIMAGE	ARCUATELY
ARBITER	ARCANIST	ARCHINE	ARCUATION
ARBITERS	ARCANISTS	ARCHINES	ARCUS
ARBITRAGE	ARCANUM	ARCHING	ARCUSES
ARBITRAL	ARCANUMS	ARCHINGS	ARD
ARBITRARY	ARCATURE	ARCHITECT	ARDEB
ARBITRATE	ARCATURES	ARCHITYPE	ARDEBS
ARBITRESS	ARCCOS	ARCHIVAL	ARDENCIES
ARBITRIUM	ARCCOSES	ARCHIVE	ARDENCY
ARBLAST	ARCCOSINE	ARCHIVED	ARDENT
ARBLASTER	ARCED	ARCHIVES	ARDENTLY
ARBLASTS	ARCH	ARCHIVING	ARDOR
ARBOR	ARCHAEA	ARCHIVIST	ARDORS
ARBOREAL	ARCHAEAL	ARCHIVOLT	ARDOUR
ARBORED	ARCHAEAN	ARCHLET	ARDOURS
ARBOREOUS	ARCHAEANS	ARCHLETS	ARDRI
ARBORES	ARCHAEI	ARCHLUTE	ARDRIGH
ARBORET	ARCHAEON	ARCHLUTES	ARDRIGHS
ARBORETA	ARCHAEUS	ARCHLY	ARDRIS
ARBORETS	ARCHAIC	ARCHNESS	ARDS
ARBORETUM	ARCHAICAL	ARCHOLOGY	ARDUOUS
ARBORIO	ARCHAISE	ARCHON	ARDUOUSLY
ARBORISE	ARCHAISED	ARCHONS	ARE
ARBORISED	ARCHAISER	ARCHONTIC	AREA
ARBORISES	ARCHAISES	ARCHOSAUR	AREACH
ARBORIST	ARCHAISM	ARCHRIVAL	AREACHED
ARBORISTS	ARCHAISMS	ARCHWAY	AREACHES
ARBORIZE	ARCHAIST	ARCHWAYS	AREACHING
ARBORIZED	ARCHAISTS	ARCHWISE	AREAD
ARBORIZES	ARCHAIZE	ARCIFORM	AREADING
ARBOROUS	ARCHAIZED	ARCING	AREADS
ARBORS	ARCHAIZER	ARCINGS	AREAE
ARBOUR	ARCHAIZES	ARCKED	AREAL
ARBOURED	ARCHANGEL	ARCKING	AREALLY
ARBOURS	ARCHDUCAL	ARCKINGS	AREAR
ARBOVIRAL	ARCHDUCHY	ARCMIN	AREAS
ARBOVIRUS	ARCHDUKE	ARCMINS	AREAWAY
ARBS	ARCHDUKES	ARCO	AREAWAYS
ARBUSCLE	ARCHEAN	ARCOGRAPH	ARECA
ARBUSCLES	ARCHED	ARCOLOGY	ARECAS
ARBUTE	ARCHEI	ARCS	ARECOLINE
ARBUTEAN	ARCHENEMY	ARCSEC	ARED
ARBUTES	ARCHER	ARCSECOND	AREDD
ARBUTUS	ARCHERESS	ARCSECS	AREDE
ARBUTUSES	ARCHERIES	ARCSIN	AREDES
ARC	ARCHERS	ARCSINE	AREDING
ARCADE	ARCHERY	ARCSINES	AREFIED
ARCADED	ARCHES	ARCSINS	AREFIES
ARCADES	ARCHEST	ARCTAN	AREFY

27

AREFYING	ARGENTOUS	ARGYRIAS	ARKED
AREG	ARGENTS	ARGYRITE	ARKING
AREIC	ARGENTUM	ARGYRITES	ARKITE
ARENA	ARGENTUMS	ARHAT	ARKITES
ARENAS	ARGHAN	ARHATS	ARKOSE
ARENATION	ARGHANS	ARHATSHIP	ARKOSES
ARENE	ARGIL	ARHYTHMIA	ARKOSIC
ARENES	ARGILLITE	ARHYTHMIC	ARKS
ARENITE	ARGILS	ARIA	ARLE
ARENITES	ARGINASE	ARIARY	ARLED
ARENITIC	ARGINASES	ARIAS	ARLES
ARENOSE	ARGININE	ARID	ARLING
ARENOUS	ARGININES	ARIDER	ARM
AREOLA	ARGLE	ARIDEST	ARMADA
AREOLAE	ARGLED	ARIDITIES	ARMADAS
AREOLAR	ARGLES	ARIDITY	ARMADILLO
AREOLAS	ARGLING	ARIDLY	ARMAGNAC
AREOLATE	ARGOL	ARIDNESS	ARMAGNACS
AREOLATED	ARGOLS	ARIEL	ARMAMENT
AREOLE	ARGON	ARIELS	ARMAMENTS
AREOLES	ARGONAUT	ARIETTA	ARMATURE
AREOLOGY	ARGONAUTS	ARIETTAS	ARMATURED
AREOMETER	ARGONON	ARIETTE	ARMATURES
AREOSTYLE	ARGONONS	ARIETTES	ARMBAND
AREPA	ARGONS	ARIGHT	ARMBANDS
AREPAS	ARGOSIES	ARIKI	ARMCHAIR
ARERE	ARGOSY	ARIL	ARMCHAIRS
ARES	ARGOT	ARILED	ARMED
ARET	ARGOTIC	ARILLARY	ARMER
ARETE	ARGOTS	ARILLATE	ARMERS
ARETES	ARGUABLE	ARILLATED	ARMET
ARETHUSA	ARGUABLY	ARILLI	ARMETS
ARETHUSAS	ARGUE	ARILLODE	ARMFUL
ARETS	ARGUED	ARILLODES	ARMFULS
ARETT	ARGUER	ARILLOID	ARMGAUNT
ARETTED	ARGUERS	ARILLUS	ARMHOLE
ARETTING	ARGUES	ARILS	ARMHOLES
ARETTS	ARGUFIED	ARIOSE	ARMIES
AREW	ARGUFIER	ARIOSI	ARMIGER
ARF	ARGUFIERS	ARIOSO	ARMIGERAL
ARFS	ARGUFIES	ARIOSOS	ARMIGERO
ARGAL	ARGUFY	ARIOT	ARMIGEROS
ARGALA	ARGUFYING	ARIPPLE	ARMIGERS
ARGALAS	ARGUING	ARIS	ARMIL
ARGALI	ARGULI	ARISE	ARMILLA
ARGALIS	ARGULUS	ARISEN	ARMILLAE
ARGALS	ARGUMENT	ARISES	ARMILLARY
ARGAN	ARGUMENTA	ARISH	ARMILLAS
ARGAND	ARGUMENTS	ARISHES	ARMILS
ARGANDS	ARGUS	ARISING	ARMING
ARGANS	ARGUSES	ARISTA	ARMINGS
ARGEMONE	ARGUTE	ARISTAE	ARMISTICE
ARGEMONES	ARGUTELY	ARISTAS	ARMLESS
ARGENT	ARGYLE	ARISTATE	ARMLET
ARGENTAL	ARGYLES	ARISTO	ARMLETS
ARGENTIC	ARGYLL	ARISTOS	ARMLIKE
ARGENTINE	ARGYLLS	ARISTOTLE	ARMLOAD
ARGENTITE	ARGYRIA	ARK	ARMLOADS

ARMLOCK	AROIDS	ARRASENE	ARRIVING
ARMLOCKED	AROINT	ARRASENES	ARRIVISME
ARMLOCKS	AROINTED	ARRASES	ARRIVISTE
ARMOIRE	AROINTING	ARRAUGHT	ARROBA
ARMOIRES	AROINTS	ARRAY	ARROBAS
ARMONICA	AROLLA	ARRAYAL	ARROGANCE
ARMONICAS	AROLLAS	ARRAYALS	ARROGANCY
ARMOR	AROMA	ARRAYED	ARROGANT
ARMORED	AROMAS	ARRAYER	ARROGATE
ARMORER	AROMATASE	ARRAYERS	ARROGATED
ARMORERS	AROMATIC	ARRAYING	ARROGATES
ARMORIAL	AROMATICS	ARRAYMENT	ARROGATOR
ARMORIALS	AROMATISE	ARRAYS	ARROW
ARMORIES	AROMATIZE	ARREAR	ARROWED
ARMORING	AROSE	ARREARAGE	ARROWHEAD
ARMORIST	AROUND	ARREARS	ARROWING
ARMORISTS	AROUSABLE	ARRECT	ARROWLESS
ARMORLESS	AROUSAL	ARREEDE	ARROWLIKE
ARMORS	AROUSALS	ARREEDES	ARROWROOT
ARMORY	AROUSE	ARREEDING	ARROWS
ARMOUR	AROUSED	ARREST	ARROWWOOD
ARMOURED	AROUSER	ARRESTANT	ARROWWORM
ARMOURER	AROUSERS	ARRESTED	ARROWY
ARMOURERS	AROUSES	ARRESTEE	ARROYO
ARMOURIES	AROUSING	ARRESTEES	ARROYOS
ARMOURING	AROW	ARRESTER	ARS
ARMOURS	AROYNT	ARRESTERS	ARSE
ARMOURY	AROYNTED	ARRESTING	ARSED
ARMOZEEN	AROYNTING	ARRESTIVE	ARSEHOLE
ARMOZEENS	AROYNTS	ARRESTOR	ARSEHOLES
ARMOZINE	ARPA	ARRESTORS	ARSENAL
ARMOZINES	ARPAS	ARRESTS	ARSENALS
ARMPIT	ARPEGGIO	ARRET	ARSENATE
ARMPITS	ARPEGGIOS	ARRETS	ARSENATES
ARMREST	ARPEN	ARRHIZAL	ARSENIATE
ARMRESTS	ARPENS	ARRIAGE	ARSENIC
ARMS	ARPENT	ARRIAGES	ARSENICAL
ARMSFUL	ARPENTS	ARRIBA	ARSENICS
ARMURE	ARPILLERA	ARRIDE	ARSENIDE
ARMURES	ARQUEBUS	ARRIDED	ARSENIDES
ARMY	ARRACACHA	ARRIDES	ARSENIOUS
ARMYWORM	ARRACK	ARRIDING	ARSENITE
ARMYWORMS	ARRACKS	ARRIERE	ARSENITES
ARNA	ARRAH	ARRIERO	ARSENO
ARNAS	ARRAIGN	ARRIEROS	ARSENOUS
ARNATTO	ARRAIGNED	ARRIS	ARSES
ARNATTOS	ARRAIGNER	ARRISES	ARSEY
ARNICA	ARRAIGNS	ARRISH	ARSHEEN
ARNICAS	ARRANGE	ARRISHES	ARSHEENS
ARNOTTO	ARRANGED	ARRIVAL	ARSHIN
ARNOTTOS	ARRANGER	ARRIVALS	ARSHINE
ARNUT	ARRANGERS	ARRIVANCE	ARSHINES
ARNUTS	ARRANGES	ARRIVANCY	ARSHINS
AROBA	ARRANGING	ARRIVE	ARSIER
AROBAS	ARRANT	ARRIVED	ARSIEST
AROHA	ARRANTLY	ARRIVER	ARSINE
AROHAS	ARRAS	ARRIVERS	ARSINES
AROID	ARRASED	ARRIVES	ARSING

ARSINO	ARTISTES	ASCENDANT	ASEXUALLY
ARSIS	ARTISTIC	ASCENDED	ASH
ARSON	ARTISTRY	ASCENDENT	ASHAKE
ARSONIST	ARTISTS	ASCENDER	ASHAME
ARSONISTS	ARTLESS	ASCENDERS	ASHAMED
ARSONITE	ARTLESSLY	ASCENDEUR	ASHAMEDLY
ARSONITES	ARTS	ASCENDING	ASHAMES
ARSONOUS	ARTSIER	ASCENDS	ASHAMING
ARSONS	ARTSIES	ASCENSION	ASHCAKE
ARSY	ARTSIEST	ASCENSIVE	ASHCAKES
ART	ARTSINESS	ASCENT	ASHCAN
ARTAL	ARTSMAN	ASCENTS	ASHCANS
ARTEFACT	ARTSMEN	ASCERTAIN	ASHED
ARTEFACTS	ARTSY	ASCESES	ASHEN
ARTEL	ARTWORK	ASCESIS	ASHERIES
ARTELS	ARTWORKS	ASCETIC	ASHERY
ARTEMISIA	ARTY	ASCETICAL	ASHES
ARTERIAL	ARUGOLA	ASCETICS	ASHET
ARTERIALS	ARUGOLAS	ASCI	ASHETS
ARTERIES	ARUGULA	ASCIAN	ASHFALL
ARTERIOLE	ARUGULAS	ASCIANS	ASHFALLS
ARTERITIS	ARUHE	ASCIDIA	ASHIER
ARTERY	ARUM	ASCIDIAN	ASHIEST
ARTESIAN	ARUMS	ASCIDIANS	ASHINE
ARTFUL	ARUSPEX	ASCIDIATE	ASHINESS
ARTFULLY	ARUSPICES	ASCIDIUM	ASHING
ARTHRITIC	ARVAL	ASCITES	ASHIVER
ARTHRITIS	ARVICOLE	ASCITIC	ASHKEY
ARTHRODIA	ARVICOLES	ASCITICAL	ASHKEYS
ARTHROPOD	ARVO	ASCLEPIAD	ASHLAR
ARTHROSES	ARVOS	ASCLEPIAS	ASHLARED
ARTHROSIS	ARY	ASCOCARP	ASHLARING
ARTI	ARYBALLOS	ASCOCARPS	ASHLARS
ARTIC	ARYL	ASCOGONIA	ASHLER
ARTICHOKE	ARYLS	ASCONCE	ASHLERED
ARTICLE	ARYTENOID	ASCORBATE	ASHLERING
ARTICLED	ARYTHMIA	ASCORBIC	ASHLERS
ARTICLES	ARYTHMIAS	ASCOSPORE	ASHLESS
ARTICLING	ARYTHMIC	ASCOT	ASHMAN
ARTICS	AS	ASCOTS	ASHMEN
ARTICULAR	ASAFETIDA	ASCRIBE	ASHORE
ARTIER	ASANA	ASCRIBED	ASHPLANT
ARTIES	ASANAS	ASCRIBES	ASHPLANTS
ARTIEST	ASAR	ASCRIBING	ASHRAF
ARTIFACT	ASARUM	ASCUS	ASHRAM
ARTIFACTS	ASARUMS	ASDIC	ASHRAMA
ARTIFICE	ASBESTIC	ASDICS	ASHRAMAS
ARTIFICER	ASBESTINE	ASEA	ASHRAMITE
ARTIFICES	ASBESTOS	ASEISMIC	ASHRAMS
ARTILLERY	ASBESTOUS	ASEITIES	ASHTRAY
ARTILY	ASBESTUS	ASEITY	ASHTRAYS
ARTINESS	ASCARED	ASEPALOUS	ASHY
ARTIS	ASCARID	ASEPSES	ASIAGO
ARTISAN	ASCARIDES	ASEPSIS	ASIAGOS
ARTISANAL	ASCARIDS	ASEPTATE	ASIDE
ARTISANS	ASCARIS	ASEPTIC	ASIDES
ARTIST	ASCAUNT	ASEPTICS	ASINICO
ARTISTE	ASCEND	ASEXUAL	ASINICOS

ASININE	ASPERGER	ASPIRIN	ASSEGAIED
ASININELY	ASPERGERS	ASPIRING	ASSEGAIS
ASININITY	ASPERGES	ASPIRINS	ASSEMBLE
ASK	ASPERGILL	ASPIS	ASSEMBLED
ASKANCE	ASPERGING	ASPISES	ASSEMBLER
ASKANCED	ASPERITY	ASPISH	ASSEMBLES
ASKANCES	ASPERMIA	ASPLENIUM	ASSEMBLY
ASKANCING	ASPERMIAS	ASPORT	ASSENT
ASKANT	ASPEROUS	ASPORTED	ASSENTED
ASKANTED	ASPERS	ASPORTING	ASSENTER
ASKANTING	ASPERSE	ASPORTS	ASSENTERS
ASKANTS	ASPERSED	ASPOUT	ASSENTING
ASKARI	ASPERSER	ASPRAWL	ASSENTIVE
ASKARIS	ASPERSERS	ASPREAD	ASSENTOR
ASKED	ASPERSES	ASPRO	ASSENTORS
ASKER	ASPERSING	ASPROS	ASSENTS
ASKERS	ASPERSION	ASPROUT	ASSERT
ASKESES	ASPERSIVE	ASPS	ASSERTED
ASKESIS	ASPERSOIR	ASQUAT	ASSERTER
ASKEW	ASPERSOR	ASQUINT	ASSERTERS
ASKEWNESS	ASPERSORS	ASRAMA	ASSERTING
ASKING	ASPERSORY	ASRAMAS	ASSERTION
ASKINGS	ASPHALT	ASS	ASSERTIVE
ASKLENT	ASPHALTED	ASSAGAI	ASSERTOR
ASKOI	ASPHALTER	ASSAGAIED	ASSERTORS
ASKOS	ASPHALTIC	ASSAGAIS	ASSERTORY
ASKS	ASPHALTS	ASSAI	ASSERTS
ASLAKE	ASPHALTUM	ASSAIL	ASSES
ASLAKED	ASPHERIC	ASSAILANT	ASSESS
ASLAKES	ASPHODEL	ASSAILED	ASSESSED
ASLAKING	ASPHODELS	ASSAILER	ASSESSES
ASLANT	ASPHYXIA	ASSAILERS	ASSESSING
ASLEEP	ASPHYXIAL	ASSAILING	ASSESSOR
ASLOPE	ASPHYXIAS	ASSAILS	ASSESSORS
ASLOSH	ASPHYXIES	ASSAIS	ASSET
ASMEAR	ASPHYXY	ASSAM	ASSETLESS
ASMOULDER	ASPIC	ASSAMS	ASSETS
ASOCIAL	ASPICK	ASSART	ASSEVER
ASOCIALS	ASPICKS	ASSARTED	ASSEVERED
ASP	ASPICS	ASSARTING	ASSEVERS
ASPARAGUS	ASPIDIA	ASSARTS	ASSEZ
ASPARKLE	ASPIDIOID	ASSASSIN	ASSHOLE
ASPARTAME	ASPIDIUM	ASSASSINS	ASSHOLES
ASPARTATE	ASPINE	ASSAULT	ASSIDUITY
ASPARTIC	ASPINES	ASSAULTED	ASSIDUOUS
ASPECT	ASPIRANT	ASSAULTER	ASSIEGE
ASPECTED	ASPIRANTS	ASSAULTS	ASSIEGED
ASPECTING	ASPIRATA	ASSAY	ASSIEGES
ASPECTS	ASPIRATAE	ASSAYABLE	ASSIEGING
ASPECTUAL	ASPIRATE	ASSAYED	ASSIENTO
ASPEN	ASPIRATED	ASSAYER	ASSIENTOS
ASPENS	ASPIRATES	ASSAYERS	ASSIGN
ASPER	ASPIRATOR	ASSAYING	ASSIGNAT
ASPERATE	ASPIRE	ASSAYINGS	ASSIGNATS
ASPERATED	ASPIRED	ASSAYS	ASSIGNED
ASPERATES	ASPIRER	ASSEGAAI	ASSIGNEE
ASPERGE	ASPIRERS	ASSEGAAIS	ASSIGNEES
ASPERGED	ASPIRES	ASSEGAI	ASSIGNER

ASSIGNERS	ASSUMEDLY	ASTERT	ASTROFELL
ASSIGNING	ASSUMER	ASTERTED	ASTROID
ASSIGNOR	ASSUMERS	ASTERTING	ASTROIDS
ASSIGNORS	ASSUMES	ASTERTS	ASTROLABE
ASSIGNS	ASSUMING	ASTHENIA	ASTROLOGY
ASSIST	ASSUMINGS	ASTHENIAS	ASTRONAUT
ASSISTANT	ASSUMPSIT	ASTHENIC	ASTRONOMY
ASSISTED	ASSURABLE	ASTHENICS	ASTROPHEL
ASSISTER	ASSURANCE	ASTHENIES	ASTRUT
ASSISTERS	ASSURE	ASTHENY	ASTUCIOUS
ASSISTING	ASSURED	ASTHMA	ASTUCITY
ASSISTIVE	ASSUREDLY	ASTHMAS	ASTUN
ASSISTOR	ASSUREDS	ASTHMATIC	ASTUNNED
ASSISTORS	ASSURER	ASTHORE	ASTUNNING
ASSISTS	ASSURERS	ASTHORES	ASTUNS
ASSIZE	ASSURES	ASTICHOUS	ASTUTE
ASSIZED	ASSURGENT	ASTIGMIA	ASTUTELY
ASSIZER	ASSURING	ASTIGMIAS	ASTUTER
ASSIZERS	ASSUROR	ASTILBE	ASTUTEST
ASSIZES	ASSURORS	ASTILBES	ASTYLAR
ASSIZING	ASSWAGE	ASTIR	ASUDDEN
ASSLIKE	ASSWAGED	ASTOMATAL	ASUNDER
ASSOCIATE	ASSWAGES	ASTOMOUS	ASWARM
ASSOIL	ASSWAGING	ASTONE	ASWAY
ASSOILED	ASTABLE	ASTONED	ASWIM
ASSOILING	ASTARE	ASTONES	ASWING
ASSOILS	ASTART	ASTONIED	ASWIRL
ASSOILZIE	ASTARTED	ASTONIES	ASWOON
ASSONANCE	ASTARTING	ASTONING	ASYLA
ASSONANT	ASTARTS	ASTONISH	ASYLLABIC
ASSONANTS	ASTASIA	ASTONY	ASYLUM
ASSONATE	ASTASIAS	ASTONYING	ASYLUMS
ASSONATED	ASTATIC	ASTOOP	ASYMMETRY
ASSONATES	ASTATIDE	ASTOUND	ASYMPTOTE
ASSORT	ASTATIDES	ASTOUNDED	ASYNAPSES
ASSORTED	ASTATINE	ASTOUNDS	ASYNAPSIS
ASSORTER	ASTATINES	ASTRACHAN	ASYNDETA
ASSORTERS	ASTATKI	ASTRADDLE	ASYNDETIC
ASSORTING	ASTATKIS	ASTRAGAL	ASYNDETON
ASSORTIVE	ASTEISM	ASTRAGALI	ASYNERGIA
ASSORTS	ASTEISMS	ASTRAGALS	ASYNERGY
ASSOT	ASTELIC	ASTRAKHAN	ASYSTOLE
ASSOTS	ASTELIES	ASTRAL	ASYSTOLES
ASSOTT	ASTELY	ASTRALLY	ASYSTOLIC
ASSOTTED	ASTER	ASTRALS	AT
ASSOTTING	ASTERIA	ASTRAND	ATAATA
ASSUAGE	ASTERIAS	ASTRANTIA	ATAATAS
ASSUAGED	ASTERID	ASTRAY	ATABAL
ASSUAGER	ASTERIDS	ASTRICT	ATABALS
ASSUAGERS	ASTERISK	ASTRICTED	ATABEG
ASSUAGES	ASTERISKS	ASTRICTS	ATABEGS
ASSUAGING	ASTERISM	ASTRIDE	ATABEK
ASSUASIVE	ASTERISMS	ASTRINGE	ATABEKS
ASSUETUDE	ASTERN	ASTRINGED	ATABRIN
ASSUMABLE	ASTERNAL	ASTRINGER	ATABRINE
ASSUMABLY	ASTEROID	ASTRINGES	ATABRINES
ASSUME	ASTEROIDS	ASTROCYTE	ATABRINS
ASSUMED	ASTERS	ASTRODOME	ATACAMITE

ATACTIC	ATHEISTIC	ATMAN	ATONED
ATAGHAN	ATHEISTS	ATMANS	ATONEMENT
ATAGHANS	ATHEIZE	ATMAS	ATONER
ATALAYA	ATHEIZED	ATMOLOGY	ATONERS
ATALAYAS	ATHEIZES	ATMOLYSE	ATONES
ATAMAN	ATHEIZING	ATMOLYSED	ATONIA
ATAMANS	ATHELING	ATMOLYSES	ATONIAS
ATAMASCO	ATHELINGS	ATMOLYSIS	ATONIC
ATAMASCOS	ATHEMATIC	ATMOLYZE	ATONICITY
ATAP	ATHENAEUM	ATMOLYZED	ATONICS
ATAPS	ATHENEUM	ATMOLYZES	ATONIES
ATARACTIC	ATHENEUMS	ATMOMETER	ATONING
ATARAXIA	ATHEOLOGY	ATMOMETRY	ATONINGLY
ATARAXIAS	ATHEOUS	ATOC	ATONY
ATARAXIC	ATHERINE	ATOCIA	ATOP
ATARAXICS	ATHERINES	ATOCIAS	ATOPIC
ATARAXIES	ATHEROMA	ATOCS	ATOPIES
ATARAXY	ATHEROMAS	ATOK	ATOPY
ATAVIC	ATHETESES	ATOKAL	ATRAMENT
ATAVISM	ATHETESIS	ATOKE	ATRAMENTS
ATAVISMS	ATHETISE	ATOKES	ATRAZINE
ATAVIST	ATHETISED	ATOKOUS	ATRAZINES
ATAVISTIC	ATHETISES	ATOKS	ATREMBLE
ATAVISTS	ATHETIZE	ATOLL	ATRESIA
ATAXIA	ATHETIZED	ATOLLS	ATRESIAS
ATAXIAS	ATHETIZES	ATOM	ATRESIC
ATAXIC	ATHETOID	ATOMIC	ATRETIC
ATAXICS	ATHETOSES	ATOMICAL	ATRIA
ATAXIES	ATHETOSIC	ATOMICITY	ATRIAL
ATAXY	ATHETOSIS	ATOMICS	ATRIP
ATCHIEVE	ATHETOTIC	ATOMIES	ATRIUM
ATCHIEVED	ATHIRST	ATOMISE	ATRIUMS
ATCHIEVES	ATHLETA	ATOMISED	ATROCIOUS
ATE	ATHLETAS	ATOMISER	ATROCITY
ATEBRIN	ATHLETE	ATOMISERS	ATROPHIA
ATEBRINS	ATHLETES	ATOMISES	ATROPHIAS
ATECHNIC	ATHLETIC	ATOMISING	ATROPHIC
ATELIC	ATHLETICS	ATOMISM	ATROPHIED
ATELIER	ATHODYD	ATOMISMS	ATROPHIES
ATELIERS	ATHODYDS	ATOMIST	ATROPHY
ATEMOYA	ATHRILL	ATOMISTIC	ATROPIA
ATEMOYAS	ATHROB	ATOMISTS	ATROPIAS
ATEMPORAL	ATHROCYTE	ATOMIZE	ATROPIN
ATENOLOL	ATHWART	ATOMIZED	ATROPINE
ATENOLOLS	ATIGI	ATOMIZER	ATROPINES
ATES	ATIGIS	ATOMIZERS	ATROPINS
ATHAME	ATILT	ATOMIZES	ATROPISM
ATHAMES	ATIMIES	ATOMIZING	ATROPISMS
ATHANASY	ATIMY	ATOMS	ATROPOUS
ATHANOR	ATINGLE	ATOMY	ATT
ATHANORS	ATISHOO	ATONABLE	ATTABOY
ATHEISE	ATISHOOS	ATONAL	ATTACH
ATHEISED	ATLANTES	ATONALISM	ATTACHE
ATHEISES	ATLAS	ATONALIST	ATTACHED
ATHEISING	ATLASES	ATONALITY	ATTACHER
ATHEISM	ATLATL	ATONALLY	ATTACHERS
ATHEISMS	ATLATLS	ATONE	ATTACHES
ATHEIST	ATMA	ATONEABLE	ATTACHING

ATTACK	ATTESTING	ATTUENT	AUDING
ATTACKED	ATTESTOR	ATTUITE	AUDINGS
ATTACKER	ATTESTORS	ATTUITED	AUDIO
ATTACKERS	ATTESTS	ATTUITES	AUDIOBOOK
ATTACKING	ATTIC	ATTUITING	AUDIOGRAM
ATTACKMAN	ATTICISE	ATTUITION	AUDIOLOGY
ATTACKMEN	ATTICISED	ATTUITIVE	AUDIOPHIL
ATTACKS	ATTICISES	ATTUNE	AUDIOS
ATTAGIRL	ATTICISM	ATTUNED	AUDIOTAPE
ATTAIN	ATTICISMS	ATTUNES	AUDIPHONE
ATTAINDER	ATTICIST	ATTUNING	AUDIT
ATTAINED	ATTICISTS	ATUA	AUDITABLE
ATTAINER	ATTICIZE	ATUAS	AUDITED
ATTAINERS	ATTICIZED	ATWAIN	AUDITEE
ATTAINING	ATTICIZES	ATWEEL	AUDITEES
ATTAINS	ATTICS	ATWEEN	AUDITING
ATTAINT	ATTIRE	ATWITTER	AUDITION
ATTAINTED	ATTIRED	ATWIXT	AUDITIONS
ATTAINTS	ATTIRES	ATYPIC	AUDITIVE
ATTAP	ATTIRING	ATYPICAL	AUDITIVES
ATTAPS	ATTIRINGS	AUA	AUDITOR
ATTAR	ATTITUDE	AUBADE	AUDITORIA
ATTARS	ATTITUDES	AUBADES	AUDITORS
ATTASK	ATTOLASER	AUBERGE	AUDITORY
ATTASKED	ATTOLLENS	AUBERGES	AUDITRESS
ATTASKING	ATTOLLENT	AUBERGINE	AUDITS
ATTASKS	ATTONCE	AUBRETIA	AUE
ATTASKT	ATTONE	AUBRETIAS	AUF
ATTEMPER	ATTONES	AUBRIETA	AUFGABE
ATTEMPERS	ATTORN	AUBRIETAS	AUFGABES
ATTEMPT	ATTORNED	AUBRIETAS	AUFS
ATTEMPTED	ATTORNEY	AUBRIETIA	AUGEND
ATTEMPTER	ATTORNEYS	AUBURN	AUGENDS
ATTEMPTS	ATTORNING	AUBURNS	AUGER
ATTEND	ATTORNS	AUCEPS	AUGERS
ATTENDANT	ATTRACT	AUCEPSES	AUGHT
ATTENDED	ATTRACTED	AUCTION	AUGHTS
ATTENDEE	ATTRACTER	AUCTIONED	AUGITE
ATTENDEES	ATTRACTOR	AUCTIONS	AUGITES
ATTENDER	ATTRACTS	AUCTORIAL	AUGITIC
ATTENDERS	ATTRAHENS	AUCUBA	AUGMENT
ATTENDING	ATTRAHENT	AUCUBAS	AUGMENTED
ATTENDS	ATTRAP	AUDACIOUS	AUGMENTER
ATTENT	ATTRAPPED	AUDACITY	AUGMENTOR
ATTENTAT	ATTRAPS	AUDAD	AUGMENTS
ATTENTATS	ATTRIBUTE	AUDADS	AUGUR
ATTENTION	ATTRIST	AUDIAL	AUGURAL
ATTENTIVE	ATTRISTED	AUDIBLE	AUGURED
ATTENTS	ATTRISTS	AUDIBLED	AUGURER
ATTENUANT	ATTRIT	AUDIBLES	AUGURERS
ATTENUATE	ATTRITE	AUDIBLING	AUGURIES
ATTERCOP	ATTRITED	AUDIBLY	AUGURING
ATTERCOPS	ATTRITES	AUDIENCE	AUGURS
ATTEST	ATTRITING	AUDIENCES	AUGURSHIP
ATTESTANT	ATTRITION	AUDIENCIA	AUGURY
ATTESTED	ATTRITIVE	AUDIENT	AUGUST
ATTESTER	ATTRITS	AUDIENTS	AUGUSTE
ATTESTERS	ATTRITTED	AUDILE	AUGUSTER
		AUDILES	

AUGUSTES	AUREITIES	AUSTRALES	AUTOCRIME
AUGUSTEST	AUREITY	AUSTRALIS	AUTOCRINE
AUGUSTLY	AURELIA	AUSTRALS	AUTOCROSS
AUGUSTS	AURELIAN	AUSUBO	AUTOCUE
AUK	AURELIANS	AUSUBOS	AUTOCUES
AUKLET	AURELIAS	AUTACOID	AUTOCUTIE
AUKLETS	AUREOLA	AUTACOIDS	AUTOCYCLE
AUKS	AUREOLAE	AUTARCH	AUTODYNE
AULA	AUREOLAS	AUTARCHIC	AUTODYNES
AULARIAN	AUREOLE	AUTARCHS	AUTOECISM
AULARIANS	AUREOLED	AUTARCHY	AUTOED
AULAS	AUREOLES	AUTARKIC	AUTOFLARE
AULD	AUREOLING	AUTARKIES	AUTOFOCUS
AULDER	AURES	AUTARKIST	AUTOGAMIC
AULDEST	AUREUS	AUTARKY	AUTOGAMY
AULIC	AURIC	AUTECIOUS	AUTOGENIC
AULNAGE	AURICLE	AUTECISM	AUTOGENY
AULNAGER	AURICLED	AUTECISMS	AUTOGIRO
AULNAGERS	AURICLES	AUTEUR	AUTOGIROS
AULNAGES	AURICULA	AUTEURISM	AUTOGRAFT
AULOI	AURICULAE	AUTEURIST	AUTOGRAPH
AULOS	AURICULAR	AUTEURS	AUTOGUIDE
AUMAIL	AURICULAS	AUTHENTIC	AUTOGYRO
AUMAILED	AURIFIED	AUTHOR	AUTOGYROS
AUMAILING	AURIFIES	AUTHORED	AUTOHARP
AUMAILS	AURIFORM	AUTHORESS	AUTOHARPS
AUMBRIES	AURIFY	AUTHORIAL	AUTOICOUS
AUMBRY	AURIFYING	AUTHORING	AUTOING
AUMIL	AURIS	AUTHORISE	AUTOLATRY
AUMILS	AURISCOPE	AUTHORISH	AUTOLOGY
AUNE	AURIST	AUTHORISM	AUTOLYSE
AUNES	AURISTS	AUTHORITY	AUTOLYSED
AUNT	AUROCHS	AUTHORIZE	AUTOLYSES
AUNTER	AUROCHSES	AUTHORS	AUTOLYSIN
AUNTERS	AURORA	AUTISM	AUTOLYSIS
AUNTHOOD	AURORAE	AUTISMS	AUTOLYTIC
AUNTHOODS	AURORAL	AUTIST	AUTOLYZE
AUNTIE	AURORALLY	AUTISTIC	AUTOLYZED
AUNTIES	AURORAS	AUTISTICS	AUTOLYZES
AUNTLIER	AUROREAN	AUTISTS	AUTOMAKER
AUNTLIEST	AUROUS	AUTO	AUTOMAN
AUNTLIKE	AURUM	AUTOBAHN	AUTOMAT
AUNTLY	AURUMS	AUTOBAHNS	AUTOMATA
AUNTS	AUSFORM	AUTOBUS	AUTOMATE
AUNTY	AUSFORMED	AUTOBUSES	AUTOMATED
AURA	AUSFORMS	AUTOCADE	AUTOMATES
AURAE	AUSLANDER	AUTOCADES	AUTOMATIC
AURAL	AUSPEX	AUTOCAR	AUTOMATON
AURALITY	AUSPICATE	AUTOCARP	AUTOMATS
AURALLY	AUSPICE	AUTOCARPS	AUTOMEN
AURAR	AUSPICES	AUTOCARS	AUTOMETER
AURAS	AUSTENITE	AUTOCIDAL	AUTONOMIC
AURATE	AUSTERE	AUTOCLAVE	AUTONOMY
AURATED	AUSTERELY	AUTOCOID	AUTONYM
AURATES	AUSTERER	AUTOCOIDS	AUTONYMS
AUREATE	AUSTEREST	AUTOCRACY	AUTOPEN
AUREATELY	AUSTERITY	AUTOCRAT	AUTOPENS
AUREI	AUSTRAL	AUTOCRATS	AUTOPHAGY

AUTOPHOBY	AUXOSPORE	AVENTRING	AVIATRESS
AUTOPHONY	AUXOTONIC	AVENTURE	AVIATRICE
AUTOPHYTE	AUXOTROPH	AVENTURES	AVIATRIX
AUTOPILOT	AVA	AVENTURIN	AVICULAR
AUTOPISTA	AVADAVAT	AVENUE	AVID
AUTOPOINT	AVADAVATS	AVENUES	AVIDER
AUTOPSIA	AVAIL	AVER	AVIDEST
AUTOPSIAS	AVAILABLE	AVERAGE	AVIDIN
AUTOPSIC	AVAILABLY	AVERAGED	AVIDINS
AUTOPSIED	AVAILE	AVERAGELY	AVIDITIES
AUTOPSIES	AVAILED	AVERAGES	AVIDITY
AUTOPSIST	AVAILES	AVERAGING	AVIDLY
AUTOPSY	AVAILFUL	AVERMENT	AVIDNESS
AUTOPTIC	AVAILING	AVERMENTS	AVIETTE
AUTOPUT	AVAILS	AVERRABLE	AVIETTES
AUTOPUTS	AVAL	AVERRED	AVIFAUNA
AUTOROUTE	AVALANCHE	AVERRING	AVIFAUNAE
AUTOS	AVALE	AVERS	AVIFAUNAL
AUTOSCOPY	AVALED	AVERSE	AVIFAUNAS
AUTOSOMAL	AVALES	AVERSELY	AVIFORM
AUTOSOME	AVALING	AVERSION	AVIGATOR
AUTOSOMES	AVANT	AVERSIONS	AVIGATORS
AUTOSPORE	AVANTI	AVERSIVE	AVINE
AUTOTELIC	AVANTIST	AVERSIVES	AVION
AUTOTIMER	AVANTISTS	AVERT	AVIONIC
AUTOTOMIC	AVARICE	AVERTABLE	AVIONICS
AUTOTOMY	AVARICES	AVERTED	AVIONS
AUTOTOXIC	AVAS	AVERTEDLY	AVIRULENT
AUTOTOXIN	AVASCULAR	AVERTER	AVISANDUM
AUTOTROPH	AVAST	AVERTERS	AVISE
AUTOTUNE	AVATAR	AVERTIBLE	AVISED
AUTOTUNES	AVATARS	AVERTING	AVISEMENT
AUTOTYPE	AVAUNT	AVERTS	AVISES
AUTOTYPED	AVAUNTED	AVES	AVISING
AUTOTYPES	AVAUNTING	AVGAS	AVISO
AUTOTYPIC	AVAUNTS	AVGASES	AVISOS
AUTOTYPY	AVE	AVGASSES	AVITAL
AUTOVAC	AVEL	AVIAN	AVIZANDUM
AUTOVACS	AVELLAN	AVIANISE	AVIZE
AUTUMN	AVELLANE	AVIANISED	AVIZED
AUTUMNAL	AVELS	AVIANISES	AVIZEFULL
AUTUMNS	AVENGE	AVIANIZE	AVIZES
AUTUMNY	AVENGED	AVIANIZED	AVIZING
AUTUNITE	AVENGEFUL	AVIANIZES	AVO
AUTUNITES	AVENGER	AVIANS	AVOCADO
AUXESES	AVENGERS	AVIARIES	AVOCADOES
AUXESIS	AVENGES	AVIARIST	AVOCADOS
AUXETIC	AVENGING	AVIARISTS	AVOCATION
AUXETICS	AVENIR	AVIARY	AVOCET
AUXILIAR	AVENIRS	AVIATE	AVOCETS
AUXILIARS	AVENS	AVIATED	AVODIRE
AUXILIARY	AVENSES	AVIATES	AVODIRES
AUXIN	AVENTAIL	AVIATIC	AVOID
AUXINIC	AVENTAILE	AVIATING	AVOIDABLE
AUXINS	AVENTAILS	AVIATION	AVOIDABLY
AUXOCYTE	AVENTRE	AVIATIONS	AVOIDANCE
AUXOCYTES	AVENTRED	AVIATOR	AVOIDANT
AUXOMETER	AVENTRES	AVIATORS	AVOIDED

AVOIDER
AVOIDERS
AVOIDING
AVOIDS
AVOISION
AVOISIONS
AVOS
AVOSET
AVOSETS
AVOUCH
AVOUCHED
AVOUCHER
AVOUCHERS
AVOUCHES
AVOUCHING
AVOURE
AVOURES
AVOUTERER
AVOUTRER
AVOUTRERS
AVOUTRIES
AVOUTRY
AVOW
AVOWABLE
AVOWABLY
AVOWAL
AVOWALS
AVOWED
AVOWEDLY
AVOWER
AVOWERS
AVOWING
AVOWRIES
AVOWRY
AVOWS
AVOYER
AVOYERS
AVRUGA
AVRUGAS
AVULSE
AVULSED
AVULSES
AVULSING
AVULSION
AVULSIONS
AVUNCULAR
AVYZE
AVYZED
AVYZES
AVYZING
AW
AWA
AWAIT
AWAITED
AWAITER
AWAITERS
AWAITING
AWAITS

AWAKE
AWAKED
AWAKEN
AWAKENED
AWAKENER
AWAKENERS
AWAKENING
AWAKENS
AWAKES
AWAKING
AWAKINGS
AWANTING
AWARD
AWARDABLE
AWARDED
AWARDEE
AWARDEES
AWARDER
AWARDERS
AWARDING
AWARDS
AWARE
AWARENESS
AWARER
AWAREST
AWARN
AWARNED
AWARNING
AWARNS
AWASH
AWATCH
AWATO
AWAVE
AWAY
AWAYDAY
AWAYDAYS
AWAYES
AWAYNESS
AWAYS
AWDL
AWDLS
AWE
AWEARIED
AWEARY
AWEATHER
AWED
AWEE
AWEEL
AWEIGH
AWEING
AWELESS
AWES
AWESOME
AWESOMELY
AWESTRIKE
AWESTRUCK
AWETO
AWETOS

AWFUL
AWFULLER
AWFULLEST
AWFULLY
AWFULNESS
AWHAPE
AWHAPED
AWHAPES
AWHAPING
AWHATO
AWHEEL
AWHEELS
AWHETO
AWHILE
AWHIRL
AWING
AWKWARD
AWKWARDER
AWKWARDLY
AWL
AWLBIRD
AWLBIRDS
AWLESS
AWLS
AWLWORT
AWLWORTS
AWMOUS
AWMRIE
AWMRIES
AWMRY
AWN
AWNED
AWNER
AWNERS
AWNIER
AWNIEST
AWNING
AWNINGED
AWNINGS
AWNLESS
AWNS
AWNY
AWOKE
AWOKEN
AWOL
AWOLS
AWORK
AWRACK
AWRONG
AWRY
AWSOME
AX
AXAL
AXE
AXEBIRD
AXEBIRDS
AXED
AXEL

AXELS
AXEMAN
AXEMEN
AXENIC
AXES
AXIAL
AXIALITY
AXIALLY
AXIL
AXILE
AXILEMMA
AXILEMMAS
AXILLA
AXILLAE
AXILLAR
AXILLARS
AXILLARY
AXILLAS
AXILS
AXING
AXINITE
AXINITES
AXIOLOGY
AXIOM
AXIOMATIC
AXIOMS
AXION
AXIONS
AXIS
AXISED
AXISES
AXITE
AXITES
AXLE
AXLED
AXLES
AXLETREE
AXLETREES
AXLIKE
AXMAN
AXMEN
AXOID
AXOIDS
AXOLEMMA
AXOLEMMAS
AXOLOTL
AXOLOTLS
AXON
AXONAL
AXONE
AXONEMAL
AXONEME
AXONEMES
AXONES
AXONIC
AXONS
AXOPLASM
AXOPLASMS

AXSEED
AXSEEDS
AY
AYAH
AYAHS
AYAHUASCA
AYAHUASCO
AYATOLLAH
AYE
AYELP
AYENBITE
AYENBITES
AYES
AYGRE
AYIN
AYINS
AYONT
AYRE
AYRES
AYRIE
AYRIES
AYS
AYU
AYURVEDA
AYURVEDAS
AYURVEDIC
AYUS
AYWORD
AYWORDS
AZALEA
AZALEAS
AZAN
AZANS
AZEDARACH
AZEOTROPE
AZEOTROPY
AZERTY
AZIDE
AZIDES
AZIDO
AZIMUTH
AZIMUTHAL
AZIMUTHS
AZINE
AZINES
AZIONE
AZIONES
AZLON
AZLONS
AZO
AZOIC
AZOLE
AZOLES
AZOLLA
AZOLLAS
AZON
AZONAL
AZONIC

AZONS
AZOTAEMIA
AZOTAEMIC
AZOTE
AZOTED
AZOTEMIA
AZOTEMIAS
AZOTEMIC
AZOTES
AZOTH
AZOTHS
AZOTIC
AZOTISE
AZOTISED
AZOTISES
AZOTISING
AZOTIZE
AZOTIZED
AZOTIZES
AZOTIZING
AZOTOUS
AZOTURIA
AZOTURIAS
AZUKI
AZUKIS
AZULEJO
AZULEJOS
AZURE
AZUREAN
AZURES
AZURINE
AZURINES
AZURITE
AZURITES
AZURN
AZURY
AZYGIES
AZYGOS
AZYGOSES
AZYGOUS
AZYGY
AZYM
AZYME
AZYMES
AZYMITE
AZYMITES
AZYMOUS
AZYMS

B

BA	BABESIAS	BACALAO	BACKBENDS
BAA	BABICHE	BACALAOS	BACKBIT
BAAED	BABICHES	BACCA	BACKBITE
BAAING	BABIED	BACCAE	BACKBITER
BAAINGS	BABIER	BACCARA	BACKBITES
BAAL	BABIES	BACCARAS	BACKBLOCK
BAALEBOS	BABIEST	BACCARAT	BACKBOARD
BAALIM	BABIRUSA	BACCARATS	BACKBOND
BAALISM	BABIRUSAS	BACCARE	BACKBONDS
BAALISMS	BABIRUSSA	BACCAS	BACKBONE
BAALS	BABKA	BACCATE	BACKBONED
BAAS	BABKAS	BACCATED	BACKBONES
BAASES	BABLAH	BACCHANAL	BACKBURN
BAASKAAP	BABLAHS	BACCHANT	BACKBURNS
BAASKAAPS	BABOO	BACCHANTE	BACKCAST
BAASKAP	BABOOL	BACCHANTS	BACKCASTS
BAASKAPS	BABOOLS	BACCHIAC	BACKCHAT
BAASSKAP	BABOON	BACCHIAN	BACKCHATS
BAASSKAPS	BABOONERY	BACCHIC	BACKCHECK
BABA	BABOONISH	BACCHII	BACKCLOTH
BABACO	BABOONS	BACCHIUS	BACKCOMB
BABACOOTE	BABOOS	BACCIES	BACKCOMBS
BABACOS	BABOOSH	BACCIFORM	BACKCOURT
BABALAS	BABOOSHES	BACCO	BACKCROSS
BABAS	BABOUCHE	BACCOES	BACKDATE
BABASSU	BABOUCHES	BACCOS	BACKDATED
BABASSUS	BABU	BACCY	BACKDATES
BABBELAS	BABUCHE	BACH	BACKDOOR
BABBITRY	BABUCHES	BACHA	BACKDOWN
BABBITT	BABUDOM	BACHARACH	BACKDOWNS
BABBITTED	BABUDOMS	BACHAS	BACKDRAFT
BABBITTRY	BABUISM	BACHCHA	BACKDROP
BABBITTS	BABUISMS	BACHCHAS	BACKDROPS
BABBLE	BABUL	BACHED	BACKDROPT
BABBLED	BABULS	BACHELOR	BACKED
BABBLER	BABUS	BACHELORS	BACKER
BABBLERS	BABUSHKA	BACHES	BACKERS
BABBLES	BABUSHKAS	BACHING	BACKET
BABBLIER	BABY	BACHS	BACKETS
BABBLIEST	BABYDOLL	BACILLAR	BACKFALL
BABBLING	BABYDOLLS	BACILLARY	BACKFALLS
BABBLINGS	BABYFOOD	BACILLI	BACKFIELD
BABBLY	BABYFOODS	BACILLUS	BACKFILE
BABE	BABYHOOD	BACK	BACKFILES
BABEL	BABYHOODS	BACKACHE	BACKFILL
BABELDOM	BABYING	BACKACHES	BACKFILLS
BABELDOMS	BABYISH	BACKARE	BACKFIRE
BABELISH	BABYISHLY	BACKBAND	BACKFIRED
BABELISM	BABYPROOF	BACKBANDS	BACKFIRES
BABELISMS	BABYSAT	BACKBEAT	BACKFISCH
BABELS	BABYSIT	BACKBEATS	BACKFIT
BABES	BABYSITS	BACKBENCH	BACKFITS
BABESIA	BAC	BACKBEND	BACKFLIP

BACKFLIPS	BACKSIDE	BACTERIAS	BAFFED
BACKFLOW	BACKSIDES	BACTERIC	BAFFIES
BACKFLOWS	BACKSIGHT	BACTERIN	BAFFING
BACKHAND	BACKSLAP	BACTERINS	BAFFLE
BACKHANDS	BACKSLAPS	BACTERISE	BAFFLED
BACKHAUL	BACKSLASH	BACTERIUM	BAFFLEGAB
BACKHAULS	BACKSLID	BACTERIZE	BAFFLER
BACKHOE	BACKSLIDE	BACTEROID	BAFFLERS
BACKHOED	BACKSPACE	BACULA	BAFFLES
BACKHOES	BACKSPEER	BACULINE	BAFFLING
BACKHOUSE	BACKSPEIR	BACULITE	BAFFS
BACKIE	BACKSPIN	BACULITES	BAFFY
BACKIES	BACKSPINS	BACULUM	BAFT
BACKING	BACKSTAB	BACULUMS	BAFTS
BACKINGS	BACKSTABS	BAD	BAG
BACKLAND	BACKSTAGE	BADASS	BAGARRE
BACKLANDS	BACKSTAIR	BADASSED	BAGARRES
BACKLASH	BACKSTALL	BADASSES	BAGASS
BACKLESS	BACKSTAMP	BADDER	BAGASSE
BACKLIFT	BACKSTAY	BADDEST	BAGASSES
BACKLIFTS	BACKSTAYS	BADDIE	BAGATELLE
BACKLIGHT	BACKSTOP	BADDIES	BAGEL
BACKLIST	BACKSTOPS	BADDISH	BAGELS
BACKLISTS	BACKSTORY	BADDY	BAGFUL
BACKLIT	BACKSWEPT	BADE	BAGFULS
BACKLOAD	BACKSWING	BADGE	BAGGAGE
BACKLOADS	BACKSWORD	BADGED	BAGGAGES
BACKLOG	BACKTRACK	BADGELESS	BAGGED
BACKLOGS	BACKUP	BADGER	BAGGER
BACKLOT	BACKUPS	BADGERED	BAGGERS
BACKLOTS	BACKVELD	BADGERING	BAGGIE
BACKMOST	BACKVELDS	BADGERLY	BAGGIER
BACKOUT	BACKWARD	BADGERS	BAGGIES
BACKOUTS	BACKWARDS	BADGES	BAGGIEST
BACKPACK	BACKWASH	BADGING	BAGGILY
BACKPACKS	BACKWATER	BADINAGE	BAGGINESS
BACKPAY	BACKWOOD	BADINAGED	BAGGING
BACKPAYS	BACKWOODS	BADINAGES	BAGGINGS
BACKPEDAL	BACKWORD	BADINERIE	BAGGIT
BACKPIECE	BACKWORDS	BADIOUS	BAGGITS
BACKRA	BACKWORK	BADLAND	BAGGY
BACKRAS	BACKWORKS	BADLANDS	BAGH
BACKREST	BACKWRAP	BADLY	BAGHOUSE
BACKRESTS	BACKWRAPS	BADMAN	BAGHOUSES
BACKROOM	BACKYARD	BADMASH	BAGHS
BACKROOMS	BACKYARDS	BADMASHES	BAGIE
BACKRUSH	BACLAVA	BADMEN	BAGIES
BACKS	BACLAVAS	BADMINTON	BAGLESS
BACKSAW	BACLOFEN	BADMOUTH	BAGLIKE
BACKSAWS	BACLOFENS	BADMOUTHS	BAGMAN
BACKSEAT	BACON	BADNESS	BAGMEN
BACKSEATS	BACONER	BADNESSES	BAGNETTE
BACKSET	BACONERS	BADS	BAGNETTES
BACKSETS	BACONS	BAEL	BAGNIO
BACKSEY	BACS	BAELS	BAGNIOS
BACKSEYS	BACTERIA	BAETYL	BAGPIPE
BACKSHISH	BACTERIAL	BAETYLS	BAGPIPED
BACKSHORE	BACTERIAN	BAFF	BAGPIPER

BAGPIPERS
BAGPIPES
BAGPIPING
BAGS
BAGSFUL
BAGUET
BAGUETS
BAGUETTE
BAGUETTES
BAGUIO
BAGUIOS
BAGWASH
BAGWASHES
BAGWIG
BAGWIGS
BAGWORM
BAGWORMS
BAH
BAHADA
BAHADAS
BAHADUR
BAHADURS
BAHT
BAHTS
BAHUT
BAHUTS
BAHUVRIHI
BAIDARKA
BAIDARKAS
BAIGNOIRE
BAIL
BAILABLE
BAILBOND
BAILBONDS
BAILED
BAILEE
BAILEES
BAILER
BAILERS
BAILEY
BAILEYS
BAILIE
BAILIES
BAILIFF
BAILIFFS
BAILING
BAILIWICK
BAILLI
BAILLIAGE
BAILLIE
BAILLIES
BAILLIS
BAILMENT
BAILMENTS
BAILOR
BAILORS
BAILOUT
BAILOUTS

BAILS
BAILSMAN
BAILSMEN
BAININ
BAININS
BAINITE
BAINITES
BAIRN
BAIRNISH
BAIRNLIER
BAIRNLIKE
BAIRNLY
BAIRNS
BAISEMAIN
BAIT
BAITED
BAITER
BAITERS
BAITFISH
BAITH
BAITING
BAITINGS
BAITS
BAIZA
BAIZAS
BAIZE
BAIZED
BAIZES
BAIZING
BAJADA
BAJADAS
BAJAN
BAJANS
BAJRA
BAJRAS
BAJREE
BAJREES
BAJRI
BAJRIS
BAJU
BAJUS
BAKE
BAKEAPPLE
BAKEBOARD
BAKED
BAKEHOUSE
BAKELITE
BAKELITES
BAKEMEAT
BAKEMEATS
BAKEN
BAKER
BAKERIES
BAKERS
BAKERY
BAKES
BAKESHOP
BAKESHOPS

BAKESTONE
BAKEWARE
BAKEWARES
BAKHSHISH
BAKING
BAKINGS
BAKKIE
BAKKIES
BAKLAVA
BAKLAVAS
BAKLAWA
BAKLAWAS
BAKRA
BAKRAS
BAKSHEESH
BAKSHISH
BAL
BALACLAVA
BALADIN
BALADINE
BALADINES
BALADINS
BALALAIKA
BALANCE
BALANCED
BALANCER
BALANCERS
BALANCES
BALANCING
BALANITIS
BALAS
BALASES
BALATA
BALATAS
BALBOA
BALBOAS
BALCONET
BALCONETS
BALCONIED
BALCONIES
BALCONY
BALD
BALDACHIN
BALDAQUIN
BALDED
BALDER
BALDEST
BALDFACED
BALDHEAD
BALDHEADS
BALDICOOT
BALDIER
BALDIES
BALDIEST
BALDING
BALDISH
BALDLY
BALDMONEY

BALDNESS
BALDPATE
BALDPATED
BALDPATES
BALDRIC
BALDRICK
BALDRICKS
BALDRICS
BALDS
BALDY
BALE
BALECTION
BALED
BALEEN
BALEENS
BALEFIRE
BALEFIRES
BALEFUL
BALEFULLY
BALER
BALERS
BALES
BALING
BALISAUR
BALISAURS
BALISTA
BALISTAE
BALISTAS
BALK
BALKANISE
BALKANIZE
BALKED
BALKER
BALKERS
BALKIER
BALKIEST
BALKILY
BALKINESS
BALKING
BALKINGLY
BALKINGS
BALKLINE
BALKLINES
BALKS
BALKY
BALL
BALLABILE
BALLABILI
BALLAD
BALLADE
BALLADED
BALLADEER
BALLADES
BALLADIC
BALLADIN
BALLADINE
BALLADING
BALLADINS

41

BALLADIST
BALLADRY
BALLADS
BALLAN
BALLANS
BALLANT
BALLANTED
BALLANTS
BALLAST
BALLASTED
BALLASTER
BALLASTS
BALLAT
BALLATED
BALLATING
BALLATS
BALLCLAY
BALLCLAYS
BALLCOCK
BALLCOCKS
BALLED
BALLER
BALLERINA
BALLERINE
BALLERS
BALLET
BALLETED
BALLETIC
BALLETING
BALLETS
BALLGAME
BALLGAMES
BALLHAWK
BALLHAWKS
BALLIES
BALLING
BALLINGS
BALLISTA
BALLISTAE
BALLISTAS
BALLISTIC
BALLIUM
BALLIUMS
BALLOCKS
BALLON
BALLONET
BALLONETS
BALLONNE
BALLONNES
BALLONS
BALLOON
BALLOONED
BALLOONS
BALLOT
BALLOTED
BALLOTEE
BALLOTEES
BALLOTER

BALLOTERS
BALLOTING
BALLOTINI
BALLOTS
BALLOW
BALLOWS
BALLPARK
BALLPARKS
BALLPOINT
BALLROOM
BALLROOMS
BALLS
BALLSIER
BALLSIEST
BALLSY
BALLUP
BALLUPS
BALLUTE
BALLUTES
BALLY
BALLYARD
BALLYARDS
BALLYHOO
BALLYHOOS
BALLYRAG
BALLYRAGS
BALM
BALMACAAN
BALMED
BALMIER
BALMIEST
BALMILY
BALMINESS
BALMING
BALMLIKE
BALMORAL
BALMORALS
BALMS
BALMY
BALNEAL
BALNEARY
BALONEY
BALONEYS
BALOO
BALOOS
BALS
BALSA
BALSAM
BALSAMED
BALSAMIC
BALSAMING
BALSAMS
BALSAMY
BALSAS
BALSAWOOD
BALTHASAR
BALTHAZAR
BALTI

BALTIS
BALU
BALUN
BALUNS
BALUS
BALUSTER
BALUSTERS
BALZARINE
BAMBI
BAMBINI
BAMBINO
BAMBINOS
BAMBIS
BAMBOO
BAMBOOS
BAMBOOZLE
BAMMED
BAMMER
BAMMERS
BAMMING
BAMPOT
BAMPOTS
BAMS
BAN
BANAK
BANAKS
BANAL
BANALER
BANALEST
BANALISE
BANALISED
BANALISES
BANALITY
BANALIZE
BANALIZED
BANALIZES
BANALLY
BANANA
BANANAS
BANAUSIAN
BANAUSIC
BANC
BANCO
BANCOS
BANCS
BAND
BANDA
BANDAGE
BANDAGED
BANDAGER
BANDAGERS
BANDAGES
BANDAGING
BANDAID
BANDALORE
BANDANA
BANDANAS

BANDANNA
BANDANNAS
BANDAR
BANDARI
BANDARIS
BANDARS
BANDAS
BANDBOX
BANDBOXES
BANDBRAKE
BANDEAU
BANDEAUS
BANDEAUX
BANDED
BANDELET
BANDELETS
BANDELIER
BANDER
BANDEROL
BANDEROLE
BANDEROLS
BANDERS
BANDH
BANDHS
BANDICOOT
BANDIED
BANDIER
BANDIES
BANDIEST
BANDINESS
BANDING
BANDINGS
BANDIT
BANDITO
BANDITOS
BANDITRY
BANDITS
BANDITTI
BANDITTIS
BANDMATE
BANDMATES
BANDOBAST
BANDOBUST
BANDOG
BANDOGS
BANDOLEER
BANDOLEON
BANDOLERO
BANDOLIER
BANDOLINE
BANDONEON
BANDONION
BANDOOK
BANDOOKS
BANDORA
BANDORAS
BANDORE
BANDORES

BANDROL
BANDROLS
BANDS
BANDSAW
BANDSAWS
BANDSHELL
BANDSMAN
BANDSMEN
BANDSTAND
BANDSTER
BANDSTERS
BANDURA
BANDURAS
BANDWAGON
BANDWIDTH
BANDY
BANDYING
BANDYINGS
BANDYMAN
BANDYMEN
BANE
BANEBERRY
BANED
BANEFUL
BANEFULLY
BANES
BANG
BANGALAY
BANGALAYS
BANGALORE
BANGALOW
BANGALOWS
BANGED
BANGER
BANGERS
BANGING
BANGINGS
BANGKOK
BANGKOKS
BANGLE
BANGLED
BANGLES
BANGS
BANGSRING
BANGSTER
BANGSTERS
BANGTAIL
BANGTAILS
BANI
BANIA
BANIAN
BANIANS
BANIAS
BANING
BANISH
BANISHED
BANISHER
BANISHERS

BANISHES
BANISHING
BANISTER
BANISTERS
BANJAX
BANJAXED
BANJAXES
BANJAXING
BANJO
BANJOES
BANJOIST
BANJOISTS
BANJOS
BANJULELE
BANK
BANKABLE
BANKBOOK
BANKBOOKS
BANKCARD
BANKCARDS
BANKED
BANKER
BANKERLY
BANKERS
BANKET
BANKETS
BANKING
BANKINGS
BANKIT
BANKITS
BANKNOTE
BANKNOTES
BANKROLL
BANKROLLS
BANKRUPT
BANKRUPTS
BANKS
BANKSIA
BANKSIAS
BANKSIDE
BANKSIDES
BANKSMAN
BANKSMEN
BANLIEUE
BANLIEUES
BANNABLE
BANNED
BANNER
BANNERALL
BANNERED
BANNERET
BANNERETS
BANNERING
BANNEROL
BANNEROLS
BANNERS
BANNET
BANNETS

BANNING
BANNISTER
BANNOCK
BANNOCKS
BANNS
BANOFFEE
BANOFFEES
BANOFFI
BANOFFIS
BANQUET
BANQUETED
BANQUETER
BANQUETS
BANQUETTE
BANS
BANSELA
BANSELAS
BANSHEE
BANSHEES
BANSHIE
BANSHIES
BANT
BANTAM
BANTAMS
BANTED
BANTENG
BANTENGS
BANTER
BANTERED
BANTERER
BANTERERS
BANTERING
BANTERS
BANTIES
BANTING
BANTINGS
BANTLING
BANTLINGS
BANTS
BANTU
BANTUS
BANTY
BANXRING
BANXRINGS
BANYAN
BANYANS
BANZAI
BANZAIS
BAOBAB
BAOBABS
BAP
BAPS
BAPTISE
BAPTISED
BAPTISER
BAPTISERS
BAPTISES
BAPTISIA

BAPTISIAS
BAPTISING
BAPTISM
BAPTISMAL
BAPTISMS
BAPTIST
BAPTISTRY
BAPTISTS
BAPTIZE
BAPTIZED
BAPTIZER
BAPTIZERS
BAPTIZES
BAPTIZING
BAPU
BAPUS
BAR
BARACAN
BARACANS
BARACHOIS
BARAGOUIN
BARASINGA
BARATHEA
BARATHEAS
BARATHRUM
BARAZA
BARAZAS
BARB
BARBAL
BARBARIAN
BARBARIC
BARBARISE
BARBARISM
BARBARITY
BARBARIZE
BARBAROUS
BARBASCO
BARBASCOS
BARBASTEL
BARBATE
BARBATED
BARBE
BARBECUE
BARBECUED
BARBECUER
BARBECUES
BARBED
BARBEL
BARBELL
BARBELLS
BARBELS
BARBEQUE
BARBEQUED
BARBEQUES
BARBER
BARBERED
BARBERING
BARBERRY

BARBERS

BARBERS
BARBES
BARBET
BARBETS
BARBETTE
BARBETTES
BARBICAN
BARBICANS
BARBICEL
BARBICELS
BARBIE
BARBIES
BARBING
BARBITAL
BARBITALS
BARBITONE
BARBLESS
BARBOLA
BARBOLAS
BARBOTINE
BARBS
BARBULE
BARBULES
BARBUT
BARBUTS
BARBWIRE
BARBWIRES
BARBY
BARCA
BARCAROLE
BARCAS
BARCHAN
BARCHANE
BARCHANES
BARCHANS
BARD
BARDASH
BARDASHES
BARDE
BARDED
BARDES
BARDIC
BARDIE
BARDIER
BARDIES
BARDIEST
BARDING
BARDISM
BARDISMS
BARDLING
BARDLINGS
BARDO
BARDOS
BARDS
BARDSHIP
BARDSHIPS
BARDY
BARE

BAREBACK
BAREBACKS
BAREBOAT
BAREBOATS
BAREBONE
BAREBONED
BAREBONES
BARED
BAREFACED
BAREFIT
BAREFOOT
BAREGE
BAREGES
BAREGINE
BAREGINES
BAREHAND
BAREHANDS
BAREHEAD
BARELY
BARENESS
BARER
BARES
BARESARK
BARESARKS
BAREST
BARF
BARFED
BARFING
BARFLIES
BARFLY
BARFS
BARFUL
BARGAIN
BARGAINED
BARGAINER
BARGAINS
BARGANDER
BARGE
BARGED
BARGEE
BARGEES
BARGEESE
BARGELLO
BARGELLOS
BARGEMAN
BARGEMEN
BARGEPOLE
BARGES
BARGEST
BARGESTS
BARGHEST
BARGHESTS
BARGING
BARGOON
BARGOONS
BARGOOSE
BARGUEST
BARGUESTS

BARHOP
BARHOPPED
BARHOPS
BARIATRIC
BARIC
BARILLA
BARILLAS
BARING
BARISH
BARISTA
BARISTAS
BARITE
BARITES
BARITONAL
BARITONE
BARITONES
BARIUM
BARIUMS
BARK
BARKAN
BARKANS
BARKED
BARKEEP
BARKEEPER
BARKEEPS
BARKEN
BARKENED
BARKENING
BARKENS
BARKER
BARKERS
BARKHAN
BARKHANS
BARKIER
BARKIEST
BARKING
BARKLESS
BARKS
BARKY
BARLEDUC
BARLEDUCS
BARLESS
BARLEY
BARLEYS
BARLOW
BARLOWS
BARM
BARMAID
BARMAIDS
BARMAN
BARMBRACK
BARMEN
BARMIE
BARMIER
BARMIEST
BARMINESS
BARMKIN
BARMKINS

BARMS
BARMY
BARN
BARNACLE
BARNACLED
BARNACLES
BARNBRACK
BARNED
BARNET
BARNETS
BARNEY
BARNEYED
BARNEYING
BARNEYS
BARNIER
BARNIEST
BARNING
BARNLIKE
BARNS
BARNSTORM
BARNY
BARNYARD
BARNYARDS
BAROCCO
BAROCCOS
BAROCK
BAROCKS
BAROGRAM
BAROGRAMS
BAROGRAPH
BAROLO
BAROLOS
BAROMETER
BAROMETRY
BAROMETZ
BARON
BARONAGE
BARONAGES
BARONESS
BARONET
BARONETCY
BARONETS
BARONG
BARONGS
BARONIAL
BARONIES
BARONNE
BARONNES
BARONS
BARONY
BAROPHILE
BAROQUE
BAROQUELY
BAROQUES
BAROSAUR
BAROSAURS
BAROSCOPE
BAROSTAT

BASK

BAROSTATS
BAROUCHE
BAROUCHES
BARP
BARPERSON
BARPS
BARQUE
BARQUES
BARQUETTE
BARRA
BARRABLE
BARRACAN
BARRACANS
BARRACE
BARRACES
BARRACK
BARRACKED
BARRACKER
BARRACKS
BARRACOON
BARRACUDA
BARRAGE
BARRAGED
BARRAGES
BARRAGING
BARRANCA
BARRANCAS
BARRANCO
BARRANCOS
BARRAS
BARRAT
BARRATER
BARRATERS
BARRATOR
BARRATORS
BARRATRY
BARRATS
BARRE
BARRED
BARREED
BARREFULL
BARREING
BARREL
BARRELAGE
BARRELED
BARRELFUL
BARRELING
BARRELLED
BARRELS
BARREN
BARRENER
BARRENEST
BARRENLY
BARRENS
BARRES
BARRET
BARRETOR
BARRETORS

BARRETRY
BARRETS
BARRETTE
BARRETTER
BARRETTES
BARRICADE
BARRICADO
BARRICO
BARRICOES
BARRICOS
BARRIE
BARRIER
BARRIERED
BARRIERS
BARRIES
BARRIEST
BARRING
BARRINGS
BARRIO
BARRIOS
BARRISTER
BARRO
BARROOM
BARROOMS
BARROW
BARROWFUL
BARROWS
BARRULET
BARRULETS
BARRY
BARS
BARSTOOL
BARSTOOLS
BARTEND
BARTENDED
BARTENDER
BARTENDS
BARTER
BARTERED
BARTERER
BARTERERS
BARTERING
BARTERS
BARTISAN
BARTISANS
BARTIZAN
BARTIZANS
BARTON
BARTONS
BARTSIA
BARTSIAS
BARWARE
BARWARES
BARWOOD
BARWOODS
BARYE
BARYES
BARYON

BARYONIC
BARYONS
BARYTA
BARYTAS
BARYTE
BARYTES
BARYTIC
BARYTON
BARYTONE
BARYTONES
BARYTONS
BAS
BASAL
BASALLY
BASALT
BASALTES
BASALTIC
BASALTINE
BASALTS
BASAN
BASANITE
BASANITES
BASANS
BASCINET
BASCINETS
BASCULE
BASCULES
BASE
BASEBALL
BASEBALLS
BASEBAND
BASEBANDS
BASEBOARD
BASEBORN
BASED
BASELARD
BASELARDS
BASELESS
BASELINE
BASELINER
BASELINES
BASELY
BASEMAN
BASEMEN
BASEMENT
BASEMENTS
BASENESS
BASENJI
BASENJIS
BASEPLATE
BASER
BASES
BASEST
BASH
BASHAW
BASHAWISM
BASHAWS
BASHED

BASHER
BASHERS
BASHES
BASHFUL
BASHFULLY
BASHING
BASHINGS
BASHLESS
BASHLIK
BASHLIKS
BASHLYK
BASHLYKS
BASHO
BASIC
BASICALLY
BASICITY
BASICS
BASIDIA
BASIDIAL
BASIDIUM
BASIFIED
BASIFIER
BASIFIERS
BASIFIES
BASIFIXED
BASIFUGAL
BASIFY
BASIFYING
BASIL
BASILAR
BASILARY
BASILECT
BASILECTS
BASILIC
BASILICA
BASILICAE
BASILICAL
BASILICAN
BASILICAS
BASILICON
BASILISK
BASILISKS
BASILS
BASIN
BASINAL
BASINED
BASINET
BASINETS
BASINFUL
BASINFULS
BASING
BASINLIKE
BASINS
BASION
BASIONS
BASIPETAL
BASIS
BASK

45

BASKED
BASKET
BASKETFUL
BASKETRY
BASKETS
BASKING
BASKS
BASMATI
BASMATIS
BASNET
BASNETS
BASOCHE
BASOCHES
BASON
BASONS
BASOPHIL
BASOPHILE
BASOPHILS
BASQUE
BASQUED
BASQUES
BASQUINE
BASQUINES
BASS
BASSE
BASSED
BASSER
BASSES
BASSEST
BASSET
BASSETED
BASSETING
BASSETS
BASSETT
BASSETTED
BASSETTS
BASSI
BASSIER
BASSIEST
BASSINET
BASSINETS
BASSING
BASSIST
BASSISTS
BASSLY
BASSNESS
BASSO
BASSOON
BASSOONS
BASSOS
BASSWOOD
BASSWOODS
BASSY
BAST
BASTA
BASTARD
BASTARDLY
BASTARDRY

BASTARDS
BASTARDY
BASTE
BASTED
BASTER
BASTERS
BASTES
BASTI
BASTIDE
BASTIDES
BASTILE
BASTILES
BASTILLE
BASTILLES
BASTINADE
BASTINADO
BASTING
BASTINGS
BASTION
BASTIONED
BASTIONS
BASTIS
BASTLE
BASTLES
BASTO
BASTOS
BASTS
BASUCO
BASUCOS
BAT
BATABLE
BATATA
BATATAS
BATAVIA
BATAVIAS
BATBOY
BATBOYS
BATCH
BATCHED
BATCHER
BATCHERS
BATCHES
BATCHING
BATCHINGS
BATE
BATEAU
BATEAUX
BATED
BATELESS
BATELEUR
BATELEURS
BATEMENT
BATEMENTS
BATES
BATFISH
BATFISHES
BATFOWL
BATFOWLED

BATFOWLER
BATFOWLS
BATGIRL
BATGIRLS
BATH
BATHCUBE
BATHCUBES
BATHE
BATHED
BATHER
BATHERS
BATHES
BATHETIC
BATHHOUSE
BATHING
BATHLESS
BATHMAT
BATHMATS
BATHMIC
BATHMISM
BATHMISMS
BATHOLITE
BATHOLITH
BATHORSE
BATHORSES
BATHOS
BATHOSES
BATHROBE
BATHROBES
BATHROOM
BATHROOMS
BATHS
BATHTUB
BATHTUBS
BATHWATER
BATHYAL
BATHYBIUS
BATHYLITE
BATHYLITH
BATIK
BATIKED
BATIKING
BATIKS
BATING
BATISTE
BATISTES
BATLER
BATLERS
BATLET
BATLETS
BATLIKE
BATMAN
BATMEN
BATOLOGY
BATON
BATONED
BATONING
BATONS

BATOON
BATOONED
BATOONING
BATOONS
BATRACHIA
BATS
BATSMAN
BATSMEN
BATSWING
BATSWOMAN
BATSWOMEN
BATT
BATTA
BATTALIA
BATTALIAS
BATTALION
BATTAS
BATTEAU
BATTEAUX
BATTED
BATTEL
BATTELED
BATTELER
BATTELERS
BATTELING
BATTELLED
BATTELS
BATTEMENT
BATTEN
BATTENED
BATTENER
BATTENERS
BATTENING
BATTENS
BATTER
BATTERED
BATTERER
BATTERERS
BATTERIE
BATTERIES
BATTERING
BATTERO
BATTEROS
BATTERS
BATTERY
BATTIER
BATTIEST
BATTIK
BATTIKS
BATTILL
BATTILLED
BATTILLS
BATTINESS
BATTING
BATTINGS
BATTLE
BATTLEBUS
BATTLED

BATTLER
BATTLERS
BATTLES
BATTLING
BATTOLOGY
BATTS
BATTU
BATTUE
BATTUES
BATTUTA
BATTUTAS
BATTY
BATWING
BATWOMAN
BATWOMEN
BAUBEE
BAUBEES
BAUBLE
BAUBLES
BAUBLING
BAUCHLE
BAUCHLED
BAUCHLES
BAUCHLING
BAUD
BAUDEKIN
BAUDEKINS
BAUDRIC
BAUDRICK
BAUDRICKE
BAUDRICKS
BAUDRICS
BAUDRONS
BAUDS
BAUERA
BAUERAS
BAUHINIA
BAUHINIAS
BAUK
BAUKED
BAUKING
BAUKS
BAULK
BAULKED
BAULKER
BAULKERS
BAULKIER
BAULKIEST
BAULKILY
BAULKING
BAULKS
BAULKY
BAUR
BAURS
BAUSOND
BAUXITE
BAUXITES
BAUXITIC

BAVARDAGE
BAVAROIS
BAVIN
BAVINS
BAWBEE
BAWBEES
BAWBLE
BAWBLES
BAWCOCK
BAWCOCKS
BAWD
BAWDIER
BAWDIES
BAWDIEST
BAWDILY
BAWDINESS
BAWDKIN
BAWDKINS
BAWDRIC
BAWDRICS
BAWDRIES
BAWDRY
BAWDS
BAWDY
BAWL
BAWLED
BAWLER
BAWLERS
BAWLEY
BAWLEYS
BAWLING
BAWLINGS
BAWLS
BAWN
BAWNEEN
BAWNEENS
BAWNS
BAWR
BAWRS
BAWSUNT
BAWTIE
BAWTIES
BAWTY
BAXTER
BAXTERS
BAY
BAYADEER
BAYADEERS
BAYADERE
BAYADERES
BAYAMO
BAYAMOS
BAYARD
BAYARDS
BAYBERRY
BAYE
BAYED
BAYES

BAYING
BAYLE
BAYLES
BAYMAN
BAYMEN
BAYONET
BAYONETED
BAYONETS
BAYOU
BAYOUS
BAYS
BAYT
BAYTED
BAYTING
BAYTS
BAYWOOD
BAYWOODS
BAYYAN
BAYYANS
BAZAAR
BAZAARS
BAZAR
BAZARS
BAZAZZ
BAZAZZES
BAZILLION
BAZOO
BAZOOKA
BAZOOKAS
BAZOOMS
BAZOOS
BAZOUKI
BAZOUKIS
BDELLIUM
BDELLIUMS
BE
BEACH
BEACHBALL
BEACHBOY
BEACHBOYS
BEACHCOMB
BEACHED
BEACHES
BEACHGOER
BEACHHEAD
BEACHIER
BEACHIEST
BEACHING
BEACHSIDE
BEACHWEAR
BEACHY
BEACON
BEACONED
BEACONING
BEACONS
BEAD
BEADBLAST
BEADED

BEADER
BEADERS
BEADHOUSE
BEADIER
BEADIEST
BEADILY
BEADINESS
BEADING
BEADINGS
BEADLE
BEADLEDOM
BEADLES
BEADLIKE
BEADMAN
BEADMEN
BEADROLL
BEADROLLS
BEADS
BEADSMAN
BEADSMEN
BEADWORK
BEADWORKS
BEADY
BEAGLE
BEAGLED
BEAGLER
BEAGLERS
BEAGLES
BEAGLING
BEAGLINGS
BEAK
BEAKED
BEAKER
BEAKERS
BEAKIER
BEAKIEST
BEAKLESS
BEAKLIKE
BEAKS
BEAKY
BEAM
BEAMED
BEAMER
BEAMERS
BEAMIER
BEAMIEST
BEAMILY
BEAMINESS
BEAMING
BEAMINGLY
BEAMINGS
BEAMISH
BEAMISHLY
BEAMLESS
BEAMLET
BEAMLETS
BEAMLIKE
BEAMS

BEAMY

BEAMY	BEARWOOD	BEAUXITE	BECKETS
BEAN	BEARWOODS	BEAUXITES	BECKING
BEANBAG	BEAST	BEAVER	BECKON
BEANBAGS	BEASTHOOD	BEAVERED	BECKONED
BEANBALL	BEASTIE	BEAVERIES	BECKONER
BEANBALLS	BEASTIES	BEAVERING	BECKONERS
BEANED	BEASTILY	BEAVERS	BECKONING
BEANERIES	BEASTINGS	BEAVERY	BECKONS
BEANERY	BEASTLIER	BEBEERINE	BECKS
BEANFEAST	BEASTLIKE	BEBEERU	BECLAMOR
BEANIE	BEASTLY	BEBEERUS	BECLAMORS
BEANIES	BEASTS	BEBLOOD	BECLASP
BEANING	BEAT	BEBLOODED	BECLASPED
BEANLIKE	BEATABLE	BEBLOODS	BECLASPS
BEANO	BEATBOX	BEBOP	BECLOAK
BEANOS	BEATBOXES	BEBOPPED	BECLOAKED
BEANPOLE	BEATEN	BEBOPPER	BECLOAKS
BEANPOLES	BEATER	BEBOPPERS	BECLOG
BEANS	BEATERS	BEBOPPING	BECLOGGED
BEANSTALK	BEATH	BEBOPS	BECLOGS
BEANY	BEATHED	BEBUNG	BECLOTHE
BEAR	BEATHING	BEBUNGS	BECLOTHED
BEARABLE	BEATHS	BECALL	BECLOTHES
BEARABLY	BEATIER	BECALLED	BECLOUD
BEARBERRY	BEATIEST	BECALLING	BECLOUDED
BEARBINE	BEATIFIC	BECALLS	BECLOUDS
BEARBINES	BEATIFIED	BECALM	BECLOWN
BEARCAT	BEATIFIES	BECALMED	BECLOWNED
BEARCATS	BEATIFY	BECALMING	BECLOWNS
BEARD	BEATING	BECALMS	BECOME
BEARDED	BEATINGS	BECAME	BECOMES
BEARDIE	BEATITUDE	BECAP	BECOMING
BEARDIER	BEATLESS	BECAPPED	BECOMINGS
BEARDIES	BEATNIK	BECAPPING	BECOWARD
BEARDIEST	BEATNIKS	BECAPS	BECOWARDS
BEARDING	BEATS	BECARPET	BECQUEREL
BEARDLESS	BEATY	BECARPETS	BECRAWL
BEARDS	BEAU	BECASSE	BECRAWLED
BEARDY	BEAUCOUP	BECASSES	BECRAWLS
BEARE	BEAUCOUPS	BECAUSE	BECRIME
BEARED	BEAUFET	BECCACCIA	BECRIMED
BEARER	BEAUFETS	BECCAFICO	BECRIMES
BEARERS	BEAUFFET	BECHALK	BECRIMING
BEARES	BEAUFFETS	BECHALKED	BECROWD
BEARGRASS	BEAUFIN	BECHALKS	BECROWDED
BEARHUG	BEAUFINS	BECHAMEL	BECROWDS
BEARHUGS	BEAUISH	BECHAMELS	BECRUST
BEARING	BEAUS	BECHANCE	BECRUSTED
BEARINGS	BEAUT	BECHANCED	BECRUSTS
BEARISH	BEAUTEOUS	BECHANCES	BECUDGEL
BEARISHLY	BEAUTIED	BECHARM	BECUDGELS
BEARLIKE	BEAUTIES	BECHARMED	BECURL
BEARNAISE	BEAUTIFUL	BECHARMS	BECURLED
BEARS	BEAUTIFY	BECK	BECURLING
BEARSKIN	BEAUTS	BECKE	BECURLS
BEARSKINS	BEAUTY	BECKED	BECURSE
BEARWARD	BEAUTYING	BECKES	BECURSED
BEARWARDS	BEAUX	BECKET	BECURSES

BECURSING	BEDELL	BEDPAN	BEDSTRAWS
BECURST	BEDELLS	BEDPANS	BEDTICK
BED	BEDELS	BEDPLATE	BEDTICKS
BEDABBLE	BEDELSHIP	BEDPLATES	BEDTIME
BEDABBLED	BEDEMAN	BEDPOST	BEDTIMES
BEDABBLES	BEDEMEN	BEDPOSTS	BEDU
BEDAD	BEDERAL	BEDQUILT	BEDUCK
BEDAGGLE	BEDERALS	BEDQUILTS	BEDUCKED
BEDAGGLED	BEDES	BEDRAGGLE	BEDUCKING
BEDAGGLES	BEDESMAN	BEDRAIL	BEDUCKS
BEDAMN	BEDESMEN	BEDRAILS	BEDUIN
BEDAMNED	BEDEVIL	BEDRAL	BEDUINS
BEDAMNING	BEDEVILED	BEDRALS	BEDUMB
BEDAMNS	BEDEVILS	BEDRAPE	BEDUMBED
BEDARKEN	BEDEW	BEDRAPED	BEDUMBING
BEDARKENS	BEDEWED	BEDRAPES	BEDUMBS
BEDASH	BEDEWING	BEDRAPING	BEDUNCE
BEDASHED	BEDEWS	BEDRENCH	BEDUNCED
BEDASHES	BEDFAST	BEDRID	BEDUNCES
BEDASHING	BEDFELLOW	BEDRIDDEN	BEDUNCING
BEDAUB	BEDFRAME	BEDRIGHT	BEDUNG
BEDAUBED	BEDFRAMES	BEDRIGHTS	BEDUNGED
BEDAUBING	BEDGOWN	BEDRIVEL	BEDUNGING
BEDAUBS	BEDGOWNS	BEDRIVELS	BEDUNGS
BEDAWIN	BEDIAPER	BEDROCK	BEDUST
BEDAWINS	BEDIAPERS	BEDROCKS	BEDUSTED
BEDAZE	BEDIDE	BEDROLL	BEDUSTING
BEDAZED	BEDIGHT	BEDROLLS	BEDUSTS
BEDAZES	BEDIGHTED	BEDROOM	BEDWARD
BEDAZING	BEDIGHTS	BEDROOMED	BEDWARDS
BEDAZZLE	BEDIM	BEDROOMS	BEDWARF
BEDAZZLED	BEDIMMED	BEDROP	BEDWARFED
BEDAZZLES	BEDIMMING	BEDROPPED	BEDWARFS
BEDBOARD	BEDIMPLE	BEDROPS	BEDWARMER
BEDBOARDS	BEDIMPLED	BEDROPT	BEDWETTER
BEDBUG	BEDIMPLES	BEDRUG	BEDYDE
BEDBUGS	BEDIMS	BEDRUGGED	BEDYE
BEDCHAIR	BEDIRTIED	BEDRUGS	BEDYED
BEDCHAIRS	BEDIRTIES	BEDS	BEDYEING
BEDCOVER	BEDIRTY	BEDSHEET	BEDYES
BEDCOVERS	BEDIZEN	BEDSHEETS	BEE
BEDDABLE	BEDIZENED	BEDSIDE	BEEBEE
BEDDED	BEDIZENS	BEDSIDES	BEEBEES
BEDDER	BEDLAM	BEDSIT	BEEBREAD
BEDDERS	BEDLAMISM	BEDSITS	BEEBREADS
BEDDING	BEDLAMITE	BEDSITTER	BEECH
BEDDINGS	BEDLAMP	BEDSOCKS	BEECHEN
BEDE	BEDLAMPS	BEDSONIA	BEECHES
BEDEAFEN	BEDLAMS	BEDSONIAS	BEECHIER
BEDEAFENS	BEDLESS	BEDSORE	BEECHIEST
BEDECK	BEDLIKE	BEDSORES	BEECHMAST
BEDECKED	BEDMAKER	BEDSPREAD	BEECHNUT
BEDECKING	BEDMAKERS	BEDSPRING	BEECHNUTS
BEDECKS	BEDMATE	BEDSTAND	BEECHWOOD
BEDEGUAR	BEDMATES	BEDSTANDS	BEECHY
BEDEGUARS	BEDOTTED	BEDSTEAD	BEEDI
BEDEHOUSE	BEDOUIN	BEDSTEADS	BEEDIES
BEDEL	BEDOUINS	BEDSTRAW	BEEF

BEEFALO
BEEFALOES
BEEFALOS
BEEFCAKE
BEEFCAKES
BEEFEATER
BEEFED
BEEFIER
BEEFIEST
BEEFILY
BEEFINESS
BEEFING
BEEFLESS
BEEFS
BEEFSTEAK
BEEFWOOD
BEEFWOODS
BEEFY
BEEGAH
BEEGAHS
BEEHIVE
BEEHIVES
BEEKEEPER
BEELIKE
BEELINE
BEELINED
BEELINES
BEELINING
BEEN
BEENAH
BEENAHS
BEENTO
BEENTOS
BEEP
BEEPED
BEEPER
BEEPERS
BEEPING
BEEPS
BEER
BEERAGE
BEERAGES
BEERHALL
BEERHALLS
BEERIER
BEERIEST
BEERILY
BEERINESS
BEERS
BEERY
BEES
BEESOME
BEESTINGS
BEESWAX
BEESWAXED
BEESWAXES
BEESWING
BEESWINGS

BEET
BEETED
BEETFLIES
BEETFLY
BEETING
BEETLE
BEETLED
BEETLER
BEETLERS
BEETLES
BEETLING
BEETROOT
BEETROOTS
BEETS
BEEVES
BEEYARD
BEEYARDS
BEEZER
BEEZERS
BEFALL
BEFALLEN
BEFALLING
BEFALLS
BEFANA
BEFANAS
BEFELD
BEFELL
BEFFANA
BEFFANAS
BEFINGER
BEFINGERS
BEFINNED
BEFIT
BEFITS
BEFITTED
BEFITTING
BEFLAG
BEFLAGGED
BEFLAGS
BEFLEA
BEFLEAED
BEFLEAING
BEFLEAS
BEFLECK
BEFLECKED
BEFLECKS
BEFLOWER
BEFLOWERS
BEFLUM
BEFLUMMED
BEFLUMS
BEFOAM
BEFOAMED
BEFOAMING
BEFOAMS
BEFOG
BEFOGGED
BEFOGGING

BEFOGS
BEFOOL
BEFOOLED
BEFOOLING
BEFOOLS
BEFORE
BEFORTUNE
BEFOUL
BEFOULED
BEFOULER
BEFOULERS
BEFOULING
BEFOULS
BEFRET
BEFRETS
BEFRETTED
BEFRIEND
BEFRIENDS
BEFRINGE
BEFRINGED
BEFRINGES
BEFUDDLE
BEFUDDLED
BEFUDDLES
BEG
BEGAD
BEGALL
BEGALLED
BEGALLING
BEGALLS
BEGAN
BEGAR
BEGARS
BEGAT
BEGAZE
BEGAZED
BEGAZES
BEGAZING
BEGEM
BEGEMMED
BEGEMMING
BEGEMS
BEGET
BEGETS
BEGETTER
BEGETTERS
BEGETTING
BEGGAR
BEGGARDOM
BEGGARED
BEGGARIES
BEGGARING
BEGGARLY
BEGGARS
BEGGARY
BEGGED
BEGGING
BEGGINGLY

BEGGINGS
BEGHARD
BEGHARDS
BEGIFT
BEGIFTED
BEGIFTING
BEGIFTS
BEGILD
BEGILDED
BEGILDING
BEGILDS
BEGILT
BEGIN
BEGINNE
BEGINNER
BEGINNERS
BEGINNES
BEGINNING
BEGINS
BEGIRD
BEGIRDED
BEGIRDING
BEGIRDLE
BEGIRDLED
BEGIRDLES
BEGIRDS
BEGIRT
BEGLAD
BEGLADDED
BEGLADS
BEGLAMOR
BEGLAMORS
BEGLAMOUR
BEGLERBEG
BEGLOOM
BEGLOOMED
BEGLOOMS
BEGNAW
BEGNAWED
BEGNAWING
BEGNAWS
BEGO
BEGOES
BEGOGGLED
BEGOING
BEGONE
BEGONIA
BEGONIAS
BEGORAH
BEGORED
BEGORRA
BEGORRAH
BEGOT
BEGOTTEN
BEGRIM
BEGRIME
BEGRIMED
BEGRIMES

BEGRIMING	BEHEST	BEJESUITS	BELAYING
BEGRIMMED	BEHESTS	BEJESUS	BELAYS
BEGRIMS	BEHIGHT	BEJEWEL	BELCH
BEGROAN	BEHIGHTS	BEJEWELED	BELCHED
BEGROANED	BEHIND	BEJEWELS	BELCHER
BEGROANS	BEHINDS	BEJUMBLE	BELCHERS
BEGRUDGE	BEHOLD	BEJUMBLED	BELCHES
BEGRUDGED	BEHOLDEN	BEJUMBLES	BELCHING
BEGRUDGER	BEHOLDER	BEKAH	BELDAM
BEGRUDGES	BEHOLDERS	BEKAHS	BELDAME
BEGS	BEHOLDING	BEKISS	BELDAMES
BEGUILE	BEHOLDS	BEKISSED	BELDAMS
BEGUILED	BEHOOF	BEKISSES	BELEAGUER
BEGUILER	BEHOOFS	BEKISSING	BELEAP
BEGUILERS	BEHOOVE	BEKNAVE	BELEAPED
BEGUILES	BEHOOVED	BEKNAVED	BELEAPING
BEGUILING	BEHOOVES	BEKNAVES	BELEAPS
BEGUIN	BEHOOVING	BEKNAVING	BELEAPT
BEGUINAGE	BEHOTE	BEKNIGHT	BELEE
BEGUINE	BEHOTES	BEKNIGHTS	BELEED
BEGUINES	BEHOTING	BEKNOT	BELEEING
BEGUINS	BEHOVE	BEKNOTS	BELEES
BEGULF	BEHOVED	BEKNOTTED	BELEMNITE
BEGULFED	BEHOVEFUL	BEKNOWN	BELEMNOID
BEGULFING	BEHOVELY	BEL	BELFRIED
BEGULFS	BEHOVES	BELABOR	BELFRIES
BEGUM	BEHOVING	BELABORED	BELFRY
BEGUMS	BEHOWL	BELABORS	BELGA
BEGUN	BEHOWLED	BELABOUR	BELGARD
BEGUNK	BEHOWLING	BELABOURS	BELGARDS
BEGUNKED	BEHOWLS	BELACE	BELGAS
BEGUNKING	BEIGE	BELACED	BELIE
BEGUNKS	BEIGEL	BELACES	BELIED
BEHALF	BEIGELS	BELACING	BELIEF
BEHALVES	BEIGES	BELADIED	BELIEFS
BEHAPPEN	BEIGNE	BELADIES	BELIER
BEHAPPENS	BEIGNES	BELADY	BELIERS
BEHATTED	BEIGNET	BELADYING	BELIES
BEHAVE	BEIGNETS	BELAH	BELIEVE
BEHAVED	BEIGY	BELAHS	BELIEVED
BEHAVER	BEIN	BELAMIES	BELIEVER
BEHAVERS	BEING	BELAMOURE	BELIEVERS
BEHAVES	BEINGLESS	BELAMY	BELIEVES
BEHAVING	BEINGNESS	BELAR	BELIEVING
BEHAVIOR	BEINGS	BELARS	BELIKE
BEHAVIORS	BEINKED	BELATE	BELIQUOR
BEHAVIOUR	BEINNESS	BELATED	BELIQUORS
BEHEAD	BEJABBERS	BELATEDLY	BELITTLE
BEHEADAL	BEJABERS	BELATES	BELITTLED
BEHEADALS	BEJADE	BELATING	BELITTLER
BEHEADED	BEJADED	BELAUD	BELITTLES
BEHEADER	BEJADES	BELAUDED	BELIVE
BEHEADERS	BEJADING	BELAUDING	BELL
BEHEADING	BEJANT	BELAUDS	BELLBIND
BEHEADS	BEJANTS	BELAY	BELLBINDS
BEHELD	BEJEEBERS	BELAYED	BELLBIRD
BEHEMOTH	BEJEEZUS	BELAYER	BELLBIRDS
BEHEMOTHS	BEJESUIT	BELAYERS	BELLBOY

BELLBOYS	BELOWS	BEMIRES	BENCHER
BELLCOTE	BELS	BEMIRING	BENCHERS
BELLCOTES	BELT	BEMIST	BENCHES
BELLE	BELTED	BEMISTED	BENCHIER
BELLED	BELTER	BEMISTING	BENCHIEST
BELLEEK	BELTERS	BEMISTS	BENCHING
BELLEEKS	BELTING	BEMIX	BENCHLAND
BELLES	BELTINGS	BEMIXED	BENCHLESS
BELLETER	BELTLESS	BEMIXES	BENCHMARK
BELLETERS	BELTLINE	BEMIXING	BENCHTOP
BELLHOP	BELTLINES	BEMIXT	BENCHY
BELLHOPS	BELTMAN	BEMOAN	BEND
BELLIBONE	BELTMEN	BEMOANED	BENDABLE
BELLICOSE	BELTS	BEMOANER	BENDAY
BELLIED	BELTWAY	BEMOANERS	BENDAYED
BELLIES	BELTWAYS	BEMOANING	BENDAYING
BELLING	BELUGA	BEMOANS	BENDAYS
BELLINGS	BELUGAS	BEMOCK	BENDED
BELLMAN	BELVEDERE	BEMOCKED	BENDEE
BELLMEN	BELYING	BEMOCKING	BENDEES
BELLOCK	BEMA	BEMOCKS	BENDER
BELLOCKED	BEMAD	BEMOIL	BENDERS
BELLOCKS	BEMADAM	BEMOILED	BENDIER
BELLOW	BEMADAMED	BEMOILING	BENDIEST
BELLOWED	BEMADAMS	BEMOILS	BENDING
BELLOWER	BEMADDED	BEMONSTER	BENDINGLY
BELLOWERS	BEMADDEN	BEMOUTH	BENDINGS
BELLOWING	BEMADDENS	BEMOUTHED	BENDLET
BELLOWS	BEMADDING	BEMOUTHS	BENDLETS
BELLPULL	BEMADS	BEMUD	BENDS
BELLPULLS	BEMAS	BEMUDDED	BENDWAYS
BELLPUSH	BEMATA	BEMUDDING	BENDWISE
BELLS	BEMAUL	BEMUDDLE	BENDY
BELLWORT	BEMAULED	BEMUDDLED	BENDYS
BELLWORTS	BEMAULING	BEMUDDLES	BENE
BELLY	BEMAULS	BEMUDS	BENEATH
BELLYACHE	BEMAZED	BEMUFFLE	BENEDICK
BELLYBAND	BEMBEX	BEMUFFLED	BENEDICKS
BELLYFUL	BEMBEXES	BEMUFFLES	BENEDICT
BELLYFULS	BEMBIX	BEMURMUR	BENEDICTS
BELLYING	BEMBIXES	BEMURMURS	BENEDIGHT
BELLYINGS	BEMEAN	BEMUSE	BENEFACT
BELLYLIKE	BEMEANED	BEMUSED	BENEFACTS
BELOMANCY	BEMEANING	BEMUSEDLY	BENEFIC
BELON	BEMEANS	BEMUSES	BENEFICE
BELONG	BEMEANT	BEMUSING	BENEFICED
BELONGED	BEMEDAL	BEMUZZLE	BENEFICES
BELONGER	BEMEDALED	BEMUZZLED	BENEFIT
BELONGERS	BEMEDALS	BEMUZZLES	BENEFITED
BELONGING	BEMETE	BEN	BENEFITER
BELONGS	BEMETED	BENADRYL	BENEFITS
BELONS	BEMETES	BENADRYLS	BENEMPT
BELOVE	BEMETING	BENAME	BENEMPTED
BELOVED	BEMINGLE	BENAMED	BENES
BELOVEDS	BEMINGLED	BENAMES	BENET
BELOVES	BEMINGLES	BENAMING	BENETS
BELOVING	BEMIRE	BENCH	BENETTED
BELOW	BEMIRED	BENCHED	BENETTING

BENGALINE	BENZAL	BEPOMMELS	BERETS
BENI	BENZALS	BEPOWDER	BERETTA
BENIGHT	BENZENE	BEPOWDERS	BERETTAS
BENIGHTED	BENZENES	BEPRAISE	BERG
BENIGHTEN	BENZENOID	BEPRAISED	BERGAMA
BENIGHTER	BENZIDIN	BEPRAISES	BERGAMAS
BENIGHTS	BENZIDINE	BEPROSE	BERGAMASK
BENIGN	BENZIDINS	BEPROSED	BERGAMOT
BENIGNANT	BENZIL	BEPROSES	BERGAMOTS
BENIGNER	BENZILS	BEPROSING	BERGANDER
BENIGNEST	BENZIN	BEPUFF	BERGEN
BENIGNITY	BENZINE	BEPUFFED	BERGENIA
BENIGNLY	BENZINES	BEPUFFING	BERGENIAS
BENIS	BENZINS	BEPUFFS	BERGENS
BENISEED	BENZOATE	BEQUEATH	BERGERE
BENISEEDS	BENZOATES	BEQUEATHS	BERGERES
BENISON	BENZOIC	BEQUEST	BERGFALL
BENISONS	BENZOIN	BEQUESTS	BERGFALLS
BENITIER	BENZOINS	BERAKE	BERGHAAN
BENITIERS	BENZOL	BERAKED	BERGHAANS
BENJ	BENZOLE	BERAKES	BERGMEHL
BENJAMIN	BENZOLES	BERAKING	BERGMEHLS
BENJAMINS	BENZOLINE	BERASCAL	BERGOMASK
BENJES	BENZOLS	BERASCALS	BERGS
BENNE	BENZOYL	BERATE	BERGYLT
BENNES	BENZOYLS	BERATED	BERGYLTS
BENNET	BENZYL	BERATES	BERHYME
BENNETS	BENZYLIC	BERATING	BERHYMED
BENNI	BENZYLS	BERAY	BERHYMES
BENNIES	BEPAINT	BERAYED	BERHYMING
BENNIS	BEPAINTED	BERAYING	BERIBERI
BENNY	BEPAINTS	BERAYS	BERIBERIS
BENOMYL	BEPAT	BERBERE	BERIMBAU
BENOMYLS	BEPATCHED	BERBERES	BERIMBAUS
BENS	BEPATS	BERBERIN	BERIME
BENT	BEPATTED	BERBERINE	BERIMED
BENTGRASS	BEPATTING	BERBERINS	BERIMES
BENTHAL	BEPEARL	BERBERIS	BERIMING
BENTHIC	BEPEARLED	BERBICE	BERINGED
BENTHOAL	BEPEARLS	BERCEAU	BERK
BENTHON	BEPELT	BERCEAUX	BERKELIUM
BENTHONIC	BEPELTED	BERCEUSE	BERKO
BENTHONS	BEPELTING	BERCEUSES	BERKS
BENTHOS	BEPELTS	BERDACHE	BERLEY
BENTHOSES	BEPEPPER	BERDACHES	BERLEYED
BENTIER	BEPEPPERS	BERDASH	BERLEYING
BENTIEST	BEPESTER	BERDASHES	BERLEYS
BENTO	BEPESTERS	BERE	BERLIN
BENTONITE	BEPIMPLE	BEREAVE	BERLINE
BENTOS	BEPIMPLED	BEREAVED	BERLINES
BENTS	BEPIMPLES	BEREAVEN	BERLINS
BENTWOOD	BEPITIED	BEREAVER	BERM
BENTWOODS	BEPITIES	BEREAVERS	BERME
BENTY	BEPITY	BEREAVES	BERMED
BENUMB	BEPITYING	BEREAVING	BERMES
BENUMBED	BEPLASTER	BEREFT	BERMING
BENUMBING	BEPLUMED	BERES	BERMS
BENUMBS	BEPOMMEL	BERET	BERMUDAS

BERNICLE
BERNICLES
BEROB
BEROBBED
BEROBBING
BEROBED
BEROBS
BEROUGED
BERRET
BERRETS
BERRETTA
BERRETTAS
BERRIED
BERRIES
BERRIGAN
BERRIGANS
BERRY
BERRYING
BERRYINGS
BERRYLESS
BERRYLIKE
BERSEEM
BERSEEMS
BERSERK
BERSERKER
BERSERKLY
BERSERKS
BERTH
BERTHA
BERTHAGE
BERTHAGES
BERTHAS
BERTHE
BERTHED
BERTHES
BERTHING
BERTHS
BERYL
BERYLINE
BERYLLIA
BERYLLIAS
BERYLLIUM
BERYLS
BES
BESAINT
BESAINTED
BESAINTS
BESANG
BESAT
BESAW
BESCATTER
BESCORCH
BESCOUR
BESCOURED
BESCOURS
BESCRAWL
BESCRAWLS
BESCREEN

BESCREENS
BESEE
BESEECH
BESEECHED
BESEECHER
BESEECHES
BESEEING
BESEEKE
BESEEKES
BESEEKING
BESEEM
BESEEMED
BESEEMING
BESEEMLY
BESEEMS
BESEEN
BESEES
BESES
BESET
BESETMENT
BESETS
BESETTER
BESETTERS
BESETTING
BESHADOW
BESHADOWS
BESHAME
BESHAMED
BESHAMES
BESHAMING
BESHINE
BESHINES
BESHINING
BESHIVER
BESHIVERS
BESHONE
BESHOUT
BESHOUTED
BESHOUTS
BESHREW
BESHREWED
BESHREWS
BESHROUD
BESHROUDS
BESIDE
BESIDES
BESIEGE
BESIEGED
BESIEGER
BESIEGERS
BESIEGES
BESIEGING
BESIGH
BESIGHED
BESIGHING
BESIGHS
BESING
BESINGING

BESINGS
BESIT
BESITS
BESITTING
BESLAVE
BESLAVED
BESLAVER
BESLAVERS
BESLAVES
BESLAVING
BESLIME
BESLIMED
BESLIMES
BESLIMING
BESLOBBER
BESLUBBER
BESMEAR
BESMEARED
BESMEARER
BESMEARS
BESMILE
BESMILED
BESMILES
BESMILING
BESMIRCH
BESMOKE
BESMOKED
BESMOKES
BESMOKING
BESMOOTH
BESMOOTHS
BESMUDGE
BESMUDGED
BESMUDGES
BESMUT
BESMUTCH
BESMUTS
BESMUTTED
BESNOW
BESNOWED
BESNOWING
BESNOWS
BESOGNIO
BESOGNIOS
BESOIN
BESOINS
BESOM
BESOMED
BESOMING
BESOMS
BESONIAN
BESONIANS
BESOOTHE
BESOOTHED
BESOOTHES
BESORT
BESORTED
BESORTING

BESORTS
BESOT
BESOTS
BESOTTED
BESOTTING
BESOUGHT
BESOULED
BESPAKE
BESPANGLE
BESPAT
BESPATE
BESPATTER
BESPEAK
BESPEAKS
BESPECKLE
BESPED
BESPEED
BESPEEDS
BESPICE
BESPICED
BESPICES
BESPICING
BESPIT
BESPITS
BESPOKE
BESPOKEN
BESPORT
BESPORTED
BESPORTS
BESPOT
BESPOTS
BESPOTTED
BESPOUSE
BESPOUSED
BESPOUSES
BESPOUT
BESPOUTED
BESPOUTS
BESPREAD
BESPREADS
BESPRENT
BEST
BESTAD
BESTADDE
BESTAIN
BESTAINED
BESTAINS
BESTAR
BESTARRED
BESTARS
BESTEAD
BESTEADED
BESTEADS
BESTED
BESTI
BESTIAL
BESTIALLY
BESTIALS

BESTIARY
BESTICK
BESTICKS
BESTILL
BESTILLED
BESTILLS
BESTING
BESTIR
BESTIRRED
BESTIRS
BESTIS
BESTORM
BESTORMED
BESTORMS
BESTOW
BESTOWAL
BESTOWALS
BESTOWED
BESTOWER
BESTOWERS
BESTOWING
BESTOWS
BESTREAK
BESTREAKS
BESTREW
BESTREWED
BESTREWN
BESTREWS
BESTRID
BESTRIDE
BESTRIDES
BESTRODE
BESTROW
BESTROWED
BESTROWN
BESTROWS
BESTS
BESTUCK
BESTUD
BESTUDDED
BESTUDS
BESUITED
BESUNG
BESWARM
BESWARMED
BESWARMS
BET
BETA
BETACISM
BETACISMS
BETAINE
BETAINES
BETAKE
BETAKEN
BETAKES
BETAKING
BETAS
BETATOPIC

BETATRON
BETATRONS
BETATTER
BETATTERS
BETAXED
BETE
BETED
BETEEM
BETEEME
BETEEMED
BETEEMES
BETEEMING
BETEEMS
BETEL
BETELNUT
BETELNUTS
BETELS
BETES
BETH
BETHANK
BETHANKED
BETHANKIT
BETHANKS
BETHEL
BETHELS
BETHESDA
BETHESDAS
BETHINK
BETHINKS
BETHORN
BETHORNED
BETHORNS
BETHOUGHT
BETHRALL
BETHRALLS
BETHS
BETHUMB
BETHUMBED
BETHUMBS
BETHUMP
BETHUMPED
BETHUMPS
BETHWACK
BETHWACKS
BETID
BETIDE
BETIDED
BETIDES
BETIDING
BETIGHT
BETIME
BETIMED
BETIMES
BETIMING
BETING
BETISE
BETISES
BETITLE

BETITLED
BETITLES
BETITLING
BETOIL
BETOILED
BETOILING
BETOILS
BETOKEN
BETOKENED
BETOKENS
BETON
BETONIES
BETONS
BETONY
BETOOK
BETOSS
BETOSSED
BETOSSES
BETOSSING
BETRAY
BETRAYAL
BETRAYALS
BETRAYED
BETRAYER
BETRAYERS
BETRAYING
BETRAYS
BETREAD
BETREADS
BETRIM
BETRIMMED
BETRIMS
BETROD
BETRODDEN
BETROTH
BETROTHAL
BETROTHED
BETROTHS
BETS
BETTA
BETTAS
BETTED
BETTER
BETTERED
BETTERING
BETTERS
BETTIES
BETTING
BETTINGS
BETTONG
BETTONGS
BETTOR
BETTORS
BETTY
BETUMBLED
BETWEEN
BETWEENS
BETWIXT

BEUNCLED
BEURRE
BEURRES
BEVATRON
BEVATRONS
BEVEL
BEVELED
BEVELER
BEVELERS
BEVELING
BEVELLED
BEVELLER
BEVELLERS
BEVELLING
BEVELMENT
BEVELS
BEVER
BEVERAGE
BEVERAGES
BEVERS
BEVIES
BEVOMIT
BEVOMITED
BEVOMITS
BEVOR
BEVORS
BEVUE
BEVUES
BEVVIED
BEVVIES
BEVVY
BEVVYING
BEVY
BEWAIL
BEWAILED
BEWAILER
BEWAILERS
BEWAILING
BEWAILS
BEWARE
BEWARED
BEWARES
BEWARING
BEWEARIED
BEWEARIES
BEWEARY
BEWEEP
BEWEEPING
BEWEEPS
BEWENT
BEWEPT
BEWET
BEWETS
BEWETTED
BEWETTING
BEWHORE
BEWHORED
BEWHORES

BEWHORING
BEWIG
BEWIGGED
BEWIGGING
BEWIGS
BEWILDER
BEWILDERS
BEWINGED
BEWITCH
BEWITCHED
BEWITCHER
BEWITCHES
BEWORM
BEWORMED
BEWORMING
BEWORMS
BEWORRIED
BEWORRIES
BEWORRY
BEWRAP
BEWRAPPED
BEWRAPS
BEWRAPT
BEWRAY
BEWRAYED
BEWRAYER
BEWRAYERS
BEWRAYING
BEWRAYS
BEY
BEYLIC
BEYLICS
BEYLIK
BEYLIKS
BEYOND
BEYONDS
BEYS
BEZ
BEZANT
BEZANTS
BEZAZZ
BEZAZZES
BEZEL
BEZELS
BEZES
BEZIL
BEZILS
BEZIQUE
BEZIQUES
BEZOAR
BEZOARDIC
BEZOARS
BEZONIAN
BEZONIANS
BEZZANT
BEZZANTS
BEZZAZZ
BEZZAZZES

BEZZLE
BEZZLED
BEZZLES
BEZZLING
BHAGEE
BHAGEES
BHAJAN
BHAJANS
BHAJEE
BHAJEES
BHAJI
BHAJIS
BHAKTA
BHAKTAS
BHAKTI
BHAKTIS
BHANG
BHANGRA
BHANGRAS
BHANGS
BHARAL
BHARALS
BHAT
BHAVAN
BHAVANS
BHAWAN
BHAWANS
BHEESTIE
BHEESTIES
BHEESTY
BHEL
BHELS
BHIKHU
BHIKHUS
BHIKKHUNI
BHINDI
BHINDIS
BHISHTI
BHISHTIS
BHISTEE
BHISTEES
BHISTI
BHISTIE
BHISTIES
BHISTIS
BHOOT
BHOOTS
BHUNA
BHUNAS
BHUT
BHUTS
BI
BIACETYL
BIACETYLS
BIALI
BIALIES
BIALIS
BIALY

BIALYS
BIANNUAL
BIANNUALS
BIAS
BIASED
BIASEDLY
BIASES
BIASING
BIASINGS
BIASNESS
BIASSED
BIASSEDLY
BIASSES
BIASSING
BIATHLETE
BIATHLON
BIATHLONS
BIAXAL
BIAXIAL
BIAXIALLY
BIB
BIBACIOUS
BIBASIC
BIBATION
BIBATIONS
BIBB
BIBBED
BIBBER
BIBBERIES
BIBBERS
BIBBERY
BIBBING
BIBBLE
BIBBLES
BIBBS
BIBCOCK
BIBCOCKS
BIBELOT
BIBELOTS
BIBLE
BIBLES
BIBLESS
BIBLICAL
BIBLICISM
BIBLICIST
BIBLIKE
BIBLIOTIC
BIBLIST
BIBLISTS
BIBS
BIBULOUS
BICAMERAL
BICARB
BICARBS
BICAUDAL
BICCIES
BICCY
BICE

BICENTRIC
BICEP
BICEPS
BICEPSES
BICES
BICHORD
BICHROME
BICIPITAL
BICKER
BICKERED
BICKERER
BICKERERS
BICKERING
BICKERS
BICKIE
BICKIES
BICOASTAL
BICOLOR
BICOLORED
BICOLORS
BICOLOUR
BICOLOURS
BICONCAVE
BICONVEX
BICORN
BICORNATE
BICORNE
BICORNES
BICORNS
BICRON
BICRONS
BICUSPID
BICUSPIDS
BICYCLE
BICYCLED
BICYCLER
BICYCLERS
BICYCLES
BICYCLIC
BICYCLING
BICYCLIST
BID
BIDARKA
BIDARKAS
BIDARKEE
BIDARKEES
BIDDABLE
BIDDABLY
BIDDEN
BIDDER
BIDDERS
BIDDIES
BIDDING
BIDDINGS
BIDDY
BIDE
BIDED
BIDENT

BIDENTAL
BIDENTALS
BIDENTATE
BIDENTS
BIDER
BIDERS
BIDES
BIDET
BIDETS
BIDI
BIDING
BIDINGS
BIDIS
BIDON
BIDONS
BIDS
BIELD
BIELDED
BIELDIER
BIELDIEST
BIELDING
BIELDS
BIELDY
BIEN
BIENNALE
BIENNALES
BIENNIA
BIENNIAL
BIENNIALS
BIENNIUM
BIENNIUMS
BIER
BIERS
BIESTINGS
BIFACE
BIFACES
BIFACIAL
BIFARIOUS
BIFF
BIFFED
BIFFER
BIFFERS
BIFFIES
BIFFIN
BIFFING
BIFFINS
BIFFO
BIFFOS
BIFFS
BIFFY
BIFID
BIFIDITY
BIFIDLY
BIFILAR
BIFILARLY
BIFLEX
BIFOCAL
BIFOCALED

BIFOCALS
BIFOLD
BIFOLIATE
BIFORATE
BIFORKED
BIFORM
BIFORMED
BIFTER
BIFTERS
BIFURCATE
BIG
BIGA
BIGAE
BIGAMIES
BIGAMIST
BIGAMISTS
BIGAMOUS
BIGAMY
BIGARADE
BIGARADES
BIGAROON
BIGAROONS
BIGARREAU
BIGEMINAL
BIGEMINY
BIGENER
BIGENERIC
BIGENERS
BIGEYE
BIGEYES
BIGFEET
BIGFOOT
BIGFOOTED
BIGFOOTS
BIGG
BIGGED
BIGGER
BIGGEST
BIGGETY
BIGGIE
BIGGIES
BIGGIN
BIGGING
BIGGINGS
BIGGINS
BIGGISH
BIGGITY
BIGGON
BIGGONS
BIGGS
BIGGY
BIGHA
BIGHAS
BIGHEAD
BIGHEADED
BIGHEADS
BIGHORN
BIGHORNS

BIGHT
BIGHTED
BIGHTING
BIGHTS
BIGLY
BIGMOUTH
BIGMOUTHS
BIGNESS
BIGNESSES
BIGNONIA
BIGNONIAS
BIGOS
BIGOSES
BIGOT
BIGOTED
BIGOTEDLY
BIGOTRIES
BIGOTRY
BIGOTS
BIGS
BIGSTICK
BIGTIME
BIGUANIDE
BIGWIG
BIGWIGS
BIHOURLY
BIJECTION
BIJECTIVE
BIJOU
BIJOUS
BIJOUX
BIJUGATE
BIJUGOUS
BIJWONER
BIJWONERS
BIKE
BIKED
BIKER
BIKERS
BIKES
BIKEWAY
BIKEWAYS
BIKIE
BIKIES
BIKING
BIKINGS
BIKINI
BIKINIED
BIKINIS
BIKKIE
BIKKIES
BILABIAL
BILABIALS
BILABIATE
BILANDER
BILANDERS
BILATERAL
BILAYER

BILAYERS
BILBERRY
BILBIES
BILBO
BILBOA
BILBOAS
BILBOES
BILBOS
BILBY
BILE
BILECTION
BILED
BILES
BILESTONE
BILEVEL
BILEVELS
BILGE
BILGED
BILGES
BILGIER
BILGIEST
BILGING
BILGY
BILHARZIA
BILIAN
BILIANS
BILIARIES
BILIARY
BILIMBI
BILIMBING
BILIMBIS
BILINEAR
BILING
BILINGUAL
BILIOUS
BILIOUSLY
BILIRUBIN
BILITERAL
BILK
BILKED
BILKER
BILKERS
BILKING
BILKS
BILL
BILLABLE
BILLABONG
BILLBOARD
BILLBOOK
BILLBOOKS
BILLBUG
BILLBUGS
BILLED
BILLER
BILLERS
BILLET
BILLETED
BILLETEE

BILLETEES	BIMAS	BINGES	BIODOTS
BILLETER	BIMBASHI	BINGHI	BIOETHIC
BILLETERS	BIMBASHIS	BINGHIS	BIOETHICS
BILLETING	BIMBETTE	BINGIES	BIOFACT
BILLETS	BIMBETTES	BINGING	BIOFACTS
BILLFISH	BIMBLE	BINGLE	BIOFILM
BILLFOLD	BIMBO	BINGLED	BIOFILMS
BILLFOLDS	BIMBOES	BINGLES	BIOFOULER
BILLHEAD	BIMBOS	BINGLING	BIOFUEL
BILLHEADS	BIMENSAL	BINGO	BIOFUELED
BILLHOOK	BIMESTER	BINGOES	BIOFUELS
BILLHOOKS	BIMESTERS	BINGOS	BIOG
BILLIARD	BIMETAL	BINGS	BIOGAS
BILLIARDS	BIMETALS	BINGY	BIOGASES
BILLIE	BIMETHYL	BINIOU	BIOGASSES
BILLIES	BIMETHYLS	BINIOUS	BIOGEN
BILLING	BIMODAL	BINIT	BIOGENIC
BILLINGS	BIMONTHLY	BINITS	BIOGENIES
BILLION	BIMORPH	BINK	BIOGENOUS
BILLIONS	BIMORPHS	BINKS	BIOGENS
BILLIONTH	BIN	BINMAN	BIOGENY
BILLMAN	BINAL	BINMEN	BIOGRAPH
BILLMEN	BINARIES	BINNACLE	BIOGRAPHS
BILLON	BINARISM	BINNACLES	BIOGRAPHY
BILLONS	BINARISMS	BINNED	BIOGS
BILLOW	BINARY	BINNING	BIOHAZARD
BILLOWED	BINATE	BINOCLE	BIOHERM
BILLOWIER	BINATELY	BINOCLES	BIOHERMS
BILLOWING	BINAURAL	BINOCS	BIOLOGIC
BILLOWS	BIND	BINOCULAR	BIOLOGICS
BILLOWY	BINDABLE	BINOMIAL	BIOLOGIES
BILLS	BINDER	BINOMIALS	BIOLOGISM
BILLY	BINDERIES	BINOMINAL	BIOLOGIST
BILLYBOY	BINDERS	BINOVULAR	BIOLOGY
BILLYBOYS	BINDERY	BINS	BIOLYSES
BILLYCAN	BINDHI	BINT	BIOLYSIS
BILLYCANS	BINDHIS	BINTS	BIOLYTIC
BILLYCOCK	BINDI	BINTURONG	BIOMARKER
BILLYO	BINDING	BINUCLEAR	BIOMASS
BILLYOH	BINDINGLY	BIO	BIOMASSES
BILLYOHS	BINDINGS	BIOACTIVE	BIOME
BILLYOS	BINDIS	BIOASSAY	BIOMES
BILOBAR	BINDLE	BIOASSAYS	BIOMETER
BILOBATE	BINDLES	BIOBLAST	BIOMETERS
BILOBATED	BINDS	BIOBLASTS	BIOMETRIC
BILOBED	BINDWEED	BIOCENOSE	BIOMETRY
BILOBULAR	BINDWEEDS	BIOCHEMIC	BIOMINING
BILOCULAR	BINE	BIOCHIP	BIOMORPH
BILSTED	BINER	BIOCHIPS	BIOMORPHS
BILSTEDS	BINERS	BIOCIDAL	BIONIC
BILTONG	BINERVATE	BIOCIDE	BIONICS
BILTONGS	BINES	BIOCIDES	BIONOMIC
BIMA	BING	BIOCLEAN	BIONOMICS
BIMAH	BINGE	BIOCYCLE	BIONOMIES
BIMAHS	BINGED	BIOCYCLES	BIONOMIST
BIMANAL	BINGEING	BIODATA	BIONOMY
BIMANOUS	BINGER	BIODIESEL	BIONT
BIMANUAL	BINGERS	BIODOT	BIONTIC

BIONTS
BIOPARENT
BIOPHILIA
BIOPHOR
BIOPHORE
BIOPHORES
BIOPHORS
BIOPIC
BIOPICS
BIOPIRACY
BIOPIRATE
BIOPLASM
BIOPLASMS
BIOPLAST
BIOPLASTS
BIOPSIC
BIOPSIED
BIOPSIES
BIOPSY
BIOPSYING
BIOPTIC
BIOREGION
BIORHYTHM
BIOS
BIOSAFETY
BIOSCOPE
BIOSCOPES
BIOSCOPY
BIOSENSOR
BIOSOCIAL
BIOSOLID
BIOSOLIDS
BIOSPHERE
BIOSTABLE
BIOSTATIC
BIOSTROME
BIOTA
BIOTAS
BIOTECH
BIOTECHS
BIOTERROR
BIOTIC
BIOTICAL
BIOTICS
BIOTIN
BIOTINS
BIOTITE
BIOTITES
BIOTITIC
BIOTOPE
BIOTOPES
BIOTOXIN
BIOTOXINS
BIOTRON
BIOTRONS
BIOTROPH
BIOTROPHS
BIOTURBED

BIOTYPE
BIOTYPES
BIOTYPIC
BIOVULAR
BIOWEAPON
BIPACK
BIPACKS
BIPAROUS
BIPARTED
BIPARTITE
BIPARTY
BIPED
BIPEDAL
BIPEDALLY
BIPEDS
BIPHASIC
BIPHENYL
BIPHENYLS
BIPINNATE
BIPLANE
BIPLANES
BIPOD
BIPODS
BIPOLAR
BIPRISM
BIPRISMS
BIPYRAMID
BIRACIAL
BIRADIAL
BIRADICAL
BIRAMOSE
BIRAMOUS
BIRCH
BIRCHBARK
BIRCHED
BIRCHEN
BIRCHES
BIRCHING
BIRD
BIRDBATH
BIRDBATHS
BIRDBRAIN
BIRDCAGE
BIRDCAGES
BIRDCALL
BIRDCALLS
BIRDDOG
BIRDDOGS
BIRDED
BIRDER
BIRDERS
BIRDFARM
BIRDFARMS
BIRDFEED
BIRDFEEDS
BIRDHOUSE
BIRDIE
BIRDIED

BIRDIEING
BIRDIES
BIRDING
BIRDINGS
BIRDLIFE
BIRDLIKE
BIRDLIME
BIRDLIMED
BIRDLIMES
BIRDMAN
BIRDMEN
BIRDS
BIRDSEED
BIRDSEEDS
BIRDSEYE
BIRDSEYES
BIRDSHOT
BIRDSHOTS
BIRDSONG
BIRDSONGS
BIRDWATCH
BIRDWING
BIRDWINGS
BIREME
BIREMES
BIRETTA
BIRETTAS
BIRIANI
BIRIANIS
BIRIYANI
BIRIYANIS
BIRK
BIRKEN
BIRKIE
BIRKIER
BIRKIES
BIRKIEST
BIRKS
BIRL
BIRLE
BIRLED
BIRLER
BIRLERS
BIRLES
BIRLIEMAN
BIRLIEMEN
BIRLING
BIRLINGS
BIRLINN
BIRLINNS
BIRLS
BIRO
BIROS
BIRR
BIRRED
BIRRETTA
BIRRETTAS
BIRRING

BIRROTCH
BIRRS
BIRSE
BIRSES
BIRSIER
BIRSIEST
BIRSLE
BIRSLED
BIRSLES
BIRSLING
BIRSY
BIRTH
BIRTHDAY
BIRTHDAYS
BIRTHDOM
BIRTHDOMS
BIRTHED
BIRTHING
BIRTHINGS
BIRTHMARK
BIRTHNAME
BIRTHRATE
BIRTHROOT
BIRTHS
BIRTHWORT
BIRYANI
BIRYANIS
BIS
BISCACHA
BISCACHAS
BISCOTTI
BISCOTTO
BISCUIT
BISCUITS
BISCUITY
BISE
BISECT
BISECTED
BISECTING
BISECTION
BISECTOR
BISECTORS
BISECTRIX
BISECTS
BISERIAL
BISERIATE
BISERRATE
BISES
BISEXUAL
BISEXUALS
BISH
BISHES
BISHOP
BISHOPDOM
BISHOPED
BISHOPESS
BISHOPING
BISHOPRIC

BISHOPS	BITEWING	BITUMENS	BLACKBALL
BISK	BITEWINGS	BIUNIQUE	BLACKBAND
BISKS	BITING	BIVALENCE	BLACKBIRD
BISMAR	BITINGLY	BIVALENCY	BLACKBODY
BISMARS	BITINGS	BIVALENT	BLACKBOY
BISMILLAH	BITLESS	BIVALENTS	BLACKBOYS
BISMUTH	BITMAP	BIVALVATE	BLACKBUCK
BISMUTHAL	BITMAPPED	BIVALVE	BLACKBUTT
BISMUTHIC	BITMAPS	BIVALVED	BLACKCAP
BISMUTHS	BITO	BIVALVES	BLACKCAPS
BISNAGA	BITONAL	BIVARIANT	BLACKCOCK
BISNAGAS	BITOS	BIVARIATE	BLACKDAMP
BISON	BITOU	BIVIA	BLACKED
BISONS	BITS	BIVINYL	BLACKEN
BISONTINE	BITSER	BIVINYLS	BLACKENED
BISQUE	BITSERS	BIVIOUS	BLACKENER
BISQUES	BITSIER	BIVIUM	BLACKENS
BISSON	BITSIEST	BIVOUAC	BLACKER
BIST	BITSTOCK	BIVOUACKS	BLACKEST
BISTABLE	BITSTOCKS	BIVOUACS	BLACKFACE
BISTABLES	BITSTREAM	BIVVIED	BLACKFIN
BISTATE	BITSY	BIVVIES	BLACKFINS
BISTER	BITT	BIVVY	BLACKFISH
BISTERED	BITTACLE	BIVVYING	BLACKFLY
BISTERS	BITTACLES	BIWEEKLY	BLACKGAME
BISTORT	BITTE	BIYEARLY	BLACKGUM
BISTORTS	BITTED	BIZ	BLACKGUMS
BISTOURY	BITTEN	BIZARRE	BLACKHEAD
BISTRE	BITTER	BIZARRELY	BLACKING
BISTRED	BITTERED	BIZARRES	BLACKINGS
BISTRES	BITTERER	BIZARRO	BLACKISH
BISTRO	BITTEREST	BIZARROS	BLACKJACK
BISTROIC	BITTERING	BIZAZZ	BLACKLAND
BISTROS	BITTERISH	BIZAZZES	BLACKLEAD
BISULCATE	BITTERLY	BIZCACHA	BLACKLEG
BISULFATE	BITTERN	BIZCACHAS	BLACKLEGS
BISULFIDE	BITTERNS	BIZE	BLACKLIST
BISULFITE	BITTERNUT	BIZES	BLACKLY
BIT	BITTERS	BIZNAGA	BLACKMAIL
BITABLE	BITTIE	BIZNAGAS	BLACKNESS
BITCH	BITTIER	BIZONAL	BLACKOUT
BITCHED	BITTIES	BIZONE	BLACKOUTS
BITCHEN	BITTIEST	BIZONES	BLACKPOLL
BITCHERY	BITTINESS	BIZZES	BLACKS
BITCHES	BITTING	BIZZIES	BLACKTAIL
BITCHFEST	BITTINGS	BIZZO	BLACKTOP
BITCHIER	BITTOCK	BIZZOS	BLACKTOPS
BITCHIEST	BITTOCKS	BIZZY	BLACKWASH
BITCHILY	BITTOR	BLAB	BLACKWOOD
BITCHING	BITTORS	BLABBED	BLAD
BITCHY	BITTOUR	BLABBER	BLADDED
BITE	BITTOURS	BLABBERED	BLADDER
BITEABLE	BITTS	BLABBERS	BLADDERED
BITEPLATE	BITTUR	BLABBING	BLADDERS
BITER	BITTURS	BLABBINGS	BLADDERY
BITERS	BITTY	BLABBY	BLADDING
BITES	BITUMED	BLABS	BLADE
BITESIZE	BITUMEN	BLACK	BLADED

BLADELESS
BLADELIKE
BLADER
BLADERS
BLADES
BLADEWORK
BLADING
BLADINGS
BLADS
BLADY
BLAE
BLAEBERRY
BLAER
BLAES
BLAEST
BLAFF
BLAFFS
BLAG
BLAGGED
BLAGGER
BLAGGERS
BLAGGING
BLAGGINGS
BLAGS
BLAGUE
BLAGUER
BLAGUERS
BLAGUES
BLAGUEUR
BLAGUEURS
BLAH
BLAHED
BLAHING
BLAHS
BLAIN
BLAINS
BLAISE
BLAIZE
BLAM
BLAMABLE
BLAMABLY
BLAME
BLAMEABLE
BLAMEABLY
BLAMED
BLAMEFUL
BLAMELESS
BLAMER
BLAMERS
BLAMES
BLAMING
BLAMS
BLANCH
BLANCHED
BLANCHER
BLANCHERS
BLANCHES
BLANCHING

BLANCO
BLANCOED
BLANCOING
BLANCOS
BLAND
BLANDER
BLANDEST
BLANDISH
BLANDLY
BLANDNESS
BLANDS
BLANK
BLANKED
BLANKER
BLANKEST
BLANKET
BLANKETED
BLANKETS
BLANKETY
BLANKIES
BLANKING
BLANKINGS
BLANKLY
BLANKNESS
BLANKS
BLANKY
BLANQUET
BLANQUETS
BLARE
BLARED
BLARES
BLARING
BLARNEY
BLARNEYED
BLARNEYS
BLART
BLARTED
BLARTING
BLARTS
BLASE
BLASH
BLASHES
BLASHIER
BLASHIEST
BLASHY
BLASPHEME
BLASPHEMY
BLAST
BLASTED
BLASTEMA
BLASTEMAL
BLASTEMAS
BLASTEMIC
BLASTER
BLASTERS
BLASTIE
BLASTIER
BLASTIES

BLASTIEST
BLASTING
BLASTINGS
BLASTMENT
BLASTOFF
BLASTOFFS
BLASTOID
BLASTOIDS
BLASTOMA
BLASTOMAS
BLASTOPOR
BLASTS
BLASTULA
BLASTULAE
BLASTULAR
BLASTULAS
BLASTY
BLAT
BLATANCY
BLATANT
BLATANTLY
BLATE
BLATER
BLATEST
BLATHER
BLATHERED
BLATHERER
BLATHERS
BLATS
BLATT
BLATTANT
BLATTED
BLATTER
BLATTERED
BLATTERS
BLATTING
BLATTS
BLAUBOK
BLAUBOKS
BLAUD
BLAUDED
BLAUDING
BLAUDS
BLAW
BLAWED
BLAWING
BLAWN
BLAWORT
BLAWORTS
BLAWS
BLAY
BLAYS
BLAZE
BLAZED
BLAZER
BLAZERED
BLAZERS
BLAZES

BLAZING
BLAZINGLY
BLAZON
BLAZONED
BLAZONER
BLAZONERS
BLAZONING
BLAZONRY
BLAZONS
BLEACH
BLEACHED
BLEACHER
BLEACHERS
BLEACHERY
BLEACHES
BLEACHING
BLEAK
BLEAKER
BLEAKEST
BLEAKISH
BLEAKLY
BLEAKNESS
BLEAKS
BLEAKY
BLEAR
BLEARED
BLEARER
BLEAREST
BLEAREYED
BLEARIER
BLEARIEST
BLEARILY
BLEARING
BLEARS
BLEARY
BLEAT
BLEATED
BLEATER
BLEATERS
BLEATING
BLEATINGS
BLEATS
BLEB
BLEBBIER
BLEBBIEST
BLEBBING
BLEBBINGS
BLEBBY
BLEBS
BLED
BLEE
BLEED
BLEEDER
BLEEDERS
BLEEDING
BLEEDINGS
BLEEDS
BLEEP

BLEEPED
BLEEPER
BLEEPERS
BLEEPING
BLEEPS
BLEES
BLELLUM
BLELLUMS
BLEMISH
BLEMISHED
BLEMISHER
BLEMISHES
BLENCH
BLENCHED
BLENCHER
BLENCHERS
BLENCHES
BLENCHING
BLEND
BLENDE
BLENDED
BLENDER
BLENDERS
BLENDES
BLENDING
BLENDINGS
BLENDS
BLENNIES
BLENNIOID
BLENNY
BLENT
BLERT
BLERTS
BLESBOK
BLESBOKS
BLESBUCK
BLESBUCKS
BLESS
BLESSED
BLESSEDER
BLESSEDLY
BLESSER
BLESSERS
BLESSES
BLESSING
BLESSINGS
BLEST
BLET
BLETHER
BLETHERED
BLETHERER
BLETHERS
BLETS
BLETTED
BLETTING
BLEUATRE
BLEW
BLEWART

BLEWARTS
BLEWITS
BLEWITSES
BLEY
BLEYS
BLIGHT
BLIGHTED
BLIGHTER
BLIGHTERS
BLIGHTIES
BLIGHTING
BLIGHTS
BLIGHTY
BLIKSEM
BLIMBING
BLIMBINGS
BLIMEY
BLIMP
BLIMPISH
BLIMPS
BLIMY
BLIN
BLIND
BLINDAGE
BLINDAGES
BLINDED
BLINDER
BLINDERS
BLINDEST
BLINDFISH
BLINDFOLD
BLINDGUT
BLINDGUTS
BLINDING
BLINDINGS
BLINDLESS
BLINDLY
BLINDNESS
BLINDS
BLINDSIDE
BLINDWORM
BLING
BLINGER
BLINGEST
BLINGING
BLINGLISH
BLINGS
BLINI
BLINIS
BLINK
BLINKARD
BLINKARDS
BLINKED
BLINKER
BLINKERED
BLINKERS
BLINKING
BLINKS

BLINNED
BLINNING
BLINS
BLINTZ
BLINTZE
BLINTZES
BLINY
BLIP
BLIPPED
BLIPPING
BLIPS
BLIPVERT
BLIPVERTS
BLISS
BLISSED
BLISSES
BLISSFUL
BLISSING
BLISSLESS
BLIST
BLISTER
BLISTERED
BLISTERS
BLISTERY
BLITE
BLITES
BLITHE
BLITHEFUL
BLITHELY
BLITHER
BLITHERED
BLITHERS
BLITHEST
BLITZ
BLITZED
BLITZER
BLITZERS
BLITZES
BLITZING
BLIVE
BLIZZARD
BLIZZARDS
BLIZZARDY
BLOAT
BLOATED
BLOATER
BLOATERS
BLOATING
BLOATINGS
BLOATS
BLOATWARE
BLOB
BLOBBED
BLOBBIER
BLOBBIEST
BLOBBING
BLOBBY
BLOBS

BLOC
BLOCK
BLOCKABLE
BLOCKADE
BLOCKADED
BLOCKADER
BLOCKADES
BLOCKAGE
BLOCKAGES
BLOCKBUST
BLOCKED
BLOCKER
BLOCKERS
BLOCKHEAD
BLOCKHOLE
BLOCKIE
BLOCKIER
BLOCKIES
BLOCKIEST
BLOCKING
BLOCKINGS
BLOCKISH
BLOCKS
BLOCKWORK
BLOCKY
BLOCS
BLOG
BLOGGER
BLOGGERS
BLOGGING
BLOGGINGS
BLOGS
BLOKE
BLOKEDOM
BLOKEDOMS
BLOKEISH
BLOKES
BLOKEY
BLOKIER
BLOKIEST
BLOKISH
BLONCKET
BLOND
BLONDE
BLONDER
BLONDES
BLONDEST
BLONDINE
BLONDINED
BLONDINES
BLONDING
BLONDINGS
BLONDISH
BLONDNESS
BLONDS
BLOOD
BLOODBATH
BLOODED

BLOODFIN	BLOTCHIER	BLOWJOBS	BLUE
BLOODFINS	BLOTCHILY	BLOWKART	BLUEBACK
BLOODHEAT	BLOTCHING	BLOWKARTS	BLUEBACKS
BLOODIED	BLOTCHY	BLOWLAMP	BLUEBALL
BLOODIER	BLOTLESS	BLOWLAMPS	BLUEBALLS
BLOODIES	BLOTS	BLOWN	BLUEBEARD
BLOODIEST	BLOTTED	BLOWOFF	BLUEBEAT
BLOODILY	BLOTTER	BLOWOFFS	BLUEBEATS
BLOODING	BLOTTERS	BLOWOUT	BLUEBELL
BLOODINGS	BLOTTIER	BLOWOUTS	BLUEBELLS
BLOODLESS	BLOTTIEST	BLOWPIPE	BLUEBERRY
BLOODLIKE	BLOTTING	BLOWPIPES	BLUEBILL
BLOODLINE	BLOTTINGS	BLOWS	BLUEBILLS
BLOODLUST	BLOTTO	BLOWSE	BLUEBIRD
BLOODRED	BLOTTY	BLOWSED	BLUEBIRDS
BLOODROOT	BLOUBOK	BLOWSES	BLUEBLOOD
BLOODS	BLOUBOKS	BLOWSIER	BLUEBOOK
BLOODSHED	BLOUSE	BLOWSIEST	BLUEBOOKS
BLOODSHOT	BLOUSED	BLOWSILY	BLUEBUCK
BLOODWOOD	BLOUSES	BLOWSY	BLUEBUCKS
BLOODWORM	BLOUSIER	BLOWTORCH	BLUEBUSH
BLOODWORT	BLOUSIEST	BLOWTUBE	BLUECAP
BLOODY	BLOUSILY	BLOWTUBES	BLUECAPS
BLOODYING	BLOUSING	BLOWUP	BLUECOAT
BLOOEY	BLOUSON	BLOWUPS	BLUECOATS
BLOOIE	BLOUSONS	BLOWY	BLUECURLS
BLOOM	BLOUSY	BLOWZE	BLUED
BLOOMED	BLOVIATE	BLOWZED	BLUEFIN
BLOOMER	BLOVIATED	BLOWZES	BLUEFINS
BLOOMERS	BLOVIATES	BLOWZIER	BLUEFISH
BLOOMERY	BLOW	BLOWZIEST	BLUEGILL
BLOOMIER	BLOWBACK	BLOWZILY	BLUEGILLS
BLOOMIEST	BLOWBACKS	BLOWZY	BLUEGOWN
BLOOMING	BLOWBALL	BLUB	BLUEGOWNS
BLOOMLESS	BLOWBALLS	BLUBBED	BLUEGRASS
BLOOMS	BLOWBY	BLUBBER	BLUEGUM
BLOOMY	BLOWBYS	BLUBBERED	BLUEGUMS
BLOOP	BLOWDOWN	BLUBBERER	BLUEHEAD
BLOOPED	BLOWDOWNS	BLUBBERS	BLUEHEADS
BLOOPER	BLOWED	BLUBBERY	BLUEING
BLOOPERS	BLOWER	BLUBBING	BLUEINGS
BLOOPING	BLOWERS	BLUBS	BLUEISH
BLOOPS	BLOWFISH	BLUCHER	BLUEJACK
BLOOSME	BLOWFLIES	BLUCHERS	BLUEJACKS
BLOOSMED	BLOWFLY	BLUDE	BLUEJAY
BLOOSMES	BLOWGUN	BLUDES	BLUEJAYS
BLOOSMING	BLOWGUNS	BLUDGE	BLUEJEANS
BLOQUISTE	BLOWHARD	BLUDGED	BLUELINE
BLORE	BLOWHARDS	BLUDGEON	BLUELINER
BLORES	BLOWHOLE	BLUDGEONS	BLUELINES
BLOSSOM	BLOWHOLES	BLUDGER	BLUELY
BLOSSOMED	BLOWIE	BLUDGERS	BLUENESS
BLOSSOMS	BLOWIER	BLUDGES	BLUENOSE
BLOSSOMY	BLOWIES	BLUDGING	BLUENOSED
BLOT	BLOWIEST	BLUDIE	BLUENOSES
BLOTCH	BLOWINESS	BLUDIER	BLUEPOINT
BLOTCHED	BLOWING	BLUDIEST	BLUEPRINT
BLOTCHES	BLOWJOB	BLUDY	BLUER

BLUES	BLUNGE	BLUSTERS	BOATHOUSE
BLUESHIFT	BLUNGED	BLUSTERY	BOATIE
BLUESIER	BLUNGER	BLUSTROUS	BOATIES
BLUESIEST	BLUNGERS	BLUTWURST	BOATING
BLUESMAN	BLUNGES	BLYPE	BOATINGS
BLUESMEN	BLUNGING	BLYPES	BOATLIFT
BLUEST	BLUNK	BO	BOATLIFTS
BLUESTEM	BLUNKED	BOA	BOATLIKE
BLUESTEMS	BLUNKER	BOAB	BOATLOAD
BLUESTONE	BLUNKERS	BOABS	BOATLOADS
BLUESY	BLUNKING	BOAK	BOATMAN
BLUET	BLUNKS	BOAKED	BOATMEN
BLUETICK	BLUNT	BOAKING	BOATNECK
BLUETICKS	BLUNTED	BOAKS	BOATNECKS
BLUETIT	BLUNTER	BOAR	BOATS
BLUETITS	BLUNTEST	BOARD	BOATSMAN
BLUETS	BLUNTHEAD	BOARDABLE	BOATSMEN
BLUETTE	BLUNTING	BOARDED	BOATSWAIN
BLUETTES	BLUNTISH	BOARDER	BOATTAIL
BLUEWEED	BLUNTLY	BOARDERS	BOATTAILS
BLUEWEEDS	BLUNTNESS	BOARDING	BOATYARD
BLUEWING	BLUNTS	BOARDINGS	BOATYARDS
BLUEWINGS	BLUR	BOARDLIKE	BOB
BLUEWOOD	BLURB	BOARDMAN	BOBA
BLUEWOODS	BLURBED	BOARDMEN	BOBAC
BLUEY	BLURBING	BOARDROOM	BOBACS
BLUEYS	BLURBIST	BOARDS	BOBAK
BLUFF	BLURBISTS	BOARDWALK	BOBAKS
BLUFFABLE	BLURBS	BOARFISH	BOBAS
BLUFFED	BLURRED	BOARHOUND	BOBBED
BLUFFER	BLURREDLY	BOARISH	BOBBEJAAN
BLUFFERS	BLURRIER	BOARISHLY	BOBBER
BLUFFEST	BLURRIEST	BOARS	BOBBERIES
BLUFFING	BLURRILY	BOART	BOBBERS
BLUFFLY	BLURRING	BOARTS	BOBBERY
BLUFFNESS	BLURRY	BOAS	BOBBIES
BLUFFS	BLURS	BOAST	BOBBIN
BLUGGIER	BLURT	BOASTED	BOBBINET
BLUGGIEST	BLURTED	BOASTER	BOBBINETS
BLUGGY	BLURTER	BOASTERS	BOBBING
BLUID	BLURTERS	BOASTFUL	BOBBINS
BLUIDIER	BLURTING	BOASTING	BOBBISH
BLUIDIEST	BLURTINGS	BOASTINGS	BOBBITT
BLUIDS	BLURTS	BOASTLESS	BOBBITTED
BLUIDY	BLUSH	BOASTS	BOBBITTS
BLUIER	BLUSHED	BOAT	BOBBLE
BLUIEST	BLUSHER	BOATABLE	BOBBLED
BLUING	BLUSHERS	BOATBILL	BOBBLES
BLUINGS	BLUSHES	BOATBILLS	BOBBLIER
BLUISH	BLUSHET	BOATED	BOBBLIEST
BLUME	BLUSHETS	BOATEL	BOBBLING
BLUMED	BLUSHFUL	BOATELS	BOBBLY
BLUMES	BLUSHING	BOATER	BOBBY
BLUMING	BLUSHINGS	BOATERS	BOBBYSOCK
BLUNDER	BLUSHLESS	BOATFUL	BOBBYSOX
BLUNDERED	BLUSTER	BOATFULS	BOBCAT
BLUNDERER	BLUSTERED	BOATHOOK	BOBCATS
BLUNDERS	BLUSTERER	BOATHOOKS	BOBECHE

BOBECHES
BOBFLOAT
BOBFLOATS
BOBLET
BOBLETS
BOBOL
BOBOLINK
BOBOLINKS
BOBOLLED
BOBOLLING
BOBOLS
BOBOTIE
BOBOTIES
BOBOWLER
BOBOWLERS
BOBS
BOBSLED
BOBSLEDS
BOBSLEIGH
BOBSTAY
BOBSTAYS
BOBTAIL
BOBTAILED
BOBTAILS
BOBWEIGHT
BOBWHEEL
BOBWHEELS
BOBWHITE
BOBWHITES
BOBWIG
BOBWIGS
BOCACCIO
BOCACCIOS
BOCAGE
BOCAGES
BOCCA
BOCCAS
BOCCE
BOCCES
BOCCI
BOCCIA
BOCCIAS
BOCCIE
BOCCIES
BOCCIS
BOCHE
BOCHES
BOCK
BOCKED
BOCKEDY
BOCKING
BOCKS
BOCONCINI
BOD
BODACH
BODACHS
BODACIOUS
BODDLE

BODDLES
BODE
BODED
BODEFUL
BODEGA
BODEGAS
BODEGUERO
BODEMENT
BODEMENTS
BODES
BODGE
BODGED
BODGER
BODGERS
BODGES
BODGIE
BODGIER
BODGIES
BODGIEST
BODGING
BODHRAN
BODHRANS
BODICE
BODICES
BODIED
BODIES
BODIKIN
BODIKINS
BODILESS
BODILY
BODING
BODINGLY
BODINGS
BODKIN
BODKINS
BODLE
BODLES
BODRAG
BODRAGS
BODS
BODY
BODYBOARD
BODYCHECK
BODYGUARD
BODYING
BODYLINE
BODYLINES
BODYSHELL
BODYSUIT
BODYSUITS
BODYSURF
BODYSURFS
BODYWORK
BODYWORKS
BOEHMITE
BOEHMITES
BOEP
BOEPS

BOERBUL
BOERBULS
BOEREWORS
BOERTJIE
BOERTJIES
BOET
BOETS
BOEUF
BOFF
BOFFED
BOFFIN
BOFFING
BOFFINS
BOFFO
BOFFOLA
BOFFOLAS
BOFFOS
BOFFS
BOG
BOGAN
BOGANS
BOGART
BOGARTED
BOGARTING
BOGARTS
BOGBEAN
BOGBEANS
BOGEY
BOGEYED
BOGEYING
BOGEYISM
BOGEYISMS
BOGEYMAN
BOGEYMEN
BOGEYS
BOGGARD
BOGGARDS
BOGGART
BOGGARTS
BOGGED
BOGGER
BOGGERS
BOGGIER
BOGGIEST
BOGGINESS
BOGGING
BOGGISH
BOGGLE
BOGGLED
BOGGLER
BOGGLERS
BOGGLES
BOGGLING
BOGGY
BOGIE
BOGIED
BOGIEING
BOGIES

BOGLAND
BOGLANDS
BOGLE
BOGLES
BOGMAN
BOGMEN
BOGOAK
BOGOAKS
BOGONG
BOGONGS
BOGS
BOGUS
BOGUSLY
BOGUSNESS
BOGWOOD
BOGWOODS
BOGY
BOGYISM
BOGYISMS
BOGYMAN
BOGYMEN
BOH
BOHEA
BOHEAS
BOHEMIA
BOHEMIAN
BOHEMIANS
BOHEMIAS
BOHO
BOHOS
BOHRIUM
BOHRIUMS
BOHS
BOHUNK
BOHUNKS
BOI
BOIL
BOILABLE
BOILED
BOILER
BOILERIES
BOILERS
BOILERY
BOILING
BOILINGLY
BOILINGS
BOILOFF
BOILOFFS
BOILOVER
BOILOVERS
BOILS
BOING
BOINGED
BOINGING
BOINGS
BOINK
BOINKED
BOINKING

BOINKS
BOIS
BOISERIE
BOISERIES
BOITE
BOITES
BOK
BOKE
BOKED
BOKES
BOKING
BOKO
BOKOS
BOKS
BOLA
BOLAR
BOLAS
BOLASES
BOLD
BOLDEN
BOLDENED
BOLDENING
BOLDENS
BOLDER
BOLDEST
BOLDFACE
BOLDFACED
BOLDFACES
BOLDLY
BOLDNESS
BOLDS
BOLE
BOLECTION
BOLERO
BOLEROS
BOLES
BOLETE
BOLETES
BOLETI
BOLETUS
BOLETUSES
BOLIDE
BOLIDES
BOLINE
BOLINES
BOLIVAR
BOLIVARES
BOLIVARS
BOLIVIA
BOLIVIANO
BOLIVIAS
BOLIX
BOLIXED
BOLIXES
BOLIXING
BOLL
BOLLARD
BOLLARDS

BOLLED
BOLLEN
BOLLETRIE
BOLLING
BOLLIX
BOLLIXED
BOLLIXES
BOLLIXING
BOLLOCK
BOLLOCKED
BOLLOCKS
BOLLOX
BOLLOXED
BOLLOXES
BOLLOXING
BOLLS
BOLLWORM
BOLLWORMS
BOLO
BOLOGNA
BOLOGNAS
BOLOGRAPH
BOLOMETER
BOLOMETRY
BOLONEY
BOLONEYS
BOLOS
BOLSHEVIK
BOLSHIE
BOLSHIER
BOLSHIES
BOLSHIEST
BOLSHY
BOLSON
BOLSONS
BOLSTER
BOLSTERED
BOLSTERER
BOLSTERS
BOLT
BOLTED
BOLTER
BOLTERS
BOLTHEAD
BOLTHEADS
BOLTHOLE
BOLTHOLES
BOLTING
BOLTINGS
BOLTLESS
BOLTLIKE
BOLTONIA
BOLTONIAS
BOLTROPE
BOLTROPES
BOLTS
BOLUS
BOLUSES

BOMA
BOMAS
BOMB
BOMBABLE
BOMBARD
BOMBARDE
BOMBARDED
BOMBARDER
BOMBARDES
BOMBARDON
BOMBARDS
BOMBASINE
BOMBAST
BOMBASTED
BOMBASTER
BOMBASTIC
BOMBASTS
BOMBAX
BOMBAXES
BOMBAZINE
BOMBE
BOMBED
BOMBER
BOMBERS
BOMBES
BOMBESIN
BOMBESINS
BOMBILATE
BOMBINATE
BOMBING
BOMBINGS
BOMBLET
BOMBLETS
BOMBLOAD
BOMBLOADS
BOMBO
BOMBORA
BOMBORAS
BOMBOS
BOMBPROOF
BOMBS
BOMBSHELL
BOMBSIGHT
BOMBSITE
BOMBSITES
BOMBYCID
BOMBYCIDS
BOMBYCOID
BOMBYX
BOMBYXES
BOMMIE
BOMMIES
BON
BONA
BONACI
BONACIS
BONAMANI
BONAMANO

BONAMIA
BONAMIAS
BONANZA
BONANZAS
BONASSUS
BONASUS
BONASUSES
BONBON
BONBONS
BONCE
BONCES
BOND
BONDABLE
BONDAGE
BONDAGER
BONDAGERS
BONDAGES
BONDED
BONDER
BONDERS
BONDING
BONDINGS
BONDLESS
BONDMAID
BONDMAIDS
BONDMAN
BONDMEN
BONDS
BONDSMAN
BONDSMEN
BONDSTONE
BONDUC
BONDUCS
BONDWOMAN
BONDWOMEN
BONE
BONEBLACK
BONED
BONEFISH
BONEHEAD
BONEHEADS
BONELESS
BONEMEAL
BONEMEALS
BONER
BONERS
BONES
BONESET
BONESETS
BONEY
BONEYARD
BONEYARDS
BONEYER
BONEYEST
BONFIRE
BONFIRES
BONG
BONGED

BONGING	BONNOCKS	BOODLING	BOOKINGS
BONGO	BONNY	BOODY	BOOKISH
BONGOES	BONOBO	BOODYING	BOOKISHLY
BONGOIST	BONOBOS	BOOED	BOOKLAND
BONGOISTS	BONSAI	BOOFHEAD	BOOKLANDS
BONGOS	BONSAIS	BOOFHEADS	BOOKLESS
BONGRACE	BONSELA	BOOFIER	BOOKLET
BONGRACES	BONSELAS	BOOFIEST	BOOKLETS
BONGS	BONSELLA	BOOFY	BOOKLICE
BONHAM	BONSELLAS	BOOGER	BOOKLIGHT
BONHAMS	BONSOIR	BOOGERMAN	BOOKLORE
BONHOMIE	BONSPELL	BOOGERMEN	BOOKLORES
BONHOMIES	BONSPELLS	BOOGERS	BOOKLOUSE
BONHOMMIE	BONSPIEL	BOOGEY	BOOKMAKER
BONHOMOUS	BONSPIELS	BOOGEYED	BOOKMAN
BONIATO	BONTEBOK	BOOGEYING	BOOKMARK
BONIATOS	BONTEBOKS	BOOGEYMAN	BOOKMARKS
BONIBELL	BONUS	BOOGEYMEN	BOOKMEN
BONIBELLS	BONUSES	BOOGEYS	BOOKOO
BONIE	BONXIE	BOOGIE	BOOKOOS
BONIER	BONXIES	BOOGIED	BOOKPLATE
BONIEST	BONY	BOOGIEING	BOOKRACK
BONIFACE	BONZA	BOOGIEMAN	BOOKRACKS
BONIFACES	BONZE	BOOGIEMEN	BOOKREST
BONILASSE	BONZER	BOOGIES	BOOKRESTS
BONINESS	BONZES	BOOGY	BOOKS
BONING	BOO	BOOGYING	BOOKSHELF
BONINGS	BOOB	BOOGYMAN	BOOKSHOP
BONISM	BOOBED	BOOGYMEN	BOOKSHOPS
BONISMS	BOOBHEAD	BOOH	BOOKSIE
BONIST	BOOBHEADS	BOOHAI	BOOKSIER
BONISTS	BOOBIALLA	BOOHAIS	BOOKSIEST
BONITA	BOOBIE	BOOHED	BOOKSTALL
BONITAS	BOOBIES	BOOHING	BOOKSTAND
BONITO	BOOBING	BOOHOO	BOOKSTORE
BONITOES	BOOBIRD	BOOHOOED	BOOKSY
BONITOS	BOOBIRDS	BOOHOOING	BOOKWORK
BONJOUR	BOOBISH	BOOHOOS	BOOKWORKS
BONK	BOOBOISIE	BOOHS	BOOKWORM
BONKED	BOOBOO	BOOING	BOOKWORMS
BONKERS	BOOBOOK	BOOJUM	BOOKY
BONKING	BOOBOOKS	BOOJUMS	BOOL
BONKINGS	BOOBOOS	BOOK	BOOLED
BONKS	BOOBS	BOOKABLE	BOOLING
BONNE	BOOBY	BOOKCASE	BOOLS
BONNES	BOOBYISH	BOOKCASES	BOOM
BONNET	BOOBYISM	BOOKED	BOOMBOX
BONNETED	BOOBYISMS	BOOKEND	BOOMBOXES
BONNETING	BOOCOO	BOOKENDS	BOOMED
BONNETS	BOOCOOS	BOOKER	BOOMER
BONNIBELL	BOODIE	BOOKERS	BOOMERANG
BONNIE	BOODIED	BOOKFUL	BOOMERS
BONNIER	BOODIES	BOOKFULS	BOOMIER
BONNIES	BOODLE	BOOKIE	BOOMIEST
BONNIEST	BOODLED	BOOKIER	BOOMING
BONNILY	BOODLER	BOOKIES	BOOMINGLY
BONNINESS	BOODLERS	BOOKIEST	BOOMINGS
BONNOCK	BOODLES	BOOKING	BOOMKIN

BOOMKINS	BOOTIKIN	BORATES	BORKED
BOOMLET	BOOTIKINS	BORATING	BORKING
BOOMLETS	BOOTING	BORAX	BORKS
BOOMS	BOOTJACK	BORAXES	BORLOTTI
BOOMSLANG	BOOTJACKS	BORAZON	BORM
BOOMTOWN	BOOTLACE	BORAZONS	BORMED
BOOMTOWNS	BOOTLACES	BORD	BORMING
BOOMY	BOOTLAST	BORDAR	BORMS
BOON	BOOTLASTS	BORDARS	BORN
BOONDOCK	BOOTLEG	BORDE	BORNA
BOONDOCKS	BOOTLEGS	BORDEAUX	BORNE
BOONER	BOOTLESS	BORDEL	BORNEOL
BOONERS	BOOTLICK	BORDELLO	BORNEOLS
BOONG	BOOTLICKS	BORDELLOS	BORNITE
BOONGA	BOOTMAKER	BORDELS	BORNITES
BOONGARY	BOOTS	BORDER	BORNITIC
BOONGAS	BOOTSTRAP	BORDEREAU	BORNYL
BOONGS	BOOTY	BORDERED	BORNYLS
BOONIES	BOOZE	BORDERER	BORON
BOONLESS	BOOZED	BORDERERS	BORONIA
BOONS	BOOZER	BORDERING	BORONIAS
BOOR	BOOZERS	BORDERS	BORONIC
BOORD	BOOZES	BORDES	BORONS
BOORDE	BOOZEY	BORDS	BOROUGH
BOORDES	BOOZIER	BORDURE	BOROUGHS
BOORDS	BOOZIEST	BORDURES	BORREL
BOORISH	BOOZILY	BORE	BORRELIA
BOORISHLY	BOOZINESS	BOREAL	BORRELIAS
BOORKA	BOOZING	BOREALIS	BORRELL
BOORKAS	BOOZINGS	BOREAS	BORROW
BOORS	BOOZY	BOREASES	BORROWED
BOORTREE	BOP	BORECOLE	BORROWER
BOORTREES	BOPEEP	BORECOLES	BORROWERS
BOOS	BOPEEPS	BORED	BORROWING
BOOSE	BOPPED	BOREDOM	BORROWS
BOOSED	BOPPER	BOREDOMS	BORS
BOOSES	BOPPERS	BOREE	BORSCH
BOOSHIT	BOPPING	BOREEN	BORSCHES
BOOSING	BOPS	BOREENS	BORSCHT
BOOST	BOR	BOREES	BORSCHTS
BOOSTED	BORA	BOREHOLE	BORSHCH
BOOSTER	BORACES	BOREHOLES	BORSHCHES
BOOSTERS	BORACHIO	BOREL	BORSHT
BOOSTING	BORACHIOS	BORER	BORSHTS
BOOSTS	BORACIC	BORERS	BORSIC
BOOT	BORACITE	BORES	BORSICS
BOOTABLE	BORACITES	BORESCOPE	BORSTAL
BOOTBLACK	BORAGE	BORESOME	BORSTALL
BOOTED	BORAGES	BORGHETTO	BORSTALLS
BOOTEE	BORAK	BORGO	BORSTALS
BOOTEES	BORAKS	BORGOS	BORT
BOOTERIES	BORAL	BORIC	BORTIER
BOOTERY	BORALS	BORIDE	BORTIEST
BOOTH	BORANE	BORIDES	BORTS
BOOTHOSE	BORANES	BORING	BORTSCH
BOOTHS	BORAS	BORINGLY	BORTSCHES
BOOTIE	BORATE	BORINGS	BORTY
BOOTIES	BORATED	BORK	BORTZ

BORTZES
BORZOI
BORZOIS
BOS
BOSBERAAD
BOSBOK
BOSBOKS
BOSCAGE
BOSCAGES
BOSCHBOK
BOSCHBOKS
BOSCHE
BOSCHES
BOSCHVARK
BOSCHVELD
BOSH
BOSHBOK
BOSHBOKS
BOSHES
BOSHTA
BOSHTER
BOSHVARK
BOSHVARKS
BOSK
BOSKAGE
BOSKAGES
BOSKER
BOSKET
BOSKETS
BOSKIER
BOSKIEST
BOSKINESS
BOSKS
BOSKY
BOSOM
BOSOMED
BOSOMIER
BOSOMIEST
BOSOMING
BOSOMS
BOSOMY
BOSON
BOSONIC
BOSONS
BOSQUE
BOSQUES
BOSQUET
BOSQUETS
BOSS
BOSSBOY
BOSSBOYS
BOSSDOM
BOSSDOMS
BOSSED
BOSSER
BOSSES
BOSSEST
BOSSET

BOSSETS
BOSSIER
BOSSIES
BOSSIEST
BOSSILY
BOSSINESS
BOSSING
BOSSISM
BOSSISMS
BOSSY
BOSTANGI
BOSTANGIS
BOSTHOON
BOSTHOONS
BOSTON
BOSTONS
BOSTRYX
BOSTRYXES
BOSUN
BOSUNS
BOT
BOTA
BOTANIC
BOTANICA
BOTANICAL
BOTANICAS
BOTANICS
BOTANIES
BOTANISE
BOTANISED
BOTANISER
BOTANISES
BOTANIST
BOTANISTS
BOTANIZE
BOTANIZED
BOTANIZER
BOTANIZES
BOTANY
BOTARGO
BOTARGOES
BOTARGOS
BOTAS
BOTCH
BOTCHED
BOTCHEDLY
BOTCHER
BOTCHERS
BOTCHERY
BOTCHES
BOTCHIER
BOTCHIEST
BOTCHILY
BOTCHING
BOTCHINGS
BOTCHY
BOTEL
BOTELS

BOTFLIES
BOTFLY
BOTH
BOTHAN
BOTHANS
BOTHER
BOTHERED
BOTHERING
BOTHERS
BOTHIE
BOTHIES
BOTHOLE
BOTHOLES
BOTHRIA
BOTHRIUM
BOTHRIUMS
BOTHY
BOTHYMAN
BOTHYMEN
BOTNET
BOTNETS
BOTONE
BOTONEE
BOTONNEE
BOTRYOID
BOTRYOSE
BOTRYTIS
BOTS
BOTT
BOTTE
BOTTED
BOTTEGA
BOTTEGAS
BOTTES
BOTTIES
BOTTINE
BOTTINES
BOTTING
BOTTLE
BOTTLED
BOTTLEFUL
BOTTLER
BOTTLERS
BOTTLES
BOTTLING
BOTTLINGS
BOTTOM
BOTTOMED
BOTTOMER
BOTTOMERS
BOTTOMING
BOTTOMRY
BOTTOMS
BOTTOMSET
BOTTONY
BOTTS
BOTTY
BOTULIN

BOTULINAL
BOTULINS
BOTULINUM
BOTULINUS
BOTULISM
BOTULISMS
BOUBOU
BOUBOUS
BOUCHE
BOUCHEE
BOUCHEES
BOUCHES
BOUCLE
BOUCLEE
BOUCLEES
BOUCLES
BOUDERIE
BOUDERIES
BOUDIN
BOUDINS
BOUDOIR
BOUDOIRS
BOUFFANT
BOUFFANTS
BOUFFE
BOUFFES
BOUGE
BOUGED
BOUGES
BOUGET
BOUGETS
BOUGH
BOUGHED
BOUGHLESS
BOUGHPOT
BOUGHPOTS
BOUGHS
BOUGHT
BOUGHTEN
BOUGHTS
BOUGIE
BOUGIES
BOUGING
BOUILLI
BOUILLIS
BOUILLON
BOUILLONS
BOUK
BOUKS
BOULDER
BOULDERED
BOULDERER
BOULDERS
BOULDERY
BOULE
BOULES
BOULEVARD
BOULLE

BOULLES	BOURKHAS	BOWATS	BOWNING
BOULT	BOURLAW	BOWBENT	BOWPOT
BOULTED	BOURLAWS	BOWED	BOWPOTS
BOULTER	BOURN	BOWEL	BOWR
BOULTERS	BOURNE	BOWELED	BOWRS
BOULTING	BOURNES	BOWELING	BOWS
BOULTINGS	BOURNS	BOWELLED	BOWSAW
BOULTS	BOURREE	BOWELLESS	BOWSAWS
BOUN	BOURREES	BOWELLING	BOWSE
BOUNCE	BOURRIDE	BOWELS	BOWSED
BOUNCED	BOURRIDES	BOWER	BOWSER
BOUNCER	BOURSE	BOWERBIRD	BOWSERS
BOUNCERS	BOURSES	BOWERED	BOWSES
BOUNCES	BOURSIER	BOWERIES	BOWSEY
BOUNCIER	BOURSIERS	BOWERING	BOWSEYS
BOUNCIEST	BOURSIN	BOWERS	BOWSHOT
BOUNCILY	BOURSINS	BOWERY	BOWSHOTS
BOUNCING	BOURTREE	BOWES	BOWSIE
BOUNCY	BOURTREES	BOWET	BOWSIES
BOUND	BOUSE	BOWETS	BOWSING
BOUNDABLE	BOUSED	BOWFIN	BOWSPRIT
BOUNDARY	BOUSES	BOWFINS	BOWSPRITS
BOUNDED	BOUSIER	BOWFRONT	BOWSTRING
BOUNDEN	BOUSIEST	BOWGET	BOWSTRUNG
BOUNDER	BOUSING	BOWGETS	BOWWOW
BOUNDERS	BOUSOUKI	BOWHEAD	BOWWOWED
BOUNDING	BOUSOUKIA	BOWHEADS	BOWWOWING
BOUNDLESS	BOUSOUKIS	BOWHUNTER	BOWWOWS
BOUNDNESS	BOUSY	BOWIE	BOWYANG
BOUNDS	BOUT	BOWING	BOWYANGS
BOUNED	BOUTADE	BOWINGLY	BOWYER
BOUNING	BOUTADES	BOWINGS	BOWYERS
BOUNS	BOUTIQUE	BOWKNOT	BOX
BOUNTEOUS	BOUTIQUES	BOWKNOTS	BOXBALL
BOUNTIED	BOUTIQUEY	BOWL	BOXBALLS
BOUNTIES	BOUTON	BOWLDER	BOXBERRY
BOUNTIFUL	BOUTONNE	BOWLDERS	BOXBOARD
BOUNTREE	BOUTONNEE	BOWLED	BOXBOARDS
BOUNTREES	BOUTONS	BOWLEG	BOXCAR
BOUNTY	BOUTS	BOWLEGGED	BOXCARS
BOUNTYHED	BOUVARDIA	BOWLEGS	BOXED
BOUQUET	BOUVIER	BOWLER	BOXEN
BOUQUETS	BOUVIERS	BOWLERS	BOXER
BOURASQUE	BOUZOUKI	BOWLESS	BOXERCISE
BOURBON	BOUZOUKIA	BOWLFUL	BOXERS
BOURBONS	BOUZOUKIS	BOWLFULS	BOXES
BOURD	BOVATE	BOWLIKE	BOXFISH
BOURDER	BOVATES	BOWLINE	BOXFISHES
BOURDERS	BOVID	BOWLINES	BOXFUL
BOURDON	BOVIDS	BOWLING	BOXFULS
BOURDONS	BOVINE	BOWLINGS	BOXHAUL
BOURDS	BOVINELY	BOWLLIKE	BOXHAULED
BOURG	BOVINES	BOWLS	BOXHAULS
BOURGEOIS	BOVINITY	BOWMAN	BOXIER
BOURGEON	BOVVER	BOWMEN	BOXIEST
BOURGEONS	BOVVERS	BOWNE	BOXILY
BOURGS	BOW	BOWNED	BOXINESS
BOURKHA	BOWAT	BOWNES	BOXING

BOXINGS
BOXKEEPER
BOXLIKE
BOXROOM
BOXROOMS
BOXTHORN
BOXTHORNS
BOXWALLAH
BOXWOOD
BOXWOODS
BOXY
BOY
BOYAR
BOYARD
BOYARDS
BOYARISM
BOYARISMS
BOYARS
BOYAU
BOYAUX
BOYCHICK
BOYCHICKS
BOYCHIK
BOYCHIKS
BOYCOTT
BOYCOTTED
BOYCOTTER
BOYCOTTS
BOYED
BOYF
BOYFRIEND
BOYFS
BOYG
BOYGS
BOYHOOD
BOYHOODS
BOYING
BOYISH
BOYISHLY
BOYLA
BOYLAS
BOYO
BOYOS
BOYS
BOYSIER
BOYSIEST
BOYSY
BOZO
BOZOS
BOZZETTI
BOZZETTO
BRA
BRAAI
BRAAIED
BRAAIING
BRAAIS
BRAATA
BRAATAS

BRAATASES
BRABBLE
BRABBLED
BRABBLER
BRABBLERS
BRABBLES
BRABBLING
BRACCATE
BRACCIA
BRACCIO
BRACE
BRACED
BRACELET
BRACELETS
BRACER
BRACERO
BRACEROS
BRACERS
BRACES
BRACH
BRACHAH
BRACHAHS
BRACHES
BRACHET
BRACHETS
BRACHIA
BRACHIAL
BRACHIALS
BRACHIATE
BRACHIUM
BRACHS
BRACING
BRACINGLY
BRACINGS
BRACIOLA
BRACIOLAS
BRACIOLE
BRACIOLES
BRACK
BRACKEN
BRACKENS
BRACKET
BRACKETED
BRACKETS
BRACKISH
BRACKS
BRACONID
BRACONIDS
BRACT
BRACTEAL
BRACTEATE
BRACTED
BRACTEOLE
BRACTLESS
BRACTLET
BRACTLETS
BRACTS
BRAD

BRADAWL
BRADAWLS
BRADDED
BRADDING
BRADOON
BRADOONS
BRADS
BRAE
BRAEHEID
BRAEHEIDS
BRAES
BRAG
BRAGGART
BRAGGARTS
BRAGGED
BRAGGER
BRAGGERS
BRAGGEST
BRAGGIER
BRAGGIEST
BRAGGING
BRAGGINGS
BRAGGY
BRAGLY
BRAGS
BRAHMA
BRAHMAN
BRAHMANI
BRAHMANIS
BRAHMANS
BRAHMAS
BRAHMIN
BRAHMINS
BRAID
BRAIDE
BRAIDED
BRAIDER
BRAIDERS
BRAIDEST
BRAIDING
BRAIDINGS
BRAIDS
BRAIL
BRAILED
BRAILING
BRAILLE
BRAILLED
BRAILLER
BRAILLERS
BRAILLES
BRAILLING
BRAILLIST
BRAILS
BRAIN
BRAINBOX
BRAINCASE
BRAINDEAD
BRAINED

BRAINFART
BRAINIAC
BRAINIACS
BRAINIER
BRAINIEST
BRAINILY
BRAINING
BRAINISH
BRAINLESS
BRAINPAN
BRAINPANS
BRAINS
BRAINSICK
BRAINSTEM
BRAINWASH
BRAINWAVE
BRAINY
BRAIRD
BRAIRDED
BRAIRDING
BRAIRDS
BRAISE
BRAISED
BRAISES
BRAISING
BRAIZE
BRAIZES
BRAK
BRAKE
BRAKEAGE
BRAKEAGES
BRAKED
BRAKELESS
BRAKEMAN
BRAKEMEN
BRAKES
BRAKESMAN
BRAKESMEN
BRAKIER
BRAKIEST
BRAKING
BRAKS
BRAKY
BRALESS
BRAMBLE
BRAMBLED
BRAMBLES
BRAMBLIER
BRAMBLING
BRAMBLY
BRAME
BRAMES
BRAN
BRANCARD
BRANCARDS
BRANCH
BRANCHED
BRANCHER

71

BRANCHERS

BRANCHERS	BRANTLES	BRATPACK	BRAWLS
BRANCHERY	BRANTS	BRATPACKS	BRAWLY
BRANCHES	BRAS	BRATS	BRAWN
BRANCHIA	BRASCO	BRATTICE	BRAWNED
BRANCHIAE	BRASCOS	BRATTICED	BRAWNIER
BRANCHIAL	BRASERO	BRATTICES	BRAWNIEST
BRANCHIER	BRASEROS	BRATTIER	BRAWNILY
BRANCHING	BRASES	BRATTIEST	BRAWNS
BRANCHLET	BRASH	BRATTISH	BRAWNY
BRANCHY	BRASHED	BRATTLE	BRAWS
BRAND	BRASHER	BRATTLED	BRAXIES
BRANDADE	BRASHES	BRATTLES	BRAXY
BRANDADES	BRASHEST	BRATTLING	BRAY
BRANDED	BRASHIER	BRATTY	BRAYED
BRANDER	BRASHIEST	BRATWURST	BRAYER
BRANDERED	BRASHING	BRAUNCH	BRAYERS
BRANDERS	BRASHLY	BRAUNCHED	BRAYING
BRANDIED	BRASHNESS	BRAUNCHES	BRAYS
BRANDIES	BRASHY	BRAUNITE	BRAZA
BRANDING	BRASIER	BRAUNITES	BRAZAS
BRANDINGS	BRASIERS	BRAVA	BRAZE
BRANDISE	BRASIL	BRAVADO	BRAZED
BRANDISES	BRASILEIN	BRAVADOED	BRAZELESS
BRANDISH	BRASILIN	BRAVADOES	BRAZEN
BRANDLESS	BRASILINS	BRAVADOS	BRAZENED
BRANDLING	BRASILS	BRAVAS	BRAZENING
BRANDRETH	BRASS	BRAVE	BRAZENLY
BRANDS	BRASSAGE	BRAVED	BRAZENRY
BRANDY	BRASSAGES	BRAVELY	BRAZENS
BRANDYING	BRASSARD	BRAVENESS	BRAZER
BRANGLE	BRASSARDS	BRAVER	BRAZERS
BRANGLED	BRASSART	BRAVERIES	BRAZES
BRANGLES	BRASSARTS	BRAVERS	BRAZIER
BRANGLING	BRASSED	BRAVERY	BRAZIERS
BRANK	BRASSERIE	BRAVES	BRAZIERY
BRANKED	BRASSES	BRAVEST	BRAZIL
BRANKIER	BRASSET	BRAVI	BRAZILEIN
BRANKIEST	BRASSETS	BRAVING	BRAZILIN
BRANKING	BRASSICA	BRAVO	BRAZILINS
BRANKS	BRASSICAS	BRAVOED	BRAZILS
BRANKY	BRASSIE	BRAVOES	BRAZING
BRANLE	BRASSIER	BRAVOING	BREACH
BRANLES	BRASSIERE	BRAVOS	BREACHED
BRANNED	BRASSIES	BRAVURA	BREACHER
BRANNER	BRASSIEST	BRAVURAS	BREACHERS
BRANNERS	BRASSILY	BRAVURE	BREACHES
BRANNIER	BRASSING	BRAW	BREACHING
BRANNIEST	BRASSISH	BRAWER	BREAD
BRANNIGAN	BRASSWARE	BRAWEST	BREADBOX
BRANNING	BRASSY	BRAWL	BREADED
BRANNY	BRAST	BRAWLED	BREADHEAD
BRANS	BRASTING	BRAWLER	BREADING
BRANSLE	BRASTS	BRAWLERS	BREADLESS
BRANSLES	BRAT	BRAWLIE	BREADLINE
BRANT	BRATCHET	BRAWLIER	BREADNUT
BRANTAIL	BRATCHETS	BRAWLIEST	BREADNUTS
BRANTAILS	BRATLING	BRAWLING	BREADROOM
BRANTLE	BRATLINGS	BRAWLINGS	BREADROOT

BREADS
BREADTH
BREADTHS
BREADY
BREAK
BREAKABLE
BREAKAGE
BREAKAGES
BREAKAWAY
BREAKBACK
BREAKBEAT
BREAKBONE
BREAKDOWN
BREAKER
BREAKERS
BREAKEVEN
BREAKFAST
BREAKING
BREAKINGS
BREAKNECK
BREAKOFF
BREAKOFFS
BREAKOUT
BREAKOUTS
BREAKS
BREAKTIME
BREAKUP
BREAKUPS
BREAKWALL
BREAM
BREAMED
BREAMING
BREAMS
BREARE
BREARES
BREASKIT
BREASKITS
BREAST
BREASTED
BREASTFED
BREASTING
BREASTPIN
BREASTS
BREATH
BREATHE
BREATHED
BREATHER
BREATHERS
BREATHES
BREATHFUL
BREATHIER
BREATHILY
BREATHING
BREATHS
BREATHY
BRECCIA
BRECCIAL
BRECCIAS

BRECCIATE
BRECHAM
BRECHAMS
BRECHAN
BRECHANS
BRED
BREDE
BREDED
BREDES
BREDIE
BREDIES
BREDING
BREDS
BREE
BREECH
BREECHED
BREECHES
BREECHING
BREED
BREEDER
BREEDERS
BREEDING
BREEDINGS
BREEDS
BREEKS
BREEM
BREENGE
BREENGED
BREENGES
BREENGING
BREER
BREERED
BREERING
BREERS
BREES
BREESE
BREESES
BREEST
BREESTS
BREEZE
BREEZED
BREEZES
BREEZEWAY
BREEZIER
BREEZIEST
BREEZILY
BREEZING
BREEZY
BREGMA
BREGMATA
BREGMATE
BREGMATIC
BREHON
BREHONS
BREI
BREID
BREIDS
BREIING

BREINGE
BREINGED
BREINGES
BREINGING
BREIS
BREIST
BREISTS
BREKKIES
BREKKY
BRELOQUE
BRELOQUES
BREME
BREN
BRENNE
BRENNES
BRENNING
BRENS
BRENT
BRENTER
BRENTEST
BRENTS
BRER
BRERE
BRERES
BRERS
BRETASCHE
BRETESSE
BRETESSES
BRETHREN
BRETON
BRETONS
BRETTICE
BRETTICED
BRETTICES
BREVE
BREVES
BREVET
BREVETCY
BREVETE
BREVETED
BREVETING
BREVETS
BREVETTED
BREVIARY
BREVIATE
BREVIATES
BREVIER
BREVIERS
BREVIS
BREVISES
BREVITIES
BREVITY
BREW
BREWAGE
BREWAGES
BREWED
BREWER
BREWERIES

BREWERS
BREWERY
BREWING
BREWINGS
BREWIS
BREWISES
BREWPUB
BREWPUBS
BREWS
BREWSKI
BREWSKIES
BREWSKIS
BREWSTER
BREWSTERS
BREY
BREYED
BREYING
BREYS
BRIAR
BRIARD
BRIARDS
BRIARED
BRIARROOT
BRIARS
BRIARWOOD
BRIARY
BRIBABLE
BRIBE
BRIBEABLE
BRIBED
BRIBEE
BRIBEES
BRIBER
BRIBERIES
BRIBERS
BRIBERY
BRIBES
BRIBING
BRICABRAC
BRICHT
BRICHTER
BRICHTEST
BRICK
BRICKBAT
BRICKBATS
BRICKCLAY
BRICKED
BRICKEN
BRICKIE
BRICKIER
BRICKIES
BRICKIEST
BRICKING
BRICKINGS
BRICKKILN
BRICKLE
BRICKLES
BRICKLIKE

BRICKS	BRIERWOOD	BRINE	BRISKNESS
BRICKWALL	BRIERY	BRINED	BRISKS
BRICKWORK	BRIES	BRINELESS	BRISKY
BRICKY	BRIG	BRINER	BRISLING
BRICKYARD	BRIGADE	BRINERS	BRISLINGS
BRICOLAGE	BRIGADED	BRINES	BRISS
BRICOLE	BRIGADES	BRING	BRISSES
BRICOLES	BRIGADIER	BRINGDOWN	BRISTLE
BRIDAL	BRIGADING	BRINGER	BRISTLED
BRIDALLY	BRIGALOW	BRINGERS	BRISTLES
BRIDALS	BRIGALOWS	BRINGING	BRISTLIER
BRIDE	BRIGAND	BRINGINGS	BRISTLING
BRIDECAKE	BRIGANDRY	BRINGS	BRISTLY
BRIDED	BRIGANDS	BRINIER	BRISTOL
BRIDEMAID	BRIGHT	BRINIES	BRISTOLS
BRIDEMAN	BRIGHTEN	BRINIEST	BRISURE
BRIDEMEN	BRIGHTENS	BRININESS	BRISURES
BRIDES	BRIGHTER	BRINING	BRIT
BRIDESMAN	BRIGHTEST	BRINISH	BRITANNIA
BRIDESMEN	BRIGHTISH	BRINJAL	BRITCHES
BRIDEWELL	BRIGHTLY	BRINJALS	BRITH
BRIDGABLE	BRIGHTS	BRINJARRY	BRITHS
BRIDGE	BRIGS	BRINK	BRITS
BRIDGED	BRIGUE	BRINKMAN	BRITSCHKA
BRIDGES	BRIGUED	BRINKMEN	BRITSKA
BRIDGING	BRIGUES	BRINKS	BRITSKAS
BRIDGINGS	BRIGUING	BRINNIES	BRITT
BRIDIE	BRIGUINGS	BRINNY	BRITTANIA
BRIDIES	BRIK	BRINS	BRITTLE
BRIDING	BRIKS	BRINY	BRITTLED
BRIDLE	BRILL	BRIO	BRITTLELY
BRIDLED	BRILLER	BRIOCHE	BRITTLER
BRIDLER	BRILLEST	BRIOCHES	BRITTLES
BRIDLERS	BRILLIANT	BRIOLETTE	BRITTLEST
BRIDLES	BRILLO	BRIONIES	BRITTLING
BRIDLEWAY	BRILLOS	BRIONY	BRITTLY
BRIDLING	BRILLS	BRIOS	BRITTS
BRIDOON	BRIM	BRIQUET	BRITZKA
BRIDOONS	BRIMFUL	BRIQUETS	BRITZKAS
BRIE	BRIMFULL	BRIQUETTE	BRITZSKA
BRIEF	BRIMFULLY	BRIS	BRITZSKAS
BRIEFCASE	BRIMING	BRISANCE	BRIZE
BRIEFED	BRIMINGS	BRISANCES	BRIZES
BRIEFER	BRIMLESS	BRISANT	BRO
BRIEFERS	BRIMMED	BRISE	BROACH
BRIEFEST	BRIMMER	BRISES	BROACHED
BRIEFING	BRIMMERS	BRISK	BROACHER
BRIEFINGS	BRIMMING	BRISKED	BROACHERS
BRIEFLESS	BRIMS	BRISKEN	BROACHES
BRIEFLY	BRIMSTONE	BRISKENED	BROACHING
BRIEFNESS	BRIMSTONY	BRISKENS	BROAD
BRIEFS	BRIN	BRISKER	BROADAX
BRIER	BRINDED	BRISKEST	BROADAXE
BRIERED	BRINDISI	BRISKET	BROADAXES
BRIERIER	BRINDISIS	BRISKETS	BROADBAND
BRIERIEST	BRINDLE	BRISKING	BROADBEAN
BRIERROOT	BRINDLED	BRISKISH	BROADBILL
BRIERS	BRINDLES	BRISKLY	BROADBRIM

BROADCAST
BROADEN
BROADENED
BROADENER
BROADENS
BROADER
BROADEST
BROADISH
BROADLEAF
BROADLINE
BROADLOOM
BROADLY
BROADNESS
BROADS
BROADSIDE
BROADTAIL
BROADWAY
BROADWAYS
BROADWISE
BROCADE
BROCADED
BROCADES
BROCADING
BROCAGE
BROCAGES
BROCARD
BROCARDS
BROCATEL
BROCATELS
BROCCOLI
BROCCOLIS
BROCH
BROCHAN
BROCHANS
BROCHE
BROCHED
BROCHES
BROCHETTE
BROCHING
BROCHO
BROCHOS
BROCHS
BROCHURE
BROCHURES
BROCK
BROCKAGE
BROCKAGES
BROCKED
BROCKET
BROCKETS
BROCKIT
BROCKRAM
BROCKRAMS
BROCKS
BROCOLI
BROCOLIS
BROD
BRODDED

BRODDING
BRODDLE
BRODDLED
BRODDLES
BRODDLING
BRODEKIN
BRODEKINS
BRODKIN
BRODKINS
BRODS
BROEKIES
BROG
BROGAN
BROGANS
BROGGED
BROGGING
BROGH
BROGHS
BROGS
BROGUE
BROGUEISH
BROGUERY
BROGUES
BROGUISH
BROIDER
BROIDERED
BROIDERER
BROIDERS
BROIDERY
BROIL
BROILED
BROILER
BROILERS
BROILING
BROILS
BROKAGE
BROKAGES
BROKE
BROKED
BROKEN
BROKENLY
BROKER
BROKERAGE
BROKERED
BROKERIES
BROKERING
BROKERS
BROKERY
BROKES
BROKING
BROKINGS
BROLGA
BROLGAS
BROLLIES
BROLLY
BROMAL
BROMALS
BROMATE

BROMATED
BROMATES
BROMATING
BROME
BROMELAIN
BROMELIA
BROMELIAD
BROMELIAS
BROMELIN
BROMELINS
BROMEOSIN
BROMES
BROMIC
BROMID
BROMIDE
BROMIDES
BROMIDIC
BROMIDS
BROMIN
BROMINATE
BROMINE
BROMINES
BROMINISM
BROMINS
BROMISE
BROMISED
BROMISES
BROMISING
BROMISM
BROMISMS
BROMIZE
BROMIZED
BROMIZES
BROMIZING
BROMMER
BROMMERS
BROMO
BROMOFORM
BROMOS
BRONC
BRONCHI
BRONCHIA
BRONCHIAL
BRONCHIUM
BRONCHO
BRONCHOS
BRONCHUS
BRONCO
BRONCOS
BRONCS
BROND
BRONDS
BRONDYRON
BRONZE
BRONZED
BRONZEN
BRONZER
BRONZERS

BRONZES
BRONZIER
BRONZIEST
BRONZIFY
BRONZING
BRONZINGS
BRONZITE
BRONZITES
BRONZY
BROO
BROOCH
BROOCHED
BROOCHES
BROOCHING
BROOD
BROODED
BROODER
BROODERS
BROODIER
BROODIEST
BROODILY
BROODING
BROODINGS
BROODLESS
BROODMARE
BROODS
BROODY
BROOK
BROOKABLE
BROOKED
BROOKIE
BROOKIES
BROOKING
BROOKITE
BROOKITES
BROOKLET
BROOKLETS
BROOKLIKE
BROOKLIME
BROOKS
BROOKWEED
BROOL
BROOLS
BROOM
BROOMBALL
BROOMCORN
BROOMED
BROOMIER
BROOMIEST
BROOMING
BROOMRAPE
BROOMS
BROOMY
BROOS
BROOSE
BROOSES
BROS
BROSE

BROSES
BROSY
BROTH
BROTHEL
BROTHELS
BROTHER
BROTHERED
BROTHERLY
BROTHERS
BROTHS
BROTHY
BROUGH
BROUGHAM
BROUGHAMS
BROUGHS
BROUGHT
BROUGHTA
BROUGHTAS
BROUHAHA
BROUHAHAS
BROUZE
BROUZES
BROW
BROWALLIA
BROWBAND
BROWBANDS
BROWBEAT
BROWBEATS
BROWED
BROWLESS
BROWN
BROWNED
BROWNER
BROWNEST
BROWNIE
BROWNIER
BROWNIES
BROWNIEST
BROWNING
BROWNINGS
BROWNISH
BROWNNESS
BROWNNOSE
BROWNOUT
BROWNOUTS
BROWNS
BROWNY
BROWRIDGE
BROWS
BROWSABLE
BROWSE
BROWSED
BROWSER
BROWSERS
BROWSES
BROWSIER
BROWSIEST
BROWSING

BROWSINGS
BROWST
BROWSTS
BROWSY
BRR
BRRR
BRU
BRUCELLA
BRUCELLAE
BRUCELLAS
BRUCHID
BRUCHIDS
BRUCIN
BRUCINE
BRUCINES
BRUCINS
BRUCITE
BRUCITES
BRUCKLE
BRUGH
BRUGHS
BRUHAHA
BRUHAHAS
BRUILZIE
BRUILZIES
BRUIN
BRUINS
BRUISE
BRUISED
BRUISER
BRUISERS
BRUISES
BRUISING
BRUISINGS
BRUIT
BRUITED
BRUITER
BRUITERS
BRUITING
BRUITS
BRULE
BRULES
BRULOT
BRULOTS
BRULYIE
BRULYIES
BRULZIE
BRULZIES
BRUMAL
BRUMBIES
BRUMBY
BRUME
BRUMES
BRUMMAGEM
BRUMMER
BRUMMERS
BRUMOUS
BRUNCH

BRUNCHED
BRUNCHER
BRUNCHERS
BRUNCHES
BRUNCHING
BRUNET
BRUNETS
BRUNETTE
BRUNETTES
BRUNG
BRUNIZEM
BRUNIZEMS
BRUNT
BRUNTED
BRUNTING
BRUNTS
BRUS
BRUSH
BRUSHBACK
BRUSHED
BRUSHER
BRUSHERS
BRUSHES
BRUSHFIRE
BRUSHIER
BRUSHIEST
BRUSHING
BRUSHINGS
BRUSHLAND
BRUSHLESS
BRUSHLIKE
BRUSHMARK
BRUSHOFF
BRUSHOFFS
BRUSHUP
BRUSHUPS
BRUSHWOOD
BRUSHWORK
BRUSHY
BRUSK
BRUSKER
BRUSKEST
BRUSQUE
BRUSQUELY
BRUSQUER
BRUSQUEST
BRUSSEN
BRUST
BRUSTING
BRUSTS
BRUT
BRUTAL
BRUTALISE
BRUTALISM
BRUTALIST
BRUTALITY
BRUTALIZE
BRUTALLY

BRUTE
BRUTED
BRUTELIKE
BRUTELY
BRUTENESS
BRUTER
BRUTERS
BRUTES
BRUTIFIED
BRUTIFIES
BRUTIFY
BRUTING
BRUTINGS
BRUTISH
BRUTISHLY
BRUTISM
BRUTISMS
BRUTS
BRUX
BRUXED
BRUXES
BRUXING
BRUXISM
BRUXISMS
BRYOLOGY
BRYONIES
BRYONY
BRYOPHYTE
BRYOZOAN
BRYOZOANS
BUAT
BUATS
BUAZE
BUAZES
BUB
BUBA
BUBAL
BUBALE
BUBALES
BUBALINE
BUBALIS
BUBALISES
BUBALS
BUBAS
BUBBA
BUBBAS
BUBBIES
BUBBLE
BUBBLED
BUBBLEGUM
BUBBLER
BUBBLERS
BUBBLES
BUBBLIER
BUBBLIES
BUBBLIEST
BUBBLING
BUBBLY

BUBBY
BUBINGA
BUBINGAS
BUBKES
BUBO
BUBOED
BUBOES
BUBONIC
BUBS
BUBU
BUBUKLE
BUBUKLES
BUBUS
BUCCAL
BUCCALLY
BUCCANEER
BUCCANIER
BUCCINA
BUCCINAS
BUCELLAS
BUCENTAUR
BUCHU
BUCHUS
BUCK
BUCKAROO
BUCKAROOS
BUCKAYRO
BUCKAYROS
BUCKBEAN
BUCKBEANS
BUCKBOARD
BUCKBRUSH
BUCKED
BUCKEEN
BUCKEENS
BUCKER
BUCKEROO
BUCKEROOS
BUCKERS
BUCKET
BUCKETED
BUCKETFUL
BUCKETING
BUCKETS
BUCKEYE
BUCKEYES
BUCKHORN
BUCKHORNS
BUCKHOUND
BUCKIE
BUCKIES
BUCKING
BUCKINGS
BUCKISH
BUCKISHLY
BUCKLE
BUCKLED
BUCKLER

BUCKLERED
BUCKLERS
BUCKLES
BUCKLING
BUCKLINGS
BUCKO
BUCKOES
BUCKOS
BUCKRA
BUCKRAKE
BUCKRAKES
BUCKRAM
BUCKRAMED
BUCKRAMS
BUCKRAS
BUCKS
BUCKSAW
BUCKSAWS
BUCKSHEE
BUCKSHEES
BUCKSHISH
BUCKSHOT
BUCKSHOTS
BUCKSKIN
BUCKSKINS
BUCKSOM
BUCKTAIL
BUCKTAILS
BUCKTEETH
BUCKTHORN
BUCKTOOTH
BUCKU
BUCKUS
BUCKWHEAT
BUCKYBALL
BUCKYTUBE
BUCOLIC
BUCOLICAL
BUCOLICS
BUD
BUDA
BUDAS
BUDDED
BUDDER
BUDDERS
BUDDHA
BUDDHAS
BUDDIED
BUDDIER
BUDDIES
BUDDIEST
BUDDING
BUDDINGS
BUDDLE
BUDDLED
BUDDLEIA
BUDDLEIAS
BUDDLES

BUDDLING
BUDDY
BUDDYING
BUDGE
BUDGED
BUDGER
BUDGEREE
BUDGERO
BUDGEROS
BUDGEROW
BUDGEROWS
BUDGERS
BUDGES
BUDGET
BUDGETARY
BUDGETED
BUDGETEER
BUDGETER
BUDGETERS
BUDGETING
BUDGETS
BUDGIE
BUDGIES
BUDGING
BUDI
BUDIS
BUDLESS
BUDLIKE
BUDMASH
BUDMASHES
BUDO
BUDOS
BUDS
BUDWORM
BUDWORMS
BUFF
BUFFA
BUFFABLE
BUFFALO
BUFFALOED
BUFFALOES
BUFFALOS
BUFFE
BUFFED
BUFFEL
BUFFER
BUFFERED
BUFFERING
BUFFERS
BUFFEST
BUFFET
BUFFETED
BUFFETER
BUFFETERS
BUFFETING
BUFFETS
BUFFI
BUFFIER

BUFFIEST
BUFFING
BUFFINGS
BUFFO
BUFFOON
BUFFOONS
BUFFOS
BUFFS
BUFFY
BUFO
BUFOS
BUFOTALIN
BUG
BUGABOO
BUGABOOS
BUGBANE
BUGBANES
BUGBEAR
BUGBEARS
BUGEYE
BUGEYES
BUGGAN
BUGGANE
BUGGANES
BUGGANS
BUGGED
BUGGER
BUGGERED
BUGGERIES
BUGGERING
BUGGERS
BUGGERY
BUGGIER
BUGGIES
BUGGIEST
BUGGIN
BUGGINESS
BUGGING
BUGGINGS
BUGGINS
BUGGY
BUGHOUSE
BUGHOUSES
BUGLE
BUGLED
BUGLER
BUGLERS
BUGLES
BUGLET
BUGLETS
BUGLEWEED
BUGLING
BUGLOSS
BUGLOSSES
BUGONG
BUGONGS
BUGOUT
BUGOUTS

BUGS	BULBOUSLY	BULLDOG	BULLRUSH
BUGSEED	BULBS	BULLDOGS	BULLS
BUGSEEDS	BULBUL	BULLDOZE	BULLSHAT
BUGSHA	BULBULS	BULLDOZED	BULLSHIT
BUGSHAS	BULGE	BULLDOZER	BULLSHITS
BUGWORT	BULGED	BULLDOZES	BULLSHOT
BUGWORTS	BULGER	BULLDUST	BULLSHOTS
BUHL	BULGERS	BULLDUSTS	BULLSNAKE
BUHLS	BULGES	BULLDYKE	BULLWADDY
BUHLWORK	BULGHUR	BULLDYKES	BULLWEED
BUHLWORKS	BULGHURS	BULLED	BULLWEEDS
BUHR	BULGIER	BULLER	BULLWHACK
BUHRS	BULGIEST	BULLERED	BULLWHIP
BUHRSTONE	BULGINE	BULLERING	BULLWHIPS
BUHUND	BULGINES	BULLERS	BULLY
BUHUNDS	BULGINESS	BULLET	BULLYBOY
BUIBUI	BULGING	BULLETED	BULLYBOYS
BUIBUIS	BULGINGLY	BULLETIN	BULLYING
BUIK	BULGUR	BULLETING	BULLYISM
BUIKS	BULGURS	BULLETINS	BULLYISMS
BUILD	BULGY	BULLETRIE	BULLYRAG
BUILDABLE	BULIMIA	BULLETS	BULLYRAGS
BUILDDOWN	BULIMIAC	BULLFIGHT	BULNBULN
BUILDED	BULIMIAS	BULLFINCH	BULNBULNS
BUILDER	BULIMIC	BULLFROG	BULRUSH
BUILDERS	BULIMICS	BULLFROGS	BULRUSHES
BUILDING	BULIMIES	BULLGINE	BULRUSHY
BUILDINGS	BULIMUS	BULLGINES	BULSE
BUILDS	BULIMUSES	BULLHEAD	BULSES
BUILDUP	BULIMY	BULLHEADS	BULWADDEE
BUILDUPS	BULK	BULLHORN	BULWADDY
BUILT	BULKAGE	BULLHORNS	BULWARK
BUIRDLIER	BULKAGES	BULLIED	BULWARKED
BUIRDLY	BULKED	BULLIER	BULWARKS
BUIST	BULKER	BULLIES	BUM
BUISTED	BULKERS	BULLIEST	BUMALO
BUISTING	BULKHEAD	BULLING	BUMALOTI
BUISTS	BULKHEADS	BULLINGS	BUMALOTIS
BUKE	BULKIER	BULLION	BUMBAG
BUKES	BULKIEST	BULLIONS	BUMBAGS
BUKKAKE	BULKILY	BULLISH	BUMBAZE
BUKKAKES	BULKINESS	BULLISHLY	BUMBAZED
BUKSHEE	BULKING	BULLNECK	BUMBAZES
BUKSHEES	BULKS	BULLNECKS	BUMBAZING
BUKSHI	BULKY	BULLNOSE	BUMBLE
BUKSHIS	BULL	BULLNOSES	BUMBLEBEE
BULB	BULLA	BULLOCK	BUMBLED
BULBAR	BULLACE	BULLOCKED	BUMBLEDOM
BULBED	BULLACES	BULLOCKS	BUMBLER
BULBEL	BULLAE	BULLOCKY	BUMBLERS
BULBELS	BULLARIES	BULLOSA	BUMBLES
BULBIL	BULLARY	BULLOUS	BUMBLING
BULBILS	BULLATE	BULLPEN	BUMBLINGS
BULBING	BULLBAR	BULLPENS	BUMBO
BULBLET	BULLBARS	BULLPOUT	BUMBOAT
BULBLETS	BULLBAT	BULLPOUTS	BUMBOATS
BULBOSITY	BULLBATS	BULLRING	BUMBOS
BULBOUS	BULLBRIER	BULLRINGS	BUMELIA

BUMELIAS
BUMF
BUMFLUFF
BUMFLUFFS
BUMFS
BUMFUZZLE
BUMKIN
BUMKINS
BUMMALO
BUMMALOS
BUMMALOTI
BUMMAREE
BUMMAREES
BUMMED
BUMMEL
BUMMELS
BUMMER
BUMMERS
BUMMEST
BUMMING
BUMMLE
BUMMLED
BUMMLES
BUMMLING
BUMMOCK
BUMMOCKS
BUMP
BUMPED
BUMPER
BUMPERED
BUMPERING
BUMPERS
BUMPH
BUMPHS
BUMPIER
BUMPIEST
BUMPILY
BUMPINESS
BUMPING
BUMPINGS
BUMPKIN
BUMPKINLY
BUMPKINS
BUMPOLOGY
BUMPS
BUMPTIOUS
BUMPY
BUMS
BUMSTERS
BUMSUCKER
BUN
BUNA
BUNAS
BUNCE
BUNCED
BUNCES
BUNCH
BUNCHED

BUNCHES
BUNCHIER
BUNCHIEST
BUNCHILY
BUNCHING
BUNCHINGS
BUNCHY
BUNCING
BUNCO
BUNCOED
BUNCOING
BUNCOMBE
BUNCOMBES
BUNCOS
BUND
BUNDE
BUNDED
BUNDH
BUNDHS
BUNDIED
BUNDIES
BUNDING
BUNDIST
BUNDISTS
BUNDLE
BUNDLED
BUNDLER
BUNDLERS
BUNDLES
BUNDLING
BUNDLINGS
BUNDOBUST
BUNDOOK
BUNDOOKS
BUNDS
BUNDT
BUNDTS
BUNDU
BUNDUS
BUNDWALL
BUNDWALLS
BUNDY
BUNDYING
BUNFIGHT
BUNFIGHTS
BUNG
BUNGALOID
BUNGALOW
BUNGALOWS
BUNGED
BUNGEE
BUNGEES
BUNGER
BUNGERS
BUNGEY
BUNGEYS
BUNGHOLE
BUNGHOLES

BUNGIE
BUNGIES
BUNGING
BUNGLE
BUNGLED
BUNGLER
BUNGLERS
BUNGLES
BUNGLING
BUNGLINGS
BUNGS
BUNGWALL
BUNGWALLS
BUNGY
BUNIA
BUNIAS
BUNION
BUNIONS
BUNJE
BUNJEE
BUNJEES
BUNJES
BUNJIE
BUNJIES
BUNJY
BUNK
BUNKED
BUNKER
BUNKERED
BUNKERING
BUNKERS
BUNKHOUSE
BUNKING
BUNKMATE
BUNKMATES
BUNKO
BUNKOED
BUNKOING
BUNKOS
BUNKS
BUNKUM
BUNKUMS
BUNN
BUNNET
BUNNETS
BUNNIA
BUNNIAS
BUNNIES
BUNNS
BUNNY
BUNODONT
BUNRAKU
BUNRAKUS
BUNS
BUNSEN
BUNSENS
BUNT
BUNTAL

BUNTALS
BUNTED
BUNTER
BUNTERS
BUNTIER
BUNTIEST
BUNTING
BUNTINGS
BUNTLINE
BUNTLINES
BUNTS
BUNTY
BUNYA
BUNYAS
BUNYIP
BUNYIPS
BUOY
BUOYAGE
BUOYAGES
BUOYANCE
BUOYANCES
BUOYANCY
BUOYANT
BUOYANTLY
BUOYED
BUOYING
BUOYS
BUPKES
BUPKUS
BUPLEVER
BUPLEVERS
BUPPIE
BUPPIES
BUPPY
BUPRESTID
BUQSHA
BUQSHAS
BUR
BURA
BURAN
BURANS
BURAS
BURB
BURBLE
BURBLED
BURBLER
BURBLERS
BURBLES
BURBLIER
BURBLIEST
BURBLING
BURBLINGS
BURBLY
BURBOT
BURBOTS
BURBS
BURD
BURDASH

BURDASHES	BURGRAVES	BURNERS	BURROWING
BURDEN	BURGS	BURNET	BURROWS
BURDENED	BURGUNDY	BURNETS	BURRS
BURDENER	BURHEL	BURNIE	BURRSTONE
BURDENERS	BURHELS	BURNIES	BURRY
BURDENING	BURIAL	BURNING	BURS
BURDENOUS	BURIALS	BURNINGLY	BURSA
BURDENS	BURIED	BURNINGS	BURSAE
BURDIE	BURIER	BURNISH	BURSAL
BURDIES	BURIERS	BURNISHED	BURSAR
BURDIZZO	BURIES	BURNISHER	BURSARIAL
BURDIZZOS	BURIN	BURNISHES	BURSARIES
BURDOCK	BURINIST	BURNOOSE	BURSARS
BURDOCKS	BURINISTS	BURNOOSED	BURSARY
BURDS	BURINS	BURNOOSES	BURSAS
BUREAU	BURITI	BURNOUS	BURSATE
BUREAUS	BURITIS	BURNOUSE	BURSE
BUREAUX	BURK	BURNOUSED	BURSEED
BURET	BURKA	BURNOUSES	BURSEEDS
BURETS	BURKAS	BURNOUT	BURSERA
BURETTE	BURKE	BURNOUTS	BURSES
BURETTES	BURKED	BURNS	BURSICON
BURG	BURKER	BURNSIDE	BURSICONS
BURGAGE	BURKERS	BURNSIDES	BURSIFORM
BURGAGES	BURKES	BURNT	BURSITIS
BURGANET	BURKING	BUROO	BURST
BURGANETS	BURKITE	BUROOS	BURSTED
BURGEE	BURKITES	BURP	BURSTEN
BURGEES	BURKS	BURPED	BURSTER
BURGEON	BURL	BURPEE	BURSTERS
BURGEONED	BURLADERO	BURPEES	BURSTING
BURGEONS	BURLAP	BURPING	BURSTONE
BURGER	BURLAPS	BURPS	BURSTONES
BURGERS	BURLED	BURQA	BURSTS
BURGESS	BURLER	BURQAS	BURTHEN
BURGESSES	BURLERS	BURR	BURTHENED
BURGH	BURLESK	BURRAMYS	BURTHENS
BURGHAL	BURLESKS	BURRAWANG	BURTON
BURGHER	BURLESQUE	BURRED	BURTONS
BURGHERS	BURLETTA	BURREL	BURWEED
BURGHS	BURLETTAS	BURRELL	BURWEEDS
BURGHUL	BURLEY	BURRELLS	BURY
BURGHULS	BURLEYCUE	BURRELS	BURYING
BURGLAR	BURLEYED	BURRER	BUS
BURGLARED	BURLEYING	BURRERS	BUSBAR
BURGLARS	BURLEYS	BURRHEL	BUSBARS
BURGLARY	BURLIER	BURRHELS	BUSBIES
BURGLE	BURLIEST	BURRIER	BUSBOY
BURGLED	BURLILY	BURRIEST	BUSBOYS
BURGLES	BURLINESS	BURRING	BUSBY
BURGLING	BURLING	BURRITO	BUSED
BURGONET	BURLS	BURRITOS	BUSERA
BURGONETS	BURLY	BURRO	BUSERAS
BURGOO	BURN	BURROS	BUSES
BURGOOS	BURNABLE	BURROW	BUSGIRL
BURGOUT	BURNABLES	BURROWED	BUSGIRLS
BURGOUTS	BURNED	BURROWER	BUSH
BURGRAVE	BURNER	BURROWERS	BUSHBABY

BUSHBUCK
BUSHBUCKS
BUSHCRAFT
BUSHED
BUSHEL
BUSHELED
BUSHELER
BUSHELERS
BUSHELING
BUSHELLED
BUSHELLER
BUSHELMAN
BUSHELMEN
BUSHELS
BUSHER
BUSHERS
BUSHES
BUSHFIRE
BUSHFIRES
BUSHFLIES
BUSHFLY
BUSHGOAT
BUSHGOATS
BUSHIDO
BUSHIDOS
BUSHIE
BUSHIER
BUSHIES
BUSHIEST
BUSHILY
BUSHINESS
BUSHING
BUSHINGS
BUSHLAND
BUSHLANDS
BUSHLESS
BUSHLIKE
BUSHMAN
BUSHMEAT
BUSHMEATS
BUSHMEN
BUSHPIG
BUSHPIGS
BUSHTIT
BUSHTITS
BUSHVELD
BUSHVELDS
BUSHWA
BUSHWAH
BUSHWAHS
BUSHWALK
BUSHWALKS
BUSHWAS
BUSHWHACK
BUSHWOMAN
BUSHWOMEN
BUSHY
BUSIED

BUSIER
BUSIES
BUSIEST
BUSILY
BUSINESS
BUSINESSY
BUSING
BUSINGS
BUSK
BUSKED
BUSKER
BUSKERS
BUSKET
BUSKETS
BUSKIN
BUSKINED
BUSKING
BUSKINGS
BUSKINS
BUSKS
BUSKY
BUSLOAD
BUSLOADS
BUSMAN
BUSMEN
BUSS
BUSSED
BUSSES
BUSSING
BUSSINGS
BUSSU
BUSSUS
BUST
BUSTARD
BUSTARDS
BUSTED
BUSTEE
BUSTEES
BUSTER
BUSTERS
BUSTI
BUSTIC
BUSTICATE
BUSTICS
BUSTIER
BUSTIERS
BUSTIEST
BUSTINESS
BUSTING
BUSTINGS
BUSTIS
BUSTLE
BUSTLED
BUSTLER
BUSTLERS
BUSTLES
BUSTLINE
BUSTLINES

BUSTLING
BUSTS
BUSTY
BUSULFAN
BUSULFANS
BUSUUTI
BUSUUTIS
BUSY
BUSYBODY
BUSYING
BUSYNESS
BUSYWORK
BUSYWORKS
BUT
BUTADIENE
BUTANE
BUTANES
BUTANOL
BUTANOLS
BUTANONE
BUTANONES
BUTCH
BUTCHER
BUTCHERED
BUTCHERER
BUTCHERLY
BUTCHERS
BUTCHERY
BUTCHES
BUTCHEST
BUTCHING
BUTCHINGS
BUTCHNESS
BUTE
BUTENE
BUTENES
BUTEO
BUTEONINE
BUTEOS
BUTES
BUTLE
BUTLED
BUTLER
BUTLERAGE
BUTLERED
BUTLERIES
BUTLERING
BUTLERS
BUTLERY
BUTLES
BUTLING
BUTMENT
BUTMENTS
BUTS
BUTSUDAN
BUTSUDANS
BUTT
BUTTALS

BUTTE
BUTTED
BUTTER
BUTTERBUR
BUTTERCUP
BUTTERED
BUTTERFAT
BUTTERFLY
BUTTERIER
BUTTERIES
BUTTERINE
BUTTERING
BUTTERNUT
BUTTERS
BUTTERY
BUTTES
BUTTHEAD
BUTTHEADS
BUTTIES
BUTTING
BUTTINSKI
BUTTINSKY
BUTTLE
BUTTLED
BUTTLES
BUTTLING
BUTTOCK
BUTTOCKED
BUTTOCKS
BUTTON
BUTTONED
BUTTONER
BUTTONERS
BUTTONING
BUTTONS
BUTTONY
BUTTRESS
BUTTS
BUTTSTOCK
BUTTY
BUTTYMAN
BUTTYMEN
BUTUT
BUTUTS
BUTYL
BUTYLATE
BUTYLATED
BUTYLATES
BUTYLENE
BUTYLENES
BUTYLS
BUTYRAL
BUTYRALS
BUTYRATE
BUTYRATES
BUTYRIC
BUTYRIN
BUTYRINS

BUTYROUS
BUTYRYL
BUTYRYLS
BUVETTE
BUVETTES
BUXOM
BUXOMER
BUXOMEST
BUXOMLY
BUXOMNESS
BUY
BUYABLE
BUYABLES
BUYBACK
BUYBACKS
BUYER
BUYERS
BUYING
BUYOFF
BUYOFFS
BUYOUT
BUYOUTS
BUYS
BUZKASHI
BUZKASHIS
BUZUKI
BUZUKIA
BUZUKIS
BUZZ
BUZZARD
BUZZARDS
BUZZCUT
BUZZCUTS
BUZZED
BUZZER
BUZZERS
BUZZES
BUZZIER
BUZZIEST
BUZZING
BUZZINGLY
BUZZINGS
BUZZWIG
BUZZWIGS
BUZZWORD
BUZZWORDS
BUZZY
BWANA
BWANAS
BWAZI
BWAZIS
BY
BYCATCH
BYCATCHES
BYCOKET
BYCOKETS
BYDE
BYDED

BYDES
BYDING
BYE
BYELAW
BYELAWS
BYES
BYGONE
BYGONES
BYKE
BYKED
BYKES
BYKING
BYLANDER
BYLANDERS
BYLANE
BYLANES
BYLAW
BYLAWS
BYLINE
BYLINED
BYLINER
BYLINERS
BYLINES
BYLINING
BYLIVE
BYNAME
BYNAMES
BYNEMPT
BYPASS
BYPASSED
BYPASSES
BYPASSING
BYPAST
BYPATH
BYPATHS
BYPLACE
BYPLACES
BYPLAY
BYPLAYS
BYPRODUCT
BYRE
BYREMAN
BYREMEN
BYRES
BYREWOMAN
BYREWOMEN
BYRL
BYRLADY
BYRLAKIN
BYRLAW
BYRLAWS
BYRLED
BYRLING
BYRLS
BYRNIE
BYRNIES
BYROAD
BYROADS

BYROOM
BYROOMS
BYS
BYSSAL
BYSSI
BYSSINE
BYSSOID
BYSSUS
BYSSUSES
BYSTANDER
BYSTREET
BYSTREETS
BYTALK
BYTALKS
BYTE
BYTES
BYTOWNITE
BYWAY
BYWAYS
BYWONER
BYWONERS
BYWORD
BYWORDS
BYWORK
BYWORKS
BYZANT
BYZANTINE
BYZANTS

C

CAA
CAAED
CAAING
CAAS
CAATINGA
CAATINGAS
CAB
CABA
CABAL
CABALA
CABALAS
CABALETTA
CABALETTE
CABALISM
CABALISMS
CABALIST
CABALISTS
CABALLED
CABALLER
CABALLERO
CABALLERS
CABALLINE
CABALLING
CABALS
CABANA
CABANAS
CABARET
CABARETS
CABAS
CABBAGE
CABBAGED
CABBAGES
CABBAGEY
CABBAGING
CABBAGY
CABBALA
CABBALAH
CABBALAHS
CABBALAS
CABBALISM
CABBALIST
CABBED
CABBIE
CABBIES
CABBING
CABBY
CABDRIVER
CABER
CABERNET
CABERNETS
CABERS
CABESTRO
CABESTROS

CABEZON
CABEZONE
CABEZONES
CABEZONS
CABILDO
CABILDOS
CABIN
CABINED
CABINET
CABINETRY
CABINETS
CABINING
CABINMATE
CABINS
CABLE
CABLECAST
CABLED
CABLEGRAM
CABLER
CABLERS
CABLES
CABLET
CABLETS
CABLEWAY
CABLEWAYS
CABLING
CABLINGS
CABMAN
CABMEN
CABOB
CABOBBED
CABOBBING
CABOBS
CABOC
CABOCEER
CABOCEERS
CABOCHED
CABOCHON
CABOCHONS
CABOCS
CABOMBA
CABOMBAS
CABOODLE
CABOODLES
CABOOSE
CABOOSES
CABOSHED
CABOTAGE
CABOTAGES
CABOVER
CABRE
CABRESTA
CABRESTAS

CABRESTO
CABRESTOS
CABRETTA
CABRETTAS
CABRIE
CABRIES
CABRILLA
CABRILLAS
CABRIO
CABRIOLE
CABRIOLES
CABRIOLET
CABRIOS
CABRIT
CABRITS
CABS
CABSTAND
CABSTANDS
CACA
CACAFOGO
CACAFOGOS
CACAFUEGO
CACAO
CACAOS
CACAS
CACHAEMIA
CACHAEMIC
CACHALOT
CACHALOTS
CACHE
CACHECTIC
CACHED
CACHEPOT
CACHEPOTS
CACHES
CACHET
CACHETED
CACHETING
CACHETS
CACHEXIA
CACHEXIAS
CACHEXIC
CACHEXIES
CACHEXY
CACHING
CACHOLONG
CACHOLOT
CACHOLOTS
CACHOU
CACHOUS
CACHUCHA
CACHUCHAS
CACIQUE

CACIQUES
CACIQUISM
CACKIER
CACKIEST
CACKLE
CACKLED
CACKLER
CACKLERS
CACKLES
CACKLING
CACKY
CACODEMON
CACODOXY
CACODYL
CACODYLIC
CACODYLS
CACOEPIES
CACOEPY
CACOETHES
CACOETHIC
CACOGENIC
CACOLET
CACOLETS
CACOLOGY
CACOMIXL
CACOMIXLE
CACOMIXLS
CACONYM
CACONYMS
CACONYMY
CACOON
CACOONS
CACOPHONY
CACOTOPIA
CACTI
CACTIFORM
CACTOID
CACTUS
CACTUSES
CACUMEN
CACUMINA
CACUMINAL
CAD
CADAGA
CADAGAS
CADAGI
CADAGIS
CADASTER
CADASTERS
CADASTRAL
CADASTRE
CADASTRES
CADAVER

83

CADAVERIC
CADAVERS
CADDICE
CADDICES
CADDIE
CADDIED
CADDIES
CADDIS
CADDISED
CADDISES
CADDISFLY
CADDISH
CADDISHLY
CADDY
CADDYING
CADDYSS
CADDYSSES
CADE
CADEAU
CADEAUX
CADEE
CADEES
CADELLE
CADELLES
CADENCE
CADENCED
CADENCES
CADENCIES
CADENCING
CADENCY
CADENT
CADENTIAL
CADENZA
CADENZAS
CADES
CADET
CADETS
CADETSHIP
CADGE
CADGED
CADGER
CADGERS
CADGES
CADGIER
CADGIEST
CADGING
CADGY
CADI
CADIE
CADIES
CADIS
CADMIC
CADMIUM
CADMIUMS
CADRANS
CADRANSES
CADRE
CADRES

CADS
CADUAC
CADUACS
CADUCEAN
CADUCEI
CADUCEUS
CADUCITY
CADUCOUS
CAECA
CAECAL
CAECALLY
CAECILIAN
CAECITIS
CAECUM
CAEOMA
CAEOMAS
CAERULE
CAERULEAN
CAESAR
CAESAREAN
CAESARIAN
CAESARISM
CAESARS
CAESE
CAESIOUS
CAESIUM
CAESIUMS
CAESTUS
CAESTUSES
CAESURA
CAESURAE
CAESURAL
CAESURAS
CAESURIC
CAFARD
CAFARDS
CAFE
CAFES
CAFETERIA
CAFETIERE
CAFETORIA
CAFF
CAFFEIN
CAFFEINE
CAFFEINES
CAFFEINIC
CAFFEINS
CAFFEISM
CAFFEISMS
CAFFILA
CAFFILAS
CAFFS
CAFILA
CAFILAS
CAFTAN
CAFTANED
CAFTANS
CAG

CAGANER
CAGANERS
CAGE
CAGEBIRD
CAGEBIRDS
CAGED
CAGEFUL
CAGEFULS
CAGELIKE
CAGELING
CAGELINGS
CAGER
CAGERS
CAGES
CAGEWORK
CAGEWORKS
CAGEY
CAGEYNESS
CAGIER
CAGIEST
CAGILY
CAGINESS
CAGING
CAGMAG
CAGMAGGED
CAGMAGS
CAGOT
CAGOTS
CAGOUL
CAGOULE
CAGOULES
CAGOULS
CAGS
CAGY
CAGYNESS
CAHIER
CAHIERS
CAHOOT
CAHOOTS
CAHOW
CAHOWS
CAID
CAIDS
CAILLACH
CAILLACHS
CAILLE
CAILLEACH
CAILLES
CAILLIACH
CAIMAC
CAIMACAM
CAIMACAMS
CAIMACS
CAIMAN
CAIMANS
CAIN
CAINS
CAIQUE

CAIQUES
CAIRD
CAIRDS
CAIRN
CAIRNED
CAIRNGORM
CAIRNS
CAIRNY
CAISSON
CAISSONS
CAITIFF
CAITIFFS
CAITIVE
CAITIVES
CAJAPUT
CAJAPUTS
CAJEPUT
CAJEPUTS
CAJOLE
CAJOLED
CAJOLER
CAJOLERS
CAJOLERY
CAJOLES
CAJOLING
CAJON
CAJONES
CAJUN
CAJUPUT
CAJUPUTS
CAKE
CAKED
CAKES
CAKEWALK
CAKEWALKS
CAKEY
CAKIER
CAKIEST
CAKINESS
CAKING
CAKINGS
CAKY
CALABASH
CALABAZA
CALABAZAS
CALABOGUS
CALABOOSE
CALABRESE
CALADIUM
CALADIUMS
CALALOO
CALALOOS
CALALU
CALALUS
CALAMANCO
CALAMAR
CALAMARI
CALAMARIS

CALAMARS
CALAMARY
CALAMATA
CALAMATAS
CALAMI
CALAMINE
CALAMINED
CALAMINES
CALAMINT
CALAMINTS
CALAMITE
CALAMITES
CALAMITY
CALAMUS
CALANDO
CALANDRIA
CALANTHE
CALANTHES
CALASH
CALASHES
CALATHEA
CALATHEAS
CALATHI
CALATHOS
CALATHUS
CALAVANCE
CALCANEA
CALCANEAL
CALCANEAN
CALCANEI
CALCANEUM
CALCANEUS
CALCAR
CALCARATE
CALCARIA
CALCARINE
CALCARS
CALCEATE
CALCEATED
CALCEATES
CALCED
CALCEDONY
CALCES
CALCIC
CALCICOLE
CALCIFIC
CALCIFIED
CALCIFIES
CALCIFUGE
CALCIFY
CALCIMINE
CALCINE
CALCINED
CALCINES
CALCINING
CALCITE
CALCITES
CALCITIC

CALCIUM
CALCIUMS
CALCRETE
CALCRETES
CALCSPAR
CALCSPARS
CALCTUFA
CALCTUFAS
CALCTUFF
CALCTUFFS
CALCULAR
CALCULARY
CALCULATE
CALCULI
CALCULOSE
CALCULOUS
CALCULUS
CALDARIA
CALDARIUM
CALDERA
CALDERAS
CALDRON
CALDRONS
CALECHE
CALECHES
CALEFIED
CALEFIES
CALEFY
CALEFYING
CALEMBOUR
CALENDAL
CALENDAR
CALENDARS
CALENDER
CALENDERS
CALENDRER
CALENDRIC
CALENDRY
CALENDS
CALENDULA
CALENTURE
CALESA
CALESAS
CALESCENT
CALF
CALFDOZER
CALFLESS
CALFLICK
CALFLICKS
CALFLIKE
CALFS
CALFSKIN
CALFSKINS
CALIATOUR
CALIBER
CALIBERED
CALIBERS
CALIBRATE

CALIBRE
CALIBRED
CALIBRES
CALICES
CALICHE
CALICHES
CALICLE
CALICLES
CALICO
CALICOES
CALICOS
CALICULAR
CALID
CALIDITY
CALIF
CALIFATE
CALIFATES
CALIFONT
CALIFONTS
CALIFS
CALIGO
CALIGOES
CALIGOS
CALIMA
CALIMAS
CALIOLOGY
CALIPASH
CALIPEE
CALIPEES
CALIPER
CALIPERED
CALIPERS
CALIPH
CALIPHAL
CALIPHATE
CALIPHS
CALISAYA
CALISAYAS
CALIVER
CALIVERS
CALIX
CALK
CALKED
CALKER
CALKERS
CALKIN
CALKING
CALKINGS
CALKINS
CALKS
CALL
CALLA
CALLABLE
CALLAIDES
CALLAIS
CALLALOO
CALLALOOS
CALLAN

CALLANS
CALLANT
CALLANTS
CALLAS
CALLBACK
CALLBACKS
CALLBOARD
CALLBOY
CALLBOYS
CALLED
CALLEE
CALLEES
CALLER
CALLERS
CALLET
CALLETS
CALLID
CALLIDITY
CALLIGRAM
CALLING
CALLINGS
CALLIOPE
CALLIOPES
CALLIPASH
CALLIPEE
CALLIPEES
CALLIPER
CALLIPERS
CALLOP
CALLOPS
CALLOSE
CALLOSES
CALLOSITY
CALLOUS
CALLOUSED
CALLOUSES
CALLOUSLY
CALLOW
CALLOWER
CALLOWEST
CALLOWS
CALLS
CALLUNA
CALLUNAS
CALLUS
CALLUSED
CALLUSES
CALLUSING
CALM
CALMANT
CALMANTS
CALMATIVE
CALMED
CALMER
CALMEST
CALMIER
CALMIEST
CALMING

CALMINGLY
CALMINGS
CALMLY
CALMNESS
CALMS
CALMSTONE
CALMY
CALO
CALOMEL
CALOMELS
CALORIC
CALORICS
CALORIE
CALORIES
CALORIFIC
CALORISE
CALORISED
CALORISES
CALORIST
CALORISTS
CALORIZE
CALORIZED
CALORIZES
CALORY
CALOS
CALOTTE
CALOTTES
CALOTYPE
CALOTYPES
CALOYER
CALOYERS
CALP
CALPA
CALPAC
CALPACK
CALPACKS
CALPACS
CALPAIN
CALPAINS
CALPAS
CALPS
CALQUE
CALQUED
CALQUES
CALQUING
CALTHA
CALTHAS
CALTHROP
CALTHROPS
CALTRAP
CALTRAPS
CALTROP
CALTROPS
CALUMBA
CALUMBAS
CALUMET
CALUMETS
CALUMNIES

CALUMNY
CALUTRON
CALUTRONS
CALVADOS
CALVARIA
CALVARIAL
CALVARIAN
CALVARIAS
CALVARIES
CALVARIUM
CALVARY
CALVE
CALVED
CALVER
CALVERED
CALVERING
CALVERS
CALVES
CALVING
CALVITIES
CALX
CALXES
CALYCATE
CALYCEAL
CALYCES
CALYCINAL
CALYCINE
CALYCLE
CALYCLED
CALYCLES
CALYCOID
CALYCULAR
CALYCULE
CALYCULES
CALYCULI
CALYCULUS
CALYPSO
CALYPSOES
CALYPSOS
CALYPTER
CALYPTERA
CALYPTERS
CALYPTRA
CALYPTRAS
CALYX
CALYXES
CALZONE
CALZONES
CALZONI
CAM
CAMA
CAMAIEU
CAMAIEUX
CAMAIL
CAMAILED
CAMAILS
CAMAN
CAMANACHD

CAMANS
CAMARILLA
CAMARON
CAMARONS
CAMAS
CAMASES
CAMASH
CAMASHES
CAMASS
CAMASSES
CAMBER
CAMBERED
CAMBERING
CAMBERS
CAMBIA
CAMBIAL
CAMBIFORM
CAMBISM
CAMBISMS
CAMBIST
CAMBISTRY
CAMBISTS
CAMBIUM
CAMBIUMS
CAMBOGE
CAMBOGES
CAMBOGIA
CAMBOGIAS
CAMBOOSE
CAMBOOSES
CAMBREL
CAMBRELS
CAMBRIC
CAMBRICS
CAMCORDER
CAME
CAMEL
CAMELBACK
CAMELEER
CAMELEERS
CAMELEON
CAMELEONS
CAMELHAIR
CAMELIA
CAMELIAS
CAMELID
CAMELIDS
CAMELINE
CAMELINES
CAMELISH
CAMELLIA
CAMELLIAS
CAMELLIKE
CAMELOID
CAMELOIDS
CAMELOT
CAMELOTS
CAMELRIES

CAMELRY
CAMELS
CAMEO
CAMEOED
CAMEOING
CAMEOS
CAMERA
CAMERAE
CAMERAL
CAMERAMAN
CAMERAMEN
CAMERAS
CAMERATED
CAMES
CAMESE
CAMESES
CAMION
CAMIONS
CAMIS
CAMISA
CAMISADE
CAMISADES
CAMISADO
CAMISADOS
CAMISAS
CAMISE
CAMISES
CAMISIA
CAMISIAS
CAMISOLE
CAMISOLES
CAMLET
CAMLETS
CAMMED
CAMMIE
CAMMIES
CAMMING
CAMO
CAMOGIE
CAMOGIES
CAMOMILE
CAMOMILES
CAMOODI
CAMOODIS
CAMORRA
CAMORRAS
CAMORRIST
CAMOS
CAMOTE
CAMOTES
CAMOUFLET
CAMP
CAMPAGNA
CAMPAGNAS
CAMPAGNE
CAMPAIGN
CAMPAIGNS
CAMPANA

CAMPANAS	CAMPUSED	CANCANS	CANEBRAKE
CAMPANERO	CAMPUSES	CANCEL	CANED
CAMPANILE	CAMPUSING	CANCELED	CANEFRUIT
CAMPANILI	CAMPY	CANCELEER	CANEH
CAMPANIST	CAMS	CANCELER	CANEHS
CAMPANULA	CAMSHAFT	CANCELERS	CANELLA
CAMPCRAFT	CAMSHAFTS	CANCELIER	CANELLAS
CAMPEADOR	CAMSHO	CANCELING	CANELLINI
CAMPED	CAMSHOCH	CANCELLED	CANEPHOR
CAMPER	CAMSTAIRY	CANCELLER	CANEPHORA
CAMPERS	CAMSTANE	CANCELLI	CANEPHORE
CAMPESINO	CAMSTANES	CANCELS	CANEPHORS
CAMPEST	CAMSTEARY	CANCER	CANER
CAMPFIRE	CAMSTONE	CANCERATE	CANERS
CAMPFIRES	CAMSTONES	CANCERED	CANES
CAMPHANE	CAMUS	CANCEROUS	CANESCENT
CAMPHANES	CAMUSES	CANCERS	CANEWARE
CAMPHENE	CAMWOOD	CANCHA	CANEWARES
CAMPHENES	CAMWOODS	CANCHAS	CANFIELD
CAMPHINE	CAN	CANCRINE	CANFIELDS
CAMPHINES	CANADA	CANCROID	CANFUL
CAMPHIRE	CANADAS	CANCROIDS	CANFULS
CAMPHIRES	CANAIGRE	CANDELA	CANG
CAMPHOL	CANAIGRES	CANDELAS	CANGLE
CAMPHOLS	CANAILLE	CANDENT	CANGLED
CAMPHOR	CANAILLES	CANDID	CANGLES
CAMPHORIC	CANAKIN	CANDIDA	CANGLING
CAMPHORS	CANAKINS	CANDIDACY	CANGS
CAMPI	CANAL	CANDIDAL	CANGUE
CAMPIER	CANALBOAT	CANDIDAS	CANGUES
CAMPIEST	CANALED	CANDIDATE	CANICULAR
CAMPILY	CANALING	CANDIDER	CANID
CAMPINESS	CANALISE	CANDIDEST	CANIDS
CAMPING	CANALISED	CANDIDLY	CANIER
CAMPINGS	CANALISES	CANDIDS	CANIEST
CAMPION	CANALIZE	CANDIE	CANIKIN
CAMPIONS	CANALIZED	CANDIED	CANIKINS
CAMPLE	CANALIZES	CANDIES	CANINE
CAMPLED	CANALLED	CANDLE	CANINES
CAMPLES	CANALLER	CANDLED	CANING
CAMPLING	CANALLERS	CANDLELIT	CANINGS
CAMPLY	CANALLING	CANDLENUT	CANINITY
CAMPNESS	CANALS	CANDLEPIN	CANISTEL
CAMPO	CANAPE	CANDLER	CANISTELS
CAMPODEID	CANAPES	CANDLERS	CANISTER
CAMPONG	CANARD	CANDLES	CANISTERS
CAMPONGS	CANARDS	CANDLING	CANITIES
CAMPOREE	CANARIED	CANDOCK	CANKER
CAMPOREES	CANARIES	CANDOCKS	CANKERED
CAMPOS	CANARY	CANDOR	CANKERING
CAMPOUT	CANARYING	CANDORS	CANKEROUS
CAMPOUTS	CANASTA	CANDOUR	CANKERS
CAMPS	CANASTAS	CANDOURS	CANKERY
CAMPSHIRT	CANASTER	CANDY	CANN
CAMPSITE	CANASTERS	CANDYGRAM	CANNA
CAMPSITES	CANBANK	CANDYING	CANNABIC
CAMPSTOOL	CANBANKS	CANDYTUFT	CANNABIN
CAMPUS	CANCAN	CANE	CANNABINS

CANNABIS
CANNACH
CANNACHS
CANNAE
CANNAS
CANNED
CANNEL
CANNELON
CANNELONI
CANNELONS
CANNELS
CANNELURE
CANNER
CANNERIES
CANNERS
CANNERY
CANNIBAL
CANNIBALS
CANNIE
CANNIER
CANNIEST
CANNIKIN
CANNIKINS
CANNILY
CANNINESS
CANNING
CANNINGS
CANNISTER
CANNOLI
CANNOLIS
CANNON
CANNONADE
CANNONED
CANNONEER
CANNONIER
CANNONING
CANNONRY
CANNONS
CANNOT
CANNS
CANNULA
CANNULAE
CANNULAR
CANNULAS
CANNULATE
CANNY
CANOE
CANOEABLE
CANOED
CANOEING
CANOEINGS
CANOEIST
CANOEISTS
CANOER
CANOERS
CANOES
CANOEWOOD
CANOLA

CANOLAS
CANON
CANONESS
CANONIC
CANONICAL
CANONISE
CANONISED
CANONISER
CANONISES
CANONIST
CANONISTS
CANONIZE
CANONIZED
CANONIZER
CANONIZES
CANONRIES
CANONRY
CANONS
CANOODLE
CANOODLED
CANOODLER
CANOODLES
CANOPIC
CANOPIED
CANOPIES
CANOPY
CANOPYING
CANOROUS
CANS
CANSFUL
CANSO
CANSOS
CANST
CANSTICK
CANSTICKS
CANT
CANTABANK
CANTABILE
CANTAL
CANTALA
CANTALAS
CANTALOUP
CANTALS
CANTAR
CANTARS
CANTATA
CANTATAS
CANTATE
CANTATES
CANTDOG
CANTDOGS
CANTED
CANTEEN
CANTEENS
CANTER
CANTERED
CANTERING
CANTERS

CANTEST
CANTHAL
CANTHARI
CANTHARID
CANTHARIS
CANTHARUS
CANTHI
CANTHITIS
CANTHOOK
CANTHOOKS
CANTHUS
CANTIC
CANTICLE
CANTICLES
CANTICO
CANTICOED
CANTICOS
CANTICOY
CANTICOYS
CANTICUM
CANTICUMS
CANTIER
CANTIEST
CANTILENA
CANTILY
CANTINA
CANTINAS
CANTINESS
CANTING
CANTINGLY
CANTINGS
CANTION
CANTIONS
CANTLE
CANTLED
CANTLES
CANTLET
CANTLETS
CANTLING
CANTO
CANTON
CANTONAL
CANTONED
CANTONING
CANTONISE
CANTONIZE
CANTONS
CANTOR
CANTORIAL
CANTORIS
CANTORS
CANTOS
CANTRAIP
CANTRAIPS
CANTRAP
CANTRAPS
CANTRED
CANTREDS

CANTREF
CANTREFS
CANTRIP
CANTRIPS
CANTS
CANTUS
CANTY
CANULA
CANULAE
CANULAR
CANULAS
CANULATE
CANULATED
CANULATES
CANVAS
CANVASED
CANVASER
CANVASERS
CANVASES
CANVASING
CANVASS
CANVASSED
CANVASSER
CANVASSES
CANY
CANYON
CANYONEER
CANYONING
CANYONS
CANZONA
CANZONAS
CANZONE
CANZONES
CANZONET
CANZONETS
CANZONI
CAP
CAPA
CAPABLE
CAPABLER
CAPABLEST
CAPABLY
CAPACIOUS
CAPACITOR
CAPACITY
CAPARISON
CAPAS
CAPE
CAPED
CAPELAN
CAPELANS
CAPELET
CAPELETS
CAPELIN
CAPELINE
CAPELINES
CAPELINS
CAPELLET

CAPELLETS
CAPELLINE
CAPELLINI
CAPER
CAPERED
CAPERER
CAPERERS
CAPERING
CAPERS
CAPES
CAPESKIN
CAPESKINS
CAPEWORK
CAPEWORKS
CAPFUL
CAPFULS
CAPH
CAPHS
CAPI
CAPIAS
CAPIASES
CAPILLARY
CAPING
CAPITA
CAPITAL
CAPITALLY
CAPITALS
CAPITAN
CAPITANI
CAPITANO
CAPITANOS
CAPITANS
CAPITATE
CAPITATED
CAPITAYN
CAPITAYNS
CAPITELLA
CAPITOL
CAPITOLS
CAPITULA
CAPITULAR
CAPITULUM
CAPIZ
CAPIZES
CAPLE
CAPLES
CAPLESS
CAPLET
CAPLETS
CAPLIN
CAPLINS
CAPMAKER
CAPMAKERS
CAPO
CAPOCCHIA
CAPOEIRA
CAPOEIRAS
CAPON

CAPONATA
CAPONATAS
CAPONIER
CAPONIERE
CAPONIERS
CAPONISE
CAPONISED
CAPONISES
CAPONIZE
CAPONIZED
CAPONIZES
CAPONS
CAPORAL
CAPORALS
CAPOS
CAPOT
CAPOTASTO
CAPOTE
CAPOTES
CAPOTS
CAPOTTED
CAPOTTING
CAPOUCH
CAPOUCHES
CAPPED
CAPPER
CAPPERS
CAPPING
CAPPINGS
CAPRATE
CAPRATES
CAPRIC
CAPRICCI
CAPRICCIO
CAPRICE
CAPRICES
CAPRID
CAPRIDS
CAPRIFIED
CAPRIFIES
CAPRIFIG
CAPRIFIGS
CAPRIFOIL
CAPRIFOLE
CAPRIFORM
CAPRIFY
CAPRINE
CAPRIOLE
CAPRIOLED
CAPRIOLES
CAPRIS
CAPROATE
CAPROATES
CAPROCK
CAPROCKS
CAPROIC
CAPRYLATE
CAPRYLIC

CAPS
CAPSAICIN
CAPSICIN
CAPSICINS
CAPSICUM
CAPSICUMS
CAPSID
CAPSIDAL
CAPSIDS
CAPSIZAL
CAPSIZALS
CAPSIZE
CAPSIZED
CAPSIZES
CAPSIZING
CAPSOMER
CAPSOMERE
CAPSOMERS
CAPSTAN
CAPSTANS
CAPSTONE
CAPSTONES
CAPSULAR
CAPSULARY
CAPSULATE
CAPSULE
CAPSULED
CAPSULES
CAPSULING
CAPSULISE
CAPSULIZE
CAPTAIN
CAPTAINCY
CAPTAINED
CAPTAINRY
CAPTAINS
CAPTAN
CAPTANS
CAPTION
CAPTIONED
CAPTIONS
CAPTIOUS
CAPTIVATE
CAPTIVE
CAPTIVED
CAPTIVES
CAPTIVING
CAPTIVITY
CAPTOPRIL
CAPTOR
CAPTORS
CAPTURE
CAPTURED
CAPTURER
CAPTURERS
CAPTURES
CAPTURING
CAPUCCIO

CAPUCCIOS
CAPUCHE
CAPUCHED
CAPUCHES
CAPUCHIN
CAPUCHINS
CAPUERA
CAPUERAS
CAPUL
CAPULS
CAPUT
CAPYBARA
CAPYBARAS
CAR
CARABAO
CARABAOS
CARABID
CARABIDS
CARABIN
CARABINE
CARABINER
CARABINES
CARABINS
CARACAL
CARACALS
CARACARA
CARACARAS
CARACK
CARACKS
CARACOL
CARACOLE
CARACOLED
CARACOLER
CARACOLES
CARACOLS
CARACT
CARACTS
CARACUL
CARACULS
CARAFE
CARAFES
CARAGANA
CARAGANAS
CARAGEEN
CARAGEENS
CARAMBA
CARAMBOLA
CARAMBOLE
CARAMEL
CARAMELS
CARANGID
CARANGIDS
CARANGOID
CARANNA
CARANNAS
CARAP
CARAPACE
CARAPACED

CARAPACES
CARAPAX
CARAPAXES
CARAPS
CARASSOW
CARASSOWS
CARAT
CARATE
CARATES
CARATS
CARAUNA
CARAUNAS
CARAVAN
CARAVANCE
CARAVANED
CARAVANER
CARAVANS
CARAVEL
CARAVELLE
CARAVELS
CARAWAY
CARAWAYS
CARB
CARBACHOL
CARBAMATE
CARBAMIC
CARBAMIDE
CARBAMINO
CARBAMOYL
CARBAMYL
CARBAMYLS
CARBANION
CARBARN
CARBARNS
CARBARYL
CARBARYLS
CARBAZOLE
CARBEEN
CARBEENS
CARBENE
CARBENES
CARBIDE
CARBIDES
CARBIES
CARBINE
CARBINEER
CARBINES
CARBINIER
CARBINOL
CARBINOLS
CARBO
CARBOLIC
CARBOLICS
CARBOLISE
CARBOLIZE
CARBON
CARBONADE
CARBONADO

CARBONARA
CARBONATE
CARBONIC
CARBONISE
CARBONIUM
CARBONIZE
CARBONOUS
CARBONS
CARBONYL
CARBONYLS
CARBORA
CARBORAS
CARBOS
CARBOXYL
CARBOXYLS
CARBOY
CARBOYED
CARBOYS
CARBS
CARBUNCLE
CARBURATE
CARBURET
CARBURETS
CARBURISE
CARBURIZE
CARBY
CARCAJOU
CARCAJOUS
CARCAKE
CARCAKES
CARCANET
CARCANETS
CARCASE
CARCASED
CARCASES
CARCASING
CARCASS
CARCASSED
CARCASSES
CARCEL
CARCELS
CARCERAL
CARCINOID
CARCINOMA
CARD
CARDAMINE
CARDAMOM
CARDAMOMS
CARDAMON
CARDAMONS
CARDAMUM
CARDAMUMS
CARDAN
CARDBOARD
CARDCASE
CARDCASES
CARDECU
CARDECUE

CARDECUES
CARDECUS
CARDED
CARDER
CARDERS
CARDI
CARDIA
CARDIAC
CARDIACAL
CARDIACS
CARDIAE
CARDIALGY
CARDIAS
CARDIE
CARDIES
CARDIGAN
CARDIGANS
CARDINAL
CARDINALS
CARDING
CARDINGS
CARDIO
CARDIOID
CARDIOIDS
CARDIS
CARDITIC
CARDITIS
CARDON
CARDONS
CARDOON
CARDOONS
CARDPHONE
CARDPUNCH
CARDS
CARDSHARP
CARDUUS
CARDUUSES
CARDY
CARE
CARED
CAREEN
CAREENAGE
CAREENED
CAREENER
CAREENERS
CAREENING
CAREENS
CAREER
CAREERED
CAREERER
CAREERERS
CAREERING
CAREERISM
CAREERIST
CAREERS
CAREFREE
CAREFUL
CAREFULLY

CAREGIVER
CARELESS
CARELINE
CARELINES
CAREME
CAREMES
CARER
CARERS
CARES
CARESS
CARESSED
CARESSER
CARESSERS
CARESSES
CARESSING
CARESSIVE
CARET
CARETAKE
CARETAKEN
CARETAKER
CARETAKES
CARETOOK
CARETS
CAREWORN
CAREX
CARFARE
CARFARES
CARFAX
CARFAXES
CARFOX
CARFOXES
CARFUFFLE
CARFUL
CARFULS
CARGEESE
CARGO
CARGOED
CARGOES
CARGOING
CARGOOSE
CARGOS
CARHOP
CARHOPPED
CARHOPS
CARIACOU
CARIACOUS
CARIAMA
CARIAMAS
CARIBE
CARIBES
CARIBOU
CARIBOUS
CARICES
CARIED
CARIERE
CARIERES
CARIES
CARILLON

CARILLONS	CARNALISE	CAROLLERS	CARPORT
CARINA	CARNALISM	CAROLLING	CARPORTS
CARINAE	CARNALIST	CAROLS	CARPS
CARINAL	CARNALITY	CAROLUS	CARPUS
CARINAS	CARNALIZE	CAROLUSES	CARR
CARINATE	CARNALLED	CAROM	CARRACK
CARINATED	CARNALLY	CAROMED	CARRACKS
CARING	CARNALS	CAROMEL	CARRACT
CARIOCA	CARNAROLI	CAROMELS	CARRACTS
CARIOCAS	CARNATION	CAROMING	CARRAGEEN
CARIOLE	CARNAUBA	CAROMS	CARRAT
CARIOLES	CARNAUBAS	CAROTENE	CARRATS
CARIOSE	CARNELIAN	CAROTENES	CARRAWAY
CARIOSITY	CARNEOUS	CAROTID	CARRAWAYS
CARIOUS	CARNET	CAROTIDAL	CARRECT
CARITAS	CARNETS	CAROTIDS	CARRECTS
CARITASES	CARNEY	CAROTIN	CARREFOUR
CARITATES	CARNEYED	CAROTINS	CARREL
CARJACK	CARNEYING	CAROUSAL	CARRELL
CARJACKED	CARNEYS	CAROUSALS	CARRELLS
CARJACKER	CARNIE	CAROUSE	CARRELS
CARJACKS	CARNIED	CAROUSED	CARRIAGE
CARJACOU	CARNIER	CAROUSEL	CARRIAGES
CARJACOUS	CARNIES	CAROUSELS	CARRICK
CARK	CARNIEST	CAROUSER	CARRIED
CARKED	CARNIFEX	CAROUSERS	CARRIER
CARKING	CARNIFIED	CAROUSES	CARRIERS
CARKS	CARNIFIES	CAROUSING	CARRIES
CARL	CARNIFY	CARP	CARRIOLE
CARLE	CARNITINE	CARPACCIO	CARRIOLES
CARLES	CARNIVAL	CARPAL	CARRION
CARLESS	CARNIVALS	CARPALE	CARRIONS
CARLIN	CARNIVORA	CARPALES	CARRITCH
CARLINE	CARNIVORE	CARPALIA	CARROCH
CARLINES	CARNIVORY	CARPALS	CARROCHES
CARLING	CARNOSAUR	CARPARK	CARROM
CARLINGS	CARNOSE	CARPARKS	CARROMED
CARLINS	CARNOSITY	CARPED	CARROMING
CARLISH	CARNOTITE	CARPEL	CARROMS
CARLOAD	CARNS	CARPELS	CARRON
CARLOADS	CARNY	CARPENTER	CARRONADE
CARLOCK	CARNYING	CARPENTRY	CARROT
CARLOCKS	CAROACH	CARPER	CARROTIER
CARLOT	CAROACHES	CARPERS	CARROTIN
CARLOTS	CAROB	CARPET	CARROTINS
CARLS	CAROBS	CARPETBAG	CARROTS
CARMAKER	CAROCH	CARPETED	CARROTTOP
CARMAKERS	CAROCHE	CARPETING	CARROTY
CARMAN	CAROCHES	CARPETS	CARROUSEL
CARMELITE	CAROL	CARPI	CARRS
CARMEN	CAROLED	CARPING	CARRY
CARMINE	CAROLER	CARPINGLY	CARRYALL
CARMINES	CAROLERS	CARPINGS	CARRYALLS
CARN	CAROLI	CARPOLOGY	CARRYBACK
CARNAGE	CAROLING	CARPOOL	CARRYCOT
CARNAGES	CAROLINGS	CARPOOLED	CARRYCOTS
CARNAHUBA	CAROLLED	CARPOOLER	CARRYING
CARNAL	CAROLLER	CARPOOLS	CARRYON

CARRYONS
CARRYOUT
CARRYOUTS
CARRYOVER
CARRYTALE
CARS
CARSE
CARSES
CARSEY
CARSEYS
CARSICK
CART
CARTA
CARTABLE
CARTAGE
CARTAGES
CARTAS
CARTE
CARTED
CARTEL
CARTELISE
CARTELISM
CARTELIST
CARTELIZE
CARTELS
CARTER
CARTERS
CARTES
CARTFUL
CARTFULS
CARTHORSE
CARTILAGE
CARTING
CARTLOAD
CARTLOADS
CARTOGRAM
CARTOLOGY
CARTON
CARTONAGE
CARTONED
CARTONING
CARTONS
CARTOON
CARTOONED
CARTOONS
CARTOONY
CARTOP
CARTOPPER
CARTOUCH
CARTOUCHE
CARTRIDGE
CARTROAD
CARTROADS
CARTS
CARTULARY
CARTWAY
CARTWAYS
CARTWHEEL

CARUCAGE
CARUCAGES
CARUCATE
CARUCATES
CARUNCLE
CARUNCLES
CARVACROL
CARVE
CARVED
CARVEL
CARVELS
CARVEN
CARVER
CARVERIES
CARVERS
CARVERY
CARVES
CARVIES
CARVING
CARVINGS
CARVY
CARWASH
CARWASHES
CARYATIC
CARYATID
CARYATIDS
CARYOPSES
CARYOPSIS
CARYOTIN
CARYOTINS
CASA
CASABA
CASABAS
CASAS
CASAVA
CASAVAS
CASBAH
CASBAHS
CASCABEL
CASCABELS
CASCABLE
CASCABLES
CASCADE
CASCADED
CASCADES
CASCADING
CASCADURA
CASCARA
CASCARAS
CASCHROM
CASCHROMS
CASCO
CASCOS
CASE
CASEASE
CASEASES
CASEATE
CASEATED

CASEATES
CASEATING
CASEATION
CASEBOOK
CASEBOOKS
CASEBOUND
CASED
CASEFIED
CASEFIES
CASEFY
CASEFYING
CASEIC
CASEIN
CASEINATE
CASEINS
CASELOAD
CASELOADS
CASEMAKER
CASEMAN
CASEMATE
CASEMATED
CASEMATES
CASEMEN
CASEMENT
CASEMENTS
CASEOSE
CASEOSES
CASEOUS
CASERN
CASERNE
CASERNES
CASERNS
CASES
CASETTE
CASETTES
CASEWORK
CASEWORKS
CASEWORM
CASEWORMS
CASH
CASHABLE
CASHAW
CASHAWS
CASHBACK
CASHBACKS
CASHBOOK
CASHBOOKS
CASHBOX
CASHBOXES
CASHED
CASHES
CASHEW
CASHEWS
CASHIER
CASHIERED
CASHIERER
CASHIERS
CASHING

CASHLESS
CASHMERE
CASHMERES
CASHOO
CASHOOS
CASHPOINT
CASIMERE
CASIMERES
CASIMIRE
CASIMIRES
CASING
CASINGS
CASINI
CASINO
CASINOS
CASITA
CASITAS
CASK
CASKED
CASKET
CASKETED
CASKETING
CASKETS
CASKING
CASKS
CASKSTAND
CASKY
CASQUE
CASQUED
CASQUES
CASSABA
CASSABAS
CASSAREEP
CASSATA
CASSATAS
CASSATION
CASSAVA
CASSAVAS
CASSENA
CASSENAS
CASSENE
CASSENES
CASSEROLE
CASSETTE
CASSETTES
CASSIA
CASSIAS
CASSIMERE
CASSINA
CASSINAS
CASSINE
CASSINES
CASSINGLE
CASSINO
CASSINOS
CASSIS
CASSISES
CASSOCK

CASSOCKED
CASSOCKS
CASSONADE
CASSONE
CASSONES
CASSOULET
CASSOWARY
CASSPIR
CASSPIRS
CAST
CASTABLE
CASTANET
CASTANETS
CASTAWAY
CASTAWAYS
CASTE
CASTED
CASTEISM
CASTEISMS
CASTELESS
CASTELLA
CASTELLAN
CASTELLUM
CASTER
CASTERS
CASTES
CASTIGATE
CASTING
CASTINGS
CASTLE
CASTLED
CASTLES
CASTLING
CASTOCK
CASTOCKS
CASTOFF
CASTOFFS
CASTOR
CASTOREUM
CASTORIES
CASTORS
CASTORY
CASTRAL
CASTRATE
CASTRATED
CASTRATER
CASTRATES
CASTRATI
CASTRATO
CASTRATOR
CASTRATOS
CASTS
CASUAL
CASUALISE
CASUALISM
CASUALIZE
CASUALLY
CASUALS

CASUALTY
CASUARINA
CASUIST
CASUISTIC
CASUISTRY
CASUISTS
CASUS
CAT
CATABASES
CATABASIS
CATABATIC
CATABOLIC
CATACLASM
CATACLYSM
CATACOMB
CATACOMBS
CATAFALCO
CATALASE
CATALASES
CATALATIC
CATALEPSY
CATALEXES
CATALEXIS
CATALO
CATALOES
CATALOG
CATALOGED
CATALOGER
CATALOGIC
CATALOGS
CATALOGUE
CATALOS
CATALPA
CATALPAS
CATALYSE
CATALYSED
CATALYSER
CATALYSES
CATALYSIS
CATALYST
CATALYSTS
CATALYTIC
CATALYZE
CATALYZED
CATALYZER
CATALYZES
CATAMARAN
CATAMENIA
CATAMITE
CATAMITES
CATAMOUNT
CATAPAN
CATAPANS
CATAPHORA
CATAPHYLL
CATAPLASM
CATAPLEXY
CATAPULT

CATAPULTS
CATARACT
CATARACTS
CATARHINE
CATARRH
CATARRHAL
CATARRHS
CATASTA
CATASTAS
CATATONIA
CATATONIC
CATATONY
CATAWBA
CATAWBAS
CATBIRD
CATBIRDS
CATBOAT
CATBOATS
CATBRIER
CATBRIERS
CATCALL
CATCALLED
CATCALLER
CATCALLS
CATCH
CATCHABLE
CATCHALL
CATCHALLS
CATCHCRY
CATCHED
CATCHEN
CATCHER
CATCHERS
CATCHES
CATCHFLY
CATCHIER
CATCHIEST
CATCHING
CATCHINGS
CATCHMENT
CATCHPOLE
CATCHPOLL
CATCHT
CATCHUP
CATCHUPS
CATCHWEED
CATCHWORD
CATCHY
CATCLAW
CATCLAWS
CATE
CATECHIN
CATECHINS
CATECHISE
CATECHISM
CATECHIST
CATECHIZE
CATECHOL

CATECHOLS
CATECHU
CATECHUS
CATEGORIC
CATEGORY
CATELOG
CATELOGS
CATENA
CATENAE
CATENANE
CATENANES
CATENARY
CATENAS
CATENATE
CATENATED
CATENATES
CATENOID
CATENOIDS
CATER
CATERAN
CATERANS
CATERED
CATERER
CATERERS
CATERESS
CATERING
CATERINGS
CATERS
CATERWAUL
CATES
CATFACE
CATFACES
CATFACING
CATFALL
CATFALLS
CATFIGHT
CATFIGHTS
CATFISH
CATFISHES
CATGUT
CATGUTS
CATHARISE
CATHARIZE
CATHARSES
CATHARSIS
CATHARTIC
CATHEAD
CATHEADS
CATHECT
CATHECTED
CATHECTIC
CATHECTS
CATHEDRA
CATHEDRAE
CATHEDRAL
CATHEDRAS
CATHEPSIN
CATHEPTIC

CATHETER
CATHETERS
CATHETUS
CATHEXES
CATHEXIS
CATHISMA
CATHISMAS
CATHODAL
CATHODE
CATHODES
CATHODIC
CATHOLE
CATHOLES
CATHOLIC
CATHOLICS
CATHOLYTE
CATHOOD
CATHOODS
CATHOUSE
CATHOUSES
CATION
CATIONIC
CATIONS
CATJANG
CATJANGS
CATKIN
CATKINATE
CATKINS
CATLIKE
CATLIN
CATLING
CATLINGS
CATLINS
CATMINT
CATMINTS
CATNAP
CATNAPER
CATNAPERS
CATNAPPED
CATNAPPER
CATNAPS
CATNEP
CATNEPS
CATNIP
CATNIPS
CATOLYTE
CATOLYTES
CATOPTRIC
CATRIGGED
CATS
CATSKIN
CATSKINS
CATSPAW
CATSPAWS
CATSUIT
CATSUITS
CATSUP
CATSUPS

CATTABU
CATTABUS
CATTAIL
CATTAILS
CATTALO
CATTALOES
CATTALOS
CATTED
CATTERIES
CATTERY
CATTIE
CATTIER
CATTIES
CATTIEST
CATTILY
CATTINESS
CATTING
CATTISH
CATTISHLY
CATTLE
CATTLEMAN
CATTLEMEN
CATTLEYA
CATTLEYAS
CATTY
CATWALK
CATWALKS
CATWORKS
CATWORM
CATWORMS
CAUCHEMAR
CAUCUS
CAUCUSED
CAUCUSES
CAUCUSING
CAUCUSSED
CAUCUSSES
CAUDA
CAUDAD
CAUDAE
CAUDAL
CAUDALLY
CAUDATE
CAUDATED
CAUDATES
CAUDATION
CAUDEX
CAUDEXES
CAUDICES
CAUDICLE
CAUDICLES
CAUDILLO
CAUDILLOS
CAUDLE
CAUDLED
CAUDLES
CAUDLING
CAUDRON

CAUDRONS
CAUF
CAUGHT
CAUK
CAUKER
CAUKERS
CAUKS
CAUL
CAULD
CAULDER
CAULDEST
CAULDRIFE
CAULDRON
CAULDRONS
CAULDS
CAULES
CAULICLE
CAULICLES
CAULICULI
CAULIFORM
CAULINARY
CAULINE
CAULIS
CAULK
CAULKED
CAULKER
CAULKERS
CAULKING
CAULKINGS
CAULKS
CAULOME
CAULOMES
CAULS
CAUM
CAUMED
CAUMING
CAUMS
CAUMSTONE
CAUP
CAUPS
CAUSA
CAUSABLE
CAUSAE
CAUSAL
CAUSALGIA
CAUSALGIC
CAUSALITY
CAUSALLY
CAUSALS
CAUSATION
CAUSATIVE
CAUSE
CAUSED
CAUSELESS
CAUSEN
CAUSER
CAUSERIE
CAUSERIES

CAUSERS
CAUSES
CAUSEWAY
CAUSEWAYS
CAUSEY
CAUSEYED
CAUSEYS
CAUSING
CAUSTIC
CAUSTICAL
CAUSTICS
CAUTEL
CAUTELOUS
CAUTELS
CAUTER
CAUTERANT
CAUTERIES
CAUTERISE
CAUTERISM
CAUTERIZE
CAUTERS
CAUTERY
CAUTION
CAUTIONED
CAUTIONER
CAUTIONRY
CAUTIONS
CAUTIOUS
CAUVES
CAVA
CAVALCADE
CAVALERO
CAVALEROS
CAVALETTI
CAVALIER
CAVALIERS
CAVALLA
CAVALLAS
CAVALLIES
CAVALLY
CAVALRIES
CAVALRY
CAVAS
CAVASS
CAVASSES
CAVATINA
CAVATINAS
CAVATINE
CAVE
CAVEAT
CAVEATED
CAVEATING
CAVEATOR
CAVEATORS
CAVEATS
CAVED
CAVEFISH
CAVEL

CAVELIKE
CAVELS
CAVEMAN
CAVEMEN
CAVENDISH
CAVER
CAVERN
CAVERNED
CAVERNING
CAVERNOUS
CAVERNS
CAVERS
CAVES
CAVESSON
CAVESSONS
CAVETTI
CAVETTO
CAVETTOS
CAVIAR
CAVIARE
CAVIARES
CAVIARIE
CAVIARIES
CAVIARS
CAVICORN
CAVICORNS
CAVIE
CAVIER
CAVIERS
CAVIES
CAVIL
CAVILED
CAVILER
CAVILERS
CAVILING
CAVILLED
CAVILLER
CAVILLERS
CAVILLING
CAVILS
CAVING
CAVINGS
CAVITARY
CAVITATE
CAVITATED
CAVITATES
CAVITIED
CAVITIES
CAVITY
CAVORT
CAVORTED
CAVORTER
CAVORTERS
CAVORTING
CAVORTS
CAVY
CAW
CAWED

CAWING
CAWINGS
CAWK
CAWKER
CAWKERS
CAWKS
CAWS
CAXON
CAXONS
CAY
CAYENNE
CAYENNED
CAYENNES
CAYMAN
CAYMANS
CAYS
CAYUSE
CAYUSES
CAZ
CAZIQUE
CAZIQUES
CEANOTHUS
CEAS
CEASE
CEASED
CEASEFIRE
CEASELESS
CEASES
CEASING
CEASINGS
CEAZE
CEAZED
CEAZES
CEAZING
CEBADILLA
CEBID
CEBIDS
CEBOID
CEBOIDS
CECA
CECAL
CECALLY
CECILS
CECITIES
CECITIS
CECITISES
CECITY
CECROPIA
CECROPIAS
CECUM
CEDAR
CEDARBIRD
CEDARED
CEDARN
CEDARS
CEDARWOOD
CEDARY
CEDE

CEDED
CEDER
CEDERS
CEDES
CEDI
CEDILLA
CEDILLAS
CEDING
CEDIS
CEDRATE
CEDRATES
CEDRINE
CEDULA
CEDULAS
CEE
CEES
CEIBA
CEIBAS
CEIL
CEILED
CEILER
CEILERS
CEILI
CEILIDH
CEILIDHS
CEILING
CEILINGED
CEILINGS
CEILIS
CEILS
CEINTURE
CEINTURES
CEL
CELADON
CELADONS
CELANDINE
CELEB
CELEBRANT
CELEBRATE
CELEBRITY
CELEBS
CELERIAC
CELERIACS
CELERIES
CELERITY
CELERY
CELESTA
CELESTAS
CELESTE
CELESTES
CELESTIAL
CELESTINE
CELESTITE
CELIAC
CELIACS
CELIBACY
CELIBATE
CELIBATES

CELIBATIC
CELL
CELLA
CELLAE
CELLAR
CELLARAGE
CELLARED
CELLARER
CELLARERS
CELLARET
CELLARETS
CELLARING
CELLARIST
CELLARMAN
CELLARMEN
CELLAROUS
CELLARS
CELLARWAY
CELLBLOCK
CELLED
CELLI
CELLING
CELLIST
CELLISTS
CELLMATE
CELLMATES
CELLO
CELLOIDIN
CELLOS
CELLOSE
CELLOSES
CELLPHONE
CELLS
CELLULAR
CELLULARS
CELLULASE
CELLULE
CELLULES
CELLULITE
CELLULOID
CELLULOSE
CELLULOUS
CELOM
CELOMATA
CELOMIC
CELOMS
CELOSIA
CELOSIAS
CELOTEX
CELOTEXES
CELS
CELSITUDE
CELT
CELTS
CEMBALI
CEMBALIST
CEMBALO
CEMBALOS

CEMBRA

CEMBRA	CENTAS	CENTRISM	CERATITIS
CEMBRAS	CENTAUR	CENTRISMS	CERATODUS
CEMENT	CENTAUREA	CENTRIST	CERATOID
CEMENTA	CENTAURIC	CENTRISTS	CERBEREAN
CEMENTED	CENTAURS	CENTRODE	CERBERIAN
CEMENTER	CENTAURY	CENTRODES	CERCAL
CEMENTERS	CENTAVO	CENTROID	CERCARIA
CEMENTING	CENTAVOS	CENTROIDS	CERCARIAE
CEMENTITE	CENTENARY	CENTRUM	CERCARIAL
CEMENTITES	CENTENIER	CENTRUMS	CERCARIAN
CEMENTS	CENTER	CENTRY	CERCARIAS
CEMENTUM	CENTERED	CENTS	CERCI
CEMENTUMS	CENTERING	CENTU	CERCIS
CEMETERY	CENTERS	CENTUM	CERCISES
CEMITARE	CENTESES	CENTUMS	CERCUS
CEMITARES	CENTESIMI	CENTUMVIR	CERE
CENACLE	CENTESIMO	CENTUPLE	CEREAL
CENACLES	CENTESIS	CENTUPLED	CEREALIST
CENDRE	CENTIARE	CENTUPLES	CEREALS
CENOBITE	CENTIARES	CENTURIAL	CEREBELLA
CENOBITES	CENTIGRAM	CENTURIES	CEREBRA
CENOBITIC	CENTILE	CENTURION	CEREBRAL
CENOTAPH	CENTILES	CENTURY	CEREBRALS
CENOTAPHS	CENTIME	CEORL	CEREBRATE
CENOTE	CENTIMES	CEORLISH	CEREBRIC
CENOTES	CENTIMO	CEORLS	CEREBROID
CENOZOIC	CENTIMOS	CEP	CEREBRUM
CENS	CENTINEL	CEPACEOUS	CEREBRUMS
CENSE	CENTINELL	CEPE	CERECLOTH
CENSED	CENTINELS	CEPES	CERED
CENSER	CENTIPEDE	CEPHALAD	CEREMENT
CENSERS	CENTNER	CEPHALATE	CEREMENTS
CENSES	CENTNERS	CEPHALIC	CEREMONY
CENSING	CENTO	CEPHALICS	CEREOUS
CENSOR	CENTOIST	CEPHALIN	CERES
CENSORED	CENTOISTS	CEPHALINS	CERESIN
CENSORIAL	CENTONATE	CEPHALOUS	CERESINE
CENSORIAN	CENTONEL	CEPHEID	CERESINES
CENSORING	CENTONELL	CEPHEIDS	CERESINS
CENSORS	CENTONELS	CEPS	CEREUS
CENSUAL	CENTONES	CERACEOUS	CEREUSES
CENSURE	CENTONIST	CERAMAL	CERGE
CENSURED	CENTOS	CERAMALS	CERGES
CENSURER	CENTRA	CERAMIC	CERIA
CENSURERS	CENTRAL	CERAMICS	CERIAS
CENSURES	CENTRALER	CERAMIDE	CERIC
CENSURING	CENTRALLY	CERAMIDES	CERING
CENSUS	CENTRALS	CERAMIST	CERIPH
CENSUSED	CENTRE	CERAMISTS	CERIPHS
CENSUSES	CENTRED	CERASIN	CERISE
CENSUSING	CENTREING	CERASINS	CERISES
CENT	CENTRES	CERASTES	CERITE
CENTAGE	CENTRIC	CERASTIUM	CERITES
CENTAGES	CENTRICAL	CERATE	CERIUM
CENTAI	CENTRIES	CERATED	CERIUMS
CENTAL	CENTRING	CERATES	CERMET
CENTALS	CENTRINGS	CERATIN	CERMETS
CENTARE	CENTRIOLE	CERATINS	CERNE
CENTARES			

CERNED	CESAREVNA	CEVICHE	CHAFFER
CERNES	CESARIAN	CEVICHES	CHAFFERED
CERNING	CESARIANS	CEYLANITE	CHAFFERER
CERNUOUS	CESIOUS	CEYLONITE	CHAFFERS
CERO	CESIUM	CH	CHAFFERY
CEROGRAPH	CESIUMS	CHA	CHAFFIER
CEROMANCY	CESPITOSE	CHABAZITE	CHAFFIEST
CEROON	CESS	CHABLIS	CHAFFINCH
CEROONS	CESSATION	CHABOUK	CHAFFING
CEROS	CESSE	CHABOUKS	CHAFFINGS
CEROTIC	CESSED	CHABUK	CHAFFRON
CEROTYPE	CESSER	CHABUKS	CHAFFRONS
CEROTYPES	CESSERS	CHACE	CHAFFS
CEROUS	CESSES	CHACED	CHAFFY
CERRIAL	CESSING	CHACES	CHAFING
CERRIS	CESSION	CHACHKA	CHAFT
CERRISES	CESSIONS	CHACHKAS	CHAFTS
CERT	CESSPIT	CHACING	CHAGAN
CERTAIN	CESSPITS	CHACK	CHAGANS
CERTAINER	CESSPOOL	CHACKED	CHAGRIN
CERTAINLY	CESSPOOLS	CHACKING	CHAGRINED
CERTAINTY	CESTA	CHACKS	CHAGRINS
CERTES	CESTAS	CHACMA	CHAI
CERTIFIED	CESTI	CHACMAS	CHAIN
CERTIFIER	CESTODE	CHACO	CHAINE
CERTIFIES	CESTODES	CHACOES	CHAINED
CERTIFY	CESTOI	CHACONNE	CHAINES
CERTITUDE	CESTOID	CHACONNES	CHAINFALL
CERTS	CESTOIDS	CHACOS	CHAINING
CERULE	CESTOS	CHAD	CHAINLESS
CERULEAN	CESTOSES	CHADAR	CHAINLET
CERULEANS	CESTUI	CHADARIM	CHAINLETS
CERULEIN	CESTUIS	CHADARS	CHAINMAN
CERULEINS	CESTUS	CHADDAR	CHAINMEN
CERULEOUS	CESTUSES	CHADDARS	CHAINS
CERUMEN	CESURA	CHADDOR	CHAINSAW
CERUMENS	CESURAE	CHADDORS	CHAINSAWS
CERUSE	CESURAL	CHADLESS	CHAINSHOT
CERUSES	CESURAS	CHADO	CHAINWORK
CERUSITE	CESURE	CHADOR	CHAIR
CERUSITES	CESURES	CHADORS	CHAIRDAYS
CERUSSITE	CETACEAN	CHADOS	CHAIRED
CERVELAS	CETACEANS	CHADRI	CHAIRING
CERVELAT	CETACEOUS	CHADS	CHAIRLIFT
CERVELATS	CETANE	CHAEBOL	CHAIRMAN
CERVEZA	CETANES	CHAEBOLS	CHAIRMANS
CERVEZAS	CETE	CHAETA	CHAIRMEN
CERVICAL	CETERACH	CHAETAE	CHAIRS
CERVICES	CETERACHS	CHAETAL	CHAIS
CERVICUM	CETES	CHAETODON	CHAISE
CERVICUMS	CETOLOGY	CHAETOPOD	CHAISES
CERVID	CETRIMIDE	CHAFE	CHAKALAKA
CERVIDS	CETYL	CHAFED	CHAKRA
CERVINE	CETYLS	CHAFER	CHAKRAS
CERVIX	CETYWALL	CHAFERS	CHAL
CERVIXES	CETYWALLS	CHAFES	CHALAH
CESAREAN	CEVADILLA	CHAFF	CHALAHS
CESAREANS	CEVAPCICI	CHAFFED	CHALAN

CHALANED	CHALUTZ	CHAMPER	CHANOYUS
CHALANING	CHALUTZES	CHAMPERS	CHANSON
CHALANS	CHALUTZIM	CHAMPERTY	CHANSONS
CHALAZA	CHALYBEAN	CHAMPING	CHANT
CHALAZAE	CHALYBITE	CHAMPION	CHANTABLE
CHALAZAL	CHAM	CHAMPIONS	CHANTAGE
CHALAZAS	CHAMADE	CHAMPLEVE	CHANTAGES
CHALAZIA	CHAMADES	CHAMPS	CHANTED
CHALAZION	CHAMBER	CHAMPY	CHANTER
CHALCID	CHAMBERED	CHAMS	CHANTERS
CHALCIDS	CHAMBERER	CHANCE	CHANTEUSE
CHALCOGEN	CHAMBERS	CHANCED	CHANTEY
CHALDER	CHAMBRAY	CHANCEFUL	CHANTEYS
CHALDERS	CHAMBRAYS	CHANCEL	CHANTIE
CHALDRON	CHAMBRE	CHANCELS	CHANTIES
CHALDRONS	CHAMELEON	CHANCER	CHANTILLY
CHALEH	CHAMELOT	CHANCERS	CHANTING
CHALEHS	CHAMELOTS	CHANCERY	CHANTOR
CHALET	CHAMETZ	CHANCES	CHANTORS
CHALETS	CHAMETZES	CHANCEY	CHANTRESS
CHALICE	CHAMFER	CHANCIER	CHANTRIES
CHALICED	CHAMFERED	CHANCIEST	CHANTRY
CHALICES	CHAMFERER	CHANCILY	CHANTS
CHALK	CHAMFERS	CHANCING	CHANTY
CHALKED	CHAMFRAIN	CHANCRE	CHANUKIAH
CHALKFACE	CHAMFRON	CHANCRES	CHAO
CHALKIER	CHAMFRONS	CHANCROID	CHAOLOGY
CHALKIEST	CHAMISA	CHANCROUS	CHAORDIC
CHALKING	CHAMISAL	CHANCY	CHAOS
CHALKLIKE	CHAMISALS	CHANDELLE	CHAOSES
CHALKPIT	CHAMISAS	CHANDLER	CHAOTIC
CHALKPITS	CHAMISE	CHANDLERS	CHAP
CHALKS	CHAMISES	CHANDLERY	CHAPARRAL
CHALKY	CHAMISO	CHANFRON	CHAPATI
CHALLA	CHAMISOS	CHANFRONS	CHAPATIES
CHALLAH	CHAMLET	CHANG	CHAPATIS
CHALLAHS	CHAMLETS	CHANGA	CHAPATTI
CHALLAN	CHAMMIED	CHANGE	CHAPATTIS
CHALLANED	CHAMMIES	CHANGED	CHAPBOOK
CHALLANS	CHAMMY	CHANGEFUL	CHAPBOOKS
CHALLAS	CHAMMYING	CHANGER	CHAPE
CHALLENGE	CHAMOIS	CHANGERS	CHAPEAU
CHALLIE	CHAMOISED	CHANGES	CHAPEAUS
CHALLIES	CHAMOISES	CHANGEUP	CHAPEAUX
CHALLIS	CHAMOIX	CHANGEUPS	CHAPEL
CHALLISES	CHAMOMILE	CHANGING	CHAPELESS
CHALLOT	CHAMP	CHANGS	CHAPELRY
CHALLOTH	CHAMPAC	CHANK	CHAPELS
CHALLY	CHAMPACA	CHANKS	CHAPERON
CHALONE	CHAMPACAS	CHANNEL	CHAPERONE
CHALONES	CHAMPACS	CHANNELED	CHAPERONS
CHALONIC	CHAMPAGNE	CHANNELER	CHAPES
CHALOT	CHAMPAIGN	CHANNELS	CHAPESS
CHALOTH	CHAMPAK	CHANNER	CHAPESSES
CHALS	CHAMPAKS	CHANNERS	CHAPITER
CHALUMEAU	CHAMPART	CHANOYO	CHAPITERS
CHALUPA	CHAMPARTS	CHANOYOS	CHAPKA
CHALUPAS	CHAMPED	CHANOYU	CHAPKAS

CHAPLAIN
CHAPLAINS
CHAPLESS
CHAPLET
CHAPLETED
CHAPLETS
CHAPMAN
CHAPMEN
CHAPPAL
CHAPPALS
CHAPPATI
CHAPPATIS
CHAPPED
CHAPPESS
CHAPPIE
CHAPPIER
CHAPPIES
CHAPPIEST
CHAPPING
CHAPPY
CHAPRASSI
CHAPS
CHAPSTICK
CHAPT
CHAPTER
CHAPTERAL
CHAPTERED
CHAPTERS
CHAPTREL
CHAPTRELS
CHAQUETA
CHAQUETAS
CHAR
CHARA
CHARABANC
CHARACID
CHARACIDS
CHARACIN
CHARACINS
CHARACT
CHARACTER
CHARACTS
CHARADE
CHARADES
CHARANGA
CHARANGAS
CHARANGO
CHARANGOS
CHARAS
CHARASES
CHARBROIL
CHARCOAL
CHARCOALS
CHARCOALY
CHARD
CHARDS
CHARE
CHARED

CHARES
CHARET
CHARETS
CHARGE
CHARGED
CHARGEFUL
CHARGER
CHARGERS
CHARGES
CHARGING
CHARGRILL
CHARIDEE
CHARIDEES
CHARIER
CHARIEST
CHARILY
CHARINESS
CHARING
CHARIOT
CHARIOTED
CHARIOTS
CHARISM
CHARISMA
CHARISMAS
CHARISMS
CHARITIES
CHARITY
CHARIVARI
CHARK
CHARKA
CHARKAS
CHARKED
CHARKHA
CHARKHAS
CHARKING
CHARKS
CHARLADY
CHARLATAN
CHARLEY
CHARLEYS
CHARLIE
CHARLIER
CHARLIES
CHARLOCK
CHARLOCKS
CHARLOTTE
CHARM
CHARMED
CHARMER
CHARMERS
CHARMEUSE
CHARMFUL
CHARMING
CHARMLESS
CHARMONIA
CHARMS
CHARNECO
CHARNECOS

CHARNEL
CHARNELS
CHAROSET
CHAROSETH
CHAROSETS
CHARPAI
CHARPAIS
CHARPIE
CHARPIES
CHARPOY
CHARPOYS
CHARQUI
CHARQUID
CHARQUIS
CHARR
CHARRED
CHARRIER
CHARRIEST
CHARRING
CHARRO
CHARROS
CHARRS
CHARRY
CHARS
CHART
CHARTA
CHARTABLE
CHARTAS
CHARTED
CHARTER
CHARTERED
CHARTERER
CHARTERS
CHARTING
CHARTISM
CHARTISMS
CHARTIST
CHARTISTS
CHARTLESS
CHARTS
CHARVER
CHARVERS
CHARWOMAN
CHARWOMEN
CHARY
CHAS
CHASE
CHASEABLE
CHASED
CHASEPORT
CHASER
CHASERS
CHASES
CHASING
CHASINGS
CHASM
CHASMAL
CHASMED

CHASMIC
CHASMIER
CHASMIEST
CHASMS
CHASMY
CHASSE
CHASSED
CHASSEED
CHASSEING
CHASSEPOT
CHASSES
CHASSEUR
CHASSEURS
CHASSIS
CHASTE
CHASTELY
CHASTEN
CHASTENED
CHASTENER
CHASTENS
CHASTER
CHASTEST
CHASTISE
CHASTISED
CHASTISER
CHASTISES
CHASTITY
CHASUBLE
CHASUBLES
CHAT
CHATBOT
CHATBOTS
CHATCHKA
CHATCHKAS
CHATCHKE
CHATCHKES
CHATEAU
CHATEAUS
CHATEAUX
CHATELAIN
CHATLINE
CHATLINES
CHATON
CHATONS
CHATOYANT
CHATROOM
CHATROOMS
CHATS
CHATTA
CHATTAS
CHATTED
CHATTEL
CHATTELS
CHATTER
CHATTERED
CHATTERER
CHATTERS
CHATTERY

CHATTI	CHAWKS	CHECKED	CHEERIEST
CHATTIER	CHAWS	CHECKER	CHEERILY
CHATTIES	CHAY	CHECKERED	CHEERING
CHATTIEST	CHAYA	CHECKERS	CHEERIO
CHATTILY	CHAYAS	CHECKING	CHEERIOS
CHATTING	CHAYOTE	CHECKLESS	CHEERLEAD
CHATTIS	CHAYOTES	CHECKLIST	CHEERLED
CHATTY	CHAYROOT	CHECKMARK	CHEERLESS
CHAUFE	CHAYROOTS	CHECKMATE	CHEERLY
CHAUFED	CHAYS	CHECKOFF	CHEERO
CHAUFER	CHAZAN	CHECKOFFS	CHEEROS
CHAUFERS	CHAZANIM	CHECKOUT	CHEERS
CHAUFES	CHAZANS	CHECKOUTS	CHEERY
CHAUFF	CHAZZAN	CHECKRAIL	CHEESE
CHAUFFED	CHAZZANIM	CHECKREIN	CHEESED
CHAUFFER	CHAZZANS	CHECKROOM	CHEESES
CHAUFFERS	CHAZZEN	CHECKROW	CHEESEVAT
CHAUFFEUR	CHAZZENIM	CHECKROWS	CHEESIER
CHAUFFING	CHAZZENS	CHECKS	CHEESIEST
CHAUFFS	CHE	CHECKSUM	CHEESILY
CHAUFING	CHEAP	CHECKSUMS	CHEESING
CHAUMER	CHEAPED	CHECKUP	CHEESY
CHAUMERS	CHEAPEN	CHECKUPS	CHEETAH
CHAUNCE	CHEAPENED	CHECKY	CHEETAHS
CHAUNCED	CHEAPENER	CHEDDAR	CHEEWINK
CHAUNCES	CHEAPENS	CHEDDARS	CHEEWINKS
CHAUNCING	CHEAPER	CHEDDARY	CHEF
CHAUNGE	CHEAPEST	CHEDDITE	CHEFDOM
CHAUNGED	CHEAPIE	CHEDDITES	CHEFDOMS
CHAUNGES	CHEAPIES	CHEDER	CHEFED
CHAUNGING	CHEAPING	CHEDERS	CHEFFED
CHAUNT	CHEAPISH	CHEDITE	CHEFFING
CHAUNTED	CHEAPJACK	CHEDITES	CHEFING
CHAUNTER	CHEAPLY	CHEECHAKO	CHEFS
CHAUNTERS	CHEAPNESS	CHEEK	CHEGOE
CHAUNTING	CHEAPO	CHEEKBONE	CHEGOES
CHAUNTRY	CHEAPOS	CHEEKED	CHEILITIS
CHAUNTS	CHEAPS	CHEEKFUL	CHEKA
CHAUSSES	CHEAPY	CHEEKFULS	CHEKAS
CHAUSSURE	CHEAT	CHEEKIER	CHEKIST
CHAUVIN	CHEATABLE	CHEEKIEST	CHEKISTS
CHAUVINS	CHEATED	CHEEKILY	CHELA
CHAV	CHEATER	CHEEKING	CHELAE
CHAVE	CHEATERS	CHEEKLESS	CHELAS
CHAVENDER	CHEATERY	CHEEKS	CHELASHIP
CHAVETTE	CHEATING	CHEEKY	CHELATE
CHAVETTES	CHEATINGS	CHEEP	CHELATED
CHAVISH	CHEATS	CHEEPED	CHELATES
CHAVS	CHEBEC	CHEEPER	CHELATING
CHAW	CHEBECS	CHEEPERS	CHELATION
CHAWBACON	CHECHAKO	CHEEPING	CHELATOR
CHAWDRON	CHECHAKOS	CHEEPS	CHELATORS
CHAWDRONS	CHECHAQUO	CHEER	CHELICERA
CHAWED	CHECHIA	CHEERED	CHELIFORM
CHAWER	CHECHIAS	CHEERER	CHELIPED
CHAWERS	CHECK	CHEERERS	CHELIPEDS
CHAWING	CHECKABLE	CHEERFUL	CHELLUP
CHAWK	CHECKBOOK	CHEERIER	CHELLUPS

CHELOID
CHELOIDAL
CHELOIDS
CHELONE
CHELONES
CHELONIAN
CHELP
CHELPED
CHELPING
CHELPS
CHEMIC
CHEMICAL
CHEMICALS
CHEMICKED
CHEMICS
CHEMISE
CHEMISES
CHEMISM
CHEMISMS
CHEMISORB
CHEMIST
CHEMISTRY
CHEMISTS
CHEMITYPE
CHEMITYPY
CHEMMIES
CHEMMY
CHEMO
CHEMOKINE
CHEMOS
CHEMOSORB
CHEMOSTAT
CHEMPADUK
CHEMURGIC
CHEMURGY
CHENAR
CHENARS
CHENET
CHENETS
CHENILLE
CHENILLES
CHENIX
CHENIXES
CHENOPOD
CHENOPODS
CHEONGSAM
CHEQUE
CHEQUER
CHEQUERED
CHEQUERS
CHEQUES
CHEQUING
CHEQUY
CHER
CHERALITE
CHERE
CHERIMOYA
CHERISH

CHERISHED
CHERISHER
CHERISHES
CHERNOZEM
CHEROOT
CHEROOTS
CHERRIED
CHERRIER
CHERRIES
CHERRIEST
CHERRY
CHERRYING
CHERT
CHERTIER
CHERTIEST
CHERTS
CHERTY
CHERUB
CHERUBIC
CHERUBIM
CHERUBIMS
CHERUBIN
CHERUBINS
CHERUBS
CHERUP
CHERUPED
CHERUPING
CHERUPS
CHERVIL
CHERVILS
CHESHIRE
CHESHIRES
CHESIL
CHESILS
CHESNUT
CHESNUTS
CHESS
CHESSEL
CHESSELS
CHESSES
CHESSMAN
CHESSMEN
CHEST
CHESTED
CHESTFUL
CHESTFULS
CHESTIER
CHESTIEST
CHESTILY
CHESTING
CHESTNUT
CHESTNUTS
CHESTS
CHESTY
CHETAH
CHETAHS
CHETH
CHETHS

CHETNIK
CHETNIKS
CHETRUM
CHETRUMS
CHEVAL
CHEVALET
CHEVALETS
CHEVALIER
CHEVELURE
CHEVEN
CHEVENS
CHEVEREL
CHEVERELS
CHEVERIL
CHEVERILS
CHEVERON
CHEVERONS
CHEVERYE
CHEVERYES
CHEVET
CHEVETS
CHEVIED
CHEVIES
CHEVILLE
CHEVILLES
CHEVIN
CHEVINS
CHEVIOT
CHEVIOTS
CHEVRE
CHEVRES
CHEVRET
CHEVRETS
CHEVRETTE
CHEVRON
CHEVRONED
CHEVRONS
CHEVRONY
CHEVY
CHEVYING
CHEW
CHEWABLE
CHEWED
CHEWER
CHEWERS
CHEWET
CHEWETS
CHEWIE
CHEWIER
CHEWIES
CHEWIEST
CHEWINESS
CHEWING
CHEWINK
CHEWINKS
CHEWS
CHEWY
CHEZ

CHI
CHIA
CHIACK
CHIACKED
CHIACKING
CHIACKS
CHIANTI
CHIANTIS
CHIAO
CHIAREZZA
CHIAREZZE
CHIAS
CHIASM
CHIASMA
CHIASMAL
CHIASMAS
CHIASMATA
CHIASMI
CHIASMIC
CHIASMS
CHIASMUS
CHIASTIC
CHIAUS
CHIAUSED
CHIAUSES
CHIAUSING
CHIB
CHIBBED
CHIBBING
CHIBOL
CHIBOLS
CHIBOUK
CHIBOUKS
CHIBOUQUE
CHIBS
CHIC
CHICA
CHICALOTE
CHICANA
CHICANAS
CHICANE
CHICANED
CHICANER
CHICANERS
CHICANERY
CHICANES
CHICANING
CHICANO
CHICANOS
CHICAS
CHICCORY
CHICER
CHICEST
CHICH
CHICHA
CHICHAS
CHICHES
CHICHI

CHICHIER
CHICHIEST
CHICHIS
CHICK
CHICKADEE
CHICKAREE
CHICKEE
CHICKEES
CHICKEN
CHICKENED
CHICKENS
CHICKLING
CHICKORY
CHICKPEA
CHICKPEAS
CHICKS
CHICKWEED
CHICLE
CHICLES
CHICLY
CHICNESS
CHICO
CHICON
CHICONS
CHICORIES
CHICORY
CHICOS
CHICS
CHID
CHIDDEN
CHIDE
CHIDED
CHIDER
CHIDERS
CHIDES
CHIDING
CHIDINGLY
CHIDINGS
CHIDLINGS
CHIEF
CHIEFDOM
CHIEFDOMS
CHIEFER
CHIEFERY
CHIEFESS
CHIEFEST
CHIEFLESS
CHIEFLING
CHIEFLY
CHIEFRIES
CHIEFRY
CHIEFS
CHIEFSHIP
CHIEFTAIN
CHIEL
CHIELD
CHIELDS
CHIELS

CHIFFON
CHIFFONS
CHIFFONY
CHIGETAI
CHIGETAIS
CHIGGA
CHIGGAS
CHIGGER
CHIGGERS
CHIGNON
CHIGNONED
CHIGNONS
CHIGOE
CHIGOES
CHIGRE
CHIGRES
CHIHUAHUA
CHIK
CHIKARA
CHIKARAS
CHIKHOR
CHIKHORS
CHIKOR
CHIKORS
CHIKS
CHILBLAIN
CHILD
CHILDBED
CHILDBEDS
CHILDCARE
CHILDE
CHILDED
CHILDER
CHILDES
CHILDHOOD
CHILDING
CHILDISH
CHILDLESS
CHILDLIER
CHILDLIKE
CHILDLY
CHILDNESS
CHILDREN
CHILDS
CHILE
CHILES
CHILI
CHILIAD
CHILIADAL
CHILIADIC
CHILIADS
CHILIAGON
CHILIARCH
CHILIASM
CHILIASMS
CHILIAST
CHILIASTS
CHILIDOG

CHILIDOGS
CHILIES
CHILIOI
CHILIOIS
CHILIS
CHILL
CHILLADA
CHILLADAS
CHILLED
CHILLER
CHILLERS
CHILLEST
CHILLI
CHILLIER
CHILLIES
CHILLIEST
CHILLILY
CHILLING
CHILLINGS
CHILLIS
CHILLNESS
CHILLS
CHILLUM
CHILLUMS
CHILLY
CHILOPOD
CHILOPODS
CHILTEPIN
CHIMAERA
CHIMAERAS
CHIMAERIC
CHIMAR
CHIMARS
CHIMB
CHIMBLEY
CHIMBLEYS
CHIMBLIES
CHIMBLY
CHIMBS
CHIME
CHIMED
CHIMER
CHIMERA
CHIMERAS
CHIMERE
CHIMERES
CHIMERIC
CHIMERID
CHIMERIDS
CHIMERISM
CHIMERS
CHIMES
CHIMING
CHIMLA
CHIMLAS
CHIMLEY
CHIMLEYS
CHIMNEY

CHIMNEYED
CHIMNEYS
CHIMO
CHIMP
CHIMPS
CHIN
CHINA
CHINAMAN
CHINAMEN
CHINAMPA
CHINAMPAS
CHINAR
CHINAROOT
CHINARS
CHINAS
CHINAWARE
CHINBONE
CHINBONES
CHINCAPIN
CHINCH
CHINCHES
CHINCHIER
CHINCHY
CHINCOUGH
CHINDIT
CHINDITS
CHINE
CHINED
CHINES
CHINESE
CHINING
CHINK
CHINKAPIN
CHINKARA
CHINKARAS
CHINKED
CHINKIE
CHINKIER
CHINKIES
CHINKIEST
CHINKING
CHINKS
CHINKY
CHINLESS
CHINNED
CHINNING
CHINO
CHINONE
CHINONES
CHINOOK
CHINOOKS
CHINOS
CHINOVNIK
CHINS
CHINSTRAP
CHINTS
CHINTSES
CHINTZ

CHINTZES
CHINTZIER
CHINTZY
CHINWAG
CHINWAGS
CHIP
CHIPBOARD
CHIPMUCK
CHIPMUCKS
CHIPMUNK
CHIPMUNKS
CHIPOCHIA
CHIPOLATA
CHIPOTLE
CHIPOTLES
CHIPPABLE
CHIPPED
CHIPPER
CHIPPERED
CHIPPERS
CHIPPIE
CHIPPIER
CHIPPIES
CHIPPIEST
CHIPPING
CHIPPINGS
CHIPPY
CHIPS
CHIPSET
CHIPSETS
CHIRAGRA
CHIRAGRAS
CHIRAGRIC
CHIRAL
CHIRALITY
CHIRIMOYA
CHIRK
CHIRKED
CHIRKER
CHIRKEST
CHIRKING
CHIRKS
CHIRL
CHIRLED
CHIRLING
CHIRLS
CHIRM
CHIRMED
CHIRMING
CHIRMS
CHIRO
CHIROLOGY
CHIRONOMY
CHIROPODY
CHIROPTER
CHIROS
CHIRP
CHIRPED

CHIRPER
CHIRPERS
CHIRPIER
CHIRPIEST
CHIRPILY
CHIRPING
CHIRPS
CHIRPY
CHIRR
CHIRRE
CHIRRED
CHIRREN
CHIRRES
CHIRRING
CHIRRS
CHIRRUP
CHIRRUPED
CHIRRUPER
CHIRRUPS
CHIRRUPY
CHIRT
CHIRTED
CHIRTING
CHIRTS
CHIRU
CHIRUS
CHIS
CHISEL
CHISELED
CHISELER
CHISELERS
CHISELING
CHISELLED
CHISELLER
CHISELS
CHIT
CHITAL
CHITALS
CHITCHAT
CHITCHATS
CHITIN
CHITINOID
CHITINOUS
CHITINS
CHITLIN
CHITLING
CHITLINGS
CHITLINS
CHITON
CHITONS
CHITOSAN
CHITOSANS
CHITS
CHITTED
CHITTER
CHITTERED
CHITTERS
CHITTIER

CHITTIES
CHITTIEST
CHITTING
CHITTY
CHIV
CHIVALRIC
CHIVALRY
CHIVAREE
CHIVAREED
CHIVAREES
CHIVARI
CHIVARIED
CHIVARIES
CHIVE
CHIVED
CHIVES
CHIVIED
CHIVIES
CHIVING
CHIVS
CHIVVED
CHIVVIED
CHIVVIES
CHIVVING
CHIVVY
CHIVVYING
CHIVY
CHIVYING
CHIYOGAMI
CHIZ
CHIZZ
CHIZZED
CHIZZES
CHIZZING
CHLAMYDES
CHLAMYDIA
CHLAMYS
CHLAMYSES
CHLOASMA
CHLOASMAS
CHLORACNE
CHLORAL
CHLORALS
CHLORATE
CHLORATES
CHLORDAN
CHLORDANE
CHLORDANS
CHLORELLA
CHLORIC
CHLORID
CHLORIDE
CHLORIDES
CHLORIDIC
CHLORIDS
CHLORIN
CHLORINE
CHLORINES

CHLORINS
CHLORITE
CHLORITES
CHLORITIC
CHLOROSES
CHLOROSIS
CHLOROTIC
CHLOROUS
CHOANA
CHOANAE
CHOBDAR
CHOBDARS
CHOC
CHOCCIER
CHOCCIES
CHOCCIEST
CHOCCY
CHOCHO
CHOCHOS
CHOCK
CHOCKED
CHOCKER
CHOCKFUL
CHOCKFULL
CHOCKING
CHOCKO
CHOCKOS
CHOCKS
CHOCO
CHOCOLATE
CHOCOLATY
CHOCOS
CHOCS
CHOCTAW
CHOCTAWS
CHODE
CHOENIX
CHOENIXES
CHOG
CHOGS
CHOICE
CHOICEFUL
CHOICELY
CHOICER
CHOICES
CHOICEST
CHOIR
CHOIRBOY
CHOIRBOYS
CHOIRED
CHOIRGIRL
CHOIRING
CHOIRLIKE
CHOIRMAN
CHOIRMEN
CHOIRS
CHOKE
CHOKEABLE

CHOKEBORE	CHOMETZES	CHOPPING	CHORIONIC
CHOKECOIL	CHOMMIE	CHOPPINGS	CHORIONS
CHOKED	CHOMMIES	CHOPPY	CHORISES
CHOKEDAMP	CHOMP	CHOPS	CHORISIS
CHOKEHOLD	CHOMPED	CHOPSOCKY	CHORISM
CHOKER	CHOMPER	CHOPSTICK	CHORISMS
CHOKERS	CHOMPERS	CHORAGI	CHORIST
CHOKES	CHOMPING	CHORAGIC	CHORISTER
CHOKEY	CHOMPS	CHORAGUS	CHORISTS
CHOKEYS	CHON	CHORAL	CHORIZO
CHOKIDAR	CHONDRAL	CHORALE	CHORIZONT
CHOKIDARS	CHONDRE	CHORALES	CHORIZOS
CHOKIER	CHONDRES	CHORALIST	CHOROID
CHOKIES	CHONDRI	CHORALLY	CHOROIDAL
CHOKIEST	CHONDRIFY	CHORALS	CHOROIDS
CHOKING	CHONDRIN	CHORD	CHOROLOGY
CHOKINGLY	CHONDRINS	CHORDA	CHORRIE
CHOKO	CHONDRITE	CHORDAE	CHORRIES
CHOKOS	CHONDROID	CHORDAL	CHORTEN
CHOKRA	CHONDROMA	CHORDATE	CHORTENS
CHOKRAS	CHONDRULE	CHORDATES	CHORTLE
CHOKRI	CHONDRUS	CHORDED	CHORTLED
CHOKRIS	CHONS	CHORDEE	CHORTLER
CHOKY	CHOOF	CHORDEES	CHORTLERS
CHOLA	CHOOFED	CHORDING	CHORTLES
CHOLAEMIA	CHOOFING	CHORDINGS	CHORTLING
CHOLAEMIC	CHOOFS	CHORDS	CHORUS
CHOLAS	CHOOK	CHORDWISE	CHORUSED
CHOLATE	CHOOKED	CHORE	CHORUSES
CHOLATES	CHOOKIE	CHOREA	CHORUSING
CHOLECYST	CHOOKIES	CHOREAL	CHORUSSED
CHOLELITH	CHOOKING	CHOREAS	CHORUSSES
CHOLEMIA	CHOOKS	CHOREATIC	CHOSE
CHOLEMIAS	CHOOM	CHORED	CHOSEN
CHOLENT	CHOOMS	CHOREE	CHOSES
CHOLENTS	CHOOSE	CHOREES	CHOTA
CHOLER	CHOOSER	CHOREGI	CHOTT
CHOLERA	CHOOSERS	CHOREGIC	CHOTTS
CHOLERAIC	CHOOSES	CHOREGUS	CHOU
CHOLERAS	CHOOSEY	CHOREIC	CHOUGH
CHOLERIC	CHOOSIER	CHOREMAN	CHOUGHS
CHOLEROID	CHOOSIEST	CHOREMEN	CHOULTRY
CHOLERS	CHOOSING	CHOREOID	CHOUNTER
CHOLI	CHOOSY	CHORES	CHOUNTERS
CHOLIAMB	CHOP	CHOREUS	CHOUSE
CHOLIAMBS	CHOPHOUSE	CHOREUSES	CHOUSED
CHOLIC	CHOPIN	CHORIA	CHOUSER
CHOLINE	CHOPINE	CHORIAL	CHOUSERS
CHOLINES	CHOPINES	CHORIAMB	CHOUSES
CHOLIS	CHOPINS	CHORIAMBI	CHOUSH
CHOLLA	CHOPLOGIC	CHORIAMBS	CHOUSHES
CHOLLAS	CHOPPED	CHORIC	CHOUSING
CHOLLERS	CHOPPER	CHORINE	CHOUT
CHOLO	CHOPPERED	CHORINES	CHOUTS
CHOLOS	CHOPPERS	CHORING	CHOUX
CHOLTRIES	CHOPPIER	CHORIOID	CHOW
CHOLTRY	CHOPPIEST	CHORIOIDS	CHOWCHOW
CHOMETZ	CHOPPILY	CHORION	CHOWCHOWS

CHOWDER
CHOWDERED
CHOWDERS
CHOWED
CHOWHOUND
CHOWING
CHOWK
CHOWKIDAR
CHOWKS
CHOWRI
CHOWRIES
CHOWRIS
CHOWRY
CHOWS
CHOWSE
CHOWSED
CHOWSES
CHOWSING
CHOWTIME
CHOWTIMES
CHRESARD
CHRESARDS
CHRISM
CHRISMA
CHRISMAL
CHRISMALS
CHRISMON
CHRISMONS
CHRISMS
CHRISOM
CHRISOMS
CHRISTEN
CHRISTENS
CHRISTIAN
CHRISTIE
CHRISTIES
CHRISTOM
CHRISTOMS
CHRISTY
CHROMA
CHROMAKEY
CHROMAS
CHROMATE
CHROMATES
CHROMATIC
CHROMATID
CHROMATIN
CHROME
CHROMED
CHROMEL
CHROMELS
CHROMENE
CHROMENES
CHROMES
CHROMIC
CHROMIDE
CHROMIDES
CHROMIDIA

CHROMIER
CHROMIEST
CHROMING
CHROMINGS
CHROMISE
CHROMISED
CHROMISES
CHROMITE
CHROMITES
CHROMIUM
CHROMIUMS
CHROMIZE
CHROMIZED
CHROMIZES
CHROMO
CHROMOGEN
CHROMOS
CHROMOUS
CHROMY
CHROMYL
CHROMYLS
CHRONAXIE
CHRONAXY
CHRONIC
CHRONICAL
CHRONICLE
CHRONICS
CHRONON
CHRONONS
CHRYSALID
CHRYSALIS
CHRYSANTH
CHTHONIAN
CHTHONIC
CHUB
CHUBASCO
CHUBASCOS
CHUBBIER
CHUBBIEST
CHUBBILY
CHUBBY
CHUBS
CHUCK
CHUCKED
CHUCKER
CHUCKERS
CHUCKHOLE
CHUCKIE
CHUCKIES
CHUCKING
CHUCKLE
CHUCKLED
CHUCKLER
CHUCKLERS
CHUCKLES
CHUCKLING
CHUCKS
CHUCKY

CHUDDAH
CHUDDAHS
CHUDDAR
CHUDDARS
CHUDDER
CHUDDERS
CHUDDIES
CHUDDY
CHUFA
CHUFAS
CHUFF
CHUFFED
CHUFFER
CHUFFEST
CHUFFIER
CHUFFIEST
CHUFFING
CHUFFS
CHUFFY
CHUG
CHUGALUG
CHUGALUGS
CHUGGED
CHUGGER
CHUGGERS
CHUGGING
CHUGS
CHUKAR
CHUKARS
CHUKKA
CHUKKAR
CHUKKARS
CHUKKAS
CHUKKER
CHUKKERS
CHUKOR
CHUKORS
CHUM
CHUMASH
CHUMASHES
CHUMLEY
CHUMLEYS
CHUMMAGE
CHUMMAGES
CHUMMED
CHUMMIER
CHUMMIES
CHUMMIEST
CHUMMILY
CHUMMING
CHUMMY
CHUMP
CHUMPED
CHUMPING
CHUMPINGS
CHUMPS
CHUMS
CHUMSHIP

CHUMSHIPS
CHUNDER
CHUNDERED
CHUNDERS
CHUNK
CHUNKED
CHUNKIER
CHUNKIEST
CHUNKILY
CHUNKING
CHUNKINGS
CHUNKS
CHUNKY
CHUNNEL
CHUNNELS
CHUNNER
CHUNNERED
CHUNNERS
CHUNTER
CHUNTERED
CHUNTERS
CHUPATI
CHUPATIS
CHUPATTI
CHUPATTIS
CHUPATTY
CHUPPA
CHUPPAH
CHUPPAHS
CHUPPAS
CHUPRASSY
CHURCH
CHURCHED
CHURCHES
CHURCHIER
CHURCHING
CHURCHISM
CHURCHLY
CHURCHMAN
CHURCHMEN
CHURCHWAY
CHURCHY
CHURIDAR
CHURIDARS
CHURINGA
CHURINGAS
CHURL
CHURLISH
CHURLS
CHURN
CHURNED
CHURNER
CHURNERS
CHURNING
CHURNINGS
CHURNMILK
CHURNS
CHURR

CHURRED	CIABATTE	CIDS	CINCHONIC
CHURRING	CIAO	CIEL	CINCINNUS
CHURRO	CIAOS	CIELED	CINCT
CHURROS	CIBATION	CIELING	CINCTURE
CHURRS	CIBATIONS	CIELINGS	CINCTURED
CHURRUS	CIBOL	CIELS	CINCTURES
CHURRUSES	CIBOLS	CIERGE	CINDER
CHUSE	CIBORIA	CIERGES	CINDERED
CHUSES	CIBORIUM	CIG	CINDERING
CHUSING	CIBOULE	CIGAR	CINDEROUS
CHUT	CIBOULES	CIGARET	CINDERS
CHUTE	CICADA	CIGARETS	CINDERY
CHUTED	CICADAE	CIGARETTE	CINE
CHUTES	CICADAS	CIGARILLO	CINEAST
CHUTING	CICALA	CIGARLIKE	CINEASTE
CHUTIST	CICALAS	CIGARS	CINEASTES
CHUTISTS	CICALE	CIGGIE	CINEASTS
CHUTNEE	CICATRICE	CIGGIES	CINEMA
CHUTNEES	CICATRISE	CIGGY	CINEMAS
CHUTNEY	CICATRIX	CIGS	CINEMATIC
CHUTNEYS	CICATRIZE	CIGUATERA	CINEOL
CHUTZPA	CICELIES	CILANTRO	CINEOLE
CHUTZPAH	CICELY	CILANTROS	CINEOLES
CHUTZPAHS	CICERO	CILIA	CINEOLS
CHUTZPAS	CICERONE	CILIARY	CINEPHILE
CHYACK	CICERONED	CILIATE	CINEPLEX
CHYACKED	CICERONES	CILIATED	CINERAMIC
CHYACKING	CICERONI	CILIATELY	CINERARIA
CHYACKS	CICEROS	CILIATES	CINERARY
CHYLDE	CICHLID	CILIATION	CINERATOR
CHYLE	CICHLIDAE	CILICE	CINEREA
CHYLES	CICHLIDS	CILICES	CINEREAL
CHYLIFIED	CICHLOID	CILICIOUS	CINEREAS
CHYLIFIES	CICINNUS	CILIOLATE	CINEREOUS
CHYLIFY	CICISBEI	CILIUM	CINERIN
CHYLOUS	CICISBEO	CILL	CINERINS
CHYLURIA	CICISBEOS	CILLS	CINES
CHYLURIAS	CICLATON	CIMAR	CINGULA
CHYME	CICLATONS	CIMARS	CINGULAR
CHYMES	CICLATOUN	CIMBALOM	CINGULATE
CHYMIC	CICOREE	CIMBALOMS	CINGULUM
CHYMICS	CICOREES	CIMELIA	CINNABAR
CHYMIFIED	CICUTA	CIMEX	CINNABARS
CHYMIFIES	CICUTAS	CIMICES	CINNAMIC
CHYMIFY	CICUTINE	CIMIER	CINNAMON
CHYMIST	CICUTINES	CIMIERS	CINNAMONS
CHYMISTRY	CID	CIMINITE	CINNAMONY
CHYMISTS	CIDARIS	CIMINITES	CINNAMYL
CHYMOSIN	CIDARISES	CIMMERIAN	CINNAMYLS
CHYMOSINS	CIDE	CIMOLITE	CINQUAIN
CHYMOUS	CIDED	CIMOLITES	CINQUAINS
CHYND	CIDER	CINCH	CINQUE
CHYPRE	CIDERKIN	CINCHED	CINQUES
CHYPRES	CIDERKINS	CINCHES	CION
CHYTRID	CIDERS	CINCHING	CIONS
CHYTRIDS	CIDERY	CINCHINGS	CIOPPINO
CIABATTA	CIDES	CINCHONA	CIOPPINOS
CIABATTAS	CIDING	CINCHONAS	CIPHER

CIPHERED	CIRRIPEDS	CITER	CITYFIES
CIPHERER	CIRROSE	CITERS	CITYFY
CIPHERERS	CIRROUS	CITES	CITYFYING
CIPHERING	CIRRUS	CITESS	CITYSCAPE
CIPHERS	CIRSOID	CITESSES	CITYWARD
CIPHONIES	CIS	CITHARA	CITYWIDE
CIPHONY	CISALPINE	CITHARAS	CIVE
CIPOLIN	CISCO	CITHARIST	CIVES
CIPOLINS	CISCOES	CITHER	CIVET
CIPOLLINO	CISCOS	CITHERN	CIVETLIKE
CIPPI	CISELEUR	CITHERNS	CIVETS
CIPPUS	CISELEURS	CITHERS	CIVIC
CIRCA	CISELURE	CITHREN	CIVICALLY
CIRCADIAN	CISELURES	CITHRENS	CIVICISM
CIRCAR	CISLUNAR	CITIED	CIVICISMS
CIRCARS	CISPADANE	CITIES	CIVICS
CIRCINATE	CISPLATIN	CITIFIED	CIVIE
CIRCITER	CISSIER	CITIFIES	CIVIES
CIRCLE	CISSIES	CITIFY	CIVIL
CIRCLED	CISSIEST	CITIFYING	CIVILIAN
CIRCLER	CISSIFIED	CITIGRADE	CIVILIANS
CIRCLERS	CISSING	CITING	CIVILISE
CIRCLES	CISSINGS	CITIZEN	CIVILISED
CIRCLET	CISSOID	CITIZENLY	CIVILISER
CIRCLETS	CISSOIDS	CITIZENRY	CIVILISES
CIRCLING	CISSUS	CITIZENS	CIVILIST
CIRCLINGS	CISSUSES	CITO	CIVILISTS
CIRCLIP	CISSY	CITOLA	CIVILITY
CIRCLIPS	CIST	CITOLAS	CIVILIZE
CIRCS	CISTED	CITOLE	CIVILIZED
CIRCUIT	CISTERN	CITOLES	CIVILIZER
CIRCUITAL	CISTERNA	CITRAL	CIVILIZES
CIRCUITED	CISTERNAE	CITRALS	CIVILLY
CIRCUITRY	CISTERNAL	CITRANGE	CIVILNESS
CIRCUITS	CISTERNS	CITRANGES	CIVISM
CIRCUITY	CISTIC	CITRATE	CIVISMS
CIRCULAR	CISTRON	CITRATED	CIVVIES
CIRCULARS	CISTRONIC	CITRATES	CIVVY
CIRCULATE	CISTRONS	CITREOUS	CIZERS
CIRCUS	CISTS	CITRIC	CLABBER
CIRCUSES	CISTUS	CITRIN	CLABBERED
CIRCUSSY	CISTUSES	CITRINE	CLABBERS
CIRCUSY	CISTVAEN	CITRINES	CLACH
CIRE	CISTVAENS	CITRININ	CLACHAN
CIRES	CIT	CITRININS	CLACHANS
CIRL	CITABLE	CITRINS	CLACHS
CIRLS	CITADEL	CITRON	CLACK
CIRQUE	CITADELS	CITRONS	CLACKBOX
CIRQUES	CITAL	CITROUS	CLACKDISH
CIRRATE	CITALS	CITRUS	CLACKED
CIRRHOSED	CITATION	CITRUSES	CLACKER
CIRRHOSES	CITATIONS	CITRUSSY	CLACKERS
CIRRHOSIS	CITATOR	CITRUSY	CLACKING
CIRRHOTIC	CITATORS	CITS	CLACKS
CIRRI	CITATORY	CITTERN	CLAD
CIRRIFORM	CITE	CITTERNS	CLADDAGH
CIRRIPED	CITEABLE	CITY	CLADDAGHS
CIRRIPEDE	CITED	CITYFIED	CLADDED

CLADDER

CLADDER	CLAMMY	CLAPPED	CLASHED
CLADDERS	CLAMOR	CLAPPER	CLASHER
CLADDIE	CLAMORED	CLAPPERED	CLASHERS
CLADDIES	CLAMORER	CLAPPERS	CLASHES
CLADDING	CLAMORERS	CLAPPING	CLASHING
CLADDINGS	CLAMORING	CLAPPINGS	CLASHINGS
CLADE	CLAMOROUS	CLAPS	CLASP
CLADES	CLAMORS	CLAPT	CLASPED
CLADISM	CLAMOUR	CLAPTRAP	CLASPER
CLADISMS	CLAMOURED	CLAPTRAPS	CLASPERS
CLADIST	CLAMOURER	CLAQUE	CLASPING
CLADISTIC	CLAMOURS	CLAQUER	CLASPINGS
CLADISTS	CLAMP	CLAQUERS	CLASPS
CLADODE	CLAMPDOWN	CLAQUES	CLASPT
CLADODES	CLAMPED	CLAQUEUR	CLASS
CLADODIAL	CLAMPER	CLAQUEURS	CLASSABLE
CLADOGRAM	CLAMPERED	CLARAIN	CLASSED
CLADS	CLAMPERS	CLARAINS	CLASSER
CLAES	CLAMPING	CLARENCE	CLASSERS
CLAFOUTI	CLAMPS	CLARENCES	CLASSES
CLAFOUTIS	CLAMS	CLARENDON	CLASSIBLE
CLAG	CLAMSHELL	CLARET	CLASSIC
CLAGGED	CLAMWORM	CLARETED	CLASSICAL
CLAGGIER	CLAMWORMS	CLARETING	CLASSICO
CLAGGIEST	CLAN	CLARETS	CLASSICS
CLAGGING	CLANG	CLARIES	CLASSIER
CLAGGY	CLANGBOX	CLARIFIED	CLASSIEST
CLAGS	CLANGED	CLARIFIER	CLASSIFIC
CLAIM	CLANGER	CLARIFIES	CLASSIFY
CLAIMABLE	CLANGERS	CLARIFY	CLASSILY
CLAIMANT	CLANGING	CLARINET	CLASSING
CLAIMANTS	CLANGINGS	CLARINETS	CLASSINGS
CLAIMED	CLANGOR	CLARINI	CLASSIS
CLAIMER	CLANGORED	CLARINO	CLASSISM
CLAIMERS	CLANGORS	CLARINOS	CLASSISMS
CLAIMING	CLANGOUR	CLARION	CLASSIST
CLAIMS	CLANGOURS	CLARIONED	CLASSISTS
CLAM	CLANGS	CLARIONET	CLASSLESS
CLAMANCY	CLANK	CLARIONS	CLASSMAN
CLAMANT	CLANKED	CLARITIES	CLASSMATE
CLAMANTLY	CLANKIER	CLARITY	CLASSMEN
CLAMBAKE	CLANKIEST	CLARKIA	CLASSON
CLAMBAKES	CLANKING	CLARKIAS	CLASSONS
CLAMBE	CLANKINGS	CLARO	CLASSROOM
CLAMBER	CLANKS	CLAROES	CLASSWORK
CLAMBERED	CLANKY	CLAROS	CLASSY
CLAMBERER	CLANNISH	CLARSACH	CLAST
CLAMBERS	CLANS	CLARSACHS	CLASTIC
CLAME	CLANSHIP	CLART	CLASTICS
CLAMES	CLANSHIPS	CLARTED	CLASTS
CLAMLIKE	CLANSMAN	CLARTHEAD	CLAT
CLAMMED	CLANSMEN	CLARTIER	CLATCH
CLAMMER	CLAP	CLARTIEST	CLATCHED
CLAMMERS	CLAPBOARD	CLARTING	CLATCHES
CLAMMIER	CLAPBREAD	CLARTS	CLATCHING
CLAMMIEST	CLAPDISH	CLARTY	CLATHRATE
CLAMMILY	CLAPNET	CLARY	CLATS
CLAMMING	CLAPNETS	CLASH	CLATTED

CLATTER	CLAWING	CLEAREST	CLEM
CLATTERED	CLAWLESS	CLEAREYED	CLEMATIS
CLATTERER	CLAWLIKE	CLEARING	CLEMENCY
CLATTERS	CLAWS	CLEARINGS	CLEMENT
CLATTERY	CLAXON	CLEARLY	CLEMENTLY
CLATTING	CLAXONS	CLEARNESS	CLEMMED
CLAUCHT	CLAY	CLEARS	CLEMMING
CLAUCHTED	CLAYBANK	CLEARSKIN	CLEMS
CLAUCHTS	CLAYBANKS	CLEARWAY	CLENCH
CLAUGHT	CLAYED	CLEARWAYS	CLENCHED
CLAUGHTED	CLAYEY	CLEARWEED	CLENCHER
CLAUGHTS	CLAYIER	CLEARWING	CLENCHERS
CLAUSAL	CLAYIEST	CLEAT	CLENCHES
CLAUSE	CLAYING	CLEATED	CLENCHING
CLAUSES	CLAYISH	CLEATING	CLEOME
CLAUSTRA	CLAYLIKE	CLEATS	CLEOMES
CLAUSTRAL	CLAYMORE	CLEAVABLE	CLEOPATRA
CLAUSTRUM	CLAYMORES	CLEAVAGE	CLEPE
CLAUSULA	CLAYPAN	CLEAVAGES	CLEPED
CLAUSULAE	CLAYPANS	CLEAVE	CLEPES
CLAUSULAR	CLAYS	CLEAVED	CLEPING
CLAUT	CLAYSTONE	CLEAVER	CLEPSYDRA
CLAUTED	CLAYTONIA	CLEAVERS	CLEPT
CLAUTING	CLAYWARE	CLEAVES	CLERGIES
CLAUTS	CLAYWARES	CLEAVING	CLERGY
CLAVATE	CLEAN	CLEAVINGS	CLERGYMAN
CLAVATED	CLEANABLE	CLECHE	CLERGYMEN
CLAVATELY	CLEANED	CLECK	CLERIC
CLAVATION	CLEANER	CLECKED	CLERICAL
CLAVE	CLEANERS	CLECKIER	CLERICALS
CLAVECIN	CLEANEST	CLECKIEST	CLERICATE
CLAVECINS	CLEANING	CLECKING	CLERICITY
CLAVER	CLEANINGS	CLECKINGS	CLERICS
CLAVERED	CLEANLIER	CLECKS	CLERID
CLAVERING	CLEANLILY	CLECKY	CLERIDS
CLAVERS	CLEANLY	CLEEK	CLERIHEW
CLAVES	CLEANNESS	CLEEKED	CLERIHEWS
CLAVI	CLEANS	CLEEKING	CLERISIES
CLAVICLE	CLEANSE	CLEEKIT	CLERISY
CLAVICLES	CLEANSED	CLEEKS	CLERK
CLAVICORN	CLEANSER	CLEEP	CLERKDOM
CLAVICULA	CLEANSERS	CLEEPED	CLERKDOMS
CLAVIE	CLEANSES	CLEEPING	CLERKED
CLAVIER	CLEANSING	CLEEPS	CLERKESS
CLAVIERS	CLEANSKIN	CLEEVE	CLERKING
CLAVIES	CLEANUP	CLEEVES	CLERKISH
CLAVIFORM	CLEANUPS	CLEF	CLERKLIER
CLAVIGER	CLEAR	CLEFS	CLERKLIKE
CLAVIGERS	CLEARABLE	CLEFT	CLERKLING
CLAVIS	CLEARAGE	CLEFTED	CLERKLY
CLAVULATE	CLEARAGES	CLEFTING	CLERKS
CLAVUS	CLEARANCE	CLEFTS	CLERKSHIP
CLAW	CLEARCOLE	CLEG	CLERUCH
CLAWBACK	CLEARCUT	CLEGS	CLERUCHIA
CLAWBACKS	CLEARCUTS	CLEIDOIC	CLERUCHS
CLAWED	CLEARED	CLEIK	CLERUCHY
CLAWER	CLEARER	CLEIKS	CLEUCH
CLAWERS	CLEARERS	CLEITHRAL	CLEUCHS

CLEUGH	CLIMATAL	CLINKING	CLOACAE
CLEUGHS	CLIMATE	CLINKS	CLOACAL
CLEVE	CLIMATED	CLINOAXES	CLOACAS
CLEVEITE	CLIMATES	CLINOAXIS	CLOACINAL
CLEVEITES	CLIMATIC	CLINOSTAT	CLOACITIS
CLEVER	CLIMATING	CLINQUANT	CLOAK
CLEVERER	CLIMATISE	CLINT	CLOAKED
CLEVEREST	CLIMATIZE	CLINTONIA	CLOAKING
CLEVERISH	CLIMATURE	CLINTS	CLOAKROOM
CLEVERLY	CLIMAX	CLIP	CLOAKS
CLEVES	CLIMAXED	CLIPART	CLOAM
CLEVIS	CLIMAXES	CLIPARTS	CLOAMS
CLEVISES	CLIMAXING	CLIPBOARD	CLOBBER
CLEW	CLIMB	CLIPE	CLOBBERED
CLEWED	CLIMBABLE	CLIPED	CLOBBERS
CLEWING	CLIMBDOWN	CLIPES	CLOCHARD
CLEWS	CLIMBED	CLIPING	CLOCHARDS
CLIANTHUS	CLIMBER	CLIPPABLE	CLOCHE
CLICHE	CLIMBERS	CLIPPED	CLOCHES
CLICHED	CLIMBING	CLIPPER	CLOCK
CLICHEED	CLIMBINGS	CLIPPERS	CLOCKED
CLICHES	CLIMBS	CLIPPIE	CLOCKER
CLICK	CLIME	CLIPPIES	CLOCKERS
CLICKABLE	CLIMES	CLIPPING	CLOCKING
CLICKED	CLINAL	CLIPPINGS	CLOCKINGS
CLICKER	CLINALLY	CLIPS	CLOCKLIKE
CLICKERS	CLINAMEN	CLIPSHEAR	CLOCKS
CLICKET	CLINAMENS	CLIPSHEET	CLOCKWISE
CLICKETED	CLINCH	CLIPT	CLOCKWORK
CLICKETS	CLINCHED	CLIQUE	CLOD
CLICKING	CLINCHER	CLIQUED	CLODDED
CLICKINGS	CLINCHERS	CLIQUES	CLODDIER
CLICKLESS	CLINCHES	CLIQUEY	CLODDIEST
CLICKS	CLINCHING	CLIQUIER	CLODDING
CLICKWRAP	CLINE	CLIQUIEST	CLODDISH
CLIED	CLINES	CLIQUING	CLODDY
CLIENT	CLING	CLIQUISH	CLODLY
CLIENTAGE	CLINGED	CLIQUISM	CLODPATE
CLIENTAL	CLINGER	CLIQUISMS	CLODPATED
CLIENTELE	CLINGERS	CLIQUY	CLODPATES
CLIENTS	CLINGFILM	CLITELLA	CLODPOLE
CLIES	CLINGFISH	CLITELLAR	CLODPOLES
CLIFF	CLINGIER	CLITELLUM	CLODPOLL
CLIFFED	CLINGIEST	CLITHRAL	CLODPOLLS
CLIFFHANG	CLINGING	CLITIC	CLODS
CLIFFHUNG	CLINGS	CLITICISE	CLOFF
CLIFFIER	CLINGY	CLITICIZE	CLOFFS
CLIFFIEST	CLINIC	CLITICS	CLOG
CLIFFLIKE	CLINICAL	CLITORAL	CLOGDANCE
CLIFFS	CLINICIAN	CLITORIC	CLOGGED
CLIFFY	CLINICS	CLITORIS	CLOGGER
CLIFT	CLINIQUE	CLITTER	CLOGGERS
CLIFTED	CLINIQUES	CLITTERED	CLOGGIER
CLIFTIER	CLINK	CLITTERS	CLOGGIEST
CLIFTIEST	CLINKED	CLIVERS	CLOGGILY
CLIFTS	CLINKER	CLIVIA	CLOGGING
CLIFTY	CLINKERED	CLIVIAS	CLOGGINGS
CLIMACTIC	CLINKERS	CLOACA	CLOGGY

CLOGS
CLOISON
CLOISONNE
CLOISONS
CLOISTER
CLOISTERS
CLOISTRAL
CLOKE
CLOKED
CLOKES
CLOKING
CLOMB
CLOMP
CLOMPED
CLOMPING
CLOMPS
CLON
CLONAL
CLONALLY
CLONE
CLONED
CLONER
CLONERS
CLONES
CLONIC
CLONICITY
CLONIDINE
CLONING
CLONINGS
CLONISM
CLONISMS
CLONK
CLONKED
CLONKING
CLONKS
CLONS
CLONUS
CLONUSES
CLOOP
CLOOPS
CLOOT
CLOOTS
CLOP
CLOPPED
CLOPPING
CLOPS
CLOQUE
CLOQUES
CLOSABLE
CLOSE
CLOSEABLE
CLOSED
CLOSEDOWN
CLOSEHEAD
CLOSELY
CLOSENESS
CLOSEOUT
CLOSEOUTS

CLOSER
CLOSERS
CLOSES
CLOSEST
CLOSET
CLOSETED
CLOSETFUL
CLOSETING
CLOSETS
CLOSEUP
CLOSEUPS
CLOSING
CLOSINGS
CLOSURE
CLOSURED
CLOSURES
CLOSURING
CLOT
CLOTBUR
CLOTBURS
CLOTE
CLOTES
CLOTH
CLOTHE
CLOTHED
CLOTHES
CLOTHIER
CLOTHIERS
CLOTHING
CLOTHINGS
CLOTHLIKE
CLOTHS
CLOTPOLL
CLOTPOLLS
CLOTS
CLOTTED
CLOTTER
CLOTTERED
CLOTTERS
CLOTTIER
CLOTTIEST
CLOTTING
CLOTTINGS
CLOTTISH
CLOTTY
CLOTURE
CLOTURED
CLOTURES
CLOTURING
CLOU
CLOUD
CLOUDAGE
CLOUDAGES
CLOUDED
CLOUDIER
CLOUDIEST
CLOUDILY
CLOUDING

CLOUDINGS
CLOUDLAND
CLOUDLESS
CLOUDLET
CLOUDLETS
CLOUDLIKE
CLOUDS
CLOUDTOWN
CLOUDY
CLOUGH
CLOUGHS
CLOUR
CLOURED
CLOURING
CLOURS
CLOUS
CLOUT
CLOUTED
CLOUTER
CLOUTERLY
CLOUTERS
CLOUTING
CLOUTS
CLOVE
CLOVEN
CLOVEPINK
CLOVER
CLOVERED
CLOVERS
CLOVERY
CLOVES
CLOVIS
CLOW
CLOWDER
CLOWDERS
CLOWN
CLOWNED
CLOWNERY
CLOWNING
CLOWNINGS
CLOWNISH
CLOWNS
CLOWS
CLOY
CLOYE
CLOYED
CLOYES
CLOYING
CLOYINGLY
CLOYLESS
CLOYMENT
CLOYMENTS
CLOYS
CLOYSOME
CLOZAPINE
CLOZE
CLOZES
CLUB

CLUBABLE
CLUBBABLE
CLUBBED
CLUBBER
CLUBBERS
CLUBBIER
CLUBBIEST
CLUBBILY
CLUBBING
CLUBBINGS
CLUBBISH
CLUBBISM
CLUBBISMS
CLUBBIST
CLUBBISTS
CLUBBY
CLUBFACE
CLUBFACES
CLUBFEET
CLUBFOOT
CLUBHAND
CLUBHANDS
CLUBHAUL
CLUBHAULS
CLUBHEAD
CLUBHEADS
CLUBHOUSE
CLUBLAND
CLUBLANDS
CLUBMAN
CLUBMEN
CLUBROOM
CLUBROOMS
CLUBROOT
CLUBROOTS
CLUBRUSH
CLUBS
CLUBWOMAN
CLUBWOMEN
CLUCK
CLUCKED
CLUCKIER
CLUCKIEST
CLUCKING
CLUCKS
CLUCKY
CLUDGIE
CLUDGIES
CLUE
CLUED
CLUEING
CLUELESS
CLUES
CLUING
CLUMBER
CLUMBERS
CLUMP
CLUMPED

CLUMPER
CLUMPERS
CLUMPIER
CLUMPIEST
CLUMPING
CLUMPISH
CLUMPLIKE
CLUMPS
CLUMPY
CLUMSIER
CLUMSIEST
CLUMSILY
CLUMSY
CLUNCH
CLUNCHES
CLUNG
CLUNK
CLUNKED
CLUNKER
CLUNKERS
CLUNKIER
CLUNKIEST
CLUNKING
CLUNKS
CLUNKY
CLUPEID
CLUPEIDS
CLUPEOID
CLUPEOIDS
CLUSIA
CLUSIAS
CLUSTER
CLUSTERED
CLUSTERS
CLUSTERY
CLUTCH
CLUTCHED
CLUTCHES
CLUTCHING
CLUTCHY
CLUTTER
CLUTTERED
CLUTTERS
CLUTTERY
CLY
CLYING
CLYPE
CLYPEAL
CLYPEATE
CLYPED
CLYPEI
CLYPES
CLYPEUS
CLYPING
CLYSTER
CLYSTERS
CNEMIAL
CNEMIDES

CNEMIS
CNIDA
CNIDAE
CNIDARIAN
COACH
COACHABLE
COACHDOG
COACHDOGS
COACHED
COACHEE
COACHEES
COACHER
COACHERS
COACHES
COACHIES
COACHING
COACHINGS
COACHLINE
COACHLOAD
COACHMAN
COACHMEN
COACHWHIP
COACHWOOD
COACHWORK
COACHY
COACT
COACTED
COACTING
COACTION
COACTIONS
COACTIVE
COACTOR
COACTORS
COACTS
COADAPTED
COADJUTOR
COADMIRE
COADMIRED
COADMIRES
COADMIT
COADMITS
COADUNATE
COAEVAL
COAEVALS
COAGENCY
COAGENT
COAGENTS
COAGULA
COAGULANT
COAGULASE
COAGULATE
COAGULUM
COAGULUMS
COAITA
COAITAS
COAL
COALA
COALAS

COALBALL
COALBALLS
COALBIN
COALBINS
COALBOX
COALBOXES
COALED
COALER
COALERS
COALESCE
COALESCED
COALESCES
COALFACE
COALFACES
COALFIELD
COALFISH
COALHOLE
COALHOLES
COALHOUSE
COALIER
COALIEST
COALIFIED
COALIFIES
COALIFY
COALING
COALISE
COALISED
COALISES
COALISING
COALITION
COALIZE
COALIZED
COALIZES
COALIZING
COALLESS
COALMAN
COALMEN
COALMINE
COALMINER
COALMINES
COALPIT
COALPITS
COALS
COALSACK
COALSACKS
COALSHED
COALSHEDS
COALTAR
COALTARS
COALY
COALYARD
COALYARDS
COAMING
COAMINGS
COANCHOR
COANCHORS
COANNEX
COANNEXED

COANNEXES
COAPPEAR
COAPPEARS
COAPT
COAPTED
COAPTING
COAPTS
COARB
COARBS
COARCTATE
COARSE
COARSELY
COARSEN
COARSENED
COARSENS
COARSER
COARSEST
COARSISH
COASSIST
COASSISTS
COASSUME
COASSUMED
COASSUMES
COAST
COASTAL
COASTALLY
COASTED
COASTER
COASTERS
COASTING
COASTINGS
COASTLAND
COASTLINE
COASTS
COASTWARD
COASTWISE
COAT
COATDRESS
COATE
COATED
COATEE
COATEES
COATER
COATERS
COATES
COATI
COATING
COATINGS
COATIS
COATLESS
COATRACK
COATRACKS
COATROOM
COATROOMS
COATS
COATSTAND
COATTAIL
COATTAILS

COATTEND
COATTENDS
COATTEST
COATTESTS
COAUTHOR
COAUTHORS
COAX
COAXAL
COAXED
COAXER
COAXERS
COAXES
COAXIAL
COAXIALLY
COAXING
COAXINGLY
COB
COBAEA
COBAEAS
COBALAMIN
COBALT
COBALTIC
COBALTINE
COBALTITE
COBALTOUS
COBALTS
COBB
COBBED
COBBER
COBBERS
COBBIER
COBBIEST
COBBING
COBBLE
COBBLED
COBBLER
COBBLERS
COBBLERY
COBBLES
COBBLING
COBBLINGS
COBBS
COBBY
COBIA
COBIAS
COBLE
COBLES
COBLOAF
COBLOAVES
COBNUT
COBNUTS
COBRA
COBRAS
COBRIC
COBRIFORM
COBS
COBURG
COBURGS

COBWEB
COBWEBBED
COBWEBBY
COBWEBS
COBZA
COBZAS
COCA
COCAIN
COCAINE
COCAINES
COCAINISE
COCAINISM
COCAINIST
COCAINIZE
COCAINS
COCAPTAIN
COCAS
COCCAL
COCCI
COCCIC
COCCID
COCCIDIA
COCCIDIUM
COCCIDS
COCCO
COCCOID
COCCOIDAL
COCCOIDS
COCCOLITE
COCCOLITH
COCCOS
COCCOUS
COCCUS
COCCYGEAL
COCCYGES
COCCYGIAN
COCCYX
COCCYXES
COCH
COCHAIR
COCHAIRED
COCHAIRS
COCHES
COCHIN
COCHINEAL
COCHINS
COCHLEA
COCHLEAE
COCHLEAR
COCHLEARE
COCHLEARS
COCHLEAS
COCHLEATE
COCINERA
COCINERAS
COCK
COCKADE
COCKADED

COCKADES
COCKAMAMY
COCKAPOO
COCKAPOOS
COCKATEEL
COCKATIEL
COCKATOO
COCKATOOS
COCKBILL
COCKBILLS
COCKBIRD
COCKBIRDS
COCKBOAT
COCKBOATS
COCKCROW
COCKCROWS
COCKED
COCKER
COCKERED
COCKEREL
COCKERELS
COCKERING
COCKERS
COCKET
COCKETS
COCKEYE
COCKEYED
COCKEYES
COCKFIGHT
COCKHORSE
COCKIER
COCKIES
COCKIEST
COCKILY
COCKINESS
COCKING
COCKISH
COCKLE
COCKLEBUR
COCKLED
COCKLEERT
COCKLEMAN
COCKLEMEN
COCKLER
COCKLERS
COCKLES
COCKLIKE
COCKLING
COCKLOFT
COCKLOFTS
COCKMATCH
COCKNEY
COCKNEYFY
COCKNEYS
COCKNIFY
COCKPIT
COCKPITS
COCKROACH

COCKS
COCKSCOMB
COCKSFOOT
COCKSHIES
COCKSHOT
COCKSHOTS
COCKSHUT
COCKSHUTS
COCKSHY
COCKSIER
COCKSIEST
COCKSPUR
COCKSPURS
COCKSURE
COCKSWAIN
COCKSY
COCKTAIL
COCKTAILS
COCKUP
COCKUPS
COCKY
COCO
COCOA
COCOANUT
COCOANUTS
COCOAS
COCOBOLA
COCOBOLAS
COCOBOLO
COCOBOLOS
COCOMAT
COCOMATS
COCONUT
COCONUTS
COCOON
COCOONED
COCOONERY
COCOONING
COCOONS
COCOPAN
COCOPANS
COCOPLUM
COCOPLUMS
COCOS
COCOTTE
COCOTTES
COCOUNSEL
COCOYAM
COCOYAMS
COCOZELLE
COCREATE
COCREATED
COCREATES
COCREATOR
COCTILE
COCTION
COCTIONS
COCULTURE

113

COCURATOR	CODIFIED	COEMPLOY	COEXERT
COCUSWOOD	CODIFIER	COEMPLOYS	COEXERTED
COD	CODIFIERS	COEMPT	COEXERTS
CODA	CODIFIES	COEMPTED	COEXIST
CODABLE	CODIFY	COEMPTING	COEXISTED
CODAS	CODIFYING	COEMPTION	COEXISTS
CODDED	CODILLA	COEMPTS	COEXTEND
CODDER	CODILLAS	COENACLE	COEXTENDS
CODDERS	CODILLE	COENACLES	COFACTOR
CODDING	CODILLES	COENACT	COFACTORS
CODDLE	CODING	COENACTED	COFEATURE
CODDLED	CODINGS	COENACTS	COFF
CODDLER	CODIRECT	COENAMOR	COFFED
CODDLERS	CODIRECTS	COENAMORS	COFFEE
CODDLES	CODIST	COENDURE	COFFEEPOT
CODDLING	CODISTS	COENDURED	COFFEES
CODE	CODLIN	COENDURES	COFFER
CODEBOOK	CODLING	COENOBIA	COFFERDAM
CODEBOOKS	CODLINGS	COENOBITE	COFFERED
CODEBTOR	CODLINS	COENOBIUM	COFFERING
CODEBTORS	CODOLOGY	COENOCYTE	COFFERS
CODEC	CODOMAIN	COENOSARC	COFFIN
CODECS	CODOMAINS	COENURE	COFFINED
CODED	CODON	COENURES	COFFING
CODEIA	CODONS	COENURI	COFFINING
CODEIAS	CODPIECE	COENURUS	COFFINITE
CODEIN	CODPIECES	COENZYME	COFFINS
CODEINA	CODRIVE	COENZYMES	COFFLE
CODEINAS	CODRIVEN	COEQUAL	COFFLED
CODEINE	CODRIVER	COEQUALLY	COFFLES
CODEINES	CODRIVERS	COEQUALS	COFFLING
CODEINS	CODRIVES	COEQUATE	COFFRET
CODELESS	CODRIVING	COEQUATED	COFFRETS
CODEN	CODROVE	COEQUATES	COFFS
CODENAME	CODS	COERCE	COFINANCE
CODENAMES	COED	COERCED	COFOUND
CODENS	COEDIT	COERCER	COFOUNDED
CODER	COEDITED	COERCERS	COFOUNDER
CODERIVE	COEDITING	COERCES	COFOUNDS
CODERIVED	COEDITOR	COERCIBLE	COFT
CODERIVES	COEDITORS	COERCIBLY	COG
CODERS	COEDITS	COERCING	COGENCE
CODES	COEDS	COERCION	COGENCES
CODESIGN	COEFFECT	COERCIONS	COGENCIES
CODESIGNS	COEFFECTS	COERCIVE	COGENCY
CODETTA	COEHORN	COERECT	COGENER
CODETTAS	COEHORNS	COERECTED	COGENERS
CODEVELOP	COELIAC	COERECTS	COGENT
CODEWORD	COELIACS	COESITE	COGENTLY
CODEWORDS	COELOM	COESITES	COGGED
CODEX	COELOMATA	COETERNAL	COGGER
CODFISH	COELOMATE	COEVAL	COGGERS
CODFISHES	COELOME	COEVALITY	COGGIE
CODGER	COELOMES	COEVALLY	COGGIES
CODGERS	COELOMIC	COEVALS	COGGING
CODICES	COELOMS	COEVOLVE	COGGINGS
CODICIL	COELOSTAT	COEVOLVED	COGGLE
CODICILS	COEMBODY	COEVOLVES	COGGLED

COGGLES	COHABITOR	COIFFEUR	COIT
COGGLIER	COHABITS	COIFFEURS	COITAL
COGGLIEST	COHABS	COIFFEUSE	COITALLY
COGGLING	COHEAD	COIFFING	COITION
COGGLY	COHEADED	COIFFURE	COITIONAL
COGIE	COHEADING	COIFFURED	COITIONS
COGIES	COHEADS	COIFFURES	COITS
COGITABLE	COHEIR	COIFING	COITUS
COGITATE	COHEIRESS	COIFS	COITUSES
COGITATED	COHEIRS	COIGN	COJOIN
COGITATES	COHERE	COIGNE	COJOINED
COGITATOR	COHERED	COIGNED	COJOINING
COGITO	COHERENCE	COIGNES	COJOINS
COGITOS	COHERENCY	COIGNING	COJONES
COGNAC	COHERENT	COIGNS	COKE
COGNACS	COHERER	COIL	COKED
COGNATE	COHERERS	COILED	COKEHEAD
COGNATELY	COHERES	COILER	COKEHEADS
COGNATES	COHERING	COILERS	COKELIKE
COGNATION	COHERITOR	COILING	COKERNUT
COGNISANT	COHESIBLE	COILS	COKERNUTS
COGNISE	COHESION	COIN	COKES
COGNISED	COHESIONS	COINABLE	COKESES
COGNISER	COHESIVE	COINAGE	COKIER
COGNISERS	COHIBIT	COINAGES	COKIEST
COGNISES	COHIBITED	COINCIDE	COKING
COGNISING	COHIBITS	COINCIDED	COKULORIS
COGNITION	COHO	COINCIDES	COKY
COGNITIVE	COHOBATE	COINED	COL
COGNIZANT	COHOBATED	COINER	COLA
COGNIZE	COHOBATES	COINERS	COLANDER
COGNIZED	COHOE	COINFECT	COLANDERS
COGNIZER	COHOES	COINFECTS	COLAS
COGNIZERS	COHOG	COINFER	COLBIES
COGNIZES	COHOGS	COINFERS	COLBY
COGNIZING	COHOLDER	COINHERE	COLBYS
COGNOMEN	COHOLDERS	COINHERED	COLCANNON
COGNOMENS	COHORN	COINHERES	COLCHICA
COGNOMINA	COHORNS	COINING	COLCHICUM
COGNOSCE	COHORT	COININGS	COLCOTHAR
COGNOSCED	COHORTS	COINMATE	COLD
COGNOSCES	COHOS	COINMATES	COLDBLOOD
COGNOVIT	COHOSH	COINS	COLDCOCK
COGNOVITS	COHOSHES	COINSURE	COLDCOCKS
COGON	COHOST	COINSURED	COLDER
COGONS	COHOSTED	COINSURER	COLDEST
COGS	COHOSTESS	COINSURES	COLDHOUSE
COGUE	COHOSTING	COINTER	COLDIE
COGUES	COHOSTS	COINTERS	COLDIES
COGWAY	COHOUSING	COINTREAU	COLDISH
COGWAYS	COHUNE	COINVENT	COLDLY
COGWHEEL	COHUNES	COINVENTS	COLDNESS
COGWHEELS	COHYPONYM	COIR	COLDS
COHAB	COIF	COIRS	COLE
COHABIT	COIFED	COISTREL	COLEAD
COHABITED	COIFFE	COISTRELS	COLEADER
COHABITEE	COIFFED	COISTRIL	COLEADERS
COHABITER	COIFFES	COISTRILS	COLEADING

COLEADS
COLECTOMY
COLED
COLEOPTER
COLES
COLESEED
COLESEEDS
COLESLAW
COLESLAWS
COLESSEE
COLESSEES
COLESSOR
COLESSORS
COLETIT
COLETITS
COLEUS
COLEUSES
COLEWORT
COLEWORTS
COLEY
COLEYS
COLIBRI
COLIBRIS
COLIC
COLICIN
COLICINE
COLICINES
COLICINS
COLICKIER
COLICKY
COLICROOT
COLICS
COLICWEED
COLIES
COLIFORM
COLIFORMS
COLIN
COLINEAR
COLINS
COLIPHAGE
COLISEUM
COLISEUMS
COLISTIN
COLISTINS
COLITIC
COLITIS
COLITISES
COLL
COLLAGE
COLLAGED
COLLAGEN
COLLAGENS
COLLAGES
COLLAGING
COLLAGIST
COLLAPSAR
COLLAPSE
COLLAPSED

COLLAPSES
COLLAR
COLLARD
COLLARDS
COLLARED
COLLARET
COLLARETS
COLLARING
COLLARS
COLLATE
COLLATED
COLLATES
COLLATING
COLLATION
COLLATIVE
COLLATOR
COLLATORS
COLLEAGUE
COLLECT
COLLECTED
COLLECTOR
COLLECTS
COLLED
COLLEEN
COLLEENS
COLLEGE
COLLEGER
COLLEGERS
COLLEGES
COLLEGIA
COLLEGIAL
COLLEGIAN
COLLEGIUM
COLLET
COLLETED
COLLETING
COLLETS
COLLICULI
COLLIDE
COLLIDED
COLLIDER
COLLIDERS
COLLIDES
COLLIDING
COLLIE
COLLIED
COLLIER
COLLIERS
COLLIERY
COLLIES
COLLIGATE
COLLIMATE
COLLINEAR
COLLING
COLLINGS
COLLINS
COLLINSES
COLLINSIA

COLLISION
COLLOCATE
COLLODION
COLLODIUM
COLLOGUE
COLLOGUED
COLLOGUES
COLLOID
COLLOIDAL
COLLOIDS
COLLOP
COLLOPS
COLLOQUE
COLLOQUED
COLLOQUES
COLLOQUIA
COLLOQUY
COLLOTYPE
COLLOTYPY
COLLS
COLLUDE
COLLUDED
COLLUDER
COLLUDERS
COLLUDES
COLLUDING
COLLUSION
COLLUSIVE
COLLUVIA
COLLUVIAL
COLLUVIES
COLLUVIUM
COLLY
COLLYING
COLLYRIA
COLLYRIUM
COLOBI
COLOBID
COLOBOMA
COLOBOMAS
COLOBUS
COLOBUSES
COLOCATE
COLOCATED
COLOCATES
COLOCYNTH
COLOG
COLOGNE
COLOGNED
COLOGNES
COLOGS
COLOMBARD
COLON
COLONE
COLONEL
COLONELCY
COLONELS
COLONES

COLONI
COLONIAL
COLONIALS
COLONIC
COLONICS
COLONIES
COLONISE
COLONISED
COLONISER
COLONISES
COLONIST
COLONISTS
COLONITIS
COLONIZE
COLONIZED
COLONIZER
COLONIZES
COLONNADE
COLONS
COLONUS
COLONY
COLOPHON
COLOPHONS
COLOPHONY
COLOR
COLORABLE
COLORABLY
COLORADO
COLORANT
COLORANTS
COLORBRED
COLORCAST
COLORED
COLOREDS
COLORER
COLORERS
COLORFAST
COLORFUL
COLORIFIC
COLORING
COLORINGS
COLORISE
COLORISED
COLORISER
COLORISES
COLORISM
COLORISMS
COLORIST
COLORISTS
COLORIZE
COLORIZED
COLORIZER
COLORIZES
COLORLESS
COLORMAN
COLORMEN
COLORS
COLORWAY

COLORWAYS
COLORY
COLOSSAL
COLOSSEUM
COLOSSI
COLOSSUS
COLOSTOMY
COLOSTRAL
COLOSTRIC
COLOSTRUM
COLOTOMY
COLOUR
COLOURANT
COLOURED
COLOUREDS
COLOURER
COLOURERS
COLOURFUL
COLOURING
COLOURISE
COLOURIST
COLOURIZE
COLOURMAN
COLOURMEN
COLOURS
COLOURWAY
COLOURY
COLPITIS
COLPOTOMY
COLS
COLT
COLTAN
COLTANS
COLTED
COLTER
COLTERS
COLTING
COLTISH
COLTISHLY
COLTS
COLTSFOOT
COLTWOOD
COLTWOODS
COLUBRIAD
COLUBRID
COLUBRIDS
COLUBRINE
COLUGO
COLUGOS
COLUMBARY
COLUMBATE
COLUMBIC
COLUMBINE
COLUMBITE
COLUMBIUM
COLUMBOUS
COLUMEL
COLUMELLA

COLUMELS
COLUMN
COLUMNAL
COLUMNAR
COLUMNEA
COLUMNEAS
COLUMNED
COLUMNIST
COLUMNS
COLURE
COLURES
COLY
COLZA
COLZAS
COMA
COMADE
COMAE
COMAKE
COMAKER
COMAKERS
COMAKES
COMAKING
COMAL
COMANAGE
COMANAGED
COMANAGER
COMANAGES
COMARB
COMARBS
COMART
COMARTS
COMAS
COMATE
COMATES
COMATIC
COMATIK
COMATIKS
COMATOSE
COMATULA
COMATULAE
COMATULID
COMB
COMBAT
COMBATANT
COMBATED
COMBATER
COMBATERS
COMBATING
COMBATIVE
COMBATS
COMBATTED
COMBE
COMBED
COMBER
COMBERS
COMBES
COMBI
COMBIER

COMBIES
COMBIEST
COMBINATE
COMBINE
COMBINED
COMBINEDS
COMBINER
COMBINERS
COMBINES
COMBING
COMBINGS
COMBINING
COMBIS
COMBLE
COMBLES
COMBLESS
COMBLIKE
COMBO
COMBOS
COMBRETUM
COMBS
COMBUST
COMBUSTED
COMBUSTOR
COMBUSTS
COMBWISE
COMBY
COME
COMEBACK
COMEBACKS
COMEDDLE
COMEDDLED
COMEDDLES
COMEDIAN
COMEDIANS
COMEDIC
COMEDIES
COMEDO
COMEDONES
COMEDOS
COMEDOWN
COMEDOWNS
COMEDY
COMELIER
COMELIEST
COMELILY
COMELY
COMEMBER
COMEMBERS
COMEOVER
COMEOVERS
COMER
COMERS
COMES
COMET
COMETARY
COMETH
COMETHER

COMETHERS
COMETIC
COMETS
COMFIER
COMFIEST
COMFINESS
COMFIT
COMFITS
COMFITURE
COMFORT
COMFORTED
COMFORTER
COMFORTS
COMFREY
COMFREYS
COMFY
COMIC
COMICAL
COMICALLY
COMICE
COMICES
COMICS
COMING
COMINGLE
COMINGLED
COMINGLES
COMINGS
COMIQUE
COMIQUES
COMITADJI
COMITAL
COMITATUS
COMITIA
COMITIAL
COMITIAS
COMITIES
COMITY
COMIX
COMM
COMMA
COMMAND
COMMANDED
COMMANDER
COMMANDO
COMMANDOS
COMMANDS
COMMAS
COMMATA
COMMENCE
COMMENCED
COMMENCER
COMMENCES
COMMEND
COMMENDAM
COMMENDED
COMMENDER
COMMENDS
COMMENSAL

COMMENT

COMMENT	COMMOVE	COMPARES	COMPLEXED
COMMENTED	COMMOVED	COMPARING	COMPLEXER
COMMENTER	COMMOVES	COMPART	COMPLEXES
COMMENTOR	COMMOVING	COMPARTED	COMPLEXLY
COMMENTS	COMMS	COMPARTS	COMPLEXUS
COMMER	COMMUNAL	COMPAS	COMPLIANT
COMMERCE	COMMUNARD	COMPASS	COMPLICE
COMMERCED	COMMUNE	COMPASSED	COMPLICES
COMMERCES	COMMUNED	COMPASSES	COMPLICIT
COMMERE	COMMUNER	COMPAST	COMPLIED
COMMERES	COMMUNERS	COMPEAR	COMPLIER
COMMERGE	COMMUNES	COMPEARED	COMPLIERS
COMMERGED	COMMUNING	COMPEARS	COMPLIES
COMMERGES	COMMUNION	COMPED	COMPLIN
COMMERS	COMMUNISE	COMPEER	COMPLINE
COMMIE	COMMUNISM	COMPEERED	COMPLINES
COMMIES	COMMUNIST	COMPEERS	COMPLINS
COMMINATE	COMMUNITY	COMPEL	COMPLISH
COMMINGLE	COMMUNIZE	COMPELLED	COMPLOT
COMMINUTE	COMMUTATE	COMPELLER	COMPLOTS
COMMIS	COMMUTE	COMPELS	COMPLUVIA
COMMISSAR	COMMUTED	COMPEND	COMPLY
COMMIT	COMMUTER	COMPENDIA	COMPLYING
COMMITS	COMMUTERS	COMPENDS	COMPO
COMMITTAL	COMMUTES	COMPER	COMPONE
COMMITTED	COMMUTING	COMPERE	COMPONENT
COMMITTEE	COMMUTUAL	COMPERED	COMPONY
COMMITTER	COMMY	COMPERES	COMPORT
COMMIX	COMODO	COMPERING	COMPORTED
COMMIXED	COMONOMER	COMPERS	COMPORTS
COMMIXES	COMORBID	COMPESCE	COMPOS
COMMIXING	COMOSE	COMPESCED	COMPOSE
COMMIXT	COMOUS	COMPESCES	COMPOSED
COMMO	COMP	COMPETE	COMPOSER
COMMODE	COMPACT	COMPETED	COMPOSERS
COMMODES	COMPACTED	COMPETENT	COMPOSES
COMMODIFY	COMPACTER	COMPETES	COMPOSING
COMMODITY	COMPACTLY	COMPETING	COMPOSITE
COMMODO	COMPACTOR	COMPILE	COMPOST
COMMODORE	COMPACTS	COMPILED	COMPOSTED
COMMON	COMPADRE	COMPILER	COMPOSTER
COMMONAGE	COMPADRES	COMPILERS	COMPOSTS
COMMONED	COMPAGE	COMPILES	COMPOSURE
COMMONER	COMPAGES	COMPILING	COMPOT
COMMONERS	COMPAND	COMPING	COMPOTE
COMMONEST	COMPANDED	COMPINGS	COMPOTES
COMMONEY	COMPANDER	COMPITAL	COMPOTIER
COMMONEYS	COMPANDOR	COMPLAIN	COMPOTS
COMMONING	COMPANDS	COMPLAINS	COMPOUND
COMMONLY	COMPANIED	COMPLAINT	COMPOUNDS
COMMONS	COMPANIES	COMPLEAT	COMPRADOR
COMMORANT	COMPANING	COMPLECT	COMPRESS
COMMOS	COMPANION	COMPLECTS	COMPRINT
COMMOT	COMPANY	COMPLETE	COMPRINTS
COMMOTE	COMPARE	COMPLETED	COMPRISAL
COMMOTES	COMPARED	COMPLETER	COMPRISE
COMMOTION	COMPARER	COMPLETES	COMPRISED
COMMOTS	COMPARERS	COMPLEX	COMPRISES

COMPRIZE
COMPRIZED
COMPRIZES
COMPS
COMPT
COMPTABLE
COMPTED
COMPTER
COMPTERS
COMPTIBLE
COMPTING
COMPTROLL
COMPTS
COMPULSE
COMPULSED
COMPULSES
COMPUTANT
COMPUTE
COMPUTED
COMPUTER
COMPUTERS
COMPUTES
COMPUTING
COMPUTIST
COMRADE
COMRADELY
COMRADERY
COMRADES
COMS
COMSYMP
COMSYMPS
COMTE
COMTES
COMUS
COMUSES
CON
CONACRE
CONACRED
CONACRES
CONACRING
CONARIA
CONARIAL
CONARIUM
CONATION
CONATIONS
CONATIVE
CONATUS
CONCAUSE
CONCAUSES
CONCAVE
CONCAVED
CONCAVELY
CONCAVES
CONCAVING
CONCAVITY
CONCEAL
CONCEALED
CONCEALER

CONCEALS
CONCEDE
CONCEDED
CONCEDER
CONCEDERS
CONCEDES
CONCEDING
CONCEDO
CONCEIT
CONCEITED
CONCEITS
CONCEITY
CONCEIVE
CONCEIVED
CONCEIVER
CONCEIVES
CONCENT
CONCENTER
CONCENTRE
CONCENTS
CONCENTUS
CONCEPT
CONCEPTI
CONCEPTS
CONCEPTUS
CONCERN
CONCERNED
CONCERNS
CONCERT
CONCERTED
CONCERTI
CONCERTO
CONCERTOS
CONCERTS
CONCETTI
CONCETTO
CONCH
CONCHA
CONCHAE
CONCHAL
CONCHAS
CONCHATE
CONCHE
CONCHED
CONCHES
CONCHIE
CONCHIES
CONCHING
CONCHITIS
CONCHO
CONCHOID
CONCHOIDS
CONCHOS
CONCHS
CONCHY
CONCIERGE
CONCILIAR
CONCISE

CONCISED
CONCISELY
CONCISER
CONCISES
CONCISEST
CONCISING
CONCISION
CONCLAVE
CONCLAVES
CONCLUDE
CONCLUDED
CONCLUDER
CONCLUDES
CONCOCT
CONCOCTED
CONCOCTER
CONCOCTOR
CONCOCTS
CONCOLOR
CONCORD
CONCORDAL
CONCORDAT
CONCORDED
CONCORDS
CONCOURS
CONCOURSE
CONCREATE
CONCRETE
CONCRETED
CONCRETES
CONCREW
CONCREWED
CONCREWS
CONCUBINE
CONCUPIES
CONCUPY
CONCUR
CONCURRED
CONCURS
CONCUSS
CONCUSSED
CONCUSSES
CONCYCLIC
COND
CONDEMN
CONDEMNED
CONDEMNER
CONDEMNOR
CONDEMNS
CONDENSE
CONDENSED
CONDENSER
CONDENSES
CONDER
CONDERS
CONDIDDLE
CONDIE
CONDIES

CONDIGN
CONDIGNLY
CONDIMENT
CONDITION
CONDO
CONDOES
CONDOLE
CONDOLED
CONDOLENT
CONDOLER
CONDOLERS
CONDOLES
CONDOLING
CONDOM
CONDOMS
CONDONE
CONDONED
CONDONER
CONDONERS
CONDONES
CONDONING
CONDOR
CONDORES
CONDORS
CONDOS
CONDUCE
CONDUCED
CONDUCER
CONDUCERS
CONDUCES
CONDUCING
CONDUCIVE
CONDUCT
CONDUCTED
CONDUCTI
CONDUCTOR
CONDUCTS
CONDUCTUS
CONDUIT
CONDUITS
CONDYLAR
CONDYLE
CONDYLES
CONDYLOID
CONDYLOMA
CONE
CONED
CONELRAD
CONELRADS
CONENOSE
CONENOSES
CONEPATE
CONEPATES
CONEPATL
CONEPATLS
CONES
CONEY
CONEYS

CONF	CONFLATED	CONGESTS	CONJECT
CONFAB	CONFLATES	CONGIARY	CONJECTED
CONFABBED	CONFLICT	CONGII	CONJECTS
CONFABS	CONFLICTS	CONGIUS	CONJEE
CONFECT	CONFLUENT	CONGLOBE	CONJEED
CONFECTED	CONFLUX	CONGLOBED	CONJEEING
CONFECTS	CONFLUXES	CONGLOBES	CONJEES
CONFER	CONFOCAL	CONGO	CONJOIN
CONFEREE	CONFORM	CONGOES	CONJOINED
CONFEREES	CONFORMAL	CONGOS	CONJOINER
CONFERRAL	CONFORMED	CONGOU	CONJOINS
CONFERRED	CONFORMER	CONGOUS	CONJOINT
CONFERREE	CONFORMS	CONGRATS	CONJUGAL
CONFERRER	CONFOUND	CONGREE	CONJUGANT
CONFERS	CONFOUNDS	CONGREED	CONJUGATE
CONFERVA	CONFRERE	CONGREES	CONJUNCT
CONFERVAE	CONFRERES	CONGREET	CONJUNCTS
CONFERVAL	CONFRERIE	CONGREETS	CONJUNTO
CONFERVAS	CONFRONT	CONGRESS	CONJUNTOS
CONFESS	CONFRONTE	CONGRUE	CONJURE
CONFESSED	CONFRONTS	CONGRUED	CONJURED
CONFESSES	CONFS	CONGRUENT	CONJURER
CONFESSOR	CONFUSE	CONGRUES	CONJURERS
CONFEST	CONFUSED	CONGRUING	CONJURES
CONFESTLY	CONFUSES	CONGRUITY	CONJURIES
CONFETTI	CONFUSING	CONGRUOUS	CONJURING
CONFETTO	CONFUSION	CONI	CONJUROR
CONFIDANT	CONFUTE	CONIA	CONJURORS
CONFIDE	CONFUTED	CONIAS	CONJURY
CONFIDED	CONFUTER	CONIC	CONK
CONFIDENT	CONFUTERS	CONICAL	CONKED
CONFIDER	CONFUTES	CONICALLY	CONKER
CONFIDERS	CONFUTING	CONICINE	CONKERS
CONFIDES	CONGA	CONICINES	CONKIER
CONFIDING	CONGAED	CONICITY	CONKIEST
CONFIGURE	CONGAING	CONICS	CONKING
CONFINE	CONGAS	CONIDIA	CONKS
CONFINED	CONGE	CONIDIAL	CONKY
CONFINER	CONGEAL	CONIDIAN	CONN
CONFINERS	CONGEALED	CONIDIUM	CONNATE
CONFINES	CONGEALER	CONIES	CONNATELY
CONFINING	CONGEALS	CONIFER	CONNATION
CONFIRM	CONGED	CONIFERS	CONNATURE
CONFIRMED	CONGEE	CONIFORM	CONNE
CONFIRMEE	CONGEED	CONIINE	CONNECT
CONFIRMER	CONGEEING	CONIINES	CONNECTED
CONFIRMOR	CONGEES	CONIMA	CONNECTER
CONFIRMS	CONGEING	CONIMAS	CONNECTOR
CONFISEUR	CONGENER	CONIN	CONNECTS
CONFIT	CONGENERS	CONINE	CONNED
CONFITEOR	CONGENIAL	CONINES	CONNER
CONFITS	CONGENIC	CONING	CONNERS
CONFITURE	CONGER	CONINS	CONNES
CONFIX	CONGERIES	CONIOLOGY	CONNEXION
CONFIXED	CONGERS	CONIOSES	CONNEXIVE
CONFIXES	CONGES	CONIOSIS	CONNING
CONFIXING	CONGEST	CONIUM	CONNINGS
CONFLATE	CONGESTED	CONIUMS	CONNIVE

CONNIVED	CONSOCIES	CONSUMER	CONTINUED
CONNIVENT	CONSOL	CONSUMERS	CONTINUER
CONNIVER	CONSOLATE	CONSUMES	CONTINUES
CONNIVERS	CONSOLE	CONSUMING	CONTINUO
CONNIVERY	CONSOLED	CONSUMPT	CONTINUOS
CONNIVES	CONSOLER	CONSUMPTS	CONTINUUM
CONNIVING	CONSOLERS	CONTACT	CONTLINE
CONNOTATE	CONSOLES	CONTACTED	CONTLINES
CONNOTE	CONSOLING	CONTACTEE	CONTO
CONNOTED	CONSOLS	CONTACTOR	CONTORNO
CONNOTES	CONSOLUTE	CONTACTS	CONTORNOS
CONNOTING	CONSOMME	CONTADINA	CONTORT
CONNOTIVE	CONSOMMES	CONTADINE	CONTORTED
CONNS	CONSONANT	CONTADINI	CONTORTS
CONNUBIAL	CONSONOUS	CONTADINO	CONTOS
CONODONT	CONSORT	CONTAGIA	CONTOUR
CONODONTS	CONSORTED	CONTAGION	CONTOURED
CONOID	CONSORTER	CONTAGIUM	CONTOURS
CONOIDAL	CONSORTIA	CONTAIN	CONTRA
CONOIDIC	CONSORTS	CONTAINED	CONTRACT
CONOIDS	CONSPIRE	CONTAINER	CONTRACTS
CONOMINEE	CONSPIRED	CONTAINS	CONTRAIL
CONQUER	CONSPIRER	CONTANGO	CONTRAILS
CONQUERED	CONSPIRES	CONTANGOS	CONTRAIR
CONQUERER	CONSTABLE	CONTE	CONTRALTI
CONQUEROR	CONSTANCY	CONTECK	CONTRALTO
CONQUERS	CONSTANT	CONTECKS	CONTRARY
CONQUEST	CONSTANTS	CONTEMN	CONTRAS
CONQUESTS	CONSTATE	CONTEMNED	CONTRAST
CONQUIAN	CONSTATED	CONTEMNER	CONTRASTS
CONQUIANS	CONSTATES	CONTEMNOR	CONTRASTY
CONS	CONSTER	CONTEMNS	CONTRAT
CONSCIENT	CONSTERED	CONTEMPER	CONTRATE
CONSCIOUS	CONSTERS	CONTEMPO	CONTRATS
CONSCRIBE	CONSTRAIN	CONTEMPT	CONTRIST
CONSCRIPT	CONSTRICT	CONTEMPTS	CONTRISTS
CONSEIL	CONSTRUAL	CONTEND	CONTRITE
CONSEILS	CONSTRUCT	CONTENDED	CONTRIVE
CONSENSUS	CONSTRUE	CONTENDER	CONTRIVED
CONSENT	CONSTRUED	CONTENDS	CONTRIVER
CONSENTED	CONSTRUER	CONTENT	CONTRIVES
CONSENTER	CONSTRUES	CONTENTED	CONTROL
CONSENTS	CONSUL	CONTENTLY	CONTROLE
CONSERVE	CONSULAGE	CONTENTS	CONTROLS
CONSERVED	CONSULAR	CONTES	CONTROUL
CONSERVER	CONSULARS	CONTESSA	CONTROULS
CONSERVES	CONSULATE	CONTESSAS	CONTUMACY
CONSIDER	CONSULS	CONTEST	CONTUMELY
CONSIDERS	CONSULT	CONTESTED	CONTUND
CONSIGN	CONSULTA	CONTESTER	CONTUNDED
CONSIGNED	CONSULTAS	CONTESTS	CONTUNDS
CONSIGNEE	CONSULTED	CONTEXT	CONTUSE
CONSIGNER	CONSULTEE	CONTEXTS	CONTUSED
CONSIGNOR	CONSULTER	CONTICENT	CONTUSES
CONSIGNS	CONSULTOR	CONTINENT	CONTUSING
CONSIST	CONSULTS	CONTINUA	CONTUSION
CONSISTED	CONSUME	CONTINUAL	CONTUSIVE
CONSISTS	CONSUMED	CONTINUE	CONUNDRUM

CONURBAN	CONVIVE	COOKIE	COOMIER
CONURBIA	CONVIVED	COOKIES	COOMIEST
CONURBIAS	CONVIVES	COOKING	COOMING
CONURE	CONVIVIAL	COOKINGS	COOMS
CONURES	CONVIVING	COOKLESS	COOMY
CONUS	CONVO	COOKMAID	COON
CONVECT	CONVOCATE	COOKMAIDS	COONCAN
CONVECTED	CONVOKE	COOKOFF	COONCANS
CONVECTOR	CONVOKED	COOKOFFS	COONDOG
CONVECTS	CONVOKER	COOKOUT	COONDOGS
CONVENE	CONVOKERS	COOKOUTS	COONHOUND
CONVENED	CONVOKES	COOKROOM	COONS
CONVENER	CONVOKING	COOKROOMS	COONSKIN
CONVENERS	CONVOLUTE	COOKS	COONSKINS
CONVENES	CONVOLVE	COOKSHACK	COONTIE
CONVENING	CONVOLVED	COOKSHOP	COONTIES
CONVENOR	CONVOLVES	COOKSHOPS	COONTY
CONVENORS	CONVOS	COOKSTOVE	COOP
CONVENT	CONVOY	COOKTOP	COOPED
CONVENTED	CONVOYED	COOKTOPS	COOPER
CONVENTS	CONVOYING	COOKWARE	COOPERAGE
CONVERGE	CONVOYS	COOKWARES	COOPERATE
CONVERGED	CONVULSE	COOKY	COOPERED
CONVERGES	CONVULSED	COOL	COOPERIES
CONVERSE	CONVULSES	COOLABAH	COOPERING
CONVERSED	CONY	COOLABAHS	COOPERS
CONVERSER	COO	COOLAMON	COOPERY
CONVERSES	COOCH	COOLAMONS	COOPING
CONVERSO	COOCHES	COOLANT	COOPS
CONVERSOS	COOCOO	COOLANTS	COOPT
CONVERT	COOED	COOLDOWN	COOPTED
CONVERTED	COOEE	COOLDOWNS	COOPTING
CONVERTER	COOEED	COOLED	COOPTION
CONVERTOR	COOEEING	COOLER	COOPTIONS
CONVERTS	COOEES	COOLERS	COOPTS
CONVEX	COOER	COOLEST	COORDINAL
CONVEXED	COOERS	COOLHOUSE	COORIE
CONVEXES	COOEY	COOLIBAH	COORIED
CONVEXING	COOEYED	COOLIBAHS	COORIEING
CONVEXITY	COOEYING	COOLIBAR	COORIES
CONVEXLY	COOEYS	COOLIBARS	COOS
CONVEY	COOF	COOLIE	COOSEN
CONVEYAL	COOFS	COOLIES	COOSENED
CONVEYALS	COOING	COOLING	COOSENING
CONVEYED	COOINGLY	COOLINGLY	COOSENS
CONVEYER	COOINGS	COOLISH	COOSER
CONVEYERS	COOK	COOLLY	COOSERS
CONVEYING	COOKABLE	COOLNESS	COOSIN
CONVEYOR	COOKBOOK	COOLS	COOSINED
CONVEYORS	COOKBOOKS	COOLTH	COOSINING
CONVEYS	COOKED	COOLTHS	COOSINS
CONVICT	COOKER	COOLY	COOST
CONVICTED	COOKERIES	COOM	COOT
CONVICTS	COOKERS	COOMB	COOTCH
CONVINCE	COOKERY	COOMBE	COOTCHED
CONVINCED	COOKEY	COOMBES	COOTCHES
CONVINCER	COOKEYS	COOMBS	COOTCHING
CONVINCES	COOKHOUSE	COOMED	COOTER

COOTERS	COPINGS	COPSHOP	COQUITOS
COOTIE	COPIOUS	COPSHOPS	COR
COOTIES	COPIOUSLY	COPSIER	CORACLE
COOTIKIN	COPITA	COPSIEST	CORACLES
COOTIKINS	COPITAS	COPSING	CORACOID
COOTS	COPLANAR	COPSY	CORACOIDS
COOZE	COPLOT	COPTER	CORAGGIO
COOZES	COPLOTS	COPTERS	CORAGGIOS
COP	COPLOTTED	COPUBLISH	CORAL
COPACETIC	COPOLYMER	COPULA	CORALLA
COPAIBA	COPOUT	COPULAE	CORALLINE
COPAIBAS	COPOUTS	COPULAR	CORALLITE
COPAIVA	COPPED	COPULAS	CORALLOID
COPAIVAS	COPPER	COPULATE	CORALLUM
COPAL	COPPERAH	COPULATED	CORALROOT
COPALM	COPPERAHS	COPULATES	CORALS
COPALMS	COPPERAS	COPURIFY	CORALWORT
COPALS	COPPERED	COPY	CORAM
COPARCENY	COPPERING	COPYABLE	CORAMINE
COPARENT	COPPERISH	COPYBOOK	CORAMINES
COPARENTS	COPPERS	COPYBOOKS	CORANACH
COPARTNER	COPPERY	COPYBOY	CORANACHS
COPASETIC	COPPICE	COPYBOYS	CORANTO
COPASTOR	COPPICED	COPYCAT	CORANTOES
COPASTORS	COPPICES	COPYCATS	CORANTOS
COPATAINE	COPPICING	COPYDESK	CORBAN
COPATRIOT	COPPIES	COPYDESKS	CORBANS
COPATRON	COPPIN	COPYEDIT	CORBE
COPATRONS	COPPING	COPYEDITS	CORBEAU
COPAY	COPPINS	COPYGIRL	CORBEAUS
COPAYMENT	COPPLE	COPYGIRLS	CORBEIL
COPAYS	COPPLES	COPYGRAPH	CORBEILLE
COPE	COPPRA	COPYHOLD	CORBEILS
COPECK	COPPRAS	COPYHOLDS	CORBEL
COPECKS	COPPY	COPYING	CORBELED
COPED	COPRA	COPYISM	CORBELING
COPEMATE	COPRAH	COPYISMS	CORBELLED
COPEMATES	COPRAHS	COPYIST	CORBELS
COPEN	COPRAS	COPYISTS	CORBES
COPENS	COPREMIA	COPYLEFT	CORBICULA
COPEPOD	COPREMIAS	COPYLEFTS	CORBIE
COPEPODS	COPREMIC	COPYREAD	CORBIES
COPER	COPRESENT	COPYREADS	CORBINA
COPERED	COPRINCE	COPYRIGHT	CORBINAS
COPERING	COPRINCES	COPYTAKER	CORBY
COPERS	COPRODUCE	COQUET	CORCASS
COPES	COPRODUCT	COQUETRY	CORCASSES
COPESETIC	COPROLITE	COQUETS	CORD
COPESTONE	COPROLITH	COQUETTE	CORDAGE
COPIED	COPROLOGY	COQUETTED	CORDAGES
COPIER	COPROSMA	COQUETTES	CORDATE
COPIERS	COPROSMAS	COQUILLA	CORDATELY
COPIES	COPROZOIC	COQUILLAS	CORDED
COPIHUE	COPS	COQUILLE	CORDELLE
COPIHUES	COPSE	COQUILLES	CORDELLED
COPILOT	COPSED	COQUINA	CORDELLES
COPILOTS	COPSES	COQUINAS	CORDER
COPING	COPSEWOOD	COQUITO	CORDERS

CORDGRASS	CORIANDER	CORNCAKE	CORNIFORM
CORDIAL	CORIES	CORNCAKES	CORNIFY
CORDIALLY	CORING	CORNCOB	CORNILY
CORDIALS	CORIOUS	CORNCOBS	CORNINESS
CORDIFORM	CORIUM	CORNCRAKE	CORNING
CORDINER	CORIUMS	CORNCRIB	CORNIST
CORDINERS	CORIVAL	CORNCRIBS	CORNISTS
CORDING	CORIVALRY	CORNEA	CORNLAND
CORDINGS	CORIVALS	CORNEAE	CORNLANDS
CORDITE	CORIXID	CORNEAL	CORNLOFT
CORDITES	CORIXIDS	CORNEAS	CORNLOFTS
CORDLESS	CORK	CORNED	CORNMEAL
CORDLIKE	CORKAGE	CORNEITIS	CORNMEALS
CORDOBA	CORKAGES	CORNEL	CORNMILL
CORDOBAS	CORKBOARD	CORNELIAN	CORNMILLS
CORDON	CORKBORER	CORNELS	CORNMOTH
CORDONED	CORKED	CORNEMUSE	CORNMOTHS
CORDONING	CORKER	CORNEOUS	CORNO
CORDONNET	CORKERS	CORNER	CORNOPEAN
CORDONS	CORKIER	CORNERED	CORNPIPE
CORDOTOMY	CORKIEST	CORNERING	CORNPIPES
CORDOVAN	CORKINESS	CORNERMAN	CORNPONE
CORDOVANS	CORKING	CORNERMEN	CORNPONES
CORDS	CORKIR	CORNERS	CORNRENT
CORDUROY	CORKIRS	CORNET	CORNRENTS
CORDUROYS	CORKLIKE	CORNETCY	CORNROW
CORDWAIN	CORKS	CORNETIST	CORNROWED
CORDWAINS	CORKSCREW	CORNETS	CORNROWS
CORDWOOD	CORKTREE	CORNETT	CORNS
CORDWOODS	CORKTREES	CORNETTI	CORNSTALK
CORDYLINE	CORKWING	CORNETTO	CORNSTONE
CORE	CORKWINGS	CORNETTS	CORNU
CORED	CORKWOOD	CORNFED	CORNUA
COREDEEM	CORKWOODS	CORNFIELD	CORNUAL
COREDEEMS	CORKY	CORNFLAG	CORNUS
COREGENT	CORM	CORNFLAGS	CORNUSES
COREGENTS	CORMEL	CORNFLAKE	CORNUTE
COREIGN	CORMELS	CORNFLIES	CORNUTED
COREIGNS	CORMIDIA	CORNFLOUR	CORNUTES
CORELATE	CORMIDIUM	CORNFLY	CORNUTING
CORELATED	CORMLIKE	CORNHUSK	CORNUTO
CORELATES	CORMOID	CORNHUSKS	CORNUTOS
CORELESS	CORMORANT	CORNI	CORNWORM
CORELLA	CORMOUS	CORNICE	CORNWORMS
CORELLAS	CORMS	CORNICED	CORNY
COREMIA	CORMUS	CORNICES	COROCORE
COREMIUM	CORMUSES	CORNICHE	COROCORES
COREOPSIS	CORN	CORNICHES	COROCORO
CORER	CORNACRE	CORNICHON	COROCOROS
CORERS	CORNACRES	CORNICING	CORODIES
CORES	CORNAGE	CORNICLE	CORODY
COREY	CORNAGES	CORNICLES	COROLLA
COREYS	CORNBALL	CORNICULA	COROLLARY
CORF	CORNBALLS	CORNIER	COROLLAS
CORFHOUSE	CORNBORER	CORNIEST	COROLLATE
CORGI	CORNBRAID	CORNIFIC	COROLLINE
CORGIS	CORNBRASH	CORNIFIED	CORONA
CORIA	CORNBREAD	CORNIFIES	CORONACH

CORONACHS	CORRECT	CORSLETS	CORYPHE
CORONAE	CORRECTED	CORSNED	CORYPHEE
CORONAL	CORRECTER	CORSNEDS	CORYPHEES
CORONALLY	CORRECTLY	CORSO	CORYPHENE
CORONALS	CORRECTOR	CORSOS	CORYPHES
CORONARY	CORRECTS	CORTEGE	CORYZA
CORONAS	CORRELATE	CORTEGES	CORYZAL
CORONATE	CORRIDA	CORTEX	CORYZAS
CORONATED	CORRIDAS	CORTEXES	COS
CORONATES	CORRIDOR	CORTICAL	COSCRIPT
CORONEL	CORRIDORS	CORTICATE	COSCRIPTS
CORONELS	CORRIE	CORTICES	COSE
CORONER	CORRIES	CORTICOID	COSEC
CORONERS	CORRIGENT	CORTICOSE	COSECANT
CORONET	CORRIVAL	CORTILE	COSECANTS
CORONETED	CORRIVALS	CORTILI	COSECH
CORONETS	CORRODANT	CORTIN	COSECHS
CORONIS	CORRODE	CORTINA	COSECS
CORONISES	CORRODED	CORTINAS	COSED
CORONIUM	CORRODENT	CORTINS	COSEISMAL
CORONIUMS	CORRODER	CORTISOL	COSEISMIC
CORONOID	CORRODERS	CORTISOLS	COSES
COROTATE	CORRODES	CORTISONE	COSET
COROTATED	CORRODIES	CORULER	COSETS
COROTATES	CORRODING	CORULERS	COSEY
COROZO	CORRODY	CORUNDUM	COSEYS
COROZOS	CORROSION	CORUNDUMS	COSH
CORPORA	CORROSIVE	CORUSCANT	COSHED
CORPORAL	CORRUGATE	CORUSCATE	COSHER
CORPORALE	CORRUPT	CORVEE	COSHERED
CORPORALS	CORRUPTED	CORVEES	COSHERER
CORPORAS	CORRUPTER	CORVES	COSHERERS
CORPORATE	CORRUPTLY	CORVET	COSHERIES
CORPOREAL	CORRUPTOR	CORVETED	COSHERING
CORPORIFY	CORRUPTS	CORVETING	COSHERS
CORPOSANT	CORS	CORVETS	COSHERY
CORPS	CORSAC	CORVETTE	COSHES
CORPSE	CORSACS	CORVETTED	COSHING
CORPSED	CORSAGE	CORVETTES	COSIE
CORPSES	CORSAGES	CORVID	COSIED
CORPSING	CORSAIR	CORVIDS	COSIER
CORPSMAN	CORSAIRS	CORVINA	COSIERS
CORPSMEN	CORSE	CORVINAS	COSIES
CORPULENT	CORSELET	CORVINE	COSIEST
CORPUS	CORSELETS	CORVUS	COSIGN
CORPUSCLE	CORSES	CORVUSES	COSIGNED
CORPUSES	CORSET	CORY	COSIGNER
CORRADE	CORSETED	CORYBANT	COSIGNERS
CORRADED	CORSETIER	CORYBANTS	COSIGNING
CORRADES	CORSETING	CORYDALIS	COSIGNS
CORRADING	CORSETRY	CORYLUS	COSILY
CORRAL	CORSETS	CORYLUSES	COSINE
CORRALLED	CORSEY	CORYMB	COSINES
CORRALS	CORSEYS	CORYMBED	COSINESS
CORRASION	CORSIVE	CORYMBOSE	COSING
CORRASIVE	CORSIVES	CORYMBOUS	COSMEA
CORREA	CORSLET	CORYMBS	COSMEAS
CORREAS	CORSLETED	CORYPHAEI	COSMESES

COSMESIS

COSMESIS	COSTERS	COTINGAS	COTYLEDON
COSMETIC	COSTES	COTININE	COTYLES
COSMETICS	COSTING	COTININES	COTYLOID
COSMIC	COSTIVE	COTISE	COTYLOIDS
COSMICAL	COSTIVELY	COTISED	COTYPE
COSMID	COSTLESS	COTISES	COTYPES
COSMIDS	COSTLIER	COTISING	COUCAL
COSMIN	COSTLIEST	COTLAND	COUCALS
COSMINE	COSTLY	COTLANDS	COUCH
COSMINES	COSTMARY	COTQUEAN	COUCHANT
COSMINS	COSTOTOMY	COTQUEANS	COUCHE
COSMISM	COSTREL	COTRUSTEE	COUCHED
COSMISMS	COSTRELS	COTS	COUCHEE
COSMIST	COSTS	COTT	COUCHEES
COSMISTS	COSTUME	COTTA	COUCHER
COSMOCRAT	COSTUMED	COTTABUS	COUCHERS
COSMOGENY	COSTUMER	COTTAE	COUCHES
COSMOGONY	COSTUMERS	COTTAGE	COUCHETTE
COSMOID	COSTUMERY	COTTAGED	COUCHING
COSMOLINE	COSTUMES	COTTAGER	COUCHINGS
COSMOLOGY	COSTUMEY	COTTAGERS	COUDE
COSMONAUT	COSTUMIER	COTTAGES	COUGAN
COSMORAMA	COSTUMING	COTTAGEY	COUGANS
COSMOS	COSTUS	COTTAGING	COUGAR
COSMOSES	COSTUSES	COTTAR	COUGARS
COSMOTRON	COSY	COTTARS	COUGH
COSPHERED	COSYING	COTTAS	COUGHED
COSPONSOR	COT	COTTED	COUGHER
COSS	COTAN	COTTER	COUGHERS
COSSACK	COTANGENT	COTTERED	COUGHING
COSSACKS	COTANS	COTTERING	COUGHINGS
COSSES	COTE	COTTERS	COUGHS
COSSET	COTEAU	COTTID	COUGUAR
COSSETED	COTEAUX	COTTIDS	COUGUARS
COSSETING	COTED	COTTIER	COULD
COSSETS	COTELETTE	COTTIERS	COULDEST
COSSIE	COTELINE	COTTING	COULDST
COSSIES	COTELINES	COTTISE	COULEE
COST	COTENANCY	COTTISED	COULEES
COSTA	COTENANT	COTTISES	COULIBIAC
COSTAE	COTENANTS	COTTISING	COULIS
COSTAL	COTERIE	COTTOID	COULISSE
COSTALGIA	COTERIES	COTTON	COULISSES
COSTALLY	COTES	COTTONADE	COULOIR
COSTALS	COTH	COTTONED	COULOIRS
COSTAR	COTHS	COTTONING	COULOMB
COSTARD	COTHURN	COTTONS	COULOMBIC
COSTARDS	COTHURNAL	COTTONY	COULOMBS
COSTARRED	COTHURNI	COTTOWN	COULTER
COSTARS	COTHURNS	COTTOWNS	COULTERS
COSTATE	COTHURNUS	COTTS	COUMARIC
COSTATED	COTICULAR	COTTUS	COUMARIN
COSTE	COTIDAL	COTTUSES	COUMARINS
COSTEAN	COTILLION	COTURNIX	COUMARONE
COSTEANED	COTILLON	COTWAL	COUMAROU
COSTEANS	COTILLONS	COTWALS	COUMAROUS
COSTED	COTING	COTYLAE	COUNCIL
COSTER	COTINGA	COTYLE	COUNCILOR

COUNCILS
COUNSEL
COUNSELED
COUNSELEE
COUNSELOR
COUNSELS
COUNT
COUNTABLE
COUNTABLY
COUNTBACK
COUNTDOWN
COUNTED
COUNTER
COUNTERED
COUNTERS
COUNTESS
COUNTIAN
COUNTIANS
COUNTIES
COUNTING
COUNTLESS
COUNTLINE
COUNTRIES
COUNTROL
COUNTROLS
COUNTRY
COUNTS
COUNTSHIP
COUNTY
COUP
COUPE
COUPED
COUPEE
COUPEES
COUPER
COUPERS
COUPES
COUPING
COUPLE
COUPLED
COUPLEDOM
COUPLER
COUPLERS
COUPLES
COUPLET
COUPLETS
COUPLING
COUPLINGS
COUPON
COUPONING
COUPONS
COUPS
COUPURE
COUPURES
COUR
COURAGE
COURAGES
COURANT

COURANTE
COURANTES
COURANTO
COURANTOS
COURANTS
COURB
COURBARIL
COURBED
COURBETTE
COURBING
COURBS
COURD
COURE
COURED
COURES
COURGETTE
COURIE
COURIED
COURIEING
COURIER
COURIERED
COURIERS
COURIES
COURING
COURLAN
COURLANS
COURS
COURSE
COURSED
COURSER
COURSERS
COURSES
COURSING
COURSINGS
COURT
COURTED
COURTEOUS
COURTER
COURTERS
COURTESAN
COURTESY
COURTEZAN
COURTIER
COURTIERS
COURTING
COURTINGS
COURTLET
COURTLETS
COURTLIER
COURTLIKE
COURTLING
COURTLY
COURTROOM
COURTS
COURTSHIP
COURTSIDE
COURTYARD
COUSCOUS

COUSIN
COUSINAGE
COUSINLY
COUSINRY
COUSINS
COUTEAU
COUTEAUX
COUTER
COUTERS
COUTH
COUTHER
COUTHEST
COUTHIE
COUTHIER
COUTHIEST
COUTHS
COUTHY
COUTIL
COUTILLE
COUTILLES
COUTILS
COUTURE
COUTURES
COUTURIER
COUVADE
COUVADES
COUVERT
COUVERTS
COUZIN
COUZINS
COVALENCE
COVALENCY
COVALENT
COVARIANT
COVARIATE
COVARIED
COVARIES
COVARY
COVARYING
COVE
COVED
COVELET
COVELETS
COVELLINE
COVELLITE
COVEN
COVENANT
COVENANTS
COVENS
COVENT
COVENTS
COVER
COVERABLE
COVERAGE
COVERAGES
COVERALL
COVERALLS
COVERED

COVERER
COVERERS
COVERING
COVERINGS
COVERLESS
COVERLET
COVERLETS
COVERLID
COVERLIDS
COVERS
COVERSED
COVERSINE
COVERSLIP
COVERT
COVERTLY
COVERTS
COVERTURE
COVERUP
COVERUPS
COVES
COVET
COVETABLE
COVETED
COVETER
COVETERS
COVETING
COVETISE
COVETISES
COVETOUS
COVETS
COVEY
COVEYS
COVIN
COVING
COVINGS
COVINOUS
COVINS
COVYNE
COVYNES
COW
COWAGE
COWAGES
COWAL
COWALS
COWAN
COWANS
COWARD
COWARDED
COWARDICE
COWARDING
COWARDLY
COWARDRY
COWARDS
COWBANE
COWBANES
COWBELL
COWBELLS
COWBERRY

COWBIND	COWLING	COXES	COZY
COWBINDS	COWLINGS	COXIER	COZYING
COWBIRD	COWLS	COXIEST	COZZES
COWBIRDS	COWLSTAFF	COXINESS	CRAAL
COWBOY	COWMAN	COXING	CRAALED
COWBOYED	COWMEN	COXITIDES	CRAALING
COWBOYING	COWORKER	COXITIS	CRAALS
COWBOYS	COWORKERS	COXLESS	CRAB
COWED	COWP	COXSWAIN	CRABAPPLE
COWEDLY	COWPAT	COXSWAINS	CRABBED
COWER	COWPATS	COXY	CRABBEDLY
COWERED	COWPEA	COY	CRABBER
COWERING	COWPEAS	COYDOG	CRABBERS
COWERS	COWPED	COYDOGS	CRABBIER
COWFEEDER	COWPIE	COYED	CRABBIEST
COWFISH	COWPIES	COYER	CRABBILY
COWFISHES	COWPING	COYEST	CRABBING
COWFLAP	COWPLOP	COYING	CRABBY
COWFLAPS	COWPLOPS	COYISH	CRABEATER
COWFLOP	COWPOKE	COYISHLY	CRABGRASS
COWFLOPS	COWPOKES	COYLY	CRABLIKE
COWGIRL	COWPOX	COYNESS	CRABMEAT
COWGIRLS	COWPOXES	COYNESSES	CRABMEATS
COWGRASS	COWPS	COYOTE	CRABS
COWHAGE	COWRIE	COYOTES	CRABSTICK
COWHAGES	COWRIES	COYOTILLO	CRABWISE
COWHAND	COWRITE	COYPOU	CRABWOOD
COWHANDS	COWRITER	COYPOUS	CRABWOODS
COWHEARD	COWRITERS	COYPU	CRACK
COWHEARDS	COWRITES	COYPUS	CRACKA
COWHEEL	COWRITING	COYS	CRACKAS
COWHEELS	COWRITTEN	COYSTREL	CRACKBACK
COWHERB	COWROTE	COYSTRELS	CRACKDOWN
COWHERBS	COWRY	COYSTRIL	CRACKED
COWHERD	COWS	COYSTRILS	CRACKER
COWHERDS	COWSHED	COZ	CRACKERS
COWHIDE	COWSHEDS	COZE	CRACKET
COWHIDED	COWSKIN	COZED	CRACKETS
COWHIDES	COWSKINS	COZEN	CRACKHEAD
COWHIDING	COWSLIP	COZENAGE	CRACKING
COWHOUSE	COWSLIPS	COZENAGES	CRACKINGS
COWHOUSES	COWTREE	COZENED	CRACKJAW
COWIER	COWTREES	COZENER	CRACKJAWS
COWIEST	COWY	COZENERS	CRACKLE
COWING	COX	COZENING	CRACKLED
COWINNER	COXA	COZENS	CRACKLES
COWINNERS	COXAE	COZES	CRACKLIER
COWISH	COXAL	COZEY	CRACKLING
COWITCH	COXALGIA	COZEYS	CRACKLY
COWITCHES	COXALGIAS	COZIE	CRACKNEL
COWK	COXALGIC	COZIED	CRACKNELS
COWKED	COXALGIES	COZIER	CRACKPOT
COWKING	COXALGY	COZIERS	CRACKPOTS
COWKS	COXCOMB	COZIES	CRACKS
COWL	COXCOMBIC	COZIEST	CRACKSMAN
COWLED	COXCOMBRY	COZILY	CRACKSMEN
COWLICK	COXCOMBS	COZINESS	CRACKUP
COWLICKS	COXED	COZING	CRACKUPS

CRACKY
CRACOWE
CRACOWES
CRADLE
CRADLED
CRADLER
CRADLERS
CRADLES
CRADLING
CRADLINGS
CRAFT
CRAFTED
CRAFTER
CRAFTERS
CRAFTIER
CRAFTIEST
CRAFTILY
CRAFTING
CRAFTLESS
CRAFTS
CRAFTSMAN
CRAFTSMEN
CRAFTWORK
CRAFTY
CRAG
CRAGFAST
CRAGGED
CRAGGIER
CRAGGIEST
CRAGGILY
CRAGGY
CRAGS
CRAGSMAN
CRAGSMEN
CRAIC
CRAICS
CRAIG
CRAIGS
CRAKE
CRAKED
CRAKES
CRAKING
CRAM
CRAMBE
CRAMBES
CRAMBO
CRAMBOES
CRAMBOS
CRAME
CRAMES
CRAMESIES
CRAMESY
CRAMMABLE
CRAMMED
CRAMMER
CRAMMERS
CRAMMING
CRAMOISIE

CRAMOISY
CRAMP
CRAMPBARK
CRAMPED
CRAMPER
CRAMPERS
CRAMPET
CRAMPETS
CRAMPFISH
CRAMPIER
CRAMPIEST
CRAMPING
CRAMPIT
CRAMPITS
CRAMPON
CRAMPONED
CRAMPONS
CRAMPOON
CRAMPOONS
CRAMPS
CRAMPY
CRAMS
CRAN
CRANAGE
CRANAGES
CRANBERRY
CRANCH
CRANCHED
CRANCHES
CRANCHING
CRANE
CRANED
CRANEFLY
CRANES
CRANIA
CRANIAL
CRANIALLY
CRANIATE
CRANIATES
CRANING
CRANIUM
CRANIUMS
CRANK
CRANKCASE
CRANKED
CRANKER
CRANKEST
CRANKIER
CRANKIEST
CRANKILY
CRANKING
CRANKISH
CRANKLE
CRANKLED
CRANKLES
CRANKLING
CRANKLY
CRANKNESS

CRANKOUS
CRANKPIN
CRANKPINS
CRANKS
CRANKY
CRANNIED
CRANNIES
CRANNOG
CRANNOGE
CRANNOGES
CRANNOGS
CRANNY
CRANNYING
CRANREUCH
CRANS
CRANTS
CRANTSES
CRAP
CRAPAUD
CRAPAUDS
CRAPE
CRAPED
CRAPELIKE
CRAPES
CRAPIER
CRAPIEST
CRAPING
CRAPLE
CRAPLES
CRAPOLA
CRAPOLAS
CRAPPED
CRAPPER
CRAPPERS
CRAPPIE
CRAPPIER
CRAPPIES
CRAPPIEST
CRAPPING
CRAPPY
CRAPS
CRAPSHOOT
CRAPULENT
CRAPULOUS
CRAPY
CRARE
CRARES
CRASES
CRASH
CRASHED
CRASHER
CRASHERS
CRASHES
CRASHING
CRASHLAND
CRASHPAD
CRASHPADS
CRASIS

CRASS
CRASSER
CRASSEST
CRASSLY
CRASSNESS
CRATCH
CRATCHES
CRATE
CRATED
CRATEFUL
CRATEFULS
CRATER
CRATERED
CRATERING
CRATERLET
CRATEROUS
CRATERS
CRATES
CRATING
CRATON
CRATONIC
CRATONS
CRATUR
CRATURS
CRAUNCH
CRAUNCHED
CRAUNCHES
CRAUNCHY
CRAVAT
CRAVATS
CRAVATTED
CRAVE
CRAVED
CRAVEN
CRAVENED
CRAVENING
CRAVENLY
CRAVENS
CRAVER
CRAVERS
CRAVES
CRAVING
CRAVINGS
CRAW
CRAWDAD
CRAWDADDY
CRAWDADS
CRAWFISH
CRAWL
CRAWLED
CRAWLER
CRAWLERS
CRAWLIER
CRAWLIEST
CRAWLING
CRAWLINGS
CRAWLS
CRAWLWAY

CRAWLWAYS	CREANCES	CREDULOUS	CREMONA
CRAWLY	CREANT	CREE	CREMONAS
CRAWS	CREASE	CREED	CREMOR
CRAY	CREASED	CREEDAL	CREMORNE
CRAYER	CREASER	CREEDS	CREMORNES
CRAYERS	CREASERS	CREEING	CREMORS
CRAYFISH	CREASES	CREEK	CREMOSIN
CRAYON	CREASIER	CREEKIER	CREMS
CRAYONED	CREASIEST	CREEKIEST	CREMSIN
CRAYONER	CREASING	CREEKS	CRENA
CRAYONERS	CREASOTE	CREEKY	CRENAS
CRAYONING	CREASOTED	CREEL	CRENATE
CRAYONIST	CREASOTES	CREELED	CRENATED
CRAYONS	CREASY	CREELING	CRENATELY
CRAYS	CREATABLE	CREELS	CRENATION
CRAYTHUR	CREATE	CREEP	CRENATURE
CRAYTHURS	CREATED	CREEPAGE	CRENEL
CRAZE	CREATES	CREEPAGES	CRENELATE
CRAZED	CREATIC	CREEPED	CRENELED
CRAZES	CREATIN	CREEPER	CRENELING
CRAZIER	CREATINE	CREEPERED	CRENELLE
CRAZIES	CREATINES	CREEPERS	CRENELLED
CRAZIEST	CREATING	CREEPIE	CRENELLES
CRAZILY	CREATINS	CREEPIER	CRENELS
CRAZINESS	CREATION	CREEPIES	CRENSHAW
CRAZING	CREATIONS	CREEPIEST	CRENSHAWS
CRAZY	CREATIVE	CREEPILY	CRENULATE
CRAZYWEED	CREATIVES	CREEPING	CREODONT
CREACH	CREATOR	CREEPS	CREODONTS
CREACHS	CREATORS	CREEPY	CREOLE
CREAGH	CREATRESS	CREES	CREOLES
CREAGHS	CREATRIX	CREESE	CREOLIAN
CREAK	CREATURAL	CREESED	CREOLIANS
CREAKED	CREATURE	CREESES	CREOLISE
CREAKIER	CREATURES	CREESH	CREOLISED
CREAKIEST	CRECHE	CREESHED	CREOLISES
CREAKILY	CRECHES	CREESHES	CREOLIST
CREAKING	CRED	CREESHIER	CREOLISTS
CREAKS	CREDAL	CREESHING	CREOLIZE
CREAKY	CREDENCE	CREESHY	CREOLIZED
CREAM	CREDENCES	CREESING	CREOLIZES
CREAMCUPS	CREDENDA	CREM	CREOPHAGY
CREAMED	CREDENDUM	CREMAINS	CREOSOL
CREAMER	CREDENT	CREMANT	CREOSOLS
CREAMERS	CREDENZA	CREMASTER	CREOSOTE
CREAMERY	CREDENZAS	CREMATE	CREOSOTED
CREAMIER	CREDIBLE	CREMATED	CREOSOTES
CREAMIEST	CREDIBLY	CREMATES	CREOSOTIC
CREAMILY	CREDIT	CREMATING	CREPANCE
CREAMING	CREDITED	CREMATION	CREPANCES
CREAMLAID	CREDITING	CREMATOR	CREPE
CREAMLIKE	CREDITOR	CREMATORS	CREPED
CREAMPUFF	CREDITORS	CREMATORY	CREPERIE
CREAMS	CREDITS	CREME	CREPERIES
CREAMWARE	CREDO	CREMES	CREPES
CREAMWOVE	CREDOS	CREMINI	CREPEY
CREAMY	CREDS	CREMINIS	CREPIER
CREANCE	CREDULITY	CREMOCARP	CREPIEST

CREPINESS	CREVICE	CRICOIDS	CRINING
CREPING	CREVICED	CRIED	CRINITE
CREPITANT	CREVICES	CRIER	CRINITES
CREPITATE	CREW	CRIERS	CRINKLE
CREPITUS	CREWCUT	CRIES	CRINKLED
CREPOLINE	CREWCUTS	CRIKEY	CRINKLES
CREPON	CREWE	CRIM	CRINKLIER
CREPONS	CREWED	CRIME	CRINKLIES
CREPT	CREWEL	CRIMED	CRINKLING
CREPUSCLE	CREWELIST	CRIMEFUL	CRINKLY
CREPY	CREWELLED	CRIMELESS	CRINOID
CRESCENDI	CREWELS	CRIMEN	CRINOIDAL
CRESCENDO	CREWES	CRIMES	CRINOIDS
CRESCENT	CREWING	CRIMEWAVE	CRINOLINE
CRESCENTS	CREWLESS	CRIMINA	CRINOSE
CRESCIVE	CREWMAN	CRIMINAL	CRINUM
CRESOL	CREWMATE	CRIMINALS	CRINUMS
CRESOLS	CREWMATES	CRIMINATE	CRIOLLO
CRESS	CREWMEN	CRIMINE	CRIOLLOS
CRESSES	CREWNECK	CRIMING	CRIOS
CRESSET	CREWNECKS	CRIMINI	CRIOSES
CRESSETS	CREWS	CRIMINIS	CRIPE
CRESSY	CRIANT	CRIMINOUS	CRIPES
CREST	CRIB	CRIMINY	CRIPPLE
CRESTA	CRIBBAGE	CRIMMER	CRIPPLED
CRESTAL	CRIBBAGES	CRIMMERS	CRIPPLER
CRESTED	CRIBBED	CRIMP	CRIPPLERS
CRESTING	CRIBBER	CRIMPED	CRIPPLES
CRESTINGS	CRIBBERS	CRIMPER	CRIPPLING
CRESTLESS	CRIBBING	CRIMPERS	CRIS
CRESTON	CRIBBINGS	CRIMPIER	CRISE
CRESTONS	CRIBBLE	CRIMPIEST	CRISES
CRESTS	CRIBBLED	CRIMPING	CRISIC
CRESYL	CRIBBLES	CRIMPLE	CRISIS
CRESYLIC	CRIBBLING	CRIMPLED	CRISP
CRESYLS	CRIBELLA	CRIMPLES	CRISPATE
CRETIC	CRIBELLAR	CRIMPLING	CRISPATED
CRETICS	CRIBELLUM	CRIMPS	CRISPED
CRETIN	CRIBLE	CRIMPY	CRISPEN
CRETINISE	CRIBRATE	CRIMS	CRISPENED
CRETINISM	CRIBROSE	CRIMSON	CRISPENS
CRETINIZE	CRIBROUS	CRIMSONED	CRISPER
CRETINOID	CRIBS	CRIMSONS	CRISPERS
CRETINOUS	CRIBWORK	CRINAL	CRISPEST
CRETINS	CRIBWORKS	CRINATE	CRISPHEAD
CRETISM	CRICETID	CRINATED	CRISPIER
CRETISMS	CRICETIDS	CRINE	CRISPIEST
CRETONNE	CRICK	CRINED	CRISPILY
CRETONNES	CRICKED	CRINES	CRISPIN
CREUTZER	CRICKET	CRINGE	CRISPING
CREUTZERS	CRICKETED	CRINGED	CRISPINS
CREVALLE	CRICKETER	CRINGER	CRISPLY
CREVALLES	CRICKETS	CRINGERS	CRISPNESS
CREVASSE	CRICKEY	CRINGES	CRISPS
CREVASSED	CRICKING	CRINGING	CRISPY
CREVASSES	CRICKS	CRINGINGS	CRISSA
CREVETTE	CRICKY	CRINGLE	CRISSAL
CREVETTES	CRICOID	CRINGLES	CRISSUM

CRISTA	CROCKETS	CROODLE	CROSSABLE
CRISTAE	CROCKING	CROODLED	CROSSARM
CRISTATE	CROCKPOT	CROODLES	CROSSARMS
CRISTATED	CROCKPOTS	CROODLING	CROSSBAND
CRIT	CROCKS	CROOK	CROSSBAR
CRITERIA	CROCODILE	CROOKBACK	CROSSBARS
CRITERIAL	CROCOITE	CROOKED	CROSSBEAM
CRITERION	CROCOITES	CROOKEDER	CROSSBILL
CRITERIUM	CROCOSMIA	CROOKEDLY	CROSSBIT
CRITH	CROCS	CROOKER	CROSSBITE
CRITHS	CROCUS	CROOKERY	CROSSBOW
CRITIC	CROCUSES	CROOKEST	CROSSBOWS
CRITICAL	CROFT	CROOKING	CROSSBRED
CRITICISE	CROFTER	CROOKNECK	CROSSBUCK
CRITICISM	CROFTERS	CROOKS	CROSSCUT
CRITICIZE	CROFTING	CROOL	CROSSCUTS
CRITICS	CROFTINGS	CROOLED	CROSSE
CRITIQUE	CROFTS	CROOLING	CROSSED
CRITIQUED	CROG	CROOLS	CROSSER
CRITIQUES	CROGGED	CROON	CROSSERS
CRITS	CROGGIES	CROONED	CROSSES
CRITTER	CROGGING	CROONER	CROSSEST
CRITTERS	CROGGY	CROONERS	CROSSETTE
CRITTUR	CROGS	CROONING	CROSSFALL
CRITTURS	CROISSANT	CROONINGS	CROSSFIRE
CRIVENS	CROJIK	CROONS	CROSSFISH
CRIVVENS	CROJIKS	CROOVE	CROSSHAIR
CROAK	CROKINOLE	CROOVES	CROSSHEAD
CROAKED	CROMACK	CROP	CROSSING
CROAKER	CROMACKS	CROPBOUND	CROSSINGS
CROAKERS	CROMB	CROPFUL	CROSSISH
CROAKIER	CROMBEC	CROPFULL	CROSSJACK
CROAKIEST	CROMBECS	CROPFULS	CROSSLET
CROAKILY	CROMBED	CROPLAND	CROSSLETS
CROAKING	CROMBING	CROPLANDS	CROSSLY
CROAKINGS	CROMBS	CROPLESS	CROSSNESS
CROAKS	CROME	CROPPED	CROSSOVER
CROAKY	CROMED	CROPPER	CROSSROAD
CROC	CROMES	CROPPERS	CROSSRUFF
CROCEATE	CROMING	CROPPIE	CROSSTALK
CROCEIN	CROMLECH	CROPPIES	CROSSTIE
CROCEINE	CROMLECHS	CROPPING	CROSSTIED
CROCEINES	CROMORNA	CROPPINGS	CROSSTIES
CROCEINS	CROMORNAS	CROPPY	CROSSTOWN
CROCEOUS	CROMORNE	CROPS	CROSSTREE
CROCHE	CROMORNES	CROPSICK	CROSSWALK
CROCHES	CRONE	CROQUANTE	CROSSWAY
CROCHET	CRONES	CROQUET	CROSSWAYS
CROCHETED	CRONET	CROQUETED	CROSSWIND
CROCHETER	CRONETS	CROQUETS	CROSSWISE
CROCHETS	CRONIES	CROQUETTE	CROSSWORD
CROCI	CRONISH	CROQUIS	CROSSWORT
CROCINE	CRONK	CRORE	CROST
CROCK	CRONKER	CRORES	CROSTINI
CROCKED	CRONKEST	CROSIER	CROSTINIS
CROCKERY	CRONY	CROSIERED	CROSTINO
CROCKET	CRONYISM	CROSIERS	CROTAL
CROCKETED	CRONYISMS	CROSS	CROTALA

CROTALINE
CROTALISM
CROTALS
CROTALUM
CROTCH
CROTCHED
CROTCHES
CROTCHET
CROTCHETS
CROTCHETY
CROTON
CROTONBUG
CROTONIC
CROTONS
CROTTLE
CROTTLES
CROUCH
CROUCHED
CROUCHES
CROUCHING
CROUP
CROUPADE
CROUPADES
CROUPE
CROUPED
CROUPER
CROUPERS
CROUPES
CROUPIER
CROUPIERS
CROUPIEST
CROUPILY
CROUPING
CROUPON
CROUPONS
CROUPOUS
CROUPS
CROUPY
CROUSE
CROUSELY
CROUSTADE
CROUT
CROUTE
CROUTES
CROUTON
CROUTONS
CROUTS
CROW
CROWBAR
CROWBARS
CROWBERRY
CROWBOOT
CROWBOOTS
CROWD
CROWDED
CROWDEDLY
CROWDER
CROWDERS

CROWDIE
CROWDIES
CROWDING
CROWDS
CROWDY
CROWEA
CROWEAS
CROWED
CROWER
CROWERS
CROWFEET
CROWFOOT
CROWFOOTS
CROWING
CROWINGLY
CROWN
CROWNED
CROWNER
CROWNERS
CROWNET
CROWNETS
CROWNING
CROWNINGS
CROWNLAND
CROWNLESS
CROWNLET
CROWNLETS
CROWNS
CROWNWORK
CROWS
CROWSFEET
CROWSFOOT
CROWSTEP
CROWSTEPS
CROZE
CROZER
CROZERS
CROZES
CROZIER
CROZIERS
CROZZLED
CRU
CRUBEEN
CRUBEENS
CRUCES
CRUCIAL
CRUCIALLY
CRUCIAN
CRUCIANS
CRUCIATE
CRUCIBLE
CRUCIBLES
CRUCIFER
CRUCIFERS
CRUCIFIED
CRUCIFIER
CRUCIFIES
CRUCIFIX

CRUCIFORM
CRUCIFY
CRUCK
CRUCKS
CRUD
CRUDDED
CRUDDIER
CRUDDIEST
CRUDDING
CRUDDLE
CRUDDLED
CRUDDLES
CRUDDLING
CRUDDY
CRUDE
CRUDELY
CRUDENESS
CRUDER
CRUDES
CRUDEST
CRUDITES
CRUDITIES
CRUDITY
CRUDS
CRUDY
CRUE
CRUEL
CRUELER
CRUELEST
CRUELLER
CRUELLEST
CRUELLS
CRUELLY
CRUELNESS
CRUELS
CRUELTIES
CRUELTY
CRUES
CRUET
CRUETS
CRUISE
CRUISED
CRUISER
CRUISERS
CRUISES
CRUISEWAY
CRUISIE
CRUISIES
CRUISING
CRUISINGS
CRUIVE
CRUIVES
CRUIZIE
CRUIZIES
CRULLER
CRULLERS
CRUMB
CRUMBED

CRUMBER
CRUMBERS
CRUMBIER
CRUMBIEST
CRUMBING
CRUMBLE
CRUMBLED
CRUMBLES
CRUMBLIER
CRUMBLIES
CRUMBLING
CRUMBLY
CRUMBS
CRUMBUM
CRUMBUMS
CRUMBY
CRUMEN
CRUMENAL
CRUMENALS
CRUMENS
CRUMHORN
CRUMHORNS
CRUMMACK
CRUMMACKS
CRUMMIE
CRUMMIER
CRUMMIES
CRUMMIEST
CRUMMOCK
CRUMMOCKS
CRUMMY
CRUMP
CRUMPED
CRUMPER
CRUMPEST
CRUMPET
CRUMPETS
CRUMPIER
CRUMPIEST
CRUMPING
CRUMPLE
CRUMPLED
CRUMPLES
CRUMPLIER
CRUMPLING
CRUMPLY
CRUMPS
CRUMPY
CRUNCH
CRUNCHED
CRUNCHER
CRUNCHERS
CRUNCHES
CRUNCHIE
CRUNCHIER
CRUNCHIES
CRUNCHILY
CRUNCHING

CRUNCHY
CRUNKLE
CRUNKLED
CRUNKLES
CRUNKLING
CRUNODAL
CRUNODE
CRUNODES
CRUOR
CRUORES
CRUORS
CRUPPER
CRUPPERS
CRURA
CRURAL
CRUS
CRUSADE
CRUSADED
CRUSADER
CRUSADERS
CRUSADES
CRUSADING
CRUSADO
CRUSADOES
CRUSADOS
CRUSE
CRUSES
CRUSET
CRUSETS
CRUSH
CRUSHABLE
CRUSHED
CRUSHER
CRUSHERS
CRUSHES
CRUSHING
CRUSIAN
CRUSIANS
CRUSIE
CRUSIES
CRUSILY
CRUST
CRUSTA
CRUSTACEA
CRUSTAE
CRUSTAL
CRUSTATE
CRUSTATED
CRUSTED
CRUSTIER
CRUSTIES
CRUSTIEST
CRUSTILY
CRUSTING
CRUSTLESS
CRUSTOSE
CRUSTS
CRUSTY

CRUSY
CRUTCH
CRUTCHED
CRUTCHES
CRUTCHING
CRUVE
CRUVES
CRUX
CRUXES
CRUZADO
CRUZADOES
CRUZADOS
CRUZEIRO
CRUZEIROS
CRUZIE
CRUZIES
CRWTH
CRWTHS
CRY
CRYBABIES
CRYBABY
CRYING
CRYINGLY
CRYINGS
CRYOBANK
CRYOBANKS
CRYOCABLE
CRYOGEN
CRYOGENIC
CRYOGENS
CRYOGENY
CRYOLITE
CRYOLITES
CRYOMETER
CRYOMETRY
CRYONIC
CRYONICS
CRYOPHYTE
CRYOPROBE
CRYOSCOPE
CRYOSCOPY
CRYOSTAT
CRYOSTATS
CRYOTRON
CRYOTRONS
CRYPT
CRYPTADIA
CRYPTAL
CRYPTIC
CRYPTICAL
CRYPTO
CRYPTOGAM
CRYPTON
CRYPTONS
CRYPTONYM
CRYPTOS
CRYPTS
CRYSTAL

CRYSTALS
CSARDAS
CSARDASES
CTENE
CTENES
CTENIDIA
CTENIDIUM
CTENIFORM
CTENOID
CUADRILLA
CUATRO
CUATROS
CUB
CUBAGE
CUBAGES
CUBANE
CUBANELLE
CUBANES
CUBATURE
CUBATURES
CUBBED
CUBBIES
CUBBING
CUBBINGS
CUBBISH
CUBBISHLY
CUBBY
CUBBYHOLE
CUBE
CUBEB
CUBEBS
CUBED
CUBER
CUBERS
CUBES
CUBHOOD
CUBHOODS
CUBIC
CUBICA
CUBICAL
CUBICALLY
CUBICAS
CUBICITY
CUBICLE
CUBICLES
CUBICLY
CUBICS
CUBICULA
CUBICULUM
CUBIFORM
CUBING
CUBISM
CUBISMS
CUBIST
CUBISTIC
CUBISTS
CUBIT
CUBITAL

CUBITI
CUBITS
CUBITUS
CUBITUSES
CUBLESS
CUBOID
CUBOIDAL
CUBOIDS
CUBS
CUCKING
CUCKOLD
CUCKOLDED
CUCKOLDLY
CUCKOLDOM
CUCKOLDRY
CUCKOLDS
CUCKOO
CUCKOOED
CUCKOOING
CUCKOOS
CUCULLATE
CUCUMBER
CUCUMBERS
CUCURBIT
CUCURBITS
CUD
CUDBEAR
CUDBEARS
CUDDEN
CUDDENS
CUDDIE
CUDDIES
CUDDIN
CUDDINS
CUDDLE
CUDDLED
CUDDLER
CUDDLERS
CUDDLES
CUDDLIER
CUDDLIEST
CUDDLING
CUDDLY
CUDDY
CUDGEL
CUDGELED
CUDGELER
CUDGELERS
CUDGELING
CUDGELLED
CUDGELLER
CUDGELS
CUDGERIE
CUDGERIES
CUDS
CUDWEED
CUDWEEDS
CUE

CUED	CULEX	CULTIGENS	CUMMINS
CUEING	CULEXES	CULTISH	CUMQUAT
CUEIST	CULICES	CULTISHLY	CUMQUATS
CUEISTS	CULICID	CULTISM	CUMSHAW
CUES	CULICIDS	CULTISMS	CUMSHAWS
CUESTA	CULICINE	CULTIST	CUMULATE
CUESTAS	CULICINES	CULTISTS	CUMULATED
CUFF	CULINARY	CULTIVAR	CUMULATES
CUFFED	CULL	CULTIVARS	CUMULET
CUFFIN	CULLAY	CULTIVATE	CUMULETS
CUFFING	CULLAYS	CULTLIKE	CUMULI
CUFFINS	CULLED	CULTRATE	CUMULOSE
CUFFLE	CULLENDER	CULTRATED	CUMULOUS
CUFFLED	CULLER	CULTS	CUMULUS
CUFFLES	CULLERS	CULTURAL	CUNABULA
CUFFLESS	CULLET	CULTURATI	CUNCTATOR
CUFFLING	CULLETS	CULTURE	CUNDIES
CUFFLINK	CULLIED	CULTURED	CUNDUM
CUFFLINKS	CULLIES	CULTURES	CUNDUMS
CUFFO	CULLING	CULTURING	CUNDY
CUFFS	CULLINGS	CULTURIST	CUNEAL
CUFFUFFLE	CULLION	CULTUS	CUNEATE
CUIF	CULLIONLY	CULTUSES	CUNEATED
CUIFS	CULLIONS	CULTY	CUNEATELY
CUING	CULLIS	CULVER	CUNEATIC
CUIRASS	CULLISES	CULVERIN	CUNEI
CUIRASSED	CULLS	CULVERINS	CUNEIFORM
CUIRASSES	CULLY	CULVERS	CUNETTE
CUISH	CULLYING	CULVERT	CUNETTES
CUISHES	CULLYISM	CULVERTS	CUNEUS
CUISINART	CULLYISMS	CUM	CUNIFORM
CUISINE	CULM	CUMACEAN	CUNIFORMS
CUISINES	CULMED	CUMACEANS	CUNJEVOI
CUISINIER	CULMEN	CUMARIC	CUNJEVOIS
CUISSE	CULMENS	CUMARIN	CUNNER
CUISSER	CULMINANT	CUMARINS	CUNNERS
CUISSERS	CULMINATE	CUMARONE	CUNNING
CUISSES	CULMING	CUMARONES	CUNNINGER
CUIT	CULMS	CUMBENT	CUNNINGLY
CUITER	CULOTTE	CUMBER	CUNNINGS
CUITERED	CULOTTES	CUMBERED	CUNT
CUITERING	CULPA	CUMBERER	CUNTS
CUITERS	CULPABLE	CUMBERERS	CUP
CUITIKIN	CULPABLY	CUMBERING	CUPBEARER
CUITIKINS	CULPAE	CUMBERS	CUPBOARD
CUITS	CULPATORY	CUMBIA	CUPBOARDS
CUITTLE	CULPRIT	CUMBIAS	CUPCAKE
CUITTLED	CULPRITS	CUMBRANCE	CUPCAKES
CUITTLES	CULT	CUMBROUS	CUPEL
CUITTLING	CULTCH	CUMBUNGI	CUPELED
CUKE	CULTCHES	CUMBUNGIS	CUPELER
CUKES	CULTER	CUMEC	CUPELERS
CULCH	CULTERS	CUMECS	CUPELING
CULCHES	CULTI	CUMIN	CUPELLED
CULCHIE	CULTIC	CUMINS	CUPELLER
CULCHIES	CULTIER	CUMMER	CUPELLERS
CULET	CULTIEST	CUMMERS	CUPELLING
CULETS	CULTIGEN	CUMMIN	CUPELS

CUPFERRON
CUPFUL
CUPFULS
CUPGALL
CUPGALLS
CUPHEAD
CUPHEADS
CUPID
CUPIDITY
CUPIDS
CUPLIKE
CUPMAN
CUPMEN
CUPOLA
CUPOLAED
CUPOLAING
CUPOLAR
CUPOLAS
CUPOLATED
CUPPA
CUPPAS
CUPPED
CUPPER
CUPPERS
CUPPIER
CUPPIEST
CUPPING
CUPPINGS
CUPPY
CUPREOUS
CUPRESSUS
CUPRIC
CUPRITE
CUPRITES
CUPROUS
CUPRUM
CUPRUMS
CUPS
CUPSFUL
CUPULA
CUPULAE
CUPULAR
CUPULATE
CUPULE
CUPULES
CUR
CURABLE
CURABLY
CURACAO
CURACAOS
CURACIES
CURACOA
CURACOAS
CURACY
CURAGH
CURAGHS
CURANDERA
CURANDERO

CURARA
CURARAS
CURARE
CURARES
CURARI
CURARINE
CURARINES
CURARIS
CURARISE
CURARISED
CURARISES
CURARIZE
CURARIZED
CURARIZES
CURASSOW
CURASSOWS
CURAT
CURATE
CURATED
CURATES
CURATING
CURATIVE
CURATIVES
CURATOR
CURATORS
CURATORY
CURATRIX
CURATS
CURB
CURBABLE
CURBED
CURBER
CURBERS
CURBING
CURBINGS
CURBLESS
CURBS
CURBSIDE
CURBSIDES
CURBSTONE
CURCH
CURCHEF
CURCHEFS
CURCHES
CURCULIO
CURCULIOS
CURCUMA
CURCUMAS
CURCUMIN
CURCUMINE
CURCUMINS
CURD
CURDED
CURDIER
CURDIEST
CURDINESS
CURDING
CURDLE

CURDLED
CURDLER
CURDLERS
CURDLES
CURDLING
CURDS
CURDY
CURE
CURED
CURELESS
CURER
CURERS
CURES
CURET
CURETS
CURETTAGE
CURETTE
CURETTED
CURETTES
CURETTING
CURF
CURFEW
CURFEWS
CURFS
CURFUFFLE
CURIA
CURIAE
CURIAL
CURIALISM
CURIALIST
CURIAS
CURIE
CURIES
CURIET
CURIETS
CURING
CURIO
CURIOS
CURIOSA
CURIOSITY
CURIOUS
CURIOUSER
CURIOUSLY
CURITE
CURITES
CURIUM
CURIUMS
CURL
CURLED
CURLER
CURLERS
CURLEW
CURLEWS
CURLI
CURLICUE
CURLICUED
CURLICUES
CURLIER

CURLIES
CURLIEST
CURLILY
CURLINESS
CURLING
CURLINGS
CURLPAPER
CURLS
CURLY
CURLYCUE
CURLYCUES
CURN
CURNEY
CURNIER
CURNIEST
CURNS
CURNY
CURPEL
CURPELS
CURR
CURRACH
CURRACHS
CURRAGH
CURRAGHS
CURRAJONG
CURRAN
CURRANS
CURRANT
CURRANTS
CURRANTY
CURRAWONG
CURRED
CURREJONG
CURRENCY
CURRENT
CURRENTLY
CURRENTS
CURRICLE
CURRICLES
CURRICULA
CURRIE
CURRIED
CURRIER
CURRIERS
CURRIERY
CURRIES
CURRIJONG
CURRING
CURRISH
CURRISHLY
CURRS
CURRY
CURRYCOMB
CURRYING
CURRYINGS
CURS
CURSAL
CURSE

CURSED	CURTSYING	CUSPIDAL	CUTCHES
CURSEDER	CURULE	CUSPIDATE	CUTDOWN
CURSEDEST	CURVATE	CUSPIDES	CUTDOWNS
CURSEDLY	CURVATED	CUSPIDOR	CUTE
CURSENARY	CURVATION	CUSPIDORE	CUTELY
CURSER	CURVATIVE	CUSPIDORS	CUTENESS
CURSERS	CURVATURE	CUSPIDS	CUTER
CURSES	CURVE	CUSPIS	CUTES
CURSI	CURVEBALL	CUSPS	CUTESIE
CURSING	CURVED	CUSS	CUTESIER
CURSINGS	CURVEDLY	CUSSED	CUTESIEST
CURSITOR	CURVES	CUSSEDLY	CUTEST
CURSITORS	CURVESOME	CUSSER	CUTESY
CURSITORY	CURVET	CUSSERS	CUTEY
CURSIVE	CURVETED	CUSSES	CUTEYS
CURSIVELY	CURVETING	CUSSING	CUTGLASS
CURSIVES	CURVETS	CUSSO	CUTGRASS
CURSOR	CURVETTED	CUSSOS	CUTICLE
CURSORARY	CURVEY	CUSSWORD	CUTICLES
CURSORES	CURVIER	CUSSWORDS	CUTICULA
CURSORIAL	CURVIEST	CUSTARD	CUTICULAE
CURSORILY	CURVIFORM	CUSTARDS	CUTICULAR
CURSORS	CURVING	CUSTARDY	CUTIE
CURSORY	CURVITAL	CUSTOCK	CUTIES
CURST	CURVITIES	CUSTOCKS	CUTIKIN
CURSTNESS	CURVITY	CUSTODE	CUTIKINS
CURSUS	CURVY	CUSTODES	CUTIN
CURT	CUSCUS	CUSTODIAL	CUTINISE
CURTAIL	CUSCUSES	CUSTODIAN	CUTINISED
CURTAILED	CUSEC	CUSTODIER	CUTINISES
CURTAILER	CUSECS	CUSTODIES	CUTINIZE
CURTAILS	CUSH	CUSTODY	CUTINIZED
CURTAIN	CUSHAT	CUSTOM	CUTINIZES
CURTAINED	CUSHATS	CUSTOMARY	CUTINS
CURTAINS	CUSHAW	CUSTOMED	CUTIS
CURTAL	CUSHAWS	CUSTOMER	CUTISES
CURTALAX	CUSHES	CUSTOMERS	CUTLAS
CURTALAXE	CUSHIE	CUSTOMISE	CUTLASES
CURTALS	CUSHIER	CUSTOMIZE	CUTLASS
CURTANA	CUSHIES	CUSTOMS	CUTLASSES
CURTANAS	CUSHIEST	CUSTOS	CUTLER
CURTATE	CUSHILY	CUSTREL	CUTLERIES
CURTATION	CUSHINESS	CUSTRELS	CUTLERS
CURTAXE	CUSHION	CUSTUMAL	CUTLERY
CURTAXES	CUSHIONED	CUSTUMALS	CUTLET
CURTER	CUSHIONET	CUSTUMARY	CUTLETS
CURTESIES	CUSHIONS	CUT	CUTLINE
CURTEST	CUSHIONY	CUTANEOUS	CUTLINES
CURTESY	CUSHTY	CUTAWAY	CUTOFF
CURTILAGE	CUSHY	CUTAWAYS	CUTOFFS
CURTLY	CUSK	CUTBACK	CUTOUT
CURTNESS	CUSKS	CUTBACKS	CUTOUTS
CURTSEY	CUSP	CUTBANK	CUTOVER
CURTSEYED	CUSPAL	CUTBANKS	CUTOVERS
CURTSEYS	CUSPATE	CUTCH	CUTPURSE
CURTSIED	CUSPATED	CUTCHA	CUTPURSES
CURTSIES	CUSPED	CUTCHERRY	CUTS
CURTSY	CUSPID	CUTCHERY	CUTTABLE

CUTTAGE	CYANISES	CYCLER	CYGNETS
CUTTAGES	CYANISING	CYCLERIES	CYLICES
CUTTER	CYANITE	CYCLERS	CYLINDER
CUTTERS	CYANITES	CYCLERY	CYLINDERS
CUTTHROAT	CYANITIC	CYCLES	CYLINDRIC
CUTTIER	CYANIZE	CYCLEWAY	CYLIX
CUTTIES	CYANIZED	CYCLEWAYS	CYMA
CUTTIEST	CYANIZES	CYCLIC	CYMAE
CUTTING	CYANIZING	CYCLICAL	CYMAGRAPH
CUTTINGLY	CYANO	CYCLICALS	CYMAR
CUTTINGS	CYANOGEN	CYCLICISM	CYMARS
CUTTLE	CYANOGENS	CYCLICITY	CYMAS
CUTTLED	CYANOSED	CYCLICLY	CYMATIA
CUTTLES	CYANOSES	CYCLIN	CYMATICS
CUTTLING	CYANOSIS	CYCLING	CYMATIUM
CUTTO	CYANOTIC	CYCLINGS	CYMBAL
CUTTOE	CYANOTYPE	CYCLINS	CYMBALEER
CUTTOES	CYANS	CYCLISE	CYMBALER
CUTTY	CYANURATE	CYCLISED	CYMBALERS
CUTUP	CYANURET	CYCLISES	CYMBALIST
CUTUPS	CYANURETS	CYCLISING	CYMBALO
CUTWATER	CYATHI	CYCLIST	CYMBALOES
CUTWATERS	CYATHIA	CYCLISTS	CYMBALOM
CUTWORK	CYATHIUM	CYCLITOL	CYMBALOMS
CUTWORKS	CYATHUS	CYCLITOLS	CYMBALOS
CUTWORM	CYBER	CYCLIZE	CYMBALS
CUTWORMS	CYBERCAFE	CYCLIZED	CYMBIDIA
CUVEE	CYBERCAST	CYCLIZES	CYMBIDIUM
CUVEES	CYBERNATE	CYCLIZINE	CYMBIFORM
CUVETTE	CYBERNAUT	CYCLIZING	CYMBLING
CUVETTES	CYBERPET	CYCLO	CYMBLINGS
CUZ	CYBERPETS	CYCLOGIRO	CYME
CUZZES	CYBERPORN	CYCLOID	CYMENE
CWM	CYBERPUNK	CYCLOIDAL	CYMENES
CWMS	CYBERSEX	CYCLOIDS	CYMES
CWTCH	CYBERWAR	CYCLOLITH	CYMLIN
CWTCHED	CYBERWARS	CYCLONAL	CYMLING
CWTCHES	CYBORG	CYCLONE	CYMLINGS
CWTCHING	CYBORGS	CYCLONES	CYMLINS
CYAN	CYBRARIAN	CYCLONIC	CYMOGENE
CYANAMID	CYBRID	CYCLONITE	CYMOGENES
CYANAMIDE	CYBRIDS	CYCLOPEAN	CYMOGRAPH
CYANAMIDS	CYCAD	CYCLOPES	CYMOID
CYANATE	CYCADEOID	CYCLOPIAN	CYMOL
CYANATES	CYCADS	CYCLOPIC	CYMOLS
CYANIC	CYCAS	CYCLOPS	CYMOPHANE
CYANID	CYCASES	CYCLORAMA	CYMOSE
CYANIDE	CYCASIN	CYCLOS	CYMOSELY
CYANIDED	CYCASINS	CYCLOSES	CYMOUS
CYANIDES	CYCLAMATE	CYCLOSIS	CYNANCHE
CYANIDING	CYCLAMEN	CYCLOTRON	CYNANCHES
CYANIDS	CYCLAMENS	CYCLUS	CYNEGETIC
CYANIN	CYCLASE	CYCLUSES	CYNIC
CYANINE	CYCLASES	CYDER	CYNICAL
CYANINES	CYCLE	CYDERS	CYNICALLY
CYANINS	CYCLECAR	CYESES	CYNICISM
CYANISE	CYCLECARS	CYESIS	CYNICISMS
CYANISED	CYCLED	CYGNET	CYNICS

CYNODONT
CYNODONTS
CYNOMOLGI
CYNOSURAL
CYNOSURE
CYNOSURES
CYPHER
CYPHERED
CYPHERING
CYPHERS
CYPRES
CYPRESES
CYPRESS
CYPRESSES
CYPRIAN
CYPRIANS
CYPRID
CYPRIDES
CYPRIDS
CYPRINE
CYPRINID
CYPRINIDS
CYPRINOID
CYPRIS
CYPRUS
CYPRUSES
CYPSELA
CYPSELAE
CYST
CYSTEIN
CYSTEINE
CYSTEINES
CYSTEINIC
CYSTEINS
CYSTIC
CYSTID
CYSTIDEAN
CYSTIDS
CYSTIFORM
CYSTINE
CYSTINES
CYSTITIS
CYSTOCARP
CYSTOCELE
CYSTOID
CYSTOIDS
CYSTOLITH
CYSTOTOMY
CYSTS
CYTASE
CYTASES
CYTASTER
CYTASTERS
CYTE
CYTES
CYTIDINE
CYTIDINES
CYTIDYLIC

CYTISI
CYTISINE
CYTISINES
CYTISUS
CYTODE
CYTODES
CYTOGENY
CYTOID
CYTOKINE
CYTOKINES
CYTOKININ
CYTOLOGIC
CYTOLOGY
CYTOLYSES
CYTOLYSIN
CYTOLYSIS
CYTOLYTIC
CYTOMETER
CYTOMETRY
CYTON
CYTONS
CYTOPENIA
CYTOPLASM
CYTOPLAST
CYTOSINE
CYTOSINES
CYTOSOL
CYTOSOLIC
CYTOSOLS
CYTOSOME
CYTOSOMES
CYTOTAXES
CYTOTAXIS
CYTOTOXIC
CYTOTOXIN
CZAPKA
CZAPKAS
CZAR
CZARDAS
CZARDASES
CZARDOM
CZARDOMS
CZAREVICH
CZAREVNA
CZAREVNAS
CZARINA
CZARINAS
CZARISM
CZARISMS
CZARIST
CZARISTS
CZARITSA
CZARITSAS
CZARITZA
CZARITZAS
CZARS

D

DA	DAD	DAFTARS	DAHOONS
DAB	DADA	DAFTER	DAHS
DABBA	DADAH	DAFTEST	DAIDLE
DABBAS	DADAHS	DAFTIE	DAIDLED
DABBED	DADAISM	DAFTIES	DAIDLES
DABBER	DADAISMS	DAFTLY	DAIDLING
DABBERS	DADAIST	DAFTNESS	DAIDZEIN
DABBING	DADAISTIC	DAG	DAIDZEINS
DABBITIES	DADAISTS	DAGABA	DAIKER
DABBITY	DADAS	DAGABAS	DAIKERED
DABBLE	DADDED	DAGGA	DAIKERING
DABBLED	DADDIES	DAGGAS	DAIKERS
DABBLER	DADDING	DAGGED	DAIKON
DABBLERS	DADDLE	DAGGER	DAIKONS
DABBLES	DADDLED	DAGGERED	DAILIES
DABBLING	DADDLES	DAGGERING	DAILINESS
DABBLINGS	DADDLING	DAGGERS	DAILY
DABCHICK	DADDOCK	DAGGIER	DAILYNESS
DABCHICKS	DADDOCKS	DAGGIEST	DAIMEN
DABS	DADDY	DAGGING	DAIMIO
DABSTER	DADGUM	DAGGINGS	DAIMIOS
DABSTERS	DADO	DAGGLE	DAIMOKU
DACE	DADOED	DAGGLED	DAIMOKUS
DACES	DADOES	DAGGLES	DAIMON
DACHA	DADOING	DAGGLING	DAIMONES
DACHAS	DADOS	DAGGY	DAIMONIC
DACHSHUND	DADS	DAGLOCK	DAIMONS
DACITE	DAE	DAGLOCKS	DAIMYO
DACITES	DAEDAL	DAGO	DAIMYOS
DACK	DAEDALEAN	DAGOBA	DAINE
DACKED	DAEDALIAN	DAGOBAS	DAINED
DACKER	DAEDALIC	DAGOES	DAINES
DACKERED	DAEING	DAGOS	DAINING
DACKERING	DAEMON	DAGS	DAINT
DACKERS	DAEMONES	DAGWOOD	DAINTIER
DACKING	DAEMONIC	DAGWOODS	DAINTIES
DACKS	DAEMONS	DAH	DAINTIEST
DACOIT	DAES	DAHABEAH	DAINTILY
DACOITAGE	DAFF	DAHABEAHS	DAINTY
DACOITIES	DAFFED	DAHABEEAH	DAIQUIRI
DACOITS	DAFFIER	DAHABIAH	DAIQUIRIS
DACOITY	DAFFIES	DAHABIAHS	DAIRIES
DACQUOISE	DAFFIEST	DAHABIEH	DAIRY
DACRON	DAFFILY	DAHABIEHS	DAIRYING
DACRONS	DAFFINESS	DAHABIYA	DAIRYINGS
DACTYL	DAFFING	DAHABIYAH	DAIRYMAID
DACTYLAR	DAFFINGS	DAHABIYAS	DAIRYMAN
DACTYLI	DAFFODIL	DAHABIYEH	DAIRYMEN
DACTYLIC	DAFFODILS	DAHL	DAIS
DACTYLICS	DAFFS	DAHLIA	DAISES
DACTYLIST	DAFFY	DAHLIAS	DAISHIKI
DACTYLS	DAFT	DAHLS	DAISHIKIS
DACTYLUS	DAFTAR	DAHOON	DAISIED

DAISIES	DALTS	DAMNINGLY	DANDIACAL
DAISY	DAM	DAMNS	DANDIER
DAK	DAMAGE	DAMOISEL	DANDIES
DAKER	DAMAGED	DAMOISELS	DANDIEST
DAKERED	DAMAGER	DAMOSEL	DANDIFIED
DAKERHEN	DAMAGERS	DAMOSELS	DANDIFIES
DAKERHENS	DAMAGES	DAMOZEL	DANDIFY
DAKERING	DAMAGING	DAMOZELS	DANDILY
DAKERS	DAMAN	DAMP	DANDIPRAT
DAKOIT	DAMANS	DAMPED	DANDLE
DAKOITI	DAMAR	DAMPEN	DANDLED
DAKOITIES	DAMARS	DAMPENED	DANDLER
DAKOITIS	DAMASCENE	DAMPENER	DANDLERS
DAKOITS	DAMASK	DAMPENERS	DANDLES
DAKOITY	DAMASKED	DAMPENING	DANDLING
DAKS	DAMASKEEN	DAMPENS	DANDRIFF
DAL	DAMASKIN	DAMPER	DANDRIFFS
DALAPON	DAMASKING	DAMPERS	DANDRUFF
DALAPONS	DAMASKINS	DAMPEST	DANDRUFFS
DALASI	DAMASKS	DAMPIER	DANDRUFFY
DALASIS	DAMASQUIN	DAMPIEST	DANDY
DALE	DAMASSIN	DAMPING	DANDYFUNK
DALED	DAMASSINS	DAMPINGS	DANDYISH
DALEDH	DAMBOARD	DAMPISH	DANDYISM
DALEDHS	DAMBOARDS	DAMPLY	DANDYISMS
DALEDS	DAMBROD	DAMPNESS	DANDYPRAT
DALES	DAMBRODS	DAMPS	DANEGELD
DALESMAN	DAME	DAMPY	DANEGELDS
DALESMEN	DAMES	DAMS	DANEGELT
DALETH	DAMEWORT	DAMSEL	DANEGELTS
DALETHS	DAMEWORTS	DAMSELFLY	DANELAGH
DALGYTE	DAMFOOL	DAMSELS	DANELAGHS
DALGYTES	DAMIANA	DAMSON	DANELAW
DALI	DAMIANAS	DAMSONS	DANELAWS
DALIS	DAMMAR	DAN	DANEWEED
DALLE	DAMMARS	DANAZOL	DANEWEEDS
DALLES	DAMME	DANAZOLS	DANEWORT
DALLIANCE	DAMMED	DANCE	DANEWORTS
DALLIED	DAMMER	DANCEABLE	DANG
DALLIER	DAMMERS	DANCED	DANGED
DALLIERS	DAMMING	DANCEHALL	DANGER
DALLIES	DAMMIT	DANCER	DANGERED
DALLOP	DAMN	DANCERS	DANGERING
DALLOPS	DAMNABLE	DANCES	DANGEROUS
DALLY	DAMNABLY	DANCETTE	DANGERS
DALLYING	DAMNATION	DANCETTEE	DANGING
DALMAHOY	DAMNATORY	DANCETTES	DANGLE
DALMAHOYS	DAMNDEST	DANCETTY	DANGLED
DALMATIAN	DAMNDESTS	DANCEY	DANGLER
DALMATIC	DAMNED	DANCIER	DANGLERS
DALMATICS	DAMNEDER	DANCIEST	DANGLES
DALS	DAMNEDEST	DANCING	DANGLIER
DALT	DAMNER	DANCINGS	DANGLIEST
DALTON	DAMNERS	DANDELION	DANGLING
DALTONIAN	DAMNIFIED	DANDER	DANGLINGS
DALTONIC	DAMNIFIES	DANDERED	DANGLY
DALTONISM	DAMNIFY	DANDERING	DANGS
DALTONS	DAMNING	DANDERS	DANIO

DANIOS
DANISH
DANISHES
DANK
DANKER
DANKEST
DANKISH
DANKLY
DANKNESS
DANKS
DANNEBROG
DANNIES
DANNY
DANS
DANSEUR
DANSEURS
DANSEUSE
DANSEUSES
DANT
DANTED
DANTHONIA
DANTING
DANTON
DANTONED
DANTONING
DANTONS
DANTS
DAP
DAPHNE
DAPHNES
DAPHNIA
DAPHNIAS
DAPHNID
DAPHNIDS
DAPPED
DAPPER
DAPPERER
DAPPEREST
DAPPERLY
DAPPERS
DAPPING
DAPPLE
DAPPLED
DAPPLES
DAPPLING
DAPS
DAPSONE
DAPSONES
DAQUIRI
DAQUIRIS
DARAF
DARAFS
DARB
DARBAR
DARBARS
DARBIES
DARBS
DARCIES

DARCY
DARCYS
DARE
DARED
DAREDEVIL
DAREFUL
DARER
DARERS
DARES
DARESAY
DARG
DARGA
DARGAH
DARGAHS
DARGAS
DARGLE
DARGLES
DARGS
DARI
DARIC
DARICS
DARING
DARINGLY
DARINGS
DARIOLE
DARIOLES
DARIS
DARK
DARKED
DARKEN
DARKENED
DARKENER
DARKENERS
DARKENING
DARKENS
DARKER
DARKEST
DARKEY
DARKEYS
DARKIE
DARKIES
DARKING
DARKISH
DARKLE
DARKLED
DARKLES
DARKLIER
DARKLIEST
DARKLING
DARKLINGS
DARKLY
DARKMANS
DARKNESS
DARKROOM
DARKROOMS
DARKS
DARKSOME
DARKY

DARLING
DARLINGLY
DARLINGS
DARN
DARNATION
DARNDEST
DARNDESTS
DARNED
DARNEDER
DARNEDEST
DARNEL
DARNELS
DARNER
DARNERS
DARNING
DARNINGS
DARNS
DAROGHA
DAROGHAS
DARRAIGN
DARRAIGNE
DARRAIGNS
DARRAIN
DARRAINE
DARRAINED
DARRAINES
DARRAINS
DARRAYN
DARRAYNED
DARRAYNS
DARRE
DARRED
DARRES
DARRING
DARSHAN
DARSHANS
DART
DARTBOARD
DARTED
DARTER
DARTERS
DARTING
DARTINGLY
DARTLE
DARTLED
DARTLES
DARTLING
DARTRE
DARTRES
DARTROUS
DARTS
DARZI
DARZIS
DAS
DASH
DASHBOARD
DASHED
DASHEEN

DASHEENS
DASHEKI
DASHEKIS
DASHER
DASHERS
DASHES
DASHI
DASHIER
DASHIEST
DASHIKI
DASHIKIS
DASHING
DASHINGLY
DASHIS
DASHPOT
DASHPOTS
DASHY
DASSIE
DASSIES
DASTARD
DASTARDLY
DASTARDS
DASTARDY
DASYMETER
DASYPOD
DASYPODS
DASYURE
DASYURES
DATA
DATABANK
DATABANKS
DATABASE
DATABASED
DATABASES
DATABLE
DATABUS
DATABUSES
DATACARD
DATACARDS
DATACOMMS
DATAFLOW
DATAGLOVE
DATAL
DATALLER
DATALLERS
DATALS
DATARIA
DATARIAS
DATARIES
DATARY
DATCHA
DATCHAS
DATE
DATEABLE
DATEBOOK
DATEBOOKS
DATED
DATEDLY

DATEDNESS	DAUNERS	DAWISH	DAYMARES
DATELESS	DAUNT	DAWK	DAYMARK
DATELINE	DAUNTED	DAWKS	DAYMARKS
DATELINED	DAUNTER	DAWN	DAYNT
DATELINES	DAUNTERS	DAWNED	DAYROOM
DATER	DAUNTING	DAWNER	DAYROOMS
DATERS	DAUNTLESS	DAWNERED	DAYS
DATES	DAUNTON	DAWNERING	DAYSACK
DATING	DAUNTONED	DAWNERS	DAYSACKS
DATINGS	DAUNTONS	DAWNEY	DAYSHELL
DATIVAL	DAUNTS	DAWNING	DAYSHELLS
DATIVE	DAUPHIN	DAWNINGS	DAYSIDE
DATIVELY	DAUPHINE	DAWNLIKE	DAYSIDES
DATIVES	DAUPHINES	DAWNS	DAYSMAN
DATO	DAUPHINS	DAWS	DAYSMEN
DATOLITE	DAUR	DAWSONITE	DAYSPRING
DATOLITES	DAURED	DAWT	DAYSTAR
DATOS	DAURING	DAWTED	DAYSTARS
DATTO	DAURS	DAWTIE	DAYTALE
DATTOS	DAUT	DAWTIES	DAYTALER
DATUM	DAUTED	DAWTING	DAYTALERS
DATUMS	DAUTIE	DAWTS	DAYTALES
DATURA	DAUTIES	DAY	DAYTIME
DATURAS	DAUTING	DAYAN	DAYTIMES
DATURIC	DAUTS	DAYANIM	DAYWORK
DATURINE	DAVEN	DAYANS	DAYWORKER
DATURINES	DAVENED	DAYBED	DAYWORKS
DAUB	DAVENING	DAYBEDS	DAZE
DAUBE	DAVENPORT	DAYBOOK	DAZED
DAUBED	DAVENS	DAYBOOKS	DAZEDLY
DAUBER	DAVIDIA	DAYBOY	DAZEDNESS
DAUBERIES	DAVIDIAS	DAYBOYS	DAZER
DAUBERS	DAVIES	DAYBREAK	DAZERS
DAUBERY	DAVIT	DAYBREAKS	DAZES
DAUBES	DAVITS	DAYCARE	DAZING
DAUBIER	DAVY	DAYCARES	DAZZLE
DAUBIEST	DAW	DAYCENTRE	DAZZLED
DAUBING	DAWAH	DAYCH	DAZZLER
DAUBINGLY	DAWAHS	DAYCHED	DAZZLERS
DAUBINGS	DAWBAKE	DAYCHES	DAZZLES
DAUBRIES	DAWBAKES	DAYCHING	DAZZLING
DAUBRY	DAWBRIES	DAYDREAM	DAZZLINGS
DAUBS	DAWBRY	DAYDREAMS	DE
DAUBY	DAWCOCK	DAYDREAMT	DEACIDIFY
DAUD	DAWCOCKS	DAYDREAMY	DEACON
DAUDED	DAWD	DAYFLIES	DEACONED
DAUDING	DAWDED	DAYFLOWER	DEACONESS
DAUDS	DAWDING	DAYFLY	DEACONING
DAUGHTER	DAWDLE	DAYGLO	DEACONRY
DAUGHTERS	DAWDLED	DAYGLOW	DEACONS
DAULT	DAWDLER	DAYGLOWS	DEAD
DAULTS	DAWDLERS	DAYLIGHT	DEADBEAT
DAUNDER	DAWDLES	DAYLIGHTS	DEADBEATS
DAUNDERED	DAWDLING	DAYLILIES	DEADBOLT
DAUNDERS	DAWDS	DAYLILY	DEADBOLTS
DAUNER	DAWED	DAYLIT	DEADBOY
DAUNERED	DAWEN	DAYLONG	DEADBOYS
DAUNERING	DAWING	DAYMARE	DEADED

DEADEN	DEALATED	DEATHBEDS	DEBATING
DEADENED	DEALATES	DEATHBLOW	DEBAUCH
DEADENER	DEALATION	DEATHCUP	DEBAUCHED
DEADENERS	DEALBATE	DEATHCUPS	DEBAUCHEE
DEADENING	DEALER	DEATHFUL	DEBAUCHER
DEADENS	DEALERS	DEATHIER	DEBAUCHES
DEADER	DEALFISH	DEATHIEST	DEBBIER
DEADERS	DEALING	DEATHLESS	DEBBIES
DEADEST	DEALINGS	DEATHLIER	DEBBIEST
DEADEYE	DEALS	DEATHLIKE	DEBBY
DEADEYES	DEALT	DEATHLY	DEBE
DEADFALL	DEAMINASE	DEATHS	DEBEAK
DEADFALLS	DEAMINATE	DEATHSMAN	DEBEAKED
DEADHEAD	DEAMINISE	DEATHSMEN	DEBEAKING
DEADHEADS	DEAMINIZE	DEATHTRAP	DEBEAKS
DEADHOUSE	DEAN	DEATHWARD	DEBEARD
DEADING	DEANED	DEATHY	DEBEARDED
DEADLIER	DEANER	DEAVE	DEBEARDS
DEADLIEST	DEANERIES	DEAVED	DEBEL
DEADLIFT	DEANERS	DEAVES	DEBELLED
DEADLIFTS	DEANERY	DEAVING	DEBELLING
DEADLIGHT	DEANING	DEAW	DEBELS
DEADLINE	DEANS	DEAWIE	DEBENTURE
DEADLINED	DEANSHIP	DEAWS	DEBES
DEADLINES	DEANSHIPS	DEAWY	DEBILE
DEADLOCK	DEAR	DEB	DEBILITY
DEADLOCKS	DEARE	DEBACLE	DEBIT
DEADLY	DEARED	DEBACLES	DEBITED
DEADMAN	DEARER	DEBAG	DEBITING
DEADMEN	DEARES	DEBAGGED	DEBITOR
DEADNESS	DEAREST	DEBAGGING	DEBITORS
DEADPAN	DEARIE	DEBAGS	DEBITS
DEADPANS	DEARIES	DEBAR	DEBONAIR
DEADS	DEARING	DEBARK	DEBONAIRE
DEADSTOCK	DEARLING	DEBARKED	DEBONE
DEADWOOD	DEARLINGS	DEBARKER	DEBONED
DEADWOODS	DEARLY	DEBARKERS	DEBONER
DEAERATE	DEARN	DEBARKING	DEBONERS
DEAERATED	DEARNESS	DEBARKS	DEBONES
DEAERATES	DEARNFUL	DEBARMENT	DEBONING
DEAERATOR	DEARNLY	DEBARRASS	DEBOSH
DEAF	DEARNS	DEBARRED	DEBOSHED
DEAFBLIND	DEARS	DEBARRING	DEBOSHES
DEAFEN	DEARTH	DEBARS	DEBOSHING
DEAFENED	DEARTHS	DEBASE	DEBOSS
DEAFENING	DEARY	DEBASED	DEBOSSED
DEAFENS	DEASH	DEBASER	DEBOSSES
DEAFER	DEASHED	DEBASERS	DEBOSSING
DEAFEST	DEASHES	DEBASES	DEBOUCH
DEAFISH	DEASHING	DEBASING	DEBOUCHE
DEAFLY	DEASIL	DEBATABLE	DEBOUCHED
DEAFNESS	DEASILS	DEBATABLY	DEBOUCHES
DEAIR	DEASIUL	DEBATE	DEBRIDE
DEAIRED	DEASIULS	DEBATED	DEBRIDED
DEAIRING	DEASOIL	DEBATEFUL	DEBRIDES
DEAIRS	DEASOILS	DEBATER	DEBRIDING
DEAL	DEATH	DEBATERS	DEBRIEF
DEALATE	DEATHBED	DEBATES	DEBRIEFED

DEBRIEFER	DECADENTS	DECAUDATE	DECIBELS
DEBRIEFS	DECADES	DECAY	DECIDABLE
DEBRIS	DECADS	DECAYABLE	DECIDE
DEBRUISE	DECAF	DECAYED	DECIDED
DEBRUISED	DECAFF	DECAYER	DECIDEDLY
DEBRUISES	DECAFFS	DECAYERS	DECIDER
DEBS	DECAFS	DECAYING	DECIDERS
DEBT	DECAGON	DECAYLESS	DECIDES
DEBTED	DECAGONAL	DECAYS	DECIDING
DEBTEE	DECAGONS	DECCIE	DECIDUA
DEBTEES	DECAGRAM	DECCIES	DECIDUAE
DEBTLESS	DECAGRAMS	DECEASE	DECIDUAL
DEBTOR	DECAHEDRA	DECEASED	DECIDUAS
DEBTORS	DECAL	DECEASES	DECIDUATE
DEBTS	DECALCIFY	DECEASING	DECIDUOUS
DEBUD	DECALED	DECEDENT	DECIGRAM
DEBUDDED	DECALING	DECEDENTS	DECIGRAMS
DEBUDDING	DECALITER	DECEIT	DECILE
DEBUDS	DECALITRE	DECEITFUL	DECILES
DEBUG	DECALLED	DECEITS	DECILITER
DEBUGGED	DECALLING	DECEIVE	DECILITRE
DEBUGGER	DECALOG	DECEIVED	DECILLION
DEBUGGERS	DECALOGS	DECEIVER	DECIMAL
DEBUGGING	DECALOGUE	DECEIVERS	DECIMALLY
DEBUGS	DECALS	DECEIVES	DECIMALS
DEBUNK	DECAMETER	DECEIVING	DECIMATE
DEBUNKED	DECAMETRE	DECELERON	DECIMATED
DEBUNKER	DECAMP	DECEMVIR	DECIMATES
DEBUNKERS	DECAMPED	DECEMVIRI	DECIMATOR
DEBUNKING	DECAMPING	DECEMVIRS	DECIME
DEBUNKS	DECAMPS	DECENARY	DECIMES
DEBURR	DECANAL	DECENCIES	DECIMETER
DEBURRED	DECANALLY	DECENCY	DECIMETRE
DEBURRING	DECANE	DECENNARY	DECIPHER
DEBURRS	DECANES	DECENNIA	DECIPHERS
DEBUS	DECANI	DECENNIAL	DECISION
DEBUSED	DECANOIC	DECENNIUM	DECISIONS
DEBUSES	DECANT	DECENT	DECISIVE
DEBUSING	DECANTATE	DECENTER	DECISORY
DEBUSSED	DECANTED	DECENTERS	DECISTERE
DEBUSSES	DECANTER	DECENTEST	DECK
DEBUSSING	DECANTERS	DECENTLY	DECKCHAIR
DEBUT	DECANTING	DECENTRE	DECKED
DEBUTANT	DECANTS	DECENTRED	DECKEL
DEBUTANTE	DECAPOD	DECENTRES	DECKELS
DEBUTANTS	DECAPODAL	DECEPTION	DECKER
DEBUTED	DECAPODAN	DECEPTIVE	DECKERS
DEBUTING	DECAPODS	DECEPTORY	DECKHAND
DEBUTS	DECARB	DECERN	DECKHANDS
DEBYE	DECARBED	DECERNED	DECKHOUSE
DEBYES	DECARBING	DECERNING	DECKING
DECACHORD	DECARBS	DECERNS	DECKINGS
DECAD	DECARE	DECERTIFY	DECKLE
DECADAL	DECARES	DECESSION	DECKLED
DECADE	DECASTERE	DECHEANCE	DECKLES
DECADENCE	DECASTICH	DECIARE	DECKO
DECADENCY	DECASTYLE	DECIARES	DECKOED
DECADENT	DECATHLON	DECIBEL	DECKOING

DECKOS
DECKS
DECLAIM
DECLAIMED
DECLAIMER
DECLAIMS
DECLARANT
DECLARE
DECLARED
DECLARER
DECLARERS
DECLARES
DECLARING
DECLASS
DECLASSE
DECLASSED
DECLASSEE
DECLASSES
DECLAW
DECLAWED
DECLAWING
DECLAWS
DECLINAL
DECLINANT
DECLINATE
DECLINE
DECLINED
DECLINER
DECLINERS
DECLINES
DECLINING
DECLINIST
DECLIVITY
DECLIVOUS
DECLUTCH
DECLUTTER
DECO
DECOCT
DECOCTED
DECOCTING
DECOCTION
DECOCTIVE
DECOCTS
DECOCTURE
DECODE
DECODED
DECODER
DECODERS
DECODES
DECODING
DECOHERER
DECOKE
DECOKED
DECOKES
DECOKING
DECOLLATE
DECOLLETE
DECOLOR

DECOLORED
DECOLORS
DECOLOUR
DECOLOURS
DECOMMIT
DECOMMITS
DECOMPLEX
DECOMPOSE
DECONGEST
DECONTROL
DECOR
DECORATE
DECORATED
DECORATES
DECORATOR
DECOROUS
DECORS
DECORUM
DECORUMS
DECOS
DECOUPAGE
DECOUPLE
DECOUPLED
DECOUPLER
DECOUPLES
DECOY
DECOYED
DECOYER
DECOYERS
DECOYING
DECOYS
DECREASE
DECREASED
DECREASES
DECREE
DECREED
DECREEING
DECREER
DECREERS
DECREES
DECREET
DECREETS
DECREMENT
DECREPIT
DECRETAL
DECRETALS
DECRETIST
DECRETIVE
DECRETORY
DECREW
DECREWED
DECREWING
DECREWS
DECRIAL
DECRIALS
DECRIED
DECRIER
DECRIERS

DECRIES
DECROWN
DECROWNED
DECROWNS
DECRY
DECRYING
DECRYPT
DECRYPTED
DECRYPTS
DECTET
DECTETS
DECUBITAL
DECUBITI
DECUBITUS
DECUMAN
DECUMANS
DECUMBENT
DECUPLE
DECUPLED
DECUPLES
DECUPLING
DECURIA
DECURIAS
DECURIES
DECURION
DECURIONS
DECURRENT
DECURSION
DECURSIVE
DECURVE
DECURVED
DECURVES
DECURVING
DECURY
DECUSSATE
DEDAL
DEDALIAN
DEDANS
DEDICANT
DEDICANTS
DEDICATE
DEDICATED
DEDICATEE
DEDICATES
DEDICATOR
DEDIMUS
DEDIMUSES
DEDUCE
DEDUCED
DEDUCES
DEDUCIBLE
DEDUCIBLY
DEDUCING
DEDUCT
DEDUCTED
DEDUCTING
DEDUCTION
DEDUCTIVE

DEDUCTS
DEE
DEED
DEEDED
DEEDER
DEEDEST
DEEDFUL
DEEDIER
DEEDIEST
DEEDILY
DEEDING
DEEDLESS
DEEDS
DEEDY
DEEING
DEEJAY
DEEJAYED
DEEJAYING
DEEJAYS
DEEK
DEELY
DEEM
DEEMED
DEEMING
DEEMS
DEEMSTER
DEEMSTERS
DEEN
DEENS
DEEP
DEEPEN
DEEPENED
DEEPENER
DEEPENERS
DEEPENING
DEEPENS
DEEPER
DEEPEST
DEEPFELT
DEEPFROZE
DEEPIE
DEEPIES
DEEPLY
DEEPMOST
DEEPNESS
DEEPS
DEEPWATER
DEER
DEERBERRY
DEERE
DEERFLIES
DEERFLY
DEERGRASS
DEERHORN
DEERHORNS
DEERHOUND
DEERLET
DEERLETS

DEERLIKE
DEERS
DEERSKIN
DEERSKINS
DEERWEED
DEERWEEDS
DEERYARD
DEERYARDS
DEES
DEET
DEETS
DEEV
DEEVE
DEEVED
DEEVES
DEEVING
DEEVS
DEEWAN
DEEWANS
DEF
DEFACE
DEFACED
DEFACER
DEFACERS
DEFACES
DEFACING
DEFAECATE
DEFALCATE
DEFAME
DEFAMED
DEFAMER
DEFAMERS
DEFAMES
DEFAMING
DEFAMINGS
DEFANG
DEFANGED
DEFANGING
DEFANGS
DEFAST
DEFASTE
DEFAT
DEFATS
DEFATTED
DEFATTING
DEFAULT
DEFAULTED
DEFAULTER
DEFAULTS
DEFEAT
DEFEATED
DEFEATER
DEFEATERS
DEFEATING
DEFEATISM
DEFEATIST
DEFEATS
DEFEATURE

DEFECATE
DEFECATED
DEFECATES
DEFECATOR
DEFECT
DEFECTED
DEFECTING
DEFECTION
DEFECTIVE
DEFECTOR
DEFECTORS
DEFECTS
DEFENCE
DEFENCED
DEFENCES
DEFENCING
DEFEND
DEFENDANT
DEFENDED
DEFENDER
DEFENDERS
DEFENDING
DEFENDS
DEFENSE
DEFENSED
DEFENSES
DEFENSING
DEFENSIVE
DEFER
DEFERABLE
DEFERENCE
DEFERENT
DEFERENTS
DEFERMENT
DEFERRAL
DEFERRALS
DEFERRED
DEFERRER
DEFERRERS
DEFERRING
DEFERS
DEFFER
DEFFEST
DEFFLY
DEFFO
DEFI
DEFIANCE
DEFIANCES
DEFIANT
DEFIANTLY
DEFICIENT
DEFICIT
DEFICITS
DEFIED
DEFIER
DEFIERS
DEFIES
DEFILADE

DEFILADED
DEFILADES
DEFILE
DEFILED
DEFILER
DEFILERS
DEFILES
DEFILING
DEFINABLE
DEFINABLY
DEFINE
DEFINED
DEFINER
DEFINERS
DEFINES
DEFINIENS
DEFINING
DEFINITE
DEFIS
DEFLATE
DEFLATED
DEFLATER
DEFLATERS
DEFLATES
DEFLATING
DEFLATION
DEFLATOR
DEFLATORS
DEFLEA
DEFLEAED
DEFLEAING
DEFLEAS
DEFLECT
DEFLECTED
DEFLECTOR
DEFLECTS
DEFLEX
DEFLEXED
DEFLEXES
DEFLEXING
DEFLEXION
DEFLEXURE
DEFLORATE
DEFLOWER
DEFLOWERS
DEFLUENT
DEFLUXION
DEFOAM
DEFOAMED
DEFOAMER
DEFOAMERS
DEFOAMING
DEFOAMS
DEFOCUS
DEFOCUSED
DEFOCUSES
DEFOG
DEFOGGED

DEFOGGER
DEFOGGERS
DEFOGGING
DEFOGS
DEFOLIANT
DEFOLIATE
DEFORCE
DEFORCED
DEFORCER
DEFORCERS
DEFORCES
DEFORCING
DEFOREST
DEFORESTS
DEFORM
DEFORMED
DEFORMER
DEFORMERS
DEFORMING
DEFORMITY
DEFORMS
DEFOUL
DEFOULED
DEFOULING
DEFOULS
DEFRAG
DEFRAGGED
DEFRAGGER
DEFRAGS
DEFRAUD
DEFRAUDED
DEFRAUDER
DEFRAUDS
DEFRAY
DEFRAYAL
DEFRAYALS
DEFRAYED
DEFRAYER
DEFRAYERS
DEFRAYING
DEFRAYS
DEFREEZE
DEFREEZES
DEFROCK
DEFROCKED
DEFROCKS
DEFROST
DEFROSTED
DEFROSTER
DEFROSTS
DEFROZE
DEFROZEN
DEFT
DEFTER
DEFTEST
DEFTLY
DEFTNESS
DEFUEL

DEFUELED	DEGRADERS	DEIFIC	DEKALOGY
DEFUELING	DEGRADES	DEIFICAL	DEKAMETER
DEFUELLED	DEGRADING	DEIFIED	DEKAMETRE
DEFUELS	DEGRAS	DEIFIER	DEKARE
DEFUNCT	DEGREASE	DEIFIERS	DEKARES
DEFUNCTS	DEGREASED	DEIFIES	DEKE
DEFUND	DEGREASER	DEIFORM	DEKED
DEFUNDED	DEGREASES	DEIFY	DEKEING
DEFUNDING	DEGREE	DEIFYING	DEKES
DEFUNDS	DEGREED	DEIGN	DEKING
DEFUSE	DEGREES	DEIGNED	DEKKO
DEFUSED	DEGS	DEIGNING	DEKKOED
DEFUSER	DEGUM	DEIGNS	DEKKOING
DEFUSERS	DEGUMMED	DEIL	DEKKOS
DEFUSES	DEGUMMING	DEILS	DEL
DEFUSING	DEGUMS	DEINDEX	DELAINE
DEFUZE	DEGUST	DEINDEXED	DELAINES
DEFUZED	DEGUSTATE	DEINDEXES	DELAPSE
DEFUZES	DEGUSTED	DEINOSAUR	DELAPSED
DEFUZING	DEGUSTING	DEIONISE	DELAPSES
DEFY	DEGUSTS	DEIONISED	DELAPSING
DEFYING	DEHISCE	DEIONISER	DELAPSION
DEG	DEHISCED	DEIONISES	DELATE
DEGAGE	DEHISCENT	DEIONIZE	DELATED
DEGAME	DEHISCES	DEIONIZED	DELATES
DEGAMES	DEHISCING	DEIONIZER	DELATING
DEGAMI	DEHORN	DEIONIZES	DELATION
DEGAMIS	DEHORNED	DEIPAROUS	DELATIONS
DEGARNISH	DEHORNER	DEISEAL	DELATOR
DEGAS	DEHORNERS	DEISEALS	DELATORS
DEGASES	DEHORNING	DEISHEAL	DELAY
DEGASSED	DEHORNS	DEISHEALS	DELAYABLE
DEGASSER	DEHORT	DEISM	DELAYED
DEGASSERS	DEHORTED	DEISMS	DELAYER
DEGASSES	DEHORTER	DEIST	DELAYERS
DEGASSING	DEHORTERS	DEISTIC	DELAYING
DEGAUSS	DEHORTING	DEISTICAL	DELAYS
DEGAUSSED	DEHORTS	DEISTS	DELE
DEGAUSSER	DEHYDRATE	DEITIES	DELEAD
DEGAUSSES	DEI	DEITY	DELEADED
DEGEARING	DEICE	DEIXES	DELEADING
DEGENDER	DEICED	DEIXIS	DELEADS
DEGENDERS	DEICER	DEIXISES	DELEAVE
DEGERM	DEICERS	DEJECT	DELEAVED
DEGERMED	DEICES	DEJECTA	DELEAVES
DEGERMING	DEICIDAL	DEJECTED	DELEAVING
DEGERMS	DEICIDE	DEJECTING	DELEBLE
DEGGED	DEICIDES	DEJECTION	DELECTATE
DEGGING	DEICING	DEJECTORY	DELED
DEGLAZE	DEICTIC	DEJECTS	DELEGABLE
DEGLAZED	DEICTICS	DEJEUNE	DELEGACY
DEGLAZES	DEID	DEJEUNER	DELEGATE
DEGLAZING	DEIDER	DEJEUNERS	DELEGATED
DEGOUT	DEIDEST	DEJEUNES	DELEGATEE
DEGOUTS	DEIDS	DEKAGRAM	DELEGATES
DEGRADE	DEIF	DEKAGRAMS	DELEGATOR
DEGRADED	DEIFER	DEKALITER	DELEING
DEGRADER	DEIFEST	DEKALITRE	DELENDA

DELES	DELIVERY	DELVING	DEMERARA
DELETABLE	DELL	DEMAGOG	DEMERARAN
DELETE	DELLIES	DEMAGOGED	DEMERARAS
DELETED	DELLS	DEMAGOGIC	DEMERGE
DELETES	DELLY	DEMAGOGS	DEMERGED
DELETING	DELO	DEMAGOGUE	DEMERGER
DELETION	DELOPE	DEMAGOGY	DEMERGERS
DELETIONS	DELOPED	DEMAIN	DEMERGES
DELETIVE	DELOPES	DEMAINE	DEMERGING
DELETORY	DELOPING	DEMAINES	DEMERIT
DELF	DELOS	DEMAINS	DEMERITED
DELFS	DELOUSE	DEMAN	DEMERITS
DELFT	DELOUSED	DEMAND	DEMERSAL
DELFTS	DELOUSER	DEMANDANT	DEMERSE
DELFTWARE	DELOUSERS	DEMANDED	DEMERSED
DELI	DELOUSES	DEMANDER	DEMERSES
DELIBATE	DELOUSING	DEMANDERS	DEMERSING
DELIBATED	DELPH	DEMANDING	DEMERSION
DELIBATES	DELPHIC	DEMANDS	DEMES
DELIBLE	DELPHIN	DEMANNED	DEMESNE
DELICACY	DELPHINIA	DEMANNING	DEMESNES
DELICATE	DELPHS	DEMANS	DEMETON
DELICATES	DELS	DEMANTOID	DEMETONS
DELICE	DELT	DEMARCATE	DEMIC
DELICES	DELTA	DEMARCHE	DEMIES
DELICIOUS	DELTAIC	DEMARCHES	DEMIGOD
DELICT	DELTAS	DEMARK	DEMIGODS
DELICTS	DELTIC	DEMARKED	DEMIJOHN
DELIGHT	DELTOID	DEMARKET	DEMIJOHNS
DELIGHTED	DELTOIDEI	DEMARKETS	DEMILUNE
DELIGHTER	DELTOIDS	DEMARKING	DEMILUNES
DELIGHTS	DELTS	DEMARKS	DEMIMONDE
DELIME	DELUBRUM	DEMAST	DEMIPIQUE
DELIMED	DELUBRUMS	DEMASTED	DEMIREP
DELIMES	DELUDABLE	DEMASTING	DEMIREPS
DELIMING	DELUDE	DEMASTS	DEMISABLE
DELIMIT	DELUDED	DEMAYNE	DEMISE
DELIMITED	DELUDER	DEMAYNES	DEMISED
DELIMITER	DELUDERS	DEME	DEMISES
DELIMITS	DELUDES	DEMEAN	DEMISING
DELINEATE	DELUDING	DEMEANE	DEMISS
DELIQUIUM	DELUGE	DEMEANED	DEMISSION
DELIRIA	DELUGED	DEMEANES	DEMISSIVE
DELIRIANT	DELUGES	DEMEANING	DEMISSLY
DELIRIOUS	DELUGING	DEMEANOR	DEMIST
DELIRIUM	DELUNDUNG	DEMEANORS	DEMISTED
DELIRIUMS	DELUSION	DEMEANOUR	DEMISTER
DELIS	DELUSIONS	DEMEANS	DEMISTERS
DELISH	DELUSIVE	DEMENT	DEMISTING
DELIST	DELUSORY	DEMENTATE	DEMISTS
DELISTED	DELUSTER	DEMENTED	DEMIT
DELISTING	DELUSTERS	DEMENTI	DEMITASSE
DELISTS	DELUXE	DEMENTIA	DEMITS
DELIVER	DELVE	DEMENTIAL	DEMITTED
DELIVERED	DELVED	DEMENTIAS	DEMITTING
DELIVERER	DELVER	DEMENTING	DEMIURGE
DELIVERLY	DELVERS	DEMENTIS	DEMIURGES
DELIVERS	DELVES	DEMENTS	DEMIURGIC

DEMIURGUS	DEMPSTERS	DENIABLY	DENTATE
DEMIVEG	DEMPT	DENIAL	DENTATED
DEMIVEGES	DEMULCENT	DENIALS	DENTATELY
DEMIVOLT	DEMULSIFY	DENIED	DENTATION
DEMIVOLTE	DEMUR	DENIER	DENTED
DEMIVOLTS	DEMURE	DENIERS	DENTEL
DEMIWORLD	DEMURED	DENIES	DENTELLE
DEMO	DEMURELY	DENIGRATE	DENTELLES
DEMOB	DEMURER	DENIM	DENTELS
DEMOBBED	DEMURES	DENIMED	DENTEX
DEMOBBING	DEMUREST	DENIMS	DENTEXES
DEMOBS	DEMURING	DENIS	DENTICLE
DEMOCRACY	DEMURRAGE	DENITRATE	DENTICLES
DEMOCRAT	DEMURRAL	DENITRIFY	DENTIFORM
DEMOCRATS	DEMURRALS	DENIZEN	DENTIL
DEMOCRATY	DEMURRED	DENIZENED	DENTILED
DEMODE	DEMURRER	DENIZENS	DENTILS
DEMODED	DEMURRERS	DENNED	DENTIN
DEMOED	DEMURRING	DENNET	DENTINAL
DEMOING	DEMURS	DENNETS	DENTINE
DEMOLISH	DEMY	DENNING	DENTINES
DEMOLOGY	DEMYSHIP	DENOMINAL	DENTING
DEMON	DEMYSHIPS	DENOTABLE	DENTINS
DEMONESS	DEMYSTIFY	DENOTATE	DENTIST
DEMONIAC	DEN	DENOTATED	DENTISTRY
DEMONIACS	DENAR	DENOTATES	DENTISTS
DEMONIAN	DENARI	DENOTE	DENTITION
DEMONIC	DENARIES	DENOTED	DENTOID
DEMONICAL	DENARII	DENOTES	DENTS
DEMONISE	DENARIUS	DENOTING	DENTULOUS
DEMONISED	DENARS	DENOTIVE	DENTURAL
DEMONISES	DENARY	DENOUNCE	DENTURE
DEMONISM	DENATURE	DENOUNCED	DENTURES
DEMONISMS	DENATURED	DENOUNCER	DENTURIST
DEMONIST	DENATURES	DENOUNCES	DENUDATE
DEMONISTS	DENAY	DENS	DENUDATED
DEMONIZE	DENAYED	DENSE	DENUDATES
DEMONIZED	DENAYING	DENSELY	DENUDE
DEMONIZES	DENAYS	DENSENESS	DENUDED
DEMONRIES	DENAZIFY	DENSER	DENUDER
DEMONRY	DENDRIMER	DENSEST	DENUDERS
DEMONS	DENDRITE	DENSIFIED	DENUDES
DEMOS	DENDRITES	DENSIFIER	DENUDING
DEMOSES	DENDRITIC	DENSIFIES	DENY
DEMOTE	DENDROID	DENSIFY	DENYING
DEMOTED	DENDRON	DENSITIES	DENYINGLY
DEMOTES	DENDRONS	DENSITY	DEODAND
DEMOTIC	DENE	DENT	DEODANDS
DEMOTICS	DENERVATE	DENTAL	DEODAR
DEMOTING	DENES	DENTALIA	DEODARA
DEMOTION	DENET	DENTALITY	DEODARAS
DEMOTIONS	DENETS	DENTALIUM	DEODARS
DEMOTIST	DENETTED	DENTALLY	DEODATE
DEMOTISTS	DENETTING	DENTALS	DEODATES
DEMOUNT	DENGUE	DENTARIA	DEODORANT
DEMOUNTED	DENGUES	DENTARIAS	DEODORISE
DEMOUNTS	DENI	DENTARIES	DEODORIZE
DEMPSTER	DENIABLE	DENTARY	DEONTIC

DEONTICS
DEORBIT
DEORBITED
DEORBITS
DEOXIDATE
DEOXIDISE
DEOXIDIZE
DEOXY
DEPAINT
DEPAINTED
DEPAINTS
DEPANNEUR
DEPART
DEPARTED
DEPARTEE
DEPARTEES
DEPARTER
DEPARTERS
DEPARTING
DEPARTS
DEPARTURE
DEPASTURE
DEPECHE
DEPECHES
DEPEINCT
DEPEINCTS
DEPEND
DEPENDANT
DEPENDED
DEPENDENT
DEPENDING
DEPENDS
DEPEOPLE
DEPEOPLED
DEPEOPLES
DEPERM
DEPERMED
DEPERMING
DEPERMS
DEPICT
DEPICTED
DEPICTER
DEPICTERS
DEPICTING
DEPICTION
DEPICTIVE
DEPICTOR
DEPICTORS
DEPICTS
DEPICTURE
DEPILATE
DEPILATED
DEPILATES
DEPILATOR
DEPLANE
DEPLANED
DEPLANES
DEPLANING

DEPLETE
DEPLETED
DEPLETER
DEPLETERS
DEPLETES
DEPLETING
DEPLETION
DEPLETIVE
DEPLETORY
DEPLORE
DEPLORED
DEPLORER
DEPLORERS
DEPLORES
DEPLORING
DEPLOY
DEPLOYED
DEPLOYER
DEPLOYERS
DEPLOYING
DEPLOYS
DEPLUME
DEPLUMED
DEPLUMES
DEPLUMING
DEPOLISH
DEPONE
DEPONED
DEPONENT
DEPONENTS
DEPONES
DEPONING
DEPORT
DEPORTED
DEPORTEE
DEPORTEES
DEPORTER
DEPORTERS
DEPORTING
DEPORTS
DEPOSABLE
DEPOSAL
DEPOSALS
DEPOSE
DEPOSED
DEPOSER
DEPOSERS
DEPOSES
DEPOSING
DEPOSIT
DEPOSITED
DEPOSITOR
DEPOSITS
DEPOT
DEPOTS
DEPRAVE
DEPRAVED
DEPRAVER

DEPRAVERS
DEPRAVES
DEPRAVING
DEPRAVITY
DEPRECATE
DEPREDATE
DEPREHEND
DEPRENYL
DEPRENYLS
DEPRESS
DEPRESSED
DEPRESSES
DEPRESSOR
DEPRIVAL
DEPRIVALS
DEPRIVE
DEPRIVED
DEPRIVER
DEPRIVERS
DEPRIVES
DEPRIVING
DEPROGRAM
DEPSIDE
DEPSIDES
DEPTH
DEPTHLESS
DEPTHS
DEPURANT
DEPURANTS
DEPURATE
DEPURATED
DEPURATES
DEPURATOR
DEPUTABLE
DEPUTE
DEPUTED
DEPUTES
DEPUTIES
DEPUTING
DEPUTISE
DEPUTISED
DEPUTISES
DEPUTIZE
DEPUTIZED
DEPUTIZES
DEPUTY
DERACINE
DERAIGN
DERAIGNED
DERAIGNS
DERAIL
DERAILED
DERAILER
DERAILERS
DERAILING
DERAILS
DERANGE
DERANGED

DERANGER
DERANGERS
DERANGES
DERANGING
DERAT
DERATE
DERATED
DERATES
DERATING
DERATINGS
DERATION
DERATIONS
DERATS
DERATTED
DERATTING
DERAY
DERAYED
DERAYING
DERAYS
DERBIES
DERBY
DERE
DERED
DERELICT
DERELICTS
DEREPRESS
DERES
DERHAM
DERHAMS
DERIDE
DERIDED
DERIDER
DERIDERS
DERIDES
DERIDING
DERIG
DERIGGED
DERIGGING
DERIGS
DERING
DERINGER
DERINGERS
DERISIBLE
DERISION
DERISIONS
DERISIVE
DERISORY
DERIVABLE
DERIVABLY
DERIVATE
DERIVATES
DERIVE
DERIVED
DERIVER
DERIVERS
DERIVES
DERIVING
DERM

DERMA

DERMA	DESCANTS	DESILVER	DESORBING
DERMAL	DESCEND	DESILVERS	DESORBS
DERMAS	DESCENDED	DESINE	DESOXY
DERMATIC	DESCENDER	DESINED	DESPAIR
DERMATOID	DESCENDS	DESINENCE	DESPAIRED
DERMATOME	DESCENT	DESINENT	DESPAIRER
DERMESTID	DESCENTS	DESINES	DESPAIRS
DERMIC	DESCHOOL	DESINING	DESPATCH
DERMIS	DESCHOOLS	DESIPIENT	DESPERADO
DERMISES	DESCRIBE	DESIRABLE	DESPERATE
DERMOID	DESCRIBED	DESIRABLY	DESPIGHT
DERMOIDS	DESCRIBER	DESIRE	DESPIGHTS
DERMS	DESCRIBES	DESIRED	DESPISAL
DERN	DESCRIED	DESIRER	DESPISALS
DERNFUL	DESCRIER	DESIRERS	DESPISE
DERNIER	DESCRIERS	DESIRES	DESPISED
DERNLY	DESCRIES	DESIRING	DESPISER
DERNS	DESCRIVE	DESIROUS	DESPISERS
DERO	DESCRIVED	DESIST	DESPISES
DEROGATE	DESCRIVES	DESISTED	DESPISING
DEROGATED	DESCRY	DESISTING	DESPITE
DEROGATES	DESCRYING	DESISTS	DESPITED
DEROS	DESECRATE	DESK	DESPITES
DERRICK	DESELECT	DESKBOUND	DESPITING
DERRICKED	DESELECTS	DESKFAST	DESPOIL
DERRICKS	DESERT	DESKFASTS	DESPOILED
DERRIERE	DESERTED	DESKILL	DESPOILER
DERRIERES	DESERTER	DESKILLED	DESPOILS
DERRIES	DESERTERS	DESKILLS	DESPOND
DERRINGER	DESERTIC	DESKMAN	DESPONDED
DERRIS	DESERTIFY	DESKMEN	DESPONDS
DERRISES	DESERTING	DESKNOTE	DESPOT
DERRO	DESERTION	DESKNOTES	DESPOTAT
DERROS	DESERTS	DESKS	DESPOTATE
DERRY	DESERVE	DESKTOP	DESPOTATS
DERTH	DESERVED	DESKTOPS	DESPOTIC
DERTHS	DESERVER	DESMAN	DESPOTISM
DERV	DESERVERS	DESMANS	DESPOTS
DERVISH	DESERVES	DESMID	DESPUMATE
DERVISHES	DESERVING	DESMIDIAN	DESSE
DERVS	DESEX	DESMIDS	DESSERT
DESALT	DESEXED	DESMINE	DESSERTS
DESALTED	DESEXES	DESMINES	DESSES
DESALTER	DESEXING	DESMODIUM	DESTAIN
DESALTERS	DESHI	DESMOID	DESTAINED
DESALTING	DESI	DESMOIDS	DESTAINS
DESALTS	DESICCANT	DESMOSOME	DESTEMPER
DESAND	DESICCATE	DESNOOD	DESTINATE
DESANDED	DESIGN	DESNOODED	DESTINE
DESANDING	DESIGNATE	DESNOODS	DESTINED
DESANDS	DESIGNED	DESOEUVRE	DESTINES
DESCALE	DESIGNEE	DESOLATE	DESTINIES
DESCALED	DESIGNEES	DESOLATED	DESTINING
DESCALES	DESIGNER	DESOLATER	DESTINY
DESCALING	DESIGNERS	DESOLATES	DESTITUTE
DESCANT	DESIGNFUL	DESOLATOR	DESTOCK
DESCANTED	DESIGNING	DESORB	DESTOCKED
DESCANTER	DESIGNS	DESORBED	DESTOCKS

DESTRIER	DETENTION	DETOURS	DEVAS
DESTRIERS	DETENTIST	DETOX	DEVASTATE
DESTROY	DETENTS	DETOXED	DEVEIN
DESTROYED	DETENU	DETOXES	DEVEINED
DESTROYER	DETENUE	DETOXIFY	DEVEINING
DESTROYS	DETENUES	DETOXING	DEVEINS
DESTRUCT	DETENUS	DETRACT	DEVEL
DESTRUCTO	DETER	DETRACTED	DEVELED
DESTRUCTS	DETERGE	DETRACTOR	DEVELING
DESUETUDE	DETERGED	DETRACTS	DEVELLED
DESUGAR	DETERGENT	DETRAIN	DEVELLING
DESUGARED	DETERGER	DETRAINED	DEVELOP
DESUGARS	DETERGERS	DETRAINS	DEVELOPE
DESULFUR	DETERGES	DETRAQUE	DEVELOPED
DESULFURS	DETERGING	DETRAQUEE	DEVELOPER
DESULPHUR	DETERMENT	DETRAQUES	DEVELOPES
DESULTORY	DETERMINE	DETRIMENT	DEVELOPPE
DESYATIN	DETERRED	DETRITAL	DEVELOPS
DESYATINS	DETERRENT	DETRITION	DEVELS
DESYNE	DETERRER	DETRITUS	DEVERBAL
DESYNED	DETERRERS	DETRUDE	DEVERBALS
DESYNES	DETERRING	DETRUDED	DEVEST
DESYNING	DETERS	DETRUDES	DEVESTED
DETACH	DETERSION	DETRUDING	DEVESTING
DETACHED	DETERSIVE	DETRUSION	DEVESTS
DETACHER	DETEST	DETUNE	DEVIANCE
DETACHERS	DETESTED	DETUNED	DEVIANCES
DETACHES	DETESTER	DETUNES	DEVIANCY
DETACHING	DETESTERS	DETUNING	DEVIANT
DETAIL	DETESTING	DEUCE	DEVIANTS
DETAILED	DETESTS	DEUCED	DEVIATE
DETAILER	DETHATCH	DEUCEDLY	DEVIATED
DETAILERS	DETHRONE	DEUCES	DEVIATES
DETAILING	DETHRONED	DEUCING	DEVIATING
DETAILS	DETHRONER	DEUDDARN	DEVIATION
DETAIN	DETHRONES	DEUDDARNS	DEVIATIVE
DETAINED	DETICK	DEUS	DEVIATOR
DETAINEE	DETICKED	DEUTERATE	DEVIATORS
DETAINEES	DETICKER	DEUTERIC	DEVIATORY
DETAINER	DETICKERS	DEUTERIDE	DEVICE
DETAINERS	DETICKING	DEUTERIUM	DEVICEFUL
DETAINING	DETICKS	DEUTERON	DEVICES
DETAINS	DETINUE	DEUTERONS	DEVIL
DETASSEL	DETINUES	DEUTON	DEVILDOM
DETASSELS	DETONABLE	DEUTONS	DEVILDOMS
DETECT	DETONATE	DEUTZIA	DEVILED
DETECTED	DETONATED	DEUTZIAS	DEVILESS
DETECTER	DETONATES	DEV	DEVILET
DETECTERS	DETONATOR	DEVA	DEVILETS
DETECTING	DETORSION	DEVALL	DEVILFISH
DETECTION	DETORT	DEVALLED	DEVILING
DETECTIVE	DETORTED	DEVALLING	DEVILINGS
DETECTOR	DETORTING	DEVALLS	DEVILISH
DETECTORS	DETORTION	DEVALUATE	DEVILISM
DETECTS	DETORTS	DEVALUE	DEVILISMS
DETENT	DETOUR	DEVALUED	DEVILKIN
DETENTE	DETOURED	DEVALUES	DEVILKINS
DETENTES	DETOURING	DEVALUING	DEVILLED

DEVILLING	DEVOURING	DEWORMERS	DHOOLIES
DEVILMENT	DEVOURS	DEWORMING	DHOOLY
DEVILRIES	DEVOUT	DEWORMS	DHOORA
DEVILRY	DEVOUTER	DEWPOINT	DHOORAS
DEVILS	DEVOUTEST	DEWPOINTS	DHOOTI
DEVILSHIP	DEVOUTLY	DEWS	DHOOTIE
DEVILTRY	DEVS	DEWY	DHOOTIES
DEVILWOOD	DEVVEL	DEX	DHOOTIS
DEVIOUS	DEVVELLED	DEXES	DHOTI
DEVIOUSLY	DEVVELS	DEXIE	DHOTIS
DEVISABLE	DEW	DEXIES	DHOURRA
DEVISAL	DEWAN	DEXTER	DHOURRAS
DEVISALS	DEWANI	DEXTERITY	DHOW
DEVISE	DEWANIS	DEXTEROUS	DHOWS
DEVISED	DEWANNIES	DEXTERS	DHURNA
DEVISEE	DEWANNY	DEXTRAL	DHURNAS
DEVISEES	DEWANS	DEXTRALLY	DHURRA
DEVISER	DEWAR	DEXTRAN	DHURRAS
DEVISERS	DEWARS	DEXTRANS	DHURRIE
DEVISES	DEWATER	DEXTRIN	DHURRIES
DEVISING	DEWATERED	DEXTRINE	DHUTI
DEVISOR	DEWATERER	DEXTRINES	DHUTIS
DEVISORS	DEWATERS	DEXTRINS	DI
DEVITRIFY	DEWAX	DEXTRO	DIABASE
DEVLING	DEWAXED	DEXTRORSE	DIABASES
DEVLINGS	DEWAXES	DEXTROSE	DIABASIC
DEVOICE	DEWAXING	DEXTROSES	DIABETES
DEVOICED	DEWBERRY	DEXTROUS	DIABETIC
DEVOICES	DEWCLAW	DEXY	DIABETICS
DEVOICING	DEWCLAWED	DEY	DIABLE
DEVOID	DEWCLAWS	DEYS	DIABLERIE
DEVOIR	DEWDROP	DEZINC	DIABLERY
DEVOIRS	DEWDROPS	DEZINCED	DIABLES
DEVOLVE	DEWED	DEZINCING	DIABOLIC
DEVOLVED	DEWFALL	DEZINCKED	DIABOLISE
DEVOLVES	DEWFALLS	DEZINCS	DIABOLISM
DEVOLVING	DEWFULL	DHAK	DIABOLIST
DEVON	DEWIER	DHAKS	DIABOLIZE
DEVONIAN	DEWIEST	DHAL	DIABOLO
DEVONPORT	DEWILY	DHALS	DIABOLOGY
DEVONS	DEWINESS	DHAMMA	DIABOLOS
DEVORE	DEWING	DHAMMAS	DIACETYL
DEVORES	DEWITT	DHANSAK	DIACETYLS
DEVOT	DEWITTED	DHANSAKS	DIACHRONY
DEVOTE	DEWITTING	DHARMA	DIACHYLON
DEVOTED	DEWITTS	DHARMAS	DIACHYLUM
DEVOTEDLY	DEWLAP	DHARMIC	DIACID
DEVOTEE	DEWLAPPED	DHARMSALA	DIACIDIC
DEVOTEES	DEWLAPS	DHARNA	DIACIDS
DEVOTES	DEWLAPT	DHARNAS	DIACODION
DEVOTING	DEWLESS	DHOBI	DIACODIUM
DEVOTION	DEWOOL	DHOBIS	DIACONAL
DEVOTIONS	DEWOOLED	DHOL	DIACONATE
DEVOTS	DEWOOLING	DHOLE	DIACRITIC
DEVOUR	DEWOOLS	DHOLES	DIACT
DEVOURED	DEWORM	DHOLL	DIACTINAL
DEVOURER	DEWORMED	DHOLLS	DIACTINE
DEVOURERS	DEWORMER	DHOLS	DIACTINIC

DIADEM
DIADEMED
DIADEMING
DIADEMS
DIADOCHI
DIADOCHY
DIADROM
DIADROMS
DIAERESES
DIAERESIS
DIAERETIC
DIAGLYPH
DIAGLYPHS
DIAGNOSE
DIAGNOSED
DIAGNOSES
DIAGNOSIS
DIAGONAL
DIAGONALS
DIAGRAM
DIAGRAMED
DIAGRAMS
DIAGRAPH
DIAGRAPHS
DIAGRID
DIAGRIDS
DIAL
DIALECT
DIALECTAL
DIALECTIC
DIALECTS
DIALED
DIALER
DIALERS
DIALING
DIALINGS
DIALIST
DIALISTS
DIALLAGE
DIALLAGES
DIALLAGIC
DIALLED
DIALLEL
DIALLER
DIALLERS
DIALLING
DIALLINGS
DIALLIST
DIALLISTS
DIALOG
DIALOGED
DIALOGER
DIALOGERS
DIALOGIC
DIALOGING
DIALOGISE
DIALOGISM
DIALOGIST

DIALOGITE
DIALOGIZE
DIALOGS
DIALOGUE
DIALOGUED
DIALOGUER
DIALOGUES
DIALS
DIALYSATE
DIALYSE
DIALYSED
DIALYSER
DIALYSERS
DIALYSES
DIALYSING
DIALYSIS
DIALYTIC
DIALYZATE
DIALYZE
DIALYZED
DIALYZER
DIALYZERS
DIALYZES
DIALYZING
DIAMAGNET
DIAMANTE
DIAMANTES
DIAMETER
DIAMETERS
DIAMETRAL
DIAMETRIC
DIAMIDE
DIAMIDES
DIAMIN
DIAMINE
DIAMINES
DIAMINS
DIAMOND
DIAMONDED
DIAMONDS
DIAMYL
DIANDRIES
DIANDROUS
DIANDRY
DIANODAL
DIANOETIC
DIANOIA
DIANOIAS
DIANTHUS
DIAPASE
DIAPASES
DIAPASON
DIAPASONS
DIAPAUSE
DIAPAUSED
DIAPAUSES
DIAPENTE
DIAPENTES

DIAPER
DIAPERED
DIAPERING
DIAPERS
DIAPHONE
DIAPHONES
DIAPHONIC
DIAPHONY
DIAPHRAGM
DIAPHYSES
DIAPHYSIS
DIAPIR
DIAPIRIC
DIAPIRISM
DIAPIRS
DIAPSID
DIAPSIDS
DIAPYESES
DIAPYESIS
DIAPYETIC
DIARCH
DIARCHAL
DIARCHIC
DIARCHIES
DIARCHY
DIARIAL
DIARIAN
DIARIES
DIARISE
DIARISED
DIARISES
DIARISING
DIARIST
DIARISTIC
DIARISTS
DIARIZE
DIARIZED
DIARIZES
DIARIZING
DIARRHEA
DIARRHEAL
DIARRHEAS
DIARRHEIC
DIARRHOEA
DIARY
DIASCOPE
DIASCOPES
DIASPORA
DIASPORAS
DIASPORE
DIASPORES
DIASPORIC
DIASTASE
DIASTASES
DIASTASIC
DIASTASIS
DIASTATIC
DIASTEM

DIASTEMA
DIASTEMAS
DIASTEMS
DIASTER
DIASTERS
DIASTOLE
DIASTOLES
DIASTOLIC
DIASTRAL
DIASTYLE
DIASTYLES
DIATHERMY
DIATHESES
DIATHESIS
DIATHETIC
DIATOM
DIATOMIC
DIATOMIST
DIATOMITE
DIATOMS
DIATONIC
DIATRETUM
DIATRIBE
DIATRIBES
DIATRON
DIATRONS
DIATROPIC
DIAXON
DIAXONS
DIAZEPAM
DIAZEPAMS
DIAZEUXES
DIAZEUXIS
DIAZIN
DIAZINE
DIAZINES
DIAZINON
DIAZINONS
DIAZINS
DIAZO
DIAZOES
DIAZOLE
DIAZOLES
DIAZONIUM
DIAZOS
DIAZOTISE
DIAZOTIZE
DIB
DIBASIC
DIBBED
DIBBER
DIBBERS
DIBBING
DIBBLE
DIBBLED
DIBBLER
DIBBLERS
DIBBLES

DIBBLING
DIBBS
DIBBUK
DIBBUKIM
DIBBUKKIM
DIBBUKS
DIBROMIDE
DIBS
DIBUTYL
DICACIOUS
DICACITY
DICACODYL
DICAMBA
DICAMBAS
DICAST
DICASTERY
DICASTIC
DICASTS
DICE
DICED
DICENTRA
DICENTRAS
DICENTRIC
DICER
DICERS
DICES
DICEY
DICH
DICHASIA
DICHASIAL
DICHASIUM
DICHOGAMY
DICHONDRA
DICHOPTIC
DICHORD
DICHORDS
DICHOTIC
DICHOTOMY
DICHROIC
DICHROISM
DICHROITE
DICHROMAT
DICHROMIC
DICHT
DICHTED
DICHTING
DICHTS
DICIER
DICIEST
DICING
DICINGS
DICK
DICKED
DICKENS
DICKENSES
DICKER
DICKERED
DICKERING

DICKERS
DICKEY
DICKEYS
DICKHEAD
DICKHEADS
DICKIE
DICKIER
DICKIES
DICKIEST
DICKING
DICKS
DICKTIER
DICKTIEST
DICKTY
DICKY
DICKYBIRD
DICLINIES
DICLINISM
DICLINOUS
DICLINY
DICOT
DICOTS
DICOTYL
DICOTYLS
DICROTAL
DICROTIC
DICROTISM
DICROTOUS
DICT
DICTA
DICTATE
DICTATED
DICTATES
DICTATING
DICTATION
DICTATOR
DICTATORS
DICTATORY
DICTATRIX
DICTATURE
DICTED
DICTIER
DICTIEST
DICTING
DICTION
DICTIONAL
DICTIONS
DICTS
DICTUM
DICTUMS
DICTY
DICTYOGEN
DICUMAROL
DICYCLIC
DICYCLIES
DICYCLY
DID
DIDACT

DIDACTIC
DIDACTICS
DIDACTS
DIDACTYL
DIDACTYLS
DIDAKAI
DIDAKAIS
DIDAKEI
DIDAKEIS
DIDAPPER
DIDAPPERS
DIDDER
DIDDERED
DIDDERING
DIDDERS
DIDDICOY
DIDDICOYS
DIDDIER
DIDDIES
DIDDIEST
DIDDLE
DIDDLED
DIDDLER
DIDDLERS
DIDDLES
DIDDLEY
DIDDLEYS
DIDDLIES
DIDDLING
DIDDLY
DIDDY
DIDELPHIC
DIDELPHID
DIDICOI
DIDICOIS
DIDICOY
DIDICOYS
DIDIE
DIDIES
DIDJERIDU
DIDO
DIDOES
DIDOS
DIDRACHM
DIDRACHMA
DIDRACHMS
DIDST
DIDY
DIDYMIUM
DIDYMIUMS
DIDYMOUS
DIDYNAMY
DIE
DIEB
DIEBACK
DIEBACKS
DIEBS
DIECIOUS

DIED
DIEDRAL
DIEDRALS
DIEDRE
DIEDRES
DIEGESES
DIEGESIS
DIEHARD
DIEHARDS
DIEING
DIEL
DIELDRIN
DIELDRINS
DIELYTRA
DIELYTRAS
DIEMAKER
DIEMAKERS
DIENE
DIENES
DIEOFF
DIEOFFS
DIERESES
DIERESIS
DIERETIC
DIES
DIESEL
DIESELED
DIESELING
DIESELISE
DIESELIZE
DIESELS
DIESES
DIESINKER
DIESIS
DIESTER
DIESTERS
DIESTOCK
DIESTOCKS
DIESTROUS
DIESTRUM
DIESTRUMS
DIESTRUS
DIET
DIETARIAN
DIETARIES
DIETARILY
DIETARY
DIETED
DIETER
DIETERS
DIETETIC
DIETETICS
DIETHER
DIETHERS
DIETHYL
DIETHYLS
DIETICIAN
DIETINE

DIETINES	DIGESTORS	DIGRESSER	DILIGENCE
DIETING	DIGESTS	DIGRESSES	DILIGENT
DIETINGS	DIGGABLE	DIGS	DILL
DIETIST	DIGGED	DIGYNIAN	DILLED
DIETISTS	DIGGER	DIGYNOUS	DILLI
DIETITIAN	DIGGERS	DIHEDRA	DILLIER
DIETS	DIGGING	DIHEDRAL	DILLIES
DIF	DIGGINGS	DIHEDRALS	DILLIEST
DIFF	DIGHT	DIHEDRON	DILLING
DIFFER	DIGHTED	DIHEDRONS	DILLINGS
DIFFERED	DIGHTING	DIHYBRID	DILLIS
DIFFERENT	DIGHTS	DIHYBRIDS	DILLS
DIFFERING	DIGICAM	DIHYDRIC	DILLY
DIFFERS	DIGICAMS	DIKA	DILTIAZEM
DIFFICILE	DIGIT	DIKAS	DILUENT
DIFFICULT	DIGITAL	DIKAST	DILUENTS
DIFFIDENT	DIGITALIN	DIKASTS	DILUTABLE
DIFFLUENT	DIGITALIS	DIKDIK	DILUTE
DIFFORM	DIGITALLY	DIKDIKS	DILUTED
DIFFRACT	DIGITALS	DIKE	DILUTEE
DIFFRACTS	DIGITATE	DIKED	DILUTEES
DIFFS	DIGITATED	DIKER	DILUTER
DIFFUSE	DIGITISE	DIKERS	DILUTERS
DIFFUSED	DIGITISED	DIKES	DILUTES
DIFFUSELY	DIGITISER	DIKEY	DILUTING
DIFFUSER	DIGITISES	DIKIER	DILUTION
DIFFUSERS	DIGITIZE	DIKIEST	DILUTIONS
DIFFUSES	DIGITIZED	DIKING	DILUTIVE
DIFFUSING	DIGITIZER	DIKKOP	DILUTOR
DIFFUSION	DIGITIZES	DIKKOPS	DILUTORS
DIFFUSIVE	DIGITONIN	DIKTAT	DILUVIA
DIFFUSOR	DIGITOXIN	DIKTATS	DILUVIAL
DIFFUSORS	DIGITRON	DILATABLE	DILUVIAN
DIFS	DIGITRONS	DILATABLY	DILUVION
DIG	DIGITS	DILATANCY	DILUVIONS
DIGAMIES	DIGITULE	DILATANT	DILUVIUM
DIGAMIST	DIGITULES	DILATANTS	DILUVIUMS
DIGAMISTS	DIGLOSSIA	DILATATE	DIM
DIGAMMA	DIGLOSSIC	DILATATOR	DIMBLE
DIGAMMAS	DIGLOT	DILATE	DIMBLES
DIGAMOUS	DIGLOTS	DILATED	DIME
DIGAMY	DIGLOTTIC	DILATER	DIMENSION
DIGASTRIC	DIGLYPH	DILATERS	DIMER
DIGENESES	DIGLYPHS	DILATES	DIMERIC
DIGENESIS	DIGNIFIED	DILATING	DIMERISE
DIGENETIC	DIGNIFIES	DILATION	DIMERISED
DIGERATI	DIGNIFY	DILATIONS	DIMERISES
DIGEST	DIGNITARY	DILATIVE	DIMERISM
DIGESTANT	DIGNITIES	DILATOR	DIMERISMS
DIGESTED	DIGNITY	DILATORS	DIMERIZE
DIGESTER	DIGONAL	DILATORY	DIMERIZED
DIGESTERS	DIGOXIN	DILDO	DIMERIZES
DIGESTIF	DIGOXINS	DILDOE	DIMEROUS
DIGESTIFS	DIGRAPH	DILDOES	DIMERS
DIGESTING	DIGRAPHIC	DILDOS	DIMES
DIGESTION	DIGRAPHS	DILEMMA	DIMETER
DIGESTIVE	DIGRESS	DILEMMAS	DIMETERS
DIGESTOR	DIGRESSED	DILEMMIC	DIMETHYL

DIMETHYLS	DINGBAT	DINNING	DIORISMS
DIMETRIC	DINGBATS	DINNLE	DIORISTIC
DIMIDIATE	DINGDONG	DINNLED	DIORITE
DIMINISH	DINGDONGS	DINNLES	DIORITES
DIMISSORY	DINGE	DINNLING	DIORITIC
DIMITIES	DINGED	DINO	DIOSGENIN
DIMITY	DINGER	DINOCERAS	DIOTA
DIMLY	DINGERS	DINOMANIA	DIOTAS
DIMMABLE	DINGES	DINOS	DIOXAN
DIMMED	DINGESES	DINOSAUR	DIOXANE
DIMMER	DINGEY	DINOSAURS	DIOXANES
DIMMERS	DINGEYS	DINOTHERE	DIOXANS
DIMMEST	DINGHIES	DINS	DIOXID
DIMMING	DINGHY	DINT	DIOXIDE
DIMMISH	DINGIER	DINTED	DIOXIDES
DIMNESS	DINGIES	DINTING	DIOXIDS
DIMNESSES	DINGIEST	DINTLESS	DIOXIN
DIMORPH	DINGILY	DINTS	DIOXINS
DIMORPHIC	DINGINESS	DIOBOL	DIP
DIMORPHS	DINGING	DIOBOLON	DIPCHICK
DIMOUT	DINGLE	DIOBOLONS	DIPCHICKS
DIMOUTS	DINGLES	DIOBOLS	DIPEPTIDE
DIMP	DINGO	DIOCESAN	DIPHASE
DIMPLE	DINGOED	DIOCESANS	DIPHASIC
DIMPLED	DINGOES	DIOCESE	DIPHENYL
DIMPLES	DINGOING	DIOCESES	DIPHENYLS
DIMPLIER	DINGS	DIODE	DIPHONE
DIMPLIEST	DINGUS	DIODES	DIPHONES
DIMPLING	DINGUSES	DIOECIES	DIPHTHONG
DIMPLY	DINGY	DIOECIOUS	DIPHYSITE
DIMPS	DINIC	DIOECISM	DIPLEGIA
DIMPSIES	DINICS	DIOECISMS	DIPLEGIAS
DIMPSY	DINING	DIOECY	DIPLEGIC
DIMS	DINITRO	DIOESTRUS	DIPLEX
DIMWIT	DINK	DIOICOUS	DIPLEXER
DIMWITS	DINKED	DIOL	DIPLEXERS
DIMWITTED	DINKER	DIOLEFIN	DIPLOE
DIMYARIAN	DINKEST	DIOLEFINS	DIPLOES
DIN	DINKEY	DIOLS	DIPLOGEN
DINAR	DINKEYS	DIONYSIAC	DIPLOGENS
DINARCHY	DINKIE	DIONYSIAN	DIPLOIC
DINARS	DINKIER	DIOPSIDE	DIPLOID
DINDLE	DINKIES	DIOPSIDES	DIPLOIDIC
DINDLED	DINKIEST	DIOPSIDIC	DIPLOIDS
DINDLES	DINKING	DIOPTASE	DIPLOIDY
DINDLING	DINKLY	DIOPTASES	DIPLOMA
DINE	DINKS	DIOPTER	DIPLOMACY
DINED	DINKUM	DIOPTERS	DIPLOMAED
DINER	DINKUMS	DIOPTRAL	DIPLOMAS
DINERIC	DINKY	DIOPTRATE	DIPLOMAT
DINERO	DINMONT	DIOPTRE	DIPLOMATA
DINEROS	DINMONTS	DIOPTRES	DIPLOMATE
DINERS	DINNA	DIOPTRIC	DIPLOMATS
DINES	DINNED	DIOPTRICS	DIPLON
DINETTE	DINNER	DIORAMA	DIPLONEMA
DINETTES	DINNERED	DIORAMAS	DIPLONS
DINFUL	DINNERING	DIORAMIC	DIPLONT
DING	DINNERS	DIORISM	DIPLONTIC

DIPLONTS	DIPTYCAS	DIRKS	DISARMS
DIPLOPIA	DIPTYCH	DIRL	DISARRAY
DIPLOPIAS	DIPTYCHS	DIRLED	DISARRAYS
DIPLOPIC	DIQUARK	DIRLING	DISAS
DIPLOPOD	DIQUARKS	DIRLS	DISASTER
DIPLOPODS	DIQUAT	DIRNDL	DISASTERS
DIPLOSES	DIQUATS	DIRNDLS	DISATTIRE
DIPLOSIS	DIRAM	DIRT	DISATTUNE
DIPLOTENE	DIRAMS	DIRTBAG	DISAVOUCH
DIPLOZOA	DIRDAM	DIRTBAGS	DISAVOW
DIPLOZOIC	DIRDAMS	DIRTED	DISAVOWAL
DIPLOZOON	DIRDUM	DIRTIED	DISAVOWED
DIPNET	DIRDUMS	DIRTIER	DISAVOWER
DIPNETS	DIRE	DIRTIES	DISAVOWS
DIPNETTED	DIRECT	DIRTIEST	DISBAND
DIPNOAN	DIRECTED	DIRTILY	DISBANDED
DIPNOANS	DIRECTER	DIRTINESS	DISBANDS
DIPNOOUS	DIRECTEST	DIRTING	DISBAR
DIPODIC	DIRECTING	DIRTS	DISBARK
DIPODIES	DIRECTION	DIRTY	DISBARKED
DIPODY	DIRECTIVE	DIRTYING	DISBARKS
DIPOLAR	DIRECTLY	DIS	DISBARRED
DIPOLE	DIRECTOR	DISA	DISBARS
DIPOLES	DIRECTORS	DISABLE	DISBELIEF
DIPPABLE	DIRECTORY	DISABLED	DISBENCH
DIPPED	DIRECTRIX	DISABLER	DISBODIED
DIPPER	DIRECTS	DISABLERS	DISBOSOM
DIPPERFUL	DIREFUL	DISABLES	DISBOSOMS
DIPPERS	DIREFULLY	DISABLING	DISBOUND
DIPPIER	DIRELY	DISABUSAL	DISBOWEL
DIPPIEST	DIREMPT	DISABUSE	DISBOWELS
DIPPINESS	DIREMPTED	DISABUSED	DISBRANCH
DIPPING	DIREMPTS	DISABUSES	DISBUD
DIPPINGS	DIRENESS	DISACCORD	DISBUDDED
DIPPY	DIRER	DISADORN	DISBUDS
DIPROTIC	DIREST	DISADORNS	DISBURDEN
DIPS	DIRGE	DISAFFECT	DISBURSAL
DIPSADES	DIRGEFUL	DISAFFIRM	DISBURSE
DIPSAS	DIRGELIKE	DISAGREE	DISBURSED
DIPSHIT	DIRGES	DISAGREED	DISBURSER
DIPSHITS	DIRHAM	DISAGREES	DISBURSES
DIPSO	DIRHAMS	DISALLIED	DISC
DIPSOS	DIRHEM	DISALLIES	DISCAGE
DIPSTICK	DIRHEMS	DISALLOW	DISCAGED
DIPSTICKS	DIRIGE	DISALLOWS	DISCAGES
DIPT	DIRIGENT	DISALLY	DISCAGING
DIPTERA	DIRIGES	DISANCHOR	DISCAL
DIPTERAL	DIRIGIBLE	DISANNEX	DISCALCED
DIPTERAN	DIRIGISM	DISANNUL	DISCANDIE
DIPTERANS	DIRIGISME	DISANNULS	DISCANDY
DIPTERAS	DIRIGISMS	DISANOINT	DISCANT
DIPTERIST	DIRIGISTE	DISAPPEAR	DISCANTED
DIPTEROI	DIRIMENT	DISAPPLY	DISCANTER
DIPTERON	DIRK	DISARM	DISCANTS
DIPTERONS	DIRKE	DISARMED	DISCARD
DIPTEROS	DIRKED	DISARMER	DISCARDED
DIPTEROUS	DIRKES	DISARMERS	DISCARDER
DIPTYCA	DIRKING	DISARMING	DISCARDS

DISCASE	DISCOURE	DISFAVOUR	DISHIER
DISCASED	DISCOURED	DISFIGURE	DISHIEST
DISCASES	DISCOURES	DISFLESH	DISHING
DISCASING	DISCOURSE	DISFLUENT	DISHINGS
DISCED	DISCOVER	DISFOREST	DISHLIKE
DISCEPT	DISCOVERS	DISFORM	DISHOME
DISCEPTED	DISCOVERT	DISFORMED	DISHOMED
DISCEPTS	DISCOVERY	DISFORMS	DISHOMES
DISCERN	DISCREDIT	DISFROCK	DISHOMING
DISCERNED	DISCREET	DISFROCKS	DISHONEST
DISCERNER	DISCRETE	DISGAVEL	DISHONOR
DISCERNS	DISCRETER	DISGAVELS	DISHONORS
DISCERP	DISCROWN	DISGEST	DISHONOUR
DISCERPED	DISCROWNS	DISGESTED	DISHORN
DISCERPS	DISCS	DISGESTS	DISHORNED
DISCHARGE	DISCUMBER	DISGODDED	DISHORNS
DISCHURCH	DISCURE	DISGORGE	DISHORSE
DISCI	DISCURED	DISGORGED	DISHORSED
DISCIDE	DISCURES	DISGORGER	DISHORSES
DISCIDED	DISCURING	DISGORGES	DISHOUSE
DISCIDES	DISCURSUS	DISGOWN	DISHOUSED
DISCIDING	DISCUS	DISGOWNED	DISHOUSES
DISCIFORM	DISCUSES	DISGOWNS	DISHPAN
DISCINCT	DISCUSS	DISGRACE	DISHPANS
DISCING	DISCUSSED	DISGRACED	DISHRAG
DISCIPLE	DISCUSSER	DISGRACER	DISHRAGS
DISCIPLED	DISCUSSES	DISGRACES	DISHTOWEL
DISCIPLES	DISDAIN	DISGRADE	DISHUMOUR
DISCLAIM	DISDAINED	DISGRADED	DISHWARE
DISCLAIMS	DISDAINS	DISGRADES	DISHWARES
DISCLIKE	DISEASE	DISGUISE	DISHWATER
DISCLIMAX	DISEASED	DISGUISED	DISHY
DISCLOSE	DISEASES	DISGUISER	DISILLUDE
DISCLOSED	DISEASING	DISGUISES	DISIMMURE
DISCLOSER	DISEDGE	DISGUST	DISINFECT
DISCLOSES	DISEDGED	DISGUSTED	DISINFEST
DISCLOST	DISEDGES	DISGUSTS	DISINFORM
DISCO	DISEDGING	DISH	DISINHUME
DISCOBOLI	DISEMBARK	DISHABIT	DISINTER
DISCOED	DISEMBODY	DISHABITS	DISINTERS
DISCOER	DISEMPLOY	DISHABLE	DISINURE
DISCOERS	DISENABLE	DISHABLED	DISINURED
DISCOID	DISENDOW	DISHABLES	DISINURES
DISCOIDAL	DISENDOWS	DISHALLOW	DISINVEST
DISCOIDS	DISENGAGE	DISHCLOTH	DISINVITE
DISCOING	DISENROL	DISHCLOUT	DISJASKIT
DISCOLOGY	DISENROLS	DISHDASHA	DISJECT
DISCOLOR	DISENTAIL	DISHED	DISJECTED
DISCOLORS	DISENTOMB	DISHELM	DISJECTS
DISCOLOUR	DISESTEEM	DISHELMED	DISJOIN
DISCOMFIT	DISEUR	DISHELMS	DISJOINED
DISCOMMON	DISEURS	DISHERIT	DISJOINS
DISCORD	DISEUSE	DISHERITS	DISJOINT
DISCORDED	DISEUSES	DISHES	DISJOINTS
DISCORDS	DISFAME	DISHEVEL	DISJUNCT
DISCOS	DISFAMES	DISHEVELS	DISJUNCTS
DISCOUNT	DISFAVOR	DISHFUL	DISJUNE
DISCOUNTS	DISFAVORS	DISHFULS	DISJUNES

DISK	DISMASTED	DISPAUPER	DISPORT
DISKED	DISMASTS	DISPEACE	DISPORTED
DISKETTE	DISMAY	DISPEACES	DISPORTS
DISKETTES	DISMAYD	DISPEL	DISPOSAL
DISKING	DISMAYED	DISPELLED	DISPOSALS
DISKLESS	DISMAYFUL	DISPELLER	DISPOSE
DISKLIKE	DISMAYING	DISPELS	DISPOSED
DISKS	DISMAYL	DISPENCE	DISPOSER
DISLEAF	DISMAYLED	DISPENCED	DISPOSERS
DISLEAFED	DISMAYLS	DISPENCES	DISPOSES
DISLEAFS	DISMAYS	DISPEND	DISPOSING
DISLEAL	DISME	DISPENDED	DISPOST
DISLEAVE	DISMEMBER	DISPENDS	DISPOSTED
DISLEAVED	DISMES	DISPENSE	DISPOSTS
DISLEAVES	DISMISS	DISPENSED	DISPOSURE
DISLIKE	DISMISSAL	DISPENSER	DISPRAD
DISLIKED	DISMISSED	DISPENSES	DISPRAISE
DISLIKEN	DISMISSES	DISPEOPLE	DISPREAD
DISLIKENS	DISMODED	DISPERSAL	DISPREADS
DISLIKER	DISMOUNT	DISPERSE	DISPRED
DISLIKERS	DISMOUNTS	DISPERSED	DISPREDS
DISLIKES	DISNEST	DISPERSER	DISPRISON
DISLIKING	DISNESTED	DISPERSES	DISPRIZE
DISLIMB	DISNESTS	DISPIRIT	DISPRIZED
DISLIMBED	DISOBEY	DISPIRITS	DISPRIZES
DISLIMBS	DISOBEYED	DISPLACE	DISPROFIT
DISLIMN	DISOBEYER	DISPLACED	DISPROOF
DISLIMNED	DISOBEYS	DISPLACER	DISPROOFS
DISLIMNS	DISOBLIGE	DISPLACES	DISPROOVE
DISLINK	DISODIUM	DISPLANT	DISPROVAL
DISLINKED	DISOMIC	DISPLANTS	DISPROVE
DISLINKS	DISOMIES	DISPLAY	DISPROVED
DISLOAD	DISOMY	DISPLAYED	DISPROVEN
DISLOADED	DISORBED	DISPLAYER	DISPROVER
DISLOADS	DISORDER	DISPLAYS	DISPROVES
DISLOCATE	DISORDERS	DISPLE	DISPUNGE
DISLODGE	DISORIENT	DISPLEASE	DISPUNGED
DISLODGED	DISOWN	DISPLED	DISPUNGES
DISLODGES	DISOWNED	DISPLES	DISPURSE
DISLOIGN	DISOWNER	DISPLING	DISPURSED
DISLOIGNS	DISOWNERS	DISPLODE	DISPURSES
DISLOYAL	DISOWNING	DISPLODED	DISPURVEY
DISLUSTRE	DISOWNS	DISPLODES	DISPUTANT
DISMAL	DISPACE	DISPLUME	DISPUTE
DISMALER	DISPACED	DISPLUMED	DISPUTED
DISMALEST	DISPACES	DISPLUMES	DISPUTER
DISMALITY	DISPACING	DISPONDEE	DISPUTERS
DISMALLER	DISPARAGE	DISPONE	DISPUTES
DISMALLY	DISPARATE	DISPONED	DISPUTING
DISMALS	DISPARITY	DISPONEE	DISQUIET
DISMAN	DISPARK	DISPONEES	DISQUIETS
DISMANNED	DISPARKED	DISPONER	DISRANK
DISMANS	DISPARKS	DISPONERS	DISRANKED
DISMANTLE	DISPART	DISPONES	DISRANKS
DISMASK	DISPARTED	DISPONGE	DISRATE
DISMASKED	DISPARTS	DISPONGED	DISRATED
DISMASKS	DISPATCH	DISPONGES	DISRATES
DISMAST	DISPATHY	DISPONING	DISRATING

DISREGARD	DISSEVERS	DISTORT	DITALS
DISRELISH	DISSHIVER	DISTORTED	DITAS
DISREPAIR	DISSIDENT	DISTORTER	DITCH
DISREPUTE	DISSIGHT	DISTORTS	DITCHED
DISROBE	DISSIGHTS	DISTRACT	DITCHER
DISROBED	DISSIMILE	DISTRACTS	DITCHERS
DISROBER	DISSING	DISTRAIL	DITCHES
DISROBERS	DISSIPATE	DISTRAILS	DITCHING
DISROBES	DISSOCIAL	DISTRAIN	DITCHLESS
DISROBING	DISSOLUTE	DISTRAINS	DITE
DISROOT	DISSOLVE	DISTRAINT	DITED
DISROOTED	DISSOLVED	DISTRAIT	DITES
DISROOTS	DISSOLVER	DISTRAITE	DITHECAL
DISRUPT	DISSOLVES	DISTRESS	DITHECOUS
DISRUPTED	DISSONANT	DISTRICT	DITHEISM
DISRUPTER	DISSUADE	DISTRICTS	DITHEISMS
DISRUPTOR	DISSUADED	DISTRIX	DITHEIST
DISRUPTS	DISSUADER	DISTRIXES	DITHEISTS
DISS	DISSUADES	DISTRUST	DITHELETE
DISSAVE	DISSUNDER	DISTRUSTS	DITHELISM
DISSAVED	DISTAFF	DISTUNE	DITHER
DISSAVES	DISTAFFS	DISTUNED	DITHERED
DISSAVING	DISTAIN	DISTUNES	DITHERER
DISSEAT	DISTAINED	DISTUNING	DITHERERS
DISSEATED	DISTAINS	DISTURB	DITHERIER
DISSEATS	DISTAL	DISTURBED	DITHERING
DISSECT	DISTALLY	DISTURBER	DITHERS
DISSECTED	DISTANCE	DISTURBS	DITHERY
DISSECTOR	DISTANCED	DISTYLE	DITHIOL
DISSECTS	DISTANCES	DISTYLES	DITHYRAMB
DISSED	DISTANT	DISULFATE	DITING
DISSEISE	DISTANTLY	DISULFID	DITOKOUS
DISSEISED	DISTASTE	DISULFIDE	DITONE
DISSEISEE	DISTASTED	DISULFIDS	DITONES
DISSEISES	DISTASTES	DISUNION	DITROCHEE
DISSEISIN	DISTAVES	DISUNIONS	DITS
DISSEISOR	DISTEMPER	DISUNITE	DITSIER
DISSEIZE	DISTEND	DISUNITED	DITSIEST
DISSEIZED	DISTENDED	DISUNITER	DITSINESS
DISSEIZEE	DISTENDER	DISUNITES	DITSY
DISSEIZES	DISTENDS	DISUNITY	DITT
DISSEIZIN	DISTENT	DISUSAGE	DITTANDER
DISSEIZOR	DISTHENE	DISUSAGES	DITTANIES
DISSEMBLE	DISTHENES	DISUSE	DITTANY
DISSEMBLY	DISTHRONE	DISUSED	DITTAY
DISSENSUS	DISTICH	DISUSES	DITTAYS
DISSENT	DISTICHAL	DISUSING	DITTED
DISSENTED	DISTICHS	DISVALUE	DITTIED
DISSENTER	DISTIL	DISVALUED	DITTIES
DISSENTS	DISTILL	DISVALUES	DITTING
DISSERT	DISTILLED	DISVOUCH	DITTIT
DISSERTED	DISTILLER	DISYOKE	DITTO
DISSERTS	DISTILLS	DISYOKED	DITTOED
DISSERVE	DISTILS	DISYOKES	DITTOING
DISSERVED	DISTINCT	DISYOKING	DITTOLOGY
DISSERVES	DISTINGUE	DIT	DITTOS
DISSES	DISTOME	DITA	DITTS
DISSEVER	DISTOMES	DITAL	DITTY

DITTYING
DITZ
DITZES
DITZIER
DITZIEST
DITZINESS
DITZY
DIURESES
DIURESIS
DIURETIC
DIURETICS
DIURNAL
DIURNALLY
DIURNALS
DIURON
DIURONS
DIUTURNAL
DIV
DIVA
DIVAGATE
DIVAGATED
DIVAGATES
DIVALENCE
DIVALENCY
DIVALENT
DIVALENTS
DIVAN
DIVANS
DIVAS
DIVE
DIVEBOMB
DIVEBOMBS
DIVED
DIVELLENT
DIVER
DIVERGE
DIVERGED
DIVERGENT
DIVERGES
DIVERGING
DIVERS
DIVERSE
DIVERSED
DIVERSELY
DIVERSES
DIVERSIFY
DIVERSING
DIVERSION
DIVERSITY
DIVERSLY
DIVERT
DIVERTED
DIVERTER
DIVERTERS
DIVERTING
DIVERTIVE
DIVERTS
DIVES

DIVEST
DIVESTED
DIVESTING
DIVESTS
DIVESTURE
DIVI
DIVIDABLE
DIVIDANT
DIVIDE
DIVIDED
DIVIDEDLY
DIVIDEND
DIVIDENDS
DIVIDER
DIVIDERS
DIVIDES
DIVIDING
DIVIDINGS
DIVIDIVI
DIVIDIVIS
DIVIDUAL
DIVIDUOUS
DIVINABLE
DIVINATOR
DIVINE
DIVINED
DIVINELY
DIVINER
DIVINERS
DIVINES
DIVINEST
DIVING
DIVINGS
DIVINIFY
DIVINING
DIVINISE
DIVINISED
DIVINISES
DIVINITY
DIVINIZE
DIVINIZED
DIVINIZES
DIVIS
DIVISIBLE
DIVISIBLY
DIVISIM
DIVISION
DIVISIONS
DIVISIVE
DIVISOR
DIVISORS
DIVORCE
DIVORCED
DIVORCEE
DIVORCEES
DIVORCER
DIVORCERS
DIVORCES

DIVORCING
DIVORCIVE
DIVOT
DIVOTS
DIVS
DIVULGATE
DIVULGE
DIVULGED
DIVULGER
DIVULGERS
DIVULGES
DIVULGING
DIVULSE
DIVULSED
DIVULSES
DIVULSING
DIVULSION
DIVULSIVE
DIVVIED
DIVVIES
DIVVY
DIVVYING
DIWAN
DIWANS
DIXI
DIXIE
DIXIES
DIXIT
DIXITS
DIXY
DIZAIN
DIZAINS
DIZEN
DIZENED
DIZENING
DIZENMENT
DIZENS
DIZYGOTIC
DIZYGOUS
DIZZARD
DIZZARDS
DIZZIED
DIZZIER
DIZZIES
DIZZIEST
DIZZILY
DIZZINESS
DIZZY
DIZZYING
DJEBEL
DJEBELS
DJELLABA
DJELLABAH
DJELLABAS
DJEMBE
DJEMBES
DJIBBAH
DJIBBAHS

DJIN
DJINN
DJINNI
DJINNS
DJINNY
DJINS
DO
DOAB
DOABLE
DOABS
DOAT
DOATED
DOATER
DOATERS
DOATING
DOATINGS
DOATS
DOB
DOBBED
DOBBER
DOBBERS
DOBBIE
DOBBIES
DOBBIN
DOBBING
DOBBINS
DOBBY
DOBCHICK
DOBCHICKS
DOBHASH
DOBHASHES
DOBIE
DOBIES
DOBLA
DOBLAS
DOBLON
DOBLONES
DOBLONS
DOBRA
DOBRAS
DOBRO
DOBROS
DOBS
DOBSON
DOBSONFLY
DOBSONS
DOBY
DOC
DOCENT
DOCENTS
DOCETIC
DOCHMIAC
DOCHMII
DOCHMIUS
DOCHT
DOCIBLE
DOCILE
DOCILELY

DOCILER
DOCILEST
DOCILITY
DOCIMASY
DOCK
DOCKAGE
DOCKAGES
DOCKED
DOCKEN
DOCKENS
DOCKER
DOCKERS
DOCKET
DOCKETED
DOCKETING
DOCKETS
DOCKHAND
DOCKHANDS
DOCKING
DOCKINGS
DOCKISE
DOCKISED
DOCKISES
DOCKISING
DOCKIZE
DOCKIZED
DOCKIZES
DOCKIZING
DOCKLAND
DOCKLANDS
DOCKS
DOCKSIDE
DOCKSIDES
DOCKYARD
DOCKYARDS
DOCO
DOCOS
DOCQUET
DOCQUETED
DOCQUETS
DOCS
DOCTOR
DOCTORAL
DOCTORAND
DOCTORATE
DOCTORED
DOCTORESS
DOCTORIAL
DOCTORING
DOCTORLY
DOCTORS
DOCTRESS
DOCTRINAL
DOCTRINE
DOCTRINES
DOCUDRAMA
DOCUMENT
DOCUMENTS

DOD
DODDARD
DODDED
DODDER
DODDERED
DODDERER
DODDERERS
DODDERIER
DODDERING
DODDERS
DODDERY
DODDIER
DODDIES
DODDIEST
DODDING
DODDIPOLL
DODDLE
DODDLES
DODDY
DODDYPOLL
DODECAGON
DODGE
DODGEBALL
DODGED
DODGEM
DODGEMS
DODGER
DODGERIES
DODGERS
DODGERY
DODGES
DODGIER
DODGIEST
DODGINESS
DODGING
DODGINGS
DODGY
DODKIN
DODKINS
DODMAN
DODMANS
DODO
DODOES
DODOISM
DODOISMS
DODOS
DODS
DOE
DOEK
DOEKS
DOEN
DOER
DOERS
DOES
DOESKIN
DOESKINS
DOEST
DOETH

DOF
DOFF
DOFFED
DOFFER
DOFFERS
DOFFING
DOFFS
DOG
DOGARESSA
DOGATE
DOGATES
DOGBANE
DOGBANES
DOGBERRY
DOGBOLT
DOGBOLTS
DOGCART
DOGCARTS
DOGDAYS
DOGDOM
DOGDOMS
DOGE
DOGEAR
DOGEARED
DOGEARING
DOGEARS
DOGEATE
DOGEATES
DOGEDOM
DOGEDOMS
DOGES
DOGESHIP
DOGESHIPS
DOGEY
DOGEYS
DOGFACE
DOGFACES
DOGFIGHT
DOGFIGHTS
DOGFISH
DOGFISHES
DOGFOUGHT
DOGFOX
DOGFOXES
DOGGED
DOGGEDER
DOGGEDEST
DOGGEDLY
DOGGER
DOGGEREL
DOGGERELS
DOGGERIES
DOGGERMAN
DOGGERMEN
DOGGERS
DOGGERY
DOGGESS
DOGGESSES

DOGGIE
DOGGIER
DOGGIES
DOGGIEST
DOGGINESS
DOGGING
DOGGINGS
DOGGISH
DOGGISHLY
DOGGO
DOGGONE
DOGGONED
DOGGONER
DOGGONES
DOGGONEST
DOGGONING
DOGGREL
DOGGRELS
DOGGY
DOGHANGED
DOGHOLE
DOGHOLES
DOGHOUSE
DOGHOUSES
DOGIE
DOGIES
DOGLEG
DOGLEGGED
DOGLEGS
DOGLIKE
DOGMA
DOGMAN
DOGMAS
DOGMATA
DOGMATIC
DOGMATICS
DOGMATISE
DOGMATISM
DOGMATIST
DOGMATIZE
DOGMATORY
DOGMEN
DOGNAP
DOGNAPED
DOGNAPER
DOGNAPERS
DOGNAPING
DOGNAPPED
DOGNAPPER
DOGNAPS
DOGROBBER
DOGS
DOGSBODY
DOGSHIP
DOGSHIPS
DOGSHORES
DOGSKIN
DOGSKINS

DOGSLED	DOLINA	DOLS	DOMINIUM
DOGSLEDS	DOLINAS	DOLT	DOMINIUMS
DOGSLEEP	DOLINE	DOLTISH	DOMINO
DOGSLEEPS	DOLINES	DOLTISHLY	DOMINOES
DOGTEETH	DOLING	DOLTS	DOMINOS
DOGTOOTH	DOLIUM	DOM	DOMS
DOGTOWN	DOLL	DOMAIN	DOMY
DOGTOWNS	DOLLAR	DOMAINAL	DON
DOGTROT	DOLLARED	DOMAINE	DONA
DOGTROTS	DOLLARISE	DOMAINES	DONAH
DOGVANE	DOLLARIZE	DOMAINS	DONAHS
DOGVANES	DOLLARS	DOMAL	DONARIES
DOGWATCH	DOLLDOM	DOMANIAL	DONARY
DOGWOOD	DOLLDOMS	DOMATIA	DONAS
DOGWOODS	DOLLED	DOMATIUM	DONATARY
DOGY	DOLLHOOD	DOME	DONATE
DOH	DOLLHOODS	DOMED	DONATED
DOHS	DOLLHOUSE	DOMELIKE	DONATES
DOHYO	DOLLIED	DOMES	DONATING
DOHYOS	DOLLIER	DOMESDAY	DONATION
DOILED	DOLLIERS	DOMESDAYS	DONATIONS
DOILIES	DOLLIES	DOMESTIC	DONATISM
DOILT	DOLLINESS	DOMESTICS	DONATISMS
DOILTER	DOLLING	DOMETT	DONATIVE
DOILTEST	DOLLISH	DOMETTS	DONATIVES
DOILY	DOLLISHLY	DOMIC	DONATOR
DOING	DOLLOP	DOMICAL	DONATORS
DOINGS	DOLLOPED	DOMICALLY	DONATORY
DOIT	DOLLOPING	DOMICIL	DONDER
DOITED	DOLLOPS	DOMICILE	DONDERED
DOITIT	DOLLS	DOMICILED	DONDERING
DOITKIN	DOLLY	DOMICILES	DONDERS
DOITKINS	DOLLYBIRD	DOMICILS	DONE
DOITS	DOLLYING	DOMIER	DONEE
DOJO	DOLMA	DOMIEST	DONEES
DOJOS	DOLMADES	DOMINANCE	DONENESS
DOL	DOLMAN	DOMINANCY	DONER
DOLABRATE	DOLMANS	DOMINANT	DONG
DOLCE	DOLMAS	DOMINANTS	DONGA
DOLCES	DOLMEN	DOMINATE	DONGAS
DOLCETTO	DOLMENIC	DOMINATED	DONGED
DOLCETTOS	DOLMENS	DOMINATES	DONGING
DOLCI	DOLOMITE	DOMINATOR	DONGLE
DOLDRUMS	DOLOMITES	DOMINE	DONGLES
DOLE	DOLOMITIC	DOMINEE	DONGOLA
DOLED	DOLOR	DOMINEER	DONGOLAS
DOLEFUL	DOLORIFIC	DOMINEERS	DONGS
DOLEFULLY	DOLOROSO	DOMINEES	DONING
DOLENT	DOLOROUS	DOMINES	DONINGS
DOLENTE	DOLORS	DOMING	DONJON
DOLERITE	DOLOS	DOMINICAL	DONJONS
DOLERITES	DOLOSSE	DOMINICK	DONKEY
DOLERITIC	DOLOSTONE	DOMINICKS	DONKEYS
DOLES	DOLOUR	DOMINIE	DONKO
DOLESOME	DOLOURS	DOMINIES	DONKOS
DOLIA	DOLPHIN	DOMINION	DONNA
DOLICHOS	DOLPHINET	DOMINIONS	DONNARD
DOLICHURI	DOLPHINS	DOMINIQUE	DONNART

DONNAS

DONNAS
DONNAT
DONNATS
DONNE
DONNED
DONNEE
DONNEES
DONNERD
DONNERED
DONNERT
DONNES
DONNICKER
DONNIES
DONNIKER
DONNIKERS
DONNING
DONNISH
DONNISHLY
DONNISM
DONNISMS
DONNOT
DONNOTS
DONNY
DONOR
DONORS
DONORSHIP
DONS
DONSHIP
DONSHIPS
DONSIE
DONSIER
DONSIEST
DONSY
DONUT
DONUTS
DONUTTED
DONUTTING
DONZEL
DONZELS
DOO
DOOB
DOOBIE
DOOBIES
DOOBS
DOOCED
DOOCOT
DOOCOTS
DOODAD
DOODADS
DOODAH
DOODAHS
DOODIES
DOODLE
DOODLEBUG
DOODLED
DOODLER
DOODLERS
DOODLES

DOODLING
DOODOO
DOODOOS
DOODY
DOOFER
DOOFERS
DOOFUS
DOOFUSES
DOOHICKEY
DOOK
DOOKED
DOOKET
DOOKETS
DOOKING
DOOKS
DOOL
DOOLALLY
DOOLAN
DOOLANS
DOOLE
DOOLEE
DOOLEES
DOOLES
DOOLIE
DOOLIES
DOOLS
DOOLY
DOOM
DOOMED
DOOMFUL
DOOMFULLY
DOOMIER
DOOMIEST
DOOMILY
DOOMING
DOOMS
DOOMSAYER
DOOMSDAY
DOOMSDAYS
DOOMSMAN
DOOMSMEN
DOOMSTER
DOOMSTERS
DOOMWATCH
DOOMY
DOON
DOONA
DOONAS
DOOR
DOORBELL
DOORBELLS
DOORCASE
DOORCASES
DOORFRAME
DOORJAMB
DOORJAMBS
DOORKNOB
DOORKNOBS

DOORKNOCK
DOORLESS
DOORMAN
DOORMAT
DOORMATS
DOORMEN
DOORN
DOORNAIL
DOORNAILS
DOORNS
DOORPLATE
DOORPOST
DOORPOSTS
DOORS
DOORSILL
DOORSILLS
DOORSMAN
DOORSMEN
DOORSTEP
DOORSTEPS
DOORSTONE
DOORSTOP
DOORSTOPS
DOORWAY
DOORWAYS
DOORWOMAN
DOORWOMEN
DOORYARD
DOORYARDS
DOOS
DOOSRA
DOOSRAS
DOOWOP
DOOWOPS
DOOZER
DOOZERS
DOOZIE
DOOZIES
DOOZY
DOP
DOPA
DOPAMINE
DOPAMINES
DOPANT
DOPANTS
DOPAS
DOPATTA
DOPATTAS
DOPE
DOPED
DOPEHEAD
DOPEHEADS
DOPER
DOPERS
DOPES
DOPESHEET
DOPESTER
DOPESTERS

DOPEY
DOPEYNESS
DOPIAZA
DOPIAZAS
DOPIER
DOPIEST
DOPILY
DOPINESS
DOPING
DOPINGS
DOPPED
DOPPER
DOPPERS
DOPPIE
DOPPIES
DOPPING
DOPPINGS
DOPPIO
DOPPIOS
DOPS
DOPY
DOR
DORAD
DORADO
DORADOS
DORADS
DORB
DORBA
DORBAS
DORBEETLE
DORBS
DORBUG
DORBUGS
DORE
DOREE
DOREES
DORHAWK
DORHAWKS
DORIC
DORIDOID
DORIDOIDS
DORIES
DORIS
DORISE
DORISED
DORISES
DORISING
DORIZE
DORIZED
DORIZES
DORIZING
DORK
DORKIER
DORKIEST
DORKINESS
DORKS
DORKY
DORLACH

DORLACHS	DORTS	DOTH	DOUBTING
DORM	DORTY	DOTIER	DOUBTINGS
DORMANCY	DORY	DOTIEST	DOUBTLESS
DORMANT	DOS	DOTING	DOUBTS
DORMANTS	DOSAGE	DOTINGLY	DOUC
DORMER	DOSAGES	DOTINGS	DOUCE
DORMERED	DOSE	DOTISH	DOUCELY
DORMERS	DOSED	DOTS	DOUCENESS
DORMICE	DOSEH	DOTTED	DOUCEPERE
DORMIE	DOSEHS	DOTTEL	DOUCER
DORMIENT	DOSEMETER	DOTTELS	DOUCEST
DORMIN	DOSER	DOTTER	DOUCET
DORMINS	DOSERS	DOTTEREL	DOUCETS
DORMITION	DOSES	DOTTERELS	DOUCEUR
DORMITIVE	DOSH	DOTTERS	DOUCEURS
DORMITORY	DOSHES	DOTTIER	DOUCHE
DORMOUSE	DOSIMETER	DOTTIEST	DOUCHEBAG
DORMS	DOSIMETRY	DOTTILY	DOUCHED
DORMY	DOSING	DOTTINESS	DOUCHES
DORNECK	DOSIOLOGY	DOTTING	DOUCHING
DORNECKS	DOSOLOGY	DOTTLE	DOUCINE
DORNICK	DOSS	DOTTLED	DOUCINES
DORNICKS	DOSSAL	DOTTLER	DOUCS
DORNOCK	DOSSALS	DOTTLES	DOUGH
DORNOCKS	DOSSED	DOTTLEST	DOUGHBOY
DORONICUM	DOSSEL	DOTTREL	DOUGHBOYS
DORP	DOSSELS	DOTTRELS	DOUGHFACE
DORPER	DOSSER	DOTTY	DOUGHIER
DORPERS	DOSSERET	DOTY	DOUGHIEST
DORPS	DOSSERETS	DOUANE	DOUGHLIKE
DORR	DOSSERS	DOUANES	DOUGHNUT
DORRED	DOSSES	DOUANIER	DOUGHNUTS
DORRING	DOSSHOUSE	DOUANIERS	DOUGHS
DORRS	DOSSIER	DOUAR	DOUGHT
DORS	DOSSIERS	DOUARS	DOUGHTIER
DORSA	DOSSIL	DOUBLE	DOUGHTILY
DORSAD	DOSSILS	DOUBLED	DOUGHTY
DORSAL	DOSSING	DOUBLER	DOUGHY
DORSALLY	DOST	DOUBLERS	DOUK
DORSALS	DOT	DOUBLES	DOUKED
DORSE	DOTAGE	DOUBLET	DOUKING
DORSEL	DOTAGES	DOUBLETON	DOUKS
DORSELS	DOTAL	DOUBLETS	DOULA
DORSER	DOTANT	DOUBLING	DOULAS
DORSERS	DOTANTS	DOUBLINGS	DOULEIA
DORSES	DOTARD	DOUBLOON	DOULEIAS
DORSIFLEX	DOTARDLY	DOUBLOONS	DOUM
DORSUM	DOTARDS	DOUBLURE	DOUMA
DORT	DOTATION	DOUBLURES	DOUMAS
DORTED	DOTATIONS	DOUBLY	DOUMS
DORTER	DOTCOM	DOUBT	DOUN
DORTERS	DOTCOMMER	DOUBTABLE	DOUP
DORTIER	DOTCOMS	DOUBTABLY	DOUPIONI
DORTIEST	DOTE	DOUBTED	DOUPIONIS
DORTINESS	DOTED	DOUBTER	DOUPPIONI
DORTING	DOTER	DOUBTERS	DOUPS
DORTOUR	DOTERS	DOUBTFUL	DOUR
DORTOURS	DOTES	DOUBTFULS	DOURA

DOURAH	DOWAR	DOWNCOURT	DOWNTHROW
DOURAHS	DOWARS	DOWNDRAFT	DOWNTICK
DOURAS	DOWD	DOWNED	DOWNTICKS
DOURER	DOWDIER	DOWNER	DOWNTIME
DOUREST	DOWDIES	DOWNERS	DOWNTIMES
DOURINE	DOWDIEST	DOWNFALL	DOWNTOWN
DOURINES	DOWDILY	DOWNFALLS	DOWNTOWNS
DOURLY	DOWDINESS	DOWNFIELD	DOWNTREND
DOURNESS	DOWDS	DOWNFLOW	DOWNTROD
DOUSE	DOWDY	DOWNFLOWS	DOWNTURN
DOUSED	DOWDYISH	DOWNFORCE	DOWNTURNS
DOUSER	DOWDYISM	DOWNGRADE	DOWNWARD
DOUSERS	DOWDYISMS	DOWNHAUL	DOWNWARDS
DOUSES	DOWED	DOWNHAULS	DOWNWASH
DOUSING	DOWEL	DOWNHILL	DOWNWIND
DOUT	DOWELED	DOWNHILLS	DOWNY
DOUTED	DOWELING	DOWNHOLE	DOWNZONE
DOUTER	DOWELLED	DOWNIER	DOWNZONED
DOUTERS	DOWELLING	DOWNIEST	DOWNZONES
DOUTING	DOWELS	DOWNINESS	DOWP
DOUTS	DOWER	DOWNING	DOWPS
DOUX	DOWERED	DOWNLAND	DOWRIES
DOUZEPER	DOWERIES	DOWNLANDS	DOWRY
DOUZEPERS	DOWERING	DOWNLESS	DOWS
DOVE	DOWERLESS	DOWNLIGHT	DOWSABEL
DOVECOT	DOWERS	DOWNLIKE	DOWSABELS
DOVECOTE	DOWERY	DOWNLINK	DOWSE
DOVECOTES	DOWF	DOWNLINKS	DOWSED
DOVECOTS	DOWFNESS	DOWNLOAD	DOWSER
DOVED	DOWIE	DOWNLOADS	DOWSERS
DOVEISH	DOWIER	DOWNMOST	DOWSES
DOVEKEY	DOWIEST	DOWNPIPE	DOWSET
DOVEKEYS	DOWING	DOWNPIPES	DOWSETS
DOVEKIE	DOWITCHER	DOWNPLAY	DOWSING
DOVEKIES	DOWL	DOWNPLAYS	DOWT
DOVELET	DOWLAS	DOWNPOUR	DOWTS
DOVELETS	DOWLASES	DOWNPOURS	DOXASTIC
DOVELIKE	DOWLE	DOWNRANGE	DOXIE
DOVEN	DOWLES	DOWNRIGHT	DOXIES
DOVENED	DOWLIER	DOWNRIVER	DOXOLOGY
DOVENING	DOWLIEST	DOWNRUSH	DOXY
DOVENS	DOWLNE	DOWNS	DOY
DOVER	DOWLNES	DOWNSCALE	DOYEN
DOVERED	DOWLNEY	DOWNSHIFT	DOYENNE
DOVERING	DOWLS	DOWNSIDE	DOYENNES
DOVERS	DOWLY	DOWNSIDES	DOYENS
DOVES	DOWN	DOWNSIZE	DOYLEY
DOVETAIL	DOWNA	DOWNSIZED	DOYLEYS
DOVETAILS	DOWNBEAT	DOWNSIZES	DOYLIES
DOVIE	DOWNBEATS	DOWNSLIDE	DOYLY
DOVIER	DOWNBOW	DOWNSLOPE	DOYS
DOVIEST	DOWNBOWS	DOWNSPIN	DOZE
DOVING	DOWNBURST	DOWNSPINS	DOZED
DOVISH	DOWNCAST	DOWNSPOUT	DOZEN
DOW	DOWNCASTS	DOWNSTAGE	DOZENED
DOWABLE	DOWNCOME	DOWNSTAIR	DOZENING
DOWAGER	DOWNCOMER	DOWNSTATE	DOZENS
DOWAGERS	DOWNCOMES	DOWNSWING	DOZENTH

DOZENTHS	DRAFFIEST	DRAGS	DRAPEABLE
DOZER	DRAFFISH	DRAGSMAN	DRAPED
DOZERS	DRAFFS	DRAGSMEN	DRAPER
DOZES	DRAFFY	DRAGSTER	DRAPERIED
DOZIER	DRAFT	DRAGSTERS	DRAPERIES
DOZIEST	DRAFTABLE	DRAGSTRIP	DRAPERS
DOZILY	DRAFTED	DRAIL	DRAPERY
DOZINESS	DRAFTEE	DRAILED	DRAPES
DOZING	DRAFTEES	DRAILING	DRAPET
DOZINGS	DRAFTER	DRAILS	DRAPETS
DOZY	DRAFTERS	DRAIN	DRAPEY
DRAB	DRAFTIER	DRAINABLE	DRAPIER
DRABBED	DRAFTIEST	DRAINAGE	DRAPIERS
DRABBER	DRAFTILY	DRAINAGES	DRAPING
DRABBERS	DRAFTING	DRAINED	DRAPPED
DRABBEST	DRAFTINGS	DRAINER	DRAPPIE
DRABBET	DRAFTS	DRAINERS	DRAPPIES
DRABBETS	DRAFTSMAN	DRAINING	DRAPPING
DRABBIER	DRAFTSMEN	DRAINPIPE	DRAPPY
DRABBIEST	DRAFTY	DRAINS	DRAPS
DRABBING	DRAG	DRAISENE	DRASTIC
DRABBISH	DRAGEE	DRAISENES	DRASTICS
DRABBLE	DRAGEES	DRAISINE	DRAT
DRABBLED	DRAGGED	DRAISINES	DRATCHELL
DRABBLER	DRAGGER	DRAKE	DRATS
DRABBLERS	DRAGGERS	DRAKES	DRATTED
DRABBLES	DRAGGIER	DRAM	DRATTING
DRABBLING	DRAGGIEST	DRAMA	DRAUGHT
DRABBY	DRAGGING	DRAMADIES	DRAUGHTED
DRABETTE	DRAGGLE	DRAMADY	DRAUGHTER
DRABETTES	DRAGGLED	DRAMAS	DRAUGHTS
DRABLER	DRAGGLES	DRAMATIC	DRAUGHTY
DRABLERS	DRAGGLING	DRAMATICS	DRAUNT
DRABLY	DRAGGY	DRAMATISE	DRAUNTED
DRABNESS	DRAGHOUND	DRAMATIST	DRAUNTING
DRABS	DRAGLINE	DRAMATIZE	DRAUNTS
DRAC	DRAGLINES	DRAMATURG	DRAVE
DRACAENA	DRAGNET	DRAMEDIES	DRAW
DRACAENAS	DRAGNETS	DRAMEDY	DRAWABLE
DRACENA	DRAGOMAN	DRAMMACH	DRAWBACK
DRACENAS	DRAGOMANS	DRAMMACHS	DRAWBACKS
DRACHM	DRAGOMEN	DRAMMED	DRAWBAR
DRACHMA	DRAGON	DRAMMING	DRAWBARS
DRACHMAE	DRAGONESS	DRAMMOCK	DRAWBORE
DRACHMAI	DRAGONET	DRAMMOCKS	DRAWBORES
DRACHMAS	DRAGONETS	DRAMS	DRAWDOWN
DRACHMS	DRAGONFLY	DRAMSHOP	DRAWDOWNS
DRACK	DRAGONISE	DRAMSHOPS	DRAWEE
DRACO	DRAGONISH	DRANGWAY	DRAWEES
DRACONE	DRAGONISM	DRANGWAYS	DRAWER
DRACONES	DRAGONIZE	DRANK	DRAWERFUL
DRACONIAN	DRAGONNE	DRANT	DRAWERS
DRACONIC	DRAGONS	DRANTED	DRAWING
DRACONISM	DRAGOON	DRANTING	DRAWINGS
DRACONTIC	DRAGOONED	DRANTS	DRAWKNIFE
DRAD	DRAGOONS	DRAP	DRAWL
DRAFF	DRAGROPE	DRAPABLE	DRAWLED
DRAFFIER	DRAGROPES	DRAPE	DRAWLER

DRAWLERS
DRAWLIER
DRAWLIEST
DRAWLING
DRAWLS
DRAWLY
DRAWN
DRAWNWORK
DRAWPLATE
DRAWS
DRAWSHAVE
DRAWTUBE
DRAWTUBES
DRAY
DRAYAGE
DRAYAGES
DRAYED
DRAYHORSE
DRAYING
DRAYMAN
DRAYMEN
DRAYS
DRAZEL
DRAZELS
DREAD
DREADED
DREADER
DREADERS
DREADFUL
DREADFULS
DREADING
DREADLESS
DREADLOCK
DREADLY
DREADS
DREAM
DREAMBOAT
DREAMED
DREAMER
DREAMERS
DREAMERY
DREAMFUL
DREAMHOLE
DREAMIER
DREAMIEST
DREAMILY
DREAMING
DREAMINGS
DREAMLAND
DREAMLESS
DREAMLIKE
DREAMS
DREAMT
DREAMTIME
DREAMY
DREAR
DREARE
DREARER

DREARES
DREAREST
DREARIER
DREARIES
DREARIEST
DREARILY
DREARING
DREARINGS
DREARS
DREARY
DRECK
DRECKIER
DRECKIEST
DRECKS
DRECKSILL
DRECKY
DREDGE
DREDGED
DREDGER
DREDGERS
DREDGES
DREDGING
DREDGINGS
DREE
DREED
DREEING
DREES
DREG
DREGGIER
DREGGIEST
DREGGISH
DREGGY
DREGS
DREICH
DREICHER
DREICHEST
DREIDEL
DREIDELS
DREIDL
DREIDLS
DREIGH
DREK
DREKS
DRENCH
DRENCHED
DRENCHER
DRENCHERS
DRENCHES
DRENCHING
DRENT
DREPANID
DREPANIDS
DREPANIUM
DRERE
DRERES
DRERIHEAD
DRESS
DRESSAGE

DRESSAGES
DRESSED
DRESSER
DRESSERS
DRESSES
DRESSIER
DRESSIEST
DRESSILY
DRESSING
DRESSINGS
DRESSMADE
DRESSMAKE
DRESSY
DREST
DREVILL
DREVILLS
DREW
DREY
DREYS
DRIB
DRIBBED
DRIBBER
DRIBBERS
DRIBBING
DRIBBLE
DRIBBLED
DRIBBLER
DRIBBLERS
DRIBBLES
DRIBBLET
DRIBBLETS
DRIBBLIER
DRIBBLING
DRIBBLY
DRIBLET
DRIBLETS
DRIBS
DRICE
DRICES
DRICKSIE
DRICKSIER
DRIED
DRIEGH
DRIER
DRIERS
DRIES
DRIEST
DRIFT
DRIFTAGE
DRIFTAGES
DRIFTED
DRIFTER
DRIFTERS
DRIFTIER
DRIFTIEST
DRIFTING
DRIFTLESS
DRIFTPIN

DRIFTPINS
DRIFTS
DRIFTWOOD
DRIFTY
DRILL
DRILLABLE
DRILLED
DRILLER
DRILLERS
DRILLING
DRILLINGS
DRILLS
DRILLSHIP
DRILY
DRINK
DRINKABLE
DRINKABLY
DRINKER
DRINKERS
DRINKING
DRINKINGS
DRINKS
DRIP
DRIPLESS
DRIPPED
DRIPPER
DRIPPERS
DRIPPIER
DRIPPIEST
DRIPPILY
DRIPPING
DRIPPINGS
DRIPPY
DRIPS
DRIPSTONE
DRIPT
DRISHEEN
DRISHEENS
DRIVABLE
DRIVE
DRIVEABLE
DRIVEL
DRIVELED
DRIVELER
DRIVELERS
DRIVELINE
DRIVELING
DRIVELLED
DRIVELLER
DRIVELS
DRIVEN
DRIVER
DRIVERS
DRIVES
DRIVEWAY
DRIVEWAYS
DRIVING
DRIVINGLY

DRIVINGS	DRONES	DROPPERS	DROWNED
DRIZZLE	DRONGO	DROPPING	DROWNER
DRIZZLED	DRONGOES	DROPPINGS	DROWNERS
DRIZZLES	DRONGOS	DROPPLE	DROWNING
DRIZZLIER	DRONIER	DROPPLES	DROWNINGS
DRIZZLING	DRONIEST	DROPS	DROWNS
DRIZZLY	DRONING	DROPSHOT	DROWS
DROGER	DRONINGLY	DROPSHOTS	DROWSE
DROGERS	DRONISH	DROPSICAL	DROWSED
DROGHER	DRONISHLY	DROPSIED	DROWSES
DROGHERS	DRONKLAP	DROPSIES	DROWSIER
DROGUE	DRONKLAPS	DROPSONDE	DROWSIEST
DROGUES	DRONY	DROPSTONE	DROWSIHED
DROGUET	DROOB	DROPSY	DROWSILY
DROGUETS	DROOBS	DROPT	DROWSING
DROICH	DROOG	DROPWISE	DROWSY
DROICHIER	DROOGISH	DROPWORT	DRUB
DROICHS	DROOGS	DROPWORTS	DRUBBED
DROICHY	DROOK	DROSERA	DRUBBER
DROID	DROOKED	DROSERAS	DRUBBERS
DROIDS	DROOKING	DROSHKIES	DRUBBING
DROIL	DROOKINGS	DROSHKY	DRUBBINGS
DROILED	DROOKIT	DROSKIES	DRUBS
DROILING	DROOKS	DROSKY	DRUCKEN
DROILS	DROOL	DROSS	DRUDGE
DROIT	DROOLED	DROSSES	DRUDGED
DROITS	DROOLIER	DROSSIER	DRUDGER
DROLE	DROOLIEST	DROSSIEST	DRUDGERS
DROLER	DROOLING	DROSSY	DRUDGERY
DROLES	DROOLS	DROSTDIES	DRUDGES
DROLEST	DROOLY	DROSTDY	DRUDGING
DROLL	DROOME	DROSTDYS	DRUDGISM
DROLLED	DROOMES	DROUGHT	DRUDGISMS
DROLLER	DROOP	DROUGHTS	DRUG
DROLLERY	DROOPED	DROUGHTY	DRUGGED
DROLLEST	DROOPIER	DROUK	DRUGGER
DROLLING	DROOPIEST	DROUKED	DRUGGERS
DROLLINGS	DROOPILY	DROUKING	DRUGGET
DROLLISH	DROOPING	DROUKINGS	DRUGGETS
DROLLNESS	DROOPS	DROUKIT	DRUGGIE
DROLLS	DROOPY	DROUKS	DRUGGIER
DROLLY	DROP	DROUTH	DRUGGIES
DROME	DROPCLOTH	DROUTHIER	DRUGGIEST
DROMEDARE	DROPFLIES	DROUTHS	DRUGGING
DROMEDARY	DROPFLY	DROUTHY	DRUGGIST
DROMES	DROPFORGE	DROVE	DRUGGISTS
DROMIC	DROPHEAD	DROVED	DRUGGY
DROMICAL	DROPHEADS	DROVER	DRUGLORD
DROMOI	DROPKICK	DROVERS	DRUGLORDS
DROMON	DROPKICKS	DROVES	DRUGMAKER
DROMOND	DROPLET	DROVING	DRUGS
DROMONDS	DROPLETS	DROVINGS	DRUGSTORE
DROMONS	DROPLIGHT	DROW	DRUID
DROMOS	DROPOUT	DROWN	DRUIDESS
DRONE	DROPOUTS	DROWND	DRUIDIC
DRONED	DROPPABLE	DROWNDED	DRUIDICAL
DRONER	DROPPED	DROWNDING	DRUIDISM
DRONERS	DROPPER	DROWNDS	DRUIDISMS

DRUIDRIES	DRYAD	DUALLED	DUCKED
DRUIDRY	DRYADES	DUALLING	DUCKER
DRUIDS	DRYADIC	DUALLY	DUCKERS
DRUM	DRYADS	DUALS	DUCKFOOT
DRUMBEAT	DRYASDUST	DUAN	DUCKIE
DRUMBEATS	DRYBEAT	DUANS	DUCKIER
DRUMBLE	DRYBEATEN	DUAR	DUCKIES
DRUMBLED	DRYBEATS	DUARCHIES	DUCKIEST
DRUMBLES	DRYER	DUARCHY	DUCKING
DRUMBLING	DRYERS	DUARS	DUCKINGS
DRUMFIRE	DRYEST	DUATHLON	DUCKLING
DRUMFIRES	DRYING	DUATHLONS	DUCKLINGS
DRUMFISH	DRYINGS	DUB	DUCKMOLE
DRUMHEAD	DRYISH	DUBBED	DUCKMOLES
DRUMHEADS	DRYLAND	DUBBER	DUCKPIN
DRUMLIER	DRYLOT	DUBBERS	DUCKPINS
DRUMLIEST	DRYLOTS	DUBBIN	DUCKS
DRUMLIKE	DRYLY	DUBBING	DUCKSHOVE
DRUMLIN	DRYMOUTH	DUBBINGS	DUCKTAIL
DRUMLINS	DRYMOUTHS	DUBBINS	DUCKTAILS
DRUMLY	DRYNESS	DUBBO	DUCKWALK
DRUMMED	DRYNESSES	DUBBOS	DUCKWALKS
DRUMMER	DRYPOINT	DUBIETIES	DUCKWEED
DRUMMERS	DRYPOINTS	DUBIETY	DUCKWEEDS
DRUMMIES	DRYS	DUBIOSITY	DUCKY
DRUMMING	DRYSALTER	DUBIOUS	DUCT
DRUMMOCK	DRYSTONE	DUBIOUSLY	DUCTAL
DRUMMOCKS	DRYWALL	DUBITABLE	DUCTED
DRUMMY	DRYWALLED	DUBITABLY	DUCTILE
DRUMROLL	DRYWALLS	DUBITANCY	DUCTILELY
DRUMROLLS	DRYWELL	DUBITATE	DUCTILITY
DRUMS	DRYWELLS	DUBITATED	DUCTING
DRUMSTICK	DSO	DUBITATES	DUCTINGS
DRUNK	DSOBO	DUBNIUM	DUCTLESS
DRUNKARD	DSOBOS	DUBNIUMS	DUCTS
DRUNKARDS	DSOMO	DUBONNET	DUCTULE
DRUNKEN	DSOMOS	DUBONNETS	DUCTULES
DRUNKENLY	DSOS	DUBS	DUCTWORK
DRUNKER	DUAD	DUCAL	DUCTWORKS
DRUNKEST	DUADS	DUCALLY	DUD
DRUNKS	DUAL	DUCAT	DUDDER
DRUPE	DUALIN	DUCATOON	DUDDERIES
DRUPEL	DUALINS	DUCATOONS	DUDDERS
DRUPELET	DUALISE	DUCATS	DUDDERY
DRUPELETS	DUALISED	DUCDAME	DUDDIE
DRUPELS	DUALISES	DUCE	DUDDIER
DRUPES	DUALISING	DUCES	DUDDIEST
DRUSE	DUALISM	DUCHESS	DUDDY
DRUSES	DUALISMS	DUCHESSE	DUDE
DRUSIER	DUALIST	DUCHESSED	DUDED
DRUSIEST	DUALISTIC	DUCHESSES	DUDEEN
DRUSY	DUALISTS	DUCHIES	DUDEENS
DRUTHERS	DUALITIES	DUCHY	DUDES
DRUXIER	DUALITY	DUCI	DUDGEON
DRUXIEST	DUALIZE	DUCK	DUDGEONS
DRUXY	DUALIZED	DUCKBILL	DUDHEEN
DRY	DUALIZES	DUCKBILLS	DUDHEENS
DRYABLE	DUALIZING	DUCKBOARD	DUDING

DUDISH	DUFFERS	DULCIMER	DUMBOS
DUDISHLY	DUFFEST	DULCIMERS	DUMBS
DUDISM	DUFFING	DULCIMORE	DUMBSHIT
DUDISMS	DUFFINGS	DULCINEA	DUMBSHITS
DUDS	DUFFLE	DULCINEAS	DUMDUM
DUE	DUFFLES	DULCITE	DUMDUMS
DUECENTO	DUFFS	DULCITES	DUMELA
DUECENTOS	DUFUS	DULCITOL	DUMFOUND
DUED	DUFUSES	DULCITOLS	DUMFOUNDS
DUEFUL	DUG	DULCITUDE	DUMKA
DUEL	DUGITE	DULCOSE	DUMKY
DUELED	DUGITES	DULCOSES	DUMMERER
DUELER	DUGONG	DULE	DUMMERERS
DUELERS	DUGONGS	DULES	DUMMIED
DUELING	DUGOUT	DULIA	DUMMIER
DUELIST	DUGOUTS	DULIAS	DUMMIES
DUELISTS	DUGS	DULL	DUMMIEST
DUELLED	DUH	DULLARD	DUMMINESS
DUELLER	DUHKHA	DULLARDS	DUMMKOPF
DUELLERS	DUHKHAS	DULLED	DUMMKOPFS
DUELLI	DUI	DULLER	DUMMY
DUELLING	DUIKER	DULLEST	DUMMYING
DUELLINGS	DUIKERBOK	DULLIER	DUMOSE
DUELLIST	DUIKERS	DULLIEST	DUMOSITY
DUELLISTS	DUING	DULLING	DUMOUS
DUELLO	DUIT	DULLISH	DUMP
DUELLOS	DUITS	DULLISHLY	DUMPBIN
DUELS	DUKA	DULLNESS	DUMPBINS
DUELSOME	DUKAS	DULLS	DUMPCART
DUENDE	DUKE	DULLY	DUMPCARTS
DUENDES	DUKED	DULNESS	DUMPED
DUENESS	DUKEDOM	DULNESSES	DUMPER
DUENESSES	DUKEDOMS	DULOCRACY	DUMPERS
DUENNA	DUKELING	DULOSES	DUMPIER
DUENNAS	DUKELINGS	DULOSIS	DUMPIES
DUES	DUKERIES	DULOTIC	DUMPIEST
DUET	DUKERY	DULSE	DUMPILY
DUETED	DUKES	DULSES	DUMPINESS
DUETING	DUKESHIP	DULY	DUMPING
DUETS	DUKESHIPS	DUMA	DUMPINGS
DUETT	DUKING	DUMAIST	DUMPISH
DUETTED	DUKKA	DUMAISTS	DUMPISHLY
DUETTI	DUKKAH	DUMAS	DUMPLE
DUETTING	DUKKAHS	DUMB	DUMPLED
DUETTINO	DUKKAS	DUMBBELL	DUMPLES
DUETTINOS	DUKKHA	DUMBBELLS	DUMPLING
DUETTIST	DUKKHAS	DUMBCANE	DUMPLINGS
DUETTISTS	DULCAMARA	DUMBCANES	DUMPS
DUETTO	DULCET	DUMBED	DUMPSITE
DUETTOS	DULCETLY	DUMBER	DUMPSITES
DUETTS	DULCETS	DUMBEST	DUMPSTER
DUFF	DULCIAN	DUMBFOUND	DUMPSTERS
DUFFED	DULCIANA	DUMBHEAD	DUMPTRUCK
DUFFEL	DULCIANAS	DUMBHEADS	DUMPY
DUFFELS	DULCIANS	DUMBING	DUN
DUFFER	DULCIFIED	DUMBLY	DUNAM
DUFFERDOM	DULCIFIES	DUMBNESS	DUNAMS
DUFFERISM	DULCIFY	DUMBO	DUNCE

DUNCEDOM
DUNCEDOMS
DUNCELIKE
DUNCERIES
DUNCERY
DUNCES
DUNCH
DUNCHED
DUNCHES
DUNCHING
DUNCICAL
DUNCISH
DUNCISHLY
DUNDER
DUNDERS
DUNE
DUNELAND
DUNELANDS
DUNELIKE
DUNES
DUNG
DUNGAREE
DUNGAREED
DUNGAREES
DUNGED
DUNGEON
DUNGEONED
DUNGEONER
DUNGEONS
DUNGER
DUNGERS
DUNGHILL
DUNGHILLS
DUNGIER
DUNGIEST
DUNGING
DUNGMERE
DUNGMERES
DUNGS
DUNGY
DUNITE
DUNITES
DUNITIC
DUNK
DUNKED
DUNKER
DUNKERS
DUNKING
DUNKS
DUNLIN
DUNLINS
DUNNAGE
DUNNAGES
DUNNAKIN
DUNNAKINS
DUNNART
DUNNARTS
DUNNED

DUNNER
DUNNESS
DUNNESSES
DUNNEST
DUNNIER
DUNNIES
DUNNIEST
DUNNING
DUNNINGS
DUNNISH
DUNNITE
DUNNITES
DUNNO
DUNNOCK
DUNNOCKS
DUNNY
DUNS
DUNSH
DUNSHED
DUNSHES
DUNSHING
DUNT
DUNTED
DUNTING
DUNTS
DUO
DUOBINARY
DUODECIMO
DUODENA
DUODENAL
DUODENARY
DUODENUM
DUODENUMS
DUOLOG
DUOLOGS
DUOLOGUE
DUOLOGUES
DUOMI
DUOMO
DUOMOS
DUOPOLIES
DUOPOLY
DUOPSONY
DUOS
DUOTONE
DUOTONES
DUP
DUPABLE
DUPATTA
DUPATTAS
DUPE
DUPED
DUPER
DUPERIES
DUPERS
DUPERY
DUPES
DUPING

DUPION
DUPIONS
DUPLE
DUPLET
DUPLETS
DUPLEX
DUPLEXED
DUPLEXER
DUPLEXERS
DUPLEXES
DUPLEXING
DUPLEXITY
DUPLICAND
DUPLICATE
DUPLICITY
DUPLIED
DUPLIES
DUPLY
DUPLYING
DUPONDII
DUPONDIUS
DUPPED
DUPPIES
DUPPING
DUPPY
DUPS
DURA
DURABLE
DURABLES
DURABLY
DURAL
DURALS
DURALUMIN
DURAMEN
DURAMENS
DURANCE
DURANCES
DURANT
DURANTS
DURAS
DURATION
DURATIONS
DURATIVE
DURATIVES
DURBAR
DURBARS
DURDUM
DURDUMS
DURE
DURED
DUREFUL
DURES
DURESS
DURESSE
DURESSES
DURGAH
DURGAHS
DURGAN

DURGANS
DURGIER
DURGIEST
DURGY
DURIAN
DURIANS
DURICRUST
DURING
DURION
DURIONS
DURMAST
DURMASTS
DURN
DURNDEST
DURNED
DURNEDER
DURNEDEST
DURNING
DURNS
DURO
DUROC
DUROCS
DUROMETER
DUROS
DUROY
DUROYS
DURR
DURRA
DURRAS
DURRIE
DURRIES
DURRS
DURRY
DURST
DURUKULI
DURUKULIS
DURUM
DURUMS
DURZI
DURZIS
DUSH
DUSHED
DUSHES
DUSHING
DUSK
DUSKED
DUSKEN
DUSKENED
DUSKENING
DUSKENS
DUSKER
DUSKEST
DUSKIER
DUSKIEST
DUSKILY
DUSKINESS
DUSKING
DUSKISH

DUSKISHLY
DUSKLY
DUSKNESS
DUSKS
DUSKY
DUST
DUSTBIN
DUSTBINS
DUSTCART
DUSTCARTS
DUSTCOVER
DUSTED
DUSTER
DUSTERS
DUSTHEAP
DUSTHEAPS
DUSTIER
DUSTIEST
DUSTILY
DUSTINESS
DUSTING
DUSTINGS
DUSTLESS
DUSTLIKE
DUSTMAN
DUSTMEN
DUSTOFF
DUSTOFFS
DUSTPAN
DUSTPANS
DUSTPROOF
DUSTRAG
DUSTRAGS
DUSTS
DUSTSHEET
DUSTSTORM
DUSTUP
DUSTUPS
DUSTY
DUTCH
DUTCHES
DUTCHMAN
DUTCHMEN
DUTEOUS
DUTEOUSLY
DUTIABLE
DUTIED
DUTIES
DUTIFUL
DUTIFULLY
DUTY
DUUMVIR
DUUMVIRAL
DUUMVIRI
DUUMVIRS
DUVET
DUVETINE
DUVETINES

DUVETS
DUVETYN
DUVETYNE
DUVETYNES
DUVETYNS
DUX
DUXELLES
DUXES
DUYKER
DUYKERS
DVANDVA
DVANDVAS
DVORNIK
DVORNIKS
DWAAL
DWAALS
DWALE
DWALES
DWALM
DWALMED
DWALMING
DWALMS
DWAM
DWAMMED
DWAMMING
DWAMS
DWANG
DWANGS
DWARF
DWARFED
DWARFER
DWARFEST
DWARFING
DWARFISH
DWARFISM
DWARFISMS
DWARFLIKE
DWARFNESS
DWARFS
DWARVES
DWAUM
DWAUMED
DWAUMING
DWAUMS
DWEEB
DWEEBIER
DWEEBIEST
DWEEBISH
DWEEBS
DWEEBY
DWELL
DWELLED
DWELLER
DWELLERS
DWELLING
DWELLINGS
DWELLS
DWELT

DWILE
DWILES
DWINDLE
DWINDLED
DWINDLES
DWINDLING
DWINE
DWINED
DWINES
DWINING
DYABLE
DYAD
DYADIC
DYADICS
DYADS
DYARCHAL
DYARCHIC
DYARCHIES
DYARCHY
DYBBUK
DYBBUKIM
DYBBUKKIM
DYBBUKS
DYE
DYEABLE
DYED
DYEING
DYEINGS
DYELINE
DYELINES
DYER
DYERS
DYES
DYESTER
DYESTERS
DYESTUFF
DYESTUFFS
DYEWEED
DYEWEEDS
DYEWOOD
DYEWOODS
DYING
DYINGLY
DYINGNESS
DYINGS
DYKE
DYKED
DYKES
DYKEY
DYKIER
DYKIEST
DYKING
DYNAMETER
DYNAMIC
DYNAMICAL
DYNAMICS
DYNAMISE
DYNAMISED

DYNAMISES
DYNAMISM
DYNAMISMS
DYNAMIST
DYNAMISTS
DYNAMITE
DYNAMITED
DYNAMITER
DYNAMITES
DYNAMITIC
DYNAMIZE
DYNAMIZED
DYNAMIZES
DYNAMO
DYNAMOS
DYNAMOTOR
DYNAST
DYNASTIC
DYNASTIES
DYNASTS
DYNASTY
DYNATRON
DYNATRONS
DYNE
DYNEIN
DYNEINS
DYNEL
DYNELS
DYNES
DYNODE
DYNODES
DYNORPHIN
DYSBINDIN
DYSCHROA
DYSCHROAS
DYSCHROIA
DYSCRASIA
DYSCRASIC
DYSCRATIC
DYSENTERY
DYSGENIC
DYSGENICS
DYSLALIA
DYSLALIAS
DYSLECTIC
DYSLEXIA
DYSLEXIAS
DYSLEXIC
DYSLEXICS
DYSLOGIES
DYSLOGY
DYSMELIA
DYSMELIAS
DYSMELIC
DYSODIL
DYSODILE
DYSODILES
DYSODILS

DYSODYLE   DZIGGETAI
DYSODYLES   DZO
DYSPATHY   DZOS
DYSPEPSIA
DYSPEPSY
DYSPEPTIC
DYSPHAGIA
DYSPHAGIC
DYSPHAGY
DYSPHASIA
DYSPHASIC
DYSPHONIA
DYSPHONIC
DYSPHORIA
DYSPHORIC
DYSPLASIA
DYSPNEA
DYSPNEAL
DYSPNEAS
DYSPNEIC
DYSPNOEA
DYSPNOEAL
DYSPNOEAS
DYSPNOEIC
DYSPNOIC
DYSPRAXIA
DYSTAXIA
DYSTAXIAS
DYSTECTIC
DYSTHESIA
DYSTHETIC
DYSTHYMIA
DYSTHYMIC
DYSTOCIA
DYSTOCIAL
DYSTOCIAS
DYSTONIA
DYSTONIAS
DYSTONIC
DYSTOPIA
DYSTOPIAN
DYSTOPIAS
DYSTROPHY
DYSURIA
DYSURIAS
DYSURIC
DYSURIES
DYSURY
DYTISCID
DYTISCIDS
DYVOUR
DYVOURIES
DYVOURS
DYVOURY
DZEREN
DZERENS
DZHO
DZHOS

— *E* —

EA	EARDS	EARRINGS	EASEL
EACH	EARED	EARS	EASELED
EACHWHERE	EARFLAP	EARSHOT	EASELESS
EADISH	EARFLAPS	EARSHOTS	EASELS
EADISHES	EARFUL	EARST	EASEMENT
EAGER	EARFULS	EARSTONE	EASEMENTS
EAGERER	EARING	EARSTONES	EASER
EAGEREST	EARINGS	EARTH	EASERS
EAGERLY	EARL	EARTHBORN	EASES
EAGERNESS	EARLAP	EARTHED	EASIED
EAGERS	EARLAPS	EARTHEN	EASIER
EAGLE	EARLDOM	EARTHFALL	EASIES
EAGLED	EARLDOMS	EARTHFAST	EASIEST
EAGLEHAWK	EARLESS	EARTHFLAX	EASILY
EAGLES	EARLIER	EARTHIER	EASINESS
EAGLET	EARLIES	EARTHIEST	EASING
EAGLETS	EARLIEST	EARTHILY	EASLE
EAGLEWOOD	EARLIKE	EARTHING	EASLES
EAGLING	EARLINESS	EARTHLIER	EASSEL
EAGRE	EARLOBE	EARTHLIES	EASSIL
EAGRES	EARLOBES	EARTHLIKE	EAST
EALDORMAN	EARLOCK	EARTHLING	EASTBOUND
EALDORMEN	EARLOCKS	EARTHLY	EASTED
EALE	EARLS	EARTHMAN	EASTER
EALES	EARLSHIP	EARTHMEN	EASTERLY
EAN	EARLSHIPS	EARTHNUT	EASTERN
EANED	EARLY	EARTHNUTS	EASTERNER
EANING	EARLYWOOD	EARTHPEA	EASTERS
EANLING	EARMARK	EARTHPEAS	EASTING
EANLINGS	EARMARKED	EARTHRISE	EASTINGS
EANS	EARMARKS	EARTHS	EASTLAND
EAR	EARMUFF	EARTHSET	EASTLIN
EARACHE	EARMUFFS	EARTHSETS	EASTLING
EARACHES	EARN	EARTHSTAR	EASTLINGS
EARBALL	EARNED	EARTHWARD	EASTLINS
EARBALLS	EARNER	EARTHWAX	EASTMOST
EARBASH	EARNERS	EARTHWOLF	EASTS
EARBASHED	EARNEST	EARTHWORK	EASTWARD
EARBASHER	EARNESTLY	EARTHWORM	EASTWARDS
EARBASHES	EARNESTS	EARTHY	EASY
EARBOB	EARNING	EARWAX	EASYGOING
EARBOBS	EARNINGS	EARWAXES	EASYING
EARBUD	EARNS	EARWIG	EAT
EARBUDS	EARPHONE	EARWIGGED	EATABLE
EARCON	EARPHONES	EARWIGGY	EATABLES
EARCONS	EARPICK	EARWIGS	EATAGE
EARD	EARPICKS	EARWORM	EATAGES
EARDED	EARPIECE	EARWORMS	EATCHE
EARDING	EARPIECES	EAS	EATCHES
EARDROP	EARPLUG	EASE	EATEN
EARDROPS	EARPLUGS	EASED	EATER
EARDRUM	EARRING	EASEFUL	EATERIE
EARDRUMS	EARRINGED	EASEFULLY	EATERIES

EATERS
EATERY
EATH
EATHE
EATHLY
EATING
EATINGS
EATS
EAU
EAUS
EAUX
EAVE
EAVED
EAVES
EAVESDRIP
EAVESDROP
EBAUCHE
EBAUCHES
EBAYER
EBAYERS
EBAYING
EBAYINGS
EBB
EBBED
EBBET
EBBETS
EBBING
EBBLESS
EBBS
EBBTIDE
EBBTIDES
EBENEZER
EBENEZERS
EBENISTE
EBENISTES
EBIONISE
EBIONISED
EBIONISES
EBIONISM
EBIONISMS
EBIONITIC
EBIONIZE
EBIONIZED
EBIONIZES
EBON
EBONICS
EBONIES
EBONISE
EBONISED
EBONISES
EBONISING
EBONIST
EBONISTS
EBONITE
EBONITES
EBONIZE
EBONIZED
EBONIZES

EBONIZING
EBONS
EBONY
EBOOK
EBOOKS
EBRIATE
EBRIATED
EBRIETIES
EBRIETY
EBRILLADE
EBRIOSE
EBRIOSITY
EBULLIENT
EBURNEAN
EBURNEOUS
ECAD
ECADS
ECARINATE
ECARTE
ECARTES
ECAUDATE
ECBOLE
ECBOLES
ECBOLIC
ECBOLICS
ECCE
ECCENTRIC
ECCLESIA
ECCLESIAE
ECCLESIAL
ECCO
ECCRINE
ECCRISES
ECCRISIS
ECCRITIC
ECCRITICS
ECDEMIC
ECDYSES
ECDYSIAL
ECDYSIAST
ECDYSIS
ECDYSON
ECDYSONE
ECDYSONES
ECDYSONS
ECESIC
ECESIS
ECESISES
ECH
ECHAPPE
ECHAPPES
ECHARD
ECHARDS
ECHE
ECHED
ECHELLE
ECHELLES
ECHELON

ECHELONED
ECHELONS
ECHES
ECHEVERIA
ECHIDNA
ECHIDNAE
ECHIDNAS
ECHIDNINE
ECHINACEA
ECHINATE
ECHINATED
ECHING
ECHINI
ECHINOID
ECHINOIDS
ECHINUS
ECHINUSES
ECHIUM
ECHIUMS
ECHIUROID
ECHO
ECHOED
ECHOER
ECHOERS
ECHOES
ECHOEY
ECHOGRAM
ECHOGRAMS
ECHOIC
ECHOING
ECHOISE
ECHOISED
ECHOISES
ECHOISING
ECHOISM
ECHOISMS
ECHOIST
ECHOISTS
ECHOIZE
ECHOIZED
ECHOIZES
ECHOIZING
ECHOLALIA
ECHOLALIC
ECHOLESS
ECHOS
ECHOVIRUS
ECHT
ECLAIR
ECLAIRS
ECLAMPSIA
ECLAMPSY
ECLAMPTIC
ECLAT
ECLATS
ECLECTIC
ECLECTICS
ECLIPSE

ECLIPSED
ECLIPSER
ECLIPSERS
ECLIPSES
ECLIPSING
ECLIPSIS
ECLIPTIC
ECLIPTICS
ECLOGITE
ECLOGITES
ECLOGUE
ECLOGUES
ECLOSE
ECLOSED
ECLOSES
ECLOSING
ECLOSION
ECLOSIONS
ECO
ECOCIDAL
ECOCIDE
ECOCIDES
ECOD
ECOFREAK
ECOFREAKS
ECOLOGIC
ECOLOGIES
ECOLOGIST
ECOLOGY
ECOMMERCE
ECONOBOX
ECONOMIC
ECONOMICS
ECONOMIES
ECONOMISE
ECONOMISM
ECONOMIST
ECONOMIZE
ECONOMY
ECONUT
ECONUTS
ECOPHOBIA
ECORCHE
ECORCHES
ECOREGION
ECOS
ECOSPHERE
ECOSSAISE
ECOSTATE
ECOSYSTEM
ECOTAGE
ECOTAGES
ECOTONAL
ECOTONE
ECOTONES
ECOTOUR
ECOTOURS
ECOTOXIC

ECOTYPE	ECUELLE	EDICTALLY	EECHES
ECOTYPES	ECUELLES	EDICTS	EECHING
ECOTYPIC	ECUMENIC	EDIFICE	EEJIT
ECRASEUR	ECUMENICS	EDIFICES	EEJITS
ECRASEURS	ECUMENISM	EDIFICIAL	EEK
ECRITOIRE	ECUMENIST	EDIFIED	EEL
ECRU	ECURIE	EDIFIER	EELFARE
ECRUS	ECURIES	EDIFIERS	EELFARES
ECSTASES	ECUS	EDIFIES	EELGRASS
ECSTASIED	ECZEMA	EDIFY	EELIER
ECSTASIES	ECZEMAS	EDIFYING	EELIEST
ECSTASIS	ED	EDILE	EELLIKE
ECSTASISE	EDACIOUS	EDILES	EELPOUT
ECSTASIZE	EDACITIES	EDIT	EELPOUTS
ECSTASY	EDACITY	EDITABLE	EELS
ECSTATIC	EDAPHIC	EDITED	EELWORM
ECSTATICS	EDDIED	EDITING	EELWORMS
ECTASES	EDDIES	EDITINGS	EELWRACK
ECTASIA	EDDISH	EDITION	EELWRACKS
ECTASIAS	EDDISHES	EDITIONED	EELY
ECTASIS	EDDO	EDITIONS	EEN
ECTATIC	EDDOES	EDITOR	EERIE
ECTHYMA	EDDY	EDITORIAL	EERIER
ECTHYMAS	EDDYING	EDITORS	EERIEST
ECTHYMATA	EDELWEISS	EDITRESS	EERILY
ECTOBLAST	EDEMA	EDITRICES	EERINESS
ECTOCRINE	EDEMAS	EDITRIX	EERY
ECTODERM	EDEMATA	EDITRIXES	EEVEN
ECTODERMS	EDEMATOSE	EDITS	EEVENS
ECTOGENIC	EDEMATOUS	EDS	EEVN
ECTOGENY	EDENIC	EDUCABLE	EEVNING
ECTOMERE	EDENTAL	EDUCABLES	EEVNINGS
ECTOMERES	EDENTATE	EDUCATE	EEVNS
ECTOMERIC	EDENTATES	EDUCATED	EF
ECTOMORPH	EDGE	EDUCATES	EFF
ECTOPHYTE	EDGEBONE	EDUCATING	EFFABLE
ECTOPIA	EDGEBONES	EDUCATION	EFFACE
ECTOPIAS	EDGED	EDUCATIVE	EFFACED
ECTOPIC	EDGELESS	EDUCATOR	EFFACER
ECTOPIES	EDGER	EDUCATORS	EFFACERS
ECTOPLASM	EDGERS	EDUCATORY	EFFACES
ECTOPROCT	EDGES	EDUCE	EFFACING
ECTOPY	EDGEWAYS	EDUCED	EFFECT
ECTOSARC	EDGEWISE	EDUCEMENT	EFFECTED
ECTOSARCS	EDGIER	EDUCES	EFFECTER
ECTOTHERM	EDGIEST	EDUCIBLE	EFFECTERS
ECTOZOA	EDGILY	EDUCING	EFFECTING
ECTOZOAN	EDGINESS	EDUCT	EFFECTIVE
ECTOZOANS	EDGING	EDUCTION	EFFECTOR
ECTOZOIC	EDGINGS	EDUCTIONS	EFFECTORS
ECTOZOON	EDGY	EDUCTIVE	EFFECTS
ECTROPIC	EDH	EDUCTOR	EFFECTUAL
ECTROPION	EDHS	EDUCTORS	EFFED
ECTROPIUM	EDIBILITY	EDUCTS	EFFEIR
ECTYPAL	EDIBLE	EDUSKUNTA	EFFEIRED
ECTYPE	EDIBLES	EE	EFFEIRING
ECTYPES	EDICT	EECH	EFFEIRS
ECU	EDICTAL	EECHED	EFFENDI

179

EFFENDIS
EFFERE
EFFERED
EFFERENCE
EFFERENT
EFFERENTS
EFFERES
EFFERING
EFFETE
EFFETELY
EFFICACY
EFFICIENT
EFFIERCE
EFFIERCED
EFFIERCES
EFFIGIAL
EFFIGIES
EFFIGY
EFFING
EFFINGS
EFFLUENCE
EFFLUENT
EFFLUENTS
EFFLUVIA
EFFLUVIAL
EFFLUVIUM
EFFLUX
EFFLUXES
EFFLUXION
EFFORCE
EFFORCED
EFFORCES
EFFORCING
EFFORT
EFFORTFUL
EFFORTS
EFFRAIDE
EFFRAY
EFFRAYS
EFFS
EFFULGE
EFFULGED
EFFULGENT
EFFULGES
EFFULGING
EFFUSE
EFFUSED
EFFUSES
EFFUSING
EFFUSION
EFFUSIONS
EFFUSIVE
EFS
EFT
EFTEST
EFTS
EFTSOON
EFTSOONS

EGAD
EGADS
EGAL
EGALITE
EGALITES
EGALITIES
EGALITY
EGALLY
EGAREMENT
EGENCE
EGENCES
EGENCIES
EGENCY
EGER
EGERS
EGEST
EGESTA
EGESTED
EGESTING
EGESTION
EGESTIONS
EGESTIVE
EGESTS
EGG
EGGAR
EGGARS
EGGBEATER
EGGCUP
EGGCUPS
EGGED
EGGER
EGGERIES
EGGERS
EGGERY
EGGFRUIT
EGGFRUITS
EGGHEAD
EGGHEADED
EGGHEADS
EGGIER
EGGIEST
EGGING
EGGLER
EGGLERS
EGGLESS
EGGMASS
EGGMASSES
EGGNOG
EGGNOGS
EGGPLANT
EGGPLANTS
EGGS
EGGSHELL
EGGSHELLS
EGGWASH
EGGWASHES
EGGWHISK
EGGWHISKS

EGGY
EGIS
EGISES
EGLANTINE
EGLATERE
EGLATERES
EGLOMISE
EGMA
EGMAS
EGO
EGOISM
EGOISMS
EGOIST
EGOISTIC
EGOISTS
EGOITIES
EGOITY
EGOLESS
EGOMANIA
EGOMANIAC
EGOMANIAS
EGOS
EGOTHEISM
EGOTISE
EGOTISED
EGOTISES
EGOTISING
EGOTISM
EGOTISMS
EGOTIST
EGOTISTIC
EGOTISTS
EGOTIZE
EGOTIZED
EGOTIZES
EGOTIZING
EGREGIOUS
EGRESS
EGRESSED
EGRESSES
EGRESSING
EGRESSION
EGRET
EGRETS
EGYPTIAN
EGYPTIANS
EH
EHED
EHING
EHS
EIDE
EIDENT
EIDER
EIDERDOWN
EIDERS
EIDETIC
EIDETICS
EIDOGRAPH

EIDOLA
EIDOLIC
EIDOLON
EIDOLONS
EIDOS
EIGENMODE
EIGENTONE
EIGHT
EIGHTBALL
EIGHTEEN
EIGHTEENS
EIGHTFOIL
EIGHTFOLD
EIGHTFOOT
EIGHTH
EIGHTHLY
EIGHTHS
EIGHTIES
EIGHTIETH
EIGHTS
EIGHTSMAN
EIGHTSMEN
EIGHTSOME
EIGHTVO
EIGHTVOS
EIGHTY
EIGNE
EIK
EIKED
EIKING
EIKON
EIKONES
EIKONS
EIKS
EILD
EILDING
EILDINGS
EILDS
EINA
EINE
EINKORN
EINKORNS
EINSTEIN
EINSTEINS
EIRACK
EIRACKS
EIRENIC
EIRENICAL
EIRENICON
EISEGESES
EISEGESIS
EISEL
EISELL
EISELLS
EISELS
EISH
EISWEIN
EISWEINS

EITHER
EJACULATE
EJECT
EJECTA
EJECTABLE
EJECTED
EJECTING
EJECTION
EJECTIONS
EJECTIVE
EJECTIVES
EJECTMENT
EJECTOR
EJECTORS
EJECTS
EKE
EKED
EKES
EKING
EKISTIC
EKISTICAL
EKISTICS
EKKA
EKKAS
EKLOGITE
EKLOGITES
EKPHRASES
EKPHRASIS
EKPWELE
EKPWELES
EKTEXINE
EKTEXINES
EKUELE
EL
ELABORATE
ELAEOLITE
ELAIN
ELAINS
ELAIOSOME
ELAN
ELANCE
ELANCED
ELANCES
ELANCING
ELAND
ELANDS
ELANET
ELANETS
ELANS
ELAPHINE
ELAPID
ELAPIDS
ELAPINE
ELAPSE
ELAPSED
ELAPSES
ELAPSING
ELASTANCE

ELASTANE
ELASTANES
ELASTASE
ELASTASES
ELASTIC
ELASTICS
ELASTIN
ELASTINS
ELASTOMER
ELATE
ELATED
ELATEDLY
ELATER
ELATERID
ELATERIDS
ELATERIN
ELATERINS
ELATERITE
ELATERIUM
ELATERS
ELATES
ELATING
ELATION
ELATIONS
ELATIVE
ELATIVES
ELBOW
ELBOWED
ELBOWING
ELBOWROOM
ELBOWS
ELCHEE
ELCHEES
ELCHI
ELCHIS
ELD
ELDER
ELDERCARE
ELDERLIES
ELDERLY
ELDERS
ELDERSHIP
ELDEST
ELDIN
ELDING
ELDINGS
ELDINS
ELDORADO
ELDORADOS
ELDRESS
ELDRESSES
ELDRICH
ELDRITCH
ELDS
ELECT
ELECTABLE
ELECTED
ELECTEE

ELECTEES
ELECTING
ELECTION
ELECTIONS
ELECTIVE
ELECTIVES
ELECTOR
ELECTORAL
ELECTORS
ELECTRESS
ELECTRET
ELECTRETS
ELECTRIC
ELECTRICS
ELECTRIFY
ELECTRISE
ELECTRIZE
ELECTRO
ELECTRODE
ELECTROED
ELECTRON
ELECTRONS
ELECTROS
ELECTRUM
ELECTRUMS
ELECTS
ELECTUARY
ELEDOISIN
ELEGANCE
ELEGANCES
ELEGANCY
ELEGANT
ELEGANTLY
ELEGIAC
ELEGIACAL
ELEGIACS
ELEGIAST
ELEGIASTS
ELEGIES
ELEGISE
ELEGISED
ELEGISES
ELEGISING
ELEGIST
ELEGISTS
ELEGIT
ELEGITS
ELEGIZE
ELEGIZED
ELEGIZES
ELEGIZING
ELEGY
ELEMENT
ELEMENTAL
ELEMENTS
ELEMI
ELEMIS
ELENCH

ELENCHI
ELENCHIC
ELENCHS
ELENCHTIC
ELENCHUS
ELENCTIC
ELEOPTENE
ELEPHANT
ELEPHANTS
ELEUTHERI
ELEVATE
ELEVATED
ELEVATEDS
ELEVATES
ELEVATING
ELEVATION
ELEVATOR
ELEVATORS
ELEVATORY
ELEVEN
ELEVENS
ELEVENSES
ELEVENTH
ELEVENTHS
ELEVON
ELEVONS
ELF
ELFED
ELFHOOD
ELFHOODS
ELFIN
ELFING
ELFINS
ELFISH
ELFISHLY
ELFLAND
ELFLANDS
ELFLIKE
ELFLOCK
ELFLOCKS
ELFS
ELHI
ELIAD
ELIADS
ELICHE
ELICHES
ELICIT
ELICITED
ELICITING
ELICITOR
ELICITORS
ELICITS
ELIDE
ELIDED
ELIDES
ELIDIBLE
ELIDING
ELIGIBLE

ELIGIBLES	ELOIGNER	ELUTE	EMBAILING
ELIGIBLY	ELOIGNERS	ELUTED	EMBAILS
ELIMINANT	ELOIGNING	ELUTES	EMBALE
ELIMINATE	ELOIGNS	ELUTING	EMBALED
ELINT	ELOIN	ELUTION	EMBALES
ELINTS	ELOINED	ELUTIONS	EMBALING
ELISION	ELOINER	ELUTOR	EMBALL
ELISIONS	ELOINERS	ELUTORS	EMBALLED
ELITE	ELOINING	ELUTRIATE	EMBALLING
ELITES	ELOINMENT	ELUVIA	EMBALLS
ELITISM	ELOINS	ELUVIAL	EMBALM
ELITISMS	ELONGATE	ELUVIATE	EMBALMED
ELITIST	ELONGATED	ELUVIATED	EMBALMER
ELITISTS	ELONGATES	ELUVIATES	EMBALMERS
ELIXIR	ELOPE	ELUVIUM	EMBALMING
ELIXIRS	ELOPED	ELUVIUMS	EMBALMS
ELK	ELOPEMENT	ELVAN	EMBANK
ELKHOUND	ELOPER	ELVANITE	EMBANKED
ELKHOUNDS	ELOPERS	ELVANITES	EMBANKER
ELKS	ELOPES	ELVANS	EMBANKERS
ELL	ELOPING	ELVER	EMBANKING
ELLAGIC	ELOPS	ELVERS	EMBANKS
ELLIPSE	ELOPSES	ELVES	EMBAR
ELLIPSES	ELOQUENCE	ELVISH	EMBARGO
ELLIPSIS	ELOQUENT	ELVISHLY	EMBARGOED
ELLIPSOID	ELPEE	ELYSIAN	EMBARGOES
ELLIPTIC	ELPEES	ELYTRA	EMBARK
ELLOPS	ELS	ELYTRAL	EMBARKED
ELLOPSES	ELSE	ELYTROID	EMBARKING
ELLS	ELSEWHERE	ELYTRON	EMBARKS
ELLWAND	ELSEWISE	ELYTROUS	EMBARRASS
ELLWANDS	ELSHIN	ELYTRUM	EMBARRED
ELM	ELSHINS	EM	EMBARRING
ELMEN	ELSIN	EMACIATE	EMBARS
ELMIER	ELSINS	EMACIATED	EMBASE
ELMIEST	ELT	EMACIATES	EMBASED
ELMS	ELTCHI	EMACS	EMBASES
ELMWOOD	ELTCHIS	EMACSEN	EMBASING
ELMWOODS	ELTS	EMAIL	EMBASSADE
ELMY	ELUANT	EMAILED	EMBASSAGE
ELOCUTE	ELUANTS	EMAILING	EMBASSIES
ELOCUTED	ELUATE	EMAILS	EMBASSY
ELOCUTES	ELUATES	EMANANT	EMBASTE
ELOCUTING	ELUCIDATE	EMANATE	EMBATHE
ELOCUTION	ELUDE	EMANATED	EMBATHED
ELOCUTORY	ELUDED	EMANATES	EMBATHES
ELODEA	ELUDER	EMANATING	EMBATHING
ELODEAS	ELUDERS	EMANATION	EMBATTLE
ELOGE	ELUDES	EMANATIST	EMBATTLED
ELOGES	ELUDIBLE	EMANATIVE	EMBATTLES
ELOGIES	ELUDING	EMANATOR	EMBAY
ELOGIST	ELUENT	EMANATORS	EMBAYED
ELOGISTS	ELUENTS	EMANATORY	EMBAYING
ELOGIUM	ELUSION	EMBACE	EMBAYLD
ELOGIUMS	ELUSIONS	EMBACES	EMBAYMENT
ELOGY	ELUSIVE	EMBACING	EMBAYS
ELOIGN	ELUSIVELY	EMBAIL	EMBED
ELOIGNED	ELUSORY	EMBAILED	EMBEDDED

EMBEDDING	EMBOLISED	EMBRASOR	EMDASHES
EMBEDMENT	EMBOLISES	EMBRASORS	EME
EMBEDS	EMBOLISM	EMBRASURE	EMEER
EMBELLISH	EMBOLISMS	EMBRAVE	EMEERATE
EMBER	EMBOLIZE	EMBRAVED	EMEERATES
EMBERS	EMBOLIZED	EMBRAVES	EMEERS
EMBEZZLE	EMBOLIZES	EMBRAVING	EMEND
EMBEZZLED	EMBOLUS	EMBRAZURE	EMENDABLE
EMBEZZLER	EMBOLUSES	EMBREAD	EMENDALS
EMBEZZLES	EMBOLY	EMBREADED	EMENDATE
EMBITTER	EMBORDER	EMBREADS	EMENDATED
EMBITTERS	EMBORDERS	EMBREATHE	EMENDATES
EMBLAZE	EMBOSCATA	EMBRITTLE	EMENDATOR
EMBLAZED	EMBOSK	EMBROCATE	EMENDED
EMBLAZER	EMBOSKED	EMBROGLIO	EMENDER
EMBLAZERS	EMBOSKING	EMBROIDER	EMENDERS
EMBLAZES	EMBOSKS	EMBROIL	EMENDING
EMBLAZING	EMBOSOM	EMBROILED	EMENDS
EMBLAZON	EMBOSOMED	EMBROILER	EMERALD
EMBLAZONS	EMBOSOMS	EMBROILS	EMERALDS
EMBLEM	EMBOSS	EMBROWN	EMERAUDE
EMBLEMA	EMBOSSED	EMBROWNED	EMERAUDES
EMBLEMATA	EMBOSSER	EMBROWNS	EMERGE
EMBLEMED	EMBOSSERS	EMBRUE	EMERGED
EMBLEMING	EMBOSSES	EMBRUED	EMERGENCE
EMBLEMISE	EMBOSSING	EMBRUES	EMERGENCY
EMBLEMIZE	EMBOST	EMBRUING	EMERGENT
EMBLEMS	EMBOUND	EMBRUTE	EMERGENTS
EMBLIC	EMBOUNDED	EMBRUTED	EMERGES
EMBLICS	EMBOUNDS	EMBRUTES	EMERGING
EMBLOOM	EMBOW	EMBRUTING	EMERIED
EMBLOOMED	EMBOWED	EMBRYO	EMERIES
EMBLOOMS	EMBOWEL	EMBRYOID	EMERITA
EMBLOSSOM	EMBOWELED	EMBRYOIDS	EMERITAE
EMBODIED	EMBOWELS	EMBRYON	EMERITAS
EMBODIER	EMBOWER	EMBRYONAL	EMERITI
EMBODIERS	EMBOWERED	EMBRYONIC	EMERITUS
EMBODIES	EMBOWERS	EMBRYONS	EMEROD
EMBODY	EMBOWING	EMBRYOS	EMERODS
EMBODYING	EMBOWMENT	EMBRYOTIC	EMEROID
EMBOG	EMBOWS	EMBUS	EMEROIDS
EMBOGGED	EMBOX	EMBUSED	EMERSED
EMBOGGING	EMBOXED	EMBUSES	EMERSION
EMBOGS	EMBOXES	EMBUSIED	EMERSIONS
EMBOGUE	EMBOXING	EMBUSIES	EMERY
EMBOGUED	EMBRACE	EMBUSING	EMERYING
EMBOGUES	EMBRACED	EMBUSQUE	EMES
EMBOGUING	EMBRACEOR	EMBUSQUES	EMESES
EMBOIL	EMBRACER	EMBUSSED	EMESIS
EMBOILED	EMBRACERS	EMBUSSES	EMETIC
EMBOILING	EMBRACERY	EMBUSSING	EMETICAL
EMBOILS	EMBRACES	EMBUSY	EMETICS
EMBOLDEN	EMBRACING	EMBUSYING	EMETIN
EMBOLDENS	EMBRACIVE	EMCEE	EMETINE
EMBOLI	EMBRAID	EMCEED	EMETINES
EMBOLIC	EMBRAIDED	EMCEEING	EMETINS
EMBOLIES	EMBRAIDS	EMCEES	EMEU
EMBOLISE	EMBRANGLE	EMDASH	EMEUS

EMEUTE	EMMEWS	EMPARES	EMPIRES
EMEUTES	EMMOVE	EMPARING	EMPIRIC
EMIC	EMMOVED	EMPARL	EMPIRICAL
EMICANT	EMMOVES	EMPARLED	EMPIRICS
EMICATE	EMMOVING	EMPARLING	EMPLACE
EMICATED	EMMY	EMPARLS	EMPLACED
EMICATES	EMMYS	EMPART	EMPLACES
EMICATING	EMO	EMPARTED	EMPLACING
EMICATION	EMODIN	EMPARTING	EMPLANE
EMICTION	EMODINS	EMPARTS	EMPLANED
EMICTIONS	EMOLLIATE	EMPATHIC	EMPLANES
EMICTORY	EMOLLIENT	EMPATHIES	EMPLANING
EMIGRANT	EMOLUMENT	EMPATHISE	EMPLASTER
EMIGRANTS	EMONG	EMPATHIST	EMPLASTIC
EMIGRATE	EMONGES	EMPATHIZE	EMPLEACH
EMIGRATED	EMONGEST	EMPATHY	EMPLECTON
EMIGRATES	EMONGST	EMPATRON	EMPLECTUM
EMIGRE	EMOS	EMPATRONS	EMPLONGE
EMIGRES	EMOTE	EMPAYRE	EMPLONGED
EMINENCE	EMOTED	EMPAYRED	EMPLONGES
EMINENCES	EMOTER	EMPAYRES	EMPLOY
EMINENCY	EMOTERS	EMPAYRING	EMPLOYE
EMINENT	EMOTES	EMPEACH	EMPLOYED
EMINENTLY	EMOTICON	EMPEACHED	EMPLOYEE
EMIR	EMOTICONS	EMPEACHES	EMPLOYEES
EMIRATE	EMOTING	EMPENNAGE	EMPLOYER
EMIRATES	EMOTION	EMPEOPLE	EMPLOYERS
EMIRS	EMOTIONAL	EMPEOPLED	EMPLOYES
EMISSARY	EMOTIONS	EMPEOPLES	EMPLOYING
EMISSILE	EMOTIVE	EMPERCE	EMPLOYS
EMISSION	EMOTIVELY	EMPERCED	EMPLUME
EMISSIONS	EMOTIVISM	EMPERCES	EMPLUMED
EMISSIVE	EMOTIVITY	EMPERCING	EMPLUMES
EMIT	EMOVE	EMPERIES	EMPLUMING
EMITS	EMOVED	EMPERISE	EMPOISON
EMITTANCE	EMOVES	EMPERISED	EMPOISONS
EMITTED	EMOVING	EMPERISES	EMPOLDER
EMITTER	EMPACKET	EMPERISH	EMPOLDERS
EMITTERS	EMPACKETS	EMPERIZE	EMPORIA
EMITTING	EMPAESTIC	EMPERIZED	EMPORIUM
EMLETS	EMPAIRE	EMPERIZES	EMPORIUMS
EMMA	EMPAIRED	EMPEROR	EMPOWER
EMMARBLE	EMPAIRES	EMPERORS	EMPOWERED
EMMARBLED	EMPAIRING	EMPERY	EMPOWERS
EMMARBLES	EMPALE	EMPHASES	EMPRESS
EMMAS	EMPALED	EMPHASIS	EMPRESSE
EMMER	EMPALER	EMPHASISE	EMPRESSES
EMMERS	EMPALERS	EMPHASIZE	EMPRISE
EMMESH	EMPALES	EMPHATIC	EMPRISES
EMMESHED	EMPALING	EMPHATICS	EMPRIZE
EMMESHES	EMPANADA	EMPHLYSES	EMPRIZES
EMMESHING	EMPANADAS	EMPHLYSIS	EMPT
EMMET	EMPANEL	EMPHYSEMA	EMPTED
EMMETROPE	EMPANELED	EMPIERCE	EMPTIABLE
EMMETS	EMPANELS	EMPIERCED	EMPTIED
EMMEW	EMPANOPLY	EMPIERCES	EMPTIER
EMMEWED	EMPARE	EMPIGHT	EMPTIERS
EMMEWING	EMPARED	EMPIRE	EMPTIES

EMPTIEST	EMULSION	ENAMOR	ENCHAFES
EMPTILY	EMULSIONS	ENAMORADO	ENCHAFING
EMPTINESS	EMULSIVE	ENAMORED	ENCHAIN
EMPTING	EMULSOID	ENAMORING	ENCHAINED
EMPTINGS	EMULSOIDS	ENAMORS	ENCHAINS
EMPTINS	EMULSOR	ENAMOUR	ENCHANT
EMPTION	EMULSORS	ENAMOURED	ENCHANTED
EMPTIONAL	EMUNCTION	ENAMOURS	ENCHANTER
EMPTIONS	EMUNCTORY	ENARCH	ENCHANTS
EMPTS	EMUNGE	ENARCHED	ENCHARGE
EMPTY	EMUNGED	ENARCHES	ENCHARGED
EMPTYING	EMUNGES	ENARCHING	ENCHARGES
EMPTYINGS	EMUNGING	ENARM	ENCHARM
EMPTYSES	EMURE	ENARMED	ENCHARMED
EMPTYSIS	EMURED	ENARMING	ENCHARMS
EMPURPLE	EMURES	ENARMS	ENCHASE
EMPURPLED	EMURING	ENATE	ENCHASED
EMPURPLES	EMUS	ENATES	ENCHASER
EMPUSA	EMYD	ENATIC	ENCHASERS
EMPUSAS	EMYDE	ENATION	ENCHASES
EMPUSE	EMYDES	ENATIONS	ENCHASING
EMPUSES	EMYDS	ENAUNTER	ENCHEASON
EMPYEMA	EMYS	ENCAENIA	ENCHEER
EMPYEMAS	EN	ENCAENIAS	ENCHEERED
EMPYEMATA	ENABLE	ENCAGE	ENCHEERS
EMPYEMIC	ENABLED	ENCAGED	ENCHILADA
EMPYESES	ENABLER	ENCAGES	ENCHORIAL
EMPYESIS	ENABLERS	ENCAGING	ENCHORIC
EMPYREAL	ENABLES	ENCALM	ENCIERRO
EMPYREAN	ENABLING	ENCALMED	ENCIERROS
EMPYREANS	ENACT	ENCALMING	ENCINA
EMPYREUMA	ENACTABLE	ENCALMS	ENCINAL
EMS	ENACTED	ENCAMP	ENCINAS
EMU	ENACTING	ENCAMPED	ENCIPHER
EMULATE	ENACTION	ENCAMPING	ENCIPHERS
EMULATED	ENACTIONS	ENCAMPS	ENCIRCLE
EMULATES	ENACTIVE	ENCANTHIS	ENCIRCLED
EMULATING	ENACTMENT	ENCAPSULE	ENCIRCLES
EMULATION	ENACTOR	ENCARPUS	ENCLASP
EMULATIVE	ENACTORS	ENCASE	ENCLASPED
EMULATOR	ENACTORY	ENCASED	ENCLASPS
EMULATORS	ENACTS	ENCASES	ENCLAVE
EMULE	ENACTURE	ENCASH	ENCLAVED
EMULED	ENACTURES	ENCASHED	ENCLAVES
EMULES	ENALAPRIL	ENCASHES	ENCLAVING
EMULGE	ENALLAGE	ENCASHING	ENCLISES
EMULGED	ENALLAGES	ENCASING	ENCLISIS
EMULGENCE	ENAMEL	ENCASTRE	ENCLITIC
EMULGENT	ENAMELED	ENCAUSTIC	ENCLITICS
EMULGES	ENAMELER	ENCAVE	ENCLOSE
EMULGING	ENAMELERS	ENCAVED	ENCLOSED
EMULING	ENAMELING	ENCAVES	ENCLOSER
EMULOUS	ENAMELIST	ENCAVING	ENCLOSERS
EMULOUSLY	ENAMELLED	ENCEINTE	ENCLOSES
EMULSIBLE	ENAMELLER	ENCEINTES	ENCLOSING
EMULSIFY	ENAMELS	ENCEPHALA	ENCLOSURE
EMULSIN	ENAMINE	ENCHAFE	ENCLOTHE
EMULSINS	ENAMINES	ENCHAFED	ENCLOTHED

ENCLOTHES

ENCLOTHES
ENCLOUD
ENCLOUDED
ENCLOUDS
ENCODABLE
ENCODE
ENCODED
ENCODER
ENCODERS
ENCODES
ENCODING
ENCOLOUR
ENCOLOURS
ENCOLPION
ENCOLPIUM
ENCOLURE
ENCOLURES
ENCOMIA
ENCOMIAST
ENCOMION
ENCOMIUM
ENCOMIUMS
ENCOMPASS
ENCORE
ENCORED
ENCORES
ENCORING
ENCOUNTER
ENCOURAGE
ENCRADLE
ENCRADLED
ENCRADLES
ENCRATIES
ENCRATY
ENCREASE
ENCREASED
ENCREASES
ENCRIMSON
ENCRINAL
ENCRINIC
ENCRINITE
ENCROACH
ENCRUST
ENCRUSTED
ENCRUSTS
ENCRYPT
ENCRYPTED
ENCRYPTS
ENCUMBER
ENCUMBERS
ENCURTAIN
ENCYCLIC
ENCYCLICS
ENCYST
ENCYSTED
ENCYSTING
ENCYSTS
END

ENDAMAGE
ENDAMAGED
ENDAMAGES
ENDAMEBA
ENDAMEBAE
ENDAMEBAS
ENDAMEBIC
ENDAMOEBA
ENDANGER
ENDANGERS
ENDARCH
ENDARCHY
ENDART
ENDARTED
ENDARTING
ENDARTS
ENDASH
ENDASHES
ENDBRAIN
ENDBRAINS
ENDEAR
ENDEARED
ENDEARING
ENDEARS
ENDEAVOR
ENDEAVORS
ENDEAVOUR
ENDECAGON
ENDED
ENDEICTIC
ENDEIXES
ENDEIXIS
ENDEMIAL
ENDEMIC
ENDEMICAL
ENDEMICS
ENDEMISM
ENDEMISMS
ENDENIZEN
ENDER
ENDERMIC
ENDERON
ENDERONS
ENDERS
ENDEW
ENDEWED
ENDEWING
ENDEWS
ENDEXINE
ENDEXINES
ENDGAME
ENDGAMES
ENDING
ENDINGS
ENDIRON
ENDIRONS
ENDITE
ENDITED

ENDITES
ENDITING
ENDIVE
ENDIVES
ENDLANG
ENDLEAF
ENDLEAFS
ENDLEAVES
ENDLESS
ENDLESSLY
ENDLONG
ENDMOST
ENDNOTE
ENDNOTES
ENDOBLAST
ENDOCARP
ENDOCARPS
ENDOCAST
ENDOCASTS
ENDOCRINE
ENDOCYTIC
ENDODERM
ENDODERMS
ENDODYNE
ENDOERGIC
ENDOGAMIC
ENDOGAMY
ENDOGEN
ENDOGENIC
ENDOGENS
ENDOGENY
ENDOLYMPH
ENDOMIXES
ENDOMIXIS
ENDOMORPH
ENDOPHAGY
ENDOPHYTE
ENDOPLASM
ENDOPOD
ENDOPODS
ENDOPROCT
ENDORPHIN
ENDORSE
ENDORSED
ENDORSEE
ENDORSEES
ENDORSER
ENDORSERS
ENDORSES
ENDORSING
ENDORSIVE
ENDORSOR
ENDORSORS
ENDOSARC
ENDOSARCS
ENDOSCOPE
ENDOSCOPY
ENDOSMOS

ENDOSMOSE
ENDOSOME
ENDOSOMES
ENDOSPERM
ENDOSPORE
ENDOSS
ENDOSSED
ENDOSSES
ENDOSSING
ENDOSTEA
ENDOSTEAL
ENDOSTEUM
ENDOSTYLE
ENDOTHERM
ENDOTOXIC
ENDOTOXIN
ENDOW
ENDOWED
ENDOWER
ENDOWERS
ENDOWING
ENDOWMENT
ENDOWS
ENDOZOA
ENDOZOIC
ENDOZOON
ENDPAPER
ENDPAPERS
ENDPLATE
ENDPLATES
ENDPLAY
ENDPLAYED
ENDPLAYS
ENDPOINT
ENDPOINTS
ENDRIN
ENDRINS
ENDS
ENDSHIP
ENDSHIPS
ENDUE
ENDUED
ENDUES
ENDUING
ENDUNGEON
ENDURABLE
ENDURABLY
ENDURANCE
ENDURE
ENDURED
ENDURER
ENDURERS
ENDURES
ENDURING
ENDURO
ENDUROS
ENDWAYS
ENDWISE

ENDYSES	ENFIERCE	ENGAGED	ENGORGE
ENDYSIS	ENFIERCED	ENGAGEDLY	ENGORGED
ENE	ENFIERCES	ENGAGEE	ENGORGES
ENEMA	ENFILADE	ENGAGER	ENGORGING
ENEMAS	ENFILADED	ENGAGERS	ENGORING
ENEMATA	ENFILADES	ENGAGES	ENGOULED
ENEMIES	ENFILED	ENGAGING	ENGOUMENT
ENEMY	ENFIRE	ENGAOL	ENGRACE
ENERGETIC	ENFIRED	ENGAOLED	ENGRACED
ENERGIC	ENFIRES	ENGAOLING	ENGRACES
ENERGID	ENFIRING	ENGAOLS	ENGRACING
ENERGIDS	ENFIX	ENGARLAND	ENGRAFF
ENERGIES	ENFIXED	ENGENDER	ENGRAFFED
ENERGISE	ENFIXES	ENGENDERS	ENGRAFFS
ENERGISED	ENFIXING	ENGENDURE	ENGRAFT
ENERGISER	ENFLAME	ENGILD	ENGRAFTED
ENERGISES	ENFLAMED	ENGILDED	ENGRAFTS
ENERGIZE	ENFLAMES	ENGILDING	ENGRAIL
ENERGIZED	ENFLAMING	ENGILDS	ENGRAILED
ENERGIZER	ENFLESH	ENGILT	ENGRAILS
ENERGIZES	ENFLESHED	ENGINE	ENGRAIN
ENERGUMEN	ENFLESHES	ENGINED	ENGRAINED
ENERGY	ENFLOWER	ENGINEER	ENGRAINER
ENERVATE	ENFLOWERS	ENGINEERS	ENGRAINS
ENERVATED	ENFOLD	ENGINER	ENGRAM
ENERVATES	ENFOLDED	ENGINERS	ENGRAMMA
ENERVATOR	ENFOLDER	ENGINERY	ENGRAMMAS
ENERVE	ENFOLDERS	ENGINES	ENGRAMME
ENERVED	ENFOLDING	ENGINING	ENGRAMMES
ENERVES	ENFOLDS	ENGINOUS	ENGRAMMIC
ENERVING	ENFORCE	ENGIRD	ENGRAMS
ENES	ENFORCED	ENGIRDED	ENGRASP
ENEW	ENFORCER	ENGIRDING	ENGRASPED
ENEWED	ENFORCERS	ENGIRDLE	ENGRASPS
ENEWING	ENFORCES	ENGIRDLED	ENGRAVE
ENEWS	ENFORCING	ENGIRDLES	ENGRAVED
ENFACE	ENFOREST	ENGIRDS	ENGRAVEN
ENFACED	ENFORESTS	ENGIRT	ENGRAVER
ENFACES	ENFORM	ENGISCOPE	ENGRAVERS
ENFACING	ENFORMED	ENGLACIAL	ENGRAVERY
ENFANT	ENFORMING	ENGLISH	ENGRAVES
ENFANTS	ENFORMS	ENGLISHED	ENGRAVING
ENFEEBLE	ENFRAME	ENGLISHES	ENGRENAGE
ENFEEBLED	ENFRAMED	ENGLOBE	ENGRIEVE
ENFEEBLER	ENFRAMES	ENGLOBED	ENGRIEVED
ENFEEBLES	ENFRAMING	ENGLOBES	ENGRIEVES
ENFELON	ENFREE	ENGLOBING	ENGROOVE
ENFELONED	ENFREED	ENGLOOM	ENGROOVED
ENFELONS	ENFREEDOM	ENGLOOMED	ENGROOVES
ENFEOFF	ENFREEING	ENGLOOMS	ENGROSS
ENFEOFFED	ENFREES	ENGLUT	ENGROSSED
ENFEOFFS	ENFREEZE	ENGLUTS	ENGROSSER
ENFESTED	ENFREEZES	ENGLUTTED	ENGROSSES
ENFETTER	ENFROSEN	ENGOBE	ENGS
ENFETTERS	ENFROZE	ENGOBES	ENGUARD
ENFEVER	ENFROZEN	ENGORE	ENGUARDED
ENFEVERED	ENG	ENGORED	ENGUARDS
ENFEVERS	ENGAGE	ENGORES	ENGULF

ENGULFED	ENKERNEL	ENMEWS	ENOUNCING
ENGULFING	ENKERNELS	ENMITIES	ENOW
ENGULFS	ENKINDLE	ENMITY	ENOWS
ENGULPH	ENKINDLED	ENMOSSED	ENPLANE
ENGULPHED	ENKINDLER	ENMOVE	ENPLANED
ENGULPHS	ENKINDLES	ENMOVED	ENPLANES
ENGYSCOPE	ENLACE	ENMOVES	ENPLANING
ENHALO	ENLACED	ENMOVING	ENPRINT
ENHALOED	ENLACES	ENNAGE	ENPRINTS
ENHALOES	ENLACING	ENNAGES	ENQUIRE
ENHALOING	ENLARD	ENNEAD	ENQUIRED
ENHALOS	ENLARDED	ENNEADIC	ENQUIRER
ENHANCE	ENLARDING	ENNEADS	ENQUIRERS
ENHANCED	ENLARDS	ENNEAGON	ENQUIRES
ENHANCER	ENLARGE	ENNEAGONS	ENQUIRIES
ENHANCERS	ENLARGED	ENNOBLE	ENQUIRING
ENHANCES	ENLARGEN	ENNOBLED	ENQUIRY
ENHANCING	ENLARGENS	ENNOBLER	ENRACE
ENHANCIVE	ENLARGER	ENNOBLERS	ENRACED
ENHEARSE	ENLARGERS	ENNOBLES	ENRACES
ENHEARSED	ENLARGES	ENNOBLING	ENRACING
ENHEARSES	ENLARGING	ENNOG	ENRAGE
ENHEARTEN	ENLEVE	ENNOGS	ENRAGED
ENHUNGER	ENLIGHT	ENNUI	ENRAGEDLY
ENHUNGERS	ENLIGHTED	ENNUIED	ENRAGES
ENHYDRITE	ENLIGHTEN	ENNUIS	ENRAGING
ENHYDROS	ENLIGHTS	ENNUYE	ENRANCKLE
ENHYDROUS	ENLINK	ENNUYED	ENRANGE
ENIAC	ENLINKED	ENNUYEE	ENRANGED
ENIACS	ENLINKING	ENNUYING	ENRANGES
ENIGMA	ENLINKS	ENODAL	ENRANGING
ENIGMAS	ENLIST	ENOKI	ENRANK
ENIGMATA	ENLISTED	ENOKIDAKE	ENRANKED
ENIGMATIC	ENLISTEE	ENOKIS	ENRANKING
ENISLE	ENLISTEES	ENOKITAKE	ENRANKS
ENISLED	ENLISTER	ENOL	ENRAPT
ENISLES	ENLISTERS	ENOLASE	ENRAPTURE
ENISLING	ENLISTING	ENOLASES	ENRAUNGE
ENJAMB	ENLISTS	ENOLIC	ENRAUNGED
ENJAMBED	ENLIT	ENOLOGIES	ENRAUNGES
ENJAMBING	ENLIVEN	ENOLOGIST	ENRAVISH
ENJAMBS	ENLIVENED	ENOLOGY	ENRHEUM
ENJOIN	ENLIVENER	ENOLS	ENRHEUMED
ENJOINDER	ENLIVENS	ENOMOTIES	ENRHEUMS
ENJOINED	ENLOCK	ENOMOTY	ENRICH
ENJOINER	ENLOCKED	ENOPHILE	ENRICHED
ENJOINERS	ENLOCKING	ENOPHILES	ENRICHER
ENJOINING	ENLOCKS	ENORM	ENRICHERS
ENJOINS	ENLUMINE	ENORMITY	ENRICHES
ENJOY	ENLUMINED	ENORMOUS	ENRICHING
ENJOYABLE	ENLUMINES	ENOSES	ENRIDGED
ENJOYABLY	ENMESH	ENOSIS	ENRING
ENJOYED	ENMESHED	ENOSISES	ENRINGED
ENJOYER	ENMESHES	ENOUGH	ENRINGING
ENJOYERS	ENMESHING	ENOUGHS	ENRINGS
ENJOYING	ENMEW	ENOUNCE	ENRIVEN
ENJOYMENT	ENMEWED	ENOUNCED	ENROBE
ENJOYS	ENMEWING	ENOUNCES	ENROBED

ENROBER
ENROBERS
ENROBES
ENROBING
ENROL
ENROLL
ENROLLED
ENROLLEE
ENROLLEES
ENROLLER
ENROLLERS
ENROLLING
ENROLLS
ENROLMENT
ENROLS
ENROOT
ENROOTED
ENROOTING
ENROOTS
ENROUGH
ENROUGHED
ENROUGHS
ENROUND
ENROUNDED
ENROUNDS
ENS
ENSAMPLE
ENSAMPLED
ENSAMPLES
ENSATE
ENSCONCE
ENSCONCED
ENSCONCES
ENSCROLL
ENSCROLLS
ENSEAL
ENSEALED
ENSEALING
ENSEALS
ENSEAM
ENSEAMED
ENSEAMING
ENSEAMS
ENSEAR
ENSEARED
ENSEARING
ENSEARS
ENSEMBLE
ENSEMBLES
ENSERF
ENSERFED
ENSERFING
ENSERFS
ENSEW
ENSEWED
ENSEWING
ENSEWS
ENSHEATH

ENSHEATHE
ENSHEATHS
ENSHELL
ENSHELLED
ENSHELLS
ENSHELTER
ENSHIELD
ENSHIELDS
ENSHRINE
ENSHRINED
ENSHRINEE
ENSHRINES
ENSHROUD
ENSHROUDS
ENSIFORM
ENSIGN
ENSIGNCY
ENSIGNED
ENSIGNING
ENSIGNS
ENSILAGE
ENSILAGED
ENSILAGES
ENSILE
ENSILED
ENSILES
ENSILING
ENSKIED
ENSKIES
ENSKY
ENSKYED
ENSKYING
ENSLAVE
ENSLAVED
ENSLAVER
ENSLAVERS
ENSLAVES
ENSLAVING
ENSNARE
ENSNARED
ENSNARER
ENSNARERS
ENSNARES
ENSNARING
ENSNARL
ENSNARLED
ENSNARLS
ENSORCEL
ENSORCELL
ENSORCELS
ENSOUL
ENSOULED
ENSOULING
ENSOULS
ENSPHERE
ENSPHERED
ENSPHERES
ENSTAMP

ENSTAMPED
ENSTAMPS
ENSTATITE
ENSTEEP
ENSTEEPED
ENSTEEPS
ENSTYLE
ENSTYLED
ENSTYLES
ENSTYLING
ENSUE
ENSUED
ENSUES
ENSUING
ENSURE
ENSURED
ENSURER
ENSURERS
ENSURES
ENSURING
ENSWATHE
ENSWATHED
ENSWATHES
ENSWEEP
ENSWEEPS
ENSWEPT
ENTAIL
ENTAILED
ENTAILER
ENTAILERS
ENTAILING
ENTAILS
ENTAME
ENTAMEBA
ENTAMEBAE
ENTAMEBAS
ENTAMED
ENTAMES
ENTAMING
ENTAMOEBA
ENTANGLE
ENTANGLED
ENTANGLER
ENTANGLES
ENTASES
ENTASIA
ENTASIAS
ENTASIS
ENTASTIC
ENTAYLE
ENTAYLED
ENTAYLES
ENTAYLING
ENTELECHY
ENTELLUS
ENTENDER
ENTENDERS
ENTENTE

ENTENTES
ENTER
ENTERA
ENTERABLE
ENTERAL
ENTERALLY
ENTERATE
ENTERED
ENTERER
ENTERERS
ENTERIC
ENTERICS
ENTERING
ENTERINGS
ENTERITIS
ENTERON
ENTERONS
ENTERS
ENTERTAIN
ENTERTAKE
ENTERTOOK
ENTETE
ENTETEE
ENTHALPY
ENTHETIC
ENTHRAL
ENTHRALL
ENTHRALLS
ENTHRALS
ENTHRONE
ENTHRONED
ENTHRONES
ENTHUSE
ENTHUSED
ENTHUSES
ENTHUSING
ENTHYMEME
ENTIA
ENTICE
ENTICED
ENTICER
ENTICERS
ENTICES
ENTICING
ENTICINGS
ENTIRE
ENTIRELY
ENTIRES
ENTIRETY
ENTITIES
ENTITLE
ENTITLED
ENTITLES
ENTITLING
ENTITY
ENTOBLAST
ENTODERM
ENTODERMS

ENTOIL	ENTRISM	ENVIABLE	ENZYM
ENTOILED	ENTRISMS	ENVIABLY	ENZYMATIC
ENTOILING	ENTRIST	ENVIED	ENZYME
ENTOILS	ENTRISTS	ENVIER	ENZYMES
ENTOMB	ENTROLD	ENVIERS	ENZYMIC
ENTOMBED	ENTROPIC	ENVIES	ENZYMS
ENTOMBING	ENTROPIES	ENVIOUS	EOAN
ENTOMBS	ENTROPION	ENVIOUSLY	EOBIONT
ENTOMIC	ENTROPIUM	ENVIRO	EOBIONTS
ENTOPHYTE	ENTROPY	ENVIRON	EOCENE
ENTOPIC	ENTRUST	ENVIRONED	EOHIPPUS
ENTOPROCT	ENTRUSTED	ENVIRONS	EOLIAN
ENTOPTIC	ENTRUSTS	ENVIROS	EOLIENNE
ENTOPTICS	ENTRY	ENVISAGE	EOLIENNES
ENTOTIC	ENTRYISM	ENVISAGED	EOLIPILE
ENTOURAGE	ENTRYISMS	ENVISAGES	EOLIPILES
ENTOZOA	ENTRYIST	ENVISION	EOLITH
ENTOZOAL	ENTRYISTS	ENVISIONS	EOLITHIC
ENTOZOAN	ENTRYWAY	ENVOI	EOLITHS
ENTOZOANS	ENTRYWAYS	ENVOIS	EOLOPILE
ENTOZOIC	ENTWINE	ENVOY	EOLOPILES
ENTOZOON	ENTWINED	ENVOYS	EON
ENTRAIL	ENTWINES	ENVOYSHIP	EONIAN
ENTRAILED	ENTWINING	ENVY	EONISM
ENTRAILS	ENTWIST	ENVYING	EONISMS
ENTRAIN	ENTWISTED	ENVYINGLY	EONS
ENTRAINED	ENTWISTS	ENVYINGS	EORL
ENTRAINER	ENUCLEATE	ENWALL	EORLS
ENTRAINS	ENUF	ENWALLED	EOSIN
ENTRALL	ENUMERATE	ENWALLING	EOSINE
ENTRALLES	ENUNCIATE	ENWALLOW	EOSINES
ENTRAMMEL	ENURE	ENWALLOWS	EOSINIC
ENTRANCE	ENURED	ENWALLS	EOSINS
ENTRANCED	ENUREMENT	ENWHEEL	EOTHEN
ENTRANCES	ENURES	ENWHEELED	EPACRID
ENTRANT	ENURESES	ENWHEELS	EPACRIDS
ENTRANTS	ENURESIS	ENWIND	EPACRIS
ENTRAP	ENURETIC	ENWINDING	EPACRISES
ENTRAPPED	ENURETICS	ENWINDS	EPACT
ENTRAPPER	ENURING	ENWOMB	EPACTS
ENTRAPS	ENVASSAL	ENWOMBED	EPAENETIC
ENTREAT	ENVASSALS	ENWOMBING	EPAGOGE
ENTREATED	ENVAULT	ENWOMBS	EPAGOGES
ENTREATS	ENVAULTED	ENWOUND	EPAGOGIC
ENTREATY	ENVAULTS	ENWRAP	EPANODOS
ENTRECHAT	ENVEIGLE	ENWRAPPED	EPARCH
ENTRECOTE	ENVEIGLED	ENWRAPS	EPARCHATE
ENTREE	ENVEIGLES	ENWREATH	EPARCHIAL
ENTREES	ENVELOP	ENWREATHE	EPARCHIES
ENTREMES	ENVELOPE	ENWREATHS	EPARCHS
ENTREMETS	ENVELOPED	ENZIAN	EPARCHY
ENTRENCH	ENVELOPER	ENZIANS	EPATANT
ENTREPOT	ENVELOPES	ENZONE	EPAULE
ENTREPOTS	ENVELOPS	ENZONED	EPAULES
ENTRESOL	ENVENOM	ENZONES	EPAULET
ENTRESOLS	ENVENOMED	ENZONING	EPAULETS
ENTREZ	ENVENOMS	ENZOOTIC	EPAULETTE
ENTRIES	ENVERMEIL	ENZOOTICS	EPAXIAL

EPAZOTE	EPIBLAST	EPIDERMS	EPILOGIZE
EPAZOTES	EPIBLASTS	EPIDICTIC	EPILOGS
EPEDAPHIC	EPIBLEM	EPIDOSITE	EPILOGUE
EPEE	EPIBLEMS	EPIDOTE	EPILOGUED
EPEEIST	EPIBOLIC	EPIDOTES	EPILOGUES
EPEEISTS	EPIBOLIES	EPIDOTIC	EPIMER
EPEES	EPIBOLY	EPIDURAL	EPIMERASE
EPEIRA	EPIC	EPIDURALS	EPIMERE
EPEIRAS	EPICAL	EPIFAUNA	EPIMERES
EPEIRIC	EPICALLY	EPIFAUNAE	EPIMERIC
EPEIRID	EPICALYX	EPIFAUNAL	EPIMERISM
EPEIRIDS	EPICANTHI	EPIFAUNAS	EPIMERS
EPENDYMA	EPICARDIA	EPIFOCAL	EPIMYSIA
EPENDYMAL	EPICARP	EPIGAEAL	EPIMYSIUM
EPENDYMAS	EPICARPS	EPIGAEAN	EPINAOI
EPEOLATRY	EPICEDE	EPIGAEOUS	EPINAOS
EPERDU	EPICEDES	EPIGAMIC	EPINASTIC
EPERDUE	EPICEDIA	EPIGEAL	EPINASTY
EPERGNE	EPICEDIAL	EPIGEAN	EPINEURAL
EPERGNES	EPICEDIAN	EPIGEIC	EPINEURIA
EPHA	EPICEDIUM	EPIGENE	EPINICIAN
EPHAH	EPICENE	EPIGENIC	EPINICION
EPHAHS	EPICENES	EPIGENIST	EPINIKIAN
EPHAS	EPICENISM	EPIGENOUS	EPINIKION
EPHEBE	EPICENTER	EPIGEOUS	EPINOSIC
EPHEBES	EPICENTRA	EPIGON	EPIPHANIC
EPHEBI	EPICENTRE	EPIGONE	EPIPHANY
EPHEBIC	EPICIER	EPIGONES	EPIPHRAGM
EPHEBOI	EPICIERS	EPIGONI	EPIPHYSES
EPHEBOS	EPICISM	EPIGONIC	EPIPHYSIS
EPHEBUS	EPICISMS	EPIGONISM	EPIPHYTAL
EPHEDRA	EPICIST	EPIGONOUS	EPIPHYTE
EPHEDRAS	EPICISTS	EPIGONS	EPIPHYTES
EPHEDRIN	EPICLESES	EPIGONUS	EPIPHYTIC
EPHEDRINE	EPICLESIS	EPIGRAM	EPIPLOIC
EPHEDRINS	EPICLIKE	EPIGRAMS	EPIPLOON
EPHELIDES	EPICOTYL	EPIGRAPH	EPIPLOONS
EPHELIS	EPICOTYLS	EPIGRAPHS	EPIPOLIC
EPHEMERA	EPICRANIA	EPIGRAPHY	EPIPOLISM
EPHEMERAE	EPICRISES	EPIGYNIES	EPIROGENY
EPHEMERAL	EPICRISIS	EPIGYNOUS	EPIRRHEMA
EPHEMERAS	EPICRITIC	EPIGYNY	EPISCIA
EPHEMERID	EPICS	EPILATE	EPISCIAS
EPHEMERIS	EPICURE	EPILATED	EPISCOPAL
EPHEMERON	EPICUREAN	EPILATES	EPISCOPE
EPHIALTES	EPICURES	EPILATING	EPISCOPES
EPHOD	EPICURISE	EPILATION	EPISCOPY
EPHODS	EPICURISM	EPILATOR	EPISEMON
EPHOR	EPICURIZE	EPILATORS	EPISEMONS
EPHORAL	EPICYCLE	EPILEPSY	EPISODAL
EPHORALTY	EPICYCLES	EPILEPTIC	EPISODE
EPHORATE	EPICYCLIC	EPILIMNIA	EPISODES
EPHORATES	EPIDEMIC	EPILITHIC	EPISODIAL
EPHORI	EPIDEMICS	EPILOBIUM	EPISODIC
EPHORS	EPIDERM	EPILOG	EPISOMAL
EPIBIOSES	EPIDERMAL	EPILOGIC	EPISOME
EPIBIOSIS	EPIDERMIC	EPILOGISE	EPISOMES
EPIBIOTIC	EPIDERMIS	EPILOGIST	EPISPERM

EPISPERMS
EPISPORE
EPISPORES
EPISTASES
EPISTASIS
EPISTASY
EPISTATIC
EPISTAXES
EPISTAXIS
EPISTEMIC
EPISTERNA
EPISTLE
EPISTLED
EPISTLER
EPISTLERS
EPISTLES
EPISTLING
EPISTOLER
EPISTOLET
EPISTOLIC
EPISTOME
EPISTOMES
EPISTYLE
EPISTYLES
EPITAPH
EPITAPHED
EPITAPHER
EPITAPHIC
EPITAPHS
EPITASES
EPITASIS
EPITAXES
EPITAXIAL
EPITAXIC
EPITAXIES
EPITAXIS
EPITAXY
EPITHECA
EPITHECAE
EPITHELIA
EPITHEM
EPITHEMA
EPITHEMS
EPITHESES
EPITHESIS
EPITHET
EPITHETED
EPITHETIC
EPITHETON
EPITHETS
EPITOME
EPITOMES
EPITOMIC
EPITOMISE
EPITOMIST
EPITOMIZE
EPITONIC
EPITOPE

EPITOPES
EPITRITE
EPITRITES
EPIZEUXES
EPIZEUXIS
EPIZOA
EPIZOAN
EPIZOANS
EPIZOIC
EPIZOISM
EPIZOISMS
EPIZOITE
EPIZOITES
EPIZOON
EPIZOOTIC
EPIZOOTY
EPOCH
EPOCHA
EPOCHAL
EPOCHALLY
EPOCHAS
EPOCHS
EPODE
EPODES
EPODIC
EPONYM
EPONYMIC
EPONYMIES
EPONYMOUS
EPONYMS
EPONYMY
EPOPEE
EPOPEES
EPOPOEIA
EPOPOEIAS
EPOPT
EPOPTS
EPOS
EPOSES
EPOXIDE
EPOXIDES
EPOXIDISE
EPOXIDIZE
EPOXIED
EPOXIES
EPOXY
EPOXYED
EPOXYING
EPRIS
EPRISE
EPROM
EPROMS
EPSILON
EPSILONIC
EPSILONS
EPSOMITE
EPSOMITES
EPUISE

EPUISEE
EPULARY
EPULATION
EPULIDES
EPULIS
EPULISES
EPULOTIC
EPULOTICS
EPURATE
EPURATED
EPURATES
EPURATING
EPURATION
EPYLLIA
EPYLLION
EPYLLIONS
EQUABLE
EQUABLY
EQUAL
EQUALED
EQUALI
EQUALING
EQUALISE
EQUALISED
EQUALISER
EQUALISES
EQUALITY
EQUALIZE
EQUALIZED
EQUALIZER
EQUALIZES
EQUALLED
EQUALLING
EQUALLY
EQUALNESS
EQUALS
EQUANT
EQUANTS
EQUATABLE
EQUATE
EQUATED
EQUATES
EQUATING
EQUATION
EQUATIONS
EQUATOR
EQUATORS
EQUERRIES
EQUERRY
EQUID
EQUIDS
EQUIMOLAL
EQUIMOLAR
EQUINAL
EQUINE
EQUINELY
EQUINES
EQUINIA

EQUINIAS
EQUINITY
EQUINOX
EQUINOXES
EQUIP
EQUIPAGE
EQUIPAGED
EQUIPAGES
EQUIPE
EQUIPES
EQUIPMENT
EQUIPOISE
EQUIPPED
EQUIPPER
EQUIPPERS
EQUIPPING
EQUIPS
EQUISETA
EQUISETIC
EQUISETUM
EQUITABLE
EQUITABLY
EQUITANT
EQUITES
EQUITIES
EQUITY
EQUIVALVE
EQUIVOCAL
EQUIVOKE
EQUIVOKES
EQUIVOQUE
ER
ERA
ERADIATE
ERADIATED
ERADIATES
ERADICANT
ERADICATE
ERAS
ERASABLE
ERASE
ERASED
ERASEMENT
ERASER
ERASERS
ERASES
ERASING
ERASION
ERASIONS
ERASURE
ERASURES
ERATHEM
ERATHEMS
ERBIA
ERBIAS
ERBIUM
ERBIUMS
ERE

ERECT	ERGONS	ERODE	ERRATA
ERECTABLE	ERGOS	ERODED	ERRATAS
ERECTED	ERGOT	ERODENT	ERRATIC
ERECTER	ERGOTIC	ERODENTS	ERRATICAL
ERECTERS	ERGOTISE	ERODES	ERRATICS
ERECTILE	ERGOTISED	ERODIBLE	ERRATUM
ERECTING	ERGOTISES	ERODING	ERRED
ERECTION	ERGOTISM	ERODIUM	ERRHINE
ERECTIONS	ERGOTISMS	ERODIUMS	ERRHINES
ERECTIVE	ERGOTIZE	EROGENIC	ERRING
ERECTLY	ERGOTIZED	EROGENOUS	ERRINGLY
ERECTNESS	ERGOTIZES	EROS	ERRINGS
ERECTOR	ERGOTS	EROSE	ERRONEOUS
ERECTORS	ERGS	EROSELY	ERROR
ERECTS	ERIACH	EROSES	ERRORIST
ERED	ERIACHS	EROSIBLE	ERRORISTS
ERELONG	ERIC	EROSION	ERRORLESS
EREMIC	ERICA	EROSIONAL	ERRORS
EREMITAL	ERICAS	EROSIONS	ERRS
EREMITE	ERICK	EROSIVE	ERS
EREMITES	ERICKS	EROSIVITY	ERSATZ
EREMITIC	ERICOID	EROSTRATE	ERSATZES
EREMITISH	ERICS	EROTEMA	ERSES
EREMITISM	ERIGERON	EROTEMAS	ERST
EREMURI	ERIGERONS	EROTEME	ERSTWHILE
EREMURUS	ERING	EROTEMES	ERUCIC
ERENOW	ERINGO	EROTESES	ERUCIFORM
EREPSIN	ERINGOES	EROTESIS	ERUCT
EREPSINS	ERINGOS	EROTETIC	ERUCTATE
ERES	ERINITE	EROTIC	ERUCTATED
ERETHIC	ERINITES	EROTICA	ERUCTATES
ERETHISM	ERINUS	EROTICAL	ERUCTED
ERETHISMS	ERINUSES	EROTICISE	ERUCTING
ERETHITIC	ERIOMETER	EROTICISM	ERUCTS
EREV	ERIONITE	EROTICIST	ERUDITE
EREVS	ERIONITES	EROTICIZE	ERUDITELY
EREWHILE	ERIOPHYID	EROTICS	ERUDITES
EREWHILES	ERISTIC	EROTISE	ERUDITION
ERF	ERISTICAL	EROTISED	ERUGO
ERG	ERISTICS	EROTISES	ERUGOS
ERGASTIC	ERK	EROTISING	ERUMPENT
ERGATANER	ERKS	EROTISM	ERUPT
ERGATE	ERLANG	EROTISMS	ERUPTED
ERGATES	ERLANGS	EROTIZE	ERUPTIBLE
ERGATIVE	ERLKING	EROTIZED	ERUPTING
ERGATIVES	ERLKINGS	EROTIZES	ERUPTION
ERGATOID	ERMELIN	EROTIZING	ERUPTIONS
ERGO	ERMELINS	EROTOLOGY	ERUPTIVE
ERGODIC	ERMINE	ERR	ERUPTIVES
ERGOGENIC	ERMINED	ERRABLE	ERUPTS
ERGOGRAM	ERMINES	ERRANCIES	ERUV
ERGOGRAMS	ERN	ERRANCY	ERUVIM
ERGOGRAPH	ERNE	ERRAND	ERUVIN
ERGOMANIA	ERNED	ERRANDS	ERUVS
ERGOMETER	ERNES	ERRANT	ERVALENTA
ERGOMETRY	ERNING	ERRANTLY	ERVEN
ERGON	ERNS	ERRANTRY	ERVIL
ERGONOMIC	ERODABLE	ERRANTS	ERVILS

ERYNGIUM
ERYNGIUMS
ERYNGO
ERYNGOES
ERYNGOS
ERYTHEMA
ERYTHEMAL
ERYTHEMAS
ERYTHEMIC
ERYTHRINA
ERYTHRISM
ERYTHRITE
ERYTHROID
ERYTHRON
ERYTHRONS
ES
ESCALADE
ESCALADED
ESCALADER
ESCALADES
ESCALADO
ESCALATE
ESCALATED
ESCALATES
ESCALATOR
ESCALIER
ESCALIERS
ESCALLOP
ESCALLOPS
ESCALOP
ESCALOPE
ESCALOPED
ESCALOPES
ESCALOPS
ESCAPABLE
ESCAPADE
ESCAPADES
ESCAPADO
ESCAPE
ESCAPED
ESCAPEE
ESCAPEES
ESCAPER
ESCAPERS
ESCAPES
ESCAPING
ESCAPISM
ESCAPISMS
ESCAPIST
ESCAPISTS
ESCAR
ESCARGOT
ESCARGOTS
ESCAROLE
ESCAROLES
ESCARP
ESCARPED
ESCARPING

ESCARPS
ESCARS
ESCHALOT
ESCHALOTS
ESCHAR
ESCHARS
ESCHEAT
ESCHEATED
ESCHEATOR
ESCHEATS
ESCHEW
ESCHEWAL
ESCHEWALS
ESCHEWED
ESCHEWER
ESCHEWERS
ESCHEWING
ESCHEWS
ESCLANDRE
ESCOLAR
ESCOLARS
ESCOPETTE
ESCORT
ESCORTAGE
ESCORTED
ESCORTING
ESCORTS
ESCOT
ESCOTED
ESCOTING
ESCOTS
ESCOTTED
ESCOTTING
ESCRIBANO
ESCRIBE
ESCRIBED
ESCRIBES
ESCRIBING
ESCROC
ESCROCS
ESCROL
ESCROLL
ESCROLLS
ESCROLS
ESCROW
ESCROWED
ESCROWING
ESCROWS
ESCUAGE
ESCUAGES
ESCUDO
ESCUDOS
ESCULENT
ESCULENTS
ESEMPLASY
ESERINE
ESERINES
ESES

ESILE
ESILES
ESKAR
ESKARS
ESKER
ESKERS
ESKIES
ESKY
ESLOIN
ESLOINED
ESLOINING
ESLOINS
ESLOYNE
ESLOYNED
ESLOYNES
ESLOYNING
ESNE
ESNECIES
ESNECY
ESNES
ESOPHAGI
ESOPHAGUS
ESOTERIC
ESOTERICA
ESOTERIES
ESOTERISM
ESOTERY
ESOTROPIA
ESOTROPIC
ESPADA
ESPADAS
ESPAGNOLE
ESPALIER
ESPALIERS
ESPANOL
ESPANOLES
ESPARTO
ESPARTOS
ESPECIAL
ESPERANCE
ESPIAL
ESPIALS
ESPIED
ESPIEGLE
ESPIER
ESPIERS
ESPIES
ESPIONAGE
ESPLANADE
ESPOUSAL
ESPOUSALS
ESPOUSE
ESPOUSED
ESPOUSER
ESPOUSERS
ESPOUSES
ESPOUSING
ESPRESSO

ESPRESSOS
ESPRIT
ESPRITS
ESPUMOSO
ESPUMOSOS
ESPY
ESPYING
ESQUIRE
ESQUIRED
ESQUIRES
ESQUIRESS
ESQUIRING
ESQUISSE
ESQUISSES
ESS
ESSAY
ESSAYED
ESSAYER
ESSAYERS
ESSAYETTE
ESSAYING
ESSAYISH
ESSAYIST
ESSAYISTS
ESSAYS
ESSE
ESSENCE
ESSENCES
ESSENTIAL
ESSES
ESSIVE
ESSIVES
ESSOIN
ESSOINER
ESSOINERS
ESSOINS
ESSONITE
ESSONITES
ESSOYNE
ESSOYNES
EST
ESTABLISH
ESTACADE
ESTACADES
ESTAFETTE
ESTAMINET
ESTANCIA
ESTANCIAS
ESTATE
ESTATED
ESTATES
ESTATING
ESTEEM
ESTEEMED
ESTEEMING
ESTEEMS
ESTER
ESTERASE

ESTERASES	ESTRICHES	ETATS	ETHERISER
ESTERIFY	ESTRIDGE	ETCETERA	ETHERISES
ESTERS	ESTRIDGES	ETCETERAS	ETHERISH
ESTHESES	ESTRILDID	ETCH	ETHERISM
ESTHESIA	ESTRIN	ETCHANT	ETHERISMS
ESTHESIAS	ESTRINS	ETCHANTS	ETHERIST
ESTHESIS	ESTRIOL	ETCHED	ETHERISTS
ESTHETE	ESTRIOLS	ETCHER	ETHERIZE
ESTHETES	ESTRO	ETCHERS	ETHERIZED
ESTHETIC	ESTROGEN	ETCHES	ETHERIZER
ESTHETICS	ESTROGENS	ETCHING	ETHERIZES
ESTIMABLE	ESTRONE	ETCHINGS	ETHERS
ESTIMABLY	ESTRONES	ETEN	ETHIC
ESTIMATE	ESTROS	ETENS	ETHICAL
ESTIMATED	ESTROUS	ETERNAL	ETHICALLY
ESTIMATES	ESTRUAL	ETERNALLY	ETHICALS
ESTIMATOR	ESTRUM	ETERNALS	ETHICIAN
ESTIVAL	ESTRUMS	ETERNE	ETHICIANS
ESTIVATE	ESTRUS	ETERNISE	ETHICISE
ESTIVATED	ESTRUSES	ETERNISED	ETHICISED
ESTIVATES	ESTS	ETERNISES	ETHICISES
ESTIVATOR	ESTUARIAL	ETERNITY	ETHICISM
ESTOC	ESTUARIAN	ETERNIZE	ETHICISMS
ESTOCS	ESTUARIES	ETERNIZED	ETHICIST
ESTOILE	ESTUARINE	ETERNIZES	ETHICISTS
ESTOILES	ESTUARY	ETESIAN	ETHICIZE
ESTOP	ESURIENCE	ETESIANS	ETHICIZED
ESTOPPAGE	ESURIENCY	ETH	ETHICIZES
ESTOPPED	ESURIENT	ETHAL	ETHICS
ESTOPPEL	ET	ETHALS	ETHINYL
ESTOPPELS	ETA	ETHANAL	ETHINYLS
ESTOPPING	ETACISM	ETHANALS	ETHION
ESTOPS	ETACISMS	ETHANE	ETHIONINE
ESTOVER	ETAERIO	ETHANES	ETHIONS
ESTOVERS	ETAERIOS	ETHANOATE	ETHIOPS
ESTRADE	ETAGE	ETHANOIC	ETHIOPSES
ESTRADES	ETAGERE	ETHANOL	ETHMOID
ESTRADIOL	ETAGERES	ETHANOLS	ETHMOIDAL
ESTRAGON	ETAGES	ETHANOYL	ETHMOIDS
ESTRAGONS	ETALAGE	ETHANOYLS	ETHNARCH
ESTRAL	ETALAGES	ETHE	ETHNARCHS
ESTRANGE	ETALON	ETHENE	ETHNARCHY
ESTRANGED	ETALONS	ETHENES	ETHNIC
ESTRANGER	ETAMIN	ETHEPHON	ETHNICAL
ESTRANGES	ETAMINE	ETHEPHONS	ETHNICISM
ESTRAPADE	ETAMINES	ETHER	ETHNICITY
ESTRAY	ETAMINS	ETHERCAP	ETHNICS
ESTRAYED	ETAPE	ETHERCAPS	ETHNOCIDE
ESTRAYING	ETAPES	ETHEREAL	ETHNOGENY
ESTRAYS	ETAS	ETHEREOUS	ETHNOLOGY
ESTREAT	ETAT	ETHERIAL	ETHNONYM
ESTREATED	ETATISM	ETHERIC	ETHNONYMS
ESTREATS	ETATISME	ETHERICAL	ETHNOS
ESTREPE	ETATISMES	ETHERIFY	ETHNOSES
ESTREPED	ETATISMS	ETHERION	ETHOGRAM
ESTREPES	ETATIST	ETHERIONS	ETHOGRAMS
ESTREPING	ETATISTE	ETHERISE	ETHOLOGIC
ESTRICH	ETATISTES	ETHERISED	ETHOLOGY

ETHONONE	ETUI	EUGENISM	EUONYMIN
ETHONONES	ETUIS	EUGENISMS	EUONYMINS
ETHOS	ETWEE	EUGENIST	EUONYMUS
ETHOSES	ETWEES	EUGENISTS	EUOUAE
ETHOXIDE	ETYMA	EUGENOL	EUOUAES
ETHOXIDES	ETYMIC	EUGENOLS	EUPAD
ETHOXIES	ETYMOLOGY	EUGH	EUPADS
ETHOXY	ETYMON	EUGHEN	EUPATRID
ETHOXYL	ETYMONS	EUGHS	EUPATRIDS
ETHOXYLS	ETYPIC	EUGLENA	EUPEPSIA
ETHS	ETYPICAL	EUGLENAS	EUPEPSIAS
ETHYL	EUCAIN	EUGLENID	EUPEPSIES
ETHYLATE	EUCAINE	EUGLENIDS	EUPEPSY
ETHYLATED	EUCAINES	EUGLENOID	EUPEPTIC
ETHYLATES	EUCAINS	EUK	EUPHAUSID
ETHYLENE	EUCALYPT	EUKARYON	EUPHEMISE
ETHYLENES	EUCALYPTI	EUKARYONS	EUPHEMISM
ETHYLENIC	EUCALYPTS	EUKARYOT	EUPHEMIST
ETHYLIC	EUCARYON	EUKARYOTE	EUPHEMIZE
ETHYLS	EUCARYONS	EUKARYOTS	EUPHENIC
ETHYNE	EUCARYOT	EUKED	EUPHENICS
ETHYNES	EUCARYOTE	EUKING	EUPHOBIA
ETHYNYL	EUCARYOTS	EUKS	EUPHOBIAS
ETHYNYLS	EUCHARIS	EULACHAN	EUPHON
ETIC	EUCHLORIC	EULACHANS	EUPHONIA
ETIOLATE	EUCHLORIN	EULACHON	EUPHONIAS
ETIOLATED	EUCHOLOGY	EULACHONS	EUPHONIC
ETIOLATES	EUCHRE	EULOGIA	EUPHONIES
ETIOLIN	EUCHRED	EULOGIAE	EUPHONISE
ETIOLINS	EUCHRES	EULOGIAS	EUPHONISM
ETIOLOGIC	EUCHRING	EULOGIES	EUPHONIUM
ETIOLOGY	EUCLASE	EULOGISE	EUPHONIZE
ETIQUETTE	EUCLASES	EULOGISED	EUPHONS
ETNA	EUCLIDEAN	EULOGISER	EUPHONY
ETNAS	EUCLIDIAN	EULOGISES	EUPHORBIA
ETOILE	EUCRITE	EULOGIST	EUPHORIA
ETOILES	EUCRITES	EULOGISTS	EUPHORIAS
ETOUFFEE	EUCRITIC	EULOGIUM	EUPHORIC
ETOUFFEES	EUCRYPHIA	EULOGIUMS	EUPHORIES
ETOURDI	EUCYCLIC	EULOGIZE	EUPHORY
ETOURDIE	EUDAEMON	EULOGIZED	EUPHOTIC
ETRANGER	EUDAEMONS	EULOGIZER	EUPHRASY
ETRANGERE	EUDAEMONY	EULOGIZES	EUPHROE
ETRANGERS	EUDAIMON	EULOGY	EUPHROES
ETRENNE	EUDAIMONS	EUMELANIN	EUPHUISE
ETRENNES	EUDEMON	EUMERISM	EUPHUISED
ETRIER	EUDEMONIA	EUMERISMS	EUPHUISES
ETRIERS	EUDEMONIC	EUMONG	EUPHUISM
ETTERCAP	EUDEMONS	EUMONGS	EUPHUISMS
ETTERCAPS	EUDIALYTE	EUMUNG	EUPHUIST
ETTIN	EUGARIE	EUMUNGS	EUPHUISTS
ETTINS	EUGARIES	EUNUCH	EUPHUIZE
ETTLE	EUGE	EUNUCHISE	EUPHUIZED
ETTLED	EUGENIA	EUNUCHISM	EUPHUIZES
ETTLES	EUGENIAS	EUNUCHIZE	EUPLASTIC
ETTLING	EUGENIC	EUNUCHOID	EUPLOID
ETUDE	EUGENICAL	EUNUCHS	EUPLOIDS
ETUDES	EUGENICS	EUOI	EUPLOIDY

EUPNEA	EUTEXIA	EVASION	EVERYDAY
EUPNEAS	EUTEXIAS	EVASIONAL	EVERYDAYS
EUPNEIC	EUTHANASY	EVASIONS	EVERYMAN
EUPNOEA	EUTHANISE	EVASIVE	EVERYMEN
EUPNOEAS	EUTHANIZE	EVASIVELY	EVERYONE
EUPNOEIC	EUTHENICS	EVE	EVERYWAY
EUREKA	EUTHENIST	EVECTION	EVERYWHEN
EUREKAS	EUTHERIAN	EVECTIONS	EVES
EURHYTHMY	EUTHYMIA	EVEJAR	EVET
EURIPI	EUTHYMIAS	EVEJARS	EVETS
EURIPUS	EUTHYROID	EVEN	EVHOE
EURIPUSES	EUTRAPELY	EVENED	EVICT
EURO	EUTROPHIC	EVENEMENT	EVICTED
EUROBOND	EUTROPHY	EVENER	EVICTEE
EUROBONDS	EUTROPIC	EVENERS	EVICTEES
EUROCRAT	EUTROPIES	EVENEST	EVICTING
EUROCRATS	EUTROPOUS	EVENFALL	EVICTION
EUROCREEP	EUTROPY	EVENFALLS	EVICTIONS
EUROKIES	EUXENITE	EVENING	EVICTOR
EUROKOUS	EUXENITES	EVENINGS	EVICTORS
EUROKY	EVACUANT	EVENLY	EVICTS
EURONOTE	EVACUANTS	EVENNESS	EVIDENCE
EURONOTES	EVACUATE	EVENS	EVIDENCED
EUROPHILE	EVACUATED	EVENSONG	EVIDENCES
EUROPIUM	EVACUATES	EVENSONGS	EVIDENT
EUROPIUMS	EVACUATOR	EVENT	EVIDENTLY
EUROS	EVACUEE	EVENTED	EVIDENTS
EURYBATH	EVACUEES	EVENTER	EVIL
EURYBATHS	EVADABLE	EVENTERS	EVILDOER
EURYOKIES	EVADE	EVENTFUL	EVILDOERS
EURYOKOUS	EVADED	EVENTIDE	EVILDOING
EURYOKY	EVADER	EVENTIDES	EVILER
EURYTHERM	EVADERS	EVENTING	EVILEST
EURYTHMIC	EVADES	EVENTINGS	EVILLER
EURYTHMY	EVADIBLE	EVENTLESS	EVILLEST
EURYTOPIC	EVADING	EVENTRATE	EVILLY
EUSOCIAL	EVADINGLY	EVENTS	EVILNESS
EUSOL	EVAGATION	EVENTUAL	EVILS
EUSOLS	EVAGINATE	EVENTUATE	EVINCE
EUSTACIES	EVALUABLE	EVER	EVINCED
EUSTACY	EVALUATE	EVERGLADE	EVINCES
EUSTASIES	EVALUATED	EVERGREEN	EVINCIBLE
EUSTASY	EVALUATES	EVERMORE	EVINCIBLY
EUSTATIC	EVALUATOR	EVERNET	EVINCING
EUSTELE	EVANESCE	EVERNETS	EVINCIVE
EUSTELES	EVANESCED	EVERSIBLE	EVIRATE
EUSTYLE	EVANESCES	EVERSION	EVIRATED
EUSTYLES	EVANGEL	EVERSIONS	EVIRATES
EUTAXIA	EVANGELIC	EVERT	EVIRATING
EUTAXIAS	EVANGELS	EVERTED	EVITABLE
EUTAXIES	EVANGELY	EVERTING	EVITATE
EUTAXITE	EVANISH	EVERTOR	EVITATED
EUTAXITES	EVANISHED	EVERTORS	EVITATES
EUTAXITIC	EVANISHES	EVERTS	EVITATING
EUTAXY	EVANITION	EVERWHERE	EVITATION
EUTECTIC	EVAPORATE	EVERWHICH	EVITE
EUTECTICS	EVAPORITE	EVERY	EVITED
EUTECTOID	EVASIBLE	EVERYBODY	EVITERNAL

EVITES	EWGHEN	EXAMS	EXCESSED
EVITING	EWHOW	EXANIMATE	EXCESSES
EVO	EWK	EXANTHEM	EXCESSING
EVOCABLE	EWKED	EXANTHEMA	EXCESSIVE
EVOCATE	EWKING	EXANTHEMS	EXCHANGE
EVOCATED	EWKS	EXAPTED	EXCHANGED
EVOCATES	EWT	EXAPTIVE	EXCHANGER
EVOCATING	EWTS	EXARATE	EXCHANGES
EVOCATION	EX	EXARATION	EXCHEAT
EVOCATIVE	EXABYTE	EXARCH	EXCHEATS
EVOCATOR	EXABYTES	EXARCHAL	EXCHEQUER
EVOCATORS	EXACT	EXARCHATE	EXCIDE
EVOCATORY	EXACTA	EXARCHIES	EXCIDED
EVOE	EXACTABLE	EXARCHIST	EXCIDES
EVOHE	EXACTAS	EXARCHS	EXCIDING
EVOKE	EXACTED	EXARCHY	EXCIMER
EVOKED	EXACTER	EXCAMB	EXCIMERS
EVOKER	EXACTERS	EXCAMBED	EXCIPIENT
EVOKERS	EXACTEST	EXCAMBING	EXCIPLE
EVOKES	EXACTING	EXCAMBION	EXCIPLES
EVOKING	EXACTION	EXCAMBIUM	EXCISABLE
EVOLUE	EXACTIONS	EXCAMBS	EXCISE
EVOLUES	EXACTLY	EXCARNATE	EXCISED
EVOLUTE	EXACTMENT	EXCAUDATE	EXCISEMAN
EVOLUTED	EXACTNESS	EXCAVATE	EXCISEMEN
EVOLUTES	EXACTOR	EXCAVATED	EXCISES
EVOLUTING	EXACTORS	EXCAVATES	EXCISING
EVOLUTION	EXACTRESS	EXCAVATOR	EXCISION
EVOLUTIVE	EXACTS	EXCEED	EXCISIONS
EVOLVABLE	EXACUM	EXCEEDED	EXCITABLE
EVOLVE	EXACUMS	EXCEEDER	EXCITABLY
EVOLVED	EXAHERTZ	EXCEEDERS	EXCITANCY
EVOLVENT	EXALT	EXCEEDING	EXCITANT
EVOLVER	EXALTED	EXCEEDS	EXCITANTS
EVOLVERS	EXALTEDLY	EXCEL	EXCITE
EVOLVES	EXALTER	EXCELLED	EXCITED
EVOLVING	EXALTERS	EXCELLENT	EXCITEDLY
EVONYMUS	EXALTING	EXCELLING	EXCITER
EVOS	EXALTS	EXCELS	EXCITERS
EVOVAE	EXAM	EXCELSIOR	EXCITES
EVOVAES	EXAMEN	EXCENTRIC	EXCITING
EVULGATE	EXAMENS	EXCEPT	EXCITON
EVULGATED	EXAMINANT	EXCEPTANT	EXCITONIC
EVULGATES	EXAMINATE	EXCEPTED	EXCITONS
EVULSE	EXAMINE	EXCEPTING	EXCITOR
EVULSED	EXAMINED	EXCEPTION	EXCITORS
EVULSES	EXAMINEE	EXCEPTIVE	EXCLAIM
EVULSING	EXAMINEES	EXCEPTOR	EXCLAIMED
EVULSION	EXAMINER	EXCEPTORS	EXCLAIMER
EVULSIONS	EXAMINERS	EXCEPTS	EXCLAIMS
EVZONE	EXAMINES	EXCERPT	EXCLAVE
EVZONES	EXAMINING	EXCERPTA	EXCLAVES
EWE	EXAMPLAR	EXCERPTED	EXCLOSURE
EWER	EXAMPLARS	EXCERPTER	EXCLUDE
EWERS	EXAMPLE	EXCERPTOR	EXCLUDED
EWES	EXAMPLED	EXCERPTS	EXCLUDEE
EWEST	EXAMPLES	EXCERPTUM	EXCLUDEES
EWFTES	EXAMPLING	EXCESS	EXCLUDER

EXCLUDERS	EXECUTING	EXERTIVE	EXILERS
EXCLUDES	EXECUTION	EXERTS	EXILES
EXCLUDING	EXECUTIVE	EXES	EXILIAN
EXCLUSION	EXECUTOR	EXEUNT	EXILIC
EXCLUSIVE	EXECUTORS	EXFOLIANT	EXILING
EXCLUSORY	EXECUTORY	EXFOLIATE	EXILITIES
EXCORIATE	EXECUTRIX	EXHALABLE	EXILITY
EXCREMENT	EXECUTRY	EXHALANT	EXIMIOUS
EXCRETA	EXED	EXHALANTS	EXINE
EXCRETAL	EXEDRA	EXHALE	EXINES
EXCRETE	EXEDRAE	EXHALED	EXING
EXCRETED	EXEEM	EXHALENT	EXIST
EXCRETER	EXEEMED	EXHALENTS	EXISTED
EXCRETERS	EXEEMING	EXHALES	EXISTENCE
EXCRETES	EXEEMS	EXHALING	EXISTENT
EXCRETING	EXEGESES	EXHAUST	EXISTENTS
EXCRETION	EXEGESIS	EXHAUSTED	EXISTING
EXCRETIVE	EXEGETE	EXHAUSTER	EXISTS
EXCRETORY	EXEGETES	EXHAUSTS	EXIT
EXCUBANT	EXEGETIC	EXHEDRA	EXITANCE
EXCUDIT	EXEGETICS	EXHEDRAE	EXITANCES
EXCULPATE	EXEGETIST	EXHIBIT	EXITED
EXCURRENT	EXEME	EXHIBITED	EXITING
EXCURSE	EXEMED	EXHIBITER	EXITLESS
EXCURSED	EXEMES	EXHIBITOR	EXITS
EXCURSES	EXEMING	EXHIBITS	EXO
EXCURSING	EXEMPLA	EXHORT	EXOCARP
EXCURSION	EXEMPLAR	EXHORTED	EXOCARPS
EXCURSIVE	EXEMPLARS	EXHORTER	EXOCRINE
EXCURSUS	EXEMPLARY	EXHORTERS	EXOCRINES
EXCUSABLE	EXEMPLE	EXHORTING	EXOCYCLIC
EXCUSABLY	EXEMPLES	EXHORTS	EXOCYTIC
EXCUSAL	EXEMPLIFY	EXHUMATE	EXOCYTOSE
EXCUSALS	EXEMPLUM	EXHUMATED	EXODE
EXCUSE	EXEMPT	EXHUMATES	EXODERM
EXCUSED	EXEMPTED	EXHUME	EXODERMAL
EXCUSER	EXEMPTING	EXHUMED	EXODERMIS
EXCUSERS	EXEMPTION	EXHUMER	EXODERMS
EXCUSES	EXEMPTIVE	EXHUMERS	EXODES
EXCUSING	EXEMPTS	EXHUMES	EXODIC
EXCUSIVE	EXEQUATUR	EXHUMING	EXODIST
EXEAT	EXEQUIAL	EXIES	EXODISTS
EXEATS	EXEQUIES	EXIGEANT	EXODOI
EXEC	EXEQUY	EXIGEANTE	EXODONTIA
EXECRABLE	EXERCISE	EXIGENCE	EXODOS
EXECRABLY	EXERCISED	EXIGENCES	EXODUS
EXECRATE	EXERCISER	EXIGENCY	EXODUSES
EXECRATED	EXERCISES	EXIGENT	EXOENZYME
EXECRATES	EXERCYCLE	EXIGENTLY	EXOERGIC
EXECRATOR	EXERGONIC	EXIGENTS	EXOGAMIC
EXECS	EXERGUAL	EXIGIBLE	EXOGAMIES
EXECUTANT	EXERGUE	EXIGUITY	EXOGAMOUS
EXECUTARY	EXERGUES	EXIGUOUS	EXOGAMY
EXECUTE	EXERT	EXILABLE	EXOGEN
EXECUTED	EXERTED	EXILE	EXOGENISM
EXECUTER	EXERTING	EXILED	EXOGENOUS
EXECUTERS	EXERTION	EXILEMENT	EXOGENS
EXECUTES	EXERTIONS	EXILER	EXOMION

EXOMIONS
EXOMIS
EXOMISES
EXON
EXONERATE
EXONIC
EXONS
EXONUMIA
EXONUMIST
EXONYM
EXONYMS
EXOPHAGY
EXOPHORIC
EXOPLANET
EXOPLASM
EXOPLASMS
EXOPOD
EXOPODITE
EXOPODS
EXORABLE
EXORATION
EXORCISE
EXORCISED
EXORCISER
EXORCISES
EXORCISM
EXORCISMS
EXORCIST
EXORCISTS
EXORCIZE
EXORCIZED
EXORCIZER
EXORCIZES
EXORDIA
EXORDIAL
EXORDIUM
EXORDIUMS
EXOSMIC
EXOSMOSE
EXOSMOSES
EXOSMOSIS
EXOSMOTIC
EXOSPHERE
EXOSPORAL
EXOSPORE
EXOSPORES
EXOSPORIA
EXOSTOSES
EXOSTOSIS
EXOTERIC
EXOTIC
EXOTICA
EXOTICISM
EXOTICIST
EXOTICS
EXOTISM
EXOTISMS
EXOTOXIC

EXOTOXIN
EXOTOXINS
EXOTROPIA
EXOTROPIC
EXPAND
EXPANDED
EXPANDER
EXPANDERS
EXPANDING
EXPANDOR
EXPANDORS
EXPANDS
EXPANSE
EXPANSES
EXPANSILE
EXPANSION
EXPANSIVE
EXPAT
EXPATIATE
EXPATS
EXPECT
EXPECTANT
EXPECTED
EXPECTER
EXPECTERS
EXPECTING
EXPECTS
EXPEDIENT
EXPEDITE
EXPEDITED
EXPEDITER
EXPEDITES
EXPEDITOR
EXPEL
EXPELLANT
EXPELLED
EXPELLEE
EXPELLEES
EXPELLENT
EXPELLER
EXPELLERS
EXPELLING
EXPELS
EXPEND
EXPENDED
EXPENDER
EXPENDERS
EXPENDING
EXPENDS
EXPENSE
EXPENSED
EXPENSES
EXPENSING
EXPENSIVE
EXPERT
EXPERTED
EXPERTING
EXPERTISE

EXPERTISM
EXPERTIZE
EXPERTLY
EXPERTS
EXPIABLE
EXPIATE
EXPIATED
EXPIATES
EXPIATING
EXPIATION
EXPIATOR
EXPIATORS
EXPIATORY
EXPIRABLE
EXPIRANT
EXPIRANTS
EXPIRE
EXPIRED
EXPIRER
EXPIRERS
EXPIRES
EXPIRIES
EXPIRING
EXPIRY
EXPISCATE
EXPLAIN
EXPLAINED
EXPLAINER
EXPLAINS
EXPLANT
EXPLANTED
EXPLANTS
EXPLETIVE
EXPLETORY
EXPLICATE
EXPLICIT
EXPLICITS
EXPLODE
EXPLODED
EXPLODER
EXPLODERS
EXPLODES
EXPLODING
EXPLOIT
EXPLOITED
EXPLOITER
EXPLOITS
EXPLORE
EXPLORED
EXPLORER
EXPLORERS
EXPLORES
EXPLORING
EXPLOSION
EXPLOSIVE
EXPO
EXPONENT
EXPONENTS

EXPONIBLE
EXPORT
EXPORTED
EXPORTER
EXPORTERS
EXPORTING
EXPORTS
EXPOS
EXPOSABLE
EXPOSAL
EXPOSALS
EXPOSE
EXPOSED
EXPOSER
EXPOSERS
EXPOSES
EXPOSING
EXPOSIT
EXPOSITED
EXPOSITOR
EXPOSITS
EXPOSTURE
EXPOSURE
EXPOSURES
EXPOUND
EXPOUNDED
EXPOUNDER
EXPOUNDS
EXPRESS
EXPRESSED
EXPRESSER
EXPRESSES
EXPRESSLY
EXPRESSO
EXPRESSOS
EXPUGN
EXPUGNED
EXPUGNING
EXPUGNS
EXPULSE
EXPULSED
EXPULSES
EXPULSING
EXPULSION
EXPULSIVE
EXPUNCT
EXPUNCTED
EXPUNCTS
EXPUNGE
EXPUNGED
EXPUNGER
EXPUNGERS
EXPUNGES
EXPUNGING
EXPURGATE
EXPURGE
EXPURGED
EXPURGES

EXPURGING
EXQUISITE
EXSCIND
EXSCINDED
EXSCINDS
EXSECANT
EXSECANTS
EXSECT
EXSECTED
EXSECTING
EXSECTION
EXSECTS
EXSERT
EXSERTED
EXSERTILE
EXSERTING
EXSERTION
EXSERTS
EXSICCANT
EXSICCATE
EXSTROPHY
EXSUCCOUS
EXTANT
EXTASIES
EXTASY
EXTATIC
EXTEMPORE
EXTEND
EXTENDANT
EXTENDED
EXTENDER
EXTENDERS
EXTENDING
EXTENDS
EXTENSE
EXTENSILE
EXTENSION
EXTENSITY
EXTENSIVE
EXTENSOR
EXTENSORS
EXTENT
EXTENTS
EXTENUATE
EXTERIOR
EXTERIORS
EXTERMINE
EXTERN
EXTERNAL
EXTERNALS
EXTERNAT
EXTERNATS
EXTERNE
EXTERNES
EXTERNS
EXTINCT
EXTINCTED
EXTINCTS

EXTINE
EXTINES
EXTIRP
EXTIRPATE
EXTIRPED
EXTIRPING
EXTIRPS
EXTOL
EXTOLD
EXTOLL
EXTOLLED
EXTOLLER
EXTOLLERS
EXTOLLING
EXTOLLS
EXTOLMENT
EXTOLS
EXTORSIVE
EXTORT
EXTORTED
EXTORTER
EXTORTERS
EXTORTING
EXTORTION
EXTORTIVE
EXTORTS
EXTRA
EXTRABOLD
EXTRACT
EXTRACTED
EXTRACTOR
EXTRACTS
EXTRADITE
EXTRADOS
EXTRAIT
EXTRAITS
EXTRALITY
EXTRANET
EXTRANETS
EXTRAPOSE
EXTRAS
EXTRAUGHT
EXTRAVERT
EXTREAT
EXTREATS
EXTREMA
EXTREMAL
EXTREMALS
EXTREME
EXTREMELY
EXTREMER
EXTREMES
EXTREMEST
EXTREMISM
EXTREMIST
EXTREMITY
EXTREMUM
EXTRICATE

EXTRINSIC
EXTRORSAL
EXTRORSE
EXTROVERT
EXTRUDE
EXTRUDED
EXTRUDER
EXTRUDERS
EXTRUDES
EXTRUDING
EXTRUSION
EXTRUSIVE
EXTRUSORY
EXTUBATE
EXTUBATED
EXTUBATES
EXUBERANT
EXUBERATE
EXUDATE
EXUDATES
EXUDATION
EXUDATIVE
EXUDE
EXUDED
EXUDES
EXUDING
EXUL
EXULS
EXULT
EXULTANCE
EXULTANCY
EXULTANT
EXULTED
EXULTING
EXULTS
EXURB
EXURBAN
EXURBIA
EXURBIAS
EXURBS
EXUVIA
EXUVIAE
EXUVIAL
EXUVIATE
EXUVIATED
EXUVIATES
EXUVIUM
EYALET
EYALETS
EYAS
EYASES
EYASS
EYASSES
EYE
EYEABLE
EYEBALL
EYEBALLED
EYEBALLS

EYEBANK
EYEBANKS
EYEBAR
EYEBARS
EYEBATH
EYEBATHS
EYEBEAM
EYEBEAMS
EYEBLACK
EYEBLACKS
EYEBLINK
EYEBLINKS
EYEBOLT
EYEBOLTS
EYEBRIGHT
EYEBROW
EYEBROWED
EYEBROWS
EYECUP
EYECUPS
EYED
EYEDNESS
EYEDROPS
EYEFOLD
EYEFOLDS
EYEFUL
EYEFULS
EYEGLASS
EYEHOLE
EYEHOLES
EYEHOOK
EYEHOOKS
EYEING
EYELASH
EYELASHES
EYELESS
EYELET
EYELETED
EYELETEER
EYELETING
EYELETS
EYELETTED
EYELEVEL
EYELIAD
EYELIADS
EYELID
EYELIDS
EYELIFT
EYELIFTS
EYELIKE
EYELINER
EYELINERS
EYEN
EYEOPENER
EYEPIECE
EYEPIECES
EYEPOINT
EYEPOINTS

EYEPOPPER
EYER
EYERS
EYES
EYESHADE
EYESHADES
EYESHADOW
EYESHINE
EYESHINES
EYESHOT
EYESHOTS
EYESIGHT
EYESIGHTS
EYESOME
EYESORE
EYESORES
EYESPOT
EYESPOTS
EYESTALK
EYESTALKS
EYESTONE
EYESTONES
EYESTRAIN
EYETEETH
EYETOOTH
EYEWASH
EYEWASHES
EYEWATER
EYEWATERS
EYEWEAR
EYEWINK
EYEWINKS
EYING
EYLIAD
EYLIADS
EYNE
EYOT
EYOTS
EYRA
EYRAS
EYRE
EYRES
EYRIE
EYRIES
EYRIR
EYRY

F

FA	FACEMAIL	FACTOIDAL	FADEINS
FAA	FACEMAILS	FACTOIDS	FADELESS
FAAING	FACEMAN	FACTOR	FADEOUT
FAAN	FACEMASK	FACTORAGE	FADEOUTS
FAAS	FACEMASKS	FACTORED	FADER
FAB	FACEMEN	FACTORIAL	FADERS
FABACEOUS	FACEPLATE	FACTORIES	FADES
FABBER	FACEPRINT	FACTORING	FADEUR
FABBEST	FACER	FACTORISE	FADEURS
FABLE	FACERS	FACTORIZE	FADGE
FABLED	FACES	FACTORS	FADGED
FABLER	FACET	FACTORY	FADGES
FABLERS	FACETE	FACTOTUM	FADGING
FABLES	FACETED	FACTOTUMS	FADIER
FABLIAU	FACETELY	FACTS	FADIEST
FABLIAUX	FACETIAE	FACTSHEET	FADING
FABLING	FACETING	FACTUAL	FADINGS
FABLINGS	FACETIOUS	FACTUALLY	FADLIKE
FABRIC	FACETS	FACTUM	FADO
FABRICANT	FACETTED	FACTUMS	FADOMETER
FABRICATE	FACETTING	FACTURE	FADOS
FABRICKED	FACEUP	FACTURES	FADS
FABRICS	FACIA	FACULA	FADY
FABS	FACIAE	FACULAE	FAE
FABULAR	FACIAL	FACULAR	FAECAL
FABULATE	FACIALLY	FACULTIES	FAECES
FABULATED	FACIALS	FACULTY	FAENA
FABULATES	FACIAS	FACUNDITY	FAENAS
FABULATOR	FACIEND	FAD	FAERIE
FABULISE	FACIENDS	FADABLE	FAERIES
FABULISED	FACIES	FADAISE	FAERY
FABULISES	FACILE	FADAISES	FAFF
FABULIST	FACILELY	FADDIER	FAFFED
FABULISTS	FACILITY	FADDIEST	FAFFING
FABULIZE	FACING	FADDINESS	FAFFS
FABULIZED	FACINGS	FADDISH	FAG
FABULIZES	FACONNE	FADDISHLY	FAGACEOUS
FABULOUS	FACONNES	FADDISM	FAGGED
FABURDEN	FACSIMILE	FADDISMS	FAGGERIES
FABURDENS	FACT	FADDIST	FAGGERY
FACADE	FACTFUL	FADDISTS	FAGGIER
FACADES	FACTICE	FADDLE	FAGGIEST
FACE	FACTICES	FADDLED	FAGGING
FACEABLE	FACTICITY	FADDLES	FAGGINGS
FACEBAR	FACTION	FADDLING	FAGGOT
FACEBARS	FACTIONAL	FADDY	FAGGOTED
FACECLOTH	FACTIONS	FADE	FAGGOTING
FACED	FACTIOUS	FADEAWAY	FAGGOTRY
FACEDOWN	FACTIS	FADEAWAYS	FAGGOTS
FACEDOWNS	FACTISES	FADED	FAGGOTY
FACELESS	FACTITIVE	FADEDLY	FAGGY
FACELIFT	FACTIVE	FADEDNESS	FAGIN
FACELIFTS	FACTOID	FADEIN	FAGINS

FAGOT	FAINTERS	FAKED	FALLALERY
FAGOTED	FAINTEST	FAKEER	FALLALS
FAGOTER	FAINTIER	FAKEERS	FALLAWAY
FAGOTERS	FAINTIEST	FAKEMENT	FALLAWAYS
FAGOTING	FAINTING	FAKEMENTS	FALLBACK
FAGOTINGS	FAINTINGS	FAKER	FALLBACKS
FAGOTS	FAINTISH	FAKERIES	FALLBOARD
FAGOTTI	FAINTLY	FAKERS	FALLEN
FAGOTTIST	FAINTNESS	FAKERY	FALLER
FAGOTTO	FAINTS	FAKES	FALLERS
FAGS	FAINTY	FAKEY	FALLFISH
FAH	FAIR	FAKING	FALLIBLE
FAHLBAND	FAIRED	FAKIR	FALLIBLY
FAHLBANDS	FAIRER	FAKIRISM	FALLING
FAHLERZ	FAIREST	FAKIRISMS	FALLINGS
FAHLERZES	FAIRFACED	FAKIRS	FALLOFF
FAHLORE	FAIRGOER	FALAFEL	FALLOFFS
FAHLORES	FAIRGOERS	FALAFELS	FALLOUT
FAHS	FAIRIES	FALAJ	FALLOUTS
FAIBLE	FAIRILY	FALANGISM	FALLOW
FAIBLES	FAIRING	FALANGIST	FALLOWED
FAIENCE	FAIRINGS	FALBALA	FALLOWER
FAIENCES	FAIRISH	FALBALAS	FALLOWEST
FAIK	FAIRISHLY	FALCADE	FALLOWING
FAIKED	FAIRLEAD	FALCADES	FALLOWS
FAIKES	FAIRLEADS	FALCATE	FALLS
FAIKING	FAIRLY	FALCATED	FALSE
FAIKS	FAIRNESS	FALCATION	FALSED
FAIL	FAIRS	FALCES	FALSEFACE
FAILED	FAIRWAY	FALCHION	FALSEHOOD
FAILING	FAIRWAYS	FALCHIONS	FALSELY
FAILINGLY	FAIRY	FALCIFORM	FALSENESS
FAILINGS	FAIRYDOM	FALCON	FALSER
FAILLE	FAIRYDOMS	FALCONER	FALSERS
FAILLES	FAIRYHOOD	FALCONERS	FALSES
FAILS	FAIRYISM	FALCONET	FALSEST
FAILURE	FAIRYISMS	FALCONETS	FALSETTO
FAILURES	FAIRYLAND	FALCONINE	FALSETTOS
FAIN	FAIRYLIKE	FALCONOID	FALSEWORK
FAINE	FAIRYTALE	FALCONRY	FALSIE
FAINEANCE	FAITH	FALCONS	FALSIES
FAINEANCY	FAITHCURE	FALCULA	FALSIFIED
FAINEANT	FAITHED	FALCULAE	FALSIFIER
FAINEANTS	FAITHER	FALCULAS	FALSIFIES
FAINED	FAITHERS	FALCULATE	FALSIFY
FAINER	FAITHFUL	FALDAGE	FALSING
FAINES	FAITHFULS	FALDAGES	FALSISH
FAINEST	FAITHING	FALDERAL	FALSISM
FAINING	FAITHLESS	FALDERALS	FALSISMS
FAINITES	FAITHS	FALDEROL	FALSITIES
FAINLY	FAITOR	FALDEROLS	FALSITY
FAINNE	FAITORS	FALDETTA	FALTBOAT
FAINNES	FAITOUR	FALDETTAS	FALTBOATS
FAINNESS	FAITOURS	FALDSTOOL	FALTER
FAINS	FAIX	FALL	FALTERED
FAINT	FAJITA	FALLACIES	FALTERER
FAINTED	FAJITAS	FALLACY	FALTERERS
FAINTER	FAKE	FALLAL	FALTERING

FALTERS	FANDED	FANNIES	FARADIC
FALX	FANDING	FANNING	FARADISE
FAME	FANDOM	FANNINGS	FARADISED
FAMED	FANDOMS	FANNY	FARADISER
FAMELESS	FANDS	FANO	FARADISES
FAMES	FANE	FANON	FARADISM
FAMILIAL	FANEGA	FANONS	FARADISMS
FAMILIAR	FANEGADA	FANOS	FARADIZE
FAMILIARS	FANEGADAS	FANS	FARADIZED
FAMILIES	FANEGAS	FANTAD	FARADIZER
FAMILISM	FANES	FANTADS	FARADIZES
FAMILISMS	FANFARADE	FANTAIL	FARADS
FAMILLE	FANFARE	FANTAILED	FARAND
FAMILLES	FANFARED	FANTAILS	FARANDINE
FAMILY	FANFARES	FANTASIA	FARANDOLE
FAMINE	FANFARING	FANTASIAS	FARAWAY
FAMINES	FANFARON	FANTASIE	FARAWAYS
FAMING	FANFARONA	FANTASIED	FARCE
FAMISH	FANFARONS	FANTASIES	FARCED
FAMISHED	FANFIC	FANTASISE	FARCEMEAT
FAMISHES	FANFICS	FANTASIST	FARCER
FAMISHING	FANFOLD	FANTASIZE	FARCERS
FAMOUS	FANFOLDED	FANTASM	FARCES
FAMOUSED	FANFOLDS	FANTASMAL	FARCEUR
FAMOUSES	FANG	FANTASMIC	FARCEURS
FAMOUSING	FANGA	FANTASMS	FARCEUSE
FAMOUSLY	FANGAS	FANTASQUE	FARCEUSES
FAMULI	FANGED	FANTAST	FARCI
FAMULUS	FANGING	FANTASTIC	FARCICAL
FAMULUSES	FANGLE	FANTASTRY	FARCIE
FAN	FANGLED	FANTASTS	FARCIED
FANAL	FANGLES	FANTASY	FARCIES
FANALS	FANGLESS	FANTEEG	FARCIFIED
FANATIC	FANGLIKE	FANTEEGS	FARCIFIES
FANATICAL	FANGLING	FANTIGUE	FARCIFY
FANATICS	FANGO	FANTIGUES	FARCIN
FANBASE	FANGOS	FANTOD	FARCING
FANBASES	FANGS	FANTODS	FARCINGS
FANCIABLE	FANION	FANTOM	FARCINS
FANCIED	FANIONS	FANTOMS	FARCY
FANCIER	FANJET	FANTOOSH	FARD
FANCIERS	FANJETS	FANUM	FARDAGE
FANCIES	FANK	FANUMS	FARDAGES
FANCIEST	FANKLE	FANWISE	FARDED
FANCIFIED	FANKLED	FANWORT	FARDEL
FANCIFIES	FANKLES	FANWORTS	FARDELS
FANCIFUL	FANKLING	FANZINE	FARDEN
FANCIFY	FANKS	FANZINES	FARDENS
FANCILESS	FANLIGHT	FAP	FARDING
FANCILY	FANLIGHTS	FAQIR	FARDINGS
FANCINESS	FANLIKE	FAQIRS	FARDS
FANCY	FANNED	FAQUIR	FARE
FANCYING	FANNEL	FAQUIRS	FAREBOX
FANCYWORK	FANNELL	FAR	FAREBOXES
FAND	FANNELLS	FARAD	FARED
FANDANGLE	FANNELS	FARADAIC	FARER
FANDANGO	FANNER	FARADAY	FARERS
FANDANGOS	FANNERS	FARADAYS	FARES

FAREWELL	FARREN	FASCISMO	FATBIRDS
FAREWELLS	FARRENS	FASCISMS	FATE
FARFAL	FARRIER	FASCIST	FATED
FARFALLE	FARRIERS	FASCISTA	FATEFUL
FARFALS	FARRIERY	FASCISTI	FATEFULLY
FARFEL	FARRING	FASCISTIC	FATES
FARFELS	FARROW	FASCISTS	FATHEAD
FARFET	FARROWED	FASCITIS	FATHEADED
FARINA	FARROWING	FASH	FATHEADS
FARINAS	FARROWS	FASHED	FATHER
FARING	FARRUCA	FASHERIES	FATHERED
FARINHA	FARRUCAS	FASHERY	FATHERING
FARINHAS	FARS	FASHES	FATHERLY
FARINOSE	FARSE	FASHING	FATHERS
FARL	FARSED	FASHION	FATHOM
FARLE	FARSEEING	FASHIONED	FATHOMED
FARLES	FARSES	FASHIONER	FATHOMER
FARLS	FARSIDE	FASHIONS	FATHOMERS
FARM	FARSIDES	FASHIONY	FATHOMING
FARMABLE	FARSING	FASHIOUS	FATHOMS
FARMED	FART	FAST	FATIDIC
FARMER	FARTED	FASTBACK	FATIDICAL
FARMERESS	FARTHEL	FASTBACKS	FATIGABLE
FARMERIES	FARTHELS	FASTBALL	FATIGATE
FARMERS	FARTHER	FASTBALLS	FATIGATED
FARMERY	FARTHEST	FASTED	FATIGATES
FARMHAND	FARTHING	FASTEN	FATIGUE
FARMHANDS	FARTHINGS	FASTENED	FATIGUED
FARMHOUSE	FARTING	FASTENER	FATIGUES
FARMING	FARTLEK	FASTENERS	FATIGUING
FARMINGS	FARTLEKS	FASTENING	FATING
FARMLAND	FARTS	FASTENS	FATISCENT
FARMLANDS	FAS	FASTER	FATLESS
FARMOST	FASCES	FASTERS	FATLIKE
FARMS	FASCI	FASTEST	FATLING
FARMSTEAD	FASCIA	FASTI	FATLINGS
FARMWIFE	FASCIAE	FASTIE	FATLY
FARMWIVES	FASCIAL	FASTIES	FATNESS
FARMWORK	FASCIAS	FASTIGIUM	FATNESSES
FARMWORKS	FASCIATE	FASTING	FATS
FARMYARD	FASCIATED	FASTINGS	FATSIA
FARMYARDS	FASCICLE	FASTISH	FATSIAS
FARNARKEL	FASCICLED	FASTLY	FATSO
FARNESOL	FASCICLES	FASTNESS	FATSOES
FARNESOLS	FASCICULE	FASTS	FATSOS
FARNESS	FASCICULI	FASTUOUS	FATSTOCK
FARNESSES	FASCIITIS	FAT	FATSTOCKS
FARO	FASCINATE	FATAL	FATTED
FAROLITO	FASCINE	FATALISM	FATTEN
FAROLITOS	FASCINES	FATALISMS	FATTENED
FAROS	FASCIO	FATALIST	FATTENER
FAROUCHE	FASCIOLA	FATALISTS	FATTENERS
FARRAGO	FASCIOLAS	FATALITY	FATTENING
FARRAGOES	FASCIOLE	FATALLY	FATTENS
FARRAGOS	FASCIOLES	FATALNESS	FATTER
FARRAND	FASCIS	FATBACK	FATTEST
FARRANT	FASCISM	FATBACKS	FATTIER
FARRED	FASCISMI	FATBIRD	FATTIES

FATTIEST	FAUNIST	FAVOSE	FEAL
FATTILY	FAUNISTIC	FAVOUR	FEALED
FATTINESS	FAUNISTS	FAVOURED	FEALING
FATTING	FAUNLIKE	FAVOURER	FEALS
FATTISH	FAUNS	FAVOURERS	FEALTIES
FATTISM	FAUNULA	FAVOURING	FEALTY
FATTISMS	FAUNULAE	FAVOURITE	FEAR
FATTIST	FAUNULE	FAVOURS	FEARE
FATTISTS	FAUNULES	FAVOUS	FEARED
FATTRELS	FAUR	FAVRILE	FEARER
FATTY	FAURD	FAVRILES	FEARERS
FATUITIES	FAURER	FAVUS	FEARES
FATUITOUS	FAUREST	FAVUSES	FEARFUL
FATUITY	FAUSTIAN	FAW	FEARFULLY
FATUOUS	FAUT	FAWN	FEARING
FATUOUSLY	FAUTED	FAWNED	FEARLESS
FATWA	FAUTEUIL	FAWNER	FEARS
FATWAED	FAUTEUILS	FAWNERS	FEARSOME
FATWAH	FAUTING	FAWNIER	FEASANCE
FATWAHED	FAUTOR	FAWNIEST	FEASANCES
FATWAHING	FAUTORS	FAWNING	FEASE
FATWAHS	FAUTS	FAWNINGLY	FEASED
FATWAING	FAUVE	FAWNINGS	FEASES
FATWAS	FAUVES	FAWNLIKE	FEASIBLE
FATWOOD	FAUVETTE	FAWNS	FEASIBLY
FATWOODS	FAUVETTES	FAWNY	FEASING
FAUBOURG	FAUVISM	FAWS	FEAST
FAUBOURGS	FAUVISMS	FAX	FEASTED
FAUCAL	FAUVIST	FAXED	FEASTER
FAUCALS	FAUVISTS	FAXES	FEASTERS
FAUCES	FAUX	FAXING	FEASTFUL
FAUCET	FAVA	FAY	FEASTING
FAUCETS	FAVAS	FAYALITE	FEASTINGS
FAUCHION	FAVE	FAYALITES	FEASTLESS
FAUCHIONS	FAVEL	FAYED	FEASTS
FAUCHON	FAVELA	FAYENCE	FEAT
FAUCHONS	FAVELAS	FAYENCES	FEATED
FAUCIAL	FAVELL	FAYER	FEATEOUS
FAUGH	FAVELLA	FAYEST	FEATER
FAULCHION	FAVELLAS	FAYING	FEATEST
FAULD	FAVEOLATE	FAYNE	FEATHER
FAULDS	FAVER	FAYNED	FEATHERED
FAULT	FAVES	FAYNES	FEATHERS
FAULTED	FAVEST	FAYNING	FEATHERY
FAULTFUL	FAVISM	FAYRE	FEATING
FAULTIER	FAVISMS	FAYRES	FEATLIER
FAULTIEST	FAVONIAN	FAYS	FEATLIEST
FAULTILY	FAVOR	FAZE	FEATLY
FAULTING	FAVORABLE	FAZED	FEATOUS
FAULTLESS	FAVORABLY	FAZENDA	FEATS
FAULTS	FAVORED	FAZENDAS	FEATUOUS
FAULTY	FAVORER	FAZES	FEATURE
FAUN	FAVORERS	FAZING	FEATURED
FAUNA	FAVORING	FE	FEATURELY
FAUNAE	FAVORITE	FEAGUE	FEATURES
FAUNAL	FAVORITES	FEAGUED	FEATURING
FAUNALLY	FAVORLESS	FEAGUES	FEAZE
FAUNAS	FAVORS	FEAGUING	FEAZED

FEAZES
FEAZING
FEBLESSE
FEBLESSES
FEBRICITY
FEBRICULA
FEBRICULE
FEBRIFIC
FEBRIFUGE
FEBRILE
FEBRILITY
FECAL
FECES
FECHT
FECHTER
FECHTERS
FECHTING
FECHTS
FECIAL
FECIALS
FECIT
FECK
FECKED
FECKIN
FECKING
FECKLESS
FECKLY
FECKS
FECULA
FECULAE
FECULAS
FECULENCE
FECULENCY
FECULENT
FECUND
FECUNDATE
FECUNDITY
FED
FEDARIE
FEDARIES
FEDAYEE
FEDAYEEN
FEDELINI
FEDELINIS
FEDERACY
FEDERAL
FEDERALLY
FEDERALS
FEDERARIE
FEDERARY
FEDERATE
FEDERATED
FEDERATES
FEDERATOR
FEDEX
FEDEXED
FEDEXES
FEDEXING

FEDORA
FEDORAS
FEDS
FEE
FEEB
FEEBLE
FEEBLED
FEEBLER
FEEBLES
FEEBLEST
FEEBLING
FEEBLISH
FEEBLY
FEEBS
FEED
FEEDABLE
FEEDBACK
FEEDBACKS
FEEDBAG
FEEDBAGS
FEEDBOX
FEEDBOXES
FEEDER
FEEDERS
FEEDGRAIN
FEEDHOLE
FEEDHOLES
FEEDING
FEEDINGS
FEEDLOT
FEEDLOTS
FEEDS
FEEDSTOCK
FEEDSTUFF
FEEDWATER
FEEDYARD
FEEDYARDS
FEEING
FEEL
FEELBAD
FEELBADS
FEELER
FEELERS
FEELESS
FEELGOOD
FEELGOODS
FEELING
FEELINGLY
FEELINGS
FEELS
FEEN
FEENS
FEER
FEERED
FEERIE
FEERIES
FEERIN
FEERING

FEERINGS
FEERINS
FEERS
FEES
FEESE
FEESED
FEESES
FEESING
FEET
FEETFIRST
FEETLESS
FEEZE
FEEZED
FEEZES
FEEZING
FEG
FEGARIES
FEGARY
FEGS
FEH
FEHM
FEHME
FEHMIC
FEHS
FEIGN
FEIGNED
FEIGNEDLY
FEIGNER
FEIGNERS
FEIGNING
FEIGNINGS
FEIGNS
FEIJOA
FEIJOAS
FEINT
FEINTED
FEINTER
FEINTEST
FEINTING
FEINTS
FEIRIE
FEIS
FEISEANNA
FEIST
FEISTIER
FEISTIEST
FEISTILY
FEISTS
FEISTY
FELAFEL
FELAFELS
FELDGRAU
FELDGRAUS
FELDSCHAR
FELDSCHER
FELDSHER
FELDSHERS
FELDSPAR

FELDSPARS
FELDSPATH
FELICIA
FELICIAS
FELICIFIC
FELICITER
FELICITY
FELID
FELIDS
FELINE
FELINELY
FELINES
FELINITY
FELL
FELLA
FELLABLE
FELLAH
FELLAHEEN
FELLAHIN
FELLAHS
FELLAS
FELLATE
FELLATED
FELLATES
FELLATING
FELLATIO
FELLATION
FELLATIOS
FELLATOR
FELLATORS
FELLATRIX
FELLED
FELLER
FELLERS
FELLEST
FELLIES
FELLING
FELLNESS
FELLOE
FELLOES
FELLOW
FELLOWED
FELLOWING
FELLOWLY
FELLOWMAN
FELLOWMEN
FELLOWS
FELLS
FELLY
FELON
FELONIES
FELONIOUS
FELONOUS
FELONRIES
FELONRY
FELONS
FELONY
FELSIC

FELSITE	FEMMIER	FENS	FERMENT
FELSITES	FEMMIEST	FENT	FERMENTED
FELSITIC	FEMMY	FENTANYL	FERMENTER
FELSPAR	FEMORA	FENTANYLS	FERMENTOR
FELSPARS	FEMORAL	FENTHION	FERMENTS
FELSTONE	FEMS	FENTHIONS	FERMI
FELSTONES	FEMUR	FENTS	FERMION
FELT	FEMURS	FENUGREEK	FERMIONIC
FELTED	FEN	FENURON	FERMIONS
FELTER	FENAGLE	FENURONS	FERMIS
FELTERED	FENAGLED	FEOD	FERMIUM
FELTERING	FENAGLES	FEODAL	FERMIUMS
FELTERS	FENAGLING	FEODARIES	FERMS
FELTIER	FENCE	FEODARY	FERN
FELTIEST	FENCED	FEODS	FERNBIRD
FELTING	FENCELESS	FEOFF	FERNBIRDS
FELTINGS	FENCELIKE	FEOFFED	FERNERIES
FELTLIKE	FENCER	FEOFFEE	FERNERY
FELTS	FENCEROW	FEOFFEES	FERNIER
FELTY	FENCEROWS	FEOFFER	FERNIEST
FELUCCA	FENCERS	FEOFFERS	FERNING
FELUCCAS	FENCES	FEOFFING	FERNINGS
FELWORT	FENCIBLE	FEOFFMENT	FERNINST
FELWORTS	FENCIBLES	FEOFFOR	FERNLESS
FEM	FENCING	FEOFFORS	FERNLIKE
FEMAL	FENCINGS	FEOFFS	FERNS
FEMALE	FEND	FER	FERNSHAW
FEMALES	FENDED	FERACIOUS	FERNSHAWS
FEMALITY	FENDER	FERACITY	FERNTICLE
FEMALS	FENDERED	FERAL	FERNY
FEME	FENDERS	FERALISED	FEROCIOUS
FEMERALL	FENDIER	FERALIZED	FEROCITY
FEMERALLS	FENDIEST	FERALS	FERRATE
FEMES	FENDING	FERBAM	FERRATES
FEMETARY	FENDS	FERBAMS	FERREL
FEMINACY	FENDY	FERE	FERRELED
FEMINAL	FENESTRA	FERER	FERRELING
FEMINAZI	FENESTRAE	FERES	FERRELLED
FEMINAZIS	FENESTRAL	FEREST	FERRELS
FEMINEITY	FENESTRAS	FERETORY	FERREOUS
FEMINIE	FENI	FERIA	FERRET
FEMININE	FENIS	FERIAE	FERRETED
FEMININES	FENITAR	FERIAL	FERRETER
FEMINISE	FENITARS	FERIAS	FERRETERS
FEMINISED	FENKS	FERINE	FERRETING
FEMINISES	FENLAND	FERITIES	FERRETS
FEMINISM	FENLANDS	FERITY	FERRETY
FEMINISMS	FENMAN	FERLIE	FERRIAGE
FEMINIST	FENMEN	FERLIED	FERRIAGES
FEMINISTS	FENNEC	FERLIER	FERRIC
FEMINITY	FENNECS	FERLIES	FERRIED
FEMINIZE	FENNEL	FERLIEST	FERRIES
FEMINIZED	FENNELS	FERLY	FERRITE
FEMINIZES	FENNIER	FERLYING	FERRITES
FEMITER	FENNIES	FERM	FERRITIC
FEMITERS	FENNIEST	FERMATA	FERRITIN
FEMME	FENNISH	FERMATAS	FERRITINS
FEMMES	FENNY	FERMATE	FERROCENE

FERROTYPE	FESTAS	FETING	FEUDIST
FERROUS	FESTER	FETISH	FEUDISTS
FERRUGO	FESTERED	FETISHES	FEUDS
FERRUGOS	FESTERING	FETISHISE	FEUED
FERRULE	FESTERS	FETISHISM	FEUILLETE
FERRULED	FESTIER	FETISHIST	FEUING
FERRULES	FESTIEST	FETISHIZE	FEUS
FERRULING	FESTILOGY	FETLOCK	FEUTRE
FERRUM	FESTINATE	FETLOCKED	FEUTRED
FERRUMS	FESTIVAL	FETLOCKS	FEUTRES
FERRY	FESTIVALS	FETOLOGY	FEUTRING
FERRYBOAT	FESTIVE	FETOR	FEVER
FERRYING	FESTIVELY	FETORS	FEVERED
FERRYMAN	FESTIVITY	FETOSCOPE	FEVERFEW
FERRYMEN	FESTIVOUS	FETOSCOPY	FEVERFEWS
FERTIGATE	FESTOLOGY	FETS	FEVERING
FERTILE	FESTOON	FETT	FEVERISH
FERTILELY	FESTOONED	FETTA	FEVERLESS
FERTILER	FESTOONS	FETTAS	FEVEROUS
FERTILEST	FESTS	FETTED	FEVERROOT
FERTILISE	FESTY	FETTER	FEVERS
FERTILITY	FET	FETTERED	FEVERWEED
FERTILIZE	FETA	FETTERER	FEVERWORT
FERULA	FETAL	FETTERERS	FEW
FERULAE	FETAS	FETTERING	FEWER
FERULAS	FETATION	FETTERS	FEWEST
FERULE	FETATIONS	FETTING	FEWMET
FERULED	FETCH	FETTLE	FEWMETS
FERULES	FETCHED	FETTLED	FEWNESS
FERULING	FETCHER	FETTLER	FEWNESSES
FERVENCY	FETCHERS	FETTLERS	FEWTER
FERVENT	FETCHES	FETTLES	FEWTERED
FERVENTER	FETCHING	FETTLING	FEWTERING
FERVENTLY	FETE	FETTLINGS	FEWTERS
FERVID	FETED	FETTS	FEWTRILS
FERVIDER	FETERITA	FETTUCINE	FEY
FERVIDEST	FETERITAS	FETTUCINI	FEYED
FERVIDITY	FETES	FETUS	FEYER
FERVIDLY	FETIAL	FETUSES	FEYEST
FERVOR	FETIALES	FETWA	FEYING
FERVOROUS	FETIALIS	FETWAS	FEYLY
FERVORS	FETIALS	FEU	FEYNESS
FERVOUR	FETICH	FEUAR	FEYNESSES
FERVOURS	FETICHE	FEUARS	FEYS
FES	FETICHES	FEUD	FEZ
FESCUE	FETICHISE	FEUDAL	FEZES
FESCUES	FETICHISM	FEUDALISE	FEZZED
FESS	FETICHIST	FEUDALISM	FEZZES
FESSE	FETICHIZE	FEUDALIST	FEZZY
FESSED	FETICIDAL	FEUDALITY	FIACRE
FESSES	FETICIDE	FEUDALIZE	FIACRES
FESSING	FETICIDES	FEUDALLY	FIANCE
FESSWISE	FETID	FEUDARIES	FIANCEE
FEST	FETIDER	FEUDARY	FIANCEES
FESTA	FETIDEST	FEUDATORY	FIANCES
FESTAL	FETIDITY	FEUDED	FIAR
FESTALLY	FETIDLY	FEUDING	FIARS
FESTALS	FETIDNESS	FEUDINGS	FIASCHI

FIASCO	FIBROS	FIDEISMS	FIERIER
FIASCOES	FIBROSE	FIDEIST	FIERIEST
FIASCOS	FIBROSED	FIDEISTIC	FIERILY
FIAT	FIBROSES	FIDEISTS	FIERINESS
FIATED	FIBROSING	FIDELISMO	FIERS
FIATING	FIBROSIS	FIDELISTA	FIERY
FIATS	FIBROTIC	FIDELITY	FIEST
FIAUNT	FIBROUS	FIDGE	FIESTA
FIAUNTS	FIBROUSLY	FIDGED	FIESTAS
FIB	FIBS	FIDGES	FIFE
FIBBED	FIBSTER	FIDGET	FIFED
FIBBER	FIBSTERS	FIDGETED	FIFER
FIBBERIES	FIBULA	FIDGETER	FIFERS
FIBBERS	FIBULAE	FIDGETERS	FIFES
FIBBERY	FIBULAR	FIDGETIER	FIFI
FIBBING	FIBULAS	FIDGETING	FIFING
FIBER	FICE	FIDGETS	FIFTEEN
FIBERED	FICES	FIDGETY	FIFTEENER
FIBERFILL	FICHE	FIDGING	FIFTEENS
FIBERISE	FICHES	FIDIBUS	FIFTEENTH
FIBERISED	FICHU	FIDIBUSES	FIFTH
FIBERISES	FICHUS	FIDO	FIFTHLY
FIBERIZE	FICIN	FIDOS	FIFTHS
FIBERIZED	FICINS	FIDS	FIFTIES
FIBERIZES	FICKLE	FIDUCIAL	FIFTIETH
FIBERLESS	FICKLED	FIDUCIARY	FIFTIETHS
FIBERLIKE	FICKLER	FIE	FIFTY
FIBERS	FICKLES	FIEF	FIFTYISH
FIBRANNE	FICKLEST	FIEFDOM	FIG
FIBRANNES	FICKLING	FIEFDOMS	FIGEATER
FIBRE	FICKLY	FIEFS	FIGEATERS
FIBRED	FICO	FIELD	FIGGED
FIBREFILL	FICOES	FIELDED	FIGGERIES
FIBRELESS	FICOS	FIELDER	FIGGERY
FIBRES	FICTILE	FIELDERS	FIGGING
FIBRIFORM	FICTION	FIELDFARE	FIGHT
FIBRIL	FICTIONAL	FIELDING	FIGHTABLE
FIBRILAR	FICTIONS	FIELDINGS	FIGHTBACK
FIBRILLA	FICTIVE	FIELDMICE	FIGHTER
FIBRILLAE	FICTIVELY	FIELDS	FIGHTERS
FIBRILLAR	FICTOR	FIELDSMAN	FIGHTING
FIBRILLIN	FICTORS	FIELDSMEN	FIGHTINGS
FIBRILS	FICUS	FIELDVOLE	FIGHTS
FIBRIN	FICUSES	FIELDWARD	FIGJAM
FIBRINOID	FID	FIELDWORK	FIGJAMS
FIBRINOUS	FIDDIOUS	FIEND	FIGMENT
FIBRINS	FIDDLE	FIENDISH	FIGMENTS
FIBRO	FIDDLED	FIENDLIKE	FIGO
FIBROCYTE	FIDDLER	FIENDS	FIGOS
FIBROID	FIDDLERS	FIENT	FIGS
FIBROIDS	FIDDLES	FIENTS	FIGULINE
FIBROIN	FIDDLEY	FIER	FIGULINES
FIBROINS	FIDDLEYS	FIERCE	FIGURABLE
FIBROLINE	FIDDLIER	FIERCELY	FIGURAL
FIBROLITE	FIDDLIEST	FIERCER	FIGURALLY
FIBROMA	FIDDLING	FIERCEST	FIGURANT
FIBROMAS	FIDDLY	FIERE	FIGURANTE
FIBROMATA	FIDEISM	FIERES	FIGURANTS

FIGURATE
FIGURE
FIGURED
FIGUREDLY
FIGURER
FIGURERS
FIGURES
FIGURINE
FIGURINES
FIGURING
FIGURIST
FIGURISTS
FIGWORT
FIGWORTS
FIKE
FIKED
FIKERIES
FIKERY
FIKES
FIKIER
FIKIEST
FIKING
FIKISH
FIKY
FIL
FILA
FILABEG
FILABEGS
FILACEOUS
FILACER
FILACERS
FILAGREE
FILAGREED
FILAGREES
FILAMENT
FILAMENTS
FILANDER
FILANDERS
FILAR
FILAREE
FILAREES
FILARIA
FILARIAE
FILARIAL
FILARIAN
FILARIAS
FILARIID
FILARIIDS
FILASSE
FILASSES
FILATORY
FILATURE
FILATURES
FILAZER
FILAZERS
FILBERD
FILBERDS
FILBERT

FILBERTS
FILCH
FILCHED
FILCHER
FILCHERS
FILCHES
FILCHING
FILCHINGS
FILE
FILEABLE
FILECARD
FILECARDS
FILED
FILEFISH
FILEMOT
FILEMOTS
FILENAME
FILENAMES
FILER
FILERS
FILES
FILET
FILETED
FILETING
FILETS
FILFOT
FILFOTS
FILIAL
FILIALLY
FILIATE
FILIATED
FILIATES
FILIATING
FILIATION
FILIBEG
FILIBEGS
FILICIDAL
FILICIDE
FILICIDES
FILIFORM
FILIGRAIN
FILIGRANE
FILIGREE
FILIGREED
FILIGREES
FILING
FILINGS
FILIOQUE
FILIOQUES
FILISTER
FILISTERS
FILL
FILLABLE
FILLAGREE
FILLE
FILLED
FILLER
FILLERS

FILLES
FILLESTER
FILLET
FILLETED
FILLETING
FILLETS
FILLIBEG
FILLIBEGS
FILLIES
FILLING
FILLINGS
FILLIP
FILLIPED
FILLIPEEN
FILLIPING
FILLIPS
FILLISTER
FILLO
FILLOS
FILLS
FILLY
FILM
FILMABLE
FILMCARD
FILMCARDS
FILMDOM
FILMDOMS
FILMED
FILMER
FILMERS
FILMGOER
FILMGOERS
FILMGOING
FILMI
FILMIC
FILMIER
FILMIEST
FILMILY
FILMINESS
FILMING
FILMIS
FILMISH
FILMLAND
FILMLANDS
FILMLESS
FILMLIKE
FILMMAKER
FILMS
FILMSET
FILMSETS
FILMSTRIP
FILMY
FILO
FILOPLUME
FILOPODIA
FILOS
FILOSE
FILOSELLE

FILOVIRUS
FILS
FILTER
FILTERED
FILTERER
FILTERERS
FILTERING
FILTERS
FILTH
FILTHIER
FILTHIEST
FILTHILY
FILTHS
FILTHY
FILTRABLE
FILTRATE
FILTRATED
FILTRATES
FILUM
FIMBLE
FIMBLES
FIMBRIA
FIMBRIAE
FIMBRIAL
FIMBRIATE
FIN
FINABLE
FINAGLE
FINAGLED
FINAGLER
FINAGLERS
FINAGLES
FINAGLING
FINAL
FINALE
FINALES
FINALIS
FINALISE
FINALISED
FINALISER
FINALISES
FINALISM
FINALISMS
FINALIST
FINALISTS
FINALITY
FINALIZE
FINALIZED
FINALIZER
FINALIZES
FINALLY
FINALS
FINANCE
FINANCED
FINANCES
FINANCIAL
FINANCIER
FINANCING

FINBACK	FINICALLY	FINOCCHIO	FIREFANGS
FINBACKS	FINICKETY	FINOCHIO	FIREFIGHT
FINCA	FINICKIER	FINOCHIOS	FIREFLIES
FINCAS	FINICKIN	FINOS	FIREFLOAT
FINCH	FINICKING	FINS	FIREFLOOD
FINCHED	FINICKY	FINSKO	FIREFLY
FINCHES	FINIKIN	FIORATURA	FIREGUARD
FIND	FINIKING	FIORD	FIREHALL
FINDABLE	FINING	FIORDS	FIREHALLS
FINDER	FININGS	FIORIN	FIREHOUSE
FINDERS	FINIS	FIORINS	FIRELESS
FINDING	FINISES	FIORITURA	FIRELIGHT
FINDINGS	FINISH	FIORITURE	FIRELIT
FINDRAM	FINISHED	FIPPENCE	FIRELOCK
FINDRAMS	FINISHER	FIPPENCES	FIRELOCKS
FINDS	FINISHERS	FIPPLE	FIREMAN
FINE	FINISHES	FIPPLES	FIREMANIC
FINEABLE	FINISHING	FIQUE	FIREMARK
FINED	FINITE	FIQUES	FIREMARKS
FINEER	FINITELY	FIR	FIREMEN
FINEERED	FINITES	FIRE	FIREPAN
FINEERING	FINITISM	FIREABLE	FIREPANS
FINEERS	FINITISMS	FIREARM	FIREPINK
FINEISH	FINITO	FIREARMED	FIREPINKS
FINELESS	FINITUDE	FIREARMS	FIREPLACE
FINELY	FINITUDES	FIREBACK	FIREPLUG
FINENESS	FINJAN	FIREBACKS	FIREPLUGS
FINER	FINJANS	FIREBALL	FIREPOT
FINERIES	FINK	FIREBALLS	FIREPOTS
FINERS	FINKED	FIREBASE	FIREPOWER
FINERY	FINKING	FIREBASES	FIREPROOF
FINES	FINKS	FIREBIRD	FIRER
FINESPUN	FINLESS	FIREBIRDS	FIREROOM
FINESSE	FINLIKE	FIREBOARD	FIREROOMS
FINESSED	FINMARK	FIREBOAT	FIRERS
FINESSER	FINMARKS	FIREBOATS	FIRES
FINESSERS	FINNAC	FIREBOMB	FIRESHIP
FINESSES	FINNACK	FIREBOMBS	FIRESHIPS
FINESSING	FINNACKS	FIREBOX	FIRESIDE
FINEST	FINNACS	FIREBOXES	FIRESIDES
FINFISH	FINNAN	FIREBRAND	FIRESTONE
FINFISHES	FINNANS	FIREBRAT	FIRESTORM
FINFOOT	FINNED	FIREBRATS	FIRETHORN
FINFOOTS	FINNER	FIREBREAK	FIRETRAP
FINGAN	FINNERS	FIREBRICK	FIRETRAPS
FINGANS	FINNESKO	FIREBUG	FIRETRUCK
FINGER	FINNICKY	FIREBUGS	FIREWALL
FINGERED	FINNIER	FIREBUSH	FIREWALLS
FINGERER	FINNIEST	FIRECLAY	FIREWATER
FINGERERS	FINNING	FIRECLAYS	FIREWEED
FINGERING	FINNMARK	FIRECREST	FIREWEEDS
FINGERS	FINNMARKS	FIRED	FIREWOMAN
FINGERTIP	FINNOCHIO	FIREDAMP	FIREWOMEN
FINI	FINNOCK	FIREDAMPS	FIREWOOD
FINIAL	FINNOCKS	FIREDOG	FIREWOODS
FINIALED	FINNSKO	FIREDOGS	FIREWORK
FINIALS	FINNY	FIREDRAKE	FIREWORKS
FINICAL	FINO	FIREFANG	FIREWORM

FIREWORMS
FIRIE
FIRIES
FIRING
FIRINGS
FIRK
FIRKED
FIRKIN
FIRKING
FIRKINS
FIRKS
FIRLOT
FIRLOTS
FIRM
FIRMAMENT
FIRMAN
FIRMANS
FIRMED
FIRMER
FIRMERS
FIRMEST
FIRMING
FIRMLESS
FIRMLY
FIRMNESS
FIRMS
FIRMWARE
FIRMWARES
FIRN
FIRNS
FIRRIER
FIRRIEST
FIRRING
FIRRINGS
FIRRY
FIRS
FIRST
FIRSTBORN
FIRSTHAND
FIRSTLING
FIRSTLY
FIRSTNESS
FIRSTS
FIRTH
FIRTHS
FISC
FISCAL
FISCALIST
FISCALLY
FISCALS
FISCS
FISGIG
FISGIGS
FISH
FISHABLE
FISHBALL
FISHBALLS
FISHBOLT

FISHBOLTS
FISHBONE
FISHBONES
FISHBOWL
FISHBOWLS
FISHCAKE
FISHCAKES
FISHED
FISHER
FISHERIES
FISHERMAN
FISHERMEN
FISHERS
FISHERY
FISHES
FISHEYE
FISHEYES
FISHFUL
FISHGIG
FISHGIGS
FISHHOOK
FISHHOOKS
FISHIER
FISHIEST
FISHIFIED
FISHIFIES
FISHIFY
FISHILY
FISHINESS
FISHING
FISHINGS
FISHKILL
FISHKILLS
FISHLESS
FISHLIKE
FISHLINE
FISHLINES
FISHMEAL
FISHMEALS
FISHNET
FISHNETS
FISHPLATE
FISHPOLE
FISHPOLES
FISHPOND
FISHPONDS
FISHSKIN
FISHSKINS
FISHTAIL
FISHTAILS
FISHWAY
FISHWAYS
FISHWIFE
FISHWIVES
FISHWORM
FISHWORMS
FISHY
FISHYBACK

FISK
FISKED
FISKING
FISKS
FISNOMIE
FISNOMIES
FISSATE
FISSILE
FISSILITY
FISSION
FISSIONAL
FISSIONED
FISSIONS
FISSIPED
FISSIPEDE
FISSIPEDS
FISSIVE
FISSLE
FISSLED
FISSLES
FISSLING
FISSURAL
FISSURE
FISSURED
FISSURES
FISSURING
FIST
FISTED
FISTFIGHT
FISTFUL
FISTFULS
FISTIANA
FISTIC
FISTICAL
FISTICUFF
FISTIER
FISTIEST
FISTING
FISTMELE
FISTMELES
FISTNOTE
FISTNOTES
FISTS
FISTULA
FISTULAE
FISTULAR
FISTULAS
FISTULATE
FISTULOSE
FISTULOUS
FISTY
FIT
FITCH
FITCHE
FITCHEE
FITCHES
FITCHET
FITCHETS

FITCHEW
FITCHEWS
FITCHY
FITFUL
FITFULLY
FITLIER
FITLIEST
FITLY
FITMENT
FITMENTS
FITNA
FITNAS
FITNESS
FITNESSES
FITS
FITT
FITTABLE
FITTE
FITTED
FITTER
FITTERS
FITTES
FITTEST
FITTING
FITTINGLY
FITTINGS
FITTS
FIVE
FIVEFOLD
FIVEPENCE
FIVEPENNY
FIVEPIN
FIVEPINS
FIVER
FIVERS
FIVES
FIX
FIXABLE
FIXATE
FIXATED
FIXATES
FIXATIF
FIXATIFS
FIXATING
FIXATION
FIXATIONS
FIXATIVE
FIXATIVES
FIXATURE
FIXATURES
FIXED
FIXEDLY
FIXEDNESS
FIXER
FIXERS
FIXES
FIXING
FIXINGS

FIXIT
FIXITIES
FIXITY
FIXIVE
FIXT
FIXTURE
FIXTURES
FIXURE
FIXURES
FIZ
FIZGIG
FIZGIGGED
FIZGIGS
FIZZ
FIZZED
FIZZEN
FIZZENS
FIZZER
FIZZERS
FIZZES
FIZZGIG
FIZZGIGS
FIZZIER
FIZZIEST
FIZZINESS
FIZZING
FIZZINGS
FIZZLE
FIZZLED
FIZZLES
FIZZLING
FIZZY
FJELD
FJELDS
FJORD
FJORDIC
FJORDS
FLAB
FLABBIER
FLABBIEST
FLABBILY
FLABBY
FLABELLA
FLABELLUM
FLABS
FLACCID
FLACCIDER
FLACCIDLY
FLACK
FLACKED
FLACKER
FLACKERED
FLACKERS
FLACKERY
FLACKET
FLACKETS
FLACKING
FLACKS

FLACON
FLACONS
FLAFF
FLAFFED
FLAFFER
FLAFFERED
FLAFFERS
FLAFFING
FLAFFS
FLAG
FLAGELLA
FLAGELLAR
FLAGELLIN
FLAGELLUM
FLAGEOLET
FLAGGED
FLAGGER
FLAGGERS
FLAGGIER
FLAGGIEST
FLAGGING
FLAGGINGS
FLAGGY
FLAGITATE
FLAGLESS
FLAGMAN
FLAGMEN
FLAGON
FLAGONS
FLAGPOLE
FLAGPOLES
FLAGRANCE
FLAGRANCY
FLAGRANT
FLAGS
FLAGSHIP
FLAGSHIPS
FLAGSTAFF
FLAGSTICK
FLAGSTONE
FLAIL
FLAILED
FLAILING
FLAILS
FLAIR
FLAIRS
FLAK
FLAKE
FLAKED
FLAKER
FLAKERS
FLAKES
FLAKEY
FLAKIER
FLAKIES
FLAKIEST
FLAKILY
FLAKINESS

FLAKING
FLAKS
FLAKY
FLAM
FLAMBE
FLAMBEAU
FLAMBEAUS
FLAMBEAUX
FLAMBEE
FLAMBEED
FLAMBEES
FLAMBEING
FLAMBES
FLAME
FLAMED
FLAMELESS
FLAMELET
FLAMELETS
FLAMELIKE
FLAMEN
FLAMENCO
FLAMENCOS
FLAMENS
FLAMEOUT
FLAMEOUTS
FLAMER
FLAMERS
FLAMES
FLAMFEW
FLAMFEWS
FLAMIER
FLAMIEST
FLAMINES
FLAMING
FLAMINGLY
FLAMINGO
FLAMINGOS
FLAMM
FLAMMABLE
FLAMMED
FLAMMING
FLAMMS
FLAMMULE
FLAMMULES
FLAMS
FLAMY
FLAN
FLANCARD
FLANCARDS
FLANCH
FLANCHED
FLANCHES
FLANCHING
FLANERIE
FLANERIES
FLANES
FLANEUR
FLANEURS

FLANGE
FLANGED
FLANGER
FLANGERS
FLANGES
FLANGING
FLANK
FLANKED
FLANKEN
FLANKER
FLANKERED
FLANKERS
FLANKING
FLANKS
FLANNEL
FLANNELED
FLANNELET
FLANNELLY
FLANNELS
FLANNEN
FLANNENS
FLANS
FLAP
FLAPERON
FLAPERONS
FLAPJACK
FLAPJACKS
FLAPLESS
FLAPPABLE
FLAPPED
FLAPPER
FLAPPERS
FLAPPIER
FLAPPIEST
FLAPPING
FLAPPINGS
FLAPPY
FLAPS
FLAPTRACK
FLARE
FLAREBACK
FLARED
FLARES
FLAREUP
FLAREUPS
FLARIER
FLARIEST
FLARING
FLARINGLY
FLARY
FLASER
FLASERS
FLASH
FLASHBACK
FLASHBULB
FLASHCARD
FLASHCUBE
FLASHED

FLASHER
FLASHERS
FLASHES
FLASHEST
FLASHGUN
FLASHGUNS
FLASHIER
FLASHIEST
FLASHILY
FLASHING
FLASHINGS
FLASHLAMP
FLASHOVER
FLASHTUBE
FLASHY
FLASK
FLASKET
FLASKETS
FLASKS
FLAT
FLATBACK
FLATBACKS
FLATBED
FLATBEDS
FLATBOAT
FLATBOATS
FLATBREAD
FLATCAP
FLATCAPS
FLATCAR
FLATCARS
FLATETTE
FLATETTES
FLATFEET
FLATFISH
FLATFOOT
FLATFOOTS
FLATHEAD
FLATHEADS
FLATIRON
FLATIRONS
FLATLAND
FLATLANDS
FLATLET
FLATLETS
FLATLINE
FLATLINED
FLATLINER
FLATLINES
FLATLING
FLATLINGS
FLATLONG
FLATLY
FLATMATE
FLATMATES
FLATNESS
FLATPACK
FLATPACKS

FLATS
FLATSHARE
FLATTED
FLATTEN
FLATTENED
FLATTENER
FLATTENS
FLATTER
FLATTERED
FLATTERER
FLATTERS
FLATTERY
FLATTEST
FLATTIE
FLATTIES
FLATTING
FLATTINGS
FLATTISH
FLATTOP
FLATTOPS
FLATTY
FLATULENT
FLATUOUS
FLATUS
FLATUSES
FLATWARE
FLATWARES
FLATWASH
FLATWAYS
FLATWISE
FLATWORK
FLATWORKS
FLATWORM
FLATWORMS
FLAUGHT
FLAUGHTED
FLAUGHTER
FLAUGHTS
FLAUNCH
FLAUNCHED
FLAUNCHES
FLAUNE
FLAUNES
FLAUNT
FLAUNTED
FLAUNTER
FLAUNTERS
FLAUNTIER
FLAUNTILY
FLAUNTING
FLAUNTS
FLAUNTY
FLAUTA
FLAUTAS
FLAUTIST
FLAUTISTS
FLAVANOL
FLAVANOLS

FLAVANONE
FLAVIN
FLAVINE
FLAVINES
FLAVINS
FLAVONE
FLAVONES
FLAVONOID
FLAVONOL
FLAVONOLS
FLAVOR
FLAVORED
FLAVORER
FLAVORERS
FLAVORFUL
FLAVORING
FLAVORIST
FLAVOROUS
FLAVORS
FLAVORY
FLAVOUR
FLAVOURED
FLAVOURER
FLAVOURS
FLAVOURY
FLAW
FLAWED
FLAWIER
FLAWIEST
FLAWING
FLAWLESS
FLAWN
FLAWNS
FLAWS
FLAWY
FLAX
FLAXEN
FLAXES
FLAXIER
FLAXIEST
FLAXSEED
FLAXSEEDS
FLAXY
FLAY
FLAYED
FLAYER
FLAYERS
FLAYING
FLAYS
FLAYSOME
FLEA
FLEABAG
FLEABAGS
FLEABANE
FLEABANES
FLEABITE
FLEABITES
FLEAM

FLEAMS
FLEAPIT
FLEAPITS
FLEAS
FLEASOME
FLEAWORT
FLEAWORTS
FLECHE
FLECHES
FLECHETTE
FLECK
FLECKED
FLECKER
FLECKERED
FLECKERS
FLECKING
FLECKLESS
FLECKS
FLECKY
FLECTION
FLECTIONS
FLED
FLEDGE
FLEDGED
FLEDGES
FLEDGIER
FLEDGIEST
FLEDGING
FLEDGLING
FLEDGY
FLEE
FLEECE
FLEECED
FLEECER
FLEECERS
FLEECES
FLEECH
FLEECHED
FLEECHES
FLEECHING
FLEECIE
FLEECIER
FLEECIES
FLEECIEST
FLEECILY
FLEECING
FLEECY
FLEEING
FLEER
FLEERED
FLEERER
FLEERERS
FLEERING
FLEERINGS
FLEERS
FLEES
FLEET
FLEETED

FLEETER	FLETCHES	FLIER	FLIPPED
FLEETEST	FLETCHING	FLIERS	FLIPPER
FLEETING	FLETTON	FLIES	FLIPPERS
FLEETLY	FLETTONS	FLIEST	FLIPPEST
FLEETNESS	FLEURET	FLIGHT	FLIPPING
FLEETS	FLEURETS	FLIGHTED	FLIPPY
FLEG	FLEURETTE	FLIGHTIER	FLIPS
FLEGGED	FLEURON	FLIGHTILY	FLIR
FLEGGING	FLEURONS	FLIGHTING	FLIRS
FLEGS	FLEURY	FLIGHTS	FLIRT
FLEHMEN	FLEW	FLIGHTY	FLIRTED
FLEHMENED	FLEWED	FLIM	FLIRTER
FLEHMENS	FLEWS	FLIMFLAM	FLIRTERS
FLEISHIG	FLEX	FLIMFLAMS	FLIRTIER
FLEISHIK	FLEXAGON	FLIMP	FLIRTIEST
FLEME	FLEXAGONS	FLIMPED	FLIRTING
FLEMES	FLEXED	FLIMPING	FLIRTINGS
FLEMING	FLEXES	FLIMPS	FLIRTISH
FLEMISH	FLEXIBLE	FLIMS	FLIRTS
FLEMISHED	FLEXIBLY	FLIMSIER	FLIRTY
FLEMISHES	FLEXILE	FLIMSIES	FLISK
FLEMIT	FLEXING	FLIMSIEST	FLISKED
FLENCH	FLEXION	FLIMSILY	FLISKIER
FLENCHED	FLEXIONAL	FLIMSY	FLISKIEST
FLENCHER	FLEXIONS	FLINCH	FLISKING
FLENCHERS	FLEXITIME	FLINCHED	FLISKS
FLENCHES	FLEXO	FLINCHER	FLISKY
FLENCHING	FLEXOR	FLINCHERS	FLIT
FLENSE	FLEXORS	FLINCHES	FLITCH
FLENSED	FLEXOS	FLINCHING	FLITCHED
FLENSER	FLEXTIME	FLINDER	FLITCHES
FLENSERS	FLEXTIMER	FLINDERS	FLITCHING
FLENSES	FLEXTIMES	FLING	FLITE
FLENSING	FLEXUOSE	FLINGER	FLITED
FLESH	FLEXUOUS	FLINGERS	FLITES
FLESHED	FLEXURAL	FLINGING	FLITING
FLESHER	FLEXURE	FLINGS	FLITS
FLESHERS	FLEXURES	FLINKITE	FLITT
FLESHES	FLEY	FLINKITES	FLITTED
FLESHHOOD	FLEYED	FLINT	FLITTER
FLESHIER	FLEYING	FLINTED	FLITTERED
FLESHIEST	FLEYS	FLINTHEAD	FLITTERN
FLESHILY	FLIBBERT	FLINTIER	FLITTERNS
FLESHING	FLIBBERTS	FLINTIEST	FLITTERS
FLESHINGS	FLIC	FLINTIFY	FLITTING
FLESHLESS	FLICHTER	FLINTILY	FLITTINGS
FLESHLIER	FLICHTERS	FLINTING	FLIVVER
FLESHLING	FLICK	FLINTLIKE	FLIVVERS
FLESHLY	FLICKABLE	FLINTLOCK	FLIX
FLESHMENT	FLICKED	FLINTS	FLIXED
FLESHPOT	FLICKER	FLINTY	FLIXES
FLESHPOTS	FLICKERED	FLIP	FLIXING
FLESHWORM	FLICKERS	FLIPBOOK	FLOAT
FLESHY	FLICKERY	FLIPBOOKS	FLOATABLE
FLETCH	FLICKING	FLIPFLOP	FLOATAGE
FLETCHED	FLICKS	FLIPFLOPS	FLOATAGES
FLETCHER	FLICS	FLIPPANCY	FLOATANT
FLETCHERS	FLIED	FLIPPANT	FLOATANTS

FLOATCUT
FLOATED
FLOATEL
FLOATELS
FLOATER
FLOATERS
FLOATIER
FLOATIEST
FLOATING
FLOATINGS
FLOATS
FLOATY
FLOC
FLOCCED
FLOCCI
FLOCCING
FLOCCOSE
FLOCCULAR
FLOCCULE
FLOCCULES
FLOCCULI
FLOCCULUS
FLOCCUS
FLOCK
FLOCKED
FLOCKIER
FLOCKIEST
FLOCKING
FLOCKINGS
FLOCKLESS
FLOCKS
FLOCKY
FLOCS
FLOE
FLOES
FLOG
FLOGGABLE
FLOGGED
FLOGGER
FLOGGERS
FLOGGING
FLOGGINGS
FLOGS
FLOKATI
FLOKATIS
FLONG
FLONGS
FLOOD
FLOODABLE
FLOODED
FLOODER
FLOODERS
FLOODGATE
FLOODING
FLOODINGS
FLOODLESS
FLOODLIT
FLOODMARK

FLOODS
FLOODTIDE
FLOODWALL
FLOODWAY
FLOODWAYS
FLOOEY
FLOOIE
FLOOR
FLOORAGE
FLOORAGES
FLOORED
FLOORER
FLOORERS
FLOORHEAD
FLOORING
FLOORINGS
FLOORLESS
FLOORS
FLOORSHOW
FLOOSIE
FLOOSIES
FLOOSY
FLOOZIE
FLOOZIES
FLOOZY
FLOP
FLOPHOUSE
FLOPOVER
FLOPOVERS
FLOPPED
FLOPPER
FLOPPERS
FLOPPIER
FLOPPIES
FLOPPIEST
FLOPPILY
FLOPPING
FLOPPY
FLOPS
FLOPTICAL
FLOR
FLORA
FLORAE
FLORAL
FLORALLY
FLORALS
FLORAS
FLOREANT
FLOREAT
FLOREATED
FLORENCE
FLORENCES
FLORET
FLORETS
FLORIATED
FLORICANE
FLORID
FLORIDEAN

FLORIDER
FLORIDEST
FLORIDITY
FLORIDLY
FLORIER
FLORIEST
FLORIFORM
FLORIGEN
FLORIGENS
FLORIN
FLORINS
FLORIST
FLORISTIC
FLORISTRY
FLORISTS
FLORS
FLORUIT
FLORUITS
FLORULA
FLORULAE
FLORULE
FLORULES
FLORY
FLOSCULAR
FLOSCULE
FLOSCULES
FLOSH
FLOSHES
FLOSS
FLOSSED
FLOSSER
FLOSSERS
FLOSSES
FLOSSIE
FLOSSIER
FLOSSIES
FLOSSIEST
FLOSSILY
FLOSSING
FLOSSINGS
FLOSSY
FLOTA
FLOTAGE
FLOTAGES
FLOTANT
FLOTAS
FLOTATION
FLOTE
FLOTEL
FLOTELS
FLOTES
FLOTILLA
FLOTILLAS
FLOTSAM
FLOTSAMS
FLOUNCE
FLOUNCED
FLOUNCES

FLOUNCIER
FLOUNCING
FLOUNCY
FLOUNDER
FLOUNDERS
FLOUR
FLOURED
FLOURIER
FLOURIEST
FLOURING
FLOURISH
FLOURISHY
FLOURLESS
FLOURS
FLOURY
FLOUSE
FLOUSED
FLOUSES
FLOUSH
FLOUSHED
FLOUSHES
FLOUSHING
FLOUSING
FLOUT
FLOUTED
FLOUTER
FLOUTERS
FLOUTING
FLOUTS
FLOW
FLOWAGE
FLOWAGES
FLOWCHART
FLOWED
FLOWER
FLOWERAGE
FLOWERBED
FLOWERED
FLOWERER
FLOWERERS
FLOWERET
FLOWERETS
FLOWERFUL
FLOWERIER
FLOWERILY
FLOWERING
FLOWERPOT
FLOWERS
FLOWERY
FLOWING
FLOWINGLY
FLOWMETER
FLOWN
FLOWS
FLOWSTONE
FLU
FLUATE
FLUATES

FLUB	FLUIDLIKE	FLUORITES	FLUXED
FLUBBED	FLUIDLY	FLUOROSES	FLUXES
FLUBBER	FLUIDNESS	FLUOROSIS	FLUXGATE
FLUBBERS	FLUIDRAM	FLUOROTIC	FLUXGATES
FLUBBING	FLUIDRAMS	FLUORS	FLUXING
FLUBDUB	FLUIDS	FLUORSPAR	FLUXION
FLUBDUBS	FLUIER	FLURR	FLUXIONAL
FLUBS	FLUIEST	FLURRED	FLUXIONS
FLUCTUANT	FLUISH	FLURRIED	FLUXIVE
FLUCTUATE	FLUKE	FLURRIES	FLUXMETER
FLUE	FLUKED	FLURRING	FLUYT
FLUED	FLUKES	FLURRS	FLUYTS
FLUELLEN	FLUKEY	FLURRY	FLY
FLUELLENS	FLUKIER	FLURRYING	FLYABLE
FLUELLIN	FLUKIEST	FLUS	FLYAWAY
FLUELLINS	FLUKILY	FLUSH	FLYAWAYS
FLUENCE	FLUKINESS	FLUSHABLE	FLYBACK
FLUENCES	FLUKING	FLUSHED	FLYBACKS
FLUENCIES	FLUKY	FLUSHER	FLYBANE
FLUENCY	FLUME	FLUSHERS	FLYBANES
FLUENT	FLUMED	FLUSHES	FLYBELT
FLUENTLY	FLUMES	FLUSHEST	FLYBELTS
FLUENTS	FLUMING	FLUSHIER	FLYBLEW
FLUERIC	FLUMMERY	FLUSHIEST	FLYBLOW
FLUERICS	FLUMMOX	FLUSHING	FLYBLOWN
FLUES	FLUMMOXED	FLUSHINGS	FLYBLOWS
FLUEWORK	FLUMMOXES	FLUSHNESS	FLYBOAT
FLUEWORKS	FLUMP	FLUSHWORK	FLYBOATS
FLUEY	FLUMPED	FLUSHY	FLYBOOK
FLUFF	FLUMPING	FLUSTER	FLYBOOKS
FLUFFED	FLUMPS	FLUSTERED	FLYBOY
FLUFFER	FLUNG	FLUSTERS	FLYBOYS
FLUFFERS	FLUNK	FLUSTERY	FLYBRIDGE
FLUFFIER	FLUNKED	FLUSTRATE	FLYBY
FLUFFIEST	FLUNKER	FLUTE	FLYBYS
FLUFFILY	FLUNKERS	FLUTED	FLYER
FLUFFING	FLUNKEY	FLUTELIKE	FLYERS
FLUFFS	FLUNKEYS	FLUTER	FLYEST
FLUFFY	FLUNKIE	FLUTERS	FLYHAND
FLUGEL	FLUNKIES	FLUTES	FLYHANDS
FLUGELMAN	FLUNKING	FLUTEY	FLYING
FLUGELMEN	FLUNKS	FLUTIER	FLYINGS
FLUGELS	FLUNKY	FLUTIEST	FLYLEAF
FLUID	FLUNKYISM	FLUTINA	FLYLEAVES
FLUIDAL	FLUOR	FLUTINAS	FLYLESS
FLUIDALLY	FLUORENE	FLUTING	FLYMAKER
FLUIDIC	FLUORENES	FLUTINGS	FLYMAKERS
FLUIDICS	FLUORESCE	FLUTIST	FLYMAN
FLUIDIFY	FLUORIC	FLUTISTS	FLYMEN
FLUIDISE	FLUORID	FLUTTER	FLYOFF
FLUIDISED	FLUORIDE	FLUTTERED	FLYOFFS
FLUIDISER	FLUORIDES	FLUTTERER	FLYOVER
FLUIDISES	FLUORIDS	FLUTTERS	FLYOVERS
FLUIDITY	FLUORIN	FLUTTERY	FLYPAPER
FLUIDIZE	FLUORINE	FLUTY	FLYPAPERS
FLUIDIZED	FLUORINES	FLUVIAL	FLYPAST
FLUIDIZER	FLUORINS	FLUVIATIC	FLYPASTS
FLUIDIZES	FLUORITE	FLUX	FLYPE

FLYPED	FOCALISES	FOGEYDOMS	FOININGLY
FLYPES	FOCALIZE	FOGEYISH	FOINS
FLYPING	FOCALIZED	FOGEYISM	FOISON
FLYPITCH	FOCALIZES	FOGEYISMS	FOISONS
FLYRODDER	FOCALLY	FOGEYS	FOIST
FLYSCH	FOCI	FOGFRUIT	FOISTED
FLYSCHES	FOCIMETER	FOGFRUITS	FOISTER
FLYSCREEN	FOCOMETER	FOGGAGE	FOISTERS
FLYSHEET	FOCUS	FOGGAGES	FOISTING
FLYSHEETS	FOCUSABLE	FOGGED	FOISTS
FLYSPECK	FOCUSED	FOGGER	FOLACIN
FLYSPECKS	FOCUSER	FOGGERS	FOLACINS
FLYSTRIKE	FOCUSERS	FOGGIER	FOLATE
FLYTE	FOCUSES	FOGGIEST	FOLATES
FLYTED	FOCUSING	FOGGILY	FOLD
FLYTES	FOCUSINGS	FOGGINESS	FOLDABLE
FLYTIER	FOCUSLESS	FOGGING	FOLDAWAY
FLYTIERS	FOCUSSED	FOGGY	FOLDAWAYS
FLYTING	FOCUSSES	FOGHORN	FOLDBACK
FLYTINGS	FOCUSSING	FOGHORNS	FOLDBACKS
FLYTRAP	FODDER	FOGIE	FOLDBOAT
FLYTRAPS	FODDERED	FOGIES	FOLDBOATS
FLYWAY	FODDERER	FOGLE	FOLDED
FLYWAYS	FODDERERS	FOGLES	FOLDER
FLYWEIGHT	FODDERING	FOGLESS	FOLDEROL
FLYWHEEL	FODDERS	FOGMAN	FOLDEROLS
FLYWHEELS	FODGEL	FOGMEN	FOLDERS
FOAL	FOE	FOGRAM	FOLDING
FOALED	FOEDARIE	FOGRAMITE	FOLDINGS
FOALFOOT	FOEDARIES	FOGRAMITY	FOLDOUT
FOALFOOTS	FOEDERATI	FOGRAMS	FOLDOUTS
FOALING	FOEHN	FOGS	FOLDS
FOALS	FOEHNS	FOGY	FOLDUP
FOAM	FOEMAN	FOGYDOM	FOLDUPS
FOAMABLE	FOEMEN	FOGYDOMS	FOLEY
FOAMED	FOEN	FOGYISH	FOLEYS
FOAMER	FOES	FOGYISM	FOLIA
FOAMERS	FOETAL	FOGYISMS	FOLIAGE
FOAMIER	FOETATION	FOH	FOLIAGED
FOAMIEST	FOETICIDE	FOHN	FOLIAGES
FOAMILY	FOETID	FOHNS	FOLIAR
FOAMINESS	FOETIDER	FOHS	FOLIATE
FOAMING	FOETIDEST	FOIBLE	FOLIATED
FOAMINGLY	FOETIDLY	FOIBLES	FOLIATES
FOAMINGS	FOETOR	FOID	FOLIATING
FOAMLESS	FOETORS	FOIDS	FOLIATION
FOAMLIKE	FOETUS	FOIL	FOLIATURE
FOAMS	FOETUSES	FOILABLE	FOLIC
FOAMY	FOG	FOILBORNE	FOLIE
FOB	FOGASH	FOILED	FOLIES
FOBBED	FOGASHES	FOILING	FOLIO
FOBBING	FOGBOUND	FOILINGS	FOLIOED
FOBS	FOGBOW	FOILS	FOLIOING
FOCACCIA	FOGBOWS	FOILSMAN	FOLIOLATE
FOCACCIAS	FOGDOG	FOILSMEN	FOLIOLE
FOCAL	FOGDOGS	FOIN	FOLIOLES
FOCALISE	FOGEY	FOINED	FOLIOLOSE
FOCALISED	FOGEYDOM	FOINING	FOLIOS

FOLIOSE
FOLIOUS
FOLIUM
FOLIUMS
FOLK
FOLKIE
FOLKIER
FOLKIES
FOLKIEST
FOLKISH
FOLKLAND
FOLKLANDS
FOLKLIFE
FOLKLIKE
FOLKLIVES
FOLKLORE
FOLKLORES
FOLKLORIC
FOLKMOOT
FOLKMOOTS
FOLKMOT
FOLKMOTE
FOLKMOTES
FOLKMOTS
FOLKS
FOLKSIER
FOLKSIEST
FOLKSILY
FOLKSONG
FOLKSONGS
FOLKSY
FOLKTALE
FOLKTALES
FOLKWAY
FOLKWAYS
FOLKY
FOLLES
FOLLICLE
FOLLICLES
FOLLIED
FOLLIES
FOLLIS
FOLLOW
FOLLOWED
FOLLOWER
FOLLOWERS
FOLLOWING
FOLLOWS
FOLLOWUP
FOLLOWUPS
FOLLY
FOLLYING
FOMENT
FOMENTED
FOMENTER
FOMENTERS
FOMENTING
FOMENTS

FOMES
FOMITE
FOMITES
FON
FOND
FONDA
FONDANT
FONDANTS
FONDAS
FONDED
FONDER
FONDEST
FONDING
FONDLE
FONDLED
FONDLER
FONDLERS
FONDLES
FONDLING
FONDLINGS
FONDLY
FONDNESS
FONDS
FONDU
FONDUE
FONDUED
FONDUEING
FONDUES
FONDUING
FONDUS
FONE
FONLY
FONNED
FONNING
FONS
FONT
FONTAL
FONTANEL
FONTANELS
FONTANGE
FONTANGES
FONTICULI
FONTINA
FONTINAS
FONTLET
FONTLETS
FONTS
FOOBAR
FOOD
FOODFUL
FOODIE
FOODIES
FOODISM
FOODISMS
FOODLESS
FOODS
FOODSTUFF
FOODWAYS

FOODY
FOOFARAW
FOOFARAWS
FOOL
FOOLED
FOOLERIES
FOOLERY
FOOLFISH
FOOLHARDY
FOOLING
FOOLINGS
FOOLISH
FOOLISHER
FOOLISHLY
FOOLPROOF
FOOLS
FOOLSCAP
FOOLSCAPS
FOOSBALL
FOOSBALLS
FOOT
FOOTAGE
FOOTAGES
FOOTBAG
FOOTBAGS
FOOTBALL
FOOTBALLS
FOOTBAR
FOOTBARS
FOOTBATH
FOOTBATHS
FOOTBOARD
FOOTBOY
FOOTBOYS
FOOTCLOTH
FOOTED
FOOTER
FOOTERED
FOOTERING
FOOTERS
FOOTFALL
FOOTFALLS
FOOTFAULT
FOOTGEAR
FOOTGEARS
FOOTHILL
FOOTHILLS
FOOTHOLD
FOOTHOLDS
FOOTIE
FOOTIER
FOOTIES
FOOTIEST
FOOTING
FOOTINGS
FOOTLE
FOOTLED
FOOTLER

FOOTLERS
FOOTLES
FOOTLESS
FOOTLIGHT
FOOTLIKE
FOOTLING
FOOTLINGS
FOOTLOOSE
FOOTMAN
FOOTMARK
FOOTMARKS
FOOTMEN
FOOTMUFF
FOOTMUFFS
FOOTNOTE
FOOTNOTED
FOOTNOTES
FOOTPACE
FOOTPACES
FOOTPAD
FOOTPADS
FOOTPAGE
FOOTPAGES
FOOTPATH
FOOTPATHS
FOOTPLATE
FOOTPOST
FOOTPOSTS
FOOTPRINT
FOOTRA
FOOTRACE
FOOTRACES
FOOTRAS
FOOTREST
FOOTRESTS
FOOTROPE
FOOTROPES
FOOTROT
FOOTROTS
FOOTRULE
FOOTRULES
FOOTS
FOOTSIE
FOOTSIES
FOOTSLOG
FOOTSLOGS
FOOTSORE
FOOTSTALK
FOOTSTALL
FOOTSTEP
FOOTSTEPS
FOOTSTOCK
FOOTSTONE
FOOTSTOOL
FOOTSY
FOOTWALL
FOOTWALLS
FOOTWAY

FOOTWAYS	FORBIDALS	FOREBODER	FOREIGN
FOOTWEAR	FORBIDDAL	FOREBODES	FOREIGNER
FOOTWEARS	FORBIDDEN	FOREBODY	FOREIGNLY
FOOTWEARY	FORBIDDER	FOREBOOM	FOREJUDGE
FOOTWELL	FORBIDS	FOREBOOMS	FOREKING
FOOTWELLS	FORBODE	FOREBRAIN	FOREKINGS
FOOTWORK	FORBODED	FOREBY	FOREKNEW
FOOTWORKS	FORBODES	FOREBYE	FOREKNOW
FOOTWORN	FORBODING	FORECABIN	FOREKNOWN
FOOTY	FORBORE	FORECAR	FOREKNOWS
FOOZLE	FORBORNE	FORECARS	FOREL
FOOZLED	FORBS	FORECAST	FORELADY
FOOZLER	FORBY	FORECASTS	FORELAID
FOOZLERS	FORBYE	FORECHECK	FORELAIN
FOOZLES	FORCAT	FORECLOSE	FORELAND
FOOZLING	FORCATS	FORECLOTH	FORELANDS
FOOZLINGS	FORCE	FORECOURT	FORELAY
FOP	FORCEABLE	FOREDATE	FORELAYS
FOPLING	FORCED	FOREDATED	FORELEG
FOPLINGS	FORCEDLY	FOREDATES	FORELEGS
FOPPED	FORCEFUL	FOREDECK	FORELEND
FOPPERIES	FORCELESS	FOREDECKS	FORELENDS
FOPPERY	FORCEMEAT	FOREDID	FORELENT
FOPPING	FORCEPS	FOREDO	FORELIE
FOPPISH	FORCEPSES	FOREDOES	FORELIES
FOPPISHLY	FORCER	FOREDOING	FORELIFT
FOPS	FORCERS	FOREDONE	FORELIFTS
FOR	FORCES	FOREDOOM	FORELIMB
FORA	FORCIBLE	FOREDOOMS	FORELIMBS
FORAGE	FORCIBLY	FOREFACE	FORELOCK
FORAGED	FORCING	FOREFACES	FORELOCKS
FORAGER	FORCINGLY	FOREFEEL	FORELS
FORAGERS	FORCIPATE	FOREFEELS	FORELYING
FORAGES	FORCIPES	FOREFEET	FOREMAN
FORAGING	FORD	FOREFELT	FOREMAST
FORAM	FORDABLE	FOREFEND	FOREMASTS
FORAMEN	FORDED	FOREFENDS	FOREMEAN
FORAMENS	FORDID	FOREFOOT	FOREMEANS
FORAMINA	FORDING	FOREFRONT	FOREMEANT
FORAMINAL	FORDLESS	FOREGLEAM	FOREMEN
FORAMS	FORDO	FOREGO	FOREMILK
FORANE	FORDOES	FOREGOER	FOREMILKS
FORASMUCH	FORDOING	FOREGOERS	FOREMOST
FORAY	FORDONE	FOREGOES	FORENAME
FORAYED	FORDS	FOREGOING	FORENAMED
FORAYER	FORE	FOREGONE	FORENAMES
FORAYERS	FOREANENT	FOREGUT	FORENIGHT
FORAYING	FOREARM	FOREGUTS	FORENOON
FORAYS	FOREARMED	FOREHAND	FORENOONS
FORB	FOREARMS	FOREHANDS	FORENSIC
FORBAD	FOREBAY	FOREHEAD	FORENSICS
FORBADE	FOREBAYS	FOREHEADS	FOREPART
FORBARE	FOREBEAR	FOREHENT	FOREPARTS
FORBEAR	FOREBEARS	FOREHENTS	FOREPAST
FORBEARER	FOREBITT	FOREHOCK	FOREPAW
FORBEARS	FOREBITTS	FOREHOCKS	FOREPAWS
FORBID	FOREBODE	FOREHOOF	FOREPEAK
FORBIDAL	FOREBODED	FOREHOOFS	FOREPEAKS

FOREPLAN
FOREPLANS
FOREPLAY
FOREPLAYS
FOREPOINT
FORERAN
FORERANK
FORERANKS
FOREREACH
FOREREAD
FOREREADS
FORERUN
FORERUNS
FORES
FORESAID
FORESAIL
FORESAILS
FORESAW
FORESAY
FORESAYS
FORESEE
FORESEEN
FORESEER
FORESEERS
FORESEES
FORESHANK
FORESHEET
FORESHEW
FORESHEWN
FORESHEWS
FORESHIP
FORESHIPS
FORESHOCK
FORESHORE
FORESHOW
FORESHOWN
FORESHOWS
FORESIDE
FORESIDES
FORESIGHT
FORESKIN
FORESKINS
FORESKIRT
FORESLACK
FORESLOW
FORESLOWS
FORESPAKE
FORESPEAK
FORESPEND
FORESPENT
FORESPOKE
FOREST
FORESTAGE
FORESTAIR
FORESTAL
FORESTALL
FORESTAY
FORESTAYS

FORESTEAL
FORESTED
FORESTER
FORESTERS
FORESTIAL
FORESTINE
FORESTING
FORESTRY
FORESTS
FORESWEAR
FORESWORE
FORESWORN
FORETASTE
FORETEACH
FORETEETH
FORETELL
FORETELLS
FORETHINK
FORETIME
FORETIMES
FORETOKEN
FORETOLD
FORETOOTH
FORETOP
FORETOPS
FOREVER
FOREVERS
FOREWARD
FOREWARDS
FOREWARN
FOREWARNS
FOREWEIGH
FOREWENT
FOREWIND
FOREWINDS
FOREWING
FOREWINGS
FOREWOMAN
FOREWOMEN
FOREWORD
FOREWORDS
FOREWORN
FOREX
FOREXES
FOREYARD
FOREYARDS
FORFAIR
FORFAIRED
FORFAIRN
FORFAIRS
FORFAITER
FORFAULT
FORFAULTS
FORFEIT
FORFEITED
FORFEITER
FORFEITS
FORFEND

FORFENDED
FORFENDS
FORFEX
FORFEXES
FORFICATE
FORFOCHEN
FORGAT
FORGATHER
FORGAVE
FORGE
FORGEABLE
FORGED
FORGEMAN
FORGEMEN
FORGER
FORGERIES
FORGERS
FORGERY
FORGES
FORGET
FORGETFUL
FORGETIVE
FORGETS
FORGETTER
FORGING
FORGINGS
FORGIVE
FORGIVEN
FORGIVER
FORGIVERS
FORGIVES
FORGIVING
FORGO
FORGOER
FORGOERS
FORGOES
FORGOING
FORGONE
FORGOT
FORGOTTEN
FORHAILE
FORHAILED
FORHAILES
FORHENT
FORHENTS
FORHOO
FORHOOED
FORHOOIE
FORHOOIED
FORHOOIES
FORHOOING
FORHOOS
FORHOW
FORHOWED
FORHOWING
FORHOWS
FORINSEC
FORINT

FORINTS
FORJASKIT
FORJESKIT
FORJUDGE
FORJUDGED
FORJUDGES
FORK
FORKBALL
FORKBALLS
FORKED
FORKEDLY
FORKER
FORKERS
FORKFUL
FORKFULS
FORKHEAD
FORKHEADS
FORKIER
FORKIEST
FORKINESS
FORKING
FORKLESS
FORKLIFT
FORKLIFTS
FORKLIKE
FORKS
FORKSFUL
FORKTAIL
FORKTAILS
FORKY
FORLANA
FORLANAS
FORLEND
FORLENDS
FORLENT
FORLESE
FORLESES
FORLESING
FORLORE
FORLORN
FORLORNER
FORLORNLY
FORLORNS
FORM
FORMABLE
FORMABLY
FORMAL
FORMALIN
FORMALINS
FORMALISE
FORMALISM
FORMALIST
FORMALITY
FORMALIZE
FORMALLY
FORMALS
FORMAMIDE
FORMANT

FORMANTS

FORMANTS
FORMAT
FORMATE
FORMATED
FORMATES
FORMATING
FORMATION
FORMATIVE
FORMATS
FORMATTED
FORMATTER
FORME
FORMED
FORMEE
FORMER
FORMERLY
FORMERS
FORMES
FORMFUL
FORMIATE
FORMIATES
FORMIC
FORMICA
FORMICANT
FORMICARY
FORMICAS
FORMICATE
FORMING
FORMINGS
FORMLESS
FORMOL
FORMOLS
FORMS
FORMULA
FORMULAE
FORMULAIC
FORMULAR
FORMULARY
FORMULAS
FORMULATE
FORMULISE
FORMULISM
FORMULIST
FORMULIZE
FORMWORK
FORMWORKS
FORMYL
FORMYLS
FORNENST
FORNENT
FORNICAL
FORNICATE
FORNICES
FORNIX
FORPET
FORPETS
FORPINE
FORPINED

FORPINES
FORPINING
FORPIT
FORPITS
FORRAD
FORRADER
FORRARDER
FORRAY
FORRAYED
FORRAYING
FORRAYS
FORREN
FORRIT
FORSAID
FORSAKE
FORSAKEN
FORSAKER
FORSAKERS
FORSAKES
FORSAKING
FORSAY
FORSAYING
FORSAYS
FORSLACK
FORSLACKS
FORSLOE
FORSLOED
FORSLOES
FORSLOW
FORSLOWED
FORSLOWS
FORSOOK
FORSOOTH
FORSPEAK
FORSPEAKS
FORSPEND
FORSPENDS
FORSPENT
FORSPOKE
FORSPOKEN
FORSWATT
FORSWEAR
FORSWEARS
FORSWINK
FORSWINKS
FORSWONCK
FORSWORE
FORSWORN
FORSWUNK
FORSYTHIA
FORT
FORTALICE
FORTE
FORTED
FORTES
FORTH
FORTHCAME
FORTHCOME

FORTHINK
FORTHINKS
FORTHWITH
FORTHY
FORTIES
FORTIETH
FORTIETHS
FORTIFIED
FORTIFIER
FORTIFIES
FORTIFY
FORTILAGE
FORTING
FORTIS
FORTITUDE
FORTLET
FORTLETS
FORTNIGHT
FORTRESS
FORTS
FORTUITY
FORTUNATE
FORTUNE
FORTUNED
FORTUNES
FORTUNING
FORTUNISE
FORTUNIZE
FORTY
FORTYISH
FORUM
FORUMS
FORWANDER
FORWARD
FORWARDED
FORWARDER
FORWARDLY
FORWARDS
FORWARN
FORWARNED
FORWARNS
FORWASTE
FORWASTED
FORWASTES
FORWEARY
FORWENT
FORWHY
FORWORN
FORZA
FORZANDI
FORZANDO
FORZANDOS
FORZATI
FORZATO
FORZATOS
FORZE
FOSCARNET
FOSS

FOSSA
FOSSAE
FOSSAS
FOSSATE
FOSSE
FOSSED
FOSSES
FOSSETTE
FOSSETTES
FOSSICK
FOSSICKED
FOSSICKER
FOSSICKS
FOSSIL
FOSSILISE
FOSSILIZE
FOSSILS
FOSSOR
FOSSORIAL
FOSSORS
FOSSULA
FOSSULAE
FOSSULATE
FOSTER
FOSTERAGE
FOSTERED
FOSTERER
FOSTERERS
FOSTERING
FOSTERS
FOSTRESS
FOTHER
FOTHERED
FOTHERING
FOTHERS
FOU
FOUAT
FOUATS
FOUD
FOUDRIE
FOUDRIES
FOUDS
FOUER
FOUEST
FOUET
FOUETS
FOUETTE
FOUETTES
FOUGADE
FOUGADES
FOUGASSE
FOUGASSES
FOUGHT
FOUGHTEN
FOUGHTIER
FOUGHTY
FOUL
FOULARD

FOULARDS
FOULBROOD
FOULDER
FOULDERED
FOULDERS
FOULE
FOULED
FOULER
FOULES
FOULEST
FOULIE
FOULIES
FOULING
FOULINGS
FOULLY
FOULMART
FOULMARTS
FOULNESS
FOULS
FOUMART
FOUMARTS
FOUND
FOUNDED
FOUNDER
FOUNDERED
FOUNDERS
FOUNDING
FOUNDINGS
FOUNDLING
FOUNDRESS
FOUNDRIES
FOUNDRY
FOUNDS
FOUNT
FOUNTAIN
FOUNTAINS
FOUNTFUL
FOUNTS
FOUR
FOURBALL
FOURBALLS
FOURCHEE
FOUREYED
FOURFOLD
FOURGON
FOURGONS
FOURPENCE
FOURPENNY
FOURPLEX
FOURS
FOURSCORE
FOURSES
FOURSOME
FOURSOMES
FOURTEEN
FOURTEENS
FOURTH
FOURTHLY

FOURTHS
FOUS
FOUSSA
FOUSSAS
FOUSTIER
FOUSTIEST
FOUSTY
FOUTER
FOUTERED
FOUTERING
FOUTERS
FOUTH
FOUTHS
FOUTRA
FOUTRAS
FOUTRE
FOUTRED
FOUTRES
FOUTRING
FOVEA
FOVEAE
FOVEAL
FOVEAS
FOVEATE
FOVEATED
FOVEIFORM
FOVEOLA
FOVEOLAE
FOVEOLAR
FOVEOLAS
FOVEOLATE
FOVEOLE
FOVEOLES
FOVEOLET
FOVEOLETS
FOWL
FOWLED
FOWLER
FOWLERS
FOWLING
FOWLINGS
FOWLPOX
FOWLPOXES
FOWLS
FOWTH
FOWTHS
FOX
FOXBERRY
FOXED
FOXES
FOXFIRE
FOXFIRES
FOXFISH
FOXFISHES
FOXGLOVE
FOXGLOVES
FOXHOLE
FOXHOLES

FOXHOUND
FOXHOUNDS
FOXHUNT
FOXHUNTED
FOXHUNTER
FOXHUNTS
FOXIE
FOXIER
FOXIES
FOXIEST
FOXILY
FOXINESS
FOXING
FOXINGS
FOXLIKE
FOXSHARK
FOXSHARKS
FOXSHIP
FOXSHIPS
FOXSKIN
FOXSKINS
FOXTAIL
FOXTAILS
FOXTROT
FOXTROTS
FOXY
FOY
FOYBOAT
FOYBOATS
FOYER
FOYERS
FOYLE
FOYLED
FOYLES
FOYLING
FOYNE
FOYNED
FOYNES
FOYNING
FOYS
FOZIER
FOZIEST
FOZINESS
FOZY
FRA
FRAB
FRABBED
FRABBING
FRABBIT
FRABJOUS
FRABS
FRACAS
FRACASES
FRACK
FRACKING
FRACKINGS
FRACT
FRACTAL

FRACTALS
FRACTED
FRACTI
FRACTING
FRACTION
FRACTIONS
FRACTIOUS
FRACTS
FRACTUR
FRACTURAL
FRACTURE
FRACTURED
FRACTURER
FRACTURES
FRACTURS
FRACTUS
FRAE
FRAENA
FRAENUM
FRAENUMS
FRAG
FRAGGED
FRAGGING
FRAGGINGS
FRAGILE
FRAGILELY
FRAGILER
FRAGILEST
FRAGILITY
FRAGMENT
FRAGMENTS
FRAGOR
FRAGORS
FRAGRANCE
FRAGRANCY
FRAGRANT
FRAGS
FRAICHEUR
FRAIL
FRAILER
FRAILEST
FRAILISH
FRAILLY
FRAILNESS
FRAILS
FRAILTEE
FRAILTEES
FRAILTIES
FRAILTY
FRAIM
FRAIMS
FRAISE
FRAISED
FRAISES
FRAISING
FRAKTUR
FRAKTURS
FRAMABLE

FRAMBESIA	FRAPPE	FRAZZLING	FREERS
FRAMBOISE	FRAPPED	FREAK	FREES
FRAME	FRAPPEE	FREAKED	FREESHEET
FRAMEABLE	FRAPPES	FREAKERY	FREESIA
FRAMED	FRAPPING	FREAKFUL	FREESIAS
FRAMELESS	FRAPS	FREAKIER	FREEST
FRAMER	FRAS	FREAKIEST	FREESTONE
FRAMERS	FRASCATI	FREAKILY	FREESTYLE
FRAMES	FRASCATIS	FREAKING	FREET
FRAMEWORK	FRASS	FREAKISH	FREETIER
FRAMING	FRASSES	FREAKOUT	FREETIEST
FRAMINGS	FRAT	FREAKOUTS	FREETS
FRAMPAL	FRATCH	FREAKS	FREETY
FRAMPLER	FRATCHES	FREAKY	FREEWARE
FRAMPLERS	FRATCHETY	FRECKLE	FREEWARES
FRAMPOLD	FRATCHIER	FRECKLED	FREEWAY
FRANC	FRATCHING	FRECKLES	FREEWAYS
FRANCHISE	FRATCHY	FRECKLIER	FREEWHEEL
FRANCISE	FRATE	FRECKLING	FREEWILL
FRANCISED	FRATER	FRECKLY	FREEWOMAN
FRANCISES	FRATERIES	FREDAINE	FREEWOMEN
FRANCIUM	FRATERNAL	FREDAINES	FREEWRITE
FRANCIUMS	FRATERS	FREE	FREEWROTE
FRANCIZE	FRATERY	FREEBASE	FREEZABLE
FRANCIZED	FRATI	FREEBASED	FREEZE
FRANCIZES	FRATRIES	FREEBASER	FREEZER
FRANCO	FRATRY	FREEBASES	FREEZERS
FRANCOLIN	FRATS	FREEBEE	FREEZES
FRANCS	FRAU	FREEBEES	FREEZING
FRANGER	FRAUD	FREEBIE	FREEZINGS
FRANGERS	FRAUDFUL	FREEBIES	FREIGHT
FRANGIBLE	FRAUDS	FREEBOARD	FREIGHTED
FRANGLAIS	FRAUDSMAN	FREEBOOT	FREIGHTER
FRANION	FRAUDSMEN	FREEBOOTS	FREIGHTS
FRANIONS	FRAUDSTER	FREEBOOTY	FREIT
FRANK	FRAUGHAN	FREEBORN	FREITIER
FRANKABLE	FRAUGHANS	FREED	FREITIEST
FRANKED	FRAUGHT	FREEDMAN	FREITS
FRANKER	FRAUGHTED	FREEDMEN	FREITY
FRANKERS	FRAUGHTER	FREEDOM	FREMD
FRANKEST	FRAUGHTS	FREEDOMS	FREMDS
FRANKFORT	FRAULEIN	FREEFORM	FREMIT
FRANKFURT	FRAULEINS	FREEGAN	FREMITS
FRANKING	FRAUS	FREEGANS	FREMITUS
FRANKLIN	FRAUTAGE	FREEHAND	FRENA
FRANKLINS	FRAUTAGES	FREEHOLD	FRENCH
FRANKLY	FRAWZEY	FREEHOLDS	FRENCHED
FRANKNESS	FRAWZEYS	FREEING	FRENCHES
FRANKS	FRAY	FREELANCE	FRENCHIFY
FRANSERIA	FRAYED	FREELOAD	FRENCHING
FRANTIC	FRAYING	FREELOADS	FRENETIC
FRANTICLY	FRAYINGS	FREELY	FRENETICS
FRANZIER	FRAYS	FREEMAN	FRENNE
FRANZIEST	FRAZIL	FREEMASON	FRENULA
FRANZY	FRAZILS	FREEMEN	FRENULAR
FRAP	FRAZZLE	FREENESS	FRENULUM
FRAPE	FRAZZLED	FREEPHONE	FRENULUMS
FRAPPANT	FRAZZLES	FREER	FRENUM

FRENUMS
FRENZICAL
FRENZIED
FRENZIES
FRENZILY
FRENZY
FRENZYING
FREON
FREONS
FREQUENCE
FREQUENCY
FREQUENT
FREQUENTS
FRERE
FRERES
FRESCADE
FRESCADES
FRESCO
FRESCOED
FRESCOER
FRESCOERS
FRESCOES
FRESCOING
FRESCOIST
FRESCOS
FRESH
FRESHED
FRESHEN
FRESHENED
FRESHENER
FRESHENS
FRESHER
FRESHERS
FRESHES
FRESHEST
FRESHET
FRESHETS
FRESHIE
FRESHIES
FRESHING
FRESHISH
FRESHLY
FRESHMAN
FRESHMEN
FRESHNESS
FRESNEL
FRESNELS
FRET
FRETBOARD
FRETFUL
FRETFULLY
FRETLESS
FRETS
FRETSAW
FRETSAWS
FRETSOME
FRETTED
FRETTER

FRETTERS
FRETTIER
FRETTIEST
FRETTING
FRETTINGS
FRETTY
FRETWORK
FRETWORKS
FRIABLE
FRIAND
FRIANDE
FRIANDES
FRIANDS
FRIAR
FRIARBIRD
FRIARIES
FRIARLY
FRIARS
FRIARY
FRIB
FRIBBLE
FRIBBLED
FRIBBLER
FRIBBLERS
FRIBBLES
FRIBBLING
FRIBBLISH
FRIBS
FRICADEL
FRICADELS
FRICANDO
FRICASSEE
FRICATIVE
FRICHT
FRICHTED
FRICHTING
FRICHTS
FRICKING
FRICTION
FRICTIONS
FRIDGE
FRIDGED
FRIDGES
FRIDGING
FRIED
FRIEDCAKE
FRIEND
FRIENDED
FRIENDING
FRIENDLY
FRIENDS
FRIER
FRIERS
FRIES
FRIEZE
FRIEZED
FRIEZES
FRIEZING

FRIG
FRIGATE
FRIGATES
FRIGATOON
FRIGES
FRIGGED
FRIGGER
FRIGGERS
FRIGGING
FRIGGINGS
FRIGHT
FRIGHTED
FRIGHTEN
FRIGHTENS
FRIGHTFUL
FRIGHTING
FRIGHTS
FRIGID
FRIGIDER
FRIGIDEST
FRIGIDITY
FRIGIDLY
FRIGOT
FRIGOTS
FRIGS
FRIJOL
FRIJOLE
FRIJOLES
FRIKKADEL
FRILL
FRILLED
FRILLER
FRILLERS
FRILLIER
FRILLIES
FRILLIEST
FRILLING
FRILLINGS
FRILLS
FRILLY
FRINGE
FRINGED
FRINGES
FRINGIER
FRINGIEST
FRINGING
FRINGY
FRIPON
FRIPONS
FRIPPER
FRIPPERER
FRIPPERS
FRIPPERY
FRIPPET
FRIPPETS
FRIS
FRISBEE
FRISBEES

FRISE
FRISEE
FRISEES
FRISES
FRISETTE
FRISETTES
FRISEUR
FRISEURS
FRISK
FRISKA
FRISKAS
FRISKED
FRISKER
FRISKERS
FRISKET
FRISKETS
FRISKFUL
FRISKIER
FRISKIEST
FRISKILY
FRISKING
FRISKINGS
FRISKS
FRISKY
FRISSON
FRISSONS
FRIST
FRISTED
FRISTING
FRISTS
FRISURE
FRISURES
FRIT
FRITES
FRITFLIES
FRITFLY
FRITH
FRITHBORH
FRITHS
FRITS
FRITT
FRITTATA
FRITTATAS
FRITTED
FRITTER
FRITTERED
FRITTERER
FRITTERS
FRITTING
FRITTS
FRITURE
FRITURES
FRITZ
FRITZES
FRIVOL
FRIVOLED
FRIVOLER
FRIVOLERS

FRIVOLING
FRIVOLITY
FRIVOLLED
FRIVOLLER
FRIVOLOUS
FRIVOLS
FRIZ
FRIZE
FRIZED
FRIZER
FRIZERS
FRIZES
FRIZETTE
FRIZETTES
FRIZING
FRIZZ
FRIZZANTE
FRIZZED
FRIZZER
FRIZZERS
FRIZZES
FRIZZIER
FRIZZIES
FRIZZIEST
FRIZZILY
FRIZZING
FRIZZLE
FRIZZLED
FRIZZLER
FRIZZLERS
FRIZZLES
FRIZZLIER
FRIZZLING
FRIZZLY
FRIZZY
FRO
FROCK
FROCKED
FROCKING
FROCKINGS
FROCKLESS
FROCKS
FROE
FROES
FROG
FROGBIT
FROGBITS
FROGEYE
FROGEYED
FROGEYES
FROGFISH
FROGGED
FROGGERY
FROGGIER
FROGGIEST
FROGGING
FROGGINGS
FROGGY

FROGLET
FROGLETS
FROGLIKE
FROGLING
FROGLINGS
FROGMAN
FROGMARCH
FROGMEN
FROGMOUTH
FROGS
FROGSPAWN
FROIDEUR
FROIDEURS
FROING
FROINGS
FROISE
FROISES
FROLIC
FROLICKED
FROLICKER
FROLICKY
FROLICS
FROM
FROMAGE
FROMAGES
FROMENTY
FROND
FRONDAGE
FRONDAGES
FRONDED
FRONDENT
FRONDEUR
FRONDEURS
FRONDLESS
FRONDOSE
FRONDOUS
FRONDS
FRONS
FRONT
FRONTAGE
FRONTAGER
FRONTAGES
FRONTAL
FRONTALLY
FRONTALS
FRONTED
FRONTENIS
FRONTER
FRONTES
FRONTIER
FRONTIERS
FRONTING
FRONTLESS
FRONTLET
FRONTLETS
FRONTLINE
FRONTLIST
FRONTMAN

FRONTMEN
FRONTON
FRONTONS
FRONTOON
FRONTOONS
FRONTPAGE
FRONTS
FRONTWARD
FRONTWAYS
FRONTWISE
FRORE
FROREN
FRORN
FRORNE
FRORY
FROS
FROSH
FROSHES
FROST
FROSTBIT
FROSTBITE
FROSTED
FROSTEDS
FROSTFISH
FROSTIER
FROSTIEST
FROSTILY
FROSTING
FROSTINGS
FROSTLESS
FROSTLIKE
FROSTLINE
FROSTNIP
FROSTNIPS
FROSTS
FROSTWORK
FROSTY
FROTH
FROTHED
FROTHER
FROTHERS
FROTHERY
FROTHIER
FROTHIEST
FROTHILY
FROTHING
FROTHLESS
FROTHS
FROTHY
FROTTAGE
FROTTAGES
FROTTEUR
FROTTEURS
FROUFROU
FROUFROUS
FROUGHIER
FROUGHY
FROUNCE

FROUNCED
FROUNCES
FROUNCING
FROUZIER
FROUZIEST
FROUZY
FROW
FROWARD
FROWARDLY
FROWARDS
FROWIE
FROWIER
FROWIEST
FROWN
FROWNED
FROWNER
FROWNERS
FROWNING
FROWNS
FROWS
FROWSIER
FROWSIEST
FROWST
FROWSTED
FROWSTER
FROWSTERS
FROWSTIER
FROWSTING
FROWSTS
FROWSTY
FROWSY
FROWY
FROWZIER
FROWZIEST
FROWZILY
FROWZY
FROZE
FROZEN
FROZENLY
FRUCTAN
FRUCTANS
FRUCTED
FRUCTIFY
FRUCTIVE
FRUCTOSE
FRUCTOSES
FRUCTUARY
FRUCTUATE
FRUCTUOUS
FRUG
FRUGAL
FRUGALIST
FRUGALITY
FRUGALLY
FRUGGED
FRUGGING
FRUGIVORE
FRUGS

FRUICT
FRUICTS
FRUIT
FRUITAGE
FRUITAGES
FRUITCAKE
FRUITED
FRUITER
FRUITERER
FRUITERS
FRUITERY
FRUITFUL
FRUITIER
FRUITIEST
FRUITILY
FRUITING
FRUITINGS
FRUITION
FRUITIONS
FRUITIVE
FRUITLESS
FRUITLET
FRUITLETS
FRUITLIKE
FRUITS
FRUITWOOD
FRUITY
FRUMENTY
FRUMP
FRUMPED
FRUMPIER
FRUMPIEST
FRUMPILY
FRUMPING
FRUMPISH
FRUMPLE
FRUMPLED
FRUMPLES
FRUMPLING
FRUMPS
FRUMPY
FRUSEMIDE
FRUSH
FRUSHED
FRUSHES
FRUSHING
FRUST
FRUSTA
FRUSTRATE
FRUSTS
FRUSTULE
FRUSTULES
FRUSTUM
FRUSTUMS
FRUTEX
FRUTICES
FRUTICOSE
FRUTIFIED

FRUTIFIES
FRUTIFY
FRY
FRYABLE
FRYBREAD
FRYBREADS
FRYER
FRYERS
FRYING
FRYINGS
FRYPAN
FRYPANS
FUB
FUBAR
FUBBED
FUBBERIES
FUBBERY
FUBBIER
FUBBIEST
FUBBING
FUBBY
FUBS
FUBSIER
FUBSIEST
FUBSY
FUCHSIA
FUCHSIAS
FUCHSIN
FUCHSINE
FUCHSINES
FUCHSINS
FUCHSITE
FUCHSITES
FUCI
FUCK
FUCKED
FUCKER
FUCKERS
FUCKING
FUCKINGS
FUCKOFF
FUCKOFFS
FUCKS
FUCKUP
FUCKUPS
FUCKWIT
FUCKWITS
FUCOID
FUCOIDAL
FUCOIDS
FUCOSE
FUCOSES
FUCOUS
FUCUS
FUCUSED
FUCUSES
FUD
FUDDIES

FUDDLE
FUDDLED
FUDDLER
FUDDLERS
FUDDLES
FUDDLING
FUDDLINGS
FUDDY
FUDGE
FUDGED
FUDGES
FUDGING
FUDS
FUEHRER
FUEHRERS
FUEL
FUELED
FUELER
FUELERS
FUELING
FUELLED
FUELLER
FUELLERS
FUELLING
FUELS
FUELWOOD
FUELWOODS
FUERO
FUEROS
FUFF
FUFFED
FUFFIER
FUFFIEST
FUFFING
FUFFS
FUFFY
FUG
FUGACIOUS
FUGACITY
FUGAL
FUGALLY
FUGATO
FUGATOS
FUGGED
FUGGIER
FUGGIEST
FUGGILY
FUGGING
FUGGY
FUGHETTA
FUGHETTAS
FUGIE
FUGIES
FUGIO
FUGIOS
FUGITIVE
FUGITIVES
FUGLE

FUGLED
FUGLEMAN
FUGLEMEN
FUGLES
FUGLIER
FUGLIEST
FUGLING
FUGLY
FUGS
FUGU
FUGUE
FUGUED
FUGUELIKE
FUGUES
FUGUING
FUGUIST
FUGUISTS
FUGUS
FUHRER
FUHRERS
FUJI
FUJIS
FULCRA
FULCRATE
FULCRUM
FULCRUMS
FULFIL
FULFILL
FULFILLED
FULFILLER
FULFILLS
FULFILS
FULGENCY
FULGENT
FULGENTLY
FULGID
FULGOR
FULGOROUS
FULGORS
FULGOUR
FULGOURS
FULGURAL
FULGURANT
FULGURATE
FULGURITE
FULGUROUS
FULHAM
FULHAMS
FULL
FULLAGE
FULLAGES
FULLAM
FULLAMS
FULLAN
FULLANS
FULLBACK
FULLBACKS
FULLBLOOD

FULLED
FULLER
FULLERED
FULLERENE
FULLERIDE
FULLERIES
FULLERING
FULLERITE
FULLERS
FULLERY
FULLEST
FULLFACE
FULLFACES
FULLING
FULLISH
FULLNESS
FULLS
FULLY
FULMAR
FULMARS
FULMINANT
FULMINATE
FULMINE
FULMINED
FULMINES
FULMINIC
FULMINING
FULMINOUS
FULNESS
FULNESSES
FULSOME
FULSOMELY
FULSOMER
FULSOMEST
FULVID
FULVOUS
FUM
FUMADO
FUMADOES
FUMADOS
FUMAGE
FUMAGES
FUMARASE
FUMARASES
FUMARATE
FUMARATES
FUMARIC
FUMAROLE
FUMAROLES
FUMAROLIC
FUMATORIA
FUMATORY
FUMBLE
FUMBLED
FUMBLER
FUMBLERS
FUMBLES
FUMBLING

FUME
FUMED
FUMELESS
FUMELIKE
FUMER
FUMEROLE
FUMEROLES
FUMERS
FUMES
FUMET
FUMETS
FUMETTE
FUMETTES
FUMETTI
FUMETTO
FUMIER
FUMIEST
FUMIGANT
FUMIGANTS
FUMIGATE
FUMIGATED
FUMIGATES
FUMIGATOR
FUMING
FUMINGLY
FUMITORY
FUMOSITY
FUMOUS
FUMS
FUMULI
FUMULUS
FUMY
FUN
FUNBOARD
FUNBOARDS
FUNCTION
FUNCTIONS
FUNCTOR
FUNCTORS
FUND
FUNDABLE
FUNDAMENT
FUNDED
FUNDER
FUNDERS
FUNDI
FUNDIC
FUNDIE
FUNDIES
FUNDING
FUNDINGS
FUNDIS
FUNDLESS
FUNDRAISE
FUNDS
FUNDUS
FUNDY
FUNEBRAL

FUNEBRE
FUNEBRIAL
FUNERAL
FUNERALS
FUNERARY
FUNEREAL
FUNEST
FUNFAIR
FUNFAIRS
FUNFEST
FUNFESTS
FUNG
FUNGAL
FUNGALS
FUNGI
FUNGIBLE
FUNGIBLES
FUNGIC
FUNGICIDE
FUNGIFORM
FUNGISTAT
FUNGO
FUNGOES
FUNGOID
FUNGOIDAL
FUNGOIDS
FUNGOSITY
FUNGOUS
FUNGS
FUNGUS
FUNGUSES
FUNHOUSE
FUNHOUSES
FUNICLE
FUNICLES
FUNICULAR
FUNICULI
FUNICULUS
FUNK
FUNKED
FUNKER
FUNKERS
FUNKHOLE
FUNKHOLES
FUNKIA
FUNKIAS
FUNKIER
FUNKIEST
FUNKILY
FUNKINESS
FUNKING
FUNKS
FUNKSTER
FUNKSTERS
FUNKY
FUNNED
FUNNEL
FUNNELED

FUNNELING
FUNNELLED
FUNNELS
FUNNER
FUNNEST
FUNNIER
FUNNIES
FUNNIEST
FUNNILY
FUNNINESS
FUNNING
FUNNY
FUNNYMAN
FUNNYMEN
FUNPLEX
FUNPLEXES
FUNS
FUNSTER
FUNSTERS
FUR
FURACIOUS
FURACITY
FURAL
FURALS
FURAN
FURANE
FURANES
FURANOSE
FURANOSES
FURANS
FURBEARER
FURBELOW
FURBELOWS
FURBISH
FURBISHED
FURBISHER
FURBISHES
FURCA
FURCAE
FURCAL
FURCATE
FURCATED
FURCATELY
FURCATES
FURCATING
FURCATION
FURCRAEA
FURCRAEAS
FURCULA
FURCULAE
FURCULAR
FURCULUM
FURDER
FUREUR
FUREURS
FURFAIR
FURFAIRS
FURFUR

FURFURAL
FURFURALS
FURFURAN
FURFURANS
FURFURES
FURFUROL
FURFUROLE
FURFUROLS
FURFUROUS
FURFURS
FURIBUND
FURIES
FURIOSITY
FURIOSO
FURIOSOS
FURIOUS
FURIOUSLY
FURKID
FURKIDS
FURL
FURLABLE
FURLANA
FURLANAS
FURLED
FURLER
FURLERS
FURLESS
FURLING
FURLONG
FURLONGS
FURLOUGH
FURLOUGHS
FURLS
FURMENTY
FURMETIES
FURMETY
FURMITIES
FURMITY
FURNACE
FURNACED
FURNACES
FURNACING
FURNIMENT
FURNISH
FURNISHED
FURNISHER
FURNISHES
FURNITURE
FUROL
FUROLE
FUROLES
FUROLS
FUROR
FURORE
FURORES
FURORS
FURPHIES
FURPHY

FURR
FURRED
FURRIER
FURRIERS
FURRIERY
FURRIES
FURRIEST
FURRILY
FURRINER
FURRINERS
FURRINESS
FURRING
FURRINGS
FURROW
FURROWED
FURROWER
FURROWERS
FURROWING
FURROWS
FURROWY
FURRS
FURRY
FURS
FURTH
FURTHER
FURTHERED
FURTHERER
FURTHERS
FURTHEST
FURTIVE
FURTIVELY
FURUNCLE
FURUNCLES
FURY
FURZE
FURZES
FURZIER
FURZIEST
FURZY
FUSAIN
FUSAINS
FUSARIA
FUSARIUM
FUSAROL
FUSAROLE
FUSAROLES
FUSAROLS
FUSC
FUSCOUS
FUSE
FUSED
FUSEE
FUSEES
FUSEL
FUSELAGE
FUSELAGES
FUSELESS
FUSELIKE

FUSELS
FUSES
FUSHION
FUSHIONS
FUSIBLE
FUSIBLY
FUSIFORM
FUSIL
FUSILE
FUSILEER
FUSILEERS
FUSILIER
FUSILIERS
FUSILLADE
FUSILLI
FUSILLIS
FUSILS
FUSING
FUSION
FUSIONAL
FUSIONISM
FUSIONIST
FUSIONS
FUSS
FUSSED
FUSSER
FUSSERS
FUSSES
FUSSIER
FUSSIEST
FUSSILY
FUSSINESS
FUSSING
FUSSPOT
FUSSPOTS
FUSSY
FUST
FUSTED
FUSTET
FUSTETS
FUSTIAN
FUSTIANS
FUSTIC
FUSTICS
FUSTIER
FUSTIEST
FUSTIGATE
FUSTILUGS
FUSTILY
FUSTINESS
FUSTING
FUSTOC
FUSTOCS
FUSTS
FUSTY
FUSULINID
FUSUMA
FUTCHEL

FUTCHELS
FUTHARC
FUTHARCS
FUTHARK
FUTHARKS
FUTHORC
FUTHORCS
FUTHORK
FUTHORKS
FUTILE
FUTILELY
FUTILER
FUTILEST
FUTILITY
FUTON
FUTONS
FUTSAL
FUTSALS
FUTTOCK
FUTTOCKS
FUTURAL
FUTURE
FUTURES
FUTURISM
FUTURISMS
FUTURIST
FUTURISTS
FUTURITY
FUTZ
FUTZED
FUTZES
FUTZING
FUZE
FUZED
FUZEE
FUZEES
FUZES
FUZIL
FUZILS
FUZING
FUZZ
FUZZED
FUZZES
FUZZIER
FUZZIEST
FUZZILY
FUZZINESS
FUZZING
FUZZLE
FUZZLED
FUZZLES
FUZZLING
FUZZTONE
FUZZTONES
FUZZY
FY
FYCE
FYCES

FYKE

FYKE
FYKED
FYKES
FYKING
FYLE
FYLES
FYLFOT
FYLFOTS
FYNBOS
FYNBOSES
FYRD
FYRDS
FYTTE
FYTTES

G

GAB	GADABOUT	GAFF	GAINERS
GABARDINE	GADABOUTS	GAFFE	GAINEST
GABBARD	GADARENE	GAFFED	GAINFUL
GABBARDS	GADDED	GAFFER	GAINFULLY
GABBART	GADDER	GAFFERS	GAINING
GABBARTS	GADDERS	GAFFES	GAININGS
GABBED	GADDI	GAFFING	GAINLESS
GABBER	GADDING	GAFFINGS	GAINLIER
GABBERS	GADDIS	GAFFS	GAINLIEST
GABBIER	GADE	GAFFSAIL	GAINLY
GABBIEST	GADES	GAFFSAILS	GAINS
GABBINESS	GADFLIES	GAG	GAINSAID
GABBING	GADFLY	GAGA	GAINSAY
GABBLE	GADGE	GAGAKU	GAINSAYER
GABBLED	GADGES	GAGAKUS	GAINSAYS
GABBLER	GADGET	GAGE	GAINST
GABBLERS	GADGETEER	GAGEABLE	GAIR
GABBLES	GADGETRY	GAGEABLY	GAIRFOWL
GABBLING	GADGETS	GAGED	GAIRFOWLS
GABBLINGS	GADGETY	GAGER	GAIRS
GABBRO	GADGIE	GAGERS	GAIT
GABBROIC	GADGIES	GAGES	GAITED
GABBROID	GADI	GAGGED	GAITER
GABBROS	GADID	GAGGER	GAITERS
GABBY	GADIDS	GAGGERIES	GAITING
GABELLE	GADIS	GAGGERS	GAITS
GABELLED	GADJE	GAGGERY	GAITT
GABELLER	GADJES	GAGGING	GAITTS
GABELLERS	GADJO	GAGGLE	GAJO
GABELLES	GADLING	GAGGLED	GAJOS
GABERDINE	GADLINGS	GAGGLES	GAL
GABFEST	GADOID	GAGGLING	GALA
GABFESTS	GADOIDS	GAGGLINGS	GALABEA
GABIES	GADOLINIC	GAGING	GALABEAH
GABION	GADROON	GAGMAN	GALABEAHS
GABIONADE	GADROONED	GAGMEN	GALABEAS
GABIONAGE	GADROONS	GAGS	GALABIA
GABIONED	GADS	GAGSTER	GALABIAH
GABIONS	GADSMAN	GAGSTERS	GALABIAHS
GABLE	GADSMEN	GAHNITE	GALABIAS
GABLED	GADSO	GAHNITES	GALABIEH
GABLELIKE	GADSOS	GAID	GALABIEHS
GABLES	GADWALL	GAIDS	GALABIYA
GABLET	GADWALLS	GAIETIES	GALABIYAH
GABLETS	GADZOOKS	GAIETY	GALABIYAS
GABLING	GAE	GAIJIN	GALACTIC
GABNASH	GAED	GAILLARD	GALACTOSE
GABNASHES	GAEING	GAILLARDE	GALAGE
GABOON	GAELICISE	GAILY	GALAGES
GABOONS	GAELICISM	GAIN	GALAGO
GABS	GAELICIZE	GAINABLE	GALAGOS
GABY	GAEN	GAINED	GALAH
GAD	GAES	GAINER	GALAHS

GALANGA
GALANGAL
GALANGALS
GALANGAS
GALANT
GALANTINE
GALANTY
GALAPAGO
GALAPAGOS
GALAS
GALATEA
GALATEAS
GALAVANT
GALAVANTS
GALAX
GALAXES
GALAXIES
GALAXY
GALBANUM
GALBANUMS
GALDRAGON
GALE
GALEA
GALEAE
GALEAS
GALEATE
GALEATED
GALEIFORM
GALENA
GALENAS
GALENGALE
GALENIC
GALENICAL
GALENITE
GALENITES
GALENOID
GALERE
GALERES
GALES
GALETTE
GALETTES
GALILEE
GALILEES
GALINGALE
GALIONGEE
GALIOT
GALIOTS
GALIPOT
GALIPOTS
GALIVANT
GALIVANTS
GALL
GALLABEA
GALLABEAH
GALLABEAS
GALLABIA
GALLABIAH
GALLABIAS

GALLABIEH
GALLABIYA
GALLAMINE
GALLANT
GALLANTED
GALLANTER
GALLANTLY
GALLANTRY
GALLANTS
GALLATE
GALLATES
GALLEASS
GALLED
GALLEIN
GALLEINS
GALLEON
GALLEONS
GALLERIA
GALLERIAS
GALLERIED
GALLERIES
GALLERIST
GALLERY
GALLET
GALLETA
GALLETAS
GALLETED
GALLETING
GALLETS
GALLEY
GALLEYS
GALLFLIES
GALLFLY
GALLIARD
GALLIARDS
GALLIASS
GALLIC
GALLICA
GALLICAN
GALLICAS
GALLICISE
GALLICISM
GALLICIZE
GALLIED
GALLIES
GALLINAZO
GALLING
GALLINGLY
GALLINULE
GALLIOT
GALLIOTS
GALLIPOT
GALLIPOTS
GALLISE
GALLISED
GALLISES
GALLISING
GALLISISE

GALLISIZE
GALLIUM
GALLIUMS
GALLIVANT
GALLIVAT
GALLIVATS
GALLIWASP
GALLIZE
GALLIZED
GALLIZES
GALLIZING
GALLNUT
GALLNUTS
GALLOCK
GALLON
GALLONAGE
GALLONS
GALLOON
GALLOONED
GALLOONS
GALLOOT
GALLOOTS
GALLOP
GALLOPADE
GALLOPED
GALLOPER
GALLOPERS
GALLOPING
GALLOPS
GALLOUS
GALLOW
GALLOWED
GALLOWING
GALLOWS
GALLOWSES
GALLS
GALLSTONE
GALLUMPH
GALLUMPHS
GALLUS
GALLUSED
GALLUSES
GALLY
GALLYING
GALOCHE
GALOCHED
GALOCHES
GALOCHING
GALOOT
GALOOTS
GALOP
GALOPADE
GALOPADES
GALOPED
GALOPIN
GALOPING
GALOPINS
GALOPPED

GALOPPING
GALOPS
GALORE
GALORES
GALOSH
GALOSHE
GALOSHED
GALOSHES
GALOSHING
GALOWSES
GALRAVAGE
GALS
GALTONIA
GALTONIAS
GALUMPH
GALUMPHED
GALUMPHER
GALUMPHS
GALUT
GALUTH
GALUTHS
GALUTS
GALVANIC
GALVANISE
GALVANISM
GALVANIST
GALVANIZE
GALVO
GALVOS
GALYAC
GALYACS
GALYAK
GALYAKS
GAM
GAMA
GAMAHUCHE
GAMARUCHE
GAMAS
GAMASH
GAMASHES
GAMAY
GAMAYS
GAMB
GAMBA
GAMBADE
GAMBADES
GAMBADO
GAMBADOED
GAMBADOES
GAMBADOS
GAMBAS
GAMBE
GAMBES
GAMBESON
GAMBESONS
GAMBET
GAMBETS
GAMBETTA

GAMBETTAS	GAMESTER	GAN	GANGWAY
GAMBIA	GAMESTERS	GANACHE	GANGWAYS
GAMBIAS	GAMESY	GANACHES	GANISTER
GAMBIER	GAMETAL	GANCH	GANISTERS
GAMBIERS	GAMETE	GANCHED	GANJA
GAMBIR	GAMETES	GANCHES	GANJAH
GAMBIRS	GAMETIC	GANCHING	GANJAHS
GAMBIST	GAMEY	GANDER	GANJAS
GAMBISTS	GAMIC	GANDERED	GANNED
GAMBIT	GAMIER	GANDERING	GANNET
GAMBITED	GAMIEST	GANDERISM	GANNETRY
GAMBITING	GAMILY	GANDERS	GANNETS
GAMBITS	GAMIN	GANDY	GANNING
GAMBLE	GAMINE	GANE	GANNISTER
GAMBLED	GAMINERIE	GANEF	GANOF
GAMBLER	GAMINES	GANEFS	GANOFS
GAMBLERS	GAMINESS	GANEV	GANOID
GAMBLES	GAMING	GANEVS	GANOIDS
GAMBLING	GAMINGS	GANG	GANOIN
GAMBLINGS	GAMINS	GANGBANG	GANOINE
GAMBO	GAMMA	GANGBANGS	GANOINES
GAMBOGE	GAMMADIA	GANGBOARD	GANOINS
GAMBOGES	GAMMADION	GANGED	GANS
GAMBOGIAN	GAMMAS	GANGER	GANSEY
GAMBOGIC	GAMMAT	GANGERS	GANSEYS
GAMBOL	GAMMATIA	GANGING	GANT
GAMBOLED	GAMMATION	GANGINGS	GANTED
GAMBOLING	GAMMATS	GANGLAND	GANTELOPE
GAMBOLLED	GAMME	GANGLANDS	GANTING
GAMBOLS	GAMMED	GANGLIA	GANTLET
GAMBOS	GAMMER	GANGLIAL	GANTLETED
GAMBREL	GAMMERS	GANGLIAR	GANTLETS
GAMBRELS	GAMMES	GANGLIATE	GANTLINE
GAMBROON	GAMMIER	GANGLIER	GANTLINES
GAMBROONS	GAMMIEST	GANGLIEST	GANTLOPE
GAMBS	GAMMING	GANGLING	GANTLOPES
GAMBUSIA	GAMMOCK	GANGLION	GANTRIES
GAMBUSIAS	GAMMOCKED	GANGLIONS	GANTRY
GAME	GAMMOCKS	GANGLY	GANTS
GAMECOCK	GAMMON	GANGPLANK	GANYMEDE
GAMECOCKS	GAMMONED	GANGPLOW	GANYMEDES
GAMED	GAMMONER	GANGPLOWS	GAOL
GAMELAN	GAMMONERS	GANGREL	GAOLBIRD
GAMELANS	GAMMONING	GANGRELS	GAOLBIRDS
GAMELIKE	GAMMONS	GANGRENE	GAOLBREAK
GAMELY	GAMMY	GANGRENED	GAOLED
GAMENESS	GAMODEME	GANGRENES	GAOLER
GAMEPLAY	GAMODEMES	GANGS	GAOLERESS
GAMEPLAYS	GAMONE	GANGSHAG	GAOLERS
GAMER	GAMONES	GANGSHAGS	GAOLING
GAMERS	GAMP	GANGSMAN	GAOLLESS
GAMES	GAMPISH	GANGSMEN	GAOLS
GAMESIER	GAMPS	GANGSTA	GAP
GAMESIEST	GAMS	GANGSTAS	GAPE
GAMESMAN	GAMUT	GANGSTER	GAPED
GAMESMEN	GAMUTS	GANGSTERS	GAPER
GAMESOME	GAMY	GANGUE	GAPERS
GAMEST	GAMYNESS	GANGUES	GAPES

GAPESEED

GAPESEED
GAPESEEDS
GAPEWORM
GAPEWORMS
GAPIER
GAPIEST
GAPING
GAPINGLY
GAPINGS
GAPLESS
GAPO
GAPOS
GAPOSIS
GAPOSISES
GAPPED
GAPPER
GAPPERS
GAPPIER
GAPPIEST
GAPPING
GAPPY
GAPS
GAPY
GAR
GARAGE
GARAGED
GARAGEMAN
GARAGEMEN
GARAGES
GARAGING
GARAGINGS
GARAGIST
GARAGISTE
GARAGISTES
GARAGISTS
GARB
GARBAGE
GARBAGES
GARBAGEY
GARBAGY
GARBANZO
GARBANZOS
GARBE
GARBED
GARBES
GARBING
GARBLE
GARBLED
GARBLER
GARBLERS
GARBLES
GARBLESS
GARBLING
GARBLINGS
GARBO
GARBOARD
GARBOARDS
GARBOIL
GARBOILS

GARBOLOGY
GARBOS
GARBS
GARBURE
GARBURES
GARCINIA
GARCINIAS
GARCON
GARCONS
GARDA
GARDAI
GARDANT
GARDANTS
GARDEN
GARDENED
GARDENER
GARDENERS
GARDENFUL
GARDENIA
GARDENIAS
GARDENING
GARDENS
GARDEROBE
GARDYLOO
GARDYLOOS
GARE
GAREFOWL
GAREFOWLS
GARFISH
GARFISHES
GARGANEY
GARGANEYS
GARGANTUA
GARGARISE
GARGARISM
GARGARIZE
GARGET
GARGETS
GARGETY
GARGLE
GARGLED
GARGLER
GARGLERS
GARGLES
GARGLING
GARGOYLE
GARGOYLED
GARGOYLES
GARI
GARIAL
GARIALS
GARIBALDI
GARIGUE
GARIGUES
GARIS
GARISH
GARISHED
GARISHES

GARISHING
GARISHLY
GARJAN
GARJANS
GARLAND
GARLANDED
GARLANDRY
GARLANDS
GARLIC
GARLICKED
GARLICKY
GARLICS
GARMENT
GARMENTED
GARMENTS
GARNER
GARNERED
GARNERING
GARNERS
GARNET
GARNETS
GARNI
GARNISH
GARNISHED
GARNISHEE
GARNISHER
GARNISHES
GARNISHRY
GARNITURE
GAROTE
GAROTED
GAROTES
GAROTING
GAROTTE
GAROTTED
GAROTTER
GAROTTERS
GAROTTES
GAROTTING
GAROUPA
GAROUPAS
GARPIKE
GARPIKES
GARRAN
GARRANS
GARRE
GARRED
GARRES
GARRET
GARRETED
GARRETEER
GARRETS
GARRIGUE
GARRIGUES
GARRING
GARRISON
GARRISONS
GARRON

GARRONS
GARROT
GARROTE
GARROTED
GARROTER
GARROTERS
GARROTES
GARROTING
GARROTS
GARROTTE
GARROTTED
GARROTTER
GARROTTES
GARRULITY
GARRULOUS
GARRYA
GARRYAS
GARRYOWEN
GARS
GART
GARTER
GARTERED
GARTERING
GARTERS
GARTH
GARTHS
GARUDA
GARUDAS
GARUM
GARUMS
GARVEY
GARVEYS
GARVIE
GARVIES
GARVOCK
GARVOCKS
GAS
GASAHOL
GASAHOLS
GASALIER
GASALIERS
GASBAG
GASBAGGED
GASBAGS
GASCON
GASCONADE
GASCONISM
GASCONS
GASEITIES
GASEITY
GASELIER
GASELIERS
GASEOUS
GASES
GASFIELD
GASFIELDS
GASH
GASHED

236

GASHER
GASHES
GASHEST
GASHFUL
GASHING
GASHLY
GASHOLDER
GASHOUSE
GASHOUSES
GASIFIED
GASIFIER
GASIFIERS
GASIFIES
GASIFORM
GASIFY
GASIFYING
GASKET
GASKETS
GASKIN
GASKING
GASKINGS
GASKINS
GASLESS
GASLIGHT
GASLIGHTS
GASLIT
GASMAN
GASMEN
GASOGENE
GASOGENES
GASOHOL
GASOHOLS
GASOLENE
GASOLENES
GASOLIER
GASOLIERS
GASOLINE
GASOLINES
GASOLINIC
GASOMETER
GASOMETRY
GASP
GASPED
GASPER
GASPEREAU
GASPERS
GASPIER
GASPIEST
GASPINESS
GASPING
GASPINGLY
GASPINGS
GASPS
GASPY
GASSED
GASSER
GASSERS
GASSES

GASSIER
GASSIEST
GASSILY
GASSINESS
GASSING
GASSINGS
GASSY
GAST
GASTED
GASTER
GASTERS
GASTFULL
GASTIGHT
GASTING
GASTNESS
GASTNESSE
GASTRAEA
GASTRAEAS
GASTRAEUM
GASTRAL
GASTREA
GASTREAS
GASTRIC
GASTRIN
GASTRINS
GASTRITIC
GASTRITIS
GASTROPOD
GASTRULA
GASTRULAE
GASTRULAR
GASTRULAS
GASTS
GASWORKS
GAT
GATE
GATEAU
GATEAUS
GATEAUX
GATECRASH
GATED
GATEFOLD
GATEFOLDS
GATEHOUSE
GATELEG
GATELESS
GATELIKE
GATEMAN
GATEMEN
GATEPOST
GATEPOSTS
GATER
GATERS
GATES
GATEWAY
GATEWAYS
GATH
GATHER

GATHERED
GATHERER
GATHERERS
GATHERING
GATHERS
GATHS
GATING
GATINGS
GATOR
GATORS
GATS
GATVOL
GAU
GAUCHE
GAUCHELY
GAUCHER
GAUCHERIE
GAUCHESCO
GAUCHEST
GAUCHO
GAUCHOS
GAUCIE
GAUCIER
GAUCIEST
GAUCY
GAUD
GAUDEAMUS
GAUDED
GAUDERIES
GAUDERY
GAUDGIE
GAUDGIES
GAUDIER
GAUDIES
GAUDIEST
GAUDILY
GAUDINESS
GAUDING
GAUDS
GAUDY
GAUFER
GAUFERS
GAUFFER
GAUFFERED
GAUFFERS
GAUFRE
GAUFRES
GAUGE
GAUGEABLE
GAUGEABLY
GAUGED
GAUGER
GAUGERS
GAUGES
GAUGING
GAUGINGS
GAUJE
GAUJES

GAULEITER
GAULT
GAULTER
GAULTERS
GAULTS
GAUM
GAUMED
GAUMIER
GAUMIEST
GAUMING
GAUMLESS
GAUMS
GAUMY
GAUN
GAUNCH
GAUNCHED
GAUNCHES
GAUNCHING
GAUNT
GAUNTED
GAUNTER
GAUNTEST
GAUNTING
GAUNTLET
GAUNTLETS
GAUNTLY
GAUNTNESS
GAUNTREE
GAUNTREES
GAUNTRIES
GAUNTRY
GAUNTS
GAUP
GAUPED
GAUPER
GAUPERS
GAUPING
GAUPS
GAUPUS
GAUPUSES
GAUR
GAURS
GAUS
GAUSS
GAUSSES
GAUSSIAN
GAUZE
GAUZELIKE
GAUZES
GAUZIER
GAUZIEST
GAUZILY
GAUZINESS
GAUZY
GAVAGE
GAVAGES
GAVE
GAVEL

GAVELED
GAVELING
GAVELKIND
GAVELLED
GAVELLING
GAVELMAN
GAVELMEN
GAVELOCK
GAVELOCKS
GAVELS
GAVIAL
GAVIALOID
GAVIALS
GAVOT
GAVOTS
GAVOTTE
GAVOTTED
GAVOTTES
GAVOTTING
GAWCIER
GAWCIEST
GAWCY
GAWD
GAWDS
GAWK
GAWKED
GAWKER
GAWKERS
GAWKIER
GAWKIES
GAWKIEST
GAWKIHOOD
GAWKILY
GAWKINESS
GAWKING
GAWKISH
GAWKISHLY
GAWKS
GAWKY
GAWP
GAWPED
GAWPER
GAWPERS
GAWPING
GAWPS
GAWPUS
GAWPUSES
GAWSIE
GAWSIER
GAWSIEST
GAWSY
GAY
GAYAL
GAYALS
GAYDAR
GAYDARS
GAYER
GAYEST

GAYETIES
GAYETY
GAYLY
GAYNESS
GAYNESSES
GAYS
GAYSOME
GAYWINGS
GAZABO
GAZABOES
GAZABOS
GAZAL
GAZALS
GAZANIA
GAZANIAS
GAZAR
GAZARS
GAZE
GAZEBO
GAZEBOES
GAZEBOS
GAZED
GAZEFUL
GAZEHOUND
GAZELLE
GAZELLES
GAZEMENT
GAZEMENTS
GAZER
GAZERS
GAZES
GAZETTE
GAZETTED
GAZETTEER
GAZETTES
GAZETTING
GAZIER
GAZIEST
GAZILLION
GAZING
GAZINGS
GAZOGENE
GAZOGENES
GAZON
GAZONS
GAZOO
GAZOOKA
GAZOOKAS
GAZOON
GAZOONS
GAZOOS
GAZPACHO
GAZPACHOS
GAZUMP
GAZUMPED
GAZUMPER
GAZUMPERS
GAZUMPING

GAZUMPS
GAZUNDER
GAZUNDERS
GAZY
GEAL
GEALED
GEALING
GEALOUS
GEALOUSY
GEALS
GEAN
GEANS
GEAR
GEARBOX
GEARBOXES
GEARCASE
GEARCASES
GEARE
GEARED
GEARES
GEARHEAD
GEARHEADS
GEARING
GEARINGS
GEARLESS
GEARS
GEARSHIFT
GEARWHEEL
GEASON
GEAT
GEATS
GEBUR
GEBURS
GECK
GECKED
GECKING
GECKO
GECKOES
GECKOS
GECKS
GED
GEDACT
GEDACTS
GEDDIT
GEDECKT
GEDECKTS
GEDS
GEE
GEEBAG
GEEBAGS
GEEBUNG
GEEBUNGS
GEECHEE
GEECHEES
GEED
GEEGAW
GEEGAWS
GEEING

GEEK
GEEKDOM
GEEKDOMS
GEEKED
GEEKIER
GEEKIEST
GEEKINESS
GEEKS
GEEKSPEAK
GEEKY
GEELBEK
GEELBEKS
GEEP
GEEPOUND
GEEPOUNDS
GEEPS
GEES
GEESE
GEEST
GEESTS
GEEZ
GEEZAH
GEEZAHS
GEEZER
GEEZERS
GEFILTE
GEFUFFLE
GEFUFFLED
GEFUFFLES
GEFULLTE
GEGGIE
GEGGIES
GEHLENITE
GEISHA
GEISHAS
GEIST
GEISTS
GEIT
GEITS
GEL
GELABLE
GELADA
GELADAS
GELANDE
GELANT
GELANTS
GELASTIC
GELATE
GELATED
GELATES
GELATI
GELATIN
GELATINE
GELATINES
GELATING
GELATINS
GELATION
GELATIONS

GELATIS
GELATO
GELATOS
GELCAP
GELCAPS
GELD
GELDED
GELDER
GELDERS
GELDING
GELDINGS
GELDS
GELEE
GELEES
GELID
GELIDER
GELIDEST
GELIDITY
GELIDLY
GELIDNESS
GELIGNITE
GELLANT
GELLANTS
GELLED
GELLIES
GELLING
GELLY
GELOSIES
GELOSY
GELS
GELSEMIA
GELSEMINE
GELSEMIUM
GELT
GELTS
GEM
GEMATRIA
GEMATRIAS
GEMCLIP
GEMCLIPS
GEMEL
GEMELS
GEMFISH
GEMFISHES
GEMINAL
GEMINALLY
GEMINATE
GEMINATED
GEMINATES
GEMINI
GEMINIES
GEMINOUS
GEMINY
GEMLIKE
GEMMA
GEMMAE
GEMMAN
GEMMATE

GEMMATED
GEMMATES
GEMMATING
GEMMATION
GEMMATIVE
GEMMED
GEMMEN
GEMMEOUS
GEMMERIES
GEMMERY
GEMMIER
GEMMIEST
GEMMILY
GEMMINESS
GEMMING
GEMMOLOGY
GEMMULE
GEMMULES
GEMMY
GEMOLOGY
GEMONY
GEMOT
GEMOTE
GEMOTES
GEMOTS
GEMS
GEMSBOK
GEMSBOKS
GEMSBUCK
GEMSBUCKS
GEMSHORN
GEMSHORNS
GEMSTONE
GEMSTONES
GEMUTLICH
GEN
GENA
GENAL
GENAPPE
GENAPPES
GENAS
GENDARME
GENDARMES
GENDER
GENDERED
GENDERING
GENDERISE
GENDERIZE
GENDERS
GENE
GENEALOGY
GENERA
GENERABLE
GENERAL
GENERALCY
GENERALE
GENERALIA
GENERALLY

GENERALS
GENERANT
GENERANTS
GENERATE
GENERATED
GENERATES
GENERATOR
GENERIC
GENERICAL
GENERICS
GENEROUS
GENES
GENESES
GENESIS
GENET
GENETIC
GENETICAL
GENETICS
GENETRIX
GENETS
GENETTE
GENETTES
GENEVA
GENEVAS
GENIAL
GENIALISE
GENIALITY
GENIALIZE
GENIALLY
GENIC
GENICALLY
GENICULAR
GENIE
GENIES
GENII
GENIP
GENIPAP
GENIPAPS
GENIPS
GENISTA
GENISTAS
GENISTEIN
GENITAL
GENITALIA
GENITALIC
GENITALLY
GENITALS
GENITIVAL
GENITIVE
GENITIVES
GENITOR
GENITORS
GENITRIX
GENITURE
GENITURES
GENIUS
GENIUSES
GENIZAH

GENIZAHS
GENIZOT
GENIZOTH
GENLOCK
GENLOCKS
GENNAKER
GENNAKERS
GENNED
GENNEL
GENNELS
GENNET
GENNETS
GENNIES
GENNING
GENNY
GENOA
GENOAS
GENOCIDAL
GENOCIDE
GENOCIDES
GENOGRAM
GENOGRAMS
GENOISE
GENOISES
GENOM
GENOME
GENOMES
GENOMIC
GENOMICS
GENOMS
GENOTYPE
GENOTYPES
GENOTYPIC
GENRE
GENRES
GENRO
GENROS
GENS
GENSENG
GENSENGS
GENT
GENTEEL
GENTEELER
GENTEELLY
GENTES
GENTIAN
GENTIANS
GENTIER
GENTIEST
GENTIL
GENTILE
GENTILES
GENTILIC
GENTILISE
GENTILISH
GENTILISM
GENTILITY
GENTILIZE

GENTLE
GENTLED
GENTLEMAN
GENTLEMEN
GENTLER
GENTLES
GENTLEST
GENTLING
GENTLY
GENTOO
GENTOOS
GENTRICE
GENTRICES
GENTRIES
GENTRIFY
GENTRY
GENTS
GENTY
GENU
GENUA
GENUFLECT
GENUINE
GENUINELY
GENUS
GENUSES
GEO
GEOBOTANY
GEOCARPIC
GEOCARPY
GEOCORONA
GEODE
GEODES
GEODESIC
GEODESICS
GEODESIES
GEODESIST
GEODESY
GEODETIC
GEODETICS
GEODIC
GEODUCK
GEODUCKS
GEOFACT
GEOFACTS
GEOGENIES
GEOGENY
GEOGNOSES
GEOGNOSIS
GEOGNOST
GEOGNOSTS
GEOGNOSY
GEOGONIC
GEOGONIES
GEOGONY
GEOGRAPHY
GEOID
GEOIDAL
GEOIDS

GEOLATRY
GEOLOGER
GEOLOGERS
GEOLOGIAN
GEOLOGIC
GEOLOGIES
GEOLOGISE
GEOLOGIST
GEOLOGIZE
GEOLOGY
GEOMANCER
GEOMANCY
GEOMANT
GEOMANTIC
GEOMANTS
GEOMETER
GEOMETERS
GEOMETRIC
GEOMETRID
GEOMETRY
GEOMYOID
GEOPHAGIA
GEOPHAGY
GEOPHILIC
GEOPHONE
GEOPHONES
GEOPHYTE
GEOPHYTES
GEOPHYTIC
GEOPONIC
GEOPONICS
GEOPROBE
GEOPROBES
GEORGETTE
GEORGIC
GEORGICAL
GEORGICS
GEOS
GEOSPHERE
GEOSTATIC
GEOTACTIC
GEOTAXES
GEOTAXIS
GEOTHERM
GEOTHERMS
GEOTROPIC
GERAH
GERAHS
GERANIAL
GERANIALS
GERANIOL
GERANIOLS
GERANIUM
GERANIUMS
GERARDIA
GERARDIAS
GERBE
GERBERA

GERBERAS
GERBES
GERBIL
GERBILLE
GERBILLES
GERBILS
GERE
GERENT
GERENTS
GERENUK
GERENUKS
GERES
GERFALCON
GERIATRIC
GERLE
GERLES
GERM
GERMAIN
GERMAINE
GERMAINES
GERMAINS
GERMAN
GERMANDER
GERMANE
GERMANELY
GERMANIC
GERMANISE
GERMANITE
GERMANIUM
GERMANIZE
GERMANOUS
GERMANS
GERMED
GERMEN
GERMENS
GERMFREE
GERMICIDE
GERMIER
GERMIEST
GERMIN
GERMINA
GERMINAL
GERMINANT
GERMINATE
GERMINESS
GERMING
GERMINS
GERMLIKE
GERMPLASM
GERMPROOF
GERMS
GERMY
GERNE
GERNED
GERNES
GERNING
GERONIMO
GERONTIC

GEROPIGA
GEROPIGAS
GERT
GERTCHA
GERUND
GERUNDIAL
GERUNDIVE
GERUNDS
GESNERIA
GESNERIAD
GESNERIAS
GESSAMINE
GESSE
GESSED
GESSES
GESSING
GESSO
GESSOED
GESSOES
GEST
GESTALT
GESTALTEN
GESTALTS
GESTANT
GESTAPO
GESTAPOS
GESTATE
GESTATED
GESTATES
GESTATING
GESTATION
GESTATIVE
GESTATORY
GESTE
GESTES
GESTIC
GESTICAL
GESTS
GESTURAL
GESTURE
GESTURED
GESTURER
GESTURERS
GESTURES
GESTURING
GET
GETA
GETABLE
GETAS
GETATABLE
GETAWAY
GETAWAYS
GETS
GETTABLE
GETTER
GETTERED
GETTERING
GETTERS

GETTING
GETTINGS
GETUP
GETUPS
GEUM
GEUMS
GEWGAW
GEWGAWED
GEWGAWS
GEY
GEYAN
GEYER
GEYEST
GEYSER
GEYSERITE
GEYSERS
GHARIAL
GHARIALS
GHARRI
GHARRIES
GHARRIS
GHARRY
GHAST
GHASTED
GHASTFUL
GHASTING
GHASTLIER
GHASTLY
GHASTNESS
GHASTS
GHAT
GHATS
GHAUT
GHAUTS
GHAZAL
GHAZALS
GHAZEL
GHAZELS
GHAZI
GHAZIES
GHAZIS
GHEE
GHEES
GHERAO
GHERAOED
GHERAOES
GHERAOING
GHERAOS
GHERKIN
GHERKINS
GHESSE
GHESSED
GHESSES
GHESSING
GHEST
GHETTO
GHETTOED
GHETTOES

GHETTOING
GHETTOISE
GHETTOIZE
GHETTOS
GHI
GHIBLI
GHIBLIS
GHILGAI
GHILGAIS
GHILLIE
GHILLIED
GHILLIES
GHILLYING
GHIS
GHOST
GHOSTED
GHOSTIER
GHOSTIEST
GHOSTING
GHOSTINGS
GHOSTLIER
GHOSTLIKE
GHOSTLY
GHOSTS
GHOSTY
GHOUL
GHOULIE
GHOULIES
GHOULISH
GHOULS
GHYLL
GHYLLS
GI
GIAMBEUX
GIANT
GIANTESS
GIANTHOOD
GIANTISM
GIANTISMS
GIANTLIER
GIANTLIKE
GIANTLY
GIANTRIES
GIANTRY
GIANTS
GIANTSHIP
GIAOUR
GIAOURS
GIARDIA
GIARDIAS
GIB
GIBBED
GIBBER
GIBBERED
GIBBERING
GIBBERISH
GIBBERS
GIBBET

GIBBETED
GIBBETING
GIBBETS
GIBBETTED
GIBBING
GIBBON
GIBBONS
GIBBOSE
GIBBOSITY
GIBBOUS
GIBBOUSLY
GIBBSITE
GIBBSITES
GIBE
GIBED
GIBEL
GIBELS
GIBER
GIBERS
GIBES
GIBING
GIBINGLY
GIBLET
GIBLETS
GIBLI
GIBLIS
GIBS
GIBSON
GIBSONS
GIBUS
GIBUSES
GID
GIDDAP
GIDDAY
GIDDIED
GIDDIER
GIDDIES
GIDDIEST
GIDDILY
GIDDINESS
GIDDUP
GIDDY
GIDDYAP
GIDDYING
GIDDYUP
GIDGEE
GIDGEES
GIDJEE
GIDJEES
GIDS
GIE
GIED
GIEING
GIEN
GIES
GIF
GIFT
GIFTABLE

GIFTABLES
GIFTED
GIFTEDLY
GIFTEE
GIFTEES
GIFTING
GIFTLESS
GIFTS
GIFTSHOP
GIFTSHOPS
GIFTWARE
GIFTWARES
GIFTWRAP
GIFTWRAPS
GIG
GIGA
GIGABIT
GIGABITS
GIGABYTE
GIGABYTES
GIGACYCLE
GIGAFLOP
GIGAFLOPS
GIGAHERTZ
GIGANTEAN
GIGANTIC
GIGANTISM
GIGAS
GIGATON
GIGATONS
GIGAWATT
GIGAWATTS
GIGGED
GIGGING
GIGGIT
GIGGITED
GIGGITING
GIGGITS
GIGGLE
GIGGLED
GIGGLER
GIGGLERS
GIGGLES
GIGGLIER
GIGGLIEST
GIGGLING
GIGGLINGS
GIGGLY
GIGHE
GIGLET
GIGLETS
GIGLOT
GIGLOTS
GIGMAN
GIGMANITY
GIGMEN
GIGOLO
GIGOLOS

GIGOT
GIGOTS
GIGS
GIGUE
GIGUES
GILA
GILAS
GILBERT
GILBERTS
GILCUP
GILCUPS
GILD
GILDED
GILDEN
GILDER
GILDERS
GILDHALL
GILDHALLS
GILDING
GILDINGS
GILDS
GILDSMAN
GILDSMEN
GILET
GILETS
GILGAI
GILGAIS
GILGIE
GILGIES
GILL
GILLAROO
GILLAROOS
GILLED
GILLER
GILLERS
GILLET
GILLETS
GILLFLIRT
GILLIE
GILLIED
GILLIES
GILLING
GILLION
GILLIONS
GILLNET
GILLNETS
GILLS
GILLY
GILLYING
GILLYVOR
GILLYVORS
GILPEY
GILPEYS
GILPIES
GILPY
GILRAVAGE
GILSONITE
GILT

GILTCUP
GILTCUPS
GILTHEAD
GILTHEADS
GILTS
GILTWOOD
GIMBAL
GIMBALED
GIMBALING
GIMBALLED
GIMBALS
GIMCRACK
GIMCRACKS
GIMEL
GIMELS
GIMLET
GIMLETED
GIMLETING
GIMLETS
GIMMAL
GIMMALLED
GIMMALS
GIMME
GIMMER
GIMMERS
GIMMES
GIMMICK
GIMMICKED
GIMMICKRY
GIMMICKS
GIMMICKY
GIMMIE
GIMMIES
GIMMOR
GIMMORS
GIMP
GIMPED
GIMPIER
GIMPIEST
GIMPING
GIMPS
GIMPY
GIN
GING
GINGAL
GINGALL
GINGALLS
GINGALS
GINGE
GINGELEY
GINGELEYS
GINGELI
GINGELIES
GINGELIS
GINGELLI
GINGELLIS
GINGELLY
GINGELY

GINGER
GINGERADE
GINGERED
GINGERING
GINGERLY
GINGEROUS
GINGERS
GINGERY
GINGES
GINGHAM
GINGHAMS
GINGILI
GINGILIS
GINGILLI
GINGILLIS
GINGIVA
GINGIVAE
GINGIVAL
GINGKO
GINGKOES
GINGKOS
GINGLE
GINGLES
GINGLYMI
GINGLYMUS
GINGS
GINHOUSE
GINHOUSES
GINK
GINKGO
GINKGOES
GINKGOS
GINKS
GINN
GINNED
GINNEL
GINNELS
GINNER
GINNERIES
GINNERS
GINNERY
GINNIER
GINNIEST
GINNING
GINNINGS
GINNY
GINORMOUS
GINS
GINSENG
GINSENGS
GINSHOP
GINSHOPS
GINZO
GINZOES
GIO
GIOCOSO
GIOS
GIP

GIPON
GIPONS
GIPPED
GIPPER
GIPPERS
GIPPIES
GIPPING
GIPPO
GIPPOES
GIPPOS
GIPPY
GIPS
GIPSEN
GIPSENS
GIPSIED
GIPSIES
GIPSY
GIPSYDOM
GIPSYDOMS
GIPSYHOOD
GIPSYING
GIPSYISH
GIPSYWORT
GIRAFFE
GIRAFFES
GIRAFFID
GIRAFFINE
GIRAFFISH
GIRAFFOID
GIRANDOLA
GIRANDOLE
GIRASOL
GIRASOLE
GIRASOLES
GIRASOLS
GIRD
GIRDED
GIRDER
GIRDERS
GIRDING
GIRDINGLY
GIRDINGS
GIRDLE
GIRDLED
GIRDLER
GIRDLERS
GIRDLES
GIRDLING
GIRDS
GIRKIN
GIRKINS
GIRL
GIRLHOOD
GIRLHOODS
GIRLIE
GIRLIER
GIRLIES
GIRLIEST

GIRLISH	GITES	GLACIATED	GLAIRIEST
GIRLISHLY	GITS	GLACIATES	GLAIRIN
GIRLOND	GITTARONE	GLACIER	GLAIRING
GIRLONDS	GITTED	GLACIERED	GLAIRINS
GIRLS	GITTERN	GLACIERS	GLAIRS
GIRLY	GITTERNED	GLACIS	GLAIRY
GIRN	GITTERNS	GLACISES	GLAIVE
GIRNED	GITTIN	GLAD	GLAIVED
GIRNEL	GITTING	GLADDED	GLAIVES
GIRNELS	GIUST	GLADDEN	GLAM
GIRNER	GIUSTED	GLADDENED	GLAMOR
GIRNERS	GIUSTING	GLADDENER	GLAMORED
GIRNIE	GIUSTO	GLADDENS	GLAMORING
GIRNIER	GIUSTS	GLADDER	GLAMORISE
GIRNIEST	GIVABLE	GLADDEST	GLAMORIZE
GIRNING	GIVE	GLADDIE	GLAMOROUS
GIRNS	GIVEABLE	GLADDIES	GLAMORS
GIRO	GIVEAWAY	GLADDING	GLAMOUR
GIROLLE	GIVEAWAYS	GLADDON	GLAMOURED
GIROLLES	GIVEBACK	GLADDONS	GLAMOURS
GIRON	GIVEBACKS	GLADE	GLAMS
GIRONIC	GIVED	GLADELIKE	GLANCE
GIRONNY	GIVEN	GLADES	GLANCED
GIRONS	GIVENNESS	GLADFUL	GLANCER
GIROS	GIVENS	GLADIATE	GLANCERS
GIROSOL	GIVER	GLADIATOR	GLANCES
GIROSOLS	GIVERS	GLADIER	GLANCING
GIRR	GIVES	GLADIEST	GLANCINGS
GIRRS	GIVING	GLADIOLA	GLAND
GIRSH	GIVINGS	GLADIOLAR	GLANDERED
GIRSHES	GIZMO	GLADIOLAS	GLANDERS
GIRT	GIZMOLOGY	GLADIOLE	GLANDES
GIRTED	GIZMOS	GLADIOLES	GLANDLESS
GIRTH	GIZZ	GLADIOLI	GLANDLIKE
GIRTHED	GIZZARD	GLADIOLUS	GLANDS
GIRTHING	GIZZARDS	GLADIUS	GLANDULAR
GIRTHLINE	GIZZEN	GLADIUSES	GLANDULE
GIRTHS	GIZZENED	GLADLIER	GLANDULES
GIRTING	GIZZENING	GLADLIEST	GLANS
GIRTLINE	GIZZENS	GLADLY	GLARE
GIRTLINES	GIZZES	GLADNESS	GLAREAL
GIRTS	GJETOST	GLADS	GLARED
GIS	GJETOSTS	GLADSOME	GLARELESS
GISARME	GJU	GLADSOMER	GLAREOUS
GISARMES	GJUS	GLADSTONE	GLARES
GISM	GLABELLA	GLADWRAP	GLARIER
GISMO	GLABELLAE	GLADWRAPS	GLARIEST
GISMOLOGY	GLABELLAR	GLADY	GLARINESS
GISMOS	GLABRATE	GLAIK	GLARING
GISMS	GLABROUS	GLAIKET	GLARINGLY
GIST	GLACE	GLAIKIT	GLARY
GISTS	GLACEED	GLAIKS	GLASNOST
GIT	GLACEING	GLAIR	GLASNOSTS
GITANA	GLACES	GLAIRE	GLASS
GITANAS	GLACIAL	GLAIRED	GLASSED
GITANO	GLACIALLY	GLAIREOUS	GLASSEN
GITANOS	GLACIALS	GLAIRES	GLASSES
GITE	GLACIATE	GLAIRIER	GLASSFUL

GLASSFULS
GLASSIE
GLASSIER
GLASSIES
GLASSIEST
GLASSIFY
GLASSILY
GLASSINE
GLASSINES
GLASSING
GLASSLESS
GLASSLIKE
GLASSMAN
GLASSMEN
GLASSWARE
GLASSWORK
GLASSWORM
GLASSWORT
GLASSY
GLAUCOMA
GLAUCOMAS
GLAUCOUS
GLAUM
GLAUMED
GLAUMING
GLAUMS
GLAUR
GLAURIER
GLAURIEST
GLAURS
GLAURY
GLAZE
GLAZED
GLAZEN
GLAZER
GLAZERS
GLAZES
GLAZIER
GLAZIERS
GLAZIERY
GLAZIEST
GLAZILY
GLAZINESS
GLAZING
GLAZINGS
GLAZY
GLEAM
GLEAMED
GLEAMER
GLEAMERS
GLEAMIER
GLEAMIEST
GLEAMING
GLEAMINGS
GLEAMS
GLEAMY
GLEAN
GLEANABLE

GLEANED
GLEANER
GLEANERS
GLEANING
GLEANINGS
GLEANS
GLEAVE
GLEAVES
GLEBA
GLEBAE
GLEBE
GLEBELESS
GLEBES
GLEBOUS
GLEBY
GLED
GLEDE
GLEDES
GLEDGE
GLEDGED
GLEDGES
GLEDGING
GLEDS
GLEE
GLEED
GLEEDS
GLEEFUL
GLEEFULLY
GLEEING
GLEEK
GLEEKED
GLEEKING
GLEEKS
GLEEMAN
GLEEMEN
GLEENIE
GLEENIES
GLEES
GLEESOME
GLEET
GLEETED
GLEETIER
GLEETIEST
GLEETING
GLEETS
GLEETY
GLEG
GLEGGER
GLEGGEST
GLEGLY
GLEGNESS
GLEI
GLEIS
GLEN
GLENGARRY
GLENLIKE
GLENOID
GLENOIDAL

GLENOIDS
GLENS
GLENT
GLENTED
GLENTING
GLENTS
GLEY
GLEYED
GLEYING
GLEYINGS
GLEYS
GLIA
GLIADIN
GLIADINE
GLIADINES
GLIADINS
GLIAL
GLIAS
GLIB
GLIBBED
GLIBBER
GLIBBERY
GLIBBEST
GLIBBING
GLIBLY
GLIBNESS
GLIBS
GLID
GLIDDER
GLIDDERY
GLIDDEST
GLIDE
GLIDED
GLIDEPATH
GLIDER
GLIDERS
GLIDES
GLIDING
GLIDINGLY
GLIDINGS
GLIFF
GLIFFING
GLIFFINGS
GLIFFS
GLIFT
GLIFTS
GLIKE
GLIKES
GLIM
GLIME
GLIMED
GLIMES
GLIMING
GLIMMER
GLIMMERED
GLIMMERS
GLIMMERY
GLIMPSE

GLIMPSED
GLIMPSER
GLIMPSERS
GLIMPSES
GLIMPSING
GLIMS
GLINT
GLINTED
GLINTIER
GLINTIEST
GLINTING
GLINTS
GLINTY
GLIOMA
GLIOMAS
GLIOMATA
GLIOSES
GLIOSIS
GLISK
GLISKS
GLISSADE
GLISSADED
GLISSADER
GLISSADES
GLISSANDI
GLISSANDO
GLISTEN
GLISTENED
GLISTENS
GLISTER
GLISTERED
GLISTERS
GLIT
GLITCH
GLITCHES
GLITCHIER
GLITCHY
GLITS
GLITTER
GLITTERED
GLITTERS
GLITTERY
GLITZ
GLITZED
GLITZES
GLITZIER
GLITZIEST
GLITZILY
GLITZING
GLITZY
GLOAM
GLOAMING
GLOAMINGS
GLOAMS
GLOAT
GLOATED
GLOATER
GLOATERS

GLOATING
GLOATS
GLOB
GLOBAL
GLOBALISE
GLOBALISM
GLOBALIST
GLOBALIZE
GLOBALLY
GLOBATE
GLOBATED
GLOBBIER
GLOBBIEST
GLOBBY
GLOBE
GLOBED
GLOBEFISH
GLOBELIKE
GLOBES
GLOBESITY
GLOBETROT
GLOBI
GLOBIN
GLOBING
GLOBINS
GLOBOID
GLOBOIDS
GLOBOSE
GLOBOSELY
GLOBOSES
GLOBOSITY
GLOBOUS
GLOBS
GLOBULAR
GLOBULARS
GLOBULE
GLOBULES
GLOBULET
GLOBULETS
GLOBULIN
GLOBULINS
GLOBULITE
GLOBULOUS
GLOBUS
GLOBY
GLOCHID
GLOCHIDIA
GLOCHIDS
GLODE
GLOGG
GLOGGS
GLOIRE
GLOIRES
GLOM
GLOMERA
GLOMERATE
GLOMERULE
GLOMERULI

GLOMMED
GLOMMING
GLOMS
GLOMUS
GLONOIN
GLONOINS
GLOOM
GLOOMED
GLOOMFUL
GLOOMIER
GLOOMIEST
GLOOMILY
GLOOMING
GLOOMINGS
GLOOMLESS
GLOOMS
GLOOMY
GLOOP
GLOOPED
GLOOPIER
GLOOPIEST
GLOOPING
GLOOPS
GLOOPY
GLOP
GLOPPED
GLOPPIER
GLOPPIEST
GLOPPING
GLOPPY
GLOPS
GLORIA
GLORIAS
GLORIED
GLORIES
GLORIFIED
GLORIFIER
GLORIFIES
GLORIFY
GLORIOLE
GLORIOLES
GLORIOSA
GLORIOSAS
GLORIOUS
GLORY
GLORYING
GLOSS
GLOSSA
GLOSSAE
GLOSSAL
GLOSSARY
GLOSSAS
GLOSSATOR
GLOSSED
GLOSSEME
GLOSSEMES
GLOSSER
GLOSSERS

GLOSSES
GLOSSIER
GLOSSIES
GLOSSIEST
GLOSSILY
GLOSSINA
GLOSSINAS
GLOSSING
GLOSSIST
GLOSSISTS
GLOSSITIC
GLOSSITIS
GLOSSLESS
GLOSSY
GLOST
GLOSTS
GLOTTAL
GLOTTIC
GLOTTIDES
GLOTTIS
GLOTTISES
GLOUT
GLOUTED
GLOUTING
GLOUTS
GLOVE
GLOVED
GLOVELESS
GLOVER
GLOVERS
GLOVES
GLOVING
GLOVINGS
GLOW
GLOWED
GLOWER
GLOWERED
GLOWERING
GLOWERS
GLOWFLIES
GLOWFLY
GLOWING
GLOWINGLY
GLOWLAMP
GLOWLAMPS
GLOWS
GLOWSTICK
GLOWWORM
GLOWWORMS
GLOXINIA
GLOXINIAS
GLOZE
GLOZED
GLOZES
GLOZING
GLOZINGS
GLUCAGON
GLUCAGONS

GLUCAN
GLUCANS
GLUCINA
GLUCINAS
GLUCINIC
GLUCINIUM
GLUCINUM
GLUCINUMS
GLUCONATE
GLUCOSE
GLUCOSES
GLUCOSIC
GLUCOSIDE
GLUE
GLUED
GLUEING
GLUELIKE
GLUEPOT
GLUEPOTS
GLUER
GLUERS
GLUES
GLUEY
GLUEYNESS
GLUG
GLUGGABLE
GLUGGED
GLUGGING
GLUGS
GLUHWEIN
GLUHWEINS
GLUIER
GLUIEST
GLUILY
GLUINESS
GLUING
GLUISH
GLUM
GLUME
GLUMELIKE
GLUMELLA
GLUMELLAS
GLUMES
GLUMLY
GLUMMER
GLUMMEST
GLUMNESS
GLUMPIER
GLUMPIEST
GLUMPILY
GLUMPISH
GLUMPS
GLUMPY
GLUMS
GLUNCH
GLUNCHED
GLUNCHES
GLUNCHING

GLUON
GLUONS
GLURGE
GLURGES
GLUT
GLUTAEAL
GLUTAEI
GLUTAEUS
GLUTAMATE
GLUTAMIC
GLUTAMINE
GLUTE
GLUTEAL
GLUTEI
GLUTELIN
GLUTELINS
GLUTEN
GLUTENIN
GLUTENINS
GLUTENOUS
GLUTENS
GLUTES
GLUTEUS
GLUTINOUS
GLUTS
GLUTTED
GLUTTING
GLUTTON
GLUTTONS
GLUTTONY
GLYCAEMIA
GLYCAEMIC
GLYCAN
GLYCANS
GLYCEMIA
GLYCEMIAS
GLYCEMIC
GLYCERIA
GLYCERIAS
GLYCERIC
GLYCERIDE
GLYCERIN
GLYCERINE
GLYCERINS
GLYCEROL
GLYCEROLS
GLYCERYL
GLYCERYLS
GLYCIN
GLYCINE
GLYCINES
GLYCINS
GLYCOCOLL
GLYCOGEN
GLYCOGENS
GLYCOL
GLYCOLIC
GLYCOLLIC

GLYCOLS
GLYCONIC
GLYCONICS
GLYCOSE
GLYCOSES
GLYCOSIDE
GLYCOSYL
GLYCOSYLS
GLYCYL
GLYCYLS
GLYPH
GLYPHIC
GLYPHS
GLYPTAL
GLYPTALS
GLYPTIC
GLYPTICS
GMELINITE
GNAMMA
GNAR
GNARL
GNARLED
GNARLIER
GNARLIEST
GNARLING
GNARLS
GNARLY
GNARR
GNARRED
GNARRING
GNARRS
GNARS
GNASH
GNASHED
GNASHER
GNASHERS
GNASHES
GNASHING
GNAT
GNATHAL
GNATHIC
GNATHION
GNATHIONS
GNATHITE
GNATHITES
GNATHONIC
GNATLIKE
GNATLING
GNATLINGS
GNATS
GNATTIER
GNATTIEST
GNATTY
GNAW
GNAWABLE
GNAWED
GNAWER
GNAWERS

GNAWING
GNAWINGLY
GNAWINGS
GNAWN
GNAWS
GNEISS
GNEISSES
GNEISSIC
GNEISSOID
GNEISSOSE
GNOCCHI
GNOCCHIS
GNOMAE
GNOME
GNOMELIKE
GNOMES
GNOMIC
GNOMICAL
GNOMISH
GNOMIST
GNOMISTS
GNOMON
GNOMONIC
GNOMONICS
GNOMONS
GNOSES
GNOSIS
GNOSTIC
GNOSTICAL
GNOSTICS
GNOW
GNOWS
GNU
GNUS
GO
GOA
GOAD
GOADED
GOADING
GOADLIKE
GOADS
GOADSMAN
GOADSMEN
GOADSTER
GOADSTERS
GOAF
GOAFS
GOAL
GOALBALL
GOALBALLS
GOALED
GOALIE
GOALIES
GOALING
GOALLESS
GOALMOUTH
GOALPOST
GOALPOSTS

GOALS
GOALWARD
GOANNA
GOANNAS
GOARY
GOAS
GOAT
GOATEE
GOATEED
GOATEES
GOATFISH
GOATHERD
GOATHERDS
GOATIER
GOATIEST
GOATISH
GOATISHLY
GOATLIKE
GOATLING
GOATLINGS
GOATS
GOATSKIN
GOATSKINS
GOATWEED
GOATWEEDS
GOATY
GOB
GOBAN
GOBANG
GOBANGS
GOBANS
GOBBED
GOBBELINE
GOBBET
GOBBETS
GOBBI
GOBBIER
GOBBIEST
GOBBING
GOBBLE
GOBBLED
GOBBLER
GOBBLERS
GOBBLES
GOBBLING
GOBBO
GOBBY
GOBIES
GOBIID
GOBIIDS
GOBIOID
GOBIOIDS
GOBLET
GOBLETS
GOBLIN
GOBLINS
GOBO
GOBOES

GOBONEE	GODSONS	GOITRE	GOLFIANAS
GOBONY	GODSOS	GOITRED	GOLFING
GOBOS	GODSPEED	GOITRES	GOLFINGS
GOBS	GODSPEEDS	GOITROGEN	GOLFS
GOBSHITE	GODSQUAD	GOITROUS	GOLGOTHA
GOBSHITES	GODSQUADS	GOLCONDA	GOLGOTHAS
GOBURRA	GODWARD	GOLCONDAS	GOLIARD
GOBURRAS	GODWARDS	GOLD	GOLIARDIC
GOBY	GODWIT	GOLDARN	GOLIARDS
GOD	GODWITS	GOLDARNS	GOLIARDY
GODCHILD	GOE	GOLDBRICK	GOLIAS
GODDAM	GOEL	GOLDBUG	GOLIASED
GODDAMMED	GOELS	GOLDBUGS	GOLIASES
GODDAMN	GOER	GOLDCREST	GOLIASING
GODDAMNED	GOERS	GOLDEN	GOLIATH
GODDAMNS	GOES	GOLDENED	GOLIATHS
GODDAMS	GOETHITE	GOLDENER	GOLLAN
GODDED	GOETHITES	GOLDENEST	GOLLAND
GODDEN	GOETIC	GOLDENEYE	GOLLANDS
GODDENS	GOETIES	GOLDENING	GOLLANS
GODDESS	GOETY	GOLDENLY	GOLLAR
GODDESSES	GOEY	GOLDENROD	GOLLARED
GODDING	GOFER	GOLDENS	GOLLARING
GODET	GOFERS	GOLDER	GOLLARS
GODETIA	GOFF	GOLDEST	GOLLER
GODETIAS	GOFFED	GOLDEYE	GOLLERED
GODETS	GOFFER	GOLDEYES	GOLLERING
GODFATHER	GOFFERED	GOLDFIELD	GOLLERS
GODHEAD	GOFFERING	GOLDFINCH	GOLLIED
GODHEADS	GOFFERS	GOLDFINNY	GOLLIES
GODHOOD	GOFFING	GOLDFISH	GOLLIWOG
GODHOODS	GOFFS	GOLDIER	GOLLIWOGG
GODLESS	GOGGA	GOLDIEST	GOLLIWOGS
GODLESSLY	GOGGAS	GOLDISH	GOLLOP
GODLIER	GOGGLE	GOLDLESS	GOLLOPED
GODLIEST	GOGGLEBOX	GOLDMINER	GOLLOPER
GODLIKE	GOGGLED	GOLDS	GOLLOPERS
GODLILY	GOGGLER	GOLDSINNY	GOLLOPING
GODLINESS	GOGGLERS	GOLDSIZE	GOLLOPS
GODLING	GOGGLES	GOLDSIZES	GOLLY
GODLINGS	GOGGLIER	GOLDSMITH	GOLLYING
GODLY	GOGGLIEST	GOLDSPINK	GOLLYWOG
GODMOTHER	GOGGLING	GOLDSTICK	GOLLYWOGS
GODOWN	GOGGLINGS	GOLDSTONE	GOLOMYNKA
GODOWNS	GOGGLY	GOLDTAIL	GOLOSH
GODPARENT	GOGLET	GOLDTONE	GOLOSHE
GODROON	GOGLETS	GOLDURN	GOLOSHED
GODROONED	GOGO	GOLDURNS	GOLOSHES
GODROONS	GOGOS	GOLDY	GOLOSHING
GODS	GOHONZON	GOLE	GOLOSHOES
GODSEND	GOHONZONS	GOLEM	GOLP
GODSENDS	GOIER	GOLEMS	GOLPE
GODSHIP	GOIEST	GOLES	GOLPES
GODSHIPS	GOING	GOLF	GOLPS
GODSLOT	GOINGS	GOLFED	GOMBEEN
GODSLOTS	GOITER	GOLFER	GOMBEENS
GODSO	GOITERED	GOLFERS	GOMBO
GODSON	GOITERS	GOLFIANA	GOMBOS

GOMBRO
GOMBROON
GOMBROONS
GOMBROS
GOMER
GOMERAL
GOMERALS
GOMEREL
GOMERELS
GOMERIL
GOMERILS
GOMERS
GOMOKU
GOMOKUS
GOMPA
GOMPAS
GOMPHOSES
GOMPHOSIS
GOMUTI
GOMUTIS
GOMUTO
GOMUTOS
GON
GONAD
GONADAL
GONADIAL
GONADIC
GONADS
GONDELAY
GONDELAYS
GONDOLA
GONDOLAS
GONDOLIER
GONE
GONEF
GONEFS
GONENESS
GONER
GONERS
GONFALON
GONFALONS
GONFANON
GONFANONS
GONG
GONGED
GONGING
GONGLIKE
GONGS
GONGSTER
GONGSTERS
GONGYO
GONGYOS
GONIA
GONIATITE
GONIDIA
GONIDIAL
GONIDIC
GONIDIUM

GONIF
GONIFF
GONIFFS
GONIFS
GONION
GONIUM
GONK
GONKS
GONNA
GONOCOCCI
GONOCYTE
GONOCYTES
GONODUCT
GONODUCTS
GONOF
GONOFS
GONOPH
GONOPHORE
GONOPHS
GONOPOD
GONOPODS
GONOPORE
GONOPORES
GONORRHEA
GONOSOME
GONOSOMES
GONS
GONYS
GONYSES
GONZO
GOO
GOOBER
GOOBERS
GOOBIES
GOOBY
GOOD
GOODBY
GOODBYE
GOODBYES
GOODBYS
GOODFACED
GOODIE
GOODIER
GOODIES
GOODIEST
GOODINESS
GOODISH
GOODLIER
GOODLIEST
GOODLY
GOODMAN
GOODMEN
GOODNESS
GOODNIGHT
GOODS
GOODSIRE
GOODSIRES
GOODTIME

GOODWIFE
GOODWILL
GOODWILLS
GOODWIVES
GOODY
GOODYEAR
GOODYEARS
GOOEY
GOOEYNESS
GOOF
GOOFBALL
GOOFBALLS
GOOFED
GOOFIER
GOOFIEST
GOOFILY
GOOFINESS
GOOFING
GOOFS
GOOFY
GOOG
GOOGLE
GOOGLED
GOOGLES
GOOGLIES
GOOGLING
GOOGLY
GOOGOL
GOOGOLS
GOOGS
GOOIER
GOOIEST
GOOILY
GOOK
GOOKS
GOOKY
GOOL
GOOLD
GOOLDS
GOOLEY
GOOLEYS
GOOLIE
GOOLIES
GOOLS
GOOLY
GOOMBAH
GOOMBAHS
GOOMBAY
GOOMBAYS
GOON
GOONDA
GOONDAS
GOONEY
GOONEYS
GOONIE
GOONIER
GOONIES
GOONIEST

GOONS
GOONY
GOOP
GOOPIER
GOOPIEST
GOOPS
GOOPY
GOOR
GOORAL
GOORALS
GOORIE
GOORIES
GOOROO
GOOROOS
GOORS
GOORY
GOOS
GOOSANDER
GOOSE
GOOSED
GOOSEFISH
GOOSEFOOT
GOOSEGOB
GOOSEGOBS
GOOSEGOG
GOOSEGOGS
GOOSEHERD
GOOSENECK
GOOSERIES
GOOSERY
GOOSES
GOOSEY
GOOSEYS
GOOSIER
GOOSIES
GOOSIEST
GOOSINESS
GOOSING
GOOSY
GOPAK
GOPAKS
GOPHER
GOPHERED
GOPHERING
GOPHERS
GOPIK
GOPURA
GOPURAM
GOPURAMS
GOPURAS
GOR
GORA
GORAL
GORALS
GORAMIES
GORAMY
GORAS
GORBELLY

GORBLIMEY
GORBLIMY
GORCOCK
GORCOCKS
GORCROW
GORCROWS
GORDITA
GORDITAS
GORE
GORED
GOREHOUND
GORES
GORGE
GORGEABLE
GORGED
GORGEDLY
GORGEOUS
GORGER
GORGERIN
GORGERINS
GORGERS
GORGES
GORGET
GORGETED
GORGETS
GORGIA
GORGIAS
GORGING
GORGIO
GORGIOS
GORGON
GORGONEIA
GORGONIAN
GORGONISE
GORGONIZE
GORGONS
GORHEN
GORHENS
GORI
GORIER
GORIEST
GORILLA
GORILLAS
GORILLIAN
GORILLINE
GORILLOID
GORILY
GORINESS
GORING
GORINGS
GORIS
GORM
GORMAND
GORMANDS
GORMED
GORMIER
GORMIEST
GORMING

GORMLESS
GORMS
GORMY
GORP
GORPED
GORPING
GORPS
GORSE
GORSEDD
GORSEDDS
GORSES
GORSIER
GORSIEST
GORSOON
GORSOONS
GORSY
GORY
GOS
GOSH
GOSHAWK
GOSHAWKS
GOSHT
GOSHTS
GOSLARITE
GOSLET
GOSLETS
GOSLING
GOSLINGS
GOSPEL
GOSPELER
GOSPELERS
GOSPELISE
GOSPELIZE
GOSPELLED
GOSPELLER
GOSPELLY
GOSPELS
GOSPODA
GOSPODAR
GOSPODARS
GOSPODIN
GOSPORT
GOSPORTS
GOSS
GOSSAMER
GOSSAMERS
GOSSAMERY
GOSSAN
GOSSANS
GOSSE
GOSSED
GOSSES
GOSSIB
GOSSIBS
GOSSING
GOSSIP
GOSSIPED
GOSSIPER

GOSSIPERS
GOSSIPING
GOSSIPPED
GOSSIPPER
GOSSIPRY
GOSSIPS
GOSSIPY
GOSSOON
GOSSOONS
GOSSYPINE
GOSSYPOL
GOSSYPOLS
GOSTER
GOSTERED
GOSTERING
GOSTERS
GOT
GOTCHA
GOTCHAS
GOTH
GOTHIC
GOTHICISE
GOTHICISM
GOTHICIZE
GOTHICS
GOTHITE
GOTHITES
GOTHS
GOTTA
GOTTEN
GOUACHE
GOUACHES
GOUGE
GOUGED
GOUGER
GOUGERE
GOUGERES
GOUGERS
GOUGES
GOUGING
GOUJEERS
GOUJON
GOUJONS
GOUK
GOUKS
GOULASH
GOULASHES
GOURA
GOURAMI
GOURAMIES
GOURAMIS
GOURAS
GOURD
GOURDE
GOURDES
GOURDIER
GOURDIEST
GOURDLIKE

GOURDS
GOURDY
GOURMAND
GOURMANDS
GOURMET
GOURMETS
GOUSTIER
GOUSTIEST
GOUSTROUS
GOUSTY
GOUT
GOUTFLIES
GOUTFLY
GOUTIER
GOUTIEST
GOUTILY
GOUTINESS
GOUTS
GOUTTE
GOUTTES
GOUTWEED
GOUTWEEDS
GOUTWORT
GOUTWORTS
GOUTY
GOV
GOVERN
GOVERNALL
GOVERNED
GOVERNESS
GOVERNING
GOVERNOR
GOVERNORS
GOVERNS
GOVS
GOWAN
GOWANED
GOWANS
GOWANY
GOWD
GOWDER
GOWDEST
GOWDS
GOWDSPINK
GOWF
GOWFED
GOWFER
GOWFERS
GOWFING
GOWFS
GOWK
GOWKS
GOWL
GOWLAN
GOWLAND
GOWLANDS
GOWLANS
GOWLED

GOWLING
GOWLS
GOWN
GOWNBOY
GOWNBOYS
GOWNED
GOWNING
GOWNMAN
GOWNMEN
GOWNS
GOWNSMAN
GOWNSMEN
GOWPEN
GOWPENFUL
GOWPENS
GOX
GOXES
GOY
GOYIM
GOYISCH
GOYISH
GOYS
GOZZAN
GOZZANS
GRAAL
GRAALS
GRAB
GRABBABLE
GRABBED
GRABBER
GRABBERS
GRABBIER
GRABBIEST
GRABBING
GRABBLE
GRABBLED
GRABBLER
GRABBLERS
GRABBLES
GRABBLING
GRABBY
GRABEN
GRABENS
GRABS
GRACE
GRACED
GRACEFUL
GRACELESS
GRACES
GRACILE
GRACILES
GRACILIS
GRACILITY
GRACING
GRACIOSO
GRACIOSOS
GRACIOUS
GRACKLE

GRACKLES
GRAD
GRADABLE
GRADABLES
GRADATE
GRADATED
GRADATES
GRADATIM
GRADATING
GRADATION
GRADATORY
GRADDAN
GRADDANED
GRADDANS
GRADE
GRADED
GRADELESS
GRADELIER
GRADELY
GRADER
GRADERS
GRADES
GRADIENT
GRADIENTS
GRADIN
GRADINE
GRADINES
GRADING
GRADINI
GRADINO
GRADINS
GRADS
GRADUAL
GRADUALLY
GRADUALS
GRADUAND
GRADUANDS
GRADUATE
GRADUATED
GRADUATES
GRADUATOR
GRADUS
GRADUSES
GRAECISE
GRAECISED
GRAECISES
GRAECIZE
GRAECIZED
GRAECIZES
GRAFF
GRAFFED
GRAFFING
GRAFFITI
GRAFFITIS
GRAFFITO
GRAFFS
GRAFT
GRAFTAGE

GRAFTAGES
GRAFTED
GRAFTER
GRAFTERS
GRAFTING
GRAFTINGS
GRAFTS
GRAHAM
GRAHAMS
GRAIL
GRAILE
GRAILES
GRAILS
GRAIN
GRAINAGE
GRAINAGES
GRAINE
GRAINED
GRAINER
GRAINERS
GRAINES
GRAINIER
GRAINIEST
GRAINING
GRAININGS
GRAINLESS
GRAINS
GRAINY
GRAIP
GRAIPS
GRAITH
GRAITHED
GRAITHING
GRAITHLY
GRAITHS
GRAKLE
GRAKLES
GRALLOCH
GRALLOCHS
GRAM
GRAMA
GRAMARIES
GRAMARY
GRAMARYE
GRAMARYES
GRAMAS
GRAMASH
GRAMASHES
GRAME
GRAMERCY
GRAMES
GRAMMA
GRAMMAGE
GRAMMAGES
GRAMMAR
GRAMMARS
GRAMMAS
GRAMMATIC

GRAMME
GRAMMES
GRAMOCHE
GRAMOCHES
GRAMP
GRAMPA
GRAMPAS
GRAMPS
GRAMPUS
GRAMPUSES
GRAMS
GRAN
GRANA
GRANARIES
GRANARY
GRAND
GRANDAD
GRANDADDY
GRANDADS
GRANDAM
GRANDAME
GRANDAMES
GRANDAMS
GRANDAUNT
GRANDBABY
GRANDDAD
GRANDDADS
GRANDDAM
GRANDDAMS
GRANDE
GRANDEE
GRANDEES
GRANDER
GRANDEST
GRANDEUR
GRANDEURS
GRANDIOSE
GRANDIOSO
GRANDKID
GRANDKIDS
GRANDLY
GRANDMA
GRANDMAMA
GRANDMAS
GRANDNESS
GRANDPA
GRANDPAPA
GRANDPAS
GRANDS
GRANDSIR
GRANDSIRE
GRANDSIRS
GRANDSON
GRANDSONS
GRANFER
GRANFERS
GRANGE
GRANGER

GRANGERS
GRANGES
GRANITA
GRANITAS
GRANITE
GRANITES
GRANITIC
GRANITISE
GRANITITE
GRANITIZE
GRANITOID
GRANIVORE
GRANNAM
GRANNAMS
GRANNIE
GRANNIED
GRANNIES
GRANNOM
GRANNOMS
GRANNY
GRANNYING
GRANNYISH
GRANOLA
GRANOLAS
GRANOLITH
GRANS
GRANT
GRANTABLE
GRANTED
GRANTEE
GRANTEES
GRANTER
GRANTERS
GRANTING
GRANTOR
GRANTORS
GRANTS
GRANTSMAN
GRANTSMEN
GRANULAR
GRANULARY
GRANULATE
GRANULE
GRANULES
GRANULITE
GRANULOMA
GRANULOSE
GRANULOUS
GRANUM
GRAPE
GRAPED
GRAPELESS
GRAPELIKE
GRAPERIES
GRAPERY
GRAPES
GRAPESEED
GRAPESHOT

GRAPETREE
GRAPEVINE
GRAPEY
GRAPH
GRAPHED
GRAPHEME
GRAPHEMES
GRAPHEMIC
GRAPHIC
GRAPHICAL
GRAPHICLY
GRAPHICS
GRAPHING
GRAPHITE
GRAPHITES
GRAPHITIC
GRAPHIUM
GRAPHIUMS
GRAPHS
GRAPIER
GRAPIEST
GRAPINESS
GRAPING
GRAPLE
GRAPLES
GRAPLIN
GRAPLINE
GRAPLINES
GRAPLINS
GRAPNEL
GRAPNELS
GRAPPA
GRAPPAS
GRAPPLE
GRAPPLED
GRAPPLER
GRAPPLERS
GRAPPLES
GRAPPLING
GRAPY
GRASP
GRASPABLE
GRASPED
GRASPER
GRASPERS
GRASPING
GRASPLESS
GRASPS
GRASS
GRASSED
GRASSER
GRASSERS
GRASSES
GRASSHOOK
GRASSIER
GRASSIEST
GRASSILY
GRASSING

GRASSINGS
GRASSLAND
GRASSLESS
GRASSLIKE
GRASSPLOT
GRASSQUIT
GRASSROOT
GRASSUM
GRASSUMS
GRASSY
GRASTE
GRAT
GRATE
GRATED
GRATEFUL
GRATELESS
GRATER
GRATERS
GRATES
GRATICULE
GRATIFIED
GRATIFIER
GRATIFIES
GRATIFY
GRATIN
GRATINATE
GRATINE
GRATINEE
GRATINEED
GRATINEES
GRATING
GRATINGLY
GRATINGS
GRATINS
GRATIS
GRATITUDE
GRATTOIR
GRATTOIRS
GRATUITY
GRATULANT
GRATULATE
GRAUNCH
GRAUNCHED
GRAUNCHER
GRAUNCHES
GRAUPEL
GRAUPELS
GRAV
GRAVADLAX
GRAVAMEN
GRAVAMENS
GRAVAMINA
GRAVE
GRAVED
GRAVEL
GRAVELED
GRAVELESS
GRAVELIKE

GRAVELING
GRAVELISH
GRAVELLED
GRAVELLY
GRAVELS
GRAVELY
GRAVEN
GRAVENESS
GRAVER
GRAVERS
GRAVES
GRAVESIDE
GRAVESITE
GRAVEST
GRAVEWARD
GRAVEYARD
GRAVID
GRAVIDA
GRAVIDAE
GRAVIDAS
GRAVIDITY
GRAVIDLY
GRAVIES
GRAVING
GRAVINGS
GRAVIS
GRAVITAS
GRAVITATE
GRAVITIES
GRAVITINO
GRAVITON
GRAVITONS
GRAVITY
GRAVLAKS
GRAVLAX
GRAVLAXES
GRAVS
GRAVURE
GRAVURES
GRAVY
GRAY
GRAYBACK
GRAYBACKS
GRAYBEARD
GRAYED
GRAYER
GRAYEST
GRAYFISH
GRAYFLIES
GRAYFLY
GRAYHOUND
GRAYING
GRAYISH
GRAYLAG
GRAYLAGS
GRAYLE
GRAYLES
GRAYLING

GRAYLINGS
GRAYLY
GRAYMAIL
GRAYMAILS
GRAYNESS
GRAYOUT
GRAYOUTS
GRAYS
GRAYSCALE
GRAYWACKE
GRAYWATER
GRAZABLE
GRAZE
GRAZEABLE
GRAZED
GRAZER
GRAZERS
GRAZES
GRAZIER
GRAZIERS
GRAZING
GRAZINGLY
GRAZINGS
GRAZIOSO
GREASE
GREASED
GREASER
GREASERS
GREASES
GREASIER
GREASIES
GREASIEST
GREASILY
GREASING
GREASY
GREAT
GREATCOAT
GREATEN
GREATENED
GREATENS
GREATER
GREATEST
GREATESTS
GREATLY
GREATNESS
GREATS
GREAVE
GREAVED
GREAVES
GREAVING
GREBE
GREBES
GRECE
GRECES
GRECIAN
GRECIANS
GRECISE
GRECISED

GRECISES
GRECISING
GRECIZE
GRECIZED
GRECIZES
GRECIZING
GRECQUE
GRECQUES
GREE
GREEBO
GREEBOES
GREECE
GREECES
GREED
GREEDIER
GREEDIEST
GREEDILY
GREEDLESS
GREEDS
GREEDSOME
GREEDY
GREEGREE
GREEGREES
GREEING
GREEK
GREEKED
GREEKING
GREEKINGS
GREEN
GREENBACK
GREENBELT
GREENBONE
GREENBUG
GREENBUGS
GREENED
GREENER
GREENERS
GREENERY
GREENEST
GREENFLY
GREENGAGE
GREENHAND
GREENHEAD
GREENHORN
GREENIE
GREENIER
GREENIES
GREENIEST
GREENING
GREENINGS
GREENISH
GREENLET
GREENLETS
GREENLING
GREENLIT
GREENLY
GREENMAIL
GREENNESS

GREENROOM
GREENS
GREENSAND
GREENSICK
GREENSOME
GREENTH
GREENTHS
GREENWASH
GREENWAY
GREENWAYS
GREENWEED
GREENWING
GREENWOOD
GREENY
GREES
GREESE
GREESES
GREESING
GREESINGS
GREET
GREETE
GREETED
GREETER
GREETERS
GREETES
GREETING
GREETINGS
GREETS
GREFFIER
GREFFIERS
GREGALE
GREGALES
GREGARIAN
GREGARINE
GREGATIM
GREGE
GREGO
GREGOS
GREIGE
GREIGES
GREIN
GREINED
GREINING
GREINS
GREISEN
GREISENS
GREISLY
GREMIAL
GREMIALS
GREMLIN
GREMLINS
GREMMIE
GREMMIES
GREMMY
GREMOLATA
GREN
GRENADE
GRENADES

GRENADIER
GRENADINE
GRENNED
GRENNING
GRENS
GRENZ
GRESE
GRESES
GRESSING
GRESSINGS
GREVE
GREVES
GREVILLEA
GREW
GREWED
GREWHOUND
GREWING
GREWS
GREWSOME
GREWSOMER
GREX
GREXES
GREY
GREYBACK
GREYBACKS
GREYBEARD
GREYED
GREYER
GREYEST
GREYHEN
GREYHENS
GREYHOUND
GREYING
GREYINGS
GREYISH
GREYLAG
GREYLAGS
GREYLIST
GREYLISTS
GREYLY
GREYNESS
GREYS
GREYSTONE
GREYWACKE
GRIBBLE
GRIBBLES
GRICE
GRICED
GRICER
GRICERS
GRICES
GRICING
GRICINGS
GRID
GRIDDED
GRIDDER
GRIDDERS
GRIDDLE

GRIDDLED
GRIDDLES
GRIDDLING
GRIDE
GRIDED
GRIDELIN
GRIDELINS
GRIDES
GRIDING
GRIDIRON
GRIDIRONS
GRIDLOCK
GRIDLOCKS
GRIDS
GRIECE
GRIECED
GRIECES
GRIEF
GRIEFER
GRIEFERS
GRIEFFUL
GRIEFLESS
GRIEFS
GRIESIE
GRIESLY
GRIESY
GRIEVANCE
GRIEVANT
GRIEVANTS
GRIEVE
GRIEVED
GRIEVER
GRIEVERS
GRIEVES
GRIEVING
GRIEVINGS
GRIEVOUS
GRIFF
GRIFFE
GRIFFES
GRIFFIN
GRIFFINS
GRIFFON
GRIFFONS
GRIFFS
GRIFT
GRIFTED
GRIFTER
GRIFTERS
GRIFTING
GRIFTS
GRIG
GRIGGED
GRIGGING
GRIGRI
GRIGRIS
GRIGS
GRIKE

GRIKES
GRILL
GRILLADE
GRILLADES
GRILLAGE
GRILLAGES
GRILLE
GRILLED
GRILLER
GRILLERS
GRILLERY
GRILLES
GRILLING
GRILLINGS
GRILLION
GRILLIONS
GRILLROOM
GRILLS
GRILLWORK
GRILSE
GRILSES
GRIM
GRIMACE
GRIMACED
GRIMACER
GRIMACERS
GRIMACES
GRIMACING
GRIMALKIN
GRIME
GRIMED
GRIMES
GRIMIER
GRIMIEST
GRIMILY
GRIMINESS
GRIMING
GRIMLY
GRIMMER
GRIMMEST
GRIMNESS
GRIMOIRE
GRIMOIRES
GRIMY
GRIN
GRINCH
GRINCHES
GRIND
GRINDED
GRINDELIA
GRINDER
GRINDERS
GRINDERY
GRINDING
GRINDINGS
GRINDS
GRINGA
GRINGAS

GRINGO
GRINGOS
GRINNED
GRINNER
GRINNERS
GRINNING
GRINNINGS
GRINS
GRIOT
GRIOTS
GRIP
GRIPE
GRIPED
GRIPER
GRIPERS
GRIPES
GRIPEY
GRIPIER
GRIPIEST
GRIPING
GRIPINGLY
GRIPLE
GRIPMAN
GRIPMEN
GRIPPE
GRIPPED
GRIPPER
GRIPPERS
GRIPPES
GRIPPIER
GRIPPIEST
GRIPPING
GRIPPLE
GRIPPLES
GRIPPY
GRIPS
GRIPSACK
GRIPSACKS
GRIPT
GRIPTAPE
GRIPTAPES
GRIPY
GRIS
GRISAILLE
GRISE
GRISED
GRISELY
GRISEOUS
GRISES
GRISETTE
GRISETTES
GRISGRIS
GRISING
GRISKIN
GRISKINS
GRISLED
GRISLIER
GRISLIES

GRISLIEST
GRISLY
GRISON
GRISONS
GRISSINI
GRIST
GRISTER
GRISTERS
GRISTLE
GRISTLES
GRISTLIER
GRISTLY
GRISTMILL
GRISTS
GRISY
GRIT
GRITH
GRITHS
GRITLESS
GRITS
GRITSTONE
GRITTED
GRITTER
GRITTERS
GRITTEST
GRITTIER
GRITTIEST
GRITTILY
GRITTING
GRITTY
GRIVATION
GRIVET
GRIVETS
GRIZE
GRIZES
GRIZZLE
GRIZZLED
GRIZZLER
GRIZZLERS
GRIZZLES
GRIZZLIER
GRIZZLIES
GRIZZLING
GRIZZLY
GROAN
GROANED
GROANER
GROANERS
GROANFUL
GROANING
GROANINGS
GROANS
GROAT
GROATS
GROCER
GROCERIES
GROCERS
GROCERY

GROCKLE
GROCKLES
GRODIER
GRODIEST
GRODY
GROG
GROGGED
GROGGERY
GROGGIER
GROGGIEST
GROGGILY
GROGGING
GROGGY
GROGRAM
GROGRAMS
GROGS
GROGSHOP
GROGSHOPS
GROIN
GROINED
GROINING
GROININGS
GROINS
GROK
GROKKED
GROKKING
GROKS
GROMA
GROMAS
GROMET
GROMETS
GROMMET
GROMMETED
GROMMETS
GROMWELL
GROMWELLS
GRONE
GRONED
GRONEFULL
GRONES
GRONING
GROOF
GROOFS
GROOLIER
GROOLIEST
GROOLY
GROOM
GROOMED
GROOMER
GROOMERS
GROOMING
GROOMINGS
GROOMS
GROOMSMAN
GROOMSMEN
GROOVE
GROOVED
GROOVER

GROOVERS
GROOVES
GROOVIER
GROOVIEST
GROOVING
GROOVY
GROPE
GROPED
GROPER
GROPERS
GROPES
GROPING
GROPINGLY
GROSBEAK
GROSBEAKS
GROSCHEN
GROSCHENS
GROSER
GROSERS
GROSERT
GROSERTS
GROSET
GROSETS
GROSGRAIN
GROSS
GROSSART
GROSSARTS
GROSSED
GROSSER
GROSSERS
GROSSES
GROSSEST
GROSSING
GROSSLY
GROSSNESS
GROSSULAR
GROSZ
GROSZE
GROSZY
GROT
GROTESQUE
GROTS
GROTTIER
GROTTIEST
GROTTO
GROTTOED
GROTTOES
GROTTOS
GROTTY
GROUCH
GROUCHED
GROUCHES
GROUCHIER
GROUCHILY
GROUCHING
GROUCHY
GROUF
GROUFS

GROUGH
GROUGHS
GROUND
GROUNDAGE
GROUNDED
GROUNDEN
GROUNDER
GROUNDERS
GROUNDHOG
GROUNDING
GROUNDMAN
GROUNDMEN
GROUNDNUT
GROUNDOUT
GROUNDS
GROUNDSEL
GROUP
GROUPABLE
GROUPAGE
GROUPAGES
GROUPED
GROUPER
GROUPERS
GROUPIE
GROUPIES
GROUPING
GROUPINGS
GROUPIST
GROUPISTS
GROUPLET
GROUPLETS
GROUPOID
GROUPOIDS
GROUPS
GROUPWARE
GROUPY
GROUSE
GROUSED
GROUSER
GROUSERS
GROUSES
GROUSEST
GROUSING
GROUT
GROUTED
GROUTER
GROUTERS
GROUTIER
GROUTIEST
GROUTING
GROUTINGS
GROUTS
GROUTY
GROVE
GROVED
GROVEL
GROVELED
GROVELER

GROVELERS
GROVELESS
GROVELING
GROVELLED
GROVELLER
GROVELS
GROVES
GROVET
GROVETS
GROW
GROWABLE
GROWER
GROWERS
GROWING
GROWINGLY
GROWINGS
GROWL
GROWLED
GROWLER
GROWLERS
GROWLERY
GROWLIER
GROWLIEST
GROWLING
GROWLINGS
GROWLS
GROWLY
GROWN
GROWNUP
GROWNUPS
GROWS
GROWTH
GROWTHIER
GROWTHIST
GROWTHS
GROWTHY
GROYNE
GROYNES
GROZING
GRUB
GRUBBED
GRUBBER
GRUBBERS
GRUBBIER
GRUBBIEST
GRUBBILY
GRUBBING
GRUBBLE
GRUBBLED
GRUBBLES
GRUBBLING
GRUBBY
GRUBS
GRUBSTAKE
GRUBWORM
GRUBWORMS
GRUDGE
GRUDGED

GRUDGEFUL
GRUDGER
GRUDGERS
GRUDGES
GRUDGING
GRUDGINGS
GRUE
GRUED
GRUEING
GRUEL
GRUELED
GRUELER
GRUELERS
GRUELING
GRUELINGS
GRUELLED
GRUELLER
GRUELLERS
GRUELLING
GRUELS
GRUES
GRUESOME
GRUESOMER
GRUFE
GRUFES
GRUFF
GRUFFED
GRUFFER
GRUFFEST
GRUFFIER
GRUFFIEST
GRUFFILY
GRUFFING
GRUFFISH
GRUFFLY
GRUFFNESS
GRUFFS
GRUFFY
GRUFTED
GRUGRU
GRUGRUS
GRUIFORM
GRUING
GRUM
GRUMBLE
GRUMBLED
GRUMBLER
GRUMBLERS
GRUMBLES
GRUMBLIER
GRUMBLING
GRUMBLY
GRUME
GRUMES
GRUMLY
GRUMMER
GRUMMEST
GRUMMET

GRUMMETED
GRUMMETS
GRUMNESS
GRUMOSE
GRUMOUS
GRUMP
GRUMPED
GRUMPH
GRUMPHED
GRUMPHIE
GRUMPHIES
GRUMPHING
GRUMPHS
GRUMPHY
GRUMPIER
GRUMPIEST
GRUMPILY
GRUMPING
GRUMPISH
GRUMPS
GRUMPY
GRUNDIES
GRUNGE
GRUNGER
GRUNGERS
GRUNGES
GRUNGIER
GRUNGIEST
GRUNGY
GRUNION
GRUNIONS
GRUNT
GRUNTED
GRUNTER
GRUNTERS
GRUNTING
GRUNTINGS
GRUNTLE
GRUNTLED
GRUNTLES
GRUNTLING
GRUNTS
GRUPPETTI
GRUPPETTO
GRUSHIE
GRUTCH
GRUTCHED
GRUTCHES
GRUTCHING
GRUTTEN
GRUYERE
GRUYERES
GRYCE
GRYCES
GRYDE
GRYDED
GRYDES
GRYDING

GRYESY
GRYFON
GRYFONS
GRYKE
GRYKES
GRYPE
GRYPES
GRYPHON
GRYPHONS
GRYPT
GRYSBOK
GRYSBOKS
GRYSELY
GRYSIE
GU
GUACAMOLE
GUACHARO
GUACHAROS
GUACO
GUACOS
GUAIAC
GUAIACOL
GUAIACOLS
GUAIACS
GUAIACUM
GUAIACUMS
GUAIOCUM
GUAIOCUMS
GUAN
GUANA
GUANABANA
GUANACO
GUANACOS
GUANAS
GUANASE
GUANASES
GUANAY
GUANAYS
GUANAZOLO
GUANGO
GUANGOS
GUANIDIN
GUANIDINE
GUANIDINS
GUANIN
GUANINE
GUANINES
GUANINS
GUANO
GUANOS
GUANOSINE
GUANS
GUANXI
GUANXIS
GUANYLIC
GUAR
GUARANA
GUARANAS

GUARANI
GUARANIES
GUARANIS
GUARANTEE
GUARANTOR
GUARANTY
GUARD
GUARDABLE
GUARDAGE
GUARDAGES
GUARDANT
GUARDANTS
GUARDDOG
GUARDDOGS
GUARDED
GUARDEDLY
GUARDEE
GUARDEES
GUARDER
GUARDERS
GUARDIAN
GUARDIANS
GUARDING
GUARDLESS
GUARDLIKE
GUARDRAIL
GUARDROOM
GUARDS
GUARDSHIP
GUARDSMAN
GUARDSMEN
GUARISH
GUARISHED
GUARISHES
GUARS
GUAVA
GUAVAS
GUAYABERA
GUAYULE
GUAYULES
GUB
GUBBAH
GUBBAHS
GUBBINS
GUBBINSES
GUBERNIYA
GUBS
GUCK
GUCKIER
GUCKIEST
GUCKS
GUCKY
GUDDLE
GUDDLED
GUDDLES
GUDDLING
GUDE
GUDEMAN

GUDEMEN
GUDES
GUDESIRE
GUDESIRES
GUDEWIFE
GUDEWIVES
GUDGEON
GUDGEONED
GUDGEONS
GUE
GUENON
GUENONS
GUERDON
GUERDONED
GUERDONER
GUERDONS
GUEREZA
GUEREZAS
GUERIDON
GUERIDONS
GUERILLA
GUERILLAS
GUERITE
GUERITES
GUERNSEY
GUERNSEYS
GUERRILLA
GUES
GUESS
GUESSABLE
GUESSED
GUESSER
GUESSERS
GUESSES
GUESSING
GUESSINGS
GUESSWORK
GUEST
GUESTED
GUESTEN
GUESTENED
GUESTENS
GUESTING
GUESTS
GUESTWISE
GUFF
GUFFAW
GUFFAWED
GUFFAWING
GUFFAWS
GUFFIE
GUFFIES
GUFFS
GUGA
GUGAS
GUGGLE
GUGGLED
GUGGLES

GUGGLING
GUGLET
GUGLETS
GUICHET
GUICHETS
GUID
GUIDABLE
GUIDAGE
GUIDAGES
GUIDANCE
GUIDANCES
GUIDE
GUIDEBOOK
GUIDED
GUIDELESS
GUIDELINE
GUIDEPOST
GUIDER
GUIDERS
GUIDES
GUIDESHIP
GUIDEWAY
GUIDEWAYS
GUIDEWORD
GUIDING
GUIDINGS
GUIDON
GUIDONS
GUIDS
GUILD
GUILDER
GUILDERS
GUILDHALL
GUILDRIES
GUILDRY
GUILDS
GUILDSHIP
GUILDSMAN
GUILDSMEN
GUILE
GUILED
GUILEFUL
GUILELESS
GUILER
GUILERS
GUILES
GUILING
GUILLEMET
GUILLEMOT
GUILLOCHE
GUILT
GUILTIER
GUILTIEST
GUILTILY
GUILTLESS
GUILTS
GUILTY
GUIMBARD

GUIMBARDS
GUIMP
GUIMPE
GUIMPED
GUIMPES
GUIMPING
GUIMPS
GUINEA
GUINEAS
GUIPURE
GUIPURES
GUIRO
GUIROS
GUISARD
GUISARDS
GUISE
GUISED
GUISER
GUISERS
GUISES
GUISING
GUISINGS
GUITAR
GUITARIST
GUITARS
GUITGUIT
GUITGUITS
GUIZER
GUIZERS
GUL
GULA
GULAG
GULAGS
GULAR
GULAS
GULCH
GULCHED
GULCHES
GULCHING
GULDEN
GULDENS
GULE
GULES
GULF
GULFED
GULFIER
GULFIEST
GULFING
GULFLIKE
GULFS
GULFWEED
GULFWEEDS
GULFY
GULL
GULLABLE
GULLABLY
GULLED
GULLER

GULLERIES
GULLERS
GULLERY
GULLET
GULLETS
GULLEY
GULLEYED
GULLEYING
GULLEYS
GULLIBLE
GULLIBLY
GULLIED
GULLIES
GULLING
GULLISH
GULLS
GULLWING
GULLY
GULLYING
GULOSITY
GULP
GULPED
GULPER
GULPERS
GULPH
GULPHS
GULPIER
GULPIEST
GULPING
GULPINGLY
GULPS
GULPY
GULS
GULY
GUM
GUMBALL
GUMBALLS
GUMBO
GUMBOIL
GUMBOILS
GUMBOOT
GUMBOOTS
GUMBOS
GUMBOTIL
GUMBOTILS
GUMDROP
GUMDROPS
GUMLANDS
GUMLESS
GUMLIKE
GUMLINE
GUMLINES
GUMMA
GUMMAS
GUMMATA
GUMMATOUS
GUMMED
GUMMER

GUMMERS
GUMMIER
GUMMIES
GUMMIEST
GUMMILY
GUMMINESS
GUMMING
GUMMINGS
GUMMITE
GUMMITES
GUMMOSE
GUMMOSES
GUMMOSIS
GUMMOSITY
GUMMOUS
GUMMY
GUMNUT
GUMNUTS
GUMP
GUMPED
GUMPHION
GUMPHIONS
GUMPING
GUMPS
GUMPTION
GUMPTIONS
GUMPTIOUS
GUMS
GUMSHIELD
GUMSHOE
GUMSHOED
GUMSHOES
GUMSUCKER
GUMTREE
GUMTREES
GUMWEED
GUMWEEDS
GUMWOOD
GUMWOODS
GUN
GUNBOAT
GUNBOATS
GUNCOTTON
GUNDIES
GUNDOG
GUNDOGS
GUNDY
GUNFIGHT
GUNFIGHTS
GUNFIRE
GUNFIRES
GUNFLINT
GUNFLINTS
GUNFOUGHT
GUNG
GUNGE
GUNGED
GUNGES

GUNGIER
GUNGIEST
GUNGING
GUNGY
GUNHOUSE
GUNHOUSES
GUNITE
GUNITES
GUNK
GUNKHOLE
GUNKHOLED
GUNKHOLES
GUNKIER
GUNKIEST
GUNKS
GUNKY
GUNLAYER
GUNLAYERS
GUNLESS
GUNLOCK
GUNLOCKS
GUNMAKER
GUNMAKERS
GUNMAN
GUNMEN
GUNMETAL
GUNMETALS
GUNNAGE
GUNNAGES
GUNNED
GUNNEL
GUNNELS
GUNNEN
GUNNER
GUNNERA
GUNNERAS
GUNNERIES
GUNNERS
GUNNERY
GUNNIES
GUNNING
GUNNINGS
GUNNY
GUNNYBAG
GUNNYBAGS
GUNNYSACK
GUNPAPER
GUNPAPERS
GUNPLAY
GUNPLAYS
GUNPOINT
GUNPOINTS
GUNPORT
GUNPORTS
GUNPOWDER
GUNROOM
GUNROOMS
GUNRUNNER

GUNS
GUNSEL
GUNSELS
GUNSHIP
GUNSHIPS
GUNSHOT
GUNSHOTS
GUNSMITH
GUNSMITHS
GUNSTICK
GUNSTICKS
GUNSTOCK
GUNSTOCKS
GUNSTONE
GUNSTONES
GUNTER
GUNTERS
GUNWALE
GUNWALES
GUNYAH
GUNYAHS
GUP
GUPPIES
GUPPY
GUPS
GUR
GURAMI
GURAMIS
GURDWARA
GURDWARAS
GURGE
GURGED
GURGES
GURGING
GURGLE
GURGLED
GURGLES
GURGLET
GURGLETS
GURGLING
GURGOYLE
GURGOYLES
GURJUN
GURJUNS
GURL
GURLED
GURLET
GURLETS
GURLIER
GURLIEST
GURLING
GURLS
GURLY
GURN
GURNARD
GURNARDS
GURNED
GURNET

GURNETS
GURNEY
GURNEYS
GURNING
GURNS
GURRAH
GURRAHS
GURRIER
GURRIERS
GURRIES
GURRY
GURS
GURSH
GURSHES
GURU
GURUDOM
GURUDOMS
GURUISM
GURUISMS
GURUS
GURUSHIP
GURUSHIPS
GUS
GUSH
GUSHED
GUSHER
GUSHERS
GUSHES
GUSHIER
GUSHIEST
GUSHILY
GUSHINESS
GUSHING
GUSHINGLY
GUSHY
GUSLA
GUSLAR
GUSLARS
GUSLAS
GUSLE
GUSLES
GUSLI
GUSLIS
GUSSET
GUSSETED
GUSSETING
GUSSETS
GUSSIE
GUSSIED
GUSSIES
GUSSY
GUSSYING
GUST
GUSTABLE
GUSTABLES
GUSTATION
GUSTATIVE
GUSTATORY

GUSTED
GUSTFUL
GUSTIE
GUSTIER
GUSTIEST
GUSTILY
GUSTINESS
GUSTING
GUSTLESS
GUSTO
GUSTOES
GUSTOS
GUSTS
GUSTY
GUT
GUTBUCKET
GUTCHER
GUTCHERS
GUTFUL
GUTFULS
GUTLESS
GUTLIKE
GUTROT
GUTROTS
GUTS
GUTSED
GUTSER
GUTSERS
GUTSES
GUTSFUL
GUTSFULS
GUTSIER
GUTSIEST
GUTSILY
GUTSINESS
GUTSING
GUTSY
GUTTA
GUTTAE
GUTTAS
GUTTATE
GUTTATED
GUTTATES
GUTTATING
GUTTATION
GUTTED
GUTTER
GUTTERED
GUTTERING
GUTTERS
GUTTERY
GUTTIER
GUTTIES
GUTTIEST
GUTTING
GUTTLE
GUTTLED
GUTTLER

GUTTLERS
GUTTLES
GUTTLING
GUTTURAL
GUTTURALS
GUTTY
GUTZER
GUTZERS
GUV
GUVS
GUY
GUYED
GUYING
GUYLE
GUYLED
GUYLER
GUYLERS
GUYLES
GUYLINE
GUYLINES
GUYLING
GUYOT
GUYOTS
GUYS
GUYSE
GUYSES
GUZZLE
GUZZLED
GUZZLER
GUZZLERS
GUZZLES
GUZZLING
GWEDUC
GWEDUCK
GWEDUCKS
GWEDUCS
GWINE
GWINIAD
GWINIADS
GWYNIAD
GWYNIADS
GYAL
GYALS
GYBE
GYBED
GYBES
GYBING
GYELD
GYELDS
GYLDEN
GYM
GYMBAL
GYMBALS
GYMKHANA
GYMKHANAS
GYMMAL
GYMMALS
GYMNASIA

GYMNASIAL
GYMNASIC
GYMNASIEN
GYMNASIUM
GYMNAST
GYMNASTIC
GYMNASTS
GYMNIC
GYMNOSOPH
GYMP
GYMPED
GYMPIE
GYMPIES
GYMPING
GYMPS
GYMS
GYMSLIP
GYMSLIPS
GYNAE
GYNAECEA
GYNAECEUM
GYNAECIA
GYNAECIUM
GYNAECOID
GYNAES
GYNANDRY
GYNARCHIC
GYNARCHY
GYNECIA
GYNECIC
GYNECIUM
GYNECOID
GYNIATRY
GYNIE
GYNIES
GYNNEY
GYNNEYS
GYNNIES
GYNNY
GYNOCRACY
GYNOECIA
GYNOECIUM
GYNOPHOBE
GYNOPHORE
GYNY
GYOZA
GYOZAS
GYP
GYPLURE
GYPLURES
GYPPED
GYPPER
GYPPERS
GYPPIE
GYPPIES
GYPPING
GYPPO
GYPPOS

GYPPY
GYPS
GYPSEIAN
GYPSEOUS
GYPSIED
GYPSIES
GYPSTER
GYPSTERS
GYPSUM
GYPSUMS
GYPSY
GYPSYDOM
GYPSYDOMS
GYPSYHOOD
GYPSYING
GYPSYISH
GYPSYISM
GYPSYISMS
GYPSYWORT
GYRAL
GYRALLY
GYRANT
GYRASE
GYRASES
GYRATE
GYRATED
GYRATES
GYRATING
GYRATION
GYRATIONS
GYRATOR
GYRATORS
GYRATORY
GYRE
GYRED
GYRENE
GYRENES
GYRES
GYRFALCON
GYRI
GYRING
GYRO
GYROCAR
GYROCARS
GYRODYNE
GYRODYNES
GYROIDAL
GYROLITE
GYROLITES
GYROMANCY
GYRON
GYRONIC
GYRONNY
GYRONS
GYROPILOT
GYROPLANE
GYROS
GYROSCOPE

GYROSE
GYROSTAT
GYROSTATS
GYROUS
GYROVAGUE
GYRUS
GYRUSES
GYTE
GYTES
GYTRASH
GYTRASHES
GYTTJA
GYTTJAS
GYVE
GYVED
GYVES
GYVING

H

HA	HACKABLE	HADDOCK	HAES
HAAF	HACKAMORE	HADDOCKS	HAET
HAAFS	HACKBERRY	HADE	HAETS
HAANEPOOT	HACKBOLT	HADED	HAFF
HAAR	HACKBOLTS	HADEDAH	HAFFET
HAARS	HACKBUT	HADEDAHS	HAFFETS
HABANERA	HACKBUTS	HADES	HAFFIT
HABANERAS	HACKED	HADING	HAFFITS
HABANERO	HACKEE	HADITH	HAFFLIN
HABANEROS	HACKEES	HADITHS	HAFFLINS
HABDABS	HACKER	HADJ	HAFFS
HABDALAH	HACKERIES	HADJEE	HAFIZ
HABDALAHS	HACKERS	HADJEES	HAFIZES
HABERDINE	HACKERY	HADJES	HAFNIUM
HABERGEON	HACKETTE	HADJI	HAFNIUMS
HABILABLE	HACKETTES	HADJIS	HAFT
HABILE	HACKIE	HADROME	HAFTARA
HABIT	HACKIES	HADROMES	HAFTARAH
HABITABLE	HACKING	HADRON	HAFTARAHS
HABITABLY	HACKINGS	HADRONIC	HAFTARAS
HABITAN	HACKLE	HADRONS	HAFTAROT
HABITANS	HACKLED	HADROSAUR	HAFTAROTH
HABITANT	HACKLER	HADS	HAFTED
HABITANTS	HACKLERS	HADST	HAFTER
HABITAT	HACKLES	HAE	HAFTERS
HABITATS	HACKLET	HAECCEITY	HAFTING
HABITED	HACKLETS	HAED	HAFTORAH
HABITING	HACKLIER	HAEING	HAFTORAHS
HABITS	HACKLIEST	HAEM	HAFTOROS
HABITUAL	HACKLING	HAEMAL	HAFTOROT
HABITUALS	HACKLY	HAEMATAL	HAFTOROTH
HABITUATE	HACKMAN	HAEMATEIN	HAFTS
HABITUDE	HACKMEN	HAEMATIC	HAG
HABITUDES	HACKNEY	HAEMATICS	HAGADIC
HABITUE	HACKNEYED	HAEMATIN	HAGADIST
HABITUES	HACKNEYS	HAEMATINS	HAGADISTS
HABITUS	HACKS	HAEMATITE	HAGBERRY
HABLE	HACKSAW	HAEMATOID	HAGBOLT
HABOOB	HACKSAWED	HAEMATOMA	HAGBOLTS
HABOOBS	HACKSAWN	HAEMIC	HAGBORN
HABU	HACKSAWS	HAEMIN	HAGBUSH
HABUS	HACKWORK	HAEMINS	HAGBUSHES
HACEK	HACKWORKS	HAEMOCOEL	HAGBUT
HACEKS	HACQUETON	HAEMOCYTE	HAGBUTEER
HACENDADO	HAD	HAEMOID	HAGBUTS
HACHIS	HADAL	HAEMONIES	HAGBUTTER
HACHURE	HADARIM	HAEMONY	HAGDEN
HACHURED	HADAWAY	HAEMOSTAT	HAGDENS
HACHURES	HADDEN	HAEMS	HAGDON
HACHURING	HADDEST	HAEN	HAGDONS
HACIENDA	HADDIE	HAEREDES	HAGDOWN
HACIENDAS	HADDIES	HAEREMAI	HAGDOWNS
HACK	HADDING	HAERES	HAGFISH

HAGFISHES	HAILERS	HAIRPIECE	HALAKHOT
HAGG	HAILIER	HAIRPIN	HALAKHOTH
HAGGADA	HAILIEST	HAIRPINS	HALAKIC
HAGGADAH	HAILING	HAIRS	HALAKIST
HAGGADAHS	HAILS	HAIRSPRAY	HALAKISTS
HAGGADAS	HAILSHOT	HAIRST	HALAKOTH
HAGGADIC	HAILSHOTS	HAIRSTED	HALAL
HAGGADIST	HAILSTONE	HAIRSTING	HALALA
HAGGADOT	HAILSTORM	HAIRSTS	HALALAH
HAGGADOTH	HAILY	HAIRSTYLE	HALALAHS
HAGGARD	HAIMISH	HAIRTAIL	HALALAS
HAGGARDLY	HAIN	HAIRTAILS	HALALLED
HAGGARDS	HAINCH	HAIRWORK	HALALLING
HAGGED	HAINCHED	HAIRWORKS	HALALS
HAGGING	HAINCHES	HAIRWORM	HALATION
HAGGIS	HAINCHING	HAIRWORMS	HALATIONS
HAGGISES	HAINED	HAIRY	HALAVAH
HAGGISH	HAINING	HAIRYBACK	HALAVAHS
HAGGISHLY	HAININGS	HAITH	HALAZONE
HAGGLE	HAINS	HAJ	HALAZONES
HAGGLED	HAINT	HAJES	HALBERD
HAGGLER	HAINTS	HAJI	HALBERDS
HAGGLERS	HAIQUE	HAJIS	HALBERT
HAGGLES	HAIQUES	HAJJ	HALBERTS
HAGGLING	HAIR	HAJJAH	HALCYON
HAGGS	HAIRBALL	HAJJAHS	HALCYONIC
HAGIARCHY	HAIRBALLS	HAJJES	HALCYONS
HAGIOLOGY	HAIRBAND	HAJJI	HALE
HAGLET	HAIRBANDS	HAJJIS	HALED
HAGLETS	HAIRBELL	HAKA	HALENESS
HAGLIKE	HAIRBELLS	HAKAM	HALER
HAGRIDDEN	HAIRBRUSH	HAKAMS	HALERS
HAGRIDE	HAIRCAP	HAKARI	HALERU
HAGRIDER	HAIRCAPS	HAKAS	HALES
HAGRIDERS	HAIRCLOTH	HAKE	HALEST
HAGRIDES	HAIRCUT	HAKEA	HALF
HAGRIDING	HAIRCUTS	HAKEAS	HALFA
HAGRODE	HAIRDO	HAKEEM	HALFAS
HAGS	HAIRDOS	HAKEEMS	HALFBACK
HAH	HAIRDRIER	HAKES	HALFBACKS
HAHA	HAIRDRYER	HAKIM	HALFBEAK
HAHAS	HAIRED	HAKIMS	HALFBEAKS
HAHNIUM	HAIRGRIP	HAKU	HALFEN
HAHNIUMS	HAIRGRIPS	HAKUS	HALFLIFE
HAHS	HAIRIER	HALACHA	HALFLIN
HAICK	HAIRIEST	HALACHAS	HALFLING
HAICKS	HAIRIF	HALACHIC	HALFLINGS
HAIDUK	HAIRIFS	HALACHIST	HALFLINS
HAIDUKS	HAIRINESS	HALACHOT	HALFLIVES
HAIK	HAIRING	HALACHOTH	HALFNESS
HAIKA	HAIRLESS	HALAKAH	HALFPACE
HAIKAI	HAIRLIKE	HALAKAHS	HALFPACES
HAIKS	HAIRLINE	HALAKHA	HALFPENCE
HAIKU	HAIRLINES	HALAKHAH	HALFPENNY
HAIKUS	HAIRLOCK	HALAKHAHS	HALFPIPE
HAIL	HAIRLOCKS	HALAKHAS	HALFPIPES
HAILED	HAIRNET	HALAKHIC	HALFS
HAILER	HAIRNETS	HALAKHIST	HALFTIME

261

HALFTIMES	HALLO	HALOUMI	HAMBURG
HALFTONE	HALLOA	HALOUMIS	HAMBURGER
HALFTONES	HALLOAED	HALSE	HAMBURGS
HALFTRACK	HALLOAING	HALSED	HAME
HALFWAY	HALLOAS	HALSER	HAMED
HALFWIT	HALLOED	HALSERS	HAMES
HALFWITS	HALLOES	HALSES	HAMEWITH
HALIBUT	HALLOING	HALSING	HAMFATTER
HALIBUTS	HALLOO	HALT	HAMING
HALICORE	HALLOOED	HALTED	HAMLET
HALICORES	HALLOOING	HALTER	HAMLETS
HALID	HALLOOS	HALTERE	HAMMADA
HALIDE	HALLOS	HALTERED	HAMMADAS
HALIDES	HALLOT	HALTERES	HAMMAL
HALIDOM	HALLOTH	HALTERING	HAMMALS
HALIDOME	HALLOUMI	HALTERS	HAMMAM
HALIDOMES	HALLOUMIS	HALTING	HAMMAMS
HALIDOMS	HALLOW	HALTINGLY	HAMMED
HALIDS	HALLOWED	HALTINGS	HAMMER
HALIEUTIC	HALLOWER	HALTLESS	HAMMERED
HALIMOT	HALLOWERS	HALTS	HAMMERER
HALIMOTE	HALLOWING	HALUTZ	HAMMERERS
HALIMOTES	HALLOWS	HALUTZIM	HAMMERING
HALIMOTS	HALLS	HALVA	HAMMERKOP
HALING	HALLSTAND	HALVAH	HAMMERMAN
HALIOTIS	HALLUCAL	HALVAHS	HAMMERMEN
HALITE	HALLUCES	HALVAS	HAMMERS
HALITES	HALLUX	HALVE	HAMMERTOE
HALITOSES	HALLWAY	HALVED	HAMMIER
HALITOSIS	HALLWAYS	HALVER	HAMMIEST
HALITOTIC	HALLYON	HALVERS	HAMMILY
HALITOUS	HALLYONS	HALVES	HAMMINESS
HALITUS	HALM	HALVING	HAMMING
HALITUSES	HALMA	HALYARD	HAMMOCK
HALL	HALMAS	HALYARDS	HAMMOCKS
HALLAH	HALMS	HAM	HAMMY
HALLAHS	HALO	HAMADA	HAMOSE
HALLAL	HALOBIONT	HAMADAS	HAMOUS
HALLALI	HALOCLINE	HAMADRYAD	HAMPER
HALLALIS	HALOED	HAMADRYAS	HAMPERED
HALLALLED	HALOES	HAMAL	HAMPERER
HALLALOO	HALOGEN	HAMALS	HAMPERERS
HALLALOOS	HALOGENS	HAMAMELIS	HAMPERING
HALLALS	HALOGETON	HAMARTIA	HAMPERS
HALLAN	HALOID	HAMARTIAS	HAMPSTER
HALLANS	HALOIDS	HAMATE	HAMPSTERS
HALLEL	HALOING	HAMATES	HAMS
HALLELS	HALOLIKE	HAMAUL	HAMSTER
HALLIAN	HALON	HAMAULS	HAMSTERS
HALLIANS	HALONS	HAMBA	HAMSTRING
HALLIARD	HALOPHILE	HAMBLE	HAMSTRUNG
HALLIARDS	HALOPHILY	HAMBLED	HAMULAR
HALLING	HALOPHOBE	HAMBLES	HAMULATE
HALLINGS	HALOPHYTE	HAMBLING	HAMULI
HALLION	HALOS	HAMBONE	HAMULOSE
HALLIONS	HALOSERE	HAMBONED	HAMULOUS
HALLMARK	HALOSERES	HAMBONES	HAMULUS
HALLMARKS	HALOTHANE	HAMBONING	HAMZA

HAMZAH	HANDICAPS	HANDSOMES	HANK
HAMZAHS	HANDIER	HANDSPIKE	HANKED
HAMZAS	HANDIEST	HANDSTAFF	HANKER
HAN	HANDILY	HANDSTAMP	HANKERED
HANAP	HANDINESS	HANDSTAND	HANKERER
HANAPER	HANDING	HANDSTURN	HANKERERS
HANAPERS	HANDISM	HANDTOWEL	HANKERING
HANAPS	HANDISMS	HANDWHEEL	HANKERS
HANCE	HANDIWORK	HANDWORK	HANKIE
HANCES	HANDJAR	HANDWORKS	HANKIES
HANCH	HANDJARS	HANDWOVEN	HANKING
HANCHED	HANDLE	HANDWRIT	HANKS
HANCHES	HANDLEBAR	HANDWRITE	HANKY
HANCHING	HANDLED	HANDWROTE	HANSA
HAND	HANDLER	HANDY	HANSAS
HANDAX	HANDLERS	HANDYMAN	HANSE
HANDAXES	HANDLES	HANDYMEN	HANSEATIC
HANDBAG	HANDLESS	HANDYWORK	HANSEL
HANDBAGS	HANDLIKE	HANEPOOT	HANSELED
HANDBALL	HANDLING	HANEPOOTS	HANSELING
HANDBALLS	HANDLINGS	HANG	HANSELLED
HANDBELL	HANDLIST	HANGABLE	HANSELS
HANDBELLS	HANDLISTS	HANGAR	HANSES
HANDBILL	HANDLOOM	HANGARED	HANSOM
HANDBILLS	HANDLOOMS	HANGARING	HANSOMS
HANDBLOWN	HANDMADE	HANGARS	HANT
HANDBOOK	HANDMAID	HANGBIRD	HANTED
HANDBOOKS	HANDMAIDS	HANGBIRDS	HANTING
HANDBRAKE	HANDOFF	HANGDOG	HANTLE
HANDCAR	HANDOFFS	HANGDOGS	HANTLES
HANDCARS	HANDOUT	HANGED	HANTS
HANDCART	HANDOUTS	HANGER	HANUKIAH
HANDCARTS	HANDOVER	HANGERS	HANUKIAHS
HANDCLAP	HANDOVERS	HANGFIRE	HANUMAN
HANDCLAPS	HANDPHONE	HANGFIRES	HANUMANS
HANDCLASP	HANDPICK	HANGI	HAO
HANDCRAFT	HANDPICKS	HANGING	HAOLE
HANDCUFF	HANDPLAY	HANGINGS	HAOLES
HANDCUFFS	HANDPLAYS	HANGIS	HAOMA
HANDED	HANDPRESS	HANGMAN	HAOMAS
HANDER	HANDPRINT	HANGMEN	HAP
HANDERS	HANDRAIL	HANGNAIL	HAPAX
HANDFAST	HANDRAILS	HANGNAILS	HAPAXES
HANDFASTS	HANDROLL	HANGNEST	HAPHAZARD
HANDFED	HANDROLLS	HANGNESTS	HAPHTARA
HANDFEED	HANDS	HANGOUT	HAPHTARAH
HANDFEEDS	HANDSAW	HANGOUTS	HAPHTARAS
HANDFUL	HANDSAWS	HANGOVER	HAPHTAROT
HANDFULS	HANDSEL	HANGOVERS	HAPKIDO
HANDGRIP	HANDSELED	HANGS	HAPKIDOS
HANDGRIPS	HANDSELS	HANGTAG	HAPLESS
HANDGUN	HANDSET	HANGTAGS	HAPLESSLY
HANDGUNS	HANDSETS	HANGUL	HAPLITE
HANDHELD	HANDSEWN	HANGUP	HAPLITES
HANDHELDS	HANDSFUL	HANGUPS	HAPLITIC
HANDHOLD	HANDSHAKE	HANIWA	HAPLOID
HANDHOLDS	HANDSOME	HANJAR	HAPLOIDIC
HANDICAP	HANDSOMER	HANJARS	HAPLOIDS

HAPLOIDY	HARANGUER	HARDHACK	HARELDS
HAPLOLOGY	HARANGUES	HARDHACKS	HARELIKE
HAPLONT	HARASS	HARDHAT	HARELIP
HAPLONTIC	HARASSED	HARDHATS	HARELIPS
HAPLONTS	HARASSER	HARDHEAD	HAREM
HAPLOPIA	HARASSERS	HARDHEADS	HAREMS
HAPLOPIAS	HARASSES	HARDIER	HARES
HAPLOSES	HARASSING	HARDIES	HARESTAIL
HAPLOSIS	HARBINGER	HARDIEST	HAREWOOD
HAPLOTYPE	HARBOR	HARDIHEAD	HAREWOODS
HAPLY	HARBORAGE	HARDIHOOD	HARIANA
HAPPED	HARBORED	HARDILY	HARIANAS
HAPPEN	HARBORER	HARDIMENT	HARICOT
HAPPENED	HARBORERS	HARDINESS	HARICOTS
HAPPENING	HARBORFUL	HARDISH	HARIGALDS
HAPPENS	HARBORING	HARDLINE	HARIGALS
HAPPIED	HARBOROUS	HARDLINER	HARIJAN
HAPPIER	HARBORS	HARDLY	HARIJANS
HAPPIES	HARBOUR	HARDMAN	HARIM
HAPPIEST	HARBOURED	HARDMEN	HARIMS
HAPPILY	HARBOURER	HARDNESS	HARING
HAPPINESS	HARBOURS	HARDNOSE	HARIOLATE
HAPPING	HARD	HARDNOSED	HARIRA
HAPPY	HARDASS	HARDNOSES	HARIRAS
HAPPYING	HARDASSES	HARDOKE	HARISH
HAPS	HARDBACK	HARDOKES	HARISSA
HAPTEN	HARDBACKS	HARDPACK	HARISSAS
HAPTENE	HARDBAG	HARDPACKS	HARK
HAPTENES	HARDBAGS	HARDPAN	HARKED
HAPTENIC	HARDBAKE	HARDPANS	HARKEN
HAPTENS	HARDBAKES	HARDPARTS	HARKENED
HAPTERON	HARDBALL	HARDROCK	HARKENER
HAPTERONS	HARDBALLS	HARDROCKS	HARKENERS
HAPTIC	HARDBEAM	HARDS	HARKENING
HAPTICAL	HARDBEAMS	HARDSET	HARKENS
HAPTICS	HARDBOARD	HARDSHELL	HARKING
HAPU	HARDBOOT	HARDSHIP	HARKS
HAPUKA	HARDBOOTS	HARDSHIPS	HARL
HAPUKAS	HARDBOUND	HARDSTAND	HARLED
HAPUKU	HARDCASE	HARDTACK	HARLEQUIN
HAPUKUS	HARDCORE	HARDTACKS	HARLING
HAPUS	HARDCORES	HARDTOP	HARLINGS
HAQUETON	HARDCOURT	HARDTOPS	HARLOT
HAQUETONS	HARDCOVER	HARDWARE	HARLOTRY
HARAKEKE	HARDEDGE	HARDWARES	HARLOTS
HARAKEKES	HARDEDGES	HARDWIRE	HARLS
HARAM	HARDEN	HARDWIRED	HARM
HARAMBEE	HARDENED	HARDWIRES	HARMALA
HARAMBEES	HARDENER	HARDWOOD	HARMALAS
HARAMDA	HARDENERS	HARDWOODS	HARMALIN
HARAMDAS	HARDENING	HARDY	HARMALINE
HARAMDI	HARDENS	HARE	HARMALINS
HARAMDIS	HARDER	HAREBELL	HARMAN
HARAMS	HARDEST	HAREBELLS	HARMANS
HARAMZADA	HARDFACE	HARED	HARMATTAN
HARAMZADI	HARDFACES	HAREEM	HARMDOING
HARANGUE	HARDGOODS	HAREEMS	HARMED
HARANGUED	HARDGRASS	HARELD	HARMEL

HARMELS	HARRIED	HASHISH	HATCHECK
HARMER	HARRIER	HASHISHES	HATCHECKS
HARMERS	HARRIERS	HASHMARK	HATCHED
HARMFUL	HARRIES	HASHMARKS	HATCHEL
HARMFULLY	HARROW	HASHY	HATCHELED
HARMIN	HARROWED	HASK	HATCHELS
HARMINE	HARROWER	HASKS	HATCHER
HARMINES	HARROWERS	HASLET	HATCHERS
HARMING	HARROWING	HASLETS	HATCHERY
HARMINS	HARROWS	HASP	HATCHES
HARMLESS	HARRUMPH	HASPED	HATCHET
HARMONIC	HARRUMPHS	HASPING	HATCHETS
HARMONICA	HARRY	HASPS	HATCHETY
HARMONICS	HARRYING	HASSAR	HATCHING
HARMONIES	HARSH	HASSARS	HATCHINGS
HARMONISE	HARSHEN	HASSEL	HATCHLING
HARMONIST	HARSHENED	HASSELS	HATCHMENT
HARMONIUM	HARSHENS	HASSIUM	HATCHWAY
HARMONIZE	HARSHER	HASSIUMS	HATCHWAYS
HARMONY	HARSHEST	HASSLE	HATE
HARMOST	HARSHLY	HASSLED	HATEABLE
HARMOSTS	HARSHNESS	HASSLES	HATED
HARMOSTY	HARSLET	HASSLING	HATEFUL
HARMOTOME	HARSLETS	HASSOCK	HATEFULLY
HARMS	HART	HASSOCKS	HATELESS
HARN	HARTAL	HASSOCKY	HATER
HARNESS	HARTALS	HAST	HATERENT
HARNESSED	HARTBEES	HASTA	HATERENTS
HARNESSER	HARTBEEST	HASTATE	HATERS
HARNESSES	HARTELY	HASTATED	HATES
HARNS	HARTEN	HASTATELY	HATFUL
HARO	HARTENED	HASTE	HATFULS
HAROS	HARTENING	HASTED	HATGUARD
HAROSET	HARTENS	HASTEFUL	HATGUARDS
HAROSETH	HARTLESSE	HASTEN	HATH
HAROSETHS	HARTS	HASTENED	HATHA
HAROSETS	HARTSHORN	HASTENER	HATING
HARP	HARUMPH	HASTENERS	HATLESS
HARPED	HARUMPHED	HASTENING	HATLIKE
HARPER	HARUMPHS	HASTENS	HATMAKER
HARPERS	HARUSPEX	HASTES	HATMAKERS
HARPIES	HARUSPICY	HASTIER	HATPEG
HARPIN	HARVEST	HASTIEST	HATPEGS
HARPING	HARVESTED	HASTILY	HATPIN
HARPINGS	HARVESTER	HASTINESS	HATPINS
HARPINS	HARVESTS	HASTING	HATRACK
HARPIST	HAS	HASTINGS	HATRACKS
HARPISTS	HASBIAN	HASTY	HATRED
HARPOON	HASBIANS	HAT	HATREDS
HARPOONED	HASH	HATABLE	HATS
HARPOONER	HASHED	HATBAND	HATSFUL
HARPOONS	HASHEESH	HATBANDS	HATSTAND
HARPS	HASHES	HATBOX	HATSTANDS
HARPY	HASHHEAD	HATBOXES	HATTED
HARPYLIKE	HASHHEADS	HATBRUSH	HATTER
HARQUEBUS	HASHIER	HATCH	HATTERED
HARRIDAN	HASHIEST	HATCHABLE	HATTERIA
HARRIDANS	HASHING	HATCHBACK	HATTERIAS

HATTERING
HATTERS
HATTING
HATTINGS
HATTOCK
HATTOCKS
HAUBERK
HAUBERKS
HAUBOIS
HAUD
HAUDING
HAUDS
HAUF
HAUFS
HAUGH
HAUGHS
HAUGHT
HAUGHTIER
HAUGHTILY
HAUGHTY
HAUL
HAULAGE
HAULAGES
HAULD
HAULDS
HAULED
HAULER
HAULERS
HAULIER
HAULIERS
HAULING
HAULM
HAULMIER
HAULMIEST
HAULMS
HAULMY
HAULS
HAULST
HAULT
HAULYARD
HAULYARDS
HAUNCH
HAUNCHED
HAUNCHES
HAUNCHING
HAUNT
HAUNTED
HAUNTER
HAUNTERS
HAUNTING
HAUNTINGS
HAUNTS
HAURIANT
HAURIENT
HAUSE
HAUSED
HAUSEN
HAUSENS

HAUSES
HAUSFRAU
HAUSFRAUS
HAUSING
HAUSTELLA
HAUSTORIA
HAUT
HAUTBOIS
HAUTBOY
HAUTBOYS
HAUTE
HAUTEUR
HAUTEURS
HAUYNE
HAUYNES
HAVARTI
HAVARTIS
HAVDALAH
HAVDALAHS
HAVDOLOH
HAVDOLOHS
HAVE
HAVELOCK
HAVELOCKS
HAVEN
HAVENED
HAVENING
HAVENLESS
HAVENS
HAVEOUR
HAVEOURS
HAVER
HAVERED
HAVEREL
HAVERELS
HAVERING
HAVERINGS
HAVERS
HAVERSACK
HAVERSINE
HAVES
HAVILDAR
HAVILDARS
HAVING
HAVINGS
HAVIOR
HAVIORS
HAVIOUR
HAVIOURS
HAVOC
HAVOCKED
HAVOCKER
HAVOCKERS
HAVOCKING
HAVOCS
HAW
HAWALA
HAWALAS

HAWBUCK
HAWBUCKS
HAWED
HAWFINCH
HAWING
HAWK
HAWKBELL
HAWKBELLS
HAWKBILL
HAWKBILLS
HAWKBIT
HAWKBITS
HAWKED
HAWKER
HAWKERS
HAWKEY
HAWKEYED
HAWKEYS
HAWKIE
HAWKIES
HAWKING
HAWKINGS
HAWKISH
HAWKISHLY
HAWKIT
HAWKLIKE
HAWKMOTH
HAWKMOTHS
HAWKNOSE
HAWKNOSES
HAWKS
HAWKSBILL
HAWKSHAW
HAWKSHAWS
HAWKWEED
HAWKWEEDS
HAWM
HAWMED
HAWMING
HAWMS
HAWS
HAWSE
HAWSED
HAWSEHOLE
HAWSEPIPE
HAWSER
HAWSERS
HAWSES
HAWSING
HAWTHORN
HAWTHORNS
HAWTHORNY
HAY
HAYBAND
HAYBANDS
HAYBOX
HAYBOXES
HAYCOCK

HAYCOCKS
HAYED
HAYER
HAYERS
HAYEY
HAYFIELD
HAYFIELDS
HAYFORK
HAYFORKS
HAYING
HAYINGS
HAYLAGE
HAYLAGES
HAYLE
HAYLES
HAYLOFT
HAYLOFTS
HAYMAKER
HAYMAKERS
HAYMAKING
HAYMOW
HAYMOWS
HAYRACK
HAYRACKS
HAYRICK
HAYRICKS
HAYRIDE
HAYRIDES
HAYS
HAYSEED
HAYSEEDS
HAYSEL
HAYSELS
HAYSTACK
HAYSTACKS
HAYWARD
HAYWARDS
HAYWIRE
HAYWIRES
HAZAN
HAZANIM
HAZANS
HAZARD
HAZARDED
HAZARDER
HAZARDERS
HAZARDING
HAZARDIZE
HAZARDOUS
HAZARDRY
HAZARDS
HAZE
HAZED
HAZEL
HAZELHEN
HAZELHENS
HAZELLY
HAZELNUT

HAZELNUTS
HAZELS
HAZER
HAZERS
HAZES
HAZIER
HAZIEST
HAZILY
HAZINESS
HAZING
HAZINGS
HAZMAT
HAZMATS
HAZY
HAZZAN
HAZZANIM
HAZZANS
HE
HEAD
HEADACHE
HEADACHES
HEADACHEY
HEADACHY
HEADAGE
HEADAGES
HEADBAND
HEADBANDS
HEADBANG
HEADBANGS
HEADBOARD
HEADCASE
HEADCASES
HEADCHAIR
HEADCLOTH
HEADCOUNT
HEADDRESS
HEADED
HEADEND
HEADENDS
HEADER
HEADERS
HEADFAST
HEADFASTS
HEADFIRST
HEADFISH
HEADFRAME
HEADFUCK
HEADFUCKS
HEADFUL
HEADFULS
HEADGATE
HEADGATES
HEADGEAR
HEADGEARS
HEADGUARD
HEADHUNT
HEADHUNTS
HEADIER

HEADIEST
HEADILY
HEADINESS
HEADING
HEADINGS
HEADLAMP
HEADLAMPS
HEADLAND
HEADLANDS
HEADLEASE
HEADLESS
HEADLIGHT
HEADLIKE
HEADLINE
HEADLINED
HEADLINER
HEADLINES
HEADLOCK
HEADLOCKS
HEADLONG
HEADMAN
HEADMARK
HEADMARKS
HEADMEN
HEADMOST
HEADNOTE
HEADNOTES
HEADPEACE
HEADPHONE
HEADPIECE
HEADPIN
HEADPINS
HEADRACE
HEADRACES
HEADRAIL
HEADRAILS
HEADREACH
HEADREST
HEADRESTS
HEADRIG
HEADRIGS
HEADRING
HEADRINGS
HEADROOM
HEADROOMS
HEADROPE
HEADROPES
HEADS
HEADSAIL
HEADSAILS
HEADSCARF
HEADSET
HEADSETS
HEADSHAKE
HEADSHIP
HEADSHIPS
HEADSHOT
HEADSHOTS

HEADSMAN
HEADSMEN
HEADSPACE
HEADSTALL
HEADSTAND
HEADSTAY
HEADSTAYS
HEADSTICK
HEADSTOCK
HEADSTONE
HEADWARD
HEADWARDS
HEADWATER
HEADWAY
HEADWAYS
HEADWIND
HEADWINDS
HEADWORD
HEADWORDS
HEADWORK
HEADWORKS
HEADY
HEAL
HEALABLE
HEALD
HEALDED
HEALDING
HEALDS
HEALED
HEALEE
HEALEES
HEALER
HEALERS
HEALING
HEALINGLY
HEALINGS
HEALS
HEALSOME
HEALTH
HEALTHFUL
HEALTHIER
HEALTHILY
HEALTHISM
HEALTHS
HEALTHY
HEAME
HEAP
HEAPED
HEAPER
HEAPERS
HEAPIER
HEAPIEST
HEAPING
HEAPS
HEAPSTEAD
HEAPY
HEAR
HEARABLE

HEARD
HEARDS
HEARE
HEARER
HEARERS
HEARES
HEARIE
HEARING
HEARINGS
HEARKEN
HEARKENED
HEARKENER
HEARKENS
HEARS
HEARSAY
HEARSAYS
HEARSE
HEARSED
HEARSES
HEARSIER
HEARSIEST
HEARSING
HEARSY
HEART
HEARTACHE
HEARTBEAT
HEARTBURN
HEARTED
HEARTEN
HEARTENED
HEARTENER
HEARTENS
HEARTFELT
HEARTFREE
HEARTH
HEARTHRUG
HEARTHS
HEARTIER
HEARTIES
HEARTIEST
HEARTIKIN
HEARTILY
HEARTING
HEARTLAND
HEARTLESS
HEARTLET
HEARTLETS
HEARTLING
HEARTLY
HEARTPEA
HEARTPEAS
HEARTS
HEARTSEED
HEARTSICK
HEARTSOME
HEARTSORE
HEARTWOOD
HEARTWORM

HEARTY
HEAST
HEASTE
HEASTES
HEASTS
HEAT
HEATABLE
HEATED
HEATEDLY
HEATER
HEATERS
HEATH
HEATHBIRD
HEATHCOCK
HEATHEN
HEATHENRY
HEATHENS
HEATHER
HEATHERED
HEATHERS
HEATHERY
HEATHFOWL
HEATHIER
HEATHIEST
HEATHLAND
HEATHLESS
HEATHLIKE
HEATHS
HEATHY
HEATING
HEATINGS
HEATLESS
HEATPROOF
HEATS
HEATSPOT
HEATSPOTS
HEAUME
HEAUMES
HEAVE
HEAVED
HEAVEN
HEAVENLY
HEAVENS
HEAVER
HEAVERS
HEAVES
HEAVIER
HEAVIES
HEAVIEST
HEAVILY
HEAVINESS
HEAVING
HEAVINGS
HEAVY
HEAVYSET
HEBDOMAD
HEBDOMADS
HEBE

HEBEN
HEBENON
HEBENONS
HEBENS
HEBES
HEBETANT
HEBETATE
HEBETATED
HEBETATES
HEBETIC
HEBETUDE
HEBETUDES
HEBONA
HEBONAS
HEBRAISE
HEBRAISED
HEBRAISES
HEBRAIZE
HEBRAIZED
HEBRAIZES
HECATOMB
HECATOMBS
HECH
HECHT
HECHTING
HECHTS
HECK
HECKLE
HECKLED
HECKLER
HECKLERS
HECKLES
HECKLING
HECKLINGS
HECKS
HECOGENIN
HECTARE
HECTARES
HECTIC
HECTICAL
HECTICLY
HECTICS
HECTOGRAM
HECTOR
HECTORED
HECTORER
HECTORERS
HECTORING
HECTORISM
HECTORLY
HECTORS
HEDDLE
HEDDLED
HEDDLES
HEDDLING
HEDER
HEDERA
HEDERAL

HEDERAS
HEDERATED
HEDERS
HEDGE
HEDGEBILL
HEDGED
HEDGEHOG
HEDGEHOGS
HEDGEHOP
HEDGEHOPS
HEDGEPIG
HEDGEPIGS
HEDGER
HEDGEROW
HEDGEROWS
HEDGERS
HEDGES
HEDGIER
HEDGIEST
HEDGING
HEDGINGLY
HEDGINGS
HEDGY
HEDONIC
HEDONICS
HEDONISM
HEDONISMS
HEDONIST
HEDONISTS
HEDYPHANE
HEED
HEEDED
HEEDER
HEEDERS
HEEDFUL
HEEDFULLY
HEEDINESS
HEEDING
HEEDLESS
HEEDS
HEEDY
HEEHAW
HEEHAWED
HEEHAWING
HEEHAWS
HEEL
HEELBALL
HEELBALLS
HEELED
HEELER
HEELERS
HEELING
HEELINGS
HEELLESS
HEELPIECE
HEELPLATE
HEELPOST
HEELPOSTS

HEELS
HEELTAP
HEELTAPS
HEEZE
HEEZED
HEEZES
HEEZIE
HEEZIES
HEEZING
HEFT
HEFTE
HEFTED
HEFTER
HEFTERS
HEFTIER
HEFTIEST
HEFTILY
HEFTINESS
HEFTING
HEFTS
HEFTY
HEGARI
HEGARIS
HEGEMON
HEGEMONIC
HEGEMONS
HEGEMONY
HEGIRA
HEGIRAS
HEGUMEN
HEGUMENE
HEGUMENES
HEGUMENOI
HEGUMENOS
HEGUMENY
HEH
HEHS
HEID
HEIDS
HEIFER
HEIFERS
HEIGH
HEIGHT
HEIGHTEN
HEIGHTENS
HEIGHTH
HEIGHTHS
HEIGHTISM
HEIGHTS
HEIL
HEILED
HEILING
HEILS
HEIMISH
HEINIE
HEINIES
HEINOUS

HEINOUSLY	HELICOPT	HELLICAT	HELPLESS
HEIR	HELICOPTS	HELLICATS	HELPLINE
HEIRDOM	HELICTITE	HELLIER	HELPLINES
HEIRDOMS	HELIDECK	HELLIERS	HELPMATE
HEIRED	HELIDECKS	HELLING	HELPMATES
HEIRESS	HELIDROME	HELLION	HELPMEET
HEIRESSES	HELILIFT	HELLIONS	HELPMEETS
HEIRING	HELILIFTS	HELLISH	HELPS
HEIRLESS	HELIMAN	HELLISHLY	HELVE
HEIRLOOM	HELIMEN	HELLKITE	HELVED
HEIRLOOMS	HELING	HELLKITES	HELVES
HEIRS	HELIO	HELLO	HELVETIUM
HEIRSHIP	HELIODOR	HELLOED	HELVING
HEIRSHIPS	HELIODORS	HELLOES	HEM
HEISHI	HELIOGRAM	HELLOING	HEMAGOG
HEIST	HELIOLOGY	HELLOS	HEMAGOGS
HEISTED	HELIOS	HELLOVA	HEMAGOGUE
HEISTER	HELIOSES	HELLS	HEMAL
HEISTERS	HELIOSIS	HELLUVA	HEMATAL
HEISTING	HELIOSTAT	HELLWARD	HEMATEIN
HEISTS	HELIOTYPE	HELLWARDS	HEMATEINS
HEITIKI	HELIOTYPY	HELM	HEMATIC
HEITIKIS	HELIOZOAN	HELMED	HEMATICS
HEJAB	HELIOZOIC	HELMER	HEMATIN
HEJABS	HELIPAD	HELMERS	HEMATINE
HEJIRA	HELIPADS	HELMET	HEMATINES
HEJIRAS	HELIPILOT	HELMETED	HEMATINIC
HEJRA	HELIPORT	HELMETING	HEMATINS
HEJRAS	HELIPORTS	HELMETS	HEMATITE
HEKETARA	HELISTOP	HELMING	HEMATITES
HEKETARAS	HELISTOPS	HELMINTH	HEMATITIC
HEKTARE	HELIUM	HELMINTHS	HEMATOID
HEKTARES	HELIUMS	HELMLESS	HEMATOMA
HEKTOGRAM	HELIX	HELMS	HEMATOMAS
HELCOID	HELIXES	HELMSMAN	HEMATOSES
HELD	HELL	HELMSMEN	HEMATOSIS
HELE	HELLBENT	HELO	HEMATOZOA
HELED	HELLBOX	HELOPHYTE	HEMATURIA
HELENIUM	HELLBOXES	HELOS	HEMATURIC
HELENIUMS	HELLBROTH	HELOT	HEME
HELES	HELLCAT	HELOTAGE	HEMELYTRA
HELIAC	HELLCATS	HELOTAGES	HEMES
HELIACAL	HELLDIVER	HELOTISM	HEMIALGIA
HELIAST	HELLEBORE	HELOTISMS	HEMIC
HELIASTS	HELLED	HELOTRIES	HEMICYCLE
HELIBORNE	HELLENISE	HELOTRY	HEMIHEDRY
HELIBUS	HELLENIZE	HELOTS	HEMIN
HELIBUSES	HELLER	HELP	HEMINA
HELICAL	HELLERI	HELPABLE	HEMINAS
HELICALLY	HELLERIES	HELPDESK	HEMINS
HELICES	HELLERIS	HELPDESKS	HEMIOLA
HELICITY	HELLERS	HELPED	HEMIOLAS
HELICLINE	HELLERY	HELPER	HEMIOLIA
HELICOID	HELLFIRE	HELPERS	HEMIOLIAS
HELICOIDS	HELLFIRES	HELPFUL	HEMIOLIC
HELICON	HELLHOLE	HELPFULLY	HEMIONE
HELICONIA	HELLHOLES	HELPING	HEMIONES
HELICONS	HELLHOUND	HELPINGS	HEMIONUS

HEMIOPIA	HENBANE	HENTS	HERBALIST
HEMIOPIAS	HENBANES	HEP	HERBALS
HEMIOPIC	HENBIT	HEPAR	HERBAR
HEMIOPSIA	HENBITS	HEPARIN	HERBARIA
HEMIPOD	HENCE	HEPARINS	HERBARIAL
HEMIPODE	HENCHMAN	HEPARS	HERBARIAN
HEMIPODES	HENCHMEN	HEPATIC	HERBARIES
HEMIPODS	HENCOOP	HEPATICA	HERBARIUM
HEMIPTER	HENCOOPS	HEPATICAE	HERBARS
HEMIPTERS	HEND	HEPATICAL	HERBARY
HEMISPACE	HENDED	HEPATICAS	HERBED
HEMISTICH	HENDIADYS	HEPATICS	HERBELET
HEMITROPE	HENDING	HEPATISE	HERBELETS
HEMITROPY	HENDS	HEPATISED	HERBICIDE
HEMLINE	HENEQUEN	HEPATISES	HERBIER
HEMLINES	HENEQUENS	HEPATITE	HERBIEST
HEMLOCK	HENEQUIN	HEPATITES	HERBIST
HEMLOCKS	HENEQUINS	HEPATITIS	HERBISTS
HEMMED	HENGE	HEPATIZE	HERBIVORA
HEMMER	HENGES	HEPATIZED	HERBIVORE
HEMMERS	HENHOUSE	HEPATIZES	HERBIVORY
HEMMING	HENHOUSES	HEPATOMA	HERBLESS
HEMOCOEL	HENIQUEN	HEPATOMAS	HERBLET
HEMOCOELS	HENIQUENS	HEPCAT	HERBLETS
HEMOCYTE	HENIQUIN	HEPCATS	HERBLIKE
HEMOCYTES	HENIQUINS	HEPPER	HERBOLOGY
HEMOID	HENLEY	HEPPEST	HERBORISE
HEMOLYMPH	HENLEYS	HEPS	HERBORIST
HEMOLYSE	HENLIKE	HEPSTER	HERBORIZE
HEMOLYSED	HENNA	HEPSTERS	HERBOSE
HEMOLYSES	HENNAED	HEPT	HERBOUS
HEMOLYSIN	HENNAING	HEPTAD	HERBS
HEMOLYSIS	HENNAS	HEPTADS	HERBY
HEMOLYTIC	HENNED	HEPTAGLOT	HERCOGAMY
HEMOLYZE	HENNER	HEPTAGON	HERCULEAN
HEMOLYZED	HENNERIES	HEPTAGONS	HERCULES
HEMOLYZES	HENNERS	HEPTANE	HERCYNITE
HEMOPHILE	HENNERY	HEPTANES	HERD
HEMOSTAT	HENNIER	HEPTAPODY	HERDBOY
HEMOSTATS	HENNIES	HEPTARCH	HERDBOYS
HEMOTOXIC	HENNIEST	HEPTARCHS	HERDED
HEMOTOXIN	HENNIN	HEPTARCHY	HERDEN
HEMP	HENNING	HEPTOSE	HERDENS
HEMPEN	HENNINS	HEPTOSES	HERDER
HEMPIE	HENNISH	HER	HERDERS
HEMPIER	HENNISHLY	HERALD	HERDESS
HEMPIES	HENNY	HERALDED	HERDESSES
HEMPIEST	HENOTIC	HERALDIC	HERDIC
HEMPLIKE	HENPECK	HERALDING	HERDICS
HEMPS	HENPECKED	HERALDIST	HERDING
HEMPSEED	HENPECKS	HERALDRY	HERDLIKE
HEMPSEEDS	HENRIES	HERALDS	HERDMAN
HEMPWEED	HENRY	HERB	HERDMEN
HEMPWEEDS	HENRYS	HERBAGE	HERDS
HEMPY	HENS	HERBAGED	HERDSMAN
HEMS	HENT	HERBAGES	HERDSMEN
HEMSTITCH	HENTED	HERBAL	HERDWICK
HEN	HENTING	HERBALISM	HERDWICKS

HERE	HERMITAGE	HERPETOID	HETAIRA
HEREABOUT	HERMITESS	HERPTILE	HETAIRAI
HEREAFTER	HERMITIC	HERRIED	HETAIRAS
HEREAT	HERMITISM	HERRIES	HETAIRIA
HEREAWAY	HERMITRY	HERRIMENT	HETAIRIAS
HEREAWAYS	HERMITS	HERRING	HETAIRIC
HEREBY	HERMS	HERRINGER	HETAIRISM
HEREDES	HERN	HERRINGS	HETAIRIST
HEREDITY	HERNIA	HERRY	HETE
HEREFROM	HERNIAE	HERRYING	HETERO
HEREIN	HERNIAL	HERRYMENT	HETERODOX
HEREINTO	HERNIAS	HERS	HETERONYM
HERENESS	HERNIATE	HERSALL	HETEROPOD
HEREOF	HERNIATED	HERSALLS	HETEROS
HEREON	HERNIATES	HERSE	HETEROSES
HERES	HERNS	HERSED	HETEROSIS
HERESIES	HERNSHAW	HERSELF	HETEROTIC
HERESY	HERNSHAWS	HERSES	HETES
HERETIC	HERO	HERSHIP	HETH
HERETICAL	HEROE	HERSHIPS	HETHER
HERETICS	HEROES	HERSTORY	HETHS
HERETO	HEROIC	HERTZ	HETING
HERETRIX	HEROICAL	HERTZES	HETMAN
HEREUNDER	HEROICISE	HERY	HETMANATE
HEREUNTO	HEROICIZE	HERYE	HETMANS
HEREUPON	HEROICLY	HERYED	HETS
HEREWITH	HEROICS	HERYES	HEUCH
HERIED	HEROIN	HERYING	HEUCHERA
HERIES	HEROINE	HES	HEUCHERAS
HERIOT	HEROINES	HESITANCE	HEUCHS
HERIOTS	HEROINISM	HESITANCY	HEUGH
HERISSE	HEROINS	HESITANT	HEUGHS
HERISSON	HEROISE	HESITATE	HEUREKA
HERISSONS	HEROISED	HESITATED	HEUREKAS
HERITABLE	HEROISES	HESITATER	HEURETIC
HERITABLY	HEROISING	HESITATES	HEURETICS
HERITAGE	HEROISM	HESITATOR	HEURISM
HERITAGES	HEROISMS	HESP	HEURISMS
HERITOR	HEROIZE	HESPED	HEURISTIC
HERITORS	HEROIZED	HESPERID	HEVEA
HERITRESS	HEROIZES	HESPERIDS	HEVEAS
HERITRIX	HEROIZING	HESPING	HEW
HERKOGAMY	HERON	HESPS	HEWABLE
HERL	HERONRIES	HESSIAN	HEWED
HERLING	HERONRY	HESSIANS	HEWER
HERLINGS	HERONS	HESSITE	HEWERS
HERLS	HERONSEW	HESSITES	HEWGH
HERM	HERONSEWS	HESSONITE	HEWING
HERMA	HERONSHAW	HEST	HEWINGS
HERMAE	HEROON	HESTERNAL	HEWN
HERMAEAN	HEROONS	HESTS	HEWS
HERMAI	HEROS	HET	HEX
HERMANDAD	HEROSHIP	HETAERA	HEXACHORD
HERMETIC	HEROSHIPS	HETAERAE	HEXACT
HERMETICS	HERPES	HETAERAS	HEXACTS
HERMETISM	HERPESES	HETAERIC	HEXAD
HERMETIST	HERPETIC	HETAERISM	HEXADE
HERMIT	HERPETICS	HETAERIST	HEXADES

HEXADIC
HEXADS
HEXAFOIL
HEXAFOILS
HEXAGLOT
HEXAGON
HEXAGONAL
HEXAGONS
HEXAGRAM
HEXAGRAMS
HEXAHEDRA
HEXAMERAL
HEXAMETER
HEXAMINE
HEXAMINES
HEXANE
HEXANES
HEXANOIC
HEXAPLA
HEXAPLAR
HEXAPLAS
HEXAPLOID
HEXAPOD
HEXAPODIC
HEXAPODS
HEXAPODY
HEXARCH
HEXARCHY
HEXASTICH
HEXASTYLE
HEXED
HEXENE
HEXENES
HEXER
HEXEREI
HEXEREIS
HEXERS
HEXES
HEXING
HEXINGS
HEXONE
HEXONES
HEXOSAN
HEXOSANS
HEXOSE
HEXOSES
HEXYL
HEXYLENE
HEXYLENES
HEXYLIC
HEXYLS
HEY
HEYDAY
HEYDAYS
HEYDEY
HEYDEYS
HEYDUCK
HEYDUCKS

HEYED
HEYING
HEYS
HI
HIANT
HIATAL
HIATUS
HIATUSES
HIBACHI
HIBACHIS
HIBAKUSHA
HIBERNAL
HIBERNATE
HIBERNISE
HIBERNIZE
HIBISCUS
HIC
HICATEE
HICATEES
HICCATEE
HICCATEES
HICCOUGH
HICCOUGHS
HICCUP
HICCUPED
HICCUPING
HICCUPPED
HICCUPS
HICCUPY
HICK
HICKEY
HICKEYS
HICKIE
HICKIES
HICKISH
HICKORIES
HICKORY
HICKS
HICKWALL
HICKWALLS
HICKYMAL
HICKYMALS
HID
HIDABLE
HIDAGE
HIDAGES
HIDALGA
HIDALGAS
HIDALGO
HIDALGOS
HIDDEN
HIDDENITE
HIDDENLY
HIDDER
HIDDERS
HIDE
HIDEAWAY
HIDEAWAYS

HIDEBOUND
HIDED
HIDELESS
HIDEOSITY
HIDEOUS
HIDEOUSLY
HIDEOUT
HIDEOUTS
HIDER
HIDERS
HIDES
HIDING
HIDINGS
HIDLING
HIDLINGS
HIDLINS
HIDROSES
HIDROSIS
HIDROTIC
HIDROTICS
HIE
HIED
HIEING
HIELAMAN
HIELAMANS
HIELAND
HIEMAL
HIEMS
HIERACIUM
HIERARCH
HIERARCHS
HIERARCHY
HIERATIC
HIERATICA
HIEROCRAT
HIERODULE
HIEROGRAM
HIEROLOGY
HIERURGY
HIES
HIFALUTIN
HIGGLE
HIGGLED
HIGGLER
HIGGLERS
HIGGLES
HIGGLING
HIGGLINGS
HIGH
HIGHBALL
HIGHBALLS
HIGHBORN
HIGHBOY
HIGHBOYS
HIGHBRED
HIGHBROW
HIGHBROWS
HIGHBUSH

HIGHCHAIR
HIGHED
HIGHER
HIGHERED
HIGHERING
HIGHERS
HIGHEST
HIGHFLIER
HIGHFLYER
HIGHING
HIGHISH
HIGHJACK
HIGHJACKS
HIGHLAND
HIGHLANDS
HIGHLIFE
HIGHLIFES
HIGHLIGHT
HIGHLY
HIGHMAN
HIGHMEN
HIGHMOST
HIGHNESS
HIGHRISE
HIGHRISES
HIGHROAD
HIGHROADS
HIGHS
HIGHSPOT
HIGHSPOTS
HIGHT
HIGHTAIL
HIGHTAILS
HIGHTED
HIGHTH
HIGHTHS
HIGHTING
HIGHTOP
HIGHTOPS
HIGHTS
HIGHVELD
HIGHVELDS
HIGHWAY
HIGHWAYS
HIJAB
HIJABS
HIJACK
HIJACKED
HIJACKER
HIJACKERS
HIJACKING
HIJACKS
HIJINKS
HIJRA
HIJRAH
HIJRAHS
HIJRAS
HIKE

HIKED	HILTLESS	HINT	HIPT
HIKER	HILTS	HINTED	HIRABLE
HIKERS	HILUM	HINTER	HIRAGANA
HIKES	HILUS	HINTERS	HIRAGANAS
HIKING	HIM	HINTING	HIRAGE
HIKOI	HIMATIA	HINTINGLY	HIRAGES
HIKOIED	HIMATION	HINTINGS	HIRCINE
HIKOIING	HIMATIONS	HINTS	HIRCOSITY
HIKOIS	HIMBO	HIOI	HIRE
HILA	HIMBOS	HIOIS	HIREABLE
HILAR	HIMS	HIP	HIREAGE
HILARIOUS	HIMSELF	HIPBONE	HIREAGES
HILARITY	HIN	HIPBONES	HIRED
HILCH	HINAHINA	HIPHUGGER	HIREE
HILCHED	HINAU	HIPLESS	HIREES
HILCHES	HIND	HIPLIKE	HIRELING
HILCHING	HINDBERRY	HIPLINE	HIRELINGS
HILD	HINDBRAIN	HIPLINES	HIRER
HILDING	HINDER	HIPLY	HIRERS
HILDINGS	HINDERED	HIPNESS	HIRES
HILI	HINDERER	HIPNESSES	HIRING
HILL	HINDERERS	HIPPARCH	HIRINGS
HILLBILLY	HINDERING	HIPPARCHS	HIRLING
HILLCREST	HINDERS	HIPPED	HIRLINGS
HILLED	HINDFEET	HIPPEN	HIRPLE
HILLER	HINDFOOT	HIPPENS	HIRPLED
HILLERS	HINDGUT	HIPPER	HIRPLES
HILLFOLK	HINDGUTS	HIPPEST	HIRPLING
HILLFORT	HINDHEAD	HIPPIATRY	HIRRIENT
HILLFORTS	HINDHEADS	HIPPIC	HIRRIENTS
HILLIER	HINDLEG	HIPPIE	HIRSEL
HILLIEST	HINDLEGS	HIPPIEDOM	HIRSELED
HILLINESS	HINDMOST	HIPPIEISH	HIRSELING
HILLING	HINDRANCE	HIPPIER	HIRSELLED
HILLMEN	HINDS	HIPPIES	HIRSELS
HILLO	HINDSHANK	HIPPIEST	HIRSLE
HILLOA	HINDSIGHT	HIPPIN	HIRSLED
HILLOAED	HINDWARD	HIPPINESS	HIRSLES
HILLOAING	HINDWING	HIPPING	HIRSLING
HILLOAS	HINDWINGS	HIPPINGS	HIRSTIE
HILLOCK	HING	HIPPINS	HIRSUTE
HILLOCKED	HINGE	HIPPISH	HIRSUTISM
HILLOCKS	HINGED	HIPPO	HIRUDIN
HILLOCKY	HINGELESS	HIPPOCRAS	HIRUDINS
HILLOED	HINGELIKE	HIPPODAME	HIRUNDINE
HILLOES	HINGER	HIPPOLOGY	HIS
HILLOING	HINGERS	HIPPOS	HISH
HILLOS	HINGES	HIPPURIC	HISHED
HILLS	HINGING	HIPPURITE	HISHES
HILLSIDE	HINGS	HIPPUS	HISHING
HILLSIDES	HINKIER	HIPPUSES	HISN
HILLSLOPE	HINKIEST	HIPPY	HISPANISM
HILLTOP	HINKY	HIPPYDOM	HISPID
HILLTOPS	HINNIED	HIPPYDOMS	HISPIDITY
HILLY	HINNIES	HIPS	HISS
HILT	HINNY	HIPSHOT	HISSED
HILTED	HINNYING	HIPSTER	HISSELF
HILTING	HINS	HIPSTERS	HISSER

HISSERS

HISSERS
HISSES
HISSIER
HISSIES
HISSIEST
HISSING
HISSINGLY
HISSINGS
HISSY
HIST
HISTAMIN
HISTAMINE
HISTAMINS
HISTED
HISTIDIN
HISTIDINE
HISTIDINS
HISTIE
HISTING
HISTIOID
HISTOGEN
HISTOGENS
HISTOGENY
HISTOGRAM
HISTOID
HISTOLOGY
HISTONE
HISTONES
HISTORIAN
HISTORIC
HISTORIED
HISTORIES
HISTORIFY
HISTORISM
HISTORY
HISTRIO
HISTRION
HISTRIONS
HISTRIOS
HISTS
HIT
HITCH
HITCHED
HITCHER
HITCHERS
HITCHES
HITCHHIKE
HITCHIER
HITCHIEST
HITCHILY
HITCHING
HITCHY
HITHE
HITHER
HITHERED
HITHERING
HITHERS
HITHERTO

HITHES
HITLESS
HITMAN
HITMEN
HITS
HITTABLE
HITTER
HITTERS
HITTING
HIVE
HIVED
HIVELESS
HIVELIKE
HIVER
HIVERS
HIVES
HIVEWARD
HIVEWARDS
HIVING
HIYA
HIZEN
HIZENS
HIZZ
HIZZED
HIZZES
HIZZING
HIZZONER
HIZZONERS
HM
HMM
HO
HOA
HOACTZIN
HOACTZINS
HOAED
HOAGIE
HOAGIES
HOAGY
HOAING
HOAR
HOARD
HOARDED
HOARDER
HOARDERS
HOARDING
HOARDINGS
HOARDS
HOARED
HOARFROST
HOARHEAD
HOARHEADS
HOARHOUND
HOARIER
HOARIEST
HOARILY
HOARINESS
HOARING
HOARS

HOARSE
HOARSELY
HOARSEN
HOARSENED
HOARSENS
HOARSER
HOARSEST
HOARY
HOAS
HOAST
HOASTED
HOASTING
HOASTMAN
HOASTMEN
HOASTS
HOATCHING
HOATZIN
HOATZINES
HOATZINS
HOAX
HOAXED
HOAXER
HOAXERS
HOAXES
HOAXING
HOB
HOBBED
HOBBER
HOBBERS
HOBBIES
HOBBING
HOBBISH
HOBBIT
HOBBITRY
HOBBITS
HOBBLE
HOBBLED
HOBBLER
HOBBLERS
HOBBLES
HOBBLING
HOBBLINGS
HOBBY
HOBBYISM
HOBBYISMS
HOBBYIST
HOBBYISTS
HOBBYLESS
HOBDAY
HOBDAYED
HOBDAYING
HOBDAYS
HOBGOBLIN
HOBJOB
HOBJOBBED
HOBJOBBER
HOBJOBS
HOBLIKE

HOBNAIL
HOBNAILED
HOBNAILS
HOBNOB
HOBNOBBED
HOBNOBBER
HOBNOBBY
HOBNOBS
HOBO
HOBODOM
HOBODOMS
HOBOED
HOBOES
HOBOING
HOBOISM
HOBOISMS
HOBOS
HOBS
HOC
HOCK
HOCKED
HOCKER
HOCKERS
HOCKEY
HOCKEYS
HOCKING
HOCKLE
HOCKLED
HOCKLES
HOCKLING
HOCKS
HOCKSHOP
HOCKSHOPS
HOCUS
HOCUSED
HOCUSES
HOCUSING
HOCUSSED
HOCUSSES
HOCUSSING
HOD
HODAD
HODADDIES
HODADDY
HODADS
HODDED
HODDEN
HODDENS
HODDIN
HODDING
HODDINS
HODDLE
HODDLED
HODDLES
HODDLING
HODIERNAL
HODJA
HODJAS

HODMAN
HODMANDOD
HODMEN
HODOGRAPH
HODOMETER
HODOMETRY
HODOSCOPE
HODS
HOE
HOECAKE
HOECAKES
HOED
HOEDOWN
HOEDOWNS
HOEING
HOELIKE
HOER
HOERS
HOES
HOG
HOGAN
HOGANS
HOGBACK
HOGBACKS
HOGEN
HOGENS
HOGFISH
HOGFISHES
HOGG
HOGGED
HOGGER
HOGGEREL
HOGGERELS
HOGGERIES
HOGGERS
HOGGERY
HOGGET
HOGGETS
HOGGIN
HOGGING
HOGGINGS
HOGGINS
HOGGISH
HOGGISHLY
HOGGS
HOGH
HOGHOOD
HOGHOODS
HOGHS
HOGLIKE
HOGMANAY
HOGMANAYS
HOGMANE
HOGMANES
HOGMENAY
HOGMENAYS
HOGNOSE
HOGNOSED

HOGNOSES
HOGNUT
HOGNUTS
HOGS
HOGSHEAD
HOGSHEADS
HOGTIE
HOGTIED
HOGTIEING
HOGTIES
HOGTYING
HOGWARD
HOGWARDS
HOGWASH
HOGWASHES
HOGWEED
HOGWEEDS
HOH
HOHA
HOHED
HOHING
HOHS
HOI
HOICK
HOICKED
HOICKING
HOICKS
HOICKSED
HOICKSES
HOICKSING
HOIDEN
HOIDENED
HOIDENING
HOIDENISH
HOIDENS
HOIK
HOIKED
HOIKING
HOIKS
HOING
HOISE
HOISED
HOISES
HOISIN
HOISING
HOISINS
HOIST
HOISTED
HOISTER
HOISTERS
HOISTING
HOISTINGS
HOISTMAN
HOISTMEN
HOISTS
HOISTWAY
HOISTWAYS
HOKA

HOKE
HOKED
HOKES
HOKEY
HOKEYNESS
HOKI
HOKIER
HOKIEST
HOKILY
HOKINESS
HOKING
HOKIS
HOKKU
HOKONUI
HOKONUIS
HOKUM
HOKUMS
HOKYPOKY
HOLANDRIC
HOLARCHY
HOLARD
HOLARDS
HOLD
HOLDABLE
HOLDALL
HOLDALLS
HOLDBACK
HOLDBACKS
HOLDDOWN
HOLDDOWNS
HOLDEN
HOLDER
HOLDERBAT
HOLDERS
HOLDFAST
HOLDFASTS
HOLDING
HOLDINGS
HOLDOUT
HOLDOUTS
HOLDOVER
HOLDOVERS
HOLDS
HOLDUP
HOLDUPS
HOLE
HOLED
HOLELESS
HOLES
HOLESOM
HOLESOME
HOLEY
HOLEYER
HOLEYEST
HOLIBUT
HOLIBUTS
HOLIDAY
HOLIDAYED

HOLIDAYER
HOLIDAYS
HOLIER
HOLIES
HOLIEST
HOLILY
HOLINESS
HOLING
HOLINGS
HOLISM
HOLISMS
HOLIST
HOLISTIC
HOLISTS
HOLK
HOLKED
HOLKING
HOLKS
HOLLA
HOLLAED
HOLLAING
HOLLAND
HOLLANDS
HOLLAS
HOLLER
HOLLERED
HOLLERING
HOLLERS
HOLLIDAM
HOLLIDAMS
HOLLIES
HOLLO
HOLLOA
HOLLOAED
HOLLOAING
HOLLOAS
HOLLOED
HOLLOES
HOLLOING
HOLLOO
HOLLOOED
HOLLOOING
HOLLOOS
HOLLOS
HOLLOW
HOLLOWARE
HOLLOWED
HOLLOWER
HOLLOWEST
HOLLOWING
HOLLOWLY
HOLLOWS
HOLLY
HOLLYHOCK
HOLM
HOLMIA
HOLMIAS
HOLMIC

HOLMIUM
HOLMIUMS
HOLMS
HOLOCAUST
HOLOCENE
HOLOCRINE
HOLOGAMY
HOLOGRAM
HOLOGRAMS
HOLOGRAPH
HOLOGYNIC
HOLOGYNY
HOLOHEDRA
HOLON
HOLONIC
HOLONS
HOLOPHOTE
HOLOPHYTE
HOLOPTIC
HOLOTYPE
HOLOTYPES
HOLOTYPIC
HOLOZOIC
HOLP
HOLPEN
HOLS
HOLSTEIN
HOLSTEINS
HOLSTER
HOLSTERED
HOLSTERS
HOLT
HOLTS
HOLY
HOLYDAM
HOLYDAME
HOLYDAMES
HOLYDAMS
HOLYDAY
HOLYDAYS
HOLYSTONE
HOLYTIDE
HOLYTIDES
HOM
HOMA
HOMAGE
HOMAGED
HOMAGER
HOMAGERS
HOMAGES
HOMAGING
HOMALOID
HOMALOIDS
HOMAS
HOMBRE
HOMBRES
HOMBURG
HOMBURGS

HOME
HOMEBIRTH
HOMEBODY
HOMEBOUND
HOMEBOY
HOMEBOYS
HOMEBRED
HOMEBREDS
HOMEBREW
HOMEBREWS
HOMEBUILT
HOMEBUYER
HOMECOMER
HOMECRAFT
HOMED
HOMEFELT
HOMEGIRL
HOMEGIRLS
HOMEGROWN
HOMELAND
HOMELANDS
HOMELESS
HOMELIER
HOMELIEST
HOMELIKE
HOMELILY
HOMELY
HOMELYN
HOMELYNS
HOMEMADE
HOMEMAKER
HOMEOBOX
HOMEOMERY
HOMEOPATH
HOMEOSES
HOMEOSIS
HOMEOTIC
HOMEOWNER
HOMEPAGE
HOMEPAGES
HOMEPLACE
HOMEPORT
HOMEPORTS
HOMER
HOMERED
HOMERIC
HOMERING
HOMEROOM
HOMEROOMS
HOMERS
HOMES
HOMESICK
HOMESITE
HOMESITES
HOMESPUN
HOMESPUNS
HOMESTALL
HOMESTAND

HOMESTAY
HOMESTAYS
HOMESTEAD
HOMETOWN
HOMETOWNS
HOMEWARD
HOMEWARDS
HOMEWARE
HOMEWARES
HOMEWORK
HOMEWORKS
HOMEY
HOMEYNESS
HOMEYS
HOMICIDAL
HOMICIDE
HOMICIDES
HOMIE
HOMIER
HOMIES
HOMIEST
HOMILETIC
HOMILIES
HOMILIST
HOMILISTS
HOMILY
HOMINES
HOMINESS
HOMING
HOMINGS
HOMINIAN
HOMINIANS
HOMINID
HOMINIDS
HOMINIES
HOMININE
HOMINISE
HOMINISED
HOMINISES
HOMINIZE
HOMINIZED
HOMINIZES
HOMINOID
HOMINOIDS
HOMINY
HOMME
HOMMES
HOMMOCK
HOMMOCKS
HOMMOS
HOMMOSES
HOMO
HOMOCERCY
HOMODONT
HOMODYNE
HOMOEOBOX
HOMOEOSES
HOMOEOSIS

HOMOEOTIC
HOMOGAMIC
HOMOGAMY
HOMOGENY
HOMOGONY
HOMOGRAFT
HOMOGRAPH
HOMOLOG
HOMOLOGIC
HOMOLOGS
HOMOLOGUE
HOMOLOGY
HOMOLYSES
HOMOLYSIS
HOMOLYTIC
HOMOMORPH
HOMONYM
HOMONYMIC
HOMONYMS
HOMONYMY
HOMOPHILE
HOMOPHOBE
HOMOPHONE
HOMOPHONY
HOMOPHYLY
HOMOPLASY
HOMOPOLAR
HOMOS
HOMOSEX
HOMOSEXES
HOMOSPORY
HOMOSTYLY
HOMOTAXES
HOMOTAXIC
HOMOTAXIS
HOMOTONIC
HOMOTONY
HOMOTYPAL
HOMOTYPE
HOMOTYPES
HOMOTYPIC
HOMOTYPY
HOMOUSIAN
HOMS
HOMUNCLE
HOMUNCLES
HOMUNCULE
HOMUNCULI
HOMY
HON
HONAN
HONANS
HONCHO
HONCHOED
HONCHOING
HONCHOS
HOND
HONDA

HONDAS
HONDLE
HONDLED
HONDLES
HONDLING
HONDS
HONE
HONED
HONER
HONERS
HONES
HONEST
HONESTER
HONESTEST
HONESTIES
HONESTLY
HONESTY
HONEWORT
HONEWORTS
HONEY
HONEYBEE
HONEYBEES
HONEYBUN
HONEYBUNS
HONEYCOMB
HONEYDEW
HONEYDEWS
HONEYED
HONEYEDLY
HONEYFUL
HONEYING
HONEYLESS
HONEYMOON
HONEYPOT
HONEYPOTS
HONEYS
HONEYTRAP
HONG
HONGI
HONGIED
HONGIES
HONGIING
HONGING
HONGIS
HONGS
HONIED
HONIEDLY
HONING
HONK
HONKED
HONKER
HONKERS
HONKEY
HONKEYS
HONKIE
HONKIES
HONKING
HONKS

HONKY
HONOR
HONORABLE
HONORABLY
HONORAND
HONORANDS
HONORARIA
HONORARY
HONORED
HONOREE
HONOREES
HONORER
HONORERS
HONORIFIC
HONORING
HONORLESS
HONORS
HONOUR
HONOURED
HONOURER
HONOURERS
HONOURING
HONOURS
HONS
HOO
HOOCH
HOOCHES
HOOCHIE
HOOCHIES
HOOD
HOODED
HOODIA
HOODIAS
HOODIE
HOODIER
HOODIES
HOODIEST
HOODING
HOODLESS
HOODLIKE
HOODLUM
HOODLUMS
HOODMAN
HOODMEN
HOODMOLD
HOODMOLDS
HOODOO
HOODOOED
HOODOOING
HOODOOISM
HOODOOS
HOODS
HOODWINK
HOODWINKS
HOODY
HOOEY
HOOEYS
HOOF

HOOFBEAT
HOOFBEATS
HOOFBOUND
HOOFED
HOOFER
HOOFERS
HOOFING
HOOFLESS
HOOFLIKE
HOOFPRINT
HOOFROT
HOOFROTS
HOOFS
HOOK
HOOKA
HOOKAH
HOOKAHS
HOOKAS
HOOKCHECK
HOOKED
HOOKER
HOOKERS
HOOKEY
HOOKEYS
HOOKIER
HOOKIES
HOOKIEST
HOOKING
HOOKLESS
HOOKLET
HOOKLETS
HOOKLIKE
HOOKNOSE
HOOKNOSED
HOOKNOSES
HOOKS
HOOKUP
HOOKUPS
HOOKWORM
HOOKWORMS
HOOKY
HOOLACHAN
HOOLEY
HOOLEYS
HOOLICAN
HOOLICANS
HOOLIE
HOOLIER
HOOLIES
HOOLIEST
HOOLIGAN
HOOLIGANS
HOOLOCK
HOOLOCKS
HOOLY
HOON
HOONS
HOOP

HOOPED
HOOPER
HOOPERS
HOOPING
HOOPLA
HOOPLAS
HOOPLESS
HOOPLIKE
HOOPOE
HOOPOES
HOOPOO
HOOPOOS
HOOPS
HOOPSKIRT
HOOPSTER
HOOPSTERS
HOORAH
HOORAHED
HOORAHING
HOORAHS
HOORAY
HOORAYED
HOORAYING
HOORAYS
HOORD
HOORDS
HOOROO
HOOSEGOW
HOOSEGOWS
HOOSGOW
HOOSGOWS
HOOSH
HOOSHED
HOOSHES
HOOSHING
HOOT
HOOTCH
HOOTCHES
HOOTED
HOOTER
HOOTERS
HOOTIER
HOOTIEST
HOOTING
HOOTNANNY
HOOTS
HOOTY
HOOVE
HOOVED
HOOVEN
HOOVER
HOOVERED
HOOVERING
HOOVERS
HOOVES
HOOVING
HOP
HOPBIND

HOPBINDS
HOPBINE
HOPBINES
HOPDOG
HOPDOGS
HOPE
HOPED
HOPEFUL
HOPEFULLY
HOPEFULS
HOPELESS
HOPER
HOPERS
HOPES
HOPHEAD
HOPHEADS
HOPING
HOPINGLY
HOPLITE
HOPLITES
HOPLITIC
HOPLOLOGY
HOPPED
HOPPER
HOPPERCAR
HOPPERS
HOPPIER
HOPPIEST
HOPPING
HOPPINGS
HOPPLE
HOPPLED
HOPPLER
HOPPLERS
HOPPLES
HOPPLING
HOPPY
HOPS
HOPSACK
HOPSACKS
HOPSCOTCH
HOPTOAD
HOPTOADS
HORA
HORAH
HORAHS
HORAL
HORARY
HORAS
HORDE
HORDED
HORDEIN
HORDEINS
HORDEOLA
HORDEOLUM
HORDES
HORDING
HORDOCK

HORDOCKS
HORE
HOREHOUND
HORI
HORIATIKI
HORIS
HORIZON
HORIZONAL
HORIZONS
HORKEY
HORKEYS
HORLICKS
HORME
HORMES
HORMIC
HORMONAL
HORMONE
HORMONES
HORMONIC
HORN
HORNBAG
HORNBAGS
HORNBEAK
HORNBEAKS
HORNBEAM
HORNBEAMS
HORNBILL
HORNBILLS
HORNBOOK
HORNBOOKS
HORNBUG
HORNBUGS
HORNED
HORNER
HORNERS
HORNET
HORNETS
HORNFELS
HORNFUL
HORNFULS
HORNGELD
HORNGELDS
HORNIER
HORNIEST
HORNILY
HORNINESS
HORNING
HORNINGS
HORNISH
HORNIST
HORNISTS
HORNITO
HORNITOS
HORNLESS
HORNLET
HORNLETS
HORNLIKE
HORNPIPE

HORNPIPES
HORNPOUT
HORNPOUTS
HORNS
HORNSTONE
HORNTAIL
HORNTAILS
HORNWORK
HORNWORKS
HORNWORM
HORNWORMS
HORNWORT
HORNWORTS
HORNWRACK
HORNY
HORNYHEAD
HORNYWINK
HOROEKA
HOROKAKA
HOROLOGE
HOROLOGER
HOROLOGES
HOROLOGIA
HOROLOGIC
HOROLOGY
HOROMETRY
HOROPITO
HOROPITOS
HOROPTER
HOROPTERS
HOROSCOPE
HOROSCOPY
HORRENT
HORRIBLE
HORRIBLES
HORRIBLY
HORRID
HORRIDER
HORRIDEST
HORRIDLY
HORRIFIC
HORRIFIED
HORRIFIES
HORRIFY
HORROR
HORRORS
HORS
HORSE
HORSEBACK
HORSEBEAN
HORSEBOX
HORSECAR
HORSECARS
HORSED
HORSEFLY
HORSEHAIR
HORSEHIDE
HORSELESS

HORSELIKE
HORSEMAN
HORSEMEAT
HORSEMEN
HORSEMINT
HORSEPLAY
HORSEPOND
HORSEPOX
HORSERACE
HORSES
HORSESHIT
HORSESHOD
HORSESHOE
HORSETAIL
HORSEWAY
HORSEWAYS
HORSEWEED
HORSEWHIP
HORSEY
HORSIER
HORSIEST
HORSILY
HORSINESS
HORSING
HORSINGS
HORSON
HORSONS
HORST
HORSTE
HORSTES
HORSTS
HORSY
HORTATION
HORTATIVE
HORTATORY
HOS
HOSANNA
HOSANNAED
HOSANNAH
HOSANNAHS
HOSANNAS
HOSE
HOSED
HOSEL
HOSELIKE
HOSELS
HOSEMAN
HOSEMEN
HOSEN
HOSEPIPE
HOSEPIPES
HOSER
HOSERS
HOSES
HOSEY
HOSEYED
HOSEYING
HOSEYS

HOSIER	HOTCAKES	HOTTIE	HOUSEKEEP
HOSIERIES	HOTCH	HOTTIES	HOUSEKEPT
HOSIERS	HOTCHED	HOTTING	HOUSEL
HOSIERY	HOTCHES	HOTTINGS	HOUSELED
HOSING	HOTCHING	HOTTISH	HOUSELEEK
HOSPICE	HOTCHPOT	HOTTY	HOUSELESS
HOSPICES	HOTCHPOTS	HOUDAH	HOUSELINE
HOSPITAGE	HOTDOG	HOUDAHS	HOUSELING
HOSPITAL	HOTDOGGED	HOUDAN	HOUSELLED
HOSPITALE	HOTDOGGER	HOUDANS	HOUSELS
HOSPITALS	HOTDOGS	HOUF	HOUSEMAID
HOSPITIA	HOTE	HOUFED	HOUSEMAN
HOSPITIUM	HOTEL	HOUFF	HOUSEMATE
HOSPODAR	HOTELDOM	HOUFFED	HOUSEMEN
HOSPODARS	HOTELDOMS	HOUFFING	HOUSER
HOSS	HOTELIER	HOUFFS	HOUSEROOM
HOSSES	HOTELIERS	HOUFING	HOUSERS
HOST	HOTELMAN	HOUFS	HOUSES
HOSTA	HOTELMEN	HOUGH	HOUSESAT
HOSTAGE	HOTELS	HOUGHED	HOUSESIT
HOSTAGES	HOTEN	HOUGHING	HOUSESITS
HOSTAS	HOTFOOT	HOUGHS	HOUSETOP
HOSTED	HOTFOOTED	HOUHERE	HOUSETOPS
HOSTEL	HOTFOOTS	HOUMMOS	HOUSEWIFE
HOSTELED	HOTHEAD	HOUMMOSES	HOUSEWORK
HOSTELER	HOTHEADED	HOUMOUS	HOUSEY
HOSTELERS	HOTHEADS	HOUMOUSES	HOUSIER
HOSTELING	HOTHOUSE	HOUMUS	HOUSIEST
HOSTELLED	HOTHOUSED	HOUMUSES	HOUSING
HOSTELLER	HOTHOUSES	HOUND	HOUSINGS
HOSTELRY	HOTLINE	HOUNDED	HOUSLING
HOSTELS	HOTLINES	HOUNDER	HOUSTONIA
HOSTESS	HOTLINK	HOUNDERS	HOUT
HOSTESSED	HOTLINKS	HOUNDFISH	HOUTED
HOSTESSES	HOTLY	HOUNDING	HOUTING
HOSTIE	HOTNESS	HOUNDS	HOUTINGS
HOSTIES	HOTNESSES	HOUNGAN	HOUTS
HOSTILE	HOTPLATE	HOUNGANS	HOVE
HOSTILELY	HOTPLATES	HOUR	HOVEA
HOSTILES	HOTPOT	HOURGLASS	HOVEAS
HOSTILITY	HOTPOTS	HOURI	HOVED
HOSTING	HOTPRESS	HOURIS	HOVEL
HOSTINGS	HOTROD	HOURLIES	HOVELED
HOSTLER	HOTRODS	HOURLONG	HOVELING
HOSTLERS	HOTS	HOURLY	HOVELLED
HOSTLESSE	HOTSHOT	HOURPLATE	HOVELLER
HOSTLY	HOTSHOTS	HOURS	HOVELLERS
HOSTRIES	HOTSPOT	HOUSE	HOVELLING
HOSTRY	HOTSPOTS	HOUSEBOAT	HOVELS
HOSTS	HOTSPUR	HOUSEBOY	HOVEN
HOT	HOTSPURS	HOUSEBOYS	HOVER
HOTBED	HOTTED	HOUSECARL	HOVERED
HOTBEDS	HOTTENTOT	HOUSECOAT	HOVERER
HOTBLOOD	HOTTER	HOUSED	HOVERERS
HOTBLOODS	HOTTERED	HOUSEFLY	HOVERFLY
HOTBOX	HOTTERING	HOUSEFUL	HOVERING
HOTBOXES	HOTTERS	HOUSEFULS	HOVERPORT
HOTCAKE	HOTTEST	HOUSEHOLD	HOVERS

HOVES
HOVING
HOW
HOWBE
HOWBEIT
HOWDAH
HOWDAHS
HOWDIE
HOWDIED
HOWDIES
HOWDY
HOWDYING
HOWE
HOWES
HOWEVER
HOWF
HOWFED
HOWFF
HOWFFED
HOWFFING
HOWFFS
HOWFING
HOWFS
HOWITZER
HOWITZERS
HOWK
HOWKED
HOWKER
HOWKERS
HOWKING
HOWKS
HOWL
HOWLBACK
HOWLBACKS
HOWLED
HOWLER
HOWLERS
HOWLET
HOWLETS
HOWLING
HOWLINGLY
HOWLINGS
HOWLROUND
HOWLS
HOWRE
HOWRES
HOWS
HOWSO
HOWSOEVER
HOWTOWDIE
HOWZAT
HOWZIT
HOX
HOXED
HOXES
HOXING
HOY
HOYA

HOYAS
HOYDEN
HOYDENED
HOYDENING
HOYDENISH
HOYDENISM
HOYDENS
HOYED
HOYING
HOYLE
HOYLES
HOYS
HRYVNA
HRYVNAS
HRYVNIA
HRYVNIAS
HRYVNYA
HRYVNYAS
HUANACO
HUANACOS
HUAQUERO
HUAQUEROS
HUARACHE
HUARACHES
HUARACHO
HUARACHOS
HUB
HUBBIES
HUBBLY
HUBBUB
HUBBUBOO
HUBBUBOOS
HUBBUBS
HUBBY
HUBCAP
HUBCAPS
HUBRIS
HUBRISES
HUBRISTIC
HUBS
HUCK
HUCKABACK
HUCKERY
HUCKLE
HUCKLES
HUCKS
HUCKSTER
HUCKSTERS
HUCKSTERY
HUDDEN
HUDDLE
HUDDLED
HUDDLER
HUDDLERS
HUDDLES
HUDDLING
HUDDUP
HUDNA

HUDNAS
HUDUD
HUDUDS
HUE
HUED
HUELESS
HUER
HUERS
HUES
HUFF
HUFFED
HUFFER
HUFFERS
HUFFIER
HUFFIEST
HUFFILY
HUFFINESS
HUFFING
HUFFINGS
HUFFISH
HUFFISHLY
HUFFKIN
HUFFKINS
HUFFS
HUFFY
HUG
HUGE
HUGELY
HUGENESS
HUGEOUS
HUGEOUSLY
HUGER
HUGEST
HUGGABLE
HUGGED
HUGGER
HUGGERS
HUGGIER
HUGGIEST
HUGGING
HUGGY
HUGS
HUGY
HUH
HUHU
HUHUS
HUI
HUIA
HUIAS
HUIC
HUIPIL
HUIPILES
HUIPILS
HUIS
HUISACHE
HUISACHES
HUISSIER
HUISSIERS

HUITAIN
HUITAINS
HULA
HULAS
HULE
HULES
HULK
HULKED
HULKIER
HULKIEST
HULKING
HULKS
HULKY
HULL
HULLED
HULLER
HULLERS
HULLIER
HULLIEST
HULLING
HULLO
HULLOA
HULLOAED
HULLOAING
HULLOAS
HULLOED
HULLOES
HULLOING
HULLOO
HULLOOED
HULLOOING
HULLOOS
HULLOS
HULLS
HULLY
HUM
HUMA
HUMAN
HUMANE
HUMANELY
HUMANER
HUMANEST
HUMANHOOD
HUMANISE
HUMANISED
HUMANISER
HUMANISES
HUMANISM
HUMANISMS
HUMANIST
HUMANISTS
HUMANITY
HUMANIZE
HUMANIZED
HUMANIZER
HUMANIZES
HUMANKIND
HUMANLIKE

HUMANLY
HUMANNESS
HUMANOID
HUMANOIDS
HUMANS
HUMAS
HUMATE
HUMATES
HUMBLE
HUMBLEBEE
HUMBLED
HUMBLER
HUMBLERS
HUMBLES
HUMBLESSE
HUMBLEST
HUMBLING
HUMBLINGS
HUMBLY
HUMBUCKER
HUMBUG
HUMBUGGED
HUMBUGGER
HUMBUGS
HUMBUZZ
HUMBUZZES
HUMDINGER
HUMDRUM
HUMDRUMS
HUMECT
HUMECTANT
HUMECTATE
HUMECTED
HUMECTING
HUMECTIVE
HUMECTS
HUMEFIED
HUMEFIES
HUMEFY
HUMEFYING
HUMERAL
HUMERALS
HUMERI
HUMERUS
HUMF
HUMFED
HUMFING
HUMFS
HUMHUM
HUMHUMS
HUMIC
HUMICOLE
HUMICOLES
HUMID
HUMIDER
HUMIDEST
HUMIDEX
HUMIDEXES

HUMIDICES
HUMIDIFY
HUMIDITY
HUMIDLY
HUMIDNESS
HUMIDOR
HUMIDORS
HUMIFIED
HUMIFIES
HUMIFY
HUMIFYING
HUMILIANT
HUMILIATE
HUMILITY
HUMINT
HUMINTS
HUMITE
HUMITES
HUMITURE
HUMITURES
HUMLIE
HUMLIES
HUMMABLE
HUMMAUM
HUMMAUMS
HUMMED
HUMMEL
HUMMELLED
HUMMELLER
HUMMELS
HUMMER
HUMMERS
HUMMING
HUMMINGS
HUMMOCK
HUMMOCKED
HUMMOCKS
HUMMOCKY
HUMMUM
HUMMUMS
HUMMUS
HUMMUSES
HUMOGEN
HUMOGENS
HUMONGOUS
HUMOR
HUMORAL
HUMORALLY
HUMORED
HUMORESK
HUMORESKS
HUMORFUL
HUMORING
HUMORIST
HUMORISTS
HUMORLESS
HUMOROUS
HUMORS

HUMORSOME
HUMOUR
HUMOURED
HUMOURFUL
HUMOURING
HUMOURS
HUMOUS
HUMP
HUMPBACK
HUMPBACKS
HUMPED
HUMPEN
HUMPENS
HUMPER
HUMPERS
HUMPH
HUMPHED
HUMPHING
HUMPHS
HUMPIER
HUMPIES
HUMPIEST
HUMPINESS
HUMPING
HUMPLESS
HUMPLIKE
HUMPS
HUMPTIES
HUMPTY
HUMPY
HUMS
HUMSTRUM
HUMSTRUMS
HUMUNGOUS
HUMUS
HUMUSES
HUMUSY
HUMVEE
HUMVEES
HUN
HUNCH
HUNCHBACK
HUNCHED
HUNCHES
HUNCHING
HUNDRED
HUNDREDER
HUNDREDOR
HUNDREDS
HUNDREDTH
HUNG
HUNGAN
HUNGANS
HUNGER
HUNGERED
HUNGERFUL
HUNGERING
HUNGERLY

HUNGERS
HUNGOVER
HUNGRIER
HUNGRIEST
HUNGRILY
HUNGRY
HUNH
HUNK
HUNKER
HUNKERED
HUNKERING
HUNKERS
HUNKEY
HUNKEYS
HUNKIE
HUNKIER
HUNKIES
HUNKIEST
HUNKS
HUNKSES
HUNKY
HUNNISH
HUNS
HUNT
HUNTABLE
HUNTAWAY
HUNTAWAYS
HUNTED
HUNTEDLY
HUNTER
HUNTERS
HUNTING
HUNTINGS
HUNTRESS
HUNTS
HUNTSMAN
HUNTSMEN
HUP
HUPIRO
HUPPAH
HUPPAHS
HUPPED
HUPPING
HUPS
HURCHEON
HURCHEONS
HURDEN
HURDENS
HURDIES
HURDLE
HURDLED
HURDLER
HURDLERS
HURDLES
HURDLING
HURDLINGS
HURDS
HURL

HURLBAT	HUSHED	HUTMENT	HYDATHODE
HURLBATS	HUSHEDLY	HUTMENTS	HYDATID
HURLED	HUSHER	HUTS	HYDATIDS
HURLER	HUSHERED	HUTTED	HYDATOID
HURLERS	HUSHERING	HUTTING	HYDRA
HURLEY	HUSHERS	HUTTINGS	HYDRACID
HURLEYS	HUSHES	HUTZPA	HYDRACIDS
HURLIES	HUSHFUL	HUTZPAH	HYDRAE
HURLING	HUSHIER	HUTZPAHS	HYDRAEMIA
HURLINGS	HUSHIEST	HUTZPAS	HYDRAGOG
HURLS	HUSHING	HUZOOR	HYDRAGOGS
HURLY	HUSHPUPPY	HUZOORS	HYDRANGEA
HURRA	HUSHY	HUZZA	HYDRANT
HURRAED	HUSK	HUZZAED	HYDRANTH
HURRAH	HUSKED	HUZZAH	HYDRANTHS
HURRAHED	HUSKER	HUZZAHED	HYDRANTS
HURRAHING	HUSKERS	HUZZAHING	HYDRAS
HURRAHS	HUSKIER	HUZZAHS	HYDRASE
HURRAING	HUSKIES	HUZZAING	HYDRASES
HURRAS	HUSKIEST	HUZZAS	HYDRASTIS
HURRAY	HUSKILY	HUZZIES	HYDRATE
HURRAYED	HUSKINESS	HUZZY	HYDRATED
HURRAYING	HUSKING	HWAN	HYDRATES
HURRAYS	HUSKINGS	HWYL	HYDRATING
HURRICANE	HUSKLIKE	HWYLS	HYDRATION
HURRICANO	HUSKS	HYACINE	HYDRATOR
HURRIED	HUSKY	HYACINES	HYDRATORS
HURRIEDLY	HUSO	HYACINTH	HYDRAULIC
HURRIER	HUSOS	HYACINTHS	HYDRAZIDE
HURRIERS	HUSS	HYAENA	HYDRAZINE
HURRIES	HUSSAR	HYAENAS	HYDRAZOIC
HURRY	HUSSARS	HYAENIC	HYDREMIA
HURRYING	HUSSES	HYALIN	HYDREMIAS
HURRYINGS	HUSSIES	HYALINE	HYDRIA
HURST	HUSSIF	HYALINES	HYDRIAE
HURSTS	HUSSIFS	HYALINISE	HYDRIC
HURT	HUSSY	HYALINIZE	HYDRID
HURTER	HUSTINGS	HYALINS	HYDRIDE
HURTERS	HUSTLE	HYALITE	HYDRIDES
HURTFUL	HUSTLED	HYALITES	HYDRIDS
HURTFULLY	HUSTLER	HYALOGEN	HYDRILLA
HURTING	HUSTLERS	HYALOGENS	HYDRILLAS
HURTLE	HUSTLES	HYALOID	HYDRIODIC
HURTLED	HUSTLING	HYALOIDS	HYDRO
HURTLES	HUSTLINGS	HYALONEMA	HYDROCAST
HURTLESS	HUSWIFE	HYBRID	HYDROCELE
HURTLING	HUSWIFES	HYBRIDISE	HYDROFOIL
HURTS	HUSWIVES	HYBRIDISM	HYDROGEL
HUSBAND	HUT	HYBRIDIST	HYDROGELS
HUSBANDED	HUTCH	HYBRIDITY	HYDROGEN
HUSBANDER	HUTCHED	HYBRIDIZE	HYDROGENS
HUSBANDLY	HUTCHES	HYBRIDOMA	HYDROID
HUSBANDRY	HUTCHIE	HYBRIDOUS	HYDROIDS
HUSBANDS	HUTCHIES	HYBRIDS	HYDROLASE
HUSH	HUTCHING	HYBRIS	HYDROLOGY
HUSHABIED	HUTIA	HYBRISES	HYDROLYSE
HUSHABIES	HUTIAS	HYBRISTIC	HYDROLYTE
HUSHABY	HUTLIKE	HYDANTOIN	HYDROLYZE

HYDROMA
HYDROMAS
HYDROMATA
HYDROMEL
HYDROMELS
HYDRONAUT
HYDRONIC
HYDRONIUM
HYDROPATH
HYDROPIC
HYDROPS
HYDROPSES
HYDROPSY
HYDROPTIC
HYDROPULT
HYDROS
HYDROSERE
HYDROSKI
HYDROSKIS
HYDROSOL
HYDROSOLS
HYDROSOMA
HYDROSOME
HYDROSTAT
HYDROUS
HYDROVANE
HYDROXIDE
HYDROXY
HYDROXYL
HYDROXYLS
HYDROZOA
HYDROZOAN
HYDROZOON
HYDYNE
HYDYNES
HYE
HYED
HYEING
HYEN
HYENA
HYENAS
HYENIC
HYENINE
HYENOID
HYENS
HYES
HYETAL
HYETOLOGY
HYGEIST
HYGEISTS
HYGIEIST
HYGIEISTS
HYGIENE
HYGIENES
HYGIENIC
HYGIENICS
HYGIENIST
HYGRISTOR

HYGRODEIK
HYGROLOGY
HYGROMA
HYGROMAS
HYGROMATA
HYGROPHIL
HYGROSTAT
HYING
HYKE
HYKES
HYLA
HYLAS
HYLDING
HYLDINGS
HYLE
HYLEG
HYLEGS
HYLES
HYLIC
HYLICISM
HYLICISMS
HYLICIST
HYLICISTS
HYLISM
HYLISMS
HYLIST
HYLISTS
HYLOBATE
HYLOBATES
HYLOIST
HYLOISTS
HYLOPHYTE
HYLOZOIC
HYLOZOISM
HYLOZOIST
HYMEN
HYMENAEAL
HYMENAEAN
HYMENAL
HYMENEAL
HYMENEALS
HYMENEAN
HYMENIA
HYMENIAL
HYMENIUM
HYMENIUMS
HYMENS
HYMN
HYMNAL
HYMNALS
HYMNARIES
HYMNARY
HYMNBOOK
HYMNBOOKS
HYMNED
HYMNIC
HYMNING
HYMNIST

HYMNISTS
HYMNLESS
HYMNLIKE
HYMNODIES
HYMNODIST
HYMNODY
HYMNOLOGY
HYMNS
HYNDE
HYNDES
HYOID
HYOIDAL
HYOIDEAN
HYOIDS
HYOSCINE
HYOSCINES
HYP
HYPALGIA
HYPALGIAS
HYPALLAGE
HYPANTHIA
HYPATE
HYPATES
HYPE
HYPED
HYPER
HYPERACID
HYPERARID
HYPERBOLA
HYPERBOLE
HYPERCUBE
HYPEREMIA
HYPEREMIC
HYPERFINE
HYPERGAMY
HYPERGOL
HYPERGOLS
HYPERICUM
HYPERLINK
HYPERMART
HYPERNOVA
HYPERNYM
HYPERNYMS
HYPERNYMY
HYPERON
HYPERONS
HYPEROPE
HYPEROPES
HYPEROPIA
HYPEROPIC
HYPERPNEA
HYPERPURE
HYPERREAL
HYPERS
HYPERTEXT
HYPES
HYPESTER
HYPESTERS

HYPETHRAL
HYPHA
HYPHAE
HYPHAL
HYPHEMIA
HYPHEMIAS
HYPHEN
HYPHENATE
HYPHENED
HYPHENIC
HYPHENING
HYPHENISE
HYPHENISM
HYPHENIZE
HYPHENS
HYPING
HYPINGS
HYPINOSES
HYPINOSIS
HYPNIC
HYPNICS
HYPNOGENY
HYPNOID
HYPNOIDAL
HYPNOLOGY
HYPNONE
HYPNONES
HYPNOSES
HYPNOSIS
HYPNOTEE
HYPNOTEES
HYPNOTIC
HYPNOTICS
HYPNOTISE
HYPNOTISM
HYPNOTIST
HYPNOTIZE
HYPNOTOID
HYPNUM
HYPNUMS
HYPO
HYPOACID
HYPOBARIC
HYPOBLAST
HYPOBOLE
HYPOBOLES
HYPOCAUST
HYPOCIST
HYPOCISTS
HYPOCOTYL
HYPOCRISY
HYPOCRITE
HYPODERM
HYPODERMA
HYPODERMS
HYPOED
HYPOGAEA
HYPOGAEAL

HYPOGAEAN
HYPOGAEUM
HYPOGEA
HYPOGEAL
HYPOGEAN
HYPOGENE
HYPOGENIC
HYPOGEOUS
HYPOGEUM
HYPOGYNY
HYPOID
HYPOING
HYPOMANIA
HYPOMANIC
HYPOMORPH
HYPONASTY
HYPONEA
HYPONEAS
HYPONOIA
HYPONOIAS
HYPONYM
HYPONYMS
HYPONYMY
HYPOPHYGE
HYPOPLOID
HYPOPNEA
HYPOPNEAS
HYPOPNEIC
HYPOPNOEA
HYPOPYON
HYPOPYONS
HYPOS
HYPOSTOME
HYPOSTYLE
HYPOTAXES
HYPOTAXIS
HYPOTHEC
HYPOTHECA
HYPOTHECS
HYPOTONIA
HYPOTONIC
HYPOXEMIA
HYPOXEMIC
HYPOXIA
HYPOXIAS
HYPOXIC
HYPPED
HYPPING
HYPS
HYPURAL
HYRACES
HYRACOID
HYRACOIDS
HYRAX
HYRAXES
HYSON
HYSONS
HYSSOP

HYSSOPS
HYSTERIA
HYSTERIAS
HYSTERIC
HYSTERICS
HYSTEROID
HYTE
HYTHE
HYTHES

I

IAMB	ICEMAN	ICONIC	IDEALNESS
IAMBI	ICEMEN	ICONICAL	IDEALOGUE
IAMBIC	ICEPACK	ICONICITY	IDEALOGY
IAMBICS	ICEPACKS	ICONIFIED	IDEALS
IAMBIST	ICER	ICONIFIES	IDEAS
IAMBISTS	ICERS	ICONIFY	IDEATA
IAMBS	ICES	ICONISE	IDEATE
IAMBUS	ICESTONE	ICONISED	IDEATED
IAMBUSES	ICESTONES	ICONISES	IDEATES
IANTHINE	ICEWINE	ICONISING	IDEATING
IATRIC	ICEWINES	ICONIZE	IDEATION
IATRICAL	ICH	ICONIZED	IDEATIONS
IATROGENY	ICHABOD	ICONIZES	IDEATIVE
IBERIS	ICHED	ICONIZING	IDEATUM
IBERISES	ICHES	ICONOLOGY	IDEE
IBEX	ICHING	ICONOSTAS	IDEES
IBEXES	ICHNEUMON	ICONS	IDEM
IBICES	ICHNITE	ICTAL	IDENT
IBIDEM	ICHNITES	ICTERIC	IDENTIC
IBIS	ICHNOLITE	ICTERICAL	IDENTICAL
IBISES	ICHNOLOGY	ICTERICS	IDENTIFY
IBOGAINE	ICHOR	ICTERID	IDENTIKIT
IBOGAINES	ICHOROUS	ICTERIDS	IDENTITY
IBUPROFEN	ICHORS	ICTERINE	IDENTS
ICE	ICHS	ICTERUS	IDEOGRAM
ICEBALL	ICHTHIC	ICTERUSES	IDEOGRAMS
ICEBALLS	ICHTHYIC	ICTIC	IDEOGRAPH
ICEBERG	ICHTHYOID	ICTUS	IDEOLOGIC
ICEBERGS	ICHTHYS	ICTUSES	IDEOLOGUE
ICEBLINK	ICHTHYSES	ICY	IDEOLOGY
ICEBLINKS	ICICLE	ID	IDEOMOTOR
ICEBOAT	ICICLED	IDANT	IDEOPHONE
ICEBOATER	ICICLES	IDANTS	IDES
ICEBOATS	ICIER	IDE	IDIOBLAST
ICEBOUND	ICIEST	IDEA	IDIOCIES
ICEBOX	ICILY	IDEAED	IDIOCY
ICEBOXES	ICINESS	IDEAL	IDIOGRAM
ICECAP	ICINESSES	IDEALESS	IDIOGRAMS
ICECAPPED	ICING	IDEALISE	IDIOGRAPH
ICECAPS	ICINGS	IDEALISED	IDIOLECT
ICED	ICK	IDEALISER	IDIOLECTS
ICEFALL	ICKER	IDEALISES	IDIOM
ICEFALLS	ICKERS	IDEALISM	IDIOMATIC
ICEFIELD	ICKIER	IDEALISMS	IDIOMS
ICEFIELDS	ICKIEST	IDEALIST	IDIOPATHY
ICEHOUSE	ICKILY	IDEALISTS	IDIOPHONE
ICEHOUSES	ICKINESS	IDEALITY	IDIOPLASM
ICEKHANA	ICKLE	IDEALIZE	IDIOT
ICEKHANAS	ICKLER	IDEALIZED	IDIOTCIES
ICELESS	ICKLEST	IDEALIZER	IDIOTCY
ICELIKE	ICKY	IDEALIZES	IDIOTIC
ICEMAKER	ICON	IDEALLESS	IDIOTICAL
ICEMAKERS	ICONES	IDEALLY	IDIOTICON

285

IDIOTISH
IDIOTISM
IDIOTISMS
IDIOTS
IDIOTYPE
IDIOTYPES
IDIOTYPIC
IDLE
IDLED
IDLEHOOD
IDLEHOODS
IDLENESS
IDLER
IDLERS
IDLES
IDLESSE
IDLESSES
IDLEST
IDLING
IDLY
IDOCRASE
IDOCRASES
IDOL
IDOLA
IDOLATER
IDOLATERS
IDOLATOR
IDOLATORS
IDOLATRY
IDOLISE
IDOLISED
IDOLISER
IDOLISERS
IDOLISES
IDOLISING
IDOLISM
IDOLISMS
IDOLIST
IDOLISTS
IDOLIZE
IDOLIZED
IDOLIZER
IDOLIZERS
IDOLIZES
IDOLIZING
IDOLS
IDOLUM
IDONEITY
IDONEOUS
IDS
IDYL
IDYLIST
IDYLISTS
IDYLL
IDYLLIAN
IDYLLIC
IDYLLIST
IDYLLISTS

IDYLLS
IDYLS
IF
IFF
IFFIER
IFFIEST
IFFINESS
IFFY
IFS
IFTAR
IFTARS
IGAD
IGAPO
IGAPOS
IGARAPE
IGARAPES
IGG
IGGED
IGGING
IGGS
IGLOO
IGLOOS
IGLU
IGLUS
IGNARO
IGNAROES
IGNAROS
IGNATIA
IGNATIAS
IGNEOUS
IGNESCENT
IGNIFIED
IGNIFIES
IGNIFY
IGNIFYING
IGNITABLE
IGNITE
IGNITED
IGNITER
IGNITERS
IGNITES
IGNITIBLE
IGNITING
IGNITION
IGNITIONS
IGNITOR
IGNITORS
IGNITRON
IGNITRONS
IGNOBLE
IGNOBLER
IGNOBLEST
IGNOBLY
IGNOMIES
IGNOMINY
IGNOMY
IGNORABLE
IGNORAMI

IGNORAMUS
IGNORANCE
IGNORANT
IGNORANTS
IGNORE
IGNORED
IGNORER
IGNORERS
IGNORES
IGNORING
IGUANA
IGUANAS
IGUANIAN
IGUANIANS
IGUANID
IGUANIDS
IGUANODON
IHRAM
IHRAMS
IJTIHAD
IJTIHADS
IKAN
IKANS
IKAT
IKATS
IKEBANA
IKEBANAS
IKON
IKONS
ILEA
ILEAC
ILEAL
ILEITIDES
ILEITIS
ILEITISES
ILEOSTOMY
ILEUM
ILEUS
ILEUSES
ILEX
ILEXES
ILIA
ILIAC
ILIACUS
ILIACUSES
ILIAD
ILIADS
ILIAL
ILICES
ILIUM
ILK
ILKA
ILKADAY
ILKADAYS
ILKS
ILL
ILLAPSE
ILLAPSED

ILLAPSES
ILLAPSING
ILLATION
ILLATIONS
ILLATIVE
ILLATIVES
ILLEGAL
ILLEGALLY
ILLEGALS
ILLEGIBLE
ILLEGIBLY
ILLER
ILLEST
ILLIAD
ILLIADS
ILLIBERAL
ILLICIT
ILLICITLY
ILLIMITED
ILLINIUM
ILLINIUMS
ILLIPE
ILLIPES
ILLIQUID
ILLISION
ILLISIONS
ILLITE
ILLITES
ILLITIC
ILLNESS
ILLNESSES
ILLOGIC
ILLOGICAL
ILLOGICS
ILLS
ILLTH
ILLTHS
ILLUDE
ILLUDED
ILLUDES
ILLUDING
ILLUME
ILLUMED
ILLUMES
ILLUMINE
ILLUMINED
ILLUMINER
ILLUMINES
ILLUMING
ILLUPI
ILLUPIS
ILLUSION
ILLUSIONS
ILLUSIVE
ILLUSORY
ILLUVIA
ILLUVIAL
ILLUVIATE

ILLUVIUM	IMBASE	IMBROWNED	IMMATURES
ILLUVIUMS	IMBASED	IMBROWNS	IMMEDIACY
ILLY	IMBASES	IMBRUE	IMMEDIATE
ILMENITE	IMBASING	IMBRUED	IMMENSE
ILMENITES	IMBATHE	IMBRUES	IMMENSELY
IMAGE	IMBATHED	IMBRUING	IMMENSER
IMAGEABLE	IMBATHES	IMBRUTE	IMMENSEST
IMAGED	IMBATHING	IMBRUTED	IMMENSITY
IMAGELESS	IMBECILE	IMBRUTES	IMMERGE
IMAGER	IMBECILES	IMBRUTING	IMMERGED
IMAGERIES	IMBECILIC	IMBUE	IMMERGES
IMAGERS	IMBED	IMBUED	IMMERGING
IMAGERY	IMBEDDED	IMBUEMENT	IMMERSE
IMAGES	IMBEDDING	IMBUES	IMMERSED
IMAGINAL	IMBEDS	IMBUING	IMMERSER
IMAGINARY	IMBIBE	IMBURSE	IMMERSERS
IMAGINE	IMBIBED	IMBURSED	IMMERSES
IMAGINED	IMBIBER	IMBURSES	IMMERSING
IMAGINER	IMBIBERS	IMBURSING	IMMERSION
IMAGINERS	IMBIBES	IMID	IMMERSIVE
IMAGINES	IMBIBING	IMIDAZOLE	IMMESH
IMAGING	IMBITTER	IMIDE	IMMESHED
IMAGINGS	IMBITTERS	IMIDES	IMMESHES
IMAGINING	IMBIZO	IMIDIC	IMMESHING
IMAGINIST	IMBIZOS	IMIDO	IMMEW
IMAGISM	IMBLAZE	IMIDS	IMMEWED
IMAGISMS	IMBLAZED	IMINAZOLE	IMMEWING
IMAGIST	IMBLAZES	IMINE	IMMEWS
IMAGISTIC	IMBLAZING	IMINES	IMMIES
IMAGISTS	IMBODIED	IMINO	IMMIGRANT
IMAGO	IMBODIES	IMINOUREA	IMMIGRATE
IMAGOES	IMBODY	IMITABLE	IMMINENCE
IMAGOS	IMBODYING	IMITANCY	IMMINENCY
IMAM	IMBOLDEN	IMITANT	IMMINENT
IMAMATE	IMBOLDENS	IMITANTS	IMMINGLE
IMAMATES	IMBORDER	IMITATE	IMMINGLED
IMAMS	IMBORDERS	IMITATED	IMMINGLES
IMARET	IMBOSK	IMITATES	IMMINUTE
IMARETS	IMBOSKED	IMITATING	IMMISSION
IMARI	IMBOSKING	IMITATION	IMMIT
IMARIS	IMBOSKS	IMITATIVE	IMMITS
IMAUM	IMBOSOM	IMITATOR	IMMITTED
IMAUMS	IMBOSOMED	IMITATORS	IMMITTING
IMBALANCE	IMBOSOMS	IMMANACLE	IMMIX
IMBALM	IMBOSS	IMMANE	IMMIXED
IMBALMED	IMBOSSED	IMMANELY	IMMIXES
IMBALMER	IMBOSSES	IMMANENCE	IMMIXING
IMBALMERS	IMBOSSING	IMMANENCY	IMMIXTURE
IMBALMING	IMBOWER	IMMANENT	IMMOBILE
IMBALMS	IMBOWERED	IMMANITY	IMMODEST
IMBAR	IMBOWERS	IMMANTLE	IMMODESTY
IMBARK	IMBRANGLE	IMMANTLED	IMMOLATE
IMBARKED	IMBRAST	IMMANTLES	IMMOLATED
IMBARKING	IMBREX	IMMASK	IMMOLATES
IMBARKS	IMBRICATE	IMMASKED	IMMOLATOR
IMBARRED	IMBRICES	IMMASKING	IMMOMENT
IMBARRING	IMBROGLIO	IMMASKS	IMMORAL
IMBARS	IMBROWN	IMMATURE	IMMORALLY

IMMORTAL
IMMORTALS
IMMOTILE
IMMOVABLE
IMMOVABLY
IMMUNE
IMMUNES
IMMUNISE
IMMUNISED
IMMUNISER
IMMUNISES
IMMUNITY
IMMUNIZE
IMMUNIZED
IMMUNIZER
IMMUNIZES
IMMUNOGEN
IMMURE
IMMURED
IMMURES
IMMURING
IMMUTABLE
IMMUTABLY
IMMY
IMP
IMPACABLE
IMPACT
IMPACTED
IMPACTER
IMPACTERS
IMPACTFUL
IMPACTING
IMPACTION
IMPACTITE
IMPACTIVE
IMPACTOR
IMPACTORS
IMPACTS
IMPAINT
IMPAINTED
IMPAINTS
IMPAIR
IMPAIRED
IMPAIRER
IMPAIRERS
IMPAIRING
IMPAIRS
IMPALA
IMPALAS
IMPALE
IMPALED
IMPALER
IMPALERS
IMPALES
IMPALING
IMPANATE
IMPANEL
IMPANELED

IMPANELS
IMPANNEL
IMPANNELS
IMPARITY
IMPARK
IMPARKED
IMPARKING
IMPARKS
IMPARL
IMPARLED
IMPARLING
IMPARLS
IMPART
IMPARTED
IMPARTER
IMPARTERS
IMPARTIAL
IMPARTING
IMPARTS
IMPASSE
IMPASSES
IMPASSION
IMPASSIVE
IMPASTE
IMPASTED
IMPASTES
IMPASTING
IMPASTO
IMPASTOED
IMPASTOS
IMPATIENS
IMPATIENT
IMPAVE
IMPAVED
IMPAVES
IMPAVID
IMPAVIDLY
IMPAVING
IMPAWN
IMPAWNED
IMPAWNING
IMPAWNS
IMPEACH
IMPEACHED
IMPEACHER
IMPEACHES
IMPEARL
IMPEARLED
IMPEARLS
IMPECCANT
IMPED
IMPEDANCE
IMPEDE
IMPEDED
IMPEDER
IMPEDERS
IMPEDES
IMPEDING

IMPEDOR
IMPEDORS
IMPEL
IMPELLED
IMPELLENT
IMPELLER
IMPELLERS
IMPELLING
IMPELLOR
IMPELLORS
IMPELS
IMPEND
IMPENDED
IMPENDENT
IMPENDING
IMPENDS
IMPENNATE
IMPERATOR
IMPERFECT
IMPERIA
IMPERIAL
IMPERIALS
IMPERIL
IMPERILED
IMPERILS
IMPERIOUS
IMPERIUM
IMPERIUMS
IMPETICOS
IMPETIGO
IMPETIGOS
IMPETRATE
IMPETUOUS
IMPETUS
IMPETUSES
IMPHEE
IMPHEES
IMPI
IMPIES
IMPIETIES
IMPIETY
IMPING
IMPINGE
IMPINGED
IMPINGENT
IMPINGER
IMPINGERS
IMPINGES
IMPINGING
IMPINGS
IMPIOUS
IMPIOUSLY
IMPIS
IMPISH
IMPISHLY
IMPLANT
IMPLANTED
IMPLANTER

IMPLANTS
IMPLATE
IMPLATED
IMPLATES
IMPLATING
IMPLEACH
IMPLEAD
IMPLEADED
IMPLEADER
IMPLEADS
IMPLED
IMPLEDGE
IMPLEDGED
IMPLEDGES
IMPLEMENT
IMPLETE
IMPLETED
IMPLETES
IMPLETING
IMPLETION
IMPLEX
IMPLEXES
IMPLEXION
IMPLICATE
IMPLICIT
IMPLICITY
IMPLIED
IMPLIEDLY
IMPLIES
IMPLODE
IMPLODED
IMPLODENT
IMPLODES
IMPLODING
IMPLORE
IMPLORED
IMPLORER
IMPLORERS
IMPLORES
IMPLORING
IMPLOSION
IMPLOSIVE
IMPLUNGE
IMPLUNGED
IMPLUNGES
IMPLUVIA
IMPLUVIUM
IMPLY
IMPLYING
IMPOCKET
IMPOCKETS
IMPOLDER
IMPOLDERS
IMPOLICY
IMPOLITE
IMPOLITER
IMPOLITIC
IMPONE

IMPONED	IMPRESSES	IMSHI	INBROUGHT
IMPONENT	IMPREST	IMSHY	INBUILT
IMPONENTS	IMPRESTS	IN	INBURNING
IMPONES	IMPRIMIS	INABILITY	INBURST
IMPONING	IMPRINT	INACTION	INBURSTS
IMPOROUS	IMPRINTED	INACTIONS	INBY
IMPORT	IMPRINTER	INACTIVE	INBYE
IMPORTANT	IMPRINTS	INAIDABLE	INCAGE
IMPORTED	IMPRISON	INAMORATA	INCAGED
IMPORTER	IMPRISONS	INAMORATO	INCAGES
IMPORTERS	IMPROBITY	INANE	INCAGING
IMPORTING	IMPROMPTU	INANELY	INCANT
IMPORTS	IMPROPER	INANENESS	INCANTED
IMPORTUNE	IMPROV	INANER	INCANTING
IMPOSABLE	IMPROVE	INANES	INCANTS
IMPOSE	IMPROVED	INANEST	INCAPABLE
IMPOSED	IMPROVER	INANGA	INCAPABLY
IMPOSER	IMPROVERS	INANGAS	INCARNATE
IMPOSERS	IMPROVES	INANIMATE	INCASE
IMPOSES	IMPROVING	INANITIES	INCASED
IMPOSING	IMPROVISE	INANITION	INCASES
IMPOST	IMPROVS	INANITY	INCASING
IMPOSTED	IMPRUDENT	INAPT	INCAUTION
IMPOSTER	IMPS	INAPTLY	INCAVE
IMPOSTERS	IMPSONITE	INAPTNESS	INCAVED
IMPOSTING	IMPUDENCE	INARABLE	INCAVES
IMPOSTOR	IMPUDENCY	INARCH	INCAVI
IMPOSTORS	IMPUDENT	INARCHED	INCAVING
IMPOSTS	IMPUGN	INARCHES	INCAVO
IMPOSTUME	IMPUGNED	INARCHING	INCEDE
IMPOSTURE	IMPUGNER	INARM	INCEDED
IMPOT	IMPUGNERS	INARMED	INCEDES
IMPOTENCE	IMPUGNING	INARMING	INCEDING
IMPOTENCY	IMPUGNS	INARMS	INCENSE
IMPOTENT	IMPULSE	INASMUCH	INCENSED
IMPOTENTS	IMPULSED	INAUDIBLE	INCENSER
IMPOTS	IMPULSES	INAUDIBLY	INCENSERS
IMPOUND	IMPULSING	INAUGURAL	INCENSES
IMPOUNDED	IMPULSION	INAURATE	INCENSING
IMPOUNDER	IMPULSIVE	INBEING	INCENSOR
IMPOUNDS	IMPUNDULU	INBEINGS	INCENSORS
IMPOWER	IMPUNITY	INBENT	INCENSORY
IMPOWERED	IMPURE	INBOARD	INCENT
IMPOWERS	IMPURELY	INBOARDS	INCENTED
IMPRECATE	IMPURER	INBORN	INCENTER
IMPRECISE	IMPUREST	INBOUND	INCENTERS
IMPREGN	IMPURITY	INBOUNDED	INCENTING
IMPREGNED	IMPURPLE	INBOUNDS	INCENTIVE
IMPREGNS	IMPURPLED	INBREAK	INCENTRE
IMPRESA	IMPURPLES	INBREAKS	INCENTRES
IMPRESARI	IMPUTABLE	INBREATHE	INCENTS
IMPRESAS	IMPUTABLY	INBRED	INCEPT
IMPRESE	IMPUTE	INBREDS	INCEPTED
IMPRESES	IMPUTED	INBREED	INCEPTING
IMPRESS	IMPUTER	INBREEDER	INCEPTION
IMPRESSE	IMPUTERS	INBREEDS	INCEPTIVE
IMPRESSED	IMPUTES	INBRING	INCEPTOR
IMPRESSER	IMPUTING	INBRINGS	INCEPTORS

INCEPTS

INCEPTS	INCLE	INCROSS	INDARTING
INCERTAIN	INCLEMENT	INCROSSED	INDARTS
INCESSANT	INCLES	INCROSSES	INDEBTED
INCEST	INCLINE	INCRUST	INDECENCY
INCESTS	INCLINED	INCRUSTED	INDECENT
INCH	INCLINER	INCRUSTS	INDECORUM
INCHASE	INCLINERS	INCUBATE	INDEED
INCHASED	INCLINES	INCUBATED	INDELIBLE
INCHASES	INCLINING	INCUBATES	INDELIBLY
INCHASING	INCLIP	INCUBATOR	INDEMNIFY
INCHED	INCLIPPED	INCUBI	INDEMNITY
INCHER	INCLIPS	INCUBOUS	INDENE
INCHERS	INCLOSE	INCUBUS	INDENES
INCHES	INCLOSED	INCUBUSES	INDENT
INCHING	INCLOSER	INCUDAL	INDENTED
INCHMEAL	INCLOSERS	INCUDATE	INDENTER
INCHOATE	INCLOSES	INCUDES	INDENTERS
INCHOATED	INCLOSING	INCULCATE	INDENTING
INCHOATES	INCLOSURE	INCULPATE	INDENTION
INCHPIN	INCLUDE	INCULT	INDENTOR
INCHPINS	INCLUDED	INCUMBENT	INDENTORS
INCHWORM	INCLUDES	INCUMBER	INDENTS
INCHWORMS	INCLUDING	INCUMBERS	INDENTURE
INCIDENCE	INCLUSION	INCUNABLE	INDEVOUT
INCIDENT	INCLUSIVE	INCUR	INDEW
INCIDENTS	INCOG	INCURABLE	INDEWED
INCIPIENT	INCOGNITA	INCURABLY	INDEWING
INCIPIT	INCOGNITO	INCURIOUS	INDEWS
INCIPITS	INCOGS	INCURRED	INDEX
INCISAL	INCOME	INCURRENT	INDEXABLE
INCISE	INCOMER	INCURRING	INDEXAL
INCISED	INCOMERS	INCURS	INDEXED
INCISES	INCOMES	INCURSION	INDEXER
INCISING	INCOMING	INCURSIVE	INDEXERS
INCISION	INCOMINGS	INCURVATE	INDEXES
INCISIONS	INCOMMODE	INCURVE	INDEXICAL
INCISIVE	INCOMPACT	INCURVED	INDEXING
INCISOR	INCONDITE	INCURVES	INDEXINGS
INCISORS	INCONIE	INCURVING	INDEXLESS
INCISORY	INCONNU	INCURVITY	INDICAN
INCISURAL	INCONNUE	INCUS	INDICANS
INCISURE	INCONNUES	INCUSE	INDICANT
INCISURES	INCONNUS	INCUSED	INDICANTS
INCITABLE	INCONY	INCUSES	INDICATE
INCITANT	INCORPSE	INCUSING	INDICATED
INCITANTS	INCORPSED	INCUT	INDICATES
INCITE	INCORPSES	INDABA	INDICATOR
INCITED	INCORRECT	INDABAS	INDICES
INCITER	INCORRUPT	INDAGATE	INDICIA
INCITERS	INCREASE	INDAGATED	INDICIAL
INCITES	INCREASED	INDAGATES	INDICIAS
INCITING	INCREASER	INDAGATOR	INDICIUM
INCIVIL	INCREASES	INDAMIN	INDICIUMS
INCIVISM	INCREATE	INDAMINE	INDICT
INCIVISMS	INCREMATE	INDAMINES	INDICTED
INCLASP	INCREMENT	INDAMINS	INDICTEE
INCLASPED	INCRETION	INDART	INDICTEES
INCLASPS	INCRETORY	INDARTED	INDICTER

INDICTERS	INDORSER	INDUNA	INEXACT
INDICTING	INDORSERS	INDUNAS	INEXACTLY
INDICTION	INDORSES	INDURATE	INEXPERT
INDICTOR	INDORSING	INDURATED	INEXPERTS
INDICTORS	INDORSOR	INDURATES	INFALL
INDICTS	INDORSORS	INDUSIA	INFALLING
INDIE	INDOW	INDUSIAL	INFALLS
INDIES	INDOWED	INDUSIATE	INFAME
INDIGEN	INDOWING	INDUSIUM	INFAMED
INDIGENCE	INDOWS	INDUSTRY	INFAMES
INDIGENCY	INDOXYL	INDUVIAE	INFAMIES
INDIGENE	INDOXYLS	INDUVIAL	INFAMING
INDIGENES	INDRAFT	INDUVIATE	INFAMISE
INDIGENS	INDRAFTS	INDWELL	INFAMISED
INDIGENT	INDRAUGHT	INDWELLER	INFAMISES
INDIGENTS	INDRAWN	INDWELLS	INFAMIZE
INDIGEST	INDRENCH	INDWELT	INFAMIZED
INDIGESTS	INDRI	INEARTH	INFAMIZES
INDIGN	INDRIS	INEARTHED	INFAMOUS
INDIGNANT	INDRISES	INEARTHS	INFAMY
INDIGNIFY	INDUBIOUS	INEBRIANT	INFANCIES
INDIGNITY	INDUCE	INEBRIATE	INFANCY
INDIGNLY	INDUCED	INEBRIETY	INFANT
INDIGO	INDUCER	INEBRIOUS	INFANTA
INDIGOES	INDUCERS	INEDIBLE	INFANTAS
INDIGOID	INDUCES	INEDIBLY	INFANTE
INDIGOIDS	INDUCIAE	INEDITA	INFANTES
INDIGOS	INDUCIBLE	INEDITED	INFANTILE
INDIGOTIC	INDUCING	INEFFABLE	INFANTINE
INDIGOTIN	INDUCT	INEFFABLY	INFANTRY
INDINAVIR	INDUCTED	INELASTIC	INFANTS
INDIRECT	INDUCTEE	INELEGANT	INFARCT
INDIRUBIN	INDUCTEES	INEPT	INFARCTED
INDISPOSE	INDUCTILE	INEPTER	INFARCTS
INDITE	INDUCTING	INEPTEST	INFARE
INDITED	INDUCTION	INEPTLY	INFARES
INDITER	INDUCTIVE	INEPTNESS	INFATUATE
INDITERS	INDUCTOR	INEQUABLE	INFAUNA
INDITES	INDUCTORS	INEQUITY	INFAUNAE
INDITING	INDUCTS	INERM	INFAUNAL
INDIUM	INDUE	INERMOUS	INFAUNAS
INDIUMS	INDUED	INERRABLE	INFAUST
INDIVIDUA	INDUES	INERRABLY	INFECT
INDOCIBLE	INDUING	INERRANCY	INFECTANT
INDOCILE	INDULGE	INERRANT	INFECTED
INDOL	INDULGED	INERT	INFECTER
INDOLE	INDULGENT	INERTER	INFECTERS
INDOLENCE	INDULGER	INERTEST	INFECTING
INDOLENCY	INDULGERS	INERTIA	INFECTION
INDOLENT	INDULGES	INERTIAE	INFECTIVE
INDOLES	INDULGING	INERTIAL	INFECTOR
INDOLS	INDULIN	INERTIAS	INFECTORS
INDOOR	INDULINE	INERTLY	INFECTS
INDOORS	INDULINES	INERTNESS	INFECUND
INDORSE	INDULINS	INERTS	INFEFT
INDORSED	INDULT	INERUDITE	INFEFTED
INDORSEE	INDULTS	INESSIVE	INFEFTING
INDORSEES	INDUMENTA	INESSIVES	INFEFTS

INFELT
INFEOFF
INFEOFFED
INFEOFFS
INFER
INFERABLE
INFERABLY
INFERE
INFERENCE
INFERIAE
INFERIBLE
INFERIOR
INFERIORS
INFERNAL
INFERNO
INFERNOS
INFERRED
INFERRER
INFERRERS
INFERRING
INFERS
INFERTILE
INFEST
INFESTANT
INFESTED
INFESTER
INFESTERS
INFESTING
INFESTS
INFICETE
INFIDEL
INFIDELIC
INFIDELS
INFIELD
INFIELDER
INFIELDS
INFIGHT
INFIGHTER
INFIGHTS
INFILL
INFILLED
INFILLING
INFILLS
INFIMA
INFIMUM
INFIMUMS
INFINITE
INFINITES
INFINITY
INFIRM
INFIRMARY
INFIRMED
INFIRMER
INFIRMEST
INFIRMING
INFIRMITY
INFIRMLY
INFIRMS

INFIX
INFIXED
INFIXES
INFIXING
INFIXION
INFIXIONS
INFLAME
INFLAMED
INFLAMER
INFLAMERS
INFLAMES
INFLAMING
INFLATE
INFLATED
INFLATER
INFLATERS
INFLATES
INFLATING
INFLATION
INFLATIVE
INFLATOR
INFLATORS
INFLATUS
INFLECT
INFLECTED
INFLECTOR
INFLECTS
INFLEXED
INFLEXION
INFLEXURE
INFLICT
INFLICTED
INFLICTER
INFLICTOR
INFLICTS
INFLIGHT
INFLOW
INFLOWING
INFLOWS
INFLUENCE
INFLUENT
INFLUENTS
INFLUENZA
INFLUX
INFLUXES
INFLUXION
INFO
INFOBAHN
INFOBAHNS
INFOLD
INFOLDED
INFOLDER
INFOLDERS
INFOLDING
INFOLDS
INFOMANIA
INFORCE
INFORCED

INFORCES
INFORCING
INFORM
INFORMAL
INFORMANT
INFORMED
INFORMER
INFORMERS
INFORMING
INFORMS
INFORTUNE
INFOS
INFOUGHT
INFRA
INFRACT
INFRACTED
INFRACTOR
INFRACTS
INFRARED
INFRAREDS
INFRINGE
INFRINGED
INFRINGER
INFRINGES
INFRUGAL
INFULA
INFULAE
INFURIATE
INFUSCATE
INFUSE
INFUSED
INFUSER
INFUSERS
INFUSES
INFUSIBLE
INFUSING
INFUSION
INFUSIONS
INFUSIVE
INFUSORIA
INFUSORY
INGAN
INGANS
INGATE
INGATES
INGATHER
INGATHERS
INGENER
INGENERS
INGENIOUS
INGENIUM
INGENIUMS
INGENU
INGENUE
INGENUES
INGENUITY
INGENUOUS
INGENUS

INGEST
INGESTA
INGESTED
INGESTING
INGESTION
INGESTIVE
INGESTS
INGINE
INGINES
INGLE
INGLENEUK
INGLENOOK
INGLES
INGLOBE
INGLOBED
INGLOBES
INGLOBING
INGLUVIAL
INGLUVIES
INGO
INGOES
INGOING
INGOINGS
INGOT
INGOTED
INGOTING
INGOTS
INGRAFT
INGRAFTED
INGRAFTS
INGRAIN
INGRAINED
INGRAINS
INGRAM
INGRATE
INGRATELY
INGRATES
INGRESS
INGRESSES
INGROOVE
INGROOVED
INGROOVES
INGROSS
INGROSSED
INGROSSES
INGROUND
INGROUP
INGROUPS
INGROWING
INGROWN
INGROWTH
INGROWTHS
INGRUM
INGUINAL
INGULF
INGULFED
INGULFING
INGULFS

INGULPH	INHOOPS	INJURING	INLIER
INGULPHED	INHUMAN	INJURIOUS	INLIERS
INGULPHS	INHUMANE	INJURY	INLOCK
INHABIT	INHUMANLY	INJUSTICE	INLOCKED
INHABITED	INHUMATE	INK	INLOCKING
INHABITER	INHUMATED	INKBERRY	INLOCKS
INHABITOR	INHUMATES	INKBLOT	INLY
INHABITS	INHUME	INKBLOTS	INLYING
INHALANT	INHUMED	INKED	INMATE
INHALANTS	INHUMER	INKER	INMATES
INHALATOR	INHUMERS	INKERS	INMESH
INHALE	INHUMES	INKHOLDER	INMESHED
INHALED	INHUMING	INKHORN	INMESHES
INHALER	INIA	INKHORNS	INMESHING
INHALERS	INIMICAL	INKIER	INMIGRANT
INHALES	INION	INKIEST	INMOST
INHALING	INIONS	INKINESS	INN
INHARMONY	INIQUITY	INKING	INNAGE
INHAUL	INISLE	INKJET	INNAGES
INHAULER	INISLED	INKLE	INNARDS
INHAULERS	INISLES	INKLED	INNATE
INHAULS	INISLING	INKLES	INNATELY
INHAUST	INITIAL	INKLESS	INNATIVE
INHAUSTED	INITIALED	INKLIKE	INNED
INHAUSTS	INITIALER	INKLING	INNER
INHEARSE	INITIALLY	INKLINGS	INNERLY
INHEARSED	INITIALS	INKPOT	INNERMOST
INHEARSES	INITIATE	INKPOTS	INNERNESS
INHERCE	INITIATED	INKS	INNERS
INHERCED	INITIATES	INKSPOT	INNERSOLE
INHERCES	INITIATOR	INKSPOTS	INNERVATE
INHERCING	INJECT	INKSTAND	INNERVE
INHERE	INJECTANT	INKSTANDS	INNERVED
INHERED	INJECTED	INKSTONE	INNERVES
INHERENCE	INJECTING	INKSTONES	INNERVING
INHERENCY	INJECTION	INKWELL	INNERWEAR
INHERENT	INJECTIVE	INKWELLS	INNING
INHERES	INJECTOR	INKWOOD	INNINGS
INHERING	INJECTORS	INKWOODS	INNKEEPER
INHERIT	INJECTS	INKY	INNLESS
INHERITED	INJELLIED	INLACE	INNOCENCE
INHERITOR	INJELLIES	INLACED	INNOCENCY
INHERITS	INJELLY	INLACES	INNOCENT
INHESION	INJERA	INLACING	INNOCENTS
INHESIONS	INJERAS	INLAID	INNOCUITY
INHIBIN	INJOINT	INLAND	INNOCUOUS
INHIBINS	INJOINTED	INLANDER	INNOVATE
INHIBIT	INJOINTS	INLANDERS	INNOVATED
INHIBITED	INJUNCT	INLANDS	INNOVATES
INHIBITER	INJUNCTED	INLAY	INNOVATOR
INHIBITOR	INJUNCTS	INLAYER	INNOXIOUS
INHIBITS	INJURABLE	INLAYERS	INNS
INHOLDER	INJURE	INLAYING	INNUENDO
INHOLDERS	INJURED	INLAYINGS	INNUENDOS
INHOLDING	INJURER	INLAYS	INNYARD
INHOOP	INJURERS	INLET	INNYARDS
INHOOPED	INJURES	INLETS	INOCULA
INHOOPING	INJURIES	INLETTING	INOCULANT

INOCULATE	INRUNS	INSETTED	INSOLES
INOCULUM	INRUSH	INSETTER	INSOLUBLE
INOCULUMS	INRUSHES	INSETTERS	INSOLUBLY
INODOROUS	INRUSHING	INSETTING	INSOLVENT
INOPINATE	INS	INSHALLAH	INSOMNIA
INORB	INSANE	INSHEATH	INSOMNIAC
INORBED	INSANELY	INSHEATHE	INSOMNIAS
INORBING	INSANER	INSHEATHS	INSOMUCH
INORBS	INSANEST	INSHELL	INSOOTH
INORGANIC	INSANIE	INSHELLED	INSOUL
INORNATE	INSANIES	INSHELLS	INSOULED
INOSINE	INSANITY	INSHELTER	INSOULING
INOSINES	INSATIATE	INSHIP	INSOULS
INOSITE	INSATIETY	INSHIPPED	INSPAN
INOSITES	INSCAPE	INSHIPS	INSPANNED
INOSITOL	INSCAPES	INSHORE	INSPANS
INOSITOLS	INSCIENCE	INSHRINE	INSPECT
INOTROPIC	INSCIENT	INSHRINED	INSPECTED
INPATIENT	INSCONCE	INSHRINES	INSPECTOR
INPAYMENT	INSCONCED	INSIDE	INSPECTS
INPHASE	INSCONCES	INSIDER	INSPHERE
INPOUR	INSCRIBE	INSIDERS	INSPHERED
INPOURED	INSCRIBED	INSIDES	INSPHERES
INPOURING	INSCRIBER	INSIDIOUS	INSPIRE
INPOURS	INSCRIBES	INSIGHT	INSPIRED
INPUT	INSCROLL	INSIGHTS	INSPIRER
INPUTS	INSCROLLS	INSIGNE	INSPIRERS
INPUTTED	INSCULP	INSIGNIA	INSPIRES
INPUTTER	INSCULPED	INSIGNIAS	INSPIRING
INPUTTERS	INSCULPS	INSINCERE	INSPIRIT
INPUTTING	INSCULPT	INSINEW	INSPIRITS
INQILAB	INSEAM	INSINEWED	INSTABLE
INQILABS	INSEAMED	INSINEWS	INSTAL
INQUERE	INSEAMING	INSINUATE	INSTALL
INQUERED	INSEAMS	INSIPID	INSTALLED
INQUERES	INSECT	INSIPIDLY	INSTALLER
INQUERING	INSECTAN	INSIPIENT	INSTALLS
INQUEST	INSECTARY	INSIST	INSTALS
INQUESTS	INSECTEAN	INSISTED	INSTANCE
INQUIET	INSECTILE	INSISTENT	INSTANCED
INQUIETED	INSECTION	INSISTER	INSTANCES
INQUIETLY	INSECTS	INSISTERS	INSTANCY
INQUIETS	INSECURE	INSISTING	INSTANT
INQUILINE	INSEEM	INSISTS	INSTANTER
INQUINATE	INSEEMED	INSNARE	INSTANTLY
INQUIRE	INSEEMING	INSNARED	INSTANTS
INQUIRED	INSEEMS	INSNARER	INSTAR
INQUIRER	INSELBERG	INSNARERS	INSTARRED
INQUIRERS	INSENSATE	INSNARES	INSTARS
INQUIRES	INSERT	INSNARING	INSTATE
INQUIRIES	INSERTED	INSOFAR	INSTATED
INQUIRING	INSERTER	INSOLATE	INSTATES
INQUIRY	INSERTERS	INSOLATED	INSTATING
INQUORATE	INSERTING	INSOLATES	INSTEAD
INRO	INSERTION	INSOLE	INSTEP
INROAD	INSERTS	INSOLENCE	INSTEPS
INROADS	INSET	INSOLENT	INSTIGATE
INRUN	INSETS	INSOLENTS	INSTIL

INSTILL	INTAGLI	INTERCOMS	INTERNAL
INSTILLED	INTAGLIO	INTERCROP	INTERNALS
INSTILLER	INTAGLIOS	INTERCUT	INTERNE
INSTILLS	INTAKE	INTERCUTS	INTERNED
INSTILS	INTAKES	INTERDASH	INTERNEE
INSTINCT	INTARSIA	INTERDEAL	INTERNEES
INSTINCTS	INTARSIAS	INTERDICT	INTERNES
INSTITUTE	INTEGER	INTERDINE	INTERNET
INSTRESS	INTEGERS	INTERESS	INTERNETS
INSTROKE	INTEGRAL	INTERESSE	INTERNING
INSTROKES	INTEGRALS	INTEREST	INTERNIST
INSTRUCT	INTEGRAND	INTERESTS	INTERNODE
INSTRUCTS	INTEGRANT	INTERFACE	INTERNS
INSUCKEN	INTEGRATE	INTERFERE	INTERPAGE
INSULA	INTEGRITY	INTERFILE	INTERPLAY
INSULAE	INTEL	INTERFIRM	INTERPLED
INSULANT	INTELLECT	INTERFLOW	INTERPONE
INSULANTS	INTELS	INTERFOLD	INTERPOSE
INSULAR	INTENABLE	INTERFUSE	INTERPRET
INSULARLY	INTEND	INTERGANG	INTERRACE
INSULARS	INTENDANT	INTERGREW	INTERRAIL
INSULAS	INTENDED	INTERGROW	INTERRED
INSULATE	INTENDEDS	INTERIM	INTERREX
INSULATED	INTENDER	INTERIMS	INTERRING
INSULATES	INTENDERS	INTERIOR	INTERROW
INSULATOR	INTENDING	INTERIORS	INTERRUPT
INSULIN	INTENDS	INTERJECT	INTERS
INSULINS	INTENIBLE	INTERJOIN	INTERSECT
INSULSE	INTENSATE	INTERKNIT	INTERSERT
INSULSITY	INTENSE	INTERKNOT	INTERSEX
INSULT	INTENSELY	INTERLACE	INTERTERM
INSULTANT	INTENSER	INTERLAID	INTERTEXT
INSULTED	INTENSEST	INTERLAP	INTERTIE
INSULTER	INTENSIFY	INTERLAPS	INTERTIES
INSULTERS	INTENSION	INTERLARD	INTERTILL
INSULTING	INTENSITY	INTERLAY	INTERUNIT
INSULTS	INTENSIVE	INTERLAYS	INTERVAL
INSURABLE	INTENT	INTERLEAF	INTERVALE
INSURANCE	INTENTION	INTERLEND	INTERVALS
INSURANT	INTENTIVE	INTERLENT	INTERVEIN
INSURANTS	INTENTLY	INTERLINE	INTERVENE
INSURE	INTENTS	INTERLINK	INTERVIEW
INSURED	INTER	INTERLOAN	INTERWAR
INSUREDS	INTERACT	INTERLOCK	INTERWIND
INSURER	INTERACTS	INTERLOOP	INTERWORK
INSURERS	INTERAGE	INTERLOPE	INTERWOVE
INSURES	INTERARCH	INTERLUDE	INTERZONE
INSURGENT	INTERBANK	INTERMALE	INTESTACY
INSURING	INTERBED	INTERMAT	INTESTATE
INSWATHE	INTERBEDS	INTERMATS	INTESTINE
INSWATHED	INTERBRED	INTERMENT	INTHRAL
INSWATHES	INTERCEDE	INTERMESH	INTHRALL
INSWEPT	INTERCELL	INTERMIT	INTHRALLS
INSWING	INTERCEPT	INTERMITS	INTHRALS
INSWINGER	INTERCITY	INTERMIX	INTHRONE
INSWINGS	INTERCLAN	INTERMONT	INTHRONED
INTACT	INTERCLUB	INTERMURE	INTHRONES
INTACTLY	INTERCOM	INTERN	INTI

INTIFADA	INTRA	INTUITING	INVALID
INTIFADAH	INTRACITY	INTUITION	INVALIDED
INTIFADAS	INTRADA	INTUITIVE	INVALIDLY
INTIFADEH	INTRADAS	INTUITS	INVALIDS
INTIL	INTRADAY	INTUMESCE	INVAR
INTIMA	INTRADOS	INTURN	INVARIANT
INTIMACY	INTRANET	INTURNED	INVARS
INTIMAE	INTRANETS	INTURNS	INVASION
INTIMAL	INTRANT	INTUSE	INVASIONS
INTIMAS	INTRANTS	INTUSES	INVASIVE
INTIMATE	INTREAT	INTWINE	INVEAGLE
INTIMATED	INTREATED	INTWINED	INVEAGLED
INTIMATER	INTREATS	INTWINES	INVEAGLES
INTIMATES	INTRENCH	INTWINING	INVECKED
INTIME	INTREPID	INTWIST	INVECTED
INTIMISM	INTRICACY	INTWISTED	INVECTIVE
INTIMISMS	INTRICATE	INTWISTS	INVEIGH
INTIMIST	INTRIGANT	INUKSHUIT	INVEIGHED
INTIMISTE	INTRIGUE	INUKSHUK	INVEIGHER
INTIMISTS	INTRIGUED	INUKSHUKS	INVEIGHS
INTIMITY	INTRIGUER	INULA	INVEIGLE
INTINE	INTRIGUES	INULAS	INVEIGLED
INTINES	INTRINCE	INULASE	INVEIGLER
INTIRE	INTRINSIC	INULASES	INVEIGLES
INTIS	INTRO	INULIN	INVENIT
INTITLE	INTRODUCE	INULINS	INVENT
INTITLED	INTROFIED	INUMBRATE	INVENTED
INTITLES	INTROFIES	INUNCTION	INVENTER
INTITLING	INTROFY	INUNDANT	INVENTERS
INTITULE	INTROIT	INUNDATE	INVENTING
INTITULED	INTROITAL	INUNDATED	INVENTION
INTITULES	INTROITS	INUNDATES	INVENTIVE
INTO	INTROITUS	INUNDATOR	INVENTOR
INTOED	INTROJECT	INURBANE	INVENTORS
INTOMB	INTROLD	INURE	INVENTORY
INTOMBED	INTROMIT	INURED	INVENTS
INTOMBING	INTROMITS	INUREMENT	INVERITY
INTOMBS	INTRON	INURES	INVERNESS
INTONACO	INTRONS	INURING	INVERSE
INTONACOS	INTRORSE	INURN	INVERSED
INTONATE	INTROS	INURNED	INVERSELY
INTONATED	INTROVERT	INURNING	INVERSES
INTONATES	INTRUDE	INURNMENT	INVERSING
INTONATOR	INTRUDED	INURNS	INVERSION
INTONE	INTRUDER	INUSITATE	INVERSIVE
INTONED	INTRUDERS	INUST	INVERT
INTONER	INTRUDES	INUSTION	INVERTASE
INTONERS	INTRUDING	INUSTIONS	INVERTED
INTONES	INTRUSION	INUTILE	INVERTER
INTONING	INTRUSIVE	INUTILELY	INVERTERS
INTONINGS	INTRUST	INUTILITY	INVERTIN
INTORSION	INTRUSTED	INVADABLE	INVERTING
INTORT	INTRUSTS	INVADE	INVERTINS
INTORTED	INTUBATE	INVADED	INVERTOR
INTORTING	INTUBATED	INVADER	INVERTORS
INTORTION	INTUBATES	INVADERS	INVERTS
INTORTS	INTUIT	INVADES	INVEST
INTOWN	INTUITED	INVADING	INVESTED

INVESTING	INWARDS	IODIZED	IPECACS
INVESTOR	INWEAVE	IODIZER	IPOMOEA
INVESTORS	INWEAVED	IODIZERS	IPOMOEAS
INVESTS	INWEAVES	IODIZES	IPPON
INVEXED	INWEAVING	IODIZING	IPPONS
INVIABLE	INWICK	IODOFORM	IPRINDOLE
INVIABLY	INWICKED	IODOFORMS	IRACUND
INVIDIOUS	INWICKING	IODOMETRY	IRADE
INVIOLACY	INWICKS	IODOPHILE	IRADES
INVIOLATE	INWIND	IODOPHOR	IRASCIBLE
INVIOUS	INWINDING	IODOPHORS	IRASCIBLY
INVIRILE	INWINDS	IODOPSIN	IRATE
INVISCID	INWIT	IODOPSINS	IRATELY
INVISIBLE	INWITH	IODOUS	IRATENESS
INVISIBLY	INWITS	IODURET	IRATER
INVITAL	INWORK	IODURETS	IRATEST
INVITE	INWORKED	IODYRITE	IRE
INVITED	INWORKING	IODYRITES	IRED
INVITEE	INWORKS	IOLITE	IREFUL
INVITEES	INWORN	IOLITES	IREFULLY
INVITER	INWOUND	ION	IRELESS
INVITERS	INWOVE	IONIC	IRENIC
INVITES	INWOVEN	IONICITY	IRENICAL
INVITING	INWRAP	IONICS	IRENICISM
INVITINGS	INWRAPPED	IONISABLE	IRENICON
INVOCABLE	INWRAPS	IONISE	IRENICONS
INVOCATE	INWREATHE	IONISED	IRENICS
INVOCATED	INWROUGHT	IONISER	IRENOLOGY
INVOCATES	INYALA	IONISERS	IRES
INVOCATOR	INYALAS	IONISES	IRID
INVOICE	IO	IONISING	IRIDAL
INVOICED	IODATE	IONIUM	IRIDEAL
INVOICES	IODATED	IONIUMS	IRIDES
INVOICING	IODATES	IONIZABLE	IRIDIAL
INVOKE	IODATING	IONIZE	IRIDIAN
INVOKED	IODATION	IONIZED	IRIDIC
INVOKER	IODATIONS	IONIZER	IRIDISE
INVOKERS	IODIC	IONIZERS	IRIDISED
INVOKES	IODID	IONIZES	IRIDISES
INVOKING	IODIDE	IONIZING	IRIDISING
INVOLUCEL	IODIDES	IONOGEN	IRIDIUM
INVOLUCRA	IODIDS	IONOGENIC	IRIDIUMS
INVOLUCRE	IODIN	IONOGENS	IRIDIZE
INVOLUTE	IODINATE	IONOMER	IRIDIZED
INVOLUTED	IODINATED	IONOMERS	IRIDIZES
INVOLUTES	IODINATES	IONONE	IRIDIZING
INVOLVE	IODINE	IONONES	IRIDOCYTE
INVOLVED	IODINES	IONOPAUSE	IRIDOLOGY
INVOLVER	IODINS	IONOPHORE	IRIDOTOMY
INVOLVERS	IODISE	IONOSONDE	IRIDS
INVOLVES	IODISED	IONOTROPY	IRING
INVOLVING	IODISER	IONS	IRIS
INWALL	IODISERS	IOS	IRISATE
INWALLED	IODISES	IOTA	IRISATED
INWALLING	IODISING	IOTACISM	IRISATES
INWALLS	IODISM	IOTACISMS	IRISATING
INWARD	IODISMS	IOTAS	IRISATION
INWARDLY	IODIZE	IPECAC	IRISCOPE

IRISCOPES	IRONWOMEN	ISCHAEMIA	ISOBRONT
IRISED	IRONWOOD	ISCHAEMIC	ISOBRONTS
IRISES	IRONWOODS	ISCHEMIA	ISOBUTANE
IRISING	IRONWORK	ISCHEMIAS	ISOBUTENE
IRITIC	IRONWORKS	ISCHEMIC	ISOBUTYL
IRITIS	IRONY	ISCHIA	ISOBUTYLS
IRITISES	IRRADIANT	ISCHIADIC	ISOCHASM
IRK	IRRADIATE	ISCHIAL	ISOCHASMS
IRKED	IRREAL	ISCHIATIC	ISOCHEIM
IRKING	IRREALITY	ISCHIUM	ISOCHEIMS
IRKS	IRREDENTA	ISCHURIA	ISOCHIMAL
IRKSOME	IRREGULAR	ISCHURIAS	ISOCHIME
IRKSOMELY	IRRELATED	ISEIKONIA	ISOCHIMES
IROKO	IRRIDENTA	ISEIKONIC	ISOCHOR
IROKOS	IRRIGABLE	ISENERGIC	ISOCHORE
IRON	IRRIGABLY	ISH	ISOCHORES
IRONBARK	IRRIGATE	ISHES	ISOCHORIC
IRONBARKS	IRRIGATED	ISINGLASS	ISOCHORS
IRONBOUND	IRRIGATES	ISIT	ISOCHRON
IRONCLAD	IRRIGATOR	ISLAND	ISOCHRONE
IRONCLADS	IRRIGUOUS	ISLANDED	ISOCHRONS
IRONE	IRRISION	ISLANDER	ISOCLINAL
IRONED	IRRISIONS	ISLANDERS	ISOCLINE
IRONER	IRRISORY	ISLANDING	ISOCLINES
IRONERS	IRRITABLE	ISLANDS	ISOCLINIC
IRONES	IRRITABLY	ISLE	ISOCRACY
IRONIC	IRRITANCY	ISLED	ISOCRATIC
IRONICAL	IRRITANT	ISLELESS	ISOCRYMAL
IRONIER	IRRITANTS	ISLEMAN	ISOCRYME
IRONIES	IRRITATE	ISLEMEN	ISOCRYMES
IRONIEST	IRRITATED	ISLES	ISOCYANIC
IRONING	IRRITATES	ISLESMAN	ISOCYCLIC
IRONINGS	IRRITATOR	ISLESMEN	ISODICA
IRONISE	IRRUPT	ISLET	ISODICON
IRONISED	IRRUPTED	ISLETED	ISODOMA
IRONISES	IRRUPTING	ISLETS	ISODOMON
IRONISING	IRRUPTION	ISLING	ISODOMONS
IRONIST	IRRUPTIVE	ISLOMANIA	ISODOMOUS
IRONISTS	IRRUPTS	ISM	ISODOMUM
IRONIZE	IS	ISMATIC	ISODONT
IRONIZED	ISABEL	ISMATICAL	ISODONTAL
IRONIZES	ISABELLA	ISMS	ISODONTS
IRONIZING	ISABELLAS	ISNA	ISODOSE
IRONLESS	ISABELS	ISNAE	ISODOSES
IRONLIKE	ISAGOGE	ISO	ISOENZYME
IRONMAN	ISAGOGES	ISOAMYL	ISOETES
IRONMEN	ISAGOGIC	ISOAMYLS	ISOFORM
IRONNESS	ISAGOGICS	ISOBAR	ISOFORMS
IRONS	ISALLOBAR	ISOBARE	ISOGAMETE
IRONSIDE	ISARITHM	ISOBARES	ISOGAMIC
IRONSIDES	ISARITHMS	ISOBARIC	ISOGAMIES
IRONSMITH	ISATIN	ISOBARISM	ISOGAMOUS
IRONSTONE	ISATINE	ISOBARS	ISOGAMY
IRONWARE	ISATINES	ISOBASE	ISOGENEIC
IRONWARES	ISATINIC	ISOBASES	ISOGENIC
IRONWEED	ISATINS	ISOBATH	ISOGENIES
IRONWEEDS	ISBA	ISOBATHIC	ISOGENOUS
IRONWOMAN	ISBAS	ISOBATHS	ISOGENY

ISOGLOSS	ISOMETRIC	ISOTRON	ITEM
ISOGON	ISOMETRY	ISOTRONS	ITEMED
ISOGONALS	ISOMORPH	ISOTROPIC	ITEMING
ISOGONALS	ISOMORPHS	ISOTROPY	ITEMISE
ISOGONE	ISONIAZID	ISOTYPE	ITEMISED
ISOGONES	ISONOME	ISOTYPES	ITEMISER
ISOGONIC	ISONOMES	ISOTYPIC	ITEMISERS
ISOGONICS	ISONOMIC	ISOZYME	ITEMISES
ISOGONIES	ISONOMIES	ISOZYMES	ITEMISING
ISOGONS	ISONOMOUS	ISOZYMIC	ITEMIZE
ISOGONY	ISONOMY	ISPAGHULA	ITEMIZED
ISOGRAFT	ISOOCTANE	ISSEI	ITEMIZER
ISOGRAFTS	ISOPACH	ISSEIS	ITEMIZERS
ISOGRAM	ISOPACHS	ISSUABLE	ITEMIZES
ISOGRAMS	ISOPHONE	ISSUABLY	ITEMIZING
ISOGRAPH	ISOPHONES	ISSUANCE	ITEMS
ISOGRAPHS	ISOPHOTAL	ISSUANCES	ITERANCE
ISOGRIV	ISOPHOTE	ISSUANT	ITERANCES
ISOGRIVS	ISOPHOTES	ISSUE	ITERANT
ISOHEL	ISOPLETH	ISSUED	ITERATE
ISOHELS	ISOPLETHS	ISSUELESS	ITERATED
ISOHYDRIC	ISOPOD	ISSUER	ITERATES
ISOHYET	ISOPODAN	ISSUERS	ITERATING
ISOHYETAL	ISOPODANS	ISSUES	ITERATION
ISOHYETS	ISOPODOUS	ISSUING	ITERATIVE
ISOKONT	ISOPODS	ISTANA	ITERUM
ISOKONTAN	ISOPOLITY	ISTANAS	ITHER
ISOKONTS	ISOPRENE	ISTHMI	ITINERACY
ISOLABLE	ISOPRENES	ISTHMIAN	ITINERANT
ISOLATE	ISOPROPYL	ISTHMIANS	ITINERARY
ISOLATED	ISOPYCNAL	ISTHMIC	ITINERATE
ISOLATES	ISOPYCNIC	ISTHMOID	ITS
ISOLATING	ISOS	ISTHMUS	ITSELF
ISOLATION	ISOSCELES	ISTHMUSES	IURE
ISOLATIVE	ISOSMOTIC	ISTLE	IVIED
ISOLATOR	ISOSPIN	ISTLES	IVIES
ISOLATORS	ISOSPINS	IT	IVORIED
ISOLEAD	ISOSPORY	ITA	IVORIES
ISOLEADS	ISOSTACY	ITACISM	IVORIST
ISOLEX	ISOSTASY	ITACISMS	IVORISTS
ISOLEXES	ISOSTATIC	ITACONIC	IVORY
ISOLINE	ISOSTERIC	ITALIC	IVORYBILL
ISOLINES	ISOTACH	ITALICISE	IVORYLIKE
ISOLOG	ISOTACHS	ITALICIZE	IVORYWOOD
ISOLOGOUS	ISOTACTIC	ITALICS	IVRESSE
ISOLOGS	ISOTHERAL	ITAS	IVRESSES
ISOLOGUE	ISOTHERE	ITCH	IVY
ISOLOGUES	ISOTHERES	ITCHED	IVYLIKE
ISOMER	ISOTHERM	ITCHES	IWI
ISOMERASE	ISOTHERMS	ITCHIER	IWIS
ISOMERE	ISOTONE	ITCHIEST	IXIA
ISOMERES	ISOTONES	ITCHILY	IXIAS
ISOMERIC	ISOTONIC	ITCHINESS	IXODIASES
ISOMERISE	ISOTOPE	ITCHING	IXODIASIS
ISOMERISM	ISOTOPES	ITCHINGS	IXODID
ISOMERIZE	ISOTOPIC	ITCHWEED	IXODIDS
ISOMEROUS	ISOTOPIES	ITCHWEEDS	IXORA
ISOMERS	ISOTOPY	ITCHY	IXORAS

IXTLE

IXTLE
IXTLES
IZAR
IZARD
IZARDS
IZARS
IZVESTIA
IZVESTIAS
IZVESTIYA
IZZARD
IZZARDS
IZZAT
IZZATS

J

JA
JAAP
JAAPS
JAB
JABBED
JABBER
JABBERED
JABBERER
JABBERERS
JABBERING
JABBERS
JABBING
JABBINGLY
JABBLE
JABBLED
JABBLES
JABBLING
JABERS
JABIRU
JABIRUS
JABORANDI
JABOT
JABOTS
JABS
JACAL
JACALES
JACALS
JACAMAR
JACAMARS
JACANA
JACANAS
JACARANDA
JACARE
JACARES
JACCHUS
JACCHUSES
JACENT
JACINTH
JACINTHE
JACINTHES
JACINTHS
JACK
JACKAL
JACKALLED
JACKALS
JACKAROO
JACKAROOS
JACKASS
JACKASSES
JACKBOOT
JACKBOOTS
JACKDAW
JACKDAWS

JACKED
JACKEEN
JACKEENS
JACKER
JACKEROO
JACKEROOS
JACKERS
JACKET
JACKETED
JACKETING
JACKETS
JACKFISH
JACKFRUIT
JACKIES
JACKING
JACKINGS
JACKKNIFE
JACKLEG
JACKLEGS
JACKLIGHT
JACKMAN
JACKMEN
JACKPLANE
JACKPOT
JACKPOTS
JACKROLL
JACKROLLS
JACKS
JACKSCREW
JACKSHAFT
JACKSIE
JACKSIES
JACKSMELT
JACKSMITH
JACKSNIPE
JACKSTAY
JACKSTAYS
JACKSTONE
JACKSTRAW
JACKSY
JACKY
JACOBIN
JACOBINS
JACOBUS
JACOBUSES
JACONET
JACONETS
JACQUARD
JACQUARDS
JACQUERIE
JACTATION
JACULATE
JACULATED

JACULATES
JACULATOR
JACUZZI
JACUZZIS
JADE
JADED
JADEDLY
JADEDNESS
JADEITE
JADEITES
JADELIKE
JADERIES
JADERY
JADES
JADING
JADISH
JADISHLY
JADITIC
JAEGER
JAEGERS
JAFA
JAFAS
JAG
JAGA
JAGAED
JAGAING
JAGAS
JAGER
JAGERS
JAGG
JAGGARIES
JAGGARY
JAGGED
JAGGEDER
JAGGEDEST
JAGGEDLY
JAGGER
JAGGERIES
JAGGERS
JAGGERY
JAGGHERY
JAGGIER
JAGGIES
JAGGIEST
JAGGING
JAGGS
JAGGY
JAGHIR
JAGHIRDAR
JAGHIRE
JAGHIRES
JAGHIRS
JAGIR

JAGIRS
JAGLESS
JAGRA
JAGRAS
JAGS
JAGUAR
JAGUARS
JAI
JAIL
JAILABLE
JAILBAIT
JAILBIRD
JAILBIRDS
JAILBREAK
JAILED
JAILER
JAILERESS
JAILERS
JAILHOUSE
JAILING
JAILLESS
JAILOR
JAILORESS
JAILORS
JAILS
JAK
JAKE
JAKES
JAKESES
JAKEY
JAKEYS
JAKFRUIT
JAKFRUITS
JAKS
JALAP
JALAPENO
JALAPENOS
JALAPIC
JALAPIN
JALAPINS
JALAPS
JALOP
JALOPIES
JALOPPIES
JALOPPY
JALOPS
JALOPY
JALOUSE
JALOUSED
JALOUSES
JALOUSIE
JALOUSIED
JALOUSIES

JALOUSING
JAM
JAMADAR
JAMADARS
JAMB
JAMBALAYA
JAMBART
JAMBARTS
JAMBE
JAMBEAU
JAMBEAUX
JAMBED
JAMBEE
JAMBEES
JAMBER
JAMBERS
JAMBES
JAMBEUX
JAMBIER
JAMBIERS
JAMBING
JAMBIYA
JAMBIYAH
JAMBIYAHS
JAMBIYAS
JAMBO
JAMBOK
JAMBOKKED
JAMBOKS
JAMBOLAN
JAMBOLANA
JAMBOLANS
JAMBONE
JAMBONES
JAMBOOL
JAMBOOLS
JAMBOREE
JAMBOREES
JAMBOS
JAMBS
JAMBU
JAMBUL
JAMBULS
JAMBUS
JAMDANI
JAMDANIS
JAMES
JAMESES
JAMJAR
JAMJARS
JAMLIKE
JAMMABLE
JAMMED
JAMMER
JAMMERS
JAMMIER
JAMMIES
JAMMIEST

JAMMING
JAMMINGS
JAMMY
JAMPACKED
JAMPAN
JAMPANEE
JAMPANEES
JAMPANI
JAMPANIS
JAMPANS
JAMPOT
JAMPOTS
JAMS
JANDAL
JANDALS
JANE
JANES
JANGLE
JANGLED
JANGLER
JANGLERS
JANGLES
JANGLIER
JANGLIEST
JANGLING
JANGLINGS
JANGLY
JANIFORM
JANISARY
JANISSARY
JANITOR
JANITORS
JANITRESS
JANITRIX
JANIZAR
JANIZARS
JANIZARY
JANKER
JANKERS
JANN
JANNIES
JANNOCK
JANNOCKS
JANNS
JANNY
JANSKY
JANSKYS
JANTEE
JANTIER
JANTIES
JANTIEST
JANTY
JAP
JAPAN
JAPANISE
JAPANISED
JAPANISES
JAPANIZE

JAPANIZED
JAPANIZES
JAPANNED
JAPANNER
JAPANNERS
JAPANNING
JAPANS
JAPE
JAPED
JAPER
JAPERIES
JAPERS
JAPERY
JAPES
JAPING
JAPINGLY
JAPINGS
JAPONICA
JAPONICAS
JAPPED
JAPPING
JAPS
JAR
JARARACA
JARARACAS
JARARAKA
JARARAKAS
JARFUL
JARFULS
JARGON
JARGONED
JARGONEER
JARGONEL
JARGONELS
JARGONING
JARGONISE
JARGONISH
JARGONIST
JARGONIZE
JARGONS
JARGONY
JARGOON
JARGOONS
JARHEAD
JARHEADS
JARINA
JARINAS
JARK
JARKMAN
JARKMEN
JARKS
JARL
JARLDOM
JARLDOMS
JARLS
JARLSBERG
JAROOL
JAROOLS

JAROSITE
JAROSITES
JAROVISE
JAROVISED
JAROVISES
JAROVIZE
JAROVIZED
JAROVIZES
JARP
JARPED
JARPING
JARPS
JARRAH
JARRAHS
JARRED
JARRING
JARRINGLY
JARRINGS
JARS
JARSFUL
JARTA
JARTAS
JARUL
JARULS
JARVEY
JARVEYS
JARVIE
JARVIES
JASEY
JASEYS
JASIES
JASMIN
JASMINE
JASMINES
JASMINS
JASP
JASPE
JASPER
JASPERISE
JASPERIZE
JASPEROUS
JASPERS
JASPERY
JASPES
JASPIDEAN
JASPILITE
JASPIS
JASPISES
JASPS
JASS
JASSES
JASSID
JASSIDS
JASY
JATAKA
JATAKAS
JATO
JATOS

JAUK	JAWING	JEDI	JELLABAH
JAUKED	JAWINGS	JEDIS	JELLABAHS
JAUKING	JAWLESS	JEE	JELLABAS
JAUKS	JAWLIKE	JEED	JELLED
JAUNCE	JAWLINE	JEEING	JELLIED
JAUNCED	JAWLINES	JEEL	JELLIES
JAUNCES	JAWS	JEELED	JELLIFIED
JAUNCING	JAXIE	JEELIE	JELLIFIES
JAUNDICE	JAXIES	JEELIED	JELLIFY
JAUNDICED	JAXY	JEELIEING	JELLING
JAUNDICES	JAY	JEELIES	JELLO
JAUNSE	JAYBIRD	JEELING	JELLOS
JAUNSED	JAYBIRDS	JEELS	JELLS
JAUNSES	JAYGEE	JEELY	JELLY
JAUNSING	JAYGEES	JEELYING	JELLYBEAN
JAUNT	JAYHAWKER	JEEP	JELLYFISH
JAUNTED	JAYS	JEEPED	JELLYING
JAUNTEE	JAYVEE	JEEPERS	JELLYLIKE
JAUNTIE	JAYVEES	JEEPING	JELLYROLL
JAUNTIER	JAYWALK	JEEPNEY	JELUTONG
JAUNTIES	JAYWALKED	JEEPNEYS	JELUTONGS
JAUNTIEST	JAYWALKER	JEEPS	JEMADAR
JAUNTILY	JAYWALKS	JEER	JEMADARS
JAUNTING	JAZERANT	JEERED	JEMBE
JAUNTS	JAZERANTS	JEERER	JEMBES
JAUNTY	JAZIES	JEERERS	JEMIDAR
JAUP	JAZY	JEERING	JEMIDARS
JAUPED	JAZZ	JEERINGLY	JEMIMA
JAUPING	JAZZBO	JEERINGS	JEMIMAS
JAUPS	JAZZBOS	JEERS	JEMMIED
JAVA	JAZZED	JEES	JEMMIER
JAVAS	JAZZER	JEEZ	JEMMIES
JAVEL	JAZZERS	JEFE	JEMMIEST
JAVELIN	JAZZES	JEFES	JEMMINESS
JAVELINA	JAZZIER	JEFF	JEMMY
JAVELINAS	JAZZIEST	JEFFED	JEMMYING
JAVELINED	JAZZILY	JEFFING	JENNET
JAVELINS	JAZZINESS	JEFFS	JENNETING
JAVELS	JAZZING	JEHAD	JENNETS
JAW	JAZZLIKE	JEHADI	JENNIES
JAWAN	JAZZMAN	JEHADIS	JENNY
JAWANS	JAZZMEN	JEHADISM	JEOFAIL
JAWARI	JAZZY	JEHADISMS	JEOFAILS
JAWARIS	JEALOUS	JEHADIST	JEON
JAWBATION	JEALOUSE	JEHADISTS	JEOPARD
JAWBONE	JEALOUSED	JEHADS	JEOPARDED
JAWBONED	JEALOUSES	JEHU	JEOPARDER
JAWBONER	JEALOUSLY	JEHUS	JEOPARDS
JAWBONERS	JEALOUSY	JEJUNA	JEOPARDY
JAWBONES	JEAN	JEJUNAL	JEQUERITY
JAWBONING	JEANED	JEJUNE	JEQUIRITY
JAWBOX	JEANETTE	JEJUNELY	JERBIL
JAWBOXES	JEANETTES	JEJUNITY	JERBILS
JAWED	JEANS	JEJUNUM	JERBOA
JAWFALL	JEAT	JELAB	JERBOAS
JAWFALLS	JEATS	JELABS	JEREED
JAWHOLE	JEBEL	JELL	JEREEDS
JAWHOLES	JEBELS	JELLABA	JEREMIAD

JEREMIADS	JESTBOOK	JETWAY	JIBES
JEREPIGO	JESTBOOKS	JETWAYS	JIBING
JEREPIGOS	JESTED	JEU	JIBINGLY
JERFALCON	JESTEE	JEUNE	JIBS
JERID	JESTEES	JEUX	JICAMA
JERIDS	JESTER	JEW	JICAMAS
JERK	JESTERS	JEWED	JICKAJOG
JERKED	JESTFUL	JEWEL	JICKAJOGS
JERKER	JESTING	JEWELED	JIFF
JERKERS	JESTINGLY	JEWELER	JIFFIES
JERKIER	JESTINGS	JEWELERS	JIFFS
JERKIES	JESTS	JEWELFISH	JIFFY
JERKIEST	JESUIT	JEWELING	JIG
JERKILY	JESUITIC	JEWELLED	JIGABOO
JERKIN	JESUITISM	JEWELLER	JIGABOOS
JERKINESS	JESUITRY	JEWELLERS	JIGAJIG
JERKING	JESUITS	JEWELLERY	JIGAJIGS
JERKINGLY	JESUS	JEWELLIKE	JIGAJOG
JERKINGS	JET	JEWELLING	JIGAJOGS
JERKINS	JETBEAD	JEWELRIES	JIGAMAREE
JERKS	JETBEADS	JEWELRY	JIGGED
JERKWATER	JETE	JEWELS	JIGGER
JERKY	JETES	JEWELWEED	JIGGERED
JEROBOAM	JETFOIL	JEWFISH	JIGGERING
JEROBOAMS	JETFOILS	JEWFISHES	JIGGERS
JERQUE	JETLAG	JEWIE	JIGGIER
JERQUED	JETLAGS	JEWIES	JIGGIEST
JERQUER	JETLIKE	JEWING	JIGGING
JERQUERS	JETLINER	JEWS	JIGGINGS
JERQUES	JETLINERS	JEZAIL	JIGGISH
JERQUING	JETON	JEZAILS	JIGGLE
JERQUINGS	JETONS	JEZEBEL	JIGGLED
JERREED	JETPLANE	JEZEBELS	JIGGLES
JERREEDS	JETPLANES	JHALA	JIGGLIER
JERRICAN	JETPORT	JHALAS	JIGGLIEST
JERRICANS	JETPORTS	JHATKA	JIGGLING
JERRID	JETS	JHATKAS	JIGGLY
JERRIDS	JETSAM	JIAO	JIGGUMBOB
JERRIES	JETSAMS	JIAOS	JIGGY
JERRY	JETSOM	JIB	JIGJIG
JERRYCAN	JETSOMS	JIBB	JIGJIGGED
JERRYCANS	JETSON	JIBBAH	JIGJIGS
JERSEY	JETSONS	JIBBAHS	JIGLIKE
JERSEYED	JETSTREAM	JIBBED	JIGOT
JERSEYS	JETTATURA	JIBBER	JIGOTS
JESS	JETTED	JIBBERED	JIGS
JESSAMIES	JETTIED	JIBBERING	JIGSAW
JESSAMINE	JETTIER	JIBBERS	JIGSAWED
JESSAMY	JETTIES	JIBBING	JIGSAWING
JESSANT	JETTIEST	JIBBINGS	JIGSAWN
JESSE	JETTINESS	JIBBONS	JIGSAWS
JESSED	JETTING	JIBBOOM	JIHAD
JESSERANT	JETTISON	JIBBOOMS	JIHADI
JESSES	JETTISONS	JIBBS	JIHADIS
JESSIE	JETTON	JIBE	JIHADISM
JESSIES	JETTONS	JIBED	JIHADISMS
JESSING	JETTY	JIBER	JIHADIST
JEST	JETTYING	JIBERS	JIHADISTS

JIHADS	JINGLIEST	JIUJITSU	JOCKEYISH
JILBAB	JINGLING	JIUJITSUS	JOCKEYISM
JILBABS	JINGLY	JIUJUTSU	JOCKEYS
JILGIE	JINGO	JIUJUTSUS	JOCKNEY
JILGIES	JINGOES	JIVE	JOCKNEYS
JILL	JINGOISH	JIVEASS	JOCKO
JILLAROO	JINGOISM	JIVED	JOCKOS
JILLAROOS	JINGOISMS	JIVER	JOCKS
JILLET	JINGOIST	JIVERS	JOCKSTRAP
JILLETS	JINGOISTS	JIVES	JOCKTELEG
JILLFLIRT	JINJILI	JIVEY	JOCO
JILLION	JINJILIS	JIVIER	JOCOSE
JILLIONS	JINK	JIVIEST	JOCOSELY
JILLIONTH	JINKED	JIVING	JOCOSITY
JILLS	JINKER	JIVY	JOCULAR
JILT	JINKERS	JIZ	JOCULARLY
JILTED	JINKING	JIZZ	JOCULATOR
JILTER	JINKS	JIZZES	JOCUND
JILTERS	JINN	JNANA	JOCUNDITY
JILTING	JINNE	JNANAS	JOCUNDLY
JILTS	JINNEE	JO	JODEL
JIMCRACK	JINNI	JOANNA	JODELLED
JIMCRACKS	JINNIS	JOANNAS	JODELLING
JIMINY	JINNS	JOANNES	JODELS
JIMJAM	JINRIKSHA	JOANNESES	JODHPUR
JIMJAMS	JINS	JOB	JODHPURS
JIMMIE	JINX	JOBATION	JOE
JIMMIED	JINXED	JOBATIONS	JOES
JIMMIES	JINXES	JOBBED	JOEY
JIMMINY	JINXING	JOBBER	JOEYS
JIMMY	JIPIJAPA	JOBBERIES	JOG
JIMMYING	JIPIJAPAS	JOBBERS	JOGGED
JIMP	JIPYAPA	JOBBERY	JOGGER
JIMPER	JIPYAPAS	JOBBIE	JOGGERS
JIMPEST	JIRBLE	JOBBIES	JOGGING
JIMPIER	JIRBLED	JOBBING	JOGGINGS
JIMPIEST	JIRBLES	JOBBINGS	JOGGLE
JIMPLY	JIRBLING	JOBCENTRE	JOGGLED
JIMPNESS	JIRD	JOBE	JOGGLER
JIMPY	JIRDS	JOBED	JOGGLERS
JIMSON	JIRGA	JOBERNOWL	JOGGLES
JIN	JIRGAS	JOBES	JOGGLING
JINGAL	JIRKINET	JOBHOLDER	JOGPANTS
JINGALL	JIRKINETS	JOBING	JOGS
JINGALLS	JIRRE	JOBLESS	JOGTROT
JINGALS	JISM	JOBNAME	JOGTROTS
JINGBANG	JISMS	JOBNAMES	JOHANNES
JINGBANGS	JISSOM	JOBS	JOHN
JINGKO	JISSOMS	JOBSEEKER	JOHNBOAT
JINGKOES	JITNEY	JOBSHARE	JOHNBOATS
JINGLE	JITNEYS	JOBSHARES	JOHNNIE
JINGLED	JITTER	JOBSWORTH	JOHNNIES
JINGLER	JITTERBUG	JOCK	JOHNNY
JINGLERS	JITTERED	JOCKETTE	JOHNS
JINGLES	JITTERIER	JOCKETTES	JOHNSON
JINGLET	JITTERING	JOCKEY	JOHNSONS
JINGLETS	JITTERS	JOCKEYED	JOIN
JINGLIER	JITTERY	JOCKEYING	JOINABLE

JOINDER	JOLLEYER	JONQUILS	JOUISANCE
JOINDERS	JOLLEYERS	JONTIES	JOUK
JOINED	JOLLEYING	JONTY	JOUKED
JOINER	JOLLEYS	JOOK	JOUKERIES
JOINERIES	JOLLIED	JOOKED	JOUKERY
JOINERS	JOLLIER	JOOKERIES	JOUKING
JOINERY	JOLLIERS	JOOKERY	JOUKS
JOINING	JOLLIES	JOOKING	JOULE
JOININGS	JOLLIEST	JOOKS	JOULED
JOINS	JOLLIFIED	JOR	JOULES
JOINT	JOLLIFIES	JORAM	JOULING
JOINTED	JOLLIFY	JORAMS	JOUNCE
JOINTEDLY	JOLLILY	JORDAN	JOUNCED
JOINTER	JOLLIMENT	JORDANS	JOUNCES
JOINTERS	JOLLINESS	JORDELOO	JOUNCIER
JOINTING	JOLLING	JORDELOOS	JOUNCIEST
JOINTLESS	JOLLITIES	JORS	JOUNCING
JOINTLY	JOLLITY	JORUM	JOUNCY
JOINTNESS	JOLLOP	JORUMS	JOUR
JOINTRESS	JOLLOPS	JOSEPH	JOURNAL
JOINTS	JOLLS	JOSEPHS	JOURNALED
JOINTURE	JOLLY	JOSH	JOURNALS
JOINTURED	JOLLYBOAT	JOSHED	JOURNEY
JOINTURES	JOLLYER	JOSHER	JOURNEYED
JOINTWEED	JOLLYERS	JOSHERS	JOURNEYER
JOINTWORM	JOLLYHEAD	JOSHES	JOURNEYS
JOIST	JOLLYING	JOSHING	JOURNO
JOISTED	JOLLYINGS	JOSHINGLY	JOURNOS
JOISTING	JOLS	JOSKIN	JOURS
JOISTS	JOLT	JOSKINS	JOUST
JOJOBA	JOLTED	JOSS	JOUSTED
JOJOBAS	JOLTER	JOSSER	JOUSTER
JOKE	JOLTERS	JOSSERS	JOUSTERS
JOKED	JOLTHEAD	JOSSES	JOUSTING
JOKER	JOLTHEADS	JOSTLE	JOUSTS
JOKERS	JOLTIER	JOSTLED	JOVIAL
JOKES	JOLTIEST	JOSTLER	JOVIALITY
JOKESMITH	JOLTILY	JOSTLERS	JOVIALLY
JOKESOME	JOLTING	JOSTLES	JOVIALTY
JOKESTER	JOLTINGLY	JOSTLING	JOW
JOKESTERS	JOLTS	JOSTLINGS	JOWAR
JOKEY	JOLTY	JOT	JOWARI
JOKIER	JOMO	JOTA	JOWARIS
JOKIEST	JOMON	JOTAS	JOWARS
JOKILY	JOMOS	JOTS	JOWED
JOKINESS	JONCANOE	JOTTED	JOWING
JOKING	JONCANOES	JOTTER	JOWL
JOKINGLY	JONES	JOTTERS	JOWLED
JOKOL	JONESED	JOTTING	JOWLER
JOKY	JONESES	JOTTINGS	JOWLERS
JOL	JONESING	JOTTY	JOWLIER
JOLE	JONG	JOTUN	JOWLIEST
JOLED	JONGLEUR	JOTUNN	JOWLINESS
JOLES	JONGLEURS	JOTUNNS	JOWLING
JOLING	JONGS	JOTUNS	JOWLS
JOLL	JONNOCK	JOUAL	JOWLY
JOLLED	JONNYCAKE	JOUALS	JOWS
JOLLEY	JONQUIL	JOUGS	JOY

JOYANCE
JOYANCES
JOYED
JOYFUL
JOYFULLER
JOYFULLY
JOYING
JOYLESS
JOYLESSLY
JOYOUS
JOYOUSLY
JOYPOP
JOYPOPPED
JOYPOPPER
JOYPOPS
JOYRIDDEN
JOYRIDE
JOYRIDER
JOYRIDERS
JOYRIDES
JOYRIDING
JOYRODE
JOYS
JOYSTICK
JOYSTICKS
JUBA
JUBAS
JUBATE
JUBBAH
JUBBAHS
JUBE
JUBES
JUBHAH
JUBHAHS
JUBILANCE
JUBILANCY
JUBILANT
JUBILATE
JUBILATED
JUBILATES
JUBILE
JUBILEE
JUBILEES
JUBILES
JUCO
JUCOS
JUD
JUDAS
JUDASES
JUDDER
JUDDERED
JUDDERING
JUDDERS
JUDGE
JUDGEABLE
JUDGED
JUDGELESS
JUDGELIKE

JUDGEMENT
JUDGER
JUDGERS
JUDGES
JUDGESHIP
JUDGING
JUDGINGLY
JUDGMATIC
JUDGMENT
JUDGMENTS
JUDICABLE
JUDICATOR
JUDICIAL
JUDICIARY
JUDICIOUS
JUDIES
JUDO
JUDOGI
JUDOGIS
JUDOIST
JUDOISTS
JUDOKA
JUDOKAS
JUDOS
JUDS
JUDY
JUG
JUGA
JUGAL
JUGALS
JUGATE
JUGFUL
JUGFULS
JUGGED
JUGGING
JUGGINGS
JUGGINS
JUGGINSES
JUGGLE
JUGGLED
JUGGLER
JUGGLERS
JUGGLERY
JUGGLES
JUGGLING
JUGGLINGS
JUGHEAD
JUGHEADS
JUGLET
JUGLETS
JUGS
JUGSFUL
JUGULA
JUGULAR
JUGULARS
JUGULATE
JUGULATED
JUGULATES

JUGULUM
JUGUM
JUGUMS
JUICE
JUICED
JUICEHEAD
JUICELESS
JUICER
JUICERS
JUICES
JUICIER
JUICIEST
JUICILY
JUICINESS
JUICING
JUICY
JUJITSU
JUJITSUS
JUJU
JUJUBE
JUJUBES
JUJUISM
JUJUISMS
JUJUIST
JUJUISTS
JUJUS
JUJUTSU
JUJUTSUS
JUKE
JUKEBOX
JUKEBOXES
JUKED
JUKES
JUKING
JUKSEI
JUKSEIS
JUKU
JUKUS
JULEP
JULEPS
JULIENNE
JULIENNED
JULIENNES
JUMAR
JUMARED
JUMARING
JUMARRED
JUMARRING
JUMARS
JUMART
JUMARTS
JUMBAL
JUMBALS
JUMBIE
JUMBIES
JUMBLE
JUMBLED
JUMBLER

JUMBLERS
JUMBLES
JUMBLIER
JUMBLIEST
JUMBLING
JUMBLY
JUMBO
JUMBOISE
JUMBOISED
JUMBOISES
JUMBOIZE
JUMBOIZED
JUMBOIZES
JUMBOS
JUMBUCK
JUMBUCKS
JUMBY
JUMELLE
JUMELLES
JUMP
JUMPABLE
JUMPED
JUMPER
JUMPERS
JUMPIER
JUMPIEST
JUMPILY
JUMPINESS
JUMPING
JUMPINGLY
JUMPINGS
JUMPOFF
JUMPOFFS
JUMPS
JUMPSUIT
JUMPSUITS
JUMPY
JUN
JUNCATE
JUNCATES
JUNCO
JUNCOES
JUNCOS
JUNCTION
JUNCTIONS
JUNCTURAL
JUNCTURE
JUNCTURES
JUNCUS
JUNCUSES
JUNEATING
JUNGLE
JUNGLED
JUNGLEGYM
JUNGLES
JUNGLI
JUNGLIER
JUNGLIEST

JUNGLIS
JUNGLIST
JUNGLISTS
JUNGLY
JUNIOR
JUNIORATE
JUNIORITY
JUNIORS
JUNIPER
JUNIPERS
JUNK
JUNKANOO
JUNKANOOS
JUNKED
JUNKER
JUNKERS
JUNKET
JUNKETED
JUNKETEER
JUNKETER
JUNKETERS
JUNKETING
JUNKETS
JUNKETTED
JUNKETTER
JUNKIE
JUNKIER
JUNKIES
JUNKIEST
JUNKINESS
JUNKING
JUNKMAN
JUNKMEN
JUNKS
JUNKY
JUNKYARD
JUNKYARDS
JUNTA
JUNTAS
JUNTO
JUNTOS
JUPATI
JUPATIS
JUPE
JUPES
JUPON
JUPONS
JURA
JURAL
JURALLY
JURANT
JURANTS
JURASSIC
JURAT
JURATORY
JURATS
JURE
JUREL

JURELS
JURIDIC
JURIDICAL
JURIED
JURIES
JURIST
JURISTIC
JURISTS
JUROR
JURORS
JURY
JURYING
JURYLESS
JURYMAN
JURYMAST
JURYMASTS
JURYMEN
JURYWOMAN
JURYWOMEN
JUS
JUSSIVE
JUSSIVES
JUST
JUSTED
JUSTER
JUSTERS
JUSTEST
JUSTICE
JUSTICER
JUSTICERS
JUSTICES
JUSTICIAR
JUSTIFIED
JUSTIFIER
JUSTIFIES
JUSTIFY
JUSTING
JUSTLE
JUSTLED
JUSTLES
JUSTLING
JUSTLY
JUSTNESS
JUSTS
JUT
JUTE
JUTELIKE
JUTES
JUTS
JUTTED
JUTTIED
JUTTIES
JUTTING
JUTTINGLY
JUTTY
JUTTYING
JUVE
JUVENAL

JUVENALS
JUVENILE
JUVENILES
JUVENILIA
JUVES
JUXTAPOSE
JYMOLD
JYNX
JYNXES

— K —

KA
KAAL
KAAMA
KAAMAS
KAAS
KAB
KABAB
KABABBED
KABABBING
KABABS
KABADDI
KABADDIS
KABAKA
KABAKAS
KABALA
KABALAS
KABALISM
KABALISMS
KABALIST
KABALISTS
KABAR
KABARS
KABAYA
KABAYAS
KABBALA
KABBALAH
KABBALAHS
KABBALAS
KABBALISM
KABBALIST
KABELE
KABELES
KABELJOU
KABELJOUS
KABELJOUW
KABIKI
KABIKIS
KABOB
KABOBBED
KABOBBING
KABOBS
KABS
KABUKI
KABUKIS
KACCHA
KACCHAS
KACHA
KACHAHRI
KACHAHRIS
KACHCHA
KACHERI
KACHERIS
KACHINA

KACHINAS
KADAITCHA
KADDISH
KADDISHES
KADDISHIM
KADE
KADES
KADI
KADIS
KAE
KAED
KAEING
KAES
KAF
KAFFIR
KAFFIRS
KAFFIYAH
KAFFIYAHS
KAFFIYEH
KAFFIYEHS
KAFILA
KAFILAS
KAFIR
KAFIRS
KAFS
KAFTAN
KAFTANS
KAGO
KAGOOL
KAGOOLS
KAGOS
KAGOUL
KAGOULE
KAGOULES
KAGOULS
KAGU
KAGUS
KAHAL
KAHALS
KAHAWAI
KAHAWAIS
KAHIKATEA
KAHIKATOA
KAHUNA
KAHUNAS
KAI
KAIAK
KAIAKED
KAIAKING
KAIAKS
KAID
KAIDS
KAIE

KAIES
KAIF
KAIFS
KAIK
KAIKA
KAIKAI
KAIKAIS
KAIKAS
KAIKAWAKA
KAIKOMAKO
KAIKS
KAIL
KAILS
KAILYAIRD
KAILYARD
KAILYARDS
KAIM
KAIMAKAM
KAIMAKAMS
KAIMS
KAIN
KAING
KAINGA
KAINGAS
KAINIT
KAINITE
KAINITES
KAINITS
KAINS
KAIROMONE
KAIS
KAISER
KAISERDOM
KAISERIN
KAISERINS
KAISERISM
KAISERS
KAIZEN
KAIZENS
KAJAWAH
KAJAWAHS
KAJEPUT
KAJEPUTS
KAK
KAKA
KAKAPO
KAKAPOS
KAKARIKI
KAKAS
KAKEMONO
KAKEMONOS
KAKI
KAKIEMON

KAKIEMONS
KAKIS
KAKODYL
KAKODYLS
KAKS
KALAM
KALAMATA
KALAMATAS
KALAMDAN
KALAMDANS
KALAMKARI
KALAMS
KALANCHOE
KALE
KALENDAR
KALENDARS
KALENDS
KALES
KALEWIFE
KALEWIVES
KALEYARD
KALEYARDS
KALI
KALIAN
KALIANS
KALIF
KALIFATE
KALIFATES
KALIFS
KALIMBA
KALIMBAS
KALINITE
KALINITES
KALIPH
KALIPHATE
KALIPHS
KALIS
KALIUM
KALIUMS
KALLIDIN
KALLIDINS
KALLITYPE
KALMIA
KALMIAS
KALONG
KALONGS
KALOTYPE
KALOTYPES
KALPA
KALPAC
KALPACS
KALPAK
KALPAKS

KALPAS
KALPIS
KALPISES
KALSOMINE
KALUMPIT
KALUMPITS
KALYPTRA
KALYPTRAS
KAM
KAMA
KAMAAINA
KAMAAINAS
KAMACITE
KAMACITES
KAMAHI
KAMALA
KAMALAS
KAMAS
KAME
KAMEES
KAMEESES
KAMEEZ
KAMEEZES
KAMELA
KAMELAS
KAMERAD
KAMERADED
KAMERADS
KAMES
KAMI
KAMICHI
KAMICHIS
KAMIK
KAMIKAZE
KAMIKAZES
KAMIKS
KAMILA
KAMILAS
KAMIS
KAMISES
KAMME
KAMOKAMO
KAMPONG
KAMPONGS
KAMSEEN
KAMSEENS
KAMSIN
KAMSINS
KANA
KANAE
KANAKA
KANAKAS
KANAMYCIN
KANAS
KANBAN
KANBANS
KANDIES
KANDY

KANE
KANEH
KANEHS
KANES
KANG
KANGA
KANGAROO
KANGAROOS
KANGAS
KANGHA
KANGHAS
KANGS
KANJI
KANJIS
KANS
KANSES
KANT
KANTAR
KANTARS
KANTED
KANTELA
KANTELAS
KANTELE
KANTELES
KANTEN
KANTENS
KANTHA
KANTHAS
KANTIKOY
KANTIKOYS
KANTING
KANTS
KANUKA
KANZU
KANZUS
KAOLIANG
KAOLIANGS
KAOLIN
KAOLINE
KAOLINES
KAOLINIC
KAOLINISE
KAOLINITE
KAOLINIZE
KAOLINS
KAON
KAONIC
KAONS
KAPA
KAPAS
KAPH
KAPHS
KAPOK
KAPOKS
KAPPA
KAPPAS
KAPUKA
KAPUT

KAPUTT
KARA
KARABINER
KARAISM
KARAISMS
KARAIT
KARAITS
KARAKA
KARAKAS
KARAKIA
KARAKIAS
KARAKUL
KARAKULS
KARAMU
KARAMUS
KARANGA
KARANGAED
KARANGAS
KARAOKE
KARAOKES
KARAS
KARAT
KARATE
KARATEIST
KARATEKA
KARATEKAS
KARATES
KARATS
KAREAREA
KARENGO
KARENGOS
KARITE
KARITES
KARK
KARKED
KARKING
KARKS
KARMA
KARMAS
KARMIC
KARN
KARNS
KARO
KAROO
KAROOS
KARORO
KAROROS
KAROSHI
KAROSHIS
KAROSS
KAROSSES
KARRI
KARRIS
KARROO
KARROOS
KARSEY
KARSEYS
KARSIES

KARST
KARSTIC
KARSTIFY
KARSTS
KARSY
KART
KARTER
KARTERS
KARTING
KARTINGS
KARTS
KARYOGAMY
KARYOGRAM
KARYOLOGY
KARYON
KARYONS
KARYOSOME
KARYOTIN
KARYOTINS
KARYOTYPE
KARZIES
KARZY
KAS
KASBAH
KASBAHS
KASHA
KASHAS
KASHER
KASHERED
KASHERING
KASHERS
KASHMIR
KASHMIRS
KASHRUS
KASHRUSES
KASHRUT
KASHRUTH
KASHRUTHS
KASHRUTS
KASME
KAT
KATA
KATABASES
KATABASIS
KATABATIC
KATABOLIC
KATAKANA
KATAKANAS
KATANA
KATANAS
KATAS
KATCHINA
KATCHINAS
KATCINA
KATCINAS
KATHAK
KATHAKALI
KATHAKS

310

KATHARSES	KAYO	KECKS	KEENEST
KATHARSIS	KAYOED	KECKSES	KEENING
KATHODAL	KAYOES	KECKSIES	KEENINGS
KATHODE	KAYOING	KECKSY	KEENLY
KATHODES	KAYOINGS	KED	KEENNESS
KATHODIC	KAYOS	KEDDAH	KEENO
KATI	KAYS	KEDDAHS	KEENOS
KATION	KAZACHKI	KEDGE	KEENS
KATIONS	KAZACHOK	KEDGED	KEEP
KATIPO	KAZATSKI	KEDGER	KEEPABLE
KATIPOS	KAZATSKY	KEDGEREE	KEEPER
KATIS	KAZATZKA	KEDGEREES	KEEPERS
KATORGA	KAZATZKAS	KEDGERS	KEEPING
KATORGAS	KAZI	KEDGES	KEEPINGS
KATS	KAZILLION	KEDGIER	KEEPNET
KATSURA	KAZIS	KEDGIEST	KEEPNETS
KATSURAS	KAZOO	KEDGING	KEEPS
KATTI	KAZOOS	KEDGY	KEEPSAKE
KATTIS	KBAR	KEDS	KEEPSAKES
KATYDID	KBARS	KEECH	KEEPSAKY
KATYDIDS	KEA	KEECHES	KEESHOND
KAUGH	KEAS	KEEF	KEESHONDS
KAUGHS	KEASAR	KEEFS	KEESTER
KAUMATUA	KEASARS	KEEK	KEESTERS
KAUMATUAS	KEAVIE	KEEKED	KEET
KAUPAPA	KEAVIES	KEEKER	KEETS
KAUPAPAS	KEB	KEEKERS	KEEVE
KAURI	KEBAB	KEEKING	KEEVES
KAURIES	KEBABBED	KEEKS	KEF
KAURIS	KEBABBING	KEEL	KEFFEL
KAURU	KEBABS	KEELAGE	KEFFELS
KAURY	KEBAR	KEELAGES	KEFFIYAH
KAVA	KEBARS	KEELBOAT	KEFFIYAHS
KAVAKAVA	KEBBED	KEELBOATS	KEFFIYEH
KAVAKAVAS	KEBBIE	KEELED	KEFFIYEHS
KAVAS	KEBBIES	KEELER	KEFIR
KAVASS	KEBBING	KEELERS	KEFIRS
KAVASSES	KEBBOCK	KEELHALE	KEFS
KAW	KEBBOCKS	KEELHALED	KEFTEDES
KAWA	KEBBUCK	KEELHALES	KEFUFFLE
KAWAKAWA	KEBBUCKS	KEELHAUL	KEFUFFLED
KAWAKAWAS	KEBELE	KEELHAULS	KEFUFFLES
KAWAS	KEBELES	KEELIE	KEG
KAWAU	KEBLAH	KEELIES	KEGELER
KAWED	KEBLAHS	KEELING	KEGELERS
KAWING	KEBOB	KEELINGS	KEGGED
KAWS	KEBOBBED	KEELIVINE	KEGGER
KAY	KEBOBBING	KEELLESS	KEGGERS
KAYAK	KEBOBS	KEELMAN	KEGGING
KAYAKED	KEBS	KEELMEN	KEGLER
KAYAKER	KECK	KEELS	KEGLERS
KAYAKERS	KECKED	KEELSON	KEGLING
KAYAKING	KECKING	KEELSONS	KEGLINGS
KAYAKINGS	KECKLE	KEELYVINE	KEGS
KAYAKS	KECKLED	KEEN	KEHUA
KAYLE	KECKLES	KEENED	KEHUAS
KAYLES	KECKLING	KEENER	KEIGHT
KAYLIED	KECKLINGS	KEENERS	KEIR

KEIRETSU
KEIRETSUS
KEIRS
KEISTER
KEISTERS
KEITLOA
KEITLOAS
KEKENO
KEKERENGU
KEKS
KEKSYE
KEKSYES
KELEP
KELEPS
KELIM
KELIMS
KELL
KELLAUT
KELLAUTS
KELLIES
KELLS
KELLY
KELOID
KELOIDAL
KELOIDS
KELP
KELPED
KELPER
KELPERS
KELPIE
KELPIES
KELPING
KELPS
KELPY
KELSON
KELSONS
KELT
KELTER
KELTERS
KELTIE
KELTIES
KELTS
KELTY
KELVIN
KELVINS
KEMB
KEMBED
KEMBING
KEMBLA
KEMBLAS
KEMBO
KEMBOED
KEMBOING
KEMBOS
KEMBS
KEMP
KEMPED
KEMPER

KEMPERS
KEMPIER
KEMPIEST
KEMPING
KEMPINGS
KEMPLE
KEMPLES
KEMPS
KEMPT
KEMPY
KEN
KENAF
KENAFS
KENCH
KENCHES
KENDO
KENDOS
KENNED
KENNEL
KENNELED
KENNELING
KENNELLED
KENNELS
KENNER
KENNERS
KENNET
KENNETS
KENNETT
KENNETTED
KENNETTS
KENNING
KENNINGS
KENO
KENOS
KENOSES
KENOSIS
KENOSISES
KENOTIC
KENOTICS
KENOTRON
KENOTRONS
KENS
KENSPECK
KENT
KENTE
KENTED
KENTES
KENTIA
KENTIAS
KENTING
KENTLEDGE
KENTS
KEP
KEPHALIC
KEPHALICS
KEPHALIN
KEPHALINS
KEPHIR

KEPHIRS
KEPI
KEPIS
KEPPED
KEPPEN
KEPPING
KEPPIT
KEPS
KEPT
KERAMIC
KERAMICS
KERATIN
KERATINS
KERATITIS
KERATOID
KERATOMA
KERATOMAS
KERATOSE
KERATOSES
KERATOSIC
KERATOSIS
KERATOTIC
KERB
KERBAYA
KERBAYAS
KERBED
KERBING
KERBINGS
KERBS
KERBSIDE
KERBSIDES
KERBSTONE
KERCHIEF
KERCHIEFS
KERCHOO
KEREL
KERELS
KERERU
KERF
KERFED
KERFING
KERFLOOEY
KERFS
KERFUFFLE
KERKIER
KERKIEST
KERKY
KERMA
KERMAS
KERMES
KERMESITE
KERMESS
KERMESSE
KERMESSES
KERMIS
KERMISES
KERN
KERNE

KERNED
KERNEL
KERNELED
KERNELING
KERNELLED
KERNELLY
KERNELS
KERNES
KERNING
KERNINGS
KERNISH
KERNITE
KERNITES
KERNS
KERO
KEROGEN
KEROGENS
KEROS
KEROSENE
KEROSENES
KEROSINE
KEROSINES
KERPLUNK
KERPLUNKS
KERRIA
KERRIAS
KERRIES
KERRY
KERSEY
KERSEYS
KERVE
KERVED
KERVES
KERVING
KERYGMA
KERYGMAS
KERYGMATA
KESAR
KESARS
KESH
KESHES
KEST
KESTING
KESTREL
KESTRELS
KESTS
KET
KETA
KETAMINE
KETAMINES
KETAS
KETCH
KETCHES
KETCHING
KETCHUP
KETCHUPS
KETE
KETENE

KETENES
KETMIA
KETMIAS
KETO
KETOGENIC
KETOL
KETOLS
KETONE
KETONEMIA
KETONES
KETONIC
KETONURIA
KETOSE
KETOSES
KETOSIS
KETOTIC
KETOXIME
KETOXIMES
KETS
KETTLE
KETTLEFUL
KETTLES
KETUBAH
KETUBAHS
KETUBOT
KETUBOTH
KEVEL
KEVELS
KEVIL
KEVILS
KEWL
KEWLER
KEWLEST
KEWPIE
KEWPIES
KEX
KEXES
KEY
KEYBOARD
KEYBOARDS
KEYBUGLE
KEYBUGLES
KEYBUTTON
KEYCARD
KEYCARDS
KEYED
KEYHOLE
KEYHOLES
KEYING
KEYINGS
KEYLESS
KEYLINE
KEYLINES
KEYLOGGER
KEYNOTE
KEYNOTED
KEYNOTER
KEYNOTERS

KEYNOTES
KEYNOTING
KEYPAD
KEYPADS
KEYPAL
KEYPALS
KEYPUNCH
KEYRING
KEYS
KEYSET
KEYSETS
KEYSTER
KEYSTERS
KEYSTONE
KEYSTONED
KEYSTONES
KEYSTROKE
KEYWAY
KEYWAYS
KEYWORD
KEYWORDS
KGOTLA
KGOTLAS
KHADDAR
KHADDARS
KHADI
KHADIS
KHAF
KHAFS
KHAKI
KHAKILIKE
KHAKIS
KHALAT
KHALATS
KHALIF
KHALIFA
KHALIFAH
KHALIFAHS
KHALIFAS
KHALIFAT
KHALIFATE
KHALIFATS
KHALIFS
KHAMSEEN
KHAMSEENS
KHAMSIN
KHAMSINS
KHAN
KHANATE
KHANATES
KHANDA
KHANDAS
KHANGA
KHANGAS
KHANJAR
KHANJARS
KHANS
KHANSAMA

KHANSAMAH
KHANSAMAS
KHANUM
KHANUMS
KHAPH
KHAPHS
KHARIF
KHARIFS
KHAT
KHATS
KHAYA
KHAYAL
KHAYALS
KHAYAS
KHAZEN
KHAZENIM
KHAZENS
KHAZI
KHAZIS
KHEDA
KHEDAH
KHEDAHS
KHEDAS
KHEDIVA
KHEDIVAL
KHEDIVAS
KHEDIVATE
KHEDIVE
KHEDIVES
KHEDIVIAL
KHET
KHETH
KHETHS
KHETS
KHI
KHILAFAT
KHILAFATS
KHILAT
KHILATS
KHILIM
KHILIMS
KHIRKAH
KHIRKAHS
KHIS
KHODJA
KHODJAS
KHOJA
KHOJAS
KHOR
KHORS
KHOTBAH
KHOTBAHS
KHOTBEH
KHOTBEHS
KHOUM
KHOUMS
KHUD
KHUDS

KHURTA
KHURTAS
KHUSKHUS
KHUTBAH
KHUTBAHS
KI
KIAAT
KIAATS
KIANG
KIANGS
KIAUGH
KIAUGHS
KIBBE
KIBBEH
KIBBEHS
KIBBES
KIBBI
KIBBIS
KIBBITZ
KIBBITZED
KIBBITZER
KIBBITZES
KIBBLE
KIBBLED
KIBBLES
KIBBLING
KIBBUTZ
KIBBUTZIM
KIBE
KIBEI
KIBEIS
KIBES
KIBITKA
KIBITKAS
KIBITZ
KIBITZED
KIBITZER
KIBITZERS
KIBITZES
KIBITZING
KIBLA
KIBLAH
KIBLAHS
KIBLAS
KIBOSH
KIBOSHED
KIBOSHES
KIBOSHING
KICK
KICKABLE
KICKABOUT
KICKBACK
KICKBACKS
KICKBALL
KICKBALLS
KICKBOARD
KICKBOX
KICKBOXED

KICKBOXER
KICKBOXES
KICKDOWN
KICKDOWNS
KICKED
KICKER
KICKERS
KICKIER
KICKIEST
KICKING
KICKOFF
KICKOFFS
KICKS
KICKSHAW
KICKSHAWS
KICKSTAND
KICKSTART
KICKUP
KICKUPS
KICKY
KID
KIDDED
KIDDER
KIDDERS
KIDDIE
KIDDIED
KIDDIER
KIDDIERS
KIDDIES
KIDDING
KIDDINGLY
KIDDISH
KIDDLE
KIDDLES
KIDDO
KIDDOES
KIDDOS
KIDDUSH
KIDDUSHES
KIDDY
KIDDYING
KIDDYWINK
KIDEL
KIDELS
KIDGE
KIDGIE
KIDGIER
KIDGIEST
KIDGLOVE
KIDLET
KIDLETS
KIDLIKE
KIDLING
KIDLINGS
KIDNAP
KIDNAPED
KIDNAPEE
KIDNAPEES

KIDNAPER
KIDNAPERS
KIDNAPING
KIDNAPPED
KIDNAPPEE
KIDNAPPER
KIDNAPS
KIDNEY
KIDNEYS
KIDOLOGY
KIDS
KIDSKIN
KIDSKINS
KIDSTAKES
KIDULT
KIDULTS
KIDVID
KIDVIDS
KIEF
KIEFS
KIEKIE
KIEKIES
KIELBASA
KIELBASAS
KIELBASI
KIELBASY
KIER
KIERIE
KIERIES
KIERS
KIESELGUR
KIESERITE
KIESTER
KIESTERS
KIEVE
KIEVES
KIF
KIFF
KIFS
KIGHT
KIGHTS
KIKE
KIKES
KIKOI
KIKOIS
KIKUMON
KIKUMONS
KIKUYU
KIKUYUS
KILD
KILDERKIN
KILERG
KILERGS
KILEY
KILEYS
KILIM
KILIMS
KILL

KILLABLE
KILLADAR
KILLADARS
KILLAS
KILLASES
KILLCOW
KILLCOWS
KILLCROP
KILLCROPS
KILLDEE
KILLDEER
KILLDEERS
KILLDEES
KILLED
KILLER
KILLERS
KILLICK
KILLICKS
KILLIE
KILLIES
KILLIFISH
KILLING
KILLINGLY
KILLINGS
KILLJOY
KILLJOYS
KILLOCK
KILLOCKS
KILLOGIE
KILLOGIES
KILLS
KILLUT
KILLUTS
KILN
KILNED
KILNING
KILNS
KILO
KILOBAR
KILOBARS
KILOBASE
KILOBASES
KILOBAUD
KILOBAUDS
KILOBIT
KILOBITS
KILOBYTE
KILOBYTES
KILOCURIE
KILOCYCLE
KILOGAUSS
KILOGRAM
KILOGRAMS
KILOGRAY
KILOGRAYS
KILOHERTZ
KILOJOULE
KILOLITER

KILOLITRE
KILOMETER
KILOMETRE
KILOMOLE
KILOMOLES
KILORAD
KILORADS
KILOS
KILOTON
KILOTONS
KILOVOLT
KILOVOLTS
KILOWATT
KILOWATTS
KILP
KILPS
KILT
KILTED
KILTER
KILTERS
KILTIE
KILTIES
KILTING
KILTINGS
KILTLIKE
KILTS
KILTY
KIMBO
KIMBOED
KIMBOING
KIMBOS
KIMCHEE
KIMCHEES
KIMCHI
KIMCHIS
KIMMER
KIMMERS
KIMONO
KIMONOED
KIMONOS
KIN
KINA
KINAKINA
KINAKINAS
KINARA
KINARAS
KINAS
KINASE
KINASES
KINCHIN
KINCHINS
KINCOB
KINCOBS
KIND
KINDA
KINDED
KINDER
KINDERS

KINDEST
KINDIE
KINDIES
KINDING
KINDLE
KINDLED
KINDLER
KINDLERS
KINDLES
KINDLESS
KINDLIER
KINDLIEST
KINDLILY
KINDLING
KINDLINGS
KINDLY
KINDNESS
KINDRED
KINDREDS
KINDS
KINDY
KINE
KINEMA
KINEMAS
KINEMATIC
KINES
KINESCOPE
KINESES
KINESIC
KINESICS
KINESIS
KINETIC
KINETICAL
KINETICS
KINETIN
KINETINS
KINFOLK
KINFOLKS
KING
KINGBIRD
KINGBIRDS
KINGBOLT
KINGBOLTS
KINGCRAFT
KINGCUP
KINGCUPS
KINGDOM
KINGDOMED
KINGDOMS
KINGED
KINGFISH
KINGHOOD
KINGHOODS
KINGING
KINGKLIP
KINGKLIPS
KINGLE
KINGLES

KINGLESS
KINGLET
KINGLETS
KINGLIER
KINGLIEST
KINGLIKE
KINGLING
KINGLINGS
KINGLY
KINGMAKER
KINGPIN
KINGPINS
KINGPOST
KINGPOSTS
KINGS
KINGSHIP
KINGSHIPS
KINGSIDE
KINGSIDES
KINGSNAKE
KINGWOOD
KINGWOODS
KININ
KININS
KINK
KINKAJOU
KINKAJOUS
KINKED
KINKIER
KINKIEST
KINKILY
KINKINESS
KINKING
KINKLE
KINKLES
KINKS
KINKY
KINLESS
KINO
KINONE
KINONES
KINOS
KINRED
KINREDS
KINS
KINSFOLK
KINSFOLKS
KINSHIP
KINSHIPS
KINSMAN
KINSMEN
KINSWOMAN
KINSWOMEN
KIORE
KIOSK
KIOSKS
KIP
KIPE

KIPES
KIPP
KIPPA
KIPPAGE
KIPPAGES
KIPPAS
KIPPED
KIPPEN
KIPPER
KIPPERED
KIPPERER
KIPPERERS
KIPPERING
KIPPERS
KIPPING
KIPPS
KIPS
KIPSKIN
KIPSKINS
KIR
KIRBEH
KIRBEHS
KIRBIGRIP
KIRBY
KIRIGAMI
KIRIGAMIS
KIRIMON
KIRIMONS
KIRK
KIRKED
KIRKING
KIRKINGS
KIRKMAN
KIRKMEN
KIRKS
KIRKTON
KIRKTONS
KIRKWARD
KIRKYAIRD
KIRKYARD
KIRKYARDS
KIRMESS
KIRMESSES
KIRN
KIRNED
KIRNING
KIRNS
KIRPAN
KIRPANS
KIRRI
KIRRIS
KIRS
KIRSCH
KIRSCHES
KIRTAN
KIRTANS
KIRTLE
KIRTLED

KIRTLES
KIS
KISAN
KISANS
KISH
KISHES
KISHKA
KISHKAS
KISHKE
KISHKES
KISMAT
KISMATS
KISMET
KISMETIC
KISMETS
KISS
KISSABLE
KISSABLY
KISSAGRAM
KISSED
KISSEL
KISSELS
KISSER
KISSERS
KISSES
KISSING
KISSOGRAM
KISSY
KIST
KISTED
KISTFUL
KISTFULS
KISTING
KISTS
KISTVAEN
KISTVAENS
KIT
KITBAG
KITBAGS
KITCHEN
KITCHENED
KITCHENER
KITCHENET
KITCHENS
KITE
KITED
KITELIKE
KITENGE
KITENGES
KITER
KITERS
KITES
KITH
KITHARA
KITHARAS
KITHE
KITHED
KITHES

KITHING
KITHS
KITING
KITINGS
KITLING
KITLINGS
KITS
KITSCH
KITSCHES
KITSCHIER
KITSCHIFY
KITSCHILY
KITSCHY
KITSET
KITSETS
KITTED
KITTEL
KITTELS
KITTEN
KITTENED
KITTENING
KITTENISH
KITTENS
KITTENY
KITTIES
KITTING
KITTIWAKE
KITTLE
KITTLED
KITTLER
KITTLES
KITTLEST
KITTLIER
KITTLIEST
KITTLING
KITTLY
KITTUL
KITTULS
KITTY
KIVA
KIVAS
KIWI
KIWIFRUIT
KIWIS
KLANG
KLANGS
KLAP
KLAPPED
KLAPPING
KLAPS
KLATCH
KLATCHES
KLATSCH
KLATSCHES
KLAVERN
KLAVERNS
KLAVIER
KLAVIERS

KLAXON
KLAXONED
KLAXONING
KLAXONS
KLEAGLE
KLEAGLES
KLEENEX
KLEENEXES
KLENDUSIC
KLEPHT
KLEPHTIC
KLEPHTISM
KLEPHTS
KLEPTO
KLEPTOS
KLETT
KLETTS
KLEZMER
KLEZMERS
KLEZMORIM
KLICK
KLICKS
KLIEG
KLIK
KLIKS
KLINKER
KLINKERS
KLINOSTAT
KLIPDAS
KLIPDASES
KLISTER
KLISTERS
KLONDIKE
KLONDIKED
KLONDIKER
KLONDIKES
KLONDYKE
KLONDYKED
KLONDYKER
KLONDYKES
KLONG
KLONGS
KLOOCH
KLOOCHES
KLOOCHMAN
KLOOCHMEN
KLOOF
KLOOFS
KLOOTCH
KLOOTCHES
KLUDGE
KLUDGED
KLUDGES
KLUDGEY
KLUDGIER
KLUDGIEST
KLUDGING
KLUDGY

KLUGE
KLUGED
KLUGES
KLUGING
KLUTZ
KLUTZES
KLUTZIER
KLUTZIEST
KLUTZY
KLYSTRON
KLYSTRONS
KNACK
KNACKED
KNACKER
KNACKERED
KNACKERS
KNACKERY
KNACKIER
KNACKIEST
KNACKING
KNACKISH
KNACKS
KNACKY
KNAG
KNAGGIER
KNAGGIEST
KNAGGY
KNAGS
KNAIDEL
KNAIDLACH
KNAP
KNAPPED
KNAPPER
KNAPPERS
KNAPPING
KNAPPLE
KNAPPLED
KNAPPLES
KNAPPLING
KNAPS
KNAPSACK
KNAPSACKS
KNAPWEED
KNAPWEEDS
KNAR
KNARL
KNARLS
KNARLY
KNARRED
KNARRIER
KNARRIEST
KNARRING
KNARRY
KNARS
KNAUR
KNAURS
KNAVE
KNAVERIES

KNAVERY
KNAVES
KNAVESHIP
KNAVISH
KNAVISHLY
KNAWE
KNAWEL
KNAWELS
KNAWES
KNEAD
KNEADABLE
KNEADED
KNEADER
KNEADERS
KNEADING
KNEADS
KNEE
KNEECAP
KNEECAPS
KNEED
KNEEHOLE
KNEEHOLES
KNEEING
KNEEJERK
KNEEL
KNEELED
KNEELER
KNEELERS
KNEELING
KNEELS
KNEEPAD
KNEEPADS
KNEEPAN
KNEEPANS
KNEEPIECE
KNEES
KNEESIES
KNEESOCK
KNEESOCKS
KNEIDEL
KNEIDLACH
KNELL
KNELLED
KNELLING
KNELLS
KNELT
KNESSET
KNESSETS
KNEVELL
KNEVELLED
KNEVELLS
KNEW
KNICKER
KNICKERED
KNICKERS
KNICKS
KNIFE
KNIFED

KNIFELESS	KNOCKED	KNOWINGER	KOBS
KNIFELIKE	KNOCKER	KNOWINGLY	KOCHIA
KNIFEMAN	KNOCKERS	KNOWINGS	KOCHIAS
KNIFEMEN	KNOCKING	KNOWLEDGE	KOEKOEA
KNIFER	KNOCKINGS	KNOWN	KOEL
KNIFEREST	KNOCKLESS	KNOWNS	KOELS
KNIFERS	KNOCKOFF	KNOWS	KOFF
KNIFES	KNOCKOFFS	KNUB	KOFFS
KNIFING	KNOCKOUT	KNUBBIER	KOFTA
KNIFINGS	KNOCKOUTS	KNUBBIEST	KOFTAS
KNIGHT	KNOCKS	KNUBBLE	KOFTGAR
KNIGHTAGE	KNOLL	KNUBBLED	KOFTGARI
KNIGHTED	KNOLLED	KNUBBLES	KOFTGARIS
KNIGHTING	KNOLLER	KNUBBLIER	KOFTGARS
KNIGHTLY	KNOLLERS	KNUBBLING	KOFTWORK
KNIGHTS	KNOLLIER	KNUBBLY	KOFTWORKS
KNIPHOFIA	KNOLLIEST	KNUBBY	KOHA
KNISH	KNOLLING	KNUBS	KOHAS
KNISHES	KNOLLS	KNUCKLE	KOHEKOHE
KNIT	KNOLLY	KNUCKLED	KOHL
KNITCH	KNOP	KNUCKLER	KOHLRABI
KNITCHES	KNOPPED	KNUCKLERS	KOHLRABIS
KNITS	KNOPS	KNUCKLES	KOHLS
KNITTABLE	KNOSP	KNUCKLIER	KOI
KNITTED	KNOSPS	KNUCKLING	KOINE
KNITTER	KNOT	KNUCKLY	KOINES
KNITTERS	KNOTGRASS	KNUR	KOIS
KNITTING	KNOTHOLE	KNURL	KOJI
KNITTINGS	KNOTHOLES	KNURLED	KOJIS
KNITTLE	KNOTLESS	KNURLIER	KOKAKO
KNITTLES	KNOTLIKE	KNURLIEST	KOKAKOS
KNITWEAR	KNOTS	KNURLING	KOKANEE
KNITWEARS	KNOTTED	KNURLINGS	KOKANEES
KNIVE	KNOTTER	KNURLS	KOKER
KNIVED	KNOTTERS	KNURLY	KOKERS
KNIVES	KNOTTIER	KNURR	KOKIRI
KNIVING	KNOTTIEST	KNURRS	KOKOBEH
KNOB	KNOTTILY	KNURS	KOKOPU
KNOBBED	KNOTTING	KNUT	KOKOWAI
KNOBBER	KNOTTINGS	KNUTS	KOKOWAIS
KNOBBERS	KNOTTY	KO	KOKRA
KNOBBIER	KNOTWEED	KOA	KOKRAS
KNOBBIEST	KNOTWEEDS	KOALA	KOKUM
KNOBBING	KNOTWORK	KOALAS	KOKUMS
KNOBBLE	KNOTWORKS	KOAN	KOLA
KNOBBLED	KNOUT	KOANS	KOLACKY
KNOBBLES	KNOUTED	KOAP	KOLAS
KNOBBLIER	KNOUTING	KOAPS	KOLBASI
KNOBBLING	KNOUTS	KOAS	KOLBASIS
KNOBBLY	KNOW	KOB	KOLBASSI
KNOBBY	KNOWABLE	KOBAN	KOLBASSIS
KNOBHEAD	KNOWE	KOBANG	KOLHOZ
KNOBHEADS	KNOWER	KOBANGS	KOLHOZES
KNOBLIKE	KNOWERS	KOBANS	KOLHOZY
KNOBS	KNOWES	KOBO	KOLINSKI
KNOBSTICK	KNOWHOW	KOBOLD	KOLINSKY
KNOCK	KNOWHOWS	KOBOLDS	KOLKHOS
KNOCKDOWN	KNOWING	KOBOS	KOLKHOSES

KOLKHOSY
KOLKHOZ
KOLKHOZES
KOLKHOZY
KOLKOZ
KOLKOZES
KOLKOZY
KOLO
KOLOS
KOMATIK
KOMATIKS
KOMBU
KOMBUS
KOMISSAR
KOMISSARS
KOMITAJI
KOMITAJIS
KOMONDOR
KOMONDORS
KON
KONAKI
KONBU
KONBUS
KOND
KONDO
KONDOS
KONEKE
KONFYT
KONFYTS
KONGONI
KONIMETER
KONINI
KONIOLOGY
KONISCOPE
KONK
KONKED
KONKING
KONKS
KONNING
KONS
KOODOO
KOODOOS
KOOK
KOOKED
KOOKIE
KOOKIER
KOOKIEST
KOOKINESS
KOOKING
KOOKS
KOOKY
KOOLAH
KOOLAHS
KOORI
KOORIES
KOORIS
KOP
KOPASETIC

KOPECK
KOPECKS
KOPEK
KOPEKS
KOPH
KOPHS
KOPIYKA
KOPIYKAS
KOPJE
KOPJES
KOPPA
KOPPAS
KOPPIE
KOPPIES
KOPS
KOR
KORA
KORAI
KORARI
KORAS
KORAT
KORATS
KORE
KORERO
KOREROED
KOREROING
KOREROS
KORES
KORFBALL
KORFBALLS
KORIMAKO
KORKIR
KORKIRS
KORMA
KORMAS
KORO
KOROMIKO
KORORA
KORORAS
KOROWAI
KORS
KORU
KORUN
KORUNA
KORUNAS
KORUNY
KORUS
KOS
KOSES
KOSHER
KOSHERED
KOSHERING
KOSHERS
KOSMOS
KOSMOSES
KOSS
KOSSES
KOTARE

KOTCH
KOTCHED
KOTCHES
KOTCHING
KOTO
KOTOS
KOTOW
KOTOWED
KOTOWER
KOTOWERS
KOTOWING
KOTOWS
KOTTABOS
KOTUKU
KOTWAL
KOTWALS
KOULAN
KOULANS
KOUMIS
KOUMISES
KOUMISS
KOUMISSES
KOUMYS
KOUMYSES
KOUMYSS
KOUMYSSES
KOUPREY
KOUPREYS
KOURA
KOURBASH
KOUROI
KOUROS
KOUSKOUS
KOUSSO
KOUSSOS
KOW
KOWHAI
KOWHAIS
KOWS
KOWTOW
KOWTOWED
KOWTOWER
KOWTOWERS
KOWTOWING
KOWTOWS
KRAAL
KRAALED
KRAALING
KRAALS
KRAB
KRABS
KRAFT
KRAFTS
KRAIT
KRAITS
KRAKEN
KRAKENS
KRAKOWIAK

KRAMERIA
KRAMERIAS
KRANG
KRANGS
KRANS
KRANSES
KRANTZ
KRANTZES
KRANZ
KRANZES
KRATER
KRATERS
KRAUT
KRAUTS
KREASOTE
KREASOTED
KREASOTES
KREATINE
KREATINES
KREEP
KREEPS
KREESE
KREESED
KREESES
KREESING
KREMLIN
KREMLINS
KRENG
KRENGS
KREOSOTE
KREOSOTED
KREOSOTES
KREPLACH
KREPLECH
KREUTZER
KREUTZERS
KREUZER
KREUZERS
KREWE
KREWES
KRILL
KRILLS
KRIMMER
KRIMMERS
KRIS
KRISED
KRISES
KRISING
KROMESKY
KRONA
KRONE
KRONEN
KRONER
KRONOR
KRONUR
KROON
KROONI
KROONS

KRUBI
KRUBIS
KRUBUT
KRUBUTS
KRULLER
KRULLERS
KRUMHORN
KRUMHORNS
KRUMKAKE
KRUMKAKES
KRUMMHOLZ
KRUMMHORN
KRYOLITE
KRYOLITES
KRYOLITH
KRYOLITHS
KRYOMETER
KRYPSES
KRYPSIS
KRYPTON
KRYPTONS
KRYTRON
KRYTRONS
KSAR
KSARS
KUCHCHA
KUCHEN
KUCHENS
KUDLIK
KUDLIKS
KUDO
KUDOS
KUDOSES
KUDU
KUDUS
KUDZU
KUDZUS
KUE
KUEH
KUES
KUFI
KUFIS
KUFIYAH
KUFIYAHS
KUGEL
KUGELS
KUIA
KUIAS
KUKRI
KUKRIS
KUKU
KUKUS
KULA
KULAK
KULAKI
KULAKS
KULAN
KULANS

KULAS
KULFI
KULFIS
KULTUR
KULTURS
KUMARA
KUMARAHOU
KUMARAS
KUMARI
KUMARIS
KUMBALOI
KUMERA
KUMERAS
KUMIKUMI
KUMISS
KUMISSES
KUMITE
KUMITES
KUMMEL
KUMMELS
KUMQUAT
KUMQUATS
KUMYS
KUMYSES
KUNA
KUNDALINI
KUNE
KUNJOOS
KUNKAR
KUNKARS
KUNKUR
KUNKURS
KUNZITE
KUNZITES
KURBASH
KURBASHED
KURBASHES
KURFUFFLE
KURGAN
KURGANS
KURI
KURIS
KURRAJONG
KURRE
KURRES
KURSAAL
KURSAALS
KURTA
KURTAS
KURTOSES
KURTOSIS
KURU
KURUS
KURVEY
KURVEYED
KURVEYING
KURVEYOR
KURVEYORS

KURVEYS
KUSSO
KUSSOS
KUTA
KUTAS
KUTCH
KUTCHA
KUTCHES
KUTI
KUTIS
KUTU
KUTUS
KUVASZ
KUVASZOK
KUZU
KUZUS
KVAS
KVASES
KVASS
KVASSES
KVELL
KVELLED
KVELLING
KVELLS
KVETCH
KVETCHED
KVETCHER
KVETCHERS
KVETCHES
KVETCHIER
KVETCHILY
KVETCHING
KVETCHY
KWACHA
KWACHAS
KWAITO
KWAITOS
KWANZA
KWANZAS
KWELA
KWELAS
KY
KYACK
KYACKS
KYAK
KYAKS
KYANG
KYANGS
KYANISE
KYANISED
KYANISES
KYANISING
KYANITE
KYANITES
KYANITIC
KYANIZE
KYANIZED
KYANIZES

KYANIZING
KYAR
KYARS
KYAT
KYATS
KYBO
KYBOS
KYBOSH
KYBOSHED
KYBOSHES
KYBOSHING
KYDST
KYE
KYES
KYLE
KYLES
KYLICES
KYLIE
KYLIES
KYLIKES
KYLIN
KYLINS
KYLIX
KYLLOSES
KYLLOSIS
KYLOE
KYLOES
KYMOGRAM
KYMOGRAMS
KYMOGRAPH
KYND
KYNDE
KYNDED
KYNDES
KYNDING
KYNDS
KYNE
KYOGEN
KYOGENS
KYPE
KYPES
KYPHOSES
KYPHOSIS
KYPHOTIC
KYRIE
KYRIELLE
KYRIELLES
KYRIES
KYTE
KYTES
KYTHE
KYTHED
KYTHES
KYTHING
KYU
KYUS

L

LA
LAAGER
LAAGERED
LAAGERING
LAAGERS
LAARI
LAARIS
LAB
LABARA
LABARUM
LABARUMS
LABDA
LABDACISM
LABDANUM
LABDANUMS
LABDAS
LABEL
LABELABLE
LABELED
LABELER
LABELERS
LABELING
LABELLA
LABELLATE
LABELLED
LABELLER
LABELLERS
LABELLING
LABELLIST
LABELLOID
LABELLUM
LABELS
LABIA
LABIAL
LABIALISE
LABIALISM
LABIALITY
LABIALIZE
LABIALLY
LABIALS
LABIATE
LABIATED
LABIATES
LABILE
LABILITY
LABIS
LABISES
LABIUM
LABLAB
LABLABS
LABOR
LABORED
LABOREDLY

LABORER
LABORERS
LABORING
LABORIOUS
LABORISM
LABORISMS
LABORIST
LABORISTS
LABORITE
LABORITES
LABORS
LABOUR
LABOURED
LABOURER
LABOURERS
LABOURING
LABOURISM
LABOURIST
LABOURS
LABRA
LABRADOR
LABRADORS
LABRET
LABRETS
LABRID
LABRIDS
LABROID
LABROIDS
LABROSE
LABRUM
LABRUMS
LABRUSCA
LABRYS
LABRYSES
LABS
LABURNUM
LABURNUMS
LABYRINTH
LAC
LACCOLITE
LACCOLITH
LACE
LACEBARK
LACEBARKS
LACED
LACELESS
LACELIKE
LACER
LACERABLE
LACERANT
LACERATE
LACERATED
LACERATES

LACERS
LACERTIAN
LACERTID
LACERTIDS
LACERTINE
LACES
LACET
LACETS
LACEWING
LACEWINGS
LACEWOOD
LACEWOODS
LACEWORK
LACEWORKS
LACEY
LACHES
LACHESES
LACHRYMAL
LACIER
LACIEST
LACILY
LACINESS
LACING
LACINGS
LACINIA
LACINIAE
LACINIATE
LACK
LACKADAY
LACKED
LACKER
LACKERED
LACKERING
LACKERS
LACKEY
LACKEYED
LACKEYING
LACKEYS
LACKING
LACKLAND
LACKLANDS
LACKS
LACMUS
LACMUSES
LACONIC
LACONICAL
LACONISM
LACONISMS
LACQUER
LACQUERED
LACQUERER
LACQUERS
LACQUEY

LACQUEYED
LACQUEYS
LACRIMAL
LACRIMALS
LACRIMOSO
LACROSSE
LACROSSES
LACRYMAL
LACRYMALS
LACS
LACTAM
LACTAMS
LACTARIAN
LACTARY
LACTASE
LACTASES
LACTATE
LACTATED
LACTATES
LACTATING
LACTATION
LACTEAL
LACTEALLY
LACTEALS
LACTEAN
LACTEOUS
LACTIC
LACTIFIC
LACTONE
LACTONES
LACTONIC
LACTOSE
LACTOSES
LACUNA
LACUNAE
LACUNAL
LACUNAR
LACUNARIA
LACUNARS
LACUNARY
LACUNAS
LACUNATE
LACUNE
LACUNES
LACUNOSE
LACY
LAD
LADANUM
LADANUMS
LADDER
LADDERED
LADDERING
LADDERS

LADDERY	LADYISM	LAGUNA	LAIRING
LADDIE	LADYISMS	LAGUNAS	LAIRISE
LADDIES	LADYKIN	LAGUNE	LAIRISED
LADDISH	LADYKINS	LAGUNES	LAIRISES
LADE	LADYLIKE	LAH	LAIRISING
LADED	LADYLOVE	LAHAR	LAIRIZE
LADEN	LADYLOVES	LAHARS	LAIRIZED
LADENED	LADYPALM	LAHS	LAIRIZES
LADENING	LADYPALMS	LAIC	LAIRIZING
LADENS	LADYSHIP	LAICAL	LAIRS
LADER	LADYSHIPS	LAICALLY	LAIRY
LADERS	LAER	LAICH	LAISSE
LADES	LAERED	LAICHS	LAISSES
LADETTE	LAERING	LAICISE	LAITANCE
LADETTES	LAERS	LAICISED	LAITANCES
LADHOOD	LAESIE	LAICISES	LAITH
LADHOODS	LAETARE	LAICISING	LAITHLY
LADIES	LAETARES	LAICISM	LAITIES
LADIFIED	LAETRILE	LAICISMS	LAITY
LADIFIES	LAETRILES	LAICITIES	LAKE
LADIFY	LAEVIGATE	LAICITY	LAKEBED
LADIFYING	LAEVO	LAICIZE	LAKEBEDS
LADING	LAEVULIN	LAICIZED	LAKED
LADINGS	LAEVULINS	LAICIZES	LAKEFRONT
LADINO	LAEVULOSE	LAICIZING	LAKELAND
LADINOS	LAG	LAICS	LAKELANDS
LADLE	LAGAN	LAID	LAKELET
LADLED	LAGANS	LAIDED	LAKELETS
LADLEFUL	LAGENA	LAIDING	LAKELIKE
LADLEFULS	LAGENAS	LAIDLY	LAKEPORT
LADLER	LAGEND	LAIDS	LAKEPORTS
LADLERS	LAGENDS	LAIGH	LAKER
LADLES	LAGER	LAIGHER	LAKERS
LADLING	LAGERED	LAIGHEST	LAKES
LADRON	LAGERING	LAIGHS	LAKESHORE
LADRONE	LAGERS	LAIK	LAKESIDE
LADRONES	LAGGARD	LAIKA	LAKESIDES
LADRONS	LAGGARDLY	LAIKAS	LAKH
LADS	LAGGARDS	LAIKED	LAKHS
LADY	LAGGED	LAIKER	LAKIER
LADYBIRD	LAGGEN	LAIKERS	LAKIEST
LADYBIRDS	LAGGENS	LAIKING	LAKIN
LADYBOY	LAGGER	LAIKS	LAKING
LADYBOYS	LAGGERS	LAIN	LAKINGS
LADYBUG	LAGGIN	LAIPSE	LAKINS
LADYBUGS	LAGGING	LAIPSED	LAKISH
LADYCOW	LAGGINGLY	LAIPSES	LAKSA
LADYCOWS	LAGGINGS	LAIPSING	LAKSAS
LADYFIED	LAGGINS	LAIR	LAKY
LADYFIES	LAGNAPPE	LAIRAGE	LALANG
LADYFISH	LAGNAPPES	LAIRAGES	LALANGS
LADYFLIES	LAGNIAPPE	LAIRD	LALDIE
LADYFLY	LAGOMORPH	LAIRDLY	LALDIES
LADYFY	LAGOON	LAIRDS	LALDY
LADYFYING	LAGOONAL	LAIRDSHIP	LALIQUE
LADYHOOD	LAGOONS	LAIRED	LALIQUES
LADYHOODS	LAGRIMOSO	LAIRIER	LALL
LADYISH	LAGS	LAIRIEST	LALLAN

LALLAND
LALLANDS
LALLANS
LALLATION
LALLED
LALLING
LALLINGS
LALLS
LALLYGAG
LALLYGAGS
LAM
LAMA
LAMAISTIC
LAMANTIN
LAMANTINS
LAMAS
LAMASERAI
LAMASERY
LAMB
LAMBADA
LAMBADAS
LAMBAST
LAMBASTE
LAMBASTED
LAMBASTES
LAMBASTS
LAMBDA
LAMBDAS
LAMBDOID
LAMBED
LAMBENCY
LAMBENT
LAMBENTLY
LAMBER
LAMBERS
LAMBERT
LAMBERTS
LAMBIE
LAMBIER
LAMBIES
LAMBIEST
LAMBING
LAMBINGS
LAMBITIVE
LAMBKILL
LAMBKILLS
LAMBKIN
LAMBKINS
LAMBLIKE
LAMBLING
LAMBLINGS
LAMBOYS
LAMBRUSCO
LAMBS
LAMBSKIN
LAMBSKINS
LAMBY
LAME

LAMEBRAIN
LAMED
LAMEDH
LAMEDHS
LAMEDS
LAMELLA
LAMELLAE
LAMELLAR
LAMELLAS
LAMELLATE
LAMELLOID
LAMELLOSE
LAMELY
LAMENESS
LAMENT
LAMENTED
LAMENTER
LAMENTERS
LAMENTING
LAMENTS
LAMER
LAMES
LAMEST
LAMETER
LAMETERS
LAMIA
LAMIAE
LAMIAS
LAMIGER
LAMIGERS
LAMINA
LAMINABLE
LAMINAE
LAMINAL
LAMINALS
LAMINAR
LAMINARIA
LAMINARIN
LAMINARY
LAMINAS
LAMINATE
LAMINATED
LAMINATES
LAMINATOR
LAMING
LAMINGTON
LAMININ
LAMININS
LAMINITIS
LAMINOSE
LAMINOUS
LAMISH
LAMISTER
LAMISTERS
LAMITER
LAMITERS
LAMMED
LAMMER

LAMMERS
LAMMIE
LAMMIES
LAMMIGER
LAMMIGERS
LAMMING
LAMMINGS
LAMMY
LAMP
LAMPAD
LAMPADARY
LAMPADIST
LAMPADS
LAMPAS
LAMPASES
LAMPASSE
LAMPASSES
LAMPBLACK
LAMPED
LAMPER
LAMPERN
LAMPERNS
LAMPERS
LAMPERSES
LAMPHOLE
LAMPHOLES
LAMPING
LAMPINGS
LAMPION
LAMPIONS
LAMPLIGHT
LAMPOON
LAMPOONED
LAMPOONER
LAMPOONS
LAMPPOST
LAMPPOSTS
LAMPREY
LAMPREYS
LAMPS
LAMPSHADE
LAMPSHELL
LAMPUKA
LAMPUKAS
LAMPUKI
LAMPUKIS
LAMPYRID
LAMPYRIDS
LAMS
LAMSTER
LAMSTERS
LANA
LANAI
LANAIS
LANAS
LANATE
LANATED
LANCE

LANCED
LANCEGAY
LANCEGAYS
LANCEJACK
LANCELET
LANCELETS
LANCEOLAR
LANCER
LANCERS
LANCES
LANCET
LANCETED
LANCETS
LANCEWOOD
LANCH
LANCHED
LANCHES
LANCHING
LANCIERS
LANCIFORM
LANCINATE
LANCING
LAND
LANDAMMAN
LANDAU
LANDAULET
LANDAUS
LANDBOARD
LANDDAMNE
LANDDROS
LANDDROST
LANDE
LANDED
LANDER
LANDERS
LANDES
LANDFALL
LANDFALLS
LANDFILL
LANDFILLS
LANDFORCE
LANDFORM
LANDFORMS
LANDGRAB
LANDGRABS
LANDGRAVE
LANDING
LANDINGS
LANDLADY
LANDLER
LANDLERS
LANDLESS
LANDLINE
LANDLINES
LANDLOPER
LANDLORD
LANDLORDS
LANDMAN

LANDMARK	LANGUAGE	LANTSKIP	LAPSE
LANDMARKS	LANGUAGED	LANTSKIPS	LAPSED
LANDMASS	LANGUAGES	LANUGO	LAPSER
LANDMEN	LANGUE	LANUGOS	LAPSERS
LANDOWNER	LANGUED	LANX	LAPSES
LANDRACE	LANGUES	LANYARD	LAPSIBLE
LANDRACES	LANGUET	LANYARDS	LAPSING
LANDRAIL	LANGUETS	LAODICEAN	LAPSTONE
LANDRAILS	LANGUETTE	LAOGAI	LAPSTONES
LANDS	LANGUID	LAOGAIS	LAPSTRAKE
LANDSCAPE	LANGUIDLY	LAP	LAPSTREAK
LANDSHARK	LANGUISH	LAPBOARD	LAPSUS
LANDSIDE	LANGUOR	LAPBOARDS	LAPTOP
LANDSIDES	LANGUORS	LAPDOG	LAPTOPS
LANDSKIP	LANGUR	LAPDOGS	LAPTRAY
LANDSKIPS	LANGURS	LAPEL	LAPTRAYS
LANDSLEIT	LANIARD	LAPELED	LAPWING
LANDSLID	LANIARDS	LAPELLED	LAPWINGS
LANDSLIDE	LANIARIES	LAPELS	LAPWORK
LANDSLIP	LANIARY	LAPFUL	LAPWORKS
LANDSLIPS	LANITAL	LAPFULS	LAQUEARIA
LANDSMAN	LANITALS	LAPHELD	LAR
LANDSMEN	LANK	LAPIDARY	LARBOARD
LANDWARD	LANKED	LAPIDATE	LARBOARDS
LANDWARDS	LANKER	LAPIDATED	LARCENER
LANDWIND	LANKEST	LAPIDATES	LARCENERS
LANDWINDS	LANKIER	LAPIDEOUS	LARCENIES
LANE	LANKIEST	LAPIDES	LARCENIST
LANELY	LANKILY	LAPIDIFIC	LARCENOUS
LANES	LANKINESS	LAPIDIFY	LARCENY
LANEWAY	LANKING	LAPIDIST	LARCH
LANEWAYS	LANKLY	LAPIDISTS	LARCHEN
LANG	LANKNESS	LAPILLI	LARCHES
LANGAHA	LANKS	LAPILLUS	LARD
LANGAHAS	LANKY	LAPIN	LARDALITE
LANGAR	LANNER	LAPINS	LARDED
LANGARS	LANNERET	LAPIS	LARDER
LANGER	LANNERETS	LAPISES	LARDERER
LANGERED	LANNERS	LAPJE	LARDERERS
LANGERS	LANOLATED	LAPJES	LARDERS
LANGEST	LANOLIN	LAPPED	LARDIER
LANGLAUF	LANOLINE	LAPPEL	LARDIEST
LANGLAUFS	LANOLINES	LAPPELS	LARDING
LANGLEY	LANOLINS	LAPPER	LARDLIKE
LANGLEYS	LANOSE	LAPPERED	LARDON
LANGOUSTE	LANOSITY	LAPPERING	LARDONS
LANGRAGE	LANT	LAPPERS	LARDOON
LANGRAGES	LANTANA	LAPPET	LARDOONS
LANGREL	LANTANAS	LAPPETED	LARDS
LANGRELS	LANTERLOO	LAPPETS	LARDY
LANGRIDGE	LANTERN	LAPPIE	LARE
LANGSHAN	LANTERNED	LAPPIES	LAREE
LANGSHANS	LANTERNS	LAPPING	LAREES
LANGSPEL	LANTHANON	LAPPINGS	LARES
LANGSPELS	LANTHANUM	LAPS	LARGANDO
LANGSPIEL	LANTHORN	LAPSABLE	LARGE
LANGSYNE	LANTHORNS	LAPSANG	LARGELY
LANGSYNES	LANTS	LAPSANGS	LARGEN

LARGENED	LARRUPS	LASSLORN	LATER
LARGENESS	LARS	LASSO	LATERAD
LARGENING	LARUM	LASSOCK	LATERAL
LARGENS	LARUMS	LASSOCKS	LATERALED
LARGER	LARVA	LASSOED	LATERALLY
LARGES	LARVAE	LASSOER	LATERALS
LARGESS	LARVAL	LASSOERS	LATERBORN
LARGESSE	LARVAS	LASSOES	LATERISE
LARGESSES	LARVATE	LASSOING	LATERISED
LARGEST	LARVATED	LASSOS	LATERISES
LARGHETTO	LARVICIDE	LASSU	LATERITE
LARGISH	LARVIFORM	LASSUS	LATERITES
LARGITION	LARVIKITE	LAST	LATERITIC
LARGO	LARYNGAL	LASTAGE	LATERIZE
LARGOS	LARYNGALS	LASTAGES	LATERIZED
LARI	LARYNGEAL	LASTBORN	LATERIZES
LARIAT	LARYNGES	LASTBORNS	LATESCENT
LARIATED	LARYNX	LASTED	LATEST
LARIATING	LARYNXES	LASTER	LATESTS
LARIATS	LAS	LASTERS	LATEWAKE
LARINE	LASAGNA	LASTING	LATEWAKES
LARIS	LASAGNAS	LASTINGLY	LATEWOOD
LARK	LASAGNE	LASTINGS	LATEWOODS
LARKED	LASAGNES	LASTLY	LATEX
LARKER	LASCAR	LASTS	LATEXES
LARKERS	LASCARS	LAT	LATH
LARKIER	LASE	LATAH	LATHE
LARKIEST	LASED	LATAHS	LATHED
LARKINESS	LASER	LATAKIA	LATHEE
LARKING	LASERDISC	LATAKIAS	LATHEES
LARKISH	LASERDISK	LATCH	LATHEN
LARKS	LASERS	LATCHED	LATHER
LARKSOME	LASERWORT	LATCHES	LATHERED
LARKSPUR	LASES	LATCHET	LATHERER
LARKSPURS	LASH	LATCHETS	LATHERERS
LARKY	LASHED	LATCHING	LATHERIER
LARMIER	LASHER	LATCHKEY	LATHERING
LARMIERS	LASHERS	LATCHKEYS	LATHERS
LARN	LASHES	LATE	LATHERY
LARNAKES	LASHING	LATECOMER	LATHES
LARNAX	LASHINGLY	LATED	LATHI
LARNED	LASHINGS	LATEEN	LATHIER
LARNEY	LASHINS	LATEENER	LATHIEST
LARNEYS	LASHKAR	LATEENERS	LATHING
LARNIER	LASHKARS	LATEENS	LATHINGS
LARNIEST	LASING	LATELY	LATHIS
LARNING	LASINGS	LATEN	LATHLIKE
LARNS	LASKET	LATENCE	LATHS
LAROID	LASKETS	LATENCES	LATHWORK
LARRIGAN	LASQUE	LATENCIES	LATHWORKS
LARRIGANS	LASQUES	LATENCY	LATHY
LARRIKIN	LASS	LATENED	LATHYRISM
LARRIKINS	LASSES	LATENESS	LATHYRUS
LARRUP	LASSI	LATENING	LATI
LARRUPED	LASSIE	LATENS	LATICES
LARRUPER	LASSIES	LATENT	LATICIFER
LARRUPERS	LASSIS	LATENTLY	LATICLAVE
LARRUPING	LASSITUDE	LATENTS	LATIFONDI

LATIGO
LATIGOES
LATIGOS
LATILLA
LATILLAS
LATIMERIA
LATINA
LATINAS
LATINISE
LATINISED
LATINISES
LATINITY
LATINIZE
LATINIZED
LATINIZES
LATINO
LATINOS
LATISH
LATITANCY
LATITANT
LATITAT
LATITATS
LATITUDE
LATITUDES
LATKE
LATKES
LATOSOL
LATOSOLIC
LATOSOLS
LATRANT
LATRATION
LATRIA
LATRIAS
LATRINE
LATRINES
LATROCINY
LATRON
LATRONS
LATS
LATTE
LATTEN
LATTENS
LATTER
LATTERLY
LATTES
LATTICE
LATTICED
LATTICES
LATTICING
LATTICINI
LATTICINO
LATTIN
LATTINS
LATU
LAUAN
LAUANS
LAUCH
LAUCHING

LAUCHS
LAUD
LAUDABLE
LAUDABLY
LAUDANUM
LAUDANUMS
LAUDATION
LAUDATIVE
LAUDATOR
LAUDATORS
LAUDATORY
LAUDED
LAUDER
LAUDERS
LAUDING
LAUDS
LAUF
LAUFS
LAUGH
LAUGHABLE
LAUGHABLY
LAUGHED
LAUGHER
LAUGHERS
LAUGHFUL
LAUGHIER
LAUGHIEST
LAUGHING
LAUGHINGS
LAUGHLINE
LAUGHS
LAUGHSOME
LAUGHTER
LAUGHTERS
LAUGHY
LAUNCE
LAUNCED
LAUNCES
LAUNCH
LAUNCHED
LAUNCHER
LAUNCHERS
LAUNCHES
LAUNCHING
LAUNCHPAD
LAUNCING
LAUND
LAUNDER
LAUNDERED
LAUNDERER
LAUNDERS
LAUNDRESS
LAUNDRIES
LAUNDRY
LAUNDS
LAURA
LAURAE
LAURAS

LAUREATE
LAUREATED
LAUREATES
LAUREL
LAURELED
LAURELING
LAURELLED
LAURELS
LAURIC
LAURYL
LAURYLS
LAUWINE
LAUWINES
LAV
LAVA
LAVABO
LAVABOES
LAVABOS
LAVAFORM
LAVAGE
LAVAGES
LAVALAVA
LAVALAVAS
LAVALIER
LAVALIERE
LAVALIERS
LAVALIKE
LAVAS
LAVASH
LAVASHES
LAVATERA
LAVATERAS
LAVATION
LAVATIONS
LAVATORY
LAVE
LAVED
LAVEER
LAVEERED
LAVEERING
LAVEERS
LAVEMENT
LAVEMENTS
LAVENDER
LAVENDERS
LAVER
LAVEROCK
LAVEROCKS
LAVERS
LAVES
LAVING
LAVISH
LAVISHED
LAVISHER
LAVISHERS
LAVISHES
LAVISHEST
LAVISHING

LAVISHLY
LAVOLT
LAVOLTA
LAVOLTAED
LAVOLTAS
LAVOLTED
LAVOLTING
LAVOLTS
LAVRA
LAVRAS
LAVROCK
LAVROCKS
LAVS
LAW
LAWBOOK
LAWBOOKS
LAWED
LAWER
LAWEST
LAWFUL
LAWFULLY
LAWGIVER
LAWGIVERS
LAWGIVING
LAWIN
LAWINE
LAWINES
LAWING
LAWINGS
LAWINS
LAWK
LAWKS
LAWLAND
LAWLANDS
LAWLESS
LAWLESSLY
LAWLIKE
LAWMAKER
LAWMAKERS
LAWMAKING
LAWMAN
LAWMEN
LAWMONGER
LAWN
LAWNIER
LAWNIEST
LAWNMOWER
LAWNS
LAWNY
LAWS
LAWSUIT
LAWSUITS
LAWYER
LAWYERED
LAWYERING
LAWYERLY
LAWYERS
LAX

LAXATION	LAYTIME	LEADED	LEAGUING
LAXATIONS	LAYTIMES	LEADEN	LEAK
LAXATIVE	LAYUP	LEADENED	LEAKAGE
LAXATIVES	LAYUPS	LEADENING	LEAKAGES
LAXATOR	LAYWOMAN	LEADENLY	LEAKED
LAXATORS	LAYWOMEN	LEADENS	LEAKER
LAXER	LAZAR	LEADER	LEAKERS
LAXES	LAZARET	LEADERENE	LEAKIER
LAXEST	LAZARETS	LEADERS	LEAKIEST
LAXISM	LAZARETTE	LEADIER	LEAKILY
LAXISMS	LAZARETTO	LEADIEST	LEAKINESS
LAXIST	LAZARS	LEADING	LEAKING
LAXISTS	LAZE	LEADINGLY	LEAKLESS
LAXITIES	LAZED	LEADINGS	LEAKPROOF
LAXITY	LAZES	LEADLESS	LEAKS
LAXLY	LAZIED	LEADMAN	LEAKY
LAXNESS	LAZIER	LEADMEN	LEAL
LAXNESSES	LAZIES	LEADOFF	LEALER
LAY	LAZIEST	LEADOFFS	LEALEST
LAYABOUT	LAZILY	LEADPLANT	LEALLY
LAYABOUTS	LAZINESS	LEADS	LEALTIES
LAYAWAY	LAZING	LEADSCREW	LEALTY
LAYAWAYS	LAZO	LEADSMAN	LEAM
LAYBACK	LAZOED	LEADSMEN	LEAMED
LAYBACKED	LAZOES	LEADWORK	LEAMING
LAYBACKS	LAZOING	LEADWORKS	LEAMS
LAYDEEZ	LAZOS	LEADWORT	LEAN
LAYED	LAZULI	LEADWORTS	LEANED
LAYER	LAZULIS	LEADY	LEANER
LAYERAGE	LAZULITE	LEAF	LEANERS
LAYERAGES	LAZULITES	LEAFAGE	LEANEST
LAYERED	LAZURITE	LEAFAGES	LEANING
LAYERING	LAZURITES	LEAFBUD	LEANINGS
LAYERINGS	LAZY	LEAFBUDS	LEANLY
LAYERS	LAZYBONES	LEAFED	LEANNESS
LAYETTE	LAZYING	LEAFERIES	LEANS
LAYETTES	LAZYISH	LEAFERY	LEANT
LAYIN	LAZZARONE	LEAFIER	LEANY
LAYING	LAZZARONI	LEAFIEST	LEAP
LAYINGS	LAZZI	LEAFINESS	LEAPED
LAYINS	LAZZO	LEAFING	LEAPER
LAYLOCK	LEA	LEAFLESS	LEAPEROUS
LAYLOCKS	LEACH	LEAFLET	LEAPERS
LAYMAN	LEACHABLE	LEAFLETED	LEAPFROG
LAYMEN	LEACHATE	LEAFLETER	LEAPFROGS
LAYOFF	LEACHATES	LEAFLETS	LEAPING
LAYOFFS	LEACHED	LEAFLIKE	LEAPOROUS
LAYOUT	LEACHER	LEAFS	LEAPROUS
LAYOUTS	LEACHERS	LEAFSTALK	LEAPS
LAYOVER	LEACHES	LEAFWORM	LEAPT
LAYOVERS	LEACHIER	LEAFWORMS	LEAR
LAYPEOPLE	LEACHIEST	LEAFY	LEARE
LAYPERSON	LEACHING	LEAGUE	LEARED
LAYS	LEACHINGS	LEAGUED	LEARES
LAYSHAFT	LEACHOUR	LEAGUER	LEARIER
LAYSHAFTS	LEACHOURS	LEAGUERED	LEARIEST
LAYSTALL	LEACHY	LEAGUERS	LEARINESS
LAYSTALLS	LEAD	LEAGUES	LEARING

LEARN
LEARNABLE
LEARNED
LEARNEDLY
LEARNER
LEARNERS
LEARNING
LEARNINGS
LEARNS
LEARNT
LEARS
LEARY
LEAS
LEASABLE
LEASE
LEASEBACK
LEASED
LEASEHOLD
LEASER
LEASERS
LEASES
LEASH
LEASHED
LEASHES
LEASHING
LEASING
LEASINGS
LEASOW
LEASOWE
LEASOWED
LEASOWES
LEASOWING
LEASOWS
LEAST
LEASTS
LEASTWAYS
LEASTWISE
LEASURE
LEASURES
LEAT
LEATHER
LEATHERED
LEATHERN
LEATHERS
LEATHERY
LEATS
LEAVE
LEAVED
LEAVEN
LEAVENED
LEAVENING
LEAVENOUS
LEAVENS
LEAVER
LEAVERS
LEAVES
LEAVIER
LEAVIEST

LEAVING
LEAVINGS
LEAVY
LEAZE
LEAZES
LEBBEK
LEBBEKS
LEBEN
LEBENS
LEBKUCHEN
LECANORA
LECANORAS
LECCIES
LECCY
LECH
LECHAIM
LECHAIMS
LECHAYIM
LECHAYIMS
LECHED
LECHER
LECHERED
LECHERIES
LECHERING
LECHEROUS
LECHERS
LECHERY
LECHES
LECHING
LECHWE
LECHWES
LECITHIN
LECITHINS
LECTERN
LECTERNS
LECTIN
LECTINS
LECTION
LECTIONS
LECTOR
LECTORATE
LECTORS
LECTOTYPE
LECTRESS
LECTURE
LECTURED
LECTURER
LECTURERS
LECTURES
LECTURING
LECTURN
LECTURNS
LECYTHI
LECYTHIS
LECYTHUS
LED
LEDDEN
LEDDENS

LEDGE
LEDGED
LEDGER
LEDGERED
LEDGERING
LEDGERS
LEDGES
LEDGIER
LEDGIEST
LEDGY
LEDUM
LEDUMS
LEE
LEEAR
LEEARS
LEEBOARD
LEEBOARDS
LEECH
LEECHDOM
LEECHDOMS
LEECHED
LEECHEE
LEECHEES
LEECHES
LEECHING
LEECHLIKE
LEED
LEEING
LEEK
LEEKS
LEEP
LEEPED
LEEPING
LEEPS
LEER
LEERED
LEERIER
LEERIEST
LEERILY
LEERINESS
LEERING
LEERINGLY
LEERINGS
LEERS
LEERY
LEES
LEESE
LEESES
LEESING
LEET
LEETLE
LEETS
LEEWARD
LEEWARDLY
LEEWARDS
LEEWAY
LEEWAYS
LEFT

LEFTE
LEFTER
LEFTEST
LEFTIE
LEFTIES
LEFTISH
LEFTISM
LEFTISMS
LEFTIST
LEFTISTS
LEFTMOST
LEFTMOSTS
LEFTOVER
LEFTOVERS
LEFTS
LEFTWARD
LEFTWARDS
LEFTWING
LEFTY
LEG
LEGACIES
LEGACY
LEGAL
LEGALESE
LEGALESES
LEGALISE
LEGALISED
LEGALISER
LEGALISES
LEGALISM
LEGALISMS
LEGALIST
LEGALISTS
LEGALITY
LEGALIZE
LEGALIZED
LEGALIZER
LEGALIZES
LEGALLY
LEGALS
LEGATARY
LEGATE
LEGATED
LEGATEE
LEGATEES
LEGATES
LEGATINE
LEGATING
LEGATION
LEGATIONS
LEGATO
LEGATOR
LEGATORS
LEGATOS
LEGEND
LEGENDARY
LEGENDISE
LEGENDIST

LEGENDIZE

LEGENDIZE	LEGUAAN	LEKVAR	LENGED
LEGENDRY	LEGUAANS	LEKVARS	LENGER
LEGENDS	LEGUME	LEKYTHI	LENGEST
LEGER	LEGUMES	LEKYTHOI	LENGING
LEGERING	LEGUMIN	LEKYTHOS	LENGS
LEGERINGS	LEGUMINS	LEKYTHUS	LENGTH
LEGERITY	LEGWARMER	LEMAN	LENGTHEN
LEGERS	LEGWEAR	LEMANS	LENGTHENS
LEGES	LEGWEARS	LEME	LENGTHFUL
LEGGE	LEGWORK	LEMED	LENGTHIER
LEGGED	LEGWORKS	LEMEL	LENGTHILY
LEGGER	LEHAIM	LEMELS	LENGTHMAN
LEGGERS	LEHAIMS	LEMES	LENGTHMEN
LEGGES	LEHAYIM	LEMING	LENGTHS
LEGGIER	LEHAYIMS	LEMMA	LENGTHY
LEGGIERO	LEHR	LEMMAS	LENIENCE
LEGGIEST	LEHRJAHRE	LEMMATA	LENIENCES
LEGGIN	LEHRS	LEMMATISE	LENIENCY
LEGGINESS	LEHUA	LEMMATIZE	LENIENT
LEGGING	LEHUAS	LEMMING	LENIENTLY
LEGGINGED	LEI	LEMMINGS	LENIENTS
LEGGINGS	LEIDGER	LEMNISCAL	LENIFIED
LEGGINS	LEIDGERS	LEMNISCI	LENIFIES
LEGGISM	LEIGER	LEMNISCUS	LENIFY
LEGGISMS	LEIGERS	LEMON	LENIFYING
LEGGY	LEIOMYOMA	LEMONADE	LENIS
LEGHORN	LEIPOA	LEMONADES	LENITE
LEGHORNS	LEIPOAS	LEMONED	LENITED
LEGIBLE	LEIR	LEMONFISH	LENITES
LEGIBLY	LEIRED	LEMONIER	LENITIES
LEGION	LEIRING	LEMONIEST	LENITING
LEGIONARY	LEIRS	LEMONING	LENITION
LEGIONED	LEIS	LEMONISH	LENITIONS
LEGIONS	LEISH	LEMONLIKE	LENITIVE
LEGISLATE	LEISHER	LEMONS	LENITIVES
LEGIST	LEISHEST	LEMONWOOD	LENITY
LEGISTS	LEISLER	LEMONY	LENO
LEGIT	LEISLERS	LEMPIRA	LENOS
LEGITIM	LEISTER	LEMPIRAS	LENS
LEGITIMS	LEISTERED	LEMUR	LENSE
LEGITS	LEISTERS	LEMURES	LENSED
LEGLAN	LEISURE	LEMURIAN	LENSES
LEGLANS	LEISURED	LEMURIANS	LENSING
LEGLEN	LEISURELY	LEMURINE	LENSLESS
LEGLENS	LEISURES	LEMURINES	LENSMAN
LEGLESS	LEISURING	LEMURLIKE	LENSMEN
LEGLET	LEITMOTIF	LEMUROID	LENT
LEGLETS	LEITMOTIV	LEMUROIDS	LENTANDO
LEGLIKE	LEK	LEMURS	LENTEN
LEGLIN	LEKE	LEND	LENTI
LEGLINS	LEKGOTLA	LENDABLE	LENTIC
LEGMAN	LEKGOTLAS	LENDER	LENTICEL
LEGMEN	LEKKED	LENDERS	LENTICELS
LEGONG	LEKKER	LENDING	LENTICLE
LEGONGS	LEKKING	LENDINGS	LENTICLES
LEGROOM	LEKKINGS	LENDS	LENTICULE
LEGROOMS	LEKS	LENES	LENTIFORM
LEGS	LEKU	LENG	LENTIGO

LENTIL	LERE	LETHIED	LEUKOCYTE
LENTILS	LERED	LETS	LEUKOMA
LENTISK	LERES	LETTABLE	LEUKOMAS
LENTISKS	LERING	LETTED	LEUKON
LENTO	LERNAEAN	LETTER	LEUKONS
LENTOID	LERNEAN	LETTERBOX	LEUKOSES
LENTOIDS	LERP	LETTERED	LEUKOSIS
LENTOR	LERPS	LETTERER	LEUKOTIC
LENTORS	LES	LETTERERS	LEUKOTOMY
LENTOS	LESBIAN	LETTERING	LEV
LENTOUS	LESBIANS	LETTERMAN	LEVA
LENVOY	LESBIC	LETTERMEN	LEVANT
LENVOYS	LESBO	LETTERN	LEVANTED
LEONE	LESBOS	LETTERNS	LEVANTER
LEONES	LESES	LETTERS	LEVANTERS
LEONINE	LESION	LETTERSET	LEVANTINE
LEOPARD	LESIONED	LETTING	LEVANTING
LEOPARDS	LESIONING	LETTINGS	LEVANTS
LEOTARD	LESIONS	LETTRE	LEVATOR
LEOTARDED	LESPEDEZA	LETTRES	LEVATORES
LEOTARDS	LESS	LETTUCE	LEVATORS
LEP	LESSEE	LETTUCES	LEVE
LEPER	LESSEES	LETUP	LEVEE
LEPERS	LESSEN	LETUPS	LEVEED
LEPID	LESSENED	LEU	LEVEEING
LEPIDOTE	LESSENING	LEUCAEMIA	LEVEES
LEPIDOTES	LESSENS	LEUCAEMIC	LEVEL
LEPORID	LESSER	LEUCEMIA	LEVELED
LEPORIDAE	LESSES	LEUCEMIAS	LEVELER
LEPORIDS	LESSON	LEUCEMIC	LEVELERS
LEPORINE	LESSONED	LEUCH	LEVELING
LEPPED	LESSONING	LEUCHEN	LEVELLED
LEPPING	LESSONS	LEUCIN	LEVELLER
LEPRA	LESSOR	LEUCINE	LEVELLERS
LEPRAS	LESSORS	LEUCINES	LEVELLEST
LEPROSE	LEST	LEUCINS	LEVELLING
LEPROSERY	LESTED	LEUCITE	LEVELLY
LEPROSIES	LESTING	LEUCITES	LEVELNESS
LEPROSITY	LESTS	LEUCITIC	LEVELS
LEPROSY	LET	LEUCO	LEVER
LEPROTIC	LETCH	LEUCOCYTE	LEVERAGE
LEPROUS	LETCHED	LEUCOMA	LEVERAGED
LEPROUSLY	LETCHES	LEUCOMAS	LEVERAGES
LEPS	LETCHING	LEUCOSIN	LEVERED
LEPT	LETCHINGS	LEUCOSINS	LEVERET
LEPTA	LETDOWN	LEUCOTOME	LEVERETS
LEPTIN	LETDOWNS	LEUCOTOMY	LEVERING
LEPTINS	LETHAL	LEUD	LEVERS
LEPTOME	LETHALITY	LEUDES	LEVIABLE
LEPTOMES	LETHALLY	LEUDS	LEVIATHAN
LEPTON	LETHALS	LEUGH	LEVIED
LEPTONIC	LETHARGIC	LEUGHEN	LEVIER
LEPTONS	LETHARGY	LEUKAEMIA	LEVIERS
LEPTOPHOS	LETHE	LEUKEMIA	LEVIES
LEPTOSOME	LETHEAN	LEUKEMIAS	LEVIGABLE
LEPTOTENE	LETHEE	LEUKEMIC	LEVIGATE
LEQUEAR	LETHEES	LEUKEMICS	LEVIGATED
LEQUEARS	LETHES	LEUKEMOID	LEVIGATES

LEVIGATOR	LEXISES	LIBEL	LIBRETTI
LEVIN	LEY	LIBELANT	LIBRETTO
LEVINS	LEYLANDI	LIBELANTS	LIBRETTOS
LEVIRATE	LEYLANDII	LIBELED	LIBRI
LEVIRATES	LEYLANDIS	LIBELEE	LIBRIFORM
LEVIRATIC	LEYS	LIBELEES	LIBS
LEVIS	LEZ	LIBELER	LICE
LEVITATE	LEZES	LIBELERS	LICENCE
LEVITATED	LEZZ	LIBELING	LICENCED
LEVITATES	LEZZA	LIBELINGS	LICENCEE
LEVITATOR	LEZZAS	LIBELIST	LICENCEES
LEVITE	LEZZES	LIBELISTS	LICENCER
LEVITES	LEZZIE	LIBELLANT	LICENCERS
LEVITIC	LEZZIES	LIBELLED	LICENCES
LEVITICAL	LEZZY	LIBELLEE	LICENCING
LEVITIES	LI	LIBELLEES	LICENSE
LEVITY	LIABILITY	LIBELLER	LICENSED
LEVO	LIABLE	LIBELLERS	LICENSEE
LEVODOPA	LIAISE	LIBELLING	LICENSEES
LEVODOPAS	LIAISED	LIBELLOUS	LICENSER
LEVOGYRE	LIAISES	LIBELOUS	LICENSERS
LEVULIN	LIAISING	LIBELS	LICENSES
LEVULINS	LIAISON	LIBER	LICENSING
LEVULOSE	LIAISONS	LIBERAL	LICENSOR
LEVULOSES	LIANA	LIBERALLY	LICENSORS
LEVY	LIANAS	LIBERALS	LICENSURE
LEVYING	LIANE	LIBERATE	LICENTE
LEW	LIANES	LIBERATED	LICH
LEWD	LIANG	LIBERATES	LICHANOS
LEWDER	LIANGS	LIBERATOR	LICHEE
LEWDEST	LIANOID	LIBERO	LICHEES
LEWDLY	LIAR	LIBEROS	LICHEN
LEWDNESS	LIARD	LIBERS	LICHENED
LEWDSBIES	LIARDS	LIBERTIES	LICHENIN
LEWDSBY	LIARS	LIBERTINE	LICHENING
LEWDSTER	LIART	LIBERTY	LICHENINS
LEWDSTERS	LIAS	LIBIDINAL	LICHENISM
LEWIS	LIASES	LIBIDO	LICHENIST
LEWISES	LIATRIS	LIBIDOS	LICHENOID
LEWISIA	LIATRISES	LIBKEN	LICHENOSE
LEWISIAS	LIB	LIBKENS	LICHENOUS
LEWISITE	LIBANT	LIBLAB	LICHENS
LEWISITES	LIBATE	LIBLABS	LICHES
LEWISSON	LIBATED	LIBRA	LICHGATE
LEWISSONS	LIBATES	LIBRAE	LICHGATES
LEX	LIBATING	LIBRAIRE	LICHI
LEXEME	LIBATION	LIBRAIRES	LICHIS
LEXEMES	LIBATIONS	LIBRAIRIE	LICHT
LEXEMIC	LIBATORY	LIBRARIAN	LICHTED
LEXES	LIBBARD	LIBRARIES	LICHTER
LEXICA	LIBBARDS	LIBRARY	LICHTEST
LEXICAL	LIBBED	LIBRAS	LICHTING
LEXICALLY	LIBBER	LIBRATE	LICHTLIED
LEXICON	LIBBERS	LIBRATED	LICHTLIES
LEXICONS	LIBBING	LIBRATES	LICHTLY
LEXIGRAM	LIBECCHIO	LIBRATING	LICHTS
LEXIGRAMS	LIBECCIO	LIBRATION	LICHWAKE
LEXIS	LIBECCIOS	LIBRATORY	LICHWAKES

LICHWAY
LICHWAYS
LICIT
LICITLY
LICITNESS
LICK
LICKED
LICKER
LICKERISH
LICKERS
LICKING
LICKINGS
LICKPENNY
LICKS
LICKSPIT
LICKSPITS
LICORICE
LICORICES
LICTOR
LICTORIAN
LICTORS
LID
LIDAR
LIDARS
LIDDED
LIDDING
LIDGER
LIDGERS
LIDLESS
LIDO
LIDOCAINE
LIDOS
LIDS
LIE
LIED
LIEDER
LIEF
LIEFER
LIEFEST
LIEFLY
LIEFS
LIEGE
LIEGEDOM
LIEGEDOMS
LIEGELESS
LIEGEMAN
LIEGEMEN
LIEGER
LIEGERS
LIEGES
LIEN
LIENABLE
LIENAL
LIENS
LIENTERIC
LIENTERY
LIER
LIERNE

LIERNES
LIERS
LIES
LIEU
LIEUS
LIEVE
LIEVER
LIEVEST
LIFE
LIFEBELT
LIFEBELTS
LIFEBLOOD
LIFEBOAT
LIFEBOATS
LIFEBUOY
LIFEBUOYS
LIFECARE
LIFECARES
LIFEFUL
LIFEGUARD
LIFEHOLD
LIFELESS
LIFELIKE
LIFELINE
LIFELINES
LIFELONG
LIFER
LIFERS
LIFES
LIFESAVER
LIFESOME
LIFESPAN
LIFESPANS
LIFESTYLE
LIFETIME
LIFETIMES
LIFEWAY
LIFEWAYS
LIFEWORK
LIFEWORKS
LIFEWORLD
LIFT
LIFTABLE
LIFTBACK
LIFTBACKS
LIFTBOY
LIFTBOYS
LIFTED
LIFTER
LIFTERS
LIFTGATE
LIFTGATES
LIFTING
LIFTMAN
LIFTMEN
LIFTOFF
LIFTOFFS
LIFTS

LIFULL
LIG
LIGAMENT
LIGAMENTS
LIGAN
LIGAND
LIGANDS
LIGANS
LIGASE
LIGASES
LIGATE
LIGATED
LIGATES
LIGATING
LIGATION
LIGATIONS
LIGATIVE
LIGATURE
LIGATURED
LIGATURES
LIGER
LIGERS
LIGGE
LIGGED
LIGGEN
LIGGER
LIGGERS
LIGGES
LIGGING
LIGGINGS
LIGHT
LIGHTBULB
LIGHTED
LIGHTEN
LIGHTENED
LIGHTENER
LIGHTENS
LIGHTER
LIGHTERED
LIGHTERS
LIGHTEST
LIGHTFACE
LIGHTFAST
LIGHTFUL
LIGHTING
LIGHTINGS
LIGHTISH
LIGHTLESS
LIGHTLIED
LIGHTLIES
LIGHTLY
LIGHTNESS
LIGHTNING
LIGHTS
LIGHTSHIP
LIGHTSOME
LIGHTWAVE
LIGHTWOOD

LIGNAGE
LIGNAGES
LIGNALOES
LIGNAN
LIGNANS
LIGNE
LIGNEOUS
LIGNES
LIGNICOLE
LIGNIFIED
LIGNIFIES
LIGNIFORM
LIGNIFY
LIGNIN
LIGNINS
LIGNITE
LIGNITES
LIGNITIC
LIGNOSE
LIGNOSES
LIGNUM
LIGNUMS
LIGROIN
LIGROINE
LIGROINES
LIGROINS
LIGS
LIGULA
LIGULAE
LIGULAR
LIGULAS
LIGULATE
LIGULATED
LIGULE
LIGULES
LIGULOID
LIGURE
LIGURES
LIKABLE
LIKE
LIKEABLE
LIKED
LIKELIER
LIKELIEST
LIKELY
LIKEN
LIKENED
LIKENESS
LIKENING
LIKENS
LIKER
LIKERS
LIKES
LIKEST
LIKEWAKE
LIKEWAKES
LIKEWALK
LIKEWALKS

LIKEWISE	LIMBI	LIMMER	LINAGE
LIKIN	LIMBIC	LIMMERS	LINAGES
LIKING	LIMBIER	LIMN	LINALOL
LIKINGS	LIMBIEST	LIMNAEID	LINALOLS
LIKINS	LIMBING	LIMNAEIDS	LINALOOL
LIKUTA	LIMBLESS	LIMNED	LINALOOLS
LILAC	LIMBMEAL	LIMNER	LINCH
LILACS	LIMBO	LIMNERS	LINCHES
LILANGENI	LIMBOS	LIMNETIC	LINCHET
LILIED	LIMBOUS	LIMNIC	LINCHETS
LILIES	LIMBS	LIMNING	LINCHPIN
LILL	LIMBUS	LIMNOLOGY	LINCHPINS
LILLED	LIMBUSES	LIMNS	LINCRUSTA
LILLING	LIMBY	LIMO	LINCTURE
LILLIPUT	LIME	LIMONENE	LINCTURES
LILLIPUTS	LIMEADE	LIMONENES	LINCTUS
LILLS	LIMEADES	LIMONITE	LINCTUSES
LILO	LIMED	LIMONITES	LIND
LILOS	LIMEKILN	LIMONITIC	LINDANE
LILT	LIMEKILNS	LIMOS	LINDANES
LILTED	LIMELESS	LIMOSES	LINDEN
LILTING	LIMELIGHT	LIMOSIS	LINDENS
LILTINGLY	LIMELIT	LIMOUS	LINDIES
LILTS	LIMEN	LIMOUSINE	LINDS
LILY	LIMENS	LIMP	LINDWORM
LILYLIKE	LIMEPIT	LIMPA	LINDWORMS
LIMA	LIMEPITS	LIMPAS	LINDY
LIMACEL	LIMERICK	LIMPED	LINE
LIMACELS	LIMERICKS	LIMPER	LINEABLE
LIMACEOUS	LIMES	LIMPERS	LINEAGE
LIMACES	LIMESCALE	LIMPEST	LINEAGES
LIMACINE	LIMESTONE	LIMPET	LINEAL
LIMACON	LIMEWASH	LIMPETS	LINEALITY
LIMACONS	LIMEWATER	LIMPID	LINEALLY
LIMAIL	LIMEY	LIMPIDITY	LINEAMENT
LIMAILS	LIMEYS	LIMPIDLY	LINEAR
LIMAN	LIMIER	LIMPING	LINEARISE
LIMANS	LIMIEST	LIMPINGLY	LINEARITY
LIMAS	LIMINA	LIMPINGS	LINEARIZE
LIMATION	LIMINAL	LIMPKIN	LINEARLY
LIMATIONS	LIMINESS	LIMPKINS	LINEATE
LIMAX	LIMING	LIMPLY	LINEATED
LIMB	LIMINGS	LIMPNESS	LINEATION
LIMBA	LIMIT	LIMPS	LINEBRED
LIMBAS	LIMITABLE	LIMPSEY	LINECUT
LIMBATE	LIMITARY	LIMPSIER	LINECUTS
LIMBEC	LIMITED	LIMPSIEST	LINED
LIMBECK	LIMITEDLY	LIMPSY	LINELESS
LIMBECKS	LIMITEDS	LIMULI	LINELIKE
LIMBECS	LIMITER	LIMULOID	LINEMAN
LIMBED	LIMITERS	LIMULOIDS	LINEMEN
LIMBER	LIMITES	LIMULUS	LINEN
LIMBERED	LIMITING	LIMULUSES	LINENS
LIMBERER	LIMITINGS	LIMY	LINENY
LIMBEREST	LIMITLESS	LIN	LINEOLATE
LIMBERING	LIMITS	LINABLE	LINER
LIMBERLY	LIMMA	LINAC	LINERLESS
LIMBERS	LIMMAS	LINACS	LINERS

LINES	LINHAYS	LINOTYPED	LIONISMS
LINESMAN	LINIER	LINOTYPER	LIONIZE
LINESMEN	LINIEST	LINOTYPES	LIONIZED
LINEUP	LINIMENT	LINS	LIONIZER
LINEUPS	LINIMENTS	LINSANG	LIONIZERS
LINEY	LININ	LINSANGS	LIONIZES
LING	LINING	LINSEED	LIONIZING
LINGA	LININGS	LINSEEDS	LIONLIKE
LINGAM	LININS	LINSEY	LIONLY
LINGAMS	LINISH	LINSEYS	LIONS
LINGAS	LINISHED	LINSTOCK	LIP
LINGBERRY	LINISHER	LINSTOCKS	LIPA
LINGCOD	LINISHERS	LINT	LIPAEMIA
LINGCODS	LINISHES	LINTED	LIPAEMIAS
LINGEL	LINISHING	LINTEL	LIPARITE
LINGELS	LINK	LINTELLED	LIPARITES
LINGER	LINKABLE	LINTELS	LIPASE
LINGERED	LINKAGE	LINTER	LIPASES
LINGERER	LINKAGES	LINTERS	LIPE
LINGERERS	LINKBOY	LINTIE	LIPECTOMY
LINGERIE	LINKBOYS	LINTIER	LIPEMIA
LINGERIES	LINKED	LINTIES	LIPEMIAS
LINGERING	LINKER	LINTIEST	LIPID
LINGERS	LINKERS	LINTING	LIPIDE
LINGIER	LINKING	LINTLESS	LIPIDES
LINGIEST	LINKMAN	LINTOL	LIPIDIC
LINGLE	LINKMEN	LINTOLS	LIPIDS
LINGLES	LINKS	LINTS	LIPIN
LINGO	LINKSLAND	LINTSEED	LIPINS
LINGOES	LINKSMAN	LINTSEEDS	LIPLESS
LINGOT	LINKSMEN	LINTSTOCK	LIPLIKE
LINGOTS	LINKSTER	LINTWHITE	LIPO
LINGS	LINKSTERS	LINTY	LIPOCYTE
LINGSTER	LINKUP	LINUM	LIPOCYTES
LINGSTERS	LINKUPS	LINUMS	LIPOGRAM
LINGUA	LINKWORK	LINURON	LIPOGRAMS
LINGUAE	LINKWORKS	LINURONS	LIPOIC
LINGUAL	LINKY	LINUX	LIPOID
LINGUALLY	LINN	LINUXES	LIPOIDAL
LINGUALS	LINNED	LINY	LIPOIDS
LINGUAS	LINNET	LION	LIPOLITIC
LINGUICA	LINNETS	LIONCEL	LIPOLYSES
LINGUICAS	LINNEY	LIONCELLE	LIPOLYSIS
LINGUINE	LINNEYS	LIONCELS	LIPOLYTIC
LINGUINES	LINNIES	LIONEL	LIPOMA
LINGUINI	LINNING	LIONELS	LIPOMAS
LINGUINIS	LINNS	LIONESS	LIPOMATA
LINGUISA	LINNY	LIONESSES	LIPOPLAST
LINGUISAS	LINO	LIONET	LIPOS
LINGUIST	LINOCUT	LIONETS	LIPOSOMAL
LINGUISTS	LINOCUTS	LIONFISH	LIPOSOME
LINGULA	LINOLEATE	LIONISE	LIPOSOMES
LINGULAE	LINOLEIC	LIONISED	LIPOSUCK
LINGULAR	LINOLENIC	LIONISER	LIPOSUCKS
LINGULAS	LINOLEUM	LIONISERS	LIPOTROPY
LINGULATE	LINOLEUMS	LIONISES	LIPPED
LINGY	LINOS	LIONISING	LIPPEN
LINHAY	LINOTYPE	LIONISM	LIPPENED

LIPPENING	LIRE	LISTINGS	LITHITE
LIPPENS	LIRI	LISTLESS	LITHITES
LIPPER	LIRIOPE	LISTS	LITHIUM
LIPPERED	LIRIOPES	LISTSERV	LITHIUMS
LIPPERING	LIRIPIPE	LISTSERVS	LITHO
LIPPERS	LIRIPIPES	LIT	LITHOCYST
LIPPIE	LIRIPOOP	LITAI	LITHOED
LIPPIER	LIRIPOOPS	LITANIES	LITHOID
LIPPIES	LIRK	LITANY	LITHOIDAL
LIPPIEST	LIRKED	LITAS	LITHOING
LIPPINESS	LIRKING	LITCHI	LITHOLOGY
LIPPING	LIRKS	LITCHIS	LITHOPONE
LIPPINGS	LIROT	LITE	LITHOPS
LIPPITUDE	LIROTH	LITED	LITHOS
LIPPY	LIS	LITENESS	LITHOSOL
LIPREAD	LISENTE	LITER	LITHOSOLS
LIPREADER	LISK	LITERACY	LITHOTOME
LIPREADS	LISKS	LITERAL	LITHOTOMY
LIPS	LISLE	LITERALLY	LITHS
LIPSTICK	LISLES	LITERALS	LITIGABLE
LIPSTICKS	LISP	LITERARY	LITIGANT
LIPURIA	LISPED	LITERATE	LITIGANTS
LIPURIAS	LISPER	LITERATES	LITIGATE
LIQUABLE	LISPERS	LITERATI	LITIGATED
LIQUATE	LISPING	LITERATIM	LITIGATES
LIQUATED	LISPINGLY	LITERATO	LITIGATOR
LIQUATES	LISPINGS	LITERATOR	LITIGIOUS
LIQUATING	LISPOUND	LITERATUS	LITING
LIQUATION	LISPOUNDS	LITEROSE	LITMUS
LIQUEFIED	LISPS	LITERS	LITMUSES
LIQUEFIER	LISPUND	LITES	LITORAL
LIQUEFIES	LISPUNDS	LITH	LITOTES
LIQUEFY	LISSES	LITHARGE	LITOTIC
LIQUESCE	LISSOM	LITHARGES	LITRE
LIQUESCED	LISSOME	LITHATE	LITRES
LIQUESCES	LISSOMELY	LITHATES	LITS
LIQUEUR	LISSOMLY	LITHE	LITTEN
LIQUEURED	LIST	LITHED	LITTER
LIQUEURS	LISTABLE	LITHELY	LITTERBAG
LIQUID	LISTED	LITHEMIA	LITTERBUG
LIQUIDATE	LISTEE	LITHEMIAS	LITTERED
LIQUIDISE	LISTEES	LITHEMIC	LITTERER
LIQUIDITY	LISTEL	LITHENESS	LITTERERS
LIQUIDIZE	LISTELS	LITHER	LITTERING
LIQUIDLY	LISTEN	LITHERLY	LITTERS
LIQUIDS	LISTENED	LITHES	LITTERY
LIQUIDUS	LISTENER	LITHESOME	LITTLE
LIQUIFIED	LISTENERS	LITHEST	LITTLER
LIQUIFIES	LISTENING	LITHIA	LITTLES
LIQUIFY	LISTENS	LITHIAS	LITTLEST
LIQUOR	LISTER	LITHIASES	LITTLIE
LIQUORED	LISTERIA	LITHIASIS	LITTLIES
LIQUORICE	LISTERIAL	LITHIC	LITTLIN
LIQUORING	LISTERIAS	LITHIFIED	LITTLING
LIQUORISH	LISTERS	LITHIFIES	LITTLINGS
LIQUORS	LISTETH	LITHIFY	LITTLINS
LIRA	LISTFUL	LITHING	LITTLISH
LIRAS	LISTING	LITHISTID	LITTORAL

LITTORALS
LITU
LITURGIC
LITURGICS
LITURGIES
LITURGISM
LITURGIST
LITURGY
LITUUS
LITUUSES
LIVABLE
LIVE
LIVEABLE
LIVED
LIVEDO
LIVEDOS
LIVELIER
LIVELIEST
LIVELILY
LIVELOD
LIVELODS
LIVELONG
LIVELONGS
LIVELOOD
LIVELOODS
LIVELY
LIVEN
LIVENED
LIVENER
LIVENERS
LIVENESS
LIVENING
LIVENS
LIVER
LIVERED
LIVERIED
LIVERIES
LIVERING
LIVERISH
LIVERLEAF
LIVERLESS
LIVERS
LIVERWORT
LIVERY
LIVERYMAN
LIVERYMEN
LIVES
LIVEST
LIVESTOCK
LIVETRAP
LIVETRAPS
LIVEWARE
LIVEWARES
LIVEYER
LIVEYERE
LIVEYERES
LIVEYERS
LIVID

LIVIDER
LIVIDEST
LIVIDITY
LIVIDLY
LIVIDNESS
LIVIER
LIVIERS
LIVING
LIVINGLY
LIVINGS
LIVOR
LIVORS
LIVRAISON
LIVRE
LIVRES
LIVYER
LIVYERS
LIXIVIA
LIXIVIAL
LIXIVIATE
LIXIVIOUS
LIXIVIUM
LIXIVIUMS
LIZARD
LIZARDS
LIZZIE
LIZZIES
LLAMA
LLAMAS
LLANERO
LLANEROS
LLANO
LLANOS
LO
LOACH
LOACHES
LOAD
LOADED
LOADEN
LOADENED
LOADENING
LOADENS
LOADER
LOADERS
LOADING
LOADINGS
LOADS
LOADSPACE
LOADSTAR
LOADSTARS
LOADSTONE
LOAF
LOAFED
LOAFER
LOAFERISH
LOAFERS
LOAFING
LOAFINGS

LOAFS
LOAM
LOAMED
LOAMIER
LOAMIEST
LOAMINESS
LOAMING
LOAMLESS
LOAMS
LOAMY
LOAN
LOANABLE
LOANBACK
LOANBACKS
LOANED
LOANER
LOANERS
LOANING
LOANINGS
LOANS
LOANSHIFT
LOANWORD
LOANWORDS
LOAST
LOATH
LOATHE
LOATHED
LOATHER
LOATHERS
LOATHES
LOATHEST
LOATHFUL
LOATHING
LOATHINGS
LOATHLY
LOATHNESS
LOATHSOME
LOATHY
LOAVE
LOAVED
LOAVES
LOAVING
LOB
LOBAR
LOBATE
LOBATED
LOBATELY
LOBATION
LOBATIONS
LOBBED
LOBBER
LOBBERS
LOBBIED
LOBBIES
LOBBING
LOBBY
LOBBYER
LOBBYERS

LOBBYGOW
LOBBYGOWS
LOBBYING
LOBBYINGS
LOBBYISM
LOBBYISMS
LOBBYIST
LOBBYISTS
LOBE
LOBECTOMY
LOBED
LOBEFIN
LOBEFINS
LOBELET
LOBELETS
LOBELIA
LOBELIAS
LOBELINE
LOBELINES
LOBES
LOBI
LOBING
LOBINGS
LOBIPED
LOBLOLLY
LOBO
LOBOLA
LOBOLAS
LOBOLO
LOBOLOS
LOBOS
LOBOSE
LOBOTOMY
LOBS
LOBSCOUSE
LOBSTER
LOBSTERED
LOBSTERER
LOBSTERS
LOBSTICK
LOBSTICKS
LOBULAR
LOBULARLY
LOBULATE
LOBULATED
LOBULE
LOBULES
LOBULI
LOBULOSE
LOBULUS
LOBUS
LOBWORM
LOBWORMS
LOCA
LOCAL
LOCALE
LOCALES
LOCALISE

335

LOCALISED	LOCKINGS	LOCUSTED	LOGANS
LOCALISER	LOCKJAW	LOCUSTING	LOGAOEDIC
LOCALISES	LOCKJAWS	LOCUSTS	LOGARITHM
LOCALISM	LOCKMAKER	LOCUTION	LOGBOARD
LOCALISMS	LOCKMAN	LOCUTIONS	LOGBOARDS
LOCALIST	LOCKMEN	LOCUTORY	LOGBOOK
LOCALISTS	LOCKNUT	LOD	LOGBOOKS
LOCALITE	LOCKNUTS	LODE	LOGE
LOCALITES	LOCKOUT	LODEN	LOGES
LOCALITY	LOCKOUTS	LODENS	LOGGAT
LOCALIZE	LOCKPICK	LODES	LOGGATS
LOCALIZED	LOCKPICKS	LODESMAN	LOGGED
LOCALIZER	LOCKRAM	LODESMEN	LOGGER
LOCALIZES	LOCKRAMS	LODESTAR	LOGGERS
LOCALLY	LOCKS	LODESTARS	LOGGETS
LOCALNESS	LOCKSET	LODESTONE	LOGGIA
LOCALS	LOCKSETS	LODGE	LOGGIAS
LOCATABLE	LOCKSMAN	LODGEABLE	LOGGIE
LOCATE	LOCKSMEN	LODGED	LOGGIER
LOCATED	LOCKSMITH	LODGEMENT	LOGGIEST
LOCATER	LOCKSTEP	LODGEPOLE	LOGGING
LOCATERS	LOCKSTEPS	LODGER	LOGGINGS
LOCATES	LOCKUP	LODGERS	LOGGISH
LOCATING	LOCKUPS	LODGES	LOGGY
LOCATION	LOCO	LODGING	LOGIA
LOCATIONS	LOCOED	LODGINGS	LOGIC
LOCATIVE	LOCOES	LODGMENT	LOGICAL
LOCATIVES	LOCOFOCO	LODGMENTS	LOGICALLY
LOCATOR	LOCOFOCOS	LODICULA	LOGICIAN
LOCATORS	LOCOING	LODICULAE	LOGICIANS
LOCELLATE	LOCOISM	LODICULE	LOGICISE
LOCH	LOCOISMS	LODICULES	LOGICISED
LOCHAN	LOCOMAN	LODS	LOGICISES
LOCHANS	LOCOMEN	LOERIE	LOGICISM
LOCHIA	LOCOMOTE	LOERIES	LOGICISMS
LOCHIAL	LOCOMOTED	LOESS	LOGICIST
LOCHS	LOCOMOTES	LOESSAL	LOGICISTS
LOCI	LOCOMOTOR	LOESSES	LOGICIZE
LOCK	LOCOPLANT	LOESSIAL	LOGICIZED
LOCKABLE	LOCOS	LOFT	LOGICIZES
LOCKAGE	LOCOWEED	LOFTED	LOGICLESS
LOCKAGES	LOCOWEEDS	LOFTER	LOGICS
LOCKAWAY	LOCULAR	LOFTERS	LOGIE
LOCKAWAYS	LOCULATE	LOFTIER	LOGIER
LOCKBOX	LOCULATED	LOFTIEST	LOGIES
LOCKBOXES	LOCULE	LOFTILY	LOGIEST
LOCKDOWN	LOCULED	LOFTINESS	LOGILY
LOCKDOWNS	LOCULES	LOFTING	LOGIN
LOCKED	LOCULI	LOFTLESS	LOGINESS
LOCKER	LOCULUS	LOFTLIKE	LOGINS
LOCKERS	LOCUM	LOFTS	LOGION
LOCKET	LOCUMS	LOFTSMAN	LOGIONS
LOCKETS	LOCUPLETE	LOFTSMEN	LOGISTIC
LOCKFAST	LOCUS	LOFTY	LOGISTICS
LOCKFUL	LOCUST	LOG	LOGJAM
LOCKFULS	LOCUSTA	LOGAN	LOGJAMMED
LOCKHOUSE	LOCUSTAE	LOGANIA	LOGJAMS
LOCKING	LOCUSTAL	LOGANIAS	LOGJUICE

LOGJUICES	LOKE	LONGANS	LONGWAYS
LOGLINE	LOKES	LONGAS	LONGWISE
LOGLINES	LOKSHEN	LONGBOARD	LONICERA
LOGLOG	LOLIGO	LONGBOAT	LONICERAS
LOGLOGS	LOLIGOS	LONGBOATS	LOO
LOGNORMAL	LOLIUM	LONGBOW	LOOBIER
LOGO	LOLIUMS	LONGBOWS	LOOBIES
LOGOFF	LOLL	LONGCASE	LOOBIEST
LOGOFFS	LOLLED	LONGCLOTH	LOOBILY
LOGOGRAM	LOLLER	LONGE	LOOBY
LOGOGRAMS	LOLLERS	LONGED	LOOED
LOGOGRAPH	LOLLIES	LONGEING	LOOEY
LOGOGRIPH	LOLLING	LONGER	LOOEYS
LOGOI	LOLLINGLY	LONGERON	LOOF
LOGOMACH	LOLLIPOP	LONGERONS	LOOFA
LOGOMACHS	LOLLIPOPS	LONGERS	LOOFAH
LOGOMACHY	LOLLOP	LONGES	LOOFAHS
LOGON	LOLLOPED	LONGEST	LOOFAS
LOGONS	LOLLOPING	LONGEVAL	LOOFFUL
LOGOPEDIC	LOLLOPS	LONGEVITY	LOOFFULS
LOGOPHILE	LOLLOPY	LONGEVOUS	LOOFS
LOGORRHEA	LOLLS	LONGHAIR	LOOIE
LOGOS	LOLLY	LONGHAIRS	LOOIES
LOGOTHETE	LOLLYGAG	LONGHAND	LOOING
LOGOTYPE	LOLLYGAGS	LONGHANDS	LOOK
LOGOTYPES	LOLLYPOP	LONGHEAD	LOOKALIKE
LOGOTYPY	LOLLYPOPS	LONGHEADS	LOOKDOWN
LOGOUT	LOLOG	LONGHORN	LOOKDOWNS
LOGOUTS	LOLOGS	LONGHORNS	LOOKED
LOGROLL	LOMA	LONGHOUSE	LOOKER
LOGROLLED	LOMAS	LONGICORN	LOOKERS
LOGROLLER	LOMATA	LONGIES	LOOKING
LOGROLLS	LOME	LONGING	LOOKISM
LOGS	LOMED	LONGINGLY	LOOKISMS
LOGWAY	LOMEIN	LONGINGS	LOOKIST
LOGWAYS	LOMEINS	LONGISH	LOOKISTS
LOGWOOD	LOMENT	LONGITUDE	LOOKOUT
LOGWOODS	LOMENTA	LONGJUMP	LOOKOUTS
LOGY	LOMENTS	LONGJUMPS	LOOKOVER
LOHAN	LOMENTUM	LONGLEAF	LOOKOVERS
LOHANS	LOMENTUMS	LONGLINE	LOOKS
LOID	LOMES	LONGLINES	LOOKSISM
LOIDED	LOMING	LONGLY	LOOKSISMS
LOIDING	LOMPISH	LONGNECK	LOOKUP
LOIDS	LONE	LONGNECKS	LOOKUPS
LOIN	LONELIER	LONGNESS	LOOM
LOINCLOTH	LONELIEST	LONGS	LOOMED
LOINS	LONELILY	LONGSHIP	LOOMING
LOIPE	LONELY	LONGSHIPS	LOOMS
LOIPEN	LONENESS	LONGSHORE	LOON
LOIR	LONER	LONGSOME	LOONEY
LOIRS	LONERS	LONGSPUR	LOONEYS
LOITER	LONESOME	LONGSPURS	LOONIE
LOITERED	LONESOMES	LONGTIME	LOONIER
LOITERER	LONG	LONGUEUR	LOONIES
LOITERERS	LONGA	LONGUEURS	LOONIEST
LOITERING	LONGAEVAL	LONGWALL	LOONILY
LOITERS	LONGAN	LONGWALLS	LOONINESS

337

LOONING	LOPING	LORETTES	LOTAH
LOONINGS	LOPOLITH	LORGNETTE	LOTAHS
LOONS	LOPOLITHS	LORGNON	LOTAS
LOONY	LOPPED	LORGNONS	LOTE
LOOP	LOPPER	LORIC	LOTES
LOOPED	LOPPERED	LORICA	LOTH
LOOPER	LOPPERING	LORICAE	LOTHARIO
LOOPERS	LOPPERS	LORICATE	LOTHARIOS
LOOPHOLE	LOPPIER	LORICATED	LOTHEFULL
LOOPHOLED	LOPPIES	LORICATES	LOTHER
LOOPHOLES	LOPPIEST	LORICS	LOTHEST
LOOPIER	LOPPING	LORIES	LOTHFULL
LOOPIEST	LOPPINGS	LORIKEET	LOTHNESS
LOOPILY	LOPPY	LORIKEETS	LOTHSOME
LOOPINESS	LOPS	LORIMER	LOTI
LOOPING	LOPSIDED	LORIMERS	LOTIC
LOOPINGS	LOPSTICK	LORINER	LOTION
LOOPS	LOPSTICKS	LORINERS	LOTIONS
LOOPY	LOQUACITY	LORING	LOTO
LOOR	LOQUAT	LORINGS	LOTOS
LOORD	LOQUATS	LORIOT	LOTOSES
LOORDS	LOQUITUR	LORIOTS	LOTS
LOOS	LOR	LORIS	LOTTE
LOOSE	LORAL	LORISES	LOTTED
LOOSEBOX	LORAN	LORN	LOTTER
LOOSED	LORANS	LORNNESS	LOTTERIES
LOOSELY	LORATE	LORRELL	LOTTERS
LOOSEN	LORAZEPAM	LORRELLS	LOTTERY
LOOSENED	LORCHA	LORRIES	LOTTES
LOOSENER	LORCHAS	LORRY	LOTTING
LOOSENERS	LORD	LORY	LOTTO
LOOSENESS	LORDED	LOS	LOTTOS
LOOSENING	LORDING	LOSABLE	LOTUS
LOOSENS	LORDINGS	LOSE	LOTUSES
LOOSER	LORDKIN	LOSED	LOTUSLAND
LOOSES	LORDKINS	LOSEL	LOU
LOOSEST	LORDLESS	LOSELS	LOUCHE
LOOSIE	LORDLIER	LOSEN	LOUCHELY
LOOSIES	LORDLIEST	LOSER	LOUD
LOOSING	LORDLIKE	LOSERS	LOUDEN
LOOSINGS	LORDLING	LOSES	LOUDENED
LOOT	LORDLINGS	LOSH	LOUDENING
LOOTED	LORDLY	LOSING	LOUDENS
LOOTEN	LORDOMA	LOSINGLY	LOUDER
LOOTER	LORDOMAS	LOSINGS	LOUDEST
LOOTERS	LORDOSES	LOSLYF	LOUDISH
LOOTING	LORDOSIS	LOSLYFS	LOUDLIER
LOOTINGS	LORDOTIC	LOSS	LOUDLIEST
LOOTS	LORDS	LOSSES	LOUDLY
LOOVES	LORDSHIP	LOSSIER	LOUDMOUTH
LOP	LORDSHIPS	LOSSIEST	LOUDNESS
LOPE	LORDY	LOSSLESS	LOUED
LOPED	LORE	LOSSMAKER	LOUGH
LOPER	LOREAL	LOSSY	LOUGHS
LOPERS	LOREL	LOST	LOUIE
LOPES	LORELS	LOSTNESS	LOUIES
LOPGRASS	LORES	LOT	LOUING
LOPHODONT	LORETTE	LOTA	LOUIS

LOUMA
LOUMAS
LOUN
LOUND
LOUNDED
LOUNDER
LOUNDERED
LOUNDERS
LOUNDING
LOUNDS
LOUNED
LOUNGE
LOUNGED
LOUNGER
LOUNGERS
LOUNGES
LOUNGING
LOUNGINGS
LOUNGY
LOUNING
LOUNS
LOUP
LOUPE
LOUPED
LOUPEN
LOUPES
LOUPING
LOUPIT
LOUPS
LOUR
LOURE
LOURED
LOURES
LOURIE
LOURIER
LOURIES
LOURIEST
LOURING
LOURINGLY
LOURINGS
LOURS
LOURY
LOUS
LOUSE
LOUSED
LOUSER
LOUSERS
LOUSES
LOUSEWORT
LOUSIER
LOUSIEST
LOUSILY
LOUSINESS
LOUSING
LOUSY
LOUT
LOUTED
LOUTING

LOUTISH
LOUTISHLY
LOUTS
LOUVAR
LOUVARS
LOUVER
LOUVERED
LOUVERS
LOUVRE
LOUVRED
LOUVRES
LOVABLE
LOVABLY
LOVAGE
LOVAGES
LOVAT
LOVATS
LOVE
LOVEABLE
LOVEABLY
LOVEBIRD
LOVEBIRDS
LOVEBITE
LOVEBITES
LOVEBUG
LOVEBUGS
LOVED
LOVEFEST
LOVEFESTS
LOVELESS
LOVELIER
LOVELIES
LOVELIEST
LOVELIGHT
LOVELILY
LOVELOCK
LOVELOCKS
LOVELORN
LOVELY
LOVEMAKER
LOVER
LOVERED
LOVERLESS
LOVERLY
LOVERS
LOVES
LOVESEAT
LOVESEATS
LOVESICK
LOVESOME
LOVEVINE
LOVEVINES
LOVEY
LOVEYS
LOVING
LOVINGLY
LOVINGS
LOW

LOWAN
LOWANS
LOWBALL
LOWBALLED
LOWBALLS
LOWBORN
LOWBOY
LOWBOYS
LOWBRED
LOWBROW
LOWBROWED
LOWBROWS
LOWDOWN
LOWDOWNS
LOWE
LOWED
LOWER
LOWERABLE
LOWERCASE
LOWERED
LOWERIER
LOWERIEST
LOWERING
LOWERINGS
LOWERMOST
LOWERS
LOWERY
LOWES
LOWEST
LOWING
LOWINGS
LOWISH
LOWLAND
LOWLANDER
LOWLANDS
LOWLIER
LOWLIEST
LOWLIFE
LOWLIFER
LOWLIFERS
LOWLIFES
LOWLIGHT
LOWLIGHTS
LOWLIHEAD
LOWLILY
LOWLINESS
LOWLIVES
LOWLY
LOWN
LOWND
LOWNDED
LOWNDING
LOWNDS
LOWNE
LOWNED
LOWNES
LOWNESS
LOWNESSES

LOWNING
LOWNS
LOWP
LOWPED
LOWPING
LOWPS
LOWRIDER
LOWRIDERS
LOWRIE
LOWRIES
LOWRY
LOWS
LOWSE
LOWSED
LOWSENING
LOWSER
LOWSES
LOWSEST
LOWSING
LOWSIT
LOWT
LOWTED
LOWTING
LOWTS
LOWVELD
LOWVELDS
LOX
LOXED
LOXES
LOXING
LOXODROME
LOXODROMY
LOXYGEN
LOXYGENS
LOY
LOYAL
LOYALER
LOYALEST
LOYALISM
LOYALISMS
LOYALIST
LOYALISTS
LOYALLER
LOYALLEST
LOYALLY
LOYALNESS
LOYALTIES
LOYALTY
LOYS
LOZELL
LOZELLS
LOZEN
LOZENGE
LOZENGED
LOZENGES
LOZENGY
LOZENS
LUACH

LUAU	LUCKINESS	LUGHOLES	LUMINED
LUAUS	LUCKING	LUGING	LUMINES
LUBBARD	LUCKLESS	LUGINGS	LUMINESCE
LUBBARDS	LUCKPENNY	LUGS	LUMINING
LUBBER	LUCKS	LUGSAIL	LUMINISM
LUBBERLY	LUCKY	LUGSAILS	LUMINISMS
LUBBERS	LUCRATIVE	LUGWORM	LUMINIST
LUBE	LUCRE	LUGWORMS	LUMINISTS
LUBED	LUCRES	LUIT	LUMINOUS
LUBES	LUCTATION	LUITEN	LUMME
LUBFISH	LUCUBRATE	LUKE	LUMMIER
LUBFISHES	LUCULENT	LUKEWARM	LUMMIEST
LUBING	LUCUMA	LULIBUB	LUMMOX
LUBRA	LUCUMAS	LULIBUBS	LUMMOXES
LUBRAS	LUCUMO	LULL	LUMMY
LUBRIC	LUCUMONES	LULLABIED	LUMP
LUBRICAL	LUCUMOS	LULLABIES	LUMPED
LUBRICANT	LUD	LULLABY	LUMPEN
LUBRICATE	LUDE	LULLED	LUMPENLY
LUBRICITY	LUDERICK	LULLER	LUMPENS
LUBRICOUS	LUDERICKS	LULLERS	LUMPER
LUCARNE	LUDES	LULLING	LUMPERS
LUCARNES	LUDIC	LULLS	LUMPFISH
LUCE	LUDICALLY	LULU	LUMPIER
LUCENCE	LUDICROUS	LULUS	LUMPIEST
LUCENCES	LUDO	LUM	LUMPILY
LUCENCIES	LUDOS	LUMA	LUMPINESS
LUCENCY	LUDS	LUMAS	LUMPING
LUCENT	LUDSHIP	LUMBAGO	LUMPINGLY
LUCENTLY	LUDSHIPS	LUMBAGOS	LUMPISH
LUCERN	LUES	LUMBANG	LUMPISHLY
LUCERNE	LUETIC	LUMBANGS	LUMPKIN
LUCERNES	LUETICS	LUMBAR	LUMPKINS
LUCERNS	LUFF	LUMBARS	LUMPS
LUCES	LUFFA	LUMBER	LUMPY
LUCHOT	LUFFAS	LUMBERED	LUMS
LUCHOTH	LUFFED	LUMBERER	LUNA
LUCID	LUFFING	LUMBERERS	LUNACIES
LUCIDER	LUFFS	LUMBERING	LUNACY
LUCIDEST	LUG	LUMBERLY	LUNANAUT
LUCIDITY	LUGE	LUMBERMAN	LUNANAUTS
LUCIDLY	LUGED	LUMBERMEN	LUNAR
LUCIDNESS	LUGEING	LUMBERS	LUNARIAN
LUCIFER	LUGEINGS	LUMBRICAL	LUNARIANS
LUCIFERIN	LUGER	LUMBRICI	LUNARIES
LUCIFERS	LUGERS	LUMBRICUS	LUNARIST
LUCIGEN	LUGES	LUMEN	LUNARISTS
LUCIGENS	LUGGABLE	LUMENAL	LUNARNAUT
LUCITE	LUGGABLES	LUMENS	LUNARS
LUCITES	LUGGAGE	LUMINA	LUNARY
LUCK	LUGGAGES	LUMINAIRE	LUNAS
LUCKED	LUGGED	LUMINAL	LUNATE
LUCKEN	LUGGER	LUMINANCE	LUNATED
LUCKIE	LUGGERS	LUMINANT	LUNATELY
LUCKIER	LUGGIE	LUMINANTS	LUNATES
LUCKIES	LUGGIES	LUMINARIA	LUNATIC
LUCKIEST	LUGGING	LUMINARY	LUNATICAL
LUCKILY	LUGHOLE	LUMINE	LUNATICS

LUNATION	LUNT	LURINGLY	LUSTRED
LUNATIONS	LUNTED	LURK	LUSTRES
LUNCH	LUNTING	LURKED	LUSTRINE
LUNCHBOX	LUNTS	LURKER	LUSTRINES
LUNCHED	LUNULA	LURKERS	LUSTRING
LUNCHEON	LUNULAE	LURKING	LUSTRINGS
LUNCHEONS	LUNULAR	LURKINGLY	LUSTROUS
LUNCHER	LUNULATE	LURKINGS	LUSTRUM
LUNCHERS	LUNULATED	LURKS	LUSTRUMS
LUNCHES	LUNULE	LURRIES	LUSTS
LUNCHING	LUNULES	LURRY	LUSTY
LUNCHMEAT	LUNY	LURS	LUSUS
LUNCHROOM	LUNYIE	LURVE	LUSUSES
LUNCHTIME	LUNYIES	LURVES	LUTANIST
LUNE	LUPANAR	LUSCIOUS	LUTANISTS
LUNES	LUPANARS	LUSER	LUTE
LUNET	LUPIN	LUSERS	LUTEA
LUNETS	LUPINE	LUSH	LUTEAL
LUNETTE	LUPINES	LUSHED	LUTECIUM
LUNETTES	LUPINS	LUSHER	LUTECIUMS
LUNG	LUPOUS	LUSHERS	LUTED
LUNGAN	LUPPEN	LUSHES	LUTEFISK
LUNGANS	LUPULIN	LUSHEST	LUTEFISKS
LUNGE	LUPULINE	LUSHIER	LUTEIN
LUNGED	LUPULINIC	LUSHIEST	LUTEINISE
LUNGEE	LUPULINS	LUSHING	LUTEINIZE
LUNGEES	LUPUS	LUSHLY	LUTEINS
LUNGEING	LUPUSES	LUSHNESS	LUTENIST
LUNGER	LUR	LUSHY	LUTENISTS
LUNGERS	LURCH	LUSK	LUTEOLIN
LUNGES	LURCHED	LUSKED	LUTEOLINS
LUNGFISH	LURCHER	LUSKING	LUTEOLOUS
LUNGFUL	LURCHERS	LUSKISH	LUTEOUS
LUNGFULS	LURCHES	LUSKS	LUTER
LUNGI	LURCHING	LUST	LUTERS
LUNGIE	LURDAN	LUSTED	LUTES
LUNGIES	LURDANE	LUSTER	LUTESCENT
LUNGING	LURDANES	LUSTERED	LUTETIUM
LUNGIS	LURDANS	LUSTERING	LUTETIUMS
LUNGS	LURDEN	LUSTERS	LUTEUM
LUNGWORM	LURDENS	LUSTFUL	LUTFISK
LUNGWORMS	LURE	LUSTFULLY	LUTFISKS
LUNGWORT	LURED	LUSTICK	LUTHERN
LUNGWORTS	LURER	LUSTIER	LUTHERNS
LUNGYI	LURERS	LUSTIEST	LUTHIER
LUNGYIS	LURES	LUSTIHEAD	LUTHIERS
LUNIER	LUREX	LUSTIHOOD	LUTING
LUNIES	LUREXES	LUSTILY	LUTINGS
LUNIEST	LURGI	LUSTINESS	LUTIST
LUNINESS	LURGIES	LUSTING	LUTISTS
LUNISOLAR	LURGIS	LUSTIQUE	LUTITE
LUNITIDAL	LURGY	LUSTLESS	LUTITES
LUNK	LURID	LUSTRA	LUTTEN
LUNKER	LURIDER	LUSTRAL	LUTZ
LUNKERS	LURIDEST	LUSTRATE	LUTZES
LUNKHEAD	LURIDLY	LUSTRATED	LUV
LUNKHEADS	LURIDNESS	LUSTRATES	LUVS
LUNKS	LURING	LUSTRE	LUVVIE

LUVVIES

LUVVIES
LUVVY
LUX
LUXATE
LUXATED
LUXATES
LUXATING
LUXATION
LUXATIONS
LUXE
LUXES
LUXMETER
LUXMETERS
LUXURIANT
LUXURIATE
LUXURIES
LUXURIOUS
LUXURIST
LUXURISTS
LUXURY
LUZ
LUZERN
LUZERNS
LUZZES
LWEI
LWEIS
LYAM
LYAMS
LYARD
LYART
LYASE
LYASES
LYCEA
LYCEE
LYCEES
LYCEUM
LYCEUMS
LYCH
LYCHEE
LYCHEES
LYCHES
LYCHGATE
LYCHGATES
LYCHNIS
LYCHNISES
LYCOPENE
LYCOPENES
LYCOPOD
LYCOPODS
LYCRA
LYCRAS
LYDDITE
LYDDITES
LYE
LYES
LYFULL
LYING
LYINGLY

LYINGS
LYKEWAKE
LYKEWAKES
LYKEWALK
LYKEWALKS
LYM
LYME
LYMES
LYMITER
LYMITERS
LYMPH
LYMPHAD
LYMPHADS
LYMPHATIC
LYMPHOID
LYMPHOMA
LYMPHOMAS
LYMPHS
LYMS
LYNAGE
LYNAGES
LYNCEAN
LYNCH
LYNCHED
LYNCHER
LYNCHERS
LYNCHES
LYNCHET
LYNCHETS
LYNCHING
LYNCHINGS
LYNCHPIN
LYNCHPINS
LYNE
LYNES
LYNX
LYNXES
LYNXLIKE
LYOLYSES
LYOLYSIS
LYOMEROUS
LYONNAISE
LYOPHIL
LYOPHILE
LYOPHILED
LYOPHILIC
LYOPHOBE
LYOPHOBIC
LYRA
LYRATE
LYRATED
LYRATELY
LYRE
LYREBIRD
LYREBIRDS
LYRES
LYRIC
LYRICAL

LYRICALLY
LYRICISE
LYRICISED
LYRICISES
LYRICISM
LYRICISMS
LYRICIST
LYRICISTS
LYRICIZE
LYRICIZED
LYRICIZES
LYRICON
LYRICONS
LYRICS
LYRIFORM
LYRISM
LYRISMS
LYRIST
LYRISTS
LYSATE
LYSATES
LYSE
LYSED
LYSERGIC
LYSERGIDE
LYSES
LYSIGENIC
LYSIMETER
LYSIN
LYSINE
LYSINES
LYSING
LYSINS
LYSIS
LYSOGEN
LYSOGENIC
LYSOGENS
LYSOGENY
LYSOL
LYSOLS
LYSOSOMAL
LYSOSOME
LYSOSOMES
LYSOZYME
LYSOZYMES
LYSSA
LYSSAS
LYTE
LYTED
LYTES
LYTHE
LYTHES
LYTIC
LYTICALLY
LYTING
LYTTA
LYTTAE
LYTTAS

M

MA	MACCHIE	MACKINAW	MACULED
MAA	MACCOBOY	MACKINAWS	MACULES
MAAED	MACCOBOYS	MACKLE	MACULING
MAAING	MACE	MACKLED	MACULOSE
MAAR	MACED	MACKLES	MACUMBA
MAARE	MACEDOINE	MACKLING	MACUMBAS
MAARS	MACER	MACKS	MAD
MAAS	MACERAL	MACLE	MADAFU
MAASES	MACERALS	MACLED	MADAFUS
MAATJES	MACERATE	MACLES	MADAM
MABE	MACERATED	MACON	MADAME
MABELA	MACERATER	MACONS	MADAMED
MABELAS	MACERATES	MACOYA	MADAMES
MABES	MACERATOR	MACOYAS	MADAMING
MAC	MACERS	MACRAME	MADAMS
MACABER	MACES	MACRAMES	MADAROSES
MACABRE	MACH	MACRAMI	MADAROSIS
MACABRELY	MACHAIR	MACRAMIS	MADBRAIN
MACACO	MACHAIRS	MACRO	MADCAP
MACACOS	MACHAN	MACROBIAN	MADCAPS
MACADAM	MACHANS	MACROCODE	MADDED
MACADAMIA	MACHE	MACROCOPY	MADDEN
MACADAMS	MACHER	MACROCOSM	MADDENED
MACAHUBA	MACHERS	MACROCYST	MADDENING
MACAHUBAS	MACHES	MACROCYTE	MADDENS
MACALLUM	MACHETE	MACRODOME	MADDER
MACALLUMS	MACHETES	MACRODONT	MADDERS
MACAQUE	MACHI	MACROGLIA	MADDEST
MACAQUES	MACHINATE	MACROLOGY	MADDING
MACARISE	MACHINE	MACROMERE	MADDINGLY
MACARISED	MACHINED	MACROMOLE	MADDISH
MACARISES	MACHINERY	MACRON	MADDOCK
MACARISM	MACHINES	MACRONS	MADDOCKS
MACARISMS	MACHINING	MACROPOD	MADE
MACARIZE	MACHINIST	MACROPODS	MADEFIED
MACARIZED	MACHISMO	MACROPSIA	MADEFIES
MACARIZES	MACHISMOS	MACROS	MADEFY
MACARONI	MACHMETER	MACROTOUS	MADEFYING
MACARONIC	MACHO	MACRURAL	MADEIRA
MACARONIS	MACHOISM	MACRURAN	MADEIRAS
MACAROON	MACHOISMS	MACRURANS	MADELEINE
MACAROONS	MACHOS	MACRUROID	MADERISE
MACASSAR	MACHREE	MACRUROUS	MADERISED
MACASSARS	MACHREES	MACS	MADERISES
MACAW	MACHS	MACTATION	MADERIZE
MACAWS	MACHZOR	MACULA	MADERIZED
MACCABAW	MACHZORIM	MACULAE	MADERIZES
MACCABAWS	MACHZORS	MACULAR	MADGE
MACCABOY	MACING	MACULAS	MADGES
MACCABOYS	MACINTOSH	MACULATE	MADHOUSE
MACCARONI	MACK	MACULATED	MADHOUSES
MACCHIA	MACKEREL	MACULATES	MADID
MACCHIATO	MACKERELS	MACULE	MADISON

MADISONS
MADLING
MADLINGS
MADLY
MADMAN
MADMEN
MADNESS
MADNESSES
MADONNA
MADONNAS
MADOQUA
MADOQUAS
MADRAS
MADRASA
MADRASAH
MADRASAHS
MADRASAS
MADRASES
MADRASSA
MADRASSAH
MADRASSAS
MADRE
MADREPORE
MADRES
MADRIGAL
MADRIGALS
MADRILENE
MADRONA
MADRONAS
MADRONE
MADRONES
MADRONO
MADRONOS
MADS
MADTOM
MADTOMS
MADURO
MADUROS
MADWOMAN
MADWOMEN
MADWORT
MADWORTS
MADZOON
MADZOONS
MAE
MAELID
MAELIDS
MAELSTROM
MAENAD
MAENADES
MAENADIC
MAENADISM
MAENADS
MAES
MAESTOSO
MAESTOSOS
MAESTRI
MAESTRO

MAESTROS
MAFFIA
MAFFIAS
MAFFICK
MAFFICKED
MAFFICKER
MAFFICKS
MAFFLED
MAFFLIN
MAFFLING
MAFFLINGS
MAFFLINS
MAFIA
MAFIAS
MAFIC
MAFICS
MAFIOSI
MAFIOSO
MAFIOSOS
MAFTED
MAFTIR
MAFTIRS
MAG
MAGAININ
MAGAININS
MAGALOG
MAGALOGS
MAGALOGUE
MAGAZINE
MAGAZINES
MAGDALEN
MAGDALENE
MAGDALENS
MAGE
MAGENTA
MAGENTAS
MAGES
MAGESHIP
MAGESHIPS
MAGG
MAGGED
MAGGIE
MAGGIES
MAGGING
MAGGOT
MAGGOTIER
MAGGOTS
MAGGOTY
MAGGS
MAGI
MAGIAN
MAGIANISM
MAGIANS
MAGIC
MAGICAL
MAGICALLY
MAGICIAN
MAGICIANS

MAGICKED
MAGICKING
MAGICS
MAGILP
MAGILPS
MAGISM
MAGISMS
MAGISTER
MAGISTERS
MAGISTERY
MAGISTRAL
MAGLEV
MAGLEVS
MAGMA
MAGMAS
MAGMATA
MAGMATIC
MAGMATISM
MAGNALIUM
MAGNATE
MAGNATES
MAGNES
MAGNESES
MAGNESIA
MAGNESIAL
MAGNESIAN
MAGNESIAS
MAGNESIC
MAGNESITE
MAGNESIUM
MAGNET
MAGNETAR
MAGNETARS
MAGNETIC
MAGNETICS
MAGNETISE
MAGNETISM
MAGNETIST
MAGNETITE
MAGNETIZE
MAGNETO
MAGNETON
MAGNETONS
MAGNETOS
MAGNETRON
MAGNETS
MAGNIFIC
MAGNIFICO
MAGNIFIED
MAGNIFIER
MAGNIFIES
MAGNIFY
MAGNITUDE
MAGNOLIA
MAGNOLIAS
MAGNON
MAGNONS
MAGNOX

MAGNOXES
MAGNUM
MAGNUMS
MAGNUS
MAGOT
MAGOTS
MAGPIE
MAGPIES
MAGS
MAGSMAN
MAGSMEN
MAGUEY
MAGUEYS
MAGUS
MAGYAR
MAHARAJA
MAHARAJAH
MAHARAJAS
MAHARANEE
MAHARANI
MAHARANIS
MAHARISHI
MAHATMA
MAHATMAS
MAHEWU
MAHEWUS
MAHIMAHI
MAHIMAHIS
MAHJONG
MAHJONGG
MAHJONGGS
MAHJONGS
MAHLSTICK
MAHMAL
MAHMALS
MAHOE
MAHOES
MAHOGANY
MAHONIA
MAHONIAS
MAHOUT
MAHOUTS
MAHSEER
MAHSEERS
MAHSIR
MAHSIRS
MAHUA
MAHUANG
MAHUANGS
MAHUAS
MAHWA
MAHWAS
MAHZOR
MAHZORIM
MAHZORS
MAIASAUR
MAIASAURA
MAIASAURS

MALAXES

MAID
MAIDAN
MAIDANS
MAIDED
MAIDEN
MAIDENISH
MAIDENLY
MAIDENS
MAIDHOOD
MAIDHOODS
MAIDING
MAIDISH
MAIDISM
MAIDISMS
MAIDLESS
MAIDS
MAIEUTIC
MAIEUTICS
MAIGRE
MAIGRES
MAIHEM
MAIHEMS
MAIK
MAIKO
MAIKOS
MAIKS
MAIL
MAILABLE
MAILBAG
MAILBAGS
MAILBOX
MAILBOXES
MAILCAR
MAILCARS
MAILCOACH
MAILE
MAILED
MAILER
MAILERS
MAILES
MAILGRAM
MAILGRAMS
MAILING
MAILINGS
MAILL
MAILLESS
MAILLOT
MAILLOTS
MAILLS
MAILMAN
MAILMEN
MAILMERGE
MAILPOUCH
MAILROOM
MAILROOMS
MAILS
MAILSACK
MAILSACKS

MAILSHOT
MAILSHOTS
MAILVAN
MAILVANS
MAIM
MAIMED
MAIMER
MAIMERS
MAIMING
MAIMINGS
MAIMS
MAIN
MAINBOOM
MAINBOOMS
MAINBRACE
MAINDOOR
MAINDOORS
MAINED
MAINER
MAINEST
MAINFRAME
MAINING
MAINLAND
MAINLANDS
MAINLINE
MAINLINED
MAINLINER
MAINLINES
MAINLY
MAINMAST
MAINMASTS
MAINOR
MAINORS
MAINOUR
MAINOURS
MAINPRISE
MAINS
MAINSAIL
MAINSAILS
MAINSHEET
MAINSTAY
MAINSTAYS
MAINTAIN
MAINTAINS
MAINTOP
MAINTOPS
MAINYARD
MAINYARDS
MAIOLICA
MAIOLICAS
MAIR
MAIRE
MAIREHAU
MAIREHAUS
MAIRES
MAIRS
MAISE
MAISES

MAIST
MAISTER
MAISTERED
MAISTERS
MAISTRIES
MAISTRING
MAISTRY
MAISTS
MAIZE
MAIZES
MAJAGUA
MAJAGUAS
MAJESTIC
MAJESTIES
MAJESTY
MAJLIS
MAJLISES
MAJOLICA
MAJOLICAS
MAJOR
MAJORAT
MAJORATS
MAJORDOMO
MAJORED
MAJORETTE
MAJORING
MAJORITY
MAJORLY
MAJORS
MAJORSHIP
MAJUSCULE
MAK
MAKABLE
MAKAR
MAKARS
MAKE
MAKEABLE
MAKEBATE
MAKEBATES
MAKEFAST
MAKEFASTS
MAKELESS
MAKEOVER
MAKEOVERS
MAKER
MAKEREADY
MAKERS
MAKES
MAKESHIFT
MAKEUP
MAKEUPS
MAKI
MAKIMONO
MAKIMONOS
MAKING
MAKINGS
MAKIS
MAKO

MAKOS
MAKS
MAKUTA
MAKUTU
MAKUTUED
MAKUTUING
MAKUTUS
MAL
MALA
MALACCA
MALACCAS
MALACHITE
MALACIA
MALACIAS
MALADIES
MALADROIT
MALADY
MALAGUENA
MALAISE
MALAISES
MALAM
MALAMS
MALAMUTE
MALAMUTES
MALANDER
MALANDERS
MALANGA
MALANGAS
MALAPERT
MALAPERTS
MALAPROP
MALAPROPS
MALAR
MALARIA
MALARIAL
MALARIAN
MALARIAS
MALARIOUS
MALARKEY
MALARKEYS
MALARKIES
MALARKY
MALAROMA
MALAROMAS
MALARS
MALAS
MALATE
MALATES
MALATHION
MALAX
MALAXAGE
MALAXAGES
MALAXATE
MALAXATED
MALAXATES
MALAXATOR
MALAXED
MALAXES

345

MALAXING	MALIST	MALTALENT	MAMELON
MALE	MALKIN	MALTASE	MAMELONS
MALEATE	MALKINS	MALTASES	MAMELUCO
MALEATES	MALL	MALTED	MAMELUCOS
MALEDICT	MALLAM	MALTEDS	MAMELUKE
MALEDICTS	MALLAMS	MALTHA	MAMELUKES
MALEFFECT	MALLANDER	MALTHAS	MAMEY
MALEFIC	MALLARD	MALTIER	MAMEYES
MALEFICE	MALLARDS	MALTIEST	MAMEYS
MALEFICES	MALLEABLE	MALTINESS	MAMIE
MALEIC	MALLEABLY	MALTING	MAMIES
MALEMIUT	MALLEATE	MALTINGS	MAMILLA
MALEMIUTS	MALLEATED	MALTMAN	MAMILLAE
MALEMUTE	MALLEATES	MALTMEN	MAMILLAR
MALEMUTES	MALLECHO	MALTOL	MAMILLARY
MALENESS	MALLECHOS	MALTOLS	MAMILLATE
MALENGINE	MALLED	MALTOSE	MAMLUK
MALES	MALLEE	MALTOSES	MAMLUKS
MALFED	MALLEES	MALTREAT	MAMMA
MALFORMED	MALLEI	MALTREATS	MAMMAE
MALGRADO	MALLEMUCK	MALTS	MAMMAL
MALGRE	MALLENDER	MALTSTER	MAMMALIAN
MALGRED	MALLEOLAR	MALTSTERS	MAMMALITY
MALGRES	MALLEOLI	MALTWORM	MAMMALOGY
MALGRING	MALLEOLUS	MALTWORMS	MAMMALS
MALI	MALLET	MALTY	MAMMARY
MALIBU	MALLETS	MALVA	MAMMAS
MALIC	MALLEUS	MALVAS	MAMMATE
MALICE	MALLEUSES	MALVASIA	MAMMATI
MALICED	MALLING	MALVASIAN	MAMMATUS
MALICES	MALLINGS	MALVASIAS	MAMMEE
MALICHO	MALLOW	MALVESIE	MAMMEES
MALICHOS	MALLOWS	MALVESIES	MAMMER
MALICING	MALLS	MALVOISIE	MAMMERED
MALICIOUS	MALM	MALWA	MAMMERING
MALIGN	MALMAG	MALWARE	MAMMERS
MALIGNANT	MALMAGS	MALWARES	MAMMET
MALIGNED	MALMIER	MALWAS	MAMMETRY
MALIGNER	MALMIEST	MAM	MAMMETS
MALIGNERS	MALMS	MAMA	MAMMEY
MALIGNING	MALMSEY	MAMAGUY	MAMMEYS
MALIGNITY	MALMSEYS	MAMAGUYED	MAMMIE
MALIGNLY	MALMSTONE	MAMAGUYS	MAMMIES
MALIGNS	MALMY	MAMAKAU	MAMMIFER
MALIHINI	MALODOR	MAMAKO	MAMMIFERS
MALIHINIS	MALODORS	MAMAKU	MAMMIFORM
MALIK	MALODOUR	MAMALIGA	MAMMILLA
MALIKS	MALODOURS	MAMALIGAS	MAMMILLAE
MALINE	MALONATE	MAMAS	MAMMITIS
MALINES	MALONATES	MAMBA	MAMMOCK
MALINGER	MALONIC	MAMBAS	MAMMOCKED
MALINGERS	MALOTI	MAMBO	MAMMOCKS
MALINGERY	MALPIGHIA	MAMBOED	MAMMOGRAM
MALIS	MALPOSED	MAMBOES	MAMMON
MALISM	MALS	MAMBOING	MAMMONISH
MALISMS	MALSTICK	MAMBOS	MAMMONISM
MALISON	MALSTICKS	MAMEE	MAMMONIST
MALISONS	MALT	MAMEES	MAMMONITE

MAMMONS	MANDAMUS	MANET	MANHOLE
MAMMOTH	MANDARIN	MANEUVER	MANHOLES
MAMMOTHS	MANDARINE	MANEUVERS	MANHOOD
MAMMY	MANDARINS	MANFUL	MANHOODS
MAMPARA	MANDATARY	MANFULLY	MANHUNT
MAMPARAS	MANDATE	MANG	MANHUNTER
MAMPOER	MANDATED	MANGA	MANHUNTS
MAMPOERS	MANDATES	MANGABEY	MANI
MAMS	MANDATING	MANGABEYS	MANIA
MAMSELLE	MANDATOR	MANGABIES	MANIAC
MAMSELLES	MANDATORS	MANGABY	MANIACAL
MAMZER	MANDATORY	MANGAL	MANIACS
MAMZERIM	MANDI	MANGALS	MANIAS
MAMZERS	MANDIBLE	MANGANATE	MANIC
MAN	MANDIBLES	MANGANESE	MANICALLY
MANA	MANDILION	MANGANIC	MANICOTTI
MANACLE	MANDIOC	MANGANIN	MANICS
MANACLED	MANDIOCA	MANGANINS	MANICURE
MANACLES	MANDIOCAS	MANGANITE	MANICURED
MANACLING	MANDIOCCA	MANGANOUS	MANICURES
MANAGE	MANDIOCS	MANGAS	MANIES
MANAGED	MANDIR	MANGE	MANIFEST
MANAGER	MANDIRA	MANGEAO	MANIFESTO
MANAGERS	MANDIRAS	MANGED	MANIFESTS
MANAGES	MANDIRS	MANGEL	MANIFOLD
MANAGING	MANDIS	MANGELS	MANIFOLDS
MANAIA	MANDOLA	MANGER	MANIFORM
MANAKIN	MANDOLAS	MANGERS	MANIHOC
MANAKINS	MANDOLIN	MANGES	MANIHOCS
MANANA	MANDOLINE	MANGETOUT	MANIHOT
MANANAS	MANDOLINS	MANGEY	MANIHOTS
MANAS	MANDOM	MANGIER	MANIKIN
MANAT	MANDOMS	MANGIEST	MANIKINS
MANATEE	MANDORA	MANGILY	MANILA
MANATEES	MANDORAS	MANGINESS	MANILAS
MANATI	MANDORLA	MANGING	MANILLA
MANATIS	MANDORLAS	MANGLE	MANILLAS
MANATOID	MANDRAKE	MANGLED	MANILLE
MANATS	MANDRAKES	MANGLER	MANILLES
MANATU	MANDREL	MANGLERS	MANIOC
MANAWA	MANDRELS	MANGLES	MANIOCA
MANAWAS	MANDRIL	MANGLING	MANIOCAS
MANCALA	MANDRILL	MANGO	MANIOCS
MANCALAS	MANDRILLS	MANGOES	MANIPLE
MANCANDO	MANDRILS	MANGOLD	MANIPLES
MANCHE	MANDUCATE	MANGOLDS	MANIPLIES
MANCHES	MANDYLION	MANGONEL	MANIPULAR
MANCHET	MANE	MANGONELS	MANIS
MANCHETS	MANED	MANGOS	MANITO
MANCIPATE	MANEGE	MANGOSTAN	MANITOS
MANCIPLE	MANEGED	MANGOUSTE	MANITOU
MANCIPLES	MANEGES	MANGROVE	MANITOUS
MANCUS	MANEGING	MANGROVES	MANITU
MANCUSES	MANEH	MANGS	MANITUS
MAND	MANEHS	MANGULATE	MANJACK
MANDALA	MANELESS	MANGY	MANJACKS
MANDALAS	MANENT	MANHANDLE	MANKIER
MANDALIC	MANES	MANHATTAN	MANKIEST

MANKIND	MANRIDING	MANTUA	MAPPEMOND
MANKINDS	MANROPE	MANTUAS	MAPPER
MANKY	MANROPES	MANTY	MAPPERIES
MANLESS	MANS	MANUAL	MAPPERS
MANLIER	MANSARD	MANUALLY	MAPPERY
MANLIEST	MANSARDED	MANUALS	MAPPING
MANLIKE	MANSARDS	MANUARY	MAPPINGS
MANLIKELY	MANSE	MANUBRIA	MAPPIST
MANLILY	MANSES	MANUBRIAL	MAPPISTS
MANLINESS	MANSHIFT	MANUBRIUM	MAPS
MANLY	MANSHIFTS	MANUHIRI	MAPSTICK
MANMADE	MANSION	MANUHIRIS	MAPSTICKS
MANNA	MANSIONS	MANUKA	MAPWISE
MANNAN	MANSLAYER	MANUKAS	MAQUETTE
MANNANS	MANSONRY	MANUL	MAQUETTES
MANNAS	MANSUETE	MANULS	MAQUI
MANNED	MANSWORN	MANUMEA	MAQUILA
MANNEQUIN	MANTA	MANUMEAS	MAQUILAS
MANNER	MANTAS	MANUMIT	MAQUIS
MANNERED	MANTEAU	MANUMITS	MAQUISARD
MANNERISM	MANTEAUS	MANURANCE	MAR
MANNERIST	MANTEAUX	MANURE	MARA
MANNERLY	MANTEEL	MANURED	MARABI
MANNERS	MANTEELS	MANURER	MARABIS
MANNIKIN	MANTEL	MANURERS	MARABOU
MANNIKINS	MANTELET	MANURES	MARABOUS
MANNING	MANTELETS	MANURIAL	MARABOUT
MANNISH	MANTELS	MANURING	MARABOUTS
MANNISHLY	MANTES	MANURINGS	MARABUNTA
MANNITE	MANTIC	MANUS	MARACA
MANNITES	MANTICORA	MANWARD	MARACAS
MANNITIC	MANTICORE	MANWARDS	MARAE
MANNITOL	MANTID	MANWISE	MARAES
MANNITOLS	MANTIDS	MANY	MARAGING
MANNOSE	MANTIES	MANYATA	MARAGINGS
MANNOSES	MANTILLA	MANYATAS	MARAH
MANO	MANTILLAS	MANYATTA	MARAHS
MANOAO	MANTIS	MANYATTAS	MARANATHA
MANOAOS	MANTISES	MANYFOLD	MARANTA
MANOEUVRE	MANTISSA	MANYPLIES	MARANTAS
MANOMETER	MANTISSAS	MANZANITA	MARARI
MANOMETRY	MANTLE	MANZELLO	MARARIS
MANOR	MANTLED	MANZELLOS	MARAS
MANORIAL	MANTLES	MAOMAO	MARASCA
MANORS	MANTLET	MAORMOR	MARASCAS
MANOS	MANTLETS	MAORMORS	MARASMIC
MANOSCOPY	MANTLING	MAP	MARASMOID
MANPACK	MANTLINGS	MAPAU	MARASMUS
MANPACKS	MANTO	MAPLE	MARATHON
MANPOWER	MANTOES	MAPLELIKE	MARATHONS
MANPOWERS	MANTOS	MAPLES	MARAUD
MANQUE	MANTRA	MAPLESS	MARAUDED
MANRED	MANTRAM	MAPLIKE	MARAUDER
MANREDS	MANTRAMS	MAPMAKER	MARAUDERS
MANRENT	MANTRAP	MAPMAKERS	MARAUDING
MANRENTS	MANTRAPS	MAPMAKING	MARAUDS
MANRIDER	MANTRAS	MAPPABLE	MARAVEDI
MANRIDERS	MANTRIC	MAPPED	MARAVEDIS

MARBELISE
MARBELIZE
MARBLE
MARBLED
MARBLEISE
MARBLEIZE
MARBLER
MARBLERS
MARBLES
MARBLIER
MARBLIEST
MARBLING
MARBLINGS
MARBLY
MARC
MARCASITE
MARCATO
MARCATOS
MARCEL
MARCELLA
MARCELLAS
MARCELLED
MARCELLER
MARCELS
MARCH
MARCHED
MARCHEN
MARCHER
MARCHERS
MARCHES
MARCHESA
MARCHESAS
MARCHESE
MARCHESES
MARCHESI
MARCHING
MARCHLAND
MARCHLIKE
MARCHMAN
MARCHMEN
MARCHPANE
MARCONI
MARCONIED
MARCONIS
MARCS
MARD
MARDIED
MARDIER
MARDIES
MARDIEST
MARDY
MARDYING
MARE
MAREMMA
MAREMMAS
MAREMME
MARENGO
MARES

MARESCHAL
MARG
MARGARIC
MARGARIN
MARGARINE
MARGARINS
MARGARITA
MARGARITE
MARGAY
MARGAYS
MARGE
MARGENT
MARGENTED
MARGENTS
MARGES
MARGIN
MARGINAL
MARGINALS
MARGINATE
MARGINED
MARGINING
MARGINS
MARGOSA
MARGOSAS
MARGRAVE
MARGRAVES
MARGS
MARIA
MARIACHI
MARIACHIS
MARIALITE
MARID
MARIDS
MARIES
MARIGOLD
MARIGOLDS
MARIGRAM
MARIGRAMS
MARIGRAPH
MARIHUANA
MARIJUANA
MARIMBA
MARIMBAS
MARIMBIST
MARINA
MARINADE
MARINADED
MARINADES
MARINARA
MARINARAS
MARINAS
MARINATE
MARINATED
MARINATES
MARINE
MARINER
MARINERA
MARINERAS

MARINERS
MARINES
MARINIERE
MARIPOSA
MARIPOSAS
MARISCHAL
MARISH
MARISHES
MARITAGE
MARITAGES
MARITAL
MARITALLY
MARITIME
MARJORAM
MARJORAMS
MARK
MARKA
MARKAS
MARKDOWN
MARKDOWNS
MARKED
MARKEDLY
MARKER
MARKERS
MARKET
MARKETED
MARKETEER
MARKETER
MARKETERS
MARKETING
MARKETS
MARKHOOR
MARKHOORS
MARKHOR
MARKHORS
MARKING
MARKINGS
MARKKA
MARKKAA
MARKKAS
MARKMAN
MARKMEN
MARKS
MARKSMAN
MARKSMEN
MARKUP
MARKUPS
MARL
MARLE
MARLED
MARLES
MARLIER
MARLIEST
MARLIN
MARLINE
MARLINES
MARLING
MARLINGS

MARLINS
MARLITE
MARLITES
MARLITIC
MARLS
MARLSTONE
MARLY
MARM
MARMALADE
MARMALISE
MARMALIZE
MARMARISE
MARMARIZE
MARMELISE
MARMELIZE
MARMITE
MARMITES
MARMOREAL
MARMOREAN
MARMOSE
MARMOSES
MARMOSET
MARMOSETS
MARMOT
MARMOTS
MARMS
MAROCAIN
MAROCAINS
MARON
MARONS
MAROON
MAROONED
MAROONER
MAROONERS
MAROONING
MAROONS
MAROQUIN
MAROQUINS
MAROR
MARORS
MARPLOT
MARPLOTS
MARQUE
MARQUEE
MARQUEES
MARQUES
MARQUESS
MARQUETRY
MARQUIS
MARQUISE
MARQUISES
MARRAM
MARRAMS
MARRANO
MARRANOS
MARRED
MARRELS
MARRER

MARRERS	MARTED	MASA	MASING
MARRI	MARTEL	MASALA	MASJID
MARRIAGE	MARTELLED	MASALAS	MASJIDS
MARRIAGES	MARTELLO	MASAS	MASK
MARRIED	MARTELLOS	MASCARA	MASKABLE
MARRIEDS	MARTELS	MASCARAED	MASKED
MARRIER	MARTEN	MASCARAS	MASKEG
MARRIERS	MARTENS	MASCARON	MASKEGS
MARRIES	MARTEXT	MASCARONS	MASKER
MARRING	MARTEXTS	MASCLE	MASKERS
MARRIS	MARTIAL	MASCLED	MASKING
MARRON	MARTIALLY	MASCLES	MASKINGS
MARRONS	MARTIALS	MASCON	MASKLIKE
MARROW	MARTIAN	MASCONS	MASKS
MARROWED	MARTIANS	MASCOT	MASLIN
MARROWFAT	MARTIN	MASCOTS	MASLINS
MARROWING	MARTINET	MASCULINE	MASOCHISM
MARROWISH	MARTINETS	MASCULIST	MASOCHIST
MARROWS	MARTING	MASCULY	MASON
MARROWSKY	MARTINGAL	MASE	MASONED
MARROWY	MARTINI	MASED	MASONIC
MARRUM	MARTINIS	MASER	MASONING
MARRUMS	MARTINS	MASERS	MASONITE
MARRY	MARTLET	MASES	MASONITES
MARRYING	MARTLETS	MASH	MASONRIED
MARRYINGS	MARTS	MASHALLAH	MASONRIES
MARS	MARTYR	MASHED	MASONRY
MARSALA	MARTYRDOM	MASHER	MASONS
MARSALAS	MARTYRED	MASHERS	MASOOLAH
MARSE	MARTYRIA	MASHES	MASOOLAHS
MARSEILLE	MARTYRIES	MASHGIACH	MASQUE
MARSES	MARTYRING	MASHGIAH	MASQUER
MARSH	MARTYRISE	MASHGIHIM	MASQUERS
MARSHAL	MARTYRIUM	MASHIACH	MASQUES
MARSHALCY	MARTYRIZE	MASHIACHS	MASS
MARSHALED	MARTYRLY	MASHIE	MASSA
MARSHALER	MARTYRS	MASHIER	MASSACRE
MARSHALL	MARTYRY	MASHIES	MASSACRED
MARSHALLS	MARVEL	MASHIEST	MASSACRER
MARSHALS	MARVELED	MASHING	MASSACRES
MARSHBUCK	MARVELING	MASHINGS	MASSAGE
MARSHES	MARVELLED	MASHLAM	MASSAGED
MARSHIER	MARVELOUS	MASHLAMS	MASSAGER
MARSHIEST	MARVELS	MASHLIM	MASSAGERS
MARSHLAND	MARVER	MASHLIMS	MASSAGES
MARSHLIKE	MARVERED	MASHLIN	MASSAGING
MARSHWORT	MARVERING	MASHLINS	MASSAGIST
MARSHY	MARVERS	MASHLOCH	MASSAS
MARSPORT	MARVY	MASHLOCHS	MASSCULT
MARSPORTS	MARXISANT	MASHLUM	MASSCULTS
MARSQUAKE	MARY	MASHLUMS	MASSE
MARSUPIA	MARYBUD	MASHMAN	MASSED
MARSUPIAL	MARYBUDS	MASHMEN	MASSEDLY
MARSUPIAN	MARYJANE	MASHUA	MASSES
MARSUPIUM	MARYJANES	MASHUAS	MASSETER
MART	MARZIPAN	MASHUP	MASSETERS
MARTAGON	MARZIPANS	MASHUPS	MASSEUR
MARTAGONS	MAS	MASHY	MASSEURS

MASSEUSE
MASSEUSES
MASSICOT
MASSICOTS
MASSIER
MASSIEST
MASSIF
MASSIFS
MASSINESS
MASSING
MASSIVE
MASSIVELY
MASSIVES
MASSLESS
MASSOOLA
MASSOOLAS
MASSY
MASSYMORE
MAST
MASTABA
MASTABAH
MASTABAHS
MASTABAS
MASTED
MASTER
MASTERATE
MASTERDOM
MASTERED
MASTERFUL
MASTERIES
MASTERING
MASTERLY
MASTERS
MASTERY
MASTFUL
MASTHEAD
MASTHEADS
MASTHOUSE
MASTIC
MASTICATE
MASTICH
MASTICHE
MASTICHES
MASTICHS
MASTICOT
MASTICOTS
MASTICS
MASTIER
MASTIEST
MASTIFF
MASTIFFS
MASTING
MASTITIC
MASTITIS
MASTIX
MASTIXES
MASTLESS
MASTLIKE

MASTODON
MASTODONS
MASTODONT
MASTOID
MASTOIDAL
MASTOIDS
MASTOPEXY
MASTS
MASTY
MASU
MASULA
MASULAS
MASURIUM
MASURIUMS
MASUS
MAT
MATACHIN
MATACHINA
MATACHINI
MATADOR
MATADORA
MATADORAS
MATADORE
MATADORES
MATADORS
MATAGOURI
MATAI
MATAIS
MATAMATA
MATAMATAS
MATAMBALA
MATATA
MATCH
MATCHABLE
MATCHBOOK
MATCHBOX
MATCHED
MATCHER
MATCHERS
MATCHES
MATCHET
MATCHETS
MATCHING
MATCHLESS
MATCHLOCK
MATCHMADE
MATCHMAKE
MATCHMARK
MATCHPLAY
MATCHUP
MATCHUPS
MATCHWOOD
MATE
MATED
MATELASSE
MATELESS
MATELOT
MATELOTE

MATELOTES
MATELOTS
MATELOTTE
MATER
MATERIAL
MATERIALS
MATERIEL
MATERIELS
MATERNAL
MATERNITY
MATERS
MATES
MATESHIP
MATESHIPS
MATEY
MATEYNESS
MATEYS
MATFELON
MATFELONS
MATGRASS
MATH
MATHESES
MATHESIS
MATHS
MATICO
MATICOS
MATIER
MATIES
MATIEST
MATILDA
MATILDAS
MATILY
MATIN
MATINAL
MATINEE
MATINEES
MATINESS
MATING
MATINGS
MATINS
MATIPO
MATIPOS
MATJES
MATLESS
MATLO
MATLOS
MATLOW
MATLOWS
MATOKE
MATOKES
MATOOKE
MATOOKES
MATRASS
MATRASSES
MATRES
MATRIARCH
MATRIC
MATRICE

MATRICES
MATRICIDE
MATRICS
MATRICULA
MATRILINY
MATRIMONY
MATRIX
MATRIXES
MATRON
MATRONAGE
MATRONAL
MATRONISE
MATRONIZE
MATRONLY
MATRONS
MATROSS
MATROSSES
MATS
MATSAH
MATSAHS
MATSURI
MATSURIS
MATSUTAKE
MATT
MATTAMORE
MATTE
MATTED
MATTEDLY
MATTER
MATTERED
MATTERFUL
MATTERING
MATTERS
MATTERY
MATTES
MATTIE
MATTIES
MATTIFIED
MATTIFIES
MATTIFY
MATTIN
MATTING
MATTINGS
MATTINS
MATTOCK
MATTOCKS
MATTOID
MATTOIDS
MATTRASS
MATTRESS
MATTS
MATURABLE
MATURATE
MATURATED
MATURATES
MATURE
MATURED
MATURELY

MATURER	MAUNDING	MAWN	MAYAS
MATURERS	MAUNDS	MAWPUS	MAYBE
MATURES	MAUNDY	MAWPUSES	MAYBES
MATUREST	MAUNGIER	MAWR	MAYBIRD
MATURING	MAUNGIEST	MAWRS	MAYBIRDS
MATURITY	MAUNGY	MAWS	MAYBUSH
MATUTINAL	MAUNNA	MAWSEED	MAYBUSHES
MATUTINE	MAURI	MAWSEEDS	MAYDAY
MATWEED	MAURIS	MAWTHER	MAYDAYS
MATWEEDS	MAUSOLEA	MAWTHERS	MAYED
MATY	MAUSOLEAN	MAX	MAYEST
MATZA	MAUSOLEUM	MAXED	MAYFLIES
MATZAH	MAUT	MAXES	MAYFLOWER
MATZAHS	MAUTHER	MAXI	MAYFLY
MATZAS	MAUTHERS	MAXICOAT	MAYHAP
MATZO	MAUTS	MAXICOATS	MAYHAPPEN
MATZOH	MAUVAIS	MAXILLA	MAYHEM
MATZOHS	MAUVAISE	MAXILLAE	MAYHEMS
MATZOON	MAUVE	MAXILLAR	MAYING
MATZOONS	MAUVEIN	MAXILLARY	MAYINGS
MATZOS	MAUVEINE	MAXILLAS	MAYO
MATZOT	MAUVEINES	MAXILLULA	MAYOR
MATZOTH	MAUVEINS	MAXIM	MAYORAL
MAUBIES	MAUVER	MAXIMA	MAYORALTY
MAUBY	MAUVES	MAXIMAL	MAYORESS
MAUD	MAUVEST	MAXIMALLY	MAYORS
MAUDLIN	MAUVIN	MAXIMALS	MAYORSHIP
MAUDLINLY	MAUVINE	MAXIMIN	MAYOS
MAUDS	MAUVINES	MAXIMINS	MAYPOLE
MAUGER	MAUVINS	MAXIMISE	MAYPOLES
MAUGRE	MAVEN	MAXIMISED	MAYPOP
MAUGRED	MAVENS	MAXIMISER	MAYPOPS
MAUGRES	MAVERICK	MAXIMISES	MAYS
MAUGRING	MAVERICKS	MAXIMIST	MAYST
MAUL	MAVIE	MAXIMISTS	MAYSTER
MAULED	MAVIES	MAXIMITE	MAYSTERS
MAULER	MAVIN	MAXIMITES	MAYVIN
MAULERS	MAVINS	MAXIMIZE	MAYVINS
MAULGRE	MAVIS	MAXIMIZED	MAYWEED
MAULGRED	MAVISES	MAXIMIZER	MAYWEEDS
MAULGRES	MAVOURNIN	MAXIMIZES	MAZAEDIA
MAULGRING	MAW	MAXIMS	MAZAEDIUM
MAULING	MAWBOUND	MAXIMUM	MAZARD
MAULS	MAWED	MAXIMUMLY	MAZARDS
MAULSTICK	MAWGER	MAXIMUMS	MAZARINE
MAULVI	MAWING	MAXIMUS	MAZARINES
MAULVIS	MAWK	MAXIMUSES	MAZE
MAUMET	MAWKIER	MAXING	MAZED
MAUMETRY	MAWKIEST	MAXIS	MAZEDLY
MAUMETS	MAWKIN	MAXIXE	MAZEDNESS
MAUN	MAWKINS	MAXIXES	MAZEFUL
MAUND	MAWKISH	MAXWELL	MAZELIKE
MAUNDED	MAWKISHLY	MAXWELLS	MAZELTOV
MAUNDER	MAWKS	MAY	MAZEMENT
MAUNDERED	MAWKY	MAYA	MAZEMENTS
MAUNDERER	MAWMET	MAYAN	MAZER
MAUNDERS	MAWMETRY	MAYAPPLE	MAZERS
MAUNDIES	MAWMETS	MAYAPPLES	MAZES

MAZEY	MEALYBUGS	MEATHES	MEDALLIST
MAZHBI	MEAN	MEATHS	MEDALS
MAZHBIS	MEANDER	MEATIER	MEDCINAL
MAZIER	MEANDERED	MEATIEST	MEDDLE
MAZIEST	MEANDERER	MEATILY	MEDDLED
MAZILY	MEANDERS	MEATINESS	MEDDLER
MAZINESS	MEANDRIAN	MEATLESS	MEDDLERS
MAZING	MEANDROUS	MEATLOAF	MEDDLES
MAZOURKA	MEANE	MEATMAN	MEDDLING
MAZOURKAS	MEANED	MEATMEN	MEDDLINGS
MAZOUT	MEANER	MEATS	MEDEVAC
MAZOUTS	MEANERS	MEATSPACE	MEDEVACED
MAZUMA	MEANES	MEATUS	MEDEVACS
MAZUMAS	MEANEST	MEATUSES	MEDFLIES
MAZURKA	MEANIE	MEATY	MEDFLY
MAZURKAS	MEANIES	MEAWES	MEDIA
MAZUT	MEANING	MEAZEL	MEDIACIES
MAZUTS	MEANINGLY	MEAZELS	MEDIACY
MAZY	MEANINGS	MEBOS	MEDIAD
MAZZARD	MEANLY	MEBOSES	MEDIAE
MAZZARDS	MEANNESS	MECCA	MEDIAEVAL
MBAQANGA	MEANS	MECCAS	MEDIAL
MBAQANGAS	MEANT	MECHANIC	MEDIALLY
MBIRA	MEANTIME	MECHANICS	MEDIALS
MBIRAS	MEANTIMES	MECHANISE	MEDIAN
ME	MEANWHILE	MECHANISM	MEDIANLY
MEACOCK	MEANY	MECHANIST	MEDIANS
MEACOCKS	MEARE	MECHANIZE	MEDIANT
MEAD	MEARES	MECHITZA	MEDIANTS
MEADOW	MEARING	MECHITZAS	MEDIAS
MEADOWS	MEASE	MECHITZOT	MEDIATE
MEADOWY	MEASED	MECK	MEDIATED
MEADS	MEASES	MECKS	MEDIATELY
MEAGER	MEASING	MECLIZINE	MEDIATES
MEAGERLY	MEASLE	MECONATE	MEDIATING
MEAGRE	MEASLED	MECONATES	MEDIATION
MEAGRELY	MEASLES	MECONIC	MEDIATISE
MEAGRER	MEASLIER	MECONIN	MEDIATIVE
MEAGRES	MEASLIEST	MECONINS	MEDIATIZE
MEAGREST	MEASLING	MECONIUM	MEDIATOR
MEAL	MEASLY	MECONIUMS	MEDIATORS
MEALED	MEASURE	MED	MEDIATORY
MEALER	MEASURED	MEDACCA	MEDIATRIX
MEALERS	MEASURER	MEDACCAS	MEDIC
MEALIE	MEASURERS	MEDAILLON	MEDICABLE
MEALIER	MEASURES	MEDAKA	MEDICABLY
MEALIES	MEASURING	MEDAKAS	MEDICAID
MEALIEST	MEAT	MEDAL	MEDICAIDS
MEALINESS	MEATAL	MEDALED	MEDICAL
MEALING	MEATAXE	MEDALET	MEDICALLY
MEALLESS	MEATAXES	MEDALETS	MEDICALS
MEALS	MEATBALL	MEDALING	MEDICANT
MEALTIME	MEATBALLS	MEDALIST	MEDICANTS
MEALTIMES	MEATED	MEDALISTS	MEDICARE
MEALWORM	MEATH	MEDALLED	MEDICARES
MEALWORMS	MEATHE	MEDALLIC	MEDICATE
MEALY	MEATHEAD	MEDALLING	MEDICATED
MEALYBUG	MEATHEADS	MEDALLION	MEDICATES

MEDICIDE
MEDICIDES
MEDICINAL
MEDICINE
MEDICINED
MEDICINER
MEDICINES
MEDICK
MEDICKS
MEDICO
MEDICOS
MEDICS
MEDIEVAL
MEDIEVALS
MEDIGAP
MEDIGAPS
MEDII
MEDINA
MEDINAS
MEDIOCRE
MEDITATE
MEDITATED
MEDITATES
MEDITATOR
MEDIUM
MEDIUMS
MEDIUS
MEDIUSES
MEDIVAC
MEDIVACED
MEDIVACS
MEDLAR
MEDLARS
MEDLE
MEDLED
MEDLES
MEDLEY
MEDLEYS
MEDLING
MEDRESE
MEDRESES
MEDRESSEH
MEDS
MEDULLA
MEDULLAE
MEDULLAR
MEDULLARY
MEDULLAS
MEDULLATE
MEDUSA
MEDUSAE
MEDUSAL
MEDUSAN
MEDUSANS
MEDUSAS
MEDUSOID
MEDUSOIDS
MEE

MEED
MEEDS
MEEK
MEEKEN
MEEKENED
MEEKENING
MEEKENS
MEEKER
MEEKEST
MEEKLY
MEEKNESS
MEEMIE
MEEMIES
MEER
MEERCAT
MEERCATS
MEERED
MEERING
MEERKAT
MEERKATS
MEERS
MEES
MEET
MEETER
MEETERS
MEETEST
MEETING
MEETINGS
MEETLY
MEETNESS
MEETS
MEFF
MEFFS
MEG
MEGA
MEGABAR
MEGABARS
MEGABIT
MEGABITS
MEGABUCK
MEGABUCKS
MEGABYTE
MEGABYTES
MEGACITY
MEGACURIE
MEGACYCLE
MEGADEAL
MEGADEALS
MEGADEATH
MEGADOSE
MEGADOSES
MEGADYNE
MEGADYNES
MEGAFARAD
MEGAFAUNA
MEGAFLOP
MEGAFLOPS
MEGAFLORA

MEGAFOG
MEGAFOGS
MEGAGAUSS
MEGAHERTZ
MEGAHIT
MEGAHITS
MEGAJOULE
MEGALITH
MEGALITHS
MEGALITRE
MEGALOPIC
MEGALOPS
MEGAPHONE
MEGAPHYLL
MEGAPIXEL
MEGAPLEX
MEGAPOD
MEGAPODE
MEGAPODES
MEGAPODS
MEGARA
MEGARAD
MEGARADS
MEGARON
MEGARONS
MEGASCOPE
MEGASPORE
MEGASS
MEGASSE
MEGASSES
MEGASTAR
MEGASTARS
MEGASTORE
MEGATHERE
MEGATON
MEGATONIC
MEGATONS
MEGAVOLT
MEGAVOLTS
MEGAWATT
MEGAWATTS
MEGILLA
MEGILLAH
MEGILLAHS
MEGILLAS
MEGILLOTH
MEGILP
MEGILPH
MEGILPHS
MEGILPS
MEGOHM
MEGOHMS
MEGRIM
MEGRIMS
MEGS
MEHNDI
MEHNDIS
MEIBOMIAN

MEIKLE
MEIN
MEINED
MEINEY
MEINEYS
MEINIE
MEINIES
MEINING
MEINS
MEINT
MEINY
MEIOCYTE
MEIOCYTES
MEIOFAUNA
MEIONITE
MEIONITES
MEIOSES
MEIOSIS
MEIOSPORE
MEIOTIC
MEISHI
MEISHIS
MEISTER
MEISTERS
MEITH
MEITHS
MEJLIS
MEJLISES
MEKKA
MEKKAS
MEKOMETER
MEL
MELA
MELALEUCA
MELAMDIM
MELAMED
MELAMINE
MELAMINES
MELAMPODE
MELANGE
MELANGES
MELANIAN
MELANIC
MELANICS
MELANIN
MELANINS
MELANISE
MELANISED
MELANISES
MELANISM
MELANISMS
MELANIST
MELANISTS
MELANITE
MELANITES
MELANITIC
MELANIZE
MELANIZED

MELANIZES	MELLOWER	MELTITH	MENAGE
MELANO	MELLOWEST	MELTITHS	MENAGED
MELANOID	MELLOWING	MELTON	MENAGERIE
MELANOIDS	MELLOWLY	MELTONS	MENAGES
MELANOMA	MELLOWS	MELTS	MENAGING
MELANOMAS	MELLOWY	MELTWATER	MENARCHE
MELANOS	MELLS	MELTY	MENARCHES
MELANOSES	MELOCOTON	MELUNGEON	MENAZON
MELANOSIS	MELODEON	MEM	MENAZONS
MELANOTIC	MELODEONS	MEMBER	MEND
MELANOUS	MELODIA	MEMBERED	MENDABLE
MELANURIA	MELODIAS	MEMBERS	MENDACITY
MELANURIC	MELODIC	MEMBRAL	MENDED
MELAPHYRE	MELODICA	MEMBRANAL	MENDER
MELAS	MELODICAS	MEMBRANE	MENDERS
MELASTOME	MELODICS	MEMBRANED	MENDICANT
MELATONIN	MELODIES	MEMBRANES	MENDICITY
MELD	MELODION	MEME	MENDIGO
MELDED	MELODIONS	MEMENTO	MENDIGOS
MELDER	MELODIOUS	MEMENTOES	MENDING
MELDERS	MELODISE	MEMENTOS	MENDINGS
MELDING	MELODISED	MEMES	MENDS
MELDS	MELODISER	MEMETICS	MENE
MELEE	MELODISES	MEMO	MENED
MELEES	MELODIST	MEMOIR	MENEER
MELENA	MELODISTS	MEMOIRISM	MENEERS
MELENAS	MELODIZE	MEMOIRIST	MENES
MELIC	MELODIZED	MEMOIRS	MENFOLK
MELICK	MELODIZER	MEMORABLE	MENFOLKS
MELICKS	MELODIZES	MEMORABLY	MENG
MELICS	MELODRAMA	MEMORANDA	MENGE
MELIK	MELODRAME	MEMORIAL	MENGED
MELIKS	MELODY	MEMORIALS	MENGES
MELILITE	MELOID	MEMORIES	MENGING
MELILITES	MELOIDS	MEMORISE	MENGS
MELILOT	MELOMANIA	MEMORISED	MENHADEN
MELILOTS	MELOMANIC	MEMORISER	MENHADENS
MELINITE	MELON	MEMORISES	MENHIR
MELINITES	MELONGENE	MEMORITER	MENHIRS
MELIORATE	MELONS	MEMORIZE	MENIAL
MELIORISM	MELPHALAN	MEMORIZED	MENIALLY
MELIORIST	MELS	MEMORIZER	MENIALS
MELIORITY	MELT	MEMORIZES	MENILITE
MELISMA	MELTABLE	MEMORY	MENILITES
MELISMAS	MELTAGE	MEMOS	MENING
MELISMATA	MELTAGES	MEMS	MENINGEAL
MELL	MELTDOWN	MEMSAHIB	MENINGES
MELLAY	MELTDOWNS	MEMSAHIBS	MENINX
MELLAYS	MELTED	MEN	MENISCAL
MELLED	MELTEMI	MENACE	MENISCATE
MELLIFIC	MELTEMIS	MENACED	MENISCI
MELLING	MELTER	MENACER	MENISCOID
MELLITE	MELTERS	MENACERS	MENISCUS
MELLITES	MELTIER	MENACES	MENO
MELLITIC	MELTIEST	MENACING	MENOLOGY
MELLOTRON	MELTING	MENAD	MENOMINEE
MELLOW	MELTINGLY	MENADIONE	MENOMINI
MELLOWED	MELTINGS	MENADS	MENOMINIS

MENOPAUSE
MENOPOLIS
MENOPOME
MENOPOMES
MENORAH
MENORAHS
MENORRHEA
MENSA
MENSAE
MENSAL
MENSAS
MENSCH
MENSCHEN
MENSCHES
MENSCHY
MENSE
MENSED
MENSEFUL
MENSELESS
MENSES
MENSH
MENSHED
MENSHEN
MENSHES
MENSHING
MENSING
MENSTRUA
MENSTRUAL
MENSTRUUM
MENSUAL
MENSURAL
MENSWEAR
MENSWEARS
MENT
MENTA
MENTAL
MENTALESE
MENTALISM
MENTALIST
MENTALITY
MENTALLY
MENTATION
MENTEE
MENTEES
MENTHENE
MENTHENES
MENTHOL
MENTHOLS
MENTICIDE
MENTION
MENTIONED
MENTIONER
MENTIONS
MENTO
MENTOR
MENTORED
MENTORIAL
MENTORING

MENTORS
MENTOS
MENTUM
MENU
MENUDO
MENUDOS
MENUISIER
MENUS
MENYIE
MENYIES
MEOU
MEOUED
MEOUING
MEOUS
MEOW
MEOWED
MEOWING
MEOWS
MEPACRINE
MEPHITIC
MEPHITIS
MEPHITISM
MERANTI
MERANTIS
MERBROMIN
MERC
MERCAPTAN
MERCAPTO
MERCAT
MERCATS
MERCENARY
MERCER
MERCERIES
MERCERISE
MERCERIZE
MERCERS
MERCERY
MERCES
MERCH
MERCHANT
MERCHANTS
MERCHES
MERCHET
MERCHETS
MERCHILD
MERCIABLE
MERCIES
MERCIFIDE
MERCIFIED
MERCIFIES
MERCIFUL
MERCIFY
MERCILESS
MERCS
MERCURATE
MERCURIAL
MERCURIC
MERCURIES

MERCURISE
MERCURIZE
MERCUROUS
MERCURY
MERCY
MERDE
MERDES
MERE
MERED
MEREL
MERELL
MERELLS
MERELS
MERELY
MERENGUE
MERENGUES
MEREOLOGY
MERER
MERES
MERESMAN
MERESMEN
MEREST
MERESTONE
MERFOLK
MERFOLKS
MERGANSER
MERGE
MERGED
MERGEE
MERGEES
MERGENCE
MERGENCES
MERGER
MERGERS
MERGES
MERGING
MERGINGS
MERI
MERICARP
MERICARPS
MERIDIAN
MERIDIANS
MERIL
MERILS
MERIMAKE
MERIMAKES
MERING
MERINGS
MERINGUE
MERINGUES
MERINO
MERINOS
MERIS
MERISES
MERISIS
MERISM
MERISMS
MERISTEM

MERISTEMS
MERISTIC
MERIT
MERITED
MERITING
MERITLESS
MERITS
MERK
MERKIN
MERKINS
MERKS
MERL
MERLE
MERLES
MERLIN
MERLING
MERLINGS
MERLINS
MERLON
MERLONS
MERLOT
MERLOTS
MERLS
MERMAID
MERMAIDEN
MERMAIDS
MERMAN
MERMEN
MEROCRINE
MEROGONY
MEROISTIC
MEROME
MEROMES
MERONYM
MERONYMS
MERONYMY
MEROPIA
MEROPIAS
MEROPIC
MEROPIDAN
MEROSOME
MEROSOMES
MEROZOITE
MERPEOPLE
MERRIER
MERRIES
MERRIEST
MERRILY
MERRIMENT
MERRINESS
MERRY
MERRYMAN
MERRYMEN
MERSALYL
MERSALYLS
MERSE
MERSES
MERSION

MERSIONS
MERYCISM
MERYCISMS
MES
MESA
MESAIL
MESAILS
MESAL
MESALLY
MESARAIC
MESARCH
MESAS
MESCAL
MESCALIN
MESCALINE
MESCALINS
MESCALISM
MESCALS
MESCLUM
MESCLUMS
MESCLUN
MESCLUNS
MESDAMES
MESE
MESEEMED
MESEEMETH
MESEEMS
MESEL
MESELED
MESELS
MESENTERA
MESENTERY
MESES
MESETA
MESETAS
MESH
MESHED
MESHES
MESHIER
MESHIEST
MESHING
MESHINGS
MESHUGA
MESHUGAAS
MESHUGAH
MESHUGAS
MESHUGGA
MESHUGGAH
MESHUGGE
MESHWORK
MESHWORKS
MESHY
MESIAD
MESIAL
MESIALLY
MESIAN
MESIC
MESICALLY

MESMERIC
MESMERISE
MESMERISM
MESMERIST
MESMERIZE
MESNALTY
MESNE
MESNES
MESOBLAST
MESOCARP
MESOCARPS
MESOCRANY
MESODERM
MESODERMS
MESOGLEA
MESOGLEAL
MESOGLEAS
MESOGLOEA
MESOLITE
MESOLITES
MESOMERE
MESOMERES
MESOMORPH
MESON
MESONIC
MESONS
MESOPAUSE
MESOPHILE
MESOPHYL
MESOPHYLL
MESOPHYLS
MESOPHYTE
MESOSCALE
MESOSOME
MESOSOMES
MESOTRON
MESOTRONS
MESOZOAN
MESOZOANS
MESOZOIC
MESPRISE
MESPRISES
MESPRIZE
MESPRIZES
MESQUIN
MESQUINE
MESQUIT
MESQUITE
MESQUITES
MESQUITS
MESS
MESSAGE
MESSAGED
MESSAGES
MESSAGING
MESSALINE
MESSAN
MESSANS

MESSED
MESSENGER
MESSES
MESSIAH
MESSIAHS
MESSIANIC
MESSIAS
MESSIASES
MESSIER
MESSIEST
MESSIEURS
MESSILY
MESSINESS
MESSING
MESSMAN
MESSMATE
MESSMATES
MESSMEN
MESSUAGE
MESSUAGES
MESSY
MESTEE
MESTEES
MESTER
MESTERS
MESTESO
MESTESOES
MESTESOS
MESTINO
MESTINOES
MESTINOS
MESTIZA
MESTIZAS
MESTIZO
MESTIZOES
MESTIZOS
MESTO
MESTOM
MESTOME
MESTOMES
MESTOMS
MESTRANOL
MET
META
METABASES
METABASIS
METABATIC
METABOLIC
METABOLY
METACARPI
METAGE
METAGENIC
METAGES
METAIRIE
METAIRIES
METAL
METALED
METALHEAD

METALING
METALISE
METALISED
METALISES
METALIST
METALISTS
METALIZE
METALIZED
METALIZES
METALLED
METALLIC
METALLICS
METALLIKE
METALLINE
METALLING
METALLISE
METALLIST
METALLIZE
METALLOID
METALLY
METALMARK
METALS
METALWARE
METALWORK
METAMALE
METAMALES
METAMER
METAMERAL
METAMERE
METAMERES
METAMERIC
METAMERS
METAMICT
METANOIA
METANOIAS
METAPELET
METAPHASE
METAPHOR
METAPHORS
METAPLASM
METAPLOT
METARCHON
METASOMA
METASOMAS
METATAG
METATAGS
METATARSI
METATE
METATES
METAXYLEM
METAYAGE
METAYAGES
METAYER
METAYERS
METAZOA
METAZOAL
METAZOAN
METAZOANS

METAZOIC	METHYL	METRIFY	MEZUZA
METAZOON	METHYLAL	METRING	MEZUZAH
METCAST	METHYLALS	METRIST	MEZUZAHS
METCASTS	METHYLASE	METRISTS	MEZUZAS
METE	METHYLATE	METRITIS	MEZUZOT
METED	METHYLENE	METRO	MEZUZOTH
METEOR	METHYLIC	METROLOGY	MEZZ
METEORIC	METHYLS	METRONOME	MEZZALUNA
METEORISM	METHYSES	METROPLEX	MEZZANINE
METEORIST	METHYSIS	METROS	MEZZE
METEORITE	METHYSTIC	METS	MEZZES
METEOROID	METIC	METTLE	MEZZO
METEOROUS	METICAIS	METTLED	MEZZOS
METEORS	METICAL	METTLES	MEZZOTINT
METEPA	METICALS	METUMP	MGANGA
METEPAS	METICS	METUMPS	MGANGAS
METER	METIER	MEU	MHO
METERAGE	METIERS	MEUNIERE	MHORR
METERAGES	METIF	MEUS	MHORRS
METERED	METIFS	MEUSE	MHOS
METERING	METING	MEUSED	MI
METERS	METIS	MEUSES	MIAOU
METES	METISSE	MEUSING	MIAOUED
METESTICK	METISSES	MEVE	MIAOUING
METESTRUS	METOL	MEVED	MIAOUS
METEWAND	METOLS	MEVES	MIAOW
METEWANDS	METONYM	MEVING	MIAOWED
METEYARD	METONYMIC	MEVROU	MIAOWING
METEYARDS	METONYMS	MEVROUS	MIAOWS
METFORMIN	METONYMY	MEW	MIASM
METH	METOPAE	MEWED	MIASMA
METHADON	METOPE	MEWING	MIASMAL
METHADONE	METOPES	MEWL	MIASMAS
METHADONS	METOPIC	MEWLED	MIASMATA
METHANAL	METOPISM	MEWLER	MIASMATIC
METHANALS	METOPISMS	MEWLERS	MIASMIC
METHANE	METOPON	MEWLING	MIASMOUS
METHANES	METOPONS	MEWLS	MIASMS
METHANOIC	METOPRYL	MEWS	MIAUL
METHANOL	METOPRYLS	MEWSED	MIAULED
METHANOLS	METRALGIA	MEWSES	MIAULING
METHEGLIN	METRAZOL	MEWSING	MIAULS
METHINK	METRAZOLS	MEYNT	MIB
METHINKS	METRE	MEZAIL	MIBS
METHO	METRED	MEZAILS	MIC
METHOD	METRES	MEZCAL	MICA
METHODIC	METRIC	MEZCALINE	MICACEOUS
METHODISE	METRICAL	MEZCALS	MICAS
METHODISM	METRICATE	MEZE	MICATE
METHODIST	METRICIAN	MEZEREON	MICATED
METHODIZE	METRICISE	MEZEREONS	MICATES
METHODS	METRICISM	MEZEREUM	MICATING
METHOS	METRICIST	MEZEREUMS	MICAWBER
METHOUGHT	METRICIZE	MEZES	MICAWBERS
METHOXIDE	METRICS	MEZQUIT	MICE
METHOXY	METRIFIED	MEZQUITE	MICELL
METHOXYL	METRIFIER	MEZQUITES	MICELLA
METHS	METRIFIES	MEZQUITS	MICELLAE

MICELLAR	MICROFILM	MIDDIES	MIDRASHOT
MICELLAS	MICROFORM	MIDDLE	MIDRIB
MICELLE	MICROGLIA	MIDDLED	MIDRIBS
MICELLES	MICROGRAM	MIDDLEMAN	MIDRIFF
MICELLS	MICROHM	MIDDLEMEN	MIDRIFFS
MICH	MICROHMS	MIDDLER	MIDS
MICHE	MICROINCH	MIDDLERS	MIDSHIP
MICHED	MICROJET	MIDDLES	MIDSHIPS
MICHER	MICROJETS	MIDDLING	MIDSIZE
MICHERS	MICROLITE	MIDDLINGS	MIDSIZED
MICHES	MICROLITH	MIDDORSAL	MIDSOLE
MICHIGAN	MICROLOAN	MIDDY	MIDSOLES
MICHIGANS	MICROLOGY	MIDFIELD	MIDSPACE
MICHING	MICROLUX	MIDFIELDS	MIDSPACES
MICHINGS	MICROMERE	MIDGE	MIDST
MICHT	MICROMESH	MIDGES	MIDSTORY
MICHTS	MICROMHO	MIDGET	MIDSTREAM
MICK	MICROMHOS	MIDGETS	MIDSTS
MICKEY	MICROMINI	MIDGIE	MIDSUMMER
MICKEYED	MICROMOLE	MIDGIER	MIDTERM
MICKEYING	MICRON	MIDGIES	MIDTERMS
MICKEYS	MICRONISE	MIDGIEST	MIDTOWN
MICKIES	MICRONIZE	MIDGUT	MIDTOWNS
MICKLE	MICRONS	MIDGUTS	MIDWATCH
MICKLER	MICROPORE	MIDGY	MIDWAY
MICKLES	MICROPSIA	MIDI	MIDWAYS
MICKLEST	MICROPUMP	MIDINETTE	MIDWEEK
MICKS	MICROPYLE	MIDIRON	MIDWEEKLY
MICKY	MICROS	MIDIRONS	MIDWEEKS
MICO	MICROSITE	MIDIS	MIDWIFE
MICOS	MICROSOME	MIDISKIRT	MIDWIFED
MICRA	MICROTOME	MIDLAND	MIDWIFERY
MICRIFIED	MICROTOMY	MIDLANDS	MIDWIFES
MICRIFIES	MICROTONE	MIDLEG	MIDWIFING
MICRIFY	MICROVOLT	MIDLEGS	MIDWINTER
MICRO	MICROWATT	MIDLIFE	MIDWIVE
MICROBAR	MICROWAVE	MIDLIFER	MIDWIVED
MICROBARS	MICROWIRE	MIDLIFERS	MIDWIVES
MICROBE	MICRURGY	MIDLINE	MIDWIVING
MICROBEAM	MICS	MIDLINES	MIDYEAR
MICROBES	MICTION	MIDLIST	MIDYEARS
MICROBIAL	MICTIONS	MIDLISTS	MIELIE
MICROBIAN	MICTURATE	MIDLIVES	MIELIES
MICROBIC	MID	MIDMONTH	MIEN
MICROBREW	MIDAIR	MIDMONTHS	MIENS
MICROBUS	MIDAIRS	MIDMOST	MIEVE
MICROCAP	MIDBRAIN	MIDMOSTS	MIEVED
MICROCAR	MIDBRAINS	MIDNIGHT	MIEVES
MICROCARD	MIDCAP	MIDNIGHTS	MIEVING
MICROCARS	MIDCOURSE	MIDNOON	MIFF
MICROCHIP	MIDCULT	MIDNOONS	MIFFED
MICROCODE	MIDCULTS	MIDPOINT	MIFFIER
MICROCOPY	MIDDAY	MIDPOINTS	MIFFIEST
MICROCOSM	MIDDAYS	MIDRANGE	MIFFILY
MICROCYTE	MIDDEN	MIDRANGES	MIFFINESS
MICRODONT	MIDDENS	MIDRASH	MIFFING
MICRODOT	MIDDEST	MIDRASHIC	MIFFS
MICRODOTS	MIDDIE	MIDRASHIM	MIFFY

MIFTY	MIL	MILITATES	MILLERS
MIG	MILADI	MILITIA	MILLES
MIGG	MILADIES	MILITIAS	MILLET
MIGGLE	MILADIS	MILIUM	MILLETS
MIGGLES	MILADY	MILK	MILLHOUSE
MIGGS	MILAGE	MILKED	MILLIARD
MIGHT	MILAGES	MILKEN	MILLIARDS
MIGHTEST	MILCH	MILKER	MILLIARE
MIGHTFUL	MILCHIG	MILKERS	MILLIARES
MIGHTIER	MILCHIK	MILKFISH	MILLIARY
MIGHTIEST	MILD	MILKIER	MILLIBAR
MIGHTILY	MILDED	MILKIEST	MILLIBARS
MIGHTS	MILDEN	MILKILY	MILLIE
MIGHTST	MILDENED	MILKINESS	MILLIEME
MIGHTY	MILDENING	MILKING	MILLIEMES
MIGMATITE	MILDENS	MILKINGS	MILLIER
MIGNON	MILDER	MILKLESS	MILLIERS
MIGNONNE	MILDEST	MILKLIKE	MILLIES
MIGNONNES	MILDEW	MILKMAID	MILLIGAL
MIGNONS	MILDEWED	MILKMAIDS	MILLIGALS
MIGRAINE	MILDEWING	MILKMAN	MILLIGRAM
MIGRAINES	MILDEWS	MILKMEN	MILLILUX
MIGRANT	MILDEWY	MILKO	MILLIME
MIGRANTS	MILDING	MILKOS	MILLIMES
MIGRATE	MILDLY	MILKS	MILLIMHO
MIGRATED	MILDNESS	MILKSHAKE	MILLIMHOS
MIGRATES	MILDS	MILKSHED	MILLIMOLE
MIGRATING	MILE	MILKSHEDS	MILLINE
MIGRATION	MILEAGE	MILKSOP	MILLINER
MIGRATOR	MILEAGES	MILKSOPPY	MILLINERS
MIGRATORS	MILEPOST	MILKSOPS	MILLINERY
MIGRATORY	MILEPOSTS	MILKTOAST	MILLINES
MIGS	MILER	MILKWEED	MILLING
MIHA	MILERS	MILKWEEDS	MILLINGS
MIHI	MILES	MILKWOOD	MILLIOHM
MIHIED	MILESIAN	MILKWOODS	MILLIOHMS
MIHIING	MILESIMO	MILKWORT	MILLION
MIHIS	MILESIMOS	MILKWORTS	MILLIONS
MIHRAB	MILESTONE	MILKY	MILLIONTH
MIHRABS	MILFOIL	MILL	MILLIPED
MIJNHEER	MILFOILS	MILLABLE	MILLIPEDE
MIJNHEERS	MILIA	MILLAGE	MILLIPEDS
MIKADO	MILIARIA	MILLAGES	MILLIREM
MIKADOS	MILIARIAL	MILLBOARD	MILLIREMS
MIKE	MILIARIAS	MILLCAKE	MILLIVOLT
MIKED	MILIARY	MILLCAKES	MILLIWATT
MIKES	MILIEU	MILLDAM	MILLOCRAT
MIKING	MILIEUS	MILLDAMS	MILLPOND
MIKRA	MILIEUX	MILLE	MILLPONDS
MIKRON	MILITANCE	MILLED	MILLRACE
MIKRONS	MILITANCY	MILLENARY	MILLRACES
MIKVAH	MILITANT	MILLENNIA	MILLRIND
MIKVAHS	MILITANTS	MILLEPED	MILLRINDS
MIKVEH	MILITAR	MILLEPEDE	MILLRUN
MIKVEHS	MILITARIA	MILLEPEDS	MILLRUNS
MIKVOS	MILITARY	MILLEPORE	MILLS
MIKVOT	MILITATE	MILLER	MILLSCALE
MIKVOTH	MILITATED	MILLERITE	MILLSTONE

MILLTAIL
MILLTAILS
MILLWHEEL
MILLWORK
MILLWORKS
MILNEB
MILNEBS
MILO
MILOMETER
MILOR
MILORD
MILORDS
MILORS
MILOS
MILPA
MILPAS
MILREIS
MILS
MILSEY
MILSEYS
MILT
MILTED
MILTER
MILTERS
MILTIER
MILTIEST
MILTING
MILTONIA
MILTONIAS
MILTS
MILTY
MILTZ
MILTZES
MILVINE
MIM
MIMBAR
MIMBARS
MIME
MIMED
MIMEO
MIMEOED
MIMEOING
MIMEOS
MIMER
MIMERS
MIMES
MIMESES
MIMESIS
MIMESISES
MIMESTER
MIMESTERS
MIMETIC
MIMETICAL
MIMETITE
MIMETITES
MIMIC
MIMICAL
MIMICKED

MIMICKER
MIMICKERS
MIMICKING
MIMICRIES
MIMICRY
MIMICS
MIMING
MIMMER
MIMMEST
MIMMICK
MIMMICKED
MIMMICKS
MIMOSA
MIMOSAS
MIMSEY
MIMSIER
MIMSIEST
MIMSY
MIMULUS
MIMULUSES
MINA
MINABLE
MINACIOUS
MINACITY
MINAE
MINAR
MINARET
MINARETED
MINARETS
MINARS
MINAS
MINATORY
MINBAR
MINBARS
MINCE
MINCED
MINCEMEAT
MINCER
MINCERS
MINCES
MINCEUR
MINCIER
MINCIEST
MINCING
MINCINGLY
MINCINGS
MINCY
MIND
MINDED
MINDER
MINDERS
MINDFUCK
MINDFUCKS
MINDFUL
MINDFULLY
MINDING
MINDINGS
MINDLESS

MINDS
MINDSET
MINDSETS
MINDSHARE
MINE
MINEABLE
MINED
MINEFIELD
MINELAYER
MINEOLA
MINEOLAS
MINER
MINERAL
MINERALS
MINERS
MINES
MINESHAFT
MINESTONE
MINETTE
MINETTES
MINEVER
MINEVERS
MING
MINGE
MINGED
MINGER
MINGERS
MINGES
MINGIER
MINGIEST
MINGIN
MINGINESS
MINGING
MINGLE
MINGLED
MINGLER
MINGLERS
MINGLES
MINGLING
MINGLINGS
MINGS
MINGY
MINI
MINIATE
MINIATED
MINIATES
MINIATING
MINIATION
MINIATURE
MINIBAR
MINIBARS
MINIBIKE
MINIBIKER
MINIBIKES
MINIBREAK
MINIBUS
MINIBUSES
MINICAB

MINICABS
MINICAM
MINICAMP
MINICAMPS
MINICAMS
MINICAR
MINICARS
MINICOM
MINICOMS
MINIDISC
MINIDISCS
MINIDISH
MINIDISK
MINIDISKS
MINIDRESS
MINIER
MINIEST
MINIFIED
MINIFIES
MINIFY
MINIFYING
MINIKIN
MINIKINS
MINILAB
MINILABS
MINIM
MINIMA
MINIMAL
MINIMALLY
MINIMALS
MINIMAX
MINIMAXED
MINIMAXES
MINIMENT
MINIMENTS
MINIMILL
MINIMILLS
MINIMISE
MINIMISED
MINIMISER
MINIMISES
MINIMISM
MINIMISMS
MINIMIST
MINIMISTS
MINIMIZE
MINIMIZED
MINIMIZER
MINIMIZES
MINIMOTO
MINIMOTOS
MINIMS
MINIMUM
MINIMUMS
MINIMUS
MINIMUSES
MINING
MININGS

MINION	MINSHUKU	MIRABLE	MIRVING
MINIONS	MINSHUKUS	MIRACIDIA	MIRVS
MINIPARK	MINSTER	MIRACLE	MIRY
MINIPARKS	MINSTERS	MIRACLES	MIRZA
MINIPILL	MINSTREL	MIRADOR	MIRZAS
MINIPILLS	MINSTRELS	MIRADORS	MIS
MINIRUGBY	MINT	MIRAGE	MISACT
MINIS	MINTAGE	MIRAGES	MISACTED
MINISCULE	MINTAGES	MIRANDISE	MISACTING
MINISH	MINTED	MIRANDIZE	MISACTS
MINISHED	MINTER	MIRBANE	MISADAPT
MINISHES	MINTERS	MIRBANES	MISADAPTS
MINISHING	MINTIER	MIRCHI	MISADD
MINISKI	MINTIEST	MIRE	MISADDED
MINISKIRT	MINTING	MIRED	MISADDING
MINISKIS	MINTS	MIREPOIX	MISADDS
MINISTATE	MINTY	MIRES	MISADJUST
MINISTER	MINUEND	MIREX	MISADVICE
MINISTERS	MINUENDS	MIREXES	MISADVISE
MINISTRY	MINUET	MIRI	MISAGENT
MINITOWER	MINUETS	MIRIER	MISAGENTS
MINITRACK	MINUS	MIRIEST	MISAIM
MINIUM	MINUSCULE	MIRIFIC	MISAIMED
MINIUMS	MINUSES	MIRIFICAL	MISAIMING
MINIVAN	MINUTE	MIRIN	MISAIMS
MINIVANS	MINUTED	MIRINESS	MISALIGN
MINIVER	MINUTELY	MIRING	MISALIGNS
MINIVERS	MINUTEMAN	MIRINS	MISALLEGE
MINIVET	MINUTEMEN	MIRITI	MISALLIED
MINIVETS	MINUTER	MIRITIS	MISALLIES
MINK	MINUTES	MIRK	MISALLOT
MINKE	MINUTEST	MIRKER	MISALLOTS
MINKES	MINUTIA	MIRKEST	MISALLY
MINKS	MINUTIAE	MIRKIER	MISALTER
MINNEOLA	MINUTIAL	MIRKIEST	MISALTERS
MINNEOLAS	MINUTING	MIRKILY	MISANDRY
MINNICK	MINUTIOSE	MIRKINESS	MISAPPLY
MINNICKED	MINX	MIRKS	MISARRAY
MINNICKS	MINXES	MIRKY	MISARRAYS
MINNIE	MINXISH	MIRLIER	MISASSAY
MINNIES	MINY	MIRLIEST	MISASSAYS
MINNOCK	MINYAN	MIRLIGOES	MISASSIGN
MINNOCKED	MINYANIM	MIRLITON	MISATE
MINNOCKS	MINYANS	MIRLITONS	MISATONE
MINNOW	MIOCENE	MIRLY	MISATONED
MINNOWS	MIOMBO	MIRO	MISATONES
MINNY	MIOMBOS	MIROMIRO	MISAUNTER
MINO	MIOSES	MIRROR	MISAVER
MINOR	MIOSIS	MIRRORED	MISAVERS
MINORCA	MIOTIC	MIRRORING	MISAVISED
MINORCAS	MIOTICS	MIRRORS	MISAWARD
MINORED	MIPS	MIRS	MISAWARDS
MINORING	MIQUELET	MIRTH	MISBECAME
MINORITY	MIQUELETS	MIRTHFUL	MISBECOME
MINORS	MIR	MIRTHLESS	MISBEGAN
MINORSHIP	MIRABELLE	MIRTHS	MISBEGIN
MINOS	MIRABILIA	MIRV	MISBEGINS
MINOXIDIL	MIRABILIS	MIRVED	MISBEGOT

MISBEGUN	MISCOINS	MISDOUBT	MISFEEDS
MISBEHAVE	MISCOLOR	MISDOUBTS	MISFEIGN
MISBELIEF	MISCOLORS	MISDRAW	MISFEIGNS
MISBESEEM	MISCOLOUR	MISDRAWN	MISFELL
MISBESTOW	MISCOOK	MISDRAWS	MISFIELD
MISBIAS	MISCOOKED	MISDREAD	MISFIELDS
MISBIASED	MISCOOKS	MISDREADS	MISFILE
MISBIASES	MISCOPIED	MISDREW	MISFILED
MISBILL	MISCOPIES	MISDRIVE	MISFILES
MISBILLED	MISCOPY	MISDRIVEN	MISFILING
MISBILLS	MISCOUNT	MISDRIVES	MISFIRE
MISBIND	MISCOUNTS	MISDROVE	MISFIRED
MISBINDS	MISCREANT	MISE	MISFIRES
MISBIRTH	MISCREATE	MISEASE	MISFIRING
MISBIRTHS	MISCREDIT	MISEASES	MISFIT
MISBORN	MISCREED	MISEAT	MISFITS
MISBOUND	MISCREEDS	MISEATEN	MISFITTED
MISBRAND	MISCUE	MISEATING	MISFOCUS
MISBRANDS	MISCUED	MISEATS	MISFORM
MISBUILD	MISCUEING	MISEDIT	MISFORMED
MISBUILDS	MISCUES	MISEDITED	MISFORMS
MISBUILT	MISCUING	MISEDITS	MISFRAME
MISBUTTON	MISCUT	MISEMPLOY	MISFRAMED
MISCALL	MISCUTS	MISENROL	MISFRAMES
MISCALLED	MISDATE	MISENROLL	MISGAUGE
MISCALLER	MISDATED	MISENROLS	MISGAUGED
MISCALLS	MISDATES	MISENTER	MISGAUGES
MISCARRY	MISDATING	MISENTERS	MISGAVE
MISCAST	MISDEAL	MISENTRY	MISGIVE
MISCASTS	MISDEALER	MISER	MISGIVEN
MISCEGEN	MISDEALS	MISERABLE	MISGIVES
MISCEGENE	MISDEALT	MISERABLY	MISGIVING
MISCEGENS	MISDEED	MISERE	MISGO
MISCEGINE	MISDEEDS	MISERERE	MISGOES
MISCH	MISDEEM	MISERERES	MISGOING
MISCHANCE	MISDEEMED	MISERES	MISGONE
MISCHANCY	MISDEEMS	MISERIES	MISGOTTEN
MISCHARGE	MISDEFINE	MISERLIER	MISGOVERN
MISCHIEF	MISDEMEAN	MISERLY	MISGRADE
MISCHIEFS	MISDEMPT	MISERS	MISGRADED
MISCHOICE	MISDESERT	MISERY	MISGRADES
MISCHOOSE	MISDIAL	MISES	MISGRAFF
MISCHOSE	MISDIALED	MISESTEEM	MISGRAFT
MISCHOSEN	MISDIALS	MISEVENT	MISGRAFTS
MISCIBLE	MISDID	MISEVENTS	MISGREW
MISCITE	MISDIET	MISFAITH	MISGROW
MISCITED	MISDIETS	MISFAITHS	MISGROWN
MISCITES	MISDIGHT	MISFALL	MISGROWS
MISCITING	MISDIRECT	MISFALLEN	MISGROWTH
MISCLAIM	MISDIVIDE	MISFALLS	MISGUESS
MISCLAIMS	MISDO	MISFALNE	MISGUGGLE
MISCLASS	MISDOER	MISFARE	MISGUIDE
MISCODE	MISDOERS	MISFARED	MISGUIDED
MISCODED	MISDOES	MISFARES	MISGUIDER
MISCODES	MISDOING	MISFARING	MISGUIDES
MISCODING	MISDOINGS	MISFEASOR	MISHANDLE
MISCOIN	MISDONE	MISFED	MISHANTER
MISCOINED	MISDONNE	MISFEED	MISHAP

MISHAPPED
MISHAPPEN
MISHAPS
MISHAPT
MISHEAR
MISHEARD
MISHEARS
MISHEGAAS
MISHEGOSS
MISHIT
MISHITS
MISHMASH
MISHMEE
MISHMEES
MISHMI
MISHMIS
MISHMOSH
MISINFER
MISINFERS
MISINFORM
MISINTEND
MISINTER
MISINTERS
MISJOIN
MISJOINED
MISJOINS
MISJUDGE
MISJUDGED
MISJUDGER
MISJUDGES
MISKAL
MISKALS
MISKEEP
MISKEEPS
MISKEN
MISKENNED
MISKENS
MISKENT
MISKEPT
MISKEY
MISKEYED
MISKEYING
MISKEYS
MISKICK
MISKICKED
MISKICKS
MISKNEW
MISKNOW
MISKNOWN
MISKNOWS
MISLABEL
MISLABELS
MISLABOR
MISLABORS
MISLAID
MISLAIN
MISLAY
MISLAYER

MISLAYERS
MISLAYING
MISLAYS
MISLEAD
MISLEADER
MISLEADS
MISLEARED
MISLEARN
MISLEARNS
MISLEARNT
MISLED
MISLEEKE
MISLEEKED
MISLEEKES
MISLETOE
MISLETOES
MISLIE
MISLIES
MISLIGHT
MISLIGHTS
MISLIKE
MISLIKED
MISLIKER
MISLIKERS
MISLIKES
MISLIKING
MISLIPPEN
MISLIT
MISLIVE
MISLIVED
MISLIVES
MISLIVING
MISLOCATE
MISLODGE
MISLODGED
MISLODGES
MISLUCK
MISLUCKED
MISLUCKS
MISLYING
MISMADE
MISMAKE
MISMAKES
MISMAKING
MISMANAGE
MISMARK
MISMARKED
MISMARKS
MISMARRY
MISMATCH
MISMATE
MISMATED
MISMATES
MISMATING
MISMEET
MISMEETS
MISMET
MISMETRE

MISMETRED
MISMETRES
MISMOVE
MISMOVED
MISMOVES
MISMOVING
MISNAME
MISNAMED
MISNAMES
MISNAMING
MISNOMER
MISNOMERS
MISNUMBER
MISO
MISOCLERE
MISOGAMIC
MISOGAMY
MISOGYNIC
MISOGYNY
MISOLOGY
MISONEISM
MISONEIST
MISORDER
MISORDERS
MISORIENT
MISOS
MISPAGE
MISPAGED
MISPAGES
MISPAGING
MISPAINT
MISPAINTS
MISPARSE
MISPARSED
MISPARSES
MISPART
MISPARTED
MISPARTS
MISPATCH
MISPEN
MISPENNED
MISPENS
MISPHRASE
MISPICKEL
MISPLACE
MISPLACED
MISPLACES
MISPLAN
MISPLANS
MISPLANT
MISPLANTS
MISPLAY
MISPLAYED
MISPLAYS
MISPLEAD
MISPLEADS
MISPLEASE
MISPLED

MISPOINT
MISPOINTS
MISPOISE
MISPOISED
MISPOISES
MISPRAISE
MISPRICE
MISPRICED
MISPRICES
MISPRINT
MISPRINTS
MISPRISE
MISPRISED
MISPRISES
MISPRIZE
MISPRIZED
MISPRIZER
MISPRIZES
MISPROUD
MISQUOTE
MISQUOTED
MISQUOTER
MISQUOTES
MISRAISE
MISRAISED
MISRAISES
MISRATE
MISRATED
MISRATES
MISRATING
MISREAD
MISREADS
MISRECKON
MISRECORD
MISREFER
MISREFERS
MISREGARD
MISRELATE
MISRELIED
MISRELIES
MISRELY
MISRENDER
MISREPORT
MISRHYMED
MISROUTE
MISROUTED
MISROUTES
MISRULE
MISRULED
MISRULES
MISRULING
MISS
MISSA
MISSABLE
MISSAE
MISSAID
MISSAL
MISSALS

MISSAW	MISSOUT	MISTENDS	MISTRYST
MISSAY	MISSOUTS	MISTER	MISTRYSTS
MISSAYING	MISSPACE	MISTERED	MISTS
MISSAYS	MISSPACED	MISTERIES	MISTUNE
MISSEAT	MISSPACES	MISTERING	MISTUNED
MISSEATED	MISSPEAK	MISTERM	MISTUNES
MISSEATS	MISSPEAKS	MISTERMED	MISTUNING
MISSED	MISSPELL	MISTERMS	MISTUTOR
MISSEE	MISSPELLS	MISTERS	MISTUTORS
MISSEEING	MISSPELT	MISTERY	MISTY
MISSEEM	MISSPEND	MISTEUK	MISTYPE
MISSEEMED	MISSPENDS	MISTFUL	MISTYPED
MISSEEMS	MISSPENT	MISTHINK	MISTYPES
MISSEEN	MISSPOKE	MISTHINKS	MISTYPING
MISSEES	MISSPOKEN	MISTHREW	MISUNION
MISSEL	MISSTAMP	MISTHROW	MISUNIONS
MISSELS	MISSTAMPS	MISTHROWN	MISUSAGE
MISSEND	MISSTART	MISTHROWS	MISUSAGES
MISSENDS	MISSTARTS	MISTICO	MISUSE
MISSENSE	MISSTATE	MISTICOS	MISUSED
MISSENSES	MISSTATED	MISTIER	MISUSER
MISSENT	MISSTATES	MISTIEST	MISUSERS
MISSES	MISSTEER	MISTIGRIS	MISUSES
MISSET	MISSTEERS	MISTILY	MISUSING
MISSETS	MISSTEP	MISTIME	MISUST
MISSHAPE	MISSTEPS	MISTIMED	MISVALUE
MISSHAPED	MISSTOP	MISTIMES	MISVALUED
MISSHAPEN	MISSTOPS	MISTIMING	MISVALUES
MISSHAPER	MISSTRIKE	MISTINESS	MISWEEN
MISSHAPES	MISSTRUCK	MISTING	MISWEENED
MISSHOD	MISSTYLE	MISTINGS	MISWEENS
MISSHOOD	MISSTYLED	MISTITLE	MISWEND
MISSHOODS	MISSTYLES	MISTITLED	MISWENDS
MISSIER	MISSUIT	MISTITLES	MISWENT
MISSIES	MISSUITED	MISTLE	MISWORD
MISSIEST	MISSUITS	MISTLED	MISWORDED
MISSILE	MISSUS	MISTLES	MISWORDS
MISSILEER	MISSUSES	MISTLETOE	MISWRIT
MISSILERY	MISSY	MISTLING	MISWRITE
MISSILES	MIST	MISTOLD	MISWRITES
MISSILRY	MISTAKE	MISTOOK	MISWROTE
MISSING	MISTAKEN	MISTOUCH	MISYOKE
MISSINGLY	MISTAKER	MISTRACE	MISYOKED
MISSION	MISTAKERS	MISTRACED	MISYOKES
MISSIONAL	MISTAKES	MISTRACES	MISYOKING
MISSIONED	MISTAKING	MISTRAIN	MITCH
MISSIONER	MISTAL	MISTRAINS	MITCHED
MISSIONS	MISTALS	MISTRAL	MITCHES
MISSIS	MISTAUGHT	MISTRALS	MITCHING
MISSISES	MISTBOW	MISTREAT	MITE
MISSISH	MISTBOWS	MISTREATS	MITER
MISSIVE	MISTEACH	MISTRESS	MITERED
MISSIVES	MISTED	MISTRIAL	MITERER
MISSORT	MISTELL	MISTRIALS	MITERERS
MISSORTED	MISTELLS	MISTRUST	MITERING
MISSORTS	MISTEMPER	MISTRUSTS	MITERS
MISSOUND	MISTEND	MISTRUTH	MITERWORT
MISSOUNDS	MISTENDED	MISTRUTHS	MITES

MITHER
MITHERED
MITHERING
MITHERS
MITICIDAL
MITICIDE
MITICIDES
MITIER
MITIEST
MITIGABLE
MITIGANT
MITIGATE
MITIGATED
MITIGATES
MITIGATOR
MITIS
MITISES
MITOGEN
MITOGENIC
MITOGENS
MITOMYCIN
MITOSES
MITOSIS
MITOTIC
MITRAILLE
MITRAL
MITRE
MITRED
MITRES
MITREWORT
MITRIFORM
MITRING
MITSVAH
MITSVAHS
MITSVOTH
MITT
MITTEN
MITTENED
MITTENS
MITTIMUS
MITTS
MITUMBA
MITUMBAS
MITY
MITZVAH
MITZVAHS
MITZVOTH
MIURUS
MIURUSES
MIX
MIXABLE
MIXDOWN
MIXDOWNS
MIXED
MIXEDLY
MIXEDNESS
MIXEN
MIXENS

MIXER
MIXERS
MIXES
MIXIBLE
MIXIER
MIXIEST
MIXING
MIXMASTER
MIXOLOGY
MIXT
MIXTE
MIXTION
MIXTIONS
MIXTURE
MIXTURES
MIXUP
MIXUPS
MIXY
MIZ
MIZEN
MIZENMAST
MIZENS
MIZMAZE
MIZMAZES
MIZUNA
MIZUNAS
MIZZ
MIZZEN
MIZZENS
MIZZES
MIZZLE
MIZZLED
MIZZLES
MIZZLIER
MIZZLIEST
MIZZLING
MIZZLINGS
MIZZLY
MIZZONITE
MIZZY
MM
MNA
MNAS
MNEME
MNEMES
MNEMIC
MNEMON
MNEMONIC
MNEMONICS
MNEMONIST
MNEMONS
MO
MOA
MOAI
MOAN
MOANED
MOANER
MOANERS

MOANFUL
MOANFULLY
MOANING
MOANINGLY
MOANINGS
MOANS
MOAS
MOAT
MOATED
MOATING
MOATLIKE
MOATS
MOB
MOBBED
MOBBER
MOBBERS
MOBBIE
MOBBIES
MOBBING
MOBBINGS
MOBBISH
MOBBISHLY
MOBBISM
MOBBISMS
MOBBLE
MOBBLED
MOBBLES
MOBBLING
MOBBY
MOBCAP
MOBCAPS
MOBE
MOBES
MOBIE
MOBIES
MOBILE
MOBILES
MOBILISE
MOBILISED
MOBILISER
MOBILISES
MOBILITY
MOBILIZE
MOBILIZED
MOBILIZER
MOBILIZES
MOBLE
MOBLED
MOBLES
MOBLING
MOBLOG
MOBLOGGER
MOBLOGS
MOBOCRACY
MOBOCRAT
MOBOCRATS
MOBS
MOBSMAN

MOBSMEN
MOBSTER
MOBSTERS
MOBY
MOC
MOCASSIN
MOCASSINS
MOCCASIN
MOCCASINS
MOCCIES
MOCH
MOCHA
MOCHAS
MOCHELL
MOCHELLS
MOCHIE
MOCHIER
MOCHIEST
MOCHILA
MOCHILAS
MOCHINESS
MOCHS
MOCHY
MOCK
MOCKABLE
MOCKADO
MOCKADOES
MOCKAGE
MOCKAGES
MOCKED
MOCKER
MOCKERED
MOCKERIES
MOCKERING
MOCKERNUT
MOCKERS
MOCKERY
MOCKING
MOCKINGLY
MOCKINGS
MOCKNEY
MOCKNEYS
MOCKS
MOCKTAIL
MOCKTAILS
MOCKUP
MOCKUPS
MOCOCK
MOCOCKS
MOCS
MOCUCK
MOCUCKS
MOCUDDUM
MOCUDDUMS
MOD
MODAL
MODALISM
MODALISMS

MODALIST
MODALISTS
MODALITY
MODALLY
MODALS
MODE
MODEL
MODELED
MODELER
MODELERS
MODELING
MODELINGS
MODELIST
MODELISTS
MODELLED
MODELLER
MODELLERS
MODELLI
MODELLING
MODELLO
MODELLOS
MODELS
MODEM
MODEMED
MODEMING
MODEMS
MODENA
MODENAS
MODER
MODERATE
MODERATED
MODERATES
MODERATO
MODERATOR
MODERATOS
MODERN
MODERNE
MODERNER
MODERNES
MODERNEST
MODERNISE
MODERNISM
MODERNIST
MODERNITY
MODERNIZE
MODERNLY
MODERNS
MODERS
MODES
MODEST
MODESTER
MODESTEST
MODESTIES
MODESTLY
MODESTY
MODGE
MODGED
MODGES

MODGING
MODI
MODICA
MODICUM
MODICUMS
MODIFIED
MODIFIER
MODIFIERS
MODIFIES
MODIFY
MODIFYING
MODII
MODILLION
MODIOLAR
MODIOLI
MODIOLUS
MODISH
MODISHLY
MODIST
MODISTE
MODISTES
MODISTS
MODIUS
MODIWORT
MODIWORTS
MODS
MODULAR
MODULARLY
MODULARS
MODULATE
MODULATED
MODULATES
MODULATOR
MODULE
MODULES
MODULI
MODULO
MODULUS
MODUS
MOE
MOELLON
MOELLONS
MOER
MOERED
MOERING
MOERS
MOES
MOFETTE
MOFETTES
MOFFETTE
MOFFETTES
MOFFIE
MOFFIES
MOFO
MOFOS
MOFUSSIL
MOFUSSILS
MOG

MOGGAN
MOGGANS
MOGGED
MOGGIE
MOGGIES
MOGGING
MOGGY
MOGHUL
MOGHULS
MOGS
MOGUL
MOGULED
MOGULS
MOHAIR
MOHAIRS
MOHALIM
MOHAWK
MOHAWKS
MOHEL
MOHELIM
MOHELS
MOHICAN
MOHICANS
MOHR
MOHRS
MOHUA
MOHUR
MOHURS
MOI
MOIDER
MOIDERED
MOIDERING
MOIDERS
MOIDORE
MOIDORES
MOIETIES
MOIETY
MOIL
MOILED
MOILER
MOILERS
MOILING
MOILINGLY
MOILS
MOINEAU
MOINEAUS
MOIRA
MOIRAI
MOIRE
MOIRES
MOISER
MOISERS
MOIST
MOISTED
MOISTEN
MOISTENED
MOISTENER
MOISTENS

MOISTER
MOISTEST
MOISTFUL
MOISTIFY
MOISTING
MOISTLY
MOISTNESS
MOISTS
MOISTURE
MOISTURES
MOIT
MOITHER
MOITHERED
MOITHERS
MOITS
MOJARRA
MOJARRAS
MOJO
MOJOES
MOJOS
MOKADDAM
MOKADDAMS
MOKE
MOKES
MOKI
MOKIHI
MOKIS
MOKO
MOKOMOKO
MOKOPUNA
MOKOPUNAS
MOKORO
MOKOROS
MOKOS
MOKSHA
MOKSHAS
MOL
MOLA
MOLAL
MOLALITY
MOLAR
MOLARITY
MOLARS
MOLAS
MOLASSE
MOLASSES
MOLD
MOLDABLE
MOLDAVITE
MOLDBOARD
MOLDED
MOLDER
MOLDERED
MOLDERING
MOLDERS
MOLDIER
MOLDIEST
MOLDINESS

MOLDING
MOLDINGS
MOLDS
MOLDWARP
MOLDWARPS
MOLDY
MOLE
MOLECAST
MOLECASTS
MOLECULAR
MOLECULE
MOLECULES
MOLEHILL
MOLEHILLS
MOLEHUNT
MOLEHUNTS
MOLERAT
MOLERATS
MOLES
MOLESKIN
MOLESKINS
MOLEST
MOLESTED
MOLESTER
MOLESTERS
MOLESTFUL
MOLESTING
MOLESTS
MOLIES
MOLIMEN
MOLIMENS
MOLINE
MOLINES
MOLINET
MOLINETS
MOLL
MOLLA
MOLLAH
MOLLAHS
MOLLAS
MOLLIE
MOLLIES
MOLLIFIED
MOLLIFIER
MOLLIFIES
MOLLIFY
MOLLITIES
MOLLS
MOLLUSC
MOLLUSCA
MOLLUSCAN
MOLLUSCS
MOLLUSCUM
MOLLUSK
MOLLUSKAN
MOLLUSKS
MOLLY
MOLLYHAWK

MOLLYMAWK
MOLOCH
MOLOCHISE
MOLOCHIZE
MOLOCHS
MOLOSSI
MOLOSSUS
MOLS
MOLT
MOLTED
MOLTEN
MOLTENLY
MOLTER
MOLTERS
MOLTING
MOLTO
MOLTS
MOLY
MOLYBDATE
MOLYBDIC
MOLYBDOUS
MOM
MOME
MOMENT
MOMENTA
MOMENTANY
MOMENTARY
MOMENTLY
MOMENTO
MOMENTOES
MOMENTOS
MOMENTOUS
MOMENTS
MOMENTUM
MOMENTUMS
MOMES
MOMI
MOMISM
MOMISMS
MOMMA
MOMMAS
MOMMET
MOMMETS
MOMMIES
MOMMY
MOMS
MOMSER
MOMSERS
MOMUS
MOMUSES
MOMZER
MOMZERIM
MOMZERS
MON
MONA
MONACHAL
MONACHISM
MONACHIST

MONACID
MONACIDIC
MONACIDS
MONACT
MONACTINE
MONAD
MONADAL
MONADES
MONADIC
MONADICAL
MONADISM
MONADISMS
MONADNOCK
MONADS
MONAL
MONALS
MONANDRY
MONARCH
MONARCHAL
MONARCHIC
MONARCHS
MONARCHY
MONARDA
MONARDAS
MONAS
MONASES
MONASTERY
MONASTIC
MONASTICS
MONATOMIC
MONAUL
MONAULS
MONAURAL
MONAXIAL
MONAXON
MONAXONIC
MONAXONS
MONAZITE
MONAZITES
MONDAIN
MONDAINE
MONDAINES
MONDAINS
MONDE
MONDES
MONDIAL
MONDO
MONDOS
MONECIAN
MONECIOUS
MONELLIN
MONELLINS
MONEME
MONEMES
MONER
MONERA
MONERAN
MONERANS

MONERGISM
MONERON
MONETARY
MONETH
MONETHS
MONETISE
MONETISED
MONETISES
MONETIZE
MONETIZED
MONETIZES
MONEY
MONEYBAG
MONEYBAGS
MONEYED
MONEYER
MONEYERS
MONEYLESS
MONEYMAN
MONEYMEN
MONEYS
MONEYWORT
MONG
MONGCORN
MONGCORNS
MONGED
MONGEESE
MONGER
MONGERED
MONGERIES
MONGERING
MONGERS
MONGERY
MONGO
MONGOE
MONGOES
MONGOL
MONGOLIAN
MONGOLISM
MONGOLOID
MONGOLS
MONGOOSE
MONGOOSES
MONGOS
MONGREL
MONGRELLY
MONGRELS
MONGS
MONGST
MONIAL
MONIALS
MONICKER
MONICKERS
MONIE
MONIED
MONIES
MONIKER
MONIKERS

MONILIA	MONOCOT	MONOMARK	MONOTONES
MONILIAL	MONOCOTS	MONOMARKS	MONOTONIC
MONILIAS	MONOCOTYL	MONOMER	MONOTONY
MONIMENT	MONOCRACY	MONOMERIC	MONOTREME
MONIMENTS	MONOCRAT	MONOMERS	MONOTROCH
MONIPLIES	MONOCRATS	MONOMETER	MONOTYPE
MONISH	MONOCULAR	MONOMIAL	MONOTYPES
MONISHED	MONOCYCLE	MONOMIALS	MONOTYPIC
MONISHES	MONOCYTE	MONOMODE	MONOVULAR
MONISHING	MONOCYTES	MONONYM	MONOXIDE
MONISM	MONOCYTIC	MONONYMS	MONOXIDES
MONISMS	MONODIC	MONOPHAGY	MONOXYLON
MONIST	MONODICAL	MONOPHASE	MONS
MONISTIC	MONODIES	MONOPHONY	MONSIEUR
MONISTS	MONODIST	MONOPHYLY	MONSIGNOR
MONITION	MONODISTS	MONOPITCH	MONSOON
MONITIONS	MONODONT	MONOPLANE	MONSOONAL
MONITIVE	MONODRAMA	MONOPLOID	MONSOONS
MONITOR	MONODY	MONOPOD	MONSTER
MONITORED	MONOECIES	MONOPODE	MONSTERA
MONITORS	MONOECISM	MONOPODES	MONSTERAS
MONITORY	MONOECY	MONOPODIA	MONSTERED
MONITRESS	MONOESTER	MONOPODS	MONSTERS
MONK	MONOFIL	MONOPODY	MONSTROUS
MONKERIES	MONOFILS	MONOPOLE	MONTADALE
MONKERY	MONOFUEL	MONOPOLES	MONTAGE
MONKEY	MONOFUELS	MONOPOLY	MONTAGED
MONKEYED	MONOGAMIC	MONOPSONY	MONTAGES
MONKEYING	MONOGAMY	MONOPTERA	MONTAGING
MONKEYISH	MONOGENIC	MONOPTOTE	MONTAN
MONKEYISM	MONOGENY	MONOPULSE	MONTANE
MONKEYPOD	MONOGERM	MONORAIL	MONTANES
MONKEYPOT	MONOGLOT	MONORAILS	MONTANT
MONKEYS	MONOGLOTS	MONORCHID	MONTANTO
MONKFISH	MONOGONY	MONORHINE	MONTANTOS
MONKHOOD	MONOGRAM	MONORHYME	MONTANTS
MONKHOODS	MONOGRAMS	MONOS	MONTARIA
MONKISH	MONOGRAPH	MONOSEMY	MONTARIAS
MONKISHLY	MONOGYNY	MONOSES	MONTE
MONKS	MONOHULL	MONOSIES	MONTEITH
MONKSHOOD	MONOHULLS	MONOSIS	MONTEITHS
MONO	MONOICOUS	MONOSKI	MONTEM
MONOACID	MONOKINE	MONOSKIER	MONTEMS
MONOACIDS	MONOKINES	MONOSKIS	MONTERO
MONOAMINE	MONOKINI	MONOSOME	MONTEROS
MONOAO	MONOKINIS	MONOSOMES	MONTES
MONOBASIC	MONOLATER	MONOSOMIC	MONTH
MONOBROW	MONOLATRY	MONOSOMY	MONTHLIES
MONOBROWS	MONOLAYER	MONOSTELE	MONTHLING
MONOCARP	MONOLITH	MONOSTELY	MONTHLONG
MONOCARPS	MONOLITHS	MONOSTICH	MONTHLY
MONOCEROS	MONOLOG	MONOSTOME	MONTHS
MONOCHORD	MONOLOGIC	MONOSTYLE	MONTICLE
MONOCLE	MONOLOGS	MONOSY	MONTICLES
MONOCLED	MONOLOGUE	MONOTINT	MONTICULE
MONOCLES	MONOLOGY	MONOTINTS	MONTIES
MONOCLINE	MONOMACHY	MONOTONE	MONTRE
MONOCOQUE	MONOMANIA	MONOTONED	MONTRES

MONTURE	MOONBOW	MOONWARDS	MOOVES
MONTURES	MOONBOWS	MOONWORT	MOOVING
MONTY	MOONCALF	MOONWORTS	MOP
MONUMENT	MOONCHILD	MOONY	MOPANE
MONUMENTS	MOONDUST	MOOP	MOPANES
MONURON	MOONDUSTS	MOOPED	MOPANI
MONURONS	MOONED	MOOPING	MOPANIS
MONY	MOONER	MOOPS	MOPBOARD
MONYPLIES	MOONERS	MOOR	MOPBOARDS
MONZONITE	MOONEYE	MOORAGE	MOPE
MOO	MOONEYES	MOORAGES	MOPED
MOOCH	MOONFACE	MOORBURN	MOPEDS
MOOCHED	MOONFACED	MOORBURNS	MOPEHAWK
MOOCHER	MOONFACES	MOORCOCK	MOPEHAWKS
MOOCHERS	MOONFISH	MOORCOCKS	MOPER
MOOCHES	MOONIER	MOORED	MOPERIES
MOOCHING	MOONIES	MOORFOWL	MOPERS
MOOD	MOONIEST	MOORFOWLS	MOPERY
MOODIED	MOONILY	MOORHEN	MOPES
MOODIER	MOONINESS	MOORHENS	MOPEY
MOODIES	MOONING	MOORIER	MOPHEAD
MOODIEST	MOONISH	MOORIEST	MOPHEADS
MOODILY	MOONISHLY	MOORILL	MOPIER
MOODINESS	MOONLESS	MOORILLS	MOPIEST
MOODS	MOONLET	MOORING	MOPINESS
MOODY	MOONLETS	MOORINGS	MOPING
MOODYING	MOONLIGHT	MOORISH	MOPINGLY
MOOED	MOONLIKE	MOORLAND	MOPISH
MOOI	MOONLIT	MOORLANDS	MOPISHLY
MOOING	MOONPHASE	MOORLOG	MOPOKE
MOOK	MOONPORT	MOORLOGS	MOPOKES
MOOKS	MOONPORTS	MOORMAN	MOPPED
MOOKTAR	MOONQUAKE	MOORMEN	MOPPER
MOOKTARS	MOONRAKER	MOORS	MOPPERS
MOOL	MOONRISE	MOORVA	MOPPET
MOOLA	MOONRISES	MOORVAS	MOPPETS
MOOLAH	MOONROCK	MOORWORT	MOPPIER
MOOLAHS	MOONROCKS	MOORWORTS	MOPPIEST
MOOLAS	MOONROOF	MOORY	MOPPING
MOOLED	MOONROOFS	MOOS	MOPPY
MOOLEY	MOONS	MOOSE	MOPS
MOOLEYS	MOONSAIL	MOOSEBIRD	MOPSIES
MOOLI	MOONSAILS	MOOSEWOOD	MOPSTICK
MOOLIES	MOONSCAPE	MOOSEYARD	MOPSTICKS
MOOLING	MOONSEED	MOOT	MOPSY
MOOLIS	MOONSEEDS	MOOTABLE	MOPUS
MOOLOO	MOONSET	MOOTED	MOPUSES
MOOLOOS	MOONSETS	MOOTER	MOPY
MOOLS	MOONSHEE	MOOTERS	MOQUETTE
MOOLVI	MOONSHEES	MOOTEST	MOQUETTES
MOOLVIE	MOONSHINE	MOOTING	MOR
MOOLVIES	MOONSHINY	MOOTINGS	MORA
MOOLVIS	MOONSHOT	MOOTMAN	MORACEOUS
MOOLY	MOONSHOTS	MOOTMEN	MORAE
MOON	MOONSTONE	MOOTNESS	MORAINAL
MOONBEAM	MOONWALK	MOOTS	MORAINE
MOONBEAMS	MOONWALKS	MOOVE	MORAINES
MOONBLIND	MOONWARD	MOOVED	MORAINIC

MORAL	MOREISH	MOROSE	MORSURE
MORALE	MOREL	MOROSELY	MORSURES
MORALES	MORELLE	MOROSER	MORT
MORALISE	MORELLES	MOROSEST	MORTAL
MORALISED	MORELLO	MOROSITY	MORTALISE
MORALISER	MORELLOS	MORPH	MORTALITY
MORALISES	MORELS	MORPHEAN	MORTALIZE
MORALISM	MORENDO	MORPHED	MORTALLY
MORALISMS	MORENESS	MORPHEME	MORTALS
MORALIST	MOREOVER	MORPHEMES	MORTAR
MORALISTS	MOREPORK	MORPHEMIC	MORTARED
MORALITY	MOREPORKS	MORPHETIC	MORTARING
MORALIZE	MORES	MORPHEW	MORTARMAN
MORALIZED	MORESQUE	MORPHEWS	MORTARMEN
MORALIZER	MORESQUES	MORPHIA	MORTARS
MORALIZES	MORGAN	MORPHIAS	MORTARY
MORALL	MORGANITE	MORPHIC	MORTBELL
MORALLED	MORGANS	MORPHIN	MORTBELLS
MORALLER	MORGAY	MORPHINE	MORTCLOTH
MORALLERS	MORGAYS	MORPHINES	MORTGAGE
MORALLING	MORGEN	MORPHING	MORTGAGED
MORALLS	MORGENS	MORPHINGS	MORTGAGEE
MORALLY	MORGUE	MORPHINIC	MORTGAGER
MORALS	MORGUES	MORPHINS	MORTGAGES
MORAS	MORIA	MORPHO	MORTGAGOR
MORASS	MORIAS	MORPHOGEN	MORTICE
MORASSES	MORIBUND	MORPHOS	MORTICED
MORASSY	MORICHE	MORPHOSES	MORTICER
MORAT	MORICHES	MORPHOSIS	MORTICERS
MORATORIA	MORION	MORPHOTIC	MORTICES
MORATORY	MORIONS	MORPHS	MORTICIAN
MORATS	MORISCO	MORRA	MORTICING
MORAY	MORISCOES	MORRAS	MORTIFIC
MORAYS	MORISCOS	MORRELL	MORTIFIED
MORBID	MORISH	MORRELLS	MORTIFIER
MORBIDER	MORKIN	MORRHUA	MORTIFIES
MORBIDEST	MORKINS	MORRHUAS	MORTIFY
MORBIDITY	MORLING	MORRICE	MORTISE
MORBIDLY	MORLINGS	MORRICES	MORTISED
MORBIFIC	MORMAOR	MORRION	MORTISER
MORBILLI	MORMAORS	MORRIONS	MORTISERS
MORBUS	MORN	MORRIS	MORTISES
MORBUSES	MORNAY	MORRISED	MORTISING
MORCEAU	MORNAYS	MORRISES	MORTLING
MORCEAUX	MORNE	MORRISING	MORTLINGS
MORCHA	MORNED	MORRO	MORTMAIN
MORCHAS	MORNES	MORROS	MORTMAINS
MORDACITY	MORNING	MORROW	MORTS
MORDANCY	MORNINGS	MORROWS	MORTSAFE
MORDANT	MORNS	MORS	MORTSAFES
MORDANTED	MOROCCO	MORSAL	MORTUARY
MORDANTLY	MOROCCOS	MORSE	MORULA
MORDANTS	MORON	MORSEL	MORULAE
MORDENT	MORONIC	MORSELED	MORULAR
MORDENTS	MORONISM	MORSELING	MORULAS
MORE	MORONISMS	MORSELLED	MORWONG
MOREEN	MORONITY	MORSELS	MORWONGS
MOREENS	MORONS	MORSES	MORYAH

MOS	MOST	MOTIVATED	MOTSERS
MOSAIC	MOSTE	MOTIVATES	MOTT
MOSAICISM	MOSTEST	MOTIVATOR	MOTTE
MOSAICIST	MOSTESTS	MOTIVE	MOTTES
MOSAICKED	MOSTLY	MOTIVED	MOTTIER
MOSAICS	MOSTS	MOTIVES	MOTTIES
MOSASAUR	MOSTWHAT	MOTIVIC	MOTTIEST
MOSASAURI	MOT	MOTIVING	MOTTLE
MOSASAURS	MOTE	MOTIVITY	MOTTLED
MOSCHATE	MOTED	MOTLEY	MOTTLER
MOSCHATEL	MOTEL	MOTLEYER	MOTTLERS
MOSE	MOTELIER	MOTLEYEST	MOTTLES
MOSED	MOTELIERS	MOTLEYS	MOTTLING
MOSELLE	MOTELS	MOTLIER	MOTTLINGS
MOSELLES	MOTEN	MOTLIEST	MOTTO
MOSES	MOTES	MOTMOT	MOTTOED
MOSEY	MOTET	MOTMOTS	MOTTOES
MOSEYED	MOTETS	MOTOCROSS	MOTTOS
MOSEYING	MOTETT	MOTOR	MOTTS
MOSEYS	MOTETTIST	MOTORABLE	MOTTY
MOSH	MOTETTS	MOTORAIL	MOTU
MOSHAV	MOTEY	MOTORAILS	MOTUCA
MOSHAVIM	MOTH	MOTORBIKE	MOTUCAS
MOSHED	MOTHBALL	MOTORBOAT	MOTUS
MOSHER	MOTHBALLS	MOTORBUS	MOTZA
MOSHERS	MOTHED	MOTORCADE	MOTZAS
MOSHES	MOTHER	MOTORCAR	MOU
MOSHING	MOTHERED	MOTORCARS	MOUCH
MOSHINGS	MOTHERESE	MOTORDOM	MOUCHARD
MOSING	MOTHERING	MOTORDOMS	MOUCHARDS
MOSK	MOTHERLY	MOTORED	MOUCHED
MOSKONFYT	MOTHERS	MOTORHOME	MOUCHER
MOSKS	MOTHERY	MOTORIAL	MOUCHERS
MOSLINGS	MOTHIER	MOTORIC	MOUCHES
MOSQUE	MOTHIEST	MOTORING	MOUCHING
MOSQUES	MOTHLIKE	MOTORINGS	MOUCHOIR
MOSQUITO	MOTHPROOF	MOTORISE	MOUCHOIRS
MOSQUITOS	MOTHS	MOTORISED	MOUDIWART
MOSS	MOTHY	MOTORISES	MOUDIWORT
MOSSBACK	MOTI	MOTORIST	MOUE
MOSSBACKS	MOTIER	MOTORISTS	MOUES
MOSSED	MOTIEST	MOTORIUM	MOUFFLON
MOSSER	MOTIF	MOTORIUMS	MOUFFLONS
MOSSERS	MOTIFIC	MOTORIZE	MOUFLON
MOSSES	MOTIFS	MOTORIZED	MOUFLONS
MOSSGROWN	MOTILE	MOTORIZES	MOUGHT
MOSSIE	MOTILES	MOTORLESS	MOUILLE
MOSSIER	MOTILITY	MOTORMAN	MOUJIK
MOSSIES	MOTION	MOTORMEN	MOUJIKS
MOSSIEST	MOTIONAL	MOTORS	MOULAGE
MOSSINESS	MOTIONED	MOTORSHIP	MOULAGES
MOSSING	MOTIONER	MOTORWAY	MOULD
MOSSLAND	MOTIONERS	MOTORWAYS	MOULDABLE
MOSSLANDS	MOTIONING	MOTORY	MOULDED
MOSSLIKE	MOTIONIST	MOTOSCAFI	MOULDER
MOSSO	MOTIONS	MOTOSCAFO	MOULDERED
MOSSPLANT	MOTIS	MOTS	MOULDERS
MOSSY	MOTIVATE	MOTSER	MOULDIER

MOULDIEST
MOULDING
MOULDINGS
MOULDS
MOULDWARP
MOULDY
MOULIN
MOULINET
MOULINETS
MOULINS
MOULS
MOULT
MOULTED
MOULTEN
MOULTER
MOULTERS
MOULTING
MOULTINGS
MOULTS
MOUND
MOUNDBIRD
MOUNDED
MOUNDING
MOUNDS
MOUNSEER
MOUNSEERS
MOUNT
MOUNTABLE
MOUNTAIN
MOUNTAINS
MOUNTAINY
MOUNTANT
MOUNTANTS
MOUNTED
MOUNTER
MOUNTERS
MOUNTING
MOUNTINGS
MOUNTS
MOUP
MOUPED
MOUPING
MOUPS
MOURN
MOURNED
MOURNER
MOURNERS
MOURNFUL
MOURNING
MOURNINGS
MOURNIVAL
MOURNS
MOUS
MOUSAKA
MOUSAKAS
MOUSE
MOUSEBIRD
MOUSED

MOUSEKIN
MOUSEKINS
MOUSELIKE
MOUSEMAT
MOUSEMATS
MOUSEOVER
MOUSEPAD
MOUSEPADS
MOUSER
MOUSERIES
MOUSERS
MOUSERY
MOUSES
MOUSETAIL
MOUSETRAP
MOUSEY
MOUSIE
MOUSIER
MOUSIES
MOUSIEST
MOUSILY
MOUSINESS
MOUSING
MOUSINGS
MOUSLE
MOUSLED
MOUSLES
MOUSLING
MOUSME
MOUSMEE
MOUSMEES
MOUSMES
MOUSSAKA
MOUSSAKAS
MOUSSE
MOUSSED
MOUSSES
MOUSSING
MOUST
MOUSTACHE
MOUSTED
MOUSTING
MOUSTS
MOUSY
MOUTAN
MOUTANS
MOUTER
MOUTERED
MOUTERER
MOUTERERS
MOUTERING
MOUTERS
MOUTH
MOUTHABLE
MOUTHED
MOUTHER
MOUTHERS
MOUTHFEEL

MOUTHFUL
MOUTHFULS
MOUTHIER
MOUTHIEST
MOUTHILY
MOUTHING
MOUTHLESS
MOUTHLIKE
MOUTHPART
MOUTHS
MOUTHWASH
MOUTHY
MOUTON
MOUTONNEE
MOUTONS
MOVABLE
MOVABLES
MOVABLY
MOVE
MOVEABLE
MOVEABLES
MOVEABLY
MOVED
MOVELESS
MOVEMENT
MOVEMENTS
MOVER
MOVERS
MOVES
MOVIE
MOVIEDOM
MOVIEDOMS
MOVIEGOER
MOVIELAND
MOVIEOKE
MOVIEOKES
MOVIEOLA
MOVIEOLAS
MOVIES
MOVING
MOVINGLY
MOVIOLA
MOVIOLAS
MOW
MOWA
MOWAS
MOWBURN
MOWBURNED
MOWBURNS
MOWBURNT
MOWDIE
MOWDIES
MOWED
MOWER
MOWERS
MOWING
MOWINGS
MOWN

MOWRA
MOWRAS
MOWS
MOXA
MOXAS
MOXIE
MOXIES
MOY
MOYA
MOYAS
MOYGASHEL
MOYITIES
MOYITY
MOYL
MOYLE
MOYLED
MOYLES
MOYLING
MOYLS
MOYS
MOZ
MOZE
MOZED
MOZES
MOZETTA
MOZETTAS
MOZETTE
MOZING
MOZO
MOZOS
MOZZ
MOZZES
MOZZETTA
MOZZETTAS
MOZZETTE
MOZZIE
MOZZIES
MOZZLE
MOZZLES
MPRET
MPRETS
MRIDAMGAM
MRIDANG
MRIDANGA
MRIDANGAM
MRIDANGAS
MRIDANGS
MU
MUCATE
MUCATES
MUCH
MUCHACHO
MUCHACHOS
MUCHEL
MUCHELL
MUCHELLS
MUCHELS
MUCHES

MUCHLY
MUCHNESS
MUCHO
MUCIC
MUCID
MUCIDITY
MUCIDNESS
MUCIGEN
MUCIGENS
MUCILAGE
MUCILAGES
MUCIN
MUCINOGEN
MUCINOID
MUCINOUS
MUCINS
MUCK
MUCKAMUCK
MUCKED
MUCKENDER
MUCKER
MUCKERED
MUCKERING
MUCKERISH
MUCKERS
MUCKHEAP
MUCKHEAPS
MUCKIER
MUCKIEST
MUCKILY
MUCKINESS
MUCKING
MUCKLE
MUCKLES
MUCKLUCK
MUCKLUCKS
MUCKRAKE
MUCKRAKED
MUCKRAKER
MUCKRAKES
MUCKS
MUCKSWEAT
MUCKWORM
MUCKWORMS
MUCKY
MUCLUC
MUCLUCS
MUCOID
MUCOIDAL
MUCOIDS
MUCOLYTIC
MUCOR
MUCORS
MUCOSA
MUCOSAE
MUCOSAL
MUCOSAS
MUCOSE

MUCOSITY
MUCOUS
MUCRO
MUCRONATE
MUCRONES
MUCROS
MUCULENT
MUCUS
MUCUSES
MUD
MUDBATH
MUDBATHS
MUDBUG
MUDBUGS
MUDCAP
MUDCAPPED
MUDCAPS
MUDCAT
MUDCATS
MUDDED
MUDDER
MUDDERS
MUDDIED
MUDDIER
MUDDIES
MUDDIEST
MUDDILY
MUDDINESS
MUDDING
MUDDLE
MUDDLED
MUDDLER
MUDDLERS
MUDDLES
MUDDLIER
MUDDLIEST
MUDDLING
MUDDLINGS
MUDDLY
MUDDY
MUDDYING
MUDEJAR
MUDEJARES
MUDEYE
MUDEYES
MUDFISH
MUDFISHES
MUDFLAP
MUDFLAPS
MUDFLAT
MUDFLATS
MUDFLOW
MUDFLOWS
MUDGE
MUDGED
MUDGER
MUDGERS
MUDGES

MUDGING
MUDGUARD
MUDGUARDS
MUDHEN
MUDHENS
MUDHOLE
MUDHOLES
MUDHOOK
MUDHOOKS
MUDIR
MUDIRIA
MUDIRIAS
MUDIRIEH
MUDIRIEHS
MUDIRS
MUDLARK
MUDLARKED
MUDLARKS
MUDLOGGER
MUDPACK
MUDPACKS
MUDPUPPY
MUDRA
MUDRAS
MUDROCK
MUDROCKS
MUDROOM
MUDROOMS
MUDS
MUDSCOW
MUDSCOWS
MUDSILL
MUDSILLS
MUDSLIDE
MUDSLIDES
MUDSTONE
MUDSTONES
MUDWORT
MUDWORTS
MUEDDIN
MUEDDINS
MUENSTER
MUENSTERS
MUESLI
MUESLIS
MUEZZIN
MUEZZINS
MUFF
MUFFED
MUFFIN
MUFFINEER
MUFFING
MUFFINS
MUFFISH
MUFFLE
MUFFLED
MUFFLER
MUFFLERED

MUFFLERS
MUFFLES
MUFFLING
MUFFS
MUFLON
MUFLONS
MUFTI
MUFTIS
MUG
MUGEARITE
MUGFUL
MUGFULS
MUGG
MUGGA
MUGGAR
MUGGARS
MUGGAS
MUGGED
MUGGEE
MUGGEES
MUGGER
MUGGERS
MUGGIER
MUGGIEST
MUGGILY
MUGGINESS
MUGGING
MUGGINGS
MUGGINS
MUGGINSES
MUGGISH
MUGGS
MUGGUR
MUGGURS
MUGGY
MUGHAL
MUGHALS
MUGS
MUGSHOT
MUGSHOTS
MUGWORT
MUGWORTS
MUGWUMP
MUGWUMPS
MUHLIES
MUHLY
MUID
MUIDS
MUIL
MUILS
MUIR
MUIRBURN
MUIRBURNS
MUIRS
MUIST
MUISTED
MUISTING
MUISTS

MUJAHEDIN	MULLEY	MULTIPAGE	MUMMIFIED
MUJAHIDIN	MULLEYS	MULTIPARA	MUMMIFIES
MUJIK	MULLIGAN	MULTIPART	MUMMIFORM
MUJIKS	MULLIGANS	MULTIPATH	MUMMIFY
MUKHTAR	MULLING	MULTIPED	MUMMING
MUKHTARS	MULLION	MULTIPEDE	MUMMINGS
MUKLUK	MULLIONED	MULTIPEDS	MUMMOCK
MUKLUKS	MULLIONS	MULTIPION	MUMMOCKS
MUKTUK	MULLITE	MULTIPLE	MUMMS
MUKTUKS	MULLITES	MULTIPLES	MUMMY
MULATTA	MULLOCK	MULTIPLET	MUMMYING
MULATTAS	MULLOCKS	MULTIPLEX	MUMP
MULATTO	MULLOCKY	MULTIPLY	MUMPED
MULATTOES	MULLOWAY	MULTIPOLE	MUMPER
MULATTOS	MULLOWAYS	MULTIPORT	MUMPERS
MULBERRY	MULLS	MULTIROLE	MUMPING
MULCH	MULMUL	MULTIROOM	MUMPISH
MULCHED	MULMULL	MULTISITE	MUMPISHLY
MULCHES	MULMULLS	MULTISIZE	MUMPS
MULCHING	MULMULS	MULTISTEP	MUMPSIMUS
MULCT	MULSE	MULTITASK	MUMS
MULCTED	MULSES	MULTITON	MUMSIER
MULCTING	MULSH	MULTITONE	MUMSIEST
MULCTS	MULSHED	MULTITUDE	MUMSY
MULE	MULSHES	MULTIUNIT	MUMU
MULED	MULSHING	MULTIUSE	MUMUS
MULES	MULTEITY	MULTIUSER	MUN
MULESED	MULTIAGE	MULTIWALL	MUNCH
MULESES	MULTIATOM	MULTIYEAR	MUNCHABLE
MULESING	MULTIBAND	MULTUM	MUNCHED
MULETA	MULTIBANK	MULTUMS	MUNCHER
MULETAS	MULTICAR	MULTURE	MUNCHERS
MULETEER	MULTICAST	MULTURED	MUNCHES
MULETEERS	MULTICELL	MULTURER	MUNCHIES
MULEY	MULTICIDE	MULTURERS	MUNCHING
MULEYS	MULTICITY	MULTURES	MUNCHKIN
MULGA	MULTICOPY	MULTURING	MUNCHKINS
MULGAS	MULTIDAY	MUM	MUNDANE
MULING	MULTIDISC	MUMBLE	MUNDANELY
MULISH	MULTIDRUG	MUMBLED	MUNDANER
MULISHLY	MULTIFID	MUMBLER	MUNDANEST
MULL	MULTIFIL	MUMBLERS	MUNDANITY
MULLA	MULTIFILS	MUMBLES	MUNDIC
MULLAH	MULTIFOIL	MUMBLING	MUNDICS
MULLAHISM	MULTIFOLD	MUMBLINGS	MUNDIFIED
MULLAHS	MULTIFORM	MUMBLY	MUNDIFIES
MULLARKY	MULTIGERM	MUMCHANCE	MUNDIFY
MULLAS	MULTIGRID	MUMM	MUNDUNGO
MULLED	MULTIGYM	MUMMED	MUNDUNGOS
MULLEIN	MULTIGYMS	MUMMER	MUNDUNGUS
MULLEINS	MULTIHUED	MUMMERIES	MUNG
MULLEN	MULTIHULL	MUMMERS	MUNGA
MULLENS	MULTIJET	MUMMERY	MUNGAS
MULLER	MULTILANE	MUMMIA	MUNGCORN
MULLERED	MULTILINE	MUMMIAS	MUNGCORNS
MULLERS	MULTILOBE	MUMMICHOG	MUNGED
MULLET	MULTIMODE	MUMMIED	MUNGING
MULLETS	MULTIPACK	MUMMIES	MUNGO

MUNGOES
MUNGOOSE
MUNGOOSES
MUNGOS
MUNGS
MUNI
MUNICIPAL
MUNIFIED
MUNIFIES
MUNIFY
MUNIFYING
MUNIMENT
MUNIMENTS
MUNIS
MUNITE
MUNITED
MUNITES
MUNITING
MUNITION
MUNITIONS
MUNNION
MUNNIONS
MUNS
MUNSHI
MUNSHIS
MUNSTER
MUNSTERS
MUNT
MUNTER
MUNTERS
MUNTIN
MUNTING
MUNTINGS
MUNTINS
MUNTJAC
MUNTJACS
MUNTJAK
MUNTJAKS
MUNTRIE
MUNTRIES
MUNTS
MUNTU
MUNTUS
MUON
MUONIC
MUONIUM
MUONIUMS
MUONS
MUPPET
MUPPETS
MUQADDAM
MUQADDAMS
MURA
MURAENA
MURAENAS
MURAENID
MURAENIDS
MURAGE

MURAGES
MURAL
MURALED
MURALIST
MURALISTS
MURALLED
MURALS
MURAS
MURDABAD
MURDER
MURDERED
MURDEREE
MURDEREES
MURDERER
MURDERERS
MURDERESS
MURDERING
MURDEROUS
MURDERS
MURE
MURED
MUREIN
MUREINS
MURENA
MURENAS
MURES
MUREX
MUREXES
MURGEON
MURGEONED
MURGEONS
MURIATE
MURIATED
MURIATES
MURIATIC
MURICATE
MURICATED
MURICES
MURID
MURIDS
MURIFORM
MURINE
MURINES
MURING
MURK
MURKER
MURKEST
MURKIER
MURKIEST
MURKILY
MURKINESS
MURKISH
MURKLY
MURKS
MURKSOME
MURKY
MURL
MURLAIN

MURLAINS
MURLAN
MURLANS
MURLED
MURLIER
MURLIEST
MURLIN
MURLING
MURLINS
MURLS
MURLY
MURMUR
MURMURED
MURMURER
MURMURERS
MURMURING
MURMUROUS
MURMURS
MURPHIES
MURPHY
MURR
MURRA
MURRAGH
MURRAGHS
MURRAIN
MURRAINED
MURRAINS
MURRAM
MURRAMS
MURRAS
MURRAY
MURRAYS
MURRE
MURREE
MURREES
MURRELET
MURRELETS
MURREN
MURRENS
MURRES
MURREY
MURREYS
MURRHA
MURRHAS
MURRHINE
MURRI
MURRIES
MURRIN
MURRINE
MURRINS
MURRION
MURRIONS
MURRIS
MURRS
MURRY
MURTHER
MURTHERED
MURTHERER

MURTHERS
MURTI
MURTIS
MURVA
MURVAS
MUS
MUSACEOUS
MUSANG
MUSANGS
MUSAR
MUSARS
MUSCA
MUSCADEL
MUSCADELS
MUSCADET
MUSCADETS
MUSCADIN
MUSCADINE
MUSCADINS
MUSCAE
MUSCARINE
MUSCAT
MUSCATEL
MUSCATELS
MUSCATS
MUSCAVADO
MUSCID
MUSCIDS
MUSCLE
MUSCLED
MUSCLEMAN
MUSCLEMEN
MUSCLES
MUSCLIER
MUSCLIEST
MUSCLING
MUSCLINGS
MUSCLY
MUSCOID
MUSCOLOGY
MUSCONE
MUSCONES
MUSCOSE
MUSCOVADO
MUSCOVITE
MUSCULAR
MUSCULOUS
MUSE
MUSED
MUSEFUL
MUSEFULLY
MUSEOLOGY
MUSER
MUSERS
MUSES
MUSET
MUSETS
MUSETTE

MUSETTES	MUSKINESS	MUSTELID	MUTILATED
MUSEUM	MUSKING	MUSTELIDS	MUTILATES
MUSEUMS	MUSKIT	MUSTELINE	MUTILATOR
MUSH	MUSKITS	MUSTER	MUTINE
MUSHA	MUSKLE	MUSTERED	MUTINED
MUSHED	MUSKLES	MUSTERER	MUTINEER
MUSHER	MUSKMELON	MUSTERERS	MUTINEERS
MUSHERS	MUSKONE	MUSTERING	MUTINES
MUSHES	MUSKONES	MUSTERS	MUTING
MUSHIER	MUSKOX	MUSTH	MUTINIED
MUSHIEST	MUSKOXEN	MUSTHS	MUTINIES
MUSHILY	MUSKRAT	MUSTIER	MUTINING
MUSHINESS	MUSKRATS	MUSTIEST	MUTINOUS
MUSHING	MUSKROOT	MUSTILY	MUTINY
MUSHMOUTH	MUSKROOTS	MUSTINESS	MUTINYING
MUSHROOM	MUSKS	MUSTING	MUTIS
MUSHROOMS	MUSKY	MUSTS	MUTISM
MUSHY	MUSLIN	MUSTY	MUTISMS
MUSIC	MUSLINED	MUT	MUTON
MUSICAL	MUSLINET	MUTABLE	MUTONS
MUSICALE	MUSLINETS	MUTABLY	MUTOSCOPE
MUSICALES	MUSLINS	MUTAGEN	MUTS
MUSICALLY	MUSMON	MUTAGENIC	MUTT
MUSICALS	MUSMONS	MUTAGENS	MUTTER
MUSICIAN	MUSO	MUTANDA	MUTTERED
MUSICIANS	MUSOS	MUTANDUM	MUTTERER
MUSICK	MUSPIKE	MUTANT	MUTTERERS
MUSICKED	MUSPIKES	MUTANTS	MUTTERING
MUSICKER	MUSQUASH	MUTASE	MUTTERS
MUSICKERS	MUSROL	MUTASES	MUTTON
MUSICKING	MUSROLS	MUTATE	MUTTONS
MUSICKS	MUSS	MUTATED	MUTTONY
MUSICLESS	MUSSE	MUTATES	MUTTS
MUSICS	MUSSED	MUTATING	MUTUAL
MUSIMON	MUSSEL	MUTATION	MUTUALISE
MUSIMONS	MUSSELLED	MUTATIONS	MUTUALISM
MUSING	MUSSELS	MUTATIVE	MUTUALIST
MUSINGLY	MUSSES	MUTATORY	MUTUALITY
MUSINGS	MUSSIER	MUTCH	MUTUALIZE
MUSIT	MUSSIEST	MUTCHED	MUTUALLY
MUSITS	MUSSILY	MUTCHES	MUTUALS
MUSIVE	MUSSINESS	MUTCHING	MUTUCA
MUSJID	MUSSING	MUTCHKIN	MUTUCAS
MUSJIDS	MUSSITATE	MUTCHKINS	MUTUEL
MUSK	MUSSY	MUTE	MUTUELS
MUSKED	MUST	MUTED	MUTULAR
MUSKEG	MUSTACHE	MUTEDLY	MUTULE
MUSKEGS	MUSTACHED	MUTELY	MUTULES
MUSKET	MUSTACHES	MUTENESS	MUTUUM
MUSKETEER	MUSTACHIO	MUTER	MUTUUMS
MUSKETOON	MUSTANG	MUTES	MUUMUU
MUSKETRY	MUSTANGS	MUTEST	MUUMUUS
MUSKETS	MUSTARD	MUTHA	MUX
MUSKIE	MUSTARDS	MUTHAS	MUXED
MUSKIER	MUSTARDY	MUTI	MUXES
MUSKIES	MUSTED	MUTICATE	MUXING
MUSKIEST	MUSTEE	MUTICOUS	MUZAKY
MUSKILY	MUSTEES	MUTILATE	MUZHIK

MUZHIKS
MUZJIK
MUZJIKS
MUZZ
MUZZED
MUZZES
MUZZIER
MUZZIEST
MUZZILY
MUZZINESS
MUZZING
MUZZLE
MUZZLED
MUZZLER
MUZZLERS
MUZZLES
MUZZLING
MUZZY
MVULE
MVULES
MWALIMU
MWALIMUS
MY
MYAL
MYALGIA
MYALGIAS
MYALGIC
MYALISM
MYALISMS
MYALIST
MYALISTS
MYALL
MYALLS
MYASES
MYASIS
MYC
MYCELE
MYCELES
MYCELIA
MYCELIAL
MYCELIAN
MYCELIUM
MYCELLA
MYCELLAS
MYCELOID
MYCETES
MYCETOMA
MYCETOMAS
MYCOBIONT
MYCOFLORA
MYCOLOGIC
MYCOLOGY
MYCOPHAGY
MYCOPHILE
MYCORHIZA
MYCOSES
MYCOSIS
MYCOTIC

MYCOTOXIN
MYCOVIRUS
MYCS
MYDRIASES
MYDRIASIS
MYDRIATIC
MYELIN
MYELINE
MYELINES
MYELINIC
MYELINS
MYELITIS
MYELOCYTE
MYELOGRAM
MYELOID
MYELOMA
MYELOMAS
MYELOMATA
MYELON
MYELONS
MYGALE
MYGALES
MYIASES
MYIASIS
MYIOPHILY
MYLAR
MYLARS
MYLODON
MYLODONS
MYLODONT
MYLODONTS
MYLOHYOID
MYLONITE
MYLONITES
MYLONITIC
MYNA
MYNAH
MYNAHS
MYNAS
MYNHEER
MYNHEERS
MYOBLAST
MYOBLASTS
MYOCARDIA
MYOCLONIC
MYOCLONUS
MYOFIBRIL
MYOGEN
MYOGENIC
MYOGENS
MYOGLOBIN
MYOGRAM
MYOGRAMS
MYOGRAPH
MYOGRAPHS
MYOGRAPHY
MYOID
MYOLOGIC

MYOLOGIES
MYOLOGIST
MYOLOGY
MYOMA
MYOMANCY
MYOMANTIC
MYOMAS
MYOMATA
MYOMATOUS
MYONEURAL
MYOPATHIC
MYOPATHY
MYOPE
MYOPES
MYOPHILY
MYOPIA
MYOPIAS
MYOPIC
MYOPICS
MYOPIES
MYOPS
MYOPSES
MYOPY
MYOSCOPE
MYOSCOPES
MYOSES
MYOSIN
MYOSINS
MYOSIS
MYOSITIS
MYOSOTE
MYOSOTES
MYOSOTIS
MYOTIC
MYOTICS
MYOTOME
MYOTOMES
MYOTONIA
MYOTONIAS
MYOTONIC
MYOTUBE
MYOTUBES
MYRBANE
MYRBANES
MYRIAD
MYRIADS
MYRIADTH
MYRIADTHS
MYRIAPOD
MYRIAPODS
MYRICA
MYRICAS
MYRINGA
MYRINGAS
MYRIOPOD
MYRIOPODS
MYRIORAMA
MYRISTIC

MYRMECOID
MYRMIDON
MYRMIDONS
MYROBALAN
MYRRH
MYRRHIC
MYRRHINE
MYRRHOL
MYRRHOLS
MYRRHS
MYRTLE
MYRTLES
MYSELF
MYSID
MYSIDS
MYSOST
MYSOSTS
MYSTAGOG
MYSTAGOGS
MYSTAGOGY
MYSTERIES
MYSTERY
MYSTIC
MYSTICAL
MYSTICETE
MYSTICISM
MYSTICLY
MYSTICS
MYSTIFIED
MYSTIFIER
MYSTIFIES
MYSTIFY
MYSTIQUE
MYSTIQUES
MYTH
MYTHI
MYTHIC
MYTHICAL
MYTHICISE
MYTHICISM
MYTHICIST
MYTHICIZE
MYTHIER
MYTHIEST
MYTHISE
MYTHISED
MYTHISES
MYTHISING
MYTHISM
MYTHISMS
MYTHIST
MYTHISTS
MYTHIZE
MYTHIZED
MYTHIZES
MYTHIZING
MYTHMAKER
MYTHOI

MYTHOLOGY
MYTHOMANE
MYTHOPEIC
MYTHOPOET
MYTHOS
MYTHS
MYTHUS
MYTHY
MYTILOID
MYXAMEBA
MYXAMEBAE
MYXAMEBAS
MYXAMOEBA
MYXEDEMA
MYXEDEMAS
MYXEDEMIC
MYXO
MYXOCYTE
MYXOCYTES
MYXOEDEMA
MYXOID
MYXOMA
MYXOMAS
MYXOMATA
MYXOS
MYXOVIRAL
MYXOVIRUS
MZEE
MZEES
MZUNGU
MZUNGUS

N

NA
NAAM
NAAMS
NAAN
NAANS
NAARTJE
NAARTJES
NAARTJIE
NAARTJIES
NAB
NABBED
NABBER
NABBERS
NABBING
NABE
NABES
NABIS
NABK
NABKS
NABLA
NABLAS
NABOB
NABOBERY
NABOBESS
NABOBISH
NABOBISM
NABOBISMS
NABOBS
NABS
NACARAT
NACARATS
NACELLE
NACELLES
NACH
NACHAS
NACHE
NACHES
NACHO
NACHOS
NACHTMAAL
NACKET
NACKETS
NACRE
NACRED
NACREOUS
NACRES
NACRITE
NACRITES
NACROUS
NADA
NADAS
NADIR
NADIRAL

NADIRS
NADORS
NADS
NAE
NAEBODIES
NAEBODY
NAETHING
NAETHINGS
NAEVE
NAEVES
NAEVI
NAEVOID
NAEVUS
NAFF
NAFFED
NAFFER
NAFFEST
NAFFING
NAFFLY
NAFFNESS
NAFFS
NAG
NAGA
NAGANA
NAGANAS
NAGAPIE
NAGAPIES
NAGARI
NAGARIS
NAGAS
NAGGED
NAGGER
NAGGERS
NAGGIER
NAGGIEST
NAGGING
NAGGINGLY
NAGGY
NAGMAAL
NAGMAALS
NAGOR
NAGORS
NAGS
NAH
NAHAL
NAHALS
NAIAD
NAIADES
NAIADS
NAIANT
NAIF
NAIFER
NAIFEST

NAIFLY
NAIFNESS
NAIFS
NAIK
NAIKS
NAIL
NAILBITER
NAILBRUSH
NAILED
NAILER
NAILERIES
NAILERS
NAILERY
NAILFILE
NAILFILES
NAILFOLD
NAILFOLDS
NAILHEAD
NAILHEADS
NAILING
NAILINGS
NAILLESS
NAILS
NAILSET
NAILSETS
NAIN
NAINSELL
NAINSELLS
NAINSOOK
NAINSOOKS
NAIRA
NAIRAS
NAIRU
NAIRUS
NAISSANCE
NAISSANT
NAIVE
NAIVELY
NAIVENESS
NAIVER
NAIVES
NAIVEST
NAIVETE
NAIVETES
NAIVETIES
NAIVETY
NAIVIST
NAKED
NAKEDER
NAKEDEST
NAKEDLY
NAKEDNESS
NAKER

NAKERS
NAKFA
NAKFAS
NALA
NALAS
NALED
NALEDS
NALLA
NALLAH
NALLAHS
NALLAS
NALOXONE
NALOXONES
NAM
NAMABLE
NAMASKAR
NAMASKARS
NAMASTE
NAMASTES
NAMAYCUSH
NAME
NAMEABLE
NAMECHECK
NAMED
NAMELESS
NAMELY
NAMEPLATE
NAMER
NAMERS
NAMES
NAMESAKE
NAMESAKES
NAMETAG
NAMETAGS
NAMETAPE
NAMETAPES
NAMING
NAMINGS
NAMMA
NAMS
NAMU
NAN
NANA
NANAS
NANCE
NANCES
NANCIES
NANCIFIED
NANCY
NANDIN
NANDINA
NANDINAS
NANDINE

NANDINES	NAPES	NARCOMA	NARRATOR
NANDINS	NAPHTHA	NARCOMAS	NARRATORS
NANDOO	NAPHTHAS	NARCOMATA	NARRATORY
NANDOOS	NAPHTHENE	NARCOS	NARRE
NANDU	NAPHTHOL	NARCOSE	NARROW
NANDUS	NAPHTHOLS	NARCOSES	NARROWED
NANE	NAPHTHOUS	NARCOSIS	NARROWER
NANISM	NAPHTHYL	NARCOTIC	NARROWEST
NANISMS	NAPHTHYLS	NARCOTICS	NARROWING
NANKEEN	NAPHTOL	NARCOTINE	NARROWISH
NANKEENS	NAPHTOLS	NARCOTISE	NARROWLY
NANKIN	NAPIFORM	NARCOTISM	NARROWS
NANKINS	NAPING	NARCOTIST	NARTHEX
NANNA	NAPKIN	NARCOTIZE	NARTHEXES
NANNAS	NAPKINS	NARCS	NARTJIE
NANNIE	NAPLESS	NARD	NARTJIES
NANNIED	NAPOLEON	NARDED	NARWAL
NANNIES	NAPOLEONS	NARDINE	NARWALS
NANNY	NAPOO	NARDING	NARWHAL
NANNYGAI	NAPOOED	NARDOO	NARWHALE
NANNYGAIS	NAPOOING	NARDOOS	NARWHALES
NANNYING	NAPOOS	NARDS	NARWHALS
NANNYISH	NAPPA	NARE	NARY
NANOBE	NAPPAS	NARES	NAS
NANOBES	NAPPE	NARGHILE	NASAL
NANODOT	NAPPED	NARGHILES	NASALISE
NANODOTS	NAPPER	NARGHILLY	NASALISED
NANOGRAM	NAPPERS	NARGHILY	NASALISES
NANOGRAMS	NAPPES	NARGILE	NASALISM
NANOMETER	NAPPIE	NARGILEH	NASALISMS
NANOMETRE	NAPPIER	NARGILEHS	NASALITY
NANOOK	NAPPIES	NARGILES	NASALIZE
NANOOKS	NAPPIEST	NARGILIES	NASALIZED
NANOSCALE	NAPPINESS	NARGILY	NASALIZES
NANOTECH	NAPPING	NARIAL	NASALLY
NANOTECHS	NAPPY	NARIC	NASALS
NANOTESLA	NAPRON	NARICORN	NASARD
NANOTUBE	NAPRONS	NARICORNS	NASARDS
NANOTUBES	NAPROXEN	NARINE	NASCENCE
NANOWATT	NAPROXENS	NARIS	NASCENCES
NANOWATTS	NAPS	NARK	NASCENCY
NANOWORLD	NARAS	NARKED	NASCENT
NANS	NARASES	NARKIER	NASEBERRY
NANUA	NARC	NARKIEST	NASHGAB
NAOI	NARCEEN	NARKING	NASHGABS
NAOS	NARCEENS	NARKS	NASHI
NAOSES	NARCEIN	NARKY	NASHIS
NAP	NARCEINE	NARQUOIS	NASIAL
NAPA	NARCEINES	NARRAS	NASION
NAPALM	NARCEINS	NARRASES	NASIONS
NAPALMED	NARCISM	NARRATE	NASSELLA
NAPALMING	NARCISMS	NARRATED	NASTALIK
NAPALMS	NARCISSI	NARRATER	NASTALIKS
NAPAS	NARCISSUS	NARRATERS	NASTIC
NAPE	NARCIST	NARRATES	NASTIER
NAPED	NARCISTIC	NARRATING	NASTIES
NAPERIES	NARCISTS	NARRATION	NASTIEST
NAPERY	NARCO	NARRATIVE	NASTILY

NASTINESS
NASTY
NASUTE
NASUTES
NAT
NATAL
NATALITY
NATANT
NATANTLY
NATATION
NATATIONS
NATATORIA
NATATORY
NATCH
NATCHES
NATES
NATHELESS
NATHEMO
NATHEMORE
NATHLESS
NATIFORM
NATION
NATIONAL
NATIONALS
NATIONS
NATIS
NATIVE
NATIVELY
NATIVES
NATIVISM
NATIVISMS
NATIVIST
NATIVISTS
NATIVITY
NATRIUM
NATRIUMS
NATROLITE
NATRON
NATRONS
NATS
NATTER
NATTERED
NATTERER
NATTERERS
NATTERING
NATTERS
NATTERY
NATTIER
NATTIEST
NATTILY
NATTINESS
NATTY
NATURA
NATURAE
NATURAL
NATURALLY
NATURALS
NATURE

NATURED
NATURES
NATURING
NATURISM
NATURISMS
NATURIST
NATURISTS
NAUCH
NAUCHES
NAUGAHYDE
NAUGHT
NAUGHTIER
NAUGHTIES
NAUGHTILY
NAUGHTS
NAUGHTY
NAUMACHIA
NAUMACHY
NAUNT
NAUNTS
NAUPLIAL
NAUPLII
NAUPLIOID
NAUPLIUS
NAUSEA
NAUSEANT
NAUSEANTS
NAUSEAS
NAUSEATE
NAUSEATED
NAUSEATES
NAUSEOUS
NAUTCH
NAUTCHES
NAUTIC
NAUTICAL
NAUTICS
NAUTILI
NAUTILOID
NAUTILUS
NAVAID
NAVAIDS
NAVAL
NAVALISM
NAVALISMS
NAVALLY
NAVAR
NAVARCH
NAVARCHS
NAVARCHY
NAVARHO
NAVARHOS
NAVARIN
NAVARINS
NAVARS
NAVE
NAVEL
NAVELS

NAVELWORT
NAVES
NAVETTE
NAVETTES
NAVEW
NAVEWS
NAVICERT
NAVICERTS
NAVICULA
NAVICULAR
NAVICULAS
NAVIES
NAVIGABLE
NAVIGABLY
NAVIGATE
NAVIGATED
NAVIGATES
NAVIGATOR
NAVVIED
NAVVIES
NAVVY
NAVVYING
NAVY
NAW
NAWAB
NAWABS
NAY
NAYS
NAYSAID
NAYSAY
NAYSAYER
NAYSAYERS
NAYSAYING
NAYSAYS
NAYTHLES
NAYWARD
NAYWARDS
NAYWORD
NAYWORDS
NAZE
NAZES
NAZI
NAZIFIED
NAZIFIES
NAZIFY
NAZIFYING
NAZIR
NAZIRS
NAZIS
NE
NEAFE
NEAFES
NEAFFE
NEAFFES
NEAL
NEALED
NEALING
NEALS

NEANIC
NEAP
NEAPED
NEAPING
NEAPS
NEAR
NEARBY
NEARED
NEARER
NEAREST
NEARING
NEARLIER
NEARLIEST
NEARLY
NEARNESS
NEARS
NEARSHORE
NEARSIDE
NEARSIDES
NEAT
NEATEN
NEATENED
NEATENING
NEATENS
NEATER
NEATEST
NEATH
NEATHERD
NEATHERDS
NEATLY
NEATNESS
NEATNIK
NEATNIKS
NEATS
NEB
NEBBED
NEBBICH
NEBBICHS
NEBBING
NEBBISH
NEBBISHE
NEBBISHER
NEBBISHES
NEBBISHY
NEBBUK
NEBBUKS
NEBECK
NEBECKS
NEBEK
NEBEKS
NEBEL
NEBELS
NEBENKERN
NEBISH
NEBISHES
NEBRIS
NEBRISES
NEBS

NEBULA
NEBULAE
NEBULAR
NEBULAS
NEBULE
NEBULES
NEBULISE
NEBULISED
NEBULISER
NEBULISES
NEBULIUM
NEBULIUMS
NEBULIZE
NEBULIZED
NEBULIZER
NEBULIZES
NEBULOSE
NEBULOUS
NEBULY
NECESSARY
NECESSITY
NECK
NECKATEE
NECKATEES
NECKBAND
NECKBANDS
NECKBEEF
NECKBEEFS
NECKCLOTH
NECKED
NECKER
NECKERS
NECKGEAR
NECKGEARS
NECKING
NECKINGS
NECKLACE
NECKLACED
NECKLACES
NECKLESS
NECKLET
NECKLETS
NECKLIKE
NECKLINE
NECKLINES
NECKPIECE
NECKS
NECKTIE
NECKTIES
NECKVERSE
NECKWEAR
NECKWEARS
NECKWEED
NECKWEEDS
NECROLOGY
NECROPHIL
NECROPOLI
NECROPSY

NECROSE
NECROSED
NECROSES
NECROSING
NECROSIS
NECROTIC
NECROTISE
NECROTIZE
NECROTOMY
NECTAR
NECTAREAL
NECTAREAN
NECTARED
NECTARIAL
NECTARIED
NECTARIES
NECTARINE
NECTAROUS
NECTARS
NECTARY
NED
NEDDIER
NEDDIES
NEDDIEST
NEDDISH
NEDDY
NEDETTE
NEDETTES
NEDS
NEE
NEED
NEEDED
NEEDER
NEEDERS
NEEDFIRE
NEEDFIRES
NEEDFUL
NEEDFULLY
NEEDFULS
NEEDIER
NEEDIEST
NEEDILY
NEEDINESS
NEEDING
NEEDLE
NEEDLED
NEEDLEFUL
NEEDLER
NEEDLERS
NEEDLES
NEEDLESS
NEEDLIER
NEEDLIEST
NEEDLING
NEEDLINGS
NEEDLY
NEEDMENT
NEEDMENTS

NEEDS
NEEDY
NEELD
NEELDS
NEELE
NEELES
NEEM
NEEMB
NEEMBS
NEEMS
NEEP
NEEPS
NEESBERRY
NEESE
NEESED
NEESES
NEESING
NEEZE
NEEZED
NEEZES
NEEZING
NEF
NEFANDOUS
NEFARIOUS
NEFAST
NEFS
NEG
NEGATE
NEGATED
NEGATER
NEGATERS
NEGATES
NEGATING
NEGATION
NEGATIONS
NEGATIVE
NEGATIVED
NEGATIVES
NEGATON
NEGATONS
NEGATOR
NEGATORS
NEGATORY
NEGATRON
NEGATRONS
NEGLECT
NEGLECTED
NEGLECTER
NEGLECTOR
NEGLECTS
NEGLIGE
NEGLIGEE
NEGLIGEES
NEGLIGENT
NEGLIGES
NEGOCIANT
NEGOTIANT
NEGOTIATE

NEGRESS
NEGRESSES
NEGRITUDE
NEGRO
NEGROES
NEGROHEAD
NEGROID
NEGROIDAL
NEGROIDS
NEGROISM
NEGROISMS
NEGRONI
NEGRONIS
NEGROPHIL
NEGS
NEGUS
NEGUSES
NEIF
NEIFS
NEIGH
NEIGHBOR
NEIGHBORS
NEIGHBOUR
NEIGHED
NEIGHING
NEIGHS
NEINEI
NEINEIS
NEIST
NEITHER
NEIVE
NEIVES
NEK
NEKS
NEKTON
NEKTONIC
NEKTONS
NELIES
NELIS
NELLIE
NELLIES
NELLY
NELSON
NELSONS
NELUMBIUM
NELUMBO
NELUMBOS
NEMA
NEMAS
NEMATIC
NEMATODE
NEMATODES
NEMATOID
NEMERTEAN
NEMERTIAN
NEMERTINE
NEMESES
NEMESIA

NEMESIAS
NEMESIS
NEMN
NEMNED
NEMNING
NEMNS
NEMOPHILA
NEMORAL
NEMOROUS
NEMPT
NENE
NENES
NENNIGAI
NENNIGAIS
NENUPHAR
NENUPHARS
NEOBLAST
NEOBLASTS
NEOCON
NEOCONS
NEOCORTEX
NEODYMIUM
NEOGENE
NEOGOTHIC
NEOLITH
NEOLITHIC
NEOLITHS
NEOLOGIAN
NEOLOGIC
NEOLOGIES
NEOLOGISE
NEOLOGISM
NEOLOGIST
NEOLOGIZE
NEOLOGY
NEOMORPH
NEOMORPHS
NEOMYCIN
NEOMYCINS
NEON
NEONATAL
NEONATE
NEONATES
NEONED
NEONOMIAN
NEONS
NEOPAGAN
NEOPAGANS
NEOPHILE
NEOPHILES
NEOPHILIA
NEOPHOBE
NEOPHOBES
NEOPHOBIA
NEOPHOBIC
NEOPHYTE
NEOPHYTES
NEOPHYTIC

NEOPILINA
NEOPLASIA
NEOPLASM
NEOPLASMS
NEOPLASTY
NEOPRENE
NEOPRENES
NEOTEINIA
NEOTENIC
NEOTENIES
NEOTENOUS
NEOTENY
NEOTERIC
NEOTERICS
NEOTERISE
NEOTERISM
NEOTERIST
NEOTERIZE
NEOTOXIN
NEOTOXINS
NEOTROPIC
NEOTYPE
NEOTYPES
NEP
NEPENTHE
NEPENTHES
NEPER
NEPERS
NEPETA
NEPETAS
NEPHALISM
NEPHALIST
NEPHELINE
NEPHELITE
NEPHEW
NEPHEWS
NEPHOGRAM
NEPHOLOGY
NEPHRALGY
NEPHRIC
NEPHRIDIA
NEPHRISM
NEPHRISMS
NEPHRITE
NEPHRITES
NEPHRITIC
NEPHRITIS
NEPHROID
NEPHRON
NEPHRONS
NEPHROSES
NEPHROSIS
NEPHROTIC
NEPIONIC
NEPIT
NEPITS
NEPOTIC
NEPOTISM

NEPOTISMS
NEPOTIST
NEPOTISTS
NEPS
NEPTUNIUM
NERAL
NERALS
NERD
NERDIER
NERDIEST
NERDINESS
NERDISH
NERDS
NERDY
NEREID
NEREIDES
NEREIDS
NEREIS
NERINE
NERINES
NERITE
NERITES
NERITIC
NERK
NERKA
NERKAS
NERKS
NEROL
NEROLI
NEROLIS
NEROLS
NERTS
NERTZ
NERVAL
NERVATE
NERVATION
NERVATURE
NERVE
NERVED
NERVELESS
NERVELET
NERVELETS
NERVER
NERVERS
NERVES
NERVIER
NERVIEST
NERVILY
NERVINE
NERVINES
NERVINESS
NERVING
NERVINGS
NERVOSITY
NERVOUS
NERVOUSLY
NERVULAR
NERVULE

NERVULES
NERVURE
NERVURES
NERVY
NESCIENCE
NESCIENT
NESCIENTS
NESH
NESHER
NESHEST
NESHNESS
NESS
NESSES
NEST
NESTABLE
NESTED
NESTER
NESTERS
NESTFUL
NESTFULS
NESTING
NESTINGS
NESTLE
NESTLED
NESTLER
NESTLERS
NESTLES
NESTLIKE
NESTLING
NESTLINGS
NESTOR
NESTORS
NESTS
NET
NETBALL
NETBALLER
NETBALLS
NETE
NETES
NETFUL
NETFULS
NETHEAD
NETHEADS
NETHELESS
NETHER
NETIZEN
NETIZENS
NETLESS
NETLIKE
NETMINDER
NETOP
NETOPS
NETS
NETSPEAK
NETSPEAKS
NETSUKE
NETSUKES
NETT

NETTABLE	NEUROMAST	NEWED	NEWSROOM
NETTED	NEUROMATA	NEWEL	NEWSROOMS
NETTER	NEURON	NEWELL	NEWSSTAND
NETTERS	NEURONAL	NEWELLED	NEWSTRADE
NETTIE	NEURONE	NEWELLS	NEWSWIRE
NETTIER	NEURONES	NEWELS	NEWSWIRES
NETTIES	NEURONIC	NEWER	NEWSWOMAN
NETTIEST	NEURONS	NEWEST	NEWSWOMEN
NETTING	NEUROPATH	NEWFANGLE	NEWSY
NETTINGS	NEUROPIL	NEWFOUND	NEWT
NETTLE	NEUROPILS	NEWIE	NEWTON
NETTLED	NEUROSAL	NEWIES	NEWTONS
NETTLER	NEUROSES	NEWING	NEWTS
NETTLERS	NEUROSIS	NEWISH	NEWWAVER
NETTLES	NEUROTIC	NEWISHLY	NEWWAVERS
NETTLIER	NEUROTICS	NEWLY	NEXT
NETTLIEST	NEUROTOMY	NEWLYWED	NEXTDOOR
NETTLING	NEURULA	NEWLYWEDS	NEXTLY
NETTLY	NEURULAE	NEWMARKET	NEXTNESS
NETTS	NEURULAR	NEWMOWN	NEXTS
NETTY	NEURULAS	NEWNESS	NEXUS
NETWORK	NEUSTIC	NEWNESSES	NEXUSES
NETWORKED	NEUSTON	NEWS	NGAIO
NETWORKER	NEUSTONIC	NEWSAGENT	NGAIOS
NETWORKS	NEUSTONS	NEWSBEAT	NGANA
NEUK	NEUTER	NEWSBEATS	NGANAS
NEUKS	NEUTERED	NEWSBOY	NGARARA
NEUM	NEUTERING	NEWSBOYS	NGATI
NEUMATIC	NEUTERS	NEWSBREAK	NGATIS
NEUME	NEUTRAL	NEWSCAST	NGOMA
NEUMES	NEUTRALLY	NEWSCASTS	NGOMAS
NEUMIC	NEUTRALS	NEWSDESK	NGULTRUM
NEUMS	NEUTRETTO	NEWSDESKS	NGULTRUMS
NEURAL	NEUTRINO	NEWSED	NGWEE
NEURALGIA	NEUTRINOS	NEWSES	NHANDU
NEURALGIC	NEUTRON	NEWSFLASH	NHANDUS
NEURALLY	NEUTRONIC	NEWSGIRL	NIACIN
NEURATION	NEUTRONS	NEWSGIRLS	NIACINS
NEURAXON	NEVE	NEWSGROUP	NIAISERIE
NEURAXONS	NEVEL	NEWSHAWK	NIALAMIDE
NEURILITY	NEVELLED	NEWSHAWKS	NIB
NEURINE	NEVELLING	NEWSHOUND	NIBBED
NEURINES	NEVELS	NEWSIE	NIBBING
NEURISM	NEVER	NEWSIER	NIBBLE
NEURISMS	NEVERMIND	NEWSIES	NIBBLED
NEURITE	NEVERMORE	NEWSIEST	NIBBLER
NEURITES	NEVES	NEWSINESS	NIBBLERS
NEURITIC	NEVI	NEWSING	NIBBLES
NEURITICS	NEVOID	NEWSLESS	NIBBLING
NEURITIS	NEVUS	NEWSMAKER	NIBBLINGS
NEUROCHIP	NEW	NEWSMAN	NIBLICK
NEUROCOEL	NEWBIE	NEWSMEN	NIBLICKS
NEUROGLIA	NEWBIES	NEWSPAPER	NIBLIKE
NEUROGRAM	NEWBORN	NEWSPEAK	NIBS
NEUROID	NEWBORNS	NEWSPEAKS	NICAD
NEUROLOGY	NEWCOME	NEWSPRINT	NICADS
NEUROMA	NEWCOMER	NEWSREEL	NICCOLITE
NEUROMAS	NEWCOMERS	NEWSREELS	NICE

NICEISH
NICELY
NICENESS
NICER
NICEST
NICETIES
NICETY
NICHE
NICHED
NICHER
NICHERED
NICHERING
NICHERS
NICHES
NICHING
NICHT
NICHTS
NICISH
NICK
NICKAR
NICKARS
NICKED
NICKEL
NICKELED
NICKELIC
NICKELINE
NICKELING
NICKELISE
NICKELIZE
NICKELLED
NICKELOUS
NICKELS
NICKER
NICKERED
NICKERING
NICKERS
NICKING
NICKLE
NICKLED
NICKLES
NICKLING
NICKNACK
NICKNACKS
NICKNAME
NICKNAMED
NICKNAMER
NICKNAMES
NICKPOINT
NICKS
NICKSTICK
NICKUM
NICKUMS
NICKY
NICOISE
NICOL
NICOLS
NICOMPOOP
NICOTIAN

NICOTIANA
NICOTIANS
NICOTIN
NICOTINE
NICOTINED
NICOTINES
NICOTINIC
NICOTINS
NICTATE
NICTATED
NICTATES
NICTATING
NICTATION
NICTITANT
NICTITATE
NID
NIDAL
NIDAMENTA
NIDATE
NIDATED
NIDATES
NIDATING
NIDATION
NIDATIONS
NIDDERING
NIDDICK
NIDDICKS
NIDE
NIDED
NIDERING
NIDERINGS
NIDERLING
NIDES
NIDGET
NIDGETS
NIDI
NIDIFIED
NIDIFIES
NIDIFY
NIDIFYING
NIDING
NIDINGS
NIDOR
NIDOROUS
NIDORS
NIDS
NIDUS
NIDUSES
NIE
NIECE
NIECES
NIED
NIEF
NIEFS
NIELLATED
NIELLI
NIELLIST
NIELLISTS

NIELLO
NIELLOED
NIELLOING
NIELLOS
NIES
NIEVE
NIEVEFUL
NIEVEFULS
NIEVES
NIFE
NIFES
NIFF
NIFFED
NIFFER
NIFFERED
NIFFERING
NIFFERS
NIFFIER
NIFFIEST
NIFFING
NIFFNAFF
NIFFNAFFS
NIFFS
NIFFY
NIFTIER
NIFTIES
NIFTIEST
NIFTILY
NIFTINESS
NIFTY
NIGELLA
NIGELLAS
NIGER
NIGERS
NIGGARD
NIGGARDED
NIGGARDLY
NIGGARDS
NIGGER
NIGGERDOM
NIGGERED
NIGGERING
NIGGERISH
NIGGERISM
NIGGERS
NIGGERY
NIGGLE
NIGGLED
NIGGLER
NIGGLERS
NIGGLES
NIGGLIER
NIGGLIEST
NIGGLING
NIGGLINGS
NIGGLY
NIGH
NIGHED

NIGHER
NIGHEST
NIGHING
NIGHLY
NIGHNESS
NIGHS
NIGHT
NIGHTBIRD
NIGHTCAP
NIGHTCAPS
NIGHTCLUB
NIGHTED
NIGHTFALL
NIGHTFIRE
NIGHTGEAR
NIGHTGLOW
NIGHTGOWN
NIGHTHAWK
NIGHTIE
NIGHTIES
NIGHTJAR
NIGHTJARS
NIGHTLESS
NIGHTLIFE
NIGHTLIKE
NIGHTLONG
NIGHTLY
NIGHTMARE
NIGHTMARY
NIGHTS
NIGHTSIDE
NIGHTSPOT
NIGHTTIDE
NIGHTTIME
NIGHTWARD
NIGHTWEAR
NIGHTY
NIGIRI
NIGIRIS
NIGRICANT
NIGRIFIED
NIGRIFIES
NIGRIFY
NIGRITUDE
NIGROSIN
NIGROSINE
NIGROSINS
NIHIL
NIHILISM
NIHILISMS
NIHILIST
NIHILISTS
NIHILITY
NIHILS
NIHONGA
NIHONGAS
NIKAU
NIKAUS

NIL	NINESCORE	NIRLED	NITRE
NILGAI	NINETEEN	NIRLIE	NITRES
NILGAIS	NINETEENS	NIRLIER	NITRIC
NILGAU	NINETIES	NIRLIEST	NITRID
NILGAUS	NINETIETH	NIRLING	NITRIDE
NILGHAI	NINETY	NIRLIT	NITRIDED
NILGHAIS	NINHYDRIN	NIRLS	NITRIDES
NILGHAU	NINJA	NIRLY	NITRIDING
NILGHAUS	NINJAS	NIRVANA	NITRIDS
NILL	NINJITSU	NIRVANAS	NITRIFIED
NILLED	NINJITSUS	NIRVANIC	NITRIFIER
NILLING	NINJUTSU	NIS	NITRIFIES
NILLS	NINJUTSUS	NISBERRY	NITRIFY
NILPOTENT	NINNIES	NISEI	NITRIL
NILS	NINNY	NISEIS	NITRILE
NIM	NINNYISH	NISGUL	NITRILES
NIMB	NINON	NISGULS	NITRILS
NIMBED	NINONS	NISH	NITRITE
NIMBI	NINTH	NISHES	NITRITES
NIMBLE	NINTHLY	NISI	NITRO
NIMBLER	NINTHS	NISSE	NITROGEN
NIMBLESSE	NIOBATE	NISSES	NITROGENS
NIMBLEST	NIOBATES	NISUS	NITROLIC
NIMBLEWIT	NIOBIC	NIT	NITROS
NIMBLY	NIOBITE	NITCHIE	NITROSO
NIMBS	NIOBITES	NITCHIES	NITROSYL
NIMBUS	NIOBIUM	NITE	NITROSYLS
NIMBUSED	NIOBIUMS	NITER	NITROUS
NIMBUSES	NIOBOUS	NITERIE	NITROXYL
NIMBYISM	NIP	NITERIES	NITROXYLS
NIMBYISMS	NIPA	NITERS	NITRY
NIMBYNESS	NIPAS	NITERY	NITRYL
NIMIETIES	NIPCHEESE	NITES	NITRYLS
NIMIETY	NIPPED	NITHER	NITS
NIMIOUS	NIPPER	NITHERED	NITTIER
NIMMED	NIPPERED	NITHERING	NITTIEST
NIMMER	NIPPERING	NITHERS	NITTY
NIMMERS	NIPPERKIN	NITHING	NITWIT
NIMMING	NIPPERS	NITHINGS	NITWITS
NIMONIC	NIPPIER	NITID	NITWITTED
NIMPS	NIPPIEST	NITINOL	NIVAL
NIMROD	NIPPILY	NITINOLS	NIVATION
NIMRODS	NIPPINESS	NITON	NIVATIONS
NIMS	NIPPING	NITONS	NIVEOUS
NINCOM	NIPPINGLY	NITPICK	NIX
NINCOMS	NIPPLE	NITPICKED	NIXE
NINCUM	NIPPLED	NITPICKER	NIXED
NINCUMS	NIPPLES	NITPICKS	NIXER
NINE	NIPPLING	NITPICKY	NIXERS
NINEBARK	NIPPY	NITRAMINE	NIXES
NINEBARKS	NIPS	NITRATE	NIXIE
NINEFOLD	NIPTER	NITRATED	NIXIES
NINEHOLES	NIPTERS	NITRATES	NIXING
NINEPENCE	NIQAB	NITRATINE	NIXY
NINEPENNY	NIQABS	NITRATING	NIZAM
NINEPIN	NIRAMIAI	NITRATION	NIZAMATE
NINEPINS	NIRAMIAIS	NITRATOR	NIZAMATES
NINES	NIRL	NITRATORS	NIZAMS

387

NKOSI
NKOSIS
NO
NOAH
NOAHS
NOB
NOBBIER
NOBBIEST
NOBBILY
NOBBINESS
NOBBLE
NOBBLED
NOBBLER
NOBBLERS
NOBBLES
NOBBLING
NOBBUT
NOBBY
NOBELIUM
NOBELIUMS
NOBILESSE
NOBILIARY
NOBILITY
NOBLE
NOBLEMAN
NOBLEMEN
NOBLENESS
NOBLER
NOBLES
NOBLESSE
NOBLESSES
NOBLEST
NOBLY
NOBODIES
NOBODY
NOBS
NOCAKE
NOCAKES
NOCENT
NOCENTLY
NOCENTS
NOCHEL
NOCHELLED
NOCHELS
NOCK
NOCKED
NOCKET
NOCKETS
NOCKING
NOCKS
NOCTILIO
NOCTILIOS
NOCTILUCA
NOCTUA
NOCTUARY
NOCTUAS
NOCTUID
NOCTUIDS

NOCTULE
NOCTULES
NOCTUOID
NOCTURIA
NOCTURIAS
NOCTURN
NOCTURNAL
NOCTURNE
NOCTURNES
NOCTURNS
NOCUOUS
NOCUOUSLY
NOD
NODAL
NODALISE
NODALISED
NODALISES
NODALITY
NODALIZE
NODALIZED
NODALIZES
NODALLY
NODATED
NODATION
NODATIONS
NODDED
NODDER
NODDERS
NODDIER
NODDIES
NODDIEST
NODDING
NODDINGLY
NODDINGS
NODDLE
NODDLED
NODDLES
NODDLING
NODDY
NODE
NODES
NODI
NODICAL
NODOSE
NODOSITY
NODOUS
NODS
NODULAR
NODULATED
NODULE
NODULED
NODULES
NODULOSE
NODULOUS
NODUS
NOEL
NOELS
NOES

NOESES
NOESIS
NOESISES
NOETIC
NOG
NOGAKU
NOGG
NOGGED
NOGGIN
NOGGING
NOGGINGS
NOGGINS
NOGGS
NOGS
NOH
NOHOW
NOHOWISH
NOIL
NOILS
NOILY
NOINT
NOINTED
NOINTER
NOINTERS
NOINTING
NOINTS
NOIR
NOIRISH
NOIRS
NOISE
NOISED
NOISEFUL
NOISELESS
NOISENIK
NOISENIKS
NOISES
NOISETTE
NOISETTES
NOISIER
NOISIEST
NOISILY
NOISINESS
NOISING
NOISOME
NOISOMELY
NOISY
NOLE
NOLES
NOLITION
NOLITIONS
NOLL
NOLLS
NOLO
NOLOS
NOM
NOMA
NOMAD
NOMADE

NOMADES
NOMADIC
NOMADIES
NOMADISE
NOMADISED
NOMADISES
NOMADISM
NOMADISMS
NOMADIZE
NOMADIZED
NOMADIZES
NOMADS
NOMADY
NOMARCH
NOMARCHS
NOMARCHY
NOMAS
NOMBLES
NOMBRIL
NOMBRILS
NOME
NOMEN
NOMES
NOMIC
NOMINA
NOMINABLE
NOMINAL
NOMINALLY
NOMINALS
NOMINATE
NOMINATED
NOMINATES
NOMINATOR
NOMINEE
NOMINEES
NOMISM
NOMISMS
NOMISTIC
NOMOCRACY
NOMOGENY
NOMOGRAM
NOMOGRAMS
NOMOGRAPH
NOMOI
NOMOLOGIC
NOMOLOGY
NOMOS
NOMOTHETE
NOMS
NON
NONA
NONACID
NONACIDIC
NONACIDS
NONACTING
NONACTION
NONACTIVE
NONACTOR

NONACTORS	NONCOLORS	NONFACTS	NONIMMUNE
NONADDICT	NONCOM	NONFADING	NONIMPACT
NONADULT	NONCOMBAT	NONFAMILY	NONINERT
NONADULTS	NONCOMS	NONFAN	NONINJURY
NONAGE	NONCONCUR	NONFANS	NONINSECT
NONAGED	NONCORE	NONFARM	NONIONIC
NONAGES	NONCOUNTY	NONFARMER	NONIRON
NONAGON	NONCREDIT	NONFAT	NONIS
NONAGONAL	NONCRIME	NONFATAL	NONISSUE
NONAGONS	NONCRIMES	NONFATTY	NONISSUES
NONANE	NONCRISES	NONFEUDAL	NONJOINER
NONANES	NONCRISIS	NONFILIAL	NONJURIES
NONANIMAL	NONCYCLIC	NONFINAL	NONJURING
NONANOIC	NONDAIRY	NONFINITE	NONJUROR
NONANSWER	NONDANCE	NONFISCAL	NONJURORS
NONARABLE	NONDANCER	NONFLUID	NONJURY
NONART	NONDANCES	NONFLUIDS	NONKOSHER
NONARTIST	NONDEGREE	NONFLYING	NONLABOR
NONARTS	NONDEMAND	NONFOCAL	NONLAWYER
NONARY	NONDESERT	NONFOOD	NONLEADED
NONAS	NONDOCTOR	NONFORMAL	NONLEAFY
NONATOMIC	NONDOLLAR	NONFOSSIL	NONLEAGUE
NONAUTHOR	NONDRIP	NONFROZEN	NONLEGAL
NONBANK	NONDRIVER	NONFUEL	NONLEGUME
NONBANKS	NONDRUG	NONFUNDED	NONLETHAL
NONBASIC	NONDRYING	NONG	NONLEVEL
NONBEING	NONE	NONGAME	NONLIABLE
NONBEINGS	NONEDIBLE	NONGAY	NONLIFE
NONBELIEF	NONEGO	NONGAYS	NONLINEAL
NONBINARY	NONEGOS	NONGHETTO	NONLINEAR
NONBITING	NONELECT	NONGLARE	NONLIQUID
NONBLACK	NONELITE	NONGLARES	NONLIVES
NONBLACKS	NONEMPTY	NONGLAZED	NONLIVING
NONBODIES	NONENDING	NONGLOSSY	NONLOCAL
NONBODY	NONENERGY	NONGOLFER	NONLOCALS
NONBONDED	NONENTITY	NONGRADED	NONLOVING
NONBOOK	NONENTRY	NONGREASY	NONLOYAL
NONBOOKS	NONEQUAL	NONGREEN	NONLYRIC
NONBRAND	NONEQUALS	NONGROWTH	NONMAJOR
NONBUYING	NONEROTIC	NONGS	NONMAJORS
NONCAKING	NONES	NONGUEST	NONMAN
NONCAMPUS	NONESUCH	NONGUESTS	NONMANUAL
NONCAREER	NONET	NONGUILT	NONMARKET
NONCASH	NONETHNIC	NONGUILTS	NONMATURE
NONCASUAL	NONETS	NONHARDY	NONMEAT
NONCAUSAL	NONETTE	NONHEME	NONMEMBER
NONCE	NONETTES	NONHERO	NONMEN
NONCEREAL	NONETTI	NONHEROES	NONMENTAL
NONCES	NONETTO	NONHEROIC	NONMETAL
NONCHURCH	NONETTOS	NONHOME	NONMETALS
NONCLASS	NONEVENT	NONHUMAN	NONMETRIC
NONCLING	NONEVENTS	NONHUMANS	NONMETRO
NONCODING	NONEXEMPT	NONHUNTER	NONMOBILE
NONCOITAL	NONEXOTIC	NONI	NONMODAL
NONCOKING	NONEXPERT	NONIDEAL	NONMODERN
NONCOLA	NONEXTANT	NONILLION	NONMONEY
NONCOLAS	NONFACT	NONIMAGE	NONMORAL
NONCOLOR	NONFACTOR	NONIMAGES	NONMORTAL

NONMOTILE
NONMOVING
NONMUSIC
NONMUSICS
NONMUTANT
NONMUTUAL
NONNASAL
NONNATIVE
NONNAVAL
NONNEURAL
NONNEWS
NONNIES
NONNOBLE
NONNORMAL
NONNOVEL
NONNOVELS
NONNY
NONOBESE
NONOHMIC
NONOILY
NONORAL
NONORALLY
NONOWNER
NONOWNERS
NONPAGAN
NONPAGANS
NONPAID
NONPAPAL
NONPAPIST
NONPAR
NONPAREIL
NONPARENT
NONPARITY
NONPAROUS
NONPARTY
NONPAST
NONPASTS
NONPAYING
NONPEAK
NONPERSON
NONPLANAR
NONPLAY
NONPLAYER
NONPLAYS
NONPLIANT
NONPLUS
NONPLUSED
NONPLUSES
NONPOETIC
NONPOINT
NONPOLAR
NONPOLICE
NONPOOR
NONPOROUS
NONPOSTAL
NONPRINT
NONPROFIT
NONPROS

NONPROVEN
NONPUBLIC
NONQUOTA
NONRACIAL
NONRANDOM
NONRATED
NONREADER
NONRETURN
NONRHOTIC
NONRIGID
NONRIOTER
NONRIVAL
NONRIVALS
NONROYAL
NONRUBBER
NONRULING
NONRURAL
NONSACRED
NONSALINE
NONSCHOOL
NONSECRET
NONSECURE
NONSELF
NONSELVES
NONSENSE
NONSENSES
NONSERIAL
NONSEXIST
NONSEXUAL
NONSHRINK
NONSIGNER
NONSKATER
NONSKED
NONSKEDS
NONSKID
NONSKIER
NONSKIERS
NONSLIP
NONSMOKER
NONSOCIAL
NONSOLAR
NONSOLID
NONSOLIDS
NONSPEECH
NONSTAPLE
NONSTATIC
NONSTEADY
NONSTICK
NONSTICKY
NONSTOP
NONSTOPS
NONSTORY
NONSTYLE
NONSTYLES
NONSUCH
NONSUCHES
NONSUGAR
NONSUGARS

NONSUIT
NONSUITED
NONSUITS
NONSYSTEM
NONTALKER
NONTARGET
NONTARIFF
NONTAX
NONTAXES
NONTHEIST
NONTIDAL
NONTITLE
NONTONAL
NONTONIC
NONTOXIC
NONTRAGIC
NONTRIBAL
NONTRUMP
NONTRUTH
NONTRUTHS
NONUNION
NONUNIONS
NONUNIQUE
NONUPLE
NONUPLES
NONUPLET
NONUPLETS
NONURBAN
NONURGENT
NONUSABLE
NONUSE
NONUSER
NONUSERS
NONUSES
NONUSING
NONVACANT
NONVALID
NONVECTOR
NONVENOUS
NONVERBAL
NONVESTED
NONVIABLE
NONVIEWER
NONVIRAL
NONVIRGIN
NONVIRILE
NONVISUAL
NONVITAL
NONVOCAL
NONVOCALS
NONVOTER
NONVOTERS
NONVOTING
NONWAGE
NONWAR
NONWARS
NONWHITE
NONWHITES

NONWINGED
NONWOODY
NONWOOL
NONWORD
NONWORDS
NONWORK
NONWORKER
NONWOVEN
NONWOVENS
NONWRITER
NONYL
NONYLS
NONZERO
NOO
NOODGE
NOODGED
NOODGES
NOODGING
NOODLE
NOODLED
NOODLEDOM
NOODLES
NOODLING
NOODLINGS
NOOGIE
NOOGIES
NOOIT
NOOK
NOOKIE
NOOKIER
NOOKIES
NOOKIEST
NOOKLIKE
NOOKS
NOOKY
NOOLOGIES
NOOLOGY
NOOMETRY
NOON
NOONDAY
NOONDAYS
NOONED
NOONER
NOONERS
NOONING
NOONINGS
NOONS
NOONTIDE
NOONTIDES
NOONTIME
NOONTIMES
NOOP
NOOPS
NOOSE
NOOSED
NOOSER
NOOSERS
NOOSES

NOOSING
NOOSPHERE
NOOTROPIC
NOPAL
NOPALES
NOPALITO
NOPALITOS
NOPALS
NOPE
NOPLACE
NOR
NORDIC
NORI
NORIA
NORIAS
NORIMON
NORIMONS
NORIS
NORITE
NORITES
NORITIC
NORK
NORKS
NORLAND
NORLANDS
NORM
NORMA
NORMAL
NORMALCY
NORMALISE
NORMALITY
NORMALIZE
NORMALLY
NORMALS
NORMAN
NORMANDE
NORMANS
NORMAS
NORMATIVE
NORMED
NORMLESS
NORMS
NORSEL
NORSELLED
NORSELLER
NORSELS
NORTENA
NORTENAS
NORTENO
NORTENOS
NORTH
NORTHEAST
NORTHED
NORTHER
NORTHERED
NORTHERLY
NORTHERN
NORTHERNS

NORTHERS
NORTHING
NORTHINGS
NORTHLAND
NORTHMOST
NORTHS
NORTHWARD
NORTHWEST
NORWARD
NORWARDS
NOS
NOSE
NOSEAN
NOSEANS
NOSEBAG
NOSEBAGS
NOSEBAND
NOSEBANDS
NOSEBLEED
NOSED
NOSEDIVE
NOSEDIVED
NOSEDIVES
NOSEDOVE
NOSEGAY
NOSEGAYS
NOSEGUARD
NOSELESS
NOSELIKE
NOSELITE
NOSELITES
NOSEPIECE
NOSER
NOSERS
NOSES
NOSEWHEEL
NOSEY
NOSEYS
NOSH
NOSHED
NOSHER
NOSHERIE
NOSHERIES
NOSHERS
NOSHERY
NOSHES
NOSHING
NOSIER
NOSIES
NOSIEST
NOSILY
NOSINESS
NOSING
NOSINGS
NOSODE
NOSODES
NOSOLOGIC
NOSOLOGY

NOSTALGIA
NOSTALGIC
NOSTOC
NOSTOCS
NOSTOI
NOSTOLOGY
NOSTOS
NOSTRIL
NOSTRILS
NOSTRO
NOSTRUM
NOSTRUMS
NOSY
NOT
NOTA
NOTABILIA
NOTABLE
NOTABLES
NOTABLY
NOTAEUM
NOTAEUMS
NOTAL
NOTANDA
NOTANDUM
NOTAPHILY
NOTARIAL
NOTARIES
NOTARISE
NOTARISED
NOTARISES
NOTARIZE
NOTARIZED
NOTARIZES
NOTARY
NOTATE
NOTATED
NOTATES
NOTATING
NOTATION
NOTATIONS
NOTCH
NOTCHBACK
NOTCHED
NOTCHEL
NOTCHELS
NOTCHER
NOTCHERS
NOTCHES
NOTCHIER
NOTCHIEST
NOTCHING
NOTCHINGS
NOTCHY
NOTE
NOTEBOOK
NOTEBOOKS
NOTECARD
NOTECARDS

NOTECASE
NOTECASES
NOTED
NOTEDLY
NOTEDNESS
NOTELESS
NOTELET
NOTELETS
NOTEPAD
NOTEPADS
NOTEPAPER
NOTER
NOTERS
NOTES
NOTHER
NOTHING
NOTHINGS
NOTICE
NOTICED
NOTICER
NOTICERS
NOTICES
NOTICING
NOTIFIED
NOTIFIER
NOTIFIERS
NOTIFIES
NOTIFY
NOTIFYING
NOTING
NOTION
NOTIONAL
NOTIONIST
NOTIONS
NOTITIA
NOTITIAE
NOTITIAS
NOTOCHORD
NOTORIETY
NOTORIOUS
NOTORNIS
NOTOUR
NOTT
NOTTURNI
NOTTURNO
NOTUM
NOUGAT
NOUGATS
NOUGHT
NOUGHTIES
NOUGHTS
NOUL
NOULD
NOULDE
NOULE
NOULES
NOULS
NOUMENA

NOUMENAL	NOVELIST	NOXIOUSLY	NUCHAL
NOUMENON	NOVELISTS	NOY	NUCHALS
NOUN	NOVELIZE	NOYADE	NUCLEAL
NOUNAL	NOVELIZED	NOYADES	NUCLEAR
NOUNALLY	NOVELIZER	NOYANCE	NUCLEASE
NOUNIER	NOVELIZES	NOYANCES	NUCLEASES
NOUNIEST	NOVELLA	NOYAU	NUCLEATE
NOUNLESS	NOVELLAE	NOYAUS	NUCLEATED
NOUNS	NOVELLAS	NOYED	NUCLEATES
NOUNY	NOVELLE	NOYES	NUCLEATOR
NOUP	NOVELLY	NOYESES	NUCLEI
NOUPS	NOVELS	NOYING	NUCLEIC
NOURICE	NOVELTIES	NOYOUS	NUCLEIDE
NOURICES	NOVELTY	NOYS	NUCLEIDES
NOURISH	NOVENA	NOYSOME	NUCLEIN
NOURISHED	NOVENAE	NOZZER	NUCLEINIC
NOURISHER	NOVENARY	NOZZERS	NUCLEINS
NOURISHES	NOVENAS	NOZZLE	NUCLEOID
NOURITURE	NOVENNIAL	NOZZLES	NUCLEOIDS
NOURSLE	NOVERCAL	NTH	NUCLEOLAR
NOURSLED	NOVERINT	NU	NUCLEOLE
NOURSLES	NOVERINTS	NUANCE	NUCLEOLES
NOURSLING	NOVICE	NUANCED	NUCLEOLI
NOUS	NOVICES	NUANCES	NUCLEOLUS
NOUSELL	NOVICIATE	NUANCING	NUCLEON
NOUSELLED	NOVITIATE	NUB	NUCLEONIC
NOUSELLS	NOVITIES	NUBBED	NUCLEONS
NOUSES	NOVITY	NUBBIER	NUCLEUS
NOUSLE	NOVOCAINE	NUBBIEST	NUCLEUSES
NOUSLED	NOVODAMUS	NUBBIN	NUCLIDE
NOUSLES	NOVUM	NUBBINESS	NUCLIDES
NOUSLING	NOVUMS	NUBBING	NUCLIDIC
NOUT	NOW	NUBBINS	NUCULE
NOUVEAU	NOWADAYS	NUBBLE	NUCULES
NOUVEAUX	NOWAY	NUBBLED	NUDATION
NOUVELLE	NOWAYS	NUBBLES	NUDATIONS
NOUVELLES	NOWED	NUBBLIER	NUDDIES
NOVA	NOWHENCE	NUBBLIEST	NUDDY
NOVAE	NOWHERE	NUBBLING	NUDE
NOVALIA	NOWHERES	NUBBLY	NUDELY
NOVALIKE	NOWHITHER	NUBBY	NUDENESS
NOVAS	NOWISE	NUBECULA	NUDER
NOVATED	NOWL	NUBECULAE	NUDES
NOVATION	NOWLS	NUBIA	NUDEST
NOVATIONS	NOWN	NUBIAS	NUDGE
NOVEL	NOWNESS	NUBIFORM	NUDGED
NOVELDOM	NOWNESSES	NUBILE	NUDGER
NOVELDOMS	NOWS	NUBILITY	NUDGERS
NOVELESE	NOWT	NUBILOSE	NUDGES
NOVELESES	NOWTIER	NUBILOUS	NUDGING
NOVELETTE	NOWTIEST	NUBS	NUDICAUL
NOVELISE	NOWTS	NUBUCK	NUDIE
NOVELISED	NOWTY	NUBUCKS	NUDIES
NOVELISER	NOWY	NUCELLAR	NUDISM
NOVELISES	NOX	NUCELLI	NUDISMS
NOVELISH	NOXAL	NUCELLUS	NUDIST
NOVELISM	NOXES	NUCHA	NUDISTS
NOVELISMS	NOXIOUS	NUCHAE	NUDITIES

NUDITY
NUDNICK
NUDNICKS
NUDNIK
NUDNIKS
NUDZH
NUDZHED
NUDZHES
NUDZHING
NUFF
NUFFIN
NUFFINS
NUFFS
NUGAE
NUGATORY
NUGGAR
NUGGARS
NUGGET
NUGGETED
NUGGETING
NUGGETS
NUGGETTED
NUGGETY
NUISANCE
NUISANCER
NUISANCES
NUKE
NUKED
NUKES
NUKING
NULL
NULLA
NULLAH
NULLAHS
NULLAS
NULLED
NULLIFIED
NULLIFIER
NULLIFIES
NULLIFY
NULLING
NULLINGS
NULLIPARA
NULLIPORE
NULLITIES
NULLITY
NULLNESS
NULLS
NUMB
NUMBAT
NUMBATS
NUMBED
NUMBER
NUMBERED
NUMBERER
NUMBERERS
NUMBERING
NUMBERS

NUMBEST
NUMBFISH
NUMBING
NUMBINGLY
NUMBLES
NUMBLY
NUMBNESS
NUMBS
NUMBSKULL
NUMCHUCK
NUMCHUCKS
NUMDAH
NUMDAHS
NUMEN
NUMERABLE
NUMERABLY
NUMERACY
NUMERAIRE
NUMERAL
NUMERALLY
NUMERALS
NUMERARY
NUMERATE
NUMERATED
NUMERATES
NUMERATOR
NUMERIC
NUMERICAL
NUMERICS
NUMEROUS
NUMINA
NUMINOUS
NUMMARY
NUMMULAR
NUMMULARY
NUMMULINE
NUMMULITE
NUMNAH
NUMNAHS
NUMPTIES
NUMPTY
NUMSKULL
NUMSKULLS
NUN
NUNATAK
NUNATAKER
NUNATAKS
NUNCHAKU
NUNCHAKUS
NUNCHEON
NUNCHEONS
NUNCIO
NUNCIOS
NUNCLE
NUNCLES
NUNCUPATE
NUNDINAL
NUNDINE

NUNDINES
NUNHOOD
NUNHOODS
NUNLIKE
NUNNATION
NUNNERIES
NUNNERY
NUNNISH
NUNNY
NUNS
NUNSHIP
NUNSHIPS
NUPTIAL
NUPTIALLY
NUPTIALS
NUR
NURAGHE
NURAGHI
NURAGHIC
NURD
NURDIER
NURDIEST
NURDISH
NURDLE
NURDLED
NURDLES
NURDLING
NURDS
NURDY
NURHAG
NURHAGS
NURL
NURLED
NURLING
NURLS
NURR
NURRS
NURS
NURSE
NURSED
NURSELIKE
NURSELING
NURSEMAID
NURSER
NURSERIES
NURSERS
NURSERY
NURSES
NURSING
NURSINGS
NURSLE
NURSLED
NURSLES
NURSLING
NURSLINGS
NURTURAL
NURTURANT
NURTURE

NURTURED
NURTURER
NURTURERS
NURTURES
NURTURING
NUS
NUT
NUTANT
NUTARIAN
NUTARIANS
NUTATE
NUTATED
NUTATES
NUTATING
NUTATION
NUTATIONS
NUTBROWN
NUTBUTTER
NUTCASE
NUTCASES
NUTGALL
NUTGALLS
NUTGRASS
NUTHATCH
NUTHOUSE
NUTHOUSES
NUTJOBBER
NUTLET
NUTLETS
NUTLIKE
NUTMEAL
NUTMEALS
NUTMEAT
NUTMEATS
NUTMEG
NUTMEGGED
NUTMEGGY
NUTMEGS
NUTPECKER
NUTPICK
NUTPICKS
NUTRIA
NUTRIAS
NUTRIENT
NUTRIENTS
NUTRIMENT
NUTRITION
NUTRITIVE
NUTS
NUTSEDGE
NUTSEDGES
NUTSHELL
NUTSHELLS
NUTSIER
NUTSIEST
NUTSO
NUTSY
NUTTED

NUTTER
NUTTERIES
NUTTERS
NUTTERY
NUTTIER
NUTTIEST
NUTTILY
NUTTINESS
NUTTING
NUTTINGS
NUTTY
NUTWOOD
NUTWOODS
NUZZER
NUZZERS
NUZZLE
NUZZLED
NUZZLER
NUZZLERS
NUZZLES
NUZZLING
NY
NYAFF
NYAFFED
NYAFFING
NYAFFS
NYALA
NYALAS
NYANZA
NYANZAS
NYAS
NYASES
NYBBLE
NYBBLES
NYCTALOPS
NYE
NYED
NYES
NYING
NYLGHAI
NYLGHAIS
NYLGHAU
NYLGHAUS
NYLON
NYLONS
NYMPH
NYMPHA
NYMPHAE
NYMPHAEA
NYMPHAEUM
NYMPHAL
NYMPHALID
NYMPHEAN
NYMPHET
NYMPHETIC
NYMPHETS
NYMPHETTE
NYMPHIC

NYMPHICAL
NYMPHISH
NYMPHLIKE
NYMPHLY
NYMPHO
NYMPHOS
NYMPHS
NYS
NYSSA
NYSSAS
NYSTAGMIC
NYSTAGMUS
NYSTATIN
NYSTATINS

O

OAF
OAFISH
OAFISHLY
OAFS
OAK
OAKED
OAKEN
OAKENSHAW
OAKER
OAKERS
OAKIER
OAKIES
OAKIEST
OAKLEAF
OAKLEAVES
OAKLIKE
OAKLING
OAKLINGS
OAKMOSS
OAKMOSSES
OAKS
OAKUM
OAKUMS
OAKY
OANSHAGH
OANSHAGHS
OAR
OARAGE
OARAGES
OARED
OARFISH
OARFISHES
OARIER
OARIEST
OARING
OARLESS
OARLIKE
OARLOCK
OARLOCKS
OARS
OARSMAN
OARSMEN
OARSWOMAN
OARSWOMEN
OARWEED
OARWEEDS
OARY
OASES
OASIS
OAST
OASTHOUSE
OASTS
OAT

OATCAKE
OATCAKES
OATEN
OATER
OATERS
OATH
OATHABLE
OATHS
OATLIKE
OATMEAL
OATMEALS
OATS
OAVES
OB
OBA
OBANG
OBANGS
OBAS
OBBLIGATI
OBBLIGATO
OBCONIC
OBCONICAL
OBCORDATE
OBDURACY
OBDURATE
OBDURATED
OBDURATES
OBDURE
OBDURED
OBDURES
OBDURING
OBE
OBEAH
OBEAHED
OBEAHING
OBEAHISM
OBEAHISMS
OBEAHS
OBECHE
OBECHES
OBEDIENCE
OBEDIENT
OBEISANCE
OBEISANT
OBEISM
OBEISMS
OBELI
OBELIA
OBELIAS
OBELION
OBELISCAL
OBELISE
OBELISED

OBELISES
OBELISING
OBELISK
OBELISKS
OBELISM
OBELISMS
OBELIZE
OBELIZED
OBELIZES
OBELIZING
OBELUS
OBENTO
OBENTOS
OBES
OBESE
OBESELY
OBESENESS
OBESER
OBESEST
OBESITIES
OBESITY
OBEY
OBEYABLE
OBEYED
OBEYER
OBEYERS
OBEYING
OBEYS
OBFUSCATE
OBI
OBIA
OBIAS
OBIED
OBIING
OBIISM
OBIISMS
OBIIT
OBIS
OBIT
OBITAL
OBITER
OBITS
OBITUAL
OBITUARY
OBJECT
OBJECTED
OBJECTIFY
OBJECTING
OBJECTION
OBJECTIVE
OBJECTOR
OBJECTORS
OBJECTS

OBJET
OBJETS
OBJURE
OBJURED
OBJURES
OBJURGATE
OBJURING
OBLAST
OBLASTI
OBLASTS
OBLATE
OBLATELY
OBLATES
OBLATION
OBLATIONS
OBLATORY
OBLIGABLE
OBLIGANT
OBLIGANTS
OBLIGATE
OBLIGATED
OBLIGATES
OBLIGATI
OBLIGATO
OBLIGATOR
OBLIGATOS
OBLIGE
OBLIGED
OBLIGEE
OBLIGEES
OBLIGER
OBLIGERS
OBLIGES
OBLIGING
OBLIGOR
OBLIGORS
OBLIQUE
OBLIQUED
OBLIQUELY
OBLIQUER
OBLIQUES
OBLIQUEST
OBLIQUID
OBLIQUING
OBLIQUITY
OBLIVION
OBLIVIONS
OBLIVIOUS
OBLONG
OBLONGLY
OBLONGS
OBLOQUIAL
OBLOQUIES

OBLOQUY
OBNOXIOUS
OBO
OBOE
OBOES
OBOIST
OBOISTS
OBOL
OBOLARY
OBOLE
OBOLES
OBOLI
OBOLS
OBOLUS
OBOS
OBOVATE
OBOVATELY
OBOVOID
OBREPTION
OBS
OBSCENE
OBSCENELY
OBSCENER
OBSCENEST
OBSCENITY
OBSCURANT
OBSCURE
OBSCURED
OBSCURELY
OBSCURER
OBSCURERS
OBSCURES
OBSCUREST
OBSCURING
OBSCURITY
OBSECRATE
OBSEQUENT
OBSEQUIAL
OBSEQUIE
OBSEQUIES
OBSEQUY
OBSERVANT
OBSERVE
OBSERVED
OBSERVER
OBSERVERS
OBSERVES
OBSERVING
OBSESS
OBSESSED
OBSESSES
OBSESSING
OBSESSION
OBSESSIVE
OBSESSOR
OBSESSORS
OBSIDIAN
OBSIDIANS

OBSIGN
OBSIGNATE
OBSIGNED
OBSIGNING
OBSIGNS
OBSOLESCE
OBSOLETE
OBSOLETED
OBSOLETES
OBSTACLE
OBSTACLES
OBSTETRIC
OBSTINACY
OBSTINATE
OBSTRUCT
OBSTRUCTS
OBSTRUENT
OBTAIN
OBTAINED
OBTAINER
OBTAINERS
OBTAINING
OBTAINS
OBTECT
OBTECTED
OBTEMPER
OBTEMPERS
OBTEND
OBTENDED
OBTENDING
OBTENDS
OBTENTION
OBTEST
OBTESTED
OBTESTING
OBTESTS
OBTRUDE
OBTRUDED
OBTRUDER
OBTRUDERS
OBTRUDES
OBTRUDING
OBTRUSION
OBTRUSIVE
OBTUND
OBTUNDED
OBTUNDENT
OBTUNDING
OBTUNDITY
OBTUNDS
OBTURATE
OBTURATED
OBTURATES
OBTURATOR
OBTUSE
OBTUSELY
OBTUSER
OBTUSEST

OBTUSITY
OBUMBRATE
OBVENTION
OBVERSE
OBVERSELY
OBVERSES
OBVERSION
OBVERT
OBVERTED
OBVERTING
OBVERTS
OBVIABLE
OBVIATE
OBVIATED
OBVIATES
OBVIATING
OBVIATION
OBVIATOR
OBVIATORS
OBVIOUS
OBVIOUSLY
OBVOLUTE
OBVOLUTED
OBVOLVENT
OCA
OCARINA
OCARINAS
OCAS
OCCAM
OCCAMIES
OCCAMS
OCCAMY
OCCASION
OCCASIONS
OCCIDENT
OCCIDENTS
OCCIES
OCCIPITA
OCCIPITAL
OCCIPUT
OCCIPUTS
OCCLUDE
OCCLUDED
OCCLUDENT
OCCLUDER
OCCLUDERS
OCCLUDES
OCCLUDING
OCCLUSAL
OCCLUSION
OCCLUSIVE
OCCLUSOR
OCCLUSORS
OCCULT
OCCULTED
OCCULTER
OCCULTERS
OCCULTING

OCCULTISM
OCCULTIST
OCCULTLY
OCCULTS
OCCUPANCE
OCCUPANCY
OCCUPANT
OCCUPANTS
OCCUPATE
OCCUPATED
OCCUPATES
OCCUPIED
OCCUPIER
OCCUPIERS
OCCUPIES
OCCUPY
OCCUPYING
OCCUR
OCCURRED
OCCURRENT
OCCURRING
OCCURS
OCCY
OCEAN
OCEANARIA
OCEANAUT
OCEANAUTS
OCEANIC
OCEANID
OCEANIDES
OCEANIDS
OCEANS
OCELLAR
OCELLATE
OCELLATED
OCELLI
OCELLUS
OCELOID
OCELOT
OCELOTS
OCH
OCHE
OCHER
OCHERED
OCHERING
OCHEROUS
OCHERS
OCHERY
OCHES
OCHIDORE
OCHIDORES
OCHLOCRAT
OCHONE
OCHRE
OCHREA
OCHREAE
OCHREATE
OCHRED

OCHREOUS
OCHRES
OCHREY
OCHRING
OCHROID
OCHROUS
OCHRY
OCICAT
OCICATS
OCKER
OCKERISM
OCKERISMS
OCKERS
OCKODOLS
OCOTILLO
OCOTILLOS
OCREA
OCREAE
OCREATE
OCTA
OCTACHORD
OCTAD
OCTADIC
OCTADS
OCTAGON
OCTAGONAL
OCTAGONS
OCTAHEDRA
OCTAL
OCTALS
OCTAMETER
OCTAN
OCTANE
OCTANES
OCTANGLE
OCTANGLES
OCTANOL
OCTANOLS
OCTANS
OCTANT
OCTANTAL
OCTANTS
OCTAPLA
OCTAPLAS
OCTAPLOID
OCTAPODIC
OCTAPODY
OCTARCHY
OCTAROON
OCTAROONS
OCTAS
OCTASTICH
OCTASTYLE
OCTAVAL
OCTAVE
OCTAVES
OCTAVO
OCTAVOS

OCTENNIAL
OCTET
OCTETS
OCTETT
OCTETTE
OCTETTES
OCTETTS
OCTILLION
OCTOFID
OCTOHEDRA
OCTONARII
OCTONARY
OCTOPI
OCTOPLOID
OCTOPOD
OCTOPODAN
OCTOPODES
OCTOPODS
OCTOPUS
OCTOPUSES
OCTOPUSH
OCTOROON
OCTOROONS
OCTOSTYLE
OCTOTHORP
OCTROI
OCTROIS
OCTUOR
OCTUORS
OCTUPLE
OCTUPLED
OCTUPLES
OCTUPLET
OCTUPLETS
OCTUPLEX
OCTUPLING
OCTUPLY
OCTYL
OCTYLS
OCULAR
OCULARIST
OCULARLY
OCULARS
OCULATE
OCULATED
OCULI
OCULIST
OCULISTS
OCULUS
OD
ODA
ODAH
ODAHS
ODAL
ODALIQUE
ODALIQUES
ODALISK
ODALISKS

ODALISQUE
ODALLER
ODALLERS
ODALS
ODAS
ODD
ODDBALL
ODDBALLS
ODDER
ODDEST
ODDISH
ODDITIES
ODDITY
ODDLY
ODDMENT
ODDMENTS
ODDNESS
ODDNESSES
ODDS
ODDSMAKER
ODDSMAN
ODDSMEN
ODE
ODEA
ODEON
ODEONS
ODES
ODEUM
ODEUMS
ODIC
ODIFEROUS
ODIOUS
ODIOUSLY
ODISM
ODISMS
ODIST
ODISTS
ODIUM
ODIUMS
ODOGRAPH
ODOGRAPHS
ODOMETER
ODOMETERS
ODOMETRY
ODONATE
ODONATES
ODONATIST
ODONTALGY
ODONTIC
ODONTIST
ODONTISTS
ODONTOID
ODONTOIDS
ODONTOMA
ODONTOMAS
ODOR
ODORANT
ODORANTS

ODORATE
ODORED
ODORFUL
ODORISE
ODORISED
ODORISES
ODORISING
ODORIZE
ODORIZED
ODORIZES
ODORIZING
ODORLESS
ODOROUS
ODOROUSLY
ODORS
ODOUR
ODOURED
ODOURFUL
ODOURLESS
ODOURS
ODS
ODSO
ODSOS
ODYL
ODYLE
ODYLES
ODYLISM
ODYLISMS
ODYLS
ODYSSEY
ODYSSEYS
ODZOOKS
OE
OECIST
OECISTS
OECOLOGY
OECUMENIC
OEDEMA
OEDEMAS
OEDEMATA
OEDIPAL
OEDIPALLY
OEDIPEAN
OEDOMETER
OEILLADE
OEILLADES
OENANTHIC
OENOLOGY
OENOMANCY
OENOMANIA
OENOMEL
OENOMELS
OENOMETER
OENOPHIL
OENOPHILE
OENOPHILS
OENOPHILY
OENOTHERA

OERLIKON	OFFHAND	OFTENNESS	OI
OERLIKONS	OFFHANDED	OFTER	OIDIA
OERSTED	OFFICE	OFTEST	OIDIOID
OERSTEDS	OFFICER	OFTTIMES	OIDIUM
OES	OFFICERED	OGAM	OIK
OESOPHAGI	OFFICERS	OGAMIC	OIKIST
OESTRAL	OFFICES	OGAMS	OIKISTS
OESTRIN	OFFICIAL	OGDOAD	OIKS
OESTRINS	OFFICIALS	OGDOADS	OIL
OESTRIOL	OFFICIANT	OGEE	OILBIRD
OESTRIOLS	OFFICIARY	OGEES	OILBIRDS
OESTROGEN	OFFICIATE	OGGIN	OILCAMP
OESTRONE	OFFICINAL	OGGINS	OILCAMPS
OESTRONES	OFFICIOUS	OGHAM	OILCAN
OESTROUS	OFFING	OGHAMIC	OILCANS
OESTRUM	OFFINGS	OGHAMIST	OILCLOTH
OESTRUMS	OFFISH	OGHAMISTS	OILCLOTHS
OESTRUS	OFFISHLY	OGHAMS	OILCUP
OESTRUSES	OFFKEY	OGIVAL	OILCUPS
OEUVRE	OFFLINE	OGIVE	OILED
OEUVRES	OFFLOAD	OGIVES	OILER
OF	OFFLOADED	OGLE	OILERIES
OFAY	OFFLOADS	OGLED	OILERS
OFAYS	OFFPEAK	OGLER	OILERY
OFF	OFFPRINT	OGLERS	OILFIELD
OFFAL	OFFPRINTS	OGLES	OILFIELDS
OFFALS	OFFPUT	OGLING	OILFIRED
OFFBEAT	OFFPUTS	OGLINGS	OILGAS
OFFBEATS	OFFRAMP	OGMIC	OILGASES
OFFCAST	OFFRAMPS	OGRE	OILHOLE
OFFCASTS	OFFS	OGREISH	OILHOLES
OFFCUT	OFFSADDLE	OGREISHLY	OILIER
OFFCUTS	OFFSCREEN	OGREISM	OILIEST
OFFED	OFFSCUM	OGREISMS	OILILY
OFFENCE	OFFSCUMS	OGRES	OILINESS
OFFENCES	OFFSEASON	OGRESS	OILING
OFFEND	OFFSET	OGRESSES	OILLET
OFFENDED	OFFSETS	OGRISH	OILLETS
OFFENDER	OFFSHOOT	OGRISHLY	OILMAN
OFFENDERS	OFFSHOOTS	OGRISM	OILMEN
OFFENDING	OFFSHORE	OGRISMS	OILNUT
OFFENDS	OFFSHORES	OH	OILNUTS
OFFENSE	OFFSIDE	OHED	OILPAPER
OFFENSES	OFFSIDER	OHIA	OILPAPERS
OFFENSIVE	OFFSIDERS	OHIAS	OILPROOF
OFFER	OFFSIDES	OHING	OILS
OFFERABLE	OFFSPRING	OHM	OILSEED
OFFERED	OFFSTAGE	OHMAGE	OILSEEDS
OFFEREE	OFFSTAGES	OHMAGES	OILSKIN
OFFEREES	OFFTAKE	OHMIC	OILSKINS
OFFERER	OFFTAKES	OHMICALLY	OILSTONE
OFFERERS	OFFTRACK	OHMMETER	OILSTONES
OFFERING	OFLAG	OHMMETERS	OILTIGHT
OFFERINGS	OFLAGS	OHMS	OILWAY
OFFEROR	OFT	OHO	OILWAYS
OFFERORS	OFTEN	OHONE	OILY
OFFERS	OFTENER	OHOS	OINK
OFFERTORY	OFTENEST	OHS	OINKED

OINKING	OLEA	OLIGOMERS	OMASA
OINKS	OLEACEOUS	OLIGOPOLY	OMASAL
OINOLOGY	OLEANDER	OLIGURIA	OMASUM
OINOMEL	OLEANDERS	OLIGURIAS	OMBER
OINOMELS	OLEARIA	OLINGO	OMBERS
OINT	OLEARIAS	OLINGOS	OMBRE
OINTED	OLEASTER	OLIO	OMBRELLA
OINTING	OLEASTERS	OLIOS	OMBRELLAS
OINTMENT	OLEATE	OLIPHANT	OMBRES
OINTMENTS	OLEATES	OLIPHANTS	OMBROPHIL
OINTS	OLECRANAL	OLITORIES	OMBU
OITICICA	OLECRANON	OLITORY	OMBUDSMAN
OITICICAS	OLEFIANT	OLIVARY	OMBUDSMEN
OJIME	OLEFIN	OLIVE	OMBUS
OJIMES	OLEFINE	OLIVENITE	OMEGA
OKA	OLEFINES	OLIVER	OMEGAS
OKAPI	OLEFINIC	OLIVERS	OMELET
OKAPIS	OLEFINS	OLIVES	OMELETS
OKAS	OLEIC	OLIVET	OMELETTE
OKAY	OLEIN	OLIVETS	OMELETTES
OKAYED	OLEINE	OLIVINE	OMEN
OKAYING	OLEINES	OLIVINES	OMENED
OKAYS	OLEINS	OLIVINIC	OMENING
OKE	OLENT	OLLA	OMENS
OKEH	OLEO	OLLAMH	OMENTA
OKEHS	OLEOGRAPH	OLLAMHS	OMENTAL
OKES	OLEORESIN	OLLAS	OMENTUM
OKEYDOKE	OLEOS	OLLAV	OMENTUMS
OKEYDOKEY	OLES	OLLAVS	OMER
OKIMONO	OLESTRA	OLLER	OMERS
OKIMONOS	OLESTRAS	OLLERS	OMERTA
OKRA	OLEUM	OLLIE	OMERTAS
OKRAS	OLEUMS	OLLIES	OMICRON
OKTA	OLFACT	OLM	OMICRONS
OKTAS	OLFACTED	OLMS	OMIGOD
OLD	OLFACTING	OLOGIES	OMIKRON
OLDEN	OLFACTION	OLOGIST	OMIKRONS
OLDENED	OLFACTIVE	OLOGISTS	OMINOUS
OLDENING	OLFACTORY	OLOGOAN	OMINOUSLY
OLDENS	OLFACTS	OLOGOANED	OMISSIBLE
OLDER	OLIBANUM	OLOGOANS	OMISSION
OLDEST	OLIBANUMS	OLOGY	OMISSIONS
OLDIE	OLICOOK	OLOLIUQUI	OMISSIVE
OLDIES	OLICOOKS	OLOROSO	OMIT
OLDISH	OLID	OLOROSOS	OMITS
OLDNESS	OLIGAEMIA	OLPAE	OMITTANCE
OLDNESSES	OLIGAEMIC	OLPE	OMITTED
OLDS	OLIGARCH	OLPES	OMITTER
OLDSQUAW	OLIGARCHS	OLYCOOK	OMITTERS
OLDSQUAWS	OLIGARCHY	OLYCOOKS	OMITTING
OLDSTER	OLIGEMIA	OLYKOEK	OMLAH
OLDSTERS	OLIGEMIAS	OLYKOEKS	OMLAHS
OLDSTYLE	OLIGEMIC	OLYMPIAD	OMMATEA
OLDSTYLES	OLIGIST	OLYMPIADS	OMMATEUM
OLDWIFE	OLIGISTS	OLYMPICS	OMMATIDIA
OLDWIVES	OLIGOCENE	OM	OMNEITIES
OLDY	OLIGOGENE	OMADHAUN	OMNEITY
OLE	OLIGOMER	OMADHAUNS	OMNIANA

OMNIARCH
OMNIARCHS
OMNIBUS
OMNIBUSES
OMNIETIES
OMNIETY
OMNIFIC
OMNIFIED
OMNIFIES
OMNIFORM
OMNIFY
OMNIFYING
OMNIMODE
OMNIRANGE
OMNIUM
OMNIUMS
OMNIVORA
OMNIVORE
OMNIVORES
OMNIVORY
OMOHYOID
OMOHYOIDS
OMOPHAGIA
OMOPHAGIC
OMOPHAGY
OMOPHORIA
OMOPLATE
OMOPLATES
OMOV
OMOVS
OMPHACITE
OMPHALI
OMPHALIC
OMPHALOID
OMPHALOS
OMRAH
OMRAHS
OMS
ON
ONAGER
ONAGERS
ONAGRI
ONANISM
ONANISMS
ONANIST
ONANISTIC
ONANISTS
ONBEAT
ONBEATS
ONBOARD
ONCE
ONCER
ONCERS
ONCES
ONCET
ONCIDIUM
ONCIDIUMS
ONCOGEN

ONCOGENE
ONCOGENES
ONCOGENIC
ONCOGENS
ONCOLOGIC
ONCOLOGY
ONCOLYSES
ONCOLYSIS
ONCOLYTIC
ONCOME
ONCOMES
ONCOMETER
ONCOMICE
ONCOMING
ONCOMINGS
ONCOMOUSE
ONCOST
ONCOSTMAN
ONCOSTMEN
ONCOSTS
ONCOTOMY
ONCOVIRUS
ONCUS
ONDATRA
ONDATRAS
ONDINE
ONDINES
ONDING
ONDINGS
ONDOGRAM
ONDOGRAMS
ONDOGRAPH
ONE
ONEFOLD
ONEIRIC
ONELY
ONENESS
ONENESSES
ONER
ONERIER
ONERIEST
ONEROUS
ONEROUSLY
ONERS
ONERY
ONES
ONESELF
ONETIME
ONEYER
ONEYERS
ONEYRE
ONEYRES
ONFALL
ONFALLS
ONFLOW
ONFLOWS
ONGAONGA
ONGAONGAS

ONGOING
ONGOINGS
ONIE
ONION
ONIONED
ONIONIER
ONIONIEST
ONIONING
ONIONS
ONIONSKIN
ONIONY
ONIRIC
ONISCOID
ONIUM
ONIUMS
ONKUS
ONLAY
ONLAYS
ONLIEST
ONLINE
ONLINER
ONLINERS
ONLOAD
ONLOADED
ONLOADING
ONLOADS
ONLOOKER
ONLOOKERS
ONLOOKING
ONLY
ONNED
ONNING
ONO
ONOMASTIC
ONOS
ONRUSH
ONRUSHES
ONRUSHING
ONS
ONSCREEN
ONSET
ONSETS
ONSETTER
ONSETTERS
ONSETTING
ONSHORE
ONSHORING
ONSIDE
ONSIDES
ONSLAUGHT
ONST
ONSTAGE
ONSTEAD
ONSTEADS
ONSTREAM
ONTIC
ONTICALLY
ONTO

ONTOGENIC
ONTOGENY
ONTOLOGIC
ONTOLOGY
ONUS
ONUSES
ONWARD
ONWARDLY
ONWARDS
ONY
ONYCHA
ONYCHAS
ONYCHIA
ONYCHIAS
ONYCHITE
ONYCHITES
ONYCHITIS
ONYCHIUM
ONYCHIUMS
ONYMOUS
ONYX
ONYXES
OO
OOBIT
OOBITS
OOCYST
OOCYSTS
OOCYTE
OOCYTES
OODLES
OODLINS
OOF
OOFIER
OOFIEST
OOFS
OOFTISH
OOFTISHES
OOFY
OOGAMETE
OOGAMETES
OOGAMIES
OOGAMOUS
OOGAMY
OOGENESES
OOGENESIS
OOGENETIC
OOGENIES
OOGENY
OOGONIA
OOGONIAL
OOGONIUM
OOGONIUMS
OOH
OOHED
OOHING
OOHS
OOIDAL
OOLACHAN

OOLACHANS
OOLAKAN
OOLAKANS
OOLITE
OOLITES
OOLITH
OOLITHS
OOLITIC
OOLOGIC
OOLOGICAL
OOLOGIES
OOLOGIST
OOLOGISTS
OOLOGY
OOLONG
OOLONGS
OOM
OOMIAC
OOMIACK
OOMIACKS
OOMIACS
OOMIAK
OOMIAKS
OOMPAH
OOMPAHED
OOMPAHING
OOMPAHS
OOMPH
OOMPHS
OOMS
OOMYCETE
OOMYCETES
OON
OONS
OONT
OONTS
OOP
OOPED
OOPHORON
OOPHORONS
OOPHYTE
OOPHYTES
OOPHYTIC
OOPING
OOPS
OOR
OORALI
OORALIS
OORIAL
OORIALS
OORIE
OORIER
OORIEST
OOS
OOSE
OOSES
OOSIER
OOSIEST

OOSPERM
OOSPERMS
OOSPHERE
OOSPHERES
OOSPORE
OOSPORES
OOSPORIC
OOSPOROUS
OOSY
OOT
OOTHECA
OOTHECAE
OOTHECAL
OOTID
OOTIDS
OOTS
OOZE
OOZED
OOZES
OOZIER
OOZIEST
OOZILY
OOZINESS
OOZING
OOZY
OP
OPACIFIED
OPACIFIER
OPACIFIES
OPACIFY
OPACITIES
OPACITY
OPACOUS
OPAH
OPAHS
OPAL
OPALED
OPALESCE
OPALESCED
OPALESCES
OPALINE
OPALINES
OPALISED
OPALIZED
OPALS
OPAQUE
OPAQUED
OPAQUELY
OPAQUER
OPAQUES
OPAQUEST
OPAQUING
OPCODE
OPCODES
OPE
OPED
OPEN
OPENABLE

OPENCAST
OPENED
OPENER
OPENERS
OPENEST
OPENING
OPENINGS
OPENLY
OPENNESS
OPENS
OPENSIDE
OPENSIDES
OPENWORK
OPENWORKS
OPEPE
OPEPES
OPERA
OPERABLE
OPERABLY
OPERAGOER
OPERAND
OPERANDS
OPERANT
OPERANTLY
OPERANTS
OPERAS
OPERATE
OPERATED
OPERATES
OPERATIC
OPERATICS
OPERATING
OPERATION
OPERATISE
OPERATIVE
OPERATIZE
OPERATOR
OPERATORS
OPERCELE
OPERCELES
OPERCULA
OPERCULAR
OPERCULE
OPERCULES
OPERCULUM
OPERETTA
OPERETTAS
OPERON
OPERONS
OPEROSE
OPEROSELY
OPEROSITY
OPES
OPGEFOK
OPHIDIAN
OPHIDIANS
OPHIOLITE
OPHIOLOGY

OPHITE
OPHITES
OPHITIC
OPHIURA
OPHIURAN
OPHIURANS
OPHIURAS
OPHIURID
OPHIURIDS
OPHIUROID
OPIATE
OPIATED
OPIATES
OPIATING
OPIFICER
OPIFICERS
OPINABLE
OPINE
OPINED
OPINES
OPING
OPINICUS
OPINING
OPINION
OPINIONED
OPINIONS
OPIOID
OPIOIDS
OPIUM
OPIUMISM
OPIUMISMS
OPIUMS
OPOBALSAM
OPODELDOC
OPOPANAX
OPORICE
OPORICES
OPOSSUM
OPOSSUMS
OPPIDAN
OPPIDANS
OPPILANT
OPPILATE
OPPILATED
OPPILATES
OPPO
OPPONENCY
OPPONENT
OPPONENTS
OPPORTUNE
OPPOS
OPPOSABLE
OPPOSABLY
OPPOSE
OPPOSED
OPPOSER
OPPOSERS
OPPOSES

OPPOSING
OPPOSITE
OPPOSITES
OPPRESS
OPPRESSED
OPPRESSES
OPPRESSOR
OPPUGN
OPPUGNANT
OPPUGNED
OPPUGNER
OPPUGNERS
OPPUGNING
OPPUGNS
OPS
OPSIMATH
OPSIMATHS
OPSIMATHY
OPSIN
OPSINS
OPSOMANIA
OPSONIC
OPSONIFY
OPSONIN
OPSONINS
OPSONISE
OPSONISED
OPSONISES
OPSONIUM
OPSONIUMS
OPSONIZE
OPSONIZED
OPSONIZES
OPT
OPTANT
OPTANTS
OPTATIVE
OPTATIVES
OPTED
OPTER
OPTERS
OPTIC
OPTICAL
OPTICALLY
OPTICIAN
OPTICIANS
OPTICIST
OPTICISTS
OPTICS
OPTIMA
OPTIMAL
OPTIMALLY
OPTIMATE
OPTIMATES
OPTIME
OPTIMES
OPTIMISE
OPTIMISED

OPTIMISER
OPTIMISES
OPTIMISM
OPTIMISMS
OPTIMIST
OPTIMISTS
OPTIMIZE
OPTIMIZED
OPTIMIZER
OPTIMIZES
OPTIMUM
OPTIMUMS
OPTING
OPTION
OPTIONAL
OPTIONALS
OPTIONED
OPTIONEE
OPTIONEES
OPTIONING
OPTIONS
OPTOLOGY
OPTOMETER
OPTOMETRY
OPTOPHONE
OPTRONICS
OPTS
OPULENCE
OPULENCES
OPULENCY
OPULENT
OPULENTLY
OPULUS
OPULUSES
OPUNTIA
OPUNTIAS
OPUS
OPUSCLE
OPUSCLES
OPUSCULA
OPUSCULAR
OPUSCULE
OPUSCULES
OPUSCULUM
OPUSES
OQUASSA
OQUASSAS
OR
ORA
ORACH
ORACHE
ORACHES
ORACIES
ORACLE
ORACLED
ORACLES
ORACLING
ORACULAR

ORACULOUS
ORACY
ORAD
ORAGIOUS
ORAL
ORALISM
ORALISMS
ORALIST
ORALISTS
ORALITIES
ORALITY
ORALLY
ORALS
ORANG
ORANGE
ORANGEADE
ORANGER
ORANGERIE
ORANGERY
ORANGES
ORANGEST
ORANGEY
ORANGIER
ORANGIEST
ORANGISH
ORANGS
ORANGUTAN
ORANGY
ORANT
ORANTS
ORARIA
ORARIAN
ORARIANS
ORARION
ORARIONS
ORARIUM
ORARIUMS
ORATE
ORATED
ORATES
ORATING
ORATION
ORATIONS
ORATOR
ORATORIAL
ORATORIAN
ORATORIES
ORATORIO
ORATORIOS
ORATORS
ORATORY
ORATRESS
ORATRICES
ORATRIX
ORATRIXES
ORB
ORBED
ORBICULAR

ORBIER
ORBIEST
ORBING
ORBIT
ORBITA
ORBITAL
ORBITALLY
ORBITALS
ORBITAS
ORBITED
ORBITER
ORBITERS
ORBITIES
ORBITING
ORBITS
ORBITY
ORBLESS
ORBS
ORBY
ORC
ORCA
ORCAS
ORCEIN
ORCEINS
ORCHARD
ORCHARDS
ORCHAT
ORCHATS
ORCHEL
ORCHELLA
ORCHELLAS
ORCHELS
ORCHESES
ORCHESIS
ORCHESTIC
ORCHESTRA
ORCHID
ORCHIDIST
ORCHIDS
ORCHIL
ORCHILLA
ORCHILLAS
ORCHILS
ORCHIS
ORCHISES
ORCHITIC
ORCHITIS
ORCIN
ORCINE
ORCINES
ORCINOL
ORCINOLS
ORCINS
ORCS
ORD
ORDAIN
ORDAINED
ORDAINER

ORDAINERS	OREPEARCH	ORGIASTS	ORISHA
ORDAINING	ORES	ORGIC	ORISHAS
ORDAINS	ORESTUNCK	ORGIES	ORISON
ORDALIAN	OREWEED	ORGILLOUS	ORISONS
ORDALIUM	OREWEEDS	ORGONE	ORIXA
ORDALIUMS	OREXIS	ORGONES	ORIXAS
ORDEAL	OREXISES	ORGUE	ORLE
ORDEALS	ORF	ORGUES	ORLEANS
ORDER	ORFE	ORGULOUS	ORLEANSES
ORDERABLE	ORFES	ORGY	ORLES
ORDERED	ORFRAY	ORIBATID	ORLON
ORDERER	ORFRAYS	ORIBATIDS	ORLONS
ORDERERS	ORFS	ORIBI	ORLOP
ORDERING	ORGAN	ORIBIS	ORLOPS
ORDERINGS	ORGANA	ORICALCHE	ORMER
ORDERLESS	ORGANDIE	ORICHALC	ORMERS
ORDERLIES	ORGANDIES	ORICHALCS	ORMOLU
ORDERLY	ORGANDY	ORIEL	ORMOLUS
ORDERS	ORGANELLE	ORIELLED	ORNAMENT
ORDINAIRE	ORGANIC	ORIELS	ORNAMENTS
ORDINAL	ORGANICAL	ORIENCIES	ORNATE
ORDINALLY	ORGANICS	ORIENCY	ORNATELY
ORDINALS	ORGANISE	ORIENT	ORNATER
ORDINANCE	ORGANISED	ORIENTAL	ORNATEST
ORDINAND	ORGANISER	ORIENTALS	ORNERIER
ORDINANDS	ORGANISES	ORIENTATE	ORNERIEST
ORDINANT	ORGANISM	ORIENTED	ORNERY
ORDINANTS	ORGANISMS	ORIENTEER	ORNIS
ORDINAR	ORGANIST	ORIENTER	ORNISES
ORDINARS	ORGANISTS	ORIENTERS	ORNITHES
ORDINARY	ORGANITY	ORIENTING	ORNITHIC
ORDINATE	ORGANIZE	ORIENTS	ORNITHINE
ORDINATED	ORGANIZED	ORIFEX	ORNITHOID
ORDINATES	ORGANIZER	ORIFEXES	OROGEN
ORDINEE	ORGANIZES	ORIFICE	OROGENIC
ORDINEES	ORGANON	ORIFICES	OROGENIES
ORDINES	ORGANONS	ORIFICIAL	OROGENS
ORDNANCE	ORGANOSOL	ORIFLAMME	OROGENY
ORDNANCES	ORGANOTIN	ORIGAMI	OROGRAPHY
ORDO	ORGANS	ORIGAMIS	OROIDE
ORDOS	ORGANUM	ORIGAN	OROIDES
ORDS	ORGANUMS	ORIGANE	OROLOGIES
ORDURE	ORGANZA	ORIGANES	OROLOGIST
ORDURES	ORGANZAS	ORIGANS	OROLOGY
ORDUROUS	ORGANZINE	ORIGANUM	OROMETER
ORE	ORGASM	ORIGANUMS	OROMETERS
OREAD	ORGASMED	ORIGIN	ORONASAL
OREADES	ORGASMIC	ORIGINAL	OROPESA
OREADS	ORGASMING	ORIGINALS	OROPESAS
ORECTIC	ORGASMS	ORIGINATE	OROTUND
ORECTIVE	ORGASTIC	ORIGINS	ORPHAN
OREGANO	ORGEAT	ORIHOU	ORPHANAGE
OREGANOS	ORGEATS	ORILLION	ORPHANED
OREIDE	ORGIA	ORILLIONS	ORPHANING
OREIDES	ORGIAC	ORINASAL	ORPHANISM
OREODONT	ORGIAS	ORINASALS	ORPHANS
OREODONTS	ORGIAST	ORIOLE	ORPHARION
OREOLOGY	ORGIASTIC	ORIOLES	ORPHIC

ORPHICAL	ORYXES	OSMOSE	OSTEOID
ORPHISM	ORZO	OSMOSED	OSTEOIDS
ORPHISMS	ORZOS	OSMOSES	OSTEOLOGY
ORPHREY	OS	OSMOSING	OSTEOMA
ORPHREYED	OSAR	OSMOSIS	OSTEOMAS
ORPHREYS	OSCAR	OSMOTIC	OSTEOMATA
ORPIMENT	OSCARS	OSMOUS	OSTEOPATH
ORPIMENTS	OSCHEAL	OSMUND	OSTEOSES
ORPIN	OSCILLATE	OSMUNDA	OSTEOSIS
ORPINE	OSCINE	OSMUNDAS	OSTEOTOME
ORPINES	OSCINES	OSMUNDINE	OSTEOTOMY
ORPINS	OSCININE	OSMUNDS	OSTIA
ORRA	OSCITANCE	OSNABURG	OSTIAL
ORRAMAN	OSCITANCY	OSNABURGS	OSTIARIES
ORRAMEN	OSCITANT	OSPREY	OSTIARY
ORRERIES	OSCITATE	OSPREYS	OSTIATE
ORRERY	OSCITATED	OSSA	OSTINATI
ORRICE	OSCITATES	OSSARIUM	OSTINATO
ORRICES	OSCULA	OSSARIUMS	OSTINATOS
ORRIS	OSCULANT	OSSATURE	OSTIOLAR
ORRISES	OSCULAR	OSSATURES	OSTIOLATE
ORRISROOT	OSCULATE	OSSEIN	OSTIOLE
ORS	OSCULATED	OSSEINS	OSTIOLES
ORSEILLE	OSCULATES	OSSELET	OSTIUM
ORSEILLES	OSCULE	OSSELETS	OSTLER
ORSELLIC	OSCULES	OSSEOUS	OSTLERESS
ORT	OSCULUM	OSSEOUSLY	OSTLERS
ORTANIQUE	OSE	OSSETER	OSTMARK
ORTHIAN	OSES	OSSETERS	OSTMARKS
ORTHICON	OSETRA	OSSETRA	OSTOMATE
ORTHICONS	OSETRAS	OSSETRAS	OSTOMATES
ORTHO	OSHAC	OSSIA	OSTOMIES
ORTHOAXES	OSHACS	OSSICLE	OSTOMY
ORTHOAXIS	OSIER	OSSICLES	OSTOSES
ORTHODOX	OSIERED	OSSICULAR	OSTOSIS
ORTHODOXY	OSIERIES	OSSIFIC	OSTOSISES
ORTHOEPIC	OSIERS	OSSIFIED	OSTRACA
ORTHOEPY	OSIERY	OSSIFIER	OSTRACEAN
ORTHOPEDY	OSMATE	OSSIFIERS	OSTRACISE
ORTHOPOD	OSMATES	OSSIFIES	OSTRACISM
ORTHOPODS	OSMATIC	OSSIFRAGA	OSTRACIZE
ORTHOPTER	OSMETERIA	OSSIFRAGE	OSTRACOD
ORTHOPTIC	OSMIATE	OSSIFY	OSTRACODE
ORTHOS	OSMIATES	OSSIFYING	OSTRACODS
ORTHOSES	OSMIC	OSSUARIES	OSTRACON
ORTHOSIS	OSMICALLY	OSSUARY	OSTRAKA
ORTHOTIC	OSMICS	OSTEAL	OSTRAKON
ORTHOTICS	OSMIOUS	OSTEITIC	OSTREGER
ORTHOTIST	OSMIUM	OSTEITIS	OSTREGERS
ORTHOTONE	OSMIUMS	OSTENSIVE	OSTRICH
ORTHROS	OSMOL	OSTENSORY	OSTRICHES
ORTHROSES	OSMOLAL	OSTENT	OTAKU
ORTOLAN	OSMOLAR	OSTENTS	OTALGIA
ORTOLANS	OSMOLE	OSTEOCYTE	OTALGIAS
ORTS	OSMOLES	OSTEODERM	OTALGIC
ORVAL	OSMOLS	OSTEOGEN	OTALGIES
ORVALS	OSMOMETER	OSTEOGENS	OTALGY
ORYX	OSMOMETRY	OSTEOGENY	OTARIES

OTARINE	OUCHING	OURARIS	OUTBAWLED
OTARY	OUCHT	OUREBI	OUTBAWLS
OTHER	OUCHTS	OUREBIS	OUTBEAM
OTHERNESS	OUD	OURIE	OUTBEAMED
OTHERS	OUDS	OURIER	OUTBEAMS
OTHERWISE	OUGHLIED	OURIEST	OUTBEG
OTIC	OUGHLIES	OURN	OUTBEGGED
OTIOSE	OUGHLY	OUROBOROS	OUTBEGS
OTIOSELY	OUGHLYING	OUROLOGY	OUTBID
OTIOSITY	OUGHT	OUROSCOPY	OUTBIDDEN
OTITIC	OUGHTED	OURS	OUTBIDDER
OTITIDES	OUGHTING	OURSELF	OUTBIDS
OTITIS	OUGHTNESS	OURSELVES	OUTBITCH
OTITISES	OUGHTS	OUS	OUTBLAZE
OTOCYST	OUGLIE	OUSEL	OUTBLAZED
OTOCYSTIC	OUGLIED	OUSELS	OUTBLAZES
OTOCYSTS	OUGLIEING	OUST	OUTBLEAT
OTOLITH	OUGLIES	OUSTED	OUTBLEATS
OTOLITHIC	OUGUIYA	OUSTER	OUTBLESS
OTOLITHS	OUGUIYAS	OUSTERS	OUTBLOOM
OTOLOGIES	OUIJA	OUSTING	OUTBLOOMS
OTOLOGIST	OUIJAS	OUSTITI	OUTBLUFF
OTOLOGY	OUISTITI	OUSTITIS	OUTBLUFFS
OTOPLASTY	OUISTITIS	OUSTS	OUTBLUSH
OTORRHOEA	OUK	OUT	OUTBOARD
OTOSCOPE	OUKS	OUTACT	OUTBOARDS
OTOSCOPES	OULACHON	OUTACTED	OUTBOAST
OTOSCOPIC	OULACHONS	OUTACTING	OUTBOASTS
OTOSCOPY	OULAKAN	OUTACTS	OUTBOUGHT
OTOTOXIC	OULAKANS	OUTADD	OUTBOUND
OTTAR	OULD	OUTADDED	OUTBOUNDS
OTTARS	OULDER	OUTADDING	OUTBOX
OTTAVA	OULDEST	OUTADDS	OUTBOXED
OTTAVAS	OULK	OUTAGE	OUTBOXES
OTTAVINO	OULKS	OUTAGES	OUTBOXING
OTTAVINOS	OULONG	OUTARGUE	OUTBRAG
OTTER	OULONGS	OUTARGUED	OUTBRAGS
OTTERED	OUMA	OUTARGUES	OUTBRAVE
OTTERING	OUMAS	OUTASIGHT	OUTBRAVED
OTTERS	OUNCE	OUTASK	OUTBRAVES
OTTO	OUNCES	OUTASKED	OUTBRAWL
OTTOMAN	OUNDY	OUTASKING	OUTBRAWLS
OTTOMANS	OUP	OUTASKS	OUTBRAZEN
OTTOS	OUPA	OUTATE	OUTBREAK
OTTRELITE	OUPAS	OUTBACK	OUTBREAKS
OU	OUPED	OUTBACKER	OUTBRED
OUABAIN	OUPH	OUTBACKS	OUTBREED
OUABAINS	OUPHE	OUTBAKE	OUTBREEDS
OUAKARI	OUPHES	OUTBAKED	OUTBRIBE
OUAKARIS	OUPHS	OUTBAKES	OUTBRIBED
OUBAAS	OUPING	OUTBAKING	OUTBRIBES
OUBAASES	OUPS	OUTBAR	OUTBROKE
OUBIT	OUR	OUTBARK	OUTBROKEN
OUBITS	OURALI	OUTBARKED	OUTBUILD
OUBLIETTE	OURALIS	OUTBARKS	OUTBUILDS
OUCH	OURANG	OUTBARRED	OUTBUILT
OUCHED	OURANGS	OUTBARS	OUTBULGE
OUCHES	OURARI	OUTBAWL	OUTBULGED

OUTBULGES	OUTCROPS	OUTDROPS	OUTFIGURE
OUTBULK	OUTCROSS	OUTDROVE	OUTFIND
OUTBULKED	OUTCROW	OUTDRUNK	OUTFINDS
OUTBULKS	OUTCROWD	OUTDUEL	OUTFIRE
OUTBULLY	OUTCROWDS	OUTDUELED	OUTFIRED
OUTBURN	OUTCROWED	OUTDUELS	OUTFIRES
OUTBURNED	OUTCROWS	OUTDURE	OUTFIRING
OUTBURNS	OUTCRY	OUTDURED	OUTFISH
OUTBURNT	OUTCRYING	OUTDURES	OUTFISHED
OUTBURST	OUTCURSE	OUTDURING	OUTFISHES
OUTBURSTS	OUTCURSED	OUTDWELL	OUTFIT
OUTBUY	OUTCURSES	OUTDWELLS	OUTFITS
OUTBUYING	OUTCURVE	OUTDWELT	OUTFITTED
OUTBUYS	OUTCURVES	OUTEARN	OUTFITTER
OUTBY	OUTDANCE	OUTEARNED	OUTFLANK
OUTBYE	OUTDANCED	OUTEARNS	OUTFLANKS
OUTCALL	OUTDANCES	OUTEAT	OUTFLASH
OUTCALLS	OUTDARE	OUTEATEN	OUTFLEW
OUTCAPER	OUTDARED	OUTEATING	OUTFLIES
OUTCAPERS	OUTDARES	OUTEATS	OUTFLING
OUTCAST	OUTDARING	OUTECHO	OUTFLINGS
OUTCASTE	OUTDATE	OUTECHOED	OUTFLOAT
OUTCASTED	OUTDATED	OUTECHOES	OUTFLOATS
OUTCASTES	OUTDATES	OUTED	OUTFLOW
OUTCASTS	OUTDATING	OUTEDGE	OUTFLOWED
OUTCATCH	OUTDAZZLE	OUTEDGES	OUTFLOWN
OUTCAUGHT	OUTDEBATE	OUTER	OUTFLOWS
OUTCAVIL	OUTDESIGN	OUTERCOAT	OUTFLUSH
OUTCAVILS	OUTDID	OUTERMOST	OUTFLY
OUTCHARGE	OUTDO	OUTERS	OUTFLYING
OUTCHARM	OUTDODGE	OUTERWEAR	OUTFOOL
OUTCHARMS	OUTDODGED	OUTFABLE	OUTFOOLED
OUTCHEAT	OUTDODGES	OUTFABLED	OUTFOOLS
OUTCHEATS	OUTDOER	OUTFABLES	OUTFOOT
OUTCHID	OUTDOERS	OUTFACE	OUTFOOTED
OUTCHIDE	OUTDOES	OUTFACED	OUTFOOTS
OUTCHIDED	OUTDOING	OUTFACES	OUTFOUGHT
OUTCHIDES	OUTDONE	OUTFACING	OUTFOUND
OUTCITIES	OUTDOOR	OUTFALL	OUTFOX
OUTCITY	OUTDOORS	OUTFALLS	OUTFOXED
OUTCLASS	OUTDOORSY	OUTFAST	OUTFOXES
OUTCLIMB	OUTDRAG	OUTFASTED	OUTFOXING
OUTCLIMBS	OUTDRAGS	OUTFASTS	OUTFROWN
OUTCLOMB	OUTDRANK	OUTFAWN	OUTFROWNS
OUTCOACH	OUTDRAW	OUTFAWNED	OUTFUMBLE
OUTCOME	OUTDRAWN	OUTFAWNS	OUTGAIN
OUTCOMES	OUTDRAWS	OUTFEAST	OUTGAINED
OUTCOOK	OUTDREAM	OUTFEASTS	OUTGAINS
OUTCOOKED	OUTDREAMS	OUTFEEL	OUTGALLOP
OUTCOOKS	OUTDREAMT	OUTFEELS	OUTGAMBLE
OUTCOUNT	OUTDRESS	OUTFELT	OUTGAS
OUTCOUNTS	OUTDREW	OUTFENCE	OUTGASES
OUTCRAFTY	OUTDRINK	OUTFENCED	OUTGASSED
OUTCRAWL	OUTDRINKS	OUTFENCES	OUTGASSES
OUTCRAWLS	OUTDRIVE	OUTFIELD	OUTGATE
OUTCRIED	OUTDRIVEN	OUTFIELDS	OUTGATES
OUTCRIES	OUTDRIVES	OUTFIGHT	OUTGAVE
OUTCROP	OUTDROP	OUTFIGHTS	OUTGAZE

OUTGAZED	OUTHIRES	OUTLAST	OUTMANS
OUTGAZES	OUTHIRING	OUTLASTED	OUTMANTLE
OUTGAZING	OUTHIT	OUTLASTS	OUTMARCH
OUTGIVE	OUTHITS	OUTLAUGH	OUTMASTER
OUTGIVEN	OUTHOMER	OUTLAUGHS	OUTMATCH
OUTGIVES	OUTHOMERS	OUTLAUNCE	OUTMODE
OUTGIVING	OUTHOUSE	OUTLAUNCH	OUTMODED
OUTGLARE	OUTHOUSES	OUTLAW	OUTMODES
OUTGLARED	OUTHOWL	OUTLAWED	OUTMODING
OUTGLARES	OUTHOWLED	OUTLAWING	OUTMOST
OUTGLEAM	OUTHOWLS	OUTLAWRY	OUTMOVE
OUTGLEAMS	OUTHUMOR	OUTLAWS	OUTMOVED
OUTGLOW	OUTHUMORS	OUTLAY	OUTMOVES
OUTGLOWED	OUTHUNT	OUTLAYING	OUTMOVING
OUTGLOWS	OUTHUNTED	OUTLAYS	OUTMUSCLE
OUTGNAW	OUTHUNTS	OUTLEAD	OUTNAME
OUTGNAWED	OUTHUSTLE	OUTLEADS	OUTNAMED
OUTGNAWN	OUTHYRE	OUTLEAP	OUTNAMES
OUTGNAWS	OUTHYRED	OUTLEAPED	OUTNAMING
OUTGO	OUTHYRES	OUTLEAPS	OUTNESS
OUTGOER	OUTHYRING	OUTLEAPT	OUTNESSES
OUTGOERS	OUTING	OUTLEARN	OUTNIGHT
OUTGOES	OUTINGS	OUTLEARNS	OUTNIGHTS
OUTGOING	OUTJEST	OUTLEARNT	OUTNUMBER
OUTGOINGS	OUTJESTED	OUTLED	OUTOFFICE
OUTGONE	OUTJESTS	OUTLER	OUTPACE
OUTGREW	OUTJET	OUTLERS	OUTPACED
OUTGRIN	OUTJETS	OUTLET	OUTPACES
OUTGRINS	OUTJINX	OUTLETS	OUTPACING
OUTGROSS	OUTJINXED	OUTLIE	OUTPAINT
OUTGROUP	OUTJINXES	OUTLIED	OUTPAINTS
OUTGROUPS	OUTJOCKEY	OUTLIER	OUTPART
OUTGROW	OUTJUGGLE	OUTLIERS	OUTPARTS
OUTGROWN	OUTJUMP	OUTLIES	OUTPASS
OUTGROWS	OUTJUMPED	OUTLINE	OUTPASSED
OUTGROWTH	OUTJUMPS	OUTLINEAR	OUTPASSES
OUTGUARD	OUTJUT	OUTLINED	OUTPEEP
OUTGUARDS	OUTJUTS	OUTLINER	OUTPEEPED
OUTGUESS	OUTJUTTED	OUTLINERS	OUTPEEPS
OUTGUIDE	OUTKEEP	OUTLINES	OUTPEER
OUTGUIDED	OUTKEEPS	OUTLINING	OUTPEERED
OUTGUIDES	OUTKEPT	OUTLIVE	OUTPEERS
OUTGUN	OUTKICK	OUTLIVED	OUTPEOPLE
OUTGUNNED	OUTKICKED	OUTLIVER	OUTPITCH
OUTGUNS	OUTKICKS	OUTLIVERS	OUTPITIED
OUTGUSH	OUTKILL	OUTLIVES	OUTPITIES
OUTGUSHED	OUTKILLED	OUTLIVING	OUTPITY
OUTGUSHES	OUTKILLS	OUTLOOK	OUTPLACE
OUTHANDLE	OUTKISS	OUTLOOKED	OUTPLACED
OUTHAUL	OUTKISSED	OUTLOOKS	OUTPLACER
OUTHAULER	OUTKISSES	OUTLOVE	OUTPLACES
OUTHAULS	OUTLAID	OUTLOVED	OUTPLAN
OUTHEAR	OUTLAIN	OUTLOVES	OUTPLANS
OUTHEARD	OUTLAND	OUTLOVING	OUTPLAY
OUTHEARS	OUTLANDER	OUTLUSTRE	OUTPLAYED
OUTHER	OUTLANDS	OUTLYING	OUTPLAYS
OUTHIRE	OUTLASH	OUTMAN	OUTPLOD
OUTHIRED	OUTLASHES	OUTMANNED	OUTPLODS

OUTPLOT	OUTRAN	OUTROLLS	OUTSET
OUTPLOTS	OUTRANCE	OUTROOP	OUTSETS
OUTPOINT	OUTRANCES	OUTROOPER	OUTSHAME
OUTPOINTS	OUTRANG	OUTROOPS	OUTSHAMED
OUTPOLL	OUTRANGE	OUTROOT	OUTSHAMES
OUTPOLLED	OUTRANGED	OUTROOTED	OUTSHINE
OUTPOLLS	OUTRANGES	OUTROOTS	OUTSHINED
OUTPORT	OUTRANK	OUTROPE	OUTSHINES
OUTPORTER	OUTRANKED	OUTROPER	OUTSHONE
OUTPORTS	OUTRANKS	OUTROPERS	OUTSHOOT
OUTPOST	OUTRATE	OUTROPES	OUTSHOOTS
OUTPOSTS	OUTRATED	OUTROS	OUTSHOT
OUTPOUR	OUTRATES	OUTROW	OUTSHOTS
OUTPOURED	OUTRATING	OUTROWED	OUTSHOUT
OUTPOURER	OUTRAVE	OUTROWING	OUTSHOUTS
OUTPOURS	OUTRAVED	OUTROWS	OUTSIDE
OUTPOWER	OUTRAVES	OUTRUN	OUTSIDER
OUTPOWERS	OUTRAVING	OUTRUNG	OUTSIDERS
OUTPRAY	OUTRE	OUTRUNNER	OUTSIDES
OUTPRAYED	OUTREACH	OUTRUNS	OUTSIGHT
OUTPRAYS	OUTREAD	OUTRUSH	OUTSIGHTS
OUTPREACH	OUTREADS	OUTRUSHED	OUTSIN
OUTPREEN	OUTREASON	OUTRUSHES	OUTSING
OUTPREENS	OUTRECKON	OUTS	OUTSINGS
OUTPRESS	OUTRED	OUTSAID	OUTSINNED
OUTPRICE	OUTREDDED	OUTSAIL	OUTSINS
OUTPRICED	OUTREDDEN	OUTSAILED	OUTSIT
OUTPRICES	OUTREDS	OUTSAILS	OUTSITS
OUTPRIZE	OUTREIGN	OUTSANG	OUTSIZE
OUTPRIZED	OUTREIGNS	OUTSAT	OUTSIZED
OUTPRIZES	OUTRELIEF	OUTSAVOR	OUTSIZES
OUTPULL	OUTREMER	OUTSAVORS	OUTSKATE
OUTPULLED	OUTREMERS	OUTSAW	OUTSKATED
OUTPULLS	OUTRIDDEN	OUTSAY	OUTSKATES
OUTPUNCH	OUTRIDE	OUTSAYING	OUTSKIRT
OUTPUPIL	OUTRIDER	OUTSAYS	OUTSKIRTS
OUTPUPILS	OUTRIDERS	OUTSCHEME	OUTSLEEP
OUTPURSUE	OUTRIDES	OUTSCOLD	OUTSLEEPS
OUTPUSH	OUTRIDING	OUTSCOLDS	OUTSLEPT
OUTPUSHED	OUTRIG	OUTSCOOP	OUTSLICK
OUTPUSHES	OUTRIGGED	OUTSCOOPS	OUTSLICKS
OUTPUT	OUTRIGGER	OUTSCORE	OUTSMART
OUTPUTS	OUTRIGHT	OUTSCORED	OUTSMARTS
OUTPUTTED	OUTRIGS	OUTSCORES	OUTSMELL
OUTQUOTE	OUTRING	OUTSCORN	OUTSMELLS
OUTQUOTED	OUTRINGS	OUTSCORNS	OUTSMELT
OUTQUOTES	OUTRIVAL	OUTSCREAM	OUTSMILE
OUTRACE	OUTRIVALS	OUTSEE	OUTSMILED
OUTRACED	OUTRO	OUTSEEING	OUTSMILES
OUTRACES	OUTROAR	OUTSEEN	OUTSMOKE
OUTRACING	OUTROARED	OUTSEES	OUTSMOKED
OUTRAGE	OUTROARS	OUTSELL	OUTSMOKES
OUTRAGED	OUTROCK	OUTSELLS	OUTSNORE
OUTRAGES	OUTROCKED	OUTSERT	OUTSNORED
OUTRAGING	OUTROCKS	OUTSERTS	OUTSNORES
OUTRAISE	OUTRODE	OUTSERVE	OUTSOAR
OUTRAISED	OUTROLL	OUTSERVED	OUTSOARED
OUTRAISES	OUTROLLED	OUTSERVES	OUTSOARS

OUTSOLD	OUTSULKED	OUTTRAVEL	OUTWELLED
OUTSOLE	OUTSULKS	OUTTRICK	OUTWELLS
OUTSOLES	OUTSUM	OUTTRICKS	OUTWENT
OUTSOURCE	OUTSUMMED	OUTTROT	OUTWEPT
OUTSPAN	OUTSUMS	OUTTROTS	OUTWHIRL
OUTSPANS	OUTSUNG	OUTTRUMP	OUTWHIRLS
OUTSPEAK	OUTSWAM	OUTTRUMPS	OUTWICK
OUTSPEAKS	OUTSWARE	OUTTURN	OUTWICKED
OUTSPED	OUTSWEAR	OUTTURNS	OUTWICKS
OUTSPEED	OUTSWEARS	OUTVALUE	OUTWILE
OUTSPEEDS	OUTSWEEP	OUTVALUED	OUTWILED
OUTSPELL	OUTSWEEPS	OUTVALUES	OUTWILES
OUTSPELLS	OUTSWELL	OUTVAUNT	OUTWILING
OUTSPELT	OUTSWELLS	OUTVAUNTS	OUTWILL
OUTSPEND	OUTSWEPT	OUTVENOM	OUTWILLED
OUTSPENDS	OUTSWIM	OUTVENOMS	OUTWILLS
OUTSPENT	OUTSWIMS	OUTVIE	OUTWIN
OUTSPOKE	OUTSWING	OUTVIED	OUTWIND
OUTSPOKEN	OUTSWINGS	OUTVIES	OUTWINDED
OUTSPORT	OUTSWORE	OUTVOICE	OUTWINDS
OUTSPORTS	OUTSWORN	OUTVOICED	OUTWING
OUTSPRANG	OUTSWUM	OUTVOICES	OUTWINGED
OUTSPREAD	OUTSWUNG	OUTVOTE	OUTWINGS
OUTSPRING	OUTTAKE	OUTVOTED	OUTWINS
OUTSPRINT	OUTTAKEN	OUTVOTER	OUTWISH
OUTSPRUNG	OUTTAKES	OUTVOTERS	OUTWISHED
OUTSTAND	OUTTAKING	OUTVOTES	OUTWISHES
OUTSTANDS	OUTTALK	OUTVOTING	OUTWIT
OUTSTARE	OUTTALKED	OUTVYING	OUTWITH
OUTSTARED	OUTTALKS	OUTWAIT	OUTWITS
OUTSTARES	OUTTASK	OUTWAITED	OUTWITTED
OUTSTART	OUTTASKED	OUTWAITS	OUTWON
OUTSTARTS	OUTTASKS	OUTWALK	OUTWORE
OUTSTATE	OUTTELL	OUTWALKED	OUTWORK
OUTSTATED	OUTTELLS	OUTWALKS	OUTWORKED
OUTSTATES	OUTTHANK	OUTWAR	OUTWORKER
OUTSTAY	OUTTHANKS	OUTWARD	OUTWORKS
OUTSTAYED	OUTTHIEVE	OUTWARDLY	OUTWORN
OUTSTAYS	OUTTHINK	OUTWARDS	OUTWORTH
OUTSTEER	OUTTHINKS	OUTWARRED	OUTWORTHS
OUTSTEERS	OUTTHREW	OUTWARS	OUTWOUND
OUTSTEP	OUTTHROB	OUTWASH	OUTWREST
OUTSTEPS	OUTTHROBS	OUTWASHES	OUTWRESTS
OUTSTOOD	OUTTHROW	OUTWASTE	OUTWRIT
OUTSTRAIN	OUTTHROWN	OUTWASTED	OUTWRITE
OUTSTRIDE	OUTTHROWS	OUTWASTES	OUTWRITES
OUTSTRIKE	OUTTHRUST	OUTWATCH	OUTWROTE
OUTSTRIP	OUTTOLD	OUTWEAR	OUTYELL
OUTSTRIPS	OUTTONGUE	OUTWEARS	OUTYELLED
OUTSTRIVE	OUTTOOK	OUTWEARY	OUTYELLS
OUTSTRODE	OUTTOP	OUTWEED	OUTYELP
OUTSTROKE	OUTTOPPED	OUTWEEDED	OUTYELPED
OUTSTROVE	OUTTOPS	OUTWEEDS	OUTYELPS
OUTSTRUCK	OUTTOWER	OUTWEEP	OUTYIELD
OUTSTUDY	OUTTOWERS	OUTWEEPS	OUTYIELDS
OUTSTUNT	OUTTRADE	OUTWEIGH	OUVERT
OUTSTUNTS	OUTTRADED	OUTWEIGHS	OUVERTE
OUTSULK	OUTTRADES	OUTWELL	OUVRAGE

OUVRAGES
OUVRIER
OUVRIERE
OUVRIERES
OUVRIERS
OUZEL
OUZELS
OUZO
OUZOS
OVA
OVAL
OVALBUMIN
OVALITIES
OVALITY
OVALLY
OVALNESS
OVALS
OVARIAL
OVARIAN
OVARIES
OVARIOLE
OVARIOLES
OVARIOUS
OVARITIS
OVARY
OVATE
OVATED
OVATELY
OVATES
OVATING
OVATION
OVATIONAL
OVATIONS
OVATOR
OVATORS
OVEL
OVELS
OVEN
OVENABLE
OVENBIRD
OVENBIRDS
OVENED
OVENING
OVENLIKE
OVENPROOF
OVENS
OVENWARE
OVENWARES
OVENWOOD
OVENWOODS
OVER
OVERABLE
OVERACT
OVERACTED
OVERACTS
OVERACUTE
OVERAGE
OVERAGED

OVERAGES
OVERALERT
OVERALL
OVERALLED
OVERALLS
OVERAPT
OVERARCH
OVERARM
OVERARMED
OVERARMS
OVERATE
OVERAWE
OVERAWED
OVERAWES
OVERAWING
OVERBAKE
OVERBAKED
OVERBAKES
OVERBEAR
OVERBEARS
OVERBEAT
OVERBEATS
OVERBED
OVERBET
OVERBETS
OVERBID
OVERBIDS
OVERBIG
OVERBILL
OVERBILLS
OVERBITE
OVERBITES
OVERBLEW
OVERBLOW
OVERBLOWN
OVERBLOWS
OVERBOARD
OVERBOIL
OVERBOILS
OVERBOLD
OVERBOOK
OVERBOOKS
OVERBOOT
OVERBOOTS
OVERBORE
OVERBORN
OVERBORNE
OVERBOUND
OVERBRAKE
OVERBRED
OVERBREED
OVERBRIEF
OVERBRIM
OVERBRIMS
OVERBROAD
OVERBROW
OVERBROWS
OVERBUILD

OVERBUILT
OVERBULK
OVERBULKS
OVERBURN
OVERBURNS
OVERBURNT
OVERBUSY
OVERBUY
OVERBUYS
OVERBY
OVERCALL
OVERCALLS
OVERCAME
OVERCARRY
OVERCAST
OVERCASTS
OVERCATCH
OVERCHEAP
OVERCHECK
OVERCHILL
OVERCIVIL
OVERCLAD
OVERCLAIM
OVERCLASS
OVERCLEAN
OVERCLEAR
OVERCLOSE
OVERCLOUD
OVERCLOY
OVERCLOYS
OVERCOACH
OVERCOAT
OVERCOATS
OVERCOLD
OVERCOLOR
OVERCOME
OVERCOMER
OVERCOMES
OVERCOOK
OVERCOOKS
OVERCOOL
OVERCOOLS
OVERCOUNT
OVERCOVER
OVERCOY
OVERCRAM
OVERCRAMS
OVERCRAW
OVERCRAWS
OVERCROP
OVERCROPS
OVERCROW
OVERCROWD
OVERCROWS
OVERCURE
OVERCURED
OVERCURES
OVERCUT

OVERCUTS
OVERDARE
OVERDARED
OVERDARES
OVERDATED
OVERDEAR
OVERDECK
OVERDECKS
OVERDID
OVERDIGHT
OVERDO
OVERDOER
OVERDOERS
OVERDOES
OVERDOG
OVERDOGS
OVERDOING
OVERDONE
OVERDOSE
OVERDOSED
OVERDOSES
OVERDRAFT
OVERDRANK
OVERDRAW
OVERDRAWN
OVERDRAWS
OVERDRESS
OVERDREW
OVERDRIED
OVERDRIES
OVERDRINK
OVERDRIVE
OVERDROVE
OVERDRUNK
OVERDRY
OVERDUB
OVERDUBS
OVERDUE
OVERDUST
OVERDUSTS
OVERDYE
OVERDYED
OVERDYER
OVERDYERS
OVERDYES
OVEREAGER
OVEREASY
OVEREAT
OVEREATEN
OVEREATER
OVEREATS
OVERED
OVEREDIT
OVEREDITS
OVEREGG
OVEREGGED
OVEREGGS
OVEREMOTE

OVEREXERT	OVERGIVES	OVERHOLY	OVERLENT
OVEREYE	OVERGLAD	OVERHONOR	OVERLET
OVEREYED	OVERGLAZE	OVERHOPE	OVERLETS
OVEREYES	OVERGLOOM	OVERHOPED	OVERLEWD
OVEREYING	OVERGO	OVERHOPES	OVERLIE
OVERFALL	OVERGOAD	OVERHOT	OVERLIER
OVERFALLS	OVERGOADS	OVERHUNG	OVERLIERS
OVERFAR	OVERGOES	OVERHUNT	OVERLIES
OVERFAST	OVERGOING	OVERHUNTS	OVERLIGHT
OVERFAT	OVERGONE	OVERHYPE	OVERLIT
OVERFAVOR	OVERGORGE	OVERHYPED	OVERLIVE
OVERFEAR	OVERGOT	OVERHYPES	OVERLIVED
OVERFEARS	OVERGRADE	OVERIDLE	OVERLIVES
OVERFED	OVERGRAIN	OVERING	OVERLOAD
OVERFEED	OVERGRASS	OVERINKED	OVERLOADS
OVERFEEDS	OVERGRAZE	OVERISSUE	OVERLOCK
OVERFELL	OVERGREAT	OVERJOY	OVERLOCKS
OVERFILL	OVERGREEN	OVERJOYED	OVERLONG
OVERFILLS	OVERGREW	OVERJOYS	OVERLOOK
OVERFINE	OVERGROW	OVERJUMP	OVERLOOKS
OVERFISH	OVERGROWN	OVERJUMPS	OVERLORD
OVERFIT	OVERGROWS	OVERJUST	OVERLORDS
OVERFLEW	OVERHAILE	OVERKEEN	OVERLOUD
OVERFLIES	OVERHAIR	OVERKEEP	OVERLOVE
OVERFLOOD	OVERHAIRS	OVERKEEPS	OVERLOVED
OVERFLOW	OVERHALE	OVERKEPT	OVERLOVES
OVERFLOWN	OVERHALED	OVERKEST	OVERLUSH
OVERFLOWS	OVERHALES	OVERKILL	OVERLUSTY
OVERFLUSH	OVERHAND	OVERKILLS	OVERLY
OVERFLY	OVERHANDS	OVERKIND	OVERLYING
OVERFOCUS	OVERHANG	OVERKING	OVERMAN
OVERFOLD	OVERHANGS	OVERKINGS	OVERMANS
OVERFOLDS	OVERHAPPY	OVERKNEE	OVERMANY
OVERFOND	OVERHARD	OVERLABOR	OVERMAST
OVERFOUL	OVERHASTE	OVERLADE	OVERMASTS
OVERFRANK	OVERHASTY	OVERLADED	OVERMATCH
OVERFREE	OVERHATE	OVERLADEN	OVERMEEK
OVERFULL	OVERHATED	OVERLADES	OVERMELT
OVERFUND	OVERHATES	OVERLAID	OVERMELTS
OVERFUNDS	OVERHAUL	OVERLAIN	OVERMEN
OVERFUSSY	OVERHAULS	OVERLAND	OVERMERRY
OVERGALL	OVERHEAD	OVERLANDS	OVERMILD
OVERGALLS	OVERHEADS	OVERLAP	OVERMILK
OVERGANG	OVERHEAP	OVERLAPS	OVERMILKS
OVERGANGS	OVERHEAPS	OVERLARD	OVERMINE
OVERGAVE	OVERHEAR	OVERLARDS	OVERMINED
OVERGEAR	OVERHEARD	OVERLARGE	OVERMINES
OVERGEARS	OVERHEARS	OVERLATE	OVERMIX
OVERGET	OVERHEAT	OVERLAX	OVERMIXED
OVERGETS	OVERHEATS	OVERLAY	OVERMIXES
OVERGILD	OVERHELD	OVERLAYS	OVERMOUNT
OVERGILDS	OVERHENT	OVERLEAF	OVERMUCH
OVERGILT	OVERHENTS	OVERLEAP	OVERNAME
OVERGIRD	OVERHIGH	OVERLEAPS	OVERNAMED
OVERGIRDS	OVERHIT	OVERLEAPT	OVERNAMES
OVERGIRT	OVERHITS	OVERLEARN	OVERNEAR
OVERGIVE	OVERHOLD	OVERLEND	OVERNEAT
OVERGIVEN	OVERHOLDS	OVERLENDS	OVERNET

OVERNETS

OVERNETS	OVERREACH	OVERSEWS	OVERSTEP
OVERNEW	OVERREACT	OVERSEXED	OVERSTEPS
OVERNICE	OVERREAD	OVERSHADE	OVERSTINK
OVERNIGHT	OVERREADS	OVERSHARP	OVERSTIR
OVERPACK	OVERRED	OVERSHINE	OVERSTIRS
OVERPACKS	OVERREDS	OVERSHIRT	OVERSTOCK
OVERPAGE	OVERREN	OVERSHOE	OVERSTOOD
OVERPAID	OVERRENS	OVERSHOES	OVERSTORY
OVERPAINT	OVERRICH	OVERSHONE	OVERSTREW
OVERPART	OVERRIDE	OVERSHOOT	OVERSTUDY
OVERPARTS	OVERRIDER	OVERSHOT	OVERSTUFF
OVERPASS	OVERRIDES	OVERSHOTS	OVERSTUNK
OVERPAST	OVERRIFE	OVERSICK	OVERSUDS
OVERPAY	OVERRIGID	OVERSIDE	OVERSUP
OVERPAYS	OVERRIPE	OVERSIDES	OVERSUPS
OVERPEDAL	OVERRIPEN	OVERSIGHT	OVERSURE
OVERPEER	OVERROAST	OVERSIZE	OVERSWAM
OVERPEERS	OVERRODE	OVERSIZED	OVERSWAY
OVERPERCH	OVERRUDE	OVERSIZES	OVERSWAYS
OVERPERT	OVERRUFF	OVERSKIP	OVERSWEAR
OVERPITCH	OVERRUFFS	OVERSKIPS	OVERSWEET
OVERPLAID	OVERRULE	OVERSKIRT	OVERSWELL
OVERPLAN	OVERRULED	OVERSLEEP	OVERSWIM
OVERPLANS	OVERRULER	OVERSLEPT	OVERSWIMS
OVERPLANT	OVERRULES	OVERSLIP	OVERSWING
OVERPLAST	OVERRUN	OVERSLIPS	OVERSWORE
OVERPLAY	OVERRUNS	OVERSLIPT	OVERSWORN
OVERPLAYS	OVERS	OVERSLOW	OVERSWUM
OVERPLIED	OVERSAD	OVERSMAN	OVERSWUNG
OVERPLIES	OVERSAIL	OVERSMEN	OVERT
OVERPLOT	OVERSAILS	OVERSMOKE	OVERTAKE
OVERPLOTS	OVERSALE	OVERSOAK	OVERTAKEN
OVERPLUS	OVERSALES	OVERSOAKS	OVERTAKES
OVERPLY	OVERSALT	OVERSOFT	OVERTALK
OVERPOISE	OVERSALTS	OVERSOLD	OVERTALKS
OVERPOST	OVERSAUCE	OVERSOON	OVERTAME
OVERPOSTS	OVERSAVE	OVERSOUL	OVERTART
OVERPOWER	OVERSAVED	OVERSOULS	OVERTASK
OVERPRESS	OVERSAVES	OVERSOW	OVERTASKS
OVERPRICE	OVERSAW	OVERSOWED	OVERTAX
OVERPRINT	OVERSCALE	OVERSOWN	OVERTAXED
OVERPRIZE	OVERSCORE	OVERSOWS	OVERTAXES
OVERPROOF	OVERSEA	OVERSPEND	OVERTEACH
OVERPROUD	OVERSEAS	OVERSPENT	OVERTEEM
OVERPUMP	OVERSEE	OVERSPICE	OVERTEEMS
OVERPUMPS	OVERSEED	OVERSPILL	OVERTHICK
OVERQUICK	OVERSEEDS	OVERSPILT	OVERTHIN
OVERRACK	OVERSEEN	OVERSPIN	OVERTHINK
OVERRACKS	OVERSEER	OVERSPINS	OVERTHREW
OVERRAKE	OVERSEERS	OVERSTAFF	OVERTHROW
OVERRAKED	OVERSEES	OVERSTAIN	OVERTIGHT
OVERRAKES	OVERSELL	OVERSTAND	OVERTIME
OVERRAN	OVERSELLS	OVERSTANK	OVERTIMED
OVERRANK	OVERSET	OVERSTARE	OVERTIMER
OVERRASH	OVERSETS	OVERSTATE	OVERTIMES
OVERRATE	OVERSEW	OVERSTAY	OVERTIMID
OVERRATED	OVERSEWED	OVERSTAYS	OVERTIP
OVERRATES	OVERSEWN	OVERSTEER	OVERTIPS

OVERTIRE	OVERWEENS	OVOLOS	OWRELAYS
OVERTIRED	OVERWEIGH	OVONIC	OWRES
OVERTIRES	OVERWENT	OVONICS	OWREWORD
OVERTLY	OVERWET	OVOTESTES	OWREWORDS
OVERTNESS	OVERWETS	OVOTESTIS	OWRIE
OVERTOIL	OVERWHELM	OVULAR	OWRIER
OVERTOILS	OVERWIDE	OVULARY	OWRIEST
OVERTONE	OVERWILY	OVULATE	OWSE
OVERTONES	OVERWIND	OVULATED	OWSEN
OVERTOOK	OVERWINDS	OVULATES	OWT
OVERTOP	OVERWING	OVULATING	OWTS
OVERTOPS	OVERWINGS	OVULATION	OX
OVERTOWER	OVERWISE	OVULATORY	OXACILLIN
OVERTRADE	OVERWORD	OVULE	OXALATE
OVERTRAIN	OVERWORDS	OVULES	OXALATED
OVERTREAT	OVERWORE	OVUM	OXALATES
OVERTRICK	OVERWORK	OW	OXALATING
OVERTRIM	OVERWORKS	OWCHE	OXALIC
OVERTRIMS	OVERWORN	OWCHES	OXALIS
OVERTRIP	OVERWOUND	OWE	OXALISES
OVERTRIPS	OVERWREST	OWED	OXAZEPAM
OVERTRUMP	OVERWRITE	OWELTIES	OXAZEPAMS
OVERTRUST	OVERWROTE	OWELTY	OXAZINE
OVERTURE	OVERYEAR	OWER	OXAZINES
OVERTURED	OVERYEARS	OWERBY	OXBLOOD
OVERTURES	OVERZEAL	OWERLOUP	OXBLOODS
OVERTURN	OVERZEALS	OWERLOUPS	OXBOW
OVERTURNS	OVIBOS	OWES	OXBOWS
OVERTYPE	OVIBOSES	OWING	OXCART
OVERTYPED	OVIBOVINE	OWL	OXCARTS
OVERTYPES	OVICIDAL	OWLED	OXEN
OVERURGE	OVICIDE	OWLER	OXER
OVERURGED	OVICIDES	OWLERIES	OXERS
OVERURGES	OVIDUCAL	OWLERS	OXES
OVERUSE	OVIDUCT	OWLERY	OXEYE
OVERUSED	OVIDUCTAL	OWLET	OXEYES
OVERUSES	OVIDUCTS	OWLETS	OXFORD
OVERUSING	OVIFEROUS	OWLIER	OXFORDS
OVERVALUE	OVIFORM	OWLIEST	OXGANG
OVERVEIL	OVIGEROUS	OWLING	OXGANGS
OVERVEILS	OVINE	OWLISH	OXGATE
OVERVIEW	OVINES	OWLISHLY	OXGATES
OVERVIEWS	OVIPARA	OWLLIKE	OXHEAD
OVERVIVID	OVIPARITY	OWLS	OXHEADS
OVERVOTE	OVIPAROUS	OWLY	OXHEART
OVERVOTED	OVIPOSIT	OWN	OXHEARTS
OVERVOTES	OVIPOSITS	OWNABLE	OXHIDE
OVERWARM	OVIRAPTOR	OWNED	OXHIDES
OVERWARMS	OVISAC	OWNER	OXID
OVERWARY	OVISACS	OWNERLESS	OXIDABLE
OVERWASH	OVIST	OWNERS	OXIDANT
OVERWATCH	OVISTS	OWNERSHIP	OXIDANTS
OVERWATER	OVOID	OWNING	OXIDASE
OVERWEAK	OVOIDAL	OWNS	OXIDASES
OVERWEAR	OVOIDALS	OWRE	OXIDASIC
OVERWEARS	OVOIDS	OWRECOME	OXIDATE
OVERWEARY	OVOLI	OWRECOMES	OXIDATED
OVERWEEN	OVOLO	OWRELAY	OXIDATES

OXIDATING
OXIDATION
OXIDATIVE
OXIDE
OXIDES
OXIDIC
OXIDISE
OXIDISED
OXIDISER
OXIDISERS
OXIDISES
OXIDISING
OXIDIZE
OXIDIZED
OXIDIZER
OXIDIZERS
OXIDIZES
OXIDIZING
OXIDS
OXIM
OXIME
OXIMES
OXIMETER
OXIMETERS
OXIMETRY
OXIMS
OXLAND
OXLANDS
OXLIKE
OXLIP
OXLIPS
OXO
OXONIUM
OXONIUMS
OXPECKER
OXPECKERS
OXSLIP
OXSLIPS
OXTAIL
OXTAILS
OXTER
OXTERED
OXTERING
OXTERS
OXTONGUE
OXTONGUES
OXY
OXYACID
OXYACIDS
OXYCODONE
OXYGEN
OXYGENASE
OXYGENATE
OXYGENIC
OXYGENISE
OXYGENIZE
OXYGENOUS
OXYGENS

OXYMEL
OXYMELS
OXYMORA
OXYMORON
OXYMORONS
OXYNTIC
OXYPHIL
OXYPHILE
OXYPHILES
OXYPHILIC
OXYPHILS
OXYSALT
OXYSALTS
OXYSOME
OXYSOMES
OXYTOCIC
OXYTOCICS
OXYTOCIN
OXYTOCINS
OXYTONE
OXYTONES
OY
OYE
OYER
OYERS
OYES
OYESES
OYESSES
OYEZ
OYEZES
OYS
OYSTER
OYSTERED
OYSTERER
OYSTERERS
OYSTERING
OYSTERMAN
OYSTERMEN
OYSTERS
OYSTRIGE
OYSTRIGES
OZAENA
OZAENAS
OZALID
OZALIDS
OZEKI
OZEKIS
OZOCERITE
OZOKERITE
OZONATE
OZONATED
OZONATES
OZONATING
OZONATION
OZONE
OZONES
OZONIC
OZONIDE

OZONIDES
OZONISE
OZONISED
OZONISER
OZONISERS
OZONISES
OZONISING
OZONIZE
OZONIZED
OZONIZER
OZONIZERS
OZONIZES
OZONIZING
OZONOUS
OZZIE
OZZIES

P

PA
PAAL
PAALS
PABLUM
PABLUMS
PABOUCHE
PABOUCHES
PABULAR
PABULOUS
PABULUM
PABULUMS
PAC
PACA
PACABLE
PACAS
PACATION
PACATIONS
PACE
PACED
PACEMAKER
PACER
PACERS
PACES
PACEWAY
PACEWAYS
PACEY
PACHA
PACHADOM
PACHADOMS
PACHAK
PACHAKS
PACHALIC
PACHALICS
PACHAS
PACHINKO
PACHINKOS
PACHISI
PACHISIS
PACHOULI
PACHOULIS
PACHUCO
PACHUCOS
PACHYDERM
PACHYTENE
PACIER
PACIEST
PACIFIC
PACIFICAL
PACIFIED
PACIFIER
PACIFIERS
PACIFIES
PACIFISM

PACIFISMS
PACIFIST
PACIFISTS
PACIFY
PACIFYING
PACING
PACK
PACKABLE
PACKAGE
PACKAGED
PACKAGER
PACKAGERS
PACKAGES
PACKAGING
PACKBOARD
PACKED
PACKER
PACKERS
PACKET
PACKETED
PACKETING
PACKETS
PACKFONG
PACKFONGS
PACKFRAME
PACKHORSE
PACKING
PACKINGS
PACKLY
PACKMAN
PACKMEN
PACKNESS
PACKS
PACKSACK
PACKSACKS
PACKSHEET
PACKSTAFF
PACKWAX
PACKWAXES
PACKWAY
PACKWAYS
PACO
PACOS
PACS
PACT
PACTA
PACTION
PACTIONAL
PACTIONED
PACTIONS
PACTS
PACTUM
PACY

PAD
PADANG
PADANGS
PADAUK
PADAUKS
PADDED
PADDER
PADDERS
PADDIES
PADDING
PADDINGS
PADDLE
PADDLED
PADDLER
PADDLERS
PADDLES
PADDLING
PADDLINGS
PADDOCK
PADDOCKED
PADDOCKS
PADDY
PADDYWACK
PADELLA
PADELLAS
PADEMELON
PADERERO
PADEREROS
PADI
PADIS
PADISHAH
PADISHAHS
PADKOS
PADLE
PADLES
PADLOCK
PADLOCKED
PADLOCKS
PADMA
PADMAS
PADNAG
PADNAGS
PADOUK
PADOUKS
PADRE
PADRES
PADRI
PADRONE
PADRONES
PADRONI
PADRONISM
PADS
PADSAW

PADSAWS
PADSHAH
PADSHAHS
PADUASOY
PADUASOYS
PADYMELON
PAEAN
PAEANISM
PAEANISMS
PAEANS
PAEDERAST
PAEDEUTIC
PAEDIATRY
PAEDOLOGY
PAELLA
PAELLAS
PAENULA
PAENULAE
PAENULAS
PAEON
PAEONIC
PAEONICS
PAEONIES
PAEONS
PAEONY
PAESAN
PAESANI
PAESANO
PAESANOS
PAESANS
PAGAN
PAGANDOM
PAGANDOMS
PAGANISE
PAGANISED
PAGANISER
PAGANISES
PAGANISH
PAGANISM
PAGANISMS
PAGANIST
PAGANISTS
PAGANIZE
PAGANIZED
PAGANIZER
PAGANIZES
PAGANS
PAGE
PAGEANT
PAGEANTRY
PAGEANTS
PAGEBOY
PAGEBOYS

PAGED	PAINCHES	PAJAMAED	PALATIAL
PAGEFUL	PAINED	PAJAMAS	PALATINE
PAGEFULS	PAINFUL	PAJOCK	PALATINES
PAGEHOOD	PAINFULLY	PAJOCKE	PALATING
PAGEHOODS	PAINIM	PAJOCKES	PALAVER
PAGER	PAINIMS	PAJOCKS	PALAVERED
PAGERS	PAINING	PAKAHI	PALAVERER
PAGES	PAINLESS	PAKAHIS	PALAVERS
PAGEVIEW	PAINS	PAKAPOO	PALAY
PAGEVIEWS	PAINT	PAKAPOOS	PALAYS
PAGINAL	PAINTABLE	PAKEHA	PALAZZI
PAGINATE	PAINTBALL	PAKEHAS	PALAZZO
PAGINATED	PAINTBOX	PAKFONG	PALAZZOS
PAGINATES	PAINTED	PAKFONGS	PALE
PAGING	PAINTER	PAKIHI	PALEA
PAGINGS	PAINTERLY	PAKIHIS	PALEAE
PAGLE	PAINTERS	PAKKA	PALEAL
PAGLES	PAINTIER	PAKOKO	PALEATE
PAGOD	PAINTIEST	PAKOKOS	PALEBUCK
PAGODA	PAINTING	PAKORA	PALEBUCKS
PAGODAS	PAINTINGS	PAKORAS	PALED
PAGODS	PAINTRESS	PAKTHONG	PALEFACE
PAGRI	PAINTS	PAKTHONGS	PALEFACES
PAGRIS	PAINTURE	PAKTONG	PALELY
PAGURIAN	PAINTURES	PAKTONGS	PALEMPORE
PAGURIANS	PAINTWORK	PAL	PALENESS
PAGURID	PAINTY	PALABRA	PALEOCENE
PAGURIDS	PAIOCK	PALABRAS	PALEOGENE
PAH	PAIOCKE	PALACE	PALEOLITH
PAHAUTEA	PAIOCKES	PALACED	PALEOLOGY
PAHLAVI	PAIOCKS	PALACES	PALEOSOL
PAHLAVIS	PAIR	PALADIN	PALEOSOLS
PAHOEHOE	PAIRE	PALADINS	PALEOZOIC
PAHOEHOES	PAIRED	PALAESTRA	PALER
PAHS	PAIRER	PALAFITTE	PALES
PAID	PAIRES	PALAGI	PALEST
PAIDEUTIC	PAIREST	PALAGIS	PALESTRA
PAIDLE	PAIRIAL	PALAIS	PALESTRAE
PAIDLES	PAIRIALS	PALAMA	PALESTRAL
PAIGLE	PAIRING	PALAMAE	PALESTRAS
PAIGLES	PAIRINGS	PALAMATE	PALET
PAIK	PAIRS	PALAMINO	PALETOT
PAIKED	PAIRWISE	PALAMINOS	PALETOTS
PAIKING	PAIS	PALAMPORE	PALETS
PAIKS	PAISA	PALANKEEN	PALETTE
PAIL	PAISAN	PALANQUIN	PALETTES
PAILFUL	PAISANA	PALAPA	PALEWAYS
PAILFULS	PAISANAS	PALAPAS	PALEWISE
PAILLARD	PAISANO	PALAS	PALFREY
PAILLARDS	PAISANOS	PALASES	PALFREYED
PAILLASSE	PAISANS	PALATABLE	PALFREYS
PAILLETTE	PAISAS	PALATABLY	PALIER
PAILLON	PAISE	PALATAL	PALIEST
PAILLONS	PAISLEY	PALATALLY	PALIFORM
PAILS	PAISLEYS	PALATALS	PALIKAR
PAILSFUL	PAITRICK	PALATE	PALIKARS
PAIN	PAITRICKS	PALATED	PALILALIA
PAINCH	PAJAMA	PALATES	PALILLOGY

PALIMONY
PALING
PALINGS
PALINKA
PALINKAS
PALINODE
PALINODES
PALINODY
PALINOPIA
PALISADE
PALISADED
PALISADES
PALISADO
PALISH
PALKEE
PALKEES
PALKI
PALKIS
PALL
PALLA
PALLADIA
PALLADIC
PALLADIUM
PALLADOUS
PALLAE
PALLAH
PALLAHS
PALLED
PALLET
PALLETED
PALLETING
PALLETISE
PALLETIZE
PALLETS
PALLETTE
PALLETTES
PALLIA
PALLIAL
PALLIARD
PALLIARDS
PALLIASSE
PALLIATE
PALLIATED
PALLIATES
PALLIATOR
PALLID
PALLIDER
PALLIDEST
PALLIDITY
PALLIDLY
PALLIER
PALLIEST
PALLING
PALLIUM
PALLIUMS
PALLONE
PALLONES
PALLOR

PALLORS
PALLS
PALLY
PALM
PALMAR
PALMARIAN
PALMARY
PALMATE
PALMATED
PALMATELY
PALMATION
PALMED
PALMER
PALMERS
PALMETTE
PALMETTES
PALMETTO
PALMETTOS
PALMFUL
PALMFULS
PALMHOUSE
PALMIE
PALMIER
PALMIES
PALMIEST
PALMIET
PALMIETS
PALMING
PALMIPED
PALMIPEDE
PALMIPEDS
PALMIST
PALMISTER
PALMISTRY
PALMISTS
PALMITATE
PALMITIC
PALMITIN
PALMITINS
PALMLIKE
PALMS
PALMTOP
PALMTOPS
PALMY
PALMYRA
PALMYRAS
PALOLO
PALOLOS
PALOMINO
PALOMINOS
PALOOKA
PALOOKAS
PALOVERDE
PALP
PALPABLE
PALPABLY
PALPAL
PALPATE

PALPATED
PALPATES
PALPATING
PALPATION
PALPATOR
PALPATORS
PALPATORY
PALPEBRA
PALPEBRAE
PALPEBRAL
PALPEBRAS
PALPED
PALPI
PALPING
PALPITANT
PALPITATE
PALPS
PALPUS
PALS
PALSGRAVE
PALSHIP
PALSHIPS
PALSIED
PALSIER
PALSIES
PALSIEST
PALSTAFF
PALSTAFFS
PALSTAVE
PALSTAVES
PALSY
PALSYING
PALSYLIKE
PALTER
PALTERED
PALTERER
PALTERERS
PALTERING
PALTERS
PALTRIER
PALTRIEST
PALTRILY
PALTRY
PALUDAL
PALUDIC
PALUDINAL
PALUDINE
PALUDISM
PALUDISMS
PALUDOSE
PALUDOUS
PALUSTRAL
PALY
PAM
PAMPA
PAMPAS
PAMPASES
PAMPEAN

PAMPEANS
PAMPER
PAMPERED
PAMPERER
PAMPERERS
PAMPERING
PAMPERO
PAMPEROS
PAMPERS
PAMPHLET
PAMPHLETS
PAMPHREY
PAMPHREYS
PAMPOEN
PAMPOENS
PAMPOOTIE
PAMS
PAN
PANACEA
PANACEAN
PANACEAS
PANACHAEA
PANACHE
PANACHES
PANADA
PANADAS
PANAMA
PANAMAS
PANARIES
PANARY
PANATELA
PANATELAS
PANATELLA
PANAX
PANAXES
PANBROIL
PANBROILS
PANCAKE
PANCAKED
PANCAKES
PANCAKING
PANCE
PANCES
PANCETTA
PANCETTAS
PANCHAX
PANCHAXES
PANCHAYAT
PANCHEON
PANCHEONS
PANCHION
PANCHIONS
PANCOSMIC
PANCRATIA
PANCRATIC
PANCREAS
PAND
PANDA

PANDANI
PANDANUS
PANDAR
PANDARED
PANDARING
PANDARS
PANDAS
PANDATION
PANDECT
PANDECTS
PANDEMIA
PANDEMIAN
PANDEMIAS
PANDEMIC
PANDEMICS
PANDER
PANDERED
PANDERER
PANDERERS
PANDERESS
PANDERING
PANDERISM
PANDERLY
PANDEROUS
PANDERS
PANDIED
PANDIES
PANDIT
PANDITS
PANDOOR
PANDOORS
PANDORA
PANDORAS
PANDORE
PANDORES
PANDOUR
PANDOURS
PANDOWDY
PANDS
PANDURA
PANDURAS
PANDURATE
PANDY
PANDYING
PANE
PANED
PANEER
PANEERS
PANEGOISM
PANEGYRIC
PANEGYRY
PANEITIES
PANEITY
PANEL
PANELED
PANELESS
PANELING
PANELINGS

PANELISED
PANELIST
PANELISTS
PANELIZED
PANELLED
PANELLING
PANELLIST
PANELS
PANES
PANETELA
PANETELAS
PANETELLA
PANETTONE
PANETTONI
PANFISH
PANFISHES
PANFRIED
PANFRIES
PANFRY
PANFRYING
PANFUL
PANFULS
PANG
PANGA
PANGAMIC
PANGAMIES
PANGAMY
PANGAS
PANGED
PANGEN
PANGENE
PANGENES
PANGENS
PANGING
PANGLESS
PANGOLIN
PANGOLINS
PANGRAM
PANGRAMS
PANGS
PANHANDLE
PANHUMAN
PANIC
PANICALLY
PANICK
PANICKED
PANICKIER
PANICKING
PANICKS
PANICKY
PANICLE
PANICLED
PANICLES
PANICS
PANICUM
PANICUMS
PANIER
PANIERS

PANIM
PANIMS
PANING
PANINI
PANINO
PANISC
PANISCS
PANISK
PANISKS
PANISLAM
PANISLAMS
PANJANDRA
PANLOGISM
PANMICTIC
PANMIXES
PANMIXIA
PANMIXIAS
PANMIXIS
PANNAGE
PANNAGES
PANNE
PANNED
PANNELLED
PANNER
PANNERS
PANNES
PANNICK
PANNICKS
PANNICLE
PANNICLES
PANNIER
PANNIERED
PANNIERS
PANNIKEL
PANNIKELL
PANNIKELS
PANNIKIN
PANNIKINS
PANNING
PANNINGS
PANNOSE
PANNUS
PANNUSES
PANOCHA
PANOCHAS
PANOCHE
PANOCHES
PANOISTIC
PANOPLIED
PANOPLIES
PANOPLY
PANOPTIC
PANORAMA
PANORAMAS
PANORAMIC
PANPIPE
PANPIPES
PANS

PANSEXUAL
PANSIED
PANSIES
PANSOPHIC
PANSOPHY
PANSPERMY
PANSY
PANT
PANTABLE
PANTABLES
PANTAGAMY
PANTALEON
PANTALET
PANTALETS
PANTALON
PANTALONE
PANTALONS
PANTALOON
PANTDRESS
PANTED
PANTER
PANTERS
PANTHEISM
PANTHEIST
PANTHENOL
PANTHEON
PANTHEONS
PANTHER
PANTHERS
PANTIE
PANTIES
PANTIHOSE
PANTILE
PANTILED
PANTILES
PANTILING
PANTINE
PANTINES
PANTING
PANTINGLY
PANTINGS
PANTLER
PANTLERS
PANTO
PANTOFFLE
PANTOFLE
PANTOFLES
PANTOMIME
PANTON
PANTONS
PANTOS
PANTOUFLE
PANTOUM
PANTOUMS
PANTRIES
PANTROPIC
PANTRY
PANTRYMAN

PANTRYMEN
PANTS
PANTSUIT
PANTSUITS
PANTUN
PANTUNS
PANTY
PANTYHOSE
PANZER
PANZERS
PANZOOTIC
PAOLI
PAOLO
PAP
PAPA
PAPABLE
PAPACIES
PAPACY
PAPADAM
PAPADAMS
PAPADOM
PAPADOMS
PAPADUM
PAPADUMS
PAPAIN
PAPAINS
PAPAL
PAPALISE
PAPALISED
PAPALISES
PAPALISM
PAPALISMS
PAPALIST
PAPALISTS
PAPALIZE
PAPALIZED
PAPALIZES
PAPALLY
PAPARAZZI
PAPARAZZO
PAPAS
PAPAUMA
PAPAW
PAPAWS
PAPAYA
PAPAYAN
PAPAYAS
PAPE
PAPER
PAPERBACK
PAPERBARK
PAPERBOY
PAPERBOYS
PAPERCLIP
PAPERED
PAPERER
PAPERERS
PAPERGIRL

PAPERIER
PAPERIEST
PAPERING
PAPERINGS
PAPERLESS
PAPERS
PAPERWARE
PAPERWORK
PAPERY
PAPES
PAPETERIE
PAPHIAN
PAPHIANS
PAPILIO
PAPILIOS
PAPILLA
PAPILLAE
PAPILLAR
PAPILLARY
PAPILLATE
PAPILLOMA
PAPILLON
PAPILLONS
PAPILLOSE
PAPILLOTE
PAPILLOUS
PAPILLULE
PAPISH
PAPISHER
PAPISHERS
PAPISHES
PAPISM
PAPISMS
PAPIST
PAPISTIC
PAPISTRY
PAPISTS
PAPOOSE
PAPOOSES
PAPPADAM
PAPPADAMS
PAPPADOM
PAPPADOMS
PAPPED
PAPPI
PAPPIER
PAPPIES
PAPPIEST
PAPPING
PAPPOOSE
PAPPOOSES
PAPPOSE
PAPPOUS
PAPPUS
PAPPUSES
PAPPY
PAPRICA
PAPRICAS

PAPRIKA
PAPRIKAS
PAPS
PAPULA
PAPULAE
PAPULAR
PAPULE
PAPULES
PAPULOSE
PAPULOUS
PAPYRAL
PAPYRI
PAPYRIAN
PAPYRINE
PAPYRUS
PAPYRUSES
PAR
PARA
PARABASES
PARABASIS
PARABEMA
PARABLAST
PARABLE
PARABLED
PARABLES
PARABLING
PARABOLA
PARABOLAS
PARABOLE
PARABOLES
PARABOLIC
PARABRAKE
PARACHOR
PARACHORS
PARACHUTE
PARACLETE
PARACME
PARACMES
PARACRINE
PARACUSES
PARACUSIS
PARADE
PARADED
PARADER
PARADERS
PARADES
PARADIGM
PARADIGMS
PARADING
PARADISAL
PARADISE
PARADISES
PARADISIC
PARADOR
PARADORES
PARADORS
PARADOS
PARADOSES

PARADOX
PARADOXAL
PARADOXER
PARADOXES
PARADOXY
PARADROP
PARADROPS
PARAE
PARAFFIN
PARAFFINE
PARAFFINS
PARAFFINY
PARAFFLE
PARAFFLES
PARAFLE
PARAFLES
PARAFOIL
PARAFOILS
PARAFORM
PARAFORMS
PARAGE
PARAGES
PARAGLIDE
PARAGOGE
PARAGOGES
PARAGOGIC
PARAGOGUE
PARAGON
PARAGONED
PARAGONS
PARAGRAM
PARAGRAMS
PARAGRAPH
PARAKEET
PARAKEETS
PARAKELIA
PARAKITE
PARAKITES
PARALALIA
PARALEGAL
PARALEXIA
PARALEXIC
PARALLAX
PARALLEL
PARALLELS
PARALOGIA
PARALOGY
PARALYSE
PARALYSED
PARALYSER
PARALYSES
PARALYSIS
PARALYTIC
PARALYZE
PARALYZED
PARALYZER
PARALYZES
PARAMATTA

PARAMECIA	PARASITE	PARDAH	PAREVE
PARAMEDIC	PARASITES	PARDAHS	PARFAIT
PARAMENT	PARASITIC	PARDAL	PARFAITS
PARAMENTA	PARASOL	PARDALE	PARFLECHE
PARAMENTS	PARASOLED	PARDALES	PARFLESH
PARAMESE	PARASOLS	PARDALIS	PARFOCAL
PARAMESES	PARATAXES	PARDALOTE	PARGANA
PARAMETER	PARATAXIS	PARDALS	PARGANAS
PARAMO	PARATHA	PARDED	PARGASITE
PARAMORPH	PARATHAS	PARDEE	PARGE
PARAMOS	PARATHION	PARDI	PARGED
PARAMOUNT	PARATONIC	PARDIE	PARGES
PARAMOUR	PARATROOP	PARDINE	PARGET
PARAMOURS	PARAVAIL	PARDNER	PARGETED
PARAMYLUM	PARAVANE	PARDNERS	PARGETER
PARANETE	PARAVANES	PARDON	PARGETERS
PARANETES	PARAVANT	PARDONED	PARGETING
PARANG	PARAVAUNT	PARDONER	PARGETS
PARANGS	PARAWING	PARDONERS	PARGETTED
PARANOEA	PARAWINGS	PARDONING	PARGING
PARANOEAS	PARAXIAL	PARDONS	PARGINGS
PARANOEIC	PARAZOA	PARDS	PARGO
PARANOIA	PARAZOAN	PARDY	PARGOS
PARANOIAC	PARAZOANS	PARE	PARGYLINE
PARANOIAS	PARAZOON	PARECIOUS	PARHELIA
PARANOIC	PARBAKE	PARECISM	PARHELIC
PARANOICS	PARBAKED	PARECISMS	PARHELION
PARANOID	PARBAKES	PARED	PARHYPATE
PARANOIDS	PARBAKING	PAREGORIC	PARIAH
PARANYM	PARBOIL	PAREIRA	PARIAHS
PARANYMPH	PARBOILED	PAREIRAS	PARIAL
PARANYMS	PARBOILS	PARELLA	PARIALS
PARAPARA	PARBREAK	PARELLAS	PARIAN
PARAPENTE	PARBREAKS	PARELLE	PARIANS
PARAPET	PARBUCKLE	PARELLES	PARIES
PARAPETED	PARCEL	PARENESES	PARIETAL
PARAPETS	PARCELED	PARENESIS	PARIETALS
PARAPH	PARCELING	PARENT	PARIETES
PARAPHED	PARCELLED	PARENTAGE	PARING
PARAPHING	PARCELS	PARENTAL	PARINGS
PARAPHS	PARCENARY	PARENTED	PARIS
PARAPODIA	PARCENER	PARENTING	PARISCHAN
PARAQUAT	PARCENERS	PARENTS	PARISES
PARAQUATS	PARCH	PAREO	PARISH
PARAQUET	PARCHED	PAREOS	PARISHAD
PARAQUETS	PARCHEDLY	PARER	PARISHADS
PARAQUITO	PARCHEESI	PARERA	PARISHEN
PARARHYME	PARCHES	PARERGA	PARISHENS
PARAS	PARCHESI	PARERGON	PARISHES
PARASAIL	PARCHESIS	PARERS	PARISON
PARASAILS	PARCHING	PARES	PARISONS
PARASANG	PARCHISI	PARESES	PARITIES
PARASANGS	PARCHISIS	PARESIS	PARITOR
PARASCEVE	PARCHMENT	PARETIC	PARITORS
PARASHAH	PARCIMONY	PARETICS	PARITY
PARASHAHS	PARCLOSE	PAREU	PARK
PARASHOT	PARCLOSES	PAREUS	PARKA
PARASHOTH	PARD	PAREV	PARKADE

PARKADES
PARKAS
PARKED
PARKEE
PARKEES
PARKER
PARKERS
PARKETTE
PARKETTES
PARKI
PARKIE
PARKIER
PARKIES
PARKIEST
PARKIN
PARKING
PARKINGS
PARKINS
PARKIS
PARKISH
PARKLAND
PARKLANDS
PARKLIKE
PARKLY
PARKOUR
PARKOURS
PARKS
PARKWARD
PARKWARDS
PARKWAY
PARKWAYS
PARKY
PARLANCE
PARLANCES
PARLANDO
PARLANTE
PARLAY
PARLAYED
PARLAYING
PARLAYS
PARLE
PARLED
PARLEMENT
PARLES
PARLEY
PARLEYED
PARLEYER
PARLEYERS
PARLEYING
PARLEYS
PARLEYVOO
PARLIES
PARLING
PARLOR
PARLORS
PARLOUR
PARLOURS
PARLOUS

PARLOUSLY
PARLY
PARMESAN
PARMESANS
PAROCHIAL
PAROCHIN
PAROCHINE
PAROCHINS
PARODIC
PARODICAL
PARODIED
PARODIES
PARODIST
PARODISTS
PARODOI
PARODOS
PARODY
PARODYING
PAROEMIA
PAROEMIAC
PAROEMIAL
PAROEMIAS
PAROICOUS
PAROL
PAROLABLE
PAROLE
PAROLED
PAROLEE
PAROLEES
PAROLES
PAROLING
PAROLS
PARONYM
PARONYMIC
PARONYMS
PARONYMY
PAROQUET
PAROQUETS
PARORE
PAROSMIA
PAROSMIAS
PAROTIC
PAROTID
PAROTIDS
PAROTIS
PAROTISES
PAROTITIC
PAROTITIS
PAROTOID
PAROTOIDS
PAROUS
PAROUSIA
PAROUSIAS
PAROXYSM
PAROXYSMS
PARP
PARPANE
PARPANES

PARPED
PARPEN
PARPEND
PARPENDS
PARPENS
PARPENT
PARPENTS
PARPING
PARPOINT
PARPOINTS
PARPS
PARQUET
PARQUETED
PARQUETRY
PARQUETS
PARR
PARRA
PARRAKEET
PARRAL
PARRALS
PARRAS
PARRED
PARREL
PARRELS
PARRHESIA
PARRICIDE
PARRIDGE
PARRIDGES
PARRIED
PARRIER
PARRIERS
PARRIES
PARRING
PARRITCH
PARROCK
PARROCKED
PARROCKS
PARROKET
PARROKETS
PARROQUET
PARROT
PARROTED
PARROTER
PARROTERS
PARROTING
PARROTRY
PARROTS
PARROTY
PARRS
PARRY
PARRYING
PARS
PARSABLE
PARSE
PARSEC
PARSECS
PARSED
PARSER

PARSERS
PARSES
PARSIMONY
PARSING
PARSINGS
PARSLEY
PARSLEYED
PARSLEYS
PARSLIED
PARSNEP
PARSNEPS
PARSNIP
PARSNIPS
PARSON
PARSONAGE
PARSONIC
PARSONISH
PARSONS
PART
PARTAKE
PARTAKEN
PARTAKER
PARTAKERS
PARTAKES
PARTAKING
PARTAN
PARTANS
PARTED
PARTER
PARTERRE
PARTERRES
PARTERS
PARTI
PARTIAL
PARTIALLY
PARTIALS
PARTIBLE
PARTICLE
PARTICLES
PARTIED
PARTIER
PARTIERS
PARTIES
PARTIM
PARTING
PARTINGS
PARTIS
PARTISAN
PARTISANS
PARTITA
PARTITAS
PARTITE
PARTITION
PARTITIVE
PARTITURA
PARTIZAN
PARTIZANS
PARTLET

PARTLETS	PASH	PASSER	PASTEUPS
PARTLY	PASHA	PASSERBY	PASTICCI
PARTNER	PASHADOM	PASSERINE	PASTICCIO
PARTNERED	PASHADOMS	PASSERS	PASTICHE
PARTNERS	PASHALIC	PASSERSBY	PASTICHES
PARTON	PASHALICS	PASSES	PASTIE
PARTONS	PASHALIK	PASSIBLE	PASTIER
PARTOOK	PASHALIKS	PASSIBLY	PASTIES
PARTRIDGE	PASHAS	PASSIM	PASTIEST
PARTS	PASHED	PASSING	PASTIL
PARTURE	PASHES	PASSINGLY	PASTILLE
PARTURES	PASHIM	PASSINGS	PASTILLES
PARTWAY	PASHIMS	PASSION	PASTILS
PARTWORK	PASHING	PASSIONAL	PASTILY
PARTWORKS	PASHKA	PASSIONED	PASTIME
PARTY	PASHKAS	PASSIONS	PASTIMES
PARTYER	PASHM	PASSIVATE	PASTINA
PARTYERS	PASHMINA	PASSIVE	PASTINAS
PARTYGOER	PASHMINAS	PASSIVELY	PASTINESS
PARTYING	PASHMS	PASSIVES	PASTING
PARTYISM	PASODOBLE	PASSIVISM	PASTINGS
PARTYISMS	PASPALUM	PASSIVIST	PASTIS
PARULIDES	PASPALUMS	PASSIVITY	PASTISES
PARULIS	PASPIES	PASSKEY	PASTITSIO
PARULISES	PASPY	PASSKEYS	PASTITSO
PARURA	PASQUIL	PASSLESS	PASTITSOS
PARURAS	PASQUILER	PASSMAN	PASTLESS
PARURE	PASQUILS	PASSMEN	PASTNESS
PARURES	PASS	PASSMENT	PASTOR
PARVE	PASSABLE	PASSMENTS	PASTORAL
PARVENU	PASSABLY	PASSOUT	PASTORALE
PARVENUE	PASSADE	PASSOUTS	PASTORALI
PARVENUES	PASSADES	PASSOVER	PASTORALS
PARVENUS	PASSADO	PASSOVERS	PASTORATE
PARVIS	PASSADOES	PASSPORT	PASTORED
PARVISE	PASSADOS	PASSPORTS	PASTORING
PARVISES	PASSAGE	PASSUS	PASTORIUM
PARVO	PASSAGED	PASSUSES	PASTORLY
PARVOLIN	PASSAGER	PASSWORD	PASTORS
PARVOLINE	PASSAGES	PASSWORDS	PASTRAMI
PARVOLINS	PASSAGING	PAST	PASTRAMIS
PARVOS	PASSALONG	PASTA	PASTRIES
PAS	PASSAMENT	PASTALIKE	PASTROMI
PASCAL	PASSANT	PASTANCE	PASTROMIS
PASCALS	PASSATA	PASTANCES	PASTRY
PASCHAL	PASSATAS	PASTAS	PASTS
PASCHALS	PASSBAND	PASTE	PASTURAGE
PASCUAL	PASSBANDS	PASTED	PASTURAL
PASE	PASSBOOK	PASTEDOWN	PASTURE
PASEAR	PASSBOOKS	PASTEL	PASTURED
PASEARED	PASSE	PASTELIST	PASTURER
PASEARING	PASSED	PASTELS	PASTURERS
PASEARS	PASSEE	PASTER	PASTURES
PASELA	PASSEL	PASTERN	PASTURING
PASELAS	PASSELS	PASTERNS	PASTY
PASEO	PASSEMENT	PASTERS	PAT
PASEOS	PASSENGER	PASTES	PATACA
PASES	PASSEPIED	PASTEUP	PATACAS

PATAGIA	PATHETICS	PATRIATE	PATTING
PATAGIAL	PATHIC	PATRIATED	PATTLE
PATAGIUM	PATHICS	PATRIATES	PATTLES
PATAKA	PATHING	PATRICIAN	PATTY
PATAMAR	PATHLESS	PATRICIDE	PATTYPAN
PATAMARS	PATHNAME	PATRICK	PATTYPANS
PATBALL	PATHNAMES	PATRICKS	PATU
PATBALLS	PATHOGEN	PATRICO	PATULENT
PATCH	PATHOGENE	PATRICOES	PATULIN
PATCHABLE	PATHOGENS	PATRILINY	PATULINS
PATCHED	PATHOGENY	PATRIMONY	PATULOUS
PATCHER	PATHOLOGY	PATRIOT	PATUS
PATCHERS	PATHOS	PATRIOTIC	PATUTUKI
PATCHERY	PATHOSES	PATRIOTS	PATUTUKIS
PATCHES	PATHS	PATRISTIC	PATY
PATCHIER	PATHWAY	PATROL	PATZER
PATCHIEST	PATHWAYS	PATROLLED	PATZERS
PATCHILY	PATIBLE	PATROLLER	PAUA
PATCHING	PATIENCE	PATROLMAN	PAUAS
PATCHINGS	PATIENCES	PATROLMEN	PAUCAL
PATCHOCKE	PATIENT	PATROLOGY	PAUCALS
PATCHOULI	PATIENTED	PATROLS	PAUCITIES
PATCHOULY	PATIENTER	PATRON	PAUCITY
PATCHWORK	PATIENTLY	PATRONAGE	PAUGHTIER
PATCHY	PATIENTS	PATRONAL	PAUGHTY
PATE	PATIKI	PATRONESS	PAUL
PATED	PATIN	PATRONISE	PAULDRON
PATELLA	PATINA	PATRONIZE	PAULDRONS
PATELLAE	PATINAE	PATRONLY	PAULIN
PATELLAR	PATINAED	PATRONNE	PAULINS
PATELLAS	PATINAS	PATRONNES	PAULOWNIA
PATELLATE	PATINATE	PATRONS	PAULS
PATEN	PATINATED	PATROON	PAUNCE
PATENCIES	PATINATES	PATROONS	PAUNCES
PATENCY	PATINE	PATS	PAUNCH
PATENS	PATINED	PATSIES	PAUNCHED
PATENT	PATINES	PATSY	PAUNCHES
PATENTED	PATINING	PATTAMAR	PAUNCHIER
PATENTEE	PATINISE	PATTAMARS	PAUNCHING
PATENTEES	PATINISED	PATTE	PAUNCHY
PATENTING	PATINISES	PATTED	PAUPER
PATENTLY	PATINIZE	PATTEE	PAUPERED
PATENTOR	PATINIZED	PATTEN	PAUPERESS
PATENTORS	PATINIZES	PATTENED	PAUPERING
PATENTS	PATINS	PATTENING	PAUPERISE
PATER	PATIO	PATTENS	PAUPERISM
PATERA	PATIOS	PATTER	PAUPERIZE
PATERAE	PATISSIER	PATTERED	PAUPERS
PATERCOVE	PATLY	PATTERER	PAUPIETTE
PATERERO	PATNESS	PATTERERS	PAUROPOD
PATEREROS	PATNESSES	PATTERING	PAUROPODS
PATERNAL	PATOIS	PATTERN	PAUSAL
PATERNITY	PATONCE	PATTERNED	PAUSE
PATERS	PATOOTIE	PATTERNS	PAUSED
PATES	PATOOTIES	PATTERS	PAUSEFUL
PATH	PATRIAL	PATTES	PAUSELESS
PATHED	PATRIALS	PATTIE	PAUSER
PATHETIC	PATRIARCH	PATTIES	PAUSERS

PAUSES
PAUSING
PAUSINGLY
PAUSINGS
PAV
PAVAGE
PAVAGES
PAVAN
PAVANE
PAVANES
PAVANS
PAVE
PAVED
PAVEED
PAVEMENT
PAVEMENTS
PAVEN
PAVENS
PAVER
PAVERS
PAVES
PAVID
PAVILION
PAVILIONS
PAVILLON
PAVILLONS
PAVIN
PAVING
PAVINGS
PAVINS
PAVIOR
PAVIORS
PAVIOUR
PAVIOURS
PAVIS
PAVISE
PAVISER
PAVISERS
PAVISES
PAVISSE
PAVISSES
PAVLOVA
PAVLOVAS
PAVONAZZO
PAVONE
PAVONES
PAVONIAN
PAVONINE
PAVS
PAW
PAWA
PAWAS
PAWAW
PAWAWED
PAWAWING
PAWAWS
PAWED
PAWER

PAWERS
PAWING
PAWK
PAWKIER
PAWKIEST
PAWKILY
PAWKINESS
PAWKS
PAWKY
PAWL
PAWLS
PAWN
PAWNABLE
PAWNAGE
PAWNAGES
PAWNCE
PAWNCES
PAWNED
PAWNEE
PAWNEES
PAWNER
PAWNERS
PAWNING
PAWNOR
PAWNORS
PAWNS
PAWNSHOP
PAWNSHOPS
PAWPAW
PAWPAWS
PAWS
PAX
PAXES
PAXIUBA
PAXIUBAS
PAXWAX
PAXWAXES
PAY
PAYABLE
PAYABLES
PAYABLY
PAYBACK
PAYBACKS
PAYCHECK
PAYCHECKS
PAYDAY
PAYDAYS
PAYED
PAYEE
PAYEES
PAYER
PAYERS
PAYFONE
PAYFONES
PAYGRADE
PAYGRADES
PAYING
PAYINGS

PAYLOAD
PAYLOADS
PAYMASTER
PAYMENT
PAYMENTS
PAYNIM
PAYNIMRY
PAYNIMS
PAYOFF
PAYOFFS
PAYOLA
PAYOLAS
PAYOR
PAYORS
PAYOUT
PAYOUTS
PAYPHONE
PAYPHONES
PAYROLL
PAYROLLS
PAYS
PAYSAGE
PAYSAGES
PAYSAGIST
PAYSD
PAYSLIP
PAYSLIPS
PAZAZZ
PAZAZZES
PAZZAZZ
PAZZAZZES
PE
PEA
PEABERRY
PEACE
PEACEABLE
PEACEABLY
PEACED
PEACEFUL
PEACELESS
PEACENIK
PEACENIKS
PEACES
PEACETIME
PEACH
PEACHBLOW
PEACHED
PEACHER
PEACHERS
PEACHES
PEACHIER
PEACHIEST
PEACHILY
PEACHING
PEACHY
PEACING
PEACOAT
PEACOATS

PEACOCK
PEACOCKED
PEACOCKS
PEACOCKY
PEACOD
PEACODS
PEAFOWL
PEAFOWLS
PEAG
PEAGE
PEAGES
PEAGS
PEAHEN
PEAHENS
PEAK
PEAKED
PEAKIER
PEAKIEST
PEAKING
PEAKISH
PEAKLESS
PEAKLIKE
PEAKS
PEAKY
PEAL
PEALED
PEALIKE
PEALING
PEALS
PEAN
PEANED
PEANING
PEANS
PEANUT
PEANUTS
PEAPOD
PEAPODS
PEAR
PEARCE
PEARCED
PEARCES
PEARCING
PEARE
PEARES
PEARL
PEARLASH
PEARLED
PEARLER
PEARLERS
PEARLIER
PEARLIES
PEARLIEST
PEARLIN
PEARLING
PEARLINGS
PEARLINS
PEARLISED
PEARLITE

PEARLITES	PEBBLE	PECTINS	PEDDERS
PEARLITIC	PEBBLED	PECTISE	PEDDLE
PEARLIZED	PEBBLES	PECTISED	PEDDLED
PEARLS	PEBBLIER	PECTISES	PEDDLER
PEARLWORT	PEBBLIEST	PECTISING	PEDDLERS
PEARLY	PEBBLING	PECTIZE	PEDDLERY
PEARMAIN	PEBBLINGS	PECTIZED	PEDDLES
PEARMAINS	PEBBLY	PECTIZES	PEDDLING
PEARS	PEBRINE	PECTIZING	PEDDLINGS
PEARST	PEBRINES	PECTOLITE	PEDERAST
PEART	PEC	PECTORAL	PEDERASTS
PEARTER	PECAN	PECTORALS	PEDERASTY
PEARTEST	PECANS	PECTOSE	PEDERERO
PEARTLY	PECCABLE	PECTOSES	PEDEREROS
PEARTNESS	PECCANCY	PECULATE	PEDES
PEARWOOD	PECCANT	PECULATED	PEDESES
PEARWOODS	PECCANTLY	PECULATES	PEDESIS
PEAS	PECCARIES	PECULATOR	PEDESTAL
PEASANT	PECCARY	PECULIA	PEDESTALS
PEASANTRY	PECCAVI	PECULIAR	PEDETIC
PEASANTS	PECCAVIS	PECULIARS	PEDIATRIC
PEASANTY	PECH	PECULIUM	PEDICAB
PEASCOD	PECHAN	PECUNIARY	PEDICABS
PEASCODS	PECHANS	PECUNIOUS	PEDICEL
PEASE	PECHED	PED	PEDICELS
PEASECOD	PECHING	PEDAGOG	PEDICLE
PEASECODS	PECHS	PEDAGOGIC	PEDICLED
PEASED	PECK	PEDAGOGS	PEDICLES
PEASEN	PECKE	PEDAGOGUE	PEDICULAR
PEASES	PECKED	PEDAGOGY	PEDICULI
PEASING	PECKER	PEDAL	PEDICULUS
PEASON	PECKERS	PEDALED	PEDICURE
PEASOUPER	PECKES	PEDALER	PEDICURED
PEAT	PECKIER	PEDALERS	PEDICURES
PEATARIES	PECKIEST	PEDALFER	PEDIFORM
PEATARY	PECKING	PEDALFERS	PEDIGREE
PEATERIES	PECKINGS	PEDALIER	PEDIGREED
PEATERY	PECKISH	PEDALIERS	PEDIGREES
PEATIER	PECKISHLY	PEDALING	PEDIMENT
PEATIEST	PECKS	PEDALLED	PEDIMENTS
PEATLAND	PECKY	PEDALLER	PEDIPALP
PEATLANDS	PECORINI	PEDALLERS	PEDIPALPI
PEATMAN	PECORINO	PEDALLING	PEDIPALPS
PEATMEN	PECORINOS	PEDALO	PEDLAR
PEATS	PECS	PEDALOES	PEDLARIES
PEATSHIP	PECTASE	PEDALOS	PEDLARS
PEATSHIPS	PECTASES	PEDALS	PEDLARY
PEATY	PECTATE	PEDANT	PEDLER
PEAVEY	PECTATES	PEDANTIC	PEDLERIES
PEAVEYS	PECTEN	PEDANTISE	PEDLERS
PEAVIES	PECTENS	PEDANTISM	PEDLERY
PEAVY	PECTIC	PEDANTIZE	PEDOCAL
PEAZE	PECTIN	PEDANTRY	PEDOCALIC
PEAZED	PECTINAL	PEDANTS	PEDOCALS
PEAZES	PECTINATE	PEDATE	PEDOGENIC
PEAZING	PECTINEAL	PEDATELY	PEDOLOGIC
PEBA	PECTINES	PEDATIFID	PEDOLOGY
PEBAS	PECTINOUS	PEDDER	PEDOMETER

PEDOPHILE	PEEPS	PEHS	PELISSES
PEDORTHIC	PEEPSHOW	PEIGNOIR	PELITE
PEDRAIL	PEEPSHOWS	PEIGNOIRS	PELITES
PEDRAILS	PEEPUL	PEIN	PELITIC
PEDRERO	PEEPULS	PEINCT	PELL
PEDREROES	PEER	PEINCTED	PELLACH
PEDREROS	PEERAGE	PEINCTING	PELLACHS
PEDRO	PEERAGES	PEINCTS	PELLACK
PEDROS	PEERED	PEINED	PELLACKS
PEDS	PEERESS	PEINING	PELLAGRA
PEDUNCLE	PEERESSES	PEINS	PELLAGRAS
PEDUNCLED	PEERIE	PEIRASTIC	PELLAGRIN
PEDUNCLES	PEERIER	PEISE	PELLET
PEE	PEERIES	PEISED	PELLETAL
PEEBEEN	PEERIEST	PEISES	PELLETED
PEEBEENS	PEERING	PEISHWA	PELLETIFY
PEECE	PEERLESS	PEISHWAH	PELLETING
PEECES	PEERS	PEISHWAHS	PELLETISE
PEED	PEERY	PEISHWAS	PELLETIZE
PEEING	PEES	PEISING	PELLETS
PEEK	PEESWEEP	PEIZE	PELLICLE
PEEKABO	PEESWEEPS	PEIZED	PELLICLES
PEEKABOO	PEETWEET	PEIZES	PELLITORY
PEEKABOOS	PEETWEETS	PEIZING	PELLMELL
PEEKABOS	PEEVE	PEJORATE	PELLMELLS
PEEKAPOO	PEEVED	PEJORATED	PELLOCK
PEEKAPOOS	PEEVER	PEJORATES	PELLOCKS
PEEKED	PEEVERS	PEKAN	PELLS
PEEKING	PEEVES	PEKANS	PELLUCID
PEEKS	PEEVING	PEKE	PELLUM
PEEL	PEEVISH	PEKEPOO	PELLUMS
PEELABLE	PEEVISHLY	PEKEPOOS	PELMA
PEELED	PEEWEE	PEKES	PELMANISM
PEELER	PEEWEES	PEKIN	PELMAS
PEELERS	PEEWIT	PEKINS	PELMATIC
PEELING	PEEWITS	PEKOE	PELMET
PEELINGS	PEG	PEKOES	PELMETS
PEELS	PEGASUS	PELA	PELOID
PEEN	PEGASUSES	PELAGE	PELOIDS
PEENED	PEGBOARD	PELAGES	PELOLOGY
PEENGE	PEGBOARDS	PELAGIAL	PELON
PEENGED	PEGBOX	PELAGIAN	PELORIA
PEENGEING	PEGBOXES	PELAGIANS	PELORIAN
PEENGES	PEGGED	PELAGIC	PELORIAS
PEENGING	PEGGIES	PELAGICS	PELORIC
PEENING	PEGGING	PELAS	PELORIES
PEENS	PEGGINGS	PELE	PELORISED
PEEOY	PEGGY	PELECYPOD	PELORISM
PEEOYS	PEGH	PELERINE	PELORISMS
PEEP	PEGHED	PELERINES	PELORIZED
PEEPE	PEGHING	PELES	PELORUS
PEEPED	PEGHS	PELF	PELORUSES
PEEPER	PEGLEGGED	PELFS	PELORY
PEEPERS	PEGLESS	PELHAM	PELOTA
PEEPES	PEGLIKE	PELHAMS	PELOTAS
PEEPHOLE	PEGMATITE	PELICAN	PELOTON
PEEPHOLES	PEGS	PELICANS	PELOTONS
PEEPING	PEH	PELISSE	PELT

PELTA
PELTAE
PELTAS
PELTAST
PELTASTS
PELTATE
PELTATELY
PELTATION
PELTED
PELTER
PELTERED
PELTERING
PELTERS
PELTING
PELTINGLY
PELTINGS
PELTLESS
PELTRIES
PELTRY
PELTS
PELVES
PELVIC
PELVICS
PELVIFORM
PELVIS
PELVISES
PEMBINA
PEMBINAS
PEMBROKE
PEMBROKES
PEMICAN
PEMICANS
PEMMICAN
PEMMICANS
PEMOLINE
PEMOLINES
PEMPHIGUS
PEMPHIX
PEMPHIXES
PEN
PENAL
PENALISE
PENALISED
PENALISES
PENALITY
PENALIZE
PENALIZED
PENALIZES
PENALLY
PENALTIES
PENALTY
PENANCE
PENANCED
PENANCES
PENANCING
PENANG
PENANGS
PENATES

PENCE
PENCEL
PENCELS
PENCES
PENCHANT
PENCHANTS
PENCIL
PENCILED
PENCILER
PENCILERS
PENCILING
PENCILLED
PENCILLER
PENCILS
PENCRAFT
PENCRAFTS
PEND
PENDANT
PENDANTLY
PENDANTS
PENDED
PENDENCY
PENDENT
PENDENTLY
PENDENTS
PENDICLE
PENDICLER
PENDICLES
PENDING
PENDRAGON
PENDS
PENDU
PENDULAR
PENDULATE
PENDULE
PENDULES
PENDULINE
PENDULOUS
PENDULUM
PENDULUMS
PENE
PENED
PENEPLAIN
PENEPLANE
PENES
PENETRANT
PENETRATE
PENFOLD
PENFOLDS
PENFUL
PENFULS
PENGO
PENGOS
PENGUIN
PENGUINRY
PENGUINS
PENHOLDER
PENI

PENIAL
PENICIL
PENICILS
PENIE
PENIES
PENILE
PENILL
PENILLION
PENING
PENINSULA
PENIS
PENISES
PENISTONE
PENITENCE
PENITENCY
PENITENT
PENITENTS
PENK
PENKNIFE
PENKNIVES
PENKS
PENLIGHT
PENLIGHTS
PENLITE
PENLITES
PENMAN
PENMEN
PENNA
PENNAE
PENNAL
PENNALISM
PENNALS
PENNAME
PENNAMES
PENNANT
PENNANTS
PENNATE
PENNATED
PENNATULA
PENNE
PENNED
PENNEECH
PENNEECHS
PENNEECK
PENNEECKS
PENNER
PENNERS
PENNES
PENNI
PENNIA
PENNIED
PENNIES
PENNIFORM
PENNILESS
PENNILL
PENNINE
PENNINES
PENNING

PENNINITE
PENNIS
PENNON
PENNONCEL
PENNONED
PENNONS
PENNY
PENNYBOY
PENNYBOYS
PENNYFEE
PENNYFEES
PENNYLAND
PENNYWISE
PENNYWORT
PENOCHE
PENOCHES
PENOLOGY
PENONCEL
PENONCELS
PENPOINT
PENPOINTS
PENPUSHER
PENS
PENSEE
PENSEES
PENSEL
PENSELS
PENSIL
PENSILE
PENSILITY
PENSILS
PENSION
PENSIONE
PENSIONED
PENSIONER
PENSIONES
PENSIONS
PENSIVE
PENSIVELY
PENSTEMON
PENSTER
PENSTERS
PENSTOCK
PENSTOCKS
PENSUM
PENSUMS
PENT
PENTACLE
PENTACLES
PENTACT
PENTACTS
PENTAD
PENTADIC
PENTADS
PENTAGON
PENTAGONS
PENTAGRAM
PENTALOGY

PENTALPHA	PENUMBRAE	PEPPIEST	PERCEABLE
PENTAMERY	PENUMBRAL	PEPPILY	PERCEANT
PENTANE	PENUMBRAS	PEPPINESS	PERCED
PENTANES	PENURIES	PEPPING	PERCEIVE
PENTANGLE	PENURIOUS	PEPPY	PERCEIVED
PENTANOIC	PENURY	PEPS	PERCEIVER
PENTANOL	PENWOMAN	PEPSIN	PERCEIVES
PENTANOLS	PENWOMEN	PEPSINATE	PERCEN
PENTAPODY	PEON	PEPSINE	PERCENT
PENTARCH	PEONAGE	PEPSINES	PERCENTAL
PENTARCHS	PEONAGES	PEPSINS	PERCENTS
PENTARCHY	PEONES	PEPTALK	PERCEPT
PENTATHLA	PEONIES	PEPTALKED	PERCEPTS
PENTEL	PEONISM	PEPTALKS	PERCES
PENTELS	PEONISMS	PEPTIC	PERCH
PENTENE	PEONS	PEPTICITY	PERCHANCE
PENTENES	PEONY	PEPTICS	PERCHED
PENTHIA	PEOPLE	PEPTID	PERCHER
PENTHIAS	PEOPLED	PEPTIDASE	PERCHERON
PENTHOUSE	PEOPLER	PEPTIDE	PERCHERS
PENTICE	PEOPLERS	PEPTIDES	PERCHERY
PENTICED	PEOPLES	PEPTIDIC	PERCHES
PENTICES	PEOPLING	PEPTIDS	PERCHING
PENTICING	PEP	PEPTISE	PERCHINGS
PENTISE	PEPERINO	PEPTISED	PERCIFORM
PENTISED	PEPERINOS	PEPTISER	PERCINE
PENTISES	PEPEROMIA	PEPTISERS	PERCING
PENTISING	PEPERONI	PEPTISES	PERCOCT
PENTITI	PEPERONIS	PEPTISING	PERCOID
PENTITO	PEPFUL	PEPTIZE	PERCOIDS
PENTODE	PEPINO	PEPTIZED	PERCOLATE
PENTODES	PEPINOS	PEPTIZER	PERCOLIN
PENTOMIC	PEPLA	PEPTIZERS	PERCOLINS
PENTOSAN	PEPLOS	PEPTIZES	PERCUSS
PENTOSANE	PEPLOSES	PEPTIZING	PERCUSSED
PENTOSANS	PEPLUM	PEPTONE	PERCUSSES
PENTOSE	PEPLUMED	PEPTONES	PERCUSSOR
PENTOSES	PEPLUMS	PEPTONIC	PERDENDO
PENTOSIDE	PEPLUS	PEPTONISE	PERDIE
PENTOXIDE	PEPLUSES	PEPTONIZE	PERDITION
PENTROOF	PEPO	PEQUISTE	PERDU
PENTROOFS	PEPONIDA	PEQUISTES	PERDUE
PENTS	PEPONIDAS	PER	PERDUES
PENTYL	PEPONIUM	PERACID	PERDURE
PENTYLENE	PEPONIUMS	PERACIDS	PERDURED
PENTYLS	PEPOS	PERACUTE	PERDURES
PENUCHE	PEPPED	PERAEA	PERDURING
PENUCHES	PEPPER	PERAEON	PERDUS
PENUCHI	PEPPERBOX	PERAEONS	PERDY
PENUCHIS	PEPPERED	PERAEOPOD	PERE
PENUCHLE	PEPPERER	PERAI	PEREA
PENUCHLES	PEPPERERS	PERAIS	PEREGAL
PENUCKLE	PEPPERIER	PERBORATE	PEREGALS
PENUCKLES	PEPPERING	PERCALE	PEREGRIN
PENULT	PEPPERONI	PERCALES	PEREGRINE
PENULTIMA	PEPPERS	PERCALINE	PEREGRINS
PENULTS	PEPPERY	PERCASE	PEREIA
PENUMBRA	PEPPIER	PERCE	PEREION

PEREIONS
PEREIOPOD
PEREIRA
PEREIRAS
PERENNATE
PERENNIAL
PERENNITY
PERENTIE
PERENTIES
PERENTY
PEREON
PEREONS
PEREOPOD
PEREOPODS
PERES
PERFAY
PERFECT
PERFECTA
PERFECTAS
PERFECTED
PERFECTER
PERFECTI
PERFECTLY
PERFECTO
PERFECTOR
PERFECTOS
PERFECTS
PERFERVID
PERFERVOR
PERFET
PERFIDIES
PERFIDY
PERFIN
PERFING
PERFINGS
PERFINS
PERFORANS
PERFORANT
PERFORATE
PERFORCE
PERFORM
PERFORMED
PERFORMER
PERFORMS
PERFUME
PERFUMED
PERFUMER
PERFUMERS
PERFUMERY
PERFUMES
PERFUMIER
PERFUMING
PERFUMY
PERFUSATE
PERFUSE
PERFUSED
PERFUSES
PERFUSING

PERFUSION
PERFUSIVE
PERGOLA
PERGOLAS
PERGUNNAH
PERHAPS
PERHAPSES
PERI
PERIAGUA
PERIAGUAS
PERIAKTOI
PERIAKTOS
PERIANTH
PERIANTHS
PERIAPSES
PERIAPSIS
PERIAPT
PERIAPTS
PERIBLAST
PERIBLEM
PERIBLEMS
PERIBOLI
PERIBOLOI
PERIBOLOS
PERIBOLUS
PERICARP
PERICARPS
PERICLASE
PERICLINE
PERICON
PERICONES
PERICOPAE
PERICOPAL
PERICOPE
PERICOPES
PERICOPIC
PERICYCLE
PERIDERM
PERIDERMS
PERIDIA
PERIDIAL
PERIDINIA
PERIDIUM
PERIDIUMS
PERIDOT
PERIDOTE
PERIDOTES
PERIDOTIC
PERIDOTS
PERIDROME
PERIGEAL
PERIGEAN
PERIGEE
PERIGEES
PERIGON
PERIGONE
PERIGONES
PERIGONIA

PERIGONS
PERIGYNY
PERIHELIA
PERIKARYA
PERIL
PERILED
PERILING
PERILLA
PERILLAS
PERILLED
PERILLING
PERILOUS
PERILS
PERILUNE
PERILUNES
PERILYMPH
PERIMETER
PERIMETRY
PERIMORPH
PERIMYSIA
PERINAEUM
PERINATAL
PERINEA
PERINEAL
PERINEUM
PERINEUMS
PERIOD
PERIODATE
PERIODED
PERIODIC
PERIODID
PERIODIDE
PERIODIDS
PERIODING
PERIODS
PERIOST
PERIOSTEA
PERIOSTS
PERIOTIC
PERIOTICS
PERIPATUS
PERIPETIA
PERIPETY
PERIPHERY
PERIPLASM
PERIPLAST
PERIPLUS
PERIPROCT
PERIPTER
PERIPTERS
PERIPTERY
PERIQUE
PERIQUES
PERIS
PERISARC
PERISARCS
PERISCIAN
PERISCOPE

PERISH
PERISHED
PERISHER
PERISHERS
PERISHES
PERISHING
PERISPERM
PERISTOME
PERISTYLE
PERITI
PERITONEA
PERITRACK
PERITRICH
PERITUS
PERIWIG
PERIWIGS
PERJINK
PERJURE
PERJURED
PERJURER
PERJURERS
PERJURES
PERJURIES
PERJURING
PERJUROUS
PERJURY
PERK
PERKED
PERKIER
PERKIEST
PERKILY
PERKIN
PERKINESS
PERKING
PERKINS
PERKISH
PERKS
PERKY
PERLEMOEN
PERLITE
PERLITES
PERLITIC
PERLOUS
PERM
PERMALLOY
PERMANENT
PERMEABLE
PERMEABLY
PERMEANCE
PERMEANT
PERMEANTS
PERMEASE
PERMEASES
PERMEATE
PERMEATED
PERMEATES
PERMEATOR
PERMED

PERMIAN
PERMIE
PERMIES
PERMING
PERMIT
PERMITS
PERMITTED
PERMITTEE
PERMITTER
PERMS
PERMUTATE
PERMUTE
PERMUTED
PERMUTES
PERMUTING
PERN
PERNANCY
PERNIO
PERNIONES
PERNOD
PERNODS
PERNS
PERONE
PERONEAL
PERONES
PERONEUS
PERORAL
PERORALLY
PERORATE
PERORATED
PERORATES
PERORATOR
PEROVSKIA
PEROXID
PEROXIDE
PEROXIDED
PEROXIDES
PEROXIDIC
PEROXIDS
PEROXO
PEROXY
PERP
PERPEND
PERPENDED
PERPENDS
PERPENT
PERPENTS
PERPETUAL
PERPLEX
PERPLEXED
PERPLEXER
PERPLEXES
PERPS
PERRADIAL
PERRADII
PERRADIUS
PERRIER
PERRIERS

PERRIES
PERRON
PERRONS
PERRUQUE
PERRUQUES
PERRY
PERSALT
PERSALTS
PERSANT
PERSAUNT
PERSE
PERSECUTE
PERSEITY
PERSELINE
PERSES
PERSEVERE
PERSICO
PERSICOS
PERSICOT
PERSICOTS
PERSIENNE
PERSIMMON
PERSING
PERSIST
PERSISTED
PERSISTER
PERSISTS
PERSON
PERSONA
PERSONAE
PERSONAGE
PERSONAL
PERSONALS
PERSONAS
PERSONATE
PERSONIFY
PERSONISE
PERSONIZE
PERSONNED
PERSONNEL
PERSONS
PERSPEX
PERSPEXES
PERSPIRE
PERSPIRED
PERSPIRES
PERSPIRY
PERST
PERSUADE
PERSUADED
PERSUADER
PERSUADES
PERSUE
PERSUED
PERSUES
PERSUING
PERSWADE
PERSWADED

PERSWADES
PERT
PERTAIN
PERTAINED
PERTAINS
PERTAKE
PERTAKEN
PERTAKES
PERTAKING
PERTER
PERTEST
PERTHITE
PERTHITES
PERTHITIC
PERTINENT
PERTLY
PERTNESS
PERTOOK
PERTS
PERTURB
PERTURBED
PERTURBER
PERTURBS
PERTUSATE
PERTUSE
PERTUSED
PERTUSION
PERTUSSAL
PERTUSSES
PERTUSSIS
PERUKE
PERUKED
PERUKES
PERUSABLE
PERUSAL
PERUSALS
PERUSE
PERUSED
PERUSER
PERUSERS
PERUSES
PERUSING
PERV
PERVADE
PERVADED
PERVADER
PERVADERS
PERVADES
PERVADING
PERVASION
PERVASIVE
PERVE
PERVED
PERVERSE
PERVERSER
PERVERT
PERVERTED
PERVERTER

PERVERTS
PERVES
PERVIATE
PERVIATED
PERVIATES
PERVICACY
PERVING
PERVIOUS
PERVS
PES
PESADE
PESADES
PESANT
PESANTE
PESANTS
PESAUNT
PESAUNTS
PESETA
PESETAS
PESEWA
PESEWAS
PESHWA
PESHWAS
PESKIER
PESKIEST
PESKILY
PESKINESS
PESKY
PESO
PESOS
PESSARIES
PESSARY
PESSIMA
PESSIMAL
PESSIMISM
PESSIMIST
PESSIMUM
PEST
PESTER
PESTERED
PESTERER
PESTERERS
PESTERING
PESTEROUS
PESTERS
PESTFUL
PESTHOLE
PESTHOLES
PESTHOUSE
PESTICIDE
PESTIER
PESTIEST
PESTILENT
PESTLE
PESTLED
PESTLES
PESTLING
PESTO

PESTOLOGY
PESTOS
PESTS
PESTY
PET
PETABYTE
PETABYTES
PETAHERTZ
PETAL
PETALED
PETALINE
PETALISM
PETALISMS
PETALLED
PETALLIKE
PETALODIC
PETALODY
PETALOID
PETALOUS
PETALS
PETANQUE
PETANQUES
PETAR
PETARA
PETARAS
PETARD
PETARDS
PETARIES
PETARS
PETARY
PETASOS
PETASOSES
PETASUS
PETASUSES
PETAURINE
PETAURIST
PETCHARY
PETCOCK
PETCOCKS
PETECHIA
PETECHIAE
PETECHIAL
PETER
PETERED
PETERING
PETERMAN
PETERMEN
PETERS
PETERSHAM
PETHER
PETHERS
PETHIDINE
PETILLANT
PETIOLAR
PETIOLATE
PETIOLE
PETIOLED
PETIOLES

PETIOLULE
PETIT
PETITE
PETITES
PETITION
PETITIONS
PETITORY
PETNAP
PETNAPER
PETNAPERS
PETNAPING
PETNAPPED
PETNAPPER
PETNAPS
PETRALE
PETRALES
PETRARIES
PETRARY
PETRE
PETREL
PETRELS
PETRES
PETRIFIC
PETRIFIED
PETRIFIER
PETRIFIES
PETRIFY
PETROGENY
PETROGRAM
PETROL
PETROLAGE
PETROLEUM
PETROLEUR
PETROLIC
PETROLLED
PETROLOGY
PETROLS
PETRONEL
PETRONELS
PETROSAL
PETROSALS
PETROUS
PETS
PETSAI
PETSAIS
PETTABLE
PETTED
PETTEDLY
PETTER
PETTERS
PETTI
PETTICOAT
PETTIER
PETTIES
PETTIEST
PETTIFOG
PETTIFOGS
PETTILY

PETTINESS
PETTING
PETTINGS
PETTISH
PETTISHLY
PETTITOES
PETTLE
PETTLED
PETTLES
PETTLING
PETTO
PETTY
PETULANCE
PETULANCY
PETULANT
PETUNIA
PETUNIAS
PETUNTSE
PETUNTSES
PETUNTZE
PETUNTZES
PEW
PEWEE
PEWEES
PEWHOLDER
PEWIT
PEWITS
PEWS
PEWTER
PEWTERER
PEWTERERS
PEWTERS
PEYOTE
PEYOTES
PEYOTISM
PEYOTISMS
PEYOTIST
PEYOTISTS
PEYOTL
PEYOTLS
PEYSE
PEYSED
PEYSES
PEYSING
PEYTRAL
PEYTRALS
PEYTREL
PEYTRELS
PEZANT
PEZANTS
PEZIZOID
PFENNIG
PFENNIGE
PFENNIGS
PFENNING
PFENNINGS
PFFT
PFUI

PHACELIA
PHACELIAS
PHACOID
PHACOIDAL
PHACOLITE
PHACOLITH
PHAEIC
PHAEISM
PHAEISMS
PHAENOGAM
PHAETON
PHAETONS
PHAGE
PHAGEDENA
PHAGES
PHAGOCYTE
PHAGOSOME
PHALANGAL
PHALANGE
PHALANGER
PHALANGES
PHALANGID
PHALANX
PHALANXES
PHALAROPE
PHALLI
PHALLIC
PHALLIN
PHALLINS
PHALLISM
PHALLISMS
PHALLIST
PHALLISTS
PHALLOID
PHALLUS
PHALLUSES
PHANG
PHANGED
PHANGING
PHANGS
PHANSIGAR
PHANTASIM
PHANTASM
PHANTASMA
PHANTASMS
PHANTAST
PHANTASTS
PHANTASY
PHANTOM
PHANTOMS
PHANTOMY
PHANTOSME
PHARAOH
PHARAOHS
PHARAONIC
PHARE
PHARES
PHARISAIC

PHARISEE
PHARISEES
PHARMA
PHARMACY
PHARMAS
PHARMING
PHARMINGS
PHAROS
PHAROSES
PHARYNGAL
PHARYNGES
PHARYNX
PHARYNXES
PHASE
PHASEAL
PHASED
PHASEDOWN
PHASELESS
PHASEOLIN
PHASEOUT
PHASEOUTS
PHASES
PHASIC
PHASING
PHASINGS
PHASIS
PHASMID
PHASMIDS
PHASOR
PHASORS
PHAT
PHATIC
PHATTER
PHATTEST
PHEASANT
PHEASANTS
PHEAZAR
PHEAZARS
PHEER
PHEERE
PHEERES
PHEERS
PHEESE
PHEESED
PHEESES
PHEESING
PHEEZE
PHEEZED
PHEEZES
PHEEZING
PHELLEM
PHELLEMS
PHELLOGEN
PHELLOID
PHELONIA
PHELONION
PHENACITE
PHENAKISM

PHENAKITE
PHENATE
PHENATES
PHENAZIN
PHENAZINE
PHENAZINS
PHENE
PHENES
PHENETIC
PHENETICS
PHENETOL
PHENETOLE
PHENETOLS
PHENGITE
PHENGITES
PHENIC
PHENIX
PHENIXES
PHENOCOPY
PHENOGAM
PHENOGAMS
PHENOL
PHENOLATE
PHENOLIC
PHENOLICS
PHENOLOGY
PHENOLS
PHENOM
PHENOMENA
PHENOMS
PHENOTYPE
PHENOXIDE
PHENOXY
PHENYL
PHENYLENE
PHENYLIC
PHENYLS
PHENYTOIN
PHEON
PHEONS
PHERESES
PHERESIS
PHEROMONE
PHESE
PHESED
PHESES
PHESING
PHEW
PHI
PHIAL
PHIALLED
PHIALLING
PHIALS
PHILABEG
PHILABEGS
PHILAMOT
PHILAMOTS
PHILANDER

PHILATELY
PHILHORSE
PHILIBEG
PHILIBEGS
PHILIPPIC
PHILISTIA
PHILLABEG
PHILLIBEG
PHILOGYNY
PHILOLOGY
PHILOMATH
PHILOMEL
PHILOMELA
PHILOMELS
PHILOMOT
PHILOMOTS
PHILOPENA
PHILTER
PHILTERED
PHILTERS
PHILTRA
PHILTRE
PHILTRED
PHILTRES
PHILTRING
PHILTRUM
PHIMOSES
PHIMOSIS
PHIMOTIC
PHINNOCK
PHINNOCKS
PHIS
PHISHING
PHISHINGS
PHISNOMY
PHIZ
PHIZES
PHIZOG
PHIZOGS
PHIZZES
PHLEBITIC
PHLEBITIS
PHLEGM
PHLEGMIER
PHLEGMON
PHLEGMONS
PHLEGMS
PHLEGMY
PHLOEM
PHLOEMS
PHLOMIS
PHLOMISES
PHLORIZIN
PHLOX
PHLOXES
PHLYCTENA
PHO
PHOBIA

PHOBIAS
PHOBIC
PHOBICS
PHOBISM
PHOBISMS
PHOBIST
PHOBISTS
PHOCA
PHOCAE
PHOCAS
PHOCINE
PHOCOMELY
PHOEBE
PHOEBES
PHOEBUS
PHOEBUSES
PHOENIX
PHOENIXES
PHOH
PHOHS
PHOLADES
PHOLAS
PHON
PHONAL
PHONATE
PHONATED
PHONATES
PHONATHON
PHONATING
PHONATION
PHONATORY
PHONE
PHONECAM
PHONECAMS
PHONECARD
PHONED
PHONEME
PHONEMES
PHONEMIC
PHONEMICS
PHONER
PHONERS
PHONES
PHONETIC
PHONETICS
PHONETISE
PHONETISM
PHONETIST
PHONETIZE
PHONEY
PHONEYED
PHONEYING
PHONEYS
PHONIC
PHONICS
PHONIED
PHONIER
PHONIES

PHONIEST
PHONILY
PHONINESS
PHONING
PHONMETER
PHONO
PHONOGRAM
PHONOLITE
PHONOLOGY
PHONON
PHONONS
PHONOPORE
PHONOS
PHONOTYPE
PHONOTYPY
PHONS
PHONY
PHONYING
PHOOEY
PHORATE
PHORATES
PHORESIES
PHORESY
PHORMINX
PHORMIUM
PHORMIUMS
PHORONID
PHORONIDS
PHOS
PHOSGENE
PHOSGENES
PHOSPHATE
PHOSPHENE
PHOSPHID
PHOSPHIDE
PHOSPHIDS
PHOSPHIN
PHOSPHINE
PHOSPHINS
PHOSPHITE
PHOSPHOR
PHOSPHORE
PHOSPHORI
PHOSPHORS
PHOSSY
PHOT
PHOTIC
PHOTICS
PHOTINIA
PHOTINIAS
PHOTISM
PHOTISMS
PHOTO
PHOTOCELL
PHOTOCOPY
PHOTOED
PHOTOFIT
PHOTOFITS

PHOTOG
PHOTOGEN
PHOTOGENE
PHOTOGENS
PHOTOGENY
PHOTOGRAM
PHOTOGS
PHOTOING
PHOTOLYSE
PHOTOLYZE
PHOTOMAP
PHOTOMAPS
PHOTOMASK
PHOTON
PHOTONIC
PHOTONICS
PHOTONS
PHOTOPHIL
PHOTOPIA
PHOTOPIAS
PHOTOPIC
PHOTOPLAY
PHOTOPSIA
PHOTOPSY
PHOTOS
PHOTOSCAN
PHOTOSET
PHOTOSETS
PHOTOSTAT
PHOTOTAXY
PHOTOTUBE
PHOTOTYPE
PHOTOTYPY
PHOTS
PHPHT
PHRASAL
PHRASALLY
PHRASE
PHRASED
PHRASEMAN
PHRASEMEN
PHRASER
PHRASERS
PHRASES
PHRASIER
PHRASIEST
PHRASING
PHRASINGS
PHRASY
PHRATRAL
PHRATRIC
PHRATRIES
PHRATRY
PHREAK
PHREAKED
PHREAKER
PHREAKERS
PHREAKING

PHREAKS
PHREATIC
PHRENESES
PHRENESIS
PHRENETIC
PHRENIC
PHRENISM
PHRENISMS
PHRENITIC
PHRENITIS
PHRENSIED
PHRENSIES
PHRENSY
PHRENTICK
PHRYGANA
PHRYGANAS
PHT
PHTHALATE
PHTHALEIN
PHTHALIC
PHTHALIN
PHTHALINS
PHTHISES
PHTHISIC
PHTHISICS
PHTHISIS
PHUT
PHUTS
PHUTTED
PHUTTING
PHYCOCYAN
PHYCOLOGY
PHYLA
PHYLAE
PHYLAR
PHYLARCH
PHYLARCHS
PHYLARCHY
PHYLAXIS
PHYLE
PHYLESES
PHYLESIS
PHYLETIC
PHYLETICS
PHYLIC
PHYLLARY
PHYLLID
PHYLLIDS
PHYLLITE
PHYLLITES
PHYLLITIC
PHYLLO
PHYLLODE
PHYLLODES
PHYLLODIA
PHYLLODY
PHYLLOID
PHYLLOIDS

PHYLLOME
PHYLLOMES
PHYLLOMIC
PHYLLOPOD
PHYLLOS
PHYLOGENY
PHYLON
PHYLUM
PHYSALIA
PHYSALIAS
PHYSALIS
PHYSED
PHYSEDS
PHYSES
PHYSETER
PHYSETERS
PHYSIATRY
PHYSIC
PHYSICAL
PHYSICALS
PHYSICIAN
PHYSICISM
PHYSICIST
PHYSICKED
PHYSICKY
PHYSICS
PHYSIO
PHYSIOS
PHYSIQUE
PHYSIQUED
PHYSIQUES
PHYSIS
PHYTANE
PHYTANES
PHYTIN
PHYTINS
PHYTOGENY
PHYTOID
PHYTOL
PHYTOLITH
PHYTOLOGY
PHYTOLS
PHYTON
PHYTONIC
PHYTONS
PHYTOSES
PHYTOSIS
PHYTOTOMY
PHYTOTRON
PI
PIA
PIACEVOLE
PIACULAR
PIAFFE
PIAFFED
PIAFFER
PIAFFERS
PIAFFES

433

PIAFFING	PICARIANS	PICKIEST	PICOWAVE
PIAL	PICARO	PICKILY	PICOWAVED
PIAN	PICAROON	PICKIN	PICOWAVES
PIANETTE	PICAROONS	PICKINESS	PICQUET
PIANETTES	PICAROS	PICKING	PICQUETED
PIANIC	PICAS	PICKINGS	PICQUETS
PIANINO	PICAYUNE	PICKINS	PICRA
PIANINOS	PICAYUNES	PICKLE	PICRAS
PIANISM	PICCADILL	PICKLED	PICRATE
PIANISMS	PICCANIN	PICKLER	PICRATED
PIANIST	PICCANINS	PICKLERS	PICRATES
PIANISTE	PICCATA	PICKLES	PICRIC
PIANISTES	PICCIES	PICKLING	PICRITE
PIANISTIC	PICCOLO	PICKLOCK	PICRITES
PIANISTS	PICCOLOS	PICKLOCKS	PICRITIC
PIANO	PICCY	PICKMAW	PICS
PIANOLIST	PICE	PICKMAWS	PICTARNIE
PIANOS	PICENE	PICKOFF	PICTOGRAM
PIANS	PICENES	PICKOFFS	PICTORIAL
PIARIST	PICEOUS	PICKPROOF	PICTURAL
PIARISTS	PICHOLINE	PICKS	PICTURALS
PIAS	PICHURIM	PICKTHANK	PICTURE
PIASABA	PICHURIMS	PICKUP	PICTURED
PIASABAS	PICIFORM	PICKUPS	PICTURES
PIASAVA	PICINE	PICKWICK	PICTURING
PIASAVAS	PICK	PICKWICKS	PICTURISE
PIASSABA	PICKABACK	PICKY	PICTURIZE
PIASSABAS	PICKABLE	PICLORAM	PICUL
PIASSAVA	PICKADIL	PICLORAMS	PICULS
PIASSAVAS	PICKADILL	PICNIC	PIDDLE
PIASTER	PICKADILS	PICNICKED	PIDDLED
PIASTERS	PICKAPACK	PICNICKER	PIDDLER
PIASTRE	PICKAROON	PICNICKY	PIDDLERS
PIASTRES	PICKAX	PICNICS	PIDDLES
PIAZZA	PICKAXE	PICOCURIE	PIDDLING
PIAZZAS	PICKAXED	PICOFARAD	PIDDLY
PIAZZE	PICKAXES	PICOGRAM	PIDDOCK
PIAZZIAN	PICKAXING	PICOGRAMS	PIDDOCKS
PIBAL	PICKBACK	PICOLIN	PIDGEON
PIBALS	PICKBACKS	PICOLINE	PIDGEONS
PIBROCH	PICKED	PICOLINES	PIDGIN
PIBROCHS	PICKEER	PICOLINIC	PIDGINISE
PIC	PICKEERED	PICOLINS	PIDGINIZE
PICA	PICKEERER	PICOMETER	PIDGINS
PICACHO	PICKEERS	PICOMETRE	PIE
PICACHOS	PICKER	PICOMOLE	PIEBALD
PICADILLO	PICKEREL	PICOMOLES	PIEBALDS
PICADOR	PICKERELS	PICONG	PIECE
PICADORES	PICKERIES	PICONGS	PIECED
PICADORS	PICKERS	PICOT	PIECELESS
PICAL	PICKERY	PICOTE	PIECEMEAL
PICAMAR	PICKET	PICOTED	PIECEN
PICAMARS	PICKETED	PICOTEE	PIECENED
PICANINNY	PICKETER	PICOTEES	PIECENER
PICANTE	PICKETERS	PICOTING	PIECENERS
PICARA	PICKETING	PICOTITE	PIECENING
PICARAS	PICKETS	PICOTITES	PIECENS
PICARIAN	PICKIER	PICOTS	PIECER

PIECERS
PIECES
PIECEWISE
PIECEWORK
PIECING
PIECINGS
PIECRUST
PIECRUSTS
PIED
PIEDFORT
PIEDFORTS
PIEDISH
PIEDISHES
PIEDMONT
PIEDMONTS
PIEDNESS
PIEFORT
PIEFORTS
PIEHOLE
PIEHOLES
PIEING
PIEMAN
PIEMEN
PIEND
PIENDS
PIEPLANT
PIEPLANTS
PIEPOWDER
PIER
PIERAGE
PIERAGES
PIERCE
PIERCED
PIERCER
PIERCERS
PIERCES
PIERCING
PIERCINGS
PIERID
PIERIDINE
PIERIDS
PIERIS
PIERISES
PIEROGI
PIEROGIES
PIERRETTE
PIERROT
PIERROTS
PIERS
PIERST
PIERT
PIERTS
PIES
PIET
PIETA
PIETAS
PIETIES
PIETISM

PIETISMS
PIETIST
PIETISTIC
PIETISTS
PIETS
PIETY
PIEZO
PIFFERARI
PIFFERARO
PIFFERO
PIFFEROS
PIFFLE
PIFFLED
PIFFLER
PIFFLERS
PIFFLES
PIFFLING
PIG
PIGBOAT
PIGBOATS
PIGEON
PIGEONED
PIGEONING
PIGEONITE
PIGEONRY
PIGEONS
PIGFACE
PIGFACES
PIGFEED
PIGFEEDS
PIGFISH
PIGFISHES
PIGGED
PIGGERIES
PIGGERY
PIGGIE
PIGGIER
PIGGIES
PIGGIEST
PIGGIN
PIGGINESS
PIGGING
PIGGINGS
PIGGINS
PIGGISH
PIGGISHLY
PIGGY
PIGGYBACK
PIGHEADED
PIGHT
PIGHTED
PIGHTING
PIGHTLE
PIGHTLES
PIGHTS
PIGLET
PIGLETS
PIGLIKE

PIGLING
PIGLINGS
PIGMAEAN
PIGMEAN
PIGMEAT
PIGMEATS
PIGMENT
PIGMENTAL
PIGMENTED
PIGMENTS
PIGMIES
PIGMOID
PIGMY
PIGNERATE
PIGNOLI
PIGNOLIA
PIGNOLIAS
PIGNOLIS
PIGNORA
PIGNORATE
PIGNUS
PIGNUT
PIGNUTS
PIGOUT
PIGOUTS
PIGPEN
PIGPENS
PIGS
PIGSCONCE
PIGSKIN
PIGSKINS
PIGSNEY
PIGSNEYS
PIGSNIE
PIGSNIES
PIGSNY
PIGSTICK
PIGSTICKS
PIGSTIES
PIGSTUCK
PIGSTY
PIGSWILL
PIGSWILLS
PIGTAIL
PIGTAILED
PIGTAILS
PIGWASH
PIGWASHES
PIGWEED
PIGWEEDS
PIHOIHOI
PIING
PIKA
PIKAKE
PIKAKES
PIKAS
PIKAU
PIKAUS

PIKE
PIKED
PIKELET
PIKELETS
PIKEMAN
PIKEMEN
PIKEPERCH
PIKER
PIKERS
PIKES
PIKESTAFF
PIKEY
PIKEYS
PIKI
PIKING
PIKINGS
PIKIS
PIKUL
PIKULS
PILA
PILAF
PILAFF
PILAFFS
PILAFS
PILAO
PILAOS
PILAR
PILASTER
PILASTERS
PILAU
PILAUS
PILAW
PILAWS
PILCH
PILCHARD
PILCHARDS
PILCHER
PILCHERS
PILCHES
PILCORN
PILCORNS
PILCROW
PILCROWS
PILE
PILEA
PILEAS
PILEATE
PILEATED
PILED
PILEI
PILELESS
PILEOUS
PILER
PILERS
PILES
PILEUM
PILEUP
PILEUPS

PILEUS
PILEWORK
PILEWORKS
PILEWORT
PILEWORTS
PILFER
PILFERAGE
PILFERED
PILFERER
PILFERERS
PILFERIES
PILFERING
PILFERS
PILFERY
PILGARLIC
PILGRIM
PILGRIMER
PILGRIMS
PILI
PILIFORM
PILING
PILINGS
PILIS
PILL
PILLAGE
PILLAGED
PILLAGER
PILLAGERS
PILLAGES
PILLAGING
PILLAR
PILLARED
PILLARING
PILLARIST
PILLARS
PILLAU
PILLAUS
PILLBOX
PILLBOXES
PILLED
PILLHEAD
PILLHEADS
PILLICOCK
PILLIE
PILLIES
PILLING
PILLINGS
PILLION
PILLIONED
PILLIONS
PILLOCK
PILLOCKS
PILLORIED
PILLORIES
PILLORISE
PILLORIZE
PILLORY
PILLOW

PILLOWED
PILLOWING
PILLOWS
PILLOWY
PILLS
PILLWORM
PILLWORMS
PILLWORT
PILLWORTS
PILOMOTOR
PILONIDAL
PILOSE
PILOSITY
PILOT
PILOTAGE
PILOTAGES
PILOTED
PILOTFISH
PILOTING
PILOTINGS
PILOTIS
PILOTLESS
PILOTMAN
PILOTMEN
PILOTS
PILOUS
PILOW
PILOWS
PILSENER
PILSENERS
PILSNER
PILSNERS
PILULA
PILULAE
PILULAR
PILULAS
PILULE
PILULES
PILUM
PILUS
PILY
PIMA
PIMAS
PIMENT
PIMENTO
PIMENTON
PIMENTONS
PIMENTOS
PIMENTS
PIMIENTO
PIMIENTOS
PIMP
PIMPED
PIMPERNEL
PIMPING
PIMPLE
PIMPLED
PIMPLES

PIMPLIER
PIMPLIEST
PIMPLY
PIMPS
PIN
PINA
PINACEOUS
PINACOID
PINACOIDS
PINAFORE
PINAFORED
PINAFORES
PINAKOID
PINAKOIDS
PINANG
PINANGS
PINAS
PINASTER
PINASTERS
PINATA
PINATAS
PINBALL
PINBALLED
PINBALLS
PINBONE
PINBONES
PINCASE
PINCASES
PINCER
PINCERED
PINCERING
PINCERS
PINCH
PINCHBECK
PINCHBUG
PINCHBUGS
PINCHCOCK
PINCHECK
PINCHECKS
PINCHED
PINCHER
PINCHERS
PINCHES
PINCHFIST
PINCHGUT
PINCHGUTS
PINCHING
PINCHINGS
PINDAN
PINDANS
PINDAREE
PINDAREES
PINDARI
PINDARIS
PINDER
PINDERS
PINDLING
PINDOWN

PINDOWNS
PINE
PINEAL
PINEALS
PINEAPPLE
PINECONE
PINECONES
PINED
PINEDROPS
PINELAND
PINELANDS
PINELIKE
PINENE
PINENES
PINERIES
PINERY
PINES
PINESAP
PINESAPS
PINETA
PINETUM
PINEWOOD
PINEWOODS
PINEY
PINFALL
PINFALLS
PINFISH
PINFISHES
PINFOLD
PINFOLDED
PINFOLDS
PING
PINGED
PINGER
PINGERS
PINGING
PINGLE
PINGLED
PINGLER
PINGLERS
PINGLES
PINGLING
PINGO
PINGOES
PINGOS
PINGPONG
PINGPONGS
PINGRASS
PINGS
PINGUEFY
PINGUID
PINGUIN
PINGUINS
PINHEAD
PINHEADED
PINHEADS
PINHOLE
PINHOLES

PINHOOKER
PINIER
PINIES
PINIEST
PINING
PINION
PINIONED
PINIONING
PINIONS
PINITE
PINITES
PINITOL
PINITOLS
PINK
PINKED
PINKEN
PINKENED
PINKENING
PINKENS
PINKER
PINKERS
PINKERTON
PINKEST
PINKEY
PINKEYE
PINKEYES
PINKEYS
PINKIE
PINKIER
PINKIES
PINKIEST
PINKINESS
PINKING
PINKINGS
PINKISH
PINKLY
PINKNESS
PINKO
PINKOES
PINKOS
PINKROOT
PINKROOTS
PINKS
PINKY
PINNA
PINNACE
PINNACES
PINNACLE
PINNACLED
PINNACLES
PINNAE
PINNAL
PINNAS
PINNATE
PINNATED
PINNATELY
PINNATION
PINNED

PINNER
PINNERS
PINNET
PINNETS
PINNIE
PINNIES
PINNING
PINNINGS
PINNIPED
PINNIPEDE
PINNIPEDS
PINNOCK
PINNOCKS
PINNOED
PINNULA
PINNULAE
PINNULAR
PINNULAS
PINNULATE
PINNULE
PINNULES
PINNY
PINOCHLE
PINOCHLES
PINOCLE
PINOCLES
PINOCYTIC
PINOLE
PINOLES
PINON
PINONES
PINONS
PINOT
PINOTS
PINPOINT
PINPOINTS
PINPRICK
PINPRICKS
PINS
PINSCHER
PINSCHERS
PINSETTER
PINSTRIPE
PINSWELL
PINSWELLS
PINT
PINTA
PINTABLE
PINTABLES
PINTADA
PINTADAS
PINTADERA
PINTADO
PINTADOES
PINTADOS
PINTAIL
PINTAILED
PINTAILS

PINTANO
PINTANOS
PINTAS
PINTLE
PINTLES
PINTO
PINTOES
PINTOS
PINTS
PINTSIZE
PINTSIZED
PINUP
PINUPS
PINWALE
PINWALES
PINWEED
PINWEEDS
PINWHEEL
PINWHEELS
PINWORK
PINWORKS
PINWORM
PINWORMS
PINWRENCH
PINXIT
PINY
PINYIN
PINYON
PINYONS
PIOLET
PIOLETS
PION
PIONED
PIONEER
PIONEERED
PIONEERS
PIONER
PIONERS
PIONEY
PIONEYS
PIONIC
PIONIES
PIONING
PIONINGS
PIONS
PIONY
PIOPIO
PIOSITIES
PIOSITY
PIOTED
PIOUS
PIOUSLY
PIOUSNESS
PIOY
PIOYE
PIOYES
PIOYS
PIP

PIPA
PIPAGE
PIPAGES
PIPAL
PIPALS
PIPAS
PIPE
PIPEAGE
PIPEAGES
PIPECLAY
PIPECLAYS
PIPED
PIPEFISH
PIPEFUL
PIPEFULS
PIPELESS
PIPELIKE
PIPELINE
PIPELINED
PIPELINES
PIPER
PIPERIC
PIPERINE
PIPERINES
PIPERONAL
PIPERS
PIPES
PIPESTEM
PIPESTEMS
PIPESTONE
PIPET
PIPETS
PIPETTE
PIPETTED
PIPETTES
PIPETTING
PIPEWORK
PIPEWORKS
PIPEWORT
PIPEWORTS
PIPI
PIPIER
PIPIEST
PIPINESS
PIPING
PIPINGLY
PIPINGS
PIPIS
PIPISTREL
PIPIT
PIPITS
PIPKIN
PIPKINS
PIPLESS
PIPPED
PIPPIER
PIPPIEST
PIPPIN

PIPPING
PIPPINS
PIPPY
PIPS
PIPSQUEAK
PIPUL
PIPULS
PIPY
PIQUANCE
PIQUANCES
PIQUANCY
PIQUANT
PIQUANTLY
PIQUE
PIQUED
PIQUES
PIQUET
PIQUETED
PIQUETING
PIQUETS
PIQUILLO
PIQUILLOS
PIQUING
PIR
PIRACETAM
PIRACIES
PIRACY
PIRAGUA
PIRAGUAS
PIRAI
PIRAIS
PIRANA
PIRANAS
PIRANHA
PIRANHAS
PIRARUCU
PIRARUCUS
PIRATE
PIRATED
PIRATES
PIRATIC
PIRATICAL
PIRATING
PIRAYA
PIRAYAS
PIRIFORM
PIRL
PIRLICUE
PIRLICUED
PIRLICUES
PIRLS
PIRN
PIRNIE
PIRNIES
PIRNIT
PIRNS
PIROG
PIROGEN

PIROGHI
PIROGI
PIROGIES
PIROGUE
PIROGUES
PIROJKI
PIROPLASM
PIROQUE
PIROQUES
PIROSHKI
PIROUETTE
PIROZHKI
PIROZHOK
PIRS
PIS
PISCARIES
PISCARY
PISCATOR
PISCATORS
PISCATORY
PISCATRIX
PISCIFORM
PISCINA
PISCINAE
PISCINAL
PISCINAS
PISCINE
PISCINES
PISCIVORE
PISCO
PISCOS
PISE
PISES
PISH
PISHED
PISHER
PISHERS
PISHES
PISHING
PISHOGE
PISHOGES
PISHOGUE
PISHOGUES
PISIFORM
PISIFORMS
PISKIES
PISKY
PISMIRE
PISMIRES
PISO
PISOLITE
PISOLITES
PISOLITH
PISOLITHS
PISOLITIC
PISOS
PISS
PISSANT

PISSANTS
PISSED
PISSER
PISSERS
PISSES
PISSHEAD
PISSHEADS
PISSING
PISSOIR
PISSOIRS
PISTACHE
PISTACHES
PISTACHIO
PISTAREEN
PISTE
PISTES
PISTIL
PISTILS
PISTOL
PISTOLE
PISTOLED
PISTOLEER
PISTOLERO
PISTOLES
PISTOLET
PISTOLETS
PISTOLIER
PISTOLING
PISTOLLED
PISTOLS
PISTON
PISTONS
PISTOU
PISTOUS
PIT
PITA
PITAHAYA
PITAHAYAS
PITAPAT
PITAPATS
PITARA
PITARAH
PITARAHS
PITARAS
PITAS
PITAYA
PITAYAS
PITCH
PITCHBEND
PITCHED
PITCHER
PITCHERS
PITCHES
PITCHFORK
PITCHIER
PITCHIEST
PITCHILY
PITCHING

PITCHINGS
PITCHMAN
PITCHMEN
PITCHOUT
PITCHOUTS
PITCHPINE
PITCHPIPE
PITCHPOLE
PITCHY
PITEOUS
PITEOUSLY
PITFALL
PITFALLS
PITH
PITHBALL
PITHBALLS
PITHEAD
PITHEADS
PITHECOID
PITHED
PITHFUL
PITHIER
PITHIEST
PITHILY
PITHINESS
PITHING
PITHLESS
PITHLIKE
PITHOI
PITHOS
PITHS
PITHY
PITIABLE
PITIABLY
PITIED
PITIER
PITIERS
PITIES
PITIFUL
PITIFULLY
PITILESS
PITMAN
PITMANS
PITMEN
PITON
PITONS
PITPROP
PITPROPS
PITS
PITSAW
PITSAWS
PITTA
PITTANCE
PITTANCES
PITTAS
PITTED
PITTEN
PITTER

PITTERED
PITTERING
PITTERS
PITTING
PITTINGS
PITTITE
PITTITES
PITUITA
PITUITARY
PITUITAS
PITUITE
PITUITES
PITUITRIN
PITURI
PITURIS
PITY
PITYING
PITYINGLY
PITYROID
PIU
PIUM
PIUMS
PIUPIU
PIUPIUS
PIVOT
PIVOTABLE
PIVOTAL
PIVOTALLY
PIVOTED
PIVOTER
PIVOTERS
PIVOTING
PIVOTINGS
PIVOTMAN
PIVOTMEN
PIVOTS
PIX
PIXEL
PIXELS
PIXES
PIXIE
PIXIEISH
PIXIES
PIXILATED
PIXINESS
PIXY
PIXYISH
PIZAZZ
PIZAZZES
PIZAZZY
PIZE
PIZED
PIZES
PIZING
PIZZA
PIZZAIOLA
PIZZALIKE
PIZZAS

PIZZAZ
PIZZAZES
PIZZAZZ
PIZZAZZES
PIZZAZZY
PIZZELLE
PIZZELLES
PIZZERIA
PIZZERIAS
PIZZICATI
PIZZICATO
PIZZLE
PIZZLES
PLAAS
PLAASES
PLACABLE
PLACABLY
PLACARD
PLACARDED
PLACARDS
PLACATE
PLACATED
PLACATER
PLACATERS
PLACATES
PLACATING
PLACATION
PLACATIVE
PLACATORY
PLACCAT
PLACCATE
PLACCATES
PLACCATS
PLACE
PLACEABLE
PLACEBO
PLACEBOES
PLACEBOS
PLACED
PLACEKICK
PLACELESS
PLACEMAN
PLACEMEN
PLACEMENT
PLACENTA
PLACENTAE
PLACENTAL
PLACENTAS
PLACER
PLACERS
PLACES
PLACET
PLACETS
PLACID
PLACIDER
PLACIDEST
PLACIDITY
PLACIDLY

PLACING
PLACINGS
PLACIT
PLACITA
PLACITORY
PLACITS
PLACITUM
PLACK
PLACKET
PLACKETS
PLACKLESS
PLACKS
PLACODERM
PLACOID
PLACOIDS
PLAFOND
PLAFONDS
PLAGAL
PLAGE
PLAGES
PLAGIARY
PLAGIUM
PLAGIUMS
PLAGUE
PLAGUED
PLAGUER
PLAGUERS
PLAGUES
PLAGUEY
PLAGUIER
PLAGUIEST
PLAGUILY
PLAGUING
PLAGUY
PLAICE
PLAICES
PLAID
PLAIDED
PLAIDING
PLAIDINGS
PLAIDMAN
PLAIDMEN
PLAIDS
PLAIN
PLAINANT
PLAINANTS
PLAINED
PLAINER
PLAINEST
PLAINFUL
PLAINING
PLAININGS
PLAINISH
PLAINLY
PLAINNESS
PLAINS
PLAINSMAN
PLAINSMEN

PLAINSONG
PLAINT
PLAINTEXT
PLAINTFUL
PLAINTIFF
PLAINTIVE
PLAINTS
PLAINWORK
PLAISTER
PLAISTERS
PLAIT
PLAITED
PLAITER
PLAITERS
PLAITING
PLAITINGS
PLAITS
PLAN
PLANAR
PLANARIA
PLANARIAN
PLANARIAS
PLANARITY
PLANATE
PLANATION
PLANCH
PLANCHE
PLANCHED
PLANCHES
PLANCHET
PLANCHETS
PLANCHING
PLANE
PLANED
PLANELOAD
PLANENESS
PLANER
PLANERS
PLANES
PLANESIDE
PLANET
PLANETARY
PLANETIC
PLANETOID
PLANETS
PLANFORM
PLANFORMS
PLANGENCY
PLANGENT
PLANING
PLANISH
PLANISHED
PLANISHER
PLANISHES
PLANK
PLANKED
PLANKING
PLANKINGS

PLANKS
PLANKTER
PLANKTERS
PLANKTON
PLANKTONS
PLANLESS
PLANNED
PLANNER
PLANNERS
PLANNING
PLANNINGS
PLANOSOL
PLANOSOLS
PLANS
PLANT
PLANTA
PLANTABLE
PLANTAE
PLANTAGE
PLANTAGES
PLANTAIN
PLANTAINS
PLANTAR
PLANTAS
PLANTED
PLANTER
PLANTERS
PLANTING
PLANTINGS
PLANTLESS
PLANTLET
PLANTLETS
PLANTLIKE
PLANTLING
PLANTS
PLANTSMAN
PLANTSMEN
PLANTULE
PLANTULES
PLANULA
PLANULAE
PLANULAR
PLANULATE
PLANULOID
PLANURIA
PLANURIAS
PLANURIES
PLANURY
PLANXTIES
PLANXTY
PLAP
PLAPPED
PLAPPING
PLAPS
PLAQUE
PLAQUES
PLAQUETTE
PLASH

PLASHED
PLASHER
PLASHERS
PLASHES
PLASHET
PLASHETS
PLASHIER
PLASHIEST
PLASHING
PLASHINGS
PLASHY
PLASM
PLASMA
PLASMAGEL
PLASMAS
PLASMASOL
PLASMATIC
PLASMIC
PLASMID
PLASMIDS
PLASMIN
PLASMINS
PLASMODIA
PLASMOID
PLASMOIDS
PLASMON
PLASMONS
PLASMS
PLAST
PLASTE
PLASTER
PLASTERED
PLASTERER
PLASTERS
PLASTERY
PLASTIC
PLASTICKY
PLASTICLY
PLASTICS
PLASTID
PLASTIDS
PLASTIQUE
PLASTISOL
PLASTRAL
PLASTRON
PLASTRONS
PLASTRUM
PLASTRUMS
PLAT
PLATAN
PLATANE
PLATANES
PLATANNA
PLATANNAS
PLATANS
PLATBAND
PLATBANDS
PLATE

PLATEASM
PLATEASMS
PLATEAU
PLATEAUED
PLATEAUS
PLATEAUX
PLATED
PLATEFUL
PLATEFULS
PLATELET
PLATELETS
PLATELIKE
PLATEMAN
PLATEMARK
PLATEMEN
PLATEN
PLATENS
PLATER
PLATERS
PLATES
PLATESFUL
PLATFORM
PLATFORMS
PLATIER
PLATIES
PLATIEST
PLATINA
PLATINAS
PLATING
PLATINGS
PLATINIC
PLATINISE
PLATINIZE
PLATINOID
PLATINOUS
PLATINUM
PLATINUMS
PLATITUDE
PLATONIC
PLATONICS
PLATONISM
PLATOON
PLATOONED
PLATOONS
PLATS
PLATTED
PLATTER
PLATTERS
PLATTING
PLATTINGS
PLATY
PLATYFISH
PLATYPI
PLATYPUS
PLATYS
PLATYSMA
PLATYSMAS
PLAUDIT

PLAUDITE
PLAUDITS
PLAUSIBLE
PLAUSIBLY
PLAUSIVE
PLAUSTRAL
PLAY
PLAYA
PLAYABLE
PLAYACT
PLAYACTED
PLAYACTOR
PLAYACTS
PLAYAS
PLAYBACK
PLAYBACKS
PLAYBILL
PLAYBILLS
PLAYBOOK
PLAYBOOKS
PLAYBOY
PLAYBOYS
PLAYBUS
PLAYBUSES
PLAYDATE
PLAYDATES
PLAYDAY
PLAYDAYS
PLAYDOWN
PLAYDOWNS
PLAYED
PLAYER
PLAYERS
PLAYFIELD
PLAYFUL
PLAYFULLY
PLAYGIRL
PLAYGIRLS
PLAYGOER
PLAYGOERS
PLAYGOING
PLAYGROUP
PLAYHOUSE
PLAYING
PLAYLAND
PLAYLANDS
PLAYLESS
PLAYLET
PLAYLETS
PLAYLIKE
PLAYLIST
PLAYLISTS
PLAYMAKER
PLAYMATE
PLAYMATES
PLAYOFF
PLAYOFFS
PLAYPEN

PLAYPENS
PLAYROOM
PLAYROOMS
PLAYS
PLAYSOME
PLAYSUIT
PLAYSUITS
PLAYTHING
PLAYTIME
PLAYTIMES
PLAYWEAR
PLAZA
PLAZAS
PLEA
PLEACH
PLEACHED
PLEACHES
PLEACHING
PLEAD
PLEADABLE
PLEADED
PLEADER
PLEADERS
PLEADING
PLEADINGS
PLEADS
PLEAED
PLEAING
PLEAS
PLEASABLE
PLEASANCE
PLEASANT
PLEASE
PLEASED
PLEASEDLY
PLEASEMAN
PLEASEMEN
PLEASER
PLEASERS
PLEASES
PLEASETH
PLEASING
PLEASINGS
PLEASURE
PLEASURED
PLEASURER
PLEASURES
PLEAT
PLEATED
PLEATER
PLEATERS
PLEATHER
PLEATHERS
PLEATING
PLEATLESS
PLEATS
PLEB
PLEBBIER

PLEBBIEST
PLEBBY
PLEBE
PLEBEAN
PLEBEIAN
PLEBEIANS
PLEBES
PLEBIFIED
PLEBIFIES
PLEBIFY
PLEBS
PLECTRA
PLECTRE
PLECTRES
PLECTRON
PLECTRONS
PLECTRUM
PLECTRUMS
PLED
PLEDGABLE
PLEDGE
PLEDGED
PLEDGEE
PLEDGEES
PLEDGEOR
PLEDGEORS
PLEDGER
PLEDGERS
PLEDGES
PLEDGET
PLEDGETS
PLEDGING
PLEDGOR
PLEDGORS
PLEIAD
PLEIADES
PLEIADS
PLEIOCENE
PLEIOMERY
PLEIOTAXY
PLENA
PLENARIES
PLENARILY
PLENARTY
PLENARY
PLENCH
PLENCHES
PLENILUNE
PLENIPO
PLENIPOES
PLENIPOS
PLENISH
PLENISHED
PLENISHER
PLENISHES
PLENISM
PLENISMS
PLENIST

PLENISTS
PLENITUDE
PLENTEOUS
PLENTIES
PLENTIFUL
PLENTY
PLENUM
PLENUMS
PLEON
PLEONAL
PLEONASM
PLEONASMS
PLEONAST
PLEONASTE
PLEONASTS
PLEONEXIA
PLEONIC
PLEONS
PLEOPOD
PLEOPODS
PLERION
PLERIONS
PLEROMA
PLEROMAS
PLEROME
PLEROMES
PLESH
PLESHES
PLESSOR
PLESSORS
PLETHORA
PLETHORAS
PLETHORIC
PLEUCH
PLEUCHED
PLEUCHING
PLEUCHS
PLEUGH
PLEUGHED
PLEUGHING
PLEUGHS
PLEURA
PLEURAE
PLEURAL
PLEURAS
PLEURISY
PLEURITIC
PLEURITIS
PLEURON
PLEUSTON
PLEUSTONS
PLEW
PLEWS
PLEX
PLEXAL
PLEXES
PLEXIFORM
PLEXOR

PLEXORS
PLEXURE
PLEXURES
PLEXUS
PLEXUSES
PLIABLE
PLIABLY
PLIANCIES
PLIANCY
PLIANT
PLIANTLY
PLICA
PLICAE
PLICAL
PLICATE
PLICATED
PLICATELY
PLICATES
PLICATING
PLICATION
PLICATURE
PLIE
PLIED
PLIER
PLIERS
PLIES
PLIGHT
PLIGHTED
PLIGHTER
PLIGHTERS
PLIGHTFUL
PLIGHTING
PLIGHTS
PLIM
PLIMMED
PLIMMING
PLIMS
PLIMSOL
PLIMSOLE
PLIMSOLES
PLIMSOLL
PLIMSOLLS
PLIMSOLS
PLING
PLINGS
PLINK
PLINKED
PLINKER
PLINKERS
PLINKING
PLINKINGS
PLINKS
PLINTH
PLINTHS
PLIOCENE
PLIOFILM
PLIOFILMS
PLIOSAUR

PLIOSAURS
PLIOTRON
PLIOTRONS
PLISKIE
PLISKIES
PLISKY
PLISSE
PLISSES
PLOAT
PLOATED
PLOATING
PLOATS
PLOD
PLODDED
PLODDER
PLODDERS
PLODDING
PLODDINGS
PLODGE
PLODGED
PLODGES
PLODGING
PLODS
PLOIDIES
PLOIDY
PLONG
PLONGD
PLONGE
PLONGED
PLONGES
PLONGING
PLONGS
PLONK
PLONKED
PLONKER
PLONKERS
PLONKIER
PLONKIEST
PLONKING
PLONKINGS
PLONKO
PLONKOS
PLONKS
PLONKY
PLOOK
PLOOKIE
PLOOKIER
PLOOKIEST
PLOOKS
PLOOKY
PLOP
PLOPPED
PLOPPING
PLOPS
PLOSION
PLOSIONS
PLOSIVE
PLOSIVES

PLOT
PLOTFUL
PLOTLESS
PLOTLINE
PLOTLINES
PLOTS
PLOTTAGE
PLOTTAGES
PLOTTED
PLOTTER
PLOTTERED
PLOTTERS
PLOTTIE
PLOTTIER
PLOTTIES
PLOTTIEST
PLOTTING
PLOTTINGS
PLOTTY
PLOTZ
PLOTZED
PLOTZES
PLOTZING
PLOUGH
PLOUGHBOY
PLOUGHED
PLOUGHER
PLOUGHERS
PLOUGHING
PLOUGHMAN
PLOUGHMEN
PLOUGHS
PLOUK
PLOUKIE
PLOUKIER
PLOUKIEST
PLOUKS
PLOUKY
PLOUTER
PLOUTERED
PLOUTERS
PLOVER
PLOVERS
PLOVERY
PLOW
PLOWABLE
PLOWBACK
PLOWBACKS
PLOWBOY
PLOWBOYS
PLOWED
PLOWER
PLOWERS
PLOWHEAD
PLOWHEADS
PLOWING
PLOWLAND
PLOWLANDS

PLOWMAN
PLOWMEN
PLOWS
PLOWSHARE
PLOWSTAFF
PLOWTER
PLOWTERED
PLOWTERS
PLOY
PLOYED
PLOYING
PLOYS
PLU
PLUCK
PLUCKED
PLUCKER
PLUCKERS
PLUCKIER
PLUCKIEST
PLUCKILY
PLUCKING
PLUCKS
PLUCKY
PLUE
PLUES
PLUFF
PLUFFED
PLUFFIER
PLUFFIEST
PLUFFING
PLUFFS
PLUFFY
PLUG
PLUGBOARD
PLUGGED
PLUGGER
PLUGGERS
PLUGGING
PLUGGINGS
PLUGHOLE
PLUGHOLES
PLUGLESS
PLUGOLA
PLUGOLAS
PLUGS
PLUGUGLY
PLUM
PLUMAGE
PLUMAGED
PLUMAGES
PLUMATE
PLUMB
PLUMBABLE
PLUMBAGO
PLUMBAGOS
PLUMBATE
PLUMBATES
PLUMBED

PLUMBEOUS
PLUMBER
PLUMBERS
PLUMBERY
PLUMBIC
PLUMBING
PLUMBINGS
PLUMBISM
PLUMBISMS
PLUMBITE
PLUMBITES
PLUMBLESS
PLUMBNESS
PLUMBOUS
PLUMBS
PLUMBUM
PLUMBUMS
PLUMCOT
PLUMCOTS
PLUMDAMAS
PLUME
PLUMED
PLUMELESS
PLUMELET
PLUMELETS
PLUMELIKE
PLUMERIA
PLUMERIAS
PLUMERIES
PLUMERY
PLUMES
PLUMIER
PLUMIEST
PLUMING
PLUMIPED
PLUMIPEDS
PLUMIST
PLUMISTS
PLUMLIKE
PLUMMER
PLUMMEST
PLUMMET
PLUMMETED
PLUMMETS
PLUMMIER
PLUMMIEST
PLUMMY
PLUMOSE
PLUMOSELY
PLUMOSITY
PLUMOUS
PLUMP
PLUMPED
PLUMPEN
PLUMPENED
PLUMPENS
PLUMPER
PLUMPERS

PLUMPEST
PLUMPIE
PLUMPIER
PLUMPIEST
PLUMPING
PLUMPISH
PLUMPLY
PLUMPNESS
PLUMPS
PLUMPY
PLUMS
PLUMULA
PLUMULAE
PLUMULAR
PLUMULATE
PLUMULE
PLUMULES
PLUMULOSE
PLUMY
PLUNDER
PLUNDERED
PLUNDERER
PLUNDERS
PLUNGE
PLUNGED
PLUNGER
PLUNGERS
PLUNGES
PLUNGING
PLUNGINGS
PLUNK
PLUNKED
PLUNKER
PLUNKERS
PLUNKIER
PLUNKIEST
PLUNKING
PLUNKS
PLUNKY
PLURAL
PLURALISE
PLURALISM
PLURALIST
PLURALITY
PLURALIZE
PLURALLY
PLURALS
PLURIPARA
PLURISIE
PLURISIES
PLURRY
PLUS
PLUSAGE
PLUSAGES
PLUSED
PLUSES
PLUSH
PLUSHER

PLUSHES
PLUSHEST
PLUSHIER
PLUSHIEST
PLUSHILY
PLUSHLY
PLUSHNESS
PLUSHY
PLUSING
PLUSSAGE
PLUSSAGES
PLUSSED
PLUSSES
PLUSSING
PLUTEAL
PLUTEI
PLUTEUS
PLUTEUSES
PLUTOCRAT
PLUTOLOGY
PLUTON
PLUTONIAN
PLUTONIC
PLUTONISM
PLUTONIUM
PLUTONOMY
PLUTONS
PLUVIAL
PLUVIALS
PLUVIAN
PLUVIOSE
PLUVIOUS
PLY
PLYER
PLYERS
PLYING
PLYINGLY
PLYWOOD
PLYWOODS
PNEUMA
PNEUMAS
PNEUMATIC
PNEUMONIA
PNEUMONIC
PO
POA
POACEOUS
POACH
POACHABLE
POACHED
POACHER
POACHERS
POACHES
POACHIER
POACHIEST
POACHING
POACHINGS
POACHY

POAKA
POAKAS
POAKE
POAKES
POAS
POBLANO
POBLANOS
POBOY
POBOYS
POCHARD
POCHARDS
POCHAY
POCHAYS
POCHETTE
POCHETTES
POCHOIR
POCHOIRS
POCK
POCKARD
POCKARDS
POCKED
POCKET
POCKETED
POCKETER
POCKETERS
POCKETFUL
POCKETING
POCKETS
POCKIER
POCKIES
POCKIEST
POCKILY
POCKING
POCKMANKY
POCKMARK
POCKMARKS
POCKPIT
POCKPITS
POCKS
POCKY
POCO
POCOSEN
POCOSENS
POCOSIN
POCOSINS
POCOSON
POCOSONS
POD
PODAGRA
PODAGRAL
PODAGRAS
PODAGRIC
PODAGROUS
PODAL
PODALIC
PODARGUS
PODCAST
PODCASTED

PODCASTER
PODCASTS
PODDED
PODDIE
PODDIER
PODDIES
PODDIEST
PODDING
PODDLE
PODDLED
PODDLES
PODDLING
PODDY
PODESTA
PODESTAS
PODEX
PODEXES
PODGE
PODGES
PODGIER
PODGIEST
PODGILY
PODGINESS
PODGY
PODIA
PODIAL
PODIATRIC
PODIATRY
PODITE
PODITES
PODITIC
PODIUM
PODIUMS
PODLEY
PODLEYS
PODLIKE
PODOCARP
PODOCARPS
PODOLOGY
PODOMERE
PODOMERES
PODS
PODSOL
PODSOLIC
PODSOLISE
PODSOLIZE
PODSOLS
PODZOL
PODZOLIC
PODZOLISE
PODZOLIZE
PODZOLS
POECHORE
POECHORES
POEM
POEMATIC
POEMS
POENOLOGY

POEP
POEPOL
POEPOLS
POEPS
POESIED
POESIES
POESY
POESYING
POET
POETASTER
POETASTRY
POETESS
POETESSES
POETIC
POETICAL
POETICALS
POETICISE
POETICISM
POETICIZE
POETICS
POETICULE
POETISE
POETISED
POETISER
POETISERS
POETISES
POETISING
POETIZE
POETIZED
POETIZER
POETIZERS
POETIZES
POETIZING
POETLESS
POETLIKE
POETRESSE
POETRIES
POETRY
POETS
POETSHIP
POETSHIPS
POFFLE
POFFLES
POGEY
POGEYS
POGGE
POGGES
POGIES
POGO
POGOED
POGOER
POGOERS
POGOING
POGONIA
POGONIAS
POGONIP
POGONIPS
POGOS

POGROM
POGROMED
POGROMING
POGROMIST
POGROMS
POGY
POH
POHIRI
POHIRIS
POI
POIGNADO
POIGNANCE
POIGNANCY
POIGNANT
POILU
POILUS
POINADO
POINADOES
POINCIANA
POIND
POINDED
POINDER
POINDERS
POINDING
POINDINGS
POINDS
POINT
POINTABLE
POINTE
POINTED
POINTEDLY
POINTEL
POINTELLE
POINTELS
POINTER
POINTERS
POINTES
POINTIER
POINTIEST
POINTILLE
POINTING
POINTINGS
POINTLESS
POINTMAN
POINTMEN
POINTS
POINTSMAN
POINTSMEN
POINTY
POIS
POISE
POISED
POISER
POISERS
POISES
POISHA
POISING
POISON

POISONED
POISONER
POISONERS
POISONING
POISONOUS
POISONS
POISSON
POISSONS
POITIN
POITINS
POITREL
POITRELS
POITRINE
POITRINES
POKABLE
POKAL
POKALS
POKE
POKEBERRY
POKED
POKEFUL
POKEFULS
POKELOGAN
POKER
POKERISH
POKEROOT
POKEROOTS
POKERS
POKERWORK
POKES
POKEWEED
POKEWEEDS
POKEY
POKEYS
POKIE
POKIER
POKIES
POKIEST
POKILY
POKINESS
POKING
POKY
POL
POLACCA
POLACCAS
POLACRE
POLACRES
POLAR
POLARISE
POLARISED
POLARISER
POLARISES
POLARITY
POLARIZE
POLARIZED
POLARIZER
POLARIZES
POLARON

POLARONS
POLARS
POLDER
POLDERED
POLDERING
POLDERS
POLE
POLEAX
POLEAXE
POLEAXED
POLEAXES
POLEAXING
POLECAT
POLECATS
POLED
POLEIS
POLELESS
POLEMARCH
POLEMIC
POLEMICAL
POLEMICS
POLEMISE
POLEMISED
POLEMISES
POLEMIST
POLEMISTS
POLEMIZE
POLEMIZED
POLEMIZES
POLENTA
POLENTAS
POLER
POLERS
POLES
POLESTAR
POLESTARS
POLEWARD
POLEY
POLEYN
POLEYNS
POLEYS
POLIANITE
POLICE
POLICED
POLICEMAN
POLICEMEN
POLICER
POLICERS
POLICES
POLICIES
POLICING
POLICINGS
POLICY
POLIES
POLING
POLINGS
POLIO
POLIOS

POLIS	POLLICY	POLONY	POLYGYNY
POLISH	POLLIES	POLOS	POLYHEDRA
POLISHED	POLLINATE	POLS	POLYIMIDE
POLISHER	POLLING	POLT	POLYLEMMA
POLISHERS	POLLINGS	POLTED	POLYMASTY
POLISHES	POLLINIA	POLTFEET	POLYMATH
POLISHING	POLLINIC	POLTFOOT	POLYMATHS
POLITBURO	POLLINISE	POLTING	POLYMATHY
POLITE	POLLINIUM	POLTROON	POLYMER
POLITELY	POLLINIZE	POLTROONS	POLYMERIC
POLITER	POLLIST	POLTS	POLYMERS
POLITESSE	POLLISTS	POLVERINE	POLYMERY
POLITEST	POLLIWIG	POLY	POLYMORPH
POLITIC	POLLIWIGS	POLYACID	POLYMYXIN
POLITICAL	POLLIWOG	POLYACT	POLYNIA
POLITICK	POLLIWOGS	POLYADIC	POLYNIAS
POLITICKS	POLLMAN	POLYAMIDE	POLYNYA
POLITICLY	POLLMEN	POLYAMINE	POLYNYAS
POLITICO	POLLOCK	POLYANDRY	POLYNYI
POLITICOS	POLLOCKS	POLYANTHA	POLYOL
POLITICS	POLLS	POLYANTHI	POLYOLS
POLITIES	POLLSTER	POLYARCH	POLYOMA
POLITIQUE	POLLSTERS	POLYARCHY	POLYOMAS
POLITY	POLLTAKER	POLYAXIAL	POLYOMINO
POLJE	POLLUCITE	POLYAXON	POLYONYM
POLJES	POLLUSION	POLYAXONS	POLYONYMS
POLK	POLLUTANT	POLYBASIC	POLYONYMY
POLKA	POLLUTE	POLYBRID	POLYP
POLKAED	POLLUTED	POLYBRIDS	POLYPARIA
POLKAING	POLLUTER	POLYCARPY	POLYPARY
POLKAS	POLLUTERS	POLYCHETE	POLYPE
POLKED	POLLUTES	POLYCONIC	POLYPED
POLKING	POLLUTING	POLYCOT	POLYPEDS
POLKS	POLLUTION	POLYCOTS	POLYPES
POLL	POLLUTIVE	POLYDEMIC	POLYPHAGY
POLLACK	POLLY	POLYENE	POLYPHASE
POLLACKS	POLLYANNA	POLYENES	POLYPHON
POLLAN	POLLYWIG	POLYENIC	POLYPHONE
POLLANS	POLLYWIGS	POLYESTER	POLYPHONS
POLLARD	POLLYWOG	POLYGALA	POLYPHONY
POLLARDED	POLLYWOGS	POLYGALAS	POLYPI
POLLARDS	POLO	POLYGAM	POLYPIDE
POLLED	POLOIDAL	POLYGAMIC	POLYPIDES
POLLEE	POLOIST	POLYGAMS	POLYPIDOM
POLLEES	POLOISTS	POLYGAMY	POLYPILL
POLLEN	POLONAISE	POLYGENE	POLYPILLS
POLLENATE	POLONIE	POLYGENES	POLYPINE
POLLENED	POLONIES	POLYGENIC	POLYPITE
POLLENING	POLONISE	POLYGENY	POLYPITES
POLLENS	POLONISED	POLYGLOT	POLYPLOID
POLLENT	POLONISES	POLYGLOTS	POLYPNEA
POLLER	POLONISM	POLYGLOTT	POLYPNEAS
POLLERS	POLONISMS	POLYGON	POLYPNEIC
POLLEX	POLONIUM	POLYGONAL	POLYPOD
POLLICAL	POLONIUMS	POLYGONS	POLYPODS
POLLICES	POLONIZE	POLYGONUM	POLYPODY
POLLICIE	POLONIZED	POLYGONY	POLYPOID
POLLICIES	POLONIZES	POLYGRAPH	POLYPORE

POLYPORES	POMEROYS	PONCHOED	PONT
POLYPOSES	POMES	PONCHOS	PONTAGE
POLYPOSIS	POMFRET	PONCIER	PONTAGES
POLYPOUS	POMFRETS	PONCIEST	PONTAL
POLYPS	POMMEE	PONCING	PONTES
POLYPTYCH	POMMEL	PONCY	PONTIANAC
POLYPUS	POMMELE	POND	PONTIANAK
POLYPUSES	POMMELED	PONDAGE	PONTIC
POLYS	POMMELING	PONDAGES	PONTIE
POLYSEME	POMMELLED	PONDED	PONTIES
POLYSEMES	POMMELS	PONDER	PONTIFEX
POLYSEMIC	POMMETTY	PONDERAL	PONTIFF
POLYSEMY	POMMIE	PONDERATE	PONTIFFS
POLYSOME	POMMIES	PONDERED	PONTIFIC
POLYSOMES	POMMY	PONDERER	PONTIFICE
POLYSOMIC	POMO	PONDERERS	PONTIFIED
POLYSOMY	POMOERIUM	PONDERING	PONTIFIES
POLYSTYLE	POMOLOGY	PONDEROSA	PONTIFY
POLYTENE	POMOS	PONDEROUS	PONTIL
POLYTENY	POMP	PONDERS	PONTILE
POLYTHENE	POMPADOUR	PONDING	PONTILES
POLYTONAL	POMPANO	PONDOK	PONTILS
POLYTYPE	POMPANOS	PONDOKKIE	PONTINE
POLYTYPES	POMPELO	PONDOKS	PONTLEVIS
POLYTYPIC	POMPELOS	PONDS	PONTON
POLYURIA	POMPEY	PONDWEED	PONTONEER
POLYURIAS	POMPEYED	PONDWEEDS	PONTONIER
POLYURIC	POMPEYING	PONE	PONTONS
POLYVINYL	POMPEYS	PONENT	PONTOON
POLYWATER	POMPHOLYX	PONES	PONTOONED
POLYZOA	POMPIER	PONEY	PONTOONER
POLYZOAN	POMPILID	PONEYS	PONTOONS
POLYZOANS	POMPILIDS	PONG	PONTS
POLYZOARY	POMPION	PONGA	PONTY
POLYZOIC	POMPIONS	PONGAS	PONY
POLYZONAL	POMPOM	PONGED	PONYING
POLYZOOID	POMPOMS	PONGEE	PONYSKIN
POLYZOON	POMPON	PONGEES	PONYSKINS
POM	POMPONS	PONGID	PONYTAIL
POMACE	POMPOON	PONGIDS	PONYTAILS
POMACEOUS	POMPOONS	PONGIER	PONZU
POMACES	POMPOSITY	PONGIEST	PONZUS
POMADE	POMPOUS	PONGING	POO
POMADED	POMPOUSLY	PONGO	POOCH
POMADES	POMPS	PONGOES	POOCHED
POMADING	POMROY	PONGOS	POOCHES
POMANDER	POMROYS	PONGS	POOCHING
POMANDERS	POMS	PONGY	POOD
POMATO	POMWATER	PONIARD	POODLE
POMATOES	POMWATERS	PONIARDED	POODLES
POMATUM	PONCE	PONIARDS	POODS
POMATUMS	PONCEAU	PONIED	POOED
POMBE	PONCEAUS	PONIES	POOF
POMBES	PONCEAUX	PONK	POOFIER
POME	PONCED	PONKED	POOFIEST
POMELO	PONCES	PONKING	POOFS
POMELOS	PONCEY	PONKS	POOFTAH
POMEROY	PONCHO	PONS	POOFTAHS

POOFTER
POOFTERS
POOFY
POOGYE
POOGYES
POOH
POOHED
POOHING
POOHS
POOING
POOJA
POOJAH
POOJAHS
POOJAS
POOK
POOKA
POOKAS
POOKING
POOKIT
POOKS
POOL
POOLED
POOLER
POOLERS
POOLHALL
POOLHALLS
POOLING
POOLROOM
POOLROOMS
POOLS
POOLSIDE
POOLSIDES
POON
POONAC
POONACS
POONCE
POONCED
POONCES
POONCING
POONS
POONTANG
POONTANGS
POOP
POOPED
POOPER
POOPERS
POOPING
POOPS
POOR
POORER
POOREST
POORHOUSE
POORI
POORIS
POORISH
POORLIER
POORLIEST
POORLY

POORMOUTH
POORNESS
POORT
POORTITH
POORTITHS
POORTS
POORWILL
POORWILLS
POOS
POOT
POOTED
POOTER
POOTERS
POOTING
POOTLE
POOTLED
POOTLES
POOTLING
POOTS
POOVE
POOVERIES
POOVERY
POOVES
POOVIER
POOVIEST
POOVY
POP
POPADUM
POPADUMS
POPCORN
POPCORNS
POPE
POPEDOM
POPEDOMS
POPEHOOD
POPEHOODS
POPELESS
POPELIKE
POPELING
POPELINGS
POPERA
POPERAS
POPERIES
POPERIN
POPERINS
POPERY
POPES
POPESEYE
POPESHIP
POPESHIPS
POPETTE
POPETTES
POPEYED
POPGUN
POPGUNS
POPINJAY
POPINJAYS
POPISH

POPISHLY
POPJOY
POPJOYED
POPJOYING
POPJOYS
POPLAR
POPLARS
POPLIN
POPLINS
POPLITEAL
POPLITEI
POPLITEUS
POPLITIC
POPOVER
POPOVERS
POPPA
POPPADOM
POPPADOMS
POPPADUM
POPPADUMS
POPPAS
POPPED
POPPER
POPPERING
POPPERS
POPPET
POPPETS
POPPIED
POPPIER
POPPIES
POPPIEST
POPPING
POPPISH
POPPIT
POPPITS
POPPLE
POPPLED
POPPLES
POPPLIER
POPPLIEST
POPPLING
POPPLY
POPPY
POPPYCOCK
POPPYHEAD
POPRIN
POPRINS
POPS
POPSICLE
POPSICLES
POPSIE
POPSIES
POPSTER
POPSTERS
POPSY
POPULACE
POPULACES
POPULAR

POPULARLY
POPULARS
POPULATE
POPULATED
POPULATES
POPULISM
POPULISMS
POPULIST
POPULISTS
POPULOUS
PORAE
PORAL
PORANGI
PORBEAGLE
PORCELAIN
PORCH
PORCHES
PORCINE
PORCINI
PORCINIS
PORCINO
PORCUPINE
PORCUPINY
PORE
PORED
PORER
PORERS
PORES
PORGE
PORGED
PORGES
PORGIE
PORGIES
PORGING
PORGY
PORIER
PORIEST
PORIFER
PORIFERAL
PORIFERAN
PORIFERS
PORINA
PORINAS
PORINESS
PORING
PORISM
PORISMS
PORISTIC
PORK
PORKED
PORKER
PORKERS
PORKIER
PORKIES
PORKIEST
PORKINESS
PORKING
PORKLING

PORKLINGS
PORKPIE
PORKPIES
PORKS
PORKWOOD
PORKWOODS
PORKY
PORN
PORNIER
PORNIEST
PORNO
PORNOMAG
PORNOMAGS
PORNOS
PORNS
PORNY
POROGAMIC
POROGAMY
POROMERIC
POROSCOPE
POROSCOPY
POROSE
POROSES
POROSIS
POROSITY
POROUS
POROUSLY
PORPESS
PORPESSE
PORPESSES
PORPHYRIA
PORPHYRIC
PORPHYRIN
PORPHYRIO
PORPHYRY
PORPOISE
PORPOISED
PORPOISES
PORPORATE
PORRECT
PORRECTED
PORRECTS
PORRENGER
PORRIDGE
PORRIDGES
PORRIDGY
PORRIGO
PORRIGOS
PORRINGER
PORT
PORTA
PORTABLE
PORTABLES
PORTABLY
PORTAGE
PORTAGED
PORTAGES
PORTAGING

PORTAGUE
PORTAGUES
PORTAL
PORTALED
PORTALS
PORTANCE
PORTANCES
PORTAPACK
PORTAPAK
PORTAPAKS
PORTAS
PORTASES
PORTATE
PORTATILE
PORTATIVE
PORTED
PORTEND
PORTENDED
PORTENDS
PORTENT
PORTENTS
PORTEOUS
PORTER
PORTERAGE
PORTERED
PORTERESS
PORTERING
PORTERLY
PORTERS
PORTESS
PORTESSE
PORTESSES
PORTFIRE
PORTFIRES
PORTFOLIO
PORTHOLE
PORTHOLES
PORTHORS
PORTHOS
PORTHOSES
PORTHOUSE
PORTICO
PORTICOED
PORTICOES
PORTICOS
PORTIER
PORTIERE
PORTIERED
PORTIERES
PORTIEST
PORTIGUE
PORTIGUES
PORTING
PORTION
PORTIONED
PORTIONER
PORTIONS
PORTLAND

PORTLANDS
PORTLAST
PORTLASTS
PORTLESS
PORTLIER
PORTLIEST
PORTLY
PORTMAN
PORTMEN
PORTOISE
PORTOISES
PORTOLAN
PORTOLANI
PORTOLANO
PORTOLANS
PORTOUS
PORTOUSES
PORTRAIT
PORTRAITS
PORTRAY
PORTRAYAL
PORTRAYED
PORTRAYER
PORTRAYS
PORTREEVE
PORTRESS
PORTS
PORTSIDE
PORTULACA
PORTULAN
PORTULANS
PORTY
PORWIGGLE
PORY
POS
POSABLE
POSADA
POSADAS
POSAUNE
POSAUNES
POSE
POSEABLE
POSED
POSER
POSERISH
POSERS
POSES
POSEUR
POSEURS
POSEUSE
POSEUSES
POSEY
POSH
POSHED
POSHER
POSHES
POSHEST
POSHING

POSHLY
POSHNESS
POSHO
POSHOS
POSHTEEN
POSHTEENS
POSIER
POSIES
POSIEST
POSIGRADE
POSING
POSINGLY
POSINGS
POSIT
POSITED
POSITIF
POSITIFS
POSITING
POSITION
POSITIONS
POSITIVE
POSITIVER
POSITIVES
POSITON
POSITONS
POSITRON
POSITRONS
POSITS
POSNET
POSNETS
POSOLE
POSOLES
POSOLOGIC
POSOLOGY
POSS
POSSE
POSSED
POSSER
POSSERS
POSSES
POSSESS
POSSESSED
POSSESSES
POSSESSOR
POSSET
POSSETED
POSSETING
POSSETS
POSSIBLE
POSSIBLER
POSSIBLES
POSSIBLY
POSSIE
POSSIES
POSSING
POSSUM
POSSUMED
POSSUMING

POSSUMS
POST
POSTAGE
POSTAGES
POSTAL
POSTALLY
POSTALS
POSTANAL
POSTAXIAL
POSTBAG
POSTBAGS
POSTBASE
POSTBOX
POSTBOXES
POSTBOY
POSTBOYS
POSTBURN
POSTBUS
POSTBUSES
POSTCARD
POSTCARDS
POSTCAVA
POSTCAVAE
POSTCAVAL
POSTCAVAS
POSTCODE
POSTCODED
POSTCODES
POSTCOUP
POSTCRASH
POSTDATE
POSTDATED
POSTDATES
POSTDIVE
POSTDOC
POSTDOCS
POSTDRUG
POSTED
POSTEEN
POSTEENS
POSTER
POSTERED
POSTERING
POSTERIOR
POSTERITY
POSTERN
POSTERNS
POSTERS
POSTFACE
POSTFACES
POSTFAULT
POSTFIRE
POSTFIX
POSTFIXAL
POSTFIXED
POSTFIXES
POSTFORM
POSTFORMS

POSTGAME
POSTGRAD
POSTGRADS
POSTHASTE
POSTHEAT
POSTHEATS
POSTHOLE
POSTHOLES
POSTHORSE
POSTHOUSE
POSTICAL
POSTICHE
POSTICHES
POSTICOUS
POSTIE
POSTIES
POSTIL
POSTILED
POSTILING
POSTILION
POSTILLED
POSTILLER
POSTILS
POSTIN
POSTING
POSTINGS
POSTINS
POSTIQUE
POSTIQUES
POSTLUDE
POSTLUDES
POSTMAN
POSTMARK
POSTMARKS
POSTMEN
POSTNASAL
POSTNATAL
POSTNATI
POSTOP
POSTOPS
POSTORAL
POSTPAID
POSTPONE
POSTPONED
POSTPONER
POSTPONES
POSTPOSE
POSTPOSED
POSTPOSES
POSTPUNK
POSTRACE
POSTRIDER
POSTRIOT
POSTS
POSTSHOW
POSTSYNC
POSTSYNCS
POSTTAX

POSTTEEN
POSTTEENS
POSTTEST
POSTTESTS
POSTTRIAL
POSTULANT
POSTULATA
POSTULATE
POSTURAL
POSTURE
POSTURED
POSTURER
POSTURERS
POSTURES
POSTURING
POSTURISE
POSTURIST
POSTURIZE
POSTVIRAL
POSTWAR
POSTWOMAN
POSTWOMEN
POSY
POT
POTABLE
POTABLES
POTAE
POTAES
POTAGE
POTAGER
POTAGERS
POTAGES
POTAMIC
POTASH
POTASHED
POTASHES
POTASHING
POTASS
POTASSA
POTASSAS
POTASSES
POTASSIC
POTASSIUM
POTATION
POTATIONS
POTATO
POTATOBUG
POTATOES
POTATORY
POTBELLY
POTBOIL
POTBOILED
POTBOILER
POTBOILS
POTBOUND
POTBOY
POTBOYS
POTCH

POTCHE
POTCHED
POTCHER
POTCHERS
POTCHES
POTCHING
POTE
POTED
POTEEN
POTEENS
POTENCE
POTENCES
POTENCIES
POTENCY
POTENT
POTENTATE
POTENTIAL
POTENTISE
POTENTIZE
POTENTLY
POTENTS
POTES
POTFUL
POTFULS
POTGUN
POTGUNS
POTHEAD
POTHEADS
POTHECARY
POTHEEN
POTHEENS
POTHER
POTHERB
POTHERBS
POTHERED
POTHERING
POTHERS
POTHERY
POTHOLDER
POTHOLE
POTHOLED
POTHOLER
POTHOLERS
POTHOLES
POTHOLING
POTHOOK
POTHOOKS
POTHOS
POTHOUSE
POTHOUSES
POTHUNTER
POTICARY
POTICHE
POTICHES
POTIN
POTING
POTINS
POTION

POTIONS

POTIONS
POTLACH
POTLACHE
POTLACHES
POTLATCH
POTLIKE
POTLINE
POTLINES
POTLUCK
POTLUCKS
POTMAN
POTMEN
POTOMETER
POTOO
POTOOS
POTOROO
POTOROOS
POTPIE
POTPIES
POTPOURRI
POTS
POTSHARD
POTSHARDS
POTSHARE
POTSHARES
POTSHERD
POTSHERDS
POTSHOP
POTSHOPS
POTSHOT
POTSHOTS
POTSIE
POTSIES
POTSTONE
POTSTONES
POTSY
POTT
POTTAGE
POTTAGES
POTTED
POTTEEN
POTTEENS
POTTER
POTTERED
POTTERER
POTTERERS
POTTERIES
POTTERING
POTTERS
POTTERY
POTTIER
POTTIES
POTTIEST
POTTINESS
POTTING
POTTINGAR
POTTINGER
POTTLE

POTTLES
POTTO
POTTOS
POTTS
POTTY
POTWALLER
POTZER
POTZERS
POUCH
POUCHED
POUCHES
POUCHFUL
POUCHFULS
POUCHIER
POUCHIEST
POUCHING
POUCHY
POUDER
POUDERS
POUDRE
POUDRES
POUF
POUFED
POUFF
POUFFE
POUFFED
POUFFES
POUFFING
POUFFS
POUFFY
POUFING
POUFS
POUFTAH
POUFTAHS
POUFTER
POUFTERS
POUK
POUKE
POUKES
POUKING
POUKIT
POUKS
POULAINE
POULAINES
POULARD
POULARDE
POULARDES
POULARDS
POULDER
POULDERS
POULDRE
POULDRES
POULDRON
POULDRONS
POULE
POULES
POULP
POULPE

POULPES
POULPS
POULT
POULTER
POULTERER
POULTERS
POULTICE
POULTICED
POULTICES
POULTRIES
POULTRY
POULTS
POUNCE
POUNCED
POUNCER
POUNCERS
POUNCES
POUNCET
POUNCETS
POUNCHING
POUNCING
POUND
POUNDAGE
POUNDAGES
POUNDAL
POUNDALS
POUNDCAKE
POUNDED
POUNDER
POUNDERS
POUNDING
POUNDS
POUPE
POUPED
POUPES
POUPING
POUPT
POUR
POURABLE
POURBOIRE
POURED
POURER
POURERS
POURIE
POURIES
POURING
POURINGLY
POURINGS
POURPOINT
POURS
POURSEW
POURSEWED
POURSEWS
POURSUE
POURSUED
POURSUES
POURSUING
POURSUIT

POURSUITS
POURTRAY
POURTRAYD
POURTRAYS
POUSOWDIE
POUSSE
POUSSES
POUSSETTE
POUSSIE
POUSSIES
POUSSIN
POUSSINS
POUT
POUTED
POUTER
POUTERS
POUTFUL
POUTHER
POUTHERED
POUTHERS
POUTIER
POUTIEST
POUTINE
POUTINES
POUTING
POUTINGLY
POUTINGS
POUTS
POUTY
POVERTIES
POVERTY
POW
POWAN
POWANS
POWDER
POWDERED
POWDERER
POWDERERS
POWDERIER
POWDERING
POWDERS
POWDERY
POWELLISE
POWELLITE
POWELLIZE
POWER
POWERBOAT
POWERED
POWERFUL
POWERING
POWERLESS
POWERPLAY
POWERS
POWFAGGED
POWHIRI
POWHIRIS
POWIN
POWINS

POWN
POWND
POWNDED
POWNDING
POWNDS
POWNEY
POWNEYS
POWNIE
POWNIES
POWNS
POWNY
POWRE
POWRED
POWRES
POWRING
POWS
POWSOWDY
POWTER
POWTERED
POWTERING
POWTERS
POWWAW
POWWOW
POWWOWED
POWWOWING
POWWOWS
POX
POXED
POXES
POXIER
POXIEST
POXING
POXVIRUS
POXY
POYNANT
POYNT
POYNTED
POYNTING
POYNTS
POYOU
POYOUS
POYSE
POYSED
POYSES
POYSING
POYSON
POYSONED
POYSONING
POYSONS
POZ
POZOLE
POZOLES
POZZ
POZZIES
POZZOLAN
POZZOLANA
POZZOLANS
POZZY

PRAAM
PRAAMS
PRABBLE
PRABBLES
PRACHARAK
PRACTIC
PRACTICAL
PRACTICE
PRACTICED
PRACTICER
PRACTICES
PRACTICK
PRACTICKS
PRACTICS
PRACTICUM
PRACTIQUE
PRACTISE
PRACTISED
PRACTISER
PRACTISES
PRACTIVE
PRACTOLOL
PRAD
PRADS
PRAEAMBLE
PRAECIPE
PRAECIPES
PRAECOCES
PRAEDIAL
PRAEDIALS
PRAEFECT
PRAEFECTS
PRAELECT
PRAELECTS
PRAELUDIA
PRAENOMEN
PRAESES
PRAESIDIA
PRAETOR
PRAETORS
PRAGMATIC
PRAHU
PRAHUS
PRAIRIE
PRAIRIED
PRAIRIES
PRAISE
PRAISEACH
PRAISED
PRAISEFUL
PRAISER
PRAISERS
PRAISES
PRAISING
PRAISINGS
PRAJNA
PRAJNAS
PRALINE

PRALINES
PRAM
PRAMS
PRANA
PRANAS
PRANAYAMA
PRANCE
PRANCED
PRANCER
PRANCERS
PRANCES
PRANCING
PRANCINGS
PRANCK
PRANCKE
PRANCKED
PRANCKES
PRANCKING
PRANCKS
PRANDIAL
PRANG
PRANGED
PRANGING
PRANGS
PRANK
PRANKED
PRANKFUL
PRANKIER
PRANKIEST
PRANKING
PRANKINGS
PRANKISH
PRANKLE
PRANKLED
PRANKLES
PRANKLING
PRANKS
PRANKSOME
PRANKSTER
PRANKY
PRAO
PRAOS
PRASE
PRASES
PRAT
PRATE
PRATED
PRATER
PRATERS
PRATES
PRATFALL
PRATFALLS
PRATFELL
PRATIE
PRATIES
PRATING
PRATINGLY
PRATINGS

PRATIQUE
PRATIQUES
PRATS
PRATT
PRATTED
PRATTING
PRATTLE
PRATTLED
PRATTLER
PRATTLERS
PRATTLES
PRATTLING
PRATTS
PRATY
PRAU
PRAUNCE
PRAUNCED
PRAUNCES
PRAUNCING
PRAUS
PRAVITIES
PRAVITY
PRAWLE
PRAWLES
PRAWLIN
PRAWLINS
PRAWN
PRAWNED
PRAWNER
PRAWNERS
PRAWNING
PRAWNS
PRAXES
PRAXIS
PRAXISES
PRAY
PRAYED
PRAYER
PRAYERFUL
PRAYERS
PRAYING
PRAYINGLY
PRAYINGS
PRAYS
PRE
PREABSORB
PREACCUSE
PREACE
PREACED
PREACES
PREACH
PREACHED
PREACHER
PREACHERS
PREACHES
PREACHIER
PREACHIFY
PREACHILY

PREACHING	PREBENDAL	PRECEPTOR	PRECREASE
PREACHY	PREBENDS	PRECEPTS	PRECRISIS
PREACING	PREBID	PRECESS	PRECURE
PREACT	PREBIDDEN	PRECESSED	PRECURED
PREACTED	PREBIDS	PRECESSES	PRECURES
PREACTING	PREBILL	PRECHARGE	PRECURING
PREACTS	PREBILLED	PRECHECK	PRECURRER
PREADAMIC	PREBILLS	PRECHECKS	PRECURSE
PREADAPT	PREBIND	PRECHILL	PRECURSES
PREADAPTS	PREBINDS	PRECHILLS	PRECURSOR
PREADJUST	PREBIOTIC	PRECHOOSE	PRECUT
PREADMIT	PREBIRTH	PRECHOSE	PRECUTS
PREADMITS	PREBIRTHS	PRECHOSEN	PREDACITY
PREADOPT	PREBLESS	PRECIEUSE	PREDATE
PREADOPTS	PREBOARD	PRECIEUX	PREDATED
PREADULT	PREBOARDS	PRECINCT	PREDATES
PREADULTS	PREBOIL	PRECINCTS	PREDATING
PREAGED	PREBOILED	PRECIOUS	PREDATION
PREALLOT	PREBOILS	PRECIPE	PREDATISM
PREALLOTS	PREBOOK	PRECIPES	PREDATIVE
PREALTER	PREBOOKED	PRECIPICE	PREDATOR
PREALTERS	PREBOOKS	PRECIS	PREDATORS
PREAMBLE	PREBOOM	PRECISE	PREDATORY
PREAMBLED	PREBORN	PRECISED	PREDAWN
PREAMBLES	PREBOUGHT	PRECISELY	PREDAWNS
PREAMP	PREBOUND	PRECISER	PREDEATH
PREAMPS	PREBUDGET	PRECISES	PREDEATHS
PREANAL	PREBUILD	PRECISEST	PREDEBATE
PREAPPLY	PREBUILDS	PRECISIAN	PREDEDUCT
PREARM	PREBUILT	PRECISING	PREDEFINE
PREARMED	PREBUTTAL	PRECISION	PREDELLA
PREARMING	PREBUY	PRECISIVE	PREDELLAS
PREARMS	PREBUYING	PRECITED	PREDELLE
PREASE	PREBUYS	PRECLEAN	PREDESIGN
PREASED	PRECANCEL	PRECLEANS	PREDEVOTE
PREASES	PRECANCER	PRECLEAR	PREDIAL
PREASING	PRECAST	PRECLEARS	PREDIALS
PREASSE	PRECASTS	PRECLUDE	PREDICANT
PREASSED	PRECATIVE	PRECLUDED	PREDICATE
PREASSES	PRECATORY	PRECLUDES	PREDICT
PREASSIGN	PRECAUDAL	PRECOCIAL	PREDICTED
PREASSING	PRECAVA	PRECOCITY	PREDICTER
PREASSURE	PRECAVAE	PRECODE	PREDICTOR
PREATOMIC	PRECAVAL	PRECODED	PREDICTS
PREATTUNE	PRECEDE	PRECODES	PREDIED
PREAUDIT	PRECEDED	PRECODING	PREDIES
PREAUDITS	PRECEDENT	PRECOITAL	PREDIGEST
PREAVER	PRECEDES	PRECONISE	PREDIKANT
PREAVERS	PRECEDING	PRECONIZE	PREDILECT
PREAXIAL	PRECEESE	PRECOOK	PREDINNER
PREBADE	PRECENSOR	PRECOOKED	PREDIVE
PREBAKE	PRECENT	PRECOOKER	PREDOOM
PREBAKED	PRECENTED	PRECOOKS	PREDOOMED
PREBAKES	PRECENTOR	PRECOOL	PREDOOMS
PREBAKING	PRECENTS	PRECOOLED	PREDRAFT
PREBASAL	PRECEPIT	PRECOOLS	PREDRIED
PREBATTLE	PRECEPITS	PRECOUP	PREDRIES
PREBEND	PRECEPT	PRECRASH	PREDRILL

PREDRILLS
PREDRY
PREDRYING
PREDUSK
PREDUSKS
PREDY
PREDYING
PREE
PREED
PREEDIT
PREEDITED
PREEDITS
PREEING
PREELECT
PREELECTS
PREEMIE
PREEMIES
PREEMPT
PREEMPTED
PREEMPTOR
PREEMPTS
PREEN
PREENACT
PREENACTS
PREENED
PREENER
PREENERS
PREENING
PREENS
PREERECT
PREERECTS
PREES
PREEVE
PREEVED
PREEVES
PREEVING
PREEXCITE
PREEXEMPT
PREEXILIC
PREEXIST
PREEXISTS
PREEXPOSE
PREFAB
PREFABBED
PREFABS
PREFACE
PREFACED
PREFACER
PREFACERS
PREFACES
PREFACIAL
PREFACING
PREFADE
PREFADED
PREFADES
PREFADING
PREFARD
PREFATORY

PREFECT
PREFECTS
PREFER
PREFERRED
PREFERRER
PREFERS
PREFEUDAL
PREFIGHT
PREFIGURE
PREFILE
PREFILED
PREFILES
PREFILING
PREFILLED
PREFIRE
PREFIRED
PREFIRES
PREFIRING
PREFIX
PREFIXAL
PREFIXED
PREFIXES
PREFIXING
PREFIXION
PREFLAME
PREFLIGHT
PREFOCUS
PREFORM
PREFORMAT
PREFORMED
PREFORMS
PREFRANK
PREFRANKS
PREFREEZE
PREFROZE
PREFROZEN
PREFUND
PREFUNDED
PREFUNDS
PREGAME
PREGAMES
PREGGERS
PREGGIER
PREGGIEST
PREGGY
PREGNABLE
PREGNANCE
PREGNANCY
PREGNANT
PREGROWTH
PREGUIDE
PREGUIDED
PREGUIDES
PREHALLUX
PREHANDLE
PREHARDEN
PREHEAT
PREHEATED

PREHEATER
PREHEATS
PREHEND
PREHENDED
PREHENDS
PREHENSOR
PREHIRING
PREHNITE
PREHNITES
PREHUMAN
PREHUMANS
PREIF
PREIFE
PREIFES
PREIFS
PREIMPOSE
PREINFORM
PREINSERT
PREINVITE
PREJINK
PREJUDGE
PREJUDGED
PREJUDGER
PREJUDGES
PREJUDICE
PREJUDIZE
PRELACIES
PRELACY
PRELATE
PRELATES
PRELATESS
PRELATIAL
PRELATIC
PRELATIES
PRELATION
PRELATISE
PRELATISH
PRELATISM
PRELATIST
PRELATIZE
PRELATURE
PRELATY
PRELAUNCH
PRELAW
PRELECT
PRELECTED
PRELECTOR
PRELECTS
PRELEGAL
PRELIFE
PRELIM
PRELIMIT
PRELIMITS
PRELIMS
PRELIVES
PRELOAD
PRELOADED
PRELOADS

PRELOCATE
PRELOVED
PRELUDE
PRELUDED
PRELUDER
PRELUDERS
PRELUDES
PRELUDI
PRELUDIAL
PRELUDING
PRELUDIO
PRELUNCH
PRELUSION
PRELUSIVE
PRELUSORY
PREM
PREMADE
PREMAN
PREMARKET
PREMATURE
PREMEAL
PREMED
PREMEDIC
PREMEDICS
PREMEDS
PREMEET
PREMEN
PREMERGER
PREMIA
PREMIE
PREMIER
PREMIERE
PREMIERED
PREMIERES
PREMIERS
PREMIES
PREMISE
PREMISED
PREMISES
PREMISING
PREMISS
PREMISSES
PREMIUM
PREMIUMS
PREMIX
PREMIXED
PREMIXES
PREMIXING
PREMIXT
PREMODERN
PREMODIFY
PREMOLAR
PREMOLARS
PREMOLD
PREMOLDED
PREMOLDS
PREMOLT
PREMONISH

453

PREMORAL
PREMORSE
PREMOSAIC
PREMOTION
PREMOVE
PREMOVED
PREMOVES
PREMOVING
PREMS
PREMUNE
PREMY
PRENAME
PRENAMES
PRENASAL
PRENASALS
PRENATAL
PRENATALS
PRENOMEN
PRENOMENS
PRENOMINA
PRENOON
PRENOTIFY
PRENOTION
PRENT
PRENTED
PRENTICE
PRENTICED
PRENTICES
PRENTING
PRENTS
PRENUBILE
PRENUMBER
PRENUP
PRENUPS
PRENZIE
PREOBTAIN
PREOCCUPY
PREOCULAR
PREOP
PREOPS
PREOPTION
PREORAL
PREORDAIN
PREORDER
PREORDERS
PREOWNED
PREP
PREPACK
PREPACKED
PREPACKS
PREPAID
PREPARE
PREPARED
PREPARER
PREPARERS
PREPARES
PREPARING
PREPASTE

PREPASTED
PREPASTES
PREPAVE
PREPAVED
PREPAVES
PREPAVING
PREPAY
PREPAYING
PREPAYS
PREPENSE
PREPENSED
PREPENSES
PREPILL
PREPLACE
PREPLACED
PREPLACES
PREPLAN
PREPLANS
PREPLANT
PREPOLLEX
PREPONE
PREPONED
PREPONES
PREPONING
PREPOSE
PREPOSED
PREPOSES
PREPOSING
PREPOSTOR
PREPOTENT
PREPPED
PREPPIE
PREPPIER
PREPPIES
PREPPIEST
PREPPILY
PREPPING
PREPPY
PREPREG
PREPREGS
PREPRESS
PREPRICE
PREPRICED
PREPRICES
PREPRINT
PREPRINTS
PREPS
PREPUBES
PREPUBIS
PREPUCE
PREPUCES
PREPUEBLO
PREPUNCH
PREPUPA
PREPUPAE
PREPUPAL
PREPUPAS
PREPUTIAL

PREQUEL
PREQUELS
PRERACE
PRERADIO
PRERECORD
PRERECTAL
PREREFORM
PRERENAL
PRERETURN
PREREVIEW
PRERINSE
PRERINSED
PRERINSES
PRERIOT
PREROCK
PRERUPT
PRESA
PRESAGE
PRESAGED
PRESAGER
PRESAGERS
PRESAGES
PRESAGING
PRESALE
PRESALES
PRESBYOPE
PRESBYOPY
PRESBYTE
PRESBYTER
PRESBYTES
PRESBYTIC
PRESCHOOL
PRESCIENT
PRESCIND
PRESCINDS
PRESCIOUS
PRESCORE
PRESCORED
PRESCORES
PRESCREEN
PRESCRIBE
PRESCRIPT
PRESCUTA
PRESCUTUM
PRESE
PRESEASON
PRESELECT
PRESELL
PRESELLS
PRESENCE
PRESENCES
PRESENILE
PRESENT
PRESENTED
PRESENTEE
PRESENTER
PRESENTLY
PRESENTS

PRESERVE
PRESERVED
PRESERVER
PRESERVES
PRESES
PRESET
PRESETS
PRESETTLE
PRESHAPE
PRESHAPED
PRESHAPES
PRESHIP
PRESHIPS
PRESHOW
PRESHOWED
PRESHOWN
PRESHOWS
PRESHRANK
PRESHRINK
PRESHRUNK
PRESIDE
PRESIDED
PRESIDENT
PRESIDER
PRESIDERS
PRESIDES
PRESIDIA
PRESIDIAL
PRESIDING
PRESIDIO
PRESIDIOS
PRESIDIUM
PRESIFT
PRESIFTED
PRESIFTS
PRESIGNAL
PRESLEEP
PRESLICE
PRESLICED
PRESLICES
PRESOAK
PRESOAKED
PRESOAKS
PRESOLD
PRESOLVE
PRESOLVED
PRESOLVES
PRESONG
PRESORT
PRESORTED
PRESORTS
PRESPLIT
PRESS
PRESSED
PRESSER
PRESSERS
PRESSES
PRESSFAT

PRESSFATS	PRETELL	PREUNITES	PREWIRING
PRESSFUL	PRETELLS	PREVAIL	PREWORK
PRESSFULS	PRETENCE	PREVAILED	PREWORKED
PRESSGANG	PRETENCES	PREVAILER	PREWORKS
PRESSIE	PRETEND	PREVAILS	PREWORN
PRESSIES	PRETENDED	PREVALENT	PREWRAP
PRESSING	PRETENDER	PREVALUE	PREWRAPS
PRESSINGS	PRETENDS	PREVALUED	PREWYN
PRESSION	PRETENSE	PREVALUES	PREWYNS
PRESSIONS	PRETENSES	PREVE	PREX
PRESSMAN	PRETERIST	PREVED	PREXES
PRESSMARK	PRETERIT	PREVENE	PREXIES
PRESSMEN	PRETERITE	PREVENED	PREXY
PRESSOR	PRETERITS	PREVENES	PREY
PRESSORS	PRETERM	PREVENING	PREYED
PRESSROOM	PRETERMIT	PREVENT	PREYER
PRESSRUN	PRETERMS	PREVENTED	PREYERS
PRESSRUNS	PRETEST	PREVENTER	PREYFUL
PRESSURE	PRETESTED	PREVENTS	PREYING
PRESSURED	PRETESTS	PREVERB	PREYS
PRESSURES	PRETEXT	PREVERBAL	PREZ
PRESSWORK	PRETEXTED	PREVERBS	PREZES
PREST	PRETEXTS	PREVES	PREZZIE
PRESTAMP	PRETOLD	PREVIABLE	PREZZIES
PRESTAMPS	PRETONIC	PREVIEW	PRIAL
PRESTED	PRETOR	PREVIEWED	PRIALS
PRESTER	PRETORIAL	PREVIEWER	PRIAPEAN
PRESTERNA	PRETORIAN	PREVIEWS	PRIAPI
PRESTERS	PRETORS	PREVING	PRIAPIC
PRESTIGE	PRETRAIN	PREVIOUS	PRIAPISM
PRESTIGES	PRETRAINS	PREVISE	PRIAPISMS
PRESTING	PRETRAVEL	PREVISED	PRIAPUS
PRESTO	PRETREAT	PREVISES	PRIAPUSES
PRESTORE	PRETREATS	PREVISING	PRIBBLE
PRESTORED	PRETRIAL	PREVISION	PRIBBLES
PRESTORES	PRETRIALS	PREVISIT	PRICE
PRESTOS	PRETRIM	PREVISITS	PRICEABLE
PRESTRESS	PRETRIMS	PREVISOR	PRICED
PRESTRIKE	PRETTIED	PREVISORS	PRICELESS
PRESTS	PRETTIER	PREVUE	PRICER
PRESUME	PRETTIES	PREVUED	PRICERS
PRESUMED	PRETTIEST	PREVUES	PRICES
PRESUMER	PRETTIFY	PREVUING	PRICEY
PRESUMERS	PRETTILY	PREWAR	PRICIER
PRESUMES	PRETTY	PREWARM	PRICIEST
PRESUMING	PRETTYING	PREWARMED	PRICILY
PRESUMMIT	PRETTYISH	PREWARMS	PRICINESS
PRESURVEY	PRETTYISM	PREWARN	PRICING
PRETAPE	PRETYPE	PREWARNED	PRICINGS
PRETAPED	PRETYPED	PREWARNS	PRICK
PRETAPES	PRETYPES	PREWASH	PRICKED
PRETAPING	PRETYPING	PREWASHED	PRICKER
PRETASTE	PRETZEL	PREWASHES	PRICKERS
PRETASTED	PRETZELS	PREWEIGH	PRICKET
PRETASTES	PREUNION	PREWEIGHS	PRICKETS
PRETAX	PREUNIONS	PREWIRE	PRICKIER
PRETEEN	PREUNITE	PREWIRED	PRICKIEST
PRETEENS	PREUNITED	PREWIRES	PRICKING

455

PRICKINGS

PRICKINGS
PRICKLE
PRICKLED
PRICKLES
PRICKLIER
PRICKLING
PRICKLY
PRICKS
PRICKWOOD
PRICKY
PRICY
PRIDE
PRIDED
PRIDEFUL
PRIDELESS
PRIDES
PRIDIAN
PRIDING
PRIED
PRIEDIEU
PRIEDIEUS
PRIEDIEUX
PRIEF
PRIEFE
PRIEFES
PRIEFS
PRIER
PRIERS
PRIES
PRIEST
PRIESTED
PRIESTESS
PRIESTING
PRIESTLY
PRIESTS
PRIEVE
PRIEVED
PRIEVES
PRIEVING
PRIG
PRIGGED
PRIGGER
PRIGGERS
PRIGGERY
PRIGGING
PRIGGINGS
PRIGGISH
PRIGGISM
PRIGGISMS
PRIGS
PRILL
PRILLED
PRILLING
PRILLS
PRIM
PRIMA
PRIMACIES
PRIMACY

PRIMAEVAL
PRIMAGE
PRIMAGES
PRIMAL
PRIMALITY
PRIMALLY
PRIMARIES
PRIMARILY
PRIMARY
PRIMAS
PRIMATAL
PRIMATALS
PRIMATE
PRIMATES
PRIMATIAL
PRIMATIC
PRIMAVERA
PRIME
PRIMED
PRIMELY
PRIMENESS
PRIMER
PRIMERO
PRIMEROS
PRIMERS
PRIMES
PRIMETIME
PRIMEUR
PRIMEURS
PRIMEVAL
PRIMI
PRIMINE
PRIMINES
PRIMING
PRIMINGS
PRIMIPARA
PRIMITIAE
PRIMITIAL
PRIMITIAS
PRIMITIVE
PRIMLY
PRIMMED
PRIMMER
PRIMMERS
PRIMMEST
PRIMMING
PRIMNESS
PRIMO
PRIMORDIA
PRIMOS
PRIMP
PRIMPED
PRIMPING
PRIMPS
PRIMROSE
PRIMROSED
PRIMROSES
PRIMROSY

PRIMS
PRIMSIE
PRIMSIER
PRIMSIEST
PRIMULA
PRIMULAS
PRIMULINE
PRIMUS
PRIMUSES
PRIMY
PRINCE
PRINCED
PRINCEDOM
PRINCEKIN
PRINCELET
PRINCELY
PRINCES
PRINCESS
PRINCESSE
PRINCING
PRINCIPAL
PRINCIPE
PRINCIPI
PRINCIPIA
PRINCIPLE
PRINCOCK
PRINCOCKS
PRINCOX
PRINCOXES
PRINK
PRINKED
PRINKER
PRINKERS
PRINKING
PRINKS
PRINT
PRINTABLE
PRINTED
PRINTER
PRINTERS
PRINTERY
PRINTHEAD
PRINTING
PRINTINGS
PRINTLESS
PRINTOUT
PRINTOUTS
PRINTS
PRION
PRIONS
PRIOR
PRIORATE
PRIORATES
PRIORESS
PRIORIES
PRIORITY
PRIORLY
PRIORS

PRIORSHIP
PRIORY
PRISAGE
PRISAGES
PRISE
PRISED
PRISER
PRISERE
PRISERES
PRISERS
PRISES
PRISING
PRISM
PRISMATIC
PRISMOID
PRISMOIDS
PRISMS
PRISMY
PRISON
PRISONED
PRISONER
PRISONERS
PRISONING
PRISONOUS
PRISONS
PRISS
PRISSED
PRISSES
PRISSIER
PRISSIES
PRISSIEST
PRISSILY
PRISSING
PRISSY
PRISTANE
PRISTANES
PRISTINE
PRITHEE
PRIVACIES
PRIVACY
PRIVADO
PRIVADOES
PRIVADOS
PRIVATE
PRIVATEER
PRIVATELY
PRIVATER
PRIVATES
PRIVATEST
PRIVATION
PRIVATISE
PRIVATISM
PRIVATIST
PRIVATIVE
PRIVATIZE
PRIVET
PRIVETS
PRIVIER

PRIVIES
PRIVIEST
PRIVILEGE
PRIVILY
PRIVITIES
PRIVITY
PRIVY
PRIZABLE
PRIZE
PRIZED
PRIZEMAN
PRIZEMEN
PRIZER
PRIZERS
PRIZES
PRIZING
PRO
PROA
PROACTION
PROACTIVE
PROAS
PROB
PROBABLE
PROBABLES
PROBABLY
PROBALL
PROBAND
PROBANDS
PROBANG
PROBANGS
PROBATE
PROBATED
PROBATES
PROBATING
PROBATION
PROBATIVE
PROBATORY
PROBE
PROBEABLE
PROBED
PROBER
PROBERS
PROBES
PROBING
PROBINGLY
PROBIOTIC
PROBIT
PROBITIES
PROBITS
PROBITY
PROBLEM
PROBLEMS
PROBOSCIS
PROBS
PROCACITY
PROCAINE
PROCAINES
PROCAMBIA

PROCARP
PROCARPS
PROCARYON
PROCEDURE
PROCEED
PROCEEDED
PROCEEDER
PROCEEDS
PROCERITY
PROCESS
PROCESSED
PROCESSER
PROCESSES
PROCESSOR
PROCHAIN
PROCHEIN
PROCHOICE
PROCHURCH
PROCIDENT
PROCINCT
PROCINCTS
PROCLAIM
PROCLAIMS
PROCLISES
PROCLISIS
PROCLITIC
PROCLIVE
PROCONSUL
PROCREANT
PROCREATE
PROCTAL
PROCTITIS
PROCTODEA
PROCTOR
PROCTORED
PROCTORS
PROCURACY
PROCURAL
PROCURALS
PROCURE
PROCURED
PROCURER
PROCURERS
PROCURES
PROCURESS
PROCUREUR
PROCURING
PROD
PRODDED
PRODDER
PRODDERS
PRODDING
PRODIGAL
PRODIGALS
PRODIGIES
PRODIGY
PRODITOR
PRODITORS

PRODITORY
PRODNOSE
PRODNOSED
PRODNOSES
PRODROMAL
PRODROME
PRODROMES
PRODROMI
PRODROMIC
PRODROMUS
PRODRUG
PRODRUGS
PRODS
PRODUCE
PRODUCED
PRODUCER
PRODUCERS
PRODUCES
PRODUCING
PRODUCT
PRODUCTS
PROEM
PROEMBRYO
PROEMIAL
PROEMS
PROENZYME
PROESTRUS
PROETTE
PROETTES
PROF
PROFACE
PROFAMILY
PROFANE
PROFANED
PROFANELY
PROFANER
PROFANERS
PROFANES
PROFANING
PROFANITY
PROFESS
PROFESSED
PROFESSES
PROFESSOR
PROFFER
PROFFERED
PROFFERER
PROFFERS
PROFILE
PROFILED
PROFILER
PROFILERS
PROFILES
PROFILING
PROFILIST
PROFIT
PROFITED
PROFITEER

PROFITER
PROFITERS
PROFITING
PROFITS
PROFLUENT
PROFORMA
PROFORMAS
PROFOUND
PROFOUNDS
PROFS
PROFUSE
PROFUSELY
PROFUSER
PROFUSERS
PROFUSION
PROFUSIVE
PROG
PROGENIES
PROGENY
PROGERIA
PROGERIAS
PROGESTIN
PROGGED
PROGGER
PROGGERS
PROGGING
PROGGINS
PROGNOSE
PROGNOSED
PROGNOSES
PROGNOSIS
PROGRADE
PROGRADED
PROGRADES
PROGRAM
PROGRAMED
PROGRAMER
PROGRAMME
PROGRAMS
PROGRESS
PROGS
PROGUN
PROHIBIT
PROHIBITS
PROIGN
PROIGNED
PROIGNING
PROIGNS
PROIN
PROINE
PROINED
PROINES
PROINING
PROINS
PROJECT
PROJECTED
PROJECTOR
PROJECTS

PROJET	PROLOGIZE	PROMPTURE	PROOTICS
PROJETS	PROLOGS	PROMS	PROP
PROKARYON	PROLOGUE	PROMULGE	PROPAGATE
PROKARYOT	PROLOGUED	PROMULGED	PROPAGE
PROKE	PROLOGUES	PROMULGES	PROPAGED
PROKED	PROLONG	PROMUSCES	PROPAGES
PROKER	PROLONGE	PROMUSCIS	PROPAGING
PROKERS	PROLONGED	PRONAOI	PROPAGULA
PROKES	PROLONGER	PRONAOS	PROPAGULE
PROKING	PROLONGES	PRONATE	PROPALE
PROLABOR	PROLONGS	PRONATED	PROPALED
PROLACTIN	PROLUSION	PRONATES	PROPALES
PROLAMIN	PROLUSORY	PRONATING	PROPALING
PROLAMINE	PROM	PRONATION	PROPANE
PROLAMINS	PROMACHOS	PRONATOR	PROPANES
PROLAN	PROMENADE	PRONATORS	PROPANOIC
PROLANS	PROMETAL	PRONE	PROPANOL
PROLAPSE	PROMETALS	PRONELY	PROPANOLS
PROLAPSED	PROMETRIC	PRONENESS	PROPANONE
PROLAPSES	PROMINE	PRONEPHRA	PROPEL
PROLAPSUS	PROMINENT	PRONER	PROPELLED
PROLATE	PROMINES	PRONES	PROPELLER
PROLATED	PROMISE	PRONEST	PROPELLOR
PROLATELY	PROMISED	PRONEUR	PROPELS
PROLATES	PROMISEE	PRONEURS	PROPEND
PROLATING	PROMISEES	PRONG	PROPENDED
PROLATION	PROMISER	PRONGBUCK	PROPENDS
PROLATIVE	PROMISERS	PRONGED	PROPENE
PROLE	PROMISES	PRONGHORN	PROPENES
PROLED	PROMISING	PRONGING	PROPENOIC
PROLEG	PROMISOR	PRONGS	PROPENOL
PROLEGS	PROMISORS	PRONK	PROPENOLS
PROLEPSES	PROMISSOR	PRONKED	PROPENSE
PROLEPSIS	PROMMER	PRONKING	PROPENYL
PROLEPTIC	PROMMERS	PRONKS	PROPER
PROLER	PROMO	PRONOTA	PROPERDIN
PROLERS	PROMODERN	PRONOTAL	PROPERER
PROLES	PROMOED	PRONOTUM	PROPEREST
PROLETARY	PROMOING	PRONOUN	PROPERLY
PROLICIDE	PROMOS	PRONOUNCE	PROPERS
PROLIFIC	PROMOTE	PRONOUNS	PROPERTY
PROLINE	PROMOTED	PRONTO	PROPHAGE
PROLINES	PROMOTER	PRONUCLEI	PROPHAGES
PROLING	PROMOTERS	PRONUNCIO	PROPHASE
PROLIX	PROMOTES	PROO	PROPHASES
PROLIXITY	PROMOTING	PROOEMION	PROPHASIC
PROLIXLY	PROMOTION	PROOEMIUM	PROPHECY
PROLL	PROMOTIVE	PROOF	PROPHESY
PROLLED	PROMOTOR	PROOFED	PROPHET
PROLLER	PROMOTORS	PROOFER	PROPHETIC
PROLLERS	PROMPT	PROOFERS	PROPHETS
PROLLING	PROMPTED	PROOFING	PROPHYLL
PROLLS	PROMPTER	PROOFINGS	PROPHYLLS
PROLOG	PROMPTERS	PROOFLESS	PROPINE
PROLOGED	PROMPTEST	PROOFREAD	PROPINED
PROLOGING	PROMPTING	PROOFROOM	PROPINES
PROLOGISE	PROMPTLY	PROOFS	PROPINING
PROLOGIST	PROMPTS	PROOTIC	PROPIONIC

PROPJET	PROS	PROSSES	PROTEST
PROPJETS	PROSAIC	PROSSIE	PROTESTED
PROPMAN	PROSAICAL	PROSSIES	PROTESTER
PROPMEN	PROSAISM	PROST	PROTESTOR
PROPODEON	PROSAISMS	PROSTATE	PROTESTS
PROPODEUM	PROSAIST	PROSTATES	PROTEUS
PROPOLIS	PROSAISTS	PROSTATIC	PROTEUSES
PROPONE	PROSATEUR	PROSTERNA	PROTHALLI
PROPONED	PROSCENIA	PROSTIE	PROTHESES
PROPONENT	PROSCRIBE	PROSTIES	PROTHESIS
PROPONES	PROSCRIPT	PROSTOMIA	PROTHETIC
PROPONING	PROSE	PROSTRATE	PROTHORAX
PROPOSAL	PROSECT	PROSTYLE	PROTHYL
PROPOSALS	PROSECTED	PROSTYLES	PROTHYLS
PROPOSE	PROSECTOR	PROSUMER	PROTIST
PROPOSED	PROSECTS	PROSUMERS	PROTISTAN
PROPOSER	PROSECUTE	PROSY	PROTISTIC
PROPOSERS	PROSED	PROTAMIN	PROTISTS
PROPOSES	PROSELIKE	PROTAMINE	PROTIUM
PROPOSING	PROSELYTE	PROTAMINS	PROTIUMS
PROPOSITA	PROSEMAN	PROTANDRY	PROTOAVIS
PROPOSITI	PROSEMEN	PROTANOPE	PROTOCOL
PROPOUND	PROSER	PROTASES	PROTOCOLS
PROPOUNDS	PROSERS	PROTASIS	PROTODERM
PROPPANT	PROSES	PROTATIC	PROTOGINE
PROPPANTS	PROSEUCHA	PROTEA	PROTOGYNY
PROPPED	PROSEUCHE	PROTEAN	PROTON
PROPPING	PROSIER	PROTEANS	PROTONATE
PROPRETOR	PROSIEST	PROTEAS	PROTONEMA
PROPRIA	PROSIFIED	PROTEASE	PROTONIC
PROPRIETY	PROSIFIES	PROTEASES	PROTONS
PROPRIUM	PROSIFY	PROTECT	PROTOPOD
PROPS	PROSILY	PROTECTED	PROTOPODS
PROPTOSES	PROSIMIAN	PROTECTER	PROTORE
PROPTOSIS	PROSINESS	PROTECTOR	PROTORES
PROPULSOR	PROSING	PROTECTS	PROTOSTAR
PROPYL	PROSINGS	PROTEGE	PROTOTYPE
PROPYLA	PROSIT	PROTEGEE	PROTOXID
PROPYLAEA	PROSO	PROTEGEES	PROTOXIDE
PROPYLENE	PROSODIAL	PROTEGES	PROTOXIDS
PROPYLIC	PROSODIAN	PROTEI	PROTOZOA
PROPYLITE	PROSODIC	PROTEID	PROTOZOAL
PROPYLON	PROSODIES	PROTEIDE	PROTOZOAN
PROPYLONS	PROSODIST	PROTEIDES	PROTOZOIC
PROPYLS	PROSODY	PROTEIDS	PROTOZOON
PRORATE	PROSOMA	PROTEIN	PROTRACT
PRORATED	PROSOMAL	PROTEINIC	PROTRACTS
PRORATES	PROSOMAS	PROTEINS	PROTRADE
PRORATING	PROSOMATA	PROTEND	PROTRUDE
PRORATION	PROSOPON	PROTENDED	PROTRUDED
PRORE	PROSOPONS	PROTENDS	PROTRUDES
PRORECTOR	PROSOS	PROTENSE	PROTYL
PROREFORM	PROSPECT	PROTENSES	PROTYLE
PRORES	PROSPECTS	PROTEOME	PROTYLES
PROROGATE	PROSPER	PROTEOMES	PROTYLS
PROROGUE	PROSPERED	PROTEOMIC	PROUD
PROROGUED	PROSPERS	PROTEOSE	PROUDER
PROROGUES	PROSS	PROTEOSES	PROUDEST

PROUDFUL
PROUDISH
PROUDLY
PROUDNESS
PROUL
PROULED
PROULER
PROULERS
PROULING
PROULS
PROUNION
PROUSTITE
PROVABLE
PROVABLY
PROVAND
PROVANDS
PROVANT
PROVE
PROVEABLE
PROVEABLY
PROVED
PROVEDOR
PROVEDORE
PROVEDORS
PROVEN
PROVEND
PROVENDER
PROVENDS
PROVENLY
PROVER
PROVERB
PROVERBED
PROVERBS
PROVERS
PROVES
PROVIANT
PROVIANTS
PROVIDE
PROVIDED
PROVIDENT
PROVIDER
PROVIDERS
PROVIDES
PROVIDING
PROVIDOR
PROVIDORS
PROVINCE
PROVINCES
PROVINE
PROVINED
PROVINES
PROVING
PROVINGS
PROVINING
PROVIRAL
PROVIRUS
PROVISION
PROVISO

PROVISOES
PROVISOR
PROVISORS
PROVISORY
PROVISOS
PROVOCANT
PROVOKE
PROVOKED
PROVOKER
PROVOKERS
PROVOKES
PROVOKING
PROVOLONE
PROVOST
PROVOSTRY
PROVOSTS
PROW
PROWAR
PROWER
PROWESS
PROWESSED
PROWESSES
PROWEST
PROWL
PROWLED
PROWLER
PROWLERS
PROWLING
PROWLINGS
PROWLS
PROWS
PROXEMIC
PROXEMICS
PROXIES
PROXIMAL
PROXIMATE
PROXIMITY
PROXIMO
PROXY
PROYN
PROYNE
PROYNED
PROYNES
PROYNING
PROYNS
PROZYMITE
PRUDE
PRUDENCE
PRUDENCES
PRUDENT
PRUDENTLY
PRUDERIES
PRUDERY
PRUDES
PRUDISH
PRUDISHLY
PRUH
PRUINA

PRUINAS
PRUINE
PRUINES
PRUINOSE
PRUNABLE
PRUNE
PRUNED
PRUNELLA
PRUNELLAS
PRUNELLE
PRUNELLES
PRUNELLO
PRUNELLOS
PRUNER
PRUNERS
PRUNES
PRUNING
PRUNINGS
PRUNT
PRUNTED
PRUNTS
PRUNUS
PRUNUSES
PRURIENCE
PRURIENCY
PRURIENT
PRURIGO
PRURIGOS
PRURITIC
PRURITUS
PRUSIK
PRUSIKED
PRUSIKING
PRUSIKS
PRUSSIATE
PRUSSIC
PRUTA
PRUTAH
PRUTOT
PRUTOTH
PRY
PRYER
PRYERS
PRYING
PRYINGLY
PRYINGS
PRYS
PRYSE
PRYSED
PRYSES
PRYSING
PRYTANEA
PRYTANEUM
PRYTHEE
PSALM
PSALMBOOK
PSALMED
PSALMIC

PSALMING
PSALMIST
PSALMISTS
PSALMODIC
PSALMODY
PSALMS
PSALTER
PSALTERIA
PSALTERS
PSALTERY
PSALTRESS
PSALTRIES
PSALTRY
PSAMMITE
PSAMMITES
PSAMMITIC
PSAMMON
PSAMMONS
PSCHENT
PSCHENTS
PSELLISM
PSELLISMS
PSEPHISM
PSEPHISMS
PSEPHITE
PSEPHITES
PSEPHITIC
PSEUD
PSEUDAXES
PSEUDAXIS
PSEUDERY
PSEUDISH
PSEUDO
PSEUDONYM
PSEUDOPOD
PSEUDOS
PSEUDS
PSHAW
PSHAWED
PSHAWING
PSHAWS
PSI
PSILOCIN
PSILOCINS
PSILOSES
PSILOSIS
PSILOTIC
PSION
PSIONIC
PSIONICS
PSIONS
PSIS
PSOAE
PSOAI
PSOAS
PSOASES
PSOATIC
PSOCID

PSOCIDS
PSORA
PSORALEA
PSORALEAS
PSORALEN
PSORALENS
PSORAS
PSORIASES
PSORIASIS
PSORIATIC
PSORIC
PSST
PST
PSYCH
PSYCHE
PSYCHED
PSYCHES
PSYCHIC
PSYCHICAL
PSYCHICS
PSYCHING
PSYCHISM
PSYCHISMS
PSYCHIST
PSYCHISTS
PSYCHO
PSYCHOGAS
PSYCHOID
PSYCHOIDS
PSYCHOS
PSYCHOSES
PSYCHOSIS
PSYCHOTIC
PSYCHS
PSYLLA
PSYLLAS
PSYLLID
PSYLLIDS
PSYLLIUM
PSYLLIUMS
PSYOP
PSYOPS
PSYWAR
PSYWARS
PTARMIC
PTARMICS
PTARMIGAN
PTERIA
PTERIDINE
PTERIN
PTERINS
PTERION
PTEROPOD
PTEROPODS
PTEROSAUR
PTERYGIA
PTERYGIAL
PTERYGIUM

PTERYGOID
PTERYLA
PTERYLAE
PTILOSES
PTILOSIS
PTISAN
PTISANS
PTOMAIN
PTOMAINE
PTOMAINES
PTOMAINIC
PTOMAINS
PTOOEY
PTOSES
PTOSIS
PTOTIC
PTUI
PTYALIN
PTYALINS
PTYALISE
PTYALISED
PTYALISES
PTYALISM
PTYALISMS
PTYALIZE
PTYALIZED
PTYALIZES
PTYXES
PTYXIS
PTYXISES
PUB
PUBBED
PUBBING
PUBE
PUBERAL
PUBERTAL
PUBERTIES
PUBERTY
PUBES
PUBESCENT
PUBIC
PUBIS
PUBISES
PUBLIC
PUBLICAN
PUBLICANS
PUBLICISE
PUBLICIST
PUBLICITY
PUBLICIZE
PUBLICLY
PUBLICS
PUBLISH
PUBLISHED
PUBLISHER
PUBLISHES
PUBS
PUCAN

PUCANS
PUCCOON
PUCCOONS
PUCE
PUCELAGE
PUCELAGES
PUCELLE
PUCELLES
PUCER
PUCES
PUCEST
PUCK
PUCKA
PUCKED
PUCKER
PUCKERED
PUCKERER
PUCKERERS
PUCKERIER
PUCKERING
PUCKEROOD
PUCKERS
PUCKERY
PUCKFIST
PUCKFISTS
PUCKING
PUCKISH
PUCKISHLY
PUCKLE
PUCKLES
PUCKS
PUD
PUDDEN
PUDDENING
PUDDENS
PUDDER
PUDDERED
PUDDERING
PUDDERS
PUDDIES
PUDDING
PUDDINGS
PUDDINGY
PUDDLE
PUDDLED
PUDDLER
PUDDLERS
PUDDLES
PUDDLIER
PUDDLIEST
PUDDLING
PUDDLINGS
PUDDLY
PUDDOCK
PUDDOCKS
PUDDY
PUDENCIES
PUDENCY

PUDENDA
PUDENDAL
PUDENDOUS
PUDENDUM
PUDENT
PUDGE
PUDGES
PUDGIER
PUDGIEST
PUDGILY
PUDGINESS
PUDGY
PUDIBUND
PUDIC
PUDICITY
PUDOR
PUDORS
PUDS
PUDSEY
PUDSIER
PUDSIEST
PUDSY
PUDU
PUDUS
PUEBLO
PUEBLOS
PUER
PUERED
PUERILE
PUERILELY
PUERILISM
PUERILITY
PUERING
PUERPERA
PUERPERAE
PUERPERAL
PUERPERIA
PUERS
PUFF
PUFFBALL
PUFFBALLS
PUFFBIRD
PUFFBIRDS
PUFFED
PUFFER
PUFFERIES
PUFFERS
PUFFERY
PUFFIER
PUFFIEST
PUFFILY
PUFFIN
PUFFINESS
PUFFING
PUFFINGLY
PUFFINGS
PUFFINS
PUFFS

PUFFY	PUKA	PULLOUT	PULSATED
PUFTALOON	PUKATEA	PULLOUTS	PULSATES
PUG	PUKATEAS	PULLOVER	PULSATILE
PUGAREE	PUKE	PULLOVERS	PULSATING
PUGAREES	PUKED	PULLS	PULSATION
PUGGAREE	PUKEKO	PULLULATE	PULSATIVE
PUGGAREES	PUKEKOS	PULLUP	PULSATOR
PUGGED	PUKER	PULLUPS	PULSATORS
PUGGERIES	PUKERS	PULLUS	PULSATORY
PUGGERY	PUKES	PULMO	PULSE
PUGGIE	PUKING	PULMONARY	PULSED
PUGGIER	PUKKA	PULMONATE	PULSEJET
PUGGIES	PUKU	PULMONES	PULSEJETS
PUGGIEST	PUKUS	PULMONIC	PULSELESS
PUGGINESS	PUL	PULMONICS	PULSER
PUGGING	PULA	PULMOTOR	PULSERS
PUGGINGS	PULAO	PULMOTORS	PULSES
PUGGISH	PULAOS	PULP	PULSIDGE
PUGGLE	PULAS	PULPAL	PULSIDGES
PUGGLED	PULDRON	PULPALLY	PULSIFIC
PUGGLES	PULDRONS	PULPBOARD	PULSING
PUGGLING	PULE	PULPED	PULSION
PUGGREE	PULED	PULPER	PULSIONS
PUGGREES	PULER	PULPERS	PULSOJET
PUGGRIES	PULERS	PULPIER	PULSOJETS
PUGGRY	PULES	PULPIEST	PULTAN
PUGGY	PULI	PULPIFIED	PULTANS
PUGH	PULICENE	PULPIFIES	PULTON
PUGIL	PULICIDE	PULPIFY	PULTONS
PUGILISM	PULICIDES	PULPILY	PULTOON
PUGILISMS	PULIER	PULPINESS	PULTOONS
PUGILIST	PULIEST	PULPING	PULTUN
PUGILISTS	PULIK	PULPIT	PULTUNS
PUGILS	PULING	PULPITAL	PULTURE
PUGMARK	PULINGLY	PULPITED	PULTURES
PUGMARKS	PULINGS	PULPITEER	PULU
PUGNACITY	PULIS	PULPITER	PULUS
PUGREE	PULK	PULPITERS	PULVER
PUGREES	PULKA	PULPITRY	PULVERED
PUGS	PULKAS	PULPITS	PULVERINE
PUH	PULKHA	PULPITUM	PULVERING
PUHA	PULKHAS	PULPITUMS	PULVERISE
PUHAS	PULKS	PULPLESS	PULVERIZE
PUIR	PULL	PULPMILL	PULVEROUS
PUIRER	PULLBACK	PULPMILLS	PULVERS
PUIREST	PULLBACKS	PULPOUS	PULVIL
PUIRTITH	PULLED	PULPS	PULVILIO
PUIRTITHS	PULLER	PULPSTONE	PULVILIOS
PUISNE	PULLERS	PULPWOOD	PULVILLAR
PUISNES	PULLET	PULPWOODS	PULVILLE
PUISNY	PULLETS	PULPY	PULVILLED
PUISSANCE	PULLEY	PULQUE	PULVILLES
PUISSANT	PULLEYS	PULQUES	PULVILLIO
PUISSAUNT	PULLI	PULS	PULVILLIO
PUJA	PULLING	PULSANT	PULVILLUS
PUJAH	PULLMAN	PULSAR	PULVILS
PUJAHS	PULLMANS	PULSARS	PULVINAR
PUJAS	PULLORUM	PULSATE	PULVINARS

PULVINATE
PULVINI
PULVINULE
PULVINUS
PULWAR
PULWARS
PULY
PUMA
PUMAS
PUMELO
PUMELOS
PUMICATE
PUMICATED
PUMICATES
PUMICE
PUMICED
PUMICEOUS
PUMICER
PUMICERS
PUMICES
PUMICING
PUMICITE
PUMICITES
PUMIE
PUMIES
PUMMEL
PUMMELED
PUMMELING
PUMMELLED
PUMMELO
PUMMELOS
PUMMELS
PUMP
PUMPED
PUMPER
PUMPERS
PUMPHOOD
PUMPHOODS
PUMPING
PUMPION
PUMPIONS
PUMPKIN
PUMPKING
PUMPKINGS
PUMPKINS
PUMPLESS
PUMPLIKE
PUMPS
PUMY
PUN
PUNA
PUNALUA
PUNALUAN
PUNALUAS
PUNAS
PUNCE
PUNCED
PUNCES

PUNCH
PUNCHBAG
PUNCHBAGS
PUNCHBALL
PUNCHBOWL
PUNCHED
PUNCHEON
PUNCHEONS
PUNCHER
PUNCHERS
PUNCHES
PUNCHIER
PUNCHIEST
PUNCHILY
PUNCHING
PUNCHLESS
PUNCHY
PUNCING
PUNCTA
PUNCTATE
PUNCTATED
PUNCTATOR
PUNCTILIO
PUNCTO
PUNCTOS
PUNCTUAL
PUNCTUATE
PUNCTULE
PUNCTULES
PUNCTUM
PUNCTURE
PUNCTURED
PUNCTURER
PUNCTURES
PUNDIT
PUNDITIC
PUNDITRY
PUNDITS
PUNDONOR
PUNG
PUNGA
PUNGAS
PUNGENCE
PUNGENCES
PUNGENCY
PUNGENT
PUNGENTLY
PUNGLE
PUNGLED
PUNGLES
PUNGLING
PUNGS
PUNIER
PUNIEST
PUNILY
PUNINESS
PUNISH
PUNISHED

PUNISHER
PUNISHERS
PUNISHES
PUNISHING
PUNITION
PUNITIONS
PUNITIVE
PUNITORY
PUNJI
PUNJIS
PUNK
PUNKA
PUNKAH
PUNKAHS
PUNKAS
PUNKER
PUNKERS
PUNKEST
PUNKEY
PUNKEYS
PUNKIE
PUNKIER
PUNKIES
PUNKIEST
PUNKIN
PUNKINESS
PUNKINS
PUNKISH
PUNKS
PUNKY
PUNNED
PUNNER
PUNNERS
PUNNET
PUNNETS
PUNNIER
PUNNIEST
PUNNING
PUNNINGLY
PUNNINGS
PUNNY
PUNS
PUNSTER
PUNSTERS
PUNT
PUNTED
PUNTEE
PUNTEES
PUNTER
PUNTERS
PUNTIES
PUNTING
PUNTO
PUNTOS
PUNTS
PUNTSMAN
PUNTSMEN
PUNTY

PUNY
PUP
PUPA
PUPAE
PUPAL
PUPARIA
PUPARIAL
PUPARIUM
PUPAS
PUPATE
PUPATED
PUPATES
PUPATING
PUPATION
PUPATIONS
PUPFISH
PUPFISHES
PUPIL
PUPILAGE
PUPILAGES
PUPILAR
PUPILARY
PUPILLAGE
PUPILLAR
PUPILLARY
PUPILLATE
PUPILS
PUPILSHIP
PUPPED
PUPPET
PUPPETEER
PUPPETRY
PUPPETS
PUPPIED
PUPPIES
PUPPING
PUPPODUM
PUPPODUMS
PUPPY
PUPPYDOM
PUPPYDOMS
PUPPYHOOD
PUPPYING
PUPPYISH
PUPPYISM
PUPPYISMS
PUPPYLIKE
PUPS
PUPU
PUPUNHA
PUPUNHAS
PUPUS
PUR
PURANA
PURANAS
PURANIC
PURBLIND
PURCHASE

PURCHASED	PURIS	PURPURIC	PURVEYOR
PURCHASER	PURISM	PURPURIN	PURVEYORS
PURCHASES	PURISMS	PURPURINS	PURVEYS
PURDA	PURIST	PURPY	PURVIEW
PURDAH	PURISTIC	PURR	PURVIEWS
PURDAHED	PURISTS	PURRED	PUS
PURDAHS	PURITAN	PURRING	PUSES
PURDAS	PURITANIC	PURRINGLY	PUSH
PURDONIUM	PURITANS	PURRINGS	PUSHBALL
PURE	PURITIES	PURRS	PUSHBALLS
PUREBLOOD	PURITY	PURS	PUSHCART
PUREBRED	PURL	PURSE	PUSHCARTS
PUREBREDS	PURLED	PURSED	PUSHCHAIR
PURED	PURLER	PURSEFUL	PUSHDOWN
PUREE	PURLERS	PURSEFULS	PUSHDOWNS
PUREED	PURLICUE	PURSELIKE	PUSHED
PUREEING	PURLICUED	PURSER	PUSHER
PUREES	PURLICUES	PURSERS	PUSHERS
PURELY	PURLIEU	PURSES	PUSHES
PURENESS	PURLIEUS	PURSEW	PUSHFUL
PURER	PURLIN	PURSEWED	PUSHFULLY
PURES	PURLINE	PURSEWING	PUSHIER
PUREST	PURLINES	PURSEWS	PUSHIEST
PURFLE	PURLING	PURSIER	PUSHILY
PURFLED	PURLINGS	PURSIEST	PUSHINESS
PURFLER	PURLINS	PURSILY	PUSHING
PURFLERS	PURLOIN	PURSINESS	PUSHINGLY
PURFLES	PURLOINED	PURSING	PUSHOVER
PURFLING	PURLOINER	PURSLAIN	PUSHOVERS
PURFLINGS	PURLOINS	PURSLAINS	PUSHPIN
PURFLY	PURLS	PURSLANE	PUSHPINS
PURGATION	PUROMYCIN	PURSLANES	PUSHROD
PURGATIVE	PURPIE	PURSUABLE	PUSHRODS
PURGATORY	PURPIES	PURSUAL	PUSHUP
PURGE	PURPLE	PURSUALS	PUSHUPS
PURGEABLE	PURPLED	PURSUANCE	PUSHY
PURGED	PURPLER	PURSUANT	PUSLE
PURGER	PURPLES	PURSUE	PUSLED
PURGERS	PURPLEST	PURSUED	PUSLES
PURGES	PURPLIER	PURSUER	PUSLEY
PURGING	PURPLIEST	PURSUERS	PUSLEYS
PURGINGS	PURPLING	PURSUES	PUSLIKE
PURI	PURPLISH	PURSUING	PUSLING
PURIFIED	PURPLY	PURSUINGS	PUSS
PURIFIER	PURPORT	PURSUIT	PUSSEL
PURIFIERS	PURPORTED	PURSUITS	PUSSELS
PURIFIES	PURPORTS	PURSY	PUSSER
PURIFY	PURPOSE	PURTIER	PUSSERS
PURIFYING	PURPOSED	PURTIEST	PUSSES
PURIM	PURPOSELY	PURTRAID	PUSSIER
PURIMS	PURPOSES	PURTRAYD	PUSSIES
PURIN	PURPOSING	PURTY	PUSSIEST
PURINE	PURPOSIVE	PURULENCE	PUSSLEY
PURINES	PURPURA	PURULENCY	PUSSLEYS
PURING	PURPURAS	PURULENT	PUSSLIES
PURINS	PURPURE	PURVEY	PUSSLIKE
PURIRI	PURPUREAL	PURVEYED	PUSSLY
PURIRIS	PURPURES	PURVEYING	PUSSY

PUSSYCAT
PUSSYCATS
PUSSYFOOT
PUSSYTOES
PUSTULANT
PUSTULAR
PUSTULATE
PUSTULE
PUSTULED
PUSTULES
PUSTULOUS
PUT
PUTAMEN
PUTAMINA
PUTATIVE
PUTCHEON
PUTCHEONS
PUTCHER
PUTCHERS
PUTCHOCK
PUTCHOCKS
PUTCHUK
PUTCHUKS
PUTDOWN
PUTDOWNS
PUTEAL
PUTEALS
PUTELI
PUTELIS
PUTID
PUTLOCK
PUTLOCKS
PUTLOG
PUTLOGS
PUTOFF
PUTOFFS
PUTOIS
PUTON
PUTONGHUA
PUTONS
PUTOUT
PUTOUTS
PUTREFIED
PUTREFIER
PUTREFIES
PUTREFY
PUTRID
PUTRIDER
PUTRIDEST
PUTRIDITY
PUTRIDLY
PUTS
PUTSCH
PUTSCHES
PUTSCHIST
PUTT
PUTTED
PUTTEE

PUTTEES
PUTTEN
PUTTER
PUTTERED
PUTTERER
PUTTERERS
PUTTERING
PUTTERS
PUTTI
PUTTIE
PUTTIED
PUTTIER
PUTTIERS
PUTTIES
PUTTING
PUTTINGS
PUTTO
PUTTOCK
PUTTOCKS
PUTTS
PUTTY
PUTTYING
PUTTYLESS
PUTTYLIKE
PUTTYROOT
PUTURE
PUTURES
PUTZ
PUTZED
PUTZES
PUTZING
PUY
PUYS
PUZEL
PUZELS
PUZZEL
PUZZELS
PUZZLE
PUZZLED
PUZZLEDLY
PUZZLEDOM
PUZZLER
PUZZLERS
PUZZLES
PUZZLING
PUZZOLANA
PYA
PYAEMIA
PYAEMIAS
PYAEMIC
PYAS
PYAT
PYATS
PYCNIC
PYCNIDIA
PYCNIDIAL
PYCNIDIUM
PYCNITE

PYCNITES
PYCNON
PYCNONS
PYCNOSES
PYCNOSIS
PYCNOTIC
PYE
PYEBALD
PYEBALDS
PYEING
PYELITIC
PYELITIS
PYELOGRAM
PYEMIA
PYEMIAS
PYEMIC
PYENGADU
PYENGADUS
PYES
PYET
PYETS
PYGAL
PYGALS
PYGARG
PYGARGS
PYGIDIA
PYGIDIAL
PYGIDIUM
PYGIDIUMS
PYGMAEAN
PYGMEAN
PYGMIES
PYGMOID
PYGMY
PYGMYISH
PYGMYISM
PYGMYISMS
PYGOSTYLE
PYIC
PYIN
PYINKADO
PYINKADOS
PYINS
PYJAMA
PYJAMAED
PYJAMAS
PYKNIC
PYKNICS
PYKNOSES
PYKNOSIS
PYKNOSOME
PYKNOTIC
PYLON
PYLONS
PYLORI
PYLORIC
PYLORUS
PYLORUSES

PYNE
PYNED
PYNES
PYNING
PYODERMA
PYODERMAS
PYODERMIC
PYOGENIC
PYOID
PYONER
PYONERS
PYONINGS
PYORRHEA
PYORRHEAL
PYORRHEAS
PYORRHEIC
PYORRHOEA
PYOSES
PYOSIS
PYOT
PYOTS
PYRACANTH
PYRAL
PYRALID
PYRALIDID
PYRALIDS
PYRALIS
PYRALISES
PYRAMID
PYRAMIDAL
PYRAMIDED
PYRAMIDES
PYRAMIDIA
PYRAMIDIC
PYRAMIDON
PYRAMIDS
PYRAMIS
PYRAMISES
PYRAN
PYRANOID
PYRANOSE
PYRANOSES
PYRANS
PYRAZOLE
PYRAZOLES
PYRE
PYRENE
PYRENEITE
PYRENES
PYRENOID
PYRENOIDS
PYRES
PYRETHRIN
PYRETHRUM
PYRETIC
PYREX
PYREXES
PYREXIA

PYREXIAL

PYREXIAL
PYREXIAS
PYREXIC
PYRIC
PYRIDIC
PYRIDINE
PYRIDINES
PYRIDOXAL
PYRIDOXIN
PYRIFORM
PYRITE
PYRITES
PYRITIC
PYRITICAL
PYRITISE
PYRITISED
PYRITISES
PYRITIZE
PYRITIZED
PYRITIZES
PYRITOUS
PYRO
PYROCERAM
PYROCLAST
PYROGEN
PYROGENIC
PYROGENS
PYROLA
PYROLAS
PYROLATER
PYROLATRY
PYROLISE
PYROLISED
PYROLISES
PYROLIZE
PYROLIZED
PYROLIZES
PYROLOGY
PYROLYSE
PYROLYSED
PYROLYSER
PYROLYSES
PYROLYSIS
PYROLYTIC
PYROLYZE
PYROLYZED
PYROLYZER
PYROLYZES
PYROMANCY
PYROMANIA
PYROMETER
PYROMETRY
PYRONE
PYRONES
PYRONINE
PYRONINES
PYROPE
PYROPES

PYROPHONE
PYROPUS
PYROPUSES
PYROS
PYROSCOPE
PYROSES
PYROSIS
PYROSISES
PYROSOME
PYROSOMES
PYROSTAT
PYROSTATS
PYROXENE
PYROXENES
PYROXENIC
PYROXYLE
PYROXYLES
PYROXYLIC
PYROXYLIN
PYRRHIC
PYRRHICS
PYRRHOUS
PYRROL
PYRROLE
PYRROLES
PYRROLIC
PYRROLS
PYRUVATE
PYRUVATES
PYRUVIC
PYTHIUM
PYTHIUMS
PYTHON
PYTHONESS
PYTHONIC
PYTHONS
PYURIA
PYURIAS
PYX
PYXED
PYXES
PYXIDES
PYXIDIA
PYXIDIUM
PYXIE
PYXIES
PYXING
PYXIS
PZAZZ
PZAZZES

Q

QABALA
QABALAH
QABALAHS
QABALAS
QABALISM
QABALISMS
QABALIST
QABALISTS
QADI
QADIS
QAID
QAIDS
QAIMAQAM
QAIMAQAMS
QALAMDAN
QALAMDANS
QANAT
QANATS
QASIDA
QASIDAS
QAT
QATS
QAWWAL
QAWWALI
QAWWALIS
QAWWALS
QI
QIBLA
QIBLAS
QIGONG
QIGONGS
QINDAR
QINDARKA
QINDARS
QINGHAOSU
QINTAR
QINTARS
QIS
QIVIUT
QIVIUTS
QOPH
QOPHS
QORMA
QORMAS
QUA
QUAALUDE
QUAALUDES
QUACK
QUACKED
QUACKER
QUACKERS
QUACKERY
QUACKIER

QUACKIEST
QUACKING
QUACKISH
QUACKISM
QUACKISMS
QUACKLE
QUACKLED
QUACKLES
QUACKLING
QUACKS
QUACKY
QUAD
QUADDED
QUADDING
QUADPLEX
QUADRANS
QUADRANT
QUADRANTS
QUADRAT
QUADRATE
QUADRATED
QUADRATES
QUADRATIC
QUADRATS
QUADRATUS
QUADRELLA
QUADRIC
QUADRICEP
QUADRICS
QUADRIFID
QUADRIGA
QUADRIGAE
QUADRIGAS
QUADRILLE
QUADRIVIA
QUADROON
QUADROONS
QUADRUMAN
QUADRUPED
QUADRUPLE
QUADRUPLY
QUADS
QUAERE
QUAERED
QUAEREING
QUAERES
QUAERITUR
QUAESITUM
QUAESTOR
QUAESTORS
QUAFF
QUAFFABLE
QUAFFED

QUAFFER
QUAFFERS
QUAFFING
QUAFFS
QUAG
QUAGGA
QUAGGAS
QUAGGIER
QUAGGIEST
QUAGGY
QUAGMIRE
QUAGMIRED
QUAGMIRES
QUAGMIRY
QUAGS
QUAHAUG
QUAHAUGS
QUAHOG
QUAHOGS
QUAI
QUAICH
QUAICHES
QUAICHS
QUAIGH
QUAIGHS
QUAIL
QUAILED
QUAILING
QUAILINGS
QUAILS
QUAINT
QUAINTER
QUAINTEST
QUAINTLY
QUAIR
QUAIRS
QUAIS
QUAKE
QUAKED
QUAKER
QUAKERS
QUAKES
QUAKIER
QUAKIEST
QUAKILY
QUAKINESS
QUAKING
QUAKINGLY
QUAKINGS
QUAKY
QUALE
QUALIA
QUALIFIED

QUALIFIER
QUALIFIES
QUALIFY
QUALITIED
QUALITIES
QUALITY
QUALM
QUALMIER
QUALMIEST
QUALMING
QUALMISH
QUALMLESS
QUALMS
QUALMY
QUAMASH
QUAMASHES
QUANDANG
QUANDANGS
QUANDARY
QUANDONG
QUANDONGS
QUANGO
QUANGOS
QUANNET
QUANNETS
QUANT
QUANTA
QUANTAL
QUANTALLY
QUANTED
QUANTIC
QUANTICAL
QUANTICS
QUANTIFY
QUANTILE
QUANTILES
QUANTING
QUANTISE
QUANTISED
QUANTISER
QUANTISES
QUANTITY
QUANTIZE
QUANTIZED
QUANTIZER
QUANTIZES
QUANTONG
QUANTONGS
QUANTS
QUANTUM
QUARE
QUARENDEN
QUARENDER

QUARER
QUAREST
QUARK
QUARKS
QUARREL
QUARRELED
QUARRELER
QUARRELS
QUARRIAN
QUARRIANS
QUARRIED
QUARRIER
QUARRIERS
QUARRIES
QUARRION
QUARRIONS
QUARRY
QUARRYING
QUARRYMAN
QUARRYMEN
QUART
QUARTAN
QUARTANS
QUARTE
QUARTER
QUARTERED
QUARTERER
QUARTERLY
QUARTERN
QUARTERNS
QUARTERS
QUARTES
QUARTET
QUARTETS
QUARTETT
QUARTETTE
QUARTETTI
QUARTETTO
QUARTETTS
QUARTIC
QUARTICS
QUARTIER
QUARTIERS
QUARTILE
QUARTILES
QUARTO
QUARTOS
QUARTS
QUARTZ
QUARTZES
QUARTZIER
QUARTZITE
QUARTZOSE
QUARTZOUS
QUARTZY
QUASAR
QUASARS
QUASH

QUASHED
QUASHEE
QUASHEES
QUASHER
QUASHERS
QUASHES
QUASHIE
QUASHIES
QUASHING
QUASI
QUASS
QUASSES
QUASSIA
QUASSIAS
QUASSIN
QUASSINS
QUAT
QUATCH
QUATCHED
QUATCHES
QUATCHING
QUATE
QUATORZE
QUATORZES
QUATRAIN
QUATRAINS
QUATRE
QUATRES
QUATS
QUAVER
QUAVERED
QUAVERER
QUAVERERS
QUAVERIER
QUAVERING
QUAVERS
QUAVERY
QUAY
QUAYAGE
QUAYAGES
QUAYD
QUAYLIKE
QUAYS
QUAYSIDE
QUAYSIDES
QUAZZIER
QUAZZIEST
QUAZZY
QUBIT
QUBITS
QUBYTE
QUBYTES
QUEACH
QUEACHES
QUEACHIER
QUEACHY
QUEAN
QUEANS

QUEASIER
QUEASIEST
QUEASILY
QUEASY
QUEAZIER
QUEAZIEST
QUEAZY
QUEBRACHO
QUEECHIER
QUEECHY
QUEEN
QUEENCAKE
QUEENDOM
QUEENDOMS
QUEENED
QUEENHOOD
QUEENIE
QUEENIER
QUEENIES
QUEENIEST
QUEENING
QUEENINGS
QUEENITE
QUEENITES
QUEENLESS
QUEENLET
QUEENLETS
QUEENLIER
QUEENLY
QUEENS
QUEENSHIP
QUEENSIDE
QUEENY
QUEER
QUEERCORE
QUEERDOM
QUEERDOMS
QUEERED
QUEERER
QUEEREST
QUEERING
QUEERISH
QUEERITY
QUEERLY
QUEERNESS
QUEERS
QUEEST
QUEESTS
QUEINT
QUELCH
QUELCHED
QUELCHES
QUELCHING
QUELEA
QUELEAS
QUELL
QUELLABLE
QUELLED

QUELLER
QUELLERS
QUELLING
QUELLS
QUEME
QUEMED
QUEMES
QUEMING
QUENA
QUENAS
QUENCH
QUENCHED
QUENCHER
QUENCHERS
QUENCHES
QUENCHING
QUENELLE
QUENELLES
QUEP
QUERCETIC
QUERCETIN
QUERCETUM
QUERCINE
QUERCITIN
QUERIDA
QUERIDAS
QUERIED
QUERIER
QUERIERS
QUERIES
QUERIMONY
QUERIST
QUERISTS
QUERN
QUERNS
QUERULOUS
QUERY
QUERYING
QUERYINGS
QUEST
QUESTANT
QUESTANTS
QUESTED
QUESTER
QUESTERS
QUESTING
QUESTINGS
QUESTION
QUESTIONS
QUESTOR
QUESTORS
QUESTRIST
QUESTS
QUETCH
QUETCHED
QUETCHES
QUETCHING
QUETHE

QUETHES
QUETHING
QUETSCH
QUETSCHES
QUETZAL
QUETZALES
QUETZALS
QUEUE
QUEUED
QUEUEING
QUEUEINGS
QUEUER
QUEUERS
QUEUES
QUEUING
QUEUINGS
QUEY
QUEYN
QUEYNIE
QUEYNIES
QUEYNS
QUEYS
QUEZAL
QUEZALES
QUEZALS
QUIBBLE
QUIBBLED
QUIBBLER
QUIBBLERS
QUIBBLES
QUIBBLING
QUIBLIN
QUIBLINS
QUICH
QUICHE
QUICHED
QUICHES
QUICHING
QUICK
QUICKBEAM
QUICKEN
QUICKENED
QUICKENER
QUICKENS
QUICKER
QUICKEST
QUICKIE
QUICKIES
QUICKLIME
QUICKLY
QUICKNESS
QUICKS
QUICKSAND
QUICKSET
QUICKSETS
QUICKSTEP
QUID
QUIDAM

QUIDAMS
QUIDDANY
QUIDDIT
QUIDDITCH
QUIDDITS
QUIDDITY
QUIDDLE
QUIDDLED
QUIDDLER
QUIDDLERS
QUIDDLES
QUIDDLING
QUIDNUNC
QUIDNUNCS
QUIDS
QUIESCE
QUIESCED
QUIESCENT
QUIESCES
QUIESCING
QUIET
QUIETED
QUIETEN
QUIETENED
QUIETENER
QUIETENS
QUIETER
QUIETERS
QUIETEST
QUIETING
QUIETINGS
QUIETISM
QUIETISMS
QUIETIST
QUIETISTS
QUIETIVE
QUIETIVES
QUIETLY
QUIETNESS
QUIETS
QUIETSOME
QUIETUDE
QUIETUDES
QUIETUS
QUIETUSES
QUIFF
QUIFFS
QUIGHT
QUIGHTED
QUIGHTING
QUIGHTS
QUILL
QUILLAI
QUILLAIA
QUILLAIAS
QUILLAIS
QUILLAJA
QUILLAJAS

QUILLBACK
QUILLED
QUILLET
QUILLETS
QUILLING
QUILLINGS
QUILLMAN
QUILLMEN
QUILLON
QUILLONS
QUILLS
QUILLWORK
QUILLWORT
QUILT
QUILTED
QUILTER
QUILTERS
QUILTING
QUILTINGS
QUILTS
QUIM
QUIMS
QUIN
QUINA
QUINARIES
QUINARY
QUINAS
QUINATE
QUINCE
QUINCES
QUINCHE
QUINCHED
QUINCHES
QUINCHING
QUINCUNX
QUINE
QUINELA
QUINELAS
QUINELLA
QUINELLAS
QUINES
QUINIC
QUINIDINE
QUINIE
QUINIELA
QUINIELAS
QUINIES
QUININ
QUININA
QUININAS
QUININE
QUININES
QUININS
QUINNAT
QUINNATS
QUINO
QUINOA
QUINOAS

QUINOID
QUINOIDAL
QUINOIDS
QUINOL
QUINOLIN
QUINOLINE
QUINOLINS
QUINOLONE
QUINOLS
QUINONE
QUINONES
QUINONOID
QUINOS
QUINQUINA
QUINS
QUINSIED
QUINSIES
QUINSY
QUINT
QUINTA
QUINTAIN
QUINTAINS
QUINTAL
QUINTALS
QUINTAN
QUINTANS
QUINTAR
QUINTARS
QUINTAS
QUINTE
QUINTES
QUINTET
QUINTETS
QUINTETT
QUINTETTE
QUINTETTI
QUINTETTO
QUINTETTS
QUINTIC
QUINTICS
QUINTILE
QUINTILES
QUINTIN
QUINTINS
QUINTROON
QUINTS
QUINTUPLE
QUINTUPLY
QUINZE
QUINZES
QUIP
QUIPO
QUIPOS
QUIPPED
QUIPPER
QUIPPERS
QUIPPIER
QUIPPIEST

QUIPPING
QUIPPISH
QUIPPU
QUIPPUS
QUIPPY
QUIPS
QUIPSTER
QUIPSTERS
QUIPU
QUIPUS
QUIRE
QUIRED
QUIRES
QUIRING
QUIRISTER
QUIRK
QUIRKED
QUIRKIER
QUIRKIEST
QUIRKILY
QUIRKING
QUIRKISH
QUIRKS
QUIRKY
QUIRT
QUIRTED
QUIRTING
QUIRTS
QUISLING
QUISLINGS
QUIST
QUISTS
QUIT
QUITCH
QUITCHED
QUITCHES
QUITCHING
QUITCLAIM
QUITE
QUITED
QUITES
QUITING
QUITRENT
QUITRENTS
QUITS
QUITTAL
QUITTALS
QUITTANCE
QUITTED
QUITTER
QUITTERS
QUITTING
QUITTOR
QUITTORS
QUIVER
QUIVERED
QUIVERER
QUIVERERS

QUIVERFUL
QUIVERIER
QUIVERING
QUIVERISH
QUIVERS
QUIVERY
QUIXOTE
QUIXOTES
QUIXOTIC
QUIXOTISM
QUIXOTRY
QUIZ
QUIZZED
QUIZZER
QUIZZERS
QUIZZERY
QUIZZES
QUIZZICAL
QUIZZIFY
QUIZZING
QUIZZINGS
QUOAD
QUOD
QUODDED
QUODDING
QUODLIBET
QUODLIN
QUODLINS
QUODS
QUOHOG
QUOHOGS
QUOIF
QUOIFED
QUOIFING
QUOIFS
QUOIN
QUOINED
QUOINING
QUOINS
QUOIST
QUOISTS
QUOIT
QUOITED
QUOITER
QUOITERS
QUOITING
QUOITS
QUOKKA
QUOKKAS
QUOLL
QUOLLS
QUOMODO
QUOMODOS
QUONDAM
QUONK
QUONKED
QUONKING
QUONKS

QUOOKE
QUOP
QUOPPED
QUOPPING
QUOPS
QUORATE
QUORUM
QUORUMS
QUOTA
QUOTABLE
QUOTABLY
QUOTAS
QUOTATION
QUOTATIVE
QUOTE
QUOTED
QUOTER
QUOTERS
QUOTES
QUOTH
QUOTHA
QUOTIDIAN
QUOTIENT
QUOTIENTS
QUOTING
QUOTITION
QUOTUM
QUOTUMS
QURSH
QURSHES
QURUSH
QURUSHES
QUYTE
QUYTED
QUYTES
QUYTING
QWERTIES
QWERTY
QWERTYS

R

RABANNA
RABANNAS
RABAT
RABATINE
RABATINES
RABATMENT
RABATO
RABATOES
RABATOS
RABATS
RABATTE
RABATTED
RABATTES
RABATTING
RABBET
RABBETED
RABBETING
RABBETS
RABBI
RABBIES
RABBIN
RABBINATE
RABBINIC
RABBINICS
RABBINISM
RABBINIST
RABBINITE
RABBINS
RABBIS
RABBIT
RABBITED
RABBITER
RABBITERS
RABBITING
RABBITO
RABBITOH
RABBITOHS
RABBITOS
RABBITRY
RABBITS
RABBITY
RABBLE
RABBLED
RABBLER
RABBLERS
RABBLES
RABBLING
RABBLINGS
RABBONI
RABBONIS
RABI
RABIC
RABID

RABIDER
RABIDEST
RABIDITY
RABIDLY
RABIDNESS
RABIES
RABIETIC
RABIS
RACA
RACAHOUT
RACAHOUTS
RACCAHOUT
RACCOON
RACCOONS
RACE
RACECARD
RACECARDS
RACED
RACEGOER
RACEGOERS
RACEGOING
RACEHORSE
RACEMATE
RACEMATES
RACEME
RACEMED
RACEMES
RACEMIC
RACEMISE
RACEMISED
RACEMISES
RACEMISM
RACEMISMS
RACEMIZE
RACEMIZED
RACEMIZES
RACEMOID
RACEMOSE
RACEMOUS
RACEPATH
RACEPATHS
RACER
RACERS
RACES
RACETRACK
RACEWALK
RACEWALKS
RACEWAY
RACEWAYS
RACH
RACHE
RACHES
RACHET

RACHETED
RACHETING
RACHETS
RACHIAL
RACHIDES
RACHIDIAL
RACHIDIAN
RACHILLA
RACHILLAE
RACHILLAS
RACHIS
RACHISES
RACHITIC
RACHITIS
RACIAL
RACIALISE
RACIALISM
RACIALIST
RACIALIZE
RACIALLY
RACIATION
RACIER
RACIEST
RACILY
RACINESS
RACING
RACINGS
RACISM
RACISMS
RACIST
RACISTS
RACK
RACKED
RACKER
RACKERS
RACKET
RACKETED
RACKETEER
RACKETER
RACKETERS
RACKETIER
RACKETING
RACKETRY
RACKETS
RACKETT
RACKETTS
RACKETY
RACKFUL
RACKFULS
RACKING
RACKINGLY
RACKINGS
RACKLE

RACKS
RACKWORK
RACKWORKS
RACLETTE
RACLETTES
RACLOIR
RACLOIRS
RACON
RACONS
RACONTEUR
RACOON
RACOONS
RACQUET
RACQUETED
RACQUETS
RACY
RAD
RADAR
RADARS
RADDED
RADDER
RADDEST
RADDING
RADDLE
RADDLED
RADDLEMAN
RADDLEMEN
RADDLES
RADDLING
RADDOCKE
RADDOCKES
RADE
RADGE
RADGER
RADGES
RADGEST
RADIABLE
RADIAL
RADIALE
RADIALIA
RADIALISE
RADIALITY
RADIALIZE
RADIALLY
RADIALS
RADIAN
RADIANCE
RADIANCES
RADIANCY
RADIANS
RADIANT
RADIANTLY
RADIANTS

RADIATA	RADULAS	RAGGEDY	RAGWORT
RADIATAS	RADULATE	RAGGEE	RAGWORTS
RADIATE	RADWASTE	RAGGEES	RAH
RADIATED	RADWASTES	RAGGERIES	RAHED
RADIATELY	RAFALE	RAGGERY	RAHING
RADIATES	RAFALES	RAGGIER	RAHS
RADIATING	RAFF	RAGGIES	RAHUI
RADIATION	RAFFIA	RAGGIEST	RAHUIS
RADIATIVE	RAFFIAS	RAGGING	RAI
RADIATOR	RAFFINATE	RAGGINGS	RAIA
RADIATORS	RAFFINOSE	RAGGLE	RAIAS
RADIATORY	RAFFISH	RAGGLED	RAID
RADICAL	RAFFISHLY	RAGGLES	RAIDED
RADICALLY	RAFFLE	RAGGLING	RAIDER
RADICALS	RAFFLED	RAGGS	RAIDERS
RADICAND	RAFFLER	RAGGY	RAIDING
RADICANDS	RAFFLERS	RAGHEAD	RAIDINGS
RADICANT	RAFFLES	RAGHEADS	RAIDS
RADICATE	RAFFLESIA	RAGI	RAIK
RADICATED	RAFFLING	RAGING	RAIKED
RADICATES	RAFFS	RAGINGLY	RAIKING
RADICCHIO	RAFT	RAGINGS	RAIKS
RADICEL	RAFTED	RAGINI	RAIL
RADICELS	RAFTER	RAGINIS	RAILBED
RADICES	RAFTERED	RAGIS	RAILBEDS
RADICLE	RAFTERING	RAGLAN	RAILBIRD
RADICLES	RAFTERS	RAGLANS	RAILBIRDS
RADICULAR	RAFTING	RAGMAN	RAILBUS
RADICULE	RAFTINGS	RAGMANS	RAILBUSES
RADICULES	RAFTMAN	RAGMEN	RAILCAR
RADII	RAFTMEN	RAGMENT	RAILCARD
RADIO	RAFTS	RAGMENTS	RAILCARDS
RADIOED	RAFTSMAN	RAGOUT	RAILCARS
RADIOGOLD	RAFTSMEN	RAGOUTED	RAILE
RADIOGRAM	RAG	RAGOUTING	RAILED
RADIOING	RAGA	RAGOUTS	RAILER
RADIOLOGY	RAGAS	RAGPICKER	RAILERS
RADIOMAN	RAGBAG	RAGS	RAILES
RADIOMEN	RAGBAGS	RAGSTONE	RAILHEAD
RADIONICS	RAGBOLT	RAGSTONES	RAILHEADS
RADIOS	RAGBOLTS	RAGTAG	RAILING
RADIOTHON	RAGDE	RAGTAGS	RAILINGLY
RADISH	RAGE	RAGTIME	RAILINGS
RADISHES	RAGED	RAGTIMER	RAILLERY
RADIUM	RAGEE	RAGTIMERS	RAILLESS
RADIUMS	RAGEES	RAGTIMES	RAILLIES
RADIUS	RAGEFUL	RAGTOP	RAILLY
RADIUSES	RAGER	RAGTOPS	RAILMAN
RADIX	RAGERS	RAGULED	RAILMEN
RADIXES	RAGES	RAGULY	RAILROAD
RADOME	RAGG	RAGWEED	RAILROADS
RADOMES	RAGGA	RAGWEEDS	RAILS
RADON	RAGGAS	RAGWHEEL	RAILWAY
RADONS	RAGGED	RAGWHEELS	RAILWAYS
RADS	RAGGEDER	RAGWORK	RAILWOMAN
RADULA	RAGGEDEST	RAGWORKS	RAILWOMEN
RADULAE	RAGGEDIER	RAGWORM	RAIMENT
RADULAR	RAGGEDLY	RAGWORMS	RAIMENTS

RAIN
RAINBAND
RAINBANDS
RAINBIRD
RAINBIRDS
RAINBOW
RAINBOWED
RAINBOWS
RAINBOWY
RAINCHECK
RAINCOAT
RAINCOATS
RAINDATE
RAINDATES
RAINDROP
RAINDROPS
RAINE
RAINED
RAINES
RAINFALL
RAINFALLS
RAINIER
RAINIEST
RAINILY
RAININESS
RAINING
RAINLESS
RAINMAKER
RAINOUT
RAINOUTS
RAINPROOF
RAINS
RAINSPOUT
RAINSTORM
RAINTIGHT
RAINWASH
RAINWATER
RAINWEAR
RAINWEARS
RAINY
RAIRD
RAIRDS
RAIS
RAISABLE
RAISE
RAISEABLE
RAISED
RAISER
RAISERS
RAISES
RAISIN
RAISING
RAISINGS
RAISINS
RAISINY
RAISONNE
RAIT
RAITA

RAITAS
RAITED
RAITING
RAITS
RAIYAT
RAIYATS
RAJ
RAJA
RAJAH
RAJAHS
RAJAHSHIP
RAJAS
RAJASHIP
RAJASHIPS
RAJES
RAKE
RAKED
RAKEE
RAKEES
RAKEHELL
RAKEHELLS
RAKEHELLY
RAKEOFF
RAKEOFFS
RAKER
RAKERIES
RAKERS
RAKERY
RAKES
RAKESHAME
RAKI
RAKING
RAKINGS
RAKIS
RAKISH
RAKISHLY
RAKSHAS
RAKSHASA
RAKSHASAS
RAKSHASES
RAKU
RAKUS
RALE
RALES
RALLIED
RALLIER
RALLIERS
RALLIES
RALLIFORM
RALLINE
RALLY
RALLYE
RALLYES
RALLYING
RALLYINGS
RALLYIST
RALLYISTS
RALPH

RALPHED
RALPHING
RALPHS
RAM
RAMADA
RAMADAS
RAMAKIN
RAMAKINS
RAMAL
RAMATE
RAMBLA
RAMBLAS
RAMBLE
RAMBLED
RAMBLER
RAMBLERS
RAMBLES
RAMBLING
RAMBLINGS
RAMBUTAN
RAMBUTANS
RAMCAT
RAMCATS
RAMEAL
RAMEE
RAMEES
RAMEKIN
RAMEKINS
RAMEN
RAMENS
RAMENTA
RAMENTUM
RAMEOUS
RAMEQUIN
RAMEQUINS
RAMET
RAMETS
RAMI
RAMIE
RAMIES
RAMIFIED
RAMIFIES
RAMIFORM
RAMIFY
RAMIFYING
RAMILIE
RAMILIES
RAMILLIE
RAMILLIES
RAMIN
RAMINS
RAMIS
RAMJET
RAMJETS
RAMMED
RAMMEL
RAMMELS
RAMMER

RAMMERS
RAMMIER
RAMMIES
RAMMIEST
RAMMING
RAMMISH
RAMMISHLY
RAMMLE
RAMMLES
RAMMY
RAMONA
RAMONAS
RAMOSE
RAMOSELY
RAMOSITY
RAMOUS
RAMOUSLY
RAMP
RAMPAGE
RAMPAGED
RAMPAGER
RAMPAGERS
RAMPAGES
RAMPAGING
RAMPANCY
RAMPANT
RAMPANTLY
RAMPART
RAMPARTED
RAMPARTS
RAMPAUGE
RAMPAUGED
RAMPAUGES
RAMPED
RAMPER
RAMPERS
RAMPICK
RAMPICKED
RAMPICKS
RAMPIKE
RAMPIKES
RAMPING
RAMPINGS
RAMPION
RAMPIONS
RAMPIRE
RAMPIRED
RAMPIRES
RAMPOLE
RAMPOLES
RAMPS
RAMPSMAN
RAMPSMEN
RAMROD
RAMRODDED
RAMRODS
RAMS
RAMSHORN

RAMSHORNS
RAMSON
RAMSONS
RAMSTAM
RAMTIL
RAMTILLA
RAMTILLAS
RAMTILS
RAMULAR
RAMULI
RAMULOSE
RAMULOUS
RAMULUS
RAMUS
RAN
RANA
RANARIAN
RANARIUM
RANARIUMS
RANAS
RANCE
RANCED
RANCEL
RANCELS
RANCES
RANCH
RANCHED
RANCHER
RANCHERIA
RANCHERIE
RANCHERO
RANCHEROS
RANCHERS
RANCHES
RANCHING
RANCHINGS
RANCHLESS
RANCHLIKE
RANCHMAN
RANCHMEN
RANCHO
RANCHOS
RANCID
RANCIDER
RANCIDEST
RANCIDITY
RANCIDLY
RANCING
RANCOR
RANCORED
RANCOROUS
RANCORS
RANCOUR
RANCOURED
RANCOURS
RAND
RANDAN
RANDANS

RANDED
RANDEM
RANDEMS
RANDIE
RANDIER
RANDIES
RANDIEST
RANDILY
RANDINESS
RANDING
RANDLORD
RANDLORDS
RANDOM
RANDOMISE
RANDOMIZE
RANDOMLY
RANDOMS
RANDON
RANDONS
RANDS
RANDY
RANEE
RANEES
RANG
RANGATIRA
RANGE
RANGED
RANGELAND
RANGER
RANGERS
RANGES
RANGI
RANGIER
RANGIEST
RANGILY
RANGINESS
RANGING
RANGINGS
RANGIORA
RANGIORAS
RANGIS
RANGOLI
RANGOLIS
RANGY
RANI
RANID
RANIDS
RANIFORM
RANINE
RANIS
RANK
RANKE
RANKED
RANKER
RANKERS
RANKES
RANKEST
RANKING

RANKINGS
RANKISH
RANKISM
RANKISMS
RANKLE
RANKLED
RANKLES
RANKLESS
RANKLING
RANKLY
RANKNESS
RANKS
RANKSHIFT
RANPIKE
RANPIKES
RANSACK
RANSACKED
RANSACKER
RANSACKS
RANSEL
RANSELS
RANSHAKLE
RANSOM
RANSOMED
RANSOMER
RANSOMERS
RANSOMING
RANSOMS
RANT
RANTED
RANTER
RANTERISM
RANTERS
RANTING
RANTINGLY
RANTINGS
RANTIPOLE
RANTS
RANULA
RANULAR
RANULAS
RANUNCULI
RANZEL
RANZELMAN
RANZELMEN
RANZELS
RAOULIA
RAOULIAS
RAP
RAPACIOUS
RAPACITY
RAPE
RAPED
RAPER
RAPERS
RAPES
RAPESEED
RAPESEEDS

RAPHAE
RAPHANIA
RAPHANIAS
RAPHE
RAPHES
RAPHIA
RAPHIAS
RAPHIDE
RAPHIDES
RAPHIS
RAPID
RAPIDER
RAPIDEST
RAPIDITY
RAPIDLY
RAPIDNESS
RAPIDS
RAPIER
RAPIERED
RAPIERS
RAPINE
RAPINES
RAPING
RAPINI
RAPIST
RAPISTS
RAPLOCH
RAPLOCHS
RAPPAREE
RAPPAREES
RAPPE
RAPPED
RAPPEE
RAPPEES
RAPPEL
RAPPELED
RAPPELING
RAPPELLED
RAPPELS
RAPPEN
RAPPER
RAPPERS
RAPPES
RAPPING
RAPPINGS
RAPPINI
RAPPORT
RAPPORTS
RAPS
RAPT
RAPTLY
RAPTNESS
RAPTOR
RAPTORIAL
RAPTORS
RAPTURE
RAPTURED
RAPTURES

RAPTURING
RAPTURISE
RAPTURIST
RAPTURIZE
RAPTUROUS
RARE
RAREBIT
RAREBITS
RARED
RAREE
RAREFIED
RAREFIER
RAREFIERS
RAREFIES
RAREFY
RAREFYING
RARELY
RARENESS
RARER
RARERIPE
RARERIPES
RARES
RAREST
RARIFIED
RARIFIES
RARIFY
RARIFYING
RARING
RARITIES
RARITY
RARK
RARKED
RARKING
RARKS
RAS
RASBORA
RASBORAS
RASCAILLE
RASCAL
RASCALDOM
RASCALISM
RASCALITY
RASCALLY
RASCALS
RASCASSE
RASCASSES
RASCHEL
RASCHELS
RASE
RASED
RASER
RASERS
RASES
RASH
RASHED
RASHER
RASHERS
RASHES

RASHEST
RASHIE
RASHIES
RASHING
RASHLIKE
RASHLY
RASHNESS
RASING
RASMALAI
RASMALAIS
RASORIAL
RASP
RASPATORY
RASPBERRY
RASPED
RASPER
RASPERS
RASPIER
RASPIEST
RASPINESS
RASPING
RASPINGLY
RASPINGS
RASPISH
RASPS
RASPY
RASSE
RASSES
RASSLE
RASSLED
RASSLES
RASSLING
RAST
RASTA
RASTAFARI
RASTER
RASTERED
RASTERING
RASTERISE
RASTERIZE
RASTERS
RASTRUM
RASTRUMS
RASURE
RASURES
RAT
RATA
RATABLE
RATABLES
RATABLY
RATAFEE
RATAFEES
RATAFIA
RATAFIAS
RATAL
RATALS
RATAN
RATANIES

RATANS
RATANY
RATAPLAN
RATAPLANS
RATAS
RATATAT
RATATATS
RATBAG
RATBAGS
RATBITE
RATCH
RATCHED
RATCHES
RATCHET
RATCHETED
RATCHETS
RATCHING
RATE
RATEABLE
RATEABLY
RATED
RATEEN
RATEENS
RATEL
RATELS
RATEMETER
RATEPAYER
RATER
RATERS
RATES
RATFINK
RATFINKS
RATFISH
RATFISHES
RATH
RATHA
RATHAS
RATHE
RATHER
RATHEREST
RATHERIPE
RATHERISH
RATHEST
RATHOLE
RATHOLES
RATHOUSE
RATHOUSES
RATHRIPE
RATHRIPES
RATHS
RATICIDE
RATICIDES
RATIFIED
RATIFIER
RATIFIERS
RATIFIES
RATIFY
RATIFYING

RATINE
RATINES
RATING
RATINGS
RATIO
RATION
RATIONAL
RATIONALE
RATIONALS
RATIONED
RATIONING
RATIONS
RATIOS
RATITE
RATITES
RATLIKE
RATLIN
RATLINE
RATLINES
RATLING
RATLINGS
RATLINS
RATO
RATOO
RATOON
RATOONED
RATOONER
RATOONERS
RATOONING
RATOONS
RATOOS
RATOS
RATPACK
RATPACKS
RATPROOF
RATS
RATSBANE
RATSBANES
RATTAIL
RATTAILED
RATTAILS
RATTAN
RATTANS
RATTED
RATTEEN
RATTEENS
RATTEN
RATTENED
RATTENER
RATTENERS
RATTENING
RATTENS
RATTER
RATTERIES
RATTERS
RATTERY
RATTIER
RATTIEST

RATTILY	RAUWOLFIA	RAWBONE	RAZMATAZ
RATTINESS	RAVAGE	RAWBONED	RAZOO
RATTING	RAVAGED	RAWER	RAZOOS
RATTINGS	RAVAGER	RAWEST	RAZOR
RATTISH	RAVAGERS	RAWHEAD	RAZORABLE
RATTLE	RAVAGES	RAWHEADS	RAZORBACK
RATTLEBAG	RAVAGING	RAWHIDE	RAZORBILL
RATTLEBOX	RAVE	RAWHIDED	RAZORED
RATTLED	RAVED	RAWHIDES	RAZORING
RATTLER	RAVEL	RAWHIDING	RAZORS
RATTLERS	RAVELED	RAWIN	RAZURE
RATTLES	RAVELER	RAWING	RAZURES
RATTLIER	RAVELERS	RAWINGS	RAZZ
RATTLIEST	RAVELIN	RAWINS	RAZZBERRY
RATTLIN	RAVELING	RAWISH	RAZZED
RATTLINE	RAVELINGS	RAWLY	RAZZES
RATTLINES	RAVELINS	RAWMAISH	RAZZIA
RATTLING	RAVELLED	RAWN	RAZZIAS
RATTLINGS	RAVELLER	RAWNESS	RAZZING
RATTLINS	RAVELLERS	RAWNESSES	RAZZLE
RATTLY	RAVELLING	RAWNS	RAZZLES
RATTON	RAVELLY	RAWS	RE
RATTONS	RAVELMENT	RAX	REABSORB
RATTOON	RAVELS	RAXED	REABSORBS
RATTOONED	RAVEN	RAXES	REACCEDE
RATTOONS	RAVENED	RAXING	REACCEDED
RATTRAP	RAVENER	RAY	REACCEDES
RATTRAPS	RAVENERS	RAYA	REACCENT
RATTY	RAVENING	RAYAH	REACCENTS
RATU	RAVENINGS	RAYAHS	REACCEPT
RATUS	RAVENLIKE	RAYAS	REACCEPTS
RAUCID	RAVENOUS	RAYED	REACCLAIM
RAUCITIES	RAVENS	RAYGRASS	REACCUSE
RAUCITY	RAVER	RAYING	REACCUSED
RAUCLE	RAVERS	RAYLE	REACCUSES
RAUCLER	RAVES	RAYLED	REACH
RAUCLEST	RAVIGOTE	RAYLES	REACHABLE
RAUCOUS	RAVIGOTES	RAYLESS	REACHED
RAUCOUSLY	RAVIGOTTE	RAYLESSLY	REACHER
RAUGHT	RAVIN	RAYLET	REACHERS
RAUN	RAVINE	RAYLETS	REACHES
RAUNCH	RAVINED	RAYLIKE	REACHING
RAUNCHED	RAVINES	RAYLING	REACHLESS
RAUNCHES	RAVING	RAYNE	REACQUIRE
RAUNCHIER	RAVINGLY	RAYNES	REACT
RAUNCHILY	RAVINGS	RAYON	REACTANCE
RAUNCHING	RAVINING	RAYONS	REACTANT
RAUNCHY	RAVINS	RAYS	REACTANTS
RAUNGE	RAVIOLI	RAZE	REACTED
RAUNGED	RAVIOLIS	RAZED	REACTING
RAUNGES	RAVISH	RAZEE	REACTION
RAUNGING	RAVISHED	RAZEED	REACTIONS
RAUNS	RAVISHER	RAZEEING	REACTIVE
RAUPATU	RAVISHERS	RAZEES	REACTOR
RAUPATUS	RAVISHES	RAZER	REACTORS
RAUPO	RAVISHING	RAZERS	REACTS
RAURIKI	RAW	RAZES	REACTUATE
RAURIKIS	RAWARU	RAZING	READ

READABLE	REAKING	REAMENDED	REARMING
READABLY	REAKS	REAMENDS	REARMOST
READAPT	REAL	REAMER	REARMOUSE
READAPTED	REALER	REAMERS	REARMS
READAPTS	REALES	REAMES	REAROSE
READD	REALEST	REAMIER	REAROUSAL
READDED	REALGAR	REAMIEST	REAROUSE
READDICT	REALGARS	REAMING	REAROUSED
READDICTS	REALIA	REAMS	REAROUSES
READDING	REALIGN	REAMY	REARRANGE
READDRESS	REALIGNED	REAN	REARREST
READDS	REALIGNS	REANALYSE	REARRESTS
READER	REALISE	REANALYZE	REARS
READERLY	REALISED	REANIMATE	REARWARD
READERS	REALISER	REANNEX	REARWARDS
READIED	REALISERS	REANNEXED	REASCEND
READIER	REALISES	REANNEXES	REASCENDS
READIES	REALISING	REANOINT	REASCENT
READIEST	REALISM	REANOINTS	REASCENTS
READILY	REALISMS	REANS	REASON
READINESS	REALIST	REANSWER	REASONED
READING	REALISTIC	REANSWERS	REASONER
READINGS	REALISTS	REAP	REASONERS
READJUST	REALITIES	REAPABLE	REASONING
READJUSTS	REALITY	REAPED	REASONS
READMIT	REALIZE	REAPER	REASSAIL
READMITS	REALIZED	REAPERS	REASSAILS
READOPT	REALIZER	REAPHOOK	REASSERT
READOPTED	REALIZERS	REAPHOOKS	REASSERTS
READOPTS	REALIZES	REAPING	REASSESS
READORN	REALIZING	REAPPAREL	REASSIGN
READORNED	REALLIE	REAPPEAR	REASSIGNS
READORNS	REALLIED	REAPPEARS	REASSORT
READOUT	REALLIES	REAPPLIED	REASSORTS
READOUTS	REALLOT	REAPPLIES	REASSUME
READS	REALLOTS	REAPPLY	REASSUMED
READVANCE	REALLY	REAPPOINT	REASSUMES
READVISE	REALLYING	REAPPROVE	REASSURE
READVISED	REALM	REAPS	REASSURED
READVISES	REALMLESS	REAR	REASSURER
READY	REALMS	REARED	REASSURES
READYING	REALNESS	REARER	REAST
READYMADE	REALO	REARERS	REASTED
REAEDIFY	REALOS	REARGUARD	REASTIER
REAEDIFYE	REALS	REARGUE	REASTIEST
REAFFIRM	REALTER	REARGUED	REASTING
REAFFIRMS	REALTERED	REARGUES	REASTS
REAFFIX	REALTERS	REARGUING	REASTY
REAFFIXED	REALTIE	REARHORSE	REATA
REAFFIXES	REALTIES	REARING	REATAS
REAGENCY	REALTIME	REARISE	REATE
REAGENT	REALTOR	REARISEN	REATES
REAGENTS	REALTORS	REARISES	REATTACH
REAGIN	REALTY	REARISING	REATTACK
REAGINIC	REAM	REARLY	REATTACKS
REAGINS	REAME	REARM	REATTAIN
REAK	REAMED	REARMED	REATTAINS
REAKED	REAMEND	REARMICE	REATTEMPT

REAVAIL
REAVAILED
REAVAILS
REAVE
REAVED
REAVER
REAVERS
REAVES
REAVING
REAVOW
REAVOWED
REAVOWING
REAVOWS
REAWAKE
REAWAKED
REAWAKEN
REAWAKENS
REAWAKES
REAWAKING
REAWOKE
REAWOKEN
REB
REBACK
REBACKED
REBACKING
REBACKS
REBADGE
REBADGED
REBADGES
REBADGING
REBAIT
REBAITED
REBAITING
REBAITS
REBALANCE
REBAPTISE
REBAPTISM
REBAPTIZE
REBAR
REBARS
REBATABLE
REBATE
REBATED
REBATER
REBATERS
REBATES
REBATING
REBATO
REBATOES
REBATOS
REBBE
REBBES
REBBETZIN
REBEC
REBECK
REBECKS
REBECS
REBEGAN

REBEGIN
REBEGINS
REBEGUN
REBEL
REBELDOM
REBELDOMS
REBELLED
REBELLER
REBELLERS
REBELLING
REBELLION
REBELLOW
REBELLOWS
REBELS
REBID
REBIDDEN
REBIDDING
REBIDS
REBILL
REBILLED
REBILLING
REBILLS
REBIND
REBINDING
REBINDS
REBIRTH
REBIRTHS
REBIT
REBITE
REBITES
REBITING
REBITTEN
REBLEND
REBLENDED
REBLENDS
REBLENT
REBLOOM
REBLOOMED
REBLOOMS
REBLOSSOM
REBOANT
REBOARD
REBOARDED
REBOARDS
REBOATION
REBODIED
REBODIES
REBODY
REBODYING
REBOIL
REBOILED
REBOILING
REBOILS
REBOOK
REBOOKED
REBOOKING
REBOOKS
REBOOT

REBOOTED
REBOOTING
REBOOTS
REBOP
REBOPS
REBORE
REBORED
REBORES
REBORING
REBORN
REBORROW
REBORROWS
REBOTTLE
REBOTTLED
REBOTTLES
REBOUGHT
REBOUND
REBOUNDED
REBOUNDER
REBOUNDS
REBOZO
REBOZOS
REBRACE
REBRACED
REBRACES
REBRACING
REBRANCH
REBRAND
REBRANDED
REBRANDS
REBRED
REBREED
REBREEDS
REBS
REBUFF
REBUFFED
REBUFFING
REBUFFS
REBUILD
REBUILDED
REBUILDS
REBUILT
REBUKABLE
REBUKE
REBUKED
REBUKEFUL
REBUKER
REBUKERS
REBUKES
REBUKING
REBURIAL
REBURIALS
REBURIED
REBURIES
REBURY
REBURYING
REBUS
REBUSES

REBUT
REBUTMENT
REBUTS
REBUTTAL
REBUTTALS
REBUTTED
REBUTTER
REBUTTERS
REBUTTING
REBUTTON
REBUTTONS
REBUY
REBUYING
REBUYS
REC
RECAL
RECALESCE
RECALL
RECALLED
RECALLER
RECALLERS
RECALLING
RECALLS
RECALMENT
RECALS
RECAMIER
RECAMIERS
RECANE
RECANED
RECANES
RECANING
RECANT
RECANTED
RECANTER
RECANTERS
RECANTING
RECANTS
RECAP
RECAPPED
RECAPPING
RECAPS
RECAPTION
RECAPTOR
RECAPTORS
RECAPTURE
RECARPET
RECARPETS
RECARRIED
RECARRIES
RECARRY
RECAST
RECASTING
RECASTS
RECATALOG
RECATCH
RECATCHES
RECAUGHT
RECAUTION

RECCE	RECHANGE	RECKON	RECODED
RECCED	RECHANGED	RECKONED	RECODES
RECCEED	RECHANGES	RECKONER	RECODIFY
RECCEING	RECHANNEL	RECKONERS	RECODING
RECCES	RECHARGE	RECKONING	RECOGNISE
RECCIED	RECHARGED	RECKONS	RECOGNIZE
RECCIES	RECHARGER	RECKS	RECOIL
RECCO	RECHARGES	RECLAD	RECOILED
RECCOS	RECHART	RECLADDED	RECOILER
RECCY	RECHARTED	RECLADS	RECOILERS
RECCYING	RECHARTER	RECLAIM	RECOILING
RECEDE	RECHARTS	RECLAIMED	RECOILS
RECEDED	RECHATE	RECLAIMER	RECOIN
RECEDES	RECHATES	RECLAIMS	RECOINAGE
RECEDING	RECHAUFFE	RECLAME	RECOINED
RECEIPT	RECHEAT	RECLAMES	RECOINING
RECEIPTED	RECHEATED	RECLASP	RECOINS
RECEIPTOR	RECHEATS	RECLASPED	RECOLLECT
RECEIPTS	RECHECK	RECLASPS	RECOLLET
RECEIVAL	RECHECKED	RECLEAN	RECOLLETS
RECEIVALS	RECHECKS	RECLEANED	RECOLOR
RECEIVE	RECHERCHE	RECLEANS	RECOLORED
RECEIVED	RECHEW	RECLIMB	RECOLORS
RECEIVER	RECHEWED	RECLIMBED	RECOMB
RECEIVERS	RECHEWING	RECLIMBS	RECOMBED
RECEIVES	RECHEWS	RECLINATE	RECOMBINE
RECEIVING	RECHIE	RECLINE	RECOMBING
RECEMENT	RECHLESSE	RECLINED	RECOMBS
RECEMENTS	RECHOOSE	RECLINER	RECOMFORT
RECENCIES	RECHOOSES	RECLINERS	RECOMMEND
RECENCY	RECHOSE	RECLINES	RECOMMIT
RECENSE	RECHOSEN	RECLINING	RECOMMITS
RECENSED	RECIPE	RECLOSE	RECOMPACT
RECENSES	RECIPES	RECLOSED	RECOMPILE
RECENSING	RECIPIENT	RECLOSES	RECOMPOSE
RECENSION	RECIRCLE	RECLOSING	RECOMPUTE
RECENSOR	RECIRCLED	RECLOTHE	RECON
RECENSORS	RECIRCLES	RECLOTHED	RECONCILE
RECENT	RECISION	RECLOTHES	RECONDITE
RECENTER	RECISIONS	RECLUSE	RECONDUCT
RECENTEST	RECIT	RECLUSELY	RECONFER
RECENTLY	RECITABLE	RECLUSES	RECONFERS
RECENTRE	RECITAL	RECLUSION	RECONFINE
RECENTRED	RECITALS	RECLUSIVE	RECONFIRM
RECENTRES	RECITE	RECLUSORY	RECONNECT
RECEPT	RECITED	RECOAL	RECONNED
RECEPTION	RECITER	RECOALED	RECONNING
RECEPTIVE	RECITERS	RECOALING	RECONQUER
RECEPTOR	RECITES	RECOALS	RECONS
RECEPTORS	RECITING	RECOAT	RECONSIGN
RECEPTS	RECITS	RECOATED	RECONSOLE
RECERTIFY	RECK	RECOATING	RECONSULT
RECESS	RECKAN	RECOATS	RECONTACT
RECESSED	RECKED	RECOCK	RECONTOUR
RECESSES	RECKING	RECOCKED	RECONVENE
RECESSING	RECKLESS	RECOCKING	RECONVERT
RECESSION	RECKLING	RECOCKS	RECONVEY
RECESSIVE	RECKLINGS	RECODE	RECONVEYS

RECONVICT
RECOOK
RECOOKED
RECOOKING
RECOOKS
RECOPIED
RECOPIES
RECOPY
RECOPYING
RECORD
RECORDED
RECORDER
RECORDERS
RECORDING
RECORDIST
RECORDS
RECORK
RECORKED
RECORKING
RECORKS
RECOUNT
RECOUNTAL
RECOUNTED
RECOUNTER
RECOUNTS
RECOUP
RECOUPE
RECOUPED
RECOUPING
RECOUPLE
RECOUPLED
RECOUPLES
RECOUPS
RECOURE
RECOURED
RECOURES
RECOURING
RECOURSE
RECOURSED
RECOURSES
RECOVER
RECOVERED
RECOVEREE
RECOVERER
RECOVEROR
RECOVERS
RECOVERY
RECOWER
RECOWERED
RECOWERS
RECOYLE
RECOYLED
RECOYLES
RECOYLING
RECRATE
RECRATED
RECRATES
RECRATING

RECREANCE
RECREANCY
RECREANT
RECREANTS
RECREATE
RECREATED
RECREATES
RECREATOR
RECREMENT
RECROSS
RECROSSED
RECROSSES
RECROWN
RECROWNED
RECROWNS
RECRUIT
RECRUITAL
RECRUITED
RECRUITER
RECRUITS
RECS
RECTA
RECTAL
RECTALLY
RECTANGLE
RECTI
RECTIFIED
RECTIFIER
RECTIFIES
RECTIFY
RECTION
RECTIONS
RECTITIC
RECTITIS
RECTITUDE
RECTO
RECTOCELE
RECTOR
RECTORAL
RECTORATE
RECTORESS
RECTORIAL
RECTORIES
RECTORS
RECTORY
RECTOS
RECTRESS
RECTRICES
RECTRIX
RECTUM
RECTUMS
RECTUS
RECUILE
RECUILED
RECUILES
RECUILING
RECULE
RECULED

RECULES
RECULING
RECUMBENT
RECUR
RECURE
RECURED
RECURES
RECURING
RECURRED
RECURRENT
RECURRING
RECURS
RECURSION
RECURSIVE
RECURVATE
RECURVE
RECURVED
RECURVES
RECURVING
RECUSAL
RECUSALS
RECUSANCE
RECUSANCY
RECUSANT
RECUSANTS
RECUSE
RECUSED
RECUSES
RECUSING
RECUT
RECUTS
RECUTTING
RECYCLATE
RECYCLE
RECYCLED
RECYCLER
RECYCLERS
RECYCLES
RECYCLING
RECYCLIST
RED
REDACT
REDACTED
REDACTING
REDACTION
REDACTOR
REDACTORS
REDACTS
REDAMAGE
REDAMAGED
REDAMAGES
REDAN
REDANS
REDARGUE
REDARGUED
REDARGUES
REDATE
REDATED

REDATES
REDATING
REDBACK
REDBACKS
REDBAIT
REDBAITED
REDBAITER
REDBAITS
REDBAY
REDBAYS
REDBELLY
REDBIRD
REDBIRDS
REDBONE
REDBONES
REDBREAST
REDBRICK
REDBRICKS
REDBUD
REDBUDS
REDBUG
REDBUGS
REDCAP
REDCAPS
REDCOAT
REDCOATS
REDD
REDDED
REDDEN
REDDENDA
REDDENDO
REDDENDOS
REDDENDUM
REDDENED
REDDENING
REDDENS
REDDER
REDDERS
REDDEST
REDDIER
REDDIEST
REDDING
REDDINGS
REDDISH
REDDISHLY
REDDLE
REDDLED
REDDLEMAN
REDDLEMEN
REDDLES
REDDLING
REDDS
REDDY
REDE
REDEAL
REDEALING
REDEALS
REDEALT

REDEAR
REDEARS
REDECIDE
REDECIDED
REDECIDES
REDECRAFT
REDED
REDEEM
REDEEMED
REDEEMER
REDEEMERS
REDEEMING
REDEEMS
REDEFEAT
REDEFEATS
REDEFECT
REDEFECTS
REDEFIED
REDEFIES
REDEFINE
REDEFINED
REDEFINES
REDEFY
REDEFYING
REDELESS
REDELIVER
REDEMAND
REDEMANDS
REDENIED
REDENIES
REDENY
REDENYING
REDEPLOY
REDEPLOYS
REDEPOSIT
REDES
REDESCEND
REDESIGN
REDESIGNS
REDEVELOP
REDEYE
REDEYES
REDFIN
REDFINS
REDFISH
REDFISHES
REDFOOT
REDFOOTS
REDHANDED
REDHEAD
REDHEADED
REDHEADS
REDHORSE
REDHORSES
REDIA
REDIAE
REDIAL
REDIALED

REDIALING
REDIALLED
REDIALS
REDIAS
REDICTATE
REDID
REDIGEST
REDIGESTS
REDIGRESS
REDING
REDINGOTE
REDIP
REDIPPED
REDIPPING
REDIPS
REDIPT
REDIRECT
REDIRECTS
REDISCUSS
REDISPLAY
REDISPOSE
REDISTIL
REDISTILL
REDISTILS
REDIVIDE
REDIVIDED
REDIVIDES
REDIVIVUS
REDIVORCE
REDLEG
REDLEGS
REDLINE
REDLINED
REDLINER
REDLINERS
REDLINES
REDLINING
REDLY
REDNECK
REDNECKED
REDNECKS
REDNESS
REDNESSES
REDO
REDOCK
REDOCKED
REDOCKING
REDOCKS
REDOES
REDOING
REDOLENCE
REDOLENCY
REDOLENT
REDON
REDONE
REDONNED
REDONNING
REDONS

REDOS
REDOUBLE
REDOUBLED
REDOUBLER
REDOUBLES
REDOUBT
REDOUBTED
REDOUBTS
REDOUND
REDOUNDED
REDOUNDS
REDOUT
REDOUTS
REDOWA
REDOWAS
REDOX
REDOXES
REDPOLL
REDPOLLS
REDRAFT
REDRAFTED
REDRAFTS
REDRAW
REDRAWER
REDRAWERS
REDRAWING
REDRAWN
REDRAWS
REDREAM
REDREAMED
REDREAMS
REDREAMT
REDRESS
REDRESSED
REDRESSER
REDRESSES
REDRESSOR
REDREW
REDRIED
REDRIES
REDRILL
REDRILLED
REDRILLS
REDRIVE
REDRIVEN
REDRIVES
REDRIVING
REDROOT
REDROOTS
REDROVE
REDRY
REDRYING
REDS
REDSEAR
REDSHANK
REDSHANKS
REDSHARE
REDSHIFT

REDSHIFTS
REDSHIRE
REDSHIRT
REDSHIRTS
REDSHORT
REDSKIN
REDSKINS
REDSTART
REDSTARTS
REDSTREAK
REDTAIL
REDTAILS
REDTOP
REDTOPS
REDUB
REDUBBED
REDUBBING
REDUBS
REDUCE
REDUCED
REDUCER
REDUCERS
REDUCES
REDUCIBLE
REDUCIBLY
REDUCING
REDUCTANT
REDUCTASE
REDUCTION
REDUCTIVE
REDUCTOR
REDUCTORS
REDUIT
REDUITS
REDUNDANT
REDUVIID
REDUVIIDS
REDUX
REDWARE
REDWARES
REDWATER
REDWATERS
REDWING
REDWINGS
REDWOOD
REDWOODS
REDYE
REDYED
REDYEING
REDYES
REE
REEARN
REEARNED
REEARNING
REEARNS
REEBOK
REEBOKS
REECH

REECHED	REEFINGS	REENJOYED	REFASHION
REECHES	REEFS	REENJOYS	REFASTEN
REECHIE	REEFY	REENLARGE	REFASTENS
REECHIER	REEJECT	REENLIST	REFECT
REECHIEST	REEJECTED	REENLISTS	REFECTED
REECHING	REEJECTS	REENROLL	REFECTING
REECHO	REEK	REENROLLS	REFECTION
REECHOED	REEKED	REENS	REFECTIVE
REECHOES	REEKER	REENSLAVE	REFECTORY
REECHOING	REEKERS	REENTER	REFECTS
REECHY	REEKIE	REENTERED	REFED
REED	REEKIER	REENTERS	REFEED
REEDBED	REEKIEST	REENTRANT	REFEEDING
REEDBEDS	REEKING	REENTRIES	REFEEDS
REEDBIRD	REEKINGLY	REENTRY	REFEEL
REEDBIRDS	REEKS	REEQUIP	REFEELING
REEDBUCK	REEKY	REEQUIPS	REFEELS
REEDBUCKS	REEL	REERECT	REFEL
REEDE	REELABLE	REERECTED	REFELL
REEDED	REELECT	REERECTS	REFELLED
REEDEN	REELECTED	REES	REFELLING
REEDER	REELECTS	REEST	REFELS
REEDERS	REELED	REESTED	REFELT
REEDES	REELER	REESTIER	REFENCE
REEDIER	REELERS	REESTIEST	REFENCED
REEDIEST	REELEVATE	REESTING	REFENCES
REEDIFIED	REELING	REESTS	REFENCING
REEDIFIES	REELINGLY	REESTY	REFER
REEDIFY	REELINGS	REEVE	REFERABLE
REEDILY	REELMAN	REEVED	REFEREE
REEDINESS	REELMEN	REEVES	REFEREED
REEDING	REELS	REEVING	REFEREES
REEDINGS	REEMBARK	REEVOKE	REFERENCE
REEDIT	REEMBARKS	REEVOKED	REFERENDA
REEDITED	REEMBODY	REEVOKES	REFERENT
REEDITING	REEMBRACE	REEVOKING	REFERENTS
REEDITION	REEMERGE	REEXAMINE	REFERRAL
REEDITS	REEMERGED	REEXECUTE	REFERRALS
REEDLIKE	REEMERGES	REEXHIBIT	REFERRED
REEDLING	REEMIT	REEXPEL	REFERRER
REEDLINGS	REEMITS	REEXPELS	REFERRERS
REEDMACE	REEMITTED	REEXPLAIN	REFERRING
REEDMACES	REEMPLOY	REEXPLORE	REFERS
REEDMAN	REEMPLOYS	REEXPORT	REFFED
REEDMEN	REEN	REEXPORTS	REFFING
REEDS	REENACT	REEXPOSE	REFFO
REEDSTOP	REENACTED	REEXPOSED	REFFOS
REEDSTOPS	REENACTOR	REEXPOSES	REFIGHT
REEDUCATE	REENACTS	REEXPRESS	REFIGHTS
REEDY	REENDOW	REF	REFIGURE
REEF	REENDOWED	REFACE	REFIGURED
REEFABLE	REENDOWS	REFACED	REFIGURES
REEFED	REENFORCE	REFACES	REFILE
REEFER	REENGAGE	REFACING	REFILED
REEFERS	REENGAGED	REFALL	REFILES
REEFIER	REENGAGES	REFALLEN	REFILING
REEFIEST	REENGRAVE	REFALLING	REFILL
REEFING	REENJOY	REFALLS	REFILLED

REFILLING	REFLEXLY	REFOUNDS	REFUSALS
REFILLS	REFLIES	REFRACT	REFUSE
REFILM	REFLOAT	REFRACTED	REFUSED
REFILMED	REFLOATED	REFRACTOR	REFUSENIK
REFILMING	REFLOATS	REFRACTS	REFUSER
REFILMS	REFLOOD	REFRAIN	REFUSERS
REFILTER	REFLOODED	REFRAINED	REFUSES
REFILTERS	REFLOODS	REFRAINER	REFUSING
REFINABLE	REFLOW	REFRAINS	REFUSION
REFINANCE	REFLOWED	REFRAME	REFUSIONS
REFIND	REFLOWER	REFRAMED	REFUSNIK
REFINDING	REFLOWERS	REFRAMES	REFUSNIKS
REFINDS	REFLOWING	REFRAMING	REFUTABLE
REFINE	REFLOWN	REFREEZE	REFUTABLY
REFINED	REFLOWS	REFREEZES	REFUTAL
REFINEDLY	REFLUENCE	REFRESH	REFUTALS
REFINER	REFLUENT	REFRESHED	REFUTE
REFINERS	REFLUX	REFRESHEN	REFUTED
REFINERY	REFLUXED	REFRESHER	REFUTER
REFINES	REFLUXES	REFRESHES	REFUTERS
REFINING	REFLUXING	REFRIED	REFUTES
REFININGS	REFLY	REFRIES	REFUTING
REFINISH	REFLYING	REFRINGE	REG
REFIRE	REFOCUS	REFRINGED	REGAIN
REFIRED	REFOCUSED	REFRINGES	REGAINED
REFIRES	REFOCUSES	REFRONT	REGAINER
REFIRING	REFOLD	REFRONTED	REGAINERS
REFIT	REFOLDED	REFRONTS	REGAINING
REFITMENT	REFOLDING	REFROZE	REGAINS
REFITS	REFOLDS	REFROZEN	REGAL
REFITTED	REFOOT	REFRY	REGALE
REFITTING	REFOOTED	REFRYING	REGALED
REFIX	REFOOTING	REFS	REGALER
REFIXED	REFOOTS	REFT	REGALERS
REFIXES	REFOREST	REFUEL	REGALES
REFIXING	REFORESTS	REFUELED	REGALIA
REFLAG	REFORGE	REFUELING	REGALIAN
REFLAGGED	REFORGED	REFUELLED	REGALIAS
REFLAGS	REFORGES	REFUELS	REGALING
REFLATE	REFORGING	REFUGE	REGALISM
REFLATED	REFORM	REFUGED	REGALISMS
REFLATES	REFORMADE	REFUGEE	REGALIST
REFLATING	REFORMADO	REFUGEES	REGALISTS
REFLATION	REFORMAT	REFUGES	REGALITY
REFLECT	REFORMATE	REFUGIA	REGALLY
REFLECTED	REFORMATS	REFUGING	REGALNESS
REFLECTER	REFORMED	REFUGIUM	REGALS
REFLECTOR	REFORMER	REFULGENT	REGAR
REFLECTS	REFORMERS	REFUND	REGARD
REFLET	REFORMING	REFUNDED	REGARDANT
REFLETS	REFORMISM	REFUNDER	REGARDED
REFLEW	REFORMIST	REFUNDERS	REGARDER
REFLEX	REFORMS	REFUNDING	REGARDERS
REFLEXED	REFORTIFY	REFUNDS	REGARDFUL
REFLEXES	REFOUGHT	REFURBISH	REGARDING
REFLEXING	REFOUND	REFURNISH	REGARDS
REFLEXION	REFOUNDED	REFUSABLE	REGARS
REFLEXIVE	REFOUNDER	REFUSAL	REGATHER

REGATHERS
REGATTA
REGATTAS
REGAUGE
REGAUGED
REGAUGES
REGAUGING
REGAVE
REGEAR
REGEARED
REGEARING
REGEARS
REGELATE
REGELATED
REGELATES
REGENCE
REGENCES
REGENCIES
REGENCY
REGENT
REGENTAL
REGENTS
REGES
REGEST
REGESTS
REGGAE
REGGAES
REGGO
REGGOS
REGICIDAL
REGICIDE
REGICIDES
REGIE
REGIES
REGILD
REGILDED
REGILDING
REGILDS
REGILT
REGIME
REGIMEN
REGIMENS
REGIMENT
REGIMENTS
REGIMES
REGIMINAL
REGINA
REGINAE
REGINAL
REGINAS
REGION
REGIONAL
REGIONALS
REGIONARY
REGIONS
REGISSEUR
REGISTER
REGISTERS

REGISTRAR
REGISTRY
REGIUS
REGIVE
REGIVEN
REGIVES
REGIVING
REGLAZE
REGLAZED
REGLAZES
REGLAZING
REGLET
REGLETS
REGLORIFY
REGLOSS
REGLOSSED
REGLOSSES
REGLOW
REGLOWED
REGLOWING
REGLOWS
REGLUE
REGLUED
REGLUES
REGLUING
REGMA
REGMAKER
REGMAKERS
REGMATA
REGNA
REGNAL
REGNANCY
REGNANT
REGNUM
REGO
REGOLITH
REGOLITHS
REGORGE
REGORGED
REGORGES
REGORGING
REGOS
REGOSOL
REGOSOLS
REGRADE
REGRADED
REGRADES
REGRADING
REGRAFT
REGRAFTED
REGRAFTS
REGRANT
REGRANTED
REGRANTS
REGRATE
REGRATED
REGRATER
REGRATERS

REGRATES
REGRATING
REGRATOR
REGRATORS
REGREDE
REGREDED
REGREDES
REGREDING
REGREEN
REGREENED
REGREENS
REGREET
REGREETED
REGREETS
REGRESS
REGRESSED
REGRESSES
REGRESSOR
REGRET
REGRETFUL
REGRETS
REGRETTED
REGRETTER
REGREW
REGRIND
REGRINDS
REGROOM
REGROOMED
REGROOMS
REGROOVE
REGROOVED
REGROOVES
REGROUND
REGROUP
REGROUPED
REGROUPS
REGROW
REGROWING
REGROWN
REGROWS
REGROWTH
REGROWTHS
REGS
REGUERDON
REGULA
REGULABLE
REGULAE
REGULAR
REGULARLY
REGULARS
REGULATE
REGULATED
REGULATES
REGULATOR
REGULI
REGULINE
REGULISE
REGULISED

REGULISES
REGULIZE
REGULIZED
REGULIZES
REGULO
REGULOS
REGULUS
REGULUSES
REGUR
REGURS
REH
REHAB
REHABBED
REHABBER
REHABBERS
REHABBING
REHABS
REHAMMER
REHAMMERS
REHANDLE
REHANDLED
REHANDLES
REHANG
REHANGED
REHANGING
REHANGS
REHARDEN
REHARDENS
REHASH
REHASHED
REHASHES
REHASHING
REHEAR
REHEARD
REHEARING
REHEARS
REHEARSAL
REHEARSE
REHEARSED
REHEARSER
REHEARSES
REHEAT
REHEATED
REHEATER
REHEATERS
REHEATING
REHEATS
REHEEL
REHEELED
REHEELING
REHEELS
REHEM
REHEMMED
REHEMMING
REHEMS
REHINGE
REHINGED
REHINGES

REHINGING	REINDEX	REINVENT	REJOICE
REHIRE	REINDEXED	REINVENTS	REJOICED
REHIRED	REINDEXES	REINVEST	REJOICER
REHIRES	REINDICT	REINVESTS	REJOICERS
REHIRING	REINDICTS	REINVITE	REJOICES
REHOBOAM	REINDUCE	REINVITED	REJOICING
REHOBOAMS	REINDUCED	REINVITES	REJOIN
REHOUSE	REINDUCES	REINVOKE	REJOINDER
REHOUSED	REINDUCT	REINVOKED	REJOINED
REHOUSES	REINDUCTS	REINVOKES	REJOINING
REHOUSING	REINED	REINVOLVE	REJOINS
REHS	REINETTE	REIRD	REJON
REHUNG	REINETTES	REIRDS	REJONEO
REHYDRATE	REINFECT	REIS	REJONEOS
REI	REINFECTS	REISES	REJONES
REIF	REINFLAME	REISSUE	REJOURN
REIFIED	REINFLATE	REISSUED	REJOURNED
REIFIER	REINFORCE	REISSUER	REJOURNS
REIFIERS	REINFORM	REISSUERS	REJUDGE
REIFIES	REINFORMS	REISSUES	REJUDGED
REIFS	REINFUND	REISSUING	REJUDGES
REIFY	REINFUNDS	REIST	REJUDGING
REIFYING	REINFUSE	REISTAFEL	REJUGGLE
REIGN	REINFUSED	REISTED	REJUGGLED
REIGNED	REINFUSES	REISTING	REJUGGLES
REIGNING	REINHABIT	REISTS	REJUSTIFY
REIGNITE	REINING	REITBOK	REKE
REIGNITED	REINJECT	REITBOKS	REKED
REIGNITES	REINJECTS	REITER	REKES
REIGNS	REINJURE	REITERANT	REKEY
REIK	REINJURED	REITERATE	REKEYED
REIKI	REINJURES	REITERS	REKEYING
REIKIS	REINJURY	REIVE	REKEYS
REIKS	REINK	REIVED	REKINDLE
REILLUME	REINKED	REIVER	REKINDLED
REILLUMED	REINKING	REIVERS	REKINDLES
REILLUMES	REINKS	REIVES	REKING
REIMAGE	REINLESS	REIVING	REKNIT
REIMAGED	REINS	REJACKET	REKNITS
REIMAGES	REINSERT	REJACKETS	REKNITTED
REIMAGINE	REINSERTS	REJECT	REKNOT
REIMAGING	REINSMAN	REJECTED	REKNOTS
REIMBURSE	REINSMEN	REJECTEE	REKNOTTED
REIMMERSE	REINSPECT	REJECTEES	RELABEL
REIMPLANT	REINSPIRE	REJECTER	RELABELED
REIMPORT	REINSTAL	REJECTERS	RELABELS
REIMPORTS	REINSTALL	REJECTING	RELACE
REIMPOSE	REINSTALS	REJECTION	RELACED
REIMPOSED	REINSTATE	REJECTIVE	RELACES
REIMPOSES	REINSURE	REJECTOR	RELACHE
REIN	REINSURED	REJECTORS	RELACHES
REINCITE	REINSURER	REJECTS	RELACING
REINCITED	REINSURES	REJIG	RELACQUER
REINCITES	REINTER	REJIGGED	RELAID
REINCUR	REINTERS	REJIGGER	RELAND
REINCURS	REINVADE	REJIGGERS	RELANDED
REINDEER	REINVADED	REJIGGING	RELANDING
REINDEERS	REINVADES	REJIGS	RELANDS

485

RELAPSE	RELEGATES	RELINES	RELUCT
RELAPSED	RELEND	RELINING	RELUCTANT
RELAPSER	RELENDING	RELINK	RELUCTATE
RELAPSERS	RELENDS	RELINKED	RELUCTED
RELAPSES	RELENT	RELINKING	RELUCTING
RELAPSING	RELENTED	RELINKS	RELUCTS
RELATA	RELENTING	RELIQUARY	RELUME
RELATABLE	RELENTS	RELIQUE	RELUMED
RELATE	RELET	RELIQUEFY	RELUMES
RELATED	RELETS	RELIQUES	RELUMINE
RELATEDLY	RELETTER	RELIQUIAE	RELUMINED
RELATER	RELETTERS	RELISH	RELUMINES
RELATERS	RELETTING	RELISHED	RELUMING
RELATES	RELEVANCE	RELISHES	RELY
RELATING	RELEVANCY	RELISHING	RELYING
RELATION	RELEVANT	RELIST	REM
RELATIONS	RELEVE	RELISTED	REMADE
RELATIVAL	RELEVES	RELISTING	REMADES
RELATIVE	RELIABLE	RELISTS	REMAIL
RELATIVES	RELIABLES	RELIT	REMAILED
RELATOR	RELIABLY	RELIVABLE	REMAILING
RELATORS	RELIANCE	RELIVE	REMAILS
RELATUM	RELIANCES	RELIVED	REMAIN
RELAUNCH	RELIANT	RELIVER	REMAINDER
RELAUNDER	RELIANTLY	RELIVERED	REMAINED
RELAX	RELIC	RELIVERS	REMAINING
RELAXABLE	RELICENSE	RELIVES	REMAINS
RELAXANT	RELICS	RELIVING	REMAKE
RELAXANTS	RELICT	RELLENO	REMAKER
RELAXED	RELICTION	RELLENOS	REMAKERS
RELAXEDLY	RELICTS	RELLIES	REMAKES
RELAXER	RELIDE	RELLISH	REMAKING
RELAXERS	RELIE	RELLISHED	REMAN
RELAXES	RELIED	RELLISHES	REMAND
RELAXIN	RELIEF	RELOAD	REMANDED
RELAXING	RELIEFS	RELOADED	REMANDING
RELAXINS	RELIER	RELOADER	REMANDS
RELAY	RELIERS	RELOADERS	REMANENCE
RELAYED	RELIES	RELOADING	REMANENCY
RELAYING	RELIEVE	RELOADS	REMANENT
RELAYS	RELIEVED	RELOAN	REMANENTS
RELEARN	RELIEVER	RELOANED	REMANET
RELEARNED	RELIEVERS	RELOANING	REMANETS
RELEARNS	RELIEVES	RELOANS	REMANIE
RELEARNT	RELIEVING	RELOCATE	REMANIES
RELEASE	RELIEVO	RELOCATED	REMANNED
RELEASED	RELIEVOS	RELOCATEE	REMANNING
RELEASEE	RELIGHT	RELOCATES	REMANS
RELEASEES	RELIGHTED	RELOCATOR	REMAP
RELEASER	RELIGHTS	RELOCK	REMAPPED
RELEASERS	RELIGIEUX	RELOCKED	REMAPPING
RELEASES	RELIGION	RELOCKING	REMAPS
RELEASING	RELIGIONS	RELOCKS	REMARK
RELEASOR	RELIGIOSE	RELOOK	REMARKED
RELEASORS	RELIGIOSO	RELOOKED	REMARKER
RELEGABLE	RELIGIOUS	RELOOKING	REMARKERS
RELEGATE	RELINE	RELOOKS	REMARKET
RELEGATED	RELINED	RELUCENT	REMARKETS

REMARKING	REMERCIED	REMNANTS	RENAGUES
REMARKS	REMERCIES	REMODEL	RENAGUING
REMARQUE	REMERCY	REMODELED	RENAIL
REMARQUED	REMERGE	REMODELER	RENAILED
REMARQUES	REMERGED	REMODELS	RENAILING
REMARRIED	REMERGES	REMODIFY	RENAILS
REMARRIES	REMERGING	REMOISTEN	RENAL
REMARRY	REMET	REMOLADE	RENAME
REMASTER	REMEX	REMOLADES	RENAMED
REMASTERS	REMIGATE	REMOLD	RENAMES
REMATCH	REMIGATED	REMOLDED	RENAMING
REMATCHED	REMIGATES	REMOLDING	RENASCENT
REMATCHES	REMIGES	REMOLDS	RENATURE
REMATE	REMIGIAL	REMONTANT	RENATURED
REMATED	REMIGRATE	REMONTOIR	RENATURES
REMATES	REMIND	REMORA	RENAY
REMATING	REMINDED	REMORAS	RENAYED
REMBLAI	REMINDER	REMORID	RENAYING
REMBLAIS	REMINDERS	REMORSE	RENAYS
REMBLE	REMINDFUL	REMORSES	RENCONTRE
REMBLED	REMINDING	REMOTE	REND
REMBLES	REMINDS	REMOTELY	RENDED
REMBLING	REMINISCE	REMOTER	RENDER
REMEAD	REMINT	REMOTES	RENDERED
REMEADED	REMINTED	REMOTEST	RENDERER
REMEADING	REMINTING	REMOTION	RENDERERS
REMEADS	REMINTS	REMOTIONS	RENDERING
REMEASURE	REMISE	REMOUD	RENDERS
REMEDE	REMISED	REMOULADE	RENDIBLE
REMEDED	REMISES	REMOULD	RENDING
REMEDES	REMISING	REMOULDED	RENDITION
REMEDIAL	REMISS	REMOULDS	RENDS
REMEDIAT	REMISSION	REMOUNT	RENDZINA
REMEDIATE	REMISSIVE	REMOUNTED	RENDZINAS
REMEDIED	REMISSLY	REMOUNTS	RENEGADE
REMEDIES	REMISSORY	REMOVABLE	RENEGADED
REMEDING	REMIT	REMOVABLY	RENEGADES
REMEDY	REMITMENT	REMOVAL	RENEGADO
REMEDYING	REMITS	REMOVALS	RENEGADOS
REMEET	REMITTAL	REMOVE	RENEGATE
REMEETING	REMITTALS	REMOVED	RENEGATES
REMEETS	REMITTED	REMOVEDLY	RENEGE
REMEID	REMITTEE	REMOVER	RENEGED
REMEIDED	REMITTEES	REMOVERS	RENEGER
REMEIDING	REMITTENT	REMOVES	RENEGERS
REMEIDS	REMITTER	REMOVING	RENEGES
REMELT	REMITTERS	REMS	RENEGING
REMELTED	REMITTING	REMUAGE	RENEGUE
REMELTING	REMITTOR	REMUAGES	RENEGUED
REMELTS	REMITTORS	REMUDA	RENEGUER
REMEMBER	REMIX	REMUDAS	RENEGUERS
REMEMBERS	REMIXED	REMUEUR	RENEGUES
REMEN	REMIXES	REMUEURS	RENEGUING
REMEND	REMIXING	REMURMUR	RENEST
REMENDED	REMIXT	REMURMURS	RENESTED
REMENDING	REMIXTURE	REN	RENESTING
REMENDS	REMNANT	RENAGUE	RENESTS
REMENS	REMNANTAL	RENAGUED	RENEW

RENEWABLE
RENEWABLY
RENEWAL
RENEWALS
RENEWED
RENEWEDLY
RENEWER
RENEWERS
RENEWING
RENEWINGS
RENEWS
RENEY
RENEYED
RENEYING
RENEYS
RENFIERST
RENFORCE
RENFORCED
RENFORCES
RENFORST
RENGA
RENGAS
RENIED
RENIES
RENIFORM
RENIG
RENIGGED
RENIGGING
RENIGS
RENIN
RENINS
RENITENCE
RENITENCY
RENITENT
RENK
RENKER
RENKEST
RENMINBI
RENMINBIS
RENNASE
RENNASES
RENNE
RENNED
RENNES
RENNET
RENNETS
RENNIN
RENNING
RENNINGS
RENNINS
RENOGRAM
RENOGRAMS
RENOTIFY
RENOUNCE
RENOUNCED
RENOUNCER
RENOUNCES
RENOVATE

RENOVATED
RENOVATES
RENOVATOR
RENOWN
RENOWNED
RENOWNER
RENOWNERS
RENOWNING
RENOWNS
RENS
RENT
RENTABLE
RENTAL
RENTALLER
RENTALS
RENTE
RENTED
RENTER
RENTERS
RENTES
RENTIER
RENTIERS
RENTING
RENTINGS
RENTS
RENUMBER
RENUMBERS
RENVERSE
RENVERSED
RENVERSES
RENVERST
RENVOI
RENVOIS
RENVOY
RENVOYS
RENY
RENYING
REO
REOBJECT
REOBJECTS
REOBSERVE
REOBTAIN
REOBTAINS
REOCCUPY
REOCCUR
REOCCURS
REOFFEND
REOFFENDS
REOFFER
REOFFERED
REOFFERS
REOIL
REOILED
REOILING
REOILS
REOPEN
REOPENED
REOPENER

REOPENERS
REOPENING
REOPENS
REOPERATE
REOPPOSE
REOPPOSED
REOPPOSES
REORDAIN
REORDAINS
REORDER
REORDERED
REORDERS
REORIENT
REORIENTS
REOS
REOUTFIT
REOUTFITS
REOVIRUS
REOXIDISE
REOXIDIZE
REP
REPACIFY
REPACK
REPACKAGE
REPACKED
REPACKING
REPACKS
REPAID
REPAINT
REPAINTED
REPAINTS
REPAIR
REPAIRED
REPAIRER
REPAIRERS
REPAIRING
REPAIRMAN
REPAIRMEN
REPAIRS
REPAND
REPANDLY
REPANEL
REPANELED
REPANELS
REPAPER
REPAPERED
REPAPERS
REPARABLE
REPARABLY
REPARK
REPARKED
REPARKING
REPARKS
REPARTEE
REPARTEED
REPARTEES
REPASS
REPASSAGE

REPASSED
REPASSES
REPASSING
REPAST
REPASTED
REPASTING
REPASTS
REPASTURE
REPATCH
REPATCHED
REPATCHES
REPATTERN
REPAVE
REPAVED
REPAVES
REPAVING
REPAY
REPAYABLE
REPAYING
REPAYMENT
REPAYS
REPEAL
REPEALED
REPEALER
REPEALERS
REPEALING
REPEALS
REPEAT
REPEATED
REPEATER
REPEATERS
REPEATING
REPEATS
REPECHAGE
REPEG
REPEGGED
REPEGGING
REPEGS
REPEL
REPELLANT
REPELLED
REPELLENT
REPELLER
REPELLERS
REPELLING
REPELS
REPENT
REPENTANT
REPENTED
REPENTER
REPENTERS
REPENTING
REPENTS
REPEOPLE
REPEOPLED
REPEOPLES
REPERCUSS
REPEREPE

REPERK	REPLEDGED	REPORTER	REPRICES
REPERKED	REPLEDGES	REPORTERS	REPRICING
REPERKING	REPLENISH	REPORTING	REPRIEFE
REPERKS	REPLETE	REPORTS	REPRIEFES
REPERTORY	REPLETED	REPOS	REPRIEVAL
REPERUSAL	REPLETELY	REPOSAL	REPRIEVE
REPERUSE	REPLETES	REPOSALL	REPRIEVED
REPERUSED	REPLETING	REPOSALLS	REPRIEVER
REPERUSES	REPLETION	REPOSALS	REPRIEVES
REPETEND	REPLEVIED	REPOSE	REPRIMAND
REPETENDS	REPLEVIES	REPOSED	REPRIME
REPHRASE	REPLEVIN	REPOSEDLY	REPRIMED
REPHRASED	REPLEVINS	REPOSEFUL	REPRIMES
REPHRASES	REPLEVY	REPOSER	REPRIMING
REPIGMENT	REPLICA	REPOSERS	REPRINT
REPIN	REPLICAS	REPOSES	REPRINTED
REPINE	REPLICASE	REPOSING	REPRINTER
REPINED	REPLICATE	REPOSIT	REPRINTS
REPINER	REPLICON	REPOSITED	REPRISAL
REPINERS	REPLICONS	REPOSITOR	REPRISALS
REPINES	REPLIED	REPOSITS	REPRISE
REPINING	REPLIER	REPOSSESS	REPRISED
REPININGS	REPLIERS	REPOST	REPRISES
REPINNED	REPLIES	REPOSTED	REPRISING
REPINNING	REPLOT	REPOSTING	REPRIVE
REPINS	REPLOTS	REPOSTS	REPRIVED
REPIQUE	REPLOTTED	REPOSURE	REPRIVES
REPIQUED	REPLOW	REPOSURES	REPRIVING
REPIQUES	REPLOWED	REPOT	REPRIZE
REPIQUING	REPLOWING	REPOTS	REPRIZED
REPLA	REPLOWS	REPOTTED	REPRIZES
REPLACE	REPLUM	REPOTTING	REPRIZING
REPLACED	REPLUMB	REPOUR	REPRO
REPLACER	REPLUMBED	REPOURED	REPROACH
REPLACERS	REPLUMBS	REPOURING	REPROBACY
REPLACES	REPLUNGE	REPOURS	REPROBATE
REPLACING	REPLUNGED	REPOUSSE	REPROBE
REPLAN	REPLUNGES	REPOUSSES	REPROBED
REPLANNED	REPLY	REPOWER	REPROBES
REPLANS	REPLYING	REPOWERED	REPROBING
REPLANT	REPO	REPOWERS	REPROCESS
REPLANTED	REPOINT	REPP	REPRODUCE
REPLANTS	REPOINTED	REPPED	REPROGRAM
REPLASTER	REPOINTS	REPPING	REPROOF
REPLATE	REPOLISH	REPPINGS	REPROOFED
REPLATED	REPOLL	REPPS	REPROOFS
REPLATES	REPOLLED	REPREEVE	REPROS
REPLATING	REPOLLING	REPREEVED	REPROVAL
REPLAY	REPOLLS	REPREEVES	REPROVALS
REPLAYED	REPOMAN	REPREHEND	REPROVE
REPLAYING	REPOMEN	REPRESENT	REPROVED
REPLAYS	REPONE	REPRESS	REPROVER
REPLEAD	REPONED	REPRESSED	REPROVERS
REPLEADED	REPONES	REPRESSER	REPROVES
REPLEADER	REPONING	REPRESSES	REPROVING
REPLEADS	REPORT	REPRESSOR	REPRYVE
REPLED	REPORTAGE	REPRICE	REPRYVED
REPLEDGE	REPORTED	REPRICED	REPRYVES

REPRYVING	REQUERING	REREDOS	RESALE
REPS	REQUEST	REREDOSES	RESALES
REPTANT	REQUESTED	REREDOSSE	RESALGAR
REPTATION	REQUESTER	RERELEASE	RESALGARS
REPTILE	REQUESTOR	REREMAI	RESALUTE
REPTILES	REQUESTS	REREMICE	RESALUTED
REPTILIA	REQUICKEN	REREMIND	RESALUTES
REPTILIAN	REQUIEM	REREMINDS	RESAMPLE
REPTILIUM	REQUIEMS	REREMOUSE	RESAMPLED
REPTILOID	REQUIGHT	RERENT	RESAMPLES
REPUBLIC	REQUIGHTS	RERENTED	RESAT
REPUBLICS	REQUIN	RERENTING	RESAW
REPUBLISH	REQUINS	RERENTS	RESAWED
REPUDIATE	REQUIRE	REREPEAT	RESAWING
REPUGN	REQUIRED	REREPEATS	RESAWN
REPUGNANT	REQUIRER	REREVIEW	RESAWS
REPUGNED	REQUIRERS	REREVIEWS	RESAY
REPUGNING	REQUIRES	REREVISE	RESAYING
REPUGNS	REQUIRING	REREVISED	RESAYS
REPULP	REQUISITE	REREVISES	RESCALE
REPULPED	REQUIT	REREWARD	RESCALED
REPULPING	REQUITAL	REREWARDS	RESCALES
REPULPS	REQUITALS	RERIG	RESCALING
REPULSE	REQUITE	RERIGGED	RESCHOOL
REPULSED	REQUITED	RERIGGING	RESCHOOLS
REPULSER	REQUITER	RERIGS	RESCIND
REPULSERS	REQUITERS	RERISE	RESCINDED
REPULSES	REQUITES	RERISEN	RESCINDER
REPULSING	REQUITING	RERISES	RESCINDS
REPULSION	REQUITS	RERISING	RESCORE
REPULSIVE	REQUITTED	REROLL	RESCORED
REPUMP	REQUOTE	REROLLED	RESCORES
REPUMPED	REQUOTED	REROLLER	RESCORING
REPUMPING	REQUOTES	REROLLERS	RESCREEN
REPUMPS	REQUOTING	REROLLING	RESCREENS
REPUNIT	REQUOYLE	REROLLS	RESCRIPT
REPUNITS	REQUOYLED	REROOF	RESCRIPTS
REPURE	REQUOYLES	REROOFED	RESCUABLE
REPURED	RERACK	REROOFING	RESCUE
REPURES	RERACKED	REROOFS	RESCUED
REPURIFY	RERACKING	REROSE	RESCUER
REPURING	RERACKS	REROUTE	RESCUERS
REPURPOSE	RERADIATE	REROUTED	RESCUES
REPURSUE	RERAIL	REROUTES	RESCUING
REPURSUED	RERAILED	REROUTING	RESCULPT
REPURSUES	RERAILING	RERUN	RESCULPTS
REPUTABLE	RERAILS	RERUNNING	RESEAL
REPUTABLY	RERAISE	RERUNS	RESEALED
REPUTE	RERAISED	RES	RESEALING
REPUTED	RERAISES	RESADDLE	RESEALS
REPUTEDLY	RERAISING	RESADDLED	RESEARCH
REPUTES	RERAN	RESADDLES	RESEASON
REPUTING	REREAD	RESAID	RESEASONS
REPUTINGS	REREADING	RESAIL	RESEAT
REQUALIFY	REREADS	RESAILED	RESEATED
REQUERE	REREBRACE	RESAILING	RESEATING
REQUERED	RERECORD	RESAILS	RESEATS
REQUERES	RERECORDS	RESALABLE	RESEAU

RESEAUS	RESERVIST	RESIANCES	RESINISED
RESEAUX	RESERVOIR	RESIANT	RESINISES
RESECT	RESES	RESIANTS	RESINIZE
RESECTED	RESET	RESID	RESINIZED
RESECTING	RESETS	RESIDE	RESINIZES
RESECTION	RESETTED	RESIDED	RESINLIKE
RESECTS	RESETTER	RESIDENCE	RESINOID
RESECURE	RESETTERS	RESIDENCY	RESINOIDS
RESECURED	RESETTING	RESIDENT	RESINOSES
RESECURES	RESETTLE	RESIDENTS	RESINOSIS
RESEDA	RESETTLED	RESIDER	RESINOUS
RESEDAS	RESETTLES	RESIDERS	RESINS
RESEE	RESEW	RESIDES	RESINY
RESEED	RESEWED	RESIDING	RESIST
RESEEDED	RESEWING	RESIDS	RESISTANT
RESEEDING	RESEWN	RESIDUA	RESISTED
RESEEDS	RESEWS	RESIDUAL	RESISTENT
RESEEING	RESH	RESIDUALS	RESISTER
RESEEK	RESHAPE	RESIDUARY	RESISTERS
RESEEKING	RESHAPED	RESIDUE	RESISTING
RESEEKS	RESHAPER	RESIDUES	RESISTIVE
RESEEN	RESHAPERS	RESIDUOUS	RESISTOR
RESEES	RESHAPES	RESIDUUM	RESISTORS
RESEIZE	RESHAPING	RESIDUUMS	RESISTS
RESEIZED	RESHARPEN	RESIFT	RESIT
RESEIZES	RESHAVE	RESIFTED	RESITE
RESEIZING	RESHAVED	RESIFTING	RESITED
RESEIZURE	RESHAVEN	RESIFTS	RESITES
RESELECT	RESHAVES	RESIGHT	RESITING
RESELECTS	RESHAVING	RESIGHTED	RESITS
RESELL	RESHES	RESIGHTS	RESITTING
RESELLER	RESHINE	RESIGN	RESITUATE
RESELLERS	RESHINED	RESIGNED	RESIZE
RESELLING	RESHINES	RESIGNER	RESIZED
RESELLS	RESHINGLE	RESIGNERS	RESIZES
RESEMBLE	RESHINING	RESIGNING	RESIZING
RESEMBLED	RESHIP	RESIGNS	RESKETCH
RESEMBLER	RESHIPPED	RESILE	RESKEW
RESEMBLES	RESHIPPER	RESILED	RESKEWED
RESEND	RESHIPS	RESILES	RESKEWING
RESENDING	RESHOD	RESILIENT	RESKEWS
RESENDS	RESHOE	RESILIN	RESKILL
RESENT	RESHOED	RESILING	RESKILLED
RESENTED	RESHOEING	RESILINS	RESKILLS
RESENTER	RESHOES	RESILVER	RESKUE
RESENTERS	RESHONE	RESILVERS	RESKUED
RESENTFUL	RESHOOT	RESIN	RESKUES
RESENTING	RESHOOTS	RESINATA	RESKUING
RESENTIVE	RESHOT	RESINATAS	RESLATE
RESENTS	RESHOW	RESINATE	RESLATED
RESERPINE	RESHOWED	RESINATED	RESLATES
RESERVE	RESHOWER	RESINATES	RESLATING
RESERVED	RESHOWERS	RESINED	RESMELT
RESERVER	RESHOWING	RESINER	RESMELTED
RESERVERS	RESHOWN	RESINERS	RESMELTS
RESERVES	RESHOWS	RESINIFY	RESMOOTH
RESERVICE	RESHUFFLE	RESINING	RESMOOTHS
RESERVING	RESIANCE	RESINISE	RESNATRON

491

RESOAK	RESOWED	RESPRAYED	RESTOCKS
RESOAKED	RESOWING	RESPRAYS	RESTOKE
RESOAKING	RESOWN	RESPREAD	RESTOKED
RESOAKS	RESOWS	RESPREADS	RESTOKES
RESOD	RESPACE	RESPRING	RESTOKING
RESODDED	RESPACED	RESPRINGS	RESTORAL
RESODDING	RESPACES	RESPROUT	RESTORALS
RESODS	RESPACING	RESPROUTS	RESTORE
RESOFTEN	RESPADE	RESPRUNG	RESTORED
RESOFTENS	RESPADED	RESSALDAR	RESTORER
RESOJET	RESPADES	REST	RESTORERS
RESOJETS	RESPADING	RESTABLE	RESTORES
RESOLD	RESPEAK	RESTABLED	RESTORING
RESOLDER	RESPEAKS	RESTABLES	RESTOS
RESOLDERS	RESPECIFY	RESTACK	RESTRAIN
RESOLE	RESPECT	RESTACKED	RESTRAINS
RESOLED	RESPECTED	RESTACKS	RESTRAINT
RESOLES	RESPECTER	RESTAFF	RESTRESS
RESOLING	RESPECTS	RESTAFFED	RESTRETCH
RESOLUBLE	RESPELL	RESTAFFS	RESTRICT
RESOLUTE	RESPELLED	RESTAGE	RESTRICTS
RESOLUTER	RESPELLS	RESTAGED	RESTRIKE
RESOLUTES	RESPELT	RESTAGES	RESTRIKES
RESOLVE	RESPIRE	RESTAGING	RESTRING
RESOLVED	RESPIRED	RESTAMP	RESTRINGE
RESOLVENT	RESPIRES	RESTAMPED	RESTRINGS
RESOLVER	RESPIRING	RESTAMPS	RESTRIVE
RESOLVERS	RESPITE	RESTART	RESTRIVEN
RESOLVES	RESPITED	RESTARTED	RESTRIVES
RESOLVING	RESPITES	RESTARTER	RESTROOM
RESONANCE	RESPITING	RESTARTS	RESTROOMS
RESONANT	RESPLEND	RESTATE	RESTROVE
RESONANTS	RESPLENDS	RESTATED	RESTRUCK
RESONATE	RESPLICE	RESTATES	RESTRUNG
RESONATED	RESPLICED	RESTATING	RESTS
RESONATES	RESPLICES	RESTATION	RESTUDIED
RESONATOR	RESPLIT	RESTED	RESTUDIES
RESORB	RESPLITS	RESTEM	RESTUDY
RESORBED	RESPOKE	RESTEMMED	RESTUFF
RESORBENT	RESPOKEN	RESTEMS	RESTUFFED
RESORBING	RESPOND	RESTER	RESTUFFS
RESORBS	RESPONDED	RESTERS	RESTUMP
RESORCIN	RESPONDER	RESTFUL	RESTUMPED
RESORCINS	RESPONDS	RESTFULLY	RESTUMPS
RESORT	RESPONSA	RESTIER	RESTY
RESORTED	RESPONSE	RESTIEST	RESTYLE
RESORTER	RESPONSER	RESTIFF	RESTYLED
RESORTERS	RESPONSES	RESTIFORM	RESTYLES
RESORTING	RESPONSOR	RESTING	RESTYLING
RESORTS	RESPONSUM	RESTINGS	RESUBJECT
RESOUGHT	RESPOOL	RESTITCH	RESUBMIT
RESOUND	RESPOOLED	RESTITUTE	RESUBMITS
RESOUNDED	RESPOOLS	RESTIVE	RESULT
RESOUNDS	RESPOT	RESTIVELY	RESULTANT
RESOURCE	RESPOTS	RESTLESS	RESULTED
RESOURCED	RESPOTTED	RESTO	RESULTFUL
RESOURCES	RESPRANG	RESTOCK	RESULTING
RESOW	RESPRAY	RESTOCKED	RESULTS

RESUMABLE
RESUME
RESUMED
RESUMER
RESUMERS
RESUMES
RESUMING
RESUMMON
RESUMMONS
RESUPINE
RESUPPLY
RESURFACE
RESURGE
RESURGED
RESURGENT
RESURGES
RESURGING
RESURRECT
RESURVEY
RESURVEYS
RESUSPEND
RESWALLOW
RET
RETABLE
RETABLES
RETACK
RETACKED
RETACKING
RETACKLE
RETACKLED
RETACKLES
RETACKS
RETAG
RETAGGED
RETAGGING
RETAGS
RETAIL
RETAILED
RETAILER
RETAILERS
RETAILING
RETAILOR
RETAILORS
RETAILS
RETAIN
RETAINED
RETAINER
RETAINERS
RETAINING
RETAINS
RETAKE
RETAKEN
RETAKER
RETAKERS
RETAKES
RETAKING
RETAKINGS
RETALIATE

RETALLIED
RETALLIES
RETALLY
RETAMA
RETAMAS
RETAPE
RETAPED
RETAPES
RETAPING
RETARD
RETARDANT
RETARDATE
RETARDED
RETARDER
RETARDERS
RETARDING
RETARDS
RETARGET
RETARGETS
RETASTE
RETASTED
RETASTES
RETASTING
RETAUGHT
RETAX
RETAXED
RETAXES
RETAXING
RETCH
RETCHED
RETCHES
RETCHING
RETCHLESS
RETE
RETEACH
RETEACHES
RETEAM
RETEAMED
RETEAMING
RETEAMS
RETEAR
RETEARING
RETEARS
RETELL
RETELLER
RETELLERS
RETELLING
RETELLS
RETEM
RETEMPER
RETEMPERS
RETEMS
RETENE
RETENES
RETENTION
RETENTIVE
RETES
RETEST

RETESTED
RETESTIFY
RETESTING
RETESTS
RETEXTURE
RETHINK
RETHINKER
RETHINKS
RETHOUGHT
RETHREAD
RETHREADS
RETIA
RETIAL
RETIARII
RETIARIUS
RETIARY
RETICELLA
RETICENCE
RETICENCY
RETICENT
RETICLE
RETICLES
RETICULA
RETICULAR
RETICULE
RETICULES
RETICULUM
RETIE
RETIED
RETIEING
RETIES
RETIFORM
RETIGHTEN
RETILE
RETILED
RETILES
RETILING
RETIME
RETIMED
RETIMES
RETIMING
RETINA
RETINAE
RETINAL
RETINALS
RETINAS
RETINE
RETINENE
RETINENES
RETINES
RETINITE
RETINITES
RETINITIS
RETINOID
RETINOIDS
RETINOL
RETINOLS
RETINT

RETINTED
RETINTING
RETINTS
RETINUE
RETINUED
RETINUES
RETINULA
RETINULAE
RETINULAR
RETINULAS
RETIRACY
RETIRAL
RETIRALS
RETIRANT
RETIRANTS
RETIRE
RETIRED
RETIREDLY
RETIREE
RETIREES
RETIRER
RETIRERS
RETIRES
RETIRING
RETITLE
RETITLED
RETITLES
RETITLING
RETOLD
RETOOK
RETOOL
RETOOLED
RETOOLING
RETOOLS
RETORE
RETORN
RETORSION
RETORT
RETORTED
RETORTER
RETORTERS
RETORTING
RETORTION
RETORTIVE
RETORTS
RETOTAL
RETOTALED
RETOTALS
RETOUCH
RETOUCHED
RETOUCHER
RETOUCHES
RETOUR
RETOURED
RETOURING
RETOURS
RETRACE
RETRACED

RETRACER
RETRACERS
RETRACES
RETRACING
RETRACK
RETRACKED
RETRACKS
RETRACT
RETRACTED
RETRACTOR
RETRACTS
RETRAICT
RETRAICTS
RETRAIN
RETRAINED
RETRAINEE
RETRAINS
RETRAIT
RETRAITE
RETRAITES
RETRAITS
RETRAITT
RETRAITTS
RETRAL
RETRALLY
RETRATE
RETRATED
RETRATES
RETRATING
RETREAD
RETREADED
RETREADS
RETREAT
RETREATED
RETREATER
RETREATS
RETREE
RETREES
RETRENCH
RETRIAL
RETRIALS
RETRIBUTE
RETRIED
RETRIES
RETRIEVAL
RETRIEVE
RETRIEVED
RETRIEVER
RETRIEVES
RETRIM
RETRIMMED
RETRIMS
RETRO
RETROACT
RETROACTS
RETROCEDE
RETROD
RETRODDEN

RETRODICT
RETROFIRE
RETROFIT
RETROFITS
RETROFLEX
RETROJECT
RETRONYM
RETRONYMS
RETROPACK
RETRORSE
RETROS
RETROUSSE
RETROVERT
RETRY
RETRYING
RETS
RETSINA
RETSINAS
RETTED
RETTERIES
RETTERY
RETTING
RETUND
RETUNDED
RETUNDING
RETUNDS
RETUNE
RETUNED
RETUNES
RETUNING
RETURF
RETURFED
RETURFING
RETURFS
RETURN
RETURNED
RETURNEE
RETURNEES
RETURNER
RETURNERS
RETURNIK
RETURNIKS
RETURNING
RETURNS
RETUSE
RETWIST
RETWISTED
RETWISTS
RETYING
RETYPE
RETYPED
RETYPES
RETYPING
REUNIFIED
REUNIFIES
REUNIFY
REUNION
REUNIONS

REUNITE
REUNITED
REUNITER
REUNITERS
REUNITES
REUNITING
REUPTAKE
REUPTAKES
REURGE
REURGED
REURGES
REURGING
REUSABLE
REUSABLES
REUSE
REUSED
REUSES
REUSING
REUTILISE
REUTILIZE
REUTTER
REUTTERED
REUTTERS
REV
REVALENTA
REVALUATE
REVALUE
REVALUED
REVALUES
REVALUING
REVAMP
REVAMPED
REVAMPER
REVAMPERS
REVAMPING
REVAMPS
REVANCHE
REVANCHES
REVARNISH
REVEAL
REVEALED
REVEALER
REVEALERS
REVEALING
REVEALS
REVEHENT
REVEILLE
REVEILLES
REVEL
REVELATOR
REVELED
REVELER
REVELERS
REVELING
REVELLED
REVELLER
REVELLERS
REVELLING

REVELMENT
REVELRIES
REVELROUS
REVELRY
REVELS
REVENANT
REVENANTS
REVENGE
REVENGED
REVENGER
REVENGERS
REVENGES
REVENGING
REVENGIVE
REVENUAL
REVENUE
REVENUED
REVENUER
REVENUERS
REVENUES
REVERABLE
REVERB
REVERBED
REVERBING
REVERBS
REVERE
REVERED
REVERENCE
REVEREND
REVERENDS
REVERENT
REVERER
REVERERS
REVERES
REVERIE
REVERIES
REVERIFY
REVERING
REVERIST
REVERISTS
REVERS
REVERSAL
REVERSALS
REVERSE
REVERSED
REVERSELY
REVERSER
REVERSERS
REVERSES
REVERSI
REVERSING
REVERSION
REVERSIS
REVERSO
REVERSOS
REVERT
REVERTANT
REVERTED

REVERTER
REVERTERS
REVERTING
REVERTIVE
REVERTS
REVERY
REVEST
REVESTED
REVESTING
REVESTRY
REVESTS
REVET
REVETMENT
REVETS
REVETTED
REVETTING
REVEUR
REVEURS
REVEUSE
REVEUSES
REVIBRATE
REVICTUAL
REVIE
REVIED
REVIES
REVIEW
REVIEWAL
REVIEWALS
REVIEWED
REVIEWER
REVIEWERS
REVIEWING
REVIEWS
REVILE
REVILED
REVILER
REVILERS
REVILES
REVILING
REVILINGS
REVIOLATE
REVISABLE
REVISAL
REVISALS
REVISE
REVISED
REVISER
REVISERS
REVISES
REVISING
REVISION
REVISIONS
REVISIT
REVISITED
REVISITS
REVISOR
REVISORS
REVISORY

REVIVABLE
REVIVABLY
REVIVAL
REVIVALS
REVIVE
REVIVED
REVIVER
REVIVERS
REVIVES
REVIVIFY
REVIVING
REVIVINGS
REVIVOR
REVIVORS
REVOCABLE
REVOCABLY
REVOICE
REVOICED
REVOICES
REVOICING
REVOKABLE
REVOKABLY
REVOKE
REVOKED
REVOKER
REVOKERS
REVOKES
REVOKING
REVOLT
REVOLTED
REVOLTER
REVOLTERS
REVOLTING
REVOLTS
REVOLUTE
REVOLVE
REVOLVED
REVOLVER
REVOLVERS
REVOLVES
REVOLVING
REVOTE
REVOTED
REVOTES
REVOTING
REVS
REVUE
REVUES
REVUIST
REVUISTS
REVULSED
REVULSION
REVULSIVE
REVVED
REVVING
REVYING
REW
REWAKE

REWAKED
REWAKEN
REWAKENED
REWAKENS
REWAKES
REWAKING
REWAN
REWARD
REWARDED
REWARDER
REWARDERS
REWARDFUL
REWARDING
REWARDS
REWAREWA
REWAREWAS
REWARM
REWARMED
REWARMING
REWARMS
REWASH
REWASHED
REWASHES
REWASHING
REWAX
REWAXED
REWAXES
REWAXING
REWEAR
REWEARING
REWEARS
REWEAVE
REWEAVED
REWEAVES
REWEAVING
REWED
REWEDDED
REWEDDING
REWEDS
REWEIGH
REWEIGHED
REWEIGHS
REWELD
REWELDED
REWELDING
REWELDS
REWET
REWETS
REWETTED
REWETTING
REWIDEN
REWIDENED
REWIDENS
REWIN
REWIND
REWINDED
REWINDER
REWINDERS

REWINDING
REWINDS
REWINNING
REWINS
REWIRABLE
REWIRE
REWIRED
REWIRES
REWIRING
REWOKE
REWOKEN
REWON
REWORD
REWORDED
REWORDING
REWORDS
REWORE
REWORK
REWORKED
REWORKING
REWORKS
REWORN
REWOUND
REWOVE
REWOVEN
REWRAP
REWRAPPED
REWRAPS
REWRAPT
REWRITE
REWRITER
REWRITERS
REWRITES
REWRITING
REWRITTEN
REWROTE
REWROUGHT
REWS
REWTH
REWTHS
REX
REXES
REXINE
REXINES
REYNARD
REYNARDS
REZ
REZERO
REZEROED
REZEROES
REZEROING
REZEROS
REZONE
REZONED
REZONES
REZONING
REZZES
RHABDOID

RHABDOIDS
RHABDOM
RHABDOMAL
RHABDOME
RHABDOMES
RHABDOMS
RHABDUS
RHABDUSES
RHACHIAL
RHACHIDES
RHACHILLA
RHACHIS
RHACHISES
RHACHITIS
RHAGADES
RHAMNOSE
RHAMNOSES
RHAMNUS
RHAMNUSES
RHAMPHOID
RHANJA
RHANJAS
RHAPHAE
RHAPHE
RHAPHES
RHAPHIDE
RHAPHIDES
RHAPHIS
RHAPONTIC
RHAPSODE
RHAPSODES
RHAPSODIC
RHAPSODY
RHATANIES
RHATANY
RHEA
RHEAS
RHEBOK
RHEBOKS
RHEMATIC
RHEME
RHEMES
RHENIUM
RHENIUMS
RHEOBASE
RHEOBASES
RHEOBASIC
RHEOCHORD
RHEOCORD
RHEOCORDS
RHEOLOGIC
RHEOLOGY
RHEOMETER
RHEOMETRY
RHEOPHIL
RHEOPHILE
RHEOSTAT
RHEOSTATS

RHEOTAXES
RHEOTAXIS
RHEOTOME
RHEOTOMES
RHEOTROPE
RHESUS
RHESUSES
RHETOR
RHETORIC
RHETORICS
RHETORISE
RHETORIZE
RHETORS
RHEUM
RHEUMATIC
RHEUMATIZ
RHEUMED
RHEUMIC
RHEUMIER
RHEUMIEST
RHEUMS
RHEUMY
RHEXES
RHEXIS
RHEXISES
RHIES
RHIGOLENE
RHIME
RHIMES
RHINAL
RHINE
RHINES
RHINITIC
RHINITIS
RHINO
RHINOCERI
RHINOLITH
RHINOLOGY
RHINOS
RHIPIDATE
RHIPIDION
RHIPIDIUM
RHIZIC
RHIZINE
RHIZINES
RHIZOBIA
RHIZOBIAL
RHIZOBIUM
RHIZOCARP
RHIZOCAUL
RHIZOID
RHIZOIDAL
RHIZOIDS
RHIZOMA
RHIZOMATA
RHIZOME
RHIZOMES
RHIZOMIC

RHIZOPI
RHIZOPOD
RHIZOPODS
RHIZOPUS
RHIZOTOMY
RHO
RHODAMIN
RHODAMINE
RHODAMINS
RHODANATE
RHODANIC
RHODANISE
RHODANIZE
RHODIC
RHODIE
RHODIES
RHODINAL
RHODINALS
RHODIUM
RHODIUMS
RHODOLITE
RHODONITE
RHODOPSIN
RHODORA
RHODORAS
RHODOUS
RHODY
RHOEADINE
RHOMB
RHOMBI
RHOMBIC
RHOMBICAL
RHOMBOI
RHOMBOID
RHOMBOIDS
RHOMBOS
RHOMBS
RHOMBUS
RHOMBUSES
RHONCHAL
RHONCHI
RHONCHIAL
RHONCHUS
RHONE
RHONES
RHOPALIC
RHOPALISM
RHOS
RHOTACISE
RHOTACISM
RHOTACIST
RHOTACIZE
RHOTIC
RHOTICITY
RHUBARB
RHUBARBED
RHUBARBS
RHUBARBY

RHUMB
RHUMBA
RHUMBAED
RHUMBAING
RHUMBAS
RHUMBS
RHUS
RHUSES
RHY
RHYME
RHYMED
RHYMELESS
RHYMER
RHYMERS
RHYMES
RHYMESTER
RHYMING
RHYMIST
RHYMISTS
RHYNE
RHYNES
RHYOLITE
RHYOLITES
RHYOLITIC
RHYTA
RHYTHM
RHYTHMAL
RHYTHMED
RHYTHMI
RHYTHMIC
RHYTHMICS
RHYTHMISE
RHYTHMIST
RHYTHMIZE
RHYTHMS
RHYTHMUS
RHYTIDOME
RHYTINA
RHYTINAS
RHYTON
RHYTONS
RIA
RIAL
RIALS
RIALTO
RIALTOS
RIANCIES
RIANCY
RIANT
RIANTLY
RIAS
RIATA
RIATAS
RIB
RIBA
RIBALD
RIBALDLY
RIBALDRY

RIBALDS
RIBAND
RIBANDS
RIBAS
RIBATTUTA
RIBAUD
RIBAUDRED
RIBAUDRY
RIBAUDS
RIBAVIRIN
RIBBAND
RIBBANDS
RIBBED
RIBBER
RIBBERS
RIBBIER
RIBBIEST
RIBBING
RIBBINGS
RIBBON
RIBBONED
RIBBONING
RIBBONRY
RIBBONS
RIBBONY
RIBBY
RIBCAGE
RIBCAGES
RIBES
RIBGRASS
RIBIBE
RIBIBES
RIBIBLE
RIBIBLES
RIBIER
RIBIERS
RIBLESS
RIBLET
RIBLETS
RIBLIKE
RIBOSE
RIBOSES
RIBOSOMAL
RIBOSOME
RIBOSOMES
RIBOZYMAL
RIBOZYME
RIBOZYMES
RIBS
RIBSTON
RIBSTONE
RIBSTONES
RIBSTONS
RIBWORK
RIBWORKS
RIBWORT
RIBWORTS
RICE

RICEBIRD
RICEBIRDS
RICED
RICER
RICERCAR
RICERCARE
RICERCARI
RICERCARS
RICERCATA
RICERS
RICES
RICEY
RICH
RICHED
RICHEN
RICHENED
RICHENING
RICHENS
RICHER
RICHES
RICHESSE
RICHESSES
RICHEST
RICHING
RICHLY
RICHNESS
RICHT
RICHTED
RICHTER
RICHTEST
RICHTING
RICHTS
RICHWEED
RICHWEEDS
RICIER
RICIEST
RICIN
RICING
RICINS
RICINUS
RICINUSES
RICK
RICKED
RICKER
RICKERS
RICKETIER
RICKETILY
RICKETS
RICKETTY
RICKETY
RICKEY
RICKEYS
RICKING
RICKLE
RICKLES
RICKLY
RICKRACK
RICKRACKS

RICKS
RICKSHA
RICKSHAS
RICKSHAW
RICKSHAWS
RICKSTAND
RICKSTICK
RICKYARD
RICKYARDS
RICOCHET
RICOCHETS
RICOTTA
RICOTTAS
RICRAC
RICRACS
RICTAL
RICTUS
RICTUSES
RICY
RID
RIDABLE
RIDDANCE
RIDDANCES
RIDDED
RIDDEN
RIDDER
RIDDERS
RIDDING
RIDDLE
RIDDLED
RIDDLER
RIDDLERS
RIDDLES
RIDDLING
RIDDLINGS
RIDE
RIDEABLE
RIDENT
RIDER
RIDERED
RIDERLESS
RIDERS
RIDERSHIP
RIDES
RIDGE
RIDGEBACK
RIDGED
RIDGEL
RIDGELIKE
RIDGELINE
RIDGELING
RIDGELS
RIDGEPOLE
RIDGER
RIDGERS
RIDGES
RIDGETOP
RIDGETOPS

RIDGETREE
RIDGEWAY
RIDGEWAYS
RIDGIER
RIDGIEST
RIDGIL
RIDGILS
RIDGING
RIDGINGS
RIDGLING
RIDGLINGS
RIDGY
RIDICULE
RIDICULED
RIDICULER
RIDICULES
RIDING
RIDINGS
RIDLEY
RIDLEYS
RIDOTTO
RIDOTTOS
RIDS
RIEL
RIELS
RIEM
RIEMPIE
RIEMPIES
RIEMS
RIESLING
RIESLINGS
RIEVE
RIEVER
RIEVERS
RIEVES
RIEVING
RIF
RIFAMPIN
RIFAMPINS
RIFAMYCIN
RIFE
RIFELY
RIFENESS
RIFER
RIFEST
RIFF
RIFFAGE
RIFFAGES
RIFFED
RIFFING
RIFFLE
RIFFLED
RIFFLER
RIFFLERS
RIFFLES
RIFFLING
RIFFOLA
RIFFOLAS

RIFFRAFF	RIGHTINGS	RIKSHAW	RIMROCKS
RIFFRAFFS	RIGHTISH	RIKSHAWS	RIMS
RIFFS	RIGHTISM	RILE	RIMSHOT
RIFLE	RIGHTISMS	RILED	RIMSHOTS
RIFLEBIRD	RIGHTIST	RILES	RIMU
RIFLED	RIGHTISTS	RILEY	RIMUS
RIFLEMAN	RIGHTLESS	RILIER	RIMY
RIFLEMEN	RIGHTLY	RILIEST	RIN
RIFLER	RIGHTMOST	RILIEVI	RIND
RIFLERIES	RIGHTNESS	RILIEVO	RINDED
RIFLERS	RIGHTO	RILING	RINDIER
RIFLERY	RIGHTOS	RILL	RINDIEST
RIFLES	RIGHTS	RILLE	RINDING
RIFLING	RIGHTSIZE	RILLED	RINDLESS
RIFLINGS	RIGHTWARD	RILLES	RINDS
RIFLIP	RIGHTY	RILLET	RINDY
RIFLIPS	RIGID	RILLETS	RINE
RIFS	RIGIDER	RILLETTES	RINES
RIFT	RIGIDEST	RILLING	RING
RIFTE	RIGIDIFY	RILLMARK	RINGBARK
RIFTED	RIGIDISE	RILLMARKS	RINGBARKS
RIFTIER	RIGIDISED	RILLS	RINGBIT
RIFTIEST	RIGIDISES	RIM	RINGBITS
RIFTING	RIGIDITY	RIMA	RINGBOLT
RIFTLESS	RIGIDIZE	RIMAE	RINGBOLTS
RIFTS	RIGIDIZED	RIMAYE	RINGBONE
RIFTY	RIGIDIZES	RIMAYES	RINGBONES
RIG	RIGIDLY	RIME	RINGDOVE
RIGADOON	RIGIDNESS	RIMED	RINGDOVES
RIGADOONS	RIGIDS	RIMELESS	RINGED
RIGATONI	RIGLIN	RIMER	RINGENT
RIGATONIS	RIGLING	RIMERS	RINGER
RIGAUDON	RIGLINGS	RIMES	RINGERS
RIGAUDONS	RIGLINS	RIMESTER	RINGGIT
RIGG	RIGMAROLE	RIMESTERS	RINGGITS
RIGGALD	RIGOL	RIMFIRE	RINGHALS
RIGGALDS	RIGOLL	RIMFIRES	RINGING
RIGGED	RIGOLLS	RIMIER	RINGINGLY
RIGGER	RIGOLS	RIMIEST	RINGINGS
RIGGERS	RIGOR	RIMINESS	RINGLESS
RIGGING	RIGORISM	RIMING	RINGLET
RIGGINGS	RIGORISMS	RIMLAND	RINGLETED
RIGGISH	RIGORIST	RIMLANDS	RINGLETS
RIGGS	RIGORISTS	RIMLESS	RINGLIKE
RIGHT	RIGOROUS	RIMMED	RINGMAN
RIGHTABLE	RIGORS	RIMMER	RINGMEN
RIGHTABLY	RIGOUR	RIMMERS	RINGNECK
RIGHTED	RIGOURS	RIMMING	RINGNECKS
RIGHTEN	RIGOUT	RIMMINGS	RINGS
RIGHTENED	RIGOUTS	RIMOSE	RINGSIDE
RIGHTENS	RIGS	RIMOSELY	RINGSIDER
RIGHTEOUS	RIGSDALER	RIMOSITY	RINGSIDES
RIGHTER	RIGWIDDIE	RIMOUS	RINGSTAND
RIGHTERS	RIGWOODIE	RIMPLE	RINGSTER
RIGHTEST	RIJSTAFEL	RIMPLED	RINGSTERS
RIGHTFUL	RIKISHA	RIMPLES	RINGTAIL
RIGHTIES	RIKISHAS	RIMPLING	RINGTAILS
RIGHTING	RIKISHI	RIMROCK	RINGTAW

RINGTAWS
RINGTONE
RINGTONES
RINGTOSS
RINGWAY
RINGWAYS
RINGWISE
RINGWOMB
RINGWOMBS
RINGWORK
RINGWORKS
RINGWORM
RINGWORMS
RINK
RINKED
RINKHALS
RINKING
RINKS
RINNING
RINS
RINSABLE
RINSE
RINSEABLE
RINSED
RINSER
RINSERS
RINSES
RINSIBLE
RINSING
RINSINGS
RIOJA
RIOJAS
RIOT
RIOTED
RIOTER
RIOTERS
RIOTING
RIOTINGS
RIOTISE
RIOTISES
RIOTIZE
RIOTIZES
RIOTOUS
RIOTOUSLY
RIOTRIES
RIOTRY
RIOTS
RIP
RIPARIAL
RIPARIAN
RIPARIANS
RIPCORD
RIPCORDS
RIPE
RIPECK
RIPECKS
RIPED
RIPELY

RIPEN
RIPENED
RIPENER
RIPENERS
RIPENESS
RIPENING
RIPENS
RIPER
RIPERS
RIPES
RIPEST
RIPIENI
RIPIENIST
RIPIENO
RIPIENOS
RIPING
RIPOFF
RIPOFFS
RIPOST
RIPOSTE
RIPOSTED
RIPOSTES
RIPOSTING
RIPOSTS
RIPP
RIPPABLE
RIPPED
RIPPER
RIPPERS
RIPPIER
RIPPIERS
RIPPING
RIPPINGLY
RIPPLE
RIPPLED
RIPPLER
RIPPLERS
RIPPLES
RIPPLET
RIPPLETS
RIPPLIER
RIPPLIEST
RIPPLING
RIPPLINGS
RIPPLY
RIPPS
RIPRAP
RIPRAPPED
RIPRAPS
RIPS
RIPSAW
RIPSAWED
RIPSAWING
RIPSAWN
RIPSAWS
RIPSTOP
RIPSTOPS
RIPT

RIPTIDE
RIPTIDES
RIRORIRO
RIRORIROS
RISALDAR
RISALDARS
RISE
RISEN
RISER
RISERS
RISES
RISHI
RISHIS
RISIBLE
RISIBLES
RISIBLY
RISING
RISINGS
RISK
RISKED
RISKER
RISKERS
RISKFUL
RISKIER
RISKIEST
RISKILY
RISKINESS
RISKING
RISKLESS
RISKS
RISKY
RISOLUTO
RISOTTO
RISOTTOS
RISP
RISPED
RISPETTI
RISPETTO
RISPING
RISPINGS
RISPS
RISQUE
RISQUES
RISSOLE
RISSOLES
RISTRA
RISTRAS
RISUS
RISUSES
RIT
RITARD
RITARDS
RITE
RITELESS
RITENUTO
RITENUTOS
RITES
RITONAVIR

RITORNEL
RITORNELL
RITORNELS
RITS
RITT
RITTED
RITTER
RITTERS
RITTING
RITTS
RITUAL
RITUALISE
RITUALISM
RITUALIST
RITUALIZE
RITUALLY
RITUALS
RITZ
RITZES
RITZIER
RITZIEST
RITZILY
RITZINESS
RITZY
RIVA
RIVAGE
RIVAGES
RIVAL
RIVALED
RIVALESS
RIVALING
RIVALISE
RIVALISED
RIVALISES
RIVALITY
RIVALIZE
RIVALIZED
RIVALIZES
RIVALLED
RIVALLESS
RIVALLING
RIVALRIES
RIVALROUS
RIVALRY
RIVALS
RIVALSHIP
RIVAS
RIVE
RIVED
RIVEL
RIVELLED
RIVELLING
RIVELS
RIVEN
RIVER
RIVERAIN
RIVERAINS
RIVERBANK

RIVERBED	RIZZOR	ROARMING	ROBUSTA
RIVERBEDS	RIZZORED	ROARS	ROBUSTAS
RIVERBOAT	RIZZORING	ROARY	ROBUSTER
RIVERED	RIZZORS	ROAST	ROBUSTEST
RIVERET	ROACH	ROASTED	ROBUSTLY
RIVERETS	ROACHED	ROASTER	ROC
RIVERHEAD	ROACHES	ROASTERS	ROCAILLE
RIVERINE	ROACHING	ROASTING	ROCAILLES
RIVERLESS	ROAD	ROASTINGS	ROCAMBOLE
RIVERLIKE	ROADBED	ROASTS	ROCH
RIVERMAN	ROADBEDS	ROATE	ROCHES
RIVERMEN	ROADBLOCK	ROATED	ROCHET
RIVERS	ROADCRAFT	ROATES	ROCHETS
RIVERSIDE	ROADEO	ROATING	ROCK
RIVERWARD	ROADEOS	ROB	ROCKABIES
RIVERWAY	ROADHOUSE	ROBALO	ROCKABLE
RIVERWAYS	ROADIE	ROBALOS	ROCKABY
RIVERWEED	ROADIES	ROBAND	ROCKABYE
RIVERY	ROADING	ROBANDS	ROCKABYES
RIVES	ROADINGS	ROBBED	ROCKAWAY
RIVET	ROADKILL	ROBBER	ROCKAWAYS
RIVETED	ROADKILLS	ROBBERIES	ROCKBOUND
RIVETER	ROADLESS	ROBBERS	ROCKCRESS
RIVETERS	ROADMAN	ROBBERY	ROCKED
RIVETING	ROADMEN	ROBBIN	ROCKER
RIVETINGS	ROADS	ROBBING	ROCKERIES
RIVETS	ROADSHOW	ROBBINS	ROCKERS
RIVETTED	ROADSHOWS	ROBE	ROCKERY
RIVETTING	ROADSIDE	ROBED	ROCKET
RIVIERA	ROADSIDES	ROBES	ROCKETED
RIVIERAS	ROADSMAN	ROBIN	ROCKETEER
RIVIERE	ROADSMEN	ROBING	ROCKETER
RIVIERES	ROADSTEAD	ROBINGS	ROCKETERS
RIVING	ROADSTER	ROBINIA	ROCKETING
RIVLIN	ROADSTERS	ROBINIAS	ROCKETRY
RIVLINS	ROADWAY	ROBINS	ROCKETS
RIVO	ROADWAYS	ROBLE	ROCKFALL
RIVOS	ROADWORK	ROBLES	ROCKFALLS
RIVULET	ROADWORKS	ROBORANT	ROCKFISH
RIVULETS	ROAM	ROBORANTS	ROCKHOUND
RIVULOSE	ROAMED	ROBOT	ROCKIER
RIYAL	ROAMER	ROBOTIC	ROCKIERS
RIYALS	ROAMERS	ROBOTICS	ROCKIEST
RIZ	ROAMING	ROBOTISE	ROCKILY
RIZA	ROAMINGS	ROBOTISED	ROCKINESS
RIZARD	ROAMS	ROBOTISES	ROCKING
RIZARDS	ROAN	ROBOTISM	ROCKINGLY
RIZAS	ROANS	ROBOTISMS	ROCKINGS
RIZZAR	ROAR	ROBOTIZE	ROCKLAY
RIZZARED	ROARED	ROBOTIZED	ROCKLAYS
RIZZARING	ROARER	ROBOTIZES	ROCKLESS
RIZZARS	ROARERS	ROBOTRIES	ROCKLIKE
RIZZART	ROARIE	ROBOTRY	ROCKLING
RIZZARTS	ROARIER	ROBOTS	ROCKLINGS
RIZZER	ROARIEST	ROBS	ROCKOON
RIZZERED	ROARING	ROBURITE	ROCKOONS
RIZZERING	ROARINGLY	ROBURITES	ROCKROSE
RIZZERS	ROARINGS	ROBUST	ROCKROSES

ROCKS
ROCKSHAFT
ROCKSLIDE
ROCKWATER
ROCKWEED
ROCKWEEDS
ROCKWORK
ROCKWORKS
ROCKY
ROCOCO
ROCOCOS
ROCQUET
ROCQUETS
ROCS
ROD
RODDED
RODDING
RODDINGS
RODE
RODED
RODENT
RODENTS
RODEO
RODEOED
RODEOING
RODEOS
RODES
RODEWAY
RODEWAYS
RODFISHER
RODGERSIA
RODING
RODINGS
RODLESS
RODLIKE
RODMAN
RODMEN
RODS
RODSMAN
RODSMEN
RODSTER
RODSTERS
ROE
ROEBUCK
ROEBUCKS
ROED
ROEMER
ROEMERS
ROENTGEN
ROENTGENS
ROES
ROESTONE
ROESTONES
ROGALLO
ROGALLOS
ROGATION
ROGATIONS
ROGATORY

ROGER
ROGERED
ROGERING
ROGERINGS
ROGERS
ROGNON
ROGNONS
ROGUE
ROGUED
ROGUEING
ROGUERIES
ROGUERY
ROGUES
ROGUESHIP
ROGUING
ROGUISH
ROGUISHLY
ROGUY
ROIL
ROILED
ROILIER
ROILIEST
ROILING
ROILS
ROILY
ROIN
ROINED
ROINING
ROINISH
ROINS
ROIST
ROISTED
ROISTER
ROISTERED
ROISTERER
ROISTERS
ROISTING
ROISTS
ROJAK
ROJAKS
ROJI
ROJIS
ROK
ROKE
ROKED
ROKELAY
ROKELAYS
ROKER
ROKERS
ROKES
ROKIER
ROKIEST
ROKING
ROKKAKU
ROKS
ROKY
ROLAG
ROLAGS

ROLAMITE
ROLAMITES
ROLE
ROLES
ROLF
ROLFED
ROLFER
ROLFERS
ROLFING
ROLFINGS
ROLFS
ROLL
ROLLABLE
ROLLAWAY
ROLLAWAYS
ROLLBACK
ROLLBACKS
ROLLBAR
ROLLBARS
ROLLED
ROLLER
ROLLERS
ROLLICK
ROLLICKED
ROLLICKS
ROLLICKY
ROLLING
ROLLINGS
ROLLMOP
ROLLMOPS
ROLLNECK
ROLLNECKS
ROLLOCK
ROLLOCKS
ROLLOUT
ROLLOUTS
ROLLOVER
ROLLOVERS
ROLLS
ROLLTOP
ROLLWAY
ROLLWAYS
ROM
ROMA
ROMAGE
ROMAGES
ROMAIKA
ROMAIKAS
ROMAINE
ROMAINES
ROMAJI
ROMAJIS
ROMAL
ROMALS
ROMAN
ROMANCE
ROMANCED
ROMANCER

ROMANCERS
ROMANCES
ROMANCING
ROMANISE
ROMANISED
ROMANISES
ROMANIZE
ROMANIZED
ROMANIZES
ROMANO
ROMANOS
ROMANS
ROMANTIC
ROMANTICS
ROMANZA
ROMANZAS
ROMAS
ROMAUNT
ROMAUNTS
ROMCOM
ROMCOMS
ROMELDALE
ROMEO
ROMEOS
ROMNEYA
ROMNEYAS
ROMP
ROMPED
ROMPER
ROMPERS
ROMPING
ROMPINGLY
ROMPISH
ROMPISHLY
ROMPS
ROMS
RONCADOR
RONCADORS
RONDACHE
RONDACHES
RONDAVEL
RONDAVELS
RONDE
RONDEAU
RONDEAUX
RONDEL
RONDELET
RONDELETS
RONDELLE
RONDELLES
RONDELS
RONDES
RONDINO
RONDINOS
RONDO
RONDOS
RONDURE
RONDURES

RONE
RONEO
RONEOED
RONEOING
RONEOS
RONEPIPE
RONEPIPES
RONES
RONG
RONGGENG
RONGGENGS
RONIN
RONINS
RONION
RONIONS
RONNE
RONNEL
RONNELS
RONNIE
RONNIES
RONNING
RONT
RONTE
RONTES
RONTGEN
RONTGENS
RONTS
RONYON
RONYONS
RONZER
RONZERS
ROO
ROOD
ROODS
ROOF
ROOFED
ROOFER
ROOFERS
ROOFIE
ROOFIER
ROOFIES
ROOFIEST
ROOFING
ROOFINGS
ROOFLESS
ROOFLIKE
ROOFLINE
ROOFLINES
ROOFS
ROOFSCAPE
ROOFTOP
ROOFTOPS
ROOFTREE
ROOFTREES
ROOFY
ROOIBOS
ROOIKAT
ROOIKATS

ROOINEK
ROOINEKS
ROOK
ROOKED
ROOKERIES
ROOKERY
ROOKIE
ROOKIER
ROOKIES
ROOKIEST
ROOKING
ROOKISH
ROOKS
ROOKY
ROOM
ROOMED
ROOMER
ROOMERS
ROOMETTE
ROOMETTES
ROOMFUL
ROOMFULS
ROOMIE
ROOMIER
ROOMIES
ROOMIEST
ROOMILY
ROOMINESS
ROOMING
ROOMMATE
ROOMMATES
ROOMS
ROOMSOME
ROOMY
ROON
ROONS
ROOP
ROOPED
ROOPIER
ROOPIEST
ROOPING
ROOPIT
ROOPS
ROOPY
ROORBACH
ROORBACHS
ROORBACK
ROORBACKS
ROOS
ROOSA
ROOSAS
ROOSE
ROOSED
ROOSER
ROOSERS
ROOSES
ROOSING
ROOST

ROOSTED
ROOSTER
ROOSTERS
ROOSTING
ROOSTS
ROOT
ROOTAGE
ROOTAGES
ROOTCAP
ROOTCAPS
ROOTED
ROOTEDLY
ROOTER
ROOTERS
ROOTHOLD
ROOTHOLDS
ROOTIER
ROOTIES
ROOTIEST
ROOTINESS
ROOTING
ROOTINGS
ROOTLE
ROOTLED
ROOTLES
ROOTLESS
ROOTLET
ROOTLETS
ROOTLIKE
ROOTLING
ROOTS
ROOTSIER
ROOTSIEST
ROOTSTALK
ROOTSTOCK
ROOTSY
ROOTWORM
ROOTWORMS
ROOTY
ROPABLE
ROPE
ROPEABLE
ROPED
ROPELIKE
ROPER
ROPERIES
ROPERS
ROPERY
ROPES
ROPEWALK
ROPEWALKS
ROPEWAY
ROPEWAYS
ROPEWORK
ROPEWORKS
ROPEY
ROPIER
ROPIEST

ROPILY
ROPINESS
ROPING
ROPINGS
ROPY
ROQUE
ROQUES
ROQUET
ROQUETED
ROQUETING
ROQUETS
ROQUETTE
ROQUETTES
RORAL
RORE
RORES
RORIC
RORID
RORIE
RORIER
RORIEST
RORQUAL
RORQUALS
RORT
RORTED
RORTER
RORTERS
RORTIER
RORTIEST
RORTING
RORTS
RORTY
RORY
ROSACE
ROSACEA
ROSACEAS
ROSACEOUS
ROSACES
ROSAKER
ROSAKERS
ROSALIA
ROSALIAS
ROSANILIN
ROSARIA
ROSARIAN
ROSARIANS
ROSARIES
ROSARIUM
ROSARIUMS
ROSARY
ROSBIF
ROSBIFS
ROSCID
ROSCOE
ROSCOES
ROSE
ROSEAL
ROSEATE

ROSEATELY
ROSEBAY
ROSEBAYS
ROSEBOWL
ROSEBOWLS
ROSEBUD
ROSEBUDS
ROSEBUSH
ROSED
ROSEFINCH
ROSEFISH
ROSEHIP
ROSEHIPS
ROSELESS
ROSELIKE
ROSELLA
ROSELLAS
ROSELLE
ROSELLES
ROSEMARY
ROSEOLA
ROSEOLAR
ROSEOLAS
ROSERIES
ROSEROOT
ROSEROOTS
ROSERY
ROSES
ROSESLUG
ROSESLUGS
ROSET
ROSETED
ROSETING
ROSETS
ROSETTE
ROSETTED
ROSETTES
ROSETTY
ROSETY
ROSEWATER
ROSEWOOD
ROSEWOODS
ROSHI
ROSHIS
ROSIED
ROSIER
ROSIERE
ROSIERES
ROSIERS
ROSIES
ROSIEST
ROSILY
ROSIN
ROSINATE
ROSINATES
ROSINED
ROSINER
ROSINERS

ROSINESS
ROSING
ROSINING
ROSINOL
ROSINOLS
ROSINOUS
ROSINS
ROSINWEED
ROSINY
ROSIT
ROSITED
ROSITING
ROSITS
ROSMARINE
ROSOGLIO
ROSOGLIOS
ROSOLIO
ROSOLIOS
ROSSER
ROSSERS
ROST
ROSTED
ROSTELLA
ROSTELLAR
ROSTELLUM
ROSTER
ROSTERED
ROSTERING
ROSTERS
ROSTI
ROSTING
ROSTIS
ROSTRA
ROSTRAL
ROSTRALLY
ROSTRATE
ROSTRATED
ROSTRUM
ROSTRUMS
ROSTS
ROSULA
ROSULAS
ROSULATE
ROSY
ROSYING
ROT
ROTA
ROTACHUTE
ROTAL
ROTAMETER
ROTAN
ROTANS
ROTAPLANE
ROTARIES
ROTARY
ROTAS
ROTATABLE
ROTATE

ROTATED
ROTATES
ROTATING
ROTATION
ROTATIONS
ROTATIVE
ROTATOR
ROTATORES
ROTATORS
ROTATORY
ROTAVATE
ROTAVATED
ROTAVATES
ROTAVATOR
ROTAVIRUS
ROTCH
ROTCHE
ROTCHES
ROTCHIE
ROTCHIES
ROTE
ROTED
ROTENONE
ROTENONES
ROTES
ROTGRASS
ROTGUT
ROTGUTS
ROTHER
ROTHERS
ROTI
ROTIFER
ROTIFERAL
ROTIFERAN
ROTIFERS
ROTIFORM
ROTING
ROTIS
ROTL
ROTLS
ROTO
ROTOGRAPH
ROTOLO
ROTOLOS
ROTON
ROTONS
ROTOR
ROTORS
ROTOS
ROTOTILL
ROTOTILLS
ROTOVATE
ROTOVATED
ROTOVATES
ROTOVATOR
ROTS
ROTTAN
ROTTANS

ROTTE
ROTTED
ROTTEN
ROTTENER
ROTTENEST
ROTTENLY
ROTTENS
ROTTER
ROTTERS
ROTTES
ROTTING
ROTULA
ROTULAE
ROTULAS
ROTUND
ROTUNDA
ROTUNDAS
ROTUNDATE
ROTUNDED
ROTUNDER
ROTUNDEST
ROTUNDING
ROTUNDITY
ROTUNDLY
ROTUNDS
ROTURIER
ROTURIERS
ROUBLE
ROUBLES
ROUCHE
ROUCHES
ROUCOU
ROUCOUS
ROUE
ROUEN
ROUENS
ROUES
ROUGE
ROUGED
ROUGES
ROUGH
ROUGHAGE
ROUGHAGES
ROUGHBACK
ROUGHCAST
ROUGHDRY
ROUGHED
ROUGHEN
ROUGHENED
ROUGHENS
ROUGHER
ROUGHERS
ROUGHEST
ROUGHHEW
ROUGHHEWN
ROUGHHEWS
ROUGHIE
ROUGHIES

ROUGHING	ROUNDSMAN	ROUTINGS	ROWNDING
ROUGHISH	ROUNDSMEN	ROUTINISE	ROWNDS
ROUGHLEG	ROUNDTRIP	ROUTINISM	ROWOVER
ROUGHLEGS	ROUNDUP	ROUTINIST	ROWOVERS
ROUGHLY	ROUNDUPS	ROUTINIZE	ROWS
ROUGHNECK	ROUNDURE	ROUTOUS	ROWT
ROUGHNESS	ROUNDURES	ROUTOUSLY	ROWTED
ROUGHS	ROUNDWOOD	ROUTS	ROWTH
ROUGHSHOD	ROUNDWORM	ROUX	ROWTHS
ROUGHT	ROUP	ROVE	ROWTING
ROUGHY	ROUPED	ROVED	ROWTS
ROUGING	ROUPET	ROVEN	ROYAL
ROUILLE	ROUPIER	ROVER	ROYALET
ROUILLES	ROUPIEST	ROVERS	ROYALETS
ROUL	ROUPILY	ROVES	ROYALISE
ROULADE	ROUPING	ROVING	ROYALISED
ROULADES	ROUPIT	ROVINGLY	ROYALISES
ROULE	ROUPS	ROVINGS	ROYALISM
ROULEAU	ROUPY	ROW	ROYALISMS
ROULEAUS	ROUSANT	ROWABLE	ROYALIST
ROULEAUX	ROUSE	ROWAN	ROYALISTS
ROULES	ROUSED	ROWANS	ROYALIZE
ROULETTE	ROUSEMENT	ROWBOAT	ROYALIZED
ROULETTED	ROUSER	ROWBOATS	ROYALIZES
ROULETTES	ROUSERS	ROWDEDOW	ROYALLER
ROULS	ROUSES	ROWDEDOWS	ROYALLEST
ROUM	ROUSING	ROWDIER	ROYALLY
ROUMING	ROUSINGLY	ROWDIES	ROYALMAST
ROUMINGS	ROUSSEAU	ROWDIEST	ROYALS
ROUMS	ROUSSEAUS	ROWDILY	ROYALTIES
ROUNCE	ROUSSETTE	ROWDINESS	ROYALTY
ROUNCES	ROUST	ROWDY	ROYNE
ROUNCEVAL	ROUSTED	ROWDYDOW	ROYNED
ROUNCIES	ROUSTER	ROWDYDOWS	ROYNES
ROUNCY	ROUSTERS	ROWDYISH	ROYNING
ROUND	ROUSTING	ROWDYISM	ROYNISH
ROUNDARCH	ROUSTS	ROWDYISMS	ROYST
ROUNDBALL	ROUT	ROWED	ROYSTED
ROUNDED	ROUTE	ROWEL	ROYSTER
ROUNDEDLY	ROUTED	ROWELED	ROYSTERED
ROUNDEL	ROUTEING	ROWELING	ROYSTERER
ROUNDELAY	ROUTEMAN	ROWELLED	ROYSTERS
ROUNDELS	ROUTEMEN	ROWELLING	ROYSTING
ROUNDER	ROUTER	ROWELS	ROYSTS
ROUNDERS	ROUTERS	ROWEN	ROZELLE
ROUNDEST	ROUTES	ROWENS	ROZELLES
ROUNDHAND	ROUTEWAY	ROWER	ROZET
ROUNDHEEL	ROUTEWAYS	ROWERS	ROZETED
ROUNDING	ROUTH	ROWING	ROZETING
ROUNDINGS	ROUTHIE	ROWINGS	ROZETS
ROUNDISH	ROUTHIER	ROWLOCK	ROZIT
ROUNDLE	ROUTHIEST	ROWLOCKS	ROZITED
ROUNDLES	ROUTHS	ROWME	ROZITING
ROUNDLET	ROUTINE	ROWMES	ROZITS
ROUNDLETS	ROUTINEER	ROWND	ROZZER
ROUNDLY	ROUTINELY	ROWNDED	ROZZERS
ROUNDNESS	ROUTINES	ROWNDELL	RUANA
ROUNDS	ROUTING	ROWNDELLS	RUANAS

RUB
RUBABOO
RUBABOOS
RUBACE
RUBACES
RUBAI
RUBAIYAT
RUBASSE
RUBASSES
RUBATI
RUBATO
RUBATOS
RUBBABOO
RUBBABOOS
RUBBED
RUBBER
RUBBERED
RUBBERIER
RUBBERING
RUBBERISE
RUBBERIZE
RUBBERS
RUBBERY
RUBBET
RUBBIDIES
RUBBIDY
RUBBIES
RUBBING
RUBBINGS
RUBBISH
RUBBISHED
RUBBISHES
RUBBISHLY
RUBBISHY
RUBBIT
RUBBITIES
RUBBITY
RUBBLE
RUBBLED
RUBBLES
RUBBLIER
RUBBLIEST
RUBBLING
RUBBLY
RUBBOARD
RUBBOARDS
RUBBY
RUBDOWN
RUBDOWNS
RUBE
RUBEFIED
RUBEFIES
RUBEFY
RUBEFYING
RUBEL
RUBELLA
RUBELLAN
RUBELLANS

RUBELLAS
RUBELLITE
RUBELS
RUBEOLA
RUBEOLAR
RUBEOLAS
RUBES
RUBESCENT
RUBICELLE
RUBICON
RUBICONED
RUBICONS
RUBICUND
RUBIDIC
RUBIDIUM
RUBIDIUMS
RUBIED
RUBIER
RUBIES
RUBIEST
RUBIFIED
RUBIFIES
RUBIFY
RUBIFYING
RUBIGO
RUBIGOS
RUBIN
RUBINE
RUBINEOUS
RUBINES
RUBINS
RUBIOUS
RUBLE
RUBLES
RUBOFF
RUBOFFS
RUBOUT
RUBOUTS
RUBRIC
RUBRICAL
RUBRICATE
RUBRICIAN
RUBRICS
RUBS
RUBSTONE
RUBSTONES
RUBUS
RUBY
RUBYING
RUBYLIKE
RUC
RUCHE
RUCHED
RUCHES
RUCHING
RUCHINGS
RUCK
RUCKED

RUCKING
RUCKLE
RUCKLED
RUCKLES
RUCKLING
RUCKMAN
RUCKMEN
RUCKS
RUCKSACK
RUCKSACKS
RUCKSEAT
RUCKSEATS
RUCKUS
RUCKUSES
RUCOLA
RUCOLAS
RUCS
RUCTATION
RUCTION
RUCTIONS
RUCTIOUS
RUD
RUDACEOUS
RUDAS
RUDASES
RUDBECKIA
RUDD
RUDDED
RUDDER
RUDDERS
RUDDIED
RUDDIER
RUDDIES
RUDDIEST
RUDDILY
RUDDINESS
RUDDING
RUDDLE
RUDDLED
RUDDLEMAN
RUDDLEMEN
RUDDLES
RUDDLING
RUDDOCK
RUDDOCKS
RUDDS
RUDDY
RUDDYING
RUDE
RUDELY
RUDENESS
RUDER
RUDERAL
RUDERALS
RUDERIES
RUDERY
RUDES
RUDESBIES

RUDESBY
RUDEST
RUDIE
RUDIES
RUDIMENT
RUDIMENTS
RUDISH
RUDS
RUE
RUED
RUEFUL
RUEFULLY
RUEING
RUEINGS
RUELLE
RUELLES
RUELLIA
RUELLIAS
RUER
RUERS
RUES
RUFESCENT
RUFF
RUFFE
RUFFED
RUFFES
RUFFIAN
RUFFIANED
RUFFIANLY
RUFFIANS
RUFFIN
RUFFING
RUFFINS
RUFFLE
RUFFLED
RUFFLER
RUFFLERS
RUFFLES
RUFFLIER
RUFFLIEST
RUFFLIKE
RUFFLING
RUFFLINGS
RUFFLY
RUFFS
RUFIYAA
RUFIYAAS
RUFOUS
RUG
RUGA
RUGAE
RUGAL
RUGALACH
RUGATE
RUGBIES
RUGBY
RUGELACH
RUGGED

RUGGEDER
RUGGEDEST
RUGGEDISE
RUGGEDIZE
RUGGEDLY
RUGGELACH
RUGGER
RUGGERS
RUGGIER
RUGGIEST
RUGGING
RUGGINGS
RUGGY
RUGLIKE
RUGOLA
RUGOLAS
RUGOSA
RUGOSAS
RUGOSE
RUGOSELY
RUGOSITY
RUGOUS
RUGS
RUGULOSE
RUIN
RUINABLE
RUINATE
RUINATED
RUINATES
RUINATING
RUINATION
RUINED
RUINER
RUINERS
RUING
RUINGS
RUINING
RUININGS
RUINOUS
RUINOUSLY
RUINS
RUKH
RUKHS
RULABLE
RULE
RULED
RULELESS
RULER
RULERED
RULERING
RULERS
RULERSHIP
RULES
RULESSE
RULIER
RULIEST
RULING
RULINGS

RULLION
RULLIONS
RULLOCK
RULLOCKS
RULY
RUM
RUMAKI
RUMAKIS
RUMAL
RUMALS
RUMBA
RUMBAED
RUMBAING
RUMBAS
RUMBELOW
RUMBELOWS
RUMBLE
RUMBLED
RUMBLER
RUMBLERS
RUMBLES
RUMBLIER
RUMBLIEST
RUMBLING
RUMBLINGS
RUMBLY
RUMBO
RUMBOS
RUME
RUMEN
RUMENS
RUMES
RUMINA
RUMINAL
RUMINANT
RUMINANTS
RUMINATE
RUMINATED
RUMINATES
RUMINATOR
RUMKIN
RUMKINS
RUMLY
RUMMAGE
RUMMAGED
RUMMAGER
RUMMAGERS
RUMMAGES
RUMMAGING
RUMMER
RUMMERS
RUMMEST
RUMMIER
RUMMIES
RUMMIEST
RUMMILY
RUMMINESS
RUMMISH

RUMMY
RUMNESS
RUMNESSES
RUMOR
RUMORED
RUMORING
RUMOROUS
RUMORS
RUMOUR
RUMOURED
RUMOURER
RUMOURERS
RUMOURING
RUMOURS
RUMP
RUMPED
RUMPIES
RUMPING
RUMPLE
RUMPLED
RUMPLES
RUMPLESS
RUMPLIER
RUMPLIEST
RUMPLING
RUMPLY
RUMPO
RUMPOS
RUMPS
RUMPUS
RUMPUSES
RUMPY
RUMRUNNER
RUMS
RUN
RUNABOUT
RUNABOUTS
RUNAGATE
RUNAGATES
RUNANGA
RUNAROUND
RUNAWAY
RUNAWAYS
RUNBACK
RUNBACKS
RUNCH
RUNCHES
RUNCIBLE
RUNCINATE
RUND
RUNDALE
RUNDALES
RUNDLE
RUNDLED
RUNDLES
RUNDLET
RUNDLETS
RUNDOWN

RUNDOWNS
RUNDS
RUNE
RUNECRAFT
RUNED
RUNELIKE
RUNES
RUNFLAT
RUNG
RUNGLESS
RUNGS
RUNIC
RUNKLE
RUNKLED
RUNKLES
RUNKLING
RUNLESS
RUNLET
RUNLETS
RUNNABLE
RUNNEL
RUNNELS
RUNNER
RUNNERS
RUNNET
RUNNETS
RUNNIER
RUNNIEST
RUNNINESS
RUNNING
RUNNINGLY
RUNNINGS
RUNNION
RUNNIONS
RUNNY
RUNOFF
RUNOFFS
RUNOUT
RUNOUTS
RUNOVER
RUNOVERS
RUNRIG
RUNRIGS
RUNROUND
RUNROUNDS
RUNS
RUNT
RUNTED
RUNTIER
RUNTIEST
RUNTINESS
RUNTISH
RUNTISHLY
RUNTS
RUNTY
RUNWAY
RUNWAYS
RUPEE

RUPEES
RUPIA
RUPIAH
RUPIAHS
RUPIAS
RUPTURE
RUPTURED
RUPTURES
RUPTURING
RURAL
RURALISE
RURALISED
RURALISES
RURALISM
RURALISMS
RURALIST
RURALISTS
RURALITE
RURALITES
RURALITY
RURALIZE
RURALIZED
RURALIZES
RURALLY
RURALNESS
RURALS
RURBAN
RURP
RURPS
RURU
RURUS
RUSA
RUSALKA
RUSALKAS
RUSAS
RUSCUS
RUSCUSES
RUSE
RUSES
RUSH
RUSHED
RUSHEE
RUSHEES
RUSHEN
RUSHER
RUSHERS
RUSHES
RUSHIER
RUSHIEST
RUSHINESS
RUSHING
RUSHINGS
RUSHLIGHT
RUSHLIKE
RUSHY
RUSINE
RUSK
RUSKS

RUSMA
RUSMAS
RUSSE
RUSSEL
RUSSELS
RUSSET
RUSSETED
RUSSETING
RUSSETS
RUSSETY
RUSSIA
RUSSIAS
RUSSIFIED
RUSSIFIES
RUSSIFY
RUSSULA
RUSSULAE
RUSSULAS
RUST
RUSTABLE
RUSTED
RUSTIC
RUSTICAL
RUSTICALS
RUSTICANA
RUSTICATE
RUSTICIAL
RUSTICISE
RUSTICISM
RUSTICITY
RUSTICIZE
RUSTICLY
RUSTICS
RUSTIER
RUSTIEST
RUSTILY
RUSTINESS
RUSTING
RUSTINGS
RUSTLE
RUSTLED
RUSTLER
RUSTLERS
RUSTLES
RUSTLESS
RUSTLING
RUSTLINGS
RUSTPROOF
RUSTRE
RUSTRED
RUSTRES
RUSTS
RUSTY
RUT
RUTABAGA
RUTABAGAS
RUTACEOUS
RUTH

RUTHENIC
RUTHENIUM
RUTHFUL
RUTHFULLY
RUTHLESS
RUTHS
RUTILANT
RUTILATED
RUTILE
RUTILES
RUTIN
RUTINS
RUTS
RUTTED
RUTTER
RUTTERS
RUTTIER
RUTTIEST
RUTTILY
RUTTINESS
RUTTING
RUTTINGS
RUTTISH
RUTTISHLY
RUTTY
RYA
RYAL
RYALS
RYAS
RYBAT
RYBATS
RYBAUDRYE
RYE
RYEBREAD
RYEBREADS
RYEFLOUR
RYEFLOURS
RYEGRASS
RYEPECK
RYEPECKS
RYES
RYFE
RYKE
RYKED
RYKES
RYKING
RYMME
RYMMED
RYMMES
RYMMING
RYND
RYNDS
RYOKAN
RYOKANS
RYOT
RYOTS
RYOTWARI
RYOTWARIS

RYPE
RYPECK
RYPECKS
RYPER

— S —

SAB
SABADILLA
SABAL
SABALS
SABATON
SABATONS
SABAYON
SABAYONS
SABBAT
SABBATH
SABBATHS
SABBATIC
SABBATICS
SABBATINE
SABBATISE
SABBATISM
SABBATIZE
SABBATS
SABBED
SABBING
SABE
SABED
SABEING
SABELLA
SABELLAS
SABER
SABERED
SABERING
SABERLIKE
SABERS
SABES
SABIN
SABINE
SABINES
SABINS
SABIR
SABIRS
SABKHA
SABKHAH
SABKHAHS
SABKHAS
SABKHAT
SABKHATS
SABLE
SABLED
SABLEFISH
SABLES
SABLING
SABOT
SABOTAGE
SABOTAGED
SABOTAGES
SABOTEUR

SABOTEURS
SABOTIER
SABOTIERS
SABOTS
SABRA
SABRAS
SABRE
SABRED
SABRES
SABREUR
SABREURS
SABRING
SABS
SABULINE
SABULOSE
SABULOUS
SABURRA
SABURRAL
SABURRAS
SAC
SACATON
SACATONS
SACBUT
SACBUTS
SACCADE
SACCADES
SACCADIC
SACCATE
SACCHARIC
SACCHARIN
SACCHARUM
SACCIFORM
SACCOI
SACCOS
SACCOSES
SACCULAR
SACCULATE
SACCULE
SACCULES
SACCULI
SACCULUS
SACELLA
SACELLUM
SACHEM
SACHEMDOM
SACHEMIC
SACHEMS
SACHET
SACHETED
SACHETS
SACK
SACKABLE
SACKAGE

SACKAGES
SACKBUT
SACKBUTS
SACKCLOTH
SACKED
SACKER
SACKERS
SACKFUL
SACKFULS
SACKING
SACKINGS
SACKLESS
SACKLIKE
SACKS
SACKSFUL
SACLESS
SACLIKE
SACQUE
SACQUES
SACRA
SACRAL
SACRALGIA
SACRALISE
SACRALIZE
SACRALS
SACRAMENT
SACRARIA
SACRARIAL
SACRARIUM
SACRED
SACREDLY
SACRIFICE
SACRIFIDE
SACRIFIED
SACRIFIES
SACRIFY
SACRILEGE
SACRING
SACRINGS
SACRIST
SACRISTAN
SACRISTS
SACRISTY
SACRUM
SACRUMS
SACS
SAD
SADDED
SADDEN
SADDENED
SADDENING
SADDENS
SADDER

SADDEST
SADDHU
SADDHUS
SADDING
SADDISH
SADDLE
SADDLEBAG
SADDLEBOW
SADDLED
SADDLER
SADDLERS
SADDLERY
SADDLES
SADDLING
SADDO
SADDOES
SADDOS
SADE
SADES
SADHANA
SADHANAS
SADHE
SADHES
SADHU
SADHUS
SADI
SADIRON
SADIRONS
SADIS
SADISM
SADISMS
SADIST
SADISTIC
SADISTS
SADLY
SADNESS
SADNESSES
SADO
SADOS
SADS
SADZA
SADZAS
SAE
SAECULUM
SAECULUMS
SAETER
SAETERS
SAFARI
SAFARIED
SAFARIING
SAFARIS
SAFARIST
SAFARISTS

SAFE
SAFED
SAFEGUARD
SAFELIGHT
SAFELY
SAFENESS
SAFER
SAFES
SAFEST
SAFETIED
SAFETIES
SAFETY
SAFETYING
SAFETYMAN
SAFETYMEN
SAFFIAN
SAFFIANS
SAFFLOWER
SAFFRON
SAFFRONED
SAFFRONS
SAFFRONY
SAFING
SAFRANIN
SAFRANINE
SAFRANINS
SAFROL
SAFROLE
SAFROLES
SAFROLS
SAFRONAL
SAFRONALS
SAFT
SAFTER
SAFTEST
SAG
SAGA
SAGACIOUS
SAGACITY
SAGAMAN
SAGAMEN
SAGAMORE
SAGAMORES
SAGANASH
SAGAPENUM
SAGAS
SAGATHIES
SAGATHY
SAGBUT
SAGBUTS
SAGE
SAGEBRUSH
SAGELY
SAGENE
SAGENES
SAGENESS
SAGENITE
SAGENITES

SAGENITIC
SAGER
SAGES
SAGEST
SAGGAR
SAGGARD
SAGGARDS
SAGGARED
SAGGARING
SAGGARS
SAGGED
SAGGER
SAGGERED
SAGGERING
SAGGERS
SAGGIER
SAGGIEST
SAGGING
SAGGINGS
SAGGY
SAGIER
SAGIEST
SAGINATE
SAGINATED
SAGINATES
SAGITTA
SAGITTAL
SAGITTARY
SAGITTAS
SAGITTATE
SAGO
SAGOIN
SAGOINS
SAGOS
SAGOUIN
SAGOUINS
SAGRADA
SAGS
SAGUARO
SAGUAROS
SAGUIN
SAGUINS
SAGUM
SAGY
SAHEB
SAHEBS
SAHIB
SAHIBA
SAHIBAH
SAHIBAHS
SAHIBAS
SAHIBS
SAHIWAL
SAHIWALS
SAHUARO
SAHUAROS
SAI
SAIBLING

SAIBLINGS
SAIC
SAICE
SAICES
SAICK
SAICKS
SAICS
SAID
SAIDEST
SAIDS
SAIDST
SAIGA
SAIGAS
SAIKEI
SAIKEIS
SAIKLESS
SAIL
SAILABLE
SAILBOARD
SAILBOAT
SAILBOATS
SAILCLOTH
SAILED
SAILER
SAILERS
SAILFISH
SAILING
SAILINGS
SAILLESS
SAILMAKER
SAILOR
SAILORING
SAILORLY
SAILORS
SAILPLANE
SAILROOM
SAILROOMS
SAILS
SAIM
SAIMIN
SAIMINS
SAIMIRI
SAIMIRIS
SAIMS
SAIN
SAINE
SAINED
SAINFOIN
SAINFOINS
SAINING
SAINS
SAINT
SAINTDOM
SAINTDOMS
SAINTED
SAINTESS
SAINTFOIN
SAINTHOOD

SAINTING
SAINTISH
SAINTISM
SAINTISMS
SAINTLESS
SAINTLIER
SAINTLIKE
SAINTLILY
SAINTLING
SAINTLY
SAINTS
SAINTSHIP
SAIQUE
SAIQUES
SAIR
SAIRED
SAIRER
SAIREST
SAIRING
SAIRS
SAIS
SAIST
SAITH
SAITHE
SAITHES
SAITHS
SAIYID
SAIYIDS
SAJOU
SAJOUS
SAKAI
SAKAIS
SAKE
SAKER
SAKERET
SAKERETS
SAKERS
SAKES
SAKI
SAKIA
SAKIAS
SAKIEH
SAKIEHS
SAKIS
SAKIYEH
SAKIYEHS
SAKKOI
SAKKOS
SAKKOSES
SAKSAUL
SAKSAULS
SAL
SALAAM
SALAAMED
SALAAMING
SALAAMS
SALABLE
SALABLY

SALACIOUS
SALACITY
SALAD
SALADANG
SALADANGS
SALADE
SALADES
SALADING
SALADINGS
SALADS
SALAL
SALALS
SALAMI
SALAMIS
SALAMON
SALAMONS
SALANGANE
SALARIAT
SALARIATS
SALARIED
SALARIES
SALARY
SALARYING
SALARYMAN
SALARYMEN
SALBAND
SALBANDS
SALCHOW
SALCHOWS
SALE
SALEABLE
SALEABLY
SALEP
SALEPS
SALERATUS
SALERING
SALERINGS
SALEROOM
SALEROOMS
SALES
SALESGIRL
SALESLADY
SALESMAN
SALESMEN
SALESROOM
SALET
SALETS
SALEWD
SALEYARD
SALEYARDS
SALFERN
SALFERNS
SALIAUNCE
SALIC
SALICES
SALICET
SALICETA
SALICETS

SALICETUM
SALICIN
SALICINE
SALICINES
SALICINS
SALICYLIC
SALIENCE
SALIENCES
SALIENCY
SALIENT
SALIENTLY
SALIENTS
SALIFIED
SALIFIES
SALIFY
SALIFYING
SALIGOT
SALIGOTS
SALIMETER
SALIMETRY
SALINA
SALINAS
SALINE
SALINES
SALINISE
SALINISED
SALINISES
SALINITY
SALINIZE
SALINIZED
SALINIZES
SALIVA
SALIVAL
SALIVARY
SALIVAS
SALIVATE
SALIVATED
SALIVATES
SALIVATOR
SALIX
SALL
SALLAD
SALLADS
SALLAL
SALLALS
SALLE
SALLEE
SALLEES
SALLES
SALLET
SALLETS
SALLIED
SALLIER
SALLIERS
SALLIES
SALLOW
SALLOWED
SALLOWER

SALLOWEST
SALLOWING
SALLOWISH
SALLOWLY
SALLOWS
SALLOWY
SALLY
SALLYING
SALLYPORT
SALMI
SALMIS
SALMON
SALMONET
SALMONETS
SALMONID
SALMONIDS
SALMONOID
SALMONS
SALOL
SALOLS
SALOMETER
SALON
SALONS
SALOON
SALOONS
SALOOP
SALOOPS
SALOP
SALOPIAN
SALOPS
SALP
SALPA
SALPAE
SALPAS
SALPIAN
SALPIANS
SALPICON
SALPICONS
SALPID
SALPIDS
SALPIFORM
SALPINGES
SALPINX
SALPINXES
SALPS
SALS
SALSA
SALSAED
SALSAING
SALSAS
SALSE
SALSES
SALSIFIES
SALSIFY
SALSILLA
SALSILLAS
SALT
SALTANDO

SALTANT
SALTANTS
SALTATE
SALTATED
SALTATES
SALTATING
SALTATION
SALTATO
SALTATORY
SALTBOX
SALTBOXES
SALTBUSH
SALTCAT
SALTCATS
SALTCHUCK
SALTED
SALTER
SALTERN
SALTERNS
SALTERS
SALTEST
SALTFISH
SALTIE
SALTIER
SALTIERS
SALTIES
SALTIEST
SALTILY
SALTINE
SALTINES
SALTINESS
SALTING
SALTINGS
SALTIRE
SALTIRES
SALTISH
SALTISHLY
SALTLESS
SALTLIKE
SALTLY
SALTNESS
SALTO
SALTOED
SALTOING
SALTOS
SALTPAN
SALTPANS
SALTPETER
SALTPETRE
SALTS
SALTUS
SALTUSES
SALTWATER
SALTWORK
SALTWORKS
SALTWORT
SALTWORTS
SALTY

SALUBRITY	SAMARITAN	SAMLORS	SANDAL
SALUE	SAMARIUM	SAMMED	SANDALED
SALUED	SAMARIUMS	SAMMIES	SANDALING
SALUES	SAMAS	SAMMING	SANDALLED
SALUING	SAMBA	SAMMY	SANDALS
SALUKI	SAMBAED	SAMNITIS	SANDARAC
SALUKIS	SAMBAING	SAMOSA	SANDARACH
SALURETIC	SAMBAL	SAMOSAS	SANDARACS
SALUTARY	SAMBALS	SAMOVAR	SANDBAG
SALUTE	SAMBAR	SAMOVARS	SANDBAGS
SALUTED	SAMBARS	SAMOYED	SANDBANK
SALUTER	SAMBAS	SAMOYEDS	SANDBANKS
SALUTERS	SAMBHAR	SAMP	SANDBAR
SALUTES	SAMBHARS	SAMPAN	SANDBARS
SALUTING	SAMBHUR	SAMPANS	SANDBLAST
SALVABLE	SAMBHURS	SAMPHIRE	SANDBOX
SALVABLY	SAMBO	SAMPHIRES	SANDBOXES
SALVAGE	SAMBOS	SAMPI	SANDBOY
SALVAGED	SAMBUCA	SAMPIRE	SANDBOYS
SALVAGEE	SAMBUCAS	SAMPIRES	SANDBUR
SALVAGEES	SAMBUKE	SAMPIS	SANDBURR
SALVAGER	SAMBUKES	SAMPLE	SANDBURRS
SALVAGERS	SAMBUR	SAMPLED	SANDBURS
SALVAGES	SAMBURS	SAMPLER	SANDCRACK
SALVAGING	SAME	SAMPLERS	SANDDAB
SALVARSAN	SAMECH	SAMPLERY	SANDDABS
SALVATION	SAMECHS	SAMPLES	SANDED
SALVATORY	SAMEK	SAMPLING	SANDEK
SALVE	SAMEKH	SAMPLINGS	SANDEKS
SALVED	SAMEKHS	SAMPS	SANDER
SALVER	SAMEKS	SAMS	SANDERS
SALVERS	SAMEL	SAMSARA	SANDERSES
SALVES	SAMELY	SAMSARAS	SANDFISH
SALVETE	SAMEN	SAMSHOO	SANDFLIES
SALVETES	SAMENESS	SAMSHOOS	SANDFLY
SALVIA	SAMES	SAMSHU	SANDGLASS
SALVIAS	SAMEY	SAMSHUS	SANDHEAP
SALVIFIC	SAMFOO	SAMURAI	SANDHEAPS
SALVING	SAMFOOS	SAMURAIS	SANDHI
SALVINGS	SAMFU	SAN	SANDHILL
SALVO	SAMFUS	SANATIVE	SANDHILLS
SALVOED	SAMIEL	SANATORIA	SANDHIS
SALVOES	SAMIELS	SANATORY	SANDHOG
SALVOING	SAMIER	SANBENITO	SANDHOGS
SALVOR	SAMIEST	SANCAI	SANDIER
SALVORS	SAMISEN	SANCAIS	SANDIEST
SALVOS	SAMISENS	SANCHO	SANDINESS
SALWAR	SAMITE	SANCHOS	SANDING
SAM	SAMITES	SANCTA	SANDINGS
SAMA	SAMITHI	SANCTIFY	SANDIVER
SAMAAN	SAMITHIS	SANCTION	SANDIVERS
SAMAANS	SAMITI	SANCTIONS	SANDLESS
SAMADHI	SAMITIS	SANCTITY	SANDLIKE
SAMADHIS	SAMIZDAT	SANCTUARY	SANDLING
SAMAN	SAMIZDATS	SANCTUM	SANDLINGS
SAMANS	SAMLET	SANCTUMS	SANDLOT
SAMARA	SAMLETS	SAND	SANDLOTS
SAMARAS	SAMLOR	SANDABLE	SANDMAN

SANDMEN

SANDMEN
SANDPAPER
SANDPEEP
SANDPEEPS
SANDPILE
SANDPILES
SANDPIPER
SANDPIT
SANDPITS
SANDPUMP
SANDPUMPS
SANDS
SANDSHOE
SANDSHOES
SANDSOAP
SANDSOAPS
SANDSPOUT
SANDSPUR
SANDSPURS
SANDSTONE
SANDSTORM
SANDWICH
SANDWORM
SANDWORMS
SANDWORT
SANDWORTS
SANDY
SANE
SANED
SANELY
SANENESS
SANER
SANES
SANEST
SANG
SANGA
SANGAR
SANGAREE
SANGAREES
SANGARS
SANGAS
SANGER
SANGERS
SANGFROID
SANGH
SANGHAT
SANGHATS
SANGHS
SANGLIER
SANGLIERS
SANGO
SANGOMA
SANGOMAS
SANGOS
SANGRIA
SANGRIAS
SANGS
SANGUIFY

SANGUINE
SANGUINED
SANGUINES
SANICLE
SANICLES
SANIDINE
SANIDINES
SANIES
SANIFIED
SANIFIES
SANIFY
SANIFYING
SANING
SANIOUS
SANITARIA
SANITARY
SANITATE
SANITATED
SANITATES
SANITIES
SANITISE
SANITISED
SANITISER
SANITISES
SANITIZE
SANITIZED
SANITIZER
SANITIZES
SANITORIA
SANITY
SANJAK
SANJAKS
SANK
SANKO
SANKOS
SANNIE
SANNIES
SANNOP
SANNOPS
SANNUP
SANNUPS
SANNYASI
SANNYASIN
SANNYASIS
SANPAN
SANPANS
SANPRO
SANPROS
SANS
SANSA
SANSAR
SANSARS
SANSAS
SANSEI
SANSEIS
SANSERIF
SANSERIFS
SANT

SANTAL
SANTALIC
SANTALIN
SANTALINS
SANTALOL
SANTALOLS
SANTALS
SANTERA
SANTERAS
SANTERIA
SANTERIAS
SANTERO
SANTEROS
SANTIMI
SANTIMS
SANTIMU
SANTIR
SANTIRS
SANTO
SANTOL
SANTOLINA
SANTOLS
SANTON
SANTONICA
SANTONIN
SANTONINS
SANTONS
SANTOOR
SANTOORS
SANTOS
SANTOUR
SANTOURS
SANTS
SANTUR
SANTURS
SANYASI
SANYASIS
SAOUARI
SAOUARIS
SAP
SAPAJOU
SAPAJOUS
SAPAN
SAPANS
SAPANWOOD
SAPEGO
SAPEGOES
SAPELE
SAPELES
SAPFUL
SAPHEAD
SAPHEADED
SAPHEADS
SAPHENA
SAPHENAE
SAPHENAS
SAPHENOUS
SAPID

SAPIDITY
SAPIDLESS
SAPIDNESS
SAPIENCE
SAPIENCES
SAPIENCY
SAPIENS
SAPIENT
SAPIENTLY
SAPIENTS
SAPLESS
SAPLING
SAPLINGS
SAPODILLA
SAPOGENIN
SAPONARIA
SAPONATED
SAPONIFY
SAPONIN
SAPONINE
SAPONINES
SAPONINS
SAPONITE
SAPONITES
SAPOR
SAPORIFIC
SAPOROUS
SAPORS
SAPOTA
SAPOTAS
SAPOTE
SAPOTES
SAPOUR
SAPOURS
SAPPAN
SAPPANS
SAPPED
SAPPER
SAPPERS
SAPPHIC
SAPPHICS
SAPPHIRE
SAPPHIRED
SAPPHIRES
SAPPHISM
SAPPHISMS
SAPPHIST
SAPPHISTS
SAPPIER
SAPPIEST
SAPPILY
SAPPINESS
SAPPING
SAPPLE
SAPPLED
SAPPLES
SAPPLING
SAPPY

SAPRAEMIA
SAPRAEMIC
SAPREMIA
SAPREMIAS
SAPREMIC
SAPROBE
SAPROBES
SAPROBIAL
SAPROBIC
SAPROLITE
SAPROPEL
SAPROPELS
SAPROZOIC
SAPS
SAPSAGO
SAPSAGOS
SAPSUCKER
SAPUCAIA
SAPUCAIAS
SAPWOOD
SAPWOODS
SAR
SARABAND
SARABANDE
SARABANDS
SARAFAN
SARAFANS
SARAN
SARANGI
SARANGIS
SARANS
SARAPE
SARAPES
SARBACANE
SARCASM
SARCASMS
SARCASTIC
SARCENET
SARCENETS
SARCINA
SARCINAE
SARCINAS
SARCOCARP
SARCODE
SARCODES
SARCODIC
SARCOID
SARCOIDS
SARCOLOGY
SARCOMA
SARCOMAS
SARCOMATA
SARCOMERE
SARCONET
SARCONETS
SARCOPTIC
SARCOSOME
SARCOUS

SARD
SARDANA
SARDANAS
SARDAR
SARDARS
SARDEL
SARDELLE
SARDELLES
SARDELS
SARDINE
SARDINED
SARDINES
SARDINING
SARDIUS
SARDIUSES
SARDONIAN
SARDONIC
SARDONYX
SARDS
SARED
SAREE
SAREES
SARGASSO
SARGASSOS
SARGASSUM
SARGE
SARGES
SARGO
SARGOS
SARGOSES
SARGUS
SARGUSES
SARI
SARIN
SARING
SARINS
SARIS
SARK
SARKIER
SARKIEST
SARKING
SARKINGS
SARKS
SARKY
SARMENT
SARMENTA
SARMENTS
SARMENTUM
SARMIE
SARMIES
SARNEY
SARNEYS
SARNIE
SARNIES
SAROD
SARODE
SARODES
SARODIST

SARODISTS
SARODS
SARONG
SARONGS
SARONIC
SAROS
SAROSES
SARPANCH
SARRASIN
SARRASINS
SARRAZIN
SARRAZINS
SARS
SARSAR
SARSARS
SARSDEN
SARSDENS
SARSEN
SARSENET
SARSENETS
SARSENS
SARSNET
SARSNETS
SARTOR
SARTORIAL
SARTORIAN
SARTORII
SARTORIUS
SARTORS
SARUS
SARUSES
SASARARA
SASARARAS
SASER
SASERS
SASH
SASHAY
SASHAYED
SASHAYING
SASHAYS
SASHED
SASHES
SASHIMI
SASHIMIS
SASHING
SASHLESS
SASIN
SASINE
SASINES
SASINS
SASKATOON
SASQUATCH
SASS
SASSABIES
SASSABY
SASSAFRAS
SASSARARA
SASSE

SASSED
SASSES
SASSIER
SASSIES
SASSIEST
SASSILY
SASSINESS
SASSING
SASSOLIN
SASSOLINS
SASSOLITE
SASSWOOD
SASSWOODS
SASSY
SASSYWOOD
SASTRA
SASTRAS
SASTRUGA
SASTRUGI
SAT
SATAI
SATAIS
SATANG
SATANGS
SATANIC
SATANICAL
SATANISM
SATANISMS
SATANIST
SATANISTS
SATANITY
SATARA
SATARAS
SATAY
SATAYS
SATCHEL
SATCHELED
SATCHELS
SATE
SATED
SATEDNESS
SATEEN
SATEENS
SATELESS
SATELLES
SATELLITE
SATEM
SATES
SATI
SATIABLE
SATIABLY
SATIATE
SATIATED
SATIATES
SATIATING
SATIATION
SATIETIES
SATIETY

SATIN
SATINED
SATINET
SATINETS
SATINETTA
SATINETTE
SATING
SATINING
SATINPOD
SATINPODS
SATINS
SATINWOOD
SATINY
SATIRE
SATIRES
SATIRIC
SATIRICAL
SATIRISE
SATIRISED
SATIRISER
SATIRISES
SATIRIST
SATIRISTS
SATIRIZE
SATIRIZED
SATIRIZER
SATIRIZES
SATIS
SATISFICE
SATISFIED
SATISFIER
SATISFIES
SATISFY
SATIVE
SATORI
SATORIS
SATRAP
SATRAPAL
SATRAPIES
SATRAPS
SATRAPY
SATSUMA
SATSUMAS
SATURABLE
SATURANT
SATURANTS
SATURATE
SATURATED
SATURATER
SATURATES
SATURATOR
SATURNIC
SATURNIID
SATURNINE
SATURNISM
SATURNIST
SATYR
SATYRA

SATYRAL
SATYRALS
SATYRAS
SATYRESS
SATYRIC
SATYRICAL
SATYRID
SATYRIDS
SATYRISK
SATYRISKS
SATYRLIKE
SATYRS
SAU
SAUBA
SAUBAS
SAUCE
SAUCEBOAT
SAUCEBOX
SAUCED
SAUCELESS
SAUCEPAN
SAUCEPANS
SAUCEPOT
SAUCEPOTS
SAUCER
SAUCERFUL
SAUCERS
SAUCES
SAUCH
SAUCHS
SAUCIER
SAUCIERS
SAUCIEST
SAUCILY
SAUCINESS
SAUCING
SAUCISSE
SAUCISSES
SAUCISSON
SAUCY
SAUFGARD
SAUFGARDS
SAUGER
SAUGERS
SAUGH
SAUGHS
SAUGHY
SAUL
SAULGE
SAULGES
SAULIE
SAULIES
SAULS
SAULT
SAULTS
SAUNA
SAUNAED
SAUNAING

SAUNAS
SAUNT
SAUNTED
SAUNTER
SAUNTERED
SAUNTERER
SAUNTERS
SAUNTING
SAUNTS
SAUREL
SAURELS
SAURIAN
SAURIANS
SAURIES
SAUROID
SAUROPOD
SAUROPODS
SAURY
SAUSAGE
SAUSAGES
SAUT
SAUTE
SAUTED
SAUTEED
SAUTEEING
SAUTEES
SAUTEING
SAUTERNE
SAUTERNES
SAUTES
SAUTING
SAUTOIR
SAUTOIRE
SAUTOIRES
SAUTOIRS
SAUTS
SAV
SAVABLE
SAVAGE
SAVAGED
SAVAGEDOM
SAVAGELY
SAVAGER
SAVAGERY
SAVAGES
SAVAGEST
SAVAGING
SAVAGISM
SAVAGISMS
SAVANNA
SAVANNAH
SAVANNAHS
SAVANNAS
SAVANT
SAVANTE
SAVANTES
SAVANTS
SAVARIN

SAVARINS
SAVATE
SAVATES
SAVE
SAVEABLE
SAVED
SAVEGARD
SAVEGARDS
SAVELOY
SAVELOYS
SAVER
SAVERS
SAVES
SAVEY
SAVEYED
SAVEYING
SAVEYS
SAVIN
SAVINE
SAVINES
SAVING
SAVINGLY
SAVINGS
SAVINS
SAVIOR
SAVIORS
SAVIOUR
SAVIOURS
SAVOR
SAVORED
SAVORER
SAVORERS
SAVORIER
SAVORIES
SAVORIEST
SAVORILY
SAVORING
SAVORLESS
SAVOROUS
SAVORS
SAVORY
SAVOUR
SAVOURED
SAVOURER
SAVOURERS
SAVOURIER
SAVOURIES
SAVOURILY
SAVOURING
SAVOURLY
SAVOURS
SAVOURY
SAVOY
SAVOYARD
SAVOYARDS
SAVOYS
SAVS
SAVVEY

SAVVEYED
SAVVEYING
SAVVEYS
SAVVIED
SAVVIER
SAVVIES
SAVVIEST
SAVVILY
SAVVINESS
SAVVY
SAVVYING
SAW
SAWAH
SAWAHS
SAWBILL
SAWBILLS
SAWBLADE
SAWBLADES
SAWBONES
SAWBUCK
SAWBUCKS
SAWDER
SAWDERED
SAWDERING
SAWDERS
SAWDUST
SAWDUSTED
SAWDUSTS
SAWDUSTY
SAWED
SAWER
SAWERS
SAWFISH
SAWFISHES
SAWFLIES
SAWFLY
SAWHORSE
SAWHORSES
SAWING
SAWINGS
SAWLIKE
SAWLOG
SAWLOGS
SAWMILL
SAWMILLS
SAWN
SAWNEY
SAWNEYS
SAWPIT
SAWPITS
SAWS
SAWSHARK
SAWSHARKS
SAWTEETH
SAWTIMBER
SAWTOOTH
SAWYER
SAWYERS

SAX
SAXATILE
SAXAUL
SAXAULS
SAXE
SAXES
SAXHORN
SAXHORNS
SAXICOLE
SAXIFRAGE
SAXITOXIN
SAXONIES
SAXONITE
SAXONITES
SAXONY
SAXOPHONE
SAXTUBA
SAXTUBAS
SAY
SAYABLE
SAYED
SAYEDS
SAYER
SAYERS
SAYEST
SAYID
SAYIDS
SAYING
SAYINGS
SAYNE
SAYON
SAYONARA
SAYONARAS
SAYONS
SAYS
SAYST
SAYYID
SAYYIDS
SAZ
SAZERAC
SAZERACS
SAZES
SAZHEN
SAZHENS
SAZZES
SBIRRI
SBIRRO
SCAB
SCABBARD
SCABBARDS
SCABBED
SCABBIER
SCABBIEST
SCABBILY
SCABBING
SCABBLE
SCABBLED
SCABBLES

SCABBLING
SCABBY
SCABIES
SCABIETIC
SCABIOSA
SCABIOSAS
SCABIOUS
SCABLAND
SCABLANDS
SCABLIKE
SCABRID
SCABROUS
SCABS
SCAD
SCADS
SCAFF
SCAFFIE
SCAFFIES
SCAFFOLD
SCAFFOLDS
SCAFFS
SCAG
SCAGGED
SCAGGING
SCAGLIA
SCAGLIAS
SCAGLIOLA
SCAGS
SCAIL
SCAILED
SCAILING
SCAILS
SCAITH
SCAITHED
SCAITHING
SCAITHS
SCALA
SCALABLE
SCALABLY
SCALADE
SCALADES
SCALADO
SCALADOS
SCALAE
SCALAGE
SCALAGES
SCALAR
SCALARE
SCALARES
SCALARS
SCALATION
SCALAWAG
SCALAWAGS
SCALD
SCALDED
SCALDER
SCALDERS
SCALDFISH

SCALDHEAD
SCALDIC
SCALDING
SCALDINGS
SCALDINI
SCALDINO
SCALDS
SCALDSHIP
SCALE
SCALED
SCALELESS
SCALELIKE
SCALENE
SCALENI
SCALENUS
SCALEPAN
SCALEPANS
SCALER
SCALERS
SCALES
SCALETAIL
SCALEUP
SCALEUPS
SCALEWORK
SCALIER
SCALIEST
SCALINESS
SCALING
SCALINGS
SCALL
SCALLAWAG
SCALLED
SCALLIES
SCALLION
SCALLIONS
SCALLOP
SCALLOPED
SCALLOPER
SCALLOPS
SCALLS
SCALLY
SCALLYWAG
SCALOGRAM
SCALP
SCALPED
SCALPEL
SCALPELS
SCALPER
SCALPERS
SCALPING
SCALPINGS
SCALPINS
SCALPLESS
SCALPRUM
SCALPRUMS
SCALPS
SCALY
SCAM

SCAMBLE
SCAMBLED
SCAMBLER
SCAMBLERS
SCAMBLES
SCAMBLING
SCAMEL
SCAMELS
SCAMMED
SCAMMER
SCAMMERS
SCAMMING
SCAMMONY
SCAMP
SCAMPED
SCAMPER
SCAMPERED
SCAMPERER
SCAMPERS
SCAMPI
SCAMPIES
SCAMPING
SCAMPINGS
SCAMPIS
SCAMPISH
SCAMPS
SCAMS
SCAMSTER
SCAMSTERS
SCAMTO
SCAMTOS
SCAN
SCAND
SCANDAL
SCANDALED
SCANDALS
SCANDENT
SCANDIA
SCANDIAS
SCANDIC
SCANDIUM
SCANDIUMS
SCANNABLE
SCANNED
SCANNER
SCANNERS
SCANNING
SCANNINGS
SCANS
SCANSION
SCANSIONS
SCANT
SCANTED
SCANTER
SCANTEST
SCANTIER
SCANTIES
SCANTIEST

SCANTILY
SCANTING
SCANTITY
SCANTLE
SCANTLED
SCANTLES
SCANTLING
SCANTLY
SCANTNESS
SCANTS
SCANTY
SCAPA
SCAPAED
SCAPAING
SCAPAS
SCAPE
SCAPED
SCAPEGOAT
SCAPELESS
SCAPEMENT
SCAPES
SCAPHOID
SCAPHOIDS
SCAPHOPOD
SCAPI
SCAPING
SCAPOLITE
SCAPOSE
SCAPPLE
SCAPPLED
SCAPPLES
SCAPPLING
SCAPULA
SCAPULAE
SCAPULAR
SCAPULARS
SCAPULARY
SCAPULAS
SCAPUS
SCAR
SCARAB
SCARABAEI
SCARABEE
SCARABEES
SCARABOID
SCARABS
SCARCE
SCARCELY
SCARCER
SCARCEST
SCARCITY
SCARE
SCARECROW
SCARED
SCAREDER
SCAREDEST
SCAREHEAD
SCARER

SCARERS
SCARES
SCAREY
SCARF
SCARFED
SCARFER
SCARFERS
SCARFING
SCARFINGS
SCARFISH
SCARFPIN
SCARFPINS
SCARFS
SCARFSKIN
SCARFWISE
SCARIER
SCARIEST
SCARIFIED
SCARIFIER
SCARIFIES
SCARIFY
SCARILY
SCARINESS
SCARING
SCARIOSE
SCARIOUS
SCARLESS
SCARLET
SCARLETED
SCARLETS
SCARMOGE
SCARMOGES
SCARP
SCARPA
SCARPAED
SCARPAING
SCARPAS
SCARPED
SCARPER
SCARPERED
SCARPERS
SCARPETTI
SCARPETTO
SCARPH
SCARPHED
SCARPHING
SCARPHS
SCARPINES
SCARPING
SCARPINGS
SCARPS
SCARRE
SCARRED
SCARRES
SCARRIER
SCARRIEST
SCARRING
SCARRINGS

SCARRY
SCARS
SCART
SCARTED
SCARTH
SCARTHS
SCARTING
SCARTS
SCARVES
SCARY
SCAT
SCATBACK
SCATBACKS
SCATCH
SCATCHES
SCATH
SCATHE
SCATHED
SCATHEFUL
SCATHES
SCATHING
SCATHS
SCATOLE
SCATOLES
SCATOLOGY
SCATS
SCATT
SCATTED
SCATTER
SCATTERED
SCATTERER
SCATTERS
SCATTERY
SCATTIER
SCATTIEST
SCATTILY
SCATTING
SCATTINGS
SCATTS
SCATTY
SCAUD
SCAUDED
SCAUDING
SCAUDS
SCAUP
SCAUPED
SCAUPER
SCAUPERS
SCAUPING
SCAUPS
SCAUR
SCAURED
SCAURIES
SCAURING
SCAURS
SCAURY
SCAVAGE
SCAVAGER

SCAVAGERS	SCEPTERED	SCHIEDAMS	SCHMALZ
SCAVAGES	SCEPTERS	SCHILLER	SCHMALZES
SCAVENGE	SCEPTIC	SCHILLERS	SCHMALZY
SCAVENGED	SCEPTICAL	SCHILLING	SCHMATTE
SCAVENGER	SCEPTICS	SCHIMMEL	SCHMATTES
SCAVENGES	SCEPTRAL	SCHIMMELS	SCHMEAR
SCAW	SCEPTRE	SCHISM	SCHMEARED
SCAWS	SCEPTRED	SCHISMA	SCHMEARS
SCAWTITE	SCEPTRES	SCHISMAS	SCHMECK
SCAWTITES	SCEPTRING	SCHISMS	SCHMECKS
SCAZON	SCEPTRY	SCHIST	SCHMEER
SCAZONS	SCERNE	SCHISTOSE	SCHMEERED
SCAZONTES	SCERNED	SCHISTOUS	SCHMEERS
SCAZONTIC	SCERNES	SCHISTS	SCHMELZ
SCEAT	SCERNING	SCHIZIER	SCHMELZE
SCEATT	SCHANSE	SCHIZIEST	SCHMELZES
SCEATTAS	SCHANSES	SCHIZO	SCHMICK
SCEDULE	SCHANTZE	SCHIZOID	SCHMO
SCEDULED	SCHANTZES	SCHIZOIDS	SCHMOCK
SCEDULES	SCHANZE	SCHIZONT	SCHMOCKS
SCEDULING	SCHANZES	SCHIZONTS	SCHMOE
SCELERAT	SCHAPPE	SCHIZOPOD	SCHMOES
SCELERATE	SCHAPPED	SCHIZOS	SCHMOOS
SCELERATS	SCHAPPES	SCHIZY	SCHMOOSE
SCENA	SCHAPSKA	SCHIZZIER	SCHMOOSED
SCENARIES	SCHAPSKAS	SCHIZZY	SCHMOOSES
SCENARIO	SCHATCHEN	SCHLAGER	SCHMOOZ
SCENARIOS	SCHAV	SCHLAGERS	SCHMOOZE
SCENARISE	SCHAVS	SCHLEMIEL	SCHMOOZED
SCENARIST	SCHECHITA	SCHLEMIHL	SCHMOOZER
SCENARIZE	SCHEDULAR	SCHLEP	SCHMOOZES
SCENARY	SCHEDULE	SCHLEPP	SCHMOOZY
SCENAS	SCHEDULED	SCHLEPPED	SCHMOS
SCEND	SCHEDULER	SCHLEPPER	SCHMUCK
SCENDED	SCHEDULES	SCHLEPPS	SCHMUCKS
SCENDING	SCHEELITE	SCHLEPPY	SCHMUTTER
SCENDS	SCHELLUM	SCHLEPS	SCHNAPPER
SCENE	SCHELLUMS	SCHLICH	SCHNAPPS
SCENED	SCHELM	SCHLICHS	SCHNAPS
SCENEMAN	SCHELMS	SCHLIERE	SCHNAPSES
SCENEMEN	SCHEMA	SCHLIEREN	SCHNAUZER
SCENERIES	SCHEMAS	SCHLIERIC	SCHNECKE
SCENERY	SCHEMATA	SCHLOCK	SCHNECKEN
SCENES	SCHEMATIC	SCHLOCKER	SCHNELL
SCENIC	SCHEME	SCHLOCKS	SCHNITZEL
SCENICAL	SCHEMED	SCHLOCKY	SCHNOOK
SCENICS	SCHEMER	SCHLONG	SCHNOOKS
SCENING	SCHEMERS	SCHLONGS	SCHNORKEL
SCENT	SCHEMES	SCHLOSS	SCHNORR
SCENTED	SCHEMIE	SCHLOSSES	SCHNORRED
SCENTFUL	SCHEMIES	SCHLUB	SCHNORRER
SCENTING	SCHEMING	SCHLUBS	SCHNORRS
SCENTINGS	SCHEMINGS	SCHLUMP	SCHNOZ
SCENTLESS	SCHERZI	SCHLUMPED	SCHNOZES
SCENTS	SCHERZO	SCHLUMPS	SCHNOZZ
SCEPSIS	SCHERZOS	SCHLUMPY	SCHNOZZES
SCEPSISES	SCHIAVONE	SCHMALTZ	SCHNOZZLE
SCEPTER	SCHIEDAM	SCHMALTZY	SCHOLAR

SCHOLARCH
SCHOLARLY
SCHOLARS
SCHOLIA
SCHOLIAST
SCHOLION
SCHOLIUM
SCHOLIUMS
SCHOOL
SCHOOLBAG
SCHOOLBOY
SCHOOLDAY
SCHOOLE
SCHOOLED
SCHOOLERY
SCHOOLES
SCHOOLIE
SCHOOLIES
SCHOOLING
SCHOOLKID
SCHOOLMAN
SCHOOLMEN
SCHOOLS
SCHOONER
SCHOONERS
SCHORL
SCHORLS
SCHOUT
SCHOUTS
SCHRIK
SCHRIKS
SCHROD
SCHRODS
SCHTICK
SCHTICKS
SCHTIK
SCHTIKS
SCHTOOK
SCHTOOKS
SCHTOOM
SCHTUCK
SCHTUCKS
SCHUIT
SCHUITS
SCHUL
SCHULN
SCHULS
SCHUSS
SCHUSSED
SCHUSSER
SCHUSSERS
SCHUSSES
SCHUSSING
SCHUYT
SCHUYTS
SCHVARTZE
SCHWA
SCHWARTZE

SCHWAS
SCIAENID
SCIAENIDS
SCIAENOID
SCIAMACHY
SCIARID
SCIARIDS
SCIATIC
SCIATICA
SCIATICAL
SCIATICAS
SCIATICS
SCIENCE
SCIENCED
SCIENCES
SCIENT
SCIENTER
SCIENTIAL
SCIENTISE
SCIENTISM
SCIENTIST
SCIENTIZE
SCILICET
SCILLA
SCILLAS
SCIMETAR
SCIMETARS
SCIMITAR
SCIMITARS
SCIMITER
SCIMITERS
SCINCOID
SCINCOIDS
SCINTILLA
SCIOLISM
SCIOLISMS
SCIOLIST
SCIOLISTS
SCIOLOUS
SCIOLTO
SCIOMACHY
SCIOMANCY
SCION
SCIONS
SCIOPHYTE
SCIOSOPHY
SCIROC
SCIROCCO
SCIROCCOS
SCIROCS
SCIRRHI
SCIRRHOID
SCIRRHOUS
SCIRRHUS
SCISSEL
SCISSELS
SCISSIL
SCISSILE

SCISSILS
SCISSION
SCISSIONS
SCISSOR
SCISSORED
SCISSORER
SCISSORS
SCISSURE
SCISSURES
SCIURID
SCIURIDS
SCIURINE
SCIURINES
SCIUROID
SCLAFF
SCLAFFED
SCLAFFER
SCLAFFERS
SCLAFFING
SCLAFFS
SCLATE
SCLATED
SCLATES
SCLATING
SCLAUNDER
SCLAVE
SCLAVES
SCLERA
SCLERAE
SCLERAL
SCLERAS
SCLERE
SCLEREID
SCLEREIDE
SCLEREIDS
SCLEREMA
SCLEREMAS
SCLERES
SCLERITE
SCLERITES
SCLERITIC
SCLERITIS
SCLEROID
SCLEROMA
SCLEROMAS
SCLEROSAL
SCLEROSE
SCLEROSED
SCLEROSES
SCLEROSIS
SCLEROTAL
SCLEROTIA
SCLEROTIC
SCLEROTIN
SCLEROUS
SCLIFF
SCLIFFS
SCLIM

SCLIMMED
SCLIMMING
SCLIMS
SCODIER
SCODIEST
SCODY
SCOFF
SCOFFED
SCOFFER
SCOFFERS
SCOFFING
SCOFFINGS
SCOFFLAW
SCOFFLAWS
SCOFFS
SCOG
SCOGGED
SCOGGING
SCOGS
SCOINSON
SCOINSONS
SCOLD
SCOLDABLE
SCOLDED
SCOLDER
SCOLDERS
SCOLDING
SCOLDINGS
SCOLDS
SCOLECES
SCOLECID
SCOLECIDS
SCOLECITE
SCOLECOID
SCOLEX
SCOLIA
SCOLICES
SCOLIOMA
SCOLIOMAS
SCOLION
SCOLIOSES
SCOLIOSIS
SCOLIOTIC
SCOLLOP
SCOLLOPED
SCOLLOPS
SCOLYTID
SCOLYTIDS
SCOLYTOID
SCOMBRID
SCOMBRIDS
SCOMBROID
SCOMFISH
SCONCE
SCONCED
SCONCES
SCONCHEON
SCONCING

SCONE	SCORCHED	SCOTOMATA	SCOWDERED
SCONES	SCORCHER	SCOTOMIA	SCOWDERS
SCONTION	SCORCHERS	SCOTOMIAS	SCOWED
SCONTIONS	SCORCHES	SCOTOMIES	SCOWING
SCOOBIES	SCORCHING	SCOTOMY	SCOWL
SCOOBY	SCORDATO	SCOTOPHIL	SCOWLED
SCOOCH	SCORE	SCOTOPIA	SCOWLER
SCOOCHED	SCORECARD	SCOTOPIAS	SCOWLERS
SCOOCHES	SCORED	SCOTOPIC	SCOWLING
SCOOCHING	SCORELESS	SCOTS	SCOWLS
SCOOG	SCORELINE	SCOTTIE	SCOWP
SCOOGED	SCOREPAD	SCOTTIES	SCOWPED
SCOOGING	SCOREPADS	SCOUG	SCOWPING
SCOOGS	SCORER	SCOUGED	SCOWPS
SCOOP	SCORERS	SCOUGING	SCOWRER
SCOOPABLE	SCORES	SCOUGS	SCOWRERS
SCOOPED	SCORIA	SCOUNDREL	SCOWRIE
SCOOPER	SCORIAC	SCOUP	SCOWRIES
SCOOPERS	SCORIAE	SCOUPED	SCOWS
SCOOPFUL	SCORIFIED	SCOUPING	SCOWTH
SCOOPFULS	SCORIFIER	SCOUPS	SCOWTHER
SCOOPING	SCORIFIES	SCOUR	SCOWTHERS
SCOOPINGS	SCORIFY	SCOURED	SCOWTHS
SCOOPS	SCORING	SCOURER	SCOZZA
SCOOPSFUL	SCORINGS	SCOURERS	SCOZZAS
SCOOSH	SCORIOUS	SCOURGE	SCRAB
SCOOSHED	SCORN	SCOURGED	SCRABBED
SCOOSHES	SCORNED	SCOURGER	SCRABBING
SCOOSHING	SCORNER	SCOURGERS	SCRABBLE
SCOOT	SCORNERS	SCOURGES	SCRABBLED
SCOOTCH	SCORNFUL	SCOURGING	SCRABBLER
SCOOTCHED	SCORNING	SCOURIE	SCRABBLES
SCOOTCHES	SCORNINGS	SCOURIES	SCRABBLY
SCOOTED	SCORNS	SCOURING	SCRABS
SCOOTER	SCORODITE	SCOURINGS	SCRAE
SCOOTERS	SCORPER	SCOURS	SCRAES
SCOOTING	SCORPERS	SCOURSE	SCRAG
SCOOTS	SCORPIOID	SCOURSED	SCRAGGED
SCOP	SCORPION	SCOURSES	SCRAGGIER
SCOPA	SCORPIONS	SCOURSING	SCRAGGILY
SCOPAE	SCORRENDO	SCOUSE	SCRAGGING
SCOPAS	SCORSE	SCOUSER	SCRAGGLY
SCOPATE	SCORSED	SCOUSERS	SCRAGGY
SCOPE	SCORSER	SCOUSES	SCRAGS
SCOPED	SCORSERS	SCOUT	SCRAICH
SCOPELID	SCORSES	SCOUTED	SCRAICHED
SCOPELIDS	SCORSING	SCOUTER	SCRAICHS
SCOPELOID	SCOT	SCOUTERS	SCRAIGH
SCOPES	SCOTCH	SCOUTH	SCRAIGHED
SCOPING	SCOTCHED	SCOUTHER	SCRAIGHS
SCOPOLINE	SCOTCHES	SCOUTHERS	SCRAM
SCOPS	SCOTCHING	SCOUTHERY	SCRAMB
SCOPULA	SCOTER	SCOUTHS	SCRAMBED
SCOPULAE	SCOTERS	SCOUTING	SCRAMBING
SCOPULAS	SCOTIA	SCOUTINGS	SCRAMBLE
SCOPULATE	SCOTIAS	SCOUTS	SCRAMBLED
SCORBUTIC	SCOTOMA	SCOW	SCRAMBLER
SCORCH	SCOTOMAS	SCOWDER	SCRAMBLES

SCRAMBS
SCRAMJET
SCRAMJETS
SCRAMMED
SCRAMMING
SCRAMS
SCRAN
SCRANCH
SCRANCHED
SCRANCHES
SCRANNEL
SCRANNELS
SCRANNIER
SCRANNY
SCRANS
SCRAP
SCRAPABLE
SCRAPBOOK
SCRAPE
SCRAPED
SCRAPEGUT
SCRAPER
SCRAPERS
SCRAPES
SCRAPHEAP
SCRAPIE
SCRAPIES
SCRAPING
SCRAPINGS
SCRAPPAGE
SCRAPPED
SCRAPPER
SCRAPPERS
SCRAPPIER
SCRAPPILY
SCRAPPING
SCRAPPLE
SCRAPPLES
SCRAPPY
SCRAPS
SCRAPYARD
SCRAT
SCRATCH
SCRATCHED
SCRATCHER
SCRATCHES
SCRATCHIE
SCRATCHY
SCRATS
SCRATTED
SCRATTING
SCRATTLE
SCRATTLED
SCRATTLES
SCRAUCH
SCRAUCHED
SCRAUCHS
SCRAUGH

SCRAUGHED
SCRAUGHS
SCRAW
SCRAWL
SCRAWLED
SCRAWLER
SCRAWLERS
SCRAWLIER
SCRAWLING
SCRAWLS
SCRAWLY
SCRAWM
SCRAWMED
SCRAWMING
SCRAWMS
SCRAWNIER
SCRAWNILY
SCRAWNY
SCRAWP
SCRAWPED
SCRAWPING
SCRAWPS
SCRAWS
SCRAY
SCRAYE
SCRAYES
SCRAYS
SCREAK
SCREAKED
SCREAKIER
SCREAKING
SCREAKS
SCREAKY
SCREAM
SCREAMED
SCREAMER
SCREAMERS
SCREAMING
SCREAMS
SCREE
SCREECH
SCREECHED
SCREECHER
SCREECHES
SCREECHY
SCREED
SCREEDED
SCREEDER
SCREEDERS
SCREEDING
SCREEDS
SCREEN
SCREENED
SCREENER
SCREENERS
SCREENFUL
SCREENIE
SCREENIES

SCREENING
SCREENS
SCREES
SCREET
SCREETED
SCREETING
SCREETS
SCREEVE
SCREEVED
SCREEVER
SCREEVERS
SCREEVES
SCREEVING
SCREICH
SCREICHED
SCREICHS
SCREIGH
SCREIGHED
SCREIGHS
SCREW
SCREWABLE
SCREWBALL
SCREWBEAN
SCREWED
SCREWER
SCREWERS
SCREWIER
SCREWIEST
SCREWING
SCREWINGS
SCREWLIKE
SCREWS
SCREWTOP
SCREWTOPS
SCREWUP
SCREWUPS
SCREWWORM
SCREWY
SCRIBABLE
SCRIBAL
SCRIBBLE
SCRIBBLED
SCRIBBLER
SCRIBBLES
SCRIBBLY
SCRIBE
SCRIBED
SCRIBER
SCRIBERS
SCRIBES
SCRIBING
SCRIBINGS
SCRIBISM
SCRIBISMS
SCRIECH
SCRIECHED
SCRIECHS
SCRIED

SCRIENE
SCRIENES
SCRIES
SCRIEVE
SCRIEVED
SCRIEVES
SCRIEVING
SCRIGGLE
SCRIGGLED
SCRIGGLES
SCRIGGLY
SCRIKE
SCRIKED
SCRIKES
SCRIKING
SCRIM
SCRIMMAGE
SCRIMP
SCRIMPED
SCRIMPER
SCRIMPERS
SCRIMPIER
SCRIMPILY
SCRIMPING
SCRIMPIT
SCRIMPLY
SCRIMPS
SCRIMPY
SCRIMS
SCRIMSHAW
SCRIMURE
SCRIMURES
SCRINE
SCRINES
SCRIP
SCRIPPAGE
SCRIPS
SCRIPT
SCRIPTED
SCRIPTER
SCRIPTERS
SCRIPTING
SCRIPTORY
SCRIPTS
SCRIPTURE
SCRITCH
SCRITCHED
SCRITCHES
SCRIVE
SCRIVED
SCRIVENER
SCRIVES
SCRIVING
SCROBE
SCROBES
SCROD
SCRODDLED
SCRODS

SCROFULA
SCROFULAS
SCROG
SCROGGIE
SCROGGIER
SCROGGIN
SCROGGINS
SCROGGY
SCROGS
SCROLL
SCROLLED
SCROLLING
SCROLLS
SCROME
SCROMED
SCROMES
SCROMING
SCROOCH
SCROOCHED
SCROOCHES
SCROOGE
SCROOGED
SCROOGES
SCROOGING
SCROOP
SCROOPED
SCROOPING
SCROOPS
SCROOTCH
SCRORP
SCRORPS
SCROTA
SCROTAL
SCROTE
SCROTES
SCROTUM
SCROTUMS
SCROUGE
SCROUGED
SCROUGER
SCROUGERS
SCROUGES
SCROUGING
SCROUNGE
SCROUNGED
SCROUNGER
SCROUNGES
SCROUNGY
SCROW
SCROWDGE
SCROWDGED
SCROWDGES
SCROWL
SCROWLE
SCROWLED
SCROWLES
SCROWLING
SCROWLS

SCROWS
SCROYLE
SCROYLES
SCRUB
SCRUBBED
SCRUBBER
SCRUBBERS
SCRUBBIER
SCRUBBILY
SCRUBBING
SCRUBBY
SCRUBLAND
SCRUBS
SCRUFF
SCRUFFIER
SCRUFFILY
SCRUFFS
SCRUFFY
SCRUM
SCRUMDOWN
SCRUMMAGE
SCRUMMED
SCRUMMIE
SCRUMMIER
SCRUMMIES
SCRUMMING
SCRUMMY
SCRUMP
SCRUMPED
SCRUMPIES
SCRUMPING
SCRUMPLE
SCRUMPLED
SCRUMPLES
SCRUMPOX
SCRUMPS
SCRUMPY
SCRUMS
SCRUNCH
SCRUNCHED
SCRUNCHES
SCRUNCHIE
SCRUNCHY
SCRUNT
SCRUNTIER
SCRUNTS
SCRUNTY
SCRUPLE
SCRUPLED
SCRUPLER
SCRUPLERS
SCRUPLES
SCRUPLING
SCRUTABLE
SCRUTATOR
SCRUTINY
SCRUTO
SCRUTOIRE

SCRUTOS
SCRUZE
SCRUZED
SCRUZES
SCRUZING
SCRY
SCRYDE
SCRYER
SCRYERS
SCRYING
SCRYINGS
SCRYNE
SCRYNES
SCUBA
SCUBAED
SCUBAING
SCUBAS
SCUCHIN
SCUCHINS
SCUD
SCUDDALER
SCUDDED
SCUDDER
SCUDDERS
SCUDDING
SCUDDLE
SCUDDLED
SCUDDLES
SCUDDLING
SCUDI
SCUDLER
SCUDLERS
SCUDO
SCUDS
SCUFF
SCUFFED
SCUFFER
SCUFFERS
SCUFFING
SCUFFLE
SCUFFLED
SCUFFLER
SCUFFLERS
SCUFFLES
SCUFFLING
SCUFFS
SCUFT
SCUFTS
SCUG
SCUGGED
SCUGGING
SCUGS
SCUL
SCULCH
SCULCHES
SCULK
SCULKED
SCULKER

SCULKERS
SCULKING
SCULKS
SCULL
SCULLE
SCULLED
SCULLER
SCULLERS
SCULLERY
SCULLES
SCULLING
SCULLINGS
SCULLION
SCULLIONS
SCULLS
SCULP
SCULPED
SCULPIN
SCULPING
SCULPINS
SCULPS
SCULPSIT
SCULPT
SCULPTED
SCULPTING
SCULPTOR
SCULPTORS
SCULPTS
SCULPTURE
SCULS
SCULTCH
SCULTCHES
SCUM
SCUMBAG
SCUMBAGS
SCUMBER
SCUMBERED
SCUMBERS
SCUMBLE
SCUMBLED
SCUMBLES
SCUMBLING
SCUMFISH
SCUMLESS
SCUMLIKE
SCUMMED
SCUMMER
SCUMMERS
SCUMMIER
SCUMMIEST
SCUMMILY
SCUMMING
SCUMMINGS
SCUMMY
SCUMS
SCUNCHEON
SCUNDERED
SCUNGE

SCUNGED
SCUNGES
SCUNGIER
SCUNGIEST
SCUNGILLI
SCUNGING
SCUNGY
SCUNNER
SCUNNERED
SCUNNERS
SCUP
SCUPPAUG
SCUPPAUGS
SCUPPER
SCUPPERED
SCUPPERS
SCUPS
SCUR
SCURF
SCURFIER
SCURFIEST
SCURFS
SCURFY
SCURRED
SCURRIED
SCURRIER
SCURRIERS
SCURRIES
SCURRIL
SCURRILE
SCURRING
SCURRIOUR
SCURRY
SCURRYING
SCURS
SCURVIER
SCURVIES
SCURVIEST
SCURVILY
SCURVY
SCUSE
SCUSED
SCUSES
SCUSING
SCUT
SCUTA
SCUTAGE
SCUTAGES
SCUTAL
SCUTATE
SCUTATION
SCUTCH
SCUTCHED
SCUTCHEON
SCUTCHER
SCUTCHERS
SCUTCHES
SCUTCHING

SCUTE
SCUTELLA
SCUTELLAR
SCUTELLUM
SCUTES
SCUTIFORM
SCUTIGER
SCUTIGERS
SCUTS
SCUTTER
SCUTTERED
SCUTTERS
SCUTTLE
SCUTTLED
SCUTTLER
SCUTTLERS
SCUTTLES
SCUTTLING
SCUTUM
SCUTWORK
SCUTWORKS
SCUZZ
SCUZZBALL
SCUZZES
SCUZZIER
SCUZZIEST
SCUZZY
SCYBALA
SCYBALOUS
SCYBALUM
SCYE
SCYES
SCYPHATE
SCYPHI
SCYPHUS
SCYTALE
SCYTALES
SCYTHE
SCYTHED
SCYTHEMAN
SCYTHEMEN
SCYTHER
SCYTHERS
SCYTHES
SCYTHING
SDAINE
SDAINED
SDAINES
SDAINING
SDAYN
SDAYNED
SDAYNING
SDAYNS
SDEIGN
SDEIGNE
SDEIGNED
SDEIGNES
SDEIGNING

SDEIGNS
SDEIN
SDEINED
SDEINING
SDEINS
SEA
SEABAG
SEABAGS
SEABANK
SEABANKS
SEABEACH
SEABED
SEABEDS
SEABIRD
SEABIRDS
SEABLITE
SEABLITES
SEABOARD
SEABOARDS
SEABOOT
SEABOOTS
SEABORNE
SEABOTTLE
SEACOAST
SEACOASTS
SEACOCK
SEACOCKS
SEACRAFT
SEACRAFTS
SEACUNNY
SEADOG
SEADOGS
SEADROME
SEADROMES
SEAFARER
SEAFARERS
SEAFARING
SEAFLOOR
SEAFLOORS
SEAFOLK
SEAFOLKS
SEAFOOD
SEAFOODS
SEAFOWL
SEAFOWLS
SEAFRONT
SEAFRONTS
SEAGIRT
SEAGOING
SEAGULL
SEAGULLS
SEAHAWK
SEAHAWKS
SEAHOG
SEAHOGS
SEAHORSE
SEAHORSES
SEAHOUND

SEAHOUNDS
SEAKALE
SEAKALES
SEAL
SEALABLE
SEALANT
SEALANTS
SEALCH
SEALCHS
SEALED
SEALER
SEALERIES
SEALERS
SEALERY
SEALGH
SEALGHS
SEALIFT
SEALIFTED
SEALIFTS
SEALINE
SEALINES
SEALING
SEALINGS
SEALLIKE
SEALPOINT
SEALS
SEALSKIN
SEALSKINS
SEALWAX
SEALWAXES
SEALYHAM
SEALYHAMS
SEAM
SEAMAID
SEAMAIDS
SEAMAN
SEAMANLY
SEAMARK
SEAMARKS
SEAME
SEAMED
SEAMEN
SEAMER
SEAMERS
SEAMES
SEAMIER
SEAMIEST
SEAMINESS
SEAMING
SEAMLESS
SEAMLIKE
SEAMOUNT
SEAMOUNTS
SEAMS
SEAMSET
SEAMSETS
SEAMSTER
SEAMSTERS

SEAMY
SEAN
SEANCE
SEANCES
SEANED
SEANING
SEANS
SEAPIECE
SEAPIECES
SEAPLANE
SEAPLANES
SEAPORT
SEAPORTS
SEAQUAKE
SEAQUAKES
SEAQUARIA
SEAR
SEARAT
SEARATS
SEARCE
SEARCED
SEARCES
SEARCH
SEARCHED
SEARCHER
SEARCHERS
SEARCHES
SEARCHING
SEARCING
SEARE
SEARED
SEARER
SEAREST
SEARING
SEARINGLY
SEARINGS
SEARNESS
SEAROBIN
SEAROBINS
SEARS
SEAS
SEASCAPE
SEASCAPES
SEASCOUT
SEASCOUTS
SEASE
SEASED
SEASES
SEASHELL
SEASHELLS
SEASHORE
SEASHORES
SEASICK
SEASICKER
SEASIDE
SEASIDES
SEASING
SEASON

SEASONAL
SEASONALS
SEASONED
SEASONER
SEASONERS
SEASONING
SEASONS
SEASPEAK
SEASPEAKS
SEASTRAND
SEASURE
SEASURES
SEAT
SEATBACK
SEATBACKS
SEATBELT
SEATBELTS
SEATED
SEATER
SEATERS
SEATING
SEATINGS
SEATLESS
SEATMATE
SEATMATES
SEATRAIN
SEATRAINS
SEATROUT
SEATROUTS
SEATS
SEATWORK
SEATWORKS
SEAWALL
SEAWALLS
SEAWAN
SEAWANS
SEAWANT
SEAWANTS
SEAWARD
SEAWARDLY
SEAWARDS
SEAWARE
SEAWARES
SEAWATER
SEAWATERS
SEAWAY
SEAWAYS
SEAWEED
SEAWEEDS
SEAWIFE
SEAWIVES
SEAWOMAN
SEAWOMEN
SEAWORM
SEAWORMS
SEAWORTHY
SEAZE
SEAZED

SEAZES
SEAZING
SEBACEOUS
SEBACIC
SEBASIC
SEBATE
SEBATES
SEBESTEN
SEBESTENS
SEBIFIC
SEBORRHEA
SEBUM
SEBUMS
SEBUNDIES
SEBUNDY
SEC
SECALOSE
SECALOSES
SECANT
SECANTLY
SECANTS
SECATEUR
SECATEURS
SECCO
SECCOS
SECEDE
SECEDED
SECEDER
SECEDERS
SECEDES
SECEDING
SECERN
SECERNED
SECERNENT
SECERNING
SECERNS
SECESH
SECESHER
SECESHERS
SECESHES
SECESSION
SECH
SECHS
SECKEL
SECKELS
SECKLE
SECKLES
SECLUDE
SECLUDED
SECLUDES
SECLUDING
SECLUSION
SECLUSIVE
SECO
SECODONT
SECODONTS
SECONAL
SECONALS

SECOND
SECONDARY
SECONDE
SECONDED
SECONDEE
SECONDEES
SECONDER
SECONDERS
SECONDES
SECONDI
SECONDING
SECONDLY
SECONDO
SECONDS
SECPAR
SECPARS
SECRECIES
SECRECY
SECRET
SECRETA
SECRETAGE
SECRETARY
SECRETE
SECRETED
SECRETER
SECRETES
SECRETEST
SECRETIN
SECRETING
SECRETINS
SECRETION
SECRETIVE
SECRETLY
SECRETOR
SECRETORS
SECRETORY
SECRETS
SECS
SECT
SECTARIAL
SECTARIAN
SECTARIES
SECTARY
SECTATOR
SECTATORS
SECTILE
SECTILITY
SECTION
SECTIONAL
SECTIONED
SECTIONS
SECTOR
SECTORAL
SECTORED
SECTORIAL
SECTORING
SECTORISE
SECTORIZE

SECTORS	SEDITIONS	SEEDY	SEEWING
SECTS	SEDITIOUS	SEEING	SEFER
SECULAR	SEDUCE	SEEINGS	SEG
SECULARLY	SEDUCED	SEEK	SEGAR
SECULARS	SEDUCER	SEEKER	SEGARS
SECULUM	SEDUCERS	SEEKERS	SEGETAL
SECULUMS	SEDUCES	SEEKING	SEGGAR
SECUND	SEDUCIBLE	SEEKS	SEGGARS
SECUNDINE	SEDUCING	SEEL	SEGHOL
SECUNDLY	SEDUCINGS	SEELD	SEGHOLATE
SECUNDUM	SEDUCIVE	SEELED	SEGHOLS
SECURABLE	SEDUCTION	SEELIE	SEGMENT
SECURANCE	SEDUCTIVE	SEELIER	SEGMENTAL
SECURE	SEDUCTOR	SEELIEST	SEGMENTED
SECURED	SEDUCTORS	SEELING	SEGMENTS
SECURELY	SEDULITY	SEELINGS	SEGNI
SECURER	SEDULOUS	SEELS	SEGNO
SECURERS	SEDUM	SEELY	SEGNOS
SECURES	SEDUMS	SEEM	SEGO
SECUREST	SEE	SEEMED	SEGOL
SECURING	SEEABLE	SEEMER	SEGOLATE
SECURITAN	SEECATCH	SEEMERS	SEGOLATES
SECURITY	SEED	SEEMING	SEGOLS
SED	SEEDBED	SEEMINGLY	SEGOS
SEDAN	SEEDBEDS	SEEMINGS	SEGREANT
SEDANS	SEEDBOX	SEEMLESS	SEGREGANT
SEDARIM	SEEDBOXES	SEEMLIER	SEGREGATE
SEDATE	SEEDCAKE	SEEMLIEST	SEGS
SEDATED	SEEDCAKES	SEEMLIHED	SEGUE
SEDATELY	SEEDCASE	SEEMLY	SEGUED
SEDATER	SEEDCASES	SEEMLYHED	SEGUEING
SEDATES	SEEDEATER	SEEMS	SEGUES
SEDATEST	SEEDED	SEEN	SEI
SEDATING	SEEDER	SEEP	SEICENTO
SEDATION	SEEDERS	SEEPAGE	SEICENTOS
SEDATIONS	SEEDIER	SEEPAGES	SEICHE
SEDATIVE	SEEDIEST	SEEPED	SEICHES
SEDATIVES	SEEDILY	SEEPIER	SEIDEL
SEDENT	SEEDINESS	SEEPIEST	SEIDELS
SEDENTARY	SEEDING	SEEPING	SEIF
SEDER	SEEDINGS	SEEPS	SEIFS
SEDERS	SEEDLESS	SEEPY	SEIGNEUR
SEDERUNT	SEEDLIKE	SEER	SEIGNEURS
SEDERUNTS	SEEDLING	SEERESS	SEIGNEURY
SEDES	SEEDLINGS	SEERESSES	SEIGNIOR
SEDGE	SEEDLIP	SEERS	SEIGNIORS
SEDGED	SEEDLIPS	SEES	SEIGNIORY
SEDGELAND	SEEDMAN	SEESAW	SEIGNORAL
SEDGES	SEEDMEN	SEESAWED	SEIGNORY
SEDGIER	SEEDNESS	SEESAWING	SEIK
SEDGIEST	SEEDPOD	SEESAWS	SEIKER
SEDGY	SEEDPODS	SEETHE	SEIKEST
SEDILE	SEEDS	SEETHED	SEIL
SEDILIA	SEEDSMAN	SEETHER	SEILED
SEDILIUM	SEEDSMEN	SEETHERS	SEILING
SEDIMENT	SEEDSTOCK	SEETHES	SEILS
SEDIMENTS	SEEDTIME	SEETHING	SEINE
SEDITION	SEEDTIMES	SEETHINGS	SEINED

SEINER	SELADANGS	SELFISTS	SEMBLE
SEINERS	SELAH	SELFLESS	SEMBLED
SEINES	SELAHS	SELFNESS	SEMBLES
SEINING	SELAMLIK	SELFS	SEMBLING
SEININGS	SELAMLIKS	SELFSAME	SEME
SEIR	SELCOUTH	SELFWARD	SEMEE
SEIRS	SELD	SELFWARDS	SEMEED
SEIS	SELDOM	SELICTAR	SEMEIA
SEISABLE	SELDOMLY	SELICTARS	SEMEION
SEISE	SELDSEEN	SELKIE	SEMEIOTIC
SEISED	SELDSHOWN	SELKIES	SEMEME
SEISER	SELE	SELL	SEMEMES
SEISERS	SELECT	SELLA	SEMEMIC
SEISES	SELECTA	SELLABLE	SEMEN
SEISIN	SELECTAS	SELLAE	SEMENS
SEISING	SELECTED	SELLAS	SEMES
SEISINGS	SELECTEE	SELLE	SEMESTER
SEISINS	SELECTEES	SELLER	SEMESTERS
SEISM	SELECTING	SELLERS	SEMESTRAL
SEISMAL	SELECTION	SELLES	SEMI
SEISMIC	SELECTIVE	SELLING	SEMIANGLE
SEISMICAL	SELECTLY	SELLOFF	SEMIARID
SEISMISM	SELECTMAN	SELLOFFS	SEMIBALD
SEISMISMS	SELECTMEN	SELLOTAPE	SEMIBOLD
SEISMS	SELECTOR	SELLOUT	SEMIBOLDS
SEISOR	SELECTORS	SELLOUTS	SEMIBREVE
SEISORS	SELECTS	SELLS	SEMIBULL
SEISURE	SELENATE	SELS	SEMIBULLS
SEISURES	SELENATES	SELSYN	SEMICOLON
SEITAN	SELENIAN	SELSYNS	SEMICOMA
SEITANS	SELENIC	SELTZER	SEMICOMAS
SEITEN	SELENIDE	SELTZERS	SEMICURED
SEITENS	SELENIDES	SELVA	SEMIDEAF
SEITIES	SELENIOUS	SELVAGE	SEMIDEIFY
SEITY	SELENITE	SELVAGED	SEMIDOME
SEIZABLE	SELENITES	SELVAGEE	SEMIDOMED
SEIZE	SELENITIC	SELVAGEES	SEMIDOMES
SEIZED	SELENIUM	SELVAGES	SEMIDRY
SEIZER	SELENIUMS	SELVAGING	SEMIDWARF
SEIZERS	SELENOSES	SELVAS	SEMIE
SEIZES	SELENOSIS	SELVEDGE	SEMIERECT
SEIZIN	SELENOUS	SELVEDGED	SEMIES
SEIZING	SELES	SELVEDGES	SEMIFINAL
SEIZINGS	SELF	SELVES	SEMIFIT
SEIZINS	SELFDOM	SEMAINIER	SEMIFLUID
SEIZOR	SELFDOMS	SEMANTEME	SEMIGALA
SEIZORS	SELFED	SEMANTIC	SEMIGLOSS
SEIZURE	SELFHEAL	SEMANTICS	SEMIGROUP
SEIZURES	SELFHEALS	SEMANTIDE	SEMIHARD
SEJANT	SELFHOOD	SEMANTRA	SEMIHIGH
SEJEANT	SELFHOODS	SEMANTRON	SEMIHOBO
SEKOS	SELFING	SEMAPHORE	SEMIHOBOS
SEKOSES	SELFINGS	SEMATIC	SEMILLON
SEKT	SELFISH	SEMBLABLE	SEMILLONS
SEKTS	SELFISHLY	SEMBLABLY	SEMILOG
SEL	SELFISM	SEMBLANCE	SEMILUNAR
SELACHIAN	SELFISMS	SEMBLANT	SEMILUNE
SELADANG	SELFIST	SEMBLANTS	SEMILUNES

525

SEMIMAT
SEMIMATT
SEMIMATTE
SEMIMETAL
SEMIMICRO
SEMIMILD
SEMIMOIST
SEMIMUTE
SEMINA
SEMINAL
SEMINALLY
SEMINAR
SEMINARS
SEMINARY
SEMINATE
SEMINATED
SEMINATES
SEMINOMA
SEMINOMAD
SEMINOMAS
SEMINUDE
SEMIOLOGY
SEMIOPEN
SEMIOSES
SEMIOSIS
SEMIOTIC
SEMIOTICS
SEMIOVAL
SEMIPED
SEMIPEDS
SEMIPIOUS
SEMIPLUME
SEMIPOLAR
SEMIPRO
SEMIPROS
SEMIRAW
SEMIRIGID
SEMIROUND
SEMIRURAL
SEMIS
SEMISES
SEMISOFT
SEMISOLID
SEMISOLUS
SEMISTIFF
SEMISWEET
SEMITAR
SEMITARS
SEMITAUR
SEMITAURS
SEMITIST
SEMITISTS
SEMITONAL
SEMITONE
SEMITONES
SEMITONIC
SEMITRUCK
SEMIURBAN

SEMIVOCAL
SEMIVOWEL
SEMIWILD
SEMIWORKS
SEMMIT
SEMMITS
SEMOLINA
SEMOLINAS
SEMPER
SEMPLE
SEMPLER
SEMPLEST
SEMPLICE
SEMPRE
SEMPSTER
SEMPSTERS
SEMSEM
SEMSEMS
SEMUNCIA
SEMUNCIAE
SEMUNCIAL
SEMUNCIAS
SEN
SENA
SENARIES
SENARII
SENARIUS
SENARY
SENAS
SENATE
SENATES
SENATOR
SENATORS
SEND
SENDABLE
SENDAL
SENDALS
SENDED
SENDER
SENDERS
SENDING
SENDINGS
SENDOFF
SENDOFFS
SENDS
SENDUP
SENDUPS
SENE
SENECA
SENECAS
SENECIO
SENECIOS
SENEGA
SENEGAS
SENESCENT
SENESCHAL
SENGI
SENGREEN

SENGREENS
SENHOR
SENHORA
SENHORAS
SENHORES
SENHORITA
SENHORS
SENILE
SENILELY
SENILES
SENILITY
SENIOR
SENIORITY
SENIORS
SENITI
SENNA
SENNACHIE
SENNAS
SENNET
SENNETS
SENNIGHT
SENNIGHTS
SENNIT
SENNITS
SENOPIA
SENOPIAS
SENOR
SENORA
SENORAS
SENORES
SENORITA
SENORITAS
SENORS
SENRYU
SENS
SENSA
SENSATE
SENSATED
SENSATELY
SENSATES
SENSATING
SENSATION
SENSE
SENSED
SENSEFUL
SENSEI
SENSEIS
SENSELESS
SENSES
SENSI
SENSIBLE
SENSIBLER
SENSIBLES
SENSIBLY
SENSILE
SENSILLA
SENSILLAE
SENSILLUM

SENSING
SENSINGS
SENSIS
SENSISM
SENSISMS
SENSIST
SENSISTS
SENSITISE
SENSITIVE
SENSITIZE
SENSOR
SENSORIA
SENSORIAL
SENSORILY
SENSORIUM
SENSORS
SENSORY
SENSUAL
SENSUALLY
SENSUM
SENSUOUS
SENT
SENTE
SENTED
SENTENCE
SENTENCED
SENTENCER
SENTENCES
SENTENTIA
SENTI
SENTIENCE
SENTIENCY
SENTIENT
SENTIENTS
SENTIMENT
SENTIMO
SENTIMOS
SENTINEL
SENTINELS
SENTING
SENTRIES
SENTRY
SENTS
SENVIES
SENVY
SENZA
SEPAD
SEPADDED
SEPADDING
SEPADS
SEPAL
SEPALED
SEPALINE
SEPALLED
SEPALODY
SEPALOID
SEPALOUS
SEPALS

SEPARABLE	SEPTUM	SERAPHIM	SERIALIST
SEPARABLY	SEPTUMS	SERAPHIMS	SERIALITY
SEPARATA	SEPTUOR	SERAPHIN	SERIALIZE
SEPARATE	SEPTUORS	SERAPHINE	SERIALLY
SEPARATED	SEPTUPLE	SERAPHINS	SERIALS
SEPARATES	SEPTUPLED	SERAPHS	SERIATE
SEPARATOR	SEPTUPLES	SERASKIER	SERIATED
SEPARATUM	SEPTUPLET	SERDAB	SERIATELY
SEPHEN	SEPULCHER	SERDABS	SERIATES
SEPHENS	SEPULCHRE	SERE	SERIATIM
SEPIA	SEPULTURE	SERED	SERIATING
SEPIAS	SEQUACITY	SEREIN	SERIATION
SEPIC	SEQUEL	SEREINS	SERIC
SEPIMENT	SEQUELA	SERENADE	SERICEOUS
SEPIMENTS	SEQUELAE	SERENADED	SERICIN
SEPIOLITE	SEQUELISE	SERENADER	SERICINS
SEPIOST	SEQUELIZE	SERENADES	SERICITE
SEPIOSTS	SEQUELS	SERENATA	SERICITES
SEPIUM	SEQUENCE	SERENATAS	SERICITIC
SEPIUMS	SEQUENCED	SERENATE	SERICON
SEPMAG	SEQUENCER	SERENATES	SERICONS
SEPOY	SEQUENCES	SERENE	SERIEMA
SEPOYS	SEQUENCY	SERENED	SERIEMAS
SEPPUKU	SEQUENT	SERENELY	SERIES
SEPPUKUS	SEQUENTLY	SERENER	SERIF
SEPS	SEQUENTS	SERENES	SERIFED
SEPSES	SEQUESTER	SERENEST	SERIFFED
SEPSIS	SEQUESTRA	SERENING	SERIFS
SEPT	SEQUIN	SERENITY	SERIGRAPH
SEPTA	SEQUINED	SERER	SERIN
SEPTAGE	SEQUINING	SERES	SERINE
SEPTAGES	SEQUINNED	SEREST	SERINES
SEPTAL	SEQUINS	SERF	SERINETTE
SEPTARIA	SEQUITUR	SERFAGE	SERING
SEPTARIAN	SEQUITURS	SERFAGES	SERINGA
SEPTARIUM	SEQUOIA	SERFDOM	SERINGAS
SEPTATE	SEQUOIAS	SERFDOMS	SERINS
SEPTATION	SER	SERFHOOD	SERIOUS
SEPTEMFID	SERA	SERFHOODS	SERIOUSLY
SEPTEMVIR	SERAC	SERFISH	SERIPH
SEPTENARY	SERACS	SERFLIKE	SERIPHS
SEPTENNIA	SERAFILE	SERFS	SERJEANCY
SEPTET	SERAFILES	SERFSHIP	SERJEANT
SEPTETS	SERAFIN	SERFSHIPS	SERJEANTS
SEPTETTE	SERAFINS	SERGE	SERJEANTY
SEPTETTES	SERAGLIO	SERGEANCY	SERK
SEPTIC	SERAGLIOS	SERGEANT	SERKALI
SEPTICAL	SERAI	SERGEANTS	SERKALIS
SEPTICITY	SERAIL	SERGEANTY	SERKS
SEPTICS	SERAILS	SERGED	SERMON
SEPTIFORM	SERAIS	SERGER	SERMONED
SEPTIMAL	SERAL	SERGERS	SERMONEER
SEPTIME	SERANG	SERGES	SERMONER
SEPTIMES	SERANGS	SERGING	SERMONERS
SEPTIMOLE	SERAPE	SERGINGS	SERMONET
SEPTLEVA	SERAPES	SERIAL	SERMONETS
SEPTLEVAS	SERAPH	SERIALISE	SERMONIC
SEPTS	SERAPHIC	SERIALISM	SERMONING

SERMONISE	SERRATUS	SERVITORS	SETNESS
SERMONIZE	SERRE	SERVITUDE	SETNESSES
SERMONS	SERRED	SERVLET	SETOFF
SEROLOGIC	SERREFILE	SERVLETS	SETOFFS
SEROLOGY	SERRES	SERVO	SETON
SERON	SERRICORN	SERVOS	SETONS
SERONS	SERRIED	SERVQUAL	SETOSE
SEROON	SERRIEDLY	SERVQUALS	SETOUS
SEROONS	SERRIES	SESAME	SETOUT
SEROPUS	SERRIFORM	SESAMES	SETOUTS
SEROPUSES	SERRING	SESAMOID	SETS
SEROSA	SERRS	SESAMOIDS	SETSCREW
SEROSAE	SERRULATE	SESE	SETSCREWS
SEROSAL	SERRY	SESELI	SETT
SEROSAS	SERRYING	SESELIS	SETTEE
SEROSITY	SERS	SESEY	SETTEES
SEROTINAL	SERUEWE	SESH	SETTER
SEROTINE	SERUEWED	SESHES	SETTERED
SEROTINES	SERUEWES	SESS	SETTERING
SEROTINY	SERUEWING	SESSA	SETTERS
SEROTONIN	SERUM	SESSES	SETTING
SEROTYPE	SERUMAL	SESSILE	SETTINGS
SEROTYPED	SERUMS	SESSILITY	SETTLE
SEROTYPES	SERVABLE	SESSION	SETTLED
SEROUS	SERVAL	SESSIONAL	SETTLER
SEROVAR	SERVALS	SESSIONS	SETTLERS
SEROVARS	SERVANT	SESSPOOL	SETTLES
SEROW	SERVANTED	SESSPOOLS	SETTLING
SEROWS	SERVANTRY	SESTERCE	SETTLINGS
SERPENT	SERVANTS	SESTERCES	SETTLOR
SERPENTRY	SERVE	SESTERTIA	SETTLORS
SERPENTS	SERVEABLE	SESTERTII	SETTS
SERPIGO	SERVED	SESTET	SETUALE
SERPIGOES	SERVER	SESTETS	SETUALES
SERPIGOS	SERVERIES	SESTETT	SETULE
SERPULA	SERVERS	SESTETTE	SETULES
SERPULAE	SERVERY	SESTETTES	SETULOSE
SERPULID	SERVES	SESTETTO	SETULOUS
SERPULIDS	SERVEWE	SESTETTOS	SETUP
SERPULITE	SERVEWED	SESTETTS	SETUPS
SERR	SERVEWES	SESTINA	SETWALL
SERRA	SERVEWING	SESTINAS	SETWALLS
SERRAE	SERVICE	SESTINE	SEVEN
SERRAN	SERVICED	SESTINES	SEVENFOLD
SERRANID	SERVICER	SESTON	SEVENS
SERRANIDS	SERVICERS	SESTONS	SEVENTEEN
SERRANO	SERVICES	SET	SEVENTH
SERRANOID	SERVICING	SETA	SEVENTHLY
SERRANOS	SERVIENT	SETACEOUS	SEVENTHS
SERRANS	SERVIETTE	SETAE	SEVENTIES
SERRAS	SERVILE	SETAL	SEVENTY
SERRATE	SERVILELY	SETBACK	SEVER
SERRATED	SERVILES	SETBACKS	SEVERABLE
SERRATES	SERVILISM	SETENANT	SEVERAL
SERRATI	SERVILITY	SETENANTS	SEVERALLY
SERRATING	SERVING	SETIFORM	SEVERALS
SERRATION	SERVINGS	SETLINE	SEVERALTY
SERRATURE	SERVITOR	SETLINES	SEVERANCE

SEVERE
SEVERED
SEVERELY
SEVERER
SEVEREST
SEVERIES
SEVERING
SEVERITY
SEVERS
SEVERY
SEVICHE
SEVICHES
SEVRUGA
SEVRUGAS
SEW
SEWABLE
SEWAGE
SEWAGES
SEWAN
SEWANS
SEWAR
SEWARS
SEWED
SEWEL
SEWELLEL
SEWELLELS
SEWELS
SEWEN
SEWENS
SEWER
SEWERAGE
SEWERAGES
SEWERED
SEWERING
SEWERINGS
SEWERLESS
SEWERLIKE
SEWERS
SEWIN
SEWING
SEWINGS
SEWINS
SEWN
SEWS
SEX
SEXAHOLIC
SEXED
SEXENNIAL
SEXER
SEXERCISE
SEXERS
SEXES
SEXFID
SEXFOIL
SEXFOILS
SEXIER
SEXIEST
SEXILY

SEXINESS
SEXING
SEXISM
SEXISMS
SEXIST
SEXISTS
SEXLESS
SEXLESSLY
SEXLINKED
SEXOLOGIC
SEXOLOGY
SEXPERT
SEXPERTS
SEXPOT
SEXPOTS
SEXT
SEXTAIN
SEXTAINS
SEXTAN
SEXTANS
SEXTANSES
SEXTANT
SEXTANTAL
SEXTANTS
SEXTARII
SEXTARIUS
SEXTET
SEXTETS
SEXTETT
SEXTETTE
SEXTETTES
SEXTETTS
SEXTILE
SEXTILES
SEXTO
SEXTOLET
SEXTOLETS
SEXTON
SEXTONESS
SEXTONS
SEXTOS
SEXTS
SEXTUOR
SEXTUORS
SEXTUPLE
SEXTUPLED
SEXTUPLES
SEXTUPLET
SEXTUPLY
SEXUAL
SEXUALISE
SEXUALISM
SEXUALIST
SEXUALITY
SEXUALIZE
SEXUALLY
SEXVALENT
SEXY

SEY
SEYEN
SEYENS
SEYS
SEYSURE
SEYSURES
SEZ
SFERICS
SFORZANDI
SFORZANDO
SFORZATI
SFORZATO
SFORZATOS
SFUMATO
SFUMATOS
SGRAFFITI
SGRAFFITO
SH
SHA
SHABASH
SHABBATOT
SHABBIER
SHABBIEST
SHABBILY
SHABBLE
SHABBLES
SHABBY
SHABRACK
SHABRACKS
SHACK
SHACKED
SHACKING
SHACKLE
SHACKLED
SHACKLER
SHACKLERS
SHACKLES
SHACKLING
SHACKO
SHACKOES
SHACKOS
SHACKS
SHAD
SHADBERRY
SHADBLOW
SHADBLOWS
SHADBUSH
SHADCHAN
SHADCHANS
SHADDOCK
SHADDOCKS
SHADE
SHADED
SHADELESS
SHADER
SHADERS
SHADES
SHADFLIES

SHADFLY
SHADIER
SHADIEST
SHADILY
SHADINESS
SHADING
SHADINGS
SHADKHAN
SHADKHANS
SHADOOF
SHADOOFS
SHADOW
SHADOWBOX
SHADOWED
SHADOWER
SHADOWERS
SHADOWIER
SHADOWILY
SHADOWING
SHADOWS
SHADOWY
SHADRACH
SHADRACHS
SHADS
SHADUF
SHADUFS
SHADY
SHAFT
SHAFTED
SHAFTER
SHAFTERS
SHAFTING
SHAFTINGS
SHAFTLESS
SHAFTS
SHAG
SHAGBARK
SHAGBARKS
SHAGGABLE
SHAGGED
SHAGGIER
SHAGGIEST
SHAGGILY
SHAGGING
SHAGGY
SHAGPILE
SHAGREEN
SHAGREENS
SHAGROON
SHAGROONS
SHAGS
SHAH
SHAHADA
SHAHADAS
SHAHDOM
SHAHDOMS
SHAHS
SHAHTOOSH

SHAIKH
SHAIKHS
SHAIRD
SHAIRDS
SHAIRN
SHAIRNS
SHAITAN
SHAITANS
SHAKABLE
SHAKE
SHAKEABLE
SHAKED
SHAKEDOWN
SHAKEN
SHAKEOUT
SHAKEOUTS
SHAKER
SHAKERS
SHAKES
SHAKEUP
SHAKEUPS
SHAKIER
SHAKIEST
SHAKILY
SHAKINESS
SHAKING
SHAKINGS
SHAKO
SHAKOES
SHAKOS
SHAKT
SHAKUDO
SHAKUDOS
SHAKY
SHALE
SHALED
SHALELIKE
SHALES
SHALEY
SHALIER
SHALIEST
SHALING
SHALL
SHALLI
SHALLIS
SHALLON
SHALLONS
SHALLOON
SHALLOONS
SHALLOP
SHALLOPS
SHALLOT
SHALLOTS
SHALLOW
SHALLOWED
SHALLOWER
SHALLOWLY
SHALLOWS

SHALM
SHALMS
SHALOM
SHALOMS
SHALOT
SHALOTS
SHALT
SHALWAR
SHALWARS
SHALY
SHAM
SHAMA
SHAMABLE
SHAMABLY
SHAMAN
SHAMANIC
SHAMANISM
SHAMANIST
SHAMANS
SHAMAS
SHAMATEUR
SHAMBA
SHAMBAS
SHAMBLE
SHAMBLED
SHAMBLES
SHAMBLIER
SHAMBLING
SHAMBLY
SHAMBOLIC
SHAME
SHAMEABLE
SHAMEABLY
SHAMED
SHAMEFAST
SHAMEFUL
SHAMELESS
SHAMER
SHAMERS
SHAMES
SHAMIANA
SHAMIANAH
SHAMIANAS
SHAMINA
SHAMINAS
SHAMING
SHAMISEN
SHAMISENS
SHAMMAS
SHAMMASH
SHAMMASIM
SHAMMED
SHAMMER
SHAMMERS
SHAMMES
SHAMMIED
SHAMMIES
SHAMMING

SHAMMOS
SHAMMOSIM
SHAMMY
SHAMMYING
SHAMOIS
SHAMOS
SHAMOSIM
SHAMOY
SHAMOYED
SHAMOYING
SHAMOYS
SHAMPOO
SHAMPOOED
SHAMPOOER
SHAMPOOS
SHAMROCK
SHAMROCKS
SHAMS
SHAMUS
SHAMUSES
SHAN
SHANACHIE
SHAND
SHANDIES
SHANDRIES
SHANDRY
SHANDS
SHANDY
SHANGHAI
SHANGHAIS
SHANK
SHANKBONE
SHANKED
SHANKING
SHANKS
SHANNIES
SHANNY
SHANS
SHANTEY
SHANTEYS
SHANTI
SHANTIES
SHANTIH
SHANTIHS
SHANTIS
SHANTUNG
SHANTUNGS
SHANTY
SHANTYMAN
SHANTYMEN
SHAPABLE
SHAPE
SHAPEABLE
SHAPED
SHAPELESS
SHAPELIER
SHAPELY
SHAPEN

SHAPER
SHAPERS
SHAPES
SHAPEUP
SHAPEUPS
SHAPEWEAR
SHAPING
SHAPINGS
SHAPS
SHARABLE
SHARD
SHARDED
SHARDS
SHARE
SHAREABLE
SHARECROP
SHARED
SHAREMAN
SHAREMEN
SHARER
SHARERS
SHARES
SHARESMAN
SHARESMEN
SHAREWARE
SHARIA
SHARIAH
SHARIAHS
SHARIAS
SHARIAT
SHARIATS
SHARIF
SHARIFIAN
SHARIFS
SHARING
SHARINGS
SHARK
SHARKED
SHARKER
SHARKERS
SHARKING
SHARKINGS
SHARKLIKE
SHARKS
SHARKSKIN
SHARN
SHARNIER
SHARNIEST
SHARNS
SHARNY
SHARON
SHARP
SHARPED
SHARPEN
SHARPENED
SHARPENER
SHARPENS
SHARPER

SHARPERS	SHAWLED	SHEATHING	SHEEPISH
SHARPEST	SHAWLEY	SHEATHS	SHEEPLE
SHARPIE	SHAWLEYS	SHEATHY	SHEEPLIKE
SHARPIES	SHAWLIE	SHEAVE	SHEEPMAN
SHARPING	SHAWLIES	SHEAVED	SHEEPMEN
SHARPINGS	SHAWLING	SHEAVES	SHEEPO
SHARPISH	SHAWLINGS	SHEAVING	SHEEPOS
SHARPLY	SHAWLLESS	SHEBANG	SHEEPSKIN
SHARPNESS	SHAWLS	SHEBANGS	SHEEPWALK
SHARPS	SHAWM	SHEBEAN	SHEEPY
SHARPY	SHAWMS	SHEBEANS	SHEER
SHASH	SHAWN	SHEBEEN	SHEERED
SHASHED	SHAWS	SHEBEENED	SHEERER
SHASHES	SHAY	SHEBEENER	SHEEREST
SHASHING	SHAYA	SHEBEENS	SHEERING
SHASHLICK	SHAYAS	SHECHITA	SHEERLEG
SHASHLIK	SHAYS	SHECHITAH	SHEERLEGS
SHASHLIKS	SHAZAM	SHECHITAS	SHEERLY
SHASLIK	SHCHI	SHED	SHEERNESS
SHASLIKS	SHCHIS	SHEDABLE	SHEERS
SHASTER	SHE	SHEDDABLE	SHEESH
SHASTERS	SHEA	SHEDDED	SHEET
SHASTRA	SHEADING	SHEDDER	SHEETED
SHASTRAS	SHEADINGS	SHEDDERS	SHEETER
SHAT	SHEAF	SHEDDING	SHEETERS
SHATTER	SHEAFED	SHEDDINGS	SHEETFED
SHATTERED	SHEAFIER	SHEDFUL	SHEETIER
SHATTERER	SHEAFIEST	SHEDFULS	SHEETIEST
SHATTERS	SHEAFING	SHEDLIKE	SHEETING
SHATTERY	SHEAFLIKE	SHEDLOAD	SHEETINGS
SHAUCHLE	SHEAFS	SHEDLOADS	SHEETLESS
SHAUCHLED	SHEAFY	SHEDS	SHEETLIKE
SHAUCHLES	SHEAL	SHEEL	SHEETROCK
SHAUCHLY	SHEALED	SHEELED	SHEETS
SHAUGH	SHEALING	SHEELING	SHEETY
SHAUGHS	SHEALINGS	SHEELS	SHEEVE
SHAUL	SHEALS	SHEEN	SHEEVES
SHAULED	SHEAR	SHEENED	SHEGETZ
SHAULING	SHEARED	SHEENEY	SHEHITA
SHAULS	SHEARER	SHEENEYS	SHEHITAH
SHAVABLE	SHEARERS	SHEENFUL	SHEHITAHS
SHAVE	SHEARING	SHEENIE	SHEHITAS
SHAVEABLE	SHEARINGS	SHEENIER	SHEIK
SHAVED	SHEARLEG	SHEENIES	SHEIKDOM
SHAVELING	SHEARLEGS	SHEENIEST	SHEIKDOMS
SHAVEN	SHEARLING	SHEENING	SHEIKH
SHAVER	SHEARMAN	SHEENS	SHEIKHA
SHAVERS	SHEARMEN	SHEENY	SHEIKHAS
SHAVES	SHEARS	SHEEP	SHEIKHDOM
SHAVETAIL	SHEAS	SHEEPCOT	SHEIKHS
SHAVIE	SHEATFISH	SHEEPCOTE	SHEIKS
SHAVIES	SHEATH	SHEEPCOTS	SHEILA
SHAVING	SHEATHE	SHEEPDOG	SHEILAS
SHAVINGS	SHEATHED	SHEEPDOGS	SHEILING
SHAW	SHEATHER	SHEEPFOLD	SHEILINGS
SHAWED	SHEATHERS	SHEEPHEAD	SHEITAN
SHAWING	SHEATHES	SHEEPIER	SHEITANS
SHAWL	SHEATHIER	SHEEPIEST	SHEKALIM

SHEKEL
SHEKELIM
SHEKELS
SHELDDUCK
SHELDRAKE
SHELDUCK
SHELDUCKS
SHELF
SHELFED
SHELFFUL
SHELFFULS
SHELFIER
SHELFIEST
SHELFING
SHELFLIKE
SHELFROOM
SHELFS
SHELFY
SHELL
SHELLAC
SHELLACK
SHELLACKS
SHELLACS
SHELLBACK
SHELLBARK
SHELLDUCK
SHELLED
SHELLER
SHELLERS
SHELLFIRE
SHELLFISH
SHELLFUL
SHELLFULS
SHELLIER
SHELLIEST
SHELLING
SHELLINGS
SHELLS
SHELLWORK
SHELLY
SHELTA
SHELTAS
SHELTER
SHELTERED
SHELTERER
SHELTERS
SHELTERY
SHELTIE
SHELTIES
SHELTY
SHELVE
SHELVED
SHELVER
SHELVERS
SHELVES
SHELVIER
SHELVIEST
SHELVING

SHELVINGS
SHELVY
SHEMOZZLE
SHEND
SHENDING
SHENDS
SHENT
SHEOL
SHEOLS
SHEPHERD
SHEPHERDS
SHEQALIM
SHEQEL
SHEQELS
SHERANG
SHERANGS
SHERBERT
SHERBERTS
SHERBET
SHERBETS
SHERD
SHERDS
SHERE
SHEREEF
SHEREEFS
SHERIA
SHERIAS
SHERIAT
SHERIATS
SHERIF
SHERIFF
SHERIFFS
SHERIFIAN
SHERIFS
SHERLOCK
SHERLOCKS
SHEROOT
SHEROOTS
SHERPA
SHERPAS
SHERRIES
SHERRIS
SHERRISES
SHERRY
SHERWANI
SHERWANIS
SHES
SHET
SHETLAND
SHETLANDS
SHETS
SHETTING
SHEUCH
SHEUCHED
SHEUCHING
SHEUCHS
SHEUGH
SHEUGHED

SHEUGHING
SHEUGHS
SHEVA
SHEVAS
SHEW
SHEWBREAD
SHEWED
SHEWEL
SHEWELS
SHEWER
SHEWERS
SHEWING
SHEWN
SHEWS
SHH
SHIAI
SHIAIS
SHIATSU
SHIATSUS
SHIATZU
SHIATZUS
SHIBAH
SHIBAHS
SHIBUICHI
SHICKER
SHICKERED
SHICKERS
SHICKSA
SHICKSAS
SHIDDER
SHIDDERS
SHIDDUCH
SHIED
SHIEL
SHIELD
SHIELDED
SHIELDER
SHIELDERS
SHIELDING
SHIELDS
SHIELED
SHIELING
SHIELINGS
SHIELS
SHIER
SHIERS
SHIES
SHIEST
SHIFT
SHIFTABLE
SHIFTED
SHIFTER
SHIFTERS
SHIFTIER
SHIFTIEST
SHIFTILY
SHIFTING
SHIFTINGS

SHIFTLESS
SHIFTS
SHIFTWORK
SHIFTY
SHIGELLA
SHIGELLAE
SHIGELLAS
SHIITAKE
SHIITAKES
SHIKAR
SHIKAREE
SHIKAREES
SHIKARI
SHIKARIS
SHIKARRED
SHIKARS
SHIKKER
SHIKKERS
SHIKSA
SHIKSAS
SHIKSE
SHIKSEH
SHIKSEHS
SHIKSES
SHILINGI
SHILL
SHILLABER
SHILLALA
SHILLALAH
SHILLALAS
SHILLED
SHILLELAH
SHILLING
SHILLINGS
SHILLS
SHILPIT
SHILY
SHIM
SHIMAAL
SHIMAALS
SHIMMED
SHIMMER
SHIMMERED
SHIMMERS
SHIMMERY
SHIMMEY
SHIMMEYS
SHIMMIED
SHIMMIES
SHIMMING
SHIMMY
SHIMMYING
SHIMOZZLE
SHIMS
SHIN
SHINBONE
SHINBONES
SHINDIES

SHINDIG	SHIPLAPS	SHIRRINGS	SHIVAREES
SHINDIGS	SHIPLESS	SHIRRS	SHIVAS
SHINDY	SHIPLOAD	SHIRS	SHIVE
SHINDYS	SHIPLOADS	SHIRT	SHIVER
SHINE	SHIPMAN	SHIRTBAND	SHIVERED
SHINED	SHIPMATE	SHIRTED	SHIVERER
SHINELESS	SHIPMATES	SHIRTIER	SHIVERERS
SHINER	SHIPMEN	SHIRTIEST	SHIVERIER
SHINERS	SHIPMENT	SHIRTILY	SHIVERING
SHINES	SHIPMENTS	SHIRTING	SHIVERS
SHINESS	SHIPOWNER	SHIRTINGS	SHIVERY
SHINESSES	SHIPPABLE	SHIRTLESS	SHIVES
SHINGLE	SHIPPED	SHIRTS	SHIVITI
SHINGLED	SHIPPEN	SHIRTTAIL	SHIVITIS
SHINGLER	SHIPPENS	SHIRTY	SHIVOO
SHINGLERS	SHIPPER	SHISH	SHIVOOS
SHINGLES	SHIPPERS	SHISHA	SHIVS
SHINGLIER	SHIPPIE	SHISHAS	SHIVVED
SHINGLING	SHIPPIES	SHISO	SHIVVING
SHINGLY	SHIPPING	SHISOS	SHKOTZIM
SHINGUARD	SHIPPINGS	SHIST	SHLEMIEHL
SHINIER	SHIPPO	SHISTS	SHLEMIEL
SHINIES	SHIPPON	SHIT	SHLEMIELS
SHINIEST	SHIPPONS	SHITAKE	SHLEP
SHINILY	SHIPPOS	SHITAKES	SHLEPP
SHININESS	SHIPPOUND	SHITE	SHLEPPED
SHINING	SHIPS	SHITED	SHLEPPER
SHININGLY	SHIPSHAPE	SHITES	SHLEPPERS
SHINJU	SHIPSIDE	SHITFACED	SHLEPPING
SHINJUS	SHIPSIDES	SHITHEAD	SHLEPPS
SHINKIN	SHIPWAY	SHITHEADS	SHLEPS
SHINKINS	SHIPWAYS	SHITHOLE	SHLIMAZEL
SHINLEAF	SHIPWORM	SHITHOLES	SHLOCK
SHINLEAFS	SHIPWORMS	SHITING	SHLOCKIER
SHINNE	SHIPWRECK	SHITLESS	SHLOCKS
SHINNED	SHIPYARD	SHITLIST	SHLOCKY
SHINNERY	SHIPYARDS	SHITLISTS	SHLOSHIM
SHINNES	SHIR	SHITLOAD	SHLOSHIMS
SHINNEY	SHIRALEE	SHITLOADS	SHLUB
SHINNEYED	SHIRALEES	SHITS	SHLUBS
SHINNEYS	SHIRE	SHITTAH	SHLUMP
SHINNIED	SHIRED	SHITTAHS	SHLUMPED
SHINNIES	SHIREMAN	SHITTED	SHLUMPING
SHINNING	SHIREMEN	SHITTIER	SHLUMPS
SHINNY	SHIRES	SHITTIEST	SHLUMPY
SHINNYING	SHIRING	SHITTILY	SHMALTZ
SHINS	SHIRK	SHITTIM	SHMALTZES
SHINTIED	SHIRKED	SHITTIMS	SHMALTZY
SHINTIES	SHIRKER	SHITTING	SHMATTE
SHINTY	SHIRKERS	SHITTY	SHMATTES
SHINTYING	SHIRKING	SHIUR	SHMEAR
SHINY	SHIRKS	SHIURIM	SHMEARS
SHIP	SHIRR	SHIV	SHMEK
SHIPBOARD	SHIRRA	SHIVA	SHMEKS
SHIPBORNE	SHIRRALEE	SHIVAH	SHMO
SHIPFUL	SHIRRAS	SHIVAHS	SHMOCK
SHIPFULS	SHIRRED	SHIVAREE	SHMOCKS
SHIPLAP	SHIRRING	SHIVAREED	SHMOES

SHMOOSE	SHOEING	SHOOGLING	SHORAN
SHMOOSED	SHOEINGS	SHOOGLY	SHORANS
SHMOOSES	SHOELACE	SHOOING	SHORE
SHMOOSING	SHOELACES	SHOOK	SHOREBIRD
SHMOOZE	SHOELESS	SHOOKS	SHORED
SHMOOZED	SHOEMAKER	SHOOL	SHORELESS
SHMOOZES	SHOEPAC	SHOOLE	SHORELINE
SHMOOZING	SHOEPACK	SHOOLED	SHOREMAN
SHMUCK	SHOEPACKS	SHOOLES	SHOREMEN
SHMUCKS	SHOEPACS	SHOOLING	SHORER
SHNAPPS	SHOER	SHOOLS	SHORERS
SHNAPS	SHOERS	SHOON	SHORES
SHNOOK	SHOES	SHOORA	SHORESIDE
SHNOOKS	SHOESHINE	SHOORAS	SHORESMAN
SHNORRER	SHOETREE	SHOOS	SHORESMEN
SHNORRERS	SHOETREES	SHOOT	SHOREWARD
SHOAL	SHOFAR	SHOOTABLE	SHOREWEED
SHOALED	SHOFARS	SHOOTDOWN	SHORING
SHOALER	SHOFROTH	SHOOTER	SHORINGS
SHOALEST	SHOG	SHOOTERS	SHORL
SHOALIER	SHOGGED	SHOOTING	SHORLS
SHOALIEST	SHOGGING	SHOOTINGS	SHORN
SHOALING	SHOGGLE	SHOOTIST	SHORT
SHOALINGS	SHOGGLED	SHOOTISTS	SHORTAGE
SHOALNESS	SHOGGLES	SHOOTOUT	SHORTAGES
SHOALS	SHOGGLIER	SHOOTOUTS	SHORTARM
SHOALWISE	SHOGGLING	SHOOTS	SHORTCAKE
SHOALY	SHOGGLY	SHOP	SHORTCUT
SHOAT	SHOGI	SHOPBOARD	SHORTCUTS
SHOATS	SHOGIS	SHOPBOY	SHORTED
SHOCHET	SHOGS	SHOPBOYS	SHORTEN
SHOCHETIM	SHOGUN	SHOPE	SHORTENED
SHOCHETS	SHOGUNAL	SHOPFRONT	SHORTENER
SHOCK	SHOGUNATE	SHOPFUL	SHORTENS
SHOCKABLE	SHOGUNS	SHOPFULS	SHORTER
SHOCKED	SHOJI	SHOPGIRL	SHORTEST
SHOCKER	SHOJIS	SHOPGIRLS	SHORTFALL
SHOCKERS	SHOLA	SHOPHAR	SHORTGOWN
SHOCKING	SHOLAS	SHOPHARS	SHORTHAIR
SHOCKS	SHOLOM	SHOPHROTH	SHORTHAND
SHOD	SHOLOMS	SHOPLIFT	SHORTHEAD
SHODDEN	SHONE	SHOPLIFTS	SHORTHOLD
SHODDIER	SHONEEN	SHOPMAN	SHORTHORN
SHODDIES	SHONEENS	SHOPMEN	SHORTIA
SHODDIEST	SHONKIER	SHOPPE	SHORTIAS
SHODDILY	SHONKIEST	SHOPPED	SHORTIE
SHODDY	SHONKY	SHOPPER	SHORTIES
SHODER	SHOO	SHOPPERS	SHORTING
SHODERS	SHOOED	SHOPPES	SHORTISH
SHOE	SHOOFLIES	SHOPPIER	SHORTLIST
SHOEBILL	SHOOFLY	SHOPPIEST	SHORTLY
SHOEBILLS	SHOOGIE	SHOPPING	SHORTNESS
SHOEBLACK	SHOOGIED	SHOPPINGS	SHORTS
SHOEBOX	SHOOGIES	SHOPPY	SHORTSTOP
SHOEBOXES	SHOOGLE	SHOPS	SHORTWAVE
SHOED	SHOOGLED	SHOPTALK	SHORTY
SHOEHORN	SHOOGLES	SHOPTALKS	SHOT
SHOEHORNS	SHOOGLIER	SHOPWORN	SHOTE

SHOTES
SHOTFIRER
SHOTGUN
SHOTGUNS
SHOTHOLE
SHOTHOLES
SHOTMAKER
SHOTPROOF
SHOTPUT
SHOTPUTS
SHOTS
SHOTT
SHOTTE
SHOTTED
SHOTTEN
SHOTTES
SHOTTING
SHOTTLE
SHOTTLES
SHOTTS
SHOUGH
SHOUGHS
SHOULD
SHOULDER
SHOULDERS
SHOULDEST
SHOULDST
SHOUSE
SHOUSES
SHOUT
SHOUTED
SHOUTER
SHOUTERS
SHOUTHER
SHOUTHERS
SHOUTIER
SHOUTIEST
SHOUTING
SHOUTINGS
SHOUTLINE
SHOUTS
SHOUTY
SHOVE
SHOVED
SHOVEL
SHOVELED
SHOVELER
SHOVELERS
SHOVELFUL
SHOVELING
SHOVELLED
SHOVELLER
SHOVELS
SHOVER
SHOVERS
SHOVES
SHOVING
SHOVINGS

SHOW
SHOWABLE
SHOWBIZ
SHOWBIZZY
SHOWBOAT
SHOWBOATS
SHOWBOX
SHOWBOXES
SHOWBREAD
SHOWCASE
SHOWCASED
SHOWCASES
SHOWD
SHOWDED
SHOWDING
SHOWDOWN
SHOWDOWNS
SHOWDS
SHOWED
SHOWER
SHOWERED
SHOWERER
SHOWERERS
SHOWERFUL
SHOWERIER
SHOWERING
SHOWERS
SHOWERY
SHOWGHE
SHOWGHES
SHOWGIRL
SHOWGIRLS
SHOWIER
SHOWIEST
SHOWILY
SHOWINESS
SHOWING
SHOWINGS
SHOWMAN
SHOWMANLY
SHOWMEN
SHOWN
SHOWOFF
SHOWOFFS
SHOWPIECE
SHOWPLACE
SHOWRING
SHOWRINGS
SHOWROOM
SHOWROOMS
SHOWS
SHOWTIME
SHOWTIMES
SHOWY
SHOWYARD
SHOWYARDS
SHOYU
SHOYUS

SHRADDHA
SHRADDHAS
SHRANK
SHRAPNEL
SHRAPNELS
SHRED
SHREDDED
SHREDDER
SHREDDERS
SHREDDIER
SHREDDING
SHREDDY
SHREDLESS
SHREDS
SHREEK
SHREEKED
SHREEKING
SHREEKS
SHREIK
SHREIKED
SHREIKING
SHREIKS
SHREW
SHREWD
SHREWDER
SHREWDEST
SHREWDIE
SHREWDIES
SHREWDLY
SHREWED
SHREWING
SHREWISH
SHREWLIKE
SHREWMICE
SHREWS
SHRI
SHRIECH
SHRIECHED
SHRIECHES
SHRIEK
SHRIEKED
SHRIEKER
SHRIEKERS
SHRIEKIER
SHRIEKING
SHRIEKS
SHRIEKY
SHRIEVAL
SHRIEVE
SHRIEVED
SHRIEVES
SHRIEVING
SHRIFT
SHRIFTS
SHRIGHT
SHRIGHTS
SHRIKE
SHRIKED

SHRIKES
SHRIKING
SHRILL
SHRILLED
SHRILLER
SHRILLEST
SHRILLIER
SHRILLING
SHRILLS
SHRILLY
SHRIMP
SHRIMPED
SHRIMPER
SHRIMPERS
SHRIMPIER
SHRIMPING
SHRIMPS
SHRIMPY
SHRINAL
SHRINE
SHRINED
SHRINES
SHRINING
SHRINK
SHRINKAGE
SHRINKER
SHRINKERS
SHRINKING
SHRINKS
SHRIS
SHRITCH
SHRITCHED
SHRITCHES
SHRIVE
SHRIVED
SHRIVEL
SHRIVELED
SHRIVELS
SHRIVEN
SHRIVER
SHRIVERS
SHRIVES
SHRIVING
SHRIVINGS
SHROFF
SHROFFAGE
SHROFFED
SHROFFING
SHROFFS
SHROOM
SHROOMED
SHROOMER
SHROOMERS
SHROOMING
SHROOMS
SHROUD
SHROUDED
SHROUDIER

SHROUDING
SHROUDS
SHROUDY
SHROVE
SHROVED
SHROVES
SHROVING
SHROW
SHROWD
SHROWED
SHROWING
SHROWS
SHRUB
SHRUBBED
SHRUBBERY
SHRUBBIER
SHRUBBING
SHRUBBY
SHRUBLAND
SHRUBLESS
SHRUBLIKE
SHRUBS
SHRUG
SHRUGGED
SHRUGGING
SHRUGS
SHRUNK
SHRUNKEN
SHTCHI
SHTCHIS
SHTETEL
SHTETELS
SHTETL
SHTETLACH
SHTETLS
SHTICK
SHTICKIER
SHTICKS
SHTICKY
SHTIK
SHTIKS
SHTOOK
SHTOOKS
SHTOOM
SHTUCK
SHTUCKS
SHTUM
SHTUMM
SHTUP
SHTUPPED
SHTUPPING
SHTUPS
SHUBUNKIN
SHUCK
SHUCKED
SHUCKER
SHUCKERS
SHUCKING

SHUCKINGS
SHUCKS
SHUDDER
SHUDDERED
SHUDDERS
SHUDDERY
SHUFFLE
SHUFFLED
SHUFFLER
SHUFFLERS
SHUFFLES
SHUFFLING
SHUFTI
SHUFTIES
SHUFTIS
SHUFTY
SHUGGIES
SHUGGY
SHUL
SHULE
SHULED
SHULES
SHULING
SHULN
SHULS
SHUN
SHUNLESS
SHUNNABLE
SHUNNED
SHUNNER
SHUNNERS
SHUNNING
SHUNPIKE
SHUNPIKED
SHUNPIKER
SHUNPIKES
SHUNS
SHUNT
SHUNTED
SHUNTER
SHUNTERS
SHUNTING
SHUNTINGS
SHUNTS
SHURA
SHURAS
SHUSH
SHUSHED
SHUSHER
SHUSHERS
SHUSHES
SHUSHING
SHUT
SHUTDOWN
SHUTDOWNS
SHUTE
SHUTED
SHUTES

SHUTEYE
SHUTEYES
SHUTING
SHUTOFF
SHUTOFFS
SHUTOUT
SHUTOUTS
SHUTS
SHUTTER
SHUTTERED
SHUTTERS
SHUTTING
SHUTTLE
SHUTTLED
SHUTTLER
SHUTTLERS
SHUTTLES
SHUTTLING
SHVARTZE
SHVARTZES
SHWA
SHWANPAN
SHWANPANS
SHWAS
SHWESHWE
SHWESHWES
SHY
SHYER
SHYERS
SHYEST
SHYING
SHYISH
SHYLOCK
SHYLOCKED
SHYLOCKS
SHYLY
SHYNESS
SHYNESSES
SHYPOO
SHYPOOS
SHYSTER
SHYSTERS
SI
SIAL
SIALIC
SIALID
SIALIDAN
SIALIDANS
SIALIDS
SIALOGRAM
SIALOID
SIALOLITH
SIALON
SIALONS
SIALS
SIAMANG
SIAMANGS
SIAMESE

SIAMESED
SIAMESES
SIAMESING
SIAMEZE
SIAMEZED
SIAMEZES
SIAMEZING
SIB
SIBB
SIBBS
SIBILANCE
SIBILANCY
SIBILANT
SIBILANTS
SIBILATE
SIBILATED
SIBILATES
SIBILATOR
SIBILOUS
SIBLING
SIBLINGS
SIBS
SIBSHIP
SIBSHIPS
SIBYL
SIBYLIC
SIBYLLIC
SIBYLLINE
SIBYLS
SIC
SICCAN
SICCAR
SICCATIVE
SICCED
SICCING
SICCITIES
SICCITY
SICE
SICES
SICH
SICHT
SICHTED
SICHTING
SICHTS
SICILIANA
SICILIANE
SICILIANO
SICK
SICKBAY
SICKBAYS
SICKBED
SICKBEDS
SICKED
SICKEE
SICKEES
SICKEN
SICKENED
SICKENER

SICKENERS
SICKENING
SICKENS
SICKER
SICKERLY
SICKEST
SICKIE
SICKIES
SICKING
SICKISH
SICKISHLY
SICKLE
SICKLED
SICKLEMAN
SICKLEMEN
SICKLEMIA
SICKLEMIC
SICKLES
SICKLIED
SICKLIER
SICKLIES
SICKLIEST
SICKLILY
SICKLING
SICKLY
SICKLYING
SICKNESS
SICKNURSE
SICKO
SICKOS
SICKOUT
SICKOUTS
SICKROOM
SICKROOMS
SICKS
SICLIKE
SICS
SIDA
SIDALCEA
SIDALCEAS
SIDAS
SIDDHA
SIDDHAS
SIDDHI
SIDDHIS
SIDDHUISM
SIDDUR
SIDDURIM
SIDDURS
SIDE
SIDEARM
SIDEARMS
SIDEBAND
SIDEBANDS
SIDEBAR
SIDEBARS
SIDEBOARD
SIDEBONES

SIDEBURNS
SIDECAR
SIDECARS
SIDECHECK
SIDED
SIDEDNESS
SIDEDRESS
SIDEHILL
SIDEHILLS
SIDEKICK
SIDEKICKS
SIDELIGHT
SIDELINE
SIDELINED
SIDELINER
SIDELINES
SIDELING
SIDELOCK
SIDELOCKS
SIDELONG
SIDEMAN
SIDEMEN
SIDENOTE
SIDENOTES
SIDEPATH
SIDEPATHS
SIDEPIECE
SIDER
SIDERAL
SIDERATE
SIDERATED
SIDERATES
SIDEREAL
SIDERITE
SIDERITES
SIDERITIC
SIDEROAD
SIDEROADS
SIDEROSES
SIDEROSIS
SIDEROTIC
SIDERS
SIDES
SIDESHOOT
SIDESHOW
SIDESHOWS
SIDESLIP
SIDESLIPS
SIDESMAN
SIDESMEN
SIDESPIN
SIDESPINS
SIDESTEP
SIDESTEPS
SIDESWIPE
SIDETRACK
SIDEWALK
SIDEWALKS

SIDEWALL
SIDEWALLS
SIDEWARD
SIDEWARDS
SIDEWAY
SIDEWAYS
SIDEWHEEL
SIDEWISE
SIDH
SIDHA
SIDHAS
SIDHE
SIDING
SIDINGS
SIDLE
SIDLED
SIDLER
SIDLERS
SIDLES
SIDLING
SIDLINGLY
SIECLE
SIECLES
SIEGE
SIEGED
SIEGER
SIEGERS
SIEGES
SIEGING
SIELD
SIEMENS
SIEN
SIENITE
SIENITES
SIENNA
SIENNAS
SIENS
SIENT
SIENTS
SIEROZEM
SIEROZEMS
SIERRA
SIERRAN
SIERRAS
SIES
SIESTA
SIESTAS
SIETH
SIETHS
SIEUR
SIEURS
SIEVE
SIEVED
SIEVELIKE
SIEVERT
SIEVERTS
SIEVES
SIEVING

SIF
SIFAKA
SIFAKAS
SIFFLE
SIFFLED
SIFFLES
SIFFLEUR
SIFFLEURS
SIFFLEUSE
SIFFLING
SIFREI
SIFT
SIFTED
SIFTER
SIFTERS
SIFTING
SIFTINGLY
SIFTINGS
SIFTS
SIGANID
SIGANIDS
SIGH
SIGHED
SIGHER
SIGHERS
SIGHFUL
SIGHING
SIGHINGLY
SIGHLESS
SIGHLIKE
SIGHS
SIGHT
SIGHTABLE
SIGHTED
SIGHTER
SIGHTERS
SIGHTING
SIGHTINGS
SIGHTLESS
SIGHTLIER
SIGHTLINE
SIGHTLY
SIGHTS
SIGHTSAW
SIGHTSEE
SIGHTSEEN
SIGHTSEER
SIGHTSEES
SIGHTSMAN
SIGHTSMEN
SIGIL
SIGILLARY
SIGILLATE
SIGILS
SIGISBEI
SIGISBEO
SIGLA
SIGLAS

SIGLOI
SIGLOS
SIGLUM
SIGMA
SIGMAS
SIGMATE
SIGMATED
SIGMATES
SIGMATIC
SIGMATING
SIGMATION
SIGMATISM
SIGMATRON
SIGMOID
SIGMOIDAL
SIGMOIDS
SIGN
SIGNA
SIGNABLE
SIGNAGE
SIGNAGES
SIGNAL
SIGNALED
SIGNALER
SIGNALERS
SIGNALING
SIGNALISE
SIGNALIZE
SIGNALLED
SIGNALLER
SIGNALLY
SIGNALMAN
SIGNALMEN
SIGNALS
SIGNARIES
SIGNARY
SIGNATORY
SIGNATURE
SIGNBOARD
SIGNED
SIGNEE
SIGNEES
SIGNER
SIGNERS
SIGNET
SIGNETED
SIGNETING
SIGNETS
SIGNEUR
SIGNEURIE
SIGNIEUR
SIGNIEURS
SIGNIFICS
SIGNIFIED
SIGNIFIER
SIGNIFIES
SIGNIFY
SIGNING

SIGNINGS
SIGNIOR
SIGNIORI
SIGNIORS
SIGNIORY
SIGNLESS
SIGNOR
SIGNORA
SIGNORAS
SIGNORE
SIGNORES
SIGNORI
SIGNORIA
SIGNORIAL
SIGNORIAS
SIGNORIES
SIGNORINA
SIGNORINE
SIGNORINI
SIGNORINO
SIGNORS
SIGNORY
SIGNPOST
SIGNPOSTS
SIGNS
SIJO
SIJOS
SIK
SIKA
SIKAS
SIKE
SIKER
SIKES
SIKORSKY
SILAGE
SILAGED
SILAGEING
SILAGES
SILAGING
SILANE
SILANES
SILASTIC
SILASTICS
SILD
SILDS
SILE
SILED
SILEN
SILENCE
SILENCED
SILENCER
SILENCERS
SILENCES
SILENCING
SILENE
SILENES
SILENI
SILENS

SILENT
SILENTER
SILENTEST
SILENTLY
SILENTS
SILENUS
SILER
SILERS
SILES
SILESIA
SILESIAS
SILEX
SILEXES
SILICA
SILICAS
SILICATE
SILICATED
SILICATES
SILICEOUS
SILICIC
SILICIDE
SILICIDES
SILICIFY
SILICIOUS
SILICIUM
SILICIUMS
SILICLE
SILICLES
SILICON
SILICONE
SILICONES
SILICONS
SILICOSES
SILICOSIS
SILICOTIC
SILICULA
SILICULAE
SILICULAS
SILICULE
SILICULES
SILING
SILIQUA
SILIQUAE
SILIQUAS
SILIQUE
SILIQUES
SILIQUOSE
SILIQUOUS
SILK
SILKALENE
SILKALINE
SILKED
SILKEN
SILKENED
SILKENING
SILKENS
SILKIE
SILKIER

SILKIES
SILKIEST
SILKILY
SILKINESS
SILKING
SILKLIKE
SILKOLINE
SILKS
SILKTAIL
SILKTAILS
SILKWEED
SILKWEEDS
SILKWORM
SILKWORMS
SILKY
SILL
SILLABUB
SILLABUBS
SILLADAR
SILLADARS
SILLER
SILLERS
SILLIBUB
SILLIBUBS
SILLIER
SILLIES
SILLIEST
SILLILY
SILLINESS
SILLOCK
SILLOCKS
SILLS
SILLY
SILO
SILOED
SILOING
SILOS
SILOXANE
SILOXANES
SILPHIA
SILPHIUM
SILPHIUMS
SILT
SILTATION
SILTED
SILTIER
SILTIEST
SILTING
SILTS
SILTSTONE
SILTY
SILURIAN
SILURID
SILURIDS
SILURIST
SILURISTS
SILUROID
SILUROIDS

SILVA
SILVAE
SILVAN
SILVANS
SILVAS
SILVATIC
SILVER
SILVERED
SILVERER
SILVERERS
SILVEREYE
SILVERIER
SILVERING
SILVERISE
SILVERIZE
SILVERLY
SILVERN
SILVERS
SILVERY
SILVEX
SILVEXES
SILVICAL
SILVICS
SIM
SIMA
SIMAR
SIMAROUBA
SIMARRE
SIMARRES
SIMARS
SIMARUBA
SIMARUBAS
SIMAS
SIMATIC
SIMAZINE
SIMAZINES
SIMBA
SIMBAS
SIMI
SIMIAL
SIMIAN
SIMIANS
SIMILAR
SIMILARLY
SIMILE
SIMILES
SIMILISE
SIMILISED
SIMILISES
SIMILIZE
SIMILIZED
SIMILIZES
SIMILOR
SIMILORS
SIMIOID
SIMIOUS
SIMIS
SIMITAR

SIMITARS
SIMKIN
SIMKINS
SIMLIN
SIMLINS
SIMMER
SIMMERED
SIMMERING
SIMMERS
SIMNEL
SIMNELS
SIMOLEON
SIMOLEONS
SIMONIAC
SIMONIACS
SIMONIES
SIMONIOUS
SIMONISE
SIMONISED
SIMONISES
SIMONIST
SIMONISTS
SIMONIZE
SIMONIZED
SIMONIZES
SIMONY
SIMOOM
SIMOOMS
SIMOON
SIMOONS
SIMORG
SIMORGS
SIMP
SIMPAI
SIMPAIS
SIMPATICO
SIMPER
SIMPERED
SIMPERER
SIMPERERS
SIMPERING
SIMPERS
SIMPKIN
SIMPKINS
SIMPLE
SIMPLED
SIMPLER
SIMPLERS
SIMPLES
SIMPLESSE
SIMPLEST
SIMPLETON
SIMPLEX
SIMPLEXES
SIMPLICES
SIMPLICIA
SIMPLIFY
SIMPLING

SIMPLINGS
SIMPLISM
SIMPLISMS
SIMPLIST
SIMPLISTE
SIMPLISTS
SIMPLY
SIMPS
SIMS
SIMUL
SIMULACRA
SIMULACRE
SIMULANT
SIMULANTS
SIMULAR
SIMULARS
SIMULATE
SIMULATED
SIMULATES
SIMULATOR
SIMULCAST
SIMULIUM
SIMULIUMS
SIMULS
SIMURG
SIMURGH
SIMURGHS
SIMURGS
SIN
SINAPISM
SINAPISMS
SINCE
SINCERE
SINCERELY
SINCERER
SINCEREST
SINCERITY
SINCIPITA
SINCIPUT
SINCIPUTS
SIND
SINDED
SINDING
SINDINGS
SINDON
SINDONS
SINDS
SINE
SINECURE
SINECURES
SINED
SINES
SINEW
SINEWED
SINEWIER
SINEWIEST
SINEWING
SINEWLESS

SINEWS
SINEWY
SINFONIA
SINFONIAS
SINFONIE
SINFUL
SINFULLY
SING
SINGABLE
SINGALONG
SINGE
SINGED
SINGEING
SINGER
SINGERS
SINGES
SINGING
SINGINGLY
SINGINGS
SINGLE
SINGLED
SINGLEDOM
SINGLES
SINGLET
SINGLETON
SINGLETS
SINGLING
SINGLINGS
SINGLY
SINGS
SINGSONG
SINGSONGS
SINGSONGY
SINGSPIEL
SINGULAR
SINGULARS
SINGULARY
SINGULT
SINGULTS
SINGULTUS
SINH
SINHS
SINICAL
SINICISE
SINICISED
SINICISES
SINICIZE
SINICIZED
SINICIZES
SINING
SINISTER
SINISTRAL
SINK
SINKABLE
SINKAGE
SINKAGES
SINKER
SINKERS

SINKHOLE

SINKHOLE
SINKHOLES
SINKIER
SINKIEST
SINKING
SINKINGS
SINKS
SINKY
SINLESS
SINLESSLY
SINNED
SINNER
SINNERED
SINNERING
SINNERS
SINNET
SINNETS
SINNING
SINNINGIA
SINOLOGUE
SINOLOGY
SINOPIA
SINOPIAS
SINOPIE
SINOPIS
SINOPISES
SINOPITE
SINOPITES
SINS
SINSYNE
SINTER
SINTERED
SINTERING
SINTERS
SINTERY
SINUATE
SINUATED
SINUATELY
SINUATES
SINUATING
SINUATION
SINUITIS
SINUOSE
SINUOSITY
SINUOUS
SINUOUSLY
SINUS
SINUSES
SINUSITIS
SINUSLIKE
SINUSOID
SINUSOIDS
SIP
SIPE
SIPED
SIPES
SIPHON
SIPHONAGE

SIPHONAL
SIPHONATE
SIPHONED
SIPHONET
SIPHONETS
SIPHONIC
SIPHONING
SIPHONS
SIPHUNCLE
SIPING
SIPPED
SIPPER
SIPPERS
SIPPET
SIPPETS
SIPPING
SIPPLE
SIPPLED
SIPPLES
SIPPLING
SIPPY
SIPS
SIR
SIRCAR
SIRCARS
SIRDAR
SIRDARS
SIRE
SIRED
SIREE
SIREES
SIREN
SIRENIAN
SIRENIANS
SIRENIC
SIRENISE
SIRENISED
SIRENISES
SIRENIZE
SIRENIZED
SIRENIZES
SIRENS
SIRES
SIRGANG
SIRGANGS
SIRI
SIRIASES
SIRIASIS
SIRIH
SIRIHS
SIRING
SIRIS
SIRKAR
SIRKARS
SIRLOIN
SIRLOINS
SIRNAME
SIRNAMED

SIRNAMES
SIRNAMING
SIROC
SIROCCO
SIROCCOS
SIROCS
SIRONISE
SIRONISED
SIRONISES
SIRONIZE
SIRONIZED
SIRONIZES
SIROSET
SIRRA
SIRRAH
SIRRAHS
SIRRAS
SIRRED
SIRREE
SIRREES
SIRRING
SIRS
SIRUP
SIRUPED
SIRUPIER
SIRUPIEST
SIRUPING
SIRUPS
SIRUPY
SIRVENTE
SIRVENTES
SIS
SISAL
SISALS
SISERARY
SISES
SISKIN
SISKINS
SISS
SISSES
SISSIER
SISSIES
SISSIEST
SISSIFIED
SISSINESS
SISSOO
SISSOOS
SISSY
SISSYISH
SISSYNESS
SIST
SISTED
SISTER
SISTERED
SISTERING
SISTERLY
SISTERS
SISTING

SISTRA
SISTROID
SISTRUM
SISTRUMS
SISTS
SIT
SITAR
SITARIST
SITARISTS
SITARS
SITATUNGA
SITCOM
SITCOMS
SITE
SITED
SITELLA
SITELLAS
SITES
SITFAST
SITFASTS
SITH
SITHE
SITHED
SITHEE
SITHEN
SITHENCE
SITHENS
SITHES
SITHING
SITING
SITIOLOGY
SITKA
SITKAMER
SITKAMERS
SITOLOGY
SITREP
SITREPS
SITS
SITTAR
SITTARS
SITTELLA
SITTELLAS
SITTEN
SITTER
SITTERS
SITTINE
SITTING
SITTINGS
SITUATE
SITUATED
SITUATES
SITUATING
SITUATION
SITULA
SITULAE
SITUP
SITUPS
SITUS

SITUSES	SIZER	SKATED	SKEIGH
SITUTUNGA	SIZERS	SKATEPARK	SKEIGHER
SITZ	SIZES	SKATER	SKEIGHEST
SITZKRIEG	SIZIER	SKATERS	SKEIN
SITZMARK	SIZIEST	SKATES	SKEINED
SITZMARKS	SIZINESS	SKATING	SKEINING
SIVER	SIZING	SKATINGS	SKEINS
SIVERS	SIZINGS	SKATOL	SKELDER
SIWASH	SIZISM	SKATOLE	SKELDERED
SIWASHED	SIZISMS	SKATOLES	SKELDERS
SIWASHES	SIZIST	SKATOLS	SKELETAL
SIWASHING	SIZISTS	SKATS	SKELETON
SIX	SIZY	SKATT	SKELETONS
SIXAIN	SIZZLE	SKATTS	SKELF
SIXAINE	SIZZLED	SKAW	SKELFS
SIXAINES	SIZZLER	SKAWS	SKELL
SIXAINS	SIZZLERS	SKEAN	SKELLIE
SIXER	SIZZLES	SKEANE	SKELLIED
SIXERS	SIZZLING	SKEANES	SKELLIER
SIXES	SIZZLINGS	SKEANS	SKELLIES
SIXFOLD	SJAMBOK	SKEAR	SKELLIEST
SIXMO	SJAMBOKED	SKEARED	SKELLOCH
SIXMOS	SJAMBOKS	SKEARIER	SKELLOCHS
SIXPENCE	SJOE	SKEARIEST	SKELLS
SIXPENCES	SKA	SKEARING	SKELLUM
SIXPENNY	SKAG	SKEARS	SKELLUMS
SIXSCORE	SKAGS	SKEARY	SKELLY
SIXSCORES	SKAIL	SKEDADDLE	SKELLYING
SIXTE	SKAILED	SKEE	SKELM
SIXTEEN	SKAILING	SKEECHAN	SKELMS
SIXTEENER	SKAILS	SKEECHANS	SKELP
SIXTEENMO	SKAITH	SKEED	SKELPED
SIXTEENS	SKAITHED	SKEEF	SKELPING
SIXTEENTH	SKAITHING	SKEEING	SKELPINGS
SIXTES	SKAITHS	SKEELIER	SKELPIT
SIXTH	SKALD	SKEELIEST	SKELPS
SIXTHLY	SKALDIC	SKEELY	SKELTER
SIXTHS	SKALDS	SKEEN	SKELTERED
SIXTIES	SKALDSHIP	SKEENS	SKELTERS
SIXTIETH	SKANGER	SKEER	SKELUM
SIXTIETHS	SKANGERS	SKEERED	SKELUMS
SIXTY	SKANK	SKEERIER	SKEN
SIXTYISH	SKANKED	SKEERIEST	SKENE
SIZABLE	SKANKER	SKEERING	SKENES
SIZABLY	SKANKERS	SKEERS	SKENNED
SIZAR	SKANKIER	SKEERY	SKENNING
SIZARS	SKANKIEST	SKEES	SKENS
SIZARSHIP	SKANKING	SKEESICKS	SKEO
SIZE	SKANKINGS	SKEET	SKEOS
SIZEABLE	SKANKS	SKEETER	SKEP
SIZEABLY	SKANKY	SKEETERS	SKEPFUL
SIZED	SKART	SKEETS	SKEPFULS
SIZEISM	SKARTH	SKEG	SKEPPED
SIZEISMS	SKARTHS	SKEGG	SKEPPING
SIZEIST	SKARTS	SKEGGER	SKEPS
SIZEISTS	SKAS	SKEGGERS	SKEPSIS
SIZEL	SKAT	SKEGGS	SKEPSISES
SIZELS	SKATE	SKEGS	SKEPTIC

SKEPTICAL
SKEPTICS
SKER
SKERRED
SKERRICK
SKERRICKS
SKERRIES
SKERRING
SKERRY
SKERS
SKET
SKETCH
SKETCHED
SKETCHER
SKETCHERS
SKETCHES
SKETCHIER
SKETCHILY
SKETCHING
SKETCHPAD
SKETCHY
SKETS
SKETTED
SKETTING
SKEW
SKEWBACK
SKEWBACKS
SKEWBALD
SKEWBALDS
SKEWED
SKEWER
SKEWERED
SKEWERING
SKEWERS
SKEWEST
SKEWING
SKEWNESS
SKEWS
SKEWWHIFF
SKI
SKIABLE
SKIAGRAM
SKIAGRAMS
SKIAGRAPH
SKIAMACHY
SKIASCOPE
SKIASCOPY
SKIATRON
SKIATRONS
SKIBOB
SKIBOBBED
SKIBOBBER
SKIBOBS
SKID
SKIDDED
SKIDDER
SKIDDERS
SKIDDIER

SKIDDIEST
SKIDDING
SKIDDOO
SKIDDOOED
SKIDDOOS
SKIDDY
SKIDLID
SKIDLIDS
SKIDOO
SKIDOOED
SKIDOOING
SKIDOOS
SKIDPAN
SKIDPANS
SKIDPROOF
SKIDS
SKIDWAY
SKIDWAYS
SKIED
SKIER
SKIERS
SKIES
SKIEY
SKIEYER
SKIEYEST
SKIFF
SKIFFED
SKIFFING
SKIFFLE
SKIFFLED
SKIFFLES
SKIFFLESS
SKIFFLING
SKIFFS
SKIING
SKIINGS
SKIJORER
SKIJORERS
SKIJORING
SKILFUL
SKILFULLY
SKILL
SKILLED
SKILLESS
SKILLET
SKILLETS
SKILLFUL
SKILLIER
SKILLIES
SKILLIEST
SKILLING
SKILLINGS
SKILLION
SKILLIONS
SKILLS
SKILLY
SKIM
SKIMBOARD

SKIMMED
SKIMMER
SKIMMERS
SKIMMIA
SKIMMIAS
SKIMMING
SKIMMINGS
SKIMO
SKIMOBILE
SKIMOS
SKIMP
SKIMPED
SKIMPIER
SKIMPIEST
SKIMPILY
SKIMPING
SKIMPS
SKIMPY
SKIMS
SKIN
SKINCARE
SKINCARES
SKINFLICK
SKINFLINT
SKINFOOD
SKINFOODS
SKINFUL
SKINFULS
SKINHEAD
SKINHEADS
SKINK
SKINKED
SKINKER
SKINKERS
SKINKING
SKINKS
SKINLESS
SKINLIKE
SKINNED
SKINNER
SKINNERS
SKINNIER
SKINNIEST
SKINNING
SKINNY
SKINS
SKINT
SKINTER
SKINTEST
SKINTIGHT
SKIO
SKIORING
SKIORINGS
SKIOS
SKIP
SKIPJACK
SKIPJACKS
SKIPLANE

SKIPLANES
SKIPPABLE
SKIPPED
SKIPPER
SKIPPERED
SKIPPERS
SKIPPET
SKIPPETS
SKIPPIER
SKIPPIEST
SKIPPING
SKIPPINGS
SKIPPY
SKIPS
SKIRL
SKIRLED
SKIRLING
SKIRLINGS
SKIRLS
SKIRMISH
SKIRR
SKIRRED
SKIRRET
SKIRRETS
SKIRRING
SKIRRS
SKIRT
SKIRTED
SKIRTER
SKIRTERS
SKIRTING
SKIRTINGS
SKIRTLESS
SKIRTLIKE
SKIRTS
SKIS
SKIT
SKITCH
SKITCHED
SKITCHES
SKITCHING
SKITE
SKITED
SKITES
SKITING
SKITS
SKITTER
SKITTERED
SKITTERS
SKITTERY
SKITTISH
SKITTLE
SKITTLED
SKITTLES
SKITTLING
SKIVE
SKIVED
SKIVER

SKIVERED
SKIVERING
SKIVERS
SKIVES
SKIVIE
SKIVIER
SKIVIEST
SKIVING
SKIVINGS
SKIVVIED
SKIVVIES
SKIVVY
SKIVVYING
SKIVY
SKIWEAR
SKLATE
SKLATED
SKLATES
SKLATING
SKLENT
SKLENTED
SKLENTING
SKLENTS
SKLIFF
SKLIFFS
SKLIM
SKLIMMED
SKLIMMING
SKLIMS
SKOAL
SKOALED
SKOALING
SKOALS
SKOFF
SKOFFED
SKOFFING
SKOFFS
SKOKIAAN
SKOKIAANS
SKOL
SKOLIA
SKOLION
SKOLLED
SKOLLIE
SKOLLIES
SKOLLING
SKOLLY
SKOLS
SKOOKUM
SKOOL
SKOOLS
SKOOSH
SKOOSHED
SKOOSHES
SKOOSHING
SKORT
SKORTS
SKOSH

SKOSHES
SKRAN
SKRANS
SKREEGH
SKREEGHED
SKREEGHS
SKREEN
SKREENS
SKREIGH
SKREIGHED
SKREIGHS
SKRIECH
SKRIECHED
SKRIECHS
SKRIED
SKRIEGH
SKRIEGHED
SKRIEGHS
SKRIES
SKRIK
SKRIKE
SKRIKED
SKRIKES
SKRIKING
SKRIKS
SKRIMMAGE
SKRIMP
SKRIMPED
SKRIMPING
SKRIMPS
SKRUMP
SKRUMPED
SKRUMPING
SKRUMPS
SKRY
SKRYER
SKRYERS
SKRYING
SKUA
SKUAS
SKUDLER
SKUDLERS
SKUG
SKUGGED
SKUGGING
SKUGS
SKULK
SKULKED
SKULKER
SKULKERS
SKULKING
SKULKINGS
SKULKS
SKULL
SKULLCAP
SKULLCAPS
SKULLED
SKULLING

SKULLS
SKULPIN
SKULPINS
SKUMMER
SKUMMERED
SKUMMERS
SKUNK
SKUNKBIRD
SKUNKED
SKUNKIER
SKUNKIEST
SKUNKING
SKUNKS
SKUNKWEED
SKUNKY
SKURRIED
SKURRIES
SKURRY
SKURRYING
SKUTTLE
SKUTTLED
SKUTTLES
SKUTTLING
SKY
SKYBOARD
SKYBOARDS
SKYBORN
SKYBORNE
SKYBOX
SKYBOXES
SKYBRIDGE
SKYCAP
SKYCAPS
SKYCLAD
SKYDIVE
SKYDIVED
SKYDIVER
SKYDIVERS
SKYDIVES
SKYDIVING
SKYDOVE
SKYED
SKYER
SKYERS
SKYEY
SKYF
SKYFED
SKYFING
SKYFS
SKYHOME
SKYHOMES
SKYHOOK
SKYHOOKS
SKYIER
SKYIEST
SKYING
SKYISH
SKYJACK

SKYJACKED
SKYJACKER
SKYJACKS
SKYLAB
SKYLABS
SKYLARK
SKYLARKED
SKYLARKER
SKYLARKS
SKYLIGHT
SKYLIGHTS
SKYLIKE
SKYLINE
SKYLINES
SKYLIT
SKYMAN
SKYMEN
SKYPHOI
SKYPHOS
SKYR
SKYRE
SKYRED
SKYRES
SKYRING
SKYROCKET
SKYRS
SKYSAIL
SKYSAILS
SKYSCAPE
SKYSCAPES
SKYSURF
SKYSURFED
SKYSURFER
SKYSURFS
SKYTE
SKYTED
SKYTES
SKYTING
SKYWALK
SKYWALKS
SKYWARD
SKYWARDS
SKYWAY
SKYWAYS
SKYWRITE
SKYWRITER
SKYWRITES
SKYWROTE
SLAB
SLABBED
SLABBER
SLABBERED
SLABBERER
SLABBERS
SLABBERY
SLABBIER
SLABBIEST
SLABBING

SLABBY	SLAMDANCE	SLASH	SLAY
SLABLIKE	SLAMMAKIN	SLASHED	SLAYABLE
SLABS	SLAMMED	SLASHER	SLAYED
SLABSTONE	SLAMMER	SLASHERS	SLAYER
SLACK	SLAMMERS	SLASHES	SLAYERS
SLACKED	SLAMMING	SLASHFEST	SLAYING
SLACKEN	SLAMMINGS	SLASHING	SLAYS
SLACKENED	SLAMS	SLASHINGS	SLEAVE
SLACKENER	SLANDER	SLAT	SLEAVED
SLACKENS	SLANDERED	SLATCH	SLEAVES
SLACKER	SLANDERER	SLATCHES	SLEAVING
SLACKERS	SLANDERS	SLATE	SLEAZE
SLACKEST	SLANE	SLATED	SLEAZEBAG
SLACKING	SLANES	SLATELIKE	SLEAZES
SLACKLY	SLANG	SLATER	SLEAZIER
SLACKNESS	SLANGED	SLATERS	SLEAZIEST
SLACKS	SLANGER	SLATES	SLEAZILY
SLADANG	SLANGERS	SLATEY	SLEAZO
SLADANGS	SLANGIER	SLATHER	SLEAZOID
SLADE	SLANGIEST	SLATHERED	SLEAZOIDS
SLADES	SLANGILY	SLATHERS	SLEAZY
SLAE	SLANGING	SLATIER	SLED
SLAES	SLANGINGS	SLATIEST	SLEDDED
SLAG	SLANGISH	SLATINESS	SLEDDER
SLAGGED	SLANGS	SLATING	SLEDDERS
SLAGGIER	SLANGUAGE	SLATINGS	SLEDDING
SLAGGIEST	SLANGULAR	SLATS	SLEDDINGS
SLAGGING	SLANGY	SLATTED	SLEDED
SLAGGINGS	SLANK	SLATTER	SLEDGE
SLAGGY	SLANT	SLATTERED	SLEDGED
SLAGS	SLANTED	SLATTERN	SLEDGER
SLAID	SLANTER	SLATTERNS	SLEDGERS
SLAIN	SLANTERS	SLATTERS	SLEDGES
SLAINTE	SLANTING	SLATTERY	SLEDGING
SLAIRG	SLANTLY	SLATTING	SLEDGINGS
SLAIRGED	SLANTS	SLATTINGS	SLEDS
SLAIRGING	SLANTWAYS	SLATY	SLEE
SLAIRGS	SLANTWISE	SLAUGHTER	SLEECH
SLAISTER	SLANTY	SLAVE	SLEECHES
SLAISTERS	SLAP	SLAVED	SLEECHIER
SLAISTERY	SLAPDASH	SLAVER	SLEECHY
SLAKABLE	SLAPHAPPY	SLAVERED	SLEEK
SLAKE	SLAPHEAD	SLAVERER	SLEEKED
SLAKEABLE	SLAPHEADS	SLAVERERS	SLEEKEN
SLAKED	SLAPJACK	SLAVERIES	SLEEKENED
SLAKELESS	SLAPJACKS	SLAVERING	SLEEKENS
SLAKER	SLAPPED	SLAVERS	SLEEKER
SLAKERS	SLAPPER	SLAVERY	SLEEKERS
SLAKES	SLAPPERS	SLAVES	SLEEKEST
SLAKING	SLAPPING	SLAVEY	SLEEKIER
SLALOM	SLAPS	SLAVEYS	SLEEKIEST
SLALOMED	SLAPSHOT	SLAVING	SLEEKING
SLALOMER	SLAPSHOTS	SLAVISH	SLEEKINGS
SLALOMERS	SLAPSTICK	SLAVISHLY	SLEEKIT
SLALOMING	SLART	SLAVOCRAT	SLEEKLY
SLALOMIST	SLARTED	SLAVOPHIL	SLEEKNESS
SLALOMS	SLARTING	SLAW	SLEEKS
SLAM	SLARTS	SLAWS	SLEEKY

SLEEP	SLEUTH	SLIGHTER	SLIOTAR
SLEEPAWAY	SLEUTHED	SLIGHTERS	SLIOTARS
SLEEPER	SLEUTHING	SLIGHTEST	SLIP
SLEEPERS	SLEUTHS	SLIGHTING	SLIPCASE
SLEEPERY	SLEW	SLIGHTISH	SLIPCASED
SLEEPIER	SLEWED	SLIGHTLY	SLIPCASES
SLEEPIEST	SLEWING	SLIGHTS	SLIPCOVER
SLEEPILY	SLEWS	SLILY	SLIPDRESS
SLEEPING	SLEY	SLIM	SLIPE
SLEEPINGS	SLEYS	SLIMDOWN	SLIPED
SLEEPLESS	SLICE	SLIMDOWNS	SLIPES
SLEEPLIKE	SLICEABLE	SLIME	SLIPFORM
SLEEPOUT	SLICED	SLIMEBALL	SLIPFORMS
SLEEPOUTS	SLICER	SLIMED	SLIPING
SLEEPOVER	SLICERS	SLIMES	SLIPKNOT
SLEEPRY	SLICES	SLIMIER	SLIPKNOTS
SLEEPS	SLICING	SLIMIEST	SLIPLESS
SLEEPSUIT	SLICINGS	SLIMILY	SLIPNOOSE
SLEEPWALK	SLICK	SLIMINESS	SLIPOUT
SLEEPWEAR	SLICKED	SLIMING	SLIPOUTS
SLEEPY	SLICKEN	SLIMLINE	SLIPOVER
SLEER	SLICKENED	SLIMLY	SLIPOVERS
SLEEST	SLICKENER	SLIMMED	SLIPPAGE
SLEET	SLICKENS	SLIMMER	SLIPPAGES
SLEETED	SLICKER	SLIMMERS	SLIPPED
SLEETIER	SLICKERED	SLIMMEST	SLIPPER
SLEETIEST	SLICKERS	SLIMMING	SLIPPERED
SLEETING	SLICKEST	SLIMMINGS	SLIPPERS
SLEETS	SLICKING	SLIMMISH	SLIPPERY
SLEETY	SLICKINGS	SLIMNESS	SLIPPIER
SLEEVE	SLICKLY	SLIMPSIER	SLIPPIEST
SLEEVED	SLICKNESS	SLIMPSY	SLIPPILY
SLEEVEEN	SLICKROCK	SLIMS	SLIPPING
SLEEVEENS	SLICKS	SLIMSIER	SLIPPY
SLEEVELET	SLICKSTER	SLIMSIEST	SLIPRAIL
SLEEVER	SLID	SLIMSY	SLIPRAILS
SLEEVERS	SLIDABLE	SLIMY	SLIPS
SLEEVES	SLIDDEN	SLING	SLIPSHEET
SLEEVING	SLIDDER	SLINGBACK	SLIPSHOD
SLEEVINGS	SLIDDERED	SLINGER	SLIPSLOP
SLEEZIER	SLIDDERS	SLINGERS	SLIPSLOPS
SLEEZIEST	SLIDDERY	SLINGING	SLIPSOLE
SLEEZY	SLIDE	SLINGS	SLIPSOLES
SLEIDED	SLIDED	SLINGSHOT	SLIPT
SLEIGH	SLIDER	SLINK	SLIPUP
SLEIGHED	SLIDERS	SLINKED	SLIPUPS
SLEIGHER	SLIDES	SLINKER	SLIPWARE
SLEIGHERS	SLIDEWAY	SLINKERS	SLIPWARES
SLEIGHING	SLIDEWAYS	SLINKIER	SLIPWAY
SLEIGHS	SLIDING	SLINKIEST	SLIPWAYS
SLEIGHT	SLIDINGLY	SLINKILY	SLISH
SLEIGHTS	SLIDINGS	SLINKING	SLISHES
SLENDER	SLIER	SLINKS	SLIT
SLENDERER	SLIEST	SLINKSKIN	SLITHER
SLENDERLY	SLIEVE	SLINKWEED	SLITHERED
SLENTER	SLIEVES	SLINKY	SLITHERS
SLENTERS	SLIGHT	SLINTER	SLITHERY
SLEPT	SLIGHTED	SLINTERS	SLITLESS

SLITLIKE
SLITS
SLITTED
SLITTER
SLITTERS
SLITTIER
SLITTIEST
SLITTING
SLITTY
SLIVE
SLIVED
SLIVEN
SLIVER
SLIVERED
SLIVERER
SLIVERERS
SLIVERING
SLIVERS
SLIVES
SLIVING
SLIVOVIC
SLIVOVICA
SLIVOVITZ
SLIVOWITZ
SLOAN
SLOANS
SLOB
SLOBBER
SLOBBERED
SLOBBERER
SLOBBERS
SLOBBERY
SLOBBIER
SLOBBIEST
SLOBBISH
SLOBBY
SLOBLAND
SLOBLANDS
SLOBS
SLOCKEN
SLOCKENED
SLOCKENS
SLOE
SLOEBUSH
SLOES
SLOETHORN
SLOETREE
SLOETREES
SLOG
SLOGAN
SLOGANEER
SLOGANISE
SLOGANIZE
SLOGANS
SLOGGED
SLOGGER
SLOGGERS
SLOGGING

SLOGS
SLOID
SLOIDS
SLOJD
SLOJDS
SLOKEN
SLOKENED
SLOKENING
SLOKENS
SLOMMOCK
SLOMMOCKS
SLOOM
SLOOMED
SLOOMIER
SLOOMIEST
SLOOMING
SLOOMS
SLOOMY
SLOOP
SLOOPS
SLOOSH
SLOOSHED
SLOOSHES
SLOOSHING
SLOOT
SLOOTS
SLOP
SLOPE
SLOPED
SLOPER
SLOPERS
SLOPES
SLOPEWISE
SLOPIER
SLOPIEST
SLOPING
SLOPINGLY
SLOPPED
SLOPPIER
SLOPPIEST
SLOPPILY
SLOPPING
SLOPPY
SLOPS
SLOPWORK
SLOPWORKS
SLOPY
SLORM
SLORMED
SLORMING
SLORMS
SLOSH
SLOSHED
SLOSHES
SLOSHIER
SLOSHIEST
SLOSHING
SLOSHINGS

SLOSHY
SLOT
SLOTBACK
SLOTBACKS
SLOTH
SLOTHED
SLOTHFUL
SLOTHING
SLOTHS
SLOTS
SLOTTED
SLOTTER
SLOTTERS
SLOTTING
SLOUCH
SLOUCHED
SLOUCHER
SLOUCHERS
SLOUCHES
SLOUCHIER
SLOUCHILY
SLOUCHING
SLOUCHY
SLOUGH
SLOUGHED
SLOUGHIER
SLOUGHING
SLOUGHS
SLOUGHY
SLOVE
SLOVEN
SLOVENLY
SLOVENRY
SLOVENS
SLOW
SLOWBACK
SLOWBACKS
SLOWCOACH
SLOWDOWN
SLOWDOWNS
SLOWED
SLOWER
SLOWEST
SLOWING
SLOWINGS
SLOWISH
SLOWLY
SLOWNESS
SLOWPOKE
SLOWPOKES
SLOWS
SLOWWORM
SLOWWORMS
SLOYD
SLOYDS
SLUB
SLUBB
SLUBBED

SLUBBER
SLUBBERED
SLUBBERS
SLUBBIER
SLUBBIEST
SLUBBING
SLUBBINGS
SLUBBS
SLUBBY
SLUBS
SLUDGE
SLUDGED
SLUDGES
SLUDGIER
SLUDGIEST
SLUDGING
SLUDGY
SLUE
SLUED
SLUEING
SLUES
SLUFF
SLUFFED
SLUFFING
SLUFFS
SLUG
SLUGABED
SLUGABEDS
SLUGFEST
SLUGFESTS
SLUGGABED
SLUGGARD
SLUGGARDS
SLUGGED
SLUGGER
SLUGGERS
SLUGGING
SLUGGISH
SLUGHORN
SLUGHORNE
SLUGHORNS
SLUGS
SLUICE
SLUICED
SLUICES
SLUICEWAY
SLUICIER
SLUICIEST
SLUICING
SLUICY
SLUING
SLUIT
SLUITS
SLUM
SLUMBER
SLUMBERED
SLUMBERER
SLUMBERS

SLUMBERY	SLUT	SMALT	SMAZE
SLUMBROUS	SLUTCH	SMALTI	SMAZES
SLUMBRY	SLUTCHES	SMALTINE	SMEAR
SLUMGUM	SLUTCHIER	SMALTINES	SMEARCASE
SLUMGUMS	SLUTCHY	SMALTITE	SMEARED
SLUMISM	SLUTS	SMALTITES	SMEARER
SLUMISMS	SLUTTERY	SMALTO	SMEARERS
SLUMLORD	SLUTTIER	SMALTOS	SMEARIER
SLUMLORDS	SLUTTIEST	SMALTS	SMEARIEST
SLUMMED	SLUTTISH	SMARAGD	SMEARILY
SLUMMER	SLUTTY	SMARAGDE	SMEARING
SLUMMERS	SLY	SMARAGDES	SMEARS
SLUMMIER	SLYBOOTS	SMARAGDS	SMEARY
SLUMMIEST	SLYER	SMARM	SMEATH
SLUMMING	SLYEST	SMARMED	SMEATHS
SLUMMINGS	SLYISH	SMARMIER	SMECTIC
SLUMMOCK	SLYLY	SMARMIEST	SMECTITE
SLUMMOCKS	SLYNESS	SMARMILY	SMECTITES
SLUMMY	SLYNESSES	SMARMING	SMECTITIC
SLUMP	SLYPE	SMARMS	SMEDDUM
SLUMPED	SLYPES	SMARMY	SMEDDUMS
SLUMPIER	SMA	SMART	SMEE
SLUMPIEST	SMAAK	SMARTARSE	SMEECH
SLUMPING	SMAAKED	SMARTASS	SMEECHED
SLUMPS	SMAAKING	SMARTED	SMEECHES
SLUMPY	SMAAKS	SMARTEN	SMEECHING
SLUMS	SMACK	SMARTENED	SMEEK
SLUNG	SMACKED	SMARTENS	SMEEKED
SLUNGSHOT	SMACKER	SMARTER	SMEEKING
SLUNK	SMACKERS	SMARTEST	SMEEKS
SLUR	SMACKHEAD	SMARTIE	SMEES
SLURB	SMACKING	SMARTIES	SMEETH
SLURBAN	SMACKINGS	SMARTING	SMEETHS
SLURBS	SMACKS	SMARTISH	SMEGMA
SLURP	SMAIK	SMARTLY	SMEGMAS
SLURPED	SMAIKS	SMARTNESS	SMELL
SLURPER	SMALL	SMARTS	SMELLED
SLURPERS	SMALLAGE	SMARTWEED	SMELLER
SLURPING	SMALLAGES	SMARTY	SMELLERS
SLURPS	SMALLBOY	SMASH	SMELLIER
SLURRED	SMALLBOYS	SMASHABLE	SMELLIES
SLURRIED	SMALLED	SMASHED	SMELLIEST
SLURRIES	SMALLER	SMASHER	SMELLING
SLURRING	SMALLEST	SMASHEROO	SMELLINGS
SLURRY	SMALLING	SMASHERS	SMELLS
SLURRYING	SMALLISH	SMASHES	SMELLY
SLURS	SMALLNESS	SMASHING	SMELT
SLUSE	SMALLPOX	SMASHINGS	SMELTED
SLUSES	SMALLS	SMASHUP	SMELTER
SLUSH	SMALLSAT	SMASHUPS	SMELTERS
SLUSHED	SMALLSATS	SMATCH	SMELTERY
SLUSHES	SMALLTIME	SMATCHED	SMELTING
SLUSHIER	SMALM	SMATCHES	SMELTINGS
SLUSHIES	SMALMED	SMATCHING	SMELTS
SLUSHIEST	SMALMILY	SMATTER	SMERK
SLUSHILY	SMALMING	SMATTERED	SMERKED
SLUSHING	SMALMS	SMATTERER	SMERKING
SLUSHY	SMALMY	SMATTERS	SMERKS

547

SMEUSE	SMIRKING	SMOKEJACK	SMOOTHIE
SMEUSES	SMIRKS	SMOKELESS	SMOOTHIES
SMEW	SMIRKY	SMOKELIKE	SMOOTHING
SMEWS	SMIRR	SMOKEPOT	SMOOTHISH
SMICKER	SMIRRED	SMOKEPOTS	SMOOTHLY
SMICKERED	SMIRRIER	SMOKER	SMOOTHS
SMICKERS	SMIRRIEST	SMOKERS	SMOOTHY
SMICKET	SMIRRING	SMOKES	SMOOTING
SMICKETS	SMIRRS	SMOKETREE	SMOOTS
SMICKLY	SMIRRY	SMOKEY	SMORBROD
SMIDDIED	SMIRS	SMOKIER	SMORBRODS
SMIDDIES	SMIRTING	SMOKIES	SMORE
SMIDDY	SMIRTINGS	SMOKIEST	SMORED
SMIDDYING	SMIT	SMOKILY	SMORES
SMIDGE	SMITE	SMOKINESS	SMORING
SMIDGEN	SMITER	SMOKING	SMORZANDO
SMIDGENS	SMITERS	SMOKINGS	SMORZATO
SMIDGEON	SMITES	SMOKO	SMOTE
SMIDGEONS	SMITH	SMOKOS	SMOTHER
SMIDGES	SMITHED	SMOKY	SMOTHERED
SMIDGIN	SMITHERS	SMOLDER	SMOTHERER
SMIDGINS	SMITHERY	SMOLDERED	SMOTHERS
SMIERCASE	SMITHIED	SMOLDERS	SMOTHERY
SMIGHT	SMITHIES	SMOLT	SMOUCH
SMIGHTING	SMITHING	SMOLTS	SMOUCHED
SMIGHTS	SMITHS	SMOOCH	SMOUCHES
SMILAX	SMITHY	SMOOCHED	SMOUCHING
SMILAXES	SMITHYING	SMOOCHER	SMOULDER
SMILE	SMITING	SMOOCHERS	SMOULDERS
SMILED	SMITS	SMOOCHES	SMOULDRY
SMILEFUL	SMITTED	SMOOCHING	SMOUSE
SMILELESS	SMITTEN	SMOOCHY	SMOUSED
SMILER	SMITTING	SMOODGE	SMOUSER
SMILERS	SMITTLE	SMOODGED	SMOUSERS
SMILES	SMOCK	SMOODGES	SMOUSES
SMILET	SMOCKED	SMOODGING	SMOUSING
SMILETS	SMOCKING	SMOOGE	SMOUT
SMILEY	SMOCKINGS	SMOOGED	SMOUTED
SMILEYS	SMOCKLIKE	SMOOGES	SMOUTING
SMILING	SMOCKS	SMOOGING	SMOUTS
SMILINGLY	SMOG	SMOOR	SMOWT
SMILINGS	SMOGGIER	SMOORED	SMOWTS
SMILODON	SMOGGIEST	SMOORING	SMOYLE
SMILODONS	SMOGGY	SMOORS	SMOYLED
SMIR	SMOGLESS	SMOOSH	SMOYLES
SMIRCH	SMOGS	SMOOSHED	SMOYLING
SMIRCHED	SMOILE	SMOOSHES	SMRITI
SMIRCHER	SMOILED	SMOOSHING	SMRITIS
SMIRCHERS	SMOILES	SMOOT	SMUDGE
SMIRCHES	SMOILING	SMOOTED	SMUDGED
SMIRCHING	SMOKABLE	SMOOTH	SMUDGEDLY
SMIRK	SMOKE	SMOOTHED	SMUDGER
SMIRKED	SMOKEABLE	SMOOTHEN	SMUDGERS
SMIRKER	SMOKEBUSH	SMOOTHENS	SMUDGES
SMIRKERS	SMOKED	SMOOTHER	SMUDGIER
SMIRKIER	SMOKEHO	SMOOTHERS	SMUDGIEST
SMIRKIEST	SMOKEHOOD	SMOOTHES	SMUDGILY
SMIRKILY	SMOKEHOS	SMOOTHEST	SMUDGING

SMUDGINGS
SMUDGY
SMUG
SMUGGED
SMUGGER
SMUGGERY
SMUGGEST
SMUGGING
SMUGGLE
SMUGGLED
SMUGGLER
SMUGGLERS
SMUGGLES
SMUGGLING
SMUGLY
SMUGNESS
SMUGS
SMUR
SMURFING
SMURFINGS
SMURRED
SMURRIER
SMURRIEST
SMURRING
SMURRY
SMURS
SMUSH
SMUSHED
SMUSHES
SMUSHING
SMUT
SMUTCH
SMUTCHED
SMUTCHES
SMUTCHIER
SMUTCHING
SMUTCHY
SMUTS
SMUTTED
SMUTTIER
SMUTTIEST
SMUTTILY
SMUTTING
SMUTTY
SMYTRIE
SMYTRIES
SNAB
SNABBLE
SNABBLED
SNABBLES
SNABBLING
SNABS
SNACK
SNACKED
SNACKER
SNACKERS
SNACKETTE
SNACKING

SNACKS
SNAFFLE
SNAFFLED
SNAFFLES
SNAFFLING
SNAFU
SNAFUED
SNAFUING
SNAFUS
SNAG
SNAGGED
SNAGGIER
SNAGGIEST
SNAGGING
SNAGGY
SNAGLIKE
SNAGS
SNAIL
SNAILED
SNAILERY
SNAILFISH
SNAILIER
SNAILIEST
SNAILING
SNAILLIKE
SNAILS
SNAILY
SNAKE
SNAKEBIRD
SNAKEBIT
SNAKEBITE
SNAKED
SNAKEFISH
SNAKEHEAD
SNAKELIKE
SNAKEPIT
SNAKEPITS
SNAKEROOT
SNAKES
SNAKESKIN
SNAKEWEED
SNAKEWISE
SNAKEWOOD
SNAKEY
SNAKIER
SNAKIEST
SNAKILY
SNAKINESS
SNAKING
SNAKISH
SNAKY
SNAP
SNAPBACK
SNAPBACKS
SNAPHANCE
SNAPLESS
SNAPLINK
SNAPLINKS

SNAPPABLE
SNAPPED
SNAPPER
SNAPPERED
SNAPPERS
SNAPPIER
SNAPPIEST
SNAPPILY
SNAPPING
SNAPPINGS
SNAPPISH
SNAPPY
SNAPS
SNAPSHOT
SNAPSHOTS
SNAPTIN
SNAPTINS
SNAPWEED
SNAPWEEDS
SNAR
SNARE
SNARED
SNARELESS
SNARER
SNARERS
SNARES
SNARF
SNARFED
SNARFING
SNARFS
SNARIER
SNARIEST
SNARING
SNARINGS
SNARK
SNARKIER
SNARKIEST
SNARKILY
SNARKS
SNARKY
SNARL
SNARLED
SNARLER
SNARLERS
SNARLIER
SNARLIEST
SNARLING
SNARLINGS
SNARLS
SNARLY
SNARRED
SNARRING
SNARS
SNARY
SNASH
SNASHED
SNASHES
SNASHING

SNASTE
SNASTES
SNATCH
SNATCHED
SNATCHER
SNATCHERS
SNATCHES
SNATCHIER
SNATCHILY
SNATCHING
SNATCHY
SNATH
SNATHE
SNATHES
SNATHS
SNAW
SNAWED
SNAWING
SNAWS
SNAZZIER
SNAZZIEST
SNAZZILY
SNAZZY
SNEAD
SNEADS
SNEAK
SNEAKED
SNEAKER
SNEAKERED
SNEAKERS
SNEAKEUP
SNEAKEUPS
SNEAKIER
SNEAKIEST
SNEAKILY
SNEAKING
SNEAKISH
SNEAKS
SNEAKSBY
SNEAKY
SNEAP
SNEAPED
SNEAPING
SNEAPS
SNEATH
SNEATHS
SNEB
SNEBBE
SNEBBED
SNEBBES
SNEBBING
SNEBS
SNECK
SNECKED
SNECKING
SNECKS
SNED
SNEDDED

SNEDDING	SNIDELY	SNIPE	SNOBBY
SNEDS	SNIDENESS	SNIPED	SNOBLING
SNEE	SNIDER	SNIPEFISH	SNOBLINGS
SNEED	SNIDES	SNIPELIKE	SNOBS
SNEEING	SNIDEST	SNIPER	SNOD
SNEER	SNIDEY	SNIPERS	SNODDED
SNEERED	SNIDIER	SNIPES	SNODDER
SNEERER	SNIDIEST	SNIPIER	SNODDEST
SNEERERS	SNIDING	SNIPIEST	SNODDING
SNEERFUL	SNIES	SNIPING	SNODDIT
SNEERIER	SNIFF	SNIPINGS	SNODS
SNEERIEST	SNIFFABLE	SNIPPED	SNOEK
SNEERING	SNIFFED	SNIPPER	SNOEKS
SNEERINGS	SNIFFER	SNIPPERS	SNOEP
SNEERS	SNIFFERS	SNIPPET	SNOG
SNEERY	SNIFFIER	SNIPPETS	SNOGGED
SNEES	SNIFFIEST	SNIPPETY	SNOGGING
SNEESH	SNIFFILY	SNIPPIER	SNOGS
SNEESHAN	SNIFFING	SNIPPIEST	SNOKE
SNEESHANS	SNIFFINGS	SNIPPILY	SNOKED
SNEESHES	SNIFFISH	SNIPPING	SNOKES
SNEESHIN	SNIFFLE	SNIPPINGS	SNOKING
SNEESHING	SNIFFLED	SNIPPY	SNOOD
SNEESHINS	SNIFFLER	SNIPS	SNOODED
SNEEZE	SNIFFLERS	SNIPY	SNOODING
SNEEZED	SNIFFLES	SNIRT	SNOODS
SNEEZER	SNIFFLIER	SNIRTLE	SNOOK
SNEEZERS	SNIFFLING	SNIRTLED	SNOOKED
SNEEZES	SNIFFLY	SNIRTLES	SNOOKER
SNEEZIER	SNIFFS	SNIRTLING	SNOOKERED
SNEEZIEST	SNIFFY	SNIRTS	SNOOKERS
SNEEZING	SNIFT	SNIT	SNOOKING
SNEEZINGS	SNIFTED	SNITCH	SNOOKS
SNEEZY	SNIFTER	SNITCHED	SNOOL
SNELL	SNIFTERED	SNITCHER	SNOOLED
SNELLED	SNIFTERS	SNITCHERS	SNOOLING
SNELLER	SNIFTIER	SNITCHES	SNOOLS
SNELLEST	SNIFTIEST	SNITCHIER	SNOOP
SNELLING	SNIFTING	SNITCHING	SNOOPED
SNELLS	SNIFTS	SNITCHY	SNOOPER
SNELLY	SNIFTY	SNITS	SNOOPERS
SNIB	SNIG	SNIVEL	SNOOPIER
SNIBBED	SNIGGED	SNIVELED	SNOOPIEST
SNIBBING	SNIGGER	SNIVELER	SNOOPILY
SNIBS	SNIGGERED	SNIVELERS	SNOOPING
SNICK	SNIGGERER	SNIVELING	SNOOPS
SNICKED	SNIGGERS	SNIVELLED	SNOOPY
SNICKER	SNIGGING	SNIVELLER	SNOOT
SNICKERED	SNIGGLE	SNIVELLY	SNOOTED
SNICKERER	SNIGGLED	SNIVELS	SNOOTFUL
SNICKERS	SNIGGLER	SNOB	SNOOTFULS
SNICKERY	SNIGGLERS	SNOBBERY	SNOOTIER
SNICKET	SNIGGLES	SNOBBIER	SNOOTIEST
SNICKETS	SNIGGLING	SNOBBIEST	SNOOTILY
SNICKING	SNIGLET	SNOBBILY	SNOOTING
SNICKS	SNIGLETS	SNOBBISH	SNOOTS
SNIDE	SNIGS	SNOBBISM	SNOOTY
SNIDED	SNIP	SNOBBISMS	SNOOZE

SNOOZED	SNOWBALL	SNOWPLOWS	SNUGGERIE
SNOOZER	SNOWBALLS	SNOWS	SNUGGERY
SNOOZERS	SNOWBANK	SNOWSCAPE	SNUGGEST
SNOOZES	SNOWBANKS	SNOWSHED	SNUGGIES
SNOOZIER	SNOWBELL	SNOWSHEDS	SNUGGING
SNOOZIEST	SNOWBELLS	SNOWSHOE	SNUGGLE
SNOOZING	SNOWBELT	SNOWSHOED	SNUGGLED
SNOOZLE	SNOWBELTS	SNOWSHOER	SNUGGLES
SNOOZLED	SNOWBERRY	SNOWSHOES	SNUGGLING
SNOOZLES	SNOWBIRD	SNOWSLIDE	SNUGLY
SNOOZLING	SNOWBIRDS	SNOWSLIP	SNUGNESS
SNOOZY	SNOWBLINK	SNOWSLIPS	SNUGS
SNORE	SNOWBOARD	SNOWSTORM	SNUSH
SNORED	SNOWBOOT	SNOWSUIT	SNUSHED
SNORER	SNOWBOOTS	SNOWSUITS	SNUSHES
SNORERS	SNOWBOUND	SNOWY	SNUSHING
SNORES	SNOWBRUSH	SNUB	SNUZZLE
SNORING	SNOWBUSH	SNUBBE	SNUZZLED
SNORINGS	SNOWCAP	SNUBBED	SNUZZLES
SNORKEL	SNOWCAPS	SNUBBER	SNUZZLING
SNORKELED	SNOWCAT	SNUBBERS	SNY
SNORKELER	SNOWCATS	SNUBBES	SNYE
SNORKELS	SNOWDRIFT	SNUBBIER	SNYES
SNORT	SNOWDROP	SNUBBIEST	SO
SNORTED	SNOWDROPS	SNUBBING	SOAK
SNORTER	SNOWED	SNUBBINGS	SOAKAGE
SNORTERS	SNOWFALL	SNUBBISH	SOAKAGES
SNORTIER	SNOWFALLS	SNUBBY	SOAKAWAY
SNORTIEST	SNOWFIELD	SNUBNESS	SOAKAWAYS
SNORTING	SNOWFLAKE	SNUBS	SOAKED
SNORTINGS	SNOWFLECK	SNUCK	SOAKEN
SNORTS	SNOWFLICK	SNUDGE	SOAKER
SNORTY	SNOWIER	SNUDGED	SOAKERS
SNOT	SNOWIEST	SNUDGES	SOAKING
SNOTS	SNOWILY	SNUDGING	SOAKINGLY
SNOTTED	SNOWINESS	SNUFF	SOAKINGS
SNOTTER	SNOWING	SNUFFBOX	SOAKS
SNOTTERED	SNOWISH	SNUFFED	SOAP
SNOTTERS	SNOWK	SNUFFER	SOAPBARK
SNOTTERY	SNOWKED	SNUFFERS	SOAPBARKS
SNOTTIE	SNOWKING	SNUFFIER	SOAPBERRY
SNOTTIER	SNOWKS	SNUFFIEST	SOAPBOX
SNOTTIES	SNOWLAND	SNUFFILY	SOAPBOXED
SNOTTIEST	SNOWLANDS	SNUFFING	SOAPBOXES
SNOTTILY	SNOWLESS	SNUFFINGS	SOAPED
SNOTTING	SNOWLIKE	SNUFFLE	SOAPER
SNOTTY	SNOWLINE	SNUFFLED	SOAPERS
SNOUT	SNOWLINES	SNUFFLER	SOAPIE
SNOUTED	SNOWMAKER	SNUFFLERS	SOAPIER
SNOUTIER	SNOWMAN	SNUFFLES	SOAPIES
SNOUTIEST	SNOWMELT	SNUFFLIER	SOAPIEST
SNOUTING	SNOWMELTS	SNUFFLING	SOAPILY
SNOUTISH	SNOWMEN	SNUFFLY	SOAPINESS
SNOUTLESS	SNOWMOLD	SNUFFS	SOAPING
SNOUTLIKE	SNOWMOLDS	SNUFFY	SOAPLAND
SNOUTS	SNOWPACK	SNUG	SOAPLANDS
SNOUTY	SNOWPACKS	SNUGGED	SOAPLESS
SNOW	SNOWPLOW	SNUGGER	SOAPLIKE

SOAPROOT	SOCAS	SODALITES	SOFTBOUND
SOAPROOTS	SOCCAGE	SODALITY	SOFTCORE
SOAPS	SOCCAGES	SODAMIDE	SOFTCOVER
SOAPSTONE	SOCCER	SODAMIDES	SOFTED
SOAPSUDS	SOCCERS	SODAS	SOFTEN
SOAPSUDSY	SOCIABLE	SODBUSTER	SOFTENED
SOAPWORT	SOCIABLES	SODDED	SOFTENER
SOAPWORTS	SOCIABLY	SODDEN	SOFTENERS
SOAPY	SOCIAL	SODDENED	SOFTENING
SOAR	SOCIALISE	SODDENING	SOFTENS
SOARAWAY	SOCIALISM	SODDENLY	SOFTER
SOARE	SOCIALIST	SODDENS	SOFTEST
SOARED	SOCIALITE	SODDIER	SOFTGOODS
SOARER	SOCIALITY	SODDIES	SOFTHEAD
SOARERS	SOCIALIZE	SODDIEST	SOFTHEADS
SOARES	SOCIALLY	SODDING	SOFTIE
SOARING	SOCIALS	SODDY	SOFTIES
SOARINGLY	SOCIATE	SODGER	SOFTING
SOARINGS	SOCIATES	SODGERED	SOFTISH
SOARS	SOCIATION	SODGERING	SOFTLING
SOAVE	SOCIATIVE	SODGERS	SOFTLINGS
SOAVES	SOCIETAL	SODIC	SOFTLY
SOB	SOCIETIES	SODICITY	SOFTNESS
SOBA	SOCIETY	SODIUM	SOFTPASTE
SOBAS	SOCIOGRAM	SODIUMS	SOFTS
SOBBED	SOCIOLECT	SODOM	SOFTSHELL
SOBBER	SOCIOLOGY	SODOMIES	SOFTWARE
SOBBERS	SOCIOPATH	SODOMISE	SOFTWARES
SOBBING	SOCK	SODOMISED	SOFTWOOD
SOBBINGLY	SOCKED	SODOMISES	SOFTWOODS
SOBBINGS	SOCKET	SODOMIST	SOFTY
SOBEIT	SOCKETED	SODOMISTS	SOG
SOBER	SOCKETING	SODOMITE	SOGER
SOBERED	SOCKETS	SODOMITES	SOGERS
SOBERER	SOCKETTE	SODOMITIC	SOGGED
SOBEREST	SOCKETTES	SODOMIZE	SOGGIER
SOBERING	SOCKEYE	SODOMIZED	SOGGIEST
SOBERISE	SOCKEYES	SODOMIZES	SOGGILY
SOBERISED	SOCKING	SODOMS	SOGGINESS
SOBERISES	SOCKLESS	SODOMY	SOGGING
SOBERIZE	SOCKMAN	SODS	SOGGINGS
SOBERIZED	SOCKMEN	SOEVER	SOGGY
SOBERIZES	SOCKO	SOFA	SOGS
SOBERLY	SOCKS	SOFABED	SOH
SOBERNESS	SOCLE	SOFABEDS	SOHO
SOBERS	SOCLES	SOFAR	SOHS
SOBFUL	SOCMAN	SOFARS	SOIGNE
SOBOLE	SOCMEN	SOFAS	SOIGNEE
SOBOLES	SOCS	SOFFIONI	SOIL
SOBRIETY	SOD	SOFFIT	SOILAGE
SOBRIQUET	SODA	SOFFITS	SOILAGES
SOBS	SODAIC	SOFT	SOILBORNE
SOC	SODAIN	SOFTA	SOILED
SOCA	SODAINE	SOFTAS	SOILIER
SOCAGE	SODALESS	SOFTBACK	SOILIEST
SOCAGER	SODALIST	SOFTBACKS	SOILINESS
SOCAGERS	SODALISTS	SOFTBALL	SOILING
SOCAGES	SODALITE	SOFTBALLS	SOILINGS

SOILLESS	SOLARISTS	SOLEMNISE	SOLILOQUY
SOILS	SOLARIUM	SOLEMNITY	SOLING
SOILURE	SOLARIUMS	SOLEMNIZE	SOLION
SOILURES	SOLARIZE	SOLEMNLY	SOLIONS
SOILY	SOLARIZED	SOLENESS	SOLIPED
SOIREE	SOLARIZES	SOLENETTE	SOLIPEDS
SOIREES	SOLARS	SOLENODON	SOLIPSISM
SOJA	SOLAS	SOLENOID	SOLIPSIST
SOJAS	SOLATE	SOLENOIDS	SOLIQUID
SOJOURN	SOLATED	SOLEPLATE	SOLIQUIDS
SOJOURNED	SOLATES	SOLEPRINT	SOLITAIRE
SOJOURNER	SOLATIA	SOLER	SOLITARY
SOJOURNS	SOLATING	SOLERA	SOLITO
SOKAH	SOLATION	SOLERAS	SOLITON
SOKAHS	SOLATIONS	SOLERET	SOLITONS
SOKAIYA	SOLATIUM	SOLERETS	SOLITUDE
SOKE	SOLD	SOLERS	SOLITUDES
SOKEMAN	SOLDADO	SOLES	SOLIVE
SOKEMANRY	SOLDADOS	SOLEUS	SOLIVES
SOKEMEN	SOLDAN	SOLEUSES	SOLLAR
SOKEN	SOLDANS	SOLFATARA	SOLLARS
SOKENS	SOLDE	SOLFEGE	SOLLER
SOKES	SOLDER	SOLFEGES	SOLLERET
SOKOL	SOLDERED	SOLFEGGI	SOLLERETS
SOKOLS	SOLDERER	SOLFEGGIO	SOLLERS
SOL	SOLDERERS	SOLFERINO	SOLLICKER
SOLA	SOLDERING	SOLGEL	SOLO
SOLACE	SOLDERS	SOLI	SOLOED
SOLACED	SOLDES	SOLICIT	SOLOING
SOLACER	SOLDI	SOLICITED	SOLOIST
SOLACERS	SOLDIER	SOLICITOR	SOLOISTIC
SOLACES	SOLDIERED	SOLICITS	SOLOISTS
SOLACING	SOLDIERLY	SOLICITY	SOLON
SOLACIOUS	SOLDIERS	SOLID	SOLONCHAK
SOLAH	SOLDIERY	SOLIDAGO	SOLONETS
SOLAHS	SOLDO	SOLIDAGOS	SOLONETZ
SOLAN	SOLDS	SOLIDARE	SOLONS
SOLAND	SOLE	SOLIDARES	SOLOS
SOLANDER	SOLECISE	SOLIDARY	SOLPUGID
SOLANDERS	SOLECISED	SOLIDATE	SOLPUGIDS
SOLANDS	SOLECISES	SOLIDATED	SOLS
SOLANIN	SOLECISM	SOLIDATES	SOLSTICE
SOLANINE	SOLECISMS	SOLIDER	SOLSTICES
SOLANINES	SOLECIST	SOLIDEST	SOLUBLE
SOLANINS	SOLECISTS	SOLIDI	SOLUBLES
SOLANO	SOLECIZE	SOLIDIFY	SOLUBLY
SOLANOS	SOLECIZED	SOLIDISH	SOLUM
SOLANS	SOLECIZES	SOLIDISM	SOLUMS
SOLANUM	SOLED	SOLIDISMS	SOLUNAR
SOLANUMS	SOLEI	SOLIDIST	SOLUS
SOLAR	SOLEIN	SOLIDISTS	SOLUTE
SOLARIA	SOLELESS	SOLIDITY	SOLUTES
SOLARISE	SOLELY	SOLIDLY	SOLUTION
SOLARISED	SOLEMN	SOLIDNESS	SOLUTIONS
SOLARISES	SOLEMNER	SOLIDS	SOLUTIVE
SOLARISM	SOLEMNESS	SOLIDUM	SOLVABLE
SOLARISMS	SOLEMNEST	SOLIDUMS	SOLVATE
SOLARIST	SOLEMNIFY	SOLIDUS	SOLVATED

SOLVATES

SOLVATES
SOLVATING
SOLVATION
SOLVE
SOLVED
SOLVENCY
SOLVENT
SOLVENTLY
SOLVENTS
SOLVER
SOLVERS
SOLVES
SOLVING
SOM
SOMA
SOMAN
SOMANS
SOMAS
SOMASCOPE
SOMATA
SOMATIC
SOMATISM
SOMATISMS
SOMATIST
SOMATISTS
SOMBER
SOMBERED
SOMBERER
SOMBEREST
SOMBERING
SOMBERLY
SOMBERS
SOMBRE
SOMBRED
SOMBRELY
SOMBRER
SOMBRERO
SOMBREROS
SOMBRES
SOMBREST
SOMBRING
SOMBROUS
SOME
SOMEBODY
SOMEDAY
SOMEDEAL
SOMEDELE
SOMEGATE
SOMEHOW
SOMEONE
SOMEONES
SOMEPLACE
SOMERSET
SOMERSETS
SOMETHING
SOMETIME
SOMETIMES
SOMEWAY

SOMEWAYS
SOMEWHAT
SOMEWHATS
SOMEWHEN
SOMEWHERE
SOMEWHILE
SOMEWHY
SOMEWISE
SOMITAL
SOMITE
SOMITES
SOMITIC
SOMMELIER
SOMNIAL
SOMNIATE
SOMNIATED
SOMNIATES
SOMNIFIC
SOMNOLENT
SOMONI
SOMS
SOMY
SON
SONANCE
SONANCES
SONANCIES
SONANCY
SONANT
SONANTAL
SONANTIC
SONANTS
SONAR
SONARMAN
SONARMEN
SONARS
SONATA
SONATAS
SONATINA
SONATINAS
SONATINE
SONCE
SONCES
SONDAGE
SONDAGES
SONDE
SONDELI
SONDELIS
SONDER
SONDERS
SONDES
SONE
SONERI
SONERIS
SONES
SONG
SONGBIRD
SONGBIRDS
SONGBOOK

SONGBOOKS
SONGCRAFT
SONGFEST
SONGFESTS
SONGFUL
SONGFULLY
SONGKOK
SONGKOKS
SONGLESS
SONGLIKE
SONGMAN
SONGMEN
SONGOLOLO
SONGS
SONGSMITH
SONGSTER
SONGSTERS
SONHOOD
SONHOODS
SONIC
SONICALLY
SONICATE
SONICATED
SONICATES
SONICATOR
SONICS
SONLESS
SONLIKE
SONLY
SONNE
SONNES
SONNET
SONNETARY
SONNETED
SONNETEER
SONNETING
SONNETISE
SONNETIZE
SONNETS
SONNETTED
SONNIES
SONNY
SONOBUOY
SONOBUOYS
SONOGRAM
SONOGRAMS
SONOGRAPH
SONOMETER
SONORANT
SONORANTS
SONORITY
SONOROUS
SONOVOX
SONOVOXES
SONS
SONSE
SONSES
SONSHIP

SONSHIPS
SONSIE
SONSIER
SONSIEST
SONSY
SONTAG
SONTAGS
SONTIES
SOOCHONG
SOOCHONGS
SOOEY
SOOGEE
SOOGEED
SOOGEEING
SOOGEES
SOOGIE
SOOGIED
SOOGIEING
SOOGIES
SOOJEY
SOOJEYS
SOOK
SOOKED
SOOKING
SOOKS
SOOL
SOOLE
SOOLED
SOOLES
SOOLING
SOOLS
SOOM
SOOMED
SOOMING
SOOMS
SOON
SOONER
SOONERS
SOONEST
SOOP
SOOPED
SOOPING
SOOPINGS
SOOPS
SOOPSTAKE
SOOT
SOOTE
SOOTED
SOOTERKIN
SOOTES
SOOTFLAKE
SOOTH
SOOTHE
SOOTHED
SOOTHER
SOOTHERED
SOOTHERS
SOOTHES

SOOTHEST	SOPRANOS	SOREDIATE	SOROSISES
SOOTHFAST	SOPS	SOREDIUM	SORPTION
SOOTHFUL	SORA	SOREE	SORPTIONS
SOOTHING	SORAGE	SOREES	SORPTIVE
SOOTHINGS	SORAGES	SOREHEAD	SORRA
SOOTHLICH	SORAL	SOREHEADS	SORRAS
SOOTHLY	SORAS	SOREHON	SORREL
SOOTHS	SORB	SOREHONS	SORRELS
SOOTHSAID	SORBABLE	SOREL	SORRIER
SOOTHSAY	SORBARIA	SORELL	SORRIEST
SOOTHSAYS	SORBARIAS	SORELLS	SORRILY
SOOTIER	SORBATE	SORELS	SORRINESS
SOOTIEST	SORBATES	SORELY	SORROW
SOOTILY	SORBED	SORENESS	SORROWED
SOOTINESS	SORBENT	SORER	SORROWER
SOOTING	SORBENTS	SORES	SORROWERS
SOOTLESS	SORBET	SOREST	SORROWFUL
SOOTS	SORBETS	SOREX	SORROWING
SOOTY	SORBIC	SOREXES	SORROWS
SOP	SORBING	SORGHO	SORRY
SOPAPILLA	SORBITE	SORGHOS	SORRYISH
SOPH	SORBITES	SORGHUM	SORT
SOPHERIC	SORBITIC	SORGHUMS	SORTA
SOPHERIM	SORBITISE	SORGO	SORTABLE
SOPHIES	SORBITIZE	SORGOS	SORTABLY
SOPHISM	SORBITOL	SORI	SORTAL
SOPHISMS	SORBITOLS	SORICINE	SORTALS
SOPHIST	SORBO	SORICOID	SORTANCE
SOPHISTER	SORBOSE	SORING	SORTANCES
SOPHISTIC	SORBOSES	SORINGS	SORTATION
SOPHISTRY	SORBS	SORITES	SORTED
SOPHISTS	SORBUS	SORITIC	SORTER
SOPHOMORE	SORBUSES	SORITICAL	SORTERS
SOPHS	SORCERER	SORN	SORTES
SOPHY	SORCERERS	SORNED	SORTIE
SOPITE	SORCERESS	SORNER	SORTIED
SOPITED	SORCERIES	SORNERS	SORTIEING
SOPITES	SORCEROUS	SORNING	SORTIES
SOPITING	SORCERY	SORNINGS	SORTILEGE
SOPOR	SORD	SORNS	SORTILEGY
SOPORIFIC	SORDA	SOROBAN	SORTING
SOPOROSE	SORDES	SOROBANS	SORTINGS
SOPOROUS	SORDID	SOROCHE	SORTITION
SOPORS	SORDIDER	SOROCHES	SORTMENT
SOPPED	SORDIDEST	SORORAL	SORTMENTS
SOPPIER	SORDIDLY	SORORALLY	SORTS
SOPPIEST	SORDINE	SORORATE	SORUS
SOPPILY	SORDINES	SORORATES	SOS
SOPPINESS	SORDINI	SORORIAL	SOSATIE
SOPPING	SORDINO	SORORISE	SOSATIES
SOPPINGS	SORDO	SORORISED	SOSS
SOPPY	SORDOR	SORORISES	SOSSED
SOPRA	SORDORS	SORORITY	SOSSES
SOPRANI	SORDS	SORORIZE	SOSSING
SOPRANINI	SORE	SORORIZED	SOSSINGS
SOPRANINO	SORED	SORORIZES	SOSTENUTI
SOPRANIST	SOREDIA	SOROSES	SOSTENUTO
SOPRANO	SOREDIAL	SOROSIS	SOT

SOTERIAL
SOTH
SOTHS
SOTOL
SOTOLS
SOTS
SOTTED
SOTTEDLY
SOTTING
SOTTINGS
SOTTISH
SOTTISHLY
SOTTISIER
SOU
SOUARI
SOUARIS
SOUBISE
SOUBISES
SOUBRETTE
SOUCAR
SOUCARS
SOUCE
SOUCED
SOUCES
SOUCHONG
SOUCHONGS
SOUCING
SOUCT
SOUDAN
SOUDANS
SOUFFLE
SOUFFLED
SOUFFLEED
SOUFFLES
SOUGH
SOUGHED
SOUGHING
SOUGHS
SOUGHT
SOUK
SOUKED
SOUKING
SOUKOUS
SOUKOUSES
SOUKS
SOUL
SOULDAN
SOULDANS
SOULDIER
SOULDIERS
SOULED
SOULFUL
SOULFULLY
SOULLESS
SOULLIKE
SOULMATE
SOULMATES
SOULS

SOUM
SOUMED
SOUMING
SOUMINGS
SOUMS
SOUND
SOUNDABLE
SOUNDBITE
SOUNDBOX
SOUNDCARD
SOUNDED
SOUNDER
SOUNDERS
SOUNDEST
SOUNDING
SOUNDINGS
SOUNDLESS
SOUNDLY
SOUNDMAN
SOUNDMEN
SOUNDNESS
SOUNDPOST
SOUNDS
SOUP
SOUPCON
SOUPCONS
SOUPED
SOUPER
SOUPERS
SOUPFIN
SOUPFINS
SOUPIER
SOUPIEST
SOUPING
SOUPLE
SOUPLED
SOUPLES
SOUPLESS
SOUPLIKE
SOUPLING
SOUPS
SOUPSPOON
SOUPY
SOUR
SOURBALL
SOURBALLS
SOURCE
SOURCED
SOURCEFUL
SOURCES
SOURCING
SOURCINGS
SOURDINE
SOURDINES
SOURDOUGH
SOURED
SOURER
SOUREST

SOURING
SOURINGS
SOURISH
SOURISHLY
SOURLY
SOURNESS
SOUROCK
SOUROCKS
SOURPUSS
SOURS
SOURSE
SOURSES
SOURSOP
SOURSOPS
SOURWOOD
SOURWOODS
SOUS
SOUSE
SOUSED
SOUSES
SOUSING
SOUSINGS
SOUSLIK
SOUSLIKS
SOUT
SOUTACHE
SOUTACHES
SOUTANE
SOUTANES
SOUTAR
SOUTARS
SOUTENEUR
SOUTER
SOUTERLY
SOUTERS
SOUTH
SOUTHEAST
SOUTHED
SOUTHER
SOUTHERED
SOUTHERLY
SOUTHERN
SOUTHERNS
SOUTHERS
SOUTHING
SOUTHINGS
SOUTHLAND
SOUTHMOST
SOUTHPAW
SOUTHPAWS
SOUTHRON
SOUTHRONS
SOUTHS
SOUTHSAID
SOUTHSAY
SOUTHSAYS
SOUTHWARD
SOUTHWEST

SOUTIE
SOUTIES
SOUTPIEL
SOUTPIELS
SOUTS
SOUVENIR
SOUVENIRS
SOUVLAKI
SOUVLAKIA
SOUVLAKIS
SOV
SOVENANCE
SOVEREIGN
SOVIET
SOVIETIC
SOVIETISE
SOVIETISM
SOVIETIST
SOVIETIZE
SOVIETS
SOVKHOZ
SOVKHOZES
SOVKHOZY
SOVRAN
SOVRANLY
SOVRANS
SOVRANTY
SOVS
SOW
SOWABLE
SOWANS
SOWAR
SOWARREE
SOWARREES
SOWARRIES
SOWARRY
SOWARS
SOWBACK
SOWBACKS
SOWBELLY
SOWBREAD
SOWBREADS
SOWCAR
SOWCARS
SOWCE
SOWCED
SOWCES
SOWCING
SOWED
SOWENS
SOWER
SOWERS
SOWF
SOWFED
SOWFF
SOWFFED
SOWFFING
SOWFFS

SOWFING	SOZZLIER	SPADING	SPALDS
SOWFS	SOZZLIEST	SPADIX	SPALE
SOWING	SOZZLING	SPADIXES	SPALES
SOWINGS	SOZZLY	SPADO	SPALL
SOWL	SPA	SPADOES	SPALLABLE
SOWLE	SPACE	SPADONES	SPALLE
SOWLED	SPACEBAND	SPADOS	SPALLED
SOWLES	SPACED	SPADROON	SPALLER
SOWLING	SPACELAB	SPADROONS	SPALLERS
SOWLS	SPACELABS	SPAE	SPALLES
SOWM	SPACELESS	SPAED	SPALLING
SOWMED	SPACEMAN	SPAEING	SPALLINGS
SOWMING	SPACEMEN	SPAEINGS	SPALLS
SOWMS	SPACEPORT	SPAEMAN	SPALPEEN
SOWN	SPACER	SPAEMEN	SPALPEENS
SOWND	SPACERS	SPAER	SPALT
SOWNDED	SPACES	SPAERS	SPALTED
SOWNDING	SPACESHIP	SPAES	SPALTING
SOWNDS	SPACESUIT	SPAETZLE	SPALTS
SOWNE	SPACEWALK	SPAETZLES	SPAM
SOWNES	SPACEWARD	SPAEWIFE	SPAMBOT
SOWP	SPACEY	SPAEWIVES	SPAMBOTS
SOWPS	SPACIAL	SPAG	SPAMMED
SOWS	SPACIALLY	SPAGERIC	SPAMMER
SOWSE	SPACIER	SPAGERICS	SPAMMERS
SOWSED	SPACIEST	SPAGERIST	SPAMMIE
SOWSES	SPACINESS	SPAGGED	SPAMMIER
SOWSING	SPACING	SPAGGING	SPAMMIES
SOWSSE	SPACINGS	SPAGHETTI	SPAMMIEST
SOWSSED	SPACIOUS	SPAGIRIC	SPAMMING
SOWSSES	SPACKLE	SPAGIRICS	SPAMMINGS
SOWSSING	SPACKLED	SPAGIRIST	SPAMMY
SOWTER	SPACKLES	SPAGS	SPAMS
SOWTERS	SPACKLING	SPAGYRIC	SPAN
SOWTH	SPACY	SPAGYRICS	SPANAEMIA
SOWTHED	SPADASSIN	SPAGYRIST	SPANAEMIC
SOWTHING	SPADE	SPAHEE	SPANCEL
SOWTHS	SPADED	SPAHEES	SPANCELED
SOX	SPADEFISH	SPAHI	SPANCELS
SOY	SPADEFUL	SPAHIS	SPANDEX
SOYA	SPADEFULS	SPAIL	SPANDEXES
SOYAS	SPADELIKE	SPAILS	SPANDREL
SOYBEAN	SPADEMAN	SPAIN	SPANDRELS
SOYBEANS	SPADEMEN	SPAINED	SPANDRIL
SOYLE	SPADER	SPAING	SPANDRILS
SOYLES	SPADERS	SPAINGS	SPANE
SOYMILK	SPADES	SPAINING	SPANED
SOYMILKS	SPADESMAN	SPAINS	SPANES
SOYS	SPADESMEN	SPAIRGE	SPANG
SOYUZ	SPADEWORK	SPAIRGED	SPANGED
SOYUZES	SPADGER	SPAIRGES	SPANGHEW
SOZIN	SPADGERS	SPAIRGING	SPANGHEWS
SOZINE	SPADICES	SPAIT	SPANGING
SOZINES	SPADILLE	SPAITS	SPANGLE
SOZINS	SPADILLES	SPAKE	SPANGLED
SOZZLE	SPADILLIO	SPALD	SPANGLER
SOZZLED	SPADILLO	SPALDEEN	SPANGLERS
SOZZLES	SPADILLOS	SPALDEENS	SPANGLES

SPANGLET

SPANGLET	SPARKER	SPARTINA	SPAWLING
SPANGLETS	SPARKERS	SPARTINAS	SPAWLS
SPANGLIER	SPARKES	SPARTS	SPAWN
SPANGLING	SPARKIE	SPAS	SPAWNED
SPANGLY	SPARKIER	SPASM	SPAWNER
SPANGS	SPARKIES	SPASMATIC	SPAWNERS
SPANIEL	SPARKIEST	SPASMED	SPAWNIER
SPANIELS	SPARKILY	SPASMIC	SPAWNIEST
SPANING	SPARKING	SPASMING	SPAWNING
SPANK	SPARKISH	SPASMODIC	SPAWNINGS
SPANKED	SPARKLE	SPASMS	SPAWNS
SPANKER	SPARKLED	SPASTIC	SPAWNY
SPANKERS	SPARKLER	SPASTICS	SPAWS
SPANKING	SPARKLERS	SPAT	SPAY
SPANKINGS	SPARKLES	SPATE	SPAYAD
SPANKS	SPARKLESS	SPATES	SPAYADS
SPANLESS	SPARKLET	SPATFALL	SPAYD
SPANNED	SPARKLETS	SPATFALLS	SPAYDS
SPANNER	SPARKLIER	SPATHAL	SPAYED
SPANNERS	SPARKLIES	SPATHE	SPAYING
SPANNING	SPARKLING	SPATHED	SPAYS
SPANS	SPARKLY	SPATHES	SPAZ
SPANSPEK	SPARKPLUG	SPATHIC	SPAZA
SPANSPEKS	SPARKS	SPATHOSE	SPAZZ
SPANSULE	SPARKY	SPATIAL	SPAZZED
SPANSULES	SPARLIKE	SPATIALLY	SPAZZES
SPANWORM	SPARLING	SPATLESE	SPAZZING
SPANWORMS	SPARLINGS	SPATLESEN	SPEAK
SPAR	SPAROID	SPATLESES	SPEAKABLE
SPARABLE	SPAROIDS	SPATS	SPEAKEASY
SPARABLES	SPARRE	SPATTED	SPEAKER
SPARAXIS	SPARRED	SPATTEE	SPEAKERS
SPARD	SPARRER	SPATTEES	SPEAKING
SPARE	SPARRERS	SPATTER	SPEAKINGS
SPAREABLE	SPARRES	SPATTERED	SPEAKOUT
SPARED	SPARRIER	SPATTERS	SPEAKOUTS
SPARELESS	SPARRIEST	SPATTING	SPEAKS
SPARELY	SPARRING	SPATULA	SPEAL
SPARENESS	SPARRINGS	SPATULAR	SPEALS
SPARER	SPARROW	SPATULAS	SPEAN
SPARERIB	SPARROWS	SPATULATE	SPEANED
SPARERIBS	SPARRY	SPATULE	SPEANING
SPARERS	SPARS	SPATULES	SPEANS
SPARES	SPARSE	SPATZLE	SPEAR
SPAREST	SPARSEDLY	SPATZLES	SPEARED
SPARGE	SPARSELY	SPAUL	SPEARER
SPARGED	SPARSER	SPAULD	SPEARERS
SPARGER	SPARSEST	SPAULDS	SPEARFISH
SPARGERS	SPARSITY	SPAULS	SPEARGUN
SPARGES	SPART	SPAVIE	SPEARGUNS
SPARGING	SPARTAN	SPAVIES	SPEARHEAD
SPARID	SPARTANS	SPAVIET	SPEARIER
SPARIDS	SPARTEINE	SPAVIN	SPEARIEST
SPARING	SPARTERIE	SPAVINED	SPEARING
SPARINGLY	SPARTH	SPAVINS	SPEARLIKE
SPARK	SPARTHE	SPAW	SPEARMAN
SPARKE	SPARTHES	SPAWL	SPEARMEN
SPARKED	SPARTHS	SPAWLED	SPEARMINT

SPEARS
SPEARWORT
SPEARY
SPEAT
SPEATS
SPEC
SPECCED
SPECCIES
SPECCING
SPECCY
SPECIAL
SPECIALER
SPECIALLY
SPECIALS
SPECIALTY
SPECIATE
SPECIATED
SPECIATES
SPECIE
SPECIES
SPECIFIC
SPECIFICS
SPECIFIED
SPECIFIER
SPECIFIES
SPECIFY
SPECIMEN
SPECIMENS
SPECIOUS
SPECK
SPECKED
SPECKIER
SPECKIEST
SPECKING
SPECKLE
SPECKLED
SPECKLES
SPECKLESS
SPECKLING
SPECKS
SPECKY
SPECS
SPECTACLE
SPECTATE
SPECTATED
SPECTATES
SPECTATOR
SPECTER
SPECTERS
SPECTRA
SPECTRAL
SPECTRE
SPECTRES
SPECTRIN
SPECTRINS
SPECTRUM
SPECTRUMS
SPECULA

SPECULAR
SPECULATE
SPECULUM
SPECULUMS
SPED
SPEECH
SPEECHED
SPEECHES
SPEECHFUL
SPEECHIFY
SPEECHING
SPEED
SPEEDBALL
SPEEDBOAT
SPEEDED
SPEEDER
SPEEDERS
SPEEDFUL
SPEEDIER
SPEEDIEST
SPEEDILY
SPEEDING
SPEEDINGS
SPEEDLESS
SPEEDO
SPEEDOS
SPEEDREAD
SPEEDS
SPEEDSTER
SPEEDUP
SPEEDUPS
SPEEDWAY
SPEEDWAYS
SPEEDWELL
SPEEDY
SPEEL
SPEELED
SPEELER
SPEELERS
SPEELING
SPEELS
SPEER
SPEERED
SPEERING
SPEERINGS
SPEERS
SPEIL
SPEILED
SPEILING
SPEILS
SPEIR
SPEIRED
SPEIRING
SPEIRINGS
SPEIRS
SPEISE
SPEISES
SPEISS

SPEISSES
SPEK
SPEKBOOM
SPEKBOOMS
SPEKS
SPELAEAN
SPELD
SPELDED
SPELDER
SPELDERED
SPELDERS
SPELDIN
SPELDING
SPELDINGS
SPELDINS
SPELDRIN
SPELDRING
SPELDRINS
SPELDS
SPELEAN
SPELK
SPELKS
SPELL
SPELLABLE
SPELLBIND
SPELLDOWN
SPELLED
SPELLER
SPELLERS
SPELLFUL
SPELLICAN
SPELLING
SPELLINGS
SPELLS
SPELT
SPELTER
SPELTERS
SPELTS
SPELTZ
SPELTZES
SPELUNK
SPELUNKED
SPELUNKER
SPELUNKS
SPENCE
SPENCER
SPENCERS
SPENCES
SPEND
SPENDABLE
SPENDALL
SPENDALLS
SPENDER
SPENDERS
SPENDIER
SPENDIEST
SPENDING
SPENDINGS

SPENDS
SPENDY
SPENSE
SPENSES
SPENT
SPEOS
SPEOSES
SPERLING
SPERLINGS
SPERM
SPERMARIA
SPERMARY
SPERMATIA
SPERMATIC
SPERMATID
SPERMIC
SPERMINE
SPERMINES
SPERMOUS
SPERMS
SPERRE
SPERRED
SPERRES
SPERRING
SPERSE
SPERSED
SPERSES
SPERSING
SPERST
SPERTHE
SPERTHES
SPET
SPETCH
SPETCHES
SPETS
SPETSNAZ
SPETTING
SPETZNAZ
SPEUG
SPEUGS
SPEW
SPEWED
SPEWER
SPEWERS
SPEWIER
SPEWIEST
SPEWINESS
SPEWING
SPEWS
SPEWY
SPHACELUS
SPHAER
SPHAERE
SPHAERES
SPHAERITE
SPHAERS
SPHAGNOUS
SPHAGNUM

SPHAGNUMS	SPICERY	SPIFFS	SPILT
SPHAIREE	SPICES	SPIFFY	SPILTH
SPHAIREES	SPICEY	SPIFFYING	SPILTHS
SPHEAR	SPICIER	SPIFS	SPIM
SPHEARE	SPICIEST	SPIGHT	SPIMS
SPHEARES	SPICILEGE	SPIGHTED	SPIN
SPHEARS	SPICILY	SPIGHTING	SPINA
SPHENDONE	SPICINESS	SPIGHTS	SPINACENE
SPHENE	SPICING	SPIGNEL	SPINACH
SPHENES	SPICK	SPIGNELS	SPINACHES
SPHENIC	SPICKER	SPIGOT	SPINACHY
SPHENODON	SPICKEST	SPIGOTS	SPINAE
SPHENOID	SPICKNEL	SPIK	SPINAGE
SPHENOIDS	SPICKNELS	SPIKE	SPINAGES
SPHERAL	SPICKS	SPIKED	SPINAL
SPHERE	SPICS	SPIKEFISH	SPINALLY
SPHERED	SPICULA	SPIKELET	SPINALS
SPHERES	SPICULAE	SPIKELETS	SPINAR
SPHERIC	SPICULAR	SPIKELIKE	SPINARS
SPHERICAL	SPICULATE	SPIKENARD	SPINAS
SPHERICS	SPICULE	SPIKER	SPINATE
SPHERIER	SPICULES	SPIKERIES	SPINDLE
SPHERIEST	SPICULUM	SPIKERS	SPINDLED
SPHERING	SPICY	SPIKERY	SPINDLER
SPHEROID	SPIDE	SPIKES	SPINDLERS
SPHEROIDS	SPIDER	SPIKEY	SPINDLES
SPHERULAR	SPIDERIER	SPIKIER	SPINDLIER
SPHERULE	SPIDERISH	SPIKIEST	SPINDLING
SPHERULES	SPIDERMAN	SPIKILY	SPINDLY
SPHERY	SPIDERMEN	SPIKINESS	SPINDRIFT
SPHINCTER	SPIDERS	SPIKING	SPINE
SPHINGES	SPIDERWEB	SPIKS	SPINED
SPHINGID	SPIDERY	SPIKY	SPINEL
SPHINGIDS	SPIDES	SPILE	SPINELESS
SPHINX	SPIE	SPILED	SPINELIKE
SPHINXES	SPIED	SPILES	SPINELLE
SPHYGMIC	SPIEGEL	SPILIKIN	SPINELLES
SPHYGMOID	SPIEGELS	SPILIKINS	SPINELS
SPHYGMUS	SPIEL	SPILING	SPINES
SPHYNX	SPIELED	SPILINGS	SPINET
SPHYNXES	SPIELER	SPILITE	SPINETS
SPIAL	SPIELERS	SPILITES	SPINETTE
SPIALS	SPIELING	SPILITIC	SPINETTES
SPIC	SPIELS	SPILL	SPINIER
SPICA	SPIER	SPILLABLE	SPINIEST
SPICAE	SPIERED	SPILLAGE	SPINIFEX
SPICAS	SPIERING	SPILLAGES	SPINIFORM
SPICATE	SPIERS	SPILLED	SPININESS
SPICATED	SPIES	SPILLER	SPINK
SPICCATO	SPIF	SPILLERS	SPINKS
SPICCATOS	SPIFF	SPILLIKIN	SPINLESS
SPICE	SPIFFED	SPILLING	SPINNAKER
SPICEBUSH	SPIFFIED	SPILLINGS	SPINNER
SPICED	SPIFFIER	SPILLOVER	SPINNERET
SPICELESS	SPIFFIES	SPILLS	SPINNERS
SPICER	SPIFFIEST	SPILLWAY	SPINNERY
SPICERIES	SPIFFILY	SPILLWAYS	SPINNET
SPICERS	SPIFFING	SPILOSITE	SPINNETS

SPINNEY	SPIRELESS	SPITING	SPLENIA
SPINNEYS	SPIRELET	SPITS	SPLENIAL
SPINNIES	SPIRELETS	SPITTED	SPLENIC
SPINNING	SPIREM	SPITTEN	SPLENII
SPINNINGS	SPIREME	SPITTER	SPLENITIS
SPINNY	SPIREMES	SPITTERS	SPLENIUM
SPINODE	SPIREMS	SPITTING	SPLENIUMS
SPINODES	SPIRES	SPITTINGS	SPLENIUS
SPINOFF	SPIREWISE	SPITTLE	SPLENT
SPINOFFS	SPIRIC	SPITTLES	SPLENTS
SPINONE	SPIRICS	SPITTOON	SPLEUCHAN
SPINONI	SPIRIER	SPITTOONS	SPLICE
SPINOR	SPIRIEST	SPITZ	SPLICED
SPINORS	SPIRILLA	SPITZES	SPLICER
SPINOSE	SPIRILLAR	SPIV	SPLICERS
SPINOSELY	SPIRILLUM	SPIVS	SPLICES
SPINOSITY	SPIRING	SPIVVERY	SPLICING
SPINOUS	SPIRIT	SPIVVIER	SPLIFF
SPINOUT	SPIRITED	SPIVVIEST	SPLIFFS
SPINOUTS	SPIRITFUL	SPIVVY	SPLINE
SPINS	SPIRITING	SPLAKE	SPLINED
SPINSTER	SPIRITISM	SPLAKES	SPLINES
SPINSTERS	SPIRITIST	SPLASH	SPLINING
SPINTEXT	SPIRITOSO	SPLASHED	SPLINT
SPINTEXTS	SPIRITOUS	SPLASHER	SPLINTED
SPINTO	SPIRITS	SPLASHERS	SPLINTER
SPINTOS	SPIRITUAL	SPLASHES	SPLINTERS
SPINULA	SPIRITUEL	SPLASHIER	SPLINTERY
SPINULAE	SPIRITUS	SPLASHILY	SPLINTING
SPINULATE	SPIRITY	SPLASHING	SPLINTS
SPINULE	SPIRLING	SPLASHY	SPLIT
SPINULES	SPIRLINGS	SPLAT	SPLITS
SPINULOSE	SPIROGRAM	SPLATCH	SPLITTED
SPINULOUS	SPIROGYRA	SPLATCHED	SPLITTER
SPINY	SPIROID	SPLATCHES	SPLITTERS
SPIRACLE	SPIRT	SPLATS	SPLITTING
SPIRACLES	SPIRTED	SPLATTED	SPLODGE
SPIRACULA	SPIRTING	SPLATTER	SPLODGED
SPIRAEA	SPIRTLE	SPLATTERS	SPLODGES
SPIRAEAS	SPIRTLES	SPLATTING	SPLODGIER
SPIRAL	SPIRTS	SPLAY	SPLODGILY
SPIRALED	SPIRULA	SPLAYED	SPLODGING
SPIRALING	SPIRULAE	SPLAYFEET	SPLODGY
SPIRALISM	SPIRULAS	SPLAYFOOT	SPLOOSH
SPIRALIST	SPIRULINA	SPLAYING	SPLOOSHED
SPIRALITY	SPIRY	SPLAYS	SPLOOSHES
SPIRALLED	SPIT	SPLEEN	SPLORE
SPIRALLY	SPITAL	SPLEENFUL	SPLORES
SPIRALS	SPITALS	SPLEENIER	SPLOSH
SPIRANT	SPITBALL	SPLEENISH	SPLOSHED
SPIRANTS	SPITBALLS	SPLEENS	SPLOSHES
SPIRASTER	SPITCHER	SPLEENY	SPLOSHING
SPIRATED	SPITE	SPLENDENT	SPLOTCH
SPIRATION	SPITED	SPLENDID	SPLOTCHED
SPIRE	SPITEFUL	SPLENDOR	SPLOTCHES
SPIREA	SPITES	SPLENDORS	SPLOTCHY
SPIREAS	SPITFIRE	SPLENDOUR	SPLURGE
SPIRED	SPITFIRES	SPLENETIC	SPLURGED

SPLURGER	SPONGEBAG	SPOOMING	SPORTED
SPLURGERS	SPONGED	SPOOMS	SPORTER
SPLURGES	SPONGEOUS	SPOON	SPORTERS
SPLURGIER	SPONGER	SPOONBAIT	SPORTFUL
SPLURGING	SPONGERS	SPOONBILL	SPORTIER
SPLURGY	SPONGES	SPOONED	SPORTIES
SPLUTTER	SPONGIER	SPOONEY	SPORTIEST
SPLUTTERS	SPONGIEST	SPOONEYS	SPORTIF
SPLUTTERY	SPONGILY	SPOONFED	SPORTILY
SPOD	SPONGIN	SPOONFUL	SPORTING
SPODDIER	SPONGING	SPOONFULS	SPORTIVE
SPODDIEST	SPONGINS	SPOONIER	SPORTLESS
SPODDY	SPONGIOSE	SPOONIES	SPORTS
SPODE	SPONGIOUS	SPOONIEST	SPORTSMAN
SPODES	SPONGOID	SPOONILY	SPORTSMEN
SPODIUM	SPONGY	SPOONING	SPORTY
SPODIUMS	SPONSAL	SPOONS	SPORULAR
SPODOGRAM	SPONSALIA	SPOONSFUL	SPORULATE
SPODOSOL	SPONSIBLE	SPOONWAYS	SPORULE
SPODOSOLS	SPONSING	SPOONWISE	SPORULES
SPODS	SPONSINGS	SPOONY	SPOSH
SPODUMENE	SPONSION	SPOOR	SPOSHES
SPOFFISH	SPONSIONS	SPOORED	SPOSHIER
SPOFFY	SPONSON	SPOORER	SPOSHIEST
SPOIL	SPONSONS	SPOORERS	SPOSHY
SPOILABLE	SPONSOR	SPOORING	SPOT
SPOILAGE	SPONSORED	SPOORS	SPOTLESS
SPOILAGES	SPONSORS	SPOOT	SPOTLIGHT
SPOILED	SPONTOON	SPOOTS	SPOTLIT
SPOILER	SPONTOONS	SPORADIC	SPOTS
SPOILERS	SPOOF	SPORAL	SPOTTABLE
SPOILFIVE	SPOOFED	SPORANGIA	SPOTTED
SPOILFUL	SPOOFER	SPORE	SPOTTER
SPOILING	SPOOFERS	SPORED	SPOTTERS
SPOILS	SPOOFERY	SPORES	SPOTTIE
SPOILSMAN	SPOOFING	SPORICIDE	SPOTTIER
SPOILSMEN	SPOOFINGS	SPORIDESM	SPOTTIES
SPOILT	SPOOFS	SPORIDIA	SPOTTIEST
SPOKE	SPOOFY	SPORIDIAL	SPOTTILY
SPOKED	SPOOK	SPORIDIUM	SPOTTING
SPOKEN	SPOOKED	SPORING	SPOTTINGS
SPOKES	SPOOKERY	SPOROCARP	SPOTTY
SPOKESMAN	SPOOKIER	SPOROCYST	SPOUSAGE
SPOKESMEN	SPOOKIEST	SPOROCYTE	SPOUSAGES
SPOKEWISE	SPOOKILY	SPOROGENY	SPOUSAL
SPOKING	SPOOKING	SPOROGONY	SPOUSALLY
SPOLIATE	SPOOKISH	SPOROID	SPOUSALS
SPOLIATED	SPOOKS	SPOROPHYL	SPOUSE
SPOLIATES	SPOOKY	SPOROZOA	SPOUSED
SPOLIATOR	SPOOL	SPOROZOAL	SPOUSES
SPONDAIC	SPOOLED	SPOROZOAN	SPOUSING
SPONDAICS	SPOOLER	SPOROZOIC	SPOUT
SPONDEE	SPOOLERS	SPOROZOON	SPOUTED
SPONDEES	SPOOLING	SPORRAN	SPOUTER
SPONDULIX	SPOOLINGS	SPORRANS	SPOUTERS
SPONDYL	SPOOLS	SPORT	SPOUTIER
SPONDYLS	SPOOM	SPORTABLE	SPOUTIEST
SPONGE	SPOOMED	SPORTANCE	SPOUTING

SPOUTINGS	SPREAGH	SPRINGES	SPRUGS
SPOUTLESS	SPREAGHS	SPRINGIER	SPRUIK
SPOUTS	SPREATHE	SPRINGILY	SPRUIKED
SPOUTY	SPREATHED	SPRINGING	SPRUIKER
SPRACK	SPREATHES	SPRINGLE	SPRUIKERS
SPRACKLE	SPREAZE	SPRINGLES	SPRUIKING
SPRACKLED	SPREAZED	SPRINGLET	SPRUIKS
SPRACKLES	SPREAZES	SPRINGS	SPRUIT
SPRAD	SPREAZING	SPRINGY	SPRUITS
SPRADDLE	SPRECHERY	SPRINKLE	SPRUNG
SPRADDLED	SPRECKLED	SPRINKLED	SPRUSH
SPRADDLES	SPRED	SPRINKLER	SPRUSHED
SPRAG	SPREDD	SPRINKLES	SPRUSHES
SPRAGGED	SPREDDE	SPRINT	SPRUSHING
SPRAGGING	SPREDDEN	SPRINTED	SPRY
SPRAGS	SPREDDES	SPRINTER	SPRYER
SPRAID	SPREDDING	SPRINTERS	SPRYEST
SPRAIN	SPREDDS	SPRINTING	SPRYLY
SPRAINED	SPREDS	SPRINTS	SPRYNESS
SPRAINING	SPREE	SPRIT	SPUD
SPRAINS	SPREED	SPRITE	SPUDDED
SPRAINT	SPREEING	SPRITEFUL	SPUDDER
SPRAINTS	SPREES	SPRITELY	SPUDDERS
SPRANG	SPREETHE	SPRITES	SPUDDIER
SPRANGLE	SPREETHED	SPRITS	SPUDDIEST
SPRANGLED	SPREETHES	SPRITSAIL	SPUDDING
SPRANGLES	SPREEZE	SPRITZ	SPUDDINGS
SPRANGS	SPREEZED	SPRITZED	SPUDDLE
SPRAT	SPREEZES	SPRITZER	SPUDDLES
SPRATS	SPREEZING	SPRITZERS	SPUDDY
SPRATTLE	SPREKELIA	SPRITZES	SPUDS
SPRATTLED	SPRENT	SPRITZIG	SPUE
SPRATTLES	SPREW	SPRITZIGS	SPUED
SPRAUCHLE	SPREWS	SPRITZING	SPUEING
SPRAUNCY	SPRIER	SPROCKET	SPUER
SPRAWL	SPRIEST	SPROCKETS	SPUERS
SPRAWLED	SPRIG	SPROD	SPUES
SPRAWLER	SPRIGGED	SPRODS	SPUG
SPRAWLERS	SPRIGGER	SPROG	SPUGGIES
SPRAWLIER	SPRIGGERS	SPROGS	SPUGGY
SPRAWLING	SPRIGGIER	SPRONG	SPUGS
SPRAWLS	SPRIGGING	SPROUT	SPUILZIE
SPRAWLY	SPRIGGY	SPROUTED	SPUILZIED
SPRAY	SPRIGHT	SPROUTING	SPUILZIES
SPRAYED	SPRIGHTED	SPROUTS	SPUING
SPRAYER	SPRIGHTLY	SPRUCE	SPULE
SPRAYERS	SPRIGHTS	SPRUCED	SPULES
SPRAYEY	SPRIGS	SPRUCELY	SPULYE
SPRAYIER	SPRIGTAIL	SPRUCER	SPULYED
SPRAYIEST	SPRING	SPRUCES	SPULYEING
SPRAYING	SPRINGAL	SPRUCEST	SPULYES
SPRAYINGS	SPRINGALD	SPRUCIER	SPULYIE
SPRAYS	SPRINGALS	SPRUCIEST	SPULYIED
SPREAD	SPRINGBOK	SPRUCING	SPULYIES
SPREADER	SPRINGE	SPRUCY	SPULZIE
SPREADERS	SPRINGED	SPRUE	SPULZIED
SPREADING	SPRINGER	SPRUES	SPULZIES
SPREADS	SPRINGERS	SPRUG	SPUMANTE

SPUMANTES	SPURRY	SQUADRON	SQUARSON
SPUME	SPURS	SQUADRONE	SQUARSONS
SPUMED	SPURT	SQUADRONS	SQUASH
SPUMES	SPURTED	SQUADS	SQUASHED
SPUMIER	SPURTER	SQUAIL	SQUASHER
SPUMIEST	SPURTERS	SQUAILED	SQUASHERS
SPUMING	SPURTING	SQUAILER	SQUASHES
SPUMONE	SPURTLE	SQUAILERS	SQUASHIER
SPUMONES	SPURTLES	SQUAILING	SQUASHILY
SPUMONI	SPURTS	SQUAILS	SQUASHING
SPUMONIS	SPURWAY	SQUALENE	SQUASHY
SPUMOUS	SPURWAYS	SQUALENES	SQUAT
SPUMY	SPUTA	SQUALID	SQUATLY
SPUN	SPUTNIK	SQUALIDER	SQUATNESS
SPUNGE	SPUTNIKS	SQUALIDLY	SQUATS
SPUNGES	SPUTTER	SQUALL	SQUATTED
SPUNK	SPUTTERED	SQUALLED	SQUATTER
SPUNKED	SPUTTERER	SQUALLER	SQUATTERS
SPUNKIE	SPUTTERS	SQUALLERS	SQUATTEST
SPUNKIER	SPUTTERY	SQUALLIER	SQUATTIER
SPUNKIES	SPUTUM	SQUALLING	SQUATTILY
SPUNKIEST	SPY	SQUALLISH	SQUATTING
SPUNKILY	SPYAL	SQUALLS	SQUATTLE
SPUNKING	SPYALS	SQUALLY	SQUATTLED
SPUNKS	SPYGLASS	SQUALOID	SQUATTLES
SPUNKY	SPYHOLE	SQUALOR	SQUATTY
SPUNYARN	SPYHOLES	SQUALORS	SQUAW
SPUNYARNS	SPYING	SQUAMA	SQUAWBUSH
SPUR	SPYINGS	SQUAMAE	SQUAWFISH
SPURGALL	SPYMASTER	SQUAMATE	SQUAWK
SPURGALLS	SPYPLANE	SQUAMATES	SQUAWKED
SPURGE	SPYPLANES	SQUAME	SQUAWKER
SPURGES	SPYRE	SQUAMELLA	SQUAWKERS
SPURIAE	SPYRES	SQUAMES	SQUAWKIER
SPURIOUS	SPYWARE	SQUAMOSAL	SQUAWKING
SPURLESS	SPYWARES	SQUAMOSE	SQUAWKS
SPURLING	SQUAB	SQUAMOUS	SQUAWKY
SPURLINGS	SQUABASH	SQUAMULA	SQUAWMAN
SPURN	SQUABBED	SQUAMULAS	SQUAWMEN
SPURNE	SQUABBER	SQUAMULE	SQUAWROOT
SPURNED	SQUABBEST	SQUAMULES	SQUAWS
SPURNER	SQUABBIER	SQUANDER	SQUEAK
SPURNERS	SQUABBING	SQUANDERS	SQUEAKED
SPURNES	SQUABBISH	SQUARE	SQUEAKER
SPURNING	SQUABBLE	SQUARED	SQUEAKERS
SPURNINGS	SQUABBLED	SQUARELY	SQUEAKERY
SPURNS	SQUABBLER	SQUARER	SQUEAKIER
SPURRED	SQUABBLES	SQUARERS	SQUEAKILY
SPURRER	SQUABBY	SQUARES	SQUEAKING
SPURRERS	SQUABS	SQUAREST	SQUEAKS
SPURREY	SQUACCO	SQUARIAL	SQUEAKY
SPURREYS	SQUACCOS	SQUARIALS	SQUEAL
SPURRIER	SQUAD	SQUARING	SQUEALED
SPURRIERS	SQUADDED	SQUARINGS	SQUEALER
SPURRIES	SQUADDIE	SQUARISH	SQUEALERS
SPURRIEST	SQUADDIES	SQUARK	SQUEALING
SPURRING	SQUADDING	SQUARKS	SQUEALS
SPURRINGS	SQUADDY	SQUARROSE	SQUEAMISH

SQUEEGEE	SQUINANCY	SQUISHED	STACKABLE
SQUEEGEED	SQUINCH	SQUISHES	STACKED
SQUEEGEES	SQUINCHED	SQUISHIER	STACKER
SQUEEZE	SQUINCHES	SQUISHING	STACKERS
SQUEEZED	SQUINIED	SQUISHY	STACKET
SQUEEZER	SQUINIES	SQUIT	STACKETS
SQUEEZERS	SQUINNIED	SQUITCH	STACKING
SQUEEZES	SQUINNIER	SQUITCHES	STACKINGS
SQUEEZIER	SQUINNIES	SQUITS	STACKLESS
SQUEEZING	SQUINNY	SQUIZ	STACKROOM
SQUEEZY	SQUINT	SQUIZZES	STACKS
SQUEG	SQUINTED	SQUOOSH	STACKUP
SQUEGGED	SQUINTER	SQUOOSHED	STACKUPS
SQUEGGER	SQUINTERS	SQUOOSHES	STACKYARD
SQUEGGERS	SQUINTEST	SQUOOSHY	STACTE
SQUEGGING	SQUINTIER	SQUUSH	STACTES
SQUEGS	SQUINTING	SQUUSHED	STADDA
SQUELCH	SQUINTS	SQUUSHES	STADDAS
SQUELCHED	SQUINTY	SQUUSHING	STADDLE
SQUELCHER	SQUINY	SRADDHA	STADDLES
SQUELCHES	SQUINYING	SRADDHAS	STADE
SQUELCHY	SQUIRAGE	SRADHA	STADES
SQUIB	SQUIRAGES	SRADHAS	STADIA
SQUIBBED	SQUIRALTY	SRI	STADIAL
SQUIBBING	SQUIRARCH	SRIS	STADIALS
SQUIBS	SQUIRE	ST	STADIAS
SQUID	SQUIREAGE	STAB	STADIUM
SQUIDDED	SQUIRED	STABBED	STADIUMS
SQUIDDING	SQUIREDOM	STABBER	STAFF
SQUIDGE	SQUIREEN	STABBERS	STAFFAGE
SQUIDGED	SQUIREENS	STABBING	STAFFAGES
SQUIDGES	SQUIRELY	STABBINGS	STAFFED
SQUIDGIER	SQUIRES	STABILATE	STAFFER
SQUIDGING	SQUIRESS	STABILE	STAFFERS
SQUIDGY	SQUIRING	STABILES	STAFFING
SQUIDS	SQUIRISH	STABILISE	STAFFMAN
SQUIER	SQUIRM	STABILITY	STAFFMEN
SQUIERS	SQUIRMED	STABILIZE	STAFFROOM
SQUIFF	SQUIRMER	STABLE	STAFFS
SQUIFFED	SQUIRMERS	STABLEBOY	STAG
SQUIFFER	SQUIRMIER	STABLED	STAGE
SQUIFFERS	SQUIRMING	STABLEMAN	STAGEABLE
SQUIFFIER	SQUIRMS	STABLEMEN	STAGED
SQUIFFY	SQUIRMY	STABLER	STAGEFUL
SQUIGGLE	SQUIRR	STABLERS	STAGEFULS
SQUIGGLED	SQUIRRED	STABLES	STAGEHAND
SQUIGGLER	SQUIRREL	STABLEST	STAGELIKE
SQUIGGLES	SQUIRRELS	STABLING	STAGER
SQUIGGLY	SQUIRRELY	STABLINGS	STAGERIES
SQUILGEE	SQUIRRING	STABLISH	STAGERS
SQUILGEED	SQUIRRS	STABLY	STAGERY
SQUILGEES	SQUIRT	STABS	STAGES
SQUILL	SQUIRTED	STACCATI	STAGEY
SQUILLA	SQUIRTER	STACCATO	STAGGARD
SQUILLAE	SQUIRTERS	STACCATOS	STAGGARDS
SQUILLAS	SQUIRTING	STACHYS	STAGGART
SQUILLION	SQUIRTS	STACHYSES	STAGGARTS
SQUILLS	SQUISH	STACK	STAGGED

STAGGER	STAITH	STAMINEAL	STANDOFFS
STAGGERED	STAITHE	STAMINODE	STANDOUT
STAGGERER	STAITHES	STAMINODY	STANDOUTS
STAGGERS	STAITHS	STAMINOID	STANDOVER
STAGGERY	STAKE	STAMMEL	STANDPAT
STAGGIE	STAKED	STAMMELS	STANDPIPE
STAGGIER	STAKEOUT	STAMMER	STANDS
STAGGIES	STAKEOUTS	STAMMERED	STANDUP
STAGGIEST	STAKES	STAMMERER	STANDUPS
STAGGING	STAKING	STAMMERS	STANE
STAGGY	STALACTIC	STAMNOI	STANED
STAGHORN	STALAG	STAMNOS	STANES
STAGHOUND	STALAGS	STAMP	STANG
STAGIER	STALE	STAMPED	STANGED
STAGIEST	STALED	STAMPEDE	STANGING
STAGILY	STALELY	STAMPEDED	STANGS
STAGINESS	STALEMATE	STAMPEDER	STANHOPE
STAGING	STALENESS	STAMPEDES	STANHOPES
STAGINGS	STALER	STAMPEDO	STANIEL
STAGNANCE	STALES	STAMPEDOS	STANIELS
STAGNANCY	STALEST	STAMPER	STANINE
STAGNANT	STALING	STAMPERS	STANINES
STAGNATE	STALK	STAMPING	STANING
STAGNATED	STALKED	STAMPINGS	STANK
STAGNATES	STALKER	STAMPLESS	STANKED
STAGS	STALKERS	STAMPS	STANKING
STAGY	STALKIER	STANCE	STANKS
STAID	STALKIEST	STANCES	STANNARY
STAIDER	STALKILY	STANCH	STANNATE
STAIDEST	STALKING	STANCHED	STANNATES
STAIDLY	STALKINGS	STANCHEL	STANNATOR
STAIDNESS	STALKLESS	STANCHELS	STANNEL
STAIG	STALKLIKE	STANCHER	STANNELS
STAIGS	STALKO	STANCHERS	STANNIC
STAIN	STALKOES	STANCHES	STANNITE
STAINABLE	STALKS	STANCHEST	STANNITES
STAINED	STALKY	STANCHING	STANNOUS
STAINER	STALL	STANCHION	STANNUM
STAINERS	STALLAGE	STANCHLY	STANNUMS
STAINING	STALLAGES	STANCK	STANOL
STAININGS	STALLED	STAND	STANOLS
STAINLESS	STALLING	STANDARD	STANYEL
STAINS	STALLINGS	STANDARDS	STANYELS
STAIR	STALLION	STANDAWAY	STANZA
STAIRCASE	STALLIONS	STANDBY	STANZAED
STAIRED	STALLMAN	STANDBYS	STANZAIC
STAIRFOOT	STALLMEN	STANDDOWN	STANZAS
STAIRHEAD	STALLS	STANDEE	STANZE
STAIRLESS	STALWART	STANDEES	STANZES
STAIRLIFT	STALWARTS	STANDEN	STANZO
STAIRLIKE	STALWORTH	STANDER	STANZOES
STAIRS	STAMEN	STANDERS	STANZOS
STAIRSTEP	STAMENED	STANDFAST	STAP
STAIRWAY	STAMENS	STANDGALE	STAPEDES
STAIRWAYS	STAMINA	STANDING	STAPEDIAL
STAIRWELL	STAMINAL	STANDINGS	STAPEDII
STAIRWISE	STAMINAS	STANDISH	STAPEDIUS
STAIRWORK	STAMINATE	STANDOFF	STAPELIA

STAPELIAS	STARKERS	STARTSY	STATIONAL
STAPES	STARKEST	STARTUP	STATIONED
STAPH	STARKING	STARTUPS	STATIONER
STAPHS	STARKLY	STARVE	STATIONS
STAPLE	STARKNESS	STARVED	STATISM
STAPLED	STARKS	STARVER	STATISMS
STAPLER	STARLESS	STARVERS	STATIST
STAPLERS	STARLET	STARVES	STATISTIC
STAPLES	STARLETS	STARVING	STATISTS
STAPLING	STARLIGHT	STARVINGS	STATIVE
STAPPED	STARLIKE	STARWORT	STATIVES
STAPPING	STARLING	STARWORTS	STATOCYST
STAPPLE	STARLINGS	STASES	STATOLITH
STAPPLES	STARLIT	STASH	STATOR
STAPS	STARN	STASHED	STATORS
STAR	STARNED	STASHES	STATS
STARAGEN	STARNIE	STASHIE	STATUA
STARAGENS	STARNIES	STASHIES	STATUARY
STARBOARD	STARNING	STASHING	STATUAS
STARBURST	STARNOSE	STASIDION	STATUE
STARCH	STARNOSES	STASIMA	STATUED
STARCHED	STARNS	STASIMON	STATUES
STARCHER	STAROSTA	STASIS	STATUETTE
STARCHERS	STAROSTAS	STAT	STATURE
STARCHES	STAROSTY	STATABLE	STATURED
STARCHIER	STARR	STATAL	STATURES
STARCHILY	STARRED	STATANT	STATUS
STARCHING	STARRIER	STATE	STATUSES
STARCHY	STARRIEST	STATEABLE	STATUSY
STARDOM	STARRILY	STATED	STATUTE
STARDOMS	STARRING	STATEDLY	STATUTES
STARDRIFT	STARRINGS	STATEHOOD	STATUTORY
STARDUST	STARRS	STATELESS	STAUMREL
STARDUSTS	STARRY	STATELET	STAUMRELS
STARE	STARS	STATELETS	STAUN
STARED	STARSHINE	STATELIER	STAUNCH
STARER	STARSHIP	STATELILY	STAUNCHED
STARERS	STARSHIPS	STATELY	STAUNCHER
STARES	STARSPOT	STATEMENT	STAUNCHES
STARETS	STARSPOTS	STATER	STAUNCHLY
STARETSES	STARSTONE	STATEROOM	STAUNING
STARETZ	START	STATERS	STAUNS
STARETZES	STARTED	STATES	STAVE
STARFISH	STARTER	STATESIDE	STAVED
STARFRUIT	STARTERS	STATESMAN	STAVES
STARGAZE	STARTFUL	STATESMEN	STAVING
STARGAZED	STARTING	STATEWIDE	STAVUDINE
STARGAZER	STARTINGS	STATIC	STAW
STARGAZES	STARTISH	STATICAL	STAWED
STARING	STARTLE	STATICE	STAWING
STARINGLY	STARTLED	STATICES	STAWS
STARINGS	STARTLER	STATICKY	STAY
STARK	STARTLERS	STATICS	STAYAWAY
STARKED	STARTLES	STATIM	STAYAWAYS
STARKEN	STARTLING	STATIN	STAYED
STARKENED	STARTLISH	STATING	STAYER
STARKENS	STARTLY	STATINS	STAYERS
STARKER	STARTS	STATION	STAYING

STAYLESS	STEAMROLL	STEEDIES	STEEPLED
STAYMAKER	STEAMS	STEEDING	STEEPLES
STAYNE	STEAMSHIP	STEEDLIKE	STEEPLY
STAYNED	STEAMY	STEEDS	STEEPNESS
STAYNES	STEAN	STEEDY	STEEPS
STAYNING	STEANE	STEEDYING	STEEPUP
STAYRE	STEANED	STEEK	STEEPY
STAYRES	STEANES	STEEKED	STEER
STAYS	STEANING	STEEKING	STEERABLE
STAYSAIL	STEANINGS	STEEKIT	STEERAGE
STAYSAILS	STEANS	STEEKS	STEERAGES
STEAD	STEAPSIN	STEEL	STEERED
STEADED	STEAPSINS	STEELBOW	STEERER
STEADFAST	STEAR	STEELBOWS	STEERERS
STEADICAM	STEARAGE	STEELD	STEERIES
STEADIED	STEARAGES	STEELED	STEERING
STEADIER	STEARATE	STEELHEAD	STEERINGS
STEADIERS	STEARATES	STEELIE	STEERLING
STEADIES	STEARD	STEELIER	STEERS
STEADIEST	STEARE	STEELIES	STEERSMAN
STEADILY	STEARED	STEELIEST	STEERSMEN
STEADING	STEARES	STEELING	STEERY
STEADINGS	STEARIC	STEELINGS	STEEVE
STEADS	STEARIN	STEELMAN	STEEVED
STEADY	STEARINE	STEELMEN	STEEVELY
STEADYING	STEARINES	STEELS	STEEVER
STEAK	STEARING	STEELWARE	STEEVES
STEAKS	STEARINS	STEELWORK	STEEVEST
STEAL	STEARS	STEELY	STEEVING
STEALABLE	STEARSMAN	STEELYARD	STEEVINGS
STEALAGE	STEARSMEN	STEEM	STEGNOSES
STEALAGES	STEATITE	STEEMED	STEGNOSIS
STEALE	STEATITES	STEEMING	STEGNOTIC
STEALED	STEATITIC	STEEMS	STEGODON
STEALER	STEATOMA	STEEN	STEGODONS
STEALERS	STEATOMAS	STEENBOK	STEGODONT
STEALES	STEATOSES	STEENBOKS	STEGOMYIA
STEALING	STEATOSIS	STEENBRAS	STEGOSAUR
STEALINGS	STED	STEENBUCK	STEIL
STEALS	STEDD	STEENED	STEILS
STEALT	STEDDE	STEENING	STEIN
STEALTH	STEDDED	STEENINGS	STEINBOCK
STEALTHED	STEDDES	STEENKIRK	STEINBOK
STEALTHS	STEDDIED	STEENS	STEINBOKS
STEALTHY	STEDDIES	STEEP	STEINED
STEAM	STEDDING	STEEPED	STEINING
STEAMBOAT	STEDDS	STEEPEN	STEININGS
STEAMED	STEDDY	STEEPENED	STEINKIRK
STEAMER	STEDDYING	STEEPENS	STEINS
STEAMERED	STEDE	STEEPER	STELA
STEAMERS	STEDED	STEEPERS	STELAE
STEAMIE	STEDES	STEEPEST	STELAI
STEAMIER	STEDFAST	STEEPEUP	STELAR
STEAMIES	STEDING	STEEPIER	STELE
STEAMIEST	STEDS	STEEPIEST	STELENE
STEAMILY	STEED	STEEPING	STELES
STEAMING	STEEDED	STEEPISH	STELIC
STEAMINGS	STEEDIED	STEEPLE	STELL

STELLA
STELLAR
STELLAS
STELLATE
STELLATED
STELLED
STELLERID
STELLIFY
STELLING
STELLION
STELLIONS
STELLITE
STELLITES
STELLS
STELLULAR
STEM
STEMBOK
STEMBOKS
STEMBUCK
STEMBUCKS
STEME
STEMED
STEMES
STEMHEAD
STEMHEADS
STEMING
STEMLESS
STEMLET
STEMLETS
STEMLIKE
STEMMA
STEMMAS
STEMMATA
STEMMATIC
STEMME
STEMMED
STEMMER
STEMMERS
STEMMERY
STEMMES
STEMMIER
STEMMIEST
STEMMING
STEMMINGS
STEMMY
STEMPEL
STEMPELS
STEMPLE
STEMPLES
STEMS
STEMSON
STEMSONS
STEMWARE
STEMWARES
STEN
STENCH
STENCHED
STENCHES

STENCHFUL
STENCHIER
STENCHING
STENCHY
STENCIL
STENCILED
STENCILER
STENCILS
STEND
STENDED
STENDING
STENDS
STENGAH
STENGAHS
STENLOCK
STENLOCKS
STENNED
STENNING
STENO
STENOBATH
STENOKIES
STENOKOUS
STENOKY
STENOPAIC
STENOS
STENOSED
STENOSES
STENOSIS
STENOTIC
STENOTYPE
STENOTYPY
STENS
STENT
STENTED
STENTING
STENTOR
STENTORS
STENTOUR
STENTOURS
STENTS
STEP
STEPBAIRN
STEPCHILD
STEPDAME
STEPDAMES
STEPHANE
STEPHANES
STEPLIKE
STEPNEY
STEPNEYS
STEPPE
STEPPED
STEPPER
STEPPERS
STEPPES
STEPPING
STEPS
STEPSON

STEPSONS
STEPSTOOL
STEPT
STEPWISE
STERADIAN
STERCORAL
STERCULIA
STERE
STEREO
STEREOED
STEREOING
STEREOME
STEREOMES
STEREOS
STERES
STERIC
STERICAL
STERIGMA
STERIGMAS
STERILANT
STERILE
STERILELY
STERILISE
STERILITY
STERILIZE
STERLET
STERLETS
STERLING
STERLINGS
STERN
STERNA
STERNAGE
STERNAGES
STERNAL
STERNEBRA
STERNED
STERNER
STERNEST
STERNFAST
STERNING
STERNITE
STERNITES
STERNITIC
STERNLY
STERNMOST
STERNNESS
STERNPORT
STERNPOST
STERNS
STERNSON
STERNSONS
STERNUM
STERNUMS
STERNWARD
STERNWAY
STERNWAYS
STEROID
STEROIDAL

STEROIDS
STEROL
STEROLS
STERTOR
STERTORS
STERVE
STERVED
STERVES
STERVING
STET
STETS
STETSON
STETSONS
STETTED
STETTING
STEVEDORE
STEVEN
STEVENS
STEW
STEWABLE
STEWARD
STEWARDED
STEWARDRY
STEWARDS
STEWARTRY
STEWBUM
STEWBUMS
STEWED
STEWER
STEWERS
STEWIER
STEWIEST
STEWING
STEWINGS
STEWPAN
STEWPANS
STEWPOND
STEWPONDS
STEWPOT
STEWPOTS
STEWS
STEWY
STEY
STEYER
STEYEST
STHENIA
STHENIAS
STHENIC
STIBBLE
STIBBLER
STIBBLERS
STIBBLES
STIBIAL
STIBINE
STIBINES
STIBIUM
STIBIUMS
STIBNITE

STIBNITES
STICCADO
STICCADOS
STICCATO
STICCATOS
STICH
STICHARIA
STICHERA
STICHERON
STICHIC
STICHIDIA
STICHOI
STICHOS
STICHS
STICK
STICKABLE
STICKBALL
STICKED
STICKER
STICKERED
STICKERS
STICKFUL
STICKFULS
STICKIED
STICKIER
STICKIES
STICKIEST
STICKILY
STICKING
STICKINGS
STICKIT
STICKJAW
STICKJAWS
STICKLE
STICKLED
STICKLER
STICKLERS
STICKLES
STICKLIKE
STICKLING
STICKMAN
STICKMEN
STICKOUT
STICKOUTS
STICKPIN
STICKPINS
STICKS
STICKSEED
STICKUM
STICKUMS
STICKUP
STICKUPS
STICKWEED
STICKWORK
STICKY
STICKYING
STICTION
STICTIONS

STIDDIE
STIDDIED
STIDDIES
STIE
STIED
STIES
STIEVE
STIEVELY
STIEVER
STIEVEST
STIFF
STIFFED
STIFFEN
STIFFENED
STIFFENER
STIFFENS
STIFFER
STIFFEST
STIFFIE
STIFFIES
STIFFING
STIFFISH
STIFFLY
STIFFNESS
STIFFS
STIFFWARE
STIFFY
STIFLE
STIFLED
STIFLER
STIFLERS
STIFLES
STIFLING
STIFLINGS
STIGMA
STIGMAL
STIGMAS
STIGMATA
STIGMATIC
STIGME
STIGMES
STILB
STILBENE
STILBENES
STILBITE
STILBITES
STILBS
STILE
STILED
STILES
STILET
STILETS
STILETTO
STILETTOS
STILING
STILL
STILLAGE
STILLAGES

STILLBORN
STILLED
STILLER
STILLERS
STILLEST
STILLIER
STILLIEST
STILLING
STILLINGS
STILLION
STILLIONS
STILLMAN
STILLMEN
STILLNESS
STILLROOM
STILLS
STILLY
STILT
STILTBIRD
STILTED
STILTEDLY
STILTER
STILTERS
STILTIER
STILTIEST
STILTING
STILTINGS
STILTISH
STILTS
STILTY
STIM
STIME
STIMED
STIMES
STIMIE
STIMIED
STIMIES
STIMING
STIMS
STIMULANT
STIMULATE
STIMULI
STIMULUS
STIMY
STIMYING
STING
STINGAREE
STINGBULL
STINGED
STINGER
STINGERS
STINGFISH
STINGIER
STINGIES
STINGIEST
STINGILY
STINGING
STINGINGS

STINGLESS
STINGO
STINGOS
STINGRAY
STINGRAYS
STINGS
STINGY
STINK
STINKARD
STINKARDS
STINKBUG
STINKBUGS
STINKER
STINKEROO
STINKERS
STINKHORN
STINKIER
STINKIEST
STINKING
STINKINGS
STINKO
STINKPOT
STINKPOTS
STINKS
STINKWEED
STINKWOOD
STINKY
STINT
STINTED
STINTEDLY
STINTER
STINTERS
STINTIER
STINTIEST
STINTING
STINTINGS
STINTLESS
STINTS
STINTY
STIPA
STIPAS
STIPE
STIPED
STIPEL
STIPELS
STIPEND
STIPENDS
STIPES
STIPIFORM
STIPITATE
STIPITES
STIPPLE
STIPPLED
STIPPLER
STIPPLERS
STIPPLES
STIPPLING
STIPULAR

STIPULARY	STOAT	STOEP	STOMACK
STIPULATE	STOATS	STOEPS	STOMACKS
STIPULE	STOB	STOGEY	STOMAL
STIPULED	STOBBED	STOGEYS	STOMAS
STIPULES	STOBBING	STOGIE	STOMATA
STIR	STOBS	STOGIES	STOMATAL
STIRABOUT	STOCCADO	STOGY	STOMATE
STIRE	STOCCADOS	STOIC	STOMATES
STIRED	STOCCATA	STOICAL	STOMATIC
STIRES	STOCCATAS	STOICALLY	STOMATOUS
STIRING	STOCIOUS	STOICISM	STOMIA
STIRK	STOCK	STOICISMS	STOMIUM
STIRKS	STOCKADE	STOICS	STOMIUMS
STIRLESS	STOCKADED	STOIT	STOMODAEA
STIRP	STOCKADES	STOITED	STOMODEA
STIRPES	STOCKAGE	STOITER	STOMODEAL
STIRPS	STOCKAGES	STOITERED	STOMODEUM
STIRRA	STOCKCAR	STOITERS	STOMP
STIRRABLE	STOCKCARS	STOITING	STOMPED
STIRRAH	STOCKED	STOITS	STOMPER
STIRRAHS	STOCKER	STOKE	STOMPERS
STIRRAS	STOCKERS	STOKED	STOMPIE
STIRRE	STOCKFISH	STOKEHOLD	STOMPIES
STIRRED	STOCKHORN	STOKEHOLE	STOMPING
STIRRER	STOCKIER	STOKER	STOMPS
STIRRERS	STOCKIEST	STOKERS	STONABLE
STIRRES	STOCKILY	STOKES	STOND
STIRRING	STOCKINET	STOKESIA	STONDS
STIRRINGS	STOCKING	STOKESIAS	STONE
STIRRUP	STOCKINGS	STOKING	STONEABLE
STIRRUPS	STOCKISH	STOKVEL	STONEBOAT
STIRS	STOCKIST	STOKVELS	STONECAST
STISHIE	STOCKISTS	STOLE	STONECHAT
STISHIES	STOCKLESS	STOLED	STONECROP
STITCH	STOCKLIST	STOLEN	STONED
STITCHED	STOCKLOCK	STOLES	STONEFISH
STITCHER	STOCKMAN	STOLID	STONEFLY
STITCHERS	STOCKMEN	STOLIDER	STONEHAND
STITCHERY	STOCKPILE	STOLIDEST	STONELESS
STITCHES	STOCKPOT	STOLIDITY	STONELIKE
STITCHING	STOCKPOTS	STOLIDLY	STONEN
STITHIED	STOCKROOM	STOLLEN	STONER
STITHIES	STOCKS	STOLLENS	STONERAG
STITHY	STOCKTAKE	STOLN	STONERAGS
STITHYING	STOCKTOOK	STOLON	STONERAW
STIVE	STOCKWORK	STOLONATE	STONERAWS
STIVED	STOCKY	STOLONIC	STONERN
STIVER	STOCKYARD	STOLONS	STONERS
STIVERS	STODGE	STOLPORT	STONES
STIVES	STODGED	STOLPORTS	STONESHOT
STIVIER	STODGER	STOMA	STONEWALL
STIVIEST	STODGERS	STOMACH	STONEWARE
STIVING	STODGES	STOMACHAL	STONEWASH
STIVY	STODGIER	STOMACHED	STONEWORK
STOA	STODGIEST	STOMACHER	STONEWORT
STOAE	STODGILY	STOMACHIC	STONEY
STOAI	STODGING	STOMACHS	STONG
STOAS	STODGY	STOMACHY	STONIED

STONIER

STONIER	STOOSHIES	STORGE	STOUP
STONIES	STOP	STORGES	STOUPS
STONIEST	STOPBANK	STORIATED	STOUR
STONILY	STOPBANKS	STORIED	STOURE
STONINESS	STOPCOCK	STORIES	STOURES
STONING	STOPCOCKS	STORIETTE	STOURIE
STONINGS	STOPE	STORING	STOURIER
STONISH	STOPED	STORK	STOURIEST
STONISHED	STOPER	STORKS	STOURS
STONISHES	STOPERS	STORM	STOURY
STONK	STOPES	STORMBIRD	STOUSH
STONKED	STOPGAP	STORMED	STOUSHED
STONKER	STOPGAPS	STORMER	STOUSHES
STONKERED	STOPING	STORMERS	STOUSHIE
STONKERS	STOPINGS	STORMFUL	STOUSHIES
STONKING	STOPLESS	STORMIER	STOUSHING
STONKS	STOPLIGHT	STORMIEST	STOUT
STONN	STOPOFF	STORMILY	STOUTEN
STONNE	STOPOFFS	STORMING	STOUTENED
STONNED	STOPOVER	STORMINGS	STOUTENS
STONNES	STOPOVERS	STORMLESS	STOUTER
STONNING	STOPPABLE	STORMLIKE	STOUTEST
STONNS	STOPPAGE	STORMS	STOUTH
STONY	STOPPAGES	STORMY	STOUTHS
STONYING	STOPPED	STORNELLI	STOUTISH
STOOD	STOPPER	STORNELLO	STOUTLY
STOODEN	STOPPERED	STORY	STOUTNESS
STOOGE	STOPPERS	STORYBOOK	STOUTS
STOOGED	STOPPING	STORYETTE	STOVAINE
STOOGES	STOPPINGS	STORYING	STOVAINES
STOOGING	STOPPLE	STORYINGS	STOVE
STOOK	STOPPLED	STORYLINE	STOVED
STOOKED	STOPPLES	STOSS	STOVEPIPE
STOOKER	STOPPLING	STOSSES	STOVER
STOOKERS	STOPS	STOT	STOVERS
STOOKIE	STOPT	STOTIN	STOVES
STOOKIES	STOPWATCH	STOTINKA	STOVETOP
STOOKING	STOPWORD	STOTINKI	STOVETOPS
STOOKS	STOPWORDS	STOTINOV	STOVIES
STOOL	STORABLE	STOTINS	STOVING
STOOLBALL	STORABLES	STOTIOUS	STOVINGS
STOOLED	STORAGE	STOTS	STOW
STOOLIE	STORAGES	STOTT	STOWABLE
STOOLIES	STORAX	STOTTED	STOWAGE
STOOLING	STORAXES	STOTTER	STOWAGES
STOOLS	STORE	STOTTERED	STOWAWAY
STOOP	STORED	STOTTERS	STOWAWAYS
STOOPBALL	STOREMAN	STOTTIE	STOWDOWN
STOOPE	STOREMEN	STOTTIES	STOWDOWNS
STOOPED	STORER	STOTTING	STOWED
STOOPER	STOREROOM	STOTTS	STOWER
STOOPERS	STORERS	STOUN	STOWERS
STOOPES	STORES	STOUND	STOWING
STOOPING	STORESHIP	STOUNDED	STOWINGS
STOOPS	STOREWIDE	STOUNDING	STOWLINS
STOOR	STOREY	STOUNDS	STOWN
STOORS	STOREYED	STOUNING	STOWND
STOOSHIE	STOREYS	STOUNS	STOWNDED

STOWNDING	STRAITING	STRATI	STREAMING
STOWNDS	STRAITLY	STRATIFY	STREAMLET
STOWNLINS	STRAITS	STRATONIC	STREAMS
STOWP	STRAKE	STRATOSE	STREAMY
STOWPS	STRAKED	STRATOUS	STREEK
STOWRE	STRAKES	STRATUM	STREEKED
STOWRES	STRAMACON	STRATUMS	STREEKER
STOWS	STRAMASH	STRATUS	STREEKERS
STRABISM	STRAMAZON	STRAUCHT	STREEKING
STRABISMS	STRAMMEL	STRAUCHTS	STREEKS
STRAD	STRAMMELS	STRAUGHT	STREEL
STRADDLE	STRAMONY	STRAUGHTS	STREELED
STRADDLED	STRAMP	STRAUNGE	STREELING
STRADDLER	STRAMPED	STRAVAGE	STREELS
STRADDLES	STRAMPING	STRAVAGED	STREET
STRADIOT	STRAMPS	STRAVAGES	STREETAGE
STRADIOTS	STRAND	STRAVAIG	STREETBOY
STRADS	STRANDED	STRAVAIGS	STREETCAR
STRAE	STRANDER	STRAW	STREETED
STRAES	STRANDERS	STRAWED	STREETFUL
STRAFE	STRANDING	STRAWEN	STREETIER
STRAFED	STRANDS	STRAWHAT	STREETING
STRAFER	STRANG	STRAWIER	STREETS
STRAFERS	STRANGE	STRAWIEST	STREETY
STRAFES	STRANGELY	STRAWING	STREIGHT
STRAFF	STRANGER	STRAWLESS	STREIGHTS
STRAFFED	STRANGERS	STRAWLIKE	STREIGNE
STRAFFING	STRANGES	STRAWN	STREIGNED
STRAFFS	STRANGEST	STRAWS	STREIGNES
STRAFING	STRANGLE	STRAWWORM	STRELITZ
STRAG	STRANGLED	STRAWY	STRELITZI
STRAGGLE	STRANGLER	STRAY	STRENE
STRAGGLED	STRANGLES	STRAYED	STRENES
STRAGGLER	STRANGURY	STRAYER	STRENGTH
STRAGGLES	STRAP	STRAYERS	STRENGTHS
STRAGGLY	STRAPHANG	STRAYING	STRENUITY
STRAGS	STRAPHUNG	STRAYINGS	STRENUOUS
STRAICHT	STRAPLESS	STRAYLING	STREP
STRAIGHT	STRAPLINE	STRAYS	STREPENT
STRAIGHTS	STRAPPADO	STRAYVE	STREPS
STRAIK	STRAPPED	STRAYVED	STRESS
STRAIKED	STRAPPER	STRAYVES	STRESSED
STRAIKING	STRAPPERS	STRAYVING	STRESSES
STRAIKS	STRAPPIER	STREAK	STRESSFUL
STRAIN	STRAPPING	STREAKED	STRESSING
STRAINED	STRAPPY	STREAKER	STRESSOR
STRAINER	STRAPS	STREAKERS	STRESSORS
STRAINERS	STRAPWORT	STREAKIER	STRETCH
STRAINING	STRASS	STREAKILY	STRETCHED
STRAINS	STRASSES	STREAKING	STRETCHER
STRAINT	STRATA	STREAKS	STRETCHES
STRAINTS	STRATAGEM	STREAKY	STRETCHY
STRAIT	STRATAL	STREAM	STRETTA
STRAITED	STRATAS	STREAMBED	STRETTAS
STRAITEN	STRATEGIC	STREAMED	STRETTE
STRAITENS	STRATEGY	STREAMER	STRETTI
STRAITER	STRATH	STREAMERS	STRETTO
STRAITEST	STRATHS	STREAMIER	STRETTOS

STREUSEL	STRIFT	STRIVING	STRONGLY
STREUSELS	STRIFTS	STRIVINGS	STRONGMAN
STREW	STRIG	STROAM	STRONGMEN
STREWAGE	STRIGA	STROAMED	STRONGYL
STREWAGES	STRIGAE	STROAMING	STRONGYLE
STREWED	STRIGATE	STROAMS	STRONGYLS
STREWER	STRIGGED	STROBE	STRONTIA
STREWERS	STRIGGING	STROBED	STRONTIAN
STREWING	STRIGIL	STROBES	STRONTIAS
STREWINGS	STRIGILS	STROBIC	STRONTIC
STREWMENT	STRIGINE	STROBIL	STRONTIUM
STREWN	STRIGOSE	STROBILA	STROOK
STREWS	STRIGS	STROBILAE	STROOKE
STREWTH	STRIKE	STROBILAR	STROOKEN
STRIA	STRIKEOUT	STROBILE	STROOKES
STRIAE	STRIKER	STROBILES	STROP
STRIATA	STRIKERS	STROBILI	STROPHE
STRIATE	STRIKES	STROBILS	STROPHES
STRIATED	STRIKING	STROBILUS	STROPHIC
STRIATES	STRIKINGS	STROBING	STROPHOID
STRIATING	STRING	STROBINGS	STROPHULI
STRIATION	STRINGED	STRODDLE	STROPPED
STRIATUM	STRINGENT	STRODDLED	STROPPER
STRIATUMS	STRINGER	STRODDLES	STROPPERS
STRIATURE	STRINGERS	STRODE	STROPPIER
STRICH	STRINGIER	STRODLE	STROPPILY
STRICHES	STRINGILY	STRODLED	STROPPING
STRICK	STRINGING	STRODLES	STROPPY
STRICKEN	STRINGS	STRODLING	STROPS
STRICKLE	STRINGY	STROKE	STROSSERS
STRICKLED	STRINKLE	STROKED	STROUD
STRICKLES	STRINKLED	STROKEN	STROUDING
STRICKS	STRINKLES	STROKER	STROUDS
STRICT	STRIP	STROKERS	STROUP
STRICTER	STRIPE	STROKES	STROUPACH
STRICTEST	STRIPED	STROKING	STROUPAN
STRICTION	STRIPER	STROKINGS	STROUPANS
STRICTISH	STRIPERS	STROLL	STROUPS
STRICTLY	STRIPES	STROLLED	STROUT
STRICTURE	STRIPEY	STROLLER	STROUTED
STRIDDEN	STRIPIER	STROLLERS	STROUTING
STRIDDLE	STRIPIEST	STROLLING	STROUTS
STRIDDLED	STRIPING	STROLLS	STROVE
STRIDDLES	STRIPINGS	STROMA	STROW
STRIDE	STRIPLING	STROMAL	STROWED
STRIDENCE	STRIPPED	STROMATA	STROWER
STRIDENCY	STRIPPER	STROMATIC	STROWERS
STRIDENT	STRIPPERS	STROMB	STROWING
STRIDER	STRIPPING	STROMBS	STROWINGS
STRIDERS	STRIPS	STROMBUS	STROWN
STRIDES	STRIPT	STROND	STROWS
STRIDING	STRIPY	STRONDS	STROY
STRIDLING	STRIVE	STRONG	STROYED
STRIDOR	STRIVED	STRONGARM	STROYER
STRIDORS	STRIVEN	STRONGBOX	STROYERS
STRIFE	STRIVER	STRONGER	STROYING
STRIFEFUL	STRIVERS	STRONGEST	STROYS
STRIFES	STRIVES	STRONGISH	STRUCK

STRUCKEN	STUCCOERS	STUKKEND	STUPED
STRUCTURE	STUCCOES	STULL	STUPEFIED
STRUDEL	STUCCOING	STULLS	STUPEFIER
STRUDELS	STUCCOS	STULM	STUPEFIES
STRUGGLE	STUCK	STULMS	STUPEFY
STRUGGLED	STUCKS	STULTIFY	STUPENT
STRUGGLER	STUD	STUM	STUPES
STRUGGLES	STUDBOOK	STUMBLE	STUPID
STRUM	STUDBOOKS	STUMBLED	STUPIDER
STRUMA	STUDDED	STUMBLER	STUPIDEST
STRUMAE	STUDDEN	STUMBLERS	STUPIDITY
STRUMAS	STUDDIE	STUMBLES	STUPIDLY
STRUMATIC	STUDDIES	STUMBLIER	STUPIDS
STRUMITIS	STUDDING	STUMBLING	STUPING
STRUMMED	STUDDINGS	STUMBLY	STUPOR
STRUMMEL	STUDDLE	STUMER	STUPOROUS
STRUMMELS	STUDDLES	STUMERS	STUPORS
STRUMMER	STUDENT	STUMM	STUPRATE
STRUMMERS	STUDENTRY	STUMMED	STUPRATED
STRUMMING	STUDENTS	STUMMEL	STUPRATES
STRUMOSE	STUDENTY	STUMMELS	STURDIED
STRUMOUS	STUDFARM	STUMMING	STURDIER
STRUMPET	STUDFARMS	STUMP	STURDIES
STRUMPETS	STUDFISH	STUMPAGE	STURDIEST
STRUMS	STUDHORSE	STUMPAGES	STURDILY
STRUNG	STUDIED	STUMPED	STURDY
STRUNT	STUDIEDLY	STUMPER	STURE
STRUNTED	STUDIER	STUMPERS	STURGEON
STRUNTING	STUDIERS	STUMPIER	STURGEONS
STRUNTS	STUDIES	STUMPIES	STURMER
STRUT	STUDIO	STUMPIEST	STURMERS
STRUTS	STUDIOS	STUMPILY	STURNINE
STRUTTED	STUDIOUS	STUMPING	STURNOID
STRUTTER	STUDLIER	STUMPS	STURNUS
STRUTTERS	STUDLIEST	STUMPWORK	STURNUSES
STRUTTING	STUDLY	STUMPY	STURT
STRYCHNIA	STUDS	STUMS	STURTED
STRYCHNIC	STUDWORK	STUN	STURTING
STUB	STUDWORKS	STUNG	STURTS
STUBBED	STUDY	STUNK	STUSHIE
STUBBIE	STUDYING	STUNKARD	STUSHIES
STUBBIER	STUFF	STUNNED	STUTTER
STUBBIES	STUFFED	STUNNER	STUTTERED
STUBBIEST	STUFFER	STUNNERS	STUTTERER
STUBBILY	STUFFERS	STUNNING	STUTTERS
STUBBING	STUFFIER	STUNNINGS	STY
STUBBLE	STUFFIEST	STUNS	STYE
STUBBLED	STUFFILY	STUNSAIL	STYED
STUBBLES	STUFFING	STUNSAILS	STYES
STUBBLIER	STUFFINGS	STUNT	STYGIAN
STUBBLY	STUFFLESS	STUNTED	STYING
STUBBORN	STUFFS	STUNTING	STYLAR
STUBBORNS	STUFFY	STUNTMAN	STYLATE
STUBBY	STUGGIER	STUNTMEN	STYLE
STUBS	STUGGIEST	STUNTS	STYLEBOOK
STUCCO	STUGGY	STUPA	STYLED
STUCCOED	STUIVER	STUPAS	STYLELESS
STUCCOER	STUIVERS	STUPE	STYLER

STYLERS	STYPTICS	SUBALPINE	SUBCLERKS
STYLES	STYRAX	SUBALTERN	SUBCLIMAX
STYLET	STYRAXES	SUBAPICAL	SUBCODE
STYLETS	STYRE	SUBAQUA	SUBCODES
STYLI	STYRED	SUBARCTIC	SUBCOLONY
STYLIE	STYRENE	SUBAREA	SUBCONSUL
STYLIER	STYRENES	SUBAREAS	SUBCOOL
STYLIEST	STYRES	SUBARID	SUBCOOLED
STYLIFORM	STYRING	SUBAS	SUBCOOLS
STYLING	STYROFOAM	SUBASTRAL	SUBCORTEX
STYLINGS	STYTE	SUBATOM	SUBCOSTA
STYLISE	STYTED	SUBATOMIC	SUBCOSTAE
STYLISED	STYTES	SUBATOMS	SUBCOSTAL
STYLISER	STYTING	SUBAUDIO	SUBCOUNTY
STYLISERS	SUABILITY	SUBAURAL	SUBCRUST
STYLISES	SUABLE	SUBAXIAL	SUBCRUSTS
STYLISH	SUABLY	SUBBASAL	SUBCULT
STYLISHLY	SUASIBLE	SUBBASE	SUBCULTS
STYLISING	SUASION	SUBBASES	SUBCUTES
STYLIST	SUASIONS	SUBBASIN	SUBCUTIS
STYLISTIC	SUASIVE	SUBBASINS	SUBDEACON
STYLISTS	SUASIVELY	SUBBASS	SUBDEALER
STYLITE	SUASORY	SUBBASSES	SUBDEAN
STYLITES	SUAVE	SUBBED	SUBDEANS
STYLITIC	SUAVELY	SUBBIE	SUBDEB
STYLITISM	SUAVENESS	SUBBIES	SUBDEBS
STYLIZE	SUAVER	SUBBING	SUBDEPOT
STYLIZED	SUAVEST	SUBBINGS	SUBDEPOTS
STYLIZER	SUAVITIES	SUBBLOCK	SUBDEPUTY
STYLIZERS	SUAVITY	SUBBLOCKS	SUBDERMAL
STYLIZES	SUB	SUBBRANCH	SUBDEW
STYLIZING	SUBA	SUBBREED	SUBDEWED
STYLO	SUBABBOT	SUBBREEDS	SUBDEWING
STYLOBATE	SUBABBOTS	SUBBUREAU	SUBDEWS
STYLOID	SUBACID	SUBBY	SUBDIVIDE
STYLOIDS	SUBACIDLY	SUBCANTOR	SUBDOLOUS
STYLOLITE	SUBACRID	SUBCASTE	SUBDORSAL
STYLOPES	SUBACT	SUBCASTES	SUBDUABLE
STYLOPISE	SUBACTED	SUBCAUDAL	SUBDUABLY
STYLOPIZE	SUBACTING	SUBCAUSE	SUBDUAL
STYLOPS	SUBACTION	SUBCAUSES	SUBDUALS
STYLOS	SUBACTS	SUBCAVITY	SUBDUCE
STYLUS	SUBACUTE	SUBCELL	SUBDUCED
STYLUSES	SUBADAR	SUBCELLAR	SUBDUCES
STYME	SUBADARS	SUBCELLS	SUBDUCING
STYMED	SUBADULT	SUBCENTER	SUBDUCT
STYMES	SUBADULTS	SUBCHASER	SUBDUCTED
STYMIE	SUBAERIAL	SUBCHIEF	SUBDUCTS
STYMIED	SUBAGENCY	SUBCHIEFS	SUBDUE
STYMIEING	SUBAGENT	SUBCHORD	SUBDUED
STYMIES	SUBAGENTS	SUBCHORDS	SUBDUEDLY
STYMING	SUBAH	SUBCLAIM	SUBDUER
STYMY	SUBAHDAR	SUBCLAIMS	SUBDUERS
STYMYING	SUBAHDARS	SUBCLAN	SUBDUES
STYPSIS	SUBAHDARY	SUBCLANS	SUBDUING
STYPSISES	SUBAHS	SUBCLASS	SUBDUPLE
STYPTIC	SUBAHSHIP	SUBCLAUSE	SUBDURAL
STYPTICAL	SUBALAR	SUBCLERK	SUBDWARF

SUBDWARFS
SUBECHO
SUBECHOES
SUBEDAR
SUBEDARS
SUBEDIT
SUBEDITED
SUBEDITOR
SUBEDITS
SUBENTIRE
SUBENTRY
SUBEPOCH
SUBEPOCHS
SUBEQUAL
SUBER
SUBERATE
SUBERATES
SUBERECT
SUBEREOUS
SUBERIC
SUBERIN
SUBERINS
SUBERISE
SUBERISED
SUBERISES
SUBERIZE
SUBERIZED
SUBERIZES
SUBEROSE
SUBEROUS
SUBERS
SUBFAMILY
SUBFEU
SUBFEUED
SUBFEUING
SUBFEUS
SUBFIELD
SUBFIELDS
SUBFILE
SUBFILES
SUBFIX
SUBFIXES
SUBFLOOR
SUBFLOORS
SUBFLUID
SUBFOSSIL
SUBFRAME
SUBFRAMES
SUBFUSC
SUBFUSCS
SUBFUSK
SUBFUSKS
SUBGENERA
SUBGENRE
SUBGENRES
SUBGENUS
SUBGOAL
SUBGOALS

SUBGRADE
SUBGRADES
SUBGRAPH
SUBGRAPHS
SUBGROUP
SUBGROUPS
SUBGUM
SUBGUMS
SUBHA
SUBHAS
SUBHEAD
SUBHEADS
SUBHEDRAL
SUBHUMAN
SUBHUMANS
SUBHUMID
SUBIDEA
SUBIDEAS
SUBIMAGO
SUBIMAGOS
SUBINCISE
SUBINDEX
SUBINFEUD
SUBITEM
SUBITEMS
SUBITISE
SUBITISED
SUBITISES
SUBITIZE
SUBITIZED
SUBITIZES
SUBITO
SUBJACENT
SUBJECT
SUBJECTED
SUBJECTS
SUBJOIN
SUBJOINED
SUBJOINS
SUBJUGATE
SUBLATE
SUBLATED
SUBLATES
SUBLATING
SUBLATION
SUBLEASE
SUBLEASED
SUBLEASES
SUBLESSEE
SUBLESSOR
SUBLET
SUBLETHAL
SUBLETS
SUBLETTER
SUBLEVEL
SUBLEVELS
SUBLIMATE
SUBLIME

SUBLIMED
SUBLIMELY
SUBLIMER
SUBLIMERS
SUBLIMES
SUBLIMEST
SUBLIMING
SUBLIMISE
SUBLIMIT
SUBLIMITS
SUBLIMITY
SUBLIMIZE
SUBLINE
SUBLINEAR
SUBLINES
SUBLOT
SUBLOTS
SUBLUNAR
SUBLUNARY
SUBLUNATE
SUBLUXATE
SUBMAN
SUBMARINE
SUBMARKET
SUBMATRIX
SUBMEN
SUBMENTA
SUBMENTAL
SUBMENTUM
SUBMENU
SUBMENUS
SUBMERGE
SUBMERGED
SUBMERGES
SUBMERSE
SUBMERSED
SUBMERSES
SUBMICRON
SUBMISS
SUBMISSLY
SUBMIT
SUBMITS
SUBMITTAL
SUBMITTED
SUBMITTER
SUBMUCOSA
SUBMUCOUS
SUBNASAL
SUBNET
SUBNETS
SUBNEURAL
SUBNICHE
SUBNICHES
SUBNIVEAL
SUBNIVEAN
SUBNODAL
SUBNORMAL
SUBNUCLEI

SUBOCEAN
SUBOCTAVE
SUBOCULAR
SUBOFFICE
SUBOPTIC
SUBORAL
SUBORDER
SUBORDERS
SUBORN
SUBORNED
SUBORNER
SUBORNERS
SUBORNING
SUBORNS
SUBOSCINE
SUBOVAL
SUBOVATE
SUBOXIDE
SUBOXIDES
SUBPANEL
SUBPANELS
SUBPAR
SUBPART
SUBPARTS
SUBPENA
SUBPENAED
SUBPENAS
SUBPERIOD
SUBPHASE
SUBPHASES
SUBPHYLA
SUBPHYLAR
SUBPHYLUM
SUBPLOT
SUBPLOTS
SUBPOENA
SUBPOENAS
SUBPOLAR
SUBPOTENT
SUBPRIOR
SUBPRIORS
SUBPUBIC
SUBRACE
SUBRACES
SUBREGION
SUBRENT
SUBRENTS
SUBRING
SUBRINGS
SUBROGATE
SUBRULE
SUBRULES
SUBS
SUBSACRAL
SUBSALE
SUBSALES
SUBSAMPLE
SUBSCALE

SUBSCALES

SUBSCALES	SUBSTAGES	SUBTLY	SUBVIRUS
SUBSCHEMA	SUBSTANCE	SUBTONE	SUBVISUAL
SUBSCRIBE	SUBSTATE	SUBTONES	SUBVOCAL
SUBSCRIPT	SUBSTATES	SUBTONIC	SUBWARDEN
SUBSEA	SUBSTRACT	SUBTONICS	SUBWAY
SUBSECIVE	SUBSTRATA	SUBTOPIA	SUBWAYED
SUBSECT	SUBSTRATE	SUBTOPIAN	SUBWAYING
SUBSECTOR	SUBSTRUCT	SUBTOPIAS	SUBWAYS
SUBSECTS	SUBSTYLAR	SUBTOPIC	SUBWOOFER
SUBSELLIA	SUBSTYLE	SUBTOPICS	SUBWORLD
SUBSENSE	SUBSTYLES	SUBTORRID	SUBWORLDS
SUBSENSES	SUBSULTUS	SUBTOTAL	SUBWRITER
SUBSERE	SUBSUME	SUBTOTALS	SUBZERO
SUBSERES	SUBSUMED	SUBTRACT	SUBZONAL
SUBSERIES	SUBSUMES	SUBTRACTS	SUBZONE
SUBSERVE	SUBSUMING	SUBTREND	SUBZONES
SUBSERVED	SUBSYSTEM	SUBTRENDS	SUCCADE
SUBSERVES	SUBTACK	SUBTRIBE	SUCCADES
SUBSET	SUBTACKS	SUBTRIBES	SUCCAH
SUBSETS	SUBTASK	SUBTRIST	SUCCAHS
SUBSHAFT	SUBTASKS	SUBTROPIC	SUCCEDENT
SUBSHAFTS	SUBTAXA	SUBTRUDE	SUCCEED
SUBSHELL	SUBTAXON	SUBTRUDED	SUCCEEDED
SUBSHELLS	SUBTAXONS	SUBTRUDES	SUCCEEDER
SUBSHRUB	SUBTEEN	SUBTUNIC	SUCCEEDS
SUBSHRUBS	SUBTEENS	SUBTUNICS	SUCCENTOR
SUBSIDE	SUBTENANT	SUBTYPE	SUCCES
SUBSIDED	SUBTEND	SUBTYPES	SUCCESS
SUBSIDER	SUBTENDED	SUBUCULA	SUCCESSES
SUBSIDERS	SUBTENDS	SUBUCULAS	SUCCESSOR
SUBSIDES	SUBTENSE	SUBULATE	SUCCI
SUBSIDIES	SUBTENSES	SUBUNIT	SUCCINATE
SUBSIDING	SUBTENURE	SUBUNITS	SUCCINCT
SUBSIDISE	SUBTEST	SUBURB	SUCCINIC
SUBSIDIZE	SUBTESTS	SUBURBAN	SUCCINITE
SUBSIDY	SUBTEXT	SUBURBANS	SUCCINYL
SUBSIST	SUBTEXTS	SUBURBED	SUCCINYLS
SUBSISTED	SUBTHEME	SUBURBIA	SUCCISE
SUBSISTER	SUBTHEMES	SUBURBIAS	SUCCOR
SUBSISTS	SUBTIDAL	SUBURBS	SUCCORED
SUBSITE	SUBTIL	SUBURSINE	SUCCORER
SUBSITES	SUBTILE	SUBVASSAL	SUCCORERS
SUBSIZAR	SUBTILELY	SUBVENE	SUCCORIES
SUBSIZARS	SUBTILER	SUBVENED	SUCCORING
SUBSKILL	SUBTILEST	SUBVENES	SUCCORS
SUBSKILLS	SUBTILIN	SUBVENING	SUCCORY
SUBSOCIAL	SUBTILINS	SUBVERSAL	SUCCOS
SUBSOIL	SUBTILISE	SUBVERSE	SUCCOSE
SUBSOILED	SUBTILITY	SUBVERSED	SUCCOT
SUBSOILER	SUBTILIZE	SUBVERSES	SUCCOTASH
SUBSOILS	SUBTILTY	SUBVERST	SUCCOTH
SUBSOLAR	SUBTITLE	SUBVERT	SUCCOUR
SUBSONG	SUBTITLED	SUBVERTED	SUCCOURED
SUBSONGS	SUBTITLES	SUBVERTER	SUCCOURER
SUBSONIC	SUBTLE	SUBVERTS	SUCCOURS
SUBSPACE	SUBTLER	SUBVICAR	SUCCOUS
SUBSPACES	SUBTLEST	SUBVICARS	SUCCUBA
SUBSTAGE	SUBTLETY	SUBVIRAL	SUCCUBAE

SUCCUBAS	SUCTIONS	SUETIER	SUGARLIKE
SUCCUBI	SUCTORIAL	SUETIEST	SUGARLOAF
SUCCUBINE	SUCTORIAN	SUETS	SUGARPLUM
SUCCUBOUS	SUCURUJU	SUETTIER	SUGARS
SUCCUBUS	SUCURUJUS	SUETTIEST	SUGARY
SUCCULENT	SUD	SUETTY	SUGGEST
SUCCUMB	SUDAMEN	SUETY	SUGGESTED
SUCCUMBED	SUDAMINA	SUFFARI	SUGGESTER
SUCCUMBER	SUDAMINAL	SUFFARIS	SUGGESTS
SUCCUMBS	SUDARIA	SUFFECT	SUGGING
SUCCURSAL	SUDARIES	SUFFER	SUGGINGS
SUCCUS	SUDARIUM	SUFFERED	SUGH
SUCCUSS	SUDARY	SUFFERER	SUGHED
SUCCUSSED	SUDATE	SUFFERERS	SUGHING
SUCCUSSES	SUDATED	SUFFERING	SUGHS
SUCH	SUDATES	SUFFERS	SUI
SUCHLIKE	SUDATING	SUFFETE	SUICIDAL
SUCHNESS	SUDATION	SUFFETES	SUICIDE
SUCHWISE	SUDATIONS	SUFFICE	SUICIDED
SUCK	SUDATORIA	SUFFICED	SUICIDES
SUCKED	SUDATORY	SUFFICER	SUICIDING
SUCKEN	SUDD	SUFFICERS	SUID
SUCKENER	SUDDEN	SUFFICES	SUIDIAN
SUCKENERS	SUDDENLY	SUFFICING	SUIDIANS
SUCKENS	SUDDENS	SUFFIX	SUIDS
SUCKER	SUDDENTY	SUFFIXAL	SUILLINE
SUCKERED	SUDDER	SUFFIXED	SUING
SUCKERING	SUDDERS	SUFFIXES	SUINGS
SUCKERS	SUDDS	SUFFIXING	SUINT
SUCKET	SUDOR	SUFFIXION	SUINTS
SUCKETS	SUDORAL	SUFFLATE	SUIPLAP
SUCKFISH	SUDORIFIC	SUFFLATED	SUIPLAPS
SUCKIER	SUDOROUS	SUFFLATES	SUIT
SUCKIEST	SUDORS	SUFFOCATE	SUITABLE
SUCKING	SUDS	SUFFRAGAN	SUITABLY
SUCKINGS	SUDSED	SUFFRAGE	SUITCASE
SUCKLE	SUDSER	SUFFRAGES	SUITCASES
SUCKLED	SUDSERS	SUFFUSE	SUITE
SUCKLER	SUDSES	SUFFUSED	SUITED
SUCKLERS	SUDSIER	SUFFUSES	SUITER
SUCKLES	SUDSIEST	SUFFUSING	SUITERS
SUCKLESS	SUDSING	SUFFUSION	SUITES
SUCKLING	SUDSLESS	SUFFUSIVE	SUITING
SUCKLINGS	SUDSY	SUGAN	SUITINGS
SUCKS	SUE	SUGANS	SUITLIKE
SUCKY	SUEABLE	SUGAR	SUITOR
SUCRALOSE	SUED	SUGARALLY	SUITORED
SUCRASE	SUEDE	SUGARBUSH	SUITORING
SUCRASES	SUEDED	SUGARCANE	SUITORS
SUCRE	SUEDES	SUGARCOAT	SUITRESS
SUCRES	SUEDETTE	SUGARED	SUITS
SUCRIER	SUEDETTES	SUGARER	SUIVANTE
SUCRIERS	SUEDING	SUGARERS	SUIVANTES
SUCROSE	SUENT	SUGARIER	SUIVEZ
SUCROSES	SUER	SUGARIEST	SUJEE
SUCTION	SUERS	SUGARING	SUJEES
SUCTIONAL	SUES	SUGARINGS	SUK
SUCTIONED	SUET	SUGARLESS	SUKH

SUKHS	SULFURYL	SULTRIER	SUMMONERS
SUKIYAKI	SULFURYLS	SULTRIEST	SUMMONING
SUKIYAKIS	SULK	SULTRILY	SUMMONS
SUKKAH	SULKED	SULTRY	SUMMONSED
SUKKAHS	SULKER	SULU	SUMMONSES
SUKKOS	SULKERS	SULUS	SUMO
SUKKOT	SULKIER	SUM	SUMOIST
SUKKOTH	SULKIES	SUMAC	SUMOISTS
SUKS	SULKIEST	SUMACH	SUMOS
SULCAL	SULKILY	SUMACHS	SUMOTORI
SULCALISE	SULKINESS	SUMACS	SUMOTORIS
SULCALIZE	SULKING	SUMATRA	SUMP
SULCATE	SULKS	SUMATRAS	SUMPH
SULCATED	SULKY	SUMLESS	SUMPHISH
SULCATION	SULLAGE	SUMMA	SUMPHS
SULCI	SULLAGES	SUMMABLE	SUMPIT
SULCUS	SULLEN	SUMMAE	SUMPITAN
SULDAN	SULLENER	SUMMAND	SUMPITANS
SULDANS	SULLENEST	SUMMANDS	SUMPITS
SULFA	SULLENLY	SUMMAR	SUMPS
SULFAS	SULLENS	SUMMARIES	SUMPSIMUS
SULFATASE	SULLIABLE	SUMMARILY	SUMPTER
SULFATE	SULLIED	SUMMARISE	SUMPTERS
SULFATED	SULLIES	SUMMARIST	SUMPTUARY
SULFATES	SULLY	SUMMARIZE	SUMPTUOUS
SULFATIC	SULLYING	SUMMARY	SUMPWEED
SULFATING	SULPHA	SUMMAS	SUMPWEEDS
SULFATION	SULPHAS	SUMMAT	SUMS
SULFID	SULPHATE	SUMMATE	SUMY
SULFIDE	SULPHATED	SUMMATED	SUN
SULFIDES	SULPHATES	SUMMATES	SUNBACK
SULFIDS	SULPHATIC	SUMMATING	SUNBAKE
SULFINYL	SULPHID	SUMMATION	SUNBAKED
SULFINYLS	SULPHIDE	SUMMATIVE	SUNBAKES
SULFITE	SULPHIDES	SUMMATS	SUNBAKING
SULFITES	SULPHIDS	SUMMED	SUNBATH
SULFITIC	SULPHINYL	SUMMER	SUNBATHE
SULFO	SULPHITE	SUMMERED	SUNBATHED
SULFONATE	SULPHITES	SUMMERIER	SUNBATHER
SULFONE	SULPHITIC	SUMMERING	SUNBATHES
SULFONES	SULPHONE	SUMMERLY	SUNBATHS
SULFONIC	SULPHONES	SUMMERS	SUNBEAM
SULFONIUM	SULPHONIC	SUMMERSET	SUNBEAMED
SULFONYL	SULPHONYL	SUMMERY	SUNBEAMS
SULFONYLS	SULPHUR	SUMMING	SUNBEAMY
SULFOXIDE	SULPHURED	SUMMINGS	SUNBEAT
SULFUR	SULPHURET	SUMMIST	SUNBEATEN
SULFURATE	SULPHURIC	SUMMISTS	SUNBED
SULFURED	SULPHURS	SUMMIT	SUNBEDS
SULFURET	SULPHURY	SUMMITAL	SUNBELT
SULFURETS	SULPHURYL	SUMMITED	SUNBELTS
SULFURIC	SULTAN	SUMMITEER	SUNBERRY
SULFURING	SULTANA	SUMMITING	SUNBIRD
SULFURISE	SULTANAS	SUMMITRY	SUNBIRDS
SULFURIZE	SULTANATE	SUMMITS	SUNBLIND
SULFUROUS	SULTANESS	SUMMON	SUNBLINDS
SULFURS	SULTANIC	SUMMONED	SUNBLOCK
SULFURY	SULTANS	SUMMONER	SUNBLOCKS

SUNBONNET
SUNBOW
SUNBOWS
SUNBRIGHT
SUNBURN
SUNBURNED
SUNBURNS
SUNBURNT
SUNBURST
SUNBURSTS
SUNCHOKE
SUNCHOKES
SUNDAE
SUNDAES
SUNDARI
SUNDARIS
SUNDECK
SUNDECKS
SUNDER
SUNDERED
SUNDERER
SUNDERERS
SUNDERING
SUNDERS
SUNDEW
SUNDEWS
SUNDIAL
SUNDIALS
SUNDOG
SUNDOGS
SUNDOWN
SUNDOWNED
SUNDOWNER
SUNDOWNS
SUNDRA
SUNDRAS
SUNDRESS
SUNDRI
SUNDRIES
SUNDRILY
SUNDRIS
SUNDROPS
SUNDRY
SUNFAST
SUNFISH
SUNFISHES
SUNFLOWER
SUNG
SUNGAR
SUNGARS
SUNGLASS
SUNGLOW
SUNGLOWS
SUNGREBE
SUNGREBES
SUNHAT
SUNHATS
SUNK

SUNKEN
SUNKET
SUNKETS
SUNKIE
SUNKIES
SUNKS
SUNLAMP
SUNLAMPS
SUNLAND
SUNLANDS
SUNLESS
SUNLESSLY
SUNLIGHT
SUNLIGHTS
SUNLIKE
SUNLIT
SUNN
SUNNA
SUNNAH
SUNNAHS
SUNNAS
SUNNED
SUNNIER
SUNNIES
SUNNIEST
SUNNILY
SUNNINESS
SUNNING
SUNNS
SUNNY
SUNPORCH
SUNPROOF
SUNRAY
SUNRAYS
SUNRISE
SUNRISES
SUNRISING
SUNROOF
SUNROOFS
SUNROOM
SUNROOMS
SUNS
SUNSCALD
SUNSCALDS
SUNSCREEN
SUNSEEKER
SUNSET
SUNSETS
SUNSHADE
SUNSHADES
SUNSHINE
SUNSHINES
SUNSHINY
SUNSPOT
SUNSPOTS
SUNSTAR
SUNSTARS
SUNSTONE

SUNSTONES
SUNSTROKE
SUNSTRUCK
SUNSUIT
SUNSUITS
SUNTAN
SUNTANNED
SUNTANS
SUNTRAP
SUNTRAPS
SUNUP
SUNUPS
SUNWARD
SUNWARDS
SUNWISE
SUP
SUPAWN
SUPAWNS
SUPE
SUPER
SUPERABLE
SUPERABLY
SUPERADD
SUPERADDS
SUPERATE
SUPERATED
SUPERATES
SUPERATOM
SUPERB
SUPERBAD
SUPERBANK
SUPERBER
SUPERBEST
SUPERBIKE
SUPERBITY
SUPERBLY
SUPERBOLD
SUPERBOMB
SUPERBRAT
SUPERBUG
SUPERBUGS
SUPERCAR
SUPERCARS
SUPERCEDE
SUPERCHIC
SUPERCITY
SUPERCLUB
SUPERCOIL
SUPERCOLD
SUPERCOOL
SUPERCOP
SUPERCOPS
SUPERCOW
SUPERCOWS
SUPERCUTE
SUPERED
SUPEREGO
SUPEREGOS

SUPERETTE
SUPERFAN
SUPERFANS
SUPERFARM
SUPERFAST
SUPERFINE
SUPERFIRM
SUPERFIT
SUPERFIX
SUPERFLUX
SUPERFUND
SUPERFUSE
SUPERGENE
SUPERGLUE
SUPERGOOD
SUPERGUN
SUPERGUNS
SUPERHEAT
SUPERHERO
SUPERHET
SUPERHETS
SUPERHIGH
SUPERHIT
SUPERHITS
SUPERHIVE
SUPERHOT
SUPERHYPE
SUPERING
SUPERIOR
SUPERIORS
SUPERJET
SUPERJETS
SUPERJOCK
SUPERLAIN
SUPERLAY
SUPERLIE
SUPERLIES
SUPERLOAD
SUPERLONG
SUPERLOO
SUPERLOOS
SUPERMALE
SUPERMAN
SUPERMART
SUPERMAX
SUPERMEN
SUPERMIND
SUPERMINI
SUPERMOM
SUPERMOMS
SUPERMOTO
SUPERNAL
SUPERNATE
SUPERNOVA
SUPERPIMP
SUPERPLUS
SUPERPORT
SUPERPOSE

SUPERPRO	SUPPLIALS	SURBED	SURFLIKE
SUPERPROS	SUPPLIANT	SURBEDDED	SURFMAN
SUPERRACE	SUPPLICAT	SURBEDS	SURFMEN
SUPERREAL	SUPPLIED	SURBET	SURFPERCH
SUPERRICH	SUPPLIER	SURCEASE	SURFRIDER
SUPERROAD	SUPPLIERS	SURCEASED	SURFS
SUPERS	SUPPLIES	SURCEASES	SURFSIDE
SUPERSAFE	SUPPLING	SURCHARGE	SURFY
SUPERSALE	SUPPLY	SURCINGLE	SURGE
SUPERSALT	SUPPLYING	SURCOAT	SURGED
SUPERSAUR	SUPPORT	SURCOATS	SURGEFUL
SUPERSEDE	SUPPORTED	SURCULI	SURGELESS
SUPERSELL	SUPPORTER	SURCULOSE	SURGENT
SUPERSEX	SUPPORTS	SURCULUS	SURGEON
SUPERSHOW	SUPPOSAL	SURD	SURGEONCY
SUPERSIZE	SUPPOSALS	SURDITIES	SURGEONS
SUPERSOFT	SUPPOSE	SURDITY	SURGER
SUPERSOLD	SUPPOSED	SURDS	SURGERIES
SUPERSPY	SUPPOSER	SURE	SURGERS
SUPERSTAR	SUPPOSERS	SURED	SURGERY
SUPERSTUD	SUPPOSES	SUREFIRE	SURGES
SUPERTAX	SUPPOSING	SURELY	SURGICAL
SUPERTHIN	SUPPRESS	SURENESS	SURGIER
SUPERVENE	SUPPURATE	SURER	SURGIEST
SUPERVISE	SUPRA	SURES	SURGING
SUPERWAIF	SUPREMACY	SUREST	SURGINGS
SUPERWAVE	SUPREME	SURETIED	SURGY
SUPERWEED	SUPREMELY	SURETIES	SURICATE
SUPERWIDE	SUPREMER	SURETY	SURICATES
SUPERWIFE	SUPREMES	SURETYING	SURIMI
SUPES	SUPREMEST	SURF	SURIMIS
SUPINATE	SUPREMITY	SURFABLE	SURING
SUPINATED	SUPREMO	SURFACE	SURLIER
SUPINATES	SUPREMOS	SURFACED	SURLIEST
SUPINATOR	SUPS	SURFACER	SURLILY
SUPINE	SUQ	SURFACERS	SURLINESS
SUPINELY	SUQS	SURFACES	SURLOIN
SUPINES	SUR	SURFACING	SURLOINS
SUPLEX	SURA	SURFBIRD	SURLY
SUPLEXES	SURAH	SURFBIRDS	SURMASTER
SUPPAWN	SURAHS	SURFBOARD	SURMISAL
SUPPAWNS	SURAL	SURFBOAT	SURMISALS
SUPPEAGO	SURAMIN	SURFBOATS	SURMISE
SUPPED	SURAMINS	SURFED	SURMISED
SUPPER	SURANCE	SURFEIT	SURMISER
SUPPERED	SURANCES	SURFEITED	SURMISERS
SUPPERING	SURAS	SURFEITER	SURMISES
SUPPERS	SURAT	SURFEITS	SURMISING
SUPPING	SURATS	SURFER	SURMOUNT
SUPPLANT	SURBAHAR	SURFERS	SURMOUNTS
SUPPLANTS	SURBAHARS	SURFFISH	SURMULLET
SUPPLE	SURBASE	SURFICIAL	SURNAME
SUPPLED	SURBASED	SURFIE	SURNAMED
SUPPLELY	SURBASES	SURFIER	SURNAMER
SUPPLER	SURBATE	SURFIES	SURNAMERS
SUPPLES	SURBATED	SURFIEST	SURNAMES
SUPPLEST	SURBATES	SURFING	SURNAMING
SUPPLIAL	SURBATING	SURFINGS	SURPASS

SURPASSED	SURVEYOR	SUTILE	SWADDLES
SURPASSER	SURVEYORS	SUTLER	SWADDLING
SURPASSES	SURVEYS	SUTLERIES	SWADDY
SURPLICE	SURVIEW	SUTLERS	SWADS
SURPLICED	SURVIEWED	SUTLERY	SWAG
SURPLICES	SURVIEWS	SUTOR	SWAGE
SURPLUS	SURVIVAL	SUTORIAL	SWAGED
SURPLUSED	SURVIVALS	SUTORIAN	SWAGER
SURPLUSES	SURVIVE	SUTORS	SWAGERS
SURPRINT	SURVIVED	SUTRA	SWAGES
SURPRINTS	SURVIVER	SUTRAS	SWAGGED
SURPRISAL	SURVIVERS	SUTTA	SWAGGER
SURPRISE	SURVIVES	SUTTAS	SWAGGERED
SURPRISED	SURVIVING	SUTTEE	SWAGGERER
SURPRISER	SURVIVOR	SUTTEEISM	SWAGGERS
SURPRISES	SURVIVORS	SUTTEES	SWAGGIE
SURPRIZE	SUS	SUTTLE	SWAGGIES
SURPRIZED	SUSCEPTOR	SUTTLED	SWAGGING
SURPRIZES	SUSCITATE	SUTTLES	SWAGING
SURQUEDRY	SUSES	SUTTLETIE	SWAGMAN
SURQUEDY	SUSHI	SUTTLING	SWAGMEN
SURRA	SUSHIS	SUTTLY	SWAGS
SURRAS	SUSLIK	SUTURAL	SWAGSHOP
SURREAL	SUSLIKS	SUTURALLY	SWAGSHOPS
SURREALLY	SUSPECT	SUTURE	SWAGSMAN
SURREBUT	SUSPECTED	SUTURED	SWAGSMEN
SURREBUTS	SUSPECTER	SUTURES	SWAIL
SURREINED	SUSPECTS	SUTURING	SWAILS
SURREJOIN	SUSPENCE	SUZERAIN	SWAIN
SURRENDER	SUSPEND	SUZERAINS	SWAINING
SURRENDRY	SUSPENDED	SVARAJ	SWAININGS
SURREY	SUSPENDER	SVARAJES	SWAINISH
SURREYS	SUSPENDS	SVASTIKA	SWAINS
SURROGACY	SUSPENS	SVASTIKAS	SWALE
SURROGATE	SUSPENSE	SVEDBERG	SWALED
SURROUND	SUSPENSER	SVEDBERGS	SWALES
SURROUNDS	SUSPENSES	SVELTE	SWALIER
SURROYAL	SUSPENSOR	SVELTELY	SWALIEST
SURROYALS	SUSPICION	SVELTER	SWALING
SURTAX	SUSPIRE	SVELTEST	SWALINGS
SURTAXED	SUSPIRED	SWAB	SWALLET
SURTAXES	SUSPIRES	SWABBED	SWALLETS
SURTAXING	SUSPIRING	SWABBER	SWALLOW
SURTITLE	SUSS	SWABBERS	SWALLOWED
SURTITLES	SUSSED	SWABBIE	SWALLOWER
SURTOUT	SUSSES	SWABBIES	SWALLOWS
SURTOUTS	SUSSING	SWABBING	SWALY
SURUCUCU	SUSTAIN	SWABBY	SWAM
SURUCUCUS	SUSTAINED	SWABS	SWAMI
SURVEIL	SUSTAINER	SWACK	SWAMIES
SURVEILED	SUSTAINS	SWACKED	SWAMIS
SURVEILLE	SUSTINENT	SWAD	SWAMP
SURVEILS	SUSU	SWADDIE	SWAMPED
SURVEY	SUSURRANT	SWADDIES	SWAMPER
SURVEYAL	SUSURRATE	SWADDLE	SWAMPERS
SURVEYALS	SUSURROUS	SWADDLED	SWAMPIER
SURVEYED	SUSURRUS	SWADDLER	SWAMPIEST
SURVEYING	SUSUS	SWADDLERS	SWAMPING

SWAMPISH	SWARDED	SWATHS	SWEDES
SWAMPLAND	SWARDIER	SWATHY	SWEDGER
SWAMPLESS	SWARDIEST	SWATS	SWEDGERS
SWAMPS	SWARDING	SWATTED	SWEE
SWAMPY	SWARDS	SWATTER	SWEED
SWAMY	SWARDY	SWATTERED	SWEEING
SWAN	SWARE	SWATTERS	SWEEL
SWANG	SWARF	SWATTING	SWEELED
SWANHERD	SWARFED	SWATTINGS	SWEELING
SWANHERDS	SWARFING	SWAY	SWEELS
SWANK	SWARFS	SWAYABLE	SWEENEY
SWANKED	SWARM	SWAYBACK	SWEENEYS
SWANKER	SWARMED	SWAYBACKS	SWEENIES
SWANKERS	SWARMER	SWAYED	SWEENY
SWANKEST	SWARMERS	SWAYER	SWEEP
SWANKEY	SWARMING	SWAYERS	SWEEPBACK
SWANKEYS	SWARMINGS	SWAYFUL	SWEEPER
SWANKIE	SWARMS	SWAYING	SWEEPERS
SWANKIER	SWART	SWAYINGS	SWEEPIER
SWANKIES	SWARTH	SWAYL	SWEEPIEST
SWANKIEST	SWARTHIER	SWAYLED	SWEEPING
SWANKILY	SWARTHILY	SWAYLING	SWEEPINGS
SWANKING	SWARTHS	SWAYLINGS	SWEEPS
SWANKPOT	SWARTHY	SWAYLS	SWEEPY
SWANKPOTS	SWARTNESS	SWAYS	SWEER
SWANKS	SWARTY	SWAZZLE	SWEERED
SWANKY	SWARVE	SWAZZLES	SWEERING
SWANLIKE	SWARVED	SWEAL	SWEERS
SWANNED	SWARVES	SWEALED	SWEERT
SWANNERY	SWARVING	SWEALING	SWEES
SWANNIE	SWASH	SWEALINGS	SWEET
SWANNIER	SWASHED	SWEALS	SWEETCORN
SWANNIES	SWASHER	SWEAR	SWEETED
SWANNIEST	SWASHERS	SWEARD	SWEETEN
SWANNING	SWASHES	SWEARDS	SWEETENED
SWANNINGS	SWASHIER	SWEARER	SWEETENER
SWANNY	SWASHIEST	SWEARERS	SWEETENS
SWANPAN	SWASHING	SWEARING	SWEETER
SWANPANS	SWASHINGS	SWEARINGS	SWEETEST
SWANS	SWASHWORK	SWEARS	SWEETFISH
SWANSDOWN	SWASHY	SWEARWORD	SWEETIE
SWANSKIN	SWASTICA	SWEAT	SWEETIES
SWANSKINS	SWASTICAS	SWEATBAND	SWEETING
SWAP	SWASTIKA	SWEATBOX	SWEETINGS
SWAPPED	SWASTIKAS	SWEATED	SWEETISH
SWAPPER	SWAT	SWEATER	SWEETLY
SWAPPERS	SWATCH	SWEATERS	SWEETMAN
SWAPPING	SWATCHES	SWEATIER	SWEETMEAL
SWAPPINGS	SWATH	SWEATIEST	SWEETMEAT
SWAPS	SWATHABLE	SWEATILY	SWEETMEN
SWAPT	SWATHE	SWEATING	SWEETNESS
SWAPTION	SWATHED	SWEATINGS	SWEETPEA
SWAPTIONS	SWATHER	SWEATLESS	SWEETPEAS
SWARAJ	SWATHERS	SWEATS	SWEETS
SWARAJES	SWATHES	SWEATSHOP	SWEETSHOP
SWARAJISM	SWATHIER	SWEATSUIT	SWEETSOP
SWARAJIST	SWATHIEST	SWEATY	SWEETSOPS
SWARD	SWATHING	SWEDE	SWEETWOOD

SWEETY	SWIFTED	SWINEPOX	SWIRLIEST
SWEIR	SWIFTER	SWINERIES	SWIRLING
SWEIRED	SWIFTERS	SWINERY	SWIRLS
SWEIRER	SWIFTEST	SWINES	SWIRLY
SWEIREST	SWIFTIE	SWING	SWISH
SWEIRING	SWIFTIES	SWINGBEAT	SWISHED
SWEIRNESS	SWIFTING	SWINGBOAT	SWISHER
SWEIRS	SWIFTLET	SWINGBY	SWISHERS
SWEIRT	SWIFTLETS	SWINGBYS	SWISHES
SWELCHIE	SWIFTLY	SWINGE	SWISHEST
SWELCHIES	SWIFTNESS	SWINGED	SWISHIER
SWELL	SWIFTS	SWINGEING	SWISHIEST
SWELLDOM	SWIFTY	SWINGER	SWISHING
SWELLDOMS	SWIG	SWINGERS	SWISHINGS
SWELLED	SWIGGED	SWINGES	SWISHY
SWELLER	SWIGGER	SWINGIER	SWISS
SWELLERS	SWIGGERS	SWINGIEST	SWISSES
SWELLEST	SWIGGING	SWINGING	SWISSING
SWELLFISH	SWIGS	SWINGINGS	SWISSINGS
SWELLHEAD	SWILER	SWINGISM	SWITCH
SWELLING	SWILERS	SWINGISMS	SWITCHED
SWELLINGS	SWILL	SWINGLE	SWITCHEL
SWELLISH	SWILLED	SWINGLED	SWITCHELS
SWELLS	SWILLER	SWINGLES	SWITCHER
SWELT	SWILLERS	SWINGLING	SWITCHERS
SWELTED	SWILLING	SWINGMAN	SWITCHES
SWELTER	SWILLINGS	SWINGMEN	SWITCHIER
SWELTERED	SWILLS	SWINGS	SWITCHING
SWELTERS	SWIM	SWINGTREE	SWITCHMAN
SWELTING	SWIMMABLE	SWINGY	SWITCHMEN
SWELTRIER	SWIMMER	SWINISH	SWITCHY
SWELTRY	SWIMMERET	SWINISHLY	SWITH
SWELTS	SWIMMERS	SWINK	SWITHE
SWEPT	SWIMMIER	SWINKED	SWITHER
SWEPTBACK	SWIMMIEST	SWINKER	SWITHERED
SWEPTWING	SWIMMILY	SWINKERS	SWITHERS
SWERF	SWIMMING	SWINKING	SWITHLY
SWERFED	SWIMMINGS	SWINKS	SWITS
SWERFING	SWIMMY	SWINNEY	SWITSES
SWERFS	SWIMS	SWINNEYS	SWIVE
SWERVABLE	SWIMSUIT	SWIPE	SWIVED
SWERVE	SWIMSUITS	SWIPED	SWIVEL
SWERVED	SWIMWEAR	SWIPER	SWIVELED
SWERVER	SWIMWEARS	SWIPERS	SWIVELING
SWERVERS	SWINDGE	SWIPES	SWIVELLED
SWERVES	SWINDGED	SWIPEY	SWIVELS
SWERVING	SWINDGES	SWIPIER	SWIVES
SWERVINGS	SWINDGING	SWIPIEST	SWIVET
SWEVEN	SWINDLE	SWIPING	SWIVETS
SWEVENS	SWINDLED	SWIPLE	SWIVING
SWEY	SWINDLER	SWIPLES	SWIZ
SWEYED	SWINDLERS	SWIPPLE	SWIZZ
SWEYING	SWINDLES	SWIPPLES	SWIZZED
SWEYS	SWINDLING	SWIRE	SWIZZES
SWIDDEN	SWINE	SWIRES	SWIZZING
SWIDDENS	SWINEHERD	SWIRL	SWIZZLE
SWIES	SWINEHOOD	SWIRLED	SWIZZLED
SWIFT	SWINELIKE	SWIRLIER	SWIZZLER

SWIZZLERS

SWIZZLERS	SWORDMAN	SYCEE	SYLVA
SWIZZLES	SWORDMEN	SYCEES	SYLVAE
SWIZZLING	SWORDPLAY	SYCES	SYLVAN
SWOB	SWORDS	SYCOMORE	SYLVANER
SWOBBED	SWORDSMAN	SYCOMORES	SYLVANERS
SWOBBER	SWORDSMEN	SYCONIA	SYLVANITE
SWOBBERS	SWORDTAIL	SYCONIUM	SYLVANS
SWOBBING	SWORE	SYCOPHANT	SYLVAS
SWOBS	SWORN	SYCOSES	SYLVATIC
SWOFFER	SWOT	SYCOSIS	SYLVIA
SWOFFERS	SWOTS	SYE	SYLVIAS
SWOFFING	SWOTTED	SYED	SYLVIINE
SWOFFINGS	SWOTTER	SYEING	SYLVIN
SWOLLEN	SWOTTERS	SYEN	SYLVINE
SWOLLENLY	SWOTTIER	SYENITE	SYLVINES
SWOLN	SWOTTIEST	SYENITES	SYLVINITE
SWONE	SWOTTING	SYENITIC	SYLVINS
SWONES	SWOTTINGS	SYENS	SYLVITE
SWOON	SWOTTY	SYES	SYLVITES
SWOONED	SWOUN	SYKE	SYMAR
SWOONER	SWOUND	SYKER	SYMARS
SWOONERS	SWOUNDED	SYKES	SYMBION
SWOONIER	SWOUNDING	SYLI	SYMBIONS
SWOONIEST	SWOUNDS	SYLIS	SYMBIONT
SWOONING	SWOUNE	SYLLABARY	SYMBIONTS
SWOONINGS	SWOUNED	SYLLABI	SYMBIOSES
SWOONS	SWOUNES	SYLLABIC	SYMBIOSIS
SWOONY	SWOUNING	SYLLABICS	SYMBIOT
SWOOP	SWOUNS	SYLLABIFY	SYMBIOTE
SWOOPED	SWOWND	SYLLABISE	SYMBIOTES
SWOOPER	SWOWNDS	SYLLABISM	SYMBIOTIC
SWOOPERS	SWOWNE	SYLLABIZE	SYMBIOTS
SWOOPIER	SWOWNES	SYLLABLE	SYMBOL
SWOOPIEST	SWOZZLE	SYLLABLED	SYMBOLE
SWOOPING	SWOZZLES	SYLLABLES	SYMBOLED
SWOOPS	SWUM	SYLLABUB	SYMBOLES
SWOOPY	SWUNG	SYLLABUBS	SYMBOLIC
SWOOSH	SWY	SYLLABUS	SYMBOLICS
SWOOSHED	SYBARITE	SYLLEPSES	SYMBOLING
SWOOSHES	SYBARITES	SYLLEPSIS	SYMBOLISE
SWOOSHING	SYBARITIC	SYLLEPTIC	SYMBOLISM
SWOP	SYBBE	SYLLOGISE	SYMBOLIST
SWOPPED	SYBBES	SYLLOGISM	SYMBOLIZE
SWOPPER	SYBIL	SYLLOGIST	SYMBOLLED
SWOPPERS	SYBILS	SYLLOGIZE	SYMBOLOGY
SWOPPING	SYBO	SYLPH	SYMBOLS
SWOPPINGS	SYBOE	SYLPHIC	SYMITAR
SWOPS	SYBOES	SYLPHID	SYMITARE
SWOPT	SYBOTIC	SYLPHIDE	SYMITARES
SWORD	SYBOTISM	SYLPHIDES	SYMITARS
SWORDBILL	SYBOTISMS	SYLPHIDS	SYMMETRAL
SWORDED	SYBOW	SYLPHIER	SYMMETRIC
SWORDER	SYBOWS	SYLPHIEST	SYMMETRY
SWORDERS	SYCAMINE	SYLPHINE	SYMPATHIN
SWORDFISH	SYCAMINES	SYLPHISH	SYMPATHY
SWORDING	SYCAMORE	SYLPHLIKE	SYMPATICO
SWORDLESS	SYCAMORES	SYLPHS	SYMPATRIC
SWORDLIKE	SYCE	SYLPHY	SYMPATRY

SYMPETALY
SYMPHILE
SYMPHILES
SYMPHILY
SYMPHONIC
SYMPHONY
SYMPHYSES
SYMPHYSIS
SYMPHYTIC
SYMPLAST
SYMPLASTS
SYMPLOCE
SYMPLOCES
SYMPODIA
SYMPODIAL
SYMPODIUM
SYMPOSIA
SYMPOSIAC
SYMPOSIAL
SYMPOSIUM
SYMPTOM
SYMPTOMS
SYMPTOSES
SYMPTOSIS
SYMPTOTIC
SYN
SYNAGOG
SYNAGOGAL
SYNAGOGS
SYNAGOGUE
SYNALEPHA
SYNANDRIA
SYNANGIA
SYNANGIUM
SYNANON
SYNANONS
SYNANTHIC
SYNANTHY
SYNAPHEA
SYNAPHEAS
SYNAPHEIA
SYNAPSE
SYNAPSED
SYNAPSES
SYNAPSID
SYNAPSIDS
SYNAPSING
SYNAPSIS
SYNAPTASE
SYNAPTE
SYNAPTES
SYNAPTIC
SYNARCHY
SYNASTRY
SYNAXARIA
SYNAXES
SYNAXIS
SYNC

SYNCARP
SYNCARPS
SYNCARPY
SYNCED
SYNCH
SYNCHED
SYNCHING
SYNCHRO
SYNCHRONY
SYNCHROS
SYNCHS
SYNCHYSES
SYNCHYSIS
SYNCING
SYNCLINAL
SYNCLINE
SYNCLINES
SYNCOM
SYNCOMS
SYNCOPAL
SYNCOPATE
SYNCOPE
SYNCOPES
SYNCOPIC
SYNCOPTIC
SYNCRETIC
SYNCS
SYNCYTIA
SYNCYTIAL
SYNCYTIUM
SYND
SYNDACTYL
SYNDED
SYNDESES
SYNDESIS
SYNDET
SYNDETIC
SYNDETON
SYNDETONS
SYNDETS
SYNDIC
SYNDICAL
SYNDICATE
SYNDICS
SYNDING
SYNDINGS
SYNDROME
SYNDROMES
SYNDROMIC
SYNDS
SYNE
SYNECHIA
SYNECHIAS
SYNECIOUS
SYNECTIC
SYNECTICS
SYNED
SYNEDRIA

SYNEDRIAL
SYNEDRION
SYNEDRIUM
SYNERESES
SYNERESIS
SYNERGIA
SYNERGIAS
SYNERGIC
SYNERGID
SYNERGIDS
SYNERGIES
SYNERGISE
SYNERGISM
SYNERGIST
SYNERGIZE
SYNERGY
SYNES
SYNESES
SYNESIS
SYNESISES
SYNFUEL
SYNFUELS
SYNGAMIC
SYNGAMIES
SYNGAMOUS
SYNGAMY
SYNGAS
SYNGASES
SYNGASSES
SYNGENEIC
SYNGENIC
SYNGRAPH
SYNGRAPHS
SYNING
SYNIZESES
SYNIZESIS
SYNKARYA
SYNKARYON
SYNOD
SYNODAL
SYNODALS
SYNODIC
SYNODICAL
SYNODS
SYNODSMAN
SYNODSMEN
SYNOECETE
SYNOECISE
SYNOECISM
SYNOECIZE
SYNOEKETE
SYNOICOUS
SYNONYM
SYNONYME
SYNONYMES
SYNONYMIC
SYNONYMS
SYNONYMY

SYNOPSES
SYNOPSIS
SYNOPSISE
SYNOPSIZE
SYNOPTIC
SYNOPTICS
SYNOPTIST
SYNOVIA
SYNOVIAL
SYNOVIAS
SYNOVITIC
SYNOVITIS
SYNROC
SYNROCS
SYNTACTIC
SYNTAGM
SYNTAGMA
SYNTAGMAS
SYNTAGMIC
SYNTAGMS
SYNTAN
SYNTANS
SYNTAX
SYNTAXES
SYNTECTIC
SYNTENIC
SYNTENIES
SYNTENY
SYNTEXIS
SYNTH
SYNTHESES
SYNTHESIS
SYNTHETIC
SYNTHON
SYNTHONS
SYNTHPOP
SYNTHPOPS
SYNTHRONI
SYNTHS
SYNTONIC
SYNTONIES
SYNTONIN
SYNTONINS
SYNTONISE
SYNTONIZE
SYNTONOUS
SYNTONY
SYNURA
SYNURAE
SYPE
SYPED
SYPES
SYPH
SYPHER
SYPHERED
SYPHERING
SYPHERS
SYPHILIS

SYPHILISE
SYPHILIZE
SYPHILOID
SYPHILOMA
SYPHON
SYPHONED
SYPHONING
SYPHONS
SYPHS
SYPING
SYRAH
SYRAHS
SYREN
SYRENS
SYRETTE
SYRETTES
SYRINGA
SYRINGAS
SYRINGE
SYRINGEAL
SYRINGED
SYRINGES
SYRINGING
SYRINX
SYRINXES
SYRPHIAN
SYRPHIANS
SYRPHID
SYRPHIDS
SYRTES
SYRTIS
SYRUP
SYRUPED
SYRUPIER
SYRUPIEST
SYRUPING
SYRUPLIKE
SYRUPS
SYRUPY
SYSADMIN
SYSADMINS
SYSOP
SYSOPS
SYSSITIA
SYSSITIAS
SYSTALTIC
SYSTEM
SYSTEMED
SYSTEMIC
SYSTEMICS
SYSTEMISE
SYSTEMIZE
SYSTEMS
SYSTOLE
SYSTOLES
SYSTOLIC
SYSTYLE
SYSTYLES

SYTHE
SYTHES
SYVER
SYVERS
SYZYGAL
SYZYGETIC
SYZYGIAL
SYZYGIES
SYZYGY

— T —

TA	TABLAS	TABOULIS	TACHISTE
TAAL	TABLATURE	TABOUR	TACHISTES
TAALS	TABLE	TABOURED	TACHISTS
TAATA	TABLEAU	TABOURER	TACHO
TAATAS	TABLEAUS	TABOURERS	TACHOGRAM
TAB	TABLEAUX	TABOURET	TACHOS
TABANID	TABLED	TABOURETS	TACHS
TABANIDS	TABLEFUL	TABOURIN	TACHYLITE
TABARD	TABLEFULS	TABOURING	TACHYLYTE
TABARDED	TABLELAND	TABOURINS	TACHYON
TABARDS	TABLELESS	TABOURS	TACHYONIC
TABARET	TABLEMATE	TABRERE	TACHYONS
TABARETS	TABLES	TABRERES	TACHYPNEA
TABASHEER	TABLESFUL	TABRET	TACIT
TABASHIR	TABLET	TABRETS	TACITLY
TABASHIRS	TABLETED	TABS	TACITNESS
TABBED	TABLETING	TABU	TACITURN
TABBIED	TABLETOP	TABUED	TACK
TABBIES	TABLETOPS	TABUING	TACKBOARD
TABBINET	TABLETS	TABULA	TACKED
TABBINETS	TABLETTED	TABULABLE	TACKER
TABBING	TABLEWARE	TABULAE	TACKERS
TABBIS	TABLEWISE	TABULAR	TACKET
TABBISES	TABLIER	TABULARLY	TACKETS
TABBOULEH	TABLIERS	TABULATE	TACKETY
TABBOULI	TABLING	TABULATED	TACKEY
TABBOULIS	TABLINGS	TABULATES	TACKIER
TABBY	TABLOID	TABULATOR	TACKIES
TABBYHOOD	TABLOIDS	TABULI	TACKIEST
TABBYING	TABLOIDY	TABULIS	TACKIFIED
TABEFIED	TABOGGAN	TABUN	TACKIFIER
TABEFIES	TABOGGANS	TABUNS	TACKIFIES
TABEFY	TABOO	TABUS	TACKIFY
TABEFYING	TABOOED	TACAHOUT	TACKILY
TABELLION	TABOOING	TACAHOUTS	TACKINESS
TABER	TABOOLEY	TACAMAHAC	TACKING
TABERD	TABOOLEYS	TACAN	TACKINGS
TABERDAR	TABOOS	TACANS	TACKLE
TABERDARS	TABOR	TACE	TACKLED
TABERDS	TABORED	TACES	TACKLER
TABERED	TABORER	TACET	TACKLERS
TABERING	TABORERS	TACETS	TACKLES
TABERS	TABORET	TACH	TACKLESS
TABES	TABORETS	TACHE	TACKLING
TABESCENT	TABORIN	TACHES	TACKLINGS
TABETIC	TABORINE	TACHINA	TACKS
TABETICS	TABORINES	TACHINID	TACKSMAN
TABI	TABORING	TACHINIDS	TACKSMEN
TABID	TABORINS	TACHISM	TACKY
TABINET	TABORS	TACHISME	TACMAHACK
TABINETS	TABOULEH	TACHISMES	TACNODE
TABIS	TABOULEHS	TACHISMS	TACNODES
TABLA	TABOULI	TACHIST	TACO

TACONITE	TAFFIES	TAHSILS	TAILORS
TACONITES	TAFFRAIL	TAI	TAILPIECE
TACOS	TAFFRAILS	TAIAHA	TAILPIPE
TACRINE	TAFFY	TAIAHAS	TAILPIPED
TACRINES	TAFIA	TAIG	TAILPIPES
TACT	TAFIAS	TAIGA	TAILPLANE
TACTFUL	TAG	TAIGAS	TAILRACE
TACTFULLY	TAGALONG	TAIGLACH	TAILRACES
TACTIC	TAGALONGS	TAIGLE	TAILS
TACTICAL	TAGAREEN	TAIGLED	TAILSKID
TACTICIAN	TAGAREENS	TAIGLES	TAILSKIDS
TACTICITY	TAGBOARD	TAIGLING	TAILSLIDE
TACTICS	TAGBOARDS	TAIGS	TAILSPIN
TACTILE	TAGETES	TAIHOA	TAILSPINS
TACTILELY	TAGGANT	TAIKONAUT	TAILSTOCK
TACTILIST	TAGGANTS	TAIL	TAILWATER
TACTILITY	TAGGED	TAILARD	TAILWHEEL
TACTION	TAGGEE	TAILARDS	TAILWIND
TACTIONS	TAGGEES	TAILBACK	TAILWINDS
TACTISM	TAGGER	TAILBACKS	TAILYE
TACTISMS	TAGGERS	TAILBOARD	TAILYES
TACTLESS	TAGGIER	TAILBONE	TAILZIE
TACTS	TAGGIEST	TAILBONES	TAILZIES
TACTUAL	TAGGING	TAILCOAT	TAIN
TACTUALLY	TAGGINGS	TAILCOATS	TAINS
TAD	TAGGY	TAILED	TAINT
TADDIE	TAGHAIRM	TAILENDER	TAINTED
TADDIES	TAGHAIRMS	TAILER	TAINTING
TADPOLE	TAGINE	TAILERON	TAINTLESS
TADPOLES	TAGINES	TAILERONS	TAINTS
TADS	TAGLIKE	TAILERS	TAINTURE
TADVANCE	TAGLINE	TAILFAN	TAINTURES
TAE	TAGLINES	TAILFANS	TAIPAN
TAED	TAGLIONI	TAILFIN	TAIPANS
TAEDIUM	TAGLIONIS	TAILFINS	TAIRA
TAEDIUMS	TAGMA	TAILFLIES	TAIRAS
TAEING	TAGMATA	TAILFLY	TAIS
TAEKWONDO	TAGMEME	TAILGATE	TAISCH
TAEL	TAGMEMES	TAILGATED	TAISCHES
TAELS	TAGMEMIC	TAILGATER	TAISH
TAENIA	TAGMEMICS	TAILGATES	TAISHES
TAENIAE	TAGRAG	TAILING	TAIT
TAENIAS	TAGRAGS	TAILINGS	TAITS
TAENIASES	TAGS	TAILLAMP	TAIVER
TAENIASIS	TAGUAN	TAILLAMPS	TAIVERED
TAENIATE	TAGUANS	TAILLE	TAIVERING
TAENIOID	TAHA	TAILLES	TAIVERS
TAES	TAHAS	TAILLESS	TAIVERT
TAFFAREL	TAHINA	TAILLEUR	TAJ
TAFFARELS	TAHINAS	TAILLEURS	TAJES
TAFFEREL	TAHINI	TAILLIE	TAJINE
TAFFERELS	TAHINIS	TAILLIES	TAJINES
TAFFETA	TAHOU	TAILLIGHT	TAK
TAFFETAS	TAHOUS	TAILLIKE	TAKA
TAFFETIES	TAHR	TAILOR	TAKABLE
TAFFETY	TAHRS	TAILORED	TAKAHE
TAFFIA	TAHSIL	TAILORESS	TAKAHES
TAFFIAS	TAHSILDAR	TAILORING	TAKAMAKA

TAKAMAKAS	TALCING	TALKIEST	TALLYHO
TAKAS	TALCKED	TALKINESS	TALLYHOED
TAKE	TALCKIER	TALKING	TALLYHOS
TAKEABLE	TALCKIEST	TALKINGS	TALLYING
TAKEAWAY	TALCKING	TALKS	TALLYMAN
TAKEAWAYS	TALCKY	TALKY	TALLYMEN
TAKEDOWN	TALCOSE	TALL	TALLYSHOP
TAKEDOWNS	TALCOUS	TALLAGE	TALMA
TAKEN	TALCS	TALLAGED	TALMAS
TAKEOFF	TALCUM	TALLAGES	TALMUD
TAKEOFFS	TALCUMS	TALLAGING	TALMUDIC
TAKEOUT	TALCY	TALLAISIM	TALMUDISM
TAKEOUTS	TALE	TALLAT	TALMUDS
TAKEOVER	TALEA	TALLATS	TALON
TAKEOVERS	TALEAE	TALLBOY	TALONED
TAKER	TALEFUL	TALLBOYS	TALONS
TAKERS	TALEGALLA	TALLENT	TALOOKA
TAKES	TALEGGIO	TALLENTS	TALOOKAS
TAKEUP	TALEGGIOS	TALLER	TALPA
TAKEUPS	TALENT	TALLEST	TALPAE
TAKHI	TALENTED	TALLET	TALPAS
TAKHIS	TALENTS	TALLETS	TALUK
TAKI	TALER	TALLGRASS	TALUKA
TAKIER	TALERS	TALLIABLE	TALUKAS
TAKIEST	TALES	TALLIATE	TALUKDAR
TAKIN	TALESMAN	TALLIATED	TALUKDARS
TAKING	TALESMEN	TALLIATES	TALUKS
TAKINGLY	TALEYSIM	TALLIED	TALUS
TAKINGS	TALI	TALLIER	TALUSES
TAKINS	TALIGRADE	TALLIERS	TALWEG
TAKIS	TALION	TALLIES	TALWEGS
TAKKIES	TALIONIC	TALLIS	TAM
TAKS	TALIONS	TALLISES	TAMABLE
TAKY	TALIPAT	TALLISH	TAMAL
TALA	TALIPATS	TALLISIM	TAMALE
TALAK	TALIPED	TALLIT	TAMALES
TALAKS	TALIPEDS	TALLITES	TAMALS
TALANT	TALIPES	TALLITH	TAMANDU
TALANTS	TALIPOT	TALLITHES	TAMANDUA
TALAPOIN	TALIPOTS	TALLITHIM	TAMANDUAS
TALAPOINS	TALISMAN	TALLITHS	TAMANDUS
TALAQ	TALISMANS	TALLITIM	TAMANOIR
TALAQS	TALK	TALLITOT	TAMANOIRS
TALAR	TALKABLE	TALLITOTH	TAMANU
TALARIA	TALKATHON	TALLITS	TAMANUS
TALARS	TALKATIVE	TALLNESS	TAMARA
TALAS	TALKBACK	TALLOL	TAMARACK
TALAUNT	TALKBACKS	TALLOLS	TAMARACKS
TALAUNTS	TALKBOX	TALLOT	TAMARAO
TALAYOT	TALKBOXES	TALLOTS	TAMARAOS
TALAYOTS	TALKED	TALLOW	TAMARAS
TALBOT	TALKER	TALLOWED	TAMARAU
TALBOTS	TALKERS	TALLOWING	TAMARAUS
TALBOTYPE	TALKFEST	TALLOWISH	TAMARI
TALC	TALKFESTS	TALLOWS	TAMARILLO
TALCED	TALKIE	TALLOWY	TAMARIN
TALCIER	TALKIER	TALLS	TAMARIND
TALCIEST	TALKIES	TALLY	TAMARINDS

TAMARINS

TAMARINS
TAMARIS
TAMARISK
TAMARISKS
TAMASHA
TAMASHAS
TAMBAC
TAMBACS
TAMBAK
TAMBAKS
TAMBALA
TAMBALAS
TAMBER
TAMBERS
TAMBOUR
TAMBOURA
TAMBOURAS
TAMBOURED
TAMBOURER
TAMBOURIN
TAMBOURS
TAMBUR
TAMBURA
TAMBURAS
TAMBURIN
TAMBURINS
TAMBURS
TAME
TAMEABLE
TAMED
TAMEIN
TAMEINS
TAMELESS
TAMELY
TAMENESS
TAMER
TAMERS
TAMES
TAMEST
TAMIN
TAMINE
TAMINES
TAMING
TAMINGS
TAMINS
TAMIS
TAMISE
TAMISES
TAMMAR
TAMMARS
TAMMIE
TAMMIED
TAMMIES
TAMMY
TAMMYING
TAMOXIFEN
TAMP
TAMPALA

TAMPALAS
TAMPAN
TAMPANS
TAMPED
TAMPER
TAMPERED
TAMPERER
TAMPERERS
TAMPERING
TAMPERS
TAMPING
TAMPINGS
TAMPION
TAMPIONS
TAMPON
TAMPONADE
TAMPONAGE
TAMPONED
TAMPONING
TAMPONS
TAMPS
TAMS
TAMWORTH
TAMWORTHS
TAN
TANA
TANADAR
TANADARS
TANAGER
TANAGERS
TANAGRA
TANAGRAS
TANAGRINE
TANAISTE
TANAISTES
TANALISED
TANALIZED
TANAS
TANBARK
TANBARKS
TANDEM
TANDEMS
TANDOOR
TANDOORI
TANDOORIS
TANDOORS
TANE
TANG
TANGA
TANGAS
TANGED
TANGELO
TANGELOS
TANGENCE
TANGENCES
TANGENCY
TANGENT
TANGENTAL

TANGENTS
TANGERINE
TANGHIN
TANGHININ
TANGHINS
TANGI
TANGIBLE
TANGIBLES
TANGIBLY
TANGIE
TANGIER
TANGIES
TANGIEST
TANGINESS
TANGING
TANGIS
TANGLE
TANGLED
TANGLER
TANGLERS
TANGLES
TANGLIER
TANGLIEST
TANGLING
TANGLINGS
TANGLY
TANGO
TANGOED
TANGOING
TANGOIST
TANGOISTS
TANGOLIKE
TANGOS
TANGRAM
TANGRAMS
TANGS
TANGUN
TANGUNS
TANGY
TANH
TANHS
TANIST
TANISTRY
TANISTS
TANIWHA
TANIWHAS
TANK
TANKA
TANKAGE
TANKAGES
TANKARD
TANKARDS
TANKAS
TANKED
TANKER
TANKERS
TANKFUL
TANKFULS

TANKIA
TANKIAS
TANKIES
TANKING
TANKINGS
TANKINI
TANKINIS
TANKLESS
TANKLIKE
TANKS
TANKSHIP
TANKSHIPS
TANKY
TANLING
TANLINGS
TANNA
TANNABLE
TANNAGE
TANNAGES
TANNAH
TANNAHS
TANNAS
TANNATE
TANNATES
TANNED
TANNER
TANNERIES
TANNERS
TANNERY
TANNEST
TANNIC
TANNIE
TANNIES
TANNIN
TANNING
TANNINGS
TANNINS
TANNISH
TANNOY
TANNOYED
TANNOYING
TANNOYS
TANREC
TANRECS
TANS
TANSIES
TANSY
TANTALATE
TANTALIC
TANTALISE
TANTALISM
TANTALITE
TANTALIZE
TANTALOUS
TANTALUM
TANTALUMS
TANTALUS
TANTARA

TANTARARA	TAPESTRY	TAQUERIA	TARIFFS
TANTARAS	TAPET	TAQUERIAS	TARING
TANTI	TAPETA	TAR	TARINGS
TANTIVIES	TAPETAL	TARA	TARLATAN
TANTIVY	TAPETI	TARAIRE	TARLATANS
TANTO	TAPETIS	TARAKIHI	TARLETAN
TANTONIES	TAPETS	TARAKIHIS	TARLETANS
TANTONY	TAPETUM	TARAMA	TARMAC
TANTRA	TAPEWORM	TARAMAS	TARMACKED
TANTRAS	TAPEWORMS	TARAMEA	TARMACS
TANTRIC	TAPHOLE	TARAMEAS	TARN
TANTRISM	TAPHOLES	TARAND	TARNAL
TANTRISMS	TAPHONOMY	TARANDS	TARNALLY
TANTRUM	TAPHOUSE	TARANTARA	TARNATION
TANTRUMS	TAPHOUSES	TARANTAS	TARNISH
TANUKI	TAPING	TARANTASS	TARNISHED
TANUKIS	TAPIOCA	TARANTISM	TARNISHER
TANYARD	TAPIOCAS	TARANTIST	TARNISHES
TANYARDS	TAPIR	TARANTULA	TARNS
TANZANITE	TAPIROID	TARAS	TARO
TAO	TAPIRS	TARAXACUM	TAROC
TAOISEACH	TAPIS	TARBOGGIN	TAROCS
TAONGA	TAPISES	TARBOOSH	TAROK
TAONGAS	TAPIST	TARBOUCHE	TAROKS
TAOS	TAPISTS	TARBOUSH	TAROS
TAP	TAPLASH	TARBOY	TAROT
TAPA	TAPLASHES	TARBOYS	TAROTS
TAPACOLO	TAPPA	TARBUSH	TARP
TAPACOLOS	TAPPABLE	TARBUSHES	TARPAN
TAPACULO	TAPPAS	TARCEL	TARPANS
TAPACULOS	TAPPED	TARCELS	TARPAPER
TAPADERA	TAPPER	TARDIED	TARPAPERS
TAPADERAS	TAPPERS	TARDIER	TARPAULIN
TAPADERO	TAPPET	TARDIES	TARPON
TAPADEROS	TAPPETS	TARDIEST	TARPONS
TAPALO	TAPPICE	TARDILY	TARPS
TAPALOS	TAPPICED	TARDINESS	TARRAGON
TAPAS	TAPPICES	TARDIVE	TARRAGONS
TAPE	TAPPICING	TARDO	TARRAS
TAPEABLE	TAPPING	TARDY	TARRASES
TAPED	TAPPINGS	TARDYING	TARRE
TAPELESS	TAPPIT	TARDYON	TARRED
TAPELIKE	TAPROOM	TARDYONS	TARRES
TAPELINE	TAPROOMS	TARE	TARRIANCE
TAPELINES	TAPROOT	TARED	TARRIED
TAPEN	TAPROOTED	TARES	TARRIER
TAPENADE	TAPROOTS	TARGE	TARRIERS
TAPENADES	TAPS	TARGED	TARRIES
TAPER	TAPSMAN	TARGES	TARRIEST
TAPERED	TAPSMEN	TARGET	TARRINESS
TAPERER	TAPSTER	TARGETED	TARRING
TAPERERS	TAPSTERS	TARGETEER	TARRINGS
TAPERING	TAPSTRESS	TARGETING	TARROCK
TAPERINGS	TAPSTRY	TARGETS	TARROCKS
TAPERNESS	TAPU	TARGING	TARROW
TAPERS	TAPUED	TARIFF	TARROWED
TAPERWISE	TAPUING	TARIFFED	TARROWING
TAPES	TAPUS	TARIFFING	TARROWS

TARRY	TARTUFES	TASTELESS	TATTLING
TARRYING	TARTUFFE	TASTER	TATTLINGS
TARS	TARTUFFES	TASTERS	TATTOO
TARSAL	TARTY	TASTES	TATTOOED
TARSALGIA	TARWEED	TASTEVIN	TATTOOER
TARSALS	TARWEEDS	TASTEVINS	TATTOOERS
TARSEAL	TARWHINE	TASTIER	TATTOOING
TARSEALS	TARWHINES	TASTIEST	TATTOOIST
TARSEL	TARZAN	TASTILY	TATTOOS
TARSELS	TARZANS	TASTINESS	TATTOW
TARSI	TAS	TASTING	TATTOWED
TARSIA	TASAR	TASTINGS	TATTOWING
TARSIAS	TASARS	TASTY	TATTOWS
TARSIER	TASER	TAT	TATTS
TARSIERS	TASERED	TATAHASH	TATTY
TARSIOID	TASERING	TATAMI	TATU
TARSIPED	TASERS	TATAMIS	TATUED
TARSIPEDS	TASH	TATAR	TATUING
TARSUS	TASHED	TATARS	TATUS
TART	TASHES	TATE	TAU
TARTAN	TASHING	TATER	TAUBE
TARTANA	TASIMETER	TATERS	TAUBES
TARTANAS	TASIMETRY	TATES	TAUGHT
TARTANE	TASK	TATH	TAUHINU
TARTANED	TASKBAR	TATHED	TAUHINUS
TARTANES	TASKBARS	TATHING	TAUHOU
TARTANRY	TASKED	TATHS	TAUIWI
TARTANS	TASKER	TATIE	TAUIWIS
TARTAR	TASKERS	TATIES	TAULD
TARTARE	TASKING	TATLER	TAUNT
TARTARES	TASKINGS	TATLERS	TAUNTED
TARTARIC	TASKLESS	TATOU	TAUNTER
TARTARISE	TASKS	TATOUAY	TAUNTERS
TARTARIZE	TASKWORK	TATOUAYS	TAUNTING
TARTARLY	TASKWORKS	TATOUS	TAUNTINGS
TARTAROUS	TASLET	TATS	TAUNTS
TARTARS	TASLETS	TATSOI	TAUON
TARTED	TASS	TATSOIS	TAUONS
TARTER	TASSE	TATT	TAUPATA
TARTEST	TASSEL	TATTED	TAUPE
TARTIER	TASSELED	TATTER	TAUPES
TARTIEST	TASSELING	TATTERED	TAUPIE
TARTILY	TASSELL	TATTERING	TAUPIES
TARTINE	TASSELLED	TATTERS	TAUREAN
TARTINES	TASSELLS	TATTERY	TAURIC
TARTINESS	TASSELLY	TATTIE	TAURIFORM
TARTING	TASSELS	TATTIER	TAURINE
TARTISH	TASSES	TATTIES	TAURINES
TARTISHLY	TASSET	TATTIEST	TAUS
TARTLET	TASSETS	TATTILY	TAUT
TARTLETS	TASSIE	TATTINESS	TAUTAUG
TARTLY	TASSIES	TATTING	TAUTAUGS
TARTNESS	TASSWAGE	TATTINGS	TAUTED
TARTRATE	TASTABLE	TATTLE	TAUTEN
TARTRATED	TASTE	TATTLED	TAUTENED
TARTRATES	TASTEABLE	TATTLER	TAUTENING
TARTS	TASTED	TATTLERS	TAUTENS
TARTUFE	TASTEFUL	TATTLES	TAUTER

TAUTEST	TAWNIEST	TAXMAN	TEACUP
TAUTING	TAWNILY	TAXMEN	TEACUPFUL
TAUTIT	TAWNINESS	TAXOL	TEACUPS
TAUTLY	TAWNY	TAXOLS	TEAD
TAUTNESS	TAWPIE	TAXON	TEADE
TAUTOG	TAWPIES	TAXONOMER	TEADES
TAUTOGS	TAWS	TAXONOMIC	TEADS
TAUTOLOGY	TAWSE	TAXONOMY	TEAED
TAUTOMER	TAWSED	TAXONS	TEAGLE
TAUTOMERS	TAWSES	TAXOR	TEAGLED
TAUTONYM	TAWSING	TAXORS	TEAGLES
TAUTONYMS	TAWT	TAXPAID	TEAGLING
TAUTONYMY	TAWTED	TAXPAYER	TEAHOUSE
TAUTS	TAWTIE	TAXPAYERS	TEAHOUSES
TAV	TAWTIER	TAXPAYING	TEAING
TAVA	TAWTIEST	TAXUS	TEAK
TAVAH	TAWTING	TAXWISE	TEAKETTLE
TAVAHS	TAWTS	TAXYING	TEAKS
TAVAS	TAX	TAY	TEAKWOOD
TAVER	TAXA	TAYASSUID	TEAKWOODS
TAVERED	TAXABLE	TAYBERRY	TEAL
TAVERING	TAXABLES	TAYRA	TEALIKE
TAVERN	TAXABLY	TAYRAS	TEALS
TAVERNA	TAXACEOUS	TAYS	TEAM
TAVERNAS	TAXAMETER	TAZZA	TEAMAKER
TAVERNER	TAXATION	TAZZAS	TEAMAKERS
TAVERNERS	TAXATIONS	TAZZE	TEAMED
TAVERNS	TAXATIVE	TCHICK	TEAMER
TAVERS	TAXED	TCHICKED	TEAMERS
TAVERT	TAXEME	TCHICKING	TEAMING
TAVS	TAXEMES	TCHICKS	TEAMINGS
TAW	TAXEMIC	TCHOTCHKE	TEAMMATE
TAWA	TAXER	TE	TEAMMATES
TAWAI	TAXERS	TEA	TEAMS
TAWAIS	TAXES	TEABERRY	TEAMSTER
TAWAS	TAXI	TEABOARD	TEAMSTERS
TAWDRIER	TAXIARCH	TEABOARDS	TEAMWISE
TAWDRIES	TAXIARCHS	TEABOWL	TEAMWORK
TAWDRIEST	TAXICAB	TEABOWLS	TEAMWORKS
TAWDRILY	TAXICABS	TEABOX	TEAPOT
TAWDRY	TAXIDERMY	TEABOXES	TEAPOTS
TAWED	TAXIED	TEABREAD	TEAPOY
TAWER	TAXIES	TEABREADS	TEAPOYS
TAWERIES	TAXIING	TEACAKE	TEAR
TAWERS	TAXIMAN	TEACAKES	TEARABLE
TAWERY	TAXIMEN	TEACART	TEARAWAY
TAWHAI	TAXIMETER	TEACARTS	TEARAWAYS
TAWHAIS	TAXING	TEACH	TEARDOWN
TAWHIRI	TAXINGLY	TEACHABLE	TEARDOWNS
TAWIE	TAXINGS	TEACHABLY	TEARDROP
TAWIER	TAXIPLANE	TEACHER	TEARDROPS
TAWIEST	TAXIS	TEACHERLY	TEARED
TAWING	TAXITE	TEACHERS	TEARER
TAWINGS	TAXITES	TEACHES	TEARERS
TAWNEY	TAXITIC	TEACHIE	TEARFUL
TAWNEYS	TAXIWAY	TEACHING	TEARFULLY
TAWNIER	TAXIWAYS	TEACHINGS	TEARGAS
TAWNIES	TAXLESS	TEACHLESS	TEARGASES

TEARIER	TEC	TEDY	TEETHED
TEARIEST	TECH	TEE	TEETHER
TEARILY	TECHED	TEED	TEETHERS
TEARINESS	TECHIE	TEEING	TEETHES
TEARING	TECHIER	TEEK	TEETHING
TEARLESS	TECHIES	TEEL	TEETHINGS
TEAROOM	TECHIEST	TEELS	TEETHLESS
TEAROOMS	TECHILY	TEEM	TEETOTAL
TEARS	TECHINESS	TEEMED	TEETOTALS
TEARSHEET	TECHNIC	TEEMER	TEETOTUM
TEARSTAIN	TECHNICAL	TEEMERS	TEETOTUMS
TEARSTRIP	TECHNICS	TEEMFUL	TEF
TEARY	TECHNIKON	TEEMING	TEFF
TEAS	TECHNIQUE	TEEMINGLY	TEFFS
TEASABLE	TECHNO	TEEMLESS	TEFILLAH
TEASE	TECHNOPOP	TEEMS	TEFILLIN
TEASED	TECHNOS	TEEN	TEFLON
TEASEL	TECHS	TEENAGE	TEFLONS
TEASELED	TECHY	TEENAGED	TEFS
TEASELER	TECKEL	TEENAGER	TEG
TEASELERS	TECKELS	TEENAGERS	TEGG
TEASELING	TECS	TEEND	TEGGS
TEASELLED	TECTA	TEENDED	TEGMEN
TEASELLER	TECTAL	TEENDING	TEGMENTA
TEASELS	TECTIFORM	TEENDS	TEGMENTAL
TEASER	TECTITE	TEENE	TEGMENTUM
TEASERS	TECTITES	TEENED	TEGMINA
TEASES	TECTONIC	TEENER	TEGMINAL
TEASHOP	TECTONICS	TEENERS	TEGS
TEASHOPS	TECTONISM	TEENES	TEGU
TEASING	TECTORIAL	TEENFUL	TEGUA
TEASINGLY	TECTRICES	TEENIER	TEGUAS
TEASINGS	TECTRIX	TEENIEST	TEGUEXIN
TEASPOON	TECTUM	TEENING	TEGUEXINS
TEASPOONS	TECTUMS	TEENS	TEGULA
TEAT	TED	TEENSIER	TEGULAE
TEATASTER	TEDDED	TEENSIEST	TEGULAR
TEATED	TEDDER	TEENSY	TEGULARLY
TEATIME	TEDDERED	TEENTIER	TEGULATED
TEATIMES	TEDDERING	TEENTIEST	TEGUMEN
TEATS	TEDDERS	TEENTSIER	TEGUMENT
TEAWARE	TEDDIE	TEENTSY	TEGUMENTS
TEAWARES	TEDDIES	TEENTY	TEGUMINA
TEAZE	TEDDING	TEENY	TEGUS
TEAZED	TEDDY	TEENYBOP	TEHR
TEAZEL	TEDESCA	TEEPEE	TEHRS
TEAZELED	TEDESCHE	TEEPEES	TEIGLACH
TEAZELING	TEDESCHI	TEER	TEIID
TEAZELLED	TEDESCO	TEERED	TEIIDS
TEAZELS	TEDIER	TEERING	TEIL
TEAZES	TEDIEST	TEERS	TEILS
TEAZING	TEDIOSITY	TEES	TEIND
TEAZLE	TEDIOUS	TEETER	TEINDED
TEAZLED	TEDIOUSLY	TEETERED	TEINDING
TEAZLES	TEDISOME	TEETERING	TEINDS
TEAZLING	TEDIUM	TEETERS	TEKKIE
TEBBAD	TEDIUMS	TEETH	TEKKIES
TEBBADS	TEDS	TEETHE	TEKNONYMY

TEKTITE	TELEPOINT	TELIUM	TELS
TEKTITES	TELEPORT	TELL	TELSON
TEKTITIC	TELEPORTS	TELLABLE	TELSONIC
TEL	TELERAN	TELLAR	TELSONS
TELA	TELERANS	TELLARED	TELT
TELAE	TELERGIC	TELLARING	TEMAZEPAM
TELAMON	TELERGIES	TELLARS	TEMBLOR
TELAMONES	TELERGY	TELLEN	TEMBLORES
TELAMONS	TELES	TELLENS	TEMBLORS
TELARY	TELESALE	TELLER	TEME
TELCO	TELESALES	TELLERED	TEMED
TELCOS	TELESCOPE	TELLERING	TEMENE
TELD	TELESCOPY	TELLERS	TEMENOS
TELE	TELESEME	TELLIES	TEMERITY
TELECAST	TELESEMES	TELLIN	TEMEROUS
TELECASTS	TELESES	TELLING	TEMES
TELECHIR	TELESHOP	TELLINGLY	TEMP
TELECHIRS	TELESHOPS	TELLINGS	TEMPED
TELECINE	TELESIS	TELLINOID	TEMPEH
TELECINES	TELESM	TELLINS	TEMPEHS
TELECOM	TELESMS	TELLS	TEMPER
TELECOMS	TELESTIC	TELLTALE	TEMPERA
TELEDU	TELESTICH	TELLTALES	TEMPERAS
TELEDUS	TELESTICS	TELLURAL	TEMPERATE
TELEFAX	TELETEX	TELLURATE	TEMPERED
TELEFAXED	TELETEXES	TELLURIAN	TEMPERER
TELEFAXES	TELETEXT	TELLURIC	TEMPERERS
TELEFILM	TELETEXTS	TELLURIDE	TEMPERING
TELEFILMS	TELETHON	TELLURION	TEMPERS
TELEGA	TELETHONS	TELLURISE	TEMPEST
TELEGAS	TELETRON	TELLURITE	TEMPESTED
TELEGENIC	TELETRONS	TELLURIUM	TEMPESTS
TELEGONIC	TELETYPE	TELLURIZE	TEMPI
TELEGONY	TELETYPED	TELLUROUS	TEMPING
TELEGRAM	TELETYPES	TELLUS	TEMPLAR
TELEGRAMS	TELEVIEW	TELLUSES	TEMPLARS
TELEGRAPH	TELEVIEWS	TELLY	TEMPLATE
TELEMAN	TELEVISE	TELLYS	TEMPLATES
TELEMARK	TELEVISED	TELNET	TEMPLE
TELEMARKS	TELEVISER	TELNETED	TEMPLED
TELEMATIC	TELEVISES	TELNETING	TEMPLES
TELEMEN	TELEVISOR	TELNETS	TEMPLET
TELEMETER	TELEX	TELNETTED	TEMPLETS
TELEMETRY	TELEXED	TELOI	TEMPO
TELEOLOGY	TELEXES	TELOME	TEMPORAL
TELEONOMY	TELEXING	TELOMERE	TEMPORALS
TELEOSAUR	TELFER	TELOMERES	TEMPORARY
TELEOST	TELFERAGE	TELOMES	TEMPORE
TELEOSTS	TELFERED	TELOMIC	TEMPORISE
TELEPATH	TELFERIC	TELOPHASE	TEMPORIZE
TELEPATHS	TELFERING	TELOS	TEMPOS
TELEPATHY	TELFERS	TELOSES	TEMPS
TELEPHEME	TELFORD	TELOTAXES	TEMPT
TELEPHONE	TELFORDS	TELOTAXIS	TEMPTABLE
TELEPHONY	TELIA	TELPHER	TEMPTED
TELEPHOTO	TELIAL	TELPHERED	TEMPTER
TELEPLAY	TELIC	TELPHERIC	TEMPTERS
TELEPLAYS	TELICALLY	TELPHERS	TEMPTING

TEMPTINGS	TENDONS	TENONING	TENTED
TEMPTRESS	TENDRE	TENONS	TENTER
TEMPTS	TENDRES	TENOR	TENTERED
TEMPURA	TENDRESSE	TENORIST	TENTERING
TEMPURAS	TENDRIL	TENORISTS	TENTERS
TEMS	TENDRILED	TENORITE	TENTFUL
TEMSE	TENDRILS	TENORITES	TENTFULS
TEMSED	TENDRON	TENORLESS	TENTH
TEMSES	TENDRONS	TENOROON	TENTHLY
TEMSING	TENDS	TENOROONS	TENTHS
TEMULENCE	TENDU	TENORS	TENTIE
TEMULENCY	TENDUS	TENOTOMY	TENTIER
TEMULENT	TENE	TENOUR	TENTIEST
TEN	TENEBRAE	TENOURS	TENTIGO
TENABLE	TENEBRIO	TENPENCE	TENTIGOS
TENABLY	TENEBRIOS	TENPENCES	TENTING
TENACE	TENEBRISM	TENPENNY	TENTINGS
TENACES	TENEBRIST	TENPIN	TENTLESS
TENACIOUS	TENEBRITY	TENPINS	TENTLIKE
TENACITY	TENEBROSE	TENREC	TENTMAKER
TENACULA	TENEBROUS	TENRECS	TENTORIA
TENACULUM	TENEMENT	TENS	TENTORIAL
TENAIL	TENEMENTS	TENSE	TENTORIUM
TENAILLE	TENENDUM	TENSED	TENTS
TENAILLES	TENENDUMS	TENSELESS	TENTWISE
TENAILLON	TENES	TENSELY	TENTY
TENAILS	TENESMIC	TENSENESS	TENUE
TENANCIES	TENESMUS	TENSER	TENUES
TENANCY	TENET	TENSES	TENUIOUS
TENANT	TENETS	TENSEST	TENUIS
TENANTED	TENFOLD	TENSIBLE	TENUITIES
TENANTING	TENFOLDS	TENSIBLY	TENUITY
TENANTRY	TENGE	TENSILE	TENUOUS
TENANTS	TENGES	TENSILELY	TENUOUSLY
TENCH	TENIA	TENSILITY	TENURABLE
TENCHES	TENIACIDE	TENSING	TENURE
TEND	TENIAE	TENSION	TENURED
TENDANCE	TENIAFUGE	TENSIONAL	TENURES
TENDANCES	TENIAS	TENSIONED	TENURIAL
TENDED	TENIASES	TENSIONER	TENURING
TENDENCE	TENIASIS	TENSIONS	TENUTI
TENDENCES	TENIOID	TENSITIES	TENUTO
TENDENCY	TENNE	TENSITY	TENUTOS
TENDENZ	TENNER	TENSIVE	TENZON
TENDENZEN	TENNERS	TENSON	TENZONS
TENDER	TENNES	TENSONS	TEOCALLI
TENDERED	TENNIES	TENSOR	TEOCALLIS
TENDERER	TENNIS	TENSORIAL	TEOPAN
TENDERERS	TENNISES	TENSORS	TEOPANS
TENDEREST	TENNIST	TENT	TEOSINTE
TENDERING	TENNISTS	TENTACLE	TEOSINTES
TENDERISE	TENNO	TENTACLED	TEPA
TENDERIZE	TENNOS	TENTACLES	TEPAL
TENDERLY	TENNY	TENTACULA	TEPALS
TENDERS	TENON	TENTAGE	TEPAS
TENDING	TENONED	TENTAGES	TEPEE
TENDINOUS	TENONER	TENTATION	TEPEES
TENDON	TENONERS	TENTATIVE	TEPEFIED

TEPEFIES	TERCELET	TERMLIES	TERRIBLES
TEPEFY	TERCELETS	TERMLY	TERRIBLY
TEPEFYING	TERCELS	TERMOR	TERRICOLE
TEPHIGRAM	TERCES	TERMORS	TERRIER
TEPHILLAH	TERCET	TERMS	TERRIERS
TEPHILLIN	TERCETS	TERMTIME	TERRIES
TEPHRA	TERCIO	TERMTIMES	TERRIFIC
TEPHRAS	TERCIOS	TERN	TERRIFIED
TEPHRITE	TEREBENE	TERNAL	TERRIFIER
TEPHRITES	TEREBENES	TERNARIES	TERRIFIES
TEPHRITIC	TEREBIC	TERNARY	TERRIFY
TEPHROITE	TEREBINTH	TERNATE	TERRINE
TEPID	TEREBRA	TERNATELY	TERRINES
TEPIDARIA	TEREBRAE	TERNE	TERRIT
TEPIDER	TEREBRANT	TERNED	TERRITORY
TEPIDEST	TEREBRAS	TERNES	TERRITS
TEPIDITY	TEREBRATE	TERNING	TERROIR
TEPIDLY	TEREDINES	TERNION	TERROIRS
TEPIDNESS	TEREDO	TERNIONS	TERROR
TEPOY	TEREDOS	TERNS	TERRORFUL
TEPOYS	TEREFA	TERPENE	TERRORISE
TEQUILA	TEREFAH	TERPENES	TERRORISM
TEQUILAS	TEREK	TERPENIC	TERRORIST
TEQUILLA	TEREKS	TERPENOID	TERRORIZE
TEQUILLAS	TERES	TERPINEOL	TERRORS
TERABYTE	TERETE	TERPINOL	TERRY
TERABYTES	TERETES	TERPINOLS	TERSE
TERAFLOP	TERF	TERRA	TERSELY
TERAFLOPS	TERFE	TERRACE	TERSENESS
TERAGLIN	TERFES	TERRACED	TERSER
TERAGLINS	TERFS	TERRACES	TERSEST
TERAHERTZ	TERGA	TERRACING	TERSION
TERAI	TERGAL	TERRAE	TERSIONS
TERAIS	TERGITE	TERRAFORM	TERTIA
TERAKIHI	TERGITES	TERRAIN	TERTIAL
TERAKIHIS	TERGUM	TERRAINS	TERTIALS
TERAOHM	TERIYAKI	TERRAMARA	TERTIAN
TERAOHMS	TERIYAKIS	TERRAMARE	TERTIANS
TERAPH	TERM	TERRANE	TERTIARY
TERAPHIM	TERMAGANT	TERRANES	TERTIAS
TERAPHIMS	TERMED	TERRAPIN	TERTIUM
TERAS	TERMER	TERRAPINS	TERTIUS
TERATA	TERMERS	TERRARIA	TERTIUSES
TERATISM	TERMINAL	TERRARIUM	TERTS
TERATISMS	TERMINALS	TERRAS	TERVALENT
TERATOGEN	TERMINATE	TERRASES	TERYLENE
TERATOID	TERMINER	TERRAZZO	TERYLENES
TERATOMA	TERMINERS	TERRAZZOS	TERZETTA
TERATOMAS	TERMING	TERREEN	TERZETTAS
TERAWATT	TERMINI	TERREENS	TERZETTI
TERAWATTS	TERMINISM	TERRELLA	TERZETTO
TERBIA	TERMINIST	TERRELLAS	TERZETTOS
TERBIAS	TERMINUS	TERRENE	TES
TERBIC	TERMITARY	TERRENELY	TESLA
TERBIUM	TERMITE	TERRENES	TESLAS
TERBIUMS	TERMITES	TERRET	TESSELATE
TERCE	TERMITIC	TERRETS	TESSELLA
TERCEL	TERMLESS	TERRIBLE	TESSELLAE

TESSELLAR
TESSERA
TESSERACT
TESSERAE
TESSERAL
TESSITURA
TESSITURE
TEST
TESTA
TESTABLE
TESTACEAN
TESTACIES
TESTACY
TESTAE
TESTAMENT
TESTAMUR
TESTAMURS
TESTATE
TESTATES
TESTATION
TESTATOR
TESTATORS
TESTATRIX
TESTATUM
TESTATUMS
TESTCROSS
TESTE
TESTED
TESTEE
TESTEES
TESTER
TESTERN
TESTERNED
TESTERNS
TESTERS
TESTES
TESTICLE
TESTICLES
TESTIER
TESTIEST
TESTIFIED
TESTIFIER
TESTIFIES
TESTIFY
TESTILY
TESTIMONY
TESTINESS
TESTING
TESTINGS
TESTIS
TESTON
TESTONS
TESTOON
TESTOONS
TESTRIL
TESTRILL
TESTRILLS
TESTRILS

TESTS
TESTUDO
TESTUDOS
TESTY
TET
TETANAL
TETANIC
TETANICAL
TETANICS
TETANIES
TETANISE
TETANISED
TETANISES
TETANIZE
TETANIZED
TETANIZES
TETANOID
TETANUS
TETANUSES
TETANY
TETCHED
TETCHIER
TETCHIEST
TETCHILY
TETCHY
TETE
TETES
TETH
TETHER
TETHERED
TETHERING
TETHERS
TETHS
TETOTUM
TETOTUMS
TETRA
TETRACID
TETRACIDS
TETRACT
TETRACTS
TETRAD
TETRADIC
TETRADITE
TETRADS
TETRAGON
TETRAGONS
TETRAGRAM
TETRALOGY
TETRAMER
TETRAMERS
TETRAPLA
TETRAPLAS
TETRAPOD
TETRAPODS
TETRAPODY
TETRARCH
TETRARCHS
TETRARCHY

TETRAS
TETRAXON
TETRAXONS
TETRI
TETRIS
TETRODE
TETRODES
TETRONAL
TETRONALS
TETROXID
TETROXIDE
TETROXIDS
TETRYL
TETRYLS
TETS
TETTER
TETTERED
TETTERING
TETTEROUS
TETTERS
TETTIX
TETTIXES
TEUCH
TEUCHAT
TEUCHATS
TEUCHER
TEUCHEST
TEUCHTER
TEUCHTERS
TEUGH
TEUGHER
TEUGHEST
TEUGHLY
TEUTONISE
TEUTONIZE
TEVATRON
TEVATRONS
TEW
TEWART
TEWARTS
TEWED
TEWEL
TEWELS
TEWHIT
TEWHITS
TEWING
TEWIT
TEWITS
TEWS
TEX
TEXAS
TEXASES
TEXES
TEXT
TEXTBOOK
TEXTBOOKS
TEXTED
TEXTER

TEXTERS
TEXTILE
TEXTILES
TEXTING
TEXTLESS
TEXTORIAL
TEXTPHONE
TEXTS
TEXTUAL
TEXTUALLY
TEXTUARY
TEXTURAL
TEXTURE
TEXTURED
TEXTURES
TEXTURING
TEXTURISE
TEXTURIZE
THACK
THACKED
THACKING
THACKS
THAE
THAGI
THAGIS
THAIM
THAIRM
THAIRMS
THALAMI
THALAMIC
THALAMUS
THALASSIC
THALER
THALERS
THALI
THALIAN
THALIS
THALLI
THALLIC
THALLINE
THALLIOUS
THALLIUM
THALLIUMS
THALLOID
THALLOUS
THALLUS
THALLUSES
THALWEG
THALWEGS
THAN
THANA
THANADAR
THANADARS
THANAGE
THANAGES
THANAH
THANAHS
THANAS

THANATISM
THANATIST
THANATOID
THANATOS
THANE
THANEDOM
THANEDOMS
THANEHOOD
THANES
THANESHIP
THANGKA
THANGKAS
THANK
THANKED
THANKEE
THANKER
THANKERS
THANKFUL
THANKING
THANKINGS
THANKLESS
THANKS
THANKYOU
THANKYOUS
THANNA
THANNAH
THANNAHS
THANNAS
THANS
THAR
THARM
THARMS
THARS
THAT
THATAWAY
THATCH
THATCHED
THATCHER
THATCHERS
THATCHES
THATCHIER
THATCHING
THATCHT
THATCHY
THATNESS
THAUMATIN
THAW
THAWED
THAWER
THAWERS
THAWIER
THAWIEST
THAWING
THAWINGS
THAWLESS
THAWS
THAWY
THE

THEACEOUS
THEANDRIC
THEARCHIC
THEARCHY
THEATER
THEATERS
THEATRAL
THEATRE
THEATRES
THEATRIC
THEATRICS
THEAVE
THEAVES
THEBAINE
THEBAINES
THEBE
THEBES
THECA
THECAE
THECAL
THECATE
THECODONT
THEE
THEED
THEEING
THEEK
THEEKED
THEEKING
THEEKS
THEELIN
THEELINS
THEELOL
THEELOLS
THEES
THEFT
THEFTLESS
THEFTS
THEFTUOUS
THEGITHER
THEGN
THEGNLY
THEGNS
THEIC
THEICS
THEIN
THEINE
THEINES
THEINS
THEIR
THEIRS
THEIRSELF
THEISM
THEISMS
THEIST
THEISTIC
THEISTS
THELEMENT
THELF

THELITIS
THELVES
THELYTOKY
THEM
THEMA
THEMATA
THEMATIC
THEMATICS
THEME
THEMED
THEMELESS
THEMES
THEMING
THEMSELF
THEN
THENABOUT
THENAGE
THENAGES
THENAL
THENAR
THENARS
THENCE
THENS
THEOCRACY
THEOCRASY
THEOCRAT
THEOCRATS
THEODICY
THEOGONIC
THEOGONY
THEOLOG
THEOLOGER
THEOLOGIC
THEOLOGS
THEOLOGUE
THEOLOGY
THEOMACHY
THEOMANCY
THEOMANIA
THEONOMY
THEOPATHY
THEOPHAGY
THEOPHANY
THEORBIST
THEORBO
THEORBOS
THEOREM
THEOREMIC
THEOREMS
THEORETIC
THEORIC
THEORICS
THEORIES
THEORIQUE
THEORISE
THEORISED
THEORISER
THEORISES

THEORIST
THEORISTS
THEORIZE
THEORIZED
THEORIZER
THEORIZES
THEORY
THEOSOPH
THEOSOPHS
THEOSOPHY
THEOTOKOI
THEOTOKOS
THEOW
THEOWS
THERALITE
THERAPIES
THERAPIST
THERAPSID
THERAPY
THERBLIG
THERBLIGS
THERE
THEREAT
THEREAWAY
THEREBY
THEREFOR
THEREFORE
THEREFROM
THEREIN
THEREINTO
THEREMIN
THEREMINS
THERENESS
THEREOF
THEREON
THEREOUT
THERES
THERETO
THEREUNTO
THEREUPON
THEREWITH
THERIAC
THERIACA
THERIACAL
THERIACAS
THERIACS
THERIAN
THERIANS
THERM
THERMAE
THERMAL
THERMALLY
THERMALS
THERME
THERMEL
THERMELS
THERMES
THERMETTE

THERMIC
THERMICAL
THERMIDOR
THERMION
THERMIONS
THERMIT
THERMITE
THERMITES
THERMITS
THERMOS
THERMOSES
THERMOSET
THERMOTIC
THERMS
THEROID
THEROLOGY
THEROPOD
THEROPODS
THESAURAL
THESAURI
THESAURUS
THESE
THESES
THESIS
THESP
THESPIAN
THESPIANS
THESPS
THETA
THETAS
THETCH
THETCHED
THETCHES
THETCHING
THETE
THETES
THETHER
THETIC
THETICAL
THEURGIC
THEURGIES
THEURGIST
THEURGY
THEW
THEWED
THEWES
THEWIER
THEWIEST
THEWLESS
THEWS
THEWY
THEY
THIAMIN
THIAMINE
THIAMINES
THIAMINS
THIASUS
THIASUSES

THIAZIDE
THIAZIDES
THIAZIN
THIAZINE
THIAZINES
THIAZINS
THIAZOL
THIAZOLE
THIAZOLES
THIAZOLS
THIBET
THIBETS
THIBLE
THIBLES
THICK
THICKED
THICKEN
THICKENED
THICKENER
THICKENS
THICKER
THICKEST
THICKET
THICKETED
THICKETS
THICKETY
THICKHEAD
THICKIE
THICKIES
THICKING
THICKISH
THICKLEAF
THICKLY
THICKNESS
THICKO
THICKOES
THICKOS
THICKS
THICKSET
THICKSETS
THICKSKIN
THICKY
THIEF
THIEVE
THIEVED
THIEVERY
THIEVES
THIEVING
THIEVINGS
THIEVISH
THIG
THIGGER
THIGGERS
THIGGING
THIGGINGS
THIGGIT
THIGH
THIGHBONE

THIGHED
THIGHS
THIGS
THILK
THILL
THILLER
THILLERS
THILLS
THIMBLE
THIMBLED
THIMBLES
THIMBLING
THIN
THINCLAD
THINCLADS
THINDOWN
THINDOWNS
THINE
THING
THINGAMY
THINGHOOD
THINGIER
THINGIES
THINGIEST
THINGNESS
THINGS
THINGUMMY
THINGY
THINK
THINKABLE
THINKABLY
THINKER
THINKERS
THINKING
THINKINGS
THINKS
THINLY
THINNED
THINNER
THINNERS
THINNESS
THINNEST
THINNING
THINNINGS
THINNISH
THINS
THIO
THIOFURAN
THIOL
THIOLIC
THIOLS
THIONATE
THIONATES
THIONIC
THIONIN
THIONINE
THIONINES
THIONINS

THIONYL
THIONYLS
THIOPHEN
THIOPHENE
THIOPHENS
THIOPHIL
THIOTEPA
THIOTEPAS
THIOUREA
THIOUREAS
THIR
THIRAM
THIRAMS
THIRD
THIRDED
THIRDHAND
THIRDING
THIRDINGS
THIRDLY
THIRDS
THIRDSMAN
THIRDSMEN
THIRL
THIRLAGE
THIRLAGES
THIRLED
THIRLING
THIRLS
THIRST
THIRSTED
THIRSTER
THIRSTERS
THIRSTFUL
THIRSTIER
THIRSTILY
THIRSTING
THIRSTS
THIRSTY
THIRTEEN
THIRTEENS
THIRTIES
THIRTIETH
THIRTY
THIRTYISH
THIS
THISAWAY
THISNESS
THISTLE
THISTLES
THISTLIER
THISTLY
THITHER
THITHERTO
THIVEL
THIVELS
THLIPSES
THLIPSIS
THO

THOFT
THOFTS
THOLE
THOLED
THOLEIITE
THOLEPIN
THOLEPINS
THOLES
THOLI
THOLING
THOLOBATE
THOLOI
THOLOS
THOLUS
THON
THONDER
THONG
THONGED
THONGS
THORACAL
THORACES
THORACIC
THORAX
THORAXES
THORIA
THORIAS
THORIC
THORITE
THORITES
THORIUM
THORIUMS
THORN
THORNBACK
THORNBILL
THORNBUSH
THORNED
THORNIER
THORNIEST
THORNILY
THORNING
THORNLESS
THORNLIKE
THORNS
THORNSET
THORNTREE
THORNY
THORO
THORON
THORONS
THOROUGH
THOROUGHS
THORP
THORPE
THORPES
THORPS
THOSE
THOTHER
THOU

THOUED
THOUGH
THOUGHT
THOUGHTED
THOUGHTEN
THOUGHTS
THOUING
THOUS
THOUSAND
THOUSANDS
THOWEL
THOWELS
THOWL
THOWLESS
THOWLS
THRAE
THRAIPING
THRALDOM
THRALDOMS
THRALL
THRALLDOM
THRALLED
THRALLING
THRALLS
THRANG
THRANGED
THRANGING
THRANGS
THRAPPLE
THRAPPLED
THRAPPLES
THRASH
THRASHED
THRASHER
THRASHERS
THRASHES
THRASHING
THRASONIC
THRAVE
THRAVES
THRAW
THRAWARD
THRAWART
THRAWED
THRAWING
THRAWN
THRAWNLY
THRAWS
THREAD
THREADED
THREADEN
THREADER
THREADERS
THREADFIN
THREADIER
THREADING
THREADS
THREADY

THREAP
THREAPED
THREAPER
THREAPERS
THREAPING
THREAPIT
THREAPS
THREAT
THREATED
THREATEN
THREATENS
THREATFUL
THREATING
THREATS
THREAVE
THREAVES
THREE
THREEFOLD
THREENESS
THREEP
THREEPED
THREEPER
THREEPERS
THREEPING
THREEPIT
THREEPS
THREES
THREESOME
THRENE
THRENES
THRENETIC
THRENODE
THRENODES
THRENODIC
THRENODY
THRENOS
THRENOSES
THREONINE
THRESH
THRESHED
THRESHEL
THRESHELS
THRESHER
THRESHERS
THRESHES
THRESHING
THRESHOLD
THRETTIES
THRETTY
THREW
THRICE
THRID
THRIDACE
THRIDACES
THRIDDED
THRIDDING
THRIDS
THRIFT

THRIFTIER
THRIFTILY
THRIFTS
THRIFTY
THRILL
THRILLANT
THRILLED
THRILLER
THRILLERS
THRILLIER
THRILLING
THRILLS
THRILLY
THRIMSA
THRIMSAS
THRIP
THRIPS
THRIPSES
THRISSEL
THRISSELS
THRIST
THRISTED
THRISTING
THRISTLE
THRISTLES
THRISTS
THRISTY
THRIVE
THRIVED
THRIVEN
THRIVER
THRIVERS
THRIVES
THRIVING
THRIVINGS
THRO
THROAT
THROATED
THROATIER
THROATILY
THROATING
THROATS
THROATY
THROB
THROBBED
THROBBER
THROBBERS
THROBBING
THROBLESS
THROBS
THROE
THROED
THROEING
THROES
THROMBI
THROMBIN
THROMBINS
THROMBOSE

THROMBUS	THRUSTS	THUNDERS	THYMOSIN
THRONE	THRUTCH	THUNDERY	THYMOSINS
THRONED	THRUTCHED	THUNDROUS	THYMUS
THRONES	THRUTCHES	THUNK	THYMUSES
THRONG	THRUWAY	THUNKED	THYMY
THRONGED	THRUWAYS	THUNKING	THYRATRON
THRONGFUL	THRYMSA	THUNKS	THYREOID
THRONGING	THRYMSAS	THURIBLE	THYREOIDS
THRONGS	THUD	THURIBLES	THYRISTOR
THRONING	THUDDED	THURIFER	THYROID
THRONNER	THUDDING	THURIFERS	THYROIDAL
THRONNERS	THUDS	THURIFIED	THYROIDS
THROPPLE	THUG	THURIFIES	THYROXIN
THROPPLED	THUGGEE	THURIFY	THYROXINE
THROPPLES	THUGGEES	THURL	THYROXINS
THROSTLE	THUGGERY	THURLS	THYRSE
THROSTLES	THUGGISH	THUS	THYRSES
THROTTLE	THUGGISM	THUSES	THYRSI
THROTTLED	THUGGISMS	THUSLY	THYRSOID
THROTTLER	THUGGO	THUSNESS	THYRSUS
THROTTLES	THUGGOS	THUSWISE	THYSELF
THROUGH	THUGS	THUYA	TI
THROUGHLY	THUJA	THUYAS	TIAR
THROVE	THUJAS	THWACK	TIARA
THROW	THULIA	THWACKED	TIARAED
THROWAWAY	THULIAS	THWACKER	TIARAS
THROWBACK	THULITE	THWACKERS	TIARS
THROWE	THULITES	THWACKING	TIBIA
THROWER	THULIUM	THWACKS	TIBIAE
THROWERS	THULIUMS	THWAITE	TIBIAL
THROWES	THUMB	THWAITES	TIBIAS
THROWING	THUMBED	THWART	TIC
THROWINGS	THUMBHOLE	THWARTED	TICAL
THROWN	THUMBIER	THWARTER	TICALS
THROWS	THUMBIEST	THWARTERS	TICCA
THROWSTER	THUMBING	THWARTING	TICCED
THRU	THUMBKIN	THWARTLY	TICCING
THRUM	THUMBKINS	THWARTS	TICE
THRUMMED	THUMBLESS	THY	TICED
THRUMMER	THUMBLIKE	THYINE	TICES
THRUMMERS	THUMBLING	THYLACINE	TICH
THRUMMIER	THUMBNAIL	THYLAKOID	TICHES
THRUMMING	THUMBNUT	THYLOSE	TICHIER
THRUMMY	THUMBNUTS	THYLOSES	TICHIEST
THRUMS	THUMBPOT	THYLOSIS	TICHY
THRUPENNY	THUMBPOTS	THYME	TICING
THRUPUT	THUMBS	THYMES	TICK
THRUPUTS	THUMBTACK	THYMEY	TICKED
THRUSH	THUMBY	THYMI	TICKEN
THRUSHES	THUMP	THYMIC	TICKENS
THRUST	THUMPED	THYMIDINE	TICKER
THRUSTED	THUMPER	THYMIER	TICKERS
THRUSTER	THUMPERS	THYMIEST	TICKET
THRUSTERS	THUMPING	THYMINE	TICKETED
THRUSTFUL	THUMPS	THYMINES	TICKETING
THRUSTING	THUNDER	THYMOCYTE	TICKETS
THRUSTOR	THUNDERED	THYMOL	TICKEY
THRUSTORS	THUNDERER	THYMOLS	TICKEYS

TICKIES	TIDEMARK	TIETAC	TIGRESS
TICKING	TIDEMARKS	TIETACK	TIGRESSES
TICKINGS	TIDEMILL	TIETACKS	TIGRIDIA
TICKLACE	TIDEMILLS	TIETACS	TIGRIDIAS
TICKLACES	TIDERIP	TIFF	TIGRINE
TICKLE	TIDERIPS	TIFFANIES	TIGRISH
TICKLED	TIDES	TIFFANY	TIGRISHLY
TICKLER	TIDESMAN	TIFFED	TIGROID
TICKLERS	TIDESMEN	TIFFIN	TIGS
TICKLES	TIDEWATER	TIFFINED	TIKA
TICKLIER	TIDEWAVE	TIFFING	TIKANGA
TICKLIEST	TIDEWAVES	TIFFINGS	TIKANGAS
TICKLING	TIDEWAY	TIFFINING	TIKAS
TICKLINGS	TIDEWAYS	TIFFINS	TIKE
TICKLISH	TIDIED	TIFFS	TIKES
TICKLY	TIDIER	TIFOSI	TIKI
TICKS	TIDIERS	TIFOSO	TIKIED
TICKSEED	TIDIES	TIFT	TIKIING
TICKSEEDS	TIDIEST	TIFTED	TIKIS
TICKTACK	TIDILY	TIFTING	TIKKA
TICKTACKS	TIDINESS	TIFTS	TIKKAS
TICKTOCK	TIDING	TIG	TIKOLOSHE
TICKTOCKS	TIDINGS	TIGE	TIL
TICKY	TIDIVATE	TIGER	TILAK
TICS	TIDIVATED	TIGEREYE	TILAKS
TICTAC	TIDIVATES	TIGEREYES	TILAPIA
TICTACKED	TIDS	TIGERISH	TILAPIAS
TICTACS	TIDY	TIGERISM	TILBURIES
TICTOC	TIDYING	TIGERISMS	TILBURY
TICTOCKED	TIDYTIPS	TIGERLIKE	TILDE
TICTOCS	TIE	TIGERLY	TILDES
TID	TIEBACK	TIGERS	TILE
TIDAL	TIEBACKS	TIGERY	TILED
TIDALLY	TIEBREAK	TIGES	TILEFISH
TIDBIT	TIEBREAKS	TIGGED	TILELIKE
TIDBITS	TIECLASP	TIGGING	TILER
TIDDIER	TIECLASPS	TIGHT	TILERIES
TIDDIES	TIED	TIGHTASS	TILERS
TIDDIEST	TIEING	TIGHTEN	TILERY
TIDDLE	TIELESS	TIGHTENED	TILES
TIDDLED	TIEPIN	TIGHTENER	TILING
TIDDLER	TIEPINS	TIGHTENS	TILINGS
TIDDLERS	TIER	TIGHTER	TILL
TIDDLES	TIERCE	TIGHTEST	TILLABLE
TIDDLEY	TIERCED	TIGHTISH	TILLAGE
TIDDLEYS	TIERCEL	TIGHTKNIT	TILLAGES
TIDDLIER	TIERCELET	TIGHTLY	TILLED
TIDDLIES	TIERCELS	TIGHTNESS	TILLER
TIDDLIEST	TIERCERON	TIGHTROPE	TILLERED
TIDDLING	TIERCES	TIGHTS	TILLERING
TIDDLY	TIERCET	TIGHTWAD	TILLERMAN
TIDDY	TIERCETS	TIGHTWADS	TILLERMEN
TIDE	TIERED	TIGHTWIRE	TILLERS
TIDED	TIERING	TIGLIC	TILLICUM
TIDELAND	TIEROD	TIGLON	TILLICUMS
TIDELANDS	TIERODS	TIGLONS	TILLIER
TIDELESS	TIERS	TIGON	TILLIEST
TIDELIKE	TIES	TIGONS	TILLING

TILLINGS
TILLITE
TILLITES
TILLS
TILLY
TILS
TILT
TILTABLE
TILTED
TILTER
TILTERS
TILTH
TILTHS
TILTING
TILTINGS
TILTMETER
TILTROTOR
TILTS
TILTYARD
TILTYARDS
TIMARAU
TIMARAUS
TIMARIOT
TIMARIOTS
TIMBAL
TIMBALE
TIMBALES
TIMBALS
TIMBER
TIMBERED
TIMBERING
TIMBERMAN
TIMBERMEN
TIMBERS
TIMBERY
TIMBO
TIMBOS
TIMBRAL
TIMBRE
TIMBREL
TIMBRELS
TIMBRES
TIME
TIMEBOMB
TIMEBOMBS
TIMECARD
TIMECARDS
TIMED
TIMEFRAME
TIMELESS
TIMELIER
TIMELIEST
TIMELINE
TIMELINES
TIMELY
TIMENOGUY
TIMEOUS
TIMEOUSLY

TIMEOUT
TIMEOUTS
TIMEPASS
TIMEPIECE
TIMER
TIMERS
TIMES
TIMESAVER
TIMESCALE
TIMETABLE
TIMEWORK
TIMEWORKS
TIMEWORN
TIMID
TIMIDER
TIMIDEST
TIMIDITY
TIMIDLY
TIMIDNESS
TIMING
TIMINGS
TIMIST
TIMISTS
TIMOCRACY
TIMOLOL
TIMOLOLS
TIMON
TIMONEER
TIMONEERS
TIMONS
TIMOROUS
TIMORSOME
TIMOTHIES
TIMOTHY
TIMOUS
TIMOUSLY
TIMPANA
TIMPANI
TIMPANIST
TIMPANO
TIMPANUM
TIMPANUMS
TIMPS
TIN
TINAJA
TINAJAS
TINAMOU
TINAMOUS
TINCAL
TINCALS
TINCHEL
TINCHELS
TINCT
TINCTED
TINCTING
TINCTS
TINCTURE
TINCTURED

TINCTURES
TIND
TINDAL
TINDALS
TINDED
TINDER
TINDERBOX
TINDERS
TINDERY
TINDING
TINDS
TINE
TINEA
TINEAL
TINEAS
TINED
TINEID
TINEIDS
TINES
TINFOIL
TINFOILS
TINFUL
TINFULS
TING
TINGE
TINGED
TINGEING
TINGES
TINGING
TINGLE
TINGLED
TINGLER
TINGLERS
TINGLES
TINGLIER
TINGLIEST
TINGLING
TINGLINGS
TINGLISH
TINGLY
TINGS
TINGUAITE
TINHORN
TINHORNS
TINIER
TINIES
TINIEST
TINILY
TININESS
TINING
TINK
TINKED
TINKER
TINKERED
TINKERER
TINKERERS
TINKERING
TINKERS

TINKERTOY
TINKING
TINKLE
TINKLED
TINKLER
TINKLERS
TINKLES
TINKLIER
TINKLIEST
TINKLING
TINKLINGS
TINKLY
TINKS
TINLIKE
TINMAN
TINMEN
TINNED
TINNER
TINNERS
TINNIE
TINNIER
TINNIES
TINNIEST
TINNILY
TINNINESS
TINNING
TINNINGS
TINNITUS
TINNY
TINPLATE
TINPLATED
TINPLATES
TINPOT
TINPOTS
TINS
TINSEL
TINSELED
TINSELING
TINSELLED
TINSELLY
TINSELRY
TINSELS
TINSEY
TINSEYS
TINSMITH
TINSMITHS
TINSNIPS
TINSTONE
TINSTONES
TINT
TINTACK
TINTACKS
TINTED
TINTER
TINTERS
TINTIER
TINTIEST
TINTINESS

TINTING	TIPSTER	TIRRIVIES	TITIAN
TINTINGS	TIPSTERS	TIRRS	TITIANS
TINTLESS	TIPSTOCK	TIS	TITILLATE
TINTOOKIE	TIPSTOCKS	TISANE	TITIS
TINTS	TIPSY	TISANES	TITIVATE
TINTY	TIPT	TISICK	TITIVATED
TINTYPE	TIPTOE	TISICKS	TITIVATES
TINTYPES	TIPTOED	TISSUAL	TITIVATOR
TINWARE	TIPTOEING	TISSUE	TITLARK
TINWARES	TIPTOES	TISSUED	TITLARKS
TINWORK	TIPTOP	TISSUES	TITLE
TINWORKS	TIPTOPS	TISSUEY	TITLED
TINY	TIPTRONIC	TISSUING	TITLELESS
TIP	TIPULA	TISSULAR	TITLER
TIPCART	TIPULAS	TISWAS	TITLERS
TIPCARTS	TIPUNA	TISWASES	TITLES
TIPCAT	TIPUNAS	TIT	TITLING
TIPCATS	TIRADE	TITAN	TITLINGS
TIPI	TIRADES	TITANATE	TITLIST
TIPIS	TIRAGE	TITANATES	TITLISTS
TIPLESS	TIRAGES	TITANESS	TITMAN
TIPOFF	TIRAMISU	TITANIA	TITMEN
TIPOFFS	TIRAMISUS	TITANIAS	TITMICE
TIPPABLE	TIRASSE	TITANIC	TITMOSE
TIPPED	TIRASSES	TITANIS	TITMOUSE
TIPPEE	TIRE	TITANISES	TITOKI
TIPPEES	TIRED	TITANISM	TITOKIS
TIPPER	TIREDER	TITANISMS	TITRABLE
TIPPERS	TIREDEST	TITANITE	TITRANT
TIPPET	TIREDLY	TITANITES	TITRANTS
TIPPETS	TIREDNESS	TITANIUM	TITRATE
TIPPIER	TIRELESS	TITANIUMS	TITRATED
TIPPIEST	TIRELING	TITANOUS	TITRATES
TIPPING	TIRELINGS	TITANS	TITRATING
TIPPINGS	TIRES	TITBIT	TITRATION
TIPPLE	TIRESOME	TITBITS	TITRATOR
TIPPLED	TIREWOMAN	TITCH	TITRATORS
TIPPLER	TIREWOMEN	TITCHES	TITRE
TIPPLERS	TIRING	TITCHIER	TITRES
TIPPLES	TIRINGS	TITCHIEST	TITS
TIPPLING	TIRITI	TITCHY	TITTED
TIPPY	TIRITIS	TITE	TITTER
TIPPYTOE	TIRL	TITELY	TITTERED
TIPPYTOED	TIRLED	TITER	TITTERER
TIPPYTOES	TIRLING	TITERS	TITTERERS
TIPS	TIRLS	TITFER	TITTERING
TIPSHEET	TIRO	TITFERS	TITTERS
TIPSHEETS	TIROES	TITHABLE	TITTIE
TIPSIER	TIRONIC	TITHE	TITTIES
TIPSIEST	TIROS	TITHED	TITTING
TIPSIFIED	TIRR	TITHER	TITTISH
TIPSIFIES	TIRRED	TITHERS	TITTIVATE
TIPSIFY	TIRRING	TITHES	TITTLE
TIPSILY	TIRRIT	TITHING	TITTLEBAT
TIPSINESS	TIRRITS	TITHINGS	TITTLED
TIPSTAFF	TIRRIVEE	TITHONIA	TITTLES
TIPSTAFFS	TIRRIVEES	TITHONIAS	TITTLING
TIPSTAVES	TIRRIVIE	TITI	TITTUP

TITTUPED	TOADYISH	TODDIES	TOFUS
TITTUPING	TOADYISM	TODDING	TOFUTTI
TITTUPPED	TOADYISMS	TODDLE	TOFUTTIS
TITTUPPY	TOAST	TODDLED	TOG
TITTUPS	TOASTED	TODDLER	TOGA
TITTUPY	TOASTER	TODDLERS	TOGAE
TITTY	TOASTERS	TODDLES	TOGAED
TITUBANCY	TOASTIE	TODDLING	TOGAS
TITUBANT	TOASTIER	TODDY	TOGATE
TITUBATE	TOASTIES	TODIES	TOGATED
TITUBATED	TOASTIEST	TODS	TOGAVIRUS
TITUBATES	TOASTING	TODY	TOGE
TITULAR	TOASTINGS	TOE	TOGED
TITULARLY	TOASTS	TOEA	TOGES
TITULARS	TOASTY	TOEAS	TOGETHER
TITULARY	TOAZE	TOEBIE	TOGGED
TITULE	TOAZED	TOEBIES	TOGGER
TITULED	TOAZES	TOECAP	TOGGERED
TITULES	TOAZING	TOECAPS	TOGGERIES
TITULI	TOBACCO	TOECLIP	TOGGERING
TITULING	TOBACCOES	TOECLIPS	TOGGERS
TITULUS	TOBACCOS	TOED	TOGGERY
TITUP	TOBIES	TOEHOLD	TOGGING
TITUPED	TOBOGGAN	TOEHOLDS	TOGGLE
TITUPING	TOBOGGANS	TOEIER	TOGGLED
TITUPPED	TOBOGGIN	TOEIEST	TOGGLER
TITUPPING	TOBOGGINS	TOEING	TOGGLERS
TITUPS	TOBY	TOELESS	TOGGLES
TITUPY	TOC	TOELIKE	TOGGLING
TIVY	TOCCATA	TOENAIL	TOGS
TIX	TOCCATAS	TOENAILED	TOGUE
TIZWAS	TOCCATE	TOENAILS	TOGUES
TIZWASES	TOCCATINA	TOEPIECE	TOHEROA
TIZZ	TOCHER	TOEPIECES	TOHEROAS
TIZZES	TOCHERED	TOEPLATE	TOHO
TIZZIES	TOCHERING	TOEPLATES	TOHOS
TIZZY	TOCHERS	TOERAG	TOHUNGA
TJANTING	TOCK	TOERAGGER	TOHUNGAS
TJANTINGS	TOCKED	TOERAGS	TOIL
TMESES	TOCKIER	TOES	TOILE
TMESIS	TOCKIEST	TOESHOE	TOILED
TO	TOCKING	TOESHOES	TOILER
TOAD	TOCKLEY	TOETOE	TOILERS
TOADEATER	TOCKLEYS	TOETOES	TOILES
TOADFISH	TOCKS	TOEY	TOILET
TOADFLAX	TOCKY	TOFF	TOILETED
TOADGRASS	TOCO	TOFFEE	TOILETING
TOADIED	TOCOLOGY	TOFFEES	TOILETRY
TOADIES	TOCOS	TOFFIER	TOILETS
TOADISH	TOCS	TOFFIES	TOILETTE
TOADLESS	TOCSIN	TOFFIEST	TOILETTES
TOADLIKE	TOCSINS	TOFFISH	TOILFUL
TOADRUSH	TOD	TOFFS	TOILFULLY
TOADS	TODAY	TOFFY	TOILINET
TOADSTONE	TODAYS	TOFORE	TOILINETS
TOADSTOOL	TODDE	TOFT	TOILING
TOADY	TODDED	TOFTS	TOILINGS
TOADYING	TODDES	TOFU	TOILLESS

TOILS
TOILSOME
TOILWORN
TOING
TOINGS
TOISE
TOISEACH
TOISEACHS
TOISECH
TOISECHS
TOISES
TOISON
TOISONS
TOIT
TOITED
TOITING
TOITOI
TOITOIS
TOITS
TOKAMAK
TOKAMAKS
TOKAY
TOKAYS
TOKE
TOKED
TOKEN
TOKENED
TOKENING
TOKENISM
TOKENISMS
TOKENS
TOKER
TOKERS
TOKES
TOKING
TOKO
TOKOLOGY
TOKOLOSHE
TOKOLOSHI
TOKOMAK
TOKOMAKS
TOKONOMA
TOKONOMAS
TOKOS
TOKOTOKO
TOKOTOKOS
TOKTOKKIE
TOLA
TOLAN
TOLANE
TOLANES
TOLANS
TOLAR
TOLARJEV
TOLARJI
TOLARS
TOLAS
TOLBOOTH

TOLBOOTHS
TOLD
TOLE
TOLED
TOLEDO
TOLEDOS
TOLERABLE
TOLERABLY
TOLERANCE
TOLERANT
TOLERATE
TOLERATED
TOLERATES
TOLERATOR
TOLES
TOLEWARE
TOLEWARES
TOLIDIN
TOLIDINE
TOLIDINES
TOLIDINS
TOLING
TOLINGS
TOLL
TOLLABLE
TOLLAGE
TOLLAGES
TOLLBAR
TOLLBARS
TOLLBOOTH
TOLLDISH
TOLLED
TOLLER
TOLLERS
TOLLGATE
TOLLGATES
TOLLHOUSE
TOLLIE
TOLLIES
TOLLING
TOLLINGS
TOLLMAN
TOLLMEN
TOLLS
TOLLWAY
TOLLWAYS
TOLLY
TOLSEL
TOLSELS
TOLSEY
TOLSEYS
TOLT
TOLTER
TOLTERED
TOLTERING
TOLTERS
TOLTS
TOLU

TOLUATE
TOLUATES
TOLUENE
TOLUENES
TOLUIC
TOLUID
TOLUIDE
TOLUIDES
TOLUIDIDE
TOLUIDIN
TOLUIDINE
TOLUIDINS
TOLUIDS
TOLUOL
TOLUOLE
TOLUOLES
TOLUOLS
TOLUS
TOLUYL
TOLUYLS
TOLYL
TOLYLS
TOLZEY
TOLZEYS
TOM
TOMAHAWK
TOMAHAWKS
TOMALLEY
TOMALLEYS
TOMAN
TOMANS
TOMATILLO
TOMATO
TOMATOES
TOMATOEY
TOMB
TOMBAC
TOMBACK
TOMBACKS
TOMBACS
TOMBAK
TOMBAKS
TOMBAL
TOMBED
TOMBIC
TOMBING
TOMBLESS
TOMBLIKE
TOMBOC
TOMBOCS
TOMBOLA
TOMBOLAS
TOMBOLO
TOMBOLOS
TOMBOY
TOMBOYISH
TOMBOYS
TOMBS

TOMBSTONE
TOMCAT
TOMCATS
TOMCATTED
TOMCOD
TOMCODS
TOME
TOMENTA
TOMENTOSE
TOMENTOUS
TOMENTUM
TOMES
TOMFOOL
TOMFOOLED
TOMFOOLS
TOMIA
TOMIAL
TOMIUM
TOMMED
TOMMIED
TOMMIES
TOMMING
TOMMY
TOMMYING
TOMMYROT
TOMMYROTS
TOMO
TOMOGRAM
TOMOGRAMS
TOMOGRAPH
TOMORROW
TOMORROWS
TOMOS
TOMPION
TOMPIONS
TOMPON
TOMPONED
TOMPONING
TOMPONS
TOMS
TOMTIT
TOMTITS
TON
TONAL
TONALITE
TONALITES
TONALITY
TONALLY
TONANT
TONDI
TONDINI
TONDINO
TONDINOS
TONDO
TONDOS
TONE
TONEARM
TONEARMS

TONED
TONELESS
TONEME
TONEMES
TONEMIC
TONEPAD
TONEPADS
TONER
TONERS
TONES
TONETIC
TONETICS
TONETTE
TONETTES
TONEY
TONG
TONGA
TONGAS
TONGED
TONGER
TONGERS
TONGING
TONGMAN
TONGMEN
TONGS
TONGSTER
TONGSTERS
TONGUE
TONGUED
TONGUELET
TONGUES
TONGUING
TONGUINGS
TONIC
TONICALLY
TONICITY
TONICS
TONIER
TONIES
TONIEST
TONIGHT
TONIGHTS
TONING
TONINGS
TONISH
TONISHLY
TONITE
TONITES
TONK
TONKA
TONKED
TONKER
TONKERS
TONKING
TONKS
TONLET
TONLETS
TONNAG

TONNAGE
TONNAGES
TONNAGS
TONNE
TONNEAU
TONNEAUS
TONNEAUX
TONNELL
TONNELLS
TONNER
TONNERS
TONNES
TONNISH
TONNISHLY
TONOMETER
TONOMETRY
TONOPLAST
TONS
TONSIL
TONSILAR
TONSILLAR
TONSILS
TONSOR
TONSORIAL
TONSORS
TONSURE
TONSURED
TONSURES
TONSURING
TONTINE
TONTINER
TONTINERS
TONTINES
TONUS
TONUSES
TONY
TOO
TOOART
TOOARTS
TOOK
TOOL
TOOLBAG
TOOLBAGS
TOOLBAR
TOOLBARS
TOOLBOX
TOOLBOXES
TOOLED
TOOLER
TOOLERS
TOOLHEAD
TOOLHEADS
TOOLHOUSE
TOOLING
TOOLINGS
TOOLKIT
TOOLKITS
TOOLLESS

TOOLMAKER
TOOLMAN
TOOLMEN
TOOLROOM
TOOLROOMS
TOOLS
TOOLSET
TOOLSETS
TOOLSHED
TOOLSHEDS
TOOM
TOOMED
TOOMER
TOOMEST
TOOMING
TOOMS
TOON
TOONIE
TOONIES
TOONS
TOORIE
TOORIES
TOOSHIE
TOOT
TOOTED
TOOTER
TOOTERS
TOOTH
TOOTHACHE
TOOTHCOMB
TOOTHED
TOOTHFISH
TOOTHFUL
TOOTHFULS
TOOTHIER
TOOTHIEST
TOOTHILY
TOOTHING
TOOTHINGS
TOOTHLESS
TOOTHLIKE
TOOTHPICK
TOOTHS
TOOTHSOME
TOOTHWASH
TOOTHWORT
TOOTHY
TOOTING
TOOTLE
TOOTLED
TOOTLER
TOOTLERS
TOOTLES
TOOTLING
TOOTS
TOOTSED
TOOTSES
TOOTSIE

TOOTSIES
TOOTSING
TOOTSY
TOP
TOPALGIA
TOPALGIAS
TOPARCH
TOPARCHS
TOPARCHY
TOPAZ
TOPAZES
TOPAZINE
TOPCOAT
TOPCOATS
TOPCROSS
TOPE
TOPECTOMY
TOPED
TOPEE
TOPEES
TOPEK
TOPEKS
TOPER
TOPERS
TOPES
TOPFLIGHT
TOPFUL
TOPFULL
TOPH
TOPHE
TOPHES
TOPHI
TOPHS
TOPHUS
TOPI
TOPIARIAN
TOPIARIES
TOPIARIST
TOPIARY
TOPIC
TOPICAL
TOPICALLY
TOPICS
TOPING
TOPIS
TOPKICK
TOPKICKS
TOPKNOT
TOPKNOTS
TOPLESS
TOPLINE
TOPLINED
TOPLINER
TOPLINERS
TOPLINES
TOPLINING
TOPLOFTY
TOPMAKER

TOPMAKERS	TOR	TORMINA	TORRIDLY
TOPMAKING	TORA	TORMINAL	TORRIFIED
TOPMAN	TORAH	TORMINOUS	TORRIFIES
TOPMAST	TORAHS	TORN	TORRIFY
TOPMASTS	TORAN	TORNADE	TORRS
TOPMEN	TORANA	TORNADES	TORS
TOPMINNOW	TORANAS	TORNADIC	TORSADE
TOPMOST	TORANS	TORNADO	TORSADES
TOPNOTCH	TORAS	TORNADOES	TORSE
TOPO	TORBANITE	TORNADOS	TORSEL
TOPOGRAPH	TORC	TORNILLO	TORSELS
TOPOI	TORCH	TORNILLOS	TORSES
TOPOLOGIC	TORCHABLE	TORO	TORSI
TOPOLOGY	TORCHED	TOROID	TORSION
TOPONYM	TORCHER	TOROIDAL	TORSIONAL
TOPONYMAL	TORCHERE	TOROIDS	TORSIONS
TOPONYMIC	TORCHERES	TOROS	TORSIVE
TOPONYMS	TORCHERS	TOROSE	TORSK
TOPONYMY	TORCHES	TOROSITY	TORSKS
TOPOS	TORCHIER	TOROT	TORSO
TOPOTYPE	TORCHIERE	TOROTH	TORSOS
TOPOTYPES	TORCHIERS	TOROUS	TORT
TOPPED	TORCHIEST	TORPEDO	TORTA
TOPPER	TORCHING	TORPEDOED	TORTAS
TOPPERS	TORCHINGS	TORPEDOER	TORTE
TOPPING	TORCHLIKE	TORPEDOES	TORTEN
TOPPINGLY	TORCHON	TORPEDOS	TORTES
TOPPINGS	TORCHONS	TORPEFIED	TORTILE
TOPPLE	TORCHWOOD	TORPEFIES	TORTILITY
TOPPLED	TORCHY	TORPEFY	TORTILLA
TOPPLES	TORCS	TORPID	TORTILLAS
TOPPLING	TORCULAR	TORPIDITY	TORTILLON
TOPS	TORCULARS	TORPIDLY	TORTIOUS
TOPSAIL	TORDION	TORPIDS	TORTIVE
TOPSAILS	TORDIONS	TORPITUDE	TORTOISE
TOPSIDE	TORE	TORPOR	TORTOISES
TOPSIDER	TOREADOR	TORPORS	TORTONI
TOPSIDERS	TOREADORS	TORQUATE	TORTONIS
TOPSIDES	TORERO	TORQUATED	TORTRICES
TOPSMAN	TOREROS	TORQUE	TORTRICID
TOPSMEN	TORES	TORQUED	TORTRIX
TOPSOIL	TOREUTIC	TORQUER	TORTRIXES
TOPSOILED	TOREUTICS	TORQUERS	TORTS
TOPSOILS	TORGOCH	TORQUES	TORTUOUS
TOPSPIN	TORGOCHS	TORQUESES	TORTURE
TOPSPINS	TORI	TORQUING	TORTURED
TOPSTITCH	TORIC	TORR	TORTURER
TOPSTONE	TORICS	TORREFIED	TORTURERS
TOPSTONES	TORIES	TORREFIES	TORTURES
TOPWORK	TORII	TORREFY	TORTURING
TOPWORKED	TORMENT	TORRENT	TORTUROUS
TOPWORKS	TORMENTA	TORRENTS	TORULA
TOQUE	TORMENTED	TORRET	TORULAE
TOQUES	TORMENTER	TORRETS	TORULAS
TOQUET	TORMENTIL	TORRID	TORULI
TOQUETS	TORMENTOR	TORRIDER	TORULIN
TOQUILLA	TORMENTS	TORRIDEST	TORULINS
TOQUILLAS	TORMENTUM	TORRIDITY	TORULOSE

TORULOSES	TOTALIZED	TOUCHED	TOURIST
TORULOSIS	TOTALIZER	TOUCHER	TOURISTA
TORULUS	TOTALIZES	TOUCHERS	TOURISTAS
TORUS	TOTALLED	TOUCHES	TOURISTED
TORY	TOTALLING	TOUCHHOLE	TOURISTIC
TOSA	TOTALLY	TOUCHIER	TOURISTS
TOSAS	TOTALS	TOUCHIEST	TOURISTY
TOSE	TOTANUS	TOUCHILY	TOURNEDOS
TOSED	TOTANUSES	TOUCHING	TOURNEY
TOSES	TOTAQUINE	TOUCHINGS	TOURNEYED
TOSH	TOTARA	TOUCHLESS	TOURNEYER
TOSHACH	TOTARAS	TOUCHLINE	TOURNEYS
TOSHACHS	TOTE	TOUCHMARK	TOURNURE
TOSHED	TOTEABLE	TOUCHPAD	TOURNURES
TOSHER	TOTED	TOUCHPADS	TOURS
TOSHERS	TOTEM	TOUCHTONE	TOURTIERE
TOSHES	TOTEMIC	TOUCHUP	TOUSE
TOSHIER	TOTEMISM	TOUCHUPS	TOUSED
TOSHIEST	TOTEMISMS	TOUCHWOOD	TOUSER
TOSHING	TOTEMIST	TOUCHY	TOUSERS
TOSHY	TOTEMISTS	TOUGH	TOUSES
TOSING	TOTEMITE	TOUGHED	TOUSIER
TOSS	TOTEMITES	TOUGHEN	TOUSIEST
TOSSED	TOTEMS	TOUGHENED	TOUSING
TOSSEN	TOTER	TOUGHENER	TOUSINGS
TOSSER	TOTERS	TOUGHENS	TOUSLE
TOSSERS	TOTES	TOUGHER	TOUSLED
TOSSES	TOTHER	TOUGHEST	TOUSLES
TOSSIER	TOTIENT	TOUGHIE	TOUSLING
TOSSIEST	TOTIENTS	TOUGHIES	TOUSTIE
TOSSILY	TOTING	TOUGHING	TOUSTIER
TOSSING	TOTITIVE	TOUGHISH	TOUSTIEST
TOSSINGS	TOTITIVES	TOUGHLY	TOUSY
TOSSPOT	TOTS	TOUGHNESS	TOUT
TOSSPOTS	TOTTED	TOUGHS	TOUTED
TOSSUP	TOTTER	TOUGHY	TOUTER
TOSSUPS	TOTTERED	TOUK	TOUTERS
TOSSY	TOTTERER	TOUKED	TOUTIE
TOST	TOTTERERS	TOUKING	TOUTIER
TOSTADA	TOTTERING	TOUKS	TOUTIEST
TOSTADAS	TOTTERS	TOUN	TOUTING
TOSTADO	TOTTERY	TOUNS	TOUTS
TOSTADOS	TOTTIE	TOUPEE	TOUZE
TOT	TOTTIER	TOUPEES	TOUZED
TOTABLE	TOTTIES	TOUPET	TOUZES
TOTAL	TOTTIEST	TOUPETS	TOUZIER
TOTALED	TOTTING	TOUR	TOUZIEST
TOTALING	TOTTINGS	TOURACO	TOUZING
TOTALISE	TOTTY	TOURACOS	TOUZLE
TOTALISED	TOUCAN	TOURED	TOUZLED
TOTALISER	TOUCANET	TOURER	TOUZLES
TOTALISES	TOUCANETS	TOURERS	TOUZLING
TOTALISM	TOUCANS	TOURIE	TOUZY
TOTALISMS	TOUCH	TOURIES	TOVARICH
TOTALIST	TOUCHABLE	TOURING	TOVARISCH
TOTALISTS	TOUCHBACK	TOURINGS	TOVARISH
TOTALITY	TOUCHDOWN	TOURISM	TOW
TOTALIZE	TOUCHE	TOURISMS	TOWABLE

TOWAGE
TOWAGES
TOWARD
TOWARDLY
TOWARDS
TOWAWAY
TOWAWAYS
TOWBAR
TOWBARS
TOWBOAT
TOWBOATS
TOWED
TOWEL
TOWELED
TOWELETTE
TOWELHEAD
TOWELING
TOWELINGS
TOWELLED
TOWELLING
TOWELS
TOWER
TOWERED
TOWERIER
TOWERIEST
TOWERING
TOWERLESS
TOWERLIKE
TOWERS
TOWERY
TOWHEAD
TOWHEADED
TOWHEADS
TOWHEE
TOWHEES
TOWIE
TOWIER
TOWIES
TOWIEST
TOWING
TOWINGS
TOWKAY
TOWKAYS
TOWLINE
TOWLINES
TOWMON
TOWMOND
TOWMONDS
TOWMONS
TOWMONT
TOWMONTS
TOWN
TOWNEE
TOWNEES
TOWNFOLK
TOWNHALL
TOWNHOME
TOWNHOMES

TOWNHOUSE
TOWNIE
TOWNIER
TOWNIES
TOWNIEST
TOWNISH
TOWNLAND
TOWNLANDS
TOWNLESS
TOWNLET
TOWNLETS
TOWNLIER
TOWNLIEST
TOWNLING
TOWNLINGS
TOWNLY
TOWNS
TOWNSCAPE
TOWNSFOLK
TOWNSHIP
TOWNSHIPS
TOWNSKIP
TOWNSKIPS
TOWNSMAN
TOWNSMEN
TOWNWEAR
TOWNY
TOWPATH
TOWPATHS
TOWPLANE
TOWPLANES
TOWROPE
TOWROPES
TOWS
TOWSACK
TOWSACKS
TOWSE
TOWSED
TOWSER
TOWSERS
TOWSES
TOWSIER
TOWSIEST
TOWSING
TOWSY
TOWT
TOWTED
TOWTING
TOWTS
TOWY
TOWZE
TOWZED
TOWZES
TOWZIER
TOWZIEST
TOWZING
TOWZY
TOXAEMIA

TOXAEMIAS
TOXAEMIC
TOXAPHENE
TOXEMIA
TOXEMIAS
TOXEMIC
TOXIC
TOXICAL
TOXICALLY
TOXICANT
TOXICANTS
TOXICITY
TOXICOSES
TOXICOSIS
TOXICS
TOXIGENIC
TOXIN
TOXINE
TOXINES
TOXINS
TOXOCARA
TOXOCARAS
TOXOID
TOXOIDS
TOXOPHILY
TOY
TOYED
TOYER
TOYERS
TOYING
TOYINGS
TOYISH
TOYISHLY
TOYLESOME
TOYLESS
TOYLIKE
TOYLSOM
TOYMAN
TOYMEN
TOYO
TOYON
TOYONS
TOYOS
TOYS
TOYSHOP
TOYSHOPS
TOYSOME
TOYTOWN
TOYWOMAN
TOYWOMEN
TOZE
TOZED
TOZES
TOZIE
TOZIES
TOZING
TRABEATE
TRABEATED

TRABECULA
TRABS
TRACE
TRACEABLE
TRACEABLY
TRACED
TRACELESS
TRACER
TRACERIED
TRACERIES
TRACERS
TRACERY
TRACES
TRACEUR
TRACEURS
TRACHEA
TRACHEAE
TRACHEAL
TRACHEARY
TRACHEAS
TRACHEATE
TRACHEID
TRACHEIDE
TRACHEIDS
TRACHEOLE
TRACHINUS
TRACHITIS
TRACHLE
TRACHLED
TRACHLES
TRACHLING
TRACHOMA
TRACHOMAS
TRACHYTE
TRACHYTES
TRACHYTIC
TRACING
TRACINGS
TRACK
TRACKABLE
TRACKAGE
TRACKAGES
TRACKBALL
TRACKED
TRACKER
TRACKERS
TRACKING
TRACKINGS
TRACKLESS
TRACKMAN
TRACKMEN
TRACKPAD
TRACKPADS
TRACKROAD
TRACKS
TRACKSIDE
TRACKSUIT
TRACKWAY

TRACKWAYS	TRAGIC	TRAJECTS	TRANECT
TRACT	TRAGICAL	TRAM	TRANECTS
TRACTABLE	TRAGICS	TRAMCAR	TRANGAM
TRACTABLY	TRAGOPAN	TRAMCARS	TRANGAMS
TRACTATE	TRAGOPANS	TRAMEL	TRANGLE
TRACTATES	TRAGULE	TRAMELED	TRANGLES
TRACTATOR	TRAGULES	TRAMELING	TRANK
TRACTED	TRAGULINE	TRAMELL	TRANKS
TRACTILE	TRAGUS	TRAMELLED	TRANKUM
TRACTING	TRAHISON	TRAMELLS	TRANKUMS
TRACTION	TRAHISONS	TRAMELS	TRANNIE
TRACTIONS	TRAIK	TRAMLESS	TRANNIES
TRACTIVE	TRAIKED	TRAMLINE	TRANNY
TRACTOR	TRAIKING	TRAMLINED	TRANQ
TRACTORS	TRAIKIT	TRAMLINES	TRANQS
TRACTRIX	TRAIKS	TRAMMED	TRANQUIL
TRACTS	TRAIL	TRAMMEL	TRANS
TRACTUS	TRAILABLE	TRAMMELED	TRANSACT
TRACTUSES	TRAILED	TRAMMELER	TRANSACTS
TRAD	TRAILER	TRAMMELS	TRANSAXLE
TRADABLE	TRAILERED	TRAMMIE	TRANSCEND
TRADE	TRAILERS	TRAMMIES	TRANSDUCE
TRADEABLE	TRAILHEAD	TRAMMING	TRANSE
TRADED	TRAILING	TRAMP	TRANSECT
TRADEFUL	TRAILLESS	TRAMPED	TRANSECTS
TRADELESS	TRAILS	TRAMPER	TRANSENNA
TRADEMARK	TRAILSIDE	TRAMPERS	TRANSEPT
TRADENAME	TRAIN	TRAMPET	TRANSEPTS
TRADEOFF	TRAINABLE	TRAMPETS	TRANSES
TRADEOFFS	TRAINBAND	TRAMPETTE	TRANSEUNT
TRADER	TRAINED	TRAMPIER	TRANSFARD
TRADERS	TRAINEE	TRAMPIEST	TRANSFECT
TRADES	TRAINEES	TRAMPING	TRANSFER
TRADESMAN	TRAINER	TRAMPINGS	TRANSFERS
TRADESMEN	TRAINERS	TRAMPISH	TRANSFIX
TRADING	TRAINFUL	TRAMPLE	TRANSFIXT
TRADINGS	TRAINFULS	TRAMPLED	TRANSFORM
TRADITION	TRAINING	TRAMPLER	TRANSFUSE
TRADITIVE	TRAININGS	TRAMPLERS	TRANSGENE
TRADITOR	TRAINLESS	TRAMPLES	TRANSHIP
TRADITORS	TRAINLOAD	TRAMPLING	TRANSHIPS
TRADS	TRAINMAN	TRAMPOLIN	TRANSHUME
TRADUCE	TRAINMEN	TRAMPS	TRANSIENT
TRADUCED	TRAINS	TRAMPY	TRANSIRE
TRADUCER	TRAINWAY	TRAMROAD	TRANSIRES
TRADUCERS	TRAINWAYS	TRAMROADS	TRANSIT
TRADUCES	TRAIPSE	TRAMS	TRANSITED
TRADUCIAN	TRAIPSED	TRAMWAY	TRANSITS
TRADUCING	TRAIPSES	TRAMWAYS	TRANSLATE
TRAFFIC	TRAIPSING	TRANCE	TRANSMEW
TRAFFICKY	TRAIT	TRANCED	TRANSMEWS
TRAFFICS	TRAITOR	TRANCEDLY	TRANSMIT
TRAGAL	TRAITORLY	TRANCES	TRANSMITS
TRAGEDIAN	TRAITORS	TRANCHE	TRANSMOVE
TRAGEDIES	TRAITRESS	TRANCHES	TRANSMUTE
TRAGEDY	TRAITS	TRANCHET	TRANSOM
TRAGELAPH	TRAJECT	TRANCHETS	TRANSOMED
TRAGI	TRAJECTED	TRANCING	TRANSOMS

TRANSONIC	TRAPPINGS	TRAVERSER	TREAGUES
TRANSPIRE	TRAPPOSE	TRAVERSES	TREASON
TRANSPORT	TRAPPOUS	TRAVERTIN	TREASONS
TRANSPOSE	TRAPPY	TRAVES	TREASURE
TRANSSHIP	TRAPROCK	TRAVESTY	TREASURED
TRANSUDE	TRAPROCKS	TRAVIS	TREASURER
TRANSUDED	TRAPS	TRAVISES	TREASURES
TRANSUDES	TRAPT	TRAVOIS	TREASURY
TRANSUME	TRAPUNTO	TRAVOISE	TREAT
TRANSUMED	TRAPUNTOS	TRAVOISES	TREATABLE
TRANSUMES	TRASH	TRAWL	TREATED
TRANSUMPT	TRASHCAN	TRAWLED	TREATER
TRANSVEST	TRASHCANS	TRAWLER	TREATERS
TRANT	TRASHED	TRAWLERS	TREATIES
TRANTED	TRASHER	TRAWLEY	TREATING
TRANTER	TRASHERS	TRAWLEYS	TREATINGS
TRANTERS	TRASHERY	TRAWLING	TREATISE
TRANTING	TRASHES	TRAWLINGS	TREATISES
TRANTS	TRASHIER	TRAWLNET	TREATMENT
TRAP	TRASHIEST	TRAWLNETS	TREATS
TRAPAN	TRASHILY	TRAWLS	TREATY
TRAPANNED	TRASHING	TRAY	TREBBIANO
TRAPANNER	TRASHMAN	TRAYBIT	TREBLE
TRAPANS	TRASHMEN	TRAYBITS	TREBLED
TRAPBALL	TRASHTRIE	TRAYFUL	TREBLES
TRAPBALLS	TRASHY	TRAYFULS	TREBLING
TRAPDOOR	TRASS	TRAYNE	TREBLY
TRAPDOORS	TRASSES	TRAYNED	TREBUCHET
TRAPE	TRAT	TRAYNES	TREBUCKET
TRAPED	TRATS	TRAYNING	TRECENTO
TRAPES	TRATT	TRAYS	TRECENTOS
TRAPESED	TRATTORIA	TRAZODONE	TRECK
TRAPESES	TRATTORIE	TREACHER	TRECKED
TRAPESING	TRATTS	TREACHERS	TRECKING
TRAPEZE	TRAUCHLE	TREACHERY	TRECKS
TRAPEZED	TRAUCHLED	TREACHOUR	TREDDLE
TRAPEZES	TRAUCHLES	TREACLE	TREDDLED
TRAPEZIA	TRAUMA	TREACLED	TREDDLES
TRAPEZIAL	TRAUMAS	TREACLES	TREDDLING
TRAPEZII	TRAUMATA	TREACLIER	TREDILLE
TRAPEZING	TRAUMATIC	TREACLING	TREDILLES
TRAPEZIST	TRAVAIL	TREACLY	TREDRILLE
TRAPEZIUM	TRAVAILED	TREAD	TREE
TRAPEZIUS	TRAVAILS	TREADED	TREED
TRAPEZOID	TRAVE	TREADER	TREEHOUSE
TRAPING	TRAVEL	TREADERS	TREEING
TRAPLIKE	TRAVELED	TREADING	TREELAWN
TRAPLINE	TRAVELER	TREADINGS	TREELAWNS
TRAPLINES	TRAVELERS	TREADLE	TREELESS
TRAPNEST	TRAVELING	TREADLED	TREELIKE
TRAPNESTS	TRAVELLED	TREADLER	TREEN
TRAPPEAN	TRAVELLER	TREADLERS	TREENAIL
TRAPPED	TRAVELOG	TREADLES	TREENAILS
TRAPPER	TRAVELOGS	TREADLESS	TREENS
TRAPPERS	TRAVELS	TREADLING	TREENWARE
TRAPPIER	TRAVERSAL	TREADMILL	TREES
TRAPPIEST	TRAVERSE	TREADS	TREESHIP
TRAPPING	TRAVERSED	TREAGUE	TREESHIPS

TREETOP
TREETOPS
TREEWARE
TREEWARES
TREEWAX
TREEWAXES
TREF
TREFA
TREFAH
TREFOIL
TREFOILED
TREFOILS
TREGETOUR
TREHALA
TREHALAS
TREHALOSE
TREIF
TREIFA
TREILLAGE
TREILLE
TREILLES
TREK
TREKKED
TREKKER
TREKKERS
TREKKING
TREKS
TRELLIS
TRELLISED
TRELLISES
TREMA
TREMAS
TREMATIC
TREMATODE
TREMATOID
TREMBLANT
TREMBLE
TREMBLED
TREMBLER
TREMBLERS
TREMBLES
TREMBLIER
TREMBLING
TREMBLY
TREMIE
TREMIES
TREMOLANT
TREMOLITE
TREMOLO
TREMOLOS
TREMOR
TREMORED
TREMORING
TREMOROUS
TREMORS
TREMULANT
TREMULATE
TREMULOUS

TRENAIL
TRENAILS
TRENCH
TRENCHAND
TRENCHANT
TRENCHARD
TRENCHED
TRENCHER
TRENCHERS
TRENCHES
TRENCHING
TREND
TRENDED
TRENDIER
TRENDIES
TRENDIEST
TRENDIFY
TRENDILY
TRENDING
TRENDOID
TRENDOIDS
TRENDS
TRENDY
TRENDYISM
TRENISE
TRENISES
TRENTAL
TRENTALS
TREPAN
TREPANG
TREPANGS
TREPANNED
TREPANNER
TREPANS
TREPHINE
TREPHINED
TREPHINER
TREPHINES
TREPID
TREPIDANT
TREPONEMA
TREPONEME
TRES
TRESPASS
TRESS
TRESSED
TRESSEL
TRESSELS
TRESSES
TRESSIER
TRESSIEST
TRESSING
TRESSOUR
TRESSOURS
TRESSURE
TRESSURED
TRESSURES
TRESSY

TREST
TRESTLE
TRESTLES
TRESTS
TRET
TRETINOIN
TRETS
TREVALLY
TREVALLYS
TREVET
TREVETS
TREVIS
TREVISES
TREVISS
TREVISSES
TREW
TREWS
TREWSMAN
TREWSMEN
TREY
TREYBIT
TREYBITS
TREYS
TREZ
TREZES
TRIABLE
TRIAC
TRIACID
TRIACIDS
TRIACS
TRIACT
TRIACTINE
TRIAD
TRIADIC
TRIADICS
TRIADISM
TRIADISMS
TRIADIST
TRIADISTS
TRIADS
TRIAGE
TRIAGED
TRIAGES
TRIAGING
TRIAL
TRIALISM
TRIALISMS
TRIALIST
TRIALISTS
TRIALITY
TRIALLED
TRIALLING
TRIALLIST
TRIALOGUE
TRIALS
TRIALWARE
TRIANGLE
TRIANGLED

TRIANGLES
TRIAPSAL
TRIARCH
TRIARCHS
TRIARCHY
TRIASSIC
TRIATHLON
TRIATIC
TRIATICS
TRIATOMIC
TRIAXIAL
TRIAXIALS
TRIAXON
TRIAXONS
TRIAZIN
TRIAZINE
TRIAZINES
TRIAZINS
TRIAZOLE
TRIAZOLES
TRIAZOLIC
TRIBADE
TRIBADES
TRIBADIC
TRIBADIES
TRIBADISM
TRIBADY
TRIBAL
TRIBALISM
TRIBALIST
TRIBALLY
TRIBALS
TRIBASIC
TRIBBLE
TRIBBLES
TRIBE
TRIBELESS
TRIBES
TRIBESMAN
TRIBESMEN
TRIBLET
TRIBLETS
TRIBOLOGY
TRIBRACH
TRIBRACHS
TRIBULATE
TRIBUNAL
TRIBUNALS
TRIBUNARY
TRIBUNATE
TRIBUNE
TRIBUNES
TRIBUTARY
TRIBUTE
TRIBUTER
TRIBUTERS
TRIBUTES
TRICAR

TRICARS
TRICE
TRICED
TRICEP
TRICEPS
TRICEPSES
TRICERION
TRICES
TRICHINA
TRICHINAE
TRICHINAL
TRICHINAS
TRICHITE
TRICHITES
TRICHITIC
TRICHOID
TRICHOME
TRICHOMES
TRICHOMIC
TRICHORD
TRICHORDS
TRICHOSES
TRICHOSIS
TRICHROIC
TRICHROME
TRICING
TRICK
TRICKED
TRICKER
TRICKERS
TRICKERY
TRICKIE
TRICKIER
TRICKIEST
TRICKILY
TRICKING
TRICKINGS
TRICKISH
TRICKLE
TRICKLED
TRICKLES
TRICKLESS
TRICKLET
TRICKLETS
TRICKLIER
TRICKLING
TRICKLY
TRICKS
TRICKSIER
TRICKSOME
TRICKSTER
TRICKSY
TRICKY
TRICLAD
TRICLADS
TRICLINIA
TRICLINIC
TRICLOSAN

TRICOLOR
TRICOLORS
TRICOLOUR
TRICORN
TRICORNE
TRICORNES
TRICORNS
TRICOT
TRICOTINE
TRICOTS
TRICROTIC
TRICTRAC
TRICTRACS
TRICUSPID
TRICYCLE
TRICYCLED
TRICYCLER
TRICYCLES
TRICYCLIC
TRIDACNA
TRIDACNAS
TRIDACTYL
TRIDARN
TRIDARNS
TRIDE
TRIDENT
TRIDENTAL
TRIDENTED
TRIDENTS
TRIDUAN
TRIDUUM
TRIDUUMS
TRIDYMITE
TRIE
TRIECIOUS
TRIED
TRIELLA
TRIELLAS
TRIENE
TRIENES
TRIENNIA
TRIENNIAL
TRIENNIUM
TRIENS
TRIENTES
TRIER
TRIERARCH
TRIERS
TRIES
TRIETERIC
TRIETHYL
TRIFACIAL
TRIFECTA
TRIFECTAS
TRIFF
TRIFFER
TRIFFEST
TRIFFIC

TRIFFID
TRIFFIDS
TRIFFIDY
TRIFID
TRIFLE
TRIFLED
TRIFLER
TRIFLERS
TRIFLES
TRIFLING
TRIFLINGS
TRIFOCAL
TRIFOCALS
TRIFOLD
TRIFOLIES
TRIFOLIUM
TRIFOLY
TRIFORIA
TRIFORIAL
TRIFORIUM
TRIFORM
TRIFORMED
TRIG
TRIGAMIES
TRIGAMIST
TRIGAMOUS
TRIGAMY
TRIGGED
TRIGGER
TRIGGERED
TRIGGERS
TRIGGEST
TRIGGING
TRIGLOT
TRIGLOTS
TRIGLY
TRIGLYPH
TRIGLYPHS
TRIGNESS
TRIGO
TRIGON
TRIGONAL
TRIGONIC
TRIGONOUS
TRIGONS
TRIGOS
TRIGRAM
TRIGRAMS
TRIGRAPH
TRIGRAPHS
TRIGS
TRIGYNIAN
TRIGYNOUS
TRIHEDRA
TRIHEDRAL
TRIHEDRON
TRIHYBRID
TRIHYDRIC

TRIJET
TRIJETS
TRIJUGATE
TRIJUGOUS
TRIKE
TRIKES
TRILBIES
TRILBY
TRILBYS
TRILD
TRILEMMA
TRILEMMAS
TRILINEAR
TRILITH
TRILITHIC
TRILITHON
TRILITHS
TRILL
TRILLED
TRILLER
TRILLERS
TRILLING
TRILLINGS
TRILLION
TRILLIONS
TRILLIUM
TRILLIUMS
TRILLO
TRILLOES
TRILLS
TRILOBAL
TRILOBATE
TRILOBE
TRILOBED
TRILOBES
TRILOBITE
TRILOGIES
TRILOGY
TRIM
TRIMARAN
TRIMARANS
TRIMER
TRIMERIC
TRIMERISM
TRIMEROUS
TRIMERS
TRIMESTER
TRIMETER
TRIMETERS
TRIMETHYL
TRIMETRIC
TRIMLY
TRIMMED
TRIMMER
TRIMMERS
TRIMMEST
TRIMMING
TRIMMINGS

TRIMNESS	TRIPACK	TRIPPLER	TRISTEZA
TRIMORPH	TRIPACKS	TRIPPLERS	TRISTEZAS
TRIMORPHS	TRIPART	TRIPPLES	TRISTFUL
TRIMOTOR	TRIPE	TRIPPLING	TRISTICH
TRIMOTORS	TRIPEDAL	TRIPPY	TRISTICHS
TRIMS	TRIPERIES	TRIPS	TRISUL
TRIMTAB	TRIPERY	TRIPSES	TRISULA
TRIMTABS	TRIPES	TRIPSIS	TRISULAS
TRIN	TRIPEY	TRIPTAN	TRISULS
TRINAL	TRIPHASE	TRIPTANE	TRITE
TRINARY	TRIPHONE	TRIPTANES	TRITELY
TRINDLE	TRIPHONES	TRIPTANS	TRITENESS
TRINDLED	TRIPIER	TRIPTOTE	TRITER
TRINDLES	TRIPIEST	TRIPTOTES	TRITES
TRINDLING	TRIPITAKA	TRIPTYCA	TRITEST
TRINE	TRIPLANE	TRIPTYCAS	TRITHEISM
TRINED	TRIPLANES	TRIPTYCH	TRITHEIST
TRINES	TRIPLE	TRIPTYCHS	TRITHING
TRINGLE	TRIPLED	TRIPTYQUE	TRITHINGS
TRINGLES	TRIPLES	TRIPUDIA	TRITIATE
TRINING	TRIPLET	TRIPUDIUM	TRITIATED
TRINITIES	TRIPLETS	TRIPWIRE	TRITIATES
TRINITRIN	TRIPLEX	TRIPWIRES	TRITICAL
TRINITY	TRIPLEXES	TRIPY	TRITICALE
TRINKET	TRIPLIED	TRIQUETRA	TRITICISM
TRINKETED	TRIPLIES	TRIRADIAL	TRITICUM
TRINKETER	TRIPLING	TRIREME	TRITICUMS
TRINKETRY	TRIPLINGS	TRIREMES	TRITIDE
TRINKETS	TRIPLITE	TRISAGION	TRITIDES
TRINKUM	TRIPLITES	TRISCELE	TRITIUM
TRINKUMS	TRIPLOID	TRISCELES	TRITIUMS
TRINODAL	TRIPLOIDS	TRISECT	TRITOMA
TRINOMIAL	TRIPLOIDY	TRISECTED	TRITOMAS
TRINS	TRIPLY	TRISECTOR	TRITON
TRIO	TRIPLYING	TRISECTS	TRITONE
TRIODE	TRIPOD	TRISEME	TRITONES
TRIODES	TRIPODAL	TRISEMES	TRITONIA
TRIOL	TRIPODIC	TRISEMIC	TRITONIAS
TRIOLEIN	TRIPODIES	TRISERIAL	TRITONS
TRIOLEINS	TRIPODS	TRISHAW	TRITURATE
TRIOLET	TRIPODY	TRISHAWS	TRIUMPH
TRIOLETS	TRIPOLI	TRISKELE	TRIUMPHAL
TRIOLS	TRIPOLIS	TRISKELES	TRIUMPHED
TRIONES	TRIPOS	TRISKELIA	TRIUMPHER
TRIONYM	TRIPOSES	TRISMIC	TRIUMPHS
TRIONYMAL	TRIPPANT	TRISMUS	TRIUMVIR
TRIONYMS	TRIPPED	TRISMUSES	TRIUMVIRI
TRIOR	TRIPPER	TRISODIUM	TRIUMVIRS
TRIORS	TRIPPERS	TRISOME	TRIUMVIRY
TRIOS	TRIPPERY	TRISOMES	TRIUNE
TRIOSE	TRIPPET	TRISOMIC	TRIUNES
TRIOSES	TRIPPETS	TRISOMICS	TRIUNITY
TRIOXID	TRIPPIER	TRISOMIES	TRIVALENT
TRIOXIDE	TRIPPIEST	TRISOMY	TRIVALVE
TRIOXIDES	TRIPPING	TRIST	TRIVALVED
TRIOXIDS	TRIPPINGS	TRISTATE	TRIVALVES
TRIOXYGEN	TRIPPLE	TRISTE	TRIVET
TRIP	TRIPPLED	TRISTESSE	TRIVETS

TRIVIA
TRIVIAL
TRIVIALLY
TRIVIUM
TRIVIUMS
TRIWEEKLY
TRIZONAL
TRIZONE
TRIZONES
TROAD
TROADE
TROADES
TROADS
TROAK
TROAKED
TROAKING
TROAKS
TROAT
TROATED
TROATING
TROATS
TROCAR
TROCARS
TROCHAIC
TROCHAICS
TROCHAL
TROCHAR
TROCHARS
TROCHE
TROCHEE
TROCHEES
TROCHES
TROCHI
TROCHIL
TROCHILI
TROCHILIC
TROCHILS
TROCHILUS
TROCHISK
TROCHISKS
TROCHITE
TROCHITES
TROCHLEA
TROCHLEAE
TROCHLEAR
TROCHLEAS
TROCHOID
TROCHOIDS
TROCHUS
TROCHUSES
TROCK
TROCKED
TROCKEN
TROCKING
TROCKS
TROD
TRODDEN
TRODE

TRODES
TRODS
TROELIE
TROELIES
TROELY
TROFFER
TROFFERS
TROG
TROGGED
TROGGING
TROGGS
TROGON
TROGONS
TROGS
TROIKA
TROIKAS
TROILISM
TROILISMS
TROILIST
TROILISTS
TROILITE
TROILITES
TROILUS
TROILUSES
TROIS
TROKE
TROKED
TROKES
TROKING
TROLAND
TROLANDS
TROLL
TROLLED
TROLLER
TROLLERS
TROLLEY
TROLLEYED
TROLLEYS
TROLLIED
TROLLIES
TROLLING
TROLLINGS
TROLLIUS
TROLLOP
TROLLOPED
TROLLOPEE
TROLLOPS
TROLLOPY
TROLLS
TROLLY
TROLLYING
TROMBONE
TROMBONES
TROMINO
TROMINOES
TROMINOS
TROMMEL
TROMMELS

TROMP
TROMPE
TROMPED
TROMPES
TROMPING
TROMPS
TRON
TRONA
TRONAS
TRONC
TRONCS
TRONE
TRONES
TRONK
TRONKS
TRONS
TROOLIE
TROOLIES
TROOP
TROOPED
TROOPER
TROOPERS
TROOPIAL
TROOPIALS
TROOPING
TROOPS
TROOPSHIP
TROOSTITE
TROOZ
TROP
TROPAEOLA
TROPARIA
TROPARION
TROPE
TROPED
TROPEOLIN
TROPES
TROPHESY
TROPHI
TROPHIC
TROPHIED
TROPHIES
TROPHY
TROPHYING
TROPIC
TROPICAL
TROPICALS
TROPICS
TROPIN
TROPINE
TROPINES
TROPING
TROPINS
TROPISM
TROPISMS
TROPIST
TROPISTIC
TROPISTS

TROPOLOGY
TROPONIN
TROPONINS
TROPPO
TROSSERS
TROT
TROTH
TROTHED
TROTHFUL
TROTHING
TROTHLESS
TROTHS
TROTLINE
TROTLINES
TROTS
TROTTED
TROTTER
TROTTERS
TROTTING
TROTTINGS
TROTTOIR
TROTTOIRS
TROTYL
TROTYLS
TROUBLE
TROUBLED
TROUBLER
TROUBLERS
TROUBLES
TROUBLING
TROUBLOUS
TROUCH
TROUCHES
TROUGH
TROUGHED
TROUGHING
TROUGHS
TROULE
TROULED
TROULES
TROULING
TROUNCE
TROUNCED
TROUNCER
TROUNCERS
TROUNCES
TROUNCING
TROUPE
TROUPED
TROUPER
TROUPERS
TROUPES
TROUPIAL
TROUPIALS
TROUPING
TROUSE
TROUSER
TROUSERED

TROUSERS
TROUSES
TROUSSEAU
TROUT
TROUTER
TROUTERS
TROUTFUL
TROUTIER
TROUTIEST
TROUTING
TROUTINGS
TROUTLESS
TROUTLET
TROUTLETS
TROUTLING
TROUTS
TROUTY
TROUVERE
TROUVERES
TROUVEUR
TROUVEURS
TROVE
TROVER
TROVERS
TROVES
TROW
TROWED
TROWEL
TROWELED
TROWELER
TROWELERS
TROWELING
TROWELLED
TROWELLER
TROWELS
TROWING
TROWS
TROWSERS
TROWTH
TROWTHS
TROY
TROYS
TRUANCIES
TRUANCY
TRUANT
TRUANTED
TRUANTING
TRUANTLY
TRUANTRY
TRUANTS
TRUCAGE
TRUCAGES
TRUCE
TRUCED
TRUCELESS
TRUCES
TRUCHMAN
TRUCHMANS

TRUCHMEN
TRUCIAL
TRUCING
TRUCK
TRUCKABLE
TRUCKAGE
TRUCKAGES
TRUCKED
TRUCKER
TRUCKERS
TRUCKFUL
TRUCKFULS
TRUCKIE
TRUCKIES
TRUCKING
TRUCKINGS
TRUCKLE
TRUCKLED
TRUCKLER
TRUCKLERS
TRUCKLES
TRUCKLINE
TRUCKLING
TRUCKLOAD
TRUCKMAN
TRUCKMEN
TRUCKS
TRUCKSTOP
TRUCULENT
TRUDGE
TRUDGED
TRUDGEN
TRUDGENS
TRUDGEON
TRUDGEONS
TRUDGER
TRUDGERS
TRUDGES
TRUDGING
TRUDGINGS
TRUE
TRUEBLUE
TRUEBLUES
TRUEBORN
TRUEBRED
TRUED
TRUEING
TRUELOVE
TRUELOVES
TRUEMAN
TRUEMEN
TRUENESS
TRUEPENNY
TRUER
TRUES
TRUEST
TRUFFE
TRUFFES

TRUFFLE
TRUFFLED
TRUFFLES
TRUFFLING
TRUG
TRUGO
TRUGOS
TRUGS
TRUING
TRUISM
TRUISMS
TRUISTIC
TRULL
TRULLS
TRULY
TRUMEAU
TRUMEAUX
TRUMP
TRUMPED
TRUMPERY
TRUMPET
TRUMPETED
TRUMPETER
TRUMPETS
TRUMPING
TRUMPINGS
TRUMPLESS
TRUMPS
TRUNCAL
TRUNCATE
TRUNCATED
TRUNCATES
TRUNCHEON
TRUNDLE
TRUNDLED
TRUNDLER
TRUNDLERS
TRUNDLES
TRUNDLING
TRUNK
TRUNKED
TRUNKFISH
TRUNKFUL
TRUNKFULS
TRUNKING
TRUNKINGS
TRUNKLESS
TRUNKS
TRUNNEL
TRUNNELS
TRUNNION
TRUNNIONS
TRUQUAGE
TRUQUAGES
TRUQUEUR
TRUQUEURS
TRUSS
TRUSSED

TRUSSER
TRUSSERS
TRUSSES
TRUSSING
TRUSSINGS
TRUST
TRUSTABLE
TRUSTED
TRUSTEE
TRUSTEED
TRUSTEES
TRUSTER
TRUSTERS
TRUSTFUL
TRUSTIER
TRUSTIES
TRUSTIEST
TRUSTILY
TRUSTING
TRUSTLESS
TRUSTOR
TRUSTORS
TRUSTS
TRUSTY
TRUTH
TRUTHFUL
TRUTHIER
TRUTHIEST
TRUTHLESS
TRUTHLIKE
TRUTHS
TRUTHY
TRY
TRYE
TRYER
TRYERS
TRYING
TRYINGLY
TRYINGS
TRYKE
TRYKES
TRYMA
TRYMATA
TRYOUT
TRYOUTS
TRYP
TRYPAN
TRYPS
TRYPSIN
TRYPSINS
TRYPTIC
TRYSAIL
TRYSAILS
TRYST
TRYSTE
TRYSTED
TRYSTER
TRYSTERS

TRYSTES
TRYSTING
TRYSTS
TRYWORKS
TSADDIK
TSADDIKIM
TSADDIKS
TSADDIQ
TSADDIQIM
TSADDIQS
TSADE
TSADES
TSADI
TSADIS
TSAMBA
TSAMBAS
TSANTSA
TSANTSAS
TSAR
TSARDOM
TSARDOMS
TSAREVICH
TSAREVNA
TSAREVNAS
TSARINA
TSARINAS
TSARISM
TSARISMS
TSARIST
TSARISTS
TSARITSA
TSARITSAS
TSARITZA
TSARITZAS
TSARS
TSATSKE
TSATSKES
TSESSEBE
TSESSEBES
TSETSE
TSETSES
TSIGANE
TSIGANES
TSIMMES
TSITSITH
TSK
TSKED
TSKING
TSKS
TSKTSK
TSKTSKED
TSKTSKING
TSKTSKS
TSOORIS
TSORES
TSORIS
TSORRISS
TSOTSI

TSOTSIS
TSOURIS
TSOURISES
TSUBA
TSUBAS
TSUNAMI
TSUNAMIC
TSUNAMIS
TSURIS
TSURISES
TSUTSUMU
TSUTSUMUS
TUAN
TUANS
TUART
TUARTS
TUATARA
TUATARAS
TUATERA
TUATERAS
TUATH
TUATHS
TUATUA
TUB
TUBA
TUBAE
TUBAGE
TUBAGES
TUBAIST
TUBAISTS
TUBAL
TUBAR
TUBAS
TUBATE
TUBBABLE
TUBBED
TUBBER
TUBBERS
TUBBIER
TUBBIEST
TUBBINESS
TUBBING
TUBBINGS
TUBBISH
TUBBY
TUBE
TUBECTOMY
TUBED
TUBEFUL
TUBEFULS
TUBELESS
TUBELIKE
TUBENOSE
TUBENOSES
TUBER
TUBERCLE
TUBERCLED
TUBERCLES

TUBERCULA
TUBERCULE
TUBEROID
TUBEROSE
TUBEROSES
TUBEROUS
TUBERS
TUBES
TUBEWORK
TUBEWORKS
TUBEWORM
TUBEWORMS
TUBFAST
TUBFASTS
TUBFISH
TUBFISHES
TUBFUL
TUBFULS
TUBICOLAR
TUBICOLE
TUBICOLES
TUBIFEX
TUBIFEXES
TUBIFICID
TUBIFORM
TUBING
TUBINGS
TUBIST
TUBISTS
TUBLIKE
TUBS
TUBULAR
TUBULARLY
TUBULATE
TUBULATED
TUBULATES
TUBULATOR
TUBULE
TUBULES
TUBULIN
TUBULINS
TUBULOSE
TUBULOUS
TUBULURE
TUBULURES
TUCHUN
TUCHUNS
TUCK
TUCKAHOE
TUCKAHOES
TUCKED
TUCKER
TUCKERBAG
TUCKERBOX
TUCKERED
TUCKERING
TUCKERS
TUCKET

TUCKETS
TUCKING
TUCKS
TUCKSHOP
TUCKSHOPS
TUCOTUCO
TUCOTUCOS
TUCUTUCO
TUCUTUCOS
TUCUTUCU
TUCUTUCUS
TUFA
TUFACEOUS
TUFAS
TUFF
TUFFE
TUFFES
TUFFET
TUFFETS
TUFFS
TUFOLI
TUFT
TUFTED
TUFTER
TUFTERS
TUFTIER
TUFTIEST
TUFTILY
TUFTING
TUFTINGS
TUFTS
TUFTY
TUG
TUGBOAT
TUGBOATS
TUGGED
TUGGER
TUGGERS
TUGGING
TUGGINGLY
TUGGINGS
TUGHRA
TUGHRAS
TUGHRIK
TUGHRIKS
TUGLESS
TUGRA
TUGRAS
TUGRIK
TUGRIKS
TUGS
TUI
TUILLE
TUILLES
TUILLETTE
TUILYIE
TUILYIED
TUILYIES

TUILZIE
TUILZIED
TUILZIES
TUINA
TUINAS
TUIS
TUISM
TUISMS
TUITION
TUITIONAL
TUITIONS
TUKTOO
TUKTOOS
TUKTU
TUKTUS
TULADI
TULADIS
TULAREMIA
TULAREMIC
TULBAN
TULBANS
TULCHAN
TULCHANS
TULE
TULES
TULIP
TULIPANT
TULIPANTS
TULIPLIKE
TULIPS
TULIPWOOD
TULLE
TULLES
TULLIBEE
TULLIBEES
TULPA
TULPAS
TULWAR
TULWARS
TUM
TUMBLE
TUMBLEBUG
TUMBLED
TUMBLER
TUMBLERS
TUMBLES
TUMBLESET
TUMBLING
TUMBLINGS
TUMBREL
TUMBRELS
TUMBRIL
TUMBRILS
TUMEFIED
TUMEFIES
TUMEFY
TUMEFYING
TUMESCE

TUMESCED
TUMESCENT
TUMESCES
TUMESCING
TUMID
TUMIDITY
TUMIDLY
TUMIDNESS
TUMMIES
TUMMLER
TUMMLERS
TUMMY
TUMOR
TUMORAL
TUMORLIKE
TUMOROUS
TUMORS
TUMOUR
TUMOURS
TUMP
TUMPED
TUMPHIES
TUMPHY
TUMPIER
TUMPIEST
TUMPING
TUMPLINE
TUMPLINES
TUMPS
TUMPY
TUMS
TUMSHIE
TUMSHIES
TUMULAR
TUMULARY
TUMULI
TUMULOSE
TUMULOUS
TUMULT
TUMULTED
TUMULTING
TUMULTS
TUMULUS
TUMULUSES
TUN
TUNA
TUNABLE
TUNABLY
TUNAS
TUNBELLY
TUND
TUNDED
TUNDING
TUNDISH
TUNDISHES
TUNDRA
TUNDRAS
TUNDS

TUNDUN
TUNDUNS
TUNE
TUNEABLE
TUNEABLY
TUNED
TUNEFUL
TUNEFULLY
TUNELESS
TUNER
TUNERS
TUNES
TUNESMITH
TUNEUP
TUNEUPS
TUNG
TUNGS
TUNGSTATE
TUNGSTEN
TUNGSTENS
TUNGSTIC
TUNGSTITE
TUNGSTOUS
TUNIC
TUNICA
TUNICAE
TUNICATE
TUNICATED
TUNICATES
TUNICIN
TUNICINS
TUNICKED
TUNICLE
TUNICLES
TUNICS
TUNIER
TUNIEST
TUNING
TUNINGS
TUNNAGE
TUNNAGES
TUNNED
TUNNEL
TUNNELED
TUNNELER
TUNNELERS
TUNNELING
TUNNELLED
TUNNELLER
TUNNELS
TUNNIES
TUNNING
TUNNINGS
TUNNY
TUNS
TUNY
TUP
TUPEK

TUPEKS
TUPELO
TUPELOS
TUPIK
TUPIKS
TUPLE
TUPLES
TUPPED
TUPPENCE
TUPPENCES
TUPPENNY
TUPPING
TUPS
TUPTOWING
TUPUNA
TUPUNAS
TUQUE
TUQUES
TURACIN
TURACINS
TURACO
TURACOS
TURACOU
TURACOUS
TURBAN
TURBAND
TURBANDS
TURBANED
TURBANNED
TURBANS
TURBANT
TURBANTS
TURBARIES
TURBARY
TURBETH
TURBETHS
TURBID
TURBIDITE
TURBIDITY
TURBIDLY
TURBINAL
TURBINALS
TURBINATE
TURBINE
TURBINED
TURBINES
TURBIT
TURBITH
TURBITHS
TURBITS
TURBO
TURBOCAR
TURBOCARS
TURBOFAN
TURBOFANS
TURBOJET
TURBOJETS
TURBOND

TURBONDS
TURBOPROP
TURBOS
TURBOT
TURBOTS
TURBULENT
TURCOPOLE
TURD
TURDINE
TURDION
TURDIONS
TURDOID
TURDS
TUREEN
TUREENS
TURF
TURFED
TURFEN
TURFGRASS
TURFIER
TURFIEST
TURFINESS
TURFING
TURFINGS
TURFITE
TURFITES
TURFLESS
TURFLIKE
TURFMAN
TURFMEN
TURFS
TURFSKI
TURFSKIS
TURFY
TURGENCY
TURGENT
TURGENTLY
TURGID
TURGIDER
TURGIDEST
TURGIDITY
TURGIDLY
TURGITE
TURGITES
TURGOR
TURGORS
TURION
TURIONS
TURISTA
TURISTAS
TURK
TURKEY
TURKEYS
TURKIES
TURKIESES
TURKIS
TURKISES
TURKOIS

TURKOISES
TURKS
TURLOUGH
TURLOUGHS
TURM
TURME
TURMERIC
TURMERICS
TURMES
TURMOIL
TURMOILED
TURMOILS
TURMS
TURN
TURNABLE
TURNABOUT
TURNAGAIN
TURNBACK
TURNBACKS
TURNCOAT
TURNCOATS
TURNCOCK
TURNCOCKS
TURNDOWN
TURNDOWNS
TURNDUN
TURNDUNS
TURNED
TURNER
TURNERIES
TURNERS
TURNERY
TURNHALL
TURNHALLS
TURNING
TURNINGS
TURNIP
TURNIPED
TURNIPING
TURNIPS
TURNKEY
TURNKEYS
TURNOFF
TURNOFFS
TURNON
TURNONS
TURNOUT
TURNOUTS
TURNOVER
TURNOVERS
TURNPIKE
TURNPIKES
TURNROUND
TURNS
TURNSKIN
TURNSKINS
TURNSOLE
TURNSOLES

TURNSPIT
TURNSPITS
TURNSTILE
TURNSTONE
TURNTABLE
TURNUP
TURNUPS
TUROPHILE
TURPETH
TURPETHS
TURPITUDE
TURPS
TURQUOIS
TURQUOISE
TURRET
TURRETED
TURRETS
TURRIBANT
TURRICAL
TURTLE
TURTLED
TURTLER
TURTLERS
TURTLES
TURTLING
TURTLINGS
TURVES
TUSCHE
TUSCHES
TUSH
TUSHED
TUSHERIES
TUSHERY
TUSHES
TUSHIE
TUSHIES
TUSHING
TUSHKAR
TUSHKARS
TUSHKER
TUSHKERS
TUSHY
TUSK
TUSKAR
TUSKARS
TUSKED
TUSKER
TUSKERS
TUSKIER
TUSKIEST
TUSKING
TUSKINGS
TUSKLESS
TUSKLIKE
TUSKS
TUSKY
TUSSAH
TUSSAHS

TUSSAL
TUSSAR
TUSSARS
TUSSEH
TUSSEHS
TUSSER
TUSSERS
TUSSES
TUSSIS
TUSSISES
TUSSIVE
TUSSLE
TUSSLED
TUSSLES
TUSSLING
TUSSOCK
TUSSOCKED
TUSSOCKS
TUSSOCKY
TUSSOR
TUSSORE
TUSSORES
TUSSORS
TUSSUCK
TUSSUCKS
TUSSUR
TUSSURS
TUT
TUTANIA
TUTANIAS
TUTEE
TUTEES
TUTELAGE
TUTELAGES
TUTELAR
TUTELARS
TUTELARY
TUTENAG
TUTENAGS
TUTIORISM
TUTIORIST
TUTMAN
TUTMEN
TUTOR
TUTORAGE
TUTORAGES
TUTORED
TUTORESS
TUTORIAL
TUTORIALS
TUTORING
TUTORINGS
TUTORISE
TUTORISED
TUTORISES
TUTORISM
TUTORISMS
TUTORIZE

TUTORIZED
TUTORIZES
TUTORS
TUTORSHIP
TUTOYED
TUTOYER
TUTOYERED
TUTOYERS
TUTRESS
TUTRESSES
TUTRICES
TUTRIX
TUTRIXES
TUTS
TUTSAN
TUTSANS
TUTSED
TUTSES
TUTSING
TUTTED
TUTTI
TUTTIES
TUTTING
TUTTINGS
TUTTIS
TUTTY
TUTU
TUTUED
TUTUS
TUTWORK
TUTWORKER
TUTWORKS
TUX
TUXEDO
TUXEDOED
TUXEDOES
TUXEDOS
TUXES
TUYER
TUYERE
TUYERES
TUYERS
TUZZ
TUZZES
TWA
TWADDLE
TWADDLED
TWADDLER
TWADDLERS
TWADDLES
TWADDLIER
TWADDLING
TWADDLY
TWAE
TWAES
TWAFALD
TWAIN
TWAINS

TWAITE
TWAITES
TWAL
TWALPENNY
TWALS
TWANG
TWANGED
TWANGER
TWANGERS
TWANGIER
TWANGIEST
TWANGING
TWANGINGS
TWANGLE
TWANGLED
TWANGLER
TWANGLERS
TWANGLES
TWANGLING
TWANGS
TWANGY
TWANK
TWANKAY
TWANKAYS
TWANKIES
TWANKS
TWANKY
TWAS
TWASOME
TWASOMES
TWAT
TWATS
TWATTLE
TWATTLED
TWATTLER
TWATTLERS
TWATTLES
TWATTLING
TWAY
TWAYBLADE
TWAYS
TWEAK
TWEAKED
TWEAKER
TWEAKERS
TWEAKIER
TWEAKIEST
TWEAKING
TWEAKINGS
TWEAKS
TWEAKY
TWEE
TWEED
TWEEDIER
TWEEDIEST
TWEEDLE
TWEEDLED
TWEEDLER

TWEEDLERS
TWEEDLES
TWEEDLING
TWEEDS
TWEEDY
TWEEL
TWEELED
TWEELING
TWEELS
TWEELY
TWEEN
TWEENAGER
TWEENER
TWEENERS
TWEENESS
TWEENIE
TWEENIES
TWEENS
TWEENY
TWEER
TWEERED
TWEERING
TWEERS
TWEEST
TWEET
TWEETED
TWEETER
TWEETERS
TWEETING
TWEETS
TWEEZE
TWEEZED
TWEEZER
TWEEZERS
TWEEZES
TWEEZING
TWELFTH
TWELFTHLY
TWELFTHS
TWELVE
TWELVEMO
TWELVEMOS
TWELVES
TWENTIES
TWENTIETH
TWENTY
TWENTYISH
TWERP
TWERPIER
TWERPIEST
TWERPS
TWERPY
TWIBIL
TWIBILL
TWIBILLS
TWIBILS
TWICE
TWICER

TWICERS
TWICHILD
TWIDDLE
TWIDDLED
TWIDDLER
TWIDDLERS
TWIDDLES
TWIDDLIER
TWIDDLING
TWIDDLY
TWIER
TWIERS
TWIFOLD
TWIFORKED
TWIFORMED
TWIG
TWIGGED
TWIGGEN
TWIGGER
TWIGGERS
TWIGGIER
TWIGGIEST
TWIGGING
TWIGGY
TWIGHT
TWIGHTED
TWIGHTING
TWIGHTS
TWIGLESS
TWIGLIKE
TWIGLOO
TWIGLOOS
TWIGS
TWIGSOME
TWILIGHT
TWILIGHTS
TWILIT
TWILL
TWILLED
TWILLIES
TWILLING
TWILLINGS
TWILLS
TWILLY
TWILT
TWILTED
TWILTING
TWILTS
TWIN
TWINBERRY
TWINBORN
TWINE
TWINED
TWINER
TWINERS
TWINES
TWINGE
TWINGED

TWINGEING	TWISTABLE	TWONIES	TYMPANIC
TWINGES	TWISTED	TWOONIE	TYMPANICS
TWINGING	TWISTER	TWOONIES	TYMPANIES
TWINIER	TWISTERS	TWOPENCE	TYMPANIST
TWINIEST	TWISTIER	TWOPENCES	TYMPANO
TWINIGHT	TWISTIEST	TWOPENNY	TYMPANS
TWINING	TWISTING	TWOS	TYMPANUM
TWININGLY	TWISTINGS	TWOSEATER	TYMPANUMS
TWININGS	TWISTOR	TWOSOME	TYMPANY
TWINJET	TWISTORS	TWOSOMES	TYMPS
TWINJETS	TWISTS	TWOSTROKE	TYND
TWINK	TWISTY	TWP	TYNDE
TWINKED	TWIT	TWYER	TYNE
TWINKIE	TWITCH	TWYERE	TYNED
TWINKIES	TWITCHED	TWYERES	TYNES
TWINKING	TWITCHER	TWYERS	TYNING
TWINKLE	TWITCHERS	TWYFOLD	TYPABLE
TWINKLED	TWITCHES	TYCHISM	TYPAL
TWINKLER	TWITCHIER	TYCHISMS	TYPE
TWINKLERS	TWITCHILY	TYCOON	TYPEABLE
TWINKLES	TWITCHING	TYCOONATE	TYPEBAR
TWINKLING	TWITCHY	TYCOONERY	TYPEBARS
TWINKLY	TWITE	TYCOONS	TYPECASE
TWINKS	TWITES	TYDE	TYPECASES
TWINLING	TWITS	TYE	TYPECAST
TWINLINGS	TWITTED	TYED	TYPECASTS
TWINNED	TWITTEN	TYEE	TYPED
TWINNING	TWITTENS	TYEES	TYPEFACE
TWINNINGS	TWITTER	TYEING	TYPEFACES
TWINS	TWITTERED	TYER	TYPES
TWINSET	TWITTERER	TYERS	TYPESET
TWINSETS	TWITTERS	TYES	TYPESETS
TWINSHIP	TWITTERY	TYG	TYPESTYLE
TWINSHIPS	TWITTING	TYGS	TYPEWRITE
TWINTER	TWITTINGS	TYIN	TYPEWROTE
TWINTERS	TWIXT	TYING	TYPEY
TWINY	TWIZZLE	TYIYN	TYPHLITIC
TWIRE	TWIZZLED	TYKE	TYPHLITIS
TWIRED	TWIZZLES	TYKES	TYPHOID
TWIRES	TWIZZLING	TYKISH	TYPHOIDAL
TWIRING	TWO	TYLECTOMY	TYPHOIDIN
TWIRL	TWOCCER	TYLER	TYPHOIDS
TWIRLED	TWOCCERS	TYLERS	TYPHON
TWIRLER	TWOCCING	TYLOPOD	TYPHONIAN
TWIRLERS	TWOCCINGS	TYLOPODS	TYPHONIC
TWIRLIER	TWOCKER	TYLOSES	TYPHONS
TWIRLIEST	TWOCKERS	TYLOSIN	TYPHOON
TWIRLING	TWOCKING	TYLOSINS	TYPHOONS
TWIRLS	TWOCKINGS	TYLOSIS	TYPHOSE
TWIRLY	TWOER	TYLOTE	TYPHOUS
TWIRP	TWOERS	TYLOTES	TYPHUS
TWIRPIER	TWOFER	TYMBAL	TYPHUSES
TWIRPIEST	TWOFERS	TYMBALS	TYPIC
TWIRPS	TWOFOLD	TYMP	TYPICAL
TWIRPY	TWOFOLDS	TYMPAN	TYPICALLY
TWISCAR	TWONESS	TYMPANA	TYPIER
TWISCARS	TWONESSES	TYMPANAL	TYPIEST
TWIST	TWONIE	TYMPANI	TYPIFIED

TYPIFIER
TYPIFIERS
TYPIFIES
TYPIFY
TYPIFYING
TYPING
TYPINGS
TYPIST
TYPISTS
TYPO
TYPOGRAPH
TYPOLOGIC
TYPOLOGY
TYPOMANIA
TYPOS
TYPP
TYPPS
TYPTO
TYPTOED
TYPTOING
TYPTOS
TYPY
TYRAMINE
TYRAMINES
TYRAN
TYRANED
TYRANING
TYRANNE
TYRANNED
TYRANNES
TYRANNESS
TYRANNIC
TYRANNIES
TYRANNING
TYRANNIS
TYRANNISE
TYRANNIZE
TYRANNOUS
TYRANNY
TYRANS
TYRANT
TYRANTED
TYRANTING
TYRANTS
TYRE
TYRED
TYRELESS
TYRES
TYRING
TYRO
TYROCIDIN
TYROES
TYRONES
TYRONIC
TYROPITTA
TYROS
TYROSINE
TYROSINES

TYSTIE
TYSTIES
TYTE
TYTHE
TYTHED
TYTHES
TYTHING
TZADDIK
TZADDIKIM
TZADDIKS
TZADDIQ
TZADDIQIM
TZADDIQS
TZAR
TZARDOM
TZARDOMS
TZAREVNA
TZAREVNAS
TZARINA
TZARINAS
TZARISM
TZARISMS
TZARIST
TZARISTS
TZARITZA
TZARITZAS
TZARS
TZATZIKI
TZATZIKIS
TZETSE
TZETSES
TZETZE
TZETZES
TZIGANE
TZIGANES
TZIGANIES
TZIGANY
TZIMMES
TZITZIS
TZITZIT
TZITZITH
TZURIS

U

UAKARI
UAKARIS
UBEROUS
UBERTIES
UBERTY
UBIETIES
UBIETY
UBIQUE
UBIQUITIN
UBIQUITY
UCKERS
UDAL
UDALLER
UDALLERS
UDALS
UDDER
UDDERED
UDDERFUL
UDDERLESS
UDDERS
UDO
UDOMETER
UDOMETERS
UDOMETRIC
UDOMETRY
UDON
UDONS
UDOS
UDS
UEY
UEYS
UFO
UFOLOGIES
UFOLOGIST
UFOLOGY
UFOS
UG
UGALI
UGALIS
UGGED
UGGING
UGH
UGHS
UGLIED
UGLIER
UGLIES
UGLIEST
UGLIFIED
UGLIFIER
UGLIFIERS
UGLIFIES
UGLIFY
UGLIFYING

UGLILY
UGLINESS
UGLY
UGLYING
UGS
UGSOME
UH
UHLAN
UHLANS
UHURU
UHURUS
UILLEAN
UINTAHITE
UINTAITE
UINTAITES
UITLANDER
UJAMAA
UJAMAAS
UKASE
UKASES
UKE
UKELELE
UKELELES
UKES
UKULELE
UKULELES
ULAMA
ULAMAS
ULAN
ULANS
ULCER
ULCERATE
ULCERATED
ULCERATES
ULCERED
ULCERING
ULCEROUS
ULCERS
ULE
ULEMA
ULEMAS
ULES
ULEX
ULEXES
ULEXITE
ULEXITES
ULICON
ULICONS
ULIGINOSE
ULIGINOUS
ULIKON
ULIKONS
ULITIS

ULITISES
ULLAGE
ULLAGED
ULLAGES
ULLAGING
ULLING
ULLINGS
ULMACEOUS
ULMIN
ULMINS
ULNA
ULNAD
ULNAE
ULNAR
ULNARE
ULNARIA
ULNAS
ULOSES
ULOSIS
ULOTRICHY
ULPAN
ULPANIM
ULSTER
ULSTERED
ULSTERS
ULTERIOR
ULTIMA
ULTIMACY
ULTIMAS
ULTIMATA
ULTIMATE
ULTIMATED
ULTIMATES
ULTIMATUM
ULTIMO
ULTION
ULTIONS
ULTRA
ULTRACHIC
ULTRACOLD
ULTRACOOL
ULTRADRY
ULTRAFAST
ULTRAFINE
ULTRAHEAT
ULTRAHIGH
ULTRAHIP
ULTRAHOT
ULTRAISM
ULTRAISMS
ULTRAIST
ULTRAISTS
ULTRALEFT

ULTRALOW
ULTRAPOSH
ULTRAPURE
ULTRARARE
ULTRARED
ULTRAREDS
ULTRARICH
ULTRAS
ULTRASAFE
ULTRASLOW
ULTRASOFT
ULTRATHIN
ULTRATINY
ULTRAWIDE
ULU
ULULANT
ULULATE
ULULATED
ULULATES
ULULATING
ULULATION
ULUS
ULVA
ULVAS
ULYIE
ULYIES
ULZIE
ULZIES
UM
UMAMI
UMAMIS
UMANGITE
UMANGITES
UMBEL
UMBELED
UMBELLAR
UMBELLATE
UMBELLED
UMBELLET
UMBELLETS
UMBELLULE
UMBELS
UMBER
UMBERED
UMBERING
UMBERS
UMBERY
UMBILICAL
UMBILICI
UMBILICUS
UMBLE
UMBLES
UMBO

UMBONAL	UMPIRAGE	UNAIMED	UNATTIRED
UMBONATE	UMPIRAGES	UNAIRED	UNATTUNED
UMBONES	UMPIRE	UNAIS	UNAU
UMBONIC	UMPIRED	UNAKIN	UNAUDITED
UMBOS	UMPIRES	UNAKING	UNAUS
UMBRA	UMPIRING	UNAKITE	UNAVENGED
UMBRACULA	UMPS	UNAKITES	UNAVERAGE
UMBRAE	UMPTEEN	UNALARMED	UNAVERTED
UMBRAGE	UMPTEENTH	UNALERTED	UNAVOIDED
UMBRAGED	UMPTIETH	UNALIGNED	UNAVOWED
UMBRAGES	UMPTY	UNALIKE	UNAWAKE
UMBRAGING	UMPY	UNALIST	UNAWAKED
UMBRAL	UMQUHILE	UNALISTS	UNAWARDED
UMBRAS	UMTEENTH	UNALIVE	UNAWARE
UMBRATED	UMU	UNALLAYED	UNAWARELY
UMBRATIC	UMWELT	UNALLEGED	UNAWARES
UMBRATILE	UMWELTS	UNALLIED	UNAWED
UMBRE	UMWHILE	UNALLOWED	UNAWESOME
UMBREL	UN	UNALLOYED	UNAXED
UMBRELLA	UNABASHED	UNALTERED	UNBACKED
UMBRELLAS	UNABATED	UNAMASSED	UNBAFFLED
UMBRELLO	UNABATING	UNAMAZED	UNBAG
UMBRELLOS	UNABETTED	UNAMENDED	UNBAGGED
UMBRELS	UNABIDING	UNAMERCED	UNBAGGING
UMBRERE	UNABJURED	UNAMIABLE	UNBAGS
UMBRERES	UNABLE	UNAMUSED	UNBAITED
UMBRES	UNABORTED	UNAMUSING	UNBAKED
UMBRETTE	UNABRADED	UNANCHOR	UNBALANCE
UMBRETTES	UNABUSED	UNANCHORS	UNBALE
UMBRIERE	UNABUSIVE	UNANELED	UNBALED
UMBRIERES	UNACCRUED	UNANIMITY	UNBALES
UMBRIL	UNACCUSED	UNANIMOUS	UNBALING
UMBRILS	UNACERBIC	UNANNEXED	UNBAN
UMBROSE	UNACHING	UNANNOYED	UNBANDAGE
UMBROUS	UNACIDIC	UNANXIOUS	UNBANDED
UMFAZI	UNACTABLE	UNAPPAREL	UNBANKED
UMFAZIS	UNACTED	UNAPPLIED	UNBANNED
UMIAC	UNACTIVE	UNAPT	UNBANNING
UMIACK	UNADAPTED	UNAPTLY	UNBANS
UMIACKS	UNADDED	UNAPTNESS	UNBAPTISE
UMIACS	UNADEPT	UNARCHED	UNBAPTIZE
UMIAK	UNADEPTLY	UNARGUED	UNBAR
UMIAKS	UNADMIRED	UNARISEN	UNBARBED
UMIAQ	UNADOPTED	UNARM	UNBARE
UMIAQS	UNADORED	UNARMED	UNBARED
UMLAUT	UNADORNED	UNARMING	UNBARES
UMLAUTED	UNADULT	UNARMORED	UNBARING
UMLAUTING	UNADVISED	UNARMS	UNBARK
UMLAUTS	UNAFRAID	UNAROUSED	UNBARKED
UMLUNGU	UNAGED	UNARRAYED	UNBARKING
UMLUNGUS	UNAGEING	UNARTFUL	UNBARKS
UMM	UNAGILE	UNARY	UNBARRED
UMP	UNAGING	UNASHAMED	UNBARRING
UMPED	UNAGREED	UNASKED	UNBARS
UMPH	UNAI	UNASSAYED	UNBASED
UMPIE	UNAIDABLE	UNASSUMED	UNBASHFUL
UMPIES	UNAIDED	UNASSURED	UNBASTED
UMPING	UNAIDEDLY	UNATONED	UNBATED

UNBATHED	UNBITT	UNBOUGHT	UNBURROW
UNBE	UNBITTED	UNBOUNCY	UNBURROWS
UNBEAR	UNBITTEN	UNBOUND	UNBURTHEN
UNBEARDED	UNBITTER	UNBOUNDED	UNBURY
UNBEARED	UNBITTING	UNBOWED	UNBURYING
UNBEARING	UNBITTS	UNBOWING	UNBUSTED
UNBEARS	UNBLAMED	UNBOX	UNBUSY
UNBEATEN	UNBLENDED	UNBOXED	UNBUTTON
UNBED	UNBLENT	UNBOXES	UNBUTTONS
UNBEDDED	UNBLESS	UNBOXING	UNCAGE
UNBEDDING	UNBLESSED	UNBRACE	UNCAGED
UNBEDS	UNBLESSES	UNBRACED	UNCAGES
UNBEEN	UNBLEST	UNBRACES	UNCAGING
UNBEGET	UNBLIND	UNBRACING	UNCAKE
UNBEGETS	UNBLINDED	UNBRAID	UNCAKED
UNBEGGED	UNBLINDS	UNBRAIDED	UNCAKES
UNBEGOT	UNBLOCK	UNBRAIDS	UNCAKING
UNBEGUILE	UNBLOCKED	UNBRAKE	UNCALLED
UNBEGUN	UNBLOCKS	UNBRAKED	UNCANDID
UNBEING	UNBLOODED	UNBRAKES	UNCANDLED
UNBEINGS	UNBLOODY	UNBRAKING	UNCANDOUR
UNBEKNOWN	UNBLOTTED	UNBRANDED	UNCANNED
UNBELIEF	UNBLOWED	UNBRASTE	UNCANNIER
UNBELIEFS	UNBLOWN	UNBRED	UNCANNILY
UNBELIEVE	UNBLUNTED	UNBREECH	UNCANNY
UNBELOVED	UNBLURRED	UNBRIDGED	UNCANONIC
UNBELT	UNBOARDED	UNBRIDLE	UNCAP
UNBELTED	UNBOBBED	UNBRIDLED	UNCAPABLE
UNBELTING	UNBODIED	UNBRIDLES	UNCAPE
UNBELTS	UNBODING	UNBRIEFED	UNCAPED
UNBEMUSED	UNBOILED	UNBRIGHT	UNCAPES
UNBEND	UNBOLT	UNBRIZZED	UNCAPING
UNBENDED	UNBOLTED	UNBROILED	UNCAPPED
UNBENDING	UNBOLTING	UNBROKE	UNCAPPING
UNBENDS	UNBOLTS	UNBROKEN	UNCAPS
UNBENIGN	UNBONDED	UNBROWNED	UNCARDED
UNBENT	UNBONE	UNBRUISED	UNCAREFUL
UNBEREFT	UNBONED	UNBRUSED	UNCARING
UNBERUFEN	UNBONES	UNBRUSHED	UNCART
UNBESEEM	UNBONING	UNBUCKLE	UNCARTED
UNBESEEMS	UNBONNET	UNBUCKLED	UNCARTING
UNBESPEAK	UNBONNETS	UNBUCKLES	UNCARTS
UNBESPOKE	UNBOOKED	UNBUDDED	UNCARVED
UNBIAS	UNBOOKISH	UNBUDGING	UNCASE
UNBIASED	UNBOOT	UNBUILD	UNCASED
UNBIASES	UNBOOTED	UNBUILDS	UNCASES
UNBIASING	UNBOOTING	UNBUILT	UNCASHED
UNBIASSED	UNBOOTS	UNBULKY	UNCASING
UNBIASSES	UNBORE	UNBUNDLE	UNCASKED
UNBID	UNBORN	UNBUNDLED	UNCAST
UNBIDDEN	UNBORNE	UNBUNDLER	UNCATCHY
UNBIGOTED	UNBOSOM	UNBUNDLES	UNCATE
UNBILLED	UNBOSOMED	UNBURDEN	UNCATERED
UNBIND	UNBOSOMER	UNBURDENS	UNCAUGHT
UNBINDING	UNBOSOMS	UNBURIED	UNCAUSED
UNBINDS	UNBOTTLE	UNBURIES	UNCE
UNBISHOP	UNBOTTLED	UNBURNED	UNCEASING
UNBISHOPS	UNBOTTLES	UNBURNT	UNCEDED

UNCERTAIN
UNCES
UNCESSANT
UNCHAIN
UNCHAINED
UNCHAINS
UNCHAIR
UNCHAIRED
UNCHAIRS
UNCHANCY
UNCHANGED
UNCHARGE
UNCHARGED
UNCHARGES
UNCHARITY
UNCHARM
UNCHARMED
UNCHARMS
UNCHARNEL
UNCHARRED
UNCHARTED
UNCHARY
UNCHASTE
UNCHASTER
UNCHECK
UNCHECKED
UNCHECKS
UNCHEERED
UNCHEWED
UNCHIC
UNCHICLY
UNCHILD
UNCHILDED
UNCHILDS
UNCHILLED
UNCHOKE
UNCHOKED
UNCHOKES
UNCHOKING
UNCHOSEN
UNCHRISOM
UNCHURCH
UNCI
UNCIA
UNCIAE
UNCIAL
UNCIALLY
UNCIALS
UNCIFORM
UNCIFORMS
UNCINAL
UNCINARIA
UNCINATE
UNCINATED
UNCINI
UNCINUS
UNCIPHER
UNCIPHERS

UNCITED
UNCIVIL
UNCIVILLY
UNCLAD
UNCLAIMED
UNCLAMP
UNCLAMPED
UNCLAMPS
UNCLARITY
UNCLASP
UNCLASPED
UNCLASPS
UNCLASSED
UNCLASSY
UNCLAWED
UNCLE
UNCLEAN
UNCLEANED
UNCLEANER
UNCLEANLY
UNCLEAR
UNCLEARED
UNCLEARER
UNCLEARLY
UNCLED
UNCLEFT
UNCLENCH
UNCLES
UNCLESHIP
UNCLEW
UNCLEWED
UNCLEWING
UNCLEWS
UNCLICHED
UNCLINCH
UNCLING
UNCLIP
UNCLIPPED
UNCLIPS
UNCLIPT
UNCLOAK
UNCLOAKED
UNCLOAKS
UNCLOG
UNCLOGGED
UNCLOGS
UNCLOSE
UNCLOSED
UNCLOSES
UNCLOSING
UNCLOTHE
UNCLOTHED
UNCLOTHES
UNCLOUD
UNCLOUDED
UNCLOUDS
UNCLOUDY
UNCLOVEN

UNCLOYED
UNCLOYING
UNCLUTCH
UNCLUTTER
UNCO
UNCOATED
UNCOATING
UNCOBBLED
UNCOCK
UNCOCKED
UNCOCKING
UNCOCKS
UNCODED
UNCOER
UNCOERCED
UNCOES
UNCOEST
UNCOFFIN
UNCOFFINS
UNCOIL
UNCOILED
UNCOILING
UNCOILS
UNCOINED
UNCOLORED
UNCOLT
UNCOLTED
UNCOLTING
UNCOLTS
UNCOMBED
UNCOMBINE
UNCOMELY
UNCOMIC
UNCOMMON
UNCONCERN
UNCONFINE
UNCONFORM
UNCONFUSE
UNCONGEAL
UNCOOKED
UNCOOL
UNCOOLED
UNCOPE
UNCOPED
UNCOPES
UNCOPING
UNCORD
UNCORDED
UNCORDIAL
UNCORDING
UNCORDS
UNCORK
UNCORKED
UNCORKING
UNCORKS
UNCORRUPT
UNCOS
UNCOSTLY

UNCOUNTED
UNCOUPLE
UNCOUPLED
UNCOUPLER
UNCOUPLES
UNCOURTLY
UNCOUTH
UNCOUTHER
UNCOUTHLY
UNCOVER
UNCOVERED
UNCOVERS
UNCOWL
UNCOWLED
UNCOWLING
UNCOWLS
UNCOY
UNCOYNED
UNCRACKED
UNCRATE
UNCRATED
UNCRATES
UNCRATING
UNCRAZY
UNCREATE
UNCREATED
UNCREATES
UNCREWED
UNCROPPED
UNCROSS
UNCROSSED
UNCROSSES
UNCROWDED
UNCROWN
UNCROWNED
UNCROWNS
UNCRUDDED
UNCRUMPLE
UNCRUSHED
UNCTION
UNCTIONS
UNCTUOUS
UNCUFF
UNCUFFED
UNCUFFING
UNCUFFS
UNCULLED
UNCURABLE
UNCURABLY
UNCURB
UNCURBED
UNCURBING
UNCURBS
UNCURDLED
UNCURED
UNCURIOUS
UNCURL
UNCURLED

UNCURLING
UNCURLS
UNCURRENT
UNCURSE
UNCURSED
UNCURSES
UNCURSING
UNCURTAIN
UNCURVED
UNCUS
UNCUT
UNCUTE
UNCYNICAL
UNDAM
UNDAMAGED
UNDAMMED
UNDAMMING
UNDAMNED
UNDAMPED
UNDAMS
UNDARING
UNDASHED
UNDATABLE
UNDATE
UNDATED
UNDAUNTED
UNDAWNING
UNDAZZLE
UNDAZZLED
UNDAZZLES
UNDE
UNDEAD
UNDEAF
UNDEAFED
UNDEAFING
UNDEAFS
UNDEALT
UNDEAR
UNDEBASED
UNDEBATED
UNDECAGON
UNDECAYED
UNDECEIVE
UNDECENT
UNDECIDED
UNDECIMAL
UNDECK
UNDECKED
UNDECKING
UNDECKS
UNDEE
UNDEEDED
UNDEFACED
UNDEFIDE
UNDEFIED
UNDEFILED
UNDEFINED
UNDEIFIED

UNDEIFIES
UNDEIFY
UNDELAYED
UNDELETED
UNDELIGHT
UNDELUDED
UNDENIED
UNDENTED
UNDER
UNDERACT
UNDERACTS
UNDERAGE
UNDERAGED
UNDERAGES
UNDERARM
UNDERARMS
UNDERATE
UNDERBAKE
UNDERBEAR
UNDERBID
UNDERBIDS
UNDERBIT
UNDERBITE
UNDERBODY
UNDERBORE
UNDERBOSS
UNDERBRED
UNDERBRIM
UNDERBUD
UNDERBUDS
UNDERBUSH
UNDERBUY
UNDERBUYS
UNDERCARD
UNDERCART
UNDERCAST
UNDERCLAD
UNDERCLAY
UNDERCLUB
UNDERCOAT
UNDERCOOK
UNDERCOOL
UNDERCUT
UNDERCUTS
UNDERDAKS
UNDERDECK
UNDERDID
UNDERDO
UNDERDOER
UNDERDOES
UNDERDOG
UNDERDOGS
UNDERDONE
UNDERDOSE
UNDERDRAW
UNDERDREW
UNDEREAT
UNDEREATS

UNDERFED
UNDERFEED
UNDERFELT
UNDERFIRE
UNDERFISH
UNDERFLOW
UNDERFONG
UNDERFOOT
UNDERFUND
UNDERFUR
UNDERFURS
UNDERGIRD
UNDERGIRT
UNDERGO
UNDERGOD
UNDERGODS
UNDERGOER
UNDERGOES
UNDERGONE
UNDERGOWN
UNDERGRAD
UNDERHAIR
UNDERHAND
UNDERHEAT
UNDERHUNG
UNDERIVED
UNDERJAW
UNDERJAWS
UNDERKEEP
UNDERKEPT
UNDERKILL
UNDERKING
UNDERLAID
UNDERLAIN
UNDERLAP
UNDERLAPS
UNDERLAY
UNDERLAYS
UNDERLEAF
UNDERLET
UNDERLETS
UNDERLIE
UNDERLIER
UNDERLIES
UNDERLINE
UNDERLING
UNDERLIP
UNDERLIPS
UNDERLIT
UNDERLOAD
UNDERMAN
UNDERMANS
UNDERMEN
UNDERMINE
UNDERMOST
UNDERN
UNDERNOTE
UNDERNS

UNDERPAID
UNDERPART
UNDERPASS
UNDERPAY
UNDERPAYS
UNDERPEEP
UNDERPIN
UNDERPINS
UNDERPLAY
UNDERPLOT
UNDERPROP
UNDERRAN
UNDERRATE
UNDERRIPE
UNDERRUN
UNDERRUNS
UNDERSAID
UNDERSAY
UNDERSAYS
UNDERSEA
UNDERSEAL
UNDERSEAS
UNDERSELF
UNDERSELL
UNDERSET
UNDERSETS
UNDERSHOT
UNDERSIDE
UNDERSIGN
UNDERSIZE
UNDERSKY
UNDERSOIL
UNDERSOLD
UNDERSONG
UNDERSPIN
UNDERTAKE
UNDERTANE
UNDERTAX
UNDERTIME
UNDERTINT
UNDERTONE
UNDERTOOK
UNDERTOW
UNDERTOWS
UNDERUSE
UNDERUSED
UNDERUSES
UNDERVEST
UNDERVOTE
UNDERWAY
UNDERWEAR
UNDERWENT
UNDERWING
UNDERWIRE
UNDERWIT
UNDERWITS
UNDERWOOD
UNDERWOOL

UNDERWORK
UNDESERT
UNDESERTS
UNDESERVE
UNDESIRED
UNDEVOUT
UNDID
UNDIES
UNDIGHT
UNDIGHTS
UNDIGNIFY
UNDILUTED
UNDIMMED
UNDINE
UNDINES
UNDINISM
UNDINISMS
UNDINTED
UNDIPPED
UNDIVIDED
UNDIVINE
UNDO
UNDOABLE
UNDOCILE
UNDOCK
UNDOCKED
UNDOCKING
UNDOCKS
UNDOER
UNDOERS
UNDOES
UNDOING
UNDOINGS
UNDONE
UNDOOMED
UNDOTTED
UNDOUBLE
UNDOUBLED
UNDOUBLES
UNDOUBTED
UNDRAINED
UNDRAPE
UNDRAPED
UNDRAPES
UNDRAPING
UNDRAW
UNDRAWING
UNDRAWN
UNDRAWS
UNDREADED
UNDREAMED
UNDREAMT
UNDRESS
UNDRESSED
UNDRESSES
UNDREST
UNDREW
UNDRIED

UNDRILLED
UNDRIVEN
UNDROSSY
UNDROWNED
UNDRUNK
UNDUBBED
UNDUE
UNDUG
UNDULANCE
UNDULANCY
UNDULANT
UNDULAR
UNDULATE
UNDULATED
UNDULATES
UNDULATOR
UNDULLED
UNDULOSE
UNDULOUS
UNDULY
UNDUTEOUS
UNDUTIFUL
UNDY
UNDYED
UNDYING
UNDYINGLY
UNDYNAMIC
UNEAGER
UNEAGERLY
UNEARED
UNEARNED
UNEARTH
UNEARTHED
UNEARTHLY
UNEARTHS
UNEASE
UNEASES
UNEASIER
UNEASIEST
UNEASILY
UNEASY
UNEATABLE
UNEATEN
UNEATH
UNEATHES
UNEDGE
UNEDGED
UNEDGES
UNEDGING
UNEDIBLE
UNEDITED
UNEFFACED
UNELATED
UNELECTED
UNEMPTIED
UNENDED
UNENDING
UNENDOWED

UNENGAGED
UNENJOYED
UNENSURED
UNENTERED
UNENVIED
UNENVIOUS
UNENVYING
UNEQUABLE
UNEQUAL
UNEQUALED
UNEQUALLY
UNEQUALS
UNERASED
UNEROTIC
UNERRING
UNESPIED
UNESSAYED
UNESSENCE
UNETH
UNETHICAL
UNEVADED
UNEVEN
UNEVENER
UNEVENEST
UNEVENLY
UNEVOLVED
UNEXALTED
UNEXCITED
UNEXCUSED
UNEXOTIC
UNEXPERT
UNEXPIRED
UNEXPOSED
UNEXTINCT
UNEXTREME
UNEYED
UNFABLED
UNFACT
UNFACTS
UNFADABLE
UNFADED
UNFADING
UNFAILING
UNFAIR
UNFAIRED
UNFAIRER
UNFAIREST
UNFAIRING
UNFAIRLY
UNFAIRS
UNFAITH
UNFAITHS
UNFAKED
UNFALLEN
UNFAMED
UNFAMOUS
UNFANCY
UNFANNED

UNFASTEN
UNFASTENS
UNFAULTY
UNFAVORED
UNFAZED
UNFEARED
UNFEARFUL
UNFEARING
UNFED
UNFEED
UNFEELING
UNFEIGNED
UNFELLED
UNFELT
UNFELTED
UNFENCE
UNFENCED
UNFENCES
UNFENCING
UNFERTILE
UNFETTER
UNFETTERS
UNFEUDAL
UNFEUED
UNFIGURED
UNFILDE
UNFILED
UNFILIAL
UNFILLED
UNFILMED
UNFINE
UNFIRED
UNFIRM
UNFISHED
UNFIT
UNFITLY
UNFITNESS
UNFITS
UNFITTED
UNFITTER
UNFITTEST
UNFITTING
UNFIX
UNFIXED
UNFIXES
UNFIXING
UNFIXITY
UNFIXT
UNFLAPPED
UNFLASHY
UNFLAWED
UNFLEDGED
UNFLESH
UNFLESHED
UNFLESHES
UNFLESHLY
UNFLEXED
UNFLOORED

UNFLUSH
UNFLUSHED
UNFLUSHES
UNFLUTED
UNFLYABLE
UNFOCUSED
UNFOILED
UNFOLD
UNFOLDED
UNFOLDER
UNFOLDERS
UNFOLDING
UNFOLDS
UNFOND
UNFOOL
UNFOOLED
UNFOOLING
UNFOOLS
UNFOOTED
UNFORBID
UNFORCED
UNFORGED
UNFORGOT
UNFORKED
UNFORM
UNFORMAL
UNFORMED
UNFORMING
UNFORMS
UNFORTUNE
UNFOUGHT
UNFOUND
UNFOUNDED
UNFRAMED
UNFRANKED
UNFRAUGHT
UNFREE
UNFREED
UNFREEDOM
UNFREEING
UNFREEMAN
UNFREEMEN
UNFREES
UNFREEZE
UNFREEZES
UNFRETTED
UNFRIEND
UNFRIENDS
UNFROCK
UNFROCKED
UNFROCKS
UNFROZE
UNFROZEN
UNFUELLED
UNFUMED
UNFUNDED
UNFUNNY
UNFURL

UNFURLED
UNFURLING
UNFURLS
UNFURNISH
UNFURRED
UNFUSED
UNFUSSIER
UNFUSSILY
UNFUSSY
UNGAG
UNGAGGED
UNGAGGING
UNGAGS
UNGAIN
UNGAINFUL
UNGAINLY
UNGALLANT
UNGALLED
UNGARBED
UNGARBLED
UNGATED
UNGAUGED
UNGAZING
UNGEAR
UNGEARED
UNGEARING
UNGEARS
UNGELDED
UNGENIAL
UNGENTEEL
UNGENTLE
UNGENTLY
UNGENUINE
UNGERMANE
UNGET
UNGETS
UNGETTING
UNGHOSTLY
UNGIFTED
UNGILD
UNGILDED
UNGILDING
UNGILDS
UNGILT
UNGIRD
UNGIRDED
UNGIRDING
UNGIRDS
UNGIRT
UNGIRTH
UNGIRTHED
UNGIRTHS
UNGIVING
UNGLAD
UNGLAZED
UNGLOSSED
UNGLOVE
UNGLOVED

UNGLOVES
UNGLOVING
UNGLUE
UNGLUED
UNGLUES
UNGLUING
UNGOD
UNGODDED
UNGODDING
UNGODLIER
UNGODLIKE
UNGODLILY
UNGODLY
UNGODS
UNGORD
UNGORED
UNGORGED
UNGOT
UNGOTTEN
UNGOWN
UNGOWNED
UNGOWNING
UNGOWNS
UNGRACED
UNGRADED
UNGRASSED
UNGRAVELY
UNGRAZED
UNGREASED
UNGREEDY
UNGROOMED
UNGROUND
UNGROUPED
UNGROWN
UNGRUDGED
UNGUAL
UNGUARD
UNGUARDED
UNGUARDS
UNGUENT
UNGUENTA
UNGUENTS
UNGUENTUM
UNGUES
UNGUESSED
UNGUIDED
UNGUIFORM
UNGUILTY
UNGUINOUS
UNGUIS
UNGULA
UNGULAE
UNGULAR
UNGULATE
UNGULATES
UNGULED
UNGUM
UNGUMMED

UNGUMMING
UNGUMS
UNGYVE
UNGYVED
UNGYVES
UNGYVING
UNHABLE
UNHACKED
UNHAILED
UNHAIR
UNHAIRED
UNHAIRER
UNHAIRERS
UNHAIRING
UNHAIRS
UNHALLOW
UNHALLOWS
UNHALSED
UNHALVED
UNHAND
UNHANDED
UNHANDIER
UNHANDILY
UNHANDING
UNHANDLED
UNHANDS
UNHANDY
UNHANG
UNHANGED
UNHANGING
UNHANGS
UNHAPPIED
UNHAPPIER
UNHAPPIES
UNHAPPILY
UNHAPPY
UNHARBOUR
UNHARDY
UNHARMED
UNHARMFUL
UNHARMING
UNHARNESS
UNHARRIED
UNHASP
UNHASPED
UNHASPING
UNHASPS
UNHASTING
UNHASTY
UNHAT
UNHATCHED
UNHATS
UNHATTED
UNHATTING
UNHAUNTED
UNHEAD
UNHEADED
UNHEADING

UNHEADS
UNHEAL
UNHEALED
UNHEALING
UNHEALS
UNHEALTH
UNHEALTHS
UNHEALTHY
UNHEARD
UNHEARSE
UNHEARSED
UNHEARSES
UNHEART
UNHEARTED
UNHEARTS
UNHEATED
UNHEDGED
UNHEEDED
UNHEEDFUL
UNHEEDILY
UNHEEDING
UNHEEDY
UNHELE
UNHELED
UNHELES
UNHELING
UNHELM
UNHELMED
UNHELMING
UNHELMS
UNHELPED
UNHELPFUL
UNHEPPEN
UNHEROIC
UNHERST
UNHEWN
UNHIDDEN
UNHINGE
UNHINGED
UNHINGES
UNHINGING
UNHIP
UNHIPPER
UNHIPPEST
UNHIRABLE
UNHIRED
UNHITCH
UNHITCHED
UNHITCHES
UNHIVE
UNHIVED
UNHIVES
UNHIVING
UNHOARD
UNHOARDED
UNHOARDS
UNHOLIER
UNHOLIEST

UNHOLILY
UNHOLPEN
UNHOLY
UNHOMELY
UNHONEST
UNHONORED
UNHOOD
UNHOODED
UNHOODING
UNHOODS
UNHOOK
UNHOOKED
UNHOOKING
UNHOOKS
UNHOOP
UNHOOPED
UNHOOPING
UNHOOPS
UNHOPED
UNHOPEFUL
UNHORSE
UNHORSED
UNHORSES
UNHORSING
UNHOSTILE
UNHOUSE
UNHOUSED
UNHOUSES
UNHOUSING
UNHUMAN
UNHUMANLY
UNHUMBLED
UNHUNG
UNHUNTED
UNHURRIED
UNHURT
UNHURTFUL
UNHUSK
UNHUSKED
UNHUSKING
UNHUSKS
UNI
UNIALGAL
UNIAXIAL
UNIBODY
UNIBROW
UNIBROWS
UNICITIES
UNICITY
UNICOLOR
UNICOLOUR
UNICORN
UNICORNS
UNICYCLE
UNICYCLED
UNICYCLES
UNIDEAED
UNIDEAL

UNIFACE
UNIFACES
UNIFIABLE
UNIFIC
UNIFIED
UNIFIER
UNIFIERS
UNIFIES
UNIFILAR
UNIFORM
UNIFORMED
UNIFORMER
UNIFORMLY
UNIFORMS
UNIFY
UNIFYING
UNIFYINGS
UNIJUGATE
UNILINEAL
UNILINEAR
UNILLUMED
UNILOBAR
UNILOBED
UNIMBUED
UNIMPEDED
UNIMPOSED
UNINCITED
UNINDEXED
UNINJURED
UNINSTALL
UNINSURED
UNINURED
UNINVITED
UNINVOKED
UNION
UNIONISE
UNIONISED
UNIONISER
UNIONISES
UNIONISM
UNIONISMS
UNIONIST
UNIONISTS
UNIONIZE
UNIONIZED
UNIONIZER
UNIONIZES
UNIONS
UNIPAROUS
UNIPED
UNIPEDS
UNIPLANAR
UNIPOD
UNIPODS
UNIPOLAR
UNIPOTENT
UNIQUE
UNIQUELY

UNIQUER
UNIQUES
UNIQUEST
UNIRAMOSE
UNIRAMOUS
UNIRONED
UNIRONIC
UNIS
UNISERIAL
UNISEX
UNISEXES
UNISEXUAL
UNISIZE
UNISON
UNISONAL
UNISONANT
UNISONOUS
UNISONS
UNISSUED
UNIT
UNITAGE
UNITAGES
UNITAL
UNITARD
UNITARDS
UNITARIAN
UNITARILY
UNITARY
UNITE
UNITED
UNITEDLY
UNITER
UNITERS
UNITES
UNITIES
UNITING
UNITINGS
UNITION
UNITIONS
UNITISE
UNITISED
UNITISER
UNITISERS
UNITISES
UNITISING
UNITIVE
UNITIVELY
UNITIZE
UNITIZED
UNITIZER
UNITIZERS
UNITIZES
UNITIZING
UNITRUST
UNITRUSTS
UNITS
UNITY
UNIVALENT

UNIVALVE	UNKNIT	UNLETTED	UNLOOSENS
UNIVALVED	UNKNITS	UNLEVEL	UNLOOSES
UNIVALVES	UNKNITTED	UNLEVELED	UNLOOSING
UNIVERSAL	UNKNOT	UNLEVELS	UNLOPPED
UNIVERSE	UNKNOTS	UNLEVIED	UNLORD
UNIVERSES	UNKNOTTED	UNLICH	UNLORDED
UNIVOCAL	UNKNOWING	UNLICKED	UNLORDING
UNIVOCALS	UNKNOWN	UNLID	UNLORDLY
UNJADED	UNKNOWNS	UNLIDDED	UNLORDS
UNJAM	UNKOSHER	UNLIDDING	UNLOSABLE
UNJAMMED	UNLABELED	UNLIDS	UNLOST
UNJAMMING	UNLABORED	UNLIGHTED	UNLOVABLE
UNJAMS	UNLACE	UNLIKABLE	UNLOVE
UNJEALOUS	UNLACED	UNLIKE	UNLOVED
UNJOINED	UNLACES	UNLIKED	UNLOVELY
UNJOINT	UNLACING	UNLIKELY	UNLOVES
UNJOINTED	UNLADE	UNLIKES	UNLOVING
UNJOINTS	UNLADED	UNLIMBER	UNLUCKIER
UNJOYFUL	UNLADEN	UNLIMBERS	UNLUCKILY
UNJOYOUS	UNLADES	UNLIME	UNLUCKY
UNJUDGED	UNLADING	UNLIMED	UNLYRICAL
UNJUST	UNLADINGS	UNLIMES	UNMACHO
UNJUSTER	UNLAID	UNLIMING	UNMADE
UNJUSTEST	UNLASH	UNLIMITED	UNMAILED
UNJUSTLY	UNLASHED	UNLINE	UNMAIMED
UNKED	UNLASHES	UNLINEAL	UNMAKABLE
UNKEELED	UNLASHING	UNLINED	UNMAKE
UNKEMPT	UNLAST	UNLINES	UNMAKER
UNKEMPTLY	UNLASTE	UNLINING	UNMAKERS
UNKEND	UNLATCH	UNLINK	UNMAKES
UNKENNED	UNLATCHED	UNLINKED	UNMAKING
UNKENNEL	UNLATCHES	UNLINKING	UNMAKINGS
UNKENNELS	UNLAW	UNLINKS	UNMAN
UNKENT	UNLAWED	UNLISTED	UNMANACLE
UNKEPT	UNLAWFUL	UNLIT	UNMANAGED
UNKET	UNLAWING	UNLIVABLE	UNMANFUL
UNKID	UNLAWS	UNLIVE	UNMANLIER
UNKIND	UNLAY	UNLIVED	UNMANLIKE
UNKINDER	UNLAYING	UNLIVELY	UNMANLY
UNKINDEST	UNLAYS	UNLIVES	UNMANNED
UNKINDLED	UNLEAD	UNLIVING	UNMANNING
UNKINDLY	UNLEADED	UNLOAD	UNMANNISH
UNKING	UNLEADEDS	UNLOADED	UNMANS
UNKINGED	UNLEADING	UNLOADER	UNMANTLE
UNKINGING	UNLEADS	UNLOADERS	UNMANTLED
UNKINGLY	UNLEAL	UNLOADING	UNMANTLES
UNKINGS	UNLEARN	UNLOADS	UNMANURED
UNKINK	UNLEARNED	UNLOBED	UNMAPPED
UNKINKED	UNLEARNS	UNLOCATED	UNMARD
UNKINKING	UNLEARNT	UNLOCK	UNMARKED
UNKINKS	UNLEASED	UNLOCKED	UNMARRED
UNKISS	UNLEASH	UNLOCKING	UNMARRIED
UNKISSED	UNLEASHED	UNLOCKS	UNMARRIES
UNKISSES	UNLEASHES	UNLOGICAL	UNMARRY
UNKISSING	UNLED	UNLOOKED	UNMASK
UNKNELLED	UNLESS	UNLOOSE	UNMASKED
UNKNIGHT	UNLET	UNLOOSED	UNMASKER
UNKNIGHTS	UNLETHAL	UNLOOSEN	UNMASKERS

UNMASKING
UNMASKS
UNMATCHED
UNMATED
UNMATTED
UNMATURED
UNMEANING
UNMEANT
UNMEEK
UNMEET
UNMEETLY
UNMELLOW
UNMELTED
UNMENDED
UNMERITED
UNMERRY
UNMESH
UNMESHED
UNMESHES
UNMESHING
UNMET
UNMETED
UNMEW
UNMEWED
UNMEWING
UNMEWS
UNMILKED
UNMILLED
UNMINDED
UNMINDFUL
UNMINED
UNMINGLE
UNMINGLED
UNMINGLES
UNMIRY
UNMISSED
UNMITER
UNMITERED
UNMITERS
UNMITRE
UNMITRED
UNMITRES
UNMITRING
UNMIX
UNMIXABLE
UNMIXED
UNMIXEDLY
UNMIXES
UNMIXING
UNMIXT
UNMOANED
UNMODISH
UNMOLD
UNMOLDED
UNMOLDING
UNMOLDS
UNMOLTEN
UNMONEYED

UNMONIED
UNMOOR
UNMOORED
UNMOORING
UNMOORS
UNMORAL
UNMORALLY
UNMORTISE
UNMOTIVED
UNMOULD
UNMOULDED
UNMOULDS
UNMOUNT
UNMOUNTED
UNMOUNTS
UNMOURNED
UNMOVABLE
UNMOVABLY
UNMOVED
UNMOVEDLY
UNMOVING
UNMOWN
UNMUFFLE
UNMUFFLED
UNMUFFLES
UNMUSICAL
UNMUZZLE
UNMUZZLED
UNMUZZLES
UNNAIL
UNNAILED
UNNAILING
UNNAILS
UNNAMABLE
UNNAMED
UNNANELD
UNNATIVE
UNNATURAL
UNNEATH
UNNEEDED
UNNEEDFUL
UNNERVE
UNNERVED
UNNERVES
UNNERVING
UNNEST
UNNESTED
UNNESTING
UNNESTS
UNNETHES
UNNETTED
UNNOBLE
UNNOBLED
UNNOBLES
UNNOBLING
UNNOISY
UNNOTED
UNNOTICED

UNNUANCED
UNOBEYED
UNOBVIOUS
UNOFFERED
UNOFTEN
UNOILED
UNOPEN
UNOPENED
UNOPPOSED
UNORDER
UNORDERED
UNORDERLY
UNORDERS
UNORNATE
UNOWED
UNOWNED
UNPACED
UNPACK
UNPACKED
UNPACKER
UNPACKERS
UNPACKING
UNPACKS
UNPADDED
UNPAGED
UNPAID
UNPAINED
UNPAINFUL
UNPAINT
UNPAINTED
UNPAINTS
UNPAIRED
UNPALSIED
UNPANEL
UNPANELS
UNPANGED
UNPANNEL
UNPANNELS
UNPAPER
UNPAPERED
UNPAPERS
UNPARED
UNPARTED
UNPARTIAL
UNPATCHED
UNPATHED
UNPAVED
UNPAY
UNPAYABLE
UNPAYING
UNPAYS
UNPEELED
UNPEERED
UNPEG
UNPEGGED
UNPEGGING
UNPEGS
UNPEN

UNPENNED
UNPENNIED
UNPENNING
UNPENS
UNPENT
UNPEOPLE
UNPEOPLED
UNPEOPLES
UNPERCH
UNPERCHED
UNPERCHES
UNPERFECT
UNPERPLEX
UNPERSON
UNPERSONS
UNPERVERT
UNPICK
UNPICKED
UNPICKING
UNPICKS
UNPIERCED
UNPILE
UNPILED
UNPILES
UNPILING
UNPILOTED
UNPIN
UNPINKED
UNPINKT
UNPINNED
UNPINNING
UNPINS
UNPITIED
UNPITIFUL
UNPITTED
UNPITYING
UNPLACE
UNPLACED
UNPLACES
UNPLACING
UNPLAGUED
UNPLAINED
UNPLAIT
UNPLAITED
UNPLAITS
UNPLANKED
UNPLANNED
UNPLANTED
UNPLAYED
UNPLEASED
UNPLEATED
UNPLEDGED
UNPLIABLE
UNPLIABLY
UNPLIANT
UNPLOWED
UNPLUCKED
UNPLUG

UNPLUGGED	UNPRUNED	UNREASON	UNRIFLED
UNPLUGS	UNPUCKER	UNREASONS	UNRIG
UNPLUMB	UNPUCKERS	UNREAVE	UNRIGGED
UNPLUMBED	UNPULLED	UNREAVED	UNRIGGING
UNPLUMBS	UNPURE	UNREAVES	UNRIGHT
UNPLUME	UNPURELY	UNREAVING	UNRIGHTS
UNPLUMED	UNPURGED	UNREBATED	UNRIGS
UNPLUMES	UNPURSE	UNREBUKED	UNRIMED
UNPLUMING	UNPURSED	UNRECKED	UNRINGED
UNPOETIC	UNPURSES	UNRED	UNRINSED
UNPOINTED	UNPURSING	UNREDREST	UNRIP
UNPOISED	UNPURSUED	UNREDUCED	UNRIPE
UNPOISON	UNPUZZLE	UNREDY	UNRIPELY
UNPOISONS	UNPUZZLED	UNREEL	UNRIPENED
UNPOLICED	UNPUZZLES	UNREELED	UNRIPER
UNPOLISH	UNQUAKING	UNREELER	UNRIPEST
UNPOLITE	UNQUALIFY	UNREELERS	UNRIPPED
UNPOLITIC	UNQUEEN	UNREELING	UNRIPPING
UNPOLLED	UNQUEENED	UNREELS	UNRIPS
UNPOPE	UNQUEENLY	UNREEVE	UNRISEN
UNPOPED	UNQUEENS	UNREEVED	UNRIVALED
UNPOPES	UNQUELLED	UNREEVES	UNRIVEN
UNPOPING	UNQUIET	UNREEVING	UNRIVET
UNPOPULAR	UNQUIETED	UNREFINED	UNRIVETED
UNPOSED	UNQUIETER	UNREFUTED	UNRIVETS
UNPOSTED	UNQUIETLY	UNREIN	UNROASTED
UNPOTABLE	UNQUIETS	UNREINED	UNROBE
UNPOTTED	UNQUOTE	UNREINING	UNROBED
UNPRAISE	UNQUOTED	UNREINS	UNROBES
UNPRAISED	UNQUOTES	UNRELATED	UNROBING
UNPRAISES	UNQUOTING	UNRELAXED	UNROLL
UNPRAY	UNRACED	UNREMOVED	UNROLLED
UNPRAYED	UNRACKED	UNRENEWED	UNROLLING
UNPRAYING	UNRAISED	UNRENT	UNROLLS
UNPRAYS	UNRAKE	UNRENTED	UNROOF
UNPREACH	UNRAKED	UNREPAID	UNROOFED
UNPRECISE	UNRAKES	UNREPAIR	UNROOFING
UNPREDICT	UNRAKING	UNREPAIRS	UNROOFS
UNPREPARE	UNRANKED	UNRESERVE	UNROOST
UNPRESSED	UNRATED	UNREST	UNROOSTED
UNPRETTY	UNRAVAGED	UNRESTED	UNROOSTS
UNPRICED	UNRAVEL	UNRESTFUL	UNROOT
UNPRIEST	UNRAVELED	UNRESTING	UNROOTED
UNPRIESTS	UNRAVELS	UNRESTS	UNROOTING
UNPRIMED	UNRAZED	UNRETIRE	UNROOTS
UNPRINTED	UNRAZORED	UNRETIRED	UNROPE
UNPRISON	UNREACHED	UNRETIRES	UNROPED
UNPRISONS	UNREAD	UNREVISED	UNROPES
UNPRIZED	UNREADIER	UNREVOKED	UNROPING
UNPROBED	UNREADILY	UNRHYMED	UNROSINED
UNPROP	UNREADY	UNRIBBED	UNROTTED
UNPROPER	UNREAL	UNRID	UNROTTEN
UNPROPPED	UNREALISE	UNRIDABLE	UNROUGED
UNPROPS	UNREALISM	UNRIDDEN	UNROUGH
UNPROVED	UNREALITY	UNRIDDLE	UNROUND
UNPROVEN	UNREALIZE	UNRIDDLED	UNROUNDED
UNPROVIDE	UNREALLY	UNRIDDLER	UNROUNDS
UNPROVOKE	UNREAPED	UNRIDDLES	UNROUSED

UNROVE	UNSCALING	UNSERIOUS	UNSHOE
UNROVEN	UNSCANNED	UNSERVED	UNSHOED
UNROYAL	UNSCARRED	UNSET	UNSHOEING
UNROYALLY	UNSCARY	UNSETS	UNSHOES
UNRUBBED	UNSCATHED	UNSETTING	UNSHOOT
UNRUDE	UNSCENTED	UNSETTLE	UNSHOOTED
UNRUFFE	UNSCOURED	UNSETTLED	UNSHOOTS
UNRUFFLE	UNSCREW	UNSETTLES	UNSHORN
UNRUFFLED	UNSCREWED	UNSEVERED	UNSHOT
UNRUFFLES	UNSCREWS	UNSEW	UNSHOUT
UNRULE	UNSCYTHED	UNSEWED	UNSHOUTED
UNRULED	UNSEAL	UNSEWING	UNSHOUTS
UNRULES	UNSEALED	UNSEWN	UNSHOWN
UNRULIER	UNSEALING	UNSEWS	UNSHOWY
UNRULIEST	UNSEALS	UNSEX	UNSHRIVED
UNRULY	UNSEAM	UNSEXED	UNSHRIVEN
UNRUMPLED	UNSEAMED	UNSEXES	UNSHROUD
UNRUSHED	UNSEAMING	UNSEXING	UNSHROUDS
UNRUSTED	UNSEAMS	UNSEXIST	UNSHRUBD
UNS	UNSEARED	UNSEXUAL	UNSHRUNK
UNSADDLE	UNSEASON	UNSEXY	UNSHUNNED
UNSADDLED	UNSEASONS	UNSHACKLE	UNSHUT
UNSADDLES	UNSEAT	UNSHADED	UNSHUTS
UNSAFE	UNSEATED	UNSHADOW	UNSHUTTER
UNSAFELY	UNSEATING	UNSHADOWS	UNSICKER
UNSAFER	UNSEATS	UNSHAKED	UNSICKLED
UNSAFEST	UNSECRET	UNSHAKEN	UNSIFTED
UNSAFETY	UNSECULAR	UNSHALE	UNSIGHING
UNSAID	UNSECURED	UNSHALED	UNSIGHT
UNSAILED	UNSEDUCED	UNSHALES	UNSIGHTED
UNSAINED	UNSEEABLE	UNSHALING	UNSIGHTLY
UNSAINT	UNSEEDED	UNSHAMED	UNSIGHTS
UNSAINTED	UNSEEING	UNSHAPE	UNSIGNED
UNSAINTLY	UNSEEL	UNSHAPED	UNSILENT
UNSAINTS	UNSEELED	UNSHAPELY	UNSIMILAR
UNSALABLE	UNSEELIE	UNSHAPEN	UNSINEW
UNSALABLY	UNSEELING	UNSHAPES	UNSINEWED
UNSALTED	UNSEELS	UNSHAPING	UNSINEWS
UNSALUTED	UNSEEMING	UNSHARED	UNSINFUL
UNSAMPLED	UNSEEMLY	UNSHARP	UNSISTING
UNSAPPED	UNSEEN	UNSHAVED	UNSIZABLE
UNSASHED	UNSEENS	UNSHAVEN	UNSIZED
UNSATABLE	UNSEIZED	UNSHEATHE	UNSKILFUL
UNSATED	UNSELDOM	UNSHED	UNSKILLED
UNSATIATE	UNSELF	UNSHELL	UNSKIMMED
UNSATING	UNSELFED	UNSHELLED	UNSKINNED
UNSAVED	UNSELFING	UNSHELLS	UNSLAIN
UNSAVORY	UNSELFISH	UNSHENT	UNSLAKED
UNSAVOURY	UNSELFS	UNSHEWN	UNSLICED
UNSAWED	UNSELL	UNSHIFT	UNSLICK
UNSAWN	UNSELLING	UNSHIFTED	UNSLING
UNSAY	UNSELLS	UNSHIFTS	UNSLINGS
UNSAYABLE	UNSELVES	UNSHIP	UNSLUICE
UNSAYING	UNSENSE	UNSHIPPED	UNSLUICED
UNSAYS	UNSENSED	UNSHIPS	UNSLUICES
UNSCALE	UNSENSES	UNSHIRTED	UNSLUNG
UNSCALED	UNSENSING	UNSHOCKED	UNSMART
UNSCALES	UNSENT	UNSHOD	UNSMILING

UNSMITTEN	UNSPARING	UNSTICK	UNSUSPECT
UNSMOKED	UNSPARRED	UNSTICKS	UNSWADDLE
UNSMOOTH	UNSPARS	UNSTIFLED	UNSWATHE
UNSMOOTHS	UNSPEAK	UNSTILLED	UNSWATHED
UNSMOTE	UNSPEAKS	UNSTINTED	UNSWATHES
UNSNAG	UNSPED	UNSTIRRED	UNSWAYED
UNSNAGGED	UNSPELL	UNSTITCH	UNSWEAR
UNSNAGS	UNSPELLED	UNSTOCK	UNSWEARS
UNSNAP	UNSPELLS	UNSTOCKED	UNSWEET
UNSNAPPED	UNSPENT	UNSTOCKS	UNSWEPT
UNSNAPS	UNSPHERE	UNSTONED	UNSWOLLEN
UNSNARL	UNSPHERED	UNSTOP	UNSWORE
UNSNARLED	UNSPHERES	UNSTOPPED	UNSWORN
UNSNARLS	UNSPIDE	UNSTOPPER	UNTACK
UNSNECK	UNSPIED	UNSTOPS	UNTACKED
UNSNECKED	UNSPILLED	UNSTOW	UNTACKING
UNSNECKS	UNSPILT	UNSTOWED	UNTACKLE
UNSNUFFED	UNSPLIT	UNSTOWING	UNTACKLED
UNSOAKED	UNSPOILED	UNSTOWS	UNTACKLES
UNSOAPED	UNSPOILT	UNSTRAP	UNTACKS
UNSOBER	UNSPOKE	UNSTRAPS	UNTACTFUL
UNSOBERLY	UNSPOKEN	UNSTRESS	UNTAGGED
UNSOCIAL	UNSPOOL	UNSTRING	UNTAILED
UNSOCKET	UNSPOOLED	UNSTRINGS	UNTAINTED
UNSOCKETS	UNSPOOLS	UNSTRIP	UNTAKEN
UNSOD	UNSPOTTED	UNSTRIPED	UNTAMABLE
UNSODDEN	UNSPRAYED	UNSTRIPS	UNTAMABLY
UNSOFT	UNSPRUNG	UNSTRUCK	UNTAME
UNSOILED	UNSPUN	UNSTRUNG	UNTAMED
UNSOLACED	UNSQUARED	UNSTUCK	UNTAMES
UNSOLD	UNSTABLE	UNSTUDIED	UNTAMING
UNSOLDER	UNSTABLER	UNSTUFFED	UNTANGLE
UNSOLDERS	UNSTABLY	UNSTUFFY	UNTANGLED
UNSOLEMN	UNSTACK	UNSTUFT	UNTANGLES
UNSOLID	UNSTACKED	UNSTUNG	UNTANNED
UNSOLIDLY	UNSTACKS	UNSTYLISH	UNTAPPED
UNSOLVED	UNSTAID	UNSUBDUED	UNTARRED
UNSONCY	UNSTAINED	UNSUBJECT	UNTASTED
UNSONSIE	UNSTALKED	UNSUBTLE	UNTAUGHT
UNSONSY	UNSTAMPED	UNSUBTLY	UNTAX
UNSOOTE	UNSTARCH	UNSUCCESS	UNTAXED
UNSOOTHED	UNSTARRED	UNSUCKED	UNTAXES
UNSORTED	UNSTARRY	UNSUIT	UNTAXING
UNSOUGHT	UNSTATE	UNSUITED	UNTEACH
UNSOUL	UNSTATED	UNSUITING	UNTEACHES
UNSOULED	UNSTATES	UNSUITS	UNTEAM
UNSOULING	UNSTATING	UNSULLIED	UNTEAMED
UNSOULS	UNSTAYED	UNSUMMED	UNTEAMING
UNSOUND	UNSTAYING	UNSUNG	UNTEAMS
UNSOUNDED	UNSTEADY	UNSUNK	UNTEMPER
UNSOUNDER	UNSTEEL	UNSUNNED	UNTEMPERS
UNSOUNDLY	UNSTEELED	UNSUNNY	UNTEMPTED
UNSOURCED	UNSTEELS	UNSUPPLE	UNTENABLE
UNSOURED	UNSTEMMED	UNSURE	UNTENABLY
UNSOWED	UNSTEP	UNSURED	UNTENANT
UNSOWN	UNSTEPPED	UNSURELY	UNTENANTS
UNSPAR	UNSTEPS	UNSURER	UNTENDED
UNSPARED	UNSTERILE	UNSUREST	UNTENDER

639

UNTENT	UNTOILING	UNTUNEFUL	UNVEXED
UNTENTED	UNTOLD	UNTUNES	UNVEXT
UNTENTING	UNTOMB	UNTUNING	UNVIABLE
UNTENTS	UNTOMBED	UNTURBID	UNVIEWED
UNTENTY	UNTOMBING	UNTURF	UNVIRTUE
UNTENURED	UNTOMBS	UNTURFED	UNVIRTUES
UNTESTED	UNTONED	UNTURFING	UNVISITED
UNTETHER	UNTORN	UNTURFS	UNVISOR
UNTETHERS	UNTOUCHED	UNTURN	UNVISORED
UNTHANKED	UNTOWARD	UNTURNED	UNVISORS
UNTHATCH	UNTRACE	UNTURNING	UNVITAL
UNTHAW	UNTRACED	UNTURNS	UNVIZARD
UNTHAWED	UNTRACES	UNTUTORED	UNVIZARDS
UNTHAWING	UNTRACING	UNTWILLED	UNVOCAL
UNTHAWS	UNTRACK	UNTWINE	UNVOICE
UNTHINK	UNTRACKED	UNTWINED	UNVOICED
UNTHINKS	UNTRACKS	UNTWINES	UNVOICES
UNTHOUGHT	UNTRADED	UNTWINING	UNVOICING
UNTHREAD	UNTRAINED	UNTWIST	UNVULGAR
UNTHREADS	UNTRAPPED	UNTWISTED	UNWAGED
UNTHRIFT	UNTREAD	UNTWISTS	UNWAKED
UNTHRIFTS	UNTREADED	UNTYING	UNWAKENED
UNTHRIFTY	UNTREADS	UNTYINGS	UNWALLED
UNTHRONE	UNTREATED	UNTYPABLE	UNWANING
UNTHRONED	UNTRENDY	UNTYPICAL	UNWANTED
UNTHRONES	UNTRESSED	UNUNBIUM	UNWARDED
UNTIDIED	UNTRIDE	UNUNBIUMS	UNWARE
UNTIDIER	UNTRIED	UNUNITED	UNWARELY
UNTIDIES	UNTRIM	UNUNUNIUM	UNWARES
UNTIDIEST	UNTRIMMED	UNURGED	UNWARIE
UNTIDILY	UNTRIMS	UNUSABLE	UNWARIER
UNTIDY	UNTROD	UNUSABLY	UNWARIEST
UNTIDYING	UNTRODDEN	UNUSED	UNWARILY
UNTIE	UNTRUE	UNUSEFUL	UNWARLIKE
UNTIED	UNTRUER	UNUSHERED	UNWARMED
UNTIEING	UNTRUEST	UNUSUAL	UNWARNED
UNTIES	UNTRUISM	UNUSUALLY	UNWARPED
UNTIL	UNTRUISMS	UNUTTERED	UNWARY
UNTILE	UNTRULY	UNVAIL	UNWASHED
UNTILED	UNTRUSS	UNVAILE	UNWASHEDS
UNTILES	UNTRUSSED	UNVAILED	UNWASHEN
UNTILING	UNTRUSSER	UNVAILES	UNWASTED
UNTILLED	UNTRUSSES	UNVAILING	UNWASTING
UNTILTED	UNTRUST	UNVAILS	UNWATCHED
UNTIMED	UNTRUSTS	UNVALUED	UNWATER
UNTIMELY	UNTRUSTY	UNVARIED	UNWATERED
UNTIMEOUS	UNTRUTH	UNVARYING	UNWATERS
UNTIN	UNTRUTHS	UNVEIL	UNWATERY
UNTINGED	UNTUCK	UNVEILED	UNWAXED
UNTINNED	UNTUCKED	UNVEILER	UNWAYED
UNTINNING	UNTUCKING	UNVEILERS	UNWEAL
UNTINS	UNTUCKS	UNVEILING	UNWEALS
UNTIPPED	UNTUFTED	UNVEILS	UNWEANED
UNTIRABLE	UNTUMBLED	UNVEINED	UNWEAPON
UNTIRED	UNTUNABLE	UNVENTED	UNWEAPONS
UNTIRING	UNTUNABLY	UNVERSED	UNWEARIED
UNTITLED	UNTUNE	UNVESTED	UNWEARY
UNTO	UNTUNED	UNVETTED	UNWEAVE

UNWEAVES	UNWITS	UNZONED	UPCASTS
UNWEAVING	UNWITTED	UP	UPCATCH
UNWEBBED	UNWITTILY	UPADAISY	UPCATCHES
UNWED	UNWITTING	UPAITHRIC	UPCAUGHT
UNWEDDED	UNWITTY	UPAS	UPCHEER
UNWEEDED	UNWIVE	UPASES	UPCHEERED
UNWEENED	UNWIVED	UPBEAR	UPCHEERS
UNWEETING	UNWIVES	UPBEARER	UPCHUCK
UNWEIGHED	UNWIVING	UPBEARERS	UPCHUCKED
UNWEIGHT	UNWOMAN	UPBEARING	UPCHUCKS
UNWEIGHTS	UNWOMANED	UPBEARS	UPCLIMB
UNWELCOME	UNWOMANLY	UPBEAT	UPCLIMBED
UNWELDED	UNWOMANS	UPBEATS	UPCLIMBS
UNWELDY	UNWON	UPBIND	UPCLOSE
UNWELL	UNWONT	UPBINDING	UPCLOSED
UNWEPT	UNWONTED	UPBINDS	UPCLOSES
UNWET	UNWOODED	UPBLEW	UPCLOSING
UNWETTED	UNWOOED	UPBLOW	UPCOAST
UNWHIPPED	UNWORDED	UPBLOWING	UPCOIL
UNWHIPT	UNWORK	UPBLOWN	UPCOILED
UNWHITE	UNWORKED	UPBLOWS	UPCOILING
UNWIELDLY	UNWORKING	UPBOIL	UPCOILS
UNWIELDY	UNWORKS	UPBOILED	UPCOME
UNWIFELY	UNWORLDLY	UPBOILING	UPCOMES
UNWIGGED	UNWORMED	UPBOILS	UPCOMING
UNWILFUL	UNWORN	UPBORE	UPCOUNTRY
UNWILL	UNWORRIED	UPBORNE	UPCOURT
UNWILLED	UNWORTH	UPBOUND	UPCURL
UNWILLING	UNWORTHS	UPBOUNDEN	UPCURLED
UNWILLS	UNWORTHY	UPBOW	UPCURLING
UNWIND	UNWOUND	UPBOWS	UPCURLS
UNWINDER	UNWOUNDED	UPBRAID	UPCURVE
UNWINDERS	UNWOVE	UPBRAIDED	UPCURVED
UNWINDING	UNWOVEN	UPBRAIDER	UPCURVES
UNWINDS	UNWRAP	UPBRAIDS	UPCURVING
UNWINGED	UNWRAPPED	UPBRAST	UPDART
UNWINKING	UNWRAPS	UPBRAY	UPDARTED
UNWIPED	UNWREAKED	UPBRAYED	UPDARTING
UNWIRE	UNWREATHE	UPBRAYING	UPDARTS
UNWIRED	UNWRINKLE	UPBRAYS	UPDATE
UNWIRES	UNWRITE	UPBREAK	UPDATED
UNWIRING	UNWRITES	UPBREAKS	UPDATER
UNWISDOM	UNWRITING	UPBRING	UPDATERS
UNWISDOMS	UNWRITTEN	UPBRINGS	UPDATES
UNWISE	UNWROTE	UPBROKE	UPDATING
UNWISELY	UNWROUGHT	UPBROKEN	UPDIVE
UNWISER	UNWRUNG	UPBROUGHT	UPDIVED
UNWISEST	UNYEANED	UPBUILD	UPDIVES
UNWISH	UNYOKE	UPBUILDER	UPDIVING
UNWISHED	UNYOKED	UPBUILDS	UPDO
UNWISHES	UNYOKES	UPBUILT	UPDOS
UNWISHFUL	UNYOKING	UPBURNING	UPDOVE
UNWISHING	UNYOUNG	UPBURST	UPDRAFT
UNWIST	UNZEALOUS	UPBURSTS	UPDRAFTS
UNWIT	UNZIP	UPBY	UPDRAG
UNWITCH	UNZIPPED	UPBYE	UPDRAGGED
UNWITCHED	UNZIPPING	UPCAST	UPDRAGS
UNWITCHES	UNZIPS	UPCASTING	UPDRAUGHT

UPDRAW
UPDRAWING
UPDRAWN
UPDRAWS
UPDREW
UPDRIED
UPDRIES
UPDRY
UPDRYING
UPEND
UPENDED
UPENDING
UPENDS
UPFIELD
UPFILL
UPFILLED
UPFILLING
UPFILLS
UPFLING
UPFLINGS
UPFLOW
UPFLOWED
UPFLOWING
UPFLOWS
UPFLUNG
UPFOLD
UPFOLDED
UPFOLDING
UPFOLDS
UPFOLLOW
UPFOLLOWS
UPFRONT
UPFURL
UPFURLED
UPFURLING
UPFURLS
UPGANG
UPGANGS
UPGATHER
UPGATHERS
UPGAZE
UPGAZED
UPGAZES
UPGAZING
UPGIRD
UPGIRDED
UPGIRDING
UPGIRDS
UPGIRT
UPGO
UPGOES
UPGOING
UPGOINGS
UPGONE
UPGRADE
UPGRADED
UPGRADER
UPGRADERS

UPGRADES
UPGRADING
UPGREW
UPGROW
UPGROWING
UPGROWN
UPGROWS
UPGROWTH
UPGROWTHS
UPGUSH
UPGUSHED
UPGUSHES
UPGUSHING
UPHAND
UPHANG
UPHANGING
UPHANGS
UPHAUD
UPHAUDING
UPHAUDS
UPHEAP
UPHEAPED
UPHEAPING
UPHEAPS
UPHEAVAL
UPHEAVALS
UPHEAVE
UPHEAVED
UPHEAVER
UPHEAVERS
UPHEAVES
UPHEAVING
UPHELD
UPHILD
UPHILL
UPHILLS
UPHOARD
UPHOARDED
UPHOARDS
UPHOIST
UPHOISTED
UPHOISTS
UPHOLD
UPHOLDER
UPHOLDERS
UPHOLDING
UPHOLDS
UPHOLSTER
UPHOORD
UPHOORDED
UPHOORDS
UPHOVE
UPHROE
UPHROES
UPHUDDEN
UPHUNG
UPHURL
UPHURLED

UPHURLING
UPHURLS
UPJET
UPJETS
UPJETTED
UPJETTING
UPKEEP
UPKEEPS
UPKNIT
UPKNITS
UPKNITTED
UPLAID
UPLAND
UPLANDER
UPLANDERS
UPLANDISH
UPLANDS
UPLAY
UPLAYING
UPLAYS
UPLEAD
UPLEADING
UPLEADS
UPLEAN
UPLEANED
UPLEANING
UPLEANS
UPLEANT
UPLEAP
UPLEAPED
UPLEAPING
UPLEAPS
UPLEAPT
UPLED
UPLIFT
UPLIFTED
UPLIFTER
UPLIFTERS
UPLIFTING
UPLIFTS
UPLIGHT
UPLIGHTED
UPLIGHTER
UPLIGHTS
UPLINK
UPLINKED
UPLINKING
UPLINKS
UPLIT
UPLOAD
UPLOADED
UPLOADING
UPLOADS
UPLOCK
UPLOCKED
UPLOCKING
UPLOCKS
UPLOOK

UPLOOKED
UPLOOKING
UPLOOKS
UPLYING
UPMAKE
UPMAKER
UPMAKERS
UPMAKES
UPMAKING
UPMAKINGS
UPMANSHIP
UPMARKET
UPMOST
UPO
UPON
UPPED
UPPER
UPPERCASE
UPPERCUT
UPPERCUTS
UPPERMOST
UPPERPART
UPPERS
UPPILE
UPPILED
UPPILES
UPPILING
UPPING
UPPINGS
UPPISH
UPPISHLY
UPPITY
UPPROP
UPPROPPED
UPPROPS
UPRAISE
UPRAISED
UPRAISER
UPRAISERS
UPRAISES
UPRAISING
UPRAN
UPRATE
UPRATED
UPRATES
UPRATING
UPREACH
UPREACHED
UPREACHES
UPREAR
UPREARED
UPREARING
UPREARS
UPREST
UPRESTS
UPRIGHT
UPRIGHTED
UPRIGHTLY

UPRIGHTS
UPRISAL
UPRISALS
UPRISE
UPRISEN
UPRISER
UPRISERS
UPRISES
UPRISING
UPRISINGS
UPRIST
UPRISTS
UPRIVER
UPRIVERS
UPROAR
UPROARED
UPROARING
UPROARS
UPROLL
UPROLLED
UPROLLING
UPROLLS
UPROOT
UPROOTAL
UPROOTALS
UPROOTED
UPROOTER
UPROOTERS
UPROOTING
UPROOTS
UPROSE
UPROUSE
UPROUSED
UPROUSES
UPROUSING
UPRUN
UPRUNNING
UPRUNS
UPRUSH
UPRUSHED
UPRUSHES
UPRUSHING
UPRYST
UPS
UPSADAISY
UPSCALE
UPSCALED
UPSCALES
UPSCALING
UPSEE
UPSEES
UPSEND
UPSENDING
UPSENDS
UPSENT
UPSET
UPSETS
UPSETTER

UPSETTERS
UPSETTING
UPSEY
UPSEYS
UPSHIFT
UPSHIFTED
UPSHIFTS
UPSHOOT
UPSHOOTS
UPSHOT
UPSHOTS
UPSIDE
UPSIDES
UPSIES
UPSILON
UPSILONS
UPSITTING
UPSIZE
UPSIZED
UPSIZES
UPSIZING
UPSKILL
UPSKILLED
UPSKILLS
UPSLOPE
UPSOAR
UPSOARED
UPSOARING
UPSOARS
UPSPAKE
UPSPEAK
UPSPEAKS
UPSPEAR
UPSPEARED
UPSPEARS
UPSPOKE
UPSPOKEN
UPSPRANG
UPSPRING
UPSPRINGS
UPSPRUNG
UPSTAGE
UPSTAGED
UPSTAGER
UPSTAGERS
UPSTAGES
UPSTAGING
UPSTAIR
UPSTAIRS
UPSTAND
UPSTANDS
UPSTARE
UPSTARED
UPSTARES
UPSTARING
UPSTART
UPSTARTED
UPSTARTS

UPSTATE
UPSTATER
UPSTATERS
UPSTATES
UPSTAY
UPSTAYED
UPSTAYING
UPSTAYS
UPSTEP
UPSTEPPED
UPSTEPS
UPSTIR
UPSTIRRED
UPSTIRS
UPSTOOD
UPSTREAM
UPSTREAMS
UPSTROKE
UPSTROKES
UPSURGE
UPSURGED
UPSURGES
UPSURGING
UPSWARM
UPSWARMED
UPSWARMS
UPSWAY
UPSWAYED
UPSWAYING
UPSWAYS
UPSWEEP
UPSWEEPS
UPSWELL
UPSWELLED
UPSWELLS
UPSWEPT
UPSWING
UPSWINGS
UPSWOLLEN
UPSWUNG
UPSY
UPTA
UPTAK
UPTAKE
UPTAKEN
UPTAKES
UPTAKING
UPTAKS
UPTALK
UPTALKED
UPTALKING
UPTALKS
UPTEAR
UPTEARING
UPTEARS
UPTEMPO
UPTEMPOS
UPTER

UPTHREW
UPTHROW
UPTHROWN
UPTHROWS
UPTHRUST
UPTHRUSTS
UPTHUNDER
UPTICK
UPTICKS
UPTIE
UPTIED
UPTIES
UPTIGHT
UPTIGHTER
UPTILT
UPTILTED
UPTILTING
UPTILTS
UPTIME
UPTIMES
UPTITLING
UPTOOK
UPTORE
UPTORN
UPTOSS
UPTOSSED
UPTOSSES
UPTOSSING
UPTOWN
UPTOWNER
UPTOWNERS
UPTOWNS
UPTRAIN
UPTRAINED
UPTRAINS
UPTREND
UPTRENDS
UPTRILLED
UPTURN
UPTURNED
UPTURNING
UPTURNS
UPTYING
UPVALUE
UPVALUED
UPVALUES
UPVALUING
UPWAFT
UPWAFTED
UPWAFTING
UPWAFTS
UPWARD
UPWARDLY
UPWARDS
UPWELL
UPWELLED
UPWELLING
UPWELLS

UPWENT
UPWHIRL
UPWHIRLED
UPWHIRLS
UPWIND
UPWINDING
UPWINDS
UPWOUND
UPWRAP
UPWRAPS
UPWROUGHT
UR
URACHI
URACHUS
URACHUSES
URACIL
URACILS
URAEI
URAEMIA
URAEMIAS
URAEMIC
URAEUS
URAEUSES
URALI
URALIS
URALITE
URALITES
URALITIC
URALITISE
URALITIZE
URANIA
URANIAN
URANIAS
URANIC
URANIDE
URANIDES
URANIN
URANINITE
URANINS
URANISCI
URANISCUS
URANISM
URANISMS
URANITE
URANITES
URANITIC
URANIUM
URANIUMS
URANOLOGY
URANOUS
URANYL
URANYLIC
URANYLS
URAO
URAOS
URARE
URARES
URARI

URARIS
URASE
URASES
URATE
URATES
URATIC
URB
URBAN
URBANE
URBANELY
URBANER
URBANEST
URBANISE
URBANISED
URBANISES
URBANISM
URBANISMS
URBANIST
URBANISTS
URBANITE
URBANITES
URBANITY
URBANIZE
URBANIZED
URBANIZES
URBIA
URBIAS
URBS
URCEOLATE
URCEOLI
URCEOLUS
URCHIN
URCHINS
URD
URDE
URDEE
URDS
URDY
URE
UREA
UREAL
UREAS
UREASE
UREASES
UREDIA
UREDIAL
UREDINE
UREDINES
UREDINIA
UREDINIAL
UREDINIUM
UREDINOUS
UREDIUM
UREDO
UREDOS
UREDOSORI
UREIC
UREIDE

UREIDES
UREMIA
UREMIAS
UREMIC
URENA
URENAS
URENT
UREOTELIC
URES
URESES
URESIS
URETER
URETERAL
URETERIC
URETERS
URETHAN
URETHANE
URETHANES
URETHANS
URETHRA
URETHRAE
URETHRAL
URETHRAS
URETIC
URGE
URGED
URGENCE
URGENCES
URGENCIES
URGENCY
URGENT
URGENTLY
URGER
URGERS
URGES
URGING
URGINGLY
URGINGS
URIAL
URIALS
URIC
URICASE
URICASES
URIDINE
URIDINES
URIDYLIC
URINAL
URINALS
URINANT
URINARIES
URINARY
URINATE
URINATED
URINATES
URINATING
URINATION
URINATIVE
URINATOR

URINATORS
URINE
URINED
URINEMIA
URINEMIAS
URINEMIC
URINES
URINING
URINOLOGY
URINOSE
URINOUS
URITE
URITES
URMAN
URMANS
URN
URNAL
URNED
URNFIELD
URNFIELDS
URNFUL
URNFULS
URNING
URNINGS
URNLIKE
URNS
UROBILIN
UROBILINS
UROCHORD
UROCHORDS
UROCHROME
URODELAN
URODELANS
URODELE
URODELES
URODELOUS
UROGENOUS
UROGRAPHY
UROKINASE
UROLAGNIA
UROLITH
UROLITHIC
UROLITHS
UROLOGIC
UROLOGIES
UROLOGIST
UROLOGY
UROMERE
UROMERES
UROPOD
UROPODAL
UROPODOUS
UROPODS
UROPYGIA
UROPYGIAL
UROPYGIUM
UROSCOPIC
UROSCOPY

UROSES
UROSIS
UROSOME
UROSOMES
UROSTEGE
UROSTEGES
UROSTOMY
UROSTYLE
UROSTYLES
URP
URPED
URPING
URPS
URSA
URSAE
URSID
URSIDS
URSIFORM
URSINE
URSON
URSONS
URTEXT
URTEXTS
URTICA
URTICANT
URTICANTS
URTICARIA
URTICAS
URTICATE
URTICATED
URTICATES
URUBU
URUBUS
URUS
URUSES
URUSHIOL
URUSHIOLS
URVA
URVAS
US
USABILITY
USABLE
USABLY
USAGE
USAGER
USAGERS
USAGES
USANCE
USANCES
USAUNCE
USAUNCES
USE
USEABLE
USEABLY
USED
USEFUL
USEFULLY
USEFULS

USELESS
USELESSLY
USER
USERNAME
USERNAMES
USERS
USES
USHER
USHERED
USHERESS
USHERETTE
USHERING
USHERINGS
USHERS
USHERSHIP
USING
USNEA
USNEAS
USQUABAE
USQUABAES
USQUE
USQUEBAE
USQUEBAES
USQUES
USTION
USTIONS
USTULATE
USUAL
USUALLY
USUALNESS
USUALS
USUCAPION
USUCAPT
USUCAPTED
USUCAPTS
USUFRUCT
USUFRUCTS
USURE
USURED
USURER
USURERS
USURES
USURESS
USURESSES
USURIES
USURING
USURIOUS
USUROUS
USURP
USURPED
USURPEDLY
USURPER
USURPERS
USURPING
USURPINGS
USURPS
USURY
USWARD

USWARDS
UT
UTA
UTAS
UTASES
UTE
UTENSIL
UTENSILS
UTERI
UTERINE
UTERITIS
UTEROTOMY
UTERUS
UTERUSES
UTES
UTILE
UTILIDOR
UTILIDORS
UTILISE
UTILISED
UTILISER
UTILISERS
UTILISES
UTILISING
UTILITIES
UTILITY
UTILIZE
UTILIZED
UTILIZER
UTILIZERS
UTILIZES
UTILIZING
UTIS
UTISES
UTMOST
UTMOSTS
UTOPIA
UTOPIAN
UTOPIANS
UTOPIAS
UTOPIAST
UTOPIASTS
UTOPISM
UTOPISMS
UTOPIST
UTOPISTIC
UTOPISTS
UTRICLE
UTRICLES
UTRICULAR
UTRICULI
UTRICULUS
UTS
UTTER
UTTERABLE
UTTERANCE
UTTERED
UTTERER

UTTERERS
UTTEREST
UTTERING
UTTERINGS
UTTERLESS
UTTERLY
UTTERMOST
UTTERNESS
UTTERS
UTU
UTUS
UVA
UVAE
UVAROVITE
UVAS
UVEA
UVEAL
UVEAS
UVEITIC
UVEITIS
UVEITISES
UVEOUS
UVULA
UVULAE
UVULAR
UVULARLY
UVULARS
UVULAS
UVULITIS
UXORIAL
UXORIALLY
UXORICIDE
UXORIOUS

— V —

VAC
VACANCE
VACANCES
VACANCIES
VACANCY
VACANT
VACANTLY
VACATABLE
VACATE
VACATED
VACATES
VACATING
VACATION
VACATIONS
VACATUR
VACATURS
VACCINA
VACCINAL
VACCINAS
VACCINATE
VACCINE
VACCINEE
VACCINEES
VACCINES
VACCINIA
VACCINIAL
VACCINIAS
VACCINIUM
VACHERIN
VACHERINS
VACILLANT
VACILLATE
VACKED
VACKING
VACS
VACUA
VACUATE
VACUATED
VACUATES
VACUATING
VACUATION
VACUIST
VACUISTS
VACUITIES
VACUITY
VACUOLAR
VACUOLATE
VACUOLE
VACUOLES
VACUOUS
VACUOUSLY
VACUUM
VACUUMED

VACUUMING
VACUUMS
VADE
VADED
VADES
VADING
VADOSE
VAE
VAES
VAG
VAGABOND
VAGABONDS
VAGAL
VAGALLY
VAGARIES
VAGARIOUS
VAGARISH
VAGARY
VAGGED
VAGGING
VAGI
VAGILE
VAGILITY
VAGINA
VAGINAE
VAGINAL
VAGINALLY
VAGINANT
VAGINAS
VAGINATE
VAGINATED
VAGINITIS
VAGINOSES
VAGINOSIS
VAGINULA
VAGINULAE
VAGINULE
VAGINULES
VAGITUS
VAGITUSES
VAGOTOMY
VAGOTONIA
VAGOTONIC
VAGRANCY
VAGRANT
VAGRANTLY
VAGRANTS
VAGROM
VAGS
VAGUE
VAGUED
VAGUELY
VAGUENESS

VAGUER
VAGUES
VAGUEST
VAGUING
VAGUS
VAHANA
VAHANAS
VAHINE
VAHINES
VAIL
VAILED
VAILING
VAILS
VAIN
VAINER
VAINESSE
VAINESSES
VAINEST
VAINGLORY
VAINLY
VAINNESS
VAIR
VAIRE
VAIRIER
VAIRIEST
VAIRS
VAIRY
VAIVODE
VAIVODES
VAKASS
VAKASSES
VAKEEL
VAKEELS
VAKIL
VAKILS
VALANCE
VALANCED
VALANCES
VALANCING
VALE
VALENCE
VALENCES
VALENCIA
VALENCIAS
VALENCIES
VALENCY
VALENTINE
VALERATE
VALERATES
VALERIAN
VALERIANS
VALERIC
VALES

VALET
VALETA
VALETAS
VALETE
VALETED
VALETES
VALETING
VALETINGS
VALETS
VALGOID
VALGOUS
VALGUS
VALGUSES
VALI
VALIANCE
VALIANCES
VALIANCY
VALIANT
VALIANTLY
VALIANTS
VALID
VALIDATE
VALIDATED
VALIDATES
VALIDER
VALIDEST
VALIDITY
VALIDLY
VALIDNESS
VALINE
VALINES
VALIS
VALISE
VALISES
VALKYR
VALKYRIE
VALKYRIES
VALKYRS
VALLAR
VALLARY
VALLATE
VALLATION
VALLECULA
VALLEY
VALLEYED
VALLEYS
VALLHUND
VALLHUNDS
VALLONIA
VALLONIAS
VALLUM
VALLUMS
VALONEA

VALONEAS
VALONIA
VALONIAS
VALOR
VALORISE
VALORISED
VALORISES
VALORIZE
VALORIZED
VALORIZES
VALOROUS
VALORS
VALOUR
VALOURS
VALPROATE
VALPROIC
VALSE
VALSED
VALSES
VALSING
VALUABLE
VALUABLES
VALUABLY
VALUATE
VALUATED
VALUATES
VALUATING
VALUATION
VALUATOR
VALUATORS
VALUE
VALUED
VALUELESS
VALUER
VALUERS
VALUES
VALUING
VALUTA
VALUTAS
VALVAL
VALVAR
VALVASSOR
VALVATE
VALVE
VALVED
VALVELESS
VALVELET
VALVELETS
VALVELIKE
VALVES
VALVING
VALVULA
VALVULAE
VALVULAR
VALVULE
VALVULES
VAMBRACE
VAMBRACED

VAMBRACES
VAMOOSE
VAMOOSED
VAMOOSES
VAMOOSING
VAMOSE
VAMOSED
VAMOSES
VAMOSING
VAMP
VAMPED
VAMPER
VAMPERS
VAMPIER
VAMPIEST
VAMPING
VAMPINGS
VAMPIRE
VAMPIRED
VAMPIRES
VAMPIRIC
VAMPIRING
VAMPIRISE
VAMPIRISH
VAMPIRISM
VAMPIRIZE
VAMPISH
VAMPISHLY
VAMPLATE
VAMPLATES
VAMPS
VAMPY
VAN
VANADATE
VANADATES
VANADIATE
VANADIC
VANADIUM
VANADIUMS
VANADOUS
VANASPATI
VANDA
VANDAL
VANDALIC
VANDALISE
VANDALISH
VANDALISM
VANDALIZE
VANDALS
VANDAS
VANDYKE
VANDYKED
VANDYKES
VANDYKING
VANE
VANED
VANELESS
VANES

VANESSA
VANESSAS
VANESSID
VANESSIDS
VANG
VANGS
VANGUARD
VANGUARDS
VANILLA
VANILLAS
VANILLIC
VANILLIN
VANILLINS
VANISH
VANISHED
VANISHER
VANISHERS
VANISHES
VANISHING
VANITAS
VANITASES
VANITIED
VANITIES
VANITORY
VANITY
VANLOAD
VANLOADS
VANMAN
VANMEN
VANNED
VANNER
VANNERS
VANNING
VANNINGS
VANPOOL
VANPOOLS
VANQUISH
VANS
VANT
VANTAGE
VANTAGED
VANTAGES
VANTAGING
VANTBRACE
VANTS
VANWARD
VAPID
VAPIDER
VAPIDEST
VAPIDITY
VAPIDLY
VAPIDNESS
VAPOR
VAPORABLE
VAPORED
VAPORER
VAPORERS
VAPORETTI

VAPORETTO
VAPORIFIC
VAPORING
VAPORINGS
VAPORISE
VAPORISED
VAPORISER
VAPORISES
VAPORISH
VAPORIZE
VAPORIZED
VAPORIZER
VAPORIZES
VAPORLESS
VAPORLIKE
VAPOROUS
VAPORS
VAPORWARE
VAPORY
VAPOUR
VAPOURED
VAPOURER
VAPOURERS
VAPOURING
VAPOURISH
VAPOURS
VAPOURY
VAPULATE
VAPULATED
VAPULATES
VAQUERO
VAQUEROS
VAR
VARA
VARACTOR
VARACTORS
VARAN
VARANS
VARAS
VARDIES
VARDY
VARE
VAREC
VARECH
VARECHS
VARECS
VARES
VAREUSE
VAREUSES
VARGUENO
VARGUENOS
VARIA
VARIABLE
VARIABLES
VARIABLY
VARIANCE
VARIANCES
VARIANT

VARIANTS

VARIANTS	VARNA	VASSALRY	VAUNT
VARIAS	VARNAS	VASSALS	VAUNTAGE
VARIATE	VARNISH	VAST	VAUNTAGES
VARIATED	VARNISHED	VASTER	VAUNTED
VARIATES	VARNISHER	VASTEST	VAUNTER
VARIATING	VARNISHES	VASTIDITY	VAUNTERS
VARIATION	VARNISHY	VASTIER	VAUNTERY
VARIATIVE	VAROOM	VASTIEST	VAUNTFUL
VARICELLA	VAROOMED	VASTITIES	VAUNTIE
VARICES	VAROOMING	VASTITUDE	VAUNTIER
VARICOID	VAROOMS	VASTITY	VAUNTIEST
VARICOSE	VARROA	VASTLY	VAUNTING
VARICOSED	VARROAS	VASTNESS	VAUNTINGS
VARICOSES	VARS	VASTS	VAUNTS
VARICOSIS	VARSAL	VASTY	VAUNTY
VARIED	VARSITIES	VAT	VAURIEN
VARIEDLY	VARSITY	VATABLE	VAURIENS
VARIEGATE	VARTABED	VATFUL	VAUS
VARIER	VARTABEDS	VATFULS	VAUT
VARIERS	VARUS	VATIC	VAUTE
VARIES	VARUSES	VATICAL	VAUTED
VARIETAL	VARVE	VATICIDE	VAUTES
VARIETALS	VARVED	VATICIDES	VAUTING
VARIETIES	VARVEL	VATICINAL	VAUTS
VARIETY	VARVELLED	VATMAN	VAV
VARIFOCAL	VARVELS	VATMEN	VAVASOR
VARIFORM	VARVES	VATS	VAVASORS
VARIOLA	VARY	VATTED	VAVASORY
VARIOLAR	VARYING	VATTER	VAVASOUR
VARIOLAS	VARYINGLY	VATTERS	VAVASOURS
VARIOLATE	VARYINGS	VATTING	VAVASSOR
VARIOLE	VAS	VATU	VAVASSORS
VARIOLES	VASA	VATUS	VAVS
VARIOLITE	VASAL	VAU	VAW
VARIOLOID	VASCULA	VAUCH	VAWARD
VARIOLOUS	VASCULAR	VAUCHED	VAWARDS
VARIORUM	VASCULUM	VAUCHES	VAWNTIE
VARIORUMS	VASCULUMS	VAUCHING	VAWS
VARIOUS	VASE	VAUDOO	VAWTE
VARIOUSLY	VASECTOMY	VAUDOOS	VAWTED
VARISCITE	VASELIKE	VAUDOUX	VAWTES
VARISIZED	VASELINE	VAULT	VAWTING
VARISTOR	VASELINES	VAULTAGE	VEAL
VARISTORS	VASES	VAULTAGES	VEALE
VARITYPE	VASIFORM	VAULTED	VEALED
VARITYPED	VASOMOTOR	VAULTER	VEALER
VARITYPES	VASOSPASM	VAULTERS	VEALERS
VARIX	VASOTOCIN	VAULTIER	VEALES
VARLET	VASOTOMY	VAULTIEST	VEALIER
VARLETESS	VASOVAGAL	VAULTING	VEALIEST
VARLETRY	VASSAIL	VAULTINGS	VEALING
VARLETS	VASSAILS	VAULTLIKE	VEALS
VARLETTO	VASSAL	VAULTS	VEALY
VARLETTOS	VASSALAGE	VAULTY	VECTOR
VARMENT	VASSALESS	VAUNCE	VECTORED
VARMENTS	VASSALISE	VAUNCED	VECTORIAL
VARMINT	VASSALIZE	VAUNCES	VECTORING
VARMINTS	VASSALLED	VAUNCING	VECTORISE

VECTORIZE
VECTORS
VEDALIA
VEDALIAS
VEDETTE
VEDETTES
VEDUTA
VEDUTE
VEDUTISTA
VEDUTISTI
VEE
VEEJAY
VEEJAYS
VEENA
VEENAS
VEEP
VEEPEE
VEEPEES
VEEPS
VEER
VEERED
VEERIES
VEERING
VEERINGLY
VEERINGS
VEERS
VEERY
VEES
VEG
VEGA
VEGAN
VEGANIC
VEGANISM
VEGANISMS
VEGANS
VEGAS
VEGELATE
VEGELATES
VEGEMITE
VEGEMITES
VEGES
VEGETABLE
VEGETABLY
VEGETAL
VEGETALLY
VEGETALS
VEGETANT
VEGETATE
VEGETATED
VEGETATES
VEGETE
VEGETIST
VEGETISTS
VEGETIVE
VEGETIVES
VEGGED
VEGGES
VEGGIE

VEGGIES
VEGGING
VEGIE
VEGIES
VEGO
VEGOS
VEHEMENCE
VEHEMENCY
VEHEMENT
VEHICLE
VEHICLES
VEHICULAR
VEHM
VEHME
VEHMIC
VEHMIQUE
VEIL
VEILED
VEILEDLY
VEILER
VEILERS
VEILIER
VEILIEST
VEILING
VEILINGS
VEILLESS
VEILLEUSE
VEILLIKE
VEILS
VEILY
VEIN
VEINAL
VEINED
VEINER
VEINERS
VEINIER
VEINIEST
VEINING
VEININGS
VEINLESS
VEINLET
VEINLETS
VEINLIKE
VEINOUS
VEINS
VEINSTONE
VEINSTUFF
VEINULE
VEINULES
VEINULET
VEINULETS
VEINY
VELA
VELAMEN
VELAMINA
VELAR
VELARIA
VELARIC

VELARISE
VELARISED
VELARISES
VELARIUM
VELARIZE
VELARIZED
VELARIZES
VELARS
VELATE
VELATED
VELATURA
VELATURAS
VELCRO
VELCROS
VELD
VELDS
VELDSKOEN
VELDT
VELDTS
VELE
VELES
VELETA
VELETAS
VELIGER
VELIGERS
VELITES
VELL
VELLEITY
VELLENAGE
VELLET
VELLETS
VELLICATE
VELLON
VELLONS
VELLS
VELLUM
VELLUMS
VELOCE
VELOCITY
VELODROME
VELOUR
VELOURS
VELOUTE
VELOUTES
VELOUTINE
VELSKOEN
VELSKOENS
VELUM
VELURE
VELURED
VELURES
VELURING
VELVERET
VELVERETS
VELVET
VELVETED
VELVETEEN
VELVETIER

VELVETING
VELVETS
VELVETY
VENA
VENAE
VENAL
VENALITY
VENALLY
VENATIC
VENATICAL
VENATION
VENATIONS
VENATOR
VENATORS
VEND
VENDABLE
VENDABLES
VENDACE
VENDACES
VENDAGE
VENDAGES
VENDANGE
VENDANGES
VENDED
VENDEE
VENDEES
VENDER
VENDERS
VENDETTA
VENDETTAS
VENDEUSE
VENDEUSES
VENDIBLE
VENDIBLES
VENDIBLY
VENDING
VENDINGS
VENDIS
VENDISES
VENDISS
VENDISSES
VENDITION
VENDOR
VENDORS
VENDS
VENDUE
VENDUES
VENEER
VENEERED
VENEERER
VENEERERS
VENEERING
VENEERS
VENEFIC
VENEFICAL
VENENATE
VENENATED
VENENATES

VENENE
VENENES
VENENOSE
VENERABLE
VENERABLY
VENERATE
VENERATED
VENERATES
VENERATOR
VENEREAL
VENEREAN
VENEREANS
VENEREOUS
VENERER
VENERERS
VENERIES
VENERY
VENETIAN
VENETIANS
VENEWE
VENEWES
VENEY
VENEYS
VENGE
VENGEABLE
VENGEABLY
VENGEANCE
VENGED
VENGEFUL
VENGEMENT
VENGER
VENGERS
VENGES
VENGING
VENIAL
VENIALITY
VENIALLY
VENIDIUM
VENIDIUMS
VENIN
VENINE
VENINES
VENINS
VENIRE
VENIREMAN
VENIREMEN
VENIRES
VENISON
VENISONS
VENITE
VENITES
VENNEL
VENNELS
VENOGRAM
VENOGRAMS
VENOLOGY
VENOM
VENOMED

VENOMER
VENOMERS
VENOMING
VENOMLESS
VENOMOUS
VENOMS
VENOSE
VENOSITY
VENOUS
VENOUSLY
VENT
VENTAGE
VENTAGES
VENTAIL
VENTAILE
VENTAILES
VENTAILS
VENTANA
VENTANAS
VENTAYLE
VENTAYLES
VENTED
VENTER
VENTERS
VENTIDUCT
VENTIFACT
VENTIGE
VENTIGES
VENTIL
VENTILATE
VENTILS
VENTING
VENTINGS
VENTLESS
VENTOSE
VENTOSITY
VENTOUSE
VENTOUSES
VENTRAL
VENTRALLY
VENTRALS
VENTRE
VENTRED
VENTRES
VENTRICLE
VENTRING
VENTRINGS
VENTROUS
VENTS
VENTURE
VENTURED
VENTURER
VENTURERS
VENTURES
VENTURI
VENTURING
VENTURIS
VENTUROUS

VENUE
VENUES
VENULAR
VENULE
VENULES
VENULOSE
VENULOUS
VENUS
VENUSES
VENVILLE
VENVILLES
VERA
VERACIOUS
VERACITY
VERANDA
VERANDAED
VERANDAH
VERANDAHS
VERANDAS
VERAPAMIL
VERATRIA
VERATRIAS
VERATRIN
VERATRINE
VERATRINS
VERATRUM
VERATRUMS
VERB
VERBAL
VERBALISE
VERBALISM
VERBALIST
VERBALITY
VERBALIZE
VERBALLED
VERBALLY
VERBALS
VERBARIAN
VERBASCUM
VERBATIM
VERBENA
VERBENAS
VERBERATE
VERBIAGE
VERBIAGES
VERBICIDE
VERBID
VERBIDS
VERBIFIED
VERBIFIES
VERBIFY
VERBILE
VERBILES
VERBING
VERBINGS
VERBLESS
VERBOSE
VERBOSELY

VERBOSER
VERBOSEST
VERBOSITY
VERBOTEN
VERBS
VERD
VERDANCY
VERDANT
VERDANTLY
VERDELHO
VERDELHOS
VERDERER
VERDERERS
VERDEROR
VERDERORS
VERDET
VERDETS
VERDICT
VERDICTS
VERDIGRIS
VERDIN
VERDINS
VERDIT
VERDITE
VERDITER
VERDITERS
VERDITES
VERDITS
VERDOY
VERDURE
VERDURED
VERDURES
VERDUROUS
VERECUND
VERGE
VERGED
VERGENCE
VERGENCES
VERGENCY
VERGER
VERGERS
VERGES
VERGING
VERGLAS
VERGLASES
VERIDIC
VERIDICAL
VERIER
VERIEST
VERIFIED
VERIFIER
VERIFIERS
VERIFIES
VERIFY
VERIFYING
VERILY
VERISM
VERISMO

VERISMOS	VERNALIZE	VERSING	VESICATED
VERISMS	VERNALLY	VERSINGS	VESICATES
VERIST	VERNANT	VERSINS	VESICLE
VERISTIC	VERNATION	VERSION	VESICLES
VERISTS	VERNICLE	VERSIONAL	VESICULA
VERITABLE	VERNICLES	VERSIONER	VESICULAE
VERITABLY	VERNIER	VERSIONS	VESICULAR
VERITAS	VERNIERS	VERSO	VESPA
VERITATES	VERNIX	VERSOS	VESPAS
VERITE	VERNIXES	VERST	VESPER
VERITES	VERONAL	VERSTE	VESPERAL
VERITIES	VERONALS	VERSTES	VESPERALS
VERITY	VERONICA	VERSTS	VESPERS
VERJUICE	VERONICAS	VERSUS	VESPIARY
VERJUICED	VERONIQUE	VERSUTE	VESPID
VERJUICES	VERQUERE	VERT	VESPIDS
VERKRAMP	VERQUERES	VERTEBRA	VESPINE
VERLAN	VERQUIRE	VERTEBRAE	VESPOID
VERLANS	VERQUIRES	VERTEBRAL	VESSAIL
VERLIG	VERRA	VERTEBRAS	VESSAILS
VERLIGTE	VERREL	VERTED	VESSEL
VERLIGTES	VERRELS	VERTEX	VESSELED
VERMAL	VERREY	VERTEXES	VESSELS
VERMEIL	VERRUCA	VERTICAL	VEST
VERMEILED	VERRUCAE	VERTICALS	VESTA
VERMEILLE	VERRUCAS	VERTICES	VESTAL
VERMEILS	VERRUCOSE	VERTICIL	VESTALLY
VERMELL	VERRUCOUS	VERTICILS	VESTALS
VERMELLS	VERRUGA	VERTICITY	VESTAS
VERMES	VERRUGAS	VERTIGO	VESTED
VERMIAN	VERRY	VERTIGOES	VESTEE
VERMICIDE	VERS	VERTIGOS	VESTEES
VERMICULE	VERSAL	VERTING	VESTIARY
VERMIFORM	VERSALS	VERTIPORT	VESTIBULA
VERMIFUGE	VERSANT	VERTS	VESTIBULE
VERMIL	VERSANTS	VERTU	VESTIGE
VERMILIES	VERSATILE	VERTUE	VESTIGES
VERMILION	VERSE	VERTUES	VESTIGIA
VERMILLED	VERSED	VERTUOUS	VESTIGIAL
VERMILS	VERSELET	VERTUS	VESTIGIUM
VERMILY	VERSELETS	VERVAIN	VESTIMENT
VERMIN	VERSEMAN	VERVAINS	VESTING
VERMINATE	VERSEMEN	VERVE	VESTINGS
VERMINED	VERSER	VERVEL	VESTITURE
VERMINOUS	VERSERS	VERVELLED	VESTLESS
VERMINS	VERSES	VERVELS	VESTLIKE
VERMINY	VERSET	VERVEN	VESTMENT
VERMIS	VERSETS	VERVENS	VESTMENTS
VERMOULU	VERSICLE	VERVES	VESTRAL
VERMOUTH	VERSICLES	VERVET	VESTRIES
VERMOUTHS	VERSIFIED	VERVETS	VESTRY
VERMUTH	VERSIFIER	VERY	VESTRYMAN
VERMUTHS	VERSIFIES	VESICA	VESTRYMEN
VERNACLE	VERSIFORM	VESICAE	VESTS
VERNACLES	VERSIFY	VESICAL	VESTURAL
VERNAL	VERSIN	VESICANT	VESTURE
VERNALISE	VERSINE	VESICANTS	VESTURED
VERNALITY	VERSINES	VESICATE	VESTURER

VESTURERS	VEZIR	VIBRATORS	VICIOUS
VESTURES	VEZIRS	VIBRATORY	VICIOUSLY
VESTURING	VIA	VIBRATOS	VICOMTE
VESUVIAN	VIABILITY	VIBRIO	VICOMTES
VESUVIANS	VIABLE	VIBRIOID	VICTIM
VET	VIABLY	VIBRION	VICTIMISE
VETCH	VIADUCT	VIBRIONIC	VICTIMIZE
VETCHES	VIADUCTS	VIBRIONS	VICTIMS
VETCHIER	VIAE	VIBRIOS	VICTOR
VETCHIEST	VIAL	VIBRIOSES	VICTORESS
VETCHLING	VIALED	VIBRIOSIS	VICTORIA
VETCHY	VIALFUL	VIBRISSA	VICTORIAS
VETERAN	VIALFULS	VIBRISSAE	VICTORIES
VETERANS	VIALING	VIBRISSAL	VICTORINE
VETIVER	VIALLED	VIBRONIC	VICTORS
VETIVERS	VIALLING	VIBS	VICTORY
VETIVERT	VIALS	VIBURNUM	VICTRESS
VETIVERTS	VIAMETER	VIBURNUMS	VICTRIX
VETKOEK	VIAMETERS	VICAR	VICTRIXES
VETKOEKS	VIAND	VICARAGE	VICTROLLA
VETO	VIANDS	VICARAGES	VICTUAL
VETOED	VIAS	VICARATE	VICTUALED
VETOER	VIATIC	VICARATES	VICTUALER
VETOERS	VIATICA	VICARESS	VICTUALS
VETOES	VIATICAL	VICARIAL	VICUGNA
VETOING	VIATICALS	VICARIANT	VICUGNAS
VETOLESS	VIATICUM	VICARIATE	VICUNA
VETS	VIATICUMS	VICARIES	VICUNAS
VETTED	VIATOR	VICARIOUS	VID
VETTER	VIATORES	VICARLY	VIDAME
VETTERS	VIATORIAL	VICARS	VIDAMES
VETTING	VIATORS	VICARSHIP	VIDE
VETTURA	VIBE	VICARY	VIDELICET
VETTURAS	VIBES	VICE	VIDENDA
VETTURINI	VIBEX	VICED	VIDENDUM
VETTURINO	VIBEY	VICEGERAL	VIDEO
VEX	VIBICES	VICELESS	VIDEODISC
VEXATION	VIBIER	VICELIKE	VIDEODISK
VEXATIONS	VIBIEST	VICENARY	VIDEOED
VEXATIOUS	VIBIST	VICENNIAL	VIDEOFIT
VEXATORY	VIBISTS	VICEREGAL	VIDEOFITS
VEXED	VIBRACULA	VICEREINE	VIDEOGRAM
VEXEDLY	VIBRAHARP	VICEROY	VIDEOING
VEXEDNESS	VIBRANCE	VICEROYS	VIDEOLAND
VEXER	VIBRANCES	VICES	VIDEOS
VEXERS	VIBRANCY	VICESIMAL	VIDEOTAPE
VEXES	VIBRANT	VICHIES	VIDEOTEX
VEXIL	VIBRANTLY	VICHY	VIDEOTEXT
VEXILLA	VIBRANTS	VICIATE	VIDETTE
VEXILLAR	VIBRATE	VICIATED	VIDETTES
VEXILLARY	VIBRATED	VICIATES	VIDICON
VEXILLATE	VIBRATES	VICIATING	VIDICONS
VEXILLUM	VIBRATILE	VICINAGE	VIDIMUS
VEXILS	VIBRATING	VICINAGES	VIDIMUSES
VEXING	VIBRATION	VICINAL	VIDS
VEXINGLY	VIBRATIVE	VICING	VIDUAGE
VEXINGS	VIBRATO	VICINITY	VIDUAGES
VEXT	VIBRATOR	VICIOSITY	VIDUAL

VIDUITIES	VIHARAS	VILLENAGE	VINIC
VIDUITY	VIHUELA	VILLI	VINIER
VIDUOUS	VIHUELAS	VILLIAGO	VINIEST
VIE	VIKING	VILLIAGOS	VINIFERA
VIED	VIKINGISM	VILLIFORM	VINIFERAS
VIELLE	VIKINGS	VILLOSE	VINIFIED
VIELLES	VILAYET	VILLOSITY	VINIFIES
VIER	VILAYETS	VILLOUS	VINIFY
VIERS	VILD	VILLOUSLY	VINIFYING
VIES	VILDE	VILLS	VINING
VIEW	VILDLY	VILLUS	VINO
VIEWABLE	VILDNESS	VIM	VINOLENT
VIEWDATA	VILE	VIMANA	VINOLOGY
VIEWDATAS	VILELY	VIMANAS	VINOS
VIEWED	VILENESS	VIMEN	VINOSITY
VIEWER	VILER	VIMINA	VINOUS
VIEWERS	VILEST	VIMINAL	VINOUSLY
VIEWIER	VILIACO	VIMINEOUS	VINS
VIEWIEST	VILIACOES	VIMS	VINT
VIEWINESS	VILIACOS	VIN	VINTAGE
VIEWING	VILIAGO	VINA	VINTAGED
VIEWINGS	VILIAGOES	VINACEOUS	VINTAGER
VIEWLESS	VILIAGOS	VINAL	VINTAGERS
VIEWLY	VILIFIED	VINALS	VINTAGES
VIEWPHONE	VILIFIER	VINAS	VINTAGING
VIEWPOINT	VILIFIERS	VINASSE	VINTED
VIEWS	VILIFIES	VINASSES	VINTING
VIEWY	VILIFY	VINCA	VINTNER
VIFDA	VILIFYING	VINCAS	VINTNERS
VIFDAS	VILIPEND	VINCIBLE	VINTRIES
VIG	VILIPENDS	VINCIBLY	VINTRY
VIGA	VILL	VINCULA	VINTS
VIGAS	VILLA	VINCULUM	VINY
VIGESIMAL	VILLADOM	VINCULUMS	VINYL
VIGIA	VILLADOMS	VINDALOO	VINYLIC
VIGIAS	VILLAE	VINDALOOS	VINYLS
VIGIL	VILLAGE	VINDEMIAL	VIOL
VIGILANCE	VILLAGER	VINDICATE	VIOLA
VIGILANT	VILLAGERS	VINE	VIOLABLE
VIGILANTE	VILLAGERY	VINEAL	VIOLABLY
VIGILS	VILLAGES	VINED	VIOLAS
VIGNERON	VILLAGIO	VINEGAR	VIOLATE
VIGNERONS	VILLAGIOS	VINEGARED	VIOLATED
VIGNETTE	VILLAGREE	VINEGARS	VIOLATER
VIGNETTED	VILLAIN	VINEGARY	VIOLATERS
VIGNETTER	VILLAINS	VINELESS	VIOLATES
VIGNETTES	VILLAINY	VINELIKE	VIOLATING
VIGOR	VILLAN	VINER	VIOLATION
VIGORISH	VILLANAGE	VINERIES	VIOLATIVE
VIGORO	VILLANIES	VINERS	VIOLATOR
VIGOROS	VILLANOUS	VINERY	VIOLATORS
VIGOROSO	VILLANS	VINES	VIOLD
VIGOROUS	VILLANY	VINEW	VIOLENCE
VIGORS	VILLAR	VINEWED	VIOLENCES
VIGOUR	VILLAS	VINEWING	VIOLENT
VIGOURS	VILLATIC	VINEWS	VIOLENTED
VIGS	VILLEIN	VINEYARD	VIOLENTLY
VIHARA	VILLEINS	VINEYARDS	VIOLENTS

VIOLER	VIRGER	VIRTUE	VISCUMS
VIOLERS	VIRGERS	VIRTUES	VISCUS
VIOLET	VIRGES	VIRTUOSA	VISE
VIOLETS	VIRGIN	VIRTUOSAS	VISED
VIOLIN	VIRGINAL	VIRTUOSE	VISEED
VIOLINIST	VIRGINALS	VIRTUOSI	VISEING
VIOLINS	VIRGINED	VIRTUOSIC	VISELIKE
VIOLIST	VIRGINIA	VIRTUOSO	VISES
VIOLISTS	VIRGINIAS	VIRTUOSOS	VISIBLE
VIOLONE	VIRGINING	VIRTUOUS	VISIBLES
VIOLONES	VIRGINITY	VIRTUS	VISIBLY
VIOLS	VIRGINIUM	VIRUCIDAL	VISIE
VIOMYCIN	VIRGINLY	VIRUCIDE	VISIED
VIOMYCINS	VIRGINS	VIRUCIDES	VISIEING
VIOSTEROL	VIRGULATE	VIRULENCE	VISIER
VIPER	VIRGULE	VIRULENCY	VISIERS
VIPERFISH	VIRGULES	VIRULENT	VISIES
VIPERINE	VIRICIDAL	VIRUS	VISILE
VIPERISH	VIRICIDE	VIRUSES	VISILES
VIPEROUS	VIRICIDES	VIRUSLIKE	VISING
VIPERS	VIRID	VIRUSOID	VISION
VIRAEMIA	VIRIDIAN	VIRUSOIDS	VISIONAL
VIRAEMIAS	VIRIDIANS	VIS	VISIONARY
VIRAEMIC	VIRIDITE	VISA	VISIONED
VIRAGO	VIRIDITES	VISAED	VISIONER
VIRAGOES	VIRIDITY	VISAGE	VISIONERS
VIRAGOISH	VIRILE	VISAGED	VISIONING
VIRAGOS	VIRILELY	VISAGES	VISIONIST
VIRAL	VIRILISE	VISAGIST	VISIONS
VIRALLY	VIRILISED	VISAGISTE	VISIT
VIRANDA	VIRILISES	VISAGISTS	VISITABLE
VIRANDAS	VIRILISM	VISAING	VISITANT
VIRANDO	VIRILISMS	VISARD	VISITANTS
VIRANDOS	VIRILITY	VISARDS	VISITATOR
VIRE	VIRILIZE	VISAS	VISITE
VIRED	VIRILIZED	VISCACHA	VISITED
VIRELAI	VIRILIZES	VISCACHAS	VISITEE
VIRELAIS	VIRILOCAL	VISCARIA	VISITEES
VIRELAY	VIRING	VISCARIAS	VISITER
VIRELAYS	VIRINO	VISCERA	VISITERS
VIREMENT	VIRINOS	VISCERAL	VISITES
VIREMENTS	VIRION	VISCERATE	VISITING
VIREMIA	VIRIONS	VISCID	VISITINGS
VIREMIAS	VIRL	VISCIDITY	VISITOR
VIREMIC	VIRLS	VISCIDLY	VISITORS
VIRENT	VIROGENE	VISCIN	VISITRESS
VIREO	VIROGENES	VISCINS	VISITS
VIREONINE	VIROID	VISCOID	VISIVE
VIREOS	VIROIDS	VISCOIDAL	VISNE
VIRES	VIROLOGIC	VISCOSE	VISNES
VIRESCENT	VIROLOGY	VISCOSES	VISNOMIE
VIRETOT	VIROSE	VISCOSITY	VISNOMIES
VIRETOTS	VIROSES	VISCOUNT	VISNOMY
VIRGA	VIROSIS	VISCOUNTS	VISON
VIRGAS	VIROUS	VISCOUNTY	VISONS
VIRGATE	VIRTU	VISCOUS	VISOR
VIRGATES	VIRTUAL	VISCOUSLY	VISORED
VIRGE	VIRTUALLY	VISCUM	VISORING

VISORLESS
VISORS
VISTA
VISTAED
VISTAING
VISTAL
VISTALESS
VISTAS
VISTO
VISTOS
VISUAL
VISUALISE
VISUALIST
VISUALITY
VISUALIZE
VISUALLY
VISUALS
VITA
VITACEOUS
VITAE
VITAL
VITALISE
VITALISED
VITALISER
VITALISES
VITALISM
VITALISMS
VITALIST
VITALISTS
VITALITY
VITALIZE
VITALIZED
VITALIZER
VITALIZES
VITALLY
VITALNESS
VITALS
VITAMER
VITAMERS
VITAMIN
VITAMINE
VITAMINES
VITAMINIC
VITAMINS
VITAS
VITASCOPE
VITATIVE
VITE
VITELLARY
VITELLI
VITELLIN
VITELLINE
VITELLINS
VITELLUS
VITESSE
VITESSES
VITEX
VITEXES

VITIABLE
VITIATE
VITIATED
VITIATES
VITIATING
VITIATION
VITIATOR
VITIATORS
VITICETA
VITICETUM
VITICIDE
VITICIDES
VITILIGO
VITILIGOS
VITIOSITY
VITRAGE
VITRAGES
VITRAIL
VITRAIN
VITRAINS
VITRAUX
VITREOUS
VITREUM
VITREUMS
VITRIC
VITRICS
VITRIFIED
VITRIFIES
VITRIFORM
VITRIFY
VITRINE
VITRINES
VITRIOL
VITRIOLED
VITRIOLIC
VITRIOLS
VITTA
VITTAE
VITTATE
VITTLE
VITTLED
VITTLES
VITTLING
VITULAR
VITULINE
VIVA
VIVACE
VIVACES
VIVACIOUS
VIVACITY
VIVAED
VIVAING
VIVAMENTE
VIVANDIER
VIVARIA
VIVARIES
VIVARIUM
VIVARIUMS

VIVARY
VIVAS
VIVAT
VIVATS
VIVDA
VIVDAS
VIVE
VIVELY
VIVENCIES
VIVENCY
VIVER
VIVERRA
VIVERRAS
VIVERRID
VIVERRIDS
VIVERRINE
VIVERS
VIVES
VIVIANITE
VIVID
VIVIDER
VIVIDEST
VIVIDITY
VIVIDLY
VIVIDNESS
VIVIFIC
VIVIFIED
VIVIFIER
VIVIFIERS
VIVIFIES
VIVIFY
VIVIFYING
VIVIPARA
VIVIPARY
VIVISECT
VIVISECTS
VIVO
VIVRES
VIXEN
VIXENISH
VIXENLY
VIXENS
VIZAMENT
VIZAMENTS
VIZARD
VIZARDED
VIZARDING
VIZARDS
VIZCACHA
VIZCACHAS
VIZIED
VIZIER
VIZIERATE
VIZIERIAL
VIZIERS
VIZIES
VIZIR
VIZIRATE

VIZIRATES
VIZIRIAL
VIZIRS
VIZIRSHIP
VIZOR
VIZORED
VIZORING
VIZORLESS
VIZORS
VIZSLA
VIZSLAS
VIZY
VIZYING
VIZZIE
VIZZIED
VIZZIEING
VIZZIES
VLEI
VLEIS
VLIES
VLY
VOAR
VOARS
VOCAB
VOCABLE
VOCABLES
VOCABLY
VOCABS
VOCABULAR
VOCAL
VOCALESE
VOCALESES
VOCALIC
VOCALICS
VOCALION
VOCALIONS
VOCALISE
VOCALISED
VOCALISER
VOCALISES
VOCALISM
VOCALISMS
VOCALIST
VOCALISTS
VOCALITY
VOCALIZE
VOCALIZED
VOCALIZER
VOCALIZES
VOCALLY
VOCALNESS
VOCALS
VOCATION
VOCATIONS
VOCATIVE
VOCATIVES
VOCES
VOCODER

VOCODERS
VOCULAR
VOCULE
VOCULES
VODKA
VODKAS
VODOU
VODOUN
VODOUNS
VODOUS
VODUN
VODUNS
VOE
VOEMA
VOEMAS
VOERTSAK
VOERTSEK
VOES
VOETSAK
VOETSEK
VOGIE
VOGIER
VOGIEST
VOGUE
VOGUED
VOGUEING
VOGUEINGS
VOGUER
VOGUERS
VOGUES
VOGUEY
VOGUIER
VOGUIEST
VOGUING
VOGUINGS
VOGUISH
VOGUISHLY
VOICE
VOICED
VOICEFUL
VOICELESS
VOICEMAIL
VOICEOVER
VOICER
VOICERS
VOICES
VOICING
VOICINGS
VOID
VOIDABLE
VOIDANCE
VOIDANCES
VOIDED
VOIDEE
VOIDEES
VOIDER
VOIDERS
VOIDING

VOIDINGS
VOIDNESS
VOIDS
VOILA
VOILE
VOILES
VOISINAGE
VOITURE
VOITURES
VOITURIER
VOIVODE
VOIVODES
VOL
VOLA
VOLABLE
VOLAE
VOLAGE
VOLANT
VOLANTE
VOLANTES
VOLAR
VOLARIES
VOLARY
VOLATIC
VOLATILE
VOLATILES
VOLCANIAN
VOLCANIC
VOLCANICS
VOLCANISE
VOLCANISM
VOLCANIST
VOLCANIZE
VOLCANO
VOLCANOES
VOLCANOS
VOLE
VOLED
VOLENS
VOLERIES
VOLERY
VOLES
VOLET
VOLETS
VOLING
VOLITANT
VOLITATE
VOLITATED
VOLITATES
VOLITIENT
VOLITION
VOLITIONS
VOLITIVE
VOLITIVES
VOLK
VOLKS
VOLKSLIED
VOLKSRAAD

VOLLEY
VOLLEYED
VOLLEYER
VOLLEYERS
VOLLEYING
VOLLEYS
VOLOST
VOLOSTS
VOLPINO
VOLPINOS
VOLPLANE
VOLPLANED
VOLPLANES
VOLS
VOLT
VOLTA
VOLTAGE
VOLTAGES
VOLTAIC
VOLTAISM
VOLTAISMS
VOLTE
VOLTES
VOLTI
VOLTIGEUR
VOLTINISM
VOLTMETER
VOLTS
VOLUBIL
VOLUBLE
VOLUBLY
VOLUCRINE
VOLUME
VOLUMED
VOLUMES
VOLUMETER
VOLUMETRY
VOLUMINAL
VOLUMING
VOLUMISE
VOLUMISED
VOLUMISES
VOLUMIST
VOLUMISTS
VOLUMIZE
VOLUMIZED
VOLUMIZES
VOLUNTARY
VOLUNTEER
VOLUSPA
VOLUSPAS
VOLUTE
VOLUTED
VOLUTES
VOLUTIN
VOLUTINS
VOLUTION
VOLUTIONS

VOLUTOID
VOLVA
VOLVAE
VOLVAS
VOLVATE
VOLVE
VOLVED
VOLVES
VOLVING
VOLVOX
VOLVOXES
VOLVULI
VOLVULUS
VOMER
VOMERINE
VOMERS
VOMICA
VOMICAE
VOMICAS
VOMIT
VOMITED
VOMITER
VOMITERS
VOMITING
VOMITINGS
VOMITIVE
VOMITIVES
VOMITO
VOMITORIA
VOMITORY
VOMITOS
VOMITOUS
VOMITS
VOMITUS
VOMITUSES
VOODOO
VOODOOED
VOODOOING
VOODOOISM
VOODOOIST
VOODOOS
VOORKAMER
VOORSKOT
VOORSKOTS
VOR
VORACIOUS
VORACITY
VORAGO
VORAGOES
VORANT
VORLAGE
VORLAGES
VORPAL
VORRED
VORRING
VORS
VORTEX
VORTEXES

VORTICAL
VORTICES
VORTICISM
VORTICIST
VORTICITY
VORTICOSE
VOSTRO
VOTABLE
VOTARESS
VOTARIES
VOTARIST
VOTARISTS
VOTARY
VOTE
VOTEABLE
VOTED
VOTEEN
VOTEENS
VOTELESS
VOTER
VOTERS
VOTES
VOTING
VOTINGS
VOTIVE
VOTIVELY
VOTIVES
VOTRESS
VOTRESSES
VOUCH
VOUCHED
VOUCHEE
VOUCHEES
VOUCHER
VOUCHERED
VOUCHERS
VOUCHES
VOUCHING
VOUCHSAFE
VOUDON
VOUDONS
VOUDOU
VOUDOUED
VOUDOUING
VOUDOUN
VOUDOUNS
VOUDOUS
VOUGE
VOUGES
VOULGE
VOULGES
VOULU
VOUSSOIR
VOUSSOIRS
VOUTSAFE
VOUTSAFED
VOUTSAFES
VOUVRAY

VOUVRAYS
VOW
VOWED
VOWEL
VOWELISE
VOWELISED
VOWELISES
VOWELIZE
VOWELIZED
VOWELIZES
VOWELLED
VOWELLESS
VOWELLING
VOWELLY
VOWELS
VOWER
VOWERS
VOWESS
VOWESSES
VOWING
VOWLESS
VOWS
VOX
VOXEL
VOXELS
VOYAGE
VOYAGED
VOYAGER
VOYAGERS
VOYAGES
VOYAGEUR
VOYAGEURS
VOYAGING
VOYEUR
VOYEURISM
VOYEURS
VOZHD
VOZHDS
VRAIC
VRAICKER
VRAICKERS
VRAICKING
VRAICS
VRIL
VRILS
VROOM
VROOMED
VROOMING
VROOMS
VROT
VROU
VROUS
VROUW
VROUWS
VROW
VROWS
VUG
VUGG

VUGGIER
VUGGIEST
VUGGS
VUGGY
VUGH
VUGHIER
VUGHIEST
VUGHS
VUGHY
VUGS
VULCAN
VULCANIAN
VULCANIC
VULCANISE
VULCANISM
VULCANIST
VULCANITE
VULCANIZE
VULCANS
VULGAR
VULGARER
VULGAREST
VULGARIAN
VULGARISE
VULGARISM
VULGARITY
VULGARIZE
VULGARLY
VULGARS
VULGATE
VULGATES
VULGO
VULGUS
VULGUSES
VULN
VULNED
VULNERARY
VULNERATE
VULNING
VULNS
VULPICIDE
VULPINE
VULPINISM
VULPINITE
VULSELLA
VULSELLAE
VULSELLUM
VULTURE
VULTURES
VULTURINE
VULTURISH
VULTURISM
VULTURN
VULTURNS
VULTUROUS
VULVA
VULVAE
VULVAL

VULVAR
VULVAS
VULVATE
VULVIFORM
VULVITIS
VUM
VUMMED
VUMMING
VUMS
VUTTIER
VUTTIEST
VUTTY
VUVUZELA
VUVUZELAS
VYING
VYINGLY
VYINGS

— W —

WAAC
WAACS
WAB
WABAIN
WABAINS
WABBIT
WABBLE
WABBLED
WABBLER
WABBLERS
WABBLES
WABBLIER
WABBLIEST
WABBLING
WABBLY
WABOOM
WABOOMS
WABS
WABSTER
WABSTERS
WACK
WACKE
WACKER
WACKERS
WACKES
WACKEST
WACKIER
WACKIEST
WACKILY
WACKINESS
WACKO
WACKOS
WACKS
WACKY
WAD
WADABLE
WADD
WADDED
WADDER
WADDERS
WADDIE
WADDIED
WADDIES
WADDING
WADDINGS
WADDLE
WADDLED
WADDLER
WADDLERS
WADDLES
WADDLIER
WADDLIEST
WADDLING

WADDLY
WADDS
WADDY
WADDYING
WADE
WADEABLE
WADED
WADER
WADERS
WADES
WADI
WADIES
WADING
WADINGS
WADIS
WADMAAL
WADMAALS
WADMAL
WADMALS
WADMEL
WADMELS
WADMOL
WADMOLL
WADMOLLS
WADMOLS
WADS
WADSET
WADSETS
WADSETT
WADSETTED
WADSETTER
WADSETTS
WADT
WADTS
WADY
WAE
WAEFUL
WAENESS
WAENESSES
WAES
WAESOME
WAESUCK
WAESUCKS
WAFER
WAFERED
WAFERING
WAFERS
WAFERY
WAFF
WAFFED
WAFFIE
WAFFIES
WAFFING

WAFFLE
WAFFLED
WAFFLER
WAFFLERS
WAFFLES
WAFFLIER
WAFFLIEST
WAFFLING
WAFFLINGS
WAFFLY
WAFFS
WAFT
WAFTAGE
WAFTAGES
WAFTED
WAFTER
WAFTERS
WAFTING
WAFTINGS
WAFTS
WAFTURE
WAFTURES
WAG
WAGE
WAGED
WAGELESS
WAGENBOOM
WAGER
WAGERED
WAGERER
WAGERERS
WAGERING
WAGERS
WAGES
WAGGA
WAGGAS
WAGGED
WAGGER
WAGGERIES
WAGGERS
WAGGERY
WAGGING
WAGGISH
WAGGISHLY
WAGGLE
WAGGLED
WAGGLER
WAGGLERS
WAGGLES
WAGGLIER
WAGGLIEST
WAGGLING
WAGGLY

WAGGON
WAGGONED
WAGGONER
WAGGONERS
WAGGONING
WAGGONS
WAGHALTER
WAGING
WAGMOIRE
WAGMOIRES
WAGON
WAGONAGE
WAGONAGES
WAGONED
WAGONER
WAGONERS
WAGONETTE
WAGONFUL
WAGONFULS
WAGONING
WAGONLESS
WAGONLOAD
WAGONS
WAGS
WAGSOME
WAGTAIL
WAGTAILS
WAHCONDA
WAHCONDAS
WAHINE
WAHINES
WAHOO
WAHOOS
WAI
WAIATA
WAIATAS
WAID
WAIDE
WAIF
WAIFED
WAIFING
WAIFISH
WAIFLIKE
WAIFS
WAIFT
WAIFTS
WAIL
WAILED
WAILER
WAILERS
WAILFUL
WAILFULLY
WAILING

WAILINGLY	WAIVING	WALING	WALLOPER
WAILINGS	WAIVODE	WALIS	WALLOPERS
WAILS	WAIVODES	WALISE	WALLOPING
WAILSOME	WAIWODE	WALISES	WALLOPS
WAIN	WAIWODES	WALK	WALLOW
WAINAGE	WAKA	WALKABLE	WALLOWED
WAINAGES	WAKAME	WALKABOUT	WALLOWER
WAINED	WAKAMES	WALKATHON	WALLOWERS
WAINING	WAKANDA	WALKAWAY	WALLOWING
WAINS	WAKANDAS	WALKAWAYS	WALLOWS
WAINSCOT	WAKANE	WALKED	WALLPAPER
WAINSCOTS	WAKANES	WALKER	WALLS
WAIR	WAKAS	WALKERS	WALLSEND
WAIRED	WAKE	WALKING	WALLSENDS
WAIRING	WAKEBOARD	WALKINGS	WALLWORT
WAIRS	WAKED	WALKMILL	WALLWORTS
WAIRSH	WAKEFUL	WALKMILLS	WALLY
WAIRSHER	WAKEFULLY	WALKOUT	WALLYBALL
WAIRSHEST	WAKELESS	WALKOUTS	WALLYDRAG
WAIRUA	WAKEMAN	WALKOVER	WALNUT
WAIRUAS	WAKEMEN	WALKOVERS	WALNUTS
WAIS	WAKEN	WALKS	WALRUS
WAIST	WAKENED	WALKUP	WALRUSES
WAISTBAND	WAKENER	WALKUPS	WALTIER
WAISTBELT	WAKENERS	WALKWAY	WALTIEST
WAISTCOAT	WAKENING	WALKWAYS	WALTY
WAISTED	WAKENINGS	WALKYRIE	WALTZ
WAISTER	WAKENS	WALKYRIES	WALTZED
WAISTERS	WAKER	WALL	WALTZER
WAISTING	WAKERIFE	WALLA	WALTZERS
WAISTINGS	WAKERS	WALLABA	WALTZES
WAISTLESS	WAKES	WALLABAS	WALTZING
WAISTLINE	WAKF	WALLABIES	WALTZINGS
WAISTS	WAKFS	WALLABY	WALTZLIKE
WAIT	WAKIKI	WALLAH	WALY
WAITE	WAKIKIS	WALLAHS	WAMBENGER
WAITED	WAKING	WALLAROO	WAMBLE
WAITER	WAKINGS	WALLAROOS	WAMBLED
WAITERAGE	WALD	WALLAS	WAMBLES
WAITERED	WALDFLUTE	WALLBOARD	WAMBLIER
WAITERING	WALDGRAVE	WALLCHART	WAMBLIEST
WAITERS	WALDHORN	WALLED	WAMBLING
WAITES	WALDHORNS	WALLER	WAMBLINGS
WAITING	WALDO	WALLERS	WAMBLY
WAITINGLY	WALDOES	WALLET	WAME
WAITINGS	WALDOS	WALLETS	WAMED
WAITLIST	WALDRAPP	WALLEYE	WAMEFOU
WAITLISTS	WALDRAPPS	WALLEYED	WAMEFOUS
WAITRESS	WALDS	WALLEYES	WAMEFUL
WAITRON	WALE	WALLFISH	WAMEFULS
WAITRONS	WALED	WALLIE	WAMES
WAITS	WALER	WALLIER	WAMMUL
WAITSTAFF	WALERS	WALLIES	WAMMULS
WAIVE	WALES	WALLIEST	WAMMUS
WAIVED	WALI	WALLING	WAMMUSES
WAIVER	WALIER	WALLINGS	WAMPEE
WAIVERS	WALIES	WALLOP	WAMPEES
WAIVES	WALIEST	WALLOPED	WAMPISH

WAMPISHED	WANKLE	WAPITI	WARDROOM
WAMPISHES	WANKS	WAPITIS	WARDROOMS
WAMPUM	WANKSTA	WAPPED	WARDROP
WAMPUMS	WANKSTAS	WAPPEND	WARDROPS
WAMPUS	WANKY	WAPPER	WARDS
WAMPUSES	WANLE	WAPPERED	WARDSHIP
WAMUS	WANLY	WAPPERING	WARDSHIPS
WAMUSES	WANNA	WAPPERS	WARE
WAN	WANNABE	WAPPING	WARED
WANCHANCY	WANNABEE	WAPS	WAREHOU
WAND	WANNABEES	WAQF	WAREHOUSE
WANDER	WANNABES	WAQFS	WARELESS
WANDERED	WANNED	WAR	WAREROOM
WANDERER	WANNEL	WARAGI	WAREROOMS
WANDERERS	WANNER	WARAGIS	WARES
WANDERING	WANNESS	WARATAH	WAREZ
WANDEROO	WANNESSES	WARATAHS	WARFARE
WANDEROOS	WANNEST	WARB	WARFARED
WANDERS	WANNIGAN	WARBIER	WARFARER
WANDLE	WANNIGANS	WARBIEST	WARFARERS
WANDLIKE	WANNING	WARBLE	WARFARES
WANDOO	WANNISH	WARBLED	WARFARIN
WANDOOS	WANS	WARBLER	WARFARING
WANDS	WANT	WARBLERS	WARFARINS
WANE	WANTAGE	WARBLES	WARHABLE
WANED	WANTAGES	WARBLING	WARHEAD
WANES	WANTED	WARBLINGS	WARHEADS
WANEY	WANTER	WARBONNET	WARHORSE
WANG	WANTERS	WARBS	WARHORSES
WANGAN	WANTHILL	WARBY	WARIBASHI
WANGANS	WANTHILLS	WARCRAFT	WARIER
WANGLE	WANTIES	WARCRAFTS	WARIEST
WANGLED	WANTING	WARD	WARILY
WANGLER	WANTINGS	WARDCORN	WARIMENT
WANGLERS	WANTON	WARDCORNS	WARIMENTS
WANGLES	WANTONED	WARDED	WARINESS
WANGLING	WANTONER	WARDEN	WARING
WANGLINGS	WANTONERS	WARDENED	WARISON
WANGS	WANTONEST	WARDENING	WARISONS
WANGUN	WANTONING	WARDENRY	WARK
WANGUNS	WANTONISE	WARDENS	WARKED
WANHOPE	WANTONIZE	WARDER	WARKING
WANHOPES	WANTONLY	WARDERED	WARKS
WANIER	WANTONS	WARDERING	WARLESS
WANIEST	WANTS	WARDERS	WARLIKE
WANIGAN	WANTY	WARDIAN	WARLING
WANIGANS	WANWORDY	WARDING	WARLINGS
WANING	WANWORTH	WARDINGS	WARLOCK
WANINGS	WANWORTHS	WARDLESS	WARLOCKRY
WANION	WANY	WARDMOTE	WARLOCKS
WANIONS	WANZE	WARDMOTES	WARLORD
WANK	WANZED	WARDOG	WARLORDS
WANKED	WANZES	WARDOGS	WARM
WANKER	WANZING	WARDRESS	WARMAKER
WANKERS	WAP	WARDROBE	WARMAKERS
WANKIER	WAPENSHAW	WARDROBED	WARMAN
WANKIEST	WAPENTAKE	WARDROBER	WARMBLOOD
WANKING	WAPINSHAW	WARDROBES	WARMED

WARMEN
WARMER
WARMERS
WARMEST
WARMING
WARMINGS
WARMISH
WARMLY
WARMNESS
WARMONGER
WARMOUTH
WARMOUTHS
WARMS
WARMTH
WARMTHS
WARMUP
WARMUPS
WARN
WARNED
WARNER
WARNERS
WARNING
WARNINGLY
WARNINGS
WARNS
WARP
WARPAGE
WARPAGES
WARPATH
WARPATHS
WARPED
WARPER
WARPERS
WARPING
WARPINGS
WARPLANE
WARPLANES
WARPOWER
WARPOWERS
WARPS
WARPWISE
WARRAGAL
WARRAGALS
WARRAGLE
WARRAGLES
WARRAGUL
WARRAGULS
WARRAN
WARRAND
WARRANDED
WARRANDS
WARRANED
WARRANING
WARRANS
WARRANT
WARRANTED
WARRANTEE
WARRANTER

WARRANTOR
WARRANTS
WARRANTY
WARRAY
WARRAYED
WARRAYING
WARRAYS
WARRE
WARRED
WARREN
WARRENER
WARRENERS
WARRENS
WARREY
WARREYED
WARREYING
WARREYS
WARRIGAL
WARRIGALS
WARRING
WARRIOR
WARRIORS
WARRISON
WARRISONS
WARS
WARSAW
WARSAWS
WARSHIP
WARSHIPS
WARSLE
WARSLED
WARSLER
WARSLERS
WARSLES
WARSLING
WARST
WARSTLE
WARSTLED
WARSTLER
WARSTLERS
WARSTLES
WARSTLING
WART
WARTED
WARTHOG
WARTHOGS
WARTIER
WARTIEST
WARTIME
WARTIMES
WARTLESS
WARTLIKE
WARTS
WARTWEED
WARTWEEDS
WARTWORT
WARTWORTS
WARTY

WARWOLF
WARWOLVES
WARWORK
WARWORKS
WARWORN
WARY
WARZONE
WARZONES
WAS
WASABI
WASABIS
WASE
WASES
WASH
WASHABLE
WASHABLES
WASHAWAY
WASHAWAYS
WASHBALL
WASHBALLS
WASHBASIN
WASHBOARD
WASHBOWL
WASHBOWLS
WASHCLOTH
WASHDAY
WASHDAYS
WASHED
WASHEN
WASHER
WASHERED
WASHERIES
WASHERING
WASHERMAN
WASHERMEN
WASHERS
WASHERY
WASHES
WASHHOUSE
WASHIER
WASHIEST
WASHILY
WASHIN
WASHINESS
WASHING
WASHINGS
WASHINS
WASHLAND
WASHLANDS
WASHOUT
WASHOUTS
WASHPOT
WASHPOTS
WASHRAG
WASHRAGS
WASHROOM
WASHROOMS
WASHSTAND

WASHTUB
WASHTUBS
WASHUP
WASHUPS
WASHWIPE
WASHWIPES
WASHWOMAN
WASHWOMEN
WASHY
WASM
WASMS
WASP
WASPIE
WASPIER
WASPIES
WASPIEST
WASPILY
WASPINESS
WASPISH
WASPISHLY
WASPLIKE
WASPNEST
WASPNESTS
WASPS
WASPY
WASSAIL
WASSAILED
WASSAILER
WASSAILRY
WASSAILS
WASSERMAN
WASSERMEN
WASSUP
WAST
WASTABLE
WASTAGE
WASTAGES
WASTE
WASTED
WASTEFUL
WASTEL
WASTELAND
WASTELOT
WASTELOTS
WASTELS
WASTENESS
WASTER
WASTERED
WASTERFUL
WASTERIE
WASTERIES
WASTERING
WASTERS
WASTERY
WASTES
WASTEWAY
WASTEWAYS
WASTEWEIR

WASTFULL	WATERHEAD	WAUFFED	WAVERIEST
WASTING	WATERHEN	WAUFFING	WAVERING
WASTINGLY	WATERHENS	WAUFFS	WAVERINGS
WASTINGS	WATERIER	WAUGH	WAVEROUS
WASTNESS	WATERIEST	WAUGHED	WAVERS
WASTREL	WATERILY	WAUGHING	WAVERY
WASTRELS	WATERING	WAUGHS	WAVES
WASTRIE	WATERINGS	WAUGHT	WAVESHAPE
WASTRIES	WATERISH	WAUGHTED	WAVESON
WASTRIFE	WATERJET	WAUGHTING	WAVESONS
WASTRIFES	WATERJETS	WAUGHTS	WAVEY
WASTRY	WATERLEAF	WAUK	WAVEYS
WASTS	WATERLESS	WAUKED	WAVICLE
WAT	WATERLILY	WAUKER	WAVICLES
WATAP	WATERLINE	WAUKERS	WAVIER
WATAPE	WATERLOG	WAUKING	WAVIES
WATAPES	WATERLOGS	WAUKMILL	WAVIEST
WATAPS	WATERLOO	WAUKMILLS	WAVILY
WATCH	WATERLOOS	WAUKRIFE	WAVINESS
WATCHABLE	WATERMAN	WAUKS	WAVING
WATCHBAND	WATERMARK	WAUL	WAVINGS
WATCHBOX	WATERMEN	WAULED	WAVY
WATCHCASE	WATERPOX	WAULING	WAW
WATCHCRY	WATERS	WAULINGS	WAWA
WATCHDOG	WATERSHED	WAULK	WAWAED
WATCHDOGS	WATERSIDE	WAULKED	WAWAING
WATCHED	WATERSKI	WAULKER	WAWAS
WATCHER	WATERSKIS	WAULKERS	WAWE
WATCHERS	WATERWAY	WAULKING	WAWES
WATCHES	WATERWAYS	WAULKMILL	WAWL
WATCHET	WATERWEED	WAULKS	WAWLED
WATCHETS	WATERWORK	WAULS	WAWLING
WATCHEYE	WATERWORN	WAUR	WAWLINGS
WATCHEYES	WATERY	WAURED	WAWLS
WATCHFUL	WATERZOOI	WAURING	WAWS
WATCHING	WATS	WAURS	WAX
WATCHLIST	WATT	WAURST	WAXABLE
WATCHMAN	WATTAGE	WAVE	WAXBERRY
WATCHMEN	WATTAGES	WAVEBAND	WAXBILL
WATCHOUT	WATTAPE	WAVEBANDS	WAXBILLS
WATCHOUTS	WATTAPES	WAVED	WAXCLOTH
WATCHWORD	WATTER	WAVEFORM	WAXCLOTHS
WATE	WATTEST	WAVEFORMS	WAXED
WATER	WATTHOUR	WAVEFRONT	WAXEN
WATERAGE	WATTHOURS	WAVEGUIDE	WAXER
WATERAGES	WATTLE	WAVELESS	WAXERS
WATERBED	WATTLED	WAVELET	WAXES
WATERBEDS	WATTLES	WAVELETS	WAXEYE
WATERBIRD	WATTLESS	WAVELIKE	WAXEYES
WATERBUCK	WATTLING	WAVELLITE	WAXFLOWER
WATERBUS	WATTLINGS	WAVEMETER	WAXIER
WATERDOG	WATTMETER	WAVEOFF	WAXIEST
WATERDOGS	WATTS	WAVEOFFS	WAXILY
WATERED	WAUCHT	WAVER	WAXINESS
WATERER	WAUCHTED	WAVERED	WAXING
WATERERS	WAUCHTING	WAVERER	WAXINGS
WATERFALL	WAUCHTS	WAVERERS	WAXLIKE
WATERFOWL	WAUFF	WAVERIER	WAXPLANT

WAXPLANTS	WAYWODE	WEAPONED	WEAZEN
WAXWEED	WAYWODES	WEAPONEER	WEAZENED
WAXWEEDS	WAYWORN	WEAPONING	WEAZENING
WAXWING	WAYZGOOSE	WEAPONISE	WEAZENS
WAXWINGS	WAZIR	WEAPONIZE	WEB
WAXWORK	WAZIRS	WEAPONRY	WEBBED
WAXWORKER	WAZOO	WEAPONS	WEBBIE
WAXWORKS	WAZOOS	WEAR	WEBBIER
WAXWORM	WAZZOCK	WEARABLE	WEBBIES
WAXWORMS	WAZZOCKS	WEARABLES	WEBBIEST
WAXY	WE	WEARED	WEBBING
WAY	WEAK	WEARER	WEBBINGS
WAYBILL	WEAKEN	WEARERS	WEBBY
WAYBILLS	WEAKENED	WEARIED	WEBCAM
WAYBOARD	WEAKENER	WEARIER	WEBCAMS
WAYBOARDS	WEAKENERS	WEARIES	WEBCAST
WAYBREAD	WEAKENING	WEARIEST	WEBCASTED
WAYBREADS	WEAKENS	WEARIFUL	WEBCASTER
WAYED	WEAKER	WEARILESS	WEBCASTS
WAYFARE	WEAKEST	WEARILY	WEBER
WAYFARED	WEAKFISH	WEARINESS	WEBERS
WAYFARER	WEAKISH	WEARING	WEBFED
WAYFARERS	WEAKISHLY	WEARINGLY	WEBFEET
WAYFARES	WEAKLIER	WEARINGS	WEBFOOT
WAYFARING	WEAKLIEST	WEARISH	WEBFOOTED
WAYGOING	WEAKLING	WEARISOME	WEBINAR
WAYGOINGS	WEAKLINGS	WEARPROOF	WEBINARS
WAYGONE	WEAKLY	WEARS	WEBLESS
WAYGOOSE	WEAKNESS	WEARY	WEBLIKE
WAYGOOSES	WEAKON	WEARYING	WEBLISH
WAYING	WEAKONS	WEASAND	WEBLISHES
WAYLAID	WEAKSIDE	WEASANDS	WEBLOG
WAYLAY	WEAKSIDES	WEASEL	WEBLOGGER
WAYLAYER	WEAL	WEASELED	WEBLOGS
WAYLAYERS	WEALD	WEASELER	WEBMAIL
WAYLAYING	WEALDS	WEASELERS	WEBMAILS
WAYLAYS	WEALS	WEASELING	WEBMASTER
WAYLEAVE	WEALSMAN	WEASELLED	WEBPAGE
WAYLEAVES	WEALSMEN	WEASELLER	WEBPAGES
WAYLEGGO	WEALTH	WEASELLY	WEBS
WAYLESS	WEALTHIER	WEASELS	WEBSITE
WAYMARK	WEALTHILY	WEASELY	WEBSITES
WAYMARKED	WEALTHS	WEASON	WEBSTER
WAYMARKS	WEALTHY	WEASONS	WEBSTERS
WAYMENT	WEAMB	WEATHER	WEBWHEEL
WAYMENTED	WEAMBS	WEATHERED	WEBWHEELS
WAYMENTS	WEAN	WEATHERER	WEBWORK
WAYPOINT	WEANED	WEATHERLY	WEBWORKS
WAYPOINTS	WEANEL	WEATHERS	WEBWORM
WAYPOST	WEANELS	WEAVE	WEBWORMS
WAYPOSTS	WEANER	WEAVED	WECHT
WAYS	WEANERS	WEAVER	WECHTS
WAYSIDE	WEANING	WEAVERS	WED
WAYSIDES	WEANINGS	WEAVES	WEDDED
WAYWARD	WEANLING	WEAVING	WEDDER
WAYWARDLY	WEANLINGS	WEAVINGS	WEDDERED
WAYWISER	WEANS	WEAZAND	WEDDERING
WAYWISERS	WEAPON	WEAZANDS	WEDDERS

663

WEDDING
WEDDINGS
WEDEL
WEDELED
WEDELING
WEDELN
WEDELNED
WEDELNING
WEDELNS
WEDELS
WEDGE
WEDGED
WEDGELIKE
WEDGES
WEDGEWISE
WEDGIE
WEDGIER
WEDGIES
WEDGIEST
WEDGING
WEDGINGS
WEDGY
WEDLOCK
WEDLOCKS
WEDS
WEE
WEED
WEEDED
WEEDER
WEEDERIES
WEEDERS
WEEDERY
WEEDICIDE
WEEDIER
WEEDIEST
WEEDILY
WEEDINESS
WEEDING
WEEDINGS
WEEDLESS
WEEDLIKE
WEEDS
WEEDY
WEEING
WEEK
WEEKDAY
WEEKDAYS
WEEKE
WEEKEND
WEEKENDED
WEEKENDER
WEEKENDS
WEEKES
WEEKLIES
WEEKLONG
WEEKLY
WEEKNIGHT
WEEKS

WEEL
WEELS
WEEM
WEEMS
WEEN
WEENED
WEENIE
WEENIER
WEENIES
WEENIEST
WEENING
WEENS
WEENSIER
WEENSIEST
WEENSY
WEENY
WEEP
WEEPER
WEEPERS
WEEPHOLE
WEEPHOLES
WEEPIE
WEEPIER
WEEPIES
WEEPIEST
WEEPILY
WEEPINESS
WEEPING
WEEPINGLY
WEEPINGS
WEEPS
WEEPY
WEER
WEES
WEEST
WEET
WEETE
WEETED
WEETEN
WEETER
WEETEST
WEETING
WEETINGLY
WEETLESS
WEETS
WEEVER
WEEVERS
WEEVIL
WEEVILED
WEEVILLED
WEEVILLY
WEEVILS
WEEVILY
WEEWEE
WEEWEED
WEEWEEING
WEEWEES
WEFT

WEFTAGE
WEFTAGES
WEFTE
WEFTED
WEFTES
WEFTING
WEFTS
WEFTWISE
WEID
WEIDS
WEIGELA
WEIGELAS
WEIGELIA
WEIGELIAS
WEIGH
WEIGHABLE
WEIGHAGE
WEIGHAGES
WEIGHED
WEIGHER
WEIGHERS
WEIGHING
WEIGHINGS
WEIGHMAN
WEIGHMEN
WEIGHS
WEIGHT
WEIGHTED
WEIGHTER
WEIGHTERS
WEIGHTIER
WEIGHTILY
WEIGHTING
WEIGHTS
WEIGHTY
WEIL
WEILS
WEINER
WEINERS
WEIR
WEIRD
WEIRDED
WEIRDER
WEIRDEST
WEIRDIE
WEIRDIES
WEIRDING
WEIRDLY
WEIRDNESS
WEIRDO
WEIRDOES
WEIRDOS
WEIRDS
WEIRDY
WEIRED
WEIRING
WEIRS
WEISE

WEISED
WEISES
WEISING
WEIZE
WEIZED
WEIZES
WEIZING
WEKA
WEKAS
WELAWAY
WELCH
WELCHED
WELCHER
WELCHERS
WELCHES
WELCHING
WELCOME
WELCOMED
WELCOMELY
WELCOMER
WELCOMERS
WELCOMES
WELCOMING
WELD
WELDABLE
WELDED
WELDER
WELDERS
WELDING
WELDINGS
WELDLESS
WELDMENT
WELDMENTS
WELDMESH
WELDOR
WELDORS
WELDS
WELFARE
WELFARES
WELFARISM
WELFARIST
WELK
WELKE
WELKED
WELKES
WELKIN
WELKING
WELKINS
WELKS
WELKT
WELL
WELLADAY
WELLADAYS
WELLANEAR
WELLAWAY
WELLAWAYS
WELLBEING
WELLBORN

WELLCURB	WENS	WETHERS	WHAKAPAPA
WELLCURBS	WENT	WETLAND	WHALE
WELLDOER	WENTS	WETLANDS	WHALEBACK
WELLDOERS	WEPT	WETLY	WHALEBOAT
WELLED	WERE	WETNESS	WHALEBONE
WELLHEAD	WEREGILD	WETNESSES	WHALED
WELLHEADS	WEREGILDS	WETPROOF	WHALELIKE
WELLHOLE	WEREWOLF	WETS	WHALEMAN
WELLHOLES	WERGELD	WETSUIT	WHALEMEN
WELLHOUSE	WERGELDS	WETSUITS	WHALER
WELLIE	WERGELT	WETTABLE	WHALERIES
WELLIES	WERGELTS	WETTED	WHALERS
WELLING	WERGILD	WETTER	WHALERY
WELLINGS	WERGILDS	WETTERS	WHALES
WELLNESS	WERNERITE	WETTEST	WHALING
WELLS	WERO	WETTIE	WHALINGS
WELLSITE	WEROS	WETTIES	WHALLY
WELLSITES	WERRIS	WETTING	WHAM
WELLY	WERRISES	WETTINGS	WHAMMED
WELSH	WERSH	WETTISH	WHAMMIES
WELSHED	WERSHER	WETWARE	WHAMMING
WELSHER	WERSHEST	WETWARES	WHAMMO
WELSHERS	WERT	WEX	WHAMMOS
WELSHES	WERWOLF	WEXE	WHAMMY
WELSHING	WERWOLVES	WEXED	WHAMO
WELT	WESAND	WEXES	WHAMPLE
WELTED	WESANDS	WEXING	WHAMPLES
WELTER	WESKIT	WEY	WHAMS
WELTERED	WESKITS	WEYARD	WHANAU
WELTERING	WESSAND	WEYS	WHANAUS
WELTERS	WESSANDS	WEYWARD	WHANG
WELTING	WEST	WEZAND	WHANGAM
WELTINGS	WESTBOUND	WEZANDS	WHANGAMS
WELTS	WESTED	WHA	WHANGED
WEM	WESTER	WHACK	WHANGEE
WEMB	WESTERED	WHACKED	WHANGEES
WEMBS	WESTERING	WHACKER	WHANGING
WEMS	WESTERLY	WHACKERS	WHANGS
WEN	WESTERN	WHACKIER	WHAP
WENA	WESTERNER	WHACKIEST	WHAPPED
WENCH	WESTERNS	WHACKING	WHAPPER
WENCHED	WESTERS	WHACKINGS	WHAPPERS
WENCHER	WESTIE	WHACKO	WHAPPING
WENCHERS	WESTIES	WHACKOES	WHAPS
WENCHES	WESTING	WHACKOS	WHARE
WENCHING	WESTINGS	WHACKS	WHARENUI
WEND	WESTLIN	WHACKY	WHARENUIS
WENDED	WESTLINS	WHAE	WHAREPUNI
WENDIGO	WESTMOST	WHAISLE	WHARES
WENDIGOS	WESTS	WHAISLED	WHARF
WENDING	WESTWARD	WHAISLES	WHARFAGE
WENDS	WESTWARDS	WHAISLING	WHARFAGES
WENGE	WET	WHAIZLE	WHARFED
WENGES	WETA	WHAIZLED	WHARFIE
WENNIER	WETAS	WHAIZLES	WHARFIES
WENNIEST	WETBACK	WHAIZLING	WHARFING
WENNISH	WETBACKS	WHAKAIRO	WHARFINGS
WENNY	WETHER	WHAKAIROS	WHARFS

665

WHARVE

WHARVE	WHEELIEST	WHELMS	WHETS
WHARVES	WHEELING	WHELP	WHETSTONE
WHAT	WHEELINGS	WHELPED	WHETTED
WHATA	WHEELLESS	WHELPING	WHETTER
WHATAS	WHEELMAN	WHELPLESS	WHETTERS
WHATEN	WHEELMEN	WHELPS	WHETTING
WHATEVER	WHEELS	WHEMMLE	WHEUGH
WHATNA	WHEELSMAN	WHEMMLED	WHEUGHED
WHATNESS	WHEELSMEN	WHEMMLES	WHEUGHING
WHATNOT	WHEELWORK	WHEMMLING	WHEUGHS
WHATNOTS	WHEELY	WHEN	WHEW
WHATS	WHEEN	WHENAS	WHEWED
WHATSIS	WHEENGE	WHENCE	WHEWING
WHATSISES	WHEENGED	WHENCES	WHEWS
WHATSIT	WHEENGES	WHENCEVER	WHEY
WHATSITS	WHEENGING	WHENEVER	WHEYEY
WHATSO	WHEENS	WHENS	WHEYFACE
WHATTEN	WHEEP	WHENUA	WHEYFACED
WHAUP	WHEEPED	WHENUAS	WHEYFACES
WHAUPS	WHEEPING	WHENWE	WHEYIER
WHAUR	WHEEPLE	WHENWES	WHEYIEST
WHAURS	WHEEPLED	WHERE	WHEYISH
WHEAL	WHEEPLES	WHEREAS	WHEYLIKE
WHEALS	WHEEPLING	WHEREASES	WHEYS
WHEAR	WHEEPS	WHEREAT	WHICH
WHEARE	WHEESH	WHEREBY	WHICHEVER
WHEAT	WHEESHED	WHEREFOR	WHICKER
WHEATEAR	WHEESHES	WHEREFORE	WHICKERED
WHEATEARS	WHEESHING	WHEREFROM	WHICKERS
WHEATEN	WHEESHT	WHEREIN	WHID
WHEATENS	WHEESHTED	WHEREINTO	WHIDAH
WHEATIER	WHEESHTS	WHERENESS	WHIDAHS
WHEATIEST	WHEEZE	WHEREOF	WHIDDED
WHEATLAND	WHEEZED	WHEREON	WHIDDER
WHEATLESS	WHEEZER	WHEREOUT	WHIDDERED
WHEATMEAL	WHEEZERS	WHERES	WHIDDERS
WHEATS	WHEEZES	WHERESO	WHIDDING
WHEATWORM	WHEEZIER	WHERETO	WHIDS
WHEATY	WHEEZIEST	WHEREUNTO	WHIFF
WHEE	WHEEZILY	WHEREUPON	WHIFFED
WHEECH	WHEEZING	WHEREVER	WHIFFER
WHEECHED	WHEEZINGS	WHEREWITH	WHIFFERS
WHEECHING	WHEEZLE	WHERRET	WHIFFET
WHEECHS	WHEEZLED	WHERRETED	WHIFFETS
WHEEDLE	WHEEZLES	WHERRETS	WHIFFIER
WHEEDLED	WHEEZLING	WHERRIED	WHIFFIEST
WHEEDLER	WHEEZY	WHERRIES	WHIFFING
WHEEDLERS	WHEFT	WHERRIT	WHIFFINGS
WHEEDLES	WHEFTS	WHERRITED	WHIFFLE
WHEEDLING	WHELK	WHERRITS	WHIFFLED
WHEEL	WHELKED	WHERRY	WHIFFLER
WHEELBASE	WHELKIER	WHERRYING	WHIFFLERS
WHEELED	WHELKIEST	WHERRYMAN	WHIFFLERY
WHEELER	WHELKS	WHERRYMEN	WHIFFLES
WHEELERS	WHELKY	WHERVE	WHIFFLING
WHEELIE	WHELM	WHERVES	WHIFFS
WHEELIER	WHELMED	WHET	WHIFFY
WHEELIES	WHELMING	WHETHER	WHIFT

WHIFTS
WHIG
WHIGGED
WHIGGING
WHIGS
WHILE
WHILED
WHILERE
WHILES
WHILING
WHILK
WHILLIED
WHILLIES
WHILLY
WHILLYING
WHILLYWHA
WHILOM
WHILST
WHIM
WHIMBERRY
WHIMBREL
WHIMBRELS
WHIMMED
WHIMMIER
WHIMMIEST
WHIMMING
WHIMMY
WHIMPER
WHIMPERED
WHIMPERER
WHIMPERS
WHIMPLE
WHIMPLED
WHIMPLES
WHIMPLING
WHIMS
WHIMSEY
WHIMSEYS
WHIMSICAL
WHIMSIED
WHIMSIER
WHIMSIES
WHIMSIEST
WHIMSILY
WHIMSY
WHIN
WHINBERRY
WHINCHAT
WHINCHATS
WHINE
WHINED
WHINER
WHINERS
WHINES
WHINEY
WHINGDING
WHINGE
WHINGED

WHINGEING
WHINGER
WHINGERS
WHINGES
WHINGING
WHINIARD
WHINIARDS
WHINIER
WHINIEST
WHININESS
WHINING
WHININGLY
WHININGS
WHINNIED
WHINNIER
WHINNIES
WHINNIEST
WHINNY
WHINNYING
WHINS
WHINSTONE
WHINY
WHINYARD
WHINYARDS
WHIO
WHIP
WHIPBIRD
WHIPBIRDS
WHIPCAT
WHIPCATS
WHIPCORD
WHIPCORDS
WHIPCORDY
WHIPJACK
WHIPJACKS
WHIPLASH
WHIPLIKE
WHIPPED
WHIPPER
WHIPPERS
WHIPPET
WHIPPETS
WHIPPIER
WHIPPIEST
WHIPPING
WHIPPINGS
WHIPPY
WHIPRAY
WHIPRAYS
WHIPS
WHIPSAW
WHIPSAWED
WHIPSAWN
WHIPSAWS
WHIPSNAKE
WHIPSTAFF
WHIPSTALL
WHIPSTER

WHIPSTERS
WHIPSTOCK
WHIPT
WHIPTAIL
WHIPTAILS
WHIPWORM
WHIPWORMS
WHIR
WHIRL
WHIRLBAT
WHIRLBATS
WHIRLED
WHIRLER
WHIRLERS
WHIRLIER
WHIRLIES
WHIRLIEST
WHIRLIGIG
WHIRLING
WHIRLINGS
WHIRLPOOL
WHIRLS
WHIRLWIND
WHIRLY
WHIRR
WHIRRED
WHIRRET
WHIRRETED
WHIRRETS
WHIRRIED
WHIRRIES
WHIRRING
WHIRRINGS
WHIRRS
WHIRRY
WHIRRYING
WHIRS
WHIRTLE
WHIRTLES
WHISH
WHISHED
WHISHES
WHISHING
WHISHT
WHISHTED
WHISHTING
WHISHTS
WHISK
WHISKED
WHISKER
WHISKERED
WHISKERS
WHISKERY
WHISKET
WHISKETS
WHISKEY
WHISKEYS
WHISKIES

WHISKING
WHISKS
WHISKY
WHISPER
WHISPERED
WHISPERER
WHISPERS
WHISPERY
WHISS
WHISSED
WHISSES
WHISSING
WHIST
WHISTED
WHISTING
WHISTLE
WHISTLED
WHISTLER
WHISTLERS
WHISTLES
WHISTLING
WHISTS
WHIT
WHITE
WHITEBAIT
WHITEBASS
WHITEBEAM
WHITECAP
WHITECAPS
WHITECOAT
WHITECOMB
WHITED
WHITEDAMP
WHITEFACE
WHITEFISH
WHITEFLY
WHITEHEAD
WHITELY
WHITEN
WHITENED
WHITENER
WHITENERS
WHITENESS
WHITENING
WHITENS
WHITEOUT
WHITEOUTS
WHITEPOT
WHITEPOTS
WHITER
WHITES
WHITEST
WHITETAIL
WHITEWALL
WHITEWARE
WHITEWASH
WHITEWING
WHITEWOOD

667

WHITEY	WHOEVER	WHOOTING	WIBBLED
WHITEYS	WHOLE	WHOOTS	WIBBLES
WHITHER	WHOLEFOOD	WHOP	WIBBLING
WHITHERED	WHOLEMEAL	WHOPPED	WICCA
WHITHERS	WHOLENESS	WHOPPER	WICCAN
WHITIER	WHOLES	WHOPPERS	WICCANS
WHITIES	WHOLESALE	WHOPPING	WICCAS
WHITIEST	WHOLESOME	WHOPPINGS	WICE
WHITING	WHOLISM	WHOPS	WICH
WHITINGS	WHOLISMS	WHORE	WICHES
WHITISH	WHOLIST	WHORED	WICK
WHITLING	WHOLISTIC	WHOREDOM	WICKAPE
WHITLINGS	WHOLISTS	WHOREDOMS	WICKAPES
WHITLOW	WHOLLY	WHORES	WICKED
WHITLOWS	WHOM	WHORESON	WICKEDER
WHITRACK	WHOMBLE	WHORESONS	WICKEDEST
WHITRACKS	WHOMBLED	WHORING	WICKEDLY
WHITRET	WHOMBLES	WHORISH	WICKEDS
WHITRETS	WHOMBLING	WHORISHLY	WICKEN
WHITRICK	WHOMEVER	WHORL	WICKENS
WHITRICKS	WHOMMLE	WHORLBAT	WICKER
WHITS	WHOMMLED	WHORLBATS	WICKERED
WHITSTER	WHOMMLES	WHORLED	WICKERS
WHITSTERS	WHOMMLING	WHORLS	WICKET
WHITTAW	WHOMP	WHORT	WICKETS
WHITTAWER	WHOMPED	WHORTLE	WICKIES
WHITTAWS	WHOMPING	WHORTLES	WICKING
WHITTER	WHOMPS	WHORTS	WICKINGS
WHITTERED	WHOMSO	WHOSE	WICKIUP
WHITTERS	WHOOBUB	WHOSEVER	WICKIUPS
WHITTLE	WHOOBUBS	WHOSIS	WICKLESS
WHITTLED	WHOOF	WHOSISES	WICKS
WHITTLER	WHOOFED	WHOSO	WICKTHING
WHITTLERS	WHOOFING	WHOSOEVER	WICKY
WHITTLES	WHOOFS	WHOT	WICKYUP
WHITTLING	WHOOP	WHOW	WICKYUPS
WHITTRET	WHOOPED	WHUMMLE	WICOPIES
WHITTRETS	WHOOPEE	WHUMMLED	WICOPY
WHITY	WHOOPEES	WHUMMLES	WIDDER
WHIZ	WHOOPER	WHUMMLING	WIDDERS
WHIZBANG	WHOOPERS	WHUMP	WIDDIE
WHIZBANGS	WHOOPIE	WHUMPED	WIDDIES
WHIZZ	WHOOPIES	WHUMPING	WIDDLE
WHIZZBANG	WHOOPING	WHUMPS	WIDDLED
WHIZZED	WHOOPINGS	WHUNSTANE	WIDDLES
WHIZZER	WHOOPLA	WHUP	WIDDLING
WHIZZERS	WHOOPLAS	WHUPPED	WIDDY
WHIZZES	WHOOPS	WHUPPING	WIDE
WHIZZIER	WHOOPSIE	WHUPS	WIDEAWAKE
WHIZZIEST	WHOOPSIES	WHY	WIDEBAND
WHIZZING	WHOOSH	WHYDAH	WIDEBODY
WHIZZINGS	WHOOSHED	WHYDAHS	WIDELY
WHIZZY	WHOOSHES	WHYDUNIT	WIDEN
WHO	WHOOSHING	WHYDUNITS	WIDENED
WHOA	WHOOSIS	WHYDUNNIT	WIDENER
WHODUNIT	WHOOSISES	WHYEVER	WIDENERS
WHODUNITS	WHOOT	WHYS	WIDENESS
WHODUNNIT	WHOOTED	WIBBLE	WIDENING

WIDENS	WIFEY	WILDCAT	WILLFULLY
WIDEOUT	WIFEYS	WILDCATS	WILLIAM
WIDEOUTS	WIFIE	WILDED	WILLIAMS
WIDER	WIFIES	WILDER	WILLIE
WIDES	WIFING	WILDERED	WILLIED
WIDEST	WIFTIER	WILDERING	WILLIES
WIDGEON	WIFTIEST	WILDERS	WILLING
WIDGEONS	WIFTY	WILDEST	WILLINGER
WIDGET	WIG	WILDFIRE	WILLINGLY
WIDGETS	WIGAN	WILDFIRES	WILLIWAU
WIDGIE	WIGANS	WILDFOWL	WILLIWAUS
WIDGIES	WIGEON	WILDFOWLS	WILLIWAW
WIDISH	WIGEONS	WILDGRAVE	WILLIWAWS
WIDOW	WIGGA	WILDING	WILLOW
WIDOWBIRD	WIGGAS	WILDINGS	WILLOWED
WIDOWED	WIGGED	WILDISH	WILLOWER
WIDOWER	WIGGER	WILDLAND	WILLOWERS
WIDOWERED	WIGGERIES	WILDLANDS	WILLOWIER
WIDOWERS	WIGGERS	WILDLIFE	WILLOWING
WIDOWHOOD	WIGGERY	WILDLIFES	WILLOWISH
WIDOWING	WIGGIER	WILDLING	WILLOWS
WIDOWMAN	WIGGIEST	WILDLINGS	WILLOWY
WIDOWMEN	WIGGING	WILDLY	WILLPOWER
WIDOWS	WIGGINGS	WILDNESS	WILLS
WIDTH	WIGGLE	WILDS	WILLY
WIDTHS	WIGGLED	WILDWOOD	WILLYARD
WIDTHWAY	WIGGLER	WILDWOODS	WILLYART
WIDTHWAYS	WIGGLERS	WILE	WILLYING
WIDTHWISE	WIGGLES	WILED	WILLYWAW
WIEL	WIGGLIER	WILEFUL	WILLYWAWS
WIELD	WIGGLIEST	WILES	WILT
WIELDABLE	WIGGLING	WILFUL	WILTED
WIELDED	WIGGLY	WILFULLY	WILTING
WIELDER	WIGGY	WILGA	WILTJA
WIELDERS	WIGHT	WILGAS	WILTJAS
WIELDIER	WIGHTED	WILI	WILTS
WIELDIEST	WIGHTING	WILIER	WILY
WIELDING	WIGHTLY	WILIEST	WIMBLE
WIELDLESS	WIGHTS	WILILY	WIMBLED
WIELDS	WIGLESS	WILINESS	WIMBLES
WIELDY	WIGLET	WILING	WIMBLING
WIELS	WIGLETS	WILIS	WIMBREL
WIENER	WIGLIKE	WILJA	WIMBRELS
WIENERS	WIGMAKER	WILJAS	WIMMIN
WIENIE	WIGMAKERS	WILL	WIMP
WIENIES	WIGS	WILLABLE	WIMPED
WIFE	WIGWAG	WILLED	WIMPIER
WIFED	WIGWAGGED	WILLEMITE	WIMPIEST
WIFEDOM	WIGWAGGER	WILLER	WIMPINESS
WIFEDOMS	WIGWAGS	WILLERS	WIMPING
WIFEHOOD	WIGWAM	WILLEST	WIMPISH
WIFEHOODS	WIGWAMS	WILLET	WIMPISHLY
WIFELESS	WIKIUP	WILLETS	WIMPLE
WIFELIER	WIKIUPS	WILLEY	WIMPLED
WIFELIEST	WILCO	WILLEYED	WIMPLES
WIFELIKE	WILD	WILLEYING	WIMPLING
WIFELY	WILDCARD	WILLEYS	WIMPS
WIFES	WILDCARDS	WILLFUL	WIMPY

WIN	WINDIGO	WINEBERRY	WINK
WINCE	WINDIGOS	WINED	WINKED
WINCED	WINDILY	WINEGLASS	WINKER
WINCER	WINDINESS	WINELESS	WINKERS
WINCERS	WINDING	WINEMAKER	WINKING
WINCES	WINDINGLY	WINEPRESS	WINKINGLY
WINCEY	WINDINGS	WINERIES	WINKINGS
WINCEYS	WINDLASS	WINERY	WINKLE
WINCH	WINDLE	WINES	WINKLED
WINCHED	WINDLED	WINESAP	WINKLER
WINCHER	WINDLES	WINESAPS	WINKLERS
WINCHERS	WINDLESS	WINESHOP	WINKLES
WINCHES	WINDLING	WINESHOPS	WINKLING
WINCHING	WINDLINGS	WINESKIN	WINKS
WINCHMAN	WINDMILL	WINESKINS	WINLESS
WINCHMEN	WINDMILLS	WINESOP	WINN
WINCING	WINDOCK	WINESOPS	WINNA
WINCINGS	WINDOCKS	WINEY	WINNABLE
WINCOPIPE	WINDORE	WING	WINNARD
WIND	WINDORES	WINGBACK	WINNARDS
WINDABLE	WINDOW	WINGBACKS	WINNED
WINDAC	WINDOWED	WINGBEAT	WINNER
WINDACS	WINDOWING	WINGBEATS	WINNERS
WINDAGE	WINDOWS	WINGBOW	WINNING
WINDAGES	WINDOWY	WINGBOWS	WINNINGLY
WINDAS	WINDPIPE	WINGCHAIR	WINNINGS
WINDASES	WINDPIPES	WINGDING	WINNLE
WINDBAG	WINDPROOF	WINGDINGS	WINNLES
WINDBAGS	WINDRING	WINGE	WINNOCK
WINDBELL	WINDROSE	WINGED	WINNOCKS
WINDBELLS	WINDROSES	WINGEDLY	WINNOW
WINDBILL	WINDROW	WINGEING	WINNOWED
WINDBILLS	WINDROWED	WINGER	WINNOWER
WINDBLAST	WINDROWER	WINGERS	WINNOWERS
WINDBLOW	WINDROWS	WINGES	WINNOWING
WINDBLOWN	WINDS	WINGIER	WINNOWS
WINDBLOWS	WINDSAIL	WINGIEST	WINNS
WINDBORNE	WINDSAILS	WINGING	WINO
WINDBOUND	WINDSES	WINGLESS	WINOES
WINDBREAK	WINDSHAKE	WINGLET	WINOS
WINDBURN	WINDSHIP	WINGLETS	WINS
WINDBURNS	WINDSHIPS	WINGLIKE	WINSEY
WINDBURNT	WINDSOCK	WINGMAN	WINSEYS
WINDCHILL	WINDSOCKS	WINGMEN	WINSOME
WINDED	WINDSTORM	WINGOVER	WINSOMELY
WINDER	WINDSURF	WINGOVERS	WINSOMER
WINDERS	WINDSURFS	WINGS	WINSOMEST
WINDFALL	WINDSWEPT	WINGSPAN	WINTER
WINDFALLS	WINDTHROW	WINGSPANS	WINTERED
WINDFLAW	WINDTIGHT	WINGSUIT	WINTERER
WINDFLAWS	WINDUP	WINGSUITS	WINTERERS
WINDGALL	WINDUPS	WINGTIP	WINTERFED
WINDGALLS	WINDWARD	WINGTIPS	WINTERIER
WINDGUN	WINDWARDS	WINGY	WINTERING
WINDGUNS	WINDWAY	WINIER	WINTERISE
WINDHOVER	WINDWAYS	WINIEST	WINTERISH
WINDIER	WINDY	WINING	WINTERIZE
WINDIEST	WINE	WINISH	WINTERLY

WINTERS	WIRINGS	WISPISH	WITHERERS
WINTERY	WIRRA	WISPLIKE	WITHERING
WINTLE	WIRRAH	WISPS	WITHERITE
WINTLED	WIRRAHS	WISPY	WITHEROD
WINTLES	WIRRICOW	WISS	WITHERODS
WINTLING	WIRRICOWS	WISSED	WITHERS
WINTRIER	WIRY	WISSES	WITHES
WINTRIEST	WIS	WISSING	WITHHAULT
WINTRILY	WISARD	WIST	WITHHELD
WINTRY	WISARDS	WISTARIA	WITHHOLD
WINY	WISDOM	WISTARIAS	WITHHOLDS
WINZE	WISDOMS	WISTED	WITHIER
WINZES	WISE	WISTERIA	WITHIES
WIPE	WISEACRE	WISTERIAS	WITHIEST
WIPED	WISEACRES	WISTFUL	WITHIN
WIPEOUT	WISEASS	WISTFULLY	WITHING
WIPEOUTS	WISEASSES	WISTING	WITHINS
WIPER	WISECRACK	WISTITI	WITHOUT
WIPERS	WISED	WISTITIS	WITHOUTEN
WIPES	WISEGUY	WISTLY	WITHOUTS
WIPING	WISEGUYS	WISTS	WITHS
WIPINGS	WISELIER	WIT	WITHSTAND
WIPPEN	WISELIEST	WITAN	WITHSTOOD
WIPPENS	WISELING	WITANS	WITHWIND
WIRABLE	WISELINGS	WITBLITS	WITHWINDS
WIRE	WISELY	WITCH	WITHY
WIRED	WISENESS	WITCHED	WITHYWIND
WIREDRAW	WISENT	WITCHEN	WITING
WIREDRAWN	WISENTS	WITCHENS	WITLESS
WIREDRAWS	WISER	WITCHERY	WITLESSLY
WIREDREW	WISES	WITCHES	WITLING
WIREGRASS	WISEST	WITCHETTY	WITLINGS
WIREHAIR	WISEWOMAN	WITCHHOOD	WITLOOF
WIREHAIRS	WISEWOMEN	WITCHIER	WITLOOFS
WIRELESS	WISH	WITCHIEST	WITNESS
WIRELIKE	WISHA	WITCHING	WITNESSED
WIREMAN	WISHBONE	WITCHINGS	WITNESSER
WIREMEN	WISHBONES	WITCHKNOT	WITNESSES
WIREPHOTO	WISHED	WITCHLIKE	WITNEY
WIRER	WISHER	WITCHWEED	WITNEYS
WIRERS	WISHERS	WITCHY	WITS
WIRES	WISHES	WITE	WITTED
WIRETAP	WISHFUL	WITED	WITTER
WIRETAPS	WISHFULLY	WITELESS	WITTERED
WIREWAY	WISHING	WITES	WITTERING
WIREWAYS	WISHINGS	WITGAT	WITTERS
WIREWORK	WISHLESS	WITGATS	WITTICISM
WIREWORKS	WISHT	WITH	WITTIER
WIREWORM	WISING	WITHAL	WITTIEST
WIREWORMS	WISKET	WITHDRAW	WITTILY
WIREWOVE	WISKETS	WITHDRAWN	WITTINESS
WIRIER	WISP	WITHDRAWS	WITTING
WIRIEST	WISPED	WITHDREW	WITTINGLY
WIRILDA	WISPIER	WITHE	WITTINGS
WIRILDAS	WISPIEST	WITHED	WITTOL
WIRILY	WISPILY	WITHER	WITTOLLY
WIRINESS	WISPINESS	WITHERED	WITTOLS
WIRING	WISPING	WITHERER	WITTY

WITWALL
WITWALLS
WITWANTON
WIVE
WIVED
WIVEHOOD
WIVEHOODS
WIVER
WIVERN
WIVERNS
WIVERS
WIVES
WIVING
WIZ
WIZARD
WIZARDLY
WIZARDRY
WIZARDS
WIZEN
WIZENED
WIZENING
WIZENS
WIZES
WIZIER
WIZIERS
WIZZEN
WIZZENS
WIZZES
WO
WOAD
WOADED
WOADS
WOADWAX
WOADWAXEN
WOADWAXES
WOALD
WOALDS
WOBBEGONG
WOBBLE
WOBBLED
WOBBLER
WOBBLERS
WOBBLES
WOBBLIER
WOBBLIES
WOBBLIEST
WOBBLING
WOBBLINGS
WOBBLY
WOBEGONE
WOCK
WOCKS
WODGE
WODGES
WOE
WOEBEGONE
WOEFUL
WOEFULLER

WOEFULLY
WOENESS
WOENESSES
WOES
WOESOME
WOF
WOFS
WOFUL
WOFULLER
WOFULLEST
WOFULLY
WOFULNESS
WOG
WOGGISH
WOGGLE
WOGGLES
WOGS
WOIWODE
WOIWODES
WOK
WOKE
WOKEN
WOKKA
WOKS
WOLD
WOLDS
WOLF
WOLFBERRY
WOLFED
WOLFER
WOLFERS
WOLFFISH
WOLFHOUND
WOLFING
WOLFINGS
WOLFISH
WOLFISHLY
WOLFKIN
WOLFKINS
WOLFLIKE
WOLFLING
WOLFLINGS
WOLFRAM
WOLFRAMS
WOLFS
WOLFSBANE
WOLFSKIN
WOLFSKINS
WOLLIES
WOLLY
WOLVE
WOLVED
WOLVER
WOLVERENE
WOLVERINE
WOLVERS
WOLVES
WOLVING

WOLVINGS
WOLVISH
WOLVISHLY
WOMAN
WOMANED
WOMANHOOD
WOMANING
WOMANISE
WOMANISED
WOMANISER
WOMANISES
WOMANISH
WOMANISM
WOMANISMS
WOMANIST
WOMANISTS
WOMANIZE
WOMANIZED
WOMANIZER
WOMANIZES
WOMANKIND
WOMANLESS
WOMANLIER
WOMANLIKE
WOMANLY
WOMANNESS
WOMANS
WOMB
WOMBAT
WOMBATS
WOMBED
WOMBIER
WOMBIEST
WOMBING
WOMBLIKE
WOMBS
WOMBY
WOMEN
WOMENFOLK
WOMENKIND
WOMERA
WOMERAS
WOMMERA
WOMMERAS
WOMMIT
WOMMITS
WOMYN
WON
WONDER
WONDERED
WONDERER
WONDERERS
WONDERFUL
WONDERING
WONDERKID
WONDEROUS
WONDERS
WONDRED

WONDROUS
WONGA
WONGAS
WONGI
WONGIED
WONGIING
WONGIS
WONING
WONINGS
WONK
WONKIER
WONKIEST
WONKS
WONKY
WONNED
WONNER
WONNERS
WONNING
WONNINGS
WONS
WONT
WONTED
WONTEDLY
WONTING
WONTLESS
WONTON
WONTONS
WONTS
WOO
WOOBUT
WOOBUTS
WOOD
WOODBIN
WOODBIND
WOODBINDS
WOODBINE
WOODBINES
WOODBINS
WOODBLOCK
WOODBORER
WOODBOX
WOODBOXES
WOODCHAT
WOODCHATS
WOODCHIP
WOODCHIPS
WOODCHOP
WOODCHOPS
WOODCHUCK
WOODCOCK
WOODCOCKS
WOODCRAFT
WOODCUT
WOODCUTS
WOODED
WOODEN
WOODENED
WOODENER

WOODENEST	WOODSKINS	WOOLFATS	WOOSELL
WOODENING	WOODSMAN	WOOLFELL	WOOSELLS
WOODENLY	WOODSMEN	WOOLFELLS	WOOSELS
WOODENS	WOODSPITE	WOOLHAT	WOOSES
WOODENTOP	WOODSTONE	WOOLHATS	WOOSH
WOODFREE	WOODSTOVE	WOOLIE	WOOSHED
WOODGRAIN	WOODSY	WOOLIER	WOOSHES
WOODHEN	WOODTONE	WOOLIES	WOOSHING
WOODHENS	WOODTONES	WOOLIEST	WOOT
WOODHOLE	WOODWALE	WOOLINESS	WOOTZ
WOODHOLES	WOODWALES	WOOLLED	WOOTZES
WOODHORSE	WOODWARD	WOOLLEN	WOOZIER
WOODHOUSE	WOODWARDS	WOOLLENS	WOOZIEST
WOODIE	WOODWAX	WOOLLIER	WOOZILY
WOODIER	WOODWAXEN	WOOLLIES	WOOZINESS
WOODIES	WOODWAXES	WOOLLIEST	WOOZY
WOODIEST	WOODWIND	WOOLLIKE	WOP
WOODINESS	WOODWINDS	WOOLLILY	WOPPED
WOODING	WOODWORK	WOOLLY	WOPPING
WOODLAND	WOODWORKS	WOOLMAN	WOPS
WOODLANDS	WOODWORM	WOOLMEN	WORCESTER
WOODLARK	WOODWORMS	WOOLPACK	WORD
WOODLARKS	WOODWOSE	WOOLPACKS	WORDAGE
WOODLESS	WOODWOSES	WOOLS	WORDAGES
WOODLICE	WOODY	WOOLSACK	WORDBOOK
WOODLORE	WOODYARD	WOOLSACKS	WORDBOOKS
WOODLORES	WOODYARDS	WOOLSEY	WORDBOUND
WOODLOT	WOOED	WOOLSEYS	WORDBREAK
WOODLOTS	WOOER	WOOLSHED	WORDED
WOODLOUSE	WOOERS	WOOLSHEDS	WORDGAME
WOODMAN	WOOF	WOOLSKIN	WORDGAMES
WOODMEAL	WOOFED	WOOLSKINS	WORDIER
WOODMEALS	WOOFER	WOOLWARD	WORDIEST
WOODMEN	WOOFERS	WOOLWORK	WORDILY
WOODMICE	WOOFIER	WOOLWORKS	WORDINESS
WOODMOUSE	WOOFIEST	WOOLY	WORDING
WOODNESS	WOOFING	WOOMERA	WORDINGS
WOODNOTE	WOOFS	WOOMERANG	WORDISH
WOODNOTES	WOOFTER	WOOMERAS	WORDLESS
WOODPILE	WOOFTERS	WOON	WORDLORE
WOODPILES	WOOFY	WOONED	WORDLORES
WOODPRINT	WOOING	WOONING	WORDPLAY
WOODREEVE	WOOINGLY	WOONS	WORDPLAYS
WOODROOF	WOOINGS	WOOPIE	WORDS
WOODROOFS	WOOL	WOOPIES	WORDSMITH
WOODRUFF	WOOLD	WOOPS	WORDY
WOODRUFFS	WOOLDED	WOOPSED	WORE
WOODRUSH	WOOLDER	WOOPSES	WORK
WOODS	WOOLDERS	WOOPSING	WORKABLE
WOODSCREW	WOOLDING	WOORALI	WORKABLY
WOODSHED	WOOLDINGS	WOORALIS	WORKADAY
WOODSHEDS	WOOLDS	WOORARA	WORKADAYS
WOODSHOCK	WOOLED	WOORARAS	WORKBAG
WOODSIA	WOOLEN	WOORARI	WORKBAGS
WOODSIAS	WOOLENS	WOORARIS	WORKBENCH
WOODSIER	WOOLER	WOOS	WORKBOAT
WOODSIEST	WOOLERS	WOOSE	WORKBOATS
WOODSKIN	WOOLFAT	WOOSEL	WORKBOOK

WORKBOOKS	WORKWOMEN	WORRITING	WOUBIT
WORKBOX	WORLD	WORRITS	WOUBITS
WORKBOXES	WORLDBEAT	WORRY	WOULD
WORKDAY	WORLDED	WORRYCOW	WOULDEST
WORKDAYS	WORLDLIER	WORRYCOWS	WOULDS
WORKED	WORLDLING	WORRYGUTS	WOULDST
WORKER	WORLDLY	WORRYING	WOUND
WORKERIST	WORLDS	WORRYINGS	WOUNDABLE
WORKERS	WORLDVIEW	WORRYWART	WOUNDED
WORKFARE	WORLDWIDE	WORSE	WOUNDEDLY
WORKFARES	WORM	WORSED	WOUNDER
WORKFLOW	WORMCAST	WORSEN	WOUNDERS
WORKFLOWS	WORMCASTS	WORSENED	WOUNDILY
WORKFOLK	WORMED	WORSENESS	WOUNDING
WORKFOLKS	WORMER	WORSENING	WOUNDINGS
WORKFORCE	WORMERIES	WORSENS	WOUNDLESS
WORKFUL	WORMERS	WORSER	WOUNDS
WORKGIRL	WORMERY	WORSES	WOUNDWORT
WORKGIRLS	WORMFLIES	WORSET	WOUNDY
WORKGROUP	WORMFLY	WORSETS	WOURALI
WORKHORSE	WORMGEAR	WORSHIP	WOURALIS
WORKHOUR	WORMGEARS	WORSHIPED	WOVE
WORKHOURS	WORMHOLE	WORSHIPER	WOVEN
WORKHOUSE	WORMHOLED	WORSHIPS	WOVENS
WORKING	WORMHOLES	WORSING	WOW
WORKINGS	WORMIER	WORST	WOWED
WORKLESS	WORMIEST	WORSTED	WOWEE
WORKLOAD	WORMIL	WORSTEDS	WOWF
WORKLOADS	WORMILS	WORSTING	WOWFER
WORKMAN	WORMINESS	WORSTS	WOWFEST
WORKMANLY	WORMING	WORT	WOWING
WORKMATE	WORMISH	WORTH	WOWS
WORKMATES	WORMLIKE	WORTHED	WOWSER
WORKMEN	WORMROOT	WORTHFUL	WOWSERS
WORKOUT	WORMROOTS	WORTHIED	WOX
WORKOUTS	WORMS	WORTHIER	WOXEN
WORKPIECE	WORMSEED	WORTHIES	WRACK
WORKPLACE	WORMSEEDS	WORTHIEST	WRACKED
WORKPRINT	WORMWOOD	WORTHILY	WRACKFUL
WORKROOM	WORMWOODS	WORTHING	WRACKING
WORKROOMS	WORMY	WORTHLESS	WRACKS
WORKS	WORN	WORTHS	WRAITH
WORKSHEET	WORNNESS	WORTHY	WRAITHS
WORKSHOP	WORRAL	WORTHYING	WRANG
WORKSHOPS	WORRALS	WORTLE	WRANGED
WORKSHY	WORREL	WORTLES	WRANGING
WORKSOME	WORRELS	WORTS	WRANGLE
WORKSPACE	WORRICOW	WOS	WRANGLED
WORKTABLE	WORRICOWS	WOSBIRD	WRANGLER
WORKTOP	WORRIED	WOSBIRDS	WRANGLERS
WORKTOPS	WORRIEDLY	WOST	WRANGLES
WORKUP	WORRIER	WOT	WRANGLING
WORKUPS	WORRIERS	WOTCHER	WRANGS
WORKWEAR	WORRIES	WOTS	WRAP
WORKWEARS	WORRIMENT	WOTTED	WRAPOVER
WORKWEEK	WORRISOME	WOTTEST	WRAPOVERS
WORKWEEKS	WORRIT	WOTTETH	WRAPPAGE
WORKWOMAN	WORRITED	WOTTING	WRAPPAGES

WRAPPED	WREATHIER	WRIGHT	WRONGEST
WRAPPER	WREATHING	WRIGHTS	WRONGFUL
WRAPPERED	WREATHS	WRING	WRONGING
WRAPPERS	WREATHY	WRINGED	WRONGLY
WRAPPING	WRECK	WRINGER	WRONGNESS
WRAPPINGS	WRECKAGE	WRINGERS	WRONGOUS
WRAPROUND	WRECKAGES	WRINGING	WRONGS
WRAPS	WRECKED	WRINGINGS	WROOT
WRAPT	WRECKER	WRINGS	WROOTED
WRASSE	WRECKERS	WRINKLE	WROOTING
WRASSES	WRECKFISH	WRINKLED	WROOTS
WRASSLE	WRECKFUL	WRINKLES	WROTE
WRASSLED	WRECKING	WRINKLIER	WROTH
WRASSLES	WRECKINGS	WRINKLIES	WROTHFUL
WRASSLING	WRECKS	WRINKLING	WROUGHT
WRAST	WREN	WRINKLY	WRUNG
WRASTED	WRENCH	WRIST	WRY
WRASTING	WRENCHED	WRISTBAND	WRYBILL
WRASTLE	WRENCHER	WRISTIER	WRYBILLS
WRASTLED	WRENCHERS	WRISTIEST	WRYER
WRASTLES	WRENCHES	WRISTLET	WRYEST
WRASTLING	WRENCHING	WRISTLETS	WRYING
WRASTS	WRENS	WRISTLOCK	WRYLY
WRATE	WREST	WRISTS	WRYNECK
WRATH	WRESTED	WRISTY	WRYNECKS
WRATHED	WRESTER	WRIT	WRYNESS
WRATHFUL	WRESTERS	WRITABLE	WRYNESSES
WRATHIER	WRESTING	WRITATIVE	WRYTHEN
WRATHIEST	WRESTLE	WRITE	WUD
WRATHILY	WRESTLED	WRITEABLE	WUDDED
WRATHING	WRESTLER	WRITER	WUDDING
WRATHLESS	WRESTLERS	WRITERESS	WUDJULA
WRATHS	WRESTLES	WRITERLY	WUDJULAS
WRATHY	WRESTLING	WRITERS	WUDS
WRAWL	WRESTS	WRITES	WUDU
WRAWLED	WRETCH	WRITHE	WUDUS
WRAWLING	WRETCHED	WRITHED	WUKKAS
WRAWLS	WRETCHES	WRITHEN	WULFENITE
WRAXLE	WRETHE	WRITHER	WULL
WRAXLED	WRETHED	WRITHERS	WULLED
WRAXLES	WRETHES	WRITHES	WULLING
WRAXLING	WRETHING	WRITHING	WULLS
WRAXLINGS	WRICK	WRITHINGS	WUNNER
WREAK	WRICKED	WRITHLED	WUNNERS
WREAKED	WRICKING	WRITING	WURLEY
WREAKER	WRICKS	WRITINGS	WURLEYS
WREAKERS	WRIED	WRITS	WURLIE
WREAKFUL	WRIER	WRITTEN	WURLIES
WREAKING	WRIES	WRIZLED	WURST
WREAKLESS	WRIEST	WROATH	WURSTS
WREAKS	WRIGGLE	WROATHS	WURTZITE
WREATH	WRIGGLED	WROKE	WURTZITES
WREATHE	WRIGGLER	WROKEN	WURZEL
WREATHED	WRIGGLERS	WRONG	WURZELS
WREATHEN	WRIGGLES	WRONGDOER	WUS
WREATHER	WRIGGLIER	WRONGED	WUSES
WREATHERS	WRIGGLING	WRONGER	WUSHU
WREATHES	WRIGGLY	WRONGERS	WUSHUS

WUSS
WUSSES
WUSSIER
WUSSIES
WUSSIEST
WUSSY
WUTHER
WUTHERED
WUTHERING
WUTHERS
WUXIA
WUXIAS
WUZZLE
WUZZLED
WUZZLES
WUZZLING
WYANDOTTE
WYCH
WYCHES
WYE
WYES
WYLE
WYLED
WYLES
WYLIECOAT
WYLING
WYN
WYND
WYNDS
WYNN
WYNNS
WYNS
WYSIWYG
WYTE
WYTED
WYTES
WYTING
WYVERN
WYVERNS

X

XANTHAM	XERANSES	XYLIDINE
XANTHAMS	XERANSIS	XYLIDINES
XANTHAN	XERANTIC	XYLIDINS
XANTHANS	XERAPHIM	XYLITOL
XANTHATE	XERAPHIMS	XYLITOLS
XANTHATES	XERARCH	XYLOCARP
XANTHEIN	XERASIA	XYLOCARPS
XANTHEINS	XERASIAS	XYLOGEN
XANTHENE	XERIC	XYLOGENS
XANTHENES	XERICALLY	XYLOGRAPH
XANTHIC	XERISCAPE	XYLOID
XANTHIN	XEROCHASY	XYLOIDIN
XANTHINE	XERODERMA	XYLOIDINE
XANTHINES	XEROMA	XYLOIDINS
XANTHINS	XEROMAS	XYLOL
XANTHISM	XEROMATA	XYLOLOGY
XANTHISMS	XEROMORPH	XYLOLS
XANTHOMA	XEROPHAGY	XYLOMA
XANTHOMAS	XEROPHILE	XYLOMAS
XANTHONE	XEROPHILY	XYLOMATA
XANTHONES	XEROPHYTE	XYLOMETER
XANTHOUS	XEROSERE	XYLONIC
XANTHOXYL	XEROSERES	XYLONITE
XEBEC	XEROSES	XYLONITES
XEBECS	XEROSIS	XYLOPHAGE
XENIA	XEROSTOMA	XYLOPHONE
XENIAL	XEROTES	XYLORIMBA
XENIAS	XEROTIC	XYLOSE
XENIC	XEROX	XYLOSES
XENIUM	XEROXED	XYLOTOMY
XENOBLAST	XEROXES	XYLYL
XENOCRYST	XEROXING	XYLYLS
XENOGAMY	XERUS	XYST
XENOGENIC	XERUSES	XYSTER
XENOGENY	XI	XYSTERS
XENOGRAFT	XIPHOID	XYSTI
XENOLITH	XIPHOIDAL	XYSTOI
XENOLITHS	XIPHOIDS	XYSTOS
XENOMANIA	XIPHOPAGI	XYSTS
XENOMENIA	XIS	XYSTUS
XENON	XOANA	
XENONS	XOANON	
XENOPHILE	XU	
XENOPHOBE	XYLAN	
XENOPHOBY	XYLANS	
XENOPHYA	XYLEM	
XENOPUS	XYLEMS	
XENOPUSES	XYLENE	
XENOTIME	XYLENES	
XENOTIMES	XYLENOL	
XENURINE	XYLENOLS	
XERAFIN	XYLIC	
XERAFINS	XYLIDIN	

—Y—

YA
YAAR
YAARS
YABA
YABBA
YABBAS
YABBER
YABBERED
YABBERING
YABBERS
YABBIE
YABBIED
YABBIES
YABBY
YABBYING
YACCA
YACCAS
YACHT
YACHTED
YACHTER
YACHTERS
YACHTIE
YACHTIES
YACHTING
YACHTINGS
YACHTMAN
YACHTMEN
YACHTS
YACHTSMAN
YACHTSMEN
YACK
YACKA
YACKAS
YACKED
YACKER
YACKERS
YACKING
YACKS
YAD
YADS
YAE
YAFF
YAFFED
YAFFING
YAFFLE
YAFFLES
YAFFS
YAG
YAGER
YAGERS
YAGGER
YAGGERS
YAGI

YAGIS
YAGS
YAH
YAHOO
YAHOOISM
YAHOOISMS
YAHOOS
YAHRZEIT
YAHRZEITS
YAHS
YAIRD
YAIRDS
YAK
YAKHDAN
YAKHDANS
YAKIMONO
YAKIMONOS
YAKITORI
YAKITORIS
YAKKA
YAKKAS
YAKKED
YAKKER
YAKKERS
YAKKING
YAKOW
YAKOWS
YAKS
YAKUZA
YALD
YALE
YALES
YAM
YAMALKA
YAMALKAS
YAMEN
YAMENS
YAMMER
YAMMERED
YAMMERER
YAMMERERS
YAMMERING
YAMMERS
YAMPIES
YAMPY
YAMS
YAMULKA
YAMULKAS
YAMUN
YAMUNS
YANG
YANGS
YANK

YANKED
YANKER
YANKERS
YANKIE
YANKIES
YANKING
YANKS
YANQUI
YANQUIS
YANTRA
YANTRAS
YAOURT
YAOURTS
YAP
YAPOCK
YAPOCKS
YAPOK
YAPOKS
YAPON
YAPONS
YAPP
YAPPED
YAPPER
YAPPERS
YAPPIE
YAPPIER
YAPPIES
YAPPIEST
YAPPING
YAPPINGLY
YAPPS
YAPPY
YAPS
YAPSTER
YAPSTERS
YAQONA
YAQONAS
YAR
YARCO
YARCOS
YARD
YARDAGE
YARDAGES
YARDANG
YARDANGS
YARDARM
YARDARMS
YARDBIRD
YARDBIRDS
YARDED
YARDER
YARDERS
YARDING

YARDINGS
YARDLAND
YARDLANDS
YARDMAN
YARDMEN
YARDS
YARDSTICK
YARDWAND
YARDWANDS
YARDWORK
YARDWORKS
YARE
YARELY
YARER
YAREST
YARFA
YARFAS
YARK
YARKED
YARKING
YARKS
YARMELKE
YARMELKES
YARMULKA
YARMULKAS
YARMULKE
YARMULKES
YARN
YARNED
YARNER
YARNERS
YARNING
YARNS
YARPHA
YARPHAS
YARR
YARRAMAN
YARRAMANS
YARRAMEN
YARRAN
YARRANS
YARROW
YARROWS
YARRS
YARTA
YARTAS
YARTO
YARTOS
YASHMAC
YASHMACS
YASHMAK
YASHMAKS
YASMAK

YASMAKS	YBORE	YEAS	YELLOWY
YATAGAN	YBOUND	YEASAYER	YELLS
YATAGANS	YBOUNDEN	YEASAYERS	YELM
YATAGHAN	YBRENT	YEAST	YELMED
YATAGHANS	YCLAD	YEASTED	YELMING
YATE	YCLED	YEASTIER	YELMS
YATES	YCLEEPE	YEASTIEST	YELP
YATTER	YCLEEPED	YEASTILY	YELPED
YATTERED	YCLEEPES	YEASTING	YELPER
YATTERING	YCLEEPING	YEASTLESS	YELPERS
YATTERS	YCLEPED	YEASTLIKE	YELPING
YAUD	YCLEPT	YEASTS	YELPINGS
YAUDS	YCOND	YEASTY	YELPS
YAULD	YDRAD	YEBO	YELT
YAUP	YDRED	YECCH	YELTS
YAUPED	YE	YECCHS	YEMMER
YAUPER	YEA	YECH	YEMMERS
YAUPERS	YEAD	YECHS	YEN
YAUPING	YEADING	YECHY	YENNED
YAUPON	YEADS	YEDE	YENNING
YAUPONS	YEAH	YEDES	YENS
YAUPS	YEAHS	YEDING	YENTA
YAUTIA	YEALDON	YEED	YENTAS
YAUTIAS	YEALDONS	YEEDING	YENTE
YAW	YEALING	YEEDS	YENTES
YAWED	YEALINGS	YEELIN	YEOMAN
YAWEY	YEALM	YEELINS	YEOMANLY
YAWING	YEALMED	YEGG	YEOMANRY
YAWL	YEALMING	YEGGMAN	YEOMEN
YAWLED	YEALMS	YEGGMEN	YEP
YAWLING	YEAN	YEGGS	YEPS
YAWLS	YEANED	YEH	YERBA
YAWMETER	YEANING	YELD	YERBAS
YAWMETERS	YEANLING	YELDRING	YERD
YAWN	YEANLINGS	YELDRINGS	YERDED
YAWNED	YEANS	YELDROCK	YERDING
YAWNER	YEAR	YELDROCKS	YERDS
YAWNERS	YEARBOOK	YELK	YERK
YAWNIER	YEARBOOKS	YELKS	YERKED
YAWNIEST	YEARD	YELL	YERKING
YAWNING	YEARDED	YELLED	YERKS
YAWNINGLY	YEARDING	YELLER	YERSINIA
YAWNINGS	YEARDS	YELLERS	YERSINIAE
YAWNS	YEAREND	YELLING	YERSINIAS
YAWNY	YEARENDS	YELLINGS	YES
YAWP	YEARLIES	YELLOCH	YESES
YAWPED	YEARLING	YELLOCHED	YESHIVA
YAWPER	YEARLINGS	YELLOCHS	YESHIVAH
YAWPERS	YEARLONG	YELLOW	YESHIVAHS
YAWPING	YEARLY	YELLOWED	YESHIVAS
YAWPINGS	YEARN	YELLOWER	YESHIVOT
YAWPS	YEARNED	YELLOWEST	YESHIVOTH
YAWS	YEARNER	YELLOWFIN	YESK
YAWY	YEARNERS	YELLOWIER	YESKED
YAY	YEARNING	YELLOWING	YESKING
YAYS	YEARNINGS	YELLOWISH	YESKS
YBET	YEARNS	YELLOWLY	YESSED
YBLENT	YEARS	YELLOWS	YESSES

679

YESSING
YEST
YESTER
YESTERDAY
YESTEREVE
YESTERN
YESTREEN
YESTREENS
YESTS
YESTY
YET
YETI
YETIS
YETT
YETTIE
YETTIES
YETTS
YEUK
YEUKED
YEUKING
YEUKS
YEUKY
YEVE
YEVEN
YEVES
YEVING
YEW
YEWEN
YEWS
YEX
YEXED
YEXES
YEXING
YFERE
YGLAUNST
YGO
YGOE
YIBBLES
YICKER
YICKERED
YICKERING
YICKERS
YID
YIDAKI
YIDAKIS
YIDS
YIELD
YIELDABLE
YIELDED
YIELDER
YIELDERS
YIELDING
YIELDINGS
YIELDS
YIKE
YIKED
YIKES
YIKING

YIKKER
YIKKERED
YIKKERING
YIKKERS
YILL
YILLS
YIN
YINCE
YINS
YIP
YIPE
YIPES
YIPPED
YIPPEE
YIPPER
YIPPERS
YIPPIE
YIPPIES
YIPPING
YIPPY
YIPS
YIRD
YIRDED
YIRDING
YIRDS
YIRK
YIRKED
YIRKING
YIRKS
YIRR
YIRRED
YIRRING
YIRRS
YIRTH
YIRTHS
YITE
YITES
YITIE
YITIES
YITTEN
YLEM
YLEMS
YLIKE
YLKE
YLKES
YMOLT
YMOLTEN
YMPE
YMPES
YMPING
YMPT
YNAMBU
YNAMBUS
YO
YOB
YOBBERIES
YOBBERY
YOBBISH

YOBBISHLY
YOBBISM
YOBBISMS
YOBBO
YOBBOES
YOBBOS
YOBS
YOCK
YOCKED
YOCKING
YOCKS
YOD
YODE
YODEL
YODELED
YODELER
YODELERS
YODELING
YODELLED
YODELLER
YODELLERS
YODELLING
YODELS
YODH
YODHS
YODLE
YODLED
YODLER
YODLERS
YODLES
YODLING
YODS
YOGA
YOGAS
YOGEE
YOGEES
YOGH
YOGHOURT
YOGHOURTS
YOGHS
YOGHURT
YOGHURTS
YOGI
YOGIC
YOGIN
YOGINI
YOGINIS
YOGINS
YOGIS
YOGISM
YOGISMS
YOGURT
YOGURTS
YOHIMBE
YOHIMBES
YOHIMBINE
YOICK
YOICKED

YOICKING
YOICKS
YOICKSED
YOICKSES
YOICKSING
YOJAN
YOJANA
YOJANAS
YOJANS
YOK
YOKE
YOKED
YOKEL
YOKELESS
YOKELISH
YOKELS
YOKEMATE
YOKEMATES
YOKER
YOKERS
YOKES
YOKING
YOKINGS
YOKKED
YOKKING
YOKOZUNA
YOKOZUNAS
YOKS
YOKUL
YOLD
YOLDRING
YOLDRINGS
YOLK
YOLKED
YOLKIER
YOLKIEST
YOLKLESS
YOLKS
YOLKY
YOM
YOMIM
YOMP
YOMPED
YOMPING
YOMPS
YON
YOND
YONDER
YONDERLY
YONDERS
YONI
YONIC
YONIS
YONKER
YONKERS
YONKS
YONNIE
YONNIES

YONT
YOOF
YOOFS
YOOP
YOOPS
YOPPER
YOPPERS
YORE
YORES
YORK
YORKED
YORKER
YORKERS
YORKIE
YORKIES
YORKING
YORKS
YORP
YORPED
YORPING
YORPS
YOS
YOTTABYTE
YOU
YOUK
YOUKED
YOUKING
YOUKS
YOUNG
YOUNGER
YOUNGERS
YOUNGEST
YOUNGISH
YOUNGLING
YOUNGLY
YOUNGNESS
YOUNGS
YOUNGSTER
YOUNGTH
YOUNGTHLY
YOUNGTHS
YOUNKER
YOUNKERS
YOUPON
YOUPONS
YOUR
YOURN
YOURS
YOURSELF
YOURT
YOURTS
YOUS
YOUSE
YOUTH
YOUTHEN
YOUTHENED
YOUTHENS
YOUTHFUL

YOUTHHEAD
YOUTHHOOD
YOUTHIER
YOUTHIEST
YOUTHLESS
YOUTHLY
YOUTHS
YOUTHSOME
YOUTHY
YOW
YOWE
YOWED
YOWES
YOWIE
YOWIES
YOWING
YOWL
YOWLED
YOWLER
YOWLERS
YOWLEY
YOWLEYS
YOWLING
YOWLINGS
YOWLS
YOWS
YPERITE
YPERITES
YPIGHT
YPLAST
YPLIGHT
YPSILOID
YPSILON
YPSILONS
YRAPT
YRAVISHED
YRENT
YRIVD
YRNEH
YRNEHS
YSAME
YSHEND
YSHENDING
YSHENDS
YSHENT
YSLAKED
YTOST
YTTERBIA
YTTERBIAS
YTTERBIC
YTTERBITE
YTTERBIUM
YTTERBOUS
YTTRIA
YTTRIAS
YTTRIC
YTTRIOUS
YTTRIUM

YTTRIUMS
YU
YUAN
YUANS
YUCA
YUCAS
YUCCA
YUCCAS
YUCCH
YUCH
YUCK
YUCKED
YUCKER
YUCKERS
YUCKIER
YUCKIEST
YUCKINESS
YUCKING
YUCKO
YUCKS
YUCKY
YUFT
YUFTS
YUG
YUGA
YUGARIE
YUGARIES
YUGAS
YUGS
YUK
YUKATA
YUKATAS
YUKE
YUKED
YUKES
YUKIER
YUKIEST
YUKING
YUKKED
YUKKIER
YUKKIEST
YUKKING
YUKKY
YUKO
YUKOS
YUKS
YUKY
YULAN
YULANS
YULE
YULES
YULETIDE
YULETIDES
YUM
YUMMIER
YUMMIES
YUMMIEST
YUMMINESS

YUMMO
YUMMY
YUMP
YUMPED
YUMPIE
YUMPIES
YUMPING
YUMPS
YUNX
YUNXES
YUP
YUPON
YUPONS
YUPPIE
YUPPIEDOM
YUPPIEISH
YUPPIES
YUPPIFIED
YUPPIFIES
YUPPIFY
YUPPY
YUPS
YURT
YURTA
YURTAS
YURTS
YUS
YUTZ
YUTZES
YUZU
YUZUS
YWIS
YWROKE

Z

ZA	ZAMBO	ZAPATEO	ZEALOTS
ZABAIONE	ZAMBOMBA	ZAPATEOS	ZEALOUS
ZABAIONES	ZAMBOMBAS	ZAPOTILLA	ZEALOUSLY
ZABAJONE	ZAMBOORAK	ZAPPED	ZEALS
ZABAJONES	ZAMBOS	ZAPPER	ZEAS
ZABETA	ZAMBUCK	ZAPPERS	ZEATIN
ZABETAS	ZAMBUCKS	ZAPPIER	ZEATINS
ZABRA	ZAMBUK	ZAPPIEST	ZEBEC
ZABRAS	ZAMBUKS	ZAPPING	ZEBECK
ZABTIEH	ZAMIA	ZAPPY	ZEBECKS
ZABTIEHS	ZAMIAS	ZAPS	ZEBECS
ZACATON	ZAMINDAR	ZAPTIAH	ZEBRA
ZACATONS	ZAMINDARI	ZAPTIAHS	ZEBRAFISH
ZACK	ZAMINDARS	ZAPTIEH	ZEBRAIC
ZACKS	ZAMINDARY	ZAPTIEHS	ZEBRANO
ZADDICK	ZAMOUSE	ZARAPE	ZEBRANOS
ZADDIK	ZAMOUSES	ZARAPES	ZEBRAS
ZADDIKIM	ZAMPOGNA	ZARATITE	ZEBRASS
ZADDIKS	ZAMPOGNAS	ZARATITES	ZEBRASSES
ZAFFAR	ZAMPONE	ZAREBA	ZEBRAWOOD
ZAFFARS	ZAMPONI	ZAREBAS	ZEBRINA
ZAFFER	ZAMZAWED	ZAREEBA	ZEBRINAS
ZAFFERS	ZANANA	ZAREEBAS	ZEBRINE
ZAFFIR	ZANANAS	ZARF	ZEBRINES
ZAFFIRS	ZANDER	ZARFS	ZEBRINNY
ZAFFRE	ZANDERS	ZARIBA	ZEBROID
ZAFFRES	ZANELLA	ZARIBAS	ZEBRULA
ZAFTIG	ZANELLAS	ZARNEC	ZEBRULAS
ZAG	ZANIED	ZARNECS	ZEBRULE
ZAGGED	ZANIER	ZARNICH	ZEBRULES
ZAGGING	ZANIES	ZARNICHS	ZEBU
ZAGS	ZANIEST	ZARZUELA	ZEBUB
ZAIBATSU	ZANILY	ZARZUELAS	ZEBUBS
ZAIKAI	ZANINESS	ZAS	ZEBUS
ZAIKAIS	ZANJA	ZASTRUGA	ZECCHIN
ZAIRE	ZANJAS	ZASTRUGI	ZECCHINE
ZAIRES	ZANJERO	ZATI	ZECCHINES
ZAITECH	ZANJEROS	ZATIS	ZECCHINI
ZAITECHS	ZANTE	ZAX	ZECCHINO
ZAKAT	ZANTES	ZAXES	ZECCHINOS
ZAKATS	ZANTHOXYL	ZAYIN	ZECCHINS
ZAKOUSKA	ZANY	ZAYINS	ZECHIN
ZAKOUSKI	ZANYING	ZAZEN	ZECHINS
ZAKUSKA	ZANYISH	ZAZENS	ZED
ZAKUSKI	ZANYISM	ZEA	ZEDOARIES
ZAMAN	ZANYISMS	ZEAL	ZEDOARY
ZAMANG	ZANZA	ZEALANT	ZEDS
ZAMANGS	ZANZAS	ZEALANTS	ZEE
ZAMANS	ZANZE	ZEALFUL	ZEES
ZAMARRA	ZANZES	ZEALLESS	ZEIN
ZAMARRAS	ZAP	ZEALOT	ZEINS
ZAMARRO	ZAPATA	ZEALOTISM	ZEITGEBER
ZAMARROS	ZAPATEADO	ZEALOTRY	ZEITGEIST

ZEK	ZEST	ZIKKURATS	ZING
ZEKS	ZESTED	ZIKURAT	ZINGANI
ZEL	ZESTER	ZIKURATS	ZINGANO
ZELANT	ZESTERS	ZILA	ZINGARA
ZELANTS	ZESTFUL	ZILAS	ZINGARE
ZELATOR	ZESTFULLY	ZILCH	ZINGARI
ZELATORS	ZESTIER	ZILCHES	ZINGARO
ZELATRICE	ZESTIEST	ZILL	ZINGED
ZELATRIX	ZESTILY	ZILLA	ZINGEL
ZELKOVA	ZESTING	ZILLAH	ZINGELS
ZELKOVAS	ZESTLESS	ZILLAHS	ZINGER
ZELOSO	ZESTS	ZILLAS	ZINGERS
ZELOTYPIA	ZESTY	ZILLION	ZINGIBER
ZELS	ZETA	ZILLIONS	ZINGIBERS
ZEMINDAR	ZETAS	ZILLIONTH	ZINGIER
ZEMINDARI	ZETETIC	ZILLS	ZINGIEST
ZEMINDARS	ZETETICS	ZIMB	ZINGING
ZEMINDARY	ZETTABYTE	ZIMBI	ZINGS
ZEMSTVA	ZEUGMA	ZIMBIS	ZINGY
ZEMSTVO	ZEUGMAS	ZIMBS	ZINKE
ZEMSTVOS	ZEUGMATIC	ZIMMER	ZINKED
ZENAIDA	ZEUXITE	ZIMMERS	ZINKENITE
ZENAIDAS	ZEUXITES	ZIMOCCA	ZINKES
ZENANA	ZEX	ZIMOCCAS	ZINKIER
ZENANAS	ZEXES	ZIN	ZINKIEST
ZENDIK	ZEZE	ZINC	ZINKIFIED
ZENDIKS	ZEZES	ZINCATE	ZINKIFIES
ZENITH	ZHO	ZINCATES	ZINKIFY
ZENITHAL	ZHOMO	ZINCED	ZINKING
ZENITHS	ZHOMOS	ZINCIC	ZINKY
ZEOLITE	ZHOS	ZINCIER	ZINNIA
ZEOLITES	ZIBELINE	ZINCIEST	ZINNIAS
ZEOLITIC	ZIBELINES	ZINCIFIED	ZINS
ZEP	ZIBELLINE	ZINCIFIES	ZIP
ZEPHYR	ZIBET	ZINCIFY	ZIPLESS
ZEPHYRS	ZIBETH	ZINCING	ZIPLOCK
ZEPPELIN	ZIBETHS	ZINCITE	ZIPPED
ZEPPELINS	ZIBETS	ZINCITES	ZIPPER
ZEPPOLE	ZIFF	ZINCKED	ZIPPERED
ZEPPOLES	ZIFFIUS	ZINCKIER	ZIPPERING
ZEPPOLI	ZIFFIUSES	ZINCKIEST	ZIPPERS
ZEPS	ZIFFS	ZINCKIFY	ZIPPIER
ZERDA	ZIG	ZINCKING	ZIPPIEST
ZERDAS	ZIGAN	ZINCKY	ZIPPING
ZEREBA	ZIGANKA	ZINCO	ZIPPO
ZEREBAS	ZIGANKAS	ZINCODE	ZIPPOS
ZERIBA	ZIGANS	ZINCODES	ZIPPY
ZERIBAS	ZIGGED	ZINCOID	ZIPS
ZERK	ZIGGING	ZINCOS	ZIPTOP
ZERKS	ZIGGURAT	ZINCOUS	ZIRAM
ZERO	ZIGGURATS	ZINCS	ZIRAMS
ZEROED	ZIGS	ZINCY	ZIRCALLOY
ZEROES	ZIGZAG	ZINDABAD	ZIRCALOY
ZEROING	ZIGZAGGED	ZINE	ZIRCALOYS
ZEROS	ZIGZAGGER	ZINEB	ZIRCON
ZEROTH	ZIGZAGGY	ZINEBS	ZIRCONIA
ZERUMBET	ZIGZAGS	ZINES	ZIRCONIAS
ZERUMBETS	ZIKKURAT	ZINFANDEL	ZIRCONIC

ZIRCONIUM	ZOECHROME	ZONULA	ZOOLATRIA
ZIRCONS	ZOECIA	ZONULAE	ZOOLATRY
ZIT	ZOECIUM	ZONULAR	ZOOLITE
ZITE	ZOEFORM	ZONULAS	ZOOLITES
ZITHER	ZOETIC	ZONULE	ZOOLITH
ZITHERIST	ZOETROPE	ZONULES	ZOOLITHIC
ZITHERN	ZOETROPES	ZONULET	ZOOLITHS
ZITHERNS	ZOETROPIC	ZONULETS	ZOOLITIC
ZITHERS	ZOFTIG	ZONURE	ZOOLOGIC
ZITI	ZOIATRIA	ZONURES	ZOOLOGIES
ZITIS	ZOIATRIAS	ZOO	ZOOLOGIST
ZITS	ZOIATRICS	ZOOBIOTIC	ZOOLOGY
ZIZ	ZOIC	ZOOBLAST	ZOOM
ZIZANIA	ZOISITE	ZOOBLASTS	ZOOMANCY
ZIZANIAS	ZOISITES	ZOOCHORE	ZOOMANIA
ZIZEL	ZOISM	ZOOCHORES	ZOOMANIAS
ZIZELS	ZOISMS	ZOOCHORY	ZOOMANTIC
ZIZIT	ZOIST	ZOOCYTIA	ZOOMED
ZIZITH	ZOISTS	ZOOCYTIUM	ZOOMETRIC
ZIZYPHUS	ZOL	ZOOEA	ZOOMETRY
ZIZZ	ZOLS	ZOOEAE	ZOOMING
ZIZZED	ZOMBI	ZOOEAL	ZOOMORPH
ZIZZES	ZOMBIE	ZOOEAS	ZOOMORPHS
ZIZZING	ZOMBIES	ZOOECIA	ZOOMORPHY
ZIZZLE	ZOMBIFIED	ZOOECIUM	ZOOMS
ZIZZLED	ZOMBIFIES	ZOOEY	ZOON
ZIZZLES	ZOMBIFY	ZOOGAMETE	ZOONAL
ZIZZLING	ZOMBIISM	ZOOGAMIES	ZOONED
ZLOTE	ZOMBIISMS	ZOOGAMOUS	ZOONIC
ZLOTIES	ZOMBIS	ZOOGAMY	ZOONING
ZLOTY	ZOMBORUK	ZOOGENIC	ZOONITE
ZLOTYCH	ZOMBORUKS	ZOOGENIES	ZOONITES
ZLOTYS	ZONA	ZOOGENOUS	ZOONITIC
ZO	ZONAE	ZOOGENY	ZOONOMIA
ZOA	ZONAL	ZOOGLEA	ZOONOMIAS
ZOAEA	ZONALLY	ZOOGLEAE	ZOONOMIC
ZOAEAE	ZONARY	ZOOGLEAL	ZOONOMIES
ZOAEAS	ZONATE	ZOOGLEAS	ZOONOMIST
ZOARIA	ZONATED	ZOOGLOEA	ZOONOMY
ZOARIAL	ZONATION	ZOOGLOEAE	ZOONOSES
ZOARIUM	ZONATIONS	ZOOGLOEAL	ZOONOSIS
ZOBO	ZONDA	ZOOGLOEAS	ZOONOTIC
ZOBOS	ZONDAS	ZOOGLOEIC	ZOONS
ZOBU	ZONE	ZOOGONIES	ZOOPATHY
ZOBUS	ZONED	ZOOGONOUS	ZOOPERAL
ZOCALO	ZONELESS	ZOOGONY	ZOOPERIES
ZOCALOS	ZONER	ZOOGRAFT	ZOOPERIST
ZOCCO	ZONERS	ZOOGRAFTS	ZOOPERY
ZOCCOLO	ZONES	ZOOGRAPHY	ZOOPHAGAN
ZOCCOLOS	ZONETIME	ZOOID	ZOOPHAGY
ZOCCOS	ZONETIMES	ZOOIDAL	ZOOPHILE
ZODIAC	ZONING	ZOOIDS	ZOOPHILES
ZODIACAL	ZONINGS	ZOOIER	ZOOPHILIA
ZODIACS	ZONK	ZOOIEST	ZOOPHILIC
ZOEA	ZONKED	ZOOKEEPER	ZOOPHILY
ZOEAE	ZONKING	ZOOKS	ZOOPHOBE
ZOEAL	ZONKS	ZOOLATER	ZOOPHOBES
ZOEAS	ZONOID	ZOOLATERS	ZOOPHOBIA

ZOOPHORI
ZOOPHORIC
ZOOPHORUS
ZOOPHYTE
ZOOPHYTES
ZOOPHYTIC
ZOOPLASTY
ZOOS
ZOOSCOPIC
ZOOSCOPY
ZOOSPERM
ZOOSPERMS
ZOOSPORE
ZOOSPORES
ZOOSPORIC
ZOOSTEROL
ZOOT
ZOOTAXIES
ZOOTAXY
ZOOTECHNY
ZOOTHECIA
ZOOTHEISM
ZOOTHOME
ZOOTHOMES
ZOOTIER
ZOOTIEST
ZOOTOMIC
ZOOTOMIES
ZOOTOMIST
ZOOTOMY
ZOOTOXIC
ZOOTOXIN
ZOOTOXINS
ZOOTROPE
ZOOTROPES
ZOOTROPHY
ZOOTY
ZOOTYPE
ZOOTYPES
ZOOTYPIC
ZOOZOO
ZOOZOOS
ZOPILOTE
ZOPILOTES
ZOPPA
ZOPPO
ZORBING
ZORBINGS
ZORBONAUT
ZORGITE
ZORGITES
ZORI
ZORIL
ZORILLA
ZORILLAS
ZORILLE
ZORILLES
ZORILLO

ZORILLOS
ZORILS
ZORINO
ZORINOS
ZORIS
ZORRO
ZORROS
ZOS
ZOSTER
ZOSTERS
ZOUAVE
ZOUAVES
ZOUK
ZOUKS
ZOUNDS
ZOWIE
ZOYSIA
ZOYSIAS
ZUCCHETTI
ZUCCHETTO
ZUCCHINI
ZUCCHINIS
ZUCHETTA
ZUCHETTAS
ZUCHETTO
ZUCHETTOS
ZUFFOLI
ZUFFOLO
ZUFOLI
ZUFOLO
ZUGZWANG
ZUGZWANGS
ZULU
ZULUS
ZUMBOORUK
ZUPA
ZUPAN
ZUPANS
ZUPAS
ZURF
ZURFS
ZUZ
ZUZIM
ZWIEBACK
ZWIEBACKS
ZYDECO
ZYDECOS
ZYGA
ZYGAENID
ZYGAENOID
ZYGAL
ZYGANTRA
ZYGANTRUM
ZYGOCACTI
ZYGODONT
ZYGOID
ZYGOMA
ZYGOMAS

ZYGOMATA
ZYGOMATIC
ZYGON
ZYGOPHYTE
ZYGOSE
ZYGOSES
ZYGOSIS
ZYGOSITY
ZYGOSPERM
ZYGOSPORE
ZYGOTE
ZYGOTENE
ZYGOTENES
ZYGOTES
ZYGOTIC
ZYLONITE
ZYLONITES
ZYMASE
ZYMASES
ZYME
ZYMES
ZYMIC
ZYMITE
ZYMITES
ZYMOGEN
ZYMOGENE
ZYMOGENES
ZYMOGENIC
ZYMOGENS
ZYMOGRAM
ZYMOGRAMS
ZYMOID
ZYMOLOGIC
ZYMOLOGY
ZYMOLYSES
ZYMOLYSIS
ZYMOLYTIC
ZYMOME
ZYMOMES
ZYMOMETER
ZYMOSAN
ZYMOSANS
ZYMOSES
ZYMOSIS
ZYMOTIC
ZYMOTICS
ZYMURGIES
ZYMURGY
ZYTHUM
ZYTHUMS
ZYZZYVA
ZYZZYVAS
ZZZ
ZZZS

COLLINS SCRABBLE
TOURNAMENT AND CLUB
WORD LIST

10-15 LETTER WORDS

A

AARDWOLVES
ABACTERIAL
ABACTINALLY
ABANDONEDLY
ABANDONEES
ABANDONERS
ABANDONING
ABANDONMENT
ABANDONMENTS
ABANDONWARE
ABANDONWARES
ABASEMENTS
ABASHMENTS
ABATEMENTS
ABBOTSHIPS
ABBREVIATE
ABBREVIATED
ABBREVIATES
ABBREVIATING
ABBREVIATION
ABBREVIATIONS
ABBREVIATOR
ABBREVIATORS
ABBREVIATORY
ABBREVIATURE
ABBREVIATURES
ABCOULOMBS
ABDICATING
ABDICATION
ABDICATIONS
ABDICATIVE
ABDICATORS
ABDOMINALLY
ABDOMINALS
ABDOMINOPLASTY
ABDOMINOUS
ABDUCENTES
ABDUCTIONS
ABDUCTORES
ABECEDARIAN
ABECEDARIANS
ABERDEVINE
ABERDEVINES
ABERNETHIES
ABERRANCES
ABERRANCIES
ABERRANTLY
ABERRATING
ABERRATION
ABERRATIONAL
ABERRATIONS
ABEYANCIES
ABHOMINABLE
ABHORRENCE

ABHORRENCES
ABHORRENCIES
ABHORRENCY
ABHORRENTLY
ABHORRINGS
ABIOGENESES
ABIOGENESIS
ABIOGENETIC
ABIOGENETICALLY
ABIOGENICALLY
ABIOGENIST
ABIOGENISTS
ABIOLOGICAL
ABIOTICALLY
ABIOTROPHIC
ABIOTROPHIES
ABIOTROPHY
ABIRRITANT
ABIRRITANTS
ABIRRITATE
ABIRRITATED
ABIRRITATES
ABIRRITATING
ABITURIENT
ABITURIENTS
ABJECTIONS
ABJECTNESS
ABJECTNESSES
ABJOINTING
ABJUNCTION
ABJUNCTIONS
ABJURATION
ABJURATIONS
ABLACTATION
ABLACTATIONS
ABLATITIOUS
ABLATIVELY
ABLUTIONARY
ABLUTOMANE
ABLUTOMANES
ABNEGATING
ABNEGATION
ABNEGATIONS
ABNEGATORS
ABNORMALISM
ABNORMALISMS
ABNORMALITIES
ABNORMALITY
ABNORMALLY
ABNORMITIES
ABODEMENTS
ABOLISHABLE
ABOLISHERS
ABOLISHING

ABOLISHMENT
ABOLISHMENTS
ABOLITIONAL
ABOLITIONARY
ABOLITIONISM
ABOLITIONISMS
ABOLITIONIST
ABOLITIONISTS
ABOLITIONS
ABOMASUSES
ABOMINABLE
ABOMINABLENESS
ABOMINABLY
ABOMINATED
ABOMINATES
ABOMINATING
ABOMINATION
ABOMINATIONS
ABOMINATOR
ABOMINATORS
ABONDANCES
ABONNEMENT
ABONNEMENTS
ABORIGINAL
ABORIGINALISM
ABORIGINALISMS
ABORIGINALITIES
ABORIGINALITY
ABORIGINALLY
ABORIGINALS
ABORIGINES
ABORTICIDE
ABORTICIDES
ABORTIFACIENT
ABORTIFACIENTS
ABORTIONAL
ABORTIONIST
ABORTIONISTS
ABORTIVELY
ABORTIVENESS
ABORTIVENESSES
ABORTUARIES
ABOVEBOARD
ABOVEGROUND
ABRACADABRA
ABRACADABRAS
ABRANCHIAL
ABRANCHIATE
ABRASIVELY
ABRASIVENESS
ABRASIVENESSES
ABREACTING
ABREACTION
ABREACTIONS

ABREACTIVE
ABRIDGABLE
ABRIDGEABLE
ABRIDGEMENT
ABRIDGEMENTS
ABRIDGMENT
ABRIDGMENTS
ABROGATING
ABROGATION
ABROGATIONS
ABROGATIVE
ABROGATORS
ABRUPTIONS
ABRUPTNESS
ABRUPTNESSES
ABSCESSING
ABSCINDING
ABSCISSINS
ABSCISSION
ABSCISSIONS
ABSCONDENCE
ABSCONDENCES
ABSCONDERS
ABSCONDING
ABSEILINGS
ABSENTEEISM
ABSENTEEISMS
ABSENTMINDED
ABSENTMINDEDLY
ABSINTHIATED
ABSINTHISM
ABSINTHISMS
ABSOLUTELY
ABSOLUTENESS
ABSOLUTENESSES
ABSOLUTEST
ABSOLUTION
ABSOLUTIONS
ABSOLUTISE
ABSOLUTISED
ABSOLUTISES
ABSOLUTISING
ABSOLUTISM
ABSOLUTISMS
ABSOLUTIST
ABSOLUTISTIC
ABSOLUTISTS
ABSOLUTIVE
ABSOLUTIZE
ABSOLUTIZED
ABSOLUTIZES
ABSOLUTIZING
ABSOLUTORY
ABSOLVABLE

ABSOLVENTS
ABSOLVITOR
ABSOLVITORS
ABSORBABILITIES
ABSORBABILITY
ABSORBABLE
ABSORBANCE
ABSORBANCES
ABSORBANCIES
ABSORBANCY
ABSORBANTS
ABSORBATES
ABSORBEDLY
ABSORBEFACIENT
ABSORBEFACIENTS
ABSORBENCIES
ABSORBENCY
ABSORBENTS
ABSORBINGLY
ABSORPTANCE
ABSORPTANCES
ABSORPTIOMETER
ABSORPTIOMETERS
ABSORPTION
ABSORPTIONS
ABSORPTIVE
ABSORPTIVENESS
ABSORPTIVITIES
ABSORPTIVITY
ABSQUATULATE
ABSQUATULATED
ABSQUATULATES
ABSQUATULATING
ABSTAINERS
ABSTAINING
ABSTEMIOUS
ABSTEMIOUSLY
ABSTEMIOUSNESS
ABSTENTION
ABSTENTIONISM
ABSTENTIONISMS
ABSTENTIONIST
ABSTENTIONISTS
ABSTENTIONS
ABSTENTIOUS
ABSTERGENT
ABSTERGENTS
ABSTERGING
ABSTERSION
ABSTERSIONS
ABSTERSIVE
ABSTERSIVES
ABSTINENCE
ABSTINENCES
ABSTINENCIES
ABSTINENCY
ABSTINENTLY
ABSTRACTABLE
ABSTRACTED

ABSTRACTEDLY
ABSTRACTEDNESS
ABSTRACTER
ABSTRACTERS
ABSTRACTEST
ABSTRACTING
ABSTRACTION
ABSTRACTIONAL
ABSTRACTIONISM
ABSTRACTIONISMS
ABSTRACTIONIST
ABSTRACTIONISTS
ABSTRACTIONS
ABSTRACTIVE
ABSTRACTIVELY
ABSTRACTIVES
ABSTRACTLY
ABSTRACTNESS
ABSTRACTNESSES
ABSTRACTOR
ABSTRACTORS
ABSTRICTED
ABSTRICTING
ABSTRICTION
ABSTRICTIONS
ABSTRUSELY
ABSTRUSENESS
ABSTRUSENESSES
ABSTRUSEST
ABSTRUSITIES
ABSTRUSITY
ABSURDISMS
ABSURDISTS
ABSURDITIES
ABSURDNESS
ABSURDNESSES
ABUNDANCES
ABUNDANCIES
ABUNDANTLY
ABUSIVENESS
ABUSIVENESSES
ABYSSOPELAGIC
ACADEMICAL
ACADEMICALISM
ACADEMICALISMS
ACADEMICALLY
ACADEMICALS
ACADEMICIAN
ACADEMICIANS
ACADEMICISM
ACADEMICISMS
ACADEMISMS
ACADEMISTS
ACALCULIAS
ACALEPHANS
ACANACEOUS
ACANTHACEOUS
ACANTHOCEPHALAN
ACANTHUSES

ACARICIDAL
ACARICIDES
ACARIDEANS
ACARIDIANS
ACARIDOMATIA
ACARIDOMATIUM
ACARODOMATIA
ACARODOMATIUM
ACAROLOGIES
ACAROLOGIST
ACAROLOGISTS
ACAROPHILIES
ACAROPHILY
ACARPELLOUS
ACARPELOUS
ACATALECTIC
ACATALECTICS
ACATALEPSIES
ACATALEPSY
ACATALEPTIC
ACATALEPTICS
ACATAMATHESIA
ACATAMATHESIAS
ACAULESCENT
ACCEDENCES
ACCELERABLE
ACCELERANDO
ACCELERANDOS
ACCELERANT
ACCELERANTS
ACCELERATE
ACCELERATED
ACCELERATES
ACCELERATING
ACCELERATINGLY
ACCELERATION
ACCELERATIONS
ACCELERATIVE
ACCELERATOR
ACCELERATORS
ACCELERATORY
ACCELEROMETER
ACCELEROMETERS
ACCENSIONS
ACCENTLESS
ACCENTUALITIES
ACCENTUALITY
ACCENTUALLY
ACCENTUATE
ACCENTUATED
ACCENTUATES
ACCENTUATING
ACCENTUATION
ACCENTUATIONS
ACCEPTABILITIES
ACCEPTABILITY
ACCEPTABLE
ACCEPTABLENESS
ACCEPTABLY

ACCEPTANCE
ACCEPTANCES
ACCEPTANCIES
ACCEPTANCY
ACCEPTANTS
ACCEPTATION
ACCEPTATIONS
ACCEPTEDLY
ACCEPTILATION
ACCEPTILATIONS
ACCEPTINGLY
ACCEPTINGNESS
ACCEPTINGNESSES
ACCEPTIVITIES
ACCEPTIVITY
ACCESSARIES
ACCESSARILY
ACCESSARINESS
ACCESSARINESSES
ACCESSIBILITIES
ACCESSIBILITY
ACCESSIBLE
ACCESSIBLENESS
ACCESSIBLY
ACCESSIONAL
ACCESSIONED
ACCESSIONING
ACCESSIONS
ACCESSORIAL
ACCESSORIES
ACCESSORII
ACCESSORILY
ACCESSORINESS
ACCESSORINESSES
ACCESSORISE
ACCESSORISED
ACCESSORISES
ACCESSORISING
ACCESSORIUS
ACCESSORIZE
ACCESSORIZED
ACCESSORIZES
ACCESSORIZING
ACCIACCATURA
ACCIACCATURAS
ACCIACCATURE
ACCIDENCES
ACCIDENTAL
ACCIDENTALISM
ACCIDENTALISMS
ACCIDENTALITIES
ACCIDENTALITY
ACCIDENTALLY
ACCIDENTALNESS
ACCIDENTALS
ACCIDENTED
ACCIDENTLY
ACCIDENTOLOGIES
ACCIDENTOLOGY

ACCIPITERS
ACCIPITRAL
ACCIPITRINE
ACCIPITRINES
ACCLAIMERS
ACCLAIMING
ACCLAMATION
ACCLAMATIONS
ACCLAMATORY
ACCLIMATABLE
ACCLIMATATION
ACCLIMATATIONS
ACCLIMATED
ACCLIMATES
ACCLIMATING
ACCLIMATION
ACCLIMATIONS
ACCLIMATISABLE
ACCLIMATISATION
ACCLIMATISE
ACCLIMATISED
ACCLIMATISER
ACCLIMATISERS
ACCLIMATISES
ACCLIMATISING
ACCLIMATIZABLE
ACCLIMATIZATION
ACCLIMATIZE
ACCLIMATIZED
ACCLIMATIZER
ACCLIMATIZERS
ACCLIMATIZES
ACCLIMATIZING
ACCLIVITIES
ACCLIVITOUS
ACCOASTING
ACCOLADING
ACCOMMODABLE
ACCOMMODATE
ACCOMMODATED
ACCOMMODATES
ACCOMMODATING
ACCOMMODATINGLY
ACCOMMODATION
ACCOMMODATIONAL
ACCOMMODATIONS
ACCOMMODATIVE
ACCOMMODATOR
ACCOMMODATORS
ACCOMPANIED
ACCOMPANIER
ACCOMPANIERS
ACCOMPANIES
ACCOMPANIMENT
ACCOMPANIMENTS
ACCOMPANIST
ACCOMPANISTS
ACCOMPANYING
ACCOMPANYIST

ACCOMPANYISTS
ACCOMPLICE
ACCOMPLICES
ACCOMPLISH
ACCOMPLISHABLE
ACCOMPLISHED
ACCOMPLISHER
ACCOMPLISHERS
ACCOMPLISHES
ACCOMPLISHING
ACCOMPLISHMENT
ACCOMPLISHMENTS
ACCOMPTABLE
ACCOMPTANT
ACCOMPTANTS
ACCOMPTING
ACCORAGING
ACCORDABLE
ACCORDANCE
ACCORDANCES
ACCORDANCIES
ACCORDANCY
ACCORDANTLY
ACCORDINGLY
ACCORDIONIST
ACCORDIONISTS
ACCORDIONS
ACCOSTABLE
ACCOUCHEMENT
ACCOUCHEMENTS
ACCOUCHEUR
ACCOUCHEURS
ACCOUCHEUSE
ACCOUCHEUSES
ACCOUNTABILITY
ACCOUNTABLE
ACCOUNTABLENESS
ACCOUNTABLY
ACCOUNTANCIES
ACCOUNTANCY
ACCOUNTANT
ACCOUNTANTS
ACCOUNTANTSHIP
ACCOUNTANTSHIPS
ACCOUNTING
ACCOUNTINGS
ACCOUPLEMENT
ACCOUPLEMENTS
ACCOURAGED
ACCOURAGES
ACCOURAGING
ACCOURTING
ACCOUSTREMENT
ACCOUSTREMENTS
ACCOUTERED
ACCOUTERING
ACCOUTERMENT
ACCOUTERMENTS
ACCOUTREMENT

ACCOUTREMENTS
ACCOUTRING
ACCREDITABLE
ACCREDITATION
ACCREDITATIONS
ACCREDITED
ACCREDITING
ACCRESCENCE
ACCRESCENCES
ACCRESCENT
ACCRETIONARY
ACCRETIONS
ACCRUEMENT
ACCRUEMENTS
ACCUBATION
ACCUBATIONS
ACCULTURAL
ACCULTURATE
ACCULTURATED
ACCULTURATES
ACCULTURATING
ACCULTURATION
ACCULTURATIONAL
ACCULTURATIONS
ACCULTURATIVE
ACCUMBENCIES
ACCUMBENCY
ACCUMULABLE
ACCUMULATE
ACCUMULATED
ACCUMULATES
ACCUMULATING
ACCUMULATION
ACCUMULATIONS
ACCUMULATIVE
ACCUMULATIVELY
ACCUMULATOR
ACCUMULATORS
ACCURACIES
ACCURATELY
ACCURATENESS
ACCURATENESSES
ACCURSEDLY
ACCURSEDNESS
ACCURSEDNESSES
ACCUSATION
ACCUSATIONS
ACCUSATIVAL
ACCUSATIVE
ACCUSATIVELY
ACCUSATIVES
ACCUSATORIAL
ACCUSATORY
ACCUSEMENT
ACCUSEMENTS
ACCUSINGLY
ACCUSTOMARY
ACCUSTOMATION
ACCUSTOMATIONS

ACCUSTOMED
ACCUSTOMEDNESS
ACCUSTOMING
ACCUSTREMENT
ACCUSTREMENTS
ACEPHALOUS
ACERACEOUS
ACERBATING
ACERBICALLY
ACERBITIES
ACERVATELY
ACERVATION
ACERVATIONS
ACESCENCES
ACESCENCIES
ACETABULAR
ACETABULUM
ACETABULUMS
ACETALDEHYDE
ACETALDEHYDES
ACETAMIDES
ACETAMINOPHEN
ACETAMINOPHENS
ACETANILID
ACETANILIDE
ACETANILIDES
ACETANILIDS
ACETAZOLAMIDE
ACETAZOLAMIDES
ACETIFICATION
ACETIFICATIONS
ACETIFIERS
ACETIFYING
ACETOMETER
ACETOMETERS
ACETONAEMIA
ACETONAEMIAS
ACETONEMIA
ACETONEMIAS
ACETONITRILE
ACETONITRILES
ACETONURIA
ACETONURIAS
ACETOPHENETIDIN
ACETYLATED
ACETYLATES
ACETYLATING
ACETYLATION
ACETYLATIONS
ACETYLATIVE
ACETYLCHOLINE
ACETYLCHOLINES
ACETYLENES
ACETYLENIC
ACETYLIDES
ACETYLSALICYLIC
ACHAENIUMS
ACHAENOCARP
ACHAENOCARPS

ACHALASIAS
ACHIEVABLE
ACHIEVEMENT
ACHIEVEMENTS
ACHINESSES
ACHLAMYDEOUS
ACHLORHYDRIA
ACHLORHYDRIAS
ACHLORHYDRIC
ACHONDRITE
ACHONDRITES
ACHONDRITIC
ACHONDROPLASIA
ACHONDROPLASIAS
ACHONDROPLASTIC
ACHROMATIC
ACHROMATICALLY
ACHROMATICITIES
ACHROMATICITY
ACHROMATIN
ACHROMATINS
ACHROMATISATION
ACHROMATISE
ACHROMATISED
ACHROMATISES
ACHROMATISING
ACHROMATISM
ACHROMATISMS
ACHROMATIZATION
ACHROMATIZE
ACHROMATIZED
ACHROMATIZES
ACHROMATIZING
ACHROMATOPSIA
ACHROMATOPSIAS
ACHROMATOUS
ACICULATED
ACIDANTHERA
ACIDANTHERAS
ACIDFREAKS
ACIDIFIABLE
ACIDIFICATION
ACIDIFICATIONS
ACIDIFIERS
ACIDIFYING
ACIDIMETER
ACIDIMETERS
ACIDIMETRIC
ACIDIMETRICAL
ACIDIMETRICALLY
ACIDIMETRIES
ACIDIMETRY
ACIDNESSES
ACIDOMETER
ACIDOMETERS
ACIDOPHILE
ACIDOPHILES
ACIDOPHILIC
ACIDOPHILOUS

ACIDOPHILS
ACIDOPHILUS
ACIDOPHILUSES
ACIDULATED
ACIDULATES
ACIDULATING
ACIDULATION
ACIDULATIONS
ACIERATING
ACIERATION
ACIERATIONS
ACINACEOUS
ACINACIFORM
ACKNOWLEDGE
ACKNOWLEDGEABLE
ACKNOWLEDGEABLY
ACKNOWLEDGED
ACKNOWLEDGEDLY
ACKNOWLEDGEMENT
ACKNOWLEDGER
ACKNOWLEDGERS
ACKNOWLEDGES
ACKNOWLEDGING
ACKNOWLEDGMENT
ACKNOWLEDGMENTS
ACOELOMATE
ACOELOMATES
ACOLOUTHIC
ACOLOUTHITE
ACOLOUTHITES
ACOLOUTHOS
ACOLOUTHOSES
ACONITINES
ACOTYLEDON
ACOTYLEDONOUS
ACOTYLEDONS
ACOUSTICAL
ACOUSTICALLY
ACOUSTICIAN
ACOUSTICIANS
ACQUAINTANCE
ACQUAINTANCES
ACQUAINTED
ACQUAINTING
ACQUIESCED
ACQUIESCENCE
ACQUIESCENCES
ACQUIESCENT
ACQUIESCENTLY
ACQUIESCENTS
ACQUIESCES
ACQUIESCING
ACQUIESCINGLY
ACQUIGHTING
ACQUIRABILITIES
ACQUIRABILITY
ACQUIRABLE
ACQUIREMENT
ACQUIREMENTS

ACQUISITION
ACQUISITIONAL
ACQUISITIONS
ACQUISITIVE
ACQUISITIVELY
ACQUISITIVENESS
ACQUISITOR
ACQUISITORS
ACQUITMENT
ACQUITMENTS
ACQUITTALS
ACQUITTANCE
ACQUITTANCED
ACQUITTANCES
ACQUITTANCING
ACQUITTERS
ACQUITTING
ACRIDITIES
ACRIDNESSES
ACRIFLAVIN
ACRIFLAVINE
ACRIFLAVINES
ACRIFLAVINS
ACRIMONIES
ACRIMONIOUS
ACRIMONIOUSLY
ACRIMONIOUSNESS
ACRITARCHS
ACROAMATIC
ACROAMATICAL
ACROBATICALLY
ACROBATICS
ACROBATISM
ACROBATISMS
ACROCARPOUS
ACROCENTRIC
ACROCENTRICS
ACROCYANOSES
ACROCYANOSIS
ACRODROMOUS
ACROGENOUS
ACROGENOUSLY
ACROLITHIC
ACROMEGALIC
ACROMEGALICS
ACROMEGALIES
ACROMEGALY
ACRONICALLY
ACRONYCALLY
ACRONYCHAL
ACRONYCHALLY
ACRONYMANIA
ACRONYMANIAS
ACRONYMICALLY
ACRONYMOUS
ACROPARESTHESIA
ACROPETALLY
ACROPHOBES
ACROPHOBIA

ACROPHOBIAS
ACROPHOBIC
ACROPHONETIC
ACROPHONIC
ACROPHONIES
ACROPOLISES
ACROSPIRES
ACROSTICAL
ACROSTICALLY
ACROTERIAL
ACROTERION
ACROTERIUM
ACROTERIUMS
ACRYLAMIDE
ACRYLAMIDES
ACRYLONITRILE
ACRYLONITRILES
ACTABILITIES
ACTABILITY
ACTINICALLY
ACTINIFORM
ACTINOBACILLI
ACTINOBACILLUS
ACTINOBIOLOGIES
ACTINOBIOLOGY
ACTINOCHEMISTRY
ACTINOLITE
ACTINOLITES
ACTINOMERE
ACTINOMERES
ACTINOMETER
ACTINOMETERS
ACTINOMETRIC
ACTINOMETRICAL
ACTINOMETRIES
ACTINOMETRY
ACTINOMORPHIC
ACTINOMORPHIES
ACTINOMORPHOUS
ACTINOMORPHY
ACTINOMYCES
ACTINOMYCETE
ACTINOMYCETES
ACTINOMYCETOUS
ACTINOMYCIN
ACTINOMYCINS
ACTINOMYCOSES
ACTINOMYCOSIS
ACTINOMYCOTIC
ACTINOPODS
ACTINOTHERAPIES
ACTINOTHERAPY
ACTINOURANIUM
ACTINOURANIUMS
ACTINOZOAN
ACTIONABLE
ACTIONABLY
ACTIONISTS
ACTIONLESS

ACTIVATING	ADAPTIVENESSES	ADHESIVELY	ADJUSTABLY
ACTIVATION	ADAPTIVITIES	ADHESIVENESS	ADJUSTMENT
ACTIVATIONS	ADAPTIVITY	ADHESIVENESSES	ADJUSTMENTAL
ACTIVATORS	ADAPTOGENIC	ADHIBITING	ADJUSTMENTS
ACTIVENESS	ADAPTOGENS	ADHIBITION	ADJUTANCIES
ACTIVENESSES	ADDERSTONE	ADHIBITIONS	ADJUVANCIES
ACTIVISING	ADDERSTONES	ADHOCRACIES	ADMEASURED
ACTIVISTIC	ADDERWORTS	ADIABATICALLY	ADMEASUREMENT
ACTIVITIES	ADDICTEDNESS	ADIABATICS	ADMEASUREMENTS
ACTIVIZING	ADDICTEDNESSES	ADIACTINIC	ADMEASURES
ACTOMYOSIN	ADDICTIONS	ADIAPHORISM	ADMEASURING
ACTOMYOSINS	ADDITAMENT	ADIAPHORISMS	ADMINICLES
ACTUALISATION	ADDITAMENTS	ADIAPHORIST	ADMINICULAR
ACTUALISATIONS	ADDITIONAL	ADIAPHORISTIC	ADMINICULATE
ACTUALISED	ADDITIONALITIES	ADIAPHORISTS	ADMINICULATED
ACTUALISES	ADDITIONALITY	ADIAPHORON	ADMINICULATES
ACTUALISING	ADDITIONALLY	ADIAPHOROUS	ADMINICULATING
ACTUALISTS	ADDITITIOUS	ADIATHERMANCIES	ADMINISTER
ACTUALITES	ADDITIVELY	ADIATHERMANCY	ADMINISTERED
ACTUALITIES	ADDITIVITIES	ADIATHERMANOUS	ADMINISTERING
ACTUALIZATION	ADDITIVITY	ADIATHERMIC	ADMINISTERS
ACTUALIZATIONS	ADDLEMENTS	ADIPOCERES	ADMINISTRABLE
ACTUALIZED	ADDLEPATED	ADIPOCEROUS	ADMINISTRANT
ACTUALIZES	ADDRESSABILITY	ADIPOCYTES	ADMINISTRANTS
ACTUALIZING	ADDRESSABLE	ADIPOSITIES	ADMINISTRATE
ACTUARIALLY	ADDRESSEES	ADJACENCES	ADMINISTRATED
ACTUATIONS	ADDRESSERS	ADJACENCIES	ADMINISTRATES
ACUMINATED	ADDRESSING	ADJACENTLY	ADMINISTRATING
ACUMINATES	ADDRESSORS	ADJECTIVAL	ADMINISTRATION
ACUMINATING	ADDUCEABLE	ADJECTIVALLY	ADMINISTRATIONS
ACUMINATION	ADDUCTIONS	ADJECTIVELY	ADMINISTRATIVE
ACUMINATIONS	ADELANTADO	ADJECTIVES	ADMINISTRATOR
ACUPRESSURE	ADELANTADOS	ADJOURNING	ADMINISTRATORS
ACUPRESSURES	ADEMPTIONS	ADJOURNMENT	ADMINISTRATRIX
ACUPUNCTURAL	ADENECTOMIES	ADJOURNMENTS	ADMIRABILITIES
ACUPUNCTURE	ADENECTOMY	ADJUDGEMENT	ADMIRABILITY
ACUPUNCTURES	ADENITISES	ADJUDGEMENTS	ADMIRABLENESS
ACUPUNCTURIST	ADENOCARCINOMA	ADJUDGMENT	ADMIRABLENESSES
ACUPUNCTURISTS	ADENOCARCINOMAS	ADJUDGMENTS	ADMIRALSHIP
ACUTENESSES	ADENOHYPOPHYSES	ADJUDICATE	ADMIRALSHIPS
ACYCLOVIRS	ADENOHYPOPHYSIS	ADJUDICATED	ADMIRALTIES
ACYLATIONS	ADENOIDECTOMIES	ADJUDICATES	ADMIRANCES
ADACTYLOUS	ADENOIDECTOMY	ADJUDICATING	ADMIRATION
ADAMANCIES	ADENOMATOUS	ADJUDICATION	ADMIRATIONS
ADAMANTEAN	ADENOPATHIES	ADJUDICATIONS	ADMIRATIVE
ADAMANTINE	ADENOPATHY	ADJUDICATIVE	ADMIRAUNCE
ADAPTABILITIES	ADENOSINES	ADJUDICATOR	ADMIRAUNCES
ADAPTABILITY	ADENOVIRAL	ADJUDICATORS	ADMIRINGLY
ADAPTABLENESS	ADENOVIRUS	ADJUDICATORY	ADMISSIBILITIES
ADAPTABLENESSES	ADENOVIRUSES	ADJUNCTION	ADMISSIBILITY
ADAPTATION	ADEPTNESSES	ADJUNCTIONS	ADMISSIBLE
ADAPTATIONAL	ADEQUACIES	ADJUNCTIVE	ADMISSIBLENESS
ADAPTATIONALLY	ADEQUATELY	ADJUNCTIVELY	ADMISSIONS
ADAPTATIONS	ADEQUATENESS	ADJURATION	ADMITTABLE
ADAPTATIVE	ADEQUATENESSES	ADJURATIONS	ADMITTANCE
ADAPTEDNESS	ADEQUATIVE	ADJURATORY	ADMITTANCES
ADAPTEDNESSES	ADHERENCES	ADJUSTABILITIES	ADMITTEDLY
ADAPTIVELY	ADHERENTLY	ADJUSTABILITY	ADMIXTURES
ADAPTIVENESS	ADHESIONAL	ADJUSTABLE	ADMONISHED

ADMONISHER
ADMONISHERS
ADMONISHES
ADMONISHING
ADMONISHINGLY
ADMONISHMENT
ADMONISHMENTS
ADMONITION
ADMONITIONS
ADMONITIVE
ADMONITORILY
ADMONITORS
ADMONITORY
ADNOMINALS
ADOLESCENCE
ADOLESCENCES
ADOLESCENT
ADOLESCENTLY
ADOLESCENTS
ADOPTABILITIES
ADOPTABILITY
ADOPTIANISM
ADOPTIANISMS
ADOPTIANIST
ADOPTIANISTS
ADOPTIONISM
ADOPTIONISMS
ADOPTIONIST
ADOPTIONISTS
ADOPTIVELY
ADORABILITIES
ADORABILITY
ADORABLENESS
ADORABLENESSES
ADORATIONS
ADORNMENTS
ADPRESSING
ADRENALECTOMIES
ADRENALECTOMY
ADRENALINE
ADRENALINES
ADRENALINS
ADRENALISED
ADRENALIZED
ADRENERGIC
ADRENERGICALLY
ADRENOCHROME
ADRENOCHROMES
ADRENOCORTICAL
ADRIAMYCIN
ADRIAMYCINS
ADROITNESS
ADROITNESSES
ADSCITITIOUS
ADSCITITIOUSLY
ADSCRIPTION
ADSCRIPTIONS
ADSORBABILITIES
ADSORBABILITY

ADSORBABLE
ADSORBATES
ADSORBENTS
ADSORPTION
ADSORPTIONS
ADSORPTIVE
ADULARESCENCE
ADULARESCENCES
ADULARESCENT
ADULATIONS
ADULTERANT
ADULTERANTS
ADULTERATE
ADULTERATED
ADULTERATES
ADULTERATING
ADULTERATION
ADULTERATIONS
ADULTERATOR
ADULTERATORS
ADULTERERS
ADULTERESS
ADULTERESSES
ADULTERIES
ADULTERINE
ADULTERINES
ADULTERISE
ADULTERISED
ADULTERISES
ADULTERISING
ADULTERIZE
ADULTERIZED
ADULTERIZES
ADULTERIZING
ADULTEROUS
ADULTEROUSLY
ADULTESCENT
ADULTESCENTS
ADULTHOODS
ADULTNESSES
ADULTRESSES
ADUMBRATED
ADUMBRATES
ADUMBRATING
ADUMBRATION
ADUMBRATIONS
ADUMBRATIVE
ADUMBRATIVELY
ADUNCITIES
ADVANCEMENT
ADVANCEMENTS
ADVANCINGLY
ADVANTAGEABLE
ADVANTAGED
ADVANTAGEOUS
ADVANTAGEOUSLY
ADVANTAGES
ADVANTAGING
ADVECTIONS

ADVENTITIA
ADVENTITIAL
ADVENTITIAS
ADVENTITIOUS
ADVENTITIOUSLY
ADVENTIVES
ADVENTURED
ADVENTUREFUL
ADVENTURER
ADVENTURERS
ADVENTURES
ADVENTURESOME
ADVENTURESS
ADVENTURESSES
ADVENTURING
ADVENTURISM
ADVENTURISMS
ADVENTURIST
ADVENTURISTIC
ADVENTURISTS
ADVENTUROUS
ADVENTUROUSLY
ADVENTUROUSNESS
ADVERBIALISE
ADVERBIALISED
ADVERBIALISES
ADVERBIALISING
ADVERBIALIZE
ADVERBIALIZED
ADVERBIALIZES
ADVERBIALIZING
ADVERBIALLY
ADVERBIALS
ADVERSARIA
ADVERSARIAL
ADVERSARIES
ADVERSARINESS
ADVERSARINESSES
ADVERSATIVE
ADVERSATIVELY
ADVERSATIVES
ADVERSENESS
ADVERSENESSES
ADVERSITIES
ADVERTENCE
ADVERTENCES
ADVERTENCIES
ADVERTENCY
ADVERTENTLY
ADVERTISED
ADVERTISEMENT
ADVERTISEMENTS
ADVERTISER
ADVERTISERS
ADVERTISES
ADVERTISING
ADVERTISINGS
ADVERTIZED
ADVERTIZEMENT

ADVERTIZEMENTS
ADVERTIZER
ADVERTIZERS
ADVERTIZES
ADVERTIZING
ADVERTORIAL
ADVERTORIALS
ADVISABILITIES
ADVISABILITY
ADVISABLENESS
ADVISABLENESSES
ADVISATORY
ADVISEDNESS
ADVISEDNESSES
ADVISEMENT
ADVISEMENTS
ADVISERSHIP
ADVISERSHIPS
ADVISORATE
ADVISORATES
ADVISORIES
ADVOCACIES
ADVOCATING
ADVOCATION
ADVOCATIONS
ADVOCATIVE
ADVOCATORS
ADVOCATORY
ADVOUTRERS
ADVOUTRIES
AECIDIOSPORE
AECIDIOSPORES
AECIDOSPORE
AECIDOSPORES
AECIOSPORE
AECIOSPORES
AEDILESHIP
AEDILESHIPS
AEOLIPILES
AEOLIPYLES
AEOLOTROPIC
AEOLOTROPIES
AEOLOTROPY
AEPYORNISES
AERENCHYMA
AERENCHYMAS
AERENCHYMATOUS
AERIALISTS
AERIALITIES
AERIFICATION
AERIFICATIONS
AEROACOUSTICS
AEROBALLISTICS
AEROBATICS
AEROBICALLY
AEROBICISE
AEROBICISED
AEROBICISES
AEROBICISING

AEROBICIST	AEROMETRIC	AEROTROPISMS	AFFECTIVELY
AEROBICISTS	AEROMETRIES	AERUGINOUS	AFFECTIVENESS
AEROBICIZE	AEROMOTORS	AESTHESIAS	AFFECTIVENESSES
AEROBICIZED	AERONAUTIC	AESTHESIOGEN	AFFECTIVITIES
AEROBICIZES	AERONAUTICAL	AESTHESIOGENIC	AFFECTIVITY
AEROBICIZING	AERONAUTICALLY	AESTHESIOGENS	AFFECTLESS
AEROBIOLOGICAL	AERONAUTICS	AESTHETICAL	AFFECTLESSNESS
AEROBIOLOGIES	AERONEUROSES	AESTHETICALLY	AFFEERMENT
AEROBIOLOGIST	AERONEUROSIS	AESTHETICIAN	AFFEERMENTS
AEROBIOLOGISTS	AERONOMERS	AESTHETICIANS	AFFENPINSCHER
AEROBIOLOGY	AERONOMICAL	AESTHETICISE	AFFENPINSCHERS
AEROBIONTS	AERONOMIES	AESTHETICISED	AFFERENTLY
AEROBIOSES	AERONOMIST	AESTHETICISES	AFFETTUOSO
AEROBIOSIS	AERONOMISTS	AESTHETICISING	AFFETTUOSOS
AEROBIOTIC	AEROPAUSES	AESTHETICISM	AFFIANCING
AEROBIOTICALLY	AEROPHAGIA	AESTHETICISMS	AFFICIONADO
AEROBRAKED	AEROPHAGIAS	AESTHETICIST	AFFICIONADOS
AEROBRAKES	AEROPHAGIES	AESTHETICISTS	AFFIDAVITS
AEROBRAKING	AEROPHOBES	AESTHETICIZE	AFFILIABLE
AEROBRAKINGS	AEROPHOBIA	AESTHETICIZED	AFFILIATED
AEROBUSSES	AEROPHOBIAS	AESTHETICIZES	AFFILIATES
AERODONETICS	AEROPHOBIC	AESTHETICIZING	AFFILIATING
AERODROMES	AEROPHONES	AESTHETICS	AFFILIATION
AERODYNAMIC	AEROPHORES	AESTIVATED	AFFILIATIONS
AERODYNAMICAL	AEROPHYTES	AESTIVATES	AFFINITIES
AERODYNAMICALLY	AEROPLANES	AESTIVATING	AFFINITIVE
AERODYNAMICIST	AEROPLANKTON	AESTIVATION	AFFIRMABLE
AERODYNAMICISTS	AEROPLANKTONS	AESTIVATIONS	AFFIRMANCE
AERODYNAMICS	AEROPULSES	AESTIVATOR	AFFIRMANCES
AEROELASTIC	AEROSCOPES	AESTIVATORS	AFFIRMANTS
AEROELASTICIAN	AEROSHELLS	AETHEREALITIES	AFFIRMATION
AEROELASTICIANS	AEROSIDERITE	AETHEREALITY	AFFIRMATIONS
AEROELASTICITY	AEROSIDERITES	AETHEREALLY	AFFIRMATIVE
AEROEMBOLISM	AEROSOLISATION	AETHRIOSCOPE	AFFIRMATIVELY
AEROEMBOLISMS	AEROSOLISATIONS	AETHRIOSCOPES	AFFIRMATIVES
AEROGENERATOR	AEROSOLISE	AETIOLOGICAL	AFFIRMATORY
AEROGENERATORS	AEROSOLISED	AETIOLOGICALLY	AFFIRMINGLY
AEROGRAMME	AEROSOLISES	AETIOLOGIES	AFFIXATION
AEROGRAMMES	AEROSOLISING	AETIOLOGIST	AFFIXATIONS
AEROGRAPHIES	AEROSOLIZATION	AETIOLOGISTS	AFFIXMENTS
AEROGRAPHS	AEROSOLIZATIONS	AFFABILITIES	AFFIXTURES
AEROGRAPHY	AEROSOLIZE	AFFABILITY	AFFLATIONS
AEROHYDROPLANE	AEROSOLIZED	AFFECTABILITIES	AFFLATUSES
AEROHYDROPLANES	AEROSOLIZES	AFFECTABILITY	AFFLICTERS
AEROLITHOLOGIES	AEROSOLIZING	AFFECTABLE	AFFLICTING
AEROLITHOLOGY	AEROSPACES	AFFECTATION	AFFLICTINGS
AEROLOGICAL	AEROSPHERE	AFFECTATIONS	AFFLICTION
AEROLOGIES	AEROSPHERES	AFFECTEDLY	AFFLICTIONS
AEROLOGIST	AEROSTATIC	AFFECTEDNESS	AFFLICTIVE
AEROLOGISTS	AEROSTATICAL	AFFECTEDNESSES	AFFLICTIVELY
AEROMAGNETIC	AEROSTATICS	AFFECTINGLY	AFFLUENCES
AEROMANCIES	AEROSTATION	AFFECTIONAL	AFFLUENCIES
AEROMECHANIC	AEROSTATIONS	AFFECTIONALLY	AFFLUENTIAL
AEROMECHANICAL	AEROSTRUCTURE	AFFECTIONATE	AFFLUENTIALS
AEROMECHANICS	AEROSTRUCTURES	AFFECTIONATELY	AFFLUENTLY
AEROMEDICAL	AEROTACTIC	AFFECTIONED	AFFLUENTNESS
AEROMEDICINE	AEROTRAINS	AFFECTIONING	AFFLUENTNESSES
AEROMEDICINES	AEROTROPIC	AFFECTIONLESS	AFFLUENZAS
AEROMETERS	AEROTROPISM	AFFECTIONS	AFFLUXIONS

AFFOORDING
AFFORCEMENT
AFFORCEMENTS
AFFORDABILITIES
AFFORDABILITY
AFFORDABLE
AFFORDABLY
AFFORESTABLE
AFFORESTATION
AFFORESTATIONS
AFFORESTED
AFFORESTING
AFFRANCHISE
AFFRANCHISED
AFFRANCHISEMENT
AFFRANCHISES
AFFRANCHISING
AFFRAPPING
AFFREIGHTMENT
AFFREIGHTMENTS
AFFRICATED
AFFRICATES
AFFRICATING
AFFRICATION
AFFRICATIONS
AFFRICATIVE
AFFRICATIVES
AFFRIGHTED
AFFRIGHTEDLY
AFFRIGHTEN
AFFRIGHTENED
AFFRIGHTENING
AFFRIGHTENS
AFFRIGHTFUL
AFFRIGHTING
AFFRIGHTMENT
AFFRIGHTMENTS
AFFRONTING
AFFRONTINGLY
AFFRONTINGS
AFFRONTIVE
AFICIONADA
AFICIONADAS
AFICIONADO
AFICIONADOS
AFLATOXINS
AFOREMENTIONED
AFORETHOUGHT
AFORETHOUGHTS
AFRORMOSIA
AFRORMOSIAS
AFTERBIRTH
AFTERBIRTHS
AFTERBODIES
AFTERBRAIN
AFTERBRAINS
AFTERBURNER
AFTERBURNERS
AFTERBURNING

AFTERBURNINGS
AFTERCARES
AFTERCLAPS
AFTERDAMPS
AFTERDECKS
AFTEREFFECT
AFTEREFFECTS
AFTEREYEING
AFTEREYING
AFTERGAMES
AFTERGLOWS
AFTERGRASS
AFTERGRASSES
AFTERGROWTH
AFTERGROWTHS
AFTERHEATS
AFTERIMAGE
AFTERIMAGES
AFTERLIFES
AFTERLIVES
AFTERMARKET
AFTERMARKETS
AFTERMATHS
AFTERNOONS
AFTERPAINS
AFTERPEAKS
AFTERPIECE
AFTERPIECES
AFTERSALES
AFTERSENSATION
AFTERSENSATIONS
AFTERSHAFT
AFTERSHAFTS
AFTERSHAVE
AFTERSHAVES
AFTERSHOCK
AFTERSHOCKS
AFTERSHOWS
AFTERSUPPER
AFTERSUPPERS
AFTERSWARM
AFTERSWARMS
AFTERTASTE
AFTERTASTES
AFTERTHOUGHT
AFTERTHOUGHTS
AFTERTIMES
AFTERWARDS
AFTERWORDS
AFTERWORLD
AFTERWORLDS
AGALACTIAS
AGALMATOLITE
AGALMATOLITES
AGAMICALLY
AGAMOGENESES
AGAMOGENESIS
AGAMOGENETIC
AGAMOGONIES

AGAMOSPERMIES
AGAMOSPERMY
AGAPANTHUS
AGAPANTHUSES
AGARICACEOUS
AGATEWARES
AGATHODAIMON
AGATHODAIMONS
AGEDNESSES
AGELESSNESS
AGELESSNESSES
AGENDALESS
AGENTIVITIES
AGENTIVITY
AGGIORNAMENTI
AGGIORNAMENTO
AGGIORNAMENTOS
AGGLOMERATE
AGGLOMERATED
AGGLOMERATES
AGGLOMERATING
AGGLOMERATION
AGGLOMERATIONS
AGGLOMERATIVE
AGGLUTINABILITY
AGGLUTINABLE
AGGLUTINANT
AGGLUTINANTS
AGGLUTINATE
AGGLUTINATED
AGGLUTINATES
AGGLUTINATING
AGGLUTINATION
AGGLUTINATIONS
AGGLUTINATIVE
AGGLUTININ
AGGLUTININS
AGGLUTINOGEN
AGGLUTINOGENIC
AGGLUTINOGENS
AGGRADATION
AGGRADATIONS
AGGRANDISE
AGGRANDISED
AGGRANDISEMENT
AGGRANDISEMENTS
AGGRANDISER
AGGRANDISERS
AGGRANDISES
AGGRANDISING
AGGRANDIZE
AGGRANDIZED
AGGRANDIZEMENT
AGGRANDIZEMENTS
AGGRANDIZER
AGGRANDIZERS
AGGRANDIZES
AGGRANDIZING
AGGRAVATED

AGGRAVATES
AGGRAVATING
AGGRAVATINGLY
AGGRAVATION
AGGRAVATIONS
AGGREGATED
AGGREGATELY
AGGREGATENESS
AGGREGATENESSES
AGGREGATES
AGGREGATING
AGGREGATION
AGGREGATIONAL
AGGREGATIONS
AGGREGATIVE
AGGREGATIVELY
AGGREGATOR
AGGREGATORS
AGGRESSING
AGGRESSION
AGGRESSIONS
AGGRESSIVE
AGGRESSIVELY
AGGRESSIVENESS
AGGRESSIVITIES
AGGRESSIVITY
AGGRESSORS
AGGRIEVEDLY
AGGRIEVEMENT
AGGRIEVEMENTS
AGGRIEVING
AGILENESSES
AGISTMENTS
AGITATEDLY
AGITATIONAL
AGITATIONS
AGNATICALLY
AGNOIOLOGIES
AGNOIOLOGY
AGNOSTICISM
AGNOSTICISMS
AGONISEDLY
AGONISINGLY
AGONISTICAL
AGONISTICALLY
AGONISTICS
AGONIZEDLY
AGONIZINGLY
AGONOTHETES
AGORAPHOBE
AGORAPHOBES
AGORAPHOBIA
AGORAPHOBIAS
AGORAPHOBIC
AGORAPHOBICS
AGRANULOCYTE
AGRANULOCYTES
AGRANULOCYTOSES
AGRANULOCYTOSIS

AGRANULOSES
AGRANULOSIS
AGRARIANISM
AGRARIANISMS
AGREEABILITIES
AGREEABILITY
AGREEABLENESS
AGREEABLENESSES
AGREEMENTS
AGREGATION
AGREGATIONS
AGRIBUSINESS
AGRIBUSINESSES
AGRIBUSINESSMAN
AGRIBUSINESSMEN
AGRICHEMICAL
AGRICHEMICALS
AGRICULTURAL
AGRICULTURALIST
AGRICULTURALLY
AGRICULTURE
AGRICULTURES
AGRICULTURIST
AGRICULTURISTS
AGRIMONIES
AGRIOLOGIES
AGRIPRODUCT
AGRIPRODUCTS
AGRITOURISM
AGRITOURISMS
AGRITOURIST
AGRITOURISTS
AGROBIOLOGICAL
AGROBIOLOGIES
AGROBIOLOGIST
AGROBIOLOGISTS
AGROBIOLOGY
AGROBUSINESS
AGROBUSINESSES
AGROCHEMICAL
AGROCHEMICALS
AGRODOLCES
AGROFORESTER
AGROFORESTERS
AGROFORESTRIES
AGROFORESTRY
AGROINDUSTRIAL
AGROINDUSTRIES
AGROINDUSTRY
AGROLOGICAL
AGROLOGIES
AGROLOGIST
AGROLOGISTS
AGRONOMIAL
AGRONOMICAL
AGRONOMICALLY
AGRONOMICS
AGRONOMIES
AGRONOMIST

AGRONOMISTS
AGROSTEMMA
AGROSTEMMAS
AGROSTEMMATA
AGROSTOLOGICAL
AGROSTOLOGIES
AGROSTOLOGIST
AGROSTOLOGISTS
AGROSTOLOGY
AGROTERRORISM
AGROTERRORISMS
AGROTOURISM
AGROTOURISMS
AGROTOURIST
AGROTOURISTS
AGRYPNOTIC
AGRYPNOTICS
AGTERSKOTS
AGUARDIENTE
AGUARDIENTES
AHISTORICAL
AHORSEBACK
AICHMOPHOBIA
AICHMOPHOBIAS
AIGUILLETTE
AIGUILLETTES
AILANTHUSES
AILOUROPHILE
AILOUROPHILES
AILOUROPHILIA
AILOUROPHILIAS
AILOUROPHILIC
AILOUROPHOBE
AILOUROPHOBES
AILOUROPHOBIA
AILOUROPHOBIAS
AILOUROPHOBIC
AILUROPHILE
AILUROPHILES
AILUROPHILIA
AILUROPHILIAS
AILUROPHILIC
AILUROPHOBE
AILUROPHOBES
AILUROPHOBIA
AILUROPHOBIAS
AILUROPHOBIC
AIMLESSNESS
AIMLESSNESSES
AIRBRUSHED
AIRBRUSHES
AIRBRUSHING
AIRCOACHES
AIRCRAFTMAN
AIRCRAFTMEN
AIRCRAFTSMAN
AIRCRAFTSMEN
AIRCRAFTSWOMAN
AIRCRAFTSWOMEN

AIRCRAFTWOMAN
AIRCRAFTWOMEN
AIRDROPPED
AIRDROPPING
AIRFREIGHT
AIRFREIGHTED
AIRFREIGHTING
AIRFREIGHTS
AIRINESSES
AIRLESSNESS
AIRLESSNESSES
AIRLIFTING
AIRMAILING
AIRMANSHIP
AIRMANSHIPS
AIRPROOFED
AIRPROOFING
AIRSICKNESS
AIRSICKNESSES
AIRSTREAMS
AIRSTRIKES
AIRTIGHTNESS
AIRTIGHTNESSES
AIRWORTHIER
AIRWORTHIEST
AIRWORTHINESS
AIRWORTHINESSES
AITCHBONES
AKATHISIAS
AKOLOUTHOS
AKOLOUTHOSES
AKOLUTHOSES
ALABAMINES
ALABANDINE
ALABANDINES
ALABANDITE
ALABANDITES
ALABASTERS
ALABASTRINE
ALABLASTER
ALABLASTERS
ALACRITIES
ALACRITOUS
ALARMINGLY
ALBARELLOS
ALBATROSSES
ALBERTITES
ALBESCENCE
ALBESCENCES
ALBESPINES
ALBESPYNES
ALBINESSES
ALBINISTIC
ALBINOISMS
ALBITISING
ALBITIZING
ALBUGINEOUS
ALBUMBLATT
ALBUMBLATTER

ALBUMBLATTS
ALBUMENISE
ALBUMENISED
ALBUMENISES
ALBUMENISING
ALBUMENIZE
ALBUMENIZED
ALBUMENIZES
ALBUMENIZING
ALBUMINATE
ALBUMINATES
ALBUMINISE
ALBUMINISED
ALBUMINISES
ALBUMINISING
ALBUMINIZE
ALBUMINIZED
ALBUMINIZES
ALBUMINIZING
ALBUMINOID
ALBUMINOIDS
ALBUMINOUS
ALBUMINURIA
ALBUMINURIAS
ALBUMINURIC
ALBUTEROLS
ALCAICERIA
ALCAICERIAS
ALCARRAZAS
ALCATRASES
ALCHEMICAL
ALCHEMICALLY
ALCHEMISED
ALCHEMISES
ALCHEMISING
ALCHEMISTIC
ALCHEMISTICAL
ALCHEMISTS
ALCHEMIZED
ALCHEMIZES
ALCHEMIZING
ALCHERINGA
ALCHERINGAS
ALCOHOLICALLY
ALCOHOLICITIES
ALCOHOLICITY
ALCOHOLICS
ALCOHOLISATION
ALCOHOLISATIONS
ALCOHOLISE
ALCOHOLISED
ALCOHOLISES
ALCOHOLISING
ALCOHOLISM
ALCOHOLISMS
ALCOHOLIZATION
ALCOHOLIZATIONS
ALCOHOLIZE
ALCOHOLIZED

ALCOHOLIZES

ALCOHOLIZES	ALGEBRAIST	ALKALIMETERS	ALLEGORIZED
ALCOHOLIZING	ALGEBRAISTS	ALKALIMETRIC	ALLEGORIZER
ALCOHOLOMETER	ALGIDITIES	ALKALIMETRIES	ALLEGORIZERS
ALCOHOLOMETERS	ALGIDNESSES	ALKALIMETRY	ALLEGORIZES
ALCOHOLOMETRIES	ALGOLAGNIA	ALKALINISATION	ALLEGORIZING
ALCOHOLOMETRY	ALGOLAGNIAC	ALKALINISATIONS	ALLEGRETTO
ALCYONARIAN	ALGOLAGNIACS	ALKALINISE	ALLEGRETTOS
ALCYONARIANS	ALGOLAGNIAS	ALKALINISED	ALLELOMORPH
ALDERFLIES	ALGOLAGNIC	ALKALINISES	ALLELOMORPHIC
ALDERMANIC	ALGOLAGNIST	ALKALINISING	ALLELOMORPHISM
ALDERMANITIES	ALGOLAGNISTS	ALKALINITIES	ALLELOMORPHISMS
ALDERMANITY	ALGOLOGICAL	ALKALINITY	ALLELOMORPHS
ALDERMANLIKE	ALGOLOGICALLY	ALKALINIZATION	ALLELOPATHIC
ALDERMANLY	ALGOLOGIES	ALKALINIZATIONS	ALLELOPATHIES
ALDERMANRIES	ALGOLOGIST	ALKALINIZE	ALLELOPATHY
ALDERMANRY	ALGOLOGISTS	ALKALINIZED	ALLELUIAHS
ALDERMANSHIP	ALGOMETERS	ALKALINIZES	ALLEMANDES
ALDERMANSHIPS	ALGOMETRIES	ALKALINIZING	ALLERGENIC
ALDERWOMAN	ALGOPHOBIA	ALKALISABLE	ALLERGENICITIES
ALDERWOMEN	ALGOPHOBIAS	ALKALISERS	ALLERGENICITY
ALDOHEXOSE	ALGORISMIC	ALKALISING	ALLERGISTS
ALDOHEXOSES	ALGORITHMIC	ALKALIZABLE	ALLETHRINS
ALDOLISATION	ALGORITHMICALLY	ALKALIZERS	ALLEVIANTS
ALDOLISATIONS	ALGORITHMS	ALKALIZING	ALLEVIATED
ALDOLIZATION	ALIENABILITIES	ALKALOIDAL	ALLEVIATES
ALDOLIZATIONS	ALIENABILITY	ALKYLATING	ALLEVIATING
ALDOPENTOSE	ALIENATING	ALKYLATION	ALLEVIATION
ALDOPENTOSES	ALIENATION	ALKYLATIONS	ALLEVIATIONS
ALDOSTERONE	ALIENATIONS	ALLANTOIDAL	ALLEVIATIVE
ALDOSTERONES	ALIENATORS	ALLANTOIDES	ALLEVIATOR
ALDOSTERONISM	ALIENNESSES	ALLANTOIDS	ALLEVIATORS
ALDOSTERONISMS	ALIGHTMENT	ALLANTOINS	ALLEVIATORY
ALEATORIES	ALIGHTMENTS	ALLANTOISES	ALLHALLOND
ALEBENCHES	ALIGNMENTS	ALLARGANDO	ALLHALLOWEN
ALECTRYONS	ALIKENESSES	ALLAYMENTS	ALLHALLOWN
ALEGGEAUNCE	ALIMENTARY	ALLEGATION	ALLHOLLOWN
ALEGGEAUNCES	ALIMENTATION	ALLEGATIONS	ALLIACEOUS
ALEMBICATED	ALIMENTATIONS	ALLEGEANCE	ALLICHOLIES
ALEMBICATION	ALIMENTATIVE	ALLEGEANCES	ALLIGARTAS
ALEMBICATIONS	ALIMENTING	ALLEGIANCE	ALLIGATING
ALEMBROTHS	ALIMENTIVENESS	ALLEGIANCES	ALLIGATION
ALERTNESSES	ALINEATION	ALLEGIANTS	ALLIGATIONS
ALEXANDERS	ALINEATIONS	ALLEGORICAL	ALLIGATORS
ALEXANDERSES	ALINEMENTS	ALLEGORICALLY	ALLINEATION
ALEXANDRINE	ALISMACEOUS	ALLEGORICALNESS	ALLINEATIONS
ALEXANDRINES	ALITERACIES	ALLEGORIES	ALLITERATE
ALEXANDRITE	ALITERATES	ALLEGORISATION	ALLITERATED
ALEXANDRITES	ALIVENESSES	ALLEGORISATIONS	ALLITERATES
ALEXIPHARMAKON	ALIZARINES	ALLEGORISE	ALLITERATING
ALEXIPHARMAKONS	ALKAHESTIC	ALLEGORISED	ALLITERATION
ALEXIPHARMIC	ALKALESCENCE	ALLEGORISER	ALLITERATIONS
ALEXIPHARMICS	ALKALESCENCES	ALLEGORISERS	ALLITERATIVE
ALFILARIAS	ALKALESCENCIES	ALLEGORISES	ALLITERATIVELY
ALFILERIAS	ALKALESCENCY	ALLEGORISING	ALLNIGHTER
ALGAECIDES	ALKALESCENT	ALLEGORIST	ALLNIGHTERS
ALGARROBAS	ALKALIFIED	ALLEGORISTS	ALLOANTIBODIES
ALGARROBOS	ALKALIFIES	ALLEGORIZATION	ALLOANTIBODY
ALGEBRAICAL	ALKALIFYING	ALLEGORIZATIONS	ALLOANTIGEN
ALGEBRAICALLY	ALKALIMETER	ALLEGORIZE	ALLOANTIGENS

ALLOCARPIES	ALLOTHEISM	ALPHABETICAL	ALTERNATION
ALLOCATABLE	ALLOTHEISMS	ALPHABETICALLY	ALTERNATIONS
ALLOCATING	ALLOTMENTS	ALPHABETIFORM	ALTERNATIVE
ALLOCATION	ALLOTRIOMORPHIC	ALPHABETING	ALTERNATIVELY
ALLOCATIONS	ALLOTROPES	ALPHABETISATION	ALTERNATIVENESS
ALLOCATORS	ALLOTROPIC	ALPHABETISE	ALTERNATIVES
ALLOCHEIRIA	ALLOTROPICALLY	ALPHABETISED	ALTERNATOR
ALLOCHEIRIAS	ALLOTROPIES	ALPHABETISER	ALTERNATORS
ALLOCHIRIA	ALLOTROPISM	ALPHABETISERS	ALTIGRAPHS
ALLOCHIRIAS	ALLOTROPISMS	ALPHABETISES	ALTIMETERS
ALLOCHTHONOUS	ALLOTROPOUS	ALPHABETISING	ALTIMETRICAL
ALLOCUTION	ALLOTTERIES	ALPHABETIZATION	ALTIMETRICALLY
ALLOCUTIONS	ALLOTYPICALLY	ALPHABETIZE	ALTIMETRIES
ALLOGAMIES	ALLOTYPIES	ALPHABETIZED	ALTIPLANOS
ALLOGAMOUS	ALLOWABILITIES	ALPHABETIZER	ALTISONANT
ALLOGENEIC	ALLOWABILITY	ALPHABETIZERS	ALTITONANT
ALLOGRAFTED	ALLOWABLENESS	ALPHABETIZES	ALTITUDINAL
ALLOGRAFTING	ALLOWABLENESSES	ALPHABETIZING	ALTITUDINARIAN
ALLOGRAFTS	ALLOWABLES	ALPHAMERIC	ALTITUDINARIANS
ALLOGRAPHIC	ALLOWANCED	ALPHAMERICAL	ALTITUDINOUS
ALLOGRAPHS	ALLOWANCES	ALPHAMERICALLY	ALTOCUMULI
ALLOIOSTROPHOS	ALLOWANCING	ALPHAMETIC	ALTOCUMULUS
ALLOMERISM	ALLUREMENT	ALPHAMETICS	ALTOGETHER
ALLOMERISMS	ALLUREMENTS	ALPHANUMERIC	ALTOGETHERS
ALLOMEROUS	ALLURINGLY	ALPHANUMERICAL	ALTORUFFLED
ALLOMETRIC	ALLUSIVELY	ALPHANUMERICS	ALTOSTRATI
ALLOMETRIES	ALLUSIVENESS	ALPHASORTED	ALTOSTRATUS
ALLOMORPHIC	ALLUSIVENESSES	ALPHASORTING	ALTRICIALS
ALLOMORPHISM	ALLYCHOLLIES	ALPHASORTS	ALTRUISTIC
ALLOMORPHISMS	ALLYCHOLLY	ALPHOSISES	ALTRUISTICALLY
ALLOMORPHS	ALMACANTAR	ALSTROEMERIA	ALUMINATES
ALLONYMOUS	ALMACANTARS	ALSTROEMERIAS	ALUMINIFEROUS
ALLOPATHIC	ALMANDINES	ALTALTISSIMO	ALUMINISED
ALLOPATHICALLY	ALMANDITES	ALTALTISSIMOS	ALUMINISES
ALLOPATHIES	ALMIGHTILY	ALTARPIECE	ALUMINISING
ALLOPATHIST	ALMIGHTINESS	ALTARPIECES	ALUMINIUMS
ALLOPATHISTS	ALMIGHTINESSES	ALTAZIMUTH	ALUMINIZED
ALLOPATRIC	ALMSGIVERS	ALTAZIMUTHS	ALUMINIZES
ALLOPATRICALLY	ALMSGIVING	ALTERABILITIES	ALUMINIZING
ALLOPATRIES	ALMSGIVINGS	ALTERABILITY	ALUMINOSILICATE
ALLOPHANES	ALMSHOUSES	ALTERATION	ALUMINOSITIES
ALLOPHONES	ALMUCANTAR	ALTERATIONS	ALUMINOSITY
ALLOPHONIC	ALMUCANTARS	ALTERATIVE	ALUMINOTHERMIES
ALLOPLASMIC	ALOGICALLY	ALTERATIVES	ALUMINOTHERMY
ALLOPLASMS	ALONENESSES	ALTERCATED	ALUMSTONES
ALLOPLASTIC	ALONGSHORE	ALTERCATES	ALVEOLARLY
ALLOPOLYPLOID	ALONGSHOREMAN	ALTERCATING	ALVEOLATION
ALLOPOLYPLOIDS	ALONGSHOREMEN	ALTERCATION	ALVEOLATIONS
ALLOPOLYPLOIDY	ALOOFNESSES	ALTERCATIONS	ALVEOLITIS
ALLOPURINOL	ALPARGATAS	ALTERCATIVE	ALVEOLITISES
ALLOPURINOLS	ALPENGLOWS	ALTERITIES	ALYCOMPAINE
ALLOSAURUS	ALPENHORNS	ALTERNANCE	ALYCOMPAINES
ALLOSAURUSES	ALPENSTOCK	ALTERNANCES	AMAKWEREKWERE
ALLOSTERIC	ALPENSTOCKS	ALTERNANTS	AMALGAMATE
ALLOSTERICALLY	ALPESTRINE	ALTERNATED	AMALGAMATED
ALLOSTERIES	ALPHABETARIAN	ALTERNATELY	AMALGAMATES
ALLOTETRAPLOID	ALPHABETARIANS	ALTERNATES	AMALGAMATING
ALLOTETRAPLOIDS	ALPHABETED	ALTERNATIM	AMALGAMATION
ALLOTETRAPLOIDY	ALPHABETIC	ALTERNATING	AMALGAMATIONS

AMALGAMATIVE	AMBIOPHONY	AMELIORATING	AMINOPHENAZONES
AMALGAMATOR	AMBISEXUAL	AMELIORATION	AMINOPHENOL
AMALGAMATORS	AMBISEXUALITIES	AMELIORATIONS	AMINOPHENOLS
AMANTADINE	AMBISEXUALITY	AMELIORATIVE	AMINOPHYLLINE
AMANTADINES	AMBISEXUALS	AMELIORATOR	AMINOPHYLLINES
AMANUENSES	AMBISONICS	AMELIORATORS	AMINOPTERIN
AMANUENSIS	AMBITIONED	AMELIORATORY	AMINOPTERINS
AMARACUSES	AMBITIONING	AMELOBLAST	AMINOPYRINE
AMARANTACEOUS	AMBITIONLESS	AMELOBLASTS	AMINOPYRINES
AMARANTHACEOUS	AMBITIOUSLY	AMELOGENESES	AMISSIBILITIES
AMARANTHINE	AMBITIOUSNESS	AMELOGENESIS	AMISSIBILITY
AMARANTINE	AMBITIOUSNESSES	AMENABILITIES	AMITOTICALLY
AMARYLLIDACEOUS	AMBIVALENCE	AMENABILITY	AMITRIPTYLINE
AMARYLLIDS	AMBIVALENCES	AMENABLENESS	AMITRIPTYLINES
AMARYLLISES	AMBIVALENCIES	AMENABLENESSES	AMITRYPTYLINE
AMASSMENTS	AMBIVALENCY	AMENAUNCES	AMITRYPTYLINES
AMATEURISH	AMBIVALENT	AMENDATORY	AMMOCOETES
AMATEURISHLY	AMBIVALENTLY	AMENDMENTS	AMMONIACAL
AMATEURISHNESS	AMBIVERSION	AMENORRHEA	AMMONIACUM
AMATEURISM	AMBIVERSIONS	AMENORRHEAS	AMMONIACUMS
AMATEURISMS	AMBLYGONITE	AMENORRHEIC	AMMONIATED
AMATEURSHIP	AMBLYGONITES	AMENORRHOEA	AMMONIATES
AMATEURSHIPS	AMBLYOPIAS	AMENORRHOEAS	AMMONIATING
AMATIVENESS	AMBOCEPTOR	AMENTACEOUS	AMMONIATION
AMATIVENESSES	AMBOCEPTORS	AMENTIFEROUS	AMMONIATIONS
AMATORIALLY	AMBOSEXUAL	AMERCEABLE	AMMONIFICATION
AMATORIOUS	AMBROSIALLY	AMERCEMENT	AMMONIFICATIONS
AMAZEDNESS	AMBROTYPES	AMERCEMENTS	AMMONIFIED
AMAZEDNESSES	AMBULACRAL	AMERCIABLE	AMMONIFIES
AMAZEMENTS	AMBULACRUM	AMERCIAMENT	AMMONIFYING
AMAZONIANS	AMBULANCEMAN	AMERCIAMENTS	AMMONOLYSES
AMAZONITES	AMBULANCEMEN	AMERICIUMS	AMMONOLYSIS
AMAZONSTONE	AMBULANCES	AMETABOLIC	AMMOPHILOUS
AMAZONSTONES	AMBULANCEWOMAN	AMETABOLISM	AMMUNITION
AMBAGITORY	AMBULANCEWOMEN	AMETABOLISMS	AMMUNITIONED
AMBASSADOR	AMBULATING	AMETABOLOUS	AMMUNITIONING
AMBASSADORIAL	AMBULATION	AMETHYSTINE	AMMUNITIONS
AMBASSADORS	AMBULATIONS	AMETROPIAS	AMNESTYING
AMBASSADORSHIP	AMBULATORIES	AMIABILITIES	AMNIOCENTESES
AMBASSADORSHIPS	AMBULATORILY	AMIABILITY	AMNIOCENTESIS
AMBASSADRESS	AMBULATORS	AMIABLENESS	AMNIOTOMIES
AMBASSADRESSES	AMBULATORY	AMIABLENESSES	AMOBARBITAL
AMBASSAGES	AMBULETTES	AMIANTHINE	AMOBARBITALS
AMBERGRISES	AMBUSCADED	AMIANTHOID	AMOEBIASES
AMBERJACKS	AMBUSCADER	AMIANTHOIDAL	AMOEBIASIS
AMBIDENTATE	AMBUSCADERS	AMIANTHUSES	AMOEBIFORM
AMBIDEXTER	AMBUSCADES	AMIANTUSES	AMOEBOCYTE
AMBIDEXTERITIES	AMBUSCADING	AMICABILITIES	AMOEBOCYTES
AMBIDEXTERITY	AMBUSCADOES	AMICABILITY	AMONTILLADO
AMBIDEXTEROUS	AMBUSCADOS	AMICABLENESS	AMONTILLADOS
AMBIDEXTERS	AMBUSHMENT	AMICABLENESSES	AMORALISMS
AMBIDEXTROUS	AMBUSHMENTS	AMINOACIDURIA	AMORALISTS
AMBIDEXTROUSLY	AMEBOCYTES	AMINOACIDURIAS	AMORALITIES
AMBIGUITIES	AMELIORABLE	AMINOBENZOIC	AMOROSITIES
AMBIGUOUSLY	AMELIORANT	AMINOBUTENE	AMOROUSNESS
AMBIGUOUSNESS	AMELIORANTS	AMINOBUTENES	AMOROUSNESSES
AMBIGUOUSNESSES	AMELIORATE	AMINOPEPTIDASE	AMORPHISMS
AMBILATERAL	AMELIORATED	AMINOPEPTIDASES	AMORPHOUSLY
AMBIOPHONIES	AMELIORATES	AMINOPHENAZONE	AMORPHOUSNESS

AMORPHOUSNESSES	AMPHIDENTATE	AMPLEXUSES	ANABAPTISTS
AMORTISABLE	AMPHIDIPLOID	AMPLIATION	ANABAPTIZE
AMORTISATION	AMPHIDIPLOIDIES	AMPLIATIONS	ANABAPTIZED
AMORTISATIONS	AMPHIDIPLOIDS	AMPLIATIVE	ANABAPTIZES
AMORTISEMENT	AMPHIDIPLOIDY	AMPLIDYNES	ANABAPTIZING
AMORTISEMENTS	AMPHIGASTRIA	AMPLIFIABLE	ANABLEPSES
AMORTISING	AMPHIGASTRIUM	AMPLIFICATION	ANABOLISMS
AMORTIZABLE	AMPHIGORIC	AMPLIFICATIONS	ANABOLITES
AMORTIZATION	AMPHIGORIES	AMPLIFIERS	ANABOLITIC
AMORTIZATIONS	AMPHIGOURI	AMPLIFYING	ANABRANCHES
AMORTIZEMENT	AMPHIGOURIS	AMPLITUDES	ANACARDIACEOUS
AMORTIZEMENTS	AMPHIMACER	AMPLOSOMES	ANACARDIUM
AMORTIZING	AMPHIMACERS	AMPULLACEAL	ANACARDIUMS
AMOURETTES	AMPHIMICTIC	AMPULLACEOUS	ANACATHARSES
AMOXICILLIN	AMPHIMIXES	AMPULLOSITIES	ANACATHARSIS
AMOXICILLINS	AMPHIMIXIS	AMPULLOSITY	ANACATHARTIC
AMOXYCILLIN	AMPHIOXUSES	AMPUTATING	ANACATHARTICS
AMOXYCILLINS	AMPHIPATHIC	AMPUTATION	ANACHARISES
AMPELOGRAPHIES	AMPHIPHILE	AMPUTATIONS	ANACHORISM
AMPELOGRAPHY	AMPHIPHILES	AMPUTATORS	ANACHORISMS
AMPELOPSES	AMPHIPHILIC	AMRITATTVA	ANACHRONIC
AMPELOPSIS	AMPHIPLOID	AMRITATTVAS	ANACHRONICAL
AMPEROMETRIC	AMPHIPLOIDIES	AMSINCKIAS	ANACHRONICALLY
AMPERSANDS	AMPHIPLOIDS	AMUSEMENTS	ANACHRONISM
AMPERZANDS	AMPHIPLOIDY	AMUSINGNESS	ANACHRONISMS
AMPHETAMINE	AMPHIPODOUS	AMUSINGNESSES	ANACHRONISTIC
AMPHETAMINES	AMPHIPROSTYLAR	AMUSIVENESS	ANACHRONOUS
AMPHIARTHROSES	AMPHIPROSTYLE	AMUSIVENESSES	ANACHRONOUSLY
AMPHIARTHROSIS	AMPHIPROSTYLES	AMYGDALACEOUS	ANACLASTIC
AMPHIASTER	AMPHIPROTIC	AMYGDALATE	ANACOLUTHA
AMPHIASTERS	AMPHISBAENA	AMYGDALINE	ANACOLUTHIA
AMPHIBIANS	AMPHISBAENAE	AMYGDALINS	ANACOLUTHIAS
AMPHIBIOTIC	AMPHISBAENAS	AMYGDALOID	ANACOLUTHIC
AMPHIBIOUS	AMPHISBAENIC	AMYGDALOIDAL	ANACOLUTHICALLY
AMPHIBIOUSLY	AMPHISCIAN	AMYGDALOIDS	ANACOLUTHON
AMPHIBIOUSNESS	AMPHISCIANS	AMYLACEOUS	ANACOLUTHONS
AMPHIBLASTIC	AMPHISTOMATAL	AMYLOIDOSES	ANACOUSTIC
AMPHIBLASTULA	AMPHISTOMATIC	AMYLOIDOSIS	ANACREONTIC
AMPHIBLASTULAE	AMPHISTOMOUS	AMYLOLYSES	ANACREONTICALLY
AMPHIBOLES	AMPHISTYLAR	AMYLOLYSIS	ANACREONTICS
AMPHIBOLIC	AMPHISTYLARS	AMYLOLYTIC	ANACRUSTIC
AMPHIBOLIES	AMPHITHEATER	AMYLOPECTIN	ANADIPLOSES
AMPHIBOLITE	AMPHITHEATERS	AMYLOPECTINS	ANADIPLOSIS
AMPHIBOLITES	AMPHITHEATRAL	AMYLOPLAST	ANADROMOUS
AMPHIBOLOGICAL	AMPHITHEATRE	AMYLOPLASTS	ANADYOMENE
AMPHIBOLOGIES	AMPHITHEATRES	AMYLOPSINS	ANAEROBICALLY
AMPHIBOLOGY	AMPHITHEATRIC	AMYOTONIAS	ANAEROBIONT
AMPHIBOLOUS	AMPHITHEATRICAL	AMYOTROPHIC	ANAEROBIONTS
AMPHIBRACH	AMPHITHECIA	AMYOTROPHIES	ANAEROBIOSES
AMPHIBRACHIC	AMPHITHECIUM	AMYOTROPHY	ANAEROBIOSIS
AMPHIBRACHS	AMPHITRICHA	ANABANTIDS	ANAEROBIOTIC
AMPHICHROIC	AMPHITRICHOUS	ANABAPTISE	ANAEROBIUM
AMPHICHROMATIC	AMPHITROPOUS	ANABAPTISED	ANAESTHESES
AMPHICOELOUS	AMPHOLYTES	ANABAPTISES	ANAESTHESIA
AMPHICTYON	AMPHOTERIC	ANABAPTISING	ANAESTHESIAS
AMPHICTYONIC	AMPICILLIN	ANABAPTISM	ANAESTHESIOLOGY
AMPHICTYONIES	AMPICILLINS	ANABAPTISMS	ANAESTHESIS
AMPHICTYONS	AMPLENESSES	ANABAPTIST	ANAESTHETIC
AMPHICTYONY	AMPLEXICAUL	ANABAPTISTIC	ANAESTHETICALLY

ANAESTHETICS

ANAESTHETICS
ANAESTHETISE
ANAESTHETISED
ANAESTHETISES
ANAESTHETISING
ANAESTHETIST
ANAESTHETISTS
ANAESTHETIZE
ANAESTHETIZED
ANAESTHETIZES
ANAESTHETIZING
ANAGENESES
ANAGENESIS
ANAGLYPHIC
ANAGLYPHICAL
ANAGLYPHIES
ANAGLYPTIC
ANAGLYPTICAL
ANAGNORISES
ANAGNORISIS
ANAGOGICAL
ANAGOGICALLY
ANAGRAMMATIC
ANAGRAMMATICAL
ANAGRAMMATISE
ANAGRAMMATISED
ANAGRAMMATISES
ANAGRAMMATISING
ANAGRAMMATISM
ANAGRAMMATISMS
ANAGRAMMATIST
ANAGRAMMATISTS
ANAGRAMMATIZE
ANAGRAMMATIZED
ANAGRAMMATIZES
ANAGRAMMATIZING
ANAGRAMMED
ANAGRAMMER
ANAGRAMMERS
ANAGRAMMING
ANALEMMATA
ANALEMMATIC
ANALEPTICS
ANALGESIAS
ANALGESICS
ANALGETICS
ANALOGICAL
ANALOGICALLY
ANALOGISED
ANALOGISES
ANALOGISING
ANALOGISMS
ANALOGISTS
ANALOGIZED
ANALOGIZES
ANALOGIZING
ANALOGOUSLY
ANALOGOUSNESS
ANALOGOUSNESSES

ANALPHABET
ANALPHABETE
ANALPHABETES
ANALPHABETIC
ANALPHABETICS
ANALPHABETISM
ANALPHABETISMS
ANALPHABETS
ANALYSABLE
ANALYSANDS
ANALYSATION
ANALYSATIONS
ANALYTICAL
ANALYTICALLY
ANALYTICITIES
ANALYTICITY
ANALYZABILITIES
ANALYZABILITY
ANALYZABLE
ANALYZATION
ANALYZATIONS
ANAMNESTIC
ANAMNESTICALLY
ANAMNIOTES
ANAMNIOTIC
ANAMORPHIC
ANAMORPHISM
ANAMORPHISMS
ANAMORPHOSCOPE
ANAMORPHOSCOPES
ANAMORPHOSES
ANAMORPHOSIS
ANAMORPHOUS
ANANDAMIDE
ANANDAMIDES
ANAPAESTIC
ANAPAESTICAL
ANAPESTICS
ANAPHORESES
ANAPHORESIS
ANAPHORICAL
ANAPHORICALLY
ANAPHRODISIA
ANAPHRODISIAC
ANAPHRODISIACS
ANAPHRODISIAS
ANAPHYLACTIC
ANAPHYLACTOID
ANAPHYLAXES
ANAPHYLAXIES
ANAPHYLAXIS
ANAPHYLAXY
ANAPLASIAS
ANAPLASMOSES
ANAPLASMOSIS
ANAPLASTIC
ANAPLASTIES
ANAPLEROSES
ANAPLEROSIS

ANAPLEROTIC
ANAPTYCTIC
ANAPTYCTICAL
ANARCHICAL
ANARCHICALLY
ANARCHISED
ANARCHISES
ANARCHISING
ANARCHISMS
ANARCHISTIC
ANARCHISTS
ANARCHIZED
ANARCHIZES
ANARCHIZING
ANARTHRIAS
ANARTHROUS
ANARTHROUSLY
ANARTHROUSNESS
ANASARCOUS
ANASTIGMAT
ANASTIGMATIC
ANASTIGMATISM
ANASTIGMATISMS
ANASTIGMATS
ANASTOMOSE
ANASTOMOSED
ANASTOMOSES
ANASTOMOSING
ANASTOMOSIS
ANASTOMOTIC
ANASTROPHE
ANASTROPHES
ANASTROZOLE
ANASTROZOLES
ANATHEMATA
ANATHEMATICAL
ANATHEMATISE
ANATHEMATISED
ANATHEMATISES
ANATHEMATISING
ANATHEMATIZE
ANATHEMATIZED
ANATHEMATIZES
ANATHEMATIZING
ANATOMICAL
ANATOMICALLY
ANATOMISATION
ANATOMISATIONS
ANATOMISED
ANATOMISER
ANATOMISERS
ANATOMISES
ANATOMISING
ANATOMISTS
ANATOMIZATION
ANATOMIZATIONS
ANATOMIZED
ANATOMIZER
ANATOMIZERS

ANATOMIZES
ANATOMIZING
ANATROPIES
ANATROPOUS
ANCESTORED
ANCESTORIAL
ANCESTORING
ANCESTRALLY
ANCESTRESS
ANCESTRESSES
ANCESTRIES
ANCHORAGES
ANCHORESSES
ANCHORETIC
ANCHORETICAL
ANCHORETTE
ANCHORETTES
ANCHORITES
ANCHORITIC
ANCHORITICAL
ANCHORITICALLY
ANCHORLESS
ANCHORPEOPLE
ANCHORPERSON
ANCHORPERSONS
ANCHORWOMAN
ANCHORWOMEN
ANCHOVETAS
ANCHOVETTA
ANCHOVETTAS
ANCHYLOSED
ANCHYLOSES
ANCHYLOSING
ANCHYLOSIS
ANCHYLOTIC
ANCIENTEST
ANCIENTNESS
ANCIENTNESSES
ANCIENTRIES
ANCILLARIES
ANCIPITOUS
ANCYLOSTOMIASES
ANCYLOSTOMIASIS
ANDALUSITE
ANDALUSITES
ANDANTINOS
ANDOUILLES
ANDOUILLETTE
ANDOUILLETTES
ANDRADITES
ANDROCENTRIC
ANDROCENTRISM
ANDROCENTRISMS
ANDROCEPHALOUS
ANDROCLINIA
ANDROCLINIUM
ANDRODIOECIOUS
ANDRODIOECISM
ANDRODIOECISMS

ANDROECIAL
ANDROECIUM
ANDROECIUMS
ANDROGENESES
ANDROGENESIS
ANDROGENETIC
ANDROGENIC
ANDROGENOUS
ANDROGYNES
ANDROGYNIES
ANDROGYNOPHORE
ANDROGYNOPHORES
ANDROGYNOUS
ANDROLOGIES
ANDROLOGIST
ANDROLOGISTS
ANDROMEDAS
ANDROMEDOTOXIN
ANDROMEDOTOXINS
ANDROMONOECIOUS
ANDROMONOECISM
ANDROMONOECISMS
ANDROPAUSE
ANDROPAUSES
ANDROPHORE
ANDROPHORES
ANDROSPHINGES
ANDROSPHINX
ANDROSPHINXES
ANDROSTERONE
ANDROSTERONES
ANECDOTAGE
ANECDOTAGES
ANECDOTALISM
ANECDOTALISMS
ANECDOTALIST
ANECDOTALISTS
ANECDOTALLY
ANECDOTICAL
ANECDOTICALLY
ANECDOTIST
ANECDOTISTS
ANELASTICITIES
ANELASTICITY
ANEMICALLY
ANEMOCHORE
ANEMOCHORES
ANEMOCHOROUS
ANEMOGRAMS
ANEMOGRAPH
ANEMOGRAPHIC
ANEMOGRAPHIES
ANEMOGRAPHS
ANEMOGRAPHY
ANEMOLOGIES
ANEMOMETER
ANEMOMETERS
ANEMOMETRIC
ANEMOMETRICAL

ANEMOMETRIES
ANEMOMETRY
ANEMOPHILIES
ANEMOPHILOUS
ANEMOPHILY
ANEMOPHOBIA
ANEMOPHOBIAS
ANEMOSCOPE
ANEMOSCOPES
ANENCEPHALIA
ANENCEPHALIAS
ANENCEPHALIC
ANENCEPHALIES
ANENCEPHALY
ANESTHESIA
ANESTHESIAS
ANESTHESIOLOGY
ANESTHETIC
ANESTHETICALLY
ANESTHETICS
ANESTHETISE
ANESTHETISED
ANESTHETISES
ANESTHETISING
ANESTHETIST
ANESTHETISTS
ANESTHETIZATION
ANESTHETIZE
ANESTHETIZED
ANESTHETIZES
ANESTHETIZING
ANEUPLOIDIES
ANEUPLOIDS
ANEUPLOIDY
ANEURISMAL
ANEURISMALLY
ANEURISMATIC
ANEURYSMAL
ANEURYSMALLY
ANEURYSMATIC
ANFRACTUOSITIES
ANFRACTUOSITY
ANFRACTUOUS
ANGASHORES
ANGELFISHES
ANGELHOODS
ANGELICALLY
ANGELOLATRIES
ANGELOLATRY
ANGELOLOGIES
ANGELOLOGIST
ANGELOLOGISTS
ANGELOLOGY
ANGELOPHANIES
ANGELOPHANY
ANGIOCARPOUS
ANGIOGENESES
ANGIOGENESIS
ANGIOGENIC

ANGIOGRAMS
ANGIOGRAPHIC
ANGIOGRAPHIES
ANGIOGRAPHY
ANGIOLOGIES
ANGIOMATOUS
ANGIOPLASTIES
ANGIOPLASTY
ANGIOSARCOMA
ANGIOSARCOMAS
ANGIOSARCOMATA
ANGIOSPERM
ANGIOSPERMAL
ANGIOSPERMOUS
ANGIOSPERMS
ANGIOSTOMATOUS
ANGIOSTOMOUS
ANGIOTENSIN
ANGIOTENSINS
ANGLEBERRIES
ANGLEBERRY
ANGLEDOZER
ANGLEDOZERS
ANGLERFISH
ANGLERFISHES
ANGLESITES
ANGLETWITCH
ANGLETWITCHES
ANGLEWORMS
ANGLICISATION
ANGLICISATIONS
ANGLICISED
ANGLICISES
ANGLICISING
ANGLICISMS
ANGLICISTS
ANGLICIZATION
ANGLICIZATIONS
ANGLICIZED
ANGLICIZES
ANGLICIZING
ANGLIFYING
ANGLISTICS
ANGLOMANIA
ANGLOMANIAC
ANGLOMANIACS
ANGLOMANIAS
ANGLOPHILE
ANGLOPHILES
ANGLOPHILIA
ANGLOPHILIAS
ANGLOPHILIC
ANGLOPHILS
ANGLOPHOBE
ANGLOPHOBES
ANGLOPHOBIA
ANGLOPHOBIAC
ANGLOPHOBIAS
ANGLOPHOBIC

ANGLOPHONE
ANGLOPHONES
ANGLOPHONIC
ANGOPHORAS
ANGOSTURAS
ANGRINESSES
ANGUIFAUNA
ANGUIFAUNAE
ANGUIFAUNAS
ANGUILLIFORM
ANGUISHING
ANGULARITIES
ANGULARITY
ANGULARNESS
ANGULARNESSES
ANGULATING
ANGULATION
ANGULATIONS
ANGUSTIFOLIATE
ANGUSTIROSTRATE
ANGWANTIBO
ANGWANTIBOS
ANHARMONIC
ANHEDONIAS
ANHELATION
ANHELATIONS
ANHIDROSES
ANHIDROSIS
ANHIDROTIC
ANHIDROTICS
ANHUNGERED
ANHYDRASES
ANHYDRIDES
ANHYDRITES
ANICONISMS
ANICONISTS
ANILINCTUS
ANILINCTUSES
ANILINGUSES
ANIMADVERSION
ANIMADVERSIONS
ANIMADVERT
ANIMADVERTED
ANIMADVERTER
ANIMADVERTERS
ANIMADVERTING
ANIMADVERTS
ANIMALCULA
ANIMALCULAR
ANIMALCULE
ANIMALCULES
ANIMALCULISM
ANIMALCULISMS
ANIMALCULIST
ANIMALCULISTS
ANIMALCULUM
ANIMALIERS
ANIMALISATION
ANIMALISATIONS

ANIMALISED	ANNALISING	ANNUNCIATOR	ANTAGONISES
ANIMALISES	ANNALISTIC	ANNUNCIATORS	ANTAGONISING
ANIMALISING	ANNALIZING	ANNUNCIATORY	ANTAGONISM
ANIMALISMS	ANNEALINGS	ANNUNTIATE	ANTAGONISMS
ANIMALISTIC	ANNELIDANS	ANNUNTIATED	ANTAGONIST
ANIMALISTS	ANNEXATION	ANNUNTIATES	ANTAGONISTIC
ANIMALITIES	ANNEXATIONAL	ANNUNTIATING	ANTAGONISTS
ANIMALIZATION	ANNEXATIONISM	ANODICALLY	ANTAGONIZABLE
ANIMALIZATIONS	ANNEXATIONISMS	ANODISATION	ANTAGONIZATION
ANIMALIZED	ANNEXATIONIST	ANODISATIONS	ANTAGONIZATIONS
ANIMALIZES	ANNEXATIONISTS	ANODIZATION	ANTAGONIZE
ANIMALIZING	ANNEXATIONS	ANODIZATIONS	ANTAGONIZED
ANIMALLIKE	ANNEXMENTS	ANODONTIAS	ANTAGONIZES
ANIMATEDLY	ANNIHILABLE	ANOESTROUS	ANTAGONIZING
ANIMATENESS	ANNIHILATE	ANOINTMENT	ANTALKALIES
ANIMATENESSES	ANNIHILATED	ANOINTMENTS	ANTALKALINE
ANIMATINGLY	ANNIHILATES	ANOMALISTIC	ANTALKALINES
ANIMATIONS	ANNIHILATING	ANOMALISTICAL	ANTALKALIS
ANIMATISMS	ANNIHILATION	ANOMALISTICALLY	ANTAPHRODISIAC
ANIMATISTS	ANNIHILATIONISM	ANOMALOUSLY	ANTAPHRODISIACS
ANIMATRONIC	ANNIHILATIONS	ANOMALOUSNESS	ANTARTHRITIC
ANIMATRONICALLY	ANNIHILATIVE	ANOMALOUSNESSES	ANTARTHRITICS
ANIMATRONICS	ANNIHILATOR	ANONACEOUS	ANTASTHMATIC
ANIMOSITIES	ANNIHILATORS	ANONYMISED	ANTASTHMATICS
ANISEIKONIA	ANNIHILATORY	ANONYMISES	ANTEBELLUM
ANISEIKONIAS	ANNIVERSARIES	ANONYMISING	ANTECEDENCE
ANISEIKONIC	ANNIVERSARY	ANONYMITIES	ANTECEDENCES
ANISOCERCAL	ANNOTATABLE	ANONYMIZED	ANTECEDENT
ANISODACTYL	ANNOTATING	ANONYMIZES	ANTECEDENTLY
ANISODACTYLOUS	ANNOTATION	ANONYMIZING	ANTECEDENTS
ANISODACTYLS	ANNOTATIONS	ANONYMOUSLY	ANTECEDING
ANISOGAMIES	ANNOTATIVE	ANONYMOUSNESS	ANTECESSOR
ANISOGAMOUS	ANNOTATORS	ANONYMOUSNESSES	ANTECESSORS
ANISOMERIC	ANNOUNCEMENT	ANOPHELINE	ANTECHAMBER
ANISOMEROUS	ANNOUNCEMENTS	ANOPHELINES	ANTECHAMBERS
ANISOMETRIC	ANNOUNCERS	ANORECTICS	ANTECHAPEL
ANISOMETROPIA	ANNOUNCING	ANOREXIGENIC	ANTECHAPELS
ANISOMETROPIAS	ANNOYANCES	ANORTHITES	ANTECHOIRS
ANISOMETROPIC	ANNOYINGLY	ANORTHITIC	ANTEDATING
ANISOMORPHIC	ANNUALISED	ANORTHOSITE	ANTEDILUVIAL
ANISOPHYLLIES	ANNUALISES	ANORTHOSITES	ANTEDILUVIALLY
ANISOPHYLLOUS	ANNUALISING	ANORTHOSITIC	ANTEDILUVIAN
ANISOPHYLLY	ANNUALIZED	ANOTHERGUESS	ANTEDILUVIANS
ANISOTROPIC	ANNUALIZES	ANOVULANTS	ANTEMERIDIAN
ANISOTROPICALLY	ANNUALIZING	ANOVULATORY	ANTEMORTEM
ANISOTROPIES	ANNUITANTS	ANOXAEMIAS	ANTEMUNDANE
ANISOTROPISM	ANNULARITIES	ANSWERABILITIES	ANTENATALLY
ANISOTROPISMS	ANNULARITY	ANSWERABILITY	ANTENATALS
ANISOTROPY	ANNULATION	ANSWERABLE	ANTENNIFEROUS
ANKLEBONES	ANNULATIONS	ANSWERABLENESS	ANTENNIFORM
ANKYLOSAUR	ANNULLABLE	ANSWERABLY	ANTENNULAR
ANKYLOSAURS	ANNULMENTS	ANSWERLESS	ANTENNULES
ANKYLOSAURUS	ANNUNCIATE	ANSWERPHONE	ANTENUPTIAL
ANKYLOSAURUSES	ANNUNCIATED	ANSWERPHONES	ANTEORBITAL
ANKYLOSING	ANNUNCIATES	ANTAGONISABLE	ANTEPENDIA
ANKYLOSTOMIASES	ANNUNCIATING	ANTAGONISATION	ANTEPENDIUM
ANKYLOSTOMIASIS	ANNUNCIATION	ANTAGONISATIONS	ANTEPENDIUMS
ANNABERGITE	ANNUNCIATIONS	ANTAGONISE	ANTEPENULT
ANNABERGITES	ANNUNCIATIVE	ANTAGONISED	ANTEPENULTIMA

ANTEPENULTIMAS
ANTEPENULTIMATE
ANTEPENULTS
ANTEPOSITION
ANTEPOSITIONS
ANTEPRANDIAL
ANTERIORITIES
ANTERIORITY
ANTERIORLY
ANTEROGRADE
ANTEVERSION
ANTEVERSIONS
ANTEVERTED
ANTEVERTING
ANTHELICES
ANTHELIONS
ANTHELIXES
ANTHELMINTHIC
ANTHELMINTHICS
ANTHELMINTIC
ANTHELMINTICS
ANTHEMWISE
ANTHERIDIA
ANTHERIDIAL
ANTHERIDIUM
ANTHEROZOID
ANTHEROZOIDS
ANTHEROZOOID
ANTHEROZOOIDS
ANTHERSMUT
ANTHERSMUTS
ANTHOCARPOUS
ANTHOCARPS
ANTHOCHLORE
ANTHOCHLORES
ANTHOCYANIN
ANTHOCYANINS
ANTHOCYANS
ANTHOLOGICAL
ANTHOLOGIES
ANTHOLOGISE
ANTHOLOGISED
ANTHOLOGISER
ANTHOLOGISERS
ANTHOLOGISES
ANTHOLOGISING
ANTHOLOGIST
ANTHOLOGISTS
ANTHOLOGIZE
ANTHOLOGIZED
ANTHOLOGIZER
ANTHOLOGIZERS
ANTHOLOGIZES
ANTHOLOGIZING
ANTHOMANIA
ANTHOMANIAC
ANTHOMANIACS
ANTHOMANIAS
ANTHOPHILOUS

ANTHOPHORE
ANTHOPHORES
ANTHOPHYLLITE
ANTHOPHYLLITES
ANTHOTAXIES
ANTHOXANTHIN
ANTHOXANTHINS
ANTHOZOANS
ANTHRACENE
ANTHRACENES
ANTHRACITE
ANTHRACITES
ANTHRACITIC
ANTHRACNOSE
ANTHRACNOSES
ANTHRACOID
ANTHRACOSES
ANTHRACOSIS
ANTHRANILATE
ANTHRANILATES
ANTHRAQUINONE
ANTHRAQUINONES
ANTHROPICAL
ANTHROPOBIOLOGY
ANTHROPOCENTRIC
ANTHROPOGENESES
ANTHROPOGENESIS
ANTHROPOGENETIC
ANTHROPOGENIC
ANTHROPOGENIES
ANTHROPOGENY
ANTHROPOGONIES
ANTHROPOGONY
ANTHROPOGRAPHY
ANTHROPOID
ANTHROPOIDAL
ANTHROPOIDS
ANTHROPOLATRIES
ANTHROPOLATRY
ANTHROPOLOGICAL
ANTHROPOLOGIES
ANTHROPOLOGIST
ANTHROPOLOGISTS
ANTHROPOLOGY
ANTHROPOMETRIC
ANTHROPOMETRIES
ANTHROPOMETRIST
ANTHROPOMETRY
ANTHROPOMORPH
ANTHROPOMORPHIC
ANTHROPOMORPHS
ANTHROPOPATHIC
ANTHROPOPATHIES
ANTHROPOPATHISM
ANTHROPOPATHY
ANTHROPOPHAGI
ANTHROPOPHAGIC
ANTHROPOPHAGIES
ANTHROPOPHAGITE

ANTHROPOPHAGOUS
ANTHROPOPHAGUS
ANTHROPOPHAGY
ANTHROPOPHOBIA
ANTHROPOPHOBIAS
ANTHROPOPHOBIC
ANTHROPOPHOBICS
ANTHROPOPHUISM
ANTHROPOPHUISMS
ANTHROPOPHYTE
ANTHROPOPHYTES
ANTHROPOPSYCHIC
ANTHROPOSOPHIC
ANTHROPOSOPHIES
ANTHROPOSOPHIST
ANTHROPOSOPHY
ANTHROPOTOMIES
ANTHROPOTOMY
ANTHURIUMS
ANTIABORTION
ANTIABORTIONIST
ANTIACADEMIC
ANTIADITIS
ANTIADITISES
ANTIAGGRESSION
ANTIAIRCRAFT
ANTIAIRCRAFTS
ANTIALCOHOL
ANTIALCOHOLISM
ANTIALCOHOLISMS
ANTIALLERGENIC
ANTIANEMIA
ANTIANXIETY
ANTIAPARTHEID
ANTIAPHRODISIAC
ANTIARRHYTHMIC
ANTIARRHYTHMICS
ANTIARTHRITIC
ANTIARTHRITICS
ANTIARTHRITIS
ANTIASTHMA
ANTIASTHMATIC
ANTIASTHMATICS
ANTIAUTHORITY
ANTIAUXINS
ANTIBACCHII
ANTIBACCHIUS
ANTIBACKLASH
ANTIBACTERIAL
ANTIBACTERIALS
ANTIBALLISTIC
ANTIBARBARUS
ANTIBARBARUSES
ANTIBARYON
ANTIBARYONS
ANTIBILIOUS
ANTIBILLBOARD
ANTIBIOSES
ANTIBIOSIS

ANTIBIOTIC
ANTIBIOTICALLY
ANTIBIOTICS
ANTIBLACKISM
ANTIBLACKISMS
ANTIBODIES
ANTIBOURGEOIS
ANTIBOYCOTT
ANTIBURGLAR
ANTIBURGLARY
ANTIBUSERS
ANTIBUSINESS
ANTIBUSING
ANTICAKING
ANTICANCER
ANTICAPITALISM
ANTICAPITALISMS
ANTICAPITALIST
ANTICAPITALISTS
ANTICARCINOGEN
ANTICARCINOGENS
ANTICARIES
ANTICATALYST
ANTICATALYSTS
ANTICATHODE
ANTICATHODES
ANTICATHOLIC
ANTICELLULITE
ANTICENSORSHIP
ANTICHLORISTIC
ANTICHLORS
ANTICHOICE
ANTICHOICER
ANTICHOICERS
ANTICHOLESTEROL
ANTICHOLINERGIC
ANTICHRIST
ANTICHRISTIAN
ANTICHRISTIANLY
ANTICHRISTS
ANTICHTHONES
ANTICHURCH
ANTICIGARETTE
ANTICIPANT
ANTICIPANTS
ANTICIPATABLE
ANTICIPATE
ANTICIPATED
ANTICIPATES
ANTICIPATING
ANTICIPATION
ANTICIPATIONS
ANTICIPATIVE
ANTICIPATIVELY
ANTICIPATOR
ANTICIPATORILY
ANTICIPATORS
ANTICIPATORY
ANTICISING

ANTICIVISM

ANTICIVISM
ANTICIVISMS
ANTICIZING
ANTICLASSICAL
ANTICLASTIC
ANTICLERICAL
ANTICLERICALISM
ANTICLERICALS
ANTICLIMACTIC
ANTICLIMACTICAL
ANTICLIMAX
ANTICLIMAXES
ANTICLINAL
ANTICLINALS
ANTICLINES
ANTICLINORIA
ANTICLINORIUM
ANTICLINORIUMS
ANTICLOCKWISE
ANTICLOTTING
ANTICOAGULANT
ANTICOAGULANTS
ANTICODONS
ANTICOINCIDENCE
ANTICOLLISION
ANTICOLONIAL
ANTICOLONIALISM
ANTICOLONIALIST
ANTICOMMERCIAL
ANTICOMMUNISM
ANTICOMMUNISMS
ANTICOMMUNIST
ANTICOMMUNISTS
ANTICOMPETITIVE
ANTICONSUMER
ANTICONVULSANT
ANTICONVULSANTS
ANTICONVULSIVE
ANTICONVULSIVES
ANTICORPORATE
ANTICORROSION
ANTICORROSIVE
ANTICORROSIVES
ANTICORRUPTION
ANTICREATIVE
ANTICRUELTY
ANTICULTURAL
ANTICYCLONE
ANTICYCLONES
ANTICYCLONIC
ANTIDANDRUFF
ANTIDAZZLE
ANTIDEFAMATION
ANTIDEMOCRATIC
ANTIDEPRESSANT
ANTIDEPRESSANTS
ANTIDEPRESSION
ANTIDERIVATIVE
ANTIDERIVATIVES

ANTIDESICCANT
ANTIDESICCANTS
ANTIDEVELOPMENT
ANTIDIABETIC
ANTIDIARRHEAL
ANTIDIARRHEALS
ANTIDILUTION
ANTIDIURETIC
ANTIDIURETICS
ANTIDOGMATIC
ANTIDOTALLY
ANTIDOTING
ANTIDROMIC
ANTIDROMICALLY
ANTIDUMPING
ANTIECONOMIC
ANTIEDUCATIONAL
ANTIEGALITARIAN
ANTIELECTRON
ANTIELECTRONS
ANTIELITES
ANTIELITISM
ANTIELITISMS
ANTIELITIST
ANTIEMETIC
ANTIEMETICS
ANTIENTROPIC
ANTIEPILEPSY
ANTIEPILEPTIC
ANTIEPILEPTICS
ANTIEROTIC
ANTIESTROGEN
ANTIESTROGENS
ANTIEVOLUTION
ANTIFAMILY
ANTIFASCISM
ANTIFASCISMS
ANTIFASCIST
ANTIFASCISTS
ANTIFASHION
ANTIFASHIONABLE
ANTIFASHIONS
ANTIFATIGUE
ANTIFEBRILE
ANTIFEBRILES
ANTIFEDERALIST
ANTIFEDERALISTS
ANTIFEMALE
ANTIFEMININE
ANTIFEMINISM
ANTIFEMINISMS
ANTIFEMINIST
ANTIFEMINISTS
ANTIFERROMAGNET
ANTIFERTILITY
ANTIFILIBUSTER
ANTIFOAMING
ANTIFOGGING
ANTIFORECLOSURE

ANTIFOREIGN
ANTIFOREIGNER
ANTIFORMALIST
ANTIFOULING
ANTIFOULINGS
ANTIFREEZE
ANTIFREEZES
ANTIFRICTION
ANTIFUNGAL
ANTIFUNGALS
ANTIGAMBLING
ANTIGENICALLY
ANTIGENICITIES
ANTIGENICITY
ANTIGLOBULIN
ANTIGLOBULINS
ANTIGOVERNMENT
ANTIGRAVITIES
ANTIGRAVITY
ANTIGROPELOES
ANTIGROPELOS
ANTIGROWTH
ANTIGUERRILLA
ANTIHALATION
ANTIHALATIONS
ANTIHELICES
ANTIHELIXES
ANTIHELMINTHIC
ANTIHELMINTHICS
ANTIHEROES
ANTIHEROIC
ANTIHEROINE
ANTIHEROINES
ANTIHERPES
ANTIHIJACK
ANTIHISTAMINE
ANTIHISTAMINES
ANTIHISTAMINIC
ANTIHISTAMINICS
ANTIHISTORICAL
ANTIHOMOSEXUAL
ANTIHUMANISM
ANTIHUMANISMS
ANTIHUMANISTIC
ANTIHUNTER
ANTIHUNTING
ANTIHYDROGEN
ANTIHYDROGENS
ANTIHYSTERIC
ANTIHYSTERICS
ANTIJACOBIN
ANTIJACOBINS
ANTIJAMMING
ANTIJAMMINGS
ANTIKICKBACK
ANTIKNOCKS
ANTILEGOMENA
ANTILEPROSY
ANTILEPTON

ANTILEPTONS
ANTILEUKEMIC
ANTILIBERAL
ANTILIBERALISM
ANTILIBERALISMS
ANTILIBERALS
ANTILIBERTARIAN
ANTILIFERS
ANTILITERATE
ANTILITTER
ANTILITTERING
ANTILOGARITHM
ANTILOGARITHMIC
ANTILOGARITHMS
ANTILOGICAL
ANTILOGIES
ANTILOGOUS
ANTILOPINE
ANTILYNCHING
ANTIMACASSAR
ANTIMACASSARS
ANTIMAGNETIC
ANTIMALARIA
ANTIMALARIAL
ANTIMALARIALS
ANTIMANAGEMENT
ANTIMARIJUANA
ANTIMARKET
ANTIMASQUE
ANTIMASQUES
ANTIMATERIALISM
ANTIMATERIALIST
ANTIMATTER
ANTIMATTERS
ANTIMECHANIST
ANTIMECHANISTS
ANTIMERGER
ANTIMERISM
ANTIMERISMS
ANTIMETABOLE
ANTIMETABOLES
ANTIMETABOLIC
ANTIMETABOLITE
ANTIMETABOLITES
ANTIMETATHESES
ANTIMETATHESIS
ANTIMICROBIAL
ANTIMICROBIALS
ANTIMILITARISM
ANTIMILITARISMS
ANTIMILITARIST
ANTIMILITARISTS
ANTIMILITARY
ANTIMISSILE
ANTIMISSILES
ANTIMITOTIC
ANTIMITOTICS
ANTIMNEMONIC
ANTIMNEMONICS

ANTIMODERN
ANTIMODERNIST
ANTIMODERNISTS
ANTIMONARCHICAL
ANTIMONARCHIST
ANTIMONARCHISTS
ANTIMONATE
ANTIMONATES
ANTIMONIAL
ANTIMONIALS
ANTIMONIATE
ANTIMONIATES
ANTIMONIDE
ANTIMONIDES
ANTIMONIES
ANTIMONIOUS
ANTIMONITE
ANTIMONITES
ANTIMONOPOLIST
ANTIMONOPOLISTS
ANTIMONOPOLY
ANTIMONOUS
ANTIMONYLS
ANTIMOSQUITO
ANTIMUSICAL
ANTIMUSICS
ANTIMUTAGEN
ANTIMUTAGENS
ANTIMYCINS
ANTIMYCOTIC
ANTINARRATIVE
ANTINARRATIVES
ANTINATIONAL
ANTINATIONALIST
ANTINATURAL
ANTINATURE
ANTINAUSEA
ANTINEOPLASTIC
ANTINEPHRITIC
ANTINEPHRITICS
ANTINEPOTISM
ANTINEUTRINO
ANTINEUTRINOS
ANTINEUTRON
ANTINEUTRONS
ANTINOMIAN
ANTINOMIANISM
ANTINOMIANISMS
ANTINOMIANS
ANTINOMICAL
ANTINOMICALLY
ANTINOMIES
ANTINOVELIST
ANTINOVELISTS
ANTINOVELS
ANTINUCLEAR
ANTINUCLEARIST
ANTINUCLEARISTS
ANTINUCLEON

ANTINUCLEONS
ANTINUKERS
ANTIOBESITY
ANTIOBSCENITY
ANTIODONTALGIC
ANTIODONTALGICS
ANTIOXIDANT
ANTIOXIDANTS
ANTIOZONANT
ANTIOZONANTS
ANTIPARALLEL
ANTIPARALLELS
ANTIPARASITIC
ANTIPARTICLE
ANTIPARTICLES
ANTIPARTIES
ANTIPASTOS
ANTIPATHETIC
ANTIPATHETICAL
ANTIPATHIC
ANTIPATHIES
ANTIPATHIST
ANTIPATHISTS
ANTIPERIODIC
ANTIPERIODICS
ANTIPERISTALSES
ANTIPERISTALSIS
ANTIPERISTALTIC
ANTIPERISTASES
ANTIPERISTASIS
ANTIPERSONNEL
ANTIPERSPIRANT
ANTIPERSPIRANTS
ANTIPESTICIDE
ANTIPETALOUS
ANTIPHLOGISTIC
ANTIPHLOGISTICS
ANTIPHONAL
ANTIPHONALLY
ANTIPHONALS
ANTIPHONARIES
ANTIPHONARY
ANTIPHONER
ANTIPHONERS
ANTIPHONIC
ANTIPHONICAL
ANTIPHONICALLY
ANTIPHONIES
ANTIPHRASES
ANTIPHRASIS
ANTIPHRASTIC
ANTIPHRASTICAL
ANTIPIRACY
ANTIPLAGUE
ANTIPLAQUE
ANTIPLEASURE
ANTIPOACHING
ANTIPODALS
ANTIPODEAN

ANTIPODEANS
ANTIPOETIC
ANTIPOLICE
ANTIPOLITICAL
ANTIPOLITICS
ANTIPOLLUTION
ANTIPOLLUTIONS
ANTIPOPULAR
ANTIPORNOGRAPHY
ANTIPOVERTY
ANTIPREDATOR
ANTIPROGRESSIVE
ANTIPROTON
ANTIPROTONS
ANTIPRURITIC
ANTIPRURITICS
ANTIPSYCHIATRY
ANTIPSYCHOTIC
ANTIPSYCHOTICS
ANTIPYRESES
ANTIPYRESIS
ANTIPYRETIC
ANTIPYRETICS
ANTIPYRINE
ANTIPYRINES
ANTIQUARIAN
ANTIQUARIANISM
ANTIQUARIANISMS
ANTIQUARIANS
ANTIQUARIES
ANTIQUARKS
ANTIQUATED
ANTIQUATEDNESS
ANTIQUATES
ANTIQUATING
ANTIQUATION
ANTIQUATIONS
ANTIQUENESS
ANTIQUENESSES
ANTIQUITARIAN
ANTIQUITARIANS
ANTIQUITIES
ANTIRABIES
ANTIRACHITIC
ANTIRACHITICS
ANTIRACISM
ANTIRACISMS
ANTIRACIST
ANTIRACISTS
ANTIRADARS
ANTIRADICAL
ANTIRADICALISM
ANTIRADICALISMS
ANTIRATIONAL
ANTIRATIONALISM
ANTIRATIONALIST
ANTIRATIONALITY
ANTIREALISM
ANTIREALISMS

ANTIREALIST
ANTIREALISTS
ANTIRECESSION
ANTIREFLECTION
ANTIREFLECTIVE
ANTIREFORM
ANTIREGULATORY
ANTIREJECTION
ANTIRELIGION
ANTIRELIGIOUS
ANTIREPUBLICAN
ANTIREPUBLICANS
ANTIRHEUMATIC
ANTIRHEUMATICS
ANTIRITUALISM
ANTIRITUALISMS
ANTIROMANTIC
ANTIROMANTICISM
ANTIROMANTICS
ANTIROYALIST
ANTIROYALISTS
ANTIRRHINUM
ANTIRRHINUMS
ANTISATELLITE
ANTISCIANS
ANTISCIENCE
ANTISCIENCES
ANTISCIENTIFIC
ANTISCORBUTIC
ANTISCORBUTICS
ANTISCRIPTURAL
ANTISECRECY
ANTISEGREGATION
ANTISEIZURE
ANTISENTIMENTAL
ANTISEPALOUS
ANTISEPARATIST
ANTISEPARATISTS
ANTISEPSES
ANTISEPSIS
ANTISEPTIC
ANTISEPTICALLY
ANTISEPTICISE
ANTISEPTICISED
ANTISEPTICISES
ANTISEPTICISING
ANTISEPTICISM
ANTISEPTICISMS
ANTISEPTICIZE
ANTISEPTICIZED
ANTISEPTICIZES
ANTISEPTICIZING
ANTISEPTICS
ANTISERUMS
ANTISEXIST
ANTISEXISTS
ANTISEXUAL
ANTISEXUALITIES
ANTISEXUALITY

ANTISHOCKS

ANTISHOCKS
ANTISHOPLIFTING
ANTISLAVERY
ANTISMOKER
ANTISMOKERS
ANTISMOKING
ANTISMUGGLING
ANTISOCIAL
ANTISOCIALISM
ANTISOCIALISMS
ANTISOCIALIST
ANTISOCIALISTS
ANTISOCIALITIES
ANTISOCIALITY
ANTISOCIALLY
ANTISPASMODIC
ANTISPASMODICS
ANTISPASTIC
ANTISPASTS
ANTISPECULATION
ANTISPECULATIVE
ANTISPENDING
ANTISTATIC
ANTISTATICS
ANTISTORIES
ANTISTRESS
ANTISTRIKE
ANTISTROPHE
ANTISTROPHES
ANTISTROPHIC
ANTISTROPHON
ANTISTROPHONS
ANTISTUDENT
ANTISTYLES
ANTISUBMARINE
ANTISUBSIDY
ANTISUBVERSION
ANTISUBVERSIVE
ANTISUICIDE
ANTISYMMETRIC
ANTISYPHILITIC
ANTISYPHILITICS
ANTISYZYGIES
ANTISYZYGY
ANTITAKEOVER
ANTITARNISH
ANTITECHNOLOGY
ANTITERRORISM
ANTITERRORISMS
ANTITERRORIST
ANTITERRORISTS
ANTITHALIAN
ANTITHEISM
ANTITHEISMS
ANTITHEIST
ANTITHEISTIC
ANTITHEISTS
ANTITHEORETICAL
ANTITHESES

ANTITHESIS
ANTITHETIC
ANTITHETICAL
ANTITHETICALLY
ANTITHROMBIN
ANTITHROMBINS
ANTITHROMBOTIC
ANTITHROMBOTICS
ANTITHYROID
ANTITOBACCO
ANTITOXINS
ANTITRADES
ANTITRADITIONAL
ANTITRAGUS
ANTITRANSPIRANT
ANTITRINITARIAN
ANTITRUSTER
ANTITRUSTERS
ANTITUBERCULAR
ANTITUBERCULOUS
ANTITUMORAL
ANTITUMORS
ANTITUSSIVE
ANTITUSSIVES
ANTITYPHOID
ANTITYPICAL
ANTITYPICALLY
ANTIUNIVERSITY
ANTIVENENE
ANTIVENENES
ANTIVENINS
ANTIVENOMS
ANTIVIOLENCE
ANTIVIRUSES
ANTIVITAMIN
ANTIVITAMINS
ANTIVIVISECTION
ANTIWELFARE
ANTIWHALING
ANTIWORLDS
ANTIWRINKLE
ANTONINIANUS
ANTONINIANUSES
ANTONOMASIA
ANTONOMASIAS
ANTONOMASTIC
ANTONYMIES
ANTONYMOUS
ANTRORSELY
ANTSINESSES
ANUCLEATED
ANXIOLYTIC
ANXIOLYTICS
ANXIOUSNESS
ANXIOUSNESSES
ANYTHINGARIAN
ANYTHINGARIANS
ANYWHITHER
AORISTICALLY

AORTITISES
AORTOGRAPHIC
AORTOGRAPHIES
AORTOGRAPHY
APAGOGICAL
APAGOGICALLY
APARTHEIDS
APARTHOTEL
APARTHOTELS
APARTMENTAL
APARTMENTS
APARTNESSES
APATHATONS
APATHETICAL
APATHETICALLY
APATOSAURS
APATOSAURUS
APATOSAURUSES
APERIODICALLY
APERIODICITIES
APERIODICITY
APERITIVES
APERTNESSES
APFELSTRUDEL
APFELSTRUDELS
APHAERESES
APHAERESIS
APHAERETIC
APHANIPTEROUS
APHELANDRA
APHELANDRAS
APHELIOTROPIC
APHELIOTROPISM
APHELIOTROPISMS
APHETICALLY
APHETISING
APHETIZING
APHIDICIDE
APHIDICIDES
APHORISERS
APHORISING
APHORISTIC
APHORISTICALLY
APHORIZERS
APHORIZING
APHRODISIA
APHRODISIAC
APHRODISIACAL
APHRODISIACS
APHRODISIAS
APHRODITES
APICULTURAL
APICULTURE
APICULTURES
APICULTURIST
APICULTURISTS
APIOLOGIES
APISHNESSES
APITHERAPIES

APITHERAPY
APLACENTAL
APLANATICALLY
APLANATISM
APLANATISMS
APLANOGAMETE
APLANOGAMETES
APLANOSPORE
APLANOSPORES
APOAPSIDES
APOCALYPSE
APOCALYPSES
APOCALYPTIC
APOCALYPTICAL
APOCALYPTICALLY
APOCALYPTICISM
APOCALYPTICISMS
APOCALYPTISM
APOCALYPTISMS
APOCALYPTIST
APOCALYPTISTS
APOCARPIES
APOCARPOUS
APOCATASTASES
APOCATASTASIS
APOCHROMAT
APOCHROMATIC
APOCHROMATISM
APOCHROMATISMS
APOCHROMATS
APOCOPATED
APOCOPATES
APOCOPATING
APOCOPATION
APOCOPATIONS
APOCRYPHAL
APOCRYPHALLY
APOCRYPHALNESS
APOCRYPHON
APOCYNACEOUS
APOCYNTHION
APOCYNTHIONS
APODEICTIC
APODEICTICAL
APODEICTICALLY
APODICTICAL
APODICTICALLY
APODYTERIUM
APODYTERIUMS
APOENZYMES
APOGAMOUSLY
APOGEOTROPIC
APOGEOTROPISM
APOGEOTROPISMS
APOLAUSTIC
APOLAUSTICS
APOLIPOPROTEIN
APOLIPOPROTEINS
APOLITICAL

APOLITICALITIES APOSIOPETIC APOTHEGMATIZED APPELLATIVE
APOLITICALITY APOSPORIES APOTHEGMATIZES APPELLATIVELY
APOLITICALLY APOSPOROUS APOTHEGMATIZING APPELLATIVES
APOLITICISM APOSTACIES APOTHEOSES APPENDAGES
APOLITICISMS APOSTASIES APOTHEOSIS APPENDANTS
APOLLONIAN APOSTATICAL APOTHEOSISE APPENDECTOMIES
APOLLONICON APOSTATISE APOTHEOSISED APPENDECTOMY
APOLLONICONS APOSTATISED APOTHEOSISES APPENDENTS
APOLOGETIC APOSTATISES APOTHEOSISING APPENDICECTOMY
APOLOGETICAL APOSTATISING APOTHEOSIZE APPENDICES
APOLOGETICALLY APOSTATIZE APOTHEOSIZED APPENDICITIS
APOLOGETICS APOSTATIZED APOTHEOSIZES APPENDICITISES
APOLOGISED APOSTATIZES APOTHEOSIZING APPENDICLE
APOLOGISER APOSTATIZING APOTROPAIC APPENDICLES
APOLOGISERS APOSTILLES APOTROPAICALLY APPENDICULAR
APOLOGISES APOSTLESHIP APOTROPAISM APPENDICULARIAN
APOLOGISING APOSTLESHIPS APOTROPAISMS APPENDICULATE
APOLOGISTS APOSTOLATE APOTROPOUS APPENDIXES
APOLOGIZED APOSTOLATES APPALLINGLY APPERCEIVE
APOLOGIZER APOSTOLICAL APPALOOSAS APPERCEIVED
APOLOGIZERS APOSTOLICALLY APPARATCHIK APPERCEIVES
APOLOGIZES APOSTOLICISM APPARATCHIKI APPERCEIVING
APOLOGIZING APOSTOLICISMS APPARATCHIKS APPERCEPTION
APOMICTICAL APOSTOLICITIES APPARATUSES APPERCEPTIONS
APOMICTICALLY APOSTOLICITY APPARELING APPERCEPTIVE
APOMORPHIA APOSTOLISE APPARELLED APPERCIPIENT
APOMORPHIAS APOSTOLISED APPARELLING APPERTAINANCE
APOMORPHINE APOSTOLISES APPARELMENT APPERTAINANCES
APOMORPHINES APOSTOLISING APPARELMENTS APPERTAINED
APONEUROSES APOSTOLIZE APPARENCIES APPERTAINING
APONEUROSIS APOSTOLIZED APPARENTLY APPERTAINMENT
APONEUROTIC APOSTOLIZES APPARENTNESS APPERTAINMENTS
APOPEMPTIC APOSTOLIZING APPARENTNESSES APPERTAINS
APOPHLEGMATIC APOSTROPHE APPARITION APPERTINENT
APOPHLEGMATICS APOSTROPHES APPARITIONAL APPERTINENTS
APOPHONIES APOSTROPHIC APPARITIONS APPETEEZEMENT
APOPHTHEGM APOSTROPHISE APPARITORS APPETEEZEMENTS
APOPHTHEGMATIC APOSTROPHISED APPARTEMENT APPETENCES
APOPHTHEGMATISE APOSTROPHISES APPARTEMENTS APPETENCIES
APOPHTHEGMATIST APOSTROPHISING APPASSIONATO APPETISEMENT
APOPHTHEGMATIZE APOSTROPHIZE APPEACHING APPETISEMENTS
APOPHTHEGMS APOSTROPHIZED APPEACHMENT APPETISERS
APOPHYLLITE APOSTROPHIZES APPEACHMENTS APPETISING
APOPHYLLITES APOSTROPHIZING APPEALABILITIES APPETISINGLY
APOPHYSATE APOSTROPHUS APPEALABILITY APPETITION
APOPHYSEAL APOSTROPHUSES APPEALABLE APPETITIONS
APOPHYSIAL APOTHECARIES APPEALINGLY APPETITIVE
APOPLECTIC APOTHECARY APPEALINGNESS APPETIZERS
APOPLECTICAL APOTHECIAL APPEALINGNESSES APPETIZING
APOPLECTICALLY APOTHECIUM APPEARANCE APPETIZINGLY
APOPLECTICS APOTHEGMATIC APPEARANCES APPLAUDABLE
APOPLEXIES APOTHEGMATICAL APPEASABLE APPLAUDABLY
APOPLEXING APOTHEGMATISE APPEASEMENT APPLAUDERS
APOPROTEIN APOTHEGMATISED APPEASEMENTS APPLAUDING
APOPROTEINS APOTHEGMATISES APPEASINGLY APPLAUDINGLY
APOSEMATIC APOTHEGMATISING APPELLANTS APPLAUSIVE
APOSEMATICALLY APOTHEGMATIST APPELLATION APPLAUSIVELY
APOSIOPESES APOTHEGMATISTS APPELLATIONAL APPLECARTS
APOSIOPESIS APOTHEGMATIZE APPELLATIONS APPLEDRAIN

APPLEDRAINS
APPLEJACKS
APPLERINGIE
APPLERINGIES
APPLESAUCE
APPLESAUCES
APPLIANCES
APPLICABILITIES
APPLICABILITY
APPLICABLE
APPLICABLENESS
APPLICABLY
APPLICANTS
APPLICATION
APPLICATIONS
APPLICATIVE
APPLICATIVELY
APPLICATOR
APPLICATORS
APPLICATORY
APPLIQUEING
APPOGGIATURA
APPOGGIATURAS
APPOGGIATURE
APPOINTEES
APPOINTERS
APPOINTING
APPOINTIVE
APPOINTMENT
APPOINTMENTS
APPOINTORS
APPORTIONABLE
APPORTIONED
APPORTIONER
APPORTIONERS
APPORTIONING
APPORTIONMENT
APPORTIONMENTS
APPORTIONS
APPOSITELY
APPOSITENESS
APPOSITENESSES
APPOSITION
APPOSITIONAL
APPOSITIONS
APPOSITIVE
APPOSITIVELY
APPOSITIVES
APPRAISABLE
APPRAISALS
APPRAISEES
APPRAISEMENT
APPRAISEMENTS
APPRAISERS
APPRAISING
APPRAISINGLY
APPRAISIVE
APPRAISIVELY
APPRECIABLE

APPRECIABLY
APPRECIATE
APPRECIATED
APPRECIATES
APPRECIATING
APPRECIATION
APPRECIATIONS
APPRECIATIVE
APPRECIATIVELY
APPRECIATOR
APPRECIATORILY
APPRECIATORS
APPRECIATORY
APPREHENDED
APPREHENDING
APPREHENDS
APPREHENSIBLE
APPREHENSIBLY
APPREHENSION
APPREHENSIONS
APPREHENSIVE
APPREHENSIVELY
APPRENTICE
APPRENTICED
APPRENTICEHOOD
APPRENTICEHOODS
APPRENTICEMENT
APPRENTICEMENTS
APPRENTICES
APPRENTICESHIP
APPRENTICESHIPS
APPRENTICING
APPRESSING
APPRESSORIA
APPRESSORIUM
APPRISINGS
APPRIZINGS
APPROACHABILITY
APPROACHABLE
APPROACHED
APPROACHES
APPROACHING
APPROBATED
APPROBATES
APPROBATING
APPROBATION
APPROBATIONS
APPROBATIVE
APPROBATORY
APPROPINQUATE
APPROPINQUATED
APPROPINQUATES
APPROPINQUATING
APPROPINQUATION
APPROPINQUE
APPROPINQUED
APPROPINQUES
APPROPINQUING
APPROPINQUITIES

APPROPINQUITY
APPROPRIABLE
APPROPRIACIES
APPROPRIACY
APPROPRIATE
APPROPRIATED
APPROPRIATELY
APPROPRIATENESS
APPROPRIATES
APPROPRIATING
APPROPRIATION
APPROPRIATIONS
APPROPRIATIVE
APPROPRIATOR
APPROPRIATORS
APPROVABLE
APPROVABLY
APPROVANCE
APPROVANCES
APPROVINGLY
APPROXIMAL
APPROXIMATE
APPROXIMATED
APPROXIMATELY
APPROXIMATES
APPROXIMATING
APPROXIMATION
APPROXIMATIONS
APPROXIMATIVE
APPULSIVELY
APPURTENANCE
APPURTENANCES
APPURTENANT
APPURTENANTS
APRICATING
APRICATION
APRICATIONS
APRIORISMS
APRIORISTS
APRIORITIES
APSIDIOLES
APTERYGIAL
APTITUDINAL
APTITUDINALLY
AQUABATICS
AQUABOARDS
AQUACEUTICAL
AQUACEUTICALS
AQUACULTURAL
AQUACULTURE
AQUACULTURES
AQUACULTURIST
AQUACULTURISTS
AQUADROMES
AQUAEROBICS
AQUAFARMED
AQUAFARMING
AQUAFITNESS
AQUAFITNESSES

AQUAFORTIS
AQUAFORTISES
AQUAFORTIST
AQUAFORTISTS
AQUALEATHER
AQUALEATHERS
AQUAMANALE
AQUAMANALES
AQUAMANILE
AQUAMANILES
AQUAMARINE
AQUAMARINES
AQUANAUTICS
AQUAPHOBES
AQUAPHOBIA
AQUAPHOBIAS
AQUAPHOBIC
AQUAPHOBICS
AQUAPLANED
AQUAPLANER
AQUAPLANERS
AQUAPLANES
AQUAPLANING
AQUAPLANINGS
AQUAPORINS
AQUARELLES
AQUARELLIST
AQUARELLISTS
AQUARIISTS
AQUAROBICS
AQUATICALLY
AQUATINTAS
AQUATINTED
AQUATINTER
AQUATINTERS
AQUATINTING
AQUATINTIST
AQUATINTISTS
AQUICULTURAL
AQUICULTURE
AQUICULTURES
AQUICULTURIST
AQUICULTURISTS
AQUIFEROUS
AQUIFOLIACEOUS
AQUILEGIAS
AQUILINITIES
AQUILINITY
ARABESQUED
ARABESQUES
ARABICISATION
ARABICISATIONS
ARABICISED
ARABICISES
ARABICISING
ARABICIZATION
ARABICIZATIONS
ARABICIZED
ARABICIZES

ARABICIZING	ARBITRATING	ARCHAEZOOLOGY	ARCHESPORIA
ARABILITIES	ARBITRATION	ARCHAICALLY	ARCHESPORIAL
ARABINOSES	ARBITRATIONAL	ARCHAICISM	ARCHESPORIUM
ARABINOSIDE	ARBITRATIONS	ARCHAICISMS	ARCHETYPAL
ARABINOSIDES	ARBITRATIVE	ARCHAISERS	ARCHETYPALLY
ARABISATION	ARBITRATOR	ARCHAISING	ARCHETYPES
ARABISATIONS	ARBITRATORS	ARCHAISTIC	ARCHETYPICAL
ARABIZATION	ARBITRATRICES	ARCHAIZERS	ARCHETYPICALLY
ARABIZATIONS	ARBITRATRIX	ARCHAIZING	ARCHFIENDS
ARACHIDONIC	ARBITRATRIXES	ARCHANGELIC	ARCHGENETHLIAC
ARACHNIDAN	ARBITREMENT	ARCHANGELS	ARCHGENETHLIACS
ARACHNIDANS	ARBITREMENTS	ARCHBISHOP	ARCHICARPS
ARACHNOIDAL	ARBITRESSES	ARCHBISHOPRIC	ARCHIDIACONAL
ARACHNOIDITIS	ARBITRIUMS	ARCHBISHOPRICS	ARCHIDIACONATE
ARACHNOIDITISES	ARBLASTERS	ARCHBISHOPS	ARCHIDIACONATES
ARACHNOIDS	ARBORACEOUS	ARCHDEACON	ARCHIEPISCOPACY
ARACHNOLOGICAL	ARBOREALLY	ARCHDEACONRIES	ARCHIEPISCOPAL
ARACHNOLOGIES	ARBORESCENCE	ARCHDEACONRY	ARCHIEPISCOPATE
ARACHNOLOGIST	ARBORESCENCES	ARCHDEACONS	ARCHILOWES
ARACHNOLOGISTS	ARBORESCENT	ARCHDIOCESAN	ARCHIMAGES
ARACHNOLOGY	ARBORETUMS	ARCHDIOCESE	ARCHIMANDRITE
ARACHNOPHOBE	ARBORICULTURAL	ARCHDIOCESES	ARCHIMANDRITES
ARACHNOPHOBES	ARBORICULTURE	ARCHDUCHESS	ARCHIPELAGIAN
ARACHNOPHOBIA	ARBORICULTURES	ARCHDUCHESSES	ARCHIPELAGIC
ARACHNOPHOBIAS	ARBORICULTURIST	ARCHDUCHIES	ARCHIPELAGO
ARAEOMETER	ARBORISATION	ARCHDUKEDOM	ARCHIPELAGOES
ARAEOMETERS	ARBORISATIONS	ARCHDUKEDOMS	ARCHIPELAGOS
ARAEOMETRIC	ARBORISING	ARCHEGONIA	ARCHIPHONEME
ARAEOMETRICAL	ARBORIZATION	ARCHEGONIAL	ARCHIPHONEMES
ARAEOMETRIES	ARBORIZATIONS	ARCHEGONIATE	ARCHIPLASM
ARAEOMETRY	ARBORIZING	ARCHEGONIATES	ARCHIPLASMIC
ARAEOSTYLE	ARBORVITAE	ARCHEGONIUM	ARCHIPLASMS
ARAEOSTYLES	ARBORVITAES	ARCHENEMIES	ARCHITECTED
ARAEOSYSTYLE	ARBOVIRUSES	ARCHENTERA	ARCHITECTING
ARAEOSYSTYLES	ARBUSCULAR	ARCHENTERIC	ARCHITECTONIC
ARAGONITES	ARCANENESS	ARCHENTERON	ARCHITECTONICS
ARAGONITIC	ARCANENESSES	ARCHENTERONS	ARCHITECTS
ARALIACEOUS	ARCCOSINES	ARCHEOASTRONOMY	ARCHITECTURAL
ARAUCARIAN	ARCHAEBACTERIA	ARCHEOBOTANIES	ARCHITECTURALLY
ARAUCARIAS	ARCHAEBACTERIUM	ARCHEOBOTANIST	ARCHITECTURE
ARBALESTER	ARCHAEOBOTANIES	ARCHEOBOTANISTS	ARCHITECTURES
ARBALESTERS	ARCHAEOBOTANIST	ARCHEOBOTANY	ARCHITRAVE
ARBALISTER	ARCHAEOBOTANY	ARCHEOLOGICAL	ARCHITRAVED
ARBALISTERS	ARCHAEOLOGICAL	ARCHEOLOGICALLY	ARCHITRAVES
ARBITRABLE	ARCHAEOLOGIES	ARCHEOLOGIES	ARCHITYPES
ARBITRAGED	ARCHAEOLOGIST	ARCHEOLOGIST	ARCHIVISTS
ARBITRAGER	ARCHAEOLOGISTS	ARCHEOLOGISTS	ARCHIVOLTS
ARBITRAGERS	ARCHAEOLOGY	ARCHEOLOGY	ARCHNESSES
ARBITRAGES	ARCHAEOMETRIC	ARCHEOMAGNETISM	ARCHOLOGIES
ARBITRAGEUR	ARCHAEOMETRIES	ARCHEOMETRIES	ARCHONSHIP
ARBITRAGEURS	ARCHAEOMETRIST	ARCHEOMETRY	ARCHONSHIPS
ARBITRAGING	ARCHAEOMETRISTS	ARCHEOZOOLOGIES	ARCHONTATE
ARBITRAMENT	ARCHAEOMETRY	ARCHEOZOOLOGIST	ARCHONTATES
ARBITRAMENTS	ARCHAEOPTERYX	ARCHEOZOOLOGY	ARCHOPLASM
ARBITRARILY	ARCHAEOPTERYXES	ARCHERESSES	ARCHOPLASMIC
ARBITRARINESS	ARCHAEORNIS	ARCHERFISH	ARCHOPLASMS
ARBITRARINESSES	ARCHAEORNISES	ARCHERFISHES	ARCHOSAURIAN
ARBITRATED	ARCHAEOZOOLOGY	ARCHESPORE	ARCHOSAURS
ARBITRATES	ARCHAEZOOLOGIES	ARCHESPORES	ARCHPRIEST

ARCHPRIESTHOOD
ARCHPRIESTHOODS
ARCHPRIESTS
ARCHPRIESTSHIP
ARCHPRIESTSHIPS
ARCHRIVALS
ARCOGRAPHS
ARCOLOGIES
ARCSECONDS
ARCTANGENT
ARCTANGENTS
ARCTICALLY
ARCTOPHILE
ARCTOPHILES
ARCTOPHILIA
ARCTOPHILIAS
ARCTOPHILIES
ARCTOPHILIST
ARCTOPHILISTS
ARCTOPHILS
ARCTOPHILY
ARCUATIONS
ARCUBALIST
ARCUBALISTS
ARDUOUSNESS
ARDUOUSNESSES
ARECOLINES
AREFACTION
AREFACTIONS
ARENACEOUS
ARENATIONS
ARENICOLOUS
AREOCENTRIC
AREOGRAPHIC
AREOGRAPHIES
AREOGRAPHY
AREOLATION
AREOLATIONS
AREOLOGIES
AREOMETERS
AREOSTYLES
AREOSYSTILE
AREOSYSTILES
ARFVEDSONITE
ARFVEDSONITES
ARGENTIFEROUS
ARGENTINES
ARGENTITES
ARGILLACEOUS
ARGILLIFEROUS
ARGILLITES
ARGILLITIC
ARGONAUTIC
ARGUMENTATION
ARGUMENTATIONS
ARGUMENTATIVE
ARGUMENTATIVELY
ARGUMENTIVE
ARGUMENTUM

ARGUMENTUMS
ARGUTENESS
ARGUTENESSES
ARGYRODITE
ARGYRODITES
ARHATSHIPS
ARHYTHMIAS
ARIBOFLAVINOSES
ARIBOFLAVINOSIS
ARIDNESSES
ARISTOCRACIES
ARISTOCRACY
ARISTOCRAT
ARISTOCRATIC
ARISTOCRATICAL
ARISTOCRATISM
ARISTOCRATISMS
ARISTOCRATS
ARISTOLOCHIA
ARISTOLOCHIAS
ARISTOLOGIES
ARISTOLOGY
ARISTOTLES
ARITHMETIC
ARITHMETICAL
ARITHMETICALLY
ARITHMETICIAN
ARITHMETICIANS
ARITHMETICS
ARITHMOMANIA
ARITHMOMANIAS
ARITHMOMETER
ARITHMOMETERS
ARITHMOPHOBIA
ARITHMOPHOBIAS
ARMADILLOS
ARMAMENTARIA
ARMAMENTARIUM
ARMAMENTARIUMS
ARMATURING
ARMIGEROUS
ARMILLARIA
ARMILLARIAS
ARMIPOTENCE
ARMIPOTENCES
ARMIPOTENT
ARMISTICES
ARMLOCKING
ARMORIALLY
ARMOURLESS
AROMATASES
AROMATHERAPIES
AROMATHERAPIST
AROMATHERAPISTS
AROMATHERAPY
AROMATICALLY
AROMATICITIES
AROMATICITY
AROMATISATION

AROMATISATIONS
AROMATISED
AROMATISES
AROMATISING
AROMATIZATION
AROMATIZATIONS
AROMATIZED
AROMATIZES
AROMATIZING
ARPEGGIATE
ARPEGGIATED
ARPEGGIATES
ARPEGGIATING
ARPEGGIATION
ARPEGGIATIONS
ARPEGGIONE
ARPEGGIONES
ARPILLERAS
ARQUEBUSADE
ARQUEBUSADES
ARQUEBUSES
ARQUEBUSIER
ARQUEBUSIERS
ARRACACHAS
ARRAGONITE
ARRAGONITES
ARRAIGNERS
ARRAIGNING
ARRAIGNINGS
ARRAIGNMENT
ARRAIGNMENTS
ARRANGEABLE
ARRANGEMENT
ARRANGEMENTS
ARRAYMENTS
ARREARAGES
ARRESTABLE
ARRESTANTS
ARRESTATION
ARRESTATIONS
ARRESTINGLY
ARRESTMENT
ARRESTMENTS
ARRHENOTOKIES
ARRHENOTOKY
ARRHYTHMIA
ARRHYTHMIAS
ARRHYTHMIC
ARRIVANCES
ARRIVANCIES
ARRIVEDERCI
ARRIVISMES
ARRIVISTES
ARROGANCES
ARROGANCIES
ARROGANTLY
ARROGATING
ARROGATION
ARROGATIONS

ARROGATIVE
ARROGATORS
ARRONDISSEMENT
ARRONDISSEMENTS
ARROWGRASS
ARROWGRASSES
ARROWHEADS
ARROWROOTS
ARROWWOODS
ARROWWORMS
ARSENIATES
ARSENICALS
ARSENOPYRITE
ARSENOPYRITES
ARSMETRICK
ARSMETRICKS
ARSPHENAMINE
ARSPHENAMINES
ARTEFACTUAL
ARTEMISIAS
ARTEMISININ
ARTEMISININS
ARTERIALISATION
ARTERIALISE
ARTERIALISED
ARTERIALISES
ARTERIALISING
ARTERIALIZATION
ARTERIALIZE
ARTERIALIZED
ARTERIALIZES
ARTERIALIZING
ARTERIALLY
ARTERIOGRAM
ARTERIOGRAMS
ARTERIOGRAPHIC
ARTERIOGRAPHIES
ARTERIOGRAPHY
ARTERIOLAR
ARTERIOLES
ARTERIOTOMIES
ARTERIOTOMY
ARTERIOVENOUS
ARTERITIDES
ARTERITISES
ARTFULNESS
ARTFULNESSES
ARTHRALGIA
ARTHRALGIAS
ARTHRALGIC
ARTHRECTOMIES
ARTHRECTOMY
ARTHRITICALLY
ARTHRITICS
ARTHRITIDES
ARTHRITISES
ARTHRODESES
ARTHRODESIS
ARTHRODIAE

ARTHRODIAL	ARTINESSES	ASCETICISM	ASPERSIONS
ARTHROGRAPHIES	ARTIODACTYL	ASCETICISMS	ASPERSIVELY
ARTHROGRAPHY	ARTIODACTYLOUS	ASCITITIOUS	ASPERSOIRS
ARTHROMERE	ARTIODACTYLS	ASCLEPIADACEOUS	ASPERSORIA
ARTHROMERES	ARTISANSHIP	ASCLEPIADS	ASPERSORIES
ARTHROMERIC	ARTISANSHIPS	ASCLEPIASES	ASPERSORIUM
ARTHROPATHIES	ARTISTICAL	ASCOCARPIC	ASPERSORIUMS
ARTHROPATHY	ARTISTICALLY	ASCOGONIUM	ASPHALTERS
ARTHROPLASTIES	ARTISTRIES	ASCOMYCETE	ASPHALTING
ARTHROPLASTY	ARTLESSNESS	ASCOMYCETES	ASPHALTITE
ARTHROPODAL	ARTLESSNESSES	ASCOMYCETOUS	ASPHALTITES
ARTHROPODAN	ARTOCARPUS	ASCORBATES	ASPHALTUMS
ARTHROPODOUS	ARTOCARPUSES	ASCOSPORES	ASPHERICAL
ARTHROPODS	ARTSINESSES	ASCOSPORIC	ASPHETERISE
ARTHROSCOPE	ARUNDINACEOUS	ASCRIBABLE	ASPHETERISED
ARTHROSCOPES	ARVICOLINE	ASCRIPTION	ASPHETERISES
ARTHROSCOPIC	ARYBALLOID	ASCRIPTIONS	ASPHETERISING
ARTHROSCOPIES	ARYBALLOSES	ASCRIPTIVE	ASPHETERISM
ARTHROSCOPY	ARYTAENOID	ASEPTICALLY	ASPHETERISMS
ARTHROSPORE	ARYTAENOIDS	ASEPTICISE	ASPHETERIZE
ARTHROSPORES	ARYTENOIDAL	ASEPTICISED	ASPHETERIZED
ARTHROSPORIC	ARYTENOIDS	ASEPTICISES	ASPHETERIZES
ARTHROSPOROUS	ASAFETIDAS	ASEPTICISING	ASPHETERIZING
ARTICHOKES	ASAFOETIDA	ASEPTICISM	ASPHYXIANT
ARTICULABLE	ASAFOETIDAS	ASEPTICISMS	ASPHYXIANTS
ARTICULACIES	ASARABACCA	ASEPTICIZE	ASPHYXIATE
ARTICULACY	ASARABACCAS	ASEPTICIZED	ASPHYXIATED
ARTICULATE	ASBESTIFORM	ASEPTICIZES	ASPHYXIATES
ARTICULATED	ASBESTOSES	ASEPTICIZING	ASPHYXIATING
ARTICULATELY	ASBESTOSIS	ASEXUALITIES	ASPHYXIATION
ARTICULATENESS	ASBESTUSES	ASEXUALITY	ASPHYXIATIONS
ARTICULATES	ASCARIASES	ASHAMEDNESS	ASPHYXIATOR
ARTICULATING	ASCARIASIS	ASHAMEDNESSES	ASPHYXIATORS
ARTICULATION	ASCENDABLE	ASHINESSES	ASPIDISTRA
ARTICULATIONS	ASCENDANCE	ASHLARINGS	ASPIDISTRAS
ARTICULATIVE	ASCENDANCES	ASHLERINGS	ASPIRATING
ARTICULATOR	ASCENDANCIES	ASHRAMITES	ASPIRATION
ARTICULATORS	ASCENDANCY	ASININITIES	ASPIRATIONAL
ARTICULATORY	ASCENDANTLY	ASKEWNESSES	ASPIRATIONS
ARTIFACTUAL	ASCENDANTS	ASPARAGINASE	ASPIRATORS
ARTIFICERS	ASCENDENCE	ASPARAGINASES	ASPIRATORY
ARTIFICIAL	ASCENDENCES	ASPARAGINE	ASPIRINGLY
ARTIFICIALISE	ASCENDENCIES	ASPARAGINES	ASPIRINGNESS
ARTIFICIALISED	ASCENDENCY	ASPARAGUSES	ASPIRINGNESSES
ARTIFICIALISES	ASCENDENTS	ASPARTAMES	ASPLANCHNIC
ARTIFICIALISING	ASCENDEURS	ASPARTATES	ASPLENIUMS
ARTIFICIALITIES	ASCENDIBLE	ASPECTABLE	ASPORTATION
ARTIFICIALITY	ASCENSIONAL	ASPERATING	ASPORTATIONS
ARTIFICIALIZE	ASCENSIONIST	ASPERGATION	ASSAFETIDA
ARTIFICIALIZED	ASCENSIONISTS	ASPERGATIONS	ASSAFETIDAS
ARTIFICIALIZES	ASCENSIONS	ASPERGILLA	ASSAFOETIDA
ARTIFICIALIZING	ASCERTAINABLE	ASPERGILLI	ASSAFOETIDAS
ARTIFICIALLY	ASCERTAINABLY	ASPERGILLOSES	ASSAGAIING
ARTIFICIALNESS	ASCERTAINED	ASPERGILLOSIS	ASSAILABLE
ARTILLERIES	ASCERTAINING	ASPERGILLS	ASSAILANTS
ARTILLERIST	ASCERTAINMENT	ASPERGILLUM	ASSAILMENT
ARTILLERISTS	ASCERTAINMENTS	ASPERGILLUMS	ASSAILMENTS
ARTILLERYMAN	ASCERTAINS	ASPERGILLUS	ASSASSINATE
ARTILLERYMEN	ASCETICALLY	ASPERITIES	ASSASSINATED

ASSASSINATES
ASSASSINATING
ASSASSINATION
ASSASSINATIONS
ASSASSINATOR
ASSASSINATORS
ASSAULTERS
ASSAULTING
ASSAULTIVE
ASSAULTIVELY
ASSAULTIVENESS
ASSEGAAIED
ASSEGAAIING
ASSEGAAIING
ASSEMBLAGE
ASSEMBLAGES
ASSEMBLAGIST
ASSEMBLAGISTS
ASSEMBLANCE
ASSEMBLANCES
ASSEMBLAUNCE
ASSEMBLAUNCES
ASSEMBLERS
ASSEMBLIES
ASSEMBLING
ASSEMBLYMAN
ASSEMBLYMEN
ASSEMBLYWOMAN
ASSEMBLYWOMEN
ASSENTANEOUS
ASSENTATION
ASSENTATIONS
ASSENTATOR
ASSENTATORS
ASSENTIENT
ASSENTIENTS
ASSENTINGLY
ASSENTIVENESS
ASSENTIVENESSES
ASSERTABLE
ASSERTEDLY
ASSERTIBLE
ASSERTIONS
ASSERTIVELY
ASSERTIVENESS
ASSERTIVENESSES
ASSERTORIC
ASSESSABLE
ASSESSMENT
ASSESSMENTS
ASSESSORIAL
ASSESSORSHIP
ASSESSORSHIPS
ASSEVERATE
ASSEVERATED
ASSEVERATES
ASSEVERATING
ASSEVERATINGLY
ASSEVERATION

ASSEVERATIONS
ASSEVERATIVE
ASSEVERING
ASSIBILATE
ASSIBILATED
ASSIBILATES
ASSIBILATING
ASSIBILATION
ASSIBILATIONS
ASSIDUITIES
ASSIDUOUSLY
ASSIDUOUSNESS
ASSIDUOUSNESSES
ASSIGNABILITIES
ASSIGNABILITY
ASSIGNABLE
ASSIGNABLY
ASSIGNATION
ASSIGNATIONS
ASSIGNMENT
ASSIGNMENTS
ASSIMILABILITY
ASSIMILABLE
ASSIMILABLY
ASSIMILATE
ASSIMILATED
ASSIMILATES
ASSIMILATING
ASSIMILATION
ASSIMILATIONISM
ASSIMILATIONIST
ASSIMILATIONS
ASSIMILATIVE
ASSIMILATIVELY
ASSIMILATOR
ASSIMILATORS
ASSIMILATORY
ASSISTANCE
ASSISTANCES
ASSISTANTS
ASSISTANTSHIP
ASSISTANTSHIPS
ASSOCIABILITIES
ASSOCIABILITY
ASSOCIABLE
ASSOCIATED
ASSOCIATES
ASSOCIATESHIP
ASSOCIATESHIPS
ASSOCIATING
ASSOCIATION
ASSOCIATIONAL
ASSOCIATIONISM
ASSOCIATIONISMS
ASSOCIATIONIST
ASSOCIATIONISTS
ASSOCIATIONS
ASSOCIATIVE
ASSOCIATIVELY

ASSOCIATIVITIES
ASSOCIATIVITY
ASSOCIATOR
ASSOCIATORS
ASSOCIATORY
ASSOILMENT
ASSOILMENTS
ASSOILZIED
ASSOILZIEING
ASSOILZIES
ASSONANCES
ASSONANTAL
ASSONATING
ASSORTATIVE
ASSORTATIVELY
ASSORTEDNESS
ASSORTEDNESSES
ASSORTMENT
ASSORTMENTS
ASSUAGEMENT
ASSUAGEMENTS
ASSUAGINGS
ASSUBJUGATE
ASSUBJUGATED
ASSUBJUGATES
ASSUBJUGATING
ASSUEFACTION
ASSUEFACTIONS
ASSUETUDES
ASSUMABILITIES
ASSUMABILITY
ASSUMINGLY
ASSUMPSITS
ASSUMPTION
ASSUMPTIONS
ASSUMPTIVE
ASSUMPTIVELY
ASSURANCES
ASSUREDNESS
ASSUREDNESSES
ASSURGENCIES
ASSURGENCY
ASSYTHMENT
ASSYTHMENTS
ASTACOLOGICAL
ASTACOLOGIES
ASTACOLOGIST
ASTACOLOGISTS
ASTACOLOGY
ASTARBOARD
ASTATICALLY
ASTATICISM
ASTATICISMS
ASTEREOGNOSES
ASTEREOGNOSIS
ASTERIATED
ASTERIDIAN
ASTERIDIANS
ASTERISKED

ASTERISKING
ASTERISKLESS
ASTEROIDAL
ASTEROIDEAN
ASTEROIDEANS
ASTHENOPIA
ASTHENOPIAS
ASTHENOPIC
ASTHENOSPHERE
ASTHENOSPHERES
ASTHENOSPHERIC
ASTHMATICAL
ASTHMATICALLY
ASTHMATICS
ASTIGMATIC
ASTIGMATICALLY
ASTIGMATICS
ASTIGMATISM
ASTIGMATISMS
ASTOMATOUS
ASTONISHED
ASTONISHES
ASTONISHING
ASTONISHINGLY
ASTONISHMENT
ASTONISHMENTS
ASTOUNDING
ASTOUNDINGLY
ASTOUNDMENT
ASTOUNDMENTS
ASTRACHANS
ASTRAGALUS
ASTRAGALUSES
ASTRAKHANS
ASTRANTIAS
ASTRAPHOBIA
ASTRAPHOBIAS
ASTRAPHOBIC
ASTRAPOPHOBIA
ASTRAPOPHOBIAS
ASTRICTING
ASTRICTION
ASTRICTIONS
ASTRICTIVE
ASTRICTIVELY
ASTRINGENCE
ASTRINGENCES
ASTRINGENCIES
ASTRINGENCY
ASTRINGENT
ASTRINGENTLY
ASTRINGENTS
ASTRINGERS
ASTRINGING
ASTROBIOLOGIES
ASTROBIOLOGIST
ASTROBIOLOGISTS
ASTROBIOLOGY
ASTROBLEME

ASTROBLEMES	ASTROPHOBIA	ATHEOLOGIES	ATROCIOUSNESSES
ASTROBOTANIES	ASTROPHOBIAS	ATHEORETICAL	ATROCITIES
ASTROBOTANY	ASTROPHOBIC	ATHERMANCIES	ATROPHYING
ASTROCHEMISTRY	ASTROPHOTOGRAPH	ATHERMANCY	ATTACHABLE
ASTROCOMPASS	ASTROPHYSICAL	ATHERMANOUS	ATTACHMENT
ASTROCOMPASSES	ASTROPHYSICALLY	ATHEROGENESES	ATTACHMENTS
ASTROCYTES	ASTROPHYSICIST	ATHEROGENESIS	ATTACKABLE
ASTROCYTIC	ASTROPHYSICISTS	ATHEROGENIC	ATTAINABILITIES
ASTROCYTOMA	ASTROPHYSICS	ATHEROMATA	ATTAINABILITY
ASTROCYTOMAS	ASTROSPHERE	ATHEROMATOUS	ATTAINABLE
ASTROCYTOMATA	ASTROSPHERES	ATHEROSCLEROSES	ATTAINABLENESS
ASTRODOMES	ASTROTOURISM	ATHEROSCLEROSIS	ATTAINDERS
ASTRODYNAMICIST	ASTROTOURISMS	ATHEROSCLEROTIC	ATTAINMENT
ASTRODYNAMICS	ASTROTOURIST	ATHETISING	ATTAINMENTS
ASTROFELLS	ASTROTOURISTS	ATHETIZING	ATTAINTING
ASTROGEOLOGIES	ASTUCIOUSLY	ATHLETICALLY	ATTAINTMENT
ASTROGEOLOGIST	ASTUCITIES	ATHLETICISM	ATTAINTMENTS
ASTROGEOLOGISTS	ASTUTENESS	ATHLETICISMS	ATTAINTURE
ASTROGEOLOGY	ASTUTENESSES	ATHROCYTES	ATTAINTURES
ASTROHATCH	ASYMMETRIC	ATHROCYTOSES	ATTEMPERED
ASTROHATCHES	ASYMMETRICAL	ATHROCYTOSIS	ATTEMPERING
ASTROLABES	ASYMMETRICALLY	ATHWARTSHIP	ATTEMPERMENT
ASTROLATRIES	ASYMMETRIES	ATHWARTSHIPS	ATTEMPERMENTS
ASTROLATRY	ASYMPTOMATIC	ATMOLOGIES	ATTEMPTABILITY
ASTROLOGER	ASYMPTOTES	ATMOLOGIST	ATTEMPTABLE
ASTROLOGERS	ASYMPTOTIC	ATMOLOGISTS	ATTEMPTERS
ASTROLOGIC	ASYMPTOTICAL	ATMOLYSING	ATTEMPTING
ASTROLOGICAL	ASYMPTOTICALLY	ATMOLYZING	ATTENDANCE
ASTROLOGICALLY	ASYNARTETE	ATMOMETERS	ATTENDANCES
ASTROLOGIES	ASYNARTETES	ATMOMETRIES	ATTENDANCIES
ASTROLOGIST	ASYNARTETIC	ATMOSPHERE	ATTENDANCY
ASTROLOGISTS	ASYNCHRONIES	ATMOSPHERED	ATTENDANTS
ASTROMETRIC	ASYNCHRONISM	ATMOSPHERES	ATTENDEMENT
ASTROMETRICAL	ASYNCHRONISMS	ATMOSPHERIC	ATTENDEMENTS
ASTROMETRIES	ASYNCHRONOUS	ATMOSPHERICAL	ATTENDINGS
ASTROMETRY	ASYNCHRONOUSLY	ATMOSPHERICALLY	ATTENDMENT
ASTRONAUTIC	ASYNCHRONY	ATMOSPHERICS	ATTENDMENTS
ASTRONAUTICAL	ASYNDETICALLY	ATOMICALLY	ATTENTIONAL
ASTRONAUTICALLY	ASYNDETONS	ATOMICITIES	ATTENTIONS
ASTRONAUTICS	ASYNERGIAS	ATOMISATION	ATTENTIVELY
ASTRONAUTS	ASYNERGIES	ATOMISATIONS	ATTENTIVENESS
ASTRONAVIGATION	ASYNTACTIC	ATOMISTICAL	ATTENTIVENESSES
ASTRONAVIGATOR	ASYSTOLISM	ATOMISTICALLY	ATTENUANTS
ASTRONAVIGATORS	ASYSTOLISMS	ATOMIZATION	ATTENUATED
ASTRONOMER	ATACAMITES	ATOMIZATIONS	ATTENUATES
ASTRONOMERS	ATARACTICS	ATONALISMS	ATTENUATING
ASTRONOMIC	ATAVISTICALLY	ATONALISTS	ATTENUATION
ASTRONOMICAL	ATCHIEVING	ATONALITIES	ATTENUATIONS
ASTRONOMICALLY	ATELECTASES	ATONEMENTS	ATTENUATOR
ASTRONOMIES	ATELECTASIS	ATONICITIES	ATTENUATORS
ASTRONOMISE	ATELECTATIC	ATRABILIAR	ATTESTABLE
ASTRONOMISED	ATELEIOSES	ATRABILIOUS	ATTESTANTS
ASTRONOMISES	ATELEIOSIS	ATRABILIOUSNESS	ATTESTATION
ASTRONOMISING	ATHANASIES	ATRACURIUM	ATTESTATIONS
ASTRONOMIZE	ATHEISTICAL	ATRACURIUMS	ATTESTATIVE
ASTRONOMIZED	ATHEISTICALLY	ATRAMENTAL	ATTESTATOR
ASTRONOMIZES	ATHEMATICALLY	ATRAMENTOUS	ATTESTATORS
ASTRONOMIZING	ATHENAEUMS	ATROCIOUSLY	ATTICISING
ASTROPHELS	ATHEOLOGICAL	ATROCIOUSNESS	ATTICIZING

ATTIREMENT	ATTRIBUTIONS	AUDIOMETRISTS	AUSCULTATORS
ATTIREMENTS	ATTRIBUTIVE	AUDIOMETRY	AUSCULTATORY
ATTITUDINAL	ATTRIBUTIVELY	AUDIOPHILE	AUSFORMING
ATTITUDINALLY	ATTRIBUTIVENESS	AUDIOPHILES	AUSLANDERS
ATTITUDINARIAN	ATTRIBUTIVES	AUDIOPHILS	AUSPICATED
ATTITUDINARIANS	ATTRIBUTOR	AUDIOTAPED	AUSPICATES
ATTITUDINISE	ATTRIBUTORS	AUDIOTAPES	AUSPICATING
ATTITUDINISED	ATTRISTING	AUDIOTAPING	AUSPICIOUS
ATTITUDINISER	ATTRITIONAL	AUDIOTYPING	AUSPICIOUSLY
ATTITUDINISERS	ATTRITIONS	AUDIOTYPINGS	AUSPICIOUSNESS
ATTITUDINISES	ATTRITTING	AUDIOTYPIST	AUSTENITES
ATTITUDINISING	ATTUITIONAL	AUDIOTYPISTS	AUSTENITIC
ATTITUDINISINGS	ATTUITIONS	AUDIOVISUAL	AUSTERENESS
ATTITUDINIZE	ATTUITIVELY	AUDIOVISUALLY	AUSTERENESSES
ATTITUDINIZED	ATTUNEMENT	AUDIOVISUALS	AUSTERITIES
ATTITUDINIZER	ATTUNEMENTS	AUDIPHONES	AUSTRALITE
ATTITUDINIZERS	ATYPICALITIES	AUDITIONED	AUSTRALITES
ATTITUDINIZES	ATYPICALITY	AUDITIONER	AUSTRINGER
ATTITUDINIZING	ATYPICALLY	AUDITIONERS	AUSTRINGERS
ATTITUDINIZINGS	AUBERGINES	AUDITIONING	AUTARCHICAL
ATTOLASERS	AUBERGISTE	AUDITORIAL	AUTARCHIES
ATTOLLENTS	AUBERGISTES	AUDITORIES	AUTARCHIST
ATTOPHYSICS	AUBRIETIAS	AUDITORILY	AUTARCHISTS
ATTORNEYDOM	AUCTIONARY	AUDITORIUM	AUTARKICAL
ATTORNEYDOMS	AUCTIONEER	AUDITORIUMS	AUTARKISTS
ATTORNEYED	AUCTIONEERED	AUDITORSHIP	AUTECOLOGIC
ATTORNEYING	AUCTIONEERING	AUDITORSHIPS	AUTECOLOGICAL
ATTORNEYISM	AUCTIONEERS	AUDITRESSES	AUTECOLOGIES
ATTORNEYISMS	AUCTIONING	AUGMENTABLE	AUTECOLOGY
ATTORNEYSHIP	AUDACIOUSLY	AUGMENTATION	AUTEURISMS
ATTORNEYSHIPS	AUDACIOUSNESS	AUGMENTATIONS	AUTEURISTS
ATTORNMENT	AUDACIOUSNESSES	AUGMENTATIVE	AUTHENTICAL
ATTORNMENTS	AUDACITIES	AUGMENTATIVELY	AUTHENTICALLY
ATTRACTABLE	AUDIBILITIES	AUGMENTATIVES	AUTHENTICATE
ATTRACTANCE	AUDIBILITY	AUGMENTERS	AUTHENTICATED
ATTRACTANCES	AUDIBLENESS	AUGMENTING	AUTHENTICATES
ATTRACTANCIES	AUDIBLENESSES	AUGMENTORS	AUTHENTICATING
ATTRACTANCY	AUDIENCIAS	AUGURSHIPS	AUTHENTICATION
ATTRACTANT	AUDIOBOOKS	AUGUSTNESS	AUTHENTICATIONS
ATTRACTANTS	AUDIOCASSETTE	AUGUSTNESSES	AUTHENTICATOR
ATTRACTERS	AUDIOCASSETTES	AURALITIES	AUTHENTICATORS
ATTRACTING	AUDIOGENIC	AUREATENESS	AUTHENTICITIES
ATTRACTINGLY	AUDIOGRAMS	AUREATENESSES	AUTHENTICITY
ATTRACTION	AUDIOGRAPH	AURICULARLY	AUTHIGENIC
ATTRACTIONS	AUDIOGRAPHS	AURICULARS	AUTHORCRAFT
ATTRACTIVE	AUDIOLOGIC	AURICULATE	AUTHORCRAFTS
ATTRACTIVELY	AUDIOLOGICAL	AURICULATED	AUTHORESSES
ATTRACTIVENESS	AUDIOLOGICALLY	AURICULATELY	AUTHORINGS
ATTRACTORS	AUDIOLOGIES	AURIFEROUS	AUTHORISABLE
ATTRAHENTS	AUDIOLOGIST	AURISCOPES	AUTHORISATION
ATTRAPPING	AUDIOLOGISTS	AURISCOPIC	AUTHORISATIONS
ATTRIBUTABLE	AUDIOMETER	AUSCULTATE	AUTHORISED
ATTRIBUTED	AUDIOMETERS	AUSCULTATED	AUTHORISER
ATTRIBUTER	AUDIOMETRIC	AUSCULTATES	AUTHORISERS
ATTRIBUTERS	AUDIOMETRICALLY	AUSCULTATING	AUTHORISES
ATTRIBUTES	AUDIOMETRICIAN	AUSCULTATION	AUTHORISING
ATTRIBUTING	AUDIOMETRICIANS	AUSCULTATIONS	AUTHORISMS
ATTRIBUTION	AUDIOMETRIES	AUSCULTATIVE	AUTHORITARIAN
ATTRIBUTIONAL	AUDIOMETRIST	AUSCULTATOR	AUTHORITARIANS

AUTHORITATIVE	AUTOCRATIC	AUTOINFECTION	AUTOMOBILIST
AUTHORITATIVELY	AUTOCRATICAL	AUTOINFECTIONS	AUTOMOBILISTS
AUTHORITIES	AUTOCRATICALLY	AUTOINOCULATION	AUTOMOBILITIES
AUTHORIZABLE	AUTOCRIMES	AUTOIONISATION	AUTOMOBILITY
AUTHORIZATION	AUTOCRITIQUE	AUTOIONISATIONS	AUTOMORPHIC
AUTHORIZATIONS	AUTOCRITIQUES	AUTOIONIZATION	AUTOMORPHICALLY
AUTHORIZED	AUTOCROSSES	AUTOIONIZATIONS	AUTOMORPHISM
AUTHORIZER	AUTOCUTIES	AUTOJUMBLE	AUTOMORPHISMS
AUTHORIZERS	AUTOCYCLES	AUTOJUMBLES	AUTOMOTIVE
AUTHORIZES	AUTODESTRUCT	AUTOKINESES	AUTONOMICAL
AUTHORIZING	AUTODESTRUCTED	AUTOKINESIS	AUTONOMICALLY
AUTHORLESS	AUTODESTRUCTING	AUTOKINETIC	AUTONOMICS
AUTHORSHIP	AUTODESTRUCTIVE	AUTOLATRIES	AUTONOMIES
AUTHORSHIPS	AUTODESTRUCTS	AUTOLOADING	AUTONOMIST
AUTISTICALLY	AUTODIDACT	AUTOLOGIES	AUTONOMISTS
AUTOALLOGAMIES	AUTODIDACTIC	AUTOLOGOUS	AUTONOMOUS
AUTOALLOGAMY	AUTODIDACTICISM	AUTOLYSATE	AUTONOMOUSLY
AUTOANTIBODIES	AUTODIDACTS	AUTOLYSATES	AUTOPHAGIA
AUTOANTIBODY	AUTOECIOUS	AUTOLYSING	AUTOPHAGIAS
AUTOBAHNEN	AUTOECIOUSLY	AUTOLYSINS	AUTOPHAGIES
AUTOBIOGRAPHER	AUTOECISMS	AUTOLYZATE	AUTOPHAGOUS
AUTOBIOGRAPHERS	AUTOEROTIC	AUTOLYZATES	AUTOPHANOUS
AUTOBIOGRAPHIC	AUTOEROTICISM	AUTOLYZING	AUTOPHOBIA
AUTOBIOGRAPHIES	AUTOEROTICISMS	AUTOMAKERS	AUTOPHOBIAS
AUTOBIOGRAPHY	AUTOEROTISM	AUTOMATABLE	AUTOPHOBIES
AUTOBUSSES	AUTOEROTISMS	AUTOMATICAL	AUTOPHONIES
AUTOCATALYSE	AUTOEXPOSURE	AUTOMATICALLY	AUTOPHYTES
AUTOCATALYSED	AUTOEXPOSURES	AUTOMATICITIES	AUTOPHYTIC
AUTOCATALYSES	AUTOFLARES	AUTOMATICITY	AUTOPHYTICALLY
AUTOCATALYSING	AUTOFOCUSES	AUTOMATICS	AUTOPILOTS
AUTOCATALYSIS	AUTOGAMIES	AUTOMATING	AUTOPISTAS
AUTOCATALYTIC	AUTOGAMOUS	AUTOMATION	AUTOPLASTIC
AUTOCATALYZE	AUTOGENESES	AUTOMATIONS	AUTOPLASTIES
AUTOCATALYZED	AUTOGENESIS	AUTOMATISATION	AUTOPLASTY
AUTOCATALYZES	AUTOGENETIC	AUTOMATISATIONS	AUTOPOINTS
AUTOCATALYZING	AUTOGENICS	AUTOMATISE	AUTOPOLYPLOID
AUTOCEPHALIC	AUTOGENIES	AUTOMATISED	AUTOPOLYPLOIDS
AUTOCEPHALIES	AUTOGENOUS	AUTOMATISES	AUTOPOLYPLOIDY
AUTOCEPHALOUS	AUTOGENOUSLY	AUTOMATISING	AUTOPSISTS
AUTOCEPHALY	AUTOGRAFTED	AUTOMATISM	AUTOPSYING
AUTOCHANGER	AUTOGRAFTING	AUTOMATISMS	AUTOPTICAL
AUTOCHANGERS	AUTOGRAFTS	AUTOMATIST	AUTOPTICALLY
AUTOCHTHON	AUTOGRAPHED	AUTOMATISTS	AUTORADIOGRAM
AUTOCHTHONAL	AUTOGRAPHIC	AUTOMATIZATION	AUTORADIOGRAMS
AUTOCHTHONES	AUTOGRAPHICAL	AUTOMATIZATIONS	AUTORADIOGRAPH
AUTOCHTHONIC	AUTOGRAPHICALLY	AUTOMATIZE	AUTORADIOGRAPHS
AUTOCHTHONIES	AUTOGRAPHIES	AUTOMATIZED	AUTORADIOGRAPHY
AUTOCHTHONISM	AUTOGRAPHING	AUTOMATIZES	AUTORICKSHAW
AUTOCHTHONISMS	AUTOGRAPHS	AUTOMATIZING	AUTORICKSHAWS
AUTOCHTHONOUS	AUTOGRAPHY	AUTOMATONS	AUTOROTATE
AUTOCHTHONOUSLY	AUTOGRAVURE	AUTOMATOUS	AUTOROTATED
AUTOCHTHONS	AUTOGRAVURES	AUTOMETERS	AUTOROTATES
AUTOCHTHONY	AUTOGUIDES	AUTOMOBILE	AUTOROTATING
AUTOCLAVED	AUTOHYPNOSES	AUTOMOBILED	AUTOROTATION
AUTOCLAVES	AUTOHYPNOSIS	AUTOMOBILES	AUTOROTATIONS
AUTOCLAVING	AUTOHYPNOTIC	AUTOMOBILIA	AUTOROUTES
AUTOCOPROPHAGY	AUTOIMMUNE	AUTOMOBILING	AUTOSCHEDIASM
AUTOCORRELATION	AUTOIMMUNITIES	AUTOMOBILISM	AUTOSCHEDIASMS
AUTOCRACIES	AUTOIMMUNITY	AUTOMOBILISMS	AUTOSCHEDIASTIC

AUTOSCHEDIAZE
AUTOSCHEDIAZED
AUTOSCHEDIAZES
AUTOSCHEDIAZING
AUTOSCOPIC
AUTOSCOPIES
AUTOSEXING
AUTOSOMALLY
AUTOSPORES
AUTOSTABILITIES
AUTOSTABILITY
AUTOSTRADA
AUTOSTRADAS
AUTOSTRADE
AUTOSUGGEST
AUTOSUGGESTED
AUTOSUGGESTING
AUTOSUGGESTION
AUTOSUGGESTIONS
AUTOSUGGESTIVE
AUTOSUGGESTS
AUTOTELLER
AUTOTELLERS
AUTOTETRAPLOID
AUTOTETRAPLOIDS
AUTOTETRAPLOIDY
AUTOTHEISM
AUTOTHEISMS
AUTOTHEIST
AUTOTHEISTS
AUTOTIMERS
AUTOTOMIES
AUTOTOMISE
AUTOTOMISED
AUTOTOMISES
AUTOTOMISING
AUTOTOMIZE
AUTOTOMIZED
AUTOTOMIZES
AUTOTOMIZING
AUTOTOMOUS
AUTOTOXAEMIA
AUTOTOXAEMIAS
AUTOTOXEMIA
AUTOTOXEMIAS
AUTOTOXINS
AUTOTRANSFORMER
AUTOTRANSFUSION
AUTOTROPHIC
AUTOTROPHICALLY
AUTOTROPHIES
AUTOTROPHS
AUTOTROPHY
AUTOTYPIES
AUTOTYPING
AUTOTYPOGRAPHY
AUTOWINDER
AUTOWINDERS
AUTOWORKER

AUTOWORKERS
AUTOXIDATION
AUTOXIDATIONS
AUTUMNALLY
AUXANOMETER
AUXANOMETERS
AUXILIARIES
AUXOCHROME
AUXOCHROMES
AUXOMETERS
AUXOSPORES
AUXOTROPHIC
AUXOTROPHIES
AUXOTROPHS
AUXOTROPHY
AVAILABILITIES
AVAILABILITY
AVAILABLENESS
AVAILABLENESSES
AVAILINGLY
AVALANCHED
AVALANCHES
AVALANCHING
AVANTURINE
AVANTURINES
AVARICIOUS
AVARICIOUSLY
AVARICIOUSNESS
AVASCULARITIES
AVASCULARITY
AVENACEOUS
AVENGEMENT
AVENGEMENTS
AVENGERESS
AVENGERESSES
AVENTAILES
AVENTURINE
AVENTURINES
AVENTURINS
AVERAGENESS
AVERAGENESSES
AVERAGINGS
AVERRUNCATE
AVERRUNCATED
AVERRUNCATES
AVERRUNCATING
AVERRUNCATION
AVERRUNCATIONS
AVERRUNCATOR
AVERRUNCATORS
AVERSENESS
AVERSENESSES
AVERSIVELY
AVERSIVENESS
AVERSIVENESSES
AVERTIMENT
AVERTIMENTS
AVGOLEMONO
AVGOLEMONOS

AVIANISING
AVIANIZING
AVIATRESSES
AVIATRICES
AVIATRIXES
AVICULTURE
AVICULTURES
AVICULTURIST
AVICULTURISTS
AVIDNESSES
AVISANDUMS
AVISEMENTS
AVITAMINOSES
AVITAMINOSIS
AVITAMINOTIC
AVIZANDUMS
AVOCATIONAL
AVOCATIONALLY
AVOCATIONS
AVOIDANCES
AVOIRDUPOIS
AVOIRDUPOISES
AVOUCHABLE
AVOUCHMENT
AVOUCHMENTS
AVOUTERERS
AVOWABLENESS
AVOWABLENESSES
AVUNCULARITIES
AVUNCULARITY
AVUNCULARLY
AVUNCULATE
AVUNCULATES
AVVOGADORE
AVVOGADORES
AWAKENINGS
AWARENESSES
AWAYNESSES
AWELESSNESS
AWELESSNESSES
AWESOMENESS
AWESOMENESSES
AWESTRICKEN
AWESTRIKES
AWESTRIKING
AWFULNESSES
AWKWARDEST
AWKWARDISH
AWKWARDNESS
AWKWARDNESSES
AXENICALLY
AXEROPHTHOL
AXEROPHTHOLS
AXIALITIES
AXILLARIES
AXINOMANCIES
AXINOMANCY
AXIOLOGICAL
AXIOLOGICALLY

AXIOLOGIES
AXIOLOGIST
AXIOLOGISTS
AXIOMATICAL
AXIOMATICALLY
AXIOMATICS
AXIOMATISATION
AXIOMATISATIONS
AXIOMATISE
AXIOMATISED
AXIOMATISES
AXIOMATISING
AXIOMATIZATION
AXIOMATIZATIONS
AXIOMATIZE
AXIOMATIZED
AXIOMATIZES
AXIOMATIZING
AXISYMMETRIC
AXISYMMETRICAL
AXISYMMETRIES
AXISYMMETRY
AXOLEMMATA
AXONOMETRIC
AXONOMETRIES
AXONOMETRY
AXOPLASMIC
AYAHUASCAS
AYAHUASCOS
AYATOLLAHS
AYUNTAMIENTO
AYUNTAMIENTOS
AYURVEDICS
AZATHIOPRINE
AZATHIOPRINES
AZEDARACHS
AZEOTROPES
AZEOTROPIC
AZEOTROPIES
AZIDOTHYMIDINE
AZIDOTHYMIDINES
AZIMUTHALLY
AZOBENZENE
AZOBENZENES
AZOOSPERMIA
AZOOSPERMIAS
AZOOSPERMIC
AZOTAEMIAS
AZOTOBACTER
AZOTOBACTERS
AZYGOSPORE
AZYGOSPORES

B

BAALEBATIM
BABACOOTES
BABBITRIES
BABBITTING
BABBITTRIES
BABBLATIVE
BABBLEMENT
BABBLEMENTS
BABELESQUE
BABESIASES
BABESIASIS
BABESIOSES
BABESIOSIS
BABINGTONITE
BABINGTONITES
BABIROUSSA
BABIROUSSAS
BABIRUSSAS
BABOONERIES
BABYPROOFED
BABYPROOFING
BABYPROOFS
BABYSITTING
BACCALAUREAN
BACCALAUREATE
BACCALAUREATES
BACCHANALIA
BACCHANALIAN
BACCHANALIANISM
BACCHANALIANS
BACCHANALS
BACCHANTES
BACCIFEROUS
BACCIVOROUS
BACHARACHS
BACHELORDOM
BACHELORDOMS
BACHELORETTE
BACHELORETTES
BACHELORHOOD
BACHELORHOODS
BACHELORISM
BACHELORISMS
BACHELORSHIP
BACHELORSHIPS
BACILLAEMIA
BACILLAEMIAS
BACILLEMIA
BACILLEMIAS
BACILLICIDE
BACILLICIDES
BACILLIFORM
BACILLURIA
BACILLURIAS

BACITRACIN
BACITRACINS
BACKBENCHER
BACKBENCHERS
BACKBENCHES
BACKBITERS
BACKBITING
BACKBITINGS
BACKBITTEN
BACKBLOCKER
BACKBLOCKERS
BACKBLOCKS
BACKBOARDS
BACKBONELESS
BACKBREAKER
BACKBREAKERS
BACKBREAKING
BACKBURNED
BACKBURNING
BACKCHATTED
BACKCHATTING
BACKCHECKED
BACKCHECKING
BACKCHECKS
BACKCLOTHS
BACKCOMBED
BACKCOMBING
BACKCOUNTRIES
BACKCOUNTRY
BACKCOURTMAN
BACKCOURTMEN
BACKCOURTS
BACKCROSSED
BACKCROSSES
BACKCROSSING
BACKDATING
BACKDRAFTS
BACKDRAUGHT
BACKDRAUGHTS
BACKDROPPED
BACKDROPPING
BACKFIELDS
BACKFILLED
BACKFILLING
BACKFIRING
BACKFISCHES
BACKFITTED
BACKFITTING
BACKFITTINGS
BACKFLIPPED
BACKFLIPPING
BACKGAMMON
BACKGAMMONED
BACKGAMMONING

BACKGAMMONS
BACKGROUND
BACKGROUNDED
BACKGROUNDER
BACKGROUNDERS
BACKGROUNDING
BACKGROUNDS
BACKHANDED
BACKHANDEDLY
BACKHANDEDNESS
BACKHANDER
BACKHANDERS
BACKHANDING
BACKHAULED
BACKHAULING
BACKHOEING
BACKHOUSES
BACKLASHED
BACKLASHER
BACKLASHERS
BACKLASHES
BACKLASHING
BACKLIGHTED
BACKLIGHTING
BACKLIGHTS
BACKLISTED
BACKLISTING
BACKLOADED
BACKLOADING
BACKLOGGED
BACKLOGGING
BACKMARKER
BACKMARKERS
BACKPACKED
BACKPACKER
BACKPACKERS
BACKPACKING
BACKPACKINGS
BACKPEDALED
BACKPEDALING
BACKPEDALLED
BACKPEDALLING
BACKPEDALS
BACKPIECES
BACKRUSHES
BACKSCATTER
BACKSCATTERED
BACKSCATTERING
BACKSCATTERINGS
BACKSCATTERS
BACKSCRATCH
BACKSCRATCHED
BACKSCRATCHER
BACKSCRATCHERS

BACKSCRATCHES
BACKSCRATCHING
BACKSCRATCHINGS
BACKSHEESH
BACKSHEESHED
BACKSHEESHES
BACKSHEESHING
BACKSHISHED
BACKSHISHES
BACKSHISHING
BACKSHORES
BACKSIGHTS
BACKSLAPPED
BACKSLAPPER
BACKSLAPPERS
BACKSLAPPING
BACKSLASHES
BACKSLIDDEN
BACKSLIDER
BACKSLIDERS
BACKSLIDES
BACKSLIDING
BACKSLIDINGS
BACKSPACED
BACKSPACER
BACKSPACERS
BACKSPACES
BACKSPACING
BACKSPEERED
BACKSPEERING
BACKSPEERS
BACKSPEIRED
BACKSPEIRING
BACKSPEIRS
BACKSPLASH
BACKSPLASHES
BACKSTABBED
BACKSTABBER
BACKSTABBERS
BACKSTABBING
BACKSTABBINGS
BACKSTAGES
BACKSTAIRS
BACKSTALLS
BACKSTAMPED
BACKSTAMPING
BACKSTAMPS
BACKSTARTING
BACKSTITCH
BACKSTITCHED
BACKSTITCHES
BACKSTITCHING
BACKSTOPPED
BACKSTOPPING

BACKSTORIES

BACKSTORIES
BACKSTREET
BACKSTREETS
BACKSTRETCH
BACKSTRETCHES
BACKSTROKE
BACKSTROKES
BACKSWINGS
BACKSWORDMAN
BACKSWORDMEN
BACKSWORDS
BACKSWORDSMAN
BACKSWORDSMEN
BACKTRACKED
BACKTRACKING
BACKTRACKINGS
BACKTRACKS
BACKVELDER
BACKVELDERS
BACKWARDATION
BACKWARDATIONS
BACKWARDLY
BACKWARDNESS
BACKWARDNESSES
BACKWASHED
BACKWASHES
BACKWASHING
BACKWATERS
BACKWOODSMAN
BACKWOODSMEN
BACKWOODSY
BACKWORKER
BACKWORKERS
BACTERAEMIA
BACTERAEMIAS
BACTEREMIA
BACTEREMIAS
BACTEREMIC
BACTERIALLY
BACTERIALS
BACTERICIDAL
BACTERICIDALLY
BACTERICIDE
BACTERICIDES
BACTERIOCIN
BACTERIOCINS
BACTERIOID
BACTERIOIDS
BACTERIOLOGIC
BACTERIOLOGICAL
BACTERIOLOGIES
BACTERIOLOGIST
BACTERIOLOGISTS
BACTERIOLOGY
BACTERIOLYSES
BACTERIOLYSIN
BACTERIOLYSINS
BACTERIOLYSIS
BACTERIOLYTIC

BACTERIOPHAGE
BACTERIOPHAGES
BACTERIOPHAGIC
BACTERIOPHAGIES
BACTERIOPHAGOUS
BACTERIOPHAGY
BACTERIOSES
BACTERIOSIS
BACTERIOSTASES
BACTERIOSTASIS
BACTERIOSTAT
BACTERIOSTATIC
BACTERIOSTATS
BACTERIOTOXIN
BACTERIOTOXINS
BACTERISATION
BACTERISATIONS
BACTERISED
BACTERISES
BACTERISING
BACTERIURIA
BACTERIURIAS
BACTERIZATION
BACTERIZATIONS
BACTERIZED
BACTERIZES
BACTERIZING
BACTEROIDS
BACTERURIA
BACTERURIAS
BACULIFORM
BACULOVIRUS
BACULOVIRUSES
BADDELEYITE
BADDELEYITES
BADDERLOCK
BADDERLOCKS
BADINAGING
BADINERIES
BADMINTONS
BADMOUTHED
BADMOUTHING
BAFFLEGABS
BAFFLEMENT
BAFFLEMENTS
BAFFLINGLY
BAGASSOSES
BAGASSOSIS
BAGATELLES
BAGGINESSES
BAGPIPINGS
BAGSWINGER
BAGSWINGERS
BAHUVRIHIS
BAIGNOIRES
BAILIESHIP
BAILIESHIPS
BAILIFFSHIP
BAILIFFSHIPS

BAILIWICKS
BAILLIAGES
BAILLIESHIP
BAILLIESHIPS
BAIRNLIEST
BAISEMAINS
BAITFISHES
BAKEAPPLES
BAKEBOARDS
BAKEHOUSES
BAKESTONES
BAKHSHISHED
BAKHSHISHES
BAKHSHISHING
BAKSHEESHED
BAKSHEESHES
BAKSHEESHING
BAKSHISHED
BAKSHISHES
BAKSHISHING
BALACLAVAS
BALALAIKAS
BALANCEABLE
BALANCINGS
BALANITISES
BALBRIGGAN
BALBRIGGANS
BALBUTIENT
BALCONETTE
BALCONETTES
BALDACHINO
BALDACHINOS
BALDACHINS
BALDAQUINS
BALDERDASH
BALDERDASHES
BALDERLOCKS
BALDERLOCKSES
BALDHEADED
BALDICOOTS
BALDMONEYS
BALDNESSES
BALECTIONS
BALEFULNESS
BALEFULNESSES
BALIBUNTAL
BALIBUNTALS
BALKANISATION
BALKANISATIONS
BALKANISED
BALKANISES
BALKANISING
BALKANIZATION
BALKANIZATIONS
BALKANIZED
BALKANIZES
BALKANIZING
BALKINESSES
BALLABILES

BALLADEERED
BALLADEERING
BALLADEERS
BALLADINES
BALLADISTS
BALLADMONGER
BALLADMONGERS
BALLADRIES
BALLANTING
BALLANWRASSE
BALLANWRASSES
BALLASTERS
BALLASTING
BALLBREAKER
BALLBREAKERS
BALLCARRIER
BALLCARRIERS
BALLERINAS
BALLETICALLY
BALLETOMANE
BALLETOMANES
BALLETOMANIA
BALLETOMANIAS
BALLFLOWER
BALLFLOWERS
BALLHANDLING
BALLHANDLINGS
BALLICATTER
BALLICATTERS
BALLISTICALLY
BALLISTICS
BALLISTITE
BALLISTITES
BALLISTOSPORE
BALLISTOSPORES
BALLOCKSED
BALLOCKSES
BALLOCKSING
BALLOONING
BALLOONINGS
BALLOONIST
BALLOONISTS
BALLOTTEMENT
BALLOTTEMENTS
BALLPLAYER
BALLPLAYERS
BALLPOINTS
BALLSINESS
BALLSINESSES
BALLYHOOED
BALLYHOOING
BALLYRAGGED
BALLYRAGGING
BALMACAANS
BALMINESSES
BALMORALITIES
BALMORALITY
BALNEARIES
BALNEATION

BALNEATIONS
BALNEOLOGICAL
BALNEOLOGIES
BALNEOLOGIST
BALNEOLOGISTS
BALNEOLOGY
BALNEOTHERAPIES
BALNEOTHERAPY
BALSAMIFEROUS
BALSAMINACEOUS
BALSAWOODS
BALTHASARS
BALTHAZARS
BALUSTERED
BALUSTRADE
BALUSTRADED
BALUSTRADES
BALZARINES
BAMBOOZLED
BAMBOOZLEMENT
BAMBOOZLEMENTS
BAMBOOZLER
BAMBOOZLERS
BAMBOOZLES
BAMBOOZLING
BANALISATION
BANALISATIONS
BANALISING
BANALITIES
BANALIZATION
BANALIZATIONS
BANALIZING
BANCASSURANCE
BANCASSURANCES
BANCASSURER
BANCASSURERS
BANDALORES
BANDBRAKES
BANDEIRANTE
BANDEIRANTES
BANDELIERS
BANDERILLA
BANDERILLAS
BANDERILLERO
BANDERILLEROS
BANDEROLES
BANDERSNATCH
BANDERSNATCHES
BANDICOOTED
BANDICOOTING
BANDICOOTS
BANDINESSES
BANDITRIES
BANDLEADER
BANDLEADERS
BANDMASTER
BANDMASTERS
BANDOBASTS
BANDOBUSTS

BANDOLEERED
BANDOLEERS
BANDOLEONS
BANDOLEROS
BANDOLIERED
BANDOLIERS
BANDOLINED
BANDOLINES
BANDOLINING
BANDONEONS
BANDONIONS
BANDSHELLS
BANDSPREADING
BANDSPREADINGS
BANDSTANDS
BANDWAGONS
BANDWIDTHS
BANEBERRIES
BANEFULNESS
BANEFULNESSES
BANGSRINGS
BANISHMENT
BANISHMENTS
BANISTERED
BANJULELES
BANKABILITIES
BANKABILITY
BANKROLLED
BANKROLLER
BANKROLLERS
BANKROLLING
BANKRUPTCIES
BANKRUPTCY
BANKRUPTED
BANKRUPTING
BANNERALLS
BANNERETTE
BANNERETTES
BANNISTERS
BANQUETEER
BANQUETEERS
BANQUETERS
BANQUETING
BANQUETINGS
BANQUETTES
BANTAMWEIGHT
BANTAMWEIGHTS
BANTERINGLY
BANTERINGS
BANTINGISM
BANTINGISMS
BAPHOMETIC
BAPTISMALLY
BAPTISTERIES
BAPTISTERY
BAPTISTRIES
BARAESTHESIA
BARAESTHESIAS
BARAGOUINS

BARASINGAS
BARASINGHA
BARASINGHAS
BARATHRUMS
BARBARESQUE
BARBARIANISM
BARBARIANISMS
BARBARIANS
BARBARICALLY
BARBARISATION
BARBARISATIONS
BARBARISED
BARBARISES
BARBARISING
BARBARISMS
BARBARITIES
BARBARIZATION
BARBARIZATIONS
BARBARIZED
BARBARIZES
BARBARIZING
BARBAROUSLY
BARBAROUSNESS
BARBAROUSNESSES
BARBASCOES
BARBASTELLE
BARBASTELLES
BARBASTELS
BARBECUERS
BARBECUING
BARBELLATE
BARBEQUING
BARBERRIES
BARBERSHOP
BARBERSHOPS
BARBITONES
BARBITURATE
BARBITURATES
BARBITURIC
BARBOTINES
BARCAROLES
BARCAROLLE
BARCAROLLES
BARDOLATER
BARDOLATERS
BARDOLATRIES
BARDOLATROUS
BARDOLATRY
BAREBACKED
BAREBACKING
BAREFACEDLY
BAREFACEDNESS
BAREFACEDNESSES
BAREFOOTED
BAREHANDED
BAREHANDING
BAREHEADED
BARELEGGED
BARENESSES

BARESTHESIA
BARESTHESIAS
BARGAINERS
BARGAINING
BARGAININGS
BARGANDERS
BARGEBOARD
BARGEBOARDS
BARGEMASTER
BARGEMASTERS
BARGEPOLES
BARHOPPING
BARKANTINE
BARKANTINES
BARKEEPERS
BARKENTINE
BARKENTINES
BARLEYCORN
BARLEYCORNS
BARMBRACKS
BARMINESSES
BARMITSVAH
BARMITSVAHS
BARMITZVAH
BARMITZVAHS
BARNBRACKS
BARNSBREAKING
BARNSBREAKINGS
BARNSTORMED
BARNSTORMER
BARNSTORMERS
BARNSTORMING
BARNSTORMINGS
BARNSTORMS
BAROCEPTOR
BAROCEPTORS
BARODYNAMICS
BAROGNOSES
BAROGNOSIS
BAROGRAPHIC
BAROGRAPHS
BAROMETERS
BAROMETRIC
BAROMETRICAL
BAROMETRICALLY
BAROMETRIES
BAROMETZES
BARONESSES
BARONETAGE
BARONETAGES
BARONETCIES
BARONETESS
BARONETESSES
BARONETICAL
BAROPHILES
BAROPHILIC
BAROPHORESES
BAROPHORESIS
BARORECEPTOR

BARORECEPTORS
BAROSCOPES
BAROSCOPIC
BAROTRAUMA
BAROTRAUMAS
BAROTRAUMATA
BARPERSONS
BARQUANTINE
BARQUANTINES
BARQUENTINE
BARQUENTINES
BARQUETTES
BARRACKERS
BARRACKING
BARRACKINGS
BARRACOONS
BARRACOOTA
BARRACOOTAS
BARRACOUTA
BARRACOUTAS
BARRACUDAS
BARRAMUNDA
BARRAMUNDAS
BARRAMUNDI
BARRAMUNDIES
BARRAMUNDIS
BARRATRIES
BARRATROUS
BARRATROUSLY
BARRELAGES
BARRELFULS
BARRELHEAD
BARRELHEADS
BARRELHOUSE
BARRELHOUSES
BARRELLING
BARRELSFUL
BARRENNESS
BARRENNESSES
BARRENWORT
BARRENWORTS
BARRETRIES
BARRETROUS
BARRETROUSLY
BARRETTERS
BARRICADED
BARRICADER
BARRICADERS
BARRICADES
BARRICADING
BARRICADOED
BARRICADOES
BARRICADOING
BARRICADOS
BARRIERING
BARRISTERIAL
BARRISTERS
BARRISTERSHIP
BARRISTERSHIPS

BARROWFULS
BARTENDERS
BARTENDING
BARTIZANED
BARYCENTRE
BARYCENTRES
BARYCENTRIC
BARYSPHERE
BARYSPHERES
BASALTWARE
BASALTWARES
BASEBALLER
BASEBALLERS
BASEBOARDS
BASEBURNER
BASEBURNERS
BASELESSLY
BASELESSNESS
BASELESSNESSES
BASELINERS
BASEMENTLESS
BASENESSES
BASEPLATES
BASERUNNER
BASERUNNERS
BASERUNNING
BASERUNNINGS
BASHAWISMS
BASHAWSHIP
BASHAWSHIPS
BASHFULNESS
BASHFULNESSES
BASHIBAZOUK
BASHIBAZOUKS
BASICITIES
BASICRANIAL
BASIDIOCARP
BASIDIOCARPS
BASIDIOMYCETE
BASIDIOMYCETES
BASIDIOMYCETOUS
BASIDIOSPORE
BASIDIOSPORES
BASIDIOSPOROUS
BASIFICATION
BASIFICATIONS
BASILICONS
BASIPETALLY
BASKETBALL
BASKETBALLS
BASKETFULS
BASKETLIKE
BASKETRIES
BASKETSFUL
BASKETWEAVE
BASKETWEAVER
BASKETWEAVERS
BASKETWEAVES
BASKETWORK

BASKETWORKS
BASMITZVAH
BASMITZVAHS
BASOPHILES
BASOPHILIA
BASOPHILIAS
BASOPHILIC
BASSETTING
BASSNESSES
BASSOONIST
BASSOONISTS
BASTARDIES
BASTARDISATION
BASTARDISATIONS
BASTARDISE
BASTARDISED
BASTARDISES
BASTARDISING
BASTARDISM
BASTARDISMS
BASTARDIZATION
BASTARDIZATIONS
BASTARDIZE
BASTARDIZED
BASTARDIZES
BASTARDIZING
BASTARDRIES
BASTINADED
BASTINADES
BASTINADING
BASTINADOED
BASTINADOES
BASTINADOING
BASTNAESITE
BASTNAESITES
BASTNASITE
BASTNASITES
BATFOWLERS
BATFOWLING
BATFOWLINGS
BATHETICALLY
BATHHOUSES
BATHMITSVAH
BATHMITSVAHS
BATHMITZVAH
BATHMITZVAHS
BATHMIZVAH
BATHMIZVAHS
BATHOCHROME
BATHOCHROMES
BATHOCHROMIC
BATHOLITES
BATHOLITHIC
BATHOLITHS
BATHOLITIC
BATHOMETER
BATHOMETERS
BATHOMETRIC
BATHOMETRICALLY

BATHOMETRIES
BATHOMETRY
BATHOPHILOUS
BATHOPHOBIA
BATHOPHOBIAS
BATHWATERS
BATHYBIUSES
BATHYGRAPHICAL
BATHYLIMNETIC
BATHYLITES
BATHYLITHIC
BATHYLITHS
BATHYLITIC
BATHYMETER
BATHYMETERS
BATHYMETRIC
BATHYMETRICAL
BATHYMETRICALLY
BATHYMETRIES
BATHYMETRY
BATHYPELAGIC
BATHYSCAPE
BATHYSCAPES
BATHYSCAPH
BATHYSCAPHE
BATHYSCAPHES
BATHYSCAPHS
BATHYSPHERE
BATHYSPHERES
BATMITZVAH
BATMITZVAHS
BATOLOGICAL
BATOLOGIES
BATOLOGIST
BATOLOGISTS
BATRACHIAN
BATRACHIANS
BATRACHOPHOBIA
BATRACHOPHOBIAS
BATRACHOPHOBIC
BATSMANSHIP
BATSMANSHIPS
BATTAILOUS
BATTALIONS
BATTEILANT
BATTELLING
BATTEMENTS
BATTENINGS
BATTERINGS
BATTILLING
BATTINESSES
BATTLEBUSES
BATTLEBUSSES
BATTLEDOOR
BATTLEDOORS
BATTLEDORE
BATTLEDORES
BATTLEDRESS
BATTLEDRESSES

BATTLEFIELD
BATTLEFIELDS
BATTLEFRONT
BATTLEFRONTS
BATTLEGROUND
BATTLEGROUNDS
BATTLEMENT
BATTLEMENTED
BATTLEMENTS
BATTLEPIECE
BATTLEPIECES
BATTLEPLANE
BATTLEPLANES
BATTLESHIP
BATTLESHIPS
BATTLEWAGON
BATTLEWAGONS
BATTOLOGICAL
BATTOLOGIES
BAUDRICKES
BAUDRONSES
BAULKINESS
BAULKINESSES
BAVARDAGES
BAVAROISES
BAWDINESSES
BAWDYHOUSE
BAWDYHOUSES
BAYBERRIES
BAYONETING
BAYONETTED
BAYONETTING
BAZILLIONS
BEACHBALLS
BEACHCOMBED
BEACHCOMBER
BEACHCOMBERS
BEACHCOMBING
BEACHCOMBINGS
BEACHCOMBS
BEACHFRONT
BEACHFRONTS
BEACHGOERS
BEACHHEADS
BEADBLASTED
BEADBLASTER
BEADBLASTERS
BEADBLASTING
BEADBLASTS
BEADHOUSES
BEADINESSES
BEADLEDOMS
BEADLEHOOD
BEADLEHOODS
BEADLESHIP
BEADLESHIPS
BEADSWOMAN
BEADSWOMEN
BEAMINESSES

BEANFEASTS
BEANSTALKS
BEARABILITIES
BEARABILITY
BEARABLENESS
BEARABLENESSES
BEARBAITING
BEARBAITINGS
BEARBERRIES
BEARDEDNESS
BEARDEDNESSES
BEARDLESSNESS
BEARDLESSNESSES
BEARDTONGUE
BEARDTONGUES
BEARGRASSES
BEARISHNESS
BEARISHNESSES
BEARNAISES
BEASTHOODS
BEASTLIEST
BEASTLINESS
BEASTLINESSES
BEATIFICAL
BEATIFICALLY
BEATIFICATION
BEATIFICATIONS
BEATIFYING
BEATITUDES
BEAUJOLAIS
BEAUJOLAISES
BEAUMONTAGE
BEAUMONTAGES
BEAUMONTAGUE
BEAUMONTAGUES
BEAUTEOUSLY
BEAUTEOUSNESS
BEAUTEOUSNESSES
BEAUTICIAN
BEAUTICIANS
BEAUTIFICATION
BEAUTIFICATIONS
BEAUTIFIED
BEAUTIFIER
BEAUTIFIERS
BEAUTIFIES
BEAUTIFULLER
BEAUTIFULLEST
BEAUTIFULLY
BEAUTIFULNESS
BEAUTIFULNESSES
BEAUTIFYING
BEAVERBOARD
BEAVERBOARDS
BEBEERINES
BEBLOODING
BEBLUBBERED
BECARPETED
BECARPETING

BECCACCIAS
BECCAFICOS
BECHALKING
BECHANCING
BECHARMING
BECKONINGS
BECLAMORED
BECLAMORING
BECLASPING
BECLOAKING
BECLOGGING
BECLOTHING
BECLOUDING
BECLOWNING
BECOMINGLY
BECOMINGNESS
BECOMINGNESSES
BECOWARDED
BECOWARDING
BECQUERELS
BECRAWLING
BECROWDING
BECRUSTING
BECUDGELED
BECUDGELING
BECUDGELLED
BECUDGELLING
BEDABBLING
BEDAGGLING
BEDARKENED
BEDARKENING
BEDAZZLEMENT
BEDAZZLEMENTS
BEDAZZLING
BEDCHAMBER
BEDCHAMBERS
BEDCLOTHES
BEDCOVERING
BEDCOVERINGS
BEDEAFENED
BEDEAFENING
BEDEHOUSES
BEDELLSHIP
BEDELLSHIPS
BEDELSHIPS
BEDEVILING
BEDEVILLED
BEDEVILLING
BEDEVILMENT
BEDEVILMENTS
BEDFELLOWS
BEDIAPERED
BEDIAPERING
BEDIGHTING
BEDIMMINGS
BEDIMPLING
BEDIRTYING
BEDIZENING
BEDIZENMENT

BEDIZENMENTS
BEDLAMISMS
BEDLAMITES
BEDPRESSER
BEDPRESSERS
BEDRAGGLED
BEDRAGGLES
BEDRAGGLING
BEDRENCHED
BEDRENCHES
BEDRENCHING
BEDRIVELED
BEDRIVELING
BEDRIVELLED
BEDRIVELLING
BEDROPPING
BEDRUGGING
BEDSITTERS
BEDSITTING
BEDSPREADS
BEDSPRINGS
BEDWARFING
BEDWARMERS
BEDWETTERS
BEECHDROPS
BEECHMASTS
BEECHWOODS
BEEFBURGER
BEEFBURGERS
BEEFEATERS
BEEFINESSES
BEEFSTEAKS
BEEKEEPERS
BEEKEEPING
BEEKEEPINGS
BEERINESSES
BEESWAXING
BEESWINGED
BEETLEBRAIN
BEETLEBRAINED
BEETLEBRAINS
BEETLEHEAD
BEETLEHEADED
BEETLEHEADS
BEETMASTER
BEETMASTERS
BEETMISTER
BEETMISTERS
BEFINGERED
BEFINGERING
BEFITTINGLY
BEFLAGGING
BEFLECKING
BEFLOWERED
BEFLOWERING
BEFLUMMING
BEFOREHAND
BEFORETIME
BEFORTUNED

BEFORTUNES
BEFORTUNING
BEFOULMENT
BEFOULMENTS
BEFRETTING
BEFRIENDED
BEFRIENDER
BEFRIENDERS
BEFRIENDING
BEFRINGING
BEFUDDLEMENT
BEFUDDLEMENTS
BEFUDDLING
BEGGARDOMS
BEGGARHOOD
BEGGARHOODS
BEGGARLINESS
BEGGARLINESSES
BEGGARWEED
BEGGARWEEDS
BEGINNINGLESS
BEGINNINGS
BEGIRDLING
BEGLADDING
BEGLAMORED
BEGLAMORING
BEGLAMOURED
BEGLAMOURING
BEGLAMOURS
BEGLERBEGS
BEGLOOMING
BEGRIMMING
BEGROANING
BEGRUDGERIES
BEGRUDGERS
BEGRUDGERY
BEGRUDGING
BEGRUDGINGLY
BEGUILEMENT
BEGUILEMENTS
BEGUILINGLY
BEGUINAGES
BEHAPPENED
BEHAPPENING
BEHAVIORAL
BEHAVIORALLY
BEHAVIORISM
BEHAVIORISMS
BEHAVIORIST
BEHAVIORISTIC
BEHAVIORISTS
BEHAVIOURAL
BEHAVIOURALLY
BEHAVIOURISM
BEHAVIOURISMS
BEHAVIOURIST
BEHAVIOURISTIC
BEHAVIOURISTS
BEHAVIOURS

BEHEADINGS
BEHIGHTING
BEHINDHAND
BEHOLDINGS
BEINGNESSES
BEINNESSES
BEJESUITED
BEJESUITING
BEJEWELING
BEJEWELLED
BEJEWELLING
BEJUMBLING
BEKNIGHTED
BEKNIGHTING
BEKNOTTING
BELABORING
BELABOURED
BELABOURING
BELAMOURES
BELATEDNESS
BELATEDNESSES
BELEAGUERED
BELEAGUERING
BELEAGUERMENT
BELEAGUERMENTS
BELEAGUERS
BELEMNITES
BELIEFLESS
BELIEVABILITIES
BELIEVABILITY
BELIEVABLE
BELIEVABLY
BELIEVINGLY
BELIEVINGS
BELIQUORED
BELIQUORING
BELITTLEMENT
BELITTLEMENTS
BELITTLERS
BELITTLING
BELITTLINGLY
BELLADONNA
BELLADONNAS
BELLAMOURE
BELLAMOURES
BELLARMINE
BELLARMINES
BELLETRISM
BELLETRISMS
BELLETRIST
BELLETRISTIC
BELLETRISTICAL
BELLETRISTS
BELLETTRIST
BELLETTRISTS
BELLFLOWER
BELLFLOWERS
BELLFOUNDER
BELLFOUNDERS

BELLFOUNDRIES
BELLFOUNDRY
BELLHANGER
BELLHANGERS
BELLIBONES
BELLICOSELY
BELLICOSITIES
BELLICOSITY
BELLIGERATI
BELLIGERENCE
BELLIGERENCES
BELLIGERENCIES
BELLIGERENCY
BELLIGERENT
BELLIGERENTLY
BELLIGERENTS
BELLOCKING
BELLPUSHES
BELLWETHER
BELLWETHERS
BELLYACHED
BELLYACHER
BELLYACHERS
BELLYACHES
BELLYACHING
BELLYBANDS
BELLYBUTTON
BELLYBUTTONS
BELOMANCIES
BELONGINGNESS
BELONGINGNESSES
BELONGINGS
BELOWDECKS
BELOWGROUND
BELOWSTAIRS
BELSHAZZAR
BELSHAZZARS
BELTCOURSE
BELTCOURSES
BELVEDERES
BEMADAMING
BEMADDENED
BEMADDENING
BEMEDALLED
BEMEDALLING
BEMINGLING
BEMOANINGS
BEMONSTERED
BEMONSTERING
BEMONSTERS
BEMOUTHING
BEMUDDLING
BEMUFFLING
BEMURMURED
BEMURMURING
BEMUSEMENT
BEMUSEMENTS
BEMUZZLING
BENCHERSHIP

BENCHERSHIPS
BENCHLANDS
BENCHMARKED
BENCHMARKING
BENCHMARKINGS
BENCHMARKS
BENCHWARMER
BENCHWARMERS
BENEDICITE
BENEDICITES
BENEDICTION
BENEDICTIONAL
BENEDICTIONS
BENEDICTIVE
BENEDICTORY
BENEDICTUS
BENEDICTUSES
BENEFACTED
BENEFACTING
BENEFACTION
BENEFACTIONS
BENEFACTOR
BENEFACTORS
BENEFACTORY
BENEFACTRESS
BENEFACTRESSES
BENEFICENCE
BENEFICENCES
BENEFICENT
BENEFICENTIAL
BENEFICENTLY
BENEFICIAL
BENEFICIALLY
BENEFICIALNESS
BENEFICIALS
BENEFICIARIES
BENEFICIARY
BENEFICIATE
BENEFICIATED
BENEFICIATES
BENEFICIATING
BENEFICIATION
BENEFICIATIONS
BENEFICING
BENEFITERS
BENEFITING
BENEFITTED
BENEFITTING
BENEPLACITO
BENEVOLENCE
BENEVOLENCES
BENEVOLENT
BENEVOLENTLY
BENEVOLENTNESS
BENGALINES
BENIGHTEDLY
BENIGHTEDNESS
BENIGHTEDNESSES
BENIGHTENED

BENIGHTENING
BENIGHTENINGS
BENIGHTENS
BENIGHTERS
BENIGHTING
BENIGHTINGS
BENIGHTMENT
BENIGHTMENTS
BENIGNANCIES
BENIGNANCY
BENIGNANTLY
BENIGNITIES
BENTGRASSES
BENTHOPELAGIC
BENTHOSCOPE
BENTHOSCOPES
BENTONITES
BENTONITIC
BENUMBEDNESS
BENUMBEDNESSES
BENUMBINGLY
BENUMBMENT
BENUMBMENTS
BENZALDEHYDE
BENZALDEHYDES
BENZANTHRACENE
BENZANTHRACENES
BENZENECARBONYL
BENZENOIDS
BENZIDINES
BENZIMIDAZOLE
BENZIMIDAZOLES
BENZOAPYRENE
BENZOAPYRENES
BENZOCAINE
BENZOCAINES
BENZODIAZEPINE
BENZODIAZEPINES
BENZOFURAN
BENZOFURANS
BENZOLINES
BENZOPHENONE
BENZOPHENONES
BENZOQUINONE
BENZOQUINONES
BENZPYRENE
BENZPYRENES
BENZYLIDINE
BENZYLIDINES
BEPAINTING
BEPEARLING
BEPEPPERED
BEPEPPERING
BEPESTERED
BEPESTERING
BEPIMPLING
BEPLASTERED
BEPLASTERING
BEPLASTERS

BEPOMMELLED
BEPOMMELLING
BEPOWDERED
BEPOWDERING
BEPRAISING
BEQUEATHABLE
BEQUEATHAL
BEQUEATHALS
BEQUEATHED
BEQUEATHER
BEQUEATHERS
BEQUEATHING
BEQUEATHMENT
BEQUEATHMENTS
BERASCALED
BERASCALING
BERBERIDACEOUS
BERBERINES
BERBERISES
BEREAVEMENT
BEREAVEMENTS
BERGAMASKS
BERGANDERS
BERGOMASKS
BERGSCHRUND
BERGSCHRUNDS
BERIBBONED
BERKELIUMS
BERRYFRUIT
BERRYFRUITS
BERSAGLIERE
BERSAGLIERI
BERSERKERS
BERTILLONAGE
BERTILLONAGES
BERYLLIOSES
BERYLLIOSIS
BERYLLIUMS
BESAINTING
BESCATTERED
BESCATTERING
BESCATTERS
BESCORCHED
BESCORCHES
BESCORCHING
BESCOURING
BESCRAWLED
BESCRAWLING
BESCREENED
BESCREENING
BESCRIBBLE
BESCRIBBLED
BESCRIBBLES
BESCRIBBLING
BESEECHERS
BESEECHING
BESEECHINGLY
BESEECHINGNESS
BESEECHINGS

BESEEMINGLY
BESEEMINGNESS
BESEEMINGNESSES
BESEEMINGS
BESETMENTS
BESHADOWED
BESHADOWING
BESHIVERED
BESHIVERING
BESHOUTING
BESHREWING
BESHROUDED
BESHROUDING
BESIEGEMENT
BESIEGEMENTS
BESIEGINGLY
BESIEGINGS
BESLAVERED
BESLAVERING
BESLOBBERED
BESLOBBERING
BESLOBBERS
BESLUBBERED
BESLUBBERING
BESLUBBERS
BESMEARERS
BESMEARING
BESMIRCHED
BESMIRCHES
BESMIRCHING
BESMOOTHED
BESMOOTHING
BESMUDGING
BESMUTCHED
BESMUTCHES
BESMUTCHING
BESMUTTING
BESOOTHING
BESOTTEDLY
BESOTTEDNESS
BESOTTEDNESSES
BESPANGLED
BESPANGLES
BESPANGLING
BESPATTERED
BESPATTERING
BESPATTERS
BESPEAKING
BESPECKLED
BESPECKLES
BESPECKLING
BESPECTACLED
BESPEEDING
BESPITTING
BESPORTING
BESPOTTEDNESS
BESPOTTEDNESSES
BESPOTTING
BESPOUSING

BESPOUTING
BESPREADING
BESPRINKLE
BESPRINKLED
BESPRINKLES
BESPRINKLING
BESTAINING
BESTARRING
BESTEADING
BESTIALISE
BESTIALISED
BESTIALISES
BESTIALISING
BESTIALISM
BESTIALISMS
BESTIALITIES
BESTIALITY
BESTIALIZE
BESTIALIZED
BESTIALIZES
BESTIALIZING
BESTIARIES
BESTICKING
BESTILLING
BESTIRRING
BESTORMING
BESTOWMENT
BESTOWMENTS
BESTRADDLE
BESTRADDLED
BESTRADDLES
BESTRADDLING
BESTRAUGHT
BESTREAKED
BESTREAKING
BESTREWING
BESTRIDABLE
BESTRIDDEN
BESTRIDING
BESTROWING
BESTSELLER
BESTSELLERDOM
BESTSELLERDOMS
BESTSELLERS
BESTSELLING
BESTUDDING
BESWARMING
BETACAROTENE
BETACAROTENES
BETACYANIN
BETACYANINS
BETATTERED
BETATTERING
BETHANKING
BETHANKITS
BETHINKING
BETHORNING
BETHRALLED
BETHRALLING

BETHUMBING	BIBLICALLY	BIBLIOTHECA	BIDIRECTIONAL
BETHUMPING	BIBLICISMS	BIBLIOTHECAE	BIDIRECTIONALLY
BETHWACKED	BIBLICISTS	BIBLIOTHECAL	BIDONVILLE
BETHWACKING	BIBLIOGRAPHER	BIBLIOTHECARIES	BIDONVILLES
BETOKENING	BIBLIOGRAPHERS	BIBLIOTHECARY	BIENNIALLY
BETREADING	BIBLIOGRAPHIC	BIBLIOTHECAS	BIENSEANCE
BETRIMMING	BIBLIOGRAPHICAL	BIBLIOTHERAPIES	BIENSEANCES
BETROTHALS	BIBLIOGRAPHIES	BIBLIOTHERAPY	BIERKELLER
BETROTHEDS	BIBLIOGRAPHY	BIBLIOTICS	BIERKELLERS
BETROTHING	BIBLIOLATER	BIBLIOTIST	BIFACIALLY
BETROTHMENT	BIBLIOLATERS	BIBLIOTISTS	BIFARIOUSLY
BETROTHMENTS	BIBLIOLATRIES	BIBULOUSLY	BIFIDITIES
BETTERINGS	BIBLIOLATRIST	BIBULOUSNESS	BIFLAGELLATE
BETTERMENT	BIBLIOLATRISTS	BIBULOUSNESSES	BIFOLIOLATE
BETTERMENTS	BIBLIOLATROUS	BICAMERALISM	BIFUNCTIONAL
BETTERMOST	BIBLIOLATRY	BICAMERALISMS	BIFURCATED
BETTERNESS	BIBLIOLOGICAL	BICAMERALIST	BIFURCATES
BETTERNESSES	BIBLIOLOGIES	BICAMERALISTS	BIFURCATING
BETULACEOUS	BIBLIOLOGIST	BICAPSULAR	BIFURCATION
BETWEENBRAIN	BIBLIOLOGISTS	BICARBONATE	BIFURCATIONS
BETWEENBRAINS	BIBLIOLOGY	BICARBONATES	BIGAMOUSLY
BETWEENITIES	BIBLIOMANCIES	BICARPELLARY	BIGARREAUS
BETWEENITY	BIBLIOMANCY	BICENTENARIES	BIGEMINIES
BETWEENNESS	BIBLIOMANE	BICENTENARY	BIGFOOTING
BETWEENNESSES	BIBLIOMANES	BICENTENNIAL	BIGHEADEDLY
BETWEENTIME	BIBLIOMANIA	BICENTENNIALS	BIGHEADEDNESS
BETWEENTIMES	BIBLIOMANIAC	BICEPHALOUS	BIGHEADEDNESSES
BETWEENWHILES	BIBLIOMANIACAL	BICHLORIDE	BIGHEARTED
BEVELLINGS	BIBLIOMANIACS	BICHLORIDES	BIGHEARTEDLY
BEVELMENTS	BIBLIOMANIAS	BICHROMATE	BIGHEARTEDNESS
BEVOMITING	BIBLIOPEGIC	BICHROMATED	BIGMOUTHED
BEWAILINGLY	BIBLIOPEGIES	BICHROMATES	BIGNONIACEOUS
BEWAILINGS	BIBLIOPEGIST	BICKERINGS	BIGUANIDES
BEWEARYING	BIBLIOPEGISTS	BICOLLATERAL	BIJECTIONS
BEWELTERED	BIBLIOPEGY	BICOLOURED	BIJOUTERIE
BEWHISKERED	BIBLIOPHAGIST	BICOMPONENT	BIJOUTERIES
BEWILDERED	BIBLIOPHAGISTS	BICONCAVITIES	BILATERALISM
BEWILDEREDLY	BIBLIOPHIL	BICONCAVITY	BILATERALISMS
BEWILDEREDNESS	BIBLIOPHILE	BICONDITIONAL	BILATERALLY
BEWILDERING	BIBLIOPHILES	BICONDITIONALS	BILBERRIES
BEWILDERINGLY	BIBLIOPHILIC	BICONVEXITIES	BILDUNGSROMAN
BEWILDERMENT	BIBLIOPHILIES	BICONVEXITY	BILDUNGSROMANS
BEWILDERMENTS	BIBLIOPHILISM	BICORNUATE	BILECTIONS
BEWITCHERIES	BIBLIOPHILISMS	BICORPORATE	BILESTONES
BEWITCHERS	BIBLIOPHILIST	BICULTURAL	BILGEWATER
BEWITCHERY	BIBLIOPHILISTIC	BICULTURALISM	BILGEWATERS
BEWITCHING	BIBLIOPHILISTS	BICULTURALISMS	BILHARZIAL
BEWITCHINGLY	BIBLIOPHILS	BICUSPIDATE	BILHARZIAS
BEWITCHMENT	BIBLIOPHILY	BICUSPIDATES	BILHARZIASES
BEWITCHMENTS	BIBLIOPHOBIA	BICYCLICAL	BILHARZIASIS
BEWORRYING	BIBLIOPHOBIAS	BICYCLISTS	BILHARZIOSES
BEWRAPPING	BIBLIOPOLE	BIDDABILITIES	BILHARZIOSIS
BHIKKHUNIS	BIBLIOPOLES	BIDDABILITY	BILIMBINGS
BIANNUALLY	BIBLIOPOLIC	BIDDABLENESS	BILINGUALISM
BIANNULATE	BIBLIOPOLICAL	BIDDABLENESSES	BILINGUALISMS
BIASNESSES	BIBLIOPOLIES	BIDENTATED	BILINGUALLY
BIATHLETES	BIBLIOPOLIST	BIDIALECTAL	BILINGUALS
BIAURICULAR	BIBLIOPOLISTS	BIDIALECTALISM	BILINGUIST
BIAURICULATE	BIBLIOPOLY	BIDIALECTALISMS	BILINGUISTS

BILIOUSNESS
BILIOUSNESSES
BILIRUBINS
BILIVERDIN
BILIVERDINS
BILLABONGS
BILLBOARDED
BILLBOARDING
BILLBOARDS
BILLFISHES
BILLINGSGATE
BILLINGSGATES
BILLIONAIRE
BILLIONAIRES
BILLIONTHS
BILLOWIEST
BILLOWINESS
BILLOWINESSES
BILLOWINGS
BILLPOSTER
BILLPOSTERS
BILLPOSTING
BILLPOSTINGS
BILLSTICKER
BILLSTICKERS
BILLSTICKING
BILLSTICKINGS
BILLYCOCKS
BILOCATION
BILOCATIONS
BILOCULATE
BIMANUALLY
BIMESTRIAL
BIMESTRIALLY
BIMETALLIC
BIMETALLICS
BIMETALLISM
BIMETALLISMS
BIMETALLIST
BIMETALLISTIC
BIMETALLISTS
BIMILLENARIES
BIMILLENARY
BIMILLENNIA
BIMILLENNIAL
BIMILLENNIALS
BIMILLENNIUM
BIMILLENNIUMS
BIMODALITIES
BIMODALITY
BIMOLECULAR
BIMOLECULARLY
BIMONTHLIES
BIMORPHEMIC
BINATIONAL
BINAURALLY
BINDINGNESS
BINDINGNESSES
BINOCULARITIES

BINOCULARITY
BINOCULARLY
BINOCULARS
BINOMIALLY
BINOMINALS
BINTURONGS
BINUCLEATE
BINUCLEATED
BIOACCUMULATE
BIOACCUMULATED
BIOACCUMULATES
BIOACCUMULATING
BIOACCUMULATION
BIOACOUSTICS
BIOACTIVITIES
BIOACTIVITY
BIOAERATION
BIOAERATIONS
BIOAERONAUTICS
BIOASSAYED
BIOASSAYING
BIOASTRONAUTICS
BIOAVAILABILITY
BIOAVAILABLE
BIOCATALYST
BIOCATALYSTS
BIOCATALYTIC
BIOCELLATE
BIOCENOLOGIES
BIOCENOLOGY
BIOCENOSES
BIOCENOSIS
BIOCENOTIC
BIOCHEMICAL
BIOCHEMICALLY
BIOCHEMICALS
BIOCHEMIST
BIOCHEMISTRIES
BIOCHEMISTRY
BIOCHEMISTS
BIOCLASTIC
BIOCLIMATIC
BIOCLIMATOLOGY
BIOCOENOLOGIES
BIOCOENOLOGY
BIOCOENOSES
BIOCOENOSIS
BIOCOENOTIC
BIOCOMPATIBLE
BIOCOMPUTING
BIOCOMPUTINGS
BIOCONTROL
BIOCONTROLS
BIOCONVERSION
BIOCONVERSIONS
BIODEGRADABLE
BIODEGRADATION
BIODEGRADATIONS
BIODEGRADE

BIODEGRADED
BIODEGRADES
BIODEGRADING
BIODESTRUCTIBLE
BIODIESELS
BIODIVERSITIES
BIODIVERSITY
BIODYNAMIC
BIODYNAMICAL
BIODYNAMICS
BIOECOLOGICAL
BIOECOLOGICALLY
BIOECOLOGIES
BIOECOLOGIST
BIOECOLOGISTS
BIOECOLOGY
BIOELECTRIC
BIOELECTRICAL
BIOELECTRICITY
BIOENERGETIC
BIOENERGETICS
BIOENGINEER
BIOENGINEERED
BIOENGINEERING
BIOENGINEERINGS
BIOENGINEERS
BIOETHICAL
BIOETHICIST
BIOETHICISTS
BIOFEEDBACK
BIOFEEDBACKS
BIOFLAVONOID
BIOFLAVONOIDS
BIOFOULERS
BIOFOULING
BIOFOULINGS
BIOGENESES
BIOGENESIS
BIOGENETIC
BIOGENETICAL
BIOGENETICALLY
BIOGENETICS
BIOGEOCHEMICAL
BIOGEOCHEMICALS
BIOGEOCHEMISTRY
BIOGEOGRAPHER
BIOGEOGRAPHERS
BIOGEOGRAPHIC
BIOGEOGRAPHICAL
BIOGEOGRAPHIES
BIOGEOGRAPHY
BIOGRAPHED
BIOGRAPHEE
BIOGRAPHEES
BIOGRAPHER
BIOGRAPHERS
BIOGRAPHIC
BIOGRAPHICAL
BIOGRAPHICALLY

BIOGRAPHIES
BIOGRAPHING
BIOGRAPHISE
BIOGRAPHISED
BIOGRAPHISES
BIOGRAPHISING
BIOGRAPHIZE
BIOGRAPHIZED
BIOGRAPHIZES
BIOGRAPHIZING
BIOHAZARDOUS
BIOHAZARDS
BIOINDUSTRIES
BIOINDUSTRY
BIOINFORMATICS
BIOLOGICAL
BIOLOGICALLY
BIOLOGICALS
BIOLOGISMS
BIOLOGISTIC
BIOLOGISTS
BIOLUMINESCENCE
BIOLUMINESCENT
BIOMAGNETICS
BIOMARKERS
BIOMATERIAL
BIOMATERIALS
BIOMATHEMATICAL
BIOMATHEMATICS
BIOMECHANICAL
BIOMECHANICALLY
BIOMECHANICS
BIOMEDICAL
BIOMEDICINE
BIOMEDICINES
BIOMETEOROLOGY
BIOMETRICAL
BIOMETRICALLY
BIOMETRICIAN
BIOMETRICIANS
BIOMETRICS
BIOMETRIES
BIOMIMETIC
BIOMIMETICS
BIOMIMICRIES
BIOMIMICRY
BIOMININGS
BIOMOLECULAR
BIOMOLECULE
BIOMOLECULES
BIOMORPHIC
BIONOMICALLY
BIONOMISTS
BIOPARENTS
BIOPESTICIDAL
BIOPESTICIDE
BIOPESTICIDES
BIOPHILIAS
BIOPHYSICAL

BIOPHYSICALLY
BIOPHYSICIST
BIOPHYSICISTS
BIOPHYSICS
BIOPIRACIES
BIOPIRATES
BIOPLASMIC
BIOPOIESES
BIOPOIESIS
BIOPOLYMER
BIOPOLYMERS
BIOPROSPECTING
BIOPROSPECTINGS
BIOPSYCHOLOGIES
BIOPSYCHOLOGY
BIOREACTOR
BIOREACTORS
BIOREAGENT
BIOREAGENTS
BIOREGIONAL
BIOREGIONALISM
BIOREGIONALISMS
BIOREGIONALIST
BIOREGIONALISTS
BIOREGIONS
BIOREMEDIATION
BIOREMEDIATIONS
BIORHYTHMIC
BIORHYTHMICALLY
BIORHYTHMICS
BIORHYTHMS
BIOSAFETIES
BIOSATELLITE
BIOSATELLITES
BIOSCIENCE
BIOSCIENCES
BIOSCIENTIFIC
BIOSCIENTIST
BIOSCIENTISTS
BIOSCOPIES
BIOSENSORS
BIOSOCIALLY
BIOSPHERES
BIOSPHERIC
BIOSTATICALLY
BIOSTATICS
BIOSTATISTICAL
BIOSTATISTICIAN
BIOSTATISTICS
BIOSTRATIGRAPHY
BIOSTROMES
BIOSURGERIES
BIOSURGERY
BIOSYNTHESES
BIOSYNTHESIS
BIOSYNTHETIC
BIOSYSTEMATIC
BIOSYSTEMATICS
BIOSYSTEMATIST

BIOSYSTEMATISTS
BIOTECHNICAL
BIOTECHNOLOGIES
BIOTECHNOLOGIST
BIOTECHNOLOGY
BIOTELEMETRIC
BIOTELEMETRIES
BIOTELEMETRY
BIOTERRORS
BIOTICALLY
BIOTURBATION
BIOTURBATIONS
BIOWEAPONS
BIPARENTAL
BIPARENTALLY
BIPARIETAL
BIPARTISAN
BIPARTISANISM
BIPARTISANISMS
BIPARTISANSHIP
BIPARTISANSHIPS
BIPARTITELY
BIPARTITION
BIPARTITIONS
BIPEDALISM
BIPEDALISMS
BIPEDALITIES
BIPEDALITY
BIPETALOUS
BIPINNARIA
BIPINNARIAS
BIPINNATELY
BIPOLARISATION
BIPOLARISATIONS
BIPOLARISE
BIPOLARISED
BIPOLARISES
BIPOLARISING
BIPOLARITIES
BIPOLARITY
BIPOLARIZATION
BIPOLARIZATIONS
BIPOLARIZE
BIPOLARIZED
BIPOLARIZES
BIPOLARIZING
BIPROPELLANT
BIPROPELLANTS
BIPYRAMIDAL
BIPYRAMIDS
BIQUADRATE
BIQUADRATES
BIQUADRATIC
BIQUADRATICS
BIQUARTERLY
BIQUINTILE
BIQUINTILES
BIRACIALISM
BIRACIALISMS

BIRACIALLY
BIRADICALS
BIRDBRAINED
BIRDBRAINS
BIRDDOGGED
BIRDDOGGING
BIRDHOUSES
BIRDLIMING
BIRDWATCHED
BIRDWATCHER
BIRDWATCHERS
BIRDWATCHES
BIRDWATCHING
BIREFRINGENCE
BIREFRINGENCES
BIREFRINGENT
BIROSTRATE
BIRTHMARKS
BIRTHNAMES
BIRTHNIGHT
BIRTHNIGHTS
BIRTHPLACE
BIRTHPLACES
BIRTHRATES
BIRTHRIGHT
BIRTHRIGHTS
BIRTHROOTS
BIRTHSTONE
BIRTHSTONES
BIRTHWORTS
BISECTIONAL
BISECTIONALLY
BISECTIONS
BISECTRICES
BISEXUALISM
BISEXUALISMS
BISEXUALITIES
BISEXUALITY
BISEXUALLY
BISHOPBIRD
BISHOPBIRDS
BISHOPDOMS
BISHOPESSES
BISHOPRICS
BISHOPWEED
BISHOPWEEDS
BISMUTHINITE
BISMUTHINITES
BISMUTHOUS
BISOCIATION
BISOCIATIONS
BISOCIATIVE
BISPHOSPHONATE
BISPHOSPHONATES
BISSEXTILE
BISSEXTILES
BISTOURIES
BISULFATES
BISULFIDES

BISULFITES
BISULPHATE
BISULPHATES
BISULPHIDE
BISULPHIDES
BISULPHITE
BISULPHITES
BISYMMETRIC
BISYMMETRICAL
BISYMMETRICALLY
BISYMMETRIES
BISYMMETRY
BITARTRATE
BITARTRATES
BITCHERIES
BITCHFESTS
BITCHINESS
BITCHINESSES
BITEPLATES
BITMAPPING
BITONALITIES
BITONALITY
BITSTREAMS
BITTERBARK
BITTERBARKS
BITTERBRUSH
BITTERBRUSHES
BITTERCRESS
BITTERCRESSES
BITTERLING
BITTERLINGS
BITTERNESS
BITTERNESSES
BITTERNUTS
BITTERROOT
BITTERROOTS
BITTERSWEET
BITTERSWEETLY
BITTERSWEETNESS
BITTERSWEETS
BITTERWEED
BITTERWEEDS
BITTERWOOD
BITTERWOODS
BITTINESSES
BITUMINATE
BITUMINATED
BITUMINATES
BITUMINATING
BITUMINISATION
BITUMINISATIONS
BITUMINISE
BITUMINISED
BITUMINISES
BITUMINISING
BITUMINIZATION
BITUMINIZATIONS
BITUMINIZE
BITUMINIZED

BITUMINIZES	BLACKGUARDISMS	BLAMABLENESS	BLASTODERMS
BITUMINIZING	BLACKGUARDLY	BLAMABLENESSES	BLASTODISC
BITUMINOUS	BLACKGUARDS	BLAMEABLENESS	BLASTODISCS
BIUNIQUENESS	BLACKHANDER	BLAMEABLENESSES	BLASTOGENESES
BIUNIQUENESSES	BLACKHANDERS	BLAMEFULLY	BLASTOGENESIS
BIVALENCES	BLACKHEADED	BLAMEFULNESS	BLASTOGENETIC
BIVALENCIES	BLACKHEADS	BLAMEFULNESSES	BLASTOGENIC
BIVALVULAR	BLACKHEART	BLAMELESSLY	BLASTOMATA
BIVARIANTS	BLACKHEARTS	BLAMELESSNESS	BLASTOMERE
BIVARIATES	BLACKISHLY	BLAMELESSNESSES	BLASTOMERES
BIVOUACKED	BLACKJACKED	BLAMEWORTHINESS	BLASTOMERIC
BIVOUACKING	BLACKJACKING	BLAMEWORTHY	BLASTOMYCOSES
BIWEEKLIES	BLACKJACKS	BLANCHISSEUSE	BLASTOMYCOSIS
BIZARRENESS	BLACKLANDS	BLANCHISSEUSES	BLASTOPORAL
BIZARRENESSES	BLACKLEADS	BLANCMANGE	BLASTOPORE
BIZARRERIE	BLACKLEGGED	BLANCMANGES	BLASTOPORES
BIZARRERIES	BLACKLEGGING	BLANDISHED	BLASTOPORIC
BLABBERING	BLACKLISTED	BLANDISHER	BLASTOPORS
BLABBERMOUTH	BLACKLISTER	BLANDISHERS	BLASTOSPHERE
BLABBERMOUTHS	BLACKLISTERS	BLANDISHES	BLASTOSPHERES
BLACKAMOOR	BLACKLISTING	BLANDISHING	BLASTOSPORE
BLACKAMOORS	BLACKLISTINGS	BLANDISHMENT	BLASTOSPORES
BLACKBALLED	BLACKLISTS	BLANDISHMENTS	BLASTULATION
BLACKBALLING	BLACKMAILED	BLANDNESSES	BLASTULATIONS
BLACKBALLINGS	BLACKMAILER	BLANKETFLOWER	BLATANCIES
BLACKBALLS	BLACKMAILERS	BLANKETFLOWERS	BLATHERERS
BLACKBANDS	BLACKMAILING	BLANKETIES	BLATHERING
BLACKBERRIED	BLACKMAILS	BLANKETING	BLATHERSKITE
BLACKBERRIES	BLACKNESSES	BLANKETINGS	BLATHERSKITES
BLACKBERRY	BLACKPOLLS	BLANKETLIKE	BLATTERING
BLACKBERRYING	BLACKSMITH	BLANKETWEED	BLAXPLOITATION
BLACKBERRYINGS	BLACKSMITHING	BLANKETWEEDS	BLAXPLOITATIONS
BLACKBIRDED	BLACKSMITHINGS	BLANKNESSES	BLAZONINGS
BLACKBIRDER	BLACKSMITHS	BLANQUETTE	BLAZONRIES
BLACKBIRDERS	BLACKSNAKE	BLANQUETTES	BLEACHABLE
BLACKBIRDING	BLACKSNAKES	BLARNEYING	BLEACHERIES
BLACKBIRDINGS	BLACKSTRAP	BLASPHEMED	BLEACHERITE
BLACKBIRDS	BLACKTAILS	BLASPHEMER	BLEACHERITES
BLACKBOARD	BLACKTHORN	BLASPHEMERS	BLEACHINGS
BLACKBOARDS	BLACKTHORNS	BLASPHEMES	BLEAKNESSES
BLACKBODIES	BLACKTOPPED	BLASPHEMIES	BLEARINESS
BLACKBUCKS	BLACKTOPPING	BLASPHEMING	BLEARINESSES
BLACKBUTTS	BLACKWASHED	BLASPHEMOUS	BLEMISHERS
BLACKCOCKS	BLACKWASHES	BLASPHEMOUSLY	BLEMISHING
BLACKCURRANT	BLACKWASHING	BLASPHEMOUSNESS	BLEMISHMENT
BLACKCURRANTS	BLACKWATER	BLASTEMATA	BLEMISHMENTS
BLACKDAMPS	BLACKWATERS	BLASTEMATIC	BLENNIOIDS
BLACKENERS	BLACKWOODS	BLASTMENTS	BLENNORRHEA
BLACKENING	BLADDERLIKE	BLASTOCHYLE	BLENNORRHEAS
BLACKENINGS	BLADDERNOSE	BLASTOCHYLES	BLENNORRHOEA
BLACKFACED	BLADDERNOSES	BLASTOCOEL	BLENNORRHOEAS
BLACKFACES	BLADDERNUT	BLASTOCOELE	BLEPHARISM
BLACKFISHES	BLADDERNUTS	BLASTOCOELES	BLEPHARISMS
BLACKFLIES	BLADDERWORT	BLASTOCOELIC	BLEPHARITIC
BLACKGAMES	BLADDERWORTS	BLASTOCOELS	BLEPHARITIS
BLACKGUARD	BLADDERWRACK	BLASTOCYST	BLEPHARITISES
BLACKGUARDED	BLADDERWRACKS	BLASTOCYSTS	BLEPHAROPLAST
BLACKGUARDING	BLADEWORKS	BLASTODERM	BLEPHAROPLASTS
BLACKGUARDISM	BLAEBERRIES	BLASTODERMIC	BLEPHAROPLASTY

BLEPHAROSPASM
BLEPHAROSPASMS
BLESSEDEST
BLESSEDNESS
BLESSEDNESSES
BLETHERANSKATE
BLETHERANSKATES
BLETHERATION
BLETHERATIONS
BLETHERERS
BLETHERING
BLETHERINGS
BLETHERSKATE
BLETHERSKATES
BLIGHTINGLY
BLIGHTINGS
BLIMPISHLY
BLIMPISHNESS
BLIMPISHNESSES
BLINDFISHES
BLINDFOLDED
BLINDFOLDING
BLINDFOLDS
BLINDINGLY
BLINDNESSES
BLINDSIDED
BLINDSIDES
BLINDSIDING
BLINDSIGHT
BLINDSIGHTS
BLINDSTOREY
BLINDSTOREYS
BLINDSTORIES
BLINDSTORY
BLINDWORMS
BLINGLISHES
BLINKERING
BLISSFULLY
BLISSFULNESS
BLISSFULNESSES
BLISTERIER
BLISTERIEST
BLISTERING
BLISTERINGLY
BLITHENESS
BLITHENESSES
BLITHERING
BLITHESOME
BLITHESOMELY
BLITHESOMENESS
BLITZKRIEG
BLITZKRIEGS
BLIZZARDLY
BLOATEDNESS
BLOATEDNESSES
BLOATWARES
BLOCKADERS
BLOCKADING
BLOCKBOARD

BLOCKBOARDS
BLOCKBUSTED
BLOCKBUSTER
BLOCKBUSTERS
BLOCKBUSTING
BLOCKBUSTINGS
BLOCKBUSTS
BLOCKHEADED
BLOCKHEADEDLY
BLOCKHEADEDNESS
BLOCKHEADS
BLOCKHOLES
BLOCKHOUSE
BLOCKHOUSES
BLOCKINESS
BLOCKINESSES
BLOCKISHLY
BLOCKISHNESS
BLOCKISHNESSES
BLOCKWORKS
BLOKEISHNESS
BLOKEISHNESSES
BLOKISHNESS
BLOKISHNESSES
BLONDENESS
BLONDENESSES
BLONDINING
BLONDNESSES
BLOODBATHS
BLOODCURDLING
BLOODCURDLINGLY
BLOODGUILT
BLOODGUILTINESS
BLOODGUILTS
BLOODGUILTY
BLOODHEATS
BLOODHOUND
BLOODHOUNDS
BLOODINESS
BLOODINESSES
BLOODLESSLY
BLOODLESSNESS
BLOODLESSNESSES
BLOODLETTER
BLOODLETTERS
BLOODLETTING
BLOODLETTINGS
BLOODLINES
BLOODLUSTS
BLOODMOBILE
BLOODMOBILES
BLOODROOTS
BLOODSHEDS
BLOODSPRENT
BLOODSTAIN
BLOODSTAINED
BLOODSTAINS
BLOODSTOCK
BLOODSTOCKS

BLOODSTONE
BLOODSTONES
BLOODSTREAM
BLOODSTREAMS
BLOODSUCKER
BLOODSUCKERS
BLOODSUCKING
BLOODTHIRSTIER
BLOODTHIRSTIEST
BLOODTHIRSTILY
BLOODTHIRSTY
BLOODWOODS
BLOODWORMS
BLOODWORTS
BLOOMERIES
BLOQUISTES
BLOSSOMING
BLOSSOMINGS
BLOSSOMLESS
BLOTCHIEST
BLOTCHINESS
BLOTCHINESSES
BLOTCHINGS
BLOTTESQUE
BLOTTESQUES
BLOVIATING
BLOVIATION
BLOVIATIONS
BLOWFISHES
BLOWINESSES
BLOWKARTING
BLOWKARTINGS
BLOWSINESS
BLOWSINESSES
BLOWTORCHED
BLOWTORCHES
BLOWTORCHING
BLOWZINESS
BLOWZINESSES
BLUBBERERS
BLUBBERIER
BLUBBERIEST
BLUBBERING
BLUDGEONED
BLUDGEONER
BLUDGEONERS
BLUDGEONING
BLUEBEARDS
BLUEBERRIES
BLUEBLOODS
BLUEBONNET
BLUEBONNETS
BLUEBOTTLE
BLUEBOTTLES
BLUEBREAST
BLUEBREASTS
BLUEBUSHES
BLUEFISHES
BLUEGRASSES

BLUEISHNESS
BLUEISHNESSES
BLUEJACKET
BLUEJACKETS
BLUEJACKING
BLUEJACKINGS
BLUELINERS
BLUENESSES
BLUEPOINTS
BLUEPRINTED
BLUEPRINTING
BLUEPRINTS
BLUESHIFTED
BLUESHIFTS
BLUESNARFING
BLUESNARFINGS
BLUESTOCKING
BLUESTOCKINGS
BLUESTONES
BLUETHROAT
BLUETHROATS
BLUETONGUE
BLUETONGUES
BLUFFNESSES
BLUISHNESS
BLUISHNESSES
BLUNDERBUSS
BLUNDERBUSSES
BLUNDERERS
BLUNDERING
BLUNDERINGLY
BLUNDERINGS
BLUNTHEADS
BLUNTNESSES
BLURREDNESS
BLURREDNESSES
BLURRINESS
BLURRINESSES
BLURRINGLY
BLUSHINGLY
BLUSHLESSLY
BLUSTERERS
BLUSTERIER
BLUSTERIEST
BLUSTERING
BLUSTERINGLY
BLUSTERINGS
BLUSTEROUS
BLUSTEROUSLY
BLUTWURSTS
BOARDINGHOUSE
BOARDINGHOUSES
BOARDROOMS
BOARDSAILING
BOARDSAILINGS
BOARDSAILOR
BOARDSAILORS
BOARDWALKS
BOARFISHES

BOARHOUNDS
BOARISHNESS
BOARISHNESSES
BOASTFULLY
BOASTFULNESS
BOASTFULNESSES
BOASTINGLY
BOATBUILDER
BOATBUILDERS
BOATBUILDING
BOATBUILDINGS
BOATHOUSES
BOATLIFTED
BOATLIFTING
BOATSWAINS
BOBBEJAANS
BOBBITTING
BOBBYSOCKS
BOBBYSOXER
BOBBYSOXERS
BOBSLEDDED
BOBSLEDDER
BOBSLEDDERS
BOBSLEDDING
BOBSLEDDINGS
BOBSLEIGHED
BOBSLEIGHING
BOBSLEIGHS
BOBTAILING
BOBWEIGHTS
BOCCONCINI
BODACIOUSLY
BODDHISATTVA
BODDHISATTVAS
BODEGUEROS
BODHISATTVA
BODHISATTVAS
BODYBOARDED
BODYBOARDING
BODYBOARDINGS
BODYBOARDS
BODYBUILDER
BODYBUILDERS
BODYBUILDING
BODYBUILDINGS
BODYCHECKED
BODYCHECKING
BODYCHECKS
BODYGUARDED
BODYGUARDING
BODYGUARDS
BODYSHELLS
BODYSURFED
BODYSURFER
BODYSURFERS
BODYSURFING
BODYSURFINGS
BODYWORKER
BODYWORKERS

BOEREMUSIEK
BOEREMUSIEKS
BOEREWORSES
BOGGINESSES
BOGTROTTER
BOGTROTTERS
BOGTROTTING
BOGTROTTINGS
BOGUSNESSES
BOHEMIANISM
BOHEMIANISMS
BOILERMAKER
BOILERMAKERS
BOILERPLATE
BOILERPLATED
BOILERPLATES
BOILERPLATING
BOILERSUIT
BOILERSUITS
BOISTEROUS
BOISTEROUSLY
BOISTEROUSNESS
BOKMAKIERIE
BOKMAKIERIES
BOLDFACING
BOLDNESSES
BOLECTIONS
BOLIVIANOS
BOLLETRIES
BOLLOCKING
BOLLOCKINGS
BOLLOCKSED
BOLLOCKSES
BOLLOCKSING
BOLOGRAPHS
BOLOMETERS
BOLOMETRIC
BOLOMETRICALLY
BOLOMETRIES
BOLSHEVIKI
BOLSHEVIKS
BOLSHEVISE
BOLSHEVISED
BOLSHEVISES
BOLSHEVISING
BOLSHEVISM
BOLSHEVISMS
BOLSHEVIST
BOLSHEVISTS
BOLSHEVIZE
BOLSHEVIZED
BOLSHEVIZES
BOLSHEVIZING
BOLSTERERS
BOLSTERING
BOLSTERINGS
BOMBACACEOUS
BOMBARDERS
BOMBARDIER

BOMBARDIERS
BOMBARDING
BOMBARDMENT
BOMBARDMENTS
BOMBARDONS
BOMBASINES
BOMBASTERS
BOMBASTICALLY
BOMBASTING
BOMBAZINES
BOMBILATED
BOMBILATES
BOMBILATING
BOMBILATION
BOMBILATIONS
BOMBINATED
BOMBINATES
BOMBINATING
BOMBINATION
BOMBINATIONS
BOMBPROOFED
BOMBPROOFING
BOMBPROOFS
BOMBSHELLS
BOMBSIGHTS
BONAMIASES
BONAMIASIS
BONASSUSES
BONBONNIERE
BONBONNIERES
BONDHOLDER
BONDHOLDERS
BONDMANSHIP
BONDMANSHIPS
BONDSERVANT
BONDSERVANTS
BONDSTONES
BONDSWOMAN
BONDSWOMEN
BONEBLACKS
BONEFISHES
BONEFISHING
BONEFISHINGS
BONEHEADED
BONEHEADEDNESS
BONESETTER
BONESETTERS
BONESHAKER
BONESHAKERS
BONHOMMIES
BONILASSES
BONINESSES
BONKBUSTER
BONKBUSTERS
BONNIBELLS
BONNILASSE
BONNILASSES
BONNINESSES
BONNYCLABBER

BONNYCLABBERS
BOOBIALLAS
BOOBOISIES
BOOKBINDER
BOOKBINDERIES
BOOKBINDERS
BOOKBINDERY
BOOKBINDING
BOOKBINDINGS
BOOKCROSSING
BOOKCROSSINGS
BOOKISHNESS
BOOKISHNESSES
BOOKKEEPER
BOOKKEEPERS
BOOKKEEPING
BOOKKEEPINGS
BOOKLIGHTS
BOOKMAKERS
BOOKMAKING
BOOKMAKINGS
BOOKMARKED
BOOKMARKER
BOOKMARKERS
BOOKMARKING
BOOKMOBILE
BOOKMOBILES
BOOKPLATES
BOOKSELLER
BOOKSELLERS
BOOKSELLING
BOOKSELLINGS
BOOKSHELVES
BOOKSTALLS
BOOKSTANDS
BOOKSTORES
BOOMERANGED
BOOMERANGING
BOOMERANGS
BOOMSLANGS
BOONDOGGLE
BOONDOGGLED
BOONDOGGLER
BOONDOGGLERS
BOONDOGGLES
BOONDOGGLING
BOONGARIES
BOORISHNESS
BOORISHNESSES
BOOSTERISH
BOOSTERISM
BOOSTERISMS
BOOTBLACKS
BOOTLEGGED
BOOTLEGGER
BOOTLEGGERS
BOOTLEGGING
BOOTLEGGINGS
BOOTLESSLY

BOOTLESSNESS
BOOTLESSNESSES
BOOTLICKED
BOOTLICKER
BOOTLICKERS
BOOTLICKING
BOOTLICKINGS
BOOTLOADER
BOOTLOADERS
BOOTMAKERS
BOOTMAKING
BOOTMAKINGS
BOOTSTRAPPED
BOOTSTRAPPING
BOOTSTRAPS
BOOTYLICIOUS
BOOZINESSES
BORAGINACEOUS
BORBORYGMAL
BORBORYGMI
BORBORYGMIC
BORBORYGMUS
BORBORYGMUSES
BORDEREAUX
BORDERLAND
BORDERLANDS
BORDERLESS
BORDERLINE
BORDERLINES
BORDRAGING
BORDRAGINGS
BORESCOPES
BORGHETTOS
BORINGNESS
BORINGNESSES
BOROHYDRIDE
BOROHYDRIDES
BOROSILICATE
BOROSILICATES
BORROWINGS
BOSBERAADS
BOSCHVARKS
BOSCHVELDS
BOSKINESSES
BOSSINESSES
BOSSYBOOTS
BOTANICALLY
BOTANICALS
BOTANISERS
BOTANISING
BOTANIZERS
BOTANIZING
BOTANOMANCIES
BOTANOMANCY
BOTCHERIES
BOTCHINESS
BOTCHINESSES
BOTHERATION
BOTHERATIONS

BOTHERSOME
BOTRYOIDAL
BOTRYTISES
BOTTLEBRUSH
BOTTLEBRUSHES
BOTTLEFULS
BOTTLENECK
BOTTLENECKED
BOTTLENECKING
BOTTLENECKS
BOTTLENOSE
BOTTOMLAND
BOTTOMLANDS
BOTTOMLESS
BOTTOMLESSLY
BOTTOMLESSNESS
BOTTOMMOST
BOTTOMNESS
BOTTOMNESSES
BOTTOMRIES
BOTULINUMS
BOTULINUSES
BOUGAINVILIA
BOUGAINVILIAS
BOUGAINVILLAEA
BOUGAINVILLAEAS
BOUGAINVILLEA
BOUGAINVILLEAS
BOUILLABAISSE
BOUILLABAISSES
BOUILLOTTE
BOUILLOTTES
BOULDERERS
BOULDERING
BOULDERINGS
BOULEVARDIER
BOULEVARDIERS
BOULEVARDS
BOULEVERSEMENT
BOULEVERSEMENTS
BOULLEWORK
BOULLEWORKS
BOUNCINESS
BOUNCINESSES
BOUNCINGLY
BOUNDARIES
BOUNDEDNESS
BOUNDEDNESSES
BOUNDERISH
BOUNDLESSLY
BOUNDLESSNESS
BOUNDLESSNESSES
BOUNDNESSES
BOUNTEOUSLY
BOUNTEOUSNESS
BOUNTEOUSNESSES
BOUNTIFULLY
BOUNTIFULNESS
BOUNTIFULNESSES

BOUNTYHEDS
BOUQUETIERE
BOUQUETIERES
BOURASQUES
BOURBONISM
BOURBONISMS
BOURGEOISE
BOURGEOISES
BOURGEOISIE
BOURGEOISIES
BOURGEOISIFIED
BOURGEOISIFIES
BOURGEOISIFY
BOURGEOISIFYING
BOURGEONED
BOURGEONING
BOURGUIGNON
BOURGUIGNONNE
BOUSINGKEN
BOUSINGKENS
BOUSTROPHEDON
BOUSTROPHEDONIC
BOUSTROPHEDONS
BOUTONNIERE
BOUTONNIERES
BOUVARDIAS
BOVINITIES
BOWDLERISATION
BOWDLERISATIONS
BOWDLERISE
BOWDLERISED
BOWDLERISER
BOWDLERISERS
BOWDLERISES
BOWDLERISING
BOWDLERISM
BOWDLERISMS
BOWDLERIZATION
BOWDLERIZATIONS
BOWDLERIZE
BOWDLERIZED
BOWDLERIZER
BOWDLERIZERS
BOWDLERIZES
BOWDLERIZING
BOWERBIRDS
BOWERWOMAN
BOWERWOMEN
BOWHUNTERS
BOWSTRINGED
BOWSTRINGING
BOWSTRINGS
BOXBERRIES
BOXERCISES
BOXHAULING
BOXINESSES
BOXKEEPERS
BOXWALLAHS
BOYCOTTERS

BOYCOTTING
BOYFRIENDS
BOYISHNESS
BOYISHNESSES
BOYSENBERRIES
BOYSENBERRY
BRAAIVLEIS
BRAAIVLEISES
BRABBLEMENT
BRABBLEMENTS
BRACHIATED
BRACHIATES
BRACHIATING
BRACHIATION
BRACHIATIONS
BRACHIATOR
BRACHIATORS
BRACHIOCEPHALIC
BRACHIOPOD
BRACHIOPODS
BRACHIOSAURUS
BRACHIOSAURUSES
BRACHISTOCHRONE
BRACHYAXES
BRACHYAXIS
BRACHYCEPHAL
BRACHYCEPHALIC
BRACHYCEPHALICS
BRACHYCEPHALIES
BRACHYCEPHALISM
BRACHYCEPHALOUS
BRACHYCEPHALS
BRACHYCEPHALY
BRACHYCEROUS
BRACHYDACTYL
BRACHYDACTYLIC
BRACHYDACTYLIES
BRACHYDACTYLISM
BRACHYDACTYLOUS
BRACHYDACTYLY
BRACHYDIAGONAL
BRACHYDIAGONALS
BRACHYDOME
BRACHYDOMES
BRACHYGRAPHIES
BRACHYGRAPHY
BRACHYLOGIES
BRACHYLOGOUS
BRACHYLOGY
BRACHYODONT
BRACHYPINAKOID
BRACHYPINAKOIDS
BRACHYPRISM
BRACHYPRISMS
BRACHYPTERISM
BRACHYPTERISMS
BRACHYPTEROUS
BRACHYTHERAPIES
BRACHYTHERAPY

BRACHYURAL
BRACHYURAN
BRACHYURANS
BRACHYUROUS
BRACKETING
BRACKETINGS
BRACKISHNESS
BRACKISHNESSES
BRACTEATES
BRACTEOLATE
BRACTEOLES
BRADYCARDIA
BRADYCARDIAC
BRADYCARDIAS
BRADYKINESIA
BRADYKINESIAS
BRADYKININ
BRADYKININS
BRADYPEPTIC
BRADYPEPTICS
BRADYSEISM
BRADYSEISMS
BRAGADISME
BRAGADISMES
BRAGGADOCIO
BRAGGADOCIOS
BRAGGADOCIOUS
BRAGGARTISM
BRAGGARTISMS
BRAGGARTLY
BRAGGINGLY
BRAHMANISM
BRAHMANISMS
BRAHMANIST
BRAHMANISTS
BRAHMINISM
BRAHMINISMS
BRAHMINIST
BRAHMINISTS
BRAILLEWRITER
BRAILLEWRITERS
BRAILLISTS
BRAINBOXES
BRAINCASES
BRAINCHILD
BRAINCHILDREN
BRAINFARTS
BRAININESS
BRAININESSES
BRAINLESSLY
BRAINLESSNESS
BRAINLESSNESSES
BRAINPOWER
BRAINPOWERS
BRAINSICKLY
BRAINSICKNESS
BRAINSICKNESSES
BRAINSTEMS
BRAINSTORM

BRAINSTORMED
BRAINSTORMER
BRAINSTORMERS
BRAINSTORMING
BRAINSTORMINGS
BRAINSTORMS
BRAINTEASER
BRAINTEASERS
BRAINWASHED
BRAINWASHER
BRAINWASHERS
BRAINWASHES
BRAINWASHING
BRAINWASHINGS
BRAINWAVES
BRAMBLIEST
BRAMBLINGS
BRANCHERIES
BRANCHIATE
BRANCHIEST
BRANCHINGS
BRANCHIOPOD
BRANCHIOPODS
BRANCHIOSTEGAL
BRANCHLESS
BRANCHLETS
BRANCHLIKE
BRANCHLINE
BRANCHLINES
BRANDERING
BRANDISHED
BRANDISHER
BRANDISHERS
BRANDISHES
BRANDISHING
BRANDLINGS
BRANDRETHS
BRANFULNESS
BRANFULNESSES
BRANGLINGS
BRANKURSINE
BRANKURSINES
BRANNIGANS
BRASHINESS
BRASHINESSES
BRASHNESSES
BRASILEINS
BRASSBOUND
BRASSERIES
BRASSFOUNDER
BRASSFOUNDERS
BRASSFOUNDING
BRASSFOUNDINGS
BRASSICACEOUS
BRASSIERES
BRASSINESS
BRASSINESSES
BRASSWARES
BRATPACKER

BRATPACKERS
BRATTICING
BRATTICINGS
BRATTINESS
BRATTINESSES
BRATTISHED
BRATTISHES
BRATTISHING
BRATTISHINGS
BRATTLINGS
BRATWURSTS
BRAUNCHING
BRAUNSCHWEIGER
BRAUNSCHWEIGERS
BRAVADOING
BRAVENESSES
BRAVISSIMO
BRAWNINESS
BRAWNINESSES
BRAZENNESS
BRAZENNESSES
BRAZENRIES
BRAZIERIES
BRAZILEINS
BRAZILWOOD
BRAZILWOODS
BREADBASKET
BREADBASKETS
BREADBERRIES
BREADBERRY
BREADBOARD
BREADBOARDED
BREADBOARDING
BREADBOARDS
BREADBOXES
BREADCRUMB
BREADCRUMBED
BREADCRUMBING
BREADCRUMBS
BREADFRUIT
BREADFRUITS
BREADHEADS
BREADLINES
BREADROOMS
BREADROOTS
BREADSTICKS
BREADSTUFF
BREADSTUFFS
BREADTHWAYS
BREADTHWISE
BREADWINNER
BREADWINNERS
BREADWINNING
BREADWINNINGS
BREAKABLENESS
BREAKABLENESSES
BREAKABLES
BREAKAWAYS
BREAKBEATS

BREAKDANCE
BREAKDANCED
BREAKDANCER
BREAKDANCERS
BREAKDANCES
BREAKDANCING
BREAKDANCINGS
BREAKDOWNS
BREAKEVENS
BREAKFASTED
BREAKFASTER
BREAKFASTERS
BREAKFASTING
BREAKFASTS
BREAKFRONT
BREAKFRONTS
BREAKPOINT
BREAKPOINTS
BREAKTHROUGH
BREAKTHROUGHS
BREAKTIMES
BREAKWALLS
BREAKWATER
BREAKWATERS
BREASTBONE
BREASTBONES
BREASTFEED
BREASTFEEDING
BREASTFEEDS
BREASTPINS
BREASTPLATE
BREASTPLATES
BREASTPLOUGH
BREASTPLOUGHS
BREASTRAIL
BREASTRAILS
BREASTSTROKE
BREASTSTROKER
BREASTSTROKERS
BREASTSTROKES
BREASTSUMMER
BREASTSUMMERS
BREASTWORK
BREASTWORKS
BREATHABILITIES
BREATHABILITY
BREATHABLE
BREATHALYSE
BREATHALYSED
BREATHALYSER
BREATHALYSERS
BREATHALYSES
BREATHALYSING
BREATHALYZE
BREATHALYZED
BREATHALYZER
BREATHALYZERS
BREATHALYZES
BREATHALYZING

BREATHARIAN
BREATHARIANISM
BREATHARIANISMS
BREATHARIANS
BREATHIEST
BREATHINESS
BREATHINESSES
BREATHINGS
BREATHLESS
BREATHLESSLY
BREATHLESSNESS
BREATHTAKING
BREATHTAKINGLY
BRECCIATED
BRECCIATES
BRECCIATING
BRECCIATION
BRECCIATIONS
BREECHBLOCK
BREECHBLOCKS
BREECHCLOTH
BREECHCLOTHS
BREECHCLOUT
BREECHCLOUTS
BREECHINGS
BREECHLESS
BREECHLOADER
BREECHLOADERS
BREEZELESS
BREEZEWAYS
BREEZINESS
BREEZINESSES
BREMSSTRAHLUNG
BREMSSTRAHLUNGS
BRESSUMMER
BRESSUMMERS
BRETASCHES
BRETTICING
BREUNNERITE
BREUNNERITES
BREVETCIES
BREVETTING
BREVIARIES
BREVIPENNATE
BREWMASTER
BREWMASTERS
BRIARROOTS
BRIARWOODS
BRICABRACS
BRICKCLAYS
BRICKEARTH
BRICKEARTHS
BRICKFIELD
BRICKFIELDER
BRICKFIELDERS
BRICKFIELDS
BRICKKILNS
BRICKLAYER
BRICKLAYERS

BRICKLAYING
BRICKLAYINGS
BRICKMAKER
BRICKMAKERS
BRICKMAKING
BRICKMAKINGS
BRICKSHAPED
BRICKWALLS
BRICKWORKS
BRICKYARDS
BRICOLAGES
BRIDECAKES
BRIDEGROOM
BRIDEGROOMS
BRIDEMAIDEN
BRIDEMAIDENS
BRIDEMAIDS
BRIDESMAID
BRIDESMAIDS
BRIDEWEALTH
BRIDEWEALTHS
BRIDEWELLS
BRIDGEABLE
BRIDGEBOARD
BRIDGEBOARDS
BRIDGEHEAD
BRIDGEHEADS
BRIDGELESS
BRIDGEWORK
BRIDGEWORKS
BRIDLEWAYS
BRIDLEWISE
BRIEFCASES
BRIEFNESSES
BRIERROOTS
BRIERWOODS
BRIGADIERS
BRIGANDAGE
BRIGANDAGES
BRIGANDINE
BRIGANDINES
BRIGANDRIES
BRIGANTINE
BRIGANTINES
BRIGHTENED
BRIGHTENER
BRIGHTENERS
BRIGHTENING
BRIGHTNESS
BRIGHTNESSES
BRIGHTSOME
BRIGHTWORK
BRIGHTWORKS
BRILLIANCE
BRILLIANCES
BRILLIANCIES
BRILLIANCY
BRILLIANTE
BRILLIANTED

BRILLIANTINE
BRILLIANTINES
BRILLIANTING
BRILLIANTLY
BRILLIANTNESS
BRILLIANTNESSES
BRILLIANTS
BRIMFULLNESS
BRIMFULLNESSES
BRIMFULNESS
BRIMFULNESSES
BRIMSTONES
BRINELLING
BRINELLINGS
BRINGDOWNS
BRININESSES
BRINJARRIES
BRINKMANSHIP
BRINKMANSHIPS
BRINKSMANSHIP
BRINKSMANSHIPS
BRIOLETTES
BRIQUETTED
BRIQUETTES
BRIQUETTING
BRISKENING
BRISKNESSES
BRISTLECONE
BRISTLECONES
BRISTLELIKE
BRISTLETAIL
BRISTLETAILS
BRISTLIEST
BRISTLINESS
BRISTLINESSES
BRITANNIAS
BRITSCHKAS
BRITTANIAS
BRITTLENESS
BRITTLENESSES
BROADBANDS
BROADBEANS
BROADBILLS
BROADBRIMS
BROADBRUSH
BROADCASTED
BROADCASTER
BROADCASTERS
BROADCASTING
BROADCASTINGS
BROADCASTS
BROADCLOTH
BROADCLOTHS
BROADENERS
BROADENING
BROADLEAVES
BROADLINES
BROADLOOMS
BROADMINDED

BROADMINDEDLY
BROADMINDEDNESS
BROADNESSES
BROADPIECE
BROADPIECES
BROADSCALE
BROADSHEET
BROADSHEETS
BROADSIDED
BROADSIDES
BROADSIDING
BROADSWORD
BROADSWORDS
BROADTAILS
BROBDINGNAGIAN
BROCATELLE
BROCATELLES
BROCHETTES
BROGUERIES
BROIDERERS
BROIDERIES
BROIDERING
BROIDERINGS
BROKENHEARTED
BROKENHEARTEDLY
BROKENNESS
BROKENNESSES
BROKERAGES
BROKERINGS
BROMEGRASS
BROMEGRASSES
BROMELAINS
BROMELIACEOUS
BROMELIADS
BROMEOSINS
BROMHIDROSES
BROMHIDROSIS
BROMIDROSES
BROMIDROSIS
BROMINATED
BROMINATES
BROMINATING
BROMINATION
BROMINATIONS
BROMINISMS
BROMOCRIPTINE
BROMOCRIPTINES
BROMOFORMS
BROMOURACIL
BROMOURACILS
BRONCHIALLY
BRONCHIECTASES
BRONCHIECTASIS
BRONCHIOLAR
BRONCHIOLE
BRONCHIOLES
BRONCHIOLITIS
BRONCHIOLITISES
BRONCHITIC

BRONCHITICS
BRONCHITIS
BRONCHITISES
BRONCHODILATOR
BRONCHODILATORS
BRONCHOGENIC
BRONCHOGRAPHIES
BRONCHOGRAPHY
BRONCHOSCOPE
BRONCHOSCOPES
BRONCHOSCOPIC
BRONCHOSCOPICAL
BRONCHOSCOPIES
BRONCHOSCOPIST
BRONCHOSCOPISTS
BRONCHOSCOPY
BRONCHOSPASM
BRONCHOSPASMS
BRONCHOSPASTIC
BRONCOBUSTER
BRONCOBUSTERS
BRONDYRONS
BRONTOBYTE
BRONTOBYTES
BRONTOSAUR
BRONTOSAURS
BRONTOSAURUS
BRONTOSAURUSES
BRONZIFIED
BRONZIFIES
BRONZIFYING
BROODINESS
BROODINESSES
BROODINGLY
BROODMARES
BROOKLIMES
BROOKWEEDS
BROOMBALLER
BROOMBALLERS
BROOMBALLS
BROOMCORNS
BROOMRAPES
BROOMSTAFF
BROOMSTAFFS
BROOMSTICK
BROOMSTICKS
BROTHERHOOD
BROTHERHOODS
BROTHERING
BROTHERLIKE
BROTHERLINESS
BROTHERLINESSES
BROUGHTASES
BROWALLIAS
BROWBEATEN
BROWBEATER
BROWBEATERS
BROWBEATING
BROWBEATINGS

BROWNFIELD
BROWNFIELDS
BROWNNESSES
BROWNNOSED
BROWNNOSER
BROWNNOSERS
BROWNNOSES
BROWNNOSING
BROWNSHIRT
BROWNSHIRTS
BROWNSTONE
BROWNSTONES
BROWRIDGES
BROWSABLES
BRUCELLOSES
BRUCELLOSIS
BRUGMANSIA
BRUGMANSIAS
BRUMMAGEMS
BRUSCHETTA
BRUSCHETTAS
BRUSCHETTE
BRUSHABILITIES
BRUSHABILITY
BRUSHBACKS
BRUSHFIRES
BRUSHLANDS
BRUSHMARKS
BRUSHWHEEL
BRUSHWHEELS
BRUSHWOODS
BRUSHWORKS
BRUSQUENESS
BRUSQUENESSES
BRUSQUERIE
BRUSQUERIES
BRUTALISATION
BRUTALISATIONS
BRUTALISED
BRUTALISES
BRUTALISING
BRUTALISMS
BRUTALISTS
BRUTALITIES
BRUTALIZATION
BRUTALIZATIONS
BRUTALIZED
BRUTALIZES
BRUTALIZING
BRUTIFYING
BRUTISHNESS
BRUTISHNESSES
BRYOLOGICAL
BRYOLOGIES
BRYOLOGIST
BRYOLOGISTS
BRYOPHYLLUM
BRYOPHYLLUMS

BRYOPHYTES
BRYOPHYTIC
BUBBLEGUMS
BUBBLEHEAD
BUBBLEHEADED
BUBBLEHEADS
BUBONOCELE
BUBONOCELES
BUCCANEERED
BUCCANEERING
BUCCANEERINGS
BUCCANEERISH
BUCCANEERS
BUCCANIERED
BUCCANIERING
BUCCANIERS
BUCCINATOR
BUCCINATORS
BUCCINATORY
BUCELLASES
BUCENTAURS
BUCKBOARDS
BUCKBRUSHES
BUCKETFULS
BUCKETINGS
BUCKETSFUL
BUCKHOUNDS
BUCKJUMPER
BUCKJUMPERS
BUCKJUMPING
BUCKJUMPINGS
BUCKLERING
BUCKRAMING
BUCKSHISHED
BUCKSHISHES
BUCKSHISHING
BUCKSKINNED
BUCKTHORNS
BUCKTOOTHED
BUCKWHEATS
BUCKYBALLS
BUCKYTUBES
BUCOLICALLY
BUDGERIGAR
BUDGERIGARS
BUDGETEERS
BUFFALOBERRIES
BUFFALOBERRY
BUFFALOFISH
BUFFALOFISHES
BUFFALOING
BUFFETINGS
BUFFLEHEAD
BUFFLEHEADS
BUFFOONERIES
BUFFOONERY
BUFFOONISH
BUFOTALINS
BUFOTENINE

BUFOTENINES
BUGGINESSES
BUGLEWEEDS
BUHRSTONES
BUILDDOWNS
BUIRDLIEST
BULBIFEROUS
BULBOSITIES
BULBOUSNESS
BULBOUSNESSES
BULGINESSES
BULKINESSES
BULLBAITING
BULLBAITINGS
BULLBRIERS
BULLDOGGED
BULLDOGGER
BULLDOGGERS
BULLDOGGING
BULLDOGGINGS
BULLDOZERS
BULLDOZING
BULLETINED
BULLETINING
BULLETPROOF
BULLETPROOFED
BULLETPROOFING
BULLETPROOFS
BULLETRIES
BULLETWOOD
BULLETWOODS
BULLFIGHTER
BULLFIGHTERS
BULLFIGHTING
BULLFIGHTINGS
BULLFIGHTS
BULLFINCHES
BULLHEADED
BULLHEADEDLY
BULLHEADEDNESS
BULLIONIST
BULLIONISTS
BULLISHNESS
BULLISHNESSES
BULLMASTIFF
BULLMASTIFFS
BULLNECKED
BULLOCKIES
BULLOCKING
BULLROARER
BULLROARERS
BULLRUSHES
BULLSHITTED
BULLSHITTER
BULLSHITTERS
BULLSHITTING
BULLSHITTINGS
BULLSNAKES
BULLTERRIER

BULLTERRIERS	BUREAUCRATESE	BURRAWANGS	BUSYBODYINGS
BULLWADDIE	BUREAUCRATESES	BURROWSTOWN	BUSYNESSES
BULLWADDIES	BUREAUCRATIC	BURROWSTOWNS	BUTADIENES
BULLWHACKED	BUREAUCRATISE	BURRSTONES	BUTCHERBIRD
BULLWHACKING	BUREAUCRATISED	BURSARSHIP	BUTCHERBIRDS
BULLWHACKS	BUREAUCRATISES	BURSARSHIPS	BUTCHERERS
BULLWHIPPED	BUREAUCRATISING	BURSERACEOUS	BUTCHERIES
BULLWHIPPING	BUREAUCRATISM	BURSICULATE	BUTCHERING
BULLYRAGGED	BUREAUCRATISMS	BURSITISES	BUTCHERINGS
BULLYRAGGING	BUREAUCRATIST	BURTHENING	BUTCHNESSES
BULWADDEES	BUREAUCRATISTS	BURTHENSOME	BUTENEDIOIC
BULWADDIES	BUREAUCRATIZE	BUSHBABIES	BUTEONINES
BULWARKING	BUREAUCRATIZED	BUSHBASHING	BUTLERAGES
BUMBAILIFF	BUREAUCRATIZES	BUSHBASHINGS	BUTLERSHIP
BUMBAILIFFS	BUREAUCRATIZING	BUSHCRAFTS	BUTLERSHIPS
BUMBERSHOOT	BUREAUCRATS	BUSHELLERS	BUTTERBALL
BUMBERSHOOTS	BURGEONING	BUSHELLING	BUTTERBALLS
BUMBLEBEES	BURGLARIES	BUSHELLINGS	BUTTERBURS
BUMBLEDOMS	BURGLARING	BUSHELWOMAN	BUTTERCUPS
BUMBLINGLY	BURGLARIOUS	BUSHELWOMEN	BUTTERDOCK
BUMFREEZER	BURGLARIOUSLY	BUSHHAMMER	BUTTERDOCKS
BUMFREEZERS	BURGLARISE	BUSHHAMMERS	BUTTERFATS
BUMFUZZLED	BURGLARISED	BUSHINESSES	BUTTERFINGERED
BUMFUZZLES	BURGLARISES	BUSHMANSHIP	BUTTERFINGERS
BUMFUZZLING	BURGLARISING	BUSHMANSHIPS	BUTTERFISH
BUMMALOTIS	BURGLARIZE	BUSHMASTER	BUTTERFISHES
BUMPINESSES	BURGLARIZED	BUSHMASTERS	BUTTERFLIED
BUMPKINISH	BURGLARIZES	BUSHRANGER	BUTTERFLIES
BUMPOLOGIES	BURGLARIZING	BUSHRANGERS	BUTTERFLYER
BUMPSADAISY	BURGLARPROOF	BUSHRANGING	BUTTERFLYERS
BUMPTIOUSLY	BURGOMASTER	BUSHRANGINGS	BUTTERFLYING
BUMPTIOUSNESS	BURGOMASTERS	BUSHWALKED	BUTTERIEST
BUMPTIOUSNESSES	BURGUNDIES	BUSHWALKER	BUTTERINES
BUMSUCKERS	BURLADEROS	BUSHWALKERS	BUTTERINESS
BUMSUCKING	BURLESQUED	BUSHWALKING	BUTTERINESSES
BUMSUCKINGS	BURLESQUELY	BUSHWALKINGS	BUTTERLESS
BUNCHBERRIES	BURLESQUER	BUSHWHACKED	BUTTERMILK
BUNCHBERRY	BURLESQUERS	BUSHWHACKER	BUTTERMILKS
BUNCHGRASS	BURLESQUES	BUSHWHACKERS	BUTTERNUTS
BUNCHGRASSES	BURLESQUING	BUSHWHACKING	BUTTERSCOTCH
BUNCHINESS	BURLEYCUES	BUSHWHACKINGS	BUTTERSCOTCHES
BUNCHINESSES	BURLINESSES	BUSHWHACKS	BUTTERWEED
BUNDOBUSTS	BURNETTISE	BUSINESSES	BUTTERWEEDS
BUNGALOIDS	BURNETTISED	BUSINESSLIKE	BUTTERWORT
BUNGLESOME	BURNETTISES	BUSINESSMAN	BUTTERWORTS
BUNGLINGLY	BURNETTISING	BUSINESSMEN	BUTTINSKIES
BUNKHOUSES	BURNETTIZE	BUSINESSPEOPLE	BUTTINSKIS
BUOYANCIES	BURNETTIZED	BUSINESSPERSON	BUTTOCKING
BUOYANTNESS	BURNETTIZES	BUSINESSPERSONS	BUTTONBALL
BUOYANTNESSES	BURNETTIZING	BUSINESSWOMAN	BUTTONBALLS
BUPIVACAINE	BURNISHABLE	BUSINESSWOMEN	BUTTONBUSH
BUPIVACAINES	BURNISHERS	BUSTICATED	BUTTONBUSHES
BUPRENORPHINE	BURNISHING	BUSTICATES	BUTTONHELD
BUPRENORPHINES	BURNISHINGS	BUSTICATING	BUTTONHOLD
BUPRESTIDS	BURNISHMENT	BUSTINESSES	BUTTONHOLDING
BURDENSOME	BURNISHMENTS	BUSTLINGLY	BUTTONHOLDS
BUREAUCRACIES	BURRAMUNDI	BUSYBODIED	BUTTONHOLE
BUREAUCRACY	BURRAMUNDIS	BUSYBODIES	BUTTONHOLED
BUREAUCRAT	BURRAMYSES	BUSYBODYING	BUTTONHOLER

BUTTONHOLERS
BUTTONHOLES
BUTTONHOLING
BUTTONHOOK
BUTTONHOOKED
BUTTONHOOKING
BUTTONHOOKS
BUTTONLESS
BUTTONMOULD
BUTTONMOULDS
BUTTONWOOD
BUTTONWOODS
BUTTRESSED
BUTTRESSES
BUTTRESSING
BUTTSTOCKS
BUTYLATING
BUTYLATION
BUTYLATIONS
BUTYRACEOUS
BUTYRALDEHYDE
BUTYRALDEHYDES
BUTYROPHENONE
BUTYROPHENONES
BUXOMNESSES
BYPRODUCTS
BYSSACEOUS
BYSSINOSES
BYSSINOSIS
BYSTANDERS
BYTOWNITES

C

CABALETTAS
CABALISTIC
CABALISTICAL
CABALLEROS
CABBAGETOWN
CABBAGETOWNS
CABBAGEWORM
CABBAGEWORMS
CABBALISMS
CABBALISTIC
CABBALISTICAL
CABBALISTS
CABDRIVERS
CABINETMAKER
CABINETMAKERS
CABINETMAKING
CABINETMAKINGS
CABINETRIES
CABINETWORK
CABINETWORKS
CABINMATES
CABLECASTED
CABLECASTING
CABLECASTS
CABLEGRAMS
CABLEVISION
CABLEVISIONS
CABRIOLETS
CACAFUEGOS
CACCIATORA
CACCIATORE
CACHAEMIAS
CACHECTICAL
CACHINNATE
CACHINNATED
CACHINNATES
CACHINNATING
CACHINNATION
CACHINNATIONS
CACHINNATORY
CACHOLONGS
CACIQUISMS
CACKERMANDER
CACKERMANDERS
CACKLEBERRIES
CACKLEBERRY
CACODAEMON
CACODAEMONS
CACODEMONIC
CACODEMONS
CACODOXIES
CACOEPISTIC
CACOGASTRIC
CACOGENICS

CACOGRAPHER
CACOGRAPHERS
CACOGRAPHIC
CACOGRAPHICAL
CACOGRAPHIES
CACOGRAPHY
CACOLOGIES
CACOMISTLE
CACOMISTLES
CACOMIXLES
CACONYMIES
CACOPHONIC
CACOPHONICAL
CACOPHONICALLY
CACOPHONIES
CACOPHONIOUS
CACOPHONOUS
CACOPHONOUSLY
CACOTOPIAN
CACOTOPIAS
CACOTROPHIES
CACOTROPHY
CACTACEOUS
CACTOBLASTES
CACTOBLASTIS
CACUMINALS
CACUMINOUS
CADASTRALLY
CADAVERINE
CADAVERINES
CADAVEROUS
CADAVEROUSLY
CADAVEROUSNESS
CADDISFLIES
CADDISHNESS
CADDISHNESSES
CADDISWORM
CADDISWORMS
CADETSHIPS
CADUCITIES
CAECILIANS
CAECITISES
CAENOGENESES
CAENOGENESIS
CAENOGENETIC
CAESALPINOID
CAESAREANS
CAESARIANS
CAESARISMS
CAESAROPAPISM
CAESAROPAPISMS
CAESPITOSE
CAESPITOSELY
CAFETERIAS

CAFETIERES
CAFETORIUM
CAFETORIUMS
CAFFEINATED
CAFFEINISM
CAFFEINISMS
CAGEYNESSES
CAGINESSES
CAGMAGGING
CAGYNESSES
CAILLEACHS
CAILLIACHS
CAINOGENESES
CAINOGENESIS
CAINOGENETIC
CAIRNGORMS
CAJOLEMENT
CAJOLEMENTS
CAJOLERIES
CAJOLINGLY
CAKEWALKED
CAKEWALKER
CAKEWALKERS
CAKEWALKING
CAKINESSES
CALABASHES
CALABOGUSES
CALABOOSES
CALABRESES
CALAMANCOES
CALAMANCOS
CALAMANDER
CALAMANDERS
CALAMARIES
CALAMINING
CALAMITIES
CALAMITOUS
CALAMITOUSLY
CALAMITOUSNESS
CALAMONDIN
CALAMONDINS
CALANDRIAS
CALAVANCES
CALAVERITE
CALAVERITES
CALCAREOUS
CALCAREOUSLY
CALCARIFEROUS
CALCARIFORM
CALCEAMENTA
CALCEAMENTUM
CALCEATING
CALCEDONIES
CALCEDONIO

CALCEDONIOS
CALCEIFORM
CALCEOLARIA
CALCEOLARIAS
CALCEOLATE
CALCICOLES
CALCICOLOUS
CALCIFEROL
CALCIFEROLS
CALCIFEROUS
CALCIFICATION
CALCIFICATIONS
CALCIFUGAL
CALCIFUGES
CALCIFUGOUS
CALCIFYING
CALCIGEROUS
CALCIMINED
CALCIMINES
CALCIMINING
CALCINABLE
CALCINATION
CALCINATIONS
CALCINOSES
CALCINOSIS
CALCITONIN
CALCITONINS
CALCSINTER
CALCSINTERS
CALCULABILITIES
CALCULABILITY
CALCULABLE
CALCULABLY
CALCULATED
CALCULATEDLY
CALCULATEDNESS
CALCULATES
CALCULATING
CALCULATINGLY
CALCULATION
CALCULATIONAL
CALCULATIONS
CALCULATIVE
CALCULATOR
CALCULATORS
CALCULUSES
CALEFACIENT
CALEFACIENTS
CALEFACTION
CALEFACTIONS
CALEFACTIVE
CALEFACTOR
CALEFACTORIES
CALEFACTORS

CALEFACTORY
CALEMBOURS
CALENDARED
CALENDARER
CALENDARERS
CALENDARING
CALENDARISATION
CALENDARISE
CALENDARISED
CALENDARISES
CALENDARISING
CALENDARIST
CALENDARISTS
CALENDARIZATION
CALENDARIZE
CALENDARIZED
CALENDARIZES
CALENDARIZING
CALENDERED
CALENDERER
CALENDERERS
CALENDERING
CALENDERINGS
CALENDRERS
CALENDRICAL
CALENDRIES
CALENDULAS
CALENTURES
CALESCENCE
CALESCENCES
CALFDOZERS
CALIATOURS
CALIBRATED
CALIBRATER
CALIBRATERS
CALIBRATES
CALIBRATING
CALIBRATION
CALIBRATIONS
CALIBRATOR
CALIBRATORS
CALIDITIES
CALIFORNIUM
CALIFORNIUMS
CALIGINOSITIES
CALIGINOSITY
CALIGINOUS
CALIOLOGIES
CALIPASHES
CALIPERING
CALIPHATES
CALISTHENIC
CALISTHENICS
CALLBOARDS
CALLIATURE
CALLIATURES
CALLIDITIES
CALLIGRAMME
CALLIGRAMMES

CALLIGRAMS
CALLIGRAPHER
CALLIGRAPHERS
CALLIGRAPHIC
CALLIGRAPHICAL
CALLIGRAPHIES
CALLIGRAPHIST
CALLIGRAPHISTS
CALLIGRAPHY
CALLIOPSIS
CALLIPASHES
CALLIPERED
CALLIPERING
CALLIPYGEAN
CALLIPYGIAN
CALLIPYGOUS
CALLISTEMON
CALLISTEMONS
CALLISTHENIC
CALLISTHENICS
CALLITHUMP
CALLITHUMPIAN
CALLITHUMPS
CALLOSITIES
CALLOUSING
CALLOUSNESS
CALLOUSNESSES
CALLOWNESS
CALLOWNESSES
CALMATIVES
CALMNESSES
CALMODULIN
CALMODULINS
CALMSTONES
CALORESCENCE
CALORESCENCES
CALORESCENT
CALORICALLY
CALORICITIES
CALORICITY
CALORIFICALLY
CALORIFICATION
CALORIFICATIONS
CALORIFIER
CALORIFIERS
CALORIMETER
CALORIMETERS
CALORIMETRIC
CALORIMETRICAL
CALORIMETRIES
CALORIMETRY
CALORISING
CALORIZING
CALOTYPIST
CALOTYPISTS
CALUMNIABLE
CALUMNIATE
CALUMNIATED
CALUMNIATES

CALUMNIATING
CALUMNIATION
CALUMNIATIONS
CALUMNIATOR
CALUMNIATORS
CALUMNIATORY
CALUMNIOUS
CALUMNIOUSLY
CALVADOSES
CALVARIUMS
CALYCANTHEMIES
CALYCANTHEMY
CALYCANTHUS
CALYCANTHUSES
CALYCIFORM
CALYCOIDEOUS
CALYCULATE
CALYPSONIAN
CALYPSONIANS
CALYPTERAS
CALYPTRATE
CALYPTROGEN
CALYPTROGENS
CAMANACHDS
CAMARADERIE
CAMARADERIES
CAMARILLAS
CAMBERINGS
CAMBISTRIES
CAMCORDERS
CAMELBACKS
CAMELEOPARD
CAMELEOPARDS
CAMELHAIRS
CAMELOPARD
CAMELOPARDS
CAMERAPERSON
CAMERAPERSONS
CAMERATION
CAMERATIONS
CAMERAWOMAN
CAMERAWOMEN
CAMERAWORK
CAMERAWORKS
CAMERLENGO
CAMERLENGOS
CAMERLINGO
CAMERLINGOS
CAMIKNICKERS
CAMIKNICKS
CAMISADOES
CAMORRISTA
CAMORRISTI
CAMORRISTS
CAMOUFLAGE
CAMOUFLAGEABLE
CAMOUFLAGED
CAMOUFLAGES
CAMOUFLAGIC

CAMOUFLAGING
CAMOUFLETS
CAMOUFLEUR
CAMOUFLEURS
CAMPAIGNED
CAMPAIGNER
CAMPAIGNERS
CAMPAIGNING
CAMPANEROS
CAMPANIFORM
CAMPANILES
CAMPANISTS
CAMPANOLOGER
CAMPANOLOGERS
CAMPANOLOGICAL
CAMPANOLOGIES
CAMPANOLOGIST
CAMPANOLOGISTS
CAMPANOLOGY
CAMPANULACEOUS
CAMPANULAR
CAMPANULAS
CAMPANULATE
CAMPCRAFTS
CAMPEADORS
CAMPESINOS
CAMPESTRAL
CAMPESTRIAN
CAMPGROUND
CAMPGROUNDS
CAMPHORACEOUS
CAMPHORATE
CAMPHORATED
CAMPHORATES
CAMPHORATING
CAMPIMETRIES
CAMPIMETRY
CAMPINESSES
CAMPNESSES
CAMPODEIDS
CAMPODEIFORM
CAMPSHIRTS
CAMPSTOOLS
CAMPYLOBACTER
CAMPYLOBACTERS
CAMPYLOTROPOUS
CAMSTEERIE
CANALBOATS
CANALICULAR
CANALICULATE
CANALICULATED
CANALICULI
CANALICULUS
CANALISATION
CANALISATIONS
CANALISING
CANALIZATION
CANALIZATIONS
CANALIZING

CANCELABLE
CANCELATION
CANCELATIONS
CANCELEERED
CANCELEERING
CANCELEERS
CANCELIERED
CANCELIERING
CANCELIERS
CANCELLABLE
CANCELLARIAL
CANCELLARIAN
CANCELLARIATE
CANCELLARIATES
CANCELLATE
CANCELLATED
CANCELLATION
CANCELLATIONS
CANCELLERS
CANCELLING
CANCELLOUS
CANCERATED
CANCERATES
CANCERATING
CANCERATION
CANCERATIONS
CANCEROPHOBIA
CANCEROPHOBIAS
CANCEROUSLY
CANCERPHOBIA
CANCERPHOBIAS
CANCIONERO
CANCIONEROS
CANCRIFORM
CANCRIZANS
CANDELABRA
CANDELABRAS
CANDELABRUM
CANDELABRUMS
CANDELILLA
CANDELILLAS
CANDESCENCE
CANDESCENCES
CANDESCENT
CANDESCENTLY
CANDIDACIES
CANDIDATES
CANDIDATESHIP
CANDIDATESHIPS
CANDIDATURE
CANDIDATURES
CANDIDIASES
CANDIDIASIS
CANDIDNESS
CANDIDNESSES
CANDLEBERRIES
CANDLEBERRY
CANDLEFISH
CANDLEFISHES

CANDLEHOLDER
CANDLEHOLDERS
CANDLELIGHT
CANDLELIGHTED
CANDLELIGHTER
CANDLELIGHTERS
CANDLELIGHTS
CANDLENUTS
CANDLEPINS
CANDLEPOWER
CANDLEPOWERS
CANDLESNUFFER
CANDLESNUFFERS
CANDLESTICK
CANDLESTICKS
CANDLEWICK
CANDLEWICKS
CANDLEWOOD
CANDLEWOODS
CANDYFLOSS
CANDYFLOSSES
CANDYGRAMS
CANDYTUFTS
CANEBRAKES
CANEFRUITS
CANEPHORAS
CANEPHORES
CANEPHORUS
CANEPHORUSES
CANESCENCE
CANESCENCES
CANINITIES
CANISTERED
CANISTERING
CANISTERISATION
CANISTERISE
CANISTERISED
CANISTERISES
CANISTERISING
CANISTERIZATION
CANISTERIZE
CANISTERIZED
CANISTERIZES
CANISTERIZING
CANKEREDLY
CANKEREDNESS
CANKEREDNESSES
CANKERWORM
CANKERWORMS
CANNABINOID
CANNABINOIDS
CANNABINOL
CANNABINOLS
CANNABISES
CANNELLINI
CANNELLONI
CANNELURES
CANNIBALISATION
CANNIBALISE

CANNIBALISED
CANNIBALISES
CANNIBALISING
CANNIBALISM
CANNIBALISMS
CANNIBALISTIC
CANNIBALIZATION
CANNIBALIZE
CANNIBALIZED
CANNIBALIZES
CANNIBALIZING
CANNIBALLY
CANNINESSES
CANNISTERS
CANNONADED
CANNONADES
CANNONADING
CANNONBALL
CANNONBALLED
CANNONBALLING
CANNONBALLS
CANNONEERS
CANNONIERS
CANNONRIES
CANNULATED
CANNULATES
CANNULATING
CANNULATION
CANNULATIONS
CANOEWOODS
CANONESSES
CANONICALLY
CANONICALS
CANONICATE
CANONICATES
CANONICITIES
CANONICITY
CANONISATION
CANONISATIONS
CANONISERS
CANONISING
CANONISTIC
CANONIZATION
CANONIZATIONS
CANONIZERS
CANONIZING
CANOODLERS
CANOODLING
CANOPHILIA
CANOPHILIAS
CANOPHILIST
CANOPHILISTS
CANOPHOBIA
CANOPHOBIAS
CANOROUSLY
CANOROUSNESS
CANOROUSNESSES
CANTABANKS
CANTABILES

CANTALOUPE
CANTALOUPES
CANTALOUPS
CANTANKEROUS
CANTANKEROUSLY
CANTATRICE
CANTATRICES
CANTATRICI
CANTERBURIES
CANTERBURY
CANTERBURYS
CANTHARIDAL
CANTHARIDES
CANTHARIDIAN
CANTHARIDIC
CANTHARIDIN
CANTHARIDINE
CANTHARIDINES
CANTHARIDINS
CANTHARIDS
CANTHAXANTHIN
CANTHAXANTHINE
CANTHAXANTHINES
CANTHAXANTHINS
CANTHITISES
CANTICOING
CANTICOYED
CANTICOYING
CANTILENAS
CANTILEVER
CANTILEVERED
CANTILEVERING
CANTILEVERS
CANTILLATE
CANTILLATED
CANTILLATES
CANTILLATING
CANTILLATION
CANTILLATIONS
CANTILLATORY
CANTINESSES
CANTONISATION
CANTONISATIONS
CANTONISED
CANTONISES
CANTONISING
CANTONIZATION
CANTONIZATIONS
CANTONIZED
CANTONIZES
CANTONIZING
CANTONMENT
CANTONMENTS
CANULATING
CANULATION
CANULATIONS
CANVASBACK
CANVASBACKS
CANVASLIKE

CANVASSERS
CANVASSING
CANVASSINGS
CANYONEERS
CANYONINGS
CANZONETTA
CANZONETTAS
CANZONETTE
CAOUTCHOUC
CAOUTCHOUCS
CAPABILITIES
CAPABILITY
CAPABLENESS
CAPABLENESSES
CAPACIOUSLY
CAPACIOUSNESS
CAPACIOUSNESSES
CAPACITANCE
CAPACITANCES
CAPACITATE
CAPACITATED
CAPACITATES
CAPACITATING
CAPACITATION
CAPACITATIONS
CAPACITIES
CAPACITIVE
CAPACITIVELY
CAPACITORS
CAPARISONED
CAPARISONING
CAPARISONS
CAPELLINES
CAPELLMEISTER
CAPELLMEISTERS
CAPERCAILLIE
CAPERCAILLIES
CAPERCAILZIE
CAPERCAILZIES
CAPERINGLY
CAPERNOITED
CAPERNOITIE
CAPERNOITIES
CAPERNOITY
CAPILLACEOUS
CAPILLAIRE
CAPILLAIRES
CAPILLARIES
CAPILLARITIES
CAPILLARITY
CAPILLITIA
CAPILLITIUM
CAPILLITIUMS
CAPITALISATION
CAPITALISATIONS
CAPITALISE
CAPITALISED
CAPITALISES
CAPITALISING

CAPITALISM
CAPITALISMS
CAPITALIST
CAPITALISTIC
CAPITALISTS
CAPITALIZATION
CAPITALIZATIONS
CAPITALIZE
CAPITALIZED
CAPITALIZES
CAPITALIZING
CAPITATION
CAPITATIONS
CAPITATIVE
CAPITELLUM
CAPITOLIAN
CAPITOLINE
CAPITULANT
CAPITULANTS
CAPITULARIES
CAPITULARLY
CAPITULARS
CAPITULARY
CAPITULATE
CAPITULATED
CAPITULATES
CAPITULATING
CAPITULATION
CAPITULATIONS
CAPITULATOR
CAPITULATORS
CAPITULATORY
CAPNOMANCIES
CAPNOMANCY
CAPOCCHIAS
CAPODASTRO
CAPODASTROS
CAPONIERES
CAPONISING
CAPONIZING
CAPOTASTOS
CAPPARIDACEOUS
CAPPELLETTI
CAPPERNOITIES
CAPPERNOITY
CAPPUCCINO
CAPPUCCINOS
CAPREOLATE
CAPRICCIOS
CAPRICCIOSO
CAPRICIOUS
CAPRICIOUSLY
CAPRICIOUSNESS
CAPRIFICATION
CAPRIFICATIONS
CAPRIFOILS
CAPRIFOLES
CAPRIFOLIACEOUS
CAPRIFYING

CAPRIOLING
CAPROLACTAM
CAPROLACTAMS
CAPRYLATES
CAPSAICINS
CAPSIZABLE
CAPSOMERES
CAPSULATED
CAPSULATION
CAPSULATIONS
CAPSULISED
CAPSULISES
CAPSULISING
CAPSULIZED
CAPSULIZES
CAPSULIZING
CAPTAINCIES
CAPTAINING
CAPTAINRIES
CAPTAINSHIP
CAPTAINSHIPS
CAPTIONING
CAPTIONLESS
CAPTIOUSLY
CAPTIOUSNESS
CAPTIOUSNESSES
CAPTIVANCE
CAPTIVANCES
CAPTIVATED
CAPTIVATES
CAPTIVATING
CAPTIVATINGLY
CAPTIVATION
CAPTIVATIONS
CAPTIVATOR
CAPTIVATORS
CAPTIVAUNCE
CAPTIVAUNCES
CAPTIVITIES
CAPTOPRILS
CARABINEER
CARABINEERS
CARABINERO
CARABINEROS
CARABINERS
CARABINIER
CARABINIERE
CARABINIERI
CARABINIERS
CARACOLERS
CARACOLING
CARACOLLED
CARACOLLING
CARAGEENAN
CARAGEENANS
CARAMBOLAS
CARAMBOLED
CARAMBOLES
CARAMBOLING

CARAMELISATION
CARAMELISATIONS
CARAMELISE
CARAMELISED
CARAMELISES
CARAMELISING
CARAMELIZATION
CARAMELIZATIONS
CARAMELIZE
CARAMELIZED
CARAMELIZES
CARAMELIZING
CARAMELLED
CARAMELLING
CARANGOIDS
CARAPACIAL
CARAVANCES
CARAVANEER
CARAVANEERS
CARAVANERS
CARAVANETTE
CARAVANETTES
CARAVANING
CARAVANINGS
CARAVANNED
CARAVANNER
CARAVANNERS
CARAVANNING
CARAVANNINGS
CARAVANSARAI
CARAVANSARAIS
CARAVANSARIES
CARAVANSARY
CARAVANSERAI
CARAVANSERAIS
CARAVELLES
CARBACHOLS
CARBAMATES
CARBAMAZEPINE
CARBAMAZEPINES
CARBAMIDES
CARBAMIDINE
CARBAMIDINES
CARBAMOYLS
CARBANIONS
CARBAZOLES
CARBIMAZOLE
CARBIMAZOLES
CARBINEERS
CARBINIERS
CARBOCYCLIC
CARBOHYDRASE
CARBOHYDRASES
CARBOHYDRATE
CARBOHYDRATES
CARBOLATED
CARBOLISED
CARBOLISES
CARBOLISING

CARBOLIZED
CARBOLIZES
CARBOLIZING
CARBONACEOUS
CARBONADES
CARBONADOED
CARBONADOES
CARBONADOING
CARBONADOS
CARBONARAS
CARBONATED
CARBONATES
CARBONATING
CARBONATION
CARBONATIONS
CARBONATITE
CARBONATITES
CARBONETTE
CARBONETTES
CARBONIFEROUS
CARBONISATION
CARBONISATIONS
CARBONISED
CARBONISER
CARBONISERS
CARBONISES
CARBONISING
CARBONIUMS
CARBONIZATION
CARBONIZATIONS
CARBONIZED
CARBONIZER
CARBONIZERS
CARBONIZES
CARBONIZING
CARBONLESS
CARBONNADE
CARBONNADES
CARBONYLATE
CARBONYLATED
CARBONYLATES
CARBONYLATING
CARBONYLATION
CARBONYLATIONS
CARBONYLIC
CARBOXYLASE
CARBOXYLASES
CARBOXYLATE
CARBOXYLATED
CARBOXYLATES
CARBOXYLATING
CARBOXYLATION
CARBOXYLATIONS
CARBOXYLIC
CARBUNCLED
CARBUNCLES
CARBUNCULAR
CARBURATED
CARBURATES

CARBURATING
CARBURATION
CARBURATIONS
CARBURETED
CARBURETER
CARBURETERS
CARBURETING
CARBURETION
CARBURETIONS
CARBURETOR
CARBURETORS
CARBURETTED
CARBURETTER
CARBURETTERS
CARBURETTING
CARBURETTOR
CARBURETTORS
CARBURISATION
CARBURISATIONS
CARBURISED
CARBURISES
CARBURISING
CARBURIZATION
CARBURIZATIONS
CARBURIZED
CARBURIZES
CARBURIZING
CARBYLAMINE
CARBYLAMINES
CARCASSING
CARCINOGEN
CARCINOGENESES
CARCINOGENESIS
CARCINOGENIC
CARCINOGENICITY
CARCINOGENS
CARCINOIDS
CARCINOLOGICAL
CARCINOLOGIES
CARCINOLOGIST
CARCINOLOGISTS
CARCINOLOGY
CARCINOMAS
CARCINOMATA
CARCINOMATOID
CARCINOMATOSES
CARCINOMATOSIS
CARCINOMATOUS
CARCINOSARCOMA
CARCINOSARCOMAS
CARCINOSES
CARCINOSIS
CARDAMINES
CARDBOARDS
CARDBOARDY
CARDCASTLE
CARDCASTLES
CARDHOLDER
CARDHOLDERS

CARDIALGIA
CARDIALGIAS
CARDIALGIC
CARDIALGIES
CARDIGANED
CARDINALATE
CARDINALATES
CARDINALATIAL
CARDINALITIAL
CARDINALITIES
CARDINALITY
CARDINALLY
CARDINALSHIP
CARDINALSHIPS
CARDIOCENTESES
CARDIOCENTESIS
CARDIOGENIC
CARDIOGRAM
CARDIOGRAMS
CARDIOGRAPH
CARDIOGRAPHER
CARDIOGRAPHERS
CARDIOGRAPHIC
CARDIOGRAPHICAL
CARDIOGRAPHIES
CARDIOGRAPHS
CARDIOGRAPHY
CARDIOLOGICAL
CARDIOLOGIES
CARDIOLOGIST
CARDIOLOGISTS
CARDIOLOGY
CARDIOMEGALIES
CARDIOMEGALY
CARDIOMOTOR
CARDIOMYOPATHY
CARDIOPATHIES
CARDIOPATHY
CARDIOPLEGIA
CARDIOPLEGIAS
CARDIOPULMONARY
CARDIOTHORACIC
CARDIOTONIC
CARDIOTONICS
CARDIOVASCULAR
CARDITISES
CARDOPHAGI
CARDOPHAGUS
CARDPHONES
CARDPLAYER
CARDPLAYERS
CARDPUNCHES
CARDSHARPER
CARDSHARPERS
CARDSHARPING
CARDSHARPINGS
CARDSHARPS
CARDUACEOUS
CAREENAGES

CAREERISMS
CAREERISTS
CAREFREENESS
CAREFREENESSES
CAREFULLER
CAREFULLEST
CAREFULNESS
CAREFULNESSES
CAREGIVERS
CAREGIVING
CAREGIVINGS
CARELESSLY
CARELESSNESS
CARELESSNESSES
CARESSINGLY
CARESSINGS
CARESSIVELY
CARETAKERS
CARETAKING
CARETAKINGS
CAREWORKER
CAREWORKERS
CARFUFFLED
CARFUFFLES
CARFUFFLING
CARHOPPING
CARICATURA
CARICATURAL
CARICATURAS
CARICATURE
CARICATURED
CARICATURES
CARICATURING
CARICATURIST
CARICATURISTS
CARILLONED
CARILLONING
CARILLONIST
CARILLONISTS
CARILLONNED
CARILLONNEUR
CARILLONNEURS
CARILLONNING
CARIOGENIC
CARIOSITIES
CARIOUSNESS
CARIOUSNESSES
CARJACKERS
CARJACKING
CARJACKINGS
CARMAGNOLE
CARMAGNOLES
CARMELITES
CARMINATIVE
CARMINATIVES
CARNAHUBAS
CARNALISED
CARNALISES
CARNALISING

CARNALISMS
CARNALISTS
CARNALITIES
CARNALIZED
CARNALIZES
CARNALIZING
CARNALLING
CARNALLITE
CARNALLITES
CARNAPTIOUS
CARNAROLIS
CARNASSIAL
CARNASSIALS
CARNATIONED
CARNATIONS
CARNELIANS
CARNIFEXES
CARNIFICATION
CARNIFICATIONS
CARNIFICIAL
CARNIFYING
CARNITINES
CARNIVALESQUE
CARNIVORES
CARNIVORIES
CARNIVOROUS
CARNIVOROUSLY
CARNIVOROUSNESS
CARNOSAURS
CARNOSITIES
CARNOTITES
CAROLLINGS
CAROMELLED
CAROMELLING
CAROTENOID
CAROTENOIDS
CAROTINOID
CAROTINOIDS
CAROUSINGLY
CARPACCIOS
CARPELLARY
CARPELLATE
CARPELLATES
CARPENTARIA
CARPENTARIAS
CARPENTERED
CARPENTERING
CARPENTERS
CARPENTRIES
CARPETBAGGED
CARPETBAGGER
CARPETBAGGERIES
CARPETBAGGERS
CARPETBAGGERY
CARPETBAGGING
CARPETBAGS
CARPETINGS
CARPETMONGER
CARPETMONGERS

CARPETWEED
CARPETWEEDS
CARPHOLOGIES
CARPHOLOGY
CARPOGONIA
CARPOGONIAL
CARPOGONIUM
CARPOLOGICAL
CARPOLOGIES
CARPOLOGIST
CARPOLOGISTS
CARPOMETACARPI
CARPOMETACARPUS
CARPOOLERS
CARPOOLING
CARPOPHAGOUS
CARPOPHORE
CARPOPHORES
CARPOSPORE
CARPOSPORES
CARRAGEENAN
CARRAGEENANS
CARRAGEENIN
CARRAGEENINS
CARRAGEENS
CARRAGHEEN
CARRAGHEENAN
CARRAGHEENANS
CARRAGHEENIN
CARRAGHEENINS
CARRAGHEENS
CARREFOURS
CARRIAGEABLE
CARRIAGEWAY
CARRIAGEWAYS
CARRITCHES
CARRIWITCHET
CARRIWITCHETS
CARRONADES
CARROTIEST
CARROTTOPPED
CARROTTOPS
CARROUSELS
CARRYBACKS
CARRYFORWARD
CARRYFORWARDS
CARRYOVERS
CARRYTALES
CARSICKNESS
CARSICKNESSES
CARTELISATION
CARTELISATIONS
CARTELISED
CARTELISES
CARTELISING
CARTELISMS
CARTELISTS
CARTELIZATION
CARTELIZATIONS

CARTELIZED
CARTELIZES
CARTELIZING
CARTHAMINE
CARTHAMINES
CARTHORSES
CARTILAGES
CARTILAGINOUS
CARTOGRAMS
CARTOGRAPHER
CARTOGRAPHERS
CARTOGRAPHIC
CARTOGRAPHICAL
CARTOGRAPHIES
CARTOGRAPHY
CARTOLOGICAL
CARTOLOGIES
CARTOMANCIES
CARTOMANCY
CARTONAGES
CARTONNAGE
CARTONNAGES
CARTOONING
CARTOONINGS
CARTOONISH
CARTOONISHLY
CARTOONIST
CARTOONISTS
CARTOONLIKE
CARTOPHILE
CARTOPHILES
CARTOPHILIC
CARTOPHILIES
CARTOPHILIST
CARTOPHILISTS
CARTOPHILY
CARTOPPERS
CARTOUCHES
CARTRIDGES
CARTULARIES
CARTWHEELED
CARTWHEELER
CARTWHEELERS
CARTWHEELING
CARTWHEELS
CARTWRIGHT
CARTWRIGHTS
CARUNCULAR
CARUNCULATE
CARUNCULATED
CARUNCULOUS
CARVACROLS
CARYATIDAL
CARYATIDEAN
CARYATIDES
CARYATIDIC
CARYOPSIDES
CARYOPTERIS
CARYOPTERISES

CASCADURAS
CASCARILLA
CASCARILLAS
CASEATIONS
CASEBEARER
CASEBEARERS
CASEINATES
CASEINOGEN
CASEINOGENS
CASEMAKERS
CASEMENTED
CASEWORKER
CASEWORKERS
CASHIERERS
CASHIERING
CASHIERINGS
CASHIERMENT
CASHIERMENTS
CASHPOINTS
CASINGHEAD
CASINGHEADS
CASKSTANDS
CASSAREEPS
CASSATIONS
CASSEROLED
CASSEROLES
CASSEROLING
CASSIMERES
CASSINGLES
CASSIOPEIUM
CASSIOPEIUMS
CASSITERITE
CASSITERITES
CASSOLETTE
CASSOLETTES
CASSONADES
CASSOULETS
CASSOWARIES
CASSUMUNAR
CASSUMUNARS
CASTABILITIES
CASTABILITY
CASTANOSPERMINE
CASTELLANS
CASTELLATED
CASTELLATION
CASTELLATIONS
CASTELLUMS
CASTIGATED
CASTIGATES
CASTIGATING
CASTIGATION
CASTIGATIONS
CASTIGATOR
CASTIGATORS
CASTIGATORY
CASTOREUMS
CASTRAMETATION
CASTRAMETATIONS

CASTRATERS
CASTRATING
CASTRATION
CASTRATIONS
CASTRATORS
CASTRATORY
CASUALISATION
CASUALISATIONS
CASUALISED
CASUALISES
CASUALISING
CASUALISMS
CASUALIZATION
CASUALIZATIONS
CASUALIZED
CASUALIZES
CASUALIZING
CASUALNESS
CASUALNESSES
CASUALTIES
CASUARINAS
CASUISTICAL
CASUISTICALLY
CASUISTRIES
CATABOLICALLY
CATABOLISE
CATABOLISED
CATABOLISES
CATABOLISING
CATABOLISM
CATABOLISMS
CATABOLITE
CATABOLITES
CATABOLIZE
CATABOLIZED
CATABOLIZES
CATABOLIZING
CATACAUSTIC
CATACAUSTICS
CATACHRESES
CATACHRESIS
CATACHRESTIC
CATACHRESTICAL
CATACLASES
CATACLASIS
CATACLASMIC
CATACLASMS
CATACLASTIC
CATACLINAL
CATACLYSMAL
CATACLYSMIC
CATACLYSMICALLY
CATACLYSMS
CATACOUSTICS
CATACUMBAL
CATADIOPTRIC
CATADIOPTRICAL
CATADROMOUS
CATAFALCOES

CATAFALQUE
CATAFALQUES
CATALECTIC
CATALECTICS
CATALEPSIES
CATALEPTIC
CATALEPTICALLY
CATALEPTICS
CATALLACTIC
CATALLACTICALLY
CATALLACTICS
CATALOGERS
CATALOGING
CATALOGISE
CATALOGISED
CATALOGISES
CATALOGISING
CATALOGIZE
CATALOGIZED
CATALOGIZES
CATALOGIZING
CATALOGUED
CATALOGUER
CATALOGUERS
CATALOGUES
CATALOGUING
CATALOGUISE
CATALOGUISED
CATALOGUISES
CATALOGUISING
CATALOGUIST
CATALOGUISTS
CATALOGUIZE
CATALOGUIZED
CATALOGUIZES
CATALOGUIZING
CATALYSERS
CATALYSING
CATALYTICAL
CATALYTICALLY
CATALYZERS
CATALYZING
CATAMARANS
CATAMENIAL
CATAMOUNTAIN
CATAMOUNTAINS
CATAMOUNTS
CATANANCHE
CATANANCHES
CATAPHONIC
CATAPHONICS
CATAPHORAS
CATAPHORESES
CATAPHORESIS
CATAPHORETIC
CATAPHORIC
CATAPHRACT
CATAPHRACTIC
CATAPHRACTS

CATAPHYLLARY
CATAPHYLLS
CATAPHYSICAL
CATAPLASIA
CATAPLASIAS
CATAPLASMS
CATAPLASTIC
CATAPLECTIC
CATAPLEXIES
CATAPULTED
CATAPULTIC
CATAPULTIER
CATAPULTIERS
CATAPULTING
CATARACTOUS
CATARRHALLY
CATARRHINE
CATARRHINES
CATARRHOUS
CATASTASES
CATASTASIS
CATASTROPHE
CATASTROPHES
CATASTROPHIC
CATASTROPHISM
CATASTROPHISMS
CATASTROPHIST
CATASTROPHISTS
CATATONIAS
CATATONICALLY
CATATONICS
CATATONIES
CATCALLERS
CATCALLING
CATCHCRIES
CATCHFLIES
CATCHINESS
CATCHINESSES
CATCHMENTS
CATCHPENNIES
CATCHPENNY
CATCHPHRASE
CATCHPHRASES
CATCHPOLES
CATCHPOLLS
CATCHWATER
CATCHWEEDS
CATCHWEIGHT
CATCHWORDS
CATECHESES
CATECHESIS
CATECHETIC
CATECHETICAL
CATECHETICALLY
CATECHETICS
CATECHISATION
CATECHISATIONS
CATECHISED
CATECHISER

CATECHISERS
CATECHISES
CATECHISING
CATECHISINGS
CATECHISMAL
CATECHISMS
CATECHISTIC
CATECHISTICAL
CATECHISTICALLY
CATECHISTS
CATECHIZATION
CATECHIZATIONS
CATECHIZED
CATECHIZER
CATECHIZERS
CATECHIZES
CATECHIZING
CATECHIZINGS
CATECHOLAMINE
CATECHOLAMINES
CATECHUMEN
CATECHUMENAL
CATECHUMENATE
CATECHUMENATES
CATECHUMENICAL
CATECHUMENISM
CATECHUMENISMS
CATECHUMENS
CATECHUMENSHIP
CATECHUMENSHIPS
CATEGOREMATIC
CATEGORIAL
CATEGORIALLY
CATEGORICAL
CATEGORICALLY
CATEGORICALNESS
CATEGORIES
CATEGORISATION
CATEGORISATIONS
CATEGORISE
CATEGORISED
CATEGORISES
CATEGORISING
CATEGORIST
CATEGORISTS
CATEGORIZATION
CATEGORIZATIONS
CATEGORIZE
CATEGORIZED
CATEGORIZES
CATEGORIZING
CATENACCIO
CATENACCIOS
CATENARIAN
CATENARIES
CATENATING
CATENATION
CATENATIONS
CATENULATE

CATERCORNER
CATERCORNERED
CATERESSES
CATERPILLAR
CATERPILLARS
CATERWAULED
CATERWAULER
CATERWAULERS
CATERWAULING
CATERWAULINGS
CATERWAULS
CATFACINGS
CATHARISED
CATHARISES
CATHARISING
CATHARIZED
CATHARIZES
CATHARIZING
CATHARTICAL
CATHARTICALLY
CATHARTICS
CATHECTING
CATHEDRALS
CATHEDRATIC
CATHEPSINS
CATHETERISATION
CATHETERISE
CATHETERISED
CATHETERISES
CATHETERISING
CATHETERISM
CATHETERISMS
CATHETERIZATION
CATHETERIZE
CATHETERIZED
CATHETERIZES
CATHETERIZING
CATHETOMETER
CATHETOMETERS
CATHETUSES
CATHODALLY
CATHODICAL
CATHODICALLY
CATHODOGRAPH
CATHODOGRAPHER
CATHODOGRAPHERS
CATHODOGRAPHIES
CATHODOGRAPHS
CATHODOGRAPHY
CATHOLICALLY
CATHOLICATE
CATHOLICATES
CATHOLICISATION
CATHOLICISE
CATHOLICISED
CATHOLICISES
CATHOLICISING
CATHOLICISM
CATHOLICISMS

CATHOLICITIES
CATHOLICITY
CATHOLICIZATION
CATHOLICIZE
CATHOLICIZED
CATHOLICIZES
CATHOLICIZING
CATHOLICLY
CATHOLICOI
CATHOLICON
CATHOLICONS
CATHOLICOS
CATHOLICOSES
CATHOLYTES
CATILINARIAN
CATIONICALLY
CATNAPPERS
CATNAPPING
CATOPTRICAL
CATOPTRICS
CATTINESSES
CATTISHNESS
CATTISHNESSES
CAUCHEMARS
CAUCUSSING
CAUDATIONS
CAUDILLISMO
CAUDILLISMOS
CAULESCENT
CAULICOLOUS
CAULICULATE
CAULICULUS
CAULICULUSES
CAULIFLORIES
CAULIFLOROUS
CAULIFLORY
CAULIFLOWER
CAULIFLOWERET
CAULIFLOWERETS
CAULIFLOWERS
CAULIGENOUS
CAUMSTONES
CAUSABILITIES
CAUSABILITY
CAUSALGIAS
CAUSALITIES
CAUSATIONAL
CAUSATIONISM
CAUSATIONISMS
CAUSATIONIST
CAUSATIONISTS
CAUSATIONS
CAUSATIVELY
CAUSATIVENESS
CAUSATIVENESSES
CAUSATIVES
CAUSELESSLY
CAUSELESSNESS
CAUSELESSNESSES

CAUSEWAYED
CAUSEWAYING
CAUSTICALLY
CAUSTICITIES
CAUSTICITY
CAUSTICNESS
CAUSTICNESSES
CAUTERANTS
CAUTERISATION
CAUTERISATIONS
CAUTERISED
CAUTERISES
CAUTERISING
CAUTERISMS
CAUTERIZATION
CAUTERIZATIONS
CAUTERIZED
CAUTERIZES
CAUTERIZING
CAUTIONARY
CAUTIONERS
CAUTIONING
CAUTIONRIES
CAUTIOUSLY
CAUTIOUSNESS
CAUTIOUSNESSES
CAVALCADED
CAVALCADES
CAVALCADING
CAVALIERED
CAVALIERING
CAVALIERISH
CAVALIERISM
CAVALIERISMS
CAVALIERLY
CAVALLETTI
CAVALRYMAN
CAVALRYMEN
CAVEFISHES
CAVENDISHES
CAVERNICOLOUS
CAVERNOUSLY
CAVERNULOUS
CAVILLATION
CAVILLATIONS
CAVILLINGS
CAVITATING
CAVITATION
CAVITATIONS
CEANOTHUSES
CEASEFIRES
CEASELESSLY
CEASELESSNESS
CEASELESSNESSES
CEBADILLAS
CECUTIENCIES
CECUTIENCY
CEDARBIRDS
CEDARWOODS

CEDRELACEOUS
CEILOMETER
CEILOMETERS
CELANDINES
CELEBRANTS
CELEBRATED
CELEBRATEDNESS
CELEBRATES
CELEBRATING
CELEBRATION
CELEBRATIONS
CELEBRATIVE
CELEBRATOR
CELEBRATORS
CELEBRATORY
CELEBRITIES
CELERITIES
CELESTIALLY
CELESTIALS
CELESTINES
CELESTITES
CELIBACIES
CELIBATARIAN
CELLARAGES
CELLARETTE
CELLARETTES
CELLARISTS
CELLARWAYS
CELLBLOCKS
CELLENTANI
CELLENTANIS
CELLIFEROUS
CELLOBIOSE
CELLOBIOSES
CELLOIDINS
CELLOPHANE
CELLOPHANES
CELLPHONES
CELLULARITIES
CELLULARITY
CELLULASES
CELLULATED
CELLULIFEROUS
CELLULITES
CELLULITIS
CELLULITISES
CELLULOIDS
CELLULOLYTIC
CELLULOSES
CELLULOSIC
CELLULOSICS
CELSITUDES
CEMBALISTS
CEMENTATION
CEMENTATIONS
CEMENTATORY
CEMENTITES
CEMENTITIOUS
CEMETERIES

CENESTHESES
CENESTHESIA
CENESTHESIAS
CENESTHESIS
CENESTHETIC
CENOBITICAL
CENOGENESES
CENOGENESIS
CENOGENETIC
CENOGENETICALLY
CENOSPECIES
CENOTAPHIC
CENSORABLE
CENSORIOUS
CENSORIOUSLY
CENSORIOUSNESS
CENSORSHIP
CENSORSHIPS
CENSURABILITIES
CENSURABILITY
CENSURABLE
CENSURABLENESS
CENSURABLY
CENTAUREAS
CENTAURIAN
CENTAURIES
CENTENARIAN
CENTENARIANISM
CENTENARIANISMS
CENTENARIANS
CENTENARIES
CENTENIERS
CENTENNIAL
CENTENNIALLY
CENTENNIALS
CENTERBOARD
CENTERBOARDS
CENTEREDNESS
CENTEREDNESSES
CENTERFOLD
CENTERFOLDS
CENTERINGS
CENTERLESS
CENTERLINE
CENTERLINES
CENTERPIECE
CENTERPIECES
CENTESIMAL
CENTESIMALLY
CENTESIMALS
CENTESIMOS
CENTIGRADE
CENTIGRAMME
CENTIGRAMMES
CENTIGRAMS
CENTILITER
CENTILITERS
CENTILITRE
CENTILITRES

CENTILLION
CENTILLIONS
CENTILLIONTH
CENTILLIONTHS
CENTIMETER
CENTIMETERS
CENTIMETRE
CENTIMETRES
CENTIMETRIC
CENTIMORGAN
CENTIMORGANS
CENTINELLS
CENTIPEDES
CENTIPOISE
CENTIPOISES
CENTONELLS
CENTONISTS
CENTRALEST
CENTRALISATION
CENTRALISATIONS
CENTRALISE
CENTRALISED
CENTRALISER
CENTRALISERS
CENTRALISES
CENTRALISING
CENTRALISM
CENTRALISMS
CENTRALIST
CENTRALISTIC
CENTRALISTS
CENTRALITIES
CENTRALITY
CENTRALIZATION
CENTRALIZATIONS
CENTRALIZE
CENTRALIZED
CENTRALIZER
CENTRALIZERS
CENTRALIZES
CENTRALIZING
CENTREBOARD
CENTREBOARDS
CENTREFOLD
CENTREFOLDS
CENTREINGS
CENTRELINE
CENTRELINES
CENTREPIECE
CENTREPIECES
CENTRICALLY
CENTRICALNESS
CENTRICALNESSES
CENTRICITIES
CENTRICITY
CENTRIFUGAL
CENTRIFUGALISE
CENTRIFUGALISED
CENTRIFUGALISES

CENTRIFUGALIZE
CENTRIFUGALIZED
CENTRIFUGALIZES
CENTRIFUGALLY
CENTRIFUGALS
CENTRIFUGATION
CENTRIFUGATIONS
CENTRIFUGE
CENTRIFUGED
CENTRIFUGENCE
CENTRIFUGENCES
CENTRIFUGES
CENTRIFUGING
CENTRIOLES
CENTRIPETAL
CENTRIPETALISM
CENTRIPETALISMS
CENTRIPETALLY
CENTROBARIC
CENTROCLINAL
CENTROIDAL
CENTROLECITHAL
CENTROMERE
CENTROMERES
CENTROMERIC
CENTROSOME
CENTROSOMES
CENTROSOMIC
CENTROSPHERE
CENTROSPHERES
CENTROSYMMETRIC
CENTUMVIRATE
CENTUMVIRATES
CENTUMVIRI
CENTUPLICATE
CENTUPLICATED
CENTUPLICATES
CENTUPLICATING
CENTUPLICATION
CENTUPLICATIONS
CENTUPLING
CENTURIATION
CENTURIATIONS
CENTURIATOR
CENTURIATORS
CENTURIONS
CEPHALAGRA
CEPHALAGRAS
CEPHALALGIA
CEPHALALGIAS
CEPHALALGIC
CEPHALEXIN
CEPHALEXINS
CEPHALICALLY
CEPHALISATION
CEPHALISATIONS
CEPHALITIS
CEPHALITISES
CEPHALIZATION

CEPHALIZATIONS
CEPHALOCELE
CEPHALOCELES
CEPHALOCHORDATE
CEPHALOMETER
CEPHALOMETERS
CEPHALOMETRIC
CEPHALOMETRIES
CEPHALOMETRY
CEPHALOPOD
CEPHALOPODAN
CEPHALOPODANS
CEPHALOPODIC
CEPHALOPODOUS
CEPHALOPODS
CEPHALORIDINE
CEPHALORIDINES
CEPHALOSPORIN
CEPHALOSPORINS
CEPHALOTHIN
CEPHALOTHINS
CEPHALOTHORACES
CEPHALOTHORACIC
CEPHALOTHORAX
CEPHALOTHORAXES
CEPHALOTOMIES
CEPHALOTOMY
CERAMICIST
CERAMICISTS
CERAMOGRAPHIES
CERAMOGRAPHY
CERARGYRITE
CERARGYRITES
CERASTIUMS
CERATITISES
CERATODUSES
CERATOPSIAN
CERATOPSIANS
CERATOPSID
CERATOPSIDS
CERCARIANS
CERCOPITHECID
CERCOPITHECIDS
CERCOPITHECOID
CERCOPITHECOIDS
CEREALISTS
CEREBELLAR
CEREBELLIC
CEREBELLOUS
CEREBELLUM
CEREBELLUMS
CEREBRALISM
CEREBRALISMS
CEREBRALIST
CEREBRALISTS
CEREBRALLY
CEREBRATED
CEREBRATES
CEREBRATING

CEREBRATION
CEREBRATIONS
CEREBRIFORM
CEREBRITIS
CEREBRITISES
CEREBROSIDE
CEREBROSIDES
CEREBROSPINAL
CEREBROTONIA
CEREBROTONIAS
CEREBROTONIC
CEREBROVASCULAR
CERECLOTHS
CEREMONIAL
CEREMONIALISM
CEREMONIALISMS
CEREMONIALIST
CEREMONIALISTS
CEREMONIALLY
CEREMONIALS
CEREMONIES
CEREMONIOUS
CEREMONIOUSLY
CEREMONIOUSNESS
CERIFEROUS
CEROGRAPHIC
CEROGRAPHICAL
CEROGRAPHIES
CEROGRAPHIST
CEROGRAPHISTS
CEROGRAPHS
CEROGRAPHY
CEROMANCIES
CEROPLASTIC
CEROPLASTICS
CERTAINEST
CERTAINTIES
CERTIFIABLE
CERTIFIABLY
CERTIFICATE
CERTIFICATED
CERTIFICATES
CERTIFICATING
CERTIFICATION
CERTIFICATIONS
CERTIFICATORIES
CERTIFICATORY
CERTIFIERS
CERTIFYING
CERTIORARI
CERTIORARIS
CERTITUDES
CERULOPLASMIN
CERULOPLASMINS
CERUMINOUS
CERUSSITES
CERVELASES
CERVICITIS
CERVICITISES

CERVICOGRAPHIES
CERVICOGRAPHY
CESAREVICH
CESAREVICHES
CESAREVITCH
CESAREVITCHES
CESAREVNAS
CESAREWICH
CESAREWICHES
CESAREWITCH
CESAREWITCHES
CESPITOSELY
CESSATIONS
CESSIONARIES
CESSIONARY
CESTOIDEAN
CESTOIDEANS
CETEOSAURUS
CETEOSAURUSES
CETOLOGICAL
CETOLOGIES
CETOLOGIST
CETOLOGISTS
CETRIMIDES
CEVADILLAS
CEYLANITES
CEYLONITES
CHABAZITES
CHAENOMELES
CHAENOMELESES
CHAETIFEROUS
CHAETODONS
CHAETOGNATH
CHAETOGNATHS
CHAETOPODS
CHAFFERERS
CHAFFERIES
CHAFFERING
CHAFFINCHES
CHAFFINGLY
CHAGRINING
CHAGRINNED
CHAGRINNING
CHAINBRAKE
CHAINBRAKES
CHAINFALLS
CHAINPLATE
CHAINPLATES
CHAINSAWED
CHAINSAWING
CHAINSHOTS
CHAINSTITCH
CHAINSTITCHES
CHAINWHEEL
CHAINWHEELS
CHAINWORKS
CHAIRBORNE
CHAIRBOUND
CHAIRLIFTS

CHAIRMANED
CHAIRMANING
CHAIRMANNED
CHAIRMANNING
CHAIRMANSHIP
CHAIRMANSHIPS
CHAIRPERSON
CHAIRPERSONS
CHAIRWOMAN
CHAIRWOMEN
CHAISELESS
CHAKALAKAS
CHALAZIONS
CHALAZOGAMIC
CHALAZOGAMIES
CHALAZOGAMY
CHALCANTHITE
CHALCANTHITES
CHALCEDONIC
CHALCEDONIES
CHALCEDONY
CHALCEDONYX
CHALCEDONYXES
CHALCOCITE
CHALCOCITES
CHALCOGENIDE
CHALCOGENIDES
CHALCOGENS
CHALCOGRAPHER
CHALCOGRAPHERS
CHALCOGRAPHIC
CHALCOGRAPHICAL
CHALCOGRAPHIES
CHALCOGRAPHIST
CHALCOGRAPHISTS
CHALCOGRAPHY
CHALCOLITHIC
CHALCOPYRITE
CHALCOPYRITES
CHALICOTHERE
CHALICOTHERES
CHALKBOARD
CHALKBOARDS
CHALKFACES
CHALKINESS
CHALKINESSES
CHALKSTONE
CHALKSTONES
CHALLANING
CHALLENGEABLE
CHALLENGED
CHALLENGER
CHALLENGERS
CHALLENGES
CHALLENGING
CHALLENGINGLY
CHALUMEAUS
CHALUMEAUX
CHALYBEATE

CHALYBEATES
CHALYBITES
CHAMAELEON
CHAMAELEONS
CHAMAEPHYTE
CHAMAEPHYTES
CHAMBERERS
CHAMBERHAND
CHAMBERHANDS
CHAMBERING
CHAMBERINGS
CHAMBERLAIN
CHAMBERLAINS
CHAMBERLAINSHIP
CHAMBERMAID
CHAMBERMAIDS
CHAMBERPOT
CHAMBERPOTS
CHAMBRANLE
CHAMBRANLES
CHAMELEONIC
CHAMELEONLIKE
CHAMELEONS
CHAMFERERS
CHAMFERING
CHAMFRAINS
CHAMOISING
CHAMOMILES
CHAMPAGNES
CHAMPAIGNS
CHAMPERTIES
CHAMPERTOUS
CHAMPIGNON
CHAMPIGNONS
CHAMPIONED
CHAMPIONESS
CHAMPIONESSES
CHAMPIONING
CHAMPIONSHIP
CHAMPIONSHIPS
CHAMPLEVES
CHANCELESS
CHANCELLERIES
CHANCELLERY
CHANCELLOR
CHANCELLORIES
CHANCELLORS
CHANCELLORSHIP
CHANCELLORSHIPS
CHANCELLORY
CHANCERIES
CHANCINESS
CHANCINESSES
CHANCROIDAL
CHANCROIDS
CHANDELIER
CHANDELIERED
CHANDELIERS
CHANDELLED

CHANDELLES	CHAOLOGISTS	CHARACTERIZED	CHARLESTON
CHANDELLING	CHAOTICALLY	CHARACTERIZER	CHARLESTONED
CHANDLERIES	CHAPARAJOS	CHARACTERIZERS	CHARLESTONING
CHANDLERING	CHAPAREJOS	CHARACTERIZES	CHARLESTONS
CHANDLERINGS	CHAPARRALS	CHARACTERIZING	CHARLOTTES
CHANDLERLY	CHAPATTIES	CHARACTERLESS	CHARMEUSES
CHANGEABILITIES	CHAPELRIES	CHARACTEROLOGY	CHARMINGER
CHANGEABILITY	CHAPERONAGE	CHARACTERS	CHARMINGEST
CHANGEABLE	CHAPERONAGES	CHARACTERY	CHARMINGLY
CHANGEABLENESS	CHAPERONED	CHARBROILED	CHARMLESSLY
CHANGEABLY	CHAPERONES	CHARBROILER	CHARMONIUM
CHANGEFULLY	CHAPERONING	CHARBROILERS	CHAROSETHS
CHANGEFULNESS	CHAPFALLEN	CHARBROILING	CHARTACEOUS
CHANGEFULNESSES	CHAPLAINCIES	CHARBROILS	CHARTERERS
CHANGELESS	CHAPLAINCY	CHARCOALED	CHARTERING
CHANGELESSLY	CHAPLAINRIES	CHARCOALING	CHARTERPARTIES
CHANGELESSNESS	CHAPLAINRY	CHARCUTERIE	CHARTERPARTY
CHANGELING	CHAPLAINSHIP	CHARCUTERIES	CHARTHOUSE
CHANGELINGS	CHAPLAINSHIPS	CHARDONNAY	CHARTHOUSES
CHANGEOVER	CHAPMANSHIP	CHARDONNAYS	CHARTOGRAPHER
CHANGEOVERS	CHAPMANSHIPS	CHARGEABILITIES	CHARTOGRAPHERS
CHANGEROUND	CHAPPESSES	CHARGEABILITY	CHARTOGRAPHIC
CHANGEROUNDS	CHAPRASSIES	CHARGEABLE	CHARTOGRAPHICAL
CHANNELERS	CHAPRASSIS	CHARGEABLENESS	CHARTOGRAPHIES
CHANNELING	CHAPSTICKS	CHARGEABLY	CHARTOGRAPHY
CHANNELISATION	CHAPTALISATION	CHARGEHAND	CHARTREUSE
CHANNELISATIONS	CHAPTALISATIONS	CHARGEHANDS	CHARTREUSES
CHANNELISE	CHAPTALISE	CHARGELESS	CHARTULARIES
CHANNELISED	CHAPTALISED	CHARGENURSE	CHARTULARY
CHANNELISES	CHAPTALISES	CHARGENURSES	CHASEPORTS
CHANNELISING	CHAPTALISING	CHARGESHEET	CHASMOGAMIC
CHANNELIZATION	CHAPTALIZATION	CHARGESHEETS	CHASMOGAMIES
CHANNELIZATIONS	CHAPTALIZATIONS	CHARGRILLED	CHASMOGAMOUS
CHANNELIZE	CHAPTALIZE	CHARGRILLING	CHASMOGAMY
CHANNELIZED	CHAPTALIZED	CHARGRILLS	CHASSEPOTS
CHANNELIZES	CHAPTALIZES	CHARINESSES	CHASTENERS
CHANNELIZING	CHAPTALIZING	CHARIOTEER	CHASTENESS
CHANNELLED	CHAPTERHOUSE	CHARIOTEERED	CHASTENESSES
CHANNELLER	CHAPTERHOUSES	CHARIOTEERING	CHASTENING
CHANNELLERS	CHAPTERING	CHARIOTEERS	CHASTENINGLY
CHANNELLING	CHARABANCS	CHARIOTING	CHASTENMENT
CHANSONETTE	CHARACINOID	CHARISMATA	CHASTENMENTS
CHANSONETTES	CHARACTERED	CHARISMATIC	CHASTISABLE
CHANSONNIER	CHARACTERFUL	CHARISMATICS	CHASTISEMENT
CHANSONNIERS	CHARACTERIES	CHARITABLE	CHASTISEMENTS
CHANTARELLE	CHARACTERING	CHARITABLENESS	CHASTISERS
CHANTARELLES	CHARACTERISABLE	CHARITABLY	CHASTISING
CHANTECLER	CHARACTERISE	CHARIVARIED	CHASTITIES
CHANTECLERS	CHARACTERISED	CHARIVARIING	CHATEAUBRIAND
CHANTERELLE	CHARACTERISER	CHARIVARIS	CHATEAUBRIANDS
CHANTERELLES	CHARACTERISERS	CHARLADIES	CHATELAINE
CHANTEUSES	CHARACTERISES	CHARLATANIC	CHATELAINES
CHANTICLEER	CHARACTERISING	CHARLATANICAL	CHATELAINS
CHANTICLEERS	CHARACTERISM	CHARLATANISM	CHATOYANCE
CHANTINGLY	CHARACTERISMS	CHARLATANISMS	CHATOYANCES
CHANTRESSES	CHARACTERISTIC	CHARLATANISTIC	CHATOYANCIES
CHANUKIAHS	CHARACTERISTICS	CHARLATANRIES	CHATOYANCY
CHAOLOGIES	CHARACTERIZABLE	CHARLATANRY	CHATOYANTS
CHAOLOGIST	CHARACTERIZE	CHARLATANS	CHATTERATI

CHATTERBOX	CHECKLISTS	CHEESEMITE	CHEMOCEPTORS
CHATTERBOXES	CHECKMARKED	CHEESEMITES	CHEMOKINES
CHATTERERS	CHECKMARKING	CHEESEMONGER	CHEMOKINESES
CHATTERING	CHECKMARKS	CHEESEMONGERS	CHEMOKINESIS
CHATTERINGS	CHECKMATED	CHEESEPARER	CHEMOLITHOTROPH
CHATTINESS	CHECKMATES	CHEESEPARERS	CHEMONASTIES
CHATTINESSES	CHECKMATING	CHEESEPARING	CHEMONASTY
CHAUDFROID	CHECKPOINT	CHEESEPARINGS	CHEMOPSYCHIATRY
CHAUDFROIDS	CHECKPOINTS	CHEESEPRESS	CHEMORECEPTION
CHAUFFEURED	CHECKRAILS	CHEESEPRESSES	CHEMORECEPTIONS
CHAUFFEURING	CHECKREINS	CHEESETASTER	CHEMORECEPTIVE
CHAUFFEURS	CHECKROOMS	CHEESETASTERS	CHEMORECEPTOR
CHAUFFEUSE	CHECKROWED	CHEESEVATS	CHEMORECEPTORS
CHAUFFEUSED	CHECKROWING	CHEESEWIRE	CHEMOSMOSES
CHAUFFEUSES	CHECKWEIGHER	CHEESEWIRES	CHEMOSMOSIS
CHAUFFEUSING	CHECKWEIGHERS	CHEESEWOOD	CHEMOSMOTIC
CHAULMOOGRA	CHEECHAKOES	CHEESEWOODS	CHEMOSORBED
CHAULMOOGRAS	CHEECHAKOS	CHEESEWRING	CHEMOSORBING
CHAULMUGRA	CHEECHALKO	CHEESEWRINGS	CHEMOSORBS
CHAULMUGRAS	CHEECHALKOES	CHEESINESS	CHEMOSPHERE
CHAUNTRESS	CHEECHALKOS	CHEESINESSES	CHEMOSPHERES
CHAUNTRESSES	CHEEKBONES	CHEILITISES	CHEMOSPHERIC
CHAUNTRIES	CHEEKINESS	CHELASHIPS	CHEMOSTATS
CHAUSSURES	CHEEKINESSES	CHELATABLE	CHEMOSURGERIES
CHAUTAUQUA	CHEEKPIECE	CHELATIONS	CHEMOSURGERY
CHAUTAUQUAS	CHEEKPIECES	CHELICERAE	CHEMOSURGICAL
CHAUVINISM	CHEEKPOUCH	CHELICERAL	CHEMOSYNTHESES
CHAUVINISMS	CHEEKPOUCHES	CHELICERATE	CHEMOSYNTHESIS
CHAUVINIST	CHEEKTEETH	CHELICERATES	CHEMOSYNTHETIC
CHAUVINISTIC	CHEEKTOOTH	CHELIFEROUS	CHEMOTACTIC
CHAUVINISTS	CHEERFULLER	CHELONIANS	CHEMOTACTICALLY
CHAVENDERS	CHEERFULLEST	CHELUVIATION	CHEMOTAXES
CHAVTASTIC	CHEERFULLY	CHELUVIATIONS	CHEMOTAXIS
CHAWBACONS	CHEERFULNESS	CHEMAUTOTROPH	CHEMOTAXONOMIC
CHEAPENERS	CHEERFULNESSES	CHEMAUTOTROPHIC	CHEMOTAXONOMIES
CHEAPENING	CHEERINESS	CHEMAUTOTROPHS	CHEMOTAXONOMIST
CHEAPISHLY	CHEERINESSES	CHEMIATRIC	CHEMOTAXONOMY
CHEAPJACKS	CHEERINGLY	CHEMICALLY	CHEMOTHERAPIES
CHEAPNESSES	CHEERISHNESS	CHEMICKING	CHEMOTHERAPIST
CHEAPSKATE	CHEERISHNESSES	CHEMIOSMOSES	CHEMOTHERAPISTS
CHEAPSKATES	CHEERLEADER	CHEMIOSMOSIS	CHEMOTHERAPY
CHEATERIES	CHEERLEADERS	CHEMIOSMOTIC	CHEMOTROPIC
CHEATINGLY	CHEERLEADING	CHEMISETTE	CHEMOTROPICALLY
CHECHAKOES	CHEERLEADS	CHEMISETTES	CHEMOTROPISM
CHECHAQUOS	CHEERLESSLY	CHEMISORBED	CHEMOTROPISMS
CHECKBOOKS	CHEERLESSNESS	CHEMISORBING	CHEMPADUKS
CHECKCLERK	CHEERLESSNESSES	CHEMISORBS	CHEMURGICAL
CHECKCLERKS	CHEESEBOARD	CHEMISORPTION	CHEMURGIES
CHECKERBERRIES	CHEESEBOARDS	CHEMISORPTIONS	CHENOPODIACEOUS
CHECKERBERRY	CHEESEBURGER	CHEMISTRIES	CHEONGSAMS
CHECKERBLOOM	CHEESEBURGERS	CHEMITYPES	CHEQUEBOOK
CHECKERBLOOMS	CHEESECAKE	CHEMITYPIES	CHEQUEBOOKS
CHECKERBOARD	CHEESECAKES	CHEMOATTRACTANT	CHEQUERBOARD
CHECKERBOARDS	CHEESECLOTH	CHEMOAUTOTROPH	CHEQUERBOARDS
CHECKERING	CHEESECLOTHS	CHEMOAUTOTROPHS	CHEQUERING
CHECKLATON	CHEESECUTTER	CHEMOAUTOTROPHY	CHEQUERWISE
CHECKLATONS	CHEESECUTTERS	CHEMOAUTROPH	CHEQUERWORK
CHECKLISTED	CHEESEHOPPER	CHEMOAUTROPHS	CHEQUERWORKS
CHECKLISTING	CHEESEHOPPERS	CHEMOCEPTOR	CHERALITES

CHERIMOYAS
CHERIMOYER
CHERIMOYERS
CHERISHABLE
CHERISHERS
CHERISHING
CHERISHINGLY
CHERISHMENT
CHERISHMENTS
CHERNOZEMIC
CHERNOZEMS
CHERRYLIKE
CHERRYSTONE
CHERRYSTONES
CHERSONESE
CHERSONESES
CHERUBICAL
CHERUBICALLY
CHERUBIMIC
CHERUBLIKE
CHERVONETS
CHESSBOARD
CHESSBOARDS
CHESSPIECE
CHESSPIECES
CHESSYLITE
CHESSYLITES
CHESTERFIELD
CHESTERFIELDS
CHESTINESS
CHESTINESSES
CHEVALIERS
CHEVELURES
CHEVESAILE
CHEVESAILES
CHEVISANCE
CHEVISANCES
CHEVRETTES
CHEVROTAIN
CHEVROTAINS
CHEWINESSES
CHIACKINGS
CHIAROSCURISM
CHIAROSCURISMS
CHIAROSCURIST
CHIAROSCURISTS
CHIAROSCURO
CHIAROSCUROS
CHIASMATIC
CHIASTOLITE
CHIASTOLITES
CHIBOUQUES
CHICALOTES
CHICANERIES
CHICANINGS
CHICCORIES
CHICKABIDDIES
CHICKABIDDY
CHICKADEES

CHICKAREES
CHICKENHEARTED
CHICKENING
CHICKENPOX
CHICKENPOXES
CHICKENSHIT
CHICKENSHITS
CHICKLINGS
CHICKORIES
CHICKWEEDS
CHICNESSES
CHIEFERIES
CHIEFESSES
CHIEFLINGS
CHIEFSHIPS
CHIEFTAINCIES
CHIEFTAINCY
CHIEFTAINESS
CHIEFTAINESSES
CHIEFTAINRIES
CHIEFTAINRY
CHIEFTAINS
CHIEFTAINSHIP
CHIEFTAINSHIPS
CHIFFCHAFF
CHIFFCHAFFS
CHIFFONADE
CHIFFONADES
CHIFFONIER
CHIFFONIERS
CHIFFONNIER
CHIFFONNIERS
CHIFFOROBE
CHIFFOROBES
CHIHUAHUAS
CHILBLAINED
CHILBLAINS
CHILDBEARING
CHILDBEARINGS
CHILDBIRTH
CHILDBIRTHS
CHILDCARES
CHILDCROWING
CHILDCROWINGS
CHILDERMAS
CHILDERMASES
CHILDHOODS
CHILDISHLY
CHILDISHNESS
CHILDISHNESSES
CHILDLESSNESS
CHILDLESSNESSES
CHILDLIEST
CHILDLIKENESS
CHILDLIKENESSES
CHILDMINDER
CHILDMINDERS
CHILDNESSES
CHILDPROOF

CHILIAGONS
CHILIAHEDRA
CHILIAHEDRON
CHILIAHEDRONS
CHILIARCHIES
CHILIARCHS
CHILIARCHY
CHILIASTIC
CHILLINESS
CHILLINESSES
CHILLINGLY
CHILLNESSES
CHILOPODAN
CHILOPODANS
CHILOPODOUS
CHILTEPINS
CHIMAERISM
CHIMAERISMS
CHIMERICAL
CHIMERICALLY
CHIMERICALNESS
CHIMERISMS
CHIMICHANGA
CHIMICHANGAS
CHIMNEYBOARD
CHIMNEYBOARDS
CHIMNEYBREAST
CHIMNEYBREASTS
CHIMNEYING
CHIMNEYLIKE
CHIMNEYPIECE
CHIMNEYPIECES
CHIMNEYPOT
CHIMNEYPOTS
CHIMPANZEE
CHIMPANZEES
CHINABERRIES
CHINABERRY
CHINACHINA
CHINACHINAS
CHINAROOTS
CHINAWARES
CHINCAPINS
CHINCHERINCHEE
CHINCHERINCHEES
CHINCHIEST
CHINCHILLA
CHINCHILLAS
CHINCOUGHS
CHINKAPINS
CHINKERINCHEE
CHINKERINCHEES
CHINOISERIE
CHINOISERIES
CHINOVNIKS
CHINQUAPIN
CHINQUAPINS
CHINSTRAPS
CHINTZIEST

CHINWAGGED
CHINWAGGING
CHIONODOXA
CHIONODOXAS
CHIPBOARDS
CHIPOCHIAS
CHIPOLATAS
CHIPPERING
CHIPPINESS
CHIPPINESSES
CHIQUICHIQUI
CHIQUICHIQUIS
CHIRAGRICAL
CHIRALITIES
CHIRIMOYAS
CHIROGNOMIES
CHIROGNOMY
CHIROGRAPH
CHIROGRAPHER
CHIROGRAPHERS
CHIROGRAPHIC
CHIROGRAPHICAL
CHIROGRAPHIES
CHIROGRAPHIST
CHIROGRAPHISTS
CHIROGRAPHS
CHIROGRAPHY
CHIROLOGIES
CHIROLOGIST
CHIROLOGISTS
CHIROMANCER
CHIROMANCERS
CHIROMANCIES
CHIROMANCY
CHIROMANTIC
CHIROMANTICAL
CHIRONOMER
CHIRONOMERS
CHIRONOMIC
CHIRONOMID
CHIRONOMIDS
CHIRONOMIES
CHIROPODIAL
CHIROPODIES
CHIROPODIST
CHIROPODISTS
CHIROPRACTIC
CHIROPRACTICS
CHIROPRACTOR
CHIROPRACTORS
CHIROPTERAN
CHIROPTERANS
CHIROPTEROUS
CHIROPTERS
CHIRPINESS
CHIRPINESSES
CHIRRUPERS
CHIRRUPING
CHIRURGEON

CHIRURGEONLY
CHIRURGEONS
CHIRURGERIES
CHIRURGERY
CHIRURGICAL
CHISELLERS
CHISELLING
CHISELLINGS
CHITARRONE
CHITARRONI
CHITCHATTED
CHITCHATTING
CHITTAGONG
CHITTAGONGS
CHITTERING
CHITTERINGS
CHITTERLING
CHITTERLINGS
CHIVALRIES
CHIVALROUS
CHIVALROUSLY
CHIVALROUSNESS
CHIVAREEING
CHIVARIING
CHIYOGAMIS
CHLAMYDATE
CHLAMYDEOUS
CHLAMYDIAE
CHLAMYDIAL
CHLAMYDIAS
CHLAMYDOMONADES
CHLAMYDOMONAS
CHLAMYDOSPORE
CHLAMYDOSPORES
CHLOANTHITE
CHLOANTHITES
CHLOASMATA
CHLORACETIC
CHLORACNES
CHLORALISM
CHLORALISMS
CHLORALOSE
CHLORALOSED
CHLORALOSES
CHLORAMBUCIL
CHLORAMBUCILS
CHLORAMINE
CHLORAMINES
CHLORAMPHENICOL
CHLORARGYRITE
CHLORARGYRITES
CHLORDANES
CHLORELLAS
CHLORENCHYMA
CHLORENCHYMAS
CHLORHEXIDINE
CHLORHEXIDINES
CHLORIDATE
CHLORIDATED

CHLORIDATES
CHLORIDATING
CHLORIDISE
CHLORIDISED
CHLORIDISES
CHLORIDISING
CHLORIDIZE
CHLORIDIZED
CHLORIDIZES
CHLORIDIZING
CHLORIMETER
CHLORIMETERS
CHLORIMETRIC
CHLORIMETRIES
CHLORIMETRY
CHLORINATE
CHLORINATED
CHLORINATES
CHLORINATING
CHLORINATION
CHLORINATIONS
CHLORINATOR
CHLORINATORS
CHLORINISE
CHLORINISED
CHLORINISES
CHLORINISING
CHLORINITIES
CHLORINITY
CHLORINIZE
CHLORINIZED
CHLORINIZES
CHLORINIZING
CHLORITISATION
CHLORITISATIONS
CHLORITIZATION
CHLORITIZATIONS
CHLOROACETIC
CHLOROARGYRITE
CHLOROBENZENE
CHLOROBENZENES
CHLOROBROMIDE
CHLOROBROMIDES
CHLOROCRUORIN
CHLOROCRUORINS
CHLORODYNE
CHLORODYNES
CHLOROFORM
CHLOROFORMED
CHLOROFORMER
CHLOROFORMERS
CHLOROFORMING
CHLOROFORMIST
CHLOROFORMISTS
CHLOROFORMS
CHLOROHYDRIN
CHLOROHYDRINS
CHLOROMETER
CHLOROMETERS

CHLOROMETHANE
CHLOROMETHANES
CHLOROMETRIC
CHLOROMETRIES
CHLOROMETRY
CHLOROPHYL
CHLOROPHYLL
CHLOROPHYLLOID
CHLOROPHYLLOUS
CHLOROPHYLLS
CHLOROPHYLS
CHLOROPHYTUM
CHLOROPHYTUMS
CHLOROPICRIN
CHLOROPICRINS
CHLOROPLAST
CHLOROPLASTAL
CHLOROPLASTIC
CHLOROPLASTS
CHLOROPRENE
CHLOROPRENES
CHLOROQUIN
CHLOROQUINE
CHLOROQUINES
CHLOROQUINS
CHLOROTHIAZIDE
CHLOROTHIAZIDES
CHLORPICRIN
CHLORPICRINS
CHLORPROMAZINE
CHLORPROMAZINES
CHLORPROPAMIDE
CHLORPROPAMIDES
CHLORTHALIDONE
CHLORTHALIDONES
CHOANOCYTE
CHOANOCYTES
CHOCAHOLIC
CHOCAHOLICS
CHOCKABLOCK
CHOCKSTONE
CHOCKSTONES
CHOCOHOLIC
CHOCOHOLICS
CHOCOLATES
CHOCOLATEY
CHOCOLATIER
CHOCOLATIERS
CHOCOLATIEST
CHOICENESS
CHOICENESSES
CHOIRGIRLS
CHOIRMASTER
CHOIRMASTERS
CHOIRSCREEN
CHOIRSCREENS
CHOIRSTALLS
CHOKEBERRIES
CHOKEBERRY

CHOKEBORES
CHOKECHERRIES
CHOKECHERRY
CHOKECOILS
CHOKEDAMPS
CHOKEHOLDS
CHOLAEMIAS
CHOLAGOGIC
CHOLAGOGUE
CHOLAGOGUES
CHOLANGIOGRAM
CHOLANGIOGRAMS
CHOLANGIOGRAPHY
CHOLECALCIFEROL
CHOLECYSTECTOMY
CHOLECYSTITIS
CHOLECYSTITISES
CHOLECYSTOKININ
CHOLECYSTOSTOMY
CHOLECYSTOTOMY
CHOLECYSTS
CHOLELITHIASES
CHOLELITHIASIS
CHOLELITHS
CHOLERICALLY
CHOLERICLY
CHOLESTASES
CHOLESTASIS
CHOLESTATIC
CHOLESTERIC
CHOLESTERIN
CHOLESTERINS
CHOLESTEROL
CHOLESTEROLEMIA
CHOLESTEROLS
CHOLESTYRAMINE
CHOLESTYRAMINES
CHOLIAMBIC
CHOLIAMBICS
CHOLINERGIC
CHOLINERGICALLY
CHOLINESTERASE
CHOLINESTERASES
CHOMOPHYTE
CHOMOPHYTES
CHONDRICHTHYAN
CHONDRICHTHYANS
CHONDRIFICATION
CHONDRIFIED
CHONDRIFIES
CHONDRIFYING
CHONDRIOSOMAL
CHONDRIOSOME
CHONDRIOSOMES
CHONDRITES
CHONDRITIC
CHONDRITIS
CHONDRITISES
CHONDROBLAST

CHONDROBLASTS
CHONDROCRANIA
CHONDROCRANIUM
CHONDROCRANIUMS
CHONDROGENESES
CHONDROGENESIS
CHONDROITIN
CHONDROITINS
CHONDROMAS
CHONDROMATA
CHONDROMATOSES
CHONDROMATOSIS
CHONDROMATOUS
CHONDROPHORINE
CHONDROPHORINES
CHONDROSKELETON
CHONDROSTIAN
CHONDROSTIANS
CHONDRULES
CHOPFALLEN
CHOPHOUSES
CHOPLOGICS
CHOPPERING
CHOPPINESS
CHOPPINESSES
CHOPSOCKIES
CHOPSTICKS
CHORAGUSES
CHORALISTS
CHORDAMESODERM
CHORDAMESODERMS
CHORDOPHONE
CHORDOPHONES
CHORDOPHONIC
CHORDOTOMIES
CHORDOTOMY
CHOREGRAPH
CHOREGRAPHED
CHOREGRAPHER
CHOREGRAPHERS
CHOREGRAPHIC
CHOREGRAPHIES
CHOREGRAPHING
CHOREGRAPHS
CHOREGRAPHY
CHOREGUSES
CHOREIFORM
CHOREODRAMA
CHOREODRAMAS
CHOREOGRAPH
CHOREOGRAPHED
CHOREOGRAPHER
CHOREOGRAPHERS
CHOREOGRAPHIC
CHOREOGRAPHIES
CHOREOGRAPHING
CHOREOGRAPHS
CHOREOGRAPHY
CHOREOLOGIES

CHOREOLOGIST
CHOREOLOGISTS
CHOREOLOGY
CHOREPISCOPAL
CHORIAMBIC
CHORIAMBICS
CHORIAMBUS
CHORIAMBUSES
CHORIOALLANTOIC
CHORIOALLANTOIS
CHORIOCARCINOMA
CHORISATION
CHORISATIONS
CHORISTERS
CHORIZATION
CHORIZATIONS
CHORIZONTIST
CHORIZONTISTS
CHORIZONTS
CHOROGRAPHER
CHOROGRAPHERS
CHOROGRAPHIC
CHOROGRAPHICAL
CHOROGRAPHIES
CHOROGRAPHY
CHOROIDITIS
CHOROIDITISES
CHOROLOGICAL
CHOROLOGIES
CHOROLOGIST
CHOROLOGISTS
CHOROPLETH
CHOROPLETHS
CHORUSMASTER
CHORUSMASTERS
CHORUSSING
CHOUCROUTE
CHOUCROUTES
CHOULTRIES
CHOUNTERED
CHOUNTERING
CHOWDERHEAD
CHOWDERHEADED
CHOWDERHEADS
CHOWDERING
CHOWHOUNDS
CHOWKIDARS
CHREMATIST
CHREMATISTIC
CHREMATISTICS
CHREMATISTS
CHRESTOMATHIC
CHRESTOMATHICAL
CHRESTOMATHIES
CHRESTOMATHY
CHRISMATION
CHRISMATIONS
CHRISMATORIES
CHRISMATORY

CHRISTCROSS
CHRISTCROSSES
CHRISTENED
CHRISTENER
CHRISTENERS
CHRISTENING
CHRISTENINGS
CHRISTIANIA
CHRISTIANIAS
CHRISTIANISE
CHRISTIANISED
CHRISTIANISER
CHRISTIANISERS
CHRISTIANISES
CHRISTIANISING
CHRISTIANIZE
CHRISTIANIZED
CHRISTIANIZER
CHRISTIANIZERS
CHRISTIANIZES
CHRISTIANIZING
CHRISTIANS
CHRISTINGLE
CHRISTINGLES
CHRISTOPHANIES
CHRISTOPHANY
CHROMAFFIN
CHROMAKEYS
CHROMATICALLY
CHROMATICISM
CHROMATICISMS
CHROMATICITIES
CHROMATICITY
CHROMATICNESS
CHROMATICNESSES
CHROMATICS
CHROMATIDS
CHROMATINIC
CHROMATINS
CHROMATIST
CHROMATISTS
CHROMATOGRAM
CHROMATOGRAMS
CHROMATOGRAPH
CHROMATOGRAPHED
CHROMATOGRAPHER
CHROMATOGRAPHIC
CHROMATOGRAPHS
CHROMATOGRAPHY
CHROMATOID
CHROMATOLOGIES
CHROMATOLOGIST
CHROMATOLOGISTS
CHROMATOLOGY
CHROMATOLYSES
CHROMATOLYSIS
CHROMATOLYTIC
CHROMATOPHORE
CHROMATOPHORES

CHROMATOPHORIC
CHROMATOPHOROUS
CHROMATOPSIA
CHROMATOPSIAS
CHROMATOSPHERE
CHROMATOSPHERES
CHROMATYPE
CHROMATYPES
CHROMIDIUM
CHROMINANCE
CHROMINANCES
CHROMISING
CHROMIZING
CHROMOCENTER
CHROMOCENTERS
CHROMODYNAMICS
CHROMOGENIC
CHROMOGENS
CHROMOGRAM
CHROMOGRAMS
CHROMOMERE
CHROMOMERES
CHROMOMERIC
CHROMONEMA
CHROMONEMAL
CHROMONEMATA
CHROMONEMATIC
CHROMONEMIC
CHROMOPHIL
CHROMOPHILIC
CHROMOPHOBE
CHROMOPHONIC
CHROMOPHORE
CHROMOPHORES
CHROMOPHORIC
CHROMOPHOROUS
CHROMOPLAST
CHROMOPLASTS
CHROMOPROTEIN
CHROMOPROTEINS
CHROMOSCOPE
CHROMOSCOPES
CHROMOSOMAL
CHROMOSOMALLY
CHROMOSOME
CHROMOSOMES
CHROMOSPHERE
CHROMOSPHERES
CHROMOSPHERIC
CHROMOTHERAPIES
CHROMOTHERAPY
CHROMOTYPE
CHROMOTYPES
CHROMOXYLOGRAPH
CHRONAXIES
CHRONICALLY
CHRONICITIES
CHRONICITY
CHRONICLED

CHRONICLER
CHRONICLERS
CHRONICLES
CHRONICLING
CHRONOBIOLOGIC
CHRONOBIOLOGIES
CHRONOBIOLOGIST
CHRONOBIOLOGY
CHRONOGRAM
CHRONOGRAMMATIC
CHRONOGRAMS
CHRONOGRAPH
CHRONOGRAPHER
CHRONOGRAPHERS
CHRONOGRAPHIC
CHRONOGRAPHIES
CHRONOGRAPHS
CHRONOGRAPHY
CHRONOLOGER
CHRONOLOGERS
CHRONOLOGIC
CHRONOLOGICAL
CHRONOLOGICALLY
CHRONOLOGIES
CHRONOLOGISE
CHRONOLOGISED
CHRONOLOGISES
CHRONOLOGISING
CHRONOLOGIST
CHRONOLOGISTS
CHRONOLOGIZE
CHRONOLOGIZED
CHRONOLOGIZES
CHRONOLOGIZING
CHRONOLOGY
CHRONOMETER
CHRONOMETERS
CHRONOMETRIC
CHRONOMETRICAL
CHRONOMETRIES
CHRONOMETRY
CHRONOSCOPE
CHRONOSCOPES
CHRONOSCOPIC
CHRONOTHERAPIES
CHRONOTHERAPY
CHRONOTRON
CHRONOTRONS
CHRYSALIDAL
CHRYSALIDES
CHRYSALIDS
CHRYSALISES
CHRYSANTHEMUM
CHRYSANTHEMUMS
CHRYSANTHS
CHRYSAROBIN
CHRYSAROBINS
CHRYSOBERYL
CHRYSOBERYLS

CHRYSOCOLLA
CHRYSOCOLLAS
CHRYSOCRACIES
CHRYSOCRACY
CHRYSOLITE
CHRYSOLITES
CHRYSOLITIC
CHRYSOMELID
CHRYSOMELIDS
CHRYSOPHAN
CHRYSOPHANS
CHRYSOPHILITE
CHRYSOPHILITES
CHRYSOPHYTE
CHRYSOPHYTES
CHRYSOPRASE
CHRYSOPRASES
CHRYSOTILE
CHRYSOTILES
CHUBBINESS
CHUBBINESSES
CHUCKAWALLA
CHUCKAWALLAS
CHUCKHOLES
CHUCKLEHEAD
CHUCKLEHEADED
CHUCKLEHEADS
CHUCKLESOME
CHUCKLINGLY
CHUCKLINGS
CHUCKWALLA
CHUCKWALLAS
CHUFFINESS
CHUFFINESSES
CHUGALUGGED
CHUGALUGGING
CHUMMINESS
CHUMMINESSES
CHUNDERING
CHUNDEROUS
CHUNKINESS
CHUNKINESSES
CHUNNERING
CHUNTERING
CHUPATTIES
CHUPRASSIES
CHURCHGOER
CHURCHGOERS
CHURCHGOING
CHURCHGOINGS
CHURCHIANITIES
CHURCHIANITY
CHURCHIEST
CHURCHINGS
CHURCHISMS
CHURCHLESS
CHURCHLIER
CHURCHLIEST
CHURCHLINESS

CHURCHLINESSES
CHURCHMANLY
CHURCHMANSHIP
CHURCHMANSHIPS
CHURCHPEOPLE
CHURCHWARD
CHURCHWARDEN
CHURCHWARDENS
CHURCHWARDS
CHURCHWAYS
CHURCHWOMAN
CHURCHWOMEN
CHURCHYARD
CHURCHYARDS
CHURLISHLY
CHURLISHNESS
CHURLISHNESSES
CHURNMILKS
CHURRIGUERESCO
CHURRIGUERESQUE
CHYLACEOUS
CHYLIFEROUS
CHYLIFICATION
CHYLIFICATIONS
CHYLIFYING
CHYLOMICRON
CHYLOMICRONS
CHYMIFEROUS
CHYMIFICATION
CHYMIFICATIONS
CHYMIFYING
CHYMISTRIES
CHYMOTRYPSIN
CHYMOTRYPSINS
CHYMOTRYPTIC
CIBACHROME
CIBACHROMES
CICADELLID
CICADELLIDS
CICATRICES
CICATRICHULE
CICATRICHULES
CICATRICIAL
CICATRICLE
CICATRICLES
CICATRICOSE
CICATRICULA
CICATRICULAS
CICATRISANT
CICATRISATION
CICATRISATIONS
CICATRISED
CICATRISER
CICATRISERS
CICATRISES
CICATRISING
CICATRIXES
CICATRIZANT
CICATRIZATION

CICATRIZATIONS
CICATRIZED
CICATRIZER
CICATRIZERS
CICATRIZES
CICATRIZING
CICERONEING
CICHORACEOUS
CICINNUSES
CICISBEISM
CICISBEISMS
CICLATOUNS
CICLOSPORIN
CICLOSPORINS
CIGARETTES
CIGARILLOS
CIGUATERAS
CILIATIONS
CIMETIDINE
CIMETIDINES
CINCHONACEOUS
CINCHONIDINE
CINCHONIDINES
CINCHONINE
CINCHONINES
CINCHONINIC
CINCHONISATION
CINCHONISATIONS
CINCHONISE
CINCHONISED
CINCHONISES
CINCHONISING
CINCHONISM
CINCHONISMS
CINCHONIZATION
CINCHONIZATIONS
CINCHONIZE
CINCHONIZED
CINCHONIZES
CINCHONIZING
CINCINNATE
CINCINNUSES
CINCTURING
CINEANGIOGRAPHY
CINEMAGOER
CINEMAGOERS
CINEMATHEQUE
CINEMATHEQUES
CINEMATICALLY
CINEMATISE
CINEMATISED
CINEMATISES
CINEMATISING
CINEMATIZE
CINEMATIZED
CINEMATIZES
CINEMATIZING
CINEMATOGRAPH
CINEMATOGRAPHED

CINEMATOGRAPHER	CIRCULARIZER	CIRCUMFERENTORS	CIRCUMPOLAR
CINEMATOGRAPHIC	CIRCULARIZERS	CIRCUMFLECT	CIRCUMPOSE
CINEMATOGRAPHS	CIRCULARIZES	CIRCUMFLECTED	CIRCUMPOSED
CINEMATOGRAPHY	CIRCULARIZING	CIRCUMFLECTING	CIRCUMPOSES
CINEMICROGRAPHY	CIRCULARLY	CIRCUMFLECTS	CIRCUMPOSING
CINEPHILES	CIRCULARNESS	CIRCUMFLEX	CIRCUMPOSITION
CINEPLEXES	CIRCULARNESSES	CIRCUMFLEXES	CIRCUMPOSITIONS
CINERARIAS	CIRCULATABLE	CIRCUMFLEXION	CIRCUMSCISSILE
CINERARIUM	CIRCULATED	CIRCUMFLEXIONS	CIRCUMSCRIBABLE
CINERATION	CIRCULATES	CIRCUMFLUENCE	CIRCUMSCRIBE
CINERATIONS	CIRCULATING	CIRCUMFLUENCES	CIRCUMSCRIBED
CINERATORS	CIRCULATINGS	CIRCUMFLUENT	CIRCUMSCRIBER
CINERITIOUS	CIRCULATION	CIRCUMFLUOUS	CIRCUMSCRIBERS
CINGULATED	CIRCULATIONS	CIRCUMFORANEAN	CIRCUMSCRIBES
CINNABARIC	CIRCULATIVE	CIRCUMFORANEOUS	CIRCUMSCRIBING
CINNABARINE	CIRCULATOR	CIRCUMFUSE	CIRCUMSCRIPTION
CINNAMONIC	CIRCULATORS	CIRCUMFUSED	CIRCUMSCRIPTIVE
CINNARIZINE	CIRCULATORY	CIRCUMFUSES	CIRCUMSOLAR
CINNARIZINES	CIRCUMAMBAGES	CIRCUMFUSILE	CIRCUMSPECT
CINQUECENTIST	CIRCUMAMBAGIOUS	CIRCUMFUSING	CIRCUMSPECTION
CINQUECENTISTS	CIRCUMAMBIENCE	CIRCUMFUSION	CIRCUMSPECTIONS
CINQUECENTO	CIRCUMAMBIENCES	CIRCUMFUSIONS	CIRCUMSPECTIVE
CINQUECENTOS	CIRCUMAMBIENCY	CIRCUMGYRATE	CIRCUMSPECTLY
CINQUEFOIL	CIRCUMAMBIENT	CIRCUMGYRATED	CIRCUMSPECTNESS
CINQUEFOILS	CIRCUMAMBIENTLY	CIRCUMGYRATES	CIRCUMSTANCE
CIPHERINGS	CIRCUMAMBULATE	CIRCUMGYRATING	CIRCUMSTANCED
CIPHERTEXT	CIRCUMAMBULATED	CIRCUMGYRATION	CIRCUMSTANCES
CIPHERTEXTS	CIRCUMAMBULATES	CIRCUMGYRATIONS	CIRCUMSTANCING
CIPOLLINOS	CIRCUMAMBULATOR	CIRCUMGYRATORY	CIRCUMSTANTIAL
CIPROFLOXACIN	CIRCUMBENDIBUS	CIRCUMINCESSION	CIRCUMSTANTIALS
CIPROFLOXACINS	CIRCUMCENTER	CIRCUMINSESSION	CIRCUMSTANTIATE
CIRCASSIAN	CIRCUMCENTERS	CIRCUMJACENCIES	CIRCUMSTELLAR
CIRCASSIANS	CIRCUMCENTRE	CIRCUMJACENCY	CIRCUMVALLATE
CIRCASSIENNE	CIRCUMCENTRES	CIRCUMJACENT	CIRCUMVALLATED
CIRCASSIENNES	CIRCUMCIRCLE	CIRCUMLITTORAL	CIRCUMVALLATES
CIRCENSIAL	CIRCUMCIRCLES	CIRCUMLOCUTE	CIRCUMVALLATING
CIRCENSIAN	CIRCUMCISE	CIRCUMLOCUTED	CIRCUMVALLATION
CIRCINATELY	CIRCUMCISED	CIRCUMLOCUTES	CIRCUMVENT
CIRCUITEER	CIRCUMCISER	CIRCUMLOCUTING	CIRCUMVENTED
CIRCUITEERS	CIRCUMCISERS	CIRCUMLOCUTION	CIRCUMVENTER
CIRCUITIES	CIRCUMCISES	CIRCUMLOCUTIONS	CIRCUMVENTERS
CIRCUITING	CIRCUMCISING	CIRCUMLOCUTORY	CIRCUMVENTING
CIRCUITOUS	CIRCUMCISION	CIRCUMLUNAR	CIRCUMVENTION
CIRCUITOUSLY	CIRCUMCISIONS	CIRCUMMURE	CIRCUMVENTIONS
CIRCUITOUSNESS	CIRCUMDUCE	CIRCUMMURED	CIRCUMVENTIVE
CIRCUITRIES	CIRCUMDUCED	CIRCUMMURES	CIRCUMVENTOR
CIRCULABLE	CIRCUMDUCES	CIRCUMMURING	CIRCUMVENTORS
CIRCULARISATION	CIRCUMDUCING	CIRCUMNAVIGABLE	CIRCUMVENTS
CIRCULARISE	CIRCUMDUCT	CIRCUMNAVIGATE	CIRCUMVOLUTION
CIRCULARISED	CIRCUMDUCTED	CIRCUMNAVIGATED	CIRCUMVOLUTIONS
CIRCULARISER	CIRCUMDUCTING	CIRCUMNAVIGATES	CIRCUMVOLUTORY
CIRCULARISERS	CIRCUMDUCTION	CIRCUMNAVIGATOR	CIRCUMVOLVE
CIRCULARISES	CIRCUMDUCTIONS	CIRCUMNUTATE	CIRCUMVOLVED
CIRCULARISING	CIRCUMDUCTORY	CIRCUMNUTATED	CIRCUMVOLVES
CIRCULARITIES	CIRCUMDUCTS	CIRCUMNUTATES	CIRCUMVOLVING
CIRCULARITY	CIRCUMFERENCE	CIRCUMNUTATING	CIRRHIPEDE
CIRCULARIZATION	CIRCUMFERENCES	CIRCUMNUTATION	CIRRHIPEDES
CIRCULARIZE	CIRCUMFERENTIAL	CIRCUMNUTATIONS	CIRRHOTICS
CIRCULARIZED	CIRCUMFERENTOR	CIRCUMNUTATORY	CIRRIGRADE

CIRRIPEDES
CIRROCUMULI
CIRROCUMULUS
CIRROSTRATI
CIRROSTRATIVE
CIRROSTRATUS
CISMONTANE
CISPLATINS
CISPONTINE
CISTACEOUS
CITATIONAL
CITHARISTIC
CITHARISTS
CITIFICATION
CITIFICATIONS
CITIZENESS
CITIZENESSES
CITIZENISE
CITIZENISED
CITIZENISES
CITIZENISING
CITIZENIZE
CITIZENIZED
CITIZENIZES
CITIZENIZING
CITIZENRIES
CITIZENSHIP
CITIZENSHIPS
CITRICULTURE
CITRICULTURES
CITRICULTURIST
CITRICULTURISTS
CITRONELLA
CITRONELLAL
CITRONELLALS
CITRONELLAS
CITRONELLOL
CITRONELLOLS
CITRULLINE
CITRULLINES
CITYFICATION
CITYFICATIONS
CITYSCAPES
CIVILIANISATION
CIVILIANISE
CIVILIANISED
CIVILIANISES
CIVILIANISING
CIVILIANIZATION
CIVILIANIZE
CIVILIANIZED
CIVILIANIZES
CIVILIANIZING
CIVILISABLE
CIVILISATION
CIVILISATIONAL
CIVILISATIONS
CIVILISERS
CIVILISING

CIVILITIES
CIVILIZABLE
CIVILIZATION
CIVILIZATIONAL
CIVILIZATIONS
CIVILIZERS
CIVILIZING
CIVILNESSES
CLABBERING
CLACKBOXES
CLACKDISHES
CLADISTICALLY
CLADISTICS
CLADOCERAN
CLADOCERANS
CLADOGENESES
CLADOGENESIS
CLADOGENETIC
CLADOGRAMS
CLADOPHYLL
CLADOPHYLLS
CLADOSPORIA
CLADOSPORIUM
CLADOSPORIUMS
CLAIRAUDIENCE
CLAIRAUDIENCES
CLAIRAUDIENT
CLAIRAUDIENTLY
CLAIRAUDIENTS
CLAIRCOLLE
CLAIRCOLLES
CLAIRSCHACH
CLAIRSCHACHS
CLAIRVOYANCE
CLAIRVOYANCES
CLAIRVOYANCIES
CLAIRVOYANCY
CLAIRVOYANT
CLAIRVOYANTLY
CLAIRVOYANTS
CLAMANCIES
CLAMATORIAL
CLAMBERERS
CLAMBERING
CLAMJAMFRIES
CLAMJAMFRY
CLAMJAMPHRIE
CLAMJAMPHRIES
CLAMMINESS
CLAMMINESSES
CLAMOROUSLY
CLAMOROUSNESS
CLAMOROUSNESSES
CLAMOURERS
CLAMOURING
CLAMPDOWNS
CLAMPERING
CLAMSHELLS
CLANDESTINE

CLANDESTINELY
CLANDESTINENESS
CLANDESTINITIES
CLANDESTINITY
CLANGBOXES
CLANGORING
CLANGOROUS
CLANGOROUSLY
CLANGOURED
CLANGOURING
CLANJAMFRAY
CLANJAMFRAYS
CLANKINGLY
CLANNISHLY
CLANNISHNESS
CLANNISHNESSES
CLANSWOMAN
CLANSWOMEN
CLAPBOARDED
CLAPBOARDING
CLAPBOARDS
CLAPBREADS
CLAPDISHES
CLAPOMETER
CLAPOMETERS
CLAPPERBOARD
CLAPPERBOARDS
CLAPPERBOY
CLAPPERBOYS
CLAPPERCLAW
CLAPPERCLAWED
CLAPPERCLAWER
CLAPPERCLAWERS
CLAPPERCLAWING
CLAPPERCLAWS
CLAPPERING
CLAPPERINGS
CLAPTRAPPERIES
CLAPTRAPPERY
CLARABELLA
CLARABELLAS
CLARENDONS
CLARIBELLA
CLARIBELLAS
CLARICHORD
CLARICHORDS
CLARIFICATION
CLARIFICATIONS
CLARIFIERS
CLARIFYING
CLARINETIST
CLARINETISTS
CLARINETTIST
CLARINETTISTS
CLARIONETS
CLARIONING
CLARTHEADS
CLASHINGLY
CLASSICALISM

CLASSICALISMS
CLASSICALIST
CLASSICALISTS
CLASSICALITIES
CLASSICALITY
CLASSICALLY
CLASSICALNESS
CLASSICALNESSES
CLASSICALS
CLASSICISE
CLASSICISED
CLASSICISES
CLASSICISING
CLASSICISM
CLASSICISMS
CLASSICIST
CLASSICISTIC
CLASSICISTS
CLASSICIZE
CLASSICIZED
CLASSICIZES
CLASSICIZING
CLASSIFIABLE
CLASSIFICATION
CLASSIFICATIONS
CLASSIFICATORY
CLASSIFIED
CLASSIFIER
CLASSIFIERS
CLASSIFIES
CLASSIFYING
CLASSINESS
CLASSINESSES
CLASSLESSNESS
CLASSLESSNESSES
CLASSMATES
CLASSROOMS
CLASSWORKS
CLATHRATES
CLATTERERS
CLATTERING
CLATTERINGLY
CLAUCHTING
CLAUDICATION
CLAUDICATIONS
CLAUGHTING
CLAUSTRATION
CLAUSTRATIONS
CLAUSTROPHOBE
CLAUSTROPHOBES
CLAUSTROPHOBIA
CLAUSTROPHOBIAS
CLAUSTROPHOBIC
CLAVATIONS
CLAVECINIST
CLAVECINISTS
CLAVICEMBALO
CLAVICEMBALOS
CLAVICHORD

CLAVICHORDIST
CLAVICHORDISTS
CLAVICHORDS
CLAVICORNS
CLAVICULAE
CLAVICULAR
CLAVICULATE
CLAVICYTHERIA
CLAVICYTHERIUM
CLAVIERIST
CLAVIERISTIC
CLAVIERISTS
CLAVIGEROUS
CLAWHAMMER
CLAYMATION
CLAYMATIONS
CLAYSTONES
CLAYTONIAS
CLEANABILITIES
CLEANABILITY
CLEANHANDED
CLEANLIEST
CLEANLINESS
CLEANLINESSES
CLEANNESSES
CLEANSABLE
CLEANSINGS
CLEANSKINS
CLEARANCES
CLEARCOLED
CLEARCOLES
CLEARCOLING
CLEARCUTTING
CLEARHEADED
CLEARHEADEDLY
CLEARHEADEDNESS
CLEARINGHOUSE
CLEARINGHOUSES
CLEARNESSES
CLEARSKINS
CLEARSTORIED
CLEARSTORIES
CLEARSTORY
CLEARWEEDS
CLEARWINGS
CLEAVABILITIES
CLEAVABILITY
CLEAVABLENESS
CLEAVABLENESSES
CLEISTOGAMIC
CLEISTOGAMIES
CLEISTOGAMOUS
CLEISTOGAMOUSLY
CLEISTOGAMY
CLEMATISES
CLEMENCIES
CLEMENTINE
CLEMENTINES
CLENBUTEROL

CLENBUTEROLS
CLEOPATRAS
CLEPSYDRAE
CLEPSYDRAS
CLEPTOCRACIES
CLEPTOCRACY
CLEPTOMANIA
CLEPTOMANIAC
CLEPTOMANIACS
CLEPTOMANIAS
CLERESTORIED
CLERESTORIES
CLERESTORY
CLERGIABLE
CLERGYABLE
CLERGYWOMAN
CLERGYWOMEN
CLERICALISM
CLERICALISMS
CLERICALIST
CLERICALISTS
CLERICALLY
CLERICATES
CLERICITIES
CLERKESSES
CLERKLIEST
CLERKLINESS
CLERKLINESSES
CLERKLINGS
CLERKSHIPS
CLEROMANCIES
CLEROMANCY
CLERUCHIAL
CLERUCHIAS
CLERUCHIES
CLEVERALITIES
CLEVERALITY
CLEVERDICK
CLEVERDICKS
CLEVERNESS
CLEVERNESSES
CLIANTHUSES
CLICKETING
CLICKSTREAM
CLICKSTREAMS
CLIENTAGES
CLIENTELES
CLIENTLESS
CLIENTSHIP
CLIENTSHIPS
CLIFFHANGER
CLIFFHANGERS
CLIFFHANGING
CLIFFHANGINGS
CLIFFHANGS
CLIMACTERIC
CLIMACTERICAL
CLIMACTERICALLY
CLIMACTERICS

CLIMACTICAL
CLIMACTICALLY
CLIMATICAL
CLIMATICALLY
CLIMATISED
CLIMATISES
CLIMATISING
CLIMATIZED
CLIMATIZES
CLIMATIZING
CLIMATOGRAPHIES
CLIMATOGRAPHY
CLIMATOLOGIC
CLIMATOLOGICAL
CLIMATOLOGIES
CLIMATOLOGIST
CLIMATOLOGISTS
CLIMATOLOGY
CLIMATURES
CLIMAXLESS
CLIMBDOWNS
CLINANDRIA
CLINANDRIUM
CLINCHINGLY
CLINDAMYCIN
CLINDAMYCINS
CLINGFILMS
CLINGFISHES
CLINGINESS
CLINGINESSES
CLINGINGLY
CLINGINGNESS
CLINGINGNESSES
CLINGSTONE
CLINGSTONES
CLINICALLY
CLINICALNESS
CLINICALNESSES
CLINICIANS
CLINKERING
CLINKSTONE
CLINKSTONES
CLINOCHLORE
CLINOCHLORES
CLINODIAGONAL
CLINODIAGONALS
CLINOMETER
CLINOMETERS
CLINOMETRIC
CLINOMETRICAL
CLINOMETRIES
CLINOMETRY
CLINOPINACOID
CLINOPINACOIDS
CLINOPINAKOID
CLINOPINAKOIDS
CLINOPYROXENE
CLINOPYROXENES
CLINOSTATS

CLINQUANTS
CLINTONIAS
CLIOMETRIC
CLIOMETRICAL
CLIOMETRICIAN
CLIOMETRICIANS
CLIOMETRICS
CLIPBOARDS
CLIPSHEARS
CLIPSHEETS
CLIQUINESS
CLIQUINESSES
CLIQUISHLY
CLIQUISHNESS
CLIQUISHNESSES
CLISHMACLAVER
CLISHMACLAVERS
CLISTOGAMIES
CLISTOGAMY
CLITICISED
CLITICISES
CLITICISING
CLITICIZED
CLITICIZES
CLITICIZING
CLITORECTOMIES
CLITORECTOMY
CLITORIDECTOMY
CLITORIDES
CLITORISES
CLITTERING
CLOACALINE
CLOACITISES
CLOAKROOMS
CLOBBERING
CLOCKMAKER
CLOCKMAKERS
CLOCKWORKS
CLODDISHLY
CLODDISHNESS
CLODDISHNESSES
CLODHOPPER
CLODHOPPERS
CLODHOPPING
CLOFIBRATE
CLOFIBRATES
CLOGDANCES
CLOGGINESS
CLOGGINESSES
CLOISONNAGE
CLOISONNAGES
CLOISONNES
CLOISTERED
CLOISTERER
CLOISTERERS
CLOISTERING
CLOISTRESS
CLOISTRESSES
CLOMIPHENE

CLOMIPHENES
CLONAZEPAM
CLONAZEPAMS
CLONICITIES
CLONIDINES
CLOSEDOWNS
CLOSEFISTED
CLOSEHEADS
CLOSEMOUTHED
CLOSENESSES
CLOSESTOOL
CLOSESTOOLS
CLOSETFULS
CLOSTRIDIA
CLOSTRIDIAL
CLOSTRIDIAN
CLOSTRIDIUM
CLOSTRIDIUMS
CLOTHBOUND
CLOTHESHORSE
CLOTHESHORSES
CLOTHESLINE
CLOTHESLINED
CLOTHESLINES
CLOTHESLINING
CLOTHESPIN
CLOTHESPINS
CLOTHESPRESS
CLOTHESPRESSES
CLOTTERING
CLOTTINESS
CLOTTINESSES
CLOUDBERRIES
CLOUDBERRY
CLOUDBURST
CLOUDBURSTS
CLOUDINESS
CLOUDINESSES
CLOUDLANDS
CLOUDLESSLY
CLOUDLESSNESS
CLOUDLESSNESSES
CLOUDSCAPE
CLOUDSCAPES
CLOUDTOWNS
CLOVEPINKS
CLOVERGRASS
CLOVERGRASSES
CLOVERLEAF
CLOVERLEAFS
CLOVERLEAVES
CLOWNERIES
CLOWNISHLY
CLOWNISHNESS
CLOWNISHNESSES
CLOXACILLIN
CLOXACILLINS
CLOZAPINES
CLUBABILITIES

CLUBABILITY
CLUBBABILITIES
CLUBBABILITY
CLUBBINESS
CLUBBINESSES
CLUBFOOTED
CLUBHAULED
CLUBHAULING
CLUBHOUSES
CLUBMANSHIP
CLUBMANSHIPS
CLUBMASTER
CLUBMASTERS
CLUBRUSHES
CLUMPINESS
CLUMPINESSES
CLUMSINESS
CLUMSINESSES
CLUSTERING
CLUSTERINGLY
CLUTTERING
CLYPEIFORM
CNIDARIANS
CNIDOBLAST
CNIDOBLASTS
COACERVATE
COACERVATED
COACERVATES
COACERVATING
COACERVATION
COACERVATIONS
COACHBUILDER
COACHBUILDERS
COACHBUILDING
COACHBUILDINGS
COACHBUILT
COACHLINES
COACHLOADS
COACHWHIPS
COACHWOODS
COACHWORKS
COACTIVELY
COACTIVITIES
COACTIVITY
COADAPTATION
COADAPTATIONS
COADJACENCIES
COADJACENCY
COADJACENT
COADJUTANT
COADJUTANTS
COADJUTORS
COADJUTORSHIP
COADJUTORSHIPS
COADJUTRESS
COADJUTRESSES
COADJUTRICES
COADJUTRIX
COADJUTRIXES

COADMIRING
COADMITTED
COADMITTING
COADUNATED
COADUNATES
COADUNATING
COADUNATION
COADUNATIONS
COADUNATIVE
COAGENCIES
COAGULABILITIES
COAGULABILITY
COAGULABLE
COAGULANTS
COAGULASES
COAGULATED
COAGULATES
COAGULATING
COAGULATION
COAGULATIONS
COAGULATIVE
COAGULATOR
COAGULATORS
COAGULATORY
COALESCENCE
COALESCENCES
COALESCENT
COALESCING
COALFIELDS
COALFISHES
COALHOUSES
COALIFICATION
COALIFICATIONS
COALIFYING
COALITIONAL
COALITIONER
COALITIONERS
COALITIONISM
COALITIONISMS
COALITIONIST
COALITIONISTS
COALITIONS
COALMASTER
COALMASTERS
COALMINERS
COANCHORED
COANCHORING
COANNEXING
COAPPEARED
COAPPEARING
COAPTATION
COAPTATIONS
COARCTATED
COARCTATES
COARCTATING
COARCTATION
COARCTATIONS
COARSENESS
COARSENESSES

COARSENING
COASSISTED
COASSISTING
COASSUMING
COASTEERING
COASTEERINGS
COASTGUARD
COASTGUARDMAN
COASTGUARDMEN
COASTGUARDS
COASTGUARDSMAN
COASTGUARDSMEN
COASTLANDS
COASTLINES
COASTWARDS
COATDRESSES
COATIMUNDI
COATIMUNDIS
COATSTANDS
COATTENDED
COATTENDING
COATTESTED
COATTESTING
COAUTHORED
COAUTHORING
COAUTHORSHIP
COAUTHORSHIPS
COBALAMINS
COBALTIFEROUS
COBALTINES
COBALTITES
COBBLERIES
COBBLESTONE
COBBLESTONED
COBBLESTONES
COBBLESTONING
COBELLIGERENT
COBELLIGERENTS
COBWEBBERIES
COBWEBBERY
COBWEBBIER
COBWEBBIEST
COBWEBBING
COCAINISATION
COCAINISATIONS
COCAINISED
COCAINISES
COCAINISING
COCAINISMS
COCAINISTS
COCAINIZATION
COCAINIZATIONS
COCAINIZED
COCAINIZES
COCAINIZING
COCAPTAINED
COCAPTAINING
COCAPTAINS
COCARBOXYLASE

COCARBOXYLASES
COCARCINOGEN
COCARCINOGENIC
COCARCINOGENS
COCATALYST
COCATALYSTS
COCCIDIOSES
COCCIDIOSIS
COCCIDIOSTAT
COCCIDIOSTATS
COCCIFEROUS
COCCINEOUS
COCCOLITES
COCCOLITHS
COCHAIRING
COCHAIRMAN
COCHAIRMEN
COCHAIRPERSON
COCHAIRPERSONS
COCHAIRWOMAN
COCHAIRWOMEN
COCHAMPION
COCHAMPIONS
COCHINEALS
COCHLEARES
COCHLEARIFORM
COCHLEATED
COCKABULLIES
COCKABULLY
COCKALEEKIE
COCKALEEKIES
COCKALORUM
COCKALORUMS
COCKAMAMIE
COCKATEELS
COCKATIELS
COCKATRICE
COCKATRICES
COCKBILLED
COCKBILLING
COCKCHAFER
COCKCHAFERS
COCKCROWING
COCKCROWINGS
COCKERNONIES
COCKERNONY
COCKEYEDLY
COCKEYEDNESS
COCKEYEDNESSES
COCKFIGHTING
COCKFIGHTINGS
COCKFIGHTS
COCKHORSES
COCKIELEEKIE
COCKIELEEKIES
COCKINESSES
COCKLEBOAT
COCKLEBOATS
COCKLEBURS

COCKLEERTS
COCKLESHELL
COCKLESHELLS
COCKMATCHES
COCKNEYDOM
COCKNEYDOMS
COCKNEYFICATION
COCKNEYFIED
COCKNEYFIES
COCKNEYFYING
COCKNEYISH
COCKNEYISM
COCKNEYISMS
COCKNIFICATION
COCKNIFICATIONS
COCKNIFIED
COCKNIFIES
COCKNIFYING
COCKROACHES
COCKSCOMBS
COCKSFOOTS
COCKSINESS
COCKSINESSES
COCKSUCKER
COCKSUCKERS
COCKSURELY
COCKSURENESS
COCKSURENESSES
COCKSWAINED
COCKSWAINING
COCKSWAINS
COCKTAILED
COCKTAILING
COCKTEASER
COCKTEASERS
COCKTHROWING
COCKTHROWINGS
COCKYLEEKIES
COCKYLEEKY
COCOMPOSER
COCOMPOSERS
COCONSCIOUS
COCONSCIOUSES
COCONSCIOUSNESS
COCONSPIRATOR
COCONSPIRATORS
COCOONERIES
COCOONINGS
COCOUNSELED
COCOUNSELING
COCOUNSELLED
COCOUNSELLING
COCOUNSELS
COCOZELLES
COCREATING
COCREATORS
COCULTIVATE
COCULTIVATED
COCULTIVATES

COCULTIVATING
COCULTIVATION
COCULTIVATIONS
COCULTURED
COCULTURES
COCULTURING
COCURATORS
COCURRICULAR
COCUSWOODS
CODECLINATION
CODECLINATIONS
CODEFENDANT
CODEFENDANTS
CODEPENDENCE
CODEPENDENCES
CODEPENDENCIES
CODEPENDENCY
CODEPENDENT
CODEPENDENTS
CODERIVING
CODESIGNED
CODESIGNING
CODETERMINATION
CODEVELOPED
CODEVELOPER
CODEVELOPERS
CODEVELOPING
CODEVELOPS
CODICILLARY
CODICOLOGICAL
CODICOLOGIES
CODICOLOGY
CODIFIABILITIES
CODIFIABILITY
CODIFICATION
CODIFICATIONS
CODIRECTED
CODIRECTING
CODIRECTION
CODIRECTIONS
CODIRECTOR
CODIRECTORS
CODISCOVER
CODISCOVERED
CODISCOVERER
CODISCOVERERS
CODISCOVERING
CODISCOVERS
CODOLOGIES
CODOMINANCE
CODOMINANCES
CODOMINANT
CODOMINANTS
CODSWALLOP
CODSWALLOPS
COEDUCATION
COEDUCATIONAL
COEDUCATIONALLY
COEDUCATIONS

COEFFICIENT
COEFFICIENTS
COELACANTH
COELACANTHIC
COELACANTHS
COELANAGLYPHIC
COELENTERA
COELENTERATE
COELENTERATES
COELENTERIC
COELENTERON
COELOMATES
COELOMATIC
COELOSTATS
COELUROSAUR
COELUROSAURS
COEMBODIED
COEMBODIES
COEMBODYING
COEMPLOYED
COEMPLOYING
COEMPTIONS
COENACTING
COENAESTHESES
COENAESTHESIA
COENAESTHESIAS
COENAESTHESIS
COENAMORED
COENAMORING
COENDURING
COENENCHYMA
COENENCHYMAS
COENENCHYMATA
COENESTHESES
COENESTHESIA
COENESTHESIAS
COENESTHESIS
COENESTHETIC
COENOBITES
COENOBITIC
COENOBITICAL
COENOBITISM
COENOBITISMS
COENOCYTES
COENOCYTIC
COENOSARCS
COENOSPECIES
COENOSTEUM
COENOSTEUMS
COENZYMATIC
COENZYMATICALLY
COEQUALITIES
COEQUALITY
COEQUALNESS
COEQUALNESSES
COEQUATING
COERCIMETER
COERCIMETERS
COERCIONIST

COERCIONISTS
COERCIVELY
COERCIVENESS
COERCIVENESSES
COERCIVITIES
COERCIVITY
COERECTING
COESSENTIAL
COESSENTIALITY
COESSENTIALLY
COESSENTIALNESS
COETANEOUS
COETANEOUSLY
COETANEOUSNESS
COETERNALLY
COETERNITIES
COETERNITY
COEVALITIES
COEVOLUTION
COEVOLUTIONARY
COEVOLUTIONS
COEVOLVING
COEXECUTOR
COEXECUTORS
COEXECUTRICES
COEXECUTRIX
COEXECUTRIXES
COEXERTING
COEXISTENCE
COEXISTENCES
COEXISTENT
COEXISTING
COEXTENDED
COEXTENDING
COEXTENSION
COEXTENSIONS
COEXTENSIVE
COEXTENSIVELY
COFAVORITE
COFAVORITES
COFEATURED
COFEATURES
COFEATURING
COFFEEHOUSE
COFFEEHOUSES
COFFEEMAKER
COFFEEMAKERS
COFFEEPOTS
COFFERDAMS
COFFINITES
COFINANCED
COFINANCES
COFINANCING
COFOUNDERS
COFOUNDING
COFUNCTION
COFUNCTIONS
COGENERATION
COGENERATIONS

COGENERATOR
COGENERATORS
COGITATING
COGITATINGLY
COGITATION
COGITATIONS
COGITATIVE
COGITATIVELY
COGITATIVENESS
COGITATORS
COGNATENESS
COGNATENESSES
COGNATIONS
COGNISABLE
COGNISABLY
COGNISANCE
COGNISANCES
COGNITIONAL
COGNITIONS
COGNITIVELY
COGNITIVISM
COGNITIVISMS
COGNITIVITIES
COGNITIVITY
COGNIZABLE
COGNIZABLY
COGNIZANCE
COGNIZANCES
COGNOMINAL
COGNOMINALLY
COGNOMINATE
COGNOMINATED
COGNOMINATES
COGNOMINATING
COGNOMINATION
COGNOMINATIONS
COGNOSCENTE
COGNOSCENTI
COGNOSCIBLE
COGNOSCING
COHABITANT
COHABITANTS
COHABITATION
COHABITATIONS
COHABITEES
COHABITERS
COHABITING
COHABITORS
COHEIRESSES
COHERENCES
COHERENCIES
COHERENTLY
COHERITORS
COHESIBILITIES
COHESIBILITY
COHESIONLESS
COHESIVELY
COHESIVENESS
COHESIVENESSES

COHIBITING
COHIBITION
COHIBITIONS
COHIBITIVE
COHOBATING
COHOMOLOGICAL
COHOMOLOGIES
COHOMOLOGY
COHORTATIVE
COHORTATIVES
COHOSTESSED
COHOSTESSES
COHOSTESSING
COHOUSINGS
COHYPONYMS
COIFFEUSES
COIFFURING
COILABILITIES
COILABILITY
COINCIDENCE
COINCIDENCES
COINCIDENCIES
COINCIDENCY
COINCIDENT
COINCIDENTAL
COINCIDENTALLY
COINCIDENTLY
COINCIDING
COINFECTED
COINFECTING
COINFERRED
COINFERRING
COINHERENCE
COINHERENCES
COINHERING
COINHERITANCE
COINHERITANCES
COINHERITOR
COINHERITORS
COINSTANTANEITY
COINSTANTANEOUS
COINSURANCE
COINSURANCES
COINSURERS
COINSURING
COINTERRED
COINTERRING
COINTREAUS
COINVENTED
COINVENTING
COINVENTOR
COINVENTORS
COINVESTIGATOR
COINVESTIGATORS
COINVESTOR
COINVESTORS
COKULORISES
COLATITUDE
COLATITUDES

COLCANNONS
COLCHICINE
COLCHICINES
COLCHICUMS
COLCOTHARS
COLDBLOODS
COLDCOCKED
COLDCOCKING
COLDHEARTED
COLDHEARTEDLY
COLDHEARTEDNESS
COLDHOUSES
COLDNESSES
COLECTOMIES
COLEMANITE
COLEMANITES
COLEOPTERA
COLEOPTERAL
COLEOPTERAN
COLEOPTERANS
COLEOPTERIST
COLEOPTERISTS
COLEOPTERON
COLEOPTERONS
COLEOPTEROUS
COLEOPTERS
COLEOPTILE
COLEOPTILES
COLEORHIZA
COLEORHIZAE
COLEORHIZAS
COLEORRHIZA
COLEORRHIZAS
COLESTIPOL
COLESTIPOLS
COLICKIEST
COLICROOTS
COLICWEEDS
COLINEARITIES
COLINEARITY
COLIPHAGES
COLLABORATE
COLLABORATED
COLLABORATES
COLLABORATING
COLLABORATION
COLLABORATIONS
COLLABORATIVE
COLLABORATIVELY
COLLABORATIVES
COLLABORATOR
COLLABORATORS
COLLAGENASE
COLLAGENASES
COLLAGENIC
COLLAGENOUS
COLLAGISTS
COLLAPSABILITY
COLLAPSABLE

COLLAPSARS	COLLECTIVIZING	COLLISIONAL	COLOMBARDS
COLLAPSIBILITY	COLLECTORATE	COLLISIONALLY	COLONELCIES
COLLAPSIBLE	COLLECTORATES	COLLISIONS	COLONELLING
COLLAPSING	COLLECTORS	COLLOCATED	COLONELLINGS
COLLARBONE	COLLECTORSHIP	COLLOCATES	COLONELSHIP
COLLARBONES	COLLECTORSHIPS	COLLOCATING	COLONELSHIPS
COLLARETTE	COLLEGIALISM	COLLOCATION	COLONIALISE
COLLARETTES	COLLEGIALISMS	COLLOCATIONAL	COLONIALISED
COLLARLESS	COLLEGIALITIES	COLLOCATIONS	COLONIALISES
COLLATABLE	COLLEGIALITY	COLLOCUTOR	COLONIALISING
COLLATERAL	COLLEGIALLY	COLLOCUTORS	COLONIALISM
COLLATERALISE	COLLEGIANER	COLLOCUTORY	COLONIALISMS
COLLATERALISED	COLLEGIANERS	COLLODIONS	COLONIALIST
COLLATERALISES	COLLEGIANS	COLLODIUMS	COLONIALISTIC
COLLATERALISING	COLLEGIATE	COLLOGUING	COLONIALISTS
COLLATERALITIES	COLLEGIATELY	COLLOIDALITIES	COLONIALIZE
COLLATERALITY	COLLEGIATES	COLLOIDALITY	COLONIALIZED
COLLATERALIZE	COLLEGIUMS	COLLOIDALLY	COLONIALIZES
COLLATERALIZED	COLLEMBOLAN	COLLOQUIAL	COLONIALIZING
COLLATERALIZES	COLLEMBOLANS	COLLOQUIALISM	COLONIALLY
COLLATERALIZING	COLLEMBOLOUS	COLLOQUIALISMS	COLONIALNESS
COLLATERALLY	COLLENCHYMA	COLLOQUIALIST	COLONIALNESSES
COLLATERALS	COLLENCHYMAS	COLLOQUIALISTS	COLONISABLE
COLLATIONS	COLLENCHYMATA	COLLOQUIALITIES	COLONISATION
COLLEAGUED	COLLENCHYMATOUS	COLLOQUIALITY	COLONISATIONIST
COLLEAGUES	COLLETERIAL	COLLOQUIALLY	COLONISATIONS
COLLEAGUESHIP	COLLICULUS	COLLOQUIALNESS	COLONISERS
COLLEAGUESHIPS	COLLICULUSES	COLLOQUIALS	COLONISING
COLLEAGUING	COLLIERIES	COLLOQUIED	COLONITISES
COLLECTABLE	COLLIESHANGIE	COLLOQUIES	COLONIZABLE
COLLECTABLES	COLLIESHANGIES	COLLOQUING	COLONIZATION
COLLECTANEA	COLLIGATED	COLLOQUISE	COLONIZATIONIST
COLLECTEDLY	COLLIGATES	COLLOQUISED	COLONIZATIONS
COLLECTEDNESS	COLLIGATING	COLLOQUISES	COLONIZERS
COLLECTEDNESSES	COLLIGATION	COLLOQUISING	COLONIZING
COLLECTIBLE	COLLIGATIONS	COLLOQUIST	COLONNADED
COLLECTIBLES	COLLIGATIVE	COLLOQUISTS	COLONNADES
COLLECTING	COLLIMATED	COLLOQUIUM	COLONOSCOPE
COLLECTINGS	COLLIMATES	COLLOQUIUMS	COLONOSCOPES
COLLECTION	COLLIMATING	COLLOQUIZE	COLONOSCOPIES
COLLECTIONS	COLLIMATION	COLLOQUIZED	COLONOSCOPY
COLLECTIVE	COLLIMATIONS	COLLOQUIZES	COLOPHONIES
COLLECTIVELY	COLLIMATOR	COLLOQUIZING	COLOQUINTIDA
COLLECTIVENESS	COLLIMATORS	COLLOQUYING	COLOQUINTIDAS
COLLECTIVES	COLLINEARITIES	COLLOTYPES	COLORATION
COLLECTIVISE	COLLINEARITY	COLLOTYPIC	COLORATIONS
COLLECTIVISED	COLLINEARLY	COLLOTYPIES	COLORATURA
COLLECTIVISES	COLLINSIAS	COLLUCTATION	COLORATURAS
COLLECTIVISING	COLLIQUABLE	COLLUCTATIONS	COLORATURE
COLLECTIVISM	COLLIQUANT	COLLUSIONS	COLORATURES
COLLECTIVISMS	COLLIQUATE	COLLUSIVELY	COLORBREED
COLLECTIVIST	COLLIQUATED	COLLUVIUMS	COLORBREEDING
COLLECTIVISTIC	COLLIQUATES	COLLYRIUMS	COLORBREEDS
COLLECTIVISTS	COLLIQUATING	COLLYWOBBLES	COLORCASTED
COLLECTIVITIES	COLLIQUATION	COLOBOMATA	COLORCASTING
COLLECTIVITY	COLLIQUATIONS	COLOCATING	COLORCASTS
COLLECTIVIZE	COLLIQUATIVE	COLOCYNTHS	COLORECTAL
COLLECTIVIZED	COLLIQUESCENCE	COLOGARITHM	COLORFASTNESS
COLLECTIVIZES	COLLIQUESCENCES	COLOGARITHMS	COLORFASTNESSES

COLORFULLY	COLOURLESSNESS	COMBINATION	COMITATIVES
COLORFULNESS	COLOURPOINT	COMBINATIONAL	COMITATUSES
COLORFULNESSES	COLOURPOINTS	COMBINATIONS	COMMANDABLE
COLORIMETER	COLOURWASH	COMBINATIVE	COMMANDANT
COLORIMETERS	COLOURWASHED	COMBINATORIAL	COMMANDANTS
COLORIMETRIC	COLOURWASHES	COMBINATORIALLY	COMMANDANTSHIP
COLORIMETRICAL	COLOURWASHING	COMBINATORICS	COMMANDANTSHIPS
COLORIMETRIES	COLOURWAYS	COMBINATORY	COMMANDEER
COLORIMETRY	COLPITISES	COMBININGS	COMMANDEERED
COLORISATION	COLPORTAGE	COMBRETUMS	COMMANDEERING
COLORISATIONS	COLPORTAGES	COMBURGESS	COMMANDEERS
COLORISERS	COLPORTEUR	COMBURGESSES	COMMANDERIES
COLORISING	COLPORTEURS	COMBUSTIBILITY	COMMANDERS
COLORISTIC	COLPOSCOPE	COMBUSTIBLE	COMMANDERSHIP
COLORISTICALLY	COLPOSCOPES	COMBUSTIBLENESS	COMMANDERSHIPS
COLORIZATION	COLPOSCOPICAL	COMBUSTIBLES	COMMANDERY
COLORIZATIONS	COLPOSCOPICALLY	COMBUSTIBLY	COMMANDING
COLORIZERS	COLPOSCOPIES	COMBUSTING	COMMANDINGLY
COLORIZING	COLPOSCOPY	COMBUSTION	COMMANDMENT
COLORLESSLY	COLPOTOMIES	COMBUSTIONS	COMMANDMENTS
COLORLESSNESS	COLTISHNESS	COMBUSTIOUS	COMMANDOES
COLORLESSNESSES	COLTISHNESSES	COMBUSTIVE	COMMEASURABLE
COLORPOINT	COLTSFOOTS	COMBUSTIVES	COMMEASURE
COLORPOINTS	COLUBRIADS	COMBUSTORS	COMMEASURED
COLOSSALLY	COLUBRIFORM	COMEDDLING	COMMEASURES
COLOSSEUMS	COLUMBARIA	COMEDICALLY	COMMEASURING
COLOSSUSES	COLUMBARIES	COMEDIENNE	COMMEMORABLE
COLOSTOMIES	COLUMBARIUM	COMEDIENNES	COMMEMORATE
COLOSTROUS	COLUMBATES	COMEDIETTA	COMMEMORATED
COLOSTRUMS	COLUMBINES	COMEDIETTAS	COMMEMORATES
COLOTOMIES	COLUMBITES	COMEDOGENIC	COMMEMORATING
COLOURABILITIES	COLUMBIUMS	COMELINESS	COMMEMORATION
COLOURABILITY	COLUMELLAE	COMELINESSES	COMMEMORATIONAL
COLOURABLE	COLUMELLAR	COMESTIBLE	COMMEMORATIONS
COLOURABLENESS	COLUMNARITIES	COMESTIBLES	COMMEMORATIVE
COLOURABLY	COLUMNARITY	COMETOGRAPHIES	COMMEMORATIVELY
COLOURANTS	COLUMNATED	COMETOGRAPHY	COMMEMORATIVES
COLOURATION	COLUMNIATED	COMETOLOGIES	COMMEMORATOR
COLOURATIONS	COLUMNIATION	COMETOLOGY	COMMEMORATORS
COLOURFAST	COLUMNIATIONS	COMEUPPANCE	COMMEMORATORY
COLOURFASTNESS	COLUMNISTIC	COMEUPPANCES	COMMENCEMENT
COLOURFULLY	COLUMNISTS	COMFINESSES	COMMENCEMENTS
COLOURFULNESS	COMANAGEMENT	COMFITURES	COMMENCERS
COLOURFULNESSES	COMANAGEMENTS	COMFORTABLE	COMMENCING
COLOURINGS	COMANAGERS	COMFORTABLENESS	COMMENDABLE
COLOURISATION	COMANAGING	COMFORTABLY	COMMENDABLENESS
COLOURISATIONS	COMANCHERO	COMFORTERS	COMMENDABLY
COLOURISED	COMANCHEROS	COMFORTING	COMMENDAMS
COLOURISES	COMATOSELY	COMFORTINGLY	COMMENDATION
COLOURISING	COMATULIDS	COMFORTLESS	COMMENDATIONS
COLOURISTIC	COMBATABLE	COMFORTLESSLY	COMMENDATOR
COLOURISTS	COMBATANTS	COMFORTLESSNESS	COMMENDATORS
COLOURIZATION	COMBATIVELY	COMICALITIES	COMMENDATORY
COLOURIZATIONS	COMBATIVENESS	COMICALITY	COMMENDERS
COLOURIZED	COMBATIVENESSES	COMICALNESS	COMMENDING
COLOURIZES	COMBATTING	COMICALNESSES	COMMENSALISM
COLOURIZING	COMBINABILITIES	COMINGLING	COMMENSALISMS
COLOURLESS	COMBINABILITY	COMITADJIS	COMMENSALITIES
COLOURLESSLY	COMBINABLE	COMITATIVE	COMMENSALITY

COMMENSALLY
COMMENSALS
COMMENSURABLE
COMMENSURABLY
COMMENSURATE
COMMENSURATELY
COMMENSURATION
COMMENSURATIONS
COMMENTARIAL
COMMENTARIAT
COMMENTARIATS
COMMENTARIES
COMMENTARY
COMMENTATE
COMMENTATED
COMMENTATES
COMMENTATING
COMMENTATION
COMMENTATIONS
COMMENTATOR
COMMENTATORIAL
COMMENTATORS
COMMENTERS
COMMENTING
COMMENTORS
COMMERCIAL
COMMERCIALESE
COMMERCIALESES
COMMERCIALISE
COMMERCIALISED
COMMERCIALISES
COMMERCIALISING
COMMERCIALISM
COMMERCIALISMS
COMMERCIALIST
COMMERCIALISTIC
COMMERCIALISTS
COMMERCIALITIES
COMMERCIALITY
COMMERCIALIZE
COMMERCIALIZED
COMMERCIALIZES
COMMERCIALIZING
COMMERCIALLY
COMMERCIALS
COMMERCING
COMMERGING
COMMINATED
COMMINATES
COMMINATING
COMMINATION
COMMINATIONS
COMMINATIVE
COMMINATORY
COMMINGLED
COMMINGLES
COMMINGLING
COMMINUTED
COMMINUTES

COMMINUTING
COMMINUTION
COMMINUTIONS
COMMISERABLE
COMMISERATE
COMMISERATED
COMMISERATES
COMMISERATING
COMMISERATINGLY
COMMISERATION
COMMISERATIONS
COMMISERATIVE
COMMISERATIVELY
COMMISERATOR
COMMISERATORS
COMMISSAIRE
COMMISSAIRES
COMMISSARIAL
COMMISSARIAT
COMMISSARIATS
COMMISSARIES
COMMISSARS
COMMISSARY
COMMISSARYSHIP
COMMISSARYSHIPS
COMMISSION
COMMISSIONAIRE
COMMISSIONAIRES
COMMISSIONAL
COMMISSIONARY
COMMISSIONED
COMMISSIONER
COMMISSIONERS
COMMISSIONING
COMMISSIONS
COMMISSURAL
COMMISSURE
COMMISSURES
COMMITMENT
COMMITMENTS
COMMITTABLE
COMMITTALS
COMMITTEEMAN
COMMITTEEMEN
COMMITTEES
COMMITTEESHIP
COMMITTEESHIPS
COMMITTEEWOMAN
COMMITTEEWOMEN
COMMITTERS
COMMITTING
COMMIXTION
COMMIXTIONS
COMMIXTURE
COMMIXTURES
COMMODIFICATION
COMMODIFIED
COMMODIFIES
COMMODIFYING

COMMODIOUS
COMMODIOUSLY
COMMODIOUSNESS
COMMODITIES
COMMODITISE
COMMODITISED
COMMODITISES
COMMODITISING
COMMODITIZE
COMMODITIZED
COMMODITIZES
COMMODITIZING
COMMODORES
COMMONABLE
COMMONAGES
COMMONALITIES
COMMONALITY
COMMONALTIES
COMMONALTY
COMMONHOLD
COMMONHOLDS
COMMONINGS
COMMONNESS
COMMONNESSES
COMMONPLACE
COMMONPLACED
COMMONPLACENESS
COMMONPLACES
COMMONPLACING
COMMONSENSE
COMMONSENSIBLE
COMMONSENSICAL
COMMONWEAL
COMMONWEALS
COMMONWEALTH
COMMONWEALTHS
COMMORANTS
COMMORIENTES
COMMOTIONAL
COMMOTIONS
COMMUNALISATION
COMMUNALISE
COMMUNALISED
COMMUNALISER
COMMUNALISERS
COMMUNALISES
COMMUNALISING
COMMUNALISM
COMMUNALISMS
COMMUNALIST
COMMUNALISTIC
COMMUNALISTS
COMMUNALITIES
COMMUNALITY
COMMUNALIZATION
COMMUNALIZE
COMMUNALIZED
COMMUNALIZER
COMMUNALIZERS

COMMUNALIZES
COMMUNALIZING
COMMUNALLY
COMMUNARDS
COMMUNAUTAIRE
COMMUNAUTAIRES
COMMUNICABILITY
COMMUNICABLE
COMMUNICABLY
COMMUNICANT
COMMUNICANTS
COMMUNICATE
COMMUNICATED
COMMUNICATEE
COMMUNICATEES
COMMUNICATES
COMMUNICATING
COMMUNICATION
COMMUNICATIONAL
COMMUNICATIONS
COMMUNICATIVE
COMMUNICATIVELY
COMMUNICATOR
COMMUNICATORS
COMMUNICATORY
COMMUNINGS
COMMUNIONAL
COMMUNIONALLY
COMMUNIONS
COMMUNIQUE
COMMUNIQUES
COMMUNISATION
COMMUNISATIONS
COMMUNISED
COMMUNISES
COMMUNISING
COMMUNISMS
COMMUNISTIC
COMMUNISTICALLY
COMMUNISTS
COMMUNITAIRE
COMMUNITAIRES
COMMUNITARIAN
COMMUNITARIANS
COMMUNITIES
COMMUNIZATION
COMMUNIZATIONS
COMMUNIZED
COMMUNIZES
COMMUNIZING
COMMUTABILITIES
COMMUTABILITY
COMMUTABLE
COMMUTABLENESS
COMMUTATED
COMMUTATES
COMMUTATING
COMMUTATION
COMMUTATIONS

COMMUTATIVE	COMPARATIVES	COMPENSABILITY	COMPLEMENT
COMMUTATIVELY	COMPARATIVIST	COMPENSABLE	COMPLEMENTAL
COMMUTATIVITIES	COMPARATIVISTS	COMPENSATE	COMPLEMENTALLY
COMMUTATIVITY	COMPARATOR	COMPENSATED	COMPLEMENTARIES
COMMUTATOR	COMPARATORS	COMPENSATES	COMPLEMENTARILY
COMMUTATORS	COMPARISON	COMPENSATING	COMPLEMENTARITY
COMONOMERS	COMPARISONS	COMPENSATION	COMPLEMENTARY
COMPACTEDLY	COMPARING	COMPENSATIONAL	COMPLEMENTATION
COMPACTEDNESS	COMPARTMENT	COMPENSATIONS	COMPLEMENTED
COMPACTEDNESSES	COMPARTMENTAL	COMPENSATIVE	COMPLEMENTING
COMPACTERS	COMPARTMENTALLY	COMPENSATOR	COMPLEMENTISER
COMPACTEST	COMPARTMENTED	COMPENSATORS	COMPLEMENTISERS
COMPACTIBLE	COMPARTMENTING	COMPENSATORY	COMPLEMENTIZER
COMPACTIFIED	COMPARTMENTS	COMPESCING	COMPLEMENTIZERS
COMPACTIFIES	COMPASSABLE	COMPETENCE	COMPLEMENTS
COMPACTIFY	COMPASSING	COMPETENCES	COMPLETABLE
COMPACTIFYING	COMPASSINGS	COMPETENCIES	COMPLETELY
COMPACTING	COMPASSION	COMPETENCY	COMPLETENESS
COMPACTION	COMPASSIONABLE	COMPETENTLY	COMPLETENESSES
COMPACTIONS	COMPASSIONATE	COMPETENTNESS	COMPLETERS
COMPACTNESS	COMPASSIONATED	COMPETENTNESSES	COMPLETEST
COMPACTNESSES	COMPASSIONATELY	COMPETITION	COMPLETING
COMPACTORS	COMPASSIONATES	COMPETITIONS	COMPLETION
COMPACTURE	COMPASSIONATING	COMPETITIVE	COMPLETIONS
COMPACTURES	COMPASSIONED	COMPETITIVELY	COMPLETIST
COMPAGINATE	COMPASSIONING	COMPETITIVENESS	COMPLETISTS
COMPAGINATED	COMPASSIONLESS	COMPETITOR	COMPLETIVE
COMPAGINATES	COMPASSIONS	COMPETITORS	COMPLETORY
COMPAGINATING	COMPATIBILITIES	COMPILATION	COMPLEXATION
COMPAGINATION	COMPATIBILITY	COMPILATIONS	COMPLEXATIONS
COMPAGINATIONS	COMPATIBLE	COMPILATOR	COMPLEXEDNESS
COMPANDERS	COMPATIBLENESS	COMPILATORS	COMPLEXEDNESSES
COMPANDING	COMPATIBLES	COMPILATORY	COMPLEXEST
COMPANDORS	COMPATIBLY	COMPILEMENT	COMPLEXIFIED
COMPANIABLE	COMPATRIOT	COMPILEMENTS	COMPLEXIFIES
COMPANIONABLE	COMPATRIOTIC	COMPLACENCE	COMPLEXIFY
COMPANIONABLY	COMPATRIOTISM	COMPLACENCES	COMPLEXIFYING
COMPANIONATE	COMPATRIOTISMS	COMPLACENCIES	COMPLEXING
COMPANIONED	COMPATRIOTS	COMPLACENCY	COMPLEXION
COMPANIONHOOD	COMPEARANCE	COMPLACENT	COMPLEXIONAL
COMPANIONHOODS	COMPEARANCES	COMPLACENTLY	COMPLEXIONED
COMPANIONING	COMPEARANT	COMPLAINANT	COMPLEXIONLESS
COMPANIONLESS	COMPEARANTS	COMPLAINANTS	COMPLEXIONS
COMPANIONS	COMPEARING	COMPLAINED	COMPLEXITIES
COMPANIONSHIP	COMPEERING	COMPLAINER	COMPLEXITY
COMPANIONSHIPS	COMPELLABLE	COMPLAINERS	COMPLEXNESS
COMPANIONWAY	COMPELLABLY	COMPLAINING	COMPLEXNESSES
COMPANIONWAYS	COMPELLATION	COMPLAININGLY	COMPLEXOMETRIC
COMPANYING	COMPELLATIONS	COMPLAININGS	COMPLEXONE
COMPARABILITIES	COMPELLATIVE	COMPLAINTS	COMPLEXONES
COMPARABILITY	COMPELLATIVES	COMPLAISANCE	COMPLEXUSES
COMPARABLE	COMPELLERS	COMPLAISANCES	COMPLIABLE
COMPARABLENESS	COMPELLING	COMPLAISANT	COMPLIABLENESS
COMPARABLY	COMPELLINGLY	COMPLAISANTLY	COMPLIABLY
COMPARATIST	COMPENDIOUS	COMPLANATE	COMPLIANCE
COMPARATISTS	COMPENDIOUSLY	COMPLANATION	COMPLIANCES
COMPARATIVE	COMPENDIOUSNESS	COMPLANATIONS	COMPLIANCIES
COMPARATIVELY	COMPENDIUM	COMPLECTED	COMPLIANCY
COMPARATIVENESS	COMPENDIUMS	COMPLECTING	COMPLIANTLY

COMPLIANTNESS

COMPLIANTNESS	COMPOSITOR	COMPRIMARIO	COMPUTATIONALLY
COMPLIANTNESSES	COMPOSITORIAL	COMPRIMARIOS	COMPUTATIONS
COMPLICACIES	COMPOSITORS	COMPRINTED	COMPUTATIVE
COMPLICACY	COMPOSITOUS	COMPRINTING	COMPUTATOR
COMPLICANT	COMPOSSIBILITY	COMPRISABLE	COMPUTATORS
COMPLICATE	COMPOSSIBLE	COMPRISALS	COMPUTERATE
COMPLICATED	COMPOSTABLE	COMPRISING	COMPUTERDOM
COMPLICATEDLY	COMPOSTERS	COMPRIZING	COMPUTERDOMS
COMPLICATEDNESS	COMPOSTING	COMPROMISE	COMPUTERESE
COMPLICATES	COMPOSTURE	COMPROMISED	COMPUTERESES
COMPLICATING	COMPOSTURED	COMPROMISER	COMPUTERISABLE
COMPLICATION	COMPOSTURES	COMPROMISERS	COMPUTERISATION
COMPLICATIONS	COMPOSTURING	COMPROMISES	COMPUTERISE
COMPLICATIVE	COMPOSURES	COMPROMISING	COMPUTERISED
COMPLICITIES	COMPOTATION	COMPROMISINGLY	COMPUTERISES
COMPLICITOUS	COMPOTATIONS	COMPROVINCIAL	COMPUTERISING
COMPLICITY	COMPOTATIONSHIP	COMPTROLLED	COMPUTERIST
COMPLIMENT	COMPOTATOR	COMPTROLLER	COMPUTERISTS
COMPLIMENTAL	COMPOTATORS	COMPTROLLERS	COMPUTERIZABLE
COMPLIMENTARILY	COMPOTATORY	COMPTROLLERSHIP	COMPUTERIZATION
COMPLIMENTARY	COMPOTIERS	COMPTROLLING	COMPUTERIZE
COMPLIMENTED	COMPOUNDABLE	COMPTROLLS	COMPUTERIZED
COMPLIMENTER	COMPOUNDED	COMPULSATIVE	COMPUTERIZES
COMPLIMENTERS	COMPOUNDER	COMPULSATORY	COMPUTERIZING
COMPLIMENTING	COMPOUNDERS	COMPULSING	COMPUTERLESS
COMPLIMENTS	COMPOUNDING	COMPULSION	COMPUTERLIKE
COMPLISHED	COMPRADORE	COMPULSIONIST	COMPUTERNIK
COMPLISHES	COMPRADORES	COMPULSIONISTS	COMPUTERNIKS
COMPLISHING	COMPRADORS	COMPULSIONS	COMPUTERPHOBE
COMPLOTTED	COMPREHEND	COMPULSITOR	COMPUTERPHOBES
COMPLOTTER	COMPREHENDED	COMPULSITORS	COMPUTERPHOBIA
COMPLOTTERS	COMPREHENDIBLE	COMPULSIVE	COMPUTERPHOBIAS
COMPLOTTING	COMPREHENDING	COMPULSIVELY	COMPUTERPHOBIC
COMPLUVIUM	COMPREHENDS	COMPULSIVENESS	COMPUTISTS
COMPLUVIUMS	COMPREHENSIBLE	COMPULSIVES	COMRADELINESS
COMPONENCIES	COMPREHENSIBLY	COMPULSIVITIES	COMRADELINESSES
COMPONENCY	COMPREHENSION	COMPULSIVITY	COMRADERIES
COMPONENTAL	COMPREHENSIONS	COMPULSORIES	COMRADESHIP
COMPONENTIAL	COMPREHENSIVE	COMPULSORILY	COMRADESHIPS
COMPONENTS	COMPREHENSIVELY	COMPULSORINESS	COMSTOCKER
COMPORTANCE	COMPREHENSIVES	COMPULSORY	COMSTOCKERIES
COMPORTANCES	COMPREHENSIVISE	COMPUNCTION	COMSTOCKERS
COMPORTING	COMPREHENSIVIZE	COMPUNCTIONS	COMSTOCKERY
COMPORTMENT	COMPRESSED	COMPUNCTIOUS	COMSTOCKISM
COMPORTMENTS	COMPRESSEDLY	COMPUNCTIOUSLY	COMSTOCKISMS
COMPOSEDLY	COMPRESSES	COMPURGATION	CONACREISM
COMPOSEDNESS	COMPRESSIBILITY	COMPURGATIONS	CONACREISMS
COMPOSEDNESSES	COMPRESSIBLE	COMPURGATOR	CONATIONAL
COMPOSITED	COMPRESSIBLY	COMPURGATORIAL	CONCANAVALIN
COMPOSITELY	COMPRESSING	COMPURGATORS	CONCANAVALINS
COMPOSITENESS	COMPRESSION	COMPURGATORY	CONCATENATE
COMPOSITENESSES	COMPRESSIONAL	COMPURSION	CONCATENATED
COMPOSITES	COMPRESSIONS	COMPURSIONS	CONCATENATES
COMPOSITING	COMPRESSIVE	COMPUTABILITIES	CONCATENATING
COMPOSITION	COMPRESSIVELY	COMPUTABILITY	CONCATENATION
COMPOSITIONAL	COMPRESSOR	COMPUTABLE	CONCATENATIONS
COMPOSITIONALLY	COMPRESSORS	COMPUTANTS	CONCAVENESS
COMPOSITIONS	COMPRESSURE	COMPUTATION	CONCAVENESSES
COMPOSITIVE	COMPRESSURES	COMPUTATIONAL	CONCAVITIES

CONCEALABLE
CONCEALERS
CONCEALING
CONCEALINGLY
CONCEALMENT
CONCEALMENTS
CONCEDEDLY
CONCEITEDLY
CONCEITEDNESS
CONCEITEDNESSES
CONCEITFUL
CONCEITING
CONCEITLESS
CONCEIVABILITY
CONCEIVABLE
CONCEIVABLENESS
CONCEIVABLY
CONCEIVERS
CONCEIVING
CONCELEBRANT
CONCELEBRANTS
CONCELEBRATE
CONCELEBRATED
CONCELEBRATES
CONCELEBRATING
CONCELEBRATION
CONCELEBRATIONS
CONCENTERED
CONCENTERING
CONCENTERS
CONCENTRATE
CONCENTRATED
CONCENTRATEDLY
CONCENTRATES
CONCENTRATING
CONCENTRATION
CONCENTRATIONS
CONCENTRATIVE
CONCENTRATIVELY
CONCENTRATOR
CONCENTRATORS
CONCENTRED
CONCENTRES
CONCENTRIC
CONCENTRICAL
CONCENTRICALLY
CONCENTRICITIES
CONCENTRICITY
CONCENTRING
CONCEPTACLE
CONCEPTACLES
CONCEPTION
CONCEPTIONAL
CONCEPTIONS
CONCEPTIOUS
CONCEPTIVE
CONCEPTUAL
CONCEPTUALISE
CONCEPTUALISED

CONCEPTUALISER
CONCEPTUALISERS
CONCEPTUALISES
CONCEPTUALISING
CONCEPTUALISM
CONCEPTUALISMS
CONCEPTUALIST
CONCEPTUALISTIC
CONCEPTUALISTS
CONCEPTUALITIES
CONCEPTUALITY
CONCEPTUALIZE
CONCEPTUALIZED
CONCEPTUALIZER
CONCEPTUALIZERS
CONCEPTUALIZES
CONCEPTUALIZING
CONCEPTUALLY
CONCEPTUSES
CONCERNANCIES
CONCERNANCY
CONCERNEDLY
CONCERNEDNESS
CONCERNEDNESSES
CONCERNING
CONCERNMENT
CONCERNMENTS
CONCERTANTE
CONCERTANTES
CONCERTANTI
CONCERTEDLY
CONCERTEDNESS
CONCERTEDNESSES
CONCERTGOER
CONCERTGOERS
CONCERTGOING
CONCERTGOINGS
CONCERTINA
CONCERTINAED
CONCERTINAING
CONCERTINAS
CONCERTING
CONCERTINI
CONCERTINIST
CONCERTINISTS
CONCERTINO
CONCERTINOS
CONCERTISE
CONCERTISED
CONCERTISES
CONCERTISING
CONCERTIZE
CONCERTIZED
CONCERTIZES
CONCERTIZING
CONCERTMASTER
CONCERTMASTERS
CONCERTMEISTER
CONCERTMEISTERS

CONCERTSTUCK
CONCERTSTUCKS
CONCESSIBLE
CONCESSION
CONCESSIONAIRE
CONCESSIONAIRES
CONCESSIONAL
CONCESSIONARIES
CONCESSIONARY
CONCESSIONER
CONCESSIONERS
CONCESSIONIST
CONCESSIONISTS
CONCESSIONNAIRE
CONCESSIONS
CONCESSIVE
CONCESSIVELY
CONCETTISM
CONCETTISMS
CONCETTIST
CONCETTISTS
CONCHIFEROUS
CONCHIFORM
CONCHIGLIE
CONCHIOLIN
CONCHIOLINS
CONCHITISES
CONCHOIDAL
CONCHOIDALLY
CONCHOLOGICAL
CONCHOLOGIES
CONCHOLOGIST
CONCHOLOGISTS
CONCHOLOGY
CONCIERGES
CONCILIABLE
CONCILIARLY
CONCILIARY
CONCILIATE
CONCILIATED
CONCILIATES
CONCILIATING
CONCILIATION
CONCILIATIONS
CONCILIATIVE
CONCILIATOR
CONCILIATORILY
CONCILIATORS
CONCILIATORY
CONCINNITIES
CONCINNITY
CONCINNOUS
CONCIPIENCIES
CONCIPIENCY
CONCIPIENT
CONCISENESS
CONCISENESSES
CONCISIONS
CONCLAMATION

CONCLAMATIONS
CONCLAVIST
CONCLAVISTS
CONCLUDERS
CONCLUDING
CONCLUSION
CONCLUSIONARY
CONCLUSIONS
CONCLUSIVE
CONCLUSIVELY
CONCLUSIVENESS
CONCLUSORY
CONCOCTERS
CONCOCTING
CONCOCTION
CONCOCTIONS
CONCOCTIVE
CONCOCTORS
CONCOLORATE
CONCOLOROUS
CONCOMITANCE
CONCOMITANCES
CONCOMITANCIES
CONCOMITANCY
CONCOMITANT
CONCOMITANTLY
CONCOMITANTS
CONCORDANCE
CONCORDANCES
CONCORDANT
CONCORDANTLY
CONCORDATS
CONCORDIAL
CONCORDING
CONCORPORATE
CONCORPORATED
CONCORPORATES
CONCORPORATING
CONCOURSES
CONCREATED
CONCREATES
CONCREATING
CONCREMATION
CONCREMATIONS
CONCRESCENCE
CONCRESCENCES
CONCRESCENT
CONCRETELY
CONCRETENESS
CONCRETENESSES
CONCRETING
CONCRETION
CONCRETIONARY
CONCRETIONS
CONCRETISATION
CONCRETISATIONS
CONCRETISE
CONCRETISED
CONCRETISES

CONCRETISING

CONCRETISING
CONCRETISM
CONCRETISMS
CONCRETIST
CONCRETISTS
CONCRETIVE
CONCRETIVELY
CONCRETIZATION
CONCRETIZATIONS
CONCRETIZE
CONCRETIZED
CONCRETIZES
CONCRETIZING
CONCREWING
CONCUBINAGE
CONCUBINAGES
CONCUBINARIES
CONCUBINARY
CONCUBINES
CONCUBITANCIES
CONCUBITANCY
CONCUBITANT
CONCUBITANTS
CONCUPISCENCE
CONCUPISCENCES
CONCUPISCENT
CONCUPISCIBLE
CONCURRENCE
CONCURRENCES
CONCURRENCIES
CONCURRENCY
CONCURRENT
CONCURRENTLY
CONCURRENTS
CONCURRING
CONCURRINGLY
CONCUSSING
CONCUSSION
CONCUSSIONS
CONCUSSIVE
CONCYCLICALLY
CONDEMNABLE
CONDEMNABLY
CONDEMNATION
CONDEMNATIONS
CONDEMNATORY
CONDEMNERS
CONDEMNING
CONDEMNINGLY
CONDEMNORS
CONDENSABILITY
CONDENSABLE
CONDENSATE
CONDENSATED
CONDENSATES
CONDENSATING
CONDENSATION
CONDENSATIONAL
CONDENSATIONS

CONDENSERIES
CONDENSERS
CONDENSERY
CONDENSIBILITY
CONDENSIBLE
CONDENSING
CONDESCEND
CONDESCENDED
CONDESCENDENCE
CONDESCENDENCES
CONDESCENDING
CONDESCENDINGLY
CONDESCENDS
CONDESCENSION
CONDESCENSIONS
CONDIDDLED
CONDIDDLES
CONDIDDLING
CONDIGNNESS
CONDIGNNESSES
CONDIMENTAL
CONDIMENTED
CONDIMENTING
CONDIMENTS
CONDISCIPLE
CONDISCIPLES
CONDITIONABLE
CONDITIONAL
CONDITIONALITY
CONDITIONALLY
CONDITIONALS
CONDITIONATE
CONDITIONATED
CONDITIONATES
CONDITIONATING
CONDITIONED
CONDITIONER
CONDITIONERS
CONDITIONING
CONDITIONINGS
CONDITIONS
CONDOLATORY
CONDOLEMENT
CONDOLEMENTS
CONDOLENCE
CONDOLENCES
CONDOLINGLY
CONDOMINIUM
CONDOMINIUMS
CONDONABLE
CONDONATION
CONDONATIONS
CONDOTTIERE
CONDOTTIERI
CONDUCEMENT
CONDUCEMENTS
CONDUCIBLE
CONDUCINGLY
CONDUCIVENESS

CONDUCIVENESSES
CONDUCTANCE
CONDUCTANCES
CONDUCTIBILITY
CONDUCTIBLE
CONDUCTIMETRIC
CONDUCTING
CONDUCTIOMETRIC
CONDUCTION
CONDUCTIONAL
CONDUCTIONS
CONDUCTIVE
CONDUCTIVELY
CONDUCTIVITIES
CONDUCTIVITY
CONDUCTOMETRIC
CONDUCTORIAL
CONDUCTORS
CONDUCTORSHIP
CONDUCTORSHIPS
CONDUCTRESS
CONDUCTRESSES
CONDUPLICATE
CONDUPLICATION
CONDUPLICATIONS
CONDYLOMAS
CONDYLOMATA
CONDYLOMATOUS
CONEFLOWER
CONEFLOWERS
CONFABBING
CONFABULAR
CONFABULATE
CONFABULATED
CONFABULATES
CONFABULATING
CONFABULATION
CONFABULATIONS
CONFABULATOR
CONFABULATORS
CONFABULATORY
CONFARREATE
CONFARREATION
CONFARREATIONS
CONFECTING
CONFECTION
CONFECTIONARIES
CONFECTIONARY
CONFECTIONER
CONFECTIONERIES
CONFECTIONERS
CONFECTIONERY
CONFECTIONS
CONFEDERACIES
CONFEDERACY
CONFEDERAL
CONFEDERATE
CONFEDERATED
CONFEDERATES

CONFEDERATING
CONFEDERATION
CONFEDERATIONS
CONFEDERATIVE
CONFERENCE
CONFERENCES
CONFERENCIER
CONFERENCIERS
CONFERENCING
CONFERENCINGS
CONFERENTIAL
CONFERMENT
CONFERMENTS
CONFERRABLE
CONFERRALS
CONFERREES
CONFERRENCE
CONFERRENCES
CONFERRERS
CONFERRING
CONFERVOID
CONFERVOIDS
CONFESSABLE
CONFESSANT
CONFESSANTS
CONFESSEDLY
CONFESSING
CONFESSION
CONFESSIONAL
CONFESSIONALISM
CONFESSIONALIST
CONFESSIONALLY
CONFESSIONALS
CONFESSIONARIES
CONFESSIONARY
CONFESSIONS
CONFESSORESS
CONFESSORESSES
CONFESSORS
CONFESSORSHIP
CONFESSORSHIPS
CONFIDANTE
CONFIDANTES
CONFIDANTS
CONFIDENCE
CONFIDENCES
CONFIDENCIES
CONFIDENCY
CONFIDENTIAL
CONFIDENTIALITY
CONFIDENTIALLY
CONFIDENTLY
CONFIDENTS
CONFIDINGLY
CONFIDINGNESS
CONFIDINGNESSES
CONFIGURATE
CONFIGURATED
CONFIGURATES

CONFIGURATING
CONFIGURATION
CONFIGURATIONAL
CONFIGURATIONS
CONFIGURATIVE
CONFIGURED
CONFIGURES
CONFIGURING
CONFINABLE
CONFINEABLE
CONFINEDLY
CONFINEDNESS
CONFINEDNESSES
CONFINELESS
CONFINEMENT
CONFINEMENTS
CONFIRMABILITY
CONFIRMABLE
CONFIRMAND
CONFIRMANDS
CONFIRMATION
CONFIRMATIONAL
CONFIRMATIONS
CONFIRMATIVE
CONFIRMATOR
CONFIRMATORS
CONFIRMATORY
CONFIRMEDLY
CONFIRMEDNESS
CONFIRMEDNESSES
CONFIRMEES
CONFIRMERS
CONFIRMING
CONFIRMINGS
CONFIRMORS
CONFISCABLE
CONFISCATABLE
CONFISCATE
CONFISCATED
CONFISCATES
CONFISCATING
CONFISCATION
CONFISCATIONS
CONFISCATOR
CONFISCATORS
CONFISCATORY
CONFISERIE
CONFISERIES
CONFISEURS
CONFITEORS
CONFITURES
CONFLAGRANT
CONFLAGRATE
CONFLAGRATED
CONFLAGRATES
CONFLAGRATING
CONFLAGRATION
CONFLAGRATIONS
CONFLAGRATIVE

CONFLATING
CONFLATION
CONFLATIONS
CONFLICTED
CONFLICTFUL
CONFLICTING
CONFLICTINGLY
CONFLICTION
CONFLICTIONS
CONFLICTIVE
CONFLICTORY
CONFLICTUAL
CONFLUENCE
CONFLUENCES
CONFLUENTLY
CONFLUENTS
CONFOCALLY
CONFORMABILITY
CONFORMABLE
CONFORMABLENESS
CONFORMABLY
CONFORMANCE
CONFORMANCES
CONFORMATION
CONFORMATIONAL
CONFORMATIONS
CONFORMERS
CONFORMING
CONFORMINGLY
CONFORMISM
CONFORMISMS
CONFORMIST
CONFORMISTS
CONFORMITIES
CONFORMITY
CONFOUNDABLE
CONFOUNDED
CONFOUNDEDLY
CONFOUNDEDNESS
CONFOUNDER
CONFOUNDERS
CONFOUNDING
CONFOUNDINGLY
CONFRATERNAL
CONFRATERNITIES
CONFRATERNITY
CONFRERIES
CONFRONTAL
CONFRONTALS
CONFRONTATION
CONFRONTATIONAL
CONFRONTATIONS
CONFRONTED
CONFRONTER
CONFRONTERS
CONFRONTING
CONFRONTMENT
CONFRONTMENTS
CONFUSABILITIES

CONFUSABILITY
CONFUSABLE
CONFUSABLES
CONFUSEDLY
CONFUSEDNESS
CONFUSEDNESSES
CONFUSIBLE
CONFUSIBLES
CONFUSINGLY
CONFUSIONAL
CONFUSIONS
CONFUTABLE
CONFUTATION
CONFUTATIONS
CONFUTATIVE
CONFUTEMENT
CONFUTEMENTS
CONGEALABLE
CONGEALABLENESS
CONGEALERS
CONGEALING
CONGEALMENT
CONGEALMENTS
CONGELATION
CONGELATIONS
CONGENERIC
CONGENERICAL
CONGENERICS
CONGENEROUS
CONGENETIC
CONGENIALITIES
CONGENIALITY
CONGENIALLY
CONGENIALNESS
CONGENIALNESSES
CONGENITAL
CONGENITALLY
CONGENITALNESS
CONGESTIBLE
CONGESTING
CONGESTION
CONGESTIONS
CONGESTIVE
CONGIARIES
CONGLOBATE
CONGLOBATED
CONGLOBATES
CONGLOBATING
CONGLOBATION
CONGLOBATIONS
CONGLOBING
CONGLOBULATE
CONGLOBULATED
CONGLOBULATES
CONGLOBULATING
CONGLOBULATION
CONGLOBULATIONS
CONGLOMERATE
CONGLOMERATED

CONGLOMERATES
CONGLOMERATEUR
CONGLOMERATEURS
CONGLOMERATIC
CONGLOMERATING
CONGLOMERATION
CONGLOMERATIONS
CONGLOMERATIVE
CONGLOMERATOR
CONGLOMERATORS
CONGLUTINANT
CONGLUTINATE
CONGLUTINATED
CONGLUTINATES
CONGLUTINATING
CONGLUTINATION
CONGLUTINATIONS
CONGLUTINATIVE
CONGLUTINATOR
CONGLUTINATORS
CONGRATTERS
CONGRATULABLE
CONGRATULANT
CONGRATULANTS
CONGRATULATE
CONGRATULATED
CONGRATULATES
CONGRATULATING
CONGRATULATION
CONGRATULATIONS
CONGRATULATIVE
CONGRATULATOR
CONGRATULATORS
CONGRATULATORY
CONGREEING
CONGREETED
CONGREETING
CONGREGANT
CONGREGANTS
CONGREGATE
CONGREGATED
CONGREGATES
CONGREGATING
CONGREGATION
CONGREGATIONAL
CONGREGATIONS
CONGREGATIVE
CONGREGATOR
CONGREGATORS
CONGRESSED
CONGRESSES
CONGRESSING
CONGRESSIONAL
CONGRESSIONALLY
CONGRESSMAN
CONGRESSMEN
CONGRESSPEOPLE
CONGRESSPERSON
CONGRESSPERSONS

CONGRESSWOMAN
CONGRESSWOMEN
CONGRUENCE
CONGRUENCES
CONGRUENCIES
CONGRUENCY
CONGRUENTLY
CONGRUITIES
CONGRUOUSLY
CONGRUOUSNESS
CONGRUOUSNESSES
CONICITIES
CONIDIOPHORE
CONIDIOPHORES
CONIDIOPHOROUS
CONIDIOSPORE
CONIDIOSPORES
CONIFEROUS
CONIOLOGIES
CONIROSTRAL
CONJECTING
CONJECTURABLE
CONJECTURABLY
CONJECTURAL
CONJECTURALLY
CONJECTURE
CONJECTURED
CONJECTURER
CONJECTURERS
CONJECTURES
CONJECTURING
CONJOINERS
CONJOINING
CONJOINTLY
CONJUGABLE
CONJUGALITIES
CONJUGALITY
CONJUGALLY
CONJUGANTS
CONJUGATED
CONJUGATELY
CONJUGATENESS
CONJUGATENESSES
CONJUGATES
CONJUGATING
CONJUGATINGS
CONJUGATION
CONJUGATIONAL
CONJUGATIONALLY
CONJUGATIONS
CONJUGATIVE
CONJUGATOR
CONJUGATORS
CONJUNCTION
CONJUNCTIONAL
CONJUNCTIONALLY
CONJUNCTIONS
CONJUNCTIVA
CONJUNCTIVAE

CONJUNCTIVAL
CONJUNCTIVAS
CONJUNCTIVE
CONJUNCTIVELY
CONJUNCTIVENESS
CONJUNCTIVES
CONJUNCTIVITIS
CONJUNCTLY
CONJUNCTURAL
CONJUNCTURE
CONJUNCTURES
CONJURATION
CONJURATIONS
CONJURATOR
CONJURATORS
CONJUREMENT
CONJUREMENTS
CONJURINGS
CONNASCENCE
CONNASCENCES
CONNASCENCIES
CONNASCENCY
CONNASCENT
CONNATENESS
CONNATENESSES
CONNATIONS
CONNATURAL
CONNATURALISE
CONNATURALISED
CONNATURALISES
CONNATURALISING
CONNATURALITIES
CONNATURALITY
CONNATURALIZE
CONNATURALIZED
CONNATURALIZES
CONNATURALIZING
CONNATURALLY
CONNATURALNESS
CONNATURES
CONNECTABLE
CONNECTEDLY
CONNECTEDNESS
CONNECTEDNESSES
CONNECTERS
CONNECTIBLE
CONNECTING
CONNECTION
CONNECTIONAL
CONNECTIONISM
CONNECTIONISMS
CONNECTIONS
CONNECTIVE
CONNECTIVELY
CONNECTIVES
CONNECTIVITIES
CONNECTIVITY
CONNECTORS
CONNEXIONAL

CONNEXIONS
CONNIPTION
CONNIPTIONS
CONNIVANCE
CONNIVANCES
CONNIVANCIES
CONNIVANCY
CONNIVENCE
CONNIVENCES
CONNIVENCIES
CONNIVENCY
CONNIVENTLY
CONNIVERIES
CONNIVINGLY
CONNOISSEUR
CONNOISSEURS
CONNOISSEURSHIP
CONNOTATED
CONNOTATES
CONNOTATING
CONNOTATION
CONNOTATIONAL
CONNOTATIONS
CONNOTATIVE
CONNOTATIVELY
CONNOTIVELY
CONNUBIALISM
CONNUBIALISMS
CONNUBIALITIES
CONNUBIALITY
CONNUBIALLY
CONNUMERATE
CONNUMERATED
CONNUMERATES
CONNUMERATING
CONNUMERATION
CONNUMERATIONS
CONOIDALLY
CONOIDICAL
CONOMINEES
CONOSCENTE
CONOSCENTI
CONQUERABLE
CONQUERABLENESS
CONQUERERS
CONQUERESS
CONQUERESSES
CONQUERING
CONQUERINGLY
CONQUERORS
CONQUISTADOR
CONQUISTADORES
CONQUISTADORS
CONSANGUINE
CONSANGUINEOUS
CONSANGUINITIES
CONSANGUINITY
CONSCIENCE
CONSCIENCELESS

CONSCIENCES
CONSCIENTIOUS
CONSCIENTIOUSLY
CONSCIENTISE
CONSCIENTISED
CONSCIENTISES
CONSCIENTISING
CONSCIENTIZE
CONSCIENTIZED
CONSCIENTIZES
CONSCIENTIZING
CONSCIONABLE
CONSCIONABLY
CONSCIOUSES
CONSCIOUSLY
CONSCIOUSNESS
CONSCIOUSNESSES
CONSCRIBED
CONSCRIBES
CONSCRIBING
CONSCRIPTED
CONSCRIPTING
CONSCRIPTION
CONSCRIPTIONAL
CONSCRIPTIONIST
CONSCRIPTIONS
CONSCRIPTS
CONSECRATE
CONSECRATED
CONSECRATEDNESS
CONSECRATES
CONSECRATING
CONSECRATION
CONSECRATIONS
CONSECRATIVE
CONSECRATOR
CONSECRATORS
CONSECRATORY
CONSECTANEOUS
CONSECTARIES
CONSECTARY
CONSECUTION
CONSECUTIONS
CONSECUTIVE
CONSECUTIVELY
CONSECUTIVENESS
CONSENESCENCE
CONSENESCENCES
CONSENESCENCIES
CONSENESCENCY
CONSENSION
CONSENSIONS
CONSENSUAL
CONSENSUALLY
CONSENSUSES
CONSENTANEITIES
CONSENTANEITY
CONSENTANEOUS
CONSENTANEOUSLY

CONSENTERS
CONSENTIENCE
CONSENTIENCES
CONSENTIENT
CONSENTING
CONSENTINGLY
CONSEQUENCE
CONSEQUENCED
CONSEQUENCES
CONSEQUENCING
CONSEQUENT
CONSEQUENTIAL
CONSEQUENTIALLY
CONSEQUENTLY
CONSEQUENTS
CONSERVABLE
CONSERVANCIES
CONSERVANCY
CONSERVANT
CONSERVATION
CONSERVATIONAL
CONSERVATIONIST
CONSERVATIONS
CONSERVATISE
CONSERVATISED
CONSERVATISES
CONSERVATISING
CONSERVATISM
CONSERVATISMS
CONSERVATIVE
CONSERVATIVELY
CONSERVATIVES
CONSERVATIZE
CONSERVATIZED
CONSERVATIZES
CONSERVATIZING
CONSERVATOIRE
CONSERVATOIRES
CONSERVATOR
CONSERVATORIA
CONSERVATORIAL
CONSERVATORIES
CONSERVATORIUM
CONSERVATORIUMS
CONSERVATORS
CONSERVATORSHIP
CONSERVATORY
CONSERVATRICES
CONSERVATRIX
CONSERVATRIXES
CONSERVERS
CONSERVING
CONSIDERABLE
CONSIDERABLES
CONSIDERABLY
CONSIDERANCE
CONSIDERANCES
CONSIDERATE
CONSIDERATELY

CONSIDERATENESS
CONSIDERATION
CONSIDERATIONS
CONSIDERATIVE
CONSIDERATIVELY
CONSIDERED
CONSIDERER
CONSIDERERS
CONSIDERING
CONSIDERINGLY
CONSIGLIERE
CONSIGLIERI
CONSIGNABLE
CONSIGNATION
CONSIGNATIONS
CONSIGNATORIES
CONSIGNATORY
CONSIGNEES
CONSIGNERS
CONSIGNIFIED
CONSIGNIFIES
CONSIGNIFY
CONSIGNIFYING
CONSIGNING
CONSIGNMENT
CONSIGNMENTS
CONSIGNORS
CONSILIENCE
CONSILIENCES
CONSILIENT
CONSIMILAR
CONSIMILARITIES
CONSIMILARITY
CONSIMILITIES
CONSIMILITUDE
CONSIMILITUDES
CONSIMILITY
CONSISTENCE
CONSISTENCES
CONSISTENCIES
CONSISTENCY
CONSISTENT
CONSISTENTLY
CONSISTING
CONSISTORIAL
CONSISTORIAN
CONSISTORIES
CONSISTORY
CONSOCIATE
CONSOCIATED
CONSOCIATES
CONSOCIATING
CONSOCIATION
CONSOCIATIONAL
CONSOCIATIONS
CONSOLABLE
CONSOLATED
CONSOLATES
CONSOLATING

CONSOLATION
CONSOLATIONS
CONSOLATORIES
CONSOLATORY
CONSOLATRICES
CONSOLATRIX
CONSOLATRIXES
CONSOLEMENT
CONSOLEMENTS
CONSOLIDATE
CONSOLIDATED
CONSOLIDATES
CONSOLIDATING
CONSOLIDATION
CONSOLIDATIONS
CONSOLIDATIVE
CONSOLIDATOR
CONSOLIDATORS
CONSOLINGLY
CONSONANCE
CONSONANCES
CONSONANCIES
CONSONANCY
CONSONANTAL
CONSONANTALLY
CONSONANTLY
CONSONANTS
CONSORTABLE
CONSORTERS
CONSORTIAL
CONSORTING
CONSORTISM
CONSORTISMS
CONSORTIUM
CONSORTIUMS
CONSPECIFIC
CONSPECIFICS
CONSPECTUITIES
CONSPECTUITY
CONSPECTUS
CONSPECTUSES
CONSPICUITIES
CONSPICUITY
CONSPICUOUS
CONSPICUOUSLY
CONSPICUOUSNESS
CONSPIRACIES
CONSPIRACY
CONSPIRANT
CONSPIRATION
CONSPIRATIONAL
CONSPIRATIONS
CONSPIRATOR
CONSPIRATORIAL
CONSPIRATORS
CONSPIRATORY
CONSPIRATRESS
CONSPIRATRESSES
CONSPIRERS

CONSPIRING
CONSPIRINGLY
CONSPURCATION
CONSPURCATIONS
CONSTABLES
CONSTABLESHIP
CONSTABLESHIPS
CONSTABLEWICK
CONSTABLEWICKS
CONSTABULARIES
CONSTABULARY
CONSTANCIES
CONSTANTAN
CONSTANTANS
CONSTANTLY
CONSTATATION
CONSTATATIONS
CONSTATING
CONSTATIVE
CONSTATIVES
CONSTELLATE
CONSTELLATED
CONSTELLATES
CONSTELLATING
CONSTELLATION
CONSTELLATIONAL
CONSTELLATIONS
CONSTELLATORY
CONSTERING
CONSTERNATE
CONSTERNATED
CONSTERNATES
CONSTERNATING
CONSTERNATION
CONSTERNATIONS
CONSTIPATE
CONSTIPATED
CONSTIPATES
CONSTIPATING
CONSTIPATION
CONSTIPATIONS
CONSTITUENCIES
CONSTITUENCY
CONSTITUENT
CONSTITUENTLY
CONSTITUENTS
CONSTITUTE
CONSTITUTED
CONSTITUTER
CONSTITUTERS
CONSTITUTES
CONSTITUTING
CONSTITUTION
CONSTITUTIONAL
CONSTITUTIONALS
CONSTITUTIONIST
CONSTITUTIONS
CONSTITUTIVE
CONSTITUTIVELY

CONSTITUTOR
CONSTITUTORS
CONSTRAINABLE
CONSTRAINED
CONSTRAINEDLY
CONSTRAINER
CONSTRAINERS
CONSTRAINING
CONSTRAINS
CONSTRAINT
CONSTRAINTS
CONSTRICTED
CONSTRICTING
CONSTRICTION
CONSTRICTIONS
CONSTRICTIVE
CONSTRICTIVELY
CONSTRICTOR
CONSTRICTORS
CONSTRICTS
CONSTRINGE
CONSTRINGED
CONSTRINGENCE
CONSTRINGENCES
CONSTRINGENCIES
CONSTRINGENCY
CONSTRINGENT
CONSTRINGES
CONSTRINGING
CONSTRUABILITY
CONSTRUABLE
CONSTRUALS
CONSTRUCTABLE
CONSTRUCTED
CONSTRUCTER
CONSTRUCTERS
CONSTRUCTIBLE
CONSTRUCTING
CONSTRUCTION
CONSTRUCTIONAL
CONSTRUCTIONISM
CONSTRUCTIONIST
CONSTRUCTIONS
CONSTRUCTIVE
CONSTRUCTIVELY
CONSTRUCTIVISM
CONSTRUCTIVISMS
CONSTRUCTIVIST
CONSTRUCTIVISTS
CONSTRUCTOR
CONSTRUCTORS
CONSTRUCTS
CONSTRUCTURE
CONSTRUCTURES
CONSTRUERS
CONSTRUING
CONSTUPRATE
CONSTUPRATED
CONSTUPRATES

CONSTUPRATING
CONSTUPRATION
CONSTUPRATIONS
CONSUBSIST
CONSUBSISTED
CONSUBSISTING
CONSUBSISTS
CONSUBSTANTIAL
CONSUBSTANTIATE
CONSUETUDE
CONSUETUDES
CONSUETUDINARY
CONSULAGES
CONSULATES
CONSULSHIP
CONSULSHIPS
CONSULTABLE
CONSULTANCIES
CONSULTANCY
CONSULTANT
CONSULTANTS
CONSULTANTSHIP
CONSULTANTSHIPS
CONSULTATION
CONSULTATIONS
CONSULTATIVE
CONSULTATIVELY
CONSULTATORY
CONSULTEES
CONSULTERS
CONSULTING
CONSULTIVE
CONSULTORS
CONSULTORY
CONSUMABLE
CONSUMABLES
CONSUMEDLY
CONSUMERISM
CONSUMERISMS
CONSUMERIST
CONSUMERISTIC
CONSUMERISTS
CONSUMERSHIP
CONSUMERSHIPS
CONSUMINGLY
CONSUMINGS
CONSUMMATE
CONSUMMATED
CONSUMMATELY
CONSUMMATES
CONSUMMATING
CONSUMMATION
CONSUMMATIONS
CONSUMMATIVE
CONSUMMATOR
CONSUMMATORS
CONSUMMATORY
CONSUMPTION
CONSUMPTIONS

CONSUMPTIVE
CONSUMPTIVELY
CONSUMPTIVENESS
CONSUMPTIVES
CONSUMPTIVITIES
CONSUMPTIVITY
CONTABESCENCE
CONTABESCENCES
CONTABESCENT
CONTACTABLE
CONTACTEES
CONTACTING
CONTACTORS
CONTACTUAL
CONTACTUALLY
CONTADINAS
CONTAGIONIST
CONTAGIONISTS
CONTAGIONS
CONTAGIOUS
CONTAGIOUSLY
CONTAGIOUSNESS
CONTAINABLE
CONTAINERBOARD
CONTAINERBOARDS
CONTAINERISE
CONTAINERISED
CONTAINERISES
CONTAINERISING
CONTAINERIZE
CONTAINERIZED
CONTAINERIZES
CONTAINERIZING
CONTAINERLESS
CONTAINERPORT
CONTAINERPORTS
CONTAINERS
CONTAINERSHIP
CONTAINERSHIPS
CONTAINING
CONTAINMENT
CONTAINMENTS
CONTAMINABLE
CONTAMINANT
CONTAMINANTS
CONTAMINATE
CONTAMINATED
CONTAMINATES
CONTAMINATING
CONTAMINATION
CONTAMINATIONS
CONTAMINATIVE
CONTAMINATOR
CONTAMINATORS
CONTANGOED
CONTANGOES
CONTANGOING
CONTEMNERS
CONTEMNIBLE

CONTEMNIBLY
CONTEMNING
CONTEMNORS
CONTEMPERATION
CONTEMPERATIONS
CONTEMPERATURE
CONTEMPERATURES
CONTEMPERED
CONTEMPERING
CONTEMPERS
CONTEMPLABLE
CONTEMPLANT
CONTEMPLANTS
CONTEMPLATE
CONTEMPLATED
CONTEMPLATES
CONTEMPLATING
CONTEMPLATION
CONTEMPLATIONS
CONTEMPLATIST
CONTEMPLATISTS
CONTEMPLATIVE
CONTEMPLATIVELY
CONTEMPLATIVES
CONTEMPLATOR
CONTEMPLATORS
CONTEMPORANEAN
CONTEMPORANEANS
CONTEMPORANEITY
CONTEMPORANEOUS
CONTEMPORARIES
CONTEMPORARILY
CONTEMPORARY
CONTEMPORISE
CONTEMPORISED
CONTEMPORISES
CONTEMPORISING
CONTEMPORIZE
CONTEMPORIZED
CONTEMPORIZES
CONTEMPORIZING
CONTEMPTIBILITY
CONTEMPTIBLE
CONTEMPTIBLY
CONTEMPTUOUS
CONTEMPTUOUSLY
CONTENDENT
CONTENDENTS
CONTENDERS
CONTENDING
CONTENDINGLY
CONTENDINGS
CONTENEMENT
CONTENEMENTS
CONTENTATION
CONTENTATIONS
CONTENTEDLY
CONTENTEDNESS
CONTENTEDNESSES

CONTENTING
CONTENTION
CONTENTIONS
CONTENTIOUS
CONTENTIOUSLY
CONTENTIOUSNESS
CONTENTLESS
CONTENTMENT
CONTENTMENTS
CONTERMINAL
CONTERMINALLY
CONTERMINANT
CONTERMINATE
CONTERMINOUS
CONTERMINOUSLY
CONTESSERATION
CONTESSERATIONS
CONTESTABILITY
CONTESTABLE
CONTESTABLENESS
CONTESTABLY
CONTESTANT
CONTESTANTS
CONTESTATION
CONTESTATIONS
CONTESTERS
CONTESTING
CONTESTINGLY
CONTEXTLESS
CONTEXTUAL
CONTEXTUALISE
CONTEXTUALISED
CONTEXTUALISES
CONTEXTUALISING
CONTEXTUALIZE
CONTEXTUALIZED
CONTEXTUALIZES
CONTEXTUALIZING
CONTEXTUALLY
CONTEXTURAL
CONTEXTURE
CONTEXTURES
CONTIGNATION
CONTIGNATIONS
CONTIGUITIES
CONTIGUITY
CONTIGUOUS
CONTIGUOUSLY
CONTIGUOUSNESS
CONTINENCE
CONTINENCES
CONTINENCIES
CONTINENCY
CONTINENTAL
CONTINENTALISM
CONTINENTALISMS
CONTINENTALIST
CONTINENTALISTS
CONTINENTALLY

CONTINENTALS
CONTINENTLY
CONTINENTS
CONTINGENCE
CONTINGENCES
CONTINGENCIES
CONTINGENCY
CONTINGENT
CONTINGENTLY
CONTINGENTS
CONTINUABLE
CONTINUALITIES
CONTINUALITY
CONTINUALLY
CONTINUALNESS
CONTINUALNESSES
CONTINUANCE
CONTINUANCES
CONTINUANT
CONTINUANTS
CONTINUATE
CONTINUATION
CONTINUATIONS
CONTINUATIVE
CONTINUATIVELY
CONTINUATIVES
CONTINUATOR
CONTINUATORS
CONTINUEDLY
CONTINUEDNESS
CONTINUEDNESSES
CONTINUERS
CONTINUING
CONTINUINGLY
CONTINUITIES
CONTINUITY
CONTINUOUS
CONTINUOUSLY
CONTINUOUSNESS
CONTINUUMS
CONTORNIATE
CONTORNIATES
CONTORTEDLY
CONTORTEDNESS
CONTORTEDNESSES
CONTORTING
CONTORTION
CONTORTIONAL
CONTORTIONATE
CONTORTIONED
CONTORTIONISM
CONTORTIONISMS
CONTORTIONIST
CONTORTIONISTIC
CONTORTIONISTS
CONTORTIONS
CONTORTIVE
CONTOURING
CONTRABAND

CONTRABANDISM
CONTRABANDISMS
CONTRABANDIST
CONTRABANDISTS
CONTRABANDS
CONTRABASS
CONTRABASSES
CONTRABASSI
CONTRABASSIST
CONTRABASSISTS
CONTRABASSO
CONTRABASSOON
CONTRABASSOONS
CONTRABASSOS
CONTRABBASSI
CONTRABBASSO
CONTRABBASSOS
CONTRACEPTION
CONTRACEPTIONS
CONTRACEPTIVE
CONTRACEPTIVES
CONTRACLOCKWISE
CONTRACTABILITY
CONTRACTABLE
CONTRACTED
CONTRACTEDLY
CONTRACTEDNESS
CONTRACTIBILITY
CONTRACTIBLE
CONTRACTIBLY
CONTRACTILE
CONTRACTILITIES
CONTRACTILITY
CONTRACTING
CONTRACTION
CONTRACTIONAL
CONTRACTIONARY
CONTRACTIONS
CONTRACTIVE
CONTRACTIVELY
CONTRACTIVENESS
CONTRACTOR
CONTRACTORS
CONTRACTUAL
CONTRACTUALLY
CONTRACTURAL
CONTRACTURE
CONTRACTURES
CONTRACYCLICAL
CONTRADANCE
CONTRADANCES
CONTRADICT
CONTRADICTABLE
CONTRADICTED
CONTRADICTER
CONTRADICTERS
CONTRADICTING
CONTRADICTION
CONTRADICTIONS

CONTRADICTIOUS
CONTRADICTIVE
CONTRADICTIVELY
CONTRADICTOR
CONTRADICTORIES
CONTRADICTORILY
CONTRADICTORS
CONTRADICTORY
CONTRADICTS
CONTRAFAGOTTO
CONTRAFAGOTTOS
CONTRAFLOW
CONTRAFLOWS
CONTRAGESTION
CONTRAGESTIONS
CONTRAGESTIVE
CONTRAGESTIVES
CONTRAHENT
CONTRAHENTS
CONTRAINDICANT
CONTRAINDICANTS
CONTRAINDICATE
CONTRAINDICATED
CONTRAINDICATES
CONTRALATERAL
CONTRALTOS
CONTRANATANT
CONTRAOCTAVE
CONTRAOCTAVES
CONTRAPLEX
CONTRAPOSITION
CONTRAPOSITIONS
CONTRAPOSITIVE
CONTRAPOSITIVES
CONTRAPPOSTO
CONTRAPPOSTOS
CONTRAPROP
CONTRAPROPELLER
CONTRAPROPS
CONTRAPTION
CONTRAPTIONS
CONTRAPUNTAL
CONTRAPUNTALIST
CONTRAPUNTALLY
CONTRAPUNTIST
CONTRAPUNTISTS
CONTRARIAN
CONTRARIANS
CONTRARIED
CONTRARIES
CONTRARIETIES
CONTRARIETY
CONTRARILY
CONTRARINESS
CONTRARINESSES
CONTRARIOUS
CONTRARIOUSLY
CONTRARIOUSNESS
CONTRARIWISE

CONTRARYING	CONTRIVEMENT	CONVALESCING	CONVERSANCY
CONTRASEXUAL	CONTRIVEMENTS	CONVECTING	CONVERSANT
CONTRASEXUALS	CONTRIVERS	CONVECTION	CONVERSANTLY
CONTRASTABLE	CONTRIVING	CONVECTIONAL	CONVERSATION
CONTRASTABLY	CONTROLLABILITY	CONVECTIONS	CONVERSATIONAL
CONTRASTED	CONTROLLABLE	CONVECTIVE	CONVERSATIONISM
CONTRASTING	CONTROLLABLY	CONVECTORS	CONVERSATIONIST
CONTRASTIVE	CONTROLLED	CONVENABLE	CONVERSATIONS
CONTRASTIVELY	CONTROLLER	CONVENANCE	CONVERSATIVE
CONTRATERRENE	CONTROLLERS	CONVENANCES	CONVERSAZIONE
CONTRAVALLATION	CONTROLLERSHIP	CONVENERSHIP	CONVERSAZIONES
CONTRAVENE	CONTROLLERSHIPS	CONVENERSHIPS	CONVERSAZIONI
CONTRAVENED	CONTROLLING	CONVENIENCE	CONVERSELY
CONTRAVENER	CONTROLMENT	CONVENIENCES	CONVERSERS
CONTRAVENERS	CONTROLMENTS	CONVENIENCIES	CONVERSING
CONTRAVENES	CONTROULED	CONVENIENCY	CONVERSION
CONTRAVENING	CONTROULING	CONVENIENT	CONVERSIONAL
CONTRAVENTION	CONTROVERSE	CONVENIENTLY	CONVERSIONARY
CONTRAVENTIONS	CONTROVERSES	CONVENORSHIP	CONVERSIONS
CONTRAYERVA	CONTROVERSIAL	CONVENORSHIPS	CONVERTAPLANE
CONTRAYERVAS	CONTROVERSIALLY	CONVENTICLE	CONVERTAPLANES
CONTRECOUP	CONTROVERSIES	CONVENTICLED	CONVERTEND
CONTRECOUPS	CONTROVERSY	CONVENTICLER	CONVERTENDS
CONTREDANCE	CONTROVERT	CONVENTICLERS	CONVERTERS
CONTREDANCES	CONTROVERTED	CONVENTICLES	CONVERTIBILITY
CONTREDANSE	CONTROVERTER	CONVENTICLING	CONVERTIBLE
CONTREDANSES	CONTROVERTERS	CONVENTING	CONVERTIBLENESS
CONTRETEMPS	CONTROVERTIBLE	CONVENTION	CONVERTIBLES
CONTRIBUTABLE	CONTROVERTIBLY	CONVENTIONAL	CONVERTIBLY
CONTRIBUTARIES	CONTROVERTING	CONVENTIONALISE	CONVERTING
CONTRIBUTARY	CONTROVERTIST	CONVENTIONALISM	CONVERTIPLANE
CONTRIBUTE	CONTROVERTISTS	CONVENTIONALIST	CONVERTIPLANES
CONTRIBUTED	CONTROVERTS	CONVENTIONALITY	CONVERTITE
CONTRIBUTES	CONTUBERNAL	CONVENTIONALIZE	CONVERTITES
CONTRIBUTING	CONTUBERNYAL	CONVENTIONALLY	CONVERTIVE
CONTRIBUTION	CONTUMACIES	CONVENTIONALS	CONVERTOPLANE
CONTRIBUTIONS	CONTUMACIOUS	CONVENTIONARY	CONVERTOPLANES
CONTRIBUTIVE	CONTUMACIOUSLY	CONVENTIONEER	CONVERTORS
CONTRIBUTIVELY	CONTUMACITIES	CONVENTIONEERS	CONVEXEDLY
CONTRIBUTOR	CONTUMACITY	CONVENTIONER	CONVEXITIES
CONTRIBUTORIES	CONTUMELIES	CONVENTIONERS	CONVEXNESS
CONTRIBUTORS	CONTUMELIOUS	CONVENTIONIST	CONVEXNESSES
CONTRIBUTORY	CONTUMELIOUSLY	CONVENTIONISTS	CONVEYABLE
CONTRISTATION	CONTUNDING	CONVENTIONS	CONVEYANCE
CONTRISTATIONS	CONTUSIONED	CONVENTUAL	CONVEYANCER
CONTRISTED	CONTUSIONS	CONVENTUALLY	CONVEYANCERS
CONTRISTING	CONUNDRUMS	CONVENTUALS	CONVEYANCES
CONTRITELY	CONURBATION	CONVERGENCE	CONVEYANCING
CONTRITENESS	CONURBATIONS	CONVERGENCES	CONVEYANCINGS
CONTRITENESSES	CONVALESCE	CONVERGENCIES	CONVEYORISATION
CONTRITION	CONVALESCED	CONVERGENCY	CONVEYORISE
CONTRITIONS	CONVALESCENCE	CONVERGENT	CONVEYORISED
CONTRITURATE	CONVALESCENCES	CONVERGING	CONVEYORISES
CONTRITURATED	CONVALESCENCIES	CONVERSABLE	CONVEYORISING
CONTRITURATES	CONVALESCENCY	CONVERSABLENESS	CONVEYORIZATION
CONTRITURATING	CONVALESCENT	CONVERSABLY	CONVEYORIZE
CONTRIVABLE	CONVALESCENTLY	CONVERSANCE	CONVEYORIZED
CONTRIVANCE	CONVALESCENTS	CONVERSANCES	CONVEYORIZES
CONTRIVANCES	CONVALESCES	CONVERSANCIES	CONVEYORIZING

CONVICINITIES	CONVULSIONISTS	COPARTNERING	COPRODUCING
CONVICINITY	CONVULSIONS	COPARTNERS	COPRODUCTION
CONVICTABLE	CONVULSIVE	COPARTNERSHIP	COPRODUCTIONS
CONVICTIBLE	CONVULSIVELY	COPARTNERSHIPS	COPRODUCTS
CONVICTING	CONVULSIVENESS	COPARTNERY	COPROLALIA
CONVICTION	COOKHOUSES	COPATRIOTS	COPROLALIAC
CONVICTIONAL	COOKSHACKS	COPAYMENTS	COPROLALIAS
CONVICTIONS	COOKSTOVES	COPESETTIC	COPROLITES
CONVICTISM	COOLHEADED	COPESTONES	COPROLITHS
CONVICTISMS	COOLHOUSES	COPINGSTONE	COPROLITIC
CONVICTIVE	COOLINGNESS	COPINGSTONES	COPROLOGIES
CONVICTIVELY	COOLINGNESSES	COPIOUSNESS	COPROMOTER
CONVINCEMENT	COOLNESSES	COPIOUSNESSES	COPROMOTERS
CONVINCEMENTS	COOMCEILED	COPLANARITIES	COPROPHAGAN
CONVINCERS	COONHOUNDS	COPLANARITY	COPROPHAGANS
CONVINCIBLE	COOPERAGES	COPLOTTING	COPROPHAGIC
CONVINCING	COOPERATED	COPOLYMERIC	COPROPHAGIES
CONVINCINGLY	COOPERATES	COPOLYMERISE	COPROPHAGIST
CONVINCINGNESS	COOPERATING	COPOLYMERISED	COPROPHAGISTS
CONVIVIALIST	COOPERATION	COPOLYMERISES	COPROPHAGOUS
CONVIVIALISTS	COOPERATIONIST	COPOLYMERISING	COPROPHAGY
CONVIVIALITIES	COOPERATIONISTS	COPOLYMERIZE	COPROPHILIA
CONVIVIALITY	COOPERATIONS	COPOLYMERIZED	COPROPHILIAC
CONVIVIALLY	COOPERATIVE	COPOLYMERIZES	COPROPHILIACS
CONVOCATED	COOPERATIVELY	COPOLYMERIZING	COPROPHILIAS
CONVOCATES	COOPERATIVENESS	COPOLYMERS	COPROPHILIC
CONVOCATING	COOPERATIVES	COPPERASES	COPROPHILOUS
CONVOCATION	COOPERATIVITIES	COPPERHEAD	COPROPRIETOR
CONVOCATIONAL	COOPERATIVITY	COPPERHEADS	COPROPRIETORS
CONVOCATIONIST	COOPERATOR	COPPERINGS	COPROSPERITIES
CONVOCATIONISTS	COOPERATORS	COPPERPLATE	COPROSPERITY
CONVOCATIONS	COOPERINGS	COPPERPLATES	COPROSTEROL
CONVOCATIVE	COOPTATION	COPPERSKIN	COPROSTEROLS
CONVOCATOR	COOPTATIONS	COPPERSKINS	COPSEWOODS
CONVOCATORS	COOPTATIVE	COPPERSMITH	COPUBLISHED
CONVOLUTED	COORDINANCE	COPPERSMITHS	COPUBLISHER
CONVOLUTEDLY	COORDINANCES	COPPERWORK	COPUBLISHERS
CONVOLUTEDNESS	COORDINATE	COPPERWORKS	COPUBLISHES
CONVOLUTELY	COORDINATED	COPPERWORM	COPUBLISHING
CONVOLUTES	COORDINATELY	COPPERWORMS	COPULATING
CONVOLUTING	COORDINATENESS	COPPICINGS	COPULATION
CONVOLUTION	COORDINATES	COPRESENCE	COPULATIONS
CONVOLUTIONAL	COORDINATING	COPRESENCES	COPULATIVE
CONVOLUTIONARY	COORDINATION	COPRESENTED	COPULATIVELY
CONVOLUTIONS	COORDINATIONS	COPRESENTING	COPULATIVES
CONVOLVING	COORDINATIVE	COPRESENTS	COPULATORY
CONVOLVULACEOUS	COORDINATOR	COPRESIDENT	COPURIFIED
CONVOLVULI	COORDINATORS	COPRESIDENTS	COPURIFIES
CONVOLVULUS	COPARCENARIES	COPRINCIPAL	COPURIFYING
CONVOLVULUSES	COPARCENARY	COPRINCIPALS	COPYCATTED
CONVULSANT	COPARCENER	COPRISONER	COPYCATTING
CONVULSANTS	COPARCENERIES	COPRISONERS	COPYEDITED
CONVULSIBLE	COPARCENERS	COPROCESSING	COPYEDITING
CONVULSING	COPARCENERY	COPROCESSOR	COPYGRAPHS
CONVULSION	COPARCENIES	COPROCESSORS	COPYHOLDER
CONVULSIONAL	COPARENTED	COPRODUCED	COPYHOLDERS
CONVULSIONARIES	COPARENTING	COPRODUCER	COPYREADER
CONVULSIONARY	COPARTNERED	COPRODUCERS	COPYREADERS
CONVULSIONIST	COPARTNERIES	COPRODUCES	COPYREADING

COPYREADINGS	CORDILLERA	CORKSCREWED	CORNUCOPIA
COPYRIGHTABLE	CORDILLERAN	CORKSCREWING	CORNUCOPIAN
COPYRIGHTED	CORDILLERAS	CORKSCREWS	CORNUCOPIAS
COPYRIGHTER	CORDLESSES	CORMOPHYTE	COROLLACEOUS
COPYRIGHTERS	CORDOCENTESES	CORMOPHYTES	COROLLARIES
COPYRIGHTING	CORDOCENTESIS	CORMOPHYTIC	COROLLIFLORAL
COPYRIGHTS	CORDONNETS	CORMORANTS	COROLLIFLOROUS
COPYTAKERS	CORDOTOMIES	CORNACEOUS	COROLLIFORM
COPYWRITER	CORDUROYED	CORNBORERS	COROMANDEL
COPYWRITERS	CORDUROYING	CORNBRAIDED	COROMANDELS
COPYWRITING	CORDWAINER	CORNBRAIDING	CORONAGRAPH
COPYWRITINGS	CORDWAINERIES	CORNBRAIDS	CORONAGRAPHS
COQUELICOT	CORDWAINERS	CORNBRANDIES	CORONARIES
COQUELICOTS	CORDWAINERY	CORNBRANDY	CORONATING
COQUETRIES	CORDYLINES	CORNBRASHES	CORONATION
COQUETTING	CORECIPIENT	CORNBREADS	CORONATIONS
COQUETTISH	CORECIPIENTS	CORNCOCKLE	CORONAVIRUS
COQUETTISHLY	COREDEEMED	CORNCOCKLES	CORONAVIRUSES
COQUETTISHNESS	COREDEEMING	CORNCRAKES	CORONERSHIP
COQUIMBITE	COREFERENTIAL	CORNEITISES	CORONERSHIPS
COQUIMBITES	COREGONINE	CORNELIANS	CORONOGRAPH
CORACIIFORM	CORELATING	CORNEMUSES	CORONOGRAPHS
CORADICATE	CORELATION	CORNERBACK	COROTATING
CORALBELLS	CORELATIONS	CORNERBACKS	COROTATION
CORALBERRIES	CORELATIVE	CORNERSTONE	COROTATIONS
CORALBERRY	CORELATIVES	CORNERSTONES	CORPORALES
CORALLACEOUS	CORELIGIONIST	CORNERWAYS	CORPORALITIES
CORALLIFEROUS	CORELIGIONISTS	CORNERWISE	CORPORALITY
CORALLIFORM	COREOPSISES	CORNETCIES	CORPORALLY
CORALLIGENOUS	COREPRESSOR	CORNETISTS	CORPORALSHIP
CORALLINES	COREPRESSORS	CORNETTINO	CORPORALSHIPS
CORALLITES	COREQUISITE	CORNETTINOS	CORPORASES
CORALLOIDAL	COREQUISITES	CORNETTIST	CORPORATELY
CORALROOTS	CORESEARCHER	CORNETTISTS	CORPORATENESS
CORALWORTS	CORESEARCHERS	CORNFIELDS	CORPORATENESSES
CORBEILLES	CORESIDENT	CORNFLAKES	CORPORATES
CORBELINGS	CORESIDENTIAL	CORNFLOURS	CORPORATION
CORBELLING	CORESIDENTS	CORNFLOWER	CORPORATIONS
CORBELLINGS	CORESPONDENT	CORNFLOWERS	CORPORATISE
CORBICULAE	CORESPONDENTS	CORNHUSKER	CORPORATISED
CORBICULATE	CORFHOUSES	CORNHUSKERS	CORPORATISES
CORDECTOMIES	CORIACEOUS	CORNHUSKING	CORPORATISING
CORDECTOMY	CORIANDERS	CORNHUSKINGS	CORPORATISM
CORDELLING	CORINTHIANISE	CORNICHONS	CORPORATISMS
CORDGRASSES	CORINTHIANISED	CORNICULATE	CORPORATIST
CORDIALISE	CORINTHIANISES	CORNICULUM	CORPORATISTS
CORDIALISED	CORINTHIANISING	CORNICULUMS	CORPORATIVE
CORDIALISES	CORINTHIANIZE	CORNIFEROUS	CORPORATIVISM
CORDIALISING	CORINTHIANIZED	CORNIFICATION	CORPORATIVISMS
CORDIALITIES	CORINTHIANIZES	CORNIFICATIONS	CORPORATIZE
CORDIALITY	CORINTHIANIZING	CORNIFYING	CORPORATIZED
CORDIALIZE	CORIVALLED	CORNIGEROUS	CORPORATIZES
CORDIALIZED	CORIVALLING	CORNINESSES	CORPORATIZING
CORDIALIZES	CORIVALRIES	CORNOPEANS	CORPORATOR
CORDIALIZING	CORIVALSHIP	CORNROWING	CORPORATORS
CORDIALNESS	CORIVALSHIPS	CORNSTALKS	CORPOREALISE
CORDIALNESSES	CORKBOARDS	CORNSTARCH	CORPOREALISED
CORDIERITE	CORKBORERS	CORNSTARCHES	CORPOREALISES
CORDIERITES	CORKINESSES	CORNSTONES	CORPOREALISING

CORPOREALISM
CORPOREALISMS
CORPOREALIST
CORPOREALISTS
CORPOREALITIES
CORPOREALITY
CORPOREALIZE
CORPOREALIZED
CORPOREALIZES
CORPOREALIZING
CORPOREALLY
CORPOREALNESS
CORPOREALNESSES
CORPOREITIES
CORPOREITY
CORPORIFICATION
CORPORIFIED
CORPORIFIES
CORPORIFYING
CORPOSANTS
CORPULENCE
CORPULENCES
CORPULENCIES
CORPULENCY
CORPULENTLY
CORPUSCLES
CORPUSCULAR
CORPUSCULARIAN
CORPUSCULARIANS
CORPUSCULARITY
CORPUSCULE
CORPUSCULES
CORRALLING
CORRASIONS
CORRECTABLE
CORRECTEST
CORRECTIBLE
CORRECTING
CORRECTION
CORRECTIONAL
CORRECTIONER
CORRECTIONERS
CORRECTIONS
CORRECTITUDE
CORRECTITUDES
CORRECTIVE
CORRECTIVELY
CORRECTIVES
CORRECTNESS
CORRECTNESSES
CORRECTORS
CORRECTORY
CORREGIDOR
CORREGIDORS
CORRELATABLE
CORRELATED
CORRELATES
CORRELATING
CORRELATION

CORRELATIONAL
CORRELATIONS
CORRELATIVE
CORRELATIVELY
CORRELATIVENESS
CORRELATIVES
CORRELATIVITIES
CORRELATIVITY
CORRELATOR
CORRELATORS
CORRELIGIONIST
CORRELIGIONISTS
CORREPTION
CORREPTIONS
CORRESPOND
CORRESPONDED
CORRESPONDENCE
CORRESPONDENCES
CORRESPONDENCY
CORRESPONDENT
CORRESPONDENTLY
CORRESPONDENTS
CORRESPONDING
CORRESPONDINGLY
CORRESPONDS
CORRESPONSIVE
CORRIGENDA
CORRIGENDUM
CORRIGENTS
CORRIGIBILITIES
CORRIGIBILITY
CORRIGIBLE
CORRIGIBLY
CORRIVALLED
CORRIVALLING
CORRIVALRIES
CORRIVALRY
CORRIVALSHIP
CORRIVALSHIPS
CORROBORABLE
CORROBORANT
CORROBORATE
CORROBORATED
CORROBORATES
CORROBORATING
CORROBORATION
CORROBORATIONS
CORROBORATIVE
CORROBORATIVELY
CORROBORATIVES
CORROBORATOR
CORROBORATORS
CORROBORATORY
CORROBOREE
CORROBOREED
CORROBOREEING
CORROBOREES
CORRODANTS
CORRODENTS

CORRODIBILITIES
CORRODIBILITY
CORRODIBLE
CORROSIBILITIES
CORROSIBILITY
CORROSIBLE
CORROSIONS
CORROSIVELY
CORROSIVENESS
CORROSIVENESSES
CORROSIVES
CORRUGATED
CORRUGATES
CORRUGATING
CORRUGATION
CORRUGATIONS
CORRUGATOR
CORRUGATORS
CORRUPTERS
CORRUPTEST
CORRUPTIBILITY
CORRUPTIBLE
CORRUPTIBLENESS
CORRUPTIBLY
CORRUPTING
CORRUPTION
CORRUPTIONIST
CORRUPTIONISTS
CORRUPTIONS
CORRUPTIVE
CORRUPTIVELY
CORRUPTNESS
CORRUPTNESSES
CORRUPTORS
CORSELETTE
CORSELETTES
CORSETIERE
CORSETIERES
CORSETIERS
CORSETRIES
CORTICALLY
CORTICATED
CORTICATION
CORTICATIONS
CORTICOIDS
CORTICOLOUS
CORTICOSTEROID
CORTICOSTEROIDS
CORTICOSTERONE
CORTICOSTERONES
CORTICOTROPHIC
CORTICOTROPHIN
CORTICOTROPHINS
CORTICOTROPIC
CORTICOTROPIN
CORTICOTROPINS
CORTISONES
CORUSCATED
CORUSCATES

CORUSCATING
CORUSCATION
CORUSCATIONS
CORVETTING
CORYBANTES
CORYBANTIC
CORYBANTISM
CORYBANTISMS
CORYDALINE
CORYDALINES
CORYDALISES
CORYLOPSES
CORYLOPSIS
CORYMBOSELY
CORYNEBACTERIA
CORYNEBACTERIAL
CORYNEBACTERIUM
CORYNEFORM
CORYPHAEUS
CORYPHENES
COSCINOMANCIES
COSCINOMANCY
COSCRIPTED
COSCRIPTING
COSEISMALS
COSEISMICS
COSENTIENT
COSHERINGS
COSIGNATORIES
COSIGNATORY
COSIGNIFICATIVE
COSINESSES
COSMECEUTICAL
COSMECEUTICALS
COSMETICAL
COSMETICALLY
COSMETICIAN
COSMETICIANS
COSMETICISE
COSMETICISED
COSMETICISES
COSMETICISING
COSMETICISM
COSMETICISMS
COSMETICIZE
COSMETICIZED
COSMETICIZES
COSMETICIZING
COSMETICOLOGIES
COSMETICOLOGY
COSMETOLOGIES
COSMETOLOGIST
COSMETOLOGISTS
COSMETOLOGY
COSMICALLY
COSMOCHEMICAL
COSMOCHEMIST
COSMOCHEMISTRY
COSMOCHEMISTS

COSMOCRATIC
COSMOCRATS
COSMODROME
COSMODROMES
COSMOGENIC
COSMOGENIES
COSMOGONAL
COSMOGONIC
COSMOGONICAL
COSMOGONIES
COSMOGONIST
COSMOGONISTS
COSMOGRAPHER
COSMOGRAPHERS
COSMOGRAPHIC
COSMOGRAPHICAL
COSMOGRAPHIES
COSMOGRAPHIST
COSMOGRAPHISTS
COSMOGRAPHY
COSMOLATRIES
COSMOLATRY
COSMOLINED
COSMOLINES
COSMOLINING
COSMOLOGIC
COSMOLOGICAL
COSMOLOGICALLY
COSMOLOGIES
COSMOLOGIST
COSMOLOGISTS
COSMONAUTICS
COSMONAUTS
COSMOPLASTIC
COSMOPOLIS
COSMOPOLISES
COSMOPOLITAN
COSMOPOLITANISM
COSMOPOLITANS
COSMOPOLITE
COSMOPOLITES
COSMOPOLITIC
COSMOPOLITICAL
COSMOPOLITICS
COSMOPOLITISM
COSMOPOLITISMS
COSMORAMAS
COSMORAMIC
COSMOSPHERE
COSMOSPHERES
COSMOTHEISM
COSMOTHEISMS
COSMOTHETIC
COSMOTHETICAL
COSMOTRONS
COSPONSORED
COSPONSORING
COSPONSORS
COSPONSORSHIP

COSPONSORSHIPS
COSTALGIAS
COSTARDMONGER
COSTARDMONGERS
COSTARRING
COSTEANING
COSTEANINGS
COSTERMONGER
COSTERMONGERS
COSTIVENESS
COSTIVENESSES
COSTLESSLY
COSTLINESS
COSTLINESSES
COSTMARIES
COSTOTOMIES
COSTUMERIES
COSTUMIERS
COSURFACTANT
COSURFACTANTS
COTANGENTIAL
COTANGENTS
COTELETTES
COTEMPORANEOUS
COTEMPORARY
COTENANCIES
COTERMINOUS
COTERMINOUSLY
COTILLIONS
COTONEASTER
COTONEASTERS
COTRANSDUCE
COTRANSDUCED
COTRANSDUCES
COTRANSDUCING
COTRANSDUCTION
COTRANSDUCTIONS
COTRANSFER
COTRANSFERS
COTRANSPORT
COTRANSPORTED
COTRANSPORTING
COTRANSPORTS
COTRUSTEES
COTTABUSES
COTTAGINGS
COTTERLESS
COTTIERISM
COTTIERISMS
COTTONADES
COTTONMOUTH
COTTONMOUTHS
COTTONOCRACIES
COTTONOCRACY
COTTONSEED
COTTONSEEDS
COTTONTAIL
COTTONTAILS
COTTONWEED

COTTONWEEDS
COTTONWOOD
COTTONWOODS
COTURNIXES
COTYLEDONAL
COTYLEDONARY
COTYLEDONOID
COTYLEDONOUS
COTYLEDONS
COTYLIFORM
COTYLOIDAL
COTYLOIDALS
COTYLOSAUR
COTYLOSAURS
COUCHETTES
COULIBIACA
COULIBIACAS
COULIBIACS
COULOMBMETER
COULOMBMETERS
COULOMETER
COULOMETERS
COULOMETRIC
COULOMETRICALLY
COULOMETRIES
COULOMETRY
COUMARILIC
COUMARONES
COUNCILLOR
COUNCILLORS
COUNCILLORSHIP
COUNCILLORSHIPS
COUNCILMAN
COUNCILMANIC
COUNCILMEN
COUNCILORS
COUNCILORSHIP
COUNCILORSHIPS
COUNCILWOMAN
COUNCILWOMEN
COUNSELABLE
COUNSELEES
COUNSELING
COUNSELINGS
COUNSELLABLE
COUNSELLED
COUNSELLING
COUNSELLINGS
COUNSELLOR
COUNSELLORS
COUNSELLORSHIP
COUNSELLORSHIPS
COUNSELORS
COUNSELORSHIP
COUNSELORSHIPS
COUNTABILITIES
COUNTABILITY
COUNTBACKS
COUNTDOWNS

COUNTENANCE
COUNTENANCED
COUNTENANCER
COUNTENANCERS
COUNTENANCES
COUNTENANCING
COUNTERACT
COUNTERACTED
COUNTERACTING
COUNTERACTION
COUNTERACTIONS
COUNTERACTIVE
COUNTERACTIVELY
COUNTERACTS
COUNTERAGENT
COUNTERAGENTS
COUNTERARGUE
COUNTERARGUED
COUNTERARGUES
COUNTERARGUING
COUNTERARGUMENT
COUNTERASSAULT
COUNTERASSAULTS
COUNTERATTACK
COUNTERATTACKED
COUNTERATTACKER
COUNTERATTACKS
COUNTERBALANCE
COUNTERBALANCED
COUNTERBALANCES
COUNTERBASE
COUNTERBASES
COUNTERBID
COUNTERBIDDER
COUNTERBIDDERS
COUNTERBIDS
COUNTERBLAST
COUNTERBLASTS
COUNTERBLOCKADE
COUNTERBLOW
COUNTERBLOWS
COUNTERBLUFF
COUNTERBLUFFS
COUNTERBOND
COUNTERBONDS
COUNTERBORE
COUNTERBORED
COUNTERBORES
COUNTERBORING
COUNTERBRACE
COUNTERBRACED
COUNTERBRACES
COUNTERBRACING
COUNTERBUFF
COUNTERBUFFED
COUNTERBUFFING
COUNTERBUFFS
COUNTERCAMPAIGN
COUNTERCHANGE

COUNTERCHANGED	COUNTERFOILS	COUNTERPACE	COUNTERPUNCHER
COUNTERCHANGES	COUNTERFORCE	COUNTERPACES	COUNTERPUNCHERS
COUNTERCHANGING	COUNTERFORCES	COUNTERPANE	COUNTERPUNCHES
COUNTERCHARGE	COUNTERFORT	COUNTERPANES	COUNTERPUNCHING
COUNTERCHARGED	COUNTERFORTS	COUNTERPART	COUNTERQUESTION
COUNTERCHARGES	COUNTERGLOW	COUNTERPARTIES	COUNTERRAID
COUNTERCHARGING	COUNTERGLOWS	COUNTERPARTS	COUNTERRAIDS
COUNTERCHARM	COUNTERGUERILLA	COUNTERPARTY	COUNTERRALLIED
COUNTERCHARMED	COUNTERIMAGE	COUNTERPEISE	COUNTERRALLIES
COUNTERCHARMING	COUNTERIMAGES	COUNTERPEISED	COUNTERRALLY
COUNTERCHARMS	COUNTERING	COUNTERPEISES	COUNTERRALLYING
COUNTERCHECK	COUNTERINSTANCE	COUNTERPEISING	COUNTERREACTION
COUNTERCHECKED	COUNTERION	COUNTERPETITION	COUNTERREFORM
COUNTERCHECKING	COUNTERIONS	COUNTERPICKET	COUNTERREFORMER
COUNTERCHECKS	COUNTERIRRITANT	COUNTERPICKETED	COUNTERREFORMS
COUNTERCLAIM	COUNTERLIGHT	COUNTERPICKETS	COUNTERRESPONSE
COUNTERCLAIMANT	COUNTERLIGHTS	COUNTERPLAN	COUNTERSANK
COUNTERCLAIMED	COUNTERMAN	COUNTERPLANS	COUNTERSCARP
COUNTERCLAIMING	COUNTERMAND	COUNTERPLAY	COUNTERSCARPS
COUNTERCLAIMS	COUNTERMANDABLE	COUNTERPLAYER	COUNTERSEAL
COUNTERCOUP	COUNTERMANDED	COUNTERPLAYERS	COUNTERSEALED
COUNTERCOUPS	COUNTERMANDING	COUNTERPLAYS	COUNTERSEALING
COUNTERCRIES	COUNTERMANDS	COUNTERPLEA	COUNTERSEALS
COUNTERCRY	COUNTERMARCH	COUNTERPLEAD	COUNTERSHADING
COUNTERCULTURAL	COUNTERMARCHED	COUNTERPLEADED	COUNTERSHADINGS
COUNTERCULTURE	COUNTERMARCHES	COUNTERPLEADING	COUNTERSHAFT
COUNTERCULTURES	COUNTERMARCHING	COUNTERPLEADS	COUNTERSHAFTS
COUNTERCURRENT	COUNTERMARK	COUNTERPLEAS	COUNTERSHOT
COUNTERCURRENTS	COUNTERMARKS	COUNTERPLED	COUNTERSHOTS
COUNTERCYCLICAL	COUNTERMEASURE	COUNTERPLOT	COUNTERSIGN
COUNTERDEMAND	COUNTERMEASURES	COUNTERPLOTS	COUNTERSIGNED
COUNTERDEMANDS	COUNTERMELODIES	COUNTERPLOTTED	COUNTERSIGNING
COUNTERDRAW	COUNTERMELODY	COUNTERPLOTTING	COUNTERSIGNS
COUNTERDRAWING	COUNTERMEMO	COUNTERPLOY	COUNTERSINK
COUNTERDRAWN	COUNTERMEMOS	COUNTERPLOYS	COUNTERSINKING
COUNTERDRAWS	COUNTERMEN	COUNTERPOINT	COUNTERSINKS
COUNTERDREW	COUNTERMINE	COUNTERPOINTED	COUNTERSNIPER
COUNTEREFFORT	COUNTERMINED	COUNTERPOINTING	COUNTERSNIPERS
COUNTEREFFORTS	COUNTERMINES	COUNTERPOINTS	COUNTERSPELL
COUNTEREVIDENCE	COUNTERMINING	COUNTERPOISE	COUNTERSPELLS
COUNTEREXAMPLE	COUNTERMOTION	COUNTERPOISED	COUNTERSPIES
COUNTEREXAMPLES	COUNTERMOTIONS	COUNTERPOISES	COUNTERSPY
COUNTERFACTUAL	COUNTERMOVE	COUNTERPOISING	COUNTERSPYING
COUNTERFACTUALS	COUNTERMOVED	COUNTERPOSE	COUNTERSPYINGS
COUNTERFECT	COUNTERMOVEMENT	COUNTERPOSED	COUNTERSTAIN
COUNTERFEISANCE	COUNTERMOVES	COUNTERPOSES	COUNTERSTAINED
COUNTERFEIT	COUNTERMOVING	COUNTERPOSING	COUNTERSTAINING
COUNTERFEITED	COUNTERMURE	COUNTERPOWER	COUNTERSTAINS
COUNTERFEITER	COUNTERMURED	COUNTERPOWERS	COUNTERSTATE
COUNTERFEITERS	COUNTERMURES	COUNTERPRESSURE	COUNTERSTATED
COUNTERFEITING	COUNTERMURING	COUNTERPROJECT	COUNTERSTATES
COUNTERFEITLY	COUNTERMYTH	COUNTERPROJECTS	COUNTERSTATING
COUNTERFEITS	COUNTERMYTHS	COUNTERPROOF	COUNTERSTEP
COUNTERFESAUNCE	COUNTEROFFER	COUNTERPROOFS	COUNTERSTEPS
COUNTERFIRE	COUNTEROFFERS	COUNTERPROPOSAL	COUNTERSTRATEGY
COUNTERFIRES	COUNTERORDER	COUNTERPROTEST	COUNTERSTREAM
COUNTERFLOW	COUNTERORDERED	COUNTERPROTESTS	COUNTERSTREAMS
COUNTERFLOWS	COUNTERORDERING	COUNTERPUNCH	COUNTERSTRICKEN
COUNTERFOIL	COUNTERORDERS	COUNTERPUNCHED	COUNTERSTRIKE

COUNTERSTRIKES
COUNTERSTRIKING
COUNTERSTROKE
COUNTERSTROKES
COUNTERSTRUCK
COUNTERSTYLE
COUNTERSTYLES
COUNTERSUBJECT
COUNTERSUBJECTS
COUNTERSUE
COUNTERSUED
COUNTERSUES
COUNTERSUING
COUNTERSUIT
COUNTERSUITS
COUNTERSUNK
COUNTERTACTIC
COUNTERTACTICS
COUNTERTENDENCY
COUNTERTENOR
COUNTERTENORS
COUNTERTERROR
COUNTERTERRORS
COUNTERTHREAT
COUNTERTHREATS
COUNTERTHRUST
COUNTERTHRUSTS
COUNTERTOP
COUNTERTOPS
COUNTERTRADE
COUNTERTRADED
COUNTERTRADES
COUNTERTRADING
COUNTERTREND
COUNTERTRENDS
COUNTERTYPE
COUNTERTYPES
COUNTERVAIL
COUNTERVAILABLE
COUNTERVAILED
COUNTERVAILING
COUNTERVAILS
COUNTERVIEW
COUNTERVIEWS
COUNTERVIOLENCE
COUNTERWEIGH
COUNTERWEIGHED
COUNTERWEIGHING
COUNTERWEIGHS
COUNTERWEIGHT
COUNTERWEIGHTED
COUNTERWEIGHTS
COUNTERWORD
COUNTERWORDS
COUNTERWORK
COUNTERWORKED
COUNTERWORKER
COUNTERWORKERS
COUNTERWORKING

COUNTERWORKS
COUNTERWORLD
COUNTERWORLDS
COUNTESSES
COUNTINGHOUSE
COUNTINGHOUSES
COUNTLESSLY
COUNTLINES
COUNTRIFIED
COUNTROLLED
COUNTROLLING
COUNTRYFIED
COUNTRYISH
COUNTRYMAN
COUNTRYMEN
COUNTRYSEAT
COUNTRYSEATS
COUNTRYSIDE
COUNTRYSIDES
COUNTRYWIDE
COUNTRYWOMAN
COUNTRYWOMEN
COUNTSHIPS
COUPLEDOMS
COUPLEMENT
COUPLEMENTS
COUPONINGS
COURAGEFUL
COURAGEOUS
COURAGEOUSLY
COURAGEOUSNESS
COURANTOES
COURBARILS
COURBETTES
COURGETTES
COURIERING
COURSEBOOK
COURSEBOOKS
COURSEWARE
COURSEWARES
COURSEWORK
COURSEWORKS
COURTCRAFT
COURTCRAFTS
COURTEOUSLY
COURTEOUSNESS
COURTEOUSNESSES
COURTESANS
COURTESIED
COURTESIES
COURTESYING
COURTEZANS
COURTHOUSE
COURTHOUSES
COURTIERISM
COURTIERISMS
COURTIERLIKE
COURTIERLY
COURTLIEST

COURTLINESS
COURTLINESSES
COURTLINGS
COURTMARTIALLED
COURTROOMS
COURTSHIPS
COURTSIDES
COURTYARDS
COUSCOUSES
COUSCOUSOU
COUSCOUSOUS
COUSINAGES
COUSINHOOD
COUSINHOODS
COUSINRIES
COUSINSHIP
COUSINSHIPS
COUTURIERE
COUTURIERES
COUTURIERS
COVALENCES
COVALENCIES
COVALENTLY
COVARIANCE
COVARIANCES
COVARIANTS
COVARIATES
COVARIATION
COVARIATIONS
COVELLINES
COVELLITES
COVENANTAL
COVENANTALLY
COVENANTED
COVENANTEE
COVENANTEES
COVENANTER
COVENANTERS
COVENANTING
COVENANTOR
COVENANTORS
COVERALLED
COVERMOUNT
COVERMOUNTED
COVERMOUNTING
COVERMOUNTS
COVERSINES
COVERSLIPS
COVERTNESS
COVERTNESSES
COVERTURES
COVETINGLY
COVETIVENESS
COVETIVENESSES
COVETOUSLY
COVETOUSNESS
COVETOUSNESSES
COWARDICES
COWARDLINESS

COWARDLINESSES
COWARDRIES
COWARDSHIP
COWARDSHIPS
COWBERRIES
COWCATCHER
COWCATCHERS
COWERINGLY
COWFEEDERS
COWFETERIA
COWFETERIAS
COWGRASSES
COWLSTAFFS
COWLSTAVES
COWPUNCHER
COWPUNCHERS
COXCOMBICAL
COXCOMBICALITY
COXCOMBICALLY
COXCOMBRIES
COXCOMICAL
COXINESSES
COXSWAINED
COXSWAINING
COYISHNESS
COYISHNESSES
COYOTILLOS
COZINESSES
CRABAPPLES
CRABBEDNESS
CRABBEDNESSES
CRABBINESS
CRABBINESSES
CRABEATERS
CRABGRASSES
CRABSTICKS
CRACKAJACK
CRACKAJACKS
CRACKBACKS
CRACKBERRIES
CRACKBERRY
CRACKBRAIN
CRACKBRAINED
CRACKBRAINS
CRACKDOWNS
CRACKERJACK
CRACKERJACKS
CRACKHEADS
CRACKLEWARE
CRACKLEWARES
CRACKLIEST
CRACKLINGS
CRACOVIENNE
CRACOVIENNES
CRADLESONG
CRADLESONGS
CRADLEWALK
CRADLEWALKS
CRAFTINESS

CRAFTINESSES
CRAFTMANSHIP
CRAFTMANSHIPS
CRAFTSMANLIKE
CRAFTSMANLY
CRAFTSMANSHIP
CRAFTSMANSHIPS
CRAFTSPEOPLE
CRAFTSPERSON
CRAFTSPERSONS
CRAFTSWOMAN
CRAFTSWOMEN
CRAFTWORKS
CRAGGEDNESS
CRAGGEDNESSES
CRAGGINESS
CRAGGINESSES
CRAIGFLUKE
CRAIGFLUKES
CRAKEBERRIES
CRAKEBERRY
CRAMBOCLINK
CRAMBOCLINKS
CRAMOISIES
CRAMPBARKS
CRAMPFISHES
CRAMPONING
CRANBERRIES
CRANEFLIES
CRANESBILL
CRANESBILLS
CRANIECTOMIES
CRANIECTOMY
CRANIOCEREBRAL
CRANIOFACIAL
CRANIOGNOMIES
CRANIOGNOMY
CRANIOLOGICAL
CRANIOLOGICALLY
CRANIOLOGIES
CRANIOLOGIST
CRANIOLOGISTS
CRANIOLOGY
CRANIOMETER
CRANIOMETERS
CRANIOMETRIC
CRANIOMETRICAL
CRANIOMETRIES
CRANIOMETRIST
CRANIOMETRISTS
CRANIOMETRY
CRANIOPAGI
CRANIOPAGUS
CRANIOSACRAL
CRANIOSCOPIES
CRANIOSCOPIST
CRANIOSCOPISTS
CRANIOSCOPY
CRANIOTOMIES

CRANIOTOMY
CRANKCASES
CRANKHANDLE
CRANKHANDLES
CRANKINESS
CRANKINESSES
CRANKNESSES
CRANKSHAFT
CRANKSHAFTS
CRANREUCHS
CRAPEHANGER
CRAPEHANGERS
CRAPEHANGING
CRAPEHANGINGS
CRAPSHOOTER
CRAPSHOOTERS
CRAPSHOOTS
CRAPULENCE
CRAPULENCES
CRAPULENTLY
CRAPULOSITIES
CRAPULOSITY
CRAPULOUSLY
CRAPULOUSNESS
CRAPULOUSNESSES
CRAQUELURE
CRAQUELURES
CRASHINGLY
CRASHLANDED
CRASHLANDING
CRASHLANDS
CRASHWORTHINESS
CRASHWORTHY
CRASSAMENTA
CRASSAMENTUM
CRASSITUDE
CRASSITUDES
CRASSNESSES
CRASSULACEAN
CRASSULACEOUS
CRATERIFORM
CRATERINGS
CRATERLESS
CRATERLETS
CRATERLIKE
CRAUNCHABLE
CRAUNCHIER
CRAUNCHIEST
CRAUNCHINESS
CRAUNCHINESSES
CRAUNCHING
CRAVATTING
CRAVENNESS
CRAVENNESSES
CRAWDADDIES
CRAWFISHED
CRAWFISHES
CRAWFISHING
CRAWLINGLY

CRAYFISHES
CRAYONISTS
CRAZINESSES
CRAZYWEEDS
CREAKINESS
CREAKINESSES
CREAKINGLY
CREAMERIES
CREAMINESS
CREAMINESSES
CREAMPUFFS
CREAMWARES
CREASELESS
CREASOTING
CREATIANISM
CREATIANISMS
CREATININE
CREATININES
CREATIONAL
CREATIONISM
CREATIONISMS
CREATIONIST
CREATIONISTIC
CREATIONISTS
CREATIVELY
CREATIVENESS
CREATIVENESSES
CREATIVITIES
CREATIVITY
CREATORSHIP
CREATORSHIPS
CREATRESSES
CREATRIXES
CREATUREHOOD
CREATUREHOODS
CREATURELINESS
CREATURELY
CREATURESHIP
CREATURESHIPS
CREDENTIAL
CREDENTIALED
CREDENTIALING
CREDENTIALISM
CREDENTIALISMS
CREDENTIALLED
CREDENTIALLING
CREDENTIALS
CREDIBILITIES
CREDIBILITY
CREDIBLENESS
CREDIBLENESSES
CREDITABILITIES
CREDITABILITY
CREDITABLE
CREDITABLENESS
CREDITABLY
CREDITLESS
CREDITWORTHY
CREDULITIES

CREDULOUSLY
CREDULOUSNESS
CREDULOUSNESSES
CREEPINESS
CREEPINESSES
CREEPINGLY
CREEPMOUSE
CREESHIEST
CREMAILLERE
CREMAILLERES
CREMASTERS
CREMATIONISM
CREMATIONISMS
CREMATIONIST
CREMATIONISTS
CREMATIONS
CREMATORIA
CREMATORIAL
CREMATORIES
CREMATORIUM
CREMATORIUMS
CREMOCARPS
CRENATIONS
CRENATURES
CRENELATED
CRENELATES
CRENELATING
CRENELATION
CRENELATIONS
CRENELLATE
CRENELLATED
CRENELLATES
CRENELLATING
CRENELLATION
CRENELLATIONS
CRENELLING
CRENULATED
CRENULATION
CRENULATIONS
CREOLISATION
CREOLISATIONS
CREOLISING
CREOLIZATION
CREOLIZATIONS
CREOLIZING
CREOPHAGIES
CREOPHAGOUS
CREOSOTING
CREPEHANGER
CREPEHANGERS
CREPEHANGING
CREPEHANGINGS
CREPINESSES
CREPITATED
CREPITATES
CREPITATING
CREPITATION
CREPITATIONS
CREPITATIVE

CREPITUSES
CREPOLINES
CREPUSCLES
CREPUSCULAR
CREPUSCULE
CREPUSCULES
CREPUSCULOUS
CRESCENDOED
CRESCENDOES
CRESCENDOING
CRESCENDOS
CRESCENTADE
CRESCENTADES
CRESCENTED
CRESCENTIC
CRESCIVELY
CRESCOGRAPH
CRESCOGRAPHS
CRESTFALLEN
CRESTFALLENLY
CRESTFALLENNESS
CRETACEOUS
CRETACEOUSES
CRETACEOUSLY
CRETINISED
CRETINISES
CRETINISING
CRETINISMS
CRETINIZED
CRETINIZES
CRETINIZING
CRETINOIDS
CREVASSING
CREWELISTS
CREWELLERIES
CREWELLERY
CREWELLING
CREWELWORK
CREWELWORKS
CRIBRATION
CRIBRATIONS
CRIBRIFORM
CRICKETERS
CRICKETING
CRICKETINGS
CRIMEWAVES
CRIMINALESE
CRIMINALESES
CRIMINALISATION
CRIMINALISE
CRIMINALISED
CRIMINALISES
CRIMINALISING
CRIMINALIST
CRIMINALISTICS
CRIMINALISTS
CRIMINALITIES
CRIMINALITY
CRIMINALIZATION

CRIMINALIZE
CRIMINALIZED
CRIMINALIZES
CRIMINALIZING
CRIMINALLY
CRIMINATED
CRIMINATES
CRIMINATING
CRIMINATION
CRIMINATIONS
CRIMINATIVE
CRIMINATOR
CRIMINATORS
CRIMINATORY
CRIMINOGENIC
CRIMINOLOGIC
CRIMINOLOGICAL
CRIMINOLOGIES
CRIMINOLOGIST
CRIMINOLOGISTS
CRIMINOLOGY
CRIMINOUSNESS
CRIMINOUSNESSES
CRIMSONING
CRIMSONNESS
CRIMSONNESSES
CRINGELING
CRINGELINGS
CRINGEWORTHY
CRINGINGLY
CRINICULTURAL
CRINIGEROUS
CRINKLEROOT
CRINKLEROOTS
CRINKLIEST
CRINOIDEAN
CRINOIDEANS
CRINOLETTE
CRINOLETTES
CRINOLINED
CRINOLINES
CRIPPLEDOM
CRIPPLEDOMS
CRIPPLEWARE
CRIPPLEWARES
CRIPPLINGLY
CRIPPLINGS
CRISPATION
CRISPATIONS
CRISPATURE
CRISPATURES
CRISPBREAD
CRISPBREADS
CRISPENING
CRISPHEADS
CRISPINESS
CRISPINESSES
CRISPNESSES
CRISSCROSS

CRISSCROSSED
CRISSCROSSES
CRISSCROSSING
CRISTIFORM
CRISTOBALITE
CRISTOBALITES
CRITERIONS
CRITERIUMS
CRITHIDIAL
CRITHOMANCIES
CRITHOMANCY
CRITICALITIES
CRITICALITY
CRITICALLY
CRITICALNESS
CRITICALNESSES
CRITICASTER
CRITICASTERS
CRITICISABLE
CRITICISED
CRITICISER
CRITICISERS
CRITICISES
CRITICISING
CRITICISINGLY
CRITICISMS
CRITICIZABLE
CRITICIZED
CRITICIZER
CRITICIZERS
CRITICIZES
CRITICIZING
CRITICIZINGLY
CRITIQUING
CROAKINESS
CROAKINESSES
CROCHETERS
CROCHETING
CROCHETINGS
CROCIDOLITE
CROCIDOLITES
CROCKERIES
CROCODILES
CROCODILIAN
CROCODILIANS
CROCOISITE
CROCOISITES
CROCOSMIAS
CROISSANTS
CROKINOLES
CROOKBACKED
CROOKBACKS
CROOKEDEST
CROOKEDNESS
CROOKEDNESSES
CROOKERIES
CROOKNECKS
CROPDUSTER
CROPDUSTERS

CROQUANTES
CROQUETING
CROQUETTES
CROQUIGNOLE
CROQUIGNOLES
CROSSABILITIES
CROSSABILITY
CROSSANDRA
CROSSANDRAS
CROSSBANDED
CROSSBANDING
CROSSBANDINGS
CROSSBANDS
CROSSBARRED
CROSSBARRING
CROSSBEAMS
CROSSBEARER
CROSSBEARERS
CROSSBENCH
CROSSBENCHER
CROSSBENCHERS
CROSSBENCHES
CROSSBILLS
CROSSBIRTH
CROSSBIRTHS
CROSSBITES
CROSSBITING
CROSSBITTEN
CROSSBONES
CROSSBOWER
CROSSBOWERS
CROSSBOWMAN
CROSSBOWMEN
CROSSBREDS
CROSSBREED
CROSSBREEDING
CROSSBREEDINGS
CROSSBREEDS
CROSSBUCKS
CROSSCHECK
CROSSCHECKED
CROSSCHECKING
CROSSCHECKS
CROSSCLAIM
CROSSCLAIMS
CROSSCOURT
CROSSCURRENT
CROSSCURRENTS
CROSSCUTTING
CROSSCUTTINGS
CROSSETTES
CROSSFALLS
CROSSFIELD
CROSSFIRES
CROSSFISHES
CROSSHAIRS
CROSSHATCH
CROSSHATCHED
CROSSHATCHES

CROSSHATCHING
CROSSHATCHINGS
CROSSHEADS
CROSSJACKS
CROSSLIGHT
CROSSLIGHTS
CROSSLINGUISTIC
CROSSNESSES
CROSSOPTERYGIAN
CROSSOVERS
CROSSPATCH
CROSSPATCHES
CROSSPIECE
CROSSPIECES
CROSSROADS
CROSSRUFFED
CROSSRUFFING
CROSSRUFFS
CROSSTALKS
CROSSTREES
CROSSWALKS
CROSSWINDS
CROSSWORDS
CROSSWORTS
CROTALARIA
CROTALARIAS
CROTALISMS
CROTCHETED
CROTCHETEER
CROTCHETEERS
CROTCHETIER
CROTCHETIEST
CROTCHETINESS
CROTCHETINESSES
CROTONBUGS
CROUPINESS
CROUPINESSES
CROUSTADES
CROWBARRED
CROWBARRING
CROWBERRIES
CROWDEDNESS
CROWDEDNESSES
CROWKEEPER
CROWKEEPERS
CROWNLANDS
CROWNPIECE
CROWNPIECES
CROWNWORKS
CROWSTEPPED
CRUCIATELY
CRUCIFEROUS
CRUCIFIERS
CRUCIFIXES
CRUCIFIXION
CRUCIFIXIONS
CRUCIFORMLY
CRUCIFORMS
CRUCIFYING

CRUCIVERBAL
CRUCIVERBALISM
CRUCIVERBALISMS
CRUCIVERBALIST
CRUCIVERBALISTS
CRUDENESSES
CRUELNESSES
CRUISERWEIGHT
CRUISERWEIGHTS
CRUISEWAYS
CRUISEWEAR
CRUISEWEARS
CRUMBCLOTH
CRUMBCLOTHS
CRUMBLIEST
CRUMBLINESS
CRUMBLINESSES
CRUMBLINGS
CRUMMINESS
CRUMMINESSES
CRUMPLIEST
CRUMPLINGS
CRUNCHABLE
CRUNCHIEST
CRUNCHINESS
CRUNCHINESSES
CRUNCHINGS
CRUSHABILITIES
CRUSHABILITY
CRUSHINGLY
CRUSHPROOF
CRUSTACEAN
CRUSTACEANS
CRUSTACEOUS
CRUSTATION
CRUSTATIONS
CRUSTINESS
CRUSTINESSES
CRUTCHINGS
CRYMOTHERAPIES
CRYMOTHERAPY
CRYOBIOLOGICAL
CRYOBIOLOGIES
CRYOBIOLOGIST
CRYOBIOLOGISTS
CRYOBIOLOGY
CRYOCABLES
CRYOCONITE
CRYOCONITES
CRYOGENICALLY
CRYOGENICS
CRYOGENIES
CRYOGLOBULIN
CRYOGLOBULINS
CRYOHYDRATE
CRYOHYDRATES
CRYOMETERS
CRYOMETRIC
CRYOMETRIES

CRYOPHILIC
CRYOPHORUS
CRYOPHORUSES
CRYOPHYSICS
CRYOPHYTES
CRYOPLANKTON
CRYOPLANKTONS
CRYOPRECIPITATE
CRYOPRESERVE
CRYOPRESERVED
CRYOPRESERVES
CRYOPRESERVING
CRYOPROBES
CRYOPROTECTANT
CRYOPROTECTANTS
CRYOPROTECTIVE
CRYOSCOPES
CRYOSCOPIC
CRYOSCOPIES
CRYOSTATIC
CRYOSURGEON
CRYOSURGEONS
CRYOSURGERIES
CRYOSURGERY
CRYOSURGICAL
CRYOTHERAPIES
CRYOTHERAPY
CRYPTAESTHESIA
CRYPTAESTHESIAS
CRYPTAESTHETIC
CRYPTANALYSES
CRYPTANALYSIS
CRYPTANALYST
CRYPTANALYSTS
CRYPTANALYTIC
CRYPTANALYTICAL
CRYPTARITHM
CRYPTARITHMS
CRYPTESTHESIA
CRYPTESTHESIAS
CRYPTICALLY
CRYPTOBIONT
CRYPTOBIONTS
CRYPTOBIOSES
CRYPTOBIOSIS
CRYPTOCLASTIC
CRYPTOCOCCAL
CRYPTOCOCCI
CRYPTOCOCCOSES
CRYPTOCOCCOSIS
CRYPTOCOCCUS
CRYPTOGAMIAN
CRYPTOGAMIC
CRYPTOGAMIES
CRYPTOGAMIST
CRYPTOGAMISTS
CRYPTOGAMOUS
CRYPTOGAMS
CRYPTOGAMY

CRYPTOGENIC
CRYPTOGRAM
CRYPTOGRAMS
CRYPTOGRAPH
CRYPTOGRAPHER
CRYPTOGRAPHERS
CRYPTOGRAPHIC
CRYPTOGRAPHICAL
CRYPTOGRAPHIES
CRYPTOGRAPHIST
CRYPTOGRAPHISTS
CRYPTOGRAPHS
CRYPTOGRAPHY
CRYPTOLOGIC
CRYPTOLOGICAL
CRYPTOLOGIES
CRYPTOLOGIST
CRYPTOLOGISTS
CRYPTOLOGY
CRYPTOMERIA
CRYPTOMERIAS
CRYPTOMETER
CRYPTOMETERS
CRYPTOMNESIA
CRYPTOMNESIAS
CRYPTOMNESIC
CRYPTONYMOUS
CRYPTONYMS
CRYPTOPHYTE
CRYPTOPHYTES
CRYPTOPHYTIC
CRYPTORCHID
CRYPTORCHIDISM
CRYPTORCHIDISMS
CRYPTORCHIDS
CRYPTORCHISM
CRYPTORCHISMS
CRYPTOSPORIDIA
CRYPTOSPORIDIUM
CRYPTOZOIC
CRYPTOZOITE
CRYPTOZOITES
CRYPTOZOOLOGIES
CRYPTOZOOLOGIST
CRYPTOZOOLOGY
CRYSTALISABLE
CRYSTALISATION
CRYSTALISATIONS
CRYSTALISE
CRYSTALISED
CRYSTALISER
CRYSTALISERS
CRYSTALISES
CRYSTALISING
CRYSTALIZABLE
CRYSTALIZATION
CRYSTALIZATIONS
CRYSTALIZE
CRYSTALIZED

779

CRYSTALIZER
CRYSTALIZERS
CRYSTALIZES
CRYSTALIZING
CRYSTALLINE
CRYSTALLINES
CRYSTALLINITIES
CRYSTALLINITY
CRYSTALLISABLE
CRYSTALLISATION
CRYSTALLISE
CRYSTALLISED
CRYSTALLISER
CRYSTALLISERS
CRYSTALLISES
CRYSTALLISING
CRYSTALLITE
CRYSTALLITES
CRYSTALLITIC
CRYSTALLITIS
CRYSTALLITISES
CRYSTALLIZABLE
CRYSTALLIZATION
CRYSTALLIZE
CRYSTALLIZED
CRYSTALLIZER
CRYSTALLIZERS
CRYSTALLIZES
CRYSTALLIZING
CRYSTALLOGRAPHY
CRYSTALLOID
CRYSTALLOIDAL
CRYSTALLOIDS
CRYSTALLOMANCY
CTENOPHORAN
CTENOPHORANS
CTENOPHORE
CTENOPHORES
CUADRILLAS
CUBANELLES
CUBBYHOLES
CUBICALNESS
CUBICALNESSES
CUBICITIES
CUBISTICALLY
CUCKOLDING
CUCKOLDISE
CUCKOLDISED
CUCKOLDISES
CUCKOLDISING
CUCKOLDIZE
CUCKOLDIZED
CUCKOLDIZES
CUCKOLDIZING
CUCKOLDOMS
CUCKOLDRIES
CUCKOOFLOWER
CUCKOOFLOWERS
CUCKOOPINT

CUCKOOPINTS
CUCULIFORM
CUCULLATED
CUCULLATELY
CUCUMIFORM
CUCURBITACEOUS
CUCURBITAL
CUDDLESOME
CUDGELLERS
CUDGELLING
CUDGELLINGS
CUFFUFFLES
CUIRASSIER
CUIRASSIERS
CUIRASSING
CUISINARTS
CUISINIERS
CULICIFORM
CULINARIAN
CULINARIANS
CULINARILY
CULLENDERS
CULMIFEROUS
CULMINATED
CULMINATES
CULMINATING
CULMINATION
CULMINATIONS
CULPABILITIES
CULPABILITY
CULPABLENESS
CULPABLENESSES
CULTISHNESS
CULTISHNESSES
CULTIVABILITIES
CULTIVABILITY
CULTIVABLE
CULTIVATABLE
CULTIVATED
CULTIVATES
CULTIVATING
CULTIVATION
CULTIVATIONS
CULTIVATOR
CULTIVATORS
CULTRIFORM
CULTURABLE
CULTURALLY
CULTURELESS
CULTURISTS
CULVERINEER
CULVERINEERS
CULVERTAGE
CULVERTAGES
CULVERTAILED
CUMBERBUND
CUMBERBUNDS
CUMBERLESS
CUMBERMENT

CUMBERMENTS
CUMBERSOME
CUMBERSOMELY
CUMBERSOMENESS
CUMBRANCES
CUMBROUSLY
CUMBROUSNESS
CUMBROUSNESSES
CUMMERBUND
CUMMERBUNDS
CUMMINGTONITE
CUMMINGTONITES
CUMULATELY
CUMULATING
CUMULATION
CUMULATIONS
CUMULATIVE
CUMULATIVELY
CUMULATIVENESS
CUMULIFORM
CUMULOCIRRI
CUMULOCIRRUS
CUMULONIMBI
CUMULONIMBUS
CUMULONIMBUSES
CUMULOSTRATI
CUMULOSTRATUS
CUNCTATION
CUNCTATIONS
CUNCTATIOUS
CUNCTATIVE
CUNCTATORS
CUNCTATORY
CUNEIFORMS
CUNNILINCTUS
CUNNILINCTUSES
CUNNILINGUS
CUNNILINGUSES
CUNNINGEST
CUNNINGNESS
CUNNINGNESSES
CUPBEARERS
CUPBOARDED
CUPBOARDING
CUPELLATION
CUPELLATIONS
CUPFERRONS
CUPIDINOUS
CUPIDITIES
CUPRAMMONIUM
CUPRAMMONIUMS
CUPRESSUSES
CUPRIFEROUS
CUPRONICKEL
CUPRONICKELS
CUPULIFEROUS
CURABILITIES
CURABILITY
CURABLENESS

CURABLENESSES
CURANDERAS
CURANDEROS
CURARISATION
CURARISATIONS
CURARISING
CURARIZATION
CURARIZATIONS
CURARIZING
CURATESHIP
CURATESHIPS
CURATIVELY
CURATIVENESS
CURATIVENESSES
CURATORIAL
CURATORSHIP
CURATORSHIPS
CURATRIXES
CURBSTONES
CURCUMINES
CURDINESSES
CURETTAGES
CURETTEMENT
CURETTEMENTS
CURFUFFLED
CURFUFFLES
CURFUFFLING
CURIALISMS
CURIALISTIC
CURIALISTS
CURIETHERAPIES
CURIETHERAPY
CURIOSITIES
CURIOUSEST
CURIOUSNESS
CURIOUSNESSES
CURLICUING
CURLIEWURLIE
CURLIEWURLIES
CURLINESSES
CURLPAPERS
CURMUDGEON
CURMUDGEONLY
CURMUDGEONS
CURMURRING
CURMURRINGS
CURNAPTIOUS
CURRAJONGS
CURRANTIER
CURRANTIEST
CURRAWONGS
CURREJONGS
CURRENCIES
CURRENTNESS
CURRENTNESSES
CURRICULAR
CURRICULUM
CURRICULUMS
CURRIERIES

CURRIJONGS
CURRISHNESS
CURRISHNESSES
CURRYCOMBED
CURRYCOMBING
CURRYCOMBS
CURSEDNESS
CURSEDNESSES
CURSELARIE
CURSIVENESS
CURSIVENESSES
CURSORINESS
CURSORINESSES
CURSTNESSES
CURTAILERS
CURTAILING
CURTAILMENT
CURTAILMENTS
CURTAINING
CURTAINLESS
CURTALAXES
CURTATIONS
CURTILAGES
CURTNESSES
CURTSEYING
CURVACEOUS
CURVACEOUSLY
CURVACIOUS
CURVATIONS
CURVATURES
CURVEBALLED
CURVEBALLING
CURVEBALLS
CURVEDNESS
CURVEDNESSES
CURVETTING
CURVICAUDATE
CURVICOSTATE
CURVIFOLIATE
CURVILINEAL
CURVILINEAR
CURVILINEARITY
CURVILINEARLY
CURVIROSTRAL
CUSHINESSES
CUSHIONETS
CUSHIONING
CUSHIONLESS
CUSPIDATED
CUSPIDATION
CUSPIDATIONS
CUSPIDORES
CUSSEDNESS
CUSSEDNESSES
CUSTODIANS
CUSTODIANSHIP
CUSTODIANSHIPS
CUSTODIERS
CUSTOMABLE

CUSTOMARIES
CUSTOMARILY
CUSTOMARINESS
CUSTOMARINESSES
CUSTOMHOUSE
CUSTOMHOUSES
CUSTOMISATION
CUSTOMISATIONS
CUSTOMISED
CUSTOMISER
CUSTOMISERS
CUSTOMISES
CUSTOMISING
CUSTOMIZATION
CUSTOMIZATIONS
CUSTOMIZED
CUSTOMIZER
CUSTOMIZERS
CUSTOMIZES
CUSTOMIZING
CUSTOMSHOUSE
CUSTOMSHOUSES
CUSTUMARIES
CUTABILITIES
CUTABILITY
CUTANEOUSLY
CUTCHERIES
CUTCHERRIES
CUTENESSES
CUTGRASSES
CUTINISATION
CUTINISATIONS
CUTINISING
CUTINIZATION
CUTINIZATIONS
CUTINIZING
CUTTHROATS
CUTTLEBONE
CUTTLEBONES
CUTTLEFISH
CUTTLEFISHES
CYANAMIDES
CYANIDATION
CYANIDATIONS
CYANIDINGS
CYANOACETYLENE
CYANOACETYLENES
CYANOACRYLATE
CYANOACRYLATES
CYANOBACTERIA
CYANOBACTERIUM
CYANOCOBALAMIN
CYANOCOBALAMINE
CYANOCOBALAMINS
CYANOETHYLATE
CYANOETHYLATED
CYANOETHYLATES
CYANOETHYLATING
CYANOETHYLATION

CYANOGENAMIDE
CYANOGENAMIDES
CYANOGENESES
CYANOGENESIS
CYANOGENETIC
CYANOGENIC
CYANOHYDRIN
CYANOHYDRINS
CYANOMETER
CYANOMETERS
CYANOPHYTE
CYANOPHYTES
CYANOTYPES
CYANURATES
CYATHIFORM
CYBERATHLETE
CYBERATHLETES
CYBERATHLETICS
CYBERCAFES
CYBERCASTS
CYBERCRIME
CYBERCRIMES
CYBERCRIMINAL
CYBERCRIMINALS
CYBERNATED
CYBERNATES
CYBERNATING
CYBERNATION
CYBERNATIONS
CYBERNAUTS
CYBERNETIC
CYBERNETICAL
CYBERNETICALLY
CYBERNETICIAN
CYBERNETICIANS
CYBERNETICIST
CYBERNETICISTS
CYBERNETICS
CYBERPHOBIA
CYBERPHOBIAS
CYBERPHOBIC
CYBERPORNS
CYBERPUNKS
CYBERSECURITIES
CYBERSECURITY
CYBERSEXES
CYBERSPACE
CYBERSPACES
CYBERSQUATTER
CYBERSQUATTERS
CYBERSQUATTING
CYBERSQUATTINGS
CYBERTERRORISM
CYBERTERRORISMS
CYBERTERRORIST
CYBERTERRORISTS
CYBRARIANS
CYCADACEOUS
CYCADEOIDS

CYCADOPHYTE
CYCADOPHYTES
CYCLAMATES
CYCLANDELATE
CYCLANDELATES
CYCLANTHACEOUS
CYCLAZOCINE
CYCLAZOCINES
CYCLICALITIES
CYCLICALITY
CYCLICALLY
CYCLICISMS
CYCLICITIES
CYCLISATION
CYCLISATIONS
CYCLIZATION
CYCLIZATIONS
CYCLIZINES
CYCLOADDITION
CYCLOADDITIONS
CYCLOALIPHATIC
CYCLOALKANE
CYCLOALKANES
CYCLOBARBITONE
CYCLOBARBITONES
CYCLODEXTRIN
CYCLODEXTRINS
CYCLODIALYSES
CYCLODIALYSIS
CYCLODIENE
CYCLODIENES
CYCLOGENESES
CYCLOGENESIS
CYCLOGIROS
CYCLOGRAPH
CYCLOGRAPHIC
CYCLOGRAPHS
CYCLOHEXANE
CYCLOHEXANES
CYCLOHEXANONE
CYCLOHEXANONES
CYCLOHEXIMIDE
CYCLOHEXIMIDES
CYCLOHEXYLAMINE
CYCLOIDALLY
CYCLOIDIAN
CYCLOIDIANS
CYCLOLITHS
CYCLOMETER
CYCLOMETERS
CYCLOMETRIES
CYCLOMETRY
CYCLONICAL
CYCLONICALLY
CYCLONITES
CYCLOOLEFIN
CYCLOOLEFINIC
CYCLOOLEFINS
CYCLOPAEDIA

CYCLOPAEDIAS
CYCLOPAEDIC
CYCLOPAEDIST
CYCLOPAEDISTS
CYCLOPARAFFIN
CYCLOPARAFFINS
CYCLOPEDIA
CYCLOPEDIAS
CYCLOPEDIC
CYCLOPEDIST
CYCLOPEDISTS
CYCLOPENTADIENE
CYCLOPENTANE
CYCLOPENTANES
CYCLOPENTOLATE
CYCLOPENTOLATES
CYCLOPLEGIA
CYCLOPLEGIAS
CYCLOPLEGIC
CYCLOPROPANE
CYCLOPROPANES
CYCLORAMAS
CYCLORAMIC
CYCLOSERINE
CYCLOSERINES
CYCLOSPERMOUS
CYCLOSPORIN
CYCLOSPORINE
CYCLOSPORINES
CYCLOSPORINS
CYCLOSTOMATE
CYCLOSTOMATOUS
CYCLOSTOME
CYCLOSTOMES
CYCLOSTOMOUS
CYCLOSTYLE
CYCLOSTYLED
CYCLOSTYLES
CYCLOSTYLING
CYCLOTHYME
CYCLOTHYMES
CYCLOTHYMIA
CYCLOTHYMIAC
CYCLOTHYMIACS
CYCLOTHYMIAS
CYCLOTHYMIC
CYCLOTHYMICS
CYCLOTOMIC
CYCLOTRONS
CYLINDERED
CYLINDERING
CYLINDRACEOUS
CYLINDRICAL
CYLINDRICALITY
CYLINDRICALLY
CYLINDRICALNESS
CYLINDRICITIES
CYLINDRICITY
CYLINDRIFORM

CYLINDRITE
CYLINDRITES
CYLINDROID
CYLINDROIDS
CYMAGRAPHS
CYMBALEERS
CYMBALISTS
CYMBIDIUMS
CYMIFEROUS
CYMOGRAPHIC
CYMOGRAPHS
CYMOPHANES
CYMOPHANOUS
CYMOTRICHIES
CYMOTRICHOUS
CYMOTRICHY
CYNGHANEDD
CYNGHANEDDS
CYNICALNESS
CYNICALNESSES
CYNOMOLGUS
CYNOPHILIA
CYNOPHILIAS
CYNOPHILIST
CYNOPHILISTS
CYNOPHOBIA
CYNOPHOBIAS
CYNOPODOUS
CYPERACEOUS
CYPRINODONT
CYPRINODONTS
CYPRINOIDS
CYPRIPEDIA
CYPRIPEDIUM
CYPRIPEDIUMS
CYPROHEPTADINE
CYPROHEPTADINES
CYPROTERONE
CYPROTERONES
CYSTEAMINE
CYSTEAMINES
CYSTECTOMIES
CYSTECTOMY
CYSTICERCI
CYSTICERCOID
CYSTICERCOIDS
CYSTICERCOSES
CYSTICERCOSIS
CYSTICERCUS
CYSTIDEANS
CYSTINOSES
CYSTINOSIS
CYSTINURIA
CYSTINURIAS
CYSTITIDES
CYSTITISES
CYSTOCARPIC
CYSTOCARPS
CYSTOCELES

CYSTOGENOUS
CYSTOGRAPHIES
CYSTOGRAPHY
CYSTOLITHIASES
CYSTOLITHIASIS
CYSTOLITHS
CYSTOSCOPE
CYSTOSCOPES
CYSTOSCOPIC
CYSTOSCOPIES
CYSTOSCOPY
CYSTOSTOMIES
CYSTOSTOMY
CYSTOTOMIES
CYTOCHALASIN
CYTOCHALASINS
CYTOCHEMICAL
CYTOCHEMISTRIES
CYTOCHEMISTRY
CYTOCHROME
CYTOCHROMES
CYTODIAGNOSES
CYTODIAGNOSIS
CYTOGENESES
CYTOGENESIS
CYTOGENETIC
CYTOGENETICAL
CYTOGENETICALLY
CYTOGENETICIST
CYTOGENETICISTS
CYTOGENETICS
CYTOGENIES
CYTOKINESES
CYTOKINESIS
CYTOKINETIC
CYTOKININS
CYTOLOGICAL
CYTOLOGICALLY
CYTOLOGIES
CYTOLOGIST
CYTOLOGISTS
CYTOLYSINS
CYTOMEGALIC
CYTOMEGALOVIRUS
CYTOMEMBRANE
CYTOMEMBRANES
CYTOMETERS
CYTOMETRIC
CYTOMETRIES
CYTOPATHIC
CYTOPATHOGENIC
CYTOPATHOLOGIES
CYTOPATHOLOGY
CYTOPENIAS
CYTOPHILIC
CYTOPHOTOMETRIC
CYTOPHOTOMETRY
CYTOPLASMIC
CYTOPLASMICALLY

CYTOPLASMS
CYTOPLASTIC
CYTOPLASTS
CYTOSKELETAL
CYTOSKELETON
CYTOSKELETONS
CYTOSTATIC
CYTOSTATICALLY
CYTOSTATICS
CYTOTAXONOMIC
CYTOTAXONOMIES
CYTOTAXONOMIST
CYTOTAXONOMISTS
CYTOTAXONOMY
CYTOTECHNOLOGY
CYTOTOXICITIES
CYTOTOXICITY
CYTOTOXINS
CZAREVICHES
CZAREVITCH
CZAREVITCHES

D

DABBLINGLY
DACHSHUNDS
DACOITAGES
DACQUOISES
DACTYLICALLY
DACTYLIOGRAPHY
DACTYLIOLOGIES
DACTYLIOLOGY
DACTYLIOMANCIES
DACTYLIOMANCY
DACTYLISTS
DACTYLOGRAM
DACTYLOGRAMS
DACTYLOGRAPHER
DACTYLOGRAPHERS
DACTYLOGRAPHIC
DACTYLOGRAPHIES
DACTYLOGRAPHY
DACTYLOLOGIES
DACTYLOLOGY
DACTYLOSCOPIES
DACTYLOSCOPY
DAFFADOWNDILLY
DAFFINESSES
DAFFODILLIES
DAFFODILLY
DAFTNESSES
DAGGERBOARD
DAGGERBOARDS
DAGGERLIKE
DAGUERREAN
DAGUERREOTYPE
DAGUERREOTYPED
DAGUERREOTYPER
DAGUERREOTYPERS
DAGUERREOTYPES
DAGUERREOTYPIES
DAGUERREOTYPING
DAGUERREOTYPIST
DAGUERREOTYPY
DAHABEEAHS
DAHABEEYAH
DAHABEEYAHS
DAHABIYAHS
DAHABIYEHS
DAILINESSES
DAILYNESSES
DAINTINESS
DAINTINESSES
DAIRYMAIDS
DAISYWHEEL
DAISYWHEELS
DALLIANCES
DALMATIANS

DALTONISMS
DAMAGEABILITIES
DAMAGEABILITY
DAMAGEABLE
DAMAGINGLY
DAMASCEENE
DAMASCEENED
DAMASCEENES
DAMASCEENING
DAMASCENED
DAMASCENES
DAMASCENING
DAMASCENINGS
DAMASKEENED
DAMASKEENING
DAMASKEENS
DAMASKINED
DAMASKINING
DAMASQUINED
DAMASQUINING
DAMASQUINS
DAMINOZIDE
DAMINOZIDES
DAMNABILITIES
DAMNABILITY
DAMNABLENESS
DAMNABLENESSES
DAMNATIONS
DAMNEDESTS
DAMNIFICATION
DAMNIFICATIONS
DAMNIFYING
DAMOISELLE
DAMOISELLES
DAMPCOURSE
DAMPCOURSES
DAMPISHNESS
DAMPISHNESSES
DAMPNESSES
DAMSELFISH
DAMSELFISHES
DAMSELFLIES
DANCEHALLS
DANDELIONS
DANDIFICATION
DANDIFICATIONS
DANDIFYING
DANDIPRATS
DANDYFUNKS
DANDYISHLY
DANDYPRATS
DANGERLESS
DANGEROUSLY
DANGEROUSNESS

DANGEROUSNESSES
DANGLINGLY
DANKNESSES
DANNEBROGS
DANTHONIAS
DAPPERLING
DAPPERLINGS
DAPPERNESS
DAPPERNESSES
DAREDEVILRIES
DAREDEVILRY
DAREDEVILS
DAREDEVILTRIES
DAREDEVILTRY
DARINGNESS
DARINGNESSES
DARKNESSES
DARLINGNESS
DARLINGNESSES
DARNATIONS
DARNEDESTS
DARRAIGNED
DARRAIGNES
DARRAIGNING
DARRAIGNMENT
DARRAIGNMENTS
DARRAINING
DARRAYNING
DARTBOARDS
DASHBOARDS
DASTARDIES
DASTARDLINESS
DASTARDLINESSES
DASTARDNESS
DASTARDNESSES
DASYMETERS
DASYPAEDAL
DASYPHYLLOUS
DATABASING
DATABUSSES
DATAGLOVES
DATAMATION
DATAMATIONS
DATEDNESSES
DATELINING
DAUGHTERHOOD
DAUGHTERHOODS
DAUGHTERLESS
DAUGHTERLINESS
DAUGHTERLING
DAUGHTERLINGS
DAUGHTERLY
DAUNDERING
DAUNOMYCIN

DAUNOMYCINS
DAUNORUBICIN
DAUNORUBICINS
DAUNTINGLY
DAUNTLESSLY
DAUNTLESSNESS
DAUNTLESSNESSES
DAUNTONING
DAUPHINESS
DAUPHINESSES
DAVENPORTS
DAWDLINGLY
DAWSONITES
DAYCENTRES
DAYDREAMED
DAYDREAMER
DAYDREAMERS
DAYDREAMING
DAYDREAMLIKE
DAYFLOWERS
DAYLIGHTED
DAYLIGHTING
DAYLIGHTINGS
DAYSPRINGS
DAYWORKERS
DAZEDNESSES
DAZZLEMENT
DAZZLEMENTS
DAZZLINGLY
DEACIDIFICATION
DEACIDIFIED
DEACIDIFIES
DEACIDIFYING
DEACONESSES
DEACONHOOD
DEACONHOODS
DEACONRIES
DEACONSHIP
DEACONSHIPS
DEACTIVATE
DEACTIVATED
DEACTIVATES
DEACTIVATING
DEACTIVATION
DEACTIVATIONS
DEACTIVATOR
DEACTIVATORS
DEADENINGLY
DEADENINGS
DEADHEADED
DEADHEADING
DEADHOUSES
DEADLIFTED
DEADLIFTING

DEADLIGHTS
DEADLINESS
DEADLINESSES
DEADLINING
DEADLOCKED
DEADLOCKING
DEADNESSES
DEADPANNED
DEADPANNER
DEADPANNERS
DEADPANNING
DEADSTOCKS
DEADSTROKE
DEADWEIGHT
DEADWEIGHTS
DEAERATING
DEAERATION
DEAERATIONS
DEAERATORS
DEAFENINGLY
DEAFENINGS
DEAFNESSES
DEALATIONS
DEALBATION
DEALBATIONS
DEALERSHIP
DEALERSHIPS
DEALFISHES
DEAMBULATORIES
DEAMBULATORY
DEAMINASES
DEAMINATED
DEAMINATES
DEAMINATING
DEAMINATION
DEAMINATIONS
DEAMINISATION
DEAMINISATIONS
DEAMINISED
DEAMINISES
DEAMINISING
DEAMINIZATION
DEAMINIZATIONS
DEAMINIZED
DEAMINIZES
DEAMINIZING
DEARBOUGHT
DEARNESSES
DEARTICULATE
DEARTICULATED
DEARTICULATES
DEARTICULATING
DEASPIRATE
DEASPIRATED
DEASPIRATES
DEASPIRATING
DEASPIRATION
DEASPIRATIONS
DEATHBLOWS

DEATHLESSLY
DEATHLESSNESS
DEATHLESSNESSES
DEATHLIEST
DEATHLINESS
DEATHLINESSES
DEATHTRAPS
DEATHWARDS
DEATHWATCH
DEATHWATCHES
DEATTRIBUTE
DEATTRIBUTED
DEATTRIBUTES
DEATTRIBUTING
DEBAGGINGS
DEBARCATION
DEBARCATIONS
DEBARKATION
DEBARKATIONS
DEBARMENTS
DEBARRASSED
DEBARRASSES
DEBARRASSING
DEBASEDNESS
DEBASEDNESSES
DEBASEMENT
DEBASEMENTS
DEBASINGLY
DEBATEABLE
DEBATEMENT
DEBATEMENTS
DEBATINGLY
DEBAUCHEDLY
DEBAUCHEDNESS
DEBAUCHEDNESSES
DEBAUCHEES
DEBAUCHERIES
DEBAUCHERS
DEBAUCHERY
DEBAUCHING
DEBAUCHMENT
DEBAUCHMENTS
DEBEARDING
DEBENTURED
DEBENTURES
DEBILITATE
DEBILITATED
DEBILITATES
DEBILITATING
DEBILITATION
DEBILITATIONS
DEBILITATIVE
DEBILITIES
DEBONAIRLY
DEBONAIRNESS
DEBONAIRNESSES
DEBONNAIRE
DEBOUCHING
DEBOUCHMENT

DEBOUCHMENTS
DEBOUCHURE
DEBOUCHURES
DEBRIDEMENT
DEBRIDEMENTS
DEBRIEFERS
DEBRIEFING
DEBRIEFINGS
DEBRUISING
DEBUTANTES
DECACHORDS
DECADENCES
DECADENCIES
DECADENTLY
DECAFFEINATE
DECAFFEINATED
DECAFFEINATES
DECAFFEINATING
DECAGONALLY
DECAGRAMME
DECAGRAMMES
DECAGYNIAN
DECAGYNOUS
DECAHEDRAL
DECAHEDRON
DECAHEDRONS
DECALCIFICATION
DECALCIFIED
DECALCIFIER
DECALCIFIERS
DECALCIFIES
DECALCIFYING
DECALCOMANIA
DECALCOMANIAS
DECALESCENCE
DECALESCENCES
DECALESCENT
DECALITERS
DECALITRES
DECALOGIST
DECALOGISTS
DECALOGUES
DECAMERONIC
DECAMEROUS
DECAMETERS
DECAMETHONIUM
DECAMETHONIUMS
DECAMETRES
DECAMETRIC
DECAMPMENT
DECAMPMENTS
DECANDRIAN
DECANDROUS
DECANEDIOIC
DECANICALLY
DECANTATED
DECANTATES
DECANTATING
DECANTATION

DECANTATIONS
DECAPITALISE
DECAPITALISED
DECAPITALISES
DECAPITALISING
DECAPITALIZE
DECAPITALIZED
DECAPITALIZES
DECAPITALIZING
DECAPITATE
DECAPITATED
DECAPITATES
DECAPITATING
DECAPITATION
DECAPITATIONS
DECAPITATOR
DECAPITATORS
DECAPODANS
DECAPODOUS
DECAPSULATE
DECAPSULATED
DECAPSULATES
DECAPSULATING
DECAPSULATION
DECAPSULATIONS
DECARBONATE
DECARBONATED
DECARBONATES
DECARBONATING
DECARBONATION
DECARBONATIONS
DECARBONATOR
DECARBONATORS
DECARBONISATION
DECARBONISE
DECARBONISED
DECARBONISER
DECARBONISERS
DECARBONISES
DECARBONISING
DECARBONIZATION
DECARBONIZE
DECARBONIZED
DECARBONIZER
DECARBONIZERS
DECARBONIZES
DECARBONIZING
DECARBOXYLASE
DECARBOXYLASES
DECARBOXYLATE
DECARBOXYLATED
DECARBOXYLATES
DECARBOXYLATING
DECARBOXYLATION
DECARBURATION
DECARBURATIONS
DECARBURISATION
DECARBURISE
DECARBURISED

DECARBURISES	DECENTRALISING	DECILITRES	DECKCHAIRS
DECARBURISING	DECENTRALIST	DECILLIONS	DECKHOUSES
DECARBURIZATION	DECENTRALISTS	DECILLIONTH	DECLAIMANT
DECARBURIZE	DECENTRALIZE	DECILLIONTHS	DECLAIMANTS
DECARBURIZED	DECENTRALIZED	DECIMALISATION	DECLAIMERS
DECARBURIZES	DECENTRALIZES	DECIMALISATIONS	DECLAIMING
DECARBURIZING	DECENTRALIZING	DECIMALISE	DECLAIMINGS
DECASTERES	DECENTRING	DECIMALISED	DECLAMATION
DECASTICHS	DECEPTIBILITIES	DECIMALISES	DECLAMATIONS
DECASTYLES	DECEPTIBILITY	DECIMALISING	DECLAMATORILY
DECASUALISATION	DECEPTIBLE	DECIMALISM	DECLAMATORY
DECASUALIZATION	DECEPTIONAL	DECIMALISMS	DECLARABLE
DECASYLLABIC	DECEPTIONS	DECIMALIST	DECLARANTS
DECASYLLABICS	DECEPTIOUS	DECIMALISTS	DECLARATION
DECASYLLABLE	DECEPTIVELY	DECIMALIZATION	DECLARATIONS
DECASYLLABLES	DECEPTIVENESS	DECIMALIZATIONS	DECLARATIVE
DECATHLETE	DECEPTIVENESSES	DECIMALIZE	DECLARATIVELY
DECATHLETES	DECEREBRATE	DECIMALIZED	DECLARATOR
DECATHLONS	DECEREBRATED	DECIMALIZES	DECLARATORILY
DECAUDATED	DECEREBRATES	DECIMALIZING	DECLARATORS
DECAUDATES	DECEREBRATING	DECIMATING	DECLARATORY
DECAUDATING	DECEREBRATION	DECIMATION	DECLAREDLY
DECEITFULLY	DECEREBRATIONS	DECIMATIONS	DECLASSIFIABLE
DECEITFULNESS	DECEREBRISE	DECIMATORS	DECLASSIFIED
DECEITFULNESSES	DECEREBRISED	DECIMETERS	DECLASSIFIES
DECEIVABILITIES	DECEREBRISES	DECIMETRES	DECLASSIFY
DECEIVABILITY	DECEREBRISING	DECIMETRIC	DECLASSIFYING
DECEIVABLE	DECEREBRIZE	DECINORMAL	DECLASSING
DECEIVABLENESS	DECEREBRIZED	DECIPHERABILITY	DECLENSION
DECEIVABLY	DECEREBRIZES	DECIPHERABLE	DECLENSIONAL
DECEIVINGLY	DECEREBRIZING	DECIPHERED	DECLENSIONALLY
DECEIVINGS	DECERTIFICATION	DECIPHERER	DECLENSIONS
DECELERATE	DECERTIFIED	DECIPHERERS	DECLINABLE
DECELERATED	DECERTIFIES	DECIPHERING	DECLINATION
DECELERATES	DECERTIFYING	DECIPHERMENT	DECLINATIONAL
DECELERATING	DECESSIONS	DECIPHERMENTS	DECLINATIONS
DECELERATION	DECHEANCES	DECISIONAL	DECLINATOR
DECELERATIONS	DECHLORINATE	DECISIONED	DECLINATORS
DECELERATOR	DECHLORINATED	DECISIONING	DECLINATORY
DECELERATORS	DECHLORINATES	DECISIVELY	DECLINATURE
DECELEROMETER	DECHLORINATING	DECISIVENESS	DECLINATURES
DECELEROMETERS	DECHLORINATION	DECISIVENESSES	DECLINISTS
DECELERONS	DECHLORINATIONS	DECISTERES	DECLINOMETER
DECEMVIRAL	DECHRISTIANISE	DECITIZENISE	DECLINOMETERS
DECEMVIRATE	DECHRISTIANISED	DECITIZENISED	DECLIVITIES
DECEMVIRATES	DECHRISTIANISES	DECITIZENISES	DECLIVITOUS
DECENARIES	DECHRISTIANIZE	DECITIZENISING	DECLUTCHED
DECENNARIES	DECHRISTIANIZED	DECITIZENIZE	DECLUTCHES
DECENNIALLY	DECHRISTIANIZES	DECITIZENIZED	DECLUTCHING
DECENNIALS	DECIDABILITIES	DECITIZENIZES	DECLUTTERED
DECENNIUMS	DECIDABILITY	DECITIZENIZING	DECLUTTERING
DECENNOVAL	DECIDEDNESS	DECIVILISE	DECLUTTERS
DECENTERED	DECIDEDNESSES	DECIVILISED	DECOCTIBLE
DECENTERING	DECIDUOUSLY	DECIVILISES	DECOCTIONS
DECENTNESS	DECIDUOUSNESS	DECIVILISING	DECOCTURES
DECENTNESSES	DECIDUOUSNESSES	DECIVILIZE	DECOHERENCE
DECENTRALISE	DECIGRAMME	DECIVILIZED	DECOHERENCES
DECENTRALISED	DECIGRAMMES	DECIVILIZES	DECOHERERS
DECENTRALISES	DECILITERS	DECIVILIZING	DECOLLATED

DECOLLATES

DECOLLATES
DECOLLATING
DECOLLATION
DECOLLATIONS
DECOLLATOR
DECOLLATORS
DECOLLETAGE
DECOLLETAGES
DECOLLETES
DECOLONISATION
DECOLONISATIONS
DECOLONISE
DECOLONISED
DECOLONISES
DECOLONISING
DECOLONIZATION
DECOLONIZATIONS
DECOLONIZE
DECOLONIZED
DECOLONIZES
DECOLONIZING
DECOLORANT
DECOLORANTS
DECOLORATE
DECOLORATED
DECOLORATES
DECOLORATING
DECOLORATION
DECOLORATIONS
DECOLORING
DECOLORISATION
DECOLORISATIONS
DECOLORISE
DECOLORISED
DECOLORISER
DECOLORISERS
DECOLORISES
DECOLORISING
DECOLORIZATION
DECOLORIZATIONS
DECOLORIZE
DECOLORIZED
DECOLORIZER
DECOLORIZERS
DECOLORIZES
DECOLORIZING
DECOLOURED
DECOLOURING
DECOLOURISATION
DECOLOURISE
DECOLOURISED
DECOLOURISES
DECOLOURISING
DECOLOURIZATION
DECOLOURIZE
DECOLOURIZED
DECOLOURIZES
DECOLOURIZING
DECOMMISSION

DECOMMISSIONED
DECOMMISSIONER
DECOMMISSIONERS
DECOMMISSIONING
DECOMMISSIONS
DECOMMITTED
DECOMMITTING
DECOMPENSATE
DECOMPENSATED
DECOMPENSATES
DECOMPENSATING
DECOMPENSATION
DECOMPENSATIONS
DECOMPOSABILITY
DECOMPOSABLE
DECOMPOSED
DECOMPOSER
DECOMPOSERS
DECOMPOSES
DECOMPOSING
DECOMPOSITE
DECOMPOSITION
DECOMPOSITIONS
DECOMPOUND
DECOMPOUNDABLE
DECOMPOUNDED
DECOMPOUNDING
DECOMPOUNDS
DECOMPRESS
DECOMPRESSED
DECOMPRESSES
DECOMPRESSING
DECOMPRESSION
DECOMPRESSIONS
DECOMPRESSIVE
DECOMPRESSOR
DECOMPRESSORS
DECONCENTRATE
DECONCENTRATED
DECONCENTRATES
DECONCENTRATING
DECONCENTRATION
DECONDITION
DECONDITIONED
DECONDITIONING
DECONDITIONS
DECONGESTANT
DECONGESTANTS
DECONGESTED
DECONGESTING
DECONGESTION
DECONGESTIONS
DECONGESTIVE
DECONGESTS
DECONSECRATE
DECONSECRATED
DECONSECRATES
DECONSECRATING
DECONSECRATION

DECONSECRATIONS
DECONSTRUCT
DECONSTRUCTED
DECONSTRUCTING
DECONSTRUCTION
DECONSTRUCTIONS
DECONSTRUCTIVE
DECONSTRUCTOR
DECONSTRUCTORS
DECONSTRUCTS
DECONTAMINANT
DECONTAMINANTS
DECONTAMINATE
DECONTAMINATED
DECONTAMINATES
DECONTAMINATING
DECONTAMINATION
DECONTAMINATIVE
DECONTAMINATOR
DECONTAMINATORS
DECONTROLLED
DECONTROLLING
DECONTROLS
DECORATING
DECORATION
DECORATIONS
DECORATIVE
DECORATIVELY
DECORATIVENESS
DECORATORS
DECOROUSLY
DECOROUSNESS
DECOROUSNESSES
DECORTICATE
DECORTICATED
DECORTICATES
DECORTICATING
DECORTICATION
DECORTICATIONS
DECORTICATOR
DECORTICATORS
DECOUPAGED
DECOUPAGES
DECOUPAGING
DECOUPLERS
DECOUPLING
DECOUPLINGS
DECRASSIFIED
DECRASSIFIES
DECRASSIFY
DECRASSIFYING
DECREASING
DECREASINGLY
DECREEABLE
DECREMENTAL
DECREMENTED
DECREMENTING
DECREMENTS
DECREPITATE

DECREPITATED
DECREPITATES
DECREPITATING
DECREPITATION
DECREPITATIONS
DECREPITLY
DECREPITNESS
DECREPITNESSES
DECREPITUDE
DECREPITUDES
DECRESCENCE
DECRESCENCES
DECRESCENDO
DECRESCENDOS
DECRESCENT
DECRETALIST
DECRETALISTS
DECRETISTS
DECRIMINALISE
DECRIMINALISED
DECRIMINALISES
DECRIMINALISING
DECRIMINALIZE
DECRIMINALIZED
DECRIMINALIZES
DECRIMINALIZING
DECROWNING
DECRUSTATION
DECRUSTATIONS
DECRYPTING
DECRYPTION
DECRYPTIONS
DECUMBENCE
DECUMBENCES
DECUMBENCIES
DECUMBENCY
DECUMBENTLY
DECUMBITURE
DECUMBITURES
DECURIONATE
DECURIONATES
DECURRENCIES
DECURRENCY
DECURRENTLY
DECURSIONS
DECURSIVELY
DECURVATION
DECURVATIONS
DECUSSATED
DECUSSATELY
DECUSSATES
DECUSSATING
DECUSSATION
DECUSSATIONS
DEDICATEDLY
DEDICATEES
DEDICATING
DEDICATION
DEDICATIONAL

DEDICATIONS
DEDICATIVE
DEDICATORIAL
DEDICATORS
DEDICATORY
DEDIFFERENTIATE
DEDRAMATISE
DEDRAMATISED
DEDRAMATISES
DEDRAMATISING
DEDRAMATIZE
DEDRAMATIZED
DEDRAMATIZES
DEDRAMATIZING
DEDUCEMENT
DEDUCEMENTS
DEDUCIBILITIES
DEDUCIBILITY
DEDUCIBLENESS
DEDUCIBLENESSES
DEDUCTIBILITIES
DEDUCTIBILITY
DEDUCTIBLE
DEDUCTIBLES
DEDUCTIONS
DEDUCTIVELY
DEEMSTERSHIP
DEEMSTERSHIPS
DEEPFREEZE
DEEPFREEZES
DEEPFREEZING
DEEPFROZEN
DEEPNESSES
DEEPWATERMAN
DEEPWATERMEN
DEERBERRIES
DEERGRASSES
DEERHOUNDS
DEERSTALKER
DEERSTALKERS
DEERSTALKING
DEERSTALKINGS
DEFACEABLE
DEFACEMENT
DEFACEMENTS
DEFACINGLY
DEFAECATED
DEFAECATES
DEFAECATING
DEFAECATION
DEFAECATIONS
DEFAECATOR
DEFAECATORS
DEFALCATED
DEFALCATES
DEFALCATING
DEFALCATION
DEFALCATIONS
DEFALCATOR

DEFALCATORS
DEFAMATION
DEFAMATIONS
DEFAMATORILY
DEFAMATORY
DEFAULTERS
DEFAULTING
DEFEASANCE
DEFEASANCED
DEFEASANCES
DEFEASIBILITIES
DEFEASIBILITY
DEFEASIBLE
DEFEASIBLENESS
DEFEATISMS
DEFEATISTS
DEFEATURED
DEFEATURES
DEFEATURING
DEFECATING
DEFECATION
DEFECATIONS
DEFECATORS
DEFECTIBILITIES
DEFECTIBILITY
DEFECTIBLE
DEFECTIONIST
DEFECTIONISTS
DEFECTIONS
DEFECTIVELY
DEFECTIVENESS
DEFECTIVENESSES
DEFECTIVES
DEFEMINISATION
DEFEMINISATIONS
DEFEMINISE
DEFEMINISED
DEFEMINISES
DEFEMINISING
DEFEMINIZATION
DEFEMINIZATIONS
DEFEMINIZE
DEFEMINIZED
DEFEMINIZES
DEFEMINIZING
DEFENCELESS
DEFENCELESSLY
DEFENCELESSNESS
DEFENCEMAN
DEFENCEMEN
DEFENDABLE
DEFENDANTS
DEFENESTRATE
DEFENESTRATED
DEFENESTRATES
DEFENESTRATING
DEFENESTRATION
DEFENESTRATIONS
DEFENSATIVE

DEFENSATIVES
DEFENSELESS
DEFENSELESSLY
DEFENSELESSNESS
DEFENSEMAN
DEFENSEMEN
DEFENSIBILITIES
DEFENSIBILITY
DEFENSIBLE
DEFENSIBLENESS
DEFENSIBLY
DEFENSIVELY
DEFENSIVENESS
DEFENSIVENESSES
DEFENSIVES
DEFERENCES
DEFERENTIAL
DEFERENTIALLY
DEFERMENTS
DEFERRABLE
DEFERRABLES
DEFERVESCENCE
DEFERVESCENCES
DEFERVESCENCIES
DEFERVESCENCY
DEFEUDALISE
DEFEUDALISED
DEFEUDALISES
DEFEUDALISING
DEFEUDALIZE
DEFEUDALIZED
DEFEUDALIZES
DEFEUDALIZING
DEFIANTNESS
DEFIANTNESSES
DEFIBRILLATE
DEFIBRILLATED
DEFIBRILLATES
DEFIBRILLATING
DEFIBRILLATION
DEFIBRILLATIONS
DEFIBRILLATOR
DEFIBRILLATORS
DEFIBRINATE
DEFIBRINATED
DEFIBRINATES
DEFIBRINATING
DEFIBRINATION
DEFIBRINATIONS
DEFIBRINISE
DEFIBRINISED
DEFIBRINISES
DEFIBRINISING
DEFIBRINIZE
DEFIBRINIZED
DEFIBRINIZES
DEFIBRINIZING
DEFICIENCE
DEFICIENCES

DEFICIENCIES
DEFICIENCY
DEFICIENTLY
DEFICIENTNESS
DEFICIENTNESSES
DEFICIENTS
DEFILADING
DEFILEMENT
DEFILEMENTS
DEFILIATION
DEFILIATIONS
DEFINABILITIES
DEFINABILITY
DEFINEMENT
DEFINEMENTS
DEFINIENDA
DEFINIENDUM
DEFINIENTIA
DEFINITELY
DEFINITENESS
DEFINITENESSES
DEFINITION
DEFINITIONAL
DEFINITIONS
DEFINITISE
DEFINITISED
DEFINITISES
DEFINITISING
DEFINITIVE
DEFINITIVELY
DEFINITIVENESS
DEFINITIVES
DEFINITIZE
DEFINITIZED
DEFINITIZES
DEFINITIZING
DEFINITUDE
DEFINITUDES
DEFLAGRABILITY
DEFLAGRABLE
DEFLAGRATE
DEFLAGRATED
DEFLAGRATES
DEFLAGRATING
DEFLAGRATION
DEFLAGRATIONS
DEFLAGRATOR
DEFLAGRATORS
DEFLATIONARY
DEFLATIONIST
DEFLATIONISTS
DEFLATIONS
DEFLECTABLE
DEFLECTING
DEFLECTION
DEFLECTIONAL
DEFLECTIONS
DEFLECTIVE
DEFLECTORS

DEFLEXIONAL

DEFLEXIONAL
DEFLEXIONS
DEFLEXURES
DEFLOCCULANT
DEFLOCCULANTS
DEFLOCCULATE
DEFLOCCULATED
DEFLOCCULATES
DEFLOCCULATING
DEFLOCCULATION
DEFLOCCULATIONS
DEFLORATED
DEFLORATES
DEFLORATING
DEFLORATION
DEFLORATIONS
DEFLOWERED
DEFLOWERER
DEFLOWERERS
DEFLOWERING
DEFLUXIONS
DEFOCUSING
DEFOCUSSED
DEFOCUSSES
DEFOCUSSING
DEFOLIANTS
DEFOLIATED
DEFOLIATES
DEFOLIATING
DEFOLIATION
DEFOLIATIONS
DEFOLIATOR
DEFOLIATORS
DEFORCEMENT
DEFORCEMENTS
DEFORCIANT
DEFORCIANTS
DEFORCIATION
DEFORCIATIONS
DEFORESTATION
DEFORESTATIONS
DEFORESTED
DEFORESTER
DEFORESTERS
DEFORESTING
DEFORMABILITIES
DEFORMABILITY
DEFORMABLE
DEFORMALISE
DEFORMALISED
DEFORMALISES
DEFORMALISING
DEFORMALIZE
DEFORMALIZED
DEFORMALIZES
DEFORMALIZING
DEFORMATION
DEFORMATIONAL
DEFORMATIONS

DEFORMATIVE
DEFORMEDLY
DEFORMEDNESS
DEFORMEDNESSES
DEFORMITIES
DEFRAGGERS
DEFRAGGING
DEFRAGMENT
DEFRAGMENTED
DEFRAGMENTING
DEFRAGMENTS
DEFRAUDATION
DEFRAUDATIONS
DEFRAUDERS
DEFRAUDING
DEFRAUDMENT
DEFRAUDMENTS
DEFRAYABLE
DEFRAYMENT
DEFRAYMENTS
DEFREEZING
DEFROCKING
DEFROSTERS
DEFROSTING
DEFTNESSES
DEFUELLING
DEFUNCTION
DEFUNCTIONS
DEFUNCTIVE
DEFUNCTNESS
DEFUNCTNESSES
DEGARNISHED
DEGARNISHES
DEGARNISHING
DEGAUSSERS
DEGAUSSING
DEGEARINGS
DEGENDERED
DEGENDERING
DEGENERACIES
DEGENERACY
DEGENERATE
DEGENERATED
DEGENERATELY
DEGENERATENESS
DEGENERATES
DEGENERATING
DEGENERATION
DEGENERATIONIST
DEGENERATIONS
DEGENERATIVE
DEGENEROUS
DEGLACIATED
DEGLACIATION
DEGLACIATIONS
DEGLAMORISATION
DEGLAMORISE
DEGLAMORISED
DEGLAMORISES

DEGLAMORISING
DEGLAMORIZATION
DEGLAMORIZE
DEGLAMORIZED
DEGLAMORIZES
DEGLAMORIZING
DEGLUTINATE
DEGLUTINATED
DEGLUTINATES
DEGLUTINATING
DEGLUTINATION
DEGLUTINATIONS
DEGLUTITION
DEGLUTITIONS
DEGLUTITIVE
DEGLUTITORY
DEGRADABILITIES
DEGRADABILITY
DEGRADABLE
DEGRADATION
DEGRADATIONS
DEGRADATIVE
DEGRADEDLY
DEGRADINGLY
DEGRADINGNESS
DEGRADINGNESSES
DEGRANULATION
DEGRANULATIONS
DEGREASANT
DEGREASANTS
DEGREASERS
DEGREASING
DEGREELESS
DEGRESSION
DEGRESSIONS
DEGRESSIVE
DEGRESSIVELY
DEGRINGOLADE
DEGRINGOLADED
DEGRINGOLADES
DEGRINGOLADING
DEGRINGOLER
DEGRINGOLERED
DEGRINGOLERING
DEGRINGOLERS
DEGUSTATED
DEGUSTATES
DEGUSTATING
DEGUSTATION
DEGUSTATIONS
DEGUSTATORY
DEHISCENCE
DEHISCENCES
DEHORTATION
DEHORTATIONS
DEHORTATIVE
DEHORTATORY
DEHUMANISATION
DEHUMANISATIONS

DEHUMANISE
DEHUMANISED
DEHUMANISES
DEHUMANISING
DEHUMANIZATION
DEHUMANIZATIONS
DEHUMANIZE
DEHUMANIZED
DEHUMANIZES
DEHUMANIZING
DEHUMIDIFIED
DEHUMIDIFIER
DEHUMIDIFIERS
DEHUMIDIFIES
DEHUMIDIFY
DEHUMIDIFYING
DEHYDRATED
DEHYDRATER
DEHYDRATERS
DEHYDRATES
DEHYDRATING
DEHYDRATION
DEHYDRATIONS
DEHYDRATOR
DEHYDRATORS
DEHYDROGENASE
DEHYDROGENASES
DEHYDROGENATE
DEHYDROGENATED
DEHYDROGENATES
DEHYDROGENATING
DEHYDROGENATION
DEHYDROGENISE
DEHYDROGENISED
DEHYDROGENISES
DEHYDROGENISING
DEHYDROGENIZE
DEHYDROGENIZED
DEHYDROGENIZES
DEHYDROGENIZING
DEHYDRORETINOL
DEHYDRORETINOLS
DEHYPNOTISATION
DEHYPNOTISE
DEHYPNOTISED
DEHYPNOTISES
DEHYPNOTISING
DEHYPNOTIZATION
DEHYPNOTIZE
DEHYPNOTIZED
DEHYPNOTIZES
DEHYPNOTIZING
DEICTICALLY
DEIFICATION
DEIFICATIONS
DEINDEXING
DEINDIVIDUATION
DEINDUSTRIALISE
DEINDUSTRIALIZE

DEINONYCHUS
DEINONYCHUSES
DEINOSAURS
DEINOTHERE
DEINOTHERES
DEINOTHERIUM
DEINOTHERIUMS
DEIONISATION
DEIONISATIONS
DEIONISERS
DEIONISING
DEIONIZATION
DEIONIZATIONS
DEIONIZERS
DEIONIZING
DEIPNOSOPHIST
DEIPNOSOPHISTS
DEISTICALLY
DEJECTEDLY
DEJECTEDNESS
DEJECTEDNESSES
DEJECTIONS
DEKALITERS
DEKALITRES
DEKALOGIES
DEKAMETERS
DEKAMETRES
DEKAMETRIC
DELAMINATE
DELAMINATED
DELAMINATES
DELAMINATING
DELAMINATION
DELAMINATIONS
DELAPSIONS
DELASSEMENT
DELASSEMENTS
DELAYERING
DELAYERINGS
DELAYINGLY
DELECTABILITIES
DELECTABILITY
DELECTABLE
DELECTABLENESS
DELECTABLES
DELECTABLY
DELECTATED
DELECTATES
DELECTATING
DELECTATION
DELECTATIONS
DELEGACIES
DELEGATEES
DELEGATING
DELEGATION
DELEGATIONS
DELEGATORS
DELEGITIMATION
DELEGITIMATIONS

DELEGITIMISE
DELEGITIMISED
DELEGITIMISES
DELEGITIMISING
DELEGITIMIZE
DELEGITIMIZED
DELEGITIMIZES
DELEGITIMIZING
DELETERIOUS
DELETERIOUSLY
DELETERIOUSNESS
DELFTWARES
DELIBATING
DELIBATION
DELIBATIONS
DELIBERATE
DELIBERATED
DELIBERATELY
DELIBERATENESS
DELIBERATES
DELIBERATING
DELIBERATION
DELIBERATIONS
DELIBERATIVE
DELIBERATIVELY
DELIBERATOR
DELIBERATORS
DELICACIES
DELICATELY
DELICATENESS
DELICATENESSES
DELICATESSEN
DELICATESSENS
DELICIOUSLY
DELICIOUSNESS
DELICIOUSNESSES
DELIGATION
DELIGATIONS
DELIGHTEDLY
DELIGHTEDNESS
DELIGHTEDNESSES
DELIGHTERS
DELIGHTFUL
DELIGHTFULLY
DELIGHTFULNESS
DELIGHTING
DELIGHTLESS
DELIGHTSOME
DELIMITATE
DELIMITATED
DELIMITATES
DELIMITATING
DELIMITATION
DELIMITATIONS
DELIMITATIVE
DELIMITERS
DELIMITING
DELINEABLE
DELINEATED

DELINEATES
DELINEATING
DELINEATION
DELINEATIONS
DELINEATIVE
DELINEATOR
DELINEATORS
DELINEAVIT
DELINQUENCIES
DELINQUENCY
DELINQUENT
DELINQUENTLY
DELINQUENTS
DELIQUESCE
DELIQUESCED
DELIQUESCENCE
DELIQUESCENCES
DELIQUESCENT
DELIQUESCES
DELIQUESCING
DELIQUIUMS
DELIRATION
DELIRATIONS
DELIRIFACIENT
DELIRIFACIENTS
DELIRIOUSLY
DELIRIOUSNESS
DELIRIOUSNESSES
DELITESCENCE
DELITESCENCES
DELITESCENT
DELIVERABILITY
DELIVERABLE
DELIVERANCE
DELIVERANCES
DELIVERERS
DELIVERIES
DELIVERING
DELIVERYMAN
DELIVERYMEN
DELOCALISATION
DELOCALISATIONS
DELOCALISE
DELOCALISED
DELOCALISES
DELOCALISING
DELOCALIZATION
DELOCALIZATIONS
DELOCALIZE
DELOCALIZED
DELOCALIZES
DELOCALIZING
DELPHICALLY
DELPHINIUM
DELPHINIUMS
DELPHINOID
DELTIOLOGIES
DELTIOLOGIST
DELTIOLOGISTS

DELTIOLOGY
DELTOIDEUS
DELUDINGLY
DELUNDUNGS
DELUSIONAL
DELUSIONARY
DELUSIONIST
DELUSIONISTS
DELUSIVELY
DELUSIVENESS
DELUSIVENESSES
DELUSTERED
DELUSTERING
DELUSTRANT
DELUSTRANTS
DEMAGNETISATION
DEMAGNETISE
DEMAGNETISED
DEMAGNETISER
DEMAGNETISERS
DEMAGNETISES
DEMAGNETISING
DEMAGNETIZATION
DEMAGNETIZE
DEMAGNETIZED
DEMAGNETIZER
DEMAGNETIZERS
DEMAGNETIZES
DEMAGNETIZING
DEMAGOGICAL
DEMAGOGICALLY
DEMAGOGIES
DEMAGOGING
DEMAGOGISM
DEMAGOGISMS
DEMAGOGUED
DEMAGOGUERIES
DEMAGOGUERY
DEMAGOGUES
DEMAGOGUING
DEMAGOGUISM
DEMAGOGUISMS
DEMANDABLE
DEMANDANTS
DEMANDINGLY
DEMANDINGNESS
DEMANDINGNESSES
DEMANNINGS
DEMANTOIDS
DEMARCATED
DEMARCATES
DEMARCATING
DEMARCATION
DEMARCATIONS
DEMARCATOR
DEMARCATORS
DEMARKATION
DEMARKATIONS
DEMARKETED

DEMARKETING	DEMIREPDOMS	DEMOGRAPHICAL	DEMONOLATRIES
DEMATERIALISE	DEMISEMIQUAVER	DEMOGRAPHICALLY	DEMONOLATRY
DEMATERIALISED	DEMISEMIQUAVERS	DEMOGRAPHICS	DEMONOLOGIC
DEMATERIALISES	DEMISSIONS	DEMOGRAPHIES	DEMONOLOGICAL
DEMATERIALISING	DEMITASSES	DEMOGRAPHIST	DEMONOLOGIES
DEMATERIALIZE	DEMIURGEOUS	DEMOGRAPHISTS	DEMONOLOGIST
DEMATERIALIZED	DEMIURGICAL	DEMOGRAPHY	DEMONOLOGISTS
DEMATERIALIZES	DEMIURGICALLY	DEMOISELLE	DEMONOLOGY
DEMATERIALIZING	DEMIURGUSES	DEMOISELLES	DEMONOMANIA
DEMEANOURS	DEMIVEGGES	DEMOLISHED	DEMONOMANIAS
DEMEASNURE	DEMIVIERGE	DEMOLISHER	DEMONSTRABILITY
DEMEASNURES	DEMIVIERGES	DEMOLISHERS	DEMONSTRABLE
DEMENTATED	DEMIVOLTES	DEMOLISHES	DEMONSTRABLY
DEMENTATES	DEMIWORLDS	DEMOLISHING	DEMONSTRATE
DEMENTATING	DEMOBILISATION	DEMOLISHMENT	DEMONSTRATED
DEMENTEDLY	DEMOBILISATIONS	DEMOLISHMENTS	DEMONSTRATES
DEMENTEDNESS	DEMOBILISE	DEMOLITION	DEMONSTRATING
DEMENTEDNESSES	DEMOBILISED	DEMOLITIONIST	DEMONSTRATION
DEMERGERED	DEMOBILISES	DEMOLITIONISTS	DEMONSTRATIONAL
DEMERGERING	DEMOBILISING	DEMOLITIONS	DEMONSTRATIONS
DEMERITING	DEMOBILIZATION	DEMOLOGIES	DEMONSTRATIVE
DEMERITORIOUS	DEMOBILIZATIONS	DEMONESSES	DEMONSTRATIVELY
DEMERITORIOUSLY	DEMOBILIZE	DEMONETARISE	DEMONSTRATIVES
DEMERSIONS	DEMOBILIZED	DEMONETARISED	DEMONSTRATOR
DEMIBASTION	DEMOBILIZES	DEMONETARISES	DEMONSTRATORS
DEMIBASTIONS	DEMOBILIZING	DEMONETARISING	DEMONSTRATORY
DEMICANTON	DEMOCRACIES	DEMONETARIZE	DEMORALISATION
DEMICANTONS	DEMOCRATIC	DEMONETARIZED	DEMORALISATIONS
DEMIGODDESS	DEMOCRATICAL	DEMONETARIZES	DEMORALISE
DEMIGODDESSES	DEMOCRATICALLY	DEMONETARIZING	DEMORALISED
DEMIGRATION	DEMOCRATIES	DEMONETISATION	DEMORALISER
DEMIGRATIONS	DEMOCRATIFIABLE	DEMONETISATIONS	DEMORALISERS
DEMILITARISE	DEMOCRATISATION	DEMONETISE	DEMORALISES
DEMILITARISED	DEMOCRATISE	DEMONETISED	DEMORALISING
DEMILITARISES	DEMOCRATISED	DEMONETISES	DEMORALISINGLY
DEMILITARISING	DEMOCRATISER	DEMONETISING	DEMORALIZATION
DEMILITARIZE	DEMOCRATISERS	DEMONETIZATION	DEMORALIZATIONS
DEMILITARIZED	DEMOCRATISES	DEMONETIZATIONS	DEMORALIZE
DEMILITARIZES	DEMOCRATISING	DEMONETIZE	DEMORALIZED
DEMILITARIZING	DEMOCRATIST	DEMONETIZED	DEMORALIZER
DEMIMONDAINE	DEMOCRATISTS	DEMONETIZES	DEMORALIZERS
DEMIMONDAINES	DEMOCRATIZATION	DEMONETIZING	DEMORALIZES
DEMIMONDES	DEMOCRATIZE	DEMONIACAL	DEMORALIZING
DEMINERALISE	DEMOCRATIZED	DEMONIACALLY	DEMORALIZINGLY
DEMINERALISED	DEMOCRATIZER	DEMONIACISM	DEMOTICIST
DEMINERALISER	DEMOCRATIZERS	DEMONIACISMS	DEMOTICISTS
DEMINERALISERS	DEMOCRATIZES	DEMONIANISM	DEMOTIVATE
DEMINERALISES	DEMOCRATIZING	DEMONIANISMS	DEMOTIVATED
DEMINERALISING	DEMODULATE	DEMONICALLY	DEMOTIVATES
DEMINERALIZE	DEMODULATED	DEMONISATION	DEMOTIVATING
DEMINERALIZED	DEMODULATES	DEMONISATIONS	DEMOUNTABLE
DEMINERALIZER	DEMODULATING	DEMONISING	DEMOUNTING
DEMINERALIZERS	DEMODULATION	DEMONIZATION	DEMULCENTS
DEMINERALIZES	DEMODULATIONS	DEMONIZATIONS	DEMULSIFICATION
DEMINERALIZING	DEMODULATOR	DEMONIZING	DEMULSIFIED
DEMIPIQUES	DEMODULATORS	DEMONOCRACIES	DEMULSIFIER
DEMIRELIEF	DEMOGRAPHER	DEMONOCRACY	DEMULSIFIERS
DEMIRELIEFS	DEMOGRAPHERS	DEMONOLATER	DEMULSIFIES
DEMIREPDOM	DEMOGRAPHIC	DEMONOLATERS	DEMULSIFYING

DEMULTIPLEXER
DEMULTIPLEXERS
DEMURENESS
DEMURENESSES
DEMURRABLE
DEMURRAGES
DEMUTUALISATION
DEMUTUALISE
DEMUTUALISED
DEMUTUALISES
DEMUTUALISING
DEMUTUALIZATION
DEMUTUALIZE
DEMUTUALIZED
DEMUTUALIZES
DEMUTUALIZING
DEMYELINATE
DEMYELINATED
DEMYELINATES
DEMYELINATING
DEMYELINATION
DEMYELINATIONS
DEMYSTIFICATION
DEMYSTIFIED
DEMYSTIFIES
DEMYSTIFYING
DEMYTHOLOGISE
DEMYTHOLOGISED
DEMYTHOLOGISER
DEMYTHOLOGISERS
DEMYTHOLOGISES
DEMYTHOLOGISING
DEMYTHOLOGIZE
DEMYTHOLOGIZED
DEMYTHOLOGIZER
DEMYTHOLOGIZERS
DEMYTHOLOGIZES
DEMYTHOLOGIZING
DENATIONALISE
DENATIONALISED
DENATIONALISES
DENATIONALISING
DENATIONALIZE
DENATIONALIZED
DENATIONALIZES
DENATIONALIZING
DENATURALISE
DENATURALISED
DENATURALISES
DENATURALISING
DENATURALIZE
DENATURALIZED
DENATURALIZES
DENATURALIZING
DENATURANT
DENATURANTS
DENATURATION
DENATURATIONS
DENATURING

DENATURISE
DENATURISED
DENATURISES
DENATURISING
DENATURIZE
DENATURIZED
DENATURIZES
DENATURIZING
DENAZIFICATION
DENAZIFICATIONS
DENAZIFIED
DENAZIFIES
DENAZIFYING
DENDRACHATE
DENDRACHATES
DENDRIFORM
DENDRIMERS
DENDRITICAL
DENDRITICALLY
DENDROBIUM
DENDROBIUMS
DENDROGLYPH
DENDROGLYPHS
DENDROGRAM
DENDROGRAMS
DENDROIDAL
DENDROLATRIES
DENDROLATRY
DENDROLOGIC
DENDROLOGICAL
DENDROLOGIES
DENDROLOGIST
DENDROLOGISTS
DENDROLOGOUS
DENDROLOGY
DENDROMETER
DENDROMETERS
DENDROPHIS
DENDROPHISES
DENEGATION
DENEGATIONS
DENERVATED
DENERVATES
DENERVATING
DENERVATION
DENERVATIONS
DENIABILITIES
DENIABILITY
DENIGRATED
DENIGRATES
DENIGRATING
DENIGRATION
DENIGRATIONS
DENIGRATIVE
DENIGRATOR
DENIGRATORS
DENIGRATORY
DENISATION
DENISATIONS

DENITRATED
DENITRATES
DENITRATING
DENITRATION
DENITRATIONS
DENITRIFICATION
DENITRIFICATOR
DENITRIFICATORS
DENITRIFIED
DENITRIFIER
DENITRIFIERS
DENITRIFIES
DENITRIFYING
DENIZATION
DENIZATIONS
DENIZENING
DENIZENSHIP
DENIZENSHIPS
DENOMINABLE
DENOMINATE
DENOMINATED
DENOMINATES
DENOMINATING
DENOMINATION
DENOMINATIONAL
DENOMINATIONS
DENOMINATIVE
DENOMINATIVELY
DENOMINATIVES
DENOMINATOR
DENOMINATORS
DENOTATING
DENOTATION
DENOTATIONS
DENOTATIVE
DENOTATIVELY
DENOTEMENT
DENOTEMENTS
DENOUEMENT
DENOUEMENTS
DENOUNCEMENT
DENOUNCEMENTS
DENOUNCERS
DENOUNCING
DENSENESSES
DENSIFICATION
DENSIFICATIONS
DENSIFIERS
DENSIFYING
DENSIMETER
DENSIMETERS
DENSIMETRIC
DENSIMETRIES
DENSIMETRY
DENSITOMETER
DENSITOMETERS
DENSITOMETRIC
DENSITOMETRIES
DENSITOMETRY

DENTALITIES
DENTALIUMS
DENTATIONS
DENTICULATE
DENTICULATED
DENTICULATELY
DENTICULATION
DENTICULATIONS
DENTIFRICE
DENTIFRICES
DENTIGEROUS
DENTILABIAL
DENTILINGUAL
DENTILINGUALS
DENTIROSTRAL
DENTISTRIES
DENTITIONS
DENTURISTS
DENUCLEARISE
DENUCLEARISED
DENUCLEARISES
DENUCLEARISING
DENUCLEARIZE
DENUCLEARIZED
DENUCLEARIZES
DENUCLEARIZING
DENUDATING
DENUDATION
DENUDATIONS
DENUDEMENT
DENUDEMENTS
DENUMERABILITY
DENUMERABLE
DENUMERABLY
DENUNCIATE
DENUNCIATED
DENUNCIATES
DENUNCIATING
DENUNCIATION
DENUNCIATIONS
DENUNCIATIVE
DENUNCIATOR
DENUNCIATORS
DENUNCIATORY
DEOBSTRUENT
DEOBSTRUENTS
DEODORANTS
DEODORISATION
DEODORISATIONS
DEODORISED
DEODORISER
DEODORISERS
DEODORISES
DEODORISING
DEODORIZATION
DEODORIZATIONS
DEODORIZED
DEODORIZER
DEODORIZERS

DEODORIZES

DEODORIZES	DEPARTMENTALISE	DEPHLOGISTICATE	DEPOLYMERISING
DEODORIZING	DEPARTMENTALISM	DEPHOSPHORYLATE	DEPOLYMERIZE
DEONTOLOGICAL	DEPARTMENTALIZE	DEPICTIONS	DEPOLYMERIZED
DEONTOLOGIES	DEPARTMENTALLY	DEPICTURED	DEPOLYMERIZES
DEONTOLOGIST	DEPARTMENTS	DEPICTURES	DEPOLYMERIZING
DEONTOLOGISTS	DEPARTURES	DEPICTURING	DEPOPULATE
DEONTOLOGY	DEPASTURED	DEPIGMENTATION	DEPOPULATED
DEOPPILATE	DEPASTURES	DEPIGMENTATIONS	DEPOPULATES
DEOPPILATED	DEPASTURING	DEPILATING	DEPOPULATING
DEOPPILATES	DEPAUPERATE	DEPILATION	DEPOPULATION
DEOPPILATING	DEPAUPERATED	DEPILATIONS	DEPOPULATIONS
DEOPPILATION	DEPAUPERATES	DEPILATORIES	DEPOPULATOR
DEOPPILATIONS	DEPAUPERATING	DEPILATORS	DEPOPULATORS
DEOPPILATIVE	DEPAUPERISE	DEPILATORY	DEPORTABLE
DEORBITING	DEPAUPERISED	DEPLETABLE	DEPORTATION
DEOXIDATED	DEPAUPERISES	DEPLETIONS	DEPORTATIONS
DEOXIDATES	DEPAUPERISING	DEPLORABILITIES	DEPORTMENT
DEOXIDATING	DEPAUPERIZE	DEPLORABILITY	DEPORTMENTS
DEOXIDATION	DEPAUPERIZED	DEPLORABLE	DEPOSITARIES
DEOXIDATIONS	DEPAUPERIZES	DEPLORABLENESS	DEPOSITARY
DEOXIDISATION	DEPAUPERIZING	DEPLORABLY	DEPOSITATION
DEOXIDISATIONS	DEPEINCTED	DEPLORATION	DEPOSITATIONS
DEOXIDISED	DEPEINCTING	DEPLORATIONS	DEPOSITING
DEOXIDISER	DEPENDABILITIES	DEPLORINGLY	DEPOSITION
DEOXIDISERS	DEPENDABILITY	DEPLOYABLE	DEPOSITIONAL
DEOXIDISES	DEPENDABLE	DEPLOYMENT	DEPOSITIONS
DEOXIDISING	DEPENDABLENESS	DEPLOYMENTS	DEPOSITIVE
DEOXIDIZATION	DEPENDABLY	DEPLUMATION	DEPOSITORIES
DEOXIDIZATIONS	DEPENDACIE	DEPLUMATIONS	DEPOSITORS
DEOXIDIZED	DEPENDACIES	DEPOLARISATION	DEPOSITORY
DEOXIDIZER	DEPENDANCE	DEPOLARISATIONS	DEPRAVATION
DEOXIDIZERS	DEPENDANCES	DEPOLARISE	DEPRAVATIONS
DEOXIDIZES	DEPENDANCIES	DEPOLARISED	DEPRAVEDLY
DEOXIDIZING	DEPENDANCY	DEPOLARISER	DEPRAVEDNESS
DEOXYCORTONE	DEPENDANTS	DEPOLARISERS	DEPRAVEDNESSES
DEOXYCORTONES	DEPENDENCE	DEPOLARISES	DEPRAVEMENT
DEOXYGENATE	DEPENDENCES	DEPOLARISING	DEPRAVEMENTS
DEOXYGENATED	DEPENDENCIES	DEPOLARIZATION	DEPRAVINGLY
DEOXYGENATES	DEPENDENCY	DEPOLARIZATIONS	DEPRAVITIES
DEOXYGENATING	DEPENDENTLY	DEPOLARIZE	DEPRECABLE
DEOXYGENATION	DEPENDENTS	DEPOLARIZED	DEPRECATED
DEOXYGENATIONS	DEPENDINGLY	DEPOLARIZER	DEPRECATES
DEOXYGENISE	DEPEOPLING	DEPOLARIZERS	DEPRECATING
DEOXYGENISED	DEPERSONALISE	DEPOLARIZES	DEPRECATINGLY
DEOXYGENISES	DEPERSONALISED	DEPOLARIZING	DEPRECATION
DEOXYGENISING	DEPERSONALISES	DEPOLISHED	DEPRECATIONS
DEOXYGENIZE	DEPERSONALISING	DEPOLISHES	DEPRECATIVE
DEOXYGENIZED	DEPERSONALIZE	DEPOLISHING	DEPRECATIVELY
DEOXYGENIZES	DEPERSONALIZED	DEPOLITICISE	DEPRECATOR
DEOXYGENIZING	DEPERSONALIZES	DEPOLITICISED	DEPRECATORILY
DEOXYRIBOSE	DEPERSONALIZING	DEPOLITICISES	DEPRECATORS
DEOXYRIBOSES	DEPHLEGMATE	DEPOLITICISING	DEPRECATORY
DEPAINTING	DEPHLEGMATED	DEPOLITICIZE	DEPRECIABLE
DEPANNEURS	DEPHLEGMATES	DEPOLITICIZED	DEPRECIATE
DEPARTEMENT	DEPHLEGMATING	DEPOLITICIZES	DEPRECIATED
DEPARTEMENTS	DEPHLEGMATION	DEPOLITICIZING	DEPRECIATES
DEPARTINGS	DEPHLEGMATIONS	DEPOLYMERISE	DEPRECIATING
DEPARTMENT	DEPHLEGMATOR	DEPOLYMERISED	DEPRECIATINGLY
DEPARTMENTAL	DEPHLEGMATORS	DEPOLYMERISES	DEPRECIATION

DEPRECIATIONS
DEPRECIATIVE
DEPRECIATOR
DEPRECIATORS
DEPRECIATORY
DEPREDATED
DEPREDATES
DEPREDATING
DEPREDATION
DEPREDATIONS
DEPREDATOR
DEPREDATORS
DEPREDATORY
DEPREHENDED
DEPREHENDING
DEPREHENDS
DEPRESSANT
DEPRESSANTS
DEPRESSIBLE
DEPRESSING
DEPRESSINGLY
DEPRESSION
DEPRESSIONS
DEPRESSIVE
DEPRESSIVELY
DEPRESSIVENESS
DEPRESSIVES
DEPRESSOMOTOR
DEPRESSOMOTORS
DEPRESSORS
DEPRESSURISE
DEPRESSURISED
DEPRESSURISES
DEPRESSURISING
DEPRESSURIZE
DEPRESSURIZED
DEPRESSURIZES
DEPRESSURIZING
DEPRIVABLE
DEPRIVATION
DEPRIVATIONS
DEPRIVATIVE
DEPRIVEMENT
DEPRIVEMENTS
DEPROGRAMED
DEPROGRAMING
DEPROGRAMME
DEPROGRAMMED
DEPROGRAMMER
DEPROGRAMMERS
DEPROGRAMMES
DEPROGRAMMING
DEPROGRAMS
DEPURATING
DEPURATION
DEPURATIONS
DEPURATIVE
DEPURATIVES
DEPURATORS

DEPURATORY
DEPUTATION
DEPUTATIONS
DEPUTISATION
DEPUTISATIONS
DEPUTISING
DEPUTIZATION
DEPUTIZATIONS
DEPUTIZING
DERACIALISE
DERACIALISED
DERACIALISES
DERACIALISING
DERACIALIZE
DERACIALIZED
DERACIALIZES
DERACIALIZING
DERACINATE
DERACINATED
DERACINATES
DERACINATING
DERACINATION
DERACINATIONS
DERAIGNING
DERAIGNMENT
DERAIGNMENTS
DERAILLEUR
DERAILLEURS
DERAILMENT
DERAILMENTS
DERANGEMENT
DERANGEMENTS
DERATIONED
DERATIONING
DEREALISATION
DEREALISATIONS
DEREALIZATION
DEREALIZATIONS
DERECOGNISE
DERECOGNISED
DERECOGNISES
DERECOGNISING
DERECOGNITION
DERECOGNITIONS
DERECOGNIZE
DERECOGNIZED
DERECOGNIZES
DERECOGNIZING
DEREGISTER
DEREGISTERED
DEREGISTERING
DEREGISTERS
DEREGISTRATION
DEREGISTRATIONS
DEREGULATE
DEREGULATED
DEREGULATES
DEREGULATING
DEREGULATION

DEREGULATIONS
DEREGULATOR
DEREGULATORS
DEREGULATORY
DERELICTION
DERELICTIONS
DERELIGIONISE
DERELIGIONISED
DERELIGIONISES
DERELIGIONISING
DERELIGIONIZE
DERELIGIONIZED
DERELIGIONIZES
DERELIGIONIZING
DEREPRESSED
DEREPRESSES
DEREPRESSING
DEREPRESSION
DEREPRESSIONS
DEREQUISITION
DEREQUISITIONED
DEREQUISITIONS
DERESTRICT
DERESTRICTED
DERESTRICTING
DERESTRICTION
DERESTRICTIONS
DERESTRICTS
DERIDINGLY
DERISIVELY
DERISIVENESS
DERISIVENESSES
DERIVATION
DERIVATIONAL
DERIVATIONIST
DERIVATIONISTS
DERIVATIONS
DERIVATISATION
DERIVATISATIONS
DERIVATISE
DERIVATISED
DERIVATISES
DERIVATISING
DERIVATIVE
DERIVATIVELY
DERIVATIVENESS
DERIVATIVES
DERIVATIZATION
DERIVATIZATIONS
DERIVATIZE
DERIVATIZED
DERIVATIZES
DERIVATIZING
DERMABRASION
DERMABRASIONS
DERMAPTERAN
DERMAPTERANS
DERMATITIS
DERMATITISES

DERMATOGEN
DERMATOGENS
DERMATOGLYPHIC
DERMATOGLYPHICS
DERMATOGRAPHIA
DERMATOGRAPHIAS
DERMATOGRAPHIC
DERMATOGRAPHIES
DERMATOGRAPHY
DERMATOLOGIC
DERMATOLOGICAL
DERMATOLOGIES
DERMATOLOGIST
DERMATOLOGISTS
DERMATOLOGY
DERMATOMAL
DERMATOMES
DERMATOMIC
DERMATOMYOSITIS
DERMATOPHYTE
DERMATOPHYTES
DERMATOPHYTIC
DERMATOPHYTOSES
DERMATOPHYTOSIS
DERMATOPLASTIC
DERMATOPLASTIES
DERMATOPLASTY
DERMATOSES
DERMATOSIS
DERMESTIDS
DERMOGRAPHIES
DERMOGRAPHY
DEROGATELY
DEROGATING
DEROGATION
DEROGATIONS
DEROGATIVE
DEROGATIVELY
DEROGATORILY
DEROGATORINESS
DEROGATORY
DERRICKING
DERRINGERS
DESACRALISATION
DESACRALISE
DESACRALISED
DESACRALISES
DESACRALISING
DESACRALIZATION
DESACRALIZE
DESACRALIZED
DESACRALIZES
DESACRALIZING
DESAGREMENT
DESAGREMENTS
DESALINATE
DESALINATED
DESALINATES
DESALINATING

DESALINATION

DESALINATION	DESCRIVING	DESEXUALIZE	DESIPIENCES
DESALINATIONS	DESECRATED	DESEXUALIZED	DESIPRAMINE
DESALINATOR	DESECRATER	DESEXUALIZES	DESIPRAMINES
DESALINATORS	DESECRATERS	DESEXUALIZING	DESIRABILITIES
DESALINISATION	DESECRATES	DESHABILLE	DESIRABILITY
DESALINISATIONS	DESECRATING	DESHABILLES	DESIRABLENESS
DESALINISE	DESECRATION	DESICCANTS	DESIRABLENESSES
DESALINISED	DESECRATIONS	DESICCATED	DESIRABLES
DESALINISES	DESECRATOR	DESICCATES	DESIRELESS
DESALINISING	DESECRATORS	DESICCATING	DESIROUSLY
DESALINIZATION	DESEGREGATE	DESICCATION	DESIROUSNESS
DESALINIZATIONS	DESEGREGATED	DESICCATIONS	DESIROUSNESSES
DESALINIZE	DESEGREGATES	DESICCATIVE	DESISTANCE
DESALINIZED	DESEGREGATING	DESICCATIVES	DESISTANCES
DESALINIZES	DESEGREGATION	DESICCATOR	DESISTENCE
DESALINIZING	DESEGREGATIONS	DESICCATORS	DESISTENCES
DESALTINGS	DESELECTED	DESIDERATA	DESKILLING
DESATURATION	DESELECTING	DESIDERATE	DESKILLINGS
DESATURATIONS	DESELECTION	DESIDERATED	DESMODIUMS
DESCANTERS	DESELECTIONS	DESIDERATES	DESMODROMIC
DESCANTING	DESENSITISATION	DESIDERATING	DESMOSOMAL
DESCENDABLE	DESENSITISE	DESIDERATION	DESMOSOMES
DESCENDANT	DESENSITISED	DESIDERATIONS	DESNOODING
DESCENDANTS	DESENSITISER	DESIDERATIVE	DESOBLIGEANTE
DESCENDENT	DESENSITISERS	DESIDERATIVES	DESOBLIGEANTES
DESCENDENTS	DESENSITISES	DESIDERATUM	DESOLATELY
DESCENDERS	DESENSITISING	DESIDERIUM	DESOLATENESS
DESCENDEUR	DESENSITIZATION	DESIDERIUMS	DESOLATENESSES
DESCENDEURS	DESENSITIZE	DESIGNABLE	DESOLATERS
DESCENDIBLE	DESENSITIZED	DESIGNATED	DESOLATING
DESCENDING	DESENSITIZER	DESIGNATES	DESOLATINGLY
DESCENDINGS	DESENSITIZERS	DESIGNATING	DESOLATION
DESCENSION	DESENSITIZES	DESIGNATION	DESOLATIONS
DESCENSIONAL	DESENSITIZING	DESIGNATIONS	DESOLATORS
DESCENSIONS	DESERPIDINE	DESIGNATIVE	DESOLATORY
DESCHOOLED	DESERPIDINES	DESIGNATOR	DESORIENTE
DESCHOOLER	DESERTIFICATION	DESIGNATORS	DESORPTION
DESCHOOLERS	DESERTIFIED	DESIGNATORY	DESORPTIONS
DESCHOOLING	DESERTIFIES	DESIGNEDLY	DESOXYRIBOSE
DESCHOOLINGS	DESERTIFYING	DESIGNINGLY	DESOXYRIBOSES
DESCRAMBLE	DESERTIONS	DESIGNINGS	DESPAIRERS
DESCRAMBLED	DESERTISATION	DESIGNLESS	DESPAIRFUL
DESCRAMBLER	DESERTISATIONS	DESIGNMENT	DESPAIRING
DESCRAMBLERS	DESERTIZATION	DESIGNMENTS	DESPAIRINGLY
DESCRAMBLES	DESERTIZATIONS	DESILVERED	DESPATCHED
DESCRAMBLING	DESERTLESS	DESILVERING	DESPATCHER
DESCRIBABLE	DESERVEDLY	DESILVERISATION	DESPATCHERS
DESCRIBERS	DESERVEDNESS	DESILVERISE	DESPATCHES
DESCRIBING	DESERVEDNESSES	DESILVERISED	DESPATCHING
DESCRIPTION	DESERVINGLY	DESILVERISES	DESPERADOES
DESCRIPTIONS	DESERVINGNESS	DESILVERISING	DESPERADOS
DESCRIPTIVE	DESERVINGNESSES	DESILVERIZATION	DESPERATELY
DESCRIPTIVELY	DESERVINGS	DESILVERIZE	DESPERATENESS
DESCRIPTIVENESS	DESEXUALISATION	DESILVERIZED	DESPERATENESSES
DESCRIPTIVISM	DESEXUALISE	DESILVERIZES	DESPERATION
DESCRIPTIVISMS	DESEXUALISED	DESILVERIZING	DESPERATIONS
DESCRIPTIVIST	DESEXUALISES	DESINENCES	DESPICABILITIES
DESCRIPTOR	DESEXUALISING	DESINENTIAL	DESPICABILITY
DESCRIPTORS	DESEXUALIZATION	DESIPIENCE	DESPICABLE

DESPICABLENESS	DESSIGNMENTS	DESULFURED	DETECTIBLE
DESPICABLY	DESSYATINE	DESULFURING	DETECTIONS
DESPIRITUALISE	DESSYATINES	DESULFURISATION	DETECTIVELIKE
DESPIRITUALISED	DESTABILISATION	DESULFURISE	DETECTIVES
DESPIRITUALISES	DESTABILISE	DESULFURISED	DETECTIVIST
DESPIRITUALIZE	DESTABILISED	DESULFURISES	DETECTIVISTS
DESPIRITUALIZED	DESTABILISER	DESULFURISING	DETECTOPHONE
DESPIRITUALIZES	DESTABILISERS	DESULFURIZATION	DETECTOPHONES
DESPISABLE	DESTABILISES	DESULFURIZE	DETECTORIST
DESPISEDNESS	DESTABILISING	DESULFURIZED	DETECTORISTS
DESPISEDNESSES	DESTABILIZATION	DESULFURIZES	DETENTIONS
DESPISEMENT	DESTABILIZE	DESULFURIZING	DETENTISTS
DESPISEMENTS	DESTABILIZED	DESULPHURATE	DETERGENCE
DESPITEFUL	DESTABILIZER	DESULPHURATED	DETERGENCES
DESPITEFULLY	DESTABILIZERS	DESULPHURATES	DETERGENCIES
DESPITEFULNESS	DESTABILIZES	DESULPHURATING	DETERGENCY
DESPITEOUS	DESTABILIZING	DESULPHURATION	DETERGENTS
DESPITEOUSLY	DESTAINING	DESULPHURATIONS	DETERIORATE
DESPOILERS	DESTEMPERED	DESULPHURED	DETERIORATED
DESPOILING	DESTEMPERING	DESULPHURING	DETERIORATES
DESPOILMENT	DESTEMPERS	DESULPHURISE	DETERIORATING
DESPOILMENTS	DESTINATED	DESULPHURISED	DETERIORATION
DESPOLIATION	DESTINATES	DESULPHURISER	DETERIORATIONS
DESPOLIATIONS	DESTINATING	DESULPHURISERS	DETERIORATIVE
DESPONDENCE	DESTINATION	DESULPHURISES	DETERIORISM
DESPONDENCES	DESTINATIONS	DESULPHURISING	DETERIORISMS
DESPONDENCIES	DESTITUTED	DESULPHURIZE	DETERIORITIES
DESPONDENCY	DESTITUTENESS	DESULPHURIZED	DETERIORITY
DESPONDENT	DESTITUTENESSES	DESULPHURIZER	DETERMENTS
DESPONDENTLY	DESTITUTES	DESULPHURIZERS	DETERMINABILITY
DESPONDING	DESTITUTING	DESULPHURIZES	DETERMINABLE
DESPONDINGLY	DESTITUTION	DESULPHURIZING	DETERMINABLY
DESPONDINGS	DESTITUTIONS	DESULPHURS	DETERMINACIES
DESPOTATES	DESTOCKING	DESULTORILY	DETERMINACY
DESPOTICAL	DESTROYABLE	DESULTORINESS	DETERMINANT
DESPOTICALLY	DESTROYERS	DESULTORINESSES	DETERMINANTAL
DESPOTICALNESS	DESTROYING	DETACHABILITIES	DETERMINANTS
DESPOTISMS	DESTRUCTED	DETACHABILITY	DETERMINATE
DESPOTOCRACIES	DESTRUCTIBILITY	DETACHABLE	DETERMINATED
DESPOTOCRACY	DESTRUCTIBLE	DETACHABLY	DETERMINATELY
DESPUMATED	DESTRUCTING	DETACHEDLY	DETERMINATENESS
DESPUMATES	DESTRUCTION	DETACHEDNESS	DETERMINATES
DESPUMATING	DESTRUCTIONAL	DETACHEDNESSES	DETERMINATING
DESPUMATION	DESTRUCTIONIST	DETACHMENT	DETERMINATION
DESPUMATIONS	DESTRUCTIONISTS	DETACHMENTS	DETERMINATIONS
DESQUAMATE	DESTRUCTIONS	DETAILEDLY	DETERMINATIVE
DESQUAMATED	DESTRUCTIVE	DETAILEDNESS	DETERMINATIVELY
DESQUAMATES	DESTRUCTIVELY	DETAILEDNESSES	DETERMINATIVES
DESQUAMATING	DESTRUCTIVENESS	DETAILINGS	DETERMINATOR
DESQUAMATION	DESTRUCTIVES	DETAINABLE	DETERMINATORS
DESQUAMATIONS	DESTRUCTIVIST	DETAINMENT	DETERMINED
DESQUAMATIVE	DESTRUCTIVISTS	DETAINMENTS	DETERMINEDLY
DESQUAMATORY	DESTRUCTIVITIES	DETASSELED	DETERMINEDNESS
DESSERTSPOON	DESTRUCTIVITY	DETASSELING	DETERMINER
DESSERTSPOONFUL	DESTRUCTOR	DETASSELLED	DETERMINERS
DESSERTSPOONS	DESTRUCTORS	DETASSELLING	DETERMINES
DESSIATINE	DESTRUCTOS	DETECTABILITIES	DETERMINING
DESSIATINES	DESUETUDES	DETECTABILITY	DETERMINISM
DESSIGNMENT	DESUGARING	DETECTABLE	DETERMINISMS

DETERMINIST
DETERMINISTIC
DETERMINISTS
DETERRABILITIES
DETERRABILITY
DETERRABLE
DETERRENCE
DETERRENCES
DETERRENTLY
DETERRENTS
DETERSIONS
DETERSIVES
DETESTABILITIES
DETESTABILITY
DETESTABLE
DETESTABLENESS
DETESTABLY
DETESTATION
DETESTATIONS
DETHATCHED
DETHATCHES
DETHATCHING
DETHRONEMENT
DETHRONEMENTS
DETHRONERS
DETHRONING
DETHRONINGS
DETONABILITIES
DETONABILITY
DETONATABLE
DETONATING
DETONATION
DETONATIONS
DETONATIVE
DETONATORS
DETORSIONS
DETORTIONS
DETOXICANT
DETOXICANTS
DETOXICATE
DETOXICATED
DETOXICATES
DETOXICATING
DETOXICATION
DETOXICATIONS
DETOXIFICATION
DETOXIFICATIONS
DETOXIFIED
DETOXIFIES
DETOXIFYING
DETRACTING
DETRACTINGLY
DETRACTINGS
DETRACTION
DETRACTIONS
DETRACTIVE
DETRACTIVELY
DETRACTORS
DETRACTORY

DETRACTRESS
DETRACTRESSES
DETRAINING
DETRAINMENT
DETRAINMENTS
DETRAQUEES
DETRIBALISATION
DETRIBALISE
DETRIBALISED
DETRIBALISES
DETRIBALISING
DETRIBALIZATION
DETRIBALIZE
DETRIBALIZED
DETRIBALIZES
DETRIBALIZING
DETRIMENTAL
DETRIMENTALLY
DETRIMENTALS
DETRIMENTS
DETRITIONS
DETRITOVORE
DETRITOVORES
DETRUNCATE
DETRUNCATED
DETRUNCATES
DETRUNCATING
DETRUNCATION
DETRUNCATIONS
DETRUSIONS
DETUMESCENCE
DETUMESCENCES
DETUMESCENT
DEUTERAGONIST
DEUTERAGONISTS
DEUTERANOMALIES
DEUTERANOMALOUS
DEUTERANOMALY
DEUTERANOPE
DEUTERANOPES
DEUTERANOPIA
DEUTERANOPIAS
DEUTERANOPIC
DEUTERATED
DEUTERATES
DEUTERATING
DEUTERATION
DEUTERATIONS
DEUTERIDES
DEUTERIUMS
DEUTEROGAMIES
DEUTEROGAMIST
DEUTEROGAMISTS
DEUTEROGAMY
DEUTEROPLASM
DEUTEROPLASMS
DEUTEROSCOPIC
DEUTEROSCOPIES
DEUTEROSCOPY

DEUTEROSTOME
DEUTEROSTOMES
DEUTEROTOKIES
DEUTEROTOKY
DEUTOPLASM
DEUTOPLASMIC
DEUTOPLASMS
DEUTOPLASTIC
DEVALORISATION
DEVALORISATIONS
DEVALORISE
DEVALORISED
DEVALORISES
DEVALORISING
DEVALORIZATION
DEVALORIZATIONS
DEVALORIZE
DEVALORIZED
DEVALORIZES
DEVALORIZING
DEVALUATED
DEVALUATES
DEVALUATING
DEVALUATION
DEVALUATIONS
DEVANAGARI
DEVANAGARIS
DEVASTATED
DEVASTATES
DEVASTATING
DEVASTATINGLY
DEVASTATION
DEVASTATIONS
DEVASTATIVE
DEVASTATOR
DEVASTATORS
DEVASTAVIT
DEVASTAVITS
DEVELOPABLE
DEVELOPERS
DEVELOPING
DEVELOPMENT
DEVELOPMENTAL
DEVELOPMENTALLY
DEVELOPMENTS
DEVELOPPES
DEVERBATIVE
DEVERBATIVES
DEVIANCIES
DEVIATIONISM
DEVIATIONISMS
DEVIATIONIST
DEVIATIONISTS
DEVIATIONS
DEVILESSES
DEVILFISHES
DEVILISHLY
DEVILISHNESS
DEVILISHNESSES

DEVILMENTS
DEVILSHIPS
DEVILTRIES
DEVILWOODS
DEVIOUSNESS
DEVIOUSNESSES
DEVITALISATION
DEVITALISATIONS
DEVITALISE
DEVITALISED
DEVITALISES
DEVITALISING
DEVITALIZATION
DEVITALIZATIONS
DEVITALIZE
DEVITALIZED
DEVITALIZES
DEVITALIZING
DEVITRIFICATION
DEVITRIFIED
DEVITRIFIES
DEVITRIFYING
DEVOCALISE
DEVOCALISED
DEVOCALISES
DEVOCALISING
DEVOCALIZE
DEVOCALIZED
DEVOCALIZES
DEVOCALIZING
DEVOLUTION
DEVOLUTIONARY
DEVOLUTIONIST
DEVOLUTIONISTS
DEVOLUTIONS
DEVOLVEMENT
DEVOLVEMENTS
DEVONPORTS
DEVOTEDNESS
DEVOTEDNESSES
DEVOTEMENT
DEVOTEMENTS
DEVOTIONAL
DEVOTIONALIST
DEVOTIONALISTS
DEVOTIONALITIES
DEVOTIONALITY
DEVOTIONALLY
DEVOTIONALNESS
DEVOTIONALS
DEVOTIONIST
DEVOTIONISTS
DEVOURINGLY
DEVOURMENT
DEVOURMENTS
DEVOUTNESS
DEVOUTNESSES
DEVVELLING
DEWATERERS

DEWATERING
DEWATERINGS
DEWBERRIES
DEWINESSES
DEXAMETHASONE
DEXAMETHASONES
DEXAMPHETAMINE
DEXAMPHETAMINES
DEXIOTROPIC
DEXTERITIES
DEXTEROUSLY
DEXTEROUSNESS
DEXTEROUSNESSES
DEXTERWISE
DEXTRALITIES
DEXTRALITY
DEXTRANASE
DEXTRANASES
DEXTROCARDIA
DEXTROCARDIAC
DEXTROCARDIACS
DEXTROCARDIAS
DEXTROGLUCOSE
DEXTROGLUCOSES
DEXTROGYRATE
DEXTROGYRE
DEXTROPHOSPHATE
DEXTROROTARY
DEXTROROTATION
DEXTROROTATIONS
DEXTROROTATORY
DEXTRORSAL
DEXTRORSELY
DEXTROUSLY
DEXTROUSNESS
DEXTROUSNESSES
DEZINCKING
DHARMSALAS
DHARMSHALA
DHARMSHALAS
DIABETICAL
DIABETOGENIC
DIABETOLOGIST
DIABETOLOGISTS
DIABLERIES
DIABOLICAL
DIABOLICALLY
DIABOLICALNESS
DIABOLISED
DIABOLISES
DIABOLISING
DIABOLISMS
DIABOLISTS
DIABOLIZED
DIABOLIZES
DIABOLIZING
DIABOLOGIES
DIABOLOLOGIES
DIABOLOLOGY

DIACATHOLICON
DIACATHOLICONS
DIACAUSTIC
DIACAUSTICS
DIACHRONIC
DIACHRONICALLY
DIACHRONIES
DIACHRONISM
DIACHRONISMS
DIACHRONISTIC
DIACHRONOUS
DIACHYLONS
DIACHYLUMS
DIACODIONS
DIACODIUMS
DIACONATES
DIACONICON
DIACONICONS
DIACOUSTIC
DIACOUSTICS
DIACRITICAL
DIACRITICALLY
DIACRITICS
DIACTINISM
DIACTINISMS
DIADELPHOUS
DIADOCHIES
DIADROMOUS
DIAGENESES
DIAGENESIS
DIAGENETIC
DIAGENETICALLY
DIAGEOTROPIC
DIAGEOTROPISM
DIAGEOTROPISMS
DIAGNOSABILITY
DIAGNOSABLE
DIAGNOSEABLE
DIAGNOSING
DIAGNOSTIC
DIAGNOSTICAL
DIAGNOSTICALLY
DIAGNOSTICIAN
DIAGNOSTICIANS
DIAGNOSTICS
DIAGOMETER
DIAGOMETERS
DIAGONALISABLE
DIAGONALISATION
DIAGONALISE
DIAGONALISED
DIAGONALISES
DIAGONALISING
DIAGONALIZABLE
DIAGONALIZATION
DIAGONALIZE
DIAGONALIZED
DIAGONALIZES
DIAGONALIZING

DIAGONALLY
DIAGRAMING
DIAGRAMMABLE
DIAGRAMMATIC
DIAGRAMMATICAL
DIAGRAMMED
DIAGRAMMING
DIAGRAPHIC
DIAHELIOTROPIC
DIAHELIOTROPISM
DIAKINESES
DIAKINESIS
DIALECTALLY
DIALECTICAL
DIALECTICALLY
DIALECTICIAN
DIALECTICIANS
DIALECTICISM
DIALECTICISMS
DIALECTICS
DIALECTOLOGICAL
DIALECTOLOGIES
DIALECTOLOGIST
DIALECTOLOGISTS
DIALECTOLOGY
DIALLAGOID
DIALOGICAL
DIALOGICALLY
DIALOGISED
DIALOGISES
DIALOGISING
DIALOGISMS
DIALOGISTIC
DIALOGISTICAL
DIALOGISTS
DIALOGITES
DIALOGIZED
DIALOGIZES
DIALOGIZING
DIALOGUERS
DIALOGUING
DIALYPETALOUS
DIALYSABILITIES
DIALYSABILITY
DIALYSABLE
DIALYSATES
DIALYSATION
DIALYSATIONS
DIALYTICALLY
DIALYZABILITIES
DIALYZABILITY
DIALYZABLE
DIALYZATES
DIALYZATION
DIALYZATIONS
DIAMAGNETIC
DIAMAGNETICALLY
DIAMAGNETISM
DIAMAGNETISMS

DIAMAGNETS
DIAMANTIFEROUS
DIAMANTINE
DIAMETRALLY
DIAMETRICAL
DIAMETRICALLY
DIAMONDBACK
DIAMONDBACKS
DIAMONDIFEROUS
DIAMONDING
DIAMORPHINE
DIAMORPHINES
DIANTHUSES
DIAPASONAL
DIAPASONIC
DIAPAUSING
DIAPEDESES
DIAPEDESIS
DIAPEDETIC
DIAPERINGS
DIAPHANEITIES
DIAPHANEITY
DIAPHANOMETER
DIAPHANOMETERS
DIAPHANOUS
DIAPHANOUSLY
DIAPHANOUSNESS
DIAPHONIES
DIAPHORASE
DIAPHORASES
DIAPHORESES
DIAPHORESIS
DIAPHORETIC
DIAPHORETICS
DIAPHOTOTROPIC
DIAPHOTOTROPIES
DIAPHOTOTROPISM
DIAPHOTOTROPY
DIAPHRAGMAL
DIAPHRAGMATIC
DIAPHRAGMATITIS
DIAPHRAGMED
DIAPHRAGMING
DIAPHRAGMS
DIAPHYSEAL
DIAPHYSIAL
DIAPIRISMS
DIAPOPHYSES
DIAPOPHYSIAL
DIAPOPHYSIS
DIAPOSITIVE
DIAPOSITIVES
DIAPYETICS
DIARCHICAL
DIARRHETIC
DIARRHOEAL
DIARRHOEAS
DIARRHOEIC
DIARTHRODIAL

DIARTHROSES
DIARTHROSIS
DIASCORDIUM
DIASCORDIUMS
DIASKEUAST
DIASKEUASTS
DIASTALSES
DIASTALSIS
DIASTALTIC
DIASTEMATA
DIASTEMATIC
DIASTEREOISOMER
DIASTEREOMER
DIASTEREOMERIC
DIASTEREOMERS
DIASTROPHIC
DIASTROPHICALLY
DIASTROPHISM
DIASTROPHISMS
DIATESSARON
DIATESSARONS
DIATHERMACIES
DIATHERMACY
DIATHERMAL
DIATHERMANCIES
DIATHERMANCY
DIATHERMANEITY
DIATHERMANOUS
DIATHERMIA
DIATHERMIAS
DIATHERMIC
DIATHERMIES
DIATHERMOUS
DIATOMACEOUS
DIATOMICITIES
DIATOMICITY
DIATOMISTS
DIATOMITES
DIATONICALLY
DIATONICISM
DIATONICISMS
DIATRETUMS
DIATRIBIST
DIATRIBISTS
DIATROPISM
DIATROPISMS
DIAZEUCTIC
DIAZOMETHANE
DIAZOMETHANES
DIAZONIUMS
DIAZOTISATION
DIAZOTISATIONS
DIAZOTISED
DIAZOTISES
DIAZOTISING
DIAZOTIZATION
DIAZOTIZATIONS
DIAZOTIZED
DIAZOTIZES

DIAZOTIZING
DIBASICITIES
DIBASICITY
DIBENZOFURAN
DIBENZOFURANS
DIBRANCHIATE
DIBRANCHIATES
DIBROMIDES
DICACITIES
DICACODYLS
DICARBOXYLIC
DICARPELLARY
DICASTERIES
DICENTRICS
DICEPHALISM
DICEPHALISMS
DICEPHALOUS
DICHASIALLY
DICHLAMYDEOUS
DICHLORACETIC
DICHLORIDE
DICHLORIDES
DICHLOROBENZENE
DICHLOROETHANE
DICHLOROETHANES
DICHLOROMETHANE
DICHLORVOS
DICHLORVOSES
DICHOGAMIC
DICHOGAMIES
DICHOGAMOUS
DICHONDRAS
DICHOTICALLY
DICHOTOMIC
DICHOTOMIES
DICHOTOMISATION
DICHOTOMISE
DICHOTOMISED
DICHOTOMISES
DICHOTOMISING
DICHOTOMIST
DICHOTOMISTS
DICHOTOMIZATION
DICHOTOMIZE
DICHOTOMIZED
DICHOTOMIZES
DICHOTOMIZING
DICHOTOMOUS
DICHOTOMOUSLY
DICHOTOMOUSNESS
DICHROISCOPE
DICHROISCOPES
DICHROISCOPIC
DICHROISMS
DICHROITES
DICHROITIC
DICHROMATE
DICHROMATES
DICHROMATIC

DICHROMATICISM
DICHROMATICISMS
DICHROMATICS
DICHROMATISM
DICHROMATISMS
DICHROMATS
DICHROMISM
DICHROMISMS
DICHROOSCOPE
DICHROOSCOPES
DICHROOSCOPIC
DICHROSCOPE
DICHROSCOPES
DICHROSCOPIC
DICKCISSEL
DICKCISSELS
DICKEYBIRD
DICKEYBIRDS
DICKYBIRDS
DICLINISMS
DICOTYLEDON
DICOTYLEDONOUS
DICOTYLEDONS
DICOUMARIN
DICOUMARINS
DICOUMAROL
DICOUMAROLS
DICROTISMS
DICTATIONAL
DICTATIONS
DICTATORIAL
DICTATORIALLY
DICTATORIALNESS
DICTATORSHIP
DICTATORSHIPS
DICTATRESS
DICTATRESSES
DICTATRICES
DICTATRIXES
DICTATURES
DICTIONALLY
DICTIONARIES
DICTIONARY
DICTYOGENS
DICTYOPTERAN
DICTYOPTERANS
DICTYOSOME
DICTYOSOMES
DICTYOSTELE
DICTYOSTELES
DICUMAROLS
DICYNODONT
DICYNODONTS
DIDACTICAL
DIDACTICALLY
DIDACTICISM
DIDACTICISMS
DIDACTYLISM
DIDACTYLISMS

DIDACTYLOUS
DIDASCALIC
DIDELPHIAN
DIDELPHIDS
DIDELPHINE
DIDELPHOUS
DIDGERIDOO
DIDGERIDOOS
DIDJERIDOO
DIDJERIDOOS
DIDJERIDUS
DIDRACHMAS
DIDYNAMIAN
DIDYNAMIES
DIDYNAMOUS
DIECIOUSLY
DIECIOUSNESS
DIECIOUSNESSES
DIEFFENBACHIA
DIEFFENBACHIAS
DIELECTRIC
DIELECTRICALLY
DIELECTRICS
DIENCEPHALA
DIENCEPHALIC
DIENCEPHALON
DIENCEPHALONS
DIESELINGS
DIESELISATION
DIESELISATIONS
DIESELISED
DIESELISES
DIESELISING
DIESELIZATION
DIESELIZATIONS
DIESELIZED
DIESELIZES
DIESELIZING
DIESINKERS
DIESTRUSES
DIETARIANS
DIETETICAL
DIETETICALLY
DIETHYLAMIDE
DIETHYLAMIDES
DIETHYLAMINE
DIETHYLAMINES
DIETHYLENE
DIETHYLENES
DIETICIANS
DIETITIANS
DIFFARREATION
DIFFARREATIONS
DIFFERENCE
DIFFERENCED
DIFFERENCES
DIFFERENCIED
DIFFERENCIES
DIFFERENCING

DIFFERENCY
DIFFERENCYING
DIFFERENTIA
DIFFERENTIABLE
DIFFERENTIAE
DIFFERENTIAL
DIFFERENTIALLY
DIFFERENTIALS
DIFFERENTIATE
DIFFERENTIATED
DIFFERENTIATES
DIFFERENTIATING
DIFFERENTIATION
DIFFERENTIATOR
DIFFERENTIATORS
DIFFERENTLY
DIFFERENTNESS
DIFFERENTNESSES
DIFFICULTIES
DIFFICULTLY
DIFFICULTY
DIFFIDENCE
DIFFIDENCES
DIFFIDENTLY
DIFFORMITIES
DIFFORMITY
DIFFRACTED
DIFFRACTING
DIFFRACTION
DIFFRACTIONS
DIFFRACTIVE
DIFFRACTIVELY
DIFFRACTIVENESS
DIFFRACTOMETER
DIFFRACTOMETERS
DIFFRACTOMETRIC
DIFFRACTOMETRY
DIFFRANGIBILITY
DIFFRANGIBLE
DIFFUSEDLY
DIFFUSEDNESS
DIFFUSEDNESSES
DIFFUSENESS
DIFFUSENESSES
DIFFUSIBILITIES
DIFFUSIBILITY
DIFFUSIBLE
DIFFUSIBLENESS
DIFFUSIONAL
DIFFUSIONISM
DIFFUSIONISMS
DIFFUSIONIST
DIFFUSIONISTS
DIFFUSIONS
DIFFUSIVELY
DIFFUSIVENESS
DIFFUSIVENESSES
DIFFUSIVITIES
DIFFUSIVITY

DIFUNCTIONAL
DIFUNCTIONALS
DIGASTRICS
DIGESTANTS
DIGESTEDLY
DIGESTIBILITIES
DIGESTIBILITY
DIGESTIBLE
DIGESTIBLENESS
DIGESTIBLY
DIGESTIONAL
DIGESTIONS
DIGESTIVELY
DIGESTIVES
DIGITALINS
DIGITALISATION
DIGITALISATIONS
DIGITALISE
DIGITALISED
DIGITALISES
DIGITALISING
DIGITALISM
DIGITALISMS
DIGITALIZATION
DIGITALIZATIONS
DIGITALIZE
DIGITALIZED
DIGITALIZES
DIGITALIZING
DIGITATELY
DIGITATION
DIGITATIONS
DIGITIFORM
DIGITIGRADE
DIGITIGRADES
DIGITISATION
DIGITISATIONS
DIGITISERS
DIGITISING
DIGITIZATION
DIGITIZATIONS
DIGITIZERS
DIGITIZING
DIGITONINS
DIGITORIUM
DIGITORIUMS
DIGITOXIGENIN
DIGITOXIGENINS
DIGITOXINS
DIGLADIATE
DIGLADIATED
DIGLADIATES
DIGLADIATING
DIGLADIATION
DIGLADIATIONS
DIGLADIATOR
DIGLADIATORS
DIGLOSSIAS
DIGLYCERIDE

DIGLYCERIDES
DIGNIFICATION
DIGNIFICATIONS
DIGNIFIEDLY
DIGNIFIEDNESS
DIGNIFIEDNESSES
DIGNIFYING
DIGNITARIES
DIGONEUTIC
DIGONEUTISM
DIGONEUTISMS
DIGRAPHICALLY
DIGRESSERS
DIGRESSING
DIGRESSION
DIGRESSIONAL
DIGRESSIONARY
DIGRESSIONS
DIGRESSIVE
DIGRESSIVELY
DIGRESSIVENESS
DIHYBRIDISM
DIHYBRIDISMS
DIHYDROGEN
DIJUDICATE
DIJUDICATED
DIJUDICATES
DIJUDICATING
DIJUDICATION
DIJUDICATIONS
DILACERATE
DILACERATED
DILACERATES
DILACERATING
DILACERATION
DILACERATIONS
DILAPIDATE
DILAPIDATED
DILAPIDATES
DILAPIDATING
DILAPIDATION
DILAPIDATIONS
DILAPIDATOR
DILAPIDATORS
DILATABILITIES
DILATABILITY
DILATABLENESS
DILATABLENESSES
DILATANCIES
DILATATION
DILATATIONAL
DILATATIONS
DILATATORS
DILATOMETER
DILATOMETERS
DILATOMETRIC
DILATOMETRIES
DILATOMETRY
DILATORILY

DILATORINESS
DILATORINESSES
DILEMMATIC
DILETTANTE
DILETTANTEISH
DILETTANTEISM
DILETTANTEISMS
DILETTANTES
DILETTANTI
DILETTANTISH
DILETTANTISM
DILETTANTISMS
DILIGENCES
DILIGENTLY
DILLYDALLIED
DILLYDALLIES
DILLYDALLY
DILLYDALLYING
DILTIAZEMS
DILUCIDATE
DILUCIDATED
DILUCIDATES
DILUCIDATING
DILUCIDATION
DILUCIDATIONS
DILUTABLES
DILUTENESS
DILUTENESSES
DILUTIONARY
DILUVIALISM
DILUVIALISMS
DILUVIALIST
DILUVIALISTS
DIMENHYDRINATE
DIMENHYDRINATES
DIMENSIONAL
DIMENSIONALITY
DIMENSIONALLY
DIMENSIONED
DIMENSIONING
DIMENSIONLESS
DIMENSIONS
DIMERCAPROL
DIMERCAPROLS
DIMERISATION
DIMERISATIONS
DIMERISING
DIMERIZATION
DIMERIZATIONS
DIMERIZING
DIMETHOATE
DIMETHOATES
DIMETHYLAMINE
DIMETHYLAMINES
DIMETHYLANILINE
DIMIDIATED
DIMIDIATES
DIMIDIATING
DIMIDIATION

DIMIDIATIONS
DIMINISHABLE
DIMINISHED
DIMINISHES
DIMINISHING
DIMINISHINGLY
DIMINISHINGS
DIMINISHMENT
DIMINISHMENTS
DIMINUENDO
DIMINUENDOES
DIMINUENDOS
DIMINUTION
DIMINUTIONS
DIMINUTIVAL
DIMINUTIVE
DIMINUTIVELY
DIMINUTIVENESS
DIMINUTIVES
DIMORPHISM
DIMORPHISMS
DIMORPHOUS
DIMPLEMENT
DIMPLEMENTS
DINANDERIE
DINANDERIES
DINARCHIES
DINGDONGED
DINGDONGING
DINGINESSES
DINGLEBERRIES
DINGLEBERRY
DINITROBENZENE
DINITROBENZENES
DINITROGEN
DINITROPHENOL
DINITROPHENOLS
DINNERLESS
DINNERTIME
DINNERTIMES
DINNERWARE
DINNERWARES
DINOCERASES
DINOFLAGELLATE
DINOFLAGELLATES
DINOMANIAS
DINOSAURIAN
DINOSAURIC
DINOTHERES
DINOTHERIUM
DINOTHERIUMS
DINOTURBATION
DINOTURBATIONS
DINUCLEOTIDE
DINUCLEOTIDES
DIOECIOUSLY
DIOECIOUSNESS
DIOECIOUSNESSES
DIOESTRUSES

DIOICOUSLY
DIOICOUSNESS
DIOICOUSNESSES
DIOPHYSITE
DIOPHYSITES
DIOPTOMETER
DIOPTOMETERS
DIOPTOMETRIES
DIOPTOMETRY
DIOPTRICAL
DIOPTRICALLY
DIORISTICAL
DIORISTICALLY
DIORTHOSES
DIORTHOSIS
DIORTHOTIC
DIOSCOREACEOUS
DIOSGENINS
DIOTHELETE
DIOTHELETES
DIOTHELETIC
DIOTHELETICAL
DIOTHELISM
DIOTHELISMS
DIOTHELITE
DIOTHELITES
DIOXONITRIC
DIPEPTIDASE
DIPEPTIDASES
DIPEPTIDES
DIPETALOUS
DIPHENHYDRAMINE
DIPHENYLAMINE
DIPHENYLAMINES
DIPHENYLENIMINE
DIPHENYLKETONE
DIPHENYLKETONES
DIPHOSGENE
DIPHOSGENES
DIPHOSPHATE
DIPHOSPHATES
DIPHTHERIA
DIPHTHERIAL
DIPHTHERIAS
DIPHTHERIC
DIPHTHERITIC
DIPHTHERITIS
DIPHTHERITISES
DIPHTHEROID
DIPHTHEROIDS
DIPHTHONGAL
DIPHTHONGALLY
DIPHTHONGED
DIPHTHONGIC
DIPHTHONGING
DIPHTHONGISE
DIPHTHONGISED
DIPHTHONGISES
DIPHTHONGISING

DIPHTHONGIZE
DIPHTHONGIZED
DIPHTHONGIZES
DIPHTHONGIZING
DIPHTHONGS
DIPHYCERCAL
DIPHYLETIC
DIPHYLLOUS
DIPHYODONT
DIPHYODONTS
DIPHYSITES
DIPHYSITISM
DIPHYSITISMS
DIPLEIDOSCOPE
DIPLEIDOSCOPES
DIPLOBIONT
DIPLOBIONTIC
DIPLOBIONTS
DIPLOBLASTIC
DIPLOCARDIAC
DIPLOCOCCAL
DIPLOCOCCI
DIPLOCOCCIC
DIPLOCOCCUS
DIPLODOCUS
DIPLODOCUSES
DIPLOGENESES
DIPLOGENESIS
DIPLOIDIES
DIPLOMACIES
DIPLOMAING
DIPLOMATED
DIPLOMATES
DIPLOMATESE
DIPLOMATESES
DIPLOMATIC
DIPLOMATICAL
DIPLOMATICALLY
DIPLOMATICS
DIPLOMATING
DIPLOMATISE
DIPLOMATISED
DIPLOMATISES
DIPLOMATISING
DIPLOMATIST
DIPLOMATISTS
DIPLOMATIZE
DIPLOMATIZED
DIPLOMATIZES
DIPLOMATIZING
DIPLOMATOLOGIES
DIPLOMATOLOGY
DIPLONEMAS
DIPLOPHASE
DIPLOPHASES
DIPLOSTEMONOUS
DIPLOTENES
DIPNETTING
DIPPERFULS

DIPPINESSES
DIPRIONIDIAN
DIPROPELLANT
DIPROPELLANTS
DIPROTODON
DIPROTODONS
DIPROTODONT
DIPROTODONTID
DIPROTODONTIDS
DIPROTODONTS
DIPSOMANIA
DIPSOMANIAC
DIPSOMANIACAL
DIPSOMANIACS
DIPSOMANIAS
DIPTERISTS
DIPTEROCARP
DIPTEROCARPOUS
DIPTEROCARPS
DIPTEROSES
DIRECTEDNESS
DIRECTEDNESSES
DIRECTIONAL
DIRECTIONALITY
DIRECTIONLESS
DIRECTIONS
DIRECTIVES
DIRECTIVITIES
DIRECTIVITY
DIRECTNESS
DIRECTNESSES
DIRECTORATE
DIRECTORATES
DIRECTORIAL
DIRECTORIALLY
DIRECTORIES
DIRECTORSHIP
DIRECTORSHIPS
DIRECTRESS
DIRECTRESSES
DIRECTRICE
DIRECTRICES
DIRECTRIXES
DIREFULNESS
DIREFULNESSES
DIREMPTING
DIREMPTION
DIREMPTIONS
DIRENESSES
DIRIGIBILITIES
DIRIGIBILITY
DIRIGIBLES
DIRIGISMES
DIRTINESSES
DISABILITIES
DISABILITY
DISABLEMENT
DISABLEMENTS
DISABUSALS

DISABUSING
DISACCHARID
DISACCHARIDASE
DISACCHARIDASES
DISACCHARIDE
DISACCHARIDES
DISACCHARIDS
DISACCOMMODATE
DISACCOMMODATED
DISACCOMMODATES
DISACCORDANT
DISACCORDED
DISACCORDING
DISACCORDS
DISACCREDIT
DISACCREDITED
DISACCREDITING
DISACCREDITS
DISACCUSTOM
DISACCUSTOMED
DISACCUSTOMING
DISACCUSTOMS
DISACKNOWLEDGE
DISACKNOWLEDGED
DISACKNOWLEDGES
DISADORNED
DISADORNING
DISADVANCE
DISADVANCED
DISADVANCES
DISADVANCING
DISADVANTAGE
DISADVANTAGED
DISADVANTAGEOUS
DISADVANTAGES
DISADVANTAGING
DISADVENTURE
DISADVENTURES
DISADVENTUROUS
DISAFFECTED
DISAFFECTEDLY
DISAFFECTEDNESS
DISAFFECTING
DISAFFECTION
DISAFFECTIONATE
DISAFFECTIONS
DISAFFECTS
DISAFFILIATE
DISAFFILIATED
DISAFFILIATES
DISAFFILIATING
DISAFFILIATION
DISAFFILIATIONS
DISAFFIRMANCE
DISAFFIRMANCES
DISAFFIRMATION
DISAFFIRMATIONS
DISAFFIRMED
DISAFFIRMING

DISAFFIRMS
DISAFFOREST
DISAFFORESTED
DISAFFORESTING
DISAFFORESTMENT
DISAFFORESTS
DISAGGREGATE
DISAGGREGATED
DISAGGREGATES
DISAGGREGATING
DISAGGREGATION
DISAGGREGATIONS
DISAGGREGATIVE
DISAGREEABILITY
DISAGREEABLE
DISAGREEABLES
DISAGREEABLY
DISAGREEING
DISAGREEMENT
DISAGREEMENTS
DISALLOWABLE
DISALLOWANCE
DISALLOWANCES
DISALLOWED
DISALLOWING
DISALLYING
DISAMBIGUATE
DISAMBIGUATED
DISAMBIGUATES
DISAMBIGUATING
DISAMBIGUATION
DISAMBIGUATIONS
DISAMENITIES
DISAMENITY
DISANALOGIES
DISANALOGOUS
DISANALOGY
DISANCHORED
DISANCHORING
DISANCHORS
DISANIMATE
DISANIMATED
DISANIMATES
DISANIMATING
DISANNEXED
DISANNEXES
DISANNEXING
DISANNULLED
DISANNULLER
DISANNULLERS
DISANNULLING
DISANNULLINGS
DISANNULMENT
DISANNULMENTS
DISANOINTED
DISANOINTING
DISANOINTS
DISAPPAREL
DISAPPARELLED

DISAPPARELLING
DISAPPARELS
DISAPPEARANCE
DISAPPEARANCES
DISAPPEARED
DISAPPEARING
DISAPPEARS
DISAPPLICATION
DISAPPLICATIONS
DISAPPLIED
DISAPPLIES
DISAPPLYING
DISAPPOINT
DISAPPOINTED
DISAPPOINTEDLY
DISAPPOINTING
DISAPPOINTINGLY
DISAPPOINTMENT
DISAPPOINTMENTS
DISAPPOINTS
DISAPPROBATION
DISAPPROBATIONS
DISAPPROBATIVE
DISAPPROBATORY
DISAPPROPRIATE
DISAPPROPRIATED
DISAPPROPRIATES
DISAPPROVAL
DISAPPROVALS
DISAPPROVE
DISAPPROVED
DISAPPROVER
DISAPPROVERS
DISAPPROVES
DISAPPROVING
DISAPPROVINGLY
DISARMAMENT
DISARMAMENTS
DISARMINGLY
DISARRANGE
DISARRANGED
DISARRANGEMENT
DISARRANGEMENTS
DISARRANGES
DISARRANGING
DISARRAYED
DISARRAYING
DISARTICULATE
DISARTICULATED
DISARTICULATES
DISARTICULATING
DISARTICULATION
DISARTICULATOR
DISARTICULATORS
DISASSEMBLE
DISASSEMBLED
DISASSEMBLER
DISASSEMBLERS
DISASSEMBLES

DISASSEMBLIES
DISASSEMBLING
DISASSEMBLY
DISASSIMILATE
DISASSIMILATED
DISASSIMILATES
DISASSIMILATING
DISASSIMILATION
DISASSIMILATIVE
DISASSOCIATE
DISASSOCIATED
DISASSOCIATES
DISASSOCIATING
DISASSOCIATION
DISASSOCIATIONS
DISASTROUS
DISASTROUSLY
DISATTIRED
DISATTIRES
DISATTIRING
DISATTRIBUTION
DISATTRIBUTIONS
DISATTUNED
DISATTUNES
DISATTUNING
DISAUTHORISE
DISAUTHORISED
DISAUTHORISES
DISAUTHORISING
DISAUTHORIZE
DISAUTHORIZED
DISAUTHORIZES
DISAUTHORIZING
DISAVAUNCE
DISAVAUNCED
DISAVAUNCES
DISAVAUNCING
DISAVENTROUS
DISAVENTURE
DISAVENTURES
DISAVOUCHED
DISAVOUCHES
DISAVOUCHING
DISAVOWABLE
DISAVOWALS
DISAVOWEDLY
DISAVOWERS
DISAVOWING
DISBANDING
DISBANDMENT
DISBANDMENTS
DISBARKING
DISBARMENT
DISBARMENTS
DISBARRING
DISBELIEFS
DISBELIEVE
DISBELIEVED
DISBELIEVER

DISBELIEVERS	DISCEPTATORS	DISCLIMAXES	DISCOMMODE
DISBELIEVES	DISCEPTING	DISCLOSERS	DISCOMMODED
DISBELIEVING	DISCERNABLE	DISCLOSING	DISCOMMODES
DISBELIEVINGLY	DISCERNABLY	DISCLOSURE	DISCOMMODING
DISBENCHED	DISCERNERS	DISCLOSURES	DISCOMMODIOUS
DISBENCHES	DISCERNIBLE	DISCOBOLOS	DISCOMMODIOUSLY
DISBENCHING	DISCERNIBLY	DISCOBOLUS	DISCOMMODITIES
DISBENEFIT	DISCERNING	DISCOBOLUSES	DISCOMMODITY
DISBENEFITS	DISCERNINGLY	DISCOGRAPHER	DISCOMMONED
DISBOSOMED	DISCERNMENT	DISCOGRAPHERS	DISCOMMONING
DISBOSOMING	DISCERNMENTS	DISCOGRAPHIC	DISCOMMONS
DISBOWELED	DISCERNS	DISCOGRAPHICAL	DISCOMMUNITIES
DISBOWELING	DISCERPIBILITY	DISCOGRAPHIES	DISCOMMUNITY
DISBOWELLED	DISCERPIBLE	DISCOGRAPHY	DISCOMPOSE
DISBOWELLING	DISCERPING	DISCOLOGIES	DISCOMPOSED
DISBRANCHED	DISCERPTIBLE	DISCOLOGIST	DISCOMPOSEDLY
DISBRANCHES	DISCERPTION	DISCOLOGISTS	DISCOMPOSES
DISBRANCHING	DISCERPTIONS	DISCOLORATION	DISCOMPOSING
DISBUDDING	DISCERPTIVE	DISCOLORATIONS	DISCOMPOSINGLY
DISBURDENED	DISCHARGEABLE	DISCOLORED	DISCOMPOSURE
DISBURDENING	DISCHARGED	DISCOLORING	DISCOMPOSURES
DISBURDENMENT	DISCHARGEE	DISCOLORMENT	DISCOMYCETE
DISBURDENMENTS	DISCHARGEES	DISCOLORMENTS	DISCOMYCETES
DISBURDENS	DISCHARGER	DISCOLOURATION	DISCOMYCETOUS
DISBURSABLE	DISCHARGERS	DISCOLOURATIONS	DISCONCERT
DISBURSALS	DISCHARGES	DISCOLOURED	DISCONCERTED
DISBURSEMENT	DISCHARGING	DISCOLOURING	DISCONCERTEDLY
DISBURSEMENTS	DISCHUFFED	DISCOLOURMENT	DISCONCERTING
DISBURSERS	DISCHURCHED	DISCOLOURMENTS	DISCONCERTINGLY
DISBURSING	DISCHURCHES	DISCOLOURS	DISCONCERTION
DISBURTHEN	DISCHURCHING	DISCOMBOBERATE	DISCONCERTIONS
DISBURTHENED	DISCIPLESHIP	DISCOMBOBERATED	DISCONCERTMENT
DISBURTHENING	DISCIPLESHIPS	DISCOMBOBERATES	DISCONCERTMENTS
DISBURTHENS	DISCIPLINABLE	DISCOMBOBULATE	DISCONCERTS
DISCALCEATE	DISCIPLINAL	DISCOMBOBULATED	DISCONFIRM
DISCALCEATES	DISCIPLINANT	DISCOMBOBULATES	DISCONFIRMATION
DISCANDERING	DISCIPLINANTS	DISCOMEDUSAN	DISCONFIRMED
DISCANDERINGS	DISCIPLINARIAN	DISCOMEDUSANS	DISCONFIRMING
DISCANDIED	DISCIPLINARIANS	DISCOMFITED	DISCONFIRMS
DISCANDIES	DISCIPLINARILY	DISCOMFITER	DISCONFORMABLE
DISCANDYING	DISCIPLINARITY	DISCOMFITERS	DISCONFORMITIES
DISCANDYINGS	DISCIPLINARIUM	DISCOMFITING	DISCONFORMITY
DISCANTERS	DISCIPLINARIUMS	DISCOMFITS	DISCONNECT
DISCANTING	DISCIPLINARY	DISCOMFITURE	DISCONNECTED
DISCAPACITATE	DISCIPLINE	DISCOMFITURES	DISCONNECTEDLY
DISCAPACITATED	DISCIPLINED	DISCOMFORT	DISCONNECTER
DISCAPACITATES	DISCIPLINER	DISCOMFORTABLE	DISCONNECTERS
DISCAPACITATING	DISCIPLINERS	DISCOMFORTED	DISCONNECTING
DISCARDABLE	DISCIPLINES	DISCOMFORTING	DISCONNECTION
DISCARDERS	DISCIPLING	DISCOMFORTS	DISCONNECTIONS
DISCARDING	DISCIPLINING	DISCOMMEND	DISCONNECTIVE
DISCARDMENT	DISCIPULAR	DISCOMMENDABLE	DISCONNECTS
DISCARDMENTS	DISCISSION	DISCOMMENDATION	DISCONNEXION
DISCARNATE	DISCISSIONS	DISCOMMENDED	DISCONNEXIONS
DISCEPTATION	DISCLAIMED	DISCOMMENDING	DISCONSENT
DISCEPTATIONS	DISCLAIMER	DISCOMMENDS	DISCONSENTED
DISCEPTATIOUS	DISCLAIMERS	DISCOMMISSION	DISCONSENTING
DISCEPTATOR	DISCLAIMING	DISCOMMISSIONED	DISCONSENTS
DISCEPTATORIAL	DISCLAMATIONS	DISCOMMISSIONS	DISCONSOLATE

DISCONSOLATELY DISCOURAGEMENTS DISCRIMINANTS DISEMBARRASSED
DISCONSOLATION DISCOURAGER DISCRIMINATE DISEMBARRASSES
DISCONSOLATIONS DISCOURAGERS DISCRIMINATED DISEMBARRASSING
DISCONTENT DISCOURAGES DISCRIMINATELY DISEMBELLISH
DISCONTENTED DISCOURAGING DISCRIMINATES DISEMBELLISHED
DISCONTENTEDLY DISCOURAGINGLY DISCRIMINATING DISEMBELLISHES
DISCONTENTFUL DISCOURAGINGS DISCRIMINATION DISEMBELLISHING
DISCONTENTING DISCOURING DISCRIMINATIONS DISEMBITTER
DISCONTENTMENT DISCOURSAL DISCRIMINATIVE DISEMBITTERED
DISCONTENTMENTS DISCOURSED DISCRIMINATOR DISEMBITTERING
DISCONTENTS DISCOURSER DISCRIMINATORS DISEMBITTERS
DISCONTIGUITIES DISCOURSERS DISCRIMINATORY DISEMBODIED
DISCONTIGUITY DISCOURSES DISCROWNED DISEMBODIES
DISCONTIGUOUS DISCOURSING DISCROWNING DISEMBODIMENT
DISCONTINUANCE DISCOURSIVE DISCULPATE DISEMBODIMENTS
DISCONTINUANCES DISCOURTEISE DISCULPATED DISEMBODYING
DISCONTINUATION DISCOURTEOUS DISCULPATES DISEMBOGUE
DISCONTINUE DISCOURTEOUSLY DISCULPATING DISEMBOGUED
DISCONTINUED DISCOURTESIES DISCUMBERED DISEMBOGUEMENT
DISCONTINUER DISCOURTESY DISCUMBERING DISEMBOGUEMENTS
DISCONTINUERS DISCOVERABLE DISCUMBERS DISEMBOGUES
DISCONTINUES DISCOVERED DISCURSION DISEMBOGUING
DISCONTINUING DISCOVERER DISCURSIONS DISEMBOSOM
DISCONTINUITIES DISCOVERERS DISCURSIST DISEMBOSOMED
DISCONTINUITY DISCOVERIES DISCURSISTS DISEMBOSOMING
DISCONTINUOUS DISCOVERING DISCURSIVE DISEMBOSOMS
DISCONTINUOUSLY DISCOVERTURE DISCURSIVELY DISEMBOWEL
DISCOPHILE DISCOVERTURES DISCURSIVENESS DISEMBOWELED
DISCOPHILES DISCREDITABLE DISCURSORY DISEMBOWELING
DISCOPHORAN DISCREDITABLY DISCURSUSES DISEMBOWELLED
DISCOPHORANS DISCREDITED DISCUSSABLE DISEMBOWELLING
DISCOPHOROUS DISCREDITING DISCUSSANT DISEMBOWELMENT
DISCORDANCE DISCREDITS DISCUSSANTS DISEMBOWELMENTS
DISCORDANCES DISCREETER DISCUSSERS DISEMBOWELS
DISCORDANCIES DISCREETEST DISCUSSIBLE DISEMBRANGLE
DISCORDANCY DISCREETLY DISCUSSING DISEMBRANGLED
DISCORDANT DISCREETNESS DISCUSSION DISEMBRANGLES
DISCORDANTLY DISCREETNESSES DISCUSSIONAL DISEMBRANGLING
DISCORDFUL DISCREPANCE DISCUSSIONS DISEMBROIL
DISCORDING DISCREPANCES DISCUSSIVE DISEMBROILED
DISCORPORATE DISCREPANCIES DISCUTIENT DISEMBROILING
DISCOTHEQUE DISCREPANCY DISCUTIENTS DISEMBROILS
DISCOTHEQUES DISCREPANT DISDAINFUL DISEMBURDEN
DISCOUNSEL DISCREPANTLY DISDAINFULLY DISEMBURDENED
DISCOUNSELLED DISCRETELY DISDAINFULNESS DISEMBURDENING
DISCOUNSELLING DISCRETENESS DISDAINING DISEMBURDENS
DISCOUNSELS DISCRETENESSES DISEASEDNESS DISEMPLOYED
DISCOUNTABLE DISCRETEST DISEASEDNESSES DISEMPLOYING
DISCOUNTED DISCRETION DISEASEFUL DISEMPLOYMENT
DISCOUNTENANCE DISCRETIONAL DISECONOMIES DISEMPLOYMENTS
DISCOUNTENANCED DISCRETIONALLY DISECONOMY DISEMPLOYS
DISCOUNTENANCES DISCRETIONARILY DISEMBARKATION DISEMPOWER
DISCOUNTER DISCRETIONARY DISEMBARKATIONS DISEMPOWERED
DISCOUNTERS DISCRETIONS DISEMBARKED DISEMPOWERING
DISCOUNTING DISCRETIVE DISEMBARKING DISEMPOWERMENT
DISCOURAGE DISCRETIVELY DISEMBARKMENT DISEMPOWERMENTS
DISCOURAGEABLE DISCRIMINABLE DISEMBARKMENTS DISEMPOWERS
DISCOURAGED DISCRIMINABLY DISEMBARKS DISENABLED
DISCOURAGEMENT DISCRIMINANT DISEMBARRASS DISENABLEMENT

803

DISENABLEMENTS

DISENABLEMENTS
DISENABLES
DISENABLING
DISENCHAIN
DISENCHAINED
DISENCHAINING
DISENCHAINS
DISENCHANT
DISENCHANTED
DISENCHANTER
DISENCHANTERS
DISENCHANTING
DISENCHANTINGLY
DISENCHANTMENT
DISENCHANTMENTS
DISENCHANTRESS
DISENCHANTS
DISENCLOSE
DISENCLOSED
DISENCLOSES
DISENCLOSING
DISENCUMBER
DISENCUMBERED
DISENCUMBERING
DISENCUMBERMENT
DISENCUMBERS
DISENCUMBRANCE
DISENCUMBRANCES
DISENDOWED
DISENDOWER
DISENDOWERS
DISENDOWING
DISENDOWMENT
DISENDOWMENTS
DISENFRANCHISE
DISENFRANCHISED
DISENFRANCHISES
DISENGAGED
DISENGAGEDNESS
DISENGAGEMENT
DISENGAGEMENTS
DISENGAGES
DISENGAGING
DISENNOBLE
DISENNOBLED
DISENNOBLES
DISENNOBLING
DISENROLLED
DISENROLLING
DISENSHROUD
DISENSHROUDED
DISENSHROUDING
DISENSHROUDS
DISENSLAVE
DISENSLAVED
DISENSLAVES
DISENSLAVING
DISENTAILED
DISENTAILING

DISENTAILMENT
DISENTAILMENTS
DISENTAILS
DISENTANGLE
DISENTANGLED
DISENTANGLEMENT
DISENTANGLES
DISENTANGLING
DISENTHRAL
DISENTHRALL
DISENTHRALLED
DISENTHRALLING
DISENTHRALLMENT
DISENTHRALLS
DISENTHRALMENT
DISENTHRALMENTS
DISENTHRALS
DISENTHRONE
DISENTHRONED
DISENTHRONES
DISENTHRONING
DISENTITLE
DISENTITLED
DISENTITLES
DISENTITLING
DISENTOMBED
DISENTOMBING
DISENTOMBS
DISENTRAIL
DISENTRAILED
DISENTRAILING
DISENTRAILS
DISENTRAIN
DISENTRAINED
DISENTRAINING
DISENTRAINMENT
DISENTRAINMENTS
DISENTRAINS
DISENTRANCE
DISENTRANCED
DISENTRANCEMENT
DISENTRANCES
DISENTRANCING
DISENTRAYLE
DISENTRAYLED
DISENTRAYLES
DISENTRAYLING
DISENTWINE
DISENTWINED
DISENTWINES
DISENTWINING
DISENVELOP
DISENVELOPED
DISENVELOPING
DISENVELOPS
DISENVIRON
DISENVIRONED
DISENVIRONING
DISENVIRONS

DISEPALOUS
DISEQUILIBRATE
DISEQUILIBRATED
DISEQUILIBRATES
DISEQUILIBRIA
DISEQUILIBRIUM
DISEQUILIBRIUMS
DISESPOUSE
DISESPOUSED
DISESPOUSES
DISESPOUSING
DISESTABLISH
DISESTABLISHED
DISESTABLISHES
DISESTABLISHING
DISESTEEMED
DISESTEEMING
DISESTEEMS
DISESTIMATION
DISESTIMATIONS
DISFAVORED
DISFAVORING
DISFAVOURED
DISFAVOURER
DISFAVOURERS
DISFAVOURING
DISFAVOURS
DISFEATURE
DISFEATURED
DISFEATUREMENT
DISFEATUREMENTS
DISFEATURES
DISFEATURING
DISFELLOWSHIP
DISFELLOWSHIPS
DISFIGURATION
DISFIGURATIONS
DISFIGURED
DISFIGUREMENT
DISFIGUREMENTS
DISFIGURER
DISFIGURERS
DISFIGURES
DISFIGURING
DISFLESHED
DISFLESHES
DISFLESHING
DISFLUENCIES
DISFLUENCY
DISFORESTATION
DISFORESTATIONS
DISFORESTED
DISFORESTING
DISFORESTS
DISFORMING
DISFRANCHISE
DISFRANCHISED
DISFRANCHISES
DISFRANCHISING

DISFROCKED
DISFROCKING
DISFUNCTION
DISFUNCTIONS
DISFURNISH
DISFURNISHED
DISFURNISHES
DISFURNISHING
DISFURNISHMENT
DISFURNISHMENTS
DISGARNISH
DISGARNISHED
DISGARNISHES
DISGARNISHING
DISGARRISON
DISGARRISONED
DISGARRISONING
DISGARRISONS
DISGAVELLED
DISGAVELLING
DISGESTING
DISGESTION
DISGESTIONS
DISGLORIFIED
DISGLORIFIES
DISGLORIFY
DISGLORIFYING
DISGORGEMENT
DISGORGEMENTS
DISGORGERS
DISGORGING
DISGOSPELLING
DISGOWNING
DISGRACEFUL
DISGRACEFULLY
DISGRACEFULNESS
DISGRACERS
DISGRACING
DISGRACIOUS
DISGRADATION
DISGRADATIONS
DISGRADING
DISGREGATION
DISGREGATIONS
DISGRUNTLE
DISGRUNTLED
DISGRUNTLEMENT
DISGRUNTLEMENTS
DISGRUNTLES
DISGRUNTLING
DISGUISABLE
DISGUISEDLY
DISGUISEDNESS
DISGUISEDNESSES
DISGUISELESS
DISGUISEMENT
DISGUISEMENTS
DISGUISERS
DISGUISING

DISGUISINGS
DISGUSTEDLY
DISGUSTEDNESS
DISGUSTEDNESSES
DISGUSTFUL
DISGUSTFULLY
DISGUSTFULNESS
DISGUSTING
DISGUSTINGLY
DISGUSTINGNESS
DISHABILITATE
DISHABILITATED
DISHABILITATES
DISHABILITATING
DISHABILITATION
DISHABILLE
DISHABILLES
DISHABITED
DISHABITING
DISHABLING
DISHALLOWED
DISHALLOWING
DISHALLOWS
DISHARMONIC
DISHARMONIES
DISHARMONIOUS
DISHARMONIOUSLY
DISHARMONISE
DISHARMONISED
DISHARMONISES
DISHARMONISING
DISHARMONIZE
DISHARMONIZED
DISHARMONIZES
DISHARMONIZING
DISHARMONY
DISHCLOTHS
DISHCLOUTS
DISHDASHAS
DISHEARTEN
DISHEARTENED
DISHEARTENING
DISHEARTENINGLY
DISHEARTENMENT
DISHEARTENMENTS
DISHEARTENS
DISHELMING
DISHERISON
DISHERISONS
DISHERITED
DISHERITING
DISHERITOR
DISHERITORS
DISHEVELED
DISHEVELING
DISHEVELLED
DISHEVELLING
DISHEVELMENT
DISHEVELMENTS

DISHONESTIES
DISHONESTLY
DISHONESTY
DISHONORABLE
DISHONORABLY
DISHONORARY
DISHONORED
DISHONORER
DISHONORERS
DISHONORING
DISHONOURABLE
DISHONOURABLY
DISHONOURED
DISHONOURER
DISHONOURERS
DISHONOURING
DISHONOURS
DISHORNING
DISHORSING
DISHOUSING
DISHTOWELS
DISHUMOURED
DISHUMOURING
DISHUMOURS
DISHWASHER
DISHWASHERS
DISHWATERS
DISILLUDED
DISILLUDES
DISILLUDING
DISILLUMINATE
DISILLUMINATED
DISILLUMINATES
DISILLUMINATING
DISILLUSION
DISILLUSIONARY
DISILLUSIONED
DISILLUSIONING
DISILLUSIONISE
DISILLUSIONISED
DISILLUSIONISES
DISILLUSIONIZE
DISILLUSIONIZED
DISILLUSIONIZES
DISILLUSIONMENT
DISILLUSIONS
DISILLUSIVE
DISIMAGINE
DISIMAGINED
DISIMAGINES
DISIMAGINING
DISIMMURED
DISIMMURES
DISIMMURING
DISIMPASSIONED
DISIMPRISON
DISIMPRISONED
DISIMPRISONING
DISIMPRISONMENT

DISIMPRISONS
DISIMPROVE
DISIMPROVED
DISIMPROVES
DISIMPROVING
DISINCARCERATE
DISINCARCERATED
DISINCARCERATES
DISINCENTIVE
DISINCENTIVES
DISINCLINATION
DISINCLINATIONS
DISINCLINE
DISINCLINED
DISINCLINES
DISINCLINING
DISINCLOSE
DISINCLOSED
DISINCLOSES
DISINCLOSING
DISINCORPORATE
DISINCORPORATED
DISINCORPORATES
DISINFECTANT
DISINFECTANTS
DISINFECTED
DISINFECTING
DISINFECTION
DISINFECTIONS
DISINFECTOR
DISINFECTORS
DISINFECTS
DISINFESTANT
DISINFESTANTS
DISINFESTATION
DISINFESTATIONS
DISINFESTED
DISINFESTING
DISINFESTS
DISINFLATION
DISINFLATIONARY
DISINFLATIONS
DISINFORMATION
DISINFORMATIONS
DISINFORMED
DISINFORMING
DISINFORMS
DISINGENUITIES
DISINGENUITY
DISINGENUOUS
DISINGENUOUSLY
DISINHERISON
DISINHERISONS
DISINHERIT
DISINHERITANCE
DISINHERITANCES
DISINHERITED
DISINHERITING
DISINHERITS

DISINHIBIT
DISINHIBITED
DISINHIBITING
DISINHIBITION
DISINHIBITIONS
DISINHIBITORY
DISINHIBITS
DISINHUMED
DISINHUMES
DISINHUMING
DISINTEGRABLE
DISINTEGRATE
DISINTEGRATED
DISINTEGRATES
DISINTEGRATING
DISINTEGRATION
DISINTEGRATIONS
DISINTEGRATIVE
DISINTEGRATOR
DISINTEGRATORS
DISINTEREST
DISINTERESTED
DISINTERESTEDLY
DISINTERESTING
DISINTERESTS
DISINTERMENT
DISINTERMENTS
DISINTERRED
DISINTERRING
DISINTHRAL
DISINTHRALLED
DISINTHRALLING
DISINTHRALS
DISINTOXICATE
DISINTOXICATED
DISINTOXICATES
DISINTOXICATING
DISINTOXICATION
DISINTRICATE
DISINTRICATED
DISINTRICATES
DISINTRICATING
DISINURING
DISINVESTED
DISINVESTING
DISINVESTITURE
DISINVESTITURES
DISINVESTMENT
DISINVESTMENTS
DISINVESTS
DISINVIGORATE
DISINVIGORATED
DISINVIGORATES
DISINVIGORATING
DISINVITED
DISINVITES
DISINVITING
DISINVOLVE
DISINVOLVED

DISINVOLVES
DISINVOLVING
DISJECTING
DISJECTION
DISJECTIONS
DISJOINABLE
DISJOINING
DISJOINTED
DISJOINTEDLY
DISJOINTEDNESS
DISJOINTING
DISJUNCTION
DISJUNCTIONS
DISJUNCTIVE
DISJUNCTIVELY
DISJUNCTIVES
DISJUNCTOR
DISJUNCTORS
DISJUNCTURE
DISJUNCTURES
DISLEAFING
DISLEAVING
DISLIKABLE
DISLIKEABLE
DISLIKEFUL
DISLIKENED
DISLIKENESS
DISLIKENESSES
DISLIKENING
DISLIMBING
DISLIMNING
DISLINKING
DISLOADING
DISLOCATED
DISLOCATEDLY
DISLOCATES
DISLOCATING
DISLOCATION
DISLOCATIONS
DISLODGEMENT
DISLODGEMENTS
DISLODGING
DISLODGMENT
DISLODGMENTS
DISLOIGNED
DISLOIGNING
DISLOYALLY
DISLOYALTIES
DISLOYALTY
DISLUSTRED
DISLUSTRES
DISLUSTRING
DISMALITIES
DISMALLEST
DISMALNESS
DISMALNESSES
DISMANNING
DISMANTLED
DISMANTLEMENT

DISMANTLEMENTS
DISMANTLER
DISMANTLERS
DISMANTLES
DISMANTLING
DISMASKING
DISMASTING
DISMASTMENT
DISMASTMENTS
DISMAYEDNESS
DISMAYEDNESSES
DISMAYFULLY
DISMAYINGLY
DISMAYLING
DISMEMBERED
DISMEMBERER
DISMEMBERERS
DISMEMBERING
DISMEMBERMENT
DISMEMBERMENTS
DISMEMBERS
DISMISSALS
DISMISSIBLE
DISMISSING
DISMISSION
DISMISSIONS
DISMISSIVE
DISMISSIVELY
DISMISSORY
DISMOUNTABLE
DISMOUNTED
DISMOUNTING
DISMUTATION
DISMUTATIONS
DISNATURALISE
DISNATURALISED
DISNATURALISES
DISNATURALISING
DISNATURALIZE
DISNATURALIZED
DISNATURALIZES
DISNATURALIZING
DISNATURED
DISNESTING
DISOBEDIENCE
DISOBEDIENCES
DISOBEDIENT
DISOBEDIENTLY
DISOBEYERS
DISOBEYING
DISOBLIGATION
DISOBLIGATIONS
DISOBLIGATORY
DISOBLIGED
DISOBLIGEMENT
DISOBLIGEMENTS
DISOBLIGES
DISOBLIGING
DISOBLIGINGLY

DISOBLIGINGNESS
DISOPERATION
DISOPERATIONS
DISORDERED
DISORDEREDLY
DISORDEREDNESS
DISORDERING
DISORDERLIES
DISORDERLINESS
DISORDERLY
DISORDINATE
DISORDINATELY
DISORGANIC
DISORGANISATION
DISORGANISE
DISORGANISED
DISORGANISER
DISORGANISERS
DISORGANISES
DISORGANISING
DISORGANIZATION
DISORGANIZE
DISORGANIZED
DISORGANIZER
DISORGANIZERS
DISORGANIZES
DISORGANIZING
DISORIENTATE
DISORIENTATED
DISORIENTATES
DISORIENTATING
DISORIENTATION
DISORIENTATIONS
DISORIENTED
DISORIENTING
DISORIENTS
DISOWNMENT
DISOWNMENTS
DISPARAGED
DISPARAGEMENT
DISPARAGEMENTS
DISPARAGER
DISPARAGERS
DISPARAGES
DISPARAGING
DISPARAGINGLY
DISPARATELY
DISPARATENESS
DISPARATENESSES
DISPARATES
DISPARITIES
DISPARKING
DISPARTING
DISPASSION
DISPASSIONATE
DISPASSIONATELY
DISPASSIONS
DISPATCHED
DISPATCHER

DISPATCHERS
DISPATCHES
DISPATCHFUL
DISPATCHING
DISPATHIES
DISPAUPERED
DISPAUPERING
DISPAUPERISE
DISPAUPERISED
DISPAUPERISES
DISPAUPERISING
DISPAUPERIZE
DISPAUPERIZED
DISPAUPERIZES
DISPAUPERIZING
DISPAUPERS
DISPELLERS
DISPELLING
DISPENCING
DISPENDING
DISPENSABILITY
DISPENSABLE
DISPENSABLENESS
DISPENSABLY
DISPENSARIES
DISPENSARY
DISPENSATION
DISPENSATIONAL
DISPENSATIONS
DISPENSATIVE
DISPENSATIVELY
DISPENSATOR
DISPENSATORIES
DISPENSATORILY
DISPENSATORS
DISPENSATORY
DISPENSERS
DISPENSING
DISPEOPLED
DISPEOPLES
DISPEOPLING
DISPERMOUS
DISPERSALS
DISPERSANT
DISPERSANTS
DISPERSEDLY
DISPERSEDNESS
DISPERSEDNESSES
DISPERSERS
DISPERSIBLE
DISPERSING
DISPERSION
DISPERSIONS
DISPERSIVE
DISPERSIVELY
DISPERSIVENESS
DISPERSOID
DISPERSOIDS
DISPIRITED

DISPIRITEDLY	DISPOSITION	DISPROVALS	DISQUISITIVE
DISPIRITEDNESS	DISPOSITIONAL	DISPROVERS	DISQUISITORY
DISPIRITING	DISPOSITIONED	DISPROVIDE	DISRANKING
DISPIRITINGLY	DISPOSITIONS	DISPROVIDED	DISREGARDED
DISPIRITMENT	DISPOSITIVE	DISPROVIDES	DISREGARDER
DISPIRITMENTS	DISPOSITIVELY	DISPROVIDING	DISREGARDERS
DISPITEOUS	DISPOSITOR	DISPROVING	DISREGARDFUL
DISPITEOUSLY	DISPOSITORS	DISPUNGING	DISREGARDFULLY
DISPITEOUSNESS	DISPOSSESS	DISPURSING	DISREGARDING
DISPLACEABLE	DISPOSSESSED	DISPURVEYANCE	DISREGARDS
DISPLACEMENT	DISPOSSESSES	DISPURVEYANCES	DISRELATED
DISPLACEMENTS	DISPOSSESSING	DISPURVEYED	DISRELATION
DISPLACERS	DISPOSSESSION	DISPURVEYING	DISRELATIONS
DISPLACING	DISPOSSESSIONS	DISPURVEYS	DISRELISHED
DISPLANTATION	DISPOSSESSOR	DISPUTABILITIES	DISRELISHES
DISPLANTATIONS	DISPOSSESSORS	DISPUTABILITY	DISRELISHING
DISPLANTED	DISPOSSESSORY	DISPUTABLE	DISREMEMBER
DISPLANTING	DISPOSTING	DISPUTABLENESS	DISREMEMBERED
DISPLAYABLE	DISPOSURES	DISPUTABLY	DISREMEMBERING
DISPLAYERS	DISPRAISED	DISPUTANTS	DISREMEMBERS
DISPLAYING	DISPRAISER	DISPUTATION	DISREPAIRS
DISPLEASANCE	DISPRAISERS	DISPUTATIONS	DISREPUTABILITY
DISPLEASANCES	DISPRAISES	DISPUTATIOUS	DISREPUTABLE
DISPLEASANT	DISPRAISING	DISPUTATIOUSLY	DISREPUTABLY
DISPLEASED	DISPRAISINGLY	DISPUTATIVE	DISREPUTATION
DISPLEASEDLY	DISPREADING	DISPUTATIVELY	DISREPUTATIONS
DISPLEASEDNESS	DISPREDDEN	DISPUTATIVENESS	DISREPUTES
DISPLEASES	DISPREDDING	DISQUALIFIABLE	DISRESPECT
DISPLEASING	DISPRINCED	DISQUALIFIED	DISRESPECTABLE
DISPLEASINGLY	DISPRISONED	DISQUALIFIER	DISRESPECTED
DISPLEASINGNESS	DISPRISONING	DISQUALIFIERS	DISRESPECTFUL
DISPLEASURE	DISPRISONS	DISQUALIFIES	DISRESPECTFULLY
DISPLEASURED	DISPRIVACIED	DISQUALIFY	DISRESPECTING
DISPLEASURES	DISPRIVILEGE	DISQUALIFYING	DISRESPECTS
DISPLEASURING	DISPRIVILEGED	DISQUANTITIED	DISROBEMENT
DISPLENISH	DISPRIVILEGES	DISQUANTITIES	DISROBEMENTS
DISPLENISHED	DISPRIVILEGING	DISQUANTITY	DISROOTING
DISPLENISHES	DISPRIZING	DISQUANTITYING	DISRUPTERS
DISPLENISHING	DISPROFESS	DISQUIETED	DISRUPTING
DISPLENISHMENT	DISPROFESSED	DISQUIETEDLY	DISRUPTION
DISPLENISHMENTS	DISPROFESSES	DISQUIETEDNESS	DISRUPTIONS
DISPLODING	DISPROFESSING	DISQUIETEN	DISRUPTIVE
DISPLOSION	DISPROFITS	DISQUIETENED	DISRUPTIVELY
DISPLOSIONS	DISPROOVED	DISQUIETENING	DISRUPTIVENESS
DISPLUMING	DISPROOVES	DISQUIETENS	DISRUPTORS
DISPONDAIC	DISPROOVING	DISQUIETFUL	DISSATISFACTION
DISPONDEES	DISPROPERTIED	DISQUIETING	DISSATISFACTORY
DISPONGING	DISPROPERTIES	DISQUIETINGLY	DISSATISFIED
DISPORTING	DISPROPERTY	DISQUIETIVE	DISSATISFIEDLY
DISPORTMENT	DISPROPERTYING	DISQUIETLY	DISSATISFIES
DISPORTMENTS	DISPROPORTION	DISQUIETNESS	DISSATISFY
DISPOSABILITIES	DISPROPORTIONAL	DISQUIETNESSES	DISSATISFYING
DISPOSABILITY	DISPROPORTIONED	DISQUIETOUS	DISSAVINGS
DISPOSABLE	DISPROPORTIONS	DISQUIETUDE	DISSEATING
DISPOSABLENESS	DISPROPRIATE	DISQUIETUDES	DISSECTIBLE
DISPOSABLES	DISPROPRIATED	DISQUISITION	DISSECTING
DISPOSEDLY	DISPROPRIATES	DISQUISITIONAL	DISSECTINGS
DISPOSINGLY	DISPROPRIATING	DISQUISITIONARY	DISSECTION
DISPOSINGS	DISPROVABLE	DISQUISITIONS	DISSECTIONS

DISSECTIVE
DISSECTORS
DISSEISEES
DISSEISING
DISSEISINS
DISSEISORS
DISSEIZEES
DISSEIZING
DISSEIZINS
DISSEIZORS
DISSELBOOM
DISSELBOOMS
DISSEMBLANCE
DISSEMBLANCES
DISSEMBLED
DISSEMBLER
DISSEMBLERS
DISSEMBLES
DISSEMBLIES
DISSEMBLING
DISSEMBLINGLY
DISSEMBLINGS
DISSEMINATE
DISSEMINATED
DISSEMINATES
DISSEMINATING
DISSEMINATION
DISSEMINATIONS
DISSEMINATIVE
DISSEMINATOR
DISSEMINATORS
DISSEMINULE
DISSEMINULES
DISSENSION
DISSENSIONS
DISSENSUSES
DISSENTERISH
DISSENTERISM
DISSENTERISMS
DISSENTERS
DISSENTIENCE
DISSENTIENCES
DISSENTIENCIES
DISSENTIENCY
DISSENTIENT
DISSENTIENTLY
DISSENTIENTS
DISSENTING
DISSENTINGLY
DISSENTION
DISSENTIONS
DISSENTIOUS
DISSEPIMENT
DISSEPIMENTAL
DISSEPIMENTS
DISSERTATE
DISSERTATED
DISSERTATES
DISSERTATING

DISSERTATION
DISSERTATIONAL
DISSERTATIONIST
DISSERTATIONS
DISSERTATIVE
DISSERTATOR
DISSERTATORS
DISSERTING
DISSERVICE
DISSERVICEABLE
DISSERVICES
DISSERVING
DISSEVERANCE
DISSEVERANCES
DISSEVERATION
DISSEVERATIONS
DISSEVERED
DISSEVERING
DISSEVERMENT
DISSEVERMENTS
DISSHEATHE
DISSHEATHED
DISSHEATHES
DISSHEATHING
DISSHIVERED
DISSHIVERING
DISSHIVERS
DISSIDENCE
DISSIDENCES
DISSIDENTLY
DISSIDENTS
DISSILIENCE
DISSILIENCES
DISSILIENT
DISSIMILAR
DISSIMILARITIES
DISSIMILARITY
DISSIMILARLY
DISSIMILARS
DISSIMILATE
DISSIMILATED
DISSIMILATES
DISSIMILATING
DISSIMILATION
DISSIMILATIONS
DISSIMILATIVE
DISSIMILATORY
DISSIMILES
DISSIMILITUDE
DISSIMILITUDES
DISSIMULATE
DISSIMULATED
DISSIMULATES
DISSIMULATING
DISSIMULATION
DISSIMULATIONS
DISSIMULATIVE
DISSIMULATOR
DISSIMULATORS

DISSIPABLE
DISSIPATED
DISSIPATEDLY
DISSIPATEDNESS
DISSIPATER
DISSIPATERS
DISSIPATES
DISSIPATING
DISSIPATION
DISSIPATIONS
DISSIPATIVE
DISSIPATOR
DISSIPATORS
DISSOCIABILITY
DISSOCIABLE
DISSOCIABLENESS
DISSOCIABLY
DISSOCIALISE
DISSOCIALISED
DISSOCIALISES
DISSOCIALISING
DISSOCIALITIES
DISSOCIALITY
DISSOCIALIZE
DISSOCIALIZED
DISSOCIALIZES
DISSOCIALIZING
DISSOCIATE
DISSOCIATED
DISSOCIATES
DISSOCIATING
DISSOCIATION
DISSOCIATIONS
DISSOCIATIVE
DISSOLUBILITIES
DISSOLUBILITY
DISSOLUBLE
DISSOLUBLENESS
DISSOLUTELY
DISSOLUTENESS
DISSOLUTENESSES
DISSOLUTES
DISSOLUTION
DISSOLUTIONISM
DISSOLUTIONISMS
DISSOLUTIONIST
DISSOLUTIONISTS
DISSOLUTIONS
DISSOLUTIVE
DISSOLVABILITY
DISSOLVABLE
DISSOLVABLENESS
DISSOLVENT
DISSOLVENTS
DISSOLVERS
DISSOLVING
DISSOLVINGS
DISSONANCE
DISSONANCES

DISSONANCIES
DISSONANCY
DISSONANTLY
DISSUADABLE
DISSUADERS
DISSUADING
DISSUASION
DISSUASIONS
DISSUASIVE
DISSUASIVELY
DISSUASIVENESS
DISSUASIVES
DISSUASORIES
DISSUASORY
DISSUNDERED
DISSUNDERING
DISSUNDERS
DISSYLLABIC
DISSYLLABLE
DISSYLLABLES
DISSYMMETRIC
DISSYMMETRICAL
DISSYMMETRIES
DISSYMMETRY
DISTAINING
DISTANCELESS
DISTANCING
DISTANTNESS
DISTANTNESSES
DISTASTEFUL
DISTASTEFULLY
DISTASTEFULNESS
DISTASTING
DISTELFINK
DISTELFINKS
DISTEMPERATE
DISTEMPERATURE
DISTEMPERATURES
DISTEMPERED
DISTEMPERING
DISTEMPERS
DISTENDERS
DISTENDING
DISTENSIBILITY
DISTENSIBLE
DISTENSILE
DISTENSION
DISTENSIONS
DISTENSIVE
DISTENTION
DISTENTIONS
DISTHRONED
DISTHRONES
DISTHRONING
DISTHRONISE
DISTHRONISED
DISTHRONISES
DISTHRONISING
DISTHRONIZE

DISTHRONIZED	DISTRACTIBLE	DISTROUBLES	DITHEISTICAL
DISTHRONIZES	DISTRACTING	DISTROUBLING	DITHELETES
DISTHRONIZING	DISTRACTINGLY	DISTRUSTED	DITHELETIC
DISTICHOUS	DISTRACTION	DISTRUSTER	DITHELETICAL
DISTICHOUSLY	DISTRACTIONS	DISTRUSTERS	DITHELETISM
DISTILLABLE	DISTRACTIVE	DISTRUSTFUL	DITHELETISMS
DISTILLAND	DISTRACTIVELY	DISTRUSTFULLY	DITHELISMS
DISTILLANDS	DISTRAINABLE	DISTRUSTFULNESS	DITHELITISM
DISTILLATE	DISTRAINED	DISTRUSTING	DITHELITISMS
DISTILLATES	DISTRAINEE	DISTRUSTLESS	DITHERIEST
DISTILLATION	DISTRAINEES	DISTURBANCE	DITHIOCARBAMATE
DISTILLATIONS	DISTRAINER	DISTURBANCES	DITHIONATE
DISTILLATORY	DISTRAINERS	DISTURBANT	DITHIONATES
DISTILLERIES	DISTRAINING	DISTURBANTS	DITHIONITE
DISTILLERS	DISTRAINMENT	DISTURBATIVE	DITHIONITES
DISTILLERY	DISTRAINMENTS	DISTURBERS	DITHIONOUS
DISTILLING	DISTRAINOR	DISTURBING	DITHYRAMBIC
DISTILLINGS	DISTRAINORS	DISTURBINGLY	DITHYRAMBICALLY
DISTILMENT	DISTRAINTS	DISUBSTITUTED	DITHYRAMBIST
DISTILMENTS	DISTRAUGHT	DISULFATES	DITHYRAMBISTS
DISTINCTER	DISTRAUGHTLY	DISULFIDES	DITHYRAMBS
DISTINCTEST	DISTRESSED	DISULFIRAM	DITRANSITIVE
DISTINCTION	DISTRESSER	DISULFIRAMS	DITRANSITIVES
DISTINCTIONS	DISTRESSERS	DISULFOTON	DITRIGLYPH
DISTINCTIVE	DISTRESSES	DISULFOTONS	DITRIGLYPHIC
DISTINCTIVELY	DISTRESSFUL	DISULPHATE	DITRIGLYPHS
DISTINCTIVENESS	DISTRESSFULLY	DISULPHATES	DITROCHEAN
DISTINCTIVES	DISTRESSFULNESS	DISULPHIDE	DITROCHEES
DISTINCTLY	DISTRESSING	DISULPHIDES	DITSINESSES
DISTINCTNESS	DISTRESSINGLY	DISULPHURET	DITTANDERS
DISTINCTNESSES	DISTRESSINGS	DISULPHURETS	DITTOGRAPHIC
DISTINCTURE	DISTRIBUEND	DISULPHURIC	DITTOGRAPHIES
DISTINCTURES	DISTRIBUENDS	DISUNIONIST	DITTOGRAPHY
DISTINGUEE	DISTRIBUTABLE	DISUNIONISTS	DITTOLOGIES
DISTINGUISH	DISTRIBUTARIES	DISUNITERS	DITZINESSES
DISTINGUISHABLE	DISTRIBUTARY	DISUNITIES	DIURETICALLY
DISTINGUISHABLY	DISTRIBUTE	DISUNITING	DIURETICALNESS
DISTINGUISHED	DISTRIBUTED	DISUTILITIES	DIURNALIST
DISTINGUISHER	DISTRIBUTEE	DISUTILITY	DIURNALISTS
DISTINGUISHERS	DISTRIBUTEES	DISVALUING	DIUTURNITIES
DISTINGUISHES	DISTRIBUTER	DISVOUCHED	DIUTURNITY
DISTINGUISHING	DISTRIBUTERS	DISVOUCHES	DIVAGATING
DISTINGUISHMENT	DISTRIBUTES	DISVOUCHING	DIVAGATION
DISTORTEDLY	DISTRIBUTING	DISWORSHIP	DIVAGATIONS
DISTORTEDNESS	DISTRIBUTION	DISWORSHIPS	DIVALENCES
DISTORTEDNESSES	DISTRIBUTIONAL	DISYLLABIC	DIVALENCIES
DISTORTERS	DISTRIBUTIONS	DISYLLABIFIED	DIVARICATE
DISTORTING	DISTRIBUTIVE	DISYLLABIFIES	DIVARICATED
DISTORTION	DISTRIBUTIVELY	DISYLLABIFY	DIVARICATELY
DISTORTIONAL	DISTRIBUTIVES	DISYLLABIFYING	DIVARICATES
DISTORTIONS	DISTRIBUTIVITY	DISYLLABISM	DIVARICATING
DISTORTIVE	DISTRIBUTOR	DISYLLABISMS	DIVARICATINGLY
DISTRACTABLE	DISTRIBUTORS	DISYLLABLE	DIVARICATION
DISTRACTED	DISTRICTED	DISYLLABLES	DIVARICATIONS
DISTRACTEDLY	DISTRICTING	DITCHDIGGER	DIVARICATOR
DISTRACTEDNESS	DISTRINGAS	DITCHDIGGERS	DIVARICATORS
DISTRACTER	DISTRINGASES	DITCHWATER	DIVEBOMBED
DISTRACTERS	DISTROUBLE	DITCHWATERS	DIVEBOMBING
DISTRACTIBILITY	DISTROUBLED	DITHEISTIC	DIVELLICATE

DIVELLICATED

DIVELLICATED
DIVELLICATES
DIVELLICATING
DIVERGEMENT
DIVERGEMENTS
DIVERGENCE
DIVERGENCES
DIVERGENCIES
DIVERGENCY
DIVERGENTLY
DIVERGINGLY
DIVERSENESS
DIVERSENESSES
DIVERSIFIABLE
DIVERSIFICATION
DIVERSIFIED
DIVERSIFIER
DIVERSIFIERS
DIVERSIFIES
DIVERSIFORM
DIVERSIFYING
DIVERSIONAL
DIVERSIONARY
DIVERSIONIST
DIVERSIONISTS
DIVERSIONS
DIVERSITIES
DIVERTIBILITIES
DIVERTIBILITY
DIVERTIBLE
DIVERTICULA
DIVERTICULAR
DIVERTICULATE
DIVERTICULATED
DIVERTICULITIS
DIVERTICULOSES
DIVERTICULOSIS
DIVERTICULUM
DIVERTIMENTI
DIVERTIMENTO
DIVERTIMENTOS
DIVERTINGLY
DIVERTISEMENT
DIVERTISEMENTS
DIVERTISSEMENT
DIVERTISSEMENTS
DIVESTIBLE
DIVESTITURE
DIVESTITURES
DIVESTMENT
DIVESTMENTS
DIVESTURES
DIVIDEDNESS
DIVIDEDNESSES
DIVIDENDLESS
DIVINATION
DIVINATIONS
DIVINATORIAL
DIVINATORS

DIVINATORY
DIVINENESS
DIVINENESSES
DIVINERESS
DIVINERESSES
DIVINIFIED
DIVINIFIES
DIVINIFYING
DIVINISATION
DIVINISATIONS
DIVINISING
DIVINITIES
DIVINIZATION
DIVINIZATIONS
DIVINIZING
DIVISIBILITIES
DIVISIBILITY
DIVISIBLENESS
DIVISIBLENESSES
DIVISIONAL
DIVISIONALLY
DIVISIONARY
DIVISIONISM
DIVISIONISMS
DIVISIONIST
DIVISIONISTS
DIVISIVELY
DIVISIVENESS
DIVISIVENESSES
DIVORCEABLE
DIVORCEMENT
DIVORCEMENTS
DIVULGATED
DIVULGATER
DIVULGATERS
DIVULGATES
DIVULGATING
DIVULGATION
DIVULGATIONS
DIVULGATOR
DIVULGATORS
DIVULGEMENT
DIVULGEMENTS
DIVULGENCE
DIVULGENCES
DIVULSIONS
DIZENMENTS
DIZZINESSES
DIZZYINGLY
DJELLABAHS
DOBSONFLIES
DOCENTSHIP
DOCENTSHIPS
DOCHMIACAL
DOCHMIUSES
DOCIBILITIES
DOCIBILITY
DOCIBLENESS
DOCIBLENESSES

DOCILITIES
DOCIMASIES
DOCIMASTIC
DOCIMOLOGIES
DOCIMOLOGY
DOCKISATION
DOCKISATIONS
DOCKIZATION
DOCKIZATIONS
DOCKMASTER
DOCKMASTERS
DOCKWORKER
DOCKWORKERS
DOCQUETING
DOCTORANDS
DOCTORATED
DOCTORATES
DOCTORATING
DOCTORESSES
DOCTORLESS
DOCTORSHIP
DOCTORSHIPS
DOCTRESSES
DOCTRINAIRE
DOCTRINAIRES
DOCTRINAIRISM
DOCTRINAIRISMS
DOCTRINALITIES
DOCTRINALITY
DOCTRINALLY
DOCTRINARIAN
DOCTRINARIANISM
DOCTRINARIANS
DOCTRINARISM
DOCTRINARISMS
DOCTRINISM
DOCTRINISMS
DOCTRINIST
DOCTRINISTS
DOCUDRAMAS
DOCUMENTABLE
DOCUMENTAL
DOCUMENTALIST
DOCUMENTALISTS
DOCUMENTARIAN
DOCUMENTARIANS
DOCUMENTARIES
DOCUMENTARILY
DOCUMENTARISE
DOCUMENTARISED
DOCUMENTARISES
DOCUMENTARISING
DOCUMENTARIST
DOCUMENTARISTS
DOCUMENTARIZE
DOCUMENTARIZED
DOCUMENTARIZES
DOCUMENTARIZING
DOCUMENTARY

DOCUMENTATION
DOCUMENTATIONAL
DOCUMENTATIONS
DOCUMENTED
DOCUMENTER
DOCUMENTERS
DOCUMENTING
DODDERIEST
DODDIPOLLS
DODDYPOLLS
DODECAGONAL
DODECAGONS
DODECAGYNIAN
DODECAGYNOUS
DODECAHEDRA
DODECAHEDRAL
DODECAHEDRON
DODECAHEDRONS
DODECANDROUS
DODECANOIC
DODECAPHONIC
DODECAPHONIES
DODECAPHONISM
DODECAPHONISMS
DODECAPHONIST
DODECAPHONISTS
DODECAPHONY
DODECASTYLE
DODECASTYLES
DODECASYLLABIC
DODECASYLLABLE
DODECASYLLABLES
DODGEBALLS
DODGINESSES
DOGARESSAS
DOGBERRIES
DOGBERRYISM
DOGBERRYISMS
DOGCATCHER
DOGCATCHERS
DOGFIGHTING
DOGGEDNESS
DOGGEDNESSES
DOGGINESSES
DOGGISHNESS
DOGGISHNESSES
DOGGONEDER
DOGGONEDEST
DOGLEGGING
DOGMATICAL
DOGMATICALLY
DOGMATICALNESS
DOGMATISATION
DOGMATISATIONS
DOGMATISED
DOGMATISER
DOGMATISERS
DOGMATISES
DOGMATISING

DOGMATISMS
DOGMATISTS
DOGMATIZATION
DOGMATIZATIONS
DOGMATIZED
DOGMATIZER
DOGMATIZERS
DOGMATIZES
DOGMATIZING
DOGMATOLOGIES
DOGMATOLOGY
DOGNAPINGS
DOGNAPPERS
DOGNAPPING
DOGNAPPINGS
DOGROBBERS
DOGSBODIED
DOGSBODIES
DOGSBODYING
DOGSLEDDED
DOGSLEDDER
DOGSLEDDERS
DOGSLEDDING
DOGTROTTED
DOGTROTTING
DOGWATCHES
DOLABRIFORM
DOLCELATTE
DOLCELATTES
DOLCEMENTE
DOLEFULLER
DOLEFULLEST
DOLEFULNESS
DOLEFULNESSES
DOLESOMELY
DOLICHOCEPHAL
DOLICHOCEPHALIC
DOLICHOCEPHALS
DOLICHOCEPHALY
DOLICHOSAURUS
DOLICHOSAURUSES
DOLICHOSES
DOLICHURUS
DOLICHURUSES
DOLLARBIRD
DOLLARBIRDS
DOLLARFISH
DOLLARFISHES
DOLLARISATION
DOLLARISATIONS
DOLLARISED
DOLLARISES
DOLLARISING
DOLLARIZATION
DOLLARIZATIONS
DOLLARIZED
DOLLARIZES
DOLLARIZING
DOLLARLESS

DOLLAROCRACIES
DOLLAROCRACY
DOLLARSHIP
DOLLARSHIPS
DOLLHOUSES
DOLLINESSES
DOLLISHNESS
DOLLISHNESSES
DOLLYBIRDS
DOLOMITISATION
DOLOMITISATIONS
DOLOMITISE
DOLOMITISED
DOLOMITISES
DOLOMITISING
DOLOMITIZATION
DOLOMITIZATIONS
DOLOMITIZE
DOLOMITIZED
DOLOMITIZES
DOLOMITIZING
DOLORIFEROUS
DOLORIMETRIES
DOLORIMETRY
DOLOROUSLY
DOLOROUSNESS
DOLOROUSNESSES
DOLOSTONES
DOLPHINARIA
DOLPHINARIUM
DOLPHINARIUMS
DOLPHINETS
DOLPHINFISH
DOLPHINFISHES
DOLTISHNESS
DOLTISHNESSES
DOMESTICABLE
DOMESTICAL
DOMESTICALLY
DOMESTICATE
DOMESTICATED
DOMESTICATES
DOMESTICATING
DOMESTICATION
DOMESTICATIONS
DOMESTICATIVE
DOMESTICATOR
DOMESTICATORS
DOMESTICISE
DOMESTICISED
DOMESTICISES
DOMESTICISING
DOMESTICITIES
DOMESTICITY
DOMESTICIZE
DOMESTICIZED
DOMESTICIZES
DOMESTICIZING
DOMICILIARY

DOMICILIATE
DOMICILIATED
DOMICILIATES
DOMICILIATING
DOMICILIATION
DOMICILIATIONS
DOMICILING
DOMINANCES
DOMINANCIES
DOMINANTLY
DOMINATING
DOMINATINGLY
DOMINATION
DOMINATIONS
DOMINATIVE
DOMINATORS
DOMINATRICES
DOMINATRIX
DOMINATRIXES
DOMINEERED
DOMINEERING
DOMINEERINGLY
DOMINEERINGNESS
DOMINICKER
DOMINICKERS
DOMINIQUES
DONATARIES
DONATISTIC
DONATISTICAL
DONATORIES
DONENESSES
DONKEYWORK
DONKEYWORKS
DONNICKERS
DONNISHNESS
DONNISHNESSES
DONNYBROOK
DONNYBROOKS
DONORSHIPS
DOODLEBUGS
DOOHICKEYS
DOOHICKIES
DOOMSAYERS
DOOMSAYING
DOOMSAYINGS
DOOMSDAYER
DOOMSDAYERS
DOOMWATCHED
DOOMWATCHER
DOOMWATCHERS
DOOMWATCHES
DOOMWATCHING
DOOMWATCHINGS
DOORFRAMES
DOORKEEPER
DOORKEEPERS
DOORKNOCKED
DOORKNOCKER
DOORKNOCKERS

DOORKNOCKING
DOORKNOCKS
DOORPLATES
DOORSTEPPED
DOORSTEPPER
DOORSTEPPERS
DOORSTEPPING
DOORSTEPPINGS
DOORSTONES
DOPAMINERGIC
DOPESHEETS
DOPEYNESSES
DOPINESSES
DOPPELGANGER
DOPPELGANGERS
DOPPLERITE
DOPPLERITES
DORBEETLES
DORKINESSES
DORMANCIES
DORMITIONS
DORMITIVES
DORMITORIES
DORONICUMS
DORSIBRANCHIATE
DORSIFEROUS
DORSIFIXED
DORSIFLEXION
DORSIFLEXIONS
DORSIGRADE
DORSIVENTRAL
DORSIVENTRALITY
DORSIVENTRALLY
DORSOLATERAL
DORSOLUMBAR
DORSOVENTRAL
DORSOVENTRALITY
DORSOVENTRALLY
DORTINESSES
DOSEMETERS
DOSIMETERS
DOSIMETRIC
DOSIMETRICIAN
DOSIMETRICIANS
DOSIMETRIES
DOSIMETRIST
DOSIMETRISTS
DOSIOLOGIES
DOSOLOGIES
DOSSHOUSES
DOTCOMMERS
DOTTINESSES
DOUBLEHEADER
DOUBLEHEADERS
DOUBLENESS
DOUBLENESSES
DOUBLESPEAK
DOUBLESPEAKER
DOUBLESPEAKERS

DOUBLESPEAKS

DOUBLESPEAKS
DOUBLETHINK
DOUBLETHINKS
DOUBLETONS
DOUBLETREE
DOUBLETREES
DOUBTFULLY
DOUBTFULNESS
DOUBTFULNESSES
DOUBTINGLY
DOUBTLESSLY
DOUBTLESSNESS
DOUBTLESSNESSES
DOUCENESSES
DOUCEPERES
DOUCHEBAGS
DOUGHFACED
DOUGHFACES
DOUGHINESS
DOUGHINESSES
DOUGHNUTLIKE
DOUGHNUTTED
DOUGHNUTTING
DOUGHNUTTINGS
DOUGHTIEST
DOUGHTINESS
DOUGHTINESSES
DOULOCRACIES
DOULOCRACY
DOUPPIONIS
DOURNESSES
DOUROUCOULI
DOUROUCOULIS
DOVEISHNESS
DOVEISHNESSES
DOVETAILED
DOVETAILING
DOVETAILINGS
DOVISHNESS
DOVISHNESSES
DOWDINESSES
DOWELLINGS
DOWFNESSES
DOWITCHERS
DOWNBURSTS
DOWNCOMERS
DOWNDRAFTS
DOWNDRAUGHT
DOWNDRAUGHTS
DOWNFALLEN
DOWNFORCES
DOWNGRADED
DOWNGRADES
DOWNGRADING
DOWNHEARTED
DOWNHEARTEDLY
DOWNHEARTEDNESS
DOWNHILLER
DOWNHILLERS

DOWNINESSES
DOWNLIGHTER
DOWNLIGHTERS
DOWNLIGHTS
DOWNLINKED
DOWNLINKING
DOWNLOADABLE
DOWNLOADED
DOWNLOADING
DOWNLOOKED
DOWNPLAYED
DOWNPLAYING
DOWNREGULATION
DOWNREGULATIONS
DOWNRIGHTLY
DOWNRIGHTNESS
DOWNRIGHTNESSES
DOWNRUSHES
DOWNSCALED
DOWNSCALES
DOWNSCALING
DOWNSHIFTED
DOWNSHIFTER
DOWNSHIFTERS
DOWNSHIFTING
DOWNSHIFTINGS
DOWNSHIFTS
DOWNSIZING
DOWNSLIDES
DOWNSPOUTS
DOWNSTAGES
DOWNSTAIRS
DOWNSTAIRSES
DOWNSTATER
DOWNSTATERS
DOWNSTATES
DOWNSTREAM
DOWNSTROKE
DOWNSTROKES
DOWNSWINGS
DOWNTHROWS
DOWNTOWNER
DOWNTOWNERS
DOWNTRENDED
DOWNTRENDING
DOWNTRENDS
DOWNTRODDEN
DOWNTURNED
DOWNWARDLY
DOWNWARDNESS
DOWNWARDNESSES
DOWNWASHES
DOWNZONING
DOXOGRAPHER
DOXOGRAPHERS
DOXOGRAPHIC
DOXOGRAPHIES
DOXOGRAPHY
DOXOLOGICAL

DOXOLOGICALLY
DOXOLOGIES
DOXORUBICIN
DOXORUBICINS
DOXYCYCLINE
DOXYCYCLINES
DOZINESSES
DRABBINESS
DRABBINESSES
DRABBLINGS
DRABNESSES
DRACONIANISM
DRACONIANISMS
DRACONICALLY
DRACONISMS
DRACONITES
DRACONTIASES
DRACONTIASIS
DRACUNCULUS
DRACUNCULUSES
DRAFTINESS
DRAFTINESSES
DRAFTSMANSHIP
DRAFTSMANSHIPS
DRAFTSPERSON
DRAFTSPERSONS
DRAGGINGLY
DRAGGLETAILED
DRAGHOUNDS
DRAGONESSES
DRAGONFLIES
DRAGONHEAD
DRAGONHEADS
DRAGONISED
DRAGONISES
DRAGONISING
DRAGONISMS
DRAGONIZED
DRAGONIZES
DRAGONIZING
DRAGONLIKE
DRAGONNADE
DRAGONNADED
DRAGONNADES
DRAGONNADING
DRAGONROOT
DRAGONROOTS
DRAGOONAGE
DRAGOONAGES
DRAGOONING
DRAGSTRIPS
DRAINLAYER
DRAINLAYERS
DRAINPIPES
DRAKESTONE
DRAKESTONES
DRAMATICAL
DRAMATICALLY
DRAMATICISM

DRAMATICISMS
DRAMATISABLE
DRAMATISATION
DRAMATISATIONS
DRAMATISED
DRAMATISER
DRAMATISERS
DRAMATISES
DRAMATISING
DRAMATISTS
DRAMATIZABLE
DRAMATIZATION
DRAMATIZATIONS
DRAMATIZED
DRAMATIZER
DRAMATIZERS
DRAMATIZES
DRAMATIZING
DRAMATURGE
DRAMATURGES
DRAMATURGIC
DRAMATURGICAL
DRAMATURGICALLY
DRAMATURGIES
DRAMATURGIST
DRAMATURGISTS
DRAMATURGS
DRAMATURGY
DRAPABILITIES
DRAPABILITY
DRAPEABILITIES
DRAPEABILITY
DRAPERYING
DRASTICALLY
DRATCHELLS
DRAUGHTBOARD
DRAUGHTBOARDS
DRAUGHTERS
DRAUGHTIER
DRAUGHTIEST
DRAUGHTILY
DRAUGHTINESS
DRAUGHTINESSES
DRAUGHTING
DRAUGHTMAN
DRAUGHTMEN
DRAUGHTSMAN
DRAUGHTSMANSHIP
DRAUGHTSMEN
DRAUGHTSWOMAN
DRAUGHTSWOMEN
DRAWBRIDGE
DRAWBRIDGES
DRAWERFULS
DRAWKNIVES
DRAWLINGLY
DRAWLINGNESS
DRAWLINGNESSES
DRAWNWORKS

DRAWPLATES
DRAWSHAVES
DRAWSTRING
DRAWSTRINGS
DRAYHORSES
DREADFULLY
DREADFULNESS
DREADFULNESSES
DREADLESSLY
DREADLESSNESS
DREADLESSNESSES
DREADLOCKS
DREADNAUGHT
DREADNAUGHTS
DREADNOUGHT
DREADNOUGHTS
DREAMBOATS
DREAMERIES
DREAMFULLY
DREAMFULNESS
DREAMFULNESSES
DREAMHOLES
DREAMINESS
DREAMINESSES
DREAMINGLY
DREAMLANDS
DREAMLESSLY
DREAMLESSNESS
DREAMLESSNESSES
DREAMTIMES
DREAMWHILE
DREAMWHILES
DREAMWORLD
DREAMWORLDS
DREARIHEAD
DREARIHEADS
DREARIHOOD
DREARIHOODS
DREARIMENT
DREARIMENTS
DREARINESS
DREARINESSES
DREARISOME
DRECKSILLS
DREGGINESS
DREGGINESSES
DREIKANTER
DREIKANTERS
DRENCHINGS
DREPANIUMS
DRERIHEADS
DRESSGUARD
DRESSGUARDS
DRESSINESS
DRESSINESSES
DRESSMAKER
DRESSMAKERS
DRESSMAKES
DRESSMAKING

DRESSMAKINGS
DRIBBLIEST
DRICKSIEST
DRIFTINGLY
DRIFTWOODS
DRILLABILITIES
DRILLABILITY
DRILLMASTER
DRILLMASTERS
DRILLSHIPS
DRILLSTOCK
DRILLSTOCKS
DRINKABILITIES
DRINKABILITY
DRINKABLENESS
DRINKABLENESSES
DRINKABLES
DRIPSTONES
DRIVABILITIES
DRIVABILITY
DRIVEABILITIES
DRIVEABILITY
DRIVELINES
DRIVELLERS
DRIVELLING
DRIVENNESS
DRIVENNESSES
DRIVERLESS
DRIVESHAFT
DRIVESHAFTS
DRIVETHROUGH
DRIVETHROUGHS
DRIVETRAIN
DRIVETRAINS
DRIZZLIEST
DRIZZLINGLY
DROICHIEST
DROLLERIES
DROLLNESSES
DROMEDARES
DROMEDARIES
DROMOPHOBIA
DROMOPHOBIAS
DRONISHNESS
DRONISHNESSES
DRONKVERDRIET
DROOPINESS
DROOPINESSES
DROOPINGLY
DROPCLOTHS
DROPFORGED
DROPFORGES
DROPFORGING
DROPKICKER
DROPKICKERS
DROPLIGHTS
DROPPERFUL
DROPPERFULS
DROPPERSFUL

DROPSICALLY
DROPSONDES
DROPSTONES
DROSERACEOUS
DROSOMETER
DROSOMETERS
DROSOPHILA
DROSOPHILAE
DROSOPHILAS
DROSSINESS
DROSSINESSES
DROUGHTIER
DROUGHTIEST
DROUGHTINESS
DROUGHTINESSES
DROUTHIEST
DROUTHINESS
DROUTHINESSES
DROWSIHEAD
DROWSIHEADS
DROWSIHEDS
DROWSINESS
DROWSINESSES
DRUCKENNESS
DRUCKENNESSES
DRUDGERIES
DRUDGINGLY
DRUGMAKERS
DRUGSTORES
DRUIDESSES
DRUMBEATER
DRUMBEATERS
DRUMBEATING
DRUMBEATINGS
DRUMBLEDOR
DRUMBLEDORS
DRUMBLEDRANE
DRUMBLEDRANES
DRUMFISHES
DRUMSTICKS
DRUNKATHON
DRUNKATHONS
DRUNKENNESS
DRUNKENNESSES
DRUPACEOUS
DRYASDUSTS
DRYBEATING
DRYOPITHECINE
DRYOPITHECINES
DRYSALTERIES
DRYSALTERS
DRYSALTERY
DRYWALLING
DUALISTICALLY
DUBIOSITIES
DUBIOUSNESS
DUBIOUSNESSES
DUBITANCIES
DUBITATING

DUBITATION
DUBITATIONS
DUBITATIVE
DUBITATIVELY
DUCHESSING
DUCKBOARDS
DUCKSHOVED
DUCKSHOVER
DUCKSHOVERS
DUCKSHOVES
DUCKSHOVING
DUCKWALKED
DUCKWALKING
DUCTILENESS
DUCTILENESSES
DUCTILITIES
DUENNASHIP
DUENNASHIPS
DUFFERDOMS
DUFFERISMS
DUIKERBOKS
DUKKERIPEN
DUKKERIPENS
DULCAMARAS
DULCETNESS
DULCETNESSES
DULCIFICATION
DULCIFICATIONS
DULCIFLUOUS
DULCIFYING
DULCILOQUIES
DULCILOQUY
DULCIMORES
DULCITUDES
DULLNESSES
DULLSVILLE
DULLSVILLES
DULOCRACIES
DUMBFOUNDED
DUMBFOUNDER
DUMBFOUNDERED
DUMBFOUNDERING
DUMBFOUNDERS
DUMBFOUNDING
DUMBFOUNDS
DUMBLEDORE
DUMBLEDORES
DUMBNESSES
DUMBSTRICKEN
DUMBSTRUCK
DUMBWAITER
DUMBWAITERS
DUMFOUNDED
DUMFOUNDER
DUMFOUNDERED
DUMFOUNDERING
DUMFOUNDERS
DUMFOUNDING
DUMMELHEAD

DUMMELHEADS
DUMMINESSES
DUMORTIERITE
DUMORTIERITES
DUMOSITIES
DUMPINESSES
DUMPISHNESS
DUMPISHNESSES
DUMPTRUCKS
DUNDERFUNK
DUNDERFUNKS
DUNDERHEAD
DUNDERHEADED
DUNDERHEADISM
DUNDERHEADISMS
DUNDERHEADS
DUNDERPATE
DUNDERPATES
DUNDREARIES
DUNGEONERS
DUNGEONING
DUNIEWASSAL
DUNIEWASSALS
DUNIWASSAL
DUNIWASSALS
DUNNIEWASSAL
DUNNIEWASSALS
DUODECENNIAL
DUODECILLION
DUODECILLIONS
DUODECIMAL
DUODECIMALLY
DUODECIMALS
DUODECIMOS
DUODENECTOMIES
DUODENECTOMY
DUODENITIS
DUODENITISES
DUOPOLISTIC
DUOPSONIES
DUPABILITIES
DUPABILITY
DUPLEXITIES
DUPLICABILITIES
DUPLICABILITY
DUPLICABLE
DUPLICANDS
DUPLICATED
DUPLICATELY
DUPLICATES
DUPLICATING
DUPLICATION
DUPLICATIONS
DUPLICATIVE
DUPLICATOR
DUPLICATORS
DUPLICATURE
DUPLICATURES
DUPLICIDENT

DUPLICITIES
DUPLICITOUS
DUPLICITOUSLY
DURABILITIES
DURABILITY
DURABLENESS
DURABLENESSES
DURALUMINIUM
DURALUMINIUMS
DURALUMINS
DURATIONAL
DURCHKOMPONIERT
DURCHKOMPONIRT
DURICRUSTS
DUROMETERS
DUSKINESSES
DUSKISHNESS
DUSKISHNESSES
DUSKNESSES
DUSTCOVERS
DUSTINESSES
DUSTSHEETS
DUSTSTORMS
DUTEOUSNESS
DUTEOUSNESSES
DUTIABILITIES
DUTIABILITY
DUTIFULNESS
DUTIFULNESSES
DUUMVIRATE
DUUMVIRATES
DWARFISHLY
DWARFISHNESS
DWARFISHNESSES
DWARFNESSES
DWINDLEMENT
DWINDLEMENTS
DYADICALLY
DYARCHICAL
DYEABILITIES
DYEABILITY
DYINGNESSES
DYNAMETERS
DYNAMICALLY
DYNAMICIST
DYNAMICISTS
DYNAMISING
DYNAMISTIC
DYNAMITARD
DYNAMITARDS
DYNAMITERS
DYNAMITING
DYNAMIZING
DYNAMOELECTRIC
DYNAMOGENESES
DYNAMOGENESIS
DYNAMOGENIES
DYNAMOGENY
DYNAMOGRAPH

DYNAMOGRAPHS
DYNAMOMETER
DYNAMOMETERS
DYNAMOMETRIC
DYNAMOMETRICAL
DYNAMOMETRIES
DYNAMOMETRY
DYNAMOTORS
DYNASTICAL
DYNASTICALLY
DYNORPHINS
DYOPHYSITE
DYOPHYSITES
DYOTHELETE
DYOTHELETES
DYOTHELETIC
DYOTHELETICAL
DYOTHELETISM
DYOTHELETISMS
DYOTHELISM
DYOTHELISMS
DYOTHELITE
DYOTHELITES
DYOTHELITIC
DYOTHELITICAL
DYSAESTHESIA
DYSAESTHESIAS
DYSAESTHETIC
DYSARTHRIA
DYSARTHRIAS
DYSBINDINS
DYSCALCULIA
DYSCALCULIAS
DYSCHROIAS
DYSCRASIAS
DYSCRASITE
DYSCRASITES
DYSENTERIC
DYSENTERIES
DYSFUNCTION
DYSFUNCTIONAL
DYSFUNCTIONS
DYSGENESES
DYSGENESIS
DYSGRAPHIA
DYSGRAPHIAS
DYSGRAPHIC
DYSHARMONIC
DYSKINESIA
DYSKINESIAS
DYSKINETIC
DYSLECTICS
DYSLOGISTIC
DYSLOGISTICALLY
DYSMENORRHEA
DYSMENORRHEAL
DYSMENORRHEAS
DYSMENORRHEIC
DYSMENORRHOEA

DYSMENORRHOEAL
DYSMENORRHOEAS
DYSMENORRHOEIC
DYSMORPHIC
DYSMORPHOPHOBIA
DYSPAREUNIA
DYSPAREUNIAS
DYSPATHETIC
DYSPATHIES
DYSPEPSIAS
DYSPEPSIES
DYSPEPTICAL
DYSPEPTICALLY
DYSPEPTICS
DYSPHAGIAS
DYSPHAGIES
DYSPHASIAS
DYSPHASICS
DYSPHEMISM
DYSPHEMISMS
DYSPHEMISTIC
DYSPHONIAS
DYSPHORIAS
DYSPLASIAS
DYSPLASTIC
DYSPRAXIAS
DYSPROSIUM
DYSPROSIUMS
DYSRHYTHMIA
DYSRHYTHMIAS
DYSRHYTHMIC
DYSSYNERGIA
DYSSYNERGIAS
DYSTELEOLOGICAL
DYSTELEOLOGIES
DYSTELEOLOGIST
DYSTELEOLOGISTS
DYSTELEOLOGY
DYSTHESIAS
DYSTHYMIAC
DYSTHYMIACS
DYSTHYMIAS
DYSTHYMICS
DYSTOPIANS
DYSTROPHIA
DYSTROPHIAS
DYSTROPHIC
DYSTROPHIES
DYSTROPHIN
DYSTROPHINS
DZIGGETAIS

EAGERNESSES
EAGLEHAWKS
EAGLESTONE
EAGLESTONES
EAGLEWOODS
EARBASHERS
EARBASHING
EARBASHINGS
EARLIERISE
EARLIERISED
EARLIERISES
EARLIERISING
EARLIERIZE
EARLIERIZED
EARLIERIZES
EARLIERIZING
EARLINESSES
EARLYWOODS
EARMARKING
EARNESTNESS
EARNESTNESSES
EARSPLITTING
EARTHBOUND
EARTHENWARE
EARTHENWARES
EARTHFALLS
EARTHFLAXES
EARTHINESS
EARTHINESSES
EARTHLIEST
EARTHLIGHT
EARTHLIGHTS
EARTHLINESS
EARTHLINESSES
EARTHLINGS
EARTHMOVER
EARTHMOVERS
EARTHMOVING
EARTHMOVINGS
EARTHQUAKE
EARTHQUAKED
EARTHQUAKES
EARTHQUAKING
EARTHRISES
EARTHSHAKER
EARTHSHAKERS
EARTHSHAKING
EARTHSHAKINGLY
EARTHSHATTERING
EARTHSHINE
EARTHSHINES
EARTHSTARS
EARTHWARDS

EARTHWAXES
EARTHWOLVES
EARTHWOMAN
EARTHWOMEN
EARTHWORKS
EARTHWORMS
EARWIGGING
EARWIGGINGS
EARWITNESS
EARWITNESSES
EASEFULNESS
EASEFULNESSES
EASINESSES
EASSELGATE
EASSELWARD
EASTERLIES
EASTERLING
EASTERLINGS
EASTERMOST
EASTERNERS
EASTERNMOST
EASTWARDLY
EASYGOINGNESS
EASYGOINGNESSES
EAVESDRIPS
EAVESDROPPED
EAVESDROPPER
EAVESDROPPERS
EAVESDROPPING
EAVESDROPPINGS
EAVESDROPS
EAVESTROUGH
EAVESTROUGHS
EBIONISING
EBIONITISM
EBIONITISMS
EBIONIZING
EBOULEMENT
EBOULEMENTS
EBRACTEATE
EBRACTEOLATE
EBRILLADES
EBRIOSITIES
EBULLIENCE
EBULLIENCES
EBULLIENCIES
EBULLIENCY
EBULLIENTLY
EBULLIOMETER
EBULLIOMETERS
EBULLIOMETRIES
EBULLIOMETRY
EBULLIOSCOPE

EBULLIOSCOPES
EBULLIOSCOPIC
EBULLIOSCOPICAL
EBULLIOSCOPIES
EBULLIOSCOPY
EBULLITION
EBULLITIONS
EBURNATION
EBURNATIONS
EBURNIFICATION
EBURNIFICATIONS
ECARDINATE
ECBLASTESES
ECBLASTESIS
ECCALEOBION
ECCALEOBIONS
ECCENTRICAL
ECCENTRICALLY
ECCENTRICITIES
ECCENTRICITY
ECCENTRICS
ECCHYMOSED
ECCHYMOSES
ECCHYMOSIS
ECCHYMOTIC
ECCLESIARCH
ECCLESIARCHS
ECCLESIAST
ECCLESIASTIC
ECCLESIASTICAL
ECCLESIASTICISM
ECCLESIASTICS
ECCLESIASTS
ECCLESIOLATER
ECCLESIOLATERS
ECCLESIOLATRIES
ECCLESIOLATRY
ECCLESIOLOGICAL
ECCLESIOLOGIES
ECCLESIOLOGIST
ECCLESIOLOGISTS
ECCLESIOLOGY
ECCOPROTIC
ECCOPROTICS
ECCREMOCARPUS
ECCREMOCARPUSES
ECCRINOLOGIES
ECCRINOLOGY
ECDYSIASTS
ECHELONING
ECHEVERIAS
ECHIDNINES
ECHINACEAS

ECHINOCOCCI
ECHINOCOCCOSES
ECHINOCOCCOSIS
ECHINOCOCCUS
ECHINODERM
ECHINODERMAL
ECHINODERMATOUS
ECHINODERMS
ECHIUROIDS
ECHOCARDIOGRAM
ECHOCARDIOGRAMS
ECHOGRAPHIES
ECHOGRAPHY
ECHOLALIAS
ECHOLOCATION
ECHOLOCATIONS
ECHOPRAXES
ECHOPRAXIA
ECHOPRAXIAS
ECHOPRAXIS
ECHOVIRUSES
ECLAIRCISSEMENT
ECLAMPSIAS
ECLAMPSIES
ECLECTICALLY
ECLECTICISM
ECLECTICISMS
ECLIPSISES
ECLIPTICALLY
ECOCATASTROPHE
ECOCATASTROPHES
ECOCENTRIC
ECOCLIMATE
ECOCLIMATES
ECOFEMINISM
ECOFEMINISMS
ECOFEMINIST
ECOFEMINISTS
ECOFRIENDLY
ECOLOGICAL
ECOLOGICALLY
ECOLOGISTS
ECOMMERCES
ECONOBOXES
ECONOMETRIC
ECONOMETRICAL
ECONOMETRICALLY
ECONOMETRICIAN
ECONOMETRICIANS
ECONOMETRICS
ECONOMETRIST
ECONOMETRISTS
ECONOMICAL

ECONOMICALLY	ECTOENZYME	EDIFICATION	EFFACEABLE
ECONOMISATION	ECTOENZYMES	EDIFICATIONS	EFFACEMENT
ECONOMISATIONS	ECTOGENESES	EDIFICATORY	EFFACEMENTS
ECONOMISED	ECTOGENESIS	EDIFYINGLY	EFFECTIBLE
ECONOMISER	ECTOGENETIC	EDITIONING	EFFECTIVELY
ECONOMISERS	ECTOGENICALLY	EDITORIALISE	EFFECTIVENESS
ECONOMISES	ECTOGENIES	EDITORIALISED	EFFECTIVENESSES
ECONOMISING	ECTOGENOUS	EDITORIALISER	EFFECTIVES
ECONOMISMS	ECTOMORPHIC	EDITORIALISERS	EFFECTIVITIES
ECONOMISTIC	ECTOMORPHIES	EDITORIALISES	EFFECTIVITY
ECONOMISTS	ECTOMORPHS	EDITORIALISING	EFFECTLESS
ECONOMIZATION	ECTOMORPHY	EDITORIALIST	EFFECTUALITIES
ECONOMIZATIONS	ECTOMYCORRHIZA	EDITORIALISTS	EFFECTUALITY
ECONOMIZED	ECTOMYCORRHIZAE	EDITORIALIZE	EFFECTUALLY
ECONOMIZER	ECTOMYCORRHIZAS	EDITORIALIZED	EFFECTUALNESS
ECONOMIZERS	ECTOPARASITE	EDITORIALIZER	EFFECTUALNESSES
ECONOMIZES	ECTOPARASITES	EDITORIALIZERS	EFFECTUATE
ECONOMIZING	ECTOPARASITIC	EDITORIALIZES	EFFECTUATED
ECOPHOBIAS	ECTOPHYTES	EDITORIALIZING	EFFECTUATES
ECOPHYSIOLOGIES	ECTOPHYTIC	EDITORIALLY	EFFECTUATING
ECOPHYSIOLOGY	ECTOPICALLY	EDITORIALS	EFFECTUATION
ECOREGIONS	ECTOPLASMIC	EDITORSHIP	EFFECTUATIONS
ECOSPECIES	ECTOPLASMS	EDITORSHIPS	EFFEMINACIES
ECOSPECIFIC	ECTOPLASTIC	EDITRESSES	EFFEMINACY
ECOSPHERES	ECTOPROCTS	EDRIOPHTHALMIAN	EFFEMINATE
ECOSSAISES	ECTOSARCOUS	EDRIOPHTHALMIC	EFFEMINATED
ECOSYSTEMS	ECTOTHERMIC	EDRIOPHTHALMOUS	EFFEMINATELY
ECOTERRORISM	ECTOTHERMS	EDUCABILITIES	EFFEMINATENESS
ECOTERRORISMS	ECTOTROPHIC	EDUCABILITY	EFFEMINATES
ECOTERRORIST	ECTROPIONS	EDUCATABILITIES	EFFEMINATING
ECOTERRORISTS	ECTROPIUMS	EDUCATABILITY	EFFEMINISE
ECOTOURISM	ECTYPOGRAPHIES	EDUCATABLE	EFFEMINISED
ECOTOURISMS	ECTYPOGRAPHY	EDUCATEDNESS	EFFEMINISES
ECOTOURIST	ECUMENICAL	EDUCATEDNESSES	EFFEMINISING
ECOTOURISTS	ECUMENICALISM	EDUCATIONAL	EFFEMINIZE
ECOTOXICOLOGIES	ECUMENICALISMS	EDUCATIONALIST	EFFEMINIZED
ECOTOXICOLOGIST	ECUMENICALLY	EDUCATIONALISTS	EFFEMINIZES
ECOTOXICOLOGY	ECUMENICISM	EDUCATIONALLY	EFFEMINIZING
ECOTYPICALLY	ECUMENICISMS	EDUCATIONESE	EFFERENCES
ECPHONESES	ECUMENICIST	EDUCATIONESES	EFFERENTLY
ECPHONESIS	ECUMENICISTS	EDUCATIONIST	EFFERVESCE
ECPHRACTIC	ECUMENICITIES	EDUCATIONISTS	EFFERVESCED
ECPHRACTICS	ECUMENICITY	EDUCATIONS	EFFERVESCENCE
ECRITOIRES	ECUMENISMS	EDUCEMENTS	EFFERVESCENCES
ECSTASISED	ECUMENISTS	EDULCORANT	EFFERVESCENCIES
ECSTASISES	ECZEMATOUS	EDULCORATE	EFFERVESCENCY
ECSTASISING	EDACIOUSLY	EDULCORATED	EFFERVESCENT
ECSTASIZED	EDACIOUSNESS	EDULCORATES	EFFERVESCENTLY
ECSTASIZES	EDACIOUSNESSES	EDULCORATING	EFFERVESCES
ECSTASIZING	EDAPHICALLY	EDULCORATION	EFFERVESCIBLE
ECSTASYING	EDAPHOLOGIES	EDULCORATIONS	EFFERVESCING
ECSTATICALLY	EDAPHOLOGY	EDULCORATIVE	EFFERVESCINGLY
ECTHLIPSES	EDELWEISSES	EDULCORATOR	EFFETENESS
ECTHLIPSIS	EDENTULATE	EDULCORATORS	EFFETENESSES
ECTOBLASTIC	EDENTULOUS	EDUSKUNTAS	EFFICACIES
ECTOBLASTS	EDGINESSES	EDUTAINMENT	EFFICACIOUS
ECTOCRINES	EDIBILITIES	EDUTAINMENTS	EFFICACIOUSLY
ECTODERMAL	EDIBLENESS	EELGRASSES	EFFICACIOUSNESS
ECTODERMIC	EDIBLENESSES	EERINESSES	EFFICACITIES

EFFICACITY
EFFICIENCE
EFFICIENCES
EFFICIENCIES
EFFICIENCY
EFFICIENTLY
EFFICIENTS
EFFIERCING
EFFIGURATE
EFFIGURATION
EFFIGURATIONS
EFFLEURAGE
EFFLEURAGED
EFFLEURAGES
EFFLEURAGING
EFFLORESCE
EFFLORESCED
EFFLORESCENCE
EFFLORESCENCES
EFFLORESCENT
EFFLORESCES
EFFLORESCING
EFFLUENCES
EFFLUVIUMS
EFFLUXIONS
EFFORTFULLY
EFFORTFULNESS
EFFORTFULNESSES
EFFORTLESS
EFFORTLESSLY
EFFORTLESSNESS
EFFRONTERIES
EFFRONTERY
EFFULGENCE
EFFULGENCES
EFFULGENTLY
EFFUSIOMETER
EFFUSIOMETERS
EFFUSIVELY
EFFUSIVENESS
EFFUSIVENESSES
EGALITARIAN
EGALITARIANISM
EGALITARIANISMS
EGALITARIANS
EGAREMENTS
EGGBEATERS
EGGHEADEDNESS
EGGHEADEDNESSES
EGLANDULAR
EGLANDULOSE
EGLANTINES
EGOCENTRIC
EGOCENTRICALLY
EGOCENTRICITIES
EGOCENTRICITY
EGOCENTRICS
EGOCENTRISM
EGOCENTRISMS

EGOISTICAL
EGOISTICALLY
EGOMANIACAL
EGOMANIACALLY
EGOMANIACS
EGOTHEISMS
EGOTISTICAL
EGOTISTICALLY
EGREGIOUSLY
EGREGIOUSNESS
EGREGIOUSNESSES
EGRESSIONS
EGURGITATE
EGURGITATED
EGURGITATES
EGURGITATING
EICOSANOID
EICOSANOIDS
EIDERDOWNS
EIDETICALLY
EIDOGRAPHS
EIGENFREQUENCY
EIGENFUNCTION
EIGENFUNCTIONS
EIGENMODES
EIGENTONES
EIGENVALUE
EIGENVALUES
EIGENVECTOR
EIGENVECTORS
EIGHTBALLS
EIGHTEENMO
EIGHTEENMOS
EIGHTEENTH
EIGHTEENTHLY
EIGHTEENTHS
EIGHTFOILS
EIGHTIETHS
EIGHTPENCE
EIGHTPENCES
EIGHTPENNY
EIGHTSCORE
EIGHTSCORES
EIGHTSOMES
EINSTEINIUM
EINSTEINIUMS
EIRENICALLY
EIRENICONS
EISTEDDFOD
EISTEDDFODAU
EISTEDDFODIC
EISTEDDFODS
EJACULATED
EJACULATES
EJACULATING
EJACULATION
EJACULATIONS
EJACULATIVE
EJACULATOR

EJACULATORS
EJACULATORY
EJECTAMENTA
EJECTIVELY
EJECTMENTS
EKISTICIAN
EKISTICIANS
ELABORATED
ELABORATELY
ELABORATENESS
ELABORATENESSES
ELABORATES
ELABORATING
ELABORATION
ELABORATIONS
ELABORATIVE
ELABORATOR
ELABORATORIES
ELABORATORS
ELABORATORY
ELAEOLITES
ELAEOPTENE
ELAEOPTENES
ELAIOSOMES
ELASMOBRANCH
ELASMOBRANCHS
ELASMOSAUR
ELASMOSAURS
ELASTANCES
ELASTICALLY
ELASTICATE
ELASTICATED
ELASTICATES
ELASTICATING
ELASTICATION
ELASTICATIONS
ELASTICISE
ELASTICISED
ELASTICISES
ELASTICISING
ELASTICITIES
ELASTICITY
ELASTICIZE
ELASTICIZED
ELASTICIZES
ELASTICIZING
ELASTICNESS
ELASTICNESSES
ELASTOMERIC
ELASTOMERS
ELATEDNESS
ELATEDNESSES
ELATERITES
ELATERIUMS
ELBOWROOMS
ELDERBERRIES
ELDERBERRY
ELDERCARES
ELDERLINESS

ELDERLINESSES
ELDERSHIPS
ELECAMPANE
ELECAMPANES
ELECTABILITIES
ELECTABILITY
ELECTIONEER
ELECTIONEERED
ELECTIONEERER
ELECTIONEERERS
ELECTIONEERING
ELECTIONEERINGS
ELECTIONEERS
ELECTIVELY
ELECTIVENESS
ELECTIVENESSES
ELECTIVITIES
ELECTIVITY
ELECTORALLY
ELECTORATE
ELECTORATES
ELECTORESS
ELECTORESSES
ELECTORIAL
ELECTORSHIP
ELECTORSHIPS
ELECTRESSES
ELECTRICAL
ELECTRICALLY
ELECTRICIAN
ELECTRICIANS
ELECTRICITIES
ELECTRICITY
ELECTRIFIABLE
ELECTRIFICATION
ELECTRIFIED
ELECTRIFIER
ELECTRIFIERS
ELECTRIFIES
ELECTRIFYING
ELECTRISATION
ELECTRISATIONS
ELECTRISED
ELECTRISES
ELECTRISING
ELECTRIZATION
ELECTRIZATIONS
ELECTRIZED
ELECTRIZES
ELECTRIZING
ELECTROACOUSTIC
ELECTROACTIVE
ELECTROACTIVITY
ELECTROANALYSES
ELECTROANALYSIS
ELECTROANALYTIC
ELECTROBIOLOGY
ELECTROCAUTERY
ELECTROCEMENT

ELECTROCEMENTS

ELECTROCEMENTS
ELECTROCHEMIC
ELECTROCHEMICAL
ELECTROCHEMIST
ELECTROCHEMISTS
ELECTROCLASH
ELECTROCLASHES
ELECTROCULTURE
ELECTROCULTURES
ELECTROCUTE
ELECTROCUTED
ELECTROCUTES
ELECTROCUTING
ELECTROCUTION
ELECTROCUTIONS
ELECTROCYTE
ELECTROCYTES
ELECTRODEPOSIT
ELECTRODEPOSITS
ELECTRODERMAL
ELECTRODES
ELECTRODIALYSES
ELECTRODIALYSIS
ELECTRODIALYTIC
ELECTRODYNAMIC
ELECTRODYNAMICS
ELECTROFISHING
ELECTROFISHINGS
ELECTROFLUOR
ELECTROFLUORS
ELECTROFORM
ELECTROFORMED
ELECTROFORMING
ELECTROFORMINGS
ELECTROFORMS
ELECTROGEN
ELECTROGENESES
ELECTROGENESIS
ELECTROGENIC
ELECTROGENS
ELECTROGILDING
ELECTROGILDINGS
ELECTROGRAM
ELECTROGRAMS
ELECTROGRAPH
ELECTROGRAPHIC
ELECTROGRAPHIES
ELECTROGRAPHS
ELECTROGRAPHY
ELECTROING
ELECTROJET
ELECTROJETS
ELECTROKINETIC
ELECTROKINETICS
ELECTROLESS
ELECTROLIER
ELECTROLIERS
ELECTROLOGIES
ELECTROLOGIST

ELECTROLOGISTS
ELECTROLOGY
ELECTROLYSATION
ELECTROLYSE
ELECTROLYSED
ELECTROLYSER
ELECTROLYSERS
ELECTROLYSES
ELECTROLYSING
ELECTROLYSIS
ELECTROLYTE
ELECTROLYTES
ELECTROLYTIC
ELECTROLYTICS
ELECTROLYZATION
ELECTROLYZE
ELECTROLYZED
ELECTROLYZER
ELECTROLYZERS
ELECTROLYZES
ELECTROLYZING
ELECTROMAGNET
ELECTROMAGNETIC
ELECTROMAGNETS
ELECTROMER
ELECTROMERIC
ELECTROMERISM
ELECTROMERISMS
ELECTROMERS
ELECTROMETER
ELECTROMETERS
ELECTROMETRIC
ELECTROMETRICAL
ELECTROMETRIES
ELECTROMETRY
ELECTROMOTANCE
ELECTROMOTANCES
ELECTROMOTIVE
ELECTROMOTOR
ELECTROMOTORS
ELECTROMYOGRAM
ELECTROMYOGRAMS
ELECTROMYOGRAPH
ELECTRONEGATIVE
ELECTRONIC
ELECTRONICA
ELECTRONICALLY
ELECTRONICAS
ELECTRONICS
ELECTRONVOLT
ELECTRONVOLTS
ELECTROOSMOSES
ELECTROOSMOSIS
ELECTROOSMOTIC
ELECTROPHILE
ELECTROPHILES
ELECTROPHILIC
ELECTROPHONE
ELECTROPHONES

ELECTROPHONIC
ELECTROPHORESE
ELECTROPHORESED
ELECTROPHORESES
ELECTROPHORESIS
ELECTROPHORETIC
ELECTROPHORI
ELECTROPHORUS
ELECTROPHORUSES
ELECTROPLATE
ELECTROPLATED
ELECTROPLATER
ELECTROPLATERS
ELECTROPLATES
ELECTROPLATING
ELECTROPLATINGS
ELECTROPOLAR
ELECTROPOSITIVE
ELECTRORECEPTOR
ELECTRORHEOLOGY
ELECTROSCOPE
ELECTROSCOPES
ELECTROSCOPIC
ELECTROSHOCK
ELECTROSHOCKS
ELECTROSONDE
ELECTROSONDES
ELECTROSTATIC
ELECTROSTATICS
ELECTROSURGERY
ELECTROSURGICAL
ELECTROTECHNICS
ELECTROTHERAPY
ELECTROTHERMAL
ELECTROTHERMIC
ELECTROTHERMICS
ELECTROTHERMIES
ELECTROTHERMY
ELECTROTINT
ELECTROTINTS
ELECTROTONIC
ELECTROTONUS
ELECTROTONUSES
ELECTROTYPE
ELECTROTYPED
ELECTROTYPER
ELECTROTYPERS
ELECTROTYPES
ELECTROTYPIC
ELECTROTYPIES
ELECTROTYPING
ELECTROTYPIST
ELECTROTYPISTS
ELECTROTYPY
ELECTROVALENCE
ELECTROVALENCES
ELECTROVALENCY
ELECTROVALENT
ELECTROVALENTLY

ELECTROWEAK
ELECTROWINNING
ELECTROWINNINGS
ELECTUARIES
ELEDOISINS
ELEEMOSYNARY
ELEGANCIES
ELEGIACALLY
ELEMENTALISM
ELEMENTALISMS
ELEMENTALLY
ELEMENTALS
ELEMENTARILY
ELEMENTARINESS
ELEMENTARY
ELEOPTENES
ELEPHANTIASES
ELEPHANTIASIC
ELEPHANTIASIS
ELEPHANTINE
ELEPHANTOID
ELEUTHERARCH
ELEUTHERARCHS
ELEUTHERIAN
ELEUTHEROCOCCI
ELEUTHEROCOCCUS
ELEUTHERODACTYL
ELEUTHEROMANIA
ELEUTHEROMANIAS
ELEUTHEROPHOBIA
ELEUTHEROPHOBIC
ELEVATIONAL
ELEVATIONS
ELEVENTHLY
ELFISHNESS
ELFISHNESSES
ELICITABLE
ELICITATION
ELICITATIONS
ELIGIBILITIES
ELIGIBILITY
ELIMINABILITIES
ELIMINABILITY
ELIMINABLE
ELIMINANTS
ELIMINATED
ELIMINATES
ELIMINATING
ELIMINATION
ELIMINATIONS
ELIMINATIVE
ELIMINATOR
ELIMINATORS
ELIMINATORY
ELLIPSOGRAPH
ELLIPSOGRAPHS
ELLIPSOIDAL
ELLIPSOIDS
ELLIPTICAL

ELLIPTICALLY	EMANCIPATE	EMBASSADOR	EMBLOSSOMS
ELLIPTICALNESS	EMANCIPATED	EMBASSADORS	EMBODIMENT
ELLIPTICALS	EMANCIPATES	EMBASSAGES	EMBODIMENTS
ELLIPTICITIES	EMANCIPATING	EMBATTLEMENT	EMBOITEMENT
ELLIPTICITY	EMANCIPATION	EMBATTLEMENTS	EMBOITEMENTS
ELOCUTIONARY	EMANCIPATIONIST	EMBATTLING	EMBOLDENED
ELOCUTIONIST	EMANCIPATIONS	EMBAYMENTS	EMBOLDENER
ELOCUTIONISTS	EMANCIPATIVE	EMBEDDINGS	EMBOLDENERS
ELOCUTIONS	EMANCIPATOR	EMBEDMENTS	EMBOLDENING
ELOIGNMENT	EMANCIPATORS	EMBELLISHED	EMBOLECTOMIES
ELOIGNMENTS	EMANCIPATORY	EMBELLISHER	EMBOLECTOMY
ELOINMENTS	EMANCIPIST	EMBELLISHERS	EMBOLISATION
ELONGATING	EMANCIPISTS	EMBELLISHES	EMBOLISATIONS
ELONGATION	EMARGINATE	EMBELLISHING	EMBOLISING
ELONGATIONS	EMARGINATED	EMBELLISHINGLY	EMBOLISMAL
ELOPEMENTS	EMARGINATELY	EMBELLISHMENT	EMBOLISMIC
ELOQUENCES	EMARGINATES	EMBELLISHMENTS	EMBOLIZATION
ELOQUENTLY	EMARGINATING	EMBEZZLEMENT	EMBOLIZATIONS
ELSEWHITHER	EMARGINATION	EMBEZZLEMENTS	EMBOLIZING
ELUCIDATED	EMARGINATIONS	EMBEZZLERS	EMBONPOINT
ELUCIDATES	EMASCULATE	EMBEZZLING	EMBONPOINTS
ELUCIDATING	EMASCULATED	EMBITTERED	EMBORDERED
ELUCIDATION	EMASCULATES	EMBITTERER	EMBORDERING
ELUCIDATIONS	EMASCULATING	EMBITTERERS	EMBOSCATAS
ELUCIDATIVE	EMASCULATION	EMBITTERING	EMBOSOMING
ELUCIDATOR	EMASCULATIONS	EMBITTERINGS	EMBOSSABLE
ELUCIDATORS	EMASCULATIVE	EMBITTERMENT	EMBOSSMENT
ELUCIDATORY	EMASCULATOR	EMBITTERMENTS	EMBOSSMENTS
ELUCUBRATE	EMASCULATORS	EMBLAZONED	EMBOTHRIUM
ELUCUBRATED	EMASCULATORY	EMBLAZONER	EMBOTHRIUMS
ELUCUBRATES	EMBALLINGS	EMBLAZONERS	EMBOUCHURE
ELUCUBRATING	EMBALMINGS	EMBLAZONING	EMBOUCHURES
ELUCUBRATION	EMBALMMENT	EMBLAZONMENT	EMBOUNDING
ELUCUBRATIONS	EMBALMMENTS	EMBLAZONMENTS	EMBOURGEOISE
ELUSIVENESS	EMBANKMENT	EMBLAZONRIES	EMBOURGEOISED
ELUSIVENESSES	EMBANKMENTS	EMBLAZONRY	EMBOURGEOISES
ELUSORINESS	EMBARCADERO	EMBLEMATIC	EMBOURGEOISING
ELUSORINESSES	EMBARCADEROS	EMBLEMATICAL	EMBOWELING
ELUTRIATED	EMBARCATION	EMBLEMATICALLY	EMBOWELLED
ELUTRIATES	EMBARCATIONS	EMBLEMATISE	EMBOWELLING
ELUTRIATING	EMBARGOING	EMBLEMATISED	EMBOWELMENT
ELUTRIATION	EMBARKATION	EMBLEMATISES	EMBOWELMENTS
ELUTRIATIONS	EMBARKATIONS	EMBLEMATISING	EMBOWERING
ELUTRIATOR	EMBARKMENT	EMBLEMATIST	EMBOWERMENT
ELUTRIATORS	EMBARKMENTS	EMBLEMATISTS	EMBOWERMENTS
ELUVIATING	EMBARQUEMENT	EMBLEMATIZE	EMBOWMENTS
ELUVIATION	EMBARQUEMENTS	EMBLEMATIZED	EMBRACEABLE
ELUVIATIONS	EMBARRASSABLE	EMBLEMATIZES	EMBRACEMENT
ELVISHNESS	EMBARRASSED	EMBLEMATIZING	EMBRACEMENTS
ELVISHNESSES	EMBARRASSEDLY	EMBLEMENTS	EMBRACEORS
ELYTRIFORM	EMBARRASSES	EMBLEMISED	EMBRACERIES
ELYTRIGEROUS	EMBARRASSING	EMBLEMISES	EMBRACINGLY
EMACIATING	EMBARRASSINGLY	EMBLEMISING	EMBRACINGNESS
EMACIATION	EMBARRASSMENT	EMBLEMIZED	EMBRACINGNESSES
EMACIATIONS	EMBARRASSMENTS	EMBLEMIZES	EMBRAIDING
EMALANGENI	EMBARRINGS	EMBLEMIZING	EMBRANCHMENT
EMANATIONAL	EMBASEMENT	EMBLOOMING	EMBRANCHMENTS
EMANATIONS	EMBASEMENTS	EMBLOSSOMED	EMBRANGLED
EMANATISTS	EMBASSADES	EMBLOSSOMING	EMBRANGLEMENT

EMBRANGLEMENTS

EMBRANGLEMENTS	EMENDATING	EMOTIONALITY	EMPHASIZES
EMBRANGLES	EMENDATION	EMOTIONALIZE	EMPHASIZING
EMBRANGLING	EMENDATIONS	EMOTIONALIZED	EMPHATICAL
EMBRASURED	EMENDATORS	EMOTIONALIZES	EMPHATICALLY
EMBRASURES	EMENDATORY	EMOTIONALIZING	EMPHATICALNESS
EMBRAZURES	EMERGENCES	EMOTIONALLY	EMPHRACTIC
EMBREADING	EMERGENCIES	EMOTIONLESS	EMPHRACTICS
EMBREATHED	EMERGENTLY	EMOTIONLESSLY	EMPHYSEMAS
EMBREATHES	EMETICALLY	EMOTIONLESSNESS	EMPHYSEMATOUS
EMBREATHING	EMETOPHOBIA	EMOTIVENESS	EMPHYSEMIC
EMBRITTLED	EMETOPHOBIAS	EMOTIVENESSES	EMPHYSEMICS
EMBRITTLEMENT	EMICATIONS	EMOTIVISMS	EMPHYTEUSES
EMBRITTLEMENTS	EMIGRATING	EMOTIVITIES	EMPHYTEUSIS
EMBRITTLES	EMIGRATION	EMPACKETED	EMPHYTEUTIC
EMBRITTLING	EMIGRATIONAL	EMPACKETING	EMPIECEMENT
EMBROCATED	EMIGRATIONIST	EMPALEMENT	EMPIECEMENTS
EMBROCATES	EMIGRATIONISTS	EMPALEMENTS	EMPIERCING
EMBROCATING	EMIGRATIONS	EMPANELING	EMPIRICALLY
EMBROCATION	EMIGRATORY	EMPANELLED	EMPIRICALNESS
EMBROCATIONS	EMINENCIES	EMPANELLING	EMPIRICALNESSES
EMBROGLIOS	EMINENTIAL	EMPANELMENT	EMPIRICISM
EMBROIDERED	EMISSARIES	EMPANELMENTS	EMPIRICISMS
EMBROIDERER	EMISSIVITIES	EMPANOPLIED	EMPIRICIST
EMBROIDERERS	EMISSIVITY	EMPANOPLIES	EMPIRICISTS
EMBROIDERIES	EMITTANCES	EMPANOPLYING	EMPIRICUTIC
EMBROIDERING	EMMARBLING	EMPARADISE	EMPLACEMENT
EMBROIDERS	EMMENAGOGIC	EMPARADISED	EMPLACEMENTS
EMBROIDERY	EMMENAGOGUE	EMPARADISES	EMPLASTERED
EMBROILERS	EMMENAGOGUES	EMPARADISING	EMPLASTERING
EMBROILING	EMMENOLOGIES	EMPARLAUNCE	EMPLASTERS
EMBROILMENT	EMMENOLOGY	EMPARLAUNCES	EMPLASTICS
EMBROILMENTS	EMMETROPES	EMPASSIONATE	EMPLASTRON
EMBROWNING	EMMETROPIA	EMPASSIONED	EMPLASTRONS
EMBRUEMENT	EMMETROPIAS	EMPATHETIC	EMPLASTRUM
EMBRUEMENTS	EMMETROPIC	EMPATHETICALLY	EMPLASTRUMS
EMBRYECTOMIES	EMOLLESCENCE	EMPATHICALLY	EMPLEACHED
EMBRYECTOMY	EMOLLESCENCES	EMPATHISED	EMPLEACHES
EMBRYOGENESES	EMOLLIATED	EMPATHISES	EMPLEACHING
EMBRYOGENESIS	EMOLLIATES	EMPATHISING	EMPLECTONS
EMBRYOGENETIC	EMOLLIATING	EMPATHISTS	EMPLECTUMS
EMBRYOGENIC	EMOLLIENCE	EMPATHIZED	EMPLONGING
EMBRYOGENIES	EMOLLIENCES	EMPATHIZES	EMPLOYABILITIES
EMBRYOGENY	EMOLLIENTS	EMPATHIZING	EMPLOYABILITY
EMBRYOLOGIC	EMOLLITION	EMPATRONED	EMPLOYABLE
EMBRYOLOGICAL	EMOLLITIONS	EMPATRONING	EMPLOYABLES
EMBRYOLOGICALLY	EMOLUMENTAL	EMPEACHING	EMPLOYMENT
EMBRYOLOGIES	EMOLUMENTARY	EMPENNAGES	EMPLOYMENTS
EMBRYOLOGIST	EMOLUMENTS	EMPEOPLING	EMPOISONED
EMBRYOLOGISTS	EMOTIONABLE	EMPERISHED	EMPOISONING
EMBRYOLOGY	EMOTIONALISE	EMPERISHES	EMPOISONMENT
EMBRYONATE	EMOTIONALISED	EMPERISHING	EMPOISONMENTS
EMBRYONATED	EMOTIONALISES	EMPERISING	EMPOLDERED
EMBRYONICALLY	EMOTIONALISING	EMPERIZING	EMPOLDERING
EMBRYOPHYTE	EMOTIONALISM	EMPERORSHIP	EMPOVERISH
EMBRYOPHYTES	EMOTIONALISMS	EMPERORSHIPS	EMPOVERISHED
EMBRYOTOMIES	EMOTIONALIST	EMPHASISED	EMPOVERISHER
EMBRYOTOMY	EMOTIONALISTIC	EMPHASISES	EMPOVERISHERS
EMBRYULCIA	EMOTIONALISTS	EMPHASISING	EMPOVERISHES
EMBRYULCIAS	EMOTIONALITIES	EMPHASIZED	EMPOVERISHING

EMPOVERISHMENT
EMPOVERISHMENTS
EMPOWERING
EMPOWERMENT
EMPOWERMENTS
EMPRESSEMENT
EMPRESSEMENTS
EMPTINESSES
EMPURPLING
EMPYREUMATA
EMPYREUMATIC
EMPYREUMATICAL
EMPYREUMATISE
EMPYREUMATISED
EMPYREUMATISES
EMPYREUMATISING
EMPYREUMATIZE
EMPYREUMATIZED
EMPYREUMATIZES
EMPYREUMATIZING
EMULATIONS
EMULATIVELY
EMULATRESS
EMULATRESSES
EMULGENCES
EMULOUSNESS
EMULOUSNESSES
EMULSIFIABLE
EMULSIFICATION
EMULSIFICATIONS
EMULSIFIED
EMULSIFIER
EMULSIFIERS
EMULSIFIES
EMULSIFYING
EMULSIONISE
EMULSIONISED
EMULSIONISES
EMULSIONISING
EMULSIONIZE
EMULSIONIZED
EMULSIONIZES
EMULSIONIZING
EMULSOIDAL
EMUNCTIONS
EMUNCTORIES
ENABLEMENT
ENABLEMENTS
ENACTMENTS
ENALAPRILS
ENAMELISTS
ENAMELLERS
ENAMELLING
ENAMELLINGS
ENAMELLIST
ENAMELLISTS
ENAMELWARE
ENAMELWARES
ENAMELWORK

ENAMELWORKS
ENAMORADOS
ENAMOURING
ENANTIODROMIA
ENANTIODROMIAS
ENANTIODROMIC
ENANTIOMER
ENANTIOMERIC
ENANTIOMERS
ENANTIOMORPH
ENANTIOMORPHIC
ENANTIOMORPHIES
ENANTIOMORPHISM
ENANTIOMORPHOUS
ENANTIOMORPHS
ENANTIOMORPHY
ENANTIOPATHIES
ENANTIOPATHY
ENANTIOSES
ENANTIOSIS
ENANTIOSTYLIES
ENANTIOSTYLOUS
ENANTIOSTYLY
ENANTIOTROPIC
ENANTIOTROPIES
ENANTIOTROPY
ENARRATION
ENARRATIONS
ENARTHRODIAL
ENARTHROSES
ENARTHROSIS
ENCAMPMENT
ENCAMPMENTS
ENCANTHISES
ENCAPSULATE
ENCAPSULATED
ENCAPSULATES
ENCAPSULATING
ENCAPSULATION
ENCAPSULATIONS
ENCAPSULED
ENCAPSULES
ENCAPSULING
ENCARNALISE
ENCARNALISED
ENCARNALISES
ENCARNALISING
ENCARNALIZE
ENCARNALIZED
ENCARNALIZES
ENCARNALIZING
ENCARPUSES
ENCASEMENT
ENCASEMENTS
ENCASHABLE
ENCASHMENT
ENCASHMENTS
ENCAUSTICALLY
ENCAUSTICS

ENCEPHALALGIA
ENCEPHALALGIAS
ENCEPHALIC
ENCEPHALIN
ENCEPHALINE
ENCEPHALINES
ENCEPHALINS
ENCEPHALITIC
ENCEPHALITIDES
ENCEPHALITIS
ENCEPHALITISES
ENCEPHALITOGEN
ENCEPHALITOGENS
ENCEPHALOCELE
ENCEPHALOCELES
ENCEPHALOGRAM
ENCEPHALOGRAMS
ENCEPHALOGRAPH
ENCEPHALOGRAPHS
ENCEPHALOGRAPHY
ENCEPHALOID
ENCEPHALOMA
ENCEPHALOMAS
ENCEPHALOMATA
ENCEPHALON
ENCEPHALONS
ENCEPHALOPATHIC
ENCEPHALOPATHY
ENCEPHALOTOMIES
ENCEPHALOTOMY
ENCEPHALOUS
ENCHAINING
ENCHAINMENT
ENCHAINMENTS
ENCHANTERS
ENCHANTING
ENCHANTINGLY
ENCHANTMENT
ENCHANTMENTS
ENCHANTRESS
ENCHANTRESSES
ENCHARGING
ENCHARMING
ENCHEASONS
ENCHEERING
ENCHEIRIDION
ENCHEIRIDIONS
ENCHILADAS
ENCHIRIDIA
ENCHIRIDION
ENCHIRIDIONS
ENCHONDROMA
ENCHONDROMAS
ENCHONDROMATA
ENCHONDROMATOUS
ENCINCTURE
ENCINCTURED
ENCINCTURES
ENCINCTURING

ENCIPHERED
ENCIPHERER
ENCIPHERERS
ENCIPHERING
ENCIPHERMENT
ENCIPHERMENTS
ENCIRCLEMENT
ENCIRCLEMENTS
ENCIRCLING
ENCIRCLINGS
ENCLASPING
ENCLITICALLY
ENCLOISTER
ENCLOISTERED
ENCLOISTERING
ENCLOISTERS
ENCLOSABLE
ENCLOSURES
ENCLOTHING
ENCLOUDING
ENCODEMENT
ENCODEMENTS
ENCOIGNURE
ENCOIGNURES
ENCOLOURED
ENCOLOURING
ENCOLPIONS
ENCOLPIUMS
ENCOMENDERO
ENCOMENDEROS
ENCOMIASTIC
ENCOMIASTICAL
ENCOMIASTICALLY
ENCOMIASTS
ENCOMIENDA
ENCOMIENDAS
ENCOMPASSED
ENCOMPASSES
ENCOMPASSING
ENCOMPASSMENT
ENCOMPASSMENTS
ENCOPRESES
ENCOPRESIS
ENCOPRETIC
ENCOUNTERED
ENCOUNTERER
ENCOUNTERERS
ENCOUNTERING
ENCOUNTERS
ENCOURAGED
ENCOURAGEMENT
ENCOURAGEMENTS
ENCOURAGER
ENCOURAGERS
ENCOURAGES
ENCOURAGING
ENCOURAGINGLY
ENCOURAGINGS
ENCRADLING

ENCREASING
ENCRIMSONED
ENCRIMSONING
ENCRIMSONS
ENCRINITAL
ENCRINITES
ENCRINITIC
ENCROACHED
ENCROACHER
ENCROACHERS
ENCROACHES
ENCROACHING
ENCROACHINGLY
ENCROACHMENT
ENCROACHMENTS
ENCRUSTATION
ENCRUSTATIONS
ENCRUSTING
ENCRUSTMENT
ENCRUSTMENTS
ENCRYPTING
ENCRYPTION
ENCRYPTIONS
ENCULTURATE
ENCULTURATED
ENCULTURATES
ENCULTURATING
ENCULTURATION
ENCULTURATIONS
ENCULTURATIVE
ENCUMBERED
ENCUMBERING
ENCUMBERINGLY
ENCUMBERMENT
ENCUMBERMENTS
ENCUMBRANCE
ENCUMBRANCER
ENCUMBRANCERS
ENCUMBRANCES
ENCURTAINED
ENCURTAINING
ENCURTAINS
ENCYCLICAL
ENCYCLICALS
ENCYCLOPAEDIA
ENCYCLOPAEDIAS
ENCYCLOPAEDIC
ENCYCLOPAEDISM
ENCYCLOPAEDISMS
ENCYCLOPAEDIST
ENCYCLOPAEDISTS
ENCYCLOPEDIA
ENCYCLOPEDIAN
ENCYCLOPEDIAS
ENCYCLOPEDIC
ENCYCLOPEDICAL
ENCYCLOPEDISM
ENCYCLOPEDISMS
ENCYCLOPEDIST

ENCYCLOPEDISTS
ENCYSTATION
ENCYSTATIONS
ENCYSTMENT
ENCYSTMENTS
ENDAMAGEMENT
ENDAMAGEMENTS
ENDAMAGING
ENDAMOEBAE
ENDAMOEBAS
ENDANGERED
ENDANGERER
ENDANGERERS
ENDANGERING
ENDANGERMENT
ENDANGERMENTS
ENDARCHIES
ENDARTERECTOMY
ENDEARINGLY
ENDEARINGNESS
ENDEARINGNESSES
ENDEARMENT
ENDEARMENTS
ENDEAVORED
ENDEAVORER
ENDEAVORERS
ENDEAVORING
ENDEAVOURED
ENDEAVOURER
ENDEAVOURERS
ENDEAVOURING
ENDEAVOURMENT
ENDEAVOURMENTS
ENDEAVOURS
ENDECAGONS
ENDEIXISES
ENDEMICALLY
ENDEMICITIES
ENDEMICITY
ENDEMIOLOGIES
ENDEMIOLOGY
ENDENIZENED
ENDENIZENING
ENDENIZENS
ENDERGONIC
ENDERMATIC
ENDERMICAL
ENDLESSNESS
ENDLESSNESSES
ENDOBIOTIC
ENDOBLASTIC
ENDOBLASTS
ENDOCARDIA
ENDOCARDIAC
ENDOCARDIAL
ENDOCARDITIC
ENDOCARDITIS
ENDOCARDITISES
ENDOCARDIUM

ENDOCARPAL
ENDOCARPIC
ENDOCENTRIC
ENDOCHONDRAL
ENDOCHYLOUS
ENDOCRANIA
ENDOCRANIAL
ENDOCRANIUM
ENDOCRINAL
ENDOCRINES
ENDOCRINIC
ENDOCRINOLOGIC
ENDOCRINOLOGIES
ENDOCRINOLOGIST
ENDOCRINOLOGY
ENDOCRINOPATHIC
ENDOCRINOPATHY
ENDOCRINOUS
ENDOCRITIC
ENDOCUTICLE
ENDOCUTICLES
ENDOCYTOSES
ENDOCYTOSIS
ENDOCYTOTIC
ENDODERMAL
ENDODERMIC
ENDODERMIS
ENDODERMISES
ENDODONTAL
ENDODONTIC
ENDODONTICALLY
ENDODONTICS
ENDODONTIST
ENDODONTISTS
ENDOENZYME
ENDOENZYMES
ENDOGAMIES
ENDOGAMOUS
ENDOGENIES
ENDOGENOUS
ENDOGENOUSLY
ENDOLITHIC
ENDOLYMPHATIC
ENDOLYMPHS
ENDOMETRIA
ENDOMETRIAL
ENDOMETRIOSES
ENDOMETRIOSIS
ENDOMETRITIS
ENDOMETRITISES
ENDOMETRIUM
ENDOMITOSES
ENDOMITOSIS
ENDOMITOTIC
ENDOMIXISES
ENDOMORPHIC
ENDOMORPHIES
ENDOMORPHISM
ENDOMORPHISMS

ENDOMORPHS
ENDOMORPHY
ENDOMYCORRHIZA
ENDONEURIA
ENDONEURIUM
ENDONUCLEASE
ENDONUCLEASES
ENDONUCLEOLYTIC
ENDOPARASITE
ENDOPARASITES
ENDOPARASITIC
ENDOPARASITISM
ENDOPARASITISMS
ENDOPEPTIDASE
ENDOPEPTIDASES
ENDOPEROXIDE
ENDOPEROXIDES
ENDOPHAGIES
ENDOPHAGOUS
ENDOPHYLLOUS
ENDOPHYTES
ENDOPHYTIC
ENDOPHYTICALLY
ENDOPLASMIC
ENDOPLASMS
ENDOPLASTIC
ENDOPLEURA
ENDOPLEURAS
ENDOPODITE
ENDOPODITES
ENDOPOLYPLOID
ENDOPOLYPLOIDY
ENDOPROCTS
ENDORADIOSONDE
ENDORADIOSONDES
ENDORHIZAL
ENDORPHINS
ENDORSABLE
ENDORSEMENT
ENDORSEMENTS
ENDOSCOPES
ENDOSCOPIC
ENDOSCOPICALLY
ENDOSCOPIES
ENDOSCOPIST
ENDOSCOPISTS
ENDOSKELETAL
ENDOSKELETON
ENDOSKELETONS
ENDOSMOMETER
ENDOSMOMETERS
ENDOSMOMETRIC
ENDOSMOSES
ENDOSMOSIS
ENDOSMOTIC
ENDOSMOTICALLY
ENDOSPERMIC
ENDOSPERMS
ENDOSPORES

ENDOSPOROUS	ENERVATION	ENGARRISONS	ENHARMONIC
ENDOSTEALLY	ENERVATIONS	ENGENDERED	ENHARMONICAL
ENDOSTOSES	ENERVATIVE	ENGENDERER	ENHARMONICALLY
ENDOSTOSIS	ENERVATORS	ENGENDERERS	ENHEARSING
ENDOSTYLES	ENFACEMENT	ENGENDERING	ENHEARTENED
ENDOSULFAN	ENFACEMENTS	ENGENDERMENT	ENHEARTENING
ENDOSULFANS	ENFEEBLEMENT	ENGENDERMENTS	ENHEARTENS
ENDOSYMBIONT	ENFEEBLEMENTS	ENGENDRURE	ENHUNGERED
ENDOSYMBIONTS	ENFEEBLERS	ENGENDRURES	ENHUNGERING
ENDOSYMBIOSES	ENFEEBLING	ENGENDURES	ENHYDRITES
ENDOSYMBIOSIS	ENFELONING	ENGINEERED	ENHYDRITIC
ENDOSYMBIOTIC	ENFEOFFING	ENGINEERING	ENHYDROSES
ENDOTHECIA	ENFEOFFMENT	ENGINEERINGS	ENHYPOSTASIA
ENDOTHECIAL	ENFEOFFMENTS	ENGINERIES	ENHYPOSTASIAS
ENDOTHECIUM	ENFESTERED	ENGIRDLING	ENHYPOSTATIC
ENDOTHELIA	ENFETTERED	ENGISCOPES	ENHYPOSTATISE
ENDOTHELIAL	ENFETTERING	ENGLACIALLY	ENHYPOSTATISED
ENDOTHELIOID	ENFEVERING	ENGLISHING	ENHYPOSTATISES
ENDOTHELIOMA	ENFIERCING	ENGLOOMING	ENHYPOSTATISING
ENDOTHELIOMAS	ENFILADING	ENGLUTTING	ENHYPOSTATIZE
ENDOTHELIOMATA	ENFLESHING	ENGORGEMENT	ENHYPOSTATIZED
ENDOTHELIUM	ENFLEURAGE	ENGORGEMENTS	ENHYPOSTATIZES
ENDOTHERMAL	ENFLEURAGES	ENGOUEMENT	ENHYPOSTATIZING
ENDOTHERMIC	ENFLOWERED	ENGOUEMENTS	ENIGMATICAL
ENDOTHERMICALLY	ENFLOWERING	ENGOUMENTS	ENIGMATICALLY
ENDOTHERMIES	ENFOLDMENT	ENGRAFFING	ENIGMATISE
ENDOTHERMISM	ENFOLDMENTS	ENGRAFTATION	ENIGMATISED
ENDOTHERMISMS	ENFORCEABILITY	ENGRAFTATIONS	ENIGMATISES
ENDOTHERMS	ENFORCEABLE	ENGRAFTING	ENIGMATISING
ENDOTHERMY	ENFORCEDLY	ENGRAFTMENT	ENIGMATIST
ENDOTOXINS	ENFORCEMENT	ENGRAFTMENTS	ENIGMATISTS
ENDOTRACHEAL	ENFORCEMENTS	ENGRAILING	ENIGMATIZE
ENDOTROPHIC	ENFORESTED	ENGRAILMENT	ENIGMATIZED
ENDOWMENTS	ENFORESTING	ENGRAILMENTS	ENIGMATIZES
ENDPLAYING	ENFOULDERED	ENGRAINEDLY	ENIGMATIZING
ENDUNGEONED	ENFRAMEMENT	ENGRAINEDNESS	ENIGMATOGRAPHY
ENDUNGEONING	ENFRAMEMENTS	ENGRAINEDNESSES	ENJAMBEMENT
ENDUNGEONS	ENFRANCHISE	ENGRAINERS	ENJAMBEMENTS
ENDURABILITIES	ENFRANCHISED	ENGRAINING	ENJAMBMENT
ENDURABILITY	ENFRANCHISEMENT	ENGRAMMATIC	ENJAMBMENTS
ENDURABLENESS	ENFRANCHISER	ENGRASPING	ENJOINDERS
ENDURABLENESSES	ENFRANCHISERS	ENGRAVERIES	ENJOINMENT
ENDURANCES	ENFRANCHISES	ENGRAVINGS	ENJOINMENTS
ENDURINGLY	ENFRANCHISING	ENGRENAGES	ENJOYABLENESS
ENDURINGNESS	ENFREEDOMED	ENGRIEVING	ENJOYABLENESSES
ENDURINGNESSES	ENFREEDOMING	ENGROOVING	ENJOYMENTS
ENERGETICAL	ENFREEDOMS	ENGROSSEDLY	ENKEPHALIN
ENERGETICALLY	ENFREEZING	ENGROSSERS	ENKEPHALINE
ENERGETICS	ENGAGEMENT	ENGROSSING	ENKEPHALINES
ENERGISATION	ENGAGEMENTS	ENGROSSINGLY	ENKEPHALINS
ENERGISATIONS	ENGAGINGLY	ENGROSSMENT	ENKERNELLED
ENERGISERS	ENGAGINGNESS	ENGROSSMENTS	ENKERNELLING
ENERGISING	ENGAGINGNESSES	ENGUARDING	ENKINDLERS
ENERGIZATION	ENGARLANDED	ENGULFMENT	ENKINDLING
ENERGIZATIONS	ENGARLANDING	ENGULFMENTS	ENLACEMENT
ENERGIZERS	ENGARLANDS	ENGULPHING	ENLACEMENTS
ENERGIZING	ENGARRISON	ENGYSCOPES	ENLARGEABLE
ENERGUMENS	ENGARRISONED	ENHANCEMENT	ENLARGEDLY
ENERVATING	ENGARRISONING	ENHANCEMENTS	ENLARGEDNESS

ENLARGEDNESSES
ENLARGEMENT
ENLARGEMENTS
ENLARGENED
ENLARGENING
ENLEVEMENT
ENLEVEMENTS
ENLIGHTENED
ENLIGHTENER
ENLIGHTENERS
ENLIGHTENING
ENLIGHTENMENT
ENLIGHTENMENTS
ENLIGHTENS
ENLIGHTING
ENLISTMENT
ENLISTMENTS
ENLIVENERS
ENLIVENING
ENLIVENMENT
ENLIVENMENTS
ENLUMINING
ENMESHMENT
ENMESHMENTS
ENNEAGONAL
ENNEAHEDRA
ENNEAHEDRAL
ENNEAHEDRON
ENNEAHEDRONS
ENNEANDRIAN
ENNEANDROUS
ENNEASTYLE
ENNOBLEMENT
ENNOBLEMENTS
ENOKIDAKES
ENOKITAKES
ENOLOGICAL
ENOLOGISTS
ENORMITIES
ENORMOUSLY
ENORMOUSNESS
ENORMOUSNESSES
ENOUNCEMENT
ENOUNCEMENTS
ENPHYTOTIC
ENQUIRATION
ENQUIRATIONS
ENRAGEMENT
ENRAGEMENTS
ENRANCKLED
ENRANCKLES
ENRANCKLING
ENRAPTURED
ENRAPTURES
ENRAPTURING
ENRAUNGING
ENRAVISHED
ENRAVISHES
ENRAVISHING

ENREGIMENT
ENREGIMENTED
ENREGIMENTING
ENREGIMENTS
ENREGISTER
ENREGISTERED
ENREGISTERING
ENREGISTERS
ENRHEUMING
ENRICHMENT
ENRICHMENTS
ENROLLMENT
ENROLLMENTS
ENROLMENTS
ENROUGHING
ENROUNDING
ENSAMPLING
ENSANGUINATED
ENSANGUINE
ENSANGUINED
ENSANGUINES
ENSANGUINING
ENSCHEDULE
ENSCHEDULED
ENSCHEDULES
ENSCHEDULING
ENSCONCING
ENSCROLLED
ENSCROLLING
ENSEPULCHRE
ENSEPULCHRED
ENSEPULCHRES
ENSEPULCHRING
ENSERFMENT
ENSERFMENTS
ENSHEATHED
ENSHEATHES
ENSHEATHING
ENSHELLING
ENSHELTERED
ENSHELTERING
ENSHELTERS
ENSHIELDED
ENSHIELDING
ENSHRINEES
ENSHRINEMENT
ENSHRINEMENTS
ENSHRINING
ENSHROUDED
ENSHROUDING
ENSIGNCIES
ENSIGNSHIP
ENSIGNSHIPS
ENSILABILITIES
ENSILABILITY
ENSILAGEING
ENSILAGING
ENSLAVEMENT
ENSLAVEMENTS

ENSNAREMENT
ENSNAREMENTS
ENSNARLING
ENSORCELED
ENSORCELING
ENSORCELLED
ENSORCELLING
ENSORCELLMENT
ENSORCELLMENTS
ENSORCELLS
ENSOULMENT
ENSOULMENTS
ENSPHERING
ENSTAMPING
ENSTATITES
ENSTEEPING
ENSTRUCTURED
ENSWATHEMENT
ENSWATHEMENTS
ENSWATHING
ENSWEEPING
ENTABLATURE
ENTABLATURES
ENTABLEMENT
ENTABLEMENTS
ENTAILMENT
ENTAILMENTS
ENTAMOEBAE
ENTAMOEBAS
ENTANGLEMENT
ENTANGLEMENTS
ENTANGLERS
ENTANGLING
ENTELECHIES
ENTELLUSES
ENTENDERED
ENTENDERING
ENTERCHAUNGE
ENTERCHAUNGED
ENTERCHAUNGES
ENTERCHAUNGING
ENTERDEALE
ENTERDEALED
ENTERDEALES
ENTERDEALING
ENTERECTOMIES
ENTERECTOMY
ENTERITIDES
ENTERITISES
ENTEROBACTERIA
ENTEROBACTERIAL
ENTEROBACTERIUM
ENTEROBIASES
ENTEROBIASIS
ENTEROCELE
ENTEROCELES
ENTEROCENTESES
ENTEROCENTESIS
ENTEROCOCCAL

ENTEROCOCCI
ENTEROCOCCUS
ENTEROCOEL
ENTEROCOELE
ENTEROCOELES
ENTEROCOELIC
ENTEROCOELOUS
ENTEROCOELS
ENTEROCOLITIS
ENTEROCOLITISES
ENTEROGASTRONE
ENTEROGASTRONES
ENTEROHEPATITIS
ENTEROKINASE
ENTEROKINASES
ENTEROLITH
ENTEROLITHS
ENTEROPATHIES
ENTEROPATHY
ENTEROPNEUST
ENTEROPNEUSTAL
ENTEROPNEUSTS
ENTEROPTOSES
ENTEROPTOSIS
ENTEROSTOMAL
ENTEROSTOMIES
ENTEROSTOMY
ENTEROTOMIES
ENTEROTOMY
ENTEROTOXIN
ENTEROTOXINS
ENTEROVIRAL
ENTEROVIRUS
ENTEROVIRUSES
ENTERPRISE
ENTERPRISED
ENTERPRISER
ENTERPRISERS
ENTERPRISES
ENTERPRISING
ENTERPRISINGLY
ENTERTAINED
ENTERTAINER
ENTERTAINERS
ENTERTAINING
ENTERTAININGLY
ENTERTAININGS
ENTERTAINMENT
ENTERTAINMENTS
ENTERTAINS
ENTERTAKEN
ENTERTAKES
ENTERTAKING
ENTERTISSUED
ENTHALPIES
ENTHRALDOM
ENTHRALDOMS
ENTHRALLED
ENTHRALLER

ENTHRALLERS
ENTHRALLING
ENTHRALLMENT
ENTHRALLMENTS
ENTHRALMENT
ENTHRALMENTS
ENTHRONEMENT
ENTHRONEMENTS
ENTHRONING
ENTHRONISATION
ENTHRONISATIONS
ENTHRONISE
ENTHRONISED
ENTHRONISES
ENTHRONISING
ENTHRONIZATION
ENTHRONIZATIONS
ENTHRONIZE
ENTHRONIZED
ENTHRONIZES
ENTHRONIZING
ENTHUSIASM
ENTHUSIASMS
ENTHUSIAST
ENTHUSIASTIC
ENTHUSIASTICAL
ENTHUSIASTS
ENTHYMEMATIC
ENTHYMEMATICAL
ENTHYMEMES
ENTICEABLE
ENTICEMENT
ENTICEMENTS
ENTICINGLY
ENTICINGNESS
ENTICINGNESSES
ENTIRENESS
ENTIRENESSES
ENTIRETIES
ENTITATIVE
ENTITLEMENT
ENTITLEMENTS
ENTOBLASTIC
ENTOBLASTS
ENTODERMAL
ENTODERMIC
ENTOILMENT
ENTOILMENTS
ENTOMBMENT
ENTOMBMENTS
ENTOMOFAUNA
ENTOMOFAUNAE
ENTOMOFAUNAS
ENTOMOLOGIC
ENTOMOLOGICAL
ENTOMOLOGICALLY
ENTOMOLOGIES
ENTOMOLOGISE
ENTOMOLOGISED

ENTOMOLOGISES
ENTOMOLOGISING
ENTOMOLOGIST
ENTOMOLOGISTS
ENTOMOLOGIZE
ENTOMOLOGIZED
ENTOMOLOGIZES
ENTOMOLOGIZING
ENTOMOLOGY
ENTOMOPHAGIES
ENTOMOPHAGOUS
ENTOMOPHAGY
ENTOMOPHILIES
ENTOMOPHILOUS
ENTOMOPHILY
ENTOMOSTRACAN
ENTOMOSTRACANS
ENTOMOSTRACOUS
ENTOPHYTAL
ENTOPHYTES
ENTOPHYTIC
ENTOPHYTOUS
ENTOPLASTRA
ENTOPLASTRAL
ENTOPLASTRON
ENTOPROCTS
ENTOURAGES
ENTRAILING
ENTRAINEMENT
ENTRAINEMENTS
ENTRAINERS
ENTRAINING
ENTRAINMENT
ENTRAINMENTS
ENTRAMMELLED
ENTRAMMELLING
ENTRAMMELS
ENTRANCEMENT
ENTRANCEMENTS
ENTRANCEWAY
ENTRANCEWAYS
ENTRANCING
ENTRAPMENT
ENTRAPMENTS
ENTRAPPERS
ENTRAPPING
ENTREASURE
ENTREASURED
ENTREASURES
ENTREASURING
ENTREATABLE
ENTREATIES
ENTREATING
ENTREATINGLY
ENTREATIVE
ENTREATMENT
ENTREATMENTS
ENTRECHATS
ENTRECOTES

ENTREMESSE
ENTREMESSES
ENTRENCHED
ENTRENCHER
ENTRENCHERS
ENTRENCHES
ENTRENCHING
ENTRENCHMENT
ENTRENCHMENTS
ENTREPRENEUR
ENTREPRENEURIAL
ENTREPRENEURS
ENTREPRENEUSE
ENTREPRENEUSES
ENTROPICALLY
ENTROPIONS
ENTROPIUMS
ENTRUSTING
ENTRUSTMENT
ENTRUSTMENTS
ENTWINEMENT
ENTWINEMENTS
ENTWISTING
ENUCLEATED
ENUCLEATES
ENUCLEATING
ENUCLEATION
ENUCLEATIONS
ENUMERABILITIES
ENUMERABILITY
ENUMERABLE
ENUMERATED
ENUMERATES
ENUMERATING
ENUMERATION
ENUMERATIONS
ENUMERATIVE
ENUMERATOR
ENUMERATORS
ENUNCIABLE
ENUNCIATED
ENUNCIATES
ENUNCIATING
ENUNCIATION
ENUNCIATIONS
ENUNCIATIVE
ENUNCIATIVELY
ENUNCIATOR
ENUNCIATORS
ENUNCIATORY
ENUREDNESS
ENUREDNESSES
ENUREMENTS
ENURESISES
ENVASSALLED
ENVASSALLING
ENVAULTING
ENVEIGLING
ENVELOPERS

ENVELOPING
ENVELOPMENT
ENVELOPMENTS
ENVENOMING
ENVENOMISATION
ENVENOMISATIONS
ENVENOMIZATION
ENVENOMIZATIONS
ENVERMEILED
ENVERMEILING
ENVERMEILS
ENVIABLENESS
ENVIABLENESSES
ENVIOUSNESS
ENVIOUSNESSES
ENVIRONICS
ENVIRONING
ENVIRONMENT
ENVIRONMENTAL
ENVIRONMENTALLY
ENVIRONMENTS
ENVISAGEMENT
ENVISAGEMENTS
ENVISAGING
ENVISIONED
ENVISIONING
ENVOYSHIPS
ENWALLOWED
ENWALLOWING
ENWHEELING
ENWRAPMENT
ENWRAPMENTS
ENWRAPPING
ENWRAPPINGS
ENWREATHED
ENWREATHES
ENWREATHING
ENZOOTICALLY
ENZYMATICALLY
ENZYMICALLY
ENZYMOLOGICAL
ENZYMOLOGIES
ENZYMOLOGIST
ENZYMOLOGISTS
ENZYMOLOGY
ENZYMOLYSES
ENZYMOLYSIS
ENZYMOLYTIC
EOHIPPUSES
EOSINOPHIL
EOSINOPHILE
EOSINOPHILES
EOSINOPHILIA
EOSINOPHILIAS
EOSINOPHILIC
EOSINOPHILOUS
EOSINOPHILS
EPAGOMENAL
EPANADIPLOSES

EPANADIPLOSIS
EPANALEPSES
EPANALEPSIS
EPANALEPTIC
EPANAPHORA
EPANAPHORAL
EPANAPHORAS
EPANODOSES
EPANORTHOSES
EPANORTHOSIS
EPANORTHOTIC
EPARCHATES
EPAULEMENT
EPAULEMENTS
EPAULETTED
EPAULETTES
EPEIROGENESES
EPEIROGENESIS
EPEIROGENETIC
EPEIROGENIC
EPEIROGENICALLY
EPEIROGENIES
EPEIROGENY
EPENCEPHALA
EPENCEPHALIC
EPENCEPHALON
EPENCEPHALONS
EPENTHESES
EPENTHESIS
EPENTHETIC
EPEOLATRIES
EPEXEGESES
EPEXEGESIS
EPEXEGETIC
EPEXEGETICAL
EPEXEGETICALLY
EPHEBOPHILIA
EPHEBOPHILIAS
EPHEDRINES
EPHEMERALITIES
EPHEMERALITY
EPHEMERALLY
EPHEMERALNESS
EPHEMERALNESSES
EPHEMERALS
EPHEMERIDES
EPHEMERIDIAN
EPHEMERIDS
EPHEMERIST
EPHEMERISTS
EPHEMERONS
EPHEMEROPTERAN
EPHEMEROPTERANS
EPHEMEROUS
EPHORALTIES
EPIBLASTIC
EPICALYCES
EPICALYXES
EPICANTHIC

EPICANTHUS
EPICARDIAC
EPICARDIAL
EPICARDIUM
EPICENISMS
EPICENTERS
EPICENTRAL
EPICENTRES
EPICENTRUM
EPICHEIREMA
EPICHEIREMAS
EPICHLOROHYDRIN
EPICONDYLE
EPICONDYLES
EPICONDYLITIS
EPICONDYLITISES
EPICONTINENTAL
EPICRANIUM
EPICUREANISM
EPICUREANISMS
EPICUREANS
EPICURISED
EPICURISES
EPICURISING
EPICURISMS
EPICURIZED
EPICURIZES
EPICURIZING
EPICUTICLE
EPICUTICLES
EPICUTICULAR
EPICYCLICAL
EPICYCLOID
EPICYCLOIDAL
EPICYCLOIDS
EPIDEICTIC
EPIDEICTICAL
EPIDEMICAL
EPIDEMICALLY
EPIDEMICITIES
EPIDEMICITY
EPIDEMIOLOGIC
EPIDEMIOLOGICAL
EPIDEMIOLOGIES
EPIDEMIOLOGIST
EPIDEMIOLOGISTS
EPIDEMIOLOGY
EPIDENDRONE
EPIDENDRONES
EPIDENDRUM
EPIDENDRUMS
EPIDERMISES
EPIDERMOID
EPIDERMOLYSES
EPIDERMOLYSIS
EPIDIASCOPE
EPIDIASCOPES
EPIDIDYMAL
EPIDIDYMIDES

EPIDIDYMIS
EPIDIDYMITIS
EPIDIDYMITISES
EPIDIORITE
EPIDIORITES
EPIDOSITES
EPIDOTISATION
EPIDOTISATIONS
EPIDOTISED
EPIDOTIZATION
EPIDOTIZATIONS
EPIDOTIZED
EPIGASTRIA
EPIGASTRIAL
EPIGASTRIC
EPIGASTRIUM
EPIGENESES
EPIGENESIS
EPIGENESIST
EPIGENESISTS
EPIGENETIC
EPIGENETICALLY
EPIGENETICIST
EPIGENETICISTS
EPIGENETICS
EPIGENISTS
EPIGLOTTAL
EPIGLOTTIC
EPIGLOTTIDES
EPIGLOTTIS
EPIGLOTTISES
EPIGNATHOUS
EPIGONISMS
EPIGRAMMATIC
EPIGRAMMATICAL
EPIGRAMMATISE
EPIGRAMMATISED
EPIGRAMMATISER
EPIGRAMMATISERS
EPIGRAMMATISES
EPIGRAMMATISING
EPIGRAMMATISM
EPIGRAMMATISMS
EPIGRAMMATIST
EPIGRAMMATISTS
EPIGRAMMATIZE
EPIGRAMMATIZED
EPIGRAMMATIZER
EPIGRAMMATIZERS
EPIGRAMMATIZES
EPIGRAMMATIZING
EPIGRAPHED
EPIGRAPHER
EPIGRAPHERS
EPIGRAPHIC
EPIGRAPHICAL
EPIGRAPHICALLY
EPIGRAPHIES
EPIGRAPHING

EPIGRAPHIST
EPIGRAPHISTS
EPILATIONS
EPILEPSIES
EPILEPTICAL
EPILEPTICALLY
EPILEPTICS
EPILEPTIFORM
EPILEPTOGENIC
EPILEPTOID
EPILIMNION
EPILIMNIONS
EPILOBIUMS
EPILOGISED
EPILOGISES
EPILOGISING
EPILOGISTIC
EPILOGISTS
EPILOGIZED
EPILOGIZES
EPILOGIZING
EPILOGUING
EPILOGUISE
EPILOGUISED
EPILOGUISES
EPILOGUISING
EPILOGUIZE
EPILOGUIZED
EPILOGUIZES
EPILOGUIZING
EPIMELETIC
EPIMERASES
EPIMERISMS
EPIMORPHIC
EPIMORPHOSES
EPIMORPHOSIS
EPINASTICALLY
EPINASTIES
EPINEPHRIN
EPINEPHRINE
EPINEPHRINES
EPINEPHRINS
EPINEURIAL
EPINEURIUM
EPINEURIUMS
EPINICIONS
EPINIKIONS
EPIPELAGIC
EPIPETALOUS
EPIPHANIES
EPIPHANOUS
EPIPHENOMENA
EPIPHENOMENAL
EPIPHENOMENALLY
EPIPHENOMENON
EPIPHONEMA
EPIPHONEMAS
EPIPHRAGMS
EPIPHYLLOUS

EPIPHYSEAL
EPIPHYSIAL
EPIPHYTICAL
EPIPHYTICALLY
EPIPHYTISM
EPIPHYTISMS
EPIPHYTOLOGIES
EPIPHYTOLOGY
EPIPHYTOTIC
EPIPHYTOTICS
EPIPLASTRA
EPIPLASTRAL
EPIPLASTRON
EPIPOLISMS
EPIROGENETIC
EPIROGENIC
EPIROGENIES
EPIRRHEMAS
EPIRRHEMATIC
EPISCOPACIES
EPISCOPACY
EPISCOPALIAN
EPISCOPALIANISM
EPISCOPALIANS
EPISCOPALISM
EPISCOPALISMS
EPISCOPALLY
EPISCOPANT
EPISCOPANTS
EPISCOPATE
EPISCOPATED
EPISCOPATES
EPISCOPATING
EPISCOPIES
EPISCOPISE
EPISCOPISED
EPISCOPISES
EPISCOPISING
EPISCOPIZE
EPISCOPIZED
EPISCOPIZES
EPISCOPIZING
EPISEMATIC
EPISEPALOUS
EPISIOTOMIES
EPISIOTOMY
EPISODICAL
EPISODICALLY
EPISOMALLY
EPISPASTIC
EPISPASTICS
EPISTASIES
EPISTAXISES
EPISTEMICALLY
EPISTEMICS
EPISTEMOLOGICAL
EPISTEMOLOGIES
EPISTEMOLOGIST
EPISTEMOLOGISTS

EPISTEMOLOGY
EPISTERNAL
EPISTERNUM
EPISTERNUMS
EPISTILBITE
EPISTILBITES
EPISTOLARIAN
EPISTOLARIANS
EPISTOLARIES
EPISTOLARY
EPISTOLATORY
EPISTOLERS
EPISTOLETS
EPISTOLICAL
EPISTOLISE
EPISTOLISED
EPISTOLISES
EPISTOLISING
EPISTOLIST
EPISTOLISTS
EPISTOLIZE
EPISTOLIZED
EPISTOLIZES
EPISTOLIZING
EPISTOLOGRAPHY
EPISTROPHE
EPISTROPHES
EPITAPHERS
EPITAPHIAL
EPITAPHIAN
EPITAPHING
EPITAPHIST
EPITAPHISTS
EPITAXIALLY
EPITHALAMIA
EPITHALAMIC
EPITHALAMION
EPITHALAMIUM
EPITHALAMIUMS
EPITHELIAL
EPITHELIALISE
EPITHELIALISED
EPITHELIALISES
EPITHELIALISING
EPITHELIALIZE
EPITHELIALIZED
EPITHELIALIZES
EPITHELIALIZING
EPITHELIOID
EPITHELIOMA
EPITHELIOMAS
EPITHELIOMATA
EPITHELIOMATOUS
EPITHELISATION
EPITHELISATIONS
EPITHELISE
EPITHELISED
EPITHELISES
EPITHELISING

EPITHELIUM
EPITHELIUMS
EPITHELIZATION
EPITHELIZATIONS
EPITHELIZE
EPITHELIZED
EPITHELIZES
EPITHELIZING
EPITHEMATA
EPITHERMAL
EPITHETICAL
EPITHETING
EPITHETONS
EPITHYMETIC
EPITOMICAL
EPITOMISATION
EPITOMISATIONS
EPITOMISED
EPITOMISER
EPITOMISERS
EPITOMISES
EPITOMISING
EPITOMISTS
EPITOMIZATION
EPITOMIZATIONS
EPITOMIZED
EPITOMIZER
EPITOMIZERS
EPITOMIZES
EPITOMIZING
EPITRACHELION
EPITRACHELIONS
EPITROCHOID
EPITROCHOIDS
EPIZEUXISES
EPIZOOTICALLY
EPIZOOTICS
EPIZOOTIES
EPIZOOTIOLOGIC
EPIZOOTIOLOGIES
EPIZOOTIOLOGY
EPONYCHIUM
EPONYCHIUMS
EPONYMOUSLY
EPOXIDATION
EPOXIDATIONS
EPOXIDISED
EPOXIDISES
EPOXIDISING
EPOXIDIZED
EPOXIDIZES
EPOXIDIZING
EPROUVETTE
EPROUVETTES
EPULATIONS
EPURATIONS
EQUABILITIES
EQUABILITY
EQUABLENESS

EQUABLENESSES
EQUALISATION
EQUALISATIONS
EQUALISERS
EQUALISING
EQUALITARIAN
EQUALITARIANISM
EQUALITARIANS
EQUALITIES
EQUALIZATION
EQUALIZATIONS
EQUALIZERS
EQUALIZING
EQUALNESSES
EQUANIMITIES
EQUANIMITY
EQUANIMOUS
EQUANIMOUSLY
EQUATABILITIES
EQUATABILITY
EQUATIONAL
EQUATIONALLY
EQUATORIAL
EQUATORIALLY
EQUATORIALS
EQUATORWARD
EQUESTRIAN
EQUESTRIANISM
EQUESTRIANISMS
EQUESTRIANS
EQUESTRIENNE
EQUESTRIENNES
EQUIANGULAR
EQUIANGULARITY
EQUIBALANCE
EQUIBALANCED
EQUIBALANCES
EQUIBALANCING
EQUICALORIC
EQUIDIFFERENT
EQUIDISTANCE
EQUIDISTANCES
EQUIDISTANT
EQUIDISTANTLY
EQUILATERAL
EQUILATERALLY
EQUILATERALS
EQUILIBRANT
EQUILIBRANTS
EQUILIBRATE
EQUILIBRATED
EQUILIBRATES
EQUILIBRATING
EQUILIBRATION
EQUILIBRATIONS
EQUILIBRATOR
EQUILIBRATORS
EQUILIBRATORY
EQUILIBRIA

EQUILIBRIST

EQUILIBRIST
EQUILIBRISTIC
EQUILIBRISTS
EQUILIBRITIES
EQUILIBRITY
EQUILIBRIUM
EQUILIBRIUMS
EQUIMOLECULAR
EQUIMULTIPLE
EQUIMULTIPLES
EQUINITIES
EQUINOCTIAL
EQUINOCTIALLY
EQUINOCTIALS
EQUINUMEROUS
EQUIPAGING
EQUIPARATE
EQUIPARATED
EQUIPARATES
EQUIPARATING
EQUIPARATION
EQUIPARATIONS
EQUIPARTITION
EQUIPARTITIONS
EQUIPMENTS
EQUIPOISED
EQUIPOISES
EQUIPOISING
EQUIPOLLENCE
EQUIPOLLENCES
EQUIPOLLENCIES
EQUIPOLLENCY
EQUIPOLLENT
EQUIPOLLENTLY
EQUIPOLLENTS
EQUIPONDERANCE
EQUIPONDERANCES
EQUIPONDERANCY
EQUIPONDERANT
EQUIPONDERATE
EQUIPONDERATED
EQUIPONDERATES
EQUIPONDERATING
EQUIPOTENT
EQUIPOTENTIAL
EQUIPROBABILITY
EQUIPROBABLE
EQUISETACEOUS
EQUISETIFORM
EQUISETUMS
EQUITABILITIES
EQUITABILITY
EQUITABLENESS
EQUITABLENESSES
EQUITATION
EQUITATIONS
EQUIVALENCE
EQUIVALENCES
EQUIVALENCIES

EQUIVALENCY
EQUIVALENT
EQUIVALENTLY
EQUIVALENTS
EQUIVOCALITIES
EQUIVOCALITY
EQUIVOCALLY
EQUIVOCALNESS
EQUIVOCALNESSES
EQUIVOCATE
EQUIVOCATED
EQUIVOCATES
EQUIVOCATING
EQUIVOCATINGLY
EQUIVOCATION
EQUIVOCATIONS
EQUIVOCATOR
EQUIVOCATORS
EQUIVOCATORY
EQUIVOQUES
ERADIATING
ERADIATION
ERADIATIONS
ERADICABLE
ERADICABLY
ERADICANTS
ERADICATED
ERADICATES
ERADICATING
ERADICATION
ERADICATIONS
ERADICATIVE
ERADICATOR
ERADICATORS
ERASABILITIES
ERASABILITY
ERASEMENTS
ERECTILITIES
ERECTILITY
ERECTNESSES
EREMACAUSES
EREMACAUSIS
EREMITICAL
EREMITISMS
EREMURUSES
ERETHISMIC
ERETHISTIC
ERGASTOPLASM
ERGASTOPLASMIC
ERGASTOPLASMS
ERGATANDROMORPH
ERGATANERS
ERGATIVITIES
ERGATIVITY
ERGATOCRACIES
ERGATOCRACY
ERGATOGYNE
ERGATOGYNES
ERGATOMORPH

ERGATOMORPHIC
ERGATOMORPHS
ERGODICITIES
ERGODICITY
ERGOGRAPHS
ERGOMANIAC
ERGOMANIACS
ERGOMANIAS
ERGOMETERS
ERGOMETRIC
ERGOMETRIES
ERGONOMICALLY
ERGONOMICS
ERGONOMIST
ERGONOMISTS
ERGONOVINE
ERGONOVINES
ERGOPHOBIA
ERGOPHOBIAS
ERGOSTEROL
ERGOSTEROLS
ERGOTAMINE
ERGOTAMINES
ERGOTISING
ERGOTIZING
ERICACEOUS
ERINACEOUS
ERIOMETERS
ERIOPHOROUS
ERIOPHORUM
ERIOPHORUMS
ERIOPHYIDS
ERIOSTEMON
ERIOSTEMONS
ERISTICALLY
ERODIBILITIES
ERODIBILITY
EROGENEITIES
EROGENEITY
EROSIONALLY
EROSIVENESS
EROSIVENESSES
EROSIVITIES
EROTICALLY
EROTICISATION
EROTICISATIONS
EROTICISED
EROTICISES
EROTICISING
EROTICISMS
EROTICISTS
EROTICIZATION
EROTICIZATIONS
EROTICIZED
EROTICIZES
EROTICIZING
EROTISATION
EROTISATIONS
EROTIZATION

EROTIZATIONS
EROTOGENIC
EROTOGENOUS
EROTOLOGICAL
EROTOLOGIES
EROTOLOGIST
EROTOLOGISTS
EROTOMANIA
EROTOMANIAC
EROTOMANIACS
EROTOMANIAS
EROTOPHOBIA
EROTOPHOBIAS
ERRANTRIES
ERRATICALLY
ERRATICISM
ERRATICISMS
ERRONEOUSLY
ERRONEOUSNESS
ERRONEOUSNESSES
ERUBESCENCE
ERUBESCENCES
ERUBESCENCIES
ERUBESCENCY
ERUBESCENT
ERUBESCITE
ERUBESCITES
ERUCTATING
ERUCTATION
ERUCTATIONS
ERUCTATIVE
ERUDITENESS
ERUDITENESSES
ERUDITIONS
ERUPTIONAL
ERUPTIVELY
ERUPTIVENESS
ERUPTIVENESSES
ERUPTIVITIES
ERUPTIVITY
ERVALENTAS
ERYSIPELAS
ERYSIPELASES
ERYSIPELATOUS
ERYSIPELOID
ERYSIPELOIDS
ERYTHEMATIC
ERYTHEMATOUS
ERYTHORBATE
ERYTHORBATES
ERYTHRAEMIA
ERYTHRAEMIAS
ERYTHREMIA
ERYTHREMIAS
ERYTHRINAS
ERYTHRISMAL
ERYTHRISMS
ERYTHRISTIC
ERYTHRITES

ERYTHRITIC
ERYTHRITOL
ERYTHRITOLS
ERYTHROBLAST
ERYTHROBLASTIC
ERYTHROBLASTS
ERYTHROCYTE
ERYTHROCYTES
ERYTHROCYTIC
ERYTHROMELALGIA
ERYTHROMYCIN
ERYTHROMYCINS
ERYTHRONIUM
ERYTHRONIUMS
ERYTHROPENIA
ERYTHROPENIAS
ERYTHROPHOBIA
ERYTHROPHOBIAS
ERYTHROPOIESES
ERYTHROPOIESIS
ERYTHROPOIETIC
ERYTHROPOIETIN
ERYTHROPOIETINS
ERYTHROPSIA
ERYTHROPSIAS
ERYTHROSIN
ERYTHROSINE
ERYTHROSINES
ERYTHROSINS
ESCADRILLE
ESCADRILLES
ESCALADERS
ESCALADING
ESCALADOES
ESCALATING
ESCALATION
ESCALATIONS
ESCALATORS
ESCALATORY
ESCALLONIA
ESCALLONIAS
ESCALLOPED
ESCALLOPING
ESCALOPING
ESCAMOTAGE
ESCAMOTAGES
ESCAPADOES
ESCAPELESS
ESCAPEMENT
ESCAPEMENTS
ESCAPOLOGIES
ESCAPOLOGIST
ESCAPOLOGISTS
ESCAPOLOGY
ESCARMOUCHE
ESCARMOUCHES
ESCARPMENT
ESCARPMENTS
ESCHAROTIC

ESCHAROTICS
ESCHATOLOGIC
ESCHATOLOGICAL
ESCHATOLOGIES
ESCHATOLOGIST
ESCHATOLOGISTS
ESCHATOLOGY
ESCHEATABLE
ESCHEATAGE
ESCHEATAGES
ESCHEATING
ESCHEATMENT
ESCHEATMENTS
ESCHEATORS
ESCHSCHOLTZIA
ESCHSCHOLTZIAS
ESCHSCHOLZIA
ESCHSCHOLZIAS
ESCLANDRES
ESCOPETTES
ESCORTAGES
ESCRIBANOS
ESCRITOIRE
ESCRITOIRES
ESCRITORIAL
ESCUTCHEON
ESCUTCHEONED
ESCUTCHEONS
ESEMPLASIES
ESEMPLASTIC
ESOPHAGEAL
ESOPHAGOSCOPE
ESOPHAGOSCOPES
ESOPHAGUSES
ESOTERICALLY
ESOTERICISM
ESOTERICISMS
ESOTERICIST
ESOTERICISTS
ESOTERISMS
ESOTROPIAS
ESPADRILLE
ESPADRILLES
ESPAGNOLES
ESPAGNOLETTE
ESPAGNOLETTES
ESPALIERED
ESPALIERING
ESPECIALLY
ESPERANCES
ESPIEGLERIE
ESPIEGLERIES
ESPIONAGES
ESPLANADES
ESPRESSIVO
ESQUIRESSES
ESSAYETTES
ESSAYISTIC
ESSENTIALISE

ESSENTIALISED
ESSENTIALISES
ESSENTIALISING
ESSENTIALISM
ESSENTIALISMS
ESSENTIALIST
ESSENTIALISTS
ESSENTIALITIES
ESSENTIALITY
ESSENTIALIZE
ESSENTIALIZED
ESSENTIALIZES
ESSENTIALIZING
ESSENTIALLY
ESSENTIALNESS
ESSENTIALNESSES
ESSENTIALS
ESTABLISHABLE
ESTABLISHED
ESTABLISHER
ESTABLISHERS
ESTABLISHES
ESTABLISHING
ESTABLISHMENT
ESTABLISHMENTS
ESTAFETTES
ESTAMINETS
ESTANCIERO
ESTANCIEROS
ESTATESMAN
ESTATESMEN
ESTERIFICATION
ESTERIFICATIONS
ESTERIFIED
ESTERIFIES
ESTERIFYING
ESTHESIOGEN
ESTHESIOGENS
ESTHESISES
ESTHETICAL
ESTHETICALLY
ESTHETICIAN
ESTHETICIANS
ESTHETICISM
ESTHETICISMS
ESTIMABLENESS
ESTIMABLENESSES
ESTIMATING
ESTIMATION
ESTIMATIONS
ESTIMATIVE
ESTIMATORS
ESTIPULATE
ESTIVATING
ESTIVATION
ESTIVATIONS
ESTIVATORS
ESTOPPAGES
ESTRADIOLS

ESTRAMAZONE
ESTRAMAZONES
ESTRANGEDNESS
ESTRANGEDNESSES
ESTRANGELO
ESTRANGELOS
ESTRANGEMENT
ESTRANGEMENTS
ESTRANGERS
ESTRANGHELO
ESTRANGHELOS
ESTRANGING
ESTRAPADES
ESTREATING
ESTREPEMENT
ESTREPEMENTS
ESTRILDIDS
ESTROGENIC
ESTROGENICALLY
ESURIENCES
ESURIENCIES
ESURIENTLY
ETEPIMELETIC
ETERNALISATION
ETERNALISATIONS
ETERNALISE
ETERNALISED
ETERNALISES
ETERNALISING
ETERNALIST
ETERNALISTS
ETERNALITIES
ETERNALITY
ETERNALIZATION
ETERNALIZATIONS
ETERNALIZE
ETERNALIZED
ETERNALIZES
ETERNALIZING
ETERNALNESS
ETERNALNESSES
ETERNISATION
ETERNISATIONS
ETERNISING
ETERNITIES
ETERNIZATION
ETERNIZATIONS
ETERNIZING
ETHAMBUTOL
ETHAMBUTOLS
ETHANEDIOIC
ETHANEDIOL
ETHANEDIOLS
ETHANOATES
ETHANOLAMINE
ETHANOLAMINES
ETHEOSTOMINE
ETHEREALISATION
ETHEREALISE

ETHEREALISED	ETHNOGRAPHER	ETYMOLOGISE	EUDIOMETRIC
ETHEREALISES	ETHNOGRAPHERS	ETYMOLOGISED	EUDIOMETRICAL
ETHEREALISING	ETHNOGRAPHIC	ETYMOLOGISES	EUDIOMETRICALLY
ETHEREALITIES	ETHNOGRAPHICA	ETYMOLOGISING	EUDIOMETRIES
ETHEREALITY	ETHNOGRAPHICAL	ETYMOLOGIST	EUDIOMETRY
ETHEREALIZATION	ETHNOGRAPHIES	ETYMOLOGISTS	EUGENECIST
ETHEREALIZE	ETHNOGRAPHY	ETYMOLOGIZE	EUGENECISTS
ETHEREALIZED	ETHNOHISTORIAN	ETYMOLOGIZED	EUGENICALLY
ETHEREALIZES	ETHNOHISTORIANS	ETYMOLOGIZES	EUGENICIST
ETHEREALIZING	ETHNOHISTORIC	ETYMOLOGIZING	EUGENICISTS
ETHEREALLY	ETHNOHISTORICAL	EUBACTERIA	EUGEOSYNCLINAL
ETHEREALNESS	ETHNOHISTORIES	EUBACTERIUM	EUGEOSYNCLINE
ETHEREALNESSES	ETHNOHISTORY	EUCALYPTOL	EUGEOSYNCLINES
ETHERIFICATION	ETHNOLINGUIST	EUCALYPTOLE	EUGLENOIDS
ETHERIFICATIONS	ETHNOLINGUISTIC	EUCALYPTOLES	EUGLOBULIN
ETHERIFIED	ETHNOLINGUISTS	EUCALYPTOLS	EUGLOBULINS
ETHERIFIES	ETHNOLOGIC	EUCALYPTUS	EUHARMONIC
ETHERIFYING	ETHNOLOGICAL	EUCALYPTUSES	EUHEMERISE
ETHERISATION	ETHNOLOGICALLY	EUCARYOTES	EUHEMERISED
ETHERISATIONS	ETHNOLOGIES	EUCARYOTIC	EUHEMERISES
ETHERISERS	ETHNOLOGIST	EUCHARISES	EUHEMERISING
ETHERISING	ETHNOLOGISTS	EUCHARISTIC	EUHEMERISM
ETHERIZATION	ETHNOMUSICOLOGY	EUCHARISTICAL	EUHEMERISMS
ETHERIZATIONS	ETHNOSCIENCE	EUCHLORINE	EUHEMERIST
ETHERIZERS	ETHNOSCIENCES	EUCHLORINES	EUHEMERISTIC
ETHERIZING	ETHOLOGICAL	EUCHLORINS	EUHEMERISTS
ETHEROMANIA	ETHOLOGICALLY	EUCHOLOGIA	EUHEMERIZE
ETHEROMANIAC	ETHOLOGIES	EUCHOLOGIES	EUHEMERIZED
ETHEROMANIACS	ETHOLOGIST	EUCHOLOGION	EUHEMERIZES
ETHEROMANIAS	ETHOLOGISTS	EUCHROMATIC	EUHEMERIZING
ETHICALITIES	ETHOXYETHANE	EUCHROMATIN	EUKARYOTES
ETHICALITY	ETHOXYETHANES	EUCHROMATINS	EUKARYOTIC
ETHICALNESS	ETHYLAMINE	EUCRYPHIAS	EULOGISERS
ETHICALNESSES	ETHYLAMINES	EUDAEMONIA	EULOGISING
ETHICISING	ETHYLATING	EUDAEMONIAS	EULOGISTIC
ETHICIZING	ETHYLATION	EUDAEMONIC	EULOGISTICAL
ETHIONAMIDE	ETHYLATIONS	EUDAEMONICS	EULOGISTICALLY
ETHIONAMIDES	ETHYLBENZENE	EUDAEMONIES	EULOGIZERS
ETHIONINES	ETHYLBENZENES	EUDAEMONISM	EULOGIZING
ETHNARCHIES	ETIOLATING	EUDAEMONISMS	EUMELANINS
ETHNICALLY	ETIOLATION	EUDAEMONIST	EUNUCHISED
ETHNICISMS	ETIOLATIONS	EUDAEMONISTIC	EUNUCHISES
ETHNICITIES	ETIOLOGICAL	EUDAEMONISTICAL	EUNUCHISING
ETHNOBIOLOGIES	ETIOLOGICALLY	EUDAEMONISTS	EUNUCHISMS
ETHNOBIOLOGY	ETIOLOGIES	EUDAIMONISM	EUNUCHIZED
ETHNOBOTANICAL	ETIOLOGIST	EUDAIMONISMS	EUNUCHIZES
ETHNOBOTANIES	ETIOLOGISTS	EUDEMONIAS	EUNUCHIZING
ETHNOBOTANIST	ETIQUETTES	EUDEMONICS	EUNUCHOIDISM
ETHNOBOTANISTS	ETONOGESTREL	EUDEMONISM	EUNUCHOIDISMS
ETHNOBOTANY	ETONOGESTRELS	EUDEMONISMS	EUNUCHOIDS
ETHNOCENTRIC	ETOURDERIE	EUDEMONIST	EUONYMUSES
ETHNOCENTRICITY	ETOURDERIES	EUDEMONISTIC	EUPATORIUM
ETHNOCENTRISM	ETRANGERES	EUDEMONISTICAL	EUPATORIUMS
ETHNOCENTRISMS	ETYMOLOGICA	EUDEMONISTS	EUPATRIDAE
ETHNOCIDES	ETYMOLOGICAL	EUDIALYTES	EUPEPTICITIES
ETHNOGENIC	ETYMOLOGICALLY	EUDICOTYLEDON	EUPEPTICITY
ETHNOGENIES	ETYMOLOGICON	EUDICOTYLEDONS	EUPHAUSIACEAN
ETHNOGENIST	ETYMOLOGICUM	EUDIOMETER	EUPHAUSIACEANS
ETHNOGENISTS	ETYMOLOGIES	EUDIOMETERS	EUPHAUSIDS

EUPHAUSIID
EUPHAUSIIDS
EUPHEMISED
EUPHEMISER
EUPHEMISERS
EUPHEMISES
EUPHEMISING
EUPHEMISMS
EUPHEMISTIC
EUPHEMISTICALLY
EUPHEMISTS
EUPHEMIZED
EUPHEMIZER
EUPHEMIZERS
EUPHEMIZES
EUPHEMIZING
EUPHONICAL
EUPHONICALLY
EUPHONIOUS
EUPHONIOUSLY
EUPHONIOUSNESS
EUPHONISED
EUPHONISES
EUPHONISING
EUPHONISMS
EUPHONIUMS
EUPHONIZED
EUPHONIZES
EUPHONIZING
EUPHORBIACEOUS
EUPHORBIAS
EUPHORBIUM
EUPHORBIUMS
EUPHORIANT
EUPHORIANTS
EUPHORICALLY
EUPHRASIES
EUPHUISING
EUPHUISTIC
EUPHUISTICAL
EUPHUISTICALLY
EUPHUIZING
EUPLASTICS
EUPLOIDIES
EURHYTHMIC
EURHYTHMICAL
EURHYTHMICS
EURHYTHMIES
EURHYTHMIST
EURHYTHMISTS
EUROCHEQUE
EUROCHEQUES
EUROCREEPS
EUROCURRENCIES
EUROCURRENCY
EURODEPOSIT
EURODEPOSITS
EURODOLLAR
EURODOLLARS

EUROMARKET
EUROMARKETS
EUROPEANISE
EUROPEANISED
EUROPEANISES
EUROPEANISING
EUROPEANIZE
EUROPEANIZED
EUROPEANIZES
EUROPEANIZING
EUROPHILES
EUROPHILIA
EUROPHILIAS
EUROPHOBIA
EUROPHOBIAS
EUROPHOBIC
EUROTERMINAL
EUROTERMINALS
EURYBATHIC
EURYHALINE
EURYPTERID
EURYPTERIDS
EURYPTEROID
EURYPTEROIDS
EURYTHERMAL
EURYTHERMIC
EURYTHERMOUS
EURYTHERMS
EURYTHMICAL
EURYTHMICS
EURYTHMIES
EUSPORANGIATE
EUSTATICALLY
EUTECTOIDS
EUTHANASIA
EUTHANASIAS
EUTHANASIAST
EUTHANASIASTS
EUTHANASIC
EUTHANASIES
EUTHANATISE
EUTHANATISED
EUTHANATISES
EUTHANATISING
EUTHANATIZE
EUTHANATIZED
EUTHANATIZES
EUTHANATIZING
EUTHANISED
EUTHANISES
EUTHANISING
EUTHANIZED
EUTHANIZES
EUTHANIZING
EUTHENISTS
EUTHERIANS
EUTHYROIDS
EUTRAPELIA
EUTRAPELIAS

EUTRAPELIES
EUTROPHICATION
EUTROPHICATIONS
EUTROPHIES
EVACUATING
EVACUATION
EVACUATIONS
EVACUATIVE
EVACUATORS
EVAGATIONS
EVAGINATED
EVAGINATES
EVAGINATING
EVAGINATION
EVAGINATIONS
EVALUATING
EVALUATION
EVALUATIONS
EVALUATIVE
EVALUATORS
EVANESCENCE
EVANESCENCES
EVANESCENT
EVANESCENTLY
EVANESCING
EVANGELIAR
EVANGELIARIES
EVANGELIARION
EVANGELIARIONS
EVANGELIARIUM
EVANGELIARIUMS
EVANGELIARS
EVANGELIARY
EVANGELICAL
EVANGELICALISM
EVANGELICALISMS
EVANGELICALLY
EVANGELICALNESS
EVANGELICALS
EVANGELICISM
EVANGELICISMS
EVANGELIES
EVANGELISATION
EVANGELISATIONS
EVANGELISE
EVANGELISED
EVANGELISER
EVANGELISERS
EVANGELISES
EVANGELISING
EVANGELISM
EVANGELISMS
EVANGELIST
EVANGELISTARIES
EVANGELISTARION
EVANGELISTARY
EVANGELISTIC
EVANGELISTS
EVANGELIZATION

EVANGELIZATIONS
EVANGELIZE
EVANGELIZED
EVANGELIZER
EVANGELIZERS
EVANGELIZES
EVANGELIZING
EVANISHING
EVANISHMENT
EVANISHMENTS
EVANITIONS
EVAPORABILITIES
EVAPORABILITY
EVAPORABLE
EVAPORATED
EVAPORATES
EVAPORATING
EVAPORATION
EVAPORATIONS
EVAPORATIVE
EVAPORATOR
EVAPORATORS
EVAPORIMETER
EVAPORIMETERS
EVAPORITES
EVAPORITIC
EVAPOROGRAPH
EVAPOROGRAPHS
EVAPOROMETER
EVAPOROMETERS
EVASIVENESS
EVASIVENESSES
EVECTIONAL
EVENEMENTS
EVENHANDED
EVENHANDEDLY
EVENHANDEDNESS
EVENNESSES
EVENTFULLY
EVENTFULNESS
EVENTFULNESSES
EVENTRATED
EVENTRATES
EVENTRATING
EVENTRATION
EVENTRATIONS
EVENTUALISE
EVENTUALISED
EVENTUALISES
EVENTUALISING
EVENTUALITIES
EVENTUALITY
EVENTUALIZE
EVENTUALIZED
EVENTUALIZES
EVENTUALIZING
EVENTUALLY
EVENTUATED
EVENTUATES

EVENTUATING
EVENTUATION
EVENTUATIONS
EVERBLOOMING
EVERDURING
EVERGLADES
EVERGREENS
EVERLASTING
EVERLASTINGLY
EVERLASTINGNESS
EVERLASTINGS
EVERYDAYNESS
EVERYDAYNESSES
EVERYPLACE
EVERYTHING
EVERYWHENCE
EVERYWHERE
EVERYWHITHER
EVERYWOMAN
EVERYWOMEN
EVIDENCING
EVIDENTIAL
EVIDENTIALLY
EVIDENTIARY
EVILDOINGS
EVILNESSES
EVINCEMENT
EVINCEMENTS
EVISCERATE
EVISCERATED
EVISCERATES
EVISCERATING
EVISCERATION
EVISCERATIONS
EVISCERATOR
EVISCERATORS
EVITATIONS
EVITERNALLY
EVITERNITIES
EVITERNITY
EVOCATIONS
EVOCATIVELY
EVOCATIVENESS
EVOCATIVENESSES
EVOLUTIONAL
EVOLUTIONARILY
EVOLUTIONARY
EVOLUTIONISM
EVOLUTIONISMS
EVOLUTIONIST
EVOLUTIONISTIC
EVOLUTIONISTS
EVOLUTIONS
EVOLVEMENT
EVOLVEMENTS
EVONYMUSES
EVULGATING
EXACERBATE
EXACERBATED

EXACERBATES
EXACERBATING
EXACERBATION
EXACERBATIONS
EXACERBESCENCE
EXACERBESCENCES
EXACTINGLY
EXACTINGNESS
EXACTINGNESSES
EXACTITUDE
EXACTITUDES
EXACTMENTS
EXACTNESSES
EXACTRESSES
EXAGGERATE
EXAGGERATED
EXAGGERATEDLY
EXAGGERATEDNESS
EXAGGERATES
EXAGGERATING
EXAGGERATINGLY
EXAGGERATION
EXAGGERATIONS
EXAGGERATIVE
EXAGGERATOR
EXAGGERATORS
EXAGGERATORY
EXAHERTZES
EXALBUMINOUS
EXALTATION
EXALTATIONS
EXALTEDNESS
EXALTEDNESSES
EXAMINABILITIES
EXAMINABILITY
EXAMINABLE
EXAMINANTS
EXAMINATES
EXAMINATION
EXAMINATIONAL
EXAMINATIONS
EXAMINATOR
EXAMINATORS
EXAMINERSHIP
EXAMINERSHIPS
EXANIMATION
EXANIMATIONS
EXANTHEMAS
EXANTHEMATA
EXANTHEMATIC
EXANTHEMATOUS
EXARATIONS
EXARCHATES
EXARCHISTS
EXASPERATE
EXASPERATED
EXASPERATEDLY
EXASPERATER
EXASPERATERS

EXASPERATES
EXASPERATING
EXASPERATINGLY
EXASPERATION
EXASPERATIONS
EXASPERATIVE
EXASPERATOR
EXASPERATORS
EXCAMBIONS
EXCAMBIUMS
EXCARNATED
EXCARNATES
EXCARNATING
EXCARNATION
EXCARNATIONS
EXCAVATING
EXCAVATION
EXCAVATIONAL
EXCAVATIONS
EXCAVATORS
EXCEEDABLE
EXCEEDINGLY
EXCELLENCE
EXCELLENCES
EXCELLENCIES
EXCELLENCY
EXCELLENTLY
EXCELSIORS
EXCENTRICS
EXCEPTANTS
EXCEPTIONABLE
EXCEPTIONABLY
EXCEPTIONAL
EXCEPTIONALISM
EXCEPTIONALISMS
EXCEPTIONALITY
EXCEPTIONALLY
EXCEPTIONALNESS
EXCEPTIONALS
EXCEPTIONS
EXCEPTIOUS
EXCEPTLESS
EXCERPTERS
EXCERPTIBLE
EXCERPTING
EXCERPTINGS
EXCERPTION
EXCERPTIONS
EXCERPTORS
EXCESSIVELY
EXCESSIVENESS
EXCESSIVENESSES
EXCHANGEABILITY
EXCHANGEABLE
EXCHANGEABLY
EXCHANGERS
EXCHANGING
EXCHEQUERED
EXCHEQUERING

EXCHEQUERS
EXCIPIENTS
EXCISIONAL
EXCITABILITIES
EXCITABILITY
EXCITABLENESS
EXCITABLENESSES
EXCITANCIES
EXCITATION
EXCITATIONS
EXCITATIVE
EXCITATORY
EXCITEDNESS
EXCITEDNESSES
EXCITEMENT
EXCITEMENTS
EXCITINGLY
EXCLAIMERS
EXCLAIMING
EXCLAMATION
EXCLAMATIONAL
EXCLAMATIONS
EXCLAMATIVE
EXCLAMATORILY
EXCLAMATORY
EXCLAUSTRATION
EXCLAUSTRATIONS
EXCLOSURES
EXCLUDABILITIES
EXCLUDABILITY
EXCLUDABLE
EXCLUDIBLE
EXCLUSIONARY
EXCLUSIONISM
EXCLUSIONISMS
EXCLUSIONIST
EXCLUSIONISTS
EXCLUSIONS
EXCLUSIVELY
EXCLUSIVENESS
EXCLUSIVENESSES
EXCLUSIVES
EXCLUSIVISM
EXCLUSIVISMS
EXCLUSIVIST
EXCLUSIVISTS
EXCLUSIVITIES
EXCLUSIVITY
EXCOGITABLE
EXCOGITATE
EXCOGITATED
EXCOGITATES
EXCOGITATING
EXCOGITATION
EXCOGITATIONS
EXCOGITATIVE
EXCOGITATOR
EXCOGITATORS
EXCOMMUNICABLE

EXCOMMUNICATE
EXCOMMUNICATED
EXCOMMUNICATES
EXCOMMUNICATING
EXCOMMUNICATION
EXCOMMUNICATIVE
EXCOMMUNICATOR
EXCOMMUNICATORS
EXCOMMUNICATORY
EXCOMMUNION
EXCOMMUNIONS
EXCORIATED
EXCORIATES
EXCORIATING
EXCORIATION
EXCORIATIONS
EXCORTICATE
EXCORTICATED
EXCORTICATES
EXCORTICATING
EXCORTICATION
EXCORTICATIONS
EXCREMENTA
EXCREMENTAL
EXCREMENTITIAL
EXCREMENTITIOUS
EXCREMENTS
EXCREMENTUM
EXCRESCENCE
EXCRESCENCES
EXCRESCENCIES
EXCRESCENCY
EXCRESCENT
EXCRESCENTIAL
EXCRESCENTLY
EXCRETIONS
EXCRETORIES
EXCRUCIATE
EXCRUCIATED
EXCRUCIATES
EXCRUCIATING
EXCRUCIATINGLY
EXCRUCIATION
EXCRUCIATIONS
EXCULPABLE
EXCULPATED
EXCULPATES
EXCULPATING
EXCULPATION
EXCULPATIONS
EXCULPATORY
EXCURSIONED
EXCURSIONING
EXCURSIONISE
EXCURSIONISED
EXCURSIONISES
EXCURSIONISING
EXCURSIONIST
EXCURSIONISTS

EXCURSIONIZE
EXCURSIONIZED
EXCURSIONIZES
EXCURSIONIZING
EXCURSIONS
EXCURSIVELY
EXCURSIVENESS
EXCURSIVENESSES
EXCURSUSES
EXCUSABLENESS
EXCUSABLENESSES
EXCUSATORY
EXECRABLENESS
EXECRABLENESSES
EXECRATING
EXECRATION
EXECRATIONS
EXECRATIVE
EXECRATIVELY
EXECRATORS
EXECRATORY
EXECUTABLE
EXECUTABLES
EXECUTANCIES
EXECUTANCY
EXECUTANTS
EXECUTARIES
EXECUTIONER
EXECUTIONERS
EXECUTIONS
EXECUTIVELY
EXECUTIVES
EXECUTORIAL
EXECUTORSHIP
EXECUTORSHIPS
EXECUTRESS
EXECUTRESSES
EXECUTRICES
EXECUTRIES
EXECUTRIXES
EXEGETICAL
EXEGETICALLY
EXEGETISTS
EXEMPLARILY
EXEMPLARINESS
EXEMPLARINESSES
EXEMPLARITIES
EXEMPLARITY
EXEMPLIFIABLE
EXEMPLIFICATION
EXEMPLIFICATIVE
EXEMPLIFIED
EXEMPLIFIER
EXEMPLIFIERS
EXEMPLIFIES
EXEMPLIFYING
EXEMPTIONS
EXENTERATE
EXENTERATED

EXENTERATES
EXENTERATING
EXENTERATION
EXENTERATIONS
EXEQUATURS
EXERCISABLE
EXERCISERS
EXERCISING
EXERCITATION
EXERCITATIONS
EXERCYCLES
EXFOLIANTS
EXFOLIATED
EXFOLIATES
EXFOLIATING
EXFOLIATION
EXFOLIATIONS
EXFOLIATIVE
EXFOLIATOR
EXFOLIATORS
EXHALATION
EXHALATIONS
EXHAUSTERS
EXHAUSTIBILITY
EXHAUSTIBLE
EXHAUSTING
EXHAUSTION
EXHAUSTIONS
EXHAUSTIVE
EXHAUSTIVELY
EXHAUSTIVENESS
EXHAUSTIVITIES
EXHAUSTIVITY
EXHAUSTLESS
EXHAUSTLESSLY
EXHAUSTLESSNESS
EXHEREDATE
EXHEREDATED
EXHEREDATES
EXHEREDATING
EXHEREDATION
EXHEREDATIONS
EXHIBITERS
EXHIBITING
EXHIBITION
EXHIBITIONER
EXHIBITIONERS
EXHIBITIONISM
EXHIBITIONISMS
EXHIBITIONIST
EXHIBITIONISTIC
EXHIBITIONISTS
EXHIBITIONS
EXHIBITIVE
EXHIBITIVELY
EXHIBITORS
EXHIBITORY
EXHILARANT
EXHILARANTS

EXHILARATE
EXHILARATED
EXHILARATES
EXHILARATING
EXHILARATINGLY
EXHILARATION
EXHILARATIONS
EXHILARATIVE
EXHILARATOR
EXHILARATORS
EXHILARATORY
EXHORTATION
EXHORTATIONS
EXHORTATIVE
EXHORTATORY
EXHUMATING
EXHUMATION
EXHUMATIONS
EXIGENCIES
EXIGUITIES
EXIGUOUSLY
EXIGUOUSNESS
EXIGUOUSNESSES
EXILEMENTS
EXIMIOUSLY
EXISTENCES
EXISTENTIAL
EXISTENTIALISM
EXISTENTIALISMS
EXISTENTIALIST
EXISTENTIALISTS
EXISTENTIALLY
EXOBIOLOGICAL
EXOBIOLOGIES
EXOBIOLOGIST
EXOBIOLOGISTS
EXOBIOLOGY
EXOCENTRIC
EXOCUTICLE
EXOCUTICLES
EXOCYTOSED
EXOCYTOSES
EXOCYTOSING
EXOCYTOSIS
EXOCYTOTIC
EXODERMISES
EXODONTIAS
EXODONTICS
EXODONTIST
EXODONTISTS
EXOENZYMES
EXOERYTHROCYTIC
EXOGENETIC
EXOGENISMS
EXOGENOUSLY
EXONERATED
EXONERATES
EXONERATING
EXONERATION

EXONERATIONS

EXONERATIONS
EXONERATIVE
EXONERATOR
EXONERATORS
EXONUCLEASE
EXONUCLEASES
EXONUMISTS
EXOPARASITE
EXOPARASITES
EXOPARASITIC
EXOPEPTIDASE
EXOPEPTIDASES
EXOPHAGIES
EXOPHAGOUS
EXOPHTHALMIA
EXOPHTHALMIAS
EXOPHTHALMIC
EXOPHTHALMOS
EXOPHTHALMOSES
EXOPHTHALMUS
EXOPHTHALMUSES
EXOPLANETS
EXOPODITES
EXOPODITIC
EXORABILITIES
EXORABILITY
EXORATIONS
EXORBITANCE
EXORBITANCES
EXORBITANCIES
EXORBITANCY
EXORBITANT
EXORBITANTLY
EXORBITATE
EXORBITATED
EXORBITATES
EXORBITATING
EXORCISERS
EXORCISING
EXORCISTIC
EXORCISTICAL
EXORCIZERS
EXORCIZING
EXOSKELETAL
EXOSKELETON
EXOSKELETONS
EXOSPHERES
EXOSPHERIC
EXOSPHERICAL
EXOSPORIUM
EXOSPOROUS
EXOTERICAL
EXOTERICALLY
EXOTERICISM
EXOTERICISMS
EXOTHERMAL
EXOTHERMALLY
EXOTHERMIC
EXOTHERMICALLY

EXOTHERMICITIES
EXOTHERMICITY
EXOTICALLY
EXOTICISMS
EXOTICISTS
EXOTICNESS
EXOTICNESSES
EXOTROPIAS
EXPANDABILITIES
EXPANDABILITY
EXPANDABLE
EXPANSIBILITIES
EXPANSIBILITY
EXPANSIBLE
EXPANSIBLY
EXPANSIONAL
EXPANSIONARY
EXPANSIONISM
EXPANSIONISMS
EXPANSIONIST
EXPANSIONISTIC
EXPANSIONISTS
EXPANSIONS
EXPANSIVELY
EXPANSIVENESS
EXPANSIVENESSES
EXPANSIVITIES
EXPANSIVITY
EXPATIATED
EXPATIATES
EXPATIATING
EXPATIATION
EXPATIATIONS
EXPATIATIVE
EXPATIATOR
EXPATIATORS
EXPATIATORY
EXPATRIATE
EXPATRIATED
EXPATRIATES
EXPATRIATING
EXPATRIATION
EXPATRIATIONS
EXPATRIATISM
EXPATRIATISMS
EXPECTABLE
EXPECTABLY
EXPECTANCE
EXPECTANCES
EXPECTANCIES
EXPECTANCY
EXPECTANTLY
EXPECTANTS
EXPECTATION
EXPECTATIONAL
EXPECTATIONS
EXPECTATIVE
EXPECTATIVES
EXPECTEDLY

EXPECTEDNESS
EXPECTEDNESSES
EXPECTINGLY
EXPECTINGS
EXPECTORANT
EXPECTORANTS
EXPECTORATE
EXPECTORATED
EXPECTORATES
EXPECTORATING
EXPECTORATION
EXPECTORATIONS
EXPECTORATIVE
EXPECTORATOR
EXPECTORATORS
EXPEDIENCE
EXPEDIENCES
EXPEDIENCIES
EXPEDIENCY
EXPEDIENTIAL
EXPEDIENTIALLY
EXPEDIENTLY
EXPEDIENTS
EXPEDITATE
EXPEDITATED
EXPEDITATES
EXPEDITATING
EXPEDITATION
EXPEDITATIONS
EXPEDITELY
EXPEDITERS
EXPEDITING
EXPEDITION
EXPEDITIONARY
EXPEDITIONS
EXPEDITIOUS
EXPEDITIOUSLY
EXPEDITIOUSNESS
EXPEDITIVE
EXPEDITORS
EXPELLABLE
EXPELLANTS
EXPELLENTS
EXPENDABILITIES
EXPENDABILITY
EXPENDABLE
EXPENDABLES
EXPENDITURE
EXPENDITURES
EXPENSIVELY
EXPENSIVENESS
EXPENSIVENESSES
EXPERIENCE
EXPERIENCEABLE
EXPERIENCED
EXPERIENCELESS
EXPERIENCES
EXPERIENCING
EXPERIENTIAL

EXPERIENTIALISM
EXPERIENTIALIST
EXPERIENTIALLY
EXPERIMENT
EXPERIMENTAL
EXPERIMENTALISE
EXPERIMENTALISM
EXPERIMENTALIST
EXPERIMENTALIZE
EXPERIMENTALLY
EXPERIMENTATION
EXPERIMENTATIVE
EXPERIMENTED
EXPERIMENTER
EXPERIMENTERS
EXPERIMENTING
EXPERIMENTIST
EXPERIMENTISTS
EXPERIMENTS
EXPERTISED
EXPERTISES
EXPERTISING
EXPERTISMS
EXPERTIZED
EXPERTIZES
EXPERTIZING
EXPERTNESS
EXPERTNESSES
EXPIATIONS
EXPIRATION
EXPIRATIONS
EXPIRATORY
EXPISCATED
EXPISCATES
EXPISCATING
EXPISCATION
EXPISCATIONS
EXPISCATORY
EXPLAINABLE
EXPLAINERS
EXPLAINING
EXPLANATION
EXPLANATIONS
EXPLANATIVE
EXPLANATIVELY
EXPLANATORILY
EXPLANATORY
EXPLANTATION
EXPLANTATIONS
EXPLANTING
EXPLETIVELY
EXPLETIVES
EXPLICABLE
EXPLICABLY
EXPLICATED
EXPLICATES
EXPLICATING
EXPLICATION
EXPLICATIONS

EXPLICATIVE	EXPOSTULATINGLY	EXPUGNATION	EXTEMPORARY
EXPLICATIVELY	EXPOSTULATION	EXPUGNATIONS	EXTEMPORES
EXPLICATOR	EXPOSTULATIONS	EXPULSIONS	EXTEMPORISATION
EXPLICATORS	EXPOSTULATIVE	EXPUNCTING	EXTEMPORISE
EXPLICATORY	EXPOSTULATOR	EXPUNCTION	EXTEMPORISED
EXPLICITLY	EXPOSTULATORS	EXPUNCTIONS	EXTEMPORISER
EXPLICITNESS	EXPOSTULATORY	EXPURGATED	EXTEMPORISERS
EXPLICITNESSES	EXPOSTURES	EXPURGATES	EXTEMPORISES
EXPLOITABLE	EXPOUNDERS	EXPURGATING	EXTEMPORISING
EXPLOITAGE	EXPOUNDING	EXPURGATION	EXTEMPORIZATION
EXPLOITAGES	EXPRESSAGE	EXPURGATIONS	EXTEMPORIZE
EXPLOITATION	EXPRESSAGES	EXPURGATOR	EXTEMPORIZED
EXPLOITATIONS	EXPRESSERS	EXPURGATORIAL	EXTEMPORIZER
EXPLOITATIVE	EXPRESSIBLE	EXPURGATORS	EXTEMPORIZERS
EXPLOITATIVELY	EXPRESSING	EXPURGATORY	EXTEMPORIZES
EXPLOITERS	EXPRESSION	EXQUISITELY	EXTEMPORIZING
EXPLOITING	EXPRESSIONAL	EXQUISITENESS	EXTENDABILITIES
EXPLOITIVE	EXPRESSIONISM	EXQUISITENESSES	EXTENDABILITY
EXPLORATION	EXPRESSIONISMS	EXQUISITES	EXTENDABLE
EXPLORATIONAL	EXPRESSIONIST	EXSANGUINATE	EXTENDEDLY
EXPLORATIONIST	EXPRESSIONISTIC	EXSANGUINATED	EXTENDEDNESS
EXPLORATIONISTS	EXPRESSIONISTS	EXSANGUINATES	EXTENDEDNESSES
EXPLORATIONS	EXPRESSIONLESS	EXSANGUINATING	EXTENDIBILITIES
EXPLORATIVE	EXPRESSIONS	EXSANGUINATION	EXTENDIBILITY
EXPLORATIVELY	EXPRESSIVE	EXSANGUINATIONS	EXTENDIBLE
EXPLORATORY	EXPRESSIVELY	EXSANGUINE	EXTENSIBILITIES
EXPLOSIBLE	EXPRESSIVENESS	EXSANGUINED	EXTENSIBILITY
EXPLOSIONS	EXPRESSIVITIES	EXSANGUINEOUS	EXTENSIBLE
EXPLOSIVELY	EXPRESSIVITY	EXSANGUINITIES	EXTENSIBLENESS
EXPLOSIVENESS	EXPRESSMAN	EXSANGUINITY	EXTENSIFICATION
EXPLOSIVENESSES	EXPRESSMEN	EXSANGUINOUS	EXTENSIMETER
EXPLOSIVES	EXPRESSNESS	EXSCINDING	EXTENSIMETERS
EXPONENTIAL	EXPRESSNESSES	EXSECTIONS	EXTENSIONAL
EXPONENTIALLY	EXPRESSURE	EXSERTIONS	EXTENSIONALISM
EXPONENTIALS	EXPRESSURES	EXSICCATED	EXTENSIONALISMS
EXPONENTIATION	EXPRESSWAY	EXSICCATES	EXTENSIONALITY
EXPONENTIATIONS	EXPRESSWAYS	EXSICCATING	EXTENSIONALLY
EXPORTABILITIES	EXPROBRATE	EXSICCATION	EXTENSIONIST
EXPORTABILITY	EXPROBRATED	EXSICCATIONS	EXTENSIONISTS
EXPORTABLE	EXPROBRATES	EXSICCATIVE	EXTENSIONS
EXPORTATION	EXPROBRATING	EXSICCATOR	EXTENSITIES
EXPORTATIONS	EXPROBRATION	EXSICCATORS	EXTENSIVELY
EXPOSEDNESS	EXPROBRATIONS	EXSOLUTION	EXTENSIVENESS
EXPOSEDNESSES	EXPROBRATIVE	EXSOLUTIONS	EXTENSIVENESSES
EXPOSITING	EXPROBRATORY	EXSTIPULATE	EXTENSIVISATION
EXPOSITION	EXPROMISSION	EXSTROPHIES	EXTENSIVIZATION
EXPOSITIONAL	EXPROMISSIONS	EXSUFFLATE	EXTENSOMETER
EXPOSITIONS	EXPROMISSOR	EXSUFFLATED	EXTENSOMETERS
EXPOSITIVE	EXPROMISSORS	EXSUFFLATES	EXTENUATED
EXPOSITIVELY	EXPROPRIABLE	EXSUFFLATING	EXTENUATES
EXPOSITORILY	EXPROPRIATE	EXSUFFLATION	EXTENUATING
EXPOSITORS	EXPROPRIATED	EXSUFFLATIONS	EXTENUATINGLY
EXPOSITORY	EXPROPRIATES	EXSUFFLICATE	EXTENUATINGS
EXPOSITRESS	EXPROPRIATING	EXTEMPORAL	EXTENUATION
EXPOSITRESSES	EXPROPRIATION	EXTEMPORALLY	EXTENUATIONS
EXPOSTULATE	EXPROPRIATIONS	EXTEMPORANEITY	EXTENUATIVE
EXPOSTULATED	EXPROPRIATOR	EXTEMPORANEOUS	EXTENUATOR
EXPOSTULATES	EXPROPRIATORS	EXTEMPORARILY	EXTENUATORS
EXPOSTULATING	EXPUGNABLE	EXTEMPORARINESS	EXTENUATORY

EXTERIORISATION

EXTERIORISATION
EXTERIORISE
EXTERIORISED
EXTERIORISES
EXTERIORISING
EXTERIORITIES
EXTERIORITY
EXTERIORIZATION
EXTERIORIZE
EXTERIORIZED
EXTERIORIZES
EXTERIORIZING
EXTERIORLY
EXTERMINABLE
EXTERMINATE
EXTERMINATED
EXTERMINATES
EXTERMINATING
EXTERMINATION
EXTERMINATIONS
EXTERMINATIVE
EXTERMINATOR
EXTERMINATORS
EXTERMINATORY
EXTERMINED
EXTERMINES
EXTERMINING
EXTERNALISATION
EXTERNALISE
EXTERNALISED
EXTERNALISES
EXTERNALISING
EXTERNALISM
EXTERNALISMS
EXTERNALIST
EXTERNALISTS
EXTERNALITIES
EXTERNALITY
EXTERNALIZATION
EXTERNALIZE
EXTERNALIZED
EXTERNALIZES
EXTERNALIZING
EXTERNALLY
EXTERNSHIP
EXTERNSHIPS
EXTEROCEPTIVE
EXTEROCEPTOR
EXTEROCEPTORS
EXTERRITORIAL
EXTERRITORIALLY
EXTINCTING
EXTINCTION
EXTINCTIONS
EXTINCTIVE
EXTINCTURE
EXTINCTURES
EXTINGUISH
EXTINGUISHABLE

EXTINGUISHANT
EXTINGUISHANTS
EXTINGUISHED
EXTINGUISHER
EXTINGUISHERS
EXTINGUISHES
EXTINGUISHING
EXTINGUISHMENT
EXTINGUISHMENTS
EXTIRPABLE
EXTIRPATED
EXTIRPATES
EXTIRPATING
EXTIRPATION
EXTIRPATIONS
EXTIRPATIVE
EXTIRPATOR
EXTIRPATORS
EXTIRPATORY
EXTOLLINGLY
EXTOLMENTS
EXTORSIVELY
EXTORTIONARY
EXTORTIONATE
EXTORTIONATELY
EXTORTIONER
EXTORTIONERS
EXTORTIONIST
EXTORTIONISTS
EXTORTIONS
EXTRABOLDS
EXTRACANONICAL
EXTRACELLULAR
EXTRACELLULARLY
EXTRACORPOREAL
EXTRACRANIAL
EXTRACTABILITY
EXTRACTABLE
EXTRACTANT
EXTRACTANTS
EXTRACTIBLE
EXTRACTING
EXTRACTION
EXTRACTIONS
EXTRACTIVE
EXTRACTIVELY
EXTRACTIVES
EXTRACTORS
EXTRACURRICULAR
EXTRADITABLE
EXTRADITED
EXTRADITES
EXTRADITING
EXTRADITION
EXTRADITIONS
EXTRADOSES
EXTRADOTAL
EXTRADURAL
EXTRAEMBRYONIC

EXTRAFLORAL
EXTRAFORANEOUS
EXTRAGALACTIC
EXTRAHEPATIC
EXTRAJUDICIAL
EXTRAJUDICIALLY
EXTRALEGAL
EXTRALEGALLY
EXTRALIMITAL
EXTRALIMITARY
EXTRALINGUISTIC
EXTRALITERARY
EXTRALITIES
EXTRALOGICAL
EXTRAMARITAL
EXTRAMETRICAL
EXTRAMUNDANE
EXTRAMURAL
EXTRAMURALLY
EXTRAMUSICAL
EXTRANEITIES
EXTRANEITY
EXTRANEOUS
EXTRANEOUSLY
EXTRANEOUSNESS
EXTRANUCLEAR
EXTRAORDINAIRE
EXTRAORDINARIES
EXTRAORDINARILY
EXTRAORDINARY
EXTRAPOLATE
EXTRAPOLATED
EXTRAPOLATES
EXTRAPOLATING
EXTRAPOLATION
EXTRAPOLATIONS
EXTRAPOLATIVE
EXTRAPOLATOR
EXTRAPOLATORS
EXTRAPOLATORY
EXTRAPOSED
EXTRAPOSES
EXTRAPOSING
EXTRAPOSITION
EXTRAPOSITIONS
EXTRAPYRAMIDAL
EXTRASENSORY
EXTRASOLAR
EXTRASYSTOLE
EXTRASYSTOLES
EXTRATEXTUAL
EXTRATROPICAL
EXTRAUTERINE
EXTRAVAGANCE
EXTRAVAGANCES
EXTRAVAGANCIES
EXTRAVAGANCY
EXTRAVAGANT
EXTRAVAGANTLY

EXTRAVAGANZA
EXTRAVAGANZAS
EXTRAVAGATE
EXTRAVAGATED
EXTRAVAGATES
EXTRAVAGATING
EXTRAVAGATION
EXTRAVAGATIONS
EXTRAVASATE
EXTRAVASATED
EXTRAVASATES
EXTRAVASATING
EXTRAVASATION
EXTRAVASATIONS
EXTRAVASCULAR
EXTRAVEHICULAR
EXTRAVERSION
EXTRAVERSIONS
EXTRAVERSIVE
EXTRAVERSIVELY
EXTRAVERTED
EXTRAVERTING
EXTRAVERTS
EXTREMENESS
EXTREMENESSES
EXTREMISMS
EXTREMISTS
EXTREMITIES
EXTREMOPHILE
EXTREMOPHILES
EXTRICABLE
EXTRICATED
EXTRICATES
EXTRICATING
EXTRICATION
EXTRICATIONS
EXTRINSICAL
EXTRINSICALITY
EXTRINSICALLY
EXTROVERSION
EXTROVERSIONS
EXTROVERSIVE
EXTROVERSIVELY
EXTROVERTED
EXTROVERTING
EXTROVERTS
EXTRUDABILITIES
EXTRUDABILITY
EXTRUDABLE
EXTRUSIBLE
EXTRUSIONS
EXTUBATING
EXUBERANCE
EXUBERANCES
EXUBERANCIES
EXUBERANCY
EXUBERANTLY
EXUBERATED
EXUBERATES

EXUBERATING
EXUDATIONS
EXULCERATE
EXULCERATED
EXULCERATES
EXULCERATING
EXULCERATION
EXULCERATIONS
EXULTANCES
EXULTANCIES
EXULTANTLY
EXULTATION
EXULTATIONS
EXULTINGLY
EXURBANITE
EXURBANITES
EXUVIATING
EXUVIATION
EXUVIATIONS
EYEBALLING
EYEBRIGHTS
EYEBROWING
EYEBROWLESS
EYEDNESSES
EYEDROPPER
EYEDROPPERS
EYEGLASSES
EYELETEERS
EYELETTING
EYEOPENERS
EYEPOPPERS
EYESHADOWS
EYESTRAINS
EYESTRINGS
EYEWITNESS
EYEWITNESSES

F

FABRICANTS
FABRICATED
FABRICATES
FABRICATING
FABRICATION
FABRICATIONS
FABRICATIVE
FABRICATOR
FABRICATORS
FABRICKING
FABULATING
FABULATORS
FABULISING
FABULISTIC
FABULIZING
FABULOSITIES
FABULOSITY
FABULOUSLY
FABULOUSNESS
FABULOUSNESSES
FACECLOTHS
FACELESSNESS
FACELESSNESSES
FACELIFTED
FACELIFTING
FACEPLATES
FACEPRINTS
FACETIOUSLY
FACETIOUSNESS
FACETIOUSNESSES
FACEWORKER
FACEWORKERS
FACILENESS
FACILENESSES
FACILITATE
FACILITATED
FACILITATES
FACILITATING
FACILITATION
FACILITATIONS
FACILITATIVE
FACILITATOR
FACILITATORS
FACILITATORY
FACILITIES
FACINERIOUS
FACINOROUS
FACINOROUSNESS
FACSIMILED
FACSIMILEING
FACSIMILES
FACSIMILIST
FACSIMILISTS
FACTICITIES

FACTIONALISM
FACTIONALISMS
FACTIONALIST
FACTIONALISTS
FACTIONALLY
FACTIONARIES
FACTIONARY
FACTIONIST
FACTIONISTS
FACTIOUSLY
FACTIOUSNESS
FACTIOUSNESSES
FACTITIOUS
FACTITIOUSLY
FACTITIOUSNESS
FACTITIVELY
FACTORABILITIES
FACTORABILITY
FACTORABLE
FACTORAGES
FACTORIALLY
FACTORIALS
FACTORINGS
FACTORISATION
FACTORISATIONS
FACTORISED
FACTORISES
FACTORISING
FACTORIZATION
FACTORIZATIONS
FACTORIZED
FACTORIZES
FACTORIZING
FACTORSHIP
FACTORSHIPS
FACTORYLIKE
FACTSHEETS
FACTUALISM
FACTUALISMS
FACTUALIST
FACTUALISTIC
FACTUALISTS
FACTUALITIES
FACTUALITY
FACTUALNESS
FACTUALNESSES
FACULTATIVE
FACULTATIVELY
FACUNDITIES
FADDINESSES
FADDISHNESS
FADDISHNESSES
FADEDNESSES
FADELESSLY

FADOMETERS
FAGGOTINGS
FAGGOTRIES
FAGOTTISTS
FAINEANCES
FAINEANCIES
FAINEANTISE
FAINEANTISES
FAINNESSES
FAINTHEARTED
FAINTHEARTEDLY
FAINTINGLY
FAINTISHNESS
FAINTISHNESSES
FAINTNESSES
FAIRGROUND
FAIRGROUNDS
FAIRLEADER
FAIRLEADERS
FAIRNESSES
FAIRNITICKLE
FAIRNITICKLES
FAIRNITICLE
FAIRNITICLES
FAIRNYTICKLE
FAIRNYTICKLES
FAIRNYTICLE
FAIRNYTICLES
FAIRYFLOSS
FAIRYFLOSSES
FAIRYHOODS
FAIRYLANDS
FAIRYTALES
FAITHCURES
FAITHFULLY
FAITHFULNESS
FAITHFULNESSES
FAITHLESSLY
FAITHLESSNESS
FAITHLESSNESSES
FAITHWORTHINESS
FAITHWORTHY
FALANGISMS
FALANGISTS
FALCATIONS
FALCONIFORM
FALCONRIES
FALDISTORIES
FALDISTORY
FALDSTOOLS
FALLACIOUS
FALLACIOUSLY
FALLACIOUSNESS
FALLALERIES

FALLALISHLY
FALLBOARDS
FALLFISHES
FALLIBILISM
FALLIBILISMS
FALLIBILIST
FALLIBILISTS
FALLIBILITIES
FALLIBILITY
FALLIBLENESS
FALLIBLENESSES
FALLOWNESS
FALLOWNESSES
FALSEFACES
FALSEHOODS
FALSENESSES
FALSEWORKS
FALSIDICAL
FALSIFIABILITY
FALSIFIABLE
FALSIFICATION
FALSIFICATIONS
FALSIFIERS
FALSIFYING
FALTERINGLY
FALTERINGS
FAMILIARISATION
FAMILIARISE
FAMILIARISED
FAMILIARISER
FAMILIARISERS
FAMILIARISES
FAMILIARISING
FAMILIARITIES
FAMILIARITY
FAMILIARIZATION
FAMILIARIZE
FAMILIARIZED
FAMILIARIZER
FAMILIARIZERS
FAMILIARIZES
FAMILIARIZING
FAMILIARLY
FAMILIARNESS
FAMILIARNESSES
FAMILISTIC
FAMISHMENT
FAMISHMENTS
FAMOUSNESS
FAMOUSNESSES
FANATICALLY
FANATICALNESS
FANATICALNESSES
FANATICISE

FANATICISED
FANATICISES
FANATICISING
FANATICISM
FANATICISMS
FANATICIZE
FANATICIZED
FANATICIZES
FANATICIZING
FANCIFULLY
FANCIFULNESS
FANCIFULNESSES
FANCIFYING
FANCINESSES
FANCYWORKS
FANDANGLES
FANDANGOES
FANFARADES
FANFARONADE
FANFARONADED
FANFARONADES
FANFARONADING
FANFARONAS
FANFOLDING
FANTABULOUS
FANTASISED
FANTASISER
FANTASISERS
FANTASISES
FANTASISING
FANTASISTS
FANTASIZED
FANTASIZER
FANTASIZERS
FANTASIZES
FANTASIZING
FANTASMALLY
FANTASMICALLY
FANTASQUES
FANTASTICAL
FANTASTICALITY
FANTASTICALLY
FANTASTICALNESS
FANTASTICATE
FANTASTICATED
FANTASTICATES
FANTASTICATING
FANTASTICATION
FANTASTICATIONS
FANTASTICISM
FANTASTICISMS
FANTASTICO
FANTASTICOES
FANTASTICS
FANTASTRIES
FANTASYING
FANTASYLAND
FANTASYLANDS
FANTOCCINI

FARADISATION
FARADISATIONS
FARADISERS
FARADISING
FARADIZATION
FARADIZATIONS
FARADIZERS
FARADIZING
FARANDINES
FARANDOLES
FARAWAYNESS
FARAWAYNESSES
FARBOROUGH
FARBOROUGHS
FARCEMEATS
FARCICALITIES
FARCICALITY
FARCICALLY
FARCICALNESS
FARCICALNESSES
FARCIFYING
FAREWELLED
FAREWELLING
FARFETCHEDNESS
FARINACEOUS
FARINOSELY
FARKLEBERRIES
FARKLEBERRY
FARMERESSES
FARMERETTE
FARMERETTES
FARMHOUSES
FARMSTEADS
FARMWORKER
FARMWORKERS
FARNARKELED
FARNARKELING
FARNARKELINGS
FARNARKELS
FARRAGINOUS
FARRANDINE
FARRANDINES
FARRIERIES
FARSIGHTED
FARSIGHTEDLY
FARSIGHTEDNESS
FARTHERMORE
FARTHERMOST
FARTHINGALE
FARTHINGALES
FARTHINGLAND
FARTHINGLANDS
FARTHINGLESS
FARTHINGSWORTH
FARTHINGSWORTHS
FASCIATELY
FASCIATION
FASCIATIONS
FASCICULAR

FASCICULARLY
FASCICULATE
FASCICULATED
FASCICULATELY
FASCICULATION
FASCICULATIONS
FASCICULES
FASCICULUS
FASCIITISES
FASCINATED
FASCINATEDLY
FASCINATES
FASCINATING
FASCINATINGLY
FASCINATION
FASCINATIONS
FASCINATIVE
FASCINATOR
FASCINATORS
FASCIOLIASES
FASCIOLIASIS
FASCISTICALLY
FASCITISES
FASHIONABILITY
FASHIONABLE
FASHIONABLENESS
FASHIONABLES
FASHIONABLY
FASHIONERS
FASHIONING
FASHIONIST
FASHIONISTA
FASHIONISTAS
FASHIONISTS
FASHIONMONGER
FASHIONMONGERS
FASHIONMONGING
FASHIOUSNESS
FASHIOUSNESSES
FASTBALLER
FASTBALLERS
FASTENINGS
FASTIDIOUS
FASTIDIOUSLY
FASTIDIOUSNESS
FASTIGIATE
FASTIGIATED
FASTIGIUMS
FASTNESSES
FATALISTIC
FATALISTICALLY
FATALITIES
FATALNESSES
FATBRAINED
FATEFULNESS
FATEFULNESSES
FATHEADEDLY
FATHEADEDNESS
FATHEADEDNESSES

FATHERHOOD
FATHERHOODS
FATHERINGS
FATHERLAND
FATHERLANDS
FATHERLESS
FATHERLESSNESS
FATHERLIKE
FATHERLINESS
FATHERLINESSES
FATHERSHIP
FATHERSHIPS
FATHOMABLE
FATHOMETER
FATHOMETERS
FATHOMLESS
FATHOMLESSLY
FATHOMLESSNESS
FATIDICALLY
FATIGABILITIES
FATIGABILITY
FATIGABLENESS
FATIGABLENESSES
FATIGATING
FATIGUABLE
FATIGUABLENESS
FATIGUELESS
FATIGUINGLY
FATISCENCE
FATISCENCES
FATSHEDERA
FATSHEDERAS
FATTENABLE
FATTENINGS
FATTINESSES
FATUOUSNESS
FATUOUSNESSES
FAULCHIONS
FAULTFINDER
FAULTFINDERS
FAULTFINDING
FAULTFINDINGS
FAULTINESS
FAULTINESSES
FAULTLESSLY
FAULTLESSNESS
FAULTLESSNESSES
FAUNISTICALLY
FAUXBOURDON
FAUXBOURDONS
FAVORABLENESS
FAVORABLENESSES
FAVOREDNESS
FAVOREDNESSES
FAVORINGLY
FAVORITISM
FAVORITISMS
FAVOURABLE
FAVOURABLENESS

FAVOURABLY
FAVOUREDNESS
FAVOUREDNESSES
FAVOURINGLY
FAVOURITES
FAVOURITISM
FAVOURITISMS
FAVOURLESS
FAWNINGNESS
FAWNINGNESSES
FAZENDEIRO
FAZENDEIROS
FEARFULLER
FEARFULLEST
FEARFULNESS
FEARFULNESSES
FEARLESSLY
FEARLESSNESS
FEARLESSNESSES
FEARNAUGHT
FEARNAUGHTS
FEARNOUGHT
FEARNOUGHTS
FEARSOMELY
FEARSOMENESS
FEARSOMENESSES
FEASIBILITIES
FEASIBILITY
FEASIBLENESS
FEASIBLENESSES
FEATEOUSLY
FEATHERBED
FEATHERBEDDED
FEATHERBEDDING
FEATHERBEDDINGS
FEATHERBEDS
FEATHERBRAIN
FEATHERBRAINED
FEATHERBRAINS
FEATHEREDGE
FEATHEREDGED
FEATHEREDGES
FEATHEREDGING
FEATHERHEAD
FEATHERHEADED
FEATHERHEADS
FEATHERIER
FEATHERIEST
FEATHERINESS
FEATHERINESSES
FEATHERING
FEATHERINGS
FEATHERLESS
FEATHERLIGHT
FEATHERSTITCH
FEATHERSTITCHED
FEATHERSTITCHES
FEATHERWEIGHT
FEATHERWEIGHTS

FEATLINESS
FEATLINESSES
FEATURELESS
FEATURELESSNESS
FEATURETTE
FEATURETTES
FEBRICITIES
FEBRICULAS
FEBRICULES
FEBRIFACIENT
FEBRIFACIENTS
FEBRIFEROUS
FEBRIFUGAL
FEBRIFUGES
FEBRILITIES
FECKLESSLY
FECKLESSNESS
FECKLESSNESSES
FECULENCES
FECULENCIES
FECUNDATED
FECUNDATES
FECUNDATING
FECUNDATION
FECUNDATIONS
FECUNDATOR
FECUNDATORS
FECUNDATORY
FECUNDITIES
FEDERACIES
FEDERALESE
FEDERALESES
FEDERALISATION
FEDERALISATIONS
FEDERALISE
FEDERALISED
FEDERALISES
FEDERALISING
FEDERALISM
FEDERALISMS
FEDERALIST
FEDERALISTIC
FEDERALISTS
FEDERALIZATION
FEDERALIZATIONS
FEDERALIZE
FEDERALIZED
FEDERALIZES
FEDERALIZING
FEDERARIES
FEDERATING
FEDERATION
FEDERATIONS
FEDERATIVE
FEDERATIVELY
FEDERATORS
FEEBLEMINDED
FEEBLEMINDEDLY
FEEBLENESS

FEEBLENESSES
FEEDGRAINS
FEEDINGSTUFF
FEEDINGSTUFFS
FEEDSTOCKS
FEEDSTUFFS
FEEDTHROUGH
FEEDTHROUGHS
FEEDWATERS
FEELINGLESS
FEELINGNESS
FEELINGNESSES
FEIGNEDNESS
FEIGNEDNESSES
FEIGNINGLY
FEISTINESS
FEISTINESSES
FELDSCHARS
FELDSCHERS
FELDSPATHIC
FELDSPATHOID
FELDSPATHOIDS
FELDSPATHOSE
FELDSPATHS
FELICITATE
FELICITATED
FELICITATES
FELICITATING
FELICITATION
FELICITATIONS
FELICITATOR
FELICITATORS
FELICITIES
FELICITOUS
FELICITOUSLY
FELICITOUSNESS
FELINENESS
FELINENESSES
FELINITIES
FELLATIONS
FELLATRICES
FELLATRIXES
FELLMONGER
FELLMONGERED
FELLMONGERIES
FELLMONGERING
FELLMONGERINGS
FELLMONGERS
FELLMONGERY
FELLNESSES
FELLOWSHIP
FELLOWSHIPED
FELLOWSHIPING
FELLOWSHIPPED
FELLOWSHIPPING
FELLOWSHIPS
FELLWALKER
FELLWALKERS
FELONIOUSLY

FELONIOUSNESS
FELONIOUSNESSES
FELSPATHIC
FELSPATHOID
FELSPATHOIDS
FELSPATHOSE
FEMALENESS
FEMALENESSES
FEMALITIES
FEMETARIES
FEMINACIES
FEMINALITIES
FEMINALITY
FEMINEITIES
FEMINILITIES
FEMINILITY
FEMININELY
FEMININENESS
FEMININENESSES
FEMINISM
FEMINISMS
FEMININITIES
FEMININITY
FEMINISATION
FEMINISATIONS
FEMINISING
FEMINISTIC
FEMINITIES
FEMINIZATION
FEMINIZATIONS
FEMINIZING
FEMTOSECOND
FEMTOSECONDS
FENCELESSNESS
FENCELESSNESSES
FENDERLESS
FENESTELLA
FENESTELLAE
FENESTELLAS
FENESTRALS
FENESTRATE
FENESTRATED
FENESTRATION
FENESTRATIONS
FENNELFLOWER
FENNELFLOWERS
FENUGREEKS
FEOFFMENTS
FERACITIES
FERETORIES
FERMENTABILITY
FERMENTABLE
FERMENTATION
FERMENTATIONS
FERMENTATIVE
FERMENTATIVELY
FERMENTERS
FERMENTESCIBLE
FERMENTING

FERMENTITIOUS
FERMENTIVE
FERMENTORS
FERNITICKLE
FERNITICKLES
FERNITICLE
FERNITICLES
FERNTICKLE
FERNTICKLED
FERNTICKLES
FERNTICLED
FERNTICLES
FERNYTICKLE
FERNYTICKLES
FERNYTICLE
FERNYTICLES
FEROCIOUSLY
FEROCIOUSNESS
FEROCIOUSNESSES
FEROCITIES
FERRANDINE
FERRANDINES
FERREDOXIN
FERREDOXINS
FERRELLING
FERRETINGS
FERRICYANIC
FERRICYANIDE
FERRICYANIDES
FERRICYANOGEN
FERRICYANOGENS
FERRIFEROUS
FERRIMAGNET
FERRIMAGNETIC
FERRIMAGNETISM
FERRIMAGNETISMS
FERRIMAGNETS
FERROCENES
FERROCHROME
FERROCHROMES
FERROCHROMIUM
FERROCHROMIUMS
FERROCONCRETE
FERROCONCRETES
FERROCYANIC
FERROCYANIDE
FERROCYANIDES
FERROCYANOGEN
FERROCYANOGENS
FERROELECTRIC
FERROELECTRICS
FERROGRAMS
FERROGRAPHIES
FERROGRAPHY
FERROMAGNESIAN
FERROMAGNET
FERROMAGNETIC
FERROMAGNETISM
FERROMAGNETISMS

FERROMAGNETS
FERROMANGANESE
FERROMANGANESES
FERROMOLYBDENUM
FERRONICKEL
FERRONICKELS
FERRONIERE
FERRONIERES
FERRONNIERE
FERRONNIERES
FERROPRUSSIATE
FERROPRUSSIATES
FERROSILICON
FERROSILICONS
FERROSOFERRIC
FERROTYPED
FERROTYPES
FERROTYPING
FERRUGINEOUS
FERRUGINOUS
FERRYBOATS
FERTIGATED
FERTIGATES
FERTIGATING
FERTIGATION
FERTIGATIONS
FERTILENESS
FERTILENESSES
FERTILISABLE
FERTILISATION
FERTILISATIONS
FERTILISED
FERTILISER
FERTILISERS
FERTILISES
FERTILISING
FERTILITIES
FERTILIZABLE
FERTILIZATION
FERTILIZATIONS
FERTILIZED
FERTILIZER
FERTILIZERS
FERTILIZES
FERTILIZING
FERULACEOUS
FERVENCIES
FERVENTEST
FERVENTNESS
FERVENTNESSES
FERVESCENT
FERVIDITIES
FERVIDNESS
FERVIDNESSES
FESCENNINE
FESTILOGIES
FESTINATED
FESTINATELY
FESTINATES

FESTINATING
FESTINATION
FESTINATIONS
FESTIVALGOER
FESTIVALGOERS
FESTIVENESS
FESTIVENESSES
FESTIVITIES
FESTOLOGIES
FESTOONERIES
FESTOONERY
FESTOONING
FESTSCHRIFT
FESTSCHRIFTEN
FESTSCHRIFTS
FETCHINGLY
FETICHISED
FETICHISES
FETICHISING
FETICHISMS
FETICHISTIC
FETICHISTS
FETICHIZED
FETICHIZES
FETICHIZING
FETIDITIES
FETIDNESSES
FETIPAROUS
FETISHISATION
FETISHISATIONS
FETISHISED
FETISHISES
FETISHISING
FETISHISMS
FETISHISTIC
FETISHISTICALLY
FETISHISTS
FETISHIZATION
FETISHIZATIONS
FETISHIZED
FETISHIZES
FETISHIZING
FETOLOGIES
FETOLOGIST
FETOLOGISTS
FETOPROTEIN
FETOPROTEINS
FETOSCOPES
FETOSCOPIES
FETTERLESS
FETTERLOCK
FETTERLOCKS
FETTUCCINE
FETTUCCINES
FETTUCCINI
FETTUCINES
FETTUCINIS
FEUDALISATION
FEUDALISATIONS

FEUDALISED
FEUDALISES
FEUDALISING
FEUDALISMS
FEUDALISTIC
FEUDALISTS
FEUDALITIES
FEUDALIZATION
FEUDALIZATIONS
FEUDALIZED
FEUDALIZES
FEUDALIZING
FEUDATORIES
FEUILLETES
FEUILLETON
FEUILLETONISM
FEUILLETONISMS
FEUILLETONIST
FEUILLETONISTIC
FEUILLETONISTS
FEUILLETONS
FEVERISHLY
FEVERISHNESS
FEVERISHNESSES
FEVEROUSLY
FEVERROOTS
FEVERWEEDS
FEVERWORTS
FIANCAILLES
FIANCHETTI
FIANCHETTO
FIANCHETTOED
FIANCHETTOES
FIANCHETTOING
FIANCHETTOS
FIBERBOARD
FIBERBOARDS
FIBERFILLS
FIBERGLASS
FIBERGLASSED
FIBERGLASSES
FIBERGLASSING
FIBERISATION
FIBERISATIONS
FIBERISING
FIBERIZATION
FIBERIZATIONS
FIBERIZING
FIBERSCOPE
FIBERSCOPES
FIBREBOARD
FIBREBOARDS
FIBREFILLS
FIBREGLASS
FIBREGLASSES
FIBREOPTIC
FIBRESCOPE
FIBRESCOPES
FIBRILLARY

FIBRILLATE
FIBRILLATED
FIBRILLATES
FIBRILLATING
FIBRILLATION
FIBRILLATIONS
FIBRILLIFORM
FIBRILLINS
FIBRILLOSE
FIBRILLOUS
FIBRINOGEN
FIBRINOGENIC
FIBRINOGENOUS
FIBRINOGENS
FIBRINOIDS
FIBRINOLYSES
FIBRINOLYSIN
FIBRINOLYSINS
FIBRINOLYSIS
FIBRINOLYTIC
FIBRINOPEPTIDE
FIBRINOPEPTIDES
FIBROBLAST
FIBROBLASTIC
FIBROBLASTS
FIBROCARTILAGE
FIBROCARTILAGES
FIBROCEMENT
FIBROCEMENTS
FIBROCYSTIC
FIBROCYTES
FIBROLINES
FIBROLITES
FIBROMATOUS
FIBROMYALGIA
FIBROMYALGIAS
FIBRONECTIN
FIBRONECTINS
FIBROSARCOMA
FIBROSARCOMAS
FIBROSARCOMATA
FIBROSITIS
FIBROSITISES
FIBROUSNESS
FIBROUSNESSES
FIBROVASCULAR
FICKLENESS
FICKLENESSES
FICTIONALISE
FICTIONALISED
FICTIONALISES
FICTIONALISING
FICTIONALITIES
FICTIONALITY
FICTIONALIZE
FICTIONALIZED
FICTIONALIZES
FICTIONALIZING
FICTIONALLY

FICTIONEER
FICTIONEERING
FICTIONEERINGS
FICTIONEERS
FICTIONISATION
FICTIONISATIONS
FICTIONISE
FICTIONISED
FICTIONISES
FICTIONISING
FICTIONIST
FICTIONISTS
FICTIONIZATION
FICTIONIZATIONS
FICTIONIZE
FICTIONIZED
FICTIONIZES
FICTIONIZING
FICTITIOUS
FICTITIOUSLY
FICTITIOUSNESS
FICTIVENESS
FICTIVENESSES
FIDDIOUSED
FIDDIOUSES
FIDDIOUSING
FIDDLEBACK
FIDDLEBACKS
FIDDLEDEDEE
FIDDLEDEEDEE
FIDDLEHEAD
FIDDLEHEADS
FIDDLENECK
FIDDLENECKS
FIDDLESTICK
FIDDLESTICKS
FIDDLEWOOD
FIDDLEWOODS
FIDEICOMMISSA
FIDEICOMMISSARY
FIDEICOMMISSUM
FIDELISMOS
FIDELISTAS
FIDELITIES
FIDGETIEST
FIDGETINESS
FIDGETINESSES
FIDGETINGLY
FIDUCIALLY
FIDUCIARIES
FIDUCIARILY
FIELDBOOTS
FIELDCRAFT
FIELDCRAFTS
FIELDFARES
FIELDMOUSE
FIELDPIECE
FIELDPIECES
FIELDSTONE

FIELDSTONES
FIELDSTRIP
FIELDSTRIPPED
FIELDSTRIPPING
FIELDSTRIPS
FIELDVOLES
FIELDWARDS
FIELDWORKER
FIELDWORKERS
FIELDWORKS
FIENDISHLY
FIENDISHNESS
FIENDISHNESSES
FIERCENESS
FIERCENESSES
FIERINESSES
FIFTEENERS
FIFTEENTHLY
FIFTEENTHS
FIGHTBACKS
FIGURABILITIES
FIGURABILITY
FIGURANTES
FIGURATELY
FIGURATION
FIGURATIONS
FIGURATIVE
FIGURATIVELY
FIGURATIVENESS
FIGUREHEAD
FIGUREHEADS
FIGURELESS
FIGUREWORK
FIGUREWORKS
FILAGREEING
FILAMENTARY
FILAMENTOUS
FILARIASES
FILARIASIS
FILATORIES
FILCHINGLY
FILEFISHES
FILIALNESS
FILIALNESSES
FILIATIONS
FILIBUSTER
FILIBUSTERED
FILIBUSTERER
FILIBUSTERERS
FILIBUSTERING
FILIBUSTERINGS
FILIBUSTERISM
FILIBUSTERISMS
FILIBUSTEROUS
FILIBUSTERS
FILICINEAN
FILIGRAINS
FILIGRANES
FILIGREEING

FILIOPIETISTIC
FILIPENDULOUS
FILLAGREED
FILLAGREEING
FILLAGREES
FILLESTERS
FILLIPEENS
FILLISTERS
FILMICALLY
FILMINESSES
FILMMAKERS
FILMMAKING
FILMMAKINGS
FILMOGRAPHIES
FILMOGRAPHY
FILMSETTER
FILMSETTERS
FILMSETTING
FILMSETTINGS
FILMSTRIPS
FILOPLUMES
FILOPODIUM
FILOSELLES
FILOVIRUSES
FILTERABILITIES
FILTERABILITY
FILTERABLE
FILTERABLENESS
FILTHINESS
FILTHINESSES
FILTRABILITIES
FILTRABILITY
FILTRATABLE
FILTRATING
FILTRATION
FILTRATIONS
FIMBRIATED
FIMBRIATES
FIMBRIATING
FIMBRIATION
FIMBRIATIONS
FIMBRILLATE
FIMICOLOUS
FINABLENESS
FINABLENESSES
FINALISATION
FINALISATIONS
FINALISERS
FINALISING
FINALISTIC
FINALITIES
FINALIZATION
FINALIZATIONS
FINALIZERS
FINALIZING
FINANCIALIST
FINANCIALISTS
FINANCIALLY
FINANCIERED

FINANCIERING
FINANCIERS
FINANCINGS
FINEABLENESS
FINEABLENESSES
FINENESSES
FINESSINGS
FINGERBOARD
FINGERBOARDS
FINGERBOWL
FINGERBOWLS
FINGERBREADTH
FINGERBREADTHS
FINGERGLASS
FINGERGLASSES
FINGERGUARD
FINGERGUARDS
FINGERHOLD
FINGERHOLDS
FINGERHOLE
FINGERHOLES
FINGERINGS
FINGERLESS
FINGERLIKE
FINGERLING
FINGERLINGS
FINGERMARK
FINGERMARKS
FINGERNAIL
FINGERNAILS
FINGERPICK
FINGERPICKED
FINGERPICKING
FINGERPICKINGS
FINGERPICKS
FINGERPLATE
FINGERPLATES
FINGERPOST
FINGERPOSTS
FINGERPRINT
FINGERPRINTED
FINGERPRINTING
FINGERPRINTINGS
FINGERPRINTS
FINGERSTALL
FINGERSTALLS
FINGERTIPS
FINICALITIES
FINICALITY
FINICALNESS
FINICALNESSES
FINICKETIER
FINICKETIEST
FINICKIEST
FINICKINESS
FINICKINESSES
FINICKINGS
FINISHINGS
FINITENESS

FINITENESSES
FINNICKIER
FINNICKIEST
FINNOCHIOS
FINOCCHIOS
FIORATURAE
FIREBALLER
FIREBALLERS
FIREBALLING
FIREBOARDS
FIREBOMBED
FIREBOMBING
FIREBRANDS
FIREBREAKS
FIREBRICKS
FIREBUSHES
FIRECRACKER
FIRECRACKERS
FIRECRESTS
FIREDRAGON
FIREDRAGONS
FIREDRAKES
FIREFANGED
FIREFANGING
FIREFIGHTER
FIREFIGHTERS
FIREFIGHTING
FIREFIGHTINGS
FIREFIGHTS
FIREFLOATS
FIREFLOODS
FIREGUARDS
FIREHOUSES
FIRELIGHTER
FIRELIGHTERS
FIRELIGHTS
FIREPLACED
FIREPLACES
FIREPOWERS
FIREPROOFED
FIREPROOFING
FIREPROOFINGS
FIREPROOFS
FIRESCREEN
FIRESCREENS
FIRESTONES
FIRESTORMS
FIRETHORNS
FIRETRUCKS
FIREWARDEN
FIREWARDENS
FIREWATERS
FIRMAMENTAL
FIRMAMENTS
FIRMNESSES
FIRSTBORNS
FIRSTFRUITS
FIRSTLINGS
FIRSTNESSES

FISCALISTS
FISHABILITIES
FISHABILITY
FISHBURGER
FISHBURGERS
FISHERFOLK
FISHERWOMAN
FISHERWOMEN
FISHFINGER
FISHFINGERS
FISHIFYING
FISHINESSES
FISHMONGER
FISHMONGERS
FISHPLATES
FISHTAILED
FISHTAILING
FISHWIFELY
FISHYBACKS
FISSICOSTATE
FISSILINGUAL
FISSILITIES
FISSIONABILITY
FISSIONABLE
FISSIONABLES
FISSIONING
FISSIPALMATE
FISSIPARISM
FISSIPARISMS
FISSIPARITIES
FISSIPARITY
FISSIPAROUS
FISSIPAROUSLY
FISSIPAROUSNESS
FISSIPEDAL
FISSIPEDES
FISSIROSTRAL
FISTFIGHTS
FISTICUFFS
FITFULNESS
FITFULNESSES
FITTINGNESS
FITTINGNESSES
FIVEFINGER
FIVEFINGERS
FIVEPENCES
FIXEDNESSES
FIXTURELESS
FIZGIGGING
FIZZENLESS
FIZZINESSES
FLABBERGAST
FLABBERGASTED
FLABBERGASTING
FLABBERGASTS
FLABBINESS
FLABBINESSES
FLABELLATE
FLABELLATION

FLABELLATIONS
FLABELLIFORM
FLABELLUMS
FLACCIDEST
FLACCIDITIES
FLACCIDITY
FLACCIDNESS
FLACCIDNESSES
FLACKERIES
FLACKERING
FLAFFERING
FLAGELLANT
FLAGELLANTISM
FLAGELLANTISMS
FLAGELLANTS
FLAGELLATE
FLAGELLATED
FLAGELLATES
FLAGELLATING
FLAGELLATION
FLAGELLATIONS
FLAGELLATOR
FLAGELLATORS
FLAGELLATORY
FLAGELLIFEROUS
FLAGELLIFORM
FLAGELLINS
FLAGELLOMANIA
FLAGELLOMANIAC
FLAGELLOMANIACS
FLAGELLOMANIAS
FLAGELLUMS
FLAGEOLETS
FLAGGINESS
FLAGGINESSES
FLAGGINGLY
FLAGITATED
FLAGITATES
FLAGITATING
FLAGITATION
FLAGITATIONS
FLAGITIOUS
FLAGITIOUSLY
FLAGITIOUSNESS
FLAGRANCES
FLAGRANCIES
FLAGRANTLY
FLAGRANTNESS
FLAGRANTNESSES
FLAGSTAFFS
FLAGSTAVES
FLAGSTICKS
FLAGSTONES
FLAKINESSES
FLAMBEEING
FLAMBOYANCE
FLAMBOYANCES
FLAMBOYANCIES
FLAMBOYANCY

FLAMBOYANT

FLAMBOYANT
FLAMBOYANTE
FLAMBOYANTES
FLAMBOYANTLY
FLAMBOYANTS
FLAMEPROOF
FLAMEPROOFED
FLAMEPROOFER
FLAMEPROOFERS
FLAMEPROOFING
FLAMEPROOFS
FLAMETHROWER
FLAMETHROWERS
FLAMINGOES
FLAMINICAL
FLAMMABILITIES
FLAMMABILITY
FLAMMABLES
FLAMMIFEROUS
FLAMMULATED
FLAMMULATION
FLAMMULATIONS
FLANCHINGS
FLANCONADE
FLANCONADES
FLANGELESS
FLANKERING
FLANNELBOARD
FLANNELBOARDS
FLANNELETS
FLANNELETTE
FLANNELETTES
FLANNELGRAPH
FLANNELGRAPHS
FLANNELING
FLANNELLED
FLANNELLING
FLANNELMOUTHED
FLAPDOODLE
FLAPDOODLES
FLAPPERHOOD
FLAPPERHOODS
FLAPPERISH
FLAPTRACKS
FLAREBACKS
FLASHBACKED
FLASHBACKING
FLASHBACKS
FLASHBOARD
FLASHBOARDS
FLASHBULBS
FLASHCARDS
FLASHCUBES
FLASHFORWARD
FLASHFORWARDED
FLASHFORWARDING
FLASHFORWARDS
FLASHINESS
FLASHINESSES

FLASHLAMPS
FLASHLIGHT
FLASHLIGHTS
FLASHMOBBING
FLASHMOBBINGS
FLASHOVERS
FLASHTUBES
FLATBREADS
FLATFISHES
FLATFOOTED
FLATFOOTING
FLATLANDER
FLATLANDERS
FLATLINERS
FLATLINING
FLATNESSES
FLATSCREEN
FLATSCREENS
FLATSHARES
FLATTENERS
FLATTENING
FLATTERABLE
FLATTERERS
FLATTERIES
FLATTERING
FLATTERINGLY
FLATTEROUS
FLATTEROUSLY
FLATULENCE
FLATULENCES
FLATULENCIES
FLATULENCY
FLATULENTLY
FLATWASHES
FLAUGHTERED
FLAUGHTERING
FLAUGHTERS
FLAUGHTING
FLAUNCHING
FLAUNCHINGS
FLAUNTIEST
FLAUNTINESS
FLAUNTINESSES
FLAUNTINGLY
FLAVANONES
FLAVESCENT
FLAVIVIRUS
FLAVIVIRUSES
FLAVONOIDS
FLAVOPROTEIN
FLAVOPROTEINS
FLAVOPURPURIN
FLAVOPURPURINS
FLAVORFULLY
FLAVORINGS
FLAVORISTS
FLAVORLESS
FLAVORSOME
FLAVOURDYNAMICS

FLAVOURERS
FLAVOURFUL
FLAVOURFULLY
FLAVOURING
FLAVOURINGS
FLAVOURLESS
FLAVOURSOME
FLAWLESSLY
FLAWLESSNESS
FLAWLESSNESSES
FLEAHOPPER
FLEAHOPPERS
FLEAMARKET
FLEAMARKETS
FLECHETTES
FLECKERING
FLECTIONAL
FLECTIONLESS
FLEDGELING
FLEDGELINGS
FLEDGLINGS
FLEECELESS
FLEECHINGS
FLEECHMENT
FLEECHMENTS
FLEECINESS
FLEECINESSES
FLEERINGLY
FLEETINGLY
FLEETINGNESS
FLEETINGNESSES
FLEETNESSES
FLEHMENING
FLEMISHING
FLESHHOODS
FLESHINESS
FLESHINESSES
FLESHLIEST
FLESHLINESS
FLESHLINESSES
FLESHLINGS
FLESHMENTS
FLESHMONGER
FLESHMONGERS
FLESHWORMS
FLETCHINGS
FLEURETTES
FLEXECUTIVE
FLEXECUTIVES
FLEXIBILITIES
FLEXIBILITY
FLEXIBLENESS
FLEXIBLENESSES
FLEXIHOURS
FLEXIONLESS
FLEXITARIAN
FLEXITARIANISM
FLEXITARIANISMS
FLEXITARIANS

FLEXITIMES
FLEXOGRAPHIC
FLEXOGRAPHIES
FLEXOGRAPHY
FLEXTIMERS
FLEXUOUSLY
FLIBBERTIGIBBET
FLICHTERED
FLICHTERING
FLICKERING
FLICKERINGLY
FLICKERTAIL
FLICKERTAILS
FLIGHTIEST
FLIGHTINESS
FLIGHTINESSES
FLIGHTLESS
FLIMFLAMMED
FLIMFLAMMER
FLIMFLAMMERIES
FLIMFLAMMERS
FLIMFLAMMERY
FLIMFLAMMING
FLIMSINESS
FLIMSINESSES
FLINCHINGLY
FLINCHINGS
FLINDERSIA
FLINDERSIAS
FLINTHEADS
FLINTIFIED
FLINTIFIES
FLINTIFYING
FLINTINESS
FLINTINESSES
FLINTLOCKS
FLIPFLOPPED
FLIPFLOPPING
FLIPPANCIES
FLIPPANTLY
FLIPPANTNESS
FLIPPANTNESSES
FLIRTATION
FLIRTATIONS
FLIRTATIOUS
FLIRTATIOUSLY
FLIRTATIOUSNESS
FLIRTINGLY
FLITTERING
FLITTERMICE
FLITTERMOUSE
FLOATABILITIES
FLOATABILITY
FLOATATION
FLOATATIONS
FLOATINGLY
FLOATPLANE
FLOATPLANES
FLOCCILLATION

FLOCCILLATIONS
FLOCCULANT
FLOCCULANTS
FLOCCULATE
FLOCCULATED
FLOCCULATES
FLOCCULATING
FLOCCULATION
FLOCCULATIONS
FLOCCULATOR
FLOCCULATORS
FLOCCULENCE
FLOCCULENCES
FLOCCULENCIES
FLOCCULENCY
FLOCCULENT
FLOCCULENTLY
FLOODGATES
FLOODLIGHT
FLOODLIGHTED
FLOODLIGHTING
FLOODLIGHTINGS
FLOODLIGHTS
FLOODMARKS
FLOODPLAIN
FLOODPLAINS
FLOODTIDES
FLOODWALLS
FLOODWATER
FLOODWATERS
FLOORBOARD
FLOORBOARDS
FLOORCLOTH
FLOORCLOTHS
FLOORHEADS
FLOORSHOWS
FLOORWALKER
FLOORWALKERS
FLOPHOUSES
FLOPPINESS
FLOPPINESSES
FLORENTINE
FLORENTINES
FLORESCENCE
FLORESCENCES
FLORESCENT
FLORIATION
FLORIATIONS
FLORIBUNDA
FLORIBUNDAS
FLORICANES
FLORICULTURAL
FLORICULTURE
FLORICULTURES
FLORICULTURIST
FLORICULTURISTS
FLORIDEANS
FLORIDEOUS
FLORIDITIES

FLORIDNESS
FLORIDNESSES
FLORIFEROUS
FLORIFEROUSNESS
FLORIGENIC
FLORILEGIA
FLORILEGIUM
FLORISTICALLY
FLORISTICS
FLORISTRIES
FLOSCULOUS
FLOTATIONS
FLOUNCIEST
FLOUNCINGS
FLOUNDERED
FLOUNDERING
FLOURISHED
FLOURISHER
FLOURISHERS
FLOURISHES
FLOURISHING
FLOURISHINGLY
FLOUTINGLY
FLOUTINGSTOCK
FLOUTINGSTOCKS
FLOWCHARTING
FLOWCHARTINGS
FLOWCHARTS
FLOWERAGES
FLOWERBEDS
FLOWERETTE
FLOWERETTES
FLOWERIEST
FLOWERINESS
FLOWERINESSES
FLOWERINGS
FLOWERLESS
FLOWERLIKE
FLOWERPOTS
FLOWINGNESS
FLOWINGNESSES
FLOWMETERS
FLOWSTONES
FLUCTUATED
FLUCTUATES
FLUCTUATING
FLUCTUATION
FLUCTUATIONAL
FLUCTUATIONS
FLUEGELHORN
FLUEGELHORNS
FLUENTNESS
FLUENTNESSES
FLUFFINESS
FLUFFINESSES
FLUGELHORN
FLUGELHORNIST
FLUGELHORNISTS
FLUGELHORNS

FLUIDEXTRACT
FLUIDEXTRACTS
FLUIDIFIED
FLUIDIFIES
FLUIDIFYING
FLUIDISATION
FLUIDISATIONS
FLUIDISERS
FLUIDISING
FLUIDITIES
FLUIDIZATION
FLUIDIZATIONS
FLUIDIZERS
FLUIDIZING
FLUIDNESSES
FLUKINESSES
FLUMMERIES
FLUMMOXING
FLUNITRAZEPAM
FLUNITRAZEPAMS
FLUNKEYDOM
FLUNKEYDOMS
FLUNKEYISH
FLUNKEYISM
FLUNKEYISMS
FLUNKYISMS
FLUORAPATITE
FLUORAPATITES
FLUORESCED
FLUORESCEIN
FLUORESCEINE
FLUORESCEINES
FLUORESCEINS
FLUORESCENCE
FLUORESCENCES
FLUORESCENT
FLUORESCENTS
FLUORESCER
FLUORESCERS
FLUORESCES
FLUORESCING
FLUORIDATE
FLUORIDATED
FLUORIDATES
FLUORIDATING
FLUORIDATION
FLUORIDATIONS
FLUORIDISE
FLUORIDISED
FLUORIDISES
FLUORIDISING
FLUORIDIZE
FLUORIDIZED
FLUORIDIZES
FLUORIDIZING
FLUORIMETER
FLUORIMETERS
FLUORIMETRIC
FLUORIMETRIES

FLUORIMETRY
FLUORINATE
FLUORINATED
FLUORINATES
FLUORINATING
FLUORINATION
FLUORINATIONS
FLUOROACETATE
FLUOROACETATES
FLUOROCARBON
FLUOROCARBONS
FLUOROCHROME
FLUOROCHROMES
FLUOROGRAPHIC
FLUOROGRAPHIES
FLUOROGRAPHY
FLUOROMETER
FLUOROMETERS
FLUOROMETRIC
FLUOROMETRIES
FLUOROMETRY
FLUOROPHORE
FLUOROPHORES
FLUOROSCOPE
FLUOROSCOPED
FLUOROSCOPES
FLUOROSCOPIC
FLUOROSCOPIES
FLUOROSCOPING
FLUOROSCOPIST
FLUOROSCOPISTS
FLUOROSCOPY
FLUOROTYPE
FLUOROTYPES
FLUOROURACIL
FLUOROURACILS
FLUORSPARS
FLUOXETINE
FLUOXETINES
FLUPHENAZINE
FLUPHENAZINES
FLUSHNESSES
FLUSHWORKS
FLUSTEREDLY
FLUSTERING
FLUSTERMENT
FLUSTERMENTS
FLUSTRATED
FLUSTRATES
FLUSTRATING
FLUSTRATION
FLUSTRATIONS
FLUTEMOUTH
FLUTEMOUTHS
FLUTTERBOARD
FLUTTERBOARDS
FLUTTERERS
FLUTTERING
FLUTTERINGLY

FLUVIALIST
FLUVIALISTS
FLUVIATILE
FLUVIOMARINE
FLUVOXAMINE
FLUVOXAMINES
FLUXIONALLY
FLUXIONARY
FLUXIONIST
FLUXIONISTS
FLUXMETERS
FLYBLOWING
FLYBRIDGES
FLYCATCHER
FLYCATCHERS
FLYPITCHER
FLYPITCHERS
FLYPITCHES
FLYPOSTING
FLYPOSTINGS
FLYRODDERS
FLYSCREENS
FLYSPECKED
FLYSPECKING
FLYSTRIKES
FLYSWATTER
FLYSWATTERS
FLYWEIGHTS
FOAMFLOWER
FOAMFLOWERS
FOAMINESSES
FOCALISATION
FOCALISATIONS
FOCALISING
FOCALIZATION
FOCALIZATIONS
FOCALIZING
FOCIMETERS
FOCOMETERS
FODDERINGS
FOEDERATUS
FOETATIONS
FOETICIDAL
FOETICIDES
FOETIDNESS
FOETIDNESSES
FOETIPAROUS
FOETOSCOPIES
FOETOSCOPY
FOGGINESSES
FOGRAMITES
FOGRAMITIES
FOISONLESS
FOLIACEOUS
FOLIATIONS
FOLIATURES
FOLKISHNESS
FOLKISHNESSES
FOLKLORISH

FOLKLORIST
FOLKLORISTIC
FOLKLORISTS
FOLKSINESS
FOLKSINESSES
FOLKSINGER
FOLKSINGERS
FOLKSINGING
FOLKSINGINGS
FOLLICULAR
FOLLICULATE
FOLLICULATED
FOLLICULIN
FOLLICULINS
FOLLICULITIS
FOLLICULITISES
FOLLICULOSE
FOLLICULOUS
FOLLOWABLE
FOLLOWERSHIP
FOLLOWERSHIPS
FOLLOWINGS
FOLLOWSHIP
FOLLOWSHIPS
FOMENTATION
FOMENTATIONS
FONCTIONNAIRE
FONCTIONNAIRES
FONDLINGLY
FONDNESSES
FONTANELLE
FONTANELLES
FONTICULUS
FONTICULUSES
FONTINALIS
FONTINALISES
FOODLESSNESS
FOODLESSNESSES
FOODSTUFFS
FOOLBEGGED
FOOLFISHES
FOOLHARDIER
FOOLHARDIEST
FOOLHARDILY
FOOLHARDINESS
FOOLHARDINESSES
FOOLHARDISE
FOOLHARDISES
FOOLHARDIZE
FOOLHARDIZES
FOOLISHEST
FOOLISHNESS
FOOLISHNESSES
FOOTBALLENE
FOOTBALLENES
FOOTBALLER
FOOTBALLERS
FOOTBALLING
FOOTBALLIST

FOOTBALLISTS
FOOTBOARDS
FOOTBREADTH
FOOTBREADTHS
FOOTBRIDGE
FOOTBRIDGES
FOOTCLOTHS
FOOTDRAGGER
FOOTDRAGGERS
FOOTFAULTED
FOOTFAULTING
FOOTFAULTS
FOOTGUARDS
FOOTLAMBERT
FOOTLAMBERTS
FOOTLESSLY
FOOTLESSNESS
FOOTLESSNESSES
FOOTLIGHTS
FOOTLOCKER
FOOTLOCKERS
FOOTNOTING
FOOTPLATEMAN
FOOTPLATEMEN
FOOTPLATES
FOOTPLATEWOMAN
FOOTPLATEWOMEN
FOOTPRINTS
FOOTSLOGGED
FOOTSLOGGER
FOOTSLOGGERS
FOOTSLOGGING
FOOTSLOGGINGS
FOOTSORENESS
FOOTSORENESSES
FOOTSTALKS
FOOTSTALLS
FOOTSTOCKS
FOOTSTONES
FOOTSTOOLED
FOOTSTOOLS
FOPPISHNESS
FOPPISHNESSES
FORAMINATED
FORAMINIFER
FORAMINIFERA
FORAMINIFERAL
FORAMINIFERAN
FORAMINIFERANS
FORAMINIFEROUS
FORAMINIFERS
FORAMINOUS
FORBEARANCE
FORBEARANCES
FORBEARANT
FORBEARERS
FORBEARING
FORBEARINGLY
FORBIDDALS

FORBIDDANCE
FORBIDDANCES
FORBIDDENLY
FORBIDDERS
FORBIDDING
FORBIDDINGLY
FORBIDDINGNESS
FORBIDDINGS
FORCEDNESS
FORCEDNESSES
FORCEFULLY
FORCEFULNESS
FORCEFULNESSES
FORCEMEATS
FORCEPSLIKE
FORCIBILITIES
FORCIBILITY
FORCIBLENESS
FORCIBLENESSES
FORCIPATED
FORCIPATION
FORCIPATIONS
FOREARMING
FOREBITTER
FOREBITTERS
FOREBODEMENT
FOREBODEMENTS
FOREBODERS
FOREBODIES
FOREBODING
FOREBODINGLY
FOREBODINGNESS
FOREBODINGS
FOREBRAINS
FORECABINS
FORECADDIE
FORECADDIES
FORECARRIAGE
FORECARRIAGES
FORECASTABLE
FORECASTED
FORECASTER
FORECASTERS
FORECASTING
FORECASTLE
FORECASTLES
FORECHECKED
FORECHECKER
FORECHECKERS
FORECHECKING
FORECHECKS
FORECHOSEN
FORECLOSABLE
FORECLOSED
FORECLOSES
FORECLOSING
FORECLOSURE
FORECLOSURES
FORECLOTHS

FORECOURSE	FOREMANSHIP	FORESHORTENINGS	FORETHINKS
FORECOURSES	FOREMANSHIPS	FORESHORTENS	FORETHOUGHT
FORECOURTS	FOREMASTMAN	FORESHOWED	FORETHOUGHTFUL
FOREDAMNED	FOREMASTMEN	FORESHOWING	FORETHOUGHTS
FOREDATING	FOREMEANING	FORESIGHTED	FORETOKENED
FOREDOOMED	FOREMENTIONED	FORESIGHTEDLY	FORETOKENING
FOREDOOMING	FOREMOTHER	FORESIGHTEDNESS	FORETOKENINGS
FOREFATHER	FOREMOTHERS	FORESIGHTFUL	FORETOKENS
FOREFATHERLY	FORENIGHTS	FORESIGHTLESS	FORETOPMAN
FOREFATHERS	FORENSICALITIES	FORESIGHTS	FORETOPMAST
FOREFEELING	FORENSICALITY	FORESIGNIFIED	FORETOPMASTS
FOREFEELINGLY	FORENSICALLY	FORESIGNIFIES	FORETOPMEN
FOREFENDED	FOREORDAIN	FORESIGNIFY	FORETRIANGLE
FOREFENDING	FOREORDAINED	FORESIGNIFYING	FORETRIANGLES
FOREFINGER	FOREORDAINING	FORESKIRTS	FOREVERMORE
FOREFINGERS	FOREORDAINMENT	FORESLACKED	FOREVERNESS
FOREFRONTS	FOREORDAINMENTS	FORESLACKING	FOREVERNESSES
FOREGATHER	FOREORDAINS	FORESLACKS	FOREVOUCHED
FOREGATHERED	FOREORDINATION	FORESLOWED	FOREWARNED
FOREGATHERING	FOREORDINATIONS	FORESLOWING	FOREWARNER
FOREGATHERS	FOREPASSED	FORESPEAKING	FOREWARNERS
FOREGLEAMS	FOREPAYMENT	FORESPEAKS	FOREWARNING
FOREGOINGS	FOREPAYMENTS	FORESPENDING	FOREWARNINGLY
FOREGONENESS	FOREPLANNED	FORESPENDS	FOREWARNINGS
FOREGONENESSES	FOREPLANNING	FORESPOKEN	FOREWEIGHED
FOREGROUND	FOREPOINTED	FORESTAGES	FOREWEIGHING
FOREGROUNDED	FOREPOINTING	FORESTAIRS	FOREWEIGHS
FOREGROUNDING	FOREPOINTS	FORESTALLED	FORFAIRING
FOREGROUNDS	FOREQUARTER	FORESTALLER	FORFAITERS
FOREHANDED	FOREQUARTERS	FORESTALLERS	FORFAITING
FOREHANDEDLY	FOREREACHED	FORESTALLING	FORFAITINGS
FOREHANDEDNESS	FOREREACHES	FORESTALLINGS	FORFEITABLE
FOREHANDING	FOREREACHING	FORESTALLMENT	FORFEITERS
FOREHENTING	FOREREADING	FORESTALLMENTS	FORFEITING
FOREHOOVES	FOREREADINGS	FORESTALLS	FORFEITURE
FOREIGNERS	FORERUNNER	FORESTALMENT	FORFEITURES
FOREIGNISM	FORERUNNERS	FORESTALMENTS	FORFENDING
FOREIGNISMS	FORERUNNING	FORESTATION	FORFEUCHEN
FOREIGNNESS	FORESAYING	FORESTATIONS	FORFICULATE
FOREIGNNESSES	FORESEEABILITY	FORESTAYSAIL	FORFOUGHEN
FOREJUDGED	FORESEEABLE	FORESTAYSAILS	FORFOUGHTEN
FOREJUDGEMENT	FORESEEING	FORESTLAND	FORGATHERED
FOREJUDGEMENTS	FORESEEINGLY	FORESTLANDS	FORGATHERING
FOREJUDGES	FORESHADOW	FORESTLESS	FORGATHERS
FOREJUDGING	FORESHADOWED	FORESTRIES	FORGEABILITIES
FOREJUDGMENT	FORESHADOWER	FORESWEARING	FORGEABILITY
FOREJUDGMENTS	FORESHADOWERS	FORESWEARS	FORGETFULLY
FOREKNOWABLE	FORESHADOWING	FORETASTED	FORGETFULNESS
FOREKNOWING	FORESHADOWINGS	FORETASTES	FORGETFULNESSES
FOREKNOWINGLY	FORESHADOWS	FORETASTING	FORGETTABLE
FOREKNOWLEDGE	FORESHANKS	FORETAUGHT	FORGETTERIES
FOREKNOWLEDGES	FORESHEETS	FORETEACHES	FORGETTERS
FORELADIES	FORESHEWED	FORETEACHING	FORGETTERY
FORELAYING	FORESHEWING	FORETELLER	FORGETTING
FORELENDING	FORESHOCKS	FORETELLERS	FORGETTINGLY
FORELIFTED	FORESHORES	FORETELLING	FORGETTINGS
FORELIFTING	FORESHORTEN	FORETHINKER	FORGIVABLE
FORELOCKED	FORESHORTENED	FORETHINKERS	FORGIVABLY
FORELOCKING	FORESHORTENING	FORETHINKING	FORGIVENESS

FORGIVENESSES
FORGIVINGLY
FORGIVINGNESS
FORGIVINGNESSES
FORGOTTENNESS
FORGOTTENNESSES
FORHAILING
FORHENTING
FORHOOIEING
FORINSECAL
FORISFAMILIATE
FORISFAMILIATED
FORISFAMILIATES
FORJUDGING
FORJUDGMENT
FORJUDGMENTS
FORKEDNESS
FORKEDNESSES
FORKINESSES
FORKLIFTED
FORKLIFTING
FORLENDING
FORLORNEST
FORLORNNESS
FORLORNNESSES
FORMABILITIES
FORMABILITY
FORMALDEHYDE
FORMALDEHYDES
FORMALISABLE
FORMALISATION
FORMALISATIONS
FORMALISED
FORMALISER
FORMALISERS
FORMALISES
FORMALISING
FORMALISMS
FORMALISTIC
FORMALISTICALLY
FORMALISTS
FORMALITER
FORMALITIES
FORMALIZABLE
FORMALIZATION
FORMALIZATIONS
FORMALIZED
FORMALIZER
FORMALIZERS
FORMALIZES
FORMALIZING
FORMALNESS
FORMALNESSES
FORMAMIDES
FORMATIONAL
FORMATIONS
FORMATIVELY
FORMATIVENESS
FORMATIVENESSES

FORMATIVES
FORMATTERS
FORMATTING
FORMFITTING
FORMICARIA
FORMICARIES
FORMICARIUM
FORMICATED
FORMICATES
FORMICATING
FORMICATION
FORMICATIONS
FORMIDABILITIES
FORMIDABILITY
FORMIDABLE
FORMIDABLENESS
FORMIDABLY
FORMLESSLY
FORMLESSNESS
FORMLESSNESSES
FORMULAICALLY
FORMULARIES
FORMULARISATION
FORMULARISE
FORMULARISED
FORMULARISER
FORMULARISERS
FORMULARISES
FORMULARISING
FORMULARISTIC
FORMULARIZATION
FORMULARIZE
FORMULARIZED
FORMULARIZER
FORMULARIZERS
FORMULARIZES
FORMULARIZING
FORMULATED
FORMULATES
FORMULATING
FORMULATION
FORMULATIONS
FORMULATOR
FORMULATORS
FORMULISED
FORMULISES
FORMULISING
FORMULISMS
FORMULISTIC
FORMULISTS
FORMULIZED
FORMULIZES
FORMULIZING
FORNICATED
FORNICATES
FORNICATING
FORNICATION
FORNICATIONS
FORNICATOR

FORNICATORS
FORNICATRESS
FORNICATRESSES
FORSAKENLY
FORSAKENNESS
FORSAKENNESSES
FORSAKINGS
FORSLACKED
FORSLACKING
FORSLOEING
FORSLOWING
FORSPEAKING
FORSPENDING
FORSTERITE
FORSTERITES
FORSWEARER
FORSWEARERS
FORSWEARING
FORSWINKED
FORSWINKING
FORSWORNNESS
FORSWORNNESSES
FORSYTHIAS
FORTALICES
FORTEPIANIST
FORTEPIANISTS
FORTEPIANO
FORTEPIANOS
FORTHCOMES
FORTHCOMING
FORTHCOMINGNESS
FORTHGOING
FORTHGOINGS
FORTHINKING
FORTHOUGHT
FORTHRIGHT
FORTHRIGHTLY
FORTHRIGHTNESS
FORTHRIGHTS
FORTIFIABLE
FORTIFICATION
FORTIFICATIONS
FORTIFIERS
FORTIFYING
FORTIFYINGLY
FORTILAGES
FORTISSIMI
FORTISSIMO
FORTISSIMOS
FORTISSISSIMO
FORTITUDES
FORTITUDINOUS
FORTNIGHTLIES
FORTNIGHTLY
FORTNIGHTS
FORTRESSED
FORTRESSES
FORTRESSING
FORTRESSLIKE

FORTUITIES
FORTUITISM
FORTUITISMS
FORTUITIST
FORTUITISTS
FORTUITOUS
FORTUITOUSLY
FORTUITOUSNESS
FORTUNATELY
FORTUNATENESS
FORTUNATENESSES
FORTUNATES
FORTUNELESS
FORTUNISED
FORTUNISES
FORTUNISING
FORTUNIZED
FORTUNIZES
FORTUNIZING
FORWANDERED
FORWANDERING
FORWANDERS
FORWARDERS
FORWARDEST
FORWARDING
FORWARDINGS
FORWARDNESS
FORWARDNESSES
FORWARNING
FORWASTING
FORWEARIED
FORWEARIES
FORWEARYING
FOSCARNETS
FOSSICKERS
FOSSICKING
FOSSICKINGS
FOSSILIFEROUS
FOSSILISABLE
FOSSILISATION
FOSSILISATIONS
FOSSILISED
FOSSILISES
FOSSILISING
FOSSILIZABLE
FOSSILIZATION
FOSSILIZATIONS
FOSSILIZED
FOSSILIZES
FOSSILIZING
FOSTERAGES
FOSTERINGLY
FOSTERINGS
FOSTERLING
FOSTERLINGS
FOSTRESSES
FOTHERGILLA
FOTHERGILLAS
FOUDROYANT

FOUGHTIEST	FRACTIONALISM	FRAGMENTING	FRANGIPANNI
FOULBROODS	FRACTIONALISMS	FRAGMENTISE	FRANKALMOIGN
FOULDERING	FRACTIONALIST	FRAGMENTISED	FRANKALMOIGNS
FOULMOUTHED	FRACTIONALISTS	FRAGMENTISES	FRANKFORTS
FOULNESSES	FRACTIONALIZE	FRAGMENTISING	FRANKFURTER
FOUNDATION	FRACTIONALIZED	FRAGMENTIZE	FRANKFURTERS
FOUNDATIONAL	FRACTIONALIZES	FRAGMENTIZED	FRANKFURTS
FOUNDATIONALLY	FRACTIONALIZING	FRAGMENTIZES	FRANKINCENSE
FOUNDATIONARY	FRACTIONALLY	FRAGMENTIZING	FRANKINCENSES
FOUNDATIONER	FRACTIONARY	FRAGRANCED	FRANKLINITE
FOUNDATIONERS	FRACTIONATE	FRAGRANCES	FRANKLINITES
FOUNDATIONLESS	FRACTIONATED	FRAGRANCIES	FRANKNESSES
FOUNDATIONS	FRACTIONATES	FRAGRANCING	FRANKPLEDGE
FOUNDERING	FRACTIONATING	FRAGRANTLY	FRANKPLEDGES
FOUNDEROUS	FRACTIONATION	FRAGRANTNESS	FRANSERIAS
FOUNDLINGS	FRACTIONATIONS	FRAGRANTNESSES	FRANTICALLY
FOUNDRESSES	FRACTIONATOR	FRAICHEURS	FRANTICNESS
FOUNTAINED	FRACTIONATORS	FRAILNESSES	FRANTICNESSES
FOUNTAINHEAD	FRACTIONED	FRAMBESIAS	FRATCHIEST
FOUNTAINHEADS	FRACTIONING	FRAMBOESIA	FRATERNALISM
FOUNTAINING	FRACTIONISATION	FRAMBOESIAS	FRATERNALISMS
FOUNTAINLESS	FRACTIONISE	FRAMBOISES	FRATERNALLY
FOURCHETTE	FRACTIONISED	FRAMESHIFT	FRATERNISATION
FOURCHETTES	FRACTIONISES	FRAMESHIFTS	FRATERNISATIONS
FOURDRINIER	FRACTIONISING	FRAMEWORKS	FRATERNISE
FOURDRINIERS	FRACTIONIZATION	FRANCHISED	FRATERNISED
FOURFOLDNESS	FRACTIONIZE	FRANCHISEE	FRATERNISER
FOURFOLDNESSES	FRACTIONIZED	FRANCHISEES	FRATERNISERS
FOURPENCES	FRACTIONIZES	FRANCHISEMENT	FRATERNISES
FOURPENNIES	FRACTIONIZING	FRANCHISEMENTS	FRATERNISING
FOURPLEXES	FRACTIONLET	FRANCHISER	FRATERNITIES
FOURRAGERE	FRACTIONLETS	FRANCHISERS	FRATERNITY
FOURRAGERES	FRACTIOUSLY	FRANCHISES	FRATERNIZATION
FOURSCORTH	FRACTIOUSNESS	FRANCHISING	FRATERNIZATIONS
FOURSQUARE	FRACTIOUSNESSES	FRANCHISOR	FRATERNIZE
FOURSQUARELY	FRACTOCUMULI	FRANCHISORS	FRATERNIZED
FOURSQUARENESS	FRACTOCUMULUS	FRANCISING	FRATERNIZER
FOURTEENER	FRACTOGRAPHIES	FRANCIZING	FRATERNIZERS
FOURTEENERS	FRACTOGRAPHY	FRANCOLINS	FRATERNIZES
FOURTEENTH	FRACTOSTRATI	FRANCOMANIA	FRATERNIZING
FOURTEENTHLY	FRACTOSTRATUS	FRANCOMANIAS	FRATRICIDAL
FOURTEENTHS	FRACTURABLE	FRANCOPHIL	FRATRICIDE
FOVEOLATED	FRACTURERS	FRANCOPHILE	FRATRICIDES
FOXBERRIES	FRACTURING	FRANCOPHILES	FRAUDFULLY
FOXHUNTERS	FRAGILENESS	FRANCOPHILS	FRAUDSTERS
FOXHUNTING	FRAGILENESSES	FRANCOPHOBE	FRAUDULENCE
FOXHUNTINGS	FRAGILITIES	FRANCOPHOBES	FRAUDULENCES
FOXINESSES	FRAGMENTAL	FRANCOPHOBIA	FRAUDULENCIES
FOXTROTTED	FRAGMENTALLY	FRANCOPHOBIAS	FRAUDULENCY
FOXTROTTING	FRAGMENTARILY	FRANCOPHONE	FRAUDULENT
FOZINESSES	FRAGMENTARINESS	FRANCOPHONES	FRAUDULENTLY
FRABJOUSLY	FRAGMENTARY	FRANGIBILITIES	FRAUDULENTNESS
FRACTALITIES	FRAGMENTATE	FRANGIBILITY	FRAUGHTAGE
FRACTALITY	FRAGMENTATED	FRANGIBLENESS	FRAUGHTAGES
FRACTIONAL	FRAGMENTATES	FRANGIBLENESSES	FRAUGHTEST
FRACTIONALISE	FRAGMENTATING	FRANGIPANE	FRAUGHTING
FRACTIONALISED	FRAGMENTATION	FRANGIPANES	FRAXINELLA
FRACTIONALISES	FRAGMENTATIONS	FRANGIPANI	FRAXINELLAS
FRACTIONALISING	FRAGMENTED	FRANGIPANIS	FREAKERIES

FREAKINESS
FREAKINESSES
FREAKISHLY
FREAKISHNESS
FREAKISHNESSES
FRECKLIEST
FRECKLINGS
FREEBASERS
FREEBASING
FREEBOARDS
FREEBOOTED
FREEBOOTER
FREEBOOTERIES
FREEBOOTERS
FREEBOOTERY
FREEBOOTIES
FREEBOOTING
FREEBOOTINGS
FREEDIVING
FREEDIVINGS
FREEDWOMAN
FREEDWOMEN
FREEHANDED
FREEHANDEDLY
FREEHANDEDNESS
FREEHEARTED
FREEHEARTEDLY
FREEHOLDER
FREEHOLDERS
FREELANCED
FREELANCER
FREELANCERS
FREELANCES
FREELANCING
FREELOADED
FREELOADER
FREELOADERS
FREELOADING
FREELOADINGS
FREEMARTIN
FREEMARTINS
FREEMASONIC
FREEMASONRIES
FREEMASONRY
FREEMASONS
FREENESSES
FREEPHONES
FREESHEETS
FREESTANDING
FREESTONES
FREESTYLER
FREESTYLERS
FREESTYLES
FREESTYLING
FREESTYLINGS
FREETHINKER
FREETHINKERS
FREETHINKING
FREETHINKINGS

FREEWHEELED
FREEWHEELER
FREEWHEELERS
FREEWHEELING
FREEWHEELINGLY
FREEWHEELINGS
FREEWHEELS
FREEWRITES
FREEWRITING
FREEWRITINGS
FREEWRITTEN
FREEZINGLY
FREIGHTAGE
FREIGHTAGES
FREIGHTERS
FREIGHTING
FREIGHTLESS
FREMESCENCE
FREMESCENCES
FREMESCENT
FREMITUSES
FRENCHIFICATION
FRENCHIFIED
FRENCHIFIES
FRENCHIFYING
FRENETICAL
FRENETICALLY
FRENETICISM
FRENETICISMS
FRENETICNESS
FRENETICNESSES
FRENZIEDLY
FREQUENCES
FREQUENCIES
FREQUENTABLE
FREQUENTATION
FREQUENTATIONS
FREQUENTATIVE
FREQUENTATIVES
FREQUENTED
FREQUENTER
FREQUENTERS
FREQUENTEST
FREQUENTING
FREQUENTLY
FREQUENTNESS
FREQUENTNESSES
FRESCOINGS
FRESCOISTS
FRESHENERS
FRESHENING
FRESHERDOM
FRESHERDOMS
FRESHMANSHIP
FRESHMANSHIPS
FRESHNESSES
FRESHWATER
FRESHWATERS
FRETBOARDS

FRETFULNESS
FRETFULNESSES
FRIABILITIES
FRIABILITY
FRIABLENESS
FRIABLENESSES
FRIARBIRDS
FRICANDEAU
FRICANDEAUS
FRICANDEAUX
FRICANDOES
FRICASSEED
FRICASSEEING
FRICASSEES
FRICATIVES
FRICTIONAL
FRICTIONALLY
FRICTIONLESS
FRICTIONLESSLY
FRIEDCAKES
FRIENDINGS
FRIENDLESS
FRIENDLESSNESS
FRIENDLIER
FRIENDLIES
FRIENDLIEST
FRIENDLILY
FRIENDLINESS
FRIENDLINESSES
FRIENDSHIP
FRIENDSHIPS
FRIEZELIKE
FRIGATOONS
FRIGHTENED
FRIGHTENER
FRIGHTENERS
FRIGHTENING
FRIGHTENINGLY
FRIGHTFULLY
FRIGHTFULNESS
FRIGHTFULNESSES
FRIGHTSOME
FRIGIDARIA
FRIGIDARIUM
FRIGIDITIES
FRIGIDNESS
FRIGIDNESSES
FRIGORIFIC
FRIGORIFICO
FRIGORIFICOS
FRIKKADELS
FRILLINESS
FRILLINESSES
FRINGELESS
FRINGILLACEOUS
FRINGILLID
FRINGILLIFORM
FRINGILLINE
FRIPONNERIE

FRIPONNERIES
FRIPPERERS
FRIPPERIES
FRISKINESS
FRISKINESSES
FRISKINGLY
FRITHBORHS
FRITHSOKEN
FRITHSOKENS
FRITHSTOOL
FRITHSTOOLS
FRITILLARIA
FRITILLARIAS
FRITILLARIES
FRITILLARY
FRITTERERS
FRITTERING
FRIVOLITIES
FRIVOLLERS
FRIVOLLING
FRIVOLOUSLY
FRIVOLOUSNESS
FRIVOLOUSNESSES
FRIZZINESS
FRIZZINESSES
FRIZZLIEST
FRIZZLINESS
FRIZZLINESSES
FROGFISHES
FROGGERIES
FROGHOPPER
FROGHOPPERS
FROGMARCHED
FROGMARCHES
FROGMARCHING
FROGMOUTHS
FROGSPAWNS
FROLICKERS
FROLICKING
FROLICSOME
FROLICSOMELY
FROLICSOMENESS
FROMENTIES
FRONDESCENCE
FRONDESCENCES
FRONDESCENT
FRONDIFEROUS
FRONTAGERS
FRONTALITIES
FRONTALITY
FRONTBENCHER
FRONTBENCHERS
FRONTCOURT
FRONTCOURTS
FRONTENISES
FRONTIERED
FRONTIERING
FRONTIERSMAN
FRONTIERSMEN

FRONTIERSWOMAN
FRONTIERSWOMEN
FRONTISPIECE
FRONTISPIECED
FRONTISPIECES
FRONTISPIECING
FRONTLESSLY
FRONTLINES
FRONTLISTS
FRONTOGENESES
FRONTOGENESIS
FRONTOGENETIC
FRONTOLYSES
FRONTOLYSIS
FRONTPAGED
FRONTPAGES
FRONTPAGING
FRONTRUNNER
FRONTRUNNERS
FRONTRUNNING
FRONTRUNNINGS
FRONTWARDS
FROSTBITES
FROSTBITING
FROSTBITINGS
FROSTBITTEN
FROSTBOUND
FROSTFISHES
FROSTINESS
FROSTINESSES
FROSTLINES
FROSTWORKS
FROTHERIES
FROTHINESS
FROTHINESSES
FROUGHIEST
FROUZINESS
FROUZINESSES
FROWARDNESS
FROWARDNESSES
FROWNINGLY
FROWSINESS
FROWSINESSES
FROWSTIEST
FROWSTINESS
FROWSTINESSES
FROWZINESS
FROWZINESSES
FROZENNESS
FROZENNESSES
FRUCTIFEROUS
FRUCTIFEROUSLY
FRUCTIFICATION
FRUCTIFICATIONS
FRUCTIFIED
FRUCTIFIER
FRUCTIFIERS
FRUCTIFIES
FRUCTIFYING

FRUCTIVOROUS
FRUCTUARIES
FRUCTUATED
FRUCTUATES
FRUCTUATING
FRUCTUATION
FRUCTUATIONS
FRUCTUOUSLY
FRUCTUOUSNESS
FRUCTUOUSNESSES
FRUGALISTS
FRUGALITIES
FRUGALNESS
FRUGALNESSES
FRUGIFEROUS
FRUGIVORES
FRUGIVOROUS
FRUITARIAN
FRUITARIANISM
FRUITARIANISMS
FRUITARIANS
FRUITCAKES
FRUITERERS
FRUITERESS
FRUITERESSES
FRUITERIES
FRUITFULLER
FRUITFULLEST
FRUITFULLY
FRUITFULNESS
FRUITFULNESSES
FRUITINESS
FRUITINESSES
FRUITLESSLY
FRUITLESSNESS
FRUITLESSNESSES
FRUITWOODS
FRUMENTACEOUS
FRUMENTARIOUS
FRUMENTATION
FRUMENTATIONS
FRUMENTIES
FRUMPINESS
FRUMPINESSES
FRUMPISHLY
FRUMPISHNESS
FRUMPISHNESSES
FRUSEMIDES
FRUSTRATED
FRUSTRATER
FRUSTRATERS
FRUSTRATES
FRUSTRATING
FRUSTRATINGLY
FRUSTRATION
FRUSTRATIONS
FRUTESCENCE
FRUTESCENCES
FRUTESCENT

FRUTIFYING
FUCIVOROUS
FUCOXANTHIN
FUCOXANTHINS
FUGACIOUSLY
FUGACIOUSNESS
FUGACIOUSNESSES
FUGACITIES
FUGITATION
FUGITATIONS
FUGITIVELY
FUGITIVENESS
FUGITIVENESSES
FUGITOMETER
FUGITOMETERS
FULFILLERS
FULFILLING
FULFILLINGS
FULFILLMENT
FULFILLMENTS
FULFILMENT
FULFILMENTS
FULGENCIES
FULGURATED
FULGURATES
FULGURATING
FULGURATION
FULGURATIONS
FULGURITES
FULIGINOSITIES
FULIGINOSITY
FULIGINOUS
FULIGINOUSLY
FULIGINOUSNESS
FULLBLOODS
FULLERENES
FULLERIDES
FULLERITES
FULLMOUTHED
FULLNESSES
FULMINANTS
FULMINATED
FULMINATES
FULMINATING
FULMINATION
FULMINATIONS
FULMINATOR
FULMINATORS
FULMINATORY
FULMINEOUS
FULSOMENESS
FULSOMENESSES
FUMATORIES
FUMATORIUM
FUMATORIUMS
FUMBLINGLY
FUMBLINGNESS
FUMBLINGNESSES
FUMIGATING

FUMIGATION
FUMIGATIONS
FUMIGATORS
FUMIGATORY
FUMITORIES
FUMOSITIES
FUNAMBULATE
FUNAMBULATED
FUNAMBULATES
FUNAMBULATING
FUNAMBULATION
FUNAMBULATIONS
FUNAMBULATOR
FUNAMBULATORS
FUNAMBULATORY
FUNAMBULISM
FUNAMBULISMS
FUNAMBULIST
FUNAMBULISTS
FUNCTIONAL
FUNCTIONALISM
FUNCTIONALISMS
FUNCTIONALIST
FUNCTIONALISTIC
FUNCTIONALISTS
FUNCTIONALITIES
FUNCTIONALITY
FUNCTIONALLY
FUNCTIONALS
FUNCTIONARIES
FUNCTIONARY
FUNCTIONATE
FUNCTIONATED
FUNCTIONATES
FUNCTIONATING
FUNCTIONED
FUNCTIONING
FUNCTIONLESS
FUNDAMENTAL
FUNDAMENTALISM
FUNDAMENTALISMS
FUNDAMENTALIST
FUNDAMENTALISTS
FUNDAMENTALITY
FUNDAMENTALLY
FUNDAMENTALNESS
FUNDAMENTALS
FUNDAMENTS
FUNDHOLDER
FUNDHOLDERS
FUNDHOLDING
FUNDRAISED
FUNDRAISER
FUNDRAISERS
FUNDRAISES
FUNDRAISING
FUNEREALLY
FUNGIBILITIES
FUNGIBILITY

FUNGICIDAL
FUNGICIDALLY
FUNGICIDES
FUNGISTATIC
FUNGISTATICALLY
FUNGISTATS
FUNGOSITIES
FUNICULARS
FUNICULATE
FUNKINESSES
FUNNELFORM
FUNNELLING
FUNNINESSES
FURACIOUSNESS
FURACIOUSNESSES
FURACITIES
FURALDEHYDE
FURALDEHYDES
FURANOSIDE
FURANOSIDES
FURAZOLIDONE
FURAZOLIDONES
FURBEARERS
FURBELOWED
FURBELOWING
FURBISHERS
FURBISHING
FURCATIONS
FURCIFEROUS
FURFURACEOUS
FURFURACEOUSLY
FURFURALDEHYDE
FURFURALDEHYDES
FURFUROLES
FURIOSITIES
FURIOUSNESS
FURIOUSNESSES
FURLOUGHED
FURLOUGHING
FURMENTIES
FURNIMENTS
FURNISHERS
FURNISHING
FURNISHINGS
FURNISHMENT
FURNISHMENTS
FURNITURES
FUROSEMIDE
FUROSEMIDES
FURRIERIES
FURRINESSES
FURROWLESS
FURSHLUGGINER
FURTHCOMING
FURTHCOMINGS
FURTHERANCE
FURTHERANCES
FURTHERERS
FURTHERING

FURTHERMORE
FURTHERMOST
FURTHERSOME
FURTIVENESS
FURTIVENESSES
FURUNCULAR
FURUNCULOSES
FURUNCULOSIS
FURUNCULOUS
FUSHIONLESS
FUSIBILITIES
FUSIBILITY
FUSIBLENESS
FUSIBLENESSES
FUSILLADED
FUSILLADES
FUSILLADING
FUSILLATION
FUSILLATIONS
FUSIONISMS
FUSIONISTS
FUSIONLESS
FUSSBUDGET
FUSSBUDGETS
FUSSBUDGETY
FUSSINESSES
FUSTANELLA
FUSTANELLAS
FUSTANELLE
FUSTANELLES
FUSTIANISE
FUSTIANISED
FUSTIANISES
FUSTIANISING
FUSTIANIST
FUSTIANISTS
FUSTIANIZE
FUSTIANIZED
FUSTIANIZES
FUSTIANIZING
FUSTIGATED
FUSTIGATES
FUSTIGATING
FUSTIGATION
FUSTIGATIONS
FUSTIGATOR
FUSTIGATORS
FUSTIGATORY
FUSTILARIAN
FUSTILARIANS
FUSTILIRIAN
FUSTILIRIANS
FUSTILLIRIAN
FUSTILLIRIANS
FUSTINESSES
FUSULINIDS
FUTILENESS
FUTILENESSES
FUTILITARIAN

FUTILITARIANISM
FUTILITARIANS
FUTILITIES
FUTURELESS
FUTURELESSNESS
FUTURISTIC
FUTURISTICALLY
FUTURISTICS
FUTURITIES
FUTURITION
FUTURITIONS
FUTUROLOGICAL
FUTUROLOGIES
FUTUROLOGIST
FUTUROLOGISTS
FUTUROLOGY
FUZZINESSES

G

GABAPENTIN
GABAPENTINS
GABARDINES
GABBINESSES
GABBLEMENT
GABBLEMENTS
GABBROITIC
GABERDINES
GABERLUNZIE
GABERLUNZIES
GABIONADES
GABIONAGES
GABIONNADE
GABIONNADES
GADGETEERS
GADGETRIES
GADOLINITE
GADOLINITES
GADOLINIUM
GADOLINIUMS
GADROONING
GADROONINGS
GADZOOKERIES
GADZOOKERY
GAELICISED
GAELICISES
GAELICISING
GAELICISMS
GAELICIZED
GAELICIZES
GAELICIZING
GAILLARDIA
GAILLARDIAS
GAINFULNESS
GAINFULNESSES
GAINGIVING
GAINGIVINGS
GAINLESSNESS
GAINLESSNESSES
GAINLINESS
GAINLINESSES
GAINSAYERS
GAINSAYING
GAINSAYINGS
GAINSTRIVE
GAINSTRIVED
GAINSTRIVEN
GAINSTRIVES
GAINSTRIVING
GAINSTROVE
GAITERLESS
GALABIYAHS
GALACTAGOGUE

GALACTAGOGUES
GALACTOMETER
GALACTOMETERS
GALACTOMETRIES
GALACTOMETRY
GALACTOPHOROUS
GALACTOPOIESES
GALACTOPOIESIS
GALACTOPOIETIC
GALACTOPOIETICS
GALACTORRHEA
GALACTORRHEAS
GALACTORRHOEA
GALACTORRHOEAS
GALACTOSAEMIA
GALACTOSAEMIAS
GALACTOSAMINE
GALACTOSAMINES
GALACTOSEMIA
GALACTOSEMIAS
GALACTOSEMIC
GALACTOSES
GALACTOSIDASE
GALACTOSIDASES
GALACTOSIDE
GALACTOSIDES
GALACTOSYL
GALACTOSYLS
GALANTAMINE
GALANTAMINES
GALANTINES
GALAVANTED
GALAVANTING
GALDRAGONS
GALENGALES
GALENICALS
GALEOPITHECINE
GALEOPITHECOID
GALIMATIAS
GALIMATIASES
GALINGALES
GALIONGEES
GALIVANTED
GALIVANTING
GALLABEAHS
GALLABIAHS
GALLABIEHS
GALLABIYAH
GALLABIYAHS
GALLABIYAS
GALLABIYEH
GALLABIYEHS
GALLAMINES

GALLANTEST
GALLANTING
GALLANTNESS
GALLANTNESSES
GALLANTRIES
GALLBLADDER
GALLBLADDERS
GALLEASSES
GALLERISTS
GALLERYGOER
GALLERYGOERS
GALLERYING
GALLERYITE
GALLERYITES
GALLIAMBIC
GALLIAMBICS
GALLIARDISE
GALLIARDISES
GALLIASSES
GALLICISATION
GALLICISATIONS
GALLICISED
GALLICISES
GALLICISING
GALLICISMS
GALLICIZATION
GALLICIZATIONS
GALLICIZED
GALLICIZES
GALLICIZING
GALLIGASKINS
GALLIMAUFRIES
GALLIMAUFRY
GALLINACEAN
GALLINACEANS
GALLINACEOUS
GALLINAZOS
GALLINIPPER
GALLINIPPERS
GALLINULES
GALLISISED
GALLISISES
GALLISISING
GALLISIZED
GALLISIZES
GALLISIZING
GALLIVANTED
GALLIVANTING
GALLIVANTS
GALLIWASPS
GALLOGLASS
GALLOGLASSES
GALLONAGES

GALLOPADED
GALLOPADES
GALLOPADING
GALLOWGLASS
GALLOWGLASSES
GALLOWSNESS
GALLOWSNESSES
GALLSICKNESS
GALLSICKNESSES
GALLSTONES
GALLUMPHED
GALLUMPHING
GALLYGASKINS
GALRAVAGED
GALRAVAGES
GALRAVAGING
GALRAVITCH
GALRAVITCHED
GALRAVITCHES
GALRAVITCHING
GALUMPHERS
GALUMPHING
GALVANICAL
GALVANICALLY
GALVANISATION
GALVANISATIONS
GALVANISED
GALVANISER
GALVANISERS
GALVANISES
GALVANISING
GALVANISMS
GALVANISTS
GALVANIZATION
GALVANIZATIONS
GALVANIZED
GALVANIZER
GALVANIZERS
GALVANIZES
GALVANIZING
GALVANOMETER
GALVANOMETERS
GALVANOMETRIC
GALVANOMETRICAL
GALVANOMETRIES
GALVANOMETRY
GALVANOPLASTIC
GALVANOPLASTIES
GALVANOPLASTY
GALVANOSCOPE
GALVANOSCOPES
GALVANOSCOPIC
GALVANOSCOPIES

GALVANOSCOPY

GALVANOSCOPY
GALVANOTROPIC
GALVANOTROPISM
GALVANOTROPISMS
GAMAHUCHED
GAMAHUCHES
GAMAHUCHING
GAMARUCHED
GAMARUCHES
GAMARUCHING
GAMBADOING
GAMBOLLING
GAMEBREAKER
GAMEBREAKERS
GAMEKEEPER
GAMEKEEPERS
GAMEKEEPING
GAMEKEEPINGS
GAMENESSES
GAMESMANSHIP
GAMESMANSHIPS
GAMESOMELY
GAMESOMENESS
GAMESOMENESSES
GAMETANGIA
GAMETANGIAL
GAMETANGIUM
GAMETICALLY
GAMETOCYTE
GAMETOCYTES
GAMETOGENESES
GAMETOGENESIS
GAMETOGENIC
GAMETOGENIES
GAMETOGENOUS
GAMETOGENY
GAMETOPHORE
GAMETOPHORES
GAMETOPHORIC
GAMETOPHYTE
GAMETOPHYTES
GAMETOPHYTIC
GAMINERIES
GAMINESQUE
GAMINESSES
GAMMERSTANG
GAMMERSTANGS
GAMMOCKING
GAMMONINGS
GAMOGENESES
GAMOGENESIS
GAMOGENETIC
GAMOGENETICAL
GAMOGENETICALLY
GAMOPETALOUS
GAMOPHYLLOUS
GAMOSEPALOUS
GAMOTROPIC
GAMOTROPISM

GAMOTROPISMS
GAMYNESSES
GANDERISMS
GANGBANGED
GANGBANGER
GANGBANGERS
GANGBANGING
GANGBOARDS
GANGBUSTER
GANGBUSTERS
GANGBUSTING
GANGBUSTINGS
GANGLIATED
GANGLIFORM
GANGLIONATED
GANGLIONIC
GANGLIOSIDE
GANGLIOSIDES
GANGPLANKS
GANGRENING
GANGRENOUS
GANGSHAGGED
GANGSHAGGING
GANGSTERDOM
GANGSTERDOMS
GANGSTERISH
GANGSTERISM
GANGSTERISMS
GANGSTERLAND
GANGSTERLANDS
GANNETRIES
GANNISTERS
GANTELOPES
GANTLETING
GAOLBREAKS
GAOLERESSES
GARAGISTES
GARBAGEMAN
GARBAGEMEN
GARBOLOGIES
GARBOLOGIST
GARBOLOGISTS
GARDENFULS
GARDENINGS
GARDENLESS
GARDEROBES
GARGANTUAN
GARGANTUAS
GARGARISED
GARGARISES
GARGARISING
GARGARISMS
GARGARIZED
GARGARIZES
GARGARIZING
GARGOYLISM
GARGOYLISMS
GARIBALDIS
GARISHNESS

GARISHNESSES
GARLANDAGE
GARLANDAGES
GARLANDING
GARLANDLESS
GARLANDRIES
GARLICKIER
GARLICKIEST
GARLICKING
GARMENTING
GARMENTLESS
GARMENTURE
GARMENTURES
GARNETIFEROUS
GARNIERITE
GARNIERITES
GARNISHEED
GARNISHEEING
GARNISHEEMENT
GARNISHEEMENTS
GARNISHEES
GARNISHERS
GARNISHING
GARNISHINGS
GARNISHMENT
GARNISHMENTS
GARNISHRIES
GARNITURES
GAROTTINGS
GARRETEERS
GARRISONED
GARRISONING
GARROTTERS
GARROTTING
GARROTTINGS
GARRULITIES
GARRULOUSLY
GARRULOUSNESS
GARRULOUSNESSES
GARRYOWENS
GASBAGGING
GASCONADED
GASCONADER
GASCONADERS
GASCONADES
GASCONADING
GASCONISMS
GASEOUSNESS
GASEOUSNESSES
GASHLINESS
GASHLINESSES
GASHOLDERS
GASIFIABLE
GASIFICATION
GASIFICATIONS
GASOMETERS
GASOMETRIC
GASOMETRICAL
GASOMETRIES

GASPEREAUS
GASPEREAUX
GASPINESSES
GASSINESSES
GASTEROPOD
GASTEROPODOUS
GASTEROPODS
GASTIGHTNESS
GASTIGHTNESSES
GASTNESSES
GASTRAEUMS
GASTRALGIA
GASTRALGIAS
GASTRALGIC
GASTRECTOMIES
GASTRECTOMY
GASTRITIDES
GASTRITISES
GASTROCNEMII
GASTROCNEMIUS
GASTROCOLIC
GASTRODUODENAL
GASTROENTERIC
GASTROENTERITIC
GASTROENTERITIS
GASTROLITH
GASTROLITHS
GASTROLOGER
GASTROLOGERS
GASTROLOGICAL
GASTROLOGIES
GASTROLOGIST
GASTROLOGISTS
GASTROLOGY
GASTROMANCIES
GASTROMANCY
GASTRONOME
GASTRONOMER
GASTRONOMERS
GASTRONOMES
GASTRONOMIC
GASTRONOMICAL
GASTRONOMICALLY
GASTRONOMIES
GASTRONOMIST
GASTRONOMISTS
GASTRONOMY
GASTROPODAN
GASTROPODANS
GASTROPODOUS
GASTROPODS
GASTROSCOPE
GASTROSCOPES
GASTROSCOPIC
GASTROSCOPIES
GASTROSCOPIST
GASTROSCOPISTS
GASTROSCOPY
GASTROSOPH

GASTROSOPHER
GASTROSOPHERS
GASTROSOPHIES
GASTROSOPHS
GASTROSOPHY
GASTROSTOMIES
GASTROSTOMY
GASTROTOMIES
GASTROTOMY
GASTROTRICH
GASTROTRICHS
GASTROVASCULAR
GASTRULATE
GASTRULATED
GASTRULATES
GASTRULATING
GASTRULATION
GASTRULATIONS
GATECRASHED
GATECRASHER
GATECRASHERS
GATECRASHES
GATECRASHING
GATEHOUSES
GATEKEEPER
GATEKEEPERS
GATEKEEPING
GATHERABLE
GATHERINGS
GAUCHENESS
GAUCHENESSES
GAUCHERIES
GAUDEAMUSES
GAUDINESSES
GAUFFERING
GAUFFERINGS
GAULEITERS
GAULTHERIA
GAULTHERIAS
GAUNTLETED
GAUNTLETING
GAUNTNESSES
GAUSSMETER
GAUSSMETERS
GAUZINESSES
GAVELKINDS
GAWKIHOODS
GAWKINESSES
GAWKISHNESS
GAWKISHNESSES
GAZEHOUNDS
GAZETTEERED
GAZETTEERING
GAZETTEERISH
GAZETTEERS
GAZILLIONAIRE
GAZILLIONAIRES
GAZILLIONS
GAZUNDERED

GAZUNDERER
GAZUNDERERS
GAZUNDERING
GEALOUSIES
GEANTICLINAL
GEANTICLINE
GEANTICLINES
GEARCHANGE
GEARCHANGES
GEARSHIFTS
GEARWHEELS
GEEKINESSES
GEEKSPEAKS
GEFUFFLING
GEGENSCHEIN
GEGENSCHEINS
GEHLENITES
GEITONOGAMIES
GEITONOGAMOUS
GEITONOGAMY
GELANDESPRUNG
GELANDESPRUNGS
GELATINATE
GELATINATED
GELATINATES
GELATINATING
GELATINATION
GELATINATIONS
GELATINISATION
GELATINISATIONS
GELATINISE
GELATINISED
GELATINISER
GELATINISERS
GELATINISES
GELATINISING
GELATINIZATION
GELATINIZATIONS
GELATINIZE
GELATINIZED
GELATINIZER
GELATINIZERS
GELATINIZES
GELATINIZING
GELATINOID
GELATINOIDS
GELATINOUS
GELATINOUSLY
GELATINOUSNESS
GELIDITIES
GELIDNESSES
GELIGNITES
GELLIFLOWRE
GELLIFLOWRES
GELSEMINES
GELSEMININE
GELSEMININES
GELSEMIUMS
GEMEINSCHAFT

GEMEINSCHAFTEN
GEMEINSCHAFTS
GEMFIBROZIL
GEMFIBROZILS
GEMINATELY
GEMINATING
GEMINATION
GEMINATIONS
GEMMACEOUS
GEMMATIONS
GEMMIFEROUS
GEMMINESSES
GEMMIPAROUS
GEMMIPAROUSLY
GEMMOLOGICAL
GEMMOLOGIES
GEMMOLOGIST
GEMMOLOGISTS
GEMMULATION
GEMMULATIONS
GEMOLOGICAL
GEMOLOGIES
GEMOLOGIST
GEMOLOGISTS
GEMUTLICHKEIT
GEMUTLICHKEITS
GENDARMERIE
GENDARMERIES
GENDARMERY
GENDERISED
GENDERISES
GENDERISING
GENDERIZED
GENDERIZES
GENDERIZING
GENDERLESS
GENEALOGIC
GENEALOGICAL
GENEALOGICALLY
GENEALOGIES
GENEALOGISE
GENEALOGISED
GENEALOGISES
GENEALOGISING
GENEALOGIST
GENEALOGISTS
GENEALOGIZE
GENEALOGIZED
GENEALOGIZES
GENEALOGIZING
GENECOLOGIES
GENECOLOGY
GENERALATE
GENERALATES
GENERALCIES
GENERALISABLE
GENERALISATION
GENERALISATIONS
GENERALISE

GENERALISED
GENERALISER
GENERALISERS
GENERALISES
GENERALISING
GENERALISSIMO
GENERALISSIMOS
GENERALIST
GENERALISTS
GENERALITIES
GENERALITY
GENERALIZABLE
GENERALIZATION
GENERALIZATIONS
GENERALIZE
GENERALIZED
GENERALIZER
GENERALIZERS
GENERALIZES
GENERALIZING
GENERALLED
GENERALLING
GENERALNESS
GENERALNESSES
GENERALSHIP
GENERALSHIPS
GENERATING
GENERATION
GENERATIONAL
GENERATIONALLY
GENERATIONISM
GENERATIONISMS
GENERATIONS
GENERATIVE
GENERATORS
GENERATRICES
GENERATRIX
GENERICALLY
GENERICNESS
GENERICNESSES
GENEROSITIES
GENEROSITY
GENEROUSLY
GENEROUSNESS
GENEROUSNESSES
GENETHLIAC
GENETHLIACAL
GENETHLIACALLY
GENETHLIACON
GENETHLIACONS
GENETHLIACS
GENETHLIALOGIC
GENETHLIALOGIES
GENETHLIALOGY
GENETICALLY
GENETICIST
GENETICISTS
GENETOTROPHIC
GENETRICES

GENETRIXES
GENEVRETTE
GENEVRETTES
GENIALISED
GENIALISES
GENIALISING
GENIALITIES
GENIALIZED
GENIALIZES
GENIALIZING
GENIALNESS
GENIALNESSES
GENICULATE
GENICULATED
GENICULATELY
GENICULATES
GENICULATING
GENICULATION
GENICULATIONS
GENISTEINS
GENITALIAL
GENITIVALLY
GENITIVELY
GENITOURINARY
GENITRICES
GENITRIXES
GENOPHOBIA
GENOPHOBIAS
GENOTYPICAL
GENOTYPICALLY
GENOTYPICITIES
GENOTYPICITY
GENOUILLERE
GENOUILLERES
GENSDARMES
GENTAMICIN
GENTAMICINS
GENTEELEST
GENTEELISE
GENTEELISED
GENTEELISES
GENTEELISH
GENTEELISING
GENTEELISM
GENTEELISMS
GENTEELIZE
GENTEELIZED
GENTEELIZES
GENTEELIZING
GENTEELNESS
GENTEELNESSES
GENTIANACEOUS
GENTIANELLA
GENTIANELLAS
GENTILESSE
GENTILESSES
GENTILHOMME
GENTILISED
GENTILISES

GENTILISING
GENTILISMS
GENTILITIAL
GENTILITIAN
GENTILITIES
GENTILITIOUS
GENTILIZED
GENTILIZES
GENTILIZING
GENTILSHOMMES
GENTLEFOLK
GENTLEFOLKS
GENTLEHOOD
GENTLEHOODS
GENTLEMANHOOD
GENTLEMANHOODS
GENTLEMANLIKE
GENTLEMANLINESS
GENTLEMANLY
GENTLEMANSHIP
GENTLEMANSHIPS
GENTLENESS
GENTLENESSE
GENTLENESSES
GENTLEPERSON
GENTLEPERSONS
GENTLEWOMAN
GENTLEWOMANLY
GENTLEWOMEN
GENTRIFICATION
GENTRIFICATIONS
GENTRIFIED
GENTRIFIER
GENTRIFIERS
GENTRIFIES
GENTRIFYING
GENUFLECTED
GENUFLECTING
GENUFLECTION
GENUFLECTIONS
GENUFLECTOR
GENUFLECTORS
GENUFLECTS
GENUFLEXION
GENUFLEXIONS
GENUINENESS
GENUINENESSES
GEOBOTANIC
GEOBOTANICAL
GEOBOTANIES
GEOBOTANIST
GEOBOTANISTS
GEOCACHING
GEOCACHINGS
GEOCARPIES
GEOCENTRIC
GEOCENTRICAL
GEOCENTRICALLY
GEOCENTRICISM

GEOCENTRICISMS
GEOCHEMICAL
GEOCHEMICALLY
GEOCHEMIST
GEOCHEMISTRIES
GEOCHEMISTRY
GEOCHEMISTS
GEOCHRONOLOGIC
GEOCHRONOLOGIES
GEOCHRONOLOGIST
GEOCHRONOLOGY
GEOCORONAE
GEOCORONAS
GEODEMOGRAPHICS
GEODESICAL
GEODESISTS
GEODETICAL
GEODETICALLY
GEODYNAMIC
GEODYNAMICAL
GEODYNAMICIST
GEODYNAMICISTS
GEODYNAMICS
GEOGNOSIES
GEOGNOSTIC
GEOGNOSTICAL
GEOGNOSTICALLY
GEOGRAPHER
GEOGRAPHERS
GEOGRAPHIC
GEOGRAPHICAL
GEOGRAPHICALLY
GEOGRAPHIES
GEOHYDROLOGIC
GEOHYDROLOGIES
GEOHYDROLOGIST
GEOHYDROLOGISTS
GEOHYDROLOGY
GEOLATRIES
GEOLINGUISTICS
GEOLOGIANS
GEOLOGICAL
GEOLOGICALLY
GEOLOGISED
GEOLOGISES
GEOLOGISING
GEOLOGISTS
GEOLOGIZED
GEOLOGIZES
GEOLOGIZING
GEOMAGNETIC
GEOMAGNETICALLY
GEOMAGNETISM
GEOMAGNETISMS
GEOMAGNETIST
GEOMAGNETISTS
GEOMANCERS
GEOMANCIES
GEOMECHANICS

GEOMEDICAL
GEOMEDICINE
GEOMEDICINES
GEOMETRICAL
GEOMETRICALLY
GEOMETRICIAN
GEOMETRICIANS
GEOMETRICS
GEOMETRIDS
GEOMETRIES
GEOMETRISATION
GEOMETRISATIONS
GEOMETRISE
GEOMETRISED
GEOMETRISES
GEOMETRISING
GEOMETRIST
GEOMETRISTS
GEOMETRIZATION
GEOMETRIZATIONS
GEOMETRIZE
GEOMETRIZED
GEOMETRIZES
GEOMETRIZING
GEOMORPHIC
GEOMORPHOGENIC
GEOMORPHOGENIES
GEOMORPHOGENIST
GEOMORPHOGENY
GEOMORPHOLOGIC
GEOMORPHOLOGIES
GEOMORPHOLOGIST
GEOMORPHOLOGY
GEOPHAGIAS
GEOPHAGIES
GEOPHAGISM
GEOPHAGISMS
GEOPHAGIST
GEOPHAGISTS
GEOPHAGOUS
GEOPHILOUS
GEOPHYSICAL
GEOPHYSICALLY
GEOPHYSICIST
GEOPHYSICISTS
GEOPHYSICS
GEOPOLITICAL
GEOPOLITICALLY
GEOPOLITICIAN
GEOPOLITICIANS
GEOPOLITICS
GEOPONICAL
GEOPRESSURED
GEORGETTES
GEOSCIENCE
GEOSCIENCES
GEOSCIENTIFIC
GEOSCIENTIST
GEOSCIENTISTS

GEOSPHERES
GEOSTATICS
GEOSTATIONARY
GEOSTRATEGIC
GEOSTRATEGICAL
GEOSTRATEGIES
GEOSTRATEGIST
GEOSTRATEGISTS
GEOSTRATEGY
GEOSTROPHIC
GEOSTROPHICALLY
GEOSYNCHRONOUS
GEOSYNCLINAL
GEOSYNCLINE
GEOSYNCLINES
GEOTACTICAL
GEOTACTICALLY
GEOTECHNIC
GEOTECHNICAL
GEOTECHNICS
GEOTECHNOLOGIES
GEOTECHNOLOGY
GEOTECTONIC
GEOTECTONICALLY
GEOTECTONICS
GEOTEXTILE
GEOTEXTILES
GEOTHERMAL
GEOTHERMALLY
GEOTHERMIC
GEOTHERMOMETER
GEOTHERMOMETERS
GEOTROPICALLY
GEOTROPISM
GEOTROPISMS
GERANIACEOUS
GERATOLOGICAL
GERATOLOGIES
GERATOLOGIST
GERATOLOGISTS
GERATOLOGY
GERFALCONS
GERIATRICIAN
GERIATRICIANS
GERIATRICS
GERIATRIST
GERIATRISTS
GERMANDERS
GERMANENESS
GERMANENESSES
GERMANISATION
GERMANISATIONS
GERMANISED
GERMANISES
GERMANISING
GERMANITES
GERMANIUMS
GERMANIZATION
GERMANIZATIONS

GERMANIZED
GERMANIZES
GERMANIZING
GERMICIDAL
GERMICIDES
GERMINABILITIES
GERMINABILITY
GERMINABLE
GERMINALLY
GERMINATED
GERMINATES
GERMINATING
GERMINATION
GERMINATIONS
GERMINATIVE
GERMINATOR
GERMINATORS
GERMINESSES
GERMPLASMS
GERONTOCRACIES
GERONTOCRACY
GERONTOCRAT
GERONTOCRATIC
GERONTOCRATS
GERONTOLOGIC
GERONTOLOGICAL
GERONTOLOGIES
GERONTOLOGIST
GERONTOLOGISTS
GERONTOLOGY
GERONTOMORPHIC
GERONTOPHIL
GERONTOPHILE
GERONTOPHILES
GERONTOPHILIA
GERONTOPHILIAS
GERONTOPHILS
GERONTOPHOBE
GERONTOPHOBES
GERONTOPHOBIA
GERONTOPHOBIAS
GERRYMANDER
GERRYMANDERED
GERRYMANDERER
GERRYMANDERERS
GERRYMANDERING
GERRYMANDERINGS
GERRYMANDERS
GERUNDIVAL
GERUNDIVELY
GERUNDIVES
GESELLSCHAFT
GESELLSCHAFTEN
GESELLSCHAFTS
GESNERIADS
GESSAMINES
GESTALTISM
GESTALTISMS
GESTALTIST

GESTALTISTS
GESTATIONAL
GESTATIONS
GESTATORIAL
GESTICULANT
GESTICULATE
GESTICULATED
GESTICULATES
GESTICULATING
GESTICULATION
GESTICULATIONS
GESTICULATIVE
GESTICULATOR
GESTICULATORS
GESTICULATORY
GESTURALLY
GESUNDHEIT
GETTERINGS
GEWURZTRAMINER
GEWURZTRAMINERS
GEYSERITES
GHASTFULLY
GHASTLIEST
GHASTLINESS
GHASTLINESSES
GHASTNESSES
GHETTOISATION
GHETTOISATIONS
GHETTOISED
GHETTOISES
GHETTOISING
GHETTOIZATION
GHETTOIZATIONS
GHETTOIZED
GHETTOIZES
GHETTOIZING
GHOSTLIEST
GHOSTLINESS
GHOSTLINESSES
GHOSTWRITE
GHOSTWRITER
GHOSTWRITERS
GHOSTWRITES
GHOSTWRITING
GHOSTWRITTEN
GHOSTWROTE
GHOULISHLY
GHOULISHNESS
GHOULISHNESSES
GIANTESSES
GIANTHOODS
GIANTLIEST
GIANTSHIPS
GIARDIASES
GIARDIASIS
GIBBERELLIC
GIBBERELLIN
GIBBERELLINS
GIBBERISHES

GIBBETTING
GIBBOSITIES
GIBBOUSNESS
GIBBOUSNESSES
GIDDINESSES
GIFTEDNESS
GIFTEDNESSES
GIFTWRAPPED
GIFTWRAPPING
GIGACYCLES
GIGAHERTZES
GIGANTESQUE
GIGANTICALLY
GIGANTICIDE
GIGANTICIDES
GIGANTICNESS
GIGANTICNESSES
GIGANTISMS
GIGANTOLOGIES
GIGANTOLOGY
GIGANTOMACHIA
GIGANTOMACHIAS
GIGANTOMACHIES
GIGANTOMACHY
GIGGLESOME
GIGGLINGLY
GIGMANITIES
GILDSWOMAN
GILDSWOMEN
GILLFLIRTS
GILLIFLOWER
GILLIFLOWERS
GILLNETTED
GILLNETTER
GILLNETTERS
GILLNETTING
GILLRAVAGE
GILLRAVAGED
GILLRAVAGES
GILLRAVAGING
GILLRAVITCH
GILLRAVITCHED
GILLRAVITCHES
GILLRAVITCHING
GILLYFLOWER
GILLYFLOWERS
GILRAVAGED
GILRAVAGER
GILRAVAGERS
GILRAVAGES
GILRAVAGING
GILRAVITCH
GILRAVITCHED
GILRAVITCHES
GILRAVITCHING
GILSONITES
GIMBALLING
GIMCRACKERIES
GIMCRACKERY

GIMMICKIER
GIMMICKIEST
GIMMICKING
GIMMICKRIES
GINGELLIES
GINGERADES
GINGERBREAD
GINGERBREADED
GINGERBREADS
GINGERBREADY
GINGERLINESS
GINGERLINESSES
GINGERROOT
GINGERROOTS
GINGERSNAP
GINGERSNAPS
GINGIVECTOMIES
GINGIVECTOMY
GINGIVITIS
GINGIVITISES
GINGLIMOID
GIPSYHOODS
GIPSYWORTS
GIRANDOLAS
GIRANDOLES
GIRDLECAKE
GIRDLECAKES
GIRDLESCONE
GIRDLESCONES
GIRDLESTEAD
GIRDLESTEADS
GIRLFRIEND
GIRLFRIENDS
GIRLISHNESS
GIRLISHNESSES
GIRTHLINES
GISMOLOGIES
GITTARONES
GITTERNING
GIVENNESSES
GIZMOLOGIES
GLABRESCENT
GLABROUSNESS
GLABROUSNESSES
GLACIALIST
GLACIALISTS
GLACIATING
GLACIATION
GLACIATIONS
GLACIOLOGIC
GLACIOLOGICAL
GLACIOLOGIES
GLACIOLOGIST
GLACIOLOGISTS
GLACIOLOGY
GLADDENERS
GLADDENING
GLADFULNESS
GLADFULNESSES

GLADIATORIAL
GLADIATORIAN
GLADIATORS
GLADIATORSHIP
GLADIATORSHIPS
GLADIATORY
GLADIOLUSES
GLADNESSES
GLADSOMELY
GLADSOMENESS
GLADSOMENESSES
GLADSOMEST
GLADSTONES
GLADWRAPPED
GLADWRAPPING
GLAIKETNESS
GLAIKETNESSES
GLAIKITNESS
GLAIKITNESSES
GLAIRINESS
GLAIRINESSES
GLAMORISATION
GLAMORISATIONS
GLAMORISED
GLAMORISER
GLAMORISERS
GLAMORISES
GLAMORISING
GLAMORIZATION
GLAMORIZATIONS
GLAMORIZED
GLAMORIZER
GLAMORIZERS
GLAMORIZES
GLAMORIZING
GLAMOROUSLY
GLAMOROUSNESS
GLAMOROUSNESSES
GLAMOURING
GLAMOURISE
GLAMOURISED
GLAMOURISES
GLAMOURISING
GLAMOURIZE
GLAMOURIZED
GLAMOURIZES
GLAMOURIZING
GLAMOURLESS
GLAMOUROUS
GLAMOUROUSLY
GLAMOUROUSNESS
GLAMOURPUSS
GLAMOURPUSSES
GLANCINGLY
GLANDEROUS
GLANDIFEROUS
GLANDIFORM
GLANDULARLY
GLANDULIFEROUS

GLANDULOUS
GLANDULOUSLY
GLARINESSES
GLARINGNESS
GLARINGNESSES
GLASNOSTIAN
GLASNOSTIC
GLASSBLOWER
GLASSBLOWERS
GLASSBLOWING
GLASSBLOWINGS
GLASSHOUSE
GLASSHOUSES
GLASSIFIED
GLASSIFIES
GLASSIFYING
GLASSINESS
GLASSINESSES
GLASSMAKER
GLASSMAKERS
GLASSMAKING
GLASSMAKINGS
GLASSPAPER
GLASSPAPERED
GLASSPAPERING
GLASSPAPERS
GLASSWARES
GLASSWORKER
GLASSWORKERS
GLASSWORKS
GLASSWORMS
GLASSWORTS
GLASSYHEADED
GLAUBERITE
GLAUBERITES
GLAUCESCENCE
GLAUCESCENCES
GLAUCESCENT
GLAUCOMATOUS
GLAUCONITE
GLAUCONITES
GLAUCONITIC
GLAUCOUSLY
GLAUCOUSNESS
GLAUCOUSNESSES
GLAZIERIES
GLAZINESSES
GLEEFULNESS
GLEEFULNESSES
GLEEMAIDEN
GLEEMAIDENS
GLEGNESSES
GLEISATION
GLEISATIONS
GLEIZATION
GLEIZATIONS
GLENDOVEER
GLENDOVEERS
GLENGARRIES

GLIBNESSES
GLIDEPATHS
GLIMMERING
GLIMMERINGLY
GLIMMERINGS
GLIOBLASTOMA
GLIOBLASTOMAS
GLIOBLASTOMATA
GLIOMATOSES
GLIOMATOSIS
GLIOMATOUS
GLISSADERS
GLISSADING
GLISSANDOS
GLISTENING
GLISTENINGLY
GLISTERING
GLISTERINGLY
GLITCHIEST
GLITTERAND
GLITTERATI
GLITTERIER
GLITTERIEST
GLITTERING
GLITTERINGLY
GLITTERINGS
GLITZINESS
GLITZINESSES
GLOATINGLY
GLOBALISATION
GLOBALISATIONS
GLOBALISED
GLOBALISES
GLOBALISING
GLOBALISMS
GLOBALISTS
GLOBALIZATION
GLOBALIZATIONS
GLOBALIZED
GLOBALIZES
GLOBALIZING
GLOBEFISHES
GLOBEFLOWER
GLOBEFLOWERS
GLOBESITIES
GLOBETROTS
GLOBETROTTED
GLOBETROTTER
GLOBETROTTERS
GLOBETROTTING
GLOBETROTTINGS
GLOBIGERINA
GLOBIGERINAE
GLOBIGERINAS
GLOBOSENESS
GLOBOSENESSES
GLOBOSITIES
GLOBULARITIES
GLOBULARITY

GLOBULARLY
GLOBULARNESS
GLOBULARNESSES
GLOBULIFEROUS
GLOBULITES
GLOCHIDIATE
GLOCHIDIUM
GLOCKENSPIEL
GLOCKENSPIELS
GLOMERATED
GLOMERATES
GLOMERATING
GLOMERATION
GLOMERATIONS
GLOMERULAR
GLOMERULATE
GLOMERULES
GLOMERULUS
GLOOMFULLY
GLOOMINESS
GLOOMINESSES
GLORIFIABLE
GLORIFICATION
GLORIFICATIONS
GLORIFIERS
GLORIFYING
GLORIOUSLY
GLORIOUSNESS
GLORIOUSNESSES
GLOSSARIAL
GLOSSARIALLY
GLOSSARIES
GLOSSARIST
GLOSSARISTS
GLOSSATORS
GLOSSECTOMIES
GLOSSECTOMY
GLOSSINESS
GLOSSINESSES
GLOSSINGLY
GLOSSITISES
GLOSSODYNIA
GLOSSODYNIAS
GLOSSOGRAPHER
GLOSSOGRAPHERS
GLOSSOGRAPHICAL
GLOSSOGRAPHIES
GLOSSOGRAPHY
GLOSSOLALIA
GLOSSOLALIAS
GLOSSOLALIST
GLOSSOLALISTS
GLOSSOLOGICAL
GLOSSOLOGIES
GLOSSOLOGIST
GLOSSOLOGISTS
GLOSSOLOGY
GLOTTIDEAN
GLOTTOGONIC

GLOTTOLOGIES
GLOTTOLOGY
GLOWERINGLY
GLOWSTICKS
GLUCINIUMS
GLUCOCORTICOID
GLUCOCORTICOIDS
GLUCOKINASE
GLUCOKINASES
GLUCONATES
GLUCONEOGENESES
GLUCONEOGENESIS
GLUCONEOGENIC
GLUCOPHORE
GLUCOPHORES
GLUCOPROTEIN
GLUCOPROTEINS
GLUCOSAMINE
GLUCOSAMINES
GLUCOSIDAL
GLUCOSIDASE
GLUCOSIDASES
GLUCOSIDES
GLUCOSIDIC
GLUCOSURIA
GLUCOSURIAS
GLUCOSURIC
GLUCURONIDASE
GLUCURONIDASES
GLUCURONIDE
GLUCURONIDES
GLUEYNESSES
GLUINESSES
GLUMACEOUS
GLUMIFEROUS
GLUMNESSES
GLUTAMATES
GLUTAMINASE
GLUTAMINASES
GLUTAMINES
GLUTAMINIC
GLUTARALDEHYDE
GLUTARALDEHYDES
GLUTATHIONE
GLUTATHIONES
GLUTETHIMIDE
GLUTETHIMIDES
GLUTINOSITIES
GLUTINOSITY
GLUTINOUSLY
GLUTINOUSNESS
GLUTINOUSNESSES
GLUTTINGLY
GLUTTONIES
GLUTTONISE
GLUTTONISED
GLUTTONISES
GLUTTONISH
GLUTTONISING

GLUTTONIZE
GLUTTONIZED
GLUTTONIZES
GLUTTONIZING
GLUTTONOUS
GLUTTONOUSLY
GLUTTONOUSNESS
GLYCAEMIAS
GLYCERALDEHYDE
GLYCERALDEHYDES
GLYCERIDES
GLYCERIDIC
GLYCERINATE
GLYCERINATED
GLYCERINATES
GLYCERINATING
GLYCERINES
GLYCOCOLLS
GLYCOGENESES
GLYCOGENESIS
GLYCOGENETIC
GLYCOGENIC
GLYCOGENOLYSES
GLYCOGENOLYSIS
GLYCOGENOLYTIC
GLYCOLIPID
GLYCOLIPIDS
GLYCOLYSES
GLYCOLYSIS
GLYCOLYTIC
GLYCONEOGENESES
GLYCONEOGENESIS
GLYCOPEPTIDE
GLYCOPEPTIDES
GLYCOPHYTE
GLYCOPHYTES
GLYCOPHYTIC
GLYCOPROTEIN
GLYCOPROTEINS
GLYCOSIDASE
GLYCOSIDASES
GLYCOSIDES
GLYCOSIDIC
GLYCOSIDICALLY
GLYCOSURIA
GLYCOSURIAS
GLYCOSURIC
GLYCOSYLATE
GLYCOSYLATED
GLYCOSYLATES
GLYCOSYLATING
GLYCOSYLATION
GLYCOSYLATIONS
GLYOXALINE
GLYOXALINES
GLYPHOGRAPH
GLYPHOGRAPHER
GLYPHOGRAPHERS
GLYPHOGRAPHIC

GLYPHOGRAPHICAL
GLYPHOCRAPHIES
GLYPHOGRAPHS
GLYPHOGRAPHY
GLYPTODONT
GLYPTODONTS
GLYPTOGRAPHER
GLYPTOGRAPHERS
GLYPTOGRAPHIC
GLYPTOGRAPHICAL
GLYPTOGRAPHIES
GLYPTOGRAPHY
GLYPTOTHECA
GLYPTOTHECAE
GMELINITES
GNAPHALIUM
GNAPHALIUMS
GNASHINGLY
GNATCATCHER
GNATCATCHERS
GNATHONICAL
GNATHONICALLY
GNATHOSTOMATOUS
GNATHOSTOME
GNATHOSTOMES
GNEISSITIC
GNETOPHYTE
GNETOPHYTES
GNOMICALLY
GNOMONICAL
GNOMONICALLY
GNOMONOLOGIES
GNOMONOLOGY
GNOSEOLOGIES
GNOSEOLOGY
GNOSIOLOGIES
GNOSIOLOGY
GNOSTICALLY
GNOSTICISM
GNOSTICISMS
GNOTOBIOLOGICAL
GNOTOBIOLOGIES
GNOTOBIOLOGY
GNOTOBIOSES
GNOTOBIOSIS
GNOTOBIOTE
GNOTOBIOTES
GNOTOBIOTIC
GNOTOBIOTICALLY
GNOTOBIOTICS
GOALKEEPER
GOALKEEPERS
GOALKEEPING
GOALKEEPINGS
GOALKICKER
GOALKICKERS
GOALKICKING
GOALKICKINGS
GOALMOUTHS

GOALTENDER
GOALTENDERS
GOALTENDING
GOALTENDINGS
GOATFISHES
GOATISHNESS
GOATISHNESSES
GOATSBEARD
GOATSBEARDS
GOATSUCKER
GOATSUCKERS
GOBBELINES
GOBBLEDEGOOK
GOBBLEDEGOOKS
GOBBLEDYGOOK
GOBBLEDYGOOKS
GOBSMACKED
GOBSTOPPER
GOBSTOPPERS
GODCHILDREN
GODDAMMING
GODDAMNDEST
GODDAMNEDEST
GODDAMNING
GODDAUGHTER
GODDAUGHTERS
GODDESSHOOD
GODDESSHOODS
GODFATHERED
GODFATHERING
GODFATHERS
GODFORSAKEN
GODLESSNESS
GODLESSNESSES
GODLIKENESS
GODLIKENESSES
GODLINESSES
GODMOTHERED
GODMOTHERING
GODMOTHERS
GODPARENTS
GODROONING
GODROONINGS
GOFFERINGS
GOGGLEBOXES
GOITROGENIC
GOITROGENICITY
GOITROGENS
GOLDBEATER
GOLDBEATERS
GOLDBRICKED
GOLDBRICKING
GOLDBRICKS
GOLDCRESTS
GOLDENBERRIES
GOLDENBERRY
GOLDENEYES
GOLDENNESS
GOLDENNESSES

GOLDENRODS
GOLDENSEAL
GOLDENSEALS
GOLDFIELDS
GOLDFINCHES
GOLDFINNIES
GOLDFISHES
GOLDILOCKS
GOLDILOCKSES
GOLDMINERS
GOLDSINNIES
GOLDSMITHERIES
GOLDSMITHERY
GOLDSMITHRIES
GOLDSMITHRY
GOLDSMITHS
GOLDSPINKS
GOLDSTICKS
GOLDSTONES
GOLDTHREAD
GOLDTHREADS
GOLIARDERIES
GOLIARDERY
GOLIARDIES
GOLIATHISE
GOLIATHISED
GOLIATHISES
GOLIATHISING
GOLIATHIZE
GOLIATHIZED
GOLIATHIZES
GOLIATHIZING
GOLLIWOGGS
GOLOMYNKAS
GOLOPTIOUS
GOLUPTIOUS
GOMBEENISM
GOMBEENISMS
GONADECTOMIES
GONADECTOMISED
GONADECTOMIZED
GONADECTOMY
GONADOTROPHIC
GONADOTROPHIN
GONADOTROPHINS
GONADOTROPIC
GONADOTROPIN
GONADOTROPINS
GONDOLIERS
GONENESSES
GONFALONIER
GONFALONIERS
GONGORISTIC
GONIATITES
GONIATITOID
GONIATITOIDS
GONIMOBLAST
GONIMOBLASTS
GONIOMETER

GONIOMETERS
GONIOMETRIC
GONIOMETRICAL
GONIOMETRICALLY
GONIOMETRIES
GONIOMETRY
GONIOSCOPE
GONIOSCOPES
GONOCOCCAL
GONOCOCCIC
GONOCOCCOID
GONOCOCCUS
GONOPHORES
GONOPHORIC
GONOPHOROUS
GONORRHEAL
GONORRHEAS
GONORRHEIC
GONORRHOEA
GONORRHOEAL
GONORRHOEAS
GONORRHOEIC
GOODFELLOW
GOODFELLOWS
GOODFELLOWSHIP
GOODFELLOWSHIPS
GOODINESSES
GOODLIHEAD
GOODLIHEADS
GOODLINESS
GOODLINESSES
GOODLYHEAD
GOODLYHEADS
GOODNESSES
GOODNIGHTS
GOODWILLED
GOOEYNESSES
GOOFINESSES
GOOGLEWHACK
GOOGLEWHACKS
GOOGOLPLEX
GOOGOLPLEXES
GOONEYBIRD
GOONEYBIRDS
GOOSANDERS
GOOSEBERRIES
GOOSEBERRY
GOOSEFISHES
GOOSEFLESH
GOOSEFLESHES
GOOSEFOOTS
GOOSEGRASS
GOOSEGRASSES
GOOSEHERDS
GOOSENECKED
GOOSENECKS
GOOSINESSES
GOPHERWOOD
GOPHERWOODS

GORBELLIES
GOREHOUNDS
GORGEOUSLY
GORGEOUSNESS
GORGEOUSNESSES
GORGONEION
GORGONIANS
GORGONISED
GORGONISES
GORGONISING
GORGONIZED
GORGONIZES
GORGONIZING
GORILLAGRAM
GORILLAGRAMS
GORINESSES
GORMANDISE
GORMANDISED
GORMANDISER
GORMANDISERS
GORMANDISES
GORMANDISING
GORMANDISINGS
GORMANDISM
GORMANDISMS
GORMANDIZE
GORMANDIZED
GORMANDIZER
GORMANDIZERS
GORMANDIZES
GORMANDIZING
GORMANDIZINGS
GOSLARITES
GOSPELISED
GOSPELISES
GOSPELISING
GOSPELIZED
GOSPELIZES
GOSPELIZING
GOSPELLERS
GOSPELLING
GOSPELLISE
GOSPELLISED
GOSPELLISES
GOSPELLISING
GOSPELLIZE
GOSPELLIZED
GOSPELLIZES
GOSPELLIZING
GOSSIPINGLY
GOSSIPINGS
GOSSIPMONGER
GOSSIPMONGERS
GOSSIPPERS
GOSSIPPING
GOSSIPRIES
GOTHICALLY
GOTHICISED
GOTHICISES

GOTHICISING
GOTHICISMS
GOTHICIZED
GOTHICIZES
GOTHICIZING
GOURDINESS
GOURDINESSES
GOURMANDISE
GOURMANDISED
GOURMANDISES
GOURMANDISING
GOURMANDISM
GOURMANDISMS
GOURMANDIZE
GOURMANDIZED
GOURMANDIZES
GOURMANDIZING
GOUTINESSES
GOUVERNANTE
GOUVERNANTES
GOVERNABILITIES
GOVERNABILITY
GOVERNABLE
GOVERNABLENESS
GOVERNALLS
GOVERNANCE
GOVERNANCES
GOVERNANTE
GOVERNANTES
GOVERNESSED
GOVERNESSES
GOVERNESSING
GOVERNESSY
GOVERNMENT
GOVERNMENTAL
GOVERNMENTALISE
GOVERNMENTALISM
GOVERNMENTALIST
GOVERNMENTALIZE
GOVERNMENTALLY
GOVERNMENTESE
GOVERNMENTESES
GOVERNMENTS
GOVERNORATE
GOVERNORATES
GOVERNORSHIP
GOVERNORSHIPS
GOWDSPINKS
GOWPENFULS
GRACEFULLER
GRACEFULLEST
GRACEFULLY
GRACEFULNESS
GRACEFULNESSES
GRACELESSLY
GRACELESSNESS
GRACELESSNESSES
GRACILENESS
GRACILENESSES

GRACILITIES
GRACIOSITIES
GRACIOSITY
GRACIOUSES
GRACIOUSLY
GRACIOUSNESS
GRACIOUSNESSES
GRADABILITIES
GRADABILITY
GRADABLENESS
GRADABLENESSES
GRADATIONAL
GRADATIONALLY
GRADATIONED
GRADATIONS
GRADDANING
GRADELIEST
GRADIENTER
GRADIENTERS
GRADIOMETER
GRADIOMETERS
GRADUALISM
GRADUALISMS
GRADUALIST
GRADUALISTIC
GRADUALISTS
GRADUALITIES
GRADUALITY
GRADUALNESS
GRADUALNESSES
GRADUATESHIP
GRADUATESHIPS
GRADUATING
GRADUATION
GRADUATIONS
GRADUATORS
GRAECISING
GRAECIZING
GRAFFITIED
GRAFFITIING
GRAFFITING
GRAFFITIST
GRAFFITISTS
GRAINFIELD
GRAINFIELDS
GRAININESS
GRAININESSES
GRALLATORIAL
GRALLOCHED
GRALLOCHING
GRAMERCIES
GRAMICIDIN
GRAMICIDINS
GRAMINACEOUS
GRAMINEOUS
GRAMINICOLOUS
GRAMINIVOROUS
GRAMINOLOGIES
GRAMINOLOGY

GRAMMALOGUE
GRAMMALOGUES
GRAMMARIAN
GRAMMARIANS
GRAMMARLESS
GRAMMATICAL
GRAMMATICALITY
GRAMMATICALLY
GRAMMATICALNESS
GRAMMATICASTER
GRAMMATICASTERS
GRAMMATICISE
GRAMMATICISED
GRAMMATICISES
GRAMMATICISING
GRAMMATICISM
GRAMMATICISMS
GRAMMATICIZE
GRAMMATICIZED
GRAMMATICIZES
GRAMMATICIZING
GRAMMATIST
GRAMMATISTS
GRAMMATOLOGIES
GRAMMATOLOGIST
GRAMMATOLOGISTS
GRAMMATOLOGY
GRAMOPHONE
GRAMOPHONES
GRAMOPHONIC
GRAMOPHONICALLY
GRAMOPHONIES
GRAMOPHONIST
GRAMOPHONISTS
GRAMOPHONY
GRANADILLA
GRANADILLAS
GRANDADDIES
GRANDAUNTS
GRANDBABIES
GRANDCHILD
GRANDCHILDREN
GRANDDADDIES
GRANDDADDY
GRANDDAUGHTER
GRANDDAUGHTERS
GRANDEESHIP
GRANDEESHIPS
GRANDFATHER
GRANDFATHERED
GRANDFATHERING
GRANDFATHERLY
GRANDFATHERS
GRANDIFLORA
GRANDIFLORAS
GRANDILOQUENCE
GRANDILOQUENCES
GRANDILOQUENT
GRANDILOQUENTLY

GRANDILOQUOUS
GRANDIOSELY
GRANDIOSENESS
GRANDIOSENESSES
GRANDIOSITIES
GRANDIOSITY
GRANDMAMAS
GRANDMAMMA
GRANDMAMMAS
GRANDMASTER
GRANDMASTERS
GRANDMOTHER
GRANDMOTHERLY
GRANDMOTHERS
GRANDNEPHEW
GRANDNEPHEWS
GRANDNESSES
GRANDNIECE
GRANDNIECES
GRANDPAPAS
GRANDPARENT
GRANDPARENTAL
GRANDPARENTHOOD
GRANDPARENTS
GRANDSIRES
GRANDSTAND
GRANDSTANDED
GRANDSTANDER
GRANDSTANDERS
GRANDSTANDING
GRANDSTANDS
GRANDSTOOD
GRANDUNCLE
GRANDUNCLES
GRANGERISATION
GRANGERISATIONS
GRANGERISE
GRANGERISED
GRANGERISER
GRANGERISERS
GRANGERISES
GRANGERISING
GRANGERISM
GRANGERISMS
GRANGERIZATION
GRANGERIZATIONS
GRANGERIZE
GRANGERIZED
GRANGERIZER
GRANGERIZERS
GRANGERIZES
GRANGERIZING
GRANITELIKE
GRANITEWARE
GRANITEWARES
GRANITIFICATION
GRANITIFORM
GRANITISATION
GRANITISATIONS

GRANITISED
GRANITISES
GRANITISING
GRANITITES
GRANITIZATION
GRANITIZATIONS
GRANITIZED
GRANITIZES
GRANITIZING
GRANIVORES
GRANIVOROUS
GRANNIEING
GRANODIORITE
GRANODIORITES
GRANODIORITIC
GRANOLITHIC
GRANOLITHICS
GRANOLITHS
GRANOPHYRE
GRANOPHYRES
GRANOPHYRIC
GRANTSMANSHIP
GRANTSMANSHIPS
GRANULARITIES
GRANULARITY
GRANULARLY
GRANULATED
GRANULATER
GRANULATERS
GRANULATES
GRANULATING
GRANULATION
GRANULATIONS
GRANULATIVE
GRANULATOR
GRANULATORS
GRANULIFEROUS
GRANULIFORM
GRANULITES
GRANULITIC
GRANULITISATION
GRANULITIZATION
GRANULOCYTE
GRANULOCYTES
GRANULOCYTIC
GRANULOMAS
GRANULOMATA
GRANULOMATOUS
GRANULOSES
GRANULOSIS
GRAPEFRUIT
GRAPEFRUITS
GRAPESEEDS
GRAPESHOTS
GRAPESTONE
GRAPESTONES
GRAPETREES
GRAPEVINES
GRAPHEMICALLY

GRAPHEMICS
GRAPHICACIES
GRAPHICACY
GRAPHICALLY
GRAPHICALNESS
GRAPHICALNESSES
GRAPHICNESS
GRAPHICNESSES
GRAPHITISABLE
GRAPHITISATION
GRAPHITISATIONS
GRAPHITISE
GRAPHITISED
GRAPHITISES
GRAPHITISING
GRAPHITIZABLE
GRAPHITIZATION
GRAPHITIZATIONS
GRAPHITIZE
GRAPHITIZED
GRAPHITIZES
GRAPHITIZING
GRAPHITOID
GRAPHOLECT
GRAPHOLECTS
GRAPHOLOGIC
GRAPHOLOGICAL
GRAPHOLOGIES
GRAPHOLOGIST
GRAPHOLOGISTS
GRAPHOLOGY
GRAPHOMANIA
GRAPHOMANIAS
GRAPHOMOTOR
GRAPHOPHOBIA
GRAPHOPHOBIAS
GRAPINESSES
GRAPLEMENT
GRAPLEMENTS
GRAPPLINGS
GRAPTOLITE
GRAPTOLITES
GRAPTOLITIC
GRASPINGLY
GRASPINGNESS
GRASPINGNESSES
GRASSFINCH
GRASSFINCHES
GRASSHOOKS
GRASSHOPPER
GRASSHOPPERS
GRASSINESS
GRASSINESSES
GRASSLANDS
GRASSPLOTS
GRASSQUITS
GRASSROOTS
GRASSWRACK
GRASSWRACKS

GRATEFULLER
GRATEFULLEST
GRATEFULLY
GRATEFULNESS
GRATEFULNESSES
GRATICULATION
GRATICULATIONS
GRATICULES
GRATIFICATION
GRATIFICATIONS
GRATIFIERS
GRATIFYING
GRATIFYINGLY
GRATILLITIES
GRATILLITY
GRATINATED
GRATINATES
GRATINATING
GRATINEEING
GRATITUDES
GRATUITIES
GRATUITOUS
GRATUITOUSLY
GRATUITOUSNESS
GRATULATED
GRATULATES
GRATULATING
GRATULATION
GRATULATIONS
GRATULATORY
GRAUNCHERS
GRAUNCHING
GRAVADLAXES
GRAVELLING
GRAVENESSES
GRAVEOLENT
GRAVESIDES
GRAVESITES
GRAVESTONE
GRAVESTONES
GRAVEYARDS
GRAVIDITIES
GRAVIDNESS
GRAVIDNESSES
GRAVIMETER
GRAVIMETERS
GRAVIMETRIC
GRAVIMETRICAL
GRAVIMETRICALLY
GRAVIMETRIES
GRAVIMETRY
GRAVIPERCEPTION
GRAVITASES
GRAVITATED
GRAVITATER
GRAVITATERS
GRAVITATES
GRAVITATING
GRAVITATION

GRAVITATIONAL
GRAVITATIONALLY
GRAVITATIONS
GRAVITATIVE
GRAVITINOS
GRAVITOMETER
GRAVITOMETERS
GRAYBEARDED
GRAYBEARDS
GRAYFISHES
GRAYHOUNDS
GRAYNESSES
GRAYWACKES
GRAYWATERS
GREASEBALL
GREASEBALLS
GREASEBAND
GREASEBANDS
GREASEBUSH
GREASEBUSHES
GREASELESS
GREASEPAINT
GREASEPAINTS
GREASEPROOF
GREASEPROOFS
GREASEWOOD
GREASEWOODS
GREASINESS
GREASINESSES
GREATCOATED
GREATCOATS
GREATENING
GREATHEARTED
GREATHEARTEDLY
GREATNESSES
GRECIANISE
GRECIANISED
GRECIANISES
GRECIANISING
GRECIANIZE
GRECIANIZED
GRECIANIZES
GRECIANIZING
GREEDINESS
GREEDINESSES
GREENBACKER
GREENBACKERS
GREENBACKISM
GREENBACKISMS
GREENBACKS
GREENBELTS
GREENBONES
GREENBOTTLE
GREENBOTTLES
GREENBRIER
GREENBRIERS
GREENCLOTH
GREENCLOTHS
GREENERIES

GREENFIELD
GREENFIELDS
GREENFINCH
GREENFINCHES
GREENFLIES
GREENGAGES
GREENGROCER
GREENGROCERIES
GREENGROCERS
GREENGROCERY
GREENHANDS
GREENHEADS
GREENHEART
GREENHEARTS
GREENHORNS
GREENHOUSE
GREENHOUSES
GREENISHNESS
GREENISHNESSES
GREENKEEPER
GREENKEEPERS
GREENLIGHT
GREENLIGHTED
GREENLIGHTING
GREENLIGHTS
GREENLINGS
GREENMAILED
GREENMAILER
GREENMAILERS
GREENMAILING
GREENMAILS
GREENNESSES
GREENOCKITE
GREENOCKITES
GREENROOMS
GREENSANDS
GREENSHANK
GREENSHANKS
GREENSICKNESS
GREENSICKNESSES
GREENSKEEPER
GREENSKEEPERS
GREENSOMES
GREENSPEAK
GREENSPEAKS
GREENSTICK
GREENSTICKS
GREENSTONE
GREENSTONES
GREENSTUFF
GREENSTUFFS
GREENSWARD
GREENSWARDS
GREENWASHED
GREENWASHES
GREENWASHING
GREENWEEDS
GREENWINGS
GREENWOODS

GREGARIANISM
GREGARIANISMS
GREGARINES
GREGARINIAN
GREGARIOUS
GREGARIOUSLY
GREGARIOUSNESS
GREISENISATION
GREISENISATIONS
GREISENISE
GREISENISED
GREISENISES
GREISENISING
GREISENIZATION
GREISENIZATIONS
GREISENIZE
GREISENIZED
GREISENIZES
GREISENIZING
GREMOLATAS
GRENADIERS
GRENADILLA
GRENADILLAS
GRENADINES
GRESSORIAL
GRESSORIOUS
GREVILLEAS
GREWHOUNDS
GREWSOMEST
GREYBEARDED
GREYBEARDS
GREYHOUNDS
GREYLISTED
GREYLISTING
GREYNESSES
GREYSTONES
GREYWACKES
GREYWETHER
GREYWETHERS
GRIDDLEBREAD
GRIDDLEBREADS
GRIDDLECAKE
GRIDDLECAKES
GRIDIRONED
GRIDIRONING
GRIDLOCKED
GRIDLOCKING
GRIEVANCES
GRIEVINGLY
GRIEVOUSLY
GRIEVOUSNESS
GRIEVOUSNESSES
GRIFFINISH
GRIFFINISM
GRIFFINISMS
GRILLERIES
GRILLROOMS
GRILLSTEAK
GRILLSTEAKS

GRILLWORKS
GRIMACINGLY
GRIMALKINS
GRIMINESSES
GRIMLOOKED
GRIMNESSES
GRINDELIAS
GRINDERIES
GRINDHOUSE
GRINDHOUSES
GRINDINGLY
GRINDSTONE
GRINDSTONES
GRINNINGLY
GRIPPINGLY
GRISAILLES
GRISEOFULVIN
GRISEOFULVINS
GRISLINESS
GRISLINESSES
GRISTLIEST
GRISTLINESS
GRISTLINESSES
GRISTMILLS
GRITSTONES
GRITTINESS
GRITTINESSES
GRIVATIONS
GRIZZLIEST
GROANINGLY
GROATSWORTH
GROATSWORTHS
GROCETERIA
GROCETERIAS
GROGGERIES
GROGGINESS
GROGGINESSES
GROMMETING
GROOVELESS
GROOVELIKE
GROSGRAINS
GROSSIERETE
GROSSIERETES
GROSSNESSES
GROSSULARITE
GROSSULARITES
GROSSULARS
GROTESQUELY
GROTESQUENESS
GROTESQUENESSES
GROTESQUER
GROTESQUERIE
GROTESQUERIES
GROTESQUERY
GROTESQUES
GROTESQUEST
GROUCHIEST
GROUCHINESS
GROUCHINESSES

GROUNDAGES
GROUNDBAIT
GROUNDBAITED
GROUNDBAITING
GROUNDBAITS
GROUNDBREAKER
GROUNDBREAKERS
GROUNDBREAKING
GROUNDBREAKINGS
GROUNDBURST
GROUNDBURSTS
GROUNDEDLY
GROUNDFISH
GROUNDFISHES
GROUNDHOGS
GROUNDINGS
GROUNDLESS
GROUNDLESSLY
GROUNDLESSNESS
GROUNDLING
GROUNDLINGS
GROUNDMASS
GROUNDMASSES
GROUNDNUTS
GROUNDOUTS
GROUNDPLOT
GROUNDPLOTS
GROUNDPROX
GROUNDPROXES
GROUNDSELL
GROUNDSELLS
GROUNDSELS
GROUNDSHARE
GROUNDSHARED
GROUNDSHARES
GROUNDSHARING
GROUNDSHEET
GROUNDSHEETS
GROUNDSILL
GROUNDSILLS
GROUNDSKEEPER
GROUNDSKEEPERS
GROUNDSMAN
GROUNDSMEN
GROUNDSPEED
GROUNDSPEEDS
GROUNDSWELL
GROUNDSWELLS
GROUNDWATER
GROUNDWATERS
GROUNDWOOD
GROUNDWOODS
GROUNDWORK
GROUNDWORKS
GROUPTHINK
GROUPTHINKS
GROUPUSCULE
GROUPUSCULES
GROUPWARES

GROUSELIKE
GROVELINGLY
GROVELLERS
GROVELLING
GROVELLINGLY
GROVELLINGS
GROWLERIES
GROWLINESS
GROWLINESSES
GROWLINGLY
GROWTHIEST
GROWTHINESS
GROWTHINESSES
GROWTHISTS
GRUBBINESS
GRUBBINESSES
GRUBSTAKED
GRUBSTAKER
GRUBSTAKERS
GRUBSTAKES
GRUBSTAKING
GRUDGELESS
GRUDGINGLY
GRUELINGLY
GRUELLINGS
GRUESOMELY
GRUESOMENESS
GRUESOMENESSES
GRUESOMEST
GRUFFNESSES
GRUMBLIEST
GRUMBLINGLY
GRUMBLINGS
GRUMMETING
GRUMNESSES
GRUMPINESS
GRUMPINESSES
GRUMPISHLY
GRUMPISHNESS
GRUMPISHNESSES
GRUNTINGLY
GUACAMOLES
GUACHAMOLE
GUACHAMOLES
GUACHAROES
GUANABANAS
GUANAZOLOS
GUANETHIDINE
GUANETHIDINES
GUANIDINES
GUANIFEROUS
GUANOSINES
GUARANTEED
GUARANTEEING
GUARANTEES
GUARANTIED
GUARANTIES
GUARANTORS
GUARANTYING

GUARDEDNESS
GUARDEDNESSES
GUARDHOUSE
GUARDHOUSES
GUARDIANSHIP
GUARDIANSHIPS
GUARDRAILS
GUARDROOMS
GUARDSHIPS
GUARISHING
GUAYABERAS
GUBERNACULA
GUBERNACULAR
GUBERNACULUM
GUBERNATION
GUBERNATIONS
GUBERNATOR
GUBERNATORIAL
GUBERNATORS
GUBERNIYAS
GUDGEONING
GUERDONERS
GUERDONING
GUERILLAISM
GUERILLAISMS
GUERRILLAISM
GUERRILLAISMS
GUERRILLAS
GUERRILLERO
GUERRILLEROS
GUESSINGLY
GUESSTIMATE
GUESSTIMATED
GUESSTIMATES
GUESSTIMATING
GUESSWORKS
GUESTENING
GUESTHOUSE
GUESTHOUSES
GUESTIMATE
GUESTIMATED
GUESTIMATES
GUESTIMATING
GUIDEBOOKS
GUIDELINES
GUIDEPOSTS
GUIDESHIPS
GUIDEWORDS
GUIDWILLIE
GUILDHALLS
GUILDSHIPS
GUILDSWOMAN
GUILDSWOMEN
GUILEFULLY
GUILEFULNESS
GUILEFULNESSES
GUILELESSLY
GUILELESSNESS
GUILELESSNESSES

GUILLEMETS
GUILLEMOTS
GUILLOCHED
GUILLOCHES
GUILLOCHING
GUILLOTINE
GUILLOTINED
GUILLOTINER
GUILLOTINERS
GUILLOTINES
GUILLOTINING
GUILTINESS
GUILTINESSES
GUILTLESSLY
GUILTLESSNESS
GUILTLESSNESSES
GUITARFISH
GUITARFISHES
GUITARISTS
GULLIBILITIES
GULLIBILITY
GULOSITIES
GUMMIFEROUS
GUMMINESSES
GUMMOSITIES
GUMSHIELDS
GUMSHOEING
GUMSUCKERS
GUNCOTTONS
GUNFIGHTER
GUNFIGHTERS
GUNFIGHTING
GUNFIGHTINGS
GUNKHOLING
GUNMANSHIP
GUNMANSHIPS
GUNNERSHIP
GUNNERSHIPS
GUNNYSACKS
GUNPOWDERS
GUNPOWDERY
GUNRUNNERS
GUNRUNNING
GUNRUNNINGS
GUNSLINGER
GUNSLINGERS
GUNSLINGING
GUNSLINGINGS
GUNSMITHING
GUNSMITHINGS
GURGITATION
GURGITATIONS
GUSHINESSES
GUSTATIONS
GUSTATORILY
GUSTINESSES
GUTBUCKETS
GUTLESSNESS
GUTLESSNESSES

GUTSINESSES
GUTTATIONS
GUTTERBLOOD
GUTTERBLOODS
GUTTERINGS
GUTTERSNIPE
GUTTERSNIPES
GUTTERSNIPISH
GUTTIFEROUS
GUTTURALISATION
GUTTURALISE
GUTTURALISED
GUTTURALISES
GUTTURALISING
GUTTURALISM
GUTTURALISMS
GUTTURALITIES
GUTTURALITY
GUTTURALIZATION
GUTTURALIZE
GUTTURALIZED
GUTTURALIZES
GUTTURALIZING
GUTTURALLY
GUTTURALNESS
GUTTURALNESSES
GYMNASIARCH
GYMNASIARCHS
GYMNASIAST
GYMNASIASTS
GYMNASIUMS
GYMNASTICAL
GYMNASTICALLY
GYMNASTICS
GYMNORHINAL
GYMNOSOPHIES
GYMNOSOPHIST
GYMNOSOPHISTS
GYMNOSOPHS
GYMNOSOPHY
GYMNOSPERM
GYMNOSPERMIES
GYMNOSPERMOUS
GYMNOSPERMS
GYMNOSPERMY
GYNAECEUMS
GYNAECOCRACIES
GYNAECOCRACY
GYNAECOCRATIC
GYNAECOLOGIC
GYNAECOLOGICAL
GYNAECOLOGIES
GYNAECOLOGIST
GYNAECOLOGISTS
GYNAECOLOGY
GYNAECOMAST
GYNAECOMASTIA
GYNAECOMASTIAS
GYNAECOMASTIES

GYNAECOMASTS
GYNAECOMASTY
GYNANDRIES
GYNANDRISM
GYNANDRISMS
GYNANDROMORPH
GYNANDROMORPHIC
GYNANDROMORPHS
GYNANDROMORPHY
GYNANDROUS
GYNARCHIES
GYNECOCRACIES
GYNECOCRACY
GYNECOCRATIC
GYNECOLOGIC
GYNECOLOGICAL
GYNECOLOGIES
GYNECOLOGIST
GYNECOLOGISTS
GYNECOLOGY
GYNECOMASTIA
GYNECOMASTIAS
GYNIATRICS
GYNIATRIES
GYNIOLATRIES
GYNIOLATRY
GYNOCRACIES
GYNOCRATIC
GYNODIOECIOUS
GYNODIOECISM
GYNODIOECISMS
GYNOGENESES
GYNOGENESIS
GYNOGENETIC
GYNOMONOECIOUS
GYNOMONOECISM
GYNOMONOECISMS
GYNOPHOBES
GYNOPHOBIA
GYNOPHOBIAS
GYNOPHOBIC
GYNOPHOBICS
GYNOPHORES
GYNOPHORIC
GYNOSTEMIA
GYNOSTEMIUM
GYPSIFEROUS
GYPSOPHILA
GYPSOPHILAS
GYPSYHOODS
GYPSYWORTS
GYRATIONAL
GYRFALCONS
GYROCOMPASS
GYROCOMPASSES
GYROCOPTER
GYROCOPTERS
GYROFREQUENCIES
GYROFREQUENCY

GYROMAGNETIC
GYROMAGNETISM
GYROMAGNETISMS
GYROMANCIES
GYROPILOTS
GYROPLANES
GYROSCOPES
GYROSCOPIC
GYROSCOPICALLY
GYROSCOPICS
GYROSTABILISER
GYROSTABILISERS
GYROSTABILIZER
GYROSTABILIZERS
GYROSTATIC
GYROSTATICALLY
GYROSTATICS
GYROVAGUES

H

HAANEPOOTS
HABERDASHER
HABERDASHERIES
HABERDASHERS
HABERDASHERY
HABERDINES
HABERGEONS
HABILATORY
HABILIMENT
HABILIMENTS
HABILITATE
HABILITATED
HABILITATES
HABILITATING
HABILITATION
HABILITATIONS
HABILITATOR
HABILITATORS
HABITABILITIES
HABITABILITY
HABITABLENESS
HABITABLENESSES
HABITATION
HABITATIONAL
HABITATIONS
HABITAUNCE
HABITAUNCES
HABITUALLY
HABITUALNESS
HABITUALNESSES
HABITUATED
HABITUATES
HABITUATING
HABITUATION
HABITUATIONS
HABITUDINAL
HACENDADOS
HACIENDADO
HACIENDADOS
HACKAMORES
HACKBERRIES
HACKBUTEER
HACKBUTEERS
HACKBUTTER
HACKBUTTERS
HACKMATACK
HACKMATACKS
HACKNEYING
HACKNEYISM
HACKNEYISMS
HACKNEYMAN
HACKNEYMEN
HACKSAWING

HACQUETONS
HADROSAURS
HADROSAURUS
HADROSAURUSES
HAECCEITIES
HAEMACHROME
HAEMACHROMES
HAEMACYTOMETER
HAEMACYTOMETERS
HAEMAGGLUTINATE
HAEMAGGLUTININ
HAEMAGGLUTININS
HAEMAGOGUE
HAEMAGOGUES
HAEMANGIOMA
HAEMANGIOMAS
HAEMANGIOMATA
HAEMATEINS
HAEMATEMESES
HAEMATEMESIS
HAEMATINIC
HAEMATINICS
HAEMATITES
HAEMATITIC
HAEMATOBLAST
HAEMATOBLASTIC
HAEMATOBLASTS
HAEMATOCELE
HAEMATOCELES
HAEMATOCRIT
HAEMATOCRITS
HAEMATOCRYAL
HAEMATOGENESES
HAEMATOGENESIS
HAEMATOGENETIC
HAEMATOGENIC
HAEMATOGENOUS
HAEMATOLOGIC
HAEMATOLOGICAL
HAEMATOLOGIES
HAEMATOLOGIST
HAEMATOLOGISTS
HAEMATOLOGY
HAEMATOLYSES
HAEMATOLYSIS
HAEMATOMAS
HAEMATOMATA
HAEMATOPHAGOUS
HAEMATOPOIESES
HAEMATOPOIESIS
HAEMATOPOIETIC
HAEMATOSES
HAEMATOSIS

HAEMATOTHERMAL
HAEMATOXYLIC
HAEMATOXYLIN
HAEMATOXYLINS
HAEMATOXYLON
HAEMATOXYLONS
HAEMATOZOA
HAEMATOZOON
HAEMATURIA
HAEMATURIAS
HAEMATURIC
HAEMOCHROME
HAEMOCHROMES
HAEMOCOELS
HAEMOCONIA
HAEMOCONIAS
HAEMOCYANIN
HAEMOCYANINS
HAEMOCYTES
HAEMOCYTOMETER
HAEMOCYTOMETERS
HAEMODIALYSER
HAEMODIALYSERS
HAEMODIALYSES
HAEMODIALYSIS
HAEMODIALYZER
HAEMODIALYZERS
HAEMOFLAGELLATE
HAEMOGLOBIN
HAEMOGLOBINS
HAEMOGLOBINURIA
HAEMOLYSES
HAEMOLYSIN
HAEMOLYSINS
HAEMOLYSIS
HAEMOLYTIC
HAEMOPHILE
HAEMOPHILES
HAEMOPHILIA
HAEMOPHILIAC
HAEMOPHILIACS
HAEMOPHILIAS
HAEMOPHILIC
HAEMOPHILIOID
HAEMOPOIESES
HAEMOPOIESIS
HAEMOPOIETIC
HAEMOPTYSES
HAEMOPTYSIS
HAEMORRHAGE
HAEMORRHAGED
HAEMORRHAGES
HAEMORRHAGIC

HAEMORRHAGING
HAEMORRHOID
HAEMORRHOIDAL
HAEMORRHOIDS
HAEMOSTASES
HAEMOSTASIA
HAEMOSTASIAS
HAEMOSTASIS
HAEMOSTATIC
HAEMOSTATICS
HAEMOSTATS
HAGBERRIES
HAGBUTEERS
HAGBUTTERS
HAGGADICAL
HAGGADISTIC
HAGGADISTS
HAGGARDNESS
HAGGARDNESSES
HAGGISHNESS
HAGGISHNESSES
HAGIARCHIES
HAGIOCRACIES
HAGIOCRACY
HAGIOGRAPHER
HAGIOGRAPHERS
HAGIOGRAPHIC
HAGIOGRAPHICAL
HAGIOGRAPHIES
HAGIOGRAPHIST
HAGIOGRAPHISTS
HAGIOGRAPHY
HAGIOLATER
HAGIOLATERS
HAGIOLATRIES
HAGIOLATROUS
HAGIOLATRY
HAGIOLOGIC
HAGIOLOGICAL
HAGIOLOGIES
HAGIOLOGIST
HAGIOLOGISTS
HAGIOSCOPE
HAGIOSCOPES
HAGIOSCOPIC
HAILSTONES
HAILSTORMS
HAIRBRAINED
HAIRBREADTH
HAIRBREADTHS
HAIRBRUSHES
HAIRCLOTHS
HAIRCUTTER

HAIRCUTTERS
HAIRCUTTING
HAIRCUTTINGS
HAIRDRESSER
HAIRDRESSERS
HAIRDRESSING
HAIRDRESSINGS
HAIRDRIERS
HAIRDRYERS
HAIRINESSES
HAIRLESSNESS
HAIRLESSNESSES
HAIRPIECES
HAIRSBREADTH
HAIRSBREADTHS
HAIRSPLITTER
HAIRSPLITTERS
HAIRSPLITTING
HAIRSPLITTINGS
HAIRSPRAYS
HAIRSPRING
HAIRSPRINGS
HAIRSTREAK
HAIRSTREAKS
HAIRSTYLES
HAIRSTYLING
HAIRSTYLINGS
HAIRSTYLIST
HAIRSTYLISTS
HAIRWEAVING
HAIRWEAVINGS
HAIRYBACKS
HALACHISTS
HALAKHISTS
HALBERDIER
HALBERDIERS
HALCYONIAN
HALENESSES
HALFENDEALE
HALFHEARTED
HALFHEARTEDLY
HALFHEARTEDNESS
HALFNESSES
HALFPENNIES
HALFPENNYWORTH
HALFPENNYWORTHS
HALFSERIOUSLY
HALFTRACKS
HALFWITTED
HALFWITTEDLY
HALFWITTEDNESS
HALIEUTICS
HALIPLANKTON
HALIPLANKTONS
HALLALLING
HALLEFLINTA
HALLEFLINTAS
HALLELUIAH
HALLELUIAHS

HALLELUJAH
HALLELUJAHS
HALLMARKED
HALLMARKING
HALLOWEDNESS
HALLOWEDNESSES
HALLOYSITE
HALLOYSITES
HALLSTANDS
HALLUCINATE
HALLUCINATED
HALLUCINATES
HALLUCINATING
HALLUCINATION
HALLUCINATIONAL
HALLUCINATIONS
HALLUCINATIVE
HALLUCINATOR
HALLUCINATORS
HALLUCINATORY
HALLUCINOGEN
HALLUCINOGENIC
HALLUCINOGENICS
HALLUCINOGENS
HALLUCINOSES
HALLUCINOSIS
HALOBIONTIC
HALOBIONTS
HALOBIOTIC
HALOCARBON
HALOCARBONS
HALOCLINES
HALOGENATE
HALOGENATED
HALOGENATES
HALOGENATING
HALOGENATION
HALOGENATIONS
HALOGENOID
HALOGENOUS
HALOGETONS
HALOMORPHIC
HALOPERIDOL
HALOPERIDOLS
HALOPHILES
HALOPHILIC
HALOPHILIES
HALOPHILOUS
HALOPHOBES
HALOPHYTES
HALOPHYTIC
HALOPHYTISM
HALOPHYTISMS
HALOTHANES
HALTERBREAK
HALTERBREAKING
HALTERBREAKS
HALTERBROKE
HALTERBROKEN

HALTERNECK
HALTERNECKS
HALTINGNESS
HALTINGNESSES
HAMADRYADES
HAMADRYADS
HAMADRYASES
HAMAMELIDACEOUS
HAMAMELISES
HAMANTASCH
HAMANTASCHEN
HAMARTHRITIS
HAMARTHRITISES
HAMARTIOLOGIES
HAMARTIOLOGY
HAMBURGERS
HAMBURGHER
HAMBURGHERS
HAMESUCKEN
HAMESUCKENS
HAMFATTERED
HAMFATTERING
HAMFATTERS
HAMMERCLOTH
HAMMERCLOTHS
HAMMERHEAD
HAMMERHEADED
HAMMERHEADS
HAMMERINGS
HAMMERKOPS
HAMMERLESS
HAMMERLOCKS
HAMMERSTONE
HAMMERSTONES
HAMMERTOES
HAMMINESSES
HAMPEREDNESS
HAMPEREDNESSES
HAMSHACKLE
HAMSHACKLED
HAMSHACKLES
HAMSHACKLING
HAMSTRINGED
HAMSTRINGING
HAMSTRINGS
HANDBAGGED
HANDBAGGING
HANDBAGGINGS
HANDBALLED
HANDBALLER
HANDBALLERS
HANDBALLING
HANDBARROW
HANDBARROWS
HANDBASKET
HANDBASKETS
HANDBRAKES
HANDBREADTH

HANDBREADTHS
HANDCLASPS
HANDCRAFTED
HANDCRAFTING
HANDCRAFTS
HANDCRAFTSMAN
HANDCRAFTSMEN
HANDCUFFED
HANDCUFFING
HANDEDNESS
HANDEDNESSES
HANDFASTED
HANDFASTING
HANDFASTINGS
HANDFEEDING
HANDICAPPED
HANDICAPPER
HANDICAPPERS
HANDICAPPING
HANDICRAFT
HANDICRAFTER
HANDICRAFTERS
HANDICRAFTS
HANDICRAFTSMAN
HANDICRAFTSMEN
HANDICUFFS
HANDINESSES
HANDIWORKS
HANDKERCHER
HANDKERCHERS
HANDKERCHIEF
HANDKERCHIEFS
HANDKERCHIEVES
HANDLANGER
HANDLANGERS
HANDLEABLE
HANDLEBARS
HANDLELESS
HANDMAIDEN
HANDMAIDENS
HANDPHONES
HANDPICKED
HANDPICKING
HANDPRESSES
HANDPRINTS
HANDSBREADTH
HANDSBREADTHS
HANDSELING
HANDSELLED
HANDSELLING
HANDSHAKES
HANDSHAKING
HANDSHAKINGS
HANDSOMELY
HANDSOMENESS
HANDSOMENESSES
HANDSOMEST
HANDSPIKES
HANDSPRING

HANDSPRINGS

HANDSPRINGS
HANDSTAFFS
HANDSTAMPED
HANDSTAMPING
HANDSTAMPS
HANDSTANDS
HANDSTAVES
HANDSTROKE
HANDSTROKES
HANDSTURNS
HANDTOWELS
HANDWHEELS
HANDWORKED
HANDWORKER
HANDWORKERS
HANDWRINGER
HANDWRINGERS
HANDWRITES
HANDWRITING
HANDWRITINGS
HANDWRITTEN
HANDWROUGHT
HANDYPERSON
HANDYPERSONS
HANDYWORKS
HANGABILITIES
HANGABILITY
HANKERINGS
HANSARDISE
HANSARDISED
HANSARDISES
HANSARDISING
HANSARDIZE
HANSARDIZED
HANSARDIZES
HANSARDIZING
HANSELLING
HANTAVIRUS
HANTAVIRUSES
HAPAXANTHIC
HAPAXANTHOUS
HAPHAZARDLY
HAPHAZARDNESS
HAPHAZARDNESSES
HAPHAZARDRIES
HAPHAZARDRY
HAPHAZARDS
HAPHTARAHS
HAPHTAROTH
HAPLESSNESS
HAPLESSNESSES
HAPLOBIONT
HAPLOBIONTIC
HAPLOBIONTS
HAPLOGRAPHIES
HAPLOGRAPHY
HAPLOIDIES
HAPLOLOGIC
HAPLOLOGIES

HAPLOSTEMONOUS
HAPLOTYPES
HAPPENCHANCE
HAPPENCHANCES
HAPPENINGS
HAPPENSTANCE
HAPPENSTANCES
HAPPINESSES
HAPTOGLOBIN
HAPTOGLOBINS
HAPTOTROPIC
HAPTOTROPISM
HAPTOTROPISMS
HARAMZADAS
HARAMZADIS
HARANGUERS
HARANGUING
HARASSEDLY
HARASSINGLY
HARASSINGS
HARASSMENT
HARASSMENTS
HARBINGERED
HARBINGERING
HARBINGERS
HARBORAGES
HARBORFULS
HARBORLESS
HARBORMASTER
HARBORMASTERS
HARBORSIDE
HARBOURAGE
HARBOURAGES
HARBOURERS
HARBOURING
HARBOURLESS
HARDBACKED
HARDBOARDS
HARDBOUNDS
HARDCOVERS
HARDENINGS
HARDFISTED
HARDGRASSES
HARDHANDED
HARDHANDEDNESS
HARDHEADED
HARDHEADEDLY
HARDHEADEDNESS
HARDHEARTED
HARDHEARTEDLY
HARDHEARTEDNESS
HARDIHEADS
HARDIHOODS
HARDIMENTS
HARDINESSES
HARDINGGRASS
HARDINGGRASSES
HARDLINERS
HARDMOUTHED

HARDNESSES
HARDSCRABBLE
HARDSTANDING
HARDSTANDINGS
HARDSTANDS
HARDWAREMAN
HARDWAREMEN
HARDWIRING
HARDWORKING
HAREBRAINED
HARELIPPED
HARESTAILS
HARIOLATED
HARIOLATES
HARIOLATING
HARIOLATION
HARIOLATIONS
HARLEQUINADE
HARLEQUINADES
HARLEQUINED
HARLEQUINING
HARLEQUINS
HARLOTRIES
HARMALINES
HARMATTANS
HARMDOINGS
HARMFULNESS
HARMFULNESSES
HARMLESSLY
HARMLESSNESS
HARMLESSNESSES
HARMOLODIC
HARMOLODICS
HARMONICAL
HARMONICALLY
HARMONICAS
HARMONICHORD
HARMONICHORDS
HARMONICIST
HARMONICISTS
HARMONICON
HARMONICONS
HARMONIOUS
HARMONIOUSLY
HARMONIOUSNESS
HARMONIPHON
HARMONIPHONE
HARMONIPHONES
HARMONIPHONS
HARMONISABLE
HARMONISATION
HARMONISATIONS
HARMONISED
HARMONISER
HARMONISERS
HARMONISES
HARMONISING
HARMONISTIC
HARMONISTICALLY

HARMONISTS
HARMONIUMIST
HARMONIUMISTS
HARMONIUMS
HARMONIZABLE
HARMONIZATION
HARMONIZATIONS
HARMONIZED
HARMONIZER
HARMONIZERS
HARMONIZES
HARMONIZING
HARMONOGRAM
HARMONOGRAMS
HARMONOGRAPH
HARMONOGRAPHS
HARMONOMETER
HARMONOMETERS
HARMOSTIES
HARMOTOMES
HARNESSERS
HARNESSING
HARNESSLESS
HARPOONEER
HARPOONEERS
HARPOONERS
HARPOONING
HARPSICHORD
HARPSICHORDIST
HARPSICHORDISTS
HARPSICHORDS
HARQUEBUSE
HARQUEBUSES
HARQUEBUSIER
HARQUEBUSIERS
HARQUEBUSS
HARQUEBUSSES
HARROWINGLY
HARROWINGS
HARROWMENT
HARROWMENTS
HARRUMPHED
HARRUMPHING
HARSHENING
HARSHNESSES
HARTBEESES
HARTBEESTS
HARTEBEEST
HARTEBEESTS
HARTSHORNS
HARUMPHING
HARUSPICAL
HARUSPICATE
HARUSPICATED
HARUSPICATES
HARUSPICATING
HARUSPICATION
HARUSPICATIONS
HARUSPICES

HARUSPICIES
HARVESTABLE
HARVESTERS
HARVESTING
HARVESTINGS
HARVESTLESS
HARVESTMAN
HARVESTMEN
HARVESTTIME
HARVESTTIMES
HASENPFEFFER
HASENPFEFFERS
HASHEESHES
HASTEFULLY
HASTINESSES
HATBRUSHES
HATCHABILITIES
HATCHABILITY
HATCHBACKS
HATCHELING
HATCHELLED
HATCHELLER
HATCHELLERS
HATCHELLING
HATCHERIES
HATCHETTITE
HATCHETTITES
HATCHLINGS
HATCHMENTS
HATEFULNESS
HATEFULNESSES
HATELESSNESS
HATELESSNESSES
HATEWORTHY
HATLESSNESS
HATLESSNESSES
HAUBERGEON
HAUBERGEONS
HAUGHTIEST
HAUGHTINESS
HAUGHTINESSES
HAUNTINGLY
HAUSFRAUEN
HAUSSMANNISE
HAUSSMANNISED
HAUSSMANNISES
HAUSSMANNISING
HAUSSMANNIZE
HAUSSMANNIZED
HAUSSMANNIZES
HAUSSMANNIZING
HAUSTELLATE
HAUSTELLUM
HAUSTORIAL
HAUSTORIUM
HAVERSACKS
HAVERSINES
HAWFINCHES
HAWKISHNESS

HAWKISHNESSES
HAWKSBEARD
HAWKSBEARDS
HAWKSBILLS
HAWSEHOLES
HAWSEPIPES
HAYMAKINGS
HAZARDABLE
HAZARDIZES
HAZARDOUSLY
HAZARDOUSNESS
HAZARDOUSNESSES
HAZARDRIES
HAZINESSES
HEADACHIER
HEADACHIEST
HEADBANGED
HEADBANGING
HEADBOARDS
HEADBOROUGH
HEADBOROUGHS
HEADCHAIRS
HEADCHEESE
HEADCHEESES
HEADCLOTHS
HEADCOUNTS
HEADDRESSES
HEADFISHES
HEADFOREMOST
HEADFRAMES
HEADGUARDS
HEADHUNTED
HEADHUNTER
HEADHUNTERS
HEADHUNTING
HEADHUNTINGS
HEADINESSES
HEADLEASES
HEADLESSNESS
HEADLESSNESSES
HEADLIGHTS
HEADLINERS
HEADLINING
HEADMASTER
HEADMASTERLY
HEADMASTERS
HEADMASTERSHIP
HEADMASTERSHIPS
HEADMISTRESS
HEADMISTRESSES
HEADMISTRESSY
HEADPEACES
HEADPHONES
HEADPIECES
HEADQUARTER
HEADQUARTERED
HEADQUARTERING
HEADQUARTERS
HEADREACHED

HEADREACHES
HEADREACHING
HEADSCARVES
HEADSHAKES
HEADSHEETS
HEADSHRINKER
HEADSHRINKERS
HEADSPACES
HEADSPRING
HEADSPRINGS
HEADSQUARE
HEADSQUARES
HEADSTALLS
HEADSTANDS
HEADSTICKS
HEADSTOCKS
HEADSTONES
HEADSTREAM
HEADSTREAMS
HEADSTRONG
HEADSTRONGLY
HEADSTRONGNESS
HEADWAITER
HEADWAITERS
HEADWATERS
HEADWORKER
HEADWORKERS
HEALTHCARE
HEALTHCARES
HEALTHFULLY
HEALTHFULNESS
HEALTHFULNESSES
HEALTHIEST
HEALTHINESS
HEALTHINESSES
HEALTHISMS
HEALTHLESS
HEALTHLESSNESS
HEALTHSOME
HEAPSTEADS
HEARKENERS
HEARKENING
HEARTACHES
HEARTBEATS
HEARTBREAK
HEARTBREAKER
HEARTBREAKERS
HEARTBREAKING
HEARTBREAKINGLY
HEARTBREAKS
HEARTBROKE
HEARTBROKEN
HEARTBROKENLY
HEARTBROKENNESS
HEARTBURNING
HEARTBURNINGS
HEARTBURNS
HEARTENERS
HEARTENING

HEARTENINGLY
HEARTHRUGS
HEARTHSTONE
HEARTHSTONES
HEARTIKINS
HEARTINESS
HEARTINESSES
HEARTLANDS
HEARTLESSLY
HEARTLESSNESS
HEARTLESSNESSES
HEARTLINGS
HEARTRENDING
HEARTRENDINGLY
HEARTSEASE
HEARTSEASES
HEARTSEEDS
HEARTSICKNESS
HEARTSICKNESSES
HEARTSOMELY
HEARTSOMENESS
HEARTSOMENESSES
HEARTSTRING
HEARTSTRINGS
HEARTTHROB
HEARTTHROBS
HEARTWARMING
HEARTWATER
HEARTWATERS
HEARTWOODS
HEARTWORMS
HEATEDNESS
HEATEDNESSES
HEATHBERRIES
HEATHBERRY
HEATHBIRDS
HEATHCOCKS
HEATHENDOM
HEATHENDOMS
HEATHENESSE
HEATHENESSES
HEATHENISE
HEATHENISED
HEATHENISES
HEATHENISH
HEATHENISHLY
HEATHENISHNESS
HEATHENISING
HEATHENISM
HEATHENISMS
HEATHENIZE
HEATHENIZED
HEATHENIZES
HEATHENIZING
HEATHENNESS
HEATHENNESSES
HEATHENRIES
HEATHERIER
HEATHERIEST

HEATHFOWLS
HEATHLANDS
HEATSTROKE
HEATSTROKES
HEAVENLIER
HEAVENLIEST
HEAVENLINESS
HEAVENLINESSES
HEAVENWARD
HEAVENWARDS
HEAVINESSES
HEAVYHEARTED
HEAVYHEARTEDLY
HEAVYWEIGHT
HEAVYWEIGHTS
HEBDOMADAL
HEBDOMADALLY
HEBDOMADAR
HEBDOMADARIES
HEBDOMADARS
HEBDOMADARY
HEBDOMADER
HEBDOMADERS
HEBEPHRENIA
HEBEPHRENIAC
HEBEPHRENIACS
HEBEPHRENIAS
HEBEPHRENIC
HEBEPHRENICS
HEBETATING
HEBETATION
HEBETATIONS
HEBETATIVE
HEBETUDINOSITY
HEBETUDINOUS
HEBRAISATION
HEBRAISATIONS
HEBRAISING
HEBRAIZATION
HEBRAIZATIONS
HEBRAIZING
HECKELPHONE
HECKELPHONES
HECOGENINS
HECTICALLY
HECTOCOTYLI
HECTOCOTYLUS
HECTOGRAMME
HECTOGRAMMES
HECTOGRAMS
HECTOGRAPH
HECTOGRAPHED
HECTOGRAPHIC
HECTOGRAPHIES
HECTOGRAPHING
HECTOGRAPHS
HECTOGRAPHY
HECTOLITER
HECTOLITERS

HECTOLITRE
HECTOLITRES
HECTOMETER
HECTOMETERS
HECTOMETRE
HECTOMETRES
HECTORINGLY
HECTORINGS
HECTORISMS
HECTORSHIP
HECTORSHIPS
HECTOSTERE
HECTOSTERES
HEDGEBILLS
HEDGEHOPPED
HEDGEHOPPER
HEDGEHOPPERS
HEDGEHOPPING
HEDGEHOPPINGS
HEDONICALLY
HEDONISTIC
HEDONISTICALLY
HEDYPHANES
HEEDFULNESS
HEEDFULNESSES
HEEDINESSES
HEEDLESSLY
HEEDLESSNESS
HEEDLESSNESSES
HEELPIECES
HEELPLATES
HEFTINESSES
HEGEMONIAL
HEGEMONICAL
HEGEMONIES
HEGEMONISM
HEGEMONISMS
HEGEMONIST
HEGEMONISTS
HEGUMENIES
HEGUMENOSES
HEIGHTENED
HEIGHTENER
HEIGHTENERS
HEIGHTENING
HEIGHTISMS
HEINOUSNESS
HEINOUSNESSES
HEKTOGRAMS
HELDENTENOR
HELDENTENORS
HELIACALLY
HELIANTHEMUM
HELIANTHEMUMS
HELIANTHUS
HELIANTHUSES
HELIBUSSES
HELICHRYSUM
HELICHRYSUMS

HELICITIES
HELICLINES
HELICOGRAPH
HELICOGRAPHS
HELICOIDAL
HELICOIDALLY
HELICONIAS
HELICOPTED
HELICOPTER
HELICOPTERED
HELICOPTERING
HELICOPTERS
HELICOPTING
HELICTITES
HELIDROMES
HELILIFTED
HELILIFTING
HELIOCENTRIC
HELIOCENTRICISM
HELIOCENTRICITY
HELIOCHROME
HELIOCHROMES
HELIOCHROMIC
HELIOCHROMIES
HELIOCHROMY
HELIOGRAMS
HELIOGRAPH
HELIOGRAPHED
HELIOGRAPHER
HELIOGRAPHERS
HELIOGRAPHIC
HELIOGRAPHICAL
HELIOGRAPHIES
HELIOGRAPHING
HELIOGRAPHS
HELIOGRAPHY
HELIOGRAVURE
HELIOGRAVURES
HELIOLATER
HELIOLATERS
HELIOLATRIES
HELIOLATROUS
HELIOLATRY
HELIOLITHIC
HELIOLOGIES
HELIOMETER
HELIOMETERS
HELIOMETRIC
HELIOMETRICAL
HELIOMETRICALLY
HELIOMETRIES
HELIOMETRY
HELIOPAUSE
HELIOPAUSES
HELIOPHILOUS
HELIOPHOBIC
HELIOPHYTE
HELIOPHYTES
HELIOSCIOPHYTE

HELIOSCIOPHYTES
HELIOSCOPE
HELIOSCOPES
HELIOSCOPIC
HELIOSPHERE
HELIOSPHERES
HELIOSTATIC
HELIOSTATS
HELIOTACTIC
HELIOTAXES
HELIOTAXIS
HELIOTHERAPIES
HELIOTHERAPY
HELIOTROPE
HELIOTROPES
HELIOTROPIC
HELIOTROPICAL
HELIOTROPICALLY
HELIOTROPIES
HELIOTROPIN
HELIOTROPINS
HELIOTROPISM
HELIOTROPISMS
HELIOTROPY
HELIOTYPED
HELIOTYPES
HELIOTYPIC
HELIOTYPIES
HELIOTYPING
HELIOZOANS
HELIPILOTS
HELISPHERIC
HELISPHERICAL
HELLACIOUS
HELLACIOUSLY
HELLBENDER
HELLBENDERS
HELLBROTHS
HELLDIVERS
HELLEBORES
HELLEBORINE
HELLEBORINES
HELLENISATION
HELLENISATIONS
HELLENISED
HELLENISES
HELLENISING
HELLENIZATION
HELLENIZATIONS
HELLENIZED
HELLENIZES
HELLENIZING
HELLGRAMITE
HELLGRAMITES
HELLGRAMMITE
HELLGRAMMITES
HELLHOUNDS
HELLISHNESS
HELLISHNESSES

HELMETLIKE	HEMATOPOIESIS	HEMIPARASITES	HEMOPHILIA
HELMINTHIASES	HEMATOPOIETIC	HEMIPARASITIC	HEMOPHILIAC
HELMINTHIASIS	HEMATOPORPHYRIN	HEMIPLEGIA	HEMOPHILIACS
HELMINTHIC	HEMATOTHERMAL	HEMIPLEGIAS	HEMOPHILIAS
HELMINTHICS	HEMATOXYLIN	HEMIPLEGIC	HEMOPHILIC
HELMINTHOID	HEMATOXYLINS	HEMIPLEGICS	HEMOPHILICS
HELMINTHOLOGIC	HEMATOZOON	HEMIPTERAL	HEMOPHILIOID
HELMINTHOLOGIES	HEMATURIAS	HEMIPTERAN	HEMOPOIESES
HELMINTHOLOGIST	HEMELYTRAL	HEMIPTERANS	HEMOPOIESIS
HELMINTHOLOGY	HEMELYTRON	HEMIPTERON	HEMOPOIETIC
HELMINTHOUS	HEMELYTRUM	HEMIPTERONS	HEMOPROTEIN
HELMSMANSHIP	HEMERALOPIA	HEMIPTEROUS	HEMOPROTEINS
HELMSMANSHIPS	HEMERALOPIAS	HEMISPACES	HEMOPTYSES
HELOPHYTES	HEMERALOPIC	HEMISPHERE	HEMOPTYSIS
HELPFULNESS	HEMEROCALLIS	HEMISPHERES	HEMORRHAGE
HELPFULNESSES	HEMEROCALLISES	HEMISPHERIC	HEMORRHAGED
HELPLESSLY	HEMERYTHRIN	HEMISPHERICAL	HEMORRHAGES
HELPLESSNESS	HEMERYTHRINS	HEMISPHEROID	HEMORRHAGIC
HELPLESSNESSES	HEMIACETAL	HEMISPHEROIDAL	HEMORRHAGING
HELVETIUMS	HEMIACETALS	HEMISPHEROIDS	HEMORRHOID
HEMACHROME	HEMIALGIAS	HEMISTICHAL	HEMORRHOIDAL
HEMACHROMES	HEMIANOPIA	HEMISTICHS	HEMORRHOIDALS
HEMACYTOMETER	HEMIANOPIAS	HEMITERPENE	HEMORRHOIDS
HEMACYTOMETERS	HEMIANOPSIA	HEMITERPENES	HEMOSIDERIN
HEMAGGLUTINATE	HEMIANOPSIAS	HEMITROPAL	HEMOSIDERINS
HEMAGGLUTINATED	HEMIANOPTIC	HEMITROPES	HEMOSTASES
HEMAGGLUTINATES	HEMICELLULOSE	HEMITROPIC	HEMOSTASIA
HEMAGGLUTININ	HEMICELLULOSES	HEMITROPIES	HEMOSTASIAS
HEMAGGLUTININS	HEMICHORDATE	HEMITROPISM	HEMOSTASIS
HEMAGOGUES	HEMICHORDATES	HEMITROPISMS	HEMOSTATIC
HEMANGIOMA	HEMICRANIA	HEMITROPOUS	HEMOSTATICS
HEMANGIOMAS	HEMICRANIAS	HEMIZYGOUS	HEMOTOXINS
HEMANGIOMATA	HEMICRYPTOPHYTE	HEMOCHROMATOSES	HEMSTITCHED
HEMATEMESES	HEMICRYSTALLINE	HEMOCHROMATOSIS	HEMSTITCHER
HEMATEMESIS	HEMICYCLES	HEMOCHROME	HEMSTITCHERS
HEMATINICS	HEMICYCLIC	HEMOCHROMES	HEMSTITCHES
HEMATOBLAST	HEMIELYTRA	HEMOCYANIN	HEMSTITCHING
HEMATOBLASTIC	HEMIELYTRAL	HEMOCYANINS	HENCEFORTH
HEMATOBLASTS	HEMIELYTRON	HEMOCYTOMETER	HENCEFORWARD
HEMATOCELE	HEMIHEDRAL	HEMOCYTOMETERS	HENCEFORWARDS
HEMATOCELES	HEMIHEDRIES	HEMODIALYSES	HENCHPERSON
HEMATOCRIT	HEMIHEDRISM	HEMODIALYSIS	HENCHPERSONS
HEMATOCRITS	HEMIHEDRISMS	HEMODILUTION	HENCHWOMAN
HEMATOCRYAL	HEMIHEDRON	HEMODILUTIONS	HENCHWOMEN
HEMATOGENESES	HEMIHEDRONS	HEMODYNAMIC	HENDECAGON
HEMATOGENESIS	HEMIHYDRATE	HEMODYNAMICALLY	HENDECAGONAL
HEMATOGENETIC	HEMIHYDRATED	HEMODYNAMICS	HENDECAGONS
HEMATOGENOUS	HEMIHYDRATES	HEMOFLAGELLATE	HENDECAHEDRA
HEMATOLOGIC	HEMIMETABOLOUS	HEMOFLAGELLATES	HENDECAHEDRON
HEMATOLOGICAL	HEMIMORPHIC	HEMOGLOBIN	HENDECAHEDRONS
HEMATOLOGIES	HEMIMORPHIES	HEMOGLOBINS	HENDECASYLLABIC
HEMATOLOGIST	HEMIMORPHISM	HEMOGLOBINURIA	HENDECASYLLABLE
HEMATOLOGISTS	HEMIMORPHISMS	HEMOGLOBINURIAS	HENDIADYSES
HEMATOLOGY	HEMIMORPHITE	HEMOGLOBINURIC	HENOTHEISM
HEMATOLYSES	HEMIMORPHITES	HEMOLYMPHS	HENOTHEISMS
HEMATOLYSIS	HEMIMORPHY	HEMOLYSING	HENOTHEIST
HEMATOMATA	HEMIONUSES	HEMOLYSINS	HENOTHEISTIC
HEMATOPHAGOUS	HEMIOPSIAS	HEMOLYZING	HENOTHEISTS
HEMATOPOIESES	HEMIPARASITE	HEMOPHILES	HENPECKERIES

HENPECKERY	HEPTAMETER	HEREDITABLE	HERMENEUTIST
HENPECKING	HEPTAMETERS	HEREDITABLY	HERMENEUTISTS
HEORTOLOGICAL	HEPTAMETRICAL	HEREDITAMENT	HERMETICAL
HEORTOLOGIES	HEPTANDROUS	HEREDITAMENTS	HERMETICALLY
HEORTOLOGIST	HEPTANGULAR	HEREDITARIAN	HERMETICISM
HEORTOLOGISTS	HEPTAPODIC	HEREDITARIANISM	HERMETICISMS
HEORTOLOGY	HEPTAPODIES	HEREDITARIANIST	HERMETICITIES
HEPARINISED	HEPTARCHAL	HEREDITARIANS	HERMETICITY
HEPARINIZED	HEPTARCHIC	HEREDITARILY	HERMETISMS
HEPARINOID	HEPTARCHIES	HEREDITARINESS	HERMETISTS
HEPATECTOMIES	HEPTARCHIST	HEREDITARY	HERMITAGES
HEPATECTOMISED	HEPTARCHISTS	HEREDITIES	HERMITESSES
HEPATECTOMIZED	HEPTASTICH	HEREDITIST	HERMITICAL
HEPATECTOMY	HEPTASTICHS	HEREDITISTS	HERMITICALLY
HEPATICOLOGICAL	HEPTASYLLABIC	HEREINABOVE	HERMITISMS
HEPATICOLOGIES	HEPTATHLETE	HEREINAFTER	HERMITRIES
HEPATICOLOGIST	HEPTATHLETES	HEREINBEFORE	HERNIATING
HEPATICOLOGISTS	HEPTATHLON	HEREINBELOW	HERNIATION
HEPATICOLOGY	HEPTATHLONS	HERENESSES	HERNIATIONS
HEPATISATION	HEPTATONIC	HERESIARCH	HERNIORRHAPHIES
HEPATISATIONS	HEPTAVALENT	HERESIARCHS	HERNIORRHAPHY
HEPATISING	HERALDICALLY	HERESIOGRAPHER	HERNIOTOMIES
HEPATITIDES	HERALDISTS	HERESIOGRAPHERS	HERNIOTOMY
HEPATITISES	HERALDRIES	HERESIOGRAPHIES	HEROICALLY
HEPATIZATION	HERALDSHIP	HERESIOGRAPHY	HEROICALNESS
HEPATIZATIONS	HERALDSHIPS	HERESIOLOGIES	HEROICALNESSES
HEPATIZING	HERBACEOUS	HERESIOLOGIST	HEROICISED
HEPATOCELLULAR	HERBACEOUSLY	HERESIOLOGISTS	HEROICISES
HEPATOCYTE	HERBALISMS	HERESIOLOGY	HEROICISING
HEPATOCYTES	HERBALISTS	HERESTHETIC	HEROICIZED
HEPATOGENOUS	HERBARIANS	HERESTHETICAL	HEROICIZES
HEPATOLOGIES	HERBARIUMS	HERESTHETICIAN	HEROICIZING
HEPATOLOGIST	HERBICIDAL	HERESTHETICIANS	HEROICNESS
HEPATOLOGISTS	HERBICIDALLY	HERESTHETICS	HEROICNESSES
HEPATOLOGY	HERBICIDES	HERETICALLY	HEROICOMIC
HEPATOMATA	HERBIVORES	HERETICATE	HEROICOMICAL
HEPATOMEGALIES	HERBIVORIES	HERETICATED	HEROINISMS
HEPATOMEGALY	HERBIVOROUS	HERETICATES	HERONSHAWS
HEPATOPANCREAS	HERBIVOROUSLY	HERETICATING	HERPESVIRUS
HEPATOSCOPIES	HERBIVOROUSNESS	HERETOFORE	HERPESVIRUSES
HEPATOSCOPY	HERBOLOGIES	HERETRICES	HERPETOFAUNA
HEPATOTOXIC	HERBORISATION	HERETRIXES	HERPETOFAUNAE
HEPATOTOXICITY	HERBORISATIONS	HERIOTABLE	HERPETOFAUNAS
HEPHTHEMIMER	HERBORISED	HERITABILITIES	HERPETOLOGIC
HEPHTHEMIMERAL	HERBORISES	HERITABILITY	HERPETOLOGICAL
HEPHTHEMIMERS	HERBORISING	HERITRESSES	HERPETOLOGIES
HEPTACHLOR	HERBORISTS	HERITRICES	HERPETOLOGIST
HEPTACHLORS	HERBORIZATION	HERITRIXES	HERPETOLOGISTS
HEPTACHORD	HERBORIZATIONS	HERKOGAMIES	HERPETOLOGY
HEPTACHORDS	HERBORIZED	HERMANDADS	HERRENVOLK
HEPTADECANOIC	HERBORIZES	HERMAPHRODITE	HERRENVOLKS
HEPTAGLOTS	HERBORIZING	HERMAPHRODITES	HERRIMENTS
HEPTAGONAL	HERCOGAMIES	HERMAPHRODITIC	HERRINGBONE
HEPTAGYNOUS	HERCOGAMOUS	HERMAPHRODITISM	HERRINGBONED
HEPTAHEDRA	HERCULESES	HERMATYPIC	HERRINGBONES
HEPTAHEDRAL	HERCYNITES	HERMENEUTIC	HERRINGBONING
HEPTAHEDRON	HEREABOUTS	HERMENEUTICAL	HERRINGERS
HEPTAHEDRONS	HEREAFTERS	HERMENEUTICALLY	HERRYMENTS
HEPTAMEROUS	HEREDITABILITY	HERMENEUTICS	HERSTORIES

HESITANCES
HESITANCIES
HESITANTLY
HESITATERS
HESITATING
HESITATINGLY
HESITATION
HESITATIONS
HESITATIVE
HESITATORS
HESITATORY
HESPERIDIA
HESPERIDIN
HESPERIDINS
HESPERIDIUM
HESPERIDIUMS
HESSONITES
HETAERISMIC
HETAERISMS
HETAERISTIC
HETAERISTS
HETAIRISMIC
HETAIRISMS
HETAIRISTIC
HETAIRISTS
HETERARCHIES
HETERARCHY
HETERAUXESES
HETERAUXESIS
HETEROATOM
HETEROATOMS
HETEROAUXIN
HETEROAUXINS
HETEROBLASTIC
HETEROBLASTIES
HETEROBLASTY
HETEROCARPOUS
HETEROCERCAL
HETEROCERCALITY
HETEROCERCIES
HETEROCERCY
HETEROCHROMATIC
HETEROCHROMATIN
HETEROCHROMOUS
HETEROCHRONIC
HETEROCHRONIES
HETEROCHRONISM
HETEROCHRONISMS
HETEROCHRONOUS
HETEROCHRONY
HETEROCLITE
HETEROCLITES
HETEROCLITIC
HETEROCLITOUS
HETEROCONT
HETEROCONTS
HETEROCYCLE
HETEROCYCLES
HETEROCYCLIC

HETEROCYCLICS
HETEROCYST
HETEROCYSTOUS
HETEROCYSTS
HETERODACTYL
HETERODACTYLOUS
HETERODACTYLS
HETERODONT
HETERODOXIES
HETERODOXY
HETERODUPLEX
HETERODUPLEXES
HETERODYNE
HETERODYNED
HETERODYNES
HETERODYNING
HETEROECIOUS
HETEROECISM
HETEROECISMS
HETEROFLEXIBLE
HETEROFLEXIBLES
HETEROGAMETE
HETEROGAMETES
HETEROGAMETIC
HETEROGAMETIES
HETEROGAMETY
HETEROGAMIES
HETEROGAMOUS
HETEROGAMY
HETEROGENEITIES
HETEROGENEITY
HETEROGENEOUS
HETEROGENEOUSLY
HETEROGENESES
HETEROGENESIS
HETEROGENETIC
HETEROGENIC
HETEROGENIES
HETEROGENOUS
HETEROGENY
HETEROGONIC
HETEROGONIES
HETEROGONOUS
HETEROGONOUSLY
HETEROGONY
HETEROGRAFT
HETEROGRAFTS
HETEROGRAPHIC
HETEROGRAPHICAL
HETEROGRAPHIES
HETEROGRAPHY
HETEROGYNOUS
HETEROKARYON
HETEROKARYONS
HETEROKARYOSES
HETEROKARYOSIS
HETEROKARYOTIC
HETEROKONT
HETEROKONTAN

HETEROKONTS
HETEROLECITHAL
HETEROLOGIES
HETEROLOGOUS
HETEROLOGOUSLY
HETEROLOGY
HETEROLYSES
HETEROLYSIS
HETEROLYTIC
HETEROMEROUS
HETEROMORPHIC
HETEROMORPHIES
HETEROMORPHISM
HETEROMORPHISMS
HETEROMORPHOUS
HETEROMORPHY
HETERONOMIES
HETERONOMOUS
HETERONOMOUSLY
HETERONOMY
HETERONYMOUS
HETERONYMOUSLY
HETERONYMS
HETEROOUSIAN
HETEROOUSIANS
HETEROPHIL
HETEROPHILE
HETEROPHONIES
HETEROPHONY
HETEROPHYLLIES
HETEROPHYLLOUS
HETEROPHYLLY
HETEROPLASIA
HETEROPLASIAS
HETEROPLASTIC
HETEROPLASTIES
HETEROPLASTY
HETEROPLOID
HETEROPLOIDIES
HETEROPLOIDS
HETEROPLOIDY
HETEROPODS
HETEROPOLAR
HETEROPOLARITY
HETEROPTERAN
HETEROPTEROUS
HETEROSCEDASTIC
HETEROSCIAN
HETEROSCIANS
HETEROSEXISM
HETEROSEXISMS
HETEROSEXIST
HETEROSEXISTS
HETEROSEXUAL
HETEROSEXUALITY
HETEROSEXUALLY
HETEROSEXUALS
HETEROSOCIAL
HETEROSOCIALITY

HETEROSOMATOUS
HETEROSPECIFIC
HETEROSPORIES
HETEROSPOROUS
HETEROSPORY
HETEROSTROPHIC
HETEROSTROPHIES
HETEROSTROPHY
HETEROSTYLED
HETEROSTYLIES
HETEROSTYLISM
HETEROSTYLISMS
HETEROSTYLOUS
HETEROSTYLY
HETEROTACTIC
HETEROTACTOUS
HETEROTAXES
HETEROTAXIA
HETEROTAXIAS
HETEROTAXIC
HETEROTAXIES
HETEROTAXIS
HETEROTAXY
HETEROTHALLIC
HETEROTHALLIES
HETEROTHALLISM
HETEROTHALLISMS
HETEROTHALLY
HETEROTHERMAL
HETEROTOPIA
HETEROTOPIAS
HETEROTOPIC
HETEROTOPIES
HETEROTOPOUS
HETEROTOPY
HETEROTROPH
HETEROTROPHIC
HETEROTROPHIES
HETEROTROPHS
HETEROTROPHY
HETEROTYPIC
HETEROTYPICAL
HETEROUSIAN
HETEROUSIANS
HETEROZYGOSES
HETEROZYGOSIS
HETEROZYGOSITY
HETEROZYGOTE
HETEROZYGOTES
HETEROZYGOUS
HETHERWARD
HETMANATES
HETMANSHIP
HETMANSHIPS
HEULANDITE
HEULANDITES
HEURISTICALLY
HEURISTICS
HEXACHLORETHANE

HEXACHLORIDE
HEXACHLORIDES
HEXACHLOROPHANE
HEXACHLOROPHENE
HEXACHORDS
HEXACOSANOIC
HEXACTINAL
HEXACTINELLID
HEXACTINELLIDS
HEXADACTYLIC
HEXADACTYLOUS
HEXADECANE
HEXADECANES
HEXADECANOIC
HEXADECIMAL
HEXADECIMALS
HEXAEMERIC
HEXAEMERON
HEXAEMERONS
HEXAFLUORIDE
HEXAFLUORIDES
HEXAGONALLY
HEXAGRAMMOID
HEXAGRAMMOIDS
HEXAGYNIAN
HEXAGYNOUS
HEXAHEDRAL
HEXAHEDRON
HEXAHEDRONS
HEXAHEMERIC
HEXAHEMERON
HEXAHEMERONS
HEXAHYDRATE
HEXAHYDRATED
HEXAHYDRATES
HEXAMERISM
HEXAMERISMS
HEXAMEROUS
HEXAMETERS
HEXAMETHONIUM
HEXAMETHONIUMS
HEXAMETRAL
HEXAMETRIC
HEXAMETRICAL
HEXAMETRISE
HEXAMETRISED
HEXAMETRISES
HEXAMETRISING
HEXAMETRIST
HEXAMETRISTS
HEXAMETRIZE
HEXAMETRIZED
HEXAMETRIZES
HEXAMETRIZING
HEXANDRIAN
HEXANDROUS
HEXANGULAR
HEXAPLARIAN
HEXAPLARIC

HEXAPLOIDIES
HEXAPLOIDS
HEXAPLOIDY
HEXAPODIES
HEXARCHIES
HEXASTICHAL
HEXASTICHIC
HEXASTICHON
HEXASTICHONS
HEXASTICHS
HEXASTYLES
HEXATEUCHAL
HEXAVALENT
HEXOBARBITAL
HEXOBARBITALS
HEXOKINASE
HEXOKINASES
HEXOSAMINIDASE
HEXOSAMINIDASES
HEXYLRESORCINOL
HIBAKUSHAS
HIBERNACLE
HIBERNACLES
HIBERNACULA
HIBERNACULUM
HIBERNATED
HIBERNATES
HIBERNATING
HIBERNATION
HIBERNATIONS
HIBERNATOR
HIBERNATORS
HIBERNICISE
HIBERNICISED
HIBERNICISES
HIBERNICISING
HIBERNICIZE
HIBERNICIZED
HIBERNICIZES
HIBERNICIZING
HIBERNISATION
HIBERNISATIONS
HIBERNISED
HIBERNISES
HIBERNISING
HIBERNIZATION
HIBERNIZATIONS
HIBERNIZED
HIBERNIZES
HIBERNIZING
HIBISCUSES
HICCOUGHED
HICCOUGHING
HICCUPPING
HIDALGOISH
HIDALGOISM
HIDALGOISMS
HIDDENITES
HIDDENMOST

HIDDENNESS
HIDDENNESSES
HIDEOSITIES
HIDEOUSNESS
HIDEOUSNESSES
HIERACIUMS
HIERACOSPHINGES
HIERACOSPHINX
HIERACOSPHINXES
HIERARCHAL
HIERARCHIC
HIERARCHICAL
HIERARCHICALLY
HIERARCHIES
HIERARCHISE
HIERARCHISED
HIERARCHISES
HIERARCHISING
HIERARCHISM
HIERARCHISMS
HIERARCHIZE
HIERARCHIZED
HIERARCHIZES
HIERARCHIZING
HIERATICAL
HIERATICALLY
HIERATICAS
HIEROCRACIES
HIEROCRACY
HIEROCRATIC
HIEROCRATICAL
HIEROCRATS
HIERODULES
HIERODULIC
HIEROGLYPH
HIEROGLYPHED
HIEROGLYPHIC
HIEROGLYPHICAL
HIEROGLYPHICS
HIEROGLYPHING
HIEROGLYPHIST
HIEROGLYPHISTS
HIEROGLYPHS
HIEROGRAMMAT
HIEROGRAMMATE
HIEROGRAMMATES
HIEROGRAMMATIC
HIEROGRAMMATIST
HIEROGRAMMATS
HIEROGRAMS
HIEROGRAPH
HIEROGRAPHER
HIEROGRAPHERS
HIEROGRAPHIC
HIEROGRAPHICAL
HIEROGRAPHIES
HIEROGRAPHS
HIEROGRAPHY
HIEROLATRIES

HIEROLATRY
HIEROLOGIC
HIEROLOGICAL
HIEROLOGIES
HIEROLOGIST
HIEROLOGISTS
HIEROMANCIES
HIEROMANCY
HIEROPHANT
HIEROPHANTIC
HIEROPHANTS
HIEROPHOBIA
HIEROPHOBIAS
HIEROPHOBIC
HIEROSCOPIES
HIEROSCOPY
HIERURGICAL
HIERURGIES
HIGHBALLED
HIGHBALLING
HIGHBINDER
HIGHBINDERS
HIGHBLOODED
HIGHBROWED
HIGHBROWISM
HIGHBROWISMS
HIGHCHAIRS
HIGHERMOST
HIGHFALUTIN
HIGHFALUTING
HIGHFALUTINGS
HIGHFALUTINS
HIGHFLIERS
HIGHFLYERS
HIGHJACKED
HIGHJACKER
HIGHJACKERS
HIGHJACKING
HIGHLANDER
HIGHLANDERS
HIGHLIGHTED
HIGHLIGHTER
HIGHLIGHTERS
HIGHLIGHTING
HIGHLIGHTS
HIGHNESSES
HIGHTAILED
HIGHTAILING
HIGHWAYMAN
HIGHWAYMEN
HIGHWROUGHT
HILARIOUSLY
HILARIOUSNESS
HILARIOUSNESSES
HILARITIES
HILLBILLIES
HILLCRESTS
HILLINESSES
HILLSLOPES

HILLWALKER	HIPPOPHAGISTS	HISTIOLOGY	HISTORIOLOGIES
HILLWALKERS	HIPPOPHAGOUS	HISTIOPHOROID	HISTORIOLOGY
HILLWALKING	HIPPOPHAGY	HISTOBLAST	HISTORISMS
HILLWALKINGS	HIPPOPHILE	HISTOBLASTS	HISTORYING
HINDBERRIES	HIPPOPHILES	HISTOCHEMICAL	HISTRIONIC
HINDBRAINS	HIPPOPHOBE	HISTOCHEMICALLY	HISTRIONICAL
HINDERANCE	HIPPOPHOBES	HISTOCHEMIST	HISTRIONICALLY
HINDERANCES	HIPPOPOTAMI	HISTOCHEMISTRY	HISTRIONICISM
HINDERINGLY	HIPPOPOTAMIAN	HISTOCHEMISTS	HISTRIONICISMS
HINDERINGS	HIPPOPOTAMIC	HISTOCOMPATIBLE	HISTRIONICS
HINDERLAND	HIPPOPOTAMUS	HISTOGENESES	HISTRIONISM
HINDERLANDS	HIPPOPOTAMUSES	HISTOGENESIS	HISTRIONISMS
HINDERLANS	HIPPURITES	HISTOGENETIC	HITCHHIKED
HINDERLINGS	HIPPURITIC	HISTOGENIC	HITCHHIKER
HINDERLINS	HIPSTERISM	HISTOGENICALLY	HITCHHIKERS
HINDERMOST	HIPSTERISMS	HISTOGENIES	HITCHHIKES
HINDFOREMOST	HIRCOCERVUS	HISTOGRAMS	HITCHHIKING
HINDQUARTER	HIRCOCERVUSES	HISTOLOGIC	HITHERMOST
HINDQUARTERS	HIRCOSITIES	HISTOLOGICAL	HITHERSIDE
HINDRANCES	HIRSELLING	HISTOLOGICALLY	HITHERSIDES
HINDSHANKS	HIRSUTENESS	HISTOLOGIES	HITHERWARD
HINDSIGHTS	HIRSUTENESSES	HISTOLOGIST	HITHERWARDS
HINTERLAND	HIRSUTISMS	HISTOLOGISTS	HOACTZINES
HINTERLANDS	HIRUDINEAN	HISTOLYSES	HOARFROSTS
HIPPEASTRUM	HIRUDINEANS	HISTOLYSIS	HOARHOUNDS
HIPPEASTRUMS	HIRUDINOID	HISTOLYTIC	HOARINESSES
HIPPIATRIC	HIRUDINOUS	HISTOLYTICALLY	HOARSENESS
HIPPIATRICS	HISPANICISE	HISTOPATHOLOGIC	HOARSENESSES
HIPPIATRIES	HISPANICISED	HISTOPATHOLOGY	HOARSENING
HIPPIATRIST	HISPANICISES	HISTOPHYSIOLOGY	HOBBITRIES
HIPPIATRISTS	HISPANICISING	HISTOPLASMOSES	HOBBLEBUSH
HIPPIEDOMS	HISPANICISM	HISTOPLASMOSIS	HOBBLEBUSHES
HIPPIENESS	HISPANICISMS	HISTORIANS	HOBBLEDEHOY
HIPPIENESSES	HISPANICIZE	HISTORIATED	HOBBLEDEHOYDOM
HIPPINESSES	HISPANICIZED	HISTORICAL	HOBBLEDEHOYDOMS
HIPPOCAMPAL	HISPANICIZES	HISTORICALLY	HOBBLEDEHOYHOOD
HIPPOCAMPI	HISPANICIZING	HISTORICALNESS	HOBBLEDEHOYISH
HIPPOCAMPUS	HISPANIDAD	HISTORICISE	HOBBLEDEHOYISM
HIPPOCENTAUR	HISPANIDADS	HISTORICISED	HOBBLEDEHOYISMS
HIPPOCENTAURS	HISPANIOLISE	HISTORICISES	HOBBLEDEHOYS
HIPPOCRASES	HISPANIOLISED	HISTORICISING	HOBBLINGLY
HIPPOCREPIAN	HISPANIOLISES	HISTORICISM	HOBBYHORSE
HIPPODAMES	HISPANIOLISING	HISTORICISMS	HOBBYHORSED
HIPPODAMIST	HISPANIOLIZE	HISTORICIST	HOBBYHORSES
HIPPODAMISTS	HISPANIOLIZED	HISTORICISTS	HOBBYHORSING
HIPPODAMOUS	HISPANIOLIZES	HISTORICITIES	HOBGOBLINISM
HIPPODROME	HISPANIOLIZING	HISTORICITY	HOBGOBLINISMS
HIPPODROMES	HISPANISMS	HISTORICIZE	HOBGOBLINRIES
HIPPODROMIC	HISPIDITIES	HISTORICIZED	HOBGOBLINRY
HIPPOGRIFF	HISTAMINASE	HISTORICIZES	HOBGOBLINS
HIPPOGRIFFS	HISTAMINASES	HISTORICIZING	HOBJOBBERS
HIPPOGRYPH	HISTAMINERGIC	HISTORIETTE	HOBJOBBING
HIPPOGRYPHS	HISTAMINES	HISTORIETTES	HOBJOBBINGS
HIPPOLOGIES	HISTAMINIC	HISTORIFIED	HOBNAILING
HIPPOLOGIST	HISTIDINES	HISTORIFIES	HOBNOBBERS
HIPPOLOGISTS	HISTIOCYTE	HISTORIFYING	HOBNOBBING
HIPPOMANES	HISTIOCYTES	HISTORIOGRAPHER	HOCHMAGANDIES
HIPPOPHAGIES	HISTIOCYTIC	HISTORIOGRAPHIC	HOCHMAGANDY
HIPPOPHAGIST	HISTIOLOGIES	HISTORIOGRAPHY	HODGEPODGE

HODGEPODGES	HOLOGYNIES	HOMEOPATHIES	HOMINIZATIONS
HODMANDODS	HOLOHEDRAL	HOMEOPATHIST	HOMINIZING
HODOGRAPHIC	HOLOHEDRISM	HOMEOPATHISTS	HOMOBLASTIC
HODOGRAPHS	HOLOHEDRISMS	HOMEOPATHS	HOMOBLASTIES
HODOMETERS	HOLOHEDRON	HOMEOPATHY	HOMOBLASTY
HODOMETRIES	HOLOHEDRONS	HOMEOSTASES	HOMOCENTRIC
HODOSCOPES	HOLOMETABOLIC	HOMEOSTASIS	HOMOCENTRICALLY
HOGGISHNESS	HOLOMETABOLISM	HOMEOSTATIC	HOMOCERCAL
HOGGISHNESSES	HOLOMETABOLISMS	HOMEOTELEUTON	HOMOCERCIES
HOIDENISHNESS	HOLOMETABOLOUS	HOMEOTELEUTONS	HOMOCHLAMYDEOUS
HOIDENISHNESSES	HOLOMORPHIC	HOMEOTHERM	HOMOCHROMATIC
HOJATOLESLAM	HOLOPHOTAL	HOMEOTHERMAL	HOMOCHROMATISM
HOJATOLESLAMS	HOLOPHOTES	HOMEOTHERMIC	HOMOCHROMATISMS
HOJATOLISLAM	HOLOPHRASE	HOMEOTHERMIES	HOMOCHROMIES
HOJATOLISLAMS	HOLOPHRASES	HOMEOTHERMOUS	HOMOCHROMOUS
HOKEYNESSES	HOLOPHRASTIC	HOMEOTHERMS	HOMOCHROMY
HOKEYPOKEY	HOLOPHYTES	HOMEOTHERMY	HOMOCYCLIC
HOKEYPOKEYS	HOLOPHYTIC	HOMEOTYPIC	HOMOCYSTEINE
HOKINESSES	HOLOPHYTISM	HOMEOTYPICAL	HOMOCYSTEINES
HOKYPOKIES	HOLOPHYTISMS	HOMEOWNERS	HOMOEOMERIC
HOLARCHIES	HOLOPLANKTON	HOMEOWNERSHIP	HOMOEOMERIES
HOLDERBATS	HOLOPLANKTONS	HOMEOWNERSHIPS	HOMOEOMEROUS
HOLDERSHIP	HOLOSTERIC	HOMEPLACES	HOMOEOMERY
HOLDERSHIPS	HOLOTHURIAN	HOMEPORTED	HOMOEOMORPH
HOLIDAYERS	HOLOTHURIANS	HOMEPORTING	HOMOEOMORPHIC
HOLIDAYING	HOLSTERING	HOMESCHOOL	HOMOEOMORPHIES
HOLIDAYMAKER	HOLYSTONED	HOMESCHOOLED	HOMOEOMORPHISM
HOLIDAYMAKERS	HOLYSTONES	HOMESCHOOLER	HOMOEOMORPHISMS
HOLINESSES	HOLYSTONING	HOMESCHOOLERS	HOMOEOMORPHOUS
HOLISTICALLY	HOMALOGRAPHIC	HOMESCHOOLING	HOMOEOMORPHS
HOLLANDAISE	HOMALOIDAL	HOMESCHOOLS	HOMOEOMORPHY
HOLLANDAISES	HOMEBIRTHS	HOMESCREETCH	HOMOEOPATH
HOLLOWARES	HOMEBODIES	HOMESCREETCHES	HOMOEOPATHIC
HOLLOWNESS	HOMEBUYERS	HOMESICKNESS	HOMOEOPATHIES
HOLLOWNESSES	HOMECOMERS	HOMESICKNESSES	HOMOEOPATHIST
HOLLOWWARE	HOMECOMING	HOMESTALLS	HOMOEOPATHISTS
HOLLOWWARES	HOMECOMINGS	HOMESTANDS	HOMOEOPATHS
HOLLYHOCKS	HOMECRAFTS	HOMESTEADED	HOMOEOPATHY
HOLOBENTHIC	HOMELESSNESS	HOMESTEADER	HOMOEOSTASES
HOLOBLASTIC	HOMELESSNESSES	HOMESTEADERS	HOMOEOSTASIS
HOLOBLASTICALLY	HOMELINESS	HOMESTEADING	HOMOEOSTATIC
HOLOCAUSTAL	HOMELINESSES	HOMESTEADINGS	HOMOEOTELEUTON
HOLOCAUSTIC	HOMEMAKERS	HOMESTEADS	HOMOEOTELEUTONS
HOLOCAUSTS	HOMEMAKING	HOMESTRETCH	HOMOEOTHERMAL
HOLOCRYSTALLINE	HOMEMAKINGS	HOMESTRETCHES	HOMOEOTHERMIC
HOLODISCUS	HOMEOBOXES	HOMEWORKER	HOMOEOTHERMOUS
HOLODISCUSES	HOMEOMERIC	HOMEWORKERS	HOMOEOTYPIC
HOLOENZYME	HOMEOMERIES	HOMEWORKING	HOMOEOTYPICAL
HOLOENZYMES	HOMEOMEROUS	HOMEWORKINGS	HOMOEROTIC
HOLOGAMIES	HOMEOMORPH	HOMEYNESSES	HOMOEROTICISM
HOLOGRAPHED	HOMEOMORPHIC	HOMICIDALLY	HOMOEROTICISMS
HOLOGRAPHER	HOMEOMORPHIES	HOMILETICAL	HOMOEROTISM
HOLOGRAPHERS	HOMEOMORPHISM	HOMILETICALLY	HOMOEROTISMS
HOLOGRAPHIC	HOMEOMORPHISMS	HOMILETICS	HOMOGAMETIC
HOLOGRAPHICALLY	HOMEOMORPHOUS	HOMINESSES	HOMOGAMIES
HOLOGRAPHIES	HOMEOMORPHS	HOMINISATION	HOMOGAMOUS
HOLOGRAPHING	HOMEOMORPHY	HOMINISATIONS	HOMOGENATE
HOLOGRAPHS	HOMEOPATHIC	HOMINISING	HOMOGENATES
HOLOGRAPHY	HOMEOPATHICALLY	HOMINIZATION	HOMOGENEITIES

HOMOGENEITY	HOMOLOGIZERS	HOMOSEXUALISTS	HONEYMONTHS
HOMOGENEOUS	HOMOLOGIZES	HOMOSEXUALITIES	HONEYMOONED
HOMOGENEOUSLY	HOMOLOGIZING	HOMOSEXUALITY	HONEYMOONER
HOMOGENEOUSNESS	HOMOLOGOUMENA	HOMOSEXUALLY	HONEYMOONERS
HOMOGENESES	HOMOLOGOUS	HOMOSEXUALS	HONEYMOONING
HOMOGENESIS	HOMOLOGRAPHIC	HOMOSOCIAL	HONEYMOONS
HOMOGENETIC	HOMOLOGUES	HOMOSOCIALITIES	HONEYSUCKER
HOMOGENETICAL	HOMOLOGUMENA	HOMOSOCIALITY	HONEYSUCKERS
HOMOGENIES	HOMOLOSINE	HOMOSPORIES	HONEYSUCKLE
HOMOGENISATION	HOMOMORPHIC	HOMOSPOROUS	HONEYSUCKLED
HOMOGENISATIONS	HOMOMORPHIES	HOMOSTYLIES	HONEYSUCKLES
HOMOGENISE	HOMOMORPHISM	HOMOTAXIAL	HONEYTRAPS
HOMOGENISED	HOMOMORPHISMS	HOMOTAXIALLY	HONORABILITIES
HOMOGENISER	HOMOMORPHOSES	HOMOTHALLIC	HONORABILITY
HOMOGENISERS	HOMOMORPHOSIS	HOMOTHALLIES	HONORABLENESS
HOMOGENISES	HOMOMORPHOUS	HOMOTHALLISM	HONORABLENESSES
HOMOGENISING	HOMOMORPHS	HOMOTHALLISMS	HONORARIES
HOMOGENIZATION	HOMOMORPHY	HOMOTHALLY	HONORARILY
HOMOGENIZATIONS	HOMONUCLEAR	HOMOTHERMAL	HONORARIUM
HOMOGENIZE	HOMONYMIES	HOMOTHERMIC	HONORARIUMS
HOMOGENIZED	HOMONYMITIES	HOMOTHERMIES	HONORIFICAL
HOMOGENIZER	HOMONYMITY	HOMOTHERMOUS	HONORIFICALLY
HOMOGENIZERS	HOMONYMOUS	HOMOTHERMY	HONORIFICS
HOMOGENIZES	HOMONYMOUSLY	HOMOTONIES	HONOURABLE
HOMOGENIZING	HOMOOUSIAN	HOMOTONOUS	HONOURABLENESS
HOMOGENOUS	HOMOOUSIANS	HOMOTRANSPLANT	HONOURABLY
HOMOGONIES	HOMOPHILES	HOMOTRANSPLANTS	HONOURLESS
HOMOGONOUS	HOMOPHOBES	HOMOTYPIES	HOODEDNESS
HOMOGONOUSLY	HOMOPHOBIA	HOMOUSIANS	HOODEDNESSES
HOMOGRAFTS	HOMOPHOBIAS	HOMOZYGOSES	HOODLUMISH
HOMOGRAPHIC	HOMOPHOBIC	HOMOZYGOSIS	HOODLUMISM
HOMOGRAPHS	HOMOPHONES	HOMOZYGOSITIES	HOODLUMISMS
HOMOIOMEROUS	HOMOPHONIC	HOMOZYGOSITY	HOODOOISMS
HOMOIOTHERM	HOMOPHONICALLY	HOMOZYGOTE	HOODWINKED
HOMOIOTHERMAL	HOMOPHONIES	HOMOZYGOTES	HOODWINKER
HOMOIOTHERMIC	HOMOPHONOUS	HOMOZYGOTIC	HOODWINKERS
HOMOIOTHERMIES	HOMOPHYLIES	HOMOZYGOUS	HOODWINKING
HOMOIOTHERMS	HOMOPHYLLIC	HOMOZYGOUSLY	HOOFPRINTS
HOMOIOTHERMY	HOMOPLASIES	HOMUNCULAR	HOOKCHECKS
HOMOIOUSIAN	HOMOPLASMIES	HOMUNCULES	HOOKEDNESS
HOMOIOUSIANS	HOMOPLASMY	HOMUNCULUS	HOOKEDNESSES
HOMOLOGATE	HOMOPLASTIC	HONESTNESS	HOOLACHANS
HOMOLOGATED	HOMOPLASTICALLY	HONESTNESSES	HOOLIGANISM
HOMOLOGATES	HOMOPLASTIES	HONEYBUNCH	HOOLIGANISMS
HOMOLOGATING	HOMOPLASTY	HONEYBUNCHES	HOOPSKIRTS
HOMOLOGATION	HOMOPOLARITIES	HONEYCOMBED	HOOTANANNIE
HOMOLOGATIONS	HOMOPOLARITY	HONEYCOMBING	HOOTANANNIES
HOMOLOGICAL	HOMOPOLYMER	HONEYCOMBINGS	HOOTANANNY
HOMOLOGICALLY	HOMOPOLYMERIC	HONEYCOMBS	HOOTENANNIE
HOMOLOGIES	HOMOPOLYMERS	HONEYCREEPER	HOOTENANNIES
HOMOLOGISE	HOMOPTERAN	HONEYCREEPERS	HOOTENANNY
HOMOLOGISED	HOMOPTERANS	HONEYDEWED	HOOTNANNIE
HOMOLOGISER	HOMOPTEROUS	HONEYEATER	HOOTNANNIES
HOMOLOGISERS	HOMORGANIC	HONEYEATERS	HOPEFULNESS
HOMOLOGISES	HOMOSCEDASTIC	HONEYGUIDE	HOPEFULNESSES
HOMOLOGISING	HOMOSEXUAL	HONEYGUIDES	HOPELESSLY
HOMOLOGIZE	HOMOSEXUALISM	HONEYMONTH	HOPELESSNESS
HOMOLOGIZED	HOMOSEXUALISMS	HONEYMONTHED	HOPELESSNESSES
HOMOLOGIZER	HOMOSEXUALIST	HONEYMONTHING	HOPLOLOGIES

HOPLOLOGIST
HOPLOLOGISTS
HOPPERCARS
HOPSACKING
HOPSACKINGS
HOPSCOTCHED
HOPSCOTCHES
HOPSCOTCHING
HOREHOUNDS
HORIATIKIS
HORIZONLESS
HORIZONTAL
HORIZONTALITIES
HORIZONTALITY
HORIZONTALLY
HORIZONTALNESS
HORIZONTALS
HORMOGONIA
HORMOGONIUM
HORMONALLY
HORMONELIKE
HORNBLENDE
HORNBLENDES
HORNBLENDIC
HORNEDNESS
HORNEDNESSES
HORNINESSES
HORNLESSNESS
HORNLESSNESSES
HORNSTONES
HORNSWOGGLE
HORNSWOGGLED
HORNSWOGGLES
HORNSWOGGLING
HORNWRACKS
HORNYHEADS
HORNYWINKS
HOROGRAPHER
HOROGRAPHERS
HOROGRAPHIES
HOROGRAPHY
HOROLOGERS
HOROLOGICAL
HOROLOGIES
HOROLOGION
HOROLOGIONS
HOROLOGIST
HOROLOGISTS
HOROLOGIUM
HOROLOGIUMS
HOROMETRICAL
HOROMETRIES
HOROSCOPES
HOROSCOPIC
HOROSCOPIES
HOROSCOPIST
HOROSCOPISTS
HORRENDOUS
HORRENDOUSLY

HORRENDOUSNESS
HORRIBLENESS
HORRIBLENESSES
HORRIDNESS
HORRIDNESSES
HORRIFICALLY
HORRIFICATION
HORRIFICATIONS
HORRIFYING
HORRIFYINGLY
HORRIPILANT
HORRIPILATE
HORRIPILATED
HORRIPILATES
HORRIPILATING
HORRIPILATION
HORRIPILATIONS
HORRISONANT
HORRISONOUS
HORSEBACKS
HORSEBEANS
HORSEBOXES
HORSEFEATHERS
HORSEFLESH
HORSEFLESHES
HORSEFLIES
HORSEHAIRS
HORSEHIDES
HORSELAUGH
HORSELAUGHS
HORSELEECH
HORSELEECHES
HORSEMANSHIP
HORSEMANSHIPS
HORSEMEATS
HORSEMINTS
HORSEPLAYER
HORSEPLAYERS
HORSEPLAYS
HORSEPONDS
HORSEPOWER
HORSEPOWERS
HORSEPOXES
HORSERACES
HORSERADISH
HORSERADISHES
HORSESHITS
HORSESHOED
HORSESHOEING
HORSESHOEINGS
HORSESHOER
HORSESHOERS
HORSESHOES
HORSETAILS
HORSEWEEDS
HORSEWHIPPED
HORSEWHIPPER
HORSEWHIPPERS
HORSEWHIPPING

HORSEWHIPS
HORSEWOMAN
HORSEWOMEN
HORSINESSES
HORTATIONS
HORTATIVELY
HORTATORILY
HORTICULTURAL
HORTICULTURALLY
HORTICULTURE
HORTICULTURES
HORTICULTURIST
HORTICULTURISTS
HOSANNAING
HOSPITABLE
HOSPITABLENESS
HOSPITABLY
HOSPITAGES
HOSPITALER
HOSPITALERS
HOSPITALES
HOSPITALISATION
HOSPITALISE
HOSPITALISED
HOSPITALISES
HOSPITALISING
HOSPITALITIES
HOSPITALITY
HOSPITALIZATION
HOSPITALIZE
HOSPITALIZED
HOSPITALIZES
HOSPITALIZING
HOSPITALLER
HOSPITALLERS
HOSTELLERS
HOSTELLING
HOSTELLINGS
HOSTELRIES
HOSTESSING
HOSTILITIES
HOTCHPOTCH
HOTCHPOTCHES
HOTDOGGERS
HOTDOGGING
HOTFOOTING
HOTHEADEDLY
HOTHEADEDNESS
HOTHEADEDNESSES
HOTHOUSING
HOTPRESSED
HOTPRESSES
HOTPRESSING
HOTTENTOTS
HOUGHMAGANDIE
HOUGHMAGANDIES
HOUNDFISHES
HOURGLASSES
HOURPLATES

HOUSEBOATER
HOUSEBOATERS
HOUSEBOATS
HOUSEBOUND
HOUSEBREAK
HOUSEBREAKER
HOUSEBREAKERS
HOUSEBREAKING
HOUSEBREAKINGS
HOUSEBREAKS
HOUSEBROKE
HOUSEBROKEN
HOUSECARLS
HOUSECLEAN
HOUSECLEANED
HOUSECLEANING
HOUSECLEANINGS
HOUSECLEANS
HOUSECOATS
HOUSECRAFT
HOUSECRAFTS
HOUSEDRESS
HOUSEDRESSES
HOUSEFATHER
HOUSEFATHERS
HOUSEFLIES
HOUSEFRONT
HOUSEFRONTS
HOUSEGUEST
HOUSEGUESTS
HOUSEHOLDER
HOUSEHOLDERS
HOUSEHOLDERSHIP
HOUSEHOLDS
HOUSEHUSBAND
HOUSEHUSBANDS
HOUSEKEEPER
HOUSEKEEPERS
HOUSEKEEPING
HOUSEKEEPINGS
HOUSEKEEPS
HOUSELEEKS
HOUSELESSNESS
HOUSELESSNESSES
HOUSELIGHTS
HOUSELINES
HOUSELLING
HOUSELLINGS
HOUSEMAIDS
HOUSEMASTER
HOUSEMASTERS
HOUSEMATES
HOUSEMISTRESS
HOUSEMISTRESSES
HOUSEMOTHER
HOUSEMOTHERS
HOUSEPAINTER
HOUSEPAINTERS
HOUSEPARENT

HOUSEPARENTS
HOUSEPERSON
HOUSEPERSONS
HOUSEPLANT
HOUSEPLANTS
HOUSEROOMS
HOUSESITTING
HOUSEWARES
HOUSEWARMING
HOUSEWARMINGS
HOUSEWIFELINESS
HOUSEWIFELY
HOUSEWIFERIES
HOUSEWIFERY
HOUSEWIFESHIP
HOUSEWIFESHIPS
HOUSEWIFESKEP
HOUSEWIFESKEPS
HOUSEWIFEY
HOUSEWIVES
HOUSEWORKER
HOUSEWORKERS
HOUSEWORKS
HOUSTONIAS
HOVERCRAFT
HOVERCRAFTS
HOVERFLIES
HOVERINGLY
HOVERPORTS
HOVERTRAIN
HOVERTRAINS
HOWLROUNDS
HOWSOMDEVER
HOWSOMEVER
HOWTOWDIES
HOYDENHOOD
HOYDENHOODS
HOYDENISHNESS
HOYDENISHNESSES
HOYDENISMS
HUBRISTICALLY
HUCKABACKS
HUCKLEBERRIES
HUCKLEBERRY
HUCKLEBERRYING
HUCKLEBERRYINGS
HUCKLEBONE
HUCKLEBONES
HUCKSTERAGE
HUCKSTERAGES
HUCKSTERED
HUCKSTERESS
HUCKSTERESSES
HUCKSTERIES
HUCKSTERING
HUCKSTERISM
HUCKSTERISMS
HUCKSTRESS
HUCKSTRESSES

HUDIBRASTIC
HUFFINESSES
HUFFISHNESS
HUFFISHNESSES
HUGENESSES
HUGEOUSNESS
HUGEOUSNESSES
HULLABALLOO
HULLABALLOOS
HULLABALOO
HULLABALOOS
HUMANENESS
HUMANENESSES
HUMANHOODS
HUMANISATION
HUMANISATIONS
HUMANISERS
HUMANISING
HUMANISTIC
HUMANISTICALLY
HUMANITARIAN
HUMANITARIANISM
HUMANITARIANIST
HUMANITARIANS
HUMANITIES
HUMANIZATION
HUMANIZATIONS
HUMANIZERS
HUMANIZING
HUMANKINDS
HUMANNESSES
HUMBLEBEES
HUMBLENESS
HUMBLENESSES
HUMBLESSES
HUMBLINGLY
HUMBUCKERS
HUMBUGGABLE
HUMBUGGERIES
HUMBUGGERS
HUMBUGGERY
HUMBUGGING
HUMDINGERS
HUMDRUMNESS
HUMDRUMNESSES
HUMDUDGEON
HUMDUDGEONS
HUMECTANTS
HUMECTATED
HUMECTATES
HUMECTATING
HUMECTATION
HUMECTATIONS
HUMECTIVES
HUMGRUFFIAN
HUMGRUFFIANS
HUMGRUFFIN
HUMGRUFFINS
HUMICOLOUS

HUMIDIFICATION
HUMIDIFICATIONS
HUMIDIFIED
HUMIDIFIER
HUMIDIFIERS
HUMIDIFIES
HUMIDIFYING
HUMIDISTAT
HUMIDISTATS
HUMIDITIES
HUMIDNESSES
HUMIFICATION
HUMIFICATIONS
HUMILIATED
HUMILIATES
HUMILIATING
HUMILIATINGLY
HUMILIATION
HUMILIATIONS
HUMILIATIVE
HUMILIATOR
HUMILIATORS
HUMILIATORY
HUMILITIES
HUMMELLERS
HUMMELLING
HUMMINGBIRD
HUMMINGBIRDS
HUMMOCKING
HUMORALISM
HUMORALISMS
HUMORALIST
HUMORALISTS
HUMORESQUE
HUMORESQUES
HUMORISTIC
HUMORLESSLY
HUMORLESSNESS
HUMORLESSNESSES
HUMOROUSLY
HUMOROUSNESS
HUMOROUSNESSES
HUMOURLESS
HUMOURLESSNESS
HUMOURSOME
HUMOURSOMENESS
HUMPBACKED
HUMPINESSES
HUNCHBACKED
HUNCHBACKS
HUNDREDERS
HUNDREDFOLD
HUNDREDFOLDS
HUNDREDORS
HUNDREDTHS
HUNDREDWEIGHT
HUNDREDWEIGHTS
HUNGERINGLY
HUNGRINESS

HUNGRINESSES
HUNTIEGOWK
HUNTIEGOWKS
HUNTRESSES
HUNTSMANSHIP
HUNTSMANSHIPS
HUPAITHRIC
HURLBARROW
HURLBARROWS
HURRICANES
HURRICANOES
HURRIEDNESS
HURRIEDNESSES
HURRYINGLY
HURTFULNESS
HURTFULNESSES
HURTLEBERRIES
HURTLEBERRY
HURTLESSLY
HURTLESSNESS
HURTLESSNESSES
HUSBANDAGE
HUSBANDAGES
HUSBANDERS
HUSBANDING
HUSBANDLAND
HUSBANDLANDS
HUSBANDLESS
HUSBANDLIKE
HUSBANDMAN
HUSBANDMEN
HUSBANDRIES
HUSHABYING
HUSHPUPPIES
HUSKINESSES
HYACINTHINE
HYALINISATION
HYALINISATIONS
HYALINISED
HYALINISES
HYALINISING
HYALINIZATION
HYALINIZATIONS
HYALINIZED
HYALINIZES
HYALINIZING
HYALOMELAN
HYALOMELANE
HYALOMELANES
HYALOMELANS
HYALONEMAS
HYALOPHANE
HYALOPHANES
HYALOPLASM
HYALOPLASMIC
HYALOPLASMS
HYALURONIC
HYALURONIDASE
HYALURONIDASES

HYBRIDISABLE	HYDROBIOLOGISTS	HYDROGENATIONS	HYDROLYZER
HYBRIDISATION	HYDROBIOLOGY	HYDROGENATOR	HYDROLYZERS
HYBRIDISATIONS	HYDROBROMIC	HYDROGENATORS	HYDROLYZES
HYBRIDISED	HYDROCARBON	HYDROGENISATION	HYDROLYZING
HYBRIDISER	HYDROCARBONS	HYDROGENISE	HYDROMAGNETIC
HYBRIDISERS	HYDROCASTS	HYDROGENISED	HYDROMAGNETICS
HYBRIDISES	HYDROCELES	HYDROGENISES	HYDROMANCER
HYBRIDISING	HYDROCELLULOSE	HYDROGENISING	HYDROMANCERS
HYBRIDISMS	HYDROCELLULOSES	HYDROGENIZATION	HYDROMANCIES
HYBRIDISTS	HYDROCEPHALIC	HYDROGENIZE	HYDROMANCY
HYBRIDITIES	HYDROCEPHALICS	HYDROGENIZED	HYDROMANIA
HYBRIDIZABLE	HYDROCEPHALIES	HYDROGENIZES	HYDROMANIAS
HYBRIDIZATION	HYDROCEPHALOID	HYDROGENIZING	HYDROMANTIC
HYBRIDIZATIONS	HYDROCEPHALOUS	HYDROGENOLYSES	HYDROMECHANICAL
HYBRIDIZED	HYDROCEPHALUS	HYDROGENOLYSIS	HYDROMECHANICS
HYBRIDIZER	HYDROCEPHALUSES	HYDROGENOUS	HYDROMEDUSA
HYBRIDIZERS	HYDROCEPHALY	HYDROGEOLOGICAL	HYDROMEDUSAE
HYBRIDIZES	HYDROCHLORIC	HYDROGEOLOGIES	HYDROMEDUSAN
HYBRIDIZING	HYDROCHLORIDE	HYDROGEOLOGIST	HYDROMEDUSANS
HYBRIDOMAS	HYDROCHLORIDES	HYDROGEOLOGISTS	HYDROMEDUSAS
HYDANTOINS	HYDROCHORE	HYDROGEOLOGY	HYDROMEDUSOID
HYDATHODES	HYDROCHORES	HYDROGRAPH	HYDROMEDUSOIDS
HYDATIDIFORM	HYDROCHORIC	HYDROGRAPHER	HYDROMETALLURGY
HYDNOCARPATE	HYDROCOLLOID	HYDROGRAPHERS	HYDROMETEOR
HYDNOCARPATES	HYDROCOLLOIDAL	HYDROGRAPHIC	HYDROMETEORS
HYDNOCARPIC	HYDROCOLLOIDS	HYDROGRAPHICAL	HYDROMETER
HYDRAEMIAS	HYDROCORAL	HYDROGRAPHIES	HYDROMETERS
HYDRAGOGUE	HYDROCORALLINE	HYDROGRAPHS	HYDROMETRIC
HYDRAGOGUES	HYDROCORALLINES	HYDROGRAPHY	HYDROMETRICAL
HYDRALAZINE	HYDROCORALS	HYDROKINETIC	HYDROMETRICALLY
HYDRALAZINES	HYDROCORTISONE	HYDROKINETICAL	HYDROMETRIES
HYDRANGEAS	HYDROCORTISONES	HYDROKINETICS	HYDROMETRY
HYDRARGYRAL	HYDROCRACK	HYDROLASES	HYDROMORPHIC
HYDRARGYRIA	HYDROCRACKED	HYDROLOGIC	HYDRONAUTS
HYDRARGYRIAS	HYDROCRACKER	HYDROLOGICAL	HYDRONEPHROSES
HYDRARGYRIC	HYDROCRACKERS	HYDROLOGICALLY	HYDRONEPHROSIS
HYDRARGYRISM	HYDROCRACKING	HYDROLOGIES	HYDRONEPHROTIC
HYDRARGYRISMS	HYDROCRACKINGS	HYDROLOGIST	HYDRONICALLY
HYDRARGYRUM	HYDROCRACKS	HYDROLOGISTS	HYDRONIUMS
HYDRARGYRUMS	HYDROCYANIC	HYDROLYSABLE	HYDROPATHIC
HYDRARTHROSES	HYDRODYNAMIC	HYDROLYSATE	HYDROPATHICAL
HYDRARTHROSIS	HYDRODYNAMICAL	HYDROLYSATES	HYDROPATHICALLY
HYDRASTINE	HYDRODYNAMICIST	HYDROLYSATION	HYDROPATHICS
HYDRASTINES	HYDRODYNAMICS	HYDROLYSATIONS	HYDROPATHIES
HYDRASTININE	HYDROELASTIC	HYDROLYSED	HYDROPATHIST
HYDRASTININES	HYDROELECTRIC	HYDROLYSER	HYDROPATHISTS
HYDRASTISES	HYDROEXTRACTOR	HYDROLYSERS	HYDROPATHS
HYDRATIONS	HYDROEXTRACTORS	HYDROLYSES	HYDROPATHY
HYDRAULICALLY	HYDROFLUORIC	HYDROLYSING	HYDROPEROXIDE
HYDRAULICKED	HYDROFOILS	HYDROLYSIS	HYDROPEROXIDES
HYDRAULICKING	HYDROFORMING	HYDROLYTES	HYDROPHANE
HYDRAULICS	HYDROFORMINGS	HYDROLYTIC	HYDROPHANES
HYDRAZIDES	HYDROGENASE	HYDROLYTICALLY	HYDROPHANOUS
HYDRAZINES	HYDROGENASES	HYDROLYZABLE	HYDROPHILE
HYDRICALLY	HYDROGENATE	HYDROLYZATE	HYDROPHILES
HYDROACOUSTICS	HYDROGENATED	HYDROLYZATES	HYDROPHILIC
HYDROBIOLOGICAL	HYDROGENATES	HYDROLYZATION	HYDROPHILICITY
HYDROBIOLOGIES	HYDROGENATING	HYDROLYZATIONS	HYDROPHILIES
HYDROBIOLOGIST	HYDROGENATION	HYDROLYZED	HYDROPHILITE

HYDROPHILITES
HYDROPHILOUS
HYDROPHILY
HYDROPHOBIA
HYDROPHOBIAS
HYDROPHOBIC
HYDROPHOBICITY
HYDROPHOBOUS
HYDROPHONE
HYDROPHONES
HYDROPHYTE
HYDROPHYTES
HYDROPHYTIC
HYDROPHYTON
HYDROPHYTONS
HYDROPHYTOUS
HYDROPLANE
HYDROPLANED
HYDROPLANES
HYDROPLANING
HYDROPNEUMATIC
HYDROPOLYP
HYDROPOLYPS
HYDROPONIC
HYDROPONICALLY
HYDROPONICS
HYDROPOWER
HYDROPOWERS
HYDROPSIES
HYDROPULTS
HYDROQUINOL
HYDROQUINOLS
HYDROQUINONE
HYDROQUINONES
HYDROSCOPE
HYDROSCOPES
HYDROSCOPIC
HYDROSCOPICAL
HYDROSERES
HYDROSOLIC
HYDROSOMAL
HYDROSOMATA
HYDROSOMATOUS
HYDROSOMES
HYDROSPACE
HYDROSPACES
HYDROSPHERE
HYDROSPHERES
HYDROSPHERIC
HYDROSTATIC
HYDROSTATICAL
HYDROSTATICALLY
HYDROSTATICS
HYDROSTATS
HYDROSULPHATE
HYDROSULPHATES
HYDROSULPHIDE
HYDROSULPHIDES
HYDROSULPHITE

HYDROSULPHITES
HYDROSULPHURIC
HYDROSULPHUROUS
HYDROTACTIC
HYDROTAXES
HYDROTAXIS
HYDROTHECA
HYDROTHECAE
HYDROTHERAPIC
HYDROTHERAPIES
HYDROTHERAPIST
HYDROTHERAPISTS
HYDROTHERAPY
HYDROTHERMAL
HYDROTHERMALLY
HYDROTHORACES
HYDROTHORACIC
HYDROTHORAX
HYDROTHORAXES
HYDROTROPIC
HYDROTROPICALLY
HYDROTROPISM
HYDROTROPISMS
HYDROVANES
HYDROXIDES
HYDROXONIUM
HYDROXONIUMS
HYDROXYAPATITE
HYDROXYAPATITES
HYDROXYBUTYRATE
HYDROXYLAMINE
HYDROXYLAMINES
HYDROXYLAPATITE
HYDROXYLASE
HYDROXYLASES
HYDROXYLATE
HYDROXYLATED
HYDROXYLATES
HYDROXYLATING
HYDROXYLATION
HYDROXYLATIONS
HYDROXYLIC
HYDROXYPROLINE
HYDROXYPROLINES
HYDROXYUREA
HYDROXYUREAS
HYDROXYZINE
HYDROXYZINES
HYDROZINCITE
HYDROZINCITES
HYDROZOANS
HYETOGRAPH
HYETOGRAPHIC
HYETOGRAPHICAL
HYETOGRAPHIES
HYETOGRAPHS
HYETOGRAPHY
HYETOLOGIES
HYETOMETER

HYETOMETERS
HYETOMETROGRAPH
HYGIENICALLY
HYGIENISTS
HYGRISTORS
HYGROCHASIES
HYGROCHASTIC
HYGROCHASY
HYGRODEIKS
HYGROGRAPH
HYGROGRAPHIC
HYGROGRAPHICAL
HYGROGRAPHS
HYGROLOGIES
HYGROMETER
HYGROMETERS
HYGROMETRIC
HYGROMETRICAL
HYGROMETRICALLY
HYGROMETRIES
HYGROMETRY
HYGROPHILE
HYGROPHILES
HYGROPHILOUS
HYGROPHOBE
HYGROPHYTE
HYGROPHYTES
HYGROPHYTIC
HYGROSCOPE
HYGROSCOPES
HYGROSCOPIC
HYGROSCOPICAL
HYGROSCOPICALLY
HYGROSCOPICITY
HYGROSTATS
HYLOGENESES
HYLOGENESIS
HYLOMORPHIC
HYLOMORPHISM
HYLOMORPHISMS
HYLOPATHISM
HYLOPATHISMS
HYLOPATHIST
HYLOPATHISTS
HYLOPHAGOUS
HYLOPHYTES
HYLOTHEISM
HYLOTHEISMS
HYLOTHEIST
HYLOTHEISTS
HYLOTOMOUS
HYLOZOICAL
HYLOZOISMS
HYLOZOISTIC
HYLOZOISTICALLY
HYLOZOISTS
HYMENEALLY
HYMENOPHORE
HYMENOPHORES

HYMENOPTERA
HYMENOPTERAN
HYMENOPTERANS
HYMENOPTERON
HYMENOPTERONS
HYMENOPTEROUS
HYMNODICAL
HYMNODISTS
HYMNOGRAPHER
HYMNOGRAPHERS
HYMNOGRAPHIES
HYMNOGRAPHY
HYMNOLOGIC
HYMNOLOGICAL
HYMNOLOGIES
HYMNOLOGIST
HYMNOLOGISTS
HYOPLASTRA
HYOPLASTRAL
HYOPLASTRON
HYOSCYAMINE
HYOSCYAMINES
HYOSCYAMUS
HYOSCYAMUSES
HYPABYSSAL
HYPABYSSALLY
HYPAESTHESIA
HYPAESTHESIAS
HYPAESTHESIC
HYPAETHRAL
HYPAETHRON
HYPAETHRONS
HYPALGESIA
HYPALGESIAS
HYPALGESIC
HYPALLACTIC
HYPALLAGES
HYPANTHIAL
HYPANTHIUM
HYPERACIDITIES
HYPERACIDITY
HYPERACTION
HYPERACTIONS
HYPERACTIVE
HYPERACTIVES
HYPERACTIVITIES
HYPERACTIVITY
HYPERACUITIES
HYPERACUITY
HYPERACUSES
HYPERACUSIS
HYPERACUTE
HYPERACUTENESS
HYPERADRENALISM
HYPERAEMIA
HYPERAEMIAS
HYPERAEMIC
HYPERAESTHESIA
HYPERAESTHESIAS

HYPERAESTHESIC	HYPERCIVILISED	HYPERFUNCTIONS	HYPERMARTS
HYPERAESTHETIC	HYPERCIVILIZED	HYPERGAMIES	HYPERMASCULINE
HYPERAGGRESSIVE	HYPERCOAGULABLE	HYPERGAMOUS	HYPERMEDIA
HYPERALERT	HYPERCOLOUR	HYPERGEOMETRIC	HYPERMEDIAS
HYPERALGESIA	HYPERCOLOURS	HYPERGLYCAEMIA	HYPERMETABOLIC
HYPERALGESIAS	HYPERCOMPLEX	HYPERGLYCAEMIAS	HYPERMETABOLISM
HYPERALGESIC	HYPERCONSCIOUS	HYPERGLYCAEMIC	HYPERMETER
HYPERAROUSAL	HYPERCORRECT	HYPERGLYCEMIA	HYPERMETERS
HYPERAROUSALS	HYPERCORRECTION	HYPERGLYCEMIAS	HYPERMETRIC
HYPERAWARE	HYPERCORRECTLY	HYPERGLYCEMIC	HYPERMETRICAL
HYPERAWARENESS	HYPERCRITIC	HYPERGOLIC	HYPERMETROPIA
HYPERBARIC	HYPERCRITICAL	HYPERGOLICALLY	HYPERMETROPIAS
HYPERBARICALLY	HYPERCRITICALLY	HYPERHIDROSES	HYPERMETROPIC
HYPERBATIC	HYPERCRITICISE	HYPERHIDROSIS	HYPERMETROPICAL
HYPERBATICALLY	HYPERCRITICISED	HYPERICUMS	HYPERMETROPIES
HYPERBATON	HYPERCRITICISES	HYPERIDROSES	HYPERMETROPY
HYPERBATONS	HYPERCRITICISM	HYPERIDROSIS	HYPERMNESIA
HYPERBOLAE	HYPERCRITICISMS	HYPERIMMUNE	HYPERMNESIAS
HYPERBOLAS	HYPERCRITICIZE	HYPERIMMUNISE	HYPERMNESIC
HYPERBOLES	HYPERCRITICIZED	HYPERIMMUNISED	HYPERMOBILITIES
HYPERBOLIC	HYPERCRITICIZES	HYPERIMMUNISES	HYPERMOBILITY
HYPERBOLICAL	HYPERCRITICS	HYPERIMMUNISING	HYPERMODERN
HYPERBOLICALLY	HYPERCUBES	HYPERIMMUNIZE	HYPERMODERNIST
HYPERBOLISE	HYPERDACTYL	HYPERIMMUNIZED	HYPERMODERNISTS
HYPERBOLISED	HYPERDACTYLIES	HYPERIMMUNIZES	HYPERMUTABILITY
HYPERBOLISES	HYPERDACTYLY	HYPERIMMUNIZING	HYPERMUTABLE
HYPERBOLISING	HYPERDORIAN	HYPERINFLATED	HYPERNATRAEMIA
HYPERBOLISM	HYPERDULIA	HYPERINFLATION	HYPERNATRAEMIAS
HYPERBOLISMS	HYPERDULIAS	HYPERINFLATIONS	HYPERNOVAE
HYPERBOLIST	HYPERDULIC	HYPERINOSES	HYPERNOVAS
HYPERBOLISTS	HYPERDULICAL	HYPERINOSIS	HYPERNYMIES
HYPERBOLIZE	HYPEREFFICIENT	HYPERINOTIC	HYPEROPIAS
HYPERBOLIZED	HYPEREMESES	HYPERINSULINISM	HYPEROREXIA
HYPERBOLIZES	HYPEREMESIS	HYPERINTENSE	HYPEROREXIAS
HYPERBOLIZING	HYPEREMETIC	HYPERINVOLUTION	HYPEROSMIA
HYPERBOLOID	HYPEREMIAS	HYPERIRRITABLE	HYPEROSMIAS
HYPERBOLOIDAL	HYPEREMOTIONAL	HYPERKERATOSES	HYPEROSTOSES
HYPERBOLOIDS	HYPERENDEMIC	HYPERKERATOSIS	HYPEROSTOSIS
HYPERBOREAN	HYPERENERGETIC	HYPERKERATOTIC	HYPEROSTOTIC
HYPERBOREANS	HYPERESTHESIA	HYPERKINESES	HYPERPARASITE
HYPERCALCAEMIA	HYPERESTHESIAS	HYPERKINESIA	HYPERPARASITES
HYPERCALCAEMIAS	HYPERESTHETIC	HYPERKINESIAS	HYPERPARASITIC
HYPERCALCEMIA	HYPEREUTECTIC	HYPERKINESIS	HYPERPARASITISM
HYPERCALCEMIAS	HYPEREUTECTOID	HYPERKINETIC	HYPERPHAGIA
HYPERCALCEMIC	HYPEREXCITABLE	HYPERLINKED	HYPERPHAGIAS
HYPERCAPNIA	HYPEREXCITED	HYPERLINKING	HYPERPHAGIC
HYPERCAPNIAS	HYPEREXCITEMENT	HYPERLINKS	HYPERPHRYGIAN
HYPERCAPNIC	HYPEREXCRETION	HYPERLIPEMIA	HYPERPHYSICAL
HYPERCARBIA	HYPEREXCRETIONS	HYPERLIPEMIAS	HYPERPHYSICALLY
HYPERCARBIAS	HYPEREXTEND	HYPERLIPEMIC	HYPERPIGMENTED
HYPERCATABOLISM	HYPEREXTENDED	HYPERLIPIDAEMIA	HYPERPITUITARY
HYPERCATALECTIC	HYPEREXTENDING	HYPERLIPIDEMIA	HYPERPLANE
HYPERCATALEXES	HYPEREXTENDS	HYPERLIPIDEMIAS	HYPERPLANES
HYPERCATALEXIS	HYPEREXTENSION	HYPERLYDIAN	HYPERPLASIA
HYPERCAUTIOUS	HYPEREXTENSIONS	HYPERMANIA	HYPERPLASIAS
HYPERCHARGE	HYPERFASTIDIOUS	HYPERMANIAS	HYPERPLASTIC
HYPERCHARGED	HYPERFOCAL	HYPERMANIC	HYPERPLOID
HYPERCHARGES	HYPERFUNCTION	HYPERMARKET	HYPERPLOIDIES
HYPERCHARGING	HYPERFUNCTIONAL	HYPERMARKETS	HYPERPLOIDS

HYPERPLOIDY	HYPERSEXUAL	HYPERURICEMIAS	HYPNOTHERAPIST
HYPERPNEAS	HYPERSEXUALITY	HYPERVELOCITIES	HYPNOTHERAPISTS
HYPERPNEIC	HYPERSOMNIA	HYPERVELOCITY	HYPNOTHERAPY
HYPERPNOEA	HYPERSOMNIAS	HYPERVENTILATE	HYPNOTICALLY
HYPERPNOEAS	HYPERSOMNOLENCE	HYPERVENTILATED	HYPNOTISABILITY
HYPERPOLARISE	HYPERSONIC	HYPERVENTILATES	HYPNOTISABLE
HYPERPOLARISED	HYPERSONICALLY	HYPERVIGILANCE	HYPNOTISATION
HYPERPOLARISES	HYPERSONICS	HYPERVIGILANCES	HYPNOTISATIONS
HYPERPOLARISING	HYPERSPACE	HYPERVIGILANT	HYPNOTISED
HYPERPOLARIZE	HYPERSPACES	HYPERVIRULENT	HYPNOTISER
HYPERPOLARIZED	HYPERSPATIAL	HYPERVISCOSITY	HYPNOTISERS
HYPERPOLARIZES	HYPERSTATIC	HYPESTHESIA	HYPNOTISES
HYPERPOLARIZING	HYPERSTHENE	HYPESTHESIAS	HYPNOTISING
HYPERPOWER	HYPERSTHENES	HYPESTHESIC	HYPNOTISMS
HYPERPOWERS	HYPERSTHENIA	HYPHENATED	HYPNOTISTIC
HYPERPRODUCER	HYPERSTHENIAS	HYPHENATES	HYPNOTISTS
HYPERPRODUCERS	HYPERSTHENIC	HYPHENATING	HYPNOTIZABILITY
HYPERPRODUCTION	HYPERSTHENITE	HYPHENATION	HYPNOTIZABLE
HYPERPROSEXIA	HYPERSTHENITES	HYPHENATIONS	HYPNOTIZATION
HYPERPROSEXIAS	HYPERSTIMULATE	HYPHENISATION	HYPNOTIZATIONS
HYPERPYRETIC	HYPERSTIMULATED	HYPHENISATIONS	HYPNOTIZED
HYPERPYREXIA	HYPERSTIMULATES	HYPHENISED	HYPNOTIZER
HYPERPYREXIAL	HYPERSTRESS	HYPHENISES	HYPNOTIZERS
HYPERPYREXIAS	HYPERSTRESSES	HYPHENISING	HYPNOTIZES
HYPERRATIONAL	HYPERSURFACE	HYPHENISMS	HYPNOTIZING
HYPERREACTIVE	HYPERSURFACES	HYPHENIZATION	HYPOACIDITIES
HYPERREACTIVITY	HYPERTENSE	HYPHENIZATIONS	HYPOACIDITY
HYPERREACTOR	HYPERTENSION	HYPHENIZED	HYPOAEOLIAN
HYPERREACTORS	HYPERTENSIONS	HYPHENIZES	HYPOALLERGENIC
HYPERREALISM	HYPERTENSIVE	HYPHENIZING	HYPOBLASTIC
HYPERREALISMS	HYPERTENSIVES	HYPHENLESS	HYPOBLASTS
HYPERREALIST	HYPERTEXTS	HYPNAGOGIC	HYPOCALCEMIA
HYPERREALISTIC	HYPERTHERMAL	HYPNOANALYSES	HYPOCALCEMIAS
HYPERREALISTS	HYPERTHERMIA	HYPNOANALYSIS	HYPOCALCEMIC
HYPERREALITIES	HYPERTHERMIAS	HYPNOANALYTIC	HYPOCAUSTS
HYPERREALITY	HYPERTHERMIC	HYPNOGENESES	HYPOCENTER
HYPERREALS	HYPERTHERMIES	HYPNOGENESIS	HYPOCENTERS
HYPERRESPONSIVE	HYPERTHERMY	HYPNOGENETIC	HYPOCENTRAL
HYPERROMANTIC	HYPERTHYMIA	HYPNOGENIC	HYPOCENTRE
HYPERROMANTICS	HYPERTHYMIAS	HYPNOGENIES	HYPOCENTRES
HYPERSALINE	HYPERTHYROID	HYPNOGENOUS	HYPOCHLORITE
HYPERSALINITIES	HYPERTHYROIDISM	HYPNOGOGIC	HYPOCHLORITES
HYPERSALINITY	HYPERTHYROIDS	HYPNOIDISE	HYPOCHLOROUS
HYPERSALIVATION	HYPERTONIA	HYPNOIDISED	HYPOCHONDRIA
HYPERSARCOMA	HYPERTONIAS	HYPNOIDISES	HYPOCHONDRIAC
HYPERSARCOMAS	HYPERTONIC	HYPNOIDISING	HYPOCHONDRIACAL
HYPERSARCOMATA	HYPERTONICITIES	HYPNOIDIZE	HYPOCHONDRIACS
HYPERSARCOSES	HYPERTONICITY	HYPNOIDIZED	HYPOCHONDRIAS
HYPERSARCOSIS	HYPERTROPHIC	HYPNOIDIZES	HYPOCHONDRIASES
HYPERSECRETION	HYPERTROPHICAL	HYPNOIDIZING	HYPOCHONDRIASIS
HYPERSECRETIONS	HYPERTROPHIED	HYPNOLOGIC	HYPOCHONDRIASM
HYPERSENSITISE	HYPERTROPHIES	HYPNOLOGICAL	HYPOCHONDRIASMS
HYPERSENSITISED	HYPERTROPHOUS	HYPNOLOGIES	HYPOCHONDRIAST
HYPERSENSITISES	HYPERTROPHY	HYPNOLOGIST	HYPOCHONDRIASTS
HYPERSENSITIVE	HYPERTROPHYING	HYPNOLOGISTS	HYPOCHONDRIUM
HYPERSENSITIZE	HYPERTYPICAL	HYPNOPAEDIA	HYPOCORISM
HYPERSENSITIZED	HYPERURBANISM	HYPNOPAEDIAS	HYPOCORISMA
HYPERSENSITIZES	HYPERURBANISMS	HYPNOPOMPIC	HYPOCORISMAS
HYPERSENSUAL	HYPERURICEMIA	HYPNOTHERAPIES	HYPOCORISMS

HYPOCORISTIC	HYPOMENORRHOEA	HYPOSTASISING	HYPOTHERMIC
HYPOCORISTICAL	HYPOMENORRHOEAS	HYPOSTASIZATION	HYPOTHESES
HYPOCOTYLOUS	HYPOMIXOLYDIAN	HYPOSTASIZE	HYPOTHESIS
HYPOCOTYLS	HYPOMORPHIC	HYPOSTASIZED	HYPOTHESISE
HYPOCRISIES	HYPOMORPHS	HYPOSTASIZES	HYPOTHESISED
HYPOCRITES	HYPONASTIC	HYPOSTASIZING	HYPOTHESISER
HYPOCRITIC	HYPONASTICALLY	HYPOSTATIC	HYPOTHESISERS
HYPOCRITICAL	HYPONASTIES	HYPOSTATICAL	HYPOTHESISES
HYPOCRITICALLY	HYPONATRAEMIA	HYPOSTATICALLY	HYPOTHESISING
HYPOCRYSTALLINE	HYPONATRAEMIAS	HYPOSTATISATION	HYPOTHESIST
HYPOCYCLOID	HYPONITRITE	HYPOSTATISE	HYPOTHESISTS
HYPOCYCLOIDAL	HYPONITRITES	HYPOSTATISED	HYPOTHESIZE
HYPOCYCLOIDS	HYPONITROUS	HYPOSTATISES	HYPOTHESIZED
HYPODERMAL	HYPONYMIES	HYPOSTATISING	HYPOTHESIZER
HYPODERMAS	HYPOPHARYNGES	HYPOSTATIZATION	HYPOTHESIZERS
HYPODERMIC	HYPOPHARYNX	HYPOSTATIZE	HYPOTHESIZES
HYPODERMICALLY	HYPOPHARYNXES	HYPOSTATIZED	HYPOTHESIZING
HYPODERMICS	HYPOPHOSPHATE	HYPOSTATIZES	HYPOTHETIC
HYPODERMIS	HYPOPHOSPHATES	HYPOSTATIZING	HYPOTHETICAL
HYPODERMISES	HYPOPHOSPHITE	HYPOSTHENIA	HYPOTHETICALLY
HYPODIPLOID	HYPOPHOSPHITES	HYPOSTHENIAS	HYPOTHETISE
HYPODIPLOIDIES	HYPOPHOSPHORIC	HYPOSTHENIC	HYPOTHETISED
HYPODIPLOIDY	HYPOPHOSPHOROUS	HYPOSTOMES	HYPOTHETISES
HYPODORIAN	HYPOPHRYGIAN	HYPOSTRESS	HYPOTHETISING
HYPOEUTECTIC	HYPOPHYGES	HYPOSTRESSES	HYPOTHETIZE
HYPOEUTECTOID	HYPOPHYSEAL	HYPOSTROPHE	HYPOTHETIZED
HYPOGAEOUS	HYPOPHYSECTOMY	HYPOSTROPHES	HYPOTHETIZES
HYPOGASTRIA	HYPOPHYSES	HYPOSTYLES	HYPOTHETIZING
HYPOGASTRIC	HYPOPHYSIAL	HYPOSULPHATE	HYPOTHYMIA
HYPOGASTRIUM	HYPOPHYSIS	HYPOSULPHATES	HYPOTHYMIAS
HYPOGENOUS	HYPOPITUITARISM	HYPOSULPHITE	HYPOTHYROIDISM
HYPOGLOSSAL	HYPOPITUITARY	HYPOSULPHITES	HYPOTHYROIDISMS
HYPOGLOSSALS	HYPOPLASIA	HYPOSULPHURIC	HYPOTHYROIDS
HYPOGLYCAEMIA	HYPOPLASIAS	HYPOSULPHUROUS	HYPOTONIAS
HYPOGLYCAEMIAS	HYPOPLASTIC	HYPOTACTIC	HYPOTONICITIES
HYPOGLYCAEMIC	HYPOPLASTIES	HYPOTENSION	HYPOTONICITY
HYPOGLYCEMIA	HYPOPLASTRA	HYPOTENSIONS	HYPOTROCHOID
HYPOGLYCEMIAS	HYPOPLASTRON	HYPOTENSIVE	HYPOTROCHOIDS
HYPOGLYCEMIC	HYPOPLASTY	HYPOTENSIVES	HYPOTYPOSES
HYPOGLYCEMICS	HYPOPLOIDIES	HYPOTENUSE	HYPOTYPOSIS
HYPOGNATHISM	HYPOPLOIDS	HYPOTENUSES	HYPOVENTILATION
HYPOGNATHISMS	HYPOPLOIDY	HYPOTHALAMI	HYPOXAEMIA
HYPOGNATHOUS	HYPOPNOEAS	HYPOTHALAMIC	HYPOXAEMIAS
HYPOGYNIES	HYPOSENSITISE	HYPOTHALAMUS	HYPOXAEMIC
HYPOGYNOUS	HYPOSENSITISED	HYPOTHECAE	HYPOXANTHINE
HYPOKALEMIA	HYPOSENSITISES	HYPOTHECARY	HYPOXANTHINES
HYPOKALEMIAS	HYPOSENSITISING	HYPOTHECATE	HYPOXEMIAS
HYPOKALEMIC	HYPOSENSITIZE	HYPOTHECATED	HYPSOCHROME
HYPOLIMNIA	HYPOSENSITIZED	HYPOTHECATES	HYPSOCHROMES
HYPOLIMNION	HYPOSENSITIZES	HYPOTHECATING	HYPSOCHROMIC
HYPOLIMNIONS	HYPOSENSITIZING	HYPOTHECATION	HYPSOGRAPHIC
HYPOLYDIAN	HYPOSPADIAS	HYPOTHECATIONS	HYPSOGRAPHICAL
HYPOMAGNESAEMIA	HYPOSPADIASES	HYPOTHECATOR	HYPSOGRAPHIES
HYPOMAGNESEMIA	HYPOSTASES	HYPOTHECATORS	HYPSOGRAPHY
HYPOMAGNESEMIAS	HYPOSTASIS	HYPOTHENUSE	HYPSOMETER
HYPOMANIAS	HYPOSTASISATION	HYPOTHENUSES	HYPSOMETERS
HYPOMANICS	HYPOSTASISE	HYPOTHERMAL	HYPSOMETRIC
HYPOMENORRHEA	HYPOSTASISED	HYPOTHERMIA	HYPSOMETRICAL
HYPOMENORRHEAS	HYPOSTASISES	HYPOTHERMIAS	

HYPSOMETRICALLY
HYPSOMETRIES
HYPSOMETRIST
HYPSOMETRISTS
HYPSOMETRY
HYPSOPHOBE
HYPSOPHOBES
HYPSOPHOBIA
HYPSOPHOBIAS
HYPSOPHYLL
HYPSOPHYLLARY
HYPSOPHYLLS
HYRACOIDEAN
HYRACOIDEANS
HYSTERANTHOUS
HYSTERECTOMIES
HYSTERECTOMISE
HYSTERECTOMISED
HYSTERECTOMISES
HYSTERECTOMIZE
HYSTERECTOMIZED
HYSTERECTOMIZES
HYSTERECTOMY
HYSTERESES
HYSTERESIAL
HYSTERESIS
HYSTERETIC
HYSTERETICALLY
HYSTERICAL
HYSTERICALLY
HYSTERICKY
HYSTERITIS
HYSTERITISES
HYSTEROGENIC
HYSTEROGENIES
HYSTEROGENY
HYSTEROIDAL
HYSTEROMANIA
HYSTEROMANIAS
HYSTEROTOMIES
HYSTEROTOMY
HYSTRICOMORPH
HYSTRICOMORPHIC
HYSTRICOMORPHS

I

IAMBICALLY	ICHTHYOPHAGOUS	ICONOPHILISMS	IDEOGRAPHICAL
IAMBOGRAPHER	ICHTHYOPHAGY	ICONOPHILIST	IDEOGRAPHICALLY
IAMBOGRAPHERS	ICHTHYOPSID	ICONOPHILISTS	IDEOGRAPHIES
IATROCHEMICAL	ICHTHYOPSIDAN	ICONOSCOPE	IDEOGRAPHS
IATROCHEMIST	ICHTHYOPSIDANS	ICONOSCOPES	IDEOGRAPHY
IATROCHEMISTRY	ICHTHYOPSIDS	ICONOSTASES	IDEOLOGICAL
IATROCHEMISTS	ICHTHYORNIS	ICONOSTASIS	IDEOLOGICALLY
IATROGENIC	ICHTHYORNISES	ICOSAHEDRA	IDEOLOGIES
IATROGENICALLY	ICHTHYOSAUR	ICOSAHEDRAL	IDEOLOGISE
IATROGENICITIES	ICHTHYOSAURI	ICOSAHEDRON	IDEOLOGISED
IATROGENICITY	ICHTHYOSAURIAN	ICOSAHEDRONS	IDEOLOGISES
IATROGENIES	ICHTHYOSAURIANS	ICOSANDRIAN	IDEOLOGISING
IBUPROFENS	ICHTHYOSAURS	ICOSANDROUS	IDEOLOGIST
ICEBOATERS	ICHTHYOSAURUS	ICOSITETRAHEDRA	IDEOLOGISTS
ICEBOATING	ICHTHYOSAURUSES	ICTERICALS	IDEOLOGIZE
ICEBOATINGS	ICHTHYOSES	ICTERITIOUS	IDEOLOGIZED
ICEBREAKER	ICHTHYOSIS	IDEALISATION	IDEOLOGIZES
ICEBREAKERS	ICHTHYOTIC	IDEALISATIONS	IDEOLOGIZING
ICEBREAKING	ICKINESSES	IDEALISERS	IDEOLOGUES
ICHNEUMONS	ICONICALLY	IDEALISING	IDEOPHONES
ICHNOFOSSIL	ICONICITIES	IDEALISTIC	IDEOPRAXIST
ICHNOFOSSILS	ICONIFYING	IDEALISTICALLY	IDEOPRAXISTS
ICHNOGRAPHIC	ICONOCLASM	IDEALITIES	IDIOBLASTIC
ICHNOGRAPHICAL	ICONOCLASMS	IDEALIZATION	IDIOBLASTS
ICHNOGRAPHIES	ICONOCLAST	IDEALIZATIONS	IDIOGLOSSIA
ICHNOGRAPHY	ICONOCLASTIC	IDEALIZERS	IDIOGLOSSIAS
ICHNOLITES	ICONOCLASTS	IDEALIZING	IDIOGRAPHIC
ICHNOLOGICAL	ICONOGRAPHER	IDEALNESSES	IDIOGRAPHS
ICHNOLOGIES	ICONOGRAPHERS	IDEALOGIES	IDIOLECTAL
ICHTHYOCOLLA	ICONOGRAPHIC	IDEALOGUES	IDIOLECTIC
ICHTHYOCOLLAS	ICONOGRAPHICAL	IDEATIONAL	IDIOMATICAL
ICHTHYODORULITE	ICONOGRAPHIES	IDEATIONALLY	IDIOMATICALLY
ICHTHYODORYLITE	ICONOGRAPHY	IDEMPOTENCIES	IDIOMATICALNESS
ICHTHYOFAUNA	ICONOLATER	IDEMPOTENCY	IDIOMATICNESS
ICHTHYOFAUNAE	ICONOLATERS	IDEMPOTENT	IDIOMATICNESSES
ICHTHYOFAUNAL	ICONOLATRIES	IDEMPOTENTS	IDIOMORPHIC
ICHTHYOFAUNAS	ICONOLATROUS	IDENTICALLY	IDIOMORPHICALLY
ICHTHYOIDAL	ICONOLATRY	IDENTICALNESS	IDIOMORPHISM
ICHTHYOIDS	ICONOLOGICAL	IDENTICALNESSES	IDIOMORPHISMS
ICHTHYOLATRIES	ICONOLOGIES	IDENTIFIABLE	IDIOPATHIC
ICHTHYOLATROUS	ICONOLOGIST	IDENTIFIABLY	IDIOPATHICALLY
ICHTHYOLATRY	ICONOLOGISTS	IDENTIFICATION	IDIOPATHIES
ICHTHYOLITE	ICONOMACHIES	IDENTIFICATIONS	IDIOPHONES
ICHTHYOLITES	ICONOMACHIST	IDENTIFIED	IDIOPHONIC
ICHTHYOLITIC	ICONOMACHISTS	IDENTIFIER	IDIOPLASMATIC
ICHTHYOLOGIC	ICONOMACHY	IDENTIFIERS	IDIOPLASMIC
ICHTHYOLOGICAL	ICONOMATIC	IDENTIFIES	IDIOPLASMS
ICHTHYOLOGIES	ICONOMATICISM	IDENTIFYING	IDIORHYTHMIC
ICHTHYOLOGIST	ICONOMATICISMS	IDENTIKITS	IDIORRHYTHMIC
ICHTHYOLOGISTS	ICONOMETER	IDENTITIES	IDIOSYNCRASIES
ICHTHYOLOGY	ICONOMETERS	IDEOGRAMIC	IDIOSYNCRASY
ICHTHYOPHAGIES	ICONOMETRIES	IDEOGRAMMATIC	IDIOSYNCRATIC
ICHTHYOPHAGIST	ICONOMETRY	IDEOGRAMMIC	IDIOSYNCRATICAL
ICHTHYOPHAGISTS	ICONOPHILISM	IDEOGRAPHIC	IDIOTHERMOUS

IDIOTICALLY	ILLAQUEABLE	ILLIMITATIONS	ILLUSTRATED
IDIOTICALNESS	ILLAQUEATE	ILLIQUATION	ILLUSTRATEDS
IDIOTICALNESSES	ILLAQUEATED	ILLIQUATIONS	ILLUSTRATES
IDIOTICONS	ILLAQUEATES	ILLIQUIDITIES	ILLUSTRATING
IDLENESSES	ILLAQUEATING	ILLIQUIDITY	ILLUSTRATION
IDOLATRESS	ILLAQUEATION	ILLITERACIES	ILLUSTRATIONAL
IDOLATRESSES	ILLAQUEATIONS	ILLITERACY	ILLUSTRATIONS
IDOLATRIES	ILLATIVELY	ILLITERATE	ILLUSTRATIVE
IDOLATRISE	ILLAUDABLE	ILLITERATELY	ILLUSTRATIVELY
IDOLATRISED	ILLAUDABLY	ILLITERATENESS	ILLUSTRATOR
IDOLATRISER	ILLEGALISATION	ILLITERATES	ILLUSTRATORS
IDOLATRISERS	ILLEGALISATIONS	ILLOCUTION	ILLUSTRATORY
IDOLATRISES	ILLEGALISE	ILLOCUTIONARY	ILLUSTRIOUS
IDOLATRISING	ILLEGALISED	ILLOCUTIONS	ILLUSTRIOUSLY
IDOLATRIZE	ILLEGALISES	ILLOGICALITIES	ILLUSTRIOUSNESS
IDOLATRIZED	ILLEGALISING	ILLOGICALITY	ILLUSTRISSIMO
IDOLATRIZER	ILLEGALITIES	ILLOGICALLY	ILLUVIATED
IDOLATRIZERS	ILLEGALITY	ILLOGICALNESS	ILLUVIATES
IDOLATRIZES	ILLEGALIZATION	ILLOGICALNESSES	ILLUVIATING
IDOLATRIZING	ILLEGALIZATIONS	ILLUMINABLE	ILLUVIATION
IDOLATROUS	ILLEGALIZE	ILLUMINANCE	ILLUVIATIONS
IDOLATROUSLY	ILLEGALIZED	ILLUMINANCES	IMAGINABLE
IDOLATROUSNESS	ILLEGALIZES	ILLUMINANT	IMAGINABLENESS
IDOLISATION	ILLEGALIZING	ILLUMINANTS	IMAGINABLY
IDOLISATIONS	ILLEGIBILITIES	ILLUMINATE	IMAGINARIES
IDOLIZATION	ILLEGIBILITY	ILLUMINATED	IMAGINARILY
IDOLIZATIONS	ILLEGIBLENESS	ILLUMINATES	IMAGINARINESS
IDOLOCLAST	ILLEGIBLENESSES	ILLUMINATI	IMAGINARINESSES
IDOLOCLASTS	ILLEGITIMACIES	ILLUMINATING	IMAGINATION
IDONEITIES	ILLEGITIMACY	ILLUMINATINGLY	IMAGINATIONAL
IDOXURIDINE	ILLEGITIMATE	ILLUMINATION	IMAGINATIONS
IDOXURIDINES	ILLEGITIMATED	ILLUMINATIONAL	IMAGINATIVE
IDYLLICALLY	ILLEGITIMATELY	ILLUMINATIONS	IMAGINATIVELY
IFFINESSES	ILLEGITIMATES	ILLUMINATIVE	IMAGINATIVENESS
IGNESCENTS	ILLEGITIMATING	ILLUMINATO	IMAGININGS
IGNIMBRITE	ILLEGITIMATION	ILLUMINATOR	IMAGINISTS
IGNIMBRITES	ILLEGITIMATIONS	ILLUMINATORS	IMAGISTICALLY
IGNIPOTENT	ILLIBERALISE	ILLUMINERS	IMBALANCED
IGNITABILITIES	ILLIBERALISED	ILLUMINING	IMBALANCES
IGNITABILITY	ILLIBERALISES	ILLUMINISM	IMBECILELY
IGNITIBILITIES	ILLIBERALISING	ILLUMINISMS	IMBECILICALLY
IGNITIBILITY	ILLIBERALISM	ILLUMINIST	IMBECILITIES
IGNOBILITIES	ILLIBERALISMS	ILLUMINISTS	IMBECILITY
IGNOBILITY	ILLIBERALITIES	ILLUSIONAL	IMBIBITION
IGNOBLENESS	ILLIBERALITY	ILLUSIONARY	IMBIBITIONAL
IGNOBLENESSES	ILLIBERALIZE	ILLUSIONED	IMBIBITIONS
IGNOMINIES	ILLIBERALIZED	ILLUSIONISM	IMBITTERED
IGNOMINIOUS	ILLIBERALIZES	ILLUSIONISMS	IMBITTERING
IGNOMINIOUSLY	ILLIBERALIZING	ILLUSIONIST	IMBOLDENED
IGNOMINIOUSNESS	ILLIBERALLY	ILLUSIONISTIC	IMBOLDENING
IGNORAMUSES	ILLIBERALNESS	ILLUSIONISTS	IMBORDERED
IGNORANCES	ILLIBERALNESSES	ILLUSIVELY	IMBORDERING
IGNORANTLY	ILLICITNESS	ILLUSIVENESS	IMBOSOMING
IGNORANTNESS	ILLICITNESSES	ILLUSIVENESSES	IMBOWERING
IGNORANTNESSES	ILLIMITABILITY	ILLUSORILY	IMBRANGLED
IGNORATION	ILLIMITABLE	ILLUSORINESS	IMBRANGLES
IGNORATIONS	ILLIMITABLENESS	ILLUSORINESSES	IMBRANGLING
IGUANODONS	ILLIMITABLY	ILLUSTRATABLE	IMBRICATED
ILEOSTOMIES	ILLIMITATION	ILLUSTRATE	IMBRICATELY

IMBRICATES
IMBRICATING
IMBRICATION
IMBRICATIONS
IMBROCCATA
IMBROCCATAS
IMBROGLIOS
IMBROWNING
IMBRUEMENT
IMBRUEMENTS
IMBUEMENTS
IMIDAZOLES
IMINAZOLES
IMINOUREAS
IMIPRAMINE
IMIPRAMINES
IMITABILITIES
IMITABILITY
IMITABLENESS
IMITABLENESSES
IMITANCIES
IMITATIONAL
IMITATIONS
IMITATIVELY
IMITATIVENESS
IMITATIVENESSES
IMMACULACIES
IMMACULACY
IMMACULATE
IMMACULATELY
IMMACULATENESS
IMMANACLED
IMMANACLES
IMMANACLING
IMMANATION
IMMANATIONS
IMMANENCES
IMMANENCIES
IMMANENTAL
IMMANENTISM
IMMANENTISMS
IMMANENTIST
IMMANENTISTIC
IMMANENTISTS
IMMANENTLY
IMMANITIES
IMMANTLING
IMMARCESCIBLE
IMMARGINATE
IMMATERIAL
IMMATERIALISE
IMMATERIALISED
IMMATERIALISES
IMMATERIALISING
IMMATERIALISM
IMMATERIALISMS
IMMATERIALIST
IMMATERIALISTS
IMMATERIALITIES

IMMATERIALITY
IMMATERIALIZE
IMMATERIALIZED
IMMATERIALIZES
IMMATERIALIZING
IMMATERIALLY
IMMATERIALNESS
IMMATURELY
IMMATURENESS
IMMATURENESSES
IMMATURITIES
IMMATURITY
IMMEASURABILITY
IMMEASURABLE
IMMEASURABLY
IMMEASURED
IMMEDIACIES
IMMEDIATELY
IMMEDIATENESS
IMMEDIATENESSES
IMMEDIATISM
IMMEDIATISMS
IMMEDICABLE
IMMEDICABLENESS
IMMEDICABLY
IMMEMORIAL
IMMEMORIALLY
IMMENSENESS
IMMENSENESSES
IMMENSITIES
IMMENSURABILITY
IMMENSURABLE
IMMERGENCE
IMMERGENCES
IMMERITOUS
IMMERSIBLE
IMMERSIONISM
IMMERSIONISMS
IMMERSIONIST
IMMERSIONISTS
IMMERSIONS
IMMETHODICAL
IMMETHODICALLY
IMMIGRANTS
IMMIGRATED
IMMIGRATES
IMMIGRATING
IMMIGRATION
IMMIGRATIONAL
IMMIGRATIONS
IMMIGRATOR
IMMIGRATORS
IMMIGRATORY
IMMINENCES
IMMINENCIES
IMMINENTLY
IMMINENTNESS
IMMINENTNESSES
IMMINGLING

IMMINUTION
IMMINUTIONS
IMMISCIBILITIES
IMMISCIBILITY
IMMISCIBLE
IMMISCIBLY
IMMISERATION
IMMISERATIONS
IMMISERISATION
IMMISERISATIONS
IMMISERISE
IMMISERISED
IMMISERISES
IMMISERISING
IMMISERIZATION
IMMISERIZATIONS
IMMISERIZE
IMMISERIZED
IMMISERIZES
IMMISERIZING
IMMISSIONS
IMMITIGABILITY
IMMITIGABLE
IMMITIGABLY
IMMITTANCE
IMMITTANCES
IMMIXTURES
IMMOBILISATION
IMMOBILISATIONS
IMMOBILISE
IMMOBILISED
IMMOBILISER
IMMOBILISERS
IMMOBILISES
IMMOBILISING
IMMOBILISM
IMMOBILISMS
IMMOBILITIES
IMMOBILITY
IMMOBILIZATION
IMMOBILIZATIONS
IMMOBILIZE
IMMOBILIZED
IMMOBILIZER
IMMOBILIZERS
IMMOBILIZES
IMMOBILIZING
IMMODERACIES
IMMODERACY
IMMODERATE
IMMODERATELY
IMMODERATENESS
IMMODERATION
IMMODERATIONS
IMMODESTIES
IMMODESTLY
IMMOLATING
IMMOLATION
IMMOLATIONS

IMMOLATORS
IMMOMENTOUS
IMMORALISM
IMMORALISMS
IMMORALIST
IMMORALISTS
IMMORALITIES
IMMORALITY
IMMORTALISATION
IMMORTALISE
IMMORTALISED
IMMORTALISER
IMMORTALISERS
IMMORTALISES
IMMORTALISING
IMMORTALITIES
IMMORTALITY
IMMORTALIZATION
IMMORTALIZE
IMMORTALIZED
IMMORTALIZER
IMMORTALIZERS
IMMORTALIZES
IMMORTALIZING
IMMORTALLY
IMMORTELLE
IMMORTELLES
IMMOTILITIES
IMMOTILITY
IMMOVABILITIES
IMMOVABILITY
IMMOVABLENESS
IMMOVABLENESSES
IMMOVABLES
IMMOVEABILITIES
IMMOVEABILITY
IMMOVEABLE
IMMOVEABLENESS
IMMOVEABLES
IMMOVEABLY
IMMUNIFACIENT
IMMUNISATION
IMMUNISATIONS
IMMUNISERS
IMMUNISING
IMMUNITIES
IMMUNIZATION
IMMUNIZATIONS
IMMUNIZERS
IMMUNIZING
IMMUNOASSAY
IMMUNOASSAYABLE
IMMUNOASSAYIST
IMMUNOASSAYISTS
IMMUNOASSAYS
IMMUNOBLOT
IMMUNOBLOTS
IMMUNOBLOTTING
IMMUNOBLOTTINGS

IMMUNOCHEMICAL	IMPALPABILITIES	IMPASSIVENESSES	IMPERATIVENESS
IMMUNOCHEMIST	IMPALPABILITY	IMPASSIVITIES	IMPERATIVES
IMMUNOCHEMISTRY	IMPALPABLE	IMPASSIVITY	IMPERATORIAL
IMMUNOCHEMISTS	IMPALPABLY	IMPASTATION	IMPERATORIALLY
IMMUNOCOMPETENT	IMPALUDISM	IMPASTATIONS	IMPERATORS
IMMUNOCOMPLEX	IMPALUDISMS	IMPATIENCE	IMPERATORSHIP
IMMUNOCOMPLEXES	IMPANATION	IMPATIENCES	IMPERATORSHIPS
IMMUNODEFICIENT	IMPANATIONS	IMPATIENTLY	IMPERCEABLE
IMMUNODIAGNOSES	IMPANELING	IMPEACHABILITY	IMPERCEIVABLE
IMMUNODIAGNOSIS	IMPANELLED	IMPEACHABLE	IMPERCEPTIBLE
IMMUNODIFFUSION	IMPANELLING	IMPEACHERS	IMPERCEPTIBLY
IMMUNOGENESES	IMPANELMENT	IMPEACHING	IMPERCEPTION
IMMUNOGENESIS	IMPANELMENTS	IMPEACHMENT	IMPERCEPTIONS
IMMUNOGENETIC	IMPANNELLED	IMPEACHMENTS	IMPERCEPTIVE
IMMUNOGENETICAL	IMPANNELLING	IMPEARLING	IMPERCEPTIVELY
IMMUNOGENETICS	IMPARADISE	IMPECCABILITIES	IMPERCEPTIVITY
IMMUNOGENIC	IMPARADISED	IMPECCABILITY	IMPERCIPIENCE
IMMUNOGENICALLY	IMPARADISES	IMPECCABLE	IMPERCIPIENCES
IMMUNOGENICITY	IMPARADISING	IMPECCABLY	IMPERCIPIENT
IMMUNOGENS	IMPARIDIGITATE	IMPECCANCIES	IMPERFECTIBLE
IMMUNOGLOBULIN	IMPARIPINNATE	IMPECCANCY	IMPERFECTION
IMMUNOGLOBULINS	IMPARISYLLABIC	IMPECUNIOSITIES	IMPERFECTIONS
IMMUNOLOGIC	IMPARITIES	IMPECUNIOSITY	IMPERFECTIVE
IMMUNOLOGICAL	IMPARKATION	IMPECUNIOUS	IMPERFECTIVELY
IMMUNOLOGICALLY	IMPARKATIONS	IMPECUNIOUSLY	IMPERFECTIVES
IMMUNOLOGIES	IMPARLANCE	IMPECUNIOUSNESS	IMPERFECTLY
IMMUNOLOGIST	IMPARLANCES	IMPEDANCES	IMPERFECTNESS
IMMUNOLOGISTS	IMPARTABLE	IMPEDIMENT	IMPERFECTNESSES
IMMUNOLOGY	IMPARTATION	IMPEDIMENTA	IMPERFECTS
IMMUNOMODULATOR	IMPARTATIONS	IMPEDIMENTAL	IMPERFORABLE
IMMUNOPATHOLOGY	IMPARTIALITIES	IMPEDIMENTARY	IMPERFORATE
IMMUNOPHORESES	IMPARTIALITY	IMPEDIMENTS	IMPERFORATED
IMMUNOPHORESIS	IMPARTIALLY	IMPEDINGLY	IMPERFORATION
IMMUNOREACTION	IMPARTIALNESS	IMPEDITIVE	IMPERFORATIONS
IMMUNOREACTIONS	IMPARTIALNESSES	IMPELLENTS	IMPERIALISE
IMMUNOREACTIVE	IMPARTIBILITIES	IMPENDENCE	IMPERIALISED
IMMUNOSORBENT	IMPARTIBILITY	IMPENDENCES	IMPERIALISES
IMMUNOSORBENTS	IMPARTIBLE	IMPENDENCIES	IMPERIALISING
IMMUNOSUPPRESS	IMPARTIBLY	IMPENDENCY	IMPERIALISM
IMMUNOTHERAPIES	IMPARTMENT	IMPENETRABILITY	IMPERIALISMS
IMMUNOTHERAPY	IMPARTMENTS	IMPENETRABLE	IMPERIALIST
IMMUNOTOXIC	IMPASSABILITIES	IMPENETRABLY	IMPERIALISTIC
IMMUNOTOXIN	IMPASSABILITY	IMPENETRATE	IMPERIALISTS
IMMUNOTOXINS	IMPASSABLE	IMPENETRATED	IMPERIALITIES
IMMUREMENT	IMPASSABLENESS	IMPENETRATES	IMPERIALITY
IMMUREMENTS	IMPASSABLY	IMPENETRATING	IMPERIALIZE
IMMUTABILITIES	IMPASSIBILITIES	IMPENETRATION	IMPERIALIZED
IMMUTABILITY	IMPASSIBILITY	IMPENETRATIONS	IMPERIALIZES
IMMUTABLENESS	IMPASSIBLE	IMPENITENCE	IMPERIALIZING
IMMUTABLENESSES	IMPASSIBLENESS	IMPENITENCES	IMPERIALLY
IMPACTIONS	IMPASSIBLY	IMPENITENCIES	IMPERIALNESS
IMPACTITES	IMPASSIONATE	IMPENITENCY	IMPERIALNESSES
IMPAINTING	IMPASSIONED	IMPENITENT	IMPERILING
IMPAIRABLE	IMPASSIONEDLY	IMPENITENTLY	IMPERILLED
IMPAIRINGS	IMPASSIONEDNESS	IMPENITENTNESS	IMPERILLING
IMPAIRMENT	IMPASSIONING	IMPENITENTS	IMPERILMENT
IMPAIRMENTS	IMPASSIONS	IMPERATIVAL	IMPERILMENTS
IMPALEMENT	IMPASSIVELY	IMPERATIVE	IMPERIOUSLY
IMPALEMENTS	IMPASSIVENESS	IMPERATIVELY	IMPERIOUSNESS

IMPERIOUSNESSES	IMPETIGINES	IMPLEMENTOR	IMPORTANTLY
IMPERISHABILITY	IMPETIGINOUS	IMPLEMENTORS	IMPORTATION
IMPERISHABLE	IMPETRATED	IMPLEMENTS	IMPORTATIONS
IMPERISHABLES	IMPETRATES	IMPLETIONS	IMPORTINGS
IMPERISHABLY	IMPETRATING	IMPLEXIONS	IMPORTUNACIES
IMPERMANENCE	IMPETRATION	IMPLEXUOUS	IMPORTUNACY
IMPERMANENCES	IMPETRATIONS	IMPLICATED	IMPORTUNATE
IMPERMANENCIES	IMPETRATIVE	IMPLICATES	IMPORTUNATELY
IMPERMANENCY	IMPETRATOR	IMPLICATING	IMPORTUNATENESS
IMPERMANENT	IMPETRATORS	IMPLICATION	IMPORTUNED
IMPERMANENTLY	IMPETRATORY	IMPLICATIONAL	IMPORTUNELY
IMPERMEABILITY	IMPETUOSITIES	IMPLICATIONS	IMPORTUNER
IMPERMEABLE	IMPETUOSITY	IMPLICATIVE	IMPORTUNERS
IMPERMEABLENESS	IMPETUOUSLY	IMPLICATIVELY	IMPORTUNES
IMPERMEABLY	IMPETUOUSNESS	IMPLICATIVENESS	IMPORTUNING
IMPERMISSIBLE	IMPETUOUSNESSES	IMPLICATURE	IMPORTUNINGS
IMPERMISSIBLY	IMPICTURED	IMPLICATURES	IMPORTUNITIES
IMPERSCRIPTIBLE	IMPIERCEABLE	IMPLICITIES	IMPORTUNITY
IMPERSEVERANT	IMPIGNORATE	IMPLICITLY	IMPOSINGLY
IMPERSISTENT	IMPIGNORATED	IMPLICITNESS	IMPOSINGNESS
IMPERSONAL	IMPIGNORATES	IMPLICITNESSES	IMPOSINGNESSES
IMPERSONALISE	IMPIGNORATING	IMPLODENTS	IMPOSITION
IMPERSONALISED	IMPIGNORATION	IMPLORATION	IMPOSITIONS
IMPERSONALISES	IMPIGNORATIONS	IMPLORATIONS	IMPOSSIBILISM
IMPERSONALISING	IMPINGEMENT	IMPLORATOR	IMPOSSIBILISMS
IMPERSONALITIES	IMPINGEMENTS	IMPLORATORS	IMPOSSIBILIST
IMPERSONALITY	IMPIOUSNESS	IMPLORATORY	IMPOSSIBILISTS
IMPERSONALIZE	IMPIOUSNESSES	IMPLORINGLY	IMPOSSIBILITIES
IMPERSONALIZED	IMPISHNESS	IMPLOSIONS	IMPOSSIBILITY
IMPERSONALIZES	IMPISHNESSES	IMPLOSIVELY	IMPOSSIBLE
IMPERSONALIZING	IMPLACABILITIES	IMPLOSIVES	IMPOSSIBLENESS
IMPERSONALLY	IMPLACABILITY	IMPLUNGING	IMPOSSIBLES
IMPERSONATE	IMPLACABLE	IMPOCKETED	IMPOSSIBLY
IMPERSONATED	IMPLACABLENESS	IMPOCKETING	IMPOSTHUMATE
IMPERSONATES	IMPLACABLY	IMPOLDERED	IMPOSTHUMATED
IMPERSONATING	IMPLACENTAL	IMPOLDERING	IMPOSTHUMATES
IMPERSONATION	IMPLANTABLE	IMPOLICIES	IMPOSTHUMATING
IMPERSONATIONS	IMPLANTATION	IMPOLITELY	IMPOSTHUMATION
IMPERSONATOR	IMPLANTATIONS	IMPOLITENESS	IMPOSTHUMATIONS
IMPERSONATORS	IMPLANTERS	IMPOLITENESSES	IMPOSTHUME
IMPERTINENCE	IMPLANTING	IMPOLITEST	IMPOSTHUMED
IMPERTINENCES	IMPLAUSIBILITY	IMPOLITICAL	IMPOSTHUMES
IMPERTINENCIES	IMPLAUSIBLE	IMPOLITICALLY	IMPOSTOROUS
IMPERTINENCY	IMPLAUSIBLENESS	IMPOLITICLY	IMPOSTROUS
IMPERTINENT	IMPLAUSIBLY	IMPOLITICNESS	IMPOSTUMATE
IMPERTINENTLY	IMPLEACHED	IMPOLITICNESSES	IMPOSTUMATED
IMPERTURBABLE	IMPLEACHES	IMPONDERABILIA	IMPOSTUMATES
IMPERTURBABLY	IMPLEACHING	IMPONDERABILITY	IMPOSTUMATING
IMPERTURBATION	IMPLEADABLE	IMPONDERABLE	IMPOSTUMATION
IMPERTURBATIONS	IMPLEADERS	IMPONDERABLES	IMPOSTUMATIONS
IMPERVIABILITY	IMPLEADING	IMPONDERABLY	IMPOSTUMED
IMPERVIABLE	IMPLEDGING	IMPONDEROUS	IMPOSTUMES
IMPERVIABLENESS	IMPLEMENTAL	IMPORTABILITIES	IMPOSTURES
IMPERVIOUS	IMPLEMENTATION	IMPORTABILITY	IMPOSTUROUS
IMPERVIOUSLY	IMPLEMENTATIONS	IMPORTABLE	IMPOTENCES
IMPERVIOUSNESS	IMPLEMENTED	IMPORTANCE	IMPOTENCIES
IMPETICOSSED	IMPLEMENTER	IMPORTANCES	IMPOTENTLY
IMPETICOSSES	IMPLEMENTERS	IMPORTANCIES	IMPOTENTNESS
IMPETICOSSING	IMPLEMENTING	IMPORTANCY	IMPOTENTNESSES

IMPOUNDABLE	IMPRESSIONABLE	IMPROVIDENT	IMPURITIES
IMPOUNDAGE	IMPRESSIONAL	IMPROVIDENTLY	IMPURPLING
IMPOUNDAGES	IMPRESSIONALLY	IMPROVINGLY	IMPUTABILITIES
IMPOUNDERS	IMPRESSIONISM	IMPROVISATE	IMPUTABILITY
IMPOUNDING	IMPRESSIONISMS	IMPROVISATED	IMPUTABLENESS
IMPOUNDMENT	IMPRESSIONIST	IMPROVISATES	IMPUTABLENESSES
IMPOUNDMENTS	IMPRESSIONISTIC	IMPROVISATING	IMPUTATION
IMPOVERISH	IMPRESSIONISTS	IMPROVISATION	IMPUTATIONS
IMPOVERISHED	IMPRESSIONS	IMPROVISATIONAL	IMPUTATIVE
IMPOVERISHER	IMPRESSIVE	IMPROVISATIONS	IMPUTATIVELY
IMPOVERISHERS	IMPRESSIVELY	IMPROVISATOR	INABILITIES
IMPOVERISHES	IMPRESSIVENESS	IMPROVISATORE	INABSTINENCE
IMPOVERISHING	IMPRESSMENT	IMPROVISATORES	INABSTINENCES
IMPOVERISHMENT	IMPRESSMENTS	IMPROVISATORI	INACCESSIBILITY
IMPOVERISHMENTS	IMPRESSURE	IMPROVISATORIAL	INACCESSIBLE
IMPOWERING	IMPRESSURES	IMPROVISATORS	INACCESSIBLY
IMPRACTICABLE	IMPRIMATUR	IMPROVISATORY	INACCURACIES
IMPRACTICABLY	IMPRIMATURS	IMPROVISATRICES	INACCURACY
IMPRACTICAL	IMPRINTERS	IMPROVISATRIX	INACCURATE
IMPRACTICALITY	IMPRINTING	IMPROVISATRIXES	INACCURATELY
IMPRACTICALLY	IMPRINTINGS	IMPROVISED	INACCURATENESS
IMPRACTICALNESS	IMPRISONABLE	IMPROVISER	INACTIVATE
IMPRECATED	IMPRISONED	IMPROVISERS	INACTIVATED
IMPRECATES	IMPRISONER	IMPROVISES	INACTIVATES
IMPRECATING	IMPRISONERS	IMPROVISING	INACTIVATING
IMPRECATION	IMPRISONING	IMPROVISOR	INACTIVATION
IMPRECATIONS	IMPRISONMENT	IMPROVISORS	INACTIVATIONS
IMPRECATORY	IMPRISONMENTS	IMPROVVISATORE	INACTIVELY
IMPRECISELY	IMPROBABILITIES	IMPROVVISATORES	INACTIVENESS
IMPRECISENESS	IMPROBABILITY	IMPROVVISATRICE	INACTIVENESSES
IMPRECISENESSES	IMPROBABLE	IMPRUDENCE	INACTIVITIES
IMPRECISION	IMPROBABLENESS	IMPRUDENCES	INACTIVITY
IMPRECISIONS	IMPROBABLY	IMPRUDENTLY	INADAPTABLE
IMPREDICATIVE	IMPROBATION	IMPSONITES	INADAPTATION
IMPREGNABILITY	IMPROBATIONS	IMPUDENCES	INADAPTATIONS
IMPREGNABLE	IMPROBITIES	IMPUDENCIES	INADAPTIVE
IMPREGNABLENESS	IMPROMPTUS	IMPUDENTLY	INADEQUACIES
IMPREGNABLY	IMPROPERLY	IMPUDENTNESS	INADEQUACY
IMPREGNANT	IMPROPERNESS	IMPUDENTNESSES	INADEQUATE
IMPREGNANTS	IMPROPERNESSES	IMPUDICITIES	INADEQUATELY
IMPREGNATABLE	IMPROPRIATE	IMPUDICITY	INADEQUATENESS
IMPREGNATE	IMPROPRIATED	IMPUGNABLE	INADEQUATES
IMPREGNATED	IMPROPRIATES	IMPUGNATION	INADMISSIBILITY
IMPREGNATES	IMPROPRIATING	IMPUGNATIONS	INADMISSIBLE
IMPREGNATING	IMPROPRIATION	IMPUGNMENT	INADMISSIBLY
IMPREGNATION	IMPROPRIATIONS	IMPUGNMENTS	INADVERTENCE
IMPREGNATIONS	IMPROPRIATOR	IMPUISSANCE	INADVERTENCES
IMPREGNATOR	IMPROPRIATORS	IMPUISSANCES	INADVERTENCIES
IMPREGNATORS	IMPROPRIETIES	IMPUISSANT	INADVERTENCY
IMPREGNING	IMPROPRIETY	IMPULSIONS	INADVERTENT
IMPRESARIO	IMPROVABILITIES	IMPULSIVELY	INADVERTENTLY
IMPRESARIOS	IMPROVABILITY	IMPULSIVENESS	INADVISABILITY
IMPRESCRIPTIBLE	IMPROVABLE	IMPULSIVENESSES	INADVISABLE
IMPRESCRIPTIBLY	IMPROVABLENESS	IMPULSIVITIES	INADVISABLENESS
IMPRESSERS	IMPROVABLY	IMPULSIVITY	INADVISABLY
IMPRESSIBILITY	IMPROVEMENT	IMPUNDULUS	INALIENABILITY
IMPRESSIBLE	IMPROVEMENTS	IMPUNITIES	INALIENABLE
IMPRESSING	IMPROVIDENCE	IMPURENESS	INALIENABLENESS
IMPRESSION	IMPROVIDENCES	IMPURENESSES	INALIENABLY

INALTERABILITY	INATTENTIVE	INCAPACIOUSNESS	INCENSEMENT
INALTERABLE	INATTENTIVELY	INCAPACITANT	INCENSEMENTS
INALTERABLENESS	INATTENTIVENESS	INCAPACITANTS	INCENSORIES
INALTERABLY	INAUDIBILITIES	INCAPACITATE	INCENTIVELY
INAMORATAS	INAUDIBILITY	INCAPACITATED	INCENTIVES
INAMORATOS	INAUDIBLENESS	INCAPACITATES	INCENTIVISATION
INANENESSES	INAUDIBLENESSES	INCAPACITATING	INCENTIVISE
INANIMATELY	INAUGURALS	INCAPACITATION	INCENTIVISED
INANIMATENESS	INAUGURATE	INCAPACITATIONS	INCENTIVISES
INANIMATENESSES	INAUGURATED	INCAPACITIES	INCENTIVISING
INANIMATION	INAUGURATES	INCAPACITY	INCENTIVIZATION
INANIMATIONS	INAUGURATING	INCAPSULATE	INCENTIVIZE
INANITIONS	INAUGURATION	INCAPSULATED	INCENTIVIZED
INAPPARENT	INAUGURATIONS	INCAPSULATES	INCENTIVIZES
INAPPARENTLY	INAUGURATOR	INCAPSULATING	INCENTIVIZING
INAPPEASABLE	INAUGURATORS	INCAPSULATION	INCEPTIONS
INAPPELLABLE	INAUGURATORY	INCAPSULATIONS	INCEPTIVELY
INAPPETENCE	INAUSPICIOUS	INCARCERATE	INCEPTIVES
INAPPETENCES	INAUSPICIOUSLY	INCARCERATED	INCERTAINTIES
INAPPETENCIES	INAUTHENTIC	INCARCERATES	INCERTAINTY
INAPPETENCY	INAUTHENTICITY	INCARCERATING	INCERTITUDE
INAPPETENT	INBOUNDING	INCARCERATION	INCERTITUDES
INAPPLICABILITY	INBREATHED	INCARCERATIONS	INCESSANCIES
INAPPLICABLE	INBREATHES	INCARCERATOR	INCESSANCY
INAPPLICABLY	INBREATHING	INCARCERATORS	INCESSANTLY
INAPPOSITE	INBREEDERS	INCARDINATE	INCESSANTNESS
INAPPOSITELY	INBREEDING	INCARDINATED	INCESSANTNESSES
INAPPOSITENESS	INBREEDINGS	INCARDINATES	INCESTUOUS
INAPPRECIABLE	INBRINGING	INCARDINATING	INCESTUOUSLY
INAPPRECIABLY	INBRINGINGS	INCARDINATION	INCESTUOUSNESS
INAPPRECIATION	INCALCULABILITY	INCARDINATIONS	INCHARITABLE
INAPPRECIATIONS	INCALCULABLE	INCARNADINE	INCHOATELY
INAPPRECIATIVE	INCALCULABLY	INCARNADINED	INCHOATENESS
INAPPREHENSIBLE	INCALESCENCE	INCARNADINES	INCHOATENESSES
INAPPREHENSION	INCALESCENCES	INCARNADINING	INCHOATING
INAPPREHENSIONS	INCALESCENT	INCARNATED	INCHOATION
INAPPREHENSIVE	INCANDESCE	INCARNATES	INCHOATIONS
INAPPROACHABLE	INCANDESCED	INCARNATING	INCHOATIVE
INAPPROACHABLY	INCANDESCENCE	INCARNATION	INCHOATIVELY
INAPPROPRIATE	INCANDESCENCES	INCARNATIONS	INCHOATIVES
INAPPROPRIATELY	INCANDESCENCIES	INCARVILLEA	INCIDENCES
INAPTITUDE	INCANDESCENCY	INCARVILLEAS	INCIDENTAL
INAPTITUDES	INCANDESCENT	INCASEMENT	INCIDENTALLY
INAPTNESSES	INCANDESCENTLY	INCASEMENTS	INCIDENTALNESS
INARGUABLE	INCANDESCENTS	INCATENATION	INCIDENTALS
INARGUABLY	INCANDESCES	INCATENATIONS	INCINERATE
INARTICULACIES	INCANDESCING	INCAUTIONS	INCINERATED
INARTICULACY	INCANTATION	INCAUTIOUS	INCINERATES
INARTICULATE	INCANTATIONAL	INCAUTIOUSLY	INCINERATING
INARTICULATELY	INCANTATIONS	INCAUTIOUSNESS	INCINERATION
INARTICULATES	INCANTATOR	INCEDINGLY	INCINERATIONS
INARTICULATION	INCANTATORS	INCENDIARIES	INCINERATOR
INARTICULATIONS	INCANTATORY	INCENDIARISM	INCINERATORS
INARTIFICIAL	INCAPABILITIES	INCENDIARISMS	INCIPIENCE
INARTIFICIALLY	INCAPABILITY	INCENDIARY	INCIPIENCES
INARTISTIC	INCAPABLENESS	INCENDIVITIES	INCIPIENCIES
INARTISTICALLY	INCAPABLENESSES	INCENDIVITY	INCIPIENCY
INATTENTION	INCAPABLES	INCENSATION	INCIPIENTLY
INATTENTIONS	INCAPACIOUS	INCENSATIONS	INCISIFORM

INCISIVELY	INCOGNIZANCES	INCOMPREHENSION	INCONSONANT
INCISIVENESS	INCOGNIZANT	INCOMPREHENSIVE	INCONSONANTLY
INCISIVENESSES	INCOHERENCE	INCOMPRESSIBLE	INCONSPICUOUS
INCISORIAL	INCOHERENCES	INCOMPRESSIBLY	INCONSPICUOUSLY
INCITATION	INCOHERENCIES	INCOMPUTABILITY	INCONSTANCIES
INCITATIONS	INCOHERENCY	INCOMPUTABLE	INCONSTANCY
INCITATIVE	INCOHERENT	INCOMPUTABLY	INCONSTANT
INCITATIVES	INCOHERENTLY	INCOMUNICADO	INCONSTANTLY
INCITEMENT	INCOHERENTNESS	INCONCEIVABLE	INCONSTRUABLE
INCITEMENTS	INCOMBUSTIBLE	INCONCEIVABLES	INCONSUMABLE
INCITINGLY	INCOMBUSTIBLES	INCONCEIVABLY	INCONSUMABLY
INCIVILITIES	INCOMBUSTIBLY	INCONCINNITIES	INCONTESTABLE
INCIVILITY	INCOMMENSURABLE	INCONCINNITY	INCONTESTABLY
INCLASPING	INCOMMENSURABLY	INCONCINNOUS	INCONTIGUOUS
INCLEMENCIES	INCOMMENSURATE	INCONCLUSION	INCONTIGUOUSLY
INCLEMENCY	INCOMMISCIBLE	INCONCLUSIONS	INCONTINENCE
INCLEMENTLY	INCOMMODED	INCONCLUSIVE	INCONTINENCES
INCLEMENTNESS	INCOMMODES	INCONCLUSIVELY	INCONTINENCIES
INCLEMENTNESSES	INCOMMODING	INCONDENSABLE	INCONTINENCY
INCLINABLE	INCOMMODIOUS	INCONDENSIBLE	INCONTINENT
INCLINABLENESS	INCOMMODIOUSLY	INCONDITELY	INCONTINENTLY
INCLINATION	INCOMMODITIES	INCONFORMITIES	INCONTROLLABLE
INCLINATIONAL	INCOMMODITY	INCONFORMITY	INCONTROLLABLY
INCLINATIONS	INCOMMUNICABLE	INCONGRUENCE	INCONVENIENCE
INCLINATORIA	INCOMMUNICABLY	INCONGRUENCES	INCONVENIENCED
INCLINATORIUM	INCOMMUNICADO	INCONGRUENT	INCONVENIENCES
INCLINATORY	INCOMMUNICATIVE	INCONGRUENTLY	INCONVENIENCIES
INCLININGS	INCOMMUTABILITY	INCONGRUITIES	INCONVENIENCING
INCLINOMETER	INCOMMUTABLE	INCONGRUITY	INCONVENIENCY
INCLINOMETERS	INCOMMUTABLY	INCONGRUOUS	INCONVENIENT
INCLIPPING	INCOMPARABILITY	INCONGRUOUSLY	INCONVENIENTLY
INCLOSABLE	INCOMPARABLE	INCONGRUOUSNESS	INCONVERSABLE
INCLOSURES	INCOMPARABLY	INCONSCIENT	INCONVERSANT
INCLUDABLE	INCOMPARED	INCONSCIENTLY	INCONVERTIBLE
INCLUDEDNESS	INCOMPATIBILITY	INCONSCIONABLE	INCONVERTIBLY
INCLUDEDNESSES	INCOMPATIBLE	INCONSCIOUS	INCONVINCIBLE
INCLUDIBLE	INCOMPATIBLES	INCONSECUTIVE	INCONVINCIBLY
INCLUSIONS	INCOMPATIBLY	INCONSECUTIVELY	INCOORDINATE
INCLUSIVELY	INCOMPETENCE	INCONSEQUENCE	INCOORDINATION
INCLUSIVENESS	INCOMPETENCES	INCONSEQUENCES	INCOORDINATIONS
INCLUSIVENESSES	INCOMPETENCIES	INCONSEQUENT	INCORONATE
INCLUSIVITIES	INCOMPETENCY	INCONSEQUENTIAL	INCORONATED
INCLUSIVITY	INCOMPETENT	INCONSEQUENTLY	INCORONATION
INCOAGULABLE	INCOMPETENTLY	INCONSIDERABLE	INCORONATIONS
INCOERCIBLE	INCOMPETENTS	INCONSIDERABLY	INCORPORABLE
INCOGITABILITY	INCOMPLETE	INCONSIDERATE	INCORPORAL
INCOGITABLE	INCOMPLETELY	INCONSIDERATELY	INCORPORALL
INCOGITANCIES	INCOMPLETENESS	INCONSIDERATION	INCORPORATE
INCOGITANCY	INCOMPLETION	INCONSISTENCE	INCORPORATED
INCOGITANT	INCOMPLETIONS	INCONSISTENCES	INCORPORATES
INCOGITATIVE	INCOMPLIANCE	INCONSISTENCIES	INCORPORATING
INCOGNISABLE	INCOMPLIANCES	INCONSISTENCY	INCORPORATION
INCOGNISANCE	INCOMPLIANCIES	INCONSISTENT	INCORPORATIONS
INCOGNISANCES	INCOMPLIANCY	INCONSISTENTLY	INCORPORATIVE
INCOGNISANT	INCOMPLIANT	INCONSOLABILITY	INCORPORATOR
INCOGNITAS	INCOMPLIANTLY	INCONSOLABLE	INCORPORATORS
INCOGNITOS	INCOMPOSED	INCONSOLABLY	INCORPOREAL
INCOGNIZABLE	INCOMPOSITE	INCONSONANCE	INCORPOREALITY
INCOGNIZANCE	INCOMPOSSIBLE	INCONSONANCES	INCORPOREALLY

INCORPOREITIES

INCORPOREITIES
INCORPOREITY
INCORPSING
INCORRECTLY
INCORRECTNESS
INCORRECTNESSES
INCORRIGIBILITY
INCORRIGIBLE
INCORRIGIBLES
INCORRIGIBLY
INCORRODIBLE
INCORROSIBLE
INCORRUPTED
INCORRUPTIBLE
INCORRUPTIBLES
INCORRUPTIBLY
INCORRUPTION
INCORRUPTIONS
INCORRUPTIVE
INCORRUPTLY
INCORRUPTNESS
INCORRUPTNESSES
INCRASSATE
INCRASSATED
INCRASSATES
INCRASSATING
INCRASSATION
INCRASSATIONS
INCRASSATIVE
INCREASABLE
INCREASEDLY
INCREASEFUL
INCREASERS
INCREASING
INCREASINGLY
INCREASINGS
INCREATELY
INCREDIBILITIES
INCREDIBILITY
INCREDIBLE
INCREDIBLENESS
INCREDIBLY
INCREDULITIES
INCREDULITY
INCREDULOUS
INCREDULOUSLY
INCREDULOUSNESS
INCREMATED
INCREMATES
INCREMATING
INCREMATION
INCREMATIONS
INCREMENTAL
INCREMENTALISM
INCREMENTALISMS
INCREMENTALIST
INCREMENTALISTS
INCREMENTALLY
INCREMENTALS

INCREMENTED
INCREMENTING
INCREMENTS
INCRESCENT
INCRETIONARY
INCRETIONS
INCRIMINATE
INCRIMINATED
INCRIMINATES
INCRIMINATING
INCRIMINATION
INCRIMINATIONS
INCRIMINATOR
INCRIMINATORS
INCRIMINATORY
INCROSSBRED
INCROSSBREDS
INCROSSBREED
INCROSSBREEDING
INCROSSBREEDS
INCROSSING
INCRUSTANT
INCRUSTANTS
INCRUSTATION
INCRUSTATIONS
INCRUSTING
INCUBATING
INCUBATION
INCUBATIONAL
INCUBATIONS
INCUBATIVE
INCUBATORS
INCUBATORY
INCULCATED
INCULCATES
INCULCATING
INCULCATION
INCULCATIONS
INCULCATIVE
INCULCATOR
INCULCATORS
INCULCATORY
INCULPABILITIES
INCULPABILITY
INCULPABLE
INCULPABLENESS
INCULPABLY
INCULPATED
INCULPATES
INCULPATING
INCULPATION
INCULPATIONS
INCULPATIVE
INCULPATORY
INCUMBENCIES
INCUMBENCY
INCUMBENTLY
INCUMBENTS
INCUMBERED

INCUMBERING
INCUMBERINGLY
INCUMBRANCE
INCUMBRANCES
INCUNABLES
INCUNABULA
INCUNABULAR
INCUNABULIST
INCUNABULISTS
INCUNABULUM
INCURABILITIES
INCURABILITY
INCURABLENESS
INCURABLENESSES
INCURABLES
INCURIOSITIES
INCURIOSITY
INCURIOUSLY
INCURIOUSNESS
INCURIOUSNESSES
INCURRABLE
INCURRENCE
INCURRENCES
INCURSIONS
INCURVATED
INCURVATES
INCURVATING
INCURVATION
INCURVATIONS
INCURVATURE
INCURVATURES
INCURVITIES
INDAGATING
INDAGATION
INDAGATIONS
INDAGATIVE
INDAGATORS
INDAGATORY
INDAPAMIDE
INDAPAMIDES
INDEBTEDNESS
INDEBTEDNESSES
INDECENCIES
INDECENTER
INDECENTEST
INDECENTLY
INDECIDUATE
INDECIDUOUS
INDECIPHERABLE
INDECIPHERABLY
INDECISION
INDECISIONS
INDECISIVE
INDECISIVELY
INDECISIVENESS
INDECLINABLE
INDECLINABLY
INDECOMPOSABLE
INDECOROUS

INDECOROUSLY
INDECOROUSNESS
INDECORUMS
INDEFATIGABLE
INDEFATIGABLY
INDEFEASIBILITY
INDEFEASIBLE
INDEFEASIBLY
INDEFECTIBILITY
INDEFECTIBLE
INDEFECTIBLY
INDEFENSIBILITY
INDEFENSIBLE
INDEFENSIBLY
INDEFINABILITY
INDEFINABLE
INDEFINABLENESS
INDEFINABLES
INDEFINABLY
INDEFINITE
INDEFINITELY
INDEFINITENESS
INDEFINITES
INDEHISCENCE
INDEHISCENCES
INDEHISCENT
INDELIBILITIES
INDELIBILITY
INDELIBLENESS
INDELIBLENESSES
INDELICACIES
INDELICACY
INDELICATE
INDELICATELY
INDELICATENESS
INDEMNIFICATION
INDEMNIFIED
INDEMNIFIER
INDEMNIFIERS
INDEMNIFIES
INDEMNIFYING
INDEMNITIES
INDEMONSTRABLE
INDEMONSTRABLY
INDENTATION
INDENTATIONS
INDENTIONS
INDENTURED
INDENTURES
INDENTURESHIP
INDENTURESHIPS
INDENTURING
INDEPENDENCE
INDEPENDENCES
INDEPENDENCIES
INDEPENDENCY
INDEPENDENT
INDEPENDENTLY
INDEPENDENTS

INDESCRIBABLE	INDIGENISE	INDISCRETIONS	INDIVIDUATES
INDESCRIBABLES	INDIGENISED	INDISCRIMINATE	INDIVIDUATING
INDESCRIBABLY	INDIGENISES	INDISPENSABLE	INDIVIDUATION
INDESIGNATE	INDIGENISING	INDISPENSABLES	INDIVIDUATIONS
INDESTRUCTIBLE	INDIGENITIES	INDISPENSABLY	INDIVIDUATOR
INDESTRUCTIBLY	INDIGENITY	INDISPOSED	INDIVIDUATORS
INDETECTABLE	INDIGENIZATION	INDISPOSEDNESS	INDIVIDUUM
INDETECTIBLE	INDIGENIZATIONS	INDISPOSES	INDIVISIBILITY
INDETERMINABLE	INDIGENIZE	INDISPOSING	INDIVISIBLE
INDETERMINABLY	INDIGENIZED	INDISPOSITION	INDIVISIBLENESS
INDETERMINACIES	INDIGENIZES	INDISPOSITIONS	INDIVISIBLES
INDETERMINACY	INDIGENIZING	INDISPUTABILITY	INDIVISIBLY
INDETERMINATE	INDIGENOUS	INDISPUTABLE	INDOCILITIES
INDETERMINATELY	INDIGENOUSLY	INDISPUTABLY	INDOCILITY
INDETERMINATION	INDIGENOUSNESS	INDISSOCIABLE	INDOCTRINATE
INDETERMINED	INDIGENTLY	INDISSOCIABLY	INDOCTRINATED
INDETERMINISM	INDIGESTED	INDISSOLUBILITY	INDOCTRINATES
INDETERMINISMS	INDIGESTIBILITY	INDISSOLUBLE	INDOCTRINATING
INDETERMINIST	INDIGESTIBLE	INDISSOLUBLY	INDOCTRINATION
INDETERMINISTIC	INDIGESTIBLES	INDISSOLVABLE	INDOCTRINATIONS
INDETERMINISTS	INDIGESTIBLY	INDISSUADABLE	INDOCTRINATOR
INDEXATION	INDIGESTION	INDISSUADABLY	INDOCTRINATORS
INDEXATIONS	INDIGESTIONS	INDISTINCT	INDOLEACETIC
INDEXICALS	INDIGESTIVE	INDISTINCTION	INDOLEBUTYRIC
INDEXTERITIES	INDIGNANCE	INDISTINCTIONS	INDOLENCES
INDEXTERITY	INDIGNANCES	INDISTINCTIVE	INDOLENCIES
INDICATABLE	INDIGNANTLY	INDISTINCTIVELY	INDOLENTLY
INDICATING	INDIGNATION	INDISTINCTLY	INDOMETHACIN
INDICATION	INDIGNATIONS	INDISTINCTNESS	INDOMETHACINS
INDICATIONAL	INDIGNIFIED	INDISTRIBUTABLE	INDOMITABILITY
INDICATIONS	INDIGNIFIES	INDITEMENT	INDOMITABLE
INDICATIVE	INDIGNIFYING	INDITEMENTS	INDOMITABLENESS
INDICATIVELY	INDIGNITIES	INDIVERTIBLE	INDOMITABLY
INDICATIVES	INDIGOLITE	INDIVERTIBLY	INDOPHENOL
INDICATORS	INDIGOLITES	INDIVIDABLE	INDOPHENOLS
INDICATORY	INDIGOTINS	INDIVIDUAL	INDORSABLE
INDICOLITE	INDINAVIRS	INDIVIDUALISE	INDORSEMENT
INDICOLITES	INDIRECTION	INDIVIDUALISED	INDORSEMENTS
INDICTABLE	INDIRECTIONS	INDIVIDUALISER	INDRAUGHTS
INDICTABLY	INDIRECTLY	INDIVIDUALISERS	INDRENCHED
INDICTIONAL	INDIRECTNESS	INDIVIDUALISES	INDRENCHES
INDICTIONS	INDIRECTNESSES	INDIVIDUALISING	INDRENCHING
INDICTMENT	INDIRUBINS	INDIVIDUALISM	INDUBITABILITY
INDICTMENTS	INDISCERNIBLE	INDIVIDUALISMS	INDUBITABLE
INDIFFERENCE	INDISCERNIBLY	INDIVIDUALIST	INDUBITABLENESS
INDIFFERENCES	INDISCERPTIBLE	INDIVIDUALISTIC	INDUBITABLY
INDIFFERENCIES	INDISCIPLINABLE	INDIVIDUALISTS	INDUCEMENT
INDIFFERENCY	INDISCIPLINE	INDIVIDUALITIES	INDUCEMENTS
INDIFFERENT	INDISCIPLINED	INDIVIDUALITY	INDUCIBILITIES
INDIFFERENTISM	INDISCIPLINES	INDIVIDUALIZE	INDUCIBILITY
INDIFFERENTISMS	INDISCOVERABLE	INDIVIDUALIZED	INDUCTANCE
INDIFFERENTIST	INDISCREET	INDIVIDUALIZER	INDUCTANCES
INDIFFERENTISTS	INDISCREETLY	INDIVIDUALIZERS	INDUCTILITIES
INDIFFERENTLY	INDISCREETNESS	INDIVIDUALIZES	INDUCTILITY
INDIFFERENTS	INDISCRETE	INDIVIDUALIZING	INDUCTIONAL
INDIGENCES	INDISCRETELY	INDIVIDUALLY	INDUCTIONS
INDIGENCIES	INDISCRETENESS	INDIVIDUALS	INDUCTIVELY
INDIGENISATION	INDISCRETION	INDIVIDUATE	INDUCTIVENESS
INDIGENISATIONS	INDISCRETIONARY	INDIVIDUATED	INDUCTIVENESSES

INDUCTIVITIES	INEFFABLENESSES	INEQUITABLE	INEXISTENT
INDUCTIVITY	INEFFACEABILITY	INEQUITABLENESS	INEXORABILITIES
INDULGENCE	INEFFACEABLE	INEQUITABLY	INEXORABILITY
INDULGENCED	INEFFACEABLY	INEQUITIES	INEXORABLE
INDULGENCES	INEFFECTIVE	INEQUIVALVE	INEXORABLENESS
INDULGENCIES	INEFFECTIVELY	INEQUIVALVED	INEXORABLY
INDULGENCING	INEFFECTIVENESS	INERADICABILITY	INEXPANSIBLE
INDULGENCY	INEFFECTUAL	INERADICABLE	INEXPECTANCIES
INDULGENTLY	INEFFECTUALITY	INERADICABLY	INEXPECTANCY
INDULGINGLY	INEFFECTUALLY	INERASABLE	INEXPECTANT
INDUMENTUM	INEFFECTUALNESS	INERASABLY	INEXPECTATION
INDUMENTUMS	INEFFICACIES	INERASIBLE	INEXPECTATIONS
INDUPLICATE	INEFFICACIOUS	INERASIBLY	INEXPEDIENCE
INDUPLICATED	INEFFICACIOUSLY	INERRABILITIES	INEXPEDIENCES
INDUPLICATION	INEFFICACITIES	INERRABILITY	INEXPEDIENCIES
INDUPLICATIONS	INEFFICACITY	INERRABLENESS	INEXPEDIENCY
INDURATING	INEFFICACY	INERRABLENESSES	INEXPEDIENT
INDURATION	INEFFICIENCIES	INERRANCIES	INEXPEDIENTLY
INDURATIONS	INEFFICIENCY	INERTIALLY	INEXPENSIVE
INDURATIVE	INEFFICIENT	INERTNESSES	INEXPENSIVELY
INDUSTRIAL	INEFFICIENTLY	INESCAPABLE	INEXPENSIVENESS
INDUSTRIALISE	INEFFICIENTS	INESCAPABLY	INEXPERIENCE
INDUSTRIALISED	INEGALITARIAN	INESCULENT	INEXPERIENCED
INDUSTRIALISES	INELABORATE	INESCUTCHEON	INEXPERIENCES
INDUSTRIALISING	INELABORATELY	INESCUTCHEONS	INEXPERTLY
INDUSTRIALISM	INELASTICALLY	INESSENTIAL	INEXPERTNESS
INDUSTRIALISMS	INELASTICITIES	INESSENTIALITY	INEXPERTNESSES
INDUSTRIALIST	INELASTICITY	INESSENTIALS	INEXPIABLE
INDUSTRIALISTS	INELEGANCE	INESTIMABILITY	INEXPIABLENESS
INDUSTRIALIZE	INELEGANCES	INESTIMABLE	INEXPIABLY
INDUSTRIALIZED	INELEGANCIES	INESTIMABLENESS	INEXPLAINABLE
INDUSTRIALIZES	INELEGANCY	INESTIMABLY	INEXPLAINABLY
INDUSTRIALIZING	INELEGANTLY	INEVITABILITIES	INEXPLICABILITY
INDUSTRIALLY	INELIGIBILITIES	INEVITABILITY	INEXPLICABLE
INDUSTRIALS	INELIGIBILITY	INEVITABLE	INEXPLICABLY
INDUSTRIES	INELIGIBLE	INEVITABLENESS	INEXPLICIT
INDUSTRIOUS	INELIGIBLENESS	INEVITABLY	INEXPLICITLY
INDUSTRIOUSLY	INELIGIBLES	INEXACTITUDE	INEXPLICITNESS
INDUSTRIOUSNESS	INELIGIBLY	INEXACTITUDES	INEXPRESSIBLE
INDUSTRYWIDE	INELOQUENCE	INEXACTNESS	INEXPRESSIBLES
INDWELLERS	INELOQUENCES	INEXACTNESSES	INEXPRESSIBLY
INDWELLING	INELOQUENT	INEXCITABLE	INEXPRESSIVE
INDWELLINGS	INELOQUENTLY	INEXCUSABILITY	INEXPRESSIVELY
INEARTHING	INELUCTABILITY	INEXCUSABLE	INEXPUGNABILITY
INEBRIANTS	INELUCTABLE	INEXCUSABLENESS	INEXPUGNABLE
INEBRIATED	INELUCTABLY	INEXCUSABLY	INEXPUGNABLY
INEBRIATES	INELUDIBILITIES	INEXECRABLE	INEXPUNGIBLE
INEBRIATING	INELUDIBILITY	INEXECUTABLE	INEXTENDED
INEBRIATION	INELUDIBLE	INEXECUTION	INEXTENSIBILITY
INEBRIATIONS	INELUDIBLY	INEXECUTIONS	INEXTENSIBLE
INEBRIETIES	INENARRABLE	INEXHAUSTED	INEXTENSION
INEDIBILITIES	INEPTITUDE	INEXHAUSTIBLE	INEXTENSIONS
INEDIBILITY	INEPTITUDES	INEXHAUSTIBLY	INEXTIRPABLE
INEDUCABILITIES	INEPTNESSES	INEXHAUSTIVE	INEXTRICABILITY
INEDUCABILITY	INEQUALITIES	INEXISTANT	INEXTRICABLE
INEDUCABLE	INEQUALITY	INEXISTENCE	INEXTRICABLY
INEFFABILITIES	INEQUATION	INEXISTENCES	INFALLIBILISM
INEFFABILITY	INEQUATIONS	INEXISTENCIES	INFALLIBILISMS
INEFFABLENESS	INEQUIPOTENT	INEXISTENCY	INFALLIBILIST

INFALLIBILISTS
INFALLIBILITIES
INFALLIBILITY
INFALLIBLE
INFALLIBLENESS
INFALLIBLES
INFALLIBLY
INFAMISING
INFAMIZING
INFAMONISE
INFAMONISED
INFAMONISES
INFAMONISING
INFAMONIZE
INFAMONIZED
INFAMONIZES
INFAMONIZING
INFAMOUSLY
INFAMOUSNESS
INFAMOUSNESSES
INFANGTHIEF
INFANGTHIEFS
INFANTHOOD
INFANTHOODS
INFANTICIDAL
INFANTICIDE
INFANTICIDES
INFANTILISATION
INFANTILISE
INFANTILISED
INFANTILISES
INFANTILISING
INFANTILISM
INFANTILISMS
INFANTILITIES
INFANTILITY
INFANTILIZATION
INFANTILIZE
INFANTILIZED
INFANTILIZES
INFANTILIZING
INFANTRIES
INFANTRYMAN
INFANTRYMEN
INFARCTION
INFARCTIONS
INFATUATED
INFATUATEDLY
INFATUATES
INFATUATING
INFATUATION
INFATUATIONS
INFEASIBILITIES
INFEASIBILITY
INFEASIBLE
INFEASIBLENESS
INFECTIONS
INFECTIOUS
INFECTIOUSLY

INFECTIOUSNESS
INFECTIVELY
INFECTIVENESS
INFECTIVENESSES
INFECTIVITIES
INFECTIVITY
INFECUNDITIES
INFECUNDITY
INFEFTMENT
INFEFTMENTS
INFELICITIES
INFELICITOUS
INFELICITOUSLY
INFELICITY
INFEOFFING
INFERENCES
INFERENCING
INFERENCINGS
INFERENTIAL
INFERENTIALLY
INFERIORITIES
INFERIORITY
INFERIORLY
INFERNALITIES
INFERNALITY
INFERNALLY
INFERRABLE
INFERRIBLE
INFERTILELY
INFERTILITIES
INFERTILITY
INFESTANTS
INFESTATION
INFESTATIONS
INFEUDATION
INFEUDATIONS
INFIBULATE
INFIBULATED
INFIBULATES
INFIBULATING
INFIBULATION
INFIBULATIONS
INFIDELITIES
INFIDELITY
INFIELDERS
INFIELDSMAN
INFIELDSMEN
INFIGHTERS
INFIGHTING
INFIGHTINGS
INFILLINGS
INFILTRATE
INFILTRATED
INFILTRATES
INFILTRATING
INFILTRATION
INFILTRATIONS
INFILTRATIVE
INFILTRATOR

INFILTRATORS
INFINITANT
INFINITARY
INFINITATE
INFINITATED
INFINITATES
INFINITATING
INFINITELY
INFINITENESS
INFINITENESSES
INFINITESIMAL
INFINITESIMALLY
INFINITESIMALS
INFINITIES
INFINITIVAL
INFINITIVALLY
INFINITIVE
INFINITIVELY
INFINITIVES
INFINITUDE
INFINITUDES
INFIRMARER
INFIRMARERS
INFIRMARIAN
INFIRMARIANS
INFIRMARIES
INFIRMITIES
INFIRMNESS
INFIRMNESSES
INFIXATION
INFIXATIONS
INFLAMABLE
INFLAMINGLY
INFLAMMABILITY
INFLAMMABLE
INFLAMMABLENESS
INFLAMMABLES
INFLAMMABLY
INFLAMMATION
INFLAMMATIONS
INFLAMMATORILY
INFLAMMATORY
INFLATABLE
INFLATABLES
INFLATEDLY
INFLATEDNESS
INFLATEDNESSES
INFLATINGLY
INFLATIONARY
INFLATIONISM
INFLATIONISMS
INFLATIONIST
INFLATIONISTS
INFLATIONS
INFLATUSES
INFLECTABLE
INFLECTEDNESS
INFLECTEDNESSES
INFLECTING

INFLECTION
INFLECTIONAL
INFLECTIONALLY
INFLECTIONLESS
INFLECTIONS
INFLECTIVE
INFLECTORS
INFLEXIBILITIES
INFLEXIBILITY
INFLEXIBLE
INFLEXIBLENESS
INFLEXIBLY
INFLEXIONAL
INFLEXIONALLY
INFLEXIONLESS
INFLEXIONS
INFLEXURES
INFLICTABLE
INFLICTERS
INFLICTING
INFLICTION
INFLICTIONS
INFLICTIVE
INFLICTORS
INFLORESCENCE
INFLORESCENCES
INFLORESCENT
INFLOWINGS
INFLUENCEABLE
INFLUENCED
INFLUENCER
INFLUENCERS
INFLUENCES
INFLUENCING
INFLUENTIAL
INFLUENTIALLY
INFLUENTIALS
INFLUENZAL
INFLUENZAS
INFLUXIONS
INFOLDMENT
INFOLDMENTS
INFOMANIAS
INFOMERCIAL
INFOMERCIALS
INFOPRENEURIAL
INFORMABLE
INFORMALITIES
INFORMALITY
INFORMALLY
INFORMANTS
INFORMATICIAN
INFORMATICIANS
INFORMATICS
INFORMATION
INFORMATIONAL
INFORMATIONALLY
INFORMATIONS
INFORMATIVE

INFORMATIVELY	INFURIATINGLY	INGRATIATING	INHAUSTING
INFORMATIVENESS	INFURIATION	INGRATIATINGLY	INHEARSING
INFORMATORILY	INFURIATIONS	INGRATIATION	INHERENCES
INFORMATORY	INFUSCATED	INGRATIATIONS	INHERENCIES
INFORMEDLY	INFUSIBILITIES	INGRATIATORY	INHERENTLY
INFORMIDABLE	INFUSIBILITY	INGRATITUDE	INHERITABILITY
INFORMINGLY	INFUSIBLENESS	INGRATITUDES	INHERITABLE
INFORTUNES	INFUSIBLENESSES	INGRAVESCENCE	INHERITABLENESS
INFOSPHERE	INFUSIONISM	INGRAVESCENCES	INHERITABLY
INFOSPHERES	INFUSIONISMS	INGRAVESCENT	INHERITANCE
INFOTAINMENT	INFUSIONIST	INGREDIENT	INHERITANCES
INFOTAINMENTS	INFUSIONISTS	INGREDIENTS	INHERITING
INFRACOSTAL	INFUSORIAL	INGRESSION	INHERITORS
INFRACTING	INFUSORIAN	INGRESSIONS	INHERITRESS
INFRACTION	INFUSORIANS	INGRESSIVE	INHERITRESSES
INFRACTIONS	INGATHERED	INGRESSIVENESS	INHERITRICES
INFRACTORS	INGATHERER	INGRESSIVES	INHERITRIX
INFRAGRANT	INGATHERERS	INGROOVING	INHERITRIXES
INFRAHUMAN	INGATHERING	INGROSSING	INHIBITABLE
INFRAHUMANS	INGATHERINGS	INGROWNNESS	INHIBITERS
INFRALAPSARIAN	INGEMINATE	INGROWNNESSES	INHIBITING
INFRALAPSARIANS	INGEMINATED	INGULFMENT	INHIBITION
INFRAMAXILLARY	INGEMINATES	INGULFMENTS	INHIBITIONS
INFRANGIBILITY	INGEMINATING	INGULPHING	INHIBITIVE
INFRANGIBLE	INGEMINATION	INGURGITATE	INHIBITORS
INFRANGIBLENESS	INGEMINATIONS	INGURGITATED	INHIBITORY
INFRANGIBLY	INGENERATE	INGURGITATES	INHOLDINGS
INFRAORBITAL	INGENERATED	INGURGITATING	INHOMOGENEITIES
INFRAPOSED	INGENERATES	INGURGITATION	INHOMOGENEITY
INFRAPOSITION	INGENERATING	INGURGITATIONS	INHOMOGENEOUS
INFRAPOSITIONS	INGENERATION	INHABITABILITY	INHOSPITABLE
INFRASONIC	INGENERATIONS	INHABITABLE	INHOSPITABLY
INFRASOUND	INGENIOUSLY	INHABITANCE	INHOSPITALITIES
INFRASOUNDS	INGENIOUSNESS	INHABITANCES	INHOSPITALITY
INFRASPECIFIC	INGENIOUSNESSES	INHABITANCIES	INHUMANELY
INFRASTRUCTURAL	INGENUITIES	INHABITANCY	INHUMANITIES
INFRASTRUCTURE	INGENUOUSLY	INHABITANT	INHUMANITY
INFRASTRUCTURES	INGENUOUSNESS	INHABITANTS	INHUMANNESS
INFREQUENCE	INGENUOUSNESSES	INHABITATION	INHUMANNESSES
INFREQUENCES	INGESTIBLE	INHABITATIONS	INHUMATING
INFREQUENCIES	INGESTIONS	INHABITERS	INHUMATION
INFREQUENCY	INGLENEUKS	INHABITING	INHUMATIONS
INFREQUENT	INGLENOOKS	INHABITIVENESS	INIMICALITIES
INFREQUENTLY	INGLORIOUS	INHABITORS	INIMICALITY
INFRINGEMENT	INGLORIOUSLY	INHABITRESS	INIMICALLY
INFRINGEMENTS	INGLORIOUSNESS	INHABITRESSES	INIMICALNESS
INFRINGERS	INGRAFTATION	INHALATION	INIMICALNESSES
INFRINGING	INGRAFTATIONS	INHALATIONAL	INIMICITIOUS
INFRUCTUOUS	INGRAFTING	INHALATIONS	INIMITABILITIES
INFRUCTUOUSLY	INGRAFTMENT	INHALATORIUM	INIMITABILITY
INFUNDIBULA	INGRAFTMENTS	INHALATORIUMS	INIMITABLE
INFUNDIBULAR	INGRAINEDLY	INHALATORS	INIMITABLENESS
INFUNDIBULATE	INGRAINEDNESS	INHARMONIC	INIMITABLY
INFUNDIBULIFORM	INGRAINEDNESSES	INHARMONICAL	INIQUITIES
INFUNDIBULUM	INGRAINING	INHARMONICITIES	INIQUITOUS
INFURIATED	INGRATEFUL	INHARMONICITY	INIQUITOUSLY
INFURIATELY	INGRATIATE	INHARMONIES	INIQUITOUSNESS
INFURIATES	INGRATIATED	INHARMONIOUS	INITIALERS
INFURIATING	INGRATIATES	INHARMONIOUSLY	INITIALING

INITIALISATION	INMIGRANTS	INOBEDIENCES	INORGANISATION
INITIALISATIONS	INNATENESS	INOBEDIENT	INORGANISATIONS
INITIALISE	INNATENESSES	INOBEDIENTLY	INORGANISED
INITIALISED	INNAVIGABLE	INOBSERVABLE	INORGANIZATION
INITIALISES	INNAVIGABLY	INOBSERVANCE	INORGANIZATIONS
INITIALISING	INNERMOSTS	INOBSERVANCES	INORGANIZED
INITIALISM	INNERNESSES	INOBSERVANT	INOSCULATE
INITIALISMS	INNERSOLES	INOBSERVANTLY	INOSCULATED
INITIALIZATION	INNERSPRING	INOBSERVATION	INOSCULATES
INITIALIZATIONS	INNERVATED	INOBSERVATIONS	INOSCULATING
INITIALIZE	INNERVATES	INOBTRUSIVE	INOSCULATION
INITIALIZED	INNERVATING	INOBTRUSIVELY	INOSCULATIONS
INITIALIZES	INNERVATION	INOBTRUSIVENESS	INPATIENTS
INITIALIZING	INNERVATIONS	INOCCUPATION	INPAYMENTS
INITIALLED	INNERWEARS	INOCCUPATIONS	INPOURINGS
INITIALLER	INNKEEPERS	INOCULABILITIES	INQUIETING
INITIALLERS	INNOCENCES	INOCULABILITY	INQUIETUDE
INITIALLING	INNOCENCIES	INOCULABLE	INQUIETUDES
INITIALNESS	INNOCENTER	INOCULANTS	INQUILINES
INITIALNESSES	INNOCENTEST	INOCULATED	INQUILINIC
INITIATING	INNOCENTLY	INOCULATES	INQUILINICS
INITIATION	INNOCUITIES	INOCULATING	INQUILINISM
INITIATIONS	INNOCUOUSLY	INOCULATION	INQUILINISMS
INITIATIVE	INNOCUOUSNESS	INOCULATIONS	INQUILINITIES
INITIATIVELY	INNOCUOUSNESSES	INOCULATIVE	INQUILINITY
INITIATIVES	INNOMINABLE	INOCULATOR	INQUILINOUS
INITIATORIES	INNOMINABLES	INOCULATORS	INQUINATED
INITIATORS	INNOMINATE	INOCULATORY	INQUINATES
INITIATORY	INNOVATING	INODOROUSLY	INQUINATING
INITIATRESS	INNOVATION	INODOROUSNESS	INQUINATION
INITIATRESSES	INNOVATIONAL	INODOROUSNESSES	INQUINATIONS
INITIATRICES	INNOVATIONIST	INOFFENSIVE	INQUIRATION
INITIATRIX	INNOVATIONISTS	INOFFENSIVELY	INQUIRATIONS
INITIATRIXES	INNOVATIONS	INOFFENSIVENESS	INQUIRENDO
INJECTABLE	INNOVATIVE	INOFFICIOUS	INQUIRENDOS
INJECTABLES	INNOVATIVELY	INOFFICIOUSLY	INQUIRINGLY
INJECTANTS	INNOVATIVENESS	INOFFICIOUSNESS	INQUISITION
INJECTIONS	INNOVATORS	INOPERABILITIES	INQUISITIONAL
INJELLYING	INNOVATORY	INOPERABILITY	INQUISITIONIST
INJOINTING	INNOXIOUSLY	INOPERABLE	INQUISITIONISTS
INJUDICIAL	INNOXIOUSNESS	INOPERABLENESS	INQUISITIONS
INJUDICIALLY	INNOXIOUSNESSES	INOPERABLY	INQUISITIVE
INJUDICIOUS	INNUENDOED	INOPERATIVE	INQUISITIVELY
INJUDICIOUSLY	INNUENDOES	INOPERATIVENESS	INQUISITIVENESS
INJUDICIOUSNESS	INNUENDOING	INOPERCULATE	INQUISITOR
INJUNCTING	INNUMERABILITY	INOPERCULATES	INQUISITORIAL
INJUNCTION	INNUMERABLE	INOPPORTUNE	INQUISITORIALLY
INJUNCTIONS	INNUMERABLENESS	INOPPORTUNELY	INQUISITORS
INJUNCTIVE	INNUMERABLY	INOPPORTUNENESS	INQUISITRESS
INJUNCTIVELY	INNUMERACIES	INOPPORTUNITIES	INQUISITRESSES
INJURIOUSLY	INNUMERACY	INOPPORTUNITY	INQUISITURIENT
INJURIOUSNESS	INNUMERATE	INORDINACIES	INRUSHINGS
INJURIOUSNESSES	INNUMERATES	INORDINACY	INSALIVATE
INJUSTICES	INNUMEROUS	INORDINATE	INSALIVATED
INKBERRIES	INNUTRIENT	INORDINATELY	INSALIVATES
INKHOLDERS	INNUTRITION	INORDINATENESS	INSALIVATING
INKINESSES	INNUTRITIONS	INORDINATION	INSALIVATION
INMARRIAGE	INNUTRITIOUS	INORDINATIONS	INSALIVATIONS
INMARRIAGES	INOBEDIENCE	INORGANICALLY	INSALUBRIOUS

INSALUBRIOUSLY	INSECTOLOGISTS	INSIGHTFUL	INSOLUBILIZING
INSALUBRITIES	INSECTOLOGY	INSIGHTFULLY	INSOLUBLENESS
INSALUBRITY	INSECURELY	INSIGNIFICANCE	INSOLUBLENESSES
INSALUTARY	INSECURENESS	INSIGNIFICANCES	INSOLUBLES
INSANENESS	INSECURENESSES	INSIGNIFICANCY	INSOLVABILITIES
INSANENESSES	INSECURITIES	INSIGNIFICANT	INSOLVABILITY
INSANITARINESS	INSECURITY	INSIGNIFICANTLY	INSOLVABLE
INSANITARY	INSELBERGE	INSIGNIFICATIVE	INSOLVABLY
INSANITATION	INSELBERGS	INSINCERELY	INSOLVENCIES
INSANITATIONS	INSEMINATE	INSINCERITIES	INSOLVENCY
INSANITIES	INSEMINATED	INSINCERITY	INSOLVENTS
INSATIABILITIES	INSEMINATES	INSINEWING	INSOMNIACS
INSATIABILITY	INSEMINATING	INSINUATED	INSOMNIOUS
INSATIABLE	INSEMINATION	INSINUATES	INSOMNOLENCE
INSATIABLENESS	INSEMINATIONS	INSINUATING	INSOMNOLENCES
INSATIABLY	INSEMINATOR	INSINUATINGLY	INSOUCIANCE
INSATIATELY	INSEMINATORS	INSINUATION	INSOUCIANCES
INSATIATENESS	INSENSATELY	INSINUATIONS	INSOUCIANT
INSATIATENESSES	INSENSATENESS	INSINUATIVE	INSOUCIANTLY
INSATIETIES	INSENSATENESSES	INSINUATOR	INSOULMENT
INSCIENCES	INSENSIBILITIES	INSINUATORS	INSOULMENTS
INSCONCING	INSENSIBILITY	INSINUATORY	INSPANNING
INSCRIBABLE	INSENSIBLE	INSIPIDITIES	INSPECTABLE
INSCRIBABLENESS	INSENSIBLENESS	INSIPIDITY	INSPECTING
INSCRIBERS	INSENSIBLY	INSIPIDNESS	INSPECTINGLY
INSCRIBING	INSENSITIVE	INSIPIDNESSES	INSPECTION
INSCRIPTION	INSENSITIVELY	INSIPIENCE	INSPECTIONAL
INSCRIPTIONAL	INSENSITIVENESS	INSIPIENCES	INSPECTIONS
INSCRIPTIONS	INSENSITIVITIES	INSIPIENTLY	INSPECTIVE
INSCRIPTIVE	INSENSITIVITY	INSISTENCE	INSPECTORAL
INSCRIPTIVELY	INSENSUOUS	INSISTENCES	INSPECTORATE
INSCROLLED	INSENTIENCE	INSISTENCIES	INSPECTORATES
INSCROLLING	INSENTIENCES	INSISTENCY	INSPECTORIAL
INSCRUTABILITY	INSENTIENCIES	INSISTENTLY	INSPECTORS
INSCRUTABLE	INSENTIENCY	INSISTINGLY	INSPECTORSHIP
INSCRUTABLENESS	INSENTIENT	INSNAREMENT	INSPECTORSHIPS
INSCRUTABLY	INSEPARABILITY	INSNAREMENTS	INSPHERING
INSCULPING	INSEPARABLE	INSOBRIETIES	INSPIRABLE
INSCULPTURE	INSEPARABLENESS	INSOBRIETY	INSPIRATION
INSCULPTURED	INSEPARABLES	INSOCIABILITIES	INSPIRATIONAL
INSCULPTURES	INSEPARABLY	INSOCIABILITY	INSPIRATIONALLY
INSCULPTURING	INSEPARATE	INSOCIABLE	INSPIRATIONISM
INSECTARIA	INSERTABLE	INSOCIABLY	INSPIRATIONISMS
INSECTARIES	INSERTIONAL	INSOLATING	INSPIRATIONIST
INSECTARIUM	INSERTIONS	INSOLATION	INSPIRATIONISTS
INSECTARIUMS	INSESSORIAL	INSOLATIONS	INSPIRATIONS
INSECTICIDAL	INSEVERABLE	INSOLENCES	INSPIRATIVE
INSECTICIDALLY	INSHEATHED	INSOLENTLY	INSPIRATOR
INSECTICIDE	INSHEATHES	INSOLIDITIES	INSPIRATORS
INSECTICIDES	INSHEATHING	INSOLIDITY	INSPIRATORY
INSECTIFORM	INSHELLING	INSOLUBILISE	INSPIRINGLY
INSECTIFUGE	INSHELTERED	INSOLUBILISED	INSPIRITED
INSECTIFUGES	INSHELTERING	INSOLUBILISES	INSPIRITER
INSECTIONS	INSHELTERS	INSOLUBILISING	INSPIRITERS
INSECTIVORE	INSHIPPING	INSOLUBILITIES	INSPIRITING
INSECTIVORES	INSHRINING	INSOLUBILITY	INSPIRITINGLY
INSECTIVOROUS	INSIDIOUSLY	INSOLUBILIZE	INSPIRITMENT
INSECTOLOGIES	INSIDIOUSNESS	INSOLUBILIZED	INSPIRITMENTS
INSECTOLOGIST	INSIDIOUSNESSES	INSOLUBILIZES	INSPISSATE

INSPISSATED	INSTINCTIVELY	INSUBSTANTIAL	INSURRECTIONS
INSPISSATES	INSTINCTIVITIES	INSUBSTANTIALLY	INSUSCEPTIBLE
INSPISSATING	INSTINCTIVITY	INSUFFERABLE	INSUSCEPTIBLY
INSPISSATION	INSTINCTUAL	INSUFFERABLY	INSUSCEPTIVE
INSPISSATIONS	INSTINCTUALLY	INSUFFICIENCE	INSUSCEPTIVELY
INSPISSATOR	INSTITORIAL	INSUFFICIENCES	INSWATHING
INSPISSATORS	INSTITUTED	INSUFFICIENCIES	INSWINGERS
INSTABILITIES	INSTITUTER	INSUFFICIENCY	INTACTNESS
INSTABILITY	INSTITUTERS	INSUFFICIENT	INTACTNESSES
INSTALLANT	INSTITUTES	INSUFFICIENTLY	INTAGLIATED
INSTALLANTS	INSTITUTING	INSUFFLATE	INTAGLIOED
INSTALLATION	INSTITUTION	INSUFFLATED	INTAGLIOING
INSTALLATIONS	INSTITUTIONAL	INSUFFLATES	INTANGIBILITIES
INSTALLERS	INSTITUTIONALLY	INSUFFLATING	INTANGIBILITY
INSTALLING	INSTITUTIONARY	INSUFFLATION	INTANGIBLE
INSTALLMENT	INSTITUTIONS	INSUFFLATIONS	INTANGIBLENESS
INSTALLMENTS	INSTITUTIST	INSUFFLATOR	INTANGIBLES
INSTALMENT	INSTITUTISTS	INSUFFLATORS	INTANGIBLY
INSTALMENTS	INSTITUTIVE	INSULARISM	INTEGRABILITIES
INSTANCIES	INSTITUTIVELY	INSULARISMS	INTEGRABILITY
INSTANCING	INSTITUTOR	INSULARITIES	INTEGRABLE
INSTANTANEITIES	INSTITUTORS	INSULARITY	INTEGRALITIES
INSTANTANEITY	INSTREAMING	INSULATING	INTEGRALITY
INSTANTANEOUS	INSTREAMINGS	INSULATION	INTEGRALLY
INSTANTANEOUSLY	INSTRESSED	INSULATIONS	INTEGRANDS
INSTANTIAL	INSTRESSES	INSULATORS	INTEGRANTS
INSTANTIATE	INSTRESSING	INSULINASE	INTEGRATED
INSTANTIATED	INSTRUCTED	INSULINASES	INTEGRATES
INSTANTIATES	INSTRUCTIBLE	INSULSITIES	INTEGRATING
INSTANTIATING	INSTRUCTING	INSULTABLE	INTEGRATION
INSTANTIATION	INSTRUCTION	INSULTINGLY	INTEGRATIONIST
INSTANTIATIONS	INSTRUCTIONAL	INSULTMENT	INTEGRATIONISTS
INSTANTNESS	INSTRUCTIONS	INSULTMENTS	INTEGRATIONS
INSTANTNESSES	INSTRUCTIVE	INSUPERABILITY	INTEGRATIVE
INSTARRING	INSTRUCTIVELY	INSUPERABLE	INTEGRATOR
INSTATEMENT	INSTRUCTIVENESS	INSUPERABLENESS	INTEGRATORS
INSTATEMENTS	INSTRUCTOR	INSUPERABLY	INTEGRITIES
INSTAURATION	INSTRUCTORS	INSUPPORTABLE	INTEGUMENT
INSTAURATIONS	INSTRUCTORSHIP	INSUPPORTABLY	INTEGUMENTAL
INSTAURATOR	INSTRUCTORSHIPS	INSUPPRESSIBLE	INTEGUMENTARY
INSTAURATORS	INSTRUCTRESS	INSUPPRESSIBLY	INTEGUMENTS
INSTIGATED	INSTRUCTRESSES	INSURABILITIES	INTELLECTED
INSTIGATES	INSTRUMENT	INSURABILITY	INTELLECTION
INSTIGATING	INSTRUMENTAL	INSURANCER	INTELLECTIONS
INSTIGATINGLY	INSTRUMENTALISM	INSURANCERS	INTELLECTIVE
INSTIGATION	INSTRUMENTALIST	INSURANCES	INTELLECTIVELY
INSTIGATIONS	INSTRUMENTALITY	INSURGENCE	INTELLECTS
INSTIGATIVE	INSTRUMENTALLY	INSURGENCES	INTELLECTUAL
INSTIGATOR	INSTRUMENTALS	INSURGENCIES	INTELLECTUALISE
INSTIGATORS	INSTRUMENTATION	INSURGENCY	INTELLECTUALISM
INSTILLATION	INSTRUMENTED	INSURGENTLY	INTELLECTUALIST
INSTILLATIONS	INSTRUMENTING	INSURGENTS	INTELLECTUALITY
INSTILLERS	INSTRUMENTS	INSURMOUNTABLE	INTELLECTUALIZE
INSTILLING	INSUBJECTION	INSURMOUNTABLY	INTELLECTUALLY
INSTILLMENT	INSUBJECTIONS	INSURRECTION	INTELLECTUALS
INSTILLMENTS	INSUBORDINATE	INSURRECTIONAL	INTELLIGENCE
INSTILMENT	INSUBORDINATELY	INSURRECTIONARY	INTELLIGENCER
INSTILMENTS	INSUBORDINATES	INSURRECTIONISM	INTELLIGENCERS
INSTINCTIVE	INSUBORDINATION	INSURRECTIONIST	INTELLIGENCES

INTELLIGENT

INTELLIGENT
INTELLIGENTIAL
INTELLIGENTLY
INTELLIGENTSIA
INTELLIGENTSIAS
INTELLIGENTZIA
INTELLIGENTZIAS
INTELLIGIBILITY
INTELLIGIBLE
INTELLIGIBLY
INTEMERATE
INTEMERATELY
INTEMERATENESS
INTEMPERANCE
INTEMPERANCES
INTEMPERANT
INTEMPERANTS
INTEMPERATE
INTEMPERATELY
INTEMPERATENESS
INTEMPESTIVE
INTEMPESTIVELY
INTEMPESTIVITY
INTENDANCE
INTENDANCES
INTENDANCIES
INTENDANCY
INTENDANTS
INTENDEDLY
INTENDERED
INTENDERING
INTENDMENT
INTENDMENTS
INTENERATE
INTENERATED
INTENERATES
INTENERATING
INTENERATION
INTENERATIONS
INTENSATED
INTENSATES
INTENSATING
INTENSATIVE
INTENSATIVES
INTENSENESS
INTENSENESSES
INTENSIFICATION
INTENSIFIED
INTENSIFIER
INTENSIFIERS
INTENSIFIES
INTENSIFYING
INTENSIONAL
INTENSIONALITY
INTENSIONALLY
INTENSIONS
INTENSITIES
INTENSITIVE
INTENSITIVES

INTENSIVELY
INTENSIVENESS
INTENSIVENESSES
INTENSIVES
INTENTIONAL
INTENTIONALITY
INTENTIONALLY
INTENTIONED
INTENTIONS
INTENTNESS
INTENTNESSES
INTERABANG
INTERABANGS
INTERACTANT
INTERACTANTS
INTERACTED
INTERACTING
INTERACTION
INTERACTIONAL
INTERACTIONISM
INTERACTIONISMS
INTERACTIONIST
INTERACTIONISTS
INTERACTIONS
INTERACTIVE
INTERACTIVELY
INTERACTIVITIES
INTERACTIVITY
INTERAGENCY
INTERALLELIC
INTERALLIED
INTERAMBULACRA
INTERAMBULACRAL
INTERAMBULACRUM
INTERANIMATION
INTERANIMATIONS
INTERANNUAL
INTERARCHED
INTERARCHES
INTERARCHING
INTERATOMIC
INTERBASIN
INTERBEDDED
INTERBEDDING
INTERBEDDINGS
INTERBEHAVIOR
INTERBEHAVIORAL
INTERBEHAVIORS
INTERBOROUGH
INTERBRAIN
INTERBRAINS
INTERBRANCH
INTERBREED
INTERBREEDING
INTERBREEDINGS
INTERBREEDS
INTERBROKER
INTERCALAR
INTERCALARILY

INTERCALARY
INTERCALATE
INTERCALATED
INTERCALATES
INTERCALATING
INTERCALATION
INTERCALATIONS
INTERCALATIVE
INTERCAMPUS
INTERCASTE
INTERCEDED
INTERCEDENT
INTERCEDER
INTERCEDERS
INTERCEDES
INTERCEDING
INTERCELLULAR
INTERCENSAL
INTERCEPTED
INTERCEPTER
INTERCEPTERS
INTERCEPTING
INTERCEPTION
INTERCEPTIONS
INTERCEPTIVE
INTERCEPTOR
INTERCEPTORS
INTERCEPTS
INTERCESSION
INTERCESSIONAL
INTERCESSIONS
INTERCESSOR
INTERCESSORIAL
INTERCESSORS
INTERCESSORY
INTERCHAIN
INTERCHAINED
INTERCHAINING
INTERCHAINS
INTERCHANGE
INTERCHANGEABLE
INTERCHANGEABLY
INTERCHANGED
INTERCHANGEMENT
INTERCHANGER
INTERCHANGERS
INTERCHANGES
INTERCHANGING
INTERCHANNEL
INTERCHAPTER
INTERCHAPTERS
INTERCHURCH
INTERCIPIENT
INTERCIPIENTS
INTERCLASS
INTERCLAVICLE
INTERCLAVICLES
INTERCLAVICULAR
INTERCLUDE

INTERCLUDED
INTERCLUDES
INTERCLUDING
INTERCLUSION
INTERCLUSIONS
INTERCLUSTER
INTERCOASTAL
INTERCOLLEGIATE
INTERCOLLINE
INTERCOLONIAL
INTERCOLONIALLY
INTERCOLUMNAR
INTERCOMMUNAL
INTERCOMMUNE
INTERCOMMUNED
INTERCOMMUNES
INTERCOMMUNING
INTERCOMMUNION
INTERCOMMUNIONS
INTERCOMMUNITY
INTERCOMPANY
INTERCOMPARE
INTERCOMPARED
INTERCOMPARES
INTERCOMPARING
INTERCOMPARISON
INTERCONNECT
INTERCONNECTED
INTERCONNECTING
INTERCONNECTION
INTERCONNECTOR
INTERCONNECTORS
INTERCONNECTS
INTERCONNEXION
INTERCONNEXIONS
INTERCONVERSION
INTERCONVERT
INTERCONVERTED
INTERCONVERTING
INTERCONVERTS
INTERCOOLED
INTERCOOLER
INTERCOOLERS
INTERCORPORATE
INTERCORRELATE
INTERCORRELATED
INTERCORRELATES
INTERCORTICAL
INTERCOSTAL
INTERCOSTALS
INTERCOUNTRY
INTERCOUNTY
INTERCOUPLE
INTERCOURSE
INTERCOURSES
INTERCRATER
INTERCROPPED
INTERCROPPING
INTERCROPS

INTERCROSS	INTERELECTRODE	INTERFOLDED	INTERIORLY
INTERCROSSED	INTERELECTRON	INTERFOLDING	INTERISLAND
INTERCROSSES	INTERELECTRONIC	INTERFOLDS	INTERJACENCIES
INTERCROSSING	INTEREPIDEMIC	INTERFOLIATE	INTERJACENCY
INTERCRURAL	INTERESSED	INTERFOLIATED	INTERJACENT
INTERCULTURAL	INTERESSES	INTERFOLIATES	INTERJACULATE
INTERCULTURALLY	INTERESSING	INTERFOLIATING	INTERJACULATED
INTERCULTURE	INTERESTED	INTERFRATERNITY	INTERJACULATES
INTERCURRENCE	INTERESTEDLY	INTERFRETTED	INTERJACULATING
INTERCURRENCES	INTERESTEDNESS	INTERFRONTAL	INTERJACULATORY
INTERCURRENT	INTERESTING	INTERFUSED	INTERJECTED
INTERCURRENTLY	INTERESTINGLY	INTERFUSES	INTERJECTING
INTERCUTTING	INTERESTINGNESS	INTERFUSING	INTERJECTION
INTERDASHED	INTERETHNIC	INTERFUSION	INTERJECTIONAL
INTERDASHES	INTERFACED	INTERFUSIONS	INTERJECTIONARY
INTERDASHING	INTERFACES	INTERGALACTIC	INTERJECTIONS
INTERDEALER	INTERFACIAL	INTERGENERATION	INTERJECTOR
INTERDEALERS	INTERFACIALLY	INTERGENERIC	INTERJECTORS
INTERDEALING	INTERFACING	INTERGLACIAL	INTERJECTORY
INTERDEALS	INTERFACINGS	INTERGLACIALS	INTERJECTS
INTERDEALT	INTERFACULTY	INTERGRADATION	INTERJECTURAL
INTERDENTAL	INTERFAITH	INTERGRADATIONS	INTERJOINED
INTERDENTALLY	INTERFAMILIAL	INTERGRADE	INTERJOINING
INTERDEPEND	INTERFAMILY	INTERGRADED	INTERJOINS
INTERDEPENDED	INTERFASCICULAR	INTERGRADES	INTERKINESES
INTERDEPENDENCE	INTERFEMORAL	INTERGRADIENT	INTERKINESIS
INTERDEPENDENCY	INTERFERED	INTERGRADING	INTERKNITS
INTERDEPENDENT	INTERFERENCE	INTERGRAFT	INTERKNITTED
INTERDEPENDING	INTERFERENCES	INTERGRAFTED	INTERKNITTING
INTERDEPENDS	INTERFERENTIAL	INTERGRAFTING	INTERKNOTS
INTERDIALECTAL	INTERFERER	INTERGRAFTS	INTERKNOTTED
INTERDICTED	INTERFERERS	INTERGRANULAR	INTERKNOTTING
INTERDICTING	INTERFERES	INTERGROUP	INTERLACED
INTERDICTION	INTERFERING	INTERGROWING	INTERLACEDLY
INTERDICTIONS	INTERFERINGLY	INTERGROWN	INTERLACEMENT
INTERDICTIVE	INTERFEROGRAM	INTERGROWS	INTERLACEMENTS
INTERDICTIVELY	INTERFEROGRAMS	INTERGROWTH	INTERLACES
INTERDICTOR	INTERFEROMETER	INTERGROWTHS	INTERLACING
INTERDICTORS	INTERFEROMETERS	INTERINDIVIDUAL	INTERLACUSTRINE
INTERDICTORY	INTERFEROMETRIC	INTERINDUSTRY	INTERLAMINAR
INTERDICTS	INTERFEROMETRY	INTERINFLUENCE	INTERLAMINATE
INTERDIFFUSE	INTERFERON	INTERINFLUENCES	INTERLAMINATED
INTERDIFFUSED	INTERFERONS	INTERINVOLVE	INTERLAMINATES
INTERDIFFUSES	INTERFERTILE	INTERINVOLVED	INTERLAMINATING
INTERDIFFUSING	INTERFERTILITY	INTERINVOLVES	INTERLAMINATION
INTERDIFFUSION	INTERFIBER	INTERINVOLVING	INTERLAPPED
INTERDIFFUSIONS	INTERFILED	INTERIONIC	INTERLAPPING
INTERDIGITAL	INTERFILES	INTERIORISATION	INTERLARDED
INTERDIGITATE	INTERFILING	INTERIORISE	INTERLARDING
INTERDIGITATED	INTERFLOWED	INTERIORISED	INTERLARDS
INTERDIGITATES	INTERFLOWING	INTERIORISES	INTERLAYER
INTERDIGITATING	INTERFLOWS	INTERIORISING	INTERLAYERED
INTERDIGITATION	INTERFLUENCE	INTERIORITIES	INTERLAYERING
INTERDINED	INTERFLUENCES	INTERIORITY	INTERLAYERS
INTERDINES	INTERFLUENT	INTERIORIZATION	INTERLAYING
INTERDINING	INTERFLUOUS	INTERIORIZE	INTERLEAVE
INTERDISTRICT	INTERFLUVE	INTERIORIZED	INTERLEAVED
INTERDIVISIONAL	INTERFLUVES	INTERIORIZES	INTERLEAVES
INTERDOMINION	INTERFLUVIAL	INTERIORIZING	INTERLEAVING

INTERLENDING
INTERLENDS
INTERLEUKIN
INTERLEUKINS
INTERLIBRARY
INTERLINEAL
INTERLINEALLY
INTERLINEAR
INTERLINEARLY
INTERLINEARS
INTERLINEATE
INTERLINEATED
INTERLINEATES
INTERLINEATING
INTERLINEATION
INTERLINEATIONS
INTERLINED
INTERLINER
INTERLINERS
INTERLINES
INTERLINGUA
INTERLINGUAL
INTERLINGUALLY
INTERLINGUAS
INTERLINING
INTERLININGS
INTERLINKED
INTERLINKING
INTERLINKS
INTERLOANS
INTERLOBULAR
INTERLOCAL
INTERLOCATION
INTERLOCATIONS
INTERLOCKED
INTERLOCKER
INTERLOCKERS
INTERLOCKING
INTERLOCKS
INTERLOCUTION
INTERLOCUTIONS
INTERLOCUTOR
INTERLOCUTORILY
INTERLOCUTORS
INTERLOCUTORY
INTERLOCUTRESS
INTERLOCUTRICE
INTERLOCUTRICES
INTERLOCUTRIX
INTERLOCUTRIXES
INTERLOOPED
INTERLOOPING
INTERLOOPS
INTERLOPED
INTERLOPER
INTERLOPERS
INTERLOPES
INTERLOPING
INTERLUDED

INTERLUDES
INTERLUDIAL
INTERLUDING
INTERLUNAR
INTERLUNARY
INTERLUNATION
INTERLUNATIONS
INTERMARGINAL
INTERMARRIAGE
INTERMARRIAGES
INTERMARRIED
INTERMARRIES
INTERMARRY
INTERMARRYING
INTERMATTED
INTERMATTING
INTERMAXILLA
INTERMAXILLAE
INTERMAXILLARY
INTERMEDDLE
INTERMEDDLED
INTERMEDDLER
INTERMEDDLERS
INTERMEDDLES
INTERMEDDLING
INTERMEDIA
INTERMEDIACIES
INTERMEDIACY
INTERMEDIAL
INTERMEDIARIES
INTERMEDIARY
INTERMEDIATE
INTERMEDIATED
INTERMEDIATELY
INTERMEDIATES
INTERMEDIATING
INTERMEDIATION
INTERMEDIATIONS
INTERMEDIATOR
INTERMEDIATORS
INTERMEDIATORY
INTERMEDIN
INTERMEDINS
INTERMEDIUM
INTERMEDIUMS
INTERMEMBRANE
INTERMENSTRUAL
INTERMENTS
INTERMESHED
INTERMESHES
INTERMESHING
INTERMETALLIC
INTERMETALLICS
INTERMEZZI
INTERMEZZO
INTERMEZZOS
INTERMIGRATION
INTERMIGRATIONS
INTERMINABILITY

INTERMINABLE
INTERMINABLY
INTERMINGLE
INTERMINGLED
INTERMINGLES
INTERMINGLING
INTERMISSION
INTERMISSIONS
INTERMISSIVE
INTERMITOTIC
INTERMITTED
INTERMITTENCE
INTERMITTENCES
INTERMITTENCIES
INTERMITTENCY
INTERMITTENT
INTERMITTENTLY
INTERMITTER
INTERMITTERS
INTERMITTING
INTERMITTINGLY
INTERMITTOR
INTERMITTORS
INTERMIXED
INTERMIXES
INTERMIXING
INTERMIXTURE
INTERMIXTURES
INTERMODAL
INTERMODULATION
INTERMOLECULAR
INTERMONTANE
INTERMOUNTAIN
INTERMUNDANE
INTERMURED
INTERMURES
INTERMURING
INTERNALISATION
INTERNALISE
INTERNALISED
INTERNALISES
INTERNALISING
INTERNALITIES
INTERNALITY
INTERNALIZATION
INTERNALIZE
INTERNALIZED
INTERNALIZES
INTERNALIZING
INTERNALLY
INTERNALNESS
INTERNALNESSES
INTERNATIONAL
INTERNATIONALLY
INTERNATIONALS
INTERNECINE
INTERNECIVE
INTERNEURAL
INTERNEURON

INTERNEURONAL
INTERNEURONS
INTERNISTS
INTERNMENT
INTERNMENTS
INTERNODAL
INTERNODES
INTERNODIAL
INTERNSHIP
INTERNSHIPS
INTERNUCLEAR
INTERNUCLEON
INTERNUCLEONIC
INTERNUCLEOTIDE
INTERNUNCIAL
INTERNUNCIO
INTERNUNCIOS
INTEROBSERVER
INTEROCEAN
INTEROCEANIC
INTEROCEPTIVE
INTEROCEPTOR
INTEROCEPTORS
INTEROCULAR
INTEROFFICE
INTEROPERABLE
INTEROPERATIVE
INTERORBITAL
INTERORGAN
INTEROSCULANT
INTEROSCULATE
INTEROSCULATED
INTEROSCULATES
INTEROSCULATING
INTEROSCULATION
INTEROSSEAL
INTEROSSEOUS
INTERPAGED
INTERPAGES
INTERPAGING
INTERPANDEMIC
INTERPARIETAL
INTERPARISH
INTERPAROCHIAL
INTERPAROXYSMAL
INTERPARTICLE
INTERPARTY
INTERPELLANT
INTERPELLANTS
INTERPELLATE
INTERPELLATED
INTERPELLATES
INTERPELLATING
INTERPELLATION
INTERPELLATIONS
INTERPELLATOR
INTERPELLATORS
INTERPENETRABLE
INTERPENETRANT

INTERPENETRATE
INTERPENETRATED
INTERPENETRATES
INTERPERCEPTUAL
INTERPERMEATE
INTERPERMEATED
INTERPERMEATES
INTERPERMEATING
INTERPERSONAL
INTERPERSONALLY
INTERPETIOLAR
INTERPHALANGEAL
INTERPHASE
INTERPHASES
INTERPHONE
INTERPHONES
INTERPILASTER
INTERPILASTERS
INTERPLANETARY
INTERPLANT
INTERPLANTED
INTERPLANTING
INTERPLANTS
INTERPLAYED
INTERPLAYING
INTERPLAYS
INTERPLEAD
INTERPLEADED
INTERPLEADER
INTERPLEADERS
INTERPLEADING
INTERPLEADS
INTERPLEURAL
INTERPLUVIAL
INTERPOINT
INTERPOLABLE
INTERPOLAR
INTERPOLATE
INTERPOLATED
INTERPOLATER
INTERPOLATERS
INTERPOLATES
INTERPOLATING
INTERPOLATION
INTERPOLATIONS
INTERPOLATIVE
INTERPOLATOR
INTERPOLATORS
INTERPONED
INTERPONES
INTERPONING
INTERPOPULATION
INTERPOSABLE
INTERPOSAL
INTERPOSALS
INTERPOSED
INTERPOSER
INTERPOSERS
INTERPOSES

INTERPOSING
INTERPOSITION
INTERPOSITIONS
INTERPRETABLE
INTERPRETABLY
INTERPRETATE
INTERPRETATED
INTERPRETATES
INTERPRETATING
INTERPRETATION
INTERPRETATIONS
INTERPRETATIVE
INTERPRETED
INTERPRETER
INTERPRETERS
INTERPRETERSHIP
INTERPRETESS
INTERPRETESSES
INTERPRETING
INTERPRETIVE
INTERPRETIVELY
INTERPRETRESS
INTERPRETRESSES
INTERPRETS
INTERPROVINCIAL
INTERPROXIMAL
INTERPSYCHIC
INTERPUNCTION
INTERPUNCTIONS
INTERPUNCTUATE
INTERPUNCTUATED
INTERPUNCTUATES
INTERPUPILLARY
INTERQUARTILE
INTERRACIAL
INTERRACIALLY
INTERRADIAL
INTERRADIALLY
INTERRADII
INTERRADIUS
INTERRADIUSES
INTERRAILED
INTERRAILER
INTERRAILERS
INTERRAILING
INTERRAILS
INTERRAMAL
INTERREGAL
INTERREGES
INTERREGIONAL
INTERREGNA
INTERREGNAL
INTERREGNUM
INTERREGNUMS
INTERRELATE
INTERRELATED
INTERRELATEDLY
INTERRELATES
INTERRELATING

INTERRELATION
INTERRELATIONS
INTERRELIGIOUS
INTERRENAL
INTERROBANG
INTERROBANGS
INTERROGABLE
INTERROGANT
INTERROGANTS
INTERROGATE
INTERROGATED
INTERROGATEE
INTERROGATEES
INTERROGATES
INTERROGATING
INTERROGATINGLY
INTERROGATION
INTERROGATIONAL
INTERROGATIONS
INTERROGATIVE
INTERROGATIVELY
INTERROGATIVES
INTERROGATOR
INTERROGATORIES
INTERROGATORILY
INTERROGATORS
INTERROGATORY
INTERROGEE
INTERROGEES
INTERRUPTED
INTERRUPTEDLY
INTERRUPTER
INTERRUPTERS
INTERRUPTIBLE
INTERRUPTING
INTERRUPTION
INTERRUPTIONS
INTERRUPTIVE
INTERRUPTIVELY
INTERRUPTOR
INTERRUPTORS
INTERRUPTS
INTERSCAPULAR
INTERSCHOLASTIC
INTERSCHOOL
INTERSCRIBE
INTERSCRIBED
INTERSCRIBES
INTERSCRIBING
INTERSECTED
INTERSECTING
INTERSECTION
INTERSECTIONAL
INTERSECTIONS
INTERSECTS
INTERSEGMENT
INTERSEGMENTAL
INTERSENSORY
INTERSEPTAL

INTERSERTAL
INTERSERTED
INTERSERTING
INTERSERTS
INTERSERVICE
INTERSESSION
INTERSESSIONS
INTERSEXES
INTERSEXUAL
INTERSEXUALISM
INTERSEXUALISMS
INTERSEXUALITY
INTERSEXUALLY
INTERSIDEREAL
INTERSOCIETAL
INTERSOCIETY
INTERSPACE
INTERSPACED
INTERSPACES
INTERSPACING
INTERSPATIAL
INTERSPATIALLY
INTERSPECIES
INTERSPECIFIC
INTERSPERSAL
INTERSPERSALS
INTERSPERSE
INTERSPERSED
INTERSPERSEDLY
INTERSPERSES
INTERSPERSING
INTERSPERSION
INTERSPERSIONS
INTERSPINAL
INTERSPINOUS
INTERSTADIAL
INTERSTADIALS
INTERSTAGE
INTERSTATE
INTERSTATES
INTERSTATION
INTERSTELLAR
INTERSTELLARY
INTERSTERILE
INTERSTERILITY
INTERSTICE
INTERSTICES
INTERSTIMULUS
INTERSTITIAL
INTERSTITIALLY
INTERSTITIALS
INTERSTRAIN
INTERSTRAND
INTERSTRATIFIED
INTERSTRATIFIES
INTERSTRATIFY
INTERSUBJECTIVE
INTERSYSTEM
INTERTANGLE

INTERTANGLED
INTERTANGLEMENT
INTERTANGLES
INTERTANGLING
INTERTARSAL
INTERTENTACULAR
INTERTERMINAL
INTERTEXTS
INTERTEXTUAL
INTERTEXTUALITY
INTERTEXTUALLY
INTERTEXTURE
INTERTEXTURES
INTERTIDAL
INTERTIDALLY
INTERTILLAGE
INTERTILLAGES
INTERTILLED
INTERTILLING
INTERTILLS
INTERTISSUED
INTERTRAFFIC
INTERTRAFFICS
INTERTRIAL
INTERTRIBAL
INTERTRIGO
INTERTRIGOS
INTERTROOP
INTERTROPICAL
INTERTWINE
INTERTWINED
INTERTWINEMENT
INTERTWINEMENTS
INTERTWINES
INTERTWINING
INTERTWININGLY
INTERTWININGS
INTERTWIST
INTERTWISTED
INTERTWISTING
INTERTWISTINGLY
INTERTWISTS
INTERUNION
INTERUNIONS
INTERUNIVERSITY
INTERURBAN
INTERVALES
INTERVALLEY
INTERVALLIC
INTERVALLUM
INTERVALLUMS
INTERVALOMETER
INTERVALOMETERS
INTERVARSITY
INTERVEINED
INTERVEINING
INTERVEINS
INTERVENED
INTERVENER

INTERVENERS
INTERVENES
INTERVENIENT
INTERVENING
INTERVENOR
INTERVENORS
INTERVENTION
INTERVENTIONAL
INTERVENTIONISM
INTERVENTIONIST
INTERVENTIONS
INTERVENTOR
INTERVENTORS
INTERVERTEBRAL
INTERVIEWED
INTERVIEWEE
INTERVIEWEES
INTERVIEWER
INTERVIEWERS
INTERVIEWING
INTERVIEWS
INTERVILLAGE
INTERVISIBILITY
INTERVISIBLE
INTERVISITATION
INTERVITAL
INTERVOCALIC
INTERVOLVE
INTERVOLVED
INTERVOLVES
INTERVOLVING
INTERWEAVE
INTERWEAVED
INTERWEAVEMENT
INTERWEAVEMENTS
INTERWEAVER
INTERWEAVERS
INTERWEAVES
INTERWEAVING
INTERWINDING
INTERWINDS
INTERWORKED
INTERWORKING
INTERWORKINGS
INTERWORKS
INTERWOUND
INTERWOVEN
INTERWREATHE
INTERWREATHED
INTERWREATHES
INTERWREATHING
INTERWROUGHT
INTERZONAL
INTERZONES
INTESTACIES
INTESTATES
INTESTINAL
INTESTINALLY
INTESTINES

INTHRALLED
INTHRALLING
INTHRONING
INTIFADAHS
INTIFADEHS
INTIMACIES
INTIMATELY
INTIMATENESS
INTIMATENESSES
INTIMATERS
INTIMATING
INTIMATION
INTIMATIONS
INTIMIDATE
INTIMIDATED
INTIMIDATES
INTIMIDATING
INTIMIDATINGLY
INTIMIDATION
INTIMIDATIONS
INTIMIDATOR
INTIMIDATORS
INTIMIDATORY
INTIMISTES
INTIMITIES
INTINCTION
INTINCTIONS
INTITULING
INTOLERABILITY
INTOLERABLE
INTOLERABLENESS
INTOLERABLY
INTOLERANCE
INTOLERANCES
INTOLERANT
INTOLERANTLY
INTOLERANTNESS
INTOLERANTS
INTOLERATION
INTOLERATIONS
INTONATING
INTONATION
INTONATIONAL
INTONATIONS
INTONATORS
INTONINGLY
INTORSIONS
INTORTIONS
INTOXICABLE
INTOXICANT
INTOXICANTS
INTOXICATE
INTOXICATED
INTOXICATEDLY
INTOXICATES
INTOXICATING
INTOXICATINGLY
INTOXICATION
INTOXICATIONS

INTOXICATIVE
INTOXICATOR
INTOXICATORS
INTOXIMETER
INTOXIMETERS
INTRACAPSULAR
INTRACARDIAC
INTRACARDIAL
INTRACARDIALLY
INTRACAVITARY
INTRACELLULAR
INTRACELLULARLY
INTRACEREBRAL
INTRACEREBRALLY
INTRACOMPANY
INTRACRANIAL
INTRACRANIALLY
INTRACTABILITY
INTRACTABLE
INTRACTABLENESS
INTRACTABLY
INTRACUTANEOUS
INTRADERMAL
INTRADERMALLY
INTRADERMIC
INTRADERMICALLY
INTRADOSES
INTRAFALLOPIAN
INTRAFASCICULAR
INTRAGALACTIC
INTRAGENIC
INTRAMEDULLARY
INTRAMERCURIAL
INTRAMOLECULAR
INTRAMUNDANE
INTRAMURAL
INTRAMURALLY
INTRAMUSCULAR
INTRAMUSCULARLY
INTRANASAL
INTRANASALLY
INTRANATIONAL
INTRANSIGEANCE
INTRANSIGEANCES
INTRANSIGEANT
INTRANSIGEANTLY
INTRANSIGEANTS
INTRANSIGENCE
INTRANSIGENCES
INTRANSIGENCIES
INTRANSIGENCY
INTRANSIGENT
INTRANSIGENTISM
INTRANSIGENTIST
INTRANSIGENTLY
INTRANSIGENTS
INTRANSITIVE
INTRANSITIVELY
INTRANSITIVITY

INTRANSMISSIBLE	INTRIGANTS	INTROVERSIONS	INTWISTING
INTRANSMUTABLE	INTRIGUANT	INTROVERSIVE	INUMBRATED
INTRANUCLEAR	INTRIGUANTE	INTROVERSIVELY	INUMBRATES
INTRAOCULAR	INTRIGUANTES	INTROVERTED	INUMBRATING
INTRAOCULARLY	INTRIGUANTS	INTROVERTING	INUNCTIONS
INTRAPARIETAL	INTRIGUERS	INTROVERTIVE	INUNDATING
INTRAPARTUM	INTRIGUING	INTROVERTS	INUNDATION
INTRAPERITONEAL	INTRIGUINGLY	INTRUDINGLY	INUNDATIONS
INTRAPERSONAL	INTRINSICAL	INTRUSIONAL	INUNDATORS
INTRAPETIOLAR	INTRINSICALITY	INTRUSIONIST	INUNDATORY
INTRAPLATE	INTRINSICALLY	INTRUSIONISTS	INURBANELY
INTRAPOPULATION	INTRINSICALNESS	INTRUSIONS	INURBANITIES
INTRAPRENEUR	INTRINSICATE	INTRUSIVELY	INURBANITY
INTRAPRENEURIAL	INTRODUCED	INTRUSIVENESS	INUREDNESS
INTRAPRENEURS	INTRODUCER	INTRUSIVENESSES	INUREDNESSES
INTRAPSYCHIC	INTRODUCERS	INTRUSIVES	INUREMENTS
INTRASEXUAL	INTRODUCES	INTRUSTING	INURNMENTS
INTRASPECIES	INTRODUCIBLE	INTRUSTMENT	INUSITATION
INTRASPECIFIC	INTRODUCING	INTRUSTMENTS	INUSITATIONS
INTRASTATE	INTRODUCTION	INTUBATING	INUTILITIES
INTRATELLURIC	INTRODUCTIONS	INTUBATION	INUTTERABLE
INTRATHECAL	INTRODUCTIVE	INTUBATIONS	INVAGINABLE
INTRATHECALLY	INTRODUCTORILY	INTUITABLE	INVAGINATE
INTRATHORACIC	INTRODUCTORY	INTUITIONAL	INVAGINATED
INTRAUTERINE	INTROFYING	INTUITIONALISM	INVAGINATES
INTRAVASATION	INTROGRESSANT	INTUITIONALISMS	INVAGINATING
INTRAVASATIONS	INTROGRESSANTS	INTUITIONALIST	INVAGINATION
INTRAVASCULAR	INTROGRESSION	INTUITIONALISTS	INVAGINATIONS
INTRAVASCULARLY	INTROGRESSIONS	INTUITIONALLY	INVALIDATE
INTRAVENOUS	INTROGRESSIVE	INTUITIONISM	INVALIDATED
INTRAVENOUSLY	INTROITUSES	INTUITIONISMS	INVALIDATES
INTRAVITAL	INTROJECTED	INTUITIONIST	INVALIDATING
INTRAVITALLY	INTROJECTING	INTUITIONISTS	INVALIDATION
INTRAVITAM	INTROJECTION	INTUITIONS	INVALIDATIONS
INTRAZONAL	INTROJECTIONS	INTUITIVELY	INVALIDATOR
INTREATFULL	INTROJECTIVE	INTUITIVENESS	INVALIDATORS
INTREATING	INTROJECTS	INTUITIVENESSES	INVALIDHOOD
INTREATINGLY	INTROMISSIBLE	INTUITIVISM	INVALIDHOODS
INTREATMENT	INTROMISSION	INTUITIVISMS	INVALIDING
INTREATMENTS	INTROMISSIONS	INTUMESCED	INVALIDINGS
INTRENCHANT	INTROMISSIVE	INTUMESCENCE	INVALIDISM
INTRENCHED	INTROMITTED	INTUMESCENCES	INVALIDISMS
INTRENCHER	INTROMITTENT	INTUMESCENCIES	INVALIDITIES
INTRENCHERS	INTROMITTER	INTUMESCENCY	INVALIDITY
INTRENCHES	INTROMITTERS	INTUMESCENT	INVALIDNESS
INTRENCHING	INTROMITTING	INTUMESCES	INVALIDNESSES
INTRENCHMENT	INTRORSELY	INTUMESCING	INVALUABLE
INTRENCHMENTS	INTROSPECT	INTURBIDATE	INVALUABLENESS
INTREPIDITIES	INTROSPECTED	INTURBIDATED	INVALUABLY
INTREPIDITY	INTROSPECTING	INTURBIDATES	INVARIABILITIES
INTREPIDLY	INTROSPECTION	INTURBIDATING	INVARIABILITY
INTREPIDNESS	INTROSPECTIONAL	INTUSSUSCEPT	INVARIABLE
INTREPIDNESSES	INTROSPECTIONS	INTUSSUSCEPTED	INVARIABLENESS
INTRICACIES	INTROSPECTIVE	INTUSSUSCEPTING	INVARIABLES
INTRICATELY	INTROSPECTIVELY	INTUSSUSCEPTION	INVARIABLY
INTRICATENESS	INTROSPECTS	INTUSSUSCEPTIVE	INVARIANCE
INTRICATENESSES	INTROSUSCEPTION	INTUSSUSCEPTS	INVARIANCES
INTRIGANTE	INTROVERSIBLE	INTWINEMENT	INVARIANCIES
INTRIGANTES	INTROVERSION	INTWINEMENTS	INVARIANCY

INVARIANTS

INVARIANTS	INVESTIGATORY	INVITATION	IODOMETRICAL
INVASIVENESS	INVESTITIVE	INVITATIONAL	IODOMETRICALLY
INVASIVENESSES	INVESTITURE	INVITATIONALS	IODOMETRIES
INVEAGLING	INVESTITURES	INVITATIONS	IONICITIES
INVECTIVELY	INVESTMENT	INVITATORIES	IONISATION
INVECTIVENESS	INVESTMENTS	INVITATORY	IONISATIONS
INVECTIVENESSES	INVETERACIES	INVITEMENT	IONIZATION
INVECTIVES	INVETERACY	INVITEMENTS	IONIZATIONS
INVEIGHERS	INVETERATE	INVITINGLY	IONOPAUSES
INVEIGHING	INVETERATELY	INVITINGNESS	IONOPHORES
INVEIGLEMENT	INVETERATENESS	INVITINGNESSES	IONOPHORESES
INVEIGLEMENTS	INVIABILITIES	INVOCATING	IONOPHORESIS
INVEIGLERS	INVIABILITY	INVOCATION	IONOSONDES
INVEIGLING	INVIABLENESS	INVOCATIONAL	IONOSPHERE
INVENDIBILITIES	INVIABLENESSES	INVOCATIONS	IONOSPHERES
INVENDIBILITY	INVIDIOUSLY	INVOCATIVE	IONOSPHERIC
INVENDIBLE	INVIDIOUSNESS	INVOCATORS	IONOSPHERICALLY
INVENTABLE	INVIDIOUSNESSES	INVOCATORY	IONOTROPIC
INVENTIBLE	INVIGILATE	INVOLUCELLA	IONOTROPIES
INVENTIONAL	INVIGILATED	INVOLUCELLATE	IONTOPHORESES
INVENTIONLESS	INVIGILATES	INVOLUCELLATED	IONTOPHORESIS
INVENTIONS	INVIGILATING	INVOLUCELLUM	IONTOPHORETIC
INVENTIVELY	INVIGILATION	INVOLUCELS	IPECACUANHA
INVENTIVENESS	INVIGILATIONS	INVOLUCRAL	IPECACUANHAS
INVENTIVENESSES	INVIGILATOR	INVOLUCRATE	IPRATROPIUM
INVENTORIABLE	INVIGILATORS	INVOLUCRES	IPRATROPIUMS
INVENTORIAL	INVIGORANT	INVOLUCRUM	IPRINDOLES
INVENTORIALLY	INVIGORANTS	INVOLUNTARILY	IPRONIAZID
INVENTORIED	INVIGORATE	INVOLUNTARINESS	IPRONIAZIDS
INVENTORIES	INVIGORATED	INVOLUNTARY	IPSELATERAL
INVENTORYING	INVIGORATES	INVOLUTEDLY	IPSILATERAL
INVENTRESS	INVIGORATING	INVOLUTELY	IPSILATERALLY
INVENTRESSES	INVIGORATINGLY	INVOLUTING	IRACUNDITIES
INVERACITIES	INVIGORATION	INVOLUTION	IRACUNDITY
INVERACITY	INVIGORATIONS	INVOLUTIONAL	IRACUNDULOUS
INVERITIES	INVIGORATIVE	INVOLUTIONS	IRASCIBILITIES
INVERNESSES	INVIGORATIVELY	INVOLVEDLY	IRASCIBILITY
INVERSIONS	INVIGORATOR	INVOLVEMENT	IRASCIBLENESS
INVERTASES	INVIGORATORS	INVOLVEMENTS	IRASCIBLENESSES
INVERTEBRAL	INVINCIBILITIES	INVULNERABILITY	IRATENESSES
INVERTEBRATE	INVINCIBILITY	INVULNERABLE	IREFULNESS
INVERTEBRATES	INVINCIBLE	INVULNERABLY	IREFULNESSES
INVERTEDLY	INVINCIBLENESS	INVULTUATION	IRENICALLY
INVERTIBILITIES	INVINCIBLY	INVULTUATIONS	IRENICISMS
INVERTIBILITY	INVIOLABILITIES	INWARDNESS	IRENOLOGIES
INVERTIBLE	INVIOLABILITY	INWARDNESSES	IRIDACEOUS
INVESTABLE	INVIOLABLE	INWORKINGS	IRIDECTOMIES
INVESTIBLE	INVIOLABLENESS	INWRAPPING	IRIDECTOMY
INVESTIGABLE	INVIOLABLY	INWREATHED	IRIDESCENCE
INVESTIGATE	INVIOLACIES	INWREATHES	IRIDESCENCES
INVESTIGATED	INVIOLATED	INWREATHING	IRIDESCENT
INVESTIGATES	INVIOLATELY	IODINATING	IRIDESCENTLY
INVESTIGATING	INVIOLATENESS	IODINATION	IRIDISATION
INVESTIGATION	INVIOLATENESSES	IODINATIONS	IRIDISATIONS
INVESTIGATIONAL	INVISIBILITIES	IODISATION	IRIDIZATION
INVESTIGATIONS	INVISIBILITY	IODISATIONS	IRIDIZATIONS
INVESTIGATIVE	INVISIBLENESS	IODIZATION	IRIDOCYTES
INVESTIGATOR	INVISIBLENESSES	IODIZATIONS	IRIDOLOGIES
INVESTIGATORS	INVISIBLES	IODOMETRIC	IRIDOLOGIST

IRIDOLOGISTS
IRIDOSMINE
IRIDOSMINES
IRIDOSMIUM
IRIDOSMIUMS
IRIDOTOMIES
IRISATIONS
IRKSOMENESS
IRKSOMENESSES
IRONFISTED
IRONHANDED
IRONHEARTED
IRONICALLY
IRONICALNESS
IRONICALNESSES
IRONMASTER
IRONMASTERS
IRONMONGER
IRONMONGERIES
IRONMONGERS
IRONMONGERY
IRONNESSES
IRONSMITHS
IRONSTONES
IRONWORKER
IRONWORKERS
IRRADIANCE
IRRADIANCES
IRRADIANCIES
IRRADIANCY
IRRADIATED
IRRADIATES
IRRADIATING
IRRADIATION
IRRADIATIONS
IRRADIATIVE
IRRADIATOR
IRRADIATORS
IRRADICABLE
IRRADICABLY
IRRADICATE
IRRADICATED
IRRADICATES
IRRADICATING
IRRATIONAL
IRRATIONALISE
IRRATIONALISED
IRRATIONALISES
IRRATIONALISING
IRRATIONALISM
IRRATIONALISMS
IRRATIONALIST
IRRATIONALISTIC
IRRATIONALISTS
IRRATIONALITIES
IRRATIONALITY
IRRATIONALIZE
IRRATIONALIZED
IRRATIONALIZES

IRRATIONALIZING
IRRATIONALLY
IRRATIONALNESS
IRRATIONALS
IRREALISABLE
IRREALITIES
IRREALIZABLE
IRREBUTTABLE
IRRECEPTIVE
IRRECIPROCAL
IRRECIPROCITIES
IRRECIPROCITY
IRRECLAIMABLE
IRRECLAIMABLY
IRRECOGNISABLE
IRRECOGNITION
IRRECOGNITIONS
IRRECOGNIZABLE
IRRECONCILABLE
IRRECONCILABLES
IRRECONCILABLY
IRRECONCILED
IRRECONCILEMENT
IRRECOVERABLE
IRRECOVERABLY
IRRECUSABLE
IRRECUSABLY
IRREDEEMABILITY
IRREDEEMABLE
IRREDEEMABLES
IRREDEEMABLY
IRREDENTAS
IRREDENTISM
IRREDENTISMS
IRREDENTIST
IRREDENTISTS
IRREDUCIBILITY
IRREDUCIBLE
IRREDUCIBLENESS
IRREDUCIBLY
IRREDUCTIBILITY
IRREDUCTION
IRREDUCTIONS
IRREFLECTION
IRREFLECTIONS
IRREFLECTIVE
IRREFLEXION
IRREFLEXIONS
IRREFLEXIVE
IRREFORMABILITY
IRREFORMABLE
IRREFORMABLY
IRREFRAGABILITY
IRREFRAGABLE
IRREFRAGABLY
IRREFRANGIBLE
IRREFRANGIBLY
IRREFUTABILITY
IRREFUTABLE

IRREFUTABLENESS
IRREFUTABLY
IRREGARDLESS
IRREGULARITIES
IRREGULARITY
IRREGULARLY
IRREGULARS
IRRELATION
IRRELATIONS
IRRELATIVE
IRRELATIVELY
IRRELATIVENESS
IRRELEVANCE
IRRELEVANCES
IRRELEVANCIES
IRRELEVANCY
IRRELEVANT
IRRELEVANTLY
IRRELIEVABLE
IRRELIGION
IRRELIGIONIST
IRRELIGIONISTS
IRRELIGIONS
IRRELIGIOUS
IRRELIGIOUSLY
IRRELIGIOUSNESS
IRREMEABLE
IRREMEABLY
IRREMEDIABLE
IRREMEDIABLY
IRREMISSIBILITY
IRREMISSIBLE
IRREMISSIBLY
IRREMISSION
IRREMISSIONS
IRREMISSIVE
IRREMOVABILITY
IRREMOVABLE
IRREMOVABLENESS
IRREMOVABLY
IRRENOWNED
IRREPAIRABLE
IRREPARABILITY
IRREPARABLE
IRREPARABLENESS
IRREPARABLY
IRREPEALABILITY
IRREPEALABLE
IRREPEALABLY
IRREPLACEABLE
IRREPLACEABLY
IRREPLEVIABLE
IRREPLEVISABLE
IRREPREHENSIBLE
IRREPREHENSIBLY
IRREPRESSIBLE
IRREPRESSIBLY
IRREPROACHABLE
IRREPROACHABLY

IRREPRODUCIBLE
IRREPROVABLE
IRREPROVABLY
IRRESISTANCE
IRRESISTANCES
IRRESISTIBILITY
IRRESISTIBLE
IRRESISTIBLY
IRRESOLUBILITY
IRRESOLUBLE
IRRESOLUBLY
IRRESOLUTE
IRRESOLUTELY
IRRESOLUTENESS
IRRESOLUTION
IRRESOLUTIONS
IRRESOLVABILITY
IRRESOLVABLE
IRRESOLVABLY
IRRESPECTIVE
IRRESPECTIVELY
IRRESPIRABLE
IRRESPONSIBLE
IRRESPONSIBLES
IRRESPONSIBLY
IRRESPONSIVE
IRRESPONSIVELY
IRRESTRAINABLE
IRRESUSCITABLE
IRRESUSCITABLY
IRRETENTION
IRRETENTIONS
IRRETENTIVE
IRRETENTIVENESS
IRRETRIEVABLE
IRRETRIEVABLY
IRREVERENCE
IRREVERENCES
IRREVERENT
IRREVERENTIAL
IRREVERENTLY
IRREVERSIBILITY
IRREVERSIBLE
IRREVERSIBLY
IRREVOCABILITY
IRREVOCABLE
IRREVOCABLENESS
IRREVOCABLY
IRRIDENTAS
IRRIGATING
IRRIGATION
IRRIGATIONAL
IRRIGATIONS
IRRIGATIVE
IRRIGATORS
IRRITABILITIES
IRRITABILITY
IRRITABLENESS
IRRITABLENESSES

IRRITANCIES
IRRITATING
IRRITATINGLY
IRRITATION
IRRITATIONS
IRRITATIVE
IRRITATORS
IRROTATIONAL
IRRUPTIONS
IRRUPTIVELY
ISABELLINE
ISABELLINES
ISALLOBARIC
ISALLOBARS
ISAPOSTOLIC
ISCHAEMIAS
ISCHURETIC
ISCHURETICS
ISEIKONIAS
ISENTROPIC
ISENTROPICALLY
ISINGLASSES
ISLOMANIAS
ISMATICALNESS
ISMATICALNESSES
ISOAGGLUTININ
ISOAGGLUTININS
ISOALLOXAZINE
ISOALLOXAZINES
ISOAMINILE
ISOAMINILES
ISOANTIBODIES
ISOANTIBODY
ISOANTIGEN
ISOANTIGENIC
ISOANTIGENS
ISOBARISMS
ISOBAROMETRIC
ISOBILATERAL
ISOBUTANES
ISOBUTENES
ISOBUTYLENE
ISOBUTYLENES
ISOCALORIC
ISOCARBOXAZID
ISOCARBOXAZIDS
ISOCHASMIC
ISOCHEIMAL
ISOCHEIMALS
ISOCHEIMENAL
ISOCHEIMENALS
ISOCHEIMIC
ISOCHIMALS
ISOCHROMATIC
ISOCHROMOSOME
ISOCHROMOSOMES
ISOCHRONAL
ISOCHRONALLY
ISOCHRONES

ISOCHRONISE
ISOCHRONISED
ISOCHRONISES
ISOCHRONISING
ISOCHRONISM
ISOCHRONISMS
ISOCHRONIZE
ISOCHRONIZED
ISOCHRONIZES
ISOCHRONIZING
ISOCHRONOUS
ISOCHRONOUSLY
ISOCHROOUS
ISOCLINALS
ISOCLINICS
ISOCRACIES
ISOCRYMALS
ISOCYANATE
ISOCYANATES
ISOCYANIDE
ISOCYANIDES
ISODIAMETRIC
ISODIAMETRICAL
ISODIAPHERE
ISODIAPHERES
ISODIMORPHIC
ISODIMORPHISM
ISODIMORPHISMS
ISODIMORPHOUS
ISODONTALS
ISODYNAMIC
ISODYNAMICS
ISOELECTRIC
ISOELECTRONIC
ISOENZYMATIC
ISOENZYMES
ISOENZYMIC
ISOFLAVONE
ISOFLAVONES
ISOGAMETES
ISOGAMETIC
ISOGENETIC
ISOGEOTHERM
ISOGEOTHERMAL
ISOGEOTHERMALS
ISOGEOTHERMIC
ISOGEOTHERMICS
ISOGEOTHERMS
ISOGLOSSAL
ISOGLOSSES
ISOGLOSSIC
ISOGLOTTAL
ISOGLOTTIC
ISOGRAFTED
ISOGRAFTING
ISOHYETALS
ISOIMMUNISATION
ISOIMMUNIZATION
ISOKINETIC

ISOKONTANS
ISOLABILITIES
ISOLABILITY
ISOLATABLE
ISOLATIONISM
ISOLATIONISMS
ISOLATIONIST
ISOLATIONISTS
ISOLATIONS
ISOLECITHAL
ISOLEUCINE
ISOLEUCINES
ISOMAGNETIC
ISOMAGNETICS
ISOMERASES
ISOMERISATION
ISOMERISATIONS
ISOMERISED
ISOMERISES
ISOMERISING
ISOMERISMS
ISOMERIZATION
ISOMERIZATIONS
ISOMERIZED
ISOMERIZES
ISOMERIZING
ISOMETRICAL
ISOMETRICALLY
ISOMETRICS
ISOMETRIES
ISOMETROPIA
ISOMETROPIAS
ISOMORPHIC
ISOMORPHICALLY
ISOMORPHISM
ISOMORPHISMS
ISOMORPHOUS
ISONIAZIDE
ISONIAZIDES
ISONIAZIDS
ISONITRILE
ISONITRILES
ISOOCTANES
ISOPACHYTE
ISOPACHYTES
ISOPERIMETER
ISOPERIMETERS
ISOPERIMETRICAL
ISOPERIMETRIES
ISOPERIMETRY
ISOPIESTIC
ISOPIESTICALLY
ISOPLETHIC
ISOPOLITIES
ISOPRENALINE
ISOPRENALINES
ISOPRENOID
ISOPROPYLS
ISOPROTERENOL

ISOPROTERENOLS
ISOPTEROUS
ISOPYCNALS
ISOPYCNICS
ISORHYTHMIC
ISOSEISMAL
ISOSEISMALS
ISOSEISMIC
ISOSEISMICS
ISOSMOTICALLY
ISOSPONDYLOUS
ISOSPORIES
ISOSPOROUS
ISOSTACIES
ISOSTASIES
ISOSTATICALLY
ISOSTEMONOUS
ISOSTHENURIA
ISOSTHENURIAS
ISOTENISCOPE
ISOTENISCOPES
ISOTHERALS
ISOTHERMAL
ISOTHERMALLY
ISOTHERMALS
ISOTONICALLY
ISOTONICITIES
ISOTONICITY
ISOTOPICALLY
ISOTRETINOIN
ISOTRETINOINS
ISOTROPICALLY
ISOTROPIES
ISOTROPISM
ISOTROPISMS
ISOTROPOUS
ISOXSUPRINE
ISOXSUPRINES
ISPAGHULAS
ITACOLUMITE
ITACOLUMITES
ITALIANATE
ITALIANATED
ITALIANATES
ITALIANATING
ITALIANISE
ITALIANISED
ITALIANISES
ITALIANISING
ITALIANIZE
ITALIANIZED
ITALIANIZES
ITALIANIZING
ITALICISATION
ITALICISATIONS
ITALICISED
ITALICISES
ITALICISING
ITALICIZATION

ITALICIZATIONS
ITALICIZED
ITALICIZES
ITALICIZING
ITCHINESSES
ITEMISATION
ITEMISATIONS
ITEMIZATION
ITEMIZATIONS
ITERATIONS
ITERATIVELY
ITERATIVENESS
ITERATIVENESSES
ITEROPARITIES
ITEROPARITY
ITEROPAROUS
ITHYPHALLI
ITHYPHALLIC
ITHYPHALLICS
ITHYPHALLUS
ITHYPHALLUSES
ITINERACIES
ITINERANCIES
ITINERANCY
ITINERANTLY
ITINERANTS
ITINERARIES
ITINERATED
ITINERATES
ITINERATING
ITINERATION
ITINERATIONS
IVERMECTIN
IVERMECTINS
IVORYBILLS
IVORYWOODS
IZVESTIYAS

— J —

JABBERINGLY
JABBERINGS
JABBERWOCK
JABBERWOCKIES
JABBERWOCKS
JABBERWOCKY
JABORANDIS
JABOTICABA
JABOTICABAS
JACARANDAS
JACKALLING
JACKANAPES
JACKANAPESES
JACKAROOED
JACKAROOING
JACKASSERIES
JACKASSERY
JACKBOOTED
JACKBOOTING
JACKEROOED
JACKEROOING
JACKETLESS
JACKFISHES
JACKFRUITS
JACKHAMMER
JACKHAMMERED
JACKHAMMERING
JACKHAMMERS
JACKKNIFED
JACKKNIFES
JACKKNIFING
JACKKNIVES
JACKLIGHTED
JACKLIGHTING
JACKLIGHTS
JACKPLANES
JACKRABBIT
JACKRABBITS
JACKROLLED
JACKROLLING
JACKSCREWS
JACKSHAFTS
JACKSMELTS
JACKSMITHS
JACKSNIPES
JACKSTONES
JACKSTRAWS
JACQUERIES
JACTATIONS
JACTITATION
JACTITATIONS
JACULATING
JACULATION
JACULATIONS

JACULATORS
JACULATORY
JADEDNESSES
JAGGEDNESS
JAGGEDNESSES
JAGGHERIES
JAGHIRDARS
JAGUARONDI
JAGUARONDIS
JAGUARUNDI
JAGUARUNDIS
JAILBREAKS
JAILERESSES
JAILHOUSES
JAILORESSES
JAMAHIRIYA
JAMAHIRIYAS
JAMBALAYAS
JAMBOKKING
JAMBOLANAS
JANISARIES
JANISSARIES
JANITORIAL
JANITORSHIP
JANITORSHIPS
JANITRESSES
JANITRIXES
JANIZARIAN
JANIZARIES
JAPANISING
JAPANIZING
JAPONAISERIE
JAPONAISERIES
JARDINIERE
JARDINIERES
JARGONEERS
JARGONELLE
JARGONELLES
JARGONISATION
JARGONISATIONS
JARGONISED
JARGONISES
JARGONISING
JARGONISTIC
JARGONISTS
JARGONIZATION
JARGONIZATIONS
JARGONIZED
JARGONIZES
JARGONIZING
JARLSBERGS
JAROVISING
JAROVIZING
JASPERISED

JASPERISES
JASPERISING
JASPERIZED
JASPERIZES
JASPERIZING
JASPERWARE
JASPERWARES
JASPIDEOUS
JASPILITES
JAUNDICING
JAUNTINESS
JAUNTINESSES
JAUNTINGLY
JAVELINING
JAWBATIONS
JAWBONINGS
JAWBREAKER
JAWBREAKERS
JAWBREAKING
JAWBREAKINGLY
JAWBREAKINGS
JAWCRUSHER
JAWCRUSHERS
JAWDROPPINGLY
JAYHAWKERS
JAYWALKERS
JAYWALKING
JAYWALKINGS
JAZZINESSES
JEALOUSHOOD
JEALOUSHOODS
JEALOUSIES
JEALOUSING
JEALOUSNESS
JEALOUSNESSES
JEISTIECOR
JEISTIECORS
JEJUNENESS
JEJUNENESSES
JEJUNITIES
JEJUNOSTOMIES
JEJUNOSTOMY
JELLIFICATION
JELLIFICATIONS
JELLIFYING
JELLYBEANS
JELLYFISHES
JELLYGRAPH
JELLYGRAPHED
JELLYGRAPHING
JELLYGRAPHS
JELLYROLLS
JEMMINESSES
JENNETINGS

JEOPARDERS
JEOPARDIED
JEOPARDIES
JEOPARDING
JEOPARDISE
JEOPARDISED
JEOPARDISES
JEOPARDISING
JEOPARDIZE
JEOPARDIZED
JEOPARDIZES
JEOPARDIZING
JEOPARDOUS
JEOPARDOUSLY
JEOPARDYING
JEQUERITIES
JEQUIRITIES
JERFALCONS
JERKINESSES
JERKINHEAD
JERKINHEADS
JERKWATERS
JERRYMANDER
JERRYMANDERED
JERRYMANDERING
JERRYMANDERS
JESSAMINES
JESSERANTS
JESUITICAL
JESUITICALLY
JESUITISMS
JESUITRIES
JETSTREAMS
JETTATURAS
JETTINESSES
JETTISONABLE
JETTISONED
JETTISONING
JEWELFISHES
JEWELLERIES
JEWELWEEDS
JICKAJOGGED
JICKAJOGGING
JIGAJIGGED
JIGAJIGGING
JIGAJOGGED
JIGAJOGGING
JIGAMAREES
JIGGERMAST
JIGGERMASTS
JIGGUMBOBS
JIGJIGGING
JILLFLIRTS
JIMPNESSES

JIMSONWEED
JIMSONWEEDS
JINGOISTIC
JINGOISTICALLY
JINRICKSHA
JINRICKSHAS
JINRICKSHAW
JINRICKSHAWS
JINRIKISHA
JINRIKISHAS
JINRIKSHAS
JITTERBUGGED
JITTERBUGGING
JITTERBUGS
JITTERIEST
JITTERINESS
JITTERINESSES
JOBCENTRES
JOBERNOWLS
JOBHOLDERS
JOBLESSNESS
JOBLESSNESSES
JOBSEEKERS
JOBSWORTHS
JOCKEYISMS
JOCKEYSHIP
JOCKEYSHIPS
JOCKSTRAPS
JOCKTELEGS
JOCOSENESS
JOCOSENESSES
JOCOSERIOUS
JOCOSITIES
JOCULARITIES
JOCULARITY
JOCULATORS
JOCUNDITIES
JOCUNDNESS
JOCUNDNESSES
JOHANNESES
JOHNNYCAKE
JOHNNYCAKES
JOHNSONGRASS
JOHNSONGRASSES
JOINTEDNESS
JOINTEDNESSES
JOINTNESSES
JOINTRESSES
JOINTURESS
JOINTURESSES
JOINTURING
JOINTWEEDS
JOINTWORMS
JOKESMITHS
JOKINESSES
JOLLEYINGS
JOLLIFICATION
JOLLIFICATIONS
JOLLIFYING

JOLLIMENTS
JOLLINESSES
JOLLYBOATS
JOLLYHEADS
JOLTERHEAD
JOLTERHEADS
JONNYCAKES
JOSEPHINITE
JOSEPHINITES
JOSTLEMENT
JOSTLEMENTS
JOUISANCES
JOURNALESE
JOURNALESES
JOURNALING
JOURNALISATION
JOURNALISATIONS
JOURNALISE
JOURNALISED
JOURNALISER
JOURNALISERS
JOURNALISES
JOURNALISING
JOURNALISM
JOURNALISMS
JOURNALIST
JOURNALISTIC
JOURNALISTS
JOURNALIZATION
JOURNALIZATIONS
JOURNALIZE
JOURNALIZED
JOURNALIZER
JOURNALIZERS
JOURNALIZES
JOURNALIZING
JOURNALLED
JOURNALLING
JOURNEYERS
JOURNEYING
JOURNEYMAN
JOURNEYMEN
JOURNEYWORK
JOURNEYWORKS
JOUYSAUNCE
JOUYSAUNCES
JOVIALITIES
JOVIALNESS
JOVIALNESSES
JOVIALTIES
JOVYSAUNCE
JOVYSAUNCES
JOWLINESSES
JOYFULLEST
JOYFULNESS
JOYFULNESSES
JOYLESSNESS
JOYLESSNESSES
JOYOUSNESS

JOYOUSNESSES
JOYPOPPERS
JOYPOPPING
JOYRIDINGS
JUBILANCES
JUBILANCIES
JUBILANTLY
JUBILARIAN
JUBILARIANS
JUBILATING
JUBILATION
JUBILATIONS
JUDGEMENTAL
JUDGEMENTS
JUDGESHIPS
JUDGMATICAL
JUDGMATICALLY
JUDGMENTAL
JUDGMENTALLY
JUDICATION
JUDICATIONS
JUDICATIVE
JUDICATORIAL
JUDICATORIES
JUDICATORS
JUDICATORY
JUDICATURE
JUDICATURES
JUDICIALLY
JUDICIARIES
JUDICIOUSLY
JUDICIOUSNESS
JUDICIOUSNESSES
JUGGERNAUT
JUGGERNAUTS
JUGGLERIES
JUGGLINGLY
JUGLANDACEOUS
JUGULATING
JUGULATION
JUGULATIONS
JUICEHEADS
JUICINESSES
JULIENNING
JUMBLINGLY
JUMBOISING
JUMBOIZING
JUMHOURIYA
JUMHOURIYAS
JUMPINESSES
JUNCACEOUS
JUNCTIONAL
JUNEATINGS
JUNGLEGYMS
JUNGLELIKE
JUNIORATES
JUNIORITIES
JUNKETEERED
JUNKETEERING

JUNKETEERS
JUNKETINGS
JUNKETTERS
JUNKETTING
JUNKINESSES
JURIDICALLY
JURISCONSULT
JURISCONSULTS
JURISDICTION
JURISDICTIONAL
JURISDICTIONS
JURISDICTIVE
JURISPRUDENCE
JURISPRUDENCES
JURISPRUDENT
JURISPRUDENTIAL
JURISPRUDENTS
JURISTICAL
JURISTICALLY
JUSTICESHIP
JUSTICESHIPS
JUSTICIABILITY
JUSTICIABLE
JUSTICIALISM
JUSTICIALISMS
JUSTICIARIES
JUSTICIARS
JUSTICIARSHIP
JUSTICIARSHIPS
JUSTICIARY
JUSTIFIABILITY
JUSTIFIABLE
JUSTIFIABLENESS
JUSTIFIABLY
JUSTIFICATION
JUSTIFICATIONS
JUSTIFICATIVE
JUSTIFICATOR
JUSTIFICATORS
JUSTIFICATORY
JUSTIFIERS
JUSTIFYING
JUSTNESSES
JUVENESCENCE
JUVENESCENCES
JUVENESCENT
JUVENILELY
JUVENILENESS
JUVENILENESSES
JUVENILITIES
JUVENILITY
JUXTAPOSED
JUXTAPOSES
JUXTAPOSING
JUXTAPOSITION
JUXTAPOSITIONAL
JUXTAPOSITIONS

K

KABALISTIC
KABARAGOYA
KABARAGOYAS
KABBALISMS
KABBALISTIC
KABBALISTS
KABELJOUWS
KADAITCHAS
KAFFEEKLATSCH
KAFFEEKLATSCHES
KAFFIRBOOM
KAFFIRBOOMS
KAHIKATEAS
KAILYAIRDS
KAINOGENESES
KAINOGENESIS
KAINOGENETIC
KAIROMONES
KAISERDOMS
KAISERISMS
KAISERSHIP
KAISERSHIPS
KAKISTOCRACIES
KAKISTOCRACY
KALAMKARIS
KALANCHOES
KALASHNIKOV
KALASHNIKOVS
KALEIDOPHONE
KALEIDOPHONES
KALEIDOSCOPE
KALEIDOSCOPES
KALEIDOSCOPIC
KALENDARED
KALENDARING
KALIPHATES
KALLIKREIN
KALLIKREINS
KALLITYPES
KALSOMINED
KALSOMINES
KALSOMINING
KAMELAUKION
KAMELAUKIONS
KAMERADING
KANAMYCINS
KANGAROOED
KANGAROOING
KANTIKOYED
KANTIKOYING
KAOLINISED
KAOLINISES
KAOLINISING

KAOLINITES
KAOLINITIC
KAOLINIZED
KAOLINIZES
KAOLINIZING
KAOLINOSES
KAOLINOSIS
KAPELLMEISTER
KAPELLMEISTERS
KARABINERS
KARANGAING
KARATEISTS
KARSTIFICATION
KARSTIFICATIONS
KARSTIFIED
KARSTIFIES
KARSTIFYING
KARUHIRUHI
KARYOGAMIC
KARYOGAMIES
KARYOGRAMS
KARYOKINESES
KARYOKINESIS
KARYOKINETIC
KARYOLOGIC
KARYOLOGICAL
KARYOLOGIES
KARYOLOGIST
KARYOLOGISTS
KARYOLYMPH
KARYOLYMPHS
KARYOLYSES
KARYOLYSIS
KARYOLYTIC
KARYOPLASM
KARYOPLASMIC
KARYOPLASMS
KARYOSOMES
KARYOTYPED
KARYOTYPES
KARYOTYPIC
KARYOTYPICAL
KARYOTYPICALLY
KARYOTYPING
KATABOLICALLY
KATABOLISM
KATABOLISMS
KATABOTHRON
KATABOTHRONS
KATADROMOUS
KATATHERMOMETER
KATAVOTHRON
KATAVOTHRONS

KATHAKALIS
KATHAREVOUSA
KATHAREVOUSAS
KATHAROMETER
KATHAROMETERS
KATZENJAMMER
KATZENJAMMERS
KAWANATANGA
KAWANATANGAS
KAZATSKIES
KAZILLIONS
KEELHALING
KEELHAULED
KEELHAULING
KEELHAULINGS
KEELIVINES
KEELYVINES
KEENNESSES
KEEPERLESS
KEEPERSHIP
KEEPERSHIPS
KEESHONDEN
KEFUFFLING
KELYPHITIC
KENNELLING
KENNETTING
KENOGENESES
KENOGENESIS
KENOGENETIC
KENOGENETICALLY
KENOPHOBIA
KENOPHOBIAS
KENOTICIST
KENOTICISTS
KENSPECKLE
KENTLEDGES
KERATECTOMIES
KERATECTOMY
KERATINISATION
KERATINISATIONS
KERATINISE
KERATINISED
KERATINISES
KERATINISING
KERATINIZATION
KERATINIZATIONS
KERATINIZE
KERATINIZED
KERATINIZES
KERATINIZING
KERATINOPHILIC
KERATINOUS
KERATITIDES

KERATITISES
KERATOGENOUS
KERATOMATA
KERATOMETER
KERATOMETERS
KERATOPHYRE
KERATOPHYRES
KERATOPLASTIC
KERATOPLASTIES
KERATOPLASTY
KERATOTOMIES
KERATOTOMY
KERAUNOGRAPH
KERAUNOGRAPHS
KERBSTONES
KERCHIEFED
KERCHIEFING
KERCHIEVES
KERFUFFLED
KERFUFFLES
KERFUFFLING
KERMESITES
KERNELLING
KERNICTERUS
KERNICTERUSES
KERNMANTEL
KERPLUNKED
KERPLUNKING
KERSANTITE
KERSANTITES
KERSEYMERE
KERSEYMERES
KERYGMATIC
KETOGENESES
KETOGENESIS
KETONAEMIA
KETONAEMIAS
KETONEMIAS
KETONURIAS
KETOSTEROID
KETOSTEROIDS
KETTLEDRUM
KETTLEDRUMMER
KETTLEDRUMMERS
KETTLEDRUMS
KETTLEFULS
KETTLESTITCH
KETTLESTITCHES
KEYBOARDED
KEYBOARDER
KEYBOARDERS
KEYBOARDING
KEYBOARDINGS

KEYBOARDIST
KEYBOARDISTS
KEYBUTTONS
KEYLOGGERS
KEYPUNCHED
KEYPUNCHER
KEYPUNCHERS
KEYPUNCHES
KEYPUNCHING
KEYSTONING
KEYSTROKED
KEYSTROKES
KEYSTROKING
KEYSTROKINGS
KHALIFATES
KHANSAMAHS
KHEDIVATES
KHEDIVIATE
KHEDIVIATES
KHIDMUTGAR
KHIDMUTGARS
KHITMUTGAR
KHITMUTGARS
KHUSKHUSES
KIBBITZERS
KIBBITZING
KIBBUTZNIK
KIBBUTZNIKS
KICKABOUTS
KICKAROUND
KICKAROUNDS
KICKBOARDS
KICKBOXERS
KICKBOXING
KICKBOXINGS
KICKSHAWSES
KICKSORTER
KICKSORTERS
KICKSTANDS
KICKSTARTED
KICKSTARTING
KICKSTARTS
KIDDIEWINK
KIDDIEWINKIE
KIDDIEWINKIES
KIDDIEWINKS
KIDDISHNESS
KIDDISHNESSES
KIDDYWINKS
KIDNAPINGS
KIDNAPPEES
KIDNAPPERS
KIDNAPPING
KIDNAPPINGS
KIDNEYLIKE
KIDOLOGIES
KIDOLOGIST
KIDOLOGISTS
KIESELGUHR

KIESELGUHRS
KIESELGURS
KIESERITES
KILDERKINS
KILLIFISHES
KILLIKINICK
KILLIKINICKS
KILOCALORIE
KILOCALORIES
KILOCURIES
KILOCYCLES
KILOGAUSSES
KILOGRAMME
KILOGRAMMES
KILOHERTZES
KILOJOULES
KILOLITERS
KILOLITRES
KILOMETERS
KILOMETRES
KILOMETRIC
KILOMETRICAL
KILOPARSEC
KILOPARSECS
KILOPASCAL
KILOPASCALS
KIMBERLITE
KIMBERLITES
KINAESTHESES
KINAESTHESIA
KINAESTHESIAS
KINAESTHESIS
KINAESTHETIC
KINDERGARTEN
KINDERGARTENER
KINDERGARTENERS
KINDERGARTENS
KINDERGARTNER
KINDERGARTNERS
KINDERSPIEL
KINDERSPIELS
KINDHEARTED
KINDHEARTEDLY
KINDHEARTEDNESS
KINDLESSLY
KINDLINESS
KINDLINESSES
KINDNESSES
KINDREDNESS
KINDREDNESSES
KINDREDSHIP
KINDREDSHIPS
KINEMATICAL
KINEMATICALLY
KINEMATICS
KINEMATOGRAPH
KINEMATOGRAPHER
KINEMATOGRAPHIC
KINEMATOGRAPHS

KINEMATOGRAPHY
KINESCOPED
KINESCOPES
KINESCOPING
KINESIATRIC
KINESIATRICS
KINESIOLOGIES
KINESIOLOGIST
KINESIOLOGISTS
KINESIOLOGY
KINESIPATH
KINESIPATHIC
KINESIPATHIES
KINESIPATHIST
KINESIPATHISTS
KINESIPATHS
KINESIPATHY
KINESITHERAPIES
KINESITHERAPY
KINESTHESES
KINESTHESIA
KINESTHESIAS
KINESTHESIS
KINESTHETIC
KINESTHETICALLY
KINETHEODOLITE
KINETHEODOLITES
KINETICALLY
KINETICIST
KINETICISTS
KINETOCHORE
KINETOCHORES
KINETOGRAPH
KINETOGRAPHS
KINETONUCLEI
KINETONUCLEUS
KINETONUCLEUSES
KINETOPLAST
KINETOPLASTS
KINETOSCOPE
KINETOSCOPES
KINETOSOME
KINETOSOMES
KINGCRAFTS
KINGDOMLESS
KINGFISHER
KINGFISHERS
KINGFISHES
KINGLIHOOD
KINGLIHOODS
KINGLINESS
KINGLINESSES
KINGMAKERS
KINGSNAKES
KINKINESSES
KINNIKINIC
KINNIKINICK
KINNIKINICKS
KINNIKINICS

KINNIKINNICK
KINNIKINNICKS
KIRBIGRIPS
KIRKYAIRDS
KIRSCHWASSER
KIRSCHWASSERS
KISSAGRAMS
KISSOGRAMS
KITCHENALIA
KITCHENALIAS
KITCHENDOM
KITCHENDOMS
KITCHENERS
KITCHENETS
KITCHENETTE
KITCHENETTES
KITCHENING
KITCHENWARE
KITCHENWARES
KITESURFING
KITESURFINGS
KITSCHIEST
KITSCHIFIED
KITSCHIFIES
KITSCHIFYING
KITSCHNESS
KITSCHNESSES
KITTENISHLY
KITTENISHNESS
KITTENISHNESSES
KITTIWAKES
KIWIFRUITS
KIWISPORTS
KLANGFARBE
KLANGFARBES
KLEBSIELLA
KLEBSIELLAS
KLEINHUISIE
KLEINHUISIES
KLENDUSITIES
KLENDUSITY
KLEPHTISMS
KLEPTOCRACIES
KLEPTOCRACY
KLEPTOCRATIC
KLEPTOMANIA
KLEPTOMANIAC
KLEPTOMANIACS
KLEPTOMANIAS
KLETTERSCHUH
KLETTERSCHUHE
KLINOSTATS
KLIPSPRINGER
KLIPSPRINGERS
KLONDIKERS
KLONDIKING
KLONDYKERS
KLONDYKING
KLOOCHMANS

KLOOTCHMAN
KLOOTCHMANS
KLOOTCHMEN
KLUTZINESS
KLUTZINESSES
KNACKERIES
KNACKERING
KNACKINESS
KNACKINESSES
KNACKWURST
KNACKWURSTS
KNAGGINESS
KNAGGINESSES
KNAPSACKED
KNAVESHIPS
KNAVISHNESS
KNAVISHNESSES
KNEECAPPED
KNEECAPPING
KNEECAPPINGS
KNEEPIECES
KNEVELLING
KNICKERBOCKER
KNICKERBOCKERS
KNICKKNACK
KNICKKNACKS
KNICKPOINT
KNICKPOINTS
KNIFEPOINT
KNIFEPOINTS
KNIFERESTS
KNIGHTAGES
KNIGHTHEAD
KNIGHTHEADS
KNIGHTHOOD
KNIGHTHOODS
KNIGHTLESS
KNIGHTLIER
KNIGHTLIEST
KNIGHTLINESS
KNIGHTLINESSES
KNIPHOFIAS
KNOBBINESS
KNOBBINESSES
KNOBBLIEST
KNOBKERRIE
KNOBKERRIES
KNOBSTICKS
KNOCKABOUT
KNOCKABOUTS
KNOCKDOWNS
KNOCKWURST
KNOCKWURSTS
KNOTGRASSES
KNOTTINESS
KNOTTINESSES
KNOWABLENESS
KNOWABLENESSES
KNOWINGEST

KNOWINGNESS
KNOWINGNESSES
KNOWLEDGABILITY
KNOWLEDGABLE
KNOWLEDGABLY
KNOWLEDGEABLE
KNOWLEDGEABLY
KNOWLEDGED
KNOWLEDGES
KNOWLEDGING
KNUBBLIEST
KNUCKLEBALL
KNUCKLEBALLER
KNUCKLEBALLERS
KNUCKLEBALLS
KNUCKLEBONE
KNUCKLEBONES
KNUCKLEDUSTER
KNUCKLEDUSTERS
KNUCKLEHEAD
KNUCKLEHEADED
KNUCKLEHEADS
KNUCKLIEST
KOEKSISTER
KOEKSISTERS
KOHLRABIES
KOHUTUHUTU
KOLINSKIES
KOLKHOZNIK
KOLKHOZNIKI
KOLKHOZNIKS
KOMONDOROCK
KOMONDOROK
KONIMETERS
KONIOLOGIES
KONISCOPES
KOOKABURRA
KOOKABURRAS
KOOKINESSES
KOTAHITANGA
KOTAHITANGAS
KOTTABOSES
KOTUKUTUKU
KOULIBIACA
KOULIBIACAS
KOURBASHED
KOURBASHES
KOURBASHING
KOUSKOUSES
KOWHAIWHAI
KOWHAIWHAIS
KRAKOWIAKS
KREASOTING
KREMLINOLOGIES
KREMLINOLOGIST
KREMLINOLOGISTS
KREMLINOLOGY
KREOSOTING
KRIEGSPIEL

KRIEGSPIELS
KRIEGSSPIEL
KRIEGSSPIELS
KROMESKIES
KRUGERRAND
KRUGERRANDS
KRUMMHORNS
KRYOMETERS
KUMARAHOUS
KUMMERBUND
KUMMERBUNDS
KUNDALINIS
KURBASHING
KURCHATOVIUM
KURCHATOVIUMS
KURDAITCHA
KURDAITCHAS
KURFUFFLED
KURFUFFLES
KURFUFFLING
KURRAJONGS
KURTOSISES
KVETCHIEST
KVETCHINESS
KVETCHINESSES
KWASHIORKOR
KWASHIORKORS
KYANISATION
KYANISATIONS
KYANIZATION
KYANIZATIONS
KYMOGRAPHIC
KYMOGRAPHIES
KYMOGRAPHS
KYMOGRAPHY

L

LABANOTATION
LABANOTATIONS
LABDACISMS
LABEFACTATION
LABEFACTATIONS
LABEFACTION
LABEFACTIONS
LABELLISTS
LABIALISATION
LABIALISATIONS
LABIALISED
LABIALISES
LABIALISING
LABIALISMS
LABIALITIES
LABIALIZATION
LABIALIZATIONS
LABIALIZED
LABIALIZES
LABIALIZING
LABILITIES
LABIODENTAL
LABIODENTALS
LABIONASAL
LABIONASALS
LABIOVELAR
LABIOVELARS
LABORATORIES
LABORATORY
LABOREDNESS
LABOREDNESSES
LABORINGLY
LABORIOUSLY
LABORIOUSNESS
LABORIOUSNESSES
LABORSAVING
LABOUREDLY
LABOUREDNESS
LABOUREDNESSES
LABOURINGLY
LABOURISMS
LABOURISTS
LABOURSOME
LABRADOODLE
LABRADOODLES
LABRADORESCENT
LABRADORITE
LABRADORITES
LABYRINTHAL
LABYRINTHIAN
LABYRINTHIC
LABYRINTHICAL
LABYRINTHICALLY
LABYRINTHINE

LABYRINTHITIS
LABYRINTHITISES
LABYRINTHODONT
LABYRINTHODONTS
LABYRINTHS
LACCOLITES
LACCOLITHIC
LACCOLITHS
LACCOLITIC
LACERABILITIES
LACERABILITY
LACERATING
LACERATION
LACERATIONS
LACERATIVE
LACERTIANS
LACERTILIAN
LACERTILIANS
LACHRYMALS
LACHRYMARIES
LACHRYMARY
LACHRYMATION
LACHRYMATIONS
LACHRYMATOR
LACHRYMATORIES
LACHRYMATORS
LACHRYMATORY
LACHRYMOSE
LACHRYMOSELY
LACHRYMOSITIES
LACHRYMOSITY
LACINESSES
LACINIATED
LACINIATION
LACINIATIONS
LACKADAISICAL
LACKADAISICALLY
LACKADAISY
LACKLUSTER
LACKLUSTERS
LACKLUSTRE
LACKLUSTRES
LACONICALLY
LACONICISM
LACONICISMS
LACQUERERS
LACQUERING
LACQUERINGS
LACQUERWARE
LACQUERWARES
LACQUERWORK
LACQUERWORKS
LACQUEYING
LACRIMATION

LACRIMATIONS
LACRIMATOR
LACRIMATORS
LACRIMATORY
LACRYMATOR
LACRYMATORS
LACRYMATORY
LACTALBUMIN
LACTALBUMINS
LACTARIANS
LACTATIONAL
LACTATIONALLY
LACTATIONS
LACTESCENCE
LACTESCENCES
LACTESCENT
LACTIFEROUS
LACTIFEROUSNESS
LACTIFLUOUS
LACTOBACILLI
LACTOBACILLUS
LACTOFLAVIN
LACTOFLAVINS
LACTOGENIC
LACTOGLOBULIN
LACTOGLOBULINS
LACTOMETER
LACTOMETERS
LACTOPROTEIN
LACTOPROTEINS
LACTOSCOPE
LACTOSCOPES
LACTOSURIA
LACTOSURIAS
LACTOVEGETARIAN
LACUNOSITIES
LACUNOSITY
LACUSTRINE
LADDERLIKE
LADDISHNESS
LADDISHNESSES
LADIESWEAR
LADIESWEARS
LADYFINGER
LADYFINGERS
LADYFISHES
LADYLIKENESS
LADYLIKENESSES
LAEOTROPIC
LAEVIGATED
LAEVIGATES
LAEVIGATING
LAEVOGYRATE
LAEVOROTARY

LAEVOROTATION
LAEVOROTATIONS
LAEVOROTATORY
LAEVULOSES
LAGENIFORM
LAGERPHONE
LAGERPHONES
LAGGARDNESS
LAGGARDNESSES
LAGNIAPPES
LAGOMORPHIC
LAGOMORPHOUS
LAGOMORPHS
LAICISATION
LAICISATIONS
LAICIZATION
LAICIZATIONS
LAIRDSHIPS
LAKEFRONTS
LAKESHORES
LALAPALOOZA
LALAPALOOZAS
LALLAPALOOZA
LALLAPALOOZAS
LALLATIONS
LALLYGAGGED
LALLYGAGGING
LAMASERAIS
LAMASERIES
LAMBASTING
LAMBDACISM
LAMBDACISMS
LAMBDOIDAL
LAMBENCIES
LAMBITIVES
LAMBREQUIN
LAMBREQUINS
LAMBRUSCOS
LAMEBRAINED
LAMEBRAINS
LAMELLARLY
LAMELLATED
LAMELLATELY
LAMELLATION
LAMELLATIONS
LAMELLIBRANCH
LAMELLIBRANCHS
LAMELLICORN
LAMELLICORNS
LAMELLIFORM
LAMELLIROSTRAL
LAMELLIROSTRATE
LAMELLOSITIES
LAMELLOSITY

LAMENESSES
LAMENTABLE
LAMENTABLENESS
LAMENTABLY
LAMENTATION
LAMENTATIONS
LAMENTEDLY
LAMENTINGLY
LAMENTINGS
LAMINARIAN
LAMINARIANS
LAMINARIAS
LAMINARINS
LAMINARISE
LAMINARISED
LAMINARISES
LAMINARISING
LAMINARIZE
LAMINARIZED
LAMINARIZES
LAMINARIZING
LAMINATING
LAMINATION
LAMINATIONS
LAMINATORS
LAMINECTOMIES
LAMINECTOMY
LAMINGTONS
LAMINITISES
LAMMERGEIER
LAMMERGEIERS
LAMMERGEYER
LAMMERGEYERS
LAMPADARIES
LAMPADEDROMIES
LAMPADEDROMY
LAMPADEPHORIA
LAMPADEPHORIAS
LAMPADISTS
LAMPADOMANCIES
LAMPADOMANCY
LAMPBLACKS
LAMPHOLDER
LAMPHOLDERS
LAMPLIGHTER
LAMPLIGHTERS
LAMPLIGHTS
LAMPOONERIES
LAMPOONERS
LAMPOONERY
LAMPOONING
LAMPOONIST
LAMPOONISTS
LAMPROPHYRE
LAMPROPHYRES
LAMPROPHYRIC
LAMPSHADES
LAMPSHELLS
LANCEJACKS

LANCEOLATE
LANCEOLATED
LANCEOLATELY
LANCEWOODS
LANCINATED
LANCINATES
LANCINATING
LANCINATION
LANCINATIONS
LANDAMMANN
LANDAMMANNS
LANDAMMANS
LANDAULETS
LANDAULETTE
LANDAULETTES
LANDBOARDING
LANDBOARDINGS
LANDBOARDS
LANDDAMNED
LANDDAMNES
LANDDAMNING
LANDDROSES
LANDDROSTS
LANDFILLED
LANDFILLING
LANDFILLINGS
LANDFORCES
LANDGRAVATE
LANDGRAVATES
LANDGRAVES
LANDGRAVIATE
LANDGRAVIATES
LANDGRAVINE
LANDGRAVINES
LANDHOLDER
LANDHOLDERS
LANDHOLDING
LANDHOLDINGS
LANDLADIES
LANDLESSNESS
LANDLESSNESSES
LANDLOCKED
LANDLOPERS
LANDLORDISM
LANDLORDISMS
LANDLUBBER
LANDLUBBERLY
LANDLUBBERS
LANDLUBBING
LANDMARKED
LANDMARKING
LANDMASSES
LANDOWNERS
LANDOWNERSHIP
LANDOWNERSHIPS
LANDOWNING
LANDOWNINGS
LANDSCAPED
LANDSCAPER

LANDSCAPERS
LANDSCAPES
LANDSCAPING
LANDSCAPIST
LANDSCAPISTS
LANDSHARKS
LANDSKIPPED
LANDSKIPPING
LANDSKNECHT
LANDSKNECHTS
LANDSLIDDEN
LANDSLIDES
LANDSLIDING
LANDWAITER
LANDWAITERS
LANGBEINITE
LANGBEINITES
LANGLAUFER
LANGLAUFERS
LANGOSTINO
LANGOSTINOS
LANGOUSTES
LANGOUSTINE
LANGOUSTINES
LANGRIDGES
LANGSPIELS
LANGUAGELESS
LANGUAGING
LANGUESCENT
LANGUETTES
LANGUIDNESS
LANGUIDNESSES
LANGUISHED
LANGUISHER
LANGUISHERS
LANGUISHES
LANGUISHING
LANGUISHINGLY
LANGUISHINGS
LANGUISHMENT
LANGUISHMENTS
LANGUOROUS
LANGUOROUSLY
LANGUOROUSNESS
LANIFEROUS
LANIGEROUS
LANKINESSES
LANKNESSES
LANOSITIES
LANSQUENET
LANSQUENETS
LANTERLOOS
LANTERNING
LANTERNIST
LANTERNISTS
LANTHANIDE
LANTHANIDES
LANTHANONS
LANTHANUMS

LANUGINOSE
LANUGINOUS
LANUGINOUSNESS
LANZKNECHT
LANZKNECHTS
LAODICEANS
LAPAROSCOPE
LAPAROSCOPES
LAPAROSCOPIC
LAPAROSCOPIES
LAPAROSCOPIST
LAPAROSCOPISTS
LAPAROSCOPY
LAPAROTOMIES
LAPAROTOMY
LAPIDARIAN
LAPIDARIES
LAPIDARIST
LAPIDARISTS
LAPIDATING
LAPIDATION
LAPIDATIONS
LAPIDESCENCE
LAPIDESCENCES
LAPIDESCENT
LAPIDICOLOUS
LAPIDIFICATION
LAPIDIFICATIONS
LAPIDIFIED
LAPIDIFIES
LAPIDIFYING
LAPILLIFORM
LAPSTRAKES
LAPSTREAKS
LARCENISTS
LARCENOUSLY
LARDACEOUS
LARDALITES
LARGEHEARTED
LARGEMOUTH
LARGEMOUTHS
LARGENESSES
LARGHETTOS
LARGITIONS
LARKINESSES
LARKISHNESS
LARKISHNESSES
LARRIKINISM
LARRIKINISMS
LARVICIDAL
LARVICIDES
LARVIKITES
LARVIPAROUS
LARYNGEALLY
LARYNGEALS
LARYNGECTOMEE
LARYNGECTOMEES
LARYNGECTOMIES
LARYNGECTOMISED

LARYNGECTOMIZED
LARYNGECTOMY
LARYNGISMUS
LARYNGISMUSES
LARYNGITIC
LARYNGITIS
LARYNGITISES
LARYNGOLOGIC
LARYNGOLOGICAL
LARYNGOLOGIES
LARYNGOLOGIST
LARYNGOLOGISTS
LARYNGOLOGY
LARYNGOPHONIES
LARYNGOPHONY
LARYNGOSCOPE
LARYNGOSCOPES
LARYNGOSCOPIC
LARYNGOSCOPIES
LARYNGOSCOPIST
LARYNGOSCOPISTS
LARYNGOSCOPY
LARYNGOSPASM
LARYNGOSPASMS
LARYNGOTOMIES
LARYNGOTOMY
LASCIVIOUS
LASCIVIOUSLY
LASCIVIOUSNESS
LASERDISCS
LASERDISKS
LASERWORTS
LASSITUDES
LASTINGNESS
LASTINGNESSES
LATCHSTRING
LATCHSTRINGS
LATECOMERS
LATEENRIGGED
LATENESSES
LATENSIFICATION
LATERALING
LATERALISATION
LATERALISATIONS
LATERALISE
LATERALISED
LATERALISES
LATERALISING
LATERALITIES
LATERALITY
LATERALIZATION
LATERALIZATIONS
LATERALIZE
LATERALIZED
LATERALIZES
LATERALIZING
LATERALLED
LATERALLING
LATERBORNS

LATERIGRADE
LATERISATION
LATERISATIONS
LATERISING
LATERITIOUS
LATERIZATION
LATERIZATIONS
LATERIZING
LATEROVERSION
LATEROVERSIONS
LATESCENCE
LATESCENCES
LATHERIEST
LATHYRISMS
LATHYRITIC
LATHYRUSES
LATICIFEROUS
LATICIFERS
LATICLAVES
LATIFUNDIA
LATIFUNDIO
LATIFUNDIOS
LATIFUNDIUM
LATIMERIAS
LATINISATION
LATINISATIONS
LATINISING
LATINITIES
LATINIZATION
LATINIZATIONS
LATINIZING
LATIROSTRAL
LATIROSTRATE
LATISEPTATE
LATITANCIES
LATITATION
LATITATIONS
LATITUDINAL
LATITUDINALLY
LATITUDINARIAN
LATITUDINARIANS
LATITUDINOUS
LATRATIONS
LATROCINIA
LATROCINIES
LATROCINIUM
LATTERMATH
LATTERMATHS
LATTERMOST
LATTICEWORK
LATTICEWORKS
LATTICINGS
LATTICINIO
LAUDABILITIES
LAUDABILITY
LAUDABLENESS
LAUDABLENESSES
LAUDATIONS
LAUDATIVES

LAUDATORIES
LAUGHABLENESS
LAUGHABLENESSES
LAUGHINGLY
LAUGHINGSTOCK
LAUGHINGSTOCKS
LAUGHLINES
LAUGHWORTHY
LAUNCEGAYE
LAUNCEGAYES
LAUNCHPADS
LAUNDERERS
LAUNDERETTE
LAUNDERETTES
LAUNDERING
LAUNDRESSES
LAUNDRETTE
LAUNDRETTES
LAUNDRYMAN
LAUNDRYMEN
LAUNDRYWOMAN
LAUNDRYWOMEN
LAURACEOUS
LAURDALITE
LAURDALITES
LAUREATESHIP
LAUREATESHIPS
LAUREATING
LAUREATION
LAUREATIONS
LAURELLING
LAURUSTINE
LAURUSTINES
LAURUSTINUS
LAURUSTINUSES
LAURVIKITE
LAURVIKITES
LAVALIERES
LAVALLIERE
LAVALLIERES
LAVATIONAL
LAVATORIAL
LAVATORIES
LAVENDERED
LAVENDERING
LAVERBREAD
LAVERBREADS
LAVEROCKED
LAVEROCKING
LAVISHMENT
LAVISHMENTS
LAVISHNESS
LAVISHNESSES
LAVOLTAING
LAWBREAKER
LAWBREAKERS
LAWBREAKING
LAWBREAKINGS
LAWFULNESS

LAWFULNESSES
LAWGIVINGS
LAWLESSNESS
LAWLESSNESSES
LAWMAKINGS
LAWMONGERS
LAWNMOWERS
LAWRENCIUM
LAWRENCIUMS
LAWYERINGS
LAWYERLIKE
LAXATIVENESS
LAXATIVENESSES
LAYBACKING
LAYPERSONS
LAZARETTES
LAZARETTOS
LAZINESSES
LEACHABILITIES
LEACHABILITY
LEADENNESS
LEADENNESSES
LEADERBOARD
LEADERBOARDS
LEADERENES
LEADERETTE
LEADERETTES
LEADERLESS
LEADERSHIP
LEADERSHIPS
LEADPLANTS
LEADSCREWS
LEAFCUTTER
LEAFHOPPER
LEAFHOPPERS
LEAFINESSES
LEAFLESSNESS
LEAFLESSNESSES
LEAFLETEER
LEAFLETEERS
LEAFLETERS
LEAFLETING
LEAFLETTED
LEAFLETTING
LEAFSTALKS
LEAGUERING
LEAKINESSES
LEANNESSES
LEAPFROGGED
LEAPFROGGING
LEARINESSES
LEARNABILITIES
LEARNABILITY
LEARNEDNESS
LEARNEDNESSES
LEASEBACKS
LEASEHOLDER
LEASEHOLDERS
LEASEHOLDS

LEASTAWAYS
LEATHERBACK
LEATHERBACKS
LEATHERETTE
LEATHERETTES
LEATHERGOODS
LEATHERHEAD
LEATHERHEADS
LEATHERIER
LEATHERIEST
LEATHERINESS
LEATHERINESSES
LEATHERING
LEATHERINGS
LEATHERJACKET
LEATHERJACKETS
LEATHERLEAF
LEATHERLEAVES
LEATHERLIKE
LEATHERNECK
LEATHERNECKS
LEATHERWOOD
LEATHERWOODS
LEAVENINGS
LEBENSRAUM
LEBENSRAUMS
LECHEROUSLY
LECHEROUSNESS
LECHEROUSNESSES
LECITHINASE
LECITHINASES
LECTIONARIES
LECTIONARY
LECTISTERNIA
LECTISTERNIUM
LECTORATES
LECTORSHIP
LECTORSHIPS
LECTOTYPES
LECTRESSES
LECTURESHIP
LECTURESHIPS
LECYTHIDACEOUS
LEDERHOSEN
LEECHCRAFT
LEECHCRAFTS
LEERINESSES
LEFTWARDLY
LEGALISATION
LEGALISATIONS
LEGALISERS
LEGALISING
LEGALISTIC
LEGALISTICALLY
LEGALITIES
LEGALIZATION
LEGALIZATIONS
LEGALIZERS
LEGALIZING

LEGATARIES
LEGATESHIP
LEGATESHIPS
LEGATIONARY
LEGATISSIMO
LEGATORIAL
LEGENDARIES
LEGENDARILY
LEGENDISED
LEGENDISES
LEGENDISING
LEGENDISTS
LEGENDIZED
LEGENDIZES
LEGENDIZING
LEGENDRIES
LEGERDEMAIN
LEGERDEMAINIST
LEGERDEMAINISTS
LEGERDEMAINS
LEGERITIES
LEGGINESSES
LEGIBILITIES
LEGIBILITY
LEGIBLENESS
LEGIBLENESSES
LEGIONARIES
LEGIONELLA
LEGIONELLAE
LEGIONNAIRE
LEGIONNAIRES
LEGISLATED
LEGISLATES
LEGISLATING
LEGISLATION
LEGISLATIONS
LEGISLATIVE
LEGISLATIVELY
LEGISLATIVES
LEGISLATOR
LEGISLATORIAL
LEGISLATORS
LEGISLATORSHIP
LEGISLATORSHIPS
LEGISLATRESS
LEGISLATRESSES
LEGISLATURE
LEGISLATURES
LEGITIMACIES
LEGITIMACY
LEGITIMATE
LEGITIMATED
LEGITIMATELY
LEGITIMATENESS
LEGITIMATES
LEGITIMATING
LEGITIMATION
LEGITIMATIONS
LEGITIMATISE

LEGITIMATISED
LEGITIMATISES
LEGITIMATISING
LEGITIMATIZE
LEGITIMATIZED
LEGITIMATIZES
LEGITIMATIZING
LEGITIMATOR
LEGITIMATORS
LEGITIMISATION
LEGITIMISATIONS
LEGITIMISE
LEGITIMISED
LEGITIMISER
LEGITIMISERS
LEGITIMISES
LEGITIMISING
LEGITIMISM
LEGITIMISMS
LEGITIMIST
LEGITIMISTIC
LEGITIMISTS
LEGITIMIZATION
LEGITIMIZATIONS
LEGITIMIZE
LEGITIMIZED
LEGITIMIZER
LEGITIMIZERS
LEGITIMIZES
LEGITIMIZING
LEGLESSNESS
LEGLESSNESSES
LEGUMINOUS
LEGWARMERS
LEIOMYOMAS
LEIOMYOMATA
LEIOTRICHIES
LEIOTRICHOUS
LEIOTRICHY
LEISHMANIA
LEISHMANIAE
LEISHMANIAL
LEISHMANIAS
LEISHMANIASES
LEISHMANIASIS
LEISHMANIOSES
LEISHMANIOSIS
LEISTERING
LEISURABLE
LEISURABLY
LEISURELINESS
LEISURELINESSES
LEITMOTIFS
LEITMOTIVS
LEMMATISATION
LEMMATISATIONS
LEMMATISED
LEMMATISES
LEMMATISING

LEMMATIZATION
LEMMATIZATIONS
LEMMATIZED
LEMMATIZES
LEMMATIZING
LEMMINGLIKE
LEMNISCATE
LEMNISCATES
LEMONFISHES
LEMONGRASS
LEMONGRASSES
LEMONWOODS
LENGTHENED
LENGTHENER
LENGTHENERS
LENGTHENING
LENGTHIEST
LENGTHINESS
LENGTHINESSES
LENGTHSMAN
LENGTHSMEN
LENGTHWAYS
LENGTHWISE
LENIENCIES
LENITIVELY
LENOCINIUM
LENOCINIUMS
LENTAMENTE
LENTICELLATE
LENTICULAR
LENTICULARLY
LENTICULES
LENTIGINES
LENTIGINOSE
LENTIGINOUS
LENTISSIMO
LENTIVIRUS
LENTIVIRUSES
LEONTIASES
LEONTIASIS
LEONTOPODIUM
LEONTOPODIUMS
LEOPARDESS
LEOPARDESSES
LEPIDODENDROID
LEPIDODENDROIDS
LEPIDOLITE
LEPIDOLITES
LEPIDOMELANE
LEPIDOMELANES
LEPIDOPTERA
LEPIDOPTERAN
LEPIDOPTERANS
LEPIDOPTERIST
LEPIDOPTERISTS
LEPIDOPTEROLOGY
LEPIDOPTERON
LEPIDOPTERONS

LEPIDOPTEROUS
LEPIDOSIREN
LEPIDOSIRENS
LEPRECHAUN
LEPRECHAUNISH
LEPRECHAUNS
LEPRECHAWN
LEPRECHAWNS
LEPROMATOUS
LEPROSARIA
LEPROSARIUM
LEPROSARIUMS
LEPROSERIE
LEPROSERIES
LEPROSITIES
LEPROUSNESS
LEPROUSNESSES
LEPTOCEPHALI
LEPTOCEPHALIC
LEPTOCEPHALOUS
LEPTOCEPHALUS
LEPTOCERCAL
LEPTODACTYL
LEPTODACTYLOUS
LEPTODACTYLS
LEPTOKURTIC
LEPTOPHOSES
LEPTOPHYLLOUS
LEPTORRHINE
LEPTOSOMATIC
LEPTOSOMES
LEPTOSOMIC
LEPTOSPIRAL
LEPTOSPIRE
LEPTOSPIRES
LEPTOSPIROSES
LEPTOSPIROSIS
LEPTOTENES
LESBIANISM
LESBIANISMS
LESPEDEZAS
LESSEESHIP
LESSEESHIPS
LESSONINGS
LETHALITIES
LETHARGICAL
LETHARGICALLY
LETHARGIED
LETHARGIES
LETHARGISE
LETHARGISED
LETHARGISES
LETHARGISING
LETHARGIZE
LETHARGIZED
LETHARGIZES
LETHARGIZING
LETHIFEROUS
LETTERBOXED

LETTERBOXES
LETTERBOXING
LETTERBOXINGS
LETTERFORM
LETTERFORMS
LETTERHEAD
LETTERHEADS
LETTERINGS
LETTERLESS
LETTERPRESS
LETTERPRESSES
LETTERSETS
LETTERSPACING
LETTERSPACINGS
LEUCAEMIAS
LEUCAEMOGEN
LEUCAEMOGENIC
LEUCAEMOGENS
LEUCHAEMIA
LEUCHAEMIAS
LEUCITOHEDRA
LEUCITOHEDRON
LEUCITOHEDRONS
LEUCOBLAST
LEUCOBLASTS
LEUCOCIDIN
LEUCOCIDINS
LEUCOCRATIC
LEUCOCYTES
LEUCOCYTHAEMIA
LEUCOCYTHAEMIAS
LEUCOCYTIC
LEUCOCYTOLYSES
LEUCOCYTOLYSIS
LEUCOCYTOPENIA
LEUCOCYTOPENIAS
LEUCOCYTOSES
LEUCOCYTOSIS
LEUCOCYTOTIC
LEUCODEPLETED
LEUCODERMA
LEUCODERMAL
LEUCODERMAS
LEUCODERMIA
LEUCODERMIAS
LEUCODERMIC
LEUCOMAINE
LEUCOMAINES
LEUCOPENIA
LEUCOPENIAS
LEUCOPENIC
LEUCOPLAKIA
LEUCOPLAKIAS
LEUCOPLAST
LEUCOPLASTID
LEUCOPLASTIDS
LEUCOPLASTS
LEUCOPOIESES
LEUCOPOIESIS

LEUCOPOIETIC
LEUCORRHOEA
LEUCORRHOEAL
LEUCORRHOEAS
LEUCOTOMES
LEUCOTOMIES
LEUKAEMIAS
LEUKAEMOGENESES
LEUKAEMOGENESIS
LEUKEMOGENESES
LEUKEMOGENESIS
LEUKEMOGENIC
LEUKOBLAST
LEUKOBLASTS
LEUKOCYTES
LEUKOCYTIC
LEUKOCYTOSES
LEUKOCYTOSIS
LEUKOCYTOTIC
LEUKODERMA
LEUKODERMAL
LEUKODERMAS
LEUKODERMIC
LEUKODYSTROPHY
LEUKOPENIA
LEUKOPENIAS
LEUKOPENIC
LEUKOPLAKIA
LEUKOPLAKIAS
LEUKOPLAKIC
LEUKOPOIESES
LEUKOPOIESIS
LEUKOPOIETIC
LEUKORRHEA
LEUKORRHEAL
LEUKORRHEAS
LEUKOTOMIES
LEUKOTRIENE
LEUKOTRIENES
LEVANTINES
LEVELHEADED
LEVELHEADEDNESS
LEVELLINGS
LEVELNESSES
LEVERAGING
LEVIATHANS
LEVIGATING
LEVIGATION
LEVIGATIONS
LEVIGATORS
LEVIRATICAL
LEVIRATION
LEVIRATIONS
LEVITATING
LEVITATION
LEVITATIONAL
LEVITATIONS
LEVITATORS
LEVITICALLY

LEVOROTARY
LEVOROTATORY
LEWDNESSES
LEXICALISATION
LEXICALISATIONS
LEXICALISE
LEXICALISED
LEXICALISES
LEXICALISING
LEXICALITIES
LEXICALITY
LEXICALIZATION
LEXICALIZATIONS
LEXICALIZE
LEXICALIZED
LEXICALIZES
LEXICALIZING
LEXICOGRAPHER
LEXICOGRAPHERS
LEXICOGRAPHIC
LEXICOGRAPHICAL
LEXICOGRAPHIES
LEXICOGRAPHIST
LEXICOGRAPHISTS
LEXICOGRAPHY
LEXICOLOGICAL
LEXICOLOGICALLY
LEXICOLOGIES
LEXICOLOGIST
LEXICOLOGISTS
LEXICOLOGY
LEXIGRAPHIC
LEXIGRAPHICAL
LEXIGRAPHIES
LEXIGRAPHY
LEYLANDIIS
LHERZOLITE
LHERZOLITES
LIABILITIES
LIABLENESS
LIABLENESSES
LIBATIONAL
LIBATIONARY
LIBECCHIOS
LIBELLANTS
LIBELLINGS
LIBELLOUSLY
LIBERALISATION
LIBERALISATIONS
LIBERALISE
LIBERALISED
LIBERALISER
LIBERALISERS
LIBERALISES
LIBERALISING
LIBERALISM
LIBERALISMS
LIBERALIST
LIBERALISTIC

LIBERALISTS
LIBERALITIES
LIBERALITY
LIBERALIZATION
LIBERALIZATIONS
LIBERALIZE
LIBERALIZED
LIBERALIZER
LIBERALIZERS
LIBERALIZES
LIBERALIZING
LIBERALNESS
LIBERALNESSES
LIBERATING
LIBERATION
LIBERATIONISM
LIBERATIONISMS
LIBERATIONIST
LIBERATIONISTS
LIBERATIONS
LIBERATORS
LIBERATORY
LIBERTARIAN
LIBERTARIANISM
LIBERTARIANISMS
LIBERTARIANS
LIBERTICIDAL
LIBERTICIDE
LIBERTICIDES
LIBERTINAGE
LIBERTINAGES
LIBERTINES
LIBERTINISM
LIBERTINISMS
LIBIDINALLY
LIBIDINIST
LIBIDINISTS
LIBIDINOSITIES
LIBIDINOSITY
LIBIDINOUS
LIBIDINOUSLY
LIBIDINOUSNESS
LIBRAIRIES
LIBRARIANS
LIBRARIANSHIP
LIBRARIANSHIPS
LIBRATIONAL
LIBRATIONS
LIBRETTIST
LIBRETTISTS
LICENSABLE
LICENSURES
LICENTIATE
LICENTIATES
LICENTIATESHIP
LICENTIATESHIPS
LICENTIATION
LICENTIATIONS
LICENTIOUS

LICENTIOUSLY
LICENTIOUSNESS
LICHANOSES
LICHENISMS
LICHENISTS
LICHENOLOGICAL
LICHENOLOGIES
LICHENOLOGIST
LICHENOLOGISTS
LICHENOLOGY
LICHTLYING
LICITNESSES
LICKERISHLY
LICKERISHNESS
LICKERISHNESSES
LICKPENNIES
LICKSPITTLE
LICKSPITTLES
LIDOCAINES
LIEBFRAUMILCH
LIEBFRAUMILCHS
LIENTERIES
LIEUTENANCIES
LIEUTENANCY
LIEUTENANT
LIEUTENANTRIES
LIEUTENANTRY
LIEUTENANTS
LIEUTENANTSHIP
LIEUTENANTSHIPS
LIFEBLOODS
LIFEGUARDED
LIFEGUARDING
LIFEGUARDS
LIFELESSLY
LIFELESSNESS
LIFELESSNESSES
LIFELIKENESS
LIFELIKENESSES
LIFEMANSHIP
LIFEMANSHIPS
LIFESAVERS
LIFESAVING
LIFESAVINGS
LIFESTYLER
LIFESTYLERS
LIFESTYLES
LIFEWORLDS
LIGAMENTAL
LIGAMENTARY
LIGAMENTOUS
LIGATURING
LIGHTBULBS
LIGHTENERS
LIGHTENING
LIGHTENINGS
LIGHTERAGE
LIGHTERAGES
LIGHTERING

LIGHTERMAN
LIGHTERMEN
LIGHTFACED
LIGHTFACES
LIGHTFASTNESS
LIGHTFASTNESSES
LIGHTHEARTED
LIGHTHEARTEDLY
LIGHTHOUSE
LIGHTHOUSEMAN
LIGHTHOUSEMEN
LIGHTHOUSES
LIGHTLYING
LIGHTNESSES
LIGHTNINGED
LIGHTNINGS
LIGHTPLANE
LIGHTPLANES
LIGHTPROOF
LIGHTSHIPS
LIGHTSOMELY
LIGHTSOMENESS
LIGHTSOMENESSES
LIGHTTIGHT
LIGHTWEIGHT
LIGHTWEIGHTS
LIGHTWOODS
LIGNICOLOUS
LIGNIFICATION
LIGNIFICATIONS
LIGNIFYING
LIGNIPERDOUS
LIGNIVOROUS
LIGNOCAINE
LIGNOCAINES
LIGNOCELLULOSE
LIGNOCELLULOSES
LIGNOCELLULOSIC
LIGNOSULFONATE
LIGNOSULFONATES
LIGULIFLORAL
LIKABILITIES
LIKABILITY
LIKABLENESS
LIKABLENESSES
LIKEABLENESS
LIKEABLENESSES
LIKELIHOOD
LIKELIHOODS
LIKELINESS
LIKELINESSES
LIKENESSES
LILIACEOUS
LILLIPUTIAN
LILLIPUTIANS
LILTINGNESS
LILTINGNESSES
LIMACIFORM
LIMACOLOGIES

LIMACOLOGIST
LIMACOLOGISTS
LIMACOLOGY
LIMBERNESS
LIMBERNESSES
LIMBURGITE
LIMBURGITES
LIMELIGHTED
LIMELIGHTER
LIMELIGHTERS
LIMELIGHTING
LIMELIGHTS
LIMESCALES
LIMESTONES
LIMEWASHES
LIMEWATERS
LIMICOLINE
LIMICOLOUS
LIMINESSES
LIMITABLENESS
LIMITABLENESSES
LIMITARIAN
LIMITARIANS
LIMITATION
LIMITATIONAL
LIMITATIONS
LIMITATIVE
LIMITEDNESS
LIMITEDNESSES
LIMITINGLY
LIMITLESSLY
LIMITLESSNESS
LIMITLESSNESSES
LIMITROPHE
LIMIVOROUS
LIMNOLOGIC
LIMNOLOGICAL
LIMNOLOGICALLY
LIMNOLOGIES
LIMNOLOGIST
LIMNOLOGISTS
LIMNOPHILOUS
LIMOUSINES
LIMPIDITIES
LIMPIDNESS
LIMPIDNESSES
LIMPNESSES
LINCOMYCIN
LINCOMYCINS
LINCRUSTAS
LINEALITIES
LINEAMENTAL
LINEAMENTS
LINEARISATION
LINEARISATIONS
LINEARISED
LINEARISES
LINEARISING
LINEARITIES

LINEARIZATION
LINEARIZATIONS
LINEARIZED
LINEARIZES
LINEARIZING
LINEATIONS
LINEBACKER
LINEBACKERS
LINEBACKING
LINEBACKINGS
LINEBREEDING
LINEBREEDINGS
LINECASTER
LINECASTERS
LINECASTING
LINECASTINGS
LINEOLATED
LINERBOARD
LINERBOARDS
LINGBERRIES
LINGERINGLY
LINGERINGS
LINGONBERRIES
LINGONBERRY
LINGUIFORM
LINGUISTER
LINGUISTERS
LINGUISTIC
LINGUISTICAL
LINGUISTICALLY
LINGUISTICIAN
LINGUISTICIANS
LINGUISTICS
LINGUISTRIES
LINGUISTRY
LINGULATED
LINISHINGS
LINKSLANDS
LINOLEATES
LINOTYPERS
LINOTYPING
LINTSTOCKS
LINTWHITES
LIONCELLES
LIONFISHES
LIONHEARTED
LIONHEARTEDNESS
LIONISATION
LIONISATIONS
LIONIZATION
LIONIZATIONS
LIPECTOMIES
LIPIDOPLAST
LIPIDOPLASTS
LIPOCHROME
LIPOCHROMES
LIPODYSTROPHIES
LIPODYSTROPHY
LIPOGENESES

LIPOGENESIS
LIPOGRAMMATIC
LIPOGRAMMATISM
LIPOGRAMMATISMS
LIPOGRAMMATIST
LIPOGRAMMATISTS
LIPOGRAPHIES
LIPOGRAPHY
LIPOMATOSES
LIPOMATOSIS
LIPOMATOUS
LIPOPHILIC
LIPOPLASTS
LIPOPROTEIN
LIPOPROTEINS
LIPOSCULPTURE
LIPOSCULPTURES
LIPOSUCKED
LIPOSUCKING
LIPOSUCTION
LIPOSUCTIONS
LIPOTROPIC
LIPOTROPIES
LIPOTROPIN
LIPOTROPINS
LIPPINESSES
LIPPITUDES
LIPREADERS
LIPREADING
LIPREADINGS
LIPSTICKED
LIPSTICKING
LIQUATIONS
LIQUEFACIENT
LIQUEFACIENTS
LIQUEFACTION
LIQUEFACTIONS
LIQUEFACTIVE
LIQUEFIABLE
LIQUEFIERS
LIQUEFYING
LIQUESCENCE
LIQUESCENCES
LIQUESCENCIES
LIQUESCENCY
LIQUESCENT
LIQUESCING
LIQUEURING
LIQUIDAMBAR
LIQUIDAMBARS
LIQUIDATED
LIQUIDATES
LIQUIDATING
LIQUIDATION
LIQUIDATIONS
LIQUIDATOR
LIQUIDATORS
LIQUIDISED
LIQUIDISER

LIQUIDISERS
LIQUIDISES
LIQUIDISING
LIQUIDITIES
LIQUIDIZED
LIQUIDIZER
LIQUIDIZERS
LIQUIDIZES
LIQUIDIZING
LIQUIDNESS
LIQUIDNESSES
LIQUIDUSES
LIQUIFYING
LIQUORICES
LIQUORISHLY
LIQUORISHNESS
LIQUORISHNESSES
LIRIODENDRA
LIRIODENDRON
LIRIODENDRONS
LISSENCEPHALOUS
LISSOMENESS
LISSOMENESSES
LISSOMNESS
LISSOMNESSES
LISSOTRICHOUS
LISTENABILITIES
LISTENABILITY
LISTENABLE
LISTENERSHIP
LISTENERSHIPS
LISTERIOSES
LISTERIOSIS
LISTLESSLY
LISTLESSNESS
LISTLESSNESSES
LITENESSES
LITERACIES
LITERALISATION
LITERALISATIONS
LITERALISE
LITERALISED
LITERALISER
LITERALISERS
LITERALISES
LITERALISING
LITERALISM
LITERALISMS
LITERALIST
LITERALISTIC
LITERALISTS
LITERALITIES
LITERALITY
LITERALIZATION
LITERALIZATIONS
LITERALIZE
LITERALIZED
LITERALIZER
LITERALIZERS

LITERALIZES
LITERALIZING
LITERALNESS
LITERALNESSES
LITERARILY
LITERARINESS
LITERARINESSES
LITERARYISM
LITERARYISMS
LITERATELY
LITERATENESS
LITERATENESSES
LITERATION
LITERATIONS
LITERATORS
LITERATURE
LITERATURED
LITERATURES
LITEROSITIES
LITEROSITY
LITHENESSES
LITHESOMENESS
LITHESOMENESSES
LITHIFICATION
LITHIFICATIONS
LITHIFYING
LITHISTIDS
LITHOCHROMATIC
LITHOCHROMATICS
LITHOCHROMIES
LITHOCHROMY
LITHOCLAST
LITHOCLASTS
LITHOCYSTS
LITHODOMOUS
LITHOGENOUS
LITHOGLYPH
LITHOGLYPHS
LITHOGRAPH
LITHOGRAPHED
LITHOGRAPHER
LITHOGRAPHERS
LITHOGRAPHIC
LITHOGRAPHICAL
LITHOGRAPHIES
LITHOGRAPHING
LITHOGRAPHS
LITHOGRAPHY
LITHOLAPAXIES
LITHOLAPAXY
LITHOLATRIES
LITHOLATROUS
LITHOLATRY
LITHOLOGIC
LITHOLOGICAL
LITHOLOGICALLY
LITHOLOGIES
LITHOLOGIST
LITHOLOGISTS

LITHOMANCIES
LITHOMANCY
LITHOMARGE
LITHOMARGES
LITHOMETEOR
LITHOMETEORS
LITHONTHRYPTIC
LITHONTHRYPTICS
LITHONTRIPTIC
LITHONTRIPTICS
LITHONTRIPTIST
LITHONTRIPTISTS
LITHONTRIPTOR
LITHONTRIPTORS
LITHOPHAGOUS
LITHOPHANE
LITHOPHANES
LITHOPHILOUS
LITHOPHYSA
LITHOPHYSAE
LITHOPHYSE
LITHOPHYSES
LITHOPHYTE
LITHOPHYTES
LITHOPHYTIC
LITHOPONES
LITHOPRINT
LITHOPRINTS
LITHOSPERMUM
LITHOSPERMUMS
LITHOSPHERE
LITHOSPHERES
LITHOSPHERIC
LITHOSTATIC
LITHOTOMES
LITHOTOMIC
LITHOTOMICAL
LITHOTOMIES
LITHOTOMIST
LITHOTOMISTS
LITHOTOMOUS
LITHOTRIPSIES
LITHOTRIPSY
LITHOTRIPTER
LITHOTRIPTERS
LITHOTRIPTIC
LITHOTRIPTICS
LITHOTRIPTIST
LITHOTRIPTISTS
LITHOTRIPTOR
LITHOTRIPTORS
LITHOTRITE
LITHOTRITES
LITHOTRITIC
LITHOTRITICS
LITHOTRITIES
LITHOTRITISE
LITHOTRITISED
LITHOTRITISES

LITHOTRITISING
LITHOTRITIST
LITHOTRITISTS
LITHOTRITIZE
LITHOTRITIZED
LITHOTRITIZES
LITHOTRITIZING
LITHOTRITOR
LITHOTRITORS
LITHOTRITY
LITIGATING
LITIGATION
LITIGATIONS
LITIGATORS
LITIGIOUSLY
LITIGIOUSNESS
LITIGIOUSNESSES
LITTERATEUR
LITTERATEURS
LITTERBAGS
LITTERBUGS
LITTERMATE
LITTERMATES
LITTLENECK
LITTLENECKS
LITTLENESS
LITTLENESSES
LITTLEWORTH
LITURGICAL
LITURGICALLY
LITURGIOLOGIES
LITURGIOLOGIST
LITURGIOLOGISTS
LITURGIOLOGY
LITURGISMS
LITURGISTIC
LITURGISTS
LIVABILITIES
LIVABILITY
LIVABLENESS
LIVABLENESSES
LIVEABILITIES
LIVEABILITY
LIVEABLENESS
LIVEABLENESSES
LIVELIHEAD
LIVELIHEADS
LIVELIHOOD
LIVELIHOODS
LIVELINESS
LIVELINESSES
LIVENESSES
LIVERISHNESS
LIVERISHNESSES
LIVERLEAVES
LIVERWORTS
LIVERWURST
LIVERWURSTS
LIVESTOCKS

LIVETRAPPED
LIVETRAPPING
LIVIDITIES
LIVIDNESSES
LIVINGNESS
LIVINGNESSES
LIVRAISONS
LIXIVIATED
LIXIVIATES
LIXIVIATING
LIXIVIATION
LIXIVIATIONS
LOADMASTER
LOADMASTERS
LOADSAMONEY
LOADSAMONEYS
LOADSAMONIES
LOADSPACES
LOADSTONES
LOAMINESSES
LOANSHIFTS
LOATHEDNESS
LOATHEDNESSES
LOATHFULNESS
LOATHFULNESSES
LOATHINGLY
LOATHLINESS
LOATHLINESSES
LOATHNESSES
LOATHSOMELY
LOATHSOMENESS
LOATHSOMENESSES
LOBECTOMIES
LOBLOLLIES
LOBOTOMIES
LOBOTOMISE
LOBOTOMISED
LOBOTOMISES
LOBOTOMISING
LOBOTOMIZE
LOBOTOMIZED
LOBOTOMIZES
LOBOTOMIZING
LOBSCOUSES
LOBSTERERS
LOBSTERING
LOBSTERINGS
LOBSTERLIKE
LOBSTERMAN
LOBSTERMEN
LOBULATION
LOBULATIONS
LOCALISABILITY
LOCALISABLE
LOCALISATION
LOCALISATIONS
LOCALISERS
LOCALISING
LOCALISTIC

LOCALITIES
LOCALIZABILITY
LOCALIZABLE
LOCALIZATION
LOCALIZATIONS
LOCALIZERS
LOCALIZING
LOCALNESSES
LOCATEABLE
LOCATIONAL
LOCATIONALLY
LOCKHOUSES
LOCKKEEPER
LOCKKEEPERS
LOCKMAKERS
LOCKSMITHERIES
LOCKSMITHERY
LOCKSMITHING
LOCKSMITHINGS
LOCKSMITHS
LOCKSTITCH
LOCKSTITCHED
LOCKSTITCHES
LOCKSTITCHING
LOCOMOBILE
LOCOMOBILES
LOCOMOBILITIES
LOCOMOBILITY
LOCOMOTING
LOCOMOTION
LOCOMOTIONS
LOCOMOTIVE
LOCOMOTIVELY
LOCOMOTIVENESS
LOCOMOTIVES
LOCOMOTIVITIES
LOCOMOTIVITY
LOCOMOTORS
LOCOMOTORY
LOCOPLANTS
LOCORESTIVE
LOCULAMENT
LOCULAMENTS
LOCULATION
LOCULATIONS
LOCULICIDAL
LOCUTIONARY
LOCUTORIES
LODESTONES
LODGEMENTS
LODGEPOLES
LOFTINESSES
LOGAGRAPHIA
LOGAGRAPHIAS
LOGANBERRIES
LOGANBERRY
LOGANIACEOUS
LOGAOEDICS
LOGARITHMIC

LOGARITHMICAL
LOGARITHMICALLY
LOGARITHMS
LOGGERHEAD
LOGGERHEADED
LOGGERHEADS
LOGICALITIES
LOGICALITY
LOGICALNESS
LOGICALNESSES
LOGICISING
LOGICIZING
LOGINESSES
LOGISTICAL
LOGISTICALLY
LOGISTICIAN
LOGISTICIANS
LOGJAMMING
LOGNORMALITIES
LOGNORMALITY
LOGNORMALLY
LOGODAEDALIC
LOGODAEDALIES
LOGODAEDALUS
LOGODAEDALUSES
LOGODAEDALY
LOGOGRAMMATIC
LOGOGRAPHER
LOGOGRAPHERS
LOGOGRAPHIC
LOGOGRAPHICAL
LOGOGRAPHICALLY
LOGOGRAPHIES
LOGOGRAPHS
LOGOGRAPHY
LOGOGRIPHIC
LOGOGRIPHS
LOGOMACHIES
LOGOMACHIST
LOGOMACHISTS
LOGOPAEDIC
LOGOPAEDICS
LOGOPEDICS
LOGOPHILES
LOGORRHEAS
LOGORRHEIC
LOGORRHOEA
LOGORRHOEAS
LOGOTHETES
LOGOTYPIES
LOGROLLERS
LOGROLLING
LOGROLLINGS
LOINCLOTHS
LOITERINGLY
LOITERINGS
LOLLAPALOOZA
LOLLAPALOOZAS
LOLLYGAGGED

LOLLYGAGGING
LOMENTACEOUS
LONELINESS
LONELINESSES
LONENESSES
LONESOMELY
LONESOMENESS
LONESOMENESSES
LONGAEVOUS
LONGANIMITIES
LONGANIMITY
LONGANIMOUS
LONGBOARDS
LONGBOWMAN
LONGBOWMEN
LONGCLOTHS
LONGEVITIES
LONGHAIRED
LONGHEADED
LONGHEADEDNESS
LONGHOUSES
LONGICAUDATE
LONGICORNS
LONGINQUITIES
LONGINQUITY
LONGIPENNATE
LONGIROSTRAL
LONGITUDES
LONGITUDINAL
LONGITUDINALLY
LONGJUMPED
LONGJUMPING
LONGLEAVES
LONGNESSES
LONGPRIMER
LONGPRIMERS
LONGSHOREMAN
LONGSHOREMEN
LONGSHORING
LONGSHORINGS
LONGSIGHTED
LONGSIGHTEDNESS
LONGSOMELY
LONGSOMENESS
LONGSOMENESSES
LONGSUFFERING
LONGSUFFERINGS
LONGWEARING
LOOKALIKES
LOONINESSES
LOOPHOLING
LOOPINESSES
LOOSEBOXES
LOOSENESSES
LOOSESTRIFE
LOOSESTRIFES
LOOYENWORK
LOOYENWORKS
LOPGRASSES

LOPHOBRANCH
LOPHOBRANCHIATE
LOPHOBRANCHS
LOPHOPHORATE
LOPHOPHORE
LOPHOPHORES
LOPSIDEDLY
LOPSIDEDNESS
LOPSIDEDNESSES
LOQUACIOUS
LOQUACIOUSLY
LOQUACIOUSNESS
LOQUACITIES
LORAZEPAMS
LORDLINESS
LORDLINESSES
LORDOLATRIES
LORDOLATRY
LORGNETTES
LORICATING
LORICATION
LORICATIONS
LORNNESSES
LOSABLENESS
LOSABLENESSES
LOSSMAKERS
LOSSMAKING
LOSTNESSES
LOTHNESSES
LOTUSLANDS
LOUDHAILER
LOUDHAILERS
LOUDMOUTHED
LOUDMOUTHS
LOUDNESSES
LOUDSPEAKER
LOUDSPEAKERS
LOUNDERING
LOUNDERINGS
LOUNGEWEAR
LOUNGEWEARS
LOUNGINGLY
LOUSEWORTS
LOUSINESSES
LOUTISHNESS
LOUTISHNESSES
LOVABILITIES
LOVABILITY
LOVABLENESS
LOVABLENESSES
LOVASTATIN
LOVASTATINS
LOVEABILITIES
LOVEABILITY
LOVEABLENESS
LOVEABLENESSES
LOVELESSLY
LOVELESSNESS
LOVELESSNESSES

LOVELIGHTS
LOVELIHEAD
LOVELIHEADS
LOVELINESS
LOVELINESSES
LOVELORNNESS
LOVELORNNESSES
LOVEMAKERS
LOVEMAKING
LOVEMAKINGS
LOVESICKNESS
LOVESICKNESSES
LOVESTRUCK
LOVEWORTHY
LOVINGNESS
LOVINGNESSES
LOWBALLING
LOWBALLINGS
LOWBROWISM
LOWBROWISMS
LOWERCASED
LOWERCASES
LOWERCASING
LOWERCLASSMAN
LOWERCLASSMEN
LOWERINGLY
LOWLANDERS
LOWLIGHTED
LOWLIGHTING
LOWLIHEADS
LOWLINESSES
LOWSENINGS
LOXODROMES
LOXODROMIC
LOXODROMICAL
LOXODROMICALLY
LOXODROMICS
LOXODROMIES
LOYALNESSES
LUBBERLINESS
LUBBERLINESSES
LUBRICANTS
LUBRICATED
LUBRICATES
LUBRICATING
LUBRICATION
LUBRICATIONAL
LUBRICATIONS
LUBRICATIVE
LUBRICATOR
LUBRICATORS
LUBRICIOUS
LUBRICIOUSLY
LUBRICITIES
LUBRICOUSLY
LUBRITORIA
LUBRITORIUM
LUBRITORIUMS
LUCIDITIES

LUCIDNESSES

LUCIDNESSES
LUCIFERASE
LUCIFERASES
LUCIFERINS
LUCIFEROUS
LUCIFUGOUS
LUCKENBOOTH
LUCKENBOOTHS
LUCKENGOWAN
LUCKENGOWANS
LUCKINESSES
LUCKLESSLY
LUCKLESSNESS
LUCKLESSNESSES
LUCKPENNIES
LUCRATIVELY
LUCRATIVENESS
LUCRATIVENESSES
LUCTATIONS
LUCUBRATED
LUCUBRATES
LUCUBRATING
LUCUBRATION
LUCUBRATIONS
LUCUBRATOR
LUCUBRATORS
LUCULENTLY
LUDICROUSLY
LUDICROUSNESS
LUDICROUSNESSES
LUETICALLY
LUFTMENSCH
LUFTMENSCHEN
LUGUBRIOUS
LUGUBRIOUSLY
LUGUBRIOUSNESS
LUKEWARMISH
LUKEWARMLY
LUKEWARMNESS
LUKEWARMNESSES
LUKEWARMTH
LUKEWARMTHS
LULLABYING
LUMBAGINOUS
LUMBERINGLY
LUMBERINGNESS
LUMBERINGNESSES
LUMBERINGS
LUMBERJACK
LUMBERJACKET
LUMBERJACKETS
LUMBERJACKS
LUMBERSOME
LUMBERSOMENESS
LUMBERYARD
LUMBERYARDS
LUMBOSACRAL
LUMBRICALES
LUMBRICALIS

LUMBRICALISES
LUMBRICALS
LUMBRICIFORM
LUMBRICOID
LUMBRICUSES
LUMINAIRES
LUMINANCES
LUMINARIAS
LUMINARIES
LUMINARISM
LUMINARISMS
LUMINARIST
LUMINARISTS
LUMINATION
LUMINATIONS
LUMINESCED
LUMINESCENCE
LUMINESCENCES
LUMINESCENT
LUMINESCES
LUMINESCING
LUMINIFEROUS
LUMINOSITIES
LUMINOSITY
LUMINOUSLY
LUMINOUSNESS
LUMINOUSNESSES
LUMISTEROL
LUMISTEROLS
LUMPECTOMIES
LUMPECTOMY
LUMPFISHES
LUMPINESSES
LUMPISHNESS
LUMPISHNESSES
LUMPSUCKER
LUMPSUCKERS
LUNARNAUTS
LUNATICALLY
LUNCHBOXES
LUNCHEONED
LUNCHEONETTE
LUNCHEONETTES
LUNCHEONING
LUNCHMEATS
LUNCHROOMS
LUNCHTIMES
LUNGFISHES
LUNINESSES
LUNKHEADED
LURIDNESSES
LUSCIOUSLY
LUSCIOUSNESS
LUSCIOUSNESSES
LUSHNESSES
LUSKISHNESS
LUSKISHNESSES
LUSTERLESS
LUSTERWARE

LUSTERWARES
LUSTFULNESS
LUSTFULNESSES
LUSTIHEADS
LUSTIHOODS
LUSTINESSES
LUSTRATING
LUSTRATION
LUSTRATIONS
LUSTRATIVE
LUSTRELESS
LUSTREWARE
LUSTREWARES
LUSTROUSLY
LUSTROUSNESS
LUSTROUSNESSES
LUTEINISATION
LUTEINISATIONS
LUTEINISED
LUTEINISES
LUTEINISING
LUTEINIZATION
LUTEINIZATIONS
LUTEINIZED
LUTEINIZES
LUTEINIZING
LUTEOTROPHIC
LUTEOTROPHIN
LUTEOTROPHINS
LUTEOTROPIC
LUTEOTROPIN
LUTEOTROPINS
LUTESTRING
LUTESTRINGS
LUXULIANITE
LUXULIANITES
LUXULLIANITE
LUXULLIANITES
LUXULYANITE
LUXULYANITES
LUXURIANCE
LUXURIANCES
LUXURIANCIES
LUXURIANCY
LUXURIANTLY
LUXURIATED
LUXURIATES
LUXURIATING
LUXURIATION
LUXURIATIONS
LUXURIOUSLY
LUXURIOUSNESS
LUXURIOUSNESSES
LYCANTHROPE
LYCANTHROPES
LYCANTHROPIC
LYCANTHROPIES
LYCANTHROPIST
LYCANTHROPISTS

LYCANTHROPY
LYCHNOSCOPE
LYCHNOSCOPES
LYCOPODIUM
LYCOPODIUMS
LYMPHADENITIS
LYMPHADENITISES
LYMPHADENOPATHY
LYMPHANGIAL
LYMPHANGIOGRAM
LYMPHANGIOGRAMS
LYMPHANGITIC
LYMPHANGITIDES
LYMPHANGITIS
LYMPHANGITISES
LYMPHATICALLY
LYMPHATICS
LYMPHOADENOMA
LYMPHOADENOMAS
LYMPHOADENOMATA
LYMPHOBLAST
LYMPHOBLASTIC
LYMPHOBLASTS
LYMPHOCYTE
LYMPHOCYTES
LYMPHOCYTIC
LYMPHOCYTOPENIA
LYMPHOCYTOSES
LYMPHOCYTOSIS
LYMPHOCYTOTIC
LYMPHOGRAM
LYMPHOGRAMS
LYMPHOGRANULOMA
LYMPHOGRAPHIC
LYMPHOGRAPHIES
LYMPHOGRAPHY
LYMPHOKINE
LYMPHOKINES
LYMPHOMATA
LYMPHOMATOID
LYMPHOMATOSES
LYMPHOMATOSIS
LYMPHOMATOUS
LYMPHOPENIA
LYMPHOPENIAS
LYMPHOPOIESES
LYMPHOPOIESIS
LYMPHOPOIETIC
LYMPHOSARCOMA
LYMPHOSARCOMAS
LYMPHOSARCOMATA
LYMPHOTROPHIC
LYOPHILISATION
LYOPHILISATIONS
LYOPHILISE
LYOPHILISED
LYOPHILISER
LYOPHILISERS
LYOPHILISES

LYOPHILISING
LYOPHILIZATION
LYOPHILIZATIONS
LYOPHILIZE
LYOPHILIZED
LYOPHILIZER
LYOPHILIZERS
LYOPHILIZES
LYOPHILIZING
LYOSORPTION
LYOSORPTIONS
LYRICALNESS
LYRICALNESSES
LYRICISING
LYRICIZING
LYSERGIDES
LYSIGENETIC
LYSIGENOUS
LYSIMETERS
LYSIMETRIC
LYSOGENICITIES
LYSOGENICITY
LYSOGENIES
LYSOGENISATION
LYSOGENISATIONS
LYSOGENISE
LYSOGENISED
LYSOGENISES
LYSOGENISING
LYSOGENIZATION
LYSOGENIZATIONS
LYSOGENIZE
LYSOGENIZED
LYSOGENIZES
LYSOGENIZING
LYSOLECITHIN
LYSOLECITHINS
LYTHRACEOUS

MACABERESQUE
MACADAMIAS
MACADAMISATION
MACADAMISATIONS
MACADAMISE
MACADAMISED
MACADAMISER
MACADAMISERS
MACADAMISES
MACADAMISING
MACADAMIZATION
MACADAMIZATIONS
MACADAMIZE
MACADAMIZED
MACADAMIZER
MACADAMIZERS
MACADAMIZES
MACADAMIZING
MACARISING
MACARIZING
MACARONICALLY
MACARONICS
MACARONIES
MACCARONIES
MACCARONIS
MACCHERONCINI
MACCHERONCINIS
MACCHIATOS
MACEBEARER
MACEBEARERS
MACEDOINES
MACERANDUBA
MACERANDUBAS
MACERATERS
MACERATING
MACERATION
MACERATIONS
MACERATIVE
MACERATORS
MACHAIRODONT
MACHAIRODONTS
MACHIAVELIAN
MACHIAVELIANS
MACHIAVELLIAN
MACHIAVELLIANS
MACHICOLATE
MACHICOLATED
MACHICOLATES
MACHICOLATING
MACHICOLATION
MACHICOLATIONS
MACHINABILITIES
MACHINABILITY
MACHINABLE

MACHINATED
MACHINATES
MACHINATING
MACHINATION
MACHINATIONS
MACHINATOR
MACHINATORS
MACHINEABILITY
MACHINEABLE
MACHINEGUN
MACHINEGUNNED
MACHINEGUNNING
MACHINEGUNS
MACHINELESS
MACHINELIKE
MACHINEMAN
MACHINEMEN
MACHINERIES
MACHININGS
MACHINISTS
MACHMETERS
MACHTPOLITIK
MACHTPOLITIKS
MACINTOSHES
MACKINTOSH
MACKINTOSHES
MACONOCHIE
MACONOCHIES
MACRENCEPHALIA
MACRENCEPHALIAS
MACRENCEPHALIES
MACRENCEPHALY
MACROAGGREGATE
MACROAGGREGATED
MACROAGGREGATES
MACROBIOTA
MACROBIOTE
MACROBIOTES
MACROBIOTIC
MACROBIOTICS
MACROCARPA
MACROCARPAS
MACROCEPHALIA
MACROCEPHALIAS
MACROCEPHALIC
MACROCEPHALIES
MACROCEPHALOUS
MACROCEPHALY
MACROCLIMATE
MACROCLIMATES
MACROCLIMATIC
MACROCODES
MACROCOPIES
MACROCOSMIC

MACROCOSMICALLY
MACROCOSMS
MACROCYCLE
MACROCYCLES
MACROCYCLIC
MACROCYSTS
MACROCYTES
MACROCYTIC
MACROCYTOSES
MACROCYTOSIS
MACRODACTYL
MACRODACTYLIC
MACRODACTYLIES
MACRODACTYLOUS
MACRODACTYLY
MACRODIAGONAL
MACRODIAGONALS
MACRODOMES
MACROECONOMIC
MACROECONOMICS
MACROEVOLUTION
MACROEVOLUTIONS
MACROFAUNA
MACROFLORA
MACROFOSSIL
MACROFOSSILS
MACROGAMETE
MACROGAMETES
MACROGLIAS
MACROGLOBULIN
MACROGLOBULINS
MACROGRAPH
MACROGRAPHIC
MACROGRAPHS
MACROLOGIES
MACROMERES
MACROMOLECULAR
MACROMOLECULE
MACROMOLECULES
MACROMOLES
MACRONUCLEAR
MACRONUCLEI
MACRONUCLEUS
MACRONUTRIENT
MACRONUTRIENTS
MACROPHAGE
MACROPHAGES
MACROPHAGIC
MACROPHAGOUS
MACROPHOTOGRAPH
MACROPHYLA
MACROPHYLUM
MACROPHYSICS
MACROPHYTE

MACROPHYTES
MACROPHYTIC
MACROPINAKOID
MACROPINAKOIDS
MACROPRISM
MACROPRISMS
MACROPSIAS
MACROPTEROUS
MACROSCALE
MACROSCALES
MACROSCOPIC
MACROSCOPICALLY
MACROSOCIOLOGY
MACROSPORANGIA
MACROSPORANGIUM
MACROSPORE
MACROSPORES
MACROSTRUCTURAL
MACROSTRUCTURE
MACROSTRUCTURES
MACROZAMIA
MACROZAMIAS
MACTATIONS
MACULATING
MACULATION
MACULATIONS
MACULATURE
MACULATURES
MADBRAINED
MADDENINGLY
MADDENINGNESS
MADDENINGNESSES
MADEFACTION
MADEFACTIONS
MADELEINES
MADEMOISELLE
MADEMOISELLES
MADERISATION
MADERISATIONS
MADERISING
MADERIZATION
MADERIZATIONS
MADERIZING
MADONNAISH
MADONNAWISE
MADRASSAHS
MADREPORAL
MADREPORES
MADREPORIAN
MADREPORIANS
MADREPORIC
MADREPORITE
MADREPORITES
MADREPORITIC

MADRIGALESQUE
MADRIGALIAN
MADRIGALIST
MADRIGALISTS
MADRILENES
MAELSTROMS
MAENADICALLY
MAENADISMS
MAFFICKERS
MAFFICKING
MAFFICKINGS
MAGALOGUES
MAGAZINIST
MAGAZINISTS
MAGDALENES
MAGGOTIEST
MAGGOTORIA
MAGGOTORIUM
MAGIANISMS
MAGISTERIAL
MAGISTERIALLY
MAGISTERIALNESS
MAGISTERIES
MAGISTERIUM
MAGISTERIUMS
MAGISTRACIES
MAGISTRACY
MAGISTRALITIES
MAGISTRALITY
MAGISTRALLY
MAGISTRALS
MAGISTRAND
MAGISTRANDS
MAGISTRATE
MAGISTRATES
MAGISTRATESHIP
MAGISTRATESHIPS
MAGISTRATIC
MAGISTRATICAL
MAGISTRATICALLY
MAGISTRATURE
MAGISTRATURES
MAGMATISMS
MAGNALIUMS
MAGNANIMITIES
MAGNANIMITY
MAGNANIMOUS
MAGNANIMOUSLY
MAGNANIMOUSNESS
MAGNATESHIP
MAGNATESHIPS
MAGNESITES
MAGNESIUMS
MAGNESSTONE
MAGNESSTONES
MAGNETICAL
MAGNETICALLY
MAGNETICIAN
MAGNETICIANS

MAGNETISABLE
MAGNETISATION
MAGNETISATIONS
MAGNETISED
MAGNETISER
MAGNETISERS
MAGNETISES
MAGNETISING
MAGNETISMS
MAGNETISTS
MAGNETITES
MAGNETITIC
MAGNETIZABLE
MAGNETIZATION
MAGNETIZATIONS
MAGNETIZED
MAGNETIZER
MAGNETIZERS
MAGNETIZES
MAGNETIZING
MAGNETOCHEMICAL
MAGNETOELECTRIC
MAGNETOGRAPH
MAGNETOGRAPHS
MAGNETOMETER
MAGNETOMETERS
MAGNETOMETRIC
MAGNETOMETRIES
MAGNETOMETRY
MAGNETOMOTIVE
MAGNETOPAUSE
MAGNETOPAUSES
MAGNETOSPHERE
MAGNETOSPHERES
MAGNETOSPHERIC
MAGNETOSTATIC
MAGNETOSTATICS
MAGNETRONS
MAGNIFIABLE
MAGNIFICAL
MAGNIFICALLY
MAGNIFICAT
MAGNIFICATION
MAGNIFICATIONS
MAGNIFICATS
MAGNIFICENCE
MAGNIFICENCES
MAGNIFICENT
MAGNIFICENTLY
MAGNIFICENTNESS
MAGNIFICOES
MAGNIFICOS
MAGNIFIERS
MAGNIFYING
MAGNILOQUENCE
MAGNILOQUENCES
MAGNILOQUENT
MAGNILOQUENTLY
MAGNITUDES

MAGNITUDINOUS
MAGNOLIACEOUS
MAHARAJAHS
MAHARANEES
MAHARISHIS
MAHATMAISM
MAHATMAISMS
MAHLSTICKS
MAHOGANIES
MAIASAURAS
MAIDENHAIR
MAIDENHAIRS
MAIDENHEAD
MAIDENHEADS
MAIDENHOOD
MAIDENHOODS
MAIDENLIKE
MAIDENLINESS
MAIDENLINESSES
MAIDENWEED
MAIDENWEEDS
MAIDISHNESS
MAIDISHNESSES
MAIDSERVANT
MAIDSERVANTS
MAIEUTICAL
MAILABILITIES
MAILABILITY
MAILCOACHES
MAILGRAMMED
MAILGRAMMING
MAILMERGED
MAILMERGES
MAILMERGING
MAILPOUCHES
MAILSHOTTED
MAILSHOTTING
MAIMEDNESS
MAIMEDNESSES
MAINBRACES
MAINFRAMES
MAINLANDER
MAINLANDERS
MAINLINERS
MAINLINING
MAINLININGS
MAINPERNOR
MAINPERNORS
MAINPRISES
MAINSHEETS
MAINSPRING
MAINSPRINGS
MAINSTREAM
MAINSTREAMED
MAINSTREAMING
MAINSTREAMS
MAINSTREETING
MAINSTREETINGS
MAINTAINABILITY

MAINTAINABLE
MAINTAINED
MAINTAINER
MAINTAINERS
MAINTAINING
MAINTENANCE
MAINTENANCED
MAINTENANCES
MAINTENANCING
MAINTOPMAST
MAINTOPMASTS
MAINTOPSAIL
MAINTOPSAILS
MAISONETTE
MAISONETTES
MAISONNETTE
MAISONNETTES
MAISTERDOME
MAISTERDOMES
MAISTERING
MAISTRINGS
MAJESTICAL
MAJESTICALLY
MAJESTICALNESS
MAJESTICNESS
MAJESTICNESSES
MAJOLICAWARE
MAJOLICAWARES
MAJORDOMOS
MAJORETTES
MAJORETTING
MAJORETTINGS
MAJORITAIRE
MAJORITAIRES
MAJORITARIAN
MAJORITARIANISM
MAJORITARIANS
MAJORITIES
MAJORSHIPS
MAJUSCULAR
MAJUSCULES
MAKEREADIES
MAKESHIFTS
MAKEWEIGHT
MAKEWEIGHTS
MAKUNOUCHI
MAKUNOUCHIS
MALABSORPTION
MALABSORPTIONS
MALACHITES
MALACOLOGICAL
MALACOLOGIES
MALACOLOGIST
MALACOLOGISTS
MALACOLOGY
MALACOPHILIES
MALACOPHILOUS
MALACOPHILY
MALACOPHYLLOUS

MALACOPTERYGIAN
MALACOSTRACAN
MALACOSTRACANS
MALACOSTRACOUS
MALADAPTATION
MALADAPTATIONS
MALADAPTED
MALADAPTIVE
MALADAPTIVELY
MALADDRESS
MALADDRESSES
MALADJUSTED
MALADJUSTIVE
MALADJUSTMENT
MALADJUSTMENTS
MALADMINISTER
MALADMINISTERED
MALADMINISTERS
MALADROITLY
MALADROITNESS
MALADROITNESSES
MALADROITS
MALAGUENAS
MALAGUETTA
MALAGUETTAS
MALAKATOONE
MALAKATOONES
MALAPERTLY
MALAPERTNESS
MALAPERTNESSES
MALAPPORTIONED
MALAPPROPRIATE
MALAPPROPRIATED
MALAPPROPRIATES
MALAPROPIAN
MALAPROPISM
MALAPROPISMS
MALAPROPIST
MALAPROPISTS
MALAPROPOS
MALARIOLOGIES
MALARIOLOGIST
MALARIOLOGISTS
MALARIOLOGY
MALASSIMILATION
MALATHIONS
MALAXATING
MALAXATION
MALAXATIONS
MALAXATORS
MALCONFORMATION
MALCONTENT
MALCONTENTED
MALCONTENTEDLY
MALCONTENTS
MALDEPLOYMENT
MALDEPLOYMENTS
MALDISTRIBUTION
MALEDICENT

MALEDICTED
MALEDICTING
MALEDICTION
MALEDICTIONS
MALEDICTIVE
MALEDICTORY
MALEFACTION
MALEFACTIONS
MALEFACTOR
MALEFACTORS
MALEFACTORY
MALEFACTRESS
MALEFACTRESSES
MALEFFECTS
MALEFICALLY
MALEFICENCE
MALEFICENCES
MALEFICENT
MALEFICIAL
MALENESSES
MALENGINES
MALENTENDU
MALENTENDUS
MALEVOLENCE
MALEVOLENCES
MALEVOLENT
MALEVOLENTLY
MALFEASANCE
MALFEASANCES
MALFEASANT
MALFEASANTS
MALFORMATION
MALFORMATIONS
MALFUNCTION
MALFUNCTIONED
MALFUNCTIONING
MALFUNCTIONINGS
MALFUNCTIONS
MALICIOUSLY
MALICIOUSNESS
MALICIOUSNESSES
MALIGNANCE
MALIGNANCES
MALIGNANCIES
MALIGNANCY
MALIGNANTLY
MALIGNANTS
MALIGNITIES
MALIGNMENT
MALIGNMENTS
MALIMPRINTED
MALIMPRINTING
MALIMPRINTINGS
MALINGERED
MALINGERER
MALINGERERS
MALINGERIES
MALINGERING
MALLANDERS

MALLEABILITIES
MALLEABILITY
MALLEABLENESS
MALLEABLENESSES
MALLEATING
MALLEATION
MALLEATIONS
MALLEIFORM
MALLEMAROKING
MALLEMAROKINGS
MALLEMUCKS
MALLENDERS
MALLEOLUSES
MALLOPHAGOUS
MALLOWPUFF
MALLOWPUFFS
MALMSTONES
MALNOURISHED
MALNUTRITION
MALNUTRITIONS
MALOCCLUDED
MALOCCLUSION
MALOCCLUSIONS
MALODOROUS
MALODOROUSLY
MALODOROUSNESS
MALOLACTIC
MALONYLUREA
MALONYLUREAS
MALPIGHIACEOUS
MALPOSITION
MALPOSITIONS
MALPRACTICE
MALPRACTICES
MALPRACTITIONER
MALPRESENTATION
MALTALENTS
MALTINESSES
MALTREATED
MALTREATER
MALTREATERS
MALTREATING
MALTREATMENT
MALTREATMENTS
MALVACEOUS
MALVERSATION
MALVERSATIONS
MALVOISIES
MAMAGUYING
MAMILLATED
MAMILLATION
MAMILLATIONS
MAMILLIFORM
MAMMALIANS
MAMMALIFEROUS
MAMMALITIES
MAMMALOGICAL
MAMMALOGIES
MAMMALOGIST

MAMMALOGISTS
MAMMECTOMIES
MAMMECTOMY
MAMMETRIES
MAMMIFEROUS
MAMMILLARIA
MAMMILLARIAS
MAMMILLARY
MAMMILLATE
MAMMILLATED
MAMMITIDES
MAMMOCKING
MAMMOGENIC
MAMMOGRAMS
MAMMOGRAPH
MAMMOGRAPHIC
MAMMOGRAPHIES
MAMMOGRAPHS
MAMMOGRAPHY
MAMMONISMS
MAMMONISTIC
MAMMONISTS
MAMMONITES
MAMMOPLASTIES
MAMMOPLASTY
MANAGEABILITIES
MANAGEABILITY
MANAGEABLE
MANAGEABLENESS
MANAGEABLY
MANAGEMENT
MANAGEMENTAL
MANAGEMENTS
MANAGERESS
MANAGERESSES
MANAGERIAL
MANAGERIALISM
MANAGERIALISMS
MANAGERIALIST
MANAGERIALISTS
MANAGERIALLY
MANAGERSHIP
MANAGERSHIPS
MANCHESTER
MANCHESTERS
MANCHINEEL
MANCHINEELS
MANCIPATED
MANCIPATES
MANCIPATING
MANCIPATION
MANCIPATIONS
MANCIPATORY
MANDAMUSED
MANDAMUSES
MANDAMUSING
MANDARINATE
MANDARINATES
MANDARINES

MANDARINIC
MANDARINISM
MANDARINISMS
MANDATARIES
MANDATORIES
MANDATORILY
MANDIBULAR
MANDIBULATE
MANDIBULATED
MANDIBULATES
MANDILIONS
MANDIOCCAS
MANDOLINES
MANDOLINIST
MANDOLINISTS
MANDRAGORA
MANDRAGORAS
MANDUCABLE
MANDUCATED
MANDUCATES
MANDUCATING
MANDUCATION
MANDUCATIONS
MANDUCATORY
MANDYLIONS
MANEUVERABILITY
MANEUVERABLE
MANEUVERED
MANEUVERER
MANEUVERERS
MANEUVERING
MANEUVERINGS
MANFULNESS
MANFULNESSES
MANGABEIRA
MANGABEIRAS
MANGALSUTRA
MANGALSUTRAS
MANGANATES
MANGANESES
MANGANESIAN
MANGANIFEROUS
MANGANITES
MANGELWURZEL
MANGELWURZELS
MANGEMANGE
MANGETOUTS
MANGINESSES
MANGOLDWURZEL
MANGOLDWURZELS
MANGOSTANS
MANGOSTEEN
MANGOSTEENS
MANGOUSTES
MANGULATED
MANGULATES
MANGULATING
MANHANDLED
MANHANDLES

MANHANDLING
MANHATTANS
MANHUNTERS
MANIACALLY
MANICOTTIS
MANICURING
MANICURIST
MANICURISTS
MANIFESTABLE
MANIFESTANT
MANIFESTANTS
MANIFESTATION
MANIFESTATIONAL
MANIFESTATIONS
MANIFESTATIVE
MANIFESTED
MANIFESTER
MANIFESTERS
MANIFESTIBLE
MANIFESTING
MANIFESTLY
MANIFESTNESS
MANIFESTNESSES
MANIFESTOED
MANIFESTOES
MANIFESTOING
MANIFESTOS
MANIFOLDED
MANIFOLDER
MANIFOLDERS
MANIFOLDING
MANIFOLDLY
MANIFOLDNESS
MANIFOLDNESSES
MANIPULABILITY
MANIPULABLE
MANIPULARS
MANIPULATABLE
MANIPULATE
MANIPULATED
MANIPULATES
MANIPULATING
MANIPULATION
MANIPULATIONS
MANIPULATIVE
MANIPULATIVELY
MANIPULATOR
MANIPULATORS
MANIPULATORY
MANLINESSES
MANNEQUINS
MANNERISMS
MANNERISTIC
MANNERISTICAL
MANNERISTICALLY
MANNERISTS
MANNERLESS
MANNERLESSNESS
MANNERLINESS

MANNERLINESSES
MANNIFEROUS
MANNISHNESS
MANNISHNESSES
MANOEUVRABILITY
MANOEUVRABLE
MANOEUVRED
MANOEUVRER
MANOEUVRERS
MANOEUVRES
MANOEUVRING
MANOEUVRINGS
MANOMETERS
MANOMETRIC
MANOMETRICAL
MANOMETRICALLY
MANOMETRIES
MANORIALISM
MANORIALISMS
MANOSCOPIES
MANRIKIGUSARI
MANRIKIGUSARIS
MANSERVANT
MANSIONARIES
MANSIONARY
MANSLAUGHTER
MANSLAUGHTERS
MANSLAYERS
MANSONRIES
MANSUETUDE
MANSUETUDES
MANTELLETTA
MANTELLETTAS
MANTELPIECE
MANTELPIECES
MANTELSHELF
MANTELSHELVES
MANTELTREE
MANTELTREES
MANTICALLY
MANTICORAS
MANTICORES
MANTLETREE
MANTLETREES
MANUBRIUMS
MANUFACTORIES
MANUFACTORY
MANUFACTURABLE
MANUFACTURAL
MANUFACTURE
MANUFACTURED
MANUFACTURER
MANUFACTURERS
MANUFACTURES
MANUFACTURING
MANUFACTURINGS
MANUMISSION
MANUMISSIONS
MANUMITTED

MANUMITTER
MANUMITTERS
MANUMITTING
MANURANCES
MANUSCRIPT
MANUSCRIPTS
MANZANILLA
MANZANILLAS
MANZANITAS
MAPMAKINGS
MAPPEMONDS
MAQUILADORA
MAQUILADORAS
MAQUILLAGE
MAQUILLAGES
MAQUISARDS
MARABUNTAS
MARANATHAS
MARASCHINO
MARASCHINOS
MARASMUSES
MARATHONER
MARATHONERS
MARATHONING
MARATHONINGS
MARBELISED
MARBELISES
MARBELISING
MARBELIZED
MARBELIZES
MARBELIZING
MARBLEISED
MARBLEISES
MARBLEISING
MARBLEIZED
MARBLEIZES
MARBLEIZING
MARBLEWOOD
MARBLEWOODS
MARCANTANT
MARCANTANTS
MARCASITES
MARCASITICAL
MARCATISSIMO
MARCELLERS
MARCELLING
MARCESCENCE
MARCESCENCES
MARCESCENT
MARCESCIBLE
MARCHANTIA
MARCHANTIAS
MARCHIONESS
MARCHIONESSES
MARCHLANDS
MARCHPANES
MARCONIGRAM
MARCONIGRAMS
MARCONIGRAPH

MARCONIGRAPHED
MARCONIGRAPHING
MARCONIGRAPHS
MARCONIING
MARESCHALS
MARGARINES
MARGARITAS
MARGARITES
MARGARITIC
MARGARITIFEROUS
MARGENTING
MARGINALIA
MARGINALISATION
MARGINALISE
MARGINALISED
MARGINALISES
MARGINALISING
MARGINALISM
MARGINALISMS
MARGINALIST
MARGINALISTS
MARGINALITIES
MARGINALITY
MARGINALIZATION
MARGINALIZE
MARGINALIZED
MARGINALIZES
MARGINALIZING
MARGINALLY
MARGINATED
MARGINATES
MARGINATING
MARGINATION
MARGINATIONS
MARGRAVATE
MARGRAVATES
MARGRAVIAL
MARGRAVIATE
MARGRAVIATES
MARGRAVINE
MARGRAVINES
MARGUERITE
MARGUERITES
MARIALITES
MARICULTURE
MARICULTURES
MARICULTURIST
MARICULTURISTS
MARIGRAPHS
MARIHUANAS
MARIJUANAS
MARIMBAPHONE
MARIMBAPHONES
MARIMBISTS
MARINADING
MARINATING
MARINATION
MARINATIONS
MARIONBERRIES

MARIONBERRY
MARIONETTE
MARIONETTES
MARISCHALLED
MARISCHALLING
MARISCHALS
MARIVAUDAGE
MARIVAUDAGES
MARKEDNESS
MARKEDNESSES
MARKETABILITIES
MARKETABILITY
MARKETABLE
MARKETABLENESS
MARKETABLY
MARKETEERS
MARKETINGS
MARKETISATION
MARKETISATIONS
MARKETIZATION
MARKETIZATIONS
MARKETPLACE
MARKETPLACES
MARKSMANSHIP
MARKSMANSHIPS
MARKSWOMAN
MARKSWOMEN
MARLACIOUS
MARLINESPIKE
MARLINESPIKES
MARLINGSPIKE
MARLINGSPIKES
MARLINSPIKE
MARLINSPIKES
MARLSTONES
MARMALADES
MARMALISED
MARMALISES
MARMALISING
MARMALIZED
MARMALIZES
MARMALIZING
MARMARISED
MARMARISES
MARMARISING
MARMARIZED
MARMARIZES
MARMARIZING
MARMAROSES
MARMAROSIS
MARMELISED
MARMELISES
MARMELISING
MARMELIZED
MARMELIZES
MARMELIZING
MARMOREALLY
MAROONINGS
MARPRELATE

MARPRELATED
MARPRELATES
MARPRELATING
MARQUESSATE
MARQUESSATES
MARQUESSES
MARQUETERIE
MARQUETERIES
MARQUETRIES
MARQUISATE
MARQUISATES
MARQUISETTE
MARQUISETTES
MARRIAGEABILITY
MARRIAGEABLE
MARROWBONE
MARROWBONES
MARROWFATS
MARROWLESS
MARROWSKIED
MARROWSKIES
MARROWSKYING
MARSEILLES
MARSHALCIES
MARSHALERS
MARSHALING
MARSHALLED
MARSHALLER
MARSHALLERS
MARSHALLING
MARSHALLINGS
MARSHALSHIP
MARSHALSHIPS
MARSHBUCKS
MARSHINESS
MARSHINESSES
MARSHLANDER
MARSHLANDERS
MARSHLANDS
MARSHLOCKS
MARSHLOCKSES
MARSHMALLOW
MARSHMALLOWS
MARSHMALLOWY
MARSHWORTS
MARSIPOBRANCH
MARSIPOBRANCHS
MARSQUAKES
MARSUPIALIAN
MARSUPIALIANS
MARSUPIALS
MARSUPIANS
MARSUPIUMS
MARTELLANDO
MARTELLANDOS
MARTELLATO
MARTELLING
MARTENSITE
MARTENSITES

MARTENSITIC
MARTENSITICALLY
MARTIALISM
MARTIALISMS
MARTIALIST
MARTIALISTS
MARTIALNESS
MARTIALNESSES
MARTINETISH
MARTINETISM
MARTINETISMS
MARTINGALE
MARTINGALES
MARTINGALS
MARTYRDOMS
MARTYRISATION
MARTYRISATIONS
MARTYRISED
MARTYRISES
MARTYRISING
MARTYRIZATION
MARTYRIZATIONS
MARTYRIZED
MARTYRIZES
MARTYRIZING
MARTYROLOGIC
MARTYROLOGICAL
MARTYROLOGIES
MARTYROLOGIST
MARTYROLOGISTS
MARTYROLOGY
MARVELLING
MARVELLOUS
MARVELLOUSLY
MARVELLOUSNESS
MARVELOUSLY
MARVELOUSNESS
MARVELOUSNESSES
MASCARAING
MASCARPONE
MASCARPONES
MASCULINELY
MASCULINENESS
MASCULINENESSES
MASCULINES
MASCULINISATION
MASCULINISE
MASCULINISED
MASCULINISES
MASCULINISING
MASCULINIST
MASCULINISTS
MASCULINITIES
MASCULINITY
MASCULINIZATION
MASCULINIZE
MASCULINIZED
MASCULINIZES
MASCULINIZING

MASCULISTS
MASHGICHIM
MASKALLONGE
MASKALLONGES
MASKALONGE
MASKALONGES
MASKANONGE
MASKANONGES
MASKINONGE
MASKINONGES
MASKIROVKA
MASKIROVKAS
MASOCHISMS
MASOCHISTIC
MASOCHISTICALLY
MASOCHISTS
MASONICALLY
MASQUERADE
MASQUERADED
MASQUERADER
MASQUERADERS
MASQUERADES
MASQUERADING
MASSACRERS
MASSACRING
MASSAGISTS
MASSARANDUBA
MASSARANDUBAS
MASSASAUGA
MASSASAUGAS
MASSERANDUBA
MASSERANDUBAS
MASSETERIC
MASSINESSES
MASSIVENESS
MASSIVENESSES
MASSOTHERAPIES
MASSOTHERAPIST
MASSOTHERAPISTS
MASSOTHERAPY
MASSPRIEST
MASSPRIESTS
MASSYMORES
MASTECTOMIES
MASTECTOMY
MASTERATES
MASTERCLASS
MASTERCLASSES
MASTERDOMS
MASTERFULLY
MASTERFULNESS
MASTERFULNESSES
MASTERHOOD
MASTERHOODS
MASTERINGS
MASTERLESS
MASTERLINESS
MASTERLINESSES
MASTERMIND

MASTERMINDED
MASTERMINDING
MASTERMINDS
MASTERPIECE
MASTERPIECES
MASTERSHIP
MASTERSHIPS
MASTERSINGER
MASTERSINGERS
MASTERSTROKE
MASTERSTROKES
MASTERWORK
MASTERWORKS
MASTERWORT
MASTERWORTS
MASTHEADED
MASTHEADING
MASTHOUSES
MASTICABLE
MASTICATED
MASTICATES
MASTICATING
MASTICATION
MASTICATIONS
MASTICATOR
MASTICATORIES
MASTICATORS
MASTICATORY
MASTIGOPHORAN
MASTIGOPHORANS
MASTIGOPHORE
MASTIGOPHORES
MASTIGOPHORIC
MASTIGOPHOROUS
MASTITIDES
MASTITISES
MASTODONIC
MASTODONTIC
MASTODONTS
MASTODYNIA
MASTODYNIAS
MASTOIDECTOMIES
MASTOIDECTOMY
MASTOIDITIS
MASTOIDITISES
MASTOPEXIES
MASTURBATE
MASTURBATED
MASTURBATES
MASTURBATING
MASTURBATION
MASTURBATIONS
MASTURBATOR
MASTURBATORS
MASTURBATORY
MATACHINAS
MATAGOURIS
MATCHBOARD
MATCHBOARDING

MATCHBOARDINGS
MATCHBOARDS
MATCHBOOKS
MATCHBOXES
MATCHLESSLY
MATCHLESSNESS
MATCHLESSNESSES
MATCHLOCKS
MATCHMAKER
MATCHMAKERS
MATCHMAKES
MATCHMAKING
MATCHMAKINGS
MATCHMARKED
MATCHMARKING
MATCHMARKS
MATCHSTICK
MATCHSTICKS
MATCHWOODS
MATELASSES
MATELLASSE
MATELLASSES
MATELOTTES
MATERFAMILIAS
MATERFAMILIASES
MATERIALISATION
MATERIALISE
MATERIALISED
MATERIALISER
MATERIALISERS
MATERIALISES
MATERIALISING
MATERIALISM
MATERIALISMS
MATERIALIST
MATERIALISTIC
MATERIALISTICAL
MATERIALISTS
MATERIALITIES
MATERIALITY
MATERIALIZATION
MATERIALIZE
MATERIALIZED
MATERIALIZER
MATERIALIZERS
MATERIALIZES
MATERIALIZING
MATERIALLY
MATERIALNESS
MATERIALNESSES
MATERNALISM
MATERNALISMS
MATERNALISTIC
MATERNALLY
MATERNITIES
MATEYNESSES
MATGRASSES
MATHEMATIC
MATHEMATICAL

MATHEMATICALLY
MATHEMATICIAN
MATHEMATICIANS
MATHEMATICISE
MATHEMATICISED
MATHEMATICISES
MATHEMATICISING
MATHEMATICISM
MATHEMATICISMS
MATHEMATICIZE
MATHEMATICIZED
MATHEMATICIZES
MATHEMATICIZING
MATHEMATICS
MATHEMATISATION
MATHEMATISE
MATHEMATISED
MATHEMATISES
MATHEMATISING
MATHEMATIZATION
MATHEMATIZE
MATHEMATIZED
MATHEMATIZES
MATHEMATIZING
MATINESSES
MATRESFAMILIAS
MATRIARCHAL
MATRIARCHALISM
MATRIARCHALISMS
MATRIARCHATE
MATRIARCHATES
MATRIARCHIC
MATRIARCHIES
MATRIARCHS
MATRIARCHY
MATRICIDAL
MATRICIDES
MATRICLINIC
MATRICLINOUS
MATRICULANT
MATRICULANTS
MATRICULAR
MATRICULAS
MATRICULATE
MATRICULATED
MATRICULATES
MATRICULATING
MATRICULATION
MATRICULATIONS
MATRICULATOR
MATRICULATORS
MATRICULATORY
MATRIFOCAL
MATRIFOCALITIES
MATRIFOCALITY
MATRILINEAL
MATRILINEALLY
MATRILINEAR
MATRILINIES

MATRILOCAL	MAVERICKED	MEANINGFULNESS	MECHANOCHEMICAL
MATRILOCALITIES	MAVERICKING	MEANINGLESS	MECHANOMORPHISM
MATRILOCALITY	MAVOURNEEN	MEANINGLESSLY	MECHANORECEPTOR
MATRILOCALLY	MAVOURNEENS	MEANINGLESSNESS	MECHANOTHERAPY
MATRIMONIAL	MAVOURNINS	MEANNESSES	MECHATRONIC
MATRIMONIALLY	MAWKISHNESS	MEANWHILES	MECHATRONICS
MATRIMONIES	MAWKISHNESSES	MEASLINESS	MECLIZINES
MATRIOSHKA	MAWMETRIES	MEASLINESSES	MECONOPSES
MATRIOSHKI	MAXILLARIES	MEASURABILITIES	MECONOPSIS
MATROCLINAL	MAXILLIPED	MEASURABILITY	MEDAILLONS
MATROCLINIC	MAXILLIPEDARY	MEASURABLE	MEDALLIONED
MATROCLINIES	MAXILLIPEDE	MEASURABLENESS	MEDALLIONING
MATROCLINOUS	MAXILLIPEDES	MEASURABLY	MEDALLIONS
MATROCLINY	MAXILLIPEDS	MEASUREDLY	MEDALLISTS
MATRONAGES	MAXILLOFACIAL	MEASUREDNESS	MEDDLESOME
MATRONHOOD	MAXILLULAE	MEASUREDNESSES	MEDDLESOMELY
MATRONHOODS	MAXIMALIST	MEASURELESS	MEDDLESOMENESS
MATRONISED	MAXIMALISTS	MEASURELESSLY	MEDDLINGLY
MATRONISES	MAXIMAPHILIES	MEASURELESSNESS	MEDEVACING
MATRONISING	MAXIMAPHILY	MEASUREMENT	MEDEVACKED
MATRONIZED	MAXIMATION	MEASUREMENTS	MEDEVACKING
MATRONIZES	MAXIMATIONS	MEASURINGS	MEDIAEVALISM
MATRONIZING	MAXIMISATION	MEATINESSES	MEDIAEVALISMS
MATRONLINESS	MAXIMISATIONS	MEATLOAVES	MEDIAEVALIST
MATRONLINESSES	MAXIMISERS	MEATPACKING	MEDIAEVALISTIC
MATRONSHIP	MAXIMISING	MEATPACKINGS	MEDIAEVALISTS
MATRONSHIPS	MAXIMIZATION	MEATSCREEN	MEDIAEVALLY
MATRONYMIC	MAXIMIZATIONS	MEATSCREENS	MEDIAEVALS
MATRONYMICS	MAXIMIZERS	MEATSPACES	MEDIAGENIC
MATROYSHKA	MAXIMIZING	MECAMYLAMINE	MEDIASTINA
MATROYSHKAS	MAYFLOWERS	MECAMYLAMINES	MEDIASTINAL
MATRYOSHKA	MAYONNAISE	MECHANICAL	MEDIASTINUM
MATRYOSHKAS	MAYONNAISES	MECHANICALISM	MEDIATENESS
MATRYOSHKI	MAYORALTIES	MECHANICALISMS	MEDIATENESSES
MATSUTAKES	MAYORESSES	MECHANICALLY	MEDIATIONAL
MATTAMORES	MAYORSHIPS	MECHANICALNESS	MEDIATIONS
MATTERLESS	MAYSTERDOME	MECHANICALS	MEDIATISATION
MATTIFYING	MAYSTERDOMES	MECHANICIAN	MEDIATISATIONS
MATTRASSES	MAZARINADE	MECHANICIANS	MEDIATISED
MATTRESSES	MAZARINADES	MECHANISABLE	MEDIATISES
MATURATING	MAZEDNESSES	MECHANISATION	MEDIATISING
MATURATION	MAZINESSES	MECHANISATIONS	MEDIATIZATION
MATURATIONAL	MEADOWLAND	MECHANISED	MEDIATIZATIONS
MATURATIONS	MEADOWLANDS	MECHANISER	MEDIATIZED
MATURATIVE	MEADOWLARK	MECHANISERS	MEDIATIZES
MATURENESS	MEADOWLARKS	MECHANISES	MEDIATIZING
MATURENESSES	MEADOWSWEET	MECHANISING	MEDIATORIAL
MATURITIES	MEADOWSWEETS	MECHANISMS	MEDIATORIALLY
MATUTINALLY	MEAGERNESS	MECHANISTIC	MEDIATORSHIP
MAUDLINISM	MEAGERNESSES	MECHANISTICALLY	MEDIATORSHIPS
MAUDLINISMS	MEAGRENESS	MECHANISTS	MEDIATRESS
MAUDLINNESS	MEAGRENESSES	MECHANIZABLE	MEDIATRESSES
MAUDLINNESSES	MEALINESSES	MECHANIZATION	MEDIATRICES
MAULSTICKS	MEALYMOUTHED	MECHANIZATIONS	MEDIATRIXES
MAUMETRIES	MEANDERERS	MECHANIZED	MEDICALISATION
MAUNDERERS	MEANDERING	MECHANIZER	MEDICALISATIONS
MAUNDERING	MEANDERINGLY	MECHANIZERS	MEDICALISE
MAUNDERINGS	MEANINGFUL	MECHANIZES	MEDICALISED
MAUSOLEUMS	MEANINGFULLY	MECHANIZING	MEDICALISES

MEDICALISING
MEDICALIZATION
MEDICALIZATIONS
MEDICALIZE
MEDICALIZED
MEDICALIZES
MEDICALIZING
MEDICAMENT
MEDICAMENTAL
MEDICAMENTALLY
MEDICAMENTARY
MEDICAMENTED
MEDICAMENTING
MEDICAMENTOUS
MEDICAMENTS
MEDICASTER
MEDICASTERS
MEDICATING
MEDICATION
MEDICATIONS
MEDICATIVE
MEDICINABLE
MEDICINALLY
MEDICINALS
MEDICINERS
MEDICINING
MEDICOLEGAL
MEDIEVALISM
MEDIEVALISMS
MEDIEVALIST
MEDIEVALISTIC
MEDIEVALISTS
MEDIEVALLY
MEDIOCRACIES
MEDIOCRACY
MEDIOCRITIES
MEDIOCRITY
MEDITATING
MEDITATION
MEDITATIONS
MEDITATIVE
MEDITATIVELY
MEDITATIVENESS
MEDITATORS
MEDITERRANEAN
MEDIUMISTIC
MEDIUMSHIP
MEDIUMSHIPS
MEDIVACING
MEDIVACKED
MEDIVACKING
MEDRESSEHS
MEDULLATED
MEDULLOBLASTOMA
MEDUSIFORM
MEEKNESSES
MEERSCHAUM
MEERSCHAUMS
MEETINGHOUSE

MEETINGHOUSES
MEETNESSES
MEFLOQUINE
MEFLOQUINES
MEGACEPHALIC
MEGACEPHALIES
MEGACEPHALOUS
MEGACEPHALY
MEGACITIES
MEGACORPORATION
MEGACURIES
MEGACYCLES
MEGADEATHS
MEGAFARADS
MEGAFAUNAE
MEGAFAUNAL
MEGAFAUNAS
MEGAFLORAE
MEGAFLORAS
MEGAGAMETE
MEGAGAMETES
MEGAGAMETOPHYTE
MEGAGAUSSES
MEGAHERBIVORE
MEGAHERBIVORES
MEGAHERTZES
MEGAJOULES
MEGAKARYOCYTE
MEGAKARYOCYTES
MEGAKARYOCYTIC
MEGALITHIC
MEGALITRES
MEGALOBLAST
MEGALOBLASTIC
MEGALOBLASTS
MEGALOCARDIA
MEGALOCARDIAS
MEGALOCEPHALIC
MEGALOCEPHALIES
MEGALOCEPHALOUS
MEGALOCEPHALY
MEGALOMANIA
MEGALOMANIAC
MEGALOMANIACAL
MEGALOMANIACS
MEGALOMANIAS
MEGALOMANIC
MEGALOPOLIS
MEGALOPOLISES
MEGALOPOLITAN
MEGALOPOLITANS
MEGALOPSES
MEGALOSAUR
MEGALOSAURIAN
MEGALOSAURIANS
MEGALOSAURS
MEGALOSAURUS
MEGALOSAURUSES
MEGANEWTON

MEGANEWTONS
MEGAPARSEC
MEGAPARSECS
MEGAPHONED
MEGAPHONES
MEGAPHONIC
MEGAPHONICALLY
MEGAPHONING
MEGAPHYLLS
MEGAPIXELS
MEGAPLEXES
MEGAPROJECT
MEGAPROJECTS
MEGASCOPES
MEGASCOPIC
MEGASCOPICALLY
MEGASPORANGIA
MEGASPORANGIUM
MEGASPORES
MEGASPORIC
MEGASPOROPHYLL
MEGASPOROPHYLLS
MEGASTORES
MEGASTRUCTURE
MEGASTRUCTURES
MEGATECHNOLOGY
MEGATHERES
MEGATHERIAN
MEGATONNAGE
MEGATONNAGES
MEGAVERTEBRATE
MEGAVERTEBRATES
MEGAVITAMIN
MEGAVITAMINS
MEIOFAUNAL
MEIOSPORES
MEIOTICALLY
MEITNERIUM
MEITNERIUMS
MEKOMETERS
MELACONITE
MELACONITES
MELALEUCAS
MELAMPODES
MELANAEMIA
MELANAEMIAS
MELANCHOLIA
MELANCHOLIAC
MELANCHOLIACS
MELANCHOLIAS
MELANCHOLIC
MELANCHOLICALLY
MELANCHOLICS
MELANCHOLIES
MELANCHOLILY
MELANCHOLINESS
MELANCHOLIOUS
MELANCHOLY
MELANISATION

MELANISATIONS
MELANISING
MELANISTIC
MELANIZATION
MELANIZATIONS
MELANIZING
MELANOBLAST
MELANOBLASTS
MELANOCHROI
MELANOCHROIC
MELANOCHROOUS
MELANOCYTE
MELANOCYTES
MELANOGENESES
MELANOGENESIS
MELANOMATA
MELANOPHORE
MELANOPHORES
MELANOSITIES
MELANOSITY
MELANOSOME
MELANOSOMES
MELANOTROPIN
MELANOTROPINS
MELANTERITE
MELANTERITES
MELANURIAS
MELAPHYRES
MELASTOMACEOUS
MELATONINS
MELIACEOUS
MELICOTTON
MELICOTTONS
MELIORABLE
MELIORATED
MELIORATES
MELIORATING
MELIORATION
MELIORATIONS
MELIORATIVE
MELIORATIVES
MELIORATOR
MELIORATORS
MELIORISMS
MELIORISTIC
MELIORISTS
MELIORITIES
MELIPHAGOUS
MELISMATIC
MELLIFEROUS
MELLIFICATION
MELLIFICATIONS
MELLIFLUENCE
MELLIFLUENCES
MELLIFLUENT
MELLIFLUENTLY
MELLIFLUOUS
MELLIFLUOUSLY
MELLIFLUOUSNESS

MELLIPHAGOUS
MELLIVOROUS
MELLOPHONE
MELLOPHONES
MELLOTRONS
MELLOWNESS
MELLOWNESSES
MELLOWSPEAK
MELLOWSPEAKS
MELOCOTONS
MELOCOTOON
MELOCOTOONS
MELODICALLY
MELODIOUSLY
MELODIOUSNESS
MELODIOUSNESSES
MELODISERS
MELODISING
MELODIZERS
MELODIZING
MELODRAMAS
MELODRAMATIC
MELODRAMATICS
MELODRAMATISE
MELODRAMATISED
MELODRAMATISES
MELODRAMATISING
MELODRAMATIST
MELODRAMATISTS
MELODRAMATIZE
MELODRAMATIZED
MELODRAMATIZES
MELODRAMATIZING
MELODRAMES
MELOMANIAC
MELOMANIACS
MELOMANIAS
MELONGENES
MELPHALANS
MELTABILITIES
MELTABILITY
MELTINGNESS
MELTINGNESSES
MELTWATERS
MELUNGEONS
MEMBERLESS
MEMBERSHIP
MEMBERSHIPS
MEMBRANACEOUS
MEMBRANEOUS
MEMBRANOUS
MEMBRANOUSLY
MEMOIRISMS
MEMOIRISTS
MEMORABILE
MEMORABILIA
MEMORABILITIES
MEMORABILITY
MEMORABLENESS

MEMORABLENESSES
MEMORANDUM
MEMORANDUMS
MEMORATIVE
MEMORIALISATION
MEMORIALISE
MEMORIALISED
MEMORIALISER
MEMORIALISERS
MEMORIALISES
MEMORIALISING
MEMORIALIST
MEMORIALISTS
MEMORIALIZATION
MEMORIALIZE
MEMORIALIZED
MEMORIALIZER
MEMORIALIZERS
MEMORIALIZES
MEMORIALIZING
MEMORIALLY
MEMORISABLE
MEMORISATION
MEMORISATIONS
MEMORISERS
MEMORISING
MEMORIZABLE
MEMORIZATION
MEMORIZATIONS
MEMORIZERS
MEMORIZING
MENACINGLY
MENADIONES
MENAGERIES
MENAQUINONE
MENAQUINONES
MENARCHEAL
MENARCHIAL
MENDACIOUS
MENDACIOUSLY
MENDACIOUSNESS
MENDACITIES
MENDELEVIUM
MENDELEVIUMS
MENDICANCIES
MENDICANCY
MENDICANTS
MENDICITIES
MENINGIOMA
MENINGIOMAS
MENINGIOMATA
MENINGITIC
MENINGITIDES
MENINGITIS
MENINGITISES
MENINGOCELE
MENINGOCELES
MENINGOCOCCAL
MENINGOCOCCI

MENINGOCOCCIC
MENINGOCOCCUS
MENISCECTOMIES
MENISCECTOMY
MENISCUSES
MENISPERMACEOUS
MENISPERMUM
MENISPERMUMS
MENOLOGIES
MENOMINEES
MENOPAUSAL
MENOPAUSES
MENOPAUSIC
MENOPOLISES
MENORRHAGIA
MENORRHAGIAS
MENORRHAGIC
MENORRHEAS
MENORRHOEA
MENORRHOEAS
MENSERVANTS
MENSTRUALLY
MENSTRUATE
MENSTRUATED
MENSTRUATES
MENSTRUATING
MENSTRUATION
MENSTRUATIONS
MENSTRUOUS
MENSTRUUMS
MENSURABILITIES
MENSURABILITY
MENSURABLE
MENSURATION
MENSURATIONAL
MENSURATIONS
MENSURATIVE
MENTALESES
MENTALISMS
MENTALISTIC
MENTALISTICALLY
MENTALISTS
MENTALITIES
MENTATIONS
MENTHACEOUS
MENTHOLATED
MENTICIDES
MENTIONABLE
MENTIONERS
MENTIONING
MENTONNIERE
MENTONNIERES
MENTORINGS
MENTORSHIP
MENTORSHIPS
MENUISIERS
MEPACRINES
MEPERIDINE
MEPERIDINES

MEPHITICAL
MEPHITICALLY
MEPHITISES
MEPHITISMS
MEPROBAMATE
MEPROBAMATES
MERBROMINS
MERCANTILE
MERCANTILISM
MERCANTILISMS
MERCANTILIST
MERCANTILISTIC
MERCANTILISTS
MERCAPTANS
MERCAPTIDE
MERCAPTIDES
MERCAPTOPURINE
MERCAPTOPURINES
MERCENARIES
MERCENARILY
MERCENARINESS
MERCENARINESSES
MERCENARISM
MERCENARISMS
MERCERISATION
MERCERISATIONS
MERCERISED
MERCERISER
MERCERISERS
MERCERISES
MERCERISING
MERCERIZATION
MERCERIZATIONS
MERCERIZED
MERCERIZER
MERCERIZERS
MERCERIZES
MERCERIZING
MERCHANDISE
MERCHANDISED
MERCHANDISER
MERCHANDISERS
MERCHANDISES
MERCHANDISING
MERCHANDISINGS
MERCHANDIZE
MERCHANDIZED
MERCHANDIZER
MERCHANDIZERS
MERCHANDIZES
MERCHANDIZING
MERCHANDIZINGS
MERCHANTABILITY
MERCHANTABLE
MERCHANTED
MERCHANTING
MERCHANTINGS
MERCHANTLIKE
MERCHANTMAN

MERCHANTMEN	MERITORIOUS	MESHUGGENEH	MESOMORPHISM
MERCHANTRIES	MERITORIOUSLY	MESHUGGENEHS	MESOMORPHISMS
MERCHANTRY	MERITORIOUSNESS	MESHUGGENER	MESOMORPHOUS
MERCHILDREN	MERMAIDENS	MESHUGGENERS	MESOMORPHS
MERCIFULLY	MEROBLASTIC	MESITYLENE	MESOMORPHY
MERCIFULNESS	MEROBLASTICALLY	MESITYLENES	MESONEPHRIC
MERCIFULNESSES	MEROGENESES	MESMERICAL	MESONEPHROI
MERCIFYING	MEROGENESIS	MESMERICALLY	MESONEPHROS
MERCILESSLY	MEROGENETIC	MESMERISATION	MESONEPHROSES
MERCILESSNESS	MEROGONIES	MESMERISATIONS	MESOPAUSES
MERCILESSNESSES	MEROMORPHIC	MESMERISED	MESOPELAGIC
MERCURATED	MEROMYOSIN	MESMERISER	MESOPHILES
MERCURATES	MEROMYOSINS	MESMERISERS	MESOPHILIC
MERCURATING	MERONYMIES	MESMERISES	MESOPHYLLIC
MERCURATION	MEROPIDANS	MESMERISING	MESOPHYLLOUS
MERCURATIONS	MEROPLANKTON	MESMERISMS	MESOPHYLLS
MERCURIALISE	MEROPLANKTONS	MESMERISTS	MESOPHYTES
MERCURIALISED	MEROZOITES	MESMERIZATION	MESOPHYTIC
MERCURIALISES	MERPEOPLES	MESMERIZATIONS	MESOSCAPHE
MERCURIALISING	MERRIMENTS	MESMERIZED	MESOSCAPHES
MERCURIALISM	MERRINESSES	MESMERIZER	MESOSPHERE
MERCURIALISMS	MERRYMAKER	MESMERIZERS	MESOSPHERES
MERCURIALIST	MERRYMAKERS	MESMERIZES	MESOSPHERIC
MERCURIALISTS	MERRYMAKING	MESMERIZING	MESOTHELIA
MERCURIALITIES	MERRYMAKINGS	MESNALTIES	MESOTHELIAL
MERCURIALITY	MERRYTHOUGHT	MESOAMERICAN	MESOTHELIOMA
MERCURIALIZE	MERRYTHOUGHTS	MESOBENTHOS	MESOTHELIOMAS
MERCURIALIZED	MERVEILLEUSE	MESOBENTHOSES	MESOTHELIOMATA
MERCURIALIZES	MERVEILLEUSES	MESOBLASTIC	MESOTHELIUM
MERCURIALIZING	MERVEILLEUX	MESOBLASTS	MESOTHELIUMS
MERCURIALLY	MERVEILLEUXES	MESOCEPHALIC	MESOTHORACES
MERCURIALNESS	MESALLIANCE	MESOCEPHALICS	MESOTHORACIC
MERCURIALNESSES	MESALLIANCES	MESOCEPHALIES	MESOTHORAX
MERCURIALS	MESATICEPHALIC	MESOCEPHALISM	MESOTHORAXES
MERCURISED	MESATICEPHALIES	MESOCEPHALISMS	MESOTHORIUM
MERCURISES	MESATICEPHALOUS	MESOCEPHALOUS	MESOTHORIUMS
MERCURISING	MESATICEPHALY	MESOCEPHALY	MESOTROPHIC
MERCURIZED	MESCALINES	MESOCRANIES	MESQUINERIE
MERCURIZES	MESCALISMS	MESOCRATIC	MESQUINERIES
MERCURIZING	MESDEMOISELLES	MESOCYCLONE	MESSAGINGS
MERDIVOROUS	MESENCEPHALA	MESOCYCLONES	MESSALINES
MEREOLOGICAL	MESENCEPHALIC	MESODERMAL	MESSEIGNEURS
MEREOLOGIES	MESENCEPHALON	MESODERMIC	MESSENGERED
MERESTONES	MESENCEPHALONS	MESOGASTRIA	MESSENGERING
MERETRICIOUS	MESENCHYMAL	MESOGASTRIC	MESSENGERS
MERETRICIOUSLY	MESENCHYMATOUS	MESOGASTRIUM	MESSIAHSHIP
MERGANSERS	MESENCHYME	MESOGLOEAS	MESSIAHSHIPS
MERIDIONAL	MESENCHYMES	MESOGNATHIES	MESSIANICALLY
MERIDIONALITIES	MESENTERIAL	MESOGNATHISM	MESSIANISM
MERIDIONALITY	MESENTERIC	MESOGNATHISMS	MESSIANISMS
MERIDIONALLY	MESENTERIES	MESOGNATHOUS	MESSINESSES
MERIDIONALS	MESENTERITIS	MESOGNATHY	MESTRANOLS
MERISTEMATIC	MESENTERITISES	MESOHIPPUS	METABOLICALLY
MERISTICALLY	MESENTERON	MESOHIPPUSES	METABOLIES
MERITOCRACIES	MESENTERONIC	MESOKURTIC	METABOLISABLE
MERITOCRACY	MESHUGAASEN	MESOMERISM	METABOLISE
MERITOCRAT	MESHUGASEN	MESOMERISMS	METABOLISED
MERITOCRATIC	MESHUGGENAH	MESOMORPHIC	METABOLISES
MERITOCRATS	MESHUGGENAHS	MESOMORPHIES	METABOLISING

METABOLISM
METABOLISMS
METABOLITE
METABOLITES
METABOLIZABLE
METABOLIZE
METABOLIZED
METABOLIZES
METABOLIZING
METABOLOME
METABOLOMES
METABOLOMICS
METABOTROPIC
METACARPAL
METACARPALS
METACARPUS
METACENTER
METACENTERS
METACENTRE
METACENTRES
METACENTRIC
METACENTRICS
METACERCARIA
METACERCARIAE
METACERCARIAL
METACHROMATIC
METACHROMATISM
METACHROMATISMS
METACHRONISM
METACHRONISMS
METACHROSES
METACHROSIS
METACINNABARITE
METACOGNITION
METACOGNITIONS
METACOMPUTER
METACOMPUTERS
METACOMPUTING
METACOMPUTINGS
METAETHICAL
METAETHICS
METAFEMALE
METAFEMALES
METAFICTION
METAFICTIONAL
METAFICTIONIST
METAFICTIONISTS
METAFICTIONS
METAGALACTIC
METAGALAXIES
METAGALAXY
METAGENESES
METAGENESIS
METAGENETIC
METAGENETICALLY
METAGNATHISM
METAGNATHISMS
METAGNATHOUS
METAGRABOLISE

METAGRABOLISED
METAGRABOLISES
METAGRABOLISING
METAGRABOLIZE
METAGRABOLIZED
METAGRABOLIZES
METAGRABOLIZING
METAGROBOLISE
METAGROBOLISED
METAGROBOLISES
METAGROBOLISING
METAGROBOLIZE
METAGROBOLIZED
METAGROBOLIZES
METAGROBOLIZING
METALANGUAGE
METALANGUAGES
METALDEHYDE
METALDEHYDES
METALEPSES
METALEPSIS
METALEPTIC
METALEPTICAL
METALHEADS
METALINGUISTIC
METALINGUISTICS
METALISING
METALIZATION
METALIZATIONS
METALIZING
METALLICALLY
METALLIDING
METALLIDINGS
METALLIFEROUS
METALLINGS
METALLISATION
METALLISATIONS
METALLISED
METALLISES
METALLISING
METALLISTS
METALLIZATION
METALLIZATIONS
METALLIZED
METALLIZES
METALLIZING
METALLOCENE
METALLOCENES
METALLOGENETIC
METALLOGENIC
METALLOGENIES
METALLOGENY
METALLOGRAPHER
METALLOGRAPHERS
METALLOGRAPHIC
METALLOGRAPHIES
METALLOGRAPHIST
METALLOGRAPHY
METALLOIDAL

METALLOIDS
METALLOPHONE
METALLOPHONES
METALLURGIC
METALLURGICAL
METALLURGICALLY
METALLURGIES
METALLURGIST
METALLURGISTS
METALLURGY
METALMARKS
METALSMITH
METALSMITHS
METALWARES
METALWORKER
METALWORKERS
METALWORKING
METALWORKINGS
METALWORKS
METAMATHEMATICS
METAMERICALLY
METAMERISM
METAMERISMS
METAMICTISATION
METAMICTIZATION
METAMORPHIC
METAMORPHICALLY
METAMORPHISM
METAMORPHISMS
METAMORPHIST
METAMORPHISTS
METAMORPHOSE
METAMORPHOSED
METAMORPHOSES
METAMORPHOSING
METAMORPHOSIS
METAMORPHOUS
METANALYSES
METANALYSIS
METANEPHRIC
METANEPHROI
METANEPHROS
METAPERIODIC
METAPHASES
METAPHORIC
METAPHORICAL
METAPHORICALLY
METAPHORIST
METAPHORISTS
METAPHOSPHATE
METAPHOSPHATES
METAPHOSPHORIC
METAPHRASE
METAPHRASED
METAPHRASES
METAPHRASING
METAPHRASIS
METAPHRAST
METAPHRASTIC

METAPHRASTICAL
METAPHRASTS
METAPHYSIC
METAPHYSICAL
METAPHYSICALLY
METAPHYSICIAN
METAPHYSICIANS
METAPHYSICISE
METAPHYSICISED
METAPHYSICISES
METAPHYSICISING
METAPHYSICIST
METAPHYSICISTS
METAPHYSICIZE
METAPHYSICIZED
METAPHYSICIZES
METAPHYSICIZING
METAPHYSICS
METAPLASES
METAPLASIA
METAPLASIAS
METAPLASIS
METAPLASMIC
METAPLASMS
METAPLASTIC
METAPOLITICAL
METAPOLITICS
METAPSYCHIC
METAPSYCHICAL
METAPSYCHICS
METAPSYCHOLOGY
METARCHONS
METASEQUOIA
METASEQUOIAS
METASILICATE
METASILICATES
METASILICIC
METASOMATA
METASOMATIC
METASOMATISM
METASOMATISMS
METASOMATOSES
METASOMATOSIS
METASTABILITIES
METASTABILITY
METASTABLE
METASTABLES
METASTABLY
METASTASES
METASTASIS
METASTASISE
METASTASISED
METASTASISES
METASTASISING
METASTASIZE
METASTASIZED
METASTASIZES
METASTASIZING
METASTATIC

METASTATICALLY
METATARSAL
METATARSALS
METATARSUS
METATHEORETICAL
METATHEORIES
METATHEORY
METATHERIAN
METATHERIANS
METATHESES
METATHESIS
METATHESISE
METATHESISED
METATHESISES
METATHESISING
METATHESIZE
METATHESIZED
METATHESIZES
METATHESIZING
METATHETIC
METATHETICAL
METATHETICALLY
METATHORACES
METATHORACIC
METATHORAX
METATHORAXES
METATUNGSTIC
METAVANADIC
METAXYLEMS
METECDYSES
METECDYSIS
METEMPIRIC
METEMPIRICAL
METEMPIRICALLY
METEMPIRICISM
METEMPIRICISMS
METEMPIRICIST
METEMPIRICISTS
METEMPIRICS
METEMPSYCHOSES
METEMPSYCHOSIS
METEMPSYCHOSIST
METENCEPHALA
METENCEPHALIC
METENCEPHALON
METENCEPHALONS
METEORICALLY
METEORISMS
METEORISTS
METEORITAL
METEORITES
METEORITIC
METEORITICAL
METEORITICIST
METEORITICISTS
METEORITICS
METEOROGRAM
METEOROGRAMS
METEOROGRAPH

METEOROGRAPHIC
METEOROGRAPHS
METEOROIDAL
METEOROIDS
METEOROLITE
METEOROLITES
METEOROLOGIC
METEOROLOGICAL
METEOROLOGIES
METEOROLOGIST
METEOROLOGISTS
METEOROLOGY
METESTICKS
METESTROUS
METESTRUSES
METFORMINS
METHACRYLATE
METHACRYLATES
METHACRYLIC
METHADONES
METHAEMOGLOBIN
METHAEMOGLOBINS
METHAMPHETAMINE
METHANATION
METHANATIONS
METHANOMETER
METHANOMETERS
METHAQUALONE
METHAQUALONES
METHEDRINE
METHEDRINES
METHEGLINS
METHEMOGLOBIN
METHEMOGLOBINS
METHENAMINE
METHENAMINES
METHICILLIN
METHICILLINS
METHINKETH
METHIONINE
METHIONINES
METHODICAL
METHODICALLY
METHODICALNESS
METHODISATION
METHODISATIONS
METHODISED
METHODISER
METHODISERS
METHODISES
METHODISING
METHODISMS
METHODISTIC
METHODISTS
METHODIZATION
METHODIZATIONS
METHODIZED
METHODIZER
METHODIZERS

METHODIZES
METHODIZING
METHODOLOGICAL
METHODOLOGIES
METHODOLOGIST
METHODOLOGISTS
METHODOLOGY
METHOMANIA
METHOMANIAS
METHOTREXATE
METHOTREXATES
METHOXIDES
METHOXYBENZENE
METHOXYBENZENES
METHOXYCHLOR
METHOXYCHLORS
METHOXYFLURANE
METHOXYFLURANES
METHYLAMINE
METHYLAMINES
METHYLASES
METHYLATED
METHYLATES
METHYLATING
METHYLATION
METHYLATIONS
METHYLATOR
METHYLATORS
METHYLCELLULOSE
METHYLDOPA
METHYLDOPAS
METHYLENES
METHYLMERCURIES
METHYLMERCURY
METHYLPHENIDATE
METHYLPHENOL
METHYLPHENOLS
METHYLTHIONINE
METHYLTHIONINES
METHYLXANTHINE
METHYLXANTHINES
METHYSERGIDE
METHYSERGIDES
METICULOSITIES
METICULOSITY
METICULOUS
METICULOUSLY
METICULOUSNESS
METOESTROUS
METOESTRUS
METOESTRUSES
METONYMICAL
METONYMICALLY
METONYMIES
METOPOSCOPIC
METOPOSCOPICAL
METOPOSCOPIES
METOPOSCOPIST
METOPOSCOPISTS

METOPOSCOPY
METRALGIAS
METRICALLY
METRICATED
METRICATES
METRICATING
METRICATION
METRICATIONS
METRICIANS
METRICISED
METRICISES
METRICISING
METRICISMS
METRICISTS
METRICIZED
METRICIZES
METRICIZING
METRIFICATION
METRIFICATIONS
METRIFIERS
METRIFYING
METRITISES
METROLOGIC
METROLOGICAL
METROLOGICALLY
METROLOGIES
METROLOGIST
METROLOGISTS
METROMANIA
METROMANIAS
METRONIDAZOLE
METRONIDAZOLES
METRONOMES
METRONOMIC
METRONOMICAL
METRONOMICALLY
METRONYMIC
METRONYMICS
METROPLEXES
METROPOLIS
METROPOLISES
METROPOLITAN
METROPOLITANATE
METROPOLITANISE
METROPOLITANISM
METROPOLITANIZE
METROPOLITANS
METROPOLITICAL
METRORRHAGIA
METRORRHAGIAS
METROSEXUAL
METROSTYLE
METROSTYLES
METTLESOME
METTLESOMENESS
MEZCALINES
MEZZALUNAS
MEZZANINES
MEZZOTINTED

MEZZOTINTER
MEZZOTINTERS
MEZZOTINTING
MEZZOTINTO
MEZZOTINTOS
MEZZOTINTS
MIAROLITIC
MIASMATICAL
MIASMATOUS
MIASMICALLY
MICRIFYING
MICROAEROPHILE
MICROAEROPHILES
MICROAEROPHILIC
MICROAMPERE
MICROAMPERES
MICROANALYSES
MICROANALYSIS
MICROANALYST
MICROANALYSTS
MICROANALYTIC
MICROANALYTICAL
MICROANATOMICAL
MICROANATOMIES
MICROANATOMY
MICROARRAY
MICROARRAYS
MICROBALANCE
MICROBALANCES
MICROBAROGRAPH
MICROBAROGRAPHS
MICROBEAMS
MICROBIOLOGIC
MICROBIOLOGICAL
MICROBIOLOGIES
MICROBIOLOGIST
MICROBIOLOGISTS
MICROBIOLOGY
MICROBIOTA
MICROBREWER
MICROBREWERIES
MICROBREWERS
MICROBREWERY
MICROBREWING
MICROBREWINGS
MICROBREWS
MICROBUBBLES
MICROBURST
MICROBURSTS
MICROBUSES
MICROBUSSES
MICROCAPSULE
MICROCAPSULES
MICROCARDS
MICROCASSETTE
MICROCASSETTES
MICROCELEBRITY
MICROCEPHAL
MICROCEPHALIC

MICROCEPHALICS
MICROCEPHALIES
MICROCEPHALOUS
MICROCEPHALS
MICROCEPHALY
MICROCHEMICAL
MICROCHEMISTRY
MICROCHIPPED
MICROCHIPPING
MICROCHIPS
MICROCIRCUIT
MICROCIRCUITRY
MICROCIRCUITS
MICROCLIMATE
MICROCLIMATES
MICROCLIMATIC
MICROCLINE
MICROCLINES
MICROCOCCAL
MICROCOCCI
MICROCOCCUS
MICROCODES
MICROCOMPONENT
MICROCOMPONENTS
MICROCOMPUTER
MICROCOMPUTERS
MICROCOMPUTING
MICROCOMPUTINGS
MICROCOPIED
MICROCOPIES
MICROCOPYING
MICROCOPYINGS
MICROCOSMIC
MICROCOSMICAL
MICROCOSMICALLY
MICROCOSMOS
MICROCOSMOSES
MICROCOSMS
MICROCRACK
MICROCRACKED
MICROCRACKING
MICROCRACKINGS
MICROCRACKS
MICROCRYSTAL
MICROCRYSTALS
MICROCULTURAL
MICROCULTURE
MICROCULTURES
MICROCURIE
MICROCURIES
MICROCYTES
MICROCYTIC
MICRODETECTION
MICRODETECTIONS
MICRODETECTOR
MICRODETECTORS
MICRODISSECTION
MICRODONTOUS
MICRODRIVE

MICRODRIVES
MICROEARTHQUAKE
MICROECONOMIC
MICROECONOMICS
MICROELECTRODE
MICROELECTRODES
MICROELECTRONIC
MICROELEMENT
MICROELEMENTS
MICROEVOLUTION
MICROEVOLUTIONS
MICROFARAD
MICROFARADS
MICROFAUNA
MICROFAUNAE
MICROFAUNAL
MICROFAUNAS
MICROFELSITIC
MICROFIBER
MICROFIBERS
MICROFIBRE
MICROFIBRES
MICROFIBRIL
MICROFIBRILLAR
MICROFIBRILS
MICROFICHE
MICROFICHES
MICROFILAMENT
MICROFILAMENTS
MICROFILARIA
MICROFILARIAE
MICROFILARIAL
MICROFILARIAS
MICROFILING
MICROFILINGS
MICROFILMABLE
MICROFILMED
MICROFILMER
MICROFILMERS
MICROFILMING
MICROFILMS
MICROFILTER
MICROFILTERS
MICROFLOPPIES
MICROFLOPPY
MICROFLORA
MICROFLORAE
MICROFLORAL
MICROFLORAS
MICROFORMS
MICROFOSSIL
MICROFOSSILS
MICROFUNGI
MICROFUNGUS
MICROGAMETE
MICROGAMETES
MICROGAMETOCYTE
MICROGLIAS
MICROGRAMS

MICROGRANITE
MICROGRANITES
MICROGRANITIC
MICROGRAPH
MICROGRAPHED
MICROGRAPHER
MICROGRAPHERS
MICROGRAPHIC
MICROGRAPHICS
MICROGRAPHIES
MICROGRAPHING
MICROGRAPHS
MICROGRAPHY
MICROGRAVITIES
MICROGRAVITY
MICROGROOVE
MICROGROOVES
MICROHABITAT
MICROHABITATS
MICROIMAGE
MICROIMAGES
MICROINCHES
MICROINJECT
MICROINJECTED
MICROINJECTING
MICROINJECTION
MICROINJECTIONS
MICROINJECTS
MICROLIGHT
MICROLIGHTING
MICROLIGHTINGS
MICROLIGHTS
MICROLITER
MICROLITERS
MICROLITES
MICROLITHIC
MICROLITHS
MICROLITIC
MICROLOANS
MICROLOGIC
MICROLOGICAL
MICROLOGICALLY
MICROLOGIES
MICROLOGIST
MICROLOGISTS
MICROLUCES
MICROLUXES
MICROMANAGE
MICROMANAGED
MICROMANAGEMENT
MICROMANAGER
MICROMANAGERS
MICROMANAGES
MICROMANAGING
MICROMARKETING
MICROMARKETINGS
MICROMERES
MICROMESHES
MICROMETEORITE

MICROMETEORITES	MICROPHOTOMETER	MICROREADER	MICROTECHNIQUE
MICROMETEORITIC	MICROPHOTOMETRY	MICROREADERS	MICROTECHNIQUES
MICROMETEOROID	MICROPHYLL	MICROSATELLITE	MICROTECHNOLOGY
MICROMETEOROIDS	MICROPHYLLOUS	MICROSATELLITES	MICROTOMES
MICROMETER	MICROPHYLLS	MICROSCALE	MICROTOMIC
MICROMETERS	MICROPHYSICAL	MICROSCALES	MICROTOMICAL
MICROMETHOD	MICROPHYSICALLY	MICROSCOPE	MICROTOMIES
MICROMETHODS	MICROPHYSICS	MICROSCOPES	MICROTOMIST
MICROMETRE	MICROPHYTE	MICROSCOPIC	MICROTOMISTS
MICROMETRES	MICROPHYTES	MICROSCOPICAL	MICROTONAL
MICROMETRIC	MICROPHYTIC	MICROSCOPICALLY	MICROTONALITIES
MICROMETRICAL	MICROPIPET	MICROSCOPIES	MICROTONALITY
MICROMETRIES	MICROPIPETS	MICROSCOPIST	MICROTONALLY
MICROMETRY	MICROPIPETTE	MICROSCOPISTS	MICROTONES
MICROMICROCURIE	MICROPIPETTES	MICROSCOPY	MICROTUBULAR
MICROMICROFARAD	MICROPLANKTON	MICROSECOND	MICROTUBULE
MICROMILLIMETRE	MICROPLANKTONS	MICROSECONDS	MICROTUBULES
MICROMINIATURE	MICROPOLIS	MICROSEISM	MICROTUNNELLING
MICROMINIS	MICROPOLISES	MICROSEISMIC	MICROVASCULAR
MICROMOLAR	MICROPORES	MICROSEISMICAL	MICROVILLAR
MICROMOLES	MICROPOROSITIES	MICROSEISMICITY	MICROVILLI
MICROMORPHOLOGY	MICROPOROSITY	MICROSEISMS	MICROVILLOUS
MICRONEEDLE	MICROPOROUS	MICROSITES	MICROVILLUS
MICRONEEDLES	MICROPOWER	MICROSKIRT	MICROVOLTS
MICRONISATION	MICROPOWERS	MICROSKIRTS	MICROWATTS
MICRONISATIONS	MICROPRINT	MICROSLEEP	MICROWAVABLE
MICRONISED	MICROPRINTED	MICROSLEEPS	MICROWAVEABLE
MICRONISES	MICROPRINTING	MICROSMATIC	MICROWAVED
MICRONISING	MICROPRINTINGS	MICROSOMAL	MICROWAVES
MICRONIZATION	MICROPRINTS	MICROSOMES	MICROWAVING
MICRONIZATIONS	MICROPRISM	MICROSPECIES	MICROWIRES
MICRONIZED	MICROPRISMS	MICROSPHERE	MICROWORLD
MICRONIZES	MICROPROBE	MICROSPHERES	MICROWORLDS
MICRONIZING	MICROPROBES	MICROSPHERICAL	MICROWRITER
MICRONUCLEI	MICROPROCESSING	MICROSPORANGIA	MICROWRITERS
MICRONUCLEUS	MICROPROCESSOR	MICROSPORANGIUM	MICRURGIES
MICRONUCLEUSES	MICROPROCESSORS	MICROSPORE	MICTURATED
MICRONUTRIENT	MICROPROGRAM	MICROSPORES	MICTURATES
MICRONUTRIENTS	MICROPROGRAMS	MICROSPORIC	MICTURATING
MICROORGANISM	MICROPROJECTION	MICROSPOROCYTE	MICTURITION
MICROORGANISMS	MICROPROJECTOR	MICROSPOROCYTES	MICTURITIONS
MICROPARASITE	MICROPROJECTORS	MICROSPOROPHYLL	MIDDELMANNETJIE
MICROPARASITES	MICROPSIAS	MICROSPOROUS	MIDDENSTEAD
MICROPARASITIC	MICROPTEROUS	MICROSTATE	MIDDENSTEADS
MICROPARTICLE	MICROPUBLISHER	MICROSTATES	MIDDLEBREAKER
MICROPARTICLES	MICROPUBLISHERS	MICROSTOMATOUS	MIDDLEBREAKERS
MICROPAYMENT	MICROPUBLISHING	MICROSTOMOUS	MIDDLEBROW
MICROPAYMENTS	MICROPULSATION	MICROSTRUCTURAL	MIDDLEBROWED
MICROPEGMATITE	MICROPULSATIONS	MICROSTRUCTURE	MIDDLEBROWISM
MICROPEGMATITES	MICROPUMPS	MICROSTRUCTURES	MIDDLEBROWISMS
MICROPEGMATITIC	MICROPUNCTURE	MICROSURGEON	MIDDLEBROWS
MICROPHAGE	MICROPUNCTURES	MICROSURGEONS	MIDDLEBUSTER
MICROPHAGES	MICROPYLAR	MICROSURGERIES	MIDDLEBUSTERS
MICROPHAGOUS	MICROPYLES	MICROSURGERY	MIDDLEMOST
MICROPHONE	MICROPYROMETER	MICROSURGICAL	MIDDLEWEIGHT
MICROPHONES	MICROPYROMETERS	MICROSWITCH	MIDDLEWEIGHTS
MICROPHONIC	MICROQUAKE	MICROSWITCHES	MIDDLINGLY
MICROPHONICS	MICROQUAKES	MICROTECHNIC	MIDFIELDER
MICROPHOTOGRAPH	MICRORADIOGRAPH	MICROTECHNICS	MIDFIELDERS

MIDINETTES
MIDISKIRTS
MIDLATITUDE
MIDLATITUDES
MIDLITTORAL
MIDLITTORALS
MIDNIGHTLY
MIDRASHOTH
MIDSAGITTAL
MIDSECTION
MIDSECTIONS
MIDSHIPMAN
MIDSHIPMATE
MIDSHIPMATES
MIDSHIPMEN
MIDSTORIES
MIDSTREAMS
MIDSUMMERS
MIDWATCHES
MIDWIFERIES
MIDWINTERS
MIFEPRISTONE
MIFEPRISTONES
MIFFINESSES
MIGHTINESS
MIGHTINESSES
MIGMATITES
MIGNONETTE
MIGNONETTES
MIGRAINEUR
MIGRAINEURS
MIGRAINOUS
MIGRATIONAL
MIGRATIONIST
MIGRATIONISTS
MIGRATIONS
MILDNESSES
MILEOMETER
MILEOMETERS
MILESTONES
MILITANCES
MILITANCIES
MILITANTLY
MILITANTNESS
MILITANTNESSES
MILITARIES
MILITARILY
MILITARISATION
MILITARISATIONS
MILITARISE
MILITARISED
MILITARISES
MILITARISING
MILITARISM
MILITARISMS
MILITARIST
MILITARISTIC
MILITARISTS
MILITARIZATION

MILITARIZATIONS
MILITARIZE
MILITARIZED
MILITARIZES
MILITARIZING
MILITATING
MILITATION
MILITATIONS
MILITIAMAN
MILITIAMEN
MILKFISHES
MILKINESSES
MILKSHAKES
MILKSOPISM
MILKSOPISMS
MILKSOPPING
MILKTOASTS
MILLBOARDS
MILLEFEUILLE
MILLEFEUILLES
MILLEFIORI
MILLEFIORIS
MILLEFLEUR
MILLEFLEURS
MILLENARIAN
MILLENARIANISM
MILLENARIANISMS
MILLENARIANS
MILLENARIES
MILLENARISM
MILLENARISMS
MILLENNIAL
MILLENNIALISM
MILLENNIALISMS
MILLENNIALIST
MILLENNIALISTS
MILLENNIALLY
MILLENNIANISM
MILLENNIANISMS
MILLENNIARISM
MILLENNIARISMS
MILLENNIUM
MILLENNIUMS
MILLEPEDES
MILLEPORES
MILLERITES
MILLESIMAL
MILLESIMALLY
MILLESIMALS
MILLHOUSES
MILLIAMPERE
MILLIAMPERES
MILLIARIES
MILLICURIE
MILLICURIES
MILLIDEGREE
MILLIDEGREES
MILLIGRAMME
MILLIGRAMMES

MILLIGRAMS
MILLIHENRIES
MILLIHENRY
MILLIHENRYS
MILLILAMBERT
MILLILAMBERTS
MILLILITER
MILLILITERS
MILLILITRE
MILLILITRES
MILLILUCES
MILLILUXES
MILLIMETER
MILLIMETERS
MILLIMETRE
MILLIMETRES
MILLIMICRON
MILLIMICRONS
MILLIMOLAR
MILLIMOLES
MILLINERIES
MILLIONAIRE
MILLIONAIRES
MILLIONAIRESS
MILLIONAIRESSES
MILLIONARY
MILLIONFOLD
MILLIONNAIRE
MILLIONNAIRES
MILLIONNAIRESS
MILLIONTHS
MILLIOSMOL
MILLIOSMOLS
MILLIPEDES
MILLIPROBE
MILLIPROBES
MILLIRADIAN
MILLIRADIANS
MILLIROENTGEN
MILLIROENTGENS
MILLISECOND
MILLISECONDS
MILLISIEVERT
MILLISIEVERTS
MILLIVOLTS
MILLIWATTS
MILLOCRACIES
MILLOCRACY
MILLOCRATS
MILLSCALES
MILLSTONES
MILLSTREAM
MILLSTREAMS
MILLWHEELS
MILLWRIGHT
MILLWRIGHTS
MILOMETERS
MILQUETOAST
MILQUETOASTS

MIMEOGRAPH
MIMEOGRAPHED
MIMEOGRAPHING
MIMEOGRAPHS
MIMETICALLY
MIMMICKING
MIMOGRAPHER
MIMOGRAPHERS
MIMOGRAPHIES
MIMOGRAPHY
MIMOSACEOUS
MINACIOUSLY
MINACITIES
MINATORIAL
MINATORIALLY
MINATORILY
MINAUDERIE
MINAUDERIES
MINAUDIERE
MINAUDIERES
MINCEMEATS
MINDBLOWER
MINDBLOWERS
MINDEDNESS
MINDEDNESSES
MINDFULNESS
MINDFULNESSES
MINDLESSLY
MINDLESSNESS
MINDLESSNESSES
MINDSHARES
MINEFIELDS
MINEHUNTER
MINEHUNTERS
MINELAYERS
MINERALISABLE
MINERALISATION
MINERALISATIONS
MINERALISE
MINERALISED
MINERALISER
MINERALISERS
MINERALISES
MINERALISING
MINERALIST
MINERALISTS
MINERALIZABLE
MINERALIZATION
MINERALIZATIONS
MINERALIZE
MINERALIZED
MINERALIZER
MINERALIZERS
MINERALIZES
MINERALIZING
MINERALOGIC
MINERALOGICAL
MINERALOGICALLY
MINERALOGIES

MINERALOGISE
MINERALOGISED
MINERALOGISES
MINERALOGISING
MINERALOGIST
MINERALOGISTS
MINERALOGIZE
MINERALOGIZED
MINERALOGIZES
MINERALOGIZING
MINERALOGY
MINESHAFTS
MINESTONES
MINESTRONE
MINESTRONES
MINESWEEPER
MINESWEEPERS
MINESWEEPING
MINESWEEPINGS
MINGIMINGI
MINGIMINGIS
MINGINESSES
MINGLEMENT
MINGLEMENTS
MINGLINGLY
MINIATIONS
MINIATURED
MINIATURES
MINIATURING
MINIATURISATION
MINIATURISE
MINIATURISED
MINIATURISES
MINIATURISING
MINIATURIST
MINIATURISTIC
MINIATURISTS
MINIATURIZATION
MINIATURIZE
MINIATURIZED
MINIATURIZES
MINIATURIZING
MINIBIKERS
MINIBREAKS
MINIBUDGET
MINIBUDGETS
MINIBUSSES
MINICABBING
MINICABBINGS
MINICOMPUTER
MINICOMPUTERS
MINICOURSE
MINICOURSES
MINIDISHES
MINIDRESSES
MINIFICATION
MINIFICATIONS
MINIFLOPPIES
MINIFLOPPY

MINIMALISM
MINIMALISMS
MINIMALIST
MINIMALISTS
MINIMAXING
MINIMISATION
MINIMISATIONS
MINIMISERS
MINIMISING
MINIMIZATION
MINIMIZATIONS
MINIMIZERS
MINIMIZING
MINIRUGBIES
MINISCHOOL
MINISCHOOLS
MINISCULES
MINISERIES
MINISKIRTED
MINISKIRTS
MINISTATES
MINISTERED
MINISTERIA
MINISTERIAL
MINISTERIALIST
MINISTERIALISTS
MINISTERIALLY
MINISTERING
MINISTERIUM
MINISTERSHIP
MINISTERSHIPS
MINISTRANT
MINISTRANTS
MINISTRATION
MINISTRATIONS
MINISTRATIVE
MINISTRESS
MINISTRESSES
MINISTRIES
MINISTROKE
MINISTROKES
MINITOWERS
MINITRACKS
MINIVOLLEY
MINIVOLLEYS
MINNESINGER
MINNESINGERS
MINNICKING
MINNOCKING
MINORITAIRE
MINORITAIRES
MINORITIES
MINORSHIPS
MINOXIDILS
MINSTRELSIES
MINSTRELSY
MINUSCULAR
MINUSCULES
MINUTENESS

MINUTENESSES
MIRABELLES
MIRABILISES
MIRACIDIAL
MIRACIDIUM
MIRACULOUS
MIRACULOUSLY
MIRACULOUSNESS
MIRANDISED
MIRANDISES
MIRANDISING
MIRANDIZED
MIRANDIZES
MIRANDIZING
MIRIFICALLY
MIRINESSES
MIRKINESSES
MIRRORLIKE
MIRRORWISE
MIRTHFULLY
MIRTHFULNESS
MIRTHFULNESSES
MIRTHLESSLY
MIRTHLESSNESS
MIRTHLESSNESSES
MISACCEPTATION
MISACCEPTATIONS
MISADAPTED
MISADAPTING
MISADDRESS
MISADDRESSED
MISADDRESSES
MISADDRESSING
MISADJUSTED
MISADJUSTING
MISADJUSTS
MISADVENTURE
MISADVENTURED
MISADVENTURER
MISADVENTURERS
MISADVENTURES
MISADVENTUROUS
MISADVERTENCE
MISADVERTENCES
MISADVICES
MISADVISED
MISADVISEDLY
MISADVISEDNESS
MISADVISES
MISADVISING
MISALIGNED
MISALIGNING
MISALIGNMENT
MISALIGNMENTS
MISALLEGED
MISALLEGES
MISALLEGING
MISALLIANCE
MISALLIANCES

MISALLOCATE
MISALLOCATED
MISALLOCATES
MISALLOCATING
MISALLOCATION
MISALLOCATIONS
MISALLOTMENT
MISALLOTMENTS
MISALLOTTED
MISALLOTTING
MISALLYING
MISALTERED
MISALTERING
MISANALYSES
MISANALYSIS
MISANDRIES
MISANDRIST
MISANDRISTS
MISANDROUS
MISANTHROPE
MISANTHROPES
MISANTHROPIC
MISANTHROPICAL
MISANTHROPIES
MISANTHROPIST
MISANTHROPISTS
MISANTHROPOS
MISANTHROPOSES
MISANTHROPY
MISAPPLICATION
MISAPPLICATIONS
MISAPPLIED
MISAPPLIES
MISAPPLYING
MISAPPRAISAL
MISAPPRAISALS
MISAPPRECIATE
MISAPPRECIATED
MISAPPRECIATES
MISAPPRECIATING
MISAPPRECIATION
MISAPPRECIATIVE
MISAPPREHEND
MISAPPREHENDED
MISAPPREHENDING
MISAPPREHENDS
MISAPPREHENSION
MISAPPREHENSIVE
MISAPPROPRIATE
MISAPPROPRIATED
MISAPPROPRIATES
MISARRANGE
MISARRANGED
MISARRANGEMENT
MISARRANGEMENTS
MISARRANGES
MISARRANGING
MISARTICULATE
MISARTICULATED

MISARTICULATES
MISARTICULATING
MISASSAYED
MISASSAYING
MISASSEMBLE
MISASSEMBLED
MISASSEMBLES
MISASSEMBLING
MISASSIGNED
MISASSIGNING
MISASSIGNS
MISASSUMPTION
MISASSUMPTIONS
MISATONING
MISATTRIBUTE
MISATTRIBUTED
MISATTRIBUTES
MISATTRIBUTING
MISATTRIBUTION
MISATTRIBUTIONS
MISAUNTERS
MISAVERRED
MISAVERRING
MISAWARDED
MISAWARDING
MISBALANCE
MISBALANCED
MISBALANCES
MISBALANCING
MISBECOMES
MISBECOMING
MISBECOMINGNESS
MISBEGINNING
MISBEGOTTEN
MISBEHAVED
MISBEHAVER
MISBEHAVERS
MISBEHAVES
MISBEHAVING
MISBEHAVIOR
MISBEHAVIORS
MISBEHAVIOUR
MISBEHAVIOURS
MISBELIEFS
MISBELIEVE
MISBELIEVED
MISBELIEVER
MISBELIEVERS
MISBELIEVES
MISBELIEVING
MISBESEEMED
MISBESEEMING
MISBESEEMS
MISBESTOWAL
MISBESTOWALS
MISBESTOWED
MISBESTOWING
MISBESTOWS
MISBIASING

MISBIASSED
MISBIASSES
MISBIASSING
MISBILLING
MISBINDING
MISBRANDED
MISBRANDING
MISBUILDING
MISBUTTONED
MISBUTTONING
MISBUTTONS
MISCALCULATE
MISCALCULATED
MISCALCULATES
MISCALCULATING
MISCALCULATION
MISCALCULATIONS
MISCALCULATOR
MISCALCULATORS
MISCALLERS
MISCALLING
MISCANTHUS
MISCANTHUSES
MISCAPTION
MISCAPTIONED
MISCAPTIONING
MISCAPTIONS
MISCARRIAGE
MISCARRIAGES
MISCARRIED
MISCARRIES
MISCARRYING
MISCASTING
MISCATALOG
MISCATALOGED
MISCATALOGING
MISCATALOGS
MISCEGENATE
MISCEGENATED
MISCEGENATES
MISCEGENATING
MISCEGENATION
MISCEGENATIONAL
MISCEGENATIONS
MISCEGENATOR
MISCEGENATORS
MISCEGENES
MISCEGENETIC
MISCEGENIST
MISCEGENISTS
MISCEGINES
MISCELLANARIAN
MISCELLANARIANS
MISCELLANEA
MISCELLANEOUS
MISCELLANEOUSLY
MISCELLANIES
MISCELLANIST
MISCELLANISTS

MISCELLANY
MISCHALLENGE
MISCHALLENGES
MISCHANCED
MISCHANCEFUL
MISCHANCES
MISCHANCING
MISCHANNEL
MISCHANNELED
MISCHANNELING
MISCHANNELLED
MISCHANNELLING
MISCHANNELS
MISCHANTER
MISCHANTERS
MISCHARACTERISE
MISCHARACTERIZE
MISCHARGED
MISCHARGES
MISCHARGING
MISCHIEFED
MISCHIEFING
MISCHIEVOUS
MISCHIEVOUSLY
MISCHIEVOUSNESS
MISCHMETAL
MISCHMETALS
MISCHOICES
MISCHOOSES
MISCHOOSING
MISCIBILITIES
MISCIBILITY
MISCITATION
MISCITATIONS
MISCLAIMED
MISCLAIMING
MISCLASSED
MISCLASSES
MISCLASSIFIED
MISCLASSIFIES
MISCLASSIFY
MISCLASSIFYING
MISCLASSING
MISCOINING
MISCOLORED
MISCOLORING
MISCOLOURED
MISCOLOURING
MISCOLOURS
MISCOMPREHEND
MISCOMPREHENDED
MISCOMPREHENDS
MISCOMPUTATION
MISCOMPUTATIONS
MISCOMPUTE
MISCOMPUTED
MISCOMPUTES
MISCOMPUTING
MISCONCEIT

MISCONCEITED
MISCONCEITING
MISCONCEITS
MISCONCEIVE
MISCONCEIVED
MISCONCEIVER
MISCONCEIVERS
MISCONCEIVES
MISCONCEIVING
MISCONCEPTION
MISCONCEPTIONS
MISCONDUCT
MISCONDUCTED
MISCONDUCTING
MISCONDUCTS
MISCONJECTURE
MISCONJECTURED
MISCONJECTURES
MISCONJECTURING
MISCONNECT
MISCONNECTED
MISCONNECTING
MISCONNECTION
MISCONNECTIONS
MISCONNECTS
MISCONSTER
MISCONSTERED
MISCONSTERING
MISCONSTERS
MISCONSTRUCT
MISCONSTRUCTED
MISCONSTRUCTING
MISCONSTRUCTION
MISCONSTRUCTS
MISCONSTRUE
MISCONSTRUED
MISCONSTRUES
MISCONSTRUING
MISCONTENT
MISCONTENTED
MISCONTENTING
MISCONTENTMENT
MISCONTENTMENTS
MISCONTENTS
MISCOOKING
MISCOPYING
MISCORRECT
MISCORRECTED
MISCORRECTING
MISCORRECTION
MISCORRECTIONS
MISCORRECTS
MISCORRELATION
MISCORRELATIONS
MISCOUNSEL
MISCOUNSELLED
MISCOUNSELLING
MISCOUNSELS
MISCOUNTED

MISCOUNTING
MISCREANCE
MISCREANCES
MISCREANCIES
MISCREANCY
MISCREANTS
MISCREATED
MISCREATES
MISCREATING
MISCREATION
MISCREATIONS
MISCREATIVE
MISCREATOR
MISCREATORS
MISCREAUNCE
MISCREAUNCES
MISCREDITED
MISCREDITING
MISCREDITS
MISCUTTING
MISDEALERS
MISDEALING
MISDEEMFUL
MISDEEMING
MISDEEMINGS
MISDEFINED
MISDEFINES
MISDEFINING
MISDEMEANANT
MISDEMEANANTS
MISDEMEANED
MISDEMEANING
MISDEMEANOR
MISDEMEANORS
MISDEMEANOUR
MISDEMEANOURS
MISDEMEANS
MISDESCRIBE
MISDESCRIBED
MISDESCRIBES
MISDESCRIBING
MISDESCRIPTION
MISDESCRIPTIONS
MISDESERTS
MISDEVELOP
MISDEVELOPED
MISDEVELOPING
MISDEVELOPS
MISDEVOTION
MISDEVOTIONS
MISDIAGNOSE
MISDIAGNOSED
MISDIAGNOSES
MISDIAGNOSING
MISDIAGNOSIS
MISDIALING
MISDIALLED
MISDIALLING
MISDIRECTED

MISDIRECTING
MISDIRECTION
MISDIRECTIONS
MISDIRECTS
MISDISTRIBUTION
MISDIVIDED
MISDIVIDES
MISDIVIDING
MISDIVISION
MISDIVISIONS
MISDOUBTED
MISDOUBTFUL
MISDOUBTING
MISDRAWING
MISDRAWINGS
MISDRIVING
MISEDITING
MISEDUCATE
MISEDUCATED
MISEDUCATES
MISEDUCATING
MISEDUCATION
MISEDUCATIONS
MISEMPHASES
MISEMPHASIS
MISEMPHASISE
MISEMPHASISED
MISEMPHASISES
MISEMPHASISING
MISEMPHASIZE
MISEMPHASIZED
MISEMPHASIZES
MISEMPHASIZING
MISEMPLOYED
MISEMPLOYING
MISEMPLOYMENT
MISEMPLOYMENTS
MISEMPLOYS
MISENROLLED
MISENROLLING
MISENROLLS
MISENTERED
MISENTERING
MISENTREAT
MISENTREATED
MISENTREATING
MISENTREATS
MISENTRIES
MISERABILISM
MISERABILISMS
MISERABILIST
MISERABILISTS
MISERABLENESS
MISERABLENESSES
MISERABLES
MISERABLISM
MISERABLISMS
MISERABLIST
MISERABLISTS

MISERICORD
MISERICORDE
MISERICORDES
MISERICORDS
MISERLIEST
MISERLINESS
MISERLINESSES
MISESTEEMED
MISESTEEMING
MISESTEEMS
MISESTIMATE
MISESTIMATED
MISESTIMATES
MISESTIMATING
MISESTIMATION
MISESTIMATIONS
MISEVALUATE
MISEVALUATED
MISEVALUATES
MISEVALUATING
MISEVALUATION
MISEVALUATIONS
MISFALLING
MISFARINGS
MISFEASANCE
MISFEASANCES
MISFEASORS
MISFEATURE
MISFEATURED
MISFEATURES
MISFEATURING
MISFEEDING
MISFEIGNED
MISFEIGNING
MISFIELDED
MISFIELDING
MISFITTING
MISFOCUSED
MISFOCUSES
MISFOCUSING
MISFOCUSSED
MISFOCUSSES
MISFOCUSSING
MISFORMATION
MISFORMATIONS
MISFORMING
MISFORTUNE
MISFORTUNED
MISFORTUNES
MISFRAMING
MISFUNCTION
MISFUNCTIONED
MISFUNCTIONING
MISFUNCTIONS
MISGAUGING
MISGIVINGS
MISGOVERNAUNCE
MISGOVERNAUNCES
MISGOVERNED

MISGOVERNING
MISGOVERNMENT
MISGOVERNMENTS
MISGOVERNOR
MISGOVERNORS
MISGOVERNS
MISGRADING
MISGRAFTED
MISGRAFTING
MISGROWING
MISGROWTHS
MISGUESSED
MISGUESSES
MISGUESSING
MISGUGGLED
MISGUGGLES
MISGUGGLING
MISGUIDANCE
MISGUIDANCES
MISGUIDEDLY
MISGUIDEDNESS
MISGUIDEDNESSES
MISGUIDERS
MISGUIDING
MISHALLOWED
MISHANDLED
MISHANDLES
MISHANDLING
MISHANTERS
MISHAPPENED
MISHAPPENING
MISHAPPENS
MISHAPPING
MISHEARING
MISHEGAASEN
MISHGUGGLE
MISHGUGGLED
MISHGUGGLES
MISHGUGGLING
MISHITTING
MISHMASHES
MISHMOSHES
MISIDENTIFIED
MISIDENTIFIES
MISIDENTIFY
MISIDENTIFYING
MISIMPRESSION
MISIMPRESSIONS
MISIMPROVE
MISIMPROVED
MISIMPROVEMENT
MISIMPROVEMENTS
MISIMPROVES
MISIMPROVING
MISINFERRED
MISINFERRING
MISINFORMANT
MISINFORMANTS
MISINFORMATION

MISINFORMATIONS
MISINFORMED
MISINFORMER
MISINFORMERS
MISINFORMING
MISINFORMS
MISINSTRUCT
MISINSTRUCTED
MISINSTRUCTING
MISINSTRUCTION
MISINSTRUCTIONS
MISINSTRUCTS
MISINTELLIGENCE
MISINTENDED
MISINTENDING
MISINTENDS
MISINTERPRET
MISINTERPRETED
MISINTERPRETER
MISINTERPRETERS
MISINTERPRETING
MISINTERPRETS
MISINTERRED
MISINTERRING
MISJOINDER
MISJOINDERS
MISJOINING
MISJUDGEMENT
MISJUDGEMENTS
MISJUDGERS
MISJUDGING
MISJUDGMENT
MISJUDGMENTS
MISKEEPING
MISKENNING
MISKICKING
MISKNOWING
MISKNOWLEDGE
MISKNOWLEDGES
MISLABELED
MISLABELING
MISLABELLED
MISLABELLING
MISLABORED
MISLABORING
MISLEADERS
MISLEADING
MISLEADINGLY
MISLEARNED
MISLEARNING
MISLEEKING
MISLIGHTED
MISLIGHTING
MISLIKINGS
MISLIPPENED
MISLIPPENING
MISLIPPENS
MISLOCATED
MISLOCATES

MISLOCATING
MISLOCATION
MISLOCATIONS
MISLODGING
MISLUCKING
MISMANAGED
MISMANAGEMENT
MISMANAGEMENTS
MISMANAGER
MISMANAGERS
MISMANAGES
MISMANAGING
MISMANNERS
MISMARKING
MISMARRIAGE
MISMARRIAGES
MISMARRIED
MISMARRIES
MISMARRYING
MISMATCHED
MISMATCHES
MISMATCHING
MISMATCHMENT
MISMATCHMENTS
MISMEASURE
MISMEASURED
MISMEASUREMENT
MISMEASUREMENTS
MISMEASURES
MISMEASURING
MISMEETING
MISMETRING
MISNOMERED
MISNOMERING
MISNUMBERED
MISNUMBERING
MISNUMBERS
MISOBSERVANCE
MISOBSERVANCES
MISOBSERVE
MISOBSERVED
MISOBSERVES
MISOBSERVING
MISOCAPNIC
MISOGAMIES
MISOGAMIST
MISOGAMISTS
MISOGYNIES
MISOGYNIST
MISOGYNISTIC
MISOGYNISTICAL
MISOGYNISTS
MISOGYNOUS
MISOLOGIES
MISOLOGIST
MISOLOGISTS
MISONEISMS
MISONEISTIC
MISONEISTS

MISORDERED
MISORDERING
MISORIENTATION
MISORIENTATIONS
MISORIENTED
MISORIENTING
MISORIENTS
MISPACKAGE
MISPACKAGED
MISPACKAGES
MISPACKAGING
MISPAINTED
MISPAINTING
MISPARSING
MISPARTING
MISPATCHED
MISPATCHES
MISPATCHING
MISPENNING
MISPERCEIVE
MISPERCEIVED
MISPERCEIVES
MISPERCEIVING
MISPERCEPTION
MISPERCEPTIONS
MISPERSUADE
MISPERSUADED
MISPERSUADES
MISPERSUADING
MISPERSUASION
MISPERSUASIONS
MISPHRASED
MISPHRASES
MISPHRASING
MISPICKELS
MISPLACEMENT
MISPLACEMENTS
MISPLACING
MISPLANNED
MISPLANNING
MISPLANTED
MISPLANTING
MISPLAYING
MISPLEADED
MISPLEADING
MISPLEADINGS
MISPLEASED
MISPLEASES
MISPLEASING
MISPOINTED
MISPOINTING
MISPOISING
MISPOSITION
MISPOSITIONED
MISPOSITIONING
MISPOSITIONS
MISPRAISED
MISPRAISES
MISPRAISING

MISPRICING
MISPRINTED
MISPRINTING
MISPRISING
MISPRISION
MISPRISIONS
MISPRIZERS
MISPRIZING
MISPROGRAM
MISPROGRAMED
MISPROGRAMING
MISPROGRAMMED
MISPROGRAMMING
MISPROGRAMS
MISPRONOUNCE
MISPRONOUNCED
MISPRONOUNCES
MISPRONOUNCING
MISPROPORTION
MISPROPORTIONED
MISPROPORTIONS
MISPUNCTUATE
MISPUNCTUATED
MISPUNCTUATES
MISPUNCTUATING
MISPUNCTUATION
MISPUNCTUATIONS
MISQUOTATION
MISQUOTATIONS
MISQUOTERS
MISQUOTING
MISRAISING
MISREADING
MISREADINGS
MISRECKONED
MISRECKONING
MISRECKONINGS
MISRECKONS
MISRECOLLECTION
MISRECORDED
MISRECORDING
MISRECORDS
MISREFERENCE
MISREFERENCES
MISREFERRED
MISREFERRING
MISREGARDS
MISREGISTER
MISREGISTERED
MISREGISTERING
MISREGISTERS
MISREGISTRATION
MISRELATED
MISRELATES
MISRELATING
MISRELATION
MISRELATIONS
MISRELYING
MISREMEMBER

MISREMEMBERED	MISSIONIZATIONS	MISTHROWING	MISWANDRED
MISREMEMBERING	MISSIONIZE	MISTIGRISES	MISWEENING
MISREMEMBERS	MISSIONIZED	MISTINESSES	MISWENDING
MISRENDERED	MISSIONIZER	MISTITLING	MISWORDING
MISRENDERING	MISSIONIZERS	MISTLETOES	MISWORDINGS
MISRENDERS	MISSIONIZES	MISTOUCHED	MISWORSHIP
MISREPORTED	MISSIONIZING	MISTOUCHES	MISWORSHIPPED
MISREPORTER	MISSISHNESS	MISTOUCHING	MISWORSHIPPING
MISREPORTERS	MISSISHNESSES	MISTRACING	MISWORSHIPS
MISREPORTING	MISSORTING	MISTRAINED	MISWRITING
MISREPORTS	MISSOUNDED	MISTRAINING	MISWRITTEN
MISREPRESENT	MISSOUNDING	MISTRANSCRIBE	MITERWORTS
MISREPRESENTED	MISSPACING	MISTRANSCRIBED	MITHRADATIC
MISREPRESENTER	MISSPEAKING	MISTRANSCRIBES	MITHRIDATE
MISREPRESENTERS	MISSPELLED	MISTRANSCRIBING	MITHRIDATES
MISREPRESENTING	MISSPELLING	MISTRANSLATE	MITHRIDATIC
MISREPRESENTS	MISSPELLINGS	MISTRANSLATED	MITHRIDATISE
MISROUTEING	MISSPENDER	MISTRANSLATES	MITHRIDATISED
MISROUTING	MISSPENDERS	MISTRANSLATING	MITHRIDATISES
MISSAYINGS	MISSPENDING	MISTRANSLATION	MITHRIDATISING
MISSEATING	MISSTAMPED	MISTRANSLATIONS	MITHRIDATISM
MISSEEMING	MISSTAMPING	MISTRAYNED	MITHRIDATISMS
MISSEEMINGS	MISSTARTED	MISTREADING	MITHRIDATIZE
MISSENDING	MISSTARTING	MISTREADINGS	MITHRIDATIZED
MISSETTING	MISSTATEMENT	MISTREATED	MITHRIDATIZES
MISSHAPENLY	MISSTATEMENTS	MISTREATING	MITHRIDATIZING
MISSHAPENNESS	MISSTATING	MISTREATMENT	MITIGATING
MISSHAPENNESSES	MISSTEERED	MISTREATMENTS	MITIGATION
MISSHAPERS	MISSTEERING	MISTRESSED	MITIGATIONS
MISSHAPING	MISSTEPPED	MISTRESSES	MITIGATIVE
MISSHEATHED	MISSTEPPING	MISTRESSLESS	MITIGATIVES
MISSILEERS	MISSTOPPED	MISTRESSLY	MITIGATORS
MISSILEMAN	MISSTOPPING	MISTRUSTED	MITIGATORY
MISSILEMEN	MISSTRICKEN	MISTRUSTER	MITOCHONDRIA
MISSILERIES	MISSTRIKES	MISTRUSTERS	MITOCHONDRIAL
MISSILRIES	MISSTRIKING	MISTRUSTFUL	MITOCHONDRION
MISSIOLOGIES	MISSTYLING	MISTRUSTFULLY	MITOGENETIC
MISSIOLOGY	MISSUITING	MISTRUSTFULNESS	MITOGENICITIES
MISSIONARIES	MISSUMMATION	MISTRUSTING	MITOGENICITY
MISSIONARISE	MISSUMMATIONS	MISTRUSTINGLY	MITOMYCINS
MISSIONARISED	MISTAKABLE	MISTRUSTLESS	MITOTICALLY
MISSIONARISES	MISTAKABLY	MISTRYSTED	MITRAILLES
MISSIONARISING	MISTAKEABLE	MISTRYSTING	MITRAILLEUR
MISSIONARIZE	MISTAKEABLY	MISTUTORED	MITRAILLEURS
MISSIONARIZED	MISTAKENLY	MISTUTORING	MITRAILLEUSE
MISSIONARIZES	MISTAKENNESS	MISUNDERSTAND	MITRAILLEUSES
MISSIONARIZING	MISTAKENNESSES	MISUNDERSTANDS	MITREWORTS
MISSIONARY	MISTAKINGS	MISUNDERSTOOD	MITTIMUSES
MISSIONERS	MISTEACHES	MISUTILISATION	MIXABILITIES
MISSIONING	MISTEACHING	MISUTILISATIONS	MIXABILITY
MISSIONISATION	MISTELLING	MISUTILIZATION	MIXEDNESSES
MISSIONISATIONS	MISTEMPERED	MISUTILIZATIONS	MIXMASTERS
MISSIONISE	MISTEMPERING	MISVALUING	MIXOBARBARIC
MISSIONISED	MISTEMPERS	MISVENTURE	MIXOLOGIES
MISSIONISER	MISTENDING	MISVENTURES	MIXOLOGIST
MISSIONISERS	MISTERMING	MISVENTUROUS	MIXOLOGISTS
MISSIONISES	MISTHINKING	MISVOCALISATION	MIXOLYDIAN
MISSIONISING	MISTHOUGHT	MISVOCALIZATION	MIXOTROPHIC
MISSIONIZATION	MISTHOUGHTS		MIZENMASTS

MIZZENMAST
MIZZENMASTS
MIZZONITES
MNEMONICAL
MNEMONICALLY
MNEMONISTS
MNEMOTECHNIC
MNEMOTECHNICS
MNEMOTECHNIST
MNEMOTECHNISTS
MOBILISABLE
MOBILISATION
MOBILISATIONS
MOBILISERS
MOBILISING
MOBILITIES
MOBILIZABLE
MOBILIZATION
MOBILIZATIONS
MOBILIZERS
MOBILIZING
MOBLOGGERS
MOBOCRACIES
MOBOCRATIC
MOBOCRATICAL
MOCHINESSES
MOCKERNUTS
MOCKINGBIRD
MOCKINGBIRDS
MOCKUMENTARIES
MOCKUMENTARY
MODALISTIC
MODALITIES
MODELLINGS
MODERATELY
MODERATENESS
MODERATENESSES
MODERATING
MODERATION
MODERATIONS
MODERATISM
MODERATISMS
MODERATORS
MODERATORSHIP
MODERATORSHIPS
MODERATRICES
MODERATRIX
MODERATRIXES
MODERNISATION
MODERNISATIONS
MODERNISED
MODERNISER
MODERNISERS
MODERNISES
MODERNISING
MODERNISMS
MODERNISTIC
MODERNISTICALLY
MODERNISTS

MODERNITIES
MODERNIZATION
MODERNIZATIONS
MODERNIZED
MODERNIZER
MODERNIZERS
MODERNIZES
MODERNIZING
MODERNNESS
MODERNNESSES
MODIFIABILITIES
MODIFIABILITY
MODIFIABLE
MODIFIABLENESS
MODIFICATION
MODIFICATIONS
MODIFICATIVE
MODIFICATORY
MODILLIONS
MODIOLUSES
MODISHNESS
MODISHNESSES
MODULABILITIES
MODULABILITY
MODULARISED
MODULARITIES
MODULARITY
MODULARIZED
MODULATING
MODULATION
MODULATIONS
MODULATIVE
MODULATORS
MODULATORY
MOISTENERS
MOISTENING
MOISTIFIED
MOISTIFIES
MOISTIFYING
MOISTNESSES
MOISTURELESS
MOISTURISE
MOISTURISED
MOISTURISER
MOISTURISERS
MOISTURISES
MOISTURISING
MOISTURIZE
MOISTURIZED
MOISTURIZER
MOISTURIZERS
MOISTURIZES
MOISTURIZING
MOITHERING
MOLALITIES
MOLARITIES
MOLASSESES
MOLDABILITIES
MOLDABILITY

MOLDAVITES
MOLDBOARDS
MOLDINESSES
MOLECATCHER
MOLECATCHERS
MOLECULARITIES
MOLECULARITY
MOLECULARLY
MOLEHUNTER
MOLEHUNTERS
MOLENDINAR
MOLENDINARIES
MOLENDINARS
MOLENDINARY
MOLESTATION
MOLESTATIONS
MOLIMINOUS
MOLLIFIABLE
MOLLIFICATION
MOLLIFICATIONS
MOLLIFIERS
MOLLIFYING
MOLLITIOUS
MOLLUSCANS
MOLLUSCICIDAL
MOLLUSCICIDE
MOLLUSCICIDES
MOLLUSCOID
MOLLUSCOIDAL
MOLLUSCOIDS
MOLLUSCOUS
MOLLUSKANS
MOLLYCODDLE
MOLLYCODDLED
MOLLYCODDLER
MOLLYCODDLERS
MOLLYCODDLES
MOLLYCODDLING
MOLLYHAWKS
MOLLYMAWKS
MOLOCHISED
MOLOCHISES
MOLOCHISING
MOLOCHIZED
MOLOCHIZES
MOLOCHIZING
MOLYBDATES
MOLYBDENITE
MOLYBDENITES
MOLYBDENOSES
MOLYBDENOSIS
MOLYBDENOUS
MOLYBDENUM
MOLYBDENUMS
MOLYBDOSES
MOLYBDOSIS
MOMENTANEOUS
MOMENTARILY
MOMENTARINESS

MOMENTARINESSES
MOMENTOUSLY
MOMENTOUSNESS
MOMENTOUSNESSES
MONACHISMS
MONACHISTS
MONACTINAL
MONADELPHOUS
MONADICALLY
MONADIFORM
MONADISTIC
MONADNOCKS
MONADOLOGIES
MONADOLOGY
MONANDRIES
MONANDROUS
MONANTHOUS
MONARCHALLY
MONARCHIAL
MONARCHICAL
MONARCHICALLY
MONARCHIES
MONARCHISE
MONARCHISED
MONARCHISES
MONARCHISING
MONARCHISM
MONARCHISMS
MONARCHIST
MONARCHISTIC
MONARCHISTS
MONARCHIZE
MONARCHIZED
MONARCHIZES
MONARCHIZING
MONASTERIAL
MONASTERIES
MONASTICAL
MONASTICALLY
MONASTICISM
MONASTICISMS
MONAURALLY
MONCHIQUITE
MONCHIQUITES
MONDEGREEN
MONDEGREENS
MONECIOUSLY
MONERGISMS
MONESTROUS
MONETARILY
MONETARISM
MONETARISMS
MONETARIST
MONETARISTS
MONETISATION
MONETISATIONS
MONETISING
MONETIZATION
MONETIZATIONS

MONETIZING
MONEYCHANGER
MONEYCHANGERS
MONEYGRUBBING
MONEYGRUBBINGS
MONEYLENDER
MONEYLENDERS
MONEYLENDING
MONEYLENDINGS
MONEYMAKER
MONEYMAKERS
MONEYMAKING
MONEYMAKINGS
MONEYSPINNING
MONEYWORTS
MONGERINGS
MONGOLISMS
MONGOLOIDS
MONGRELISATION
MONGRELISATIONS
MONGRELISE
MONGRELISED
MONGRELISER
MONGRELISERS
MONGRELISES
MONGRELISING
MONGRELISM
MONGRELISMS
MONGRELIZATION
MONGRELIZATIONS
MONGRELIZE
MONGRELIZED
MONGRELIZER
MONGRELIZERS
MONGRELIZES
MONGRELIZING
MONILIASES
MONILIASIS
MONILIFORM
MONISTICAL
MONISTICALLY
MONITORIAL
MONITORIALLY
MONITORIES
MONITORING
MONITORSHIP
MONITORSHIPS
MONITRESSES
MONKEYGLAND
MONKEYISMS
MONKEYPODS
MONKEYPOTS
MONKEYSHINE
MONKEYSHINES
MONKFISHES
MONKISHNESS
MONKISHNESSES
MONKSHOODS
MONOACIDIC

MONOAMINERGIC
MONOAMINES
MONOATOMIC
MONOBLEPSES
MONOBLEPSIS
MONOCARBOXYLIC
MONOCARDIAN
MONOCARPELLARY
MONOCARPIC
MONOCARPOUS
MONOCEROSES
MONOCEROUS
MONOCHASIA
MONOCHASIAL
MONOCHASIUM
MONOCHLAMYDEOUS
MONOCHLORIDE
MONOCHLORIDES
MONOCHORDS
MONOCHROIC
MONOCHROICS
MONOCHROMASIES
MONOCHROMASY
MONOCHROMAT
MONOCHROMATE
MONOCHROMATES
MONOCHROMATIC
MONOCHROMATICS
MONOCHROMATISM
MONOCHROMATISMS
MONOCHROMATOR
MONOCHROMATORS
MONOCHROMATS
MONOCHROME
MONOCHROMES
MONOCHROMIC
MONOCHROMICAL
MONOCHROMIES
MONOCHROMIST
MONOCHROMISTS
MONOCHROMY
MONOCLINAL
MONOCLINALLY
MONOCLINALS
MONOCLINES
MONOCLINIC
MONOCLINISM
MONOCLINISMS
MONOCLINOUS
MONOCLONAL
MONOCLONALS
MONOCOQUES
MONOCOTYLEDON
MONOCOTYLEDONS
MONOCOTYLS
MONOCRACIES
MONOCRATIC
MONOCRYSTAL
MONOCRYSTALLINE

MONOCRYSTALS
MONOCULARLY
MONOCULARS
MONOCULOUS
MONOCULTURAL
MONOCULTURE
MONOCULTURES
MONOCYCLES
MONOCYCLIC
MONOCYTOID
MONODACTYLOUS
MONODELPHIAN
MONODELPHIC
MONODELPHOUS
MONODICALLY
MONODISPERSE
MONODRAMAS
MONODRAMATIC
MONOECIOUS
MONOECIOUSLY
MONOECISMS
MONOESTERS
MONOFILAMENT
MONOFILAMENTS
MONOGAMIES
MONOGAMIST
MONOGAMISTIC
MONOGAMISTS
MONOGAMOUS
MONOGAMOUSLY
MONOGAMOUSNESS
MONOGASTRIC
MONOGENEAN
MONOGENEANS
MONOGENESES
MONOGENESIS
MONOGENETIC
MONOGENICALLY
MONOGENIES
MONOGENISM
MONOGENISMS
MONOGENIST
MONOGENISTIC
MONOGENISTS
MONOGENOUS
MONOGLYCERIDE
MONOGLYCERIDES
MONOGONIES
MONOGRAMED
MONOGRAMING
MONOGRAMMATIC
MONOGRAMMED
MONOGRAMMER
MONOGRAMMERS
MONOGRAMMING
MONOGRAPHED
MONOGRAPHER
MONOGRAPHERS
MONOGRAPHIC

MONOGRAPHICAL
MONOGRAPHICALLY
MONOGRAPHIES
MONOGRAPHING
MONOGRAPHIST
MONOGRAPHISTS
MONOGRAPHS
MONOGRAPHY
MONOGYNIAN
MONOGYNIES
MONOGYNIST
MONOGYNISTS
MONOGYNOUS
MONOHYBRID
MONOHYBRIDS
MONOHYDRATE
MONOHYDRATED
MONOHYDRATES
MONOHYDRIC
MONOHYDROGEN
MONOHYDROXY
MONOICOUSLY
MONOLATERS
MONOLATRIES
MONOLATRIST
MONOLATRISTS
MONOLATROUS
MONOLAYERS
MONOLINGUAL
MONOLINGUALISM
MONOLINGUALISMS
MONOLINGUALS
MONOLINGUIST
MONOLINGUISTS
MONOLITHIC
MONOLITHICALLY
MONOLOGGED
MONOLOGGING
MONOLOGICAL
MONOLOGIES
MONOLOGISE
MONOLOGISED
MONOLOGISES
MONOLOGISING
MONOLOGIST
MONOLOGISTS
MONOLOGIZE
MONOLOGIZED
MONOLOGIZES
MONOLOGIZING
MONOLOGUED
MONOLOGUES
MONOLOGUING
MONOLOGUISE
MONOLOGUISED
MONOLOGUISES
MONOLOGUISING
MONOLOGUIST
MONOLOGUISTS

MONOLOGUIZE
MONOLOGUIZED
MONOLOGUIZES
MONOLOGUIZING
MONOMACHIA
MONOMACHIAS
MONOMACHIES
MONOMANIAC
MONOMANIACAL
MONOMANIACALLY
MONOMANIACS
MONOMANIAS
MONOMEROUS
MONOMETALLIC
MONOMETALLISM
MONOMETALLISMS
MONOMETALLIST
MONOMETALLISTS
MONOMETERS
MONOMETRIC
MONOMETRICAL
MONOMOLECULAR
MONOMOLECULARLY
MONOMORPHEMIC
MONOMORPHIC
MONOMORPHISM
MONOMORPHISMS
MONOMORPHOUS
MONOMYARIAN
MONONUCLEAR
MONONUCLEARS
MONONUCLEATE
MONONUCLEATED
MONONUCLEOSES
MONONUCLEOSIS
MONONUCLEOTIDE
MONONUCLEOTIDES
MONOPETALOUS
MONOPHAGIES
MONOPHAGOUS
MONOPHASIC
MONOPHOBIA
MONOPHOBIAS
MONOPHOBIC
MONOPHOBICS
MONOPHONIC
MONOPHONICALLY
MONOPHONIES
MONOPHOSPHATE
MONOPHOSPHATES
MONOPHTHONG
MONOPHTHONGAL
MONOPHTHONGISE
MONOPHTHONGISED
MONOPHTHONGISES
MONOPHTHONGIZE
MONOPHTHONGIZED
MONOPHTHONGIZES
MONOPHTHONGS

MONOPHYLETIC
MONOPHYLIES
MONOPHYLLOUS
MONOPHYODONT
MONOPHYODONTS
MONOPHYSITE
MONOPHYSITES
MONOPHYSITIC
MONOPHYSITISM
MONOPHYSITISMS
MONOPLANES
MONOPLEGIA
MONOPLEGIAS
MONOPLEGIC
MONOPLOIDS
MONOPODIAL
MONOPODIALLY
MONOPODIES
MONOPODIUM
MONOPOLIES
MONOPOLISATION
MONOPOLISATIONS
MONOPOLISE
MONOPOLISED
MONOPOLISER
MONOPOLISERS
MONOPOLISES
MONOPOLISING
MONOPOLISM
MONOPOLISMS
MONOPOLIST
MONOPOLISTIC
MONOPOLISTS
MONOPOLIZATION
MONOPOLIZATIONS
MONOPOLIZE
MONOPOLIZED
MONOPOLIZER
MONOPOLIZERS
MONOPOLIZES
MONOPOLIZING
MONOPRIONIDIAN
MONOPROPELLANT
MONOPROPELLANTS
MONOPSONIES
MONOPSONIST
MONOPSONISTIC
MONOPSONISTS
MONOPTERAL
MONOPTEROI
MONOPTERON
MONOPTEROS
MONOPTEROSES
MONOPTOTES
MONOPULSES
MONORCHIDISM
MONORCHIDISMS
MONORCHIDS
MONORCHISM

MONORCHISMS
MONORHINAL
MONORHYMED
MONORHYMES
MONOSACCHARIDE
MONOSACCHARIDES
MONOSATURATED
MONOSEMIES
MONOSEPALOUS
MONOSKIERS
MONOSKIING
MONOSKIINGS
MONOSODIUM
MONOSOMICS
MONOSOMIES
MONOSPACED
MONOSPECIFIC
MONOSPECIFICITY
MONOSPERMAL
MONOSPERMOUS
MONOSTABLE
MONOSTELES
MONOSTELIC
MONOSTELIES
MONOSTICHIC
MONOSTICHOUS
MONOSTICHS
MONOSTOMOUS
MONOSTROPHE
MONOSTROPHES
MONOSTROPHIC
MONOSTROPHICS
MONOSTYLAR
MONOSTYLOUS
MONOSYLLABIC
MONOSYLLABICITY
MONOSYLLABISM
MONOSYLLABISMS
MONOSYLLABLE
MONOSYLLABLES
MONOSYMMETRIC
MONOSYMMETRICAL
MONOSYMMETRIES
MONOSYMMETRY
MONOSYNAPTIC
MONOTELEPHONE
MONOTELEPHONES
MONOTERPENE
MONOTERPENES
MONOTHALAMIC
MONOTHALAMOUS
MONOTHECAL
MONOTHECOUS
MONOTHEISM
MONOTHEISMS
MONOTHEIST
MONOTHEISTIC
MONOTHEISTICAL
MONOTHEISTS

MONOTHELETE
MONOTHELETES
MONOTHELETIC
MONOTHELETICAL
MONOTHELETISM
MONOTHELETISMS
MONOTHELISM
MONOTHELISMS
MONOTHELITE
MONOTHELITES
MONOTHELITISM
MONOTHELITISMS
MONOTOCOUS
MONOTONICALLY
MONOTONICITIES
MONOTONICITY
MONOTONIES
MONOTONING
MONOTONISE
MONOTONISED
MONOTONISES
MONOTONISING
MONOTONIZE
MONOTONIZED
MONOTONIZES
MONOTONIZING
MONOTONOUS
MONOTONOUSLY
MONOTONOUSNESS
MONOTREMATOUS
MONOTREMES
MONOTRICHIC
MONOTRICHOUS
MONOTROCHS
MONOUNSATURATE
MONOUNSATURATED
MONOUNSATURATES
MONOVALENCE
MONOVALENCES
MONOVALENCIES
MONOVALENCY
MONOVALENT
MONOXYLONS
MONOXYLOUS
MONOZYGOTIC
MONOZYGOUS
MONSEIGNEUR
MONSIGNORI
MONSIGNORIAL
MONSIGNORS
MONSTERING
MONSTERINGS
MONSTRANCE
MONSTRANCES
MONSTROSITIES
MONSTROSITY
MONSTROUSLY
MONSTROUSNESS
MONSTROUSNESSES

MONSTRUOSITIES	MOONSHINERS	MORIBUNDLY	MORTALIZES
MONSTRUOSITY	MOONSHINES	MORIGERATE	MORTALIZING
MONSTRUOUS	MOONSHINING	MORIGERATION	MORTARBOARD
MONTADALES	MOONSTONES	MORIGERATIONS	MORTARBOARDS
MONTAGNARD	MOONSTRICKEN	MORIGEROUS	MORTARLESS
MONTAGNARDS	MOONSTRIKE	MORONICALLY	MORTCLOTHS
MONTBRETIA	MOONSTRIKES	MORONITIES	MORTGAGEABLE
MONTBRETIAS	MOONSTRUCK	MOROSENESS	MORTGAGEES
MONTELIMAR	MOONWALKED	MOROSENESSES	MORTGAGERS
MONTELIMARS	MOONWALKER	MOROSITIES	MORTGAGING
MONTGOLFIER	MOONWALKERS	MORPHACTIN	MORTGAGORS
MONTGOLFIERS	MOONWALKING	MORPHACTINS	MORTICIANS
MONTHLINGS	MOORBUZZARD	MORPHALLAXES	MORTIFEROUS
MONTICELLITE	MOORBUZZARDS	MORPHALLAXIS	MORTIFEROUSNESS
MONTICELLITES	MOOSEBIRDS	MORPHEMICALLY	MORTIFICATION
MONTICOLOUS	MOOSEWOODS	MORPHEMICS	MORTIFICATIONS
MONTICULATE	MOOSEYARDS	MORPHINISM	MORTIFIERS
MONTICULES	MOOTNESSES	MORPHINISMS	MORTIFYING
MONTICULOUS	MOPINESSES	MORPHINOMANIA	MORTIFYINGLY
MONTICULUS	MOPISHNESS	MORPHINOMANIAC	MORTIFYINGS
MONTICULUSES	MOPISHNESSES	MORPHINOMANIACS	MORTUARIES
MONTMORILLONITE	MORALISATION	MORPHINOMANIAS	MORULATION
MONUMENTAL	MORALISATIONS	MORPHOGENESES	MORULATIONS
MONUMENTALISE	MORALISERS	MORPHOGENESIS	MOSAICALLY
MONUMENTALISED	MORALISING	MORPHOGENETIC	MOSAICISMS
MONUMENTALISES	MORALISTIC	MORPHOGENIC	MOSAICISTS
MONUMENTALISING	MORALISTICALLY	MORPHOGENIES	MOSAICKING
MONUMENTALITIES	MORALITIES	MORPHOGENS	MOSAICLIKE
MONUMENTALITY	MORALIZATION	MORPHOGENY	MOSASAURUS
MONUMENTALIZE	MORALIZATIONS	MORPHOGRAPHER	MOSBOLLETJIE
MONUMENTALIZED	MORALIZERS	MORPHOGRAPHERS	MOSBOLLETJIES
MONUMENTALIZES	MORALIZING	MORPHOGRAPHIES	MOSCHATELS
MONUMENTALIZING	MORATORIUM	MORPHOGRAPHY	MOSCHIFEROUS
MONUMENTALLY	MORATORIUMS	MORPHOLOGIC	MOSKONFYTS
MONUMENTED	MORBIDEZZA	MORPHOLOGICAL	MOSQUITOES
MONUMENTING	MORBIDEZZAS	MORPHOLOGICALLY	MOSQUITOEY
MONZONITES	MORBIDITIES	MORPHOLOGIES	MOSSBACKED
MONZONITIC	MORBIDNESS	MORPHOLOGIST	MOSSBLUITER
MOODINESSES	MORBIDNESSES	MORPHOLOGISTS	MOSSBLUITERS
MOONCALVES	MORBIFEROUS	MORPHOLOGY	MOSSBUNKER
MOONCHILDREN	MORBIFICALLY	MORPHOMETRIC	MOSSBUNKERS
MOONFISHES	MORBILLIFORM	MORPHOMETRICS	MOSSINESSES
MOONFLOWER	MORBILLIVIRUS	MORPHOMETRIES	MOSSPLANTS
MOONFLOWERS	MORBILLIVIRUSES	MORPHOMETRY	MOSSTROOPER
MOONINESSES	MORBILLOUS	MORPHOPHONEME	MOSSTROOPERS
MOONLIGHTED	MORDACIOUS	MORPHOPHONEMES	MOTETTISTS
MOONLIGHTER	MORDACIOUSLY	MORPHOPHONEMIC	MOTHBALLED
MOONLIGHTERS	MORDACIOUSNESS	MORPHOPHONEMICS	MOTHBALLING
MOONLIGHTING	MORDACITIES	MORPHOTROPIC	MOTHERBOARD
MOONLIGHTINGS	MORDANCIES	MORPHOTROPIES	MOTHERBOARDS
MOONLIGHTS	MORDANTING	MORPHOTROPY	MOTHERCRAFT
MOONPHASES	MORENESSES	MORSELLING	MOTHERCRAFTS
MOONQUAKES	MORGANATIC	MORTADELLA	MOTHERESES
MOONRAKERS	MORGANATICALLY	MORTADELLAS	MOTHERFUCKER
MOONRAKING	MORGANITES	MORTALISED	MOTHERFUCKERS
MOONRAKINGS	MORGENSTERN	MORTALISES	MOTHERFUCKING
MOONSCAPES	MORGENSTERNS	MORTALISING	MOTHERHOOD
MOONSHINED	MORIBUNDITIES	MORTALITIES	MOTHERHOODS
MOONSHINER	MORIBUNDITY	MORTALIZED	MOTHERHOUSE

MOTHERHOUSES
MOTHERINGS
MOTHERLAND
MOTHERLANDS
MOTHERLESS
MOTHERLESSNESS
MOTHERLINESS
MOTHERLINESSES
MOTHERWORT
MOTHERWORTS
MOTHPROOFED
MOTHPROOFER
MOTHPROOFERS
MOTHPROOFING
MOTHPROOFS
MOTILITIES
MOTIONISTS
MOTIONLESS
MOTIONLESSLY
MOTIONLESSNESS
MOTIVATING
MOTIVATION
MOTIVATIONAL
MOTIVATIONALLY
MOTIVATIONS
MOTIVATIVE
MOTIVATORS
MOTIVELESS
MOTIVELESSLY
MOTIVELESSNESS
MOTIVITIES
MOTOCROSSES
MOTONEURON
MOTONEURONAL
MOTONEURONS
MOTORBICYCLE
MOTORBICYCLES
MOTORBIKED
MOTORBIKES
MOTORBIKING
MOTORBOATED
MOTORBOATER
MOTORBOATERS
MOTORBOATING
MOTORBOATINGS
MOTORBOATS
MOTORBUSES
MOTORBUSSES
MOTORCADED
MOTORCADES
MOTORCADING
MOTORCOACH
MOTORCOACHES
MOTORCYCLE
MOTORCYCLED
MOTORCYCLES
MOTORCYCLING
MOTORCYCLIST
MOTORCYCLISTS

MOTORHOMES
MOTORICALLY
MOTORISATION
MOTORISATIONS
MOTORISING
MOTORIZATION
MOTORIZATIONS
MOTORIZING
MOTORMOUTH
MOTORMOUTHS
MOTORSHIPS
MOTORTRUCK
MOTORTRUCKS
MOUCHARABIES
MOUCHARABY
MOUDIEWART
MOUDIEWARTS
MOUDIEWORT
MOUDIEWORTS
MOUDIWARTS
MOUDIWORTS
MOULDABILITIES
MOULDABILITY
MOULDBOARD
MOULDBOARDS
MOULDERING
MOULDINESS
MOULDINESSES
MOULDWARPS
MOULDYWARP
MOULDYWARPS
MOUNDBIRDS
MOUNTAINBOARD
MOUNTAINBOARDER
MOUNTAINBOARDS
MOUNTAINED
MOUNTAINEER
MOUNTAINEERED
MOUNTAINEERING
MOUNTAINEERINGS
MOUNTAINEERS
MOUNTAINOUS
MOUNTAINOUSLY
MOUNTAINOUSNESS
MOUNTAINSIDE
MOUNTAINSIDES
MOUNTAINTOP
MOUNTAINTOPS
MOUNTEBANK
MOUNTEBANKED
MOUNTEBANKERIES
MOUNTEBANKERY
MOUNTEBANKING
MOUNTEBANKINGS
MOUNTEBANKISM
MOUNTEBANKISMS
MOUNTEBANKS
MOUNTENANCE
MOUNTENANCES

MOUNTENAUNCE
MOUNTENAUNCES
MOURNFULLER
MOURNFULLEST
MOURNFULLY
MOURNFULNESS
MOURNFULNESSES
MOURNINGLY
MOURNIVALS
MOUSEBIRDS
MOUSEOVERS
MOUSEPIECE
MOUSEPIECES
MOUSETAILS
MOUSETRAPPED
MOUSETRAPPING
MOUSETRAPS
MOUSINESSES
MOUSQUETAIRE
MOUSQUETAIRES
MOUSSELINE
MOUSSELINES
MOUSTACHED
MOUSTACHES
MOUSTACHIAL
MOUSTACHIO
MOUSTACHIOS
MOUTHBREATHER
MOUTHBREATHERS
MOUTHBREEDER
MOUTHBREEDERS
MOUTHBROODER
MOUTHBROODERS
MOUTHFEELS
MOUTHPARTS
MOUTHPIECE
MOUTHPIECES
MOUTHWASHES
MOUTHWATERING
MOUTHWATERINGLY
MOUVEMENTE
MOVABILITIES
MOVABILITY
MOVABLENESS
MOVABLENESSES
MOVEABILITIES
MOVEABILITY
MOVEABLENESS
MOVEABLENESSES
MOVELESSLY
MOVELESSNESS
MOVELESSNESSES
MOVIEGOERS
MOVIEGOING
MOVIEGOINGS
MOVIELANDS
MOVIEMAKER
MOVIEMAKERS
MOVIEMAKING

MOVIEMAKINGS
MOWBURNING
MOWDIEWART
MOWDIEWARTS
MOWDIEWORT
MOWDIEWORTS
MOXIBUSTION
MOXIBUSTIONS
MOYGASHELS
MOZZARELLA
MOZZARELLAS
MRIDAMGAMS
MRIDANGAMS
MUCEDINOUS
MUCHNESSES
MUCIDITIES
MUCIDNESSES
MUCIFEROUS
MUCILAGINOUS
MUCILAGINOUSLY
MUCINOGENS
MUCKAMUCKED
MUCKAMUCKING
MUCKAMUCKS
MUCKENDERS
MUCKINESSES
MUCKRAKERS
MUCKRAKING
MUCKRAKINGS
MUCKSPREAD
MUCKSPREADER
MUCKSPREADERS
MUCKSPREADING
MUCKSPREADS
MUCKSWEATS
MUCOCUTANEOUS
MUCOMEMBRANOUS
MUCOPEPTIDE
MUCOPEPTIDES
MUCOPROTEIN
MUCOPROTEINS
MUCOPURULENT
MUCOSANGUINEOUS
MUCOSITIES
MUCOVISCIDOSES
MUCOVISCIDOSIS
MUCRONATED
MUCRONATION
MUCRONATIONS
MUDCAPPING
MUDDINESSES
MUDDLEDNESS
MUDDLEDNESSES
MUDDLEHEAD
MUDDLEHEADED
MUDDLEHEADEDLY
MUDDLEHEADS
MUDDLEMENT
MUDDLEMENTS

MUDDLINGLY
MUDLARKING
MUDLOGGERS
MUDLOGGING
MUDLOGGINGS
MUDPUPPIES
MUDSKIPPER
MUDSKIPPERS
MUDSLINGER
MUDSLINGERS
MUDSLINGING
MUDSLINGINGS
MUFFINEERS
MUGEARITES
MUGGINESSES
MUGWUMPERIES
MUGWUMPERY
MUGWUMPISH
MUGWUMPISM
MUGWUMPISMS
MUJAHEDDIN
MUJAHEDEEN
MUJAHIDEEN
MULATTRESS
MULATTRESSES
MULBERRIES
MULIEBRITIES
MULIEBRITY
MULISHNESS
MULISHNESSES
MULLAHISMS
MULLARKIES
MULLIGATAWNIES
MULLIGATAWNY
MULLIGRUBS
MULLIONING
MULTANGULAR
MULTANIMOUS
MULTARTICULATE
MULTEITIES
MULTIACCESS
MULTIACCESSES
MULTIAGENCY
MULTIANGULAR
MULTIARMED
MULTIARTICULATE
MULTIAUTHOR
MULTIAXIAL
MULTIBARREL
MULTIBARRELED
MULTIBILLION
MULTIBLADED
MULTIBRANCHED
MULTIBUILDING
MULTICAMERATE
MULTICAMPUS
MULTICAPITATE
MULTICARBON
MULTICASTS

MULTICAULINE
MULTICAUSAL
MULTICELLED
MULTICELLULAR
MULTICENTER
MULTICENTRAL
MULTICENTRIC
MULTICHAIN
MULTICHAMBERED
MULTICHANNEL
MULTICHARACTER
MULTICIDES
MULTICIPITAL
MULTICLIENT
MULTICOATED
MULTICOLOR
MULTICOLORED
MULTICOLORS
MULTICOLOUR
MULTICOLOURED
MULTICOLOURS
MULTICOLUMN
MULTICOMPONENT
MULTICONDUCTOR
MULTICOSTATE
MULTICOUNTY
MULTICOURSE
MULTICULTURAL
MULTICURIE
MULTICURRENCIES
MULTICURRENCY
MULTICUSPID
MULTICUSPIDATE
MULTICUSPIDS
MULTICYCLE
MULTICYCLES
MULTIDENTATE
MULTIDIALECTAL
MULTIDIGITATE
MULTIDISCIPLINE
MULTIDIVISIONAL
MULTIDOMAIN
MULTIELECTRODE
MULTIELEMENT
MULTIEMPLOYER
MULTIEMPLOYERS
MULTIENGINE
MULTIENZYME
MULTIETHNIC
MULTIETHNICS
MULTIFACED
MULTIFACETED
MULTIFACTOR
MULTIFACTORIAL
MULTIFAMILY
MULTIFARIOUS
MULTIFARIOUSLY
MULTIFIDLY
MULTIFIDOUS

MULTIFILAMENT
MULTIFILAMENTS
MULTIFLASH
MULTIFLORA
MULTIFLOROUS
MULTIFOCAL
MULTIFOILS
MULTIFOLIATE
MULTIFOLIOLATE
MULTIFORMITIES
MULTIFORMITY
MULTIFORMS
MULTIFREQUENCY
MULTIFUNCTION
MULTIFUNCTIONAL
MULTIGENIC
MULTIGRADE
MULTIGRAIN
MULTIGRAVIDA
MULTIGRAVIDAE
MULTIGRAVIDAS
MULTIGROUP
MULTIHEADED
MULTIHOSPITAL
MULTIHULLS
MULTIJUGATE
MULTIJUGOUS
MULTILANES
MULTILATERAL
MULTILATERALISM
MULTILATERALIST
MULTILATERALLY
MULTILAYER
MULTILAYERED
MULTILEVEL
MULTILEVELED
MULTILINEAL
MULTILINEAR
MULTILINGUAL
MULTILINGUALISM
MULTILINGUALLY
MULTILINGUIST
MULTILINGUISTS
MULTILOBATE
MULTILOBED
MULTILOBES
MULTILOBULAR
MULTILOBULATE
MULTILOCATIONAL
MULTILOCULAR
MULTILOCULATE
MULTILOQUENCE
MULTILOQUENCES
MULTILOQUENT
MULTILOQUIES
MULTILOQUOUS
MULTILOQUY
MULTIMANNED
MULTIMEDIA

MULTIMEDIAS
MULTIMEGATON
MULTIMEGAWATT
MULTIMEGAWATTS
MULTIMEMBER
MULTIMETALLIC
MULTIMETER
MULTIMETERS
MULTIMILLENNIAL
MULTIMILLION
MULTIMODAL
MULTIMOLECULAR
MULTINATION
MULTINATIONAL
MULTINATIONALS
MULTINOMIAL
MULTINOMIALS
MULTINOMINAL
MULTINUCLEAR
MULTINUCLEATE
MULTINUCLEATED
MULTINUCLEOLATE
MULTIORGASMIC
MULTIPACKS
MULTIPANED
MULTIPARAE
MULTIPARAMETER
MULTIPARAS
MULTIPARITIES
MULTIPARITY
MULTIPAROUS
MULTIPARTICLE
MULTIPARTITE
MULTIPARTY
MULTIPARTYISM
MULTIPARTYISMS
MULTIPEDES
MULTIPHASE
MULTIPHASIC
MULTIPHOTON
MULTIPICTURE
MULTIPIECE
MULTIPISTON
MULTIPLANE
MULTIPLANES
MULTIPLANT
MULTIPLAYER
MULTIPLAYERS
MULTIPLETS
MULTIPLEXED
MULTIPLEXER
MULTIPLEXERS
MULTIPLEXES
MULTIPLEXING
MULTIPLEXOR
MULTIPLEXORS
MULTIPLIABLE
MULTIPLICABLE
MULTIPLICAND

MULTIPLICANDS

MULTIPLICANDS
MULTIPLICATE
MULTIPLICATES
MULTIPLICATION
MULTIPLICATIONS
MULTIPLICATIVE
MULTIPLICATOR
MULTIPLICATORS
MULTIPLICITIES
MULTIPLICITY
MULTIPLIED
MULTIPLIER
MULTIPLIERS
MULTIPLIES
MULTIPLYING
MULTIPOLAR
MULTIPOLARITIES
MULTIPOLARITY
MULTIPOLES
MULTIPOTENT
MULTIPOTENTIAL
MULTIPOWER
MULTIPRESENCE
MULTIPRESENCES
MULTIPRESENT
MULTIPROBLEM
MULTIPROCESSING
MULTIPROCESSOR
MULTIPROCESSORS
MULTIPRODUCT
MULTIPRONGED
MULTIPURPOSE
MULTIRACIAL
MULTIRACIALISM
MULTIRACIALISMS
MULTIRAMIFIED
MULTIRANGE
MULTIREGIONAL
MULTIRELIGIOUS
MULTISCIENCE
MULTISCIENCES
MULTISCREEN
MULTISENSE
MULTISENSORY
MULTISEPTATE
MULTISERIAL
MULTISERIATE
MULTISERVICE
MULTISIDED
MULTISKILL
MULTISKILLED
MULTISKILLING
MULTISKILLINGS
MULTISKILLS
MULTISONANT
MULTISOURCE
MULTISPECIES
MULTISPECTRAL
MULTISPEED

MULTISPIRAL
MULTISPORT
MULTISTAGE
MULTISTATE
MULTISTEMMED
MULTISTOREY
MULTISTOREYS
MULTISTORIED
MULTISTORY
MULTISTRANDED
MULTISTRIKE
MULTISTRIKES
MULTISULCATE
MULTISYLLABIC
MULTISYSTEM
MULTITALENTED
MULTITASKED
MULTITASKING
MULTITASKINGS
MULTITASKS
MULTITERMINAL
MULTITHREADING
MULTITHREADINGS
MULTITIERED
MULTITONES
MULTITOWERED
MULTITRACK
MULTITRILLION
MULTITUDES
MULTITUDINARY
MULTITUDINOUS
MULTITUDINOUSLY
MULTIUNION
MULTIVALENCE
MULTIVALENCES
MULTIVALENCIES
MULTIVALENCY
MULTIVALENT
MULTIVALENTS
MULTIVARIABLE
MULTIVARIATE
MULTIVARIOUS
MULTIVERSE
MULTIVERSES
MULTIVERSITIES
MULTIVERSITY
MULTIVIBRATOR
MULTIVIBRATORS
MULTIVIOUS
MULTIVITAMIN
MULTIVITAMINS
MULTIVOCAL
MULTIVOCALS
MULTIVOLTINE
MULTIVOLUME
MULTIWARHEAD
MULTIWAVELENGTH
MULTIWINDOW
MULTIWINDOWS

MULTOCULAR
MULTUNGULATE
MULTUNGULATES
MUMBLEMENT
MUMBLEMENTS
MUMBLETYPEG
MUMBLETYPEGS
MUMBLINGLY
MUMCHANCES
MUMMICHOGS
MUMMIFICATION
MUMMIFICATIONS
MUMMIFYING
MUMPISHNESS
MUMPISHNESSES
MUMPSIMUSES
MUNCHABLES
MUNDANENESS
MUNDANENESSES
MUNDANITIES
MUNDIFICATION
MUNDIFICATIONS
MUNDIFICATIVE
MUNDIFYING
MUNDUNGUSES
MUNICIPALISE
MUNICIPALISED
MUNICIPALISES
MUNICIPALISING
MUNICIPALISM
MUNICIPALISMS
MUNICIPALIST
MUNICIPALISTS
MUNICIPALITIES
MUNICIPALITY
MUNICIPALIZE
MUNICIPALIZED
MUNICIPALIZES
MUNICIPALIZING
MUNICIPALLY
MUNICIPALS
MUNIFICENCE
MUNIFICENCES
MUNIFICENT
MUNIFICENTLY
MUNIFICENTNESS
MUNIFIENCE
MUNIFIENCES
MUNITIONED
MUNITIONEER
MUNITIONEERS
MUNITIONER
MUNITIONERS
MUNITIONETTE
MUNITIONETTES
MUNITIONING
MURDERESSES
MURDEROUSLY
MURDEROUSNESS

MURDEROUSNESSES
MURGEONING
MURKINESSES
MURMURATION
MURMURATIONS
MURMURINGLY
MURMURINGS
MURMUROUSLY
MURTHERERS
MURTHERING
MUSCADELLE
MUSCADELLES
MUSCADINES
MUSCARDINE
MUSCARDINES
MUSCARINES
MUSCARINIC
MUSCATORIA
MUSCATORIUM
MUSCAVADOS
MUSCOLOGIES
MUSCOVADOS
MUSCOVITES
MUSCULARITIES
MUSCULARITY
MUSCULARLY
MUSCULATION
MUSCULATIONS
MUSCULATURE
MUSCULATURES
MUSCULOSKELETAL
MUSEOLOGICAL
MUSEOLOGIES
MUSEOLOGIST
MUSEOLOGISTS
MUSHINESSES
MUSHMOUTHS
MUSHROOMED
MUSHROOMER
MUSHROOMERS
MUSHROOMING
MUSICALISATION
MUSICALISATIONS
MUSICALISE
MUSICALISED
MUSICALISES
MUSICALISING
MUSICALITIES
MUSICALITY
MUSICALIZATION
MUSICALIZATIONS
MUSICALIZE
MUSICALIZED
MUSICALIZES
MUSICALIZING
MUSICALNESS
MUSICALNESSES
MUSICIANER
MUSICIANERS

MUSICIANLY
MUSICIANSHIP
MUSICIANSHIPS
MUSICOLOGICAL
MUSICOLOGICALLY
MUSICOLOGIES
MUSICOLOGIST
MUSICOLOGISTS
MUSICOLOGY
MUSICOTHERAPIES
MUSICOTHERAPY
MUSKELLUNGE
MUSKELLUNGES
MUSKETEERS
MUSKETOONS
MUSKETRIES
MUSKINESSES
MUSKMELONS
MUSQUASHES
MUSQUETOON
MUSQUETOONS
MUSSELCRACKER
MUSSELCRACKERS
MUSSINESSES
MUSSITATED
MUSSITATES
MUSSITATING
MUSSITATION
MUSSITATIONS
MUSTACHIOED
MUSTACHIOS
MUSTELINES
MUSTINESSES
MUTABILITIES
MUTABILITY
MUTABLENESS
MUTABLENESSES
MUTAGENESES
MUTAGENESIS
MUTAGENICALLY
MUTAGENICITIES
MUTAGENICITY
MUTAGENISE
MUTAGENISED
MUTAGENISES
MUTAGENISING
MUTAGENIZE
MUTAGENIZED
MUTAGENIZES
MUTAGENIZING
MUTATIONAL
MUTATIONALLY
MUTATIONIST
MUTATIONISTS
MUTENESSES
MUTESSARIF
MUTESSARIFAT
MUTESSARIFATS
MUTESSARIFS

MUTILATING
MUTILATION
MUTILATIONS
MUTILATIVE
MUTILATORS
MUTINEERED
MUTINEERING
MUTINOUSLY
MUTINOUSNESS
MUTINOUSNESSES
MUTOSCOPES
MUTTERATION
MUTTERATIONS
MUTTERINGLY
MUTTERINGS
MUTTONBIRD
MUTTONBIRDS
MUTTONCHOPS
MUTTONFISH
MUTTONFISHES
MUTTONHEAD
MUTTONHEADED
MUTTONHEADS
MUTUALISATION
MUTUALISATIONS
MUTUALISED
MUTUALISES
MUTUALISING
MUTUALISMS
MUTUALISTIC
MUTUALISTS
MUTUALITIES
MUTUALIZATION
MUTUALIZATIONS
MUTUALIZED
MUTUALIZES
MUTUALIZING
MUTUALNESS
MUTUALNESSES
MUZZINESSES
MYASTHENIA
MYASTHENIAS
MYASTHENIC
MYASTHENICS
MYCETOLOGIES
MYCETOLOGY
MYCETOMATA
MYCETOMATOUS
MYCETOPHAGOUS
MYCETOZOAN
MYCETOZOANS
MYCOBACTERIA
MYCOBACTERIAL
MYCOBACTERIUM
MYCOBIONTS
MYCODOMATIA
MYCODOMATIUM
MYCOFLORAE
MYCOFLORAS

MYCOLOGICAL
MYCOLOGICALLY
MYCOLOGIES
MYCOLOGIST
MYCOLOGISTS
MYCOPHAGIES
MYCOPHAGIST
MYCOPHAGISTS
MYCOPHAGOUS
MYCOPHILES
MYCOPLASMA
MYCOPLASMAL
MYCOPLASMAS
MYCOPLASMATA
MYCOPLASMOSES
MYCOPLASMOSIS
MYCORHIZAE
MYCORHIZAL
MYCORHIZAS
MYCORRHIZA
MYCORRHIZAE
MYCORRHIZAL
MYCORRHIZAS
MYCOTOXICOSES
MYCOTOXICOSIS
MYCOTOXINS
MYCOTOXOLOGIES
MYCOTOXOLOGY
MYCOTROPHIC
MYCOVIRUSES
MYDRIATICS
MYELENCEPHALA
MYELENCEPHALIC
MYELENCEPHALON
MYELENCEPHALONS
MYELINATED
MYELITIDES
MYELITISES
MYELOBLAST
MYELOBLASTIC
MYELOBLASTS
MYELOCYTES
MYELOCYTIC
MYELOFIBROSES
MYELOFIBROSIS
MYELOFIBROTIC
MYELOGENOUS
MYELOGRAMS
MYELOGRAPHIES
MYELOGRAPHY
MYELOMATOID
MYELOMATOUS
MYELOPATHIC
MYELOPATHIES
MYELOPATHY
MYIOPHILIES
MYIOPHILOUS
MYLOHYOIDS
MYLONITISATION

MYLONITISATIONS
MYLONITISE
MYLONITISED
MYLONITISES
MYLONITISING
MYLONITIZATION
MYLONITIZATIONS
MYLONITIZE
MYLONITIZED
MYLONITIZES
MYLONITIZING
MYOBLASTIC
MYOCARDIAL
MYOCARDIOGRAPH
MYOCARDIOGRAPHS
MYOCARDIOPATHY
MYOCARDITIS
MYOCARDITISES
MYOCARDIUM
MYOCARDIUMS
MYOCLONUSES
MYOELECTRIC
MYOELECTRICAL
MYOFIBRILLAR
MYOFIBRILS
MYOFILAMENT
MYOFILAMENTS
MYOGLOBINS
MYOGRAPHIC
MYOGRAPHICAL
MYOGRAPHICALLY
MYOGRAPHIES
MYOGRAPHIST
MYOGRAPHISTS
MYOINOSITOL
MYOINOSITOLS
MYOLOGICAL
MYOLOGISTS
MYOMANCIES
MYOMECTOMIES
MYOMECTOMY
MYOPATHIES
MYOPHILIES
MYOPHILOUS
MYOPICALLY
MYOSITISES
MYOSOTISES
MYRIADFOLD
MYRIADFOLDS
MYRIAPODAN
MYRIAPODOUS
MYRINGITIS
MYRINGITISES
MYRINGOSCOPE
MYRINGOSCOPES
MYRINGOTOMIES
MYRINGOTOMY
MYRIORAMAS
MYRIOSCOPE

MYRIOSCOPES
MYRISTICIVOROUS
MYRMECOCHORIES
MYRMECOCHORY
MYRMECOLOGIC
MYRMECOLOGICAL
MYRMECOLOGIES
MYRMECOLOGIST
MYRMECOLOGISTS
MYRMECOLOGY
MYRMECOPHAGOUS
MYRMECOPHILE
MYRMECOPHILES
MYRMECOPHILIES
MYRMECOPHILOUS
MYRMECOPHILY
MYRMIDONES
MYRMIDONIAN
MYROBALANS
MYRTACEOUS
MYSOPHOBIA
MYSOPHOBIAS
MYSTAGOGIC
MYSTAGOGICAL
MYSTAGOGICALLY
MYSTAGOGIES
MYSTAGOGUE
MYSTAGOGUES
MYSTAGOGUS
MYSTAGOGUSES
MYSTERIOUS
MYSTERIOUSLY
MYSTERIOUSNESS
MYSTICALLY
MYSTICALNESS
MYSTICALNESSES
MYSTICETES
MYSTICISMS
MYSTIFICATION
MYSTIFICATIONS
MYSTIFIERS
MYSTIFYING
MYSTIFYINGLY
MYTHICALLY
MYTHICISATION
MYTHICISATIONS
MYTHICISED
MYTHICISER
MYTHICISERS
MYTHICISES
MYTHICISING
MYTHICISMS
MYTHICISTS
MYTHICIZATION
MYTHICIZATIONS
MYTHICIZED
MYTHICIZER
MYTHICIZERS
MYTHICIZES

MYTHICIZING
MYTHMAKERS
MYTHMAKING
MYTHMAKINGS
MYTHOGENESES
MYTHOGENESIS
MYTHOGRAPHER
MYTHOGRAPHERS
MYTHOGRAPHIES
MYTHOGRAPHY
MYTHOLOGER
MYTHOLOGERS
MYTHOLOGIAN
MYTHOLOGIANS
MYTHOLOGIC
MYTHOLOGICAL
MYTHOLOGICALLY
MYTHOLOGIES
MYTHOLOGISATION
MYTHOLOGISE
MYTHOLOGISED
MYTHOLOGISER
MYTHOLOGISERS
MYTHOLOGISES
MYTHOLOGISING
MYTHOLOGIST
MYTHOLOGISTS
MYTHOLOGIZATION
MYTHOLOGIZE
MYTHOLOGIZED
MYTHOLOGIZER
MYTHOLOGIZERS
MYTHOLOGIZES
MYTHOLOGIZING
MYTHOMANES
MYTHOMANIA
MYTHOMANIAC
MYTHOMANIACS
MYTHOMANIAS
MYTHOPOEIA
MYTHOPOEIAS
MYTHOPOEIC
MYTHOPOEISM
MYTHOPOEISMS
MYTHOPOEIST
MYTHOPOEISTS
MYTHOPOESES
MYTHOPOESIS
MYTHOPOETIC
MYTHOPOETICAL
MYTHOPOETS
MYTILIFORM
MYXAMOEBAE
MYXAMOEBAS
MYXEDEMATOUS
MYXOEDEMAS
MYXOEDEMATOUS
MYXOEDEMIC
MYXOMATOSES

MYXOMATOSIS
MYXOMATOUS
MYXOMYCETE
MYXOMYCETES
MYXOMYCETOUS
MYXOVIRUSES

N

NABOBERIES
NABOBESSES
NACHTMAALS
NAFFNESSES
NAIFNESSES
NAILBITERS
NAILBRUSHES
NAISSANCES
NAIVENESSES
NAKEDNESSES
NALBUPHINE
NALBUPHINES
NALORPHINE
NALORPHINES
NALTREXONE
NALTREXONES
NAMAYCUSHES
NAMECHECKED
NAMECHECKING
NAMECHECKS
NAMELESSLY
NAMELESSNESS
NAMELESSNESSES
NAMEPLATES
NAMEWORTHY
NANDROLONE
NANDROLONES
NANISATION
NANISATIONS
NANIZATION
NANIZATIONS
NANNOPLANKTON
NANNOPLANKTONS
NANOGRAMME
NANOGRAMMES
NANOMATERIAL
NANOMATERIALS
NANOMETERS
NANOMETRES
NANOPARTICLE
NANOPARTICLES
NANOPHYSICS
NANOPLANKTON
NANOPLANKTONS
NANOSECOND
NANOSECONDS
NANOTECHNOLOGY
NANOTESLAS
NANOWORLDS
NAPHTHALENE
NAPHTHALENES
NAPHTHALIC
NAPHTHALIN

NAPHTHALINE
NAPHTHALINES
NAPHTHALINS
NAPHTHALISE
NAPHTHALISED
NAPHTHALISES
NAPHTHALISING
NAPHTHALIZE
NAPHTHALIZED
NAPHTHALIZES
NAPHTHALIZING
NAPHTHENES
NAPHTHENIC
NAPHTHYLAMINE
NAPHTHYLAMINES
NAPOLEONITE
NAPOLEONITES
NAPPINESSES
NAPRAPATHIES
NAPRAPATHY
NARCISSISM
NARCISSISMS
NARCISSIST
NARCISSISTIC
NARCISSISTS
NARCISSUSES
NARCOANALYSES
NARCOANALYSIS
NARCOCATHARSES
NARCOCATHARSIS
NARCOHYPNOSES
NARCOHYPNOSIS
NARCOLEPSIES
NARCOLEPSY
NARCOLEPTIC
NARCOLEPTICS
NARCOSYNTHESES
NARCOSYNTHESIS
NARCOTERRORISM
NARCOTERRORISMS
NARCOTERRORIST
NARCOTERRORISTS
NARCOTICALLY
NARCOTINES
NARCOTISATION
NARCOTISATIONS
NARCOTISED
NARCOTISES
NARCOTISING
NARCOTISMS
NARCOTISTS
NARCOTIZATION
NARCOTIZATIONS

NARCOTIZED
NARCOTIZES
NARCOTIZING
NARGHILIES
NARGHILLIES
NARRATABLE
NARRATIONAL
NARRATIONS
NARRATIVELY
NARRATIVES
NARRATOLOGICAL
NARRATOLOGIES
NARRATOLOGIST
NARRATOLOGISTS
NARRATOLOGY
NARROWBAND
NARROWBANDS
NARROWCAST
NARROWCASTED
NARROWCASTING
NARROWCASTINGS
NARROWCASTS
NARROWINGS
NARROWNESS
NARROWNESSES
NASALISATION
NASALISATIONS
NASALISING
NASALITIES
NASALIZATION
NASALIZATIONS
NASALIZING
NASCENCIES
NASEBERRIES
NASOFRONTAL
NASOGASTRIC
NASOLACRYMAL
NASOPHARYNGEAL
NASOPHARYNGES
NASOPHARYNX
NASOPHARYNXES
NASTINESSES
NASTURTIUM
NASTURTIUMS
NATALITIAL
NATALITIES
NATATIONAL
NATATORIAL
NATATORIUM
NATATORIUMS
NATHELESSE
NATIONALISATION
NATIONALISE

NATIONALISED
NATIONALISER
NATIONALISERS
NATIONALISES
NATIONALISING
NATIONALISM
NATIONALISMS
NATIONALIST
NATIONALISTIC
NATIONALISTS
NATIONALITIES
NATIONALITY
NATIONALIZATION
NATIONALIZE
NATIONALIZED
NATIONALIZER
NATIONALIZERS
NATIONALIZES
NATIONALIZING
NATIONALLY
NATIONHOOD
NATIONHOODS
NATIONLESS
NATIONWIDE
NATIVENESS
NATIVENESSES
NATIVISTIC
NATIVITIES
NATRIURESES
NATRIURESIS
NATRIURETIC
NATRIURETICS
NATROLITES
NATTERJACK
NATTERJACKS
NATTINESSES
NATURALISATION
NATURALISATIONS
NATURALISE
NATURALISED
NATURALISES
NATURALISING
NATURALISM
NATURALISMS
NATURALIST
NATURALISTIC
NATURALISTS
NATURALIZATION
NATURALIZATIONS
NATURALIZE
NATURALIZED
NATURALIZES
NATURALIZING

NATURALNESS
NATURALNESSES
NATURISTIC
NATUROPATH
NATUROPATHIC
NATUROPATHIES
NATUROPATHS
NATUROPATHY
NAUGAHYDES
NAUGHTIEST
NAUGHTINESS
NAUGHTINESSES
NAUMACHIAE
NAUMACHIAS
NAUMACHIES
NAUPLIIFORM
NAUSEATING
NAUSEATINGLY
NAUSEATION
NAUSEATIONS
NAUSEATIVE
NAUSEOUSLY
NAUSEOUSNESS
NAUSEOUSNESSES
NAUTICALLY
NAUTILOIDS
NAUTILUSES
NAVARCHIES
NAVELWORTS
NAVICULARE
NAVICULARES
NAVICULARS
NAVIGABILITIES
NAVIGABILITY
NAVIGABLENESS
NAVIGABLENESSES
NAVIGATING
NAVIGATION
NAVIGATIONAL
NAVIGATIONALLY
NAVIGATIONS
NAVIGATORS
NAYSAYINGS
NAZIFICATION
NAZIFICATIONS
NEANDERTAL
NEANDERTALER
NEANDERTALERS
NEANDERTALS
NEANDERTHAL
NEANDERTHALER
NEANDERTHALERS
NEANDERTHALOID
NEANDERTHALS
NEAPOLITAN
NEAPOLITANS
NEARNESSES
NEARSIGHTED
NEARSIGHTEDLY

NEARSIGHTEDNESS
NEARTHROSES
NEARTHROSIS
NEATNESSES
NEBBISHERS
NEBENKERNS
NEBUCHADNEZZAR
NEBUCHADNEZZARS
NEBULISATION
NEBULISATIONS
NEBULISERS
NEBULISING
NEBULIZATION
NEBULIZATIONS
NEBULIZERS
NEBULIZING
NEBULOSITIES
NEBULOSITY
NEBULOUSLY
NEBULOUSNESS
NEBULOUSNESSES
NECESSAIRE
NECESSAIRES
NECESSARIAN
NECESSARIANISM
NECESSARIANISMS
NECESSARIANS
NECESSARIES
NECESSARILY
NECESSARINESS
NECESSARINESSES
NECESSITARIAN
NECESSITARIANS
NECESSITATE
NECESSITATED
NECESSITATES
NECESSITATING
NECESSITATION
NECESSITATIONS
NECESSITATIVE
NECESSITIED
NECESSITIES
NECESSITOUS
NECESSITOUSLY
NECESSITOUSNESS
NECKCLOTHS
NECKERCHIEF
NECKERCHIEFS
NECKERCHIEVES
NECKLACING
NECKLACINGS
NECKPIECES
NECKVERSES
NECROBIOSES
NECROBIOSIS
NECROBIOTIC
NECROGRAPHER
NECROGRAPHERS
NECROLATER

NECROLATERS
NECROLATRIES
NECROLATRY
NECROLOGIC
NECROLOGICAL
NECROLOGIES
NECROLOGIST
NECROLOGISTS
NECROMANCER
NECROMANCERS
NECROMANCIES
NECROMANCY
NECROMANIA
NECROMANIAC
NECROMANIACS
NECROMANIAS
NECROMANTIC
NECROMANTICAL
NECROMANTICALLY
NECROPHAGOUS
NECROPHILE
NECROPHILES
NECROPHILIA
NECROPHILIAC
NECROPHILIACS
NECROPHILIAS
NECROPHILIC
NECROPHILIES
NECROPHILISM
NECROPHILISMS
NECROPHILOUS
NECROPHILS
NECROPHILY
NECROPHOBE
NECROPHOBES
NECROPHOBIA
NECROPHOBIAS
NECROPHOBIC
NECROPHOROUS
NECROPOLEIS
NECROPOLES
NECROPOLIS
NECROPOLISES
NECROPSIED
NECROPSIES
NECROPSYING
NECROSCOPIC
NECROSCOPICAL
NECROSCOPIES
NECROSCOPY
NECROTISED
NECROTISES
NECROTISING
NECROTIZED
NECROTIZES
NECROTIZING
NECROTOMIES
NECROTROPH
NECROTROPHIC

NECROTROPHS
NECTAREOUS
NECTAREOUSNESS
NECTARIFEROUS
NECTARINES
NECTARIVOROUS
NECTOCALYCES
NECTOCALYX
NEEDCESSITIES
NEEDCESSITY
NEEDFULNESS
NEEDFULNESSES
NEEDINESSES
NEEDLECORD
NEEDLECORDS
NEEDLECRAFT
NEEDLECRAFTS
NEEDLEFISH
NEEDLEFISHES
NEEDLEFULS
NEEDLELIKE
NEEDLEPOINT
NEEDLEPOINTS
NEEDLESSLY
NEEDLESSNESS
NEEDLESSNESSES
NEEDLESTICK
NEEDLEWOMAN
NEEDLEWOMEN
NEEDLEWORK
NEEDLEWORKER
NEEDLEWORKERS
NEEDLEWORKS
NEESBERRIES
NEFARIOUSLY
NEFARIOUSNESS
NEFARIOUSNESSES
NEGATIONAL
NEGATIONIST
NEGATIONISTS
NEGATIVELY
NEGATIVENESS
NEGATIVENESSES
NEGATIVING
NEGATIVISM
NEGATIVISMS
NEGATIVIST
NEGATIVISTIC
NEGATIVISTS
NEGATIVITIES
NEGATIVITY
NEGLECTABLE
NEGLECTEDNESS
NEGLECTEDNESSES
NEGLECTERS
NEGLECTFUL
NEGLECTFULLY
NEGLECTFULNESS
NEGLECTING

NEGLECTINGLY
NEGLECTION
NEGLECTIONS
NEGLECTIVE
NEGLECTORS
NEGLIGEABLE
NEGLIGENCE
NEGLIGENCES
NEGLIGENTLY
NEGLIGIBILITIES
NEGLIGIBILITY
NEGLIGIBLE
NEGLIGIBLENESS
NEGLIGIBLY
NEGOCIANTS
NEGOTIABILITIES
NEGOTIABILITY
NEGOTIABLE
NEGOTIANTS
NEGOTIATED
NEGOTIATES
NEGOTIATING
NEGOTIATION
NEGOTIATIONS
NEGOTIATOR
NEGOTIATORS
NEGOTIATORY
NEGOTIATRESS
NEGOTIATRESSES
NEGOTIATRICES
NEGOTIATRIX
NEGOTIATRIXES
NEGRITUDES
NEGROHEADS
NEGROPHILE
NEGROPHILES
NEGROPHILISM
NEGROPHILISMS
NEGROPHILIST
NEGROPHILISTS
NEGROPHILS
NEGROPHOBE
NEGROPHOBES
NEGROPHOBIA
NEGROPHOBIAS
NEIGHBORED
NEIGHBORHOOD
NEIGHBORHOODS
NEIGHBORING
NEIGHBORLESS
NEIGHBORLINESS
NEIGHBORLY
NEIGHBOURED
NEIGHBOURHOOD
NEIGHBOURHOODS
NEIGHBOURING
NEIGHBOURLESS
NEIGHBOURLINESS
NEIGHBOURLY

NEIGHBOURS
NELUMBIUMS
NEMATHELMINTH
NEMATHELMINTHIC
NEMATHELMINTHS
NEMATICIDAL
NEMATICIDE
NEMATICIDES
NEMATOBLAST
NEMATOBLASTS
NEMATOCIDAL
NEMATOCIDE
NEMATOCIDES
NEMATOCYST
NEMATOCYSTIC
NEMATOCYSTS
NEMATODIRIASES
NEMATODIRIASIS
NEMATODIRUS
NEMATODIRUSES
NEMATOLOGICAL
NEMATOLOGIES
NEMATOLOGIST
NEMATOLOGISTS
NEMATOLOGY
NEMATOPHORE
NEMATOPHORES
NEMERTEANS
NEMERTIANS
NEMERTINES
NEMOPHILAS
NEOANTHROPIC
NEOARSPHENAMINE
NEOCLASSIC
NEOCLASSICAL
NEOCLASSICISM
NEOCLASSICISMS
NEOCLASSICIST
NEOCLASSICISTS
NEOCOLONIAL
NEOCOLONIALISM
NEOCOLONIALISMS
NEOCOLONIALIST
NEOCOLONIALISTS
NEOCONSERVATISM
NEOCONSERVATIVE
NEOCORTEXES
NEOCORTICAL
NEOCORTICES
NEODYMIUMS
NEOGENESES
NEOGENESIS
NEOGENETIC
NEOGOTHICS
NEOGRAMMARIAN
NEOGRAMMARIANS
NEOLIBERAL
NEOLIBERALISM
NEOLIBERALISMS

NEOLIBERALS
NEOLOGIANS
NEOLOGICAL
NEOLOGICALLY
NEOLOGISED
NEOLOGISES
NEOLOGISING
NEOLOGISMS
NEOLOGISTIC
NEOLOGISTICAL
NEOLOGISTICALLY
NEOLOGISTS
NEOLOGIZED
NEOLOGIZES
NEOLOGIZING
NEONATALLY
NEONATICIDE
NEONATICIDES
NEONATOLOGIES
NEONATOLOGIST
NEONATOLOGISTS
NEONATOLOGY
NEONOMIANISM
NEONOMIANISMS
NEONOMIANS
NEOORTHODOX
NEOORTHODOXIES
NEOORTHODOXY
NEOPAGANISE
NEOPAGANISED
NEOPAGANISES
NEOPAGANISING
NEOPAGANISM
NEOPAGANISMS
NEOPAGANIZE
NEOPAGANIZED
NEOPAGANIZES
NEOPAGANIZING
NEOPHILIAC
NEOPHILIACS
NEOPHILIAS
NEOPHOBIAS
NEOPILINAS
NEOPLASIAS
NEOPLASTIC
NEOPLASTICISM
NEOPLASTICISMS
NEOPLASTICIST
NEOPLASTICISTS
NEOPLASTIES
NEOREALISM
NEOREALISMS
NEOREALIST
NEOREALISTIC
NEOREALISTS
NEOSTIGMINE
NEOSTIGMINES
NEOTEINIAS
NEOTERICAL

NEOTERICALLY
NEOTERICALS
NEOTERISED
NEOTERISES
NEOTERISING
NEOTERISMS
NEOTERISTS
NEOTERIZED
NEOTERIZES
NEOTERIZING
NEOTROPICS
NEOVITALISM
NEOVITALISMS
NEOVITALIST
NEOVITALISTS
NEPENTHEAN
NEPHALISMS
NEPHALISTS
NEPHELINES
NEPHELINIC
NEPHELINITE
NEPHELINITES
NEPHELINITIC
NEPHELITES
NEPHELOMETER
NEPHELOMETERS
NEPHELOMETRIC
NEPHELOMETRIES
NEPHELOMETRY
NEPHOGRAMS
NEPHOGRAPH
NEPHOGRAPHS
NEPHOLOGIC
NEPHOLOGICAL
NEPHOLOGIES
NEPHOLOGIST
NEPHOLOGISTS
NEPHOSCOPE
NEPHOSCOPES
NEPHRALGIA
NEPHRALGIAS
NEPHRALGIC
NEPHRALGIES
NEPHRECTOMIES
NEPHRECTOMISE
NEPHRECTOMISED
NEPHRECTOMISES
NEPHRECTOMISING
NEPHRECTOMIZE
NEPHRECTOMIZED
NEPHRECTOMIZES
NEPHRECTOMIZING
NEPHRECTOMY
NEPHRIDIAL
NEPHRIDIUM
NEPHRITICAL
NEPHRITICS
NEPHRITIDES
NEPHRITISES

NEPHROBLASTOMA
NEPHROBLASTOMAS
NEPHROLEPIS
NEPHROLEPISES
NEPHROLOGICAL
NEPHROLOGIES
NEPHROLOGIST
NEPHROLOGISTS
NEPHROLOGY
NEPHROPATHIC
NEPHROPATHIES
NEPHROPATHY
NEPHROPEXIES
NEPHROPEXY
NEPHROPTOSES
NEPHROPTOSIS
NEPHROSCOPE
NEPHROSCOPES
NEPHROSCOPIES
NEPHROSCOPY
NEPHROSTOME
NEPHROSTOMES
NEPHROTICS
NEPHROTOMIES
NEPHROTOMY
NEPHROTOXIC
NEPHROTOXICITY
NEPOTISTIC
NEPTUNIUMS
NERDINESSES
NERVATIONS
NERVATURES
NERVELESSLY
NERVELESSNESS
NERVELESSNESSES
NERVINESSES
NERVOSITIES
NERVOUSNESS
NERVOUSNESSES
NERVURATION
NERVURATIONS
NESCIENCES
NESHNESSES
NESSELRODE
NESSELRODES
NETBALLERS
NETHERLINGS
NETHERMORE
NETHERMOST
NETHERSTOCK
NETHERSTOCKS
NETHERWARD
NETHERWARDS
NETHERWORLD
NETHERWORLDS
NETIQUETTE
NETIQUETTES
NETMINDERS
NETTLELIKE

NETTLESOME
NETWORKERS
NETWORKING
NETWORKINGS
NEURALGIAS
NEURAMINIDASE
NEURAMINIDASES
NEURASTHENIA
NEURASTHENIAC
NEURASTHENIACS
NEURASTHENIAS
NEURASTHENIC
NEURASTHENICS
NEURATIONS
NEURECTOMIES
NEURECTOMY
NEURILEMMA
NEURILEMMAL
NEURILEMMAS
NEURILITIES
NEURITIDES
NEURITISES
NEUROACTIVE
NEUROANATOMIC
NEUROANATOMICAL
NEUROANATOMIES
NEUROANATOMIST
NEUROANATOMISTS
NEUROANATOMY
NEUROBIOLOGICAL
NEUROBIOLOGIES
NEUROBIOLOGIST
NEUROBIOLOGISTS
NEUROBIOLOGY
NEUROBLAST
NEUROBLASTOMA
NEUROBLASTOMAS
NEUROBLASTOMATA
NEUROBLASTS
NEUROCHEMICAL
NEUROCHEMICALS
NEUROCHEMIST
NEUROCHEMISTRY
NEUROCHEMISTS
NEUROCHIPS
NEUROCOELE
NEUROCOELES
NEUROCOELS
NEUROCOGNITIVE
NEUROCOMPUTER
NEUROCOMPUTERS
NEUROCOMPUTING
NEUROCOMPUTINGS
NEUROENDOCRINE
NEUROETHOLOGIES
NEUROETHOLOGY
NEUROFEEDBACK
NEUROFEEDBACKS
NEUROFIBRIL

NEUROFIBRILAR
NEUROFIBRILLAR
NEUROFIBRILLARY
NEUROFIBRILS
NEUROFIBROMA
NEUROFIBROMAS
NEUROFIBROMATA
NEUROGENESES
NEUROGENESIS
NEUROGENIC
NEUROGENICALLY
NEUROGLIAL
NEUROGLIAS
NEUROGRAMS
NEUROHORMONAL
NEUROHORMONE
NEUROHORMONES
NEUROHUMOR
NEUROHUMORAL
NEUROHUMORS
NEUROHYPNOLOGY
NEUROHYPOPHYSES
NEUROHYPOPHYSIS
NEUROLEMMA
NEUROLEMMAS
NEUROLEPTIC
NEUROLEPTICS
NEUROLINGUIST
NEUROLINGUISTIC
NEUROLINGUISTS
NEUROLOGIC
NEUROLOGICAL
NEUROLOGICALLY
NEUROLOGIES
NEUROLOGIST
NEUROLOGISTS
NEUROLYSES
NEUROLYSIS
NEUROMARKETING
NEUROMARKETINGS
NEUROMASTS
NEUROMATOUS
NEUROMUSCULAR
NEUROPATHIC
NEUROPATHICAL
NEUROPATHICALLY
NEUROPATHIES
NEUROPATHIST
NEUROPATHISTS
NEUROPATHOLOGIC
NEUROPATHOLOGY
NEUROPATHS
NEUROPATHY
NEUROPEPTIDE
NEUROPEPTIDES
NEUROPHYSIOLOGY
NEUROPLASM
NEUROPLASMS
NEUROPSYCHIATRY

NEUROPSYCHOLOGY
NEUROPTERA
NEUROPTERAN
NEUROPTERANS
NEUROPTERIST
NEUROPTERISTS
NEUROPTERON
NEUROPTEROUS
NEURORADIOLOGY
NEUROSCIENCE
NEUROSCIENCES
NEUROSCIENTIFIC
NEUROSCIENTIST
NEUROSCIENTISTS
NEUROSECRETION
NEUROSECRETIONS
NEUROSECRETORY
NEUROSENSORY
NEUROSPORA
NEUROSPORAS
NEUROSURGEON
NEUROSURGEONS
NEUROSURGERIES
NEUROSURGERY
NEUROSURGICAL
NEUROSURGICALLY
NEUROTICALLY
NEUROTICISM
NEUROTICISMS
NEUROTOMIES
NEUROTOMIST
NEUROTOMISTS
NEUROTOXIC
NEUROTOXICITIES
NEUROTOXICITY
NEUROTOXIN
NEUROTOXINS
NEUROTROPHIC
NEUROTROPHIES
NEUROTROPHY
NEUROTROPIC
NEUROVASCULAR
NEURULATION
NEURULATIONS
NEURYPNOLOGIES
NEURYPNOLOGY
NEUTRALISATION
NEUTRALISATIONS
NEUTRALISE
NEUTRALISED
NEUTRALISER
NEUTRALISERS
NEUTRALISES
NEUTRALISING
NEUTRALISM
NEUTRALISMS
NEUTRALIST
NEUTRALISTIC
NEUTRALISTS

NEUTRALITIES
NEUTRALITY
NEUTRALIZATION
NEUTRALIZATIONS
NEUTRALIZE
NEUTRALIZED
NEUTRALIZER
NEUTRALIZERS
NEUTRALIZES
NEUTRALIZING
NEUTRALNESS
NEUTRALNESSES
NEUTRETTOS
NEUTRINOLESS
NEUTROPENIA
NEUTROPENIAS
NEUTROPHIL
NEUTROPHILE
NEUTROPHILES
NEUTROPHILIC
NEUTROPHILS
NEVERMINDS
NEVERTHELESS
NEVERTHEMORE
NEWFANGLED
NEWFANGLEDLY
NEWFANGLEDNESS
NEWFANGLENESS
NEWFANGLENESSES
NEWISHNESS
NEWISHNESSES
NEWMARKETS
NEWSAGENCIES
NEWSAGENCY
NEWSAGENTS
NEWSBREAKS
NEWSCASTER
NEWSCASTERS
NEWSCASTING
NEWSCASTINGS
NEWSDEALER
NEWSDEALERS
NEWSFLASHES
NEWSGROUPS
NEWSHOUNDS
NEWSINESSES
NEWSLETTER
NEWSLETTERS
NEWSMAGAZINE
NEWSMAGAZINES
NEWSMAKERS
NEWSMONGER
NEWSMONGERS
NEWSPAPERDOM
NEWSPAPERDOMS
NEWSPAPERED
NEWSPAPERING
NEWSPAPERISM
NEWSPAPERISMS

NEWSPAPERMAN
NEWSPAPERMEN
NEWSPAPERS
NEWSPAPERWOMAN
NEWSPAPERWOMEN
NEWSPEOPLE
NEWSPERSON
NEWSPERSONS
NEWSPRINTS
NEWSREADER
NEWSREADERS
NEWSSTANDS
NEWSTRADES
NEWSWEEKLIES
NEWSWEEKLY
NEWSWORTHINESS
NEWSWORTHY
NEWSWRITING
NEWSWRITINGS
NEXTNESSES
NIACINAMIDE
NIACINAMIDES
NIAISERIES
NIALAMIDES
NIBBLINGLY
NICCOLITES
NICENESSES
NICKELIFEROUS
NICKELINES
NICKELISED
NICKELISES
NICKELISING
NICKELIZED
NICKELIZES
NICKELIZING
NICKELLING
NICKELODEON
NICKELODEONS
NICKNAMERS
NICKNAMING
NICKPOINTS
NICKSTICKS
NICKUMPOOP
NICKUMPOOPS
NICOMPOOPS
NICOTIANAS
NICOTINAMIDE
NICOTINAMIDES
NICOTINISM
NICOTINISMS
NICROSILAL
NICROSILALS
NICTATIONS
NICTITATED
NICTITATES
NICTITATING
NICTITATION
NICTITATIONS
NIDAMENTAL

NIDAMENTUM
NIDDERINGS
NIDDERLING
NIDDERLINGS
NIDERLINGS
NIDICOLOUS
NIDIFICATE
NIDIFICATED
NIDIFICATES
NIDIFICATING
NIDIFICATION
NIDIFICATIONS
NIDIFUGOUS
NIDULATION
NIDULATIONS
NIFEDIPINE
NIFEDIPINES
NIFFNAFFED
NIFFNAFFING
NIFTINESSES
NIGGARDING
NIGGARDISE
NIGGARDISES
NIGGARDIZE
NIGGARDIZES
NIGGARDLINESS
NIGGARDLINESSES
NIGGERDOMS
NIGGERHEAD
NIGGERHEADS
NIGGERISMS
NIGGERLING
NIGGERLINGS
NIGGLINGLY
NIGHNESSES
NIGHTBIRDS
NIGHTBLIND
NIGHTCLASS
NIGHTCLASSES
NIGHTCLOTHES
NIGHTCLUBBED
NIGHTCLUBBER
NIGHTCLUBBERS
NIGHTCLUBBING
NIGHTCLUBBINGS
NIGHTCLUBS
NIGHTDRESS
NIGHTDRESSES
NIGHTFALLS
NIGHTFARING
NIGHTFIRES
NIGHTGEARS
NIGHTGLOWS
NIGHTGOWNS
NIGHTHAWKS
NIGHTINGALE
NIGHTINGALES
NIGHTLIFES
NIGHTLIVES

NIGHTMARES
NIGHTMARISH
NIGHTMARISHLY
NIGHTMARISHNESS
NIGHTPIECE
NIGHTPIECES
NIGHTRIDER
NIGHTRIDERS
NIGHTRIDING
NIGHTRIDINGS
NIGHTSCOPE
NIGHTSCOPES
NIGHTSHADE
NIGHTSHADES
NIGHTSHIRT
NIGHTSHIRTS
NIGHTSIDES
NIGHTSPOTS
NIGHTSTAND
NIGHTSTANDS
NIGHTSTICK
NIGHTSTICKS
NIGHTTIDES
NIGHTTIMES
NIGHTWALKER
NIGHTWALKERS
NIGHTWEARS
NIGRESCENCE
NIGRESCENCES
NIGRESCENT
NIGRIFYING
NIGRITUDES
NIGROMANCIES
NIGROMANCY
NIGROSINES
NIHILISTIC
NIHILITIES
NIKETHAMIDE
NIKETHAMIDES
NILPOTENTS
NIMBLENESS
NIMBLENESSES
NIMBLESSES
NIMBLEWITS
NIMBLEWITTED
NIMBOSTRATI
NIMBOSTRATUS
NIMBYNESSES
NINCOMPOOP
NINCOMPOOPERIES
NINCOMPOOPERY
NINCOMPOOPS
NINEPENCES
NINEPENNIES
NINESCORES
NINETEENTH
NINETEENTHLY
NINETEENTHS
NINETIETHS

NINHYDRINS

NINHYDRINS
NINNYHAMMER
NINNYHAMMERS
NIPCHEESES
NIPPERKINS
NIPPINESSES
NIPPLEWORT
NIPPLEWORTS
NISBERRIES
NITPICKERS
NITPICKIER
NITPICKIEST
NITPICKING
NITRAMINES
NITRANILINE
NITRANILINES
NITRATINES
NITRATIONS
NITRAZEPAM
NITRAZEPAMS
NITRIDINGS
NITRIFIABLE
NITRIFICATION
NITRIFICATIONS
NITRIFIERS
NITRIFYING
NITROBACTERIA
NITROBACTERIUM
NITROBENZENE
NITROBENZENES
NITROCELLULOSE
NITROCELLULOSES
NITROCHLOROFORM
NITROCOTTON
NITROCOTTONS
NITROFURAN
NITROFURANS
NITROGENASE
NITROGENASES
NITROGENISATION
NITROGENISE
NITROGENISED
NITROGENISES
NITROGENISING
NITROGENIZATION
NITROGENIZE
NITROGENIZED
NITROGENIZES
NITROGENIZING
NITROGENOUS
NITROGLYCERIN
NITROGLYCERINE
NITROGLYCERINES
NITROGLYCERINS
NITROMETER
NITROMETERS
NITROMETHANE
NITROMETHANES
NITROMETRIC

NITROPARAFFIN
NITROPARAFFINS
NITROPHILOUS
NITROSAMINE
NITROSAMINES
NITROSATION
NITROSATIONS
NITROTOLUENE
NITROTOLUENES
NITWITTEDNESS
NITWITTEDNESSES
NITWITTERIES
NITWITTERY
NOBBINESSES
NOBILESSES
NOBILITATE
NOBILITATED
NOBILITATES
NOBILITATING
NOBILITATION
NOBILITATIONS
NOBILITIES
NOBLENESSES
NOBLEWOMAN
NOBLEWOMEN
NOCHELLING
NOCICEPTIVE
NOCICEPTOR
NOCICEPTORS
NOCIRECEPTOR
NOCIRECEPTORS
NOCTAMBULATION
NOCTAMBULATIONS
NOCTAMBULISM
NOCTAMBULISMS
NOCTAMBULIST
NOCTAMBULISTS
NOCTILUCAE
NOCTILUCAS
NOCTILUCENCE
NOCTILUCENCES
NOCTILUCENT
NOCTILUCOUS
NOCTIVAGANT
NOCTIVAGATION
NOCTIVAGATIONS
NOCTIVAGOUS
NOCTUARIES
NOCTURNALITIES
NOCTURNALITY
NOCTURNALLY
NOCTURNALS
NOCUOUSNESS
NOCUOUSNESSES
NODALISING
NODALITIES
NODALIZING
NODOSITIES
NODULATION

NODULATIONS
NOEMATICAL
NOEMATICALLY
NOISELESSLY
NOISELESSNESS
NOISELESSNESSES
NOISEMAKER
NOISEMAKERS
NOISEMAKING
NOISEMAKINGS
NOISINESSES
NOISOMENESS
NOISOMENESSES
NOMADICALLY
NOMADISATION
NOMADISATIONS
NOMADISING
NOMADIZATION
NOMADIZATIONS
NOMADIZING
NOMARCHIES
NOMENCLATIVE
NOMENCLATOR
NOMENCLATORIAL
NOMENCLATORS
NOMENCLATURAL
NOMENCLATURE
NOMENCLATURES
NOMENKLATURA
NOMENKLATURAS
NOMINALISATION
NOMINALISATIONS
NOMINALISE
NOMINALISED
NOMINALISES
NOMINALISING
NOMINALISM
NOMINALISMS
NOMINALIST
NOMINALISTIC
NOMINALISTS
NOMINALIZATION
NOMINALIZATIONS
NOMINALIZE
NOMINALIZED
NOMINALIZES
NOMINALIZING
NOMINATELY
NOMINATING
NOMINATION
NOMINATIONS
NOMINATIVAL
NOMINATIVALLY
NOMINATIVE
NOMINATIVELY
NOMINATIVES
NOMINATORS
NOMOCRACIES
NOMOGENIES

NOMOGRAPHER
NOMOGRAPHERS
NOMOGRAPHIC
NOMOGRAPHICAL
NOMOGRAPHICALLY
NOMOGRAPHIES
NOMOGRAPHS
NOMOGRAPHY
NOMOLOGICAL
NOMOLOGICALLY
NOMOLOGIES
NOMOLOGIST
NOMOLOGISTS
NOMOTHETES
NOMOTHETIC
NOMOTHETICAL
NONABRASIVE
NONABSORBABLE
NONABSORBENT
NONABSORPTIVE
NONABSTRACT
NONACADEMIC
NONACADEMICS
NONACCEPTANCE
NONACCEPTANCES
NONACCIDENTAL
NONACCOUNTABLE
NONACCREDITED
NONACCRUAL
NONACHIEVEMENT
NONACHIEVEMENTS
NONACQUISITIVE
NONACTIONS
NONACTIVATED
NONADAPTIVE
NONADDICTIVE
NONADDICTS
NONADDITIVE
NONADDITIVITIES
NONADDITIVITY
NONADHESIVE
NONADIABATIC
NONADJACENT
NONADMIRER
NONADMIRERS
NONADMISSION
NONADMISSIONS
NONAESTHETIC
NONAFFILIATED
NONAFFLUENT
NONAGENARIAN
NONAGENARIANS
NONAGESIMAL
NONAGESIMALS
NONAGGRESSION
NONAGGRESSIONS
NONAGGRESSIVE
NONAGRICULTURAL
NONALCOHOLIC

NONALIGNED
NONALIGNMENT
NONALIGNMENTS
NONALLELIC
NONALLERGENIC
NONALLERGIC
NONALPHABETIC
NONALUMINUM
NONAMBIGUOUS
NONANALYTIC
NONANATOMIC
NONANSWERS
NONANTAGONISTIC
NONANTIBIOTIC
NONANTIBIOTICS
NONANTIGENIC
NONAPPEARANCE
NONAPPEARANCES
NONAQUATIC
NONAQUEOUS
NONARBITRARY
NONARCHITECT
NONARCHITECTS
NONARCHITECTURE
NONARGUMENT
NONARGUMENTS
NONARISTOCRATIC
NONAROMATIC
NONAROMATICS
NONARTISTIC
NONARTISTS
NONASCETIC
NONASPIRIN
NONASSERTIVE
NONASSOCIATED
NONASTRONOMICAL
NONATHLETE
NONATHLETES
NONATHLETIC
NONATTACHED
NONATTACHMENT
NONATTACHMENTS
NONATTENDANCE
NONATTENDANCES
NONATTENDER
NONATTENDERS
NONAUDITORY
NONAUTHORS
NONAUTOMATED
NONAUTOMATIC
NONAUTOMOTIVE
NONAUTONOMOUS
NONAVAILABILITY
NONBACTERIAL
NONBANKING
NONBARBITURATE
NONBARBITURATES
NONBEARING
NONBEHAVIORAL

NONBELIEFS
NONBELIEVER
NONBELIEVERS
NONBELLIGERENCY
NONBELLIGERENT
NONBELLIGERENTS
NONBETTING
NONBINDING
NONBIOGRAPHICAL
NONBIOLOGICAL
NONBIOLOGICALLY
NONBIOLOGIST
NONBIOLOGISTS
NONBONDING
NONBOTANIST
NONBOTANISTS
NONBREAKABLE
NONBREATHING
NONBREEDER
NONBREEDERS
NONBREEDING
NONBROADCAST
NONBUILDING
NONBURNABLE
NONBUSINESS
NONCABINET
NONCALLABLE
NONCALORIC
NONCANCELABLE
NONCANCEROUS
NONCANDIDACIES
NONCANDIDACY
NONCANDIDATE
NONCANDIDATES
NONCAPITAL
NONCAPITALIST
NONCAPITALISTS
NONCARCINOGEN
NONCARCINOGENIC
NONCARCINOGENS
NONCARDIAC
NONCARRIER
NONCARRIERS
NONCELEBRATION
NONCELEBRATIONS
NONCELEBRITIES
NONCELEBRITY
NONCELLULAR
NONCELLULOSIC
NONCENTRAL
NONCERTIFICATED
NONCERTIFIED
NONCHALANCE
NONCHALANCES
NONCHALANT
NONCHALANTLY
NONCHARACTER
NONCHARACTERS
NONCHARISMATIC

NONCHARISMATICS
NONCHAUVINIST
NONCHEMICAL
NONCHEMICALS
NONCHROMOSOMAL
NONCHURCHGOER
NONCHURCHGOERS
NONCIRCULAR
NONCIRCULATING
NONCITIZEN
NONCITIZENS
NONCLANDESTINE
NONCLASSES
NONCLASSICAL
NONCLASSIFIED
NONCLASSROOM
NONCLERICAL
NONCLINICAL
NONCLOGGING
NONCOERCIVE
NONCOGNITIVE
NONCOGNITIVISM
NONCOGNITIVISMS
NONCOHERENT
NONCOINCIDENCE
NONCOINCIDENCES
NONCOLLECTOR
NONCOLLECTORS
NONCOLLEGE
NONCOLLEGIATE
NONCOLLINEAR
NONCOLORED
NONCOLORFAST
NONCOMBATANT
NONCOMBATANTS
NONCOMBATIVE
NONCOMBUSTIBLE
NONCOMMERCIAL
NONCOMMISSIONED
NONCOMMITMENT
NONCOMMITMENTS
NONCOMMITTAL
NONCOMMITTALLY
NONCOMMITTED
NONCOMMUNIST
NONCOMMUNISTS
NONCOMMUNITY
NONCOMMUTATIVE
NONCOMPARABLE
NONCOMPATIBLE
NONCOMPETITION
NONCOMPETITIVE
NONCOMPETITOR
NONCOMPETITORS
NONCOMPLEX
NONCOMPLIANCE
NONCOMPLIANCES
NONCOMPLICATED
NONCOMPLYING

NONCOMPOSER
NONCOMPOSERS
NONCOMPOUND
NONCOMPRESSIBLE
NONCOMPUTER
NONCOMPUTERISED
NONCOMPUTERIZED
NONCONCEPTUAL
NONCONCERN
NONCONCERNS
NONCONCLUSION
NONCONCLUSIONS
NONCONCURRED
NONCONCURRENCE
NONCONCURRENCES
NONCONCURRENT
NONCONCURRING
NONCONCURS
NONCONDENSABLE
NONCONDITIONED
NONCONDUCTING
NONCONDUCTION
NONCONDUCTIVE
NONCONDUCTOR
NONCONDUCTORS
NONCONFERENCE
NONCONFIDENCE
NONCONFIDENCES
NONCONFIDENTIAL
NONCONFLICTING
NONCONFORM
NONCONFORMANCE
NONCONFORMANCES
NONCONFORMED
NONCONFORMER
NONCONFORMERS
NONCONFORMING
NONCONFORMISM
NONCONFORMISMS
NONCONFORMIST
NONCONFORMISTS
NONCONFORMITIES
NONCONFORMITY
NONCONFORMS
NONCONGRUENT
NONCONJUGATED
NONCONNECTION
NONCONNECTIONS
NONCONSCIOUS
NONCONSECUTIVE
NONCONSENSUAL
NONCONSERVATION
NONCONSERVATIVE
NONCONSOLIDATED
NONCONSTANT
NONCONSTRUCTION
NONCONSTRUCTIVE
NONCONSUMER
NONCONSUMERS

NONCONSUMING

NONCONSUMING	NONDEDUCTIBLE	NONDIVIDING	NONEQUIVALENCES
NONCONSUMPTION	NONDEDUCTIVE	NONDOCTORS	NONEQUIVALENT
NONCONSUMPTIONS	NONDEFENSE	NONDOCTRINAIRE	NONESSENTIAL
NONCONSUMPTIVE	NONDEFERRABLE	NONDOCUMENTARY	NONESSENTIALS
NONCONTACT	NONDEFORMING	NONDOGMATIC	NONESTABLISHED
NONCONTAGIOUS	NONDEGENERATE	NONDOMESTIC	NONESTERIFIED
NONCONTEMPORARY	NONDEGRADABLE	NONDOMICILED	NONESUCHES
NONCONTIGUOUS	NONDELEGATE	NONDOMINANT	NONETHELESS
NONCONTINGENT	NONDELEGATES	NONDORMANT	NONETHICAL
NONCONTINUOUS	NONDELIBERATE	NONDRAMATIC	NONETHNICS
NONCONTRACT	NONDELINQUENT	NONDRINKER	NONEVALUATIVE
NONCONTRACTUAL	NONDELINQUENTS	NONDRINKERS	NONEVIDENCE
NONCONTRIBUTORY	NONDELIVERIES	NONDRINKING	NONEVIDENCES
NONCONTROLLABLE	NONDELIVERY	NONDRIVERS	NONEXCLUSIVE
NONCONTROLLED	NONDEMANDING	NONDURABLE	NONEXECUTIVE
NONCONTROLLING	NONDEMANDS	NONEARNING	NONEXECUTIVES
NONCONVENTIONAL	NONDEMOCRATIC	NONECONOMIC	NONEXEMPTS
NONCONVERTIBLE	NONDEPARTMENTAL	NONECONOMIST	NONEXISTENCE
NONCOOPERATION	NONDEPENDENT	NONECONOMISTS	NONEXISTENCES
NONCOOPERATIONS	NONDEPENDENTS	NONEDIBLES	NONEXISTENT
NONCOOPERATIVE	NONDEPLETABLE	NONEDITORIAL	NONEXISTENTIAL
NONCOOPERATOR	NONDEPLETING	NONEDUCATION	NONEXPENDABLE
NONCOOPERATORS	NONDEPOSITION	NONEDUCATIONAL	NONEXPERIMENTAL
NONCOPLANAR	NONDEPOSITIONS	NONEFFECTIVE	NONEXPERTS
NONCORPORATE	NONDEPRESSED	NONEFFECTIVES	NONEXPLANATORY
NONCORRELATION	NONDERIVATIVE	NONELASTIC	NONEXPLOITATION
NONCORRELATIONS	NONDESCRIPT	NONELECTED	NONEXPLOITATIVE
NONCORRODIBLE	NONDESCRIPTIVE	NONELECTION	NONEXPLOITIVE
NONCORRODING	NONDESCRIPTLY	NONELECTIONS	NONEXPLOSIVE
NONCORROSIVE	NONDESCRIPTNESS	NONELECTIVE	NONEXPOSED
NONCOUNTRY	NONDESCRIPTS	NONELECTRIC	NONFACTORS
NONCOVERAGE	NONDESTRUCTIVE	NONELECTRICAL	NONFACTUAL
NONCOVERAGES	NONDETACHABLE	NONELECTROLYTE	NONFACULTY
NONCREATIVE	NONDEVELOPMENT	NONELECTROLYTES	NONFAMILIAL
NONCREATIVITIES	NONDEVELOPMENTS	NONELECTRONIC	NONFAMILIES
NONCREATIVITY	NONDEVIANT	NONELEMENTARY	NONFARMERS
NONCREDENTIALED	NONDIABETIC	NONEMERGENCIES	NONFATTENING
NONCRIMINAL	NONDIABETICS	NONEMERGENCY	NONFEASANCE
NONCRIMINALS	NONDIALYSABLE	NONEMOTIONAL	NONFEASANCES
NONCRITICAL	NONDIALYZABLE	NONEMPHATIC	NONFEDERAL
NONCROSSOVER	NONDIAPAUSING	NONEMPIRICAL	NONFEDERATED
NONCRUSHABLE	NONDIDACTIC	NONEMPLOYEE	NONFEMINIST
NONCRYSTALLINE	NONDIFFUSIBLE	NONEMPLOYEES	NONFEMINISTS
NONCULINARY	NONDIMENSIONAL	NONEMPLOYMENT	NONFERROUS
NONCULTIVATED	NONDIPLOMATIC	NONEMPLOYMENTS	NONFICTION
NONCULTIVATION	NONDIRECTED	NONENCAPSULATED	NONFICTIONAL
NONCULTIVATIONS	NONDIRECTIONAL	NONENFORCEMENT	NONFICTIONALLY
NONCULTURAL	NONDIRECTIVE	NONENFORCEMENTS	NONFICTIONS
NONCUMULATIVE	NONDISABLED	NONENGAGEMENT	NONFIGURATIVE
NONCURRENT	NONDISCLOSURE	NONENGAGEMENTS	NONFILAMENTOUS
NONCUSTODIAL	NONDISCLOSURES	NONENGINEERING	NONFILTERABLE
NONCUSTOMER	NONDISCOUNT	NONENTITIES	NONFINANCIAL
NONCUSTOMERS	NONDISCURSIVE	NONENTRIES	NONFISSIONABLE
NONCYCLICAL	NONDISJUNCTION	NONENZYMATIC	NONFLAMMABILITY
NONDANCERS	NONDISJUNCTIONS	NONENZYMIC	NONFLAMMABLE
NONDECEPTIVE	NONDISPERSIVE	NONEQUILIBRIA	NONFLOWERING
NONDECISION	NONDISRUPTIVE	NONEQUILIBRIUM	NONFLUENCIES
NONDECISIONS	NONDISTINCTIVE	NONEQUILIBRIUMS	NONFLUENCY
NONDECREASING	NONDIVERSIFIED	NONEQUIVALENCE	NONFLUORESCENT

NONFORFEITABLE	NONIMPLICATION	NONIONIZING	NONMETAMERIC
NONFORFEITURE	NONIMPLICATIONS	NONIRRADIATED	NONMETAPHORICAL
NONFORFEITURES	NONIMPORTATION	NONIRRIGATED	NONMETRICAL
NONFREEZING	NONIMPORTATIONS	NONIRRITANT	NONMETROPOLITAN
NONFRIVOLOUS	NONINCLUSION	NONIRRITANTS	NONMICROBIAL
NONFULFILLMENT	NONINCLUSIONS	NONIRRITATING	NONMIGRANT
NONFULFILLMENTS	NONINCREASING	NONJOINDER	NONMIGRATORY
NONFUNCTIONAL	NONINCUMBENT	NONJOINDERS	NONMILITANT
NONFUNCTIONING	NONINCUMBENTS	NONJOINERS	NONMILITANTS
NONGASEOUS	NONINDEPENDENCE	NONJUDGEMENTAL	NONMILITARY
NONGENETIC	NONINDIGENOUS	NONJUDGMENTAL	NONMIMETIC
NONGENITAL	NONINDIVIDUAL	NONJUDICIAL	NONMINORITIES
NONGEOMETRICAL	NONINDUCTIVE	NONJUSTICIABLE	NONMINORITY
NONGLAMOROUS	NONINDUSTRIAL	NONKOSHERS	NONMODERNS
NONGOLFERS	NONINDUSTRY	NONLANDOWNER	NONMOLECULAR
NONGONOCOCCAL	NONINFECTED	NONLANDOWNERS	NONMONETARIST
NONGOVERNMENT	NONINFECTIOUS	NONLANGUAGE	NONMONETARISTS
NONGOVERNMENTAL	NONINFECTIVE	NONLANGUAGES	NONMONETARY
NONGRADUATE	NONINFESTED	NONLAWYERS	NONMONOGAMOUS
NONGRADUATES	NONINFLAMMABLE	NONLEGUMES	NONMORTALS
NONGRAMMATICAL	NONINFLAMMATORY	NONLEGUMINOUS	NONMOTILITIES
NONGRANULAR	NONINFLATIONARY	NONLEXICAL	NONMOTILITY
NONGREGARIOUS	NONINFLECTIONAL	NONLIBRARIAN	NONMOTORISED
NONGROWING	NONINFLUENCE	NONLIBRARIANS	NONMOTORIZED
NONHALOGENATED	NONINFLUENCES	NONLIBRARY	NONMUNICIPAL
NONHANDICAPPED	NONINFORMATION	NONLINEARITIES	NONMUSICAL
NONHAPPENING	NONINFORMATIONS	NONLINEARITY	NONMUSICALS
NONHAPPENINGS	NONINFRINGEMENT	NONLINGUISTIC	NONMUSICIAN
NONHARMONIC	NONINITIAL	NONLIQUIDS	NONMUSICIANS
NONHAZARDOUS	NONINITIATE	NONLITERAL	NONMUTANTS
NONHEMOLYTIC	NONINITIATES	NONLITERARY	NONMYELINATED
NONHEREDITARY	NONINSECTICIDAL	NONLITERATE	NONMYSTICAL
NONHIERARCHICAL	NONINSECTS	NONLITERATES	NONNARRATIVE
NONHISTONE	NONINSTALLMENT	NONLIVINGS	NONNATIONAL
NONHISTORICAL	NONINSTALLMENTS	NONLOGICAL	NONNATIONALS
NONHOMOGENEOUS	NONINSTRUMENTAL	NONLUMINOUS	NONNATIVES
NONHOMOLOGOUS	NONINSURANCE	NONMAGNETIC	NONNATURAL
NONHOMOSEXUAL	NONINSURED	NONMAINSTREAM	NONNECESSITIES
NONHOMOSEXUALS	NONINTEGRAL	NONMALIGNANT	NONNECESSITY
NONHORMONAL	NONINTEGRATED	NONMALLEABLE	NONNEGATIVE
NONHOSPITAL	NONINTELLECTUAL	NONMANAGEMENT	NONNEGLIGENT
NONHOSPITALISED	NONINTERACTING	NONMANAGERIAL	NONNEGOTIABLE
NONHOSPITALIZED	NONINTERACTIVE	NONMARITAL	NONNEGOTIABLES
NONHOSTILE	NONINTERCOURSE	NONMARKETS	NONNETWORK
NONHOUSING	NONINTERCOURSES	NONMATERIAL	NONNITROGENOUS
NONHUNTERS	NONINTEREST	NONMATHEMATICAL	NONNORMATIVE
NONHUNTING	NONINTERFERENCE	NONMATRICULATED	NONNUCLEAR
NONHYGROSCOPIC	NONINTERSECTING	NONMEANINGFUL	NONNUCLEATED
NONHYSTERICAL	NONINTERVENTION	NONMEASURABLE	NONNUMERICAL
NONIDENTICAL	NONINTIMIDATING	NONMECHANICAL	NONNUTRITIOUS
NONIDENTITIES	NONINTOXICANT	NONMECHANISTIC	NONNUTRITIVE
NONIDENTITY	NONINTOXICANTS	NONMEDICAL	NONOBJECTIVE
NONIDEOLOGICAL	NONINTOXICATING	NONMEETING	NONOBJECTIVISM
NONILLIONS	NONINTRUSIVE	NONMEETINGS	NONOBJECTIVISMS
NONILLIONTH	NONINTUITIVE	NONMEMBERS	NONOBJECTIVIST
NONILLIONTHS	NONINVASIVE	NONMEMBERSHIP	NONOBJECTIVISTS
NONIMITATIVE	NONINVOLVED	NONMEMBERSHIPS	NONOBJECTIVITY
NONIMMIGRANT	NONINVOLVEMENT	NONMERCURIAL	NONOBSCENE
NONIMMIGRANTS	NONINVOLVEMENTS	NONMETALLIC	NONOBSERVANCE

NONOBSERVANCES

NONOBSERVANCES	NONPHYSICIANS	NONREALISTIC	NONRIOTERS
NONOBSERVANT	NONPLASTIC	NONRECEIPT	NONRIOTING
NONOBVIOUS	NONPLASTICS	NONRECEIPTS	NONROTATING
NONOCCUPATIONAL	NONPLAYERS	NONRECIPROCAL	NONROUTINE
NONOCCURRENCE	NONPLAYING	NONRECOGNITION	NONRUMINANT
NONOCCURRENCES	NONPLUSING	NONRECOGNITIONS	NONRUMINANTS
NONOFFICIAL	NONPLUSSED	NONRECOMBINANT	NONSALABLE
NONOFFICIALS	NONPLUSSES	NONRECOMBINANTS	NONSAPONIFIABLE
NONOPERATIC	NONPLUSSING	NONRECOURSE	NONSCHEDULED
NONOPERATING	NONPOISONOUS	NONRECURRENT	NONSCIENCE
NONOPERATIONAL	NONPOLARISABLE	NONRECURRING	NONSCIENCES
NONOPERATIVE	NONPOLARIZABLE	NONRECYCLABLE	NONSCIENTIFIC
NONOPTIMAL	NONPOLITICAL	NONRECYCLABLES	NONSCIENTIST
NONORGANIC	NONPOLITICALLY	NONREDUCING	NONSCIENTISTS
NONORGASMIC	NONPOLITICIAN	NONREDUNDANT	NONSEASONAL
NONORTHODOX	NONPOLITICIANS	NONREFILLABLE	NONSECRETOR
NONOVERLAPPING	NONPOLLUTING	NONREFLECTING	NONSECRETORS
NONOXIDISING	NONPOSSESSION	NONREFLEXIVE	NONSECRETORY
NONOXIDIZING	NONPOSSESSIONS	NONREFUNDABLE	NONSECRETS
NONPAPISTS	NONPRACTICAL	NONREGULATED	NONSECTARIAN
NONPARALLEL	NONPRACTICING	NONREGULATION	NONSEDIMENTABLE
NONPARAMETRIC	NONPRACTISING	NONRELATIVE	NONSEGREGATED
NONPARASITIC	NONPREGNANT	NONRELATIVES	NONSEGREGATION
NONPAREILS	NONPRESCRIPTION	NONRELATIVISTIC	NONSEGREGATIONS
NONPARENTS	NONPROBLEM	NONRELEVANT	NONSELECTED
NONPARITIES	NONPROBLEMS	NONRELIGIOUS	NONSELECTIVE
NONPARTICIPANT	NONPRODUCING	NONRENEWABLE	NONSENSATIONAL
NONPARTICIPANTS	NONPRODUCTIVE	NONRENEWAL	NONSENSICAL
NONPARTIES	NONPRODUCTIVITY	NONREPAYABLE	NONSENSICALITY
NONPARTISAN	NONPROFESSIONAL	NONREPRODUCTIVE	NONSENSICALLY
NONPARTISANSHIP	NONPROFESSORIAL	NONRESIDENCE	NONSENSICALNESS
NONPARTIZAN	NONPROFITS	NONRESIDENCES	NONSENSITIVE
NONPARTIZANSHIP	NONPROGRAM	NONRESIDENCIES	NONSENSUOUS
NONPASSERINE	NONPROGRAMMER	NONRESIDENCY	NONSENTENCE
NONPASSIVE	NONPROGRAMMERS	NONRESIDENT	NONSENTENCES
NONPATHOGENIC	NONPROGRESSIVE	NONRESIDENTIAL	NONSEPTATE
NONPAYMENT	NONPROPRIETARY	NONRESIDENTS	NONSEQUENTIAL
NONPAYMENTS	NONPROSSED	NONRESISTANCE	NONSERIALS
NONPERFORMANCE	NONPROSSES	NONRESISTANCES	NONSERIOUS
NONPERFORMANCES	NONPROSSING	NONRESISTANT	NONSHRINKABLE
NONPERFORMER	NONPROTEIN	NONRESISTANTS	NONSIGNERS
NONPERFORMERS	NONPSYCHIATRIC	NONRESONANT	NONSIGNIFICANT
NONPERFORMING	NONPSYCHIATRIST	NONRESPONDENT	NONSIMULTANEOUS
NONPERISHABLE	NONPSYCHOTIC	NONRESPONDENTS	NONSINKABLE
NONPERISHABLES	NONPUNITIVE	NONRESPONDER	NONSKATERS
NONPERMANENT	NONPURPOSIVE	NONRESPONDERS	NONSKELETAL
NONPERMISSIVE	NONQUANTIFIABLE	NONRESPONSE	NONSMOKERS
NONPERSISTENT	NONQUANTITATIVE	NONRESPONSES	NONSMOKING
NONPERSONAL	NONRACIALLY	NONRESPONSIVE	NONSOCIALIST
NONPERSONS	NONRADIOACTIVE	NONRESTRICTED	NONSOCIALISTS
NONPETROLEUM	NONRAILROAD	NONRESTRICTIVE	NONSOLUTION
NONPHILOSOPHER	NONRANDOMNESS	NONRETRACTILE	NONSOLUTIONS
NONPHILOSOPHERS	NONRANDOMNESSES	NONRETROACTIVE	NONSPATIAL
NONPHONEMIC	NONRATIONAL	NONRETURNABLE	NONSPEAKER
NONPHONETIC	NONREACTIVE	NONRETURNABLES	NONSPEAKERS
NONPHOSPHATE	NONREACTOR	NONREUSABLE	NONSPEAKING
NONPHOTOGRAPHIC	NONREACTORS	NONREVERSIBLE	NONSPECIALIST
NONPHYSICAL	NONREADERS	NONRHOTICITIES	NONSPECIALISTS
NONPHYSICIAN	NONREADING	NONRHOTICITY	NONSPECIFIC

NONSPECIFICALLY NONTHEORETICAL NONWORKING NORTHEASTWARDS
NONSPECTACULAR NONTHERAPEUTIC NONWRITERS NORTHERING
NONSPECULAR NONTHERMAL NONYELLOWING NORTHERLIES
NONSPECULATIVE NONTHINKING NOODLEDOMS NORTHERLINESS
NONSPHERICAL NONTHREATENING NOOGENESES NORTHERLINESSES
NONSPORTING NONTOBACCO NOOGENESIS NORTHERMOST
NONSTANDARD NONTOTALITARIAN NOOMETRIES NORTHERNER
NONSTAPLES NONTRADITIONAL NOOSPHERES NORTHERNERS
NONSTARTER NONTRANSFERABLE NOOTROPICS NORTHERNISE
NONSTARTERS NONTRANSITIVE NORADRENALIN NORTHERNISED
NONSTATIONARY NONTREATMENT NORADRENALINE NORTHERNISES
NONSTATISTICAL NONTREATMENTS NORADRENALINES NORTHERNISING
NONSTATIVE NONTRIVIAL NORADRENALINS NORTHERNISM
NONSTATIVES NONTROPICAL NORADRENERGIC NORTHERNISMS
NONSTEROID NONTURBULENT NOREPINEPHRINE NORTHERNIZE
NONSTEROIDAL NONTYPICAL NOREPINEPHRINES NORTHERNIZED
NONSTEROIDS NONUNANIMOUS NORETHINDRONE NORTHERNIZES
NONSTORIES NONUNIFORM NORETHINDRONES NORTHERNIZING
NONSTRATEGIC NONUNIFORMITIES NORETHISTERONE NORTHERNMOST
NONSTRIATED NONUNIFORMITY NORETHISTERONES NORTHLANDS
NONSTRUCTURAL NONUNIONISED NORMALCIES NORTHWARDLY
NONSTRUCTURED NONUNIONISM NORMALISABLE NORTHWARDS
NONSTUDENT NONUNIONISMS NORMALISATION NORTHWESTER
NONSTUDENTS NONUNIONIST NORMALISATIONS NORTHWESTERLIES
NONSUBJECT NONUNIONISTS NORMALISED NORTHWESTERLY
NONSUBJECTIVE NONUNIONIZED NORMALISER NORTHWESTERN
NONSUBJECTS NONUNIQUENESS NORMALISERS NORTHWESTERS
NONSUBSIDISED NONUNIQUENESSES NORMALISES NORTHWESTS
NONSUBSIDIZED NONUNIVERSAL NORMALISING NORTHWESTWARD
NONSUCCESS NONUNIVERSITY NORMALITIES NORTHWESTWARDLY
NONSUCCESSES NONUTILITARIAN NORMALIZABLE NORTHWESTWARDS
NONSUITING NONUTILITIES NORMALIZATION NORTRIPTYLINE
NONSUPERVISORY NONUTILITY NORMALIZATIONS NORTRIPTYLINES
NONSUPPORT NONUTOPIAN NORMALIZED NOSEBANDED
NONSUPPORTS NONVALIDITIES NORMALIZER NOSEBLEEDING
NONSURGICAL NONVALIDITY NORMALIZERS NOSEBLEEDINGS
NONSWIMMER NONVANISHING NORMALIZES NOSEBLEEDS
NONSWIMMERS NONVASCULAR NORMALIZING NOSEDIVING
NONSYLLABIC NONVECTORS NORMATIVELY NOSEGUARDS
NONSYMBOLIC NONVEGETARIAN NORMATIVENESS NOSEPIECES
NONSYMMETRIC NONVEGETARIANS NORMATIVENESSES NOSEWHEELS
NONSYMMETRICAL NONVENOMOUS NORMOTENSIVE NOSINESSES
NONSYNCHRONOUS NONVERBALLY NORMOTENSIVES NOSOCOMIAL
NONSYSTEMATIC NONVETERAN NORMOTHERMIA NOSOGRAPHER
NONSYSTEMIC NONVETERANS NORMOTHERMIAS NOSOGRAPHERS
NONSYSTEMS NONVIEWERS NORMOTHERMIC NOSOGRAPHIC
NONTALKERS NONVINTAGE NORSELLERS NOSOGRAPHIES
NONTAXABLE NONVIOLENCE NORSELLING NOSOGRAPHY
NONTEACHING NONVIOLENCES NORTHBOUND NOSOLOGICAL
NONTECHNICAL NONVIOLENT NORTHCOUNTRYMAN NOSOLOGICALLY
NONTEMPORAL NONVIOLENTLY NORTHCOUNTRYMEN NOSOLOGIES
NONTENURED NONVIRGINS NORTHEASTER NOSOLOGIST
NONTERMINAL NONVISCOUS NORTHEASTERLIES NOSOLOGISTS
NONTERMINALS NONVOCATIONAL NORTHEASTERLY NOSOPHOBIA
NONTERMINATING NONVOLATILE NORTHEASTERN NOSOPHOBIAS
NONTHEATRICAL NONVOLCANIC NORTHEASTERS NOSTALGIAS
NONTHEISTIC NONVOLUNTARY NORTHEASTS NOSTALGICALLY
NONTHEISTS NONWINNING NORTHEASTWARD NOSTALGICS
NONTHEOLOGICAL NONWORKERS NORTHEASTWARDLY NOSTALGIST

NOSTALGISTS
NOSTOLOGIC
NOSTOLOGICAL
NOSTOLOGIES
NOSTOMANIA
NOSTOMANIAS
NOSTOPATHIES
NOSTOPATHY
NOSTRADAMIC
NOTABILITIES
NOTABILITY
NOTABLENESS
NOTABLENESSES
NOTAPHILIC
NOTAPHILIES
NOTAPHILISM
NOTAPHILISMS
NOTAPHILIST
NOTAPHILISTS
NOTARIALLY
NOTARISATION
NOTARISATIONS
NOTARISING
NOTARIZATION
NOTARIZATIONS
NOTARIZING
NOTARYSHIP
NOTARYSHIPS
NOTATIONAL
NOTCHBACKS
NOTCHELLED
NOTCHELLING
NOTEDNESSES
NOTEPAPERS
NOTEWORTHILY
NOTEWORTHINESS
NOTEWORTHY
NOTHINGARIAN
NOTHINGARIANISM
NOTHINGARIANS
NOTHINGISM
NOTHINGISMS
NOTHINGNESS
NOTHINGNESSES
NOTICEABILITIES
NOTICEABILITY
NOTICEABLE
NOTICEABLY
NOTIFIABLE
NOTIFICATION
NOTIFICATIONS
NOTIONALIST
NOTIONALISTS
NOTIONALITIES
NOTIONALITY
NOTIONALLY
NOTIONISTS
NOTOCHORDAL
NOTOCHORDS

NOTODONTID
NOTODONTIDS
NOTONECTAL
NOTORIETIES
NOTORIOUSLY
NOTORIOUSNESS
NOTORIOUSNESSES
NOTORNISES
NOTOTHERIUM
NOTOTHERIUMS
NOTOUNGULATE
NOTOUNGULATES
NOTUNGULATE
NOTUNGULATES
NOTWITHSTANDING
NOUMENALISM
NOUMENALISMS
NOUMENALIST
NOUMENALISTS
NOUMENALITIES
NOUMENALITY
NOUMENALLY
NOURISHABLE
NOURISHERS
NOURISHING
NOURISHINGLY
NOURISHMENT
NOURISHMENTS
NOURITURES
NOURRITURE
NOURRITURES
NOUSELLING
NOVACULITE
NOVACULITES
NOVELETTES
NOVELETTISH
NOVELETTIST
NOVELETTISTS
NOVELISATION
NOVELISATIONS
NOVELISERS
NOVELISING
NOVELISTIC
NOVELISTICALLY
NOVELIZATION
NOVELIZATIONS
NOVELIZERS
NOVELIZING
NOVEMDECILLION
NOVEMDECILLIONS
NOVENARIES
NOVICEHOOD
NOVICEHOODS
NOVICESHIP
NOVICESHIPS
NOVICIATES
NOVITIATES
NOVOBIOCIN
NOVOBIOCINS

NOVOCAINES
NOVOCENTENARIES
NOVOCENTENARY
NOVODAMUSES
NOWCASTING
NOWCASTINGS
NOXIOUSNESS
NOXIOUSNESSES
NUBBINESSES
NUBIFEROUS
NUBIGENOUS
NUBILITIES
NUCIFEROUS
NUCIVOROUS
NUCLEARISATION
NUCLEARISATIONS
NUCLEARISE
NUCLEARISED
NUCLEARISES
NUCLEARISING
NUCLEARIZATION
NUCLEARIZATIONS
NUCLEARIZE
NUCLEARIZED
NUCLEARIZES
NUCLEARIZING
NUCLEATING
NUCLEATION
NUCLEATIONS
NUCLEATORS
NUCLEOCAPSID
NUCLEOCAPSIDS
NUCLEOLATE
NUCLEOLATED
NUCLEONICALLY
NUCLEONICS
NUCLEOPHILE
NUCLEOPHILES
NUCLEOPHILIC
NUCLEOPHILICITY
NUCLEOPLASM
NUCLEOPLASMATIC
NUCLEOPLASMIC
NUCLEOPLASMS
NUCLEOPROTEIN
NUCLEOPROTEINS
NUCLEOSIDE
NUCLEOSIDES
NUCLEOSOMAL
NUCLEOSOME
NUCLEOSOMES
NUCLEOSYNTHESES
NUCLEOSYNTHESIS
NUCLEOSYNTHETIC
NUCLEOTIDASE
NUCLEOTIDASES
NUCLEOTIDE
NUCLEOTIDES
NUDENESSES

NUDIBRANCH
NUDIBRANCHIATE
NUDIBRANCHIATES
NUDIBRANCHS
NUDICAUDATE
NUDICAULOUS
NUGATORINESS
NUGATORINESSES
NUGGETTING
NUISANCERS
NULLIFICATION
NULLIFICATIONS
NULLIFIDIAN
NULLIFIDIANS
NULLIFIERS
NULLIFYING
NULLIPARAE
NULLIPARAS
NULLIPARITIES
NULLIPARITY
NULLIPAROUS
NULLIPORES
NULLNESSES
NUMBERABLE
NUMBERINGS
NUMBERLESS
NUMBERLESSLY
NUMBERLESSNESS
NUMBERPLATE
NUMBERPLATES
NUMBFISHES
NUMBNESSES
NUMBSKULLS
NUMERABILITIES
NUMERABILITY
NUMERACIES
NUMERAIRES
NUMERATING
NUMERATION
NUMERATIONS
NUMERATIVE
NUMERATORS
NUMERICALLY
NUMEROLOGICAL
NUMEROLOGIES
NUMEROLOGIST
NUMEROLOGISTS
NUMEROLOGY
NUMEROSITIES
NUMEROSITY
NUMEROUSLY
NUMEROUSNESS
NUMEROUSNESSES
NUMINOUSNESS
NUMINOUSNESSES
NUMISMATIC
NUMISMATICALLY
NUMISMATICS

NUMISMATIST
NUMISMATISTS
NUMISMATOLOGIES
NUMISMATOLOGIST
NUMISMATOLOGY
NUMMULATED
NUMMULATION
NUMMULATIONS
NUMMULITES
NUMMULITIC
NUMSKULLED
NUNCIATURE
NUNCIATURES
NUNCUPATED
NUNCUPATES
NUNCUPATING
NUNCUPATION
NUNCUPATIONS
NUNCUPATIVE
NUNCUPATORY
NUNNATIONS
NUNNISHNESS
NUNNISHNESSES
NUPTIALITIES
NUPTIALITY
NURSEHOUND
NURSEHOUNDS
NURSELINGS
NURSEMAIDED
NURSEMAIDING
NURSEMAIDS
NURSERYMAID
NURSERYMAIDS
NURSERYMAN
NURSERYMEN
NURTURABLE
NURTURANCE
NURTURANCES
NUTATIONAL
NUTBUTTERS
NUTCRACKER
NUTCRACKERS
NUTGRASSES
NUTHATCHES
NUTJOBBERS
NUTMEGGING
NUTPECKERS
NUTRACEUTICAL
NUTRACEUTICALS
NUTRIMENTAL
NUTRIMENTS
NUTRITIONAL
NUTRITIONALLY
NUTRITIONARY
NUTRITIONIST
NUTRITIONISTS
NUTRITIONS
NUTRITIOUS
NUTRITIOUSLY

NUTRITIOUSNESS
NUTRITIVELY
NUTRITIVES
NUTTINESSES
NYCHTHEMERAL
NYCHTHEMERON
NYCHTHEMERONS
NYCTAGINACEOUS
NYCTALOPES
NYCTALOPIA
NYCTALOPIAS
NYCTALOPIC
NYCTANTHOUS
NYCTINASTIC
NYCTINASTIES
NYCTINASTY
NYCTITROPIC
NYCTITROPISM
NYCTITROPISMS
NYCTOPHOBIA
NYCTOPHOBIAS
NYCTOPHOBIC
NYMPHAEACEOUS
NYMPHAEUMS
NYMPHALIDS
NYMPHETTES
NYMPHOLEPSIES
NYMPHOLEPSY
NYMPHOLEPT
NYMPHOLEPTIC
NYMPHOLEPTS
NYMPHOMANIA
NYMPHOMANIAC
NYMPHOMANIACAL
NYMPHOMANIACS
NYMPHOMANIAS
NYSTAGMOID
NYSTAGMUSES

O

OAFISHNESS	OBJECTIVISED	OBLITERATED	OBSERVABLE
OAFISHNESSES	OBJECTIVISES	OBLITERATES	OBSERVABLENESS
OAKENSHAWS	OBJECTIVISING	OBLITERATING	OBSERVABLES
OARSMANSHIP	OBJECTIVISM	OBLITERATION	OBSERVABLY
OARSMANSHIPS	OBJECTIVISMS	OBLITERATIONS	OBSERVANCE
OASTHOUSES	OBJECTIVIST	OBLITERATIVE	OBSERVANCES
OBBLIGATOS	OBJECTIVISTIC	OBLITERATOR	OBSERVANCIES
OBCOMPRESSED	OBJECTIVISTS	OBLITERATORS	OBSERVANCY
OBDURACIES	OBJECTIVITIES	OBLIVIOUSLY	OBSERVANTLY
OBDURATELY	OBJECTIVITY	OBLIVIOUSNESS	OBSERVANTS
OBDURATENESS	OBJECTIVIZE	OBLIVIOUSNESSES	OBSERVATION
OBDURATENESSES	OBJECTIVIZED	OBLIVISCENCE	OBSERVATIONAL
OBDURATING	OBJECTIVIZES	OBLIVISCENCES	OBSERVATIONALLY
OBDURATION	OBJECTIVIZING	OBMUTESCENCE	OBSERVATIONS
OBDURATIONS	OBJECTLESS	OBMUTESCENCES	OBSERVATIVE
OBEDIENCES	OBJECTLESSNESS	OBMUTESCENT	OBSERVATOR
OBEDIENTIAL	OBJURATION	OBNOXIOUSLY	OBSERVATORIES
OBEDIENTIARIES	OBJURATIONS	OBNOXIOUSNESS	OBSERVATORS
OBEDIENTIARY	OBJURGATED	OBNOXIOUSNESSES	OBSERVATORY
OBEDIENTLY	OBJURGATES	OBNUBILATE	OBSERVINGLY
OBEISANCES	OBJURGATING	OBNUBILATED	OBSESSIONAL
OBEISANTLY	OBJURGATION	OBNUBILATES	OBSESSIONALLY
OBELISCOID	OBJURGATIONS	OBNUBILATING	OBSESSIONIST
OBELISKOID	OBJURGATIVE	OBNUBILATION	OBSESSIONISTS
OBESENESSES	OBJURGATOR	OBNUBILATIONS	OBSESSIONS
OBFUSCATED	OBJURGATORS	OBREPTIONS	OBSESSIVELY
OBFUSCATES	OBJURGATORY	OBREPTITIOUS	OBSESSIVENESS
OBFUSCATING	OBLANCEOLATE	OBSCENENESS	OBSESSIVENESSES
OBFUSCATION	OBLATENESS	OBSCENENESSES	OBSESSIVES
OBFUSCATIONS	OBLATENESSES	OBSCENITIES	OBSIDIONAL
OBFUSCATORY	OBLATIONAL	OBSCURANTIC	OBSIDIONARY
OBITUARIES	OBLIGATELY	OBSCURANTISM	OBSIGNATED
OBITUARIST	OBLIGATING	OBSCURANTISMS	OBSIGNATES
OBITUARISTS	OBLIGATION	OBSCURANTIST	OBSIGNATING
OBJECTIFICATION	OBLIGATIONAL	OBSCURANTISTS	OBSIGNATION
OBJECTIFIED	OBLIGATIONS	OBSCURANTS	OBSIGNATIONS
OBJECTIFIES	OBLIGATIVE	OBSCURATION	OBSIGNATORY
OBJECTIFYING	OBLIGATORILY	OBSCURATIONS	OBSOLESCED
OBJECTIONABLE	OBLIGATORINESS	OBSCUREMENT	OBSOLESCENCE
OBJECTIONABLY	OBLIGATORS	OBSCUREMENTS	OBSOLESCENCES
OBJECTIONS	OBLIGATORY	OBSCURENESS	OBSOLESCENT
OBJECTIVAL	OBLIGEMENT	OBSCURENESSES	OBSOLESCENTLY
OBJECTIVATE	OBLIGEMENTS	OBSCURITIES	OBSOLESCES
OBJECTIVATED	OBLIGINGLY	OBSECRATED	OBSOLESCING
OBJECTIVATES	OBLIGINGNESS	OBSECRATES	OBSOLETELY
OBJECTIVATING	OBLIGINGNESSES	OBSECRATING	OBSOLETENESS
OBJECTIVATION	OBLIQUATION	OBSECRATION	OBSOLETENESSES
OBJECTIVATIONS	OBLIQUATIONS	OBSECRATIONS	OBSOLETING
OBJECTIVELY	OBLIQUENESS	OBSEQUIOUS	OBSOLETION
OBJECTIVENESS	OBLIQUENESSES	OBSEQUIOUSLY	OBSOLETIONS
OBJECTIVENESSES	OBLIQUITIES	OBSEQUIOUSNESS	OBSOLETISM
OBJECTIVES	OBLIQUITOUS	OBSERVABILITIES	OBSOLETISMS
OBJECTIVISE	OBLITERATE	OBSERVABILITY	OBSTETRICAL

OBSTETRICALLY	OBTRUSIVELY	OCCULTATION	OCTANDRIAN
OBSTETRICIAN	OBTRUSIVENESS	OCCULTATIONS	OCTANDROUS
OBSTETRICIANS	OBTRUSIVENESSES	OCCULTISMS	OCTANEDIOIC
OBSTETRICS	OBTUNDENTS	OCCULTISTS	OCTANGULAR
OBSTINACIES	OBTUNDITIES	OCCULTNESS	OCTAPEPTIDE
OBSTINATELY	OBTURATING	OCCULTNESSES	OCTAPEPTIDES
OBSTINATENESS	OBTURATION	OCCUPANCES	OCTAPLOIDIES
OBSTINATENESSES	OBTURATIONS	OCCUPANCIES	OCTAPLOIDS
OBSTIPATION	OBTURATORS	OCCUPATING	OCTAPLOIDY
OBSTIPATIONS	OBTUSENESS	OCCUPATION	OCTAPODIES
OBSTREPERATE	OBTUSENESSES	OCCUPATIONAL	OCTARCHIES
OBSTREPERATED	OBTUSITIES	OCCUPATIONALLY	OCTASTICHON
OBSTREPERATES	OBUMBRATED	OCCUPATIONS	OCTASTICHONS
OBSTREPERATING	OBUMBRATES	OCCUPATIVE	OCTASTICHOUS
OBSTREPEROUS	OBUMBRATING	OCCURRENCE	OCTASTICHS
OBSTREPEROUSLY	OBUMBRATION	OCCURRENCES	OCTASTROPHIC
OBSTRICTION	OBUMBRATIONS	OCCURRENTS	OCTASTYLES
OBSTRICTIONS	OBVENTIONS	OCEANARIUM	OCTAVALENT
OBSTROPALOUS	OBVERSIONS	OCEANARIUMS	OCTENNIALLY
OBSTROPULOUS	OBVIATIONS	OCEANFRONT	OCTILLIONS
OBSTRUCTED	OBVIOUSNESS	OCEANFRONTS	OCTILLIONTH
OBSTRUCTER	OBVIOUSNESSES	OCEANGOING	OCTILLIONTHS
OBSTRUCTERS	OBVOLUTION	OCEANOGRAPHER	OCTINGENARIES
OBSTRUCTING	OBVOLUTIONS	OCEANOGRAPHERS	OCTINGENARY
OBSTRUCTION	OBVOLUTIVE	OCEANOGRAPHIC	OCTINGENTENARY
OBSTRUCTIONAL	OCCASIONAL	OCEANOGRAPHICAL	OCTOCENTENARIES
OBSTRUCTIONALLY	OCCASIONALISM	OCEANOGRAPHIES	OCTOCENTENARY
OBSTRUCTIONISM	OCCASIONALISMS	OCEANOGRAPHY	OCTODECILLION
OBSTRUCTIONISMS	OCCASIONALIST	OCEANOLOGICAL	OCTODECILLIONS
OBSTRUCTIONIST	OCCASIONALISTS	OCEANOLOGIES	OCTODECIMO
OBSTRUCTIONISTS	OCCASIONALITIES	OCEANOLOGIST	OCTODECIMOS
OBSTRUCTIONS	OCCASIONALITY	OCEANOLOGISTS	OCTOGENARIAN
OBSTRUCTIVE	OCCASIONALLY	OCEANOLOGY	OCTOGENARIANS
OBSTRUCTIVELY	OCCASIONED	OCELLATION	OCTOGENARIES
OBSTRUCTIVENESS	OCCASIONER	OCELLATIONS	OCTOGENARY
OBSTRUCTIVES	OCCASIONERS	OCHLOCRACIES	OCTOGYNOUS
OBSTRUCTOR	OCCASIONING	OCHLOCRACY	OCTOHEDRON
OBSTRUCTORS	OCCIDENTAL	OCHLOCRATIC	OCTOHEDRONS
OBSTRUENTS	OCCIDENTALISE	OCHLOCRATICAL	OCTONARIAN
OBTAINABILITIES	OCCIDENTALISED	OCHLOCRATICALLY	OCTONARIANS
OBTAINABILITY	OCCIDENTALISES	OCHLOCRATS	OCTONARIES
OBTAINABLE	OCCIDENTALISING	OCHLOPHOBIA	OCTONARIUS
OBTAINMENT	OCCIDENTALISM	OCHLOPHOBIAC	OCTONOCULAR
OBTAINMENTS	OCCIDENTALISMS	OCHLOPHOBIACS	OCTOPETALOUS
OBTEMPERATE	OCCIDENTALIST	OCHLOPHOBIAS	OCTOPLOIDS
OBTEMPERATED	OCCIDENTALISTS	OCHLOPHOBIC	OCTOPODANS
OBTEMPERATES	OCCIDENTALIZE	OCHRACEOUS	OCTOPODOUS
OBTEMPERATING	OCCIDENTALIZED	OCHROLEUCOUS	OCTOPUSHER
OBTEMPERED	OCCIDENTALIZES	OCTACHORDAL	OCTOPUSHERS
OBTEMPERING	OCCIDENTALIZING	OCTACHORDS	OCTOPUSHES
OBTENTIONS	OCCIDENTALLY	OCTAGONALLY	OCTOSEPALOUS
OBTESTATION	OCCIDENTALS	OCTAHEDRAL	OCTOSTICHOUS
OBTESTATIONS	OCCIPITALLY	OCTAHEDRALLY	OCTOSTYLES
OBTRUDINGS	OCCIPITALS	OCTAHEDRITE	OCTOSYLLABIC
OBTRUNCATE	OCCLUDENTS	OCTAHEDRITES	OCTOSYLLABICS
OBTRUNCATED	OCCLUSIONS	OCTAHEDRON	OCTOSYLLABLE
OBTRUNCATES	OCCLUSIVENESS	OCTAHEDRONS	OCTOSYLLABLES
OBTRUNCATING	OCCLUSIVENESSES	OCTAMEROUS	OCTOTHORPS
OBTRUSIONS	OCCLUSIVES	OCTAMETERS	OCTUPLICATE

OCTUPLICATES
OCULARISTS
OCULOMOTOR
ODALISQUES
ODDSMAKERS
ODIOUSNESS
ODIOUSNESSES
ODOMETRIES
ODONATISTS
ODONATOLOGIES
ODONATOLOGIST
ODONATOLOGISTS
ODONATOLOGY
ODONTALGIA
ODONTALGIAS
ODONTALGIC
ODONTALGIES
ODONTOBLAST
ODONTOBLASTIC
ODONTOBLASTS
ODONTOCETE
ODONTOCETES
ODONTOGENIC
ODONTOGENIES
ODONTOGENY
ODONTOGLOSSUM
ODONTOGLOSSUMS
ODONTOGRAPH
ODONTOGRAPHIES
ODONTOGRAPHS
ODONTOGRAPHY
ODONTOLITE
ODONTOLITES
ODONTOLOGIC
ODONTOLOGICAL
ODONTOLOGIES
ODONTOLOGIST
ODONTOLOGISTS
ODONTOLOGY
ODONTOMATA
ODONTOMATOUS
ODONTOPHOBIA
ODONTOPHOBIAS
ODONTOPHORAL
ODONTOPHORAN
ODONTOPHORE
ODONTOPHORES
ODONTOPHOROUS
ODONTORHYNCHOUS
ODONTORNITHES
ODONTOSTOMATOUS
ODORIFEROUS
ODORIFEROUSLY
ODORIFEROUSNESS
ODORIMETRIES
ODORIMETRY
ODORIPHORE
ODORIPHORES
ODOROUSNESS

ODOROUSNESSES
OECOLOGICAL
OECOLOGICALLY
OECOLOGIES
OECOLOGIST
OECOLOGISTS
OECUMENICAL
OECUMENICALLY
OEDEMATOSE
OEDEMATOUS
OEDOMETERS
OENOLOGICAL
OENOLOGIES
OENOLOGIST
OENOLOGISTS
OENOMANCIES
OENOMANIAS
OENOMETERS
OENOPHILES
OENOPHILIES
OENOPHILIST
OENOPHILISTS
OENOTHERAS
OESOPHAGEAL
OESOPHAGITIS
OESOPHAGITISES
OESOPHAGOSCOPE
OESOPHAGOSCOPES
OESOPHAGOSCOPY
OESOPHAGUS
OESTRADIOL
OESTRADIOLS
OESTROGENIC
OESTROGENICALLY
OESTROGENS
OFFENCEFUL
OFFENCELESS
OFFENDEDLY
OFFENDRESS
OFFENDRESSES
OFFENSELESS
OFFENSIVELY
OFFENSIVENESS
OFFENSIVENESSES
OFFENSIVES
OFFERTORIES
OFFHANDEDLY
OFFHANDEDNESS
OFFHANDEDNESSES
OFFICEHOLDER
OFFICEHOLDERS
OFFICERING
OFFICIALDOM
OFFICIALDOMS
OFFICIALESE
OFFICIALESES
OFFICIALISM
OFFICIALISMS
OFFICIALITIES

OFFICIALITY
OFFICIALLY
OFFICIALTIES
OFFICIALTY
OFFICIANTS
OFFICIARIES
OFFICIATED
OFFICIATES
OFFICIATING
OFFICIATION
OFFICIATIONS
OFFICIATOR
OFFICIATORS
OFFICINALLY
OFFICINALS
OFFICIOUSLY
OFFICIOUSNESS
OFFICIOUSNESSES
OFFISHNESS
OFFISHNESSES
OFFLOADING
OFFPRINTED
OFFPRINTING
OFFSADDLED
OFFSADDLES
OFFSADDLING
OFFSCOURING
OFFSCOURINGS
OFFSEASONS
OFFSETABLE
OFFSETTING
OFFSHORING
OFFSHORINGS
OFFSPRINGS
OFTENNESSES
OFTENTIMES
OILINESSES
OINOLOGIES
OLDFANGLED
OLEAGINOUS
OLEAGINOUSLY
OLEAGINOUSNESS
OLEANDOMYCIN
OLEANDOMYCINS
OLECRANONS
OLEIFEROUS
OLEOGRAPHIC
OLEOGRAPHIES
OLEOGRAPHS
OLEOGRAPHY
OLEOMARGARIN
OLEOMARGARINE
OLEOMARGARINES
OLEOMARGARINS
OLEOPHILIC
OLEORESINOUS
OLEORESINS
OLERACEOUS
OLFACTIBLE

OLFACTIONS
OLFACTOLOGIES
OLFACTOLOGIST
OLFACTOLOGISTS
OLFACTOLOGY
OLFACTOMETER
OLFACTOMETERS
OLFACTOMETRIES
OLFACTOMETRY
OLFACTORIES
OLFACTRONICS
OLIGAEMIAS
OLIGARCHAL
OLIGARCHIC
OLIGARCHICAL
OLIGARCHICALLY
OLIGARCHIES
OLIGOCHAETE
OLIGOCHAETES
OLIGOCHROME
OLIGOCHROMES
OLIGOCLASE
OLIGOCLASES
OLIGOCYTHAEMIA
OLIGOCYTHAEMIAS
OLIGODENDROCYTE
OLIGODENDROGLIA
OLIGOGENES
OLIGOMERIC
OLIGOMERISATION
OLIGOMERIZATION
OLIGOMEROUS
OLIGONUCLEOTIDE
OLIGOPEPTIDE
OLIGOPEPTIDES
OLIGOPHAGIES
OLIGOPHAGOUS
OLIGOPHAGY
OLIGOPOLIES
OLIGOPOLISTIC
OLIGOPSONIES
OLIGOPSONISTIC
OLIGOPSONY
OLIGOSACCHARIDE
OLIGOSPERMIA
OLIGOSPERMIAS
OLIGOTROPHIC
OLIGOTROPHIES
OLIGOTROPHY
OLIGURESES
OLIGURESIS
OLIGURETIC
OLIVACEOUS
OLIVENITES
OLIVINITIC
OLOGOANING
OLOLIUQUIS
OMBROGENOUS
OMBROMETER

OMBROMETERS
OMBROPHILE
OMBROPHILES
OMBROPHILOUS
OMBROPHILS
OMBROPHOBE
OMBROPHOBES
OMBROPHOBOUS
OMBUDSMANSHIP
OMBUDSMANSHIPS
OMINOUSNESS
OMINOUSNESSES
OMISSIVENESS
OMISSIVENESSES
OMITTANCES
OMMATIDIAL
OMMATIDIUM
OMMATOPHORE
OMMATOPHORES
OMMATOPHOROUS
OMNIBENEVOLENCE
OMNIBENEVOLENT
OMNIBUSSES
OMNICOMPETENCE
OMNICOMPETENCES
OMNICOMPETENT
OMNIDIRECTIONAL
OMNIFARIOUS
OMNIFARIOUSLY
OMNIFARIOUSNESS
OMNIFEROUS
OMNIFICENCE
OMNIFICENCES
OMNIFICENT
OMNIFORMITIES
OMNIFORMITY
OMNIGENOUS
OMNIPARITIES
OMNIPARITY
OMNIPAROUS
OMNIPATIENT
OMNIPOTENCE
OMNIPOTENCES
OMNIPOTENCIES
OMNIPOTENCY
OMNIPOTENT
OMNIPOTENTLY
OMNIPOTENTS
OMNIPRESENCE
OMNIPRESENCES
OMNIPRESENT
OMNIRANGES
OMNISCIENCE
OMNISCIENCES
OMNISCIENT
OMNISCIENTLY
OMNIVORIES
OMNIVOROUS
OMNIVOROUSLY

OMNIVOROUSNESS
OMOPHAGIAS
OMOPHAGIES
OMOPHAGOUS
OMOPHORION
OMOPLATOSCOPIES
OMOPLATOSCOPY
OMPHACITES
OMPHALOMANCIES
OMPHALOMANCY
OMPHALOSKEPSES
OMPHALOSKEPSIS
ONAGRACEOUS
ONCHOCERCIASES
ONCHOCERCIASIS
ONCOGENESES
ONCOGENESIS
ONCOGENETICIST
ONCOGENETICISTS
ONCOGENICITIES
ONCOGENICITY
ONCOGENOUS
ONCOLOGICAL
ONCOLOGIES
ONCOLOGIST
ONCOLOGISTS
ONCOLYTICS
ONCOMETERS
ONCORNAVIRUS
ONCORNAVIRUSES
ONCOTOMIES
ONCOVIRUSES
ONDOGRAPHS
ONEIRICALLY
ONEIROCRITIC
ONEIROCRITICAL
ONEIROCRITICISM
ONEIROCRITICS
ONEIRODYNIA
ONEIRODYNIAS
ONEIROLOGIES
ONEIROLOGY
ONEIROMANCER
ONEIROMANCERS
ONEIROMANCIES
ONEIROMANCY
ONEIROSCOPIES
ONEIROSCOPIST
ONEIROSCOPISTS
ONEIROSCOPY
ONEROUSNESS
ONEROUSNESSES
ONGOINGNESS
ONGOINGNESSES
ONIONSKINS
ONOCENTAUR
ONOCENTAURS
ONOMASIOLOGIES
ONOMASIOLOGY

ONOMASTICALLY
ONOMASTICIAN
ONOMASTICIANS
ONOMASTICON
ONOMASTICONS
ONOMASTICS
ONOMATOLOGIES
ONOMATOLOGIST
ONOMATOLOGISTS
ONOMATOLOGY
ONOMATOPOEIA
ONOMATOPOEIAS
ONOMATOPOEIC
ONOMATOPOESES
ONOMATOPOESIS
ONOMATOPOETIC
ONOMATOPOIESES
ONOMATOPOIESIS
ONSETTINGS
ONSHORINGS
ONSLAUGHTS
ONTOGENESES
ONTOGENESIS
ONTOGENETIC
ONTOGENETICALLY
ONTOGENICALLY
ONTOGENIES
ONTOLOGICAL
ONTOLOGICALLY
ONTOLOGIES
ONTOLOGIST
ONTOLOGISTS
ONYCHITISES
ONYCHOCRYPTOSES
ONYCHOCRYPTOSIS
ONYCHOMANCIES
ONYCHOMANCY
ONYCHOPHAGIES
ONYCHOPHAGIST
ONYCHOPHAGISTS
ONYCHOPHAGY
ONYCHOPHORAN
ONYCHOPHORANS
OOPHORECTOMIES
OOPHORECTOMISE
OOPHORECTOMISED
OOPHORECTOMISES
OOPHORECTOMIZE
OOPHORECTOMIZED
OOPHORECTOMIZES
OOPHORECTOMY
OOPHORITIC
OOPHORITIS
OOPHORITISES
OOZINESSES
OPACIFIERS
OPACIFYING
OPALESCENCE
OPALESCENCES

OPALESCENT
OPALESCENTLY
OPALESCING
OPAQUENESS
OPAQUENESSES
OPEIDOSCOPE
OPEIDOSCOPES
OPENABILITIES
OPENABILITY
OPENHANDED
OPENHANDEDLY
OPENHANDEDNESS
OPENHEARTED
OPENHEARTEDLY
OPENHEARTEDNESS
OPENMOUTHED
OPENMOUTHEDLY
OPENMOUTHEDNESS
OPENNESSES
OPERABILITIES
OPERABILITY
OPERAGOERS
OPERAGOING
OPERAGOINGS
OPERATICALLY
OPERATIONAL
OPERATIONALISM
OPERATIONALISMS
OPERATIONALIST
OPERATIONALISTS
OPERATIONALLY
OPERATIONISM
OPERATIONISMS
OPERATIONIST
OPERATIONISTS
OPERATIONS
OPERATISED
OPERATISES
OPERATISING
OPERATIVELY
OPERATIVENESS
OPERATIVENESSES
OPERATIVES
OPERATIVITIES
OPERATIVITY
OPERATIZED
OPERATIZES
OPERATIZING
OPERATORLESS
OPERCULARS
OPERCULATE
OPERCULATED
OPERCULUMS
OPERETTIST
OPERETTISTS
OPEROSENESS
OPEROSENESSES
OPEROSITIES
OPHICALCITE

OPHICALCITES
OPHICLEIDE
OPHICLEIDES
OPHIDIARIA
OPHIDIARIUM
OPHIDIARIUMS
OPHIOLATER
OPHIOLATERS
OPHIOLATRIES
OPHIOLATROUS
OPHIOLATRY
OPHIOLITES
OPHIOLITIC
OPHIOLOGIC
OPHIOLOGICAL
OPHIOLOGIES
OPHIOLOGIST
OPHIOLOGISTS
OPHIOMORPH
OPHIOMORPHIC
OPHIOMORPHOUS
OPHIOMORPHS
OPHIOPHAGOUS
OPHIOPHILIST
OPHIOPHILISTS
OPHIUROIDS
OPHTHALMIA
OPHTHALMIAS
OPHTHALMIC
OPHTHALMIST
OPHTHALMISTS
OPHTHALMITIS
OPHTHALMITISES
OPHTHALMOLOGIC
OPHTHALMOLOGIES
OPHTHALMOLOGIST
OPHTHALMOLOGY
OPHTHALMOMETER
OPHTHALMOMETERS
OPHTHALMOMETRY
OPHTHALMOPHOBIA
OPHTHALMOPLEGIA
OPHTHALMOSCOPE
OPHTHALMOSCOPES
OPHTHALMOSCOPIC
OPHTHALMOSCOPY
OPINICUSES
OPINIONATED
OPINIONATEDLY
OPINIONATEDNESS
OPINIONATELY
OPINIONATIVE
OPINIONATIVELY
OPINIONATOR
OPINIONATORS
OPINIONIST
OPINIONISTS
OPISOMETER
OPISOMETERS

OPISTHOBRANCH
OPISTHOBRANCHS
OPISTHOCOELIAN
OPISTHOCOELOUS
OPISTHODOMOI
OPISTHODOMOS
OPISTHOGLOSSAL
OPISTHOGNATHISM
OPISTHOGNATHOUS
OPISTHOGRAPH
OPISTHOGRAPHIC
OPISTHOGRAPHIES
OPISTHOGRAPHS
OPISTHOGRAPHY
OPISTHOSOMA
OPISTHOSOMATA
OPISTHOTONIC
OPISTHOTONOS
OPISTHOTONOSES
OPOBALSAMS
OPODELDOCS
OPOPANAXES
OPOTHERAPIES
OPOTHERAPY
OPPIGNERATE
OPPIGNERATED
OPPIGNERATES
OPPIGNERATING
OPPIGNORATE
OPPIGNORATED
OPPIGNORATES
OPPIGNORATING
OPPIGNORATION
OPPIGNORATIONS
OPPILATING
OPPILATION
OPPILATIONS
OPPILATIVE
OPPONENCIES
OPPORTUNELY
OPPORTUNENESS
OPPORTUNENESSES
OPPORTUNISM
OPPORTUNISMS
OPPORTUNIST
OPPORTUNISTIC
OPPORTUNISTS
OPPORTUNITIES
OPPORTUNITY
OPPOSABILITIES
OPPOSABILITY
OPPOSELESS
OPPOSINGLY
OPPOSITELY
OPPOSITENESS
OPPOSITENESSES
OPPOSITION
OPPOSITIONAL
OPPOSITIONIST

OPPOSITIONISTS
OPPOSITIONLESS
OPPOSITIONS
OPPOSITIVE
OPPRESSING
OPPRESSINGLY
OPPRESSION
OPPRESSIONS
OPPRESSIVE
OPPRESSIVELY
OPPRESSIVENESS
OPPRESSORS
OPPROBRIOUS
OPPROBRIOUSLY
OPPROBRIOUSNESS
OPPROBRIUM
OPPROBRIUMS
OPPUGNANCIES
OPPUGNANCY
OPPUGNANTLY
OPPUGNANTS
OPSIMATHIES
OPSIOMETER
OPSIOMETERS
OPSOMANIAC
OPSOMANIACS
OPSOMANIAS
OPSONIFICATION
OPSONIFICATIONS
OPSONIFIED
OPSONIFIES
OPSONIFYING
OPSONISATION
OPSONISATIONS
OPSONISING
OPSONIZATION
OPSONIZATIONS
OPSONIZING
OPTATIVELY
OPTIMALISATION
OPTIMALISATIONS
OPTIMALISE
OPTIMALISED
OPTIMALISES
OPTIMALISING
OPTIMALITIES
OPTIMALITY
OPTIMALIZATION
OPTIMALIZATIONS
OPTIMALIZE
OPTIMALIZED
OPTIMALIZES
OPTIMALIZING
OPTIMISATION
OPTIMISATIONS
OPTIMISERS
OPTIMISING
OPTIMISTIC
OPTIMISTICAL

OPTIMISTICALLY
OPTIMIZATION
OPTIMIZATIONS
OPTIMIZERS
OPTIMIZING
OPTIONALITIES
OPTIONALITY
OPTIONALLY
OPTOACOUSTIC
OPTOELECTRONIC
OPTOELECTRONICS
OPTOKINETIC
OPTOLOGIES
OPTOLOGIST
OPTOLOGISTS
OPTOMETERS
OPTOMETRIC
OPTOMETRICAL
OPTOMETRIES
OPTOMETRIST
OPTOMETRISTS
OPTOPHONES
OPULENCIES
ORACULARITIES
ORACULARITY
ORACULARLY
ORACULARNESS
ORACULARNESSES
ORACULOUSLY
ORACULOUSNESS
ORACULOUSNESSES
ORANGEADES
ORANGERIES
ORANGEWOOD
ORANGEWOODS
ORANGUTANS
ORATORIANS
ORATORICAL
ORATORICALLY
ORATRESSES
ORBICULARES
ORBICULARIS
ORBICULARITIES
ORBICULARITY
ORBICULARLY
ORBICULATE
ORBICULATED
ORCHARDING
ORCHARDINGS
ORCHARDIST
ORCHARDISTS
ORCHARDMAN
ORCHARDMEN
ORCHESOGRAPHIES
ORCHESOGRAPHY
ORCHESTICS
ORCHESTRAL
ORCHESTRALIST
ORCHESTRALISTS

ORCHESTRALLY
ORCHESTRAS
ORCHESTRATE
ORCHESTRATED
ORCHESTRATER
ORCHESTRATERS
ORCHESTRATES
ORCHESTRATING
ORCHESTRATION
ORCHESTRATIONAL
ORCHESTRATIONS
ORCHESTRATOR
ORCHESTRATORS
ORCHESTRIC
ORCHESTRINA
ORCHESTRINAS
ORCHESTRION
ORCHESTRIONS
ORCHIDACEOUS
ORCHIDECTOMIES
ORCHIDECTOMY
ORCHIDEOUS
ORCHIDISTS
ORCHIDLIKE
ORCHIDOLOGIES
ORCHIDOLOGIST
ORCHIDOLOGISTS
ORCHIDOLOGY
ORCHIDOMANIA
ORCHIDOMANIAC
ORCHIDOMANIACS
ORCHIDOMANIAS
ORCHIECTOMIES
ORCHIECTOMY
ORCHITISES
ORDAINABLE
ORDAINMENT
ORDAINMENTS
ORDERLINESS
ORDERLINESSES
ORDINAIRES
ORDINANCES
ORDINARIER
ORDINARIES
ORDINARIEST
ORDINARILY
ORDINARINESS
ORDINARINESSES
ORDINATELY
ORDINATING
ORDINATION
ORDINATIONS
ORDONNANCE
ORDONNANCES
ORECCHIETTE
ORECCHIETTI
OREOGRAPHIC
OREOGRAPHICAL
OREOGRAPHIES

OREOGRAPHY
OREOLOGICAL
OREOLOGIES
OREOLOGIST
OREOLOGISTS
OREPEARCHED
OREPEARCHES
OREPEARCHING
ORGANELLES
ORGANICALLY
ORGANICISM
ORGANICISMS
ORGANICIST
ORGANICISTIC
ORGANICISTS
ORGANICITIES
ORGANICITY
ORGANISABILITY
ORGANISABLE
ORGANISATION
ORGANISATIONAL
ORGANISATIONS
ORGANISERS
ORGANISING
ORGANISMAL
ORGANISMALLY
ORGANISMIC
ORGANISMICALLY
ORGANISTRUM
ORGANISTRUMS
ORGANITIES
ORGANIZABILITY
ORGANIZABLE
ORGANIZATION
ORGANIZATIONAL
ORGANIZATIONS
ORGANIZERS
ORGANIZING
ORGANOCHLORINE
ORGANOCHLORINES
ORGANOGENESES
ORGANOGENESIS
ORGANOGENETIC
ORGANOGENIES
ORGANOGENY
ORGANOGRAM
ORGANOGRAMS
ORGANOGRAPHIC
ORGANOGRAPHICAL
ORGANOGRAPHIES
ORGANOGRAPHIST
ORGANOGRAPHISTS
ORGANOGRAPHY
ORGANOLEPTIC
ORGANOLOGICAL
ORGANOLOGIES
ORGANOLOGIST
ORGANOLOGISTS
ORGANOLOGY

ORGANOMERCURIAL
ORGANOMETALLIC
ORGANOMETALLICS
ORGANOPHOSPHATE
ORGANOSOLS
ORGANOTHERAPIES
ORGANOTHERAPY
ORGANZINES
ORGIASTICALLY
ORICALCHES
ORICHALCEOUS
ORIENTALISE
ORIENTALISED
ORIENTALISES
ORIENTALISING
ORIENTALISM
ORIENTALISMS
ORIENTALIST
ORIENTALISTS
ORIENTALITIES
ORIENTALITY
ORIENTALIZE
ORIENTALIZED
ORIENTALIZES
ORIENTALIZING
ORIENTALLY
ORIENTATED
ORIENTATES
ORIENTATING
ORIENTATION
ORIENTATIONAL
ORIENTATIONALLY
ORIENTATIONS
ORIENTATOR
ORIENTATORS
ORIENTEERED
ORIENTEERING
ORIENTEERINGS
ORIENTEERS
ORIFLAMMES
ORIGINALITIES
ORIGINALITY
ORIGINALLY
ORIGINATED
ORIGINATES
ORIGINATING
ORIGINATION
ORIGINATIONS
ORIGINATIVE
ORIGINATIVELY
ORIGINATOR
ORIGINATORS
ORINASALLY
ORISMOLOGICAL
ORISMOLOGIES
ORISMOLOGY
ORNAMENTAL
ORNAMENTALLY
ORNAMENTALS

ORNAMENTATION
ORNAMENTATIONS
ORNAMENTED
ORNAMENTER
ORNAMENTERS
ORNAMENTING
ORNAMENTIST
ORNAMENTISTS
ORNATENESS
ORNATENESSES
ORNERINESS
ORNERINESSES
ORNITHICHNITE
ORNITHICHNITES
ORNITHINES
ORNITHISCHIAN
ORNITHISCHIANS
ORNITHODELPHIAN
ORNITHODELPHIC
ORNITHODELPHOUS
ORNITHOGALUM
ORNITHOGALUMS
ORNITHOLOGIC
ORNITHOLOGICAL
ORNITHOLOGIES
ORNITHOLOGIST
ORNITHOLOGISTS
ORNITHOLOGY
ORNITHOMANCIES
ORNITHOMANCY
ORNITHOMANTIC
ORNITHOMORPH
ORNITHOMORPHIC
ORNITHOMORPHS
ORNITHOPHILIES
ORNITHOPHILOUS
ORNITHOPHILY
ORNITHOPHOBIA
ORNITHOPHOBIAS
ORNITHOPOD
ORNITHOPODS
ORNITHOPTER
ORNITHOPTERS
ORNITHORHYNCHUS
ORNITHOSAUR
ORNITHOSAURS
ORNITHOSCOPIES
ORNITHOSCOPY
ORNITHOSES
ORNITHOSIS
OROBANCHACEOUS
OROGENESES
OROGENESIS
OROGENETIC
OROGENETICALLY
OROGENICALLY
OROGRAPHER
OROGRAPHERS
OROGRAPHIC

OROGRAPHICAL
OROGRAPHICALLY
OROGRAPHIES
OROLOGICAL
OROLOGICALLY
OROLOGISTS
OROPHARYNGEAL
OROPHARYNGES
OROPHARYNX
OROPHARYNXES
OROROTUNDITIES
OROROTUNDITY
OROTUNDITIES
OROTUNDITY
ORPHANAGES
ORPHANHOOD
ORPHANHOODS
ORPHANISMS
ORPHARIONS
ORPHEOREON
ORPHEOREONS
ORPHICALLY
ORRISROOTS
ORTANIQUES
ORTHOBORATE
ORTHOBORATES
ORTHOBORIC
ORTHOCAINE
ORTHOCAINES
ORTHOCENTER
ORTHOCENTERS
ORTHOCENTRE
ORTHOCENTRES
ORTHOCEPHALIC
ORTHOCEPHALIES
ORTHOCEPHALOUS
ORTHOCEPHALY
ORTHOCHROMATIC
ORTHOCHROMATISM
ORTHOCLASE
ORTHOCLASES
ORTHOCOUSINS
ORTHODIAGONAL
ORTHODIAGONALS
ORTHODONTIA
ORTHODONTIAS
ORTHODONTIC
ORTHODONTICALLY
ORTHODONTICS
ORTHODONTIST
ORTHODONTISTS
ORTHODOXES
ORTHODOXIES
ORTHODOXLY
ORTHODROMIC
ORTHODROMICS
ORTHODROMIES
ORTHODROMY
ORTHOEPICAL

ORTHOEPICALLY
ORTHOEPIES
ORTHOEPIST
ORTHOEPISTS
ORTHOGENESES
ORTHOGENESIS
ORTHOGENETIC
ORTHOGENIC
ORTHOGENICALLY
ORTHOGENICS
ORTHOGNATHIC
ORTHOGNATHIES
ORTHOGNATHISM
ORTHOGNATHISMS
ORTHOGNATHOUS
ORTHOGNATHY
ORTHOGONAL
ORTHOGONALISE
ORTHOGONALISED
ORTHOGONALISES
ORTHOGONALISING
ORTHOGONALITIES
ORTHOGONALITY
ORTHOGONALIZE
ORTHOGONALIZED
ORTHOGONALIZES
ORTHOGONALIZING
ORTHOGONALLY
ORTHOGRADE
ORTHOGRAPH
ORTHOGRAPHER
ORTHOGRAPHERS
ORTHOGRAPHIC
ORTHOGRAPHICAL
ORTHOGRAPHIES
ORTHOGRAPHIST
ORTHOGRAPHISTS
ORTHOGRAPHS
ORTHOGRAPHY
ORTHOHYDROGEN
ORTHOHYDROGENS
ORTHOMOLECULAR
ORTHOMORPHIC
ORTHONORMAL
ORTHOPAEDIC
ORTHOPAEDICAL
ORTHOPAEDICS
ORTHOPAEDIES
ORTHOPAEDIST
ORTHOPAEDISTS
ORTHOPAEDY
ORTHOPEDIA
ORTHOPEDIAS
ORTHOPEDIC
ORTHOPEDICAL
ORTHOPEDICALLY
ORTHOPEDICS
ORTHOPEDIES
ORTHOPEDIST

ORTHOPEDISTS
ORTHOPHOSPHATE
ORTHOPHOSPHATES
ORTHOPHOSPHORIC
ORTHOPHYRE
ORTHOPHYRES
ORTHOPHYRIC
ORTHOPINAKOID
ORTHOPINAKOIDS
ORTHOPNOEA
ORTHOPNOEAS
ORTHOPRAXES
ORTHOPRAXIES
ORTHOPRAXIS
ORTHOPRAXY
ORTHOPRISM
ORTHOPRISMS
ORTHOPSYCHIATRY
ORTHOPTERA
ORTHOPTERAN
ORTHOPTERANS
ORTHOPTERIST
ORTHOPTERISTS
ORTHOPTEROID
ORTHOPTEROIDS
ORTHOPTEROLOGY
ORTHOPTERON
ORTHOPTEROUS
ORTHOPTERS
ORTHOPTICS
ORTHOPTIST
ORTHOPTISTS
ORTHOPYROXENE
ORTHOPYROXENES
ORTHORHOMBIC
ORTHOSCOPE
ORTHOSCOPES
ORTHOSCOPIC
ORTHOSILICATE
ORTHOSILICATES
ORTHOSTATIC
ORTHOSTICHIES
ORTHOSTICHOUS
ORTHOSTICHY
ORTHOTISTS
ORTHOTONES
ORTHOTONESES
ORTHOTONESIS
ORTHOTONIC
ORTHOTOPIC
ORTHOTROPIC
ORTHOTROPIES
ORTHOTROPISM
ORTHOTROPISMS
ORTHOTROPOUS
ORTHOTROPY
ORTHOTUNGSTIC
ORTHOVANADIC
ORYCTOLOGIES

ORYCTOLOGY
OSCILLATED
OSCILLATES
OSCILLATING
OSCILLATION
OSCILLATIONAL
OSCILLATIONS
OSCILLATIVE
OSCILLATOR
OSCILLATORS
OSCILLATORY
OSCILLOGRAM
OSCILLOGRAMS
OSCILLOGRAPH
OSCILLOGRAPHIC
OSCILLOGRAPHIES
OSCILLOGRAPHS
OSCILLOGRAPHY
OSCILLOSCOPE
OSCILLOSCOPES
OSCILLOSCOPIC
OSCITANCES
OSCITANCIES
OSCITANTLY
OSCITATING
OSCITATION
OSCITATIONS
OSCULATING
OSCULATION
OSCULATIONS
OSCULATORIES
OSCULATORY
OSMETERIUM
OSMIDROSES
OSMIDROSIS
OSMIRIDIUM
OSMIRIDIUMS
OSMOLALITIES
OSMOLALITY
OSMOLARITIES
OSMOLARITY
OSMOMETERS
OSMOMETRIC
OSMOMETRICALLY
OSMOMETRIES
OSMOREGULATION
OSMOREGULATIONS
OSMOREGULATORY
OSMOTICALLY
OSMUNDINES
OSSIFEROUS
OSSIFICATION
OSSIFICATIONS
OSSIFRAGAS
OSSIFRAGES
OSSIVOROUS
OSTEICHTHYAN
OSTEICHTHYANS
OSTEITIDES

OSTEITISES
OSTENSIBILITIES
OSTENSIBILITY
OSTENSIBLE
OSTENSIBLY
OSTENSIVELY
OSTENSORIA
OSTENSORIES
OSTENSORIUM
OSTENTATION
OSTENTATIONS
OSTENTATIOUS
OSTENTATIOUSLY
OSTEOARTHRITIC
OSTEOARTHRITICS
OSTEOARTHRITIS
OSTEOARTHROSES
OSTEOARTHROSIS
OSTEOBLAST
OSTEOBLASTIC
OSTEOBLASTS
OSTEOCLASES
OSTEOCLASIS
OSTEOCLAST
OSTEOCLASTIC
OSTEOCLASTS
OSTEOCOLLA
OSTEOCOLLAS
OSTEOCYTES
OSTEODERMAL
OSTEODERMATOUS
OSTEODERMIC
OSTEODERMOUS
OSTEODERMS
OSTEOFIBROSES
OSTEOFIBROSIS
OSTEOGENESES
OSTEOGENESIS
OSTEOGENETIC
OSTEOGENIC
OSTEOGENIES
OSTEOGENOUS
OSTEOGRAPHIES
OSTEOGRAPHY
OSTEOLOGICAL
OSTEOLOGICALLY
OSTEOLOGIES
OSTEOLOGIST
OSTEOLOGISTS
OSTEOMALACIA
OSTEOMALACIAL
OSTEOMALACIAS
OSTEOMALACIC
OSTEOMYELITIS
OSTEOMYELITISES
OSTEOPATHIC
OSTEOPATHICALLY
OSTEOPATHIES
OSTEOPATHIST

OSTEOPATHISTS
OSTEOPATHS
OSTEOPATHY
OSTEOPETROSES
OSTEOPETROSIS
OSTEOPHYTE
OSTEOPHYTES
OSTEOPHYTIC
OSTEOPLASTIC
OSTEOPLASTIES
OSTEOPLASTY
OSTEOPOROSES
OSTEOPOROSIS
OSTEOPOROTIC
OSTEOSARCOMA
OSTEOSARCOMAS
OSTEOSARCOMATA
OSTEOSISES
OSTEOTOMES
OSTEOTOMIES
OSTLERESSES
OSTRACEOUS
OSTRACISABLE
OSTRACISED
OSTRACISER
OSTRACISERS
OSTRACISES
OSTRACISING
OSTRACISMS
OSTRACIZABLE
OSTRACIZED
OSTRACIZER
OSTRACIZERS
OSTRACIZES
OSTRACIZING
OSTRACODAN
OSTRACODERM
OSTRACODERMS
OSTRACODES
OSTRACODOUS
OSTREACEOUS
OSTREICULTURE
OSTREICULTURES
OSTREICULTURIST
OSTREOPHAGE
OSTREOPHAGES
OSTREOPHAGIES
OSTREOPHAGOUS
OSTREOPHAGY
OSTRICHISM
OSTRICHISMS
OSTRICHLIKE
OTHERGATES
OTHERGUESS
OTHERNESSES
OTHERWHERE
OTHERWHILE
OTHERWHILES
OTHERWORLD

OTHERWORLDISH
OTHERWORLDLY
OTHERWORLDS
OTIOSENESS
OTIOSENESSES
OTIOSITIES
OTOLARYNGOLOGY
OTOLOGICAL
OTOLOGISTS
OTOPLASTIES
OTORRHOEAS
OTOSCLEROSES
OTOSCLEROSIS
OTOSCOPIES
OTOTOXICITIES
OTOTOXICITY
OTTRELITES
OUANANICHE
OUANANICHES
OUBLIETTES
OUGHTLINGS
OUGHTNESSES
OUROBOROSES
OUROLOGIES
OUROSCOPIES
OUTACHIEVE
OUTACHIEVED
OUTACHIEVES
OUTACHIEVING
OUTARGUING
OUTBACKERS
OUTBALANCE
OUTBALANCED
OUTBALANCES
OUTBALANCING
OUTBARGAIN
OUTBARGAINED
OUTBARGAINING
OUTBARGAINS
OUTBARKING
OUTBARRING
OUTBAWLING
OUTBEAMING
OUTBEGGING
OUTBIDDERS
OUTBIDDING
OUTBITCHED
OUTBITCHES
OUTBITCHING
OUTBLAZING
OUTBLEATED
OUTBLEATING
OUTBLESSED
OUTBLESSES
OUTBLESSING
OUTBLOOMED
OUTBLOOMING
OUTBLUFFED
OUTBLUFFING

OUTBLUSHED
OUTBLUSHES
OUTBLUSHING
OUTBLUSTER
OUTBLUSTERED
OUTBLUSTERING
OUTBLUSTERS
OUTBOASTED
OUTBOASTING
OUTBRAGGED
OUTBRAGGING
OUTBRAVING
OUTBRAWLED
OUTBRAWLING
OUTBRAZENED
OUTBRAZENING
OUTBRAZENS
OUTBREAKING
OUTBREATHE
OUTBREATHED
OUTBREATHES
OUTBREATHING
OUTBREEDING
OUTBREEDINGS
OUTBRIBING
OUTBUILDING
OUTBUILDINGS
OUTBULGING
OUTBULKING
OUTBULLIED
OUTBULLIES
OUTBULLYING
OUTBURNING
OUTBURSTING
OUTCAPERED
OUTCAPERING
OUTCASTING
OUTCATCHES
OUTCATCHING
OUTCAVILED
OUTCAVILING
OUTCAVILLED
OUTCAVILLING
OUTCHARGED
OUTCHARGES
OUTCHARGING
OUTCHARMED
OUTCHARMING
OUTCHEATED
OUTCHEATING
OUTCHIDDEN
OUTCHIDING
OUTCLASSED
OUTCLASSES
OUTCLASSING
OUTCLIMBED
OUTCLIMBING
OUTCOACHED
OUTCOACHES

OUTCOACHING
OUTCOMPETE
OUTCOMPETED
OUTCOMPETES
OUTCOMPETING
OUTCOOKING
OUTCOUNTED
OUTCOUNTING
OUTCRAFTIED
OUTCRAFTIES
OUTCRAFTYING
OUTCRAWLED
OUTCRAWLING
OUTCROPPED
OUTCROPPING
OUTCROPPINGS
OUTCROSSED
OUTCROSSES
OUTCROSSING
OUTCROSSINGS
OUTCROWDED
OUTCROWDING
OUTCROWING
OUTCURSING
OUTDACIOUS
OUTDANCING
OUTDATEDLY
OUTDATEDNESS
OUTDATEDNESSES
OUTDAZZLED
OUTDAZZLES
OUTDAZZLING
OUTDEBATED
OUTDEBATES
OUTDEBATING
OUTDELIVER
OUTDELIVERED
OUTDELIVERING
OUTDELIVERS
OUTDESIGNED
OUTDESIGNING
OUTDESIGNS
OUTDISTANCE
OUTDISTANCED
OUTDISTANCES
OUTDISTANCING
OUTDODGING
OUTDOORSMAN
OUTDOORSMANSHIP
OUTDOORSMEN
OUTDRAGGED
OUTDRAGGING
OUTDRAWING
OUTDREAMED
OUTDREAMING
OUTDRESSED
OUTDRESSES
OUTDRESSING
OUTDRINKING

OUTDRIVING
OUTDROPPED
OUTDROPPING
OUTDUELING
OUTDUELLED
OUTDUELLING
OUTDWELLED
OUTDWELLING
OUTEARNING
OUTECHOING
OUTERCOATS
OUTERCOURSE
OUTERCOURSES
OUTERWEARS
OUTFABLING
OUTFANGTHIEF
OUTFANGTHIEVES
OUTFASTING
OUTFAWNING
OUTFEASTED
OUTFEASTING
OUTFEELING
OUTFENCING
OUTFIELDER
OUTFIELDERS
OUTFIGHTING
OUTFIGURED
OUTFIGURES
OUTFIGURING
OUTFINDING
OUTFISHING
OUTFITTERS
OUTFITTING
OUTFITTINGS
OUTFLANKED
OUTFLANKING
OUTFLASHED
OUTFLASHES
OUTFLASHING
OUTFLOATED
OUTFLOATING
OUTFLOWING
OUTFLOWINGS
OUTFLUSHED
OUTFLUSHES
OUTFLUSHING
OUTFOOLING
OUTFOOTING
OUTFROWNED
OUTFROWNING
OUTFUMBLED
OUTFUMBLES
OUTFUMBLING
OUTGAINING
OUTGALLOPED
OUTGALLOPING
OUTGALLOPS
OUTGAMBLED
OUTGAMBLES

OUTGAMBLING
OUTGASSING
OUTGASSINGS
OUTGENERAL
OUTGENERALED
OUTGENERALING
OUTGENERALLED
OUTGENERALLING
OUTGENERALS
OUTGIVINGS
OUTGLARING
OUTGLEAMED
OUTGLEAMING
OUTGLITTER
OUTGLITTERED
OUTGLITTERING
OUTGLITTERS
OUTGLOWING
OUTGNAWING
OUTGOINGNESS
OUTGOINGNESSES
OUTGRINNED
OUTGRINNING
OUTGROSSED
OUTGROSSES
OUTGROSSING
OUTGROWING
OUTGROWTHS
OUTGUESSED
OUTGUESSES
OUTGUESSING
OUTGUIDING
OUTGUNNING
OUTGUSHING
OUTHANDLED
OUTHANDLES
OUTHANDLING
OUTHAULERS
OUTHEARING
OUTHITTING
OUTHOMERED
OUTHOMERING
OUTHOWLING
OUTHUMORED
OUTHUMORING
OUTHUNTING
OUTHUSTLED
OUTHUSTLES
OUTHUSTLING
OUTINTRIGUE
OUTINTRIGUED
OUTINTRIGUES
OUTINTRIGUING
OUTJESTING
OUTJETTING
OUTJETTINGS
OUTJINXING
OUTJOCKEYED
OUTJOCKEYING

OUTJOCKEYS
OUTJUGGLED
OUTJUGGLES
OUTJUGGLING
OUTJUMPING
OUTJUTTING
OUTJUTTINGS
OUTKEEPING
OUTKICKING
OUTKILLING
OUTKISSING
OUTLANDERS
OUTLANDISH
OUTLANDISHLY
OUTLANDISHNESS
OUTLASTING
OUTLAUGHED
OUTLAUGHING
OUTLAUNCED
OUTLAUNCES
OUTLAUNCHED
OUTLAUNCHES
OUTLAUNCHING
OUTLAUNCING
OUTLAWRIES
OUTLEADING
OUTLEAPING
OUTLEARNED
OUTLEARNING
OUTLODGING
OUTLODGINGS
OUTLOOKING
OUTLUSTRED
OUTLUSTRES
OUTLUSTRING
OUTMANEUVER
OUTMANEUVERED
OUTMANEUVERING
OUTMANEUVERS
OUTMANIPULATE
OUTMANIPULATED
OUTMANIPULATES
OUTMANIPULATING
OUTMANNING
OUTMANOEUVRE
OUTMANOEUVRED
OUTMANOEUVRES
OUTMANOEUVRING
OUTMANTLED
OUTMANTLES
OUTMANTLING
OUTMARCHED
OUTMARCHES
OUTMARCHING
OUTMARRIAGE
OUTMARRIAGES
OUTMASTERED
OUTMASTERING
OUTMASTERS

OUTMATCHED
OUTMATCHES
OUTMATCHING
OUTMEASURE
OUTMEASURED
OUTMEASURES
OUTMEASURING
OUTMODEDLY
OUTMODEDNESS
OUTMODEDNESSES
OUTMUSCLED
OUTMUSCLES
OUTMUSCLING
OUTNIGHTED
OUTNIGHTING
OUTNUMBERED
OUTNUMBERING
OUTNUMBERS
OUTOFFICES
OUTORGANISE
OUTORGANISED
OUTORGANISES
OUTORGANISING
OUTORGANIZE
OUTORGANIZED
OUTORGANIZES
OUTORGANIZING
OUTPAINTED
OUTPAINTING
OUTPASSING
OUTPASSION
OUTPASSIONED
OUTPASSIONING
OUTPASSIONS
OUTPATIENT
OUTPATIENTS
OUTPEEPING
OUTPEERING
OUTPEOPLED
OUTPEOPLES
OUTPEOPLING
OUTPERFORM
OUTPERFORMED
OUTPERFORMING
OUTPERFORMS
OUTPITCHED
OUTPITCHES
OUTPITCHING
OUTPITYING
OUTPLACEMENT
OUTPLACEMENTS
OUTPLACERS
OUTPLACING
OUTPLANNED
OUTPLANNING
OUTPLAYING
OUTPLODDED
OUTPLODDING
OUTPLOTTED

OUTPLOTTING
OUTPOINTED
OUTPOINTING
OUTPOLITICK
OUTPOLITICKED
OUTPOLITICKING
OUTPOLITICKS
OUTPOLLING
OUTPOPULATE
OUTPOPULATED
OUTPOPULATES
OUTPOPULATING
OUTPORTERS
OUTPOURERS
OUTPOURING
OUTPOURINGS
OUTPOWERED
OUTPOWERING
OUTPRAYING
OUTPREACHED
OUTPREACHES
OUTPREACHING
OUTPREENED
OUTPREENING
OUTPRESSED
OUTPRESSES
OUTPRESSING
OUTPRICING
OUTPRIZING
OUTPRODUCE
OUTPRODUCED
OUTPRODUCES
OUTPRODUCING
OUTPROMISE
OUTPROMISED
OUTPROMISES
OUTPROMISING
OUTPULLING
OUTPUNCHED
OUTPUNCHES
OUTPUNCHING
OUTPURSUED
OUTPURSUES
OUTPURSUING
OUTPUSHING
OUTPUTTING
OUTQUARTERS
OUTQUOTING
OUTRAGEOUS
OUTRAGEOUSLY
OUTRAGEOUSNESS
OUTRAISING
OUTRANGING
OUTRANKING
OUTREACHED
OUTREACHES
OUTREACHING
OUTREADING
OUTREASONED

OUTREASONING
OUTREASONS
OUTREBOUND
OUTREBOUNDED
OUTREBOUNDING
OUTREBOUNDS
OUTRECKONED
OUTRECKONING
OUTRECKONS
OUTRECUIDANCE
OUTRECUIDANCES
OUTREDDENED
OUTREDDENING
OUTREDDENS
OUTREDDING
OUTREIGNED
OUTREIGNING
OUTRELIEFS
OUTREPRODUCE
OUTREPRODUCED
OUTREPRODUCES
OUTREPRODUCING
OUTRIGGERS
OUTRIGGING
OUTRIGHTLY
OUTRINGING
OUTRIVALED
OUTRIVALING
OUTRIVALLED
OUTRIVALLING
OUTROARING
OUTROCKING
OUTROLLING
OUTROOPERS
OUTROOTING
OUTRUNNERS
OUTRUNNING
OUTRUSHING
OUTSAILING
OUTSAVORED
OUTSAVORING
OUTSCHEMED
OUTSCHEMES
OUTSCHEMING
OUTSCOLDED
OUTSCOLDING
OUTSCOOPED
OUTSCOOPING
OUTSCORING
OUTSCORNED
OUTSCORNING
OUTSCREAMED
OUTSCREAMING
OUTSCREAMS
OUTSELLING
OUTSERVING
OUTSETTING
OUTSETTINGS
OUTSETTLEMENT

OUTSETTLEMENTS
OUTSHAMING
OUTSHINING
OUTSHOOTING
OUTSHOUTED
OUTSHOUTING
OUTSIDERNESS
OUTSIDERNESSES
OUTSINGING
OUTSINNING
OUTSITTING
OUTSKATING
OUTSLEEPING
OUTSLICKED
OUTSLICKING
OUTSMARTED
OUTSMARTING
OUTSMELLED
OUTSMELLING
OUTSMILING
OUTSMOKING
OUTSNORING
OUTSOARING
OUTSOURCED
OUTSOURCES
OUTSOURCING
OUTSOURCINGS
OUTSPANNED
OUTSPANNING
OUTSPARKLE
OUTSPARKLED
OUTSPARKLES
OUTSPARKLING
OUTSPEAKING
OUTSPECKLE
OUTSPECKLES
OUTSPEEDED
OUTSPEEDING
OUTSPELLED
OUTSPELLING
OUTSPENDING
OUTSPOKENLY
OUTSPOKENNESS
OUTSPOKENNESSES
OUTSPORTED
OUTSPORTING
OUTSPREADING
OUTSPREADS
OUTSPRINGING
OUTSPRINGS
OUTSPRINTED
OUTSPRINTING
OUTSPRINTS
OUTSTANDING
OUTSTANDINGLY
OUTSTARING
OUTSTARTED
OUTSTARTING
OUTSTATING

OUTSTATION
OUTSTATIONS
OUTSTAYING
OUTSTEERED
OUTSTEERING
OUTSTEPPED
OUTSTEPPING
OUTSTRAINED
OUTSTRAINING
OUTSTRAINS
OUTSTRETCH
OUTSTRETCHED
OUTSTRETCHES
OUTSTRETCHING
OUTSTRIDDEN
OUTSTRIDES
OUTSTRIDING
OUTSTRIKES
OUTSTRIKING
OUTSTRIPPED
OUTSTRIPPING
OUTSTRIVEN
OUTSTRIVES
OUTSTRIVING
OUTSTROKES
OUTSTUDIED
OUTSTUDIES
OUTSTUDYING
OUTSTUNTED
OUTSTUNTING
OUTSULKING
OUTSUMMING
OUTSWEARING
OUTSWEEPING
OUTSWEETEN
OUTSWEETENED
OUTSWEETENING
OUTSWEETENS
OUTSWELLED
OUTSWELLING
OUTSWIMMING
OUTSWINGER
OUTSWINGERS
OUTSWINGING
OUTSWOLLEN
OUTTALKING
OUTTASKING
OUTTELLING
OUTTHANKED
OUTTHANKING
OUTTHIEVED
OUTTHIEVES
OUTTHIEVING
OUTTHINKING
OUTTHOUGHT
OUTTHROBBED
OUTTHROBBING
OUTTHROWING
OUTTHRUSTED

OUTTHRUSTING
OUTTHRUSTS
OUTTONGUED
OUTTONGUES
OUTTONGUING
OUTTOPPING
OUTTOWERED
OUTTOWERING
OUTTRADING
OUTTRAVELED
OUTTRAVELING
OUTTRAVELLED
OUTTRAVELLING
OUTTRAVELS
OUTTRICKED
OUTTRICKING
OUTTROTTED
OUTTROTTING
OUTTRUMPED
OUTTRUMPING
OUTVALUING
OUTVAUNTED
OUTVAUNTING
OUTVENOMED
OUTVENOMING
OUTVILLAIN
OUTVILLAINED
OUTVILLAINING
OUTVILLAINS
OUTVOICING
OUTWAITING
OUTWALKING
OUTWARDNESS
OUTWARDNESSES
OUTWARRING
OUTWASTING
OUTWATCHED
OUTWATCHES
OUTWATCHING
OUTWEARIED
OUTWEARIES
OUTWEARING
OUTWEARYING
OUTWEEDING
OUTWEEPING
OUTWEIGHED
OUTWEIGHING
OUTWELLING
OUTWHIRLED
OUTWHIRLING
OUTWICKING
OUTWILLING
OUTWINDING
OUTWINGING
OUTWINNING
OUTWISHING
OUTWITTING
OUTWORKERS
OUTWORKING

OUTWORTHED
OUTWORTHING
OUTWRESTED
OUTWRESTING
OUTWRESTLE
OUTWRESTLED
OUTWRESTLES
OUTWRESTLING
OUTWRITING
OUTWRITTEN
OUTWROUGHT
OUTYELLING
OUTYELPING
OUTYIELDED
OUTYIELDING
OUVIRANDRA
OUVIRANDRAS
OVALBUMINS
OVALNESSES
OVARIECTOMIES
OVARIECTOMISED
OVARIECTOMIZED
OVARIECTOMY
OVARIOTOMIES
OVARIOTOMIST
OVARIOTOMISTS
OVARIOTOMY
OVARITIDES
OVARITISES
OVERABOUND
OVERABOUNDED
OVERABOUNDING
OVERABOUNDS
OVERABSTRACT
OVERABUNDANCE
OVERABUNDANCES
OVERABUNDANT
OVERACCENTUATE
OVERACCENTUATED
OVERACCENTUATES
OVERACHIEVE
OVERACHIEVED
OVERACHIEVEMENT
OVERACHIEVER
OVERACHIEVERS
OVERACHIEVES
OVERACHIEVING
OVERACTING
OVERACTION
OVERACTIONS
OVERACTIVE
OVERACTIVITIES
OVERACTIVITY
OVERADJUSTMENT
OVERADJUSTMENTS
OVERADVERTISE
OVERADVERTISED
OVERADVERTISES
OVERADVERTISING

OVERAGGRESSIVE
OVERAMBITIOUS
OVERAMPLIFIED
OVERANALYSE
OVERANALYSED
OVERANALYSES
OVERANALYSING
OVERANALYSIS
OVERANALYTICAL
OVERANALYZE
OVERANALYZED
OVERANALYZES
OVERANALYZING
OVERANXIETIES
OVERANXIETY
OVERANXIOUS
OVERAPPLICATION
OVERARCHED
OVERARCHES
OVERARCHING
OVERARMING
OVERAROUSAL
OVERAROUSALS
OVERARRANGE
OVERARRANGED
OVERARRANGES
OVERARRANGING
OVERARTICULATE
OVERARTICULATED
OVERARTICULATES
OVERASSERT
OVERASSERTED
OVERASSERTING
OVERASSERTION
OVERASSERTIONS
OVERASSERTIVE
OVERASSERTS
OVERASSESSMENT
OVERASSESSMENTS
OVERATTENTION
OVERATTENTIONS
OVERATTENTIVE
OVERBAKING
OVERBALANCE
OVERBALANCED
OVERBALANCES
OVERBALANCING
OVERBEARING
OVERBEARINGLY
OVERBEARINGNESS
OVERBEATEN
OVERBEATING
OVERBEJEWELED
OVERBETTED
OVERBETTING
OVERBIDDEN
OVERBIDDER
OVERBIDDERS
OVERBIDDING

OVERBIDDINGS
OVERBILLED
OVERBILLING
OVERBLANKET
OVERBLANKETS
OVERBLEACH
OVERBLEACHED
OVERBLEACHES
OVERBLEACHING
OVERBLOUSE
OVERBLOUSES
OVERBLOWING
OVERBOILED
OVERBOILING
OVERBOLDLY
OVERBOOKED
OVERBOOKING
OVERBORROW
OVERBORROWED
OVERBORROWING
OVERBORROWS
OVERBOUGHT
OVERBOUNDED
OVERBOUNDING
OVERBOUNDS
OVERBRAKED
OVERBRAKES
OVERBRAKING
OVERBREATHING
OVERBREATHINGS
OVERBREEDING
OVERBREEDS
OVERBRIDGE
OVERBRIDGED
OVERBRIDGES
OVERBRIDGING
OVERBRIEFED
OVERBRIEFING
OVERBRIEFS
OVERBRIGHT
OVERBRIMMED
OVERBRIMMING
OVERBROWED
OVERBROWING
OVERBROWSE
OVERBROWSED
OVERBROWSES
OVERBROWSING
OVERBRUTAL
OVERBUILDING
OVERBUILDS
OVERBULKED
OVERBULKING
OVERBURDEN
OVERBURDENED
OVERBURDENING
OVERBURDENS
OVERBURDENSOME
OVERBURNED

OVERBURNING
OVERBURTHEN
OVERBURTHENED
OVERBURTHENING
OVERBURTHENS
OVERBUSIED
OVERBUSIES
OVERBUSYING
OVERBUYING
OVERCALLED
OVERCALLING
OVERCANOPIED
OVERCANOPIES
OVERCANOPY
OVERCANOPYING
OVERCAPACITIES
OVERCAPACITY
OVERCAPITALISE
OVERCAPITALISED
OVERCAPITALISES
OVERCAPITALIZE
OVERCAPITALIZED
OVERCAPITALIZES
OVERCAREFUL
OVERCARRIED
OVERCARRIES
OVERCARRYING
OVERCASTED
OVERCASTING
OVERCASTINGS
OVERCATCHES
OVERCATCHING
OVERCAUGHT
OVERCAUTION
OVERCAUTIONS
OVERCAUTIOUS
OVERCENTRALISE
OVERCENTRALISED
OVERCENTRALISES
OVERCENTRALIZE
OVERCENTRALIZED
OVERCENTRALIZES
OVERCHARGE
OVERCHARGED
OVERCHARGES
OVERCHARGING
OVERCHECKS
OVERCHILLED
OVERCHILLING
OVERCHILLS
OVERCIVILISED
OVERCIVILIZED
OVERCLAIMED
OVERCLAIMING
OVERCLAIMS
OVERCLASSES
OVERCLASSIFIED
OVERCLASSIFIES
OVERCLASSIFY

OVERCLASSIFYING
OVERCLEANED
OVERCLEANING
OVERCLEANS
OVERCLEARED
OVERCLEARING
OVERCLEARS
OVERCLOUDED
OVERCLOUDING
OVERCLOUDS
OVERCLOYED
OVERCLOYING
OVERCOACHED
OVERCOACHES
OVERCOACHING
OVERCOATING
OVERCOATINGS
OVERCOLORED
OVERCOLORING
OVERCOLORS
OVERCOLOUR
OVERCOLOURED
OVERCOLOURING
OVERCOLOURS
OVERCOMERS
OVERCOMING
OVERCOMMIT
OVERCOMMITMENT
OVERCOMMITMENTS
OVERCOMMITS
OVERCOMMITTED
OVERCOMMITTING
OVERCOMMUNICATE
OVERCOMPENSATE
OVERCOMPENSATED
OVERCOMPENSATES
OVERCOMPLEX
OVERCOMPLIANCE
OVERCOMPLIANCES
OVERCOMPLICATE
OVERCOMPLICATED
OVERCOMPLICATES
OVERCOMPRESS
OVERCOMPRESSED
OVERCOMPRESSES
OVERCOMPRESSING
OVERCONCERN
OVERCONCERNED
OVERCONCERNING
OVERCONCERNS
OVERCONFIDENCE
OVERCONFIDENCES
OVERCONFIDENT
OVERCONFIDENTLY
OVERCONSCIOUS
OVERCONSTRUCT
OVERCONSTRUCTED
OVERCONSTRUCTS
OVERCONSUME

OVERCONSUMED
OVERCONSUMES
OVERCONSUMING
OVERCONSUMPTION
OVERCONTROL
OVERCONTROLLED
OVERCONTROLLING
OVERCONTROLS
OVERCOOKED
OVERCOOKING
OVERCOOLED
OVERCOOLING
OVERCORRECT
OVERCORRECTED
OVERCORRECTING
OVERCORRECTION
OVERCORRECTIONS
OVERCORRECTS
OVERCOUNTED
OVERCOUNTING
OVERCOUNTS
OVERCOVERED
OVERCOVERING
OVERCOVERS
OVERCRAMMED
OVERCRAMMING
OVERCRAWED
OVERCRAWING
OVERCREDULITIES
OVERCREDULITY
OVERCREDULOUS
OVERCRITICAL
OVERCROPPED
OVERCROPPING
OVERCROWDED
OVERCROWDING
OVERCROWDINGS
OVERCROWDS
OVERCROWED
OVERCROWING
OVERCULTIVATION
OVERCURING
OVERCUTTING
OVERDARING
OVERDECKED
OVERDECKING
OVERDECORATE
OVERDECORATED
OVERDECORATES
OVERDECORATING
OVERDECORATION
OVERDECORATIONS
OVERDEMANDING
OVERDEPENDENCE
OVERDEPENDENCES
OVERDEPENDENT
OVERDESIGN
OVERDESIGNED
OVERDESIGNING

OVERDESIGNS

OVERDESIGNS
OVERDETERMINED
OVERDEVELOP
OVERDEVELOPED
OVERDEVELOPING
OVERDEVELOPMENT
OVERDEVELOPS
OVERDEVIATE
OVERDEVIATED
OVERDEVIATES
OVERDEVIATING
OVERDIRECT
OVERDIRECTED
OVERDIRECTING
OVERDIRECTS
OVERDISCOUNT
OVERDISCOUNTED
OVERDISCOUNTING
OVERDISCOUNTS
OVERDIVERSITIES
OVERDIVERSITY
OVERDOCUMENT
OVERDOCUMENTED
OVERDOCUMENTING
OVERDOCUMENTS
OVERDOMINANCE
OVERDOMINANCES
OVERDOMINANT
OVERDOSAGE
OVERDOSAGES
OVERDOSING
OVERDRAFTS
OVERDRAMATIC
OVERDRAMATISE
OVERDRAMATISED
OVERDRAMATISES
OVERDRAMATISING
OVERDRAMATIZE
OVERDRAMATIZED
OVERDRAMATIZES
OVERDRAMATIZING
OVERDRAUGHT
OVERDRAUGHTS
OVERDRAWING
OVERDRESSED
OVERDRESSES
OVERDRESSING
OVERDRINKING
OVERDRINKS
OVERDRIVEN
OVERDRIVES
OVERDRIVING
OVERDRYING
OVERDUBBED
OVERDUBBING
OVERDUSTED
OVERDUSTING
OVERDYEING
OVEREAGERNESS

OVEREAGERNESSES
OVEREARNEST
OVEREATERS
OVEREATING
OVEREDITED
OVEREDITING
OVEREDUCATE
OVEREDUCATED
OVEREDUCATES
OVEREDUCATING
OVEREDUCATION
OVEREDUCATIONS
OVEREGGING
OVERELABORATE
OVERELABORATED
OVERELABORATES
OVERELABORATING
OVERELABORATION
OVEREMBELLISH
OVEREMBELLISHED
OVEREMBELLISHES
OVEREMOTED
OVEREMOTES
OVEREMOTING
OVEREMOTIONAL
OVEREMPHASES
OVEREMPHASIS
OVEREMPHASISE
OVEREMPHASISED
OVEREMPHASISES
OVEREMPHASISING
OVEREMPHASIZE
OVEREMPHASIZED
OVEREMPHASIZES
OVEREMPHASIZING
OVEREMPHATIC
OVERENAMORED
OVERENCOURAGE
OVERENCOURAGED
OVERENCOURAGES
OVERENCOURAGING
OVERENERGETIC
OVERENGINEER
OVERENGINEERED
OVERENGINEERING
OVERENGINEERS
OVERENROLLED
OVERENTERTAINED
OVERENTHUSIASM
OVERENTHUSIASMS
OVEREQUIPPED
OVERESTIMATE
OVERESTIMATED
OVERESTIMATES
OVERESTIMATING
OVERESTIMATION
OVERESTIMATIONS
OVEREVALUATION
OVEREVALUATIONS

OVEREXAGGERATE
OVEREXAGGERATED
OVEREXAGGERATES
OVEREXCITABLE
OVEREXCITE
OVEREXCITED
OVEREXCITES
OVEREXCITING
OVEREXERCISE
OVEREXERCISED
OVEREXERCISES
OVEREXERCISING
OVEREXERTED
OVEREXERTING
OVEREXERTION
OVEREXERTIONS
OVEREXERTS
OVEREXPAND
OVEREXPANDED
OVEREXPANDING
OVEREXPANDS
OVEREXPANSION
OVEREXPANSIONS
OVEREXPECTATION
OVEREXPLAIN
OVEREXPLAINED
OVEREXPLAINING
OVEREXPLAINS
OVEREXPLICIT
OVEREXPLOIT
OVEREXPLOITED
OVEREXPLOITING
OVEREXPLOITS
OVEREXPOSE
OVEREXPOSED
OVEREXPOSES
OVEREXPOSING
OVEREXPOSURE
OVEREXPOSURES
OVEREXTEND
OVEREXTENDED
OVEREXTENDING
OVEREXTENDS
OVEREXTENSION
OVEREXTENSIONS
OVEREXTRACTION
OVEREXTRACTIONS
OVEREXTRAVAGANT
OVEREXUBERANT
OVEREYEING
OVERFACILE
OVERFALLEN
OVERFALLING
OVERFAMILIAR
OVERFAMILIARITY
OVERFASTIDIOUS
OVERFATIGUE
OVERFATIGUED
OVERFATIGUES

OVERFAVORED
OVERFAVORING
OVERFAVORS
OVERFEARED
OVERFEARING
OVERFEEDING
OVERFERTILISE
OVERFERTILISED
OVERFERTILISES
OVERFERTILISING
OVERFERTILIZE
OVERFERTILIZED
OVERFERTILIZES
OVERFERTILIZING
OVERFILLED
OVERFILLING
OVERFINENESS
OVERFINENESSES
OVERFINISHED
OVERFISHED
OVERFISHES
OVERFISHING
OVERFLIGHT
OVERFLIGHTS
OVERFLOODED
OVERFLOODING
OVERFLOODS
OVERFLOURISH
OVERFLOURISHED
OVERFLOURISHES
OVERFLOURISHING
OVERFLOWED
OVERFLOWING
OVERFLOWINGLY
OVERFLOWINGS
OVERFLUSHES
OVERFLYING
OVERFOCUSED
OVERFOCUSES
OVERFOCUSING
OVERFOCUSSED
OVERFOCUSSES
OVERFOCUSSING
OVERFOLDED
OVERFOLDING
OVERFONDLY
OVERFONDNESS
OVERFONDNESSES
OVERFORWARD
OVERFORWARDNESS
OVERFRAUGHT
OVERFREEDOM
OVERFREEDOMS
OVERFREELY
OVERFREIGHT
OVERFREIGHTING
OVERFREIGHTS
OVERFULFILL
OVERFULFILLED

OVERFULFILLING	OVERGRADED	OVERHOMOGENIZES	OVERISSUANCE
OVERFULFILLS	OVERGRADES	OVERHONORED	OVERISSUANCES
OVERFULLNESS	OVERGRADING	OVERHONORING	OVERISSUED
OVERFULLNESSES	OVERGRAINED	OVERHONORS	OVERISSUES
OVERFULNESS	OVERGRAINER	OVERHOPING	OVERISSUING
OVERFULNESSES	OVERGRAINERS	OVERHUNTED	OVERJOYING
OVERFUNDED	OVERGRAINING	OVERHUNTING	OVERJUMPED
OVERFUNDING	OVERGRAINS	OVERHUNTINGS	OVERJUMPING
OVERFUNDINGS	OVERGRASSED	OVERHYPING	OVERKEEPING
OVERGALLED	OVERGRASSES	OVERIDEALISE	OVERKILLED
OVERGALLING	OVERGRASSING	OVERIDEALISED	OVERKILLING
OVERGANGING	OVERGRAZED	OVERIDEALISES	OVERKINDNESS
OVERGARMENT	OVERGRAZES	OVERIDEALISING	OVERKINDNESSES
OVERGARMENTS	OVERGRAZING	OVERIDEALIZE	OVERLABORED
OVERGEARED	OVERGRAZINGS	OVERIDEALIZED	OVERLABORING
OVERGEARING	OVERGREEDY	OVERIDEALIZES	OVERLABORS
OVERGENERALISE	OVERGREENED	OVERIDEALIZING	OVERLABOUR
OVERGENERALISED	OVERGREENING	OVERIDENTIFIED	OVERLABOURED
OVERGENERALISES	OVERGREENS	OVERIDENTIFIES	OVERLABOURING
OVERGENERALIZE	OVERGROUND	OVERIDENTIFY	OVERLABOURS
OVERGENERALIZED	OVERGROWING	OVERIDENTIFYING	OVERLADING
OVERGENERALIZES	OVERGROWTH	OVERIMAGINATIVE	OVERLANDED
OVERGENEROSITY	OVERGROWTHS	OVERIMPRESS	OVERLANDER
OVERGENEROUS	OVERHAILED	OVERIMPRESSED	OVERLANDERS
OVERGENEROUSLY	OVERHAILES	OVERIMPRESSES	OVERLANDING
OVERGETTING	OVERHAILING	OVERIMPRESSING	OVERLAPPED
OVERGILDED	OVERHALING	OVERINCLINED	OVERLAPPING
OVERGILDING	OVERHANDED	OVERINDULGE	OVERLARDED
OVERGIRDED	OVERHANDING	OVERINDULGED	OVERLARDING
OVERGIRDING	OVERHANDLE	OVERINDULGENCE	OVERLAUNCH
OVERGIVING	OVERHANDLED	OVERINDULGENCES	OVERLAUNCHED
OVERGLAMORISE	OVERHANDLES	OVERINDULGENT	OVERLAUNCHES
OVERGLAMORISED	OVERHANDLING	OVERINDULGES	OVERLAUNCHING
OVERGLAMORISES	OVERHANGING	OVERINDULGING	OVERLAVISH
OVERGLAMORISING	OVERHARVEST	OVERINFLATE	OVERLAYING
OVERGLAMORIZE	OVERHARVESTED	OVERINFLATED	OVERLAYINGS
OVERGLAMORIZED	OVERHARVESTING	OVERINFLATES	OVERLEAPED
OVERGLAMORIZES	OVERHARVESTS	OVERINFLATING	OVERLEAPING
OVERGLAMORIZING	OVERHASTES	OVERINFLATION	OVERLEARNED
OVERGLANCE	OVERHASTILY	OVERINFLATIONS	OVERLEARNING
OVERGLANCED	OVERHASTINESS	OVERINFORM	OVERLEARNS
OVERGLANCES	OVERHASTINESSES	OVERINFORMED	OVERLEARNT
OVERGLANCING	OVERHATING	OVERINFORMING	OVERLEATHER
OVERGLAZED	OVERHAULED	OVERINFORMS	OVERLEATHERS
OVERGLAZES	OVERHAULING	OVERINGENIOUS	OVERLEAVEN
OVERGLAZING	OVERHEAPED	OVERINGENUITIES	OVERLEAVENED
OVERGLOOMED	OVERHEAPING	OVERINGENUITY	OVERLEAVENING
OVERGLOOMING	OVERHEARING	OVERINSISTENT	OVERLEAVENS
OVERGLOOMS	OVERHEATED	OVERINSURANCE	OVERLENDING
OVERGOADED	OVERHEATING	OVERINSURANCES	OVERLENGTH
OVERGOADING	OVERHEATINGS	OVERINSURE	OVERLENGTHEN
OVERGOINGS	OVERHENTING	OVERINSURED	OVERLENGTHENED
OVERGORGED	OVERHITTING	OVERINSURES	OVERLENGTHENING
OVERGORGES	OVERHOLDING	OVERINSURING	OVERLENGTHENS
OVERGORGING	OVERHOMOGENISE	OVERINTENSE	OVERLENGTHS
OVERGOVERN	OVERHOMOGENISED	OVERINTENSITIES	OVERLETTING
OVERGOVERNED	OVERHOMOGENISES	OVERINTENSITY	OVERLIGHTED
OVERGOVERNING	OVERHOMOGENIZE	OVERINVESTMENT	OVERLIGHTING
OVERGOVERNS	OVERHOMOGENIZED	OVERINVESTMENTS	OVERLIGHTS

OVERLITERAL
OVERLITERARY
OVERLIVING
OVERLOADED
OVERLOADING
OVERLOCKED
OVERLOCKER
OVERLOCKERS
OVERLOCKING
OVERLOCKINGS
OVERLOOKED
OVERLOOKER
OVERLOOKERS
OVERLOOKING
OVERLORDED
OVERLORDING
OVERLORDSHIP
OVERLORDSHIPS
OVERLOVING
OVERMANAGE
OVERMANAGED
OVERMANAGES
OVERMANAGING
OVERMANNED
OVERMANNERED
OVERMANNING
OVERMANTEL
OVERMANTELS
OVERMASTED
OVERMASTER
OVERMASTERED
OVERMASTERING
OVERMASTERS
OVERMASTING
OVERMATCHED
OVERMATCHES
OVERMATCHING
OVERMATTER
OVERMATTERS
OVERMATURE
OVERMATURITIES
OVERMATURITY
OVERMEASURE
OVERMEASURED
OVERMEASURES
OVERMEASURING
OVERMEDICATE
OVERMEDICATED
OVERMEDICATES
OVERMEDICATING
OVERMEDICATION
OVERMEDICATIONS
OVERMELTED
OVERMELTING
OVERMIGHTY
OVERMILKED
OVERMILKING
OVERMINING
OVERMIXING

OVERMODEST
OVERMODESTLY
OVERMOUNTED
OVERMOUNTING
OVERMOUNTS
OVERMUCHES
OVERMULTIPLIED
OVERMULTIPLIES
OVERMULTIPLY
OVERMULTIPLYING
OVERMULTITUDE
OVERMULTITUDED
OVERMULTITUDES
OVERMULTITUDING
OVERMUSCLED
OVERNAMING
OVERNETTED
OVERNETTING
OVERNICELY
OVERNICENESS
OVERNICENESSES
OVERNIGHTED
OVERNIGHTER
OVERNIGHTERS
OVERNIGHTING
OVERNIGHTS
OVERNOURISH
OVERNOURISHED
OVERNOURISHES
OVERNOURISHING
OVERNUTRITION
OVERNUTRITIONS
OVEROBVIOUS
OVEROFFICE
OVEROFFICED
OVEROFFICES
OVEROFFICING
OVEROPERATE
OVEROPERATED
OVEROPERATES
OVEROPERATING
OVEROPINIONATED
OVEROPTIMISM
OVEROPTIMISMS
OVEROPTIMIST
OVEROPTIMISTIC
OVEROPTIMISTS
OVERORCHESTRATE
OVERORGANISE
OVERORGANISED
OVERORGANISES
OVERORGANISING
OVERORGANIZE
OVERORGANIZED
OVERORGANIZES
OVERORGANIZING
OVERORNAMENT
OVERORNAMENTED
OVERORNAMENTING

OVERORNAMENTS
OVERPACKAGE
OVERPACKAGED
OVERPACKAGES
OVERPACKAGING
OVERPACKED
OVERPACKING
OVERPAINTED
OVERPAINTING
OVERPAINTS
OVERPARTED
OVERPARTICULAR
OVERPARTING
OVERPASSED
OVERPASSES
OVERPASSING
OVERPAYING
OVERPAYMENT
OVERPAYMENTS
OVERPEDALED
OVERPEDALING
OVERPEDALLED
OVERPEDALLING
OVERPEDALS
OVERPEERED
OVERPEERING
OVERPEOPLE
OVERPEOPLED
OVERPEOPLES
OVERPEOPLING
OVERPERCHED
OVERPERCHES
OVERPERCHING
OVERPERSUADE
OVERPERSUADED
OVERPERSUADES
OVERPERSUADING
OVERPERSUASION
OVERPERSUASIONS
OVERPICTURE
OVERPICTURED
OVERPICTURES
OVERPICTURING
OVERPITCHED
OVERPITCHES
OVERPITCHING
OVERPLACED
OVERPLAIDED
OVERPLAIDS
OVERPLANNED
OVERPLANNING
OVERPLANTED
OVERPLANTING
OVERPLANTS
OVERPLAYED
OVERPLAYING
OVERPLOTTED
OVERPLOTTING
OVERPLUSES

OVERPLUSSES
OVERPLYING
OVERPOISED
OVERPOISES
OVERPOISING
OVERPOPULATE
OVERPOPULATED
OVERPOPULATES
OVERPOPULATING
OVERPOPULATION
OVERPOPULATIONS
OVERPOSTED
OVERPOSTING
OVERPOTENT
OVERPOWERED
OVERPOWERING
OVERPOWERINGLY
OVERPOWERS
OVERPRAISE
OVERPRAISED
OVERPRAISES
OVERPRAISING
OVERPRECISE
OVERPREPARATION
OVERPREPARE
OVERPREPARED
OVERPREPARES
OVERPREPARING
OVERPRESCRIBE
OVERPRESCRIBED
OVERPRESCRIBES
OVERPRESCRIBING
OVERPRESSED
OVERPRESSES
OVERPRESSING
OVERPRESSURE
OVERPRESSURES
OVERPRICED
OVERPRICES
OVERPRICING
OVERPRINTED
OVERPRINTING
OVERPRINTS
OVERPRIVILEGED
OVERPRIZED
OVERPRIZES
OVERPRIZING
OVERPROCESS
OVERPROCESSED
OVERPROCESSES
OVERPROCESSING
OVERPRODUCE
OVERPRODUCED
OVERPRODUCES
OVERPRODUCING
OVERPRODUCTION
OVERPRODUCTIONS
OVERPROGRAM
OVERPROGRAMED

OVERPROGRAMING
OVERPROGRAMMED
OVERPROGRAMMING
OVERPROGRAMS
OVERPROMISE
OVERPROMISED
OVERPROMISES
OVERPROMISING
OVERPROMOTE
OVERPROMOTED
OVERPROMOTES
OVERPROMOTING
OVERPROPORTION
OVERPROPORTIONS
OVERPROTECT
OVERPROTECTED
OVERPROTECTING
OVERPROTECTION
OVERPROTECTIONS
OVERPROTECTIVE
OVERPROTECTS
OVERPUMPED
OVERPUMPING
OVERQUALIFIED
OVERRACKED
OVERRACKING
OVERRAKING
OVERRASHLY
OVERRASHNESS
OVERRASHNESSES
OVERRATING
OVERRAUGHT
OVERREACHED
OVERREACHER
OVERREACHERS
OVERREACHES
OVERREACHING
OVERREACTED
OVERREACTING
OVERREACTION
OVERREACTIONS
OVERREACTS
OVERREADING
OVERRECKON
OVERRECKONED
OVERRECKONING
OVERRECKONS
OVERREDDED
OVERREDDING
OVERREFINE
OVERREFINED
OVERREFINEMENT
OVERREFINEMENTS
OVERREFINES
OVERREFINING
OVERREGULATE
OVERREGULATED
OVERREGULATES
OVERREGULATING

OVERREGULATION
OVERREGULATIONS
OVERRELIANCE
OVERRELIANCES
OVERRENNING
OVERREPORT
OVERREPORTED
OVERREPORTING
OVERREPORTS
OVERREPRESENTED
OVERRESPOND
OVERRESPONDED
OVERRESPONDING
OVERRESPONDS
OVERRIDDEN
OVERRIDERS
OVERRIDING
OVERRIPENED
OVERRIPENESS
OVERRIPENESSES
OVERRIPENING
OVERRIPENS
OVERROASTED
OVERROASTING
OVERROASTS
OVERRUFFED
OVERRUFFING
OVERRULERS
OVERRULING
OVERRULINGS
OVERRUNNER
OVERRUNNERS
OVERRUNNING
OVERSAILED
OVERSAILING
OVERSALTED
OVERSALTING
OVERSANGUINE
OVERSATURATE
OVERSATURATED
OVERSATURATES
OVERSATURATING
OVERSATURATION
OVERSATURATIONS
OVERSAUCED
OVERSAUCES
OVERSAUCING
OVERSAVING
OVERSCALED
OVERSCHUTCHT
OVERSCORED
OVERSCORES
OVERSCORING
OVERSCRUPULOUS
OVERSCUTCHED
OVERSECRETION
OVERSECRETIONS
OVERSEEDED
OVERSEEDING

OVERSEEING
OVERSELLING
OVERSENSITIVE
OVERSENSITIVITY
OVERSERIOUS
OVERSERIOUSLY
OVERSERVICE
OVERSERVICED
OVERSERVICES
OVERSERVICING
OVERSETTING
OVERSEWING
OVERSHADED
OVERSHADES
OVERSHADING
OVERSHADOW
OVERSHADOWED
OVERSHADOWING
OVERSHADOWS
OVERSHINES
OVERSHINING
OVERSHIRTS
OVERSHOOTING
OVERSHOOTS
OVERSHOWER
OVERSHOWERED
OVERSHOWERING
OVERSHOWERS
OVERSIGHTS
OVERSIMPLE
OVERSIMPLIFIED
OVERSIMPLIFIES
OVERSIMPLIFY
OVERSIMPLIFYING
OVERSIMPLISTIC
OVERSIMPLY
OVERSIZING
OVERSKIPPED
OVERSKIPPING
OVERSKIRTS
OVERSLAUGH
OVERSLAUGHED
OVERSLAUGHING
OVERSLAUGHS
OVERSLEEPING
OVERSLEEPS
OVERSLEEVE
OVERSLEEVES
OVERSLIPPED
OVERSLIPPING
OVERSMOKED
OVERSMOKES
OVERSMOKING
OVERSOAKED
OVERSOAKING
OVERSOLICITOUS
OVERSOWING
OVERSPECIALISE
OVERSPECIALISED

OVERSPECIALISES
OVERSPECIALIZE
OVERSPECIALIZED
OVERSPECIALIZES
OVERSPECULATE
OVERSPECULATED
OVERSPECULATES
OVERSPECULATING
OVERSPECULATION
OVERSPENDER
OVERSPENDERS
OVERSPENDING
OVERSPENDS
OVERSPICED
OVERSPICES
OVERSPICING
OVERSPILLED
OVERSPILLING
OVERSPILLS
OVERSPREAD
OVERSPREADING
OVERSPREADS
OVERSTABILITIES
OVERSTABILITY
OVERSTAFFED
OVERSTAFFING
OVERSTAFFS
OVERSTAINED
OVERSTAINING
OVERSTAINS
OVERSTANDING
OVERSTANDS
OVERSTARED
OVERSTARES
OVERSTARING
OVERSTATED
OVERSTATEMENT
OVERSTATEMENTS
OVERSTATES
OVERSTATING
OVERSTAYED
OVERSTAYER
OVERSTAYERS
OVERSTAYING
OVERSTEERED
OVERSTEERING
OVERSTEERS
OVERSTEPPED
OVERSTEPPING
OVERSTIMULATE
OVERSTIMULATED
OVERSTIMULATES
OVERSTIMULATING
OVERSTIMULATION
OVERSTINKING
OVERSTINKS
OVERSTIRRED
OVERSTIRRING
OVERSTOCKED

OVERSTOCKING
OVERSTOCKS
OVERSTORIES
OVERSTRAIN
OVERSTRAINED
OVERSTRAINING
OVERSTRAINS
OVERSTRESS
OVERSTRESSED
OVERSTRESSES
OVERSTRESSING
OVERSTRETCH
OVERSTRETCHED
OVERSTRETCHES
OVERSTRETCHING
OVERSTREWED
OVERSTREWING
OVERSTREWN
OVERSTREWS
OVERSTRIDDEN
OVERSTRIDE
OVERSTRIDES
OVERSTRIDING
OVERSTRIKE
OVERSTRIKES
OVERSTRIKING
OVERSTRODE
OVERSTRONG
OVERSTROOKE
OVERSTRUCK
OVERSTRUCTURED
OVERSTRUNG
OVERSTUDIED
OVERSTUDIES
OVERSTUDYING
OVERSTUFFED
OVERSTUFFING
OVERSTUFFS
OVERSUBSCRIBE
OVERSUBSCRIBED
OVERSUBSCRIBES
OVERSUBSCRIBING
OVERSUBTLE
OVERSUBTLETIES
OVERSUBTLETY
OVERSUDSED
OVERSUDSES
OVERSUDSING
OVERSUPPED
OVERSUPPING
OVERSUPPLIED
OVERSUPPLIES
OVERSUPPLY
OVERSUPPLYING
OVERSUSPICIOUS
OVERSWAYED
OVERSWAYING
OVERSWEARING
OVERSWEARS

OVERSWEETEN
OVERSWEETENED
OVERSWEETENING
OVERSWEETENS
OVERSWEETNESS
OVERSWEETNESSES
OVERSWELLED
OVERSWELLING
OVERSWELLS
OVERSWIMMING
OVERSWINGING
OVERSWINGS
OVERSWOLLEN
OVERTAKING
OVERTALKATIVE
OVERTALKED
OVERTALKING
OVERTASKED
OVERTASKING
OVERTAUGHT
OVERTAXATION
OVERTAXATIONS
OVERTAXING
OVERTEACHES
OVERTEACHING
OVERTEDIOUS
OVERTEEMED
OVERTEEMING
OVERTHINKING
OVERTHINKS
OVERTHOUGHT
OVERTHROWER
OVERTHROWERS
OVERTHROWING
OVERTHROWN
OVERTHROWS
OVERTHRUST
OVERTHRUSTS
OVERTHWART
OVERTHWARTED
OVERTHWARTING
OVERTHWARTS
OVERTIGHTEN
OVERTIGHTENED
OVERTIGHTENING
OVERTIGHTENS
OVERTIMELY
OVERTIMERS
OVERTIMING
OVERTIPPED
OVERTIPPING
OVERTIRING
OVERTNESSES
OVERTOILED
OVERTOILING
OVERTOPPED
OVERTOPPING
OVERTOWERED
OVERTOWERING

OVERTOWERS
OVERTRADED
OVERTRADES
OVERTRADING
OVERTRAINED
OVERTRAINING
OVERTRAINS
OVERTREATED
OVERTREATING
OVERTREATMENT
OVERTREATMENTS
OVERTREATS
OVERTRICKS
OVERTRIMMED
OVERTRIMMING
OVERTRIPPED
OVERTRIPPING
OVERTRUMPED
OVERTRUMPING
OVERTRUMPS
OVERTRUSTED
OVERTRUSTING
OVERTRUSTS
OVERTURING
OVERTURNED
OVERTURNER
OVERTURNERS
OVERTURNING
OVERTYPING
OVERURGING
OVERUTILISATION
OVERUTILISE
OVERUTILISED
OVERUTILISES
OVERUTILISING
OVERUTILIZATION
OVERUTILIZE
OVERUTILIZED
OVERUTILIZES
OVERUTILIZING
OVERVALUATION
OVERVALUATIONS
OVERVALUED
OVERVALUES
OVERVALUING
OVERVEILED
OVERVEILING
OVERVIOLENT
OVERVOLTAGE
OVERVOLTAGES
OVERVOTING
OVERWARMED
OVERWARMING
OVERWASHES
OVERWATCHED
OVERWATCHES
OVERWATCHING
OVERWATERED
OVERWATERING

OVERWATERS
OVERWEARIED
OVERWEARIES
OVERWEARING
OVERWEARYING
OVERWEATHER
OVERWEATHERED
OVERWEATHERING
OVERWEATHERS
OVERWEENED
OVERWEENING
OVERWEENINGLY
OVERWEENINGNESS
OVERWEENINGS
OVERWEIGHED
OVERWEIGHING
OVERWEIGHS
OVERWEIGHT
OVERWEIGHTED
OVERWEIGHTING
OVERWEIGHTS
OVERWETTED
OVERWETTING
OVERWHELMED
OVERWHELMING
OVERWHELMINGLY
OVERWHELMINGS
OVERWHELMS
OVERWINDING
OVERWINGED
OVERWINGING
OVERWINTER
OVERWINTERED
OVERWINTERING
OVERWINTERS
OVERWISELY
OVERWITHHELD
OVERWITHHOLD
OVERWITHHOLDING
OVERWITHHOLDS
OVERWORKED
OVERWORKING
OVERWRESTED
OVERWRESTING
OVERWRESTLE
OVERWRESTLED
OVERWRESTLES
OVERWRESTLING
OVERWRESTS
OVERWRITES
OVERWRITING
OVERWRITTEN
OVERWROUGHT
OVERYEARED
OVERYEARING
OVERZEALOUS
OVERZEALOUSNESS
OVIPARITIES
OVIPAROUSLY

OVIPOSITED
OVIPOSITING
OVIPOSITION
OVIPOSITIONAL
OVIPOSITIONS
OVIPOSITOR
OVIPOSITORS
OVIRAPTORS
OVOVIVIPARITIES
OVOVIVIPARITY
OVOVIVIPAROUS
OVOVIVIPAROUSLY
OVULATIONS
OVULIFEROUS
OWERLOUPEN
OWERLOUPING
OWERLOUPIT
OWLISHNESS
OWLISHNESSES
OWNERSHIPS
OXACILLINS
OXALACETATE
OXALACETATES
OXALOACETATE
OXALOACETATES
OXIDATIONAL
OXIDATIONS
OXIDATIVELY
OXIDIMETRIC
OXIDIMETRIES
OXIDIMETRY
OXIDISABLE
OXIDISATION
OXIDISATIONS
OXIDIZABLE
OXIDIZATION
OXIDIZATIONS
OXIDOREDUCTASE
OXIDOREDUCTASES
OXIMETRIES
OXYACETYLENE
OXYACETYLENES
OXYCEPHALIC
OXYCEPHALIES
OXYCEPHALOUS
OXYCEPHALY
OXYCODONES
OXYGENASES
OXYGENATED
OXYGENATES
OXYGENATING
OXYGENATION
OXYGENATIONS
OXYGENATOR
OXYGENATORS
OXYGENISED
OXYGENISER
OXYGENISERS
OXYGENISES

OXYGENISING
OXYGENIZED
OXYGENIZER
OXYGENIZERS
OXYGENIZES
OXYGENIZING
OXYGENLESS
OXYHAEMOGLOBIN
OXYHAEMOGLOBINS
OXYHEMOGLOBIN
OXYHEMOGLOBINS
OXYHYDROGEN
OXYMORONIC
OXYMORONICALLY
OXYPHENBUTAZONE
OXYRHYNCHUS
OXYRHYNCHUSES
OXYSULPHIDE
OXYSULPHIDES
OXYTETRACYCLINE
OXYURIASES
OXYURIASIS
OYSTERCATCHER
OYSTERCATCHERS
OYSTERINGS
OZOCERITES
OZOKERITES
OZONATIONS
OZONIFEROUS
OZONISATION
OZONISATIONS
OZONIZATION
OZONIZATIONS
OZONOLYSES
OZONOLYSIS
OZONOSPHERE
OZONOSPHERES

P

PACEMAKERS
PACEMAKING
PACEMAKINGS
PACESETTER
PACESETTERS
PACESETTING
PACHYCARPOUS
PACHYDACTYL
PACHYDACTYLOUS
PACHYDERMAL
PACHYDERMATOUS
PACHYDERMIA
PACHYDERMIAS
PACHYDERMIC
PACHYDERMOUS
PACHYDERMS
PACHYMENINGITIS
PACHYMETER
PACHYMETERS
PACHYSANDRA
PACHYSANDRAS
PACHYTENES
PACIFIABLE
PACIFICALLY
PACIFICATE
PACIFICATED
PACIFICATES
PACIFICATING
PACIFICATION
PACIFICATIONS
PACIFICATOR
PACIFICATORS
PACIFICATORY
PACIFICISM
PACIFICISMS
PACIFICIST
PACIFICISTS
PACIFISTIC
PACIFISTICALLY
PACKABILITIES
PACKABILITY
PACKAGINGS
PACKBOARDS
PACKFRAMES
PACKHORSES
PACKINGHOUSE
PACKINGHOUSES
PACKNESSES
PACKSADDLE
PACKSADDLES
PACKSHEETS
PACKSTAFFS
PACKTHREAD

PACKTHREADS
PACLITAXEL
PACLITAXELS
PACTIONING
PADDLEBALL
PADDLEBALLS
PADDLEBOARD
PADDLEBOARDS
PADDLEBOAT
PADDLEBOATS
PADDLEFISH
PADDLEFISHES
PADDOCKING
PADDYMELON
PADDYMELONS
PADDYWACKED
PADDYWACKING
PADDYWACKS
PADDYWHACK
PADDYWHACKS
PADEMELONS
PADEREROES
PADLOCKING
PADRONISMS
PADYMELONS
PAEDAGOGIC
PAEDAGOGUE
PAEDAGOGUES
PAEDERASTIC
PAEDERASTIES
PAEDERASTS
PAEDERASTY
PAEDEUTICS
PAEDIATRIC
PAEDIATRICIAN
PAEDIATRICIANS
PAEDIATRICS
PAEDIATRIES
PAEDIATRIST
PAEDIATRISTS
PAEDOBAPTISM
PAEDOBAPTISMS
PAEDOBAPTIST
PAEDOBAPTISTS
PAEDODONTIC
PAEDODONTICS
PAEDOGENESES
PAEDOGENESIS
PAEDOGENETIC
PAEDOGENIC
PAEDOLOGICAL
PAEDOLOGIES
PAEDOLOGIST

PAEDOLOGISTS
PAEDOMORPHIC
PAEDOMORPHISM
PAEDOMORPHISMS
PAEDOMORPHOSES
PAEDOMORPHOSIS
PAEDOPHILE
PAEDOPHILES
PAEDOPHILIA
PAEDOPHILIAC
PAEDOPHILIACS
PAEDOPHILIAS
PAEDOPHILIC
PAEDOPHILICS
PAEDOTRIBE
PAEDOTRIBES
PAEDOTROPHIES
PAEDOTROPHY
PAGANISATION
PAGANISATIONS
PAGANISERS
PAGANISING
PAGANISTIC
PAGANISTICALLY
PAGANIZATION
PAGANIZATIONS
PAGANIZERS
PAGANIZING
PAGEANTRIES
PAGINATING
PAGINATION
PAGINATIONS
PAIDEUTICS
PAILLASSES
PAILLETTES
PAINFULLER
PAINFULLEST
PAINFULNESS
PAINFULNESSES
PAINKILLER
PAINKILLERS
PAINKILLING
PAINLESSLY
PAINLESSNESS
PAINLESSNESSES
PAINSTAKER
PAINSTAKERS
PAINSTAKING
PAINSTAKINGLY
PAINSTAKINGNESS
PAINSTAKINGS
PAINTBALLS
PAINTBOXES

PAINTBRUSH
PAINTBRUSHES
PAINTERLINESS
PAINTERLINESSES
PAINTINESS
PAINTINESSES
PAINTRESSES
PAINTWORKS
PAKIRIKIRI
PAKIRIKIRIS
PALAEANTHROPIC
PALAEBIOLOGIES
PALAEBIOLOGIST
PALAEBIOLOGISTS
PALAEBIOLOGY
PALAEETHNOLOGY
PALAEOANTHROPIC
PALAEOBIOLOGIC
PALAEOBIOLOGIES
PALAEOBIOLOGIST
PALAEOBIOLOGY
PALAEOBOTANIC
PALAEOBOTANICAL
PALAEOBOTANIES
PALAEOBOTANIST
PALAEOBOTANISTS
PALAEOBOTANY
PALAEOCLIMATE
PALAEOCLIMATES
PALAEOCLIMATIC
PALAEOCRYSTIC
PALAEOCURRENT
PALAEOCURRENTS
PALAEOECOLOGIC
PALAEOECOLOGIES
PALAEOECOLOGIST
PALAEOECOLOGY
PALAEOETHNOLOGY
PALAEOGAEA
PALAEOGAEAS
PALAEOGEOGRAPHY
PALAEOGRAPHER
PALAEOGRAPHERS
PALAEOGRAPHIC
PALAEOGRAPHICAL
PALAEOGRAPHIES
PALAEOGRAPHIST
PALAEOGRAPHISTS
PALAEOGRAPHY
PALAEOLIMNOLOGY
PALAEOLITH
PALAEOLITHIC
PALAEOLITHS

PALAEOMAGNETIC	PALEOBOTANICAL	PALINGENESISTS	PALMHOUSES
PALAEOMAGNETISM	PALEOBOTANIES	PALINGENESY	PALMIFICATION
PALAEONTOGRAPHY	PALEOBOTANIST	PALINGENETIC	PALMIFICATIONS
PALAEONTOLOGIES	PALEOBOTANISTS	PALINGENETICAL	PALMIPEDES
PALAEONTOLOGIST	PALEOBOTANY	PALINODIES	PALMISTERS
PALAEONTOLOGY	PALEOECOLOGIC	PALINOPIAS	PALMISTRIES
PALAEOPATHOLOGY	PALEOECOLOGICAL	PALINOPSIA	PALMITATES
PALAEOPEDOLOGY	PALEOECOLOGIES	PALINOPSIAS	PALOVERDES
PALAEOPHYTOLOGY	PALEOECOLOGIST	PALISADING	PALPABILITIES
PALAEOTYPE	PALEOECOLOGISTS	PALISADOED	PALPABILITY
PALAEOTYPES	PALEOECOLOGY	PALISADOES	PALPABLENESS
PALAEOTYPIC	PALEOGEOGRAPHIC	PALISADOING	PALPABLENESSES
PALAEOZOOLOGIES	PALEOGEOGRAPHY	PALISANDER	PALPATIONS
PALAEOZOOLOGIST	PALEOGRAPHER	PALISANDERS	PALPEBRATE
PALAEOZOOLOGY	PALEOGRAPHERS	PALLADIOUS	PALPEBRATED
PALAESTRAE	PALEOGRAPHIC	PALLADIUMS	PALPEBRATES
PALAESTRAL	PALEOGRAPHICAL	PALLBEARER	PALPEBRATING
PALAESTRAS	PALEOGRAPHIES	PALLBEARERS	PALPITATED
PALAESTRIC	PALEOGRAPHY	PALLESCENCE	PALPITATES
PALAESTRICAL	PALEOLITHS	PALLESCENCES	PALPITATING
PALAFITTES	PALEOLOGIES	PALLESCENT	PALPITATION
PALAGONITE	PALEOMAGNETIC	PALLETISATION	PALPITATIONS
PALAGONITES	PALEOMAGNETISM	PALLETISATIONS	PALSGRAVES
PALAMPORES	PALEOMAGNETISMS	PALLETISED	PALSGRAVINE
PALANKEENS	PALEOMAGNETIST	PALLETISER	PALSGRAVINES
PALANQUINS	PALEOMAGNETISTS	PALLETISERS	PALTRINESS
PALATABILITIES	PALEONTOLOGIC	PALLETISES	PALTRINESSES
PALATABILITY	PALEONTOLOGICAL	PALLETISING	PALUDAMENT
PALATABLENESS	PALEONTOLOGIES	PALLETIZATION	PALUDAMENTA
PALATABLENESSES	PALEONTOLOGIST	PALLETIZATIONS	PALUDAMENTS
PALATALISATION	PALEONTOLOGISTS	PALLETIZED	PALUDAMENTUM
PALATALISATIONS	PALEONTOLOGY	PALLETIZER	PALUDAMENTUMS
PALATALISE	PALEOPATHOLOGY	PALLETIZERS	PALUDICOLOUS
PALATALISED	PALEOZOOLOGICAL	PALLETIZES	PALUDINOUS
PALATALISES	PALEOZOOLOGIES	PALLETIZING	PALUSTRIAN
PALATALISING	PALEOZOOLOGIST	PALLIAMENT	PALUSTRINE
PALATALIZATION	PALEOZOOLOGISTS	PALLIAMENTS	PALYNOLOGIC
PALATALIZATIONS	PALEOZOOLOGY	PALLIASSES	PALYNOLOGICAL
PALATALIZE	PALFRENIER	PALLIATING	PALYNOLOGICALLY
PALATALIZED	PALFRENIERS	PALLIATION	PALYNOLOGIES
PALATALIZES	PALIFICATION	PALLIATIONS	PALYNOLOGIST
PALATALIZING	PALIFICATIONS	PALLIATIVE	PALYNOLOGISTS
PALATIALLY	PALILALIAS	PALLIATIVELY	PALYNOLOGY
PALATIALNESS	PALILLOGIES	PALLIATIVES	PAMPELMOOSE
PALATIALNESSES	PALIMONIES	PALLIATORS	PAMPELMOOSES
PALATINATE	PALIMPSEST	PALLIATORY	PAMPELMOUSE
PALATINATES	PALIMPSESTS	PALLIDITIES	PAMPELMOUSES
PALAVERERS	PALINDROME	PALLIDNESS	PAMPEREDNESS
PALAVERING	PALINDROMES	PALLIDNESSES	PAMPEREDNESSES
PALEACEOUS	PALINDROMIC	PALMACEOUS	PAMPHLETEER
PALEMPORES	PALINDROMICAL	PALMATIFID	PAMPHLETEERED
PALENESSES	PALINDROMIST	PALMATIONS	PAMPHLETEERING
PALEOBIOLOGIC	PALINDROMISTS	PALMATIPARTITE	PAMPHLETEERINGS
PALEOBIOLOGICAL	PALINGENESES	PALMATISECT	PAMPHLETEERS
PALEOBIOLOGIES	PALINGENESIA	PALMCORDER	PAMPOOTIES
PALEOBIOLOGIST	PALINGENESIAS	PALMCORDERS	PANACHAEAS
PALEOBIOLOGISTS	PALINGENESIES	PALMERWORM	PANAESTHESIA
PALEOBIOLOGY	PALINGENESIS	PALMERWORMS	PANAESTHESIAS
PALEOBOTANIC	PALINGENESIST	PALMETTOES	PANAESTHETISM

PANAESTHETISMS
PANARITIUM
PANARITIUMS
PANARTHRITIS
PANARTHRITISES
PANATELLAS
PANBROILED
PANBROILING
PANCHAYATS
PANCHROMATIC
PANCHROMATISM
PANCHROMATISMS
PANCOSMISM
PANCOSMISMS
PANCRATIAN
PANCRATIAST
PANCRATIASTS
PANCRATIST
PANCRATISTS
PANCRATIUM
PANCRATIUMS
PANCREASES
PANCREATECTOMY
PANCREATIC
PANCREATIN
PANCREATINS
PANCREATITIDES
PANCREATITIS
PANCREATITISES
PANCREOZYMIN
PANCREOZYMINS
PANCYTOPENIA
PANCYTOPENIAS
PANDAEMONIUM
PANDAEMONIUMS
PANDANACEOUS
PANDANUSES
PANDATIONS
PANDECTIST
PANDECTISTS
PANDEMONIAC
PANDEMONIACAL
PANDEMONIAN
PANDEMONIC
PANDEMONIUM
PANDEMONIUMS
PANDERESSES
PANDERISMS
PANDERMITE
PANDERMITES
PANDICULATION
PANDICULATIONS
PANDOWDIES
PANDURATED
PANDURIFORM
PANEGOISMS
PANEGYRICA
PANEGYRICAL
PANEGYRICALLY

PANEGYRICON
PANEGYRICS
PANEGYRIES
PANEGYRISE
PANEGYRISED
PANEGYRISES
PANEGYRISING
PANEGYRIST
PANEGYRISTS
PANEGYRIZE
PANEGYRIZED
PANEGYRIZES
PANEGYRIZING
PANELLINGS
PANELLISTS
PANENTHEISM
PANENTHEISMS
PANENTHEIST
PANENTHEISTS
PANESTHESIA
PANESTHESIAS
PANETELLAS
PANETTONES
PANGENESES
PANGENESIS
PANGENETIC
PANGENETICALLY
PANGRAMMATIST
PANGRAMMATISTS
PANHANDLED
PANHANDLER
PANHANDLERS
PANHANDLES
PANHANDLING
PANHARMONICON
PANHARMONICONS
PANHELLENIC
PANHELLENION
PANHELLENIONS
PANHELLENIUM
PANHELLENIUMS
PANICKIEST
PANICMONGER
PANICMONGERS
PANICULATE
PANICULATED
PANICULATELY
PANIDIOMORPHIC
PANIFICATION
PANIFICATIONS
PANISLAMIC
PANISLAMISM
PANISLAMISMS
PANISLAMIST
PANISLAMISTS
PANJANDARUM
PANJANDARUMS
PANJANDRUM
PANJANDRUMS

PANLEUCOPENIA
PANLEUCOPENIAS
PANLEUKOPENIA
PANLEUKOPENIAS
PANLOGISMS
PANMIXISES
PANNICULUS
PANNICULUSES
PANNIKELLS
PANOMPHAEAN
PANOPHOBIA
PANOPHOBIAS
PANOPHTHALMIA
PANOPHTHALMIAS
PANOPHTHALMITIS
PANOPTICAL
PANOPTICALLY
PANOPTICON
PANOPTICONS
PANORAMICALLY
PANPHARMACON
PANPHARMACONS
PANPSYCHISM
PANPSYCHISMS
PANPSYCHIST
PANPSYCHISTIC
PANPSYCHISTS
PANRADIOMETER
PANRADIOMETERS
PANSEXUALISM
PANSEXUALISMS
PANSEXUALIST
PANSEXUALISTS
PANSEXUALITIES
PANSEXUALITY
PANSEXUALS
PANSOPHICAL
PANSOPHICALLY
PANSOPHIES
PANSOPHISM
PANSOPHISMS
PANSOPHIST
PANSOPHISTS
PANSPERMATIC
PANSPERMATISM
PANSPERMATISMS
PANSPERMATIST
PANSPERMATISTS
PANSPERMIA
PANSPERMIAS
PANSPERMIC
PANSPERMIES
PANSPERMISM
PANSPERMISMS
PANSPERMIST
PANSPERMISTS
PANTAGAMIES
PANTAGRAPH
PANTAGRAPHS

PANTALEONS
PANTALETTED
PANTALETTES
PANTALONES
PANTALOONED
PANTALOONERIES
PANTALOONERY
PANTALOONS
PANTDRESSES
PANTECHNICON
PANTECHNICONS
PANTHEISMS
PANTHEISTIC
PANTHEISTICAL
PANTHEISTICALLY
PANTHEISTS
PANTHENOLS
PANTHEOLOGIES
PANTHEOLOGIST
PANTHEOLOGISTS
PANTHEOLOGY
PANTHERESS
PANTHERESSES
PANTHERINE
PANTHERISH
PANTILINGS
PANTISOCRACIES
PANTISOCRACY
PANTISOCRAT
PANTISOCRATIC
PANTISOCRATICAL
PANTISOCRATIST
PANTISOCRATISTS
PANTISOCRATS
PANTOFFLES
PANTOGRAPH
PANTOGRAPHER
PANTOGRAPHERS
PANTOGRAPHIC
PANTOGRAPHICAL
PANTOGRAPHIES
PANTOGRAPHS
PANTOGRAPHY
PANTOMIMED
PANTOMIMES
PANTOMIMIC
PANTOMIMICAL
PANTOMIMICALLY
PANTOMIMING
PANTOMIMIST
PANTOMIMISTS
PANTOPHAGIES
PANTOPHAGIST
PANTOPHAGISTS
PANTOPHAGOUS
PANTOPHAGY
PANTOPHOBIA
PANTOPHOBIAS
PANTOPRAGMATIC

PANTOPRAGMATICS
PANTOSCOPE
PANTOSCOPES
PANTOSCOPIC
PANTOTHENATE
PANTOTHENATES
PANTOTHENIC
PANTOUFLES
PANTROPICAL
PANTRYMAID
PANTRYMAIDS
PANTSUITED
PANTYWAIST
PANTYWAISTS
PANZOOTICS
PAPALISING
PAPALIZING
PAPAPRELATIST
PAPAPRELATISTS
PAPAVERACEOUS
PAPAVERINE
PAPAVERINES
PAPAVEROUS
PAPERBACKED
PAPERBACKER
PAPERBACKERS
PAPERBACKING
PAPERBACKS
PAPERBARKS
PAPERBOARD
PAPERBOARDS
PAPERBOUND
PAPERBOUNDS
PAPERCLIPS
PAPERGIRLS
PAPERHANGER
PAPERHANGERS
PAPERHANGING
PAPERHANGINGS
PAPERINESS
PAPERINESSES
PAPERKNIFE
PAPERKNIVES
PAPERMAKER
PAPERMAKERS
PAPERMAKING
PAPERMAKINGS
PAPERWARES
PAPERWEIGHT
PAPERWEIGHTS
PAPERWORKS
PAPETERIES
PAPILIONACEOUS
PAPILLATED
PAPILLIFEROUS
PAPILLIFORM
PAPILLITIS
PAPILLITISES
PAPILLOMAS

PAPILLOMATA
PAPILLOMATOSES
PAPILLOMATOSIS
PAPILLOMATOUS
PAPILLOMAVIRUS
PAPILLOTES
PAPILLULATE
PAPILLULES
PAPISTICAL
PAPISTICALLY
PAPISTRIES
PAPOVAVIRUS
PAPOVAVIRUSES
PAPULATION
PAPULATIONS
PAPULIFEROUS
PAPYRACEOUS
PAPYROLOGICAL
PAPYROLOGIES
PAPYROLOGIST
PAPYROLOGISTS
PAPYROLOGY
PARABAPTISM
PARABAPTISMS
PARABEMATA
PARABEMATIC
PARABIOSES
PARABIOSIS
PARABIOTIC
PARABIOTICALLY
PARABLASTIC
PARABLASTS
PARABLEPSES
PARABLEPSIES
PARABLEPSIS
PARABLEPSY
PARABLEPTIC
PARABOLANUS
PARABOLANUSES
PARABOLICAL
PARABOLICALLY
PARABOLISATION
PARABOLISATIONS
PARABOLISE
PARABOLISED
PARABOLISES
PARABOLISING
PARABOLIST
PARABOLISTS
PARABOLIZATION
PARABOLIZATIONS
PARABOLIZE
PARABOLIZED
PARABOLIZES
PARABOLIZING
PARABOLOID
PARABOLOIDAL
PARABOLOIDS
PARABRAKES

PARACASEIN
PARACASEINS
PARACENTESES
PARACENTESIS
PARACETAMOL
PARACETAMOLS
PARACHRONISM
PARACHRONISMS
PARACHUTED
PARACHUTES
PARACHUTIC
PARACHUTING
PARACHUTIST
PARACHUTISTS
PARACLETES
PARACROSTIC
PARACROSTICS
PARACYANOGEN
PARACYANOGENS
PARADIDDLE
PARADIDDLES
PARADIGMATIC
PARADIGMATICAL
PARADISAIC
PARADISAICAL
PARADISAICALLY
PARADISEAN
PARADISIAC
PARADISIACAL
PARADISIACALLY
PARADISIAL
PARADISIAN
PARADISICAL
PARADOCTOR
PARADOCTORS
PARADOXERS
PARADOXICAL
PARADOXICALITY
PARADOXICALLY
PARADOXICALNESS
PARADOXIDIAN
PARADOXIES
PARADOXIST
PARADOXISTS
PARADOXOLOGIES
PARADOXOLOGY
PARADOXURE
PARADOXURES
PARADOXURINE
PARADROPPED
PARADROPPING
PARAENESES
PARAENESIS
PARAENETIC
PARAENETICAL
PARAESTHESIA
PARAESTHESIAS
PARAESTHETIC
PARAFFINED

PARAFFINES
PARAFFINIC
PARAFFINING
PARAFFINOID
PARAGENESES
PARAGENESIA
PARAGENESIAS
PARAGENESIS
PARAGENETIC
PARAGENETICALLY
PARAGLIDED
PARAGLIDER
PARAGLIDERS
PARAGLIDES
PARAGLIDING
PARAGLIDINGS
PARAGLOSSA
PARAGLOSSAE
PARAGLOSSAL
PARAGLOSSATE
PARAGNATHISM
PARAGNATHISMS
PARAGNATHOUS
PARAGNOSES
PARAGNOSIS
PARAGOGICAL
PARAGOGICALLY
PARAGOGUES
PARAGONING
PARAGONITE
PARAGONITES
PARAGRAMMATIST
PARAGRAMMATISTS
PARAGRAPHED
PARAGRAPHER
PARAGRAPHERS
PARAGRAPHIA
PARAGRAPHIAS
PARAGRAPHIC
PARAGRAPHICAL
PARAGRAPHICALLY
PARAGRAPHING
PARAGRAPHIST
PARAGRAPHISTS
PARAGRAPHS
PARAHELIOTROPIC
PARAHYDROGEN
PARAHYDROGENS
PARAINFLUENZA
PARAINFLUENZAS
PARAJOURNALISM
PARAJOURNALISMS
PARAKEELYA
PARAKEELYAS
PARAKELIAS
PARAKITING
PARAKITINGS
PARALALIAS
PARALANGUAGE

PARALANGUAGES

PARALANGUAGES
PARALDEHYDE
PARALDEHYDES
PARALEGALS
PARALEIPOMENA
PARALEIPOMENON
PARALEIPSES
PARALEIPSIS
PARALEXIAS
PARALIMNION
PARALIMNIONS
PARALINGUISTIC
PARALINGUISTICS
PARALIPOMENA
PARALIPOMENON
PARALIPSES
PARALIPSIS
PARALLACTIC
PARALLACTICAL
PARALLACTICALLY
PARALLAXES
PARALLELED
PARALLELEPIPED
PARALLELEPIPEDA
PARALLELEPIPEDS
PARALLELING
PARALLELINGS
PARALLELISE
PARALLELISED
PARALLELISES
PARALLELISING
PARALLELISM
PARALLELISMS
PARALLELIST
PARALLELISTIC
PARALLELISTS
PARALLELIZE
PARALLELIZED
PARALLELIZES
PARALLELIZING
PARALLELLED
PARALLELLING
PARALLELLY
PARALLELOGRAM
PARALLELOGRAMS
PARALLELOPIPED
PARALLELOPIPEDA
PARALLELOPIPEDS
PARALLELWISE
PARALOGIAS
PARALOGIES
PARALOGISE
PARALOGISED
PARALOGISES
PARALOGISING
PARALOGISM
PARALOGISMS
PARALOGIST
PARALOGISTIC

PARALOGISTS
PARALOGIZE
PARALOGIZED
PARALOGIZES
PARALOGIZING
PARALYMPIC
PARALYMPICS
PARALYSATION
PARALYSATIONS
PARALYSERS
PARALYSING
PARALYSINGLY
PARALYTICALLY
PARALYTICS
PARALYZATION
PARALYZATIONS
PARALYZERS
PARALYZING
PARALYZINGLY
PARAMAECIA
PARAMAECIUM
PARAMAGNET
PARAMAGNETIC
PARAMAGNETISM
PARAMAGNETISMS
PARAMAGNETS
PARAMASTOID
PARAMASTOIDS
PARAMATTAS
PARAMECIUM
PARAMECIUMS
PARAMEDICAL
PARAMEDICALS
PARAMEDICO
PARAMEDICOS
PARAMEDICS
PARAMENSTRUA
PARAMENSTRUUM
PARAMENSTRUUMS
PARAMETERISE
PARAMETERISED
PARAMETERISES
PARAMETERISING
PARAMETERIZE
PARAMETERIZED
PARAMETERIZES
PARAMETERIZING
PARAMETERS
PARAMETRAL
PARAMETRIC
PARAMETRICAL
PARAMETRICALLY
PARAMETRISATION
PARAMETRISE
PARAMETRISED
PARAMETRISES
PARAMETRISING
PARAMETRIZATION
PARAMETRIZE

PARAMETRIZED
PARAMETRIZES
PARAMETRIZING
PARAMILITARIES
PARAMILITARY
PARAMNESIA
PARAMNESIAS
PARAMOECIA
PARAMOECIUM
PARAMORPHIC
PARAMORPHINE
PARAMORPHINES
PARAMORPHISM
PARAMORPHISMS
PARAMORPHOUS
PARAMORPHS
PARAMOUNCIES
PARAMOUNCY
PARAMOUNTCIES
PARAMOUNTCY
PARAMOUNTLY
PARAMOUNTS
PARAMYLUMS
PARAMYXOVIRUS
PARAMYXOVIRUSES
PARANEPHRIC
PARANEPHROS
PARANEPHROSES
PARANOEICS
PARANOIACS
PARANOICALLY
PARANOIDAL
PARANORMAL
PARANORMALITIES
PARANORMALITY
PARANORMALLY
PARANORMALS
PARANTHELIA
PARANTHELION
PARANTHROPUS
PARANTHROPUSES
PARANYMPHS
PARAPARESES
PARAPARESIS
PARAPARETIC
PARAPENTES
PARAPENTING
PARAPENTINGS
PARAPERIODIC
PARAPHASIA
PARAPHASIAS
PARAPHASIC
PARAPHERNALIA
PARAPHILIA
PARAPHILIAC
PARAPHILIACS
PARAPHILIAS
PARAPHIMOSES
PARAPHIMOSIS

PARAPHONIA
PARAPHONIAS
PARAPHONIC
PARAPHRASABLE
PARAPHRASE
PARAPHRASED
PARAPHRASER
PARAPHRASERS
PARAPHRASES
PARAPHRASING
PARAPHRAST
PARAPHRASTIC
PARAPHRASTICAL
PARAPHRASTS
PARAPHRAXES
PARAPHRAXIA
PARAPHRAXIAS
PARAPHRAXIS
PARAPHRENIA
PARAPHRENIAS
PARAPHYSATE
PARAPHYSES
PARAPHYSIS
PARAPINEAL
PARAPLEGIA
PARAPLEGIAS
PARAPLEGIC
PARAPLEGICS
PARAPODIAL
PARAPODIUM
PARAPOPHYSES
PARAPOPHYSIAL
PARAPOPHYSIS
PARAPRAXES
PARAPRAXIS
PARAPSYCHIC
PARAPSYCHICAL
PARAPSYCHISM
PARAPSYCHISMS
PARAPSYCHOLOGY
PARAPSYCHOSES
PARAPSYCHOSIS
PARAQUADRATE
PARAQUADRATES
PARAQUITOS
PARARHYMES
PARAROSANILINE
PARAROSANILINES
PARARTHRIA
PARARTHRIAS
PARASAILED
PARASAILING
PARASAILINGS
PARASCENDER
PARASCENDERS
PARASCENDING
PARASCENDINGS
PARASCENIA
PARASCENIUM

PARASCEVES
PARASCIENCE
PARASCIENCES
PARASELENAE
PARASELENE
PARASELENIC
PARASEXUAL
PARASEXUALITIES
PARASEXUALITY
PARASHIOTH
PARASITAEMIA
PARASITAEMIAS
PARASITICAL
PARASITICALLY
PARASITICALNESS
PARASITICIDAL
PARASITICIDE
PARASITICIDES
PARASITISATION
PARASITISATIONS
PARASITISE
PARASITISED
PARASITISES
PARASITISING
PARASITISM
PARASITISMS
PARASITIZATION
PARASITIZATIONS
PARASITIZE
PARASITIZED
PARASITIZES
PARASITIZING
PARASITOID
PARASITOIDS
PARASITOLOGIC
PARASITOLOGICAL
PARASITOLOGIES
PARASITOLOGIST
PARASITOLOGISTS
PARASITOLOGY
PARASITOSES
PARASITOSIS
PARASKIING
PARASKIINGS
PARASPHENOID
PARASPHENOIDS
PARASTATAL
PARASTATALS
PARASTICHIES
PARASTICHOUS
PARASTICHY
PARASUICIDE
PARASUICIDES
PARASYMBIONT
PARASYMBIONTS
PARASYMBIOSES
PARASYMBIOSIS
PARASYMBIOTIC
PARASYMPATHETIC

PARASYNAPSES
PARASYNAPSIS
PARASYNAPTIC
PARASYNTHESES
PARASYNTHESIS
PARASYNTHETA
PARASYNTHETIC
PARASYNTHETON
PARATACTIC
PARATACTICAL
PARATACTICALLY
PARATANIWHA
PARATHESES
PARATHESIS
PARATHIONS
PARATHORMONE
PARATHORMONES
PARATHYROID
PARATHYROIDS
PARATROOPER
PARATROOPERS
PARATROOPS
PARATUNGSTIC
PARATYPHOID
PARATYPHOIDS
PARAWALKER
PARAWALKERS
PARBOILING
PARBREAKED
PARBREAKING
PARBUCKLED
PARBUCKLES
PARBUCKLING
PARCELLING
PARCELWISE
PARCENARIES
PARCHEDNESS
PARCHEDNESSES
PARCHEESIS
PARCHMENTISE
PARCHMENTISED
PARCHMENTISES
PARCHMENTISING
PARCHMENTIZE
PARCHMENTIZED
PARCHMENTIZES
PARCHMENTIZING
PARCHMENTS
PARCHMENTY
PARCIMONIES
PARDALISES
PARDALOTES
PARDONABLE
PARDONABLENESS
PARDONABLY
PARDONINGS
PARDONLESS
PAREGORICS
PARENCEPHALA

PARENCEPHALON
PARENCHYMA
PARENCHYMAL
PARENCHYMAS
PARENCHYMATA
PARENCHYMATOUS
PARENTAGES
PARENTALLY
PARENTERAL
PARENTERALLY
PARENTHESES
PARENTHESIS
PARENTHESISE
PARENTHESISED
PARENTHESISES
PARENTHESISING
PARENTHESIZE
PARENTHESIZED
PARENTHESIZES
PARENTHESIZING
PARENTHETIC
PARENTHETICAL
PARENTHETICALLY
PARENTHOOD
PARENTHOODS
PARENTINGS
PARENTLESS
PARESTHESIA
PARESTHESIAS
PARESTHETIC
PARFLECHES
PARFLESHES
PARFOCALISE
PARFOCALISED
PARFOCALISES
PARFOCALISING
PARFOCALITIES
PARFOCALITY
PARFOCALIZE
PARFOCALIZED
PARFOCALIZES
PARFOCALIZING
PARGASITES
PARGETINGS
PARGETTING
PARGETTINGS
PARGYLINES
PARHELIACAL
PARHYPATES
PARIPINNATE
PARISCHANE
PARISCHANES
PARISCHANS
PARISHIONER
PARISHIONERS
PARISYLLABIC
PARKINSONIAN
PARKINSONISM
PARKINSONISMS

PARKLEAVES
PARLEMENTS
PARLEYVOOED
PARLEYVOOING
PARLEYVOOS
PARLIAMENT
PARLIAMENTARIAN
PARLIAMENTARILY
PARLIAMENTARISM
PARLIAMENTARY
PARLIAMENTING
PARLIAMENTINGS
PARLIAMENTS
PARLOUSNESS
PARLOUSNESSES
PARMACITIE
PARMACITIES
PARMIGIANA
PARMIGIANO
PAROCCIPITAL
PAROCHIALISE
PAROCHIALISED
PAROCHIALISES
PAROCHIALISING
PAROCHIALISM
PAROCHIALISMS
PAROCHIALITIES
PAROCHIALITY
PAROCHIALIZE
PAROCHIALIZED
PAROCHIALIZES
PAROCHIALIZING
PAROCHIALLY
PAROCHINES
PARODISTIC
PAROECIOUS
PAROEMIACS
PAROEMIOGRAPHER
PAROEMIOGRAPHY
PAROEMIOLOGIES
PAROEMIOLOGY
PARONOMASIA
PARONOMASIAS
PARONOMASIES
PARONOMASTIC
PARONOMASTICAL
PARONOMASY
PARONYCHIA
PARONYCHIAL
PARONYCHIAS
PARONYMIES
PARONYMOUS
PARONYMOUSLY
PAROTIDITIC
PAROTIDITIS
PAROTIDITISES
PAROTITISES
PAROXETINE
PAROXETINES

PAROXYSMAL
PAROXYSMALLY
PAROXYSMIC
PAROXYTONE
PAROXYTONES
PAROXYTONIC
PARQUETING
PARQUETRIES
PARQUETTED
PARQUETTING
PARRAKEETS
PARRAMATTA
PARRAMATTAS
PARRHESIAS
PARRICIDAL
PARRICIDES
PARRITCHES
PARROCKING
PARROQUETS
PARROTFISH
PARROTFISHES
PARROTRIES
PARSIMONIES
PARSIMONIOUS
PARSIMONIOUSLY
PARSONAGES
PARSONICAL
PARTAKINGS
PARTHENOCARPIC
PARTHENOCARPIES
PARTHENOCARPOUS
PARTHENOCARPY
PARTHENOGENESES
PARTHENOGENESIS
PARTHENOGENETIC
PARTHENOSPORE
PARTHENOSPORES
PARTIALISE
PARTIALISED
PARTIALISES
PARTIALISING
PARTIALISM
PARTIALISMS
PARTIALIST
PARTIALISTS
PARTIALITIES
PARTIALITY
PARTIALIZE
PARTIALIZED
PARTIALIZES
PARTIALIZING
PARTIALNESS
PARTIALNESSES
PARTIBILITIES
PARTIBILITY
PARTICIPABLE
PARTICIPANT
PARTICIPANTLY
PARTICIPANTS

PARTICIPATE
PARTICIPATED
PARTICIPATES
PARTICIPATING
PARTICIPATION
PARTICIPATIONAL
PARTICIPATIONS
PARTICIPATIVE
PARTICIPATOR
PARTICIPATORS
PARTICIPATORY
PARTICIPIAL
PARTICIPIALLY
PARTICIPIALS
PARTICIPLE
PARTICIPLES
PARTICLEBOARD
PARTICLEBOARDS
PARTICULAR
PARTICULARISE
PARTICULARISED
PARTICULARISER
PARTICULARISERS
PARTICULARISES
PARTICULARISING
PARTICULARISM
PARTICULARISMS
PARTICULARIST
PARTICULARISTIC
PARTICULARISTS
PARTICULARITIES
PARTICULARITY
PARTICULARIZE
PARTICULARIZED
PARTICULARIZER
PARTICULARIZERS
PARTICULARIZES
PARTICULARIZING
PARTICULARLY
PARTICULARNESS
PARTICULARS
PARTICULATE
PARTICULATES
PARTISANLY
PARTISANSHIP
PARTISANSHIPS
PARTITIONED
PARTITIONER
PARTITIONERS
PARTITIONING
PARTITIONIST
PARTITIONISTS
PARTITIONMENT
PARTITIONMENTS
PARTITIONS
PARTITIVELY
PARTITIVES
PARTITURAS
PARTIZANSHIP

PARTIZANSHIPS
PARTNERING
PARTNERLESS
PARTNERSHIP
PARTNERSHIPS
PARTRIDGEBERRY
PARTRIDGES
PARTURIENCIES
PARTURIENCY
PARTURIENT
PARTURIENTS
PARTURIFACIENT
PARTURITION
PARTURITIONS
PARTYGOERS
PARVANIMITIES
PARVANIMITY
PARVIFOLIATE
PARVOLINES
PARVOVIRUS
PARVOVIRUSES
PASIGRAPHIC
PASIGRAPHICAL
PASIGRAPHIES
PASIGRAPHY
PASODOBLES
PASQUEFLOWER
PASQUEFLOWERS
PASQUILANT
PASQUILANTS
PASQUILERS
PASQUILLED
PASQUILLING
PASQUINADE
PASQUINADED
PASQUINADER
PASQUINADERS
PASQUINADES
PASQUINADING
PASSABLENESS
PASSABLENESSES
PASSACAGLIA
PASSACAGLIAS
PASSAGEWAY
PASSAGEWAYS
PASSAGEWORK
PASSAGEWORKS
PASSALONGS
PASSAMENTED
PASSAMENTING
PASSAMENTS
PASSAMEZZO
PASSAMEZZOS
PASSEMEASURE
PASSEMEASURES
PASSEMENTED
PASSEMENTERIE
PASSEMENTERIES
PASSEMENTING

PASSEMENTS
PASSENGERS
PASSEPIEDS
PASSERINES
PASSIBILITIES
PASSIBILITY
PASSIBLENESS
PASSIBLENESSES
PASSIFLORA
PASSIFLORACEOUS
PASSIFLORAS
PASSIMETER
PASSIMETERS
PASSIONALS
PASSIONARIES
PASSIONARY
PASSIONATE
PASSIONATED
PASSIONATELY
PASSIONATENESS
PASSIONATES
PASSIONATING
PASSIONFLOWER
PASSIONFLOWERS
PASSIONING
PASSIONLESS
PASSIONLESSLY
PASSIONLESSNESS
PASSIVATED
PASSIVATES
PASSIVATING
PASSIVATION
PASSIVATIONS
PASSIVENESS
PASSIVENESSES
PASSIVISMS
PASSIVISTS
PASSIVITIES
PASSMENTED
PASSMENTING
PASTEBOARD
PASTEBOARDS
PASTEDOWNS
PASTELISTS
PASTELLIST
PASTELLISTS
PASTEURELLA
PASTEURELLAE
PASTEURELLAS
PASTEURISATION
PASTEURISATIONS
PASTEURISE
PASTEURISED
PASTEURISER
PASTEURISERS
PASTEURISES
PASTEURISING
PASTEURISM
PASTEURISMS

PASTEURIZATION
PASTEURIZATIONS
PASTEURIZE
PASTEURIZED
PASTEURIZER
PASTEURIZERS
PASTEURIZES
PASTEURIZING
PASTICCIOS
PASTICHEUR
PASTICHEURS
PASTINESSES
PASTITSIOS
PASTMASTER
PASTMASTERS
PASTNESSES
PASTORALES
PASTORALISM
PASTORALISMS
PASTORALIST
PASTORALISTS
PASTORALLY
PASTORALNESS
PASTORALNESSES
PASTORATES
PASTORIUMS
PASTORSHIP
PASTORSHIPS
PASTOURELLE
PASTOURELLES
PASTRYCOOK
PASTRYCOOKS
PASTURABLE
PASTURAGES
PASTURELAND
PASTURELANDS
PASTURELESS
PATAPHYSICS
PATCHBOARD
PATCHBOARDS
PATCHCOCKE
PATCHCOCKES
PATCHERIES
PATCHINESS
PATCHINESSES
PATCHOCKES
PATCHOULIES
PATCHOULIS
PATCHWORKED
PATCHWORKING
PATCHWORKS
PATELLECTOMIES
PATELLECTOMY
PATELLIFORM
PATENTABILITIES
PATENTABILITY
PATENTABLE
PATERCOVES
PATEREROES

PATERFAMILIAS
PATERFAMILIASES
PATERNALISM
PATERNALISMS
PATERNALIST
PATERNALISTIC
PATERNALISTS
PATERNALLY
PATERNITIES
PATERNOSTER
PATERNOSTERS
PATHBREAKING
PATHETICAL
PATHETICALLY
PATHFINDER
PATHFINDERS
PATHFINDING
PATHFINDINGS
PATHLESSNESS
PATHLESSNESSES
PATHOBIOLOGIES
PATHOBIOLOGY
PATHOGENES
PATHOGENESES
PATHOGENESIS
PATHOGENETIC
PATHOGENIC
PATHOGENICITIES
PATHOGENICITY
PATHOGENIES
PATHOGENOUS
PATHOGNOMIES
PATHOGNOMONIC
PATHOGNOMY
PATHOGRAPHIES
PATHOGRAPHY
PATHOLOGIC
PATHOLOGICAL
PATHOLOGICALLY
PATHOLOGIES
PATHOLOGISE
PATHOLOGISED
PATHOLOGISES
PATHOLOGISING
PATHOLOGIST
PATHOLOGISTS
PATHOLOGIZE
PATHOLOGIZED
PATHOLOGIZES
PATHOLOGIZING
PATHOPHOBIA
PATHOPHOBIAS
PATHOPHYSIOLOGY
PATIBULARY
PATIENTEST
PATIENTING
PATINATING
PATINATION
PATINATIONS

PATINISING
PATINIZING
PATISSERIE
PATISSERIES
PATISSIERS
PATRESFAMILIAS
PATRIALISATION
PATRIALISATIONS
PATRIALISE
PATRIALISED
PATRIALISES
PATRIALISING
PATRIALISM
PATRIALISMS
PATRIALITIES
PATRIALITY
PATRIALIZATION
PATRIALIZATIONS
PATRIALIZE
PATRIALIZED
PATRIALIZES
PATRIALIZING
PATRIARCHAL
PATRIARCHALISM
PATRIARCHALISMS
PATRIARCHALLY
PATRIARCHATE
PATRIARCHATES
PATRIARCHIES
PATRIARCHISM
PATRIARCHISMS
PATRIARCHS
PATRIARCHY
PATRIATING
PATRIATION
PATRIATIONS
PATRICIANLY
PATRICIANS
PATRICIATE
PATRICIATES
PATRICIDAL
PATRICIDES
PATRICLINIC
PATRICLINOUS
PATRIFOCAL
PATRIFOCALITIES
PATRIFOCALITY
PATRILINEAGE
PATRILINEAGES
PATRILINEAL
PATRILINEALLY
PATRILINEAR
PATRILINEARLY
PATRILINIES
PATRILOCAL
PATRILOCALLY
PATRIMONIAL
PATRIMONIALLY
PATRIMONIES

PATRIOTICALLY
PATRIOTISM
PATRIOTISMS
PATRISTICAL
PATRISTICALLY
PATRISTICISM
PATRISTICISMS
PATRISTICS
PATROCLINAL
PATROCLINIC
PATROCLINIES
PATROCLINOUS
PATROCLINY
PATROLLERS
PATROLLING
PATROLOGICAL
PATROLOGIES
PATROLOGIST
PATROLOGISTS
PATROLWOMAN
PATROLWOMEN
PATRONAGED
PATRONAGES
PATRONAGING
PATRONESSES
PATRONISATION
PATRONISATIONS
PATRONISED
PATRONISER
PATRONISERS
PATRONISES
PATRONISING
PATRONISINGLY
PATRONIZATION
PATRONIZATIONS
PATRONIZED
PATRONIZER
PATRONIZERS
PATRONIZES
PATRONIZING
PATRONIZINGLY
PATRONLESS
PATRONYMIC
PATRONYMICS
PATROONSHIP
PATROONSHIPS
PATTERNING
PATTERNINGS
PATTERNLESS
PATULOUSLY
PATULOUSNESS
PATULOUSNESSES
PAUCILOQUENT
PAUGHTIEST
PAULOWNIAS
PAUNCHIEST
PAUNCHINESS
PAUNCHINESSES
PAUPERESSES

PAUPERISATION
PAUPERISATIONS
PAUPERISED
PAUPERISES
PAUPERISING
PAUPERISMS
PAUPERIZATION
PAUPERIZATIONS
PAUPERIZED
PAUPERIZES
PAUPERIZING
PAUPIETTES
PAUSEFULLY
PAUSELESSLY
PAVEMENTED
PAVEMENTING
PAVILIONED
PAVILIONING
PAVONAZZOS
PAWKINESSES
PAWNBROKER
PAWNBROKERS
PAWNBROKING
PAWNBROKINGS
PAWNTICKET
PAWNTICKETS
PAYMASTERS
PAYNIMRIES
PAYSAGISTS
PEABERRIES
PEACEABLENESS
PEACEABLENESSES
PEACEFULLER
PEACEFULLEST
PEACEFULLY
PEACEFULNESS
PEACEFULNESSES
PEACEKEEPER
PEACEKEEPERS
PEACEKEEPING
PEACEKEEPINGS
PEACELESSNESS
PEACELESSNESSES
PEACEMAKER
PEACEMAKERS
PEACEMAKING
PEACEMAKINGS
PEACETIMES
PEACHBLOWS
PEACHERINO
PEACHERINOS
PEACHINESS
PEACHINESSES
PEACOCKERIES
PEACOCKERY
PEACOCKIER
PEACOCKIEST
PEACOCKING
PEACOCKISH

PEAKEDNESS
PEAKEDNESSES
PEARLASHES
PEARLESCENCE
PEARLESCENCES
PEARLESCENT
PEARLINESS
PEARLINESSES
PEARLWORTS
PEARMONGER
PEARMONGERS
PEARTNESSES
PEASANTRIES
PEASHOOTER
PEASHOOTERS
PEASOUPERS
PEBBLEDASH
PEBBLEDASHED
PEBBLEDASHES
PEBBLEDASHING
PECCABILITIES
PECCABILITY
PECCADILLO
PECCADILLOES
PECCADILLOS
PECCANCIES
PECKERWOOD
PECKERWOODS
PECKISHNESS
PECKISHNESSES
PECTINACEOUS
PECTINATED
PECTINATELY
PECTINATION
PECTINATIONS
PECTINESTERASE
PECTINESTERASES
PECTISABLE
PECTISATION
PECTISATIONS
PECTIZABLE
PECTIZATION
PECTIZATIONS
PECTOLITES
PECTORALLY
PECTORILOQUIES
PECTORILOQUY
PECULATING
PECULATION
PECULATIONS
PECULATORS
PECULIARISE
PECULIARISED
PECULIARISES
PECULIARISING
PECULIARITIES
PECULIARITY
PECULIARIZE
PECULIARIZED

PECULIARIZES
PECULIARIZING
PECULIARLY
PECUNIARILY
PEDAGOGICAL
PEDAGOGICALLY
PEDAGOGICS
PEDAGOGIES
PEDAGOGISM
PEDAGOGISMS
PEDAGOGUED
PEDAGOGUERIES
PEDAGOGUERY
PEDAGOGUES
PEDAGOGUING
PEDAGOGUISH
PEDAGOGUISHNESS
PEDAGOGUISM
PEDAGOGUISMS
PEDALLINGS
PEDANTICAL
PEDANTICALLY
PEDANTICISE
PEDANTICISED
PEDANTICISES
PEDANTICISING
PEDANTICISM
PEDANTICISMS
PEDANTICIZE
PEDANTICIZED
PEDANTICIZES
PEDANTICIZING
PEDANTISED
PEDANTISES
PEDANTISING
PEDANTISMS
PEDANTIZED
PEDANTIZES
PEDANTIZING
PEDANTOCRACIES
PEDANTOCRACY
PEDANTOCRAT
PEDANTOCRATIC
PEDANTOCRATS
PEDANTRIES
PEDDLERIES
PEDERASTIC
PEDERASTIES
PEDEREROES
PEDESTALED
PEDESTALING
PEDESTALLED
PEDESTALLING
PEDESTRIAN
PEDESTRIANISE
PEDESTRIANISED
PEDESTRIANISES
PEDESTRIANISING
PEDESTRIANISM

PEDESTRIANISMS
PEDESTRIANIZE
PEDESTRIANIZED
PEDESTRIANIZES
PEDESTRIANIZING
PEDESTRIANS
PEDETENTOUS
PEDIATRICIAN
PEDIATRICIANS
PEDIATRICS
PEDIATRIST
PEDIATRISTS
PEDICELLARIA
PEDICELLARIAE
PEDICELLATE
PEDICULATE
PEDICULATED
PEDICULATES
PEDICULATION
PEDICULATIONS
PEDICULOSES
PEDICULOSIS
PEDICULOUS
PEDICURING
PEDICURIST
PEDICURISTS
PEDIMENTAL
PEDIMENTED
PEDIPALPUS
PEDOGENESES
PEDOGENESIS
PEDOGENETIC
PEDOLOGICAL
PEDOLOGIES
PEDOLOGIST
PEDOLOGISTS
PEDOMETERS
PEDOPHILES
PEDOPHILIA
PEDOPHILIAC
PEDOPHILIACS
PEDOPHILIAS
PEDOPHILIC
PEDUNCULAR
PEDUNCULATE
PEDUNCULATED
PEDUNCULATION
PEDUNCULATIONS
PEELGARLIC
PEELGARLICS
PEERLESSLY
PEERLESSNESS
PEERLESSNESSES
PEEVISHNESS
PEEVISHNESSES
PEGMATITES
PEGMATITIC
PEIRASTICALLY
PEJORATING

PEJORATION
PEJORATIONS
PEJORATIVE
PEJORATIVELY
PEJORATIVES
PELARGONIC
PELARGONIUM
PELARGONIUMS
PELECYPODS
PELLAGRINS
PELLAGROUS
PELLETIFIED
PELLETIFIES
PELLETIFYING
PELLETISATION
PELLETISATIONS
PELLETISED
PELLETISER
PELLETISERS
PELLETISES
PELLETISING
PELLETIZATION
PELLETIZATIONS
PELLETIZED
PELLETIZER
PELLETIZERS
PELLETIZES
PELLETIZING
PELLICULAR
PELLITORIES
PELLUCIDITIES
PELLUCIDITY
PELLUCIDLY
PELLUCIDNESS
PELLUCIDNESSES
PELMANISMS
PELOLOGIES
PELOTHERAPIES
PELOTHERAPY
PELTATIONS
PELTMONGER
PELTMONGERS
PELVIMETER
PELVIMETERS
PELVIMETRIES
PELVIMETRY
PELYCOSAUR
PELYCOSAURS
PEMPHIGOID
PEMPHIGOUS
PEMPHIGUSES
PENALISATION
PENALISATIONS
PENALISING
PENALITIES
PENALIZATION
PENALIZATIONS
PENALIZING
PENANNULAR

PENCILINGS
PENCILLERS
PENCILLING
PENCILLINGS
PENDENCIES
PENDENTIVE
PENDENTIVES
PENDICLERS
PENDRAGONS
PENDRAGONSHIP
PENDRAGONSHIPS
PENDULATED
PENDULATES
PENDULATING
PENDULOSITIES
PENDULOSITY
PENDULOUSLY
PENDULOUSNESS
PENDULOUSNESSES
PENELOPISE
PENELOPISED
PENELOPISES
PENELOPISING
PENELOPIZE
PENELOPIZED
PENELOPIZES
PENELOPIZING
PENEPLAINS
PENEPLANATION
PENEPLANATIONS
PENEPLANES
PENETRABILITIES
PENETRABILITY
PENETRABLE
PENETRABLENESS
PENETRABLY
PENETRALIA
PENETRALIAN
PENETRANCE
PENETRANCES
PENETRANCIES
PENETRANCY
PENETRANTS
PENETRATED
PENETRATES
PENETRATING
PENETRATINGLY
PENETRATION
PENETRATIONS
PENETRATIVE
PENETRATIVELY
PENETRATIVENESS
PENETRATOR
PENETRATORS
PENETROMETER
PENETROMETERS
PENGUINERIES
PENGUINERY
PENGUINRIES

PENHOLDERS
PENICILLAMINE
PENICILLAMINES
PENICILLATE
PENICILLATELY
PENICILLATION
PENICILLATIONS
PENICILLIA
PENICILLIFORM
PENICILLIN
PENICILLINASE
PENICILLINASES
PENICILLINS
PENICILLIUM
PENICILLIUMS
PENINSULAR
PENINSULARITIES
PENINSULARITY
PENINSULAS
PENINSULATE
PENINSULATED
PENINSULATES
PENINSULATING
PENISTONES
PENITENCES
PENITENCIES
PENITENTIAL
PENITENTIALLY
PENITENTIALS
PENITENTIARIES
PENITENTIARY
PENITENTLY
PENMANSHIP
PENMANSHIPS
PENNACEOUS
PENNALISMS
PENNATULACEOUS
PENNATULAE
PENNATULAS
PENNILESSLY
PENNILESSNESS
PENNILESSNESSES
PENNILLION
PENNINITES
PENNONCELLE
PENNONCELLES
PENNONCELS
PENNYCRESS
PENNYCRESSES
PENNYLANDS
PENNYROYAL
PENNYROYALS
PENNYWEIGHT
PENNYWEIGHTS
PENNYWHISTLE
PENNYWHISTLES
PENNYWINKLE
PENNYWINKLES
PENNYWORTH

PENNYWORTHS
PENNYWORTS
PENOLOGICAL
PENOLOGICALLY
PENOLOGIES
PENOLOGIST
PENOLOGISTS
PENONCELLE
PENONCELLES
PENPUSHERS
PENPUSHING
PENPUSHINGS
PENSIEROSO
PENSILENESS
PENSILENESSES
PENSILITIES
PENSIONABLE
PENSIONARIES
PENSIONARY
PENSIONEER
PENSIONERS
PENSIONING
PENSIONLESS
PENSIONNAT
PENSIONNATS
PENSIVENESS
PENSIVENESSES
PENSTEMONS
PENTABARBITAL
PENTABARBITALS
PENTACHORD
PENTACHORDS
PENTACRINOID
PENTACRINOIDS
PENTACTINAL
PENTACYCLIC
PENTADACTYL
PENTADACTYLE
PENTADACTYLES
PENTADACTYLIC
PENTADACTYLIES
PENTADACTYLISM
PENTADACTYLISMS
PENTADACTYLOUS
PENTADACTYLS
PENTADACTYLY
PENTADELPHOUS
PENTAGONAL
PENTAGONALLY
PENTAGONALS
PENTAGRAMS
PENTAGRAPH
PENTAGRAPHS
PENTAGYNIAN
PENTAGYNOUS
PENTAHEDRA
PENTAHEDRAL
PENTAHEDRON
PENTAHEDRONS

PENTALOGIES

PENTALOGIES
PENTALPHAS
PENTAMERIES
PENTAMERISM
PENTAMERISMS
PENTAMEROUS
PENTAMETER
PENTAMETERS
PENTAMIDINE
PENTAMIDINES
PENTANDRIAN
PENTANDROUS
PENTANGLES
PENTANGULAR
PENTAPEPTIDE
PENTAPEPTIDES
PENTAPLOID
PENTAPLOIDIES
PENTAPLOIDS
PENTAPLOIDY
PENTAPODIC
PENTAPODIES
PENTAPOLIS
PENTAPOLISES
PENTAPOLITAN
PENTAPRISM
PENTAPRISMS
PENTAQUARK
PENTAQUARKS
PENTARCHICAL
PENTARCHIES
PENTASTICH
PENTASTICHOUS
PENTASTICHS
PENTASTYLE
PENTASTYLES
PENTASYLLABIC
PENTATEUCHAL
PENTATHLETE
PENTATHLETES
PENTATHLON
PENTATHLONS
PENTATHLUM
PENTATHLUMS
PENTATOMIC
PENTATONIC
PENTAVALENT
PENTAZOCINE
PENTAZOCINES
PENTECONTER
PENTECONTERS
PENTETERIC
PENTHEMIMER
PENTHEMIMERAL
PENTHEMIMERS
PENTHOUSED
PENTHOUSES
PENTHOUSING
PENTIMENTI

PENTIMENTO
PENTLANDITE
PENTLANDITES
PENTOBARBITAL
PENTOBARBITALS
PENTOBARBITONE
PENTOBARBITONES
PENTOSANES
PENTOSIDES
PENTOXIDES
PENTSTEMON
PENTSTEMONS
PENTYLENES
PENULTIMAS
PENULTIMATE
PENULTIMATELY
PENULTIMATES
PENUMBROUS
PENURIOUSLY
PENURIOUSNESS
PENURIOUSNESSES
PEOPLEHOOD
PEOPLEHOODS
PEOPLELESS
PEPEROMIAS
PEPPERBOXES
PEPPERCORN
PEPPERCORNS
PEPPERCORNY
PEPPERGRASS
PEPPERGRASSES
PEPPERIDGE
PEPPERIDGES
PEPPERIEST
PEPPERINESS
PEPPERINESSES
PEPPERINGS
PEPPERMILL
PEPPERMILLS
PEPPERMINT
PEPPERMINTS
PEPPERMINTY
PEPPERONIS
PEPPERTREE
PEPPERTREES
PEPPERWORT
PEPPERWORTS
PEPPINESSES
PEPSINATED
PEPSINATES
PEPSINATING
PEPSINOGEN
PEPSINOGENS
PEPTALKING
PEPTICITIES
PEPTIDASES
PEPTIDOGLYCAN
PEPTIDOGLYCANS
PEPTISABLE

PEPTISATION
PEPTISATIONS
PEPTIZABLE
PEPTIZATION
PEPTIZATIONS
PEPTONISATION
PEPTONISATIONS
PEPTONISED
PEPTONISER
PEPTONISERS
PEPTONISES
PEPTONISING
PEPTONIZATION
PEPTONIZATIONS
PEPTONIZED
PEPTONIZER
PEPTONIZERS
PEPTONIZES
PEPTONIZING
PERACIDITIES
PERACIDITY
PERADVENTURE
PERADVENTURES
PERAEOPODS
PERAMBULATE
PERAMBULATED
PERAMBULATES
PERAMBULATING
PERAMBULATION
PERAMBULATIONS
PERAMBULATOR
PERAMBULATORS
PERAMBULATORY
PERBORATES
PERCALINES
PERCEIVABILITY
PERCEIVABLE
PERCEIVABLY
PERCEIVERS
PERCEIVING
PERCEIVINGS
PERCENTAGE
PERCENTAGES
PERCENTILE
PERCENTILES
PERCEPTIBILITY
PERCEPTIBLE
PERCEPTIBLY
PERCEPTION
PERCEPTIONAL
PERCEPTIONS
PERCEPTIVE
PERCEPTIVELY
PERCEPTIVENESS
PERCEPTIVITIES
PERCEPTIVITY
PERCEPTUAL
PERCEPTUALLY
PERCHERIES

PERCHERONS
PERCHLORATE
PERCHLORATES
PERCHLORIC
PERCHLORIDE
PERCHLORIDES
PERCHLOROETHENE
PERCIPIENCE
PERCIPIENCES
PERCIPIENCIES
PERCIPIENCY
PERCIPIENT
PERCIPIENTLY
PERCIPIENTS
PERCOIDEAN
PERCOIDEANS
PERCOLABLE
PERCOLATED
PERCOLATES
PERCOLATING
PERCOLATION
PERCOLATIONS
PERCOLATIVE
PERCOLATOR
PERCOLATORS
PERCURRENT
PERCURSORY
PERCUSSANT
PERCUSSING
PERCUSSION
PERCUSSIONAL
PERCUSSIONIST
PERCUSSIONISTS
PERCUSSIONS
PERCUSSIVE
PERCUSSIVELY
PERCUSSIVENESS
PERCUSSORS
PERCUTANEOUS
PERCUTANEOUSLY
PERCUTIENT
PERCUTIENTS
PERDENDOSI
PERDITIONABLE
PERDITIONS
PERDUELLION
PERDUELLIONS
PERDURABILITIES
PERDURABILITY
PERDURABLE
PERDURABLY
PERDURANCE
PERDURANCES
PERDURATION
PERDURATIONS
PEREGRINATE
PEREGRINATED
PEREGRINATES
PEREGRINATING

PEREGRINATION
PEREGRINATIONS
PEREGRINATOR
PEREGRINATORS
PEREGRINATORY
PEREGRINES
PEREGRINITIES
PEREGRINITY
PEREIOPODS
PEREMPTORILY
PEREMPTORINESS
PEREMPTORY
PERENNATED
PERENNATES
PERENNATING
PERENNATION
PERENNATIONS
PERENNIALITIES
PERENNIALITY
PERENNIALLY
PERENNIALS
PERENNIBRANCH
PERENNIBRANCHS
PERENNITIES
PERESTROIKA
PERESTROIKAS
PERFECTATION
PERFECTATIONS
PERFECTERS
PERFECTEST
PERFECTIBILIAN
PERFECTIBILIANS
PERFECTIBILISM
PERFECTIBILISMS
PERFECTIBILIST
PERFECTIBILISTS
PERFECTIBILITY
PERFECTIBLE
PERFECTING
PERFECTION
PERFECTIONATE
PERFECTIONATED
PERFECTIONATES
PERFECTIONATING
PERFECTIONISM
PERFECTIONISMS
PERFECTIONIST
PERFECTIONISTIC
PERFECTIONISTS
PERFECTIONS
PERFECTIVE
PERFECTIVELY
PERFECTIVENESS
PERFECTIVES
PERFECTIVITIES
PERFECTIVITY
PERFECTNESS
PERFECTNESSES
PERFECTORS

PERFERVIDITIES
PERFERVIDITY
PERFERVIDLY
PERFERVIDNESS
PERFERVIDNESSES
PERFERVORS
PERFERVOUR
PERFERVOURS
PERFICIENT
PERFIDIOUS
PERFIDIOUSLY
PERFIDIOUSNESS
PERFLUOROCARBON
PERFOLIATE
PERFOLIATION
PERFOLIATIONS
PERFORABLE
PERFORANSES
PERFORATED
PERFORATES
PERFORATING
PERFORATION
PERFORATIONS
PERFORATIVE
PERFORATOR
PERFORATORS
PERFORATORY
PERFORATUS
PERFORATUSES
PERFORMABILITY
PERFORMABLE
PERFORMANCE
PERFORMANCES
PERFORMATIVE
PERFORMATIVELY
PERFORMATIVES
PERFORMATORY
PERFORMERS
PERFORMING
PERFORMINGS
PERFUMELESS
PERFUMERIES
PERFUMIERS
PERFUNCTORILY
PERFUNCTORINESS
PERFUNCTORY
PERFUSATES
PERFUSIONIST
PERFUSIONISTS
PERFUSIONS
PERGAMENEOUS
PERGAMENTACEOUS
PERGUNNAHS
PERIASTRON
PERIASTRONS
PERIBLASTS
PERICARDIA
PERICARDIAC
PERICARDIAL

PERICARDIAN
PERICARDITIC
PERICARDITIS
PERICARDITISES
PERICARDIUM
PERICARDIUMS
PERICARPIAL
PERICARPIC
PERICENTER
PERICENTERS
PERICENTRAL
PERICENTRE
PERICENTRES
PERICENTRIC
PERICHAETIA
PERICHAETIAL
PERICHAETIUM
PERICHONDRAL
PERICHONDRIA
PERICHONDRIAL
PERICHONDRIUM
PERICHORESES
PERICHORESIS
PERICHYLOUS
PERICLASES
PERICLASTIC
PERICLINAL
PERICLINES
PERICLITATE
PERICLITATED
PERICLITATES
PERICLITATING
PERICRANIA
PERICRANIAL
PERICRANIUM
PERICRANIUMS
PERICULOUS
PERICYCLES
PERICYCLIC
PERICYNTHIA
PERICYNTHION
PERICYNTHIONS
PERIDERMAL
PERIDERMIC
PERIDESMIA
PERIDESMIUM
PERIDINIAN
PERIDINIANS
PERIDINIUM
PERIDINIUMS
PERIDOTITE
PERIDOTITES
PERIDOTITIC
PERIDROMES
PERIEGESES
PERIEGESIS
PERIGASTRIC
PERIGASTRITIS
PERIGASTRITISES

PERIGENESES
PERIGENESIS
PERIGLACIAL
PERIGONIAL
PERIGONIUM
PERIGYNIES
PERIGYNOUS
PERIHELIAL
PERIHELION
PERIHEPATIC
PERIHEPATITIS
PERIHEPATITISES
PERIKARYAL
PERIKARYON
PERILOUSLY
PERILOUSNESS
PERILOUSNESSES
PERILYMPHS
PERIMENOPAUSAL
PERIMENOPAUSE
PERIMENOPAUSES
PERIMETERS
PERIMETRAL
PERIMETRIC
PERIMETRICAL
PERIMETRICALLY
PERIMETRIES
PERIMORPHIC
PERIMORPHISM
PERIMORPHISMS
PERIMORPHOUS
PERIMORPHS
PERIMYSIUM
PERIMYSIUMS
PERINAEUMS
PERINATALLY
PERINEPHRIA
PERINEPHRIC
PERINEPHRITIS
PERINEPHRITISES
PERINEPHRIUM
PERINEURAL
PERINEURIA
PERINEURIAL
PERINEURITIC
PERINEURITIS
PERINEURITISES
PERINEURIUM
PERIODATES
PERIODICAL
PERIODICALIST
PERIODICALISTS
PERIODICALLY
PERIODICALS
PERIODICITIES
PERIODICITY
PERIODIDES
PERIODISATION
PERIODISATIONS

PERIODIZATION

PERIODIZATION
PERIODIZATIONS
PERIODONTAL
PERIODONTALLY
PERIODONTIA
PERIODONTIAS
PERIODONTIC
PERIODONTICALLY
PERIODONTICS
PERIODONTIST
PERIODONTISTS
PERIODONTITIS
PERIODONTITISES
PERIODONTOLOGY
PERIONYCHIA
PERIONYCHIUM
PERIOSTEAL
PERIOSTEUM
PERIOSTITIC
PERIOSTITIS
PERIOSTITISES
PERIOSTRACUM
PERIOSTRACUMS
PERIPATETIC
PERIPATETICAL
PERIPATETICALLY
PERIPATETICISM
PERIPATETICISMS
PERIPATETICS
PERIPATUSES
PERIPETEIA
PERIPETEIAN
PERIPETEIAS
PERIPETIAN
PERIPETIAS
PERIPETIES
PERIPHERAL
PERIPHERALITIES
PERIPHERALITY
PERIPHERALLY
PERIPHERALS
PERIPHERIC
PERIPHERICAL
PERIPHERIES
PERIPHONIC
PERIPHRASE
PERIPHRASED
PERIPHRASES
PERIPHRASING
PERIPHRASIS
PERIPHRASTIC
PERIPHRASTICAL
PERIPHYTIC
PERIPHYTON
PERIPHYTONS
PERIPLASMS
PERIPLASTS
PERIPLUSES
PERIPROCTS

PERIPTERAL
PERIPTERIES
PERISARCAL
PERISARCOUS
PERISCIANS
PERISCOPES
PERISCOPIC
PERISCOPICALLY
PERISELENIA
PERISELENIUM
PERISHABILITIES
PERISHABILITY
PERISHABLE
PERISHABLENESS
PERISHABLES
PERISHABLY
PERISHINGLY
PERISPERMAL
PERISPERMIC
PERISPERMS
PERISPOMENON
PERISPOMENONS
PERISSODACTYL
PERISSODACTYLE
PERISSODACTYLES
PERISSODACTYLIC
PERISSODACTYLS
PERISSOLOGIES
PERISSOLOGY
PERISSOSYLLABIC
PERISTALITH
PERISTALITHS
PERISTALSES
PERISTALSIS
PERISTALTIC
PERISTALTICALLY
PERISTERITE
PERISTERITES
PERISTERONIC
PERISTOMAL
PERISTOMATIC
PERISTOMES
PERISTOMIAL
PERISTREPHIC
PERISTYLAR
PERISTYLES
PERITECTIC
PERITHECIA
PERITHECIAL
PERITHECIUM
PERITONAEA
PERITONAEAL
PERITONAEUM
PERITONAEUMS
PERITONEAL
PERITONEALLY
PERITONEOSCOPY
PERITONEUM
PERITONEUMS

PERITONITIC
PERITONITIS
PERITONITISES
PERITRACKS
PERITRICHA
PERITRICHOUS
PERITRICHOUSLY
PERITRICHS
PERITYPHLITIS
PERITYPHLITISES
PERIVITELLINE
PERIWIGGED
PERIWIGGING
PERIWINKLE
PERIWINKLES
PERJINKETY
PERJINKITIES
PERJINKITY
PERJURIOUS
PERJURIOUSLY
PERKINESSES
PERLEMOENS
PERLOCUTION
PERLOCUTIONARY
PERLOCUTIONS
PERLUSTRATE
PERLUSTRATED
PERLUSTRATES
PERLUSTRATING
PERLUSTRATION
PERLUSTRATIONS
PERMACULTURE
PERMACULTURES
PERMAFROST
PERMAFROSTS
PERMALLOYS
PERMANENCE
PERMANENCES
PERMANENCIES
PERMANENCY
PERMANENTLY
PERMANENTNESS
PERMANENTNESSES
PERMANENTS
PERMANGANATE
PERMANGANATES
PERMANGANIC
PERMEABILITIES
PERMEABILITY
PERMEABLENESS
PERMEABLENESSES
PERMEAMETER
PERMEAMETERS
PERMEANCES
PERMEATING
PERMEATION
PERMEATIONS
PERMEATIVE
PERMEATORS

PERMETHRIN
PERMETHRINS
PERMILLAGE
PERMILLAGES
PERMISSIBILITY
PERMISSIBLE
PERMISSIBLENESS
PERMISSIBLY
PERMISSION
PERMISSIONS
PERMISSIVE
PERMISSIVELY
PERMISSIVENESS
PERMITTANCE
PERMITTANCES
PERMITTEES
PERMITTERS
PERMITTING
PERMITTIVITIES
PERMITTIVITY
PERMUTABILITIES
PERMUTABILITY
PERMUTABLE
PERMUTABLENESS
PERMUTABLY
PERMUTATED
PERMUTATES
PERMUTATING
PERMUTATION
PERMUTATIONAL
PERMUTATIONS
PERNANCIES
PERNICIOUS
PERNICIOUSLY
PERNICIOUSNESS
PERNICKETINESS
PERNICKETY
PERNOCTATE
PERNOCTATED
PERNOCTATES
PERNOCTATING
PERNOCTATION
PERNOCTATIONS
PERONEUSES
PERORATING
PERORATION
PERORATIONAL
PERORATIONS
PERORATORS
PEROVSKIAS
PEROVSKITE
PEROVSKITES
PEROXIDASE
PEROXIDASES
PEROXIDATION
PEROXIDATIONS
PEROXIDING
PEROXIDISE
PEROXIDISED

PEROXIDISES
PEROXIDISING
PEROXIDIZE
PEROXIDIZED
PEROXIDIZES
PEROXIDIZING
PEROXISOMAL
PEROXISOME
PEROXISOMES
PEROXYSULPHURIC
PERPENDICULAR
PERPENDICULARLY
PERPENDICULARS
PERPENDING
PERPETRABLE
PERPETRATE
PERPETRATED
PERPETRATES
PERPETRATING
PERPETRATION
PERPETRATIONS
PERPETRATOR
PERPETRATORS
PERPETUABLE
PERPETUALISM
PERPETUALISMS
PERPETUALIST
PERPETUALISTS
PERPETUALITIES
PERPETUALITY
PERPETUALLY
PERPETUALS
PERPETUANCE
PERPETUANCES
PERPETUATE
PERPETUATED
PERPETUATES
PERPETUATING
PERPETUATION
PERPETUATIONS
PERPETUATOR
PERPETUATORS
PERPETUITIES
PERPETUITY
PERPHENAZINE
PERPHENAZINES
PERPLEXEDLY
PERPLEXEDNESS
PERPLEXEDNESSES
PERPLEXERS
PERPLEXING
PERPLEXINGLY
PERPLEXITIES
PERPLEXITY
PERQUISITE
PERQUISITES
PERQUISITION
PERQUISITIONS
PERQUISITOR

PERQUISITORS
PERRUQUIER
PERRUQUIERS
PERSCRUTATION
PERSCRUTATIONS
PERSECUTED
PERSECUTEE
PERSECUTEES
PERSECUTES
PERSECUTING
PERSECUTION
PERSECUTIONS
PERSECUTIVE
PERSECUTOR
PERSECUTORS
PERSECUTORY
PERSEITIES
PERSELINES
PERSEVERANCE
PERSEVERANCES
PERSEVERANT
PERSEVERATE
PERSEVERATED
PERSEVERATES
PERSEVERATING
PERSEVERATION
PERSEVERATIONS
PERSEVERATIVE
PERSEVERATOR
PERSEVERATORS
PERSEVERED
PERSEVERES
PERSEVERING
PERSEVERINGLY
PERSICARIA
PERSICARIAS
PERSIENNES
PERSIFLAGE
PERSIFLAGES
PERSIFLEUR
PERSIFLEURS
PERSIMMONS
PERSISTENCE
PERSISTENCES
PERSISTENCIES
PERSISTENCY
PERSISTENT
PERSISTENTLY
PERSISTENTS
PERSISTERS
PERSISTING
PERSISTINGLY
PERSISTIVE
PERSNICKETINESS
PERSNICKETY
PERSONABLE
PERSONABLENESS
PERSONABLY
PERSONAGES

PERSONALIA
PERSONALISATION
PERSONALISE
PERSONALISED
PERSONALISES
PERSONALISING
PERSONALISM
PERSONALISMS
PERSONALIST
PERSONALISTIC
PERSONALISTS
PERSONALITIES
PERSONALITY
PERSONALIZATION
PERSONALIZE
PERSONALIZED
PERSONALIZES
PERSONALIZING
PERSONALLY
PERSONALTIES
PERSONALTY
PERSONATED
PERSONATES
PERSONATING
PERSONATINGS
PERSONATION
PERSONATIONS
PERSONATIVE
PERSONATOR
PERSONATORS
PERSONHOOD
PERSONHOODS
PERSONIFIABLE
PERSONIFICATION
PERSONIFIED
PERSONIFIER
PERSONIFIERS
PERSONIFIES
PERSONIFYING
PERSONISED
PERSONISES
PERSONISING
PERSONIZED
PERSONIZES
PERSONIZING
PERSONNELS
PERSONPOWER
PERSONPOWERS
PERSPECTIVAL
PERSPECTIVE
PERSPECTIVELY
PERSPECTIVES
PERSPECTIVISM
PERSPECTIVISMS
PERSPECTIVIST
PERSPECTIVISTS
PERSPICACIOUS
PERSPICACIOUSLY
PERSPICACITIES

PERSPICACITY
PERSPICUITIES
PERSPICUITY
PERSPICUOUS
PERSPICUOUSLY
PERSPICUOUSNESS
PERSPIRABLE
PERSPIRATE
PERSPIRATED
PERSPIRATES
PERSPIRATING
PERSPIRATION
PERSPIRATIONS
PERSPIRATORY
PERSPIRING
PERSPIRINGLY
PERSTRINGE
PERSTRINGED
PERSTRINGES
PERSTRINGING
PERSUADABILITY
PERSUADABLE
PERSUADERS
PERSUADING
PERSUASIBILITY
PERSUASIBLE
PERSUASION
PERSUASIONS
PERSUASIVE
PERSUASIVELY
PERSUASIVENESS
PERSUASIVES
PERSUASORY
PERSULFURIC
PERSULPHATE
PERSULPHATES
PERSULPHURIC
PERSWADING
PERTAINING
PERTINACIOUS
PERTINACIOUSLY
PERTINACITIES
PERTINACITY
PERTINENCE
PERTINENCES
PERTINENCIES
PERTINENCY
PERTINENTLY
PERTINENTS
PERTNESSES
PERTURBABLE
PERTURBABLY
PERTURBANCE
PERTURBANCES
PERTURBANT
PERTURBANTS
PERTURBATE
PERTURBATED
PERTURBATES

PERTURBATING

PERTURBATING
PERTURBATION
PERTURBATIONAL
PERTURBATIONS
PERTURBATIVE
PERTURBATOR
PERTURBATORIES
PERTURBATORS
PERTURBATORY
PERTURBEDLY
PERTURBERS
PERTURBING
PERTURBINGLY
PERTUSIONS
PERTUSSISES
PERVASIONS
PERVASIVELY
PERVASIVENESS
PERVASIVENESSES
PERVERSELY
PERVERSENESS
PERVERSENESSES
PERVERSEST
PERVERSION
PERVERSIONS
PERVERSITIES
PERVERSITY
PERVERSIVE
PERVERTEDLY
PERVERTEDNESS
PERVERTEDNESSES
PERVERTERS
PERVERTIBLE
PERVERTING
PERVIATING
PERVICACIES
PERVICACIOUS
PERVICACITIES
PERVICACITY
PERVIOUSLY
PERVIOUSNESS
PERVIOUSNESSES
PESKINESSES
PESSIMISMS
PESSIMISTIC
PESSIMISTICAL
PESSIMISTICALLY
PESSIMISTS
PESTERINGLY
PESTERMENT
PESTERMENTS
PESTHOUSES
PESTICIDAL
PESTICIDES
PESTIFEROUS
PESTIFEROUSLY
PESTIFEROUSNESS
PESTILENCE
PESTILENCES

PESTILENTIAL
PESTILENTIALLY
PESTILENTLY
PESTOLOGICAL
PESTOLOGIES
PESTOLOGIST
PESTOLOGISTS
PETAHERTZES
PETALIFEROUS
PETALODIES
PETALOMANIA
PETALOMANIAS
PETAURISTS
PETCHARIES
PETERSHAMS
PETHIDINES
PETIOLATED
PETIOLULES
PETITENESS
PETITENESSES
PETITIONARY
PETITIONED
PETITIONER
PETITIONERS
PETITIONING
PETITIONINGS
PETITIONIST
PETITIONISTS
PETNAPINGS
PETNAPPERS
PETNAPPING
PETRIFACTION
PETRIFACTIONS
PETRIFACTIVE
PETRIFICATION
PETRIFICATIONS
PETRIFIERS
PETRIFYING
PETRISSAGE
PETRISSAGES
PETROCHEMICAL
PETROCHEMICALLY
PETROCHEMICALS
PETROCHEMISTRY
PETROCURRENCIES
PETROCURRENCY
PETRODOLLAR
PETRODOLLARS
PETRODROME
PETRODROMES
PETROGENESES
PETROGENESIS
PETROGENETIC
PETROGENIES
PETROGLYPH
PETROGLYPHIC
PETROGLYPHIES
PETROGLYPHS
PETROGLYPHY

PETROGRAMS
PETROGRAPHER
PETROGRAPHERS
PETROGRAPHIC
PETROGRAPHICAL
PETROGRAPHIES
PETROGRAPHY
PETROLAGES
PETROLATUM
PETROLATUMS
PETROLEOUS
PETROLEUMS
PETROLEURS
PETROLEUSE
PETROLEUSES
PETROLHEAD
PETROLHEADS
PETROLIFEROUS
PETROLLING
PETROLOGIC
PETROLOGICAL
PETROLOGICALLY
PETROLOGIES
PETROLOGIST
PETROLOGISTS
PETROMONEY
PETROMONEYS
PETROMONIES
PETRONELLA
PETRONELLAS
PETROPHYSICAL
PETROPHYSICIST
PETROPHYSICISTS
PETROPHYSICS
PETROPOUNDS
PETTEDNESS
PETTEDNESSES
PETTICHAPS
PETTICHAPSES
PETTICOATED
PETTICOATS
PETTIFOGGED
PETTIFOGGER
PETTIFOGGERIES
PETTIFOGGERS
PETTIFOGGERY
PETTIFOGGING
PETTIFOGGINGS
PETTINESSES
PETTISHNESS
PETTISHNESSES
PETULANCES
PETULANCIES
PETULANTLY
PEWHOLDERS
PHACOLITES
PHACOLITHS
PHAELONION
PHAELONIONS

PHAENOGAMIC
PHAENOGAMOUS
PHAENOGAMS
PHAENOLOGIES
PHAENOLOGY
PHAENOMENA
PHAENOMENON
PHAENOTYPE
PHAENOTYPED
PHAENOTYPES
PHAENOTYPING
PHAEOMELANIN
PHAEOMELANINS
PHAGEDAENA
PHAGEDAENAS
PHAGEDAENIC
PHAGEDENAS
PHAGEDENIC
PHAGOCYTES
PHAGOCYTIC
PHAGOCYTICAL
PHAGOCYTISE
PHAGOCYTISED
PHAGOCYTISES
PHAGOCYTISING
PHAGOCYTISM
PHAGOCYTISMS
PHAGOCYTIZE
PHAGOCYTIZED
PHAGOCYTIZES
PHAGOCYTIZING
PHAGOCYTOSE
PHAGOCYTOSED
PHAGOCYTOSES
PHAGOCYTOSING
PHAGOCYTOSIS
PHAGOCYTOTIC
PHAGOMANIA
PHAGOMANIAC
PHAGOMANIACS
PHAGOMANIAS
PHAGOPHOBIA
PHAGOPHOBIAS
PHAGOSOMES
PHALANGEAL
PHALANGERS
PHALANGIDS
PHALANGIST
PHALANGISTS
PHALANSTERIAN
PHALANSTERIES
PHALANSTERISM
PHALANSTERISMS
PHALANSTERIST
PHALANSTERISTS
PHALANSTERY
PHALAROPES
PHALLICALLY
PHALLICISM

PHALLICISMS
PHALLICIST
PHALLICISTS
PHALLOCENTRIC
PHALLOCENTRISM
PHALLOCENTRISMS
PHALLOCRAT
PHALLOCRATIC
PHALLOCRATS
PHALLOIDIN
PHALLOIDINS
PHANEROGAM
PHANEROGAMIC
PHANEROGAMOUS
PHANEROGAMS
PHANEROPHYTE
PHANEROPHYTES
PHANSIGARS
PHANTASIAST
PHANTASIASTS
PHANTASIED
PHANTASIES
PHANTASIME
PHANTASIMES
PHANTASIMS
PHANTASMAGORIA
PHANTASMAGORIAL
PHANTASMAGORIAS
PHANTASMAGORIC
PHANTASMAGORIES
PHANTASMAGORY
PHANTASMAL
PHANTASMALIAN
PHANTASMALITIES
PHANTASMALITY
PHANTASMALLY
PHANTASMATA
PHANTASMIC
PHANTASMICAL
PHANTASMICALLY
PHANTASTIC
PHANTASTICS
PHANTASTRIES
PHANTASTRY
PHANTASYING
PHANTOMATIC
PHANTOMISH
PHANTOMLIKE
PHANTOSMES
PHARISAICAL
PHARISAICALLY
PHARISAICALNESS
PHARISAISM
PHARISAISMS
PHARISEEISM
PHARISEEISMS
PHARMACEUTIC
PHARMACEUTICAL
PHARMACEUTICALS

PHARMACEUTICS
PHARMACEUTIST
PHARMACEUTISTS
PHARMACIES
PHARMACIST
PHARMACISTS
PHARMACODYNAMIC
PHARMACOGENOMIC
PHARMACOGNOSIES
PHARMACOGNOSIST
PHARMACOGNOSTIC
PHARMACOGNOSY
PHARMACOKINETIC
PHARMACOLOGIC
PHARMACOLOGICAL
PHARMACOLOGIES
PHARMACOLOGIST
PHARMACOLOGISTS
PHARMACOLOGY
PHARMACOPEIA
PHARMACOPEIAL
PHARMACOPEIAS
PHARMACOPOEIA
PHARMACOPOEIAL
PHARMACOPOEIAN
PHARMACOPOEIAS
PHARMACOPOEIC
PHARMACOPOEIST
PHARMACOPOEISTS
PHARMACOPOLIST
PHARMACOPOLISTS
PHARMACOTHERAPY
PHARYNGALS
PHARYNGEAL
PHARYNGITIC
PHARYNGITIDES
PHARYNGITIS
PHARYNGITISES
PHARYNGOLOGICAL
PHARYNGOLOGIES
PHARYNGOLOGIST
PHARYNGOLOGISTS
PHARYNGOLOGY
PHARYNGOSCOPE
PHARYNGOSCOPES
PHARYNGOSCOPIC
PHARYNGOSCOPIES
PHARYNGOSCOPY
PHARYNGOTOMIES
PHARYNGOTOMY
PHASCOGALE
PHASCOGALES
PHASEDOWNS
PHASEOLINS
PHATICALLY
PHEASANTRIES
PHEASANTRY
PHELLODERM
PHELLODERMAL

PHELLODERMS
PHELLOGENETIC
PHELLOGENIC
PHELLOGENS
PHELLOPLASTIC
PHELLOPLASTICS
PHELONIONS
PHENACAINE
PHENACAINES
PHENACETIN
PHENACETINS
PHENACITES
PHENAKISMS
PHENAKISTOSCOPE
PHENAKITES
PHENANTHRENE
PHENANTHRENES
PHENARSAZINE
PHENARSAZINES
PHENAZINES
PHENCYCLIDINE
PHENCYCLIDINES
PHENETICIST
PHENETICISTS
PHENETIDINE
PHENETIDINES
PHENETOLES
PHENFORMIN
PHENFORMINS
PHENGOPHOBIA
PHENGOPHOBIAS
PHENMETRAZINE
PHENMETRAZINES
PHENOBARBITAL
PHENOBARBITALS
PHENOBARBITONE
PHENOBARBITONES
PHENOCOPIES
PHENOCRYST
PHENOCRYSTIC
PHENOCRYSTS
PHENOLATED
PHENOLATES
PHENOLATING
PHENOLOGICAL
PHENOLOGICALLY
PHENOLOGIES
PHENOLOGIST
PHENOLOGISTS
PHENOLPHTHALEIN
PHENOMENAL
PHENOMENALISE
PHENOMENALISED
PHENOMENALISES
PHENOMENALISING
PHENOMENALISM
PHENOMENALISMS
PHENOMENALIST
PHENOMENALISTIC

PHENOMENALISTS
PHENOMENALITIES
PHENOMENALITY
PHENOMENALIZE
PHENOMENALIZED
PHENOMENALIZES
PHENOMENALIZING
PHENOMENALLY
PHENOMENAS
PHENOMENISE
PHENOMENISED
PHENOMENISES
PHENOMENISING
PHENOMENISM
PHENOMENISMS
PHENOMENIST
PHENOMENISTS
PHENOMENIZE
PHENOMENIZED
PHENOMENIZES
PHENOMENIZING
PHENOMENOLOGIES
PHENOMENOLOGIST
PHENOMENOLOGY
PHENOMENON
PHENOMENONS
PHENOTHIAZINE
PHENOTHIAZINES
PHENOTYPED
PHENOTYPES
PHENOTYPIC
PHENOTYPICAL
PHENOTYPICALLY
PHENOTYPING
PHENOXIDES
PHENTOLAMINE
PHENTOLAMINES
PHENYLALANIN
PHENYLALANINE
PHENYLALANINES
PHENYLALANINS
PHENYLAMINE
PHENYLAMINES
PHENYLBUTAZONE
PHENYLBUTAZONES
PHENYLENES
PHENYLEPHRINE
PHENYLEPHRINES
PHENYLKETONURIA
PHENYLKETONURIC
PHENYLMETHYL
PHENYLMETHYLS
PHENYLTHIOUREA
PHENYLTHIOUREAS
PHENYTOINS
PHEROMONAL
PHEROMONES
PHIALIFORM
PHILADELPHUS

PHILADELPHUSES

PHILADELPHUSES
PHILANDERED
PHILANDERER
PHILANDERERS
PHILANDERING
PHILANDERINGS
PHILANDERS
PHILANTHROPE
PHILANTHROPES
PHILANTHROPIC
PHILANTHROPICAL
PHILANTHROPIES
PHILANTHROPIST
PHILANTHROPISTS
PHILANTHROPOID
PHILANTHROPOIDS
PHILANTHROPY
PHILATELIC
PHILATELICALLY
PHILATELIES
PHILATELIST
PHILATELISTS
PHILHARMONIC
PHILHARMONICS
PHILHELLENE
PHILHELLENES
PHILHELLENIC
PHILHELLENISM
PHILHELLENISMS
PHILHELLENIST
PHILHELLENISTS
PHILHORSES
PHILIPPICS
PHILIPPINA
PHILIPPINAS
PHILIPPINE
PHILIPPINES
PHILISTIAS
PHILISTINE
PHILISTINES
PHILISTINISM
PHILISTINISMS
PHILLABEGS
PHILLIBEGS
PHILLIPSITE
PHILLIPSITES
PHILLUMENIES
PHILLUMENIST
PHILLUMENISTS
PHILLUMENY
PHILODENDRA
PHILODENDRON
PHILODENDRONS
PHILOGYNIES
PHILOGYNIST
PHILOGYNISTS
PHILOGYNOUS
PHILOLOGER
PHILOLOGERS

PHILOLOGIAN
PHILOLOGIANS
PHILOLOGIC
PHILOLOGICAL
PHILOLOGICALLY
PHILOLOGIES
PHILOLOGIST
PHILOLOGISTS
PHILOLOGUE
PHILOLOGUES
PHILOMATHIC
PHILOMATHICAL
PHILOMATHIES
PHILOMATHS
PHILOMATHY
PHILOMELAS
PHILOPENAS
PHILOPOENA
PHILOPOENAS
PHILOSOPHASTER
PHILOSOPHASTERS
PHILOSOPHE
PHILOSOPHER
PHILOSOPHERESS
PHILOSOPHERS
PHILOSOPHES
PHILOSOPHESS
PHILOSOPHESSES
PHILOSOPHIC
PHILOSOPHICAL
PHILOSOPHICALLY
PHILOSOPHIES
PHILOSOPHISE
PHILOSOPHISED
PHILOSOPHISER
PHILOSOPHISERS
PHILOSOPHISES
PHILOSOPHISING
PHILOSOPHISM
PHILOSOPHISMS
PHILOSOPHIST
PHILOSOPHISTIC
PHILOSOPHISTS
PHILOSOPHIZE
PHILOSOPHIZED
PHILOSOPHIZER
PHILOSOPHIZERS
PHILOSOPHIZES
PHILOSOPHIZING
PHILOSOPHY
PHILOXENIA
PHILOXENIAS
PHILTERING
PHISNOMIES
PHLEBECTOMIES
PHLEBECTOMY
PHLEBITIDES
PHLEBITISES
PHLEBOGRAM

PHLEBOGRAMS
PHLEBOGRAPHIC
PHLEBOGRAPHIES
PHLEBOGRAPHY
PHLEBOLITE
PHLEBOLITES
PHLEBOLOGIES
PHLEBOLOGY
PHLEBOSCLEROSES
PHLEBOSCLEROSIS
PHLEBOTOMIC
PHLEBOTOMICAL
PHLEBOTOMIES
PHLEBOTOMISE
PHLEBOTOMISED
PHLEBOTOMISES
PHLEBOTOMISING
PHLEBOTOMIST
PHLEBOTOMISTS
PHLEBOTOMIZE
PHLEBOTOMIZED
PHLEBOTOMIZES
PHLEBOTOMIZING
PHLEBOTOMY
PHLEGMAGOGIC
PHLEGMAGOGUE
PHLEGMAGOGUES
PHLEGMASIA
PHLEGMASIAS
PHLEGMATIC
PHLEGMATICAL
PHLEGMATICALLY
PHLEGMATICNESS
PHLEGMIEST
PHLEGMONIC
PHLEGMONOID
PHLEGMONOUS
PHLOGISTIC
PHLOGISTICATE
PHLOGISTICATED
PHLOGISTICATES
PHLOGISTICATING
PHLOGISTON
PHLOGISTONS
PHLOGOPITE
PHLOGOPITES
PHLORIZINS
PHLYCTAENA
PHLYCTAENAE
PHLYCTENAE
PHOCOMELIA
PHOCOMELIAS
PHOCOMELIC
PHOENIXISM
PHOENIXISMS
PHOENIXLIKE
PHOLIDOSES
PHOLIDOSIS
PHONASTHENIA

PHONASTHENIAS
PHONATHONS
PHONATIONS
PHONAUTOGRAPH
PHONAUTOGRAPHIC
PHONAUTOGRAPHS
PHONECARDS
PHONEMATIC
PHONEMATICALLY
PHONEMICALLY
PHONEMICISATION
PHONEMICISE
PHONEMICISED
PHONEMICISES
PHONEMICISING
PHONEMICIST
PHONEMICISTS
PHONEMICIZATION
PHONEMICIZE
PHONEMICIZED
PHONEMICIZES
PHONEMICIZING
PHONENDOSCOPE
PHONENDOSCOPES
PHONETICAL
PHONETICALLY
PHONETICIAN
PHONETICIANS
PHONETICISATION
PHONETICISE
PHONETICISED
PHONETICISES
PHONETICISING
PHONETICISM
PHONETICISMS
PHONETICIST
PHONETICISTS
PHONETICIZATION
PHONETICIZE
PHONETICIZED
PHONETICIZES
PHONETICIZING
PHONETISATION
PHONETISATIONS
PHONETISED
PHONETISES
PHONETISING
PHONETISMS
PHONETISTS
PHONETIZATION
PHONETIZATIONS
PHONETIZED
PHONETIZES
PHONETIZING
PHONEYNESS
PHONEYNESSES
PHONICALLY
PHONINESSES
PHONMETERS

PHONOCAMPTIC
PHONOCAMPTICS
PHONOCARDIOGRAM
PHONOCHEMISTRY
PHONOFIDDLE
PHONOFIDDLES
PHONOGRAMIC
PHONOGRAMICALLY
PHONOGRAMMIC
PHONOGRAMS
PHONOGRAPH
PHONOGRAPHER
PHONOGRAPHERS
PHONOGRAPHIC
PHONOGRAPHIES
PHONOGRAPHIST
PHONOGRAPHISTS
PHONOGRAPHS
PHONOGRAPHY
PHONOLITES
PHONOLITIC
PHONOLOGIC
PHONOLOGICAL
PHONOLOGICALLY
PHONOLOGIES
PHONOLOGIST
PHONOLOGISTS
PHONOMETER
PHONOMETERS
PHONOMETRIC
PHONOMETRICAL
PHONOPHOBIA
PHONOPHOBIAS
PHONOPHORE
PHONOPHORES
PHONOPORES
PHONOSCOPE
PHONOSCOPES
PHONOTACTIC
PHONOTACTICS
PHONOTYPED
PHONOTYPER
PHONOTYPERS
PHONOTYPES
PHONOTYPIC
PHONOTYPICAL
PHONOTYPIES
PHONOTYPING
PHONOTYPIST
PHONOTYPISTS
PHORMINGES
PHOSGENITE
PHOSGENITES
PHOSPHATASE
PHOSPHATASES
PHOSPHATED
PHOSPHATES
PHOSPHATIC
PHOSPHATIDE

PHOSPHATIDES
PHOSPHATIDIC
PHOSPHATIDYL
PHOSPHATIDYLS
PHOSPHATING
PHOSPHATISATION
PHOSPHATISE
PHOSPHATISED
PHOSPHATISES
PHOSPHATISING
PHOSPHATIZATION
PHOSPHATIZE
PHOSPHATIZED
PHOSPHATIZES
PHOSPHATIZING
PHOSPHATURIA
PHOSPHATURIAS
PHOSPHATURIC
PHOSPHENES
PHOSPHIDES
PHOSPHINES
PHOSPHITES
PHOSPHOCREATIN
PHOSPHOCREATINE
PHOSPHOCREATINS
PHOSPHOKINASE
PHOSPHOKINASES
PHOSPHOLIPASE
PHOSPHOLIPASES
PHOSPHOLIPID
PHOSPHOLIPIDS
PHOSPHONIC
PHOSPHONIUM
PHOSPHONIUMS
PHOSPHOPROTEIN
PHOSPHOPROTEINS
PHOSPHORATE
PHOSPHORATED
PHOSPHORATES
PHOSPHORATING
PHOSPHORES
PHOSPHORESCE
PHOSPHORESCED
PHOSPHORESCENCE
PHOSPHORESCENT
PHOSPHORESCES
PHOSPHORESCING
PHOSPHORET
PHOSPHORETS
PHOSPHORETTED
PHOSPHORIC
PHOSPHORISE
PHOSPHORISED
PHOSPHORISES
PHOSPHORISING
PHOSPHORISM
PHOSPHORISMS
PHOSPHORITE
PHOSPHORITES

PHOSPHORITIC
PHOSPHORIZE
PHOSPHORIZED
PHOSPHORIZES
PHOSPHORIZING
PHOSPHOROLYSES
PHOSPHOROLYSIS
PHOSPHOROLYTIC
PHOSPHOROSCOPE
PHOSPHOROSCOPES
PHOSPHOROUS
PHOSPHORUS
PHOSPHORUSES
PHOSPHORYL
PHOSPHORYLASE
PHOSPHORYLASES
PHOSPHORYLATE
PHOSPHORYLATED
PHOSPHORYLATES
PHOSPHORYLATING
PHOSPHORYLATION
PHOSPHORYLATIVE
PHOSPHORYLS
PHOSPHURET
PHOSPHURETS
PHOSPHURETTED
PHOTICALLY
PHOTOACTINIC
PHOTOACTIVE
PHOTOAUTOTROPH
PHOTOAUTOTROPHS
PHOTOBATHIC
PHOTOBIOLOGIC
PHOTOBIOLOGICAL
PHOTOBIOLOGIES
PHOTOBIOLOGIST
PHOTOBIOLOGISTS
PHOTOBIOLOGY
PHOTOCATALYSES
PHOTOCATALYSIS
PHOTOCATALYTIC
PHOTOCATHODE
PHOTOCATHODES
PHOTOCELLS
PHOTOCHEMICAL
PHOTOCHEMICALLY
PHOTOCHEMIST
PHOTOCHEMISTRY
PHOTOCHEMISTS
PHOTOCHROMIC
PHOTOCHROMICS
PHOTOCHROMIES
PHOTOCHROMISM
PHOTOCHROMISMS
PHOTOCHROMY
PHOTOCOMPOSE
PHOTOCOMPOSED
PHOTOCOMPOSER
PHOTOCOMPOSERS

PHOTOCOMPOSES
PHOTOCOMPOSING
PHOTOCONDUCTING
PHOTOCONDUCTION
PHOTOCONDUCTIVE
PHOTOCONDUCTOR
PHOTOCONDUCTORS
PHOTOCOPIABLE
PHOTOCOPIED
PHOTOCOPIER
PHOTOCOPIERS
PHOTOCOPIES
PHOTOCOPYING
PHOTOCOPYINGS
PHOTOCURRENT
PHOTOCURRENTS
PHOTODEGRADABLE
PHOTODETECTOR
PHOTODETECTORS
PHOTODIODE
PHOTODIODES
PHOTODISSOCIATE
PHOTODUPLICATE
PHOTODUPLICATED
PHOTODUPLICATES
PHOTODYNAMIC
PHOTODYNAMICS
PHOTOELASTIC
PHOTOELASTICITY
PHOTOELECTRIC
PHOTOELECTRICAL
PHOTOELECTRODE
PHOTOELECTRODES
PHOTOELECTRON
PHOTOELECTRONIC
PHOTOELECTRONS
PHOTOEMISSION
PHOTOEMISSIONS
PHOTOEMISSIVE
PHOTOENGRAVE
PHOTOENGRAVED
PHOTOENGRAVER
PHOTOENGRAVERS
PHOTOENGRAVES
PHOTOENGRAVING
PHOTOENGRAVINGS
PHOTOEXCITATION
PHOTOEXCITED
PHOTOFINISHER
PHOTOFINISHERS
PHOTOFINISHING
PHOTOFINISHINGS
PHOTOFISSION
PHOTOFISSIONS
PHOTOFLASH
PHOTOFLASHES
PHOTOFLOOD
PHOTOFLOODS
PHOTOFLUOROGRAM

PHOTOGELATINE

PHOTOGELATINE
PHOTOGENES
PHOTOGENIC
PHOTOGENICALLY
PHOTOGENIES
PHOTOGEOLOGIC
PHOTOGEOLOGICAL
PHOTOGEOLOGIES
PHOTOGEOLOGIST
PHOTOGEOLOGISTS
PHOTOGEOLOGY
PHOTOGLYPH
PHOTOGLYPHIC
PHOTOGLYPHIES
PHOTOGLYPHS
PHOTOGLYPHY
PHOTOGRAMMETRIC
PHOTOGRAMMETRY
PHOTOGRAMS
PHOTOGRAPH
PHOTOGRAPHED
PHOTOGRAPHER
PHOTOGRAPHERS
PHOTOGRAPHIC
PHOTOGRAPHICAL
PHOTOGRAPHIES
PHOTOGRAPHING
PHOTOGRAPHIST
PHOTOGRAPHISTS
PHOTOGRAPHS
PHOTOGRAPHY
PHOTOGRAVURE
PHOTOGRAVURES
PHOTOINDUCED
PHOTOINDUCTION
PHOTOINDUCTIONS
PHOTOINDUCTIVE
PHOTOIONISATION
PHOTOIONISE
PHOTOIONISED
PHOTOIONISES
PHOTOIONISING
PHOTOIONIZATION
PHOTOIONIZE
PHOTOIONIZED
PHOTOIONIZES
PHOTOIONIZING
PHOTOJOURNALISM
PHOTOJOURNALIST
PHOTOKINESES
PHOTOKINESIS
PHOTOKINETIC
PHOTOLITHO
PHOTOLITHOGRAPH
PHOTOLITHOS
PHOTOLUMINESCE
PHOTOLUMINESCED
PHOTOLUMINESCES
PHOTOLYSABLE

PHOTOLYSED
PHOTOLYSES
PHOTOLYSING
PHOTOLYSIS
PHOTOLYTIC
PHOTOLYTICALLY
PHOTOLYZABLE
PHOTOLYZED
PHOTOLYZES
PHOTOLYZING
PHOTOMACROGRAPH
PHOTOMAPPED
PHOTOMAPPING
PHOTOMASKS
PHOTOMECHANICAL
PHOTOMETER
PHOTOMETERS
PHOTOMETRIC
PHOTOMETRICALLY
PHOTOMETRIES
PHOTOMETRIST
PHOTOMETRISTS
PHOTOMETRY
PHOTOMICROGRAPH
PHOTOMONTAGE
PHOTOMONTAGES
PHOTOMOSAIC
PHOTOMOSAICS
PHOTOMULTIPLIER
PHOTOMURAL
PHOTOMURALS
PHOTONASTIC
PHOTONASTIES
PHOTONASTY
PHOTONEGATIVE
PHOTONEUTRON
PHOTONEUTRONS
PHOTONOVEL
PHOTONOVELS
PHOTONUCLEAR
PHOTOOXIDATION
PHOTOOXIDATIONS
PHOTOOXIDATIVE
PHOTOOXIDISE
PHOTOOXIDISED
PHOTOOXIDISES
PHOTOOXIDISING
PHOTOOXIDIZE
PHOTOOXIDIZED
PHOTOOXIDIZES
PHOTOOXIDIZING
PHOTOPERIOD
PHOTOPERIODIC
PHOTOPERIODISM
PHOTOPERIODISMS
PHOTOPERIODS
PHOTOPHASE
PHOTOPHASES
PHOTOPHILIC

PHOTOPHILIES
PHOTOPHILOUS
PHOTOPHILS
PHOTOPHILY
PHOTOPHOBE
PHOTOPHOBES
PHOTOPHOBIA
PHOTOPHOBIAS
PHOTOPHOBIC
PHOTOPHONE
PHOTOPHONES
PHOTOPHONIC
PHOTOPHONIES
PHOTOPHONY
PHOTOPHORE
PHOTOPHORES
PHOTOPHORESES
PHOTOPHORESIS
PHOTOPLAYS
PHOTOPOLYMER
PHOTOPOLYMERS
PHOTOPOSITIVE
PHOTOPRODUCT
PHOTOPRODUCTION
PHOTOPRODUCTS
PHOTOPSIAS
PHOTOPSIES
PHOTOREACTION
PHOTOREACTIONS
PHOTOREALISM
PHOTOREALISMS
PHOTOREALIST
PHOTOREALISTIC
PHOTOREALISTS
PHOTORECEPTION
PHOTORECEPTIONS
PHOTORECEPTIVE
PHOTORECEPTOR
PHOTORECEPTORS
PHOTOREDUCE
PHOTOREDUCED
PHOTOREDUCES
PHOTOREDUCING
PHOTOREDUCTION
PHOTOREDUCTIONS
PHOTOREFRACTIVE
PHOTORESIST
PHOTORESISTS
PHOTOSCANNED
PHOTOSCANNING
PHOTOSCANS
PHOTOSENSITISE
PHOTOSENSITISED
PHOTOSENSITISER
PHOTOSENSITISES
PHOTOSENSITIVE
PHOTOSENSITIZE
PHOTOSENSITIZED
PHOTOSENSITIZER

PHOTOSENSITIZES
PHOTOSETTER
PHOTOSETTERS
PHOTOSETTING
PHOTOSETTINGS
PHOTOSHOOT
PHOTOSHOOTS
PHOTOSPHERE
PHOTOSPHERES
PHOTOSPHERIC
PHOTOSTATED
PHOTOSTATIC
PHOTOSTATING
PHOTOSTATS
PHOTOSTATTED
PHOTOSTATTING
PHOTOSYNTHATE
PHOTOSYNTHATES
PHOTOSYNTHESES
PHOTOSYNTHESIS
PHOTOSYNTHESISE
PHOTOSYNTHESIZE
PHOTOSYNTHETIC
PHOTOSYSTEM
PHOTOSYSTEMS
PHOTOTACTIC
PHOTOTACTICALLY
PHOTOTAXES
PHOTOTAXIES
PHOTOTAXIS
PHOTOTELEGRAPH
PHOTOTELEGRAPHS
PHOTOTELEGRAPHY
PHOTOTHERAPIES
PHOTOTHERAPY
PHOTOTHERMAL
PHOTOTHERMALLY
PHOTOTHERMIC
PHOTOTONIC
PHOTOTONUS
PHOTOTONUSES
PHOTOTOPOGRAPHY
PHOTOTOXIC
PHOTOTOXICITIES
PHOTOTOXICITY
PHOTOTRANSISTOR
PHOTOTROPE
PHOTOTROPES
PHOTOTROPH
PHOTOTROPHIC
PHOTOTROPHS
PHOTOTROPIC
PHOTOTROPICALLY
PHOTOTROPIES
PHOTOTROPISM
PHOTOTROPISMS
PHOTOTROPY
PHOTOTUBES
PHOTOTYPED

PHOTOTYPES
PHOTOTYPESET
PHOTOTYPESETS
PHOTOTYPESETTER
PHOTOTYPIC
PHOTOTYPICALLY
PHOTOTYPIES
PHOTOTYPING
PHOTOTYPOGRAPHY
PHOTOVOLTAIC
PHOTOVOLTAICS
PHOTOXYLOGRAPHY
PHOTOZINCOGRAPH
PHRAGMOPLAST
PHRAGMOPLASTS
PHRASELESS
PHRASEMAKER
PHRASEMAKERS
PHRASEMAKING
PHRASEMAKINGS
PHRASEMONGER
PHRASEMONGERING
PHRASEMONGERS
PHRASEOGRAM
PHRASEOGRAMS
PHRASEOGRAPH
PHRASEOGRAPHIC
PHRASEOGRAPHIES
PHRASEOGRAPHS
PHRASEOGRAPHY
PHRASEOLOGIC
PHRASEOLOGICAL
PHRASEOLOGIES
PHRASEOLOGIST
PHRASEOLOGISTS
PHRASEOLOGY
PHREAKINGS
PHREATOPHYTE
PHREATOPHYTES
PHREATOPHYTIC
PHRENESIAC
PHRENETICAL
PHRENETICALLY
PHRENETICNESS
PHRENETICNESSES
PHRENETICS
PHRENITIDES
PHRENITISES
PHRENOLOGIC
PHRENOLOGICAL
PHRENOLOGICALLY
PHRENOLOGIES
PHRENOLOGISE
PHRENOLOGISED
PHRENOLOGISES
PHRENOLOGISING
PHRENOLOGIST
PHRENOLOGISTS
PHRENOLOGIZE

PHRENOLOGIZED
PHRENOLOGIZES
PHRENOLOGIZING
PHRENOLOGY
PHRENSICAL
PHRENSYING
PHRONTISTERIES
PHRONTISTERY
PHTHALATES
PHTHALEINS
PHTHALOCYANIN
PHTHALOCYANINE
PHTHALOCYANINES
PHTHALOCYANINS
PHTHIRIASES
PHTHIRIASIS
PHTHISICAL
PHTHISICKY
PHYCOBILIN
PHYCOBILINS
PHYCOBIONT
PHYCOBIONTS
PHYCOCYANIN
PHYCOCYANINS
PHYCOCYANS
PHYCOERYTHRIN
PHYCOERYTHRINS
PHYCOLOGICAL
PHYCOLOGIES
PHYCOLOGIST
PHYCOLOGISTS
PHYCOMYCETE
PHYCOMYCETES
PHYCOMYCETOUS
PHYCOPHAEIN
PHYCOPHAEINS
PHYCOXANTHIN
PHYCOXANTHINS
PHYLACTERIC
PHYLACTERICAL
PHYLACTERIES
PHYLACTERY
PHYLARCHIES
PHYLAXISES
PHYLESISES
PHYLETICALLY
PHYLLARIES
PHYLLOCLAD
PHYLLOCLADE
PHYLLOCLADES
PHYLLOCLADS
PHYLLODIAL
PHYLLODIES
PHYLLODIUM
PHYLLOMANIA
PHYLLOMANIAS
PHYLLOPHAGOUS
PHYLLOPLANE
PHYLLOPLANES

PHYLLOPODS
PHYLLOQUINONE
PHYLLOQUINONES
PHYLLOSILICATE
PHYLLOSILICATES
PHYLLOSPHERE
PHYLLOSPHERES
PHYLLOTACTIC
PHYLLOTACTICAL
PHYLLOTAXES
PHYLLOTAXIES
PHYLLOTAXIS
PHYLLOTAXY
PHYLLOXERA
PHYLLOXERAE
PHYLLOXERAS
PHYLOGENESES
PHYLOGENESIS
PHYLOGENETIC
PHYLOGENIC
PHYLOGENIES
PHYSALISES
PHYSHARMONICA
PHYSHARMONICAS
PHYSIATRIC
PHYSIATRICAL
PHYSIATRICS
PHYSIATRIES
PHYSIATRIST
PHYSIATRISTS
PHYSICALISM
PHYSICALISMS
PHYSICALIST
PHYSICALISTIC
PHYSICALISTS
PHYSICALITIES
PHYSICALITY
PHYSICALLY
PHYSICALNESS
PHYSICALNESSES
PHYSICIANCIES
PHYSICIANCY
PHYSICIANER
PHYSICIANERS
PHYSICIANS
PHYSICIANSHIP
PHYSICIANSHIPS
PHYSICISMS
PHYSICISTS
PHYSICKING
PHYSICOCHEMICAL
PHYSIOCRACIES
PHYSIOCRACY
PHYSIOCRAT
PHYSIOCRATIC
PHYSIOCRATS
PHYSIOGNOMIC
PHYSIOGNOMICAL
PHYSIOGNOMIES

PHYSIOGNOMIST
PHYSIOGNOMISTS
PHYSIOGNOMY
PHYSIOGRAPHER
PHYSIOGRAPHERS
PHYSIOGRAPHIC
PHYSIOGRAPHICAL
PHYSIOGRAPHIES
PHYSIOGRAPHY
PHYSIOLATER
PHYSIOLATERS
PHYSIOLATRIES
PHYSIOLATRY
PHYSIOLOGIC
PHYSIOLOGICAL
PHYSIOLOGICALLY
PHYSIOLOGIES
PHYSIOLOGIST
PHYSIOLOGISTS
PHYSIOLOGUS
PHYSIOLOGUSES
PHYSIOLOGY
PHYSIOPATHOLOGY
PHYSIOTHERAPIES
PHYSIOTHERAPIST
PHYSIOTHERAPY
PHYSITHEISM
PHYSITHEISMS
PHYSITHEISTIC
PHYSOCLISTOUS
PHYSOSTIGMIN
PHYSOSTIGMINE
PHYSOSTIGMINES
PHYSOSTIGMINS
PHYSOSTOMOUS
PHYTOALEXIN
PHYTOALEXINS
PHYTOBENTHOS
PHYTOBENTHOSES
PHYTOCHEMICAL
PHYTOCHEMICALLY
PHYTOCHEMICALS
PHYTOCHEMIST
PHYTOCHEMISTRY
PHYTOCHEMISTS
PHYTOCHROME
PHYTOCHROMES
PHYTOESTROGEN
PHYTOESTROGENS
PHYTOFLAGELLATE
PHYTOGENESES
PHYTOGENESIS
PHYTOGENETIC
PHYTOGENETICAL
PHYTOGENIC
PHYTOGENIES
PHYTOGEOGRAPHER
PHYTOGEOGRAPHIC
PHYTOGEOGRAPHY

PHYTOGRAPHER

PHYTOGRAPHER
PHYTOGRAPHERS
PHYTOGRAPHIC
PHYTOGRAPHIES
PHYTOGRAPHY
PHYTOHORMONE
PHYTOHORMONES
PHYTOLITHS
PHYTOLOGICAL
PHYTOLOGICALLY
PHYTOLOGIES
PHYTOLOGIST
PHYTOLOGISTS
PHYTONADIONE
PHYTONADIONES
PHYTOPATHOGEN
PHYTOPATHOGENIC
PHYTOPATHOGENS
PHYTOPATHOLOGY
PHYTOPHAGIC
PHYTOPHAGIES
PHYTOPHAGOUS
PHYTOPHAGY
PHYTOPLANKTER
PHYTOPLANKTERS
PHYTOPLANKTON
PHYTOPLANKTONIC
PHYTOPLANKTONS
PHYTOSOCIOLOGY
PHYTOSTEROL
PHYTOSTEROLS
PHYTOTHERAPIES
PHYTOTHERAPY
PHYTOTOMIES
PHYTOTOMIST
PHYTOTOMISTS
PHYTOTOXIC
PHYTOTOXICITIES
PHYTOTOXICITY
PHYTOTOXIN
PHYTOTOXINS
PHYTOTRONS
PIACULARITIES
PIACULARITY
PIANISSIMI
PIANISSIMO
PIANISSIMOS
PIANISSISSIMO
PIANISTICALLY
PIANOFORTE
PIANOFORTES
PIANOLISTS
PICADILLOS
PICANINNIES
PICARESQUE
PICARESQUES
PICAROONED
PICAROONING
PICAYUNISH

PICAYUNISHLY
PICAYUNISHNESS
PICCADILLIES
PICCADILLO
PICCADILLOES
PICCADILLS
PICCADILLY
PICCALILLI
PICCALILLIS
PICCANINNIES
PICCANINNY
PICCOLOIST
PICCOLOISTS
PICHICIAGO
PICHICIAGOS
PICHICIEGO
PICHICIEGOS
PICHOLINES
PICKABACKED
PICKABACKING
PICKABACKS
PICKADILLIES
PICKADILLO
PICKADILLOES
PICKADILLS
PICKADILLY
PICKANINNIES
PICKANINNY
PICKAPACKS
PICKAROONS
PICKEDNESS
PICKEDNESSES
PICKEERERS
PICKEERING
PICKELHAUBE
PICKELHAUBES
PICKERELWEED
PICKERELWEEDS
PICKETBOAT
PICKETBOATS
PICKETINGS
PICKINESSES
PICKPOCKET
PICKPOCKETS
PICKTHANKS
PICNICKERS
PICNICKING
PICOCURIES
PICOFARADS
PICOMETERS
PICOMETRES
PICORNAVIRUS
PICORNAVIRUSES
PICOSECOND
PICOSECONDS
PICOWAVING
PICQUETING
PICROCARMINE
PICROCARMINES

PICROTOXIN
PICROTOXINS
PICTARNIES
PICTOGRAMS
PICTOGRAPH
PICTOGRAPHIC
PICTOGRAPHIES
PICTOGRAPHS
PICTOGRAPHY
PICTORIALISE
PICTORIALISED
PICTORIALISES
PICTORIALISING
PICTORIALISM
PICTORIALISMS
PICTORIALIST
PICTORIALISTS
PICTORIALIZE
PICTORIALIZED
PICTORIALIZES
PICTORIALIZING
PICTORIALLY
PICTORIALNESS
PICTORIALNESSES
PICTORIALS
PICTORICAL
PICTORICALLY
PICTUREGOER
PICTUREGOERS
PICTUREPHONE
PICTUREPHONES
PICTURESQUE
PICTURESQUELY
PICTURESQUENESS
PICTURISATION
PICTURISATIONS
PICTURISED
PICTURISES
PICTURISING
PICTURIZATION
PICTURIZATIONS
PICTURIZED
PICTURIZES
PICTURIZING
PIDDLINGLY
PIDGINISATION
PIDGINISATIONS
PIDGINISED
PIDGINISES
PIDGINISING
PIDGINIZATION
PIDGINIZATIONS
PIDGINIZED
PIDGINIZES
PIDGINIZING
PIECEMEALED
PIECEMEALING
PIECEMEALS
PIECEWORKER

PIECEWORKERS
PIECEWORKS
PIEDMONTITE
PIEDMONTITES
PIEDNESSES
PIEMONTITE
PIEMONTITES
PIEPOWDERS
PIERCEABLE
PIERCINGLY
PIERCINGNESS
PIERCINGNESSES
PIERRETTES
PIETISTICAL
PIETISTICALLY
PIEZOCHEMISTRY
PIEZOELECTRIC
PIEZOMAGNETIC
PIEZOMAGNETISM
PIEZOMAGNETISMS
PIEZOMETER
PIEZOMETERS
PIEZOMETRIC
PIEZOMETRICALLY
PIEZOMETRIES
PIEZOMETRY
PIGEONHOLE
PIGEONHOLED
PIGEONHOLER
PIGEONHOLERS
PIGEONHOLES
PIGEONHOLING
PIGEONITES
PIGEONRIES
PIGEONWING
PIGEONWINGS
PIGGINESSES
PIGGISHNESS
PIGGISHNESSES
PIGGYBACKED
PIGGYBACKING
PIGGYBACKS
PIGHEADEDLY
PIGHEADEDNESS
PIGHEADEDNESSES
PIGMENTARY
PIGMENTATION
PIGMENTATIONS
PIGMENTING
PIGNERATED
PIGNERATES
PIGNERATING
PIGNORATED
PIGNORATES
PIGNORATING
PIGNORATION
PIGNORATIONS
PIGSCONCES
PIGSTICKED

PIGSTICKER
PIGSTICKERS
PIGSTICKING
PIKEPERCHES
PIKESTAFFS
PIKESTAVES
PILASTERED
PILEORHIZA
PILEORHIZAS
PILFERABLE
PILFERAGES
PILFERINGLY
PILFERINGS
PILFERPROOF
PILGARLICK
PILGARLICKS
PILGARLICKY
PILGARLICS
PILGRIMAGE
PILGRIMAGED
PILGRIMAGER
PILGRIMAGERS
PILGRIMAGES
PILGRIMAGING
PILGRIMERS
PILGRIMISE
PILGRIMISED
PILGRIMISES
PILGRIMISING
PILGRIMIZE
PILGRIMIZED
PILGRIMIZES
PILGRIMIZING
PILIFEROUS
PILLARISTS
PILLARLESS
PILLICOCKS
PILLIONING
PILLIONIST
PILLIONISTS
PILLIWINKS
PILLORISED
PILLORISES
PILLORISING
PILLORIZED
PILLORIZES
PILLORIZING
PILLORYING
PILLOWCASE
PILLOWCASES
PILLOWSLIP
PILLOWSLIPS
PILNIEWINKS
PILOCARPIN
PILOCARPINE
PILOCARPINES
PILOCARPINS
PILOSITIES
PILOTFISHES

PILOTHOUSE
PILOTHOUSES
PIMPERNELS
PIMPLINESS
PIMPLINESSES
PIMPMOBILE
PIMPMOBILES
PINACOIDAL
PINACOTHECA
PINACOTHECAE
PINAKOIDAL
PINAKOTHEK
PINAKOTHEKS
PINBALLING
PINCERLIKE
PINCHBECKS
PINCHCOCKS
PINCHCOMMONS
PINCHCOMMONSES
PINCHFISTS
PINCHINGLY
PINCHPENNIES
PINCHPENNY
PINCHPOINT
PINCHPOINTS
PINCUSHION
PINCUSHIONS
PINEALECTOMIES
PINEALECTOMISE
PINEALECTOMISED
PINEALECTOMISES
PINEALECTOMIZE
PINEALECTOMIZED
PINEALECTOMIZES
PINEALECTOMY
PINEAPPLES
PINFEATHER
PINFEATHERS
PINFOLDING
PINGRASSES
PINGUEFIED
PINGUEFIES
PINGUEFYING
PINGUIDITIES
PINGUIDITY
PINGUITUDE
PINGUITUDES
PINHEADEDNESS
PINHEADEDNESSES
PINHOOKERS
PINKERTONS
PINKINESSES
PINKISHNESS
PINKISHNESSES
PINKNESSES
PINNACLING
PINNATIFID
PINNATIFIDLY
PINNATIONS

PINNATIPARTITE
PINNATIPED
PINNATISECT
PINNIEWINKLE
PINNIEWINKLES
PINNIPEDES
PINNIPEDIAN
PINNIPEDIANS
PINNULATED
PINNYWINKLE
PINNYWINKLES
PINOCYTOSES
PINOCYTOSIS
PINOCYTOTIC
PINOCYTOTICALLY
PINPOINTED
PINPOINTING
PINPRICKED
PINPRICKING
PINSETTERS
PINSPOTTER
PINSPOTTERS
PINSTRIPES
PINTADERAS
PINWHEELED
PINWHEELING
PINWRENCHES
PIONEERING
PIOUSNESSES
PIPECLAYED
PIPECLAYING
PIPEFISHES
PIPEFITTER
PIPEFITTERS
PIPEFITTING
PIPEFITTINGS
PIPELINING
PIPELININGS
PIPERACEOUS
PIPERAZINE
PIPERAZINES
PIPERIDINE
PIPERIDINES
PIPERONALS
PIPESTONES
PIPINESSES
PIPISTRELLE
PIPISTRELLES
PIPISTRELS
PIPIWHARAUROA
PIPIWHARAUROAS
PIPSISSEWA
PIPSISSEWAS
PIPSQUEAKS
PIQUANCIES
PIQUANTNESS
PIQUANTNESSES
PIRACETAMS
PIRATICALLY

PIRLICUING
PIROPLASMA
PIROPLASMATA
PIROPLASMS
PIROUETTED
PIROUETTER
PIROUETTERS
PIROUETTES
PIROUETTING
PISCATORIAL
PISCATORIALLY
PISCATRIXES
PISCICOLOUS
PISCICULTURAL
PISCICULTURALLY
PISCICULTURE
PISCICULTURES
PISCICULTURIST
PISCICULTURISTS
PISCIFAUNA
PISCIFAUNAE
PISCIFAUNAS
PISCIVORES
PISCIVOROUS
PISSASPHALT
PISSASPHALTS
PISTACHIOS
PISTAREENS
PISTILLARY
PISTILLATE
PISTILLODE
PISTILLODES
PISTOLEERS
PISTOLEROS
PISTOLIERS
PISTOLLING
PITAPATTED
PITAPATTING
PITCHBENDS
PITCHBLENDE
PITCHBLENDES
PITCHERFUL
PITCHERFULS
PITCHERSFUL
PITCHFORKED
PITCHFORKING
PITCHFORKS
PITCHINESS
PITCHINESSES
PITCHOMETER
PITCHOMETERS
PITCHPERSON
PITCHPERSONS
PITCHPINES
PITCHPIPES
PITCHPOLED
PITCHPOLES
PITCHPOLING
PITCHSTONE

PITCHSTONES

PITCHSTONES
PITCHWOMAN
PITCHWOMEN
PITEOUSNESS
PITEOUSNESSES
PITHECANTHROPI
PITHECANTHROPUS
PITHINESSES
PITIABLENESS
PITIABLENESSES
PITIFULLER
PITIFULLEST
PITIFULNESS
PITIFULNESSES
PITILESSLY
PITILESSNESS
PITILESSNESSES
PITTOSPORUM
PITTOSPORUMS
PITUITARIES
PITUITRINS
PITYRIASES
PITYRIASIS
PITYROSPORUM
PITYROSPORUMS
PIWAKAWAKA
PIXELATION
PIXELATIONS
PIXELLATED
PIXILATION
PIXILATIONS
PIXILLATED
PIXILLATION
PIXILLATIONS
PIXINESSES
PIZZICATOS
PLACABILITIES
PLACABILITY
PLACABLENESS
PLACABLENESSES
PLACARDING
PLACATINGLY
PLACATIONS
PLACEHOLDER
PLACEHOLDERS
PLACEKICKED
PLACEKICKER
PLACEKICKERS
PLACEKICKING
PLACEKICKS
PLACELESSLY
PLACEMENTS
PLACENTALS
PLACENTATE
PLACENTATION
PLACENTATIONS
PLACENTIFORM
PLACENTOLOGIES
PLACENTOLOGY

PLACIDITIES
PLACIDNESS
PLACIDNESSES
PLACODERMS
PLAGIARIES
PLAGIARISE
PLAGIARISED
PLAGIARISER
PLAGIARISERS
PLAGIARISES
PLAGIARISING
PLAGIARISM
PLAGIARISMS
PLAGIARIST
PLAGIARISTIC
PLAGIARISTS
PLAGIARIZE
PLAGIARIZED
PLAGIARIZER
PLAGIARIZERS
PLAGIARIZES
PLAGIARIZING
PLAGIOCEPHALIES
PLAGIOCEPHALY
PLAGIOCLASE
PLAGIOCLASES
PLAGIOCLASTIC
PLAGIOCLIMAX
PLAGIOCLIMAXES
PLAGIOSTOMATOUS
PLAGIOSTOME
PLAGIOSTOMES
PLAGIOSTOMOUS
PLAGIOTROPIC
PLAGIOTROPISM
PLAGIOTROPISMS
PLAGIOTROPOUS
PLAGUESOME
PLAINCHANT
PLAINCHANTS
PLAINCLOTHES
PLAINCLOTHESMAN
PLAINCLOTHESMEN
PLAINNESSES
PLAINSONGS
PLAINSPOKEN
PLAINSPOKENNESS
PLAINSTANES
PLAINSTONES
PLAINTEXTS
PLAINTIFFS
PLAINTIVELY
PLAINTIVENESS
PLAINTIVENESSES
PLAINTLESS
PLAINWORKS
PLAISTERED
PLAISTERING
PLANARIANS

PLANARITIES
PLANATIONS
PLANCHETTE
PLANCHETTES
PLANELOADS
PLANENESSES
PLANESIDES
PLANETARIA
PLANETARIES
PLANETARIUM
PLANETARIUMS
PLANETESIMAL
PLANETESIMALS
PLANETICAL
PLANETLIKE
PLANETOIDAL
PLANETOIDS
PLANETOLOGICAL
PLANETOLOGIES
PLANETOLOGIST
PLANETOLOGISTS
PLANETOLOGY
PLANETWIDE
PLANGENCIES
PLANGENTLY
PLANIGRAPH
PLANIGRAPHS
PLANIMETER
PLANIMETERS
PLANIMETRIC
PLANIMETRICAL
PLANIMETRICALLY
PLANIMETRIES
PLANIMETRY
PLANISHERS
PLANISHING
PLANISPHERE
PLANISPHERES
PLANISPHERIC
PLANKTONIC
PLANLESSLY
PLANLESSNESS
PLANLESSNESSES
PLANOBLAST
PLANOBLASTS
PLANOGAMETE
PLANOGAMETES
PLANOGRAPHIC
PLANOGRAPHIES
PLANOGRAPHY
PLANOMETER
PLANOMETERS
PLANOMETRIC
PLANOMETRICALLY
PLANOMETRIES
PLANOMETRY
PLANTAGINACEOUS
PLANTATION
PLANTATIONS

PLANTIGRADE
PLANTIGRADES
PLANTLINGS
PLANTOCRACIES
PLANTOCRACY
PLANTSWOMAN
PLANTSWOMEN
PLANULIFORM
PLAQUETTES
PLASMAGELS
PLASMAGENE
PLASMAGENES
PLASMAGENIC
PLASMALEMMA
PLASMALEMMAS
PLASMAPHERESES
PLASMAPHERESIS
PLASMASOLS
PLASMATICAL
PLASMINOGEN
PLASMINOGENS
PLASMODESM
PLASMODESMA
PLASMODESMAS
PLASMODESMATA
PLASMODESMS
PLASMODIAL
PLASMODIUM
PLASMOGAMIES
PLASMOGAMY
PLASMOLYSE
PLASMOLYSED
PLASMOLYSES
PLASMOLYSING
PLASMOLYSIS
PLASMOLYTIC
PLASMOLYTICALLY
PLASMOLYZE
PLASMOLYZED
PLASMOLYZES
PLASMOLYZING
PLASMOSOMA
PLASMOSOMATA
PLASMOSOME
PLASMOSOMES
PLASTERBOARD
PLASTERBOARDS
PLASTERERS
PLASTERINESS
PLASTERINESSES
PLASTERING
PLASTERINGS
PLASTERSTONE
PLASTERSTONES
PLASTERWORK
PLASTERWORKS
PLASTICALLY
PLASTICENE
PLASTICENES

PLASTICINE	PLATINISED	PLAYACTINGS	PLEBEIANLY
PLASTICINES	PLATINISES	PLAYACTORS	PLEBIFICATION
PLASTICISATION	PLATINISING	PLAYBUSSES	PLEBIFICATIONS
PLASTICISATIONS	PLATINIZATION	PLAYFELLOW	PLEBIFYING
PLASTICISE	PLATINIZATIONS	PLAYFELLOWS	PLEBISCITARY
PLASTICISED	PLATINIZED	PLAYFIELDS	PLEBISCITE
PLASTICISER	PLATINIZES	PLAYFULNESS	PLEBISCITES
PLASTICISERS	PLATINIZING	PLAYFULNESSES	PLECOPTERAN
PLASTICISES	PLATINOCYANIC	PLAYGOINGS	PLECOPTERANS
PLASTICISING	PLATINOCYANIDE	PLAYGROUND	PLECOPTEROUS
PLASTICITIES	PLATINOCYANIDES	PLAYGROUNDS	PLECTOGNATH
PLASTICITY	PLATINOIDS	PLAYGROUPS	PLECTOGNATHIC
PLASTICIZATION	PLATINOTYPE	PLAYHOUSES	PLECTOGNATHOUS
PLASTICIZATIONS	PLATINOTYPES	PLAYLEADER	PLECTOGNATHS
PLASTICIZE	PLATITUDES	PLAYLEADERS	PLECTOPTEROUS
PLASTICIZED	PLATITUDINAL	PLAYLISTED	PLEDGEABLE
PLASTICIZER	PLATITUDINARIAN	PLAYLISTING	PLEINAIRISM
PLASTICIZERS	PLATITUDINISE	PLAYMAKERS	PLEINAIRISMS
PLASTICIZES	PLATITUDINISED	PLAYMAKING	PLEINAIRIST
PLASTICIZING	PLATITUDINISER	PLAYMAKINGS	PLEINAIRISTS
PLASTIDIAL	PLATITUDINISERS	PLAYSCHOOL	PLEIOCHASIA
PLASTIDULE	PLATITUDINISES	PLAYSCHOOLS	PLEIOCHASIUM
PLASTIDULES	PLATITUDINISING	PLAYTHINGS	PLEIOMERIES
PLASTILINA	PLATITUDINIZE	PLAYWRIGHT	PLEIOMEROUS
PLASTILINAS	PLATITUDINIZED	PLAYWRIGHTING	PLEIOTAXIES
PLASTIQUES	PLATITUDINIZER	PLAYWRIGHTINGS	PLEIOTROPIC
PLASTISOLS	PLATITUDINIZERS	PLAYWRIGHTS	PLEIOTROPIES
PLASTOCYANIN	PLATITUDINIZES	PLAYWRITING	PLEIOTROPISM
PLASTOCYANINS	PLATITUDINIZING	PLAYWRITINGS	PLEIOTROPISMS
PLASTOGAMIES	PLATITUDINOUS	PLEADINGLY	PLEIOTROPY
PLASTOGAMY	PLATITUDINOUSLY	PLEASANCES	PLENARTIES
PLASTOMETER	PLATONICALLY	PLEASANTER	PLENILUNAR
PLASTOMETERS	PLATONISMS	PLEASANTEST	PLENILUNES
PLASTOMETRIC	PLATOONING	PLEASANTLY	PLENIPOTENCE
PLASTOMETRIES	PLATTELAND	PLEASANTNESS	PLENIPOTENCES
PLASTOMETRY	PLATTELANDS	PLEASANTNESSES	PLENIPOTENCIES
PLASTOQUINONE	PLATTERFUL	PLEASANTRIES	PLENIPOTENCY
PLASTOQUINONES	PLATTERFULS	PLEASANTRY	PLENIPOTENT
PLATANACEOUS	PLATTERSFUL	PLEASINGLY	PLENIPOTENTIAL
PLATEAUING	PLATYCEPHALIC	PLEASINGNESS	PLENIPOTENTIARY
PLATEGLASS	PLATYCEPHALOUS	PLEASINGNESSES	PLENISHERS
PLATELAYER	PLATYFISHES	PLEASURABILITY	PLENISHING
PLATELAYERS	PLATYHELMINTH	PLEASURABLE	PLENISHINGS
PLATEMAKER	PLATYHELMINTHIC	PLEASURABLENESS	PLENISHMENT
PLATEMAKERS	PLATYHELMINTHS	PLEASURABLY	PLENISHMENTS
PLATEMAKING	PLATYKURTIC	PLEASUREFUL	PLENITUDES
PLATEMAKINGS	PLATYPUSES	PLEASURELESS	PLENITUDINOUS
PLATEMARKED	PLATYRRHINE	PLEASURERS	PLENTEOUSLY
PLATEMARKING	PLATYRRHINES	PLEASURING	PLENTEOUSNESS
PLATEMARKS	PLATYRRHINIAN	PLEBEIANISE	PLENTEOUSNESSES
PLATERESQUE	PLATYRRHINIANS	PLEBEIANISED	PLENTIFULLY
PLATFORMED	PLAUDITORY	PLEBEIANISES	PLENTIFULNESS
PLATFORMING	PLAUSIBILITIES	PLEBEIANISING	PLENTIFULNESSES
PLATFORMINGS	PLAUSIBILITY	PLEBEIANISM	PLENTITUDE
PLATINIFEROUS	PLAUSIBLENESS	PLEBEIANISMS	PLENTITUDES
PLATINIRIDIUM	PLAUSIBLENESSES	PLEBEIANIZE	PLEOCHROIC
PLATINIRIDIUMS	PLAYABILITIES	PLEBEIANIZED	PLEOCHROISM
PLATINISATION	PLAYABILITY	PLEBEIANIZES	PLEOCHROISMS
PLATINISATIONS	PLAYACTING	PLEBEIANIZING	PLEOMORPHIC

PLEOMORPHIES

PLEOMORPHIES
PLEOMORPHISM
PLEOMORPHISMS
PLEOMORPHOUS
PLEOMORPHY
PLEONASTES
PLEONASTIC
PLEONASTICAL
PLEONASTICALLY
PLEONECTIC
PLEONEXIAS
PLEROCERCOID
PLEROCERCOIDS
PLEROMATIC
PLEROPHORIA
PLEROPHORIAS
PLEROPHORIES
PLEROPHORY
PLESIOSAUR
PLESIOSAURIAN
PLESIOSAURS
PLESSIMETER
PLESSIMETERS
PLESSIMETRIC
PLESSIMETRIES
PLESSIMETRY
PLETHORICAL
PLETHORICALLY
PLETHYSMOGRAM
PLETHYSMOGRAMS
PLETHYSMOGRAPH
PLETHYSMOGRAPHS
PLETHYSMOGRAPHY
PLEURAPOPHYSES
PLEURAPOPHYSIS
PLEURISIES
PLEURITICAL
PLEURITICS
PLEURITISES
PLEUROCARPOUS
PLEUROCENTESES
PLEUROCENTESIS
PLEURODONT
PLEURODONTS
PLEURODYNIA
PLEURODYNIAS
PLEUROPNEUMONIA
PLEUROTOMIES
PLEUROTOMY
PLEUSTONIC
PLEXIGLASS
PLEXIGLASSES
PLEXIMETER
PLEXIMETERS
PLEXIMETRIC
PLEXIMETRIES
PLEXIMETRY
PLIABILITIES
PLIABILITY

PLIABLENESS
PLIABLENESSES
PLIANTNESS
PLIANTNESSES
PLICATENESS
PLICATENESSES
PLICATIONS
PLICATURES
PLODDINGLY
PLODDINGNESS
PLODDINGNESSES
PLOTLESSNESS
PLOTLESSNESSES
PLOTTERING
PLOTTINGLY
PLOUGHABLE
PLOUGHBOYS
PLOUGHGATE
PLOUGHGATES
PLOUGHINGS
PLOUGHLAND
PLOUGHLANDS
PLOUGHMANSHIP
PLOUGHMANSHIPS
PLOUGHSHARE
PLOUGHSHARES
PLOUGHSTAFF
PLOUGHSTAFFS
PLOUGHTAIL
PLOUGHTAILS
PLOUGHWISE
PLOUGHWRIGHT
PLOUGHWRIGHTS
PLOUTERING
PLOWMANSHIP
PLOWMANSHIPS
PLOWSHARES
PLOWSTAFFS
PLOWTERING
PLUCKINESS
PLUCKINESSES
PLUGBOARDS
PLUGUGLIES
PLUMASSIER
PLUMASSIERS
PLUMBAGINACEOUS
PLUMBAGINOUS
PLUMBERIES
PLUMBIFEROUS
PLUMBISOLVENCY
PLUMBISOLVENT
PLUMBNESSES
PLUMBOSOLVENCY
PLUMBOSOLVENT
PLUMDAMASES
PLUMIGEROUS
PLUMMETING
PLUMOSITIES
PLUMPENING

PLUMPNESSES
PLUMULACEOUS
PLUMULARIAN
PLUMULARIANS
PLUNDERABLE
PLUNDERAGE
PLUNDERAGES
PLUNDERERS
PLUNDERING
PLUNDEROUS
PLUPERFECT
PLUPERFECTS
PLURALISATION
PLURALISATIONS
PLURALISED
PLURALISER
PLURALISERS
PLURALISES
PLURALISING
PLURALISMS
PLURALISTIC
PLURALISTICALLY
PLURALISTS
PLURALITIES
PLURALIZATION
PLURALIZATIONS
PLURALIZED
PLURALIZER
PLURALIZERS
PLURALIZES
PLURALIZING
PLURILITERAL
PLURILOCULAR
PLURIPARAE
PLURIPARAS
PLURIPOTENT
PLURIPRESENCE
PLURIPRESENCES
PLURISERIAL
PLURISERIATE
PLUSHINESS
PLUSHINESSES
PLUSHNESSES
PLUTOCRACIES
PLUTOCRACY
PLUTOCRATIC
PLUTOCRATICAL
PLUTOCRATICALLY
PLUTOCRATS
PLUTOLATRIES
PLUTOLATRY
PLUTOLOGIES
PLUTOLOGIST
PLUTOLOGISTS
PLUTONISMS
PLUTONIUMS
PLUTONOMIES
PLUTONOMIST
PLUTONOMISTS

PLUVIOMETER
PLUVIOMETERS
PLUVIOMETRIC
PLUVIOMETRICAL
PLUVIOMETRIES
PLUVIOMETRY
PLYOMETRIC
PLYOMETRICS
PNEUMATHODE
PNEUMATHODES
PNEUMATICAL
PNEUMATICALLY
PNEUMATICITIES
PNEUMATICITY
PNEUMATICS
PNEUMATOLOGICAL
PNEUMATOLOGIES
PNEUMATOLOGIST
PNEUMATOLOGISTS
PNEUMATOLOGY
PNEUMATOLYSES
PNEUMATOLYSIS
PNEUMATOLYTIC
PNEUMATOMETER
PNEUMATOMETERS
PNEUMATOMETRIES
PNEUMATOMETRY
PNEUMATOPHORE
PNEUMATOPHORES
PNEUMECTOMIES
PNEUMECTOMY
PNEUMOBACILLI
PNEUMOBACILLUS
PNEUMOCOCCAL
PNEUMOCOCCI
PNEUMOCOCCUS
PNEUMOCONIOSES
PNEUMOCONIOSIS
PNEUMOCONIOTIC
PNEUMOCONIOTICS
PNEUMOCYSTIS
PNEUMOCYSTISES
PNEUMODYNAMICS
PNEUMOGASTRIC
PNEUMOGASTRICS
PNEUMOGRAM
PNEUMOGRAMS
PNEUMOGRAPH
PNEUMOGRAPHS
PNEUMOKONIOSES
PNEUMOKONIOSIS
PNEUMONECTOMIES
PNEUMONECTOMY
PNEUMONIAS
PNEUMONICS
PNEUMONITIS
PNEUMONITISES
PNEUMOTHORACES
PNEUMOTHORAX

PNEUMOTHORAXES
POACHINESS
POACHINESSES
POCKETABLE
POCKETBIKE
POCKETBIKES
POCKETBOOK
POCKETBOOKS
POCKETFULS
POCKETKNIFE
POCKETKNIVES
POCKETLESS
POCKETPHONE
POCKETPHONES
POCKETSFUL
POCKMANKIES
POCKMANTIE
POCKMANTIES
POCKMARKED
POCKMARKING
POCKPITTED
POCOCURANTE
POCOCURANTEISM
POCOCURANTEISMS
POCOCURANTES
POCOCURANTISM
POCOCURANTISMS
POCOCURANTIST
POCOCURANTISTS
POCULIFORM
PODAGRICAL
PODARGUSES
PODCASTERS
PODCASTING
PODCASTINGS
PODGINESSES
PODIATRIES
PODIATRIST
PODIATRISTS
PODOCONIOSES
PODOCONIOSIS
PODOLOGIES
PODOLOGIST
PODOLOGISTS
PODOPHTHALMOUS
PODOPHYLIN
PODOPHYLINS
PODOPHYLLI
PODOPHYLLIN
PODOPHYLLINS
PODOPHYLLUM
PODOPHYLLUMS
PODSOLISATION
PODSOLISATIONS
PODSOLISED
PODSOLISES
PODSOLISING
PODSOLIZATION
PODSOLIZATIONS

PODSOLIZED
PODSOLIZES
PODSOLIZING
PODZOLISATION
PODZOLISATIONS
PODZOLISED
PODZOLISES
PODZOLISING
PODZOLIZATION
PODZOLIZATIONS
PODZOLIZED
PODZOLIZES
PODZOLIZING
POENOLOGIES
POETASTERIES
POETASTERING
POETASTERINGS
POETASTERS
POETASTERY
POETASTRIES
POETICALLY
POETICALNESS
POETICALNESSES
POETICISED
POETICISES
POETICISING
POETICISMS
POETICIZED
POETICIZES
POETICIZING
POETICULES
POETRESSES
POGONOPHORAN
POGONOPHORANS
POGONOTOMIES
POGONOTOMY
POGROMISTS
POHUTUKAWA
POHUTUKAWAS
POIGNADOES
POIGNANCES
POIGNANCIES
POIGNANTLY
POIKILITIC
POIKILOCYTE
POIKILOCYTES
POIKILOTHERM
POIKILOTHERMAL
POIKILOTHERMIC
POIKILOTHERMIES
POIKILOTHERMISM
POIKILOTHERMS
POIKILOTHERMY
POINCIANAS
POINSETTIA
POINSETTIAS
POINTEDNESS
POINTEDNESSES
POINTELLES

POINTILLISM
POINTILLISME
POINTILLISMES
POINTILLISMS
POINTILLIST
POINTILLISTE
POINTILLISTES
POINTILLISTIC
POINTILLISTS
POINTLESSLY
POINTLESSNESS
POINTLESSNESSES
POISONABLE
POISONOUSLY
POISONOUSNESS
POISONOUSNESSES
POISONWOOD
POISONWOODS
POKEBERRIES
POKELOGANS
POKERISHLY
POKERWORKS
POKINESSES
POLARIMETER
POLARIMETERS
POLARIMETRIC
POLARIMETRIES
POLARIMETRY
POLARISABLE
POLARISATION
POLARISATIONS
POLARISCOPE
POLARISCOPES
POLARISCOPIC
POLARISERS
POLARISING
POLARITIES
POLARIZABILITY
POLARIZABLE
POLARIZATION
POLARIZATIONS
POLARIZERS
POLARIZING
POLAROGRAM
POLAROGRAMS
POLAROGRAPH
POLAROGRAPHIC
POLAROGRAPHIES
POLAROGRAPHS
POLAROGRAPHY
POLEMARCHS
POLEMICALLY
POLEMICISE
POLEMICISED
POLEMICISES
POLEMICISING
POLEMICIST
POLEMICISTS
POLEMICIZE

POLEMICIZED
POLEMICIZES
POLEMICIZING
POLEMISING
POLEMIZING
POLEMONIACEOUS
POLEMONIUM
POLEMONIUMS
POLIANITES
POLICEWOMAN
POLICEWOMEN
POLICYHOLDER
POLICYHOLDERS
POLIOMYELITIDES
POLIOMYELITIS
POLIOMYELITISES
POLIORCETIC
POLIORCETICS
POLIOVIRUS
POLIOVIRUSES
POLISHABLE
POLISHINGS
POLISHMENT
POLISHMENTS
POLITBUROS
POLITENESS
POLITENESSES
POLITESSES
POLITICALISE
POLITICALISED
POLITICALISES
POLITICALISING
POLITICALIZE
POLITICALIZED
POLITICALIZES
POLITICALIZING
POLITICALLY
POLITICASTER
POLITICASTERS
POLITICIAN
POLITICIANS
POLITICISATION
POLITICISATIONS
POLITICISE
POLITICISED
POLITICISES
POLITICISING
POLITICIZATION
POLITICIZATIONS
POLITICIZE
POLITICIZED
POLITICIZES
POLITICIZING
POLITICKED
POLITICKER
POLITICKERS
POLITICKING
POLITICKINGS
POLITICOES

POLITIQUES
POLLARDING
POLLENATED
POLLENATES
POLLENATING
POLLENIFEROUS
POLLENISER
POLLENISERS
POLLENIZER
POLLENIZERS
POLLENOSES
POLLENOSIS
POLLICITATION
POLLICITATIONS
POLLINATED
POLLINATES
POLLINATING
POLLINATION
POLLINATIONS
POLLINATOR
POLLINATORS
POLLINIFEROUS
POLLINISED
POLLINISER
POLLINISERS
POLLINISES
POLLINISING
POLLINIZED
POLLINIZER
POLLINIZERS
POLLINIZES
POLLINIZING
POLLINOSES
POLLINOSIS
POLLTAKERS
POLLUCITES
POLLUSIONS
POLLUTANTS
POLLUTEDLY
POLLUTEDNESS
POLLUTEDNESSES
POLLUTIONS
POLLYANNAISH
POLLYANNAISM
POLLYANNAISMS
POLLYANNAS
POLLYANNISH
POLONAISES
POLONISING
POLONIZING
POLTERGEIST
POLTERGEISTS
POLTROONERIES
POLTROONERY
POLVERINES
POLYACRYLAMIDE
POLYACRYLAMIDES
POLYACTINAL
POLYACTINE

POLYADELPHOUS
POLYALCOHOL
POLYALCOHOLS
POLYAMIDES
POLYAMINES
POLYANDRIES
POLYANDROUS
POLYANTHAS
POLYANTHUS
POLYANTHUSES
POLYARCHIES
POLYATOMIC
POLYAXIALS
POLYAXONIC
POLYBASITE
POLYBASITES
POLYBUTADIENE
POLYBUTADIENES
POLYCARBONATE
POLYCARBONATES
POLYCARBOXYLATE
POLYCARBOXYLIC
POLYCARPELLARY
POLYCARPIC
POLYCARPIES
POLYCARPOUS
POLYCENTRIC
POLYCENTRISM
POLYCENTRISMS
POLYCHAETE
POLYCHAETES
POLYCHAETOUS
POLYCHASIA
POLYCHASIUM
POLYCHETES
POLYCHLORINATED
POLYCHLOROPRENE
POLYCHOTOMIES
POLYCHOTOMOUS
POLYCHOTOMY
POLYCHREST
POLYCHRESTS
POLYCHROIC
POLYCHROISM
POLYCHROISMS
POLYCHROMATIC
POLYCHROMATISM
POLYCHROMATISMS
POLYCHROME
POLYCHROMED
POLYCHROMES
POLYCHROMIC
POLYCHROMIES
POLYCHROMING
POLYCHROMOUS
POLYCHROMY
POLYCISTRONIC
POLYCLINIC
POLYCLINICS

POLYCLONAL
POLYCOTTON
POLYCOTTONS
POLYCOTYLEDON
POLYCOTYLEDONS
POLYCROTIC
POLYCROTISM
POLYCROTISMS
POLYCRYSTAL
POLYCRYSTALLINE
POLYCRYSTALS
POLYCULTURE
POLYCULTURES
POLYCYCLIC
POLYCYCLICS
POLYCYSTIC
POLYCYTHAEMIA
POLYCYTHAEMIAS
POLYCYTHEMIA
POLYCYTHEMIAS
POLYCYTHEMIC
POLYDACTYL
POLYDACTYLIES
POLYDACTYLISM
POLYDACTYLISMS
POLYDACTYLOUS
POLYDACTYLS
POLYDACTYLY
POLYDAEMONISM
POLYDAEMONISMS
POLYDEMONISM
POLYDEMONISMS
POLYDIPSIA
POLYDIPSIAS
POLYDIPSIC
POLYDISPERSE
POLYDISPERSITY
POLYELECTROLYTE
POLYEMBRYONATE
POLYEMBRYONIC
POLYEMBRYONIES
POLYEMBRYONY
POLYESTERS
POLYESTROUS
POLYETHENE
POLYETHENES
POLYETHYLENE
POLYETHYLENES
POLYGALACEOUS
POLYGAMIES
POLYGAMISE
POLYGAMISED
POLYGAMISES
POLYGAMISING
POLYGAMIST
POLYGAMISTS
POLYGAMIZE
POLYGAMIZED
POLYGAMIZES

POLYGAMIZING
POLYGAMOUS
POLYGAMOUSLY
POLYGENESES
POLYGENESIS
POLYGENETIC
POLYGENETICALLY
POLYGENIES
POLYGENISM
POLYGENISMS
POLYGENIST
POLYGENISTS
POLYGENOUS
POLYGLOTISM
POLYGLOTISMS
POLYGLOTTAL
POLYGLOTTIC
POLYGLOTTISM
POLYGLOTTISMS
POLYGLOTTOUS
POLYGLOTTS
POLYGONACEOUS
POLYGONALLY
POLYGONATUM
POLYGONATUMS
POLYGONIES
POLYGONUMS
POLYGRAPHED
POLYGRAPHER
POLYGRAPHERS
POLYGRAPHIC
POLYGRAPHICALLY
POLYGRAPHIES
POLYGRAPHING
POLYGRAPHIST
POLYGRAPHISTS
POLYGRAPHS
POLYGRAPHY
POLYGYNIAN
POLYGYNIES
POLYGYNIST
POLYGYNISTS
POLYGYNOUS
POLYHALITE
POLYHALITES
POLYHEDRAL
POLYHEDRIC
POLYHEDRON
POLYHEDRONS
POLYHEDROSES
POLYHEDROSIS
POLYHISTOR
POLYHISTORIAN
POLYHISTORIANS
POLYHISTORIC
POLYHISTORIES
POLYHISTORS
POLYHISTORY
POLYHYBRID

POLYHYBRIDS
POLYHYDRIC
POLYHYDROXY
POLYIMIDES
POLYISOPRENE
POLYISOPRENES
POLYLEMMAS
POLYLYSINE
POLYLYSINES
POLYMASTIA
POLYMASTIAS
POLYMASTIC
POLYMASTIES
POLYMASTISM
POLYMASTISMS
POLYMATHIC
POLYMATHIES
POLYMERASE
POLYMERASES
POLYMERIDE
POLYMERIDES
POLYMERIES
POLYMERISATION
POLYMERISATIONS
POLYMERISE
POLYMERISED
POLYMERISES
POLYMERISING
POLYMERISM
POLYMERISMS
POLYMERIZATION
POLYMERIZATIONS
POLYMERIZE
POLYMERIZED
POLYMERIZES
POLYMERIZING
POLYMEROUS
POLYMORPHIC
POLYMORPHICALLY
POLYMORPHISM
POLYMORPHISMS
POLYMORPHOUS
POLYMORPHOUSLY
POLYMORPHS
POLYMYOSITIS
POLYMYOSITISES
POLYMYXINS
POLYNEURITIS
POLYNEURITISES
POLYNOMIAL
POLYNOMIALISM
POLYNOMIALISMS
POLYNOMIALS
POLYNUCLEAR
POLYNUCLEATE
POLYNUCLEOTIDE
POLYNUCLEOTIDES
POLYOLEFIN
POLYOLEFINS

POLYOMINOS
POLYONYMIC
POLYONYMIES
POLYONYMOUS
POLYPARIES
POLYPARIUM
POLYPEPTIDE
POLYPEPTIDES
POLYPEPTIDIC
POLYPETALOUS
POLYPHAGIA
POLYPHAGIAS
POLYPHAGIES
POLYPHAGOUS
POLYPHARMACIES
POLYPHARMACY
POLYPHASIC
POLYPHENOL
POLYPHENOLIC
POLYPHENOLS
POLYPHLOESBOEAN
POLYPHLOISBIC
POLYPHONES
POLYPHONIC
POLYPHONICALLY
POLYPHONIES
POLYPHONIST
POLYPHONISTS
POLYPHONOUS
POLYPHONOUSLY
POLYPHOSPHORIC
POLYPHYLETIC
POLYPHYLLOUS
POLYPHYODONT
POLYPIDOMS
POLYPLOIDAL
POLYPLOIDIC
POLYPLOIDIES
POLYPLOIDS
POLYPLOIDY
POLYPODIES
POLYPODOUS
POLYPROPENE
POLYPROPENES
POLYPROPYLENE
POLYPROPYLENES
POLYPROTODONT
POLYPROTODONTS
POLYPTYCHS
POLYRHYTHM
POLYRHYTHMIC
POLYRHYTHMS
POLYRIBOSOMAL
POLYRIBOSOME
POLYRIBOSOMES
POLYSACCHARIDE
POLYSACCHARIDES
POLYSACCHAROSE
POLYSACCHAROSES

POLYSEMANT
POLYSEMANTS
POLYSEMIES
POLYSEMOUS
POLYSEPALOUS
POLYSILOXANE
POLYSILOXANES
POLYSOMICS
POLYSOMIES
POLYSORBATE
POLYSORBATES
POLYSTICHOUS
POLYSTYLAR
POLYSTYRENE
POLYSTYRENES
POLYSULFIDE
POLYSULFIDES
POLYSULPHIDE
POLYSULPHIDES
POLYSYLLABIC
POLYSYLLABICAL
POLYSYLLABICISM
POLYSYLLABISM
POLYSYLLABISMS
POLYSYLLABLE
POLYSYLLABLES
POLYSYLLOGISM
POLYSYLLOGISMS
POLYSYNAPTIC
POLYSYNDETON
POLYSYNDETONS
POLYSYNTHESES
POLYSYNTHESIS
POLYSYNTHESISM
POLYSYNTHESISMS
POLYSYNTHETIC
POLYSYNTHETICAL
POLYSYNTHETISM
POLYSYNTHETISMS
POLYTECHNIC
POLYTECHNICAL
POLYTECHNICS
POLYTENIES
POLYTHALAMOUS
POLYTHEISM
POLYTHEISMS
POLYTHEIST
POLYTHEISTIC
POLYTHEISTICAL
POLYTHEISTS
POLYTHENES
POLYTOCOUS
POLYTONALISM
POLYTONALISMS
POLYTONALIST
POLYTONALISTS
POLYTONALITIES
POLYTONALITY
POLYTONALLY

POLYTROPHIC
POLYTUNNEL
POLYTUNNELS
POLYTYPICAL
POLYUNSATURATED
POLYURETHAN
POLYURETHANE
POLYURETHANES
POLYURETHANS
POLYVALENCE
POLYVALENCES
POLYVALENCIES
POLYVALENCY
POLYVALENT
POLYVINYLIDENE
POLYVINYLIDENES
POLYVINYLS
POLYWATERS
POLYZOARIA
POLYZOARIAL
POLYZOARIES
POLYZOARIUM
POMEGRANATE
POMEGRANATES
POMICULTURE
POMICULTURES
POMIFEROUS
POMMELLING
POMOERIUMS
POMOLOGICAL
POMOLOGICALLY
POMOLOGIES
POMOLOGIST
POMOLOGISTS
POMOSEXUAL
POMOSEXUALS
POMPADOURED
POMPADOURS
POMPELMOOSE
POMPELMOOSES
POMPELMOUSE
POMPELMOUSE
POMPELMOUSES
POMPHOLYGOUS
POMPHOLYXES
POMPOSITIES
POMPOUSNESS
POMPOUSNESSES
PONDERABILITIES
PONDERABILITY
PONDERABLE
PONDERABLES
PONDERABLY
PONDERANCE
PONDERANCES
PONDERANCIES
PONDERANCY
PONDERATED
PONDERATES

PONDERATING
PONDERATION
PONDERATIONS
PONDERINGLY
PONDERMENT
PONDERMENTS
PONDEROSAS
PONDEROSITIES
PONDEROSITY
PONDEROUSLY
PONDEROUSNESS
PONDEROUSNESSES
PONDOKKIES
PONEROLOGIES
PONEROLOGY
PONIARDING
PONTIANACS
PONTIANAKS
PONTICELLO
PONTICELLOS
PONTIFICAL
PONTIFICALITIES
PONTIFICALITY
PONTIFICALLY
PONTIFICALS
PONTIFICATE
PONTIFICATED
PONTIFICATES
PONTIFICATING
PONTIFICATION
PONTIFICATIONS
PONTIFICATOR
PONTIFICATORS
PONTIFICES
PONTIFYING
PONTLEVISES
PONTONEERS
PONTONIERS
PONTONNIER
PONTONNIERS
PONTOONERS
PONTOONING
PONYTAILED
POORHOUSES
POORMOUTHED
POORMOUTHING
POORMOUTHS
POORNESSES
POPLINETTE
POPLINETTES
POPMOBILITIES
POPMOBILITY
POPPERINGS
POPPYCOCKS
POPPYHEADS
POPULARISATION
POPULARISATIONS
POPULARISE
POPULARISED

POPULARISER
POPULARISERS
POPULARISES
POPULARISING
POPULARITIES
POPULARITY
POPULARIZATION
POPULARIZATIONS
POPULARIZE
POPULARIZED
POPULARIZER
POPULARIZERS
POPULARIZES
POPULARIZING
POPULATING
POPULATION
POPULATIONAL
POPULATIONS
POPULISTIC
POPULOUSLY
POPULOUSNESS
POPULOUSNESSES
PORBEAGLES
PORCELAINEOUS
PORCELAINISE
PORCELAINISED
PORCELAINISES
PORCELAINISING
PORCELAINIZE
PORCELAINIZED
PORCELAINIZES
PORCELAINIZING
PORCELAINLIKE
PORCELAINOUS
PORCELAINS
PORCELANEOUS
PORCELLANEOUS
PORCELLANISE
PORCELLANISED
PORCELLANISES
PORCELLANISING
PORCELLANITE
PORCELLANITES
PORCELLANIZE
PORCELLANIZED
PORCELLANIZES
PORCELLANIZING
PORCELLANOUS
PORCUPINES
PORCUPINISH
PORIFERANS
PORIFEROUS
PORINESSES
PORISMATIC
PORISMATICAL
PORISTICAL
PORKINESSES
PORLOCKING
PORLOCKINGS

PORNOCRACIES
PORNOCRACY
PORNOGRAPHER
PORNOGRAPHERS
PORNOGRAPHIC
PORNOGRAPHIES
PORNOGRAPHY
PORNOTOPIA
PORNOTOPIAN
PORNOTOPIAS
POROGAMIES
POROMERICS
POROSCOPES
POROSCOPIC
POROSCOPIES
POROSITIES
POROUSNESS
POROUSNESSES
PORPENTINE
PORPENTINES
PORPHYRIAS
PORPHYRIES
PORPHYRINS
PORPHYRIOS
PORPHYRITE
PORPHYRITES
PORPHYRITIC
PORPHYROGENITE
PORPHYROGENITES
PORPHYROID
PORPHYROIDS
PORPHYROPSIN
PORPHYROPSINS
PORPHYROUS
PORPOISING
PORRACEOUS
PORRECTING
PORRECTION
PORRECTIONS
PORRENGERS
PORRIGINOUS
PORRINGERS
PORTABELLA
PORTABELLAS
PORTABELLO
PORTABELLOS
PORTABILITIES
PORTABILITY
PORTAMENTI
PORTAMENTO
PORTAPACKS
PORTATIVES
PORTCULLIS
PORTCULLISED
PORTCULLISES
PORTCULLISING
PORTENDING
PORTENTOUS
PORTENTOUSLY

PORTENTOUSNESS
PORTEOUSES
PORTERAGES
PORTERESSES
PORTERHOUSE
PORTERHOUSES
PORTFOLIOS
PORTHORSES
PORTHOUSES
PORTIONERS
PORTIONING
PORTIONIST
PORTIONISTS
PORTIONLESS
PORTLINESS
PORTLINESSES
PORTMANTEAU
PORTMANTEAUS
PORTMANTEAUX
PORTMANTLE
PORTMANTLES
PORTMANTUA
PORTMANTUAS
PORTOBELLO
PORTOBELLOS
PORTOLANOS
PORTRAITED
PORTRAITING
PORTRAITIST
PORTRAITISTS
PORTRAITURE
PORTRAITURES
PORTRAYABLE
PORTRAYALS
PORTRAYERS
PORTRAYING
PORTREEVES
PORTRESSES
PORTULACACEOUS
PORTULACAS
PORWIGGLES
POSHNESSES
POSITIONAL
POSITIONALLY
POSITIONED
POSITIONING
POSITIVELY
POSITIVENESS
POSITIVENESSES
POSITIVEST
POSITIVISM
POSITIVISMS
POSITIVIST
POSITIVISTIC
POSITIVISTS
POSITIVITIES
POSITIVITY
POSITRONIUM
POSITRONIUMS

POSTSTIMULATORY

POSOLOGICAL
POSOLOGIES
POSSESSABLE
POSSESSEDLY
POSSESSEDNESS
POSSESSEDNESSES
POSSESSING
POSSESSION
POSSESSIONAL
POSSESSIONARY
POSSESSIONATE
POSSESSIONATES
POSSESSIONED
POSSESSIONLESS
POSSESSIONS
POSSESSIVE
POSSESSIVELY
POSSESSIVENESS
POSSESSIVES
POSSESSORS
POSSESSORSHIP
POSSESSORSHIPS
POSSESSORY
POSSIBILISM
POSSIBILISMS
POSSIBILIST
POSSIBILISTS
POSSIBILITIES
POSSIBILITY
POSSIBLEST
POSTABORTION
POSTACCIDENT
POSTADOLESCENT
POSTAMPUTATION
POSTAPOCALYPTIC
POSTARREST
POSTATOMIC
POSTATTACK
POSTBELLUM
POSTBIBLICAL
POSTBOURGEOIS
POSTBUSSES
POSTCAPITALIST
POSTCARDED
POSTCARDING
POSTCARDLIKE
POSTCLASSIC
POSTCLASSICAL
POSTCODING
POSTCOITAL
POSTCOLLEGE
POSTCOLLEGIATE
POSTCOLONIAL
POSTCONCEPTION
POSTCONCERT
POSTCONQUEST
POSTCONSONANTAL
POSTCONVENTION
POSTCOPULATORY

POSTCORONARY
POSTCRANIAL
POSTCRANIALLY
POSTCRISIS
POSTDATING
POSTDEADLINE
POSTDEBATE
POSTDEBUTANTE
POSTDELIVERY
POSTDEPRESSION
POSTDEVALUATION
POSTDILUVIAL
POSTDILUVIAN
POSTDILUVIANS
POSTDIVESTITURE
POSTDIVORCE
POSTDOCTORAL
POSTDOCTORATE
POSTEDITING
POSTELECTION
POSTEMBRYONAL
POSTEMBRYONIC
POSTEMERGENCE
POSTEMERGENCY
POSTEPILEPTIC
POSTERIORITIES
POSTERIORITY
POSTERIORLY
POSTERIORS
POSTERISATION
POSTERISATIONS
POSTERITIES
POSTERIZATION
POSTERIZATIONS
POSTEROLATERAL
POSTERUPTIVE
POSTEXERCISE
POSTEXILIAN
POSTEXILIC
POSTEXPERIENCE
POSTEXPOSURE
POSTFEMINISM
POSTFEMINISMS
POSTFEMINIST
POSTFEMINISTS
POSTFIXING
POSTFLIGHT
POSTFORMED
POSTFORMING
POSTFRACTURE
POSTFREEZE
POSTGANGLIONIC
POSTGLACIAL
POSTGRADUATE
POSTGRADUATES
POSTGRADUATION
POSTHARVEST
POSTHASTES
POSTHEMORRHAGIC

POSTHOLDER
POSTHOLDERS
POSTHOLIDAY
POSTHOLOCAUST
POSTHORSES
POSTHOSPITAL
POSTHOUSES
POSTHUMOUS
POSTHUMOUSLY
POSTHUMOUSNESS
POSTHYPNOTIC
POSTILIONS
POSTILLATE
POSTILLATED
POSTILLATES
POSTILLATING
POSTILLATION
POSTILLATIONS
POSTILLATOR
POSTILLATORS
POSTILLERS
POSTILLING
POSTILLION
POSTILLIONS
POSTIMPACT
POSTIMPERIAL
POSTINAUGURAL
POSTINDUSTRIAL
POSTINFECTION
POSTINJECTION
POSTINOCULATION
POSTIRRADIATION
POSTISCHEMIC
POSTISOLATION
POSTLANDING
POSTLAPSARIAN
POSTLAUNCH
POSTLIBERATION
POSTLIMINARY
POSTLIMINIA
POSTLIMINIARY
POSTLIMINIES
POSTLIMINIOUS
POSTLIMINIUM
POSTLIMINOUS
POSTLIMINY
POSTLITERATE
POSTMARITAL
POSTMARKED
POSTMARKING
POSTMASTECTOMY
POSTMASTER
POSTMASTERS
POSTMASTERSHIP
POSTMASTERSHIPS
POSTMATING
POSTMEDIEVAL
POSTMENOPAUSAL
POSTMENSTRUAL

POSTMERIDIAN
POSTMIDNIGHT
POSTMILLENARIAN
POSTMILLENNIAL
POSTMISTRESS
POSTMISTRESSES
POSTMODERN
POSTMODERNISM
POSTMODERNISMS
POSTMODERNIST
POSTMODERNISTS
POSTMORTEM
POSTMORTEMS
POSTNATALLY
POSTNEONATAL
POSTNUPTIAL
POSTOCULAR
POSTOPERATIVE
POSTOPERATIVELY
POSTORBITAL
POSTORGASMIC
POSTPARTUM
POSTPERSON
POSTPERSONS
POSTPOLLINATION
POSTPONABLE
POSTPONEMENT
POSTPONEMENTS
POSTPONENCE
POSTPONENCES
POSTPONERS
POSTPONING
POSTPOSING
POSTPOSITION
POSTPOSITIONAL
POSTPOSITIONS
POSTPOSITIVE
POSTPOSITIVELY
POSTPOSITIVES
POSTPRANDIAL
POSTPRIMARY
POSTPRISON
POSTPRODUCTION
POSTPRODUCTIONS
POSTPUBERTY
POSTPUBESCENT
POSTRECESSION
POSTRETIREMENT
POSTRIDERS
POSTROMANTIC
POSTSCENIUM
POSTSCENIUMS
POSTSCRIPT
POSTSCRIPTS
POSTSEASON
POSTSEASONS
POSTSECONDARY
POSTSTIMULATION
POSTSTIMULATORY

POSTSTIMULUS
POSTSTRIKE
POSTSURGICAL
POSTSYNAPTIC
POSTSYNCED
POSTSYNCING
POSTTENSION
POSTTENSIONED
POSTTENSIONING
POSTTENSIONS
POSTTRANSFUSION
POSTTRAUMATIC
POSTTREATMENT
POSTULANCIES
POSTULANCY
POSTULANTS
POSTULANTSHIP
POSTULANTSHIPS
POSTULATED
POSTULATES
POSTULATING
POSTULATION
POSTULATIONAL
POSTULATIONALLY
POSTULATIONS
POSTULATOR
POSTULATORS
POSTULATORY
POSTULATUM
POSTURISED
POSTURISES
POSTURISING
POSTURISTS
POSTURIZED
POSTURIZES
POSTURIZING
POSTVACCINAL
POSTVACCINATION
POSTVAGOTOMY
POSTVASECTOMY
POSTVOCALIC
POSTWEANING
POSTWORKSHOP
POTABILITIES
POTABILITY
POTABLENESS
POTABLENESSES
POTAMOGETON
POTAMOGETONS
POTAMOLOGICAL
POTAMOLOGIES
POTAMOLOGIST
POTAMOLOGISTS
POTAMOLOGY
POTASSIUMS
POTATOBUGS
POTBELLIED
POTBELLIES
POTBOILERS

POTBOILING
POTENTATES
POTENTIALITIES
POTENTIALITY
POTENTIALLY
POTENTIALS
POTENTIARIES
POTENTIARY
POTENTIATE
POTENTIATED
POTENTIATES
POTENTIATING
POTENTIATION
POTENTIATIONS
POTENTIATOR
POTENTIATORS
POTENTILLA
POTENTILLAS
POTENTIOMETER
POTENTIOMETERS
POTENTIOMETRIC
POTENTIOMETRIES
POTENTIOMETRY
POTENTISED
POTENTISES
POTENTISING
POTENTIZED
POTENTIZES
POTENTIZING
POTENTNESS
POTENTNESSES
POTHECARIES
POTHOLDERS
POTHOLINGS
POTHUNTERS
POTHUNTING
POTHUNTINGS
POTICARIES
POTICHOMANIA
POTICHOMANIAS
POTLATCHED
POTLATCHES
POTLATCHING
POTOMETERS
POTPOURRIS
POTSHOTTING
POTTERINGLY
POTTERINGS
POTTINESSES
POTTINGARS
POTTINGERS
POTTYMOUTH
POTTYMOUTHS
POTWALLERS
POULTERERS
POULTICING
POULTROONE
POULTROONES
POULTRYMAN

POULTRYMEN
POUNDCAKES
POURBOIRES
POURPARLER
POURPARLERS
POURPOINTS
POURSEWING
POURTRAHED
POURTRAICT
POURTRAICTS
POURTRAYED
POURTRAYING
POUSOWDIES
POUSSETTED
POUSSETTES
POUSSETTING
POUTHERING
POWDERIEST
POWDERLESS
POWDERLIKE
POWELLISED
POWELLISES
POWELLISING
POWELLITES
POWELLIZED
POWELLIZES
POWELLIZING
POWERBOATING
POWERBOATINGS
POWERBOATS
POWERFULLY
POWERFULNESS
POWERFULNESSES
POWERHOUSE
POWERHOUSES
POWERLESSLY
POWERLESSNESS
POWERLESSNESSES
POWERLIFTER
POWERLIFTERS
POWERLIFTING
POWERLIFTINGS
POWERPLAYS
POWERTRAIN
POWERTRAINS
POWSOWDIES
POXVIRUSES
POZZOLANAS
POZZOLANIC
POZZUOLANA
POZZUOLANAS
PRACHARAKS
PRACTICABILITY
PRACTICABLE
PRACTICABLENESS
PRACTICABLY
PRACTICALISM
PRACTICALISMS
PRACTICALIST

PRACTICALISTS
PRACTICALITIES
PRACTICALITY
PRACTICALLY
PRACTICALNESS
PRACTICALNESSES
PRACTICALS
PRACTICERS
PRACTICIAN
PRACTICIANS
PRACTICING
PRACTICUMS
PRACTIQUES
PRACTISANT
PRACTISANTS
PRACTISERS
PRACTISING
PRACTITIONER
PRACTITIONERS
PRACTOLOLS
PRAEAMBLES
PRAECOCIAL
PRAECORDIAL
PRAEDIALITIES
PRAEDIALITY
PRAEFECTORIAL
PRAELECTED
PRAELECTING
PRAELUDIUM
PRAEMUNIRE
PRAEMUNIRES
PRAENOMENS
PRAENOMINA
PRAENOMINAL
PRAENOMINALLY
PRAEPOSTOR
PRAEPOSTORS
PRAESIDIUM
PRAESIDIUMS
PRAETORIAL
PRAETORIAN
PRAETORIANS
PRAETORIUM
PRAETORIUMS
PRAETORSHIP
PRAETORSHIPS
PRAGMATICAL
PRAGMATICALITY
PRAGMATICALLY
PRAGMATICALNESS
PRAGMATICISM
PRAGMATICISMS
PRAGMATICIST
PRAGMATICISTS
PRAGMATICS
PRAGMATISATION
PRAGMATISATIONS
PRAGMATISE
PRAGMATISED

PRAGMATISER
PRAGMATISERS
PRAGMATISES
PRAGMATISING
PRAGMATISM
PRAGMATISMS
PRAGMATIST
PRAGMATISTIC
PRAGMATISTS
PRAGMATIZATION
PRAGMATIZATIONS
PRAGMATIZE
PRAGMATIZED
PRAGMATIZER
PRAGMATIZERS
PRAGMATIZES
PRAGMATIZING
PRAISEACHS
PRAISELESS
PRAISEWORTHILY
PRAISEWORTHY
PRAISINGLY
PRALLTRILLER
PRALLTRILLERS
PRANAYAMAS
PRANCINGLY
PRANDIALLY
PRANKINGLY
PRANKISHLY
PRANKISHNESS
PRANKISHNESSES
PRANKSTERS
PRASEODYMIUM
PRASEODYMIUMS
PRATFALLEN
PRATFALLING
PRATINCOLE
PRATINCOLES
PRATTLEBOX
PRATTLEBOXES
PRATTLEMENT
PRATTLEMENTS
PRATTLINGLY
PRAXEOLOGICAL
PRAXEOLOGIES
PRAXEOLOGY
PRAXINOSCOPE
PRAXINOSCOPES
PRAYERFULLY
PRAYERFULNESS
PRAYERFULNESSES
PRAYERLESS
PRAYERLESSLY
PRAYERLESSNESS
PREABSORBED
PREABSORBING
PREABSORBS
PREACCUSED
PREACCUSES

PREACCUSING
PREACHABLE
PREACHERSHIP
PREACHERSHIPS
PREACHIEST
PREACHIFIED
PREACHIFIES
PREACHIFYING
PREACHIFYINGS
PREACHINESS
PREACHINESSES
PREACHINGLY
PREACHINGS
PREACHMENT
PREACHMENTS
PREACQUAINT
PREACQUAINTANCE
PREACQUAINTED
PREACQUAINTING
PREACQUAINTS
PREACQUISITION
PREADAMITE
PREADAMITES
PREADAPTATION
PREADAPTATIONS
PREADAPTED
PREADAPTING
PREADAPTIVE
PREADJUSTED
PREADJUSTING
PREADJUSTS
PREADMISSION
PREADMISSIONS
PREADMITTED
PREADMITTING
PREADMONISH
PREADMONISHED
PREADMONISHES
PREADMONISHING
PREADMONITION
PREADMONITIONS
PREADOLESCENCE
PREADOLESCENCES
PREADOLESCENT
PREADOLESCENTS
PREADOPTED
PREADOPTING
PREAGRICULTURAL
PREALLOTTED
PREALLOTTING
PREALTERED
PREALTERING
PREAMBLING
PREAMBULARY
PREAMBULATE
PREAMBULATED
PREAMBULATES
PREAMBULATING
PREAMBULATORY

PREAMPLIFIER
PREAMPLIFIERS
PREANESTHETIC
PREANNOUNCE
PREANNOUNCED
PREANNOUNCES
PREANNOUNCING
PREAPPLIED
PREAPPLIES
PREAPPLYING
PREAPPOINT
PREAPPOINTED
PREAPPOINTING
PREAPPOINTS
PREAPPROVE
PREAPPROVED
PREAPPROVES
PREAPPROVING
PREARRANGE
PREARRANGED
PREARRANGEMENT
PREARRANGEMENTS
PREARRANGES
PREARRANGING
PREASSEMBLED
PREASSIGNED
PREASSIGNING
PREASSIGNS
PREASSURANCE
PREASSURANCES
PREASSURED
PREASSURES
PREASSURING
PREATTUNED
PREATTUNES
PREATTUNING
PREAUDIENCE
PREAUDIENCES
PREAVERRED
PREAVERRING
PREAXIALLY
PREBENDARIES
PREBENDARY
PREBIBLICAL
PREBIDDING
PREBILLING
PREBINDING
PREBIOLOGIC
PREBIOLOGICAL
PREBLESSED
PREBLESSES
PREBLESSING
PREBOARDED
PREBOARDING
PREBOILING
PREBOOKING
PREBREAKFAST
PREBUDGETS
PREBUILDING

PREBUTTALS
PRECALCULI
PRECALCULUS
PRECALCULUSES
PRECANCELED
PRECANCELING
PRECANCELLATION
PRECANCELLED
PRECANCELLING
PRECANCELS
PRECANCEROUS
PRECANCERS
PRECAPITALIST
PRECARIOUS
PRECARIOUSLY
PRECARIOUSNESS
PRECASTING
PRECAUTION
PRECAUTIONAL
PRECAUTIONARY
PRECAUTIONED
PRECAUTIONING
PRECAUTIONS
PRECAUTIOUS
PRECEDENCE
PRECEDENCES
PRECEDENCIES
PRECEDENCY
PRECEDENTED
PRECEDENTIAL
PRECEDENTIALLY
PRECEDENTLY
PRECEDENTS
PRECENSORED
PRECENSORING
PRECENSORS
PRECENTING
PRECENTORIAL
PRECENTORS
PRECENTORSHIP
PRECENTORSHIPS
PRECENTRESS
PRECENTRESSES
PRECENTRICES
PRECENTRIX
PRECENTRIXES
PRECEPTIAL
PRECEPTIVE
PRECEPTIVELY
PRECEPTORAL
PRECEPTORATE
PRECEPTORATES
PRECEPTORIAL
PRECEPTORIALS
PRECEPTORIES
PRECEPTORS
PRECEPTORSHIP
PRECEPTORSHIPS
PRECEPTORY

PRECEPTRESS
PRECEPTRESSES
PRECESSING
PRECESSION
PRECESSIONAL
PRECESSIONALLY
PRECESSIONS
PRECHARGED
PRECHARGES
PRECHARGING
PRECHECKED
PRECHECKING
PRECHILLED
PRECHILLING
PRECHOOSES
PRECHOOSING
PRECHRISTIAN
PRECIEUSES
PRECIOSITIES
PRECIOSITY
PRECIOUSES
PRECIOUSLY
PRECIOUSNESS
PRECIOUSNESSES
PRECIPICED
PRECIPICES
PRECIPITABILITY
PRECIPITABLE
PRECIPITANCE
PRECIPITANCES
PRECIPITANCIES
PRECIPITANCY
PRECIPITANT
PRECIPITANTLY
PRECIPITANTNESS
PRECIPITANTS
PRECIPITATE
PRECIPITATED
PRECIPITATELY
PRECIPITATENESS
PRECIPITATES
PRECIPITATING
PRECIPITATION
PRECIPITATIONS
PRECIPITATIVE
PRECIPITATOR
PRECIPITATORS
PRECIPITIN
PRECIPITINOGEN
PRECIPITINOGENS
PRECIPITINS
PRECIPITOUS
PRECIPITOUSLY
PRECIPITOUSNESS
PRECISENESS
PRECISENESSES
PRECISIANISM
PRECISIANISMS
PRECISIANIST

PRECISIANISTS
PRECISIANS
PRECISIONISM
PRECISIONISMS
PRECISIONIST
PRECISIONISTS
PRECISIONS
PRECLASSICAL
PRECLEANED
PRECLEANING
PRECLEARANCE
PRECLEARANCES
PRECLEARED
PRECLEARING
PRECLINICAL
PRECLINICALLY
PRECLUDABLE
PRECLUDING
PRECLUSION
PRECLUSIONS
PRECLUSIVE
PRECLUSIVELY
PRECOCIALS
PRECOCIOUS
PRECOCIOUSLY
PRECOCIOUSNESS
PRECOCITIES
PRECOGNISANT
PRECOGNISE
PRECOGNISED
PRECOGNISES
PRECOGNISING
PRECOGNITION
PRECOGNITIONS
PRECOGNITIVE
PRECOGNIZANT
PRECOGNIZE
PRECOGNIZED
PRECOGNIZES
PRECOGNIZING
PRECOGNOSCE
PRECOGNOSCED
PRECOGNOSCES
PRECOGNOSCING
PRECOLLEGE
PRECOLLEGIATE
PRECOLONIAL
PRECOMBUSTION
PRECOMBUSTIONS
PRECOMMITMENT
PRECOMMITMENTS
PRECOMPETITIVE
PRECOMPOSE
PRECOMPOSED
PRECOMPOSES
PRECOMPOSING
PRECOMPUTE
PRECOMPUTED
PRECOMPUTER

PRECOMPUTES
PRECOMPUTING
PRECONCEIT
PRECONCEITS
PRECONCEIVE
PRECONCEIVED
PRECONCEIVES
PRECONCEIVING
PRECONCEPTION
PRECONCEPTIONS
PRECONCERT
PRECONCERTED
PRECONCERTEDLY
PRECONCERTING
PRECONCERTS
PRECONCILIAR
PRECONDEMN
PRECONDEMNED
PRECONDEMNING
PRECONDEMNS
PRECONDITION
PRECONDITIONED
PRECONDITIONING
PRECONDITIONS
PRECONISATION
PRECONISATIONS
PRECONISED
PRECONISES
PRECONISING
PRECONIZATION
PRECONIZATIONS
PRECONIZED
PRECONIZES
PRECONIZING
PRECONQUEST
PRECONSCIOUS
PRECONSCIOUSES
PRECONSCIOUSLY
PRECONSONANTAL
PRECONSTRUCT
PRECONSTRUCTED
PRECONSTRUCTING
PRECONSTRUCTION
PRECONSTRUCTS
PRECONSUME
PRECONSUMED
PRECONSUMES
PRECONSUMING
PRECONTACT
PRECONTRACT
PRECONTRACTED
PRECONTRACTING
PRECONTRACTS
PRECONVENTION
PRECONVICTION
PRECONVICTIONS
PRECOOKERS
PRECOOKING
PRECOOLING

PRECOPULATORY
PRECORDIAL
PRECREASED
PRECREASES
PRECREASING
PRECRITICAL
PRECURRERS
PRECURSIVE
PRECURSORS
PRECURSORY
PRECUTTING
PREDACEOUS
PREDACEOUSNESS
PREDACIOUS
PREDACIOUSNESS
PREDACITIES
PREDATIONS
PREDATISMS
PREDATORILY
PREDATORINESS
PREDATORINESSES
PREDECEASE
PREDECEASED
PREDECEASES
PREDECEASING
PREDECESSOR
PREDECESSORS
PREDEDUCTED
PREDEDUCTING
PREDEDUCTS
PREDEFINED
PREDEFINES
PREDEFINING
PREDEFINITION
PREDEFINITIONS
PREDELIVERY
PREDENTATE
PREDEPARTURE
PREDEPOSIT
PREDEPOSITED
PREDEPOSITING
PREDEPOSITS
PREDESIGNATE
PREDESIGNATED
PREDESIGNATES
PREDESIGNATING
PREDESIGNATION
PREDESIGNATIONS
PREDESIGNATORY
PREDESIGNED
PREDESIGNING
PREDESIGNS
PREDESTINABLE
PREDESTINARIAN
PREDESTINARIANS
PREDESTINATE
PREDESTINATED
PREDESTINATES
PREDESTINATING

PREDESTINATION
PREDESTINATIONS
PREDESTINATIVE
PREDESTINATOR
PREDESTINATORS
PREDESTINE
PREDESTINED
PREDESTINES
PREDESTINIES
PREDESTINING
PREDESTINY
PREDETERMINABLE
PREDETERMINATE
PREDETERMINE
PREDETERMINED
PREDETERMINER
PREDETERMINERS
PREDETERMINES
PREDETERMINING
PREDETERMINISM
PREDETERMINISMS
PREDEVALUATION
PREDEVELOP
PREDEVELOPED
PREDEVELOPING
PREDEVELOPMENT
PREDEVELOPMENTS
PREDEVELOPS
PREDIABETES
PREDIABETESES
PREDIABETIC
PREDIABETICS
PREDIALITIES
PREDIALITY
PREDICABILITIES
PREDICABILITY
PREDICABLE
PREDICABLENESS
PREDICABLES
PREDICAMENT
PREDICAMENTAL
PREDICAMENTS
PREDICANTS
PREDICATED
PREDICATES
PREDICATING
PREDICATION
PREDICATIONS
PREDICATIVE
PREDICATIVELY
PREDICATOR
PREDICATORS
PREDICATORY
PREDICTABILITY
PREDICTABLE
PREDICTABLENESS
PREDICTABLY
PREDICTERS
PREDICTING

PREDICTION
PREDICTIONS
PREDICTIVE
PREDICTIVELY
PREDICTORS
PREDIGESTED
PREDIGESTING
PREDIGESTION
PREDIGESTIONS
PREDIGESTS
PREDIKANTS
PREDILECTED
PREDILECTION
PREDILECTIONS
PREDINNERS
PREDISCHARGE
PREDISCOVERIES
PREDISCOVERY
PREDISPOSAL
PREDISPOSALS
PREDISPOSE
PREDISPOSED
PREDISPOSES
PREDISPOSING
PREDISPOSITION
PREDISPOSITIONS
PREDNISOLONE
PREDNISOLONES
PREDNISONE
PREDNISONES
PREDOCTORAL
PREDOMINANCE
PREDOMINANCES
PREDOMINANCIES
PREDOMINANCY
PREDOMINANT
PREDOMINANTLY
PREDOMINATE
PREDOMINATED
PREDOMINATELY
PREDOMINATES
PREDOMINATING
PREDOMINATION
PREDOMINATIONS
PREDOMINATOR
PREDOMINATORS
PREDOOMING
PREDRILLED
PREDRILLING
PREDYNASTIC
PREECLAMPSIA
PREECLAMPSIAS
PREECLAMPTIC
PREEDITING
PREELECTED
PREELECTING
PREELECTION
PREELECTRIC
PREEMBARGO

PREEMERGENCE
PREEMERGENT
PREEMINENCE
PREEMINENCES
PREEMINENT
PREEMINENTLY
PREEMPLOYMENT
PREEMPTING
PREEMPTION
PREEMPTIONS
PREEMPTIVE
PREEMPTIVELY
PREEMPTORS
PREENACTED
PREENACTING
PREENROLLMENT
PREERECTED
PREERECTING
PREESTABLISH
PREESTABLISHED
PREESTABLISHES
PREESTABLISHING
PREETHICAL
PREEXCITED
PREEXCITES
PREEXCITING
PREEXEMPTED
PREEXEMPTING
PREEXEMPTS
PREEXISTED
PREEXISTENCE
PREEXISTENCES
PREEXISTENT
PREEXISTING
PREEXPERIMENT
PREEXPOSED
PREEXPOSES
PREEXPOSING
PREFABBING
PREFABRICATE
PREFABRICATED
PREFABRICATES
PREFABRICATING
PREFABRICATION
PREFABRICATIONS
PREFABRICATOR
PREFABRICATORS
PREFASCIST
PREFATORIAL
PREFATORIALLY
PREFATORILY
PREFECTORIAL
PREFECTSHIP
PREFECTSHIPS
PREFECTURAL
PREFECTURE
PREFECTURES
PREFERABILITIES
PREFERABILITY

PREFERABLE
PREFERABLENESS
PREFERABLY
PREFERENCE
PREFERENCES
PREFERENTIAL
PREFERENTIALISM
PREFERENTIALIST
PREFERENTIALITY
PREFERENTIALLY
PREFERMENT
PREFERMENTS
PREFERRABLE
PREFERRERS
PREFERRING
PREFIGURATE
PREFIGURATED
PREFIGURATES
PREFIGURATING
PREFIGURATION
PREFIGURATIONS
PREFIGURATIVE
PREFIGURATIVELY
PREFIGURED
PREFIGUREMENT
PREFIGUREMENTS
PREFIGURES
PREFIGURING
PREFINANCE
PREFINANCED
PREFINANCES
PREFINANCING
PREFIXALLY
PREFIXIONS
PREFIXTURE
PREFIXTURES
PREFLIGHTED
PREFLIGHTING
PREFLIGHTS
PREFLORATION
PREFLORATIONS
PREFOCUSED
PREFOCUSES
PREFOCUSING
PREFOCUSSED
PREFOCUSSES
PREFOCUSSING
PREFOLIATION
PREFOLIATIONS
PREFORMATION
PREFORMATIONISM
PREFORMATIONIST
PREFORMATIONS
PREFORMATIVE
PREFORMATS
PREFORMATTED
PREFORMATTING
PREFORMING
PREFORMULATE

PREFORMULATED

PREFORMULATED
PREFORMULATES
PREFORMULATING
PREFRANKED
PREFRANKING
PREFREEZES
PREFREEZING
PREFRESHMAN
PREFRONTAL
PREFRONTALS
PREFULGENT
PREFUNDING
PREGANGLIONIC
PREGENITAL
PREGLACIAL
PREGNABILITIES
PREGNABILITY
PREGNANCES
PREGNANCIES
PREGNANTLY
PREGNENOLONE
PREGNENOLONES
PREGROWTHS
PREGUIDING
PREGUSTATION
PREGUSTATIONS
PREHALLUCES
PREHANDLED
PREHANDLES
PREHANDLING
PREHARDENED
PREHARDENING
PREHARDENS
PREHARVEST
PREHEADACHE
PREHEATERS
PREHEATING
PREHEMINENCE
PREHEMINENCES
PREHENDING
PREHENSIBLE
PREHENSILE
PREHENSILITIES
PREHENSILITY
PREHENSION
PREHENSIONS
PREHENSIVE
PREHENSORIAL
PREHENSORS
PREHENSORY
PREHISTORIAN
PREHISTORIANS
PREHISTORIC
PREHISTORICAL
PREHISTORICALLY
PREHISTORIES
PREHISTORY
PREHOLIDAY
PREHOMINID

PREHOMINIDS
PREIGNITION
PREIGNITIONS
PREIMPLANTATION
PREIMPOSED
PREIMPOSES
PREIMPOSING
PREINAUGURAL
PREINDUCTION
PREINDUSTRIAL
PREINFORMED
PREINFORMING
PREINFORMS
PREINSERTED
PREINSERTING
PREINSERTS
PREINTERVIEW
PREINTERVIEWED
PREINTERVIEWING
PREINTERVIEWS
PREINVASION
PREINVITED
PREINVITES
PREINVITING
PREJUDGEMENT
PREJUDGEMENTS
PREJUDGERS
PREJUDGING
PREJUDGMENT
PREJUDGMENTS
PREJUDICANT
PREJUDICATE
PREJUDICATED
PREJUDICATES
PREJUDICATING
PREJUDICATION
PREJUDICATIONS
PREJUDICATIVE
PREJUDICED
PREJUDICES
PREJUDICIAL
PREJUDICIALLY
PREJUDICIALNESS
PREJUDICING
PREJUDIZES
PREKINDERGARTEN
PRELAPSARIAN
PRELATESHIP
PRELATESHIPS
PRELATESSES
PRELATICAL
PRELATICALLY
PRELATIONS
PRELATISED
PRELATISES
PRELATISING
PRELATISMS
PRELATISTS
PRELATIZED

PRELATIZES
PRELATIZING
PRELATURES
PRELAUNCHED
PRELAUNCHES
PRELAUNCHING
PRELECTING
PRELECTION
PRELECTIONS
PRELECTORS
PRELEXICAL
PRELIBATION
PRELIBATIONS
PRELIMINARIES
PRELIMINARILY
PRELIMINARY
PRELIMITED
PRELIMITING
PRELINGUAL
PRELINGUALLY
PRELITERACIES
PRELITERACY
PRELITERARY
PRELITERATE
PRELITERATES
PRELOADING
PRELOCATED
PRELOCATES
PRELOCATING
PRELOGICAL
PRELUDIOUS
PRELUNCHEON
PRELUSIONS
PRELUSIVELY
PRELUSORILY
PREMALIGNANT
PREMANDIBULAR
PREMANDIBULARS
PREMANUFACTURE
PREMANUFACTURED
PREMANUFACTURES
PREMARITAL
PREMARITALLY
PREMARKETED
PREMARKETING
PREMARKETS
PREMARRIAGE
PREMATURELY
PREMATURENESS
PREMATURENESSES
PREMATURES
PREMATURITIES
PREMATURITY
PREMAXILLA
PREMAXILLAE
PREMAXILLARIES
PREMAXILLARY
PREMAXILLAS
PREMEASURE

PREMEASURED
PREMEASURES
PREMEASURING
PREMEDICAL
PREMEDICALLY
PREMEDICATE
PREMEDICATED
PREMEDICATES
PREMEDICATING
PREMEDICATION
PREMEDICATIONS
PREMEDIEVAL
PREMEDITATE
PREMEDITATED
PREMEDITATEDLY
PREMEDITATES
PREMEDITATING
PREMEDITATION
PREMEDITATIONS
PREMEDITATIVE
PREMEDITATOR
PREMEDITATORS
PREMEIOTIC
PREMENOPAUSAL
PREMENSTRUAL
PREMENSTRUALLY
PREMIERING
PREMIERSHIP
PREMIERSHIPS
PREMIGRATION
PREMILLENARIAN
PREMILLENARIANS
PREMILLENNIAL
PREMILLENNIALLY
PREMODIFICATION
PREMODIFIED
PREMODIFIES
PREMODIFYING
PREMOISTEN
PREMOISTENED
PREMOISTENING
PREMOISTENS
PREMOLDING
PREMONISHED
PREMONISHES
PREMONISHING
PREMONISHMENT
PREMONISHMENTS
PREMONITION
PREMONITIONS
PREMONITIVE
PREMONITOR
PREMONITORILY
PREMONITORS
PREMONITORY
PREMOTIONS
PREMOVEMENT
PREMOVEMENTS
PREMUNITION

PREMUNITIONS
PREMYCOTIC
PRENATALLY
PRENEGOTIATE
PRENEGOTIATED
PRENEGOTIATES
PRENEGOTIATING
PRENEGOTIATION
PRENEGOTIATIONS
PRENOMINAL
PRENOMINATE
PRENOMINATED
PRENOMINATES
PRENOMINATING
PRENOMINATION
PRENOMINATIONS
PRENOTIFICATION
PRENOTIFIED
PRENOTIFIES
PRENOTIFYING
PRENOTIONS
PRENTICESHIP
PRENTICESHIPS
PRENTICING
PRENUMBERED
PRENUMBERING
PRENUMBERS
PRENUPTIAL
PREOBTAINED
PREOBTAINING
PREOBTAINS
PREOCCUPANCIES
PREOCCUPANCY
PREOCCUPANT
PREOCCUPANTS
PREOCCUPATE
PREOCCUPATED
PREOCCUPATES
PREOCCUPATING
PREOCCUPATION
PREOCCUPATIONS
PREOCCUPIED
PREOCCUPIES
PREOCCUPYING
PREOPENING
PREOPERATIONAL
PREOPERATIVE
PREOPERATIVELY
PREOPTIONS
PREORDAINED
PREORDAINING
PREORDAINMENT
PREORDAINMENTS
PREORDAINS
PREORDERED
PREORDERING
PREORDINANCE
PREORDINANCES
PREORDINATION

PREORDINATIONS
PREOVULATORY
PREPACKAGE
PREPACKAGED
PREPACKAGES
PREPACKAGING
PREPACKING
PREPARATION
PREPARATIONS
PREPARATIVE
PREPARATIVELY
PREPARATIVES
PREPARATOR
PREPARATORILY
PREPARATORS
PREPARATORY
PREPAREDLY
PREPAREDNESS
PREPAREDNESSES
PREPASTING
PREPATELLAR
PREPAYABLE
PREPAYMENT
PREPAYMENTS
PREPENSELY
PREPENSING
PREPENSIVE
PREPERFORMANCE
PREPLACING
PREPLANNED
PREPLANNING
PREPLANTING
PREPOLLENCE
PREPOLLENCES
PREPOLLENCIES
PREPOLLENCY
PREPOLLENT
PREPOLLICES
PREPONDERANCE
PREPONDERANCES
PREPONDERANCIES
PREPONDERANCY
PREPONDERANT
PREPONDERANTLY
PREPONDERATE
PREPONDERATED
PREPONDERATELY
PREPONDERATES
PREPONDERATING
PREPONDERATION
PREPONDERATIONS
PREPORTION
PREPORTIONED
PREPORTIONING
PREPORTIONS
PREPOSITION
PREPOSITIONAL
PREPOSITIONALLY
PREPOSITIONS

PREPOSITIVE
PREPOSITIVELY
PREPOSITIVES
PREPOSITOR
PREPOSITORS
PREPOSSESS
PREPOSSESSED
PREPOSSESSES
PREPOSSESSING
PREPOSSESSINGLY
PREPOSSESSION
PREPOSSESSIONS
PREPOSTEROUS
PREPOSTEROUSLY
PREPOSTORS
PREPOTENCE
PREPOTENCES
PREPOTENCIES
PREPOTENCY
PREPOTENTLY
PREPPINESS
PREPPINESSES
PREPRANDIAL
PREPREPARED
PREPRESIDENTIAL
PREPRICING
PREPRIMARIES
PREPRIMARY
PREPRINTED
PREPRINTING
PREPROCESS
PREPROCESSED
PREPROCESSES
PREPROCESSING
PREPROCESSOR
PREPROCESSORS
PREPRODUCTION
PREPRODUCTIONS
PREPROFESSIONAL
PREPROGRAM
PREPROGRAMED
PREPROGRAMING
PREPROGRAMMED
PREPROGRAMMING
PREPROGRAMS
PREPSYCHEDELIC
PREPUBERAL
PREPUBERTAL
PREPUBERTIES
PREPUBERTY
PREPUBESCENCE
PREPUBESCENCES
PREPUBESCENT
PREPUBESCENTS
PREPUBLICATION
PREPUBLICATIONS
PREPUNCHED
PREPUNCHES
PREPUNCHING

PREPUNCTUAL
PREPURCHASE
PREPURCHASED
PREPURCHASES
PREPURCHASING
PREQUALIFIED
PREQUALIFIES
PREQUALIFY
PREQUALIFYING
PREREADING
PRERECESSION
PRERECORDED
PRERECORDING
PRERECORDS
PREREGISTER
PREREGISTERED
PREREGISTERING
PREREGISTERS
PREREGISTRATION
PREREHEARSAL
PRERELEASE
PRERELEASED
PRERELEASES
PRERELEASING
PREREQUIRE
PREREQUIRED
PREREQUIRES
PREREQUIRING
PREREQUISITE
PREREQUISITES
PRERETIREMENT
PREREVISIONIST
PREREVOLUTION
PRERINSING
PREROGATIVE
PREROGATIVED
PREROGATIVELY
PREROGATIVES
PREROMANTIC
PRESAGEFUL
PRESAGEFULLY
PRESAGEMENT
PRESAGEMENTS
PRESANCTIFIED
PRESANCTIFIES
PRESANCTIFY
PRESANCTIFYING
PRESBYACOUSES
PRESBYACOUSIS
PRESBYACUSES
PRESBYACUSIS
PRESBYCOUSES
PRESBYCOUSIS
PRESBYCUSES
PRESBYCUSIS
PRESBYOPES
PRESBYOPIA
PRESBYOPIAS
PRESBYOPIC

PRESBYOPICS

PRESBYOPICS
PRESBYOPIES
PRESBYTERAL
PRESBYTERATE
PRESBYTERATES
PRESBYTERIAL
PRESBYTERIALLY
PRESBYTERIALS
PRESBYTERIAN
PRESBYTERIANISE
PRESBYTERIANISM
PRESBYTERIANIZE
PRESBYTERIANS
PRESBYTERIES
PRESBYTERS
PRESBYTERSHIP
PRESBYTERSHIPS
PRESBYTERY
PRESBYTISM
PRESBYTISMS
PRESCHEDULE
PRESCHEDULED
PRESCHEDULES
PRESCHEDULING
PRESCHOOLER
PRESCHOOLERS
PRESCHOOLS
PRESCIENCE
PRESCIENCES
PRESCIENTIFIC
PRESCIENTLY
PRESCINDED
PRESCINDENT
PRESCINDING
PRESCISSION
PRESCISSIONS
PRESCORING
PRESCREENED
PRESCREENING
PRESCREENS
PRESCRIBED
PRESCRIBER
PRESCRIBERS
PRESCRIBES
PRESCRIBING
PRESCRIBINGS
PRESCRIPTIBLE
PRESCRIPTION
PRESCRIPTIONS
PRESCRIPTIVE
PRESCRIPTIVELY
PRESCRIPTIVISM
PRESCRIPTIVISMS
PRESCRIPTIVIST
PRESCRIPTIVISTS
PRESCRIPTS
PRESEASONS
PRESELECTED
PRESELECTING

PRESELECTION
PRESELECTIONS
PRESELECTOR
PRESELECTORS
PRESELECTS
PRESELLING
PRESENSION
PRESENSIONS
PRESENTABILITY
PRESENTABLE
PRESENTABLENESS
PRESENTABLY
PRESENTATION
PRESENTATIONAL
PRESENTATIONISM
PRESENTATIONIST
PRESENTATIONS
PRESENTATIVE
PRESENTEEISM
PRESENTEEISMS
PRESENTEES
PRESENTENCE
PRESENTENCED
PRESENTENCES
PRESENTENCING
PRESENTERS
PRESENTIAL
PRESENTIALITIES
PRESENTIALITY
PRESENTIALLY
PRESENTIENT
PRESENTIMENT
PRESENTIMENTAL
PRESENTIMENTS
PRESENTING
PRESENTISM
PRESENTISMS
PRESENTIST
PRESENTIVE
PRESENTIVENESS
PRESENTMENT
PRESENTMENTS
PRESENTNESS
PRESENTNESSES
PRESERVABILITY
PRESERVABLE
PRESERVABLY
PRESERVATION
PRESERVATIONIST
PRESERVATIONS
PRESERVATIVE
PRESERVATIVES
PRESERVATORIES
PRESERVATORY
PRESERVERS
PRESERVICE
PRESERVING
PRESETTING
PRESETTLED

PRESETTLEMENT
PRESETTLES
PRESETTLING
PRESHAPING
PRESHIPPED
PRESHIPPING
PRESHOWING
PRESHRINKING
PRESHRINKS
PRESHRUNKEN
PRESIDENCIES
PRESIDENCY
PRESIDENTESS
PRESIDENTESSES
PRESIDENTIAL
PRESIDENTIALLY
PRESIDENTS
PRESIDENTSHIP
PRESIDENTSHIPS
PRESIDIARY
PRESIDIUMS
PRESIFTING
PRESIGNALED
PRESIGNALING
PRESIGNALLED
PRESIGNALLING
PRESIGNALS
PRESIGNIFIED
PRESIGNIFIES
PRESIGNIFY
PRESIGNIFYING
PRESLAUGHTER
PRESLICING
PRESOAKING
PRESOLVING
PRESORTING
PRESPECIFIED
PRESPECIFIES
PRESPECIFY
PRESPECIFYING
PRESSBOARD
PRESSBOARDS
PRESSGANGS
PRESSINGLY
PRESSINGNESS
PRESSINGNESSES
PRESSMARKS
PRESSROOMS
PRESSURELESS
PRESSURING
PRESSURISATION
PRESSURISATIONS
PRESSURISE
PRESSURISED
PRESSURISER
PRESSURISERS
PRESSURISES
PRESSURISING
PRESSURIZATION

PRESSURIZATIONS
PRESSURIZE
PRESSURIZED
PRESSURIZER
PRESSURIZERS
PRESSURIZES
PRESSURIZING
PRESSWOMAN
PRESSWOMEN
PRESSWORKS
PRESTAMPED
PRESTAMPING
PRESTATION
PRESTATIONS
PRESTERILISE
PRESTERILISED
PRESTERILISES
PRESTERILISING
PRESTERILIZE
PRESTERILIZED
PRESTERILIZES
PRESTERILIZING
PRESTERNUM
PRESTERNUMS
PRESTIDIGITATOR
PRESTIGEFUL
PRESTIGIATOR
PRESTIGIATORS
PRESTIGIOUS
PRESTIGIOUSLY
PRESTIGIOUSNESS
PRESTISSIMO
PRESTISSIMOS
PRESTORAGE
PRESTORING
PRESTRESSED
PRESTRESSES
PRESTRESSING
PRESTRICTION
PRESTRICTIONS
PRESTRUCTURE
PRESTRUCTURED
PRESTRUCTURES
PRESTRUCTURING
PRESUMABLE
PRESUMABLY
PRESUMEDLY
PRESUMINGLY
PRESUMMITS
PRESUMPTION
PRESUMPTIONS
PRESUMPTIVE
PRESUMPTIVELY
PRESUMPTIVENESS
PRESUMPTUOUS
PRESUMPTUOUSLY
PRESUPPOSE
PRESUPPOSED
PRESUPPOSES

PRESUPPOSING
PRESUPPOSITION
PRESUPPOSITIONS
PRESURGERY
PRESURMISE
PRESURMISES
PRESURVEYED
PRESURVEYING
PRESURVEYS
PRESWEETEN
PRESWEETENED
PRESWEETENING
PRESWEETENS
PRESYMPTOMATIC
PRESYNAPTIC
PRESYNAPTICALLY
PRETASTING
PRETELEVISION
PRETELLING
PRETENCELESS
PRETENDANT
PRETENDANTS
PRETENDEDLY
PRETENDENT
PRETENDENTS
PRETENDERS
PRETENDERSHIP
PRETENDERSHIPS
PRETENDING
PRETENDINGLY
PRETENSION
PRETENSIONED
PRETENSIONING
PRETENSIONLESS
PRETENSIONS
PRETENSIVE
PRETENTIOUS
PRETENTIOUSLY
PRETENTIOUSNESS
PRETERHUMAN
PRETERISTS
PRETERITENESS
PRETERITENESSES
PRETERITES
PRETERITION
PRETERITIONS
PRETERITIVE
PRETERMINAL
PRETERMINATION
PRETERMINATIONS
PRETERMISSION
PRETERMISSIONS
PRETERMITS
PRETERMITTED
PRETERMITTER
PRETERMITTERS
PRETERMITTING
PRETERNATURAL
PRETERNATURALLY

PRETERPERFECT
PRETERPERFECTS
PRETESTING
PRETEXTING
PRETHEATER
PRETORIANS
PRETORSHIP
PRETORSHIPS
PRETOURNAMENT
PRETRAINED
PRETRAINING
PRETREATED
PRETREATING
PRETREATMENT
PRETREATMENTS
PRETRIMMED
PRETRIMMING
PRETTIFICATION
PRETTIFICATIONS
PRETTIFIED
PRETTIFIER
PRETTIFIERS
PRETTIFIES
PRETTIFYING
PRETTINESS
PRETTINESSES
PRETTYISMS
PREUNIFICATION
PREUNITING
PREUNIVERSITY
PREVAILERS
PREVAILING
PREVAILINGLY
PREVAILMENT
PREVAILMENTS
PREVALENCE
PREVALENCES
PREVALENCIES
PREVALENCY
PREVALENTLY
PREVALENTNESS
PREVALENTNESSES
PREVALENTS
PREVALUING
PREVARICATE
PREVARICATED
PREVARICATES
PREVARICATING
PREVARICATION
PREVARICATIONS
PREVARICATOR
PREVARICATORS
PREVENANCIES
PREVENANCY
PREVENIENCE
PREVENIENCES
PREVENIENT
PREVENIENTLY
PREVENTABILITY

PREVENTABLE
PREVENTABLY
PREVENTATIVE
PREVENTATIVES
PREVENTERS
PREVENTIBILITY
PREVENTIBLE
PREVENTIBLY
PREVENTING
PREVENTION
PREVENTIONS
PREVENTIVE
PREVENTIVELY
PREVENTIVENESS
PREVENTIVES
PREVIEWERS
PREVIEWING
PREVIOUSLY
PREVIOUSNESS
PREVIOUSNESSES
PREVISIONAL
PREVISIONARY
PREVISIONED
PREVISIONING
PREVISIONS
PREVISITED
PREVISITING
PREVOCALIC
PREVOCALICALLY
PREVOCATIONAL
PREWARMING
PREWARNING
PREWASHING
PREWEANING
PREWEIGHED
PREWEIGHING
PREWORKING
PREWRAPPED
PREWRAPPING
PREWRITING
PREWRITINGS
PRICELESSLY
PRICELESSNESS
PRICELESSNESSES
PRICINESSES
PRICKLIEST
PRICKLINESS
PRICKLINESSES
PRICKLINGS
PRICKWOODS
PRIDEFULLY
PRIDEFULNESS
PRIDEFULNESSES
PRIESTCRAFT
PRIESTCRAFTS
PRIESTESSES
PRIESTHOOD
PRIESTHOODS
PRIESTLIER

PRIESTLIEST
PRIESTLIKE
PRIESTLINESS
PRIESTLINESSES
PRIESTLING
PRIESTLINGS
PRIESTSHIP
PRIESTSHIPS
PRIGGERIES
PRIGGISHLY
PRIGGISHNESS
PRIGGISHNESSES
PRIMAEVALLY
PRIMALITIES
PRIMAQUINE
PRIMAQUINES
PRIMARINESS
PRIMARINESSES
PRIMATESHIP
PRIMATESHIPS
PRIMATIALS
PRIMATICAL
PRIMATOLOGICAL
PRIMATOLOGIES
PRIMATOLOGIST
PRIMATOLOGISTS
PRIMATOLOGY
PRIMAVERAS
PRIMENESSES
PRIMEVALLY
PRIMIGENIAL
PRIMIGRAVIDA
PRIMIGRAVIDAE
PRIMIGRAVIDAS
PRIMIPARAE
PRIMIPARAS
PRIMIPARITIES
PRIMIPARITY
PRIMIPAROUS
PRIMITIVELY
PRIMITIVENESS
PRIMITIVENESSES
PRIMITIVES
PRIMITIVISM
PRIMITIVISMS
PRIMITIVIST
PRIMITIVISTIC
PRIMITIVISTS
PRIMITIVITIES
PRIMITIVITY
PRIMNESSES
PRIMOGENIAL
PRIMOGENIT
PRIMOGENITAL
PRIMOGENITARY
PRIMOGENITIVE
PRIMOGENITIVES
PRIMOGENITOR
PRIMOGENITORS

PRIMOGENITRICES	PRINTWHEEL	PRIVATIZING	PROCAMBIUM
PRIMOGENITRIX	PRINTWHEELS	PRIVILEGED	PROCAMBIUMS
PRIMOGENITRIXES	PRINTWORKS	PRIVILEGES	PROCAPITALIST
PRIMOGENITS	PRIORESSES	PRIVILEGING	PROCARBAZINE
PRIMOGENITURE	PRIORITIES	PRIZEFIGHT	PROCARBAZINES
PRIMOGENITURES	PRIORITISATION	PRIZEFIGHTER	PROCARYONS
PRIMORDIAL	PRIORITISATIONS	PRIZEFIGHTERS	PROCARYOTE
PRIMORDIALISM	PRIORITISE	PRIZEFIGHTING	PROCARYOTES
PRIMORDIALISMS	PRIORITISED	PRIZEFIGHTINGS	PROCARYOTIC
PRIMORDIALITIES	PRIORITISES	PRIZEFIGHTS	PROCATHEDRAL
PRIMORDIALITY	PRIORITISING	PRIZEWINNER	PROCATHEDRALS
PRIMORDIALLY	PRIORITIZATION	PRIZEWINNERS	PROCEDURAL
PRIMORDIALS	PRIORITIZATIONS	PRIZEWINNING	PROCEDURALLY
PRIMORDIUM	PRIORITIZE	PRIZEWOMAN	PROCEDURALS
PRIMROSING	PRIORITIZED	PRIZEWOMEN	PROCEDURES
PRIMULACEOUS	PRIORITIZES	PROABORTION	PROCEEDERS
PRIMULINES	PRIORITIZING	PROACTIONS	PROCEEDING
PRINCEDOMS	PRIORSHIPS	PROAIRESES	PROCEEDINGS
PRINCEHOOD	PRISMATICAL	PROAIRESIS	PROCELEUSMATIC
PRINCEHOODS	PRISMATICALLY	PROBABILIORISM	PROCELEUSMATICS
PRINCEKINS	PRISMATOID	PROBABILIORISMS	PROCELLARIAN
PRINCELETS	PRISMATOIDAL	PROBABILIORIST	PROCEPHALIC
PRINCELIER	PRISMATOIDS	PROBABILIORISTS	PROCERCOID
PRINCELIEST	PRISMOIDAL	PROBABILISM	PROCERCOIDS
PRINCELIKE	PRISONMENT	PROBABILISMS	PROCEREBRA
PRINCELINESS	PRISONMENTS	PROBABILIST	PROCEREBRAL
PRINCELINESSES	PRISSINESS	PROBABILISTIC	PROCEREBRUM
PRINCELING	PRISSINESSES	PROBABILISTS	PROCEREBRUMS
PRINCELINGS	PRISTINELY	PROBABILITIES	PROCERITIES
PRINCESHIP	PRIVATDOCENT	PROBABILITY	PROCESSABILITY
PRINCESHIPS	PRIVATDOCENTS	PROBATIONAL	PROCESSABLE
PRINCESSES	PRIVATDOZENT	PROBATIONALLY	PROCESSERS
PRINCESSLY	PRIVATDOZENTS	PROBATIONARIES	PROCESSIBILITY
PRINCIFIED	PRIVATEERED	PROBATIONARY	PROCESSIBLE
PRINCIPALITIES	PRIVATEERING	PROBATIONER	PROCESSING
PRINCIPALITY	PRIVATEERINGS	PROBATIONERS	PROCESSINGS
PRINCIPALLY	PRIVATEERS	PROBATIONERSHIP	PROCESSION
PRINCIPALNESS	PRIVATEERSMAN	PROBATIONS	PROCESSIONAL
PRINCIPALNESSES	PRIVATEERSMEN	PROBATIVELY	PROCESSIONALIST
PRINCIPALS	PRIVATENESS	PROBENECID	PROCESSIONALLY
PRINCIPALSHIP	PRIVATENESSES	PROBENECIDS	PROCESSIONALS
PRINCIPALSHIPS	PRIVATIONS	PROBIOTICS	PROCESSIONARY
PRINCIPATE	PRIVATISATION	PROBLEMATIC	PROCESSIONED
PRINCIPATES	PRIVATISATIONS	PROBLEMATICAL	PROCESSIONER
PRINCIPIAL	PRIVATISED	PROBLEMATICALLY	PROCESSIONERS
PRINCIPIUM	PRIVATISER	PROBLEMATICS	PROCESSIONING
PRINCIPLED	PRIVATISERS	PROBLEMIST	PROCESSIONINGS
PRINCIPLES	PRIVATISES	PROBLEMISTS	PROCESSIONS
PRINCIPLING	PRIVATISING	PROBOSCIDEAN	PROCESSORS
PRINTABILITIES	PRIVATISMS	PROBOSCIDEANS	PROCESSUAL
PRINTABILITY	PRIVATISTS	PROBOSCIDES	PROCHRONISM
PRINTABLENESS	PRIVATIVELY	PROBOSCIDIAN	PROCHRONISMS
PRINTABLENESSES	PRIVATIVES	PROBOSCIDIANS	PROCIDENCE
PRINTERIES	PRIVATIZATION	PROBOSCISES	PROCIDENCES
PRINTHEADS	PRIVATIZATIONS	PROBOULEUTIC	PROCLAIMANT
PRINTMAKER	PRIVATIZED	PROBUSINESS	PROCLAIMANTS
PRINTMAKERS	PRIVATIZER	PROCACIOUS	PROCLAIMED
PRINTMAKING	PRIVATIZERS	PROCACITIES	PROCLAIMER
PRINTMAKINGS	PRIVATIZES	PROCAMBIAL	PROCLAIMERS

PROCLAIMING
PROCLAMATION
PROCLAMATIONS
PROCLAMATORY
PROCLITICS
PROCLIVITIES
PROCLIVITY
PROCOELOUS
PROCONSULAR
PROCONSULATE
PROCONSULATES
PROCONSULS
PROCONSULSHIP
PROCONSULSHIPS
PROCRASTINATE
PROCRASTINATED
PROCRASTINATES
PROCRASTINATING
PROCRASTINATION
PROCRASTINATIVE
PROCRASTINATOR
PROCRASTINATORS
PROCRASTINATORY
PROCREANTS
PROCREATED
PROCREATES
PROCREATING
PROCREATION
PROCREATIONAL
PROCREATIONS
PROCREATIVE
PROCREATIVENESS
PROCREATOR
PROCREATORS
PROCRUSTEAN
PROCRYPSES
PROCRYPSIS
PROCRYPTIC
PROCRYPTICALLY
PROCTALGIA
PROCTALGIAS
PROCTITIDES
PROCTITISES
PROCTODAEA
PROCTODAEAL
PROCTODAEUM
PROCTODAEUMS
PROCTODEUM
PROCTODEUMS
PROCTOLOGIC
PROCTOLOGICAL
PROCTOLOGIES
PROCTOLOGIST
PROCTOLOGISTS
PROCTOLOGY
PROCTORAGE
PROCTORAGES
PROCTORIAL
PROCTORIALLY

PROCTORING
PROCTORISE
PROCTORISED
PROCTORISES
PROCTORISING
PROCTORIZE
PROCTORIZED
PROCTORIZES
PROCTORIZING
PROCTORSHIP
PROCTORSHIPS
PROCTOSCOPE
PROCTOSCOPES
PROCTOSCOPIC
PROCTOSCOPIES
PROCTOSCOPY
PROCUMBENT
PROCURABLE
PROCURACIES
PROCURANCE
PROCURANCES
PROCURATION
PROCURATIONS
PROCURATOR
PROCURATORIAL
PROCURATORIES
PROCURATORS
PROCURATORSHIP
PROCURATORSHIPS
PROCURATORY
PROCUREMENT
PROCUREMENTS
PROCURESSES
PROCUREURS
PRODIGALISE
PRODIGALISED
PRODIGALISES
PRODIGALISING
PRODIGALITIES
PRODIGALITY
PRODIGALIZE
PRODIGALIZED
PRODIGALIZES
PRODIGALIZING
PRODIGALLY
PRODIGIOSITIES
PRODIGIOSITY
PRODIGIOUS
PRODIGIOUSLY
PRODIGIOUSNESS
PRODITORIOUS
PRODNOSING
PRODROMATA
PRODUCEMENT
PRODUCEMENTS
PRODUCIBILITIES
PRODUCIBILITY
PRODUCIBLE
PRODUCTIBILITY

PRODUCTILE
PRODUCTION
PRODUCTIONAL
PRODUCTIONS
PRODUCTIVE
PRODUCTIVELY
PRODUCTIVENESS
PRODUCTIVITIES
PRODUCTIVITY
PROEMBRYOS
PROENZYMES
PROESTRUSES
PROFANATION
PROFANATIONS
PROFANATORY
PROFANENESS
PROFANENESSES
PROFANITIES
PROFASCIST
PROFECTITIOUS
PROFEMINIST
PROFESSEDLY
PROFESSING
PROFESSION
PROFESSIONAL
PROFESSIONALISE
PROFESSIONALISM
PROFESSIONALIST
PROFESSIONALIZE
PROFESSIONALLY
PROFESSIONALS
PROFESSIONS
PROFESSORATE
PROFESSORATES
PROFESSORESS
PROFESSORESSES
PROFESSORIAL
PROFESSORIALLY
PROFESSORIAT
PROFESSORIATE
PROFESSORIATES
PROFESSORIATS
PROFESSORS
PROFESSORSHIP
PROFESSORSHIPS
PROFFERERS
PROFFERING
PROFICIENCE
PROFICIENCES
PROFICIENCIES
PROFICIENCY
PROFICIENT
PROFICIENTLY
PROFICIENTS
PROFILINGS
PROFILISTS
PROFITABILITIES
PROFITABILITY
PROFITABLE

PROFITABLENESS
PROFITABLY
PROFITEERED
PROFITEERING
PROFITEERINGS
PROFITEERS
PROFITEROLE
PROFITEROLES
PROFITINGS
PROFITLESS
PROFITLESSLY
PROFITWISE
PROFLIGACIES
PROFLIGACY
PROFLIGATE
PROFLIGATELY
PROFLIGATES
PROFLUENCE
PROFLUENCES
PROFOUNDER
PROFOUNDEST
PROFOUNDLY
PROFOUNDNESS
PROFOUNDNESSES
PROFULGENT
PROFUNDITIES
PROFUNDITY
PROFUSENESS
PROFUSENESSES
PROFUSIONS
PROGENITIVE
PROGENITIVENESS
PROGENITOR
PROGENITORIAL
PROGENITORS
PROGENITORSHIP
PROGENITORSHIPS
PROGENITRESS
PROGENITRESSES
PROGENITRICES
PROGENITRIX
PROGENITRIXES
PROGENITURE
PROGENITURES
PROGESTATIONAL
PROGESTERONE
PROGESTERONES
PROGESTINS
PROGESTOGEN
PROGESTOGENIC
PROGESTOGENS
PROGGINSES
PROGLOTTIC
PROGLOTTID
PROGLOTTIDEAN
PROGLOTTIDES
PROGLOTTIDS
PROGLOTTIS
PROGNATHIC

PROGNATHISM
PROGNATHISMS
PROGNATHOUS
PROGNOSING
PROGNOSTIC
PROGNOSTICATE
PROGNOSTICATED
PROGNOSTICATES
PROGNOSTICATING
PROGNOSTICATION
PROGNOSTICATIVE
PROGNOSTICATOR
PROGNOSTICATORS
PROGNOSTICS
PROGRADATION
PROGRADATIONS
PROGRADING
PROGRAMABLE
PROGRAMERS
PROGRAMING
PROGRAMINGS
PROGRAMMABILITY
PROGRAMMABLE
PROGRAMMABLES
PROGRAMMATIC
PROGRAMMED
PROGRAMMER
PROGRAMMERS
PROGRAMMES
PROGRAMMING
PROGRAMMINGS
PROGRESSED
PROGRESSES
PROGRESSING
PROGRESSION
PROGRESSIONAL
PROGRESSIONALLY
PROGRESSIONARY
PROGRESSIONISM
PROGRESSIONISMS
PROGRESSIONIST
PROGRESSIONISTS
PROGRESSIONS
PROGRESSISM
PROGRESSISMS
PROGRESSIST
PROGRESSISTS
PROGRESSIVE
PROGRESSIVELY
PROGRESSIVENESS
PROGRESSIVES
PROGRESSIVISM
PROGRESSIVISMS
PROGRESSIVIST
PROGRESSIVISTIC
PROGRESSIVISTS
PROGRESSIVITIES
PROGRESSIVITY
PROGYMNASIA

PROGYMNASIUM
PROGYMNASIUMS
PROHIBITED
PROHIBITER
PROHIBITERS
PROHIBITING
PROHIBITION
PROHIBITIONARY
PROHIBITIONISM
PROHIBITIONISMS
PROHIBITIONIST
PROHIBITIONISTS
PROHIBITIONS
PROHIBITIVE
PROHIBITIVELY
PROHIBITIVENESS
PROHIBITOR
PROHIBITORS
PROHIBITORY
PROINSULIN
PROINSULINS
PROJECTABLE
PROJECTILE
PROJECTILES
PROJECTING
PROJECTINGS
PROJECTION
PROJECTIONAL
PROJECTIONIST
PROJECTIONISTS
PROJECTIONS
PROJECTISATION
PROJECTISATIONS
PROJECTIVE
PROJECTIVELY
PROJECTIVITIES
PROJECTIVITY
PROJECTIZATION
PROJECTIZATIONS
PROJECTMENT
PROJECTMENTS
PROJECTORS
PROJECTURE
PROJECTURES
PROKARYONS
PROKARYOTE
PROKARYOTES
PROKARYOTIC
PROKARYOTS
PROLACTINS
PROLAMINES
PROLAPSING
PROLAPSUSES
PROLATENESS
PROLATENESSES
PROLATIONS
PROLEGOMENA
PROLEGOMENAL
PROLEGOMENARY

PROLEGOMENON
PROLEGOMENOUS
PROLEPTICAL
PROLEPTICALLY
PROLETARIAN
PROLETARIANISE
PROLETARIANISED
PROLETARIANISES
PROLETARIANISM
PROLETARIANISMS
PROLETARIANIZE
PROLETARIANIZED
PROLETARIANIZES
PROLETARIANNESS
PROLETARIANS
PROLETARIAT
PROLETARIATE
PROLETARIATES
PROLETARIATS
PROLETARIES
PROLICIDAL
PROLICIDES
PROLIFERATE
PROLIFERATED
PROLIFERATES
PROLIFERATING
PROLIFERATION
PROLIFERATIONS
PROLIFERATIVE
PROLIFEROUS
PROLIFEROUSLY
PROLIFICACIES
PROLIFICACY
PROLIFICAL
PROLIFICALLY
PROLIFICATION
PROLIFICATIONS
PROLIFICITIES
PROLIFICITY
PROLIFICNESS
PROLIFICNESSES
PROLIXIOUS
PROLIXITIES
PROLIXNESS
PROLIXNESSES
PROLOCUTION
PROLOCUTIONS
PROLOCUTOR
PROLOCUTORS
PROLOCUTORSHIP
PROLOCUTORSHIPS
PROLOCUTRICES
PROLOCUTRIX
PROLOCUTRIXES
PROLOGISED
PROLOGISES
PROLOGISING
PROLOGISTS
PROLOGIZED

PROLOGIZES
PROLOGIZING
PROLOGUING
PROLOGUISE
PROLOGUISED
PROLOGUISES
PROLOGUISING
PROLOGUIZE
PROLOGUIZED
PROLOGUIZES
PROLOGUIZING
PROLONGABLE
PROLONGATE
PROLONGATED
PROLONGATES
PROLONGATING
PROLONGATION
PROLONGATIONS
PROLONGERS
PROLONGING
PROLONGMENT
PROLONGMENTS
PROLUSIONS
PROMACHOSES
PROMENADED
PROMENADER
PROMENADERS
PROMENADES
PROMENADING
PROMETHAZINE
PROMETHAZINES
PROMETHEUM
PROMETHEUMS
PROMETHIUM
PROMETHIUMS
PROMILITARY
PROMINENCE
PROMINENCES
PROMINENCIES
PROMINENCY
PROMINENTLY
PROMINENTNESS
PROMINENTNESSES
PROMISCUITIES
PROMISCUITY
PROMISCUOUS
PROMISCUOUSLY
PROMISCUOUSNESS
PROMISEFUL
PROMISELESS
PROMISINGLY
PROMISSIVE
PROMISSORILY
PROMISSORS
PROMISSORY
PROMONARCHIST
PROMONTORIES
PROMONTORY
PROMOTABILITIES

PROMOTABILITY
PROMOTABLE
PROMOTIONAL
PROMOTIONS
PROMOTIVENESS
PROMOTIVENESSES
PROMPTBOOK
PROMPTBOOKS
PROMPTINGS
PROMPTITUDE
PROMPTITUDES
PROMPTNESS
PROMPTNESSES
PROMPTUARIES
PROMPTUARY
PROMPTURES
PROMULGATE
PROMULGATED
PROMULGATES
PROMULGATING
PROMULGATION
PROMULGATIONS
PROMULGATOR
PROMULGATORS
PROMULGING
PROMUSCIDATE
PROMUSCIDES
PROMYCELIA
PROMYCELIAL
PROMYCELIUM
PRONATIONS
PRONATORES
PRONENESSES
PRONEPHRIC
PRONEPHROI
PRONEPHROS
PRONEPHROSES
PRONGBUCKS
PRONGHORNS
PRONOMINAL
PRONOMINALISE
PRONOMINALISED
PRONOMINALISES
PRONOMINALISING
PRONOMINALIZE
PRONOMINALIZED
PRONOMINALIZES
PRONOMINALIZING
PRONOMINALLY
PRONOUNCEABLE
PRONOUNCED
PRONOUNCEDLY
PRONOUNCEMENT
PRONOUNCEMENTS
PRONOUNCER
PRONOUNCERS
PRONOUNCES
PRONOUNCING
PRONOUNCINGS

PRONUCLEAR
PRONUCLEARIST
PRONUCLEARISTS
PRONUCLEUS
PRONUCLEUSES
PRONUNCIAMENTO
PRONUNCIAMENTOS
PRONUNCIATION
PRONUNCIATIONAL
PRONUNCIATIONS
PRONUNCIOS
PROOEMIONS
PROOEMIUMS
PROOFREADER
PROOFREADERS
PROOFREADING
PROOFREADINGS
PROOFREADS
PROOFROOMS
PROPAEDEUTIC
PROPAEDEUTICAL
PROPAEDEUTICS
PROPAGABILITIES
PROPAGABILITY
PROPAGABLE
PROPAGABLENESS
PROPAGANDA
PROPAGANDAS
PROPAGANDISE
PROPAGANDISED
PROPAGANDISER
PROPAGANDISERS
PROPAGANDISES
PROPAGANDISING
PROPAGANDISM
PROPAGANDISMS
PROPAGANDIST
PROPAGANDISTIC
PROPAGANDISTS
PROPAGANDIZE
PROPAGANDIZED
PROPAGANDIZER
PROPAGANDIZERS
PROPAGANDIZES
PROPAGANDIZING
PROPAGATED
PROPAGATES
PROPAGATING
PROPAGATION
PROPAGATIONAL
PROPAGATIONS
PROPAGATIVE
PROPAGATOR
PROPAGATORS
PROPAGULES
PROPAGULUM
PROPANEDIOIC
PROPANONES
PROPAROXYTONE

PROPAROXYTONES
PROPELLANT
PROPELLANTS
PROPELLENT
PROPELLENTS
PROPELLERS
PROPELLING
PROPELLORS
PROPELMENT
PROPELMENTS
PROPENDENT
PROPENDING
PROPENSELY
PROPENSENESS
PROPENSENESSES
PROPENSION
PROPENSIONS
PROPENSITIES
PROPENSITY
PROPENSIVE
PROPERDINS
PROPERISPOMENON
PROPERNESS
PROPERNESSES
PROPERTIED
PROPERTIES
PROPERTYING
PROPERTYLESS
PROPHECIES
PROPHESIABLE
PROPHESIED
PROPHESIER
PROPHESIERS
PROPHESIES
PROPHESYING
PROPHESYINGS
PROPHETESS
PROPHETESSES
PROPHETHOOD
PROPHETHOODS
PROPHETICAL
PROPHETICALLY
PROPHETICISM
PROPHETICISMS
PROPHETISM
PROPHETISMS
PROPHETSHIP
PROPHETSHIPS
PROPHYLACTIC
PROPHYLACTICS
PROPHYLAXES
PROPHYLAXIS
PROPINQUITIES
PROPINQUITY
PROPIONATE
PROPIONATES
PROPITIABLE
PROPITIATE
PROPITIATED

PROPITIATES
PROPITIATING
PROPITIATION
PROPITIATIONS
PROPITIATIOUS
PROPITIATIVE
PROPITIATOR
PROPITIATORIES
PROPITIATORILY
PROPITIATORS
PROPITIATORY
PROPITIOUS
PROPITIOUSLY
PROPITIOUSNESS
PROPLASTID
PROPLASTIDS
PROPODEONS
PROPODEUMS
PROPOLISES
PROPONENTS
PROPORTION
PROPORTIONABLE
PROPORTIONABLY
PROPORTIONAL
PROPORTIONALITY
PROPORTIONALLY
PROPORTIONALS
PROPORTIONATE
PROPORTIONATED
PROPORTIONATELY
PROPORTIONATES
PROPORTIONATING
PROPORTIONED
PROPORTIONING
PROPORTIONINGS
PROPORTIONLESS
PROPORTIONMENT
PROPORTIONMENTS
PROPORTIONS
PROPOSABLE
PROPOSITAE
PROPOSITION
PROPOSITIONAL
PROPOSITIONALLY
PROPOSITIONED
PROPOSITIONING
PROPOSITIONS
PROPOSITUS
PROPOUNDED
PROPOUNDER
PROPOUNDERS
PROPOUNDING
PROPOXYPHENE
PROPOXYPHENES
PROPRAETOR
PROPRAETORIAL
PROPRAETORIAN
PROPRAETORS
PROPRANOLOL

PROPRANOLOLS
PROPRETORS
PROPRIETARIES
PROPRIETARILY
PROPRIETARY
PROPRIETIES
PROPRIETOR
PROPRIETORIAL
PROPRIETORIALLY
PROPRIETORS
PROPRIETORSHIP
PROPRIETORSHIPS
PROPRIETRESS
PROPRIETRESSES
PROPRIETRICES
PROPRIETRIX
PROPRIETRIXES
PROPRIOCEPTION
PROPRIOCEPTIONS
PROPRIOCEPTIVE
PROPRIOCEPTOR
PROPRIOCEPTORS
PROPROCTOR
PROPROCTORS
PROPUGNATION
PROPUGNATIONS
PROPULSION
PROPULSIONS
PROPULSIVE
PROPULSORS
PROPULSORY
PROPYLAEUM
PROPYLAMINE
PROPYLAMINES
PROPYLENES
PROPYLITES
PROPYLITISATION
PROPYLITISE
PROPYLITISED
PROPYLITISES
PROPYLITISING
PROPYLITIZATION
PROPYLITIZE
PROPYLITIZED
PROPYLITIZES
PROPYLITIZING
PRORATABLE
PRORATIONS
PRORECTORS
PROROGATED
PROROGATES
PROROGATING
PROROGATION
PROROGATIONS
PROROGUING
PROSAICALLY
PROSAICALNESS
PROSAICALNESSES
PROSAICISM

PROSAICISMS
PROSAICNESS
PROSAICNESSES
PROSATEURS
PROSAUROPOD
PROSAUROPODS
PROSCENIUM
PROSCENIUMS
PROSCIUTTI
PROSCIUTTO
PROSCIUTTOS
PROSCRIBED
PROSCRIBER
PROSCRIBERS
PROSCRIBES
PROSCRIBING
PROSCRIPTION
PROSCRIPTIONS
PROSCRIPTIVE
PROSCRIPTIVELY
PROSCRIPTS
PROSECTING
PROSECTORIAL
PROSECTORS
PROSECTORSHIP
PROSECTORSHIPS
PROSECUTABLE
PROSECUTED
PROSECUTES
PROSECUTING
PROSECUTION
PROSECUTIONS
PROSECUTOR
PROSECUTORIAL
PROSECUTORS
PROSECUTRICES
PROSECUTRIX
PROSECUTRIXES
PROSELYTED
PROSELYTES
PROSELYTIC
PROSELYTING
PROSELYTISATION
PROSELYTISE
PROSELYTISED
PROSELYTISER
PROSELYTISERS
PROSELYTISES
PROSELYTISING
PROSELYTISM
PROSELYTISMS
PROSELYTIZATION
PROSELYTIZE
PROSELYTIZED
PROSELYTIZER
PROSELYTIZERS
PROSELYTIZES
PROSELYTIZING
PROSEMINAR

PROSEMINARS
PROSENCEPHALA
PROSENCEPHALIC
PROSENCEPHALON
PROSENCHYMA
PROSENCHYMAS
PROSENCHYMATA
PROSENCHYMATOUS
PROSEUCHAE
PROSIFYING
PROSILIENCIES
PROSILIENCY
PROSILIENT
PROSIMIANS
PROSINESSES
PROSLAMBANOMENE
PROSLAVERY
PROSOBRANCH
PROSOBRANCHS
PROSODIANS
PROSODICAL
PROSODICALLY
PROSODISTS
PROSOPAGNOSIA
PROSOPAGNOSIAS
PROSOPOGRAPHER
PROSOPOGRAPHERS
PROSOPOGRAPHIES
PROSOPOGRAPHY
PROSOPOPEIA
PROSOPOPEIAL
PROSOPOPEIAS
PROSOPOPOEIA
PROSOPOPOEIAL
PROSOPOPOEIAS
PROSPECTED
PROSPECTING
PROSPECTINGS
PROSPECTION
PROSPECTIONS
PROSPECTIVE
PROSPECTIVELY
PROSPECTIVENESS
PROSPECTIVES
PROSPECTLESS
PROSPECTOR
PROSPECTORS
PROSPECTUS
PROSPECTUSES
PROSPERING
PROSPERITIES
PROSPERITY
PROSPEROUS
PROSPEROUSLY
PROSPEROUSNESS
PROSTACYCLIN
PROSTACYCLINS
PROSTAGLANDIN
PROSTAGLANDINS

PROSTANTHERA
PROSTANTHERAS
PROSTATECTOMIES
PROSTATECTOMY
PROSTATISM
PROSTATISMS
PROSTATITIS
PROSTATITISES
PROSTERNUM
PROSTERNUMS
PROSTHESES
PROSTHESIS
PROSTHETIC
PROSTHETICALLY
PROSTHETICS
PROSTHETIST
PROSTHETISTS
PROSTHODONTIA
PROSTHODONTIAS
PROSTHODONTICS
PROSTHODONTIST
PROSTHODONTISTS
PROSTITUTE
PROSTITUTED
PROSTITUTES
PROSTITUTING
PROSTITUTION
PROSTITUTIONS
PROSTITUTOR
PROSTITUTORS
PROSTOMIAL
PROSTOMIUM
PROSTOMIUMS
PROSTRATED
PROSTRATES
PROSTRATING
PROSTRATION
PROSTRATIONS
PROSYLLOGISM
PROSYLLOGISMS
PROTACTINIUM
PROTACTINIUMS
PROTAGONISM
PROTAGONISMS
PROTAGONIST
PROTAGONISTS
PROTAMINES
PROTANDRIES
PROTANDROUS
PROTANOMALIES
PROTANOMALOUS
PROTANOMALY
PROTANOPES
PROTANOPIA
PROTANOPIAS
PROTANOPIC
PROTEACEOUS
PROTECTANT
PROTECTANTS

PROTECTERS
PROTECTING
PROTECTINGLY
PROTECTION
PROTECTIONISM
PROTECTIONISMS
PROTECTIONIST
PROTECTIONISTS
PROTECTIONS
PROTECTIVE
PROTECTIVELY
PROTECTIVENESS
PROTECTIVES
PROTECTORAL
PROTECTORATE
PROTECTORATES
PROTECTORIAL
PROTECTORIES
PROTECTORLESS
PROTECTORS
PROTECTORSHIP
PROTECTORSHIPS
PROTECTORY
PROTECTRESS
PROTECTRESSES
PROTECTRICES
PROTECTRIX
PROTECTRIXES
PROTEIFORM
PROTEINACEOUS
PROTEINASE
PROTEINASES
PROTEINOUS
PROTEINURIA
PROTEINURIAS
PROTENDING
PROTENSION
PROTENSIONS
PROTENSITIES
PROTENSITY
PROTENSIVE
PROTENSIVELY
PROTEOCLASTIC
PROTEOGLYCAN
PROTEOGLYCANS
PROTEOLYSE
PROTEOLYSED
PROTEOLYSES
PROTEOLYSING
PROTEOLYSIS
PROTEOLYTIC
PROTEOLYTICALLY
PROTEOMICS
PROTERANDRIES
PROTERANDROUS
PROTERANDRY
PROTEROGYNIES
PROTEROGYNOUS
PROTEROGYNY

PROTERVITIES
PROTERVITY
PROTESTANT
PROTESTANTS
PROTESTATION
PROTESTATIONS
PROTESTERS
PROTESTING
PROTESTINGLY
PROTESTORS
PROTHALAMIA
PROTHALAMION
PROTHALAMIUM
PROTHALLIA
PROTHALLIAL
PROTHALLIC
PROTHALLIUM
PROTHALLOID
PROTHALLUS
PROTHALLUSES
PROTHETICALLY
PROTHONOTARIAL
PROTHONOTARIAT
PROTHONOTARIATS
PROTHONOTARIES
PROTHONOTARY
PROTHORACES
PROTHORACIC
PROTHORAXES
PROTHROMBIN
PROTHROMBINS
PROTISTANS
PROTISTOLOGIES
PROTISTOLOGIST
PROTISTOLOGISTS
PROTISTOLOGY
PROTOACTINIUM
PROTOACTINIUMS
PROTOAVISES
PROTOCHORDATE
PROTOCHORDATES
PROTOCOCCAL
PROTOCOLED
PROTOCOLIC
PROTOCOLING
PROTOCOLISE
PROTOCOLISED
PROTOCOLISES
PROTOCOLISING
PROTOCOLIST
PROTOCOLISTS
PROTOCOLIZE
PROTOCOLIZED
PROTOCOLIZES
PROTOCOLIZING
PROTOCOLLED
PROTOCOLLING
PROTOCTIST
PROTOCTISTS

PROTODERMS
PROTOGALAXIES
PROTOGALAXY
PROTOGENIC
PROTOGINES
PROTOGYNIES
PROTOGYNOUS
PROTOHISTORIAN
PROTOHISTORIANS
PROTOHISTORIC
PROTOHISTORIES
PROTOHISTORY
PROTOHUMAN
PROTOHUMANS
PROTOLANGUAGE
PROTOLANGUAGES
PROTOLITHIC
PROTOMARTYR
PROTOMARTYRS
PROTOMORPHIC
PROTONATED
PROTONATES
PROTONATING
PROTONATION
PROTONATIONS
PROTONEMAL
PROTONEMATA
PROTONEMATAL
PROTONOTARIAL
PROTONOTARIAT
PROTONOTARIATS
PROTONOTARIES
PROTONOTARY
PROTOPATHIC
PROTOPATHIES
PROTOPATHY
PROTOPHILIC
PROTOPHLOEM
PROTOPHLOEMS
PROTOPHYTE
PROTOPHYTES
PROTOPHYTIC
PROTOPLANET
PROTOPLANETARY
PROTOPLANETS
PROTOPLASM
PROTOPLASMAL
PROTOPLASMATIC
PROTOPLASMIC
PROTOPLASMS
PROTOPLAST
PROTOPLASTIC
PROTOPLASTS
PROTOPORPHYRIN
PROTOPORPHYRINS
PROTOSPATAIRE
PROTOSPATAIRES
PROTOSPATHAIRE
PROTOSPATHAIRES

PROTOSPATHARIUS
PROTOSTARS
PROTOSTELE
PROTOSTELES
PROTOSTELIC
PROTOSTOME
PROTOSTOMES
PROTOTHERIAN
PROTOTHERIANS
PROTOTROPH
PROTOTROPHIC
PROTOTROPHIES
PROTOTROPHS
PROTOTROPHY
PROTOTYPAL
PROTOTYPED
PROTOTYPES
PROTOTYPIC
PROTOTYPICAL
PROTOTYPICALLY
PROTOTYPING
PROTOXIDES
PROTOXYLEM
PROTOXYLEMS
PROTOZOANS
PROTOZOOLOGICAL
PROTOZOOLOGIES
PROTOZOOLOGIST
PROTOZOOLOGISTS
PROTOZOOLOGY
PROTOZOONS
PROTRACTED
PROTRACTEDLY
PROTRACTEDNESS
PROTRACTIBLE
PROTRACTILE
PROTRACTING
PROTRACTION
PROTRACTIONS
PROTRACTIVE
PROTRACTOR
PROTRACTORS
PROTREPTIC
PROTREPTICAL
PROTREPTICS
PROTRUDABLE
PROTRUDENT
PROTRUDING
PROTRUSIBLE
PROTRUSILE
PROTRUSION
PROTRUSIONS
PROTRUSIVE
PROTRUSIVELY
PROTRUSIVENESS
PROTUBERANCE
PROTUBERANCES
PROTUBERANCIES
PROTUBERANCY

PROTUBERANT
PROTUBERANTLY
PROTUBERATE
PROTUBERATED
PROTUBERATES
PROTUBERATING
PROTUBERATION
PROTUBERATIONS
PROUDHEARTED
PROUDNESSES
PROUSTITES
PROVABILITIES
PROVABILITY
PROVABLENESS
PROVABLENESSES
PROVASCULAR
PROVECTION
PROVECTIONS
PROVEDITOR
PROVEDITORE
PROVEDITORES
PROVEDITORS
PROVEDORES
PROVENANCE
PROVENANCES
PROVENDERED
PROVENDERING
PROVENDERS
PROVENIENCE
PROVENIENCES
PROVENTRICULAR
PROVENTRICULI
PROVENTRICULUS
PROVERBIAL
PROVERBIALISE
PROVERBIALISED
PROVERBIALISES
PROVERBIALISING
PROVERBIALISM
PROVERBIALISMS
PROVERBIALIST
PROVERBIALISTS
PROVERBIALIZE
PROVERBIALIZED
PROVERBIALIZES
PROVERBIALIZING
PROVERBIALLY
PROVERBING
PROVIDABLE
PROVIDENCE
PROVIDENCES
PROVIDENTIAL
PROVIDENTIALLY
PROVIDENTLY
PROVINCEWIDE
PROVINCIAL
PROVINCIALISE
PROVINCIALISED
PROVINCIALISES

PROVINCIALISING
PROVINCIALISM
PROVINCIALISMS
PROVINCIALIST
PROVINCIALISTS
PROVINCIALITIES
PROVINCIALITY
PROVINCIALIZE
PROVINCIALIZED
PROVINCIALIZES
PROVINCIALIZING
PROVINCIALLY
PROVINCIALS
PROVIRUSES
PROVISIONAL
PROVISIONALLY
PROVISIONALS
PROVISIONARIES
PROVISIONARY
PROVISIONED
PROVISIONER
PROVISIONERS
PROVISIONING
PROVISIONS
PROVISORILY
PROVITAMIN
PROVITAMINS
PROVOCABLE
PROVOCANTS
PROVOCATEUR
PROVOCATEURS
PROVOCATION
PROVOCATIONS
PROVOCATIVE
PROVOCATIVELY
PROVOCATIVENESS
PROVOCATIVES
PROVOCATOR
PROVOCATORS
PROVOCATORY
PROVOKABLE
PROVOKEMENT
PROVOKEMENTS
PROVOKINGLY
PROVOLONES
PROVOSTRIES
PROVOSTSHIP
PROVOSTSHIPS
PROWLINGLY
PROXIMALLY
PROXIMATELY
PROXIMATENESS
PROXIMATENESSES
PROXIMATION
PROXIMATIONS
PROXIMITIES
PROZYMITES
PRUDENTIAL
PRUDENTIALISM

PRUDENTIALISMS
PRUDENTIALIST
PRUDENTIALISTS
PRUDENTIALITIES
PRUDENTIALITY
PRUDENTIALLY
PRUDENTIALS
PRUDISHNESS
PRUDISHNESSES
PRURIENCES
PRURIENCIES
PRURIENTLY
PRURIGINOUS
PRURITUSES
PRUSSIANISATION
PRUSSIANISE
PRUSSIANISED
PRUSSIANISES
PRUSSIANISING
PRUSSIANIZATION
PRUSSIANIZE
PRUSSIANIZED
PRUSSIANIZES
PRUSSIANIZING
PRUSSIATES
PSALIGRAPHIES
PSALIGRAPHY
PSALMBOOKS
PSALMODICAL
PSALMODIES
PSALMODISE
PSALMODISED
PSALMODISES
PSALMODISING
PSALMODIST
PSALMODISTS
PSALMODIZE
PSALMODIZED
PSALMODIZES
PSALMODIZING
PSALTERIAN
PSALTERIES
PSALTERIUM
PSALTRESSES
PSAMMOPHIL
PSAMMOPHILE
PSAMMOPHILES
PSAMMOPHILOUS
PSAMMOPHILS
PSAMMOPHYTE
PSAMMOPHYTES
PSAMMOPHYTIC
PSELLISMUS
PSELLISMUSES
PSEPHOANALYSES
PSEPHOANALYSIS
PSEPHOLOGICAL
PSEPHOLOGICALLY
PSEPHOLOGIES

PSEPHOLOGIST
PSEPHOLOGISTS
PSEPHOLOGY
PSEUDAESTHESIA
PSEUDAESTHESIAS
PSEUDARTHROSES
PSEUDARTHROSIS
PSEUDEPIGRAPH
PSEUDEPIGRAPHA
PSEUDEPIGRAPHIC
PSEUDEPIGRAPHON
PSEUDEPIGRAPHS
PSEUDEPIGRAPHY
PSEUDERIES
PSEUDIMAGINES
PSEUDIMAGO
PSEUDIMAGOS
PSEUDOACID
PSEUDOACIDS
PSEUDOALLELE
PSEUDOALLELES
PSEUDOARTHROSES
PSEUDOARTHROSIS
PSEUDOBULB
PSEUDOBULBS
PSEUDOCARP
PSEUDOCARPOUS
PSEUDOCARPS
PSEUDOCLASSIC
PSEUDOCLASSICS
PSEUDOCODE
PSEUDOCODES
PSEUDOCOEL
PSEUDOCOELOMATE
PSEUDOCOELS
PSEUDOCYESES
PSEUDOCYESIS
PSEUDOEPHEDRINE
PSEUDOGRAPH
PSEUDOGRAPHIES
PSEUDOGRAPHS
PSEUDOGRAPHY
PSEUDOLOGIA
PSEUDOLOGIAS
PSEUDOLOGIES
PSEUDOLOGUE
PSEUDOLOGUES
PSEUDOLOGY
PSEUDOMARTYR
PSEUDOMARTYRS
PSEUDOMEMBRANE
PSEUDOMEMBRANES
PSEUDOMONAD
PSEUDOMONADES
PSEUDOMONADS
PSEUDOMONAS
PSEUDOMORPH
PSEUDOMORPHIC
PSEUDOMORPHISM

PSEUDOMORPHISMS
PSEUDOMORPHOUS
PSEUDOMORPHS
PSEUDOMUTUALITY
PSEUDONYMITIES
PSEUDONYMITY
PSEUDONYMOUS
PSEUDONYMOUSLY
PSEUDONYMS
PSEUDOPODAL
PSEUDOPODIA
PSEUDOPODIAL
PSEUDOPODIUM
PSEUDOPODS
PSEUDOPREGNANCY
PSEUDOPREGNANT
PSEUDORANDOM
PSEUDOSCALAR
PSEUDOSCALARS
PSEUDOSCIENCE
PSEUDOSCIENCES
PSEUDOSCIENTIST
PSEUDOSCOPE
PSEUDOSCOPES
PSEUDOSCORPION
PSEUDOSCORPIONS
PSEUDOSOLUTION
PSEUDOSOLUTIONS
PSEUDOSYMMETRY
PSEUDOVECTOR
PSEUDOVECTORS
PSILANTHROPIC
PSILANTHROPIES
PSILANTHROPISM
PSILANTHROPISMS
PSILANTHROPIST
PSILANTHROPISTS
PSILANTHROPY
PSILOCYBIN
PSILOCYBINS
PSILOMELANE
PSILOMELANES
PSILOPHYTE
PSILOPHYTES
PSILOPHYTIC
PSITTACINE
PSITTACINES
PSITTACOSES
PSITTACOSIS
PSITTACOTIC
PSORIATICS
PSYCHAGOGUE
PSYCHAGOGUES
PSYCHASTHENIA
PSYCHASTHENIAS
PSYCHASTHENIC
PSYCHASTHENICS
PSYCHEDELIA
PSYCHEDELIAS

PSYCHEDELIC
PSYCHEDELICALLY
PSYCHEDELICS
PSYCHIATER
PSYCHIATERS
PSYCHIATRIC
PSYCHIATRICAL
PSYCHIATRICALLY
PSYCHIATRIES
PSYCHIATRIST
PSYCHIATRISTS
PSYCHIATRY
PSYCHICALLY
PSYCHICISM
PSYCHICISMS
PSYCHICIST
PSYCHICISTS
PSYCHOACOUSTIC
PSYCHOACOUSTICS
PSYCHOACTIVE
PSYCHOANALYSE
PSYCHOANALYSED
PSYCHOANALYSER
PSYCHOANALYSERS
PSYCHOANALYSES
PSYCHOANALYSING
PSYCHOANALYSIS
PSYCHOANALYST
PSYCHOANALYSTS
PSYCHOANALYTIC
PSYCHOANALYZE
PSYCHOANALYZED
PSYCHOANALYZER
PSYCHOANALYZERS
PSYCHOANALYZES
PSYCHOANALYZING
PSYCHOBABBLE
PSYCHOBABBLER
PSYCHOBABBLERS
PSYCHOBABBLES
PSYCHOBILLIES
PSYCHOBILLY
PSYCHOBIOGRAPHY
PSYCHOBIOLOGIC
PSYCHOBIOLOGIES
PSYCHOBIOLOGIST
PSYCHOBIOLOGY
PSYCHOCHEMICAL
PSYCHOCHEMICALS
PSYCHOCHEMISTRY
PSYCHODELIA
PSYCHODELIAS
PSYCHODELIC
PSYCHODELICALLY
PSYCHODRAMA
PSYCHODRAMAS
PSYCHODRAMATIC
PSYCHODYNAMIC
PSYCHODYNAMICS

PSYCHOGALVANIC
PSYCHOGASES
PSYCHOGENESES
PSYCHOGENESIS
PSYCHOGENETIC
PSYCHOGENETICAL
PSYCHOGENETICS
PSYCHOGENIC
PSYCHOGENICALLY
PSYCHOGERIATRIC
PSYCHOGNOSES
PSYCHOGNOSIS
PSYCHOGNOSTIC
PSYCHOGONIES
PSYCHOGONY
PSYCHOGRAM
PSYCHOGRAMS
PSYCHOGRAPH
PSYCHOGRAPHIC
PSYCHOGRAPHICAL
PSYCHOGRAPHICS
PSYCHOGRAPHIES
PSYCHOGRAPHS
PSYCHOGRAPHY
PSYCHOHISTORIAN
PSYCHOHISTORIES
PSYCHOHISTORY
PSYCHOKINESES
PSYCHOKINESIS
PSYCHOKINETIC
PSYCHOLINGUIST
PSYCHOLINGUISTS
PSYCHOLOGIC
PSYCHOLOGICAL
PSYCHOLOGICALLY
PSYCHOLOGIES
PSYCHOLOGISE
PSYCHOLOGISED
PSYCHOLOGISES
PSYCHOLOGISING
PSYCHOLOGISM
PSYCHOLOGISMS
PSYCHOLOGIST
PSYCHOLOGISTIC
PSYCHOLOGISTS
PSYCHOLOGIZE
PSYCHOLOGIZED
PSYCHOLOGIZES
PSYCHOLOGIZING
PSYCHOLOGY
PSYCHOMACHIA
PSYCHOMACHIAS
PSYCHOMACHIES
PSYCHOMACHY
PSYCHOMETER
PSYCHOMETERS
PSYCHOMETRIC
PSYCHOMETRICAL
PSYCHOMETRICIAN

PSYCHOMETRICS
PSYCHOMETRIES
PSYCHOMETRIST
PSYCHOMETRISTS
PSYCHOMETRY
PSYCHOMOTOR
PSYCHONEUROSES
PSYCHONEUROSIS
PSYCHONEUROTIC
PSYCHONEUROTICS
PSYCHONOMIC
PSYCHONOMICS
PSYCHOPATH
PSYCHOPATHIC
PSYCHOPATHICS
PSYCHOPATHIES
PSYCHOPATHIST
PSYCHOPATHISTS
PSYCHOPATHOLOGY
PSYCHOPATHS
PSYCHOPATHY
PSYCHOPHILIES
PSYCHOPHILY
PSYCHOPHYSICAL
PSYCHOPHYSICIST
PSYCHOPHYSICS
PSYCHOPOMP
PSYCHOPOMPS
PSYCHOSEXUAL
PSYCHOSEXUALITY
PSYCHOSEXUALLY
PSYCHOSOCIAL
PSYCHOSOCIALLY
PSYCHOSOMATIC
PSYCHOSOMATICS
PSYCHOSOMIMETIC
PSYCHOSURGEON
PSYCHOSURGEONS
PSYCHOSURGERIES
PSYCHOSURGERY
PSYCHOSURGICAL
PSYCHOSYNTHESES
PSYCHOSYNTHESIS
PSYCHOTECHNICS
PSYCHOTHERAPIES
PSYCHOTHERAPIST
PSYCHOTHERAPY
PSYCHOTICALLY
PSYCHOTICISM
PSYCHOTICISMS
PSYCHOTICS
PSYCHOTOMIMETIC
PSYCHOTOXIC
PSYCHOTROPIC
PSYCHOTROPICS
PSYCHROMETER
PSYCHROMETERS
PSYCHROMETRIC
PSYCHROMETRICAL

PSYCHROMETRIES	PUBLICIZES	PULSATANCES	PUNCHINESS
PSYCHROMETRY	PUBLICIZING	PULSATILITIES	PUNCHINESSES
PSYCHROPHILIC	PUBLICNESS	PULSATILITY	PUNCTATION
PTARMIGANS	PUBLICNESSES	PULSATILLA	PUNCTATIONS
PTERANODON	PUBLISHABLE	PULSATILLAS	PUNCTATORS
PTERANODONS	PUBLISHERS	PULSATIONS	PUNCTILIOS
PTERIDINES	PUBLISHING	PULSATIVELY	PUNCTILIOUS
PTERIDOLOGICAL	PUBLISHINGS	PULSELESSNESS	PUNCTILIOUSLY
PTERIDOLOGIES	PUBLISHMENT	PULSELESSNESSES	PUNCTILIOUSNESS
PTERIDOLOGIST	PUBLISHMENTS	PULSIMETER	PUNCTUALIST
PTERIDOLOGISTS	PUCCINIACEOUS	PULSIMETERS	PUNCTUALISTS
PTERIDOLOGY	PUCKERIEST	PULSOMETER	PUNCTUALITIES
PTERIDOMANIA	PUCKISHNESS	PULSOMETERS	PUNCTUALITY
PTERIDOMANIAS	PUCKISHNESSES	PULTACEOUS	PUNCTUALLY
PTERIDOPHILIST	PUDDENINGS	PULTRUSION	PUNCTUATED
PTERIDOPHILISTS	PUDGINESSES	PULTRUSIONS	PUNCTUATES
PTERIDOPHYTE	PUDIBUNDITIES	PULVERABLE	PUNCTUATING
PTERIDOPHYTES	PUDIBUNDITY	PULVERATION	PUNCTUATION
PTERIDOPHYTIC	PUDICITIES	PULVERATIONS	PUNCTUATIONIST
PTERIDOPHYTOUS	PUERILISMS	PULVERINES	PUNCTUATIONISTS
PTERIDOSPERM	PUERILITIES	PULVERISABLE	PUNCTUATIONS
PTERIDOSPERMS	PUERPERALLY	PULVERISATION	PUNCTUATIVE
PTERODACTYL	PUERPERIUM	PULVERISATIONS	PUNCTUATOR
PTERODACTYLE	PUERPERIUMS	PULVERISED	PUNCTUATORS
PTERODACTYLES	PUFFINESSES	PULVERISER	PUNCTULATE
PTERODACTYLS	PUFFTALOONAS	PULVERISERS	PUNCTULATED
PTEROSAURIAN	PUFTALOONIES	PULVERISES	PUNCTULATION
PTEROSAURIANS	PUFTALOONS	PULVERISING	PUNCTULATIONS
PTEROSAURS	PUGGINESSES	PULVERIZABLE	PUNCTURABLE
PTERYGIALS	PUGILISTIC	PULVERIZATION	PUNCTURATION
PTERYGIUMS	PUGILISTICAL	PULVERIZATIONS	PUNCTURATIONS
PTERYGOIDS	PUGILISTICALLY	PULVERIZED	PUNCTURERS
PTERYLOGRAPHIC	PUGNACIOUS	PULVERIZER	PUNCTURING
PTERYLOGRAPHIES	PUGNACIOUSLY	PULVERIZERS	PUNDIGRION
PTERYLOGRAPHY	PUGNACIOUSNESS	PULVERIZES	PUNDIGRIONS
PTERYLOSES	PUGNACITIES	PULVERIZING	PUNDITRIES
PTERYLOSIS	PUISSANCES	PULVERULENCE	PUNDONORES
PTOCHOCRACIES	PUISSANTLY	PULVERULENCES	PUNGENCIES
PTOCHOCRACY	PUISSAUNCE	PULVERULENT	PUNICACEOUS
PTYALAGOGIC	PUISSAUNCES	PULVILISED	PUNINESSES
PTYALAGOGUE	PULCHRITUDE	PULVILIZED	PUNISHABILITIES
PTYALAGOGUES	PULCHRITUDES	PULVILLIFORM	PUNISHABILITY
PTYALISING	PULCHRITUDINOUS	PULVILLING	PUNISHABLE
PTYALIZING	PULLULATED	PULVILLIOS	PUNISHINGLY
PUBCRAWLER	PULLULATES	PULVINATED	PUNISHMENT
PUBCRAWLERS	PULLULATING	PULVINULES	PUNISHMENTS
PUBERULENT	PULLULATION	PUMICATING	PUNITIVELY
PUBERULOUS	PULLULATIONS	PUMMELLING	PUNITIVENESS
PUBESCENCE	PULMOBRANCH	PUMPERNICKEL	PUNITIVENESSES
PUBESCENCES	PULMOBRANCHIATE	PUMPERNICKELS	PUNKINESSES
PUBLICALLY	PULMOBRANCHS	PUMPKINSEED	PUPIGEROUS
PUBLICATION	PULMONATES	PUMPKINSEEDS	PUPILABILITIES
PUBLICATIONS	PULPBOARDS	PUNCHBALLS	PUPILABILITY
PUBLICISED	PULPIFYING	PUNCHBOARD	PUPILARITIES
PUBLICISES	PULPINESSES	PUNCHBOARDS	PUPILARITY
PUBLICISING	PULPITEERS	PUNCHBOWLS	PUPILLAGES
PUBLICISTS	PULPITRIES	PUNCHINELLO	PUPILLARITIES
PUBLICITIES	PULPSTONES	PUNCHINELLOES	PUPILLARITY
PUBLICIZED	PULSATANCE	PUNCHINELLOS	PUPILSHIPS

PUPIPAROUS
PUPPETEERED
PUPPETEERING
PUPPETEERS
PUPPETLIKE
PUPPETRIES
PUPPYHOODS
PURBLINDLY
PURBLINDNESS
PURBLINDNESSES
PURCHASABILITY
PURCHASABLE
PURCHASERS
PURCHASING
PURDONIUMS
PUREBLOODS
PURENESSES
PURGATIONS
PURGATIVELY
PURGATIVES
PURGATORIAL
PURGATORIALLY
PURGATORIAN
PURGATORIES
PURIFICATION
PURIFICATIONS
PURIFICATIVE
PURIFICATOR
PURIFICATORS
PURIFICATORY
PURISTICAL
PURISTICALLY
PURITANICAL
PURITANICALLY
PURITANICALNESS
PURITANISE
PURITANISED
PURITANISES
PURITANISING
PURITANISM
PURITANISMS
PURITANIZE
PURITANIZED
PURITANIZES
PURITANIZING
PURLICUING
PURLOINERS
PURLOINING
PUROMYCINS
PURPLEHEART
PURPLEHEARTS
PURPLENESS
PURPLENESSES
PURPORTEDLY
PURPORTING
PURPORTLESS
PURPOSEFUL
PURPOSEFULLY
PURPOSEFULNESS

PURPOSELESS
PURPOSELESSLY
PURPOSELESSNESS
PURPOSIVELY
PURPOSIVENESS
PURPOSIVENESSES
PURPRESTURE
PURPRESTURES
PURSERSHIP
PURSERSHIPS
PURSINESSES
PURSUANCES
PURSUANTLY
PURSUINGLY
PURSUIVANT
PURSUIVANTS
PURTENANCE
PURTENANCES
PURULENCES
PURULENCIES
PURULENTLY
PURVEYANCE
PURVEYANCES
PUSCHKINIA
PUSCHKINIAS
PUSHCHAIRS
PUSHFULNESS
PUSHFULNESSES
PUSHINESSES
PUSHINGNESS
PUSHINGNESSES
PUSILLANIMITIES
PUSILLANIMITY
PUSILLANIMOUS
PUSILLANIMOUSLY
PUSSYFOOTED
PUSSYFOOTER
PUSSYFOOTERS
PUSSYFOOTING
PUSSYFOOTS
PUSTULANTS
PUSTULATED
PUSTULATES
PUSTULATING
PUSTULATION
PUSTULATIONS
PUTANGITANGI
PUTATIVELY
PUTONGHUAS
PUTREFACIENT
PUTREFACTION
PUTREFACTIONS
PUTREFACTIVE
PUTREFIABLE
PUTREFIERS
PUTREFYING
PUTRESCENCE
PUTRESCENCES
PUTRESCENT

PUTRESCIBILITY
PUTRESCIBLE
PUTRESCIBLES
PUTRESCINE
PUTRESCINES
PUTRIDITIES
PUTRIDNESS
PUTRIDNESSES
PUTSCHISTS
PUTTYROOTS
PUZZLEDOMS
PUZZLEHEADED
PUZZLEMENT
PUZZLEMENTS
PUZZLINGLY
PUZZOLANAS
PYCNIDIOSPORE
PYCNIDIOSPORES
PYCNOCONIDIA
PYCNOCONIDIUM
PYCNODYSOSTOSES
PYCNODYSOSTOSIS
PYCNOGONID
PYCNOGONIDS
PYCNOGONOID
PYCNOMETER
PYCNOMETERS
PYCNOMETRIC
PYCNOSPORE
PYCNOSPORES
PYCNOSTYLE
PYCNOSTYLES
PYELITISES
PYELOGRAMS
PYELOGRAPHIC
PYELOGRAPHIES
PYELOGRAPHY
PYELONEPHRITIC
PYELONEPHRITIS
PYGOSTYLES
PYKNODYSOSTOSES
PYKNODYSOSTOSIS
PYKNOMETER
PYKNOMETERS
PYKNOSOMES
PYLORECTOMIES
PYLORECTOMY
PYOGENESES
PYOGENESIS
PYORRHOEAL
PYORRHOEAS
PYORRHOEIC
PYRACANTHA
PYRACANTHAS
PYRACANTHS
PYRALIDIDS
PYRAMIDALLY
PYRAMIDICAL
PYRAMIDICALLY

PYRAMIDING
PYRAMIDION
PYRAMIDIONS
PYRAMIDIST
PYRAMIDISTS
PYRAMIDOLOGIES
PYRAMIDOLOGIST
PYRAMIDOLOGISTS
PYRAMIDOLOGY
PYRAMIDONS
PYRANOMETER
PYRANOMETERS
PYRANOSIDE
PYRANOSIDES
PYRARGYRITE
PYRARGYRITES
PYRENEITES
PYRENOCARP
PYRENOCARPS
PYRENOMYCETOUS
PYRETHRINS
PYRETHROID
PYRETHROIDS
PYRETHRUMS
PYRETOLOGIES
PYRETOLOGY
PYRETOTHERAPIES
PYRETOTHERAPY
PYRGEOMETER
PYRGEOMETERS
PYRHELIOMETER
PYRHELIOMETERS
PYRHELIOMETRIC
PYRIDOXALS
PYRIDOXAMINE
PYRIDOXAMINES
PYRIDOXINE
PYRIDOXINES
PYRIDOXINS
PYRIMETHAMINE
PYRIMETHAMINES
PYRIMIDINE
PYRIMIDINES
PYRITHIAMINE
PYRITHIAMINES
PYRITIFEROUS
PYRITISING
PYRITIZING
PYRITOHEDRA
PYRITOHEDRAL
PYRITOHEDRON
PYROBALLOGIES
PYROBALLOGY
PYROCATECHIN
PYROCATECHINS
PYROCATECHOL
PYROCATECHOLS
PYROCERAMS
PYROCHEMICAL

PYROCHEMICALLY
PYROCLASTIC
PYROCLASTICS
PYROCLASTS
PYROELECTRIC
PYROELECTRICITY
PYROELECTRICS
PYROGALLATE
PYROGALLATES
PYROGALLIC
PYROGALLOL
PYROGALLOLS
PYROGENETIC
PYROGENICITIES
PYROGENICITY
PYROGENOUS
PYROGNOSTIC
PYROGNOSTICS
PYROGRAPHER
PYROGRAPHERS
PYROGRAPHIC
PYROGRAPHIES
PYROGRAPHY
PYROGRAVURE
PYROGRAVURES
PYROKINESES
PYROKINESIS
PYROLATERS
PYROLATRIES
PYROLIGNEOUS
PYROLIGNIC
PYROLISING
PYROLIZING
PYROLOGIES
PYROLUSITE
PYROLUSITES
PYROLYSABLE
PYROLYSATE
PYROLYSATES
PYROLYSERS
PYROLYSING
PYROLYTICALLY
PYROLYZABLE
PYROLYZATE
PYROLYZATES
PYROLYZERS
PYROLYZING
PYROMAGNETIC
PYROMANCER
PYROMANCERS
PYROMANCIES
PYROMANIAC
PYROMANIACAL
PYROMANIACS
PYROMANIAS
PYROMANTIC
PYROMERIDE
PYROMERIDES
PYROMETALLURGY

PYROMETERS
PYROMETRIC
PYROMETRICAL
PYROMETRICALLY
PYROMETRIES
PYROMORPHITE
PYROMORPHITES
PYRONINOPHILIC
PYROPHOBIA
PYROPHOBIAS
PYROPHOBIC
PYROPHOBICS
PYROPHONES
PYROPHORIC
PYROPHOROUS
PYROPHORUS
PYROPHORUSES
PYROPHOSPHATE
PYROPHOSPHATES
PYROPHOSPHORIC
PYROPHOTOGRAPH
PYROPHOTOGRAPHS
PYROPHOTOGRAPHY
PYROPHOTOMETER
PYROPHOTOMETERS
PYROPHOTOMETRY
PYROPHYLLITE
PYROPHYLLITES
PYROSCOPES
PYROSTATIC
PYROSULPHATE
PYROSULPHATES
PYROSULPHURIC
PYROTARTRATE
PYROTARTRATES
PYROTECHNIC
PYROTECHNICAL
PYROTECHNICALLY
PYROTECHNICIAN
PYROTECHNICIANS
PYROTECHNICS
PYROTECHNIES
PYROTECHNIST
PYROTECHNISTS
PYROTECHNY
PYROVANADIC
PYROXENITE
PYROXENITES
PYROXENITIC
PYROXENOID
PYROXENOIDS
PYROXYLINE
PYROXYLINES
PYROXYLINS
PYRRHICIST
PYRRHICISTS
PYRRHOTINE
PYRRHOTINES
PYRRHOTITE

PYRRHOTITES
PYRRHULOXIA
PYRRHULOXIAS
PYRROLIDINE
PYRROLIDINES
PYTHOGENIC
PYTHONESSES
PYTHONOMORPH
PYTHONOMORPHS

Q

QABALISTIC	QUADRIGEMINOUS	QUADRUMANE	QUALIFIERS
QINGHAOSUS	QUADRILATERAL	QUADRUMANES	QUALIFYING
QUACKERIES	QUADRILATERALS	QUADRUMANOUS	QUALIFYINGS
QUACKSALVER	QUADRILINGUAL	QUADRUMANS	QUALITATIVE
QUACKSALVERS	QUADRILITERAL	QUADRUMVIR	QUALITATIVELY
QUACKSALVING	QUADRILITERALS	QUADRUMVIRATE	QUALMISHLY
QUADPLEXES	QUADRILLED	QUADRUMVIRATES	QUALMISHNESS
QUADRAGENARIAN	QUADRILLER	QUADRUMVIRS	QUALMISHNESSES
QUADRAGENARIANS	QUADRILLERS	QUADRUPEDAL	QUANDARIES
QUADRAGESIMAL	QUADRILLES	QUADRUPEDS	QUANGOCRACIES
QUADRANGLE	QUADRILLING	QUADRUPLED	QUANGOCRACY
QUADRANGLES	QUADRILLION	QUADRUPLES	QUANTIFIABLE
QUADRANGULAR	QUADRILLIONS	QUADRUPLET	QUANTIFICATION
QUADRANGULARLY	QUADRILLIONTH	QUADRUPLETS	QUANTIFICATIONS
QUADRANTAL	QUADRILLIONTHS	QUADRUPLEX	QUANTIFIED
QUADRANTES	QUADRILOCULAR	QUADRUPLEXED	QUANTIFIER
QUADRAPHONIC	QUADRINGENARIES	QUADRUPLEXES	QUANTIFIERS
QUADRAPHONICS	QUADRINGENARY	QUADRUPLEXING	QUANTIFIES
QUADRAPHONIES	QUADRINOMIAL	QUADRUPLICATE	QUANTIFYING
QUADRAPHONY	QUADRINOMIALS	QUADRUPLICATED	QUANTISATION
QUADRAPLEGIA	QUADRIPARTITE	QUADRUPLICATES	QUANTISATIONS
QUADRAPLEGIAS	QUADRIPARTITION	QUADRUPLICATING	QUANTISERS
QUADRAPLEGIC	QUADRIPHONIC	QUADRUPLICATION	QUANTISING
QUADRAPLEGICS	QUADRIPHONICS	QUADRUPLICITIES	QUANTITATE
QUADRATICAL	QUADRIPLEGIA	QUADRUPLICITY	QUANTITATED
QUADRATICALLY	QUADRIPLEGIAS	QUADRUPLIES	QUANTITATES
QUADRATICS	QUADRIPLEGIC	QUADRUPLING	QUANTITATING
QUADRATING	QUADRIPLEGICS	QUADRUPOLE	QUANTITATION
QUADRATRIX	QUADRIPOLE	QUADRUPOLES	QUANTITATIONS
QUADRATRIXES	QUADRIPOLES	QUAESITUMS	QUANTITATIVE
QUADRATURA	QUADRIREME	QUAESTIONARIES	QUANTITATIVELY
QUADRATURE	QUADRIREMES	QUAESTIONARY	QUANTITIES
QUADRATURES	QUADRISECT	QUAESTORIAL	QUANTITIVE
QUADRATUSES	QUADRISECTED	QUAESTORSHIP	QUANTITIVELY
QUADRELLAS	QUADRISECTING	QUAESTORSHIPS	QUANTIVALENCE
QUADRENNIA	QUADRISECTION	QUAESTUARIES	QUANTIVALENCES
QUADRENNIAL	QUADRISECTIONS	QUAESTUARY	QUANTIVALENT
QUADRENNIALLY	QUADRISECTS	QUAGGINESS	QUANTIZATION
QUADRENNIALS	QUADRISYLLABIC	QUAGGINESSES	QUANTIZATIONS
QUADRENNIUM	QUADRISYLLABLE	QUAGMIRIER	QUANTIZERS
QUADRENNIUMS	QUADRISYLLABLES	QUAGMIRIEST	QUANTIZING
QUADRICEPS	QUADRIVALENCE	QUAGMIRING	QUANTOMETER
QUADRICEPSES	QUADRIVALENCES	QUAINTNESS	QUANTOMETERS
QUADRICIPITAL	QUADRIVALENCIES	QUAINTNESSES	QUAQUAVERSAL
QUADRICONE	QUADRIVALENCY	QUAKINESSES	QUAQUAVERSALLY
QUADRICONES	QUADRIVALENT	QUALIFIABLE	QUARANTINE
QUADRIENNIA	QUADRIVALENTS	QUALIFICATION	QUARANTINED
QUADRIENNIAL	QUADRIVIAL	QUALIFICATIONS	QUARANTINES
QUADRIENNIUM	QUADRIVIUM	QUALIFICATIVE	QUARANTINING
QUADRIFARIOUS	QUADRIVIUMS	QUALIFICATIVES	QUARENDENS
QUADRIFOLIATE	QUADROPHONIC	QUALIFICATOR	QUARENDERS
QUADRIFORM	QUADROPHONICS	QUALIFICATORS	QUARRELERS
QUADRIGEMINAL	QUADROPHONIES	QUALIFICATORY	QUARRELING
QUADRIGEMINATE	QUADROPHONY	QUALIFIEDLY	QUARRELLED

QUARRELLER	QUASICRYSTALS	QUERIMONIOUSLY	QUIDDITIES
QUARRELLERS	QUASIPARTICLE	QUERNSTONE	QUIESCENCE
QUARRELLING	QUASIPARTICLES	QUERNSTONES	QUIESCENCES
QUARRELLINGS	QUASIPERIODIC	QUERSPRUNG	QUIESCENCIES
QUARRELLOUS	QUATERCENTENARY	QUERSPRUNGS	QUIESCENCY
QUARRELSOME	QUATERNARIES	QUERULOUSLY	QUIESCENTLY
QUARRELSOMELY	QUATERNARY	QUERULOUSNESS	QUIETENERS
QUARRELSOMENESS	QUATERNATE	QUERULOUSNESSES	QUIETENING
QUARRENDER	QUATERNION	QUERYINGLY	QUIETENINGS
QUARRENDERS	QUATERNIONIST	QUESADILLA	QUIETISTIC
QUARRIABLE	QUATERNIONISTS	QUESADILLAS	QUIETNESSES
QUARRINGTON	QUATERNIONS	QUESTINGLY	QUILLBACKS
QUARRINGTONS	QUATERNITIES	QUESTIONABILITY	QUILLWORKS
QUARRYINGS	QUATERNITY	QUESTIONABLE	QUILLWORTS
QUARRYMASTER	QUATORZAIN	QUESTIONABLY	QUINACRINE
QUARRYMASTERS	QUATORZAINS	QUESTIONARIES	QUINACRINES
QUARTATION	QUATREFEUILLE	QUESTIONARY	QUINAQUINA
QUARTATIONS	QUATREFEUILLES	QUESTIONED	QUINAQUINAS
QUARTERAGE	QUATREFOIL	QUESTIONEE	QUINCENTENARIES
QUARTERAGES	QUATREFOILS	QUESTIONEES	QUINCENTENARY
QUARTERBACK	QUATTROCENTISM	QUESTIONER	QUINCENTENNIAL
QUARTERBACKED	QUATTROCENTISMS	QUESTIONERS	QUINCENTENNIALS
QUARTERBACKING	QUATTROCENTIST	QUESTIONING	QUINCUNCIAL
QUARTERBACKS	QUATTROCENTISTS	QUESTIONINGLY	QUINCUNCIALLY
QUARTERDECK	QUATTROCENTO	QUESTIONINGS	QUINCUNXES
QUARTERDECKER	QUATTROCENTOS	QUESTIONIST	QUINCUNXIAL
QUARTERDECKERS	QUAVERIEST	QUESTIONISTS	QUINDECAGON
QUARTERDECKS	QUAVERINGLY	QUESTIONLESS	QUINDECAGONS
QUARTERERS	QUAVERINGS	QUESTIONLESSLY	QUINDECAPLET
QUARTERFINAL	QUEACHIEST	QUESTIONNAIRE	QUINDECAPLETS
QUARTERFINALIST	QUEASINESS	QUESTIONNAIRES	QUINDECENNIAL
QUARTERFINALS	QUEASINESSES	QUESTORIAL	QUINDECENNIALS
QUARTERING	QUEBRACHOS	QUESTORSHIP	QUINDECILLION
QUARTERINGS	QUEECHIEST	QUESTORSHIPS	QUINDECILLIONS
QUARTERLIES	QUEENCAKES	QUESTRISTS	QUINGENTENARIES
QUARTERLIFE	QUEENCRAFT	QUIBBLINGLY	QUINGENTENARY
QUARTERLIGHT	QUEENCRAFTS	QUIBBLINGS	QUINIDINES
QUARTERLIGHTS	QUEENHOODS	QUICKBEAMS	QUINOLINES
QUARTERMASTER	QUEENLIEST	QUICKENERS	QUINOLONES
QUARTERMASTERS	QUEENLINESS	QUICKENING	QUINQUAGENARIAN
QUARTERMISTRESS	QUEENLINESSES	QUICKENINGS	QUINQUAGESIMAL
QUARTEROON	QUEENSHIPS	QUICKLIMES	QUINQUECOSTATE
QUARTEROONS	QUEENSIDES	QUICKNESSES	QUINQUEFARIOUS
QUARTERSAW	QUEERCORES	QUICKSANDS	QUINQUEFOLIATE
QUARTERSAWED	QUEERITIES	QUICKSILVER	QUINQUENNIA
QUARTERSAWING	QUEERNESSES	QUICKSILVERED	QUINQUENNIAD
QUARTERSAWN	QUELQUECHOSE	QUICKSILVERING	QUINQUENNIADS
QUARTERSAWS	QUELQUECHOSES	QUICKSILVERINGS	QUINQUENNIAL
QUARTERSTAFF	QUENCHABLE	QUICKSILVERISH	QUINQUENNIALLY
QUARTERSTAFFS	QUENCHINGS	QUICKSILVERS	QUINQUENNIALS
QUARTERSTAVES	QUENCHLESS	QUICKSILVERY	QUINQUENNIUM
QUARTETTES	QUENCHLESSLY	QUICKSTEPPED	QUINQUENNIUMS
QUARTODECIMAN	QUERCETINS	QUICKSTEPPING	QUINQUEPARTITE
QUARTODECIMANS	QUERCETUMS	QUICKSTEPS	QUINQUEREME
QUARTZIEST	QUERCITINS	QUICKTHORN	QUINQUEREMES
QUARTZIFEROUS	QUERCITRON	QUICKTHORNS	QUINQUEVALENCE
QUARTZITES	QUERCITRONS	QUIDDANIES	QUINQUEVALENCES
QUARTZITIC	QUERIMONIES	QUIDDITATIVE	QUINQUEVALENCY
QUASICRYSTAL	QUERIMONIOUS	QUIDDITCHES	QUINQUEVALENT

QUINQUINAS
QUINQUIVALENT
QUINTESSENCE
QUINTESSENCES
QUINTESSENTIAL
QUINTETTES
QUINTILLION
QUINTILLIONS
QUINTILLIONTH
QUINTILLIONTHS
QUINTROONS
QUINTUPLED
QUINTUPLES
QUINTUPLET
QUINTUPLETS
QUINTUPLICATE
QUINTUPLICATED
QUINTUPLICATES
QUINTUPLICATING
QUINTUPLICATION
QUINTUPLING
QUIRISTERS
QUIRKINESS
QUIRKINESSES
QUISLINGISM
QUISLINGISMS
QUITCLAIMED
QUITCLAIMING
QUITCLAIMS
QUITTANCED
QUITTANCES
QUITTANCING
QUIVERFULS
QUIVERIEST
QUIVERINGLY
QUIVERINGS
QUIXOTICAL
QUIXOTICALLY
QUIXOTISMS
QUIXOTRIES
QUIZMASTER
QUIZMASTERS
QUIZZERIES
QUIZZICALITIES
QUIZZICALITY
QUIZZICALLY
QUIZZIFICATION
QUIZZIFICATIONS
QUIZZIFIED
QUIZZIFIES
QUIZZIFYING
QUIZZINESS
QUIZZINESSES
QUODLIBETARIAN
QUODLIBETARIANS
QUODLIBETIC
QUODLIBETICAL
QUODLIBETICALLY
QUODLIBETS

QUOTABILITIES
QUOTABILITY
QUOTABLENESS
QUOTABLENESSES
QUOTATIONS
QUOTATIOUS
QUOTATIVES
QUOTEWORTHY
QUOTIDIANS
QUOTITIONS

R

RABATMENTS
RABATTEMENT
RABATTEMENTS
RABATTINGS
RABBINATES
RABBINICAL
RABBINICALLY
RABBINISMS
RABBINISTIC
RABBINISTS
RABBINITES
RABBITBRUSH
RABBITBRUSHES
RABBITFISH
RABBITFISHES
RABBITRIES
RABBLEMENT
RABBLEMENTS
RABIDITIES
RABIDNESSES
RACCAHOUTS
RACECOURSE
RACECOURSES
RACEGOINGS
RACEHORSES
RACEMATION
RACEMATIONS
RACEMISATION
RACEMISATIONS
RACEMISING
RACEMIZATION
RACEMIZATIONS
RACEMIZING
RACEMOSELY
RACEMOUSLY
RACETRACKER
RACETRACKERS
RACETRACKS
RACEWALKED
RACEWALKER
RACEWALKERS
RACEWALKING
RACEWALKINGS
RACHIOTOMIES
RACHIOTOMY
RACHISCHISES
RACHISCHISIS
RACHITIDES
RACHITISES
RACIALISED
RACIALISES
RACIALISING
RACIALISMS
RACIALISTIC

RACIALISTS
RACIALIZED
RACIALIZES
RACIALIZING
RACIATIONS
RACINESSES
RACKABONES
RACKETEERED
RACKETEERING
RACKETEERINGS
RACKETEERS
RACKETIEST
RACKETRIES
RACONTEURING
RACONTEURINGS
RACONTEURS
RACONTEUSE
RACONTEUSES
RACQUETBALL
RACQUETBALLS
RACQUETING
RADARSCOPE
RADARSCOPES
RADIALISATION
RADIALISATIONS
RADIALISED
RADIALISES
RADIALISING
RADIALITIES
RADIALIZATION
RADIALIZATIONS
RADIALIZED
RADIALIZES
RADIALIZING
RADIANCIES
RADIATIONAL
RADIATIONLESS
RADIATIONS
RADICALISATION
RADICALISATIONS
RADICALISE
RADICALISED
RADICALISES
RADICALISING
RADICALISM
RADICALISMS
RADICALISTIC
RADICALITIES
RADICALITY
RADICALIZATION
RADICALIZATIONS
RADICALIZE
RADICALIZED
RADICALIZES

RADICALIZING
RADICALNESS
RADICALNESSES
RADICATING
RADICATION
RADICATIONS
RADICCHIOS
RADICELLOSE
RADICICOLOUS
RADICIFORM
RADICIVOROUS
RADICULOSE
RADIESTHESIA
RADIESTHESIAS
RADIESTHESIST
RADIESTHESISTS
RADIESTHETIC
RADIOACTIVATE
RADIOACTIVATED
RADIOACTIVATES
RADIOACTIVATING
RADIOACTIVATION
RADIOACTIVE
RADIOACTIVELY
RADIOACTIVITIES
RADIOACTIVITY
RADIOAUTOGRAPH
RADIOAUTOGRAPHS
RADIOAUTOGRAPHY
RADIOBIOLOGIC
RADIOBIOLOGICAL
RADIOBIOLOGIES
RADIOBIOLOGIST
RADIOBIOLOGISTS
RADIOBIOLOGY
RADIOCARBON
RADIOCARBONS
RADIOCHEMICAL
RADIOCHEMICALLY
RADIOCHEMIST
RADIOCHEMISTRY
RADIOCHEMISTS
RADIOECOLOGIES
RADIOECOLOGY
RADIOELEMENT
RADIOELEMENTS
RADIOGENIC
RADIOGOLDS
RADIOGONIOMETER
RADIOGRAMS
RADIOGRAPH
RADIOGRAPHED
RADIOGRAPHER
RADIOGRAPHERS

RADIOGRAPHIC
RADIOGRAPHIES
RADIOGRAPHING
RADIOGRAPHS
RADIOGRAPHY
RADIOIODINE
RADIOIODINES
RADIOISOTOPE
RADIOISOTOPES
RADIOISOTOPIC
RADIOLABEL
RADIOLABELED
RADIOLABELING
RADIOLABELLED
RADIOLABELLING
RADIOLABELS
RADIOLARIAN
RADIOLARIANS
RADIOLOCATION
RADIOLOCATIONAL
RADIOLOCATIONS
RADIOLOGIC
RADIOLOGICAL
RADIOLOGICALLY
RADIOLOGIES
RADIOLOGIST
RADIOLOGISTS
RADIOLUCENCIES
RADIOLUCENCY
RADIOLUCENT
RADIOLYSES
RADIOLYSIS
RADIOLYTIC
RADIOMETER
RADIOMETERS
RADIOMETRIC
RADIOMETRICALLY
RADIOMETRIES
RADIOMETRY
RADIOMICROMETER
RADIOMIMETIC
RADIONUCLIDE
RADIONUCLIDES
RADIOPACITIES
RADIOPACITY
RADIOPAGER
RADIOPAGERS
RADIOPAGING
RADIOPAGINGS
RADIOPAQUE
RADIOPHONE
RADIOPHONES
RADIOPHONIC
RADIOPHONICALLY

RADIOPHONICS
RADIOPHONIES
RADIOPHONIST
RADIOPHONISTS
RADIOPHONY
RADIOPHOSPHORUS
RADIOPHOTO
RADIOPHOTOS
RADIOPROTECTION
RADIOPROTECTIVE
RADIORESISTANT
RADIOSCOPE
RADIOSCOPES
RADIOSCOPIC
RADIOSCOPICALLY
RADIOSCOPIES
RADIOSCOPY
RADIOSENSITISE
RADIOSENSITISED
RADIOSENSITISES
RADIOSENSITIVE
RADIOSENSITIZE
RADIOSENSITIZED
RADIOSENSITIZES
RADIOSONDE
RADIOSONDES
RADIOSTRONTIUM
RADIOSTRONTIUMS
RADIOTELEGRAM
RADIOTELEGRAMS
RADIOTELEGRAPH
RADIOTELEGRAPHS
RADIOTELEGRAPHY
RADIOTELEMETER
RADIOTELEMETERS
RADIOTELEMETRIC
RADIOTELEMETRY
RADIOTELEPHONE
RADIOTELEPHONES
RADIOTELEPHONIC
RADIOTELEPHONY
RADIOTELETYPE
RADIOTELETYPES
RADIOTHERAPIES
RADIOTHERAPIST
RADIOTHERAPISTS
RADIOTHERAPY
RADIOTHERMIES
RADIOTHERMY
RADIOTHONS
RADIOTHORIUM
RADIOTHORIUMS
RADIOTOXIC
RADIOTRACER
RADIOTRACERS
RADULIFORM
RAFFINATES
RAFFINOSES
RAFFISHNESS

RAFFISHNESSES
RAFFLESIAS
RAFTERINGS
RAGAMUFFIN
RAGAMUFFINS
RAGGAMUFFIN
RAGGAMUFFINS
RAGGEDIEST
RAGGEDNESS
RAGGEDNESSES
RAGMATICAL
RAGPICKERS
RAILBUSSES
RAILLERIES
RAILROADED
RAILROADER
RAILROADERS
RAILROADING
RAILROADINGS
RAILWAYMAN
RAILWAYMEN
RAINBOWLIKE
RAINCHECKS
RAINFOREST
RAINFORESTS
RAININESSES
RAINMAKERS
RAINMAKING
RAINMAKINGS
RAINPROOFED
RAINPROOFING
RAINPROOFS
RAINSPOUTS
RAINSQUALL
RAINSQUALLS
RAINSTORMS
RAINWASHED
RAINWASHES
RAINWASHING
RAINWATERS
RAISONNEUR
RAISONNEURS
RAIYATWARI
RAIYATWARIS
RAJAHSHIPS
RAJPRAMUKH
RAJPRAMUKHS
RAKESHAMES
RAKISHNESS
RAKISHNESSES
RALLENTANDO
RALLENTANDOS
RALLYCROSS
RALLYCROSSES
RALLYINGLY
RAMAPITHECINE
RAMAPITHECINES
RAMBLINGLY
RAMBOUILLET

RAMBOUILLETS
RAMBUNCTIOUS
RAMBUNCTIOUSLY
RAMENTACEOUS
RAMGUNSHOCH
RAMIFICATION
RAMIFICATIONS
RAMMISHNESS
RAMMISHNESSES
RAMOSITIES
RAMPACIOUS
RAMPAGEOUS
RAMPAGEOUSLY
RAMPAGEOUSNESS
RAMPAGINGS
RAMPALLIAN
RAMPALLIANS
RAMPANCIES
RAMPARTING
RAMPAUGING
RAMRODDING
RAMSHACKLE
RANCHERIAS
RANCHERIES
RANCIDITIES
RANCIDNESS
RANCIDNESSES
RANCOROUSLY
RANCOROUSNESS
RANCOROUSNESSES
RANDINESSES
RANDOMISATION
RANDOMISATIONS
RANDOMISED
RANDOMISER
RANDOMISERS
RANDOMISES
RANDOMISING
RANDOMIZATION
RANDOMIZATIONS
RANDOMIZED
RANDOMIZER
RANDOMIZERS
RANDOMIZES
RANDOMIZING
RANDOMNESS
RANDOMNESSES
RANDOMWISE
RANGATIRAS
RANGATIRATANGA
RANGATIRATANGAS
RANGEFINDER
RANGEFINDERS
RANGEFINDING
RANGEFINDINGS
RANGELANDS
RANGERSHIP
RANGERSHIPS
RANGINESSES

RANIVOROUS
RANKNESSES
RANKSHIFTED
RANKSHIFTING
RANKSHIFTS
RANSACKERS
RANSACKING
RANSHACKLE
RANSHACKLED
RANSHACKLES
RANSHACKLING
RANSHAKLED
RANSHAKLES
RANSHAKLING
RANSOMABLE
RANSOMLESS
RANTERISMS
RANTIPOLED
RANTIPOLES
RANTIPOLING
RANUNCULACEOUS
RANUNCULUS
RANUNCULUSES
RAPACIOUSLY
RAPACIOUSNESS
RAPACIOUSNESSES
RAPACITIES
RAPIDITIES
RAPIDNESSES
RAPIERLIKE
RAPPELLING
RAPPELLINGS
RAPPORTAGE
RAPPORTAGES
RAPPORTEUR
RAPPORTEURS
RAPPROCHEMENT
RAPPROCHEMENTS
RAPSCALLION
RAPSCALLIONS
RAPTATORIAL
RAPTNESSES
RAPTURELESS
RAPTURISED
RAPTURISES
RAPTURISING
RAPTURISTS
RAPTURIZED
RAPTURIZES
RAPTURIZING
RAPTUROUSLY
RAPTUROUSNESS
RAPTUROUSNESSES
RAREFACTION
RAREFACTIONAL
RAREFACTIONS
RAREFACTIVE
RAREFIABLE
RAREFICATION

RAREFICATIONAL
RAREFICATIONS
RARENESSES
RASCAILLES
RASCALDOMS
RASCALISMS
RASCALITIES
RASCALLIEST
RASCALLION
RASCALLIONS
RASHNESSES
RASPATORIES
RASPBERRIES
RASPINESSES
RASTAFARIAN
RASTAFARIANS
RASTERISED
RASTERISES
RASTERISING
RASTERIZED
RASTERIZES
RASTERIZING
RATABILITIES
RATABILITY
RATABLENESS
RATABLENESSES
RATAPLANNED
RATAPLANNING
RATATOUILLE
RATATOUILLES
RATBAGGERIES
RATBAGGERY
RATCHETING
RATEABILITIES
RATEABILITY
RATEABLENESS
RATEABLENESSES
RATEMETERS
RATEPAYERS
RATHERIPES
RATHSKELLER
RATHSKELLERS
RATIFIABLE
RATIFICATION
RATIFICATIONS
RATIOCINATE
RATIOCINATED
RATIOCINATES
RATIOCINATING
RATIOCINATION
RATIOCINATIONS
RATIOCINATIVE
RATIOCINATOR
RATIOCINATORS
RATIOCINATORY
RATIONALES
RATIONALISABLE
RATIONALISATION
RATIONALISE

RATIONALISED
RATIONALISER
RATIONALISERS
RATIONALISES
RATIONALISING
RATIONALISM
RATIONALISMS
RATIONALIST
RATIONALISTIC
RATIONALISTS
RATIONALITIES
RATIONALITY
RATIONALIZABLE
RATIONALIZATION
RATIONALIZE
RATIONALIZED
RATIONALIZER
RATIONALIZERS
RATIONALIZES
RATIONALIZING
RATIONALLY
RATIONALNESS
RATIONALNESSES
RATTENINGS
RATTINESSES
RATTLEBAGS
RATTLEBOXES
RATTLEBRAIN
RATTLEBRAINED
RATTLEBRAINS
RATTLESNAKE
RATTLESNAKES
RATTLETRAP
RATTLETRAPS
RATTLINGLY
RATTOONING
RAUCOUSNESS
RAUCOUSNESSES
RAUNCHIEST
RAUNCHINESS
RAUNCHINESSES
RAUWOLFIAS
RAVAGEMENT
RAVAGEMENTS
RAVELLINGS
RAVELMENTS
RAVENINGLY
RAVENOUSLY
RAVENOUSNESS
RAVENOUSNESSES
RAVIGOTTES
RAVISHINGLY
RAVISHMENT
RAVISHMENTS
RAWINSONDE
RAWINSONDES
RAWMAISHES
RAYGRASSES
RAYLESSNESS

RAYLESSNESSES
RAZMATAZES
RAZORBACKS
RAZORBILLS
RAZZAMATAZZ
RAZZAMATAZZES
RAZZBERRIES
RAZZMATAZZ
RAZZMATAZZES
REABSORBED
REABSORBING
REABSORPTION
REABSORPTIONS
REACCEDING
REACCELERATE
REACCELERATED
REACCELERATES
REACCELERATING
REACCENTED
REACCENTING
REACCEPTED
REACCEPTING
REACCESSION
REACCESSIONS
REACCLAIMED
REACCLAIMING
REACCLAIMS
REACCLIMATISE
REACCLIMATISED
REACCLIMATISES
REACCLIMATISING
REACCLIMATIZE
REACCLIMATIZED
REACCLIMATIZES
REACCLIMATIZING
REACCREDIT
REACCREDITATION
REACCREDITED
REACCREDITING
REACCREDITS
REACCUSING
REACCUSTOM
REACCUSTOMED
REACCUSTOMING
REACCUSTOMS
REACQUAINT
REACQUAINTANCE
REACQUAINTANCES
REACQUAINTED
REACQUAINTING
REACQUAINTS
REACQUIRED
REACQUIRES
REACQUIRING
REACQUISITION
REACQUISITIONS
REACTANCES
REACTIONAL
REACTIONARIES

REACTIONARISM
REACTIONARISMS
REACTIONARIST
REACTIONARISTS
REACTIONARY
REACTIONARYISM
REACTIONARYISMS
REACTIONISM
REACTIONISMS
REACTIONIST
REACTIONISTS
REACTIVATE
REACTIVATED
REACTIVATES
REACTIVATING
REACTIVATION
REACTIVATIONS
REACTIVELY
REACTIVENESS
REACTIVENESSES
REACTIVITIES
REACTIVITY
REACTUATED
REACTUATES
REACTUATING
READABILITIES
READABILITY
READABLENESS
READABLENESSES
READAPTATION
READAPTATIONS
READAPTING
READDICTED
READDICTING
READDRESSED
READDRESSES
READDRESSING
READERSHIP
READERSHIPS
READINESSES
READJUSTABLE
READJUSTED
READJUSTER
READJUSTERS
READJUSTING
READJUSTMENT
READJUSTMENTS
READMISSION
READMISSIONS
READMITTANCE
READMITTANCES
READMITTED
READMITTING
READOPTING
READOPTION
READOPTIONS
READORNING
READVANCED
READVANCES

READVANCING
READVERTISE
READVERTISED
READVERTISEMENT
READVERTISES
READVERTISING
READVISING
READYMADES
REAEDIFIED
REAEDIFIES
REAEDIFYED
REAEDIFYES
REAEDIFYING
REAFFIRMATION
REAFFIRMATIONS
REAFFIRMED
REAFFIRMING
REAFFIXING
REAFFOREST
REAFFORESTATION
REAFFORESTED
REAFFORESTING
REAFFORESTS
REAGENCIES
REAGGREGATE
REAGGREGATED
REAGGREGATES
REAGGREGATING
REAGGREGATION
REAGGREGATIONS
REALIGNING
REALIGNMENT
REALIGNMENTS
REALISABILITIES
REALISABILITY
REALISABLE
REALISABLY
REALISATION
REALISATIONS
REALISTICALLY
REALIZABILITIES
REALIZABILITY
REALIZABLE
REALIZABLY
REALIZATION
REALIZATIONS
REALLOCATE
REALLOCATED
REALLOCATES
REALLOCATING
REALLOCATION
REALLOCATIONS
REALLOTMENT
REALLOTMENTS
REALLOTTED
REALLOTTING
REALNESSES
REALPOLITIK
REALPOLITIKER

REALPOLITIKERS
REALPOLITIKS
REALTERING
REAMENDING
REAMENDMENT
REAMENDMENTS
REANALYSED
REANALYSES
REANALYSING
REANALYSIS
REANALYZED
REANALYZES
REANALYZING
REANIMATED
REANIMATES
REANIMATING
REANIMATION
REANIMATIONS
REANNEXATION
REANNEXATIONS
REANNEXING
REANOINTED
REANOINTING
REANSWERED
REANSWERING
REAPPARELLED
REAPPARELLING
REAPPARELS
REAPPEARANCE
REAPPEARANCES
REAPPEARED
REAPPEARING
REAPPLICATION
REAPPLICATIONS
REAPPLYING
REAPPOINTED
REAPPOINTING
REAPPOINTMENT
REAPPOINTMENTS
REAPPOINTS
REAPPORTION
REAPPORTIONED
REAPPORTIONING
REAPPORTIONMENT
REAPPORTIONS
REAPPRAISAL
REAPPRAISALS
REAPPRAISE
REAPPRAISED
REAPPRAISEMENT
REAPPRAISEMENTS
REAPPRAISER
REAPPRAISERS
REAPPRAISES
REAPPRAISING
REAPPROPRIATE
REAPPROPRIATED
REAPPROPRIATES
REAPPROPRIATING

REAPPROVED
REAPPROVES
REAPPROVING
REARGUARDS
REARGUMENT
REARGUMENTS
REARHORSES
REARMAMENT
REARMAMENTS
REAROUSALS
REAROUSING
REARRANGED
REARRANGEMENT
REARRANGEMENTS
REARRANGER
REARRANGERS
REARRANGES
REARRANGING
REARRESTED
REARRESTING
REARTICULATE
REARTICULATED
REARTICULATES
REARTICULATING
REASCENDED
REASCENDING
REASCENSION
REASCENSIONS
REASONABILITIES
REASONABILITY
REASONABLE
REASONABLENESS
REASONABLY
REASONEDLY
REASONINGS
REASONLESS
REASONLESSLY
REASSAILED
REASSAILING
REASSEMBLAGE
REASSEMBLAGES
REASSEMBLE
REASSEMBLED
REASSEMBLES
REASSEMBLIES
REASSEMBLING
REASSEMBLY
REASSERTED
REASSERTING
REASSERTION
REASSERTIONS
REASSESSED
REASSESSES
REASSESSING
REASSESSMENT
REASSESSMENTS
REASSIGNED
REASSIGNING
REASSIGNMENT

REASSIGNMENTS
REASSORTED
REASSORTING
REASSORTMENT
REASSORTMENTS
REASSUMING
REASSUMPTION
REASSUMPTIONS
REASSURANCE
REASSURANCES
REASSURERS
REASSURING
REASSURINGLY
REASTINESS
REASTINESSES
REATTACHED
REATTACHES
REATTACHING
REATTACHMENT
REATTACHMENTS
REATTACKED
REATTACKING
REATTAINED
REATTAINING
REATTEMPTED
REATTEMPTING
REATTEMPTS
REATTRIBUTE
REATTRIBUTED
REATTRIBUTES
REATTRIBUTING
REATTRIBUTION
REATTRIBUTIONS
REAUTHORISATION
REAUTHORISE
REAUTHORISED
REAUTHORISES
REAUTHORISING
REAUTHORIZATION
REAUTHORIZE
REAUTHORIZED
REAUTHORIZES
REAUTHORIZING
REAVAILING
REAWAKENED
REAWAKENING
REAWAKENINGS
REBALANCED
REBALANCES
REBALANCING
REBAPTISED
REBAPTISES
REBAPTISING
REBAPTISMS
REBAPTIZED
REBAPTIZES
REBAPTIZING
REBARBATIVE
REBARBATIVELY

REBATEABLE

REBATEABLE
REBATEMENT
REBATEMENTS
REBBETZINS
REBEGINNING
REBELLIONS
REBELLIOUS
REBELLIOUSLY
REBELLIOUSNESS
REBELLOWED
REBELLOWING
REBIRTHING
REBIRTHINGS
REBLENDING
REBLOOMING
REBLOSSOMED
REBLOSSOMING
REBLOSSOMS
REBOARDING
REBOATIONS
REBORROWED
REBORROWING
REBOTTLING
REBOUNDERS
REBOUNDING
REBRANCHED
REBRANCHES
REBRANCHING
REBRANDING
REBREEDING
REBROADCAST
REBROADCASTED
REBROADCASTING
REBROADCASTS
REBUILDING
REBUKEFULLY
REBUKINGLY
REBUTMENTS
REBUTTABLE
REBUTTONED
REBUTTONING
RECALCITRANCE
RECALCITRANCES
RECALCITRANCIES
RECALCITRANCY
RECALCITRANT
RECALCITRANTS
RECALCITRATE
RECALCITRATED
RECALCITRATES
RECALCITRATING
RECALCITRATION
RECALCITRATIONS
RECALCULATE
RECALCULATED
RECALCULATES
RECALCULATING
RECALCULATION
RECALCULATIONS

RECALESCED
RECALESCENCE
RECALESCENCES
RECALESCENT
RECALESCES
RECALESCING
RECALIBRATE
RECALIBRATED
RECALIBRATES
RECALIBRATING
RECALIBRATION
RECALIBRATIONS
RECALLABILITIES
RECALLABILITY
RECALLABLE
RECALLMENT
RECALLMENTS
RECALMENTS
RECANALISATION
RECANALISATIONS
RECANALISE
RECANALISED
RECANALISES
RECANALISING
RECANALIZATION
RECANALIZATIONS
RECANALIZE
RECANALIZED
RECANALIZES
RECANALIZING
RECANTATION
RECANTATIONS
RECAPITALISE
RECAPITALISED
RECAPITALISES
RECAPITALISING
RECAPITALIZE
RECAPITALIZED
RECAPITALIZES
RECAPITALIZING
RECAPITULATE
RECAPITULATED
RECAPITULATES
RECAPITULATING
RECAPITULATION
RECAPITULATIONS
RECAPITULATIVE
RECAPITULATORY
RECAPPABLE
RECAPTIONS
RECAPTURED
RECAPTURER
RECAPTURERS
RECAPTURES
RECAPTURING
RECARPETED
RECARPETING
RECARRYING
RECATALOGED

RECATALOGING
RECATALOGS
RECATCHING
RECAUTIONED
RECAUTIONING
RECAUTIONS
RECEIPTING
RECEIPTORS
RECEIVABILITIES
RECEIVABILITY
RECEIVABLE
RECEIVABLENESS
RECEIVABLES
RECEIVERSHIP
RECEIVERSHIPS
RECEIVINGS
RECEMENTED
RECEMENTING
RECENSIONS
RECENSORED
RECENSORING
RECENTNESS
RECENTNESSES
RECENTRIFUGE
RECENTRIFUGED
RECENTRIFUGES
RECENTRIFUGING
RECENTRING
RECEPTACLE
RECEPTACLES
RECEPTACULA
RECEPTACULAR
RECEPTACULUM
RECEPTIBILITIES
RECEPTIBILITY
RECEPTIBLE
RECEPTIONIST
RECEPTIONISTS
RECEPTIONS
RECEPTIVELY
RECEPTIVENESS
RECEPTIVENESSES
RECEPTIVITIES
RECEPTIVITY
RECERTIFICATION
RECERTIFIED
RECERTIFIES
RECERTIFYING
RECESSIONAL
RECESSIONALS
RECESSIONARY
RECESSIONS
RECESSIVELY
RECESSIVENESS
RECESSIVENESSES
RECESSIVES
RECHALLENGE
RECHALLENGED
RECHALLENGES

RECHALLENGING
RECHANGING
RECHANNELED
RECHANNELING
RECHANNELLED
RECHANNELLING
RECHANNELS
RECHARGEABLE
RECHARGERS
RECHARGING
RECHARTERED
RECHARTERING
RECHARTERS
RECHARTING
RECHAUFFES
RECHEATING
RECHECKING
RECHOOSING
RECHOREOGRAPH
RECHOREOGRAPHED
RECHOREOGRAPHS
RECHRISTEN
RECHRISTENED
RECHRISTENING
RECHRISTENS
RECHROMATOGRAPH
RECIDIVISM
RECIDIVISMS
RECIDIVIST
RECIDIVISTIC
RECIDIVISTS
RECIDIVOUS
RECIPIENCE
RECIPIENCES
RECIPIENCIES
RECIPIENCY
RECIPIENTS
RECIPROCAL
RECIPROCALITIES
RECIPROCALITY
RECIPROCALLY
RECIPROCALS
RECIPROCANT
RECIPROCANTS
RECIPROCATE
RECIPROCATED
RECIPROCATES
RECIPROCATING
RECIPROCATION
RECIPROCATIONS
RECIPROCATIVE
RECIPROCATOR
RECIPROCATORS
RECIPROCATORY
RECIPROCITIES
RECIPROCITY
RECIRCLING
RECIRCULATE
RECIRCULATED

RECIRCULATES
RECIRCULATING
RECIRCULATION
RECIRCULATIONS
RECITALIST
RECITALISTS
RECITATION
RECITATIONIST
RECITATIONISTS
RECITATIONS
RECITATIVE
RECITATIVES
RECITATIVI
RECITATIVO
RECITATIVOS
RECKLESSLY
RECKLESSNESS
RECKLESSNESSES
RECKONINGS
RECLADDING
RECLAIMABLE
RECLAIMABLY
RECLAIMANT
RECLAIMANTS
RECLAIMERS
RECLAIMING
RECLAMATION
RECLAMATIONS
RECLASPING
RECLASSIFIED
RECLASSIFIES
RECLASSIFY
RECLASSIFYING
RECLEANING
RECLIMBING
RECLINABLE
RECLINATION
RECLINATIONS
RECLOSABLE
RECLOTHING
RECLUSENESS
RECLUSENESSES
RECLUSIONS
RECLUSIVELY
RECLUSIVENESS
RECLUSIVENESSES
RECLUSORIES
RECODIFICATION
RECODIFICATIONS
RECODIFIED
RECODIFIES
RECODIFYING
RECOGNISABILITY
RECOGNISABLE
RECOGNISABLY
RECOGNISANCE
RECOGNISANCES
RECOGNISANT
RECOGNISED

RECOGNISEE
RECOGNISEES
RECOGNISER
RECOGNISERS
RECOGNISES
RECOGNISING
RECOGNISOR
RECOGNISORS
RECOGNITION
RECOGNITIONS
RECOGNITIVE
RECOGNITORY
RECOGNIZABILITY
RECOGNIZABLE
RECOGNIZABLY
RECOGNIZANCE
RECOGNIZANCES
RECOGNIZANT
RECOGNIZED
RECOGNIZEE
RECOGNIZEES
RECOGNIZER
RECOGNIZERS
RECOGNIZES
RECOGNIZING
RECOGNIZOR
RECOGNIZORS
RECOILLESS
RECOINAGES
RECOLLECTED
RECOLLECTEDLY
RECOLLECTEDNESS
RECOLLECTING
RECOLLECTION
RECOLLECTIONS
RECOLLECTIVE
RECOLLECTIVELY
RECOLLECTS
RECOLONISATION
RECOLONISATIONS
RECOLONISE
RECOLONISED
RECOLONISES
RECOLONISING
RECOLONIZATION
RECOLONIZATIONS
RECOLONIZE
RECOLONIZED
RECOLONIZES
RECOLONIZING
RECOLORING
RECOMBINANT
RECOMBINANTS
RECOMBINATION
RECOMBINATIONAL
RECOMBINATIONS
RECOMBINED
RECOMBINES
RECOMBINING

RECOMFORTED
RECOMFORTING
RECOMFORTLESS
RECOMFORTS
RECOMFORTURE
RECOMFORTURES
RECOMMENCE
RECOMMENCED
RECOMMENCEMENT
RECOMMENCEMENTS
RECOMMENCES
RECOMMENCING
RECOMMENDABLE
RECOMMENDABLY
RECOMMENDATION
RECOMMENDATIONS
RECOMMENDATORY
RECOMMENDED
RECOMMENDER
RECOMMENDERS
RECOMMENDING
RECOMMENDS
RECOMMISSION
RECOMMISSIONED
RECOMMISSIONING
RECOMMISSIONS
RECOMMITMENT
RECOMMITMENTS
RECOMMITTAL
RECOMMITTALS
RECOMMITTED
RECOMMITTING
RECOMPACTED
RECOMPACTING
RECOMPACTS
RECOMPENCE
RECOMPENCES
RECOMPENSABLE
RECOMPENSE
RECOMPENSED
RECOMPENSER
RECOMPENSERS
RECOMPENSES
RECOMPENSING
RECOMPILATION
RECOMPILATIONS
RECOMPILED
RECOMPILES
RECOMPILING
RECOMPOSED
RECOMPOSES
RECOMPOSING
RECOMPOSITION
RECOMPOSITIONS
RECOMPRESS
RECOMPRESSED
RECOMPRESSES
RECOMPRESSING
RECOMPRESSION

RECOMPRESSIONS
RECOMPUTATION
RECOMPUTATIONS
RECOMPUTED
RECOMPUTES
RECOMPUTING
RECONCEIVE
RECONCEIVED
RECONCEIVES
RECONCEIVING
RECONCENTRATE
RECONCENTRATED
RECONCENTRATES
RECONCENTRATING
RECONCENTRATION
RECONCEPTION
RECONCEPTIONS
RECONCEPTUALISE
RECONCEPTUALIZE
RECONCILABILITY
RECONCILABLE
RECONCILABLY
RECONCILED
RECONCILEMENT
RECONCILEMENTS
RECONCILER
RECONCILERS
RECONCILES
RECONCILIATION
RECONCILIATIONS
RECONCILIATORY
RECONCILING
RECONDENSATION
RECONDENSATIONS
RECONDENSE
RECONDENSED
RECONDENSES
RECONDENSING
RECONDITELY
RECONDITENESS
RECONDITENESSES
RECONDITION
RECONDITIONED
RECONDITIONING
RECONDITIONS
RECONDUCTED
RECONDUCTING
RECONDUCTS
RECONFERRED
RECONFERRING
RECONFIGURATION
RECONFIGURE
RECONFIGURED
RECONFIGURES
RECONFIGURING
RECONFINED
RECONFINES
RECONFINING
RECONFIRMATION

RECONFIRMATIONS

RECONFIRMATIONS
RECONFIRMED
RECONFIRMING
RECONFIRMS
RECONNAISSANCE
RECONNAISSANCES
RECONNECTED
RECONNECTING
RECONNECTION
RECONNECTIONS
RECONNECTS
RECONNOISSANCE
RECONNOISSANCES
RECONNOITER
RECONNOITERED
RECONNOITERER
RECONNOITERERS
RECONNOITERING
RECONNOITERS
RECONNOITRE
RECONNOITRED
RECONNOITRER
RECONNOITRERS
RECONNOITRES
RECONNOITRING
RECONQUERED
RECONQUERING
RECONQUERS
RECONQUEST
RECONQUESTS
RECONSECRATE
RECONSECRATED
RECONSECRATES
RECONSECRATING
RECONSECRATION
RECONSECRATIONS
RECONSIDER
RECONSIDERATION
RECONSIDERED
RECONSIDERING
RECONSIDERS
RECONSIGNED
RECONSIGNING
RECONSIGNS
RECONSOLED
RECONSOLES
RECONSOLIDATE
RECONSOLIDATED
RECONSOLIDATES
RECONSOLIDATING
RECONSOLIDATION
RECONSOLING
RECONSTITUENT
RECONSTITUENTS
RECONSTITUTABLE
RECONSTITUTE
RECONSTITUTED
RECONSTITUTES
RECONSTITUTING

RECONSTITUTION
RECONSTITUTIONS
RECONSTRUCT
RECONSTRUCTED
RECONSTRUCTIBLE
RECONSTRUCTING
RECONSTRUCTION
RECONSTRUCTIONS
RECONSTRUCTIVE
RECONSTRUCTOR
RECONSTRUCTORS
RECONSTRUCTS
RECONSULTED
RECONSULTING
RECONSULTS
RECONTACTED
RECONTACTING
RECONTACTS
RECONTAMINATE
RECONTAMINATED
RECONTAMINATES
RECONTAMINATING
RECONTAMINATION
RECONTEXTUALISE
RECONTEXTUALIZE
RECONTINUE
RECONTINUED
RECONTINUES
RECONTINUING
RECONTOURED
RECONTOURING
RECONTOURS
RECONVALESCENCE
RECONVENED
RECONVENES
RECONVENING
RECONVERSION
RECONVERSIONS
RECONVERTED
RECONVERTING
RECONVERTS
RECONVEYANCE
RECONVEYANCES
RECONVEYED
RECONVEYING
RECONVICTED
RECONVICTING
RECONVICTION
RECONVICTIONS
RECONVICTS
RECONVINCE
RECONVINCED
RECONVINCES
RECONVINCING
RECORDABLE
RECORDATION
RECORDATIONS
RECORDERSHIP
RECORDERSHIPS

RECORDINGS
RECORDISTS
RECOUNTALS
RECOUNTERS
RECOUNTING
RECOUNTMENT
RECOUNTMENTS
RECOUPABLE
RECOUPLING
RECOUPMENT
RECOUPMENTS
RECOURSING
RECOVERABILITY
RECOVERABLE
RECOVERABLENESS
RECOVEREES
RECOVERERS
RECOVERIES
RECOVERING
RECOVERORS
RECOWERING
RECREANCES
RECREANCIES
RECREANTLY
RECREATING
RECREATION
RECREATIONAL
RECREATIONIST
RECREATIONISTS
RECREATIONS
RECREATIVE
RECREATIVELY
RECREATORS
RECREMENTAL
RECREMENTITIAL
RECREMENTITIOUS
RECREMENTS
RECRIMINATE
RECRIMINATED
RECRIMINATES
RECRIMINATING
RECRIMINATION
RECRIMINATIONS
RECRIMINATIVE
RECRIMINATOR
RECRIMINATORS
RECRIMINATORY
RECROSSING
RECROWNING
RECRUDESCE
RECRUDESCED
RECRUDESCENCE
RECRUDESCENCES
RECRUDESCENCIES
RECRUDESCENCY
RECRUDESCENT
RECRUDESCES
RECRUDESCING
RECRUITABLE

RECRUITALS
RECRUITERS
RECRUITING
RECRUITMENT
RECRUITMENTS
RECRYSTALLISE
RECRYSTALLISED
RECRYSTALLISES
RECRYSTALLISING
RECRYSTALLIZE
RECRYSTALLIZED
RECRYSTALLIZES
RECRYSTALLIZING
RECTANGLED
RECTANGLES
RECTANGULAR
RECTANGULARITY
RECTANGULARLY
RECTIFIABILITY
RECTIFIABLE
RECTIFICATION
RECTIFICATIONS
RECTIFIERS
RECTIFYING
RECTILINEAL
RECTILINEALLY
RECTILINEAR
RECTILINEARITY
RECTILINEARLY
RECTIPETALIES
RECTIPETALITIES
RECTIPETALITY
RECTIPETALY
RECTIROSTRAL
RECTISERIAL
RECTITISES
RECTITUDES
RECTITUDINOUS
RECTOCELES
RECTORATES
RECTORESSES
RECTORIALS
RECTORSHIP
RECTORSHIPS
RECTRESSES
RECTRICIAL
RECULTIVATE
RECULTIVATED
RECULTIVATES
RECULTIVATING
RECUMBENCE
RECUMBENCES
RECUMBENCIES
RECUMBENCY
RECUMBENTLY
RECUPERABLE
RECUPERATE
RECUPERATED
RECUPERATES

RECUPERATING
RECUPERATION
RECUPERATIONS
RECUPERATIVE
RECUPERATOR
RECUPERATORS
RECUPERATORY
RECURELESS
RECURRENCE
RECURRENCES
RECURRENCIES
RECURRENCY
RECURRENTLY
RECURRINGLY
RECURSIONS
RECURSIVELY
RECURSIVENESS
RECURSIVENESSES
RECURVIROSTRAL
RECUSANCES
RECUSANCIES
RECUSATION
RECUSATIONS
RECYCLABLE
RECYCLABLES
RECYCLATES
RECYCLEABLE
RECYCLISTS
REDACTIONAL
REDACTIONS
REDACTORIAL
REDAMAGING
REDARGUING
REDBAITERS
REDBAITING
REDBELLIES
REDBREASTS
REDCURRANT
REDCURRANTS
REDDISHNESS
REDDISHNESSES
REDECIDING
REDECORATE
REDECORATED
REDECORATES
REDECORATING
REDECORATION
REDECORATIONS
REDECORATOR
REDECORATORS
REDECRAFTS
REDEDICATE
REDEDICATED
REDEDICATES
REDEDICATING
REDEDICATION
REDEDICATIONS
REDEEMABILITIES
REDEEMABILITY

REDEEMABLE
REDEEMABLENESS
REDEEMABLY
REDEEMLESS
REDEFEATED
REDEFEATING
REDEFECTED
REDEFECTING
REDEFINING
REDEFINITION
REDEFINITIONS
REDELIVERANCE
REDELIVERANCES
REDELIVERED
REDELIVERER
REDELIVERERS
REDELIVERIES
REDELIVERING
REDELIVERS
REDELIVERY
REDEMANDED
REDEMANDING
REDEMPTIBLE
REDEMPTION
REDEMPTIONAL
REDEMPTIONER
REDEMPTIONERS
REDEMPTIONS
REDEMPTIVE
REDEMPTIVELY
REDEMPTORY
REDEPLOYED
REDEPLOYING
REDEPLOYMENT
REDEPLOYMENTS
REDEPOSITED
REDEPOSITING
REDEPOSITS
REDESCENDED
REDESCENDING
REDESCENDS
REDESCRIBE
REDESCRIBED
REDESCRIBES
REDESCRIBING
REDESCRIPTION
REDESCRIPTIONS
REDESIGNED
REDESIGNING
REDETERMINATION
REDETERMINE
REDETERMINED
REDETERMINES
REDETERMINING
REDEVELOPED
REDEVELOPER
REDEVELOPERS
REDEVELOPING
REDEVELOPMENT

REDEVELOPMENTS
REDEVELOPS
REDIALLING
REDICTATED
REDICTATES
REDICTATING
REDIGESTED
REDIGESTING
REDIGESTION
REDIGESTIONS
REDIGRESSED
REDIGRESSES
REDIGRESSING
REDINGOTES
REDINTEGRATE
REDINTEGRATED
REDINTEGRATES
REDINTEGRATING
REDINTEGRATION
REDINTEGRATIONS
REDINTEGRATIVE
REDIRECTED
REDIRECTING
REDIRECTION
REDIRECTIONS
REDISBURSE
REDISBURSED
REDISBURSES
REDISBURSING
REDISCOUNT
REDISCOUNTABLE
REDISCOUNTED
REDISCOUNTING
REDISCOUNTS
REDISCOVER
REDISCOVERED
REDISCOVERER
REDISCOVERERS
REDISCOVERIES
REDISCOVERING
REDISCOVERS
REDISCOVERY
REDISCUSSED
REDISCUSSES
REDISCUSSING
REDISPLAYED
REDISPLAYING
REDISPLAYS
REDISPOSED
REDISPOSES
REDISPOSING
REDISPOSITION
REDISPOSITIONS
REDISSOLUTION
REDISSOLUTIONS
REDISSOLVE
REDISSOLVED
REDISSOLVES
REDISSOLVING

REDISTILLATION
REDISTILLATIONS
REDISTILLED
REDISTILLING
REDISTILLS
REDISTRIBUTE
REDISTRIBUTED
REDISTRIBUTES
REDISTRIBUTING
REDISTRIBUTION
REDISTRIBUTIONS
REDISTRIBUTIVE
REDISTRICT
REDISTRICTED
REDISTRICTING
REDISTRICTS
REDIVIDING
REDIVISION
REDIVISIONS
REDIVORCED
REDIVORCES
REDIVORCING
REDLININGS
REDOLENCES
REDOLENCIES
REDOLENTLY
REDOUBLEMENT
REDOUBLEMENTS
REDOUBLERS
REDOUBLING
REDOUBTABLE
REDOUBTABLENESS
REDOUBTABLY
REDOUBTING
REDOUNDING
REDOUNDINGS
REDRAFTING
REDREAMING
REDRESSABLE
REDRESSERS
REDRESSIBLE
REDRESSING
REDRESSIVE
REDRESSORS
REDRILLING
REDRUTHITE
REDRUTHITES
REDSHIFTED
REDSHIRTED
REDSHIRTING
REDSTREAKS
REDUCIBILITIES
REDUCIBILITY
REDUCIBLENESS
REDUCIBLENESSES
REDUCTANTS
REDUCTASES
REDUCTIONAL
REDUCTIONISM

REDUCTIONISMS

REDUCTIONISMS
REDUCTIONIST
REDUCTIONISTIC
REDUCTIONISTS
REDUCTIONS
REDUCTIVELY
REDUCTIVENESS
REDUCTIVENESSES
REDUNDANCE
REDUNDANCES
REDUNDANCIES
REDUNDANCY
REDUNDANTLY
REDUPLICATE
REDUPLICATED
REDUPLICATES
REDUPLICATING
REDUPLICATION
REDUPLICATIONS
REDUPLICATIVE
REDUPLICATIVELY
REEDIFYING
REEDINESSES
REEDITIONS
REEDUCATED
REEDUCATES
REEDUCATING
REEDUCATION
REEDUCATIONS
REEDUCATIVE
REEJECTING
REELECTING
REELECTION
REELECTIONS
REELEVATED
REELEVATES
REELEVATING
REELIGIBILITIES
REELIGIBILITY
REELIGIBLE
REEMBARKED
REEMBARKING
REEMBODIED
REEMBODIES
REEMBODYING
REEMBRACED
REEMBRACES
REEMBRACING
REEMBROIDER
REEMBROIDERED
REEMBROIDERING
REEMBROIDERS
REEMERGENCE
REEMERGENCES
REEMERGING
REEMISSION
REEMISSIONS
REEMITTING
REEMPHASES

REEMPHASIS
REEMPHASISE
REEMPHASISED
REEMPHASISES
REEMPHASISING
REEMPHASIZE
REEMPHASIZED
REEMPHASIZES
REEMPHASIZING
REEMPLOYED
REEMPLOYING
REEMPLOYMENT
REEMPLOYMENTS
REENACTING
REENACTMENT
REENACTMENTS
REENACTORS
REENCOUNTER
REENCOUNTERED
REENCOUNTERING
REENCOUNTERS
REENDOWING
REENERGISE
REENERGISED
REENERGISES
REENERGISING
REENERGIZE
REENERGIZED
REENERGIZES
REENERGIZING
REENFORCED
REENFORCES
REENFORCING
REENGAGEMENT
REENGAGEMENTS
REENGAGING
REENGINEER
REENGINEERED
REENGINEERING
REENGINEERS
REENGRAVED
REENGRAVES
REENGRAVING
REENJOYING
REENLARGED
REENLARGES
REENLARGING
REENLISTED
REENLISTING
REENLISTMENT
REENLISTMENTS
REENROLLED
REENROLLING
REENSLAVED
REENSLAVES
REENSLAVING
REENTERING
REENTHRONE
REENTHRONED

REENTHRONES
REENTHRONING
REENTRANCE
REENTRANCES
REENTRANTS
REEQUIPMENT
REEQUIPMENTS
REEQUIPPED
REEQUIPPING
REERECTING
REESCALATE
REESCALATED
REESCALATES
REESCALATING
REESCALATION
REESCALATIONS
REESTABLISH
REESTABLISHED
REESTABLISHES
REESTABLISHING
REESTABLISHMENT
REESTIMATE
REESTIMATED
REESTIMATES
REESTIMATING
REEVALUATE
REEVALUATED
REEVALUATES
REEVALUATING
REEVALUATION
REEVALUATIONS
REEXAMINATION
REEXAMINATIONS
REEXAMINED
REEXAMINES
REEXAMINING
REEXECUTED
REEXECUTES
REEXECUTING
REEXHIBITED
REEXHIBITING
REEXHIBITS
REEXPELLED
REEXPELLING
REEXPERIENCE
REEXPERIENCED
REEXPERIENCES
REEXPERIENCING
REEXPLAINED
REEXPLAINING
REEXPLAINS
REEXPLORED
REEXPLORES
REEXPLORING
REEXPORTATION
REEXPORTATIONS
REEXPORTED
REEXPORTING
REEXPOSING

REEXPOSURE
REEXPOSURES
REEXPRESSED
REEXPRESSES
REEXPRESSING
REFASHIONED
REFASHIONING
REFASHIONMENT
REFASHIONMENTS
REFASHIONS
REFASTENED
REFASTENING
REFECTIONER
REFECTIONERS
REFECTIONS
REFECTORIAN
REFECTORIANS
REFECTORIES
REFEREEING
REFERENCED
REFERENCER
REFERENCERS
REFERENCES
REFERENCING
REFERENDARIES
REFERENDARY
REFERENDUM
REFERENDUMS
REFERENTIAL
REFERENTIALITY
REFERENTIALLY
REFERRABLE
REFERRIBLE
REFIGHTING
REFIGURING
REFILLABLE
REFILTERED
REFILTERING
REFINANCED
REFINANCES
REFINANCING
REFINANCINGS
REFINEDNESS
REFINEDNESSES
REFINEMENT
REFINEMENTS
REFINERIES
REFINISHED
REFINISHER
REFINISHERS
REFINISHES
REFINISHING
REFITMENTS
REFITTINGS
REFLAGGING
REFLATIONARY
REFLATIONS
REFLECTANCE
REFLECTANCES

REFLECTERS
REFLECTING
REFLECTINGLY
REFLECTION
REFLECTIONAL
REFLECTIONLESS
REFLECTIONS
REFLECTIVE
REFLECTIVELY
REFLECTIVENESS
REFLECTIVITIES
REFLECTIVITY
REFLECTOGRAM
REFLECTOGRAMS
REFLECTOGRAPH
REFLECTOGRAPHS
REFLECTOGRAPHY
REFLECTOMETER
REFLECTOMETERS
REFLECTOMETRIES
REFLECTOMETRY
REFLECTORISE
REFLECTORISED
REFLECTORISES
REFLECTORISING
REFLECTORIZE
REFLECTORIZED
REFLECTORIZES
REFLECTORIZING
REFLECTORS
REFLEXIBILITIES
REFLEXIBILITY
REFLEXIBLE
REFLEXIONAL
REFLEXIONS
REFLEXIVELY
REFLEXIVENESS
REFLEXIVENESSES
REFLEXIVES
REFLEXIVITIES
REFLEXIVITY
REFLEXOLOGICAL
REFLEXOLOGIES
REFLEXOLOGIST
REFLEXOLOGISTS
REFLEXOLOGY
REFLOATING
REFLOODING
REFLOWERED
REFLOWERING
REFLOWERINGS
REFLOWINGS
REFLUENCES
REFOCILLATE
REFOCILLATED
REFOCILLATES
REFOCILLATING
REFOCILLATION
REFOCILLATIONS

REFOCUSING
REFOCUSSED
REFOCUSSES
REFOCUSSING
REFORESTATION
REFORESTATIONS
REFORESTED
REFORESTING
REFORMABILITIES
REFORMABILITY
REFORMABLE
REFORMADES
REFORMADOES
REFORMADOS
REFORMATES
REFORMATION
REFORMATIONAL
REFORMATIONIST
REFORMATIONISTS
REFORMATIONS
REFORMATIVE
REFORMATORIES
REFORMATORY
REFORMATTED
REFORMATTING
REFORMINGS
REFORMISMS
REFORMISTS
REFORMULATE
REFORMULATED
REFORMULATES
REFORMULATING
REFORMULATION
REFORMULATIONS
REFORTIFICATION
REFORTIFIED
REFORTIFIES
REFORTIFYING
REFOUNDATION
REFOUNDATIONS
REFOUNDERS
REFOUNDING
REFRACTABLE
REFRACTARIES
REFRACTARY
REFRACTILE
REFRACTING
REFRACTION
REFRACTIONS
REFRACTIVE
REFRACTIVELY
REFRACTIVENESS
REFRACTIVITIES
REFRACTIVITY
REFRACTOMETER
REFRACTOMETERS
REFRACTOMETRIC
REFRACTOMETRIES
REFRACTOMETRY

REFRACTORIES
REFRACTORILY
REFRACTORINESS
REFRACTORS
REFRACTORY
REFRACTURE
REFRACTURES
REFRAINERS
REFRAINING
REFRAINMENT
REFRAINMENTS
REFRANGIBILITY
REFRANGIBLE
REFRANGIBLENESS
REFREEZING
REFRESHENED
REFRESHENER
REFRESHENERS
REFRESHENING
REFRESHENS
REFRESHERS
REFRESHFUL
REFRESHFULLY
REFRESHING
REFRESHINGLY
REFRESHMENT
REFRESHMENTS
REFRIGERANT
REFRIGERANTS
REFRIGERATE
REFRIGERATED
REFRIGERATES
REFRIGERATING
REFRIGERATION
REFRIGERATIONS
REFRIGERATIVE
REFRIGERATOR
REFRIGERATORIES
REFRIGERATORS
REFRIGERATORY
REFRINGENCE
REFRINGENCES
REFRINGENCIES
REFRINGENCY
REFRINGENT
REFRINGING
REFRONTING
REFUELABLE
REFUELLABLE
REFUELLING
REFUGEEISM
REFUGEEISMS
REFULGENCE
REFULGENCES
REFULGENCIES
REFULGENCY
REFULGENTLY
REFUNDABILITIES
REFUNDABILITY

REFUNDABLE
REFUNDMENT
REFUNDMENTS
REFURBISHED
REFURBISHER
REFURBISHERS
REFURBISHES
REFURBISHING
REFURBISHINGS
REFURBISHMENT
REFURBISHMENTS
REFURNISHED
REFURNISHES
REFURNISHING
REFUSENIKS
REFUTABILITIES
REFUTABILITY
REFUTATION
REFUTATIONS
REGAINABLE
REGAINMENT
REGAINMENTS
REGALEMENT
REGALEMENTS
REGALITIES
REGALNESSES
REGARDABLE
REGARDFULLY
REGARDFULNESS
REGARDFULNESSES
REGARDLESS
REGARDLESSLY
REGARDLESSNESS
REGATHERED
REGATHERING
REGELATING
REGELATION
REGELATIONS
REGENERABLE
REGENERACIES
REGENERACY
REGENERATE
REGENERATED
REGENERATELY
REGENERATENESS
REGENERATES
REGENERATING
REGENERATION
REGENERATIONS
REGENERATIVE
REGENERATIVELY
REGENERATOR
REGENERATORS
REGENERATORY
REGENTSHIP
REGENTSHIPS
REGIMENTAL
REGIMENTALLY
REGIMENTALS

REGIMENTATION

REGIMENTATION
REGIMENTATIONS
REGIMENTED
REGIMENTING
REGIONALISATION
REGIONALISE
REGIONALISED
REGIONALISES
REGIONALISING
REGIONALISM
REGIONALISMS
REGIONALIST
REGIONALISTIC
REGIONALISTS
REGIONALIZATION
REGIONALIZE
REGIONALIZED
REGIONALIZES
REGIONALIZING
REGIONALLY
REGISSEURS
REGISTERABLE
REGISTERED
REGISTERER
REGISTERERS
REGISTERING
REGISTRABLE
REGISTRANT
REGISTRANTS
REGISTRARIES
REGISTRARS
REGISTRARSHIP
REGISTRARSHIPS
REGISTRARY
REGISTRATION
REGISTRATIONAL
REGISTRATIONS
REGISTRIES
REGLORIFIED
REGLORIFIES
REGLORIFYING
REGLOSSING
REGNANCIES
REGRAFTING
REGRANTING
REGRATINGS
REGREDIENCE
REGREDIENCES
REGREENING
REGREETING
REGRESSING
REGRESSION
REGRESSIONS
REGRESSIVE
REGRESSIVELY
REGRESSIVENESS
REGRESSIVITIES
REGRESSIVITY
REGRESSORS

REGRETFULLY
REGRETFULNESS
REGRETFULNESSES
REGRETTABLE
REGRETTABLY
REGRETTERS
REGRETTING
REGRINDING
REGROOMING
REGROOVING
REGROUPING
REGUERDONED
REGUERDONING
REGUERDONS
REGULARISATION
REGULARISATIONS
REGULARISE
REGULARISED
REGULARISES
REGULARISING
REGULARITIES
REGULARITY
REGULARIZATION
REGULARIZATIONS
REGULARIZE
REGULARIZED
REGULARIZES
REGULARIZING
REGULATING
REGULATION
REGULATIONS
REGULATIVE
REGULATIVELY
REGULATORS
REGULATORY
REGULISING
REGULIZING
REGURGITANT
REGURGITANTS
REGURGITATE
REGURGITATED
REGURGITATES
REGURGITATING
REGURGITATION
REGURGITATIONS
REHABILITANT
REHABILITANTS
REHABILITATE
REHABILITATED
REHABILITATES
REHABILITATING
REHABILITATION
REHABILITATIONS
REHABILITATIVE
REHABILITATOR
REHABILITATORS
REHAMMERED
REHAMMERING
REHANDLING

REHANDLINGS
REHARDENED
REHARDENING
REHEARINGS
REHEARSALS
REHEARSERS
REHEARSING
REHEARSINGS
REHEATINGS
REHOSPITALISE
REHOSPITALISED
REHOSPITALISES
REHOSPITALISING
REHOSPITALIZE
REHOSPITALIZED
REHOSPITALIZES
REHOSPITALIZING
REHOUSINGS
REHUMANISE
REHUMANISED
REHUMANISES
REHUMANISING
REHUMANIZE
REHUMANIZED
REHUMANIZES
REHUMANIZING
REHYDRATABLE
REHYDRATED
REHYDRATES
REHYDRATING
REHYDRATION
REHYDRATIONS
REHYPNOTISE
REHYPNOTISED
REHYPNOTISES
REHYPNOTISING
REHYPNOTIZE
REHYPNOTIZED
REHYPNOTIZES
REHYPNOTIZING
REICHSMARK
REICHSMARKS
REIDENTIFIED
REIDENTIFIES
REIDENTIFY
REIDENTIFYING
REIFICATION
REIFICATIONS
REIFICATORY
REIGNITING
REIGNITION
REIGNITIONS
REILLUMINE
REILLUMINED
REILLUMINES
REILLUMING
REILLUMINING
REIMAGINED
REIMAGINES

REIMAGINING
REIMBURSABLE
REIMBURSED
REIMBURSEMENT
REIMBURSEMENTS
REIMBURSER
REIMBURSERS
REIMBURSES
REIMBURSING
REIMMERSED
REIMMERSES
REIMMERSING
REIMPLANTATION
REIMPLANTATIONS
REIMPLANTED
REIMPLANTING
REIMPLANTS
REIMPORTATION
REIMPORTATIONS
REIMPORTED
REIMPORTER
REIMPORTERS
REIMPORTING
REIMPOSING
REIMPOSITION
REIMPOSITIONS
REIMPRESSION
REIMPRESSIONS
REINCARNATE
REINCARNATED
REINCARNATES
REINCARNATING
REINCARNATION
REINCARNATIONS
REINCITING
REINCORPORATE
REINCORPORATED
REINCORPORATES
REINCORPORATING
REINCORPORATION
REINCREASE
REINCREASED
REINCREASES
REINCREASING
REINCURRED
REINCURRING
REINDEXING
REINDICTED
REINDICTING
REINDICTMENT
REINDICTMENTS
REINDUCING
REINDUCTED
REINDUCTING
REINDUSTRIALISE
REINDUSTRIALIZE
REINFECTED
REINFECTING
REINFECTION

REINFECTIONS
REINFESTATION
REINFESTATIONS
REINFLAMED
REINFLAMES
REINFLAMING
REINFLATED
REINFLATES
REINFLATING
REINFLATION
REINFLATIONS
REINFORCEABLE
REINFORCED
REINFORCEMENT
REINFORCEMENTS
REINFORCER
REINFORCERS
REINFORCES
REINFORCING
REINFORMED
REINFORMING
REINFUNDED
REINFUNDING
REINFUSING
REINHABITED
REINHABITING
REINHABITS
REINITIATE
REINITIATED
REINITIATES
REINITIATING
REINJECTED
REINJECTING
REINJECTION
REINJECTIONS
REINJURIES
REINJURING
REINNERVATE
REINNERVATED
REINNERVATES
REINNERVATING
REINNERVATION
REINNERVATIONS
REINOCULATE
REINOCULATED
REINOCULATES
REINOCULATING
REINOCULATION
REINOCULATIONS
REINSERTED
REINSERTING
REINSERTION
REINSERTIONS
REINSPECTED
REINSPECTING
REINSPECTION
REINSPECTIONS
REINSPECTS
REINSPIRED

REINSPIRES
REINSPIRING
REINSPIRIT
REINSPIRITED
REINSPIRITING
REINSPIRITS
REINSTALLATION
REINSTALLATIONS
REINSTALLED
REINSTALLING
REINSTALLS
REINSTALMENT
REINSTALMENTS
REINSTATED
REINSTATEMENT
REINSTATEMENTS
REINSTATES
REINSTATING
REINSTATION
REINSTATIONS
REINSTATOR
REINSTATORS
REINSTITUTE
REINSTITUTED
REINSTITUTES
REINSTITUTING
REINSURANCE
REINSURANCES
REINSURERS
REINSURING
REINTEGRATE
REINTEGRATED
REINTEGRATES
REINTEGRATING
REINTEGRATION
REINTEGRATIONS
REINTEGRATIVE
REINTERMENT
REINTERMENTS
REINTERPRET
REINTERPRETED
REINTERPRETING
REINTERPRETS
REINTERRED
REINTERRING
REINTERROGATE
REINTERROGATED
REINTERROGATES
REINTERROGATING
REINTERROGATION
REINTERVIEW
REINTERVIEWED
REINTERVIEWING
REINTERVIEWS
REINTRODUCE
REINTRODUCED
REINTRODUCES
REINTRODUCING
REINTRODUCTION

REINTRODUCTIONS
REINVADING
REINVASION
REINVASIONS
REINVENTED
REINVENTING
REINVENTION
REINVENTIONS
REINVESTED
REINVESTIGATE
REINVESTIGATED
REINVESTIGATES
REINVESTIGATING
REINVESTIGATION
REINVESTING
REINVESTMENT
REINVESTMENTS
REINVIGORATE
REINVIGORATED
REINVIGORATES
REINVIGORATING
REINVIGORATION
REINVIGORATIONS
REINVIGORATOR
REINVIGORATORS
REINVITING
REINVOKING
REINVOLVED
REINVOLVES
REINVOLVING
REIOYNDURE
REIOYNDURES
REISSUABLE
REISTAFELS
REITERANCE
REITERANCES
REITERATED
REITERATEDLY
REITERATES
REITERATING
REITERATION
REITERATIONS
REITERATIVE
REITERATIVELY
REITERATIVES
REJACKETED
REJACKETING
REJECTABLE
REJECTAMENTA
REJECTIBLE
REJECTINGLY
REJECTIONIST
REJECTIONISTS
REJECTIONS
REJIGGERED
REJIGGERING
REJOICEFUL
REJOICEMENT
REJOICEMENTS

REJOICINGLY
REJOICINGS
REJOINDERS
REJOINDURE
REJOINDURES
REJONEADOR
REJONEADORA
REJONEADORAS
REJONEADORES
REJOURNING
REJUGGLING
REJUSTIFIED
REJUSTIFIES
REJUSTIFYING
REJUVENATE
REJUVENATED
REJUVENATES
REJUVENATING
REJUVENATION
REJUVENATIONS
REJUVENATOR
REJUVENATORS
REJUVENESCE
REJUVENESCED
REJUVENESCENCE
REJUVENESCENCES
REJUVENESCENT
REJUVENESCES
REJUVENESCING
REJUVENISE
REJUVENISED
REJUVENISES
REJUVENISING
REJUVENIZE
REJUVENIZED
REJUVENIZES
REJUVENIZING
REKEYBOARD
REKEYBOARDED
REKEYBOARDING
REKEYBOARDS
REKINDLING
REKNITTING
REKNOTTING
RELABELING
RELABELLED
RELABELLING
RELACQUERED
RELACQUERING
RELACQUERS
RELANDSCAPE
RELANDSCAPED
RELANDSCAPES
RELANDSCAPING
RELATEDNESS
RELATEDNESSES
RELATIONAL
RELATIONALLY
RELATIONISM

RELATIONISMS
RELATIONIST
RELATIONISTS
RELATIONLESS
RELATIONSHIP
RELATIONSHIPS
RELATIVELY
RELATIVENESS
RELATIVENESSES
RELATIVISATION
RELATIVISATIONS
RELATIVISE
RELATIVISED
RELATIVISES
RELATIVISING
RELATIVISM
RELATIVISMS
RELATIVIST
RELATIVISTIC
RELATIVISTS
RELATIVITIES
RELATIVITIST
RELATIVITISTS
RELATIVITY
RELATIVIZATION
RELATIVIZATIONS
RELATIVIZE
RELATIVIZED
RELATIVIZES
RELATIVIZING
RELAUNCHED
RELAUNCHES
RELAUNCHING
RELAUNDERED
RELAUNDERING
RELAUNDERS
RELAXATION
RELAXATIONS
RELAXATIVE
RELAXEDNESS
RELAXEDNESSES
RELEARNING
RELEASABLE
RELEASEMENT
RELEASEMENTS
RELEGATABLE
RELEGATING
RELEGATION
RELEGATIONS
RELENTINGS
RELENTLESS
RELENTLESSLY
RELENTLESSNESS
RELENTMENT
RELENTMENTS
RELETTERED
RELETTERING
RELEVANCES
RELEVANCIES

RELEVANTLY
RELIABILITIES
RELIABILITY
RELIABLENESS
RELIABLENESSES
RELICENSED
RELICENSES
RELICENSING
RELICENSURE
RELICENSURES
RELICTIONS
RELIEFLESS
RELIEVABLE
RELIEVEDLY
RELIGHTING
RELIGIEUSE
RELIGIEUSES
RELIGIONARIES
RELIGIONARY
RELIGIONER
RELIGIONERS
RELIGIONISE
RELIGIONISED
RELIGIONISES
RELIGIONISING
RELIGIONISM
RELIGIONISMS
RELIGIONIST
RELIGIONISTS
RELIGIONIZE
RELIGIONIZED
RELIGIONIZES
RELIGIONIZING
RELIGIONLESS
RELIGIOSELY
RELIGIOSITIES
RELIGIOSITY
RELIGIOUSES
RELIGIOUSLY
RELIGIOUSNESS
RELIGIOUSNESSES
RELINQUISH
RELINQUISHED
RELINQUISHER
RELINQUISHERS
RELINQUISHES
RELINQUISHING
RELINQUISHMENT
RELINQUISHMENTS
RELIQUAIRE
RELIQUAIRES
RELIQUARIES
RELIQUEFIED
RELIQUEFIES
RELIQUEFYING
RELISHABLE
RELIVERING
RELLISHING
RELOCATABLE

RELOCATEES
RELOCATING
RELOCATION
RELOCATIONS
RELOCATORS
RELUBRICATE
RELUBRICATED
RELUBRICATES
RELUBRICATING
RELUBRICATION
RELUBRICATIONS
RELUCTANCE
RELUCTANCES
RELUCTANCIES
RELUCTANCY
RELUCTANTLY
RELUCTATED
RELUCTATES
RELUCTATING
RELUCTATION
RELUCTATIONS
RELUCTIVITIES
RELUCTIVITY
RELUMINING
REMAINDERED
REMAINDERING
REMAINDERMAN
REMAINDERMEN
REMAINDERS
REMANDMENT
REMANDMENTS
REMANENCES
REMANENCIES
REMANUFACTURE
REMANUFACTURED
REMANUFACTURER
REMANUFACTURERS
REMANUFACTURES
REMANUFACTURING
REMARKABILITIES
REMARKABILITY
REMARKABLE
REMARKABLENESS
REMARKABLES
REMARKABLY
REMARKETED
REMARKETING
REMARRIAGE
REMARRIAGES
REMARRYING
REMASTERED
REMASTERING
REMATCHING
REMATERIALISE
REMATERIALISED
REMATERIALISES
REMATERIALISING
REMATERIALIZE
REMATERIALIZED

REMATERIALIZES
REMATERIALIZING
REMEASURED
REMEASUREMENT
REMEASUREMENTS
REMEASURES
REMEASURING
REMEDIABILITIES
REMEDIABILITY
REMEDIABLE
REMEDIABLY
REMEDIALLY
REMEDIATED
REMEDIATES
REMEDIATING
REMEDIATION
REMEDIATIONS
REMEDILESS
REMEDILESSLY
REMEDILESSNESS
REMEMBERABILITY
REMEMBERABLE
REMEMBERABLY
REMEMBERED
REMEMBERER
REMEMBERERS
REMEMBERING
REMEMBRANCE
REMEMBRANCER
REMEMBRANCERS
REMEMBRANCES
REMERCYING
REMIGATING
REMIGATION
REMIGATIONS
REMIGRATED
REMIGRATES
REMIGRATING
REMIGRATION
REMIGRATIONS
REMILITARISE
REMILITARISED
REMILITARISES
REMILITARISING
REMILITARIZE
REMILITARIZED
REMILITARIZES
REMILITARIZING
REMINERALISE
REMINERALISED
REMINERALISES
REMINERALISING
REMINERALIZE
REMINERALIZED
REMINERALIZES
REMINERALIZING
REMINISCED
REMINISCENCE
REMINISCENCES

REMINISCENT
REMINISCENTIAL
REMINISCENTLY
REMINISCENTS
REMINISCER
REMINISCERS
REMINISCES
REMINISCING
REMISSIBILITIES
REMISSIBILITY
REMISSIBLE
REMISSIBLENESS
REMISSIBLY
REMISSIONS
REMISSIVELY
REMISSNESS
REMISSNESSES
REMITMENTS
REMITTABLE
REMITTANCE
REMITTANCES
REMITTENCE
REMITTENCES
REMITTENCIES
REMITTENCY
REMITTENTLY
REMIXTURES
REMOBILISATION
REMOBILISATIONS
REMOBILISE
REMOBILISED
REMOBILISES
REMOBILISING
REMOBILIZATION
REMOBILIZATIONS
REMOBILIZE
REMOBILIZED
REMOBILIZES
REMOBILIZING
REMODELERS
REMODELING
REMODELLED
REMODELLING
REMODIFIED
REMODIFIES
REMODIFYING
REMOISTENED
REMOISTENING
REMOISTENS
REMONETISATION
REMONETISATIONS
REMONETISE
REMONETISED
REMONETISES
REMONETISING
REMONETIZATION
REMONETIZATIONS
REMONETIZE
REMONETIZED

REMONETIZES
REMONETIZING
REMONSTRANCE
REMONSTRANCES
REMONSTRANT
REMONSTRANTLY
REMONSTRANTS
REMONSTRATE
REMONSTRATED
REMONSTRATES
REMONSTRATING
REMONSTRATINGLY
REMONSTRATION
REMONSTRATIONS
REMONSTRATIVE
REMONSTRATIVELY
REMONSTRATOR
REMONSTRATORS
REMONSTRATORY
REMONTANTS
REMONTOIRE
REMONTOIRES
REMONTOIRS
REMORALISATION
REMORALISATIONS
REMORALISE
REMORALISED
REMORALISES
REMORALISING
REMORALIZATION
REMORALIZATIONS
REMORALIZE
REMORALIZED
REMORALIZES
REMORALIZING
REMORSEFUL
REMORSEFULLY
REMORSEFULNESS
REMORSELESS
REMORSELESSLY
REMORSELESSNESS
REMORTGAGE
REMORTGAGED
REMORTGAGES
REMORTGAGING
REMOTENESS
REMOTENESSES
REMOTIVATE
REMOTIVATED
REMOTIVATES
REMOTIVATING
REMOTIVATION
REMOTIVATIONS
REMOULADES
REMOULDING
REMOUNTING
REMOVABILITIES
REMOVABILITY
REMOVABLENESS

REMOVABLENESSES
REMOVALIST
REMOVALISTS
REMOVEABLE
REMOVEDNESS
REMOVEDNESSES
REMUNERABILITY
REMUNERABLE
REMUNERATE
REMUNERATED
REMUNERATES
REMUNERATING
REMUNERATION
REMUNERATIONS
REMUNERATIVE
REMUNERATIVELY
REMUNERATOR
REMUNERATORS
REMUNERATORY
REMURMURED
REMURMURING
REMYTHOLOGISE
REMYTHOLOGISED
REMYTHOLOGISES
REMYTHOLOGISING
REMYTHOLOGIZE
REMYTHOLOGIZED
REMYTHOLOGIZES
REMYTHOLOGIZING
RENAISSANCE
RENAISSANCES
RENASCENCE
RENASCENCES
RENATIONALISE
RENATIONALISED
RENATIONALISES
RENATIONALISING
RENATIONALIZE
RENATIONALIZED
RENATIONALIZES
RENATIONALIZING
RENATURATION
RENATURATIONS
RENATURING
RENCONTRES
RENCOUNTER
RENCOUNTERED
RENCOUNTERING
RENCOUNTERS
RENDERABLE
RENDERINGS
RENDEZVOUS
RENDEZVOUSED
RENDEZVOUSES
RENDEZVOUSING
RENDITIONS
RENEGADING
RENEGADOES
RENEGATION

RENEGATIONS
RENEGOTIABLE
RENEGOTIATE
RENEGOTIATED
RENEGOTIATES
RENEGOTIATING
RENEGOTIATION
RENEGOTIATIONS
RENEWABILITIES
RENEWABILITY
RENEWABLES
RENEWEDNESS
RENEWEDNESSES
RENFORCING
RENITENCES
RENITENCIES
RENOGRAPHIC
RENOGRAPHIES
RENOGRAPHY
RENOMINATE
RENOMINATED
RENOMINATES
RENOMINATING
RENOMINATION
RENOMINATIONS
RENORMALISATION
RENORMALISE
RENORMALISED
RENORMALISES
RENORMALISING
RENORMALIZATION
RENORMALIZE
RENORMALIZED
RENORMALIZES
RENORMALIZING
RENOSTERVELD
RENOSTERVELDS
RENOTIFIED
RENOTIFIES
RENOTIFYING
RENOUNCEABLE
RENOUNCEMENT
RENOUNCEMENTS
RENOUNCERS
RENOUNCING
RENOVASCULAR
RENOVATING
RENOVATION
RENOVATIONS
RENOVATIVE
RENOVATORS
RENSSELAERITE
RENSSELAERITES
RENTABILITIES
RENTABILITY
RENTALLERS
RENUMBERED
RENUMBERING
RENUNCIATE

RENUNCIATES

RENUNCIATES
RENUNCIATION
RENUNCIATIONS
RENUNCIATIVE
RENUNCIATORY
RENVERSEMENT
RENVERSEMENTS
RENVERSING
REOBJECTED
REOBJECTING
REOBSERVED
REOBSERVES
REOBSERVING
REOBTAINED
REOBTAINING
REOCCUPATION
REOCCUPATIONS
REOCCUPIED
REOCCUPIES
REOCCUPYING
REOCCURRED
REOCCURRENCE
REOCCURRENCES
REOCCURRING
REOFFENDED
REOFFENDER
REOFFENDERS
REOFFENDING
REOFFERING
REOPERATED
REOPERATES
REOPERATING
REOPERATION
REOPERATIONS
REOPPOSING
REORCHESTRATE
REORCHESTRATED
REORCHESTRATES
REORCHESTRATING
REORCHESTRATION
REORDAINED
REORDAINING
REORDERING
REORDINATION
REORDINATIONS
REORGANISATION
REORGANISATIONS
REORGANISE
REORGANISED
REORGANISER
REORGANISERS
REORGANISES
REORGANISING
REORGANIZATION
REORGANIZATIONS
REORGANIZE
REORGANIZED
REORGANIZER
REORGANIZERS

REORGANIZES
REORGANIZING
REORIENTATE
REORIENTATED
REORIENTATES
REORIENTATING
REORIENTATION
REORIENTATIONS
REORIENTED
REORIENTING
REOUTFITTED
REOUTFITTING
REOVIRUSES
REOXIDATION
REOXIDATIONS
REOXIDISED
REOXIDISES
REOXIDISING
REOXIDIZED
REOXIDIZES
REOXIDIZING
REPACIFIED
REPACIFIES
REPACIFYING
REPACKAGED
REPACKAGER
REPACKAGERS
REPACKAGES
REPACKAGING
REPAGINATE
REPAGINATED
REPAGINATES
REPAGINATING
REPAGINATION
REPAGINATIONS
REPAINTING
REPAINTINGS
REPAIRABILITIES
REPAIRABILITY
REPAIRABLE
REPANELING
REPANELLED
REPANELLING
REPAPERING
REPARABILITIES
REPARABILITY
REPARATION
REPARATIONS
REPARATIVE
REPARATORY
REPARTEEING
REPARTITION
REPARTITIONED
REPARTITIONING
REPARTITIONS
REPASSAGES
REPASTURES
REPATCHING
REPATRIATE

REPATRIATED
REPATRIATES
REPATRIATING
REPATRIATION
REPATRIATIONS
REPATRIATOR
REPATRIATORS
REPATTERNED
REPATTERNING
REPATTERNS
REPAYMENTS
REPEALABLE
REPEATABILITIES
REPEATABILITY
REPEATABLE
REPEATEDLY
REPEATINGS
REPECHAGES
REPELLANCE
REPELLANCES
REPELLANCIES
REPELLANCY
REPELLANTLY
REPELLANTS
REPELLENCE
REPELLENCES
REPELLENCIES
REPELLENCY
REPELLENTLY
REPELLENTS
REPELLINGLY
REPENTANCE
REPENTANCES
REPENTANTLY
REPENTANTS
REPENTINGLY
REPEOPLING
REPERCUSSED
REPERCUSSES
REPERCUSSING
REPERCUSSION
REPERCUSSIONS
REPERCUSSIVE
REPERTOIRE
REPERTOIRES
REPERTORIAL
REPERTORIES
REPERUSALS
REPERUSING
REPETITEUR
REPETITEURS
REPETITEUSE
REPETITEUSES
REPETITION
REPETITIONAL
REPETITIONARY
REPETITIONS
REPETITIOUS
REPETITIOUSLY

REPETITIOUSNESS
REPETITIVE
REPETITIVELY
REPETITIVENESS
REPHOTOGRAPH
REPHOTOGRAPHED
REPHOTOGRAPHING
REPHOTOGRAPHS
REPHRASING
REPIGMENTED
REPIGMENTING
REPIGMENTS
REPINEMENT
REPINEMENTS
REPININGLY
REPLACEABILITY
REPLACEABLE
REPLACEMENT
REPLACEMENTS
REPLANNING
REPLANTATION
REPLANTATIONS
REPLANTING
REPLASTERED
REPLASTERING
REPLASTERS
REPLEADERS
REPLEADING
REPLEDGING
REPLENISHABLE
REPLENISHED
REPLENISHER
REPLENISHERS
REPLENISHES
REPLENISHING
REPLENISHMENT
REPLENISHMENTS
REPLETENESS
REPLETENESSES
REPLETIONS
REPLEVIABLE
REPLEVINED
REPLEVINING
REPLEVISABLE
REPLEVYING
REPLICABILITIES
REPLICABILITY
REPLICABLE
REPLICASES
REPLICATED
REPLICATES
REPLICATING
REPLICATION
REPLICATIONS
REPLICATIVE
REPLICATOR
REPLICATORS
REPLOTTING
REPLUMBING

REPLUNGING
REPOINTING
REPOLARISATION
REPOLARISATIONS
REPOLARISE
REPOLARISED
REPOLARISES
REPOLARISING
REPOLARIZATION
REPOLARIZATIONS
REPOLARIZE
REPOLARIZED
REPOLARIZES
REPOLARIZING
REPOLISHED
REPOLISHES
REPOLISHING
REPOPULARISE
REPOPULARISED
REPOPULARISES
REPOPULARISING
REPOPULARIZE
REPOPULARIZED
REPOPULARIZES
REPOPULARIZING
REPOPULATE
REPOPULATED
REPOPULATES
REPOPULATING
REPOPULATION
REPOPULATIONS
REPORTABLE
REPORTAGES
REPORTEDLY
REPORTINGLY
REPORTINGS
REPORTORIAL
REPORTORIALLY
REPOSEDNESS
REPOSEDNESSES
REPOSEFULLY
REPOSEFULNESS
REPOSEFULNESSES
REPOSITING
REPOSITION
REPOSITIONED
REPOSITIONING
REPOSITIONS
REPOSITORIES
REPOSITORS
REPOSITORY
REPOSSESSED
REPOSSESSES
REPOSSESSING
REPOSSESSION
REPOSSESSIONS
REPOSSESSOR
REPOSSESSORS
REPOTTINGS

REPOUSSAGE
REPOUSSAGES
REPOUSSOIR
REPOUSSOIRS
REPOWERING
REPREEVING
REPREHENDABLE
REPREHENDED
REPREHENDER
REPREHENDERS
REPREHENDING
REPREHENDS
REPREHENSIBLE
REPREHENSIBLY
REPREHENSION
REPREHENSIONS
REPREHENSIVE
REPREHENSIVELY
REPREHENSORY
REPRESENTABLE
REPRESENTAMEN
REPRESENTAMENS
REPRESENTANT
REPRESENTANTS
REPRESENTATION
REPRESENTATIONS
REPRESENTATIVE
REPRESENTATIVES
REPRESENTED
REPRESENTEE
REPRESENTEES
REPRESENTER
REPRESENTERS
REPRESENTING
REPRESENTMENT
REPRESENTMENTS
REPRESENTOR
REPRESENTORS
REPRESENTS
REPRESSERS
REPRESSIBILITY
REPRESSIBLE
REPRESSIBLY
REPRESSING
REPRESSION
REPRESSIONIST
REPRESSIONS
REPRESSIVE
REPRESSIVELY
REPRESSIVENESS
REPRESSORS
REPRESSURISE
REPRESSURISED
REPRESSURISES
REPRESSURISING
REPRESSURIZE
REPRESSURIZED
REPRESSURIZES
REPRESSURIZING

REPRIEVABLE
REPRIEVALS
REPRIEVERS
REPRIEVING
REPRIMANDED
REPRIMANDING
REPRIMANDS
REPRINTERS
REPRINTING
REPRISTINATE
REPRISTINATED
REPRISTINATES
REPRISTINATING
REPRISTINATION
REPRISTINATIONS
REPRIVATISATION
REPRIVATISE
REPRIVATISED
REPRIVATISES
REPRIVATISING
REPRIVATIZATION
REPRIVATIZE
REPRIVATIZED
REPRIVATIZES
REPRIVATIZING
REPROACHABLE
REPROACHABLY
REPROACHED
REPROACHER
REPROACHERS
REPROACHES
REPROACHFUL
REPROACHFULLY
REPROACHFULNESS
REPROACHING
REPROACHINGLY
REPROACHLESS
REPROBACIES
REPROBANCE
REPROBANCES
REPROBATED
REPROBATER
REPROBATERS
REPROBATES
REPROBATING
REPROBATION
REPROBATIONARY
REPROBATIONS
REPROBATIVE
REPROBATIVELY
REPROBATOR
REPROBATORS
REPROBATORY
REPROCESSED
REPROCESSES
REPROCESSING
REPRODUCED
REPRODUCER
REPRODUCERS

REPRODUCES
REPRODUCIBILITY
REPRODUCIBLE
REPRODUCIBLES
REPRODUCIBLY
REPRODUCING
REPRODUCTION
REPRODUCTIONS
REPRODUCTIVE
REPRODUCTIVELY
REPRODUCTIVES
REPRODUCTIVITY
REPROGRAMED
REPROGRAMING
REPROGRAMMABLE
REPROGRAMME
REPROGRAMMED
REPROGRAMMES
REPROGRAMMING
REPROGRAMS
REPROGRAPHER
REPROGRAPHERS
REPROGRAPHIC
REPROGRAPHICS
REPROGRAPHIES
REPROGRAPHY
REPROOFING
REPROVABLE
REPROVINGLY
REPROVINGS
REPROVISION
REPROVISIONED
REPROVISIONING
REPROVISIONS
REPTATIONS
REPTILIANLY
REPTILIANS
REPTILIFEROUS
REPTILIOUS
REPUBLICAN
REPUBLICANISE
REPUBLICANISED
REPUBLICANISES
REPUBLICANISING
REPUBLICANISM
REPUBLICANISMS
REPUBLICANIZE
REPUBLICANIZED
REPUBLICANIZES
REPUBLICANIZING
REPUBLICANS
REPUBLICATION
REPUBLICATIONS
REPUBLISHED
REPUBLISHER
REPUBLISHERS
REPUBLISHES
REPUBLISHING
REPUDIABLE

REPUDIATED

REPUDIATED
REPUDIATES
REPUDIATING
REPUDIATION
REPUDIATIONIST
REPUDIATIONISTS
REPUDIATIONS
REPUDIATIVE
REPUDIATOR
REPUDIATORS
REPUGNANCE
REPUGNANCES
REPUGNANCIES
REPUGNANCY
REPUGNANTLY
REPULSIONS
REPULSIVELY
REPULSIVENESS
REPULSIVENESSES
REPUNCTUATION
REPUNCTUATIONS
REPURCHASE
REPURCHASED
REPURCHASES
REPURCHASING
REPURIFIED
REPURIFIES
REPURIFYING
REPURPOSED
REPURPOSES
REPURPOSING
REPURSUING
REPUTABILITIES
REPUTABILITY
REPUTATION
REPUTATIONAL
REPUTATIONLESS
REPUTATIONS
REPUTATIVE
REPUTATIVELY
REPUTELESS
REQUALIFIED
REQUALIFIES
REQUALIFYING
REQUESTERS
REQUESTING
REQUESTORS
REQUICKENED
REQUICKENING
REQUICKENS
REQUIESCAT
REQUIESCATS
REQUIGHTED
REQUIGHTING
REQUIRABLE
REQUIREMENT
REQUIREMENTS
REQUIRINGS
REQUISITELY

REQUISITENESS
REQUISITENESSES
REQUISITES
REQUISITION
REQUISITIONARY
REQUISITIONED
REQUISITIONING
REQUISITIONIST
REQUISITIONISTS
REQUISITIONS
REQUISITOR
REQUISITORS
REQUISITORY
REQUITABLE
REQUITEFUL
REQUITELESS
REQUITEMENT
REQUITEMENTS
REQUITTING
REQUOYLING
RERADIATED
RERADIATES
RERADIATING
RERADIATION
RERADIATIONS
REREADINGS
REREBRACES
RERECORDED
RERECORDING
REREDORTER
REREDORTERS
REREDOSSES
REREGISTER
REREGISTERED
REREGISTERING
REREGISTERS
REREGISTRATION
REREGISTRATIONS
REREGULATE
REREGULATED
REREGULATES
REREGULATING
REREGULATION
REREGULATIONS
RERELEASED
RERELEASES
RERELEASING
REREMINDED
REREMINDING
REREPEATED
REREPEATING
REREVIEWED
REREVIEWING
REREVISING
REROUTEING
RESADDLING
RESALEABLE
RESALUTING
RESAMPLING

RESCHEDULE
RESCHEDULED
RESCHEDULES
RESCHEDULING
RESCHEDULINGS
RESCHOOLED
RESCHOOLING
RESCINDABLE
RESCINDERS
RESCINDING
RESCINDMENT
RESCINDMENTS
RESCISSIBLE
RESCISSION
RESCISSIONS
RESCISSORY
RESCREENED
RESCREENING
RESCRIPTED
RESCRIPTING
RESCULPTED
RESCULPTING
RESEALABLE
RESEARCHABLE
RESEARCHED
RESEARCHER
RESEARCHERS
RESEARCHES
RESEARCHFUL
RESEARCHING
RESEARCHIST
RESEARCHISTS
RESEASONED
RESEASONING
RESECTABILITIES
RESECTABILITY
RESECTABLE
RESECTIONAL
RESECTIONS
RESECURING
RESEGREGATE
RESEGREGATED
RESEGREGATES
RESEGREGATING
RESEGREGATION
RESEGREGATIONS
RESEIZURES
RESELECTED
RESELECTING
RESELECTION
RESELECTIONS
RESEMBLANCE
RESEMBLANCES
RESEMBLANT
RESEMBLERS
RESEMBLING
RESENSITISE
RESENSITISED
RESENSITISES

RESENSITISING
RESENSITIZE
RESENSITIZED
RESENSITIZES
RESENSITIZING
RESENTENCE
RESENTENCED
RESENTENCES
RESENTENCING
RESENTFULLY
RESENTFULNESS
RESENTFULNESSES
RESENTINGLY
RESENTMENT
RESENTMENTS
RESERPINES
RESERVABLE
RESERVATION
RESERVATIONIST
RESERVATIONISTS
RESERVATIONS
RESERVATORIES
RESERVATORY
RESERVEDLY
RESERVEDNESS
RESERVEDNESSES
RESERVICED
RESERVICES
RESERVICING
RESERVISTS
RESERVOIRED
RESERVOIRING
RESERVOIRS
RESETTABLE
RESETTLEMENT
RESETTLEMENTS
RESETTLING
RESHARPENED
RESHARPENING
RESHARPENS
RESHINGLED
RESHINGLES
RESHINGLING
RESHIPMENT
RESHIPMENTS
RESHIPPERS
RESHIPPING
RESHOOTING
RESHOWERED
RESHOWERING
RESHUFFLED
RESHUFFLES
RESHUFFLING
RESIDENCES
RESIDENCIES
RESIDENTER
RESIDENTERS
RESIDENTIAL
RESIDENTIALLY

RESIDENTIARIES
RESIDENTIARY
RESIDENTSHIP
RESIDENTSHIPS
RESIDUALLY
RESIGHTING
RESIGNATION
RESIGNATIONS
RESIGNEDLY
RESIGNEDNESS
RESIGNEDNESSES
RESIGNMENT
RESIGNMENTS
RESILEMENT
RESILEMENTS
RESILIENCE
RESILIENCES
RESILIENCIES
RESILIENCY
RESILIENTLY
RESILVERED
RESILVERING
RESINATING
RESINIFEROUS
RESINIFICATION
RESINIFICATIONS
RESINIFIED
RESINIFIES
RESINIFYING
RESINISING
RESINIZING
RESINOUSLY
RESINOUSNESS
RESINOUSNESSES
RESIPISCENCE
RESIPISCENCES
RESIPISCENCIES
RESIPISCENCY
RESIPISCENT
RESISTANCE
RESISTANCES
RESISTANTS
RESISTENTS
RESISTIBILITIES
RESISTIBILITY
RESISTIBLE
RESISTIBLY
RESISTINGLY
RESISTIVELY
RESISTIVENESS
RESISTIVENESSES
RESISTIVITIES
RESISTIVITY
RESISTLESS
RESISTLESSLY
RESISTLESSNESS
RESITTINGS
RESITUATED
RESITUATES

RESITUATING
RESKETCHED
RESKETCHES
RESKETCHING
RESKILLING
RESKILLINGS
RESMELTING
RESMOOTHED
RESMOOTHING
RESNATRONS
RESOCIALISATION
RESOCIALISE
RESOCIALISED
RESOCIALISES
RESOCIALISING
RESOCIALIZATION
RESOCIALIZE
RESOCIALIZED
RESOCIALIZES
RESOCIALIZING
RESOFTENED
RESOFTENING
RESOLDERED
RESOLDERING
RESOLIDIFIED
RESOLIDIFIES
RESOLIDIFY
RESOLIDIFYING
RESOLUBILITIES
RESOLUBILITY
RESOLUBLENESS
RESOLUBLENESSES
RESOLUTELY
RESOLUTENESS
RESOLUTENESSES
RESOLUTEST
RESOLUTION
RESOLUTIONER
RESOLUTIONERS
RESOLUTIONIST
RESOLUTIONISTS
RESOLUTIONS
RESOLUTIVE
RESOLVABILITIES
RESOLVABILITY
RESOLVABLE
RESOLVABLENESS
RESOLVEDLY
RESOLVEDNESS
RESOLVEDNESSES
RESOLVENTS
RESONANCES
RESONANTLY
RESONATING
RESONATION
RESONATIONS
RESONATORS
RESORBENCE
RESORBENCES

RESORCINAL
RESORCINOL
RESORCINOLS
RESORPTION
RESORPTIONS
RESORPTIVE
RESOUNDING
RESOUNDINGLY
RESOURCEFUL
RESOURCEFULLY
RESOURCEFULNESS
RESOURCELESS
RESOURCING
RESPEAKING
RESPECIFIED
RESPECIFIES
RESPECIFYING
RESPECTABILISE
RESPECTABILISED
RESPECTABILISES
RESPECTABILITY
RESPECTABILIZE
RESPECTABILIZED
RESPECTABILIZES
RESPECTABLE
RESPECTABLENESS
RESPECTABLES
RESPECTABLY
RESPECTANT
RESPECTERS
RESPECTFUL
RESPECTFULLY
RESPECTFULNESS
RESPECTING
RESPECTIVE
RESPECTIVELY
RESPECTIVENESS
RESPECTLESS
RESPELLING
RESPELLINGS
RESPIRABILITIES
RESPIRABILITY
RESPIRABLE
RESPIRATION
RESPIRATIONAL
RESPIRATIONS
RESPIRATOR
RESPIRATORS
RESPIRATORY
RESPIRITUALISE
RESPIRITUALISED
RESPIRITUALISES
RESPIRITUALIZE
RESPIRITUALIZED
RESPIRITUALIZES
RESPIROMETER
RESPIROMETERS
RESPIROMETRIC
RESPIROMETRIES

RESPIROMETRY
RESPITELESS
RESPLENDED
RESPLENDENCE
RESPLENDENCES
RESPLENDENCIES
RESPLENDENCY
RESPLENDENT
RESPLENDENTLY
RESPLENDING
RESPLICING
RESPLITTING
RESPONDENCE
RESPONDENCES
RESPONDENCIES
RESPONDENCY
RESPONDENT
RESPONDENTIA
RESPONDENTIAS
RESPONDENTS
RESPONDERS
RESPONDING
RESPONSELESS
RESPONSERS
RESPONSIBILITY
RESPONSIBLE
RESPONSIBLENESS
RESPONSIBLY
RESPONSIONS
RESPONSIVE
RESPONSIVELY
RESPONSIVENESS
RESPONSORIAL
RESPONSORIALS
RESPONSORIES
RESPONSORS
RESPONSORY
RESPONSUMS
RESPOOLING
RESPOTTING
RESPRAYING
RESPREADING
RESPRINGING
RESPROUTED
RESPROUTING
RESSALDARS
RESSENTIMENT
RESSENTIMENTS
RESTABILISE
RESTABILISED
RESTABILISES
RESTABILISING
RESTABILIZE
RESTABILIZED
RESTABILIZES
RESTABILIZING
RESTABLING
RESTACKING
RESTAFFING

RESTAMPING
RESTARTABLE
RESTARTERS
RESTARTING
RESTATEMENT
RESTATEMENTS
RESTATIONED
RESTATIONING
RESTATIONS
RESTAURANT
RESTAURANTEUR
RESTAURANTEURS
RESTAURANTS
RESTAURATEUR
RESTAURATEURS
RESTAURATION
RESTAURATIONS
RESTEMMING
RESTFULLER
RESTFULLEST
RESTFULNESS
RESTFULNESSES
RESTHARROW
RESTHARROWS
RESTIMULATE
RESTIMULATED
RESTIMULATES
RESTIMULATING
RESTIMULATION
RESTIMULATIONS
RESTITCHED
RESTITCHES
RESTITCHING
RESTITUTED
RESTITUTES
RESTITUTING
RESTITUTION
RESTITUTIONISM
RESTITUTIONISMS
RESTITUTIONIST
RESTITUTIONISTS
RESTITUTIONS
RESTITUTIVE
RESTITUTOR
RESTITUTORS
RESTITUTORY
RESTIVENESS
RESTIVENESSES
RESTLESSLY
RESTLESSNESS
RESTLESSNESSES
RESTOCKING
RESTORABLE
RESTORABLENESS
RESTORATION
RESTORATIONISM
RESTORATIONISMS
RESTORATIONIST
RESTORATIONISTS

RESTORATIONS
RESTORATIVE
RESTORATIVELY
RESTORATIVES
RESTRAINABLE
RESTRAINED
RESTRAINEDLY
RESTRAINEDNESS
RESTRAINER
RESTRAINERS
RESTRAINING
RESTRAININGS
RESTRAINTS
RESTRENGTHEN
RESTRENGTHENED
RESTRENGTHENING
RESTRENGTHENS
RESTRESSED
RESTRESSES
RESTRESSING
RESTRETCHED
RESTRETCHES
RESTRETCHING
RESTRICKEN
RESTRICTED
RESTRICTEDLY
RESTRICTEDNESS
RESTRICTING
RESTRICTION
RESTRICTIONISM
RESTRICTIONISMS
RESTRICTIONIST
RESTRICTIONISTS
RESTRICTIONS
RESTRICTIVE
RESTRICTIVELY
RESTRICTIVENESS
RESTRICTIVES
RESTRIKING
RESTRINGED
RESTRINGEING
RESTRINGENT
RESTRINGENTS
RESTRINGES
RESTRINGING
RESTRIVING
RESTRUCTURE
RESTRUCTURED
RESTRUCTURES
RESTRUCTURING
RESTRUCTURINGS
RESTUDYING
RESTUFFING
RESTUMPING
RESUBJECTED
RESUBJECTING
RESUBJECTS
RESUBMISSION
RESUBMISSIONS

RESUBMITTED
RESUBMITTING
RESULTANTLY
RESULTANTS
RESULTATIVE
RESULTLESS
RESULTLESSNESS
RESUMMONED
RESUMMONING
RESUMPTION
RESUMPTIONS
RESUMPTIVE
RESUMPTIVELY
RESUPINATE
RESUPINATION
RESUPINATIONS
RESUPPLIED
RESUPPLIES
RESUPPLYING
RESURFACED
RESURFACER
RESURFACERS
RESURFACES
RESURFACING
RESURGENCE
RESURGENCES
RESURRECTED
RESURRECTING
RESURRECTION
RESURRECTIONAL
RESURRECTIONARY
RESURRECTIONISE
RESURRECTIONISM
RESURRECTIONIST
RESURRECTIONIZE
RESURRECTIONS
RESURRECTIVE
RESURRECTOR
RESURRECTORS
RESURRECTS
RESURVEYED
RESURVEYING
RESUSCITABLE
RESUSCITANT
RESUSCITANTS
RESUSCITATE
RESUSCITATED
RESUSCITATES
RESUSCITATING
RESUSCITATION
RESUSCITATIONS
RESUSCITATIVE
RESUSCITATOR
RESUSCITATORS
RESUSPENDED
RESUSPENDING
RESUSPENDS
RESVERATROL
RESVERATROLS

RESWALLOWED
RESWALLOWING
RESWALLOWS
RESYNCHRONISE
RESYNCHRONISED
RESYNCHRONISES
RESYNCHRONISING
RESYNCHRONIZE
RESYNCHRONIZED
RESYNCHRONIZES
RESYNCHRONIZING
RESYNTHESES
RESYNTHESIS
RESYNTHESISE
RESYNTHESISED
RESYNTHESISES
RESYNTHESISING
RESYNTHESIZE
RESYNTHESIZED
RESYNTHESIZES
RESYNTHESIZING
RESYSTEMATISE
RESYSTEMATISED
RESYSTEMATISES
RESYSTEMATISING
RESYSTEMATIZE
RESYSTEMATIZED
RESYSTEMATIZES
RESYSTEMATIZING
RETACKLING
RETAILINGS
RETAILMENT
RETAILMENTS
RETAILORED
RETAILORING
RETAINABLE
RETAINERSHIP
RETAINERSHIPS
RETAINMENT
RETAINMENTS
RETALIATED
RETALIATES
RETALIATING
RETALIATION
RETALIATIONIST
RETALIATIONISTS
RETALIATIONS
RETALIATIVE
RETALIATOR
RETALIATORS
RETALIATORY
RETALLYING
RETARDANTS
RETARDATES
RETARDATION
RETARDATIONS
RETARDATIVE
RETARDATORY
RETARDMENT

RETARDMENTS
RETARGETED
RETARGETING
RETEACHING
RETELLINGS
RETEMPERED
RETEMPERING
RETENTIONIST
RETENTIONISTS
RETENTIONS
RETENTIVELY
RETENTIVENESS
RETENTIVENESSES
RETENTIVITIES
RETENTIVITY
RETESTIFIED
RETESTIFIES
RETESTIFYING
RETEXTURED
RETEXTURES
RETEXTURING
RETHINKERS
RETHINKING
RETHREADED
RETHREADING
RETIARIUSES
RETICELLAS
RETICENCES
RETICENCIES
RETICENTLY
RETICULARLY
RETICULARY
RETICULATE
RETICULATED
RETICULATELY
RETICULATES
RETICULATING
RETICULATION
RETICULATIONS
RETICULOCYTE
RETICULOCYTES
RETICULUMS
RETIGHTENED
RETIGHTENING
RETIGHTENS
RETINACULA
RETINACULAR
RETINACULUM
RETINALITE
RETINALITES
RETINISPORA
RETINISPORAS
RETINITIDES
RETINITISES
RETINOBLASTOMA
RETINOBLASTOMAS
RETINOPATHIES
RETINOPATHY
RETINOSCOPE

RETINOSCOPES
RETINOSCOPIC
RETINOSCOPIES
RETINOSCOPIST
RETINOSCOPISTS
RETINOSCOPY
RETINOSPORA
RETINOSPORAS
RETINOTECTAL
RETIRACIES
RETIREDNESS
RETIREDNESSES
RETIREMENT
RETIREMENTS
RETIRINGLY
RETIRINGNESS
RETIRINGNESSES
RETORSIONS
RETORTIONS
RETOTALING
RETOTALLED
RETOTALLING
RETOUCHABLE
RETOUCHERS
RETOUCHING
RETRACEABLE
RETRACEMENT
RETRACEMENTS
RETRACKING
RETRACTABILITY
RETRACTABLE
RETRACTATION
RETRACTATIONS
RETRACTIBILITY
RETRACTIBLE
RETRACTILE
RETRACTILITIES
RETRACTILITY
RETRACTING
RETRACTION
RETRACTIONS
RETRACTIVE
RETRACTIVELY
RETRACTORS
RETRAINABLE
RETRAINEES
RETRAINING
RETRANSFER
RETRANSFERRED
RETRANSFERRING
RETRANSFERS
RETRANSFORM
RETRANSFORMED
RETRANSFORMING
RETRANSFORMS
RETRANSLATE
RETRANSLATED
RETRANSLATES
RETRANSLATING

RETRANSLATION
RETRANSLATIONS
RETRANSMISSION
RETRANSMISSIONS
RETRANSMIT
RETRANSMITS
RETRANSMITTED
RETRANSMITTING
RETREADING
RETREATANT
RETREATANTS
RETREATERS
RETREATING
RETRENCHABLE
RETRENCHED
RETRENCHES
RETRENCHING
RETRENCHMENT
RETRENCHMENTS
RETRIBUTED
RETRIBUTES
RETRIBUTING
RETRIBUTION
RETRIBUTIONS
RETRIBUTIVE
RETRIBUTIVELY
RETRIBUTOR
RETRIBUTORS
RETRIBUTORY
RETRIEVABILITY
RETRIEVABLE
RETRIEVABLENESS
RETRIEVABLY
RETRIEVALS
RETRIEVEMENT
RETRIEVEMENTS
RETRIEVERS
RETRIEVING
RETRIEVINGS
RETRIMMING
RETROACTED
RETROACTING
RETROACTION
RETROACTIONS
RETROACTIVE
RETROACTIVELY
RETROACTIVENESS
RETROACTIVITIES
RETROACTIVITY
RETROBULBAR
RETROCEDED
RETROCEDENCE
RETROCEDENCES
RETROCEDENT
RETROCEDES
RETROCEDING
RETROCESSION
RETROCESSIONS
RETROCESSIVE

RETROCHOIR
RETROCHOIRS
RETROCOGNITION
RETROCOGNITIONS
RETRODICTED
RETRODICTING
RETRODICTION
RETRODICTIONS
RETRODICTIVE
RETRODICTS
RETROFIRED
RETROFIRES
RETROFIRING
RETROFITTED
RETROFITTING
RETROFITTINGS
RETROFLECTED
RETROFLECTION
RETROFLECTIONS
RETROFLEXED
RETROFLEXES
RETROFLEXION
RETROFLEXIONS
RETROGRADATION
RETROGRADATIONS
RETROGRADE
RETROGRADED
RETROGRADELY
RETROGRADES
RETROGRADING
RETROGRESS
RETROGRESSED
RETROGRESSES
RETROGRESSING
RETROGRESSION
RETROGRESSIONAL
RETROGRESSIONS
RETROGRESSIVE
RETROGRESSIVELY
RETROJECTED
RETROJECTING
RETROJECTION
RETROJECTIONS
RETROJECTS
RETROLENTAL
RETROMINGENCIES
RETROMINGENCY
RETROMINGENT
RETROMINGENTS
RETROPACKS
RETROPERITONEAL
RETROPHILIA
RETROPHILIAC
RETROPHILIACS
RETROPHILIAS
RETROPULSION
RETROPULSIONS
RETROPULSIVE
RETROREFLECTION

RETROREFLECTIVE
RETROREFLECTOR
RETROREFLECTORS
RETROROCKET
RETROROCKETS
RETRORSELY
RETROSEXUAL
RETROSEXUALS
RETROSPECT
RETROSPECTED
RETROSPECTING
RETROSPECTION
RETROSPECTIONS
RETROSPECTIVE
RETROSPECTIVELY
RETROSPECTIVES
RETROSPECTS
RETROUSSAGE
RETROUSSAGES
RETROVERSE
RETROVERSION
RETROVERSIONS
RETROVERTED
RETROVERTING
RETROVERTS
RETROVIRAL
RETROVIRUS
RETROVIRUSES
RETURNABILITIES
RETURNABILITY
RETURNABLE
RETURNABLES
RETURNLESS
RETWISTING
REUNIFICATION
REUNIFICATIONS
REUNIFYING
REUNIONISM
REUNIONISMS
REUNIONIST
REUNIONISTIC
REUNIONISTS
REUNITABLE
REUPHOLSTER
REUPHOLSTERED
REUPHOLSTERING
REUPHOLSTERS
REUSABILITIES
REUSABILITY
REUTILISATION
REUTILISATIONS
REUTILISED
REUTILISES
REUTILISING
REUTILIZATION
REUTILIZATIONS
REUTILIZED
REUTILIZES
REUTILIZING

REUTTERING
REVACCINATE
REVACCINATED
REVACCINATES
REVACCINATING
REVACCINATION
REVACCINATIONS
REVALENTAS
REVALIDATE
REVALIDATED
REVALIDATES
REVALIDATING
REVALIDATION
REVALIDATIONS
REVALORISATION
REVALORISATIONS
REVALORISE
REVALORISED
REVALORISES
REVALORISING
REVALORIZATION
REVALORIZATIONS
REVALORIZE
REVALORIZED
REVALORIZES
REVALORIZING
REVALUATED
REVALUATES
REVALUATING
REVALUATION
REVALUATIONS
REVAMPINGS
REVANCHISM
REVANCHISMS
REVANCHIST
REVANCHISTS
REVARNISHED
REVARNISHES
REVARNISHING
REVEALABILITIES
REVEALABILITY
REVEALABLE
REVEALINGLY
REVEALINGNESS
REVEALINGNESSES
REVEALINGS
REVEALMENT
REVEALMENTS
REVEGETATE
REVEGETATED
REVEGETATES
REVEGETATING
REVEGETATION
REVEGETATIONS
REVELATION
REVELATIONAL
REVELATIONIST
REVELATIONISTS
REVELATIONS

REVELATIVE
REVELATORS
REVELATORY
REVELLINGS
REVELMENTS
REVENDICATE
REVENDICATED
REVENDICATES
REVENDICATING
REVENDICATION
REVENDICATIONS
REVENGEFUL
REVENGEFULLY
REVENGEFULNESS
REVENGELESS
REVENGEMENT
REVENGEMENTS
REVENGINGLY
REVENGINGS
REVERBERANT
REVERBERANTLY
REVERBERATE
REVERBERATED
REVERBERATES
REVERBERATING
REVERBERATION
REVERBERATIONS
REVERBERATIVE
REVERBERATOR
REVERBERATORIES
REVERBERATORS
REVERBERATORY
REVERENCED
REVERENCER
REVERENCERS
REVERENCES
REVERENCING
REVERENTIAL
REVERENTIALLY
REVERENTLY
REVERENTNESS
REVERENTNESSES
REVERIFIED
REVERIFIES
REVERIFYING
REVERSEDLY
REVERSELESS
REVERSIBILITIES
REVERSIBILITY
REVERSIBLE
REVERSIBLES
REVERSIBLY
REVERSINGS
REVERSIONAL
REVERSIONALLY
REVERSIONARIES
REVERSIONARY
REVERSIONER
REVERSIONERS

REVERSIONS
REVERSISES
REVERTANTS
REVERTIBLE
REVESTIARIES
REVESTIARY
REVESTRIES
REVETMENTS
REVIBRATED
REVIBRATES
REVIBRATING
REVICTUALED
REVICTUALING
REVICTUALLED
REVICTUALLING
REVICTUALS
REVIEWABLE
REVILEMENT
REVILEMENTS
REVILINGLY
REVINDICATE
REVINDICATED
REVINDICATES
REVINDICATING
REVINDICATION
REVINDICATIONS
REVIOLATED
REVIOLATES
REVIOLATING
REVISIONAL
REVISIONARY
REVISIONISM
REVISIONISMS
REVISIONIST
REVISIONISTS
REVISITANT
REVISITANTS
REVISITATION
REVISITATIONS
REVISITING
REVISUALISATION
REVISUALIZATION
REVITALISATION
REVITALISATIONS
REVITALISE
REVITALISED
REVITALISES
REVITALISING
REVITALIZATION
REVITALIZATIONS
REVITALIZE
REVITALIZED
REVITALIZES
REVITALIZING
REVIVABILITIES
REVIVABILITY
REVIVALISM
REVIVALISMS
REVIVALIST

REVIVALISTIC
REVIVALISTS
REVIVEMENT
REVIVEMENTS
REVIVESCENCE
REVIVESCENCES
REVIVESCENCIES
REVIVESCENCY
REVIVESCENT
REVIVIFICATION
REVIVIFICATIONS
REVIVIFIED
REVIVIFIES
REVIVIFYING
REVIVINGLY
REVIVISCENCE
REVIVISCENCES
REVIVISCENCIES
REVIVISCENCY
REVIVISCENT
REVOCABILITIES
REVOCABILITY
REVOCABLENESS
REVOCABLENESSES
REVOCATION
REVOCATIONS
REVOCATORY
REVOKABILITIES
REVOKABILITY
REVOKEMENT
REVOKEMENTS
REVOLTINGLY
REVOLUTION
REVOLUTIONAL
REVOLUTIONARIES
REVOLUTIONARILY
REVOLUTIONARY
REVOLUTIONER
REVOLUTIONERS
REVOLUTIONISE
REVOLUTIONISED
REVOLUTIONISER
REVOLUTIONISERS
REVOLUTIONISES
REVOLUTIONISING
REVOLUTIONISM
REVOLUTIONISMS
REVOLUTIONIST
REVOLUTIONISTS
REVOLUTIONIZE
REVOLUTIONIZED
REVOLUTIONIZER
REVOLUTIONIZERS
REVOLUTIONIZES
REVOLUTIONIZING
REVOLUTIONS
REVOLVABLE
REVOLVABLY
REVOLVENCIES

REVOLVENCY
REVOLVINGLY
REVOLVINGS
REVULSIONARY
REVULSIONS
REVULSIVELY
REVULSIVES
REWAKENING
REWARDABLE
REWARDABLENESS
REWARDINGLY
REWARDLESS
REWEIGHING
REWIDENING
REWRAPPING
RHABDOCOELE
RHABDOCOELES
RHABDOLITH
RHABDOLITHS
RHABDOMANCER
RHABDOMANCERS
RHABDOMANCIES
RHABDOMANCY
RHABDOMANTIST
RHABDOMANTISTS
RHABDOMERE
RHABDOMERES
RHABDOMYOMA
RHABDOMYOMAS
RHABDOMYOMATA
RHABDOSPHERE
RHABDOSPHERES
RHABDOVIRUS
RHABDOVIRUSES
RHACHIDIAL
RHACHILLAS
RHACHITISES
RHADAMANTHINE
RHAGADIFORM
RHAMNACEOUS
RHAMPHOTHECA
RHAMPHOTHECAE
RHAPONTICS
RHAPSODICAL
RHAPSODICALLY
RHAPSODIES
RHAPSODISE
RHAPSODISED
RHAPSODISES
RHAPSODISING
RHAPSODIST
RHAPSODISTIC
RHAPSODISTS
RHAPSODIZE
RHAPSODIZED
RHAPSODIZES
RHAPSODIZING
RHEOCHORDS
RHEOLOGICAL

RHEOLOGICALLY
RHEOLOGIES
RHEOLOGIST
RHEOLOGISTS
RHEOMETERS
RHEOMETRIC
RHEOMETRICAL
RHEOMETRIES
RHEOMORPHIC
RHEOMORPHISM
RHEOMORPHISMS
RHEOPHILES
RHEORECEPTOR
RHEORECEPTORS
RHEOSTATIC
RHEOTACTIC
RHEOTROPES
RHEOTROPIC
RHEOTROPISM
RHEOTROPISMS
RHETORICAL
RHETORICALLY
RHETORICIAN
RHETORICIANS
RHETORISED
RHETORISES
RHETORISING
RHETORIZED
RHETORIZES
RHETORIZING
RHEUMATEESE
RHEUMATEESES
RHEUMATICAL
RHEUMATICALLY
RHEUMATICKY
RHEUMATICS
RHEUMATISE
RHEUMATISES
RHEUMATISM
RHEUMATISMAL
RHEUMATISMS
RHEUMATIZE
RHEUMATIZES
RHEUMATOID
RHEUMATOIDALLY
RHEUMATOLOGICAL
RHEUMATOLOGIES
RHEUMATOLOGIST
RHEUMATOLOGISTS
RHEUMATOLOGY
RHIGOLENES
RHINENCEPHALA
RHINENCEPHALIC
RHINENCEPHALON
RHINENCEPHALONS
RHINESTONE
RHINESTONED
RHINESTONES
RHINITIDES

RHINITISES
RHINOCERICAL
RHINOCEROS
RHINOCEROSES
RHINOCEROT
RHINOCEROTE
RHINOCEROTES
RHINOCEROTIC
RHINOLALIA
RHINOLALIAS
RHINOLITHS
RHINOLOGICAL
RHINOLOGIES
RHINOLOGIST
RHINOLOGISTS
RHINOPHYMA
RHINOPHYMAS
RHINOPLASTIC
RHINOPLASTIES
RHINOPLASTY
RHINORRHAGIA
RHINORRHAGIAS
RHINORRHOEA
RHINORRHOEAL
RHINORRHOEAS
RHINOSCLEROMA
RHINOSCLEROMAS
RHINOSCLEROMATA
RHINOSCOPE
RHINOSCOPES
RHINOSCOPIC
RHINOSCOPIES
RHINOSCOPY
RHINOTHECA
RHINOTHECAE
RHINOVIRUS
RHINOVIRUSES
RHIPIDIONS
RHIPIDIUMS
RHIZANTHOUS
RHIZOCARPIC
RHIZOCARPOUS
RHIZOCARPS
RHIZOCAULS
RHIZOCEPHALAN
RHIZOCEPHALANS
RHIZOCEPHALOUS
RHIZOCTONIA
RHIZOCTONIAS
RHIZOGENETIC
RHIZOGENIC
RHIZOGENOUS
RHIZOMATOUS
RHIZOMORPH
RHIZOMORPHOUS
RHIZOMORPHS
RHIZOPHAGOUS
RHIZOPHILOUS
RHIZOPHORE

RHIZOPHORES

RHIZOPHORES
RHIZOPLANE
RHIZOPLANES
RHIZOPODAN
RHIZOPODANS
RHIZOPODOUS
RHIZOPUSES
RHIZOSPHERE
RHIZOSPHERES
RHIZOTOMIES
RHODAMINES
RHODANATES
RHODANISED
RHODANISES
RHODANISING
RHODANIZED
RHODANIZES
RHODANIZING
RHODOCHROSITE
RHODOCHROSITES
RHODODAPHNE
RHODODAPHNES
RHODODENDRON
RHODODENDRONS
RHODOLITES
RHODOMONTADE
RHODOMONTADED
RHODOMONTADES
RHODOMONTADING
RHODONITES
RHODOPHANE
RHODOPHANES
RHODOPSINS
RHOEADINES
RHOICISSUS
RHOICISSUSES
RHOMBENCEPHALA
RHOMBENCEPHALON
RHOMBENPORPHYR
RHOMBENPORPHYRS
RHOMBENPORPHYRY
RHOMBOHEDRA
RHOMBOHEDRAL
RHOMBOHEDRON
RHOMBOHEDRONS
RHOMBOIDAL
RHOMBOIDEI
RHOMBOIDES
RHOMBOIDEUS
RHOMBPORPHYRIES
RHOMBPORPHYRY
RHOPALISMS
RHOPALOCERAL
RHOPALOCEROUS
RHOTACISED
RHOTACISES
RHOTACISING
RHOTACISMS
RHOTACISTIC

RHOTACISTS
RHOTACIZED
RHOTACIZES
RHOTACIZING
RHOTICITIES
RHUBARBING
RHUBARBINGS
RHUMBATRON
RHUMBATRONS
RHYMESTERS
RHYNCHOCOEL
RHYNCHOCOELS
RHYNCHODONT
RHYNCHOPHORE
RHYNCHOPHORES
RHYNCHOPHOROUS
RHYPAROGRAPHER
RHYPAROGRAPHERS
RHYPAROGRAPHIC
RHYPAROGRAPHIES
RHYPAROGRAPHY
RHYTHMICAL
RHYTHMICALLY
RHYTHMICITIES
RHYTHMICITY
RHYTHMISATION
RHYTHMISATIONS
RHYTHMISED
RHYTHMISES
RHYTHMISING
RHYTHMISTS
RHYTHMIZATION
RHYTHMIZATIONS
RHYTHMIZED
RHYTHMIZES
RHYTHMIZING
RHYTHMLESS
RHYTHMOMETER
RHYTHMOMETERS
RHYTHMOPOEIA
RHYTHMOPOEIAS
RHYTHMUSES
RHYTIDECTOMIES
RHYTIDECTOMY
RHYTIDOMES
RIBALDRIES
RIBATTUTAS
RIBAUDRIES
RIBAVIRINS
RIBBONFISH
RIBBONFISHES
RIBBONLIKE
RIBBONRIES
RIBBONWOOD
RIBBONWOODS
RIBGRASSES
RIBOFLAVIN
RIBOFLAVINE
RIBOFLAVINES

RIBOFLAVINS
RIBONUCLEASE
RIBONUCLEASES
RIBONUCLEIC
RIBONUCLEOSIDE
RIBONUCLEOSIDES
RIBONUCLEOTIDE
RIBONUCLEOTIDES
RICERCARES
RICERCATAS
RICHNESSES
RICINOLEIC
RICKBURNER
RICKBURNERS
RICKETIEST
RICKETINESS
RICKETINESSES
RICKETTIER
RICKETTIEST
RICKETTSIA
RICKETTSIAE
RICKETTSIAL
RICKETTSIAS
RICKSTANDS
RICKSTICKS
RICOCHETED
RICOCHETING
RICOCHETTED
RICOCHETTING
RIDABILITIES
RIDABILITY
RIDDLINGLY
RIDERSHIPS
RIDGEBACKS
RIDGELINES
RIDGELINGS
RIDGEPOLES
RIDGETREES
RIDICULERS
RIDICULING
RIDICULOUS
RIDICULOUSLY
RIDICULOUSNESS
RIEBECKITE
RIEBECKITES
RIFACIMENTI
RIFACIMENTO
RIFAMPICIN
RIFAMPICINS
RIFAMYCINS
RIFENESSES
RIFLEBIRDS
RIGAMAROLE
RIGAMAROLES
RIGHTABLENESS
RIGHTABLENESSES
RIGHTENING
RIGHTEOUSLY
RIGHTEOUSNESS

RIGHTEOUSNESSES
RIGHTFULLY
RIGHTFULNESS
RIGHTFULNESSES
RIGHTNESSES
RIGHTSIZED
RIGHTSIZES
RIGHTSIZING
RIGHTWARDS
RIGIDIFICATION
RIGIDIFICATIONS
RIGIDIFIED
RIGIDIFIES
RIGIDIFYING
RIGIDISING
RIGIDITIES
RIGIDIZING
RIGIDNESSES
RIGMAROLES
RIGORISTIC
RIGOROUSLY
RIGOROUSNESS
RIGOROUSNESSES
RIGSDALERS
RIGWIDDIES
RIGWOODIES
RIJKSDAALER
RIJKSDAALERS
RIJSTAFELS
RIJSTTAFEL
RIJSTTAFELS
RIMINESSES
RIMOSITIES
RINDERPEST
RINDERPESTS
RINFORZANDO
RINGBARKED
RINGBARKING
RINGHALSES
RINGLEADER
RINGLEADERS
RINGMASTER
RINGMASTERS
RINGSIDERS
RINGSTANDS
RINGSTRAKED
RINGTOSSES
RINKHALSES
RINSABILITIES
RINSABILITY
RINSIBILITIES
RINSIBILITY
RINTHEREOUT
RINTHEREOUTS
RIOTOUSNESS
RIOTOUSNESSES
RIPENESSES
RIPIDOLITE
RIPIDOLITES

RIPIENISTS
RIPPLINGLY
RIPRAPPING
RIPSNORTER
RIPSNORTERS
RIPSNORTING
RISIBILITIES
RISIBILITY
RISKINESSES
RISORGIMENTO
RISORGIMENTOS
RITARDANDO
RITARDANDOS
RITONAVIRS
RITORNELLE
RITORNELLES
RITORNELLI
RITORNELLO
RITORNELLOS
RITORNELLS
RITOURNELLE
RITOURNELLES
RITUALISATION
RITUALISATIONS
RITUALISED
RITUALISES
RITUALISING
RITUALISMS
RITUALISTIC
RITUALISTICALLY
RITUALISTS
RITUALIZATION
RITUALIZATIONS
RITUALIZED
RITUALIZES
RITUALIZING
RITZINESSES
RIVALESSES
RIVALISING
RIVALITIES
RIVALIZING
RIVALSHIPS
RIVERBANKS
RIVERBOATS
RIVERCRAFT
RIVERCRAFTS
RIVERFRONT
RIVERFRONTS
RIVERHEADS
RIVERSCAPE
RIVERSCAPES
RIVERSIDES
RIVERWARDS
RIVERWEEDS
RIVERWORTHINESS
RIVERWORTHY
RIVETINGLY
ROADABILITIES
ROADABILITY

ROADBLOCKED
ROADBLOCKING
ROADBLOCKS
ROADCRAFTS
ROADHEADER
ROADHEADERS
ROADHOLDING
ROADHOLDINGS
ROADHOUSES
ROADROLLER
ROADROLLERS
ROADRUNNER
ROADRUNNERS
ROADSTEADS
ROADWORTHIES
ROADWORTHINESS
ROADWORTHY
ROBERDSMAN
ROBERDSMEN
ROBERTSMAN
ROBERTSMEN
ROBORATING
ROBOTICALLY
ROBOTISATION
ROBOTISATIONS
ROBOTISING
ROBOTIZATION
ROBOTIZATIONS
ROBOTIZING
ROBUSTIOUS
ROBUSTIOUSLY
ROBUSTIOUSNESS
ROBUSTNESS
ROBUSTNESSES
ROCAMBOLES
ROCKABILLIES
ROCKABILLY
ROCKCRESSES
ROCKETEERS
ROCKETRIES
ROCKFISHES
ROCKHOPPER
ROCKHOPPERS
ROCKHOUNDING
ROCKHOUNDINGS
ROCKHOUNDS
ROCKINESSES
ROCKSHAFTS
ROCKSLIDES
ROCKSTEADIES
ROCKSTEADY
ROCKWATERS
RODENTICIDE
RODENTICIDES
RODFISHERS
RODFISHING
RODFISHINGS
RODGERSIAS
RODOMONTADE

RODOMONTADED
RODOMONTADER
RODOMONTADERS
RODOMONTADES
RODOMONTADING
ROENTGENISATION
ROENTGENISE
ROENTGENISED
ROENTGENISES
ROENTGENISING
ROENTGENIZATION
ROENTGENIZE
ROENTGENIZED
ROENTGENIZES
ROENTGENIZING
ROENTGENOGRAM
ROENTGENOGRAMS
ROENTGENOGRAPH
ROENTGENOGRAPHS
ROENTGENOGRAPHY
ROENTGENOLOGIC
ROENTGENOLOGIES
ROENTGENOLOGIST
ROENTGENOLOGY
ROENTGENOPAQUE
ROENTGENOSCOPE
ROENTGENOSCOPES
ROENTGENOSCOPIC
ROENTGENOSCOPY
ROGUESHIPS
ROGUISHNESS
ROGUISHNESSES
ROISTERERS
ROISTERING
ROISTERINGS
ROISTEROUS
ROISTEROUSLY
ROLLCOLLAR
ROLLCOLLARS
ROLLERBALL
ROLLERBALLS
ROLLERBLADE
ROLLERBLADED
ROLLERBLADER
ROLLERBLADERS
ROLLERBLADES
ROLLERBLADING
ROLLERBLADINGS
ROLLERCOASTER
ROLLERCOASTERED
ROLLERCOASTERS
ROLLICKING
ROLLICKINGS
ROLLOCKING
ROLLOCKINGS
ROMANCICAL
ROMANCINGS
ROMANICITE
ROMANICITES

ROMANISATION
ROMANISATIONS
ROMANISING
ROMANIZATION
ROMANIZATIONS
ROMANIZING
ROMANTICAL
ROMANTICALITIES
ROMANTICALITY
ROMANTICALLY
ROMANTICISATION
ROMANTICISE
ROMANTICISED
ROMANTICISES
ROMANTICISING
ROMANTICISM
ROMANTICISMS
ROMANTICIST
ROMANTICISTS
ROMANTICIZATION
ROMANTICIZE
ROMANTICIZED
ROMANTICIZES
ROMANTICIZING
ROMELDALES
ROMPISHNESS
ROMPISHNESSES
RONDOLETTO
RONDOLETTOS
RONTGENISATION
RONTGENISATIONS
RONTGENISE
RONTGENISED
RONTGENISES
RONTGENISING
RONTGENIZATION
RONTGENIZATIONS
RONTGENIZE
RONTGENIZED
RONTGENIZES
RONTGENIZING
RONTGENOGRAM
RONTGENOGRAMS
RONTGENOGRAPH
RONTGENOGRAPHS
RONTGENOGRAPHY
RONTGENOLOGICAL
RONTGENOLOGIES
RONTGENOLOGIST
RONTGENOLOGISTS
RONTGENOLOGY
RONTGENOPAQUE
RONTGENOSCOPE
RONTGENOSCOPES
RONTGENOSCOPIC
RONTGENOSCOPIES
RONTGENOSCOPY
RONTGENOTHERAPY
ROOFLESSNESS

ROOFLESSNESSES
ROOFSCAPES
ROOMINESSES
ROOTEDNESS
ROOTEDNESSES
ROOTINESSES
ROOTLESSNESS
ROOTLESSNESSES
ROOTSERVER
ROOTSERVERS
ROOTSINESS
ROOTSINESSES
ROOTSTALKS
ROOTSTOCKS
ROPEDANCER
ROPEDANCERS
ROPEDANCING
ROPEDANCINGS
ROPEWALKER
ROPEWALKERS
ROPINESSES
ROQUELAURE
ROQUELAURES
ROSANILINE
ROSANILINES
ROSANILINS
ROSEBUSHES
ROSEFINCHES
ROSEFISHES
ROSEMALING
ROSEMALINGS
ROSEMARIES
ROSEWATERS
ROSINESSES
ROSINWEEDS
ROSMARINES
ROSTELLATE
ROSTELLUMS
ROSTERINGS
ROSTROCARINATE
ROSTROCARINATES
ROTACHUTES
ROTAMETERS
ROTAPLANES
ROTATIONAL
ROTATIVELY
ROTAVATING
ROTAVATORS
ROTAVIRUSES
ROTGRASSES
ROTIFERANS
ROTIFEROUS
ROTISSERIE
ROTISSERIES
ROTOGRAPHED
ROTOGRAPHING
ROTOGRAPHS
ROTOGRAVURE
ROTOGRAVURES

ROTORCRAFT
ROTORCRAFTS
ROTOTILLED
ROTOTILLER
ROTOTILLERS
ROTOTILLING
ROTOVATING
ROTOVATORS
ROTTENNESS
ROTTENNESSES
ROTTENSTONE
ROTTENSTONED
ROTTENSTONES
ROTTENSTONING
ROTTWEILER
ROTTWEILERS
ROTUNDITIES
ROTUNDNESS
ROTUNDNESSES
ROUGHBACKS
ROUGHCASTED
ROUGHCASTER
ROUGHCASTERS
ROUGHCASTING
ROUGHCASTS
ROUGHDRIED
ROUGHDRIES
ROUGHDRYING
ROUGHENING
ROUGHHEWED
ROUGHHEWING
ROUGHHOUSE
ROUGHHOUSED
ROUGHHOUSES
ROUGHHOUSING
ROUGHNECKED
ROUGHNECKING
ROUGHNECKS
ROUGHNESSES
ROUGHRIDER
ROUGHRIDERS
ROULETTING
ROUNCEVALS
ROUNDABOUT
ROUNDABOUTATION
ROUNDABOUTED
ROUNDABOUTEDLY
ROUNDABOUTILITY
ROUNDABOUTING
ROUNDABOUTLY
ROUNDABOUTNESS
ROUNDABOUTS
ROUNDARCHED
ROUNDBALLS
ROUNDEDNESS
ROUNDEDNESSES
ROUNDELAYS
ROUNDHANDS
ROUNDHEADED

ROUNDHEADEDNESS
ROUNDHEELS
ROUNDHOUSE
ROUNDHOUSES
ROUNDNESSES
ROUNDTABLE
ROUNDTABLES
ROUNDTRIPPING
ROUNDTRIPPINGS
ROUNDTRIPS
ROUNDWOODS
ROUNDWORMS
ROUSEABOUT
ROUSEABOUTS
ROUSEDNESS
ROUSEDNESSES
ROUSEMENTS
ROUSSETTES
ROUSTABOUT
ROUSTABOUTS
ROUTEMARCH
ROUTEMARCHED
ROUTEMARCHES
ROUTEMARCHING
ROUTINEERS
ROUTINISATION
ROUTINISATIONS
ROUTINISED
ROUTINISES
ROUTINISING
ROUTINISMS
ROUTINISTS
ROUTINIZATION
ROUTINIZATIONS
ROUTINIZED
ROUTINIZES
ROUTINIZING
ROWANBERRIES
ROWANBERRY
ROWDINESSES
ROYALISING
ROYALISTIC
ROYALIZING
ROYALMASTS
ROYSTERERS
ROYSTERING
ROYSTEROUS
RUBBERIEST
RUBBERISED
RUBBERISES
RUBBERISING
RUBBERIZED
RUBBERIZES
RUBBERIZING
RUBBERLIKE
RUBBERNECK
RUBBERNECKED
RUBBERNECKER
RUBBERNECKERS

RUBBERNECKING
RUBBERNECKS
RUBBERWEAR
RUBBERWEARS
RUBBISHING
RUBBLEWORK
RUBBLEWORKS
RUBEFACIENT
RUBEFACIENTS
RUBEFACTION
RUBEFACTIONS
RUBELLITES
RUBESCENCE
RUBESCENCES
RUBIACEOUS
RUBICELLES
RUBICONING
RUBICUNDITIES
RUBICUNDITY
RUBIGINOSE
RUBIGINOUS
RUBRICALLY
RUBRICATED
RUBRICATES
RUBRICATING
RUBRICATION
RUBRICATIONS
RUBRICATOR
RUBRICATORS
RUBRICIANS
RUBYTHROAT
RUBYTHROATS
RUCTATIONS
RUDBECKIAS
RUDDERHEAD
RUDDERHEADS
RUDDERLESS
RUDDERPOST
RUDDERPOSTS
RUDDERSTOCK
RUDDERSTOCKS
RUDDINESSES
RUDENESSES
RUDIMENTAL
RUDIMENTALLY
RUDIMENTARILY
RUDIMENTARINESS
RUDIMENTARY
RUEFULNESS
RUEFULNESSES
RUFESCENCE
RUFESCENCES
RUFFIANING
RUFFIANISH
RUFFIANISM
RUFFIANISMS
RUGGEDISATION
RUGGEDISATIONS
RUGGEDISED

RUGGEDISES
RUGGEDISING
RUGGEDIZATION
RUGGEDIZATIONS
RUGGEDIZED
RUGGEDIZES
RUGGEDIZING
RUGGEDNESS
RUGGEDNESSES
RUGOSITIES
RUINATIONS
RUINOUSNESS
RUINOUSNESSES
RULERSHIPS
RUMBLEDETHUMP
RUMBLEDETHUMPS
RUMBLEGUMPTION
RUMBLEGUMPTIONS
RUMBLINGLY
RUMBULLION
RUMBULLIONS
RUMBUSTICAL
RUMBUSTIOUS
RUMBUSTIOUSLY
RUMBUSTIOUSNESS
RUMELGUMPTION
RUMELGUMPTIONS
RUMFUSTIAN
RUMFUSTIANS
RUMGUMPTION
RUMGUMPTIONS
RUMINANTLY
RUMINATING
RUMINATINGLY
RUMINATION
RUMINATIONS
RUMINATIVE
RUMINATIVELY
RUMINATORS
RUMLEGUMPTION
RUMLEGUMPTIONS
RUMMELGUMPTION
RUMMELGUMPTIONS
RUMMINESSES
RUMMLEGUMPTION
RUMMLEGUMPTIONS
RUMORMONGER
RUMORMONGERING
RUMORMONGERINGS
RUMORMONGERS
RUMRUNNERS
RUNAROUNDS
RUNECRAFTS
RUNNINESSES
RUNTINESSES
RUPESTRIAN
RUPICOLINE
RUPICOLOUS
RUPTURABLE

RUPTUREWORT
RUPTUREWORTS
RURALISATION
RURALISATIONS
RURALISING
RURALITIES
RURALIZATION
RURALIZATIONS
RURALIZING
RURALNESSES
RURIDECANAL
RUSHINESSES
RUSHLIGHTS
RUSSETINGS
RUSSETTING
RUSSETTINGS
RUSSIFYING
RUSTBUCKET
RUSTICALLY
RUSTICATED
RUSTICATES
RUSTICATING
RUSTICATINGS
RUSTICATION
RUSTICATIONS
RUSTICATOR
RUSTICATORS
RUSTICISED
RUSTICISES
RUSTICISING
RUSTICISMS
RUSTICITIES
RUSTICIZED
RUSTICIZES
RUSTICIZING
RUSTICWORK
RUSTICWORKS
RUSTINESSES
RUSTLINGLY
RUSTPROOFED
RUSTPROOFING
RUSTPROOFS
RUTHENIOUS
RUTHENIUMS
RUTHERFORD
RUTHERFORDIUM
RUTHERFORDIUMS
RUTHERFORDS
RUTHFULNESS
RUTHFULNESSES
RUTHLESSLY
RUTHLESSNESS
RUTHLESSNESSES
RUTTINESSES
RUTTISHNESS
RUTTISHNESSES
RYBAUDRYES
RYEGRASSES

S

SABADILLAS
SABBATARIAN
SABBATICAL
SABBATICALS
SABBATISED
SABBATISES
SABBATISING
SABBATISMS
SABBATIZED
SABBATIZES
SABBATIZING
SABERMETRICIAN
SABERMETRICIANS
SABERMETRICS
SABLEFISHES
SABOTAGING
SABRETACHE
SABRETACHES
SABULOSITIES
SABULOSITY
SABURRATION
SABURRATIONS
SACAHUISTA
SACAHUISTAS
SACAHUISTE
SACAHUISTES
SACCADICALLY
SACCHARASE
SACCHARASES
SACCHARATE
SACCHARATED
SACCHARATES
SACCHARIDE
SACCHARIDES
SACCHARIFEROUS
SACCHARIFIED
SACCHARIFIES
SACCHARIFY
SACCHARIFYING
SACCHARIMETER
SACCHARIMETERS
SACCHARIMETRIES
SACCHARIMETRY
SACCHARINE
SACCHARINELY
SACCHARINES
SACCHARINITIES
SACCHARINITY
SACCHARINS
SACCHARISATION
SACCHARISATIONS
SACCHARISE
SACCHARISED

SACCHARISES
SACCHARISING
SACCHARIZATION
SACCHARIZATIONS
SACCHARIZE
SACCHARIZED
SACCHARIZES
SACCHARIZING
SACCHAROID
SACCHAROIDAL
SACCHAROIDS
SACCHAROMETER
SACCHAROMETERS
SACCHAROMYCES
SACCHAROMYCETES
SACCHAROSE
SACCHAROSES
SACCHARUMS
SACCULATED
SACCULATION
SACCULATIONS
SACCULIFORM
SACERDOTAL
SACERDOTALISE
SACERDOTALISED
SACERDOTALISES
SACERDOTALISING
SACERDOTALISM
SACERDOTALISMS
SACERDOTALIST
SACERDOTALISTS
SACERDOTALIZE
SACERDOTALIZED
SACERDOTALIZES
SACERDOTALIZING
SACERDOTALLY
SACHEMDOMS
SACHEMSHIP
SACHEMSHIPS
SACKCLOTHS
SACRALGIAS
SACRALISATION
SACRALISATIONS
SACRALISED
SACRALISES
SACRALISING
SACRALIZATION
SACRALIZATIONS
SACRALIZED
SACRALIZES
SACRALIZING
SACRAMENTAL
SACRAMENTALISM

SACRAMENTALISMS
SACRAMENTALIST
SACRAMENTALISTS
SACRAMENTALITY
SACRAMENTALLY
SACRAMENTALNESS
SACRAMENTALS
SACRAMENTARIAN
SACRAMENTARIANS
SACRAMENTARIES
SACRAMENTARY
SACRAMENTED
SACRAMENTING
SACRAMENTS
SACREDNESS
SACREDNESSES
SACRIFICEABLE
SACRIFICED
SACRIFICER
SACRIFICERS
SACRIFICES
SACRIFICIAL
SACRIFICIALLY
SACRIFICING
SACRIFYING
SACRILEGES
SACRILEGIOUS
SACRILEGIOUSLY
SACRILEGIST
SACRILEGISTS
SACRISTANS
SACRISTIES
SACROCOCCYGEAL
SACROCOSTAL
SACROCOSTALS
SACROILIAC
SACROILIACS
SACROILIITIS
SACROILIITISES
SACROSANCT
SACROSANCTITIES
SACROSANCTITY
SACROSANCTNESS
SADDLEBACK
SADDLEBACKED
SADDLEBACKS
SADDLEBAGS
SADDLEBILL
SADDLEBILLS
SADDLEBOWS
SADDLEBRED
SADDLEBREDS
SADDLECLOTH

SADDLECLOTHS
SADDLELESS
SADDLERIES
SADDLEROOM
SADDLEROOMS
SADDLETREE
SADDLETREES
SADISTICALLY
SADOMASOCHISM
SADOMASOCHISMS
SADOMASOCHIST
SADOMASOCHISTIC
SADOMASOCHISTS
SAFECRACKER
SAFECRACKERS
SAFECRACKING
SAFECRACKINGS
SAFEGUARDED
SAFEGUARDING
SAFEGUARDS
SAFEKEEPING
SAFEKEEPINGS
SAFELIGHTS
SAFENESSES
SAFFLOWERS
SAFRANINES
SAGACIOUSLY
SAGACIOUSNESS
SAGACIOUSNESSES
SAGACITIES
SAGANASHES
SAGAPENUMS
SAGEBRUSHES
SAGENESSES
SAGINATING
SAGINATION
SAGINATIONS
SAGITTALLY
SAGITTARIAN
SAGITTARIANS
SAGITTARIES
SAGITTIFORM
SAILBOARDED
SAILBOARDER
SAILBOARDERS
SAILBOARDING
SAILBOARDINGS
SAILBOARDS
SAILBOATER
SAILBOATERS
SAILBOATING
SAILBOATINGS
SAILCLOTHS

SAILFISHES
SAILMAKERS
SAILORINGS
SAILORLESS
SAILORLIKE
SAILPLANED
SAILPLANER
SAILPLANERS
SAILPLANES
SAILPLANING
SAINTESSES
SAINTFOINS
SAINTHOODS
SAINTLIEST
SAINTLINESS
SAINTLINESSES
SAINTLINGS
SAINTPAULIA
SAINTPAULIAS
SAINTSHIPS
SALABILITIES
SALABILITY
SALABLENESS
SALABLENESSES
SALACIOUSLY
SALACIOUSNESS
SALACIOUSNESSES
SALACITIES
SALAMANDER
SALAMANDERS
SALAMANDRIAN
SALAMANDRINE
SALAMANDROID
SALAMANDROIDS
SALANGANES
SALBUTAMOL
SALBUTAMOLS
SALEABILITIES
SALEABILITY
SALEABLENESS
SALEABLENESSES
SALERATUSES
SALESCLERK
SALESCLERKS
SALESGIRLS
SALESLADIES
SALESMANSHIP
SALESMANSHIPS
SALESPEOPLE
SALESPERSON
SALESPERSONS
SALESROOMS
SALESWOMAN
SALESWOMEN
SALIAUNCES
SALICACEOUS
SALICETUMS
SALICIONAL
SALICIONALS

SALICORNIA
SALICORNIAS
SALICYLAMIDE
SALICYLAMIDES
SALICYLATE
SALICYLATED
SALICYLATES
SALICYLATING
SALICYLISM
SALICYLISMS
SALIENCIES
SALIENTIAN
SALIENTIANS
SALIFEROUS
SALIFIABLE
SALIFICATION
SALIFICATIONS
SALIMETERS
SALIMETRIC
SALIMETRIES
SALINISATION
SALINISATIONS
SALINISING
SALINITIES
SALINIZATION
SALINIZATIONS
SALINIZING
SALINOMETER
SALINOMETERS
SALINOMETRIC
SALINOMETRIES
SALINOMETRY
SALIVATING
SALIVATION
SALIVATIONS
SALIVATORS
SALLENDERS
SALLOWNESS
SALLOWNESSES
SALLYPORTS
SALMAGUNDI
SALMAGUNDIES
SALMAGUNDIS
SALMAGUNDY
SALMANASER
SALMANASERS
SALMANAZAR
SALMANAZARS
SALMONBERRIES
SALMONBERRY
SALMONELLA
SALMONELLAE
SALMONELLAS
SALMONELLOSES
SALMONELLOSIS
SALMONOIDS
SALOMETERS
SALOPETTES
SALPIGLOSSES

SALPIGLOSSIS
SALPIGLOSSISES
SALPINGECTOMIES
SALPINGECTOMY
SALPINGIAN
SALPINGITIC
SALPINGITIS
SALPINGITISES
SALSOLACEOUS
SALSUGINOUS
SALTARELLI
SALTARELLO
SALTARELLOS
SALTATIONISM
SALTATIONISMS
SALTATIONIST
SALTATIONISTS
SALTATIONS
SALTATORIAL
SALTATORIOUS
SALTBUSHES
SALTCELLAR
SALTCELLARS
SALTCHUCKER
SALTCHUCKERS
SALTCHUCKS
SALTFISHES
SALTIGRADE
SALTIGRADES
SALTIMBANCO
SALTIMBANCOS
SALTIMBOCCA
SALTIMBOCCAS
SALTINESSES
SALTIREWISE
SALTISHNESS
SALTISHNESSES
SALTNESSES
SALTPETERS
SALTPETREMAN
SALTPETREMEN
SALTPETRES
SALTSHAKER
SALTSHAKERS
SALUBRIOUS
SALUBRIOUSLY
SALUBRIOUSNESS
SALUBRITIES
SALURETICS
SALUTARILY
SALUTARINESS
SALUTARINESSES
SALUTATION
SALUTATIONAL
SALUTATIONS
SALUTATORIAN
SALUTATORIANS
SALUTATORIES
SALUTATORILY

SALUTATORY
SALUTIFEROUS
SALVABILITIES
SALVABILITY
SALVABLENESS
SALVABLENESSES
SALVAGEABILITY
SALVAGEABLE
SALVARSANS
SALVATIONAL
SALVATIONISM
SALVATIONISMS
SALVATIONIST
SALVATIONISTS
SALVATIONS
SALVATORIES
SALVERFORM
SALVIFICAL
SALVIFICALLY
SALVINIACEOUS
SAMARIFORM
SAMARITANS
SAMARSKITE
SAMARSKITES
SAMENESSES
SAMNITISES
SAMPLERIES
SANATORIUM
SANATORIUMS
SANBENITOS
SANCTIFIABLE
SANCTIFICATION
SANCTIFICATIONS
SANCTIFIED
SANCTIFIEDLY
SANCTIFIER
SANCTIFIERS
SANCTIFIES
SANCTIFYING
SANCTIFYINGLY
SANCTIFYINGS
SANCTIMONIES
SANCTIMONIOUS
SANCTIMONIOUSLY
SANCTIMONY
SANCTIONABLE
SANCTIONED
SANCTIONEER
SANCTIONEERS
SANCTIONER
SANCTIONERS
SANCTIONING
SANCTIONLESS
SANCTITIES
SANCTITUDE
SANCTITUDES
SANCTUARIES
SANCTUARISE
SANCTUARISED

SANCTUARISES
SANCTUARISING
SANCTUARIZE
SANCTUARIZED
SANCTUARIZES
SANCTUARIZING
SANDALLING
SANDALWOOD
SANDALWOODS
SANDARACHS
SANDBAGGED
SANDBAGGER
SANDBAGGERS
SANDBAGGING
SANDBLASTED
SANDBLASTER
SANDBLASTERS
SANDBLASTING
SANDBLASTINGS
SANDBLASTS
SANDCASTLE
SANDCASTLES
SANDCRACKS
SANDERLING
SANDERLINGS
SANDERSWOOD
SANDERSWOODS
SANDFISHES
SANDGLASSES
SANDGROPER
SANDGROPERS
SANDGROUSE
SANDGROUSES
SANDINESSES
SANDLOTTER
SANDLOTTERS
SANDPAINTING
SANDPAINTINGS
SANDPAPERED
SANDPAPERING
SANDPAPERS
SANDPAPERY
SANDPIPERS
SANDSPOUTS
SANDSTONES
SANDSTORMS
SANDSUCKER
SANDSUCKERS
SANDWICHED
SANDWICHES
SANDWICHING
SANENESSES
SANGFROIDS
SANGUIFEROUS
SANGUIFICATION
SANGUIFICATIONS
SANGUIFIED
SANGUIFIES
SANGUIFYING

SANGUINARIA
SANGUINARIAS
SANGUINARILY
SANGUINARINESS
SANGUINARY
SANGUINELY
SANGUINENESS
SANGUINENESSES
SANGUINEOUS
SANGUINEOUSNESS
SANGUINING
SANGUINITIES
SANGUINITY
SANGUINIVOROUS
SANGUINOLENCIES
SANGUINOLENCY
SANGUINOLENT
SANGUIVOROUS
SANITARIAN
SANITARIANISM
SANITARIANISMS
SANITARIANS
SANITARIES
SANITARILY
SANITARINESS
SANITARINESSES
SANITARIST
SANITARISTS
SANITARIUM
SANITARIUMS
SANITATING
SANITATION
SANITATIONIST
SANITATIONISTS
SANITATIONS
SANITISATION
SANITISATIONS
SANITISERS
SANITISING
SANITIZATION
SANITIZATIONS
SANITIZERS
SANITIZING
SANITORIUM
SANITORIUMS
SANNYASINS
SANSCULOTTE
SANSCULOTTERIE
SANSCULOTTERIES
SANSCULOTTES
SANSCULOTTIC
SANSCULOTTIDES
SANSCULOTTISH
SANSCULOTTISM
SANSCULOTTISMS
SANSCULOTTIST
SANSCULOTTISTS
SANSEVIERIA
SANSEVIERIAS

SANTALACEOUS
SANTOLINAS
SANTONICAS
SAPANWOODS
SAPIDITIES
SAPIDNESSES
SAPIENCIES
SAPIENTIAL
SAPIENTIALLY
SAPINDACEOUS
SAPLESSNESS
SAPLESSNESSES
SAPODILLAS
SAPOGENINS
SAPONACEOUS
SAPONACEOUSNESS
SAPONARIAS
SAPONIFIABLE
SAPONIFICATION
SAPONIFICATIONS
SAPONIFIED
SAPONIFIER
SAPONIFIERS
SAPONIFIES
SAPONIFYING
SAPOTACEOUS
SAPPANWOOD
SAPPANWOODS
SAPPERMENT
SAPPHIRINE
SAPPHIRINES
SAPPINESSES
SAPRAEMIAS
SAPROBIONT
SAPROBIONTS
SAPROBIOTIC
SAPROGENIC
SAPROGENICITIES
SAPROGENICITY
SAPROGENOUS
SAPROLEGNIA
SAPROLEGNIAS
SAPROLITES
SAPROLITIC
SAPROPELIC
SAPROPELITE
SAPROPELITES
SAPROPHAGOUS
SAPROPHYTE
SAPROPHYTES
SAPROPHYTIC
SAPROPHYTICALLY
SAPROPHYTISM
SAPROPHYTISMS
SAPROTROPH
SAPROTROPHIC
SAPROTROPHS
SAPSUCKERS
SARABANDES

SARBACANES
SARCASTICALLY
SARCENCHYMATOUS
SARCENCHYME
SARCENCHYMES
SARCOCARPS
SARCOCOLLA
SARCOCOLLAS
SARCOCYSTIS
SARCOCYSTISES
SARCOIDOSES
SARCOIDOSIS
SARCOLEMMA
SARCOLEMMAL
SARCOLEMMAS
SARCOLEMMATA
SARCOLOGIES
SARCOMATOID
SARCOMATOSES
SARCOMATOSIS
SARCOMATOUS
SARCOMERES
SARCOPHAGAL
SARCOPHAGI
SARCOPHAGOUS
SARCOPHAGUS
SARCOPHAGUSES
SARCOPLASM
SARCOPLASMIC
SARCOPLASMS
SARCOSOMAL
SARCOSOMES
SARDONICAL
SARDONICALLY
SARDONICISM
SARDONICISMS
SARDONYXES
SARGASSUMS
SARMENTACEOUS
SARMENTOSE
SARMENTOUS
SARPANCHES
SARRACENIA
SARRACENIACEOUS
SARRACENIAS
SARRUSOPHONE
SARRUSOPHONES
SARSAPARILLA
SARSAPARILLAS
SARTORIALLY
SARTORIUSES
SASKATOONS
SASQUATCHES
SASSAFRASES
SASSARARAS
SASSINESSES
SASSOLITES
SASSYWOODS
SATANICALLY

SATANICALNESS
SATANICALNESSES
SATANITIES
SATANOLOGIES
SATANOLOGY
SATANOPHANIES
SATANOPHANY
SATANOPHOBIA
SATANOPHOBIAS
SATCHELFUL
SATCHELFULS
SATCHELLED
SATCHELSFUL
SATEDNESSES
SATELLITED
SATELLITES
SATELLITIC
SATELLITING
SATELLITISE
SATELLITISED
SATELLITISES
SATELLITISING
SATELLITIUM
SATELLITIUMS
SATELLITIZE
SATELLITIZED
SATELLITIZES
SATELLITIZING
SATIABILITIES
SATIABILITY
SATIATIONS
SATINETTAS
SATINETTES
SATINFLOWER
SATINFLOWERS
SATINWOODS
SATIRICALLY
SATIRICALNESS
SATIRICALNESSES
SATIRISABLE
SATIRISATION
SATIRISATIONS
SATIRISERS
SATIRISING
SATIRIZABLE
SATIRIZATION
SATIRIZATIONS
SATIRIZERS
SATIRIZING
SATISFACTION
SATISFACTIONS
SATISFACTORILY
SATISFACTORY
SATISFIABLE
SATISFICED
SATISFICER
SATISFICERS
SATISFICES
SATISFICING

SATISFICINGS
SATISFIERS
SATISFYING
SATISFYINGLY
SATURABILITIES
SATURABILITY
SATURATERS
SATURATING
SATURATION
SATURATIONS
SATURATORS
SATURNALIA
SATURNALIAN
SATURNALIANLY
SATURNALIAS
SATURNIIDS
SATURNINELY
SATURNINITIES
SATURNINITY
SATURNISMS
SATURNISTS
SATYAGRAHA
SATYAGRAHAS
SATYAGRAHI
SATYAGRAHIS
SATYRESQUE
SATYRESSES
SATYRIASES
SATYRIASIS
SAUCEBOATS
SAUCEBOXES
SAUCERFULS
SAUCERLESS
SAUCERLIKE
SAUCINESSES
SAUCISSONS
SAUERBRATEN
SAUERBRATENS
SAUERKRAUT
SAUERKRAUTS
SAUNTERERS
SAUNTERING
SAUNTERINGLY
SAUNTERINGS
SAURISCHIAN
SAURISCHIANS
SAUROGNATHOUS
SAUROPODOUS
SAUROPSIDAN
SAUROPSIDANS
SAUROPTERYGIAN
SAUSSURITE
SAUSSURITES
SAUSSURITIC
SAVABLENESS
SAVABLENESSES
SAVAGEDOMS
SAVAGENESS
SAVAGENESSES

SAVAGERIES
SAVEABLENESS
SAVEABLENESSES
SAVEGARDED
SAVEGARDING
SAVINGNESS
SAVINGNESSES
SAVORINESS
SAVORINESSES
SAVOURIEST
SAVOURINESS
SAVOURINESSES
SAVOURLESS
SAVVINESSES
SAWBONESES
SAWDUSTING
SAWTIMBERS
SAXICAVOUS
SAXICOLINE
SAXICOLOUS
SAXIFRAGACEOUS
SAXIFRAGES
SAXITOXINS
SAXOPHONES
SAXOPHONIC
SAXOPHONIST
SAXOPHONISTS
SCABBARDED
SCABBARDING
SCABBARDLESS
SCABBEDNESS
SCABBEDNESSES
SCABBINESS
SCABBINESSES
SCABERULOUS
SCABIOUSES
SCABRIDITIES
SCABRIDITY
SCABROUSLY
SCABROUSNESS
SCABROUSNESSES
SCAFFOLAGE
SCAFFOLAGES
SCAFFOLDAGE
SCAFFOLDAGES
SCAFFOLDED
SCAFFOLDER
SCAFFOLDERS
SCAFFOLDING
SCAFFOLDINGS
SCAGLIOLAS
SCAITHLESS
SCALABILITIES
SCALABILITY
SCALABLENESS
SCALABLENESSES
SCALARIFORM
SCALARIFORMLY
SCALATIONS

SCALDBERRIES
SCALDBERRY
SCALDFISHES
SCALDHEADS
SCALDSHIPS
SCALEBOARD
SCALEBOARDS
SCALENOHEDRA
SCALENOHEDRON
SCALENOHEDRONS
SCALETAILS
SCALEWORKS
SCALINESSES
SCALLAWAGS
SCALLOPERS
SCALLOPING
SCALLOPINGS
SCALLOPINI
SCALLOPINIS
SCALLYWAGS
SCALOGRAMS
SCALOPPINE
SCALOPPINES
SCALOPPINI
SCALPELLIC
SCALPELLIFORM
SCALPRIFORM
SCAMBAITING
SCAMBAITINGS
SCAMBLINGLY
SCAMBLINGS
SCAMMONIATE
SCAMMONIES
SCAMPERERS
SCAMPERING
SCAMPISHLY
SCAMPISHNESS
SCAMPISHNESSES
SCANDALING
SCANDALISATION
SCANDALISATIONS
SCANDALISE
SCANDALISED
SCANDALISER
SCANDALISERS
SCANDALISES
SCANDALISING
SCANDALIZATION
SCANDALIZATIONS
SCANDALIZE
SCANDALIZED
SCANDALIZER
SCANDALIZERS
SCANDALIZES
SCANDALIZING
SCANDALLED
SCANDALLING
SCANDALMONGER
SCANDALMONGERS

SCANDALOUS
SCANDALOUSLY
SCANDALOUSNESS
SCANSORIAL
SCANTINESS
SCANTINESSES
SCANTITIES
SCANTLINGS
SCANTNESSES
SCAPEGALLOWS
SCAPEGALLOWSES
SCAPEGOATED
SCAPEGOATING
SCAPEGOATINGS
SCAPEGOATISM
SCAPEGOATISMS
SCAPEGOATS
SCAPEGRACE
SCAPEGRACES
SCAPEMENTS
SCAPEWHEEL
SCAPEWHEELS
SCAPHOCEPHALI
SCAPHOCEPHALIC
SCAPHOCEPHALIES
SCAPHOCEPHALISM
SCAPHOCEPHALOUS
SCAPHOCEPHALUS
SCAPHOCEPHALY
SCAPHOPODS
SCAPIGEROUS
SCAPOLITES
SCAPULARIES
SCAPULATED
SCAPULIMANCIES
SCAPULIMANCY
SCAPULIMANTIC
SCAPULOMANCIES
SCAPULOMANCY
SCAPULOMANTIC
SCARABAEAN
SCARABAEANS
SCARABAEID
SCARABAEIDS
SCARABAEIST
SCARABAEISTS
SCARABAEOID
SCARABAEOIDS
SCARABAEUS
SCARABAEUSES
SCARABOIDS
SCARAMOUCH
SCARAMOUCHE
SCARAMOUCHES
SCARCEMENT
SCARCEMENTS
SCARCENESS
SCARCENESSES
SCARCITIES

SCARECROWS
SCAREHEADS
SCAREMONGER
SCAREMONGERING
SCAREMONGERINGS
SCAREMONGERS
SCARFISHES
SCARFSKINS
SCARIFICATION
SCARIFICATIONS
SCARIFICATOR
SCARIFICATORS
SCARIFIERS
SCARIFYING
SCARIFYINGLY
SCARINESSES
SCARLATINA
SCARLATINAL
SCARLATINAS
SCARLETING
SCARPERING
SCATHEFULNESS
SCATHEFULNESSES
SCATHELESS
SCATHINGLY
SCATOLOGIC
SCATOLOGICAL
SCATOLOGIES
SCATOLOGIST
SCATOLOGISTS
SCATOPHAGIES
SCATOPHAGOUS
SCATOPHAGY
SCATTERABLE
SCATTERATION
SCATTERATIONS
SCATTERBRAIN
SCATTERBRAINED
SCATTERBRAINS
SCATTEREDLY
SCATTERERS
SCATTERGOOD
SCATTERGOODS
SCATTERGRAM
SCATTERGRAMS
SCATTERGUN
SCATTERGUNS
SCATTERING
SCATTERINGLY
SCATTERINGS
SCATTERLING
SCATTERLINGS
SCATTERMOUCH
SCATTERMOUCHES
SCATTERSHOT
SCATTINESS
SCATTINESSES
SCATURIENT
SCAVENGERED

SCAVENGERIES
SCAVENGERING
SCAVENGERINGS
SCAVENGERS
SCAVENGERY
SCAVENGING
SCAVENGINGS
SCAZONTICS
SCELERATES
SCENARISATION
SCENARISATIONS
SCENARISED
SCENARISES
SCENARISING
SCENARISTS
SCENARIZATION
SCENARIZATIONS
SCENARIZED
SCENARIZES
SCENARIZING
SCENESHIFTER
SCENESHIFTERS
SCENICALLY
SCENOGRAPHER
SCENOGRAPHERS
SCENOGRAPHIC
SCENOGRAPHICAL
SCENOGRAPHIES
SCENOGRAPHY
SCENTLESSNESS
SCENTLESSNESSES
SCEPTERING
SCEPTERLESS
SCEPTICALLY
SCEPTICISM
SCEPTICISMS
SCEPTRELESS
SCEUOPHYLACIA
SCEUOPHYLACIUM
SCEUOPHYLAX
SCEUOPHYLAXES
SCHADENFREUDE
SCHADENFREUDES
SCHALSTEIN
SCHALSTEINS
SCHAPPEING
SCHATCHENS
SCHECHITAH
SCHECHITAHS
SCHECHITAS
SCHECKLATON
SCHECKLATONS
SCHEDULERS
SCHEDULING
SCHEELITES
SCHEFFLERA
SCHEFFLERAS
SCHEMATICAL
SCHEMATICALLY

SCHEMATICS
SCHEMATISATION
SCHEMATISATIONS
SCHEMATISE
SCHEMATISED
SCHEMATISES
SCHEMATISING
SCHEMATISM
SCHEMATISMS
SCHEMATIST
SCHEMATISTS
SCHEMATIZATION
SCHEMATIZATIONS
SCHEMATIZE
SCHEMATIZED
SCHEMATIZES
SCHEMATIZING
SCHEMINGLY
SCHEMOZZLE
SCHEMOZZLED
SCHEMOZZLES
SCHEMOZZLING
SCHERZANDI
SCHERZANDO
SCHERZANDOS
SCHIAVONES
SCHILLERISATION
SCHILLERISE
SCHILLERISED
SCHILLERISES
SCHILLERISING
SCHILLERIZATION
SCHILLERIZE
SCHILLERIZED
SCHILLERIZES
SCHILLERIZING
SCHILLINGS
SCHINDYLESES
SCHINDYLESIS
SCHINDYLETIC
SCHIPPERKE
SCHIPPERKES
SCHISMATIC
SCHISMATICAL
SCHISMATICALLY
SCHISMATICALS
SCHISMATICS
SCHISMATISE
SCHISMATISED
SCHISMATISES
SCHISMATISING
SCHISMATIZE
SCHISMATIZED
SCHISMATIZES
SCHISMATIZING
SCHISTOSITIES
SCHISTOSITY
SCHISTOSOMAL
SCHISTOSOME

SCHISTOSOMES
SCHISTOSOMIASES
SCHISTOSOMIASIS
SCHIZAEACEOUS
SCHIZANTHUS
SCHIZANTHUSES
SCHIZOCARP
SCHIZOCARPIC
SCHIZOCARPOUS
SCHIZOCARPS
SCHIZOGENESES
SCHIZOGENESIS
SCHIZOGENETIC
SCHIZOGENIC
SCHIZOGNATHOUS
SCHIZOGONIC
SCHIZOGONIES
SCHIZOGONOUS
SCHIZOGONY
SCHIZOIDAL
SCHIZOMYCETE
SCHIZOMYCETES
SCHIZOMYCETIC
SCHIZOMYCETOUS
SCHIZOPHRENE
SCHIZOPHRENES
SCHIZOPHRENETIC
SCHIZOPHRENIA
SCHIZOPHRENIAS
SCHIZOPHRENIC
SCHIZOPHRENICS
SCHIZOPHYCEOUS
SCHIZOPHYTE
SCHIZOPHYTES
SCHIZOPHYTIC
SCHIZOPODAL
SCHIZOPODOUS
SCHIZOPODS
SCHIZOTHYMIA
SCHIZOTHYMIAS
SCHIZOTHYMIC
SCHIZZIEST
SCHLEMIELS
SCHLEMIHLS
SCHLEPPERS
SCHLEPPIER
SCHLEPPIEST
SCHLEPPING
SCHLIMAZEL
SCHLIMAZELS
SCHLOCKERS
SCHLOCKIER
SCHLOCKIEST
SCHLUMBERGERA
SCHLUMBERGERAS
SCHLUMPIER
SCHLUMPIEST
SCHLUMPING
SCHMALTZES

SCHMALTZIER
SCHMALTZIEST
SCHMALZIER
SCHMALZIEST
SCHMEARING
SCHMEERING
SCHMOOSING
SCHMOOZERS
SCHMOOZIER
SCHMOOZIEST
SCHMOOZING
SCHMUTTERS
SCHNAPPERS
SCHNAPPSES
SCHNAUZERS
SCHNITZELS
SCHNORKELED
SCHNORKELING
SCHNORKELLED
SCHNORKELLING
SCHNORKELS
SCHNORRERS
SCHNORRING
SCHNOZZLES
SCHOLARCHS
SCHOLARLIER
SCHOLARLIEST
SCHOLARLINESS
SCHOLARLINESSES
SCHOLARSHIP
SCHOLARSHIPS
SCHOLASTIC
SCHOLASTICAL
SCHOLASTICALLY
SCHOLASTICATE
SCHOLASTICATES
SCHOLASTICISM
SCHOLASTICISMS
SCHOLASTICS
SCHOLIASTIC
SCHOLIASTS
SCHOOLBAGS
SCHOOLBOOK
SCHOOLBOOKS
SCHOOLBOYISH
SCHOOLBOYS
SCHOOLCHILD
SCHOOLCHILDREN
SCHOOLCRAFT
SCHOOLCRAFTS
SCHOOLDAYS
SCHOOLERIES
SCHOOLFELLOW
SCHOOLFELLOWS
SCHOOLGIRL
SCHOOLGIRLISH
SCHOOLGIRLS
SCHOOLGOING
SCHOOLGOINGS

SCHOOLHOUSE
SCHOOLHOUSES
SCHOOLINGS
SCHOOLKIDS
SCHOOLMAID
SCHOOLMAIDS
SCHOOLMARM
SCHOOLMARMISH
SCHOOLMARMS
SCHOOLMASTER
SCHOOLMASTERED
SCHOOLMASTERING
SCHOOLMASTERISH
SCHOOLMASTERLY
SCHOOLMASTERS
SCHOOLMATE
SCHOOLMATES
SCHOOLMISTRESS
SCHOOLMISTRESSY
SCHOOLROOM
SCHOOLROOMS
SCHOOLTEACHER
SCHOOLTEACHERS
SCHOOLTEACHING
SCHOOLTEACHINGS
SCHOOLTIDE
SCHOOLTIDES
SCHOOLTIME
SCHOOLTIMES
SCHOOLWARD
SCHOOLWARDS
SCHOOLWORK
SCHOOLWORKS
SCHORLACEOUS
SCHORLOMITE
SCHORLOMITES
SCHOTTISCHE
SCHOTTISCHES
SCHRECKLICH
SCHUSSBOOMER
SCHUSSBOOMERS
SCHUTZSTAFFEL
SCHUTZSTAFFELS
SCHVARTZES
SCHWARMEREI
SCHWARMEREIS
SCHWARMERISCH
SCHWARTZES
SCHWARZLOT
SCHWARZLOTS
SCIAENOIDS
SCIAMACHIES
SCIENTIFIC
SCIENTIFICAL
SCIENTIFICALLY
SCIENTISED
SCIENTISES
SCIENTISING
SCIENTISMS

SCIENTISTIC
SCIENTISTS
SCIENTIZED
SCIENTIZES
SCIENTIZING
SCINCOIDIAN
SCINCOIDIANS
SCINDAPSUS
SCINDAPSUSES
SCINTIGRAM
SCINTIGRAMS
SCINTIGRAPHIC
SCINTIGRAPHIES
SCINTIGRAPHY
SCINTILLAE
SCINTILLANT
SCINTILLANTLY
SCINTILLAS
SCINTILLASCOPE
SCINTILLASCOPES
SCINTILLATE
SCINTILLATED
SCINTILLATES
SCINTILLATING
SCINTILLATINGLY
SCINTILLATION
SCINTILLATIONS
SCINTILLATOR
SCINTILLATORS
SCINTILLISCAN
SCINTILLISCANS
SCINTILLOMETER
SCINTILLOMETERS
SCINTILLON
SCINTILLONS
SCINTILLOSCOPE
SCINTILLOSCOPES
SCINTISCAN
SCINTISCANNER
SCINTISCANNERS
SCINTISCANS
SCIOLISTIC
SCIOMACHIES
SCIOMANCER
SCIOMANCERS
SCIOMANCIES
SCIOMANTIC
SCIOPHYTES
SCIOPHYTIC
SCIOSOPHIES
SCIRRHOSITIES
SCIRRHOSITY
SCIRRHUSES
SCISSIPARITIES
SCISSIPARITY
SCISSORERS
SCISSORING
SCISSORTAIL
SCISSORTAILS

SCISSORWISE
SCITAMINEOUS
SCLAUNDERS
SCLEREIDES
SCLERENCHYMA
SCLERENCHYMAS
SCLERENCHYMATA
SCLERIASES
SCLERIASIS
SCLERITISES
SCLEROCAULIES
SCLEROCAULOUS
SCLEROCAULY
SCLERODERM
SCLERODERMA
SCLERODERMAS
SCLERODERMATA
SCLERODERMATOUS
SCLERODERMIA
SCLERODERMIAS
SCLERODERMIC
SCLERODERMITE
SCLERODERMITES
SCLERODERMOUS
SCLERODERMS
SCLEROMALACIA
SCLEROMALACIAS
SCLEROMATA
SCLEROMETER
SCLEROMETERS
SCLEROMETRIC
SCLEROPHYLL
SCLEROPHYLLIES
SCLEROPHYLLOUS
SCLEROPHYLLS
SCLEROPHYLLY
SCLEROPROTEIN
SCLEROPROTEINS
SCLEROSING
SCLEROTALS
SCLEROTIAL
SCLEROTICS
SCLEROTINS
SCLEROTIOID
SCLEROTISATION
SCLEROTISATIONS
SCLEROTISE
SCLEROTISED
SCLEROTISES
SCLEROTISING
SCLEROTITIS
SCLEROTITISES
SCLEROTIUM
SCLEROTIZATION
SCLEROTIZATIONS
SCLEROTIZE
SCLEROTIZED
SCLEROTIZES
SCLEROTIZING

SCLEROTOMIES
SCLEROTOMY
SCOFFINGLY
SCOLDINGLY
SCOLECIFORM
SCOLECITES
SCOLLOPING
SCOLOPACEOUS
SCOLOPENDRA
SCOLOPENDRAS
SCOLOPENDRID
SCOLOPENDRIDS
SCOLOPENDRIFORM
SCOLOPENDRINE
SCOLOPENDRIUM
SCOLOPENDRIUMS
SCOLYTOIDS
SCOMBROIDS
SCOMFISHED
SCOMFISHES
SCOMFISHING
SCONCHEONS
SCOOTCHING
SCOOTERIST
SCOOTERISTS
SCOPELOIDS
SCOPOLAMINE
SCOPOLAMINES
SCOPOLINES
SCOPOPHILIA
SCOPOPHILIAC
SCOPOPHILIACS
SCOPOPHILIAS
SCOPOPHILIC
SCOPOPHOBIA
SCOPOPHOBIAS
SCOPTOPHILIA
SCOPTOPHILIAS
SCOPTOPHOBIA
SCOPTOPHOBIAS
SCORBUTICALLY
SCORCHINGLY
SCORCHINGNESS
SCORCHINGNESSES
SCORCHINGS
SCORDATURA
SCORDATURAS
SCOREBOARD
SCOREBOARDS
SCORECARDS
SCOREKEEPER
SCOREKEEPERS
SCORELINES
SCORESHEET
SCORESHEETS
SCORIACEOUS
SCORIFICATION
SCORIFICATIONS
SCORIFIERS

SCORIFYING
SCORNFULLY
SCORNFULNESS
SCORNFULNESSES
SCORODITES
SCORPAENID
SCORPAENIDS
SCORPAENOID
SCORPAENOIDS
SCORPIOIDS
SCORPIONIC
SCORZONERA
SCORZONERAS
SCOTODINIA
SCOTODINIAS
SCOTOMATOUS
SCOTOMETER
SCOTOMETERS
SCOUNDRELLY
SCOUNDRELS
SCOUTCRAFT
SCOUTCRAFTS
SCOUTHERED
SCOUTHERING
SCOUTHERINGS
SCOUTMASTER
SCOUTMASTERS
SCOWDERING
SCOWDERINGS
SCOWLINGLY
SCOWTHERED
SCOWTHERING
SCRABBLERS
SCRABBLIER
SCRABBLIEST
SCRABBLING
SCRAGGEDNESS
SCRAGGEDNESSES
SCRAGGIEST
SCRAGGINESS
SCRAGGINESSES
SCRAGGLIER
SCRAGGLIEST
SCRAGGLING
SCRAICHING
SCRAIGHING
SCRAMBLERS
SCRAMBLING
SCRAMBLINGLY
SCRAMBLINGS
SCRANCHING
SCRANNIEST
SCRAPBOOKS
SCRAPEGOOD
SCRAPEGOODS
SCRAPEGUTS
SCRAPEPENNIES
SCRAPEPENNY
SCRAPERBOARD

SCRAPERBOARDS
SCRAPHEAPS
SCRAPPAGES
SCRAPPIEST
SCRAPPINESS
SCRAPPINESSES
SCRAPYARDS
SCRATCHBACK
SCRATCHBACKS
SCRATCHBOARD
SCRATCHBOARDS
SCRATCHBUILD
SCRATCHBUILDER
SCRATCHBUILDERS
SCRATCHBUILDING
SCRATCHBUILDS
SCRATCHBUILT
SCRATCHCARD
SCRATCHCARDS
SCRATCHERS
SCRATCHIER
SCRATCHIES
SCRATCHIEST
SCRATCHILY
SCRATCHINESS
SCRATCHINESSES
SCRATCHING
SCRATCHINGLY
SCRATCHINGS
SCRATCHLESS
SCRATCHPLATE
SCRATCHPLATES
SCRATTLING
SCRAUCHING
SCRAUGHING
SCRAWLIEST
SCRAWLINGLY
SCRAWLINGS
SCRAWNIEST
SCRAWNINESS
SCRAWNINESSES
SCREAKIEST
SCREAMINGLY
SCREECHERS
SCREECHIER
SCREECHIEST
SCREECHING
SCREEDINGS
SCREENABLE
SCREENAGER
SCREENAGERS
SCREENCRAFT
SCREENCRAFTS
SCREENFULS
SCREENINGS
SCREENLAND
SCREENLANDS
SCREENLIKE
SCREENPLAY

SCREENPLAYS
SCREENSAVER
SCREENSAVERS
SCREENSHOT
SCREENSHOTS
SCREENWRITER
SCREENWRITERS
SCREEVINGS
SCREICHING
SCREIGHING
SCREWBALLS
SCREWBEANS
SCREWDRIVER
SCREWDRIVERS
SCREWINESS
SCREWINESSES
SCREWWORMS
SCRIBACIOUS
SCRIBACIOUSNESS
SCRIBBLEMENT
SCRIBBLEMENTS
SCRIBBLERS
SCRIBBLIER
SCRIBBLIEST
SCRIBBLING
SCRIBBLINGLY
SCRIBBLINGS
SCRIECHING
SCRIEVEBOARD
SCRIEVEBOARDS
SCRIGGLIER
SCRIGGLIEST
SCRIGGLING
SCRIMMAGED
SCRIMMAGER
SCRIMMAGERS
SCRIMMAGES
SCRIMMAGING
SCRIMPIEST
SCRIMPINESS
SCRIMPINESSES
SCRIMPNESS
SCRIMPNESSES
SCRIMSHANDER
SCRIMSHANDERED
SCRIMSHANDERING
SCRIMSHANDERS
SCRIMSHANDIED
SCRIMSHANDIES
SCRIMSHANDY
SCRIMSHANDYING
SCRIMSHANK
SCRIMSHANKED
SCRIMSHANKING
SCRIMSHANKS
SCRIMSHAWED
SCRIMSHAWING
SCRIMSHAWS
SCRIMSHONER

SCRIMSHONERS
SCRIPOPHILE
SCRIPOPHILES
SCRIPOPHILIES
SCRIPOPHILIST
SCRIPOPHILISTS
SCRIPOPHILY
SCRIPPAGES
SCRIPTORIA
SCRIPTORIAL
SCRIPTORIUM
SCRIPTORIUMS
SCRIPTURAL
SCRIPTURALISM
SCRIPTURALISMS
SCRIPTURALIST
SCRIPTURALISTS
SCRIPTURALLY
SCRIPTURES
SCRIPTURISM
SCRIPTURISMS
SCRIPTURIST
SCRIPTURISTS
SCRIPTWRITER
SCRIPTWRITERS
SCRIPTWRITING
SCRIPTWRITINGS
SCRITCHING
SCRIVEBOARD
SCRIVEBOARDS
SCRIVENERS
SCRIVENERSHIP
SCRIVENERSHIPS
SCRIVENING
SCRIVENINGS
SCROBICULAR
SCROBICULATE
SCROBICULATED
SCROBICULE
SCROBICULES
SCROFULOUS
SCROFULOUSLY
SCROFULOUSNESS
SCROGGIEST
SCROLLABLE
SCROLLWISE
SCROLLWORK
SCROLLWORKS
SCROOCHING
SCROOTCHED
SCROOTCHES
SCROOTCHING
SCROPHULARIA
SCROPHULARIAS
SCROUNGERS
SCROUNGIER
SCROUNGIEST
SCROUNGING
SCROUNGINGS

SCROWDGING
SCRUBBABLE
SCRUBBIEST
SCRUBBINESS
SCRUBBINESSES
SCRUBBINGS
SCRUBLANDS
SCRUBWOMAN
SCRUBWOMEN
SCRUFFIEST
SCRUFFINESS
SCRUFFINESSES
SCRUMDOWNS
SCRUMMAGED
SCRUMMAGER
SCRUMMAGERS
SCRUMMAGES
SCRUMMAGING
SCRUMMIEST
SCRUMPLING
SCRUMPOXES
SCRUMPTIOUS
SCRUMPTIOUSLY
SCRUMPTIOUSNESS
SCRUNCHEON
SCRUNCHEONS
SCRUNCHIER
SCRUNCHIES
SCRUNCHIEST
SCRUNCHING
SCRUNCHION
SCRUNCHIONS
SCRUNTIEST
SCRUPLELESS
SCRUPULOSITIES
SCRUPULOSITY
SCRUPULOUS
SCRUPULOUSLY
SCRUPULOUSNESS
SCRUTABILITIES
SCRUTABILITY
SCRUTATORS
SCRUTINEER
SCRUTINEERS
SCRUTINIES
SCRUTINISE
SCRUTINISED
SCRUTINISER
SCRUTINISERS
SCRUTINISES
SCRUTINISING
SCRUTINISINGLY
SCRUTINIZE
SCRUTINIZED
SCRUTINIZER
SCRUTINIZERS
SCRUTINIZES
SCRUTINIZING
SCRUTINIZINGLY

SCRUTINOUS
SCRUTINOUSLY
SCRUTOIRES
SCUDDALERS
SCULDUDDERIES
SCULDUDDERY
SCULDUDDRIES
SCULDUDDRY
SCULDUGGERIES
SCULDUGGERY
SCULLERIES
SCULPTRESS
SCULPTRESSES
SCULPTURAL
SCULPTURALLY
SCULPTURED
SCULPTURES
SCULPTURESQUE
SCULPTURESQUELY
SCULPTURING
SCULPTURINGS
SCUMBERING
SCUMBLINGS
SCUMFISHED
SCUMFISHES
SCUMFISHING
SCUNCHEONS
SCUNGILLIS
SCUNNERING
SCUPPERING
SCUPPERNONG
SCUPPERNONGS
SCURFINESS
SCURFINESSES
SCURRILITIES
SCURRILITY
SCURRILOUS
SCURRILOUSLY
SCURRILOUSNESS
SCURRIOURS
SCURVINESS
SCURVINESSES
SCUTATIONS
SCUTCHEONLESS
SCUTCHEONS
SCUTCHINGS
SCUTELLATE
SCUTELLATED
SCUTELLATION
SCUTELLATIONS
SCUTTERING
SCUTTLEBUTT
SCUTTLEBUTTS
SCUTTLEFUL
SCUTTLEFULS
SCUZZBALLS
SCYPHIFORM
SCYPHISTOMA
SCYPHISTOMAE

SCYPHISTOMAS
SCYPHOZOAN
SCYPHOZOANS
SCYTHELIKE
SDEIGNFULL
SDEIGNFULLY
SDRUCCIOLA
SEABEACHES
SEABORGIUM
SEABORGIUMS
SEABOTTLES
SEACUNNIES
SEAFARINGS
SEALIFTING
SEALPOINTS
SEAMANLIKE
SEAMANSHIP
SEAMANSHIPS
SEAMINESSES
SEAMLESSLY
SEAMLESSNESS
SEAMLESSNESSES
SEAMSTRESS
SEAMSTRESSES
SEAMSTRESSIES
SEAMSTRESSY
SEANNACHIE
SEANNACHIES
SEAQUARIUM
SEAQUARIUMS
SEARCHABLE
SEARCHINGLY
SEARCHINGNESS
SEARCHINGNESSES
SEARCHLESS
SEARCHLIGHT
SEARCHLIGHTS
SEAREDNESS
SEAREDNESSES
SEARNESSES
SEASICKEST
SEASICKNESS
SEASICKNESSES
SEASONABLE
SEASONABLENESS
SEASONABLY
SEASONALITIES
SEASONALITY
SEASONALLY
SEASONALNESS
SEASONALNESSES
SEASONINGS
SEASONLESS
SEASTRANDS
SEAWORTHIER
SEAWORTHIEST
SEAWORTHINESS
SEAWORTHINESSES
SEBIFEROUS

SEBORRHEAL
SEBORRHEAS
SEBORRHEIC
SEBORRHOEA
SEBORRHOEAL
SEBORRHOEAS
SEBORRHOEIC
SECERNENTS
SECERNMENT
SECERNMENTS
SECESSIONAL
SECESSIONISM
SECESSIONISMS
SECESSIONIST
SECESSIONISTS
SECESSIONS
SECLUDEDLY
SECLUDEDNESS
SECLUDEDNESSES
SECLUSIONIST
SECLUSIONISTS
SECLUSIONS
SECLUSIVELY
SECLUSIVENESS
SECLUSIVENESSES
SECOBARBITAL
SECOBARBITALS
SECONDARIES
SECONDARILY
SECONDARINESS
SECONDARINESSES
SECONDHAND
SECONDMENT
SECONDMENTS
SECRETAGES
SECRETAGOGIC
SECRETAGOGUE
SECRETAGOGUES
SECRETAIRE
SECRETAIRES
SECRETARIAL
SECRETARIAT
SECRETARIATE
SECRETARIATES
SECRETARIATS
SECRETARIES
SECRETARYSHIP
SECRETARYSHIPS
SECRETIONAL
SECRETIONARY
SECRETIONS
SECRETIVELY
SECRETIVENESS
SECRETIVENESSES
SECRETNESS
SECRETNESSES
SECRETORIES
SECTARIANISE
SECTARIANISED

SECTARIANISES
SECTARIANISING
SECTARIANISM
SECTARIANISMS
SECTARIANIZE
SECTARIANIZED
SECTARIANIZES
SECTARIANIZING
SECTARIANS
SECTILITIES
SECTIONALISE
SECTIONALISED
SECTIONALISES
SECTIONALISING
SECTIONALISM
SECTIONALISMS
SECTIONALIST
SECTIONALISTS
SECTIONALIZE
SECTIONALIZED
SECTIONALIZES
SECTIONALIZING
SECTIONALLY
SECTIONALS
SECTIONING
SECTIONISATION
SECTIONISATIONS
SECTIONISE
SECTIONISED
SECTIONISES
SECTIONISING
SECTIONIZATION
SECTIONIZATIONS
SECTIONIZE
SECTIONIZED
SECTIONIZES
SECTIONIZING
SECTORIALS
SECTORISATION
SECTORISATIONS
SECTORISED
SECTORISES
SECTORISING
SECTORIZATION
SECTORIZATIONS
SECTORIZED
SECTORIZES
SECTORIZING
SECULARISATION
SECULARISATIONS
SECULARISE
SECULARISED
SECULARISER
SECULARISERS
SECULARISES
SECULARISING
SECULARISM
SECULARISMS
SECULARIST

SECULARISTIC
SECULARISTS
SECULARITIES
SECULARITY
SECULARIZATION
SECULARIZATIONS
SECULARIZE
SECULARIZED
SECULARIZER
SECULARIZERS
SECULARIZES
SECULARIZING
SECUNDINES
SECUNDOGENITURE
SECURANCES
SECUREMENT
SECUREMENTS
SECURENESS
SECURENESSES
SECURIFORM
SECURITANS
SECURITIES
SECURITISATION
SECURITISATIONS
SECURITISE
SECURITISED
SECURITISES
SECURITISING
SECURITIZATION
SECURITIZATIONS
SECURITIZE
SECURITIZED
SECURITIZES
SECURITIZING
SECUROCRAT
SECUROCRATS
SEDATENESS
SEDATENESSES
SEDENTARILY
SEDENTARINESS
SEDENTARINESSES
SEDGELANDS
SEDIGITATED
SEDIMENTABLE
SEDIMENTARILY
SEDIMENTARY
SEDIMENTATION
SEDIMENTATIONS
SEDIMENTED
SEDIMENTING
SEDIMENTOLOGIC
SEDIMENTOLOGIES
SEDIMENTOLOGIST
SEDIMENTOLOGY
SEDIMENTOUS
SEDITIONARIES
SEDITIONARY
SEDITIOUSLY
SEDITIOUSNESS

SEDITIOUSNESSES
SEDUCEABLE
SEDUCEMENT
SEDUCEMENTS
SEDUCINGLY
SEDUCTIONS
SEDUCTIVELY
SEDUCTIVENESS
SEDUCTIVENESSES
SEDUCTRESS
SEDUCTRESSES
SEDULITIES
SEDULOUSLY
SEDULOUSNESS
SEDULOUSNESSES
SEECATCHIE
SEEDEATERS
SEEDINESSES
SEEDNESSES
SEEDSTOCKS
SEEMELESSE
SEEMINGNESS
SEEMINGNESSES
SEEMLIHEAD
SEEMLIHEADS
SEEMLIHEDS
SEEMLINESS
SEEMLINESSES
SEEMLYHEDS
SEERSUCKER
SEERSUCKERS
SEETHINGLY
SEGHOLATES
SEGMENTALLY
SEGMENTARY
SEGMENTATE
SEGMENTATION
SEGMENTATIONS
SEGMENTING
SEGREGABLE
SEGREGANTS
SEGREGATED
SEGREGATES
SEGREGATING
SEGREGATION
SEGREGATIONAL
SEGREGATIONIST
SEGREGATIONISTS
SEGREGATIONS
SEGREGATIVE
SEGREGATOR
SEGREGATORS
SEGUIDILLA
SEGUIDILLAS
SEIGNEURIAL
SEIGNEURIE
SEIGNEURIES
SEIGNIORAGE
SEIGNIORAGES

SEIGNIORALTIES
SEIGNIORALTY
SEIGNIORIAL
SEIGNIORIES
SEIGNIORSHIP
SEIGNIORSHIPS
SEIGNORAGE
SEIGNORAGES
SEIGNORIAL
SEIGNORIES
SEISMICALLY
SEISMICITIES
SEISMICITY
SEISMOGRAM
SEISMOGRAMS
SEISMOGRAPH
SEISMOGRAPHER
SEISMOGRAPHERS
SEISMOGRAPHIC
SEISMOGRAPHICAL
SEISMOGRAPHIES
SEISMOGRAPHS
SEISMOGRAPHY
SEISMOLOGIC
SEISMOLOGICAL
SEISMOLOGICALLY
SEISMOLOGIES
SEISMOLOGIST
SEISMOLOGISTS
SEISMOLOGY
SEISMOMETER
SEISMOMETERS
SEISMOMETRIC
SEISMOMETRICAL
SEISMOMETRIES
SEISMOMETRY
SEISMONASTIC
SEISMONASTIES
SEISMONASTY
SEISMOSCOPE
SEISMOSCOPES
SEISMOSCOPIC
SELACHIANS
SELAGINELLA
SELAGINELLAS
SELDOMNESS
SELDOMNESSES
SELECTABLE
SELECTIONIST
SELECTIONISTS
SELECTIONS
SELECTIVELY
SELECTIVENESS
SELECTIVENESSES
SELECTIVITIES
SELECTIVITY
SELECTNESS
SELECTNESSES
SELECTORATE

SELECTORATES
SELECTORIAL
SELEGILINE
SELEGILINES
SELENIFEROUS
SELENOCENTRIC
SELENODONT
SELENODONTS
SELENOGRAPH
SELENOGRAPHER
SELENOGRAPHERS
SELENOGRAPHIC
SELENOGRAPHICAL
SELENOGRAPHIES
SELENOGRAPHIST
SELENOGRAPHISTS
SELENOGRAPHS
SELENOGRAPHY
SELENOLOGICAL
SELENOLOGIES
SELENOLOGIST
SELENOLOGISTS
SELENOLOGY
SELFISHNESS
SELFISHNESSES
SELFLESSLY
SELFLESSNESS
SELFLESSNESSES
SELFNESSES
SELFSAMENESS
SELFSAMENESSES
SELLOTAPED
SELLOTAPES
SELLOTAPING
SELTZOGENE
SELTZOGENES
SELVEDGING
SEMAINIERS
SEMANTEMES
SEMANTICAL
SEMANTICALLY
SEMANTICIST
SEMANTICISTS
SEMANTIDES
SEMAPHORED
SEMAPHORES
SEMAPHORIC
SEMAPHORICAL
SEMAPHORICALLY
SEMAPHORING
SEMASIOLOGICAL
SEMASIOLOGIES
SEMASIOLOGIST
SEMASIOLOGISTS
SEMASIOLOGY
SEMATOLOGIES
SEMATOLOGY
SEMBLABLES
SEMBLANCES

SEMBLATIVE
SEMEIOLOGIC
SEMEIOLOGICAL
SEMEIOLOGIES
SEMEIOLOGIST
SEMEIOLOGISTS
SEMEIOLOGY
SEMEIOTICIAN
SEMEIOTICIANS
SEMEIOTICS
SEMELPARITIES
SEMELPARITY
SEMELPAROUS
SEMESTRIAL
SEMIABSTRACT
SEMIABSTRACTION
SEMIANGLES
SEMIANNUAL
SEMIANNUALLY
SEMIAQUATIC
SEMIARBOREAL
SEMIARIDITIES
SEMIARIDITY
SEMIAUTOMATIC
SEMIAUTOMATICS
SEMIAUTONOMOUS
SEMIBREVES
SEMICARBAZIDE
SEMICARBAZIDES
SEMICARBAZONE
SEMICARBAZONES
SEMICENTENNIAL
SEMICENTENNIALS
SEMICHORUS
SEMICHORUSES
SEMICIRCLE
SEMICIRCLED
SEMICIRCLES
SEMICIRCULAR
SEMICIRCULARLY
SEMICIRQUE
SEMICIRQUES
SEMICIVILISED
SEMICIVILIZED
SEMICLASSIC
SEMICLASSICAL
SEMICLASSICS
SEMICOLONIAL
SEMICOLONIALISM
SEMICOLONIES
SEMICOLONS
SEMICOLONY
SEMICOMATOSE
SEMICOMMERCIAL
SEMICONDUCTING
SEMICONDUCTION
SEMICONDUCTIONS
SEMICONDUCTOR
SEMICONDUCTORS

SEMICONSCIOUS
SEMICONSCIOUSLY
SEMICRYSTALLIC
SEMICRYSTALLINE
SEMICYLINDER
SEMICYLINDERS
SEMICYLINDRICAL
SEMIDARKNESS
SEMIDARKNESSES
SEMIDEIFIED
SEMIDEIFIES
SEMIDEIFYING
SEMIDEPONENT
SEMIDEPONENTS
SEMIDESERT
SEMIDESERTS
SEMIDETACHED
SEMIDIAMETER
SEMIDIAMETERS
SEMIDIURNAL
SEMIDIVINE
SEMIDOCUMENTARY
SEMIDOMINANT
SEMIDRYING
SEMIDWARFS
SEMIDWARVES
SEMIELLIPTICAL
SEMIEMPIRICAL
SEMIEVERGREEN
SEMIFEUDAL
SEMIFINALIST
SEMIFINALISTS
SEMIFINALS
SEMIFINISHED
SEMIFITTED
SEMIFLEXIBLE
SEMIFLUIDIC
SEMIFLUIDITIES
SEMIFLUIDITY
SEMIFLUIDS
SEMIFORMAL
SEMIFREDDO
SEMIFREDDOS
SEMIGLOBULAR
SEMIGLOSSES
SEMIGROUPS
SEMIHOBOES
SEMILEGENDARY
SEMILETHAL
SEMILETHALS
SEMILIQUID
SEMILIQUIDS
SEMILITERATE
SEMILITERATES
SEMILOGARITHMIC
SEMILUCENT
SEMILUNATE
SEMILUSTROUS
SEMIMANUFACTURE

SEMIMENSTRUAL
SEMIMETALLIC
SEMIMETALS
SEMIMONASTIC
SEMIMONTHLIES
SEMIMONTHLY
SEMIMYSTICAL
SEMINALITIES
SEMINALITY
SEMINARIAL
SEMINARIAN
SEMINARIANS
SEMINARIES
SEMINARIST
SEMINARISTS
SEMINATING
SEMINATION
SEMINATIONS
SEMINATURAL
SEMINIFEROUS
SEMINOMADIC
SEMINOMADS
SEMINOMATA
SEMINUDITIES
SEMINUDITY
SEMIOCHEMICAL
SEMIOCHEMICALS
SEMIOFFICIAL
SEMIOFFICIALLY
SEMIOLOGIC
SEMIOLOGICAL
SEMIOLOGICALLY
SEMIOLOGIES
SEMIOLOGIST
SEMIOLOGISTS
SEMIOPAQUE
SEMIOTICIAN
SEMIOTICIANS
SEMIOTICIST
SEMIOTICISTS
SEMIOVIPAROUS
SEMIPALMATE
SEMIPALMATED
SEMIPALMATION
SEMIPALMATIONS
SEMIPARASITE
SEMIPARASITES
SEMIPARASITIC
SEMIPARASITISM
SEMIPARASITISMS
SEMIPELLUCID
SEMIPERIMETER
SEMIPERIMETERS
SEMIPERMANENT
SEMIPERMEABLE
SEMIPLUMES
SEMIPOLITICAL
SEMIPOPULAR
SEMIPORCELAIN

SEMIPORCELAINS
SEMIPORNOGRAPHY
SEMIPOSTAL
SEMIPOSTALS
SEMIPRECIOUS
SEMIPRIVATE
SEMIPUBLIC
SEMIQUAVER
SEMIQUAVERS
SEMIRELIGIOUS
SEMIRETIRED
SEMIRETIREMENT
SEMIRETIREMENTS
SEMIROUNDS
SEMISACRED
SEMISECRET
SEMISEDENTARY
SEMISHRUBBY
SEMISKILLED
SEMISOLIDS
SEMISOLUSES
SEMISUBMERSIBLE
SEMISYNTHETIC
SEMITERETE
SEMITERRESTRIAL
SEMITONALLY
SEMITONICALLY
SEMITRAILER
SEMITRAILERS
SEMITRANSLUCENT
SEMITRANSPARENT
SEMITROPIC
SEMITROPICAL
SEMITROPICS
SEMITRUCKS
SEMIVITREOUS
SEMIVOCALIC
SEMIVOWELS
SEMIWEEKLIES
SEMIWEEKLY
SEMIYEARLY
SEMPERVIVUM
SEMPERVIVUMS
SEMPITERNAL
SEMPITERNALLY
SEMPITERNITIES
SEMPITERNITY
SEMPITERNUM
SEMPITERNUMS
SEMPSTERING
SEMPSTERINGS
SEMPSTRESS
SEMPSTRESSES
SEMPSTRESSING
SEMPSTRESSINGS
SENARMONTITE
SENARMONTITES
SENATORIAL
SENATORIALLY

SENATORIAN
SENATORSHIP
SENATORSHIPS
SENECTITUDE
SENECTITUDES
SENESCENCE
SENESCENCES
SENESCHALS
SENESCHALSHIP
SENESCHALSHIPS
SENHORITAS
SENILITIES
SENIORITIES
SENNACHIES
SENSATIONAL
SENSATIONALISE
SENSATIONALISED
SENSATIONALISES
SENSATIONALISM
SENSATIONALISMS
SENSATIONALIST
SENSATIONALISTS
SENSATIONALIZE
SENSATIONALIZED
SENSATIONALIZES
SENSATIONALLY
SENSATIONISM
SENSATIONISMS
SENSATIONIST
SENSATIONISTS
SENSATIONLESS
SENSATIONS
SENSELESSLY
SENSELESSNESS
SENSELESSNESSES
SENSIBILIA
SENSIBILITIES
SENSIBILITY
SENSIBLENESS
SENSIBLENESSES
SENSIBLEST
SENSITISATION
SENSITISATIONS
SENSITISED
SENSITISER
SENSITISERS
SENSITISES
SENSITISING
SENSITIVELY
SENSITIVENESS
SENSITIVENESSES
SENSITIVES
SENSITIVITIES
SENSITIVITY
SENSITIZATION
SENSITIZATIONS
SENSITIZED
SENSITIZER
SENSITIZERS

SENSITIZES	SENTIMENTALIZED	SEPTENTRIONALLY	SEQUENTIALITY
SENSITIZING	SENTIMENTALIZES	SEPTENTRIONES	SEQUENTIALLY
SENSITOMETER	SENTIMENTALLY	SEPTENTRIONS	SEQUESTERED
SENSITOMETERS	SENTIMENTS	SEPTICAEMIA	SEQUESTERING
SENSITOMETRIC	SENTINELED	SEPTICAEMIAS	SEQUESTERS
SENSITOMETRIES	SENTINELING	SEPTICAEMIC	SEQUESTRABLE
SENSITOMETRY	SENTINELLED	SEPTICALLY	SEQUESTRAL
SENSOMOTOR	SENTINELLING	SEPTICEMIA	SEQUESTRANT
SENSORIALLY	SEPALODIES	SEPTICEMIAS	SEQUESTRANTS
SENSORIMOTOR	SEPARABILITIES	SEPTICEMIC	SEQUESTRATE
SENSORINEURAL	SEPARABILITY	SEPTICIDAL	SEQUESTRATED
SENSORIUMS	SEPARABLENESS	SEPTICIDALLY	SEQUESTRATES
SENSUALISATION	SEPARABLENESSES	SEPTICITIES	SEQUESTRATING
SENSUALISATIONS	SEPARATELY	SEPTIFEROUS	SEQUESTRATION
SENSUALISE	SEPARATENESS	SEPTIFRAGAL	SEQUESTRATIONS
SENSUALISED	SEPARATENESSES	SEPTILATERAL	SEQUESTRATOR
SENSUALISES	SEPARATING	SEPTILLION	SEQUESTRATORS
SENSUALISING	SEPARATION	SEPTILLIONS	SEQUESTRUM
SENSUALISM	SEPARATIONISM	SEPTILLIONTH	SEQUESTRUMS
SENSUALISMS	SEPARATIONISMS	SEPTILLIONTHS	SERAPHICAL
SENSUALIST	SEPARATIONIST	SEPTIMOLES	SERAPHICALLY
SENSUALISTIC	SEPARATIONISTS	SEPTIVALENT	SERAPHINES
SENSUALISTS	SEPARATIONS	SEPTUAGENARIAN	SERASKIERATE
SENSUALITIES	SEPARATISM	SEPTUAGENARIANS	SERASKIERATES
SENSUALITY	SEPARATISMS	SEPTUAGENARIES	SERASKIERS
SENSUALIZATION	SEPARATIST	SEPTUAGENARY	SERENADERS
SENSUALIZATIONS	SEPARATISTIC	SEPTUPLETS	SERENADING
SENSUALIZE	SEPARATISTS	SEPTUPLICATE	SERENDIPITIES
SENSUALIZED	SEPARATIVE	SEPTUPLICATES	SERENDIPITIST
SENSUALIZES	SEPARATIVELY	SEPTUPLING	SERENDIPITISTS
SENSUALIZING	SEPARATIVENESS	SEPULCHERED	SERENDIPITOUS
SENSUALNESS	SEPARATORIES	SEPULCHERING	SERENDIPITOUSLY
SENSUALNESSES	SEPARATORS	SEPULCHERS	SERENDIPITY
SENSUOSITIES	SEPARATORY	SEPULCHRAL	SERENENESS
SENSUOSITY	SEPARATRICES	SEPULCHRALLY	SERENENESSES
SENSUOUSLY	SEPARATRIX	SEPULCHRED	SERENITIES
SENSUOUSNESS	SEPARATUMS	SEPULCHRES	SERGEANCIES
SENSUOUSNESSES	SEPIOLITES	SEPULCHRING	SERGEANTIES
SENTENCERS	SEPIOSTAIRE	SEPULCHROUS	SERGEANTSHIP
SENTENCING	SEPIOSTAIRES	SEPULTURAL	SERGEANTSHIPS
SENTENTIAE	SEPTATIONS	SEPULTURED	SERIALISATION
SENTENTIAL	SEPTAVALENT	SEPULTURES	SERIALISATIONS
SENTENTIALLY	SEPTEMVIRATE	SEPULTURING	SERIALISED
SENTENTIOUS	SEPTEMVIRATES	SEQUACIOUS	SERIALISES
SENTENTIOUSLY	SEPTEMVIRI	SEQUACIOUSLY	SERIALISING
SENTENTIOUSNESS	SEPTEMVIRS	SEQUACIOUSNESS	SERIALISMS
SENTIENCES	SEPTENARIES	SEQUACITIES	SERIALISTS
SENTIENCIES	SEPTENARII	SEQUELISED	SERIALITIES
SENTIENTLY	SEPTENARIUS	SEQUELISES	SERIALIZATION
SENTIMENTAL	SEPTENDECILLION	SEQUELISING	SERIALIZATIONS
SENTIMENTALISE	SEPTENNATE	SEQUELIZED	SERIALIZED
SENTIMENTALISED	SEPTENNATES	SEQUELIZES	SERIALIZES
SENTIMENTALISES	SEPTENNIAL	SEQUELIZING	SERIALIZING
SENTIMENTALISM	SEPTENNIALLY	SEQUENCERS	SERIATIONS
SENTIMENTALISMS	SEPTENNIUM	SEQUENCIES	SERICICULTURE
SENTIMENTALIST	SEPTENNIUMS	SEQUENCING	SERICICULTURES
SENTIMENTALISTS	SEPTENTRIAL	SEQUENCINGS	SERICICULTURIST
SENTIMENTALITY	SEPTENTRION	SEQUENTIAL	SERICITISATION
SENTIMENTALIZE	SEPTENTRIONAL	SEQUENTIALITIES	SERICITISATIONS

SERICITIZATION
SERICITIZATIONS
SERICTERIA
SERICTERIUM
SERICULTURAL
SERICULTURE
SERICULTURES
SERICULTURIST
SERICULTURISTS
SERIGRAPHER
SERIGRAPHERS
SERIGRAPHIC
SERIGRAPHIES
SERIGRAPHS
SERIGRAPHY
SERINETTES
SERIOCOMIC
SERIOCOMICAL
SERIOCOMICALLY
SERIOUSNESS
SERIOUSNESSES
SERJEANCIES
SERJEANTIES
SERJEANTRIES
SERJEANTRY
SERJEANTSHIP
SERJEANTSHIPS
SERMONEERS
SERMONETTE
SERMONETTES
SERMONICAL
SERMONINGS
SERMONISED
SERMONISER
SERMONISERS
SERMONISES
SERMONISING
SERMONIZED
SERMONIZER
SERMONIZERS
SERMONIZES
SERMONIZING
SEROCONVERSION
SEROCONVERSIONS
SEROCONVERT
SEROCONVERTED
SEROCONVERTING
SEROCONVERTS
SERODIAGNOSES
SERODIAGNOSIS
SERODIAGNOSTIC
SEROLOGICAL
SEROLOGICALLY
SEROLOGIES
SEROLOGIST
SEROLOGISTS
SERONEGATIVE
SERONEGATIVITY
SEROPOSITIVE

SEROPOSITIVITY
SEROPURULENT
SEROSITIES
SEROTAXONOMIES
SEROTAXONOMY
SEROTHERAPIES
SEROTHERAPY
SEROTINIES
SEROTINOUS
SEROTONERGIC
SEROTONINERGIC
SEROTONINS
SEROTYPING
SEROTYPINGS
SEROUSNESS
SEROUSNESSES
SERPENTIFORM
SERPENTINE
SERPENTINED
SERPENTINELY
SERPENTINES
SERPENTINIC
SERPENTINING
SERPENTININGLY
SERPENTININGS
SERPENTINISE
SERPENTINISED
SERPENTINISES
SERPENTINISING
SERPENTINITE
SERPENTINITES
SERPENTINIZE
SERPENTINIZED
SERPENTINIZES
SERPENTINIZING
SERPENTINOUS
SERPENTISE
SERPENTISED
SERPENTISES
SERPENTISING
SERPENTIZE
SERPENTIZED
SERPENTIZES
SERPENTIZING
SERPENTLIKE
SERPENTRIES
SERPIGINES
SERPIGINOUS
SERPIGINOUSLY
SERPULITES
SERRADELLA
SERRADELLAS
SERRADILLA
SERRADILLAS
SERRANOIDS
SERRASALMO
SERRASALMOS
SERRATIONS
SERRATIROSTRAL

SERRATULATE
SERRATURES
SERRATUSES
SERREFILES
SERRIEDNESS
SERRIEDNESSES
SERRULATED
SERRULATION
SERRULATIONS
SERTULARIAN
SERTULARIANS
SERVANTHOOD
SERVANTHOODS
SERVANTING
SERVANTLESS
SERVANTRIES
SERVANTSHIP
SERVANTSHIPS
SERVICEABILITY
SERVICEABLE
SERVICEABLENESS
SERVICEABLY
SERVICEBERRIES
SERVICEBERRY
SERVICELESS
SERVICEMAN
SERVICEMEN
SERVICEWOMAN
SERVICEWOMEN
SERVIETTES
SERVILENESS
SERVILENESSES
SERVILISMS
SERVILITIES
SERVITORIAL
SERVITORSHIP
SERVITORSHIPS
SERVITRESS
SERVITRESSES
SERVITUDES
SERVOCONTROL
SERVOCONTROLS
SERVOMECHANICAL
SERVOMECHANISM
SERVOMECHANISMS
SERVOMOTOR
SERVOMOTORS
SESQUIALTER
SESQUIALTERA
SESQUIALTERAS
SESQUICARBONATE
SESQUICENTENARY
SESQUIOXIDE
SESQUIOXIDES
SESQUIPEDAL
SESQUIPEDALIAN
SESQUIPEDALITY
SESQUIPLICATE
SESQUISULPHIDE

SESQUISULPHIDES
SESQUITERPENE
SESQUITERPENES
SESQUITERTIA
SESQUITERTIAS
SESSILITIES
SESSIONALLY
SESTERTIUM
SESTERTIUS
SETACEOUSLY
SETIFEROUS
SETIGEROUS
SETTERWORT
SETTERWORTS
SETTLEABLE
SETTLEDNESS
SETTLEDNESSES
SETTLEMENT
SETTLEMENTS
SEVENPENCE
SEVENPENCES
SEVENPENNIES
SEVENPENNY
SEVENTEENS
SEVENTEENTH
SEVENTEENTHLY
SEVENTEENTHS
SEVENTIETH
SEVENTIETHS
SEVERABILITIES
SEVERABILITY
SEVERALFOLD
SEVERALTIES
SEVERANCES
SEVERENESS
SEVERENESSES
SEVERITIES
SEWABILITIES
SEWABILITY
SEXAGENARIAN
SEXAGENARIANS
SEXAGENARIES
SEXAGENARY
SEXAGESIMAL
SEXAGESIMALLY
SEXAGESIMALS
SEXAHOLICS
SEXANGULAR
SEXANGULARLY
SEXAVALENT
SEXCENTENARIES
SEXCENTENARY
SEXDECILLION
SEXDECILLIONS
SEXENNIALLY
SEXENNIALS
SEXERCISES
SEXINESSES
SEXIVALENT

SEXLESSNESS	SHADOWGRAPHS	SHANGHAIERS	SHEATHBILL
SEXLESSNESSES	SHADOWGRAPHY	SHANGHAIING	SHEATHBILLS
SEXLOCULAR	SHADOWIEST	SHANKBONES	SHEATHFISH
SEXOLOGICAL	SHADOWINESS	SHANKPIECE	SHEATHFISHES
SEXOLOGIES	SHADOWINESSES	SHANKPIECES	SHEATHIEST
SEXOLOGIST	SHADOWINGS	SHANTYTOWN	SHEATHINGS
SEXOLOGISTS	SHADOWLESS	SHANTYTOWNS	SHEATHLESS
SEXPARTITE	SHADOWLIKE	SHAPELESSLY	SHEBEENERS
SEXPLOITATION	SHAGGEDNESS	SHAPELESSNESS	SHEBEENING
SEXPLOITATIONS	SHAGGEDNESSES	SHAPELESSNESSES	SHEBEENINGS
SEXTILLION	SHAGGINESS	SHAPELIEST	SHECHITAHS
SEXTILLIONS	SHAGGINESSES	SHAPELINESS	SHECKLATON
SEXTILLIONTH	SHAGGYMANE	SHAPELINESSES	SHECKLATONS
SEXTILLIONTHS	SHAGGYMANES	SHARAWADGI	SHEEPBERRIES
SEXTODECIMO	SHAGREENED	SHARAWADGIS	SHEEPBERRY
SEXTODECIMOS	SHAGTASTIC	SHARAWAGGI	SHEEPCOTES
SEXTONESSES	SHAHTOOSHES	SHARAWAGGIS	SHEEPFOLDS
SEXTONSHIP	SHAKEDOWNS	SHAREABILITIES	SHEEPHEADS
SEXTONSHIPS	SHAKINESSES	SHAREABILITY	SHEEPHERDER
SEXTUPLETS	SHAKUHACHI	SHARECROPPED	SHEEPHERDERS
SEXTUPLICATE	SHAKUHACHIS	SHARECROPPER	SHEEPHERDING
SEXTUPLICATED	SHALLOWEST	SHARECROPPERS	SHEEPHERDINGS
SEXTUPLICATES	SHALLOWING	SHARECROPPING	SHEEPISHLY
SEXTUPLICATING	SHALLOWINGS	SHARECROPS	SHEEPISHNESS
SEXTUPLING	SHALLOWNESS	SHAREFARMER	SHEEPISHNESSES
SEXUALISATION	SHALLOWNESSES	SHAREFARMERS	SHEEPSHANK
SEXUALISATIONS	SHAMANISMS	SHAREHOLDER	SHEEPSHANKS
SEXUALISED	SHAMANISTIC	SHAREHOLDERS	SHEEPSHEAD
SEXUALISES	SHAMANISTS	SHAREHOLDING	SHEEPSHEADS
SEXUALISING	SHAMATEURISM	SHAREHOLDINGS	SHEEPSHEARER
SEXUALISMS	SHAMATEURISMS	SHAREMILKER	SHEEPSHEARERS
SEXUALISTS	SHAMATEURS	SHAREMILKERS	SHEEPSHEARING
SEXUALITIES	SHAMBLIEST	SHAREWARES	SHEEPSHEARINGS
SEXUALIZATION	SHAMBLINGS	SHARKSKINS	SHEEPSKINS
SEXUALIZATIONS	SHAMEFACED	SHARKSUCKER	SHEEPTRACK
SEXUALIZED	SHAMEFACEDLY	SHARKSUCKERS	SHEEPTRACKS
SEXUALIZES	SHAMEFACEDNESS	SHARPBENDER	SHEEPWALKS
SEXUALIZING	SHAMEFASTNESS	SHARPBENDERS	SHEERNESSES
SFORZANDOS	SHAMEFASTNESSES	SHARPENERS	SHEETROCKED
SHABBINESS	SHAMEFULLY	SHARPENING	SHEETROCKING
SHABBINESSES	SHAMEFULNESS	SHARPNESSES	SHEETROCKS
SHABRACQUE	SHAMEFULNESSES	SHARPSHOOTER	SHEIKHDOMS
SHABRACQUES	SHAMELESSLY	SHARPSHOOTERS	SHELDDUCKS
SHACKLEBONE	SHAMELESSNESS	SHARPSHOOTING	SHELDRAKES
SHACKLEBONES	SHAMELESSNESSES	SHARPSHOOTINGS	SHELFROOMS
SHADBERRIES	SHAMEWORTHY	SHASHLICKS	SHELFTALKER
SHADBUSHES	SHAMIANAHS	SHATTERERS	SHELFTALKERS
SHADCHANIM	SHAMIYANAH	SHATTERING	SHELLACKED
SHADINESSES	SHAMIYANAHS	SHATTERINGLY	SHELLACKER
SHADKHANIM	SHAMMASHIM	SHATTERPROOF	SHELLACKERS
SHADOWBOXED	SHAMPOOERS	SHAUCHLIER	SHELLACKING
SHADOWBOXES	SHAMPOOING	SHAUCHLIEST	SHELLACKINGS
SHADOWBOXING	SHANACHIES	SHAUCHLING	SHELLBACKS
SHADOWCAST	SHANDRYDAN	SHAVELINGS	SHELLBARKS
SHADOWCASTING	SHANDRYDANS	SHAVETAILS	SHELLBOUND
SHADOWCASTINGS	SHANDYGAFF	SHEARLINGS	SHELLCRACKER
SHADOWCASTS	SHANDYGAFFS	SHEARWATER	SHELLCRACKERS
SHADOWGRAPH	SHANGHAIED	SHEARWATERS	SHELLDRAKE
SHADOWGRAPHIES	SHANGHAIER	SHEATFISHES	SHELLDRAKES

SHELLDUCKS
SHELLFIRES
SHELLFISHERIES
SHELLFISHERY
SHELLFISHES
SHELLINESS
SHELLINESSES
SHELLPROOF
SHELLSHOCK
SHELLSHOCKED
SHELLSHOCKS
SHELLWORKS
SHELLYCOAT
SHELLYCOATS
SHELTERBELT
SHELTERBELTS
SHELTERERS
SHELTERING
SHELTERINGS
SHELTERLESS
SHEMOZZLED
SHEMOZZLES
SHEMOZZLING
SHENANIGAN
SHENANIGANS
SHEPHERDED
SHEPHERDESS
SHEPHERDESSES
SHEPHERDING
SHEPHERDLESS
SHEPHERDLING
SHEPHERDLINGS
SHERARDISATION
SHERARDISATIONS
SHERARDISE
SHERARDISED
SHERARDISES
SHERARDISING
SHERARDIZATION
SHERARDIZATIONS
SHERARDIZE
SHERARDIZED
SHERARDIZES
SHERARDIZING
SHEREEFIAN
SHERGOTTITE
SHERGOTTITES
SHERIFFALTIES
SHERIFFALTY
SHERIFFDOM
SHERIFFDOMS
SHERIFFSHIP
SHERIFFSHIPS
SHEWBREADS
SHIBBOLETH
SHIBBOLETHS
SHIBUICHIS
SHIDDUCHIM
SHIELDINGS

SHIELDLESS
SHIELDLIKE
SHIELDLING
SHIELDLINGS
SHIELDRAKE
SHIELDRAKES
SHIELDWALL
SHIELDWALLS
SHIFTINESS
SHIFTINESSES
SHIFTLESSLY
SHIFTLESSNESS
SHIFTLESSNESSES
SHIFTWORKS
SHIGELLOSES
SHIGELLOSIS
SHIKARRING
SHILLABERS
SHILLALAHS
SHILLELAGH
SHILLELAGHS
SHILLELAHS
SHILLINGLESS
SHILLINGSWORTH
SHILLINGSWORTHS
SHILLYSHALLIED
SHILLYSHALLIER
SHILLYSHALLIERS
SHILLYSHALLIES
SHILLYSHALLY
SHILLYSHALLYING
SHIMMERING
SHIMMERINGLY
SHIMMERINGS
SHIMOZZLES
SHINGLIEST
SHINGLINGS
SHINGUARDS
SHININESSES
SHININGNESS
SHININGNESSES
SHINLEAVES
SHINNERIES
SHINNEYING
SHINPLASTER
SHINPLASTERS
SHINSPLINTS
SHIPBOARDS
SHIPBROKER
SHIPBROKERS
SHIPBUILDER
SHIPBUILDERS
SHIPBUILDING
SHIPBUILDINGS
SHIPFITTER
SHIPFITTERS
SHIPLAPPED
SHIPLAPPING
SHIPMASTER

SHIPMASTERS
SHIPOWNERS
SHIPPOUNDS
SHIPWRECKED
SHIPWRECKING
SHIPWRECKS
SHIPWRIGHT
SHIPWRIGHTS
SHIRRALEES
SHIRTBANDS
SHIRTDRESS
SHIRTDRESSES
SHIRTFRONT
SHIRTFRONTS
SHIRTINESS
SHIRTINESSES
SHIRTLIFTER
SHIRTLIFTERS
SHIRTMAKER
SHIRTMAKERS
SHIRTSLEEVE
SHIRTSLEEVED
SHIRTSLEEVES
SHIRTTAILED
SHIRTTAILING
SHIRTTAILS
SHIRTWAIST
SHIRTWAISTER
SHIRTWAISTERS
SHIRTWAISTS
SHITTIMWOOD
SHITTIMWOODS
SHITTINESS
SHITTINESSES
SHIVAREEING
SHIVERIEST
SHIVERINGLY
SHIVERINGS
SHLEMIEHLS
SHLEMOZZLE
SHLEMOZZLED
SHLEMOZZLES
SHLEMOZZLING
SHLIMAZELS
SHLOCKIEST
SHMALTZIER
SHMALTZIEST
SHOALINESS
SHOALINESSES
SHOALNESSES
SHOCKABILITIES
SHOCKABILITY
SHOCKHEADED
SHOCKINGLY
SHOCKINGNESS
SHOCKINGNESSES
SHOCKPROOF
SHOCKSTALL
SHOCKSTALLS

SHOCKUMENTARIES
SHOCKUMENTARY
SHODDINESS
SHODDINESSES
SHOEBLACKS
SHOEHORNED
SHOEHORNING
SHOEMAKERS
SHOEMAKING
SHOEMAKINGS
SHOESHINES
SHOESTRING
SHOESTRINGS
SHOGGLIEST
SHOGUNATES
SHONGOLOLO
SHONGOLOLOS
SHOOGIEING
SHOOGLIEST
SHOOTAROUND
SHOOTAROUNDS
SHOOTDOWNS
SHOPAHOLIC
SHOPAHOLICS
SHOPAHOLISM
SHOPAHOLISMS
SHOPBOARDS
SHOPBREAKER
SHOPBREAKERS
SHOPBREAKING
SHOPBREAKINGS
SHOPFRONTS
SHOPKEEPER
SHOPKEEPERS
SHOPKEEPING
SHOPKEEPINGS
SHOPLIFTED
SHOPLIFTER
SHOPLIFTERS
SHOPLIFTING
SHOPSOILED
SHOPWALKER
SHOPWALKERS
SHOPWINDOW
SHOPWINDOWS
SHOREBIRDS
SHOREFRONT
SHOREFRONTS
SHORELINES
SHOREWARDS
SHOREWEEDS
SHORTBOARD
SHORTBOARDS
SHORTBREAD
SHORTBREADS
SHORTCAKES
SHORTCHANGE
SHORTCHANGED
SHORTCHANGER

SHORTCHANGERS	SHOWBOATING	SHRIVELLING	SICCATIVES
SHORTCHANGES	SHOWBREADS	SHROFFAGES	SICILIANOS
SHORTCHANGING	SHOWCASING	SHROUDIEST	SICILIENNE
SHORTCOMING	SHOWERHEAD	SHROUDINGS	SICILIENNES
SHORTCOMINGS	SHOWERHEADS	SHROUDLESS	SICKENINGLY
SHORTCRUST	SHOWERIEST	SHRUBBERIED	SICKENINGS
SHORTCUTTING	SHOWERINESS	SHRUBBERIES	SICKERNESS
SHORTENERS	SHOWERINESSES	SHRUBBIEST	SICKERNESSES
SHORTENING	SHOWERINGS	SHRUBBINESS	SICKISHNESS
SHORTENINGS	SHOWERLESS	SHRUBBINESSES	SICKISHNESSES
SHORTFALLS	SHOWERPROOF	SHRUBLANDS	SICKLEBILL
SHORTGOWNS	SHOWERPROOFED	SHTETELACH	SICKLEBILLS
SHORTHAIRED	SHOWERPROOFING	SHTICKIEST	SICKLEMIAS
SHORTHAIRS	SHOWERPROOFINGS	SHUBUNKINS	SICKLINESS
SHORTHANDED	SHOWERPROOFS	SHUDDERING	SICKLINESSES
SHORTHANDS	SHOWGROUND	SHUDDERINGLY	SICKNESSES
SHORTHEADS	SHOWGROUNDS	SHUDDERINGS	SICKNURSES
SHORTHORNS	SHOWINESSES	SHUDDERSOME	SICKNURSING
SHORTLISTED	SHOWJUMPER	SHUFFLEBOARD	SICKNURSINGS
SHORTLISTING	SHOWJUMPERS	SHUFFLEBOARDS	SIDDHUISMS
SHORTLISTS	SHOWJUMPING	SHUFFLINGLY	SIDEBOARDS
SHORTNESSES	SHOWJUMPINGS	SHUFFLINGS	SIDEBURNED
SHORTSIGHTED	SHOWMANSHIP	SHUNAMITISM	SIDECHECKS
SHORTSIGHTEDLY	SHOWMANSHIPS	SHUNAMITISMS	SIDEDNESSES
SHORTSTOPS	SHOWPIECES	SHUNPIKERS	SIDEDRESSES
SHORTSWORD	SHOWPLACES	SHUNPIKING	SIDELEVERS
SHORTSWORDS	SHOWSTOPPER	SHUNPIKINGS	SIDELIGHTS
SHORTWAVED	SHOWSTOPPERS	SHUTTERBUG	SIDELINERS
SHORTWAVES	SHOWSTOPPING	SHUTTERBUGS	SIDELINING
SHORTWAVING	SHREDDIEST	SHUTTERING	SIDEPIECES
SHOTFIRERS	SHREDDINGS	SHUTTERINGS	SIDERATING
SHOTGUNNED	SHREWDNESS	SHUTTERLESS	SIDERATION
SHOTGUNNER	SHREWDNESSES	SHUTTLECOCK	SIDERATIONS
SHOTGUNNERS	SHREWISHLY	SHUTTLECOCKED	SIDEREALLY
SHOTGUNNING	SHREWISHNESS	SHUTTLECOCKING	SIDEROLITE
SHOTMAKERS	SHREWISHNESSES	SHUTTLECOCKS	SIDEROLITES
SHOTMAKING	SHREWMOUSE	SHUTTLELESS	SIDEROPENIA
SHOTMAKINGS	SHRIECHING	SHUTTLEWISE	SIDEROPENIAS
SHOULDERED	SHRIEKIEST	SHYLOCKING	SIDEROPHILE
SHOULDERING	SHRIEKINGLY	SIALAGOGIC	SIDEROPHILES
SHOULDERINGS	SHRIEKINGS	SIALAGOGUE	SIDEROPHILIC
SHOUTHERED	SHRIEVALTIES	SIALAGOGUES	SIDEROPHILIN
SHOUTHERING	SHRIEVALTY	SIALOGOGIC	SIDEROPHILINS
SHOUTINGLY	SHRILLIEST	SIALOGOGUE	SIDEROSTAT
SHOUTLINES	SHRILLINGS	SIALOGOGUES	SIDEROSTATIC
SHOVELBOARD	SHRILLNESS	SIALOGRAMS	SIDEROSTATS
SHOVELBOARDS	SHRILLNESSES	SIALOGRAPHIES	SIDESADDLE
SHOVELFULS	SHRIMPIEST	SIALOGRAPHY	SIDESADDLES
SHOVELHEAD	SHRIMPINGS	SIALOLITHS	SIDESHOOTS
SHOVELHEADS	SHRIMPLIKE	SIALORRHOEA	SIDESLIPPED
SHOVELLERS	SHRINELIKE	SIALORRHOEAS	SIDESLIPPING
SHOVELLING	SHRINKABLE	SIBILANCES	SIDESPLITTING
SHOVELNOSE	SHRINKAGES	SIBILANCIES	SIDESPLITTINGLY
SHOVELNOSES	SHRINKINGLY	SIBILANTLY	SIDESTEPPED
SHOVELSFUL	SHRINKPACK	SIBILATING	SIDESTEPPER
SHOWBIZZES	SHRINKPACKS	SIBILATION	SIDESTEPPERS
SHOWBOATED	SHRITCHING	SIBILATIONS	SIDESTEPPING
SHOWBOATER	SHRIVELING	SIBILATORS	SIDESTREAM
SHOWBOATERS	SHRIVELLED	SIBILATORY	SIDESTREET

SIDESTREETS
SIDESTROKE
SIDESTROKES
SIDESWIPED
SIDESWIPER
SIDESWIPERS
SIDESWIPES
SIDESWIPING
SIDETRACKED
SIDETRACKING
SIDETRACKS
SIDEWHEELER
SIDEWHEELERS
SIDEWHEELS
SIDEWINDER
SIDEWINDERS
SIEGECRAFT
SIEGECRAFTS
SIEGEWORKS
SIFFLEUSES
SIGHTLESSLY
SIGHTLESSNESS
SIGHTLESSNESSES
SIGHTLIEST
SIGHTLINES
SIGHTLINESS
SIGHTLINESSES
SIGHTSCREEN
SIGHTSCREENS
SIGHTSEEING
SIGHTSEEINGS
SIGHTSEERS
SIGHTWORTHY
SIGILLARIAN
SIGILLARIANS
SIGILLARID
SIGILLARIDS
SIGILLATION
SIGILLATIONS
SIGMATIONS
SIGMATISMS
SIGMATRONS
SIGMOIDALLY
SIGMOIDECTOMIES
SIGMOIDECTOMY
SIGMOIDOSCOPE
SIGMOIDOSCOPES
SIGMOIDOSCOPIC
SIGMOIDOSCOPIES
SIGMOIDOSCOPY
SIGNALINGS
SIGNALISATION
SIGNALISATIONS
SIGNALISED
SIGNALISES
SIGNALISING
SIGNALIZATION
SIGNALIZATIONS
SIGNALIZED

SIGNALIZES
SIGNALIZING
SIGNALLERS
SIGNALLING
SIGNALLINGS
SIGNALMENT
SIGNALMENTS
SIGNATORIES
SIGNATURES
SIGNBOARDS
SIGNEURIES
SIGNIFIABLE
SIGNIFICANCE
SIGNIFICANCES
SIGNIFICANCIES
SIGNIFICANCY
SIGNIFICANT
SIGNIFICANTLY
SIGNIFICANTS
SIGNIFICATE
SIGNIFICATES
SIGNIFICATION
SIGNIFICATIONS
SIGNIFICATIVE
SIGNIFICATIVELY
SIGNIFICATOR
SIGNIFICATORS
SIGNIFICATORY
SIGNIFIEDS
SIGNIFIERS
SIGNIFYING
SIGNIFYINGS
SIGNIORIES
SIGNORINAS
SIGNPOSTED
SIGNPOSTING
SIKORSKIES
SILENTIARIES
SILENTIARY
SILENTNESS
SILENTNESSES
SILHOUETTE
SILHOUETTED
SILHOUETTES
SILHOUETTING
SILHOUETTIST
SILHOUETTISTS
SILICATING
SILICICOLOUS
SILICIFEROUS
SILICIFICATION
SILICIFICATIONS
SILICIFIED
SILICIFIES
SILICIFYING
SILICONISED
SILICONIZED
SILICOTICS
SILICULOSE

SILIQUACEOUS
SILKALENES
SILKALINES
SILKGROWER
SILKGROWERS
SILKINESSES
SILKOLINES
SILKSCREEN
SILKSCREENS
SILLIMANITE
SILLIMANITES
SILLINESSES
SILTATIONS
SILTSTONES
SILVERBACK
SILVERBACKS
SILVERBERRIES
SILVERBERRY
SILVERBILL
SILVERBILLS
SILVEREYES
SILVERFISH
SILVERFISHES
SILVERHORN
SILVERHORNS
SILVERIEST
SILVERINESS
SILVERINESSES
SILVERINGS
SILVERISED
SILVERISES
SILVERISING
SILVERIZED
SILVERIZES
SILVERIZING
SILVERLING
SILVERLINGS
SILVERPOINT
SILVERPOINTS
SILVERSIDE
SILVERSIDES
SILVERSIDESES
SILVERSKIN
SILVERSKINS
SILVERSMITH
SILVERSMITHING
SILVERSMITHINGS
SILVERSMITHS
SILVERTAIL
SILVERTAILS
SILVERWARE
SILVERWARES
SILVERWEED
SILVERWEEDS
SILVESTRIAN
SILVICULTURAL
SILVICULTURALLY
SILVICULTURE
SILVICULTURES

SILVICULTURIST
SILVICULTURISTS
SIMAROUBACEOUS
SIMAROUBAS
SIMARUBACEOUS
SIMILARITIES
SIMILARITY
SIMILATIVE
SIMILISING
SIMILITUDE
SIMILITUDES
SIMILIZING
SIMILLIMUM
SIMILLIMUMS
SIMONIACAL
SIMONIACALLY
SIMONISING
SIMONIZING
SIMPERINGLY
SIMPERINGS
SIMPLEMINDED
SIMPLEMINDEDLY
SIMPLENESS
SIMPLENESSES
SIMPLESSES
SIMPLETONS
SIMPLICIAL
SIMPLICIALLY
SIMPLICIDENTATE
SIMPLICITER
SIMPLICITIES
SIMPLICITY
SIMPLIFICATION
SIMPLIFICATIONS
SIMPLIFICATIVE
SIMPLIFICATOR
SIMPLIFICATORS
SIMPLIFIED
SIMPLIFIER
SIMPLIFIERS
SIMPLIFIES
SIMPLIFYING
SIMPLISTIC
SIMPLISTICALLY
SIMULACRES
SIMULACRUM
SIMULACRUMS
SIMULATING
SIMULATION
SIMULATIONS
SIMULATIVE
SIMULATIVELY
SIMULATORS
SIMULATORY
SIMULCASTED
SIMULCASTING
SIMULCASTS
SIMULTANEITIES
SIMULTANEITY

SIMULTANEOUS	SINGULARITY	SIPHONOPHOROUS	SKATEBOARDER
SIMULTANEOUSES	SINGULARIZATION	SIPHONOSTELE	SKATEBOARDERS
SIMULTANEOUSLY	SINGULARIZE	SIPHONOSTELES	SKATEBOARDING
SINANTHROPUS	SINGULARIZED	SIPHONOSTELIC	SKATEBOARDINGS
SINANTHROPUSES	SINGULARIZES	SIPHUNCLES	SKATEBOARDS
SINARCHISM	SINGULARIZING	SIPUNCULID	SKATEPARKS
SINARCHISMS	SINGULARLY	SIPUNCULIDS	SKEDADDLED
SINARCHIST	SINGULARNESS	SIPUNCULOID	SKEDADDLER
SINARCHISTS	SINGULARNESSES	SIPUNCULOIDS	SKEDADDLERS
SINARQUISM	SINGULTUSES	SIRENISING	SKEDADDLES
SINARQUISMS	SINICISING	SIRENIZING	SKEDADDLING
SINARQUIST	SINICIZING	SIRONISING	SKELDERING
SINARQUISTS	SINISTERITIES	SIRONIZING	SKELETALLY
SINCERENESS	SINISTERITY	SISERARIES	SKELETOGENOUS
SINCERENESSES	SINISTERLY	SISSINESSES	SKELETONIC
SINCERITIES	SINISTERNESS	SISSYNESSES	SKELETONISE
SINCIPITAL	SINISTERNESSES	SISTERHOOD	SKELETONISED
SINDONOLOGIES	SINISTERWISE	SISTERHOODS	SKELETONISER
SINDONOLOGIST	SINISTRALITIES	SISTERLESS	SKELETONISERS
SINDONOLOGISTS	SINISTRALITY	SISTERLIKE	SKELETONISES
SINDONOLOGY	SINISTRALLY	SISTERLINESS	SKELETONISING
SINDONOPHANIES	SINISTRALS	SISTERLINESSES	SKELETONIZE
SINDONOPHANY	SINISTRODEXTRAL	SITATUNGAS	SKELETONIZED
SINECURISM	SINISTRORSAL	SITIOLOGIES	SKELETONIZER
SINECURISMS	SINISTRORSALLY	SITIOPHOBIA	SKELETONIZERS
SINECURIST	SINISTRORSE	SITIOPHOBIAS	SKELETONIZES
SINECURISTS	SINISTRORSELY	SITOLOGIES	SKELETONIZING
SINEWINESS	SINISTROUS	SITOPHOBIA	SKELLOCHED
SINEWINESSES	SINISTROUSLY	SITOPHOBIAS	SKELLOCHING
SINFONIETTA	SINLESSNESS	SITOSTEROL	SKELTERING
SINFONIETTAS	SINLESSNESSES	SITOSTEROLS	SKEPTICALLY
SINFULNESS	SINNINGIAS	SITUATIONAL	SKEPTICALNESS
SINFULNESSES	SINOATRIAL	SITUATIONALLY	SKEPTICALNESSES
SINGABLENESS	SINOLOGICAL	SITUATIONISM	SKEPTICISM
SINGABLENESSES	SINOLOGIES	SITUATIONISMS	SKEPTICISMS
SINGALONGS	SINOLOGIST	SITUATIONS	SKETCHABILITIES
SINGLEDOMS	SINOLOGISTS	SITUTUNGAS	SKETCHABILITY
SINGLEHOOD	SINOLOGUES	SITZKRIEGS	SKETCHABLE
SINGLEHOODS	SINSEMILLA	SIXPENNIES	SKETCHBOOK
SINGLENESS	SINSEMILLAS	SIXTEENERS	SKETCHBOOKS
SINGLENESSES	SINTERABILITIES	SIXTEENMOS	SKETCHIEST
SINGLESTICK	SINTERABILITY	SIXTEENTHLY	SKETCHINESS
SINGLESTICKS	SINUATIONS	SIXTEENTHS	SKETCHINESSES
SINGLETONS	SINUITISES	SIZABLENESS	SKETCHPADS
SINGLETREE	SINUOSITIES	SIZABLENESSES	SKEUOMORPH
SINGLETREES	SINUOUSNESS	SIZARSHIPS	SKEUOMORPHIC
SINGSONGED	SINUOUSNESSES	SIZEABLENESS	SKEUOMORPHISM
SINGSONGING	SINUPALLIAL	SIZEABLENESSES	SKEUOMORPHISMS
SINGSPIELS	SINUPALLIATE	SIZINESSES	SKEUOMORPHS
SINGULARISATION	SINUSITISES	SIZZLINGLY	SKEWBACKED
SINGULARISE	SINUSOIDAL	SJAMBOKING	SKEWNESSES
SINGULARISED	SINUSOIDALLY	SJAMBOKKED	SKIAGRAPHS
SINGULARISES	SIPHONAGES	SJAMBOKKING	SKIAMACHIES
SINGULARISING	SIPHONOGAM	SKAITHLESS	SKIASCOPES
SINGULARISM	SIPHONOGAMIES	SKALDSHIPS	SKIASCOPIES
SINGULARISMS	SIPHONOGAMS	SKANKINESS	SKIBOBBERS
SINGULARIST	SIPHONOGAMY	SKANKINESSES	SKIBOBBING
SINGULARISTS	SIPHONOPHORE	SKATEBOARD	SKIBOBBINGS
SINGULARITIES	SIPHONOPHORES	SKATEBOARDED	SKIDDOOING

SKIJORINGS
SKIKJORING
SKIKJORINGS
SKILFULNESS
SKILFULNESSES
SKILLCENTRE
SKILLCENTRES
SKILLESSNESS
SKILLESSNESSES
SKILLFULLY
SKILLFULNESS
SKILLFULNESSES
SKILLIGALEE
SKILLIGALEES
SKILLIGOLEE
SKILLIGOLEES
SKIMBOARDED
SKIMBOARDER
SKIMBOARDERS
SKIMBOARDING
SKIMBOARDS
SKIMMINGLY
SKIMMINGTON
SKIMMINGTONS
SKIMOBILED
SKIMOBILES
SKIMOBILING
SKIMPINESS
SKIMPINESSES
SKIMPINGLY
SKINFLICKS
SKINFLINTS
SKINFLINTY
SKINNINESS
SKINNINESSES
SKIPPERING
SKIPPERINGS
SKIPPINGLY
SKIRMISHED
SKIRMISHER
SKIRMISHERS
SKIRMISHES
SKIRMISHING
SKIRMISHINGS
SKITTERIER
SKITTERIEST
SKITTERING
SKITTISHLY
SKITTISHNESS
SKITTISHNESSES
SKREEGHING
SKREIGHING
SKRIECHING
SKRIEGHING
SKRIMMAGED
SKRIMMAGES
SKRIMMAGING
SKRIMSHANK
SKRIMSHANKED

SKRIMSHANKER
SKRIMSHANKERS
SKRIMSHANKING
SKRIMSHANKS
SKULDUDDERIES
SKULDUDDERY
SKULDUGGERIES
SKULDUGGERY
SKULKINGLY
SKULLDUGGERIES
SKULLDUGGERY
SKUMMERING
SKUNKBIRDS
SKUNKWEEDS
SKUTTERUDITE
SKUTTERUDITES
SKYBRIDGES
SKYDIVINGS
SKYJACKERS
SKYJACKING
SKYJACKINGS
SKYLARKERS
SKYLARKING
SKYLARKINGS
SKYLIGHTED
SKYROCKETED
SKYROCKETING
SKYROCKETS
SKYSCRAPER
SKYSCRAPERS
SKYSURFERS
SKYSURFING
SKYSURFINGS
SKYWRITERS
SKYWRITING
SKYWRITINGS
SKYWRITTEN
SLABBERERS
SLABBERING
SLABBINESS
SLABBINESSES
SLABSTONES
SLACKENERS
SLACKENING
SLACKENINGS
SLACKNESSES
SLAISTERED
SLAISTERIES
SLAISTERING
SLALOMISTS
SLAMDANCED
SLAMDANCES
SLAMDANCING
SLAMMAKINS
SLAMMERKIN
SLAMMERKINS
SLANDERERS
SLANDERING
SLANDEROUS

SLANDEROUSLY
SLANDEROUSNESS
SLANGINESS
SLANGINESSES
SLANGINGLY
SLANGUAGES
SLANTENDICULAR
SLANTINDICULAR
SLANTINGLY
SLANTINGWAYS
SLAPDASHES
SLAPHAPPIER
SLAPHAPPIEST
SLAPSTICKS
SLASHFESTS
SLASHINGLY
SLATHERING
SLATINESSES
SLATTERING
SLATTERNLINESS
SLATTERNLY
SLAUGHTERABLE
SLAUGHTERED
SLAUGHTERER
SLAUGHTERERS
SLAUGHTERHOUSE
SLAUGHTERHOUSES
SLAUGHTERIES
SLAUGHTERING
SLAUGHTERMAN
SLAUGHTERMEN
SLAUGHTEROUS
SLAUGHTEROUSLY
SLAUGHTERS
SLAUGHTERY
SLAVEHOLDER
SLAVEHOLDERS
SLAVEHOLDING
SLAVEHOLDINGS
SLAVERINGLY
SLAVISHNESS
SLAVISHNESSES
SLAVOCRACIES
SLAVOCRACY
SLAVOCRATS
SLAVOPHILE
SLAVOPHILES
SLAVOPHILS
SLEAZEBAGS
SLEAZEBALL
SLEAZEBALLS
SLEAZINESS
SLEAZINESSES
SLEDGEHAMMER
SLEDGEHAMMERED
SLEDGEHAMMERING
SLEDGEHAMMERS
SLEECHIEST
SLEEKENING

SLEEKNESSES
SLEEKSTONE
SLEEKSTONES
SLEEPINESS
SLEEPINESSES
SLEEPLESSLY
SLEEPLESSNESS
SLEEPLESSNESSES
SLEEPOVERS
SLEEPSUITS
SLEEPWALKED
SLEEPWALKER
SLEEPWALKERS
SLEEPWALKING
SLEEPWALKINGS
SLEEPWALKS
SLEEPYHEAD
SLEEPYHEADED
SLEEPYHEADS
SLEETINESS
SLEETINESSES
SLEEVEHAND
SLEEVEHANDS
SLEEVELESS
SLEEVELETS
SLEEVELIKE
SLEIGHINGS
SLENDEREST
SLENDERISE
SLENDERISED
SLENDERISES
SLENDERISING
SLENDERIZE
SLENDERIZED
SLENDERIZES
SLENDERIZING
SLENDERNESS
SLENDERNESSES
SLEUTHHOUND
SLEUTHHOUNDS
SLICKENERS
SLICKENING
SLICKENSIDE
SLICKENSIDED
SLICKENSIDES
SLICKNESSES
SLICKROCKS
SLICKSTERS
SLICKSTONE
SLICKSTONES
SLIDDERING
SLIGHTINGLY
SLIGHTNESS
SLIGHTNESSES
SLIMEBALLS
SLIMINESSES
SLIMNASTICS
SLIMNESSES
SLIMPSIEST

SLINGBACKS
SLINGSHOTS
SLINGSTONE
SLINGSTONES
SLINKINESS
SLINKINESSES
SLINKSKINS
SLINKWEEDS
SLIPCOVERED
SLIPCOVERING
SLIPCOVERS
SLIPDRESSES
SLIPFORMED
SLIPFORMING
SLIPNOOSES
SLIPPERIER
SLIPPERIEST
SLIPPERILY
SLIPPERINESS
SLIPPERINESSES
SLIPPERING
SLIPPERWORT
SLIPPERWORTS
SLIPPINESS
SLIPPINESSES
SLIPSHEETED
SLIPSHEETING
SLIPSHEETS
SLIPSHODDINESS
SLIPSHODNESS
SLIPSHODNESSES
SLIPSLOPPY
SLIPSTREAM
SLIPSTREAMED
SLIPSTREAMING
SLIPSTREAMS
SLITHERIER
SLITHERIEST
SLITHERING
SLIVOVICAS
SLIVOVICES
SLIVOVITZES
SLIVOWITZES
SLOBBERERS
SLOBBERIER
SLOBBERIEST
SLOBBERING
SLOBBISHNESS
SLOBBISHNESSES
SLOCKDOLAGER
SLOCKDOLAGERS
SLOCKDOLIGER
SLOCKDOLIGERS
SLOCKDOLOGER
SLOCKDOLOGERS
SLOCKENING
SLOEBUSHES
SLOETHORNS
SLOGANEERED

SLOGANEERING
SLOGANEERINGS
SLOGANEERS
SLOGANISED
SLOGANISES
SLOGANISING
SLOGANISINGS
SLOGANIZED
SLOGANIZES
SLOGANIZING
SLOGANIZINGS
SLOMMOCKED
SLOMMOCKING
SLOPINGNESS
SLOPINGNESSES
SLOPPINESS
SLOPPINESSES
SLOPWORKER
SLOPWORKERS
SLOTHFULLY
SLOTHFULNESS
SLOTHFULNESSES
SLOUCHIEST
SLOUCHINESS
SLOUCHINESSES
SLOUCHINGLY
SLOUGHIEST
SLOVENLIER
SLOVENLIEST
SLOVENLIKE
SLOVENLINESS
SLOVENLINESSES
SLOVENRIES
SLOWCOACHES
SLOWNESSES
SLUBBERING
SLUBBERINGLY
SLUBBERINGS
SLUGGABEDS
SLUGGARDISE
SLUGGARDISED
SLUGGARDISES
SLUGGARDISING
SLUGGARDIZE
SLUGGARDIZED
SLUGGARDIZES
SLUGGARDIZING
SLUGGARDLINESS
SLUGGARDLY
SLUGGARDNESS
SLUGGARDNESSES
SLUGGISHLY
SLUGGISHNESS
SLUGGISHNESSES
SLUGHORNES
SLUICEGATE
SLUICEGATES
SLUICELIKE
SLUICEWAYS

SLUMBERERS
SLUMBERFUL
SLUMBERING
SLUMBERINGLY
SLUMBERINGS
SLUMBERLAND
SLUMBERLANDS
SLUMBERLESS
SLUMBEROUS
SLUMBEROUSLY
SLUMBEROUSNESS
SLUMBERSOME
SLUMBROUSLY
SLUMGULLION
SLUMGULLIONS
SLUMMOCKED
SLUMMOCKING
SLUMPFLATION
SLUMPFLATIONARY
SLUMPFLATIONS
SLUNGSHOTS
SLUSHINESS
SLUSHINESSES
SLUTCHIEST
SLUTTERIES
SLUTTISHLY
SLUTTISHNESS
SLUTTISHNESSES
SMACKHEADS
SMALLCLOTHES
SMALLHOLDER
SMALLHOLDERS
SMALLHOLDING
SMALLHOLDINGS
SMALLMOUTH
SMALLMOUTHS
SMALLNESSES
SMALLPOXES
SMALLSWORD
SMALLSWORDS
SMALMINESS
SMALMINESSES
SMARAGDINE
SMARAGDITE
SMARAGDITES
SMARMINESS
SMARMINESSES
SMARTARSED
SMARTARSES
SMARTASSES
SMARTENING
SMARTMOUTH
SMARTMOUTHS
SMARTNESSES
SMARTPHONE
SMARTPHONES
SMARTWEEDS
SMARTYPANTS
SMASHEROOS

SMASHINGLY
SMATTERERS
SMATTERING
SMATTERINGLY
SMATTERINGS
SMEARCASES
SMEARINESS
SMEARINESSES
SMELLINESS
SMELLINESSES
SMELTERIES
SMICKERING
SMICKERINGS
SMIERCASES
SMIFLIGATE
SMIFLIGATED
SMIFLIGATES
SMIFLIGATING
SMILACACEOUS
SMILINGNESS
SMILINGNESSES
SMIRKINGLY
SMITHCRAFT
SMITHCRAFTS
SMITHEREEN
SMITHEREENED
SMITHEREENING
SMITHEREENS
SMITHERIES
SMITHSONITE
SMITHSONITES
SMOKEBOARD
SMOKEBOARDS
SMOKEBUSHES
SMOKEHOODS
SMOKEHOUSE
SMOKEHOUSES
SMOKEJACKS
SMOKELESSLY
SMOKELESSNESS
SMOKELESSNESSES
SMOKEPROOF
SMOKESCREEN
SMOKESCREENS
SMOKESTACK
SMOKESTACKS
SMOKETIGHT
SMOKETREES
SMOKINESSES
SMOLDERING
SMOOTHABLE
SMOOTHBORE
SMOOTHBORED
SMOOTHBORES
SMOOTHENED
SMOOTHENING
SMOOTHINGS
SMOOTHNESS
SMOOTHNESSES

SMOOTHPATE
SMOOTHPATES
SMORGASBORD
SMORGASBORDS
SMORREBROD
SMORREBRODS
SMOTHERERS
SMOTHERINESS
SMOTHERINESSES
SMOTHERING
SMOTHERINGLY
SMOTHERINGS
SMOULDERED
SMOULDERING
SMOULDERINGS
SMUDGELESS
SMUDGINESS
SMUDGINESSES
SMUGGERIES
SMUGGLINGS
SMUGNESSES
SMUTCHIEST
SMUTTINESS
SMUTTINESSES
SNACKETTES
SNAGGLETEETH
SNAGGLETOOTH
SNAGGLETOOTHED
SNAILERIES
SNAILFISHES
SNAKEBIRDS
SNAKEBITES
SNAKEBITTEN
SNAKEFISHES
SNAKEHEADS
SNAKEMOUTH
SNAKEMOUTHS
SNAKEROOTS
SNAKESKINS
SNAKESTONE
SNAKESTONES
SNAKEWEEDS
SNAKEWOODS
SNAKINESSES
SNAKISHNESS
SNAKISHNESSES
SNAPDRAGON
SNAPDRAGONS
SNAPHANCES
SNAPHAUNCE
SNAPHAUNCES
SNAPHAUNCH
SNAPHAUNCHES
SNAPPERING
SNAPPINESS
SNAPPINESSES
SNAPPINGLY
SNAPPISHLY
SNAPPISHNESS

SNAPPISHNESSES
SNAPSHOOTER
SNAPSHOOTERS
SNAPSHOOTING
SNAPSHOOTINGS
SNAPSHOTTED
SNAPSHOTTING
SNARLINGLY
SNATCHIEST
SNATCHINGLY
SNATCHINGS
SNAZZINESS
SNAZZINESSES
SNEAKINESS
SNEAKINESSES
SNEAKINGLY
SNEAKINGNESS
SNEAKINGNESSES
SNEAKISHLY
SNEAKISHNESS
SNEAKISHNESSES
SNEAKSBIES
SNEERINGLY
SNEESHINGS
SNEEZELESS
SNEEZEWEED
SNEEZEWEEDS
SNEEZEWOOD
SNEEZEWOODS
SNEEZEWORT
SNEEZEWORTS
SNICKERERS
SNICKERING
SNICKERSNEE
SNICKERSNEED
SNICKERSNEEING
SNICKERSNEES
SNIDENESSES
SNIFFINESS
SNIFFINESSES
SNIFFINGLY
SNIFFISHLY
SNIFFISHNESS
SNIFFISHNESSES
SNIFFLIEST
SNIFTERING
SNIGGERERS
SNIGGERING
SNIGGERINGLY
SNIGGERINGS
SNIGGLINGS
SNIPEFISHES
SNIPERSCOPE
SNIPERSCOPES
SNIPPERSNAPPER
SNIPPERSNAPPERS
SNIPPETIER
SNIPPETIEST
SNIPPETINESS

SNIPPETINESSES
SNIPPINESS
SNIPPINESSES
SNITCHIEST
SNIVELLERS
SNIVELLING
SNIVELLINGS
SNOBBERIES
SNOBBISHLY
SNOBBISHNESS
SNOBBISHNESSES
SNOBBOCRACIES
SNOBBOCRACY
SNOBOCRACIES
SNOBOCRACY
SNOBOGRAPHER
SNOBOGRAPHERS
SNOBOGRAPHIES
SNOBOGRAPHY
SNOLLYGOSTER
SNOLLYGOSTERS
SNOOKERING
SNOOPERSCOPE
SNOOPERSCOPES
SNOOTINESS
SNOOTINESSES
SNORKELERS
SNORKELING
SNORKELLED
SNORKELLING
SNORKELLINGS
SNORTINGLY
SNOTTERIES
SNOTTERING
SNOTTINESS
SNOTTINESSES
SNOWBALLED
SNOWBALLING
SNOWBERRIES
SNOWBLADER
SNOWBLADERS
SNOWBLADES
SNOWBLADING
SNOWBLADINGS
SNOWBLINKS
SNOWBLOWER
SNOWBLOWERS
SNOWBOARDED
SNOWBOARDER
SNOWBOARDERS
SNOWBOARDING
SNOWBOARDINGS
SNOWBOARDS
SNOWBRUSHES
SNOWBUSHES
SNOWCAPPED
SNOWDRIFTS
SNOWFIELDS
SNOWFLAKES

SNOWFLECKS
SNOWFLICKS
SNOWINESSES
SNOWMAKERS
SNOWMAKING
SNOWMOBILE
SNOWMOBILER
SNOWMOBILERS
SNOWMOBILES
SNOWMOBILING
SNOWMOBILINGS
SNOWMOBILIST
SNOWMOBILISTS
SNOWPLOUGH
SNOWPLOUGHED
SNOWPLOUGHING
SNOWPLOUGHS
SNOWPLOWED
SNOWPLOWING
SNOWSCAPES
SNOWSHOEING
SNOWSHOERS
SNOWSLIDES
SNOWSTORMS
SNOWSURFING
SNOWSURFINGS
SNOWTUBING
SNOWTUBINGS
SNUBBINESS
SNUBBINESSES
SNUBBINGLY
SNUBNESSES
SNUFFBOXES
SNUFFINESS
SNUFFINESSES
SNUFFLIEST
SNUFFLINGS
SNUGGERIES
SNUGNESSES
SOAPBERRIES
SOAPBOXING
SOAPINESSES
SOAPOLALLIE
SOAPOLALLIES
SOAPSTONES
SOBERINGLY
SOBERISING
SOBERIZING
SOBERNESSES
SOBERSIDED
SOBERSIDEDNESS
SOBERSIDES
SOBOLIFEROUS
SOBRIETIES
SOBRIQUETS
SOCDOLAGER
SOCDOLAGERS
SOCDOLIGER
SOCDOLIGERS

SOCDOLOGER	SOCIOMETRIST	SOLARISING	SOLICITIES
SOCDOLOGERS	SOCIOMETRISTS	SOLARIZATION	SOLICITING
SOCIABILITIES	SOCIOMETRY	SOLARIZATIONS	SOLICITINGS
SOCIABILITY	SOCIOPATHIC	SOLARIZING	SOLICITORS
SOCIABLENESS	SOCIOPATHIES	SOLDATESQUE	SOLICITORSHIP
SOCIABLENESSES	SOCIOPATHS	SOLDERABILITIES	SOLICITORSHIPS
SOCIALISABLE	SOCIOPATHY	SOLDERABILITY	SOLICITOUS
SOCIALISATION	SOCIOPOLITICAL	SOLDERABLE	SOLICITOUSLY
SOCIALISATIONS	SOCIORELIGIOUS	SOLDERINGS	SOLICITOUSNESS
SOCIALISED	SOCIOSEXUAL	SOLDIERIES	SOLICITUDE
SOCIALISER	SOCKDOLAGER	SOLDIERING	SOLICITUDES
SOCIALISERS	SOCKDOLAGERS	SOLDIERINGS	SOLIDARISM
SOCIALISES	SOCKDOLIGER	SOLDIERLIKE	SOLIDARISMS
SOCIALISING	SOCKDOLIGERS	SOLDIERLINESS	SOLIDARIST
SOCIALISMS	SOCKDOLOGER	SOLDIERLINESSES	SOLIDARISTIC
SOCIALISTIC	SOCKDOLOGERS	SOLDIERSHIP	SOLIDARISTS
SOCIALISTICALLY	SODALITIES	SOLDIERSHIPS	SOLIDARITIES
SOCIALISTS	SODBUSTERS	SOLECISING	SOLIDARITY
SOCIALITES	SODDENNESS	SOLECISTIC	SOLIDATING
SOCIALITIES	SODDENNESSES	SOLECISTICAL	SOLIDIFIABLE
SOCIALIZABLE	SODICITIES	SOLECISTICALLY	SOLIDIFICATION
SOCIALIZATION	SODOMISING	SOLECIZING	SOLIDIFICATIONS
SOCIALIZATIONS	SODOMITICAL	SOLEMNESSES	SOLIDIFIED
SOCIALIZED	SODOMITICALLY	SOLEMNIFICATION	SOLIDIFIER
SOCIALIZER	SODOMIZING	SOLEMNIFIED	SOLIDIFIERS
SOCIALIZERS	SOFTBALLER	SOLEMNIFIES	SOLIDIFIES
SOCIALIZES	SOFTBALLERS	SOLEMNIFYING	SOLIDIFYING
SOCIALIZING	SOFTBOUNDS	SOLEMNISATION	SOLIDITIES
SOCIALNESS	SOFTCOVERS	SOLEMNISATIONS	SOLIDNESSES
SOCIALNESSES	SOFTENINGS	SOLEMNISED	SOLIDUNGULATE
SOCIATIONS	SOFTHEADED	SOLEMNISER	SOLIDUNGULOUS
SOCIETALLY	SOFTHEADEDLY	SOLEMNISERS	SOLIFIDIAN
SOCIOBIOLOGICAL	SOFTHEADEDNESS	SOLEMNISES	SOLIFIDIANISM
SOCIOBIOLOGIES	SOFTHEARTED	SOLEMNISING	SOLIFIDIANISMS
SOCIOBIOLOGIST	SOFTHEARTEDLY	SOLEMNITIES	SOLIFIDIANS
SOCIOBIOLOGISTS	SOFTHEARTEDNESS	SOLEMNIZATION	SOLIFLUCTION
SOCIOBIOLOGY	SOFTNESSES	SOLEMNIZATIONS	SOLIFLUCTIONS
SOCIOCULTURAL	SOFTSHELLS	SOLEMNIZED	SOLIFLUXION
SOCIOCULTURALLY	SOGDOLAGER	SOLEMNIZER	SOLIFLUXIONS
SOCIOECONOMIC	SOGDOLAGERS	SOLEMNIZERS	SOLILOQUIES
SOCIOGRAMS	SOGDOLIGER	SOLEMNIZES	SOLILOQUISE
SOCIOHISTORICAL	SOGDOLIGERS	SOLEMNIZING	SOLILOQUISED
SOCIOLECTS	SOGDOLOGER	SOLEMNNESS	SOLILOQUISER
SOCIOLINGUIST	SOGDOLOGERS	SOLEMNNESSES	SOLILOQUISERS
SOCIOLINGUISTIC	SOGGINESSES	SOLENESSES	SOLILOQUISES
SOCIOLINGUISTS	SOILINESSES	SOLENETTES	SOLILOQUISING
SOCIOLOGESE	SOJOURNERS	SOLENODONS	SOLILOQUIST
SOCIOLOGESES	SOJOURNING	SOLENOIDAL	SOLILOQUISTS
SOCIOLOGIC	SOJOURNINGS	SOLENOIDALLY	SOLILOQUIZE
SOCIOLOGICAL	SOJOURNMENT	SOLEPLATES	SOLILOQUIZED
SOCIOLOGICALLY	SOJOURNMENTS	SOLEPRINTS	SOLILOQUIZER
SOCIOLOGIES	SOKEMANRIES	SOLFATARAS	SOLILOQUIZERS
SOCIOLOGISM	SOLACEMENT	SOLFATARIC	SOLILOQUIZES
SOCIOLOGISMS	SOLACEMENTS	SOLFEGGIOS	SOLILOQUIZING
SOCIOLOGIST	SOLANACEOUS	SOLFERINOS	SOLIPEDOUS
SOCIOLOGISTIC	SOLARIMETER	SOLICITANT	SOLIPSISMS
SOCIOLOGISTS	SOLARIMETERS	SOLICITANTS	SOLIPSISTIC
SOCIOMETRIC	SOLARISATION	SOLICITATION	SOLIPSISTICALLY
SOCIOMETRIES	SOLARISATIONS	SOLICITATIONS	SOLIPSISTS

SOLITAIRES

SOLITAIRES
SOLITARIAN
SOLITARIANS
SOLITARIES
SOLITARILY
SOLITARINESS
SOLITARINESSES
SOLITUDINARIAN
SOLITUDINARIANS
SOLITUDINOUS
SOLIVAGANT
SOLIVAGANTS
SOLLICKERS
SOLMISATION
SOLMISATIONS
SOLMIZATION
SOLMIZATIONS
SOLONCHAKS
SOLONETSES
SOLONETZES
SOLONETZIC
SOLONISATION
SOLONISATIONS
SOLONIZATION
SOLONIZATIONS
SOLSTITIAL
SOLSTITIALLY
SOLUBILISATION
SOLUBILISATIONS
SOLUBILISE
SOLUBILISED
SOLUBILISES
SOLUBILISING
SOLUBILITIES
SOLUBILITY
SOLUBILIZATION
SOLUBILIZATIONS
SOLUBILIZE
SOLUBILIZED
SOLUBILIZES
SOLUBILIZING
SOLUBLENESS
SOLUBLENESSES
SOLUTIONAL
SOLUTIONED
SOLUTIONING
SOLUTIONIST
SOLUTIONISTS
SOLVABILITIES
SOLVABILITY
SOLVABLENESS
SOLVABLENESSES
SOLVATIONS
SOLVENCIES
SOLVENTLESS
SOLVOLYSES
SOLVOLYSIS
SOLVOLYTIC
SOMAESTHESIA

SOMAESTHESIAS
SOMAESTHESIS
SOMAESTHESISES
SOMAESTHETIC
SOMASCOPES
SOMATICALLY
SOMATOGENIC
SOMATOLOGIC
SOMATOLOGICAL
SOMATOLOGICALLY
SOMATOLOGIES
SOMATOLOGIST
SOMATOLOGISTS
SOMATOLOGY
SOMATOMEDIN
SOMATOMEDINS
SOMATOPLASM
SOMATOPLASMS
SOMATOPLASTIC
SOMATOPLEURAL
SOMATOPLEURE
SOMATOPLEURES
SOMATOPLEURIC
SOMATOSENSORY
SOMATOSTATIN
SOMATOSTATINS
SOMATOTENSIC
SOMATOTONIA
SOMATOTONIAS
SOMATOTONIC
SOMATOTROPHIC
SOMATOTROPHIN
SOMATOTROPHINS
SOMATOTROPIC
SOMATOTROPIN
SOMATOTROPINS
SOMATOTYPE
SOMATOTYPED
SOMATOTYPES
SOMATOTYPING
SOMBERNESS
SOMBERNESSES
SOMBRENESS
SOMBRENESSES
SOMBRERITE
SOMBRERITES
SOMEBODIES
SOMEPLACES
SOMERSAULT
SOMERSAULTED
SOMERSAULTING
SOMERSAULTS
SOMERSETED
SOMERSETING
SOMERSETTED
SOMERSETTING
SOMESTHESIA
SOMESTHESIAS
SOMESTHESIS

SOMESTHESISES
SOMESTHETIC
SOMETHINGS
SOMEWHENCE
SOMEWHERES
SOMEWHILES
SOMEWHITHER
SOMMELIERS
SOMNAMBULANCE
SOMNAMBULANCES
SOMNAMBULANT
SOMNAMBULANTS
SOMNAMBULAR
SOMNAMBULARY
SOMNAMBULATE
SOMNAMBULATED
SOMNAMBULATES
SOMNAMBULATING
SOMNAMBULATION
SOMNAMBULATIONS
SOMNAMBULATOR
SOMNAMBULATORS
SOMNAMBULE
SOMNAMBULES
SOMNAMBULIC
SOMNAMBULISM
SOMNAMBULISMS
SOMNAMBULIST
SOMNAMBULISTIC
SOMNAMBULISTS
SOMNIATING
SOMNIATIVE
SOMNIATORY
SOMNIFACIENT
SOMNIFACIENTS
SOMNIFEROUS
SOMNIFEROUSLY
SOMNILOQUENCE
SOMNILOQUENCES
SOMNILOQUIES
SOMNILOQUISE
SOMNILOQUISED
SOMNILOQUISES
SOMNILOQUISING
SOMNILOQUISM
SOMNILOQUISMS
SOMNILOQUIST
SOMNILOQUISTS
SOMNILOQUIZE
SOMNILOQUIZED
SOMNILOQUIZES
SOMNILOQUIZING
SOMNILOQUOUS
SOMNILOQUY
SOMNOLENCE
SOMNOLENCES
SOMNOLENCIES
SOMNOLENCY
SOMNOLENTLY

SOMNOLESCENT
SONGCRAFTS
SONGFULNESS
SONGFULNESSES
SONGLESSLY
SONGOLOLOS
SONGSMITHS
SONGSTRESS
SONGSTRESSES
SONGWRITER
SONGWRITERS
SONGWRITING
SONGWRITINGS
SONICATING
SONICATION
SONICATIONS
SONICATORS
SONIFEROUS
SONNETEERING
SONNETEERINGS
SONNETEERS
SONNETISES
SONNETISING
SONNETIZED
SONNETIZES
SONNETIZING
SONNETTING
SONOFABITCH
SONOGRAPHER
SONOGRAPHERS
SONOGRAPHIES
SONOGRAPHS
SONOGRAPHY
SONOMETERS
SONORITIES
SONOROUSLY
SONOROUSNESS
SONOROUSNESSES
SOOTERKINS
SOOTFLAKES
SOOTHERING
SOOTHFASTLY
SOOTHFASTNESS
SOOTHFASTNESSES
SOOTHINGLY
SOOTHINGNESS
SOOTHINGNESSES
SOOTHSAYER
SOOTHSAYERS
SOOTHSAYING
SOOTHSAYINGS
SOOTINESSES
SOPAIPILLA
SOPAIPILLAS
SOPAPILLAS
SOPHISTERS
SOPHISTICAL
SOPHISTICALLY

SOPHISTICATE	SORTILEGES	SOUSAPHONIST	SOVEREIGNTIST
SOPHISTICATED	SORTILEGIES	SOUSAPHONISTS	SOVEREIGNTISTS
SOPHISTICATEDLY	SORTITIONS	SOUTENEURS	SOVEREIGNTY
SOPHISTICATES	SOSTENUTOS	SOUTERRAIN	SOVIETISATION
SOPHISTICATING	SOTERIOLOGIC	SOUTERRAINS	SOVIETISATIONS
SOPHISTICATION	SOTERIOLOGICAL	SOUTHBOUND	SOVIETISED
SOPHISTICATIONS	SOTERIOLOGIES	SOUTHEASTER	SOVIETISES
SOPHISTICATOR	SOTERIOLOGY	SOUTHEASTERLIES	SOVIETISING
SOPHISTICATORS	SOTTISHNESS	SOUTHEASTERLY	SOVIETISMS
SOPHISTRIES	SOTTISHNESSES	SOUTHEASTERN	SOVIETISTIC
SOPHOMORES	SOTTISIERS	SOUTHEASTERS	SOVIETISTS
SOPHOMORIC	SOUBRETTES	SOUTHEASTS	SOVIETIZATION
SOPHOMORICAL	SOUBRETTISH	SOUTHEASTWARD	SOVIETIZATIONS
SOPORIFEROUS	SOUBRIQUET	SOUTHEASTWARDS	SOVIETIZED
SOPORIFEROUSLY	SOUBRIQUETS	SOUTHERING	SOVIETIZES
SOPORIFICALLY	SOULDIERED	SOUTHERLIES	SOVIETIZING
SOPORIFICS	SOULDIERING	SOUTHERLINESS	SOVIETOLOGICAL
SOPPINESSES	SOULFULNESS	SOUTHERLINESSES	SOVIETOLOGIST
SOPRANINOS	SOULFULNESSES	SOUTHERMOST	SOVIETOLOGISTS
SOPRANISTS	SOULLESSLY	SOUTHERNER	SOVRANTIES
SORBABILITIES	SOULLESSNESS	SOUTHERNERS	SOWBELLIES
SORBABILITY	SOULLESSNESSES	SOUTHERNISE	SPACEBANDS
SORBEFACIENT	SOUNDALIKE	SOUTHERNISED	SPACEBORNE
SORBEFACIENTS	SOUNDALIKES	SOUTHERNISES	SPACECRAFT
SORBITISATION	SOUNDBITES	SOUTHERNISING	SPACECRAFTS
SORBITISATIONS	SOUNDBOARD	SOUTHERNISM	SPACEFARING
SORBITISED	SOUNDBOARDS	SOUTHERNISMS	SPACEFARINGS
SORBITISES	SOUNDBOXES	SOUTHERNIZE	SPACEFLIGHT
SORBITISING	SOUNDCARDS	SOUTHERNIZED	SPACEFLIGHTS
SORBITIZATION	SOUNDINGLY	SOUTHERNIZES	SPACEPLANE
SORBITIZATIONS	SOUNDLESSLY	SOUTHERNIZING	SPACEPLANES
SORBITIZED	SOUNDLESSNESS	SOUTHERNLY	SPACEPORTS
SORBITIZES	SOUNDLESSNESSES	SOUTHERNMOST	SPACESHIPS
SORBITIZING	SOUNDNESSES	SOUTHERNNESS	SPACESUITS
SORCERESSES	SOUNDPOSTS	SOUTHERNNESSES	SPACEWALKED
SORDAMENTE	SOUNDPROOF	SOUTHERNWOOD	SPACEWALKER
SORDIDNESS	SOUNDPROOFED	SOUTHERNWOODS	SPACEWALKERS
SORDIDNESSES	SOUNDPROOFING	SOUTHLANDER	SPACEWALKING
SOREHEADED	SOUNDPROOFINGS	SOUTHLANDERS	SPACEWALKS
SOREHEADEDLY	SOUNDPROOFS	SOUTHLANDS	SPACEWOMAN
SOREHEADEDNESS	SOUNDSCAPE	SOUTHSAYING	SPACEWOMEN
SORENESSES	SOUNDSCAPES	SOUTHWARDLY	SPACINESSES
SORICIDENT	SOUNDSTAGE	SOUTHWARDS	SPACIOUSLY
SORORIALLY	SOUNDSTAGES	SOUTHWESTER	SPACIOUSNESS
SORORICIDAL	SOUNDTRACK	SOUTHWESTERLIES	SPACIOUSNESSES
SORORICIDE	SOUNDTRACKED	SOUTHWESTERLY	SPADASSINS
SORORICIDES	SOUNDTRACKING	SOUTHWESTERN	SPADEFISHES
SORORISING	SOUNDTRACKS	SOUTHWESTERS	SPADEWORKS
SORORITIES	SOUPSPOONS	SOUTHWESTS	SPADICEOUS
SORORIZING	SOURCEBOOK	SOUTHWESTWARD	SPADICIFLORAL
SORRINESSES	SOURCEBOOKS	SOUTHWESTWARDLY	SPADILLIOS
SORROWFULLY	SOURCELESS	SOUTHWESTWARDS	SPAGERISTS
SORROWFULNESS	SOURDELINE	SOUVENIRED	SPAGHETTILIKE
SORROWFULNESSES	SOURDELINES	SOUVENIRING	SPAGHETTINI
SORROWINGS	SOURDOUGHS	SOUVLAKIAS	SPAGHETTINIS
SORROWLESS	SOURNESSES	SOVENANCES	SPAGHETTIS
SORTATIONS	SOURPUSSES	SOVEREIGNLY	SPAGIRISTS
SORTILEGER	SOUSAPHONE	SOVEREIGNS	SPAGYRICAL
SORTILEGERS	SOUSAPHONES	SOVEREIGNTIES	SPAGYRICALLY

SPAGYRISTS	SPASMATICAL	SPECIALISTS	SPECTATING
SPALLATION	SPASMODICAL	SPECIALITIES	SPECTATORIAL
SPALLATIONS	SPASMODICALLY	SPECIALITY	SPECTATORS
SPANAEMIAS	SPASMODIST	SPECIALIZATION	SPECTATORSHIP
SPANAKOPITA	SPASMODISTS	SPECIALIZATIONS	SPECTATORSHIPS
SPANAKOPITAS	SPASMOLYTIC	SPECIALIZE	SPECTATRESS
SPANCELING	SPASMOLYTICS	SPECIALIZED	SPECTATRESSES
SPANCELLED	SPASTICALLY	SPECIALIZER	SPECTATRICES
SPANCELLING	SPASTICITIES	SPECIALIZERS	SPECTATRIX
SPANGHEWED	SPASTICITY	SPECIALIZES	SPECTATRIXES
SPANGHEWING	SPATANGOID	SPECIALIZING	SPECTINOMYCIN
SPANGLIEST	SPATANGOIDS	SPECIALLED	SPECTINOMYCINS
SPANGLINGS	SPATCHCOCK	SPECIALLING	SPECTRALITIES
SPANIELLED	SPATCHCOCKED	SPECIALNESS	SPECTRALITY
SPANIELLING	SPATCHCOCKING	SPECIALNESSES	SPECTRALLY
SPANIOLATE	SPATCHCOCKS	SPECIALOGUE	SPECTRALNESS
SPANIOLATED	SPATHACEOUS	SPECIALOGUES	SPECTRALNESSES
SPANIOLATES	SPATHIPHYLLUM	SPECIALTIES	SPECTROGRAM
SPANIOLATING	SPATHIPHYLLUMS	SPECIATING	SPECTROGRAMS
SPANIOLISE	SPATHULATE	SPECIATION	SPECTROGRAPH
SPANIOLISED	SPATIALITIES	SPECIATIONAL	SPECTROGRAPHIC
SPANIOLISES	SPATIALITY	SPECIATIONS	SPECTROGRAPHIES
SPANIOLISING	SPATIOTEMPORAL	SPECIESISM	SPECTROGRAPHS
SPANIOLIZE	SPATTERDASH	SPECIESISMS	SPECTROGRAPHY
SPANIOLIZED	SPATTERDASHES	SPECIESIST	SPECTROLOGICAL
SPANIOLIZES	SPATTERDOCK	SPECIESISTS	SPECTROLOGIES
SPANIOLIZING	SPATTERDOCKS	SPECIFIABLE	SPECTROLOGY
SPANKINGLY	SPATTERING	SPECIFICAL	SPECTROMETER
SPANOKOPITA	SPATTERWORK	SPECIFICALLY	SPECTROMETERS
SPANOKOPITAS	SPATTERWORKS	SPECIFICATE	SPECTROMETRIC
SPARAGMATIC	SPEAKEASIES	SPECIFICATED	SPECTROMETRIES
SPARAGRASS	SPEAKERINE	SPECIFICATES	SPECTROMETRY
SPARAGRASSES	SPEAKERINES	SPECIFICATING	SPECTROSCOPE
SPARAXISES	SPEAKERPHONE	SPECIFICATION	SPECTROSCOPES
SPARENESSES	SPEAKERPHONES	SPECIFICATIONS	SPECTROSCOPIC
SPARGANIUM	SPEAKERSHIP	SPECIFICATIVE	SPECTROSCOPICAL
SPARGANIUMS	SPEAKERSHIPS	SPECIFICITIES	SPECTROSCOPIES
SPARINGNESS	SPEAKINGLY	SPECIFICITY	SPECTROSCOPIST
SPARINGNESSES	SPEARFISHED	SPECIFIERS	SPECTROSCOPISTS
SPARKISHLY	SPEARFISHES	SPECIFYING	SPECTROSCOPY
SPARKLESSLY	SPEARFISHING	SPECIOCIDE	SPECULARITIES
SPARKLIEST	SPEARHEADED	SPECIOCIDES	SPECULARITY
SPARKLINGLY	SPEARHEADING	SPECIOSITIES	SPECULARLY
SPARKLINGS	SPEARHEADS	SPECIOSITY	SPECULATED
SPARKPLUGGED	SPEARMINTS	SPECIOUSLY	SPECULATES
SPARKPLUGGING	SPEARWORTS	SPECIOUSNESS	SPECULATING
SPARKPLUGS	SPECIALEST	SPECIOUSNESSES	SPECULATION
SPARROWFART	SPECIALISATION	SPECKLEDNESS	SPECULATIONS
SPARROWFARTS	SPECIALISATIONS	SPECKLEDNESSES	SPECULATIST
SPARROWGRASS	SPECIALISE	SPECKSIONEER	SPECULATISTS
SPARROWGRASSES	SPECIALISED	SPECKSIONEERS	SPECULATIVE
SPARROWHAWK	SPECIALISER	SPECKTIONEER	SPECULATIVELY
SPARROWHAWKS	SPECIALISERS	SPECKTIONEERS	SPECULATIVENESS
SPARROWLIKE	SPECIALISES	SPECTACLED	SPECULATOR
SPARSENESS	SPECIALISING	SPECTACLES	SPECULATORS
SPARSENESSES	SPECIALISM	SPECTACULAR	SPECULATORY
SPARSITIES	SPECIALISMS	SPECTACULARITY	SPECULATRICES
SPARTEINES	SPECIALIST	SPECTACULARLY	SPECULATRIX
SPARTERIES	SPECIALISTIC	SPECTACULARS	SPECULATRIXES

SPEECHCRAFT
SPEECHCRAFTS
SPEECHFULNESS
SPEECHFULNESSES
SPEECHIFICATION
SPEECHIFIED
SPEECHIFIER
SPEECHIFIERS
SPEECHIFIES
SPEECHIFYING
SPEECHLESS
SPEECHLESSLY
SPEECHLESSNESS
SPEECHMAKER
SPEECHMAKERS
SPEECHMAKING
SPEECHMAKINGS
SPEECHWRITER
SPEECHWRITERS
SPEEDBALLED
SPEEDBALLING
SPEEDBALLINGS
SPEEDBALLS
SPEEDBOATING
SPEEDBOATINGS
SPEEDBOATS
SPEEDFREAK
SPEEDFREAKS
SPEEDFULLY
SPEEDINESS
SPEEDINESSES
SPEEDOMETER
SPEEDOMETERS
SPEEDREADING
SPEEDREADS
SPEEDSKATING
SPEEDSKATINGS
SPEEDSTERS
SPEEDWELLS
SPELAEOLOGICAL
SPELAEOLOGIES
SPELAEOLOGIST
SPELAEOLOGISTS
SPELAEOLOGY
SPELAEOTHEM
SPELAEOTHEMS
SPELDERING
SPELDRINGS
SPELEOLOGICAL
SPELEOLOGIES
SPELEOLOGIST
SPELEOLOGISTS
SPELEOLOGY
SPELEOTHEM
SPELEOTHEMS
SPELEOTHERAPIES
SPELEOTHERAPY
SPELLBINDER
SPELLBINDERS

SPELLBINDING
SPELLBINDINGLY
SPELLBINDS
SPELLBOUND
SPELLCHECK
SPELLCHECKER
SPELLCHECKERS
SPELLCHECKS
SPELLDOWNS
SPELLICANS
SPELLINGLY
SPELLSTOPT
SPELUNKERS
SPELUNKING
SPELUNKINGS
SPENDTHRIFT
SPENDTHRIFTS
SPERMACETI
SPERMACETIS
SPERMADUCT
SPERMADUCTS
SPERMAGONIA
SPERMAGONIUM
SPERMAPHYTE
SPERMAPHYTES
SPERMAPHYTIC
SPERMARIES
SPERMARIUM
SPERMATHECA
SPERMATHECAE
SPERMATHECAL
SPERMATIAL
SPERMATICAL
SPERMATICALLY
SPERMATICS
SPERMATIDS
SPERMATIUM
SPERMATOBLAST
SPERMATOBLASTIC
SPERMATOBLASTS
SPERMATOCELE
SPERMATOCELES
SPERMATOCIDAL
SPERMATOCIDE
SPERMATOCIDES
SPERMATOCYTE
SPERMATOCYTES
SPERMATOGENESES
SPERMATOGENESIS
SPERMATOGENETIC
SPERMATOGENIC
SPERMATOGENIES
SPERMATOGENOUS
SPERMATOGENY
SPERMATOGONIA
SPERMATOGONIAL
SPERMATOGONIUM
SPERMATOPHORAL
SPERMATOPHORE

SPERMATOPHORES
SPERMATOPHYTE
SPERMATOPHYTES
SPERMATOPHYTIC
SPERMATORRHEA
SPERMATORRHEAS
SPERMATORRHOEA
SPERMATORRHOEAS
SPERMATOTHECA
SPERMATOTHECAE
SPERMATOZOA
SPERMATOZOAL
SPERMATOZOAN
SPERMATOZOANS
SPERMATOZOIC
SPERMATOZOID
SPERMATOZOIDS
SPERMATOZOON
SPERMICIDAL
SPERMICIDE
SPERMICIDES
SPERMIDUCT
SPERMIDUCTS
SPERMIOGENESES
SPERMIOGENESIS
SPERMIOGENETIC
SPERMOGONE
SPERMOGONES
SPERMOGONIA
SPERMOGONIUM
SPERMOPHILE
SPERMOPHILES
SPERMOPHYTE
SPERMOPHYTES
SPERMOPHYTIC
SPERRYLITE
SPERRYLITES
SPESSARTINE
SPESSARTINES
SPESSARTITE
SPESSARTITES
SPETSNAZES
SPETZNAZES
SPEWINESSES
SPHACELATE
SPHACELATED
SPHACELATES
SPHACELATING
SPHACELATION
SPHACELATIONS
SPHACELUSES
SPHAERIDIA
SPHAERIDIUM
SPHAERITES
SPHAEROCRYSTAL
SPHAEROCRYSTALS
SPHAEROSIDERITE
SPHAGNICOLOUS
SPHAGNOLOGIES

SPHAGNOLOGIST
SPHAGNOLOGISTS
SPHAGNOLOGY
SPHAIRISTIKE
SPHAIRISTIKES
SPHALERITE
SPHALERITES
SPHENDONES
SPHENODONS
SPHENODONT
SPHENOGRAM
SPHENOGRAMS
SPHENOIDAL
SPHENOPSID
SPHENOPSIDS
SPHERELESS
SPHERELIKE
SPHERICALITIES
SPHERICALITY
SPHERICALLY
SPHERICALNESS
SPHERICALNESSES
SPHERICITIES
SPHERICITY
SPHERISTERION
SPHERISTERIONS
SPHEROCYTE
SPHEROCYTES
SPHEROCYTOSES
SPHEROCYTOSIS
SPHEROIDAL
SPHEROIDALLY
SPHEROIDICALLY
SPHEROIDICITIES
SPHEROIDICITY
SPHEROIDISATION
SPHEROIDISE
SPHEROIDISED
SPHEROIDISES
SPHEROIDISING
SPHEROIDIZATION
SPHEROIDIZE
SPHEROIDIZED
SPHEROIDIZES
SPHEROIDIZING
SPHEROMETER
SPHEROMETERS
SPHEROPLAST
SPHEROPLASTS
SPHERULITE
SPHERULITES
SPHERULITIC
SPHINCTERAL
SPHINCTERIAL
SPHINCTERIC
SPHINCTERS
SPHINGOMYELIN
SPHINGOMYELINS
SPHINGOSINE

SPHINGOSINES

SPHINGOSINES
SPHINXLIKE
SPHRAGISTIC
SPHRAGISTICS
SPHYGMOGRAM
SPHYGMOGRAMS
SPHYGMOGRAPH
SPHYGMOGRAPHIC
SPHYGMOGRAPHIES
SPHYGMOGRAPHS
SPHYGMOGRAPHY
SPHYGMOLOGIES
SPHYGMOLOGY
SPHYGMOMETER
SPHYGMOMETERS
SPHYGMOPHONE
SPHYGMOPHONES
SPHYGMOSCOPE
SPHYGMOSCOPES
SPHYGMUSES
SPICEBERRIES
SPICEBERRY
SPICEBUSHES
SPICILEGES
SPICINESSES
SPICULATION
SPICULATIONS
SPIDERIEST
SPIDERLIKE
SPIDERWEBS
SPIDERWOOD
SPIDERWOODS
SPIDERWORK
SPIDERWORKS
SPIDERWORT
SPIDERWORTS
SPIEGELEISEN
SPIEGELEISENS
SPIFFINESS
SPIFFINESSES
SPIFFLICATE
SPIFFLICATED
SPIFFLICATES
SPIFFLICATING
SPIFFLICATION
SPIFFLICATIONS
SPIFLICATE
SPIFLICATED
SPIFLICATES
SPIFLICATING
SPIFLICATION
SPIFLICATIONS
SPIKEFISHES
SPIKENARDS
SPIKINESSES
SPILLIKINS
SPILLOVERS
SPILOSITES
SPINACENES

SPINACEOUS
SPINACHLIKE
SPINDLELEGS
SPINDLESHANKS
SPINDLIEST
SPINDLINGS
SPINDRIFTS
SPINELESSLY
SPINELESSNESS
SPINELESSNESSES
SPINESCENCE
SPINESCENCES
SPINESCENT
SPINIFEROUS
SPINIFEXES
SPINIGEROUS
SPINIGRADE
SPININESSES
SPINMEISTER
SPINMEISTERS
SPINNAKERS
SPINNERETS
SPINNERETTE
SPINNERETTES
SPINNERIES
SPINNERULE
SPINNERULES
SPINOSITIES
SPINSTERDOM
SPINSTERDOMS
SPINSTERHOOD
SPINSTERHOODS
SPINSTERIAL
SPINSTERIAN
SPINSTERISH
SPINSTERLY
SPINSTERSHIP
SPINSTERSHIPS
SPINSTRESS
SPINSTRESSES
SPINTHARISCOPE
SPINTHARISCOPES
SPINULESCENT
SPINULIFEROUS
SPIRACULAR
SPIRACULATE
SPIRACULUM
SPIRALIFORM
SPIRALISMS
SPIRALISTS
SPIRALITIES
SPIRALLING
SPIRASTERS
SPIRATIONS
SPIRIFEROUS
SPIRILLOSES
SPIRILLOSIS
SPIRITEDLY
SPIRITEDNESS

SPIRITEDNESSES
SPIRITINGS
SPIRITISMS
SPIRITISTIC
SPIRITISTS
SPIRITLESS
SPIRITLESSLY
SPIRITLESSNESS
SPIRITOUSNESS
SPIRITOUSNESSES
SPIRITUALISE
SPIRITUALISED
SPIRITUALISER
SPIRITUALISERS
SPIRITUALISES
SPIRITUALISING
SPIRITUALISM
SPIRITUALISMS
SPIRITUALIST
SPIRITUALISTIC
SPIRITUALISTS
SPIRITUALITIES
SPIRITUALITY
SPIRITUALIZE
SPIRITUALIZED
SPIRITUALIZER
SPIRITUALIZERS
SPIRITUALIZES
SPIRITUALIZING
SPIRITUALLY
SPIRITUALNESS
SPIRITUALNESSES
SPIRITUALS
SPIRITUALTIES
SPIRITUALTY
SPIRITUELLE
SPIRITUOSITIES
SPIRITUOSITY
SPIRITUOUS
SPIRITUOUSNESS
SPIRITUSES
SPIRKETTING
SPIRKETTINGS
SPIROCHAETAEMIA
SPIROCHAETE
SPIROCHAETES
SPIROCHAETOSES
SPIROCHAETOSIS
SPIROCHETAL
SPIROCHETE
SPIROCHETES
SPIROCHETOSES
SPIROCHETOSIS
SPIROGRAMS
SPIROGRAPH
SPIROGRAPHIC
SPIROGRAPHIES
SPIROGRAPHS
SPIROGRAPHY

SPIROGYRAS
SPIROMETER
SPIROMETERS
SPIROMETRIC
SPIROMETRIES
SPIROMETRY
SPIRONOLACTONE
SPIRONOLACTONES
SPIROPHORE
SPIROPHORES
SPIRULINAS
SPISSITUDE
SPISSITUDES
SPITCHCOCK
SPITCHCOCKED
SPITCHCOCKING
SPITCHCOCKS
SPITEFULLER
SPITEFULLEST
SPITEFULLY
SPITEFULNESS
SPITEFULNESSES
SPITSTICKER
SPITSTICKERS
SPITTLEBUG
SPITTLEBUGS
SPIVVERIES
SPLANCHNIC
SPLANCHNOCELE
SPLANCHNOCELES
SPLANCHNOLOGIES
SPLANCHNOLOGY
SPLASHBACK
SPLASHBACKS
SPLASHBOARD
SPLASHBOARDS
SPLASHDOWN
SPLASHDOWNS
SPLASHIEST
SPLASHINESS
SPLASHINESSES
SPLASHINGS
SPLASHPROOF
SPLATCHING
SPLATTERED
SPLATTERING
SPLATTERPUNK
SPLATTERPUNKS
SPLATTINGS
SPLAYFOOTED
SPLAYFOOTEDLY
SPLEENFULLY
SPLEENIEST
SPLEENLESS
SPLEENSTONE
SPLEENSTONES
SPLEENWORT
SPLEENWORTS
SPLENATIVE

SPLENDIDER
SPLENDIDEST
SPLENDIDIOUS
SPLENDIDLY
SPLENDIDNESS
SPLENDIDNESSES
SPLENDIDOUS
SPLENDIFEROUS
SPLENDIFEROUSLY
SPLENDOROUS
SPLENDOURS
SPLENDROUS
SPLENECTOMIES
SPLENECTOMISE
SPLENECTOMISED
SPLENECTOMISES
SPLENECTOMISING
SPLENECTOMIZE
SPLENECTOMIZED
SPLENECTOMIZES
SPLENECTOMIZING
SPLENECTOMY
SPLENETICAL
SPLENETICALLY
SPLENETICS
SPLENISATION
SPLENISATIONS
SPLENITISES
SPLENIUSES
SPLENIZATION
SPLENIZATIONS
SPLENOMEGALIES
SPLENOMEGALY
SPLEUCHANS
SPLINTERED
SPLINTERIER
SPLINTERIEST
SPLINTERING
SPLINTLIKE
SPLINTWOOD
SPLINTWOODS
SPLODGIEST
SPLODGINESS
SPLODGINESSES
SPLOOSHING
SPLOTCHIER
SPLOTCHIEST
SPLOTCHILY
SPLOTCHINESS
SPLOTCHINESSES
SPLOTCHING
SPLURGIEST
SPLUTTERED
SPLUTTERER
SPLUTTERERS
SPLUTTERING
SPLUTTERINGLY
SPLUTTERINGS
SPODOGRAMS

SPODOMANCIES
SPODOMANCY
SPODOMANTIC
SPODUMENES
SPOILFIVES
SPOILSPORT
SPOILSPORTS
SPOKESHAVE
SPOKESHAVES
SPOKESMANSHIP
SPOKESMANSHIPS
SPOKESPEOPLE
SPOKESPERSON
SPOKESPERSONS
SPOKESWOMAN
SPOKESWOMEN
SPOLIATING
SPOLIATION
SPOLIATIONS
SPOLIATIVE
SPOLIATORS
SPOLIATORY
SPONDAICAL
SPONDOOLICKS
SPONDULICKS
SPONDYLITIC
SPONDYLITICS
SPONDYLITIS
SPONDYLITISES
SPONDYLOLYSES
SPONDYLOLYSIS
SPONDYLOSES
SPONDYLOSIS
SPONDYLOUS
SPONGEABLE
SPONGEBAGS
SPONGELIKE
SPONGEWARE
SPONGEWARES
SPONGEWOOD
SPONGEWOODS
SPONGICOLOUS
SPONGIFORM
SPONGINESS
SPONGINESSES
SPONGIOBLAST
SPONGIOBLASTIC
SPONGIOBLASTS
SPONGOLOGIES
SPONGOLOGIST
SPONGOLOGISTS
SPONGOLOGY
SPONSIONAL
SPONSORIAL
SPONSORING
SPONSORSHIP
SPONSORSHIPS
SPONTANEITIES
SPONTANEITY

SPONTANEOUS
SPONTANEOUSLY
SPONTANEOUSNESS
SPOOFERIES
SPOOKERIES
SPOOKINESS
SPOOKINESSES
SPOONBAITS
SPOONBILLS
SPOONDRIFT
SPOONDRIFTS
SPOONERISM
SPOONERISMS
SPORADICAL
SPORADICALLY
SPORADICALNESS
SPORANGIAL
SPORANGIOLA
SPORANGIOLE
SPORANGIOLES
SPORANGIOLUM
SPORANGIOPHORE
SPORANGIOPHORES
SPORANGIOSPORE
SPORANGIOSPORES
SPORANGIUM
SPORICIDAL
SPORICIDES
SPORIDESMS
SPOROCARPS
SPOROCYSTIC
SPOROCYSTS
SPOROCYTES
SPOROGENESES
SPOROGENESIS
SPOROGENIC
SPOROGENIES
SPOROGENOUS
SPOROGONIA
SPOROGONIAL
SPOROGONIC
SPOROGONIES
SPOROGONIUM
SPOROPHORE
SPOROPHORES
SPOROPHORIC
SPOROPHOROUS
SPOROPHYLL
SPOROPHYLLS
SPOROPHYLS
SPOROPHYTE
SPOROPHYTES
SPOROPHYTIC
SPOROPOLLENIN
SPOROPOLLENINS
SPOROTRICHOSES
SPOROTRICHOSIS
SPOROZOANS
SPOROZOITE

SPOROZOITES
SPORTABILITIES
SPORTABILITY
SPORTANCES
SPORTCASTER
SPORTCASTERS
SPORTFISHERMAN
SPORTFISHERMEN
SPORTFISHING
SPORTFISHINGS
SPORTFULLY
SPORTFULNESS
SPORTFULNESSES
SPORTINESS
SPORTINESSES
SPORTINGLY
SPORTIVELY
SPORTIVENESS
SPORTIVENESSES
SPORTSCAST
SPORTSCASTER
SPORTSCASTERS
SPORTSCASTS
SPORTSMANLIKE
SPORTSMANLY
SPORTSMANSHIP
SPORTSMANSHIPS
SPORTSPEOPLE
SPORTSPERSON
SPORTSPERSONS
SPORTSWEAR
SPORTSWEARS
SPORTSWOMAN
SPORTSWOMEN
SPORTSWRITER
SPORTSWRITERS
SPORTSWRITING
SPORTSWRITINGS
SPORULATED
SPORULATES
SPORULATING
SPORULATION
SPORULATIONS
SPORULATIVE
SPOTLESSLY
SPOTLESSNESS
SPOTLESSNESSES
SPOTLIGHTED
SPOTLIGHTING
SPOTLIGHTS
SPOTTEDNESS
SPOTTEDNESSES
SPOTTINESS
SPOTTINESSES
SPOUSELESS
SPOYLEFULL
SPRACHGEFUHL
SPRACHGEFUHLS
SPRACKLING

SPRADDLING	SPRINGLETS	SQUADRONAL	SQUAWKIEST
SPRANGLING	SPRINGLIKE	SQUADRONED	SQUAWKINGS
SPRATTLING	SPRINGTAIL	SQUADRONES	SQUAWROOTS
SPRAUCHLED	SPRINGTAILS	SQUADRONING	SQUEAKERIES
SPRAUCHLES	SPRINGTIDE	SQUAILINGS	SQUEAKIEST
SPRAUCHLING	SPRINGTIDES	SQUALIDEST	SQUEAKINESS
SPRAUNCIER	SPRINGTIME	SQUALIDITIES	SQUEAKINESSES
SPRAUNCIEST	SPRINGTIMES	SQUALIDITY	SQUEAKINGLY
SPRAWLIEST	SPRINGWATER	SQUALIDNESS	SQUEAKINGS
SPREADABILITIES	SPRINGWATERS	SQUALIDNESSES	SQUEALINGS
SPREADABILITY	SPRINGWOOD	SQUALLIEST	SQUEAMISHLY
SPREADABLE	SPRINGWOODS	SQUALLINGS	SQUEAMISHNESS
SPREADINGLY	SPRINGWORT	SQUAMATION	SQUEAMISHNESSES
SPREADINGS	SPRINGWORTS	SQUAMATIONS	SQUEEGEEING
SPREADSHEET	SPRINKLERED	SQUAMELLAS	SQUEEZABILITIES
SPREADSHEETS	SPRINKLERING	SQUAMIFORM	SQUEEZABILITY
SPREAGHERIES	SPRINKLERS	SQUAMOSALS	SQUEEZABLE
SPREAGHERY	SPRINKLING	SQUAMOSELY	SQUEEZIEST
SPREATHING	SPRINKLINGS	SQUAMOSENESS	SQUEEZINGS
SPRECHERIES	SPRINTINGS	SQUAMOSENESSES	SQUEGGINGS
SPRECHGESANG	SPRITELIER	SQUAMOSITIES	SQUELCHERS
SPRECHGESANGS	SPRITELIEST	SQUAMOSITY	SQUELCHIER
SPRECHSTIMME	SPRITSAILS	SQUAMOUSLY	SQUELCHIEST
SPRECHSTIMMES	SPROUTINGS	SQUAMOUSNESS	SQUELCHING
SPREETHING	SPRUCENESS	SQUAMOUSNESSES	SQUELCHINGS
SPREKELIAS	SPRUCENESSES	SQUAMULOSE	SQUETEAGUE
SPRIGGIEST	SPRYNESSES	SQUANDERED	SQUETEAGUES
SPRIGHTFUL	SPUILZIEING	SQUANDERER	SQUIBBINGS
SPRIGHTFULLY	SPULEBLADE	SQUANDERERS	SQUIDGIEST
SPRIGHTFULNESS	SPULEBLADES	SQUANDERING	SQUIFFIEST
SPRIGHTING	SPULYIEING	SQUANDERINGLY	SQUIGGLERS
SPRIGHTLESS	SPULZIEING	SQUANDERINGS	SQUIGGLIER
SPRIGHTLIER	SPUMESCENCE	SQUANDERMANIA	SQUIGGLIEST
SPRIGHTLIEST	SPUMESCENCES	SQUANDERMANIAS	SQUIGGLING
SPRIGHTLINESS	SPUMESCENT	SQUAREHEAD	SQUILGEEING
SPRIGHTLINESSES	SPUNBONDED	SQUAREHEADS	SQUILLIONS
SPRIGTAILS	SPUNKINESS	SQUARENESS	SQUINANCIES
SPRINGALDS	SPUNKINESSES	SQUARENESSES	SQUINCHING
SPRINGBOARD	SPURGALLED	SQUAREWISE	SQUINNIEST
SPRINGBOARDS	SPURGALLING	SQUARISHLY	SQUINNYING
SPRINGBOKS	SPURIOSITIES	SQUARISHNESS	SQUINTIEST
SPRINGBUCK	SPURIOSITY	SQUARISHNESSES	SQUINTINGLY
SPRINGBUCKS	SPURIOUSLY	SQUARSONAGE	SQUINTINGS
SPRINGEING	SPURIOUSNESS	SQUARSONAGES	SQUIRALITIES
SPRINGHAAS	SPURIOUSNESSES	SQUASHABLE	SQUIRALITY
SPRINGHALT	SPUTTERERS	SQUASHIEST	SQUIRALTIES
SPRINGHALTS	SPUTTERING	SQUASHINESS	SQUIRARCHAL
SPRINGHASE	SPUTTERINGLY	SQUASHINESSES	SQUIRARCHICAL
SPRINGHEAD	SPUTTERINGS	SQUATNESSES	SQUIRARCHIES
SPRINGHEADS	SPYGLASSES	SQUATTERED	SQUIRARCHS
SPRINGHOUSE	SPYMASTERS	SQUATTERING	SQUIRARCHY
SPRINGHOUSES	SQUABASHED	SQUATTIEST	SQUIREAGES
SPRINGIEST	SQUABASHER	SQUATTINESS	SQUIREARCH
SPRINGINESS	SQUABASHERS	SQUATTINESSES	SQUIREARCHAL
SPRINGINESSES	SQUABASHES	SQUATTLING	SQUIREARCHICAL
SPRINGINGS	SQUABASHING	SQUATTOCRACIES	SQUIREARCHIES
SPRINGKEEPER	SQUABBIEST	SQUATTOCRACY	SQUIREARCHS
SPRINGKEEPERS	SQUABBLERS	SQUAWBUSHES	SQUIREARCHY
SPRINGLESS	SQUABBLING	SQUAWFISHES	SQUIREDOMS

QUIREHOOD
QUIREHOODS
QUIRELIKE
QUIRELING
QUIRELINGS
QUIRESHIP
QUIRESHIPS
QUIRESSES
QUIRMIEST
QUIRMINGLY
QUIRRELED
QUIRRELFISH
QUIRRELFISHES
QUIRRELING
QUIRRELLED
QUIRRELLING
QUIRRELLY
QUIRTINGS
QUISHIEST
QUISHINESS
QUISHINESSES
QUOOSHIER
QUOOSHIEST
QUOOSHING
TABBINGLY
TABILATES
TABILISATION
TABILISATIONS
TABILISATOR
TABILISATORS
TABILISED
TABILISER
TABILISERS
TABILISES
TABILISING
TABILITIES
TABILIZATION
TABILIZATIONS
TABILIZATOR
TABILIZATORS
TABILIZED
TABILIZER
TABILIZERS
TABILIZES
TABILIZING
TABLEBOYS
TABLEMATE
TABLEMATES
TABLENESS
TABLENESSES
TABLISHED
TABLISHES
TABLISHING
TABLISHMENT
TABLISHMENTS
TACCATISSIMO
TACKROOMS
TACKYARDS
TACTOMETER

STACTOMETERS
STADDLESTONE
STADDLESTONES
STADHOLDER
STADHOLDERATE
STADHOLDERATES
STADHOLDERS
STADHOLDERSHIP
STADHOLDERSHIPS
STADIOMETER
STADIOMETERS
STADTHOLDER
STADTHOLDERATE
STADTHOLDERATES
STADTHOLDERS
STADTHOLDERSHIP
STAFFROOMS
STAGECOACH
STAGECOACHES
STAGECOACHING
STAGECOACHINGS
STAGECOACHMAN
STAGECOACHMEN
STAGECRAFT
STAGECRAFTS
STAGEHANDS
STAGESTRUCK
STAGFLATION
STAGFLATIONARY
STAGFLATIONS
STAGGERBUSH
STAGGERBUSHES
STAGGERERS
STAGGERING
STAGGERINGLY
STAGGERINGS
STAGHOUNDS
STAGINESSES
STAGNANCES
STAGNANCIES
STAGNANTLY
STAGNATING
STAGNATION
STAGNATIONS
STAIDNESSES
STAINABILITIES
STAINABILITY
STAINLESSES
STAINLESSLY
STAINLESSNESS
STAINLESSNESSES
STAINPROOF
STAIRCASED
STAIRCASES
STAIRCASING
STAIRCASINGS
STAIRFOOTS
STAIRHEADS
STAIRLIFTS

STAIRSTEPPED
STAIRSTEPPING
STAIRSTEPS
STAIRWELLS
STAIRWORKS
STAKEHOLDER
STAKEHOLDERS
STAKHANOVISM
STAKHANOVISMS
STAKHANOVITE
STAKHANOVITES
STAKTOMETER
STAKTOMETERS
STALACTICAL
STALACTIFORM
STALACTITAL
STALACTITE
STALACTITED
STALACTITES
STALACTITIC
STALACTITICAL
STALACTITICALLY
STALACTITIFORM
STALACTITIOUS
STALAGMITE
STALAGMITES
STALAGMITIC
STALAGMITICAL
STALAGMITICALLY
STALAGMOMETER
STALAGMOMETERS
STALAGMOMETRIES
STALAGMOMETRY
STALEMATED
STALEMATES
STALEMATING
STALENESSES
STALKINESS
STALKINESSES
STALLENGER
STALLENGERS
STALLHOLDER
STALLHOLDERS
STALLINGER
STALLINGERS
STALLMASTER
STALLMASTERS
STALWARTLY
STALWARTNESS
STALWARTNESSES
STALWORTHS
STAMINEOUS
STAMINIFEROUS
STAMINODES
STAMINODIA
STAMINODIES
STAMINODIUM
STAMMERERS
STAMMERING

STAMMERINGLY
STAMMERINGS
STAMPEDERS
STAMPEDING
STAMPEDOED
STAMPEDOING
STANCHABLE
STANCHELLED
STANCHELLING
STANCHERED
STANCHERING
STANCHINGS
STANCHIONED
STANCHIONING
STANCHIONS
STANCHLESS
STANCHNESS
STANCHNESSES
STANDARDBRED
STANDARDBREDS
STANDARDISATION
STANDARDISE
STANDARDISED
STANDARDISER
STANDARDISERS
STANDARDISES
STANDARDISING
STANDARDIZATION
STANDARDIZE
STANDARDIZED
STANDARDIZER
STANDARDIZERS
STANDARDIZES
STANDARDIZING
STANDARDLESS
STANDARDLY
STANDDOWNS
STANDFASTS
STANDFIRST
STANDFIRSTS
STANDGALES
STANDISHES
STANDOFFISH
STANDOFFISHLY
STANDOFFISHNESS
STANDOVERS
STANDPATTER
STANDPATTERS
STANDPATTISM
STANDPATTISMS
STANDPIPES
STANDPOINT
STANDPOINTS
STANDSTILL
STANDSTILLS
STANNARIES
STANNATORS
STANNIFEROUS
STANNOTYPE

STANNOTYPES
STAPEDECTOMIES
STAPEDECTOMY
STAPEDIUSES
STAPHYLINE
STAPHYLINID
STAPHYLINIDS
STAPHYLITIS
STAPHYLITISES
STAPHYLOCOCCAL
STAPHYLOCOCCI
STAPHYLOCOCCIC
STAPHYLOCOCCUS
STAPHYLOMA
STAPHYLOMAS
STAPHYLOMATA
STAPHYLOPLASTIC
STAPHYLOPLASTY
STAPHYLORRHAPHY
STARBOARDED
STARBOARDING
STARBOARDS
STARBURSTS
STARCHEDLY
STARCHEDNESS
STARCHEDNESSES
STARCHIEST
STARCHINESS
STARCHINESSES
STARCHLIKE
STARDRIFTS
STARFISHED
STARFISHES
STARFLOWER
STARFLOWERS
STARFRUITS
STARFUCKER
STARFUCKERS
STARFUCKING
STARFUCKINGS
STARGAZERS
STARGAZING
STARGAZINGS
STARKENING
STARKNESSES
STARLIGHTED
STARLIGHTS
STARMONGER
STARMONGERS
STAROSTIES
STARRINESS
STARRINESSES
STARSHINES
STARSTONES
STARSTRUCK
STARTINGLY
STARTLEMENT
STARTLEMENTS
STARTLINGLY

STARTLINGS
STARVATION
STARVATIONS
STARVELING
STARVELINGS
STASIDIONS
STASIMORPHIES
STASIMORPHY
STATECRAFT
STATECRAFTS
STATEHOODS
STATEHOUSE
STATEHOUSES
STATELESSNESS
STATELESSNESSES
STATELIEST
STATELINESS
STATELINESSES
STATEMENTED
STATEMENTING
STATEMENTINGS
STATEMENTS
STATEROOMS
STATESMANLIKE
STATESMANLY
STATESMANSHIP
STATESMANSHIPS
STATESPEOPLE
STATESPERSON
STATESPERSONS
STATESWOMAN
STATESWOMEN
STATICALLY
STATIONARIES
STATIONARILY
STATIONARINESS
STATIONARY
STATIONERIES
STATIONERS
STATIONERY
STATIONING
STATIONMASTER
STATIONMASTERS
STATISTICAL
STATISTICALLY
STATISTICIAN
STATISTICIANS
STATISTICS
STATOBLAST
STATOBLASTS
STATOCYSTS
STATOLATRIES
STATOLATRY
STATOLITHIC
STATOLITHS
STATOSCOPE
STATOSCOPES
STATUARIES
STATUESQUE

STATUESQUELY
STATUESQUENESS
STATUETTES
STATUTABLE
STATUTABLY
STATUTORILY
STAUNCHABLE
STAUNCHERS
STAUNCHEST
STAUNCHING
STAUNCHINGS
STAUNCHLESS
STAUNCHNESS
STAUNCHNESSES
STAUROLITE
STAUROLITES
STAUROLITIC
STAUROSCOPE
STAUROSCOPES
STAUROSCOPIC
STAVESACRE
STAVESACRES
STAVUDINES
STAYMAKERS
STEADFASTLY
STEADFASTNESS
STEADFASTNESSES
STEADICAMS
STEADINESS
STEADINESSES
STEAKHOUSE
STEAKHOUSES
STEALINGLY
STEALTHFUL
STEALTHIER
STEALTHIEST
STEALTHILY
STEALTHINESS
STEALTHINESSES
STEALTHING
STEALTHINGS
STEAMBOATS
STEAMERING
STEAMFITTER
STEAMFITTERS
STEAMINESS
STEAMINESSES
STEAMROLLED
STEAMROLLER
STEAMROLLERED
STEAMROLLERING
STEAMROLLERS
STEAMROLLING
STEAMROLLS
STEAMSHIPS
STEAMTIGHT
STEAMTIGHTNESS
STEAROPTENE
STEAROPTENES

STEARSMATE
STEARSMATES
STEATOCELE
STEATOCELES
STEATOLYSES
STEATOLYSIS
STEATOMATOUS
STEATOPYGA
STEATOPYGAS
STEATOPYGIA
STEATOPYGIAS
STEATOPYGIC
STEATOPYGOUS
STEATORRHEA
STEATORRHEAS
STEATORRHOEA
STEATORRHOEAS
STEDFASTLY
STEDFASTNESS
STEDFASTNESSES
STEELHEADS
STEELINESS
STEELINESSES
STEELMAKER
STEELMAKERS
STEELMAKING
STEELMAKINGS
STEELWARES
STEELWORKER
STEELWORKERS
STEELWORKING
STEELWORKINGS
STEELWORKS
STEELYARDS
STEENBRASES
STEENBUCKS
STEENKIRKS
STEEPDOWNE
STEEPEDOWNE
STEEPENING
STEEPINESS
STEEPINESSES
STEEPLEBUSH
STEEPLEBUSHES
STEEPLECHASE
STEEPLECHASED
STEEPLECHASER
STEEPLECHASERS
STEEPLECHASES
STEEPLECHASING
STEEPLECHASINGS
STEEPLEJACK
STEEPLEJACKS
STEEPNESSES
STEERAGEWAY
STEERAGEWAYS
STEERLINGS
STEERSMATE
STEERSMATES

STEGANOGRAM	STENOCHROME	STEPMOTHERLY	STEREOLOGIES
STEGANOGRAMS	STENOCHROMES	STEPMOTHERS	STEREOLOGY
STEGANOGRAPH	STENOCHROMIES	STEPPARENT	STEREOMETER
STEGANOGRAPHER	STENOCHROMY	STEPPARENTING	STEREOMETERS
STEGANOGRAPHERS	STENOGRAPH	STEPPARENTINGS	STEREOMETRIC
STEGANOGRAPHIC	STENOGRAPHED	STEPPARENTS	STEREOMETRICAL
STEGANOGRAPHIES	STENOGRAPHER	STEPSISTER	STEREOMETRIES
STEGANOGRAPHIST	STENOGRAPHERS	STEPSISTERS	STEREOMETRY
STEGANOGRAPHS	STENOGRAPHIC	STEPSTOOLS	STEREOPHONIC
STEGANOGRAPHY	STENOGRAPHICAL	STERADIANS	STEREOPHONIES
STEGANOPOD	STENOGRAPHIES	STERCORACEOUS	STEREOPHONY
STEGANOPODOUS	STENOGRAPHING	STERCORANISM	STEREOPSIS
STEGANOPODS	STENOGRAPHIST	STERCORANISMS	STEREOPTICON
STEGOCARPOUS	STENOGRAPHISTS	STERCORANIST	STEREOPTICONS
STEGOCEPHALIAN	STENOGRAPHS	STERCORANISTS	STEREOPTICS
STEGOCEPHALIANS	STENOGRAPHY	STERCORARIOUS	STEREOREGULAR
STEGOCEPHALOUS	STENOHALINE	STERCORARY	STEREOSCOPE
STEGODONTS	STENOPAEIC	STERCORATE	STEREOSCOPES
STEGOMYIAS	STENOPETALOUS	STERCORATED	STEREOSCOPIC
STEGOPHILIST	STENOPHAGOUS	STERCORATES	STEREOSCOPICAL
STEGOPHILISTS	STENOPHYLLOUS	STERCORATING	STEREOSCOPIES
STEGOSAURIAN	STENOTHERM	STERCORICOLOUS	STEREOSCOPIST
STEGOSAURS	STENOTHERMAL	STERCULIACEOUS	STEREOSCOPISTS
STEGOSAURUS	STENOTHERMS	STERCULIAS	STEREOSCOPY
STEGOSAURUSES	STENOTOPIC	STEREOACUITIES	STEREOSONIC
STEINBOCKS	STENOTROPIC	STEREOACUITY	STEREOSPECIFIC
STEINKIRKS	STENOTYPED	STEREOBATE	STEREOTACTIC
STELLARATOR	STENOTYPER	STEREOBATES	STEREOTACTICAL
STELLARATORS	STENOTYPERS	STEREOBATIC	STEREOTAXES
STELLATELY	STENOTYPES	STEREOBLIND	STEREOTAXIA
STELLERIDAN	STENOTYPIC	STEREOCARD	STEREOTAXIAS
STELLERIDANS	STENOTYPIES	STEREOCARDS	STEREOTAXIC
STELLERIDS	STENOTYPING	STEREOCHEMICAL	STEREOTAXICALLY
STELLIFEROUS	STENOTYPIST	STEREOCHEMISTRY	STEREOTAXIS
STELLIFIED	STENOTYPISTS	STEREOCHROME	STEREOTOMIES
STELLIFIES	STENTMASTER	STEREOCHROMED	STEREOTOMY
STELLIFORM	STENTMASTERS	STEREOCHROMES	STEREOTROPIC
STELLIFYING	STENTORIAN	STEREOCHROMIES	STEREOTROPISM
STELLIFYINGS	STEPBAIRNS	STEREOCHROMING	STEREOTROPISMS
STELLIONATE	STEPBROTHER	STEREOCHROMY	STEREOTYPE
STELLIONATES	STEPBROTHERS	STEREOGNOSES	STEREOTYPED
STELLULARLY	STEPCHILDREN	STEREOGNOSIS	STEREOTYPER
STELLULATE	STEPDANCER	STEREOGRAM	STEREOTYPERS
STEMMATOUS	STEPDANCERS	STEREOGRAMS	STEREOTYPES
STEMMERIES	STEPDANCING	STEREOGRAPH	STEREOTYPIC
STEMWINDER	STEPDANCINGS	STEREOGRAPHED	STEREOTYPICAL
STEMWINDERS	STEPDAUGHTER	STEREOGRAPHIC	STEREOTYPICALLY
STENCHIEST	STEPDAUGHTERS	STEREOGRAPHICAL	STEREOTYPIES
STENCILERS	STEPFAMILIES	STEREOGRAPHIES	STEREOTYPING
STENCILING	STEPFAMILY	STEREOGRAPHING	STEREOTYPINGS
STENCILLED	STEPFATHER	STEREOGRAPHS	STEREOTYPIST
STENCILLER	STEPFATHERS	STEREOGRAPHY	STEREOTYPISTS
STENCILLERS	STEPHANITE	STEREOISOMER	STEREOTYPY
STENCILLING	STEPHANITES	STEREOISOMERIC	STEREOVISION
STENCILLINGS	STEPHANOTIS	STEREOISOMERISM	STEREOVISIONS
STENOBATHIC	STEPHANOTISES	STEREOISOMERS	STERICALLY
STENOBATHS	STEPLADDER	STEREOISOMETRIC	STERIGMATA
STENOCARDIA	STEPLADDERS	STEREOLOGICAL	STERILANTS
STENOCARDIAS	STEPMOTHER	STEREOLOGICALLY	STERILANTS

STERILISABLE
STERILISATION
STERILISATIONS
STERILISED
STERILISER
STERILISERS
STERILISES
STERILISING
STERILITIES
STERILIZABLE
STERILIZATION
STERILIZATIONS
STERILIZED
STERILIZER
STERILIZERS
STERILIZES
STERILIZING
STERLINGLY
STERLINGNESS
STERLINGNESSES
STERNALGIA
STERNALGIAS
STERNALGIC
STERNBOARD
STERNBOARDS
STERNEBRAE
STERNFASTS
STERNFOREMOST
STERNNESSES
STERNOCOSTAL
STERNOTRIBE
STERNPORTS
STERNPOSTS
STERNSHEET
STERNSHEETS
STERNUTATION
STERNUTATIONS
STERNUTATIVE
STERNUTATIVES
STERNUTATOR
STERNUTATORIES
STERNUTATORS
STERNUTATORY
STERNWARDS
STERNWORKS
STEROIDOGENESES
STEROIDOGENESIS
STEROIDOGENIC
STERTOROUS
STERTOROUSLY
STERTOROUSNESS
STETHOSCOPE
STETHOSCOPES
STETHOSCOPIC
STETHOSCOPIES
STETHOSCOPIST
STETHOSCOPISTS
STETHOSCOPY
STEVEDORED

STEVEDORES
STEVEDORING
STEVENGRAPH
STEVENGRAPHS
STEWARDESS
STEWARDESSES
STEWARDING
STEWARDRIES
STEWARDSHIP
STEWARDSHIPS
STEWARTRIES
STIACCIATO
STIACCIATOS
STIBIALISM
STIBIALISMS
STICCADOES
STICCATOES
STICHARION
STICHARIONS
STICHICALLY
STICHIDIUM
STICHOLOGIES
STICHOLOGY
STICHOMETRIC
STICHOMETRICAL
STICHOMETRIES
STICHOMETRY
STICHOMYTHIA
STICHOMYTHIAS
STICHOMYTHIC
STICHOMYTHIES
STICHOMYTHY
STICKABILITIES
STICKABILITY
STICKBALLS
STICKERING
STICKHANDLE
STICKHANDLED
STICKHANDLER
STICKHANDLERS
STICKHANDLES
STICKHANDLING
STICKINESS
STICKINESSES
STICKLEADER
STICKLEADERS
STICKLEBACK
STICKLEBACKS
STICKSEEDS
STICKTIGHT
STICKTIGHTS
STICKWEEDS
STICKWORKS
STICKYBEAK
STICKYBEAKED
STICKYBEAKING
STICKYBEAKS
STIDDIEING
STIFFENERS

STIFFENING
STIFFENINGS
STIFFNESSES
STIFFWARES
STIFLINGLY
STIGMARIAN
STIGMARIANS
STIGMASTEROL
STIGMASTEROLS
STIGMATICAL
STIGMATICALLY
STIGMATICS
STIGMATIFEROUS
STIGMATISATION
STIGMATISATIONS
STIGMATISE
STIGMATISED
STIGMATISER
STIGMATISERS
STIGMATISES
STIGMATISING
STIGMATISM
STIGMATISMS
STIGMATIST
STIGMATISTS
STIGMATIZATION
STIGMATIZATIONS
STIGMATIZE
STIGMATIZED
STIGMATIZER
STIGMATIZERS
STIGMATIZES
STIGMATIZING
STIGMATOPHILIA
STIGMATOPHILIAS
STIGMATOPHILIST
STIGMATOSE
STILBESTROL
STILBESTROLS
STILBOESTROL
STILBOESTROLS
STILETTOED
STILETTOES
STILETTOING
STILLATORIES
STILLATORY
STILLBIRTH
STILLBIRTHS
STILLBORNS
STILLHOUSE
STILLHOUSES
STILLICIDE
STILLICIDES
STILLIFORM
STILLNESSES
STILLROOMS
STILPNOSIDERITE
STILTBIRDS
STILTEDNESS

STILTEDNESSES
STILTINESS
STILTINESSES
STIMPMETER
STIMPMETERS
STIMULABLE
STIMULANCIES
STIMULANCY
STIMULANTS
STIMULATED
STIMULATER
STIMULATERS
STIMULATES
STIMULATING
STIMULATINGLY
STIMULATION
STIMULATIONS
STIMULATIVE
STIMULATIVES
STIMULATOR
STIMULATORS
STIMULATORY
STINGAREES
STINGBULLS
STINGFISHES
STINGINESS
STINGINESSES
STINGINGLY
STINGINGNESS
STINGINGNESSES
STINKEROOS
STINKHORNS
STINKINGLY
STINKINGNESS
STINKINGNESSES
STINKSTONE
STINKSTONES
STINKWEEDS
STINKWOODS
STINTEDNESS
STINTEDNESSES
STINTINGLY
STIPELLATE
STIPENDIARIES
STIPENDIARY
STIPENDIATE
STIPENDIATED
STIPENDIATES
STIPENDIATING
STIPITIFORM
STIPPLINGS
STIPULABLE
STIPULACEOUS
STIPULATED
STIPULATES
STIPULATING
STIPULATION
STIPULATIONS
STIPULATOR

STIPULATORS
STIPULATORY
STIRABOUTS
STIRPICULTURE
STIRPICULTURES
STIRRINGLY
STITCHCRAFT
STITCHCRAFTS
STITCHERIES
STITCHINGS
STITCHWORK
STITCHWORKS
STITCHWORT
STITCHWORTS
STOCHASTIC
STOCHASTICALLY
STOCKADING
STOCKBREEDER
STOCKBREEDERS
STOCKBREEDING
STOCKBREEDINGS
STOCKBROKER
STOCKBROKERAGE
STOCKBROKERAGES
STOCKBROKERS
STOCKBROKING
STOCKBROKINGS
STOCKFISHES
STOCKHOLDER
STOCKHOLDERS
STOCKHOLDING
STOCKHOLDINGS
STOCKHORNS
STOCKHORSE
STOCKHORSES
STOCKINESS
STOCKINESSES
STOCKINETS
STOCKINETTE
STOCKINETTES
STOCKINGED
STOCKINGER
STOCKINGERS
STOCKINGLESS
STOCKISHLY
STOCKISHNESS
STOCKISHNESSES
STOCKJOBBER
STOCKJOBBERIES
STOCKJOBBERS
STOCKJOBBERY
STOCKJOBBING
STOCKJOBBINGS
STOCKKEEPER
STOCKKEEPERS
STOCKLISTS
STOCKLOCKS
STOCKPILED
STOCKPILER

STOCKPILERS
STOCKPILES
STOCKPILING
STOCKPILINGS
STOCKPUNISHT
STOCKROOMS
STOCKROUTE
STOCKROUTES
STOCKTAKEN
STOCKTAKES
STOCKTAKING
STOCKTAKINGS
STOCKWORKS
STOCKYARDS
STODGINESS
STODGINESSES
STOECHIOLOGICAL
STOECHIOLOGIES
STOECHIOLOGY
STOECHIOMETRIC
STOECHIOMETRIES
STOECHIOMETRY
STOICALNESS
STOICALNESSES
STOICHEIOLOGIES
STOICHEIOLOGY
STOICHEIOMETRIC
STOICHEIOMETRY
STOICHIOLOGICAL
STOICHIOLOGIES
STOICHIOLOGY
STOICHIOMETRIC
STOICHIOMETRIES
STOICHIOMETRY
STOITERING
STOKEHOLDS
STOKEHOLES
STOLENWISE
STOLIDITIES
STOLIDNESS
STOLIDNESSES
STOLONIFEROUS
STOMACHACHE
STOMACHACHES
STOMACHERS
STOMACHFUL
STOMACHFULNESS
STOMACHFULS
STOMACHICAL
STOMACHICS
STOMACHING
STOMACHLESS
STOMACHOUS
STOMATITIC
STOMATITIDES
STOMATITIS
STOMATITISES
STOMATODAEA
STOMATODAEUM

STOMATOGASTRIC
STOMATOLOGICAL
STOMATOLOGIES
STOMATOLOGY
STOMATOPLASTIES
STOMATOPLASTY
STOMATOPOD
STOMATOPODS
STOMODAEAL
STOMODAEUM
STOMODAEUMS
STOMODEUMS
STONEBOATS
STONEBORER
STONEBORERS
STONEBRASH
STONEBRASHES
STONEBREAK
STONEBREAKS
STONECASTS
STONECHATS
STONECROPS
STONECUTTER
STONECUTTERS
STONECUTTING
STONECUTTINGS
STONEFISHES
STONEFLIES
STONEGROUND
STONEHANDS
STONEHORSE
STONEHORSES
STONELESSNESS
STONELESSNESSES
STONEMASON
STONEMASONRIES
STONEMASONRY
STONEMASONS
STONESHOTS
STONEWALLED
STONEWALLER
STONEWALLERS
STONEWALLING
STONEWALLINGS
STONEWALLS
STONEWARES
STONEWASHED
STONEWASHES
STONEWASHING
STONEWORKER
STONEWORKERS
STONEWORKS
STONEWORTS
STONINESSES
STONISHING
STONKERING
STONYHEARTED
STOOLBALLS
STOOPBALLS

STOOPINGLY
STOPLIGHTS
STOPPERING
STOPWATCHES
STOREFRONT
STOREFRONTS
STOREHOUSE
STOREHOUSES
STOREKEEPER
STOREKEEPERS
STOREKEEPING
STOREKEEPINGS
STOREROOMS
STORESHIPS
STORIETTES
STORIOLOGIES
STORIOLOGIST
STORIOLOGISTS
STORIOLOGY
STORKSBILL
STORKSBILLS
STORMBIRDS
STORMBOUND
STORMFULLY
STORMFULNESS
STORMFULNESSES
STORMINESS
STORMINESSES
STORMPROOF
STORYBOARD
STORYBOARDED
STORYBOARDING
STORYBOARDS
STORYBOOKS
STORYETTES
STORYLINES
STORYTELLER
STORYTELLERS
STORYTELLING
STORYTELLINGS
STOTTERING
STOUTENING
STOUTHEARTED
STOUTHEARTEDLY
STOUTHERIE
STOUTHERIES
STOUTHRIEF
STOUTHRIEFS
STOUTNESSES
STOVEPIPES
STRABISMAL
STRABISMIC
STRABISMICAL
STRABISMOMETER
STRABISMOMETERS
STRABISMUS
STRABISMUSES
STRABOMETER
STRABOMETERS

STRABOTOMIES

STRABOTOMIES
STRABOTOMY
STRACCHINI
STRACCHINO
STRADDLEBACK
STRADDLERS
STRADDLING
STRAGGLERS
STRAGGLIER
STRAGGLIEST
STRAGGLING
STRAGGLINGLY
STRAGGLINGS
STRAICHTER
STRAICHTEST
STRAIGHTAWAY
STRAIGHTAWAYS
STRAIGHTBRED
STRAIGHTBREDS
STRAIGHTED
STRAIGHTEDGE
STRAIGHTEDGED
STRAIGHTEDGES
STRAIGHTEN
STRAIGHTENED
STRAIGHTENER
STRAIGHTENERS
STRAIGHTENING
STRAIGHTENS
STRAIGHTER
STRAIGHTEST
STRAIGHTFORTH
STRAIGHTFORWARD
STRAIGHTING
STRAIGHTISH
STRAIGHTJACKET
STRAIGHTJACKETS
STRAIGHTLACED
STRAIGHTLY
STRAIGHTNESS
STRAIGHTNESSES
STRAIGHTWAY
STRAIGHTWAYS
STRAINEDLY
STRAININGS
STRAITENED
STRAITENING
STRAITJACKET
STRAITJACKETED
STRAITJACKETING
STRAITJACKETS
STRAITLACED
STRAITLACEDLY
STRAITLACEDNESS
STRAITNESS
STRAITNESSES
STRAITWAISTCOAT
STRAMACONS
STRAMASHED

STRAMASHES
STRAMASHING
STRAMAZONS
STRAMINEOUS
STRAMONIES
STRAMONIUM
STRAMONIUMS
STRANDEDNESS
STRANDEDNESSES
STRANDFLAT
STRANDFLATS
STRANDLINE
STRANDLINES
STRANDWOLF
STRANDWOLVES
STRANGENESS
STRANGENESSES
STRANGERED
STRANGERING
STRANGLEHOLD
STRANGLEHOLDS
STRANGLEMENT
STRANGLEMENTS
STRANGLERS
STRANGLING
STRANGULATE
STRANGULATED
STRANGULATES
STRANGULATING
STRANGULATION
STRANGULATIONS
STRANGURIES
STRAPHANGED
STRAPHANGER
STRAPHANGERS
STRAPHANGING
STRAPHANGINGS
STRAPHANGS
STRAPLESSES
STRAPLINES
STRAPONTIN
STRAPONTINS
STRAPPADOED
STRAPPADOES
STRAPPADOING
STRAPPADOS
STRAPPIEST
STRAPPINGS
STRAPWORTS
STRATAGEMS
STRATEGETIC
STRATEGETICAL
STRATEGICAL
STRATEGICALLY
STRATEGICS
STRATEGIES
STRATEGISE
STRATEGISED
STRATEGISES

STRATEGISING
STRATEGIST
STRATEGISTS
STRATEGIZE
STRATEGIZED
STRATEGIZES
STRATEGIZING
STRATHSPEY
STRATHSPEYS
STRATICULATE
STRATICULATION
STRATICULATIONS
STRATIFICATION
STRATIFICATIONS
STRATIFIED
STRATIFIES
STRATIFORM
STRATIFYING
STRATIGRAPHER
STRATIGRAPHERS
STRATIGRAPHIC
STRATIGRAPHICAL
STRATIGRAPHIES
STRATIGRAPHIST
STRATIGRAPHISTS
STRATIGRAPHY
STRATOCRACIES
STRATOCRACY
STRATOCRAT
STRATOCRATIC
STRATOCRATS
STRATOCUMULI
STRATOCUMULUS
STRATOPAUSE
STRATOPAUSES
STRATOSPHERE
STRATOSPHERES
STRATOSPHERIC
STRATOSPHERICAL
STRATOTANKER
STRATOTANKERS
STRATOVOLCANO
STRATOVOLCANOES
STRATOVOLCANOS
STRAUCHTED
STRAUCHTER
STRAUCHTEST
STRAUCHTING
STRAUGHTED
STRAUGHTER
STRAUGHTEST
STRAUGHTING
STRAVAGING
STRAVAIGED
STRAVAIGER
STRAVAIGERS
STRAVAIGING
STRAWBERRIES
STRAWBERRY

STRAWBOARD
STRAWBOARDS
STRAWFLOWER
STRAWFLOWERS
STRAWWEIGHT
STRAWWEIGHTS
STRAWWORMS
STRAYLINGS
STREAKIEST
STREAKINESS
STREAKINESSES
STREAKINGS
STREAKLIKE
STREAMBEDS
STREAMERED
STREAMIEST
STREAMINESS
STREAMINESSES
STREAMINGLY
STREAMINGS
STREAMLESS
STREAMLETS
STREAMLIKE
STREAMLINE
STREAMLINED
STREAMLINER
STREAMLINERS
STREAMLINES
STREAMLING
STREAMLINGS
STREAMLINING
STREAMSIDE
STREAMSIDES
STREETAGES
STREETBOYS
STREETCARS
STREETFULS
STREETIEST
STREETKEEPER
STREETKEEPERS
STREETLAMP
STREETLAMPS
STREETLIGHT
STREETLIGHTS
STREETROOM
STREETROOMS
STREETSCAPE
STREETSCAPES
STREETSMART
STREETWALKER
STREETWALKERS
STREETWALKING
STREETWALKINGS
STREETWARD
STREETWARDS
STREETWEAR
STREETWEARS
STREETWISE
STREIGNING

STRELITZES
STRELITZIA
STRELITZIAS
STRENGTHEN
STRENGTHENED
STRENGTHENER
STRENGTHENERS
STRENGTHENING
STRENGTHENINGS
STRENGTHENS
STRENGTHFUL
STRENGTHLESS
STRENUITIES
STRENUOSITIES
STRENUOSITY
STRENUOUSLY
STRENUOUSNESS
STRENUOUSNESSES
STREPEROUS
STREPHOSYMBOLIA
STREPITANT
STREPITATION
STREPITATIONS
STREPITOSO
STREPITOUS
STREPSIPTEROUS
STREPTOBACILLI
STREPTOBACILLUS
STREPTOCARPUS
STREPTOCARPUSES
STREPTOCOCCAL
STREPTOCOCCI
STREPTOCOCCIC
STREPTOCOCCUS
STREPTOKINASE
STREPTOKINASES
STREPTOLYSIN
STREPTOLYSINS
STREPTOMYCES
STREPTOMYCETE
STREPTOMYCETES
STREPTOMYCIN
STREPTOMYCINS
STREPTOSOLEN
STREPTOSOLENS
STREPTOTHRICIN
STREPTOTHRICINS
STRESSBUSTER
STRESSBUSTERS
STRESSBUSTING
STRESSFULLY
STRESSFULNESS
STRESSFULNESSES
STRESSLESS
STRESSLESSNESS
STRETCHABILITY
STRETCHABLE
STRETCHERED
STRETCHERING

STRETCHERS
STRETCHIER
STRETCHIEST
STRETCHINESS
STRETCHINESSES
STRETCHING
STRETCHINGS
STRETCHLESS
STRETCHMARKS
STREWMENTS
STRIATIONS
STRIATURES
STRICKENLY
STRICKLING
STRICTIONS
STRICTNESS
STRICTNESSES
STRICTURED
STRICTURES
STRIDDLING
STRIDELEGGED
STRIDELEGS
STRIDENCES
STRIDENCIES
STRIDENTLY
STRIDEWAYS
STRIDULANCE
STRIDULANCES
STRIDULANT
STRIDULANTLY
STRIDULATE
STRIDULATED
STRIDULATES
STRIDULATING
STRIDULATION
STRIDULATIONS
STRIDULATOR
STRIDULATORS
STRIDULATORY
STRIDULOUS
STRIDULOUSLY
STRIDULOUSNESS
STRIFELESS
STRIGIFORM
STRIKEBOUND
STRIKEBREAKER
STRIKEBREAKERS
STRIKEBREAKING
STRIKEBREAKINGS
STRIKELESS
STRIKEOUTS
STRIKEOVER
STRIKEOVERS
STRIKINGLY
STRIKINGNESS
STRIKINGNESSES
STRINGBOARD
STRINGBOARDS
STRINGCOURSE

STRINGCOURSES
STRINGENCIES
STRINGENCY
STRINGENDO
STRINGENTLY
STRINGENTNESS
STRINGENTNESSES
STRINGHALT
STRINGHALTED
STRINGHALTS
STRINGIEST
STRINGINESS
STRINGINESSES
STRINGINGS
STRINGLESS
STRINGLIKE
STRINGPIECE
STRINGPIECES
STRINGYBARK
STRINGYBARKS
STRINKLING
STRINKLINGS
STRIPAGRAM
STRIPAGRAMS
STRIPELESS
STRIPINESS
STRIPINESSES
STRIPLINGS
STRIPPABLE
STRIPPERGRAM
STRIPPERGRAMS
STRIPPINGS
STRIPTEASE
STRIPTEASER
STRIPTEASERS
STRIPTEASES
STRIVINGLY
STROBILACEOUS
STROBILATE
STROBILATED
STROBILATES
STROBILATING
STROBILATION
STROBILATIONS
STROBILIFORM
STROBILINE
STROBILISATION
STROBILISATIONS
STROBILIZATION
STROBILIZATIONS
STROBILOID
STROBILUSES
STROBOSCOPE
STROBOSCOPES
STROBOSCOPIC
STROBOSCOPICAL
STROBOTRON
STROBOTRONS
STRODDLING

STROGANOFF
STROGANOFFS
STROKEPLAY
STROLLINGS
STROMATOLITE
STROMATOLITES
STROMATOLITIC
STROMATOUS
STROMBULIFEROUS
STROMBULIFORM
STROMBUSES
STRONGARMED
STRONGARMING
STRONGARMS
STRONGBOXES
STRONGHOLD
STRONGHOLDS
STRONGNESS
STRONGNESSES
STRONGPOINT
STRONGPOINTS
STRONGROOM
STRONGROOMS
STRONGYLES
STRONGYLOID
STRONGYLOIDOSES
STRONGYLOIDOSIS
STRONGYLOIDS
STRONGYLOSES
STRONGYLOSIS
STRONTIANITE
STRONTIANITES
STRONTIANS
STRONTIUMS
STROPHANTHIN
STROPHANTHINS
STROPHANTHUS
STROPHANTHUSES
STROPHICAL
STROPHIOLATE
STROPHIOLATED
STROPHIOLE
STROPHIOLES
STROPHOIDS
STROPHULUS
STROPPIEST
STROPPINESS
STROPPINESSES
STROUDINGS
STROUPACHS
STRUCTURAL
STRUCTURALISE
STRUCTURALISED
STRUCTURALISES
STRUCTURALISING
STRUCTURALISM
STRUCTURALISMS
STRUCTURALIST
STRUCTURALISTS

STRUCTURALIZE	STULTIFICATIONS	STYLOGRAPHIES	SUBALTERNITY
STRUCTURALIZED	STULTIFIED	STYLOGRAPHS	SUBALTERNS
STRUCTURALIZES	STULTIFIER	STYLOGRAPHY	SUBANGULAR
STRUCTURALIZING	STULTIFIERS	STYLOLITES	SUBANTARCTIC
STRUCTURALLY	STULTIFIES	STYLOLITIC	SUBAPOSTOLIC
STRUCTURATION	STULTIFYING	STYLOMETRIES	SUBAPPEARANCE
STRUCTURATIONS	STUMBLEBUM	STYLOMETRY	SUBAPPEARANCES
STRUCTURED	STUMBLEBUMS	STYLOPHONE	SUBAQUATIC
STRUCTURELESS	STUMBLIEST	STYLOPHONES	SUBAQUEOUS
STRUCTURES	STUMBLINGLY	STYLOPISED	SUBARACHNOID
STRUCTURING	STUMPINESS	STYLOPISES	SUBARACHNOIDAL
STRUGGLERS	STUMPINESSES	STYLOPISING	SUBARBOREAL
STRUGGLING	STUMPWORKS	STYLOPIZED	SUBARBORESCENT
STRUGGLINGLY	STUNNINGLY	STYLOPIZES	SUBARCTICS
STRUGGLINGS	STUNTEDNESS	STYLOPIZING	SUBARCUATE
STRUMITISES	STUNTEDNESSES	STYLOPODIA	SUBARCUATION
STRUMPETED	STUNTWOMAN	STYLOPODIUM	SUBARCUATIONS
STRUMPETING	STUNTWOMEN	STYLOSTIXES	SUBARRATION
STRUTHIOID	STUPEFACIENT	STYLOSTIXIS	SUBARRATIONS
STRUTHIOIDS	STUPEFACIENTS	STYPTICITIES	SUBARRHATION
STRUTHIOUS	STUPEFACTION	STYPTICITY	SUBARRHATIONS
STRUTTINGLY	STUPEFACTIONS	STYRACACEOUS	SUBARTICLE
STRUTTINGS	STUPEFACTIVE	STYROFOAMS	SUBARTICLES
STRYCHNIAS	STUPEFIERS	SUABILITIES	SUBASSEMBLE
STRYCHNINE	STUPEFYING	SUASIVENESS	SUBASSEMBLED
STRYCHNINED	STUPEFYINGLY	SUASIVENESSES	SUBASSEMBLES
STRYCHNINES	STUPENDIOUS	SUAVENESSES	SUBASSEMBLIES
STRYCHNINING	STUPENDOUS	SUAVEOLENT	SUBASSEMBLING
STRYCHNINISM	STUPENDOUSLY	SUBABDOMINAL	SUBASSEMBLY
STRYCHNINISMS	STUPENDOUSNESS	SUBACETATE	SUBASSOCIATION
STRYCHNISM	STUPIDITIES	SUBACETATES	SUBASSOCIATIONS
STRYCHNISMS	STUPIDNESS	SUBACIDITIES	SUBATMOSPHERIC
STUBBINESS	STUPIDNESSES	SUBACIDITY	SUBATOMICS
STUBBINESSES	STUPRATING	SUBACIDNESS	SUBAUDIBLE
STUBBLIEST	STUPRATION	SUBACIDNESSES	SUBAUDITION
STUBBORNED	STUPRATIONS	SUBACTIONS	SUBAUDITIONS
STUBBORNER	STURDINESS	SUBACUTELY	SUBAURICULAR
STUBBORNEST	STURDINESSES	SUBADOLESCENT	SUBAVERAGE
STUBBORNING	STUTTERERS	SUBADOLESCENTS	SUBAXILLARY
STUBBORNLY	STUTTERING	SUBAERIALLY	SUBBASEMENT
STUBBORNNESS	STUTTERINGLY	SUBAFFLUENT	SUBBASEMENTS
STUBBORNNESSES	STUTTERINGS	SUBAGENCIES	SUBBITUMINOUS
STUCCOWORK	STYLEBOOKS	SUBAGGREGATE	SUBBRANCHES
STUCCOWORKS	STYLELESSNESS	SUBAGGREGATES	SUBBUREAUS
STUDDINGSAIL	STYLELESSNESSES	SUBAGGREGATION	SUBBUREAUX
STUDDINGSAILS	STYLIFEROUS	SUBAGGREGATIONS	SUBCABINET
STUDENTRIES	STYLISATION	SUBAHDARIES	SUBCABINETS
STUDENTSHIP	STYLISATIONS	SUBAHSHIPS	SUBCALIBER
STUDENTSHIPS	STYLISHNESS	SUBALLIANCE	SUBCALIBRE
STUDFISHES	STYLISHNESSES	SUBALLIANCES	SUBCANTORS
STUDHORSES	STYLISTICALLY	SUBALLOCATION	SUBCAPSULAR
STUDIEDNESS	STYLISTICS	SUBALLOCATIONS	SUBCARDINAL
STUDIEDNESSES	STYLITISMS	SUBALTERNANT	SUBCARDINALS
STUDIOUSLY	STYLIZATION	SUBALTERNANTS	SUBCARRIER
STUDIOUSNESS	STYLIZATIONS	SUBALTERNATE	SUBCARRIERS
STUDIOUSNESSES	STYLOBATES	SUBALTERNATES	SUBCATEGORIES
STUFFINESS	STYLOGRAPH	SUBALTERNATION	SUBCATEGORISE
STUFFINESSES	STYLOGRAPHIC	SUBALTERNATIONS	SUBCATEGORISED
STULTIFICATION	STYLOGRAPHICAL	SUBALTERNITIES	SUBCATEGORISES

SUBCATEGORISING
SUBCATEGORIZE
SUBCATEGORIZED
SUBCATEGORIZES
SUBCATEGORIZING
SUBCATEGORY
SUBCAVITIES
SUBCEILING
SUBCEILINGS
SUBCELESTIAL
SUBCELESTIALS
SUBCELLARS
SUBCELLULAR
SUBCENTERS
SUBCENTRAL
SUBCENTRALLY
SUBCEPTION
SUBCEPTIONS
SUBCHANTER
SUBCHANTERS
SUBCHAPTER
SUBCHAPTERS
SUBCHARTER
SUBCHARTERS
SUBCHASERS
SUBCHELATE
SUBCHLORIDE
SUBCHLORIDES
SUBCIRCUIT
SUBCIRCUITS
SUBCIVILISATION
SUBCIVILISED
SUBCIVILIZATION
SUBCIVILIZED
SUBCLASSED
SUBCLASSES
SUBCLASSIFIED
SUBCLASSIFIES
SUBCLASSIFY
SUBCLASSIFYING
SUBCLASSING
SUBCLAUSES
SUBCLAVIAN
SUBCLAVIANS
SUBCLAVICULAR
SUBCLIMACTIC
SUBCLIMAXES
SUBCLINICAL
SUBCLINICALLY
SUBCLUSTER
SUBCLUSTERED
SUBCLUSTERING
SUBCLUSTERS
SUBCOLLECTION
SUBCOLLECTIONS
SUBCOLLEGE
SUBCOLLEGIATE
SUBCOLONIES
SUBCOMMISSION

SUBCOMMISSIONED
SUBCOMMISSIONER
SUBCOMMISSIONS
SUBCOMMITTEE
SUBCOMMITTEES
SUBCOMMUNITIES
SUBCOMMUNITY
SUBCOMPACT
SUBCOMPACTS
SUBCOMPONENT
SUBCOMPONENTS
SUBCONSCIOUS
SUBCONSCIOUSES
SUBCONSCIOUSLY
SUBCONSULS
SUBCONTIGUOUS
SUBCONTINENT
SUBCONTINENTAL
SUBCONTINENTS
SUBCONTINUOUS
SUBCONTRACT
SUBCONTRACTED
SUBCONTRACTING
SUBCONTRACTINGS
SUBCONTRACTOR
SUBCONTRACTORS
SUBCONTRACTS
SUBCONTRAOCTAVE
SUBCONTRARIES
SUBCONTRARIETY
SUBCONTRARY
SUBCOOLING
SUBCORDATE
SUBCORIACEOUS
SUBCORTEXES
SUBCORTICAL
SUBCORTICES
SUBCOSTALS
SUBCOUNTIES
SUBCRANIAL
SUBCRITICAL
SUBCRUSTAL
SUBCULTURAL
SUBCULTURALLY
SUBCULTURE
SUBCULTURED
SUBCULTURES
SUBCULTURING
SUBCURATIVE
SUBCUTANEOUS
SUBCUTANEOUSLY
SUBCUTISES
SUBDEACONATE
SUBDEACONATES
SUBDEACONRIES
SUBDEACONRY
SUBDEACONS
SUBDEACONSHIP
SUBDEACONSHIPS

SUBDEALERS
SUBDEANERIES
SUBDEANERY
SUBDEBUTANTE
SUBDEBUTANTES
SUBDECANAL
SUBDECISION
SUBDECISIONS
SUBDELIRIA
SUBDELIRIOUS
SUBDELIRIUM
SUBDELIRIUMS
SUBDEPARTMENT
SUBDEPARTMENTS
SUBDEPUTIES
SUBDERMALLY
SUBDEVELOPMENT
SUBDEVELOPMENTS
SUBDIACONAL
SUBDIACONATE
SUBDIACONATES
SUBDIALECT
SUBDIALECTS
SUBDIRECTOR
SUBDIRECTORS
SUBDISCIPLINE
SUBDISCIPLINES
SUBDISTRICT
SUBDISTRICTS
SUBDIVIDABLE
SUBDIVIDED
SUBDIVIDER
SUBDIVIDERS
SUBDIVIDES
SUBDIVIDING
SUBDIVISIBLE
SUBDIVISION
SUBDIVISIONAL
SUBDIVISIONS
SUBDIVISIVE
SUBDOMINANT
SUBDOMINANTS
SUBDUCTING
SUBDUCTION
SUBDUCTIONS
SUBDUEDNESS
SUBDUEDNESSES
SUBDUEMENT
SUBDUEMENTS
SUBDUPLICATE
SUBECONOMIC
SUBECONOMIES
SUBECONOMY
SUBEDITING
SUBEDITORIAL
SUBEDITORS
SUBEDITORSHIP
SUBEDITORSHIPS
SUBEMPLOYED

SUBEMPLOYMENT
SUBEMPLOYMENTS
SUBENTRIES
SUBEPIDERMAL
SUBEQUATORIAL
SUBERISATION
SUBERISATIONS
SUBERISING
SUBERIZATION
SUBERIZATIONS
SUBERIZING
SUBFACTORIAL
SUBFACTORIALS
SUBFAMILIES
SUBFERTILE
SUBFERTILITIES
SUBFERTILITY
SUBFEUDATION
SUBFEUDATIONS
SUBFEUDATORY
SUBFOSSILS
SUBFREEZING
SUBFUSCOUS
SUBGENERATION
SUBGENERATIONS
SUBGENERIC
SUBGENERICALLY
SUBGENUSES
SUBGLACIAL
SUBGLACIALLY
SUBGLOBOSE
SUBGLOBULAR
SUBGOVERNMENT
SUBGOVERNMENTS
SUBGROUPED
SUBGROUPING
SUBHARMONIC
SUBHARMONICS
SUBHASTATION
SUBHASTATIONS
SUBHEADING
SUBHEADINGS
SUBIMAGINAL
SUBIMAGINES
SUBIMAGOES
SUBINCISED
SUBINCISES
SUBINCISING
SUBINCISION
SUBINCISIONS
SUBINDEXES
SUBINDICATE
SUBINDICATED
SUBINDICATES
SUBINDICATING
SUBINDICATION
SUBINDICATIONS
SUBINDICATIVE
SUBINDICES

SUBINDUSTRIES
SUBINDUSTRY
SUBINFEUDATE
SUBINFEUDATED
SUBINFEUDATES
SUBINFEUDATING
SUBINFEUDATION
SUBINFEUDATIONS
SUBINFEUDATORY
SUBINFEUDED
SUBINFEUDING
SUBINFEUDS
SUBINHIBITORY
SUBINSINUATION
SUBINSINUATIONS
SUBINSPECTOR
SUBINSPECTORS
SUBINTELLECTION
SUBINTELLIGENCE
SUBINTELLIGITUR
SUBINTERVAL
SUBINTERVALS
SUBINTRANT
SUBINTRODUCE
SUBINTRODUCED
SUBINTRODUCES
SUBINTRODUCING
SUBINVOLUTION
SUBINVOLUTIONS
SUBIRRIGATE
SUBIRRIGATED
SUBIRRIGATES
SUBIRRIGATING
SUBIRRIGATION
SUBIRRIGATIONS
SUBITANEOUS
SUBITISING
SUBITIZING
SUBJACENCIES
SUBJACENCY
SUBJACENTLY
SUBJECTABILITY
SUBJECTABLE
SUBJECTIFIED
SUBJECTIFIES
SUBJECTIFY
SUBJECTIFYING
SUBJECTING
SUBJECTION
SUBJECTIONS
SUBJECTIVE
SUBJECTIVELY
SUBJECTIVENESS
SUBJECTIVES
SUBJECTIVISE
SUBJECTIVISED
SUBJECTIVISES
SUBJECTIVISING
SUBJECTIVISM

SUBJECTIVISMS
SUBJECTIVIST
SUBJECTIVISTIC
SUBJECTIVISTS
SUBJECTIVITIES
SUBJECTIVITY
SUBJECTIVIZE
SUBJECTIVIZED
SUBJECTIVIZES
SUBJECTIVIZING
SUBJECTLESS
SUBJECTSHIP
SUBJECTSHIPS
SUBJOINDER
SUBJOINDERS
SUBJOINING
SUBJUGABLE
SUBJUGATED
SUBJUGATES
SUBJUGATING
SUBJUGATION
SUBJUGATIONS
SUBJUGATOR
SUBJUGATORS
SUBJUNCTION
SUBJUNCTIONS
SUBJUNCTIVE
SUBJUNCTIVELY
SUBJUNCTIVES
SUBKINGDOM
SUBKINGDOMS
SUBLANCEOLATE
SUBLANGUAGE
SUBLANGUAGES
SUBLAPSARIAN
SUBLAPSARIANISM
SUBLAPSARIANS
SUBLATIONS
SUBLEASING
SUBLESSEES
SUBLESSORS
SUBLETHALLY
SUBLETTERS
SUBLETTING
SUBLETTINGS
SUBLIBRARIAN
SUBLIBRARIANS
SUBLICENSE
SUBLICENSED
SUBLICENSES
SUBLICENSING
SUBLIEUTENANCY
SUBLIEUTENANT
SUBLIEUTENANTS
SUBLIMABLE
SUBLIMATED
SUBLIMATES
SUBLIMATING
SUBLIMATION

SUBLIMATIONS
SUBLIMENESS
SUBLIMENESSES
SUBLIMINAL
SUBLIMINALLY
SUBLIMINALS
SUBLIMINGS
SUBLIMISED
SUBLIMISES
SUBLIMISING
SUBLIMITIES
SUBLIMIZED
SUBLIMIZES
SUBLIMIZING
SUBLINEATION
SUBLINEATIONS
SUBLINGUAL
SUBLITERACIES
SUBLITERACY
SUBLITERARY
SUBLITERATE
SUBLITERATES
SUBLITERATURE
SUBLITERATURES
SUBLITTORAL
SUBLITTORALS
SUBLUXATED
SUBLUXATES
SUBLUXATING
SUBLUXATION
SUBLUXATIONS
SUBMANAGER
SUBMANAGERS
SUBMANDIBULAR
SUBMANDIBULARS
SUBMARGINAL
SUBMARGINALLY
SUBMARINED
SUBMARINER
SUBMARINERS
SUBMARINES
SUBMARINING
SUBMARKETS
SUBMATRICES
SUBMATRIXES
SUBMAXILLARIES
SUBMAXILLARY
SUBMAXIMAL
SUBMEDIANT
SUBMEDIANTS
SUBMERGEMENT
SUBMERGEMENTS
SUBMERGENCE
SUBMERGENCES
SUBMERGIBILITY
SUBMERGIBLE
SUBMERGIBLES
SUBMERGING
SUBMERSIBILITY

SUBMERSIBLE
SUBMERSIBLES
SUBMERSING
SUBMERSION
SUBMERSIONS
SUBMETACENTRIC
SUBMETACENTRICS
SUBMICROGRAM
SUBMICRONS
SUBMICROSCOPIC
SUBMILLIMETER
SUBMINIATURE
SUBMINIATURES
SUBMINIATURISE
SUBMINIATURISED
SUBMINIATURISES
SUBMINIATURIZE
SUBMINIATURIZED
SUBMINIATURIZES
SUBMINIMAL
SUBMINISTER
SUBMINISTERS
SUBMISSIBLE
SUBMISSION
SUBMISSIONS
SUBMISSIVE
SUBMISSIVELY
SUBMISSIVENESS
SUBMISSNESS
SUBMISSNESSES
SUBMITTABLE
SUBMITTALS
SUBMITTERS
SUBMITTING
SUBMITTINGS
SUBMOLECULE
SUBMOLECULES
SUBMONTANE
SUBMONTANELY
SUBMUCOSAE
SUBMUCOSAL
SUBMUCOSAS
SUBMULTIPLE
SUBMULTIPLES
SUBMUNITION
SUBMUNITIONS
SUBNASCENT
SUBNATIONAL
SUBNATURAL
SUBNETWORK
SUBNETWORKED
SUBNETWORKING
SUBNETWORKS
SUBNORMALITIES
SUBNORMALITY
SUBNORMALLY
SUBNORMALS
SUBNUCLEAR
SUBNUCLEUS

SUBNUCLEUSES
SUBOCCIPITAL
SUBOCEANIC
SUBOCTAVES
SUBOCTUPLE
SUBOFFICER
SUBOFFICERS
SUBOFFICES
SUBOPERCULA
SUBOPERCULAR
SUBOPERCULUM
SUBOPTIMAL
SUBOPTIMISATION
SUBOPTIMISE
SUBOPTIMISED
SUBOPTIMISES
SUBOPTIMISING
SUBOPTIMIZATION
SUBOPTIMIZE
SUBOPTIMIZED
SUBOPTIMIZES
SUBOPTIMIZING
SUBOPTIMUM
SUBORBICULAR
SUBORBITAL
SUBORDINAL
SUBORDINANCIES
SUBORDINANCY
SUBORDINARIES
SUBORDINARY
SUBORDINATE
SUBORDINATED
SUBORDINATELY
SUBORDINATENESS
SUBORDINATES
SUBORDINATING
SUBORDINATION
SUBORDINATIONS
SUBORDINATIVE
SUBORDINATOR
SUBORDINATORS
SUBORGANISATION
SUBORGANIZATION
SUBORNATION
SUBORNATIONS
SUBORNATIVE
SUBOSCINES
SUBPANATION
SUBPANATIONS
SUBPARAGRAPH
SUBPARAGRAPHS
SUBPARALLEL
SUBPENAING
SUBPERIODS
SUBPHRENIC
SUBPOENAED
SUBPOENAING
SUBPOPULATION
SUBPOPULATIONS

SUBPOTENCIES
SUBPOTENCY
SUBPREFECT
SUBPREFECTS
SUBPREFECTURE
SUBPREFECTURES
SUBPRIMATE
SUBPRIMATES
SUBPRINCIPAL
SUBPRINCIPALS
SUBPRIORESS
SUBPRIORESSES
SUBPROBLEM
SUBPROBLEMS
SUBPROCESS
SUBPROCESSES
SUBPRODUCT
SUBPRODUCTS
SUBPROFESSIONAL
SUBPROGRAM
SUBPROGRAMS
SUBPROJECT
SUBPROJECTS
SUBPROLETARIAT
SUBPROLETARIATS
SUBRATIONAL
SUBREFERENCE
SUBREFERENCES
SUBREGIONAL
SUBREGIONS
SUBREPTION
SUBREPTIONS
SUBREPTITIOUS
SUBREPTITIOUSLY
SUBREPTIVE
SUBROGATED
SUBROGATES
SUBROGATING
SUBROGATION
SUBROGATIONS
SUBROUTINE
SUBROUTINES
SUBSAMPLED
SUBSAMPLES
SUBSAMPLING
SUBSATELLITE
SUBSATELLITES
SUBSATURATED
SUBSATURATION
SUBSATURATIONS
SUBSCAPULAR
SUBSCAPULARS
SUBSCHEMATA
SUBSCIENCE
SUBSCIENCES
SUBSCRIBABLE
SUBSCRIBED
SUBSCRIBER
SUBSCRIBERS

SUBSCRIBES
SUBSCRIBING
SUBSCRIBINGS
SUBSCRIPTION
SUBSCRIPTIONS
SUBSCRIPTIVE
SUBSCRIPTS
SUBSECRETARIES
SUBSECRETARY
SUBSECTION
SUBSECTIONS
SUBSECTORS
SUBSEGMENT
SUBSEGMENTS
SUBSEIZURE
SUBSEIZURES
SUBSELLIUM
SUBSENSIBLE
SUBSENTENCE
SUBSENTENCES
SUBSEQUENCE
SUBSEQUENCES
SUBSEQUENT
SUBSEQUENTIAL
SUBSEQUENTLY
SUBSEQUENTNESS
SUBSEQUENTS
SUBSERVIENCE
SUBSERVIENCES
SUBSERVIENCIES
SUBSERVIENCY
SUBSERVIENT
SUBSERVIENTLY
SUBSERVIENTS
SUBSERVING
SUBSESSILE
SUBSHRUBBY
SUBSIDENCE
SUBSIDENCES
SUBSIDENCIES
SUBSIDENCY
SUBSIDIARIES
SUBSIDIARILY
SUBSIDIARINESS
SUBSIDIARITIES
SUBSIDIARITY
SUBSIDIARY
SUBSIDISABLE
SUBSIDISATION
SUBSIDISATIONS
SUBSIDISED
SUBSIDISER
SUBSIDISERS
SUBSIDISES
SUBSIDISING
SUBSIDIZABLE
SUBSIDIZATION
SUBSIDIZATIONS
SUBSIDIZED

SUBSIDIZER
SUBSIDIZERS
SUBSIDIZES
SUBSIDIZING
SUBSISTENCE
SUBSISTENCES
SUBSISTENT
SUBSISTENTIAL
SUBSISTERS
SUBSISTING
SUBSOCIALLY
SUBSOCIETIES
SUBSOCIETY
SUBSOILERS
SUBSOILING
SUBSOILINGS
SUBSONICALLY
SUBSPECIALISE
SUBSPECIALISED
SUBSPECIALISES
SUBSPECIALISING
SUBSPECIALIST
SUBSPECIALISTS
SUBSPECIALITIES
SUBSPECIALITY
SUBSPECIALIZE
SUBSPECIALIZED
SUBSPECIALIZES
SUBSPECIALIZING
SUBSPECIALTIES
SUBSPECIALTY
SUBSPECIES
SUBSPECIFIC
SUBSPECIFICALLY
SUBSPINOUS
SUBSPONTANEOUS
SUBSTANCELESS
SUBSTANCES
SUBSTANDARD
SUBSTANTIAL
SUBSTANTIALISE
SUBSTANTIALISED
SUBSTANTIALISES
SUBSTANTIALISM
SUBSTANTIALISMS
SUBSTANTIALIST
SUBSTANTIALISTS
SUBSTANTIALITY
SUBSTANTIALIZE
SUBSTANTIALIZED
SUBSTANTIALIZES
SUBSTANTIALLY
SUBSTANTIALNESS
SUBSTANTIALS
SUBSTANTIATE
SUBSTANTIATED
SUBSTANTIATES
SUBSTANTIATING
SUBSTANTIATION

SUBSTANTIATIONS
SUBSTANTIATIVE
SUBSTANTIATOR
SUBSTANTIATORS
SUBSTANTIVAL
SUBSTANTIVALLY
SUBSTANTIVE
SUBSTANTIVELY
SUBSTANTIVENESS
SUBSTANTIVES
SUBSTANTIVISE
SUBSTANTIVISED
SUBSTANTIVISES
SUBSTANTIVISING
SUBSTANTIVITIES
SUBSTANTIVITY
SUBSTANTIVIZE
SUBSTANTIVIZED
SUBSTANTIVIZES
SUBSTANTIVIZING
SUBSTATION
SUBSTATIONS
SUBSTELLAR
SUBSTERNAL
SUBSTITUENT
SUBSTITUENTS
SUBSTITUTABLE
SUBSTITUTE
SUBSTITUTED
SUBSTITUTES
SUBSTITUTING
SUBSTITUTION
SUBSTITUTIONAL
SUBSTITUTIONARY
SUBSTITUTIONS
SUBSTITUTIVE
SUBSTITUTIVELY
SUBSTITUTIVITY
SUBSTRACTED
SUBSTRACTING
SUBSTRACTION
SUBSTRACTIONS
SUBSTRACTOR
SUBSTRACTORS
SUBSTRACTS
SUBSTRATAL
SUBSTRATES
SUBSTRATIVE
SUBSTRATOSPHERE
SUBSTRATUM
SUBSTRATUMS
SUBSTRUCTED
SUBSTRUCTING
SUBSTRUCTION
SUBSTRUCTIONS
SUBSTRUCTS
SUBSTRUCTURAL
SUBSTRUCTURE
SUBSTRUCTURES

SUBSULTIVE
SUBSULTORILY
SUBSULTORY
SUBSULTUSES
SUBSUMABLE
SUBSUMPTION
SUBSUMPTIONS
SUBSUMPTIVE
SUBSURFACE
SUBSURFACES
SUBSYSTEMS
SUBTACKSMAN
SUBTACKSMEN
SUBTANGENT
SUBTANGENTS
SUBTEMPERATE
SUBTENANCIES
SUBTENANCY
SUBTENANTS
SUBTENDING
SUBTENURES
SUBTERFUGE
SUBTERFUGES
SUBTERMINAL
SUBTERNATURAL
SUBTERRAIN
SUBTERRAINS
SUBTERRANE
SUBTERRANEAN
SUBTERRANEANLY
SUBTERRANEANS
SUBTERRANEOUS
SUBTERRANEOUSLY
SUBTERRANES
SUBTERRENE
SUBTERRENES
SUBTERRESTRIAL
SUBTERRESTRIALS
SUBTEXTUAL
SUBTHERAPEUTIC
SUBTHRESHOLD
SUBTILENESS
SUBTILENESSES
SUBTILISATION
SUBTILISATIONS
SUBTILISED
SUBTILISER
SUBTILISERS
SUBTILISES
SUBTILISIN
SUBTILISING
SUBTILISINS
SUBTILITIES
SUBTILIZATION
SUBTILIZATIONS
SUBTILIZED
SUBTILIZER
SUBTILIZERS
SUBTILIZES

SUBTILIZING
SUBTILTIES
SUBTITLING
SUBTITULAR
SUBTLENESS
SUBTLENESSES
SUBTLETIES
SUBTOTALED
SUBTOTALING
SUBTOTALLED
SUBTOTALLING
SUBTOTALLY
SUBTRACTED
SUBTRACTER
SUBTRACTERS
SUBTRACTING
SUBTRACTION
SUBTRACTIONS
SUBTRACTIVE
SUBTRACTOR
SUBTRACTORS
SUBTRAHEND
SUBTRAHENDS
SUBTREASURER
SUBTREASURERS
SUBTREASURIES
SUBTREASURY
SUBTRIANGULAR
SUBTRIPLICATE
SUBTROPICAL
SUBTROPICALLY
SUBTROPICS
SUBTRUDING
SUBTYPICAL
SUBUMBRELLA
SUBUMBRELLAR
SUBUMBRELLAS
SUBUNGULATE
SUBUNGULATES
SUBURBANISATION
SUBURBANISE
SUBURBANISED
SUBURBANISES
SUBURBANISING
SUBURBANISM
SUBURBANISMS
SUBURBANITE
SUBURBANITES
SUBURBANITIES
SUBURBANITY
SUBURBANIZATION
SUBURBANIZE
SUBURBANIZED
SUBURBANIZES
SUBURBANIZING
SUBURBICARIAN
SUBVARIETIES
SUBVARIETY
SUBVASSALS

SUBVENTION
SUBVENTIONARY
SUBVENTIONS
SUBVERSALS
SUBVERSING
SUBVERSION
SUBVERSIONARIES
SUBVERSIONARY
SUBVERSIONS
SUBVERSIVE
SUBVERSIVELY
SUBVERSIVENESS
SUBVERSIVES
SUBVERTEBRAL
SUBVERTERS
SUBVERTICAL
SUBVERTING
SUBVIRUSES
SUBVISIBLE
SUBVITREOUS
SUBVOCALISATION
SUBVOCALISE
SUBVOCALISED
SUBVOCALISES
SUBVOCALISING
SUBVOCALIZATION
SUBVOCALIZE
SUBVOCALIZED
SUBVOCALIZES
SUBVOCALIZING
SUBVOCALLY
SUBWARDENS
SUBWOOFERS
SUBWRITERS
SUCCEDANEA
SUCCEDANEOUS
SUCCEDANEUM
SUCCEDANEUMS
SUCCEEDABLE
SUCCEEDERS
SUCCEEDING
SUCCEEDINGLY
SUCCENTORS
SUCCENTORSHIP
SUCCENTORSHIPS
SUCCESSANTLY
SUCCESSFUL
SUCCESSFULLY
SUCCESSFULNESS
SUCCESSION
SUCCESSIONAL
SUCCESSIONALLY
SUCCESSIONIST
SUCCESSIONISTS
SUCCESSIONLESS
SUCCESSIONS
SUCCESSIVE
SUCCESSIVELY
SUCCESSIVENESS

SUCCESSLESS	SUDORIFEROUS	SUGARALLIE	SULFADIMIDINE
SUCCESSLESSLY	SUDORIFICS	SUGARALLIES	SULFADIMIDINES
SUCCESSLESSNESS	SUDORIPAROUS	SUGARBERRIES	SULFADOXINE
SUCCESSORAL	SUEABILITIES	SUGARBERRY	SULFADOXINES
SUCCESSORS	SUEABILITY	SUGARBUSHES	SULFAMETHAZINE
SUCCESSORSHIP	SUFFERABLE	SUGARCANES	SULFAMETHAZINES
SUCCESSORSHIPS	SUFFERABLENESS	SUGARCOATED	SULFANILAMIDE
SUCCINATES	SUFFERABLY	SUGARCOATING	SULFANILAMIDES
SUCCINCTER	SUFFERANCE	SUGARCOATS	SULFATASES
SUCCINCTEST	SUFFERANCES	SUGARHOUSE	SULFATHIAZOLE
SUCCINCTLY	SUFFERINGLY	SUGARHOUSES	SULFATHIAZOLES
SUCCINCTNESS	SUFFERINGS	SUGARINESS	SULFATIONS
SUCCINCTNESSES	SUFFICIENCE	SUGARINESSES	SULFHYDRYL
SUCCINCTORIA	SUFFICIENCES	SUGARLOAVES	SULFHYDRYLS
SUCCINCTORIES	SUFFICIENCIES	SUGARPLUMS	SULFINPYRAZONE
SUCCINCTORIUM	SUFFICIENCY	SUGGESTERS	SULFINPYRAZONES
SUCCINCTORY	SUFFICIENT	SUGGESTIBILITY	SULFONAMIDE
SUCCINITES	SUFFICIENTLY	SUGGESTIBLE	SULFONAMIDES
SUCCINYLCHOLINE	SUFFICIENTS	SUGGESTIBLENESS	SULFONATED
SUCCORABLE	SUFFICINGNESS	SUGGESTIBLY	SULFONATES
SUCCORLESS	SUFFICINGNESSES	SUGGESTING	SULFONATING
SUCCOTASHES	SUFFIGANCE	SUGGESTION	SULFONATION
SUCCOURABLE	SUFFIGANCES	SUGGESTIONISE	SULFONATIONS
SUCCOURERS	SUFFISANCE	SUGGESTIONISED	SULFONIUMS
SUCCOURING	SUFFISANCES	SUGGESTIONISES	SULFONYLUREA
SUCCOURLESS	SUFFIXATION	SUGGESTIONISING	SULFONYLUREAS
SUCCUBUSES	SUFFIXATIONS	SUGGESTIONISM	SULFOXIDES
SUCCULENCE	SUFFIXIONS	SUGGESTIONISMS	SULFURATED
SUCCULENCES	SUFFLATING	SUGGESTIONIST	SULFURATES
SUCCULENCIES	SUFFLATION	SUGGESTIONISTS	SULFURATING
SUCCULENCY	SUFFLATIONS	SUGGESTIONIZE	SULFURETED
SUCCULENTLY	SUFFOCATED	SUGGESTIONIZED	SULFURETING
SUCCULENTS	SUFFOCATES	SUGGESTIONIZES	SULFURETTED
SUCCUMBERS	SUFFOCATING	SUGGESTIONIZING	SULFURETTING
SUCCUMBING	SUFFOCATINGLY	SUGGESTIONS	SULFURISATION
SUCCURSALE	SUFFOCATINGS	SUGGESTIVE	SULFURISATIONS
SUCCURSALES	SUFFOCATION	SUGGESTIVELY	SULFURISED
SUCCURSALS	SUFFOCATIONS	SUGGESTIVENESS	SULFURISES
SUCCUSSATION	SUFFOCATIVE	SUICIDALLY	SULFURISING
SUCCUSSATIONS	SUFFRAGANS	SUICIDOLOGIES	SULFURIZED
SUCCUSSING	SUFFRAGANSHIP	SUICIDOLOGIST	SULFURIZES
SUCCUSSION	SUFFRAGANSHIPS	SUICIDOLOGISTS	SULFURIZING
SUCCUSSIONS	SUFFRAGETTE	SUICIDOLOGY	SULFUROUSLY
SUCCUSSIVE	SUFFRAGETTES	SUITABILITIES	SULFUROUSNESS
SUCHNESSES	SUFFRAGETTISM	SUITABILITY	SULFUROUSNESSES
SUCKERFISH	SUFFRAGETTISMS	SUITABLENESS	SULKINESSES
SUCKERFISHES	SUFFRAGISM	SUITABLENESSES	SULLENNESS
SUCKFISHES	SUFFRAGISMS	SUITRESSES	SULLENNESSES
SUCRALFATE	SUFFRAGIST	SULCALISED	SULPHACETAMIDE
SUCRALFATES	SUFFRAGISTS	SULCALISES	SULPHACETAMIDES
SUCRALOSES	SUFFRUTESCENT	SULCALISING	SULPHADIAZINE
SUCTIONING	SUFFRUTICOSE	SULCALIZED	SULPHADIAZINES
SUCTORIANS	SUFFUMIGATE	SULCALIZES	SULPHANILAMIDE
SUDATORIES	SUFFUMIGATED	SULCALIZING	SULPHANILAMIDES
SUDATORIUM	SUFFUMIGATES	SULCATIONS	SULPHATASE
SUDATORIUMS	SUFFUMIGATING	SULFACETAMIDE	SULPHATASES
SUDDENNESS	SUFFUMIGATION	SULFACETAMIDES	SULPHATHIAZOLE
SUDDENNESSES	SUFFUMIGATIONS	SULFADIAZINE	SULPHATHIAZOLES
SUDDENTIES	SUFFUSIONS	SULFADIAZINES	SULPHATING

SULPHATION
SULPHATIONS
SULPHHYDRYL
SULPHHYDRYLS
SULPHINPYRAZONE
SULPHINYLS
SULPHONAMIDE
SULPHONAMIDES
SULPHONATE
SULPHONATED
SULPHONATES
SULPHONATING
SULPHONATION
SULPHONATIONS
SULPHONIUM
SULPHONIUMS
SULPHONMETHANE
SULPHONMETHANES
SULPHONYLS
SULPHONYLUREA
SULPHONYLUREAS
SULPHURATE
SULPHURATED
SULPHURATES
SULPHURATING
SULPHURATION
SULPHURATIONS
SULPHURATOR
SULPHURATORS
SULPHUREOUS
SULPHUREOUSLY
SULPHUREOUSNESS
SULPHURETED
SULPHURETING
SULPHURETS
SULPHURETTED
SULPHURETTING
SULPHURING
SULPHURISATION
SULPHURISATIONS
SULPHURISE
SULPHURISED
SULPHURISES
SULPHURISING
SULPHURIZATION
SULPHURIZATIONS
SULPHURIZE
SULPHURIZED
SULPHURIZES
SULPHURIZING
SULPHUROUS
SULPHUROUSLY
SULPHUROUSNESS
SULPHURWORT
SULPHURWORTS
SULPHURYLS
SULTANATES
SULTANESSES
SULTANSHIP

SULTANSHIPS
SULTRINESS
SULTRINESSES
SUMMABILITIES
SUMMABILITY
SUMMARINESS
SUMMARINESSES
SUMMARISABLE
SUMMARISATION
SUMMARISATIONS
SUMMARISED
SUMMARISER
SUMMARISERS
SUMMARISES
SUMMARISING
SUMMARISTS
SUMMARIZABLE
SUMMARIZATION
SUMMARIZATIONS
SUMMARIZED
SUMMARIZER
SUMMARIZERS
SUMMARIZES
SUMMARIZING
SUMMATIONAL
SUMMATIONS
SUMMERHOUSE
SUMMERHOUSES
SUMMERIEST
SUMMERINESS
SUMMERINESSES
SUMMERINGS
SUMMERLESS
SUMMERLIKE
SUMMERLONG
SUMMERSAULT
SUMMERSAULTED
SUMMERSAULTING
SUMMERSAULTS
SUMMERSETS
SUMMERSETTED
SUMMERSETTING
SUMMERTIDE
SUMMERTIDES
SUMMERTIME
SUMMERTIMES
SUMMERWEIGHT
SUMMERWOOD
SUMMERWOODS
SUMMITEERS
SUMMITLESS
SUMMITRIES
SUMMONABLE
SUMMONSING
SUMPHISHNESS
SUMPHISHNESSES
SUMPSIMUSES
SUMPTUOSITIES
SUMPTUOSITY

SUMPTUOUSLY
SUMPTUOUSNESS
SUMPTUOUSNESSES
SUNBATHERS
SUNBATHING
SUNBATHINGS
SUNBERRIES
SUNBONNETED
SUNBONNETS
SUNBURNING
SUNDERABLE
SUNDERANCE
SUNDERANCES
SUNDERINGS
SUNDERMENT
SUNDERMENTS
SUNDOWNERS
SUNDOWNING
SUNDRENCHED
SUNDRESSES
SUNFLOWERS
SUNGLASSES
SUNLESSNESS
SUNLESSNESSES
SUNLOUNGER
SUNLOUNGERS
SUNNINESSES
SUNPORCHES
SUNRISINGS
SUNSCREENING
SUNSCREENS
SUNSEEKERS
SUNSETTING
SUNSETTINGS
SUNSPOTTED
SUNSTROKES
SUNTANNING
SUNWORSHIPPER
SUNWORSHIPPERS
SUOVETAURILIA
SUPERABILITIES
SUPERABILITY
SUPERABLENESS
SUPERABLENESSES
SUPERABOUND
SUPERABOUNDED
SUPERABOUNDING
SUPERABOUNDS
SUPERABSORBENT
SUPERABSORBENTS
SUPERABUNDANCE
SUPERABUNDANCES
SUPERABUNDANT
SUPERABUNDANTLY
SUPERACHIEVER
SUPERACHIEVERS
SUPERACTIVE
SUPERACTIVITIES
SUPERACTIVITY

SUPERACUTE
SUPERADDED
SUPERADDING
SUPERADDITION
SUPERADDITIONAL
SUPERADDITIONS
SUPERAGENCIES
SUPERAGENCY
SUPERAGENT
SUPERAGENTS
SUPERALLOY
SUPERALLOYS
SUPERALTAR
SUPERALTARS
SUPERALTERN
SUPERALTERNS
SUPERAMBITIOUS
SUPERANNUABLE
SUPERANNUATE
SUPERANNUATED
SUPERANNUATES
SUPERANNUATING
SUPERANNUATION
SUPERANNUATIONS
SUPERATHLETE
SUPERATHLETES
SUPERATING
SUPERATION
SUPERATIONS
SUPERATOMS
SUPERBANKS
SUPERBAZAAR
SUPERBAZAARS
SUPERBAZAR
SUPERBAZARS
SUPERBIKES
SUPERBITCH
SUPERBITCHES
SUPERBITIES
SUPERBLOCK
SUPERBLOCKS
SUPERBNESS
SUPERBNESSES
SUPERBOARD
SUPERBOARDS
SUPERBOMBER
SUPERBOMBERS
SUPERBOMBS
SUPERBRAIN
SUPERBRAINS
SUPERBRATS
SUPERBRIGHT
SUPERBUREAUCRAT
SUPERCABINET
SUPERCABINETS
SUPERCALENDER
SUPERCALENDERED
SUPERCALENDERS
SUPERCARGO

SUPERCARGOES
SUPERCARGOS
SUPERCARGOSHIP
SUPERCARGOSHIPS
SUPERCARRIER
SUPERCARRIERS
SUPERCAUTIOUS
SUPERCEDED
SUPERCEDES
SUPERCEDING
SUPERCELESTIAL
SUPERCENTER
SUPERCENTERS
SUPERCHARGE
SUPERCHARGED
SUPERCHARGER
SUPERCHARGERS
SUPERCHARGES
SUPERCHARGING
SUPERCHERIE
SUPERCHERIES
SUPERCHURCH
SUPERCHURCHES
SUPERCILIARIES
SUPERCILIARY
SUPERCILIOUS
SUPERCILIOUSLY
SUPERCITIES
SUPERCIVILISED
SUPERCIVILIZED
SUPERCLASS
SUPERCLASSES
SUPERCLEAN
SUPERCLUBS
SUPERCLUSTER
SUPERCLUSTERS
SUPERCOILED
SUPERCOILING
SUPERCOILS
SUPERCOLLIDER
SUPERCOLLIDERS
SUPERCOLOSSAL
SUPERCOLUMNAR
SUPERCOMPUTER
SUPERCOMPUTERS
SUPERCOMPUTING
SUPERCOMPUTINGS
SUPERCONDUCT
SUPERCONDUCTED
SUPERCONDUCTING
SUPERCONDUCTION
SUPERCONDUCTIVE
SUPERCONDUCTOR
SUPERCONDUCTORS
SUPERCONDUCTS
SUPERCONFIDENCE
SUPERCONFIDENT
SUPERCONTINENT
SUPERCONTINENTS

SUPERCONVENIENT
SUPERCOOLED
SUPERCOOLING
SUPERCOOLS
SUPERCRIMINAL
SUPERCRIMINALS
SUPERCRITICAL
SUPERCURRENT
SUPERCURRENTS
SUPERDAINTY
SUPERDELUXE
SUPERDENSE
SUPERDIPLOMAT
SUPERDIPLOMATS
SUPERDOMINANT
SUPERDOMINANTS
SUPEREFFECTIVE
SUPEREFFICIENCY
SUPEREFFICIENT
SUPEREGOIST
SUPEREGOISTS
SUPERELASTIC
SUPERELEVATE
SUPERELEVATED
SUPERELEVATES
SUPERELEVATING
SUPERELEVATION
SUPERELEVATIONS
SUPERELITE
SUPEREMINENCE
SUPEREMINENCES
SUPEREMINENT
SUPEREMINENTLY
SUPEREROGANT
SUPEREROGATE
SUPEREROGATED
SUPEREROGATES
SUPEREROGATING
SUPEREROGATION
SUPEREROGATIONS
SUPEREROGATIVE
SUPEREROGATOR
SUPEREROGATORS
SUPEREROGATORY
SUPERESSENTIAL
SUPERETTES
SUPEREVIDENT
SUPEREXALT
SUPEREXALTATION
SUPEREXALTED
SUPEREXALTING
SUPEREXALTS
SUPEREXCELLENCE
SUPEREXCELLENT
SUPEREXPENSIVE
SUPEREXPRESS
SUPEREXPRESSES
SUPERFAMILIES
SUPERFAMILY

SUPERFARMS
SUPERFATTED
SUPERFECTA
SUPERFECTAS
SUPERFEMALE
SUPERFEMALES
SUPERFETATE
SUPERFETATED
SUPERFETATES
SUPERFETATING
SUPERFETATION
SUPERFETATIONS
SUPERFICIAL
SUPERFICIALISE
SUPERFICIALISED
SUPERFICIALISES
SUPERFICIALITY
SUPERFICIALIZE
SUPERFICIALIZED
SUPERFICIALIZES
SUPERFICIALLY
SUPERFICIALNESS
SUPERFICIALS
SUPERFICIES
SUPERFINENESS
SUPERFINENESSES
SUPERFIRMS
SUPERFIXES
SUPERFLACK
SUPERFLACKS
SUPERFLUID
SUPERFLUIDITIES
SUPERFLUIDITY
SUPERFLUIDS
SUPERFLUITIES
SUPERFLUITY
SUPERFLUOUS
SUPERFLUOUSLY
SUPERFLUOUSNESS
SUPERFLUXES
SUPERFOETATION
SUPERFOETATIONS
SUPERFRONTAL
SUPERFRONTALS
SUPERFUNDS
SUPERFUSED
SUPERFUSES
SUPERFUSING
SUPERFUSION
SUPERFUSIONS
SUPERGENES
SUPERGIANT
SUPERGIANTS
SUPERGLACIAL
SUPERGLUED
SUPERGLUES
SUPERGLUING
SUPERGOVERNMENT
SUPERGRAPHICS

SUPERGRASS
SUPERGRASSES
SUPERGRAVITIES
SUPERGRAVITY
SUPERGROUP
SUPERGROUPS
SUPERGROWTH
SUPERGROWTHS
SUPERHARDEN
SUPERHARDENED
SUPERHARDENING
SUPERHARDENS
SUPERHEATED
SUPERHEATER
SUPERHEATERS
SUPERHEATING
SUPERHEATS
SUPERHEAVIES
SUPERHEAVY
SUPERHELICAL
SUPERHELICES
SUPERHELIX
SUPERHELIXES
SUPERHEROES
SUPERHEROINE
SUPERHEROINES
SUPERHETERODYNE
SUPERHIGHWAY
SUPERHIGHWAYS
SUPERHIVES
SUPERHUMAN
SUPERHUMANISE
SUPERHUMANISED
SUPERHUMANISES
SUPERHUMANISING
SUPERHUMANITIES
SUPERHUMANITY
SUPERHUMANIZE
SUPERHUMANIZED
SUPERHUMANIZES
SUPERHUMANIZING
SUPERHUMANLY
SUPERHUMANNESS
SUPERHUMERAL
SUPERHUMERALS
SUPERHYPED
SUPERHYPES
SUPERHYPING
SUPERIMPORTANT
SUPERIMPOSABLE
SUPERIMPOSE
SUPERIMPOSED
SUPERIMPOSES
SUPERIMPOSING
SUPERIMPOSITION
SUPERINCUMBENCE
SUPERINCUMBENCY
SUPERINCUMBENT
SUPERINDIVIDUAL

SUPERINDUCE
SUPERINDUCED
SUPERINDUCEMENT
SUPERINDUCES
SUPERINDUCING
SUPERINDUCTION
SUPERINDUCTIONS
SUPERINFECT
SUPERINFECTED
SUPERINFECTING
SUPERINFECTION
SUPERINFECTIONS
SUPERINFECTS
SUPERINSULATED
SUPERINTEND
SUPERINTENDED
SUPERINTENDENCE
SUPERINTENDENCY
SUPERINTENDENT
SUPERINTENDENTS
SUPERINTENDING
SUPERINTENDS
SUPERINTENSITY
SUPERIORESS
SUPERIORESSES
SUPERIORITIES
SUPERIORITY
SUPERIORLY
SUPERIORSHIP
SUPERIORSHIPS
SUPERJACENT
SUPERJOCKS
SUPERJUMBO
SUPERJUMBOS
SUPERKINGDOM
SUPERKINGDOMS
SUPERLARGE
SUPERLATIVE
SUPERLATIVELY
SUPERLATIVENESS
SUPERLATIVES
SUPERLAWYER
SUPERLAWYERS
SUPERLIGHT
SUPERLINER
SUPERLINERS
SUPERLOADS
SUPERLOBBYIST
SUPERLOBBYISTS
SUPERLOYALIST
SUPERLOYALISTS
SUPERLUMINAL
SUPERLUNAR
SUPERLUNARY
SUPERLUXURIOUS
SUPERLUXURY
SUPERLYING
SUPERMACHO
SUPERMAJORITIES

SUPERMAJORITY
SUPERMALES
SUPERMARKET
SUPERMARKETS
SUPERMARTS
SUPERMASCULINE
SUPERMASSIVE
SUPERMAXES
SUPERMEMBRANE
SUPERMEMBRANES
SUPERMICRO
SUPERMICROS
SUPERMILITANT
SUPERMILITANTS
SUPERMINDS
SUPERMINIS
SUPERMINISTER
SUPERMINISTERS
SUPERMODEL
SUPERMODELS
SUPERMODERN
SUPERMOTOS
SUPERMUNDANE
SUPERNACULA
SUPERNACULAR
SUPERNACULUM
SUPERNALLY
SUPERNATANT
SUPERNATANTS
SUPERNATATION
SUPERNATATIONS
SUPERNATES
SUPERNATION
SUPERNATIONAL
SUPERNATIONALLY
SUPERNATIONS
SUPERNATURAL
SUPERNATURALISE
SUPERNATURALISM
SUPERNATURALIST
SUPERNATURALIZE
SUPERNATURALLY
SUPERNATURALS
SUPERNATURE
SUPERNATURES
SUPERNORMAL
SUPERNORMALITY
SUPERNORMALLY
SUPERNOVAE
SUPERNOVAS
SUPERNUMERARIES
SUPERNUMERARY
SUPERNURSE
SUPERNURSES
SUPERNUTRIENT
SUPERNUTRIENTS
SUPERNUTRITION
SUPERNUTRITIONS
SUPEROCTAVE

SUPEROCTAVES
SUPERORDER
SUPERORDERS
SUPERORDINAL
SUPERORDINARY
SUPERORDINATE
SUPERORDINATED
SUPERORDINATES
SUPERORDINATING
SUPERORDINATION
SUPERORGANIC
SUPERORGANICISM
SUPERORGANICIST
SUPERORGANISM
SUPERORGANISMS
SUPERORGASM
SUPERORGASMS
SUPEROVULATE
SUPEROVULATED
SUPEROVULATES
SUPEROVULATING
SUPEROVULATION
SUPEROVULATIONS
SUPEROXIDE
SUPEROXIDES
SUPERPARASITISM
SUPERPARTICLE
SUPERPARTICLES
SUPERPATRIOT
SUPERPATRIOTIC
SUPERPATRIOTISM
SUPERPATRIOTS
SUPERPERSON
SUPERPERSONAL
SUPERPERSONS
SUPERPHENOMENA
SUPERPHENOMENON
SUPERPHOSPHATE
SUPERPHOSPHATES
SUPERPHYLA
SUPERPHYLUM
SUPERPHYSICAL
SUPERPIMPS
SUPERPLANE
SUPERPLANES
SUPERPLASTIC
SUPERPLASTICITY
SUPERPLASTICS
SUPERPLAYER
SUPERPLAYERS
SUPERPLUSES
SUPERPOLITE
SUPERPOLYMER
SUPERPOLYMERS
SUPERPORTS
SUPERPOSABLE
SUPERPOSED
SUPERPOSES
SUPERPOSING

SUPERPOSITION
SUPERPOSITIONS
SUPERPOWER
SUPERPOWERED
SUPERPOWERFUL
SUPERPOWERS
SUPERPRAISE
SUPERPRAISED
SUPERPRAISES
SUPERPRAISING
SUPERPREMIUM
SUPERPREMIUMS
SUPERPROFIT
SUPERPROFITS
SUPERQUALITY
SUPERRACES
SUPERREALISM
SUPERREALISMS
SUPERREALIST
SUPERREALISTS
SUPERREFINE
SUPERREFINED
SUPERREFINES
SUPERREFINING
SUPERREGIONAL
SUPERREGIONALS
SUPERROADS
SUPERROMANTIC
SUPERSAFETIES
SUPERSAFETY
SUPERSALES
SUPERSALESMAN
SUPERSALESMEN
SUPERSALTS
SUPERSATURATE
SUPERSATURATED
SUPERSATURATES
SUPERSATURATING
SUPERSATURATION
SUPERSAURS
SUPERSAVER
SUPERSAVERS
SUPERSCALAR
SUPERSCALE
SUPERSCHOOL
SUPERSCHOOLS
SUPERSCOUT
SUPERSCOUTS
SUPERSCREEN
SUPERSCREENS
SUPERSCRIBE
SUPERSCRIBED
SUPERSCRIBES
SUPERSCRIBING
SUPERSCRIPT
SUPERSCRIPTION
SUPERSCRIPTIONS
SUPERSCRIPTS
SUPERSECRECIES

SUPERSECRECY	SUPERSTATES	SUPERTITLES	SUPPLANTER
SUPERSECRET	SUPERSTATION	SUPERTONIC	SUPPLANTERS
SUPERSEDABLE	SUPERSTATIONS	SUPERTONICS	SUPPLANTING
SUPERSEDEAS	SUPERSTIMULATE	SUPERTRUCK	SUPPLEJACK
SUPERSEDEASES	SUPERSTIMULATED	SUPERTRUCKS	SUPPLEJACKS
SUPERSEDED	SUPERSTIMULATES	SUPERTWIST	SUPPLEMENT
SUPERSEDENCE	SUPERSTITION	SUPERTWISTS	SUPPLEMENTAL
SUPERSEDENCES	SUPERSTITIONS	SUPERVENED	SUPPLEMENTALLY
SUPERSEDER	SUPERSTITIOUS	SUPERVENES	SUPPLEMENTALS
SUPERSEDERE	SUPERSTITIOUSLY	SUPERVENIENCE	SUPPLEMENTARIES
SUPERSEDERES	SUPERSTOCK	SUPERVENIENCES	SUPPLEMENTARILY
SUPERSEDERS	SUPERSTOCKS	SUPERVENIENT	SUPPLEMENTARY
SUPERSEDES	SUPERSTORE	SUPERVENING	SUPPLEMENTATION
SUPERSEDING	SUPERSTORES	SUPERVENTION	SUPPLEMENTED
SUPERSEDURE	SUPERSTRATA	SUPERVENTIONS	SUPPLEMENTER
SUPERSEDURES	SUPERSTRATUM	SUPERVIRILE	SUPPLEMENTERS
SUPERSELLER	SUPERSTRATUMS	SUPERVIRTUOSI	SUPPLEMENTING
SUPERSELLERS	SUPERSTRENGTH	SUPERVIRTUOSO	SUPPLEMENTS
SUPERSELLING	SUPERSTRENGTHS	SUPERVIRTUOSOS	SUPPLENESS
SUPERSELLS	SUPERSTRIKE	SUPERVIRULENT	SUPPLENESSES
SUPERSENSIBLE	SUPERSTRIKES	SUPERVISAL	SUPPLETION
SUPERSENSIBLY	SUPERSTRING	SUPERVISALS	SUPPLETIONS
SUPERSENSITIVE	SUPERSTRINGS	SUPERVISED	SUPPLETIVE
SUPERSENSORY	SUPERSTRONG	SUPERVISEE	SUPPLETIVES
SUPERSENSUAL	SUPERSTRUCT	SUPERVISEES	SUPPLETORILY
SUPERSESSION	SUPERSTRUCTED	SUPERVISES	SUPPLETORY
SUPERSESSIONS	SUPERSTRUCTING	SUPERVISING	SUPPLIABLE
SUPERSEXES	SUPERSTRUCTION	SUPERVISION	SUPPLIANCE
SUPERSEXUALITY	SUPERSTRUCTIONS	SUPERVISIONS	SUPPLIANCES
SUPERSHARP	SUPERSTRUCTIVE	SUPERVISOR	SUPPLIANTLY
SUPERSHOWS	SUPERSTRUCTS	SUPERVISORS	SUPPLIANTS
SUPERSINGER	SUPERSTRUCTURAL	SUPERVISORSHIP	SUPPLICANT
SUPERSINGERS	SUPERSTRUCTURE	SUPERVISORSHIPS	SUPPLICANTS
SUPERSIZED	SUPERSTRUCTURES	SUPERVISORY	SUPPLICATE
SUPERSIZES	SUPERSTUDS	SUPERVOLUTE	SUPPLICATED
SUPERSIZING	SUPERSUBTILE	SUPERWAIFS	SUPPLICATES
SUPERSLEUTH	SUPERSUBTLE	SUPERWAVES	SUPPLICATING
SUPERSLEUTHS	SUPERSUBTLETIES	SUPERWEAPON	SUPPLICATINGLY
SUPERSLICK	SUPERSUBTLETY	SUPERWEAPONS	SUPPLICATION
SUPERSMART	SUPERSURGEON	SUPERWEEDS	SUPPLICATIONS
SUPERSMOOTH	SUPERSURGEONS	SUPERWIDES	SUPPLICATORY
SUPERSONIC	SUPERSWEET	SUPERWIVES	SUPPLICATS
SUPERSONICALLY	SUPERSYMMETRIC	SUPERWOMAN	SUPPLICAVIT
SUPERSONICS	SUPERSYMMETRIES	SUPERWOMEN	SUPPLICAVITS
SUPERSOUND	SUPERSYMMETRY	SUPINATING	SUPPLYMENT
SUPERSOUNDS	SUPERSYSTEM	SUPINATION	SUPPLYMENTS
SUPERSPECIAL	SUPERSYSTEMS	SUPINATIONS	SUPPORTABILITY
SUPERSPECIALIST	SUPERTANKER	SUPINATORS	SUPPORTABLE
SUPERSPECIALS	SUPERTANKERS	SUPINENESS	SUPPORTABLENESS
SUPERSPECIES	SUPERTAXES	SUPINENESSES	SUPPORTABLY
SUPERSPECTACLE	SUPERTEACHER	SUPPEAGOES	SUPPORTANCE
SUPERSPECTACLES	SUPERTEACHERS	SUPPEDANEA	SUPPORTANCES
SUPERSPEED	SUPERTERRANEAN	SUPPEDANEUM	SUPPORTERS
SUPERSPEEDS	SUPERTERRIFIC	SUPPERLESS	SUPPORTING
SUPERSPIES	SUPERTHICK	SUPPERTIME	SUPPORTINGS
SUPERSTARDOM	SUPERTHRILLER	SUPPERTIMES	SUPPORTIVE
SUPERSTARDOMS	SUPERTHRILLERS	SUPPLANTATION	SUPPORTIVELY
SUPERSTARS	SUPERTIGHT	SUPPLANTATIONS	SUPPORTIVENESS
SUPERSTATE	SUPERTITLE	SUPPLANTED	SUPPORTLESS

SUPPORTMENT
SUPPORTMENTS
SUPPORTRESS
SUPPORTRESSES
SUPPORTURE
SUPPORTURES
SUPPOSABLE
SUPPOSABLY
SUPPOSEDLY
SUPPOSINGS
SUPPOSITION
SUPPOSITIONAL
SUPPOSITIONALLY
SUPPOSITIONARY
SUPPOSITIONLESS
SUPPOSITIONS
SUPPOSITIOUS
SUPPOSITIOUSLY
SUPPOSITITIOUS
SUPPOSITIVE
SUPPOSITIVELY
SUPPOSITIVES
SUPPOSITORIES
SUPPOSITORY
SUPPRESSANT
SUPPRESSANTS
SUPPRESSED
SUPPRESSEDLY
SUPPRESSER
SUPPRESSERS
SUPPRESSES
SUPPRESSIBILITY
SUPPRESSIBLE
SUPPRESSING
SUPPRESSION
SUPPRESSIONS
SUPPRESSIVE
SUPPRESSIVENESS
SUPPRESSOR
SUPPRESSORS
SUPPURATED
SUPPURATES
SUPPURATING
SUPPURATION
SUPPURATIONS
SUPPURATIVE
SUPPURATIVES
SUPRACHIASMIC
SUPRACILIARY
SUPRACOSTAL
SUPRACRUSTAL
SUPRAGLOTTAL
SUPRALAPSARIAN
SUPRALAPSARIANS
SUPRALIMINAL
SUPRALIMINALLY
SUPRALUNAR
SUPRAMAXILLARY
SUPRAMOLECULAR

SUPRAMOLECULE
SUPRAMOLECULES
SUPRAMUNDANE
SUPRANATIONAL
SUPRANATIONALLY
SUPRAOPTIC
SUPRAORBITAL
SUPRAPUBIC
SUPRARATIONAL
SUPRARENAL
SUPRARENALS
SUPRASEGMENTAL
SUPRASENSIBLE
SUPRATEMPORAL
SUPRAVITAL
SUPRAVITALLY
SUPREMACIES
SUPREMACISM
SUPREMACISMS
SUPREMACIST
SUPREMACISTS
SUPREMATISM
SUPREMATISMS
SUPREMATIST
SUPREMATISTS
SUPREMENESS
SUPREMENESSES
SUPREMITIES
SURADDITION
SURADDITIONS
SURBASEMENT
SURBASEMENTS
SURBEDDING
SURCEASING
SURCHARGED
SURCHARGEMENT
SURCHARGEMENTS
SURCHARGER
SURCHARGERS
SURCHARGES
SURCHARGING
SURCINGLED
SURCINGLES
SURCINGLING
SURCULUSES
SUREFOOTED
SUREFOOTEDLY
SUREFOOTEDNESS
SURENESSES
SURETYSHIP
SURETYSHIPS
SURFACELESS
SURFACEMAN
SURFACEMEN
SURFACINGS
SURFACTANT
SURFACTANTS
SURFBOARDED
SURFBOARDER

SURFBOARDERS
SURFBOARDING
SURFBOARDINGS
SURFBOARDS
SURFCASTER
SURFCASTERS
SURFCASTING
SURFCASTINGS
SURFEITERS
SURFEITING
SURFEITINGS
SURFFISHES
SURFPERCHES
SURFRIDERS
SURGEONCIES
SURGEONFISH
SURGEONFISHES
SURGEONSHIP
SURGEONSHIPS
SURGICALLY
SURJECTION
SURJECTIONS
SURJECTIVE
SURLINESSES
SURMASTERS
SURMISABLE
SURMISINGS
SURMISTRESS
SURMISTRESSES
SURMOUNTABLE
SURMOUNTED
SURMOUNTER
SURMOUNTERS
SURMOUNTING
SURMOUNTINGS
SURMULLETS
SURNOMINAL
SURPASSABLE
SURPASSERS
SURPASSING
SURPASSINGLY
SURPASSINGNESS
SURPLUSAGE
SURPLUSAGES
SURPLUSING
SURPLUSSED
SURPLUSSES
SURPLUSSING
SURPRINTED
SURPRINTING
SURPRISALS
SURPRISEDLY
SURPRISERS
SURPRISING
SURPRISINGLY
SURPRISINGNESS
SURPRISINGS
SURPRIZING
SURQUEDIES

SURQUEDRIES
SURREALISM
SURREALISMS
SURREALIST
SURREALISTIC
SURREALISTS
SURREBUTTAL
SURREBUTTALS
SURREBUTTED
SURREBUTTER
SURREBUTTERS
SURREBUTTING
SURREJOINDER
SURREJOINDERS
SURREJOINED
SURREJOINING
SURREJOINS
SURRENDERED
SURRENDEREE
SURRENDEREES
SURRENDERER
SURRENDERERS
SURRENDERING
SURRENDEROR
SURRENDERORS
SURRENDERS
SURRENDRIES
SURREPTITIOUS
SURREPTITIOUSLY
SURROGACIES
SURROGATED
SURROGATES
SURROGATESHIP
SURROGATESHIPS
SURROGATING
SURROGATION
SURROGATIONS
SURROGATUM
SURROGATUMS
SURROUNDED
SURROUNDING
SURROUNDINGS
SURTARBRAND
SURTARBRANDS
SURTURBRAND
SURTURBRANDS
SURVEILING
SURVEILLANCE
SURVEILLANCES
SURVEILLANT
SURVEILLANTS
SURVEILLED
SURVEILLES
SURVEILLING
SURVEYABLE
SURVEYANCE
SURVEYANCES
SURVEYINGS
SURVEYORSHIP

SURVEYORSHIPS	SUSPENSORIAL	SUZERAINTY	SWEEPINGNESS
SURVIEWING	SUSPENSORIES	SVARABHAKTI	SWEEPINGNESSES
SURVIVABILITIES	SUSPENSORIUM	SVARABHAKTIS	SWEEPSTAKE
SURVIVABILITY	SUSPENSORS	SVELTENESS	SWEEPSTAKES
SURVIVABLE	SUSPENSORY	SVELTENESSES	SWEETBREAD
SURVIVALISM	SUSPERCOLLATE	SWAGGERERS	SWEETBREADS
SURVIVALISMS	SUSPERCOLLATED	SWAGGERING	SWEETBRIAR
SURVIVALIST	SUSPERCOLLATES	SWAGGERINGLY	SWEETBRIARS
SURVIVALISTS	SUSPERCOLLATING	SWAGGERINGS	SWEETBRIER
SURVIVANCE	SUSPICIONAL	SWAINISHNESS	SWEETBRIERS
SURVIVANCES	SUSPICIONED	SWAINISHNESSES	SWEETCORNS
SURVIVORSHIP	SUSPICIONING	SWALLOWABLE	SWEETENERS
SURVIVORSHIPS	SUSPICIONLESS	SWALLOWERS	SWEETENING
SUSCEPTANCE	SUSPICIONS	SWALLOWING	SWEETENINGS
SUSCEPTANCES	SUSPICIOUS	SWALLOWTAIL	SWEETFISHES
SUSCEPTIBILITY	SUSPICIOUSLY	SWALLOWTAILS	SWEETHEART
SUSCEPTIBLE	SUSPICIOUSNESS	SWALLOWWORT	SWEETHEARTED
SUSCEPTIBLENESS	SUSPIRATION	SWALLOWWORTS	SWEETHEARTING
SUSCEPTIBLY	SUSPIRATIONS	SWAMPINESS	SWEETHEARTS
SUSCEPTIVE	SUSPIRIOUS	SWAMPINESSES	SWEETIEWIFE
SUSCEPTIVENESS	SUSTAINABILITY	SWAMPLANDS	SWEETIEWIVES
SUSCEPTIVITIES	SUSTAINABLE	SWANKINESS	SWEETISHLY
SUSCEPTIVITY	SUSTAINEDLY	SWANKINESSES	SWEETISHNESS
SUSCEPTORS	SUSTAINERS	SWANNERIES	SWEETISHNESSES
SUSCIPIENT	SUSTAINING	SWANSDOWNS	SWEETMEATS
SUSCIPIENTS	SUSTAININGLY	SWARAJISMS	SWEETNESSES
SUSCITATED	SUSTAININGS	SWARAJISTS	SWEETSHOPS
SUSCITATES	SUSTAINMENT	SWARTHIEST	SWEETWATER
SUSCITATING	SUSTAINMENTS	SWARTHINESS	SWEETWATERS
SUSCITATION	SUSTENANCE	SWARTHINESSES	SWEETWOODS
SUSCITATIONS	SUSTENANCES	SWARTHNESS	SWEIRNESSES
SUSPECTABLE	SUSTENTACULA	SWARTHNESSES	SWELLFISHES
SUSPECTEDLY	SUSTENTACULAR	SWARTNESSES	SWELLHEADED
SUSPECTEDNESS	SUSTENTACULUM	SWASHBUCKLE	SWELLHEADEDNESS
SUSPECTEDNESSES	SUSTENTATE	SWASHBUCKLED	SWELLHEADS
SUSPECTERS	SUSTENTATED	SWASHBUCKLER	SWELLINGLY
SUSPECTFUL	SUSTENTATES	SWASHBUCKLERS	SWELTERING
SUSPECTING	SUSTENTATING	SWASHBUCKLES	SWELTERINGLY
SUSPECTLESS	SUSTENTATION	SWASHBUCKLING	SWELTERINGS
SUSPENDERED	SUSTENTATIONS	SWASHWORKS	SWELTRIEST
SUSPENDERS	SUSTENTATIVE	SWATCHBOOK	SWEPTWINGS
SUSPENDIBILITY	SUSTENTATOR	SWATCHBOOKS	SWERVELESS
SUSPENDIBLE	SUSTENTATORS	SWATHEABLE	SWIFTNESSES
SUSPENDING	SUSTENTION	SWATTERING	SWIMFEEDER
SUSPENSEFUL	SUSTENTIONS	SWAYBACKED	SWIMFEEDERS
SUSPENSEFULLY	SUSTENTIVE	SWEARWORDS	SWIMMERETS
SUSPENSEFULNESS	SUSURRATED	SWEATBANDS	SWIMMINGLY
SUSPENSELESS	SUSURRATES	SWEATBOXES	SWIMMINGNESS
SUSPENSERS	SUSURRATING	SWEATERDRESS	SWIMMINGNESSES
SUSPENSIBILITY	SUSURRATION	SWEATERDRESSES	SWINDLINGS
SUSPENSIBLE	SUSURRATIONS	SWEATINESS	SWINEHERDS
SUSPENSION	SUSURRUSES	SWEATINESSES	SWINEHOODS
SUSPENSIONS	SUTLERSHIP	SWEATPANTS	SWINEPOXES
SUSPENSIVE	SUTLERSHIPS	SWEATSHIRT	SWINESTONE
SUSPENSIVELY	SUTTEEISMS	SWEATSHIRTS	SWINESTONES
SUSPENSIVENESS	SUTTLETIES	SWEATSHOPS	SWINGBEATS
SUSPENSOID	SUTURATION	SWEATSUITS	SWINGBOATS
SUSPENSOIDS	SUTURATIONS	SWEEPBACKS	SWINGEINGLY
SUSPENSORIA	SUZERAINTIES	SWEEPINGLY	SWINGINGEST

SWINGINGLY
SWINGLETREE
SWINGLETREES
SWINGLINGS
SWINGOMETER
SWINGOMETERS
SWINGTREES
SWINISHNESS
SWINISHNESSES
SWIRLINGLY
SWISHINGLY
SWITCHABLE
SWITCHBACK
SWITCHBACKED
SWITCHBACKING
SWITCHBACKS
SWITCHBLADE
SWITCHBLADES
SWITCHBOARD
SWITCHBOARDS
SWITCHEROO
SWITCHEROOS
SWITCHGEAR
SWITCHGEARS
SWITCHGIRL
SWITCHGIRLS
SWITCHGRASS
SWITCHGRASSES
SWITCHIEST
SWITCHINGS
SWITCHLIKE
SWITCHOVER
SWITCHOVERS
SWITCHYARD
SWITCHYARDS
SWITHERING
SWIVELBLOCK
SWIVELBLOCKS
SWIVELLING
SWOLLENNESS
SWOLLENNESSES
SWOONINGLY
SWOOPSTAKE
SWORDBEARER
SWORDBEARERS
SWORDBILLS
SWORDCRAFT
SWORDCRAFTS
SWORDFISHES
SWORDPLAYER
SWORDPLAYERS
SWORDPLAYS
SWORDPROOF
SWORDSMANSHIP
SWORDSMANSHIPS
SWORDSTICK
SWORDSTICKS
SWORDTAILS
SYBARITICAL

SYBARITICALLY
SYBARITISH
SYBARITISM
SYBARITISMS
SYCOPHANCIES
SYCOPHANCY
SYCOPHANTIC
SYCOPHANTICAL
SYCOPHANTICALLY
SYCOPHANTISE
SYCOPHANTISED
SYCOPHANTISES
SYCOPHANTISH
SYCOPHANTISHLY
SYCOPHANTISING
SYCOPHANTISM
SYCOPHANTISMS
SYCOPHANTIZE
SYCOPHANTIZED
SYCOPHANTIZES
SYCOPHANTIZING
SYCOPHANTLY
SYCOPHANTRIES
SYCOPHANTRY
SYCOPHANTS
SYLLABARIA
SYLLABARIES
SYLLABARIUM
SYLLABICAL
SYLLABICALLY
SYLLABICATE
SYLLABICATED
SYLLABICATES
SYLLABICATING
SYLLABICATION
SYLLABICATIONS
SYLLABICITIES
SYLLABICITY
SYLLABIFICATION
SYLLABIFIED
SYLLABIFIES
SYLLABIFYING
SYLLABISED
SYLLABISES
SYLLABISING
SYLLABISMS
SYLLABIZED
SYLLABIZES
SYLLABIZING
SYLLABLING
SYLLABOGRAM
SYLLABOGRAMS
SYLLABOGRAPHIES
SYLLABOGRAPHY
SYLLABUSES
SYLLEPTICAL
SYLLEPTICALLY
SYLLOGISATION
SYLLOGISATIONS

SYLLOGISED
SYLLOGISER
SYLLOGISERS
SYLLOGISES
SYLLOGISING
SYLLOGISMS
SYLLOGISTIC
SYLLOGISTICAL
SYLLOGISTICALLY
SYLLOGISTICS
SYLLOGISTS
SYLLOGIZATION
SYLLOGIZATIONS
SYLLOGIZED
SYLLOGIZER
SYLLOGIZERS
SYLLOGIZES
SYLLOGIZING
SYLPHIDINE
SYLVANITES
SYLVESTRAL
SYLVESTRIAN
SYLVICULTURAL
SYLVICULTURE
SYLVICULTURES
SYLVINITES
SYMBIONTIC
SYMBIONTICALLY
SYMBIOTICAL
SYMBIOTICALLY
SYMBOLICAL
SYMBOLICALLY
SYMBOLICALNESS
SYMBOLISATION
SYMBOLISATIONS
SYMBOLISED
SYMBOLISER
SYMBOLISERS
SYMBOLISES
SYMBOLISING
SYMBOLISMS
SYMBOLISTIC
SYMBOLISTICAL
SYMBOLISTICALLY
SYMBOLISTS
SYMBOLIZATION
SYMBOLIZATIONS
SYMBOLIZED
SYMBOLIZER
SYMBOLIZERS
SYMBOLIZES
SYMBOLIZING
SYMBOLLING
SYMBOLOGICAL
SYMBOLOGIES
SYMBOLOGIST
SYMBOLOGISTS
SYMBOLOGRAPHIES
SYMBOLOGRAPHY

SYMBOLOLATRIES
SYMBOLOLATRY
SYMBOLOLOGIES
SYMBOLOLOGY
SYMMETALISM
SYMMETALISMS
SYMMETALLIC
SYMMETALLISM
SYMMETALLISMS
SYMMETRIAN
SYMMETRIANS
SYMMETRICAL
SYMMETRICALLY
SYMMETRICALNESS
SYMMETRIES
SYMMETRISATION
SYMMETRISATIONS
SYMMETRISE
SYMMETRISED
SYMMETRISES
SYMMETRISING
SYMMETRIZATION
SYMMETRIZATIONS
SYMMETRIZE
SYMMETRIZED
SYMMETRIZES
SYMMETRIZING
SYMMETROPHOBIA
SYMMETROPHOBIAS
SYMPATHECTOMIES
SYMPATHECTOMY
SYMPATHETIC
SYMPATHETICAL
SYMPATHETICALLY
SYMPATHETICS
SYMPATHIES
SYMPATHINS
SYMPATHIQUE
SYMPATHISE
SYMPATHISED
SYMPATHISER
SYMPATHISERS
SYMPATHISES
SYMPATHISING
SYMPATHIZE
SYMPATHIZED
SYMPATHIZER
SYMPATHIZERS
SYMPATHIZES
SYMPATHIZING
SYMPATHOLYTIC
SYMPATHOLYTICS
SYMPATHOMIMETIC
SYMPATRICALLY
SYMPATRIES
SYMPETALIES
SYMPETALOUS
SYMPHILIES
SYMPHILISM

SYMPHILISMS
SYMPHILOUS
SYMPHONICALLY
SYMPHONIES
SYMPHONION
SYMPHONIONS
SYMPHONIOUS
SYMPHONIOUSLY
SYMPHONIST
SYMPHONISTS
SYMPHYLOUS
SYMPHYSEAL
SYMPHYSEOTOMIES
SYMPHYSEOTOMY
SYMPHYSIAL
SYMPHYSIOTOMIES
SYMPHYSIOTOMY
SYMPHYSTIC
SYMPIESOMETER
SYMPIESOMETERS
SYMPLASTIC
SYMPODIALLY
SYMPOSIACS
SYMPOSIARCH
SYMPOSIARCHS
SYMPOSIAST
SYMPOSIASTS
SYMPOSIUMS
SYMPTOMATIC
SYMPTOMATICAL
SYMPTOMATICALLY
SYMPTOMATISE
SYMPTOMATISED
SYMPTOMATISES
SYMPTOMATISING
SYMPTOMATIZE
SYMPTOMATIZED
SYMPTOMATIZES
SYMPTOMATIZING
SYMPTOMATOLOGIC
SYMPTOMATOLOGY
SYMPTOMLESS
SYMPTOMOLOGICAL
SYMPTOMOLOGIES
SYMPTOMOLOGY
SYNADELPHITE
SYNADELPHITES
SYNAERESES
SYNAERESIS
SYNAESTHESES
SYNAESTHESIA
SYNAESTHESIAS
SYNAESTHESIS
SYNAESTHETIC
SYNAGOGICAL
SYNAGOGUES
SYNALEPHAS
SYNALLAGMATIC
SYNALOEPHA

SYNALOEPHAS
SYNANDRIUM
SYNANDROUS
SYNANTHEROUS
SYNANTHESES
SYNANTHESIS
SYNANTHETIC
SYNANTHIES
SYNANTHOUS
SYNAPHEIAS
SYNAPOSEMATIC
SYNAPOSEMATISM
SYNAPOSEMATISMS
SYNAPTASES
SYNAPTICAL
SYNAPTICALLY
SYNAPTOSOMAL
SYNAPTOSOME
SYNAPTOSOMES
SYNARCHIES
SYNARTHRODIAL
SYNARTHRODIALLY
SYNARTHROSES
SYNARTHROSIS
SYNASTRIES
SYNAXARION
SYNCARPIES
SYNCARPOUS
SYNCHONDROSES
SYNCHONDROSIS
SYNCHORESES
SYNCHORESIS
SYNCHROFLASH
SYNCHROFLASHES
SYNCHROMESH
SYNCHROMESHES
SYNCHRONAL
SYNCHRONEITIES
SYNCHRONEITY
SYNCHRONIC
SYNCHRONICAL
SYNCHRONICALLY
SYNCHRONICITIES
SYNCHRONICITY
SYNCHRONIES
SYNCHRONISATION
SYNCHRONISE
SYNCHRONISED
SYNCHRONISER
SYNCHRONISERS
SYNCHRONISES
SYNCHRONISING
SYNCHRONISM
SYNCHRONISMS
SYNCHRONISTIC
SYNCHRONISTICAL
SYNCHRONIZATION
SYNCHRONIZE
SYNCHRONIZED

SYNCHRONIZER
SYNCHRONIZERS
SYNCHRONIZES
SYNCHRONIZING
SYNCHRONOLOGIES
SYNCHRONOLOGY
SYNCHRONOSCOPE
SYNCHRONOSCOPES
SYNCHRONOUS
SYNCHRONOUSLY
SYNCHRONOUSNESS
SYNCHROSCOPE
SYNCHROSCOPES
SYNCHROTRON
SYNCHROTRONS
SYNCLASTIC
SYNCLINALS
SYNCLINORIA
SYNCLINORIUM
SYNCOPATED
SYNCOPATES
SYNCOPATING
SYNCOPATION
SYNCOPATIONS
SYNCOPATIVE
SYNCOPATOR
SYNCOPATORS
SYNCRETISATION
SYNCRETISATIONS
SYNCRETISE
SYNCRETISED
SYNCRETISES
SYNCRETISING
SYNCRETISM
SYNCRETISMS
SYNCRETIST
SYNCRETISTIC
SYNCRETISTS
SYNCRETIZATION
SYNCRETIZATIONS
SYNCRETIZE
SYNCRETIZED
SYNCRETIZES
SYNCRETIZING
SYNDACTYLIES
SYNDACTYLISM
SYNDACTYLISMS
SYNDACTYLOUS
SYNDACTYLS
SYNDACTYLY
SYNDERESES
SYNDERESIS
SYNDESISES
SYNDESMOSES
SYNDESMOSIS
SYNDESMOTIC
SYNDETICAL
SYNDETICALLY
SYNDICALISM

SYNDICALISMS
SYNDICALIST
SYNDICALISTIC
SYNDICALISTS
SYNDICATED
SYNDICATES
SYNDICATING
SYNDICATION
SYNDICATIONS
SYNDICATOR
SYNDICATORS
SYNDICSHIP
SYNDICSHIPS
SYNDIOTACTIC
SYNDYASMIAN
SYNECDOCHE
SYNECDOCHES
SYNECDOCHIC
SYNECDOCHICAL
SYNECDOCHICALLY
SYNECDOCHISM
SYNECDOCHISMS
SYNECOLOGIC
SYNECOLOGICAL
SYNECOLOGICALLY
SYNECOLOGIES
SYNECOLOGIST
SYNECOLOGISTS
SYNECOLOGY
SYNECPHONESES
SYNECPHONESIS
SYNECTICALLY
SYNEIDESES
SYNEIDESIS
SYNERGETIC
SYNERGETICALLY
SYNERGICALLY
SYNERGISED
SYNERGISES
SYNERGISING
SYNERGISMS
SYNERGISTIC
SYNERGISTICALLY
SYNERGISTS
SYNERGIZED
SYNERGIZES
SYNERGIZING
SYNESTHESIA
SYNESTHESIAS
SYNESTHETIC
SYNGENESES
SYNGENESIOUS
SYNGENESIS
SYNGENETIC
SYNGNATHOUS
SYNKARYONIC
SYNKARYONS
SYNODICALLY
SYNOECETES

SYNOECIOSES

SYNOECIOSES
SYNOECIOSIS
SYNOECIOUS
SYNOECISED
SYNOECISES
SYNOECISING
SYNOECISMS
SYNOECIZED
SYNOECIZES
SYNOECIZING
SYNOECOLOGIES
SYNOECOLOGY
SYNOEKETES
SYNONYMATIC
SYNONYMICAL
SYNONYMICON
SYNONYMICONS
SYNONYMIES
SYNONYMISE
SYNONYMISED
SYNONYMISES
SYNONYMISING
SYNONYMIST
SYNONYMISTS
SYNONYMITIES
SYNONYMITY
SYNONYMIZE
SYNONYMIZED
SYNONYMIZES
SYNONYMIZING
SYNONYMOUS
SYNONYMOUSLY
SYNONYMOUSNESS
SYNOPSISED
SYNOPSISES
SYNOPSISING
SYNOPSIZED
SYNOPSIZES
SYNOPSIZING
SYNOPTICAL
SYNOPTICALLY
SYNOPTISTIC
SYNOPTISTS
SYNOSTOSES
SYNOSTOSIS
SYNOVIALLY
SYNOVITISES
SYNSEPALOUS
SYNTACTICAL
SYNTACTICALLY
SYNTACTICS
SYNTAGMATA
SYNTAGMATIC
SYNTAGMATITE
SYNTAGMATITES
SYNTECTICAL
SYNTENOSES
SYNTENOSIS
SYNTERESES

SYNTERESIS
SYNTEXISES
SYNTHESISATION
SYNTHESISATIONS
SYNTHESISE
SYNTHESISED
SYNTHESISER
SYNTHESISERS
SYNTHESISES
SYNTHESISING
SYNTHESIST
SYNTHESISTS
SYNTHESIZATION
SYNTHESIZATIONS
SYNTHESIZE
SYNTHESIZED
SYNTHESIZER
SYNTHESIZERS
SYNTHESIZES
SYNTHESIZING
SYNTHESPIAN
SYNTHESPIANS
SYNTHETASE
SYNTHETASES
SYNTHETICAL
SYNTHETICALLY
SYNTHETICISM
SYNTHETICISMS
SYNTHETICS
SYNTHETISATION
SYNTHETISATIONS
SYNTHETISE
SYNTHETISED
SYNTHETISER
SYNTHETISERS
SYNTHETISES
SYNTHETISING
SYNTHETISM
SYNTHETISMS
SYNTHETIST
SYNTHETISTS
SYNTHETIZATION
SYNTHETIZATIONS
SYNTHETIZE
SYNTHETIZED
SYNTHETIZER
SYNTHETIZERS
SYNTHETIZES
SYNTHETIZING
SYNTHRONUS
SYNTONICALLY
SYNTONISED
SYNTONISES
SYNTONISING
SYNTONIZED
SYNTONIZES
SYNTONIZING
SYPHERINGS
SYPHILISATION

SYPHILISATIONS
SYPHILISED
SYPHILISES
SYPHILISING
SYPHILITIC
SYPHILITICALLY
SYPHILITICS
SYPHILIZATION
SYPHILIZATIONS
SYPHILIZED
SYPHILIZES
SYPHILIZING
SYPHILOLOGIES
SYPHILOLOGIST
SYPHILOLOGISTS
SYPHILOLOGY
SYPHILOMAS
SYPHILOMATA
SYPHILOPHOBIA
SYPHILOPHOBIAS
SYRINGITIS
SYRINGITISES
SYRINGOMYELIA
SYRINGOMYELIAS
SYRINGOMYELIC
SYRINGOTOMIES
SYRINGOTOMY
SYSSARCOSES
SYSSARCOSIS
SYSSARCOTIC
SYSTEMATIC
SYSTEMATICAL
SYSTEMATICALLY
SYSTEMATICIAN
SYSTEMATICIANS
SYSTEMATICNESS
SYSTEMATICS
SYSTEMATISATION
SYSTEMATISE
SYSTEMATISED
SYSTEMATISER
SYSTEMATISERS
SYSTEMATISES
SYSTEMATISING
SYSTEMATISM
SYSTEMATISMS
SYSTEMATIST
SYSTEMATISTS
SYSTEMATIZATION
SYSTEMATIZE
SYSTEMATIZED
SYSTEMATIZER
SYSTEMATIZERS
SYSTEMATIZES
SYSTEMATIZING
SYSTEMATOLOGIES
SYSTEMATOLOGY
SYSTEMICALLY
SYSTEMISATION

SYSTEMISATIONS
SYSTEMISED
SYSTEMISER
SYSTEMISERS
SYSTEMISES
SYSTEMISING
SYSTEMIZATION
SYSTEMIZATIONS
SYSTEMIZED
SYSTEMIZER
SYSTEMIZERS
SYSTEMIZES
SYSTEMIZING
SYSTEMLESS
SYZYGETICALLY

T

TABASHEERS
TABBOULEHS
TABBYHOODS
TABEFACTION
TABEFACTIONS
TABELLIONS
TABERNACLE
TABERNACLED
TABERNACLES
TABERNACLING
TABERNACULAR
TABESCENCE
TABESCENCES
TABLANETTE
TABLANETTES
TABLATURES
TABLECLOTH
TABLECLOTHS
TABLELANDS
TABLEMATES
TABLESPOON
TABLESPOONFUL
TABLESPOONFULS
TABLESPOONS
TABLESPOONSFUL
TABLETOPPED
TABLETTING
TABLEWARES
TABOGGANED
TABOGGANING
TABOPARESES
TABOPARESIS
TABULARISATION
TABULARISATIONS
TABULARISE
TABULARISED
TABULARISES
TABULARISING
TABULARIZATION
TABULARIZATIONS
TABULARIZE
TABULARIZED
TABULARIZES
TABULARIZING
TABULATING
TABULATION
TABULATIONS
TABULATORS
TABULATORY
TACAMAHACS
TACHEOMETER
TACHEOMETERS
TACHEOMETRIC
TACHEOMETRICAL

TACHEOMETRIES
TACHEOMETRY
TACHISTOSCOPE
TACHISTOSCOPES
TACHISTOSCOPIC
TACHOGRAMS
TACHOGRAPH
TACHOGRAPHS
TACHOMETER
TACHOMETERS
TACHOMETRIC
TACHOMETRICAL
TACHOMETRICALLY
TACHOMETRIES
TACHOMETRY
TACHYARRHYTHMIA
TACHYCARDIA
TACHYCARDIAC
TACHYCARDIAS
TACHYGRAPH
TACHYGRAPHER
TACHYGRAPHERS
TACHYGRAPHIC
TACHYGRAPHICAL
TACHYGRAPHIES
TACHYGRAPHIST
TACHYGRAPHISTS
TACHYGRAPHS
TACHYGRAPHY
TACHYLITES
TACHYLITIC
TACHYLYTES
TACHYLYTIC
TACHYMETER
TACHYMETERS
TACHYMETRIC
TACHYMETRICAL
TACHYMETRICALLY
TACHYMETRIES
TACHYMETRY
TACHYPHASIA
TACHYPHASIAS
TACHYPHRASIA
TACHYPHRASIAS
TACHYPHYLAXES
TACHYPHYLAXIS
TACHYPNEAS
TACHYPNOEA
TACHYPNOEAS
TACITNESSES
TACITURNITIES
TACITURNITY
TACITURNLY
TACKBOARDS

TACKIFIERS
TACKIFYING
TACKINESSES
TACMAHACKS
TACTFULNESS
TACTFULNESSES
TACTICALLY
TACTICIANS
TACTICITIES
TACTILISTS
TACTILITIES
TACTLESSLY
TACTLESSNESS
TACTLESSNESSES
TACTUALITIES
TACTUALITY
TAEKWONDOS
TAENIACIDE
TAENIACIDES
TAENIAFUGE
TAENIAFUGES
TAFFETASES
TAFFETIZED
TAGLIARINI
TAGLIARINIS
TAGLIATELLE
TAGLIATELLES
TAHSILDARS
TAIKONAUTS
TAILBOARDS
TAILCOATED
TAILENDERS
TAILGATERS
TAILGATING
TAILLESSLY
TAILLESSNESS
TAILLESSNESSES
TAILLIGHTS
TAILORBIRD
TAILORBIRDS
TAILORESSES
TAILORINGS
TAILORMADE
TAILORMAKE
TAILORMAKES
TAILORMAKING
TAILPIECES
TAILPIPING
TAILPLANES
TAILSLIDES
TAILSPINNED
TAILSPINNING
TAILSTOCKS
TAILWATERS

TAILWHEELS
TAINTLESSLY
TAKINGNESS
TAKINGNESSES
TALBOTYPES
TALEBEARER
TALEBEARERS
TALEBEARING
TALEBEARINGS
TALEGALLAS
TALENTLESS
TALISMANIC
TALISMANICAL
TALISMANICALLY
TALKABILITIES
TALKABILITY
TALKATHONS
TALKATIVELY
TALKATIVENESS
TALKATIVENESSES
TALKINESSES
TALLGRASSES
TALLIATING
TALLNESSES
TALLYHOING
TALLYSHOPS
TALLYWOMAN
TALLYWOMEN
TALMUDISMS
TAMABILITIES
TAMABILITY
TAMABLENESS
TAMABLENESSES
TAMARILLOS
TAMBOURERS
TAMBOURINE
TAMBOURINES
TAMBOURING
TAMBOURINIST
TAMBOURINISTS
TAMBOURINS
TAMEABILITIES
TAMEABILITY
TAMEABLENESS
TAMEABLENESSES
TAMELESSNESS
TAMELESSNESSES
TAMENESSES
TAMOXIFENS
TAMPERINGS
TAMPERPROOF
TAMPONADES
TAMPONAGES
TANDEMWISE

TANGENCIES

TANGENCIES
TANGENTALLY
TANGENTIAL
TANGENTIALITIES
TANGENTIALITY
TANGENTIALLY
TANGERINES
TANGHININS
TANGIBILITIES
TANGIBILITY
TANGIBLENESS
TANGIBLENESSES
TANGINESSES
TANGLEFOOT
TANGLEFOOTS
TANGLEMENT
TANGLEMENTS
TANGLESOME
TANGLEWEED
TANGLEWEEDS
TANGLINGLY
TANISTRIES
TANKBUSTER
TANKBUSTERS
TANKBUSTING
TANKBUSTINGS
TANTALATES
TANTALISATION
TANTALISATIONS
TANTALISED
TANTALISER
TANTALISERS
TANTALISES
TANTALISING
TANTALISINGLY
TANTALISINGS
TANTALISMS
TANTALITES
TANTALIZATION
TANTALIZATIONS
TANTALIZED
TANTALIZER
TANTALIZERS
TANTALIZES
TANTALIZING
TANTALIZINGLY
TANTALIZINGS
TANTALUSES
TANTAMOUNT
TANTARARAS
TANZANITES
TAOISEACHS
TAPERINGLY
TAPERNESSES
TAPERSTICK
TAPERSTICKS
TAPESCRIPT
TAPESCRIPTS
TAPESTRIED

TAPESTRIES
TAPESTRYING
TAPHEPHOBIA
TAPHEPHOBIAS
TAPHEPHOBIC
TAPHONOMIC
TAPHONOMICAL
TAPHONOMIES
TAPHONOMIST
TAPHONOMISTS
TAPHOPHOBIA
TAPHOPHOBIAS
TAPHROGENESES
TAPHROGENESIS
TAPOTEMENT
TAPOTEMENTS
TAPSALTEERIE
TAPSALTEERIES
TAPSIETEERIE
TAPSIETEERIES
TAPSTRESSES
TARADIDDLE
TARADIDDLES
TARAMASALATA
TARAMASALATAS
TARANTARAED
TARANTARAING
TARANTARAS
TARANTASES
TARANTASSES
TARANTELLA
TARANTELLAS
TARANTISMS
TARANTISTS
TARANTULAE
TARANTULAS
TARATANTARA
TARATANTARAED
TARATANTARAING
TARATANTARAS
TARAXACUMS
TARBOGGINED
TARBOGGINING
TARBOGGINS
TARBOOSHES
TARBOUCHES
TARBOUSHES
TARDIGRADE
TARDIGRADES
TARDINESSES
TARGETABLE
TARGETEERS
TARGETITIS
TARGETITISES
TARGETLESS
TARIFFICATION
TARIFFICATIONS
TARIFFLESS
TARMACADAM

TARMACADAMS
TARMACKING
TARNATIONS
TARNISHABLE
TARNISHERS
TARNISHING
TARPAULING
TARPAULINGS
TARPAULINS
TARRADIDDLE
TARRADIDDLES
TARRIANCES
TARRINESSES
TARSALGIAS
TARSOMETATARSAL
TARSOMETATARSI
TARSOMETATARSUS
TARTANALIA
TARTANALIAS
TARTANRIES
TARTAREOUS
TARTARISATION
TARTARISATIONS
TARTARISED
TARTARISES
TARTARISING
TARTARIZATION
TARTARIZATIONS
TARTARIZED
TARTARIZES
TARTARIZING
TARTINESSES
TARTNESSES
TARTRAZINE
TARTRAZINES
TASEOMETER
TASEOMETERS
TASIMETERS
TASIMETRIC
TASIMETRIES
TASKMASTER
TASKMASTERS
TASKMISTRESS
TASKMISTRESSES
TASSELLING
TASSELLINGS
TASTEFULLY
TASTEFULNESS
TASTEFULNESSES
TASTELESSLY
TASTELESSNESS
TASTELESSNESSES
TASTEMAKER
TASTEMAKERS
TASTINESSES
TATAHASHES
TATPURUSHA
TATPURUSHAS
TATTERDEMALION

TATTERDEMALIONS
TATTERDEMALLION
TATTERSALL
TATTERSALLS
TATTINESSES
TATTLETALE
TATTLETALES
TATTLINGLY
TATTOOISTS
TAUNTINGLY
TAUROBOLIA
TAUROBOLIUM
TAUROMACHIAN
TAUROMACHIES
TAUROMACHY
TAUROMORPHOUS
TAUTNESSES
TAUTOCHRONE
TAUTOCHRONES
TAUTOCHRONISM
TAUTOCHRONISMS
TAUTOCHRONOUS
TAUTOLOGIC
TAUTOLOGICAL
TAUTOLOGICALLY
TAUTOLOGIES
TAUTOLOGISE
TAUTOLOGISED
TAUTOLOGISES
TAUTOLOGISING
TAUTOLOGISM
TAUTOLOGISMS
TAUTOLOGIST
TAUTOLOGISTS
TAUTOLOGIZE
TAUTOLOGIZED
TAUTOLOGIZES
TAUTOLOGIZING
TAUTOLOGOUS
TAUTOLOGOUSLY
TAUTOMERIC
TAUTOMERISM
TAUTOMERISMS
TAUTOMETRIC
TAUTOMETRICAL
TAUTONYMIC
TAUTONYMIES
TAUTONYMOUS
TAUTOPHONIC
TAUTOPHONICAL
TAUTOPHONIES
TAUTOPHONY
TAWDRINESS
TAWDRINESSES
TAWHEOWHEO
TAWHEOWHEOS
TAWNINESSES
TAXABILITIES
TAXABILITY

TAXABLENESS
TAXABLENESSES
TAXAMETERS
TAXATIONAL
TAXIDERMAL
TAXIDERMIC
TAXIDERMIES
TAXIDERMISE
TAXIDERMISED
TAXIDERMISES
TAXIDERMISING
TAXIDERMIST
TAXIDERMISTS
TAXIDERMIZE
TAXIDERMIZED
TAXIDERMIZES
TAXIDERMIZING
TAXIMETERS
TAXIPLANES
TAXONOMERS
TAXONOMICAL
TAXONOMICALLY
TAXONOMIES
TAXONOMIST
TAXONOMISTS
TAXPAYINGS
TAYASSUIDS
TAYBERRIES
TCHOTCHKES
TCHOUKBALL
TCHOUKBALLS
TEABERRIES
TEACHABILITIES
TEACHABILITY
TEACHABLENESS
TEACHABLENESSES
TEACHERLESS
TEACHERSHIP
TEACHERSHIPS
TEACUPFULS
TEACUPSFUL
TEAKETTLES
TEARFULNESS
TEARFULNESSES
TEARGASSED
TEARGASSES
TEARGASSING
TEARINESSES
TEARJERKER
TEARJERKERS
TEARSHEETS
TEARSTAINED
TEARSTAINS
TEARSTRIPS
TEASELINGS
TEASELLERS
TEASELLING
TEASELLINGS
TEASPOONFUL

TEASPOONFULS
TEASPOONSFUL
TEATASTERS
TEAZELLING
TECHINESSES
TECHNETIUM
TECHNETIUMS
TECHNETRONIC
TECHNICALISE
TECHNICALISED
TECHNICALISES
TECHNICALISING
TECHNICALITIES
TECHNICALITY
TECHNICALIZE
TECHNICALIZED
TECHNICALIZES
TECHNICALIZING
TECHNICALLY
TECHNICALNESS
TECHNICALNESSES
TECHNICALS
TECHNICIAN
TECHNICIANS
TECHNICISE
TECHNICISED
TECHNICISES
TECHNICISING
TECHNICISM
TECHNICISMS
TECHNICIST
TECHNICISTS
TECHNICIZE
TECHNICIZED
TECHNICIZES
TECHNICIZING
TECHNICOLOUR
TECHNICOLOURED
TECHNIKONS
TECHNIQUES
TECHNOBABBLE
TECHNOBABBLES
TECHNOCRACIES
TECHNOCRACY
TECHNOCRAT
TECHNOCRATIC
TECHNOCRATS
TECHNOFEAR
TECHNOFEARS
TECHNOGRAPHIES
TECHNOGRAPHY
TECHNOJUNKIE
TECHNOJUNKIES
TECHNOLOGIC
TECHNOLOGICAL
TECHNOLOGICALLY
TECHNOLOGIES
TECHNOLOGISE
TECHNOLOGISED

TECHNOLOGISES
TECHNOLOGISING
TECHNOLOGIST
TECHNOLOGISTS
TECHNOLOGIZE
TECHNOLOGIZED
TECHNOLOGIZES
TECHNOLOGIZING
TECHNOLOGY
TECHNOMANIA
TECHNOMANIAC
TECHNOMANIACS
TECHNOMANIAS
TECHNOMUSIC
TECHNOMUSICS
TECHNOPHILE
TECHNOPHILES
TECHNOPHOBE
TECHNOPHOBES
TECHNOPHOBIA
TECHNOPHOBIAS
TECHNOPHOBIC
TECHNOPHOBICS
TECHNOPOLE
TECHNOPOLES
TECHNOPOLIS
TECHNOPOLISES
TECHNOPOLITAN
TECHNOPOLITANS
TECHNOPOPS
TECHNOSPEAK
TECHNOSPEAKS
TECHNOSTRESS
TECHNOSTRESSES
TECHNOSTRUCTURE
TECTIBRANCH
TECTIBRANCHIATE
TECTIBRANCHS
TECTONICALLY
TECTONISMS
TECTRICIAL
TEDIOSITIES
TEDIOUSNESS
TEDIOUSNESSES
TEDIOUSOME
TEEMINGNESS
TEEMINGNESSES
TEENTSIEST
TEENYBOPPER
TEENYBOPPERS
TEETERBOARD
TEETERBOARDS
TEETHRIDGE
TEETHRIDGES
TEETOTALED
TEETOTALER
TEETOTALERS
TEETOTALING
TEETOTALISM

TEETOTALISMS
TEETOTALIST
TEETOTALISTS
TEETOTALLED
TEETOTALLER
TEETOTALLERS
TEETOTALLING
TEETOTALLY
TEGUMENTAL
TEGUMENTARY
TEICHOPSIA
TEICHOPSIAS
TEINOSCOPE
TEINOSCOPES
TEKNONYMIES
TEKNONYMOUS
TELAESTHESIA
TELAESTHESIAS
TELAESTHETIC
TELANGIECTASES
TELANGIECTASIA
TELANGIECTASIAS
TELANGIECTASIS
TELANGIECTATIC
TELAUTOGRAPHIC
TELAUTOGRAPHIES
TELAUTOGRAPHY
TELEARCHICS
TELEBANKING
TELEBANKINGS
TELEBRIDGE
TELEBRIDGES
TELECAMERA
TELECAMERAS
TELECASTED
TELECASTER
TELECASTERS
TELECASTING
TELECHIRIC
TELECOMMAND
TELECOMMANDS
TELECOMMUTE
TELECOMMUTED
TELECOMMUTER
TELECOMMUTERS
TELECOMMUTING
TELECOMMUTINGS
TELECONFERENCE
TELECONFERENCES
TELECONNECTION
TELECONNECTIONS
TELECONTROL
TELECONTROLS
TELECONVERTER
TELECONVERTERS
TELECOTTAGE
TELECOTTAGES
TELECOTTAGING

TELECOTTAGINGS

TELECOTTAGINGS
TELECOURSE
TELECOURSES
TELEDILDONICS
TELEFACSIMILE
TELEFACSIMILES
TELEFAXING
TELEFERIQUE
TELEFERIQUES
TELEGENICALLY
TELEGNOSES
TELEGNOSIS
TELEGNOSTIC
TELEGONIES
TELEGONOUS
TELEGRAMMATIC
TELEGRAMMED
TELEGRAMMIC
TELEGRAMMING
TELEGRAPHED
TELEGRAPHER
TELEGRAPHERS
TELEGRAPHESE
TELEGRAPHESES
TELEGRAPHIC
TELEGRAPHICALLY
TELEGRAPHIES
TELEGRAPHING
TELEGRAPHIST
TELEGRAPHISTS
TELEGRAPHS
TELEGRAPHY
TELEHEALTH
TELEHEALTHS
TELEJOURNALISM
TELEJOURNALISMS
TELEJOURNALIST
TELEJOURNALISTS
TELEKINESES
TELEKINESIS
TELEKINETIC
TELEKINETICALLY
TELEMARKED
TELEMARKETER
TELEMARKETERS
TELEMARKETING
TELEMARKETINGS
TELEMARKING
TELEMATICS
TELEMEDICINE
TELEMEDICINES
TELEMETERED
TELEMETERING
TELEMETERS
TELEMETRIC
TELEMETRICAL
TELEMETRICALLY
TELEMETRIES
TELENCEPHALA

TELENCEPHALIC
TELENCEPHALON
TELENCEPHALONS
TELEOLOGIC
TELEOLOGICAL
TELEOLOGICALLY
TELEOLOGIES
TELEOLOGISM
TELEOLOGISMS
TELEOLOGIST
TELEOLOGISTS
TELEONOMIC
TELEONOMIES
TELEOSAURIAN
TELEOSAURIANS
TELEOSAURS
TELEOSTEAN
TELEOSTEANS
TELEOSTOME
TELEOSTOMES
TELEOSTOMOUS
TELEPATHED
TELEPATHIC
TELEPATHICALLY
TELEPATHIES
TELEPATHING
TELEPATHISE
TELEPATHISED
TELEPATHISES
TELEPATHISING
TELEPATHIST
TELEPATHISTS
TELEPATHIZE
TELEPATHIZED
TELEPATHIZES
TELEPATHIZING
TELEPHEMES
TELEPHERIQUE
TELEPHERIQUES
TELEPHONED
TELEPHONER
TELEPHONERS
TELEPHONES
TELEPHONIC
TELEPHONICALLY
TELEPHONIES
TELEPHONING
TELEPHONIST
TELEPHONISTS
TELEPHOTOGRAPH
TELEPHOTOGRAPHS
TELEPHOTOGRAPHY
TELEPHOTOS
TELEPOINTS
TELEPORTATION
TELEPORTATIONS
TELEPORTED
TELEPORTING
TELEPRESENCE

TELEPRESENCES
TELEPRINTER
TELEPRINTERS
TELEPROCESSING
TELEPROCESSINGS
TELEPROMPTER
TELEPROMPTERS
TELERECORD
TELERECORDED
TELERECORDING
TELERECORDINGS
TELERECORDS
TELERGICALLY
TELESCIENCE
TELESCIENCES
TELESCOPED
TELESCOPES
TELESCOPIC
TELESCOPICAL
TELESCOPICALLY
TELESCOPIES
TELESCOPIFORM
TELESCOPING
TELESCOPIST
TELESCOPISTS
TELESCREEN
TELESCREENS
TELESELLING
TELESELLINGS
TELESERVICES
TELESHOPPED
TELESHOPPING
TELESHOPPINGS
TELESMATIC
TELESMATICAL
TELESMATICALLY
TELESOFTWARE
TELESOFTWARES
TELESTEREOSCOPE
TELESTHESIA
TELESTHESIAS
TELESTHETIC
TELESTICHS
TELESURGERIES
TELESURGERY
TELETYPESETTING
TELETYPEWRITER
TELETYPEWRITERS
TELETYPING
TELEUTOSPORE
TELEUTOSPORES
TELEUTOSPORIC
TELEVANGELICAL
TELEVANGELISM
TELEVANGELISMS
TELEVANGELIST
TELEVANGELISTS
TELEVERITE
TELEVERITES

TELEVIEWED
TELEVIEWER
TELEVIEWERS
TELEVIEWING
TELEVISERS
TELEVISING
TELEVISION
TELEVISIONAL
TELEVISIONALLY
TELEVISIONARY
TELEVISIONS
TELEVISORS
TELEVISUAL
TELEVISUALLY
TELEWORKER
TELEWORKERS
TELEWORKING
TELEWORKINGS
TELEWRITER
TELEWRITERS
TELFERAGES
TELIOSPORE
TELIOSPORES
TELLERSHIP
TELLERSHIPS
TELLURATES
TELLURETTED
TELLURIANS
TELLURIDES
TELLURIONS
TELLURISED
TELLURISES
TELLURISING
TELLURITES
TELLURIUMS
TELLURIZED
TELLURIZES
TELLURIZING
TELLUROMETER
TELLUROMETERS
TELNETTING
TELOCENTRIC
TELOCENTRICS
TELOMERASE
TELOMERASES
TELOMERISATION
TELOMERISATIONS
TELOMERIZATION
TELOMERIZATIONS
TELOPHASES
TELOPHASIC
TELPHERAGE
TELPHERAGES
TELPHERING
TELPHERLINE
TELPHERLINES
TELPHERMAN
TELPHERMEN
TELPHERWAY

TELPHERWAYS
TEMAZEPAMS
TEMERARIOUS
TEMERARIOUSLY
TEMERARIOUSNESS
TEMERITIES
TEMEROUSLY
TEMPERABILITIES
TEMPERABILITY
TEMPERABLE
TEMPERALITIE
TEMPERALITIES
TEMPERAMENT
TEMPERAMENTAL
TEMPERAMENTALLY
TEMPERAMENTFUL
TEMPERAMENTS
TEMPERANCE
TEMPERANCES
TEMPERATED
TEMPERATELY
TEMPERATENESS
TEMPERATENESSES
TEMPERATES
TEMPERATING
TEMPERATIVE
TEMPERATURE
TEMPERATURES
TEMPERINGS
TEMPESTING
TEMPESTIVE
TEMPESTUOUS
TEMPESTUOUSLY
TEMPESTUOUSNESS
TEMPOLABILE
TEMPORALISE
TEMPORALISED
TEMPORALISES
TEMPORALISING
TEMPORALITIES
TEMPORALITY
TEMPORALIZE
TEMPORALIZED
TEMPORALIZES
TEMPORALIZING
TEMPORALLY
TEMPORALNESS
TEMPORALNESSES
TEMPORALTIES
TEMPORALTY
TEMPORANEOUS
TEMPORARIES
TEMPORARILY
TEMPORARINESS
TEMPORARINESSES
TEMPORISATION
TEMPORISATIONS
TEMPORISED
TEMPORISER

TEMPORISERS
TEMPORISES
TEMPORISING
TEMPORISINGLY
TEMPORISINGS
TEMPORIZATION
TEMPORIZATIONS
TEMPORIZED
TEMPORIZER
TEMPORIZERS
TEMPORIZES
TEMPORIZING
TEMPORIZINGLY
TEMPORIZINGS
TEMPTABILITIES
TEMPTABILITY
TEMPTABLENESS
TEMPTABLENESSES
TEMPTATION
TEMPTATIONS
TEMPTATIOUS
TEMPTINGLY
TEMPTINGNESS
TEMPTINGNESSES
TEMPTRESSES
TEMULENCES
TEMULENCIES
TEMULENTLY
TENABILITIES
TENABILITY
TENABLENESS
TENABLENESSES
TENACIOUSLY
TENACIOUSNESS
TENACIOUSNESSES
TENACITIES
TENACULUMS
TENAILLONS
TENANTABLE
TENANTLESS
TENANTRIES
TENANTSHIP
TENANTSHIPS
TENDENCIALLY
TENDENCIES
TENDENCIOUS
TENDENCIOUSLY
TENDENCIOUSNESS
TENDENTIAL
TENDENTIALLY
TENDENTIOUS
TENDENTIOUSLY
TENDENTIOUSNESS
TENDERABLE
TENDERFEET
TENDERFOOT
TENDERFOOTS
TENDERHEARTED
TENDERHEARTEDLY

TENDERINGS
TENDERISATION
TENDERISATIONS
TENDERISED
TENDERISER
TENDERISERS
TENDERISES
TENDERISING
TENDERIZATION
TENDERIZATIONS
TENDERIZED
TENDERIZER
TENDERIZERS
TENDERIZES
TENDERIZING
TENDERLING
TENDERLINGS
TENDERLOIN
TENDERLOINS
TENDERNESS
TENDERNESSES
TENDEROMETER
TENDEROMETERS
TENDINITIS
TENDINITISES
TENDONITIS
TENDONITISES
TENDOVAGINITIS
TENDRESSES
TENDRILLAR
TENDRILLED
TENDRILLOUS
TENDRILOUS
TENEBRIFIC
TENEBRIONID
TENEBRIONIDS
TENEBRIOUS
TENEBRIOUSNESS
TENEBRISMS
TENEBRISTS
TENEBRITIES
TENEBROSITIES
TENEBROSITY
TENEBROUSNESS
TENEBROUSNESSES
TENEMENTAL
TENEMENTARY
TENEMENTED
TENESMUSES
TENIACIDES
TENIAFUGES
TENNANTITE
TENNANTITES
TENORRHAPHIES
TENORRHAPHY
TENOSYNOVITIS
TENOSYNOVITISES
TENOTOMIES
TENOTOMIST

TENOTOMISTS
TENOVAGINITIS
TENOVAGINITISES
TENPOUNDER
TENPOUNDERS
TENSENESSES
TENSIBILITIES
TENSIBILITY
TENSIBLENESS
TENSIBLENESSES
TENSILENESS
TENSILENESSES
TENSILITIES
TENSIMETER
TENSIMETERS
TENSIOMETER
TENSIOMETERS
TENSIOMETRIC
TENSIOMETRIES
TENSIOMETRY
TENSIONALLY
TENSIONERS
TENSIONING
TENSIONLESS
TENTACULAR
TENTACULATE
TENTACULIFEROUS
TENTACULITE
TENTACULITES
TENTACULOID
TENTACULUM
TENTATIONS
TENTATIVELY
TENTATIVENESS
TENTATIVENESSES
TENTATIVES
TENTERHOOK
TENTERHOOKS
TENTIGINOUS
TENTMAKERS
TENTORIUMS
TENUIROSTRAL
TENUOUSNESS
TENUOUSNESSES
TENURIALLY
TEPEFACTION
TEPEFACTIONS
TEPHIGRAMS
TEPHROITES
TEPHROMANCIES
TEPHROMANCY
TEPIDARIUM
TEPIDITIES
TEPIDNESSES
TERAHERTZES
TERATOCARCINOMA
TERATOGENESES
TERATOGENESIS
TERATOGENIC

TERATOGENICIST
TERATOGENICISTS
TERATOGENICITY
TERATOGENIES
TERATOGENS
TERATOGENY
TERATOLOGIC
TERATOLOGICAL
TERATOLOGIES
TERATOLOGIST
TERATOLOGISTS
TERATOLOGY
TERATOMATA
TERATOMATOUS
TERATOPHOBIA
TERATOPHOBIAS
TERCENTENARIES
TERCENTENARY
TERCENTENNIAL
TERCENTENNIALS
TEREBINTHINE
TEREBINTHS
TEREBRANTS
TEREBRATED
TEREBRATES
TEREBRATING
TEREBRATION
TEREBRATIONS
TEREBRATULA
TEREBRATULAE
TEREBRATULAS
TEREPHTHALATE
TEREPHTHALATES
TEREPHTHALIC
TERGIVERSANT
TERGIVERSANTS
TERGIVERSATE
TERGIVERSATED
TERGIVERSATES
TERGIVERSATING
TERGIVERSATION
TERGIVERSATIONS
TERGIVERSATOR
TERGIVERSATORS
TERGIVERSATORY
TERMAGANCIES
TERMAGANCY
TERMAGANTLY
TERMAGANTS
TERMINABILITIES
TERMINABILITY
TERMINABLE
TERMINABLENESS
TERMINABLY
TERMINALLY
TERMINATED
TERMINATES
TERMINATING
TERMINATION

TERMINATIONAL
TERMINATIONS
TERMINATIVE
TERMINATIVELY
TERMINATOR
TERMINATORS
TERMINATORY
TERMINISMS
TERMINISTS
TERMINOLOGICAL
TERMINOLOGIES
TERMINOLOGIST
TERMINOLOGISTS
TERMINOLOGY
TERMINUSES
TERMITARIA
TERMITARIES
TERMITARIUM
TERMITARIUMS
TERNEPLATE
TERNEPLATES
TEROTECHNOLOGY
TERPENELESS
TERPENOIDS
TERPINEOLS
TERPOLYMER
TERPOLYMERS
TERPSICHOREAL
TERPSICHOREAN
TERRACELESS
TERRACETTE
TERRACETTES
TERRACINGS
TERRACOTTA
TERRACOTTAS
TERRAFORMED
TERRAFORMING
TERRAFORMINGS
TERRAFORMS
TERRAMARES
TERRAQUEOUS
TERRARIUMS
TERREMOTIVE
TERREPLEIN
TERREPLEINS
TERRESTRIAL
TERRESTRIALLY
TERRESTRIALNESS
TERRESTRIALS
TERRIBILITIES
TERRIBILITY
TERRIBLENESS
TERRIBLENESSES
TERRICOLES
TERRICOLOUS
TERRIFICALLY
TERRIFIERS
TERRIFYING
TERRIFYINGLY

TERRIGENOUS
TERRITORIAL
TERRITORIALISE
TERRITORIALISED
TERRITORIALISES
TERRITORIALISM
TERRITORIALISMS
TERRITORIALIST
TERRITORIALISTS
TERRITORIALITY
TERRITORIALIZE
TERRITORIALIZED
TERRITORIALIZES
TERRITORIALLY
TERRITORIALS
TERRITORIED
TERRITORIES
TERRORISATION
TERRORISATIONS
TERRORISED
TERRORISER
TERRORISERS
TERRORISES
TERRORISING
TERRORISMS
TERRORISTIC
TERRORISTS
TERRORIZATION
TERRORIZATIONS
TERRORIZED
TERRORIZER
TERRORIZERS
TERRORIZES
TERRORIZING
TERRORLESS
TERSANCTUS
TERSANCTUSES
TERSENESSES
TERTIARIES
TERVALENCIES
TERVALENCY
TESCHENITE
TESCHENITES
TESSARAGLOT
TESSELATED
TESSELATES
TESSELATING
TESSELLATE
TESSELLATED
TESSELLATES
TESSELLATING
TESSELLATION
TESSELLATIONS
TESSERACTS
TESSITURAS
TESTABILITIES
TESTABILITY
TESTACEANS
TESTACEOUS

TESTAMENTAL
TESTAMENTAR
TESTAMENTARILY
TESTAMENTARY
TESTAMENTS
TESTATIONS
TESTATRICES
TESTATRIXES
TESTCROSSED
TESTCROSSES
TESTCROSSING
TESTERNING
TESTICULAR
TESTICULATE
TESTICULATED
TESTIFICATE
TESTIFICATES
TESTIFICATION
TESTIFICATIONS
TESTIFICATOR
TESTIFICATORS
TESTIFICATORY
TESTIFIERS
TESTIFYING
TESTIMONIAL
TESTIMONIALISE
TESTIMONIALISED
TESTIMONIALISES
TESTIMONIALIZE
TESTIMONIALIZED
TESTIMONIALIZES
TESTIMONIALS
TESTIMONIED
TESTIMONIES
TESTIMONYING
TESTINESSES
TESTOSTERONE
TESTOSTERONES
TESTUDINAL
TESTUDINARY
TESTUDINEOUS
TESTUDINES
TETANICALLY
TETANISATION
TETANISATIONS
TETANISING
TETANIZATION
TETANIZATIONS
TETANIZING
TETARTOHEDRAL
TETARTOHEDRALLY
TETARTOHEDRISM
TETARTOHEDRISMS
TETCHINESS
TETCHINESSES
TETHERBALL
TETHERBALLS
TETRABASIC
TETRABASICITIES

TETRABASICITY	TETRAMETER	TETRAZZINI	THANATOGNOMONIC
TETRABRACH	TETRAMETERS	TETRODOTOXIN	THANATOGRAPHIES
TETRABRACHS	TETRAMETHYLLEAD	TETRODOTOXINS	THANATOGRAPHY
TETRABRANCHIATE	TETRAMORPHIC	TETROTOXIN	THANATOLOGICAL
TETRACAINE	TETRANDRIAN	TETROTOXINS	THANATOLOGIES
TETRACAINES	TETRANDROUS	TETROXIDES	THANATOLOGIST
TETRACHLORIDE	TETRAPLEGIA	TEUTONISED	THANATOLOGISTS
TETRACHLORIDES	TETRAPLEGIAS	TEUTONISES	THANATOLOGY
TETRACHORD	TETRAPLEGIC	TEUTONISING	THANATOPHOBIA
TETRACHORDAL	TETRAPLOID	TEUTONIZED	THANATOPHOBIAS
TETRACHORDS	TETRAPLOIDIES	TEUTONIZES	THANATOPSES
TETRACHOTOMIES	TETRAPLOIDS	TEUTONIZING	THANATOPSIS
TETRACHOTOMOUS	TETRAPLOIDY	TEXTBOOKISH	THANATOSES
TETRACHOTOMY	TETRAPODIC	TEXTPHONES	THANATOSIS
TETRACTINAL	TETRAPODIES	TEXTUALISM	THANEHOODS
TETRACTINE	TETRAPODOUS	TEXTUALISMS	THANESHIPS
TETRACYCLIC	TETRAPOLIS	TEXTUALIST	THANKFULLER
TETRACYCLINE	TETRAPOLISES	TEXTUALISTS	THANKFULLEST
TETRACYCLINES	TETRAPOLITAN	TEXTUARIES	THANKFULLY
TETRADACTYL	TETRAPTERAN	TEXTURALLY	THANKFULNESS
TETRADACTYLIES	TETRAPTEROUS	TEXTURELESS	THANKFULNESSES
TETRADACTYLOUS	TETRAPTOTE	TEXTURISED	THANKLESSLY
TETRADACTYLS	TETRAPTOTES	TEXTURISES	THANKLESSNESS
TETRADACTYLY	TETRAPYRROLE	TEXTURISING	THANKLESSNESSES
TETRADITES	TETRAPYRROLES	TEXTURIZED	THANKSGIVER
TETRADRACHM	TETRARCHATE	TEXTURIZES	THANKSGIVERS
TETRADRACHMS	TETRARCHATES	TEXTURIZING	THANKSGIVING
TETRADYMITE	TETRARCHIC	THALAMENCEPHALA	THANKSGIVINGS
TETRADYMITES	TETRARCHICAL	THALAMICALLY	THANKWORTHILY
TETRADYNAMOUS	TETRARCHIES	THALAMIFLORAL	THANKWORTHINESS
TETRAETHYL	TETRASEMIC	THALASSAEMIA	THANKWORTHY
TETRAETHYLS	TETRASPORANGIA	THALASSAEMIAS	THARBOROUGH
TETRAFLUORIDE	TETRASPORANGIUM	THALASSAEMIC	THARBOROUGHS
TETRAFLUORIDES	TETRASPORE	THALASSEMIA	THATCHIEST
TETRAGONAL	TETRASPORES	THALASSEMIAS	THATCHINGS
TETRAGONALLY	TETRASPORIC	THALASSEMIC	THATCHLESS
TETRAGONALNESS	TETRASPOROUS	THALASSEMICS	THATNESSES
TETRAGONOUS	TETRASTICH	THALASSIAN	THAUMASITE
TETRAGRAMMATON	TETRASTICHAL	THALASSIANS	THAUMASITES
TETRAGRAMMATONS	TETRASTICHIC	THALASSOCRACIES	THAUMATINS
TETRAGRAMS	TETRASTICHOUS	THALASSOCRACY	THAUMATOGENIES
TETRAGYNIAN	TETRASTICHS	THALASSOCRAT	THAUMATOGENY
TETRAGYNOUS	TETRASTYLE	THALASSOCRATS	THAUMATOGRAPHY
TETRAHEDRA	TETRASTYLES	THALASSOGRAPHER	THAUMATOLATRIES
TETRAHEDRAL	TETRASYLLABIC	THALASSOGRAPHIC	THAUMATOLATRY
TETRAHEDRALLY	TETRASYLLABICAL	THALASSOGRAPHY	THAUMATOLOGIES
TETRAHEDRITE	TETRASYLLABLE	THALASSOTHERAPY	THAUMATOLOGY
TETRAHEDRITES	TETRASYLLABLES	THALATTOCRACIES	THAUMATROPE
TETRAHEDRON	TETRATHEISM	THALATTOCRACY	THAUMATROPES
TETRAHEDRONS	TETRATHEISMS	THALICTRUM	THAUMATROPICAL
TETRAHYDROFURAN	TETRATHLON	THALICTRUMS	THAUMATURGES
TETRAHYMENA	TETRATHLONS	THALIDOMIDE	THAUMATURGES
TETRAHYMENAS	TETRATOMIC	THALIDOMIDES	THAUMATURGIC
TETRALOGIES	TETRAVALENCIES	THALLIFORM	THAUMATURGICAL
TETRAMERAL	TETRAVALENCY	THALLOPHYTE	THAUMATURGICS
TETRAMERIC	TETRAVALENT	THALLOPHYTES	THAUMATURGIES
TETRAMERISM	TETRAVALENTS	THALLOPHYTIC	THAUMATURGISM
TETRAMERISMS	TETRAZOLIUM	THANATISMS	THAUMATURGISMS
TETRAMEROUS	TETRAZOLIUMS	THANATISTS	THAUMATURGIST

THAUMATURGISTS
THAUMATURGUS
THAUMATURGUSES
THAUMATURGY
THEANTHROPIC
THEANTHROPIES
THEANTHROPISM
THEANTHROPISMS
THEANTHROPIST
THEANTHROPISTS
THEANTHROPY
THEARCHIES
THEATERGOER
THEATERGOERS
THEATERGOING
THEATERGOINGS
THEATRICAL
THEATRICALISE
THEATRICALISED
THEATRICALISES
THEATRICALISING
THEATRICALISM
THEATRICALISMS
THEATRICALITIES
THEATRICALITY
THEATRICALIZE
THEATRICALIZED
THEATRICALIZES
THEATRICALIZING
THEATRICALLY
THEATRICALNESS
THEATRICALS
THEATRICISE
THEATRICISED
THEATRICISES
THEATRICISING
THEATRICISM
THEATRICISMS
THEATRICIZE
THEATRICIZED
THEATRICIZES
THEATRICIZING
THEATROMANIA
THEATROMANIAS
THEATROPHONE
THEATROPHONES
THECODONTS
THEFTUOUSLY
THEIRSELVES
THEISTICAL
THEISTICALLY
THELEMENTS
THELITISES
THELYTOKIES
THELYTOKOUS
THEMATICALLY
THEMATISATION
THEMATISATIONS
THEMATIZATION

THEMATIZATIONS
THEMSELVES
THENABOUTS
THENARDITE
THENARDITES
THENCEFORTH
THENCEFORWARD
THENCEFORWARDS
THEOBROMINE
THEOBROMINES
THEOCENTRIC
THEOCENTRICISM
THEOCENTRICISMS
THEOCENTRICITY
THEOCENTRISM
THEOCENTRISMS
THEOCRACIES
THEOCRASIES
THEOCRATIC
THEOCRATICAL
THEOCRATICALLY
THEODICEAN
THEODICEANS
THEODICIES
THEODOLITE
THEODOLITES
THEODOLITIC
THEOGONICAL
THEOGONIES
THEOGONIST
THEOGONISTS
THEOLOGASTER
THEOLOGASTERS
THEOLOGATE
THEOLOGATES
THEOLOGERS
THEOLOGIAN
THEOLOGIANS
THEOLOGICAL
THEOLOGICALLY
THEOLOGIES
THEOLOGISATION
THEOLOGISATIONS
THEOLOGISE
THEOLOGISED
THEOLOGISER
THEOLOGISERS
THEOLOGISES
THEOLOGISING
THEOLOGIST
THEOLOGISTS
THEOLOGIZATION
THEOLOGIZATIONS
THEOLOGIZE
THEOLOGIZED
THEOLOGIZER
THEOLOGIZERS
THEOLOGIZES
THEOLOGIZING

THEOLOGOUMENA
THEOLOGOUMENON
THEOLOGUES
THEOMACHIES
THEOMACHIST
THEOMACHISTS
THEOMANCIES
THEOMANIAC
THEOMANIACS
THEOMANIAS
THEOMANTIC
THEOMORPHIC
THEOMORPHISM
THEOMORPHISMS
THEONOMIES
THEONOMOUS
THEOPATHETIC
THEOPATHIC
THEOPATHIES
THEOPHAGIES
THEOPHAGOUS
THEOPHANIC
THEOPHANIES
THEOPHANOUS
THEOPHOBIA
THEOPHOBIAC
THEOPHOBIACS
THEOPHOBIAS
THEOPHOBIST
THEOPHOBISTS
THEOPHORIC
THEOPHYLLINE
THEOPHYLLINES
THEOPNEUST
THEOPNEUSTIC
THEOPNEUSTIES
THEOPNEUSTY
THEORBISTS
THEOREMATIC
THEOREMATICAL
THEOREMATICALLY
THEOREMATIST
THEOREMATISTS
THEORETICAL
THEORETICALLY
THEORETICIAN
THEORETICIANS
THEORETICS
THEORIQUES
THEORISATION
THEORISATIONS
THEORISERS
THEORISING
THEORIZATION
THEORIZATIONS
THEORIZERS
THEORIZING
THEOSOPHER
THEOSOPHERS

THEOSOPHIC
THEOSOPHICAL
THEOSOPHICALLY
THEOSOPHIES
THEOSOPHISE
THEOSOPHISED
THEOSOPHISES
THEOSOPHISING
THEOSOPHISM
THEOSOPHISMS
THEOSOPHIST
THEOSOPHISTICAL
THEOSOPHISTS
THEOSOPHIZE
THEOSOPHIZED
THEOSOPHIZES
THEOSOPHIZING
THEOTECHNIC
THEOTECHNIES
THEOTECHNY
THERALITES
THERAPEUSES
THERAPEUSIS
THERAPEUTIC
THERAPEUTICALLY
THERAPEUTICS
THERAPEUTIST
THERAPEUTISTS
THERAPISTS
THERAPSIDS
THEREABOUT
THEREABOUTS
THEREAFTER
THEREAGAINST
THEREAMONG
THEREANENT
THEREBESIDE
THEREINAFTER
THEREINBEFORE
THERENESSES
THERETHROUGH
THERETOFORE
THEREUNDER
THEREWITHAL
THEREWITHIN
THERIANTHROPIC
THERIANTHROPISM
THERIOLATRIES
THERIOLATRY
THERIOMORPH
THERIOMORPHIC
THERIOMORPHISM
THERIOMORPHISMS
THERIOMORPHOSES
THERIOMORPHOSIS
THERIOMORPHOUS
THERIOMORPHS
THERMAESTHESIA
THERMAESTHESIAS

THERMALISATION	THERMOGRAMS	THERMOSPHERE	THIGMOTAXES
THERMALISATIONS	THERMOGRAPH	THERMOSPHERES	THIGMOTAXIS
THERMALISE	THERMOGRAPHER	THERMOSPHERIC	THIGMOTROPIC
THERMALISED	THERMOGRAPHERS	THERMOSTABILITY	THIGMOTROPISM
THERMALISES	THERMOGRAPHIC	THERMOSTABLE	THIGMOTROPISMS
THERMALISING	THERMOGRAPHIES	THERMOSTAT	THIMBLEBERRIES
THERMALIZATION	THERMOGRAPHS	THERMOSTATED	THIMBLEBERRY
THERMALIZATIONS	THERMOGRAPHY	THERMOSTATIC	THIMBLEFUL
THERMALIZE	THERMOHALINE	THERMOSTATICS	THIMBLEFULS
THERMALIZED	THERMOJUNCTION	THERMOSTATING	THIMBLERIG
THERMALIZES	THERMOJUNCTIONS	THERMOSTATS	THIMBLERIGGED
THERMALIZING	THERMOLABILE	THERMOSTATTED	THIMBLERIGGER
THERMESTHESIA	THERMOLABILITY	THERMOSTATTING	THIMBLERIGGERS
THERMESTHESIAS	THERMOLOGIES	THERMOTACTIC	THIMBLERIGGING
THERMETTES	THERMOLOGY	THERMOTAXES	THIMBLERIGGINGS
THERMICALLY	THERMOLYSES	THERMOTAXIC	THIMBLERIGS
THERMIDORS	THERMOLYSIS	THERMOTAXIS	THIMBLESFUL
THERMIONIC	THERMOLYTIC	THERMOTENSILE	THIMBLEWEED
THERMIONICS	THERMOMAGNETIC	THERMOTHERAPIES	THIMBLEWEEDS
THERMISTOR	THERMOMETER	THERMOTHERAPY	THIMBLEWIT
THERMISTORS	THERMOMETERS	THERMOTICAL	THIMBLEWITS
THERMOBALANCE	THERMOMETRIC	THERMOTICS	THIMBLEWITTED
THERMOBALANCES	THERMOMETRICAL	THERMOTOLERANT	THIMEROSAL
THERMOBARIC	THERMOMETRIES	THERMOTROPIC	THIMEROSALS
THERMOBAROGRAPH	THERMOMETRY	THERMOTROPICS	THINGAMABOB
THERMOBAROMETER	THERMOMOTOR	THERMOTROPISM	THINGAMABOBS
THERMOCHEMICAL	THERMOMOTORS	THERMOTROPISMS	THINGAMAJIG
THERMOCHEMIST	THERMONASTIES	THEROLOGIES	THINGAMAJIGS
THERMOCHEMISTRY	THERMONASTY	THEROPHYTE	THINGAMIES
THERMOCHEMISTS	THERMONUCLEAR	THEROPHYTES	THINGAMYBOB
THERMOCHROMIC	THERMOPERIODIC	THEROPODAN	THINGAMYBOBS
THERMOCHROMIES	THERMOPERIODISM	THEROPODANS	THINGAMYJIG
THERMOCHROMISM	THERMOPHIL	THERSITICAL	THINGAMYJIGS
THERMOCHROMISMS	THERMOPHILE	THESAURUSES	THINGHOODS
THERMOCHROMY	THERMOPHILES	THESMOTHETE	THINGINESS
THERMOCLINE	THERMOPHILIC	THESMOTHETES	THINGINESSES
THERMOCLINES	THERMOPHILOUS	THETICALLY	THINGLINESS
THERMOCOUPLE	THERMOPHILS	THEURGICAL	THINGLINESSES
THERMOCOUPLES	THERMOPHYLLOUS	THEURGICALLY	THINGNESSES
THERMODURIC	THERMOPILE	THEURGISTS	THINGUMABOB
THERMODYNAMIC	THERMOPILES	THIABENDAZOLE	THINGUMABOBS
THERMODYNAMICAL	THERMOPLASTIC	THIABENDAZOLES	THINGUMAJIG
THERMODYNAMICS	THERMOPLASTICS	THIAMINASE	THINGUMAJIGS
THERMOELECTRIC	THERMORECEPTOR	THIAMINASES	THINGUMBOB
THERMOELECTRON	THERMORECEPTORS	THICKENERS	THINGUMBOBS
THERMOELECTRONS	THERMOREGULATE	THICKENING	THINGUMMIES
THERMOELEMENT	THERMOREGULATED	THICKENINGS	THINGUMMYBOB
THERMOELEMENTS	THERMOREGULATES	THICKHEADED	THINGUMMYBOBS
THERMOFORM	THERMOREGULATOR	THICKHEADEDNESS	THINGUMMYJIG
THERMOFORMABLE	THERMOREMANENCE	THICKHEADS	THINGUMMYJIGS
THERMOFORMED	THERMOREMANENT	THICKLEAVES	THINKABLENESS
THERMOFORMING	THERMOSCOPE	THICKNESSES	THINKABLENESSES
THERMOFORMS	THERMOSCOPES	THICKSKINS	THINKINGLY
THERMOGENESES	THERMOSCOPIC	THIEVERIES	THINKINGNESS
THERMOGENESIS	THERMOSCOPICAL	THIEVISHLY	THINKINGNESSES
THERMOGENETIC	THERMOSETS	THIEVISHNESS	THINKPIECE
THERMOGENIC	THERMOSETTING	THIEVISHNESSES	THINKPIECES
THERMOGENOUS	THERMOSIPHON	THIGHBONES	THINNESSES
THERMOGRAM	THERMOSIPHONS	THIGMOTACTIC	THIOALCOHOL

THIOALCOHOLS

THIOALCOHOLS	THORACOCENTESES	THRALLDOMS	THROATIEST
THIOBACILLI	THORACOCENTESIS	THRAPPLING	THROATINESS
THIOBACILLUS	THORACOPLASTIES	THRASHINGS	THROATINESSES
THIOBARBITURATE	THORACOPLASTY	THRASONICAL	THROATLASH
THIOCARBAMIDE	THORACOSCOPE	THRASONICALLY	THROATLASHES
THIOCARBAMIDES	THORACOSCOPES	THREADBARE	THROATLATCH
THIOCYANATE	THORACOSTOMIES	THREADBARENESS	THROATLATCHES
THIOCYANATES	THORACOSTOMY	THREADFINS	THROATWORT
THIOCYANIC	THORACOTOMIES	THREADIEST	THROATWORTS
THIODIGLYCOL	THORACOTOMY	THREADINESS	THROBBINGLY
THIODIGLYCOLS	THORIANITE	THREADINESSES	THROBBINGS
THIOFURANS	THORIANITES	THREADLESS	THROMBOCYTE
THIOPENTAL	THORNBACKS	THREADLIKE	THROMBOCYTES
THIOPENTALS	THORNBILLS	THREADMAKER	THROMBOCYTIC
THIOPENTONE	THORNBUSHES	THREADMAKERS	THROMBOEMBOLIC
THIOPENTONES	THORNHEDGE	THREADWORM	THROMBOEMBOLISM
THIOPHENES	THORNHEDGES	THREADWORMS	THROMBOGEN
THIORIDAZINE	THORNINESS	THREATENED	THROMBOGENS
THIORIDAZINES	THORNINESSES	THREATENER	THROMBOKINASE
THIOSINAMINE	THORNPROOFS	THREATENERS	THROMBOKINASES
THIOSINAMINES	THORNTREES	THREATENING	THROMBOLYSES
THIOSULFATE	THOROUGHBASS	THREATENINGLY	THROMBOLYSIS
THIOSULFATES	THOROUGHBASSES	THREATENINGS	THROMBOLYTIC
THIOSULPHATE	THOROUGHBRACE	THREEFOLDNESS	THROMBOLYTICS
THIOSULPHATES	THOROUGHBRACED	THREEFOLDNESSES	THROMBOPHILIA
THIOSULPHURIC	THOROUGHBRACES	THREENESSES	THROMBOPHILIAS
THIOURACIL	THOROUGHBRED	THREEPENCE	THROMBOPLASTIC
THIOURACILS	THOROUGHBREDS	THREEPENCES	THROMBOPLASTIN
THIRDBOROUGH	THOROUGHER	THREEPENCEWORTH	THROMBOPLASTINS
THIRDBOROUGHS	THOROUGHEST	THREEPENNIES	THROMBOSED
THIRDSTREAM	THOROUGHFARE	THREEPENNY	THROMBOSES
THIRDSTREAMS	THOROUGHFARES	THREEPENNYWORTH	THROMBOSING
THIRSTIEST	THOROUGHGOING	THREESCORE	THROMBOSIS
THIRSTINESS	THOROUGHGOINGLY	THREESCORES	THROMBOTIC
THIRSTINESSES	THOROUGHLY	THREESOMES	THROMBOXANE
THIRSTLESS	THOROUGHNESS	THREMMATOLOGIES	THROMBOXANES
THIRTEENTH	THOROUGHNESSES	THREMMATOLOGY	THRONELESS
THIRTEENTHLY	THOROUGHPACED	THRENETICAL	THRONGINGS
THIRTEENTHS	THOROUGHPIN	THRENODIAL	THROPPLING
THIRTIETHS	THOROUGHPINS	THRENODIES	THROTTLEABLE
THIRTYFOLD	THOROUGHWAX	THRENODIST	THROTTLEHOLD
THIRTYSOMETHING	THOROUGHWAXES	THRENODISTS	THROTTLEHOLDS
THISNESSES	THOROUGHWORT	THREONINES	THROTTLERS
THISTLEDOWN	THOROUGHWORTS	THRESHINGS	THROTTLING
THISTLEDOWNS	THOUGHTCAST	THRESHOLDS	THROTTLINGS
THISTLIEST	THOUGHTCASTS	THRIFTIEST	THROUGHFARE
THITHERWARD	THOUGHTFUL	THRIFTINESS	THROUGHFARES
THITHERWARDS	THOUGHTFULLY	THRIFTINESSES	THROUGHGAUN
THIXOTROPE	THOUGHTFULNESS	THRIFTLESS	THROUGHGAUNS
THIXOTROPES	THOUGHTLESS	THRIFTLESSLY	THROUGHITHER
THIXOTROPIC	THOUGHTLESSLY	THRIFTLESSNESS	THROUGHOTHER
THIXOTROPIES	THOUGHTLESSNESS	THRILLIEST	THROUGHOUT
THIXOTROPY	THOUGHTWAY	THRILLINGLY	THROUGHPUT
THOLEIITES	THOUGHTWAYS	THRILLINGNESS	THROUGHPUTS
THOLEIITIC	THOUSANDFOLD	THRILLINGNESSES	THROUGHWAY
THOLOBATES	THOUSANDFOLDS	THRIVELESS	THROUGHWAYS
THORACENTESES	THOUSANDTH	THRIVINGLY	THROWAWAYS
THORACENTESIS	THOUSANDTHS	THRIVINGNESS	THROWBACKS
THORACICALLY	THRAIPINGS	THRIVINGNESSES	THROWSTERS

THRUMMIEST	THUNDERSTORM	THYSANURANS	TIGRISHNESSES
THRUMMINGLY	THUNDERSTORMS	THYSANUROUS	TIKOLOSHES
THRUMMINGS	THUNDERSTRICKEN	TIBIOFIBULA	TILEFISHES
THRUPPENCE	THUNDERSTRIKE	TIBIOFIBULAE	TILIACEOUS
THRUPPENCES	THUNDERSTRIKES	TIBIOFIBULAS	TILLANDSIA
THRUPPENNIES	THUNDERSTRIKING	TIBIOTARSI	TILLANDSIAS
THRUPPENNY	THUNDERSTROKE	TIBIOTARSUS	TILLERLESS
THRUSTINGS	THUNDERSTROKES	TIBOUCHINA	TILTMETERS
THRUTCHING	THUNDERSTRUCK	TIBOUCHINAS	TILTROTORS
THUDDINGLY	THURIFEROUS	TICHORRHINE	TIMBERDOODLE
THUGGERIES	THURIFICATION	TICKETINGS	TIMBERDOODLES
THUMBHOLES	THURIFICATIONS	TICKETLESS	TIMBERHEAD
THUMBIKINS	THURIFYING	TICKETTYBOO	TIMBERHEADS
THUMBLINGS	THUSNESSES	TICKLISHLY	TIMBERINGS
THUMBNAILS	THWACKINGS	TICKLISHNESS	TIMBERLAND
THUMBPIECE	THWARTEDLY	TICKLISHNESSES	TIMBERLANDS
THUMBPIECES	THWARTINGLY	TICKTACKED	TIMBERLINE
THUMBPRINT	THWARTINGS	TICKTACKING	TIMBERLINES
THUMBPRINTS	THWARTSHIP	TICKTACKTOE	TIMBERWORK
THUMBSCREW	THWARTSHIPS	TICKTACKTOES	TIMBERWORKS
THUMBSCREWS	THWARTWAYS	TICKTOCKED	TIMBERYARD
THUMBSTALL	THWARTWISE	TICKTOCKING	TIMBERYARDS
THUMBSTALLS	THYLACINES	TICTACKING	TIMBRELLED
THUMBTACKED	THYLAKOIDS	TICTOCKING	TIMBROLOGIES
THUMBTACKING	THYMECTOMIES	TIDDLEDYWINK	TIMBROLOGIST
THUMBTACKS	THYMECTOMISE	TIDDLEDYWINKS	TIMBROLOGISTS
THUMBWHEEL	THYMECTOMISED	TIDDLEYWINK	TIMBROLOGY
THUMBWHEELS	THYMECTOMISES	TIDDLEYWINKS	TIMBROMANIA
THUMPINGLY	THYMECTOMISING	TIDDLYWINK	TIMBROMANIAC
THUNBERGIA	THYMECTOMIZE	TIDDLYWINKS	TIMBROMANIACS
THUNBERGIAS	THYMECTOMIZED	TIDEWAITER	TIMBROMANIAS
THUNDERBIRD	THYMECTOMIZES	TIDEWAITERS	TIMBROPHILIES
THUNDERBIRDS	THYMECTOMIZING	TIDEWATERS	TIMBROPHILIST
THUNDERBOLT	THYMECTOMY	TIDINESSES	TIMBROPHILISTS
THUNDERBOLTS	THYMELAEACEOUS	TIDIVATING	TIMBROPHILY
THUNDERBOX	THYMIDINES	TIDIVATION	TIMEFRAMES
THUNDERBOXES	THYMIDYLIC	TIDIVATIONS	TIMEKEEPER
THUNDERCLAP	THYMOCYTES	TIEBREAKER	TIMEKEEPERS
THUNDERCLAPS	THYRATRONS	TIEBREAKERS	TIMEKEEPING
THUNDERCLOUD	THYRISTORS	TIEMANNITE	TIMEKEEPINGS
THUNDERCLOUDS	THYROCALCITONIN	TIEMANNITES	TIMELESSLY
THUNDERERS	THYROGLOBULIN	TIERCELETS	TIMELESSNESS
THUNDERFLASH	THYROGLOBULINS	TIERCERONS	TIMELESSNESSES
THUNDERFLASHES	THYROIDECTOMIES	TIGERISHLY	TIMELINESS
THUNDERHEAD	THYROIDECTOMY	TIGERISHNESS	TIMELINESSES
THUNDERHEADS	THYROIDITIS	TIGERISHNESSES	TIMENOGUYS
THUNDERIER	THYROIDITISES	TIGGYWINKLE	TIMEPASSED
THUNDERIEST	THYROTOXICOSES	TIGGYWINKLES	TIMEPASSES
THUNDERING	THYROTOXICOSIS	TIGHTASSED	TIMEPASSING
THUNDERINGLY	THYROTROPHIC	TIGHTASSES	TIMEPIECES
THUNDERINGS	THYROTROPHIN	TIGHTENERS	TIMEPLEASER
THUNDERLESS	THYROTROPHINS	TIGHTENING	TIMEPLEASERS
THUNDEROUS	THYROTROPIC	TIGHTFISTED	TIMESAVERS
THUNDEROUSLY	THYROTROPIN	TIGHTFISTEDNESS	TIMESAVING
THUNDEROUSNESS	THYROTROPINS	TIGHTISHLY	TIMESCALES
THUNDERSHOWER	THYROXINES	TIGHTNESSES	TIMESERVER
THUNDERSHOWERS	THYRSOIDAL	TIGHTROPES	TIMESERVERS
THUNDERSTONE	THYSANOPTEROUS	TIGHTWIRES	TIMESERVING
THUNDERSTONES	THYSANURAN	TIGRISHNESS	TIMESERVINGS

TIMETABLED
TIMETABLES
TIMETABLING
TIMEWORKER
TIMEWORKERS
TIMIDITIES
TIMIDNESSES
TIMOCRACIES
TIMOCRATIC
TIMOCRATICAL
TIMOROUSLY
TIMOROUSNESS
TIMOROUSNESSES
TIMPANISTS
TINCTORIAL
TINCTORIALLY
TINCTURING
TINDERBOXES
TINGLINGLY
TINGUAITES
TININESSES
TINKERINGS
TINKERTOYS
TINKLINGLY
TINNINESSES
TINNITUSES
TINPLATING
TINSELLING
TINSELRIES
TINSMITHING
TINSMITHINGS
TINTINESSES
TINTINNABULA
TINTINNABULANT
TINTINNABULAR
TINTINNABULARY
TINTINNABULATE
TINTINNABULATED
TINTINNABULATES
TINTINNABULOUS
TINTINNABULUM
TINTOMETER
TINTOMETERS
TINTOOKIES
TIPPYTOEING
TIPSIFYING
TIPSINESSES
TIPTRONICS
TIRAILLEUR
TIRAILLEURS
TIREDNESSES
TIRELESSLY
TIRELESSNESS
TIRELESSNESSES
TIRESOMELY
TIRESOMENESS
TIRESOMENESSES
TIROCINIUM
TIROCINIUMS

TITANESSES
TITANICALLY
TITANIFEROUS
TITANOSAUR
TITANOSAURS
TITANOTHERE
TITANOTHERES
TITARAKURA
TITARAKURAS
TITHINGMAN
TITHINGMEN
TITILLATED
TITILLATES
TITILLATING
TITILLATINGLY
TITILLATION
TITILLATIONS
TITILLATIVE
TITILLATOR
TITILLATORS
TITIPOUNAMU
TITIVATING
TITIVATION
TITIVATIONS
TITIVATORS
TITLEHOLDER
TITLEHOLDERS
TITLEHOLDING
TITRATABLE
TITRATIONS
TITRIMETRIC
TITTERINGLY
TITTERINGS
TITTIVATED
TITTIVATES
TITTIVATING
TITTIVATION
TITTIVATIONS
TITTIVATOR
TITTIVATORS
TITTLEBATS
TITTUPPING
TITUBANCIES
TITUBATING
TITUBATION
TITUBATIONS
TITULARIES
TITULARITIES
TITULARITY
TOADEATERS
TOADFISHES
TOADFLAXES
TOADGRASSES
TOADRUSHES
TOADSTONES
TOADSTOOLS
TOASTMASTER
TOASTMASTERS
TOASTMISTRESS

TOASTMISTRESSES
TOBACCANALIAN
TOBACCANALIANS
TOBACCOLESS
TOBACCONIST
TOBACCONISTS
TOBOGGANED
TOBOGGANER
TOBOGGANERS
TOBOGGANING
TOBOGGANINGS
TOBOGGANIST
TOBOGGANISTS
TOBOGGINED
TOBOGGINING
TOCCATELLA
TOCCATELLAS
TOCCATINAS
TOCHERLESS
TOCOLOGIES
TOCOPHEROL
TOCOPHEROLS
TODDLERHOOD
TODDLERHOODS
TOENAILING
TOERAGGERS
TOFFISHNESS
TOFFISHNESSES
TOGAVIRUSES
TOGETHERNESS
TOGETHERNESSES
TOILETRIES
TOILFULNESS
TOILFULNESSES
TOILINETTE
TOILINETTES
TOILSOMELY
TOILSOMENESS
TOILSOMENESSES
TOKENISTIC
TOKOLOGIES
TOKOLOSHES
TOKOLOSHIS
TOKTOKKIES
TOLBUTAMIDE
TOLBUTAMIDES
TOLERABILITIES
TOLERABILITY
TOLERABLENESS
TOLERABLENESSES
TOLERANCES
TOLERANTLY
TOLERATING
TOLERATION
TOLERATIONISM
TOLERATIONISMS
TOLERATIONIST
TOLERATIONISTS
TOLERATIONS

TOLERATIVE
TOLERATORS
TOLLBOOTHS
TOLLBRIDGE
TOLLBRIDGES
TOLLDISHES
TOLLHOUSES
TOLUIDIDES
TOLUIDINES
TOMAHAWKED
TOMAHAWKING
TOMATILLOES
TOMATILLOS
TOMBOYISHLY
TOMBOYISHNESS
TOMBOYISHNESSES
TOMBSTONES
TOMCATTING
TOMFOOLERIES
TOMFOOLERY
TOMFOOLING
TOMFOOLISH
TOMFOOLISHNESS
TOMOGRAPHIC
TOMOGRAPHIES
TOMOGRAPHS
TOMOGRAPHY
TONALITIES
TONALITIVE
TONELESSLY
TONELESSNESS
TONELESSNESSES
TONETICALLY
TONGUELESS
TONGUELETS
TONGUELIKE
TONGUESTER
TONGUESTERS
TONICITIES
TONISHNESS
TONISHNESSES
TONNISHNESS
TONNISHNESSES
TONOMETERS
TONOMETRIC
TONOMETRIES
TONOPLASTS
TONSILITIS
TONSILITISES
TONSILLARY
TONSILLECTOMIES
TONSILLECTOMY
TONSILLITIC
TONSILLITIS
TONSILLITISES
TONSILLOTOMIES
TONSILLOTOMY
TOOLHOLDER
TOOLHOLDERS

TOOLHOUSES	TOPOGRAPHERS	TORREFACTIONS	TOTALIZATORS
TOOLMAKERS	TOPOGRAPHIC	TORREFYING	TOTALIZERS
TOOLMAKING	TOPOGRAPHICAL	TORRENTIAL	TOTALIZING
TOOLMAKINGS	TOPOGRAPHICALLY	TORRENTIALITIES	TOTAQUINES
TOOLPUSHER	TOPOGRAPHIES	TORRENTIALITY	TOTEMICALLY
TOOLPUSHERS	TOPOGRAPHS	TORRENTIALLY	TOTEMISTIC
TOOTHACHES	TOPOGRAPHY	TORRENTUOUS	TOTIPALMATE
TOOTHBRUSH	TOPOLOGICAL	TORRIDITIES	TOTIPALMATION
TOOTHBRUSHES	TOPOLOGICALLY	TORRIDNESS	TOTIPALMATIONS
TOOTHBRUSHING	TOPOLOGIES	TORRIDNESSES	TOTIPOTENCIES
TOOTHBRUSHINGS	TOPOLOGIST	TORRIFYING	TOTIPOTENCY
TOOTHCOMBS	TOPOLOGISTS	TORSIBILITIES	TOTIPOTENT
TOOTHFISHES	TOPONYMICAL	TORSIBILITY	TOTTERINGLY
TOOTHINESS	TOPONYMICS	TORSIOGRAPH	TOTTERINGS
TOOTHINESSES	TOPONYMIES	TORSIOGRAPHS	TOUCHABLENESS
TOOTHPASTE	TOPONYMIST	TORSIONALLY	TOUCHABLENESSES
TOOTHPASTES	TOPONYMISTS	TORTELLINI	TOUCHBACKS
TOOTHPICKS	TOPOPHILIA	TORTELLINIS	TOUCHDOWNS
TOOTHSHELL	TOPOPHILIAS	TORTFEASOR	TOUCHHOLES
TOOTHSHELLS	TOPSOILING	TORTFEASORS	TOUCHINESS
TOOTHSOMELY	TOPSOILINGS	TORTICOLLAR	TOUCHINESSES
TOOTHSOMENESS	TOPSTITCHED	TORTICOLLIS	TOUCHINGLY
TOOTHSOMENESSES	TOPSTITCHES	TORTICOLLISES	TOUCHINGNESS
TOOTHWASHES	TOPSTITCHING	TORTILITIES	TOUCHINGNESSES
TOOTHWORTS	TOPWORKING	TORTILLONS	TOUCHLINES
TOPAGNOSES	TORBANITES	TORTIOUSLY	TOUCHMARKS
TOPAGNOSIA	TORBERNITE	TORTOISESHELL	TOUCHPAPER
TOPAGNOSIAS	TORBERNITES	TORTOISESHELLS	TOUCHPAPERS
TOPAGNOSIS	TORCHBEARER	TORTRICIDS	TOUCHSTONE
TOPARCHIES	TORCHBEARERS	TORTUOSITIES	TOUCHSTONES
TOPAZOLITE	TORCHIERES	TORTUOSITY	TOUCHTONES
TOPAZOLITES	TORCHLIGHT	TORTUOUSLY	TOUCHWOODS
TOPCROSSES	TORCHLIGHTS	TORTUOUSNESS	TOUGHENERS
TOPDRESSING	TORCHWOODS	TORTUOUSNESSES	TOUGHENING
TOPDRESSINGS	TORMENTEDLY	TORTUREDLY	TOUGHENINGS
TOPECTOMIES	TORMENTERS	TORTURESOME	TOUGHNESSES
TOPGALLANT	TORMENTILS	TORTURINGLY	TOURBILLION
TOPGALLANTS	TORMENTING	TORTURINGS	TOURBILLIONS
TOPHACEOUS	TORMENTINGLY	TORTUROUSLY	TOURBILLON
TOPIARISTS	TORMENTINGS	TOSSICATED	TOURBILLONS
TOPICALITIES	TORMENTORS	TOSTICATED	TOURISTICALLY
TOPICALITY	TORMENTUMS	TOSTICATION	TOURMALINE
TOPKNOTTED	TOROIDALLY	TOSTICATIONS	TOURMALINES
TOPLESSNESS	TOROSITIES	TOTALISATION	TOURMALINIC
TOPLESSNESSES	TORPEDINOUS	TOTALISATIONS	TOURNAMENT
TOPLOFTICAL	TORPEDOERS	TOTALISATOR	TOURNAMENTS
TOPLOFTIER	TORPEDOING	TOTALISATORS	TOURNEYERS
TOPLOFTIEST	TORPEDOIST	TOTALISERS	TOURNEYING
TOPLOFTILY	TORPEDOISTS	TOTALISING	TOURNIQUET
TOPLOFTINESS	TORPEFYING	TOTALISTIC	TOURNIQUETS
TOPLOFTINESSES	TORPESCENCE	TOTALITARIAN	TOURTIERES
TOPMAKINGS	TORPESCENCES	TOTALITARIANISE	TOVARICHES
TOPMINNOWS	TORPESCENT	TOTALITARIANISM	TOVARISCHES
TOPNOTCHER	TORPIDITIES	TOTALITARIANIZE	TOVARISHES
TOPNOTCHERS	TORPIDNESS	TOTALITARIANS	TOWARDLINESS
TOPOCENTRIC	TORPIDNESSES	TOTALITIES	TOWARDLINESSES
TOPOCHEMISTRIES	TORPITUDES	TOTALIZATION	TOWARDNESS
TOPOCHEMISTRY	TORPORIFIC	TOTALIZATIONS	TOWARDNESSES
TOPOGRAPHER	TORREFACTION	TOTALIZATOR	TOWELETTES

TOWELHEADS
TOWELLINGS
TOWERINGLY
TOWNHOUSES
TOWNSCAPED
TOWNSCAPES
TOWNSCAPING
TOWNSCAPINGS
TOWNSFOLKS
TOWNSPEOPLE
TOWNSPEOPLES
TOWNSWOMAN
TOWNSWOMEN
TOXALBUMIN
TOXALBUMINS
TOXAPHENES
TOXICATION
TOXICATIONS
TOXICITIES
TOXICOGENIC
TOXICOLOGIC
TOXICOLOGICAL
TOXICOLOGICALLY
TOXICOLOGIES
TOXICOLOGIST
TOXICOLOGISTS
TOXICOLOGY
TOXICOMANIA
TOXICOMANIAS
TOXICOPHAGOUS
TOXICOPHOBIA
TOXICOPHOBIAS
TOXIGENICITIES
TOXIGENICITY
TOXIPHAGOUS
TOXIPHOBIA
TOXIPHOBIAC
TOXIPHOBIACS
TOXIPHOBIAS
TOXOCARIASES
TOXOCARIASIS
TOXOPHILIES
TOXOPHILITE
TOXOPHILITES
TOXOPHILITIC
TOXOPLASMA
TOXOPLASMAS
TOXOPLASMIC
TOXOPLASMOSES
TOXOPLASMOSIS
TOYISHNESS
TOYISHNESSES
TRABEATION
TRABEATIONS
TRABECULAE
TRABECULAR
TRABECULAS
TRABECULATE
TRABECULATED

TRACASSERIE
TRACASSERIES
TRACEABILITIES
TRACEABILITY
TRACEABLENESS
TRACEABLENESSES
TRACELESSLY
TRACHEARIAN
TRACHEARIANS
TRACHEARIES
TRACHEATED
TRACHEATES
TRACHEIDAL
TRACHEIDES
TRACHEITIS
TRACHEITISES
TRACHELATE
TRACHEOLAR
TRACHEOLES
TRACHEOPHYTE
TRACHEOPHYTES
TRACHEOSCOPIES
TRACHEOSCOPY
TRACHEOSTOMIES
TRACHEOSTOMY
TRACHEOTOMIES
TRACHEOTOMY
TRACHINUSES
TRACHITISES
TRACHOMATOUS
TRACHYPTERUS
TRACHYPTERUSES
TRACHYTOID
TRACKBALLS
TRACKERBALL
TRACKERBALLS
TRACKLAYER
TRACKLAYERS
TRACKLAYING
TRACKLAYINGS
TRACKLEMENT
TRACKLEMENTS
TRACKLESSLY
TRACKLESSNESS
TRACKLESSNESSES
TRACKROADS
TRACKSIDES
TRACKSUITS
TRACKWALKER
TRACKWALKERS
TRACTABILITIES
TRACTABILITY
TRACTABLENESS
TRACTABLENESSES
TRACTARIAN
TRACTARIANS
TRACTATORS
TRACTILITIES
TRACTILITY

TRACTIONAL
TRACTORATION
TRACTORATIONS
TRACTORFEED
TRACTORFEEDS
TRACTRICES
TRADECRAFT
TRADECRAFTS
TRADEMARKED
TRADEMARKING
TRADEMARKS
TRADENAMES
TRADERSHIP
TRADERSHIPS
TRADESCANTIA
TRADESCANTIAS
TRADESFOLK
TRADESFOLKS
TRADESMANLIKE
TRADESPEOPLE
TRADESPEOPLES
TRADESWOMAN
TRADESWOMEN
TRADITIONAL
TRADITIONALISE
TRADITIONALISED
TRADITIONALISES
TRADITIONALISM
TRADITIONALISMS
TRADITIONALIST
TRADITIONALISTS
TRADITIONALITY
TRADITIONALIZE
TRADITIONALIZED
TRADITIONALIZES
TRADITIONALLY
TRADITIONARILY
TRADITIONARY
TRADITIONER
TRADITIONERS
TRADITIONIST
TRADITIONISTS
TRADITIONLESS
TRADITIONS
TRADITORES
TRADUCEMENT
TRADUCEMENTS
TRADUCIANISM
TRADUCIANISMS
TRADUCIANIST
TRADUCIANISTIC
TRADUCIANISTS
TRADUCIANS
TRADUCIBLE
TRADUCINGLY
TRADUCINGS
TRADUCTION
TRADUCTIONS
TRADUCTIVE

TRAFFICABILITY
TRAFFICABLE
TRAFFICATOR
TRAFFICATORS
TRAFFICKED
TRAFFICKER
TRAFFICKERS
TRAFFICKING
TRAFFICKINGS
TRAFFICLESS
TRAGACANTH
TRAGACANTHS
TRAGEDIANS
TRAGEDIENNE
TRAGEDIENNES
TRAGELAPHINE
TRAGELAPHS
TRAGICALLY
TRAGICALNESS
TRAGICALNESSES
TRAGICOMEDIES
TRAGICOMEDY
TRAGICOMIC
TRAGICOMICAL
TRAGICOMICALLY
TRAILBASTON
TRAILBASTONS
TRAILBLAZER
TRAILBLAZERS
TRAILBLAZING
TRAILBLAZINGS
TRAILBREAKER
TRAILBREAKERS
TRAILERABLE
TRAILERING
TRAILERINGS
TRAILERIST
TRAILERISTS
TRAILERITE
TRAILERITES
TRAILHEADS
TRAILINGLY
TRAINABILITIES
TRAINABILITY
TRAINBANDS
TRAINBEARER
TRAINBEARERS
TRAINEESHIP
TRAINEESHIPS
TRAINLOADS
TRAINSPOTTERISH
TRAIPSINGS
TRAITORESS
TRAITORESSES
TRAITORHOOD
TRAITORHOODS
TRAITORISM
TRAITORISMS
TRAITOROUS

TRAITOROUSLY
TRAITOROUSNESS
TRAITORSHIP
TRAITORSHIPS
TRAITRESSES
TRAJECTILE
TRAJECTING
TRAJECTION
TRAJECTIONS
TRAJECTORIES
TRAJECTORY
TRALATICIOUS
TRALATITIOUS
TRAMELLING
TRAMMELERS
TRAMMELING
TRAMMELLED
TRAMMELLER
TRAMMELLERS
TRAMMELLING
TRAMONTANA
TRAMONTANAS
TRAMONTANE
TRAMONTANES
TRAMPETTES
TRAMPLINGS
TRAMPOLINE
TRAMPOLINED
TRAMPOLINER
TRAMPOLINERS
TRAMPOLINES
TRAMPOLINING
TRAMPOLININGS
TRAMPOLINIST
TRAMPOLINISTS
TRAMPOLINS
TRANCELIKE
TRANQUILER
TRANQUILEST
TRANQUILISATION
TRANQUILISE
TRANQUILISED
TRANQUILISER
TRANQUILISERS
TRANQUILISES
TRANQUILISING
TRANQUILISINGLY
TRANQUILITIES
TRANQUILITY
TRANQUILIZATION
TRANQUILIZE
TRANQUILIZED
TRANQUILIZER
TRANQUILIZERS
TRANQUILIZES
TRANQUILIZING
TRANQUILIZINGLY
TRANQUILLER
TRANQUILLEST

TRANQUILLISE
TRANQUILLISED
TRANQUILLISER
TRANQUILLISERS
TRANQUILLISES
TRANQUILLISING
TRANQUILLITIES
TRANQUILLITY
TRANQUILLIZE
TRANQUILLIZED
TRANQUILLIZER
TRANQUILLIZERS
TRANQUILLIZES
TRANQUILLIZING
TRANQUILLY
TRANQUILNESS
TRANQUILNESSES
TRANSACTED
TRANSACTING
TRANSACTINIDE
TRANSACTINIDES
TRANSACTION
TRANSACTIONAL
TRANSACTIONALLY
TRANSACTIONS
TRANSACTOR
TRANSACTORS
TRANSALPINE
TRANSALPINES
TRANSAMINASE
TRANSAMINASES
TRANSAMINATION
TRANSAMINATIONS
TRANSANDEAN
TRANSANDINE
TRANSATLANTIC
TRANSAXLES
TRANSCALENCIES
TRANSCALENCY
TRANSCALENT
TRANSCAUCASIAN
TRANSCEIVER
TRANSCEIVERS
TRANSCENDED
TRANSCENDENCE
TRANSCENDENCES
TRANSCENDENCIES
TRANSCENDENCY
TRANSCENDENT
TRANSCENDENTAL
TRANSCENDENTALS
TRANSCENDENTLY
TRANSCENDENTS
TRANSCENDING
TRANSCENDINGLY
TRANSCENDS
TRANSCRANIAL

TRANSCRIPTIONAL
TRANSCRIPTIONS
TRANSCRIPTIVE
TRANSCRIPTIVELY
TRANSCRIPTS
TRANSCULTURAL
TRANSCURRENT
TRANSCUTANEOUS
TRANSDERMAL
TRANSDUCED
TRANSDUCER
TRANSDUCERS
TRANSDUCES
TRANSDUCING
TRANSDUCTANT
TRANSDUCTANTS
TRANSDUCTION
TRANSDUCTIONAL
TRANSDUCTIONS
TRANSDUCTOR
TRANSDUCTORS
TRANSECTED
TRANSECTING
TRANSECTION
TRANSECTIONS
TRANSENNAS
TRANSEPTAL
TRANSEPTATE
TRANSEXUAL
TRANSEXUALISM
TRANSEXUALISMS
TRANSEXUALS
TRANSFECTED
TRANSFECTING
TRANSFECTION
TRANSFECTIONS
TRANSFECTS
TRANSFERABILITY
TRANSFERABLE
TRANSFERAL
TRANSFERALS
TRANSFERASE
TRANSFERASES
TRANSFEREE
TRANSFEREES
TRANSFERENCE
TRANSFERENCES
TRANSFERENTIAL
TRANSFEROR
TRANSFERORS

TRANSFERRABLE
TRANSFERRAL
TRANSFERRALS
TRANSFERRED
TRANSFERRER
TRANSFERRERS
TRANSFERRIBLE
TRANSFERRIN
TRANSFERRING
TRANSFERRINS
TRANSFIGURATION
TRANSFIGURE
TRANSFIGURED
TRANSFIGUREMENT
TRANSFIGURES
TRANSFIGURING
TRANSFINITE
TRANSFIXED
TRANSFIXES
TRANSFIXING
TRANSFIXION
TRANSFIXIONS
TRANSFORMABLE
TRANSFORMATION
TRANSFORMATIONS
TRANSFORMATIVE
TRANSFORMED
TRANSFORMER
TRANSFORMERS
TRANSFORMING
TRANSFORMINGS
TRANSFORMISM
TRANSFORMISMS
TRANSFORMIST
TRANSFORMISTIC
TRANSFORMISTS
TRANSFORMS
TRANSFUSABLE
TRANSFUSED
TRANSFUSER
TRANSFUSERS
TRANSFUSES
TRANSFUSIBLE
TRANSFUSING
TRANSFUSION
TRANSFUSIONAL
TRANSFUSIONIST
TRANSFUSIONISTS
TRANSFUSIONS
TRANSFUSIVE
TRANSFUSIVELY
TRANSGENDER
TRANSGENDERED
TRANSGENDERS
TRANSGENES
TRANSGENESES
TRANSGENESIS
TRANSGENIC
TRANSGENICS

TRANSGRESS	TRANSITIVE	TRANSMIGRATING	TRANSPARENCIES
TRANSGRESSED	TRANSITIVELY	TRANSMIGRATION	TRANSPARENCY
TRANSGRESSES	TRANSITIVENESS	TRANSMIGRATIONS	TRANSPARENT
TRANSGRESSING	TRANSITIVES	TRANSMIGRATIVE	TRANSPARENTISE
TRANSGRESSION	TRANSITIVITIES	TRANSMIGRATOR	TRANSPARENTISED
TRANSGRESSIONAL	TRANSITIVITY	TRANSMIGRATORS	TRANSPARENTISES
TRANSGRESSIONS	TRANSITORILY	TRANSMIGRATORY	TRANSPARENTIZE
TRANSGRESSIVE	TRANSITORINESS	TRANSMISSIBLE	TRANSPARENTIZED
TRANSGRESSIVELY	TRANSITORY	TRANSMISSION	TRANSPARENTIZES
TRANSGRESSOR	TRANSLATABILITY	TRANSMISSIONAL	TRANSPARENTLY
TRANSGRESSORS	TRANSLATABLE	TRANSMISSIONS	TRANSPARENTNESS
TRANSHIPMENT	TRANSLATED	TRANSMISSIVE	TRANSPERSONAL
TRANSHIPMENTS	TRANSLATES	TRANSMISSIVELY	TRANSPICUOUS
TRANSHIPPED	TRANSLATING	TRANSMISSIVITY	TRANSPICUOUSLY
TRANSHIPPER	TRANSLATION	TRANSMISSOMETER	TRANSPIERCE
TRANSHIPPERS	TRANSLATIONAL	TRANSMITTABLE	TRANSPIERCED
TRANSHIPPING	TRANSLATIONALLY	TRANSMITTAL	TRANSPIERCES
TRANSHIPPINGS	TRANSLATIONS	TRANSMITTALS	TRANSPIERCING
TRANSHISTORICAL	TRANSLATIVE	TRANSMITTANCE	TRANSPIRABLE
TRANSHUMANCE	TRANSLATIVES	TRANSMITTANCES	TRANSPIRATION
TRANSHUMANCES	TRANSLATOR	TRANSMITTANCIES	TRANSPIRATIONAL
TRANSHUMANT	TRANSLATORIAL	TRANSMITTANCY	TRANSPIRATIONS
TRANSHUMANTS	TRANSLATORS	TRANSMITTED	TRANSPIRATORY
TRANSHUMED	TRANSLATORY	TRANSMITTER	TRANSPIRED
TRANSHUMES	TRANSLEITHAN	TRANSMITTERS	TRANSPIRES
TRANSHUMING	TRANSLITERATE	TRANSMITTIBLE	TRANSPIRING
TRANSIENCE	TRANSLITERATED	TRANSMITTING	TRANSPLACENTAL
TRANSIENCES	TRANSLITERATES	TRANSMITTIVITY	TRANSPLANT
TRANSIENCIES	TRANSLITERATING	TRANSMOGRIFIED	TRANSPLANTABLE
TRANSIENCY	TRANSLITERATION	TRANSMOGRIFIES	TRANSPLANTATION
TRANSIENTLY	TRANSLITERATOR	TRANSMOGRIFY	TRANSPLANTED
TRANSIENTNESS	TRANSLITERATORS	TRANSMOGRIFYING	TRANSPLANTER
TRANSIENTNESSES	TRANSLOCATE	TRANSMONTANE	TRANSPLANTERS
TRANSIENTS	TRANSLOCATED	TRANSMONTANES	TRANSPLANTING
TRANSILIENCE	TRANSLOCATES	TRANSMOUNTAIN	TRANSPLANTINGS
TRANSILIENCES	TRANSLOCATING	TRANSMOVED	TRANSPLANTS
TRANSILIENCIES	TRANSLOCATION	TRANSMOVES	TRANSPOLAR
TRANSILIENCY	TRANSLOCATIONS	TRANSMOVING	TRANSPONDER
TRANSILIENT	TRANSLUCENCE	TRANSMUNDANE	TRANSPONDERS
TRANSILLUMINATE	TRANSLUCENCES	TRANSMUTABILITY	TRANSPONDOR
TRANSISTHMIAN	TRANSLUCENCIES	TRANSMUTABLE	TRANSPONDORS
TRANSISTOR	TRANSLUCENCY	TRANSMUTABLY	TRANSPONTINE
TRANSISTORISE	TRANSLUCENT	TRANSMUTATION	TRANSPORTABLE
TRANSISTORISED	TRANSLUCENTLY	TRANSMUTATIONAL	TRANSPORTAL
TRANSISTORISES	TRANSLUCID	TRANSMUTATIONS	TRANSPORTALS
TRANSISTORISING	TRANSLUCIDITIES	TRANSMUTATIVE	TRANSPORTANCE
TRANSISTORIZE	TRANSLUCIDITY	TRANSMUTED	TRANSPORTANCES
TRANSISTORIZED	TRANSLUNAR	TRANSMUTER	TRANSPORTATION
TRANSISTORIZES	TRANSLUNARY	TRANSMUTERS	TRANSPORTATIONS
TRANSISTORIZING	TRANSMANCHE	TRANSMUTES	TRANSPORTED
TRANSISTORS	TRANSMARINE	TRANSMUTING	TRANSPORTEDLY
TRANSITABLE	TRANSMEMBRANE	TRANSNATIONAL	TRANSPORTEDNESS
TRANSITING	TRANSMEWED	TRANSNATURAL	TRANSPORTER
TRANSITION	TRANSMEWING	TRANSOCEANIC	TRANSPORTERS
TRANSITIONAL	TRANSMIGRANT	TRANSONICS	TRANSPORTING
TRANSITIONALLY	TRANSMIGRANTS	TRANSPACIFIC	TRANSPORTINGLY
TRANSITIONALS	TRANSMIGRATE	TRANSPADANE	TRANSPORTINGS
TRANSITIONARY	TRANSMIGRATED	TRANSPARENCE	TRANSPORTIVE
TRANSITIONS	TRANSMIGRATES	TRANSPARENCES	TRANSPORTS

TRANSPOSABILITY	TRANSVALUATIONS	TRAUCHLING	TREACLINESSES
TRANSPOSABLE	TRANSVALUE	TRAUMATICALLY	TREADLINGS
TRANSPOSAL	TRANSVALUED	TRAUMATISATION	TREADMILLS
TRANSPOSALS	TRANSVALUER	TRAUMATISATIONS	TREADWHEEL
TRANSPOSED	TRANSVALUERS	TRAUMATISE	TREADWHEELS
TRANSPOSER	TRANSVALUES	TRAUMATISED	TREASONABLE
TRANSPOSERS	TRANSVALUING	TRAUMATISES	TREASONABLENESS
TRANSPOSES	TRANSVERSAL	TRAUMATISING	TREASONABLY
TRANSPOSING	TRANSVERSALITY	TRAUMATISM	TREASONOUS
TRANSPOSINGS	TRANSVERSALLY	TRAUMATISMS	TREASURABLE
TRANSPOSITION	TRANSVERSALS	TRAUMATIZATION	TREASURELESS
TRANSPOSITIONAL	TRANSVERSE	TRAUMATIZATIONS	TREASURERS
TRANSPOSITIONS	TRANSVERSED	TRAUMATIZE	TREASURERSHIP
TRANSPOSITIVE	TRANSVERSELY	TRAUMATIZED	TREASURERSHIPS
TRANSPOSON	TRANSVERSENESS	TRAUMATIZES	TREASURIES
TRANSPOSONS	TRANSVERSES	TRAUMATIZING	TREASURING
TRANSPUTER	TRANSVERSING	TRAUMATOLOGICAL	TREATABILITIES
TRANSPUTERS	TRANSVERSION	TRAUMATOLOGIES	TREATABILITY
TRANSSEXUAL	TRANSVERSIONS	TRAUMATOLOGY	TREATMENTS
TRANSSEXUALISM	TRANSVERTER	TRAUMATONASTIES	TREATYLESS
TRANSSEXUALISMS	TRANSVERTERS	TRAUMATONASTY	TREBBIANOS
TRANSSEXUALITY	TRANSVESTED	TRAVAILING	TREBLENESS
TRANSSEXUALS	TRANSVESTIC	TRAVELATOR	TREBLENESSES
TRANSSHAPE	TRANSVESTING	TRAVELATORS	TREBUCHETS
TRANSSHAPED	TRANSVESTISM	TRAVELINGS	TREBUCKETS
TRANSSHAPES	TRANSVESTISMS	TRAVELLERS	TRECENTIST
TRANSSHAPING	TRANSVESTIST	TRAVELLING	TRECENTISTS
TRANSSHIPMENT	TRANSVESTISTS	TRAVELLINGS	TREDECILLION
TRANSSHIPMENTS	TRANSVESTITE	TRAVELOGUE	TREDECILLIONS
TRANSSHIPPED	TRANSVESTITES	TRAVELOGUES	TREDRILLES
TRANSSHIPPER	TRANSVESTITISM	TRAVERSABLE	TREEHOPPER
TRANSSHIPPERS	TRANSVESTITISMS	TRAVERSALS	TREEHOPPERS
TRANSSHIPPING	TRANSVESTS	TRAVERSERS	TREEHOUSES
TRANSSHIPPINGS	TRAPANNERS	TRAVERSING	TREELESSNESS
TRANSSHIPS	TRAPANNING	TRAVERSINGS	TREELESSNESSES
TRANSSONIC	TRAPESINGS	TRAVERTINE	TREENWARES
TRANSTHORACIC	TRAPEZIFORM	TRAVERTINES	TREGETOURS
TRANSUBSTANTIAL	TRAPEZISTS	TRAVERTINS	TREHALOSES
TRANSUDATE	TRAPEZIUMS	TRAVESTIED	TREILLAGED
TRANSUDATES	TRAPEZIUSES	TRAVESTIES	TREILLAGES
TRANSUDATION	TRAPEZOHEDRA	TRAVESTYING	TREKSCHUIT
TRANSUDATIONS	TRAPEZOHEDRAL	TRAVOLATOR	TREKSCHUITS
TRANSUDATORY	TRAPEZOHEDRON	TRAVOLATORS	TRELLISING
TRANSUDING	TRAPEZOHEDRONS	TRAWLERMAN	TRELLISWORK
TRANSUMING	TRAPEZOIDAL	TRAWLERMEN	TRELLISWORKS
TRANSUMPTION	TRAPEZOIDS	TRAYMOBILE	TREMATODES
TRANSUMPTIONS	TRAPNESTED	TRAYMOBILES	TREMATOIDS
TRANSUMPTIVE	TRAPNESTING	TRAZODONES	TREMBLEMENT
TRANSUMPTS	TRAPPINESS	TREACHERER	TREMBLEMENTS
TRANSURANIAN	TRAPPINESSES	TREACHERERS	TREMBLIEST
TRANSURANIC	TRAPSHOOTER	TREACHERIES	TREMBLINGLY
TRANSURANICS	TRAPSHOOTERS	TREACHEROUS	TREMBLINGS
TRANSURANIUM	TRAPSHOOTING	TREACHEROUSLY	TREMENDOUS
TRANSVAGINAL	TRAPSHOOTINGS	TREACHEROUSNESS	TREMENDOUSLY
TRANSVALUATE	TRASHERIES	TREACHETOUR	TREMENDOUSNESS
TRANSVALUATED	TRASHINESS	TREACHETOURS	TREMOLANDI
TRANSVALUATES	TRASHINESSES	TREACHOURS	TREMOLANDO
TRANSVALUATING	TRASHTRIES	TREACLIEST	TREMOLANDOS
TRANSVALUATION	TRATTORIAS	TREACLINESS	TREMOLANTS

TREMOLITES	TRIACETATE	TRIBUNESHIP	TRICHOCYSTS
TREMOLITIC	TRIACETATES	TRIBUNESHIPS	TRICHOGYNE
TREMORLESS	TRIACONTER	TRIBUNICIAL	TRICHOGYNES
TREMULANTS	TRIACONTERS	TRIBUNICIAN	TRICHOGYNIAL
TREMULATED	TRIACTINAL	TRIBUNITIAL	TRICHOGYNIC
TREMULATES	TRIADELPHOUS	TRIBUNITIAN	TRICHOLOGICAL
TREMULATING	TRIADICALLY	TRIBUTARIES	TRICHOLOGIES
TREMULOUSLY	TRIALITIES	TRIBUTARILY	TRICHOLOGIST
TREMULOUSNESS	TRIALLINGS	TRIBUTARINESS	TRICHOLOGISTS
TREMULOUSNESSES	TRIALLISTS	TRIBUTARINESSES	TRICHOLOGY
TRENCHANCIES	TRIALOGUES	TRICAMERAL	TRICHOMONACIDAL
TRENCHANCY	TRIALWARES	TRICARBOXYLIC	TRICHOMONACIDE
TRENCHANTLY	TRIAMCINOLONE	TRICARPELLARY	TRICHOMONACIDES
TRENCHARDS	TRIAMCINOLONES	TRICENTENARIES	TRICHOMONAD
TRENCHERMAN	TRIANDRIAN	TRICENTENARY	TRICHOMONADAL
TRENCHERMEN	TRIANDROUS	TRICENTENNIAL	TRICHOMONADS
TRENDIFIED	TRIANGULAR	TRICENTENNIALS	TRICHOMONAL
TRENDIFIES	TRIANGULARITIES	TRICEPHALOUS	TRICHOMONIASES
TRENDIFYING	TRIANGULARITY	TRICERATOPS	TRICHOMONIASIS
TRENDINESS	TRIANGULARLY	TRICERATOPSES	TRICHOPHYTON
TRENDINESSES	TRIANGULATE	TRICERIONS	TRICHOPHYTONS
TRENDSETTER	TRIANGULATED	TRICHIASES	TRICHOPHYTOSES
TRENDSETTERS	TRIANGULATELY	TRICHIASIS	TRICHOPHYTOSIS
TRENDSETTING	TRIANGULATES	TRICHINELLA	TRICHOPTERAN
TRENDSETTINGS	TRIANGULATING	TRICHINELLAE	TRICHOPTERANS
TRENDYISMS	TRIANGULATION	TRICHINELLAS	TRICHOPTERIST
TREPANATION	TRIANGULATIONS	TRICHINIASES	TRICHOPTERISTS
TREPANATIONS	TRIAPSIDAL	TRICHINIASIS	TRICHOPTEROUS
TREPANNERS	TRIARCHIES	TRICHINISATION	TRICHOTHECENE
TREPANNING	TRIATHLETE	TRICHINISATIONS	TRICHOTHECENES
TREPANNINGS	TRIATHLETES	TRICHINISE	TRICHOTOMIC
TREPHINATION	TRIATHLONS	TRICHINISED	TRICHOTOMIES
TREPHINATIONS	TRIATOMICALLY	TRICHINISES	TRICHOTOMISE
TREPHINERS	TRIAXIALITIES	TRICHINISING	TRICHOTOMISED
TREPHINING	TRIAXIALITY	TRICHINIZATION	TRICHOTOMISES
TREPHININGS	TRIBADISMS	TRICHINIZATIONS	TRICHOTOMISING
TREPIDATION	TRIBALISMS	TRICHINIZE	TRICHOTOMIZE
TREPIDATIONS	TRIBALISTIC	TRICHINIZED	TRICHOTOMIZED
TREPIDATORY	TRIBALISTS	TRICHINIZES	TRICHOTOMIZES
TREPONEMAL	TRIBESPEOPLE	TRICHINIZING	TRICHOTOMIZING
TREPONEMAS	TRIBESWOMAN	TRICHINOSE	TRICHOTOMOUS
TREPONEMATA	TRIBESWOMEN	TRICHINOSED	TRICHOTOMOUSLY
TREPONEMATOSES	TRIBOELECTRIC	TRICHINOSES	TRICHOTOMY
TREPONEMATOSIS	TRIBOLOGICAL	TRICHINOSING	TRICHROISM
TREPONEMATOUS	TRIBOLOGIES	TRICHINOSIS	TRICHROISMS
TREPONEMES	TRIBOLOGIST	TRICHINOTIC	TRICHROMAT
TRESPASSED	TRIBOLOGISTS	TRICHINOUS	TRICHROMATIC
TRESPASSER	TRIBOMETER	TRICHLORACETIC	TRICHROMATISM
TRESPASSERS	TRIBOMETERS	TRICHLORFON	TRICHROMATISMS
TRESPASSES	TRIBRACHIAL	TRICHLORFONS	TRICHROMATS
TRESPASSING	TRIBRACHIC	TRICHLORIDE	TRICHROMIC
TRESTLETREE	TRIBROMOETHANOL	TRICHLORIDES	TRICHROMICS
TRESTLETREES	TRIBROMOMETHANE	TRICHLOROACETIC	TRICHRONOUS
TRESTLEWORK	TRIBULATED	TRICHLOROETHANE	TRICHURIASES
TRESTLEWORKS	TRIBULATES	TRICHLORPHON	TRICHURIASIS
TRETINOINS	TRIBULATING	TRICHLORPHONS	TRICKERIES
TREVALLIES	TRIBULATION	TRICHOBACTERIA	TRICKINESS
TRIABLENESS	TRIBULATIONS	TRICHOCYST	TRICKINESSES
TRIABLENESSES	TRIBUNATES	TRICHOCYSTIC	TRICKISHLY

TRICKISHNESS	TRIFLINGLY	TRILATERATIONS	TRINKETING
TRICKISHNESSES	TRIFLINGNESS	TRILINEATE	TRINKETINGS
TRICKLIEST	TRIFLINGNESSES	TRILINGUAL	TRINKETRIES
TRICKLINGLY	TRIFLUOPERAZINE	TRILINGUALISM	TRINOCULAR
TRICKLINGS	TRIFLURALIN	TRILINGUALISMS	TRINOMIALISM
TRICKSIEST	TRIFLURALINS	TRILINGUALLY	TRINOMIALISMS
TRICKSINESS	TRIFOLIATE	TRILITERAL	TRINOMIALIST
TRICKSINESSES	TRIFOLIATED	TRILITERALISM	TRINOMIALISTS
TRICKSTERING	TRIFOLIOLATE	TRILITERALISMS	TRINOMIALLY
TRICKSTERINGS	TRIFOLIUMS	TRILITERALS	TRINOMIALS
TRICKSTERS	TRIFURCATE	TRILITHONS	TRINUCLEOTIDE
TRICKTRACK	TRIFURCATED	TRILLIONAIRE	TRINUCLEOTIDES
TRICKTRACKS	TRIFURCATES	TRILLIONAIRES	TRIOECIOUS
TRICLINIUM	TRIFURCATING	TRILLIONTH	TRIOXOBORIC
TRICLOSANS	TRIFURCATION	TRILLIONTHS	TRIOXYGENS
TRICOLETTE	TRIFURCATIONS	TRILOBATED	TRIPALMITIN
TRICOLETTES	TRIGAMISTS	TRILOBITES	TRIPALMITINS
TRICOLORED	TRIGEMINAL	TRILOBITIC	TRIPARTISM
TRICOLOURED	TRIGEMINALS	TRILOCULAR	TRIPARTISMS
TRICOLOURS	TRIGGERFISH	TRIMERISMS	TRIPARTITE
TRICONSONANTAL	TRIGGERFISHES	TRIMESTERS	TRIPARTITELY
TRICONSONANTIC	TRIGGERING	TRIMESTRAL	TRIPARTITION
TRICORNERED	TRIGGERLESS	TRIMESTRIAL	TRIPARTITIONS
TRICORPORATE	TRIGGERMAN	TRIMETHADIONE	TRIPEHOUND
TRICORPORATED	TRIGGERMEN	TRIMETHADIONES	TRIPEHOUNDS
TRICOSTATE	TRIGLYCERIDE	TRIMETHOPRIM	TRIPERSONAL
TRICOTEUSE	TRIGLYCERIDES	TRIMETHOPRIMS	TRIPERSONALISM
TRICOTEUSES	TRIGLYPHIC	TRIMETHYLAMINE	TRIPERSONALISMS
TRICOTINES	TRIGLYPHICAL	TRIMETHYLAMINES	TRIPERSONALIST
TRICROTISM	TRIGNESSES	TRIMETHYLENE	TRIPERSONALISTS
TRICROTISMS	TRIGONALLY	TRIMETHYLENES	TRIPERSONALITY
TRICROTOUS	TRIGONOMETER	TRIMETRICAL	TRIPETALOUS
TRICUSPIDAL	TRIGONOMETERS	TRIMETROGON	TRIPHAMMER
TRICUSPIDATE	TRIGONOMETRIC	TRIMETROGONS	TRIPHAMMERS
TRICUSPIDS	TRIGONOMETRICAL	TRIMMINGLY	TRIPHENYLAMINE
TRICYCLERS	TRIGONOMETRIES	TRIMNESSES	TRIPHENYLAMINES
TRICYCLICS	TRIGONOMETRY	TRIMOLECULAR	TRIPHIBIOUS
TRICYCLING	TRIGRAMMATIC	TRIMONTHLY	TRIPHOSPHATE
TRICYCLINGS	TRIGRAMMIC	TRIMORPHIC	TRIPHOSPHATES
TRICYCLIST	TRIGRAPHIC	TRIMORPHISM	TRIPHTHONG
TRICYCLISTS	TRIHALOMETHANE	TRIMORPHISMS	TRIPHTHONGAL
TRIDACTYLOUS	TRIHALOMETHANES	TRIMORPHOUS	TRIPHTHONGS
TRIDENTATE	TRIHEDRALS	TRINACRIAN	TRIPHYLITE
TRIDIMENSIONAL	TRIHEDRONS	TRINACRIFORM	TRIPHYLITES
TRIDOMINIA	TRIHYBRIDS	TRINISCOPE	TRIPHYLLOUS
TRIDOMINIUM	TRIHYDRATE	TRINISCOPES	TRIPINNATE
TRIDYMITES	TRIHYDRATED	TRINITARIAN	TRIPINNATELY
TRIENNIALLY	TRIHYDRATES	TRINITRATE	TRIPITAKAS
TRIENNIALS	TRIHYDROXY	TRINITRATES	TRIPLENESS
TRIENNIUMS	TRIIODOMETHANE	TRINITRINS	TRIPLENESSES
TRIERARCHAL	TRIIODOMETHANES	TRINITROBENZENE	TRIPLETAIL
TRIERARCHIES	TRILATERAL	TRINITROCRESOL	TRIPLETAILS
TRIERARCHS	TRILATERALISM	TRINITROCRESOLS	TRIPLICATE
TRIERARCHY	TRILATERALISMS	TRINITROPHENOL	TRIPLICATED
TRIETHYLAMINE	TRILATERALIST	TRINITROPHENOLS	TRIPLICATES
TRIETHYLAMINES	TRILATERALISTS	TRINITROTOLUENE	TRIPLICATING
TRIFACIALS	TRILATERALLY	TRINITROTOLUOL	TRIPLICATION
TRIFARIOUS	TRILATERALS	TRINITROTOLUOLS	TRIPLICATIONS
TRIFFIDIAN	TRILATERATION	TRINKETERS	TRIPLICITIES

TRIPLICITY
TRIPLOBLASTIC
TRIPLOIDIES
TRIPPERISH
TRIPPINGLY
TRIPTEROUS
TRIPTYQUES
TRIPUDIARY
TRIPUDIATE
TRIPUDIATED
TRIPUDIATES
TRIPUDIATING
TRIPUDIATION
TRIPUDIATIONS
TRIPUDIUMS
TRIQUETRAL
TRIQUETRAS
TRIQUETROUS
TRIQUETROUSLY
TRIQUETRUM
TRIRADIATE
TRIRADIATELY
TRISACCHARIDE
TRISACCHARIDES
TRISAGIONS
TRISECTING
TRISECTION
TRISECTIONS
TRISECTORS
TRISECTRICES
TRISECTRIX
TRISKELION
TRISKELIONS
TRISOCTAHEDRA
TRISOCTAHEDRAL
TRISOCTAHEDRON
TRISOCTAHEDRONS
TRISTEARIN
TRISTEARINS
TRISTESSES
TRISTFULLY
TRISTFULNESS
TRISTFULNESSES
TRISTICHIC
TRISTICHOUS
TRISTIMULUS
TRISUBSTITUTED
TRISULCATE
TRISULFIDE
TRISULFIDES
TRISULPHIDE
TRISULPHIDES
TRISYLLABIC
TRISYLLABICAL
TRISYLLABICALLY
TRISYLLABLE
TRISYLLABLES
TRITAGONIST
TRITAGONISTS

TRITANOPIA
TRITANOPIAS
TRITANOPIC
TRITENESSES
TRITERNATE
TRITHEISMS
TRITHEISTIC
TRITHEISTICAL
TRITHEISTS
TRITHIONATE
TRITHIONATES
TRITHIONIC
TRITIATING
TRITIATION
TRITIATIONS
TRITICALES
TRITICALLY
TRITICALNESS
TRITICALNESSES
TRITICEOUS
TRITICISMS
TRITUBERCULAR
TRITUBERCULATE
TRITUBERCULIES
TRITUBERCULISM
TRITUBERCULISMS
TRITUBERCULY
TRITURABLE
TRITURATED
TRITURATES
TRITURATING
TRITURATION
TRITURATIONS
TRITURATOR
TRITURATORS
TRIUMPHALISM
TRIUMPHALISMS
TRIUMPHALIST
TRIUMPHALISTS
TRIUMPHALS
TRIUMPHANT
TRIUMPHANTLY
TRIUMPHERIES
TRIUMPHERS
TRIUMPHERY
TRIUMPHING
TRIUMPHINGS
TRIUMVIRAL
TRIUMVIRATE
TRIUMVIRATES
TRIUMVIRIES
TRIUNITIES
TRIVALENCE
TRIVALENCES
TRIVALENCIES
TRIVALENCY
TRIVALVULAR
TRIVIALISATION
TRIVIALISATIONS

TRIVIALISE
TRIVIALISED
TRIVIALISES
TRIVIALISING
TRIVIALISM
TRIVIALISMS
TRIVIALIST
TRIVIALISTS
TRIVIALITIES
TRIVIALITY
TRIVIALIZATION
TRIVIALIZATIONS
TRIVIALIZE
TRIVIALIZED
TRIVIALIZES
TRIVIALIZING
TRIVIALNESS
TRIVIALNESSES
TRIWEEKLIES
TROCHAICALLY
TROCHANTER
TROCHANTERAL
TROCHANTERIC
TROCHANTERS
TROCHEAMETER
TROCHEAMETERS
TROCHELMINTH
TROCHELMINTHS
TROCHILUSES
TROCHISCUS
TROCHISCUSES
TROCHLEARS
TROCHOIDAL
TROCHOIDALLY
TROCHOMETER
TROCHOMETERS
TROCHOPHORE
TROCHOPHORES
TROCHOSPHERE
TROCHOSPHERES
TROCHOTRON
TROCHOTRONS
TROCTOLITE
TROCTOLITES
TROGLODYTE
TROGLODYTES
TROGLODYTIC
TROGLODYTICAL
TROGLODYTISM
TROGLODYTISMS
TROLLEYBUS
TROLLEYBUSES
TROLLEYBUSSES
TROLLEYING
TROLLIUSES
TROLLOPEES
TROLLOPING
TROLLOPISH
TROMBICULID

TROMBICULIDS
TROMBIDIASES
TROMBIDIASIS
TROMBONIST
TROMBONISTS
TROMOMETER
TROMOMETERS
TROMOMETRIC
TROOPSHIPS
TROOSTITES
TROPAEOLIN
TROPAEOLINS
TROPAEOLUM
TROPAEOLUMS
TROPEOLINS
TROPHALLACTIC
TROPHALLAXES
TROPHALLAXIS
TROPHESIAL
TROPHESIES
TROPHICALLY
TROPHOBIOSES
TROPHOBIOSIS
TROPHOBIOTIC
TROPHOBLAST
TROPHOBLASTIC
TROPHOBLASTS
TROPHOLOGIES
TROPHOLOGY
TROPHONEUROSES
TROPHONEUROSIS
TROPHOPLASM
TROPHOPLASMS
TROPHOTACTIC
TROPHOTAXES
TROPHOTAXIS
TROPHOTROPIC
TROPHOTROPISM
TROPHOTROPISMS
TROPHOZOITE
TROPHOZOITES
TROPICALISATION
TROPICALISE
TROPICALISED
TROPICALISES
TROPICALISING
TROPICALITIES
TROPICALITY
TROPICALIZATION
TROPICALIZE
TROPICALIZED
TROPICALIZES
TROPICALIZING
TROPICALLY
TROPICBIRD
TROPICBIRDS
TROPISMATIC
TROPOCOLLAGEN
TROPOCOLLAGENS

TROPOLOGIC	TRUANTSHIP	TRUSTLESSNESSES	TUBERCULATELY
TROPOLOGICAL	TRUANTSHIPS	TRUSTWORTHILY	TUBERCULATION
TROPOLOGICALLY	TRUCKLINES	TRUSTWORTHINESS	TUBERCULATIONS
TROPOLOGIES	TRUCKLINGS	TRUSTWORTHY	TUBERCULES
TROPOMYOSIN	TRUCKLOADS	TRUTHFULLY	TUBERCULIN
TROPOMYOSINS	TRUCKMASTER	TRUTHFULNESS	TUBERCULINS
TROPOPAUSE	TRUCKMASTERS	TRUTHFULNESSES	TUBERCULISATION
TROPOPAUSES	TRUCKSTOPS	TRUTHLESSNESS	TUBERCULISE
TROPOPHILOUS	TRUCULENCE	TRUTHLESSNESSES	TUBERCULISED
TROPOPHYTE	TRUCULENCES	TRYINGNESS	TUBERCULISES
TROPOPHYTES	TRUCULENCIES	TRYINGNESSES	TUBERCULISING
TROPOPHYTIC	TRUCULENCY	TRYPAFLAVINE	TUBERCULIZATION
TROPOSCATTER	TRUCULENTLY	TRYPAFLAVINES	TUBERCULIZE
TROPOSCATTERS	TRUEHEARTED	TRYPANOCIDAL	TUBERCULIZED
TROPOSPHERE	TRUEHEARTEDNESS	TRYPANOCIDE	TUBERCULIZES
TROPOSPHERES	TRUENESSES	TRYPANOCIDES	TUBERCULIZING
TROPOSPHERIC	TRUEPENNIES	TRYPANOSOMAL	TUBERCULOID
TROPOTAXES	TRUFFLINGS	TRYPANOSOME	TUBERCULOMA
TROPOTAXIS	TRUMPERIES	TRYPANOSOMES	TUBERCULOMAS
TROTHPLIGHT	TRUMPETERS	TRYPANOSOMIASES	TUBERCULOMATA
TROTHPLIGHTED	TRUMPETING	TRYPANOSOMIASIS	TUBERCULOSE
TROTHPLIGHTING	TRUMPETINGS	TRYPANOSOMIC	TUBERCULOSED
TROTHPLIGHTS	TRUMPETLIKE	TRYPARSAMIDE	TUBERCULOSES
TROUBADOUR	TRUMPETWEED	TRYPARSAMIDES	TUBERCULOSIS
TROUBADOURS	TRUMPETWEEDS	TRYPSINOGEN	TUBERCULOUS
TROUBLEDLY	TRUNCATELY	TRYPSINOGENS	TUBERCULOUSLY
TROUBLEFREE	TRUNCATING	TRYPTAMINE	TUBERCULUM
TROUBLEMAKER	TRUNCATION	TRYPTAMINES	TUBERIFEROUS
TROUBLEMAKERS	TRUNCATIONS	TRYPTOPHAN	TUBERIFORM
TROUBLEMAKING	TRUNCHEONED	TRYPTOPHANE	TUBEROSITIES
TROUBLEMAKINGS	TRUNCHEONER	TRYPTOPHANES	TUBEROSITY
TROUBLESHOOT	TRUNCHEONERS	TRYPTOPHANS	TUBICOLOUS
TROUBLESHOOTER	TRUNCHEONING	TSAREVICHES	TUBIFICIDS
TROUBLESHOOTERS	TRUNCHEONS	TSAREVITCH	TUBIFLOROUS
TROUBLESHOOTING	TRUNKFISHES	TSAREVITCHES	TUBOCURARINE
TROUBLESHOOTS	TRUNKSLEEVE	TSCHERNOSEM	TUBOCURARINES
TROUBLESHOT	TRUNKSLEEVES	TSCHERNOSEMS	TUBOPLASTIES
TROUBLESOME	TRUNNIONED	TSESAREVICH	TUBOPLASTY
TROUBLESOMELY	TRUSTABILITIES	TSESAREVICHES	TUBULARIAN
TROUBLESOMENESS	TRUSTABILITY	TSESAREVITCH	TUBULARIANS
TROUBLINGS	TRUSTAFARIAN	TSESAREVITCHES	TUBULARITIES
TROUBLOUSLY	TRUSTAFARIANS	TSESAREVNA	TUBULARITY
TROUBLOUSNESS	TRUSTBUSTER	TSESAREVNAS	TUBULATING
TROUBLOUSNESSES	TRUSTBUSTERS	TSESAREWICH	TUBULATION
TROUGHLIKE	TRUSTBUSTING	TSESAREWICHES	TUBULATIONS
TROUNCINGS	TRUSTBUSTINGS	TSESAREWITCH	TUBULATORS
TROUSERING	TRUSTEEING	TSESAREWITCHES	TUBULATURE
TROUSERINGS	TRUSTEESHIP	TSOTSITAAL	TUBULATURES
TROUSERLESS	TRUSTEESHIPS	TSOTSITAALS	TUBULIFLORAL
TROUSSEAUS	TRUSTFULLY	TSUTSUGAMUSHI	TUBULIFLOROUS
TROUSSEAUX	TRUSTFULNESS	TSUTSUGAMUSHIS	TUBULOUSLY
TROUTLINGS	TRUSTFULNESSES	TUBBINESSES	TUCKERBAGS
TROUTSTONE	TRUSTINESS	TUBECTOMIES	TUCKERBOXES
TROUTSTONES	TRUSTINESSES	TUBERACEOUS	TUFFACEOUS
TROUVAILLE	TRUSTINGLY	TUBERCULAR	TUFFTAFFETA
TROUVAILLES	TRUSTINGNESS	TUBERCULARLY	TUFFTAFFETAS
TROWELLERS	TRUSTINGNESSES	TUBERCULARS	TUFFTAFFETIES
TROWELLING	TRUSTLESSLY	TUBERCULATE	TUFFTAFFETY
TRUANTRIES	TRUSTLESSNESS	TUBERCULATED	TUFTAFFETA

TUFTAFFETAS	TUNELESSLY	TURGESCENCE	TWANGLINGLY
TUFTAFFETIES	TUNELESSNESS	TURGESCENCES	TWANGLINGS
TUFTAFFETY	TUNELESSNESSES	TURGESCENCIES	TWATTLINGS
TUILLETTES	TUNESMITHS	TURGESCENCY	TWAYBLADES
TUILYIEING	TUNGSTATES	TURGESCENT	TWEEDINESS
TUILZIEING	TUNGSTITES	TURGIDITIES	TWEEDINESSES
TUITIONARY	TUNNELINGS	TURGIDNESS	TWEEDLEDEE
TULARAEMIA	TUNNELLERS	TURGIDNESSES	TWEEDLEDEED
TULARAEMIAS	TUNNELLIKE	TURMOILING	TWEEDLEDEEING
TULARAEMIC	TUNNELLING	TURNABOUTS	TWEEDLEDEES
TULAREMIAS	TUNNELLINGS	TURNAGAINS	TWEENAGERS
TULIPOMANIA	TUPPENNIES	TURNAROUND	TWEENESSES
TULIPOMANIAS	TURACOVERDIN	TURNAROUNDS	TWELVEFOLD
TULIPWOODS	TURACOVERDINS	TURNBROACH	TWELVEMONTH
TUMATAKURU	TURANGAWAEWAE	TURNBROACHES	TWELVEMONTHS
TUMBLEBUGS	TURANGAWAEWAES	TURNBUCKLE	TWENTIETHS
TUMBLEDOWN	TURBELLARIAN	TURNBUCKLES	TWENTYFOLD
TUMBLEHOME	TURBELLARIANS	TURNROUNDS	TWENTYFOLDS
TUMBLEHOMES	TURBIDIMETER	TURNSTILES	TWICHILDREN
TUMBLERFUL	TURBIDIMETERS	TURNSTONES	TWIDDLIEST
TUMBLERFULS	TURBIDIMETRIC	TURNTABLES	TWIDDLINGS
TUMBLERSFUL	TURBIDIMETRIES	TURNVEREIN	TWILIGHTED
TUMBLESETS	TURBIDIMETRY	TURNVEREINS	TWILIGHTING
TUMBLEWEED	TURBIDITES	TUROPHILES	TWINBERRIES
TUMBLEWEEDS	TURBIDITIES	TURPENTINE	TWINFLOWER
TUMEFACIENT	TURBIDNESS	TURPENTINED	TWINFLOWERS
TUMEFACTION	TURBIDNESSES	TURPENTINES	TWINKLINGS
TUMEFACTIONS	TURBINACIOUS	TURPENTINING	TWISTABILITIES
TUMESCENCE	TURBINATED	TURPENTINY	TWISTABILITY
TUMESCENCES	TURBINATES	TURPITUDES	TWITCHIEST
TUMIDITIES	TURBINATION	TURQUOISES	TWITCHINGS
TUMIDNESSES	TURBINATIONS	TURRIBANTS	TWITTERERS
TUMORGENIC	TURBOCHARGED	TURRICULATE	TWITTERING
TUMORGENICITIES	TURBOCHARGER	TURRICULATED	TWITTERINGLY
TUMORGENICITY	TURBOCHARGERS	TURTLEBACK	TWITTERINGS
TUMORIGENESES	TURBOCHARGING	TURTLEBACKS	TWITTINGLY
TUMORIGENESIS	TURBOCHARGINGS	TURTLEDOVE	TWOFOLDNESS
TUMORIGENIC	TURBOELECTRIC	TURTLEDOVES	TWOFOLDNESSES
TUMORIGENICITY	TURBOGENERATOR	TURTLEHEAD	TWOPENCEWORTH
TUMULOSITIES	TURBOGENERATORS	TURTLEHEADS	TWOPENCEWORTHS
TUMULOSITY	TURBOMACHINERY	TURTLENECK	TWOPENNIES
TUMULTUARY	TURBOPROPS	TURTLENECKED	TWOSEATERS
TUMULTUATE	TURBOSHAFT	TURTLENECKS	TYCOONATES
TUMULTUATED	TURBOSHAFTS	TUTELARIES	TYCOONERIES
TUMULTUATES	TURBULATOR	TUTIORISMS	TYLECTOMIES
TUMULTUATING	TURBULATORS	TUTIORISTS	TYMPANIFORM
TUMULTUATION	TURBULENCE	TUTORESSES	TYMPANISTS
TUMULTUATIONS	TURBULENCES	TUTORIALLY	TYMPANITES
TUMULTUOUS	TURBULENCIES	TUTORISING	TYMPANITESES
TUMULTUOUSLY	TURBULENCY	TUTORIZING	TYMPANITIC
TUMULTUOUSNESS	TURBULENTLY	TUTORSHIPS	TYMPANITIS
TUNABILITIES	TURCOPOLES	TUTOYERING	TYMPANITISES
TUNABILITY	TURCOPOLIER	TUTWORKERS	TYNDALLIMETRIES
TUNABLENESS	TURCOPOLIERS	TUTWORKMAN	TYNDALLIMETRY
TUNABLENESSES	TURFGRASSES	TUTWORKMEN	TYPECASTER
TUNBELLIED	TURFINESSES	TWADDLIEST	TYPECASTERS
TUNBELLIES	TURFSKIING	TWADDLINGS	TYPECASTING
TUNEFULNESS	TURFSKIINGS	TWALPENNIES	TYPEFOUNDER
TUNEFULNESSES	TURGENCIES	TWANGINGLY	TYPEFOUNDERS

TYPEFOUNDING
TYPEFOUNDINGS
TYPESCRIPT
TYPESCRIPTS
TYPESETTER
TYPESETTERS
TYPESETTING
TYPESETTINGS
TYPESTYLES
TYPEWRITER
TYPEWRITERS
TYPEWRITES
TYPEWRITING
TYPEWRITINGS
TYPEWRITTEN
TYPHACEOUS
TYPHLITISES
TYPHLOLOGIES
TYPHLOLOGY
TYPHLOSOLE
TYPHLOSOLES
TYPHOGENIC
TYPHOIDINS
TYPICALITIES
TYPICALITY
TYPICALNESS
TYPICALNESSES
TYPIFICATION
TYPIFICATIONS
TYPOGRAPHED
TYPOGRAPHER
TYPOGRAPHERS
TYPOGRAPHIA
TYPOGRAPHIC
TYPOGRAPHICAL
TYPOGRAPHICALLY
TYPOGRAPHIES
TYPOGRAPHING
TYPOGRAPHIST
TYPOGRAPHISTS
TYPOGRAPHS
TYPOGRAPHY
TYPOLOGICAL
TYPOLOGICALLY
TYPOLOGIES
TYPOLOGIST
TYPOLOGISTS
TYPOMANIAS
TYPOTHETAE
TYRANNESSES
TYRANNICAL
TYRANNICALLY
TYRANNICALNESS
TYRANNICIDAL
TYRANNICIDE
TYRANNICIDES
TYRANNISED
TYRANNISER
TYRANNISERS

TYRANNISES
TYRANNISING
TYRANNIZED
TYRANNIZER
TYRANNIZERS
TYRANNIZES
TYRANNIZING
TYRANNOSAUR
TYRANNOSAURS
TYRANNOSAURUS
TYRANNOSAURUSES
TYRANNOUSLY
TYRANNOUSNESS
TYRANNOUSNESSES
TYROCIDINE
TYROCIDINES
TYROCIDINS
TYROGLYPHID
TYROGLYPHIDS
TYROPITTAS
TYROSINASE
TYROSINASES
TYROTHRICIN
TYROTHRICINS

U

UBIQUARIAN
UBIQUINONE
UBIQUINONES
UBIQUITARIAN
UBIQUITARIANISM
UBIQUITARIANS
UBIQUITARY
UBIQUITIES
UBIQUITINATION
UBIQUITINATIONS
UBIQUITINS
UBIQUITOUS
UBIQUITOUSLY
UBIQUITOUSNESS
UDOMETRIES
UFOLOGICAL
UFOLOGISTS
UGLIFICATION
UGLIFICATIONS
UGLINESSES
UGSOMENESS
UGSOMENESSES
UINTAHITES
UINTATHERE
UINTATHERES
UITLANDERS
ULCERATING
ULCERATION
ULCERATIONS
ULCERATIVE
ULCEROGENIC
ULCEROUSLY
ULCEROUSNESS
ULCEROUSNESSES
ULOTRICHIES
ULOTRICHOUS
ULSTERETTE
ULSTERETTES
ULTERIORLY
ULTIMACIES
ULTIMATELY
ULTIMATENESS
ULTIMATENESSES
ULTIMATING
ULTIMATUMS
ULTIMOGENITURE
ULTIMOGENITURES
ULTRABASIC
ULTRABASICS
ULTRACAREFUL
ULTRACASUAL
ULTRACAUTIOUS
ULTRACENTRIFUGE
ULTRACIVILISED
ULTRACIVILIZED

ULTRACLEAN
ULTRACOMMERCIAL
ULTRACOMPACT
ULTRACOMPETENT
ULTRACONVENIENT
ULTRACREPIDATE
ULTRACREPIDATED
ULTRACREPIDATES
ULTRACRITICAL
ULTRADEMOCRATIC
ULTRADENSE
ULTRADISTANCE
ULTRADISTANT
ULTRAEFFICIENT
ULTRAENERGETIC
ULTRAEXCLUSIVE
ULTRAFAMILIAR
ULTRAFASTIDIOUS
ULTRAFEMININE
ULTRAFICHE
ULTRAFICHES
ULTRAFILTER
ULTRAFILTERED
ULTRAFILTERING
ULTRAFILTERS
ULTRAFILTRATE
ULTRAFILTRATES
ULTRAFILTRATION
ULTRAGLAMOROUS
ULTRAHAZARDOUS
ULTRAHEATED
ULTRAHEATING
ULTRAHEATS
ULTRAHEAVY
ULTRAHUMAN
ULTRAISTIC
ULTRALARGE
ULTRALEFTISM
ULTRALEFTISMS
ULTRALEFTIST
ULTRALEFTISTS
ULTRALIBERAL
ULTRALIBERALISM
ULTRALIBERALS
ULTRALIGHT
ULTRALIGHTS
ULTRAMAFIC
ULTRAMARATHON
ULTRAMARATHONER
ULTRAMARATHONS
ULTRAMARINE
ULTRAMARINES
ULTRAMASCULINE
ULTRAMICRO
ULTRAMICROMETER

ULTRAMICROSCOPE
ULTRAMICROSCOPY
ULTRAMICROTOME
ULTRAMICROTOMES
ULTRAMICROTOMY
ULTRAMILITANT
ULTRAMILITANTS
ULTRAMINIATURE
ULTRAMODERN
ULTRAMODERNISM
ULTRAMODERNISMS
ULTRAMODERNIST
ULTRAMODERNISTS
ULTRAMONTANE
ULTRAMONTANES
ULTRAMONTANISM
ULTRAMONTANISMS
ULTRAMONTANIST
ULTRAMONTANISTS
ULTRAMUNDANE
ULTRANATIONAL
ULTRAORTHODOX
ULTRAPATRIOTIC
ULTRAPHYSICAL
ULTRAPOWERFUL
ULTRAPRACTICAL
ULTRAPRECISE
ULTRAPRECISION
ULTRAQUIET
ULTRARADICAL
ULTRARADICALS
ULTRARAPID
ULTRARAREFIED
ULTRARATIONAL
ULTRAREALISM
ULTRAREALISMS
ULTRAREALIST
ULTRAREALISTIC
ULTRAREALISTS
ULTRAREFINED
ULTRARELIABLE
ULTRARIGHT
ULTRARIGHTIST
ULTRARIGHTISTS
ULTRAROMANTIC
ULTRAROYALIST
ULTRAROYALISTS
ULTRASECRET
ULTRASENSITIVE
ULTRASENSUAL
ULTRASERIOUS
ULTRASHARP
ULTRASHORT
ULTRASIMPLE
ULTRASLICK

ULTRASMALL
ULTRASMART
ULTRASMOOTH
ULTRASONIC
ULTRASONICALLY
ULTRASONICS
ULTRASONOGRAPHY
ULTRASOUND
ULTRASOUNDS
ULTRASTRUCTURAL
ULTRASTRUCTURE
ULTRASTRUCTURES
ULTRAVACUA
ULTRAVACUUM
ULTRAVACUUMS
ULTRAVIOLENCE
ULTRAVIOLENCES
ULTRAVIOLENT
ULTRAVIOLET
ULTRAVIOLETS
ULTRAVIRILE
ULTRAVIRILITIES
ULTRAVIRILITY
ULTRAVIRUS
ULTRAVIRUSES
ULTRAWIDEBAND
ULTRAWIDEBANDS
ULTRONEOUS
ULTRONEOUSLY
ULTRONEOUSNESS
ULULATIONS
UMBELLATED
UMBELLATELY
UMBELLIFER
UMBELLIFEROUS
UMBELLIFERS
UMBELLULATE
UMBELLULES
UMBILICALLY
UMBILICALS
UMBILICATE
UMBILICATED
UMBILICATION
UMBILICATIONS
UMBILICUSES
UMBILIFORM
UMBONATION
UMBONATIONS
UMBRACULATE
UMBRACULIFORM
UMBRACULUM
UMBRAGEOUS
UMBRAGEOUSLY
UMBRAGEOUSNESS
UMBRATICAL

UMBRATILOUS	UNADULTERATE	UNANCHORING	UNARGUABLY
UMBRELLAED	UNADULTERATED	UNANESTHETISED	UNARMOURED
UMBRELLAING	UNADULTERATEDLY	UNANESTHETIZED	UNARRANGED
UMBRELLOES	UNADVENTROUS	UNANIMATED	UNARROGANT
UMBRIFEROUS	UNADVENTUROUS	UNANIMITIES	UNARTFULLY
UMPIRESHIP	UNADVERTISED	UNANIMOUSLY	UNARTICULATE
UMPIRESHIPS	UNADVISABLE	UNANIMOUSNESS	UNARTICULATED
UMPTEENTHS	UNADVISABLENESS	UNANIMOUSNESSES	UNARTIFICIAL
UNABASHEDLY	UNADVISABLY	UNANNEALED	UNARTIFICIALLY
UNABATEDLY	UNADVISEDLY	UNANNOTATED	UNARTISTIC
UNABBREVIATED	UNADVISEDNESS	UNANNOUNCED	UNARTISTLIKE
UNABOLISHED	UNADVISEDNESSES	UNANSWERABILITY	UNASCENDABLE
UNABRIDGED	UNAESTHETIC	UNANSWERABLE	UNASCENDED
UNABROGATED	UNAFFECTED	UNANSWERABLY	UNASCENDIBLE
UNABSOLVED	UNAFFECTEDLY	UNANSWERED	UNASCERTAINABLE
UNABSORBED	UNAFFECTEDNESS	UNANTICIPATED	UNASCERTAINED
UNABSORBENT	UNAFFECTING	UNANTICIPATEDLY	UNASHAMEDLY
UNACADEMIC	UNAFFECTIONATE	UNAPOLOGETIC	UNASHAMEDNESS
UNACADEMICALLY	UNAFFILIATED	UNAPOLOGISING	UNASHAMEDNESSES
UNACCENTED	UNAFFLUENT	UNAPOLOGIZING	UNASPIRATED
UNACCENTUATED	UNAFFORDABLE	UNAPOSTOLIC	UNASPIRING
UNACCEPTABILITY	UNAGGRESSIVE	UNAPOSTOLICAL	UNASPIRINGLY
UNACCEPTABLE	UNAGREEABLE	UNAPOSTOLICALLY	UNASPIRINGNESS
UNACCEPTABLY	UNALIENABLE	UNAPPALLED	UNASSAILABILITY
UNACCEPTANCE	UNALIENABLY	UNAPPARELLED	UNASSAILABLE
UNACCEPTANCES	UNALIENATED	UNAPPARELLING	UNASSAILABLY
UNACCEPTED	UNALLEVIATED	UNAPPARELS	UNASSAILED
UNACCLIMATED	UNALLOCATED	UNAPPARENT	UNASSEMBLED
UNACCLIMATISED	UNALLOTTED	UNAPPEALABLE	UNASSERTIVE
UNACCLIMATIZED	UNALLOWABLE	UNAPPEALABLY	UNASSERTIVELY
UNACCOMMODATED	UNALLURING	UNAPPEALING	UNASSIGNABLE
UNACCOMMODATING	UNALTERABILITY	UNAPPEALINGLY	UNASSIGNED
UNACCOMPANIED	UNALTERABLE	UNAPPEASABLE	UNASSIMILABLE
UNACCOMPLISHED	UNALTERABLENESS	UNAPPEASABLY	UNASSIMILATED
UNACCOUNTABLE	UNALTERABLY	UNAPPEASED	UNASSISTED
UNACCOUNTABLY	UNALTERING	UNAPPETISING	UNASSISTEDLY
UNACCOUNTED	UNAMBIGUOUS	UNAPPETISINGLY	UNASSISTING
UNACCREDITED	UNAMBIGUOUSLY	UNAPPETIZING	UNASSOCIATED
UNACCULTURATED	UNAMBITIOUS	UNAPPETIZINGLY	UNASSUAGEABLE
UNACCUSABLE	UNAMBITIOUSLY	UNAPPLAUSIVE	UNASSUAGED
UNACCUSABLY	UNAMBIVALENT	UNAPPLICABLE	UNASSUMING
UNACCUSTOMED	UNAMBIVALENTLY	UNAPPOINTED	UNASSUMINGLY
UNACCUSTOMEDLY	UNAMENABLE	UNAPPRECIATED	UNASSUMINGNESS
UNACHIEVABLE	UNAMENDABLE	UNAPPRECIATION	UNATHLETIC
UNACHIEVED	UNAMIABILITIES	UNAPPRECIATIONS	UNATONABLE
UNACKNOWLEDGED	UNAMIABILITY	UNAPPRECIATIVE	UNATTACHED
UNACQUAINT	UNAMIABLENESS	UNAPPREHENDED	UNATTAINABLE
UNACQUAINTANCE	UNAMIABLENESSES	UNAPPREHENSIBLE	UNATTAINABLY
UNACQUAINTANCES	UNAMORTISED	UNAPPREHENSIVE	UNATTAINTED
UNACQUAINTED	UNAMORTIZED	UNAPPRISED	UNATTEMPTED
UNACTORISH	UNAMPLIFIED	UNAPPROACHABLE	UNATTENDED
UNACTUATED	UNAMUSABLE	UNAPPROACHABLY	UNATTENDING
UNADAPTABLE	UNAMUSINGLY	UNAPPROACHED	UNATTENTIVE
UNADDRESSED	UNANALYSABLE	UNAPPROPRIATE	UNATTENUATED
UNADJUDICATED	UNANALYSED	UNAPPROPRIATED	UNATTESTED
UNADJUSTED	UNANALYTIC	UNAPPROVED	UNATTRACTIVE
UNADMIRING	UNANALYTICAL	UNAPPROVING	UNATTRACTIVELY
UNADMITTED	UNANALYZABLE	UNAPPROVINGLY	UNATTRIBUTABLE
UNADMONISHED	UNANALYZED	UNAPTNESSES	UNATTRIBUTED
UNADOPTABLE	UNANCHORED	UNARGUABLE	UNAUGMENTED

UNAUSPICIOUS
UNAUTHENTIC
UNAUTHENTICATED
UNAUTHENTICITY
UNAUTHORISED
UNAUTHORITATIVE
UNAUTHORIZED
UNAUTOMATED
UNAVAILABILITY
UNAVAILABLE
UNAVAILABLENESS
UNAVAILABLY
UNAVAILING
UNAVAILINGLY
UNAVAILINGNESS
UNAVERTABLE
UNAVERTIBLE
UNAVOIDABILITY
UNAVOIDABLE
UNAVOIDABLENESS
UNAVOIDABLY
UNAVOWEDLY
UNAWAKENED
UNAWAKENING
UNAWARENESS
UNAWARENESSES
UNBAILABLE
UNBALANCED
UNBALANCES
UNBALANCING
UNBALLASTED
UNBANDAGED
UNBANDAGES
UNBANDAGING
UNBAPTISED
UNBAPTISES
UNBAPTISING
UNBAPTIZED
UNBAPTIZES
UNBAPTIZING
UNBARBERED
UNBARRICADE
UNBARRICADED
UNBARRICADES
UNBARRICADING
UNBATTERED
UNBEARABLE
UNBEARABLENESS
UNBEARABLY
UNBEATABLE
UNBEATABLY
UNBEAUTIFUL
UNBEAUTIFULLY
UNBEAVERED
UNBECOMING
UNBECOMINGLY
UNBECOMINGNESS
UNBECOMINGS
UNBEDIMMED
UNBEDINNED

UNBEFITTING
UNBEFRIENDED
UNBEGETTING
UNBEGINNING
UNBEGOTTEN
UNBEGUILED
UNBEGUILES
UNBEGUILING
UNBEHOLDEN
UNBEKNOWNST
UNBELIEVABILITY
UNBELIEVABLE
UNBELIEVABLY
UNBELIEVED
UNBELIEVER
UNBELIEVERS
UNBELIEVES
UNBELIEVING
UNBELIEVINGLY
UNBELIEVINGNESS
UNBELLIGERENT
UNBENDABLE
UNBENDINGLY
UNBENDINGNESS
UNBENDINGNESSES
UNBENDINGS
UNBENEFICED
UNBENEFICIAL
UNBENEFITED
UNBENIGHTED
UNBENIGNANT
UNBENIGNLY
UNBESEEMED
UNBESEEMING
UNBESEEMINGLY
UNBESOUGHT
UNBESPEAKING
UNBESPEAKS
UNBESPOKEN
UNBESTOWED
UNBETRAYED
UNBETTERABLE
UNBETTERED
UNBEWAILED
UNBIASEDLY
UNBIASEDNESS
UNBIASEDNESSES
UNBIASSEDLY
UNBIASSEDNESS
UNBIASSEDNESSES
UNBIASSING
UNBIBLICAL
UNBINDINGS
UNBIRTHDAY
UNBIRTHDAYS
UNBISHOPED
UNBISHOPING
UNBLAMABLE
UNBLAMABLY
UNBLAMEABLE

UNBLAMEABLY
UNBLEACHED
UNBLEMISHED
UNBLENCHED
UNBLENCHING
UNBLESSEDNESS
UNBLESSEDNESSES
UNBLESSING
UNBLINDFOLD
UNBLINDFOLDED
UNBLINDFOLDING
UNBLINDFOLDS
UNBLINDING
UNBLINKING
UNBLINKINGLY
UNBLISSFUL
UNBLOCKING
UNBLOODIED
UNBLUSHING
UNBLUSHINGLY
UNBLUSHINGNESS
UNBOASTFUL
UNBONNETED
UNBONNETING
UNBORROWED
UNBOSOMERS
UNBOSOMING
UNBOTTLING
UNBOTTOMED
UNBOUNDEDLY
UNBOUNDEDNESS
UNBOUNDEDNESSES
UNBOWDLERISED
UNBOWDLERIZED
UNBRACKETED
UNBRAIDING
UNBRANCHED
UNBREACHABLE
UNBREACHED
UNBREAKABLE
UNBREATHABLE
UNBREATHED
UNBREATHING
UNBREECHED
UNBREECHES
UNBREECHING
UNBRIBABLE
UNBRIBABLE
UNBRIDGEABLE
UNBRIDLEDLY
UNBRIDLEDNESS
UNBRIDLEDNESSES
UNBRIDLING
UNBRILLIANT
UNBROKENLY
UNBROKENNESS
UNBROKENNESSES
UNBROTHERLIKE
UNBROTHERLY
UNBUCKLING
UNBUDGEABLE

UNBUDGEABLY
UNBUDGETED
UNBUDGINGLY
UNBUFFERED
UNBUILDABLE
UNBUILDING
UNBUNDLERS
UNBUNDLING
UNBUNDLINGS
UNBURDENED
UNBURDENING
UNBUREAUCRATIC
UNBURNABLE
UNBURNISHED
UNBURROWED
UNBURROWING
UNBURTHENED
UNBURTHENING
UNBURTHENS
UNBUSINESSLIKE
UNBUTTERED
UNBUTTONED
UNBUTTONING
UNCALCIFIED
UNCALCINED
UNCALCULATED
UNCALCULATING
UNCALIBRATED
UNCALLOUSED
UNCANCELED
UNCANDIDLY
UNCANDIDNESS
UNCANDIDNESSES
UNCANDOURS
UNCANNIEST
UNCANNINESS
UNCANNINESSES
UNCANONICAL
UNCANONICALNESS
UNCANONISE
UNCANONISED
UNCANONISES
UNCANONISING
UNCANONIZE
UNCANONIZED
UNCANONIZES
UNCANONIZING
UNCAPITALISED
UNCAPITALIZED
UNCAPSIZABLE
UNCAPTIONED
UNCAPTURABLE
UNCARPETED
UNCASTRATED
UNCATALOGED
UNCATALOGUED
UNCATCHABLE
UNCATEGORISABLE
UNCATEGORIZABLE
UNCEASINGLY

UNCEASINGNESS
UNCEASINGNESSES
UNCELEBRATED
UNCENSORED
UNCENSORIOUS
UNCENSURED
UNCEREBRAL
UNCEREMONIOUS
UNCEREMONIOUSLY
UNCERTAINLY
UNCERTAINNESS
UNCERTAINNESSES
UNCERTAINTIES
UNCERTAINTY
UNCERTIFICATED
UNCERTIFIED
UNCHAINING
UNCHAIRING
UNCHALLENGEABLE
UNCHALLENGEABLY
UNCHALLENGED
UNCHALLENGING
UNCHANCIER
UNCHANCIEST
UNCHANGEABILITY
UNCHANGEABLE
UNCHANGEABLY
UNCHANGING
UNCHANGINGLY
UNCHANGINGNESS
UNCHANNELED
UNCHAPERONED
UNCHARGING
UNCHARISMATIC
UNCHARITABLE
UNCHARITABLY
UNCHARITIES
UNCHARMING
UNCHARNELLED
UNCHARNELLING
UNCHARNELS
UNCHARTERED
UNCHASTELY
UNCHASTENED
UNCHASTENESS
UNCHASTENESSES
UNCHASTEST
UNCHASTISABLE
UNCHASTISED
UNCHASTITIES
UNCHASTITY
UNCHASTIZABLE
UNCHASTIZED
UNCHAUVINISTIC
UNCHECKABLE
UNCHECKING
UNCHEERFUL
UNCHEERFULLY
UNCHEERFULNESS
UNCHEWABLE

UNCHILDING
UNCHILDLIKE
UNCHIVALROUS
UNCHIVALROUSLY
UNCHLORINATED
UNCHOREOGRAPHED
UNCHRISTEN
UNCHRISTENED
UNCHRISTENING
UNCHRISTENS
UNCHRISTIAN
UNCHRISTIANED
UNCHRISTIANING
UNCHRISTIANISE
UNCHRISTIANISED
UNCHRISTIANISES
UNCHRISTIANIZE
UNCHRISTIANIZED
UNCHRISTIANIZES
UNCHRISTIANLIKE
UNCHRISTIANLY
UNCHRISTIANS
UNCHRONICLED
UNCHRONOLOGICAL
UNCHURCHED
UNCHURCHES
UNCHURCHING
UNCHURCHLY
UNCILIATED
UNCINARIAS
UNCINARIASES
UNCINARIASIS
UNCINEMATIC
UNCIPHERED
UNCIPHERING
UNCIRCULATED
UNCIRCUMCISED
UNCIRCUMCISION
UNCIRCUMCISIONS
UNCIRCUMSCRIBED
UNCIVILISED
UNCIVILISEDLY
UNCIVILISEDNESS
UNCIVILITIES
UNCIVILITY
UNCIVILIZED
UNCIVILIZEDLY
UNCIVILIZEDNESS
UNCIVILNESS
UNCIVILNESSES
UNCLAMPING
UNCLARIFIED
UNCLARITIES
UNCLASPING
UNCLASSICAL
UNCLASSIFIABLE
UNCLASSIFIED
UNCLEANEST
UNCLEANLIER
UNCLEANLIEST

UNCLEANLINESS
UNCLEANLINESSES
UNCLEANNESS
UNCLEANNESSES
UNCLEANSED
UNCLEAREST
UNCLEARNESS
UNCLEARNESSES
UNCLENCHED
UNCLENCHES
UNCLENCHING
UNCLERICAL
UNCLESHIPS
UNCLIMBABLE
UNCLIMBABLENESS
UNCLINCHED
UNCLINCHES
UNCLINCHING
UNCLIPPING
UNCLOAKING
UNCLOGGING
UNCLOISTER
UNCLOISTERED
UNCLOISTERING
UNCLOISTERS
UNCLOTHING
UNCLOUDEDLY
UNCLOUDEDNESS
UNCLOUDEDNESSES
UNCLOUDING
UNCLUBABLE
UNCLUBBABLE
UNCLUTCHED
UNCLUTCHES
UNCLUTCHING
UNCLUTTERED
UNCLUTTERING
UNCLUTTERS
UNCOALESCE
UNCOALESCED
UNCOALESCES
UNCOALESCING
UNCOATINGS
UNCODIFIED
UNCOERCIVE
UNCOERCIVELY
UNCOFFINED
UNCOFFINING
UNCOLLECTED
UNCOLLECTIBLE
UNCOLLECTIBLES
UNCOLOURED
UNCOMATABLE
UNCOMBATIVE
UNCOMBINED
UNCOMBINES
UNCOMBINING
UNCOMEATABLE
UNCOMELINESS
UNCOMELINESSES

UNCOMFORTABLE
UNCOMFORTABLY
UNCOMFORTED
UNCOMMENDABLE
UNCOMMENDABLY
UNCOMMENDED
UNCOMMERCIAL
UNCOMMITTED
UNCOMMONER
UNCOMMONEST
UNCOMMONLY
UNCOMMONNESS
UNCOMMONNESSES
UNCOMMUNICABLE
UNCOMMUNICATED
UNCOMMUNICATIVE
UNCOMMUTED
UNCOMPACTED
UNCOMPANIED
UNCOMPANIONABLE
UNCOMPANIONED
UNCOMPASSIONATE
UNCOMPELLED
UNCOMPELLING
UNCOMPENSATED
UNCOMPETITIVE
UNCOMPLACENT
UNCOMPLAINING
UNCOMPLAININGLY
UNCOMPLAISANT
UNCOMPLAISANTLY
UNCOMPLETED
UNCOMPLIANT
UNCOMPLICATED
UNCOMPLIMENTARY
UNCOMPLYING
UNCOMPOSABLE
UNCOMPOUNDED
UNCOMPREHENDED
UNCOMPREHENDING
UNCOMPREHENSIVE
UNCOMPROMISABLE
UNCOMPROMISING
UNCOMPUTERISED
UNCOMPUTERIZED
UNCONCEALABLE
UNCONCEALED
UNCONCEALING
UNCONCEIVABLE
UNCONCEIVABLY
UNCONCEIVED
UNCONCERNED
UNCONCERNEDLY
UNCONCERNEDNESS
UNCONCERNING
UNCONCERNMENT
UNCONCERNMENTS
UNCONCERNS
UNCONCERTED
UNCONCILIATORY

UNCONCLUSIVE
UNCONCOCTED
UNCONDITIONAL
UNCONDITIONALLY
UNCONDITIONED
UNCONFEDERATED
UNCONFESSED
UNCONFINABLE
UNCONFINED
UNCONFINEDLY
UNCONFINES
UNCONFINING
UNCONFIRMED
UNCONFORMABLE
UNCONFORMABLY
UNCONFORMING
UNCONFORMITIES
UNCONFORMITY
UNCONFOUNDED
UNCONFUSED
UNCONFUSEDLY
UNCONFUSES
UNCONFUSING
UNCONGEALED
UNCONGEALING
UNCONGEALS
UNCONGENIAL
UNCONGENIALITY
UNCONJECTURED
UNCONJUGAL
UNCONJUGATED
UNCONJUNCTIVE
UNCONNECTED
UNCONNECTEDLY
UNCONNECTEDNESS
UNCONNIVING
UNCONQUERABLE
UNCONQUERABLY
UNCONQUERED
UNCONSCIENTIOUS
UNCONSCIONABLE
UNCONSCIONABLY
UNCONSCIOUS
UNCONSCIOUSES
UNCONSCIOUSLY
UNCONSCIOUSNESS
UNCONSECRATE
UNCONSECRATED
UNCONSECRATES
UNCONSECRATING
UNCONSENTANEOUS
UNCONSENTING
UNCONSIDERED
UNCONSIDERING
UNCONSOLED
UNCONSOLIDATED
UNCONSTANT
UNCONSTRAINABLE
UNCONSTRAINED
UNCONSTRAINEDLY

UNCONSTRAINT
UNCONSTRAINTS
UNCONSTRICTED
UNCONSTRUCTED
UNCONSTRUCTIVE
UNCONSUMED
UNCONSUMMATED
UNCONTAINABLE
UNCONTAMINATED
UNCONTEMNED
UNCONTEMPLATED
UNCONTEMPORARY
UNCONTENTIOUS
UNCONTESTABLE
UNCONTESTED
UNCONTRACTED
UNCONTRADICTED
UNCONTRIVED
UNCONTROLLABLE
UNCONTROLLABLY
UNCONTROLLED
UNCONTROLLEDLY
UNCONTROVERSIAL
UNCONTROVERTED
UNCONVENTIONAL
UNCONVERSABLE
UNCONVERSANT
UNCONVERTED
UNCONVERTIBLE
UNCONVICTED
UNCONVINCED
UNCONVINCING
UNCONVINCINGLY
UNCONVOYED
UNCOOPERATIVE
UNCOOPERATIVELY
UNCOORDINATED
UNCOPYRIGHTABLE
UNCOQUETTISH
UNCORRECTABLE
UNCORRECTED
UNCORRELATED
UNCORROBORATED
UNCORRUPTED
UNCORSETED
UNCOUNSELLED
UNCOUNTABLE
UNCOUPLERS
UNCOUPLING
UNCOURAGEOUS
UNCOURTEOUS
UNCOURTLINESS
UNCOURTLINESSES
UNCOUTHEST
UNCOUTHNESS
UNCOUTHNESSES
UNCOVENANTED
UNCOVERING
UNCREATEDNESS
UNCREATEDNESSES

UNCREATING
UNCREATIVE
UNCREDENTIALED
UNCREDIBLE
UNCREDITABLE
UNCREDITED
UNCRIPPLED
UNCRITICAL
UNCRITICALLY
UNCROSSABLE
UNCROSSING
UNCROWNING
UNCRUMPLED
UNCRUMPLES
UNCRUMPLING
UNCRUSHABLE
UNCRYSTALLISED
UNCRYSTALLIZED
UNCTIONLESS
UNCTUOSITIES
UNCTUOSITY
UNCTUOUSLY
UNCTUOUSNESS
UNCTUOUSNESSES
UNCUCKOLDED
UNCULTIVABLE
UNCULTIVATABLE
UNCULTIVATED
UNCULTURED
UNCUMBERED
UNCURBABLE
UNCURTAILED
UNCURTAINED
UNCURTAINING
UNCURTAINS
UNCUSTOMARILY
UNCUSTOMARY
UNCUSTOMED
UNCYNICALLY
UNDANCEABLE
UNDAUNTABLE
UNDAUNTEDLY
UNDAUNTEDNESS
UNDAUNTEDNESSES
UNDAZZLING
UNDEBARRED
UNDEBATABLE
UNDEBATABLY
UNDEBAUCHED
UNDECADENT
UNDECAGONS
UNDECEIVABLE
UNDECEIVED
UNDECEIVER
UNDECEIVERS
UNDECEIVES
UNDECEIVING
UNDECIDABILITY
UNDECIDABLE
UNDECIDEDLY

UNDECIDEDNESS
UNDECIDEDNESSES
UNDECIDEDS
UNDECILLION
UNDECILLIONS
UNDECIMOLE
UNDECIMOLES
UNDECIPHERABLE
UNDECIPHERED
UNDECISIVE
UNDECLARED
UNDECLINING
UNDECOMPOSABLE
UNDECOMPOSED
UNDECORATED
UNDEDICATED
UNDEFEATED
UNDEFENDED
UNDEFINABLE
UNDEFOLIATED
UNDEFORMED
UNDEIFYING
UNDELAYING
UNDELECTABLE
UNDELEGATED
UNDELIBERATE
UNDELIGHTED
UNDELIGHTFUL
UNDELIGHTS
UNDELIVERABLE
UNDELIVERED
UNDEMANDING
UNDEMOCRATIC
UNDEMONSTRABLE
UNDEMONSTRATIVE
UNDENIABLE
UNDENIABLENESS
UNDENIABLY
UNDEPENDABLE
UNDEPENDING
UNDEPLORED
UNDEPRAVED
UNDEPRECIATED
UNDEPRESSED
UNDEPRIVED
UNDERACHIEVE
UNDERACHIEVED
UNDERACHIEVER
UNDERACHIEVERS
UNDERACHIEVES
UNDERACHIEVING
UNDERACTED
UNDERACTING
UNDERACTION
UNDERACTIONS
UNDERACTIVE
UNDERACTIVITIES
UNDERACTIVITY
UNDERACTOR
UNDERACTORS

UNDERAGENT
UNDERAGENTS
UNDERBAKED
UNDERBAKES
UNDERBAKING
UNDERBEARER
UNDERBEARERS
UNDERBEARING
UNDERBEARINGS
UNDERBEARS
UNDERBELLIES
UNDERBELLY
UNDERBIDDER
UNDERBIDDERS
UNDERBIDDING
UNDERBITES
UNDERBITING
UNDERBITTEN
UNDERBLANKET
UNDERBLANKETS
UNDERBODIES
UNDERBORNE
UNDERBOSSES
UNDERBOUGH
UNDERBOUGHS
UNDERBOUGHT
UNDERBREATH
UNDERBREATHS
UNDERBREEDING
UNDERBREEDINGS
UNDERBRIDGE
UNDERBRIDGES
UNDERBRIMS
UNDERBRUSH
UNDERBRUSHED
UNDERBRUSHES
UNDERBRUSHING
UNDERBUDDED
UNDERBUDDING
UNDERBUDGET
UNDERBUDGETED
UNDERBUDGETING
UNDERBUDGETS
UNDERBUILD
UNDERBUILDER
UNDERBUILDERS
UNDERBUILDING
UNDERBUILDS
UNDERBUILT
UNDERBURNT
UNDERBUSHED
UNDERBUSHES
UNDERBUSHING
UNDERBUYING
UNDERCAPITALISE
UNDERCAPITALIZE
UNDERCARDS
UNDERCARRIAGE
UNDERCARRIAGES
UNDERCARTS

UNDERCASTS
UNDERCHARGE
UNDERCHARGED
UNDERCHARGES
UNDERCHARGING
UNDERCLASS
UNDERCLASSES
UNDERCLASSMAN
UNDERCLASSMEN
UNDERCLAYS
UNDERCLIFF
UNDERCLIFFS
UNDERCLOTHE
UNDERCLOTHED
UNDERCLOTHES
UNDERCLOTHING
UNDERCLOTHINGS
UNDERCLUBBED
UNDERCLUBBING
UNDERCLUBS
UNDERCOATED
UNDERCOATING
UNDERCOATINGS
UNDERCOATS
UNDERCOOKED
UNDERCOOKING
UNDERCOOKS
UNDERCOOLED
UNDERCOOLING
UNDERCOOLS
UNDERCOUNT
UNDERCOUNTED
UNDERCOUNTING
UNDERCOUNTS
UNDERCOVER
UNDERCOVERT
UNDERCOVERTS
UNDERCREST
UNDERCRESTED
UNDERCRESTING
UNDERCRESTS
UNDERCROFT
UNDERCROFTS
UNDERCURRENT
UNDERCURRENTS
UNDERCUTTING
UNDERDAMPER
UNDERDAMPERS
UNDERDECKS
UNDERDEVELOP
UNDERDEVELOPED
UNDERDEVELOPING
UNDERDEVELOPS
UNDERDOERS
UNDERDOING
UNDERDOSED
UNDERDOSES
UNDERDOSING
UNDERDRAIN
UNDERDRAINAGE

UNDERDRAINAGES
UNDERDRAINED
UNDERDRAINING
UNDERDRAINS
UNDERDRAWERS
UNDERDRAWING
UNDERDRAWINGS
UNDERDRAWN
UNDERDRAWS
UNDERDRESS
UNDERDRESSED
UNDERDRESSES
UNDERDRESSING
UNDERDRIVE
UNDERDRIVES
UNDEREARTH
UNDEREATEN
UNDEREATING
UNDEREDUCATED
UNDEREMPHASES
UNDEREMPHASIS
UNDEREMPHASISE
UNDEREMPHASISED
UNDEREMPHASISES
UNDEREMPHASIZE
UNDEREMPHASIZED
UNDEREMPHASIZES
UNDEREMPLOYED
UNDEREMPLOYMENT
UNDERESTIMATE
UNDERESTIMATED
UNDERESTIMATES
UNDERESTIMATING
UNDERESTIMATION
UNDEREXPOSE
UNDEREXPOSED
UNDEREXPOSES
UNDEREXPOSING
UNDEREXPOSURE
UNDEREXPOSURES
UNDERFEEDING
UNDERFEEDS
UNDERFELTS
UNDERFINANCED
UNDERFINISHED
UNDERFIRED
UNDERFIRES
UNDERFIRING
UNDERFISHED
UNDERFISHES
UNDERFISHING
UNDERFLOOR
UNDERFLOWS
UNDERFONGED
UNDERFONGING
UNDERFONGS
UNDERFOOTED
UNDERFOOTING
UNDERFOOTS
UNDERFULFIL

UNDERFULFILLED
UNDERFULFILLING
UNDERFULFILS
UNDERFUNDED
UNDERFUNDING
UNDERFUNDINGS
UNDERFUNDS
UNDERGARMENT
UNDERGARMENTS
UNDERGIRDED
UNDERGIRDING
UNDERGIRDS
UNDERGLAZE
UNDERGLAZES
UNDERGOERS
UNDERGOING
UNDERGOWNS
UNDERGRADS
UNDERGRADUATE
UNDERGRADUATES
UNDERGRADUETTE
UNDERGRADUETTES
UNDERGROUND
UNDERGROUNDER
UNDERGROUNDERS
UNDERGROUNDS
UNDERGROVE
UNDERGROVES
UNDERGROWN
UNDERGROWTH
UNDERGROWTHS
UNDERHAIRS
UNDERHANDED
UNDERHANDEDLY
UNDERHANDEDNESS
UNDERHANDS
UNDERHEATED
UNDERHEATING
UNDERHEATS
UNDERHONEST
UNDERINFLATED
UNDERINFLATION
UNDERINFLATIONS
UNDERINSURED
UNDERINVESTMENT
UNDERJAWED
UNDERKEEPER
UNDERKEEPERS
UNDERKEEPING
UNDERKEEPS
UNDERKILLS
UNDERKINGDOM
UNDERKINGDOMS
UNDERKINGS
UNDERLAPPED
UNDERLAPPING
UNDERLAYER
UNDERLAYERS
UNDERLAYING
UNDERLAYMENT

UNDERLAYMENTS

UNDERLAYMENTS
UNDERLEASE
UNDERLEASED
UNDERLEASES
UNDERLEASING
UNDERLEAVES
UNDERLETTER
UNDERLETTERS
UNDERLETTING
UNDERLETTINGS
UNDERLIERS
UNDERLINED
UNDERLINEN
UNDERLINENS
UNDERLINES
UNDERLINGS
UNDERLINING
UNDERLOADED
UNDERLOADING
UNDERLOADS
UNDERLOOKER
UNDERLOOKERS
UNDERLYING
UNDERLYINGLY
UNDERMANNED
UNDERMANNING
UNDERMASTED
UNDERMEANING
UNDERMEANINGS
UNDERMENTIONED
UNDERMINDE
UNDERMINDED
UNDERMINDES
UNDERMINDING
UNDERMINED
UNDERMINER
UNDERMINERS
UNDERMINES
UNDERMINING
UNDERMININGS
UNDERNAMED
UNDERNEATH
UNDERNEATHS
UNDERNICENESS
UNDERNICENESSES
UNDERNOTED
UNDERNOTES
UNDERNOTING
UNDERNOURISH
UNDERNOURISHED
UNDERNOURISHES
UNDERNOURISHING
UNDERNTIME
UNDERNTIMES
UNDERNUTRITION
UNDERNUTRITIONS
UNDERPAINTING
UNDERPAINTINGS
UNDERPANTS
UNDERPARTS

UNDERPASSES
UNDERPASSION
UNDERPASSIONS
UNDERPAYING
UNDERPAYMENT
UNDERPAYMENTS
UNDERPEEPED
UNDERPEEPING
UNDERPEEPS
UNDERPEOPLED
UNDERPERFORM
UNDERPERFORMED
UNDERPERFORMING
UNDERPERFORMS
UNDERPINNED
UNDERPINNING
UNDERPINNINGS
UNDERPITCH
UNDERPLANT
UNDERPLANTED
UNDERPLANTING
UNDERPLANTS
UNDERPLAYED
UNDERPLAYING
UNDERPLAYS
UNDERPLOTS
UNDERPOPULATED
UNDERPOWERED
UNDERPRAISE
UNDERPRAISED
UNDERPRAISES
UNDERPRAISING
UNDERPREPARED
UNDERPRICE
UNDERPRICED
UNDERPRICES
UNDERPRICING
UNDERPRISE
UNDERPRISED
UNDERPRISES
UNDERPRISING
UNDERPRIVILEGED
UNDERPRIZE
UNDERPRIZED
UNDERPRIZES
UNDERPRIZING
UNDERPRODUCTION
UNDERPROOF
UNDERPROPPED
UNDERPROPPER
UNDERPROPPERS
UNDERPROPPING
UNDERPROPS
UNDERPUBLICISED
UNDERPUBLICIZED
UNDERQUOTE
UNDERQUOTED
UNDERQUOTES
UNDERQUOTING
UNDERRATED

UNDERRATES
UNDERRATING
UNDERREACT
UNDERREACTED
UNDERREACTING
UNDERREACTS
UNDERREPORT
UNDERREPORTED
UNDERREPORTING
UNDERREPORTS
UNDERRUNNING
UNDERRUNNINGS
UNDERSATURATED
UNDERSAYING
UNDERSCORE
UNDERSCORED
UNDERSCORES
UNDERSCORING
UNDERSCRUB
UNDERSCRUBS
UNDERSEALED
UNDERSEALING
UNDERSEALINGS
UNDERSEALS
UNDERSECRETARY
UNDERSELLER
UNDERSELLERS
UNDERSELLING
UNDERSELLS
UNDERSELVES
UNDERSENSE
UNDERSENSES
UNDERSERVED
UNDERSETTING
UNDERSEXED
UNDERSHAPEN
UNDERSHERIFF
UNDERSHERIFFS
UNDERSHIRT
UNDERSHIRTED
UNDERSHIRTS
UNDERSHOOT
UNDERSHOOTING
UNDERSHOOTS
UNDERSHORTS
UNDERSHRUB
UNDERSHRUBS
UNDERSIDES
UNDERSIGNED
UNDERSIGNING
UNDERSIGNS
UNDERSIZED
UNDERSKIES
UNDERSKINKER
UNDERSKINKERS
UNDERSKIRT
UNDERSKIRTS
UNDERSLEEVE
UNDERSLEEVES
UNDERSLUNG

UNDERSOILS
UNDERSONGS
UNDERSPEND
UNDERSPENDING
UNDERSPENDS
UNDERSPENT
UNDERSPINS
UNDERSTAFFED
UNDERSTAFFING
UNDERSTAFFINGS
UNDERSTAND
UNDERSTANDABLE
UNDERSTANDABLY
UNDERSTANDED
UNDERSTANDER
UNDERSTANDERS
UNDERSTANDING
UNDERSTANDINGLY
UNDERSTANDINGS
UNDERSTANDS
UNDERSTATE
UNDERSTATED
UNDERSTATEDLY
UNDERSTATEMENT
UNDERSTATEMENTS
UNDERSTATES
UNDERSTATING
UNDERSTEER
UNDERSTEERED
UNDERSTEERING
UNDERSTEERS
UNDERSTOCK
UNDERSTOCKED
UNDERSTOCKING
UNDERSTOCKS
UNDERSTOOD
UNDERSTOREY
UNDERSTOREYS
UNDERSTORIES
UNDERSTORY
UNDERSTRAPPER
UNDERSTRAPPERS
UNDERSTRAPPING
UNDERSTRATA
UNDERSTRATUM
UNDERSTRENGTH
UNDERSTUDIED
UNDERSTUDIES
UNDERSTUDY
UNDERSTUDYING
UNDERSUPPLIED
UNDERSUPPLIES
UNDERSUPPLY
UNDERSUPPLYING
UNDERSURFACE
UNDERSURFACES
UNDERTAKABLE
UNDERTAKEN
UNDERTAKER
UNDERTAKERS

UNDERTAKES
UNDERTAKING
UNDERTAKINGS
UNDERTAXED
UNDERTAXES
UNDERTAXING
UNDERTENANCIES
UNDERTENANCY
UNDERTENANT
UNDERTENANTS
UNDERTHINGS
UNDERTHIRST
UNDERTHIRSTS
UNDERTHRUST
UNDERTHRUSTING
UNDERTHRUSTS
UNDERTIMED
UNDERTIMES
UNDERTINTS
UNDERTONED
UNDERTONES
UNDERTRICK
UNDERTRICKS
UNDERTRUMP
UNDERTRUMPED
UNDERTRUMPING
UNDERTRUMPS
UNDERUSING
UNDERUTILISE
UNDERUTILISED
UNDERUTILISES
UNDERUTILISING
UNDERUTILIZE
UNDERUTILIZED
UNDERUTILIZES
UNDERUTILIZING
UNDERVALUATION
UNDERVALUATIONS
UNDERVALUE
UNDERVALUED
UNDERVALUER
UNDERVALUERS
UNDERVALUES
UNDERVALUING
UNDERVESTS
UNDERVIEWER
UNDERVIEWERS
UNDERVOICE
UNDERVOICES
UNDERVOTES
UNDERWATER
UNDERWATERS
UNDERWEARS
UNDERWEIGHT
UNDERWEIGHTS
UNDERWHELM
UNDERWHELMED
UNDERWHELMING
UNDERWHELMS
UNDERWINGS

UNDERWIRED
UNDERWIRES
UNDERWIRING
UNDERWIRINGS
UNDERWOODS
UNDERWOOLS
UNDERWORKED
UNDERWORKER
UNDERWORKERS
UNDERWORKING
UNDERWORKS
UNDERWORLD
UNDERWORLDS
UNDERWRITE
UNDERWRITER
UNDERWRITERS
UNDERWRITES
UNDERWRITING
UNDERWRITINGS
UNDERWRITTEN
UNDERWROTE
UNDERWROUGHT
UNDESCENDABLE
UNDESCENDED
UNDESCENDIBLE
UNDESCRIBABLE
UNDESCRIBED
UNDESCRIED
UNDESERVED
UNDESERVEDLY
UNDESERVEDNESS
UNDESERVER
UNDESERVERS
UNDESERVES
UNDESERVING
UNDESERVINGLY
UNDESIGNATED
UNDESIGNED
UNDESIGNEDLY
UNDESIGNEDNESS
UNDESIGNING
UNDESIRABILITY
UNDESIRABLE
UNDESIRABLENESS
UNDESIRABLES
UNDESIRABLY
UNDESIRING
UNDESIROUS
UNDESPAIRING
UNDESPAIRINGLY
UNDESPOILED
UNDESTROYED
UNDETECTABLE
UNDETECTED
UNDETERMINABLE
UNDETERMINATE
UNDETERMINATION
UNDETERMINED
UNDETERRED
UNDEVELOPED

UNDEVIATING
UNDEVIATINGLY
UNDIAGNOSABLE
UNDIAGNOSED
UNDIALECTICAL
UNDIDACTIC
UNDIFFERENCED
UNDIGESTED
UNDIGESTIBLE
UNDIGHTING
UNDIGNIFIED
UNDIGNIFIES
UNDIGNIFYING
UNDIMINISHABLE
UNDIMINISHED
UNDIPLOMATIC
UNDIRECTED
UNDISAPPOINTING
UNDISCERNED
UNDISCERNEDLY
UNDISCERNIBLE
UNDISCERNIBLY
UNDISCERNING
UNDISCERNINGS
UNDISCHARGED
UNDISCIPLINABLE
UNDISCIPLINE
UNDISCIPLINED
UNDISCIPLINES
UNDISCLOSED
UNDISCOMFITED
UNDISCORDANT
UNDISCORDING
UNDISCOURAGED
UNDISCOVERABLE
UNDISCOVERABLY
UNDISCOVERED
UNDISCUSSABLE
UNDISCUSSED
UNDISCUSSIBLE
UNDISGUISABLE
UNDISGUISED
UNDISGUISEDLY
UNDISHONOURED
UNDISMANTLED
UNDISMAYED
UNDISORDERED
UNDISPATCHED
UNDISPENSED
UNDISPOSED
UNDISPUTABLE
UNDISPUTED
UNDISPUTEDLY
UNDISSEMBLED
UNDISSOCIATED
UNDISSOLVED
UNDISSOLVING
UNDISTEMPERED
UNDISTILLED
UNDISTINCTIVE

UNDISTINGUISHED
UNDISTORTED
UNDISTRACTED
UNDISTRACTEDLY
UNDISTRACTING
UNDISTRIBUTED
UNDISTURBED
UNDISTURBEDLY
UNDISTURBING
UNDIVERSIFIED
UNDIVERTED
UNDIVERTING
UNDIVESTED
UNDIVESTEDLY
UNDIVIDABLE
UNDIVIDEDLY
UNDIVIDEDNESS
UNDIVIDEDNESSES
UNDIVORCED
UNDIVULGED
UNDOCTORED
UNDOCTRINAIRE
UNDOCUMENTED
UNDOGMATIC
UNDOGMATICALLY
UNDOMESTIC
UNDOMESTICATE
UNDOMESTICATED
UNDOMESTICATES
UNDOMESTICATING
UNDOUBLING
UNDOUBTABLE
UNDOUBTEDLY
UNDOUBTFUL
UNDOUBTING
UNDOUBTINGLY
UNDRAINABLE
UNDRAMATIC
UNDRAMATICALLY
UNDRAMATISED
UNDRAMATIZED
UNDREADING
UNDREAMING
UNDRESSING
UNDRESSINGS
UNDRINKABLE
UNDRIVEABLE
UNDROOPING
UNDULANCES
UNDULANCIES
UNDULATELY
UNDULATING
UNDULATINGLY
UNDULATION
UNDULATIONIST
UNDULATIONISTS
UNDULATIONS
UNDULATORS
UNDULATORY
UNDUPLICATED

UNDUTIFULLY
UNDUTIFULNESS
UNDUTIFULNESSES
UNDYINGNESS
UNDYINGNESSES
UNEARMARKED
UNEARTHING
UNEARTHLIER
UNEARTHLIEST
UNEARTHLINESS
UNEARTHLINESSES
UNEASINESS
UNEASINESSES
UNEATABLENESS
UNEATABLENESSES
UNECCENTRIC
UNECLIPSED
UNECOLOGICAL
UNECONOMIC
UNECONOMICAL
UNEDIFYING
UNEDUCABLE
UNEDUCATED
UNEFFECTED
UNELABORATE
UNELABORATED
UNELECTABLE
UNELECTRIFIED
UNEMBARRASSED
UNEMBELLISHED
UNEMBITTERED
UNEMBODIED
UNEMOTIONAL
UNEMOTIONALLY
UNEMOTIONED
UNEMPHATIC
UNEMPHATICALLY
UNEMPIRICAL
UNEMPLOYABILITY
UNEMPLOYABLE
UNEMPLOYABLES
UNEMPLOYED
UNEMPLOYEDS
UNEMPLOYMENT
UNEMPLOYMENTS
UNENCHANTED
UNENCLOSED
UNENCOURAGING
UNENCUMBERED
UNENDANGERED
UNENDEARED
UNENDEARING
UNENDINGLY
UNENDINGNESS
UNENDINGNESSES
UNENDURABLE
UNENDURABLENESS
UNENDURABLY
UNENFORCEABLE
UNENFORCED

UNENJOYABLE
UNENLARGED
UNENLIGHTENED
UNENLIGHTENING
UNENQUIRING
UNENRICHED
UNENSLAVED
UNENTAILED
UNENTERPRISING
UNENTERTAINED
UNENTERTAINING
UNENTHRALLED
UNENTHUSIASTIC
UNENTITLED
UNENVIABLE
UNENVIABLY
UNEQUALLED
UNEQUIPPED
UNEQUITABLE
UNEQUIVOCABLY
UNEQUIVOCAL
UNEQUIVOCALLY
UNEQUIVOCALNESS
UNERASABLE
UNERRINGLY
UNERRINGNESS
UNERRINGNESSES
UNESCAPABLE
UNESCORTED
UNESSENCED
UNESSENCES
UNESSENCING
UNESSENTIAL
UNESSENTIALLY
UNESSENTIALS
UNESTABLISHED
UNEVALUATED
UNEVANGELICAL
UNEVENNESS
UNEVENNESSES
UNEVENTFUL
UNEVENTFULLY
UNEVENTFULNESS
UNEVIDENCED
UNEXACTING
UNEXAGGERATED
UNEXAMINED
UNEXAMPLED
UNEXCAVATED
UNEXCELLED
UNEXCEPTIONABLE
UNEXCEPTIONABLY
UNEXCEPTIONAL
UNEXCEPTIONALLY
UNEXCITABLE
UNEXCITING
UNEXCLUDED
UNEXCLUSIVE
UNEXCLUSIVELY
UNEXECUTED

UNEXEMPLIFIED
UNEXERCISED
UNEXHAUSTED
UNEXPANDED
UNEXPECTANT
UNEXPECTED
UNEXPECTEDLY
UNEXPECTEDNESS
UNEXPENDED
UNEXPENSIVE
UNEXPENSIVELY
UNEXPERIENCED
UNEXPERIENT
UNEXPIATED
UNEXPLAINABLE
UNEXPLAINED
UNEXPLODED
UNEXPLOITED
UNEXPLORED
UNEXPRESSED
UNEXPRESSIBLE
UNEXPRESSIVE
UNEXPUGNABLE
UNEXPURGATED
UNEXTENDED
UNEXTENUATED
UNEXTINGUISHED
UNEXTRAORDINARY
UNFADINGLY
UNFADINGNESS
UNFADINGNESSES
UNFAILINGLY
UNFAILINGNESS
UNFAILINGNESSES
UNFAIRNESS
UNFAIRNESSES
UNFAITHFUL
UNFAITHFULLY
UNFAITHFULNESS
UNFALLIBLE
UNFALSIFIABLE
UNFALTERING
UNFALTERINGLY
UNFAMILIAR
UNFAMILIARITIES
UNFAMILIARITY
UNFAMILIARLY
UNFASHIONABLE
UNFASHIONABLY
UNFASHIONED
UNFASTENED
UNFASTENING
UNFASTIDIOUS
UNFATHERED
UNFATHERLY
UNFATHOMABLE
UNFATHOMABLY
UNFATHOMED
UNFAVORABLE
UNFAVORABLENESS

UNFAVORABLY
UNFAVORITE
UNFAVOURABLE
UNFAVOURABLY
UNFAVOURED
UNFEARFULLY
UNFEASIBLE
UNFEATHERED
UNFEATURED
UNFEELINGLY
UNFEELINGNESS
UNFEELINGNESSES
UNFEIGNEDLY
UNFEIGNEDNESS
UNFEIGNEDNESSES
UNFEIGNING
UNFELLOWED
UNFEMININE
UNFERMENTED
UNFERTILISED
UNFERTILIZED
UNFETTERED
UNFETTERING
UNFEUDALISE
UNFEUDALISED
UNFEUDALISES
UNFEUDALISING
UNFEUDALIZE
UNFEUDALIZED
UNFEUDALIZES
UNFEUDALIZING
UNFILIALLY
UNFILLABLE
UNFILLETED
UNFILTERABLE
UNFILTERED
UNFILTRABLE
UNFINDABLE
UNFINISHED
UNFINISHING
UNFINISHINGS
UNFITNESSES
UNFITTEDNESS
UNFITTEDNESSES
UNFITTINGLY
UNFIXEDNESS
UNFIXEDNESSES
UNFIXITIES
UNFLAGGING
UNFLAGGINGLY
UNFLAMBOYANT
UNFLAPPABILITY
UNFLAPPABLE
UNFLAPPABLENESS
UNFLAPPABLY
UNFLATTERING
UNFLATTERINGLY
UNFLAVOURED
UNFLESHING
UNFLINCHING

UNFLINCHINGLY	UNFREQUENTED	UNGODLIEST	UNHARMFULLY
UNFLUSHING	UNFREQUENTLY	UNGODLINESS	UNHARMONIOUS
UNFLUSTERED	UNFRIENDED	UNGODLINESSES	UNHARNESSED
UNFOCUSSED	UNFRIENDEDNESS	UNGOVERNABLE	UNHARNESSES
UNFOLDINGS	UNFRIENDLIER	UNGOVERNABLY	UNHARNESSING
UNFOLDMENT	UNFRIENDLIEST	UNGOVERNED	UNHARVESTED
UNFOLDMENTS	UNFRIENDLILY	UNGRACEFUL	UNHATTINGS
UNFORBIDDEN	UNFRIENDLINESS	UNGRACEFULLY	UNHAZARDED
UNFORCEDLY	UNFRIENDLY	UNGRACEFULNESS	UNHAZARDOUS
UNFORCIBLE	UNFRIENDSHIP	UNGRACIOUS	UNHEALABLE
UNFORDABLE	UNFRIENDSHIPS	UNGRACIOUSLY	UNHEALTHFUL
UNFOREBODING	UNFRIGHTED	UNGRACIOUSNESS	UNHEALTHFULLY
UNFOREKNOWABLE	UNFRIGHTENED	UNGRAMMATIC	UNHEALTHFULNESS
UNFOREKNOWN	UNFRIVOLOUS	UNGRAMMATICAL	UNHEALTHIER
UNFORESEEABLE	UNFROCKING	UNGRAMMATICALLY	UNHEALTHIEST
UNFORESEEING	UNFRUCTUOUS	UNGRASPABLE	UNHEALTHILY
UNFORESEEN	UNFRUITFUL	UNGRATEFUL	UNHEALTHINESS
UNFORESKINNED	UNFRUITFULLY	UNGRATEFULLY	UNHEALTHINESSES
UNFORESTED	UNFRUITFULNESS	UNGRATEFULNESS	UNHEARSING
UNFORETOLD	UNFULFILLABLE	UNGRATIFIED	UNHEARTING
UNFOREWARNED	UNFULFILLED	UNGROUNDED	UNHEEDEDLY
UNFORFEITED	UNFURNISHED	UNGROUNDEDLY	UNHEEDFULLY
UNFORGETTABLE	UNFURNISHES	UNGROUNDEDNESS	UNHEEDINGLY
UNFORGETTABLY	UNFURNISHING	UNGRUDGING	UNHELMETED
UNFORGIVABLE	UNFURROWED	UNGRUDGINGLY	UNHELPABLE
UNFORGIVEN	UNFUSSIEST	UNGUARDEDLY	UNHELPFULLY
UNFORGIVENESS	UNGAINLIER	UNGUARDEDNESS	UNHERALDED
UNFORGIVENESSES	UNGAINLIEST	UNGUARDEDNESSES	UNHEROICAL
UNFORGIVING	UNGAINLINESS	UNGUARDING	UNHEROICALLY
UNFORGIVINGNESS	UNGAINLINESSES	UNGUENTARIA	UNHESITATING
UNFORGOTTEN	UNGAINSAID	UNGUENTARIES	UNHESITATINGLY
UNFORMALISED	UNGAINSAYABLE	UNGUENTARIUM	UNHIDEBOUND
UNFORMALIZED	UNGALLANTLY	UNGUENTARY	UNHINDERED
UNFORMATTED	UNGARMENTED	UNGUERDONED	UNHINGEMENT
UNFORMIDABLE	UNGARNERED	UNGUESSABLE	UNHINGEMENTS
UNFORMULATED	UNGARNISHED	UNGUICULATE	UNHISTORIC
UNFORSAKEN	UNGARTERED	UNGUICULATED	UNHISTORICAL
UNFORTHCOMING	UNGATHERED	UNGUICULATES	UNHITCHING
UNFORTIFIED	UNGENEROSITIES	UNGULIGRADE	UNHOARDING
UNFORTUNATE	UNGENEROSITY	UNHABITABLE	UNHOLINESS
UNFORTUNATELY	UNGENEROUS	UNHABITUATED	UNHOLINESSES
UNFORTUNATENESS	UNGENEROUSLY	UNHACKNEYED	UNHOMELIKE
UNFORTUNATES	UNGENITURED	UNHALLOWED	UNHOMOGENISED
UNFORTUNED	UNGENTEELLY	UNHALLOWING	UNHOMOGENIZED
UNFORTUNES	UNGENTILITIES	UNHAMPERED	UNHONOURED
UNFOSSILIFEROUS	UNGENTILITY	UNHANDIEST	UNHOPEFULLY
UNFOSSILISED	UNGENTLEMANLIKE	UNHANDINESS	UNHOSPITABLE
UNFOSSILIZED	UNGENTLEMANLY	UNHANDINESSES	UNHOUSELED
UNFOSTERED	UNGENTLENESS	UNHANDSELED	UNHOUZZLED
UNFOUGHTEN	UNGENTLENESSES	UNHANDSOME	UNHUMANISE
UNFOUNDEDLY	UNGENTRIFIED	UNHANDSOMELY	UNHUMANISED
UNFOUNDEDNESS	UNGENUINENESS	UNHANDSOMENESS	UNHUMANISES
UNFOUNDEDNESSES	UNGENUINENESSES	UNHAPPIEST	UNHUMANISING
UNFRANCHISED	UNGERMINATED	UNHAPPINESS	UNHUMANIZE
UNFRAUGHTED	UNGETATABLE	UNHAPPINESSES	UNHUMANIZED
UNFRAUGHTING	UNGIMMICKY	UNHAPPYING	UNHUMANIZES
UNFRAUGHTS	UNGIRTHING	UNHARBOURED	UNHUMANIZING
UNFREEDOMS	UNGLAMORISED	UNHARBOURING	UNHUMOROUS
UNFREEZING	UNGLAMORIZED	UNHARBOURS	UNHURRIEDLY
UNFREQUENT	UNGLAMOROUS	UNHARDENED	UNHURRYING

UNHURTFULLY	UNILATERALITY	UNINFORMATIVELY	UNIONISATION
UNHURTFULNESS	UNILATERALLY	UNINFORMED	UNIONISATIONS
UNHURTFULNESSES	UNILINGUAL	UNINFORMING	UNIONISERS
UNHUSBANDED	UNILINGUALISM	UNINGRATIATING	UNIONISING
UNHYDROLYSED	UNILINGUALISMS	UNINHABITABLE	UNIONISTIC
UNHYDROLYZED	UNILINGUALS	UNINHABITED	UNIONIZATION
UNHYGIENIC	UNILITERAL	UNINHIBITED	UNIONIZATIONS
UNHYPHENATED	UNILLUMINATED	UNINHIBITEDLY	UNIONIZERS
UNHYSTERICAL	UNILLUMINATING	UNINHIBITEDNESS	UNIONIZING
UNHYSTERICALLY	UNILLUMINED	UNINITIATE	UNIPARENTAL
UNIAXIALLY	UNILLUSIONED	UNINITIATED	UNIPARENTALLY
UNICAMERAL	UNILLUSTRATED	UNINITIATES	UNIPARTITE
UNICAMERALISM	UNILOBULAR	UNINOCULATED	UNIPERSONAL
UNICAMERALISMS	UNILOCULAR	UNINQUIRING	UNIPERSONALITY
UNICAMERALIST	UNIMAGINABLE	UNINQUISITIVE	UNIPOLARITIES
UNICAMERALISTS	UNIMAGINABLY	UNINSCRIBED	UNIPOLARITY
UNICAMERALLY	UNIMAGINATIVE	UNINSPECTED	UNIQUENESS
UNICELLULAR	UNIMAGINATIVELY	UNINSPIRED	UNIQUENESSES
UNICELLULARITY	UNIMAGINED	UNINSPIRING	UNIRONICALLY
UNICENTRAL	UNIMMORTAL	UNINSTALLED	UNIRRADIATED
UNICOLORATE	UNIMMUNISED	UNINSTALLING	UNIRRIGATED
UNICOLOROUS	UNIMMUNIZED	UNINSTALLS	UNISEPTATE
UNICOLOURED	UNIMOLECULAR	UNINSTRUCTED	UNISERIALLY
UNICOSTATE	UNIMPAIRED	UNINSTRUCTIVE	UNISERIATE
UNICYCLING	UNIMPARTED	UNINSULATED	UNISERIATELY
UNICYCLIST	UNIMPASSIONED	UNINSURABLE	UNISEXUALITIES
UNICYCLISTS	UNIMPEACHABLE	UNINSUREDS	UNISEXUALITY
UNIDEALISM	UNIMPEACHABLY	UNINTEGRATED	UNISEXUALLY
UNIDEALISMS	UNIMPEACHED	UNINTELLECTUAL	UNISONALLY
UNIDEALISTIC	UNIMPEDEDLY	UNINTELLIGENCE	UNISONANCE
UNIDENTIFIABLE	UNIMPLORED	UNINTELLIGENCES	UNISONANCES
UNIDENTIFIED	UNIMPORTANCE	UNINTELLIGENT	UNITARIANISM
UNIDEOLOGICAL	UNIMPORTANCES	UNINTELLIGENTLY	UNITARIANISMS
UNIDIMENSIONAL	UNIMPORTANT	UNINTELLIGIBLE	UNITARIANS
UNIDIOMATIC	UNIMPORTUNED	UNINTELLIGIBLY	UNITEDNESS
UNIDIOMATICALLY	UNIMPOSING	UNINTENDED	UNITEDNESSES
UNIDIRECTIONAL	UNIMPREGNATED	UNINTENTIONAL	UNITHOLDER
UNIFICATION	UNIMPRESSED	UNINTENTIONALLY	UNITHOLDERS
UNIFICATIONS	UNIMPRESSIBLE	UNINTEREST	UNITISATION
UNIFLOROUS	UNIMPRESSIVE	UNINTERESTED	UNITISATIONS
UNIFOLIATE	UNIMPRISONED	UNINTERESTEDLY	UNITIZATION
UNIFOLIOLATE	UNIMPROVED	UNINTERESTING	UNITIZATIONS
UNIFORMEST	UNIMPUGNABLE	UNINTERESTINGLY	UNIVALENCE
UNIFORMING	UNINAUGURATED	UNINTERESTS	UNIVALENCES
UNIFORMITARIAN	UNINCHANTED	UNINTERMITTED	UNIVALENCIES
UNIFORMITARIANS	UNINCLOSED	UNINTERMITTEDLY	UNIVALENCY
UNIFORMITIES	UNINCORPORATED	UNINTERMITTING	UNIVALENTS
UNIFORMITY	UNINCUMBERED	UNINTERPRETABLE	UNIVALVULAR
UNIFORMNESS	UNINDEARED	UNINTERRUPTED	UNIVARIANT
UNIFORMNESSES	UNINDICTED	UNINTERRUPTEDLY	UNIVARIATE
UNIGENITURE	UNINFECTED	UNINTIMIDATED	UNIVERSALISED
UNIGENITURES	UNINFLAMED	UNINTOXICATING	UNIVERSALISED
UNIGNORABLE	UNINFLAMMABLE	UNINTRODUCED	UNIVERSALISES
UNILABIATE	UNINFLATED	UNINUCLEAR	UNIVERSALISING
UNILATERAL	UNINFLECTED	UNINUCLEATE	UNIVERSALISM
UNILATERALISM	UNINFLUENCED	UNINVENTIVE	UNIVERSALISMS
UNILATERALISMS	UNINFLUENTIAL	UNINVESTED	UNIVERSALIST
UNILATERALIST	UNINFORCEABLE	UNINVIDIOUS	UNIVERSALISTIC
UNILATERALISTS	UNINFORCED	UNINVITING	UNIVERSALISTS
UNILATERALITIES	UNINFORMATIVE	UNINVOLVED	UNIVERSALITIES

UNIVERSALITY
UNIVERSALIZE
UNIVERSALIZED
UNIVERSALIZES
UNIVERSALIZING
UNIVERSALLY
UNIVERSALNESS
UNIVERSALNESSES
UNIVERSALS
UNIVERSITARIAN
UNIVERSITIES
UNIVERSITY
UNIVOCALLY
UNIVOLTINE
UNJAUNDICED
UNJOINTING
UNJUSTIFIABLE
UNJUSTIFIABLY
UNJUSTIFIED
UNJUSTNESS
UNJUSTNESSES
UNKEMPTNESS
UNKEMPTNESSES
UNKENNELED
UNKENNELING
UNKENNELLED
UNKENNELLING
UNKINDLIER
UNKINDLIEST
UNKINDLINESS
UNKINDLINESSES
UNKINDNESS
UNKINDNESSES
UNKINGLIER
UNKINGLIEST
UNKINGLIKE
UNKNIGHTED
UNKNIGHTING
UNKNIGHTLINESS
UNKNIGHTLY
UNKNITTING
UNKNOTTING
UNKNOWABILITIES
UNKNOWABILITY
UNKNOWABLE
UNKNOWABLENESS
UNKNOWABLES
UNKNOWABLY
UNKNOWINGLY
UNKNOWINGNESS
UNKNOWINGNESSES
UNKNOWINGS
UNKNOWLEDGEABLE
UNKNOWNNESS
UNKNOWNNESSES
UNLABELLED
UNLABORIOUS
UNLABOURED
UNLABOURING
UNLADYLIKE

UNLAMENTED
UNLATCHING
UNLAUNDERED
UNLAWFULLY
UNLAWFULNESS
UNLAWFULNESSES
UNLEARNABLE
UNLEARNEDLY
UNLEARNEDNESS
UNLEARNEDNESSES
UNLEARNING
UNLEASHING
UNLEAVENED
UNLEISURED
UNLEISURELY
UNLESSONED
UNLETTABLE
UNLETTERED
UNLEVELING
UNLEVELLED
UNLEVELLING
UNLIBERATED
UNLIBIDINOUS
UNLICENSED
UNLIFELIKE
UNLIGHTENED
UNLIGHTSOME
UNLIKEABLE
UNLIKELIER
UNLIKELIEST
UNLIKELIHOOD
UNLIKELIHOODS
UNLIKELINESS
UNLIKELINESSES
UNLIKENESS
UNLIKENESSES
UNLIMBERED
UNLIMBERING
UNLIMITEDLY
UNLIMITEDNESS
UNLIMITEDNESSES
UNLIQUEFIED
UNLIQUIDATED
UNLIQUORED
UNLISTENABLE
UNLISTENED
UNLISTENING
UNLITERARY
UNLIVEABLE
UNLIVELINESS
UNLIVELINESSES
UNLOADINGS
UNLOCALISED
UNLOCALIZED
UNLOCKABLE
UNLOOSENED
UNLOOSENING
UNLOVEABLE
UNLOVELIER
UNLOVELIEST

UNLOVELINESS
UNLOVELINESSES
UNLOVERLIKE
UNLOVINGLY
UNLOVINGNESS
UNLOVINGNESSES
UNLUCKIEST
UNLUCKINESS
UNLUCKINESSES
UNLUXURIANT
UNLUXURIOUS
UNMACADAMISED
UNMACADAMIZED
UNMAGNIFIED
UNMAIDENLY
UNMAILABLE
UNMAINTAINABLE
UNMAINTAINED
UNMALICIOUS
UNMALICIOUSLY
UNMALLEABILITY
UNMALLEABLE
UNMANACLED
UNMANACLES
UNMANACLING
UNMANAGEABLE
UNMANAGEABLY
UNMANFULLY
UNMANIPULATED
UNMANLIEST
UNMANLINESS
UNMANLINESSES
UNMANNERED
UNMANNEREDLY
UNMANNERLINESS
UNMANNERLY
UNMANTLING
UNMANUFACTURED
UNMARKETABLE
UNMARRIABLE
UNMARRIAGEABLE
UNMARRIEDS
UNMARRYING
UNMASCULINE
UNMASKINGS
UNMASTERED
UNMATCHABLE
UNMATERIAL
UNMATERIALISED
UNMATERIALIZED
UNMATERNAL
UNMATHEMATICAL
UNMATRICULATED
UNMEANINGLY
UNMEANINGNESS
UNMEANINGNESSES
UNMEASURABLE
UNMEASURABLY
UNMEASURED
UNMEASUREDLY

UNMECHANIC
UNMECHANICAL
UNMECHANISE
UNMECHANISED
UNMECHANISES
UNMECHANISING
UNMECHANIZE
UNMECHANIZED
UNMECHANIZES
UNMECHANIZING
UNMEDIATED
UNMEDICATED
UNMEDICINABLE
UNMEDITATED
UNMEETNESS
UNMEETNESSES
UNMELLOWED
UNMELODIOUS
UNMELODIOUSNESS
UNMEMORABLE
UNMEMORABLY
UNMENTIONABLE
UNMENTIONABLES
UNMENTIONABLY
UNMENTIONED
UNMERCENARY
UNMERCHANTABLE
UNMERCIFUL
UNMERCIFULLY
UNMERCIFULNESS
UNMERITABLE
UNMERITEDLY
UNMERITING
UNMETABOLISED
UNMETABOLIZED
UNMETALLED
UNMETAPHORICAL
UNMETAPHYSICAL
UNMETHODICAL
UNMETHODISED
UNMETHODIZED
UNMETRICAL
UNMILITARY
UNMINDFULLY
UNMINDFULNESS
UNMINDFULNESSES
UNMINGLING
UNMINISTERIAL
UNMIRACULOUS
UNMISSABLE
UNMISTAKABLE
UNMISTAKABLY
UNMISTAKEABLE
UNMISTAKEABLY
UNMISTRUSTFUL
UNMITERING
UNMITIGABLE
UNMITIGABLY
UNMITIGATED
UNMITIGATEDLY

UNMITIGATEDNESS
UNMODERATED
UNMODERNISED
UNMODERNIZED
UNMODIFIABLE
UNMODIFIED
UNMODULATED
UNMOISTENED
UNMOLESTED
UNMONITORED
UNMORALISED
UNMORALISING
UNMORALITIES
UNMORALITY
UNMORALIZED
UNMORALIZING
UNMORTGAGED
UNMORTIFIED
UNMORTISED
UNMORTISES
UNMORTISING
UNMOTHERLY
UNMOTIVATED
UNMOULDING
UNMOUNTING
UNMOVEABLE
UNMOVEABLY
UNMUFFLING
UNMUNITIONED
UNMURMURING
UNMURMURINGLY
UNMUSICALLY
UNMUSICALNESS
UNMUSICALNESSES
UNMUTILATED
UNMUZZLING
UNMUZZLINGS
UNMYELINATED
UNNAMEABLE
UNNATURALISE
UNNATURALISED
UNNATURALISES
UNNATURALISING
UNNATURALIZE
UNNATURALIZED
UNNATURALIZES
UNNATURALIZING
UNNATURALLY
UNNATURALNESS
UNNATURALNESSES
UNNAVIGABLE
UNNAVIGATED
UNNECESSARILY
UNNECESSARINESS
UNNECESSARY
UNNEEDFULLY
UNNEGOTIABLE
UNNEIGHBOURED
UNNEIGHBOURLY
UNNERVINGLY

UNNEUROTIC
UNNEWSWORTHY
UNNILHEXIUM
UNNILHEXIUMS
UNNILPENTIUM
UNNILPENTIUMS
UNNILQUADIUM
UNNILQUADIUMS
UNNILSEPTIUM
UNNILSEPTIUMS
UNNOTICEABLE
UNNOTICEABLY
UNNOTICING
UNNOURISHED
UNNOURISHING
UNNUMBERED
UNNURTURED
UNOBEDIENT
UNOBJECTIONABLE
UNOBJECTIONABLY
UNOBNOXIOUS
UNOBSCURED
UNOBSERVABLE
UNOBSERVANCE
UNOBSERVANCES
UNOBSERVANT
UNOBSERVED
UNOBSERVEDLY
UNOBSERVING
UNOBSTRUCTED
UNOBSTRUCTIVE
UNOBTAINABLE
UNOBTAINED
UNOBTRUSIVE
UNOBTRUSIVELY
UNOBTRUSIVENESS
UNOCCUPIED
UNOFFENDED
UNOFFENDING
UNOFFENSIVE
UNOFFICERED
UNOFFICIAL
UNOFFICIALLY
UNOFFICIOUS
UNOPENABLE
UNOPERATIVE
UNOPPRESSIVE
UNORDAINED
UNORDERING
UNORDINARY
UNORGANISED
UNORGANIZED
UNORIGINAL
UNORIGINALITIES
UNORIGINALITY
UNORIGINATE
UNORIGINATED
UNORNAMENTAL
UNORNAMENTED
UNORTHODOX

UNORTHODOXIES
UNORTHODOXLY
UNORTHODOXY
UNOSSIFIED
UNOSTENTATIOUS
UNOVERCOME
UNOVERTHROWN
UNOXIDISED
UNOXIDIZED
UNOXYGENATED
UNPACIFIED
UNPACKINGS
UNPAINTABLE
UNPAINTING
UNPALATABILITY
UNPALATABLE
UNPALATABLY
UNPAMPERED
UNPANELLED
UNPANELLING
UNPANNELLED
UNPANNELLING
UNPAPERING
UNPARADISE
UNPARADISED
UNPARADISES
UNPARADISING
UNPARAGONED
UNPARALLEL
UNPARALLELED
UNPARASITISED
UNPARASITIZED
UNPARDONABLE
UNPARDONABLY
UNPARDONED
UNPARDONING
UNPARENTAL
UNPARENTED
UNPARLIAMENTARY
UNPASSABLE
UNPASSABLENESS
UNPASSIONATE
UNPASSIONED
UNPASTEURISED
UNPASTEURIZED
UNPASTORAL
UNPASTURED
UNPATENTABLE
UNPATENTED
UNPATHETIC
UNPATHWAYED
UNPATRIOTIC
UNPATRIOTICALLY
UNPATRONISED
UNPATRONIZED
UNPATTERNED
UNPAVILIONED
UNPEACEABLE
UNPEACEABLENESS
UNPEACEFUL

UNPEACEFULLY
UNPEDANTIC
UNPEDIGREED
UNPEERABLE
UNPENSIONED
UNPEOPLING
UNPEPPERED
UNPERCEIVABLE
UNPERCEIVABLY
UNPERCEIVED
UNPERCEIVEDLY
UNPERCEPTIVE
UNPERCHING
UNPERFECTION
UNPERFECTIONS
UNPERFECTLY
UNPERFECTNESS
UNPERFECTNESSES
UNPERFORATED
UNPERFORMABLE
UNPERFORMED
UNPERFORMING
UNPERFUMED
UNPERILOUS
UNPERISHABLE
UNPERISHED
UNPERISHING
UNPERJURED
UNPERPETRATED
UNPERPLEXED
UNPERPLEXES
UNPERPLEXING
UNPERSECUTED
UNPERSONED
UNPERSONING
UNPERSUADABLE
UNPERSUADED
UNPERSUASIVE
UNPERTURBED
UNPERVERTED
UNPERVERTING
UNPERVERTS
UNPHILOSOPHIC
UNPHILOSOPHICAL
UNPHONETIC
UNPICKABLE
UNPICTURESQUE
UNPILLARED
UNPILLOWED
UNPITIFULLY
UNPITIFULNESS
UNPITIFULNESSES
UNPITYINGLY
UNPLAITING
UNPLASTERED
UNPLAUSIBLE
UNPLAUSIBLY
UNPLAUSIVE
UNPLAYABLE
UNPLEASANT

UNPLEASANTLY
UNPLEASANTNESS
UNPLEASANTRIES
UNPLEASANTRY
UNPLEASING
UNPLEASINGLY
UNPLEASURABLE
UNPLEASURABLY
UNPLOUGHED
UNPLUGGING
UNPLUMBING
UNPOETICAL
UNPOETICALLY
UNPOETICALNESS
UNPOISONED
UNPOISONING
UNPOLARISABLE
UNPOLARISED
UNPOLARIZABLE
UNPOLARIZED
UNPOLICIED
UNPOLISHABLE
UNPOLISHED
UNPOLISHES
UNPOLISHING
UNPOLITELY
UNPOLITENESS
UNPOLITENESSES
UNPOLITICAL
UNPOLLUTED
UNPOPULARITIES
UNPOPULARITY
UNPOPULARLY
UNPOPULATED
UNPOPULOUS
UNPORTIONED
UNPOSSESSED
UNPOSSESSING
UNPOSSIBLE
UNPOWDERED
UNPRACTICABLE
UNPRACTICAL
UNPRACTICALITY
UNPRACTICALLY
UNPRACTICALNESS
UNPRACTICED
UNPRACTISED
UNPRACTISEDNESS
UNPRAISEWORTHY
UNPRAISING
UNPREACHED
UNPREACHES
UNPREACHING
UNPRECEDENTED
UNPRECEDENTEDLY
UNPREDICTABLE
UNPREDICTABLES
UNPREDICTABLY
UNPREDICTED
UNPREDICTING

UNPREDICTS
UNPREFERRED
UNPREGNANT
UNPREJUDICED
UNPREJUDICEDLY
UNPRELATICAL
UNPREMEDITABLE
UNPREMEDITATED
UNPREMEDITATION
UNPREOCCUPIED
UNPREPARED
UNPREPAREDLY
UNPREPAREDNESS
UNPREPARES
UNPREPARING
UNPREPOSSESSED
UNPREPOSSESSING
UNPRESCRIBED
UNPRESENTABLE
UNPRESSURED
UNPRESSURISED
UNPRESSURIZED
UNPRESUMING
UNPRESUMPTUOUS
UNPRETENDING
UNPRETENDINGLY
UNPRETENTIOUS
UNPRETENTIOUSLY
UNPRETTINESS
UNPRETTINESSES
UNPREVAILING
UNPREVENTABLE
UNPREVENTED
UNPRIESTED
UNPRIESTING
UNPRIESTLY
UNPRINCELY
UNPRINCIPLED
UNPRINTABLE
UNPRINTABLENESS
UNPRINTABLY
UNPRISABLE
UNPRISONED
UNPRISONING
UNPRIVILEGED
UNPRIZABLE
UNPROBLEMATIC
UNPROCEDURAL
UNPROCESSED
UNPROCLAIMED
UNPROCURABLE
UNPRODUCED
UNPRODUCTIVE
UNPRODUCTIVELY
UNPRODUCTIVITY
UNPROFANED
UNPROFESSED
UNPROFESSIONAL
UNPROFESSIONALS
UNPROFITABILITY

UNPROFITABLE
UNPROFITABLY
UNPROFITED
UNPROFITING
UNPROGRAMMABLE
UNPROGRAMMED
UNPROGRESSIVE
UNPROGRESSIVELY
UNPROHIBITED
UNPROJECTED
UNPROLIFIC
UNPROMISED
UNPROMISING
UNPROMISINGLY
UNPROMPTED
UNPRONOUNCEABLE
UNPRONOUNCED
UNPROPERLY
UNPROPERTIED
UNPROPHETIC
UNPROPHETICAL
UNPROPITIOUS
UNPROPITIOUSLY
UNPROPORTIONATE
UNPROPORTIONED
UNPROPOSED
UNPROPPING
UNPROSPEROUS
UNPROSPEROUSLY
UNPROTECTED
UNPROTECTEDNESS
UNPROTESTANTISE
UNPROTESTANTIZE
UNPROTESTED
UNPROTESTING
UNPROVABLE
UNPROVIDED
UNPROVIDEDLY
UNPROVIDENT
UNPROVIDES
UNPROVIDING
UNPROVISIONED
UNPROVOCATIVE
UNPROVOKED
UNPROVOKEDLY
UNPROVOKES
UNPROVOKING
UNPUBLICISED
UNPUBLICIZED
UNPUBLISHABLE
UNPUBLISHED
UNPUCKERED
UNPUCKERING
UNPUNCTUAL
UNPUNCTUALITIES
UNPUNCTUALITY
UNPUNCTUATED
UNPUNISHABLE
UNPUNISHABLY
UNPUNISHED

UNPURCHASABLE
UNPURCHASEABLE
UNPURCHASED
UNPURIFIED
UNPURPOSED
UNPURVAIDE
UNPURVEYED
UNPUTDOWNABLE
UNPUZZLING
UNQUALIFIABLE
UNQUALIFIED
UNQUALIFIEDLY
UNQUALIFIEDNESS
UNQUALIFIES
UNQUALIFYING
UNQUALITED
UNQUALITIED
UNQUANTIFIABLE
UNQUANTIFIED
UNQUANTISED
UNQUANTIZED
UNQUARRIED
UNQUEENING
UNQUEENLIER
UNQUEENLIEST
UNQUEENLIKE
UNQUENCHABLE
UNQUENCHABLY
UNQUENCHED
UNQUESTIONABLE
UNQUESTIONABLY
UNQUESTIONED
UNQUESTIONING
UNQUESTIONINGLY
UNQUICKENED
UNQUIETEST
UNQUIETING
UNQUIETNESS
UNQUIETNESSES
UNQUOTABLE
UNRANSOMED
UNRATIFIED
UNRAVELING
UNRAVELLED
UNRAVELLER
UNRAVELLERS
UNRAVELLING
UNRAVELLINGS
UNRAVELMENT
UNRAVELMENTS
UNRAVISHED
UNREACHABLE
UNREACTIVE
UNREADABILITIES
UNREADABILITY
UNREADABLE
UNREADABLENESS
UNREADABLY
UNREADIEST
UNREADINESS

UNREADINESSES
UNREALISABLE
UNREALISED
UNREALISES
UNREALISING
UNREALISMS
UNREALISTIC
UNREALISTICALLY
UNREALITIES
UNREALIZABLE
UNREALIZED
UNREALIZES
UNREALIZING
UNREASONABLE
UNREASONABLY
UNREASONED
UNREASONING
UNREASONINGLY
UNRECALLABLE
UNRECALLED
UNRECALLING
UNRECAPTURABLE
UNRECEIPTED
UNRECEIVED
UNRECEPTIVE
UNRECIPROCATED
UNRECKONABLE
UNRECKONED
UNRECLAIMABLE
UNRECLAIMABLY
UNRECLAIMED
UNRECOGNISABLE
UNRECOGNISABLY
UNRECOGNISED
UNRECOGNISING
UNRECOGNIZABLE
UNRECOGNIZABLY
UNRECOGNIZED
UNRECOGNIZING
UNRECOLLECTED
UNRECOMMENDABLE
UNRECOMMENDED
UNRECOMPENSED
UNRECONCILABLE
UNRECONCILABLY
UNRECONCILED
UNRECONCILIABLE
UNRECONSTRUCTED
UNRECORDED
UNRECOUNTED
UNRECOVERABLE
UNRECOVERABLY
UNRECOVERED
UNRECTIFIED
UNRECURING
UNRECYCLABLE
UNREDEEMABLE
UNREDEEMED
UNREDRESSED
UNREDUCIBLE

UNREFLECTED
UNREFLECTING
UNREFLECTINGLY
UNREFLECTIVE
UNREFLECTIVELY
UNREFORMABLE
UNREFORMED
UNREFRACTED
UNREFRESHED
UNREFRESHING
UNREFRIGERATED
UNREGARDED
UNREGARDING
UNREGENERACIES
UNREGENERACY
UNREGENERATE
UNREGENERATED
UNREGENERATELY
UNREGENERATES
UNREGIMENTED
UNREGISTERED
UNREGULATED
UNREHEARSED
UNREINFORCED
UNREJOICED
UNREJOICING
UNRELATIVE
UNRELENTING
UNRELENTINGLY
UNRELENTINGNESS
UNRELENTOR
UNRELENTORS
UNRELIABILITIES
UNRELIABILITY
UNRELIABLE
UNRELIABLENESS
UNRELIEVABLE
UNRELIEVED
UNRELIEVEDLY
UNRELIGIOUS
UNRELIGIOUSLY
UNRELISHED
UNRELUCTANT
UNREMAINING
UNREMARKABLE
UNREMARKABLY
UNREMARKED
UNREMEDIED
UNREMEMBERED
UNREMEMBERING
UNREMINISCENT
UNREMITTED
UNREMITTEDLY
UNREMITTENT
UNREMITTENTLY
UNREMITTING
UNREMITTINGLY
UNREMITTINGNESS
UNREMORSEFUL
UNREMORSEFULLY

UNREMORSELESS
UNREMOVABLE
UNREMUNERATIVE
UNRENDERED
UNREPAIRABLE
UNREPAIRED
UNREPEALABLE
UNREPEALED
UNREPEATABLE
UNREPEATED
UNREPELLED
UNREPENTANCE
UNREPENTANCES
UNREPENTANT
UNREPENTANTLY
UNREPENTED
UNREPENTING
UNREPENTINGLY
UNREPINING
UNREPININGLY
UNREPLACEABLE
UNREPLENISHED
UNREPORTABLE
UNREPORTED
UNREPOSEFUL
UNREPOSING
UNREPRESENTED
UNREPRESSED
UNREPRIEVABLE
UNREPRIEVED
UNREPRIMANDED
UNREPROACHED
UNREPROACHFUL
UNREPROACHING
UNREPRODUCIBLE
UNREPROVABLE
UNREPROVED
UNREPROVING
UNREPUGNANT
UNREPULSABLE
UNREQUIRED
UNREQUISITE
UNREQUITED
UNREQUITEDLY
UNRESCINDED
UNRESENTED
UNRESENTFUL
UNRESENTING
UNRESERVED
UNRESERVEDLY
UNRESERVEDNESS
UNRESERVES
UNRESISTANT
UNRESISTED
UNRESISTIBLE
UNRESISTING
UNRESISTINGLY
UNRESOLVABLE
UNRESOLVED
UNRESOLVEDNESS

UNRESPECTABLE
UNRESPECTED
UNRESPECTIVE
UNRESPITED
UNRESPONSIVE
UNRESPONSIVELY
UNRESTFULNESS
UNRESTFULNESSES
UNRESTINGLY
UNRESTINGNESS
UNRESTINGNESSES
UNRESTORED
UNRESTRAINABLE
UNRESTRAINED
UNRESTRAINEDLY
UNRESTRAINT
UNRESTRAINTS
UNRESTRICTED
UNRESTRICTEDLY
UNRETARDED
UNRETENTIVE
UNRETIRING
UNRETOUCHED
UNRETURNABLE
UNRETURNED
UNRETURNING
UNRETURNINGLY
UNREVEALABLE
UNREVEALED
UNREVEALING
UNREVENGED
UNREVENGEFUL
UNREVEREND
UNREVERENT
UNREVERSED
UNREVERTED
UNREVIEWABLE
UNREVIEWED
UNREVOLUTIONARY
UNREWARDED
UNREWARDEDLY
UNREWARDING
UNRHETORICAL
UNRHYTHMIC
UNRHYTHMICAL
UNRHYTHMICALLY
UNRIDDLEABLE
UNRIDDLERS
UNRIDDLING
UNRIDEABLE
UNRIGHTEOUS
UNRIGHTEOUSLY
UNRIGHTEOUSNESS
UNRIGHTFUL
UNRIGHTFULLY
UNRIGHTFULNESS
UNRIPENESS
UNRIPENESSES
UNRIPPINGS
UNRIVALLED

UNRIVETING	UNSAVORINESSES	UNSEGREGATED	UNSHEATHING
UNROMANISED	UNSAVOURILY	UNSEISABLE	UNSHELLING
UNROMANIZED	UNSAVOURINESS	UNSEIZABLE	UNSHELTERED
UNROMANTIC	UNSAVOURINESSES	UNSELECTED	UNSHIELDED
UNROMANTICAL	UNSAYABLES	UNSELECTIVE	UNSHIFTING
UNROMANTICALLY	UNSCABBARD	UNSELECTIVELY	UNSHINGLED
UNROMANTICISED	UNSCABBARDED	UNSELFCONSCIOUS	UNSHIPPING
UNROMANTICIZED	UNSCABBARDING	UNSELFISHLY	UNSHOCKABLE
UNROOSTING	UNSCABBARDS	UNSELFISHNESS	UNSHOOTING
UNROUNDING	UNSCALABLE	UNSELFISHNESSES	UNSHOUTING
UNRUFFABLE	UNSCAVENGERED	UNSELLABLE	UNSHOWERED
UNRUFFLEDNESS	UNSCEPTRED	UNSEMINARIED	UNSHRINKABLE
UNRUFFLEDNESSES	UNSCHEDULED	UNSENSATIONAL	UNSHRINKING
UNRUFFLING	UNSCHOLARLIKE	UNSENSIBLE	UNSHRINKINGLY
UNRULIMENT	UNSCHOLARLY	UNSENSIBLY	UNSHROUDED
UNRULIMENTS	UNSCHOOLED	UNSENSITISED	UNSHROUDING
UNRULINESS	UNSCIENTIFIC	UNSENSITIVE	UNSHRUBBED
UNRULINESSES	UNSCISSORED	UNSENSITIZED	UNSHUNNABLE
UNSADDLING	UNSCORCHED	UNSENSUALISE	UNSHUTTERED
UNSAFENESS	UNSCOTTIFIED	UNSENSUALISED	UNSHUTTERING
UNSAFENESSES	UNSCRAMBLE	UNSENSUALISES	UNSHUTTERS
UNSAFETIES	UNSCRAMBLED	UNSENSUALISING	UNSHUTTING
UNSAILORLIKE	UNSCRAMBLER	UNSENSUALIZE	UNSIGHTEDLY
UNSAINTING	UNSCRAMBLERS	UNSENSUALIZED	UNSIGHTING
UNSAINTLIER	UNSCRAMBLES	UNSENSUALIZES	UNSIGHTLIER
UNSAINTLIEST	UNSCRAMBLING	UNSENSUALIZING	UNSIGHTLIEST
UNSAINTLINESS	UNSCRATCHED	UNSENTENCED	UNSIGHTLINESS
UNSAINTLINESSES	UNSCREENED	UNSENTIMENTAL	UNSIGHTLINESSES
UNSALABILITIES	UNSCREWING	UNSEPARABLE	UNSINEWING
UNSALABILITY	UNSCRIPTED	UNSEPARATED	UNSINKABLE
UNSALARIED	UNSCRIPTURAL	UNSEPULCHRED	UNSINNOWED
UNSALEABILITIES	UNSCRIPTURALLY	UNSERIOUSNESS	UNSISTERED
UNSALEABILITY	UNSCRUPLED	UNSERIOUSNESSES	UNSISTERLINESS
UNSALEABLE	UNSCRUPULOSITY	UNSERVICEABLE	UNSISTERLY
UNSALVAGEABLE	UNSCRUPULOUS	UNSETTLEDLY	UNSIZEABLE
UNSANCTIFIED	UNSCRUPULOUSLY	UNSETTLEDNESS	UNSKILFULLY
UNSANCTIFIES	UNSCRUTINISED	UNSETTLEDNESSES	UNSKILFULNESS
UNSANCTIFY	UNSCRUTINIZED	UNSETTLEMENT	UNSKILFULNESSES
UNSANCTIFYING	UNSCULPTURED	UNSETTLEMENTS	UNSKILLFUL
UNSANCTIONED	UNSEALABLE	UNSETTLING	UNSKILLFULLY
UNSANDALLED	UNSEARCHABLE	UNSETTLINGLY	UNSKILLFULNESS
UNSANITARY	UNSEARCHABLY	UNSETTLINGS	UNSLAKABLE
UNSATIABLE	UNSEARCHED	UNSHACKLED	UNSLEEPING
UNSATIATED	UNSEASONABLE	UNSHACKLES	UNSLINGING
UNSATIATING	UNSEASONABLY	UNSHACKLING	UNSLIPPING
UNSATIRICAL	UNSEASONED	UNSHADOWABLE	UNSLUICING
UNSATISFACTION	UNSEASONEDNESS	UNSHADOWED	UNSLUMBERING
UNSATISFACTIONS	UNSEASONING	UNSHADOWING	UNSLUMBROUS
UNSATISFACTORY	UNSEAWORTHINESS	UNSHAKABLE	UNSMILINGLY
UNSATISFIABLE	UNSEAWORTHY	UNSHAKABLENESS	UNSMIRCHED
UNSATISFIED	UNSECONDED	UNSHAKABLY	UNSMOOTHED
UNSATISFIEDNESS	UNSECTARIAN	UNSHAKEABLE	UNSMOOTHING
UNSATISFYING	UNSECTARIANISM	UNSHAKEABLENESS	UNSMOTHERABLE
UNSATURATE	UNSECTARIANISMS	UNSHAKEABLY	UNSNAGGING
UNSATURATED	UNSEEMINGS	UNSHAKENLY	UNSNAPPING
UNSATURATES	UNSEEMLIER	UNSHAPELIER	UNSNARLING
UNSATURATION	UNSEEMLIEST	UNSHAPELIEST	UNSNECKING
UNSATURATIONS	UNSEEMLINESS	UNSHARPENED	UNSOCIABILITIES
UNSAVORILY	UNSEEMLINESSES	UNSHEATHED	UNSOCIABILITY
UNSAVORINESS	UNSEGMENTED	UNSHEATHES	UNSOCIABLE

UNSOCIABLENESS
UNSOCIABLY
UNSOCIALISED
UNSOCIALISM
UNSOCIALISMS
UNSOCIALITIES
UNSOCIALITY
UNSOCIALIZED
UNSOCIALLY
UNSOCKETED
UNSOCKETING
UNSOFTENED
UNSOFTENING
UNSOLDERED
UNSOLDERING
UNSOLDIERLIKE
UNSOLDIERLY
UNSOLICITED
UNSOLICITOUS
UNSOLIDITIES
UNSOLIDITY
UNSOLVABLE
UNSOPHISTICATE
UNSOPHISTICATED
UNSOUNDABLE
UNSOUNDEST
UNSOUNDNESS
UNSOUNDNESSES
UNSPARINGLY
UNSPARINGNESS
UNSPARINGNESSES
UNSPARRING
UNSPEAKABLE
UNSPEAKABLENESS
UNSPEAKABLY
UNSPEAKING
UNSPECIALISED
UNSPECIALIZED
UNSPECIFIABLE
UNSPECIFIC
UNSPECIFIED
UNSPECTACLED
UNSPECTACULAR
UNSPECULATIVE
UNSPELLING
UNSPHERING
UNSPIRITED
UNSPIRITUAL
UNSPIRITUALISE
UNSPIRITUALISED
UNSPIRITUALISES
UNSPIRITUALIZE
UNSPIRITUALIZED
UNSPIRITUALIZES
UNSPIRITUALLY
UNSPLINTERABLE
UNSPOOLING
UNSPORTING
UNSPORTSMANLIKE
UNSPOTTEDNESS

UNSPOTTEDNESSES
UNSPRINKLED
UNSTABLENESS
UNSTABLENESSES
UNSTABLEST
UNSTACKING
UNSTAIDNESS
UNSTAIDNESSES
UNSTAINABLE
UNSTANCHABLE
UNSTANCHED
UNSTANDARDISED
UNSTANDARDIZED
UNSTARCHED
UNSTARCHES
UNSTARCHING
UNSTARTLING
UNSTATESMANLIKE
UNSTATUTABLE
UNSTATUTABLY
UNSTAUNCHABLE
UNSTAUNCHED
UNSTEADFAST
UNSTEADFASTLY
UNSTEADFASTNESS
UNSTEADIED
UNSTEADIER
UNSTEADIES
UNSTEADIEST
UNSTEADILY
UNSTEADINESS
UNSTEADINESSES
UNSTEADYING
UNSTEELING
UNSTEPPING
UNSTERCORATED
UNSTERILISED
UNSTERILIZED
UNSTICKING
UNSTIGMATISED
UNSTIGMATIZED
UNSTIMULATED
UNSTINTING
UNSTINTINGLY
UNSTITCHED
UNSTITCHES
UNSTITCHING
UNSTOCKING
UNSTOCKINGED
UNSTOOPING
UNSTOPPABLE
UNSTOPPABLY
UNSTOPPERED
UNSTOPPERING
UNSTOPPERS
UNSTOPPING
UNSTRAINED
UNSTRAPPED
UNSTRAPPING
UNSTRATIFIED

UNSTREAMED
UNSTRENGTHENED
UNSTRESSED
UNSTRESSES
UNSTRIATED
UNSTRINGED
UNSTRINGING
UNSTRIPPED
UNSTRIPPING
UNSTRUCTURED
UNSUBDUABLE
UNSUBJECTED
UNSUBLIMATED
UNSUBLIMED
UNSUBMERGED
UNSUBMISSIVE
UNSUBMITTING
UNSUBSCRIBE
UNSUBSCRIBED
UNSUBSCRIBES
UNSUBSCRIBING
UNSUBSIDISED
UNSUBSIDIZED
UNSUBSTANTIAL
UNSUBSTANTIALLY
UNSUBSTANTIATED
UNSUCCEEDED
UNSUCCESSES
UNSUCCESSFUL
UNSUCCESSFULLY
UNSUCCESSIVE
UNSUCCOURED
UNSUFFERABLE
UNSUFFICIENT
UNSUITABILITIES
UNSUITABILITY
UNSUITABLE
UNSUITABLENESS
UNSUITABLY
UNSUMMERED
UNSUMMONED
UNSUPERFLUOUS
UNSUPERVISED
UNSUPPLENESS
UNSUPPLENESSES
UNSUPPLIED
UNSUPPORTABLE
UNSUPPORTED
UNSUPPORTEDLY
UNSUPPOSABLE
UNSUPPRESSED
UNSURFACED
UNSURMISED
UNSURMOUNTABLE
UNSURPASSABLE
UNSURPASSABLY
UNSURPASSED
UNSURPRISED
UNSURPRISING
UNSURPRISINGLY

UNSURVEYED
UNSUSCEPTIBLE
UNSUSPECTED
UNSUSPECTEDLY
UNSUSPECTEDNESS
UNSUSPECTING
UNSUSPECTINGLY
UNSUSPENDED
UNSUSPICION
UNSUSPICIONS
UNSUSPICIOUS
UNSUSPICIOUSLY
UNSUSTAINABLE
UNSUSTAINED
UNSUSTAINING
UNSWADDLED
UNSWADDLES
UNSWADDLING
UNSWALLOWED
UNSWATHING
UNSWAYABLE
UNSWEARING
UNSWEARINGS
UNSWEETENED
UNSWERVING
UNSWERVINGLY
UNSYLLABLED
UNSYMMETRICAL
UNSYMMETRICALLY
UNSYMMETRIES
UNSYMMETRISED
UNSYMMETRIZED
UNSYMMETRY
UNSYMPATHETIC
UNSYMPATHIES
UNSYMPATHISING
UNSYMPATHIZING
UNSYMPATHY
UNSYNCHRONISED
UNSYNCHRONIZED
UNSYSTEMATIC
UNSYSTEMATICAL
UNSYSTEMATISED
UNSYSTEMATIZED
UNTACKLING
UNTAINTEDLY
UNTAINTEDNESS
UNTAINTEDNESSES
UNTAINTING
UNTALENTED
UNTAMABLENESS
UNTAMABLENESSES
UNTAMEABLE
UNTAMEABLENESS
UNTAMEABLY
UNTAMEDNESS
UNTAMEDNESSES
UNTANGIBLE
UNTANGLING
UNTARNISHED

UNTASTEFUL
UNTEACHABLE
UNTEACHABLENESS
UNTEACHING
UNTEARABLE
UNTECHNICAL
UNTELLABLE
UNTEMPERED
UNTEMPERING
UNTENABILITIES
UNTENABILITY
UNTENABLENESS
UNTENABLENESSES
UNTENANTABLE
UNTENANTED
UNTENANTING
UNTENDERED
UNTENDERLY
UNTERMINATED
UNTERRESTRIAL
UNTERRIFIED
UNTERRIFYING
UNTESTABLE
UNTETHERED
UNTETHERING
UNTHANKFUL
UNTHANKFULLY
UNTHANKFULNESS
UNTHATCHED
UNTHATCHES
UNTHATCHING
UNTHEOLOGICAL
UNTHEORETICAL
UNTHICKENED
UNTHINKABILITY
UNTHINKABLE
UNTHINKABLENESS
UNTHINKABLY
UNTHINKING
UNTHINKINGLY
UNTHINKINGNESS
UNTHOROUGH
UNTHOUGHTFUL
UNTHOUGHTFULLY
UNTHREADED
UNTHREADING
UNTHREATENED
UNTHREATENING
UNTHRIFTILY
UNTHRIFTINESS
UNTHRIFTINESSES
UNTHRIFTYHEAD
UNTHRIFTYHEADS
UNTHRIFTYHED
UNTHRIFTYHEDS
UNTHRONING
UNTIDINESS
UNTIDINESSES
UNTILLABLE
UNTIMBERED

UNTIMELIER
UNTIMELIEST
UNTIMELINESS
UNTIMELINESSES
UNTIMEOUSLY
UNTINCTURED
UNTIRINGLY
UNTOCHERED
UNTOGETHER
UNTORMENTED
UNTORTURED
UNTOUCHABILITY
UNTOUCHABLE
UNTOUCHABLES
UNTOWARDLINESS
UNTOWARDLY
UNTOWARDNESS
UNTOWARDNESSES
UNTRACEABLE
UNTRACKING
UNTRACTABLE
UNTRACTABLENESS
UNTRADITIONAL
UNTRADITIONALLY
UNTRAMMELED
UNTRAMMELLED
UNTRAMPLED
UNTRANQUIL
UNTRANSFERABLE
UNTRANSFERRABLE
UNTRANSFORMED
UNTRANSLATABLE
UNTRANSLATABLY
UNTRANSLATED
UNTRANSMIGRATED
UNTRANSMISSIBLE
UNTRANSMITTED
UNTRANSMUTABLE
UNTRANSMUTED
UNTRANSPARENT
UNTRAVELED
UNTRAVELLED
UNTRAVERSABLE
UNTRAVERSED
UNTREADING
UNTREASURE
UNTREASURED
UNTREASURES
UNTREASURING
UNTREATABLE
UNTREMBLING
UNTREMBLINGLY
UNTREMENDOUS
UNTREMULOUS
UNTRENCHED
UNTRESPASSING
UNTRIMMING
UNTROUBLED
UNTROUBLEDLY
UNTRUENESS

UNTRUENESSES
UNTRUSSERS
UNTRUSSING
UNTRUSSINGS
UNTRUSTFUL
UNTRUSTINESS
UNTRUSTINESSES
UNTRUSTING
UNTRUSTWORTHILY
UNTRUSTWORTHY
UNTRUTHFUL
UNTRUTHFULLY
UNTRUTHFULNESS
UNTUCKERED
UNTUMULTUOUS
UNTUNABLENESS
UNTUNABLENESSES
UNTUNEABLE
UNTUNEFULLY
UNTUNEFULNESS
UNTUNEFULNESSES
UNTURNABLE
UNTWISTING
UNTWISTINGS
UNTYPICALLY
UNTYREABLE
UNUNUNIUMS
UNUPLIFTED
UNUSEFULLY
UNUSEFULNESS
UNUSEFULNESSES
UNUSUALNESS
UNUSUALNESSES
UNUTILISED
UNUTILIZED
UNUTTERABLE
UNUTTERABLENESS
UNUTTERABLES
UNUTTERABLY
UNVACCINATED
UNVALUABLE
UNVANQUISHABLE
UNVANQUISHED
UNVARIABLE
UNVARIEGATED
UNVARNISHED
UNVEILINGS
UNVENDIBLE
UNVENERABLE
UNVENTILATED
UNVERACIOUS
UNVERACITIES
UNVERACITY
UNVERBALISED
UNVERBALIZED
UNVERIFIABILITY
UNVERIFIABLE
UNVERIFIED
UNVIOLATED
UNVIRTUOUS

UNVIRTUOUSLY
UNVISITABLE
UNVISORING
UNVITIATED
UNVITRIFIABLE
UNVITRIFIED
UNVIZARDED
UNVIZARDING
UNVOCALISED
UNVOCALIZED
UNVOICINGS
UNVOYAGEABLE
UNVULGARISE
UNVULGARISED
UNVULGARISES
UNVULGARISING
UNVULGARIZE
UNVULGARIZED
UNVULGARIZES
UNVULGARIZING
UNVULNERABLE
UNWANDERING
UNWARENESS
UNWARENESSES
UNWARINESS
UNWARINESSES
UNWARRANTABLE
UNWARRANTABLY
UNWARRANTED
UNWARRANTEDLY
UNWASHEDNESS
UNWASHEDNESSES
UNWATCHABLE
UNWATCHFUL
UNWATCHFULLY
UNWATCHFULNESS
UNWATERING
UNWAVERING
UNWAVERINGLY
UNWEAKENED
UNWEAPONED
UNWEAPONING
UNWEARABLE
UNWEARIABLE
UNWEARIABLY
UNWEARIEDLY
UNWEARIEDNESS
UNWEARIEDNESSES
UNWEARYING
UNWEARYINGLY
UNWEATHERED
UNWEDGABLE
UNWEDGEABLE
UNWEETINGLY
UNWEIGHING
UNWEIGHTED
UNWEIGHTING
UNWELCOMED
UNWELCOMELY
UNWELCOMENESS

UNWELCOMENESSES
UNWELLNESS
UNWELLNESSES
UNWHISTLEABLE
UNWHOLESOME
UNWHOLESOMELY
UNWHOLESOMENESS
UNWIELDIER
UNWIELDIEST
UNWIELDILY
UNWIELDINESS
UNWIELDINESSES
UNWIELDLILY
UNWIELDLINESS
UNWIELDLINESSES
UNWIFELIER
UNWIFELIEST
UNWIFELIKE
UNWILLINGLY
UNWILLINGNESS
UNWILLINGNESSES
UNWINDABLE
UNWINDINGS
UNWINKINGLY
UNWINNABLE
UNWINNOWED
UNWISENESS
UNWISENESSES
UNWITCHING
UNWITHDRAWING
UNWITHERED
UNWITHERING
UNWITHHELD
UNWITHHOLDEN
UNWITHHOLDING
UNWITHSTOOD
UNWITNESSED
UNWITTINGLY
UNWITTINGNESS
UNWITTINGNESSES
UNWOMANING
UNWOMANLIER
UNWOMANLIEST
UNWOMANLINESS
UNWOMANLINESSES
UNWONTEDLY
UNWONTEDNESS
UNWONTEDNESSES
UNWORKABILITIES
UNWORKABILITY
UNWORKABLE
UNWORKMANLIKE
UNWORLDLIER
UNWORLDLIEST
UNWORLDLINESS
UNWORLDLINESSES
UNWORSHIPFUL
UNWORSHIPPED
UNWORTHIER
UNWORTHIES

UNWORTHIEST
UNWORTHILY
UNWORTHINESS
UNWORTHINESSES
UNWOUNDABLE
UNWRAPPING
UNWREATHED
UNWREATHES
UNWREATHING
UNWRINKLED
UNWRINKLES
UNWRINKLING
UNYIELDING
UNYIELDINGLY
UNYIELDINGNESS
UPBRAIDERS
UPBRAIDING
UPBRAIDINGLY
UPBRAIDINGS
UPBREAKING
UPBRINGING
UPBRINGINGS
UPBUILDERS
UPBUILDING
UPBUILDINGS
UPBUOYANCE
UPBUOYANCES
UPBURSTING
UPCATCHING
UPCHEERING
UPCHUCKING
UPCLIMBING
UPCOUNTRIES
UPDATEABLE
UPDRAGGING
UPDRAUGHTS
UPFILLINGS
UPFLASHING
UPFLINGING
UPFOLLOWED
UPFOLLOWING
UPGATHERED
UPGATHERING
UPGRADABILITIES
UPGRADABILITY
UPGRADABLE
UPGRADATION
UPGRADATIONS
UPGRADEABILITY
UPGRADEABLE
UPGROWINGS
UPHEAPINGS
UPHILLWARD
UPHOARDING
UPHOISTING
UPHOLDINGS
UPHOLSTERED
UPHOLSTERER
UPHOLSTERERS
UPHOLSTERIES

UPHOLSTERING
UPHOLSTERS
UPHOLSTERY
UPHOLSTRESS
UPHOLSTRESSES
UPHOORDING
UPKNITTING
UPLIFTINGLY
UPLIFTINGS
UPLIGHTERS
UPLIGHTING
UPLINKINGS
UPMANSHIPS
UPPERCASED
UPPERCASES
UPPERCASING
UPPERCLASSMAN
UPPERCLASSMEN
UPPERCUTTING
UPPERPARTS
UPPERWORKS
UPPISHNESS
UPPISHNESSES
UPPITINESS
UPPITINESSES
UPPITYNESS
UPPITYNESSES
UPPROPPING
UPREACHING
UPRIGHTEOUSLY
UPRIGHTING
UPRIGHTNESS
UPRIGHTNESSES
UPROARIOUS
UPROARIOUSLY
UPROARIOUSNESS
UPROOTEDNESS
UPROOTEDNESSES
UPROOTINGS
UPSETTABLE
UPSETTINGLY
UPSETTINGS
UPSHIFTING
UPSHOOTING
UPSIDEOWNE
UPSITTINGS
UPSKILLING
UPSPEAKING
UPSPEARING
UPSPRINGING
UPSTANDING
UPSTANDINGNESS
UPSTARTING
UPSTEPPING
UPSTIRRING
UPSTREAMED
UPSTREAMING
UPSTRETCHED
UPSURGENCE
UPSURGENCES

UPSWARMING
UPSWEEPING
UPSWELLING
UPSWINGING
UPTHROWING
UPTHRUSTED
UPTHRUSTING
UPTHUNDERED
UPTHUNDERING
UPTHUNDERS
UPTIGHTEST
UPTIGHTNESS
UPTIGHTNESSES
UPTITLINGS
UPTRAINING
UPTURNINGS
UPVALUATION
UPVALUATIONS
UPWARDNESS
UPWARDNESSES
UPWELLINGS
UPWHIRLING
URALITISATION
URALITISATIONS
URALITISED
URALITISES
URALITISING
URALITIZATION
URALITIZATIONS
URALITIZED
URALITIZES
URALITIZING
URANALYSES
URANALYSIS
URANINITES
URANOGRAPHER
URANOGRAPHERS
URANOGRAPHIC
URANOGRAPHICAL
URANOGRAPHIES
URANOGRAPHIST
URANOGRAPHISTS
URANOGRAPHY
URANOLOGIES
URANOMETRIES
URANOMETRY
URANOPLASTIES
URANOPLASTY
URBANENESS
URBANENESSES
URBANISATION
URBANISATIONS
URBANISING
URBANISTIC
URBANISTICALLY
URBANITIES
URBANIZATION
URBANIZATIONS
URBANIZING
URBANOLOGIES

URBANOLOGIST
URBANOLOGISTS
URBANOLOGY
URCEOLUSES
UREDINIOSPORE
UREDINIOSPORES
UREDIOSPORE
UREDIOSPORES
UREDOSORUS
UREDOSPORE
UREDOSPORES
UREOTELISM
UREOTELISMS
URETERITIS
URETERITISES
URETHRITIC
URETHRITIS
URETHRITISES
URETHROSCOPE
URETHROSCOPES
URETHROSCOPIC
URETHROSCOPIES
URETHROSCOPY
URICOSURIC
URICOTELIC
URICOTELISM
URICOTELISMS
URINALYSES
URINALYSIS
URINATIONS
URINIFEROUS
URINIPAROUS
URINOGENITAL
URINOLOGIES
URINOMETER
URINOMETERS
URINOSCOPIES
URINOSCOPY
UROBILINOGEN
UROBILINOGENS
UROCHORDAL
UROCHORDATE
UROCHORDATES
UROCHROMES
URODYNAMICS
UROGENITAL
UROGRAPHIC
UROGRAPHIES
UROKINASES
UROLAGNIAS
UROLITHIASES
UROLITHIASIS
UROLOGICAL
UROLOGISTS
UROPOIESES
UROPOIESIS
UROPYGIUMS
UROSCOPIES
UROSCOPIST
UROSCOPISTS

UROSTEGITE
UROSTEGITES
UROSTHENIC
UROSTOMIES
URTICACEOUS
URTICARIAL
URTICARIAS
URTICARIOUS
URTICATING
URTICATION
URTICATIONS
USABILITIES
USABLENESS
USABLENESSES
USEABILITIES
USEABILITY
USEABLENESS
USEABLENESSES
USEFULNESS
USEFULNESSES
USELESSNESS
USELESSNESSES
USHERESSES
USHERETTES
USHERSHIPS
USQUEBAUGH
USQUEBAUGHS
USTILAGINEOUS
USTILAGINOUS
USTULATION
USTULATIONS
USUALNESSES
USUCAPIENT
USUCAPIENTS
USUCAPIONS
USUCAPTIBLE
USUCAPTING
USUCAPTION
USUCAPTIONS
USUFRUCTED
USUFRUCTING
USUFRUCTUARIES
USUFRUCTUARY
USURIOUSLY
USURIOUSNESS
USURIOUSNESSES
USURPATION
USURPATIONS
USURPATIVE
USURPATORY
USURPATURE
USURPATURES
USURPINGLY
UTERECTOMIES
UTERECTOMY
UTERITISES
UTEROGESTATION
UTEROGESTATIONS
UTEROTOMIES
UTILISABLE

UTILISATION
UTILISATIONS
UTILITARIAN
UTILITARIANISE
UTILITARIANISED
UTILITARIANISES
UTILITARIANISM
UTILITARIANISMS
UTILITARIANIZE
UTILITARIANIZED
UTILITARIANIZES
UTILITARIANS
UTILIZABLE
UTILIZATION
UTILIZATIONS
UTOPIANISE
UTOPIANISED
UTOPIANISER
UTOPIANISERS
UTOPIANISES
UTOPIANISING
UTOPIANISM
UTOPIANISMS
UTOPIANIZE
UTOPIANIZED
UTOPIANIZER
UTOPIANIZERS
UTOPIANIZES
UTOPIANIZING
UTRICULARIA
UTRICULARIAS
UTRICULATE
UTRICULITIS
UTRICULITISES
UTTERABLENESS
UTTERABLENESSES
UTTERANCES
UTTERMOSTS
UTTERNESSES
UVAROVITES
UVULITISES
UXORICIDAL
UXORICIDES
UXORILOCAL
UXORIOUSLY
UXORIOUSNESS
UXORIOUSNESSES

V

VACANTNESS
VACANTNESSES
VACATIONED
VACATIONER
VACATIONERS
VACATIONING
VACATIONIST
VACATIONISTS
VACATIONLAND
VACATIONLANDS
VACATIONLESS
VACCINATED
VACCINATES
VACCINATING
VACCINATION
VACCINATIONS
VACCINATOR
VACCINATORS
VACCINATORY
VACCINIUMS
VACILLATED
VACILLATES
VACILLATING
VACILLATINGLY
VACILLATION
VACILLATIONS
VACILLATOR
VACILLATORS
VACILLATORY
VACUATIONS
VACUOLATED
VACUOLATION
VACUOLATIONS
VACUOLISATION
VACUOLISATIONS
VACUOLIZATION
VACUOLIZATIONS
VACUOUSNESS
VACUOUSNESSES
VAGABONDAGE
VAGABONDAGES
VAGABONDED
VAGABONDING
VAGABONDISE
VAGABONDISED
VAGABONDISES
VAGABONDISH
VAGABONDISING
VAGABONDISM
VAGABONDISMS
VAGABONDIZE
VAGABONDIZED
VAGABONDIZES
VAGABONDIZING

VAGARIOUSLY
VAGILITIES
VAGINECTOMIES
VAGINECTOMY
VAGINICOLINE
VAGINICOLOUS
VAGINISMUS
VAGINISMUSES
VAGINITISES
VAGOTOMIES
VAGOTONIAS
VAGOTROPIC
VAGRANCIES
VAGRANTNESS
VAGRANTNESSES
VAGUENESSES
VAINGLORIED
VAINGLORIES
VAINGLORIOUS
VAINGLORIOUSLY
VAINGLORYING
VAINNESSES
VAIVODESHIP
VAIVODESHIPS
VALEDICTION
VALEDICTIONS
VALEDICTORIAN
VALEDICTORIANS
VALEDICTORIES
VALEDICTORY
VALENTINES
VALERIANACEOUS
VALETUDINARIAN
VALETUDINARIANS
VALETUDINARIES
VALETUDINARY
VALIANCIES
VALIANTNESS
VALIANTNESSES
VALIDATING
VALIDATION
VALIDATIONS
VALIDATORY
VALIDITIES
VALIDNESSES
VALLATIONS
VALLECULAE
VALLECULAR
VALLECULATE
VALORISATION
VALORISATIONS
VALORISING
VALORIZATION
VALORIZATIONS

VALORIZING
VALOROUSLY
VALPOLICELLA
VALPOLICELLAS
VALPROATES
VALUABLENESS
VALUABLENESSES
VALUATIONAL
VALUATIONALLY
VALUATIONS
VALUELESSNESS
VALUELESSNESSES
VALVASSORS
VALVULITIS
VALVULITISES
VAMPIRISED
VAMPIRISES
VAMPIRISING
VAMPIRISMS
VAMPIRIZED
VAMPIRIZES
VAMPIRIZING
VANADIATES
VANADINITE
VANADINITES
VANASPATIS
VANCOMYCIN
VANCOMYCINS
VANDALISATION
VANDALISATIONS
VANDALISED
VANDALISES
VANDALISING
VANDALISMS
VANDALISTIC
VANDALIZATION
VANDALIZATIONS
VANDALIZED
VANDALIZES
VANDALIZING
VANGUARDISM
VANGUARDISMS
VANGUARDIST
VANGUARDISTS
VANISHINGLY
VANISHINGS
VANISHMENT
VANISHMENTS
VANITORIES
VANPOOLING
VANPOOLINGS
VANQUISHABLE
VANQUISHED
VANQUISHER

VANQUISHERS
VANQUISHES
VANQUISHING
VANQUISHMENT
VANQUISHMENTS
VANTAGELESS
VANTBRACES
VAPIDITIES
VAPIDNESSES
VAPORABILITIES
VAPORABILITY
VAPORESCENCE
VAPORESCENCES
VAPORESCENT
VAPORETTOS
VAPORIFORM
VAPORIMETER
VAPORIMETERS
VAPORISABLE
VAPORISATION
VAPORISATIONS
VAPORISERS
VAPORISHNESS
VAPORISHNESSES
VAPORISING
VAPORIZABLE
VAPORIZATION
VAPORIZATIONS
VAPORIZERS
VAPORIZING
VAPOROSITIES
VAPOROSITY
VAPOROUSLY
VAPOROUSNESS
VAPOROUSNESSES
VAPORWARES
VAPOURABILITIES
VAPOURABILITY
VAPOURABLE
VAPOURINGLY
VAPOURINGS
VAPOURISHNESS
VAPOURISHNESSES
VAPOURLESS
VAPOURWARE
VAPOURWARES
VAPULATING
VAPULATION
VAPULATIONS
VARIABILITIES
VARIABILITY
VARIABLENESS
VARIABLENESSES
VARIATIONAL

VARIATIONALLY
VARIATIONIST
VARIATIONISTS
VARIATIONS
VARICELLAR
VARICELLAS
VARICELLATE
VARICELLOID
VARICELLOUS
VARICOCELE
VARICOCELES
VARICOLORED
VARICOLOURED
VARICOSITIES
VARICOSITY
VARICOTOMIES
VARICOTOMY
VARIEDNESS
VARIEDNESSES
VARIEGATED
VARIEGATES
VARIEGATING
VARIEGATION
VARIEGATIONS
VARIEGATOR
VARIEGATORS
VARIETALLY
VARIFOCALS
VARIFORMLY
VARIOLATED
VARIOLATES
VARIOLATING
VARIOLATION
VARIOLATIONS
VARIOLATOR
VARIOLATORS
VARIOLISATION
VARIOLISATIONS
VARIOLITES
VARIOLITIC
VARIOLIZATION
VARIOLIZATIONS
VARIOLOIDS
VARIOMETER
VARIOMETERS
VARIOUSNESS
VARIOUSNESSES
VARISCITES
VARITYPING
VARITYPIST
VARITYPISTS
VARLETESSES
VARLETRIES
VARNISHERS
VARNISHING
VARNISHINGS
VARSOVIENNE
VARSOVIENNES
VASCULARISATION

VASCULARISE
VASCULARISED
VASCULARISES
VASCULARISING
VASCULARITIES
VASCULARITY
VASCULARIZATION
VASCULARIZE
VASCULARIZED
VASCULARIZES
VASCULARIZING
VASCULARLY
VASCULATURE
VASCULATURES
VASCULIFORM
VASCULITIDES
VASCULITIS
VASECTOMIES
VASECTOMISE
VASECTOMISED
VASECTOMISES
VASECTOMISING
VASECTOMIZE
VASECTOMIZED
VASECTOMIZES
VASECTOMIZING
VASOACTIVE
VASOACTIVITIES
VASOACTIVITY
VASOCONSTRICTOR
VASODILATATION
VASODILATATIONS
VASODILATATORY
VASODILATION
VASODILATIONS
VASODILATOR
VASODILATORS
VASODILATORY
VASOINHIBITOR
VASOINHIBITORS
VASOINHIBITORY
VASOPRESSIN
VASOPRESSINS
VASOPRESSOR
VASOPRESSORS
VASOSPASMS
VASOSPASTIC
VASOTOCINS
VASOTOMIES
VASSALAGES
VASSALESSES
VASSALISED
VASSALISES
VASSALISING
VASSALIZED
VASSALIZES
VASSALIZING
VASSALLING
VASSALRIES

VASTIDITIES
VASTITUDES
VASTNESSES
VATICINATE
VATICINATED
VATICINATES
VATICINATING
VATICINATION
VATICINATIONS
VATICINATOR
VATICINATORS
VATICINATORY
VAUDEVILLE
VAUDEVILLEAN
VAUDEVILLEANS
VAUDEVILLES
VAUDEVILLIAN
VAUDEVILLIANS
VAUDEVILLIST
VAUDEVILLISTS
VAULTINGLY
VAUNTERIES
VAUNTINGLY
VAVASORIES
VECTOGRAPH
VECTOGRAPHS
VECTORIALLY
VECTORINGS
VECTORISATION
VECTORISATIONS
VECTORISED
VECTORISES
VECTORISING
VECTORIZATION
VECTORIZATIONS
VECTORIZED
VECTORIZES
VECTORIZING
VECTORSCOPE
VECTORSCOPES
VEGEBURGER
VEGEBURGERS
VEGETABLES
VEGETARIAN
VEGETARIANISM
VEGETARIANISMS
VEGETARIANS
VEGETATING
VEGETATINGS
VEGETATION
VEGETATIONAL
VEGETATIONS
VEGETATIOUS
VEGETATIVE
VEGETATIVELY
VEGETATIVENESS
VEGGIEBURGER
VEGGIEBURGERS
VEHEMENCES

VEHEMENCIES
VEHEMENTLY
VEILLEUSES
VEINSTONES
VEINSTUFFS
VELARISATION
VELARISATIONS
VELARISING
VELARIZATION
VELARIZATIONS
VELARIZING
VELDSCHOEN
VELDSCHOENS
VELDSKOENS
VELITATION
VELITATIONS
VELLEITIES
VELLENAGES
VELLICATED
VELLICATES
VELLICATING
VELLICATION
VELLICATIONS
VELLICATIVE
VELOCIMETER
VELOCIMETERS
VELOCIMETRIES
VELOCIMETRY
VELOCIPEDE
VELOCIPEDEAN
VELOCIPEDEANS
VELOCIPEDED
VELOCIPEDER
VELOCIPEDERS
VELOCIPEDES
VELOCIPEDIAN
VELOCIPEDIANS
VELOCIPEDING
VELOCIPEDIST
VELOCIPEDISTS
VELOCIRAPTOR
VELOCIRAPTORS
VELOCITIES
VELODROMES
VELOUTINES
VELUTINOUS
VELVETEENED
VELVETEENS
VELVETIEST
VELVETINESS
VELVETINESSES
VELVETINGS
VELVETLIKE
VENALITIES
VENATICALLY
VENATIONAL
VENATORIAL
VENDETTIST
VENDETTISTS

VENDIBILITIES
VENDIBILITY
VENDIBLENESS
VENDIBLENESSES
VENDITATION
VENDITATIONS
VENDITIONS
VENEERINGS
VENEFICALLY
VENEFICIOUS
VENEFICIOUSLY
VENEFICOUS
VENEFICOUSLY
VENENATING
VENEPUNCTURE
VENEPUNCTURES
VENERABILITIES
VENERABILITY
VENERABLENESS
VENERABLENESSES
VENERABLES
VENERATING
VENERATION
VENERATIONAL
VENERATIONS
VENERATIVENESS
VENERATORS
VENEREOLOGICAL
VENEREOLOGIES
VENEREOLOGIST
VENEREOLOGISTS
VENEREOLOGY
VENESECTION
VENESECTIONS
VENGEANCES
VENGEFULLY
VENGEFULNESS
VENGEFULNESSES
VENGEMENTS
VENIALITIES
VENIALNESS
VENIALNESSES
VENIPUNCTURE
VENIPUNCTURES
VENISECTION
VENISECTIONS
VENOGRAPHIC
VENOGRAPHICAL
VENOGRAPHIES
VENOGRAPHY
VENOLOGIES
VENOMOUSLY
VENOMOUSNESS
VENOMOUSNESSES
VENOSCLEROSES
VENOSCLEROSIS
VENOSITIES
VENOUSNESS
VENOUSNESSES

VENTIDUCTS
VENTIFACTS
VENTILABLE
VENTILATED
VENTILATES
VENTILATING
VENTILATION
VENTILATIONS
VENTILATIVE
VENTILATOR
VENTILATORS
VENTILATORY
VENTOSITIES
VENTRICLES
VENTRICOSE
VENTRICOSITIES
VENTRICOSITY
VENTRICOUS
VENTRICULAR
VENTRICULE
VENTRICULES
VENTRICULI
VENTRICULUS
VENTRILOQUAL
VENTRILOQUIAL
VENTRILOQUIALLY
VENTRILOQUIES
VENTRILOQUISE
VENTRILOQUISED
VENTRILOQUISES
VENTRILOQUISING
VENTRILOQUISM
VENTRILOQUISMS
VENTRILOQUIST
VENTRILOQUISTIC
VENTRILOQUISTS
VENTRILOQUIZE
VENTRILOQUIZED
VENTRILOQUIZES
VENTRILOQUIZING
VENTRILOQUOUS
VENTRILOQUY
VENTRIPOTENT
VENTROLATERAL
VENTROMEDIAL
VENTURESOME
VENTURESOMELY
VENTURESOMENESS
VENTURINGLY
VENTURINGS
VENTUROUSLY
VENTUROUSNESS
VENTUROUSNESSES
VERACIOUSLY
VERACIOUSNESS
VERACIOUSNESSES
VERACITIES
VERANDAHED
VERAPAMILS

VERATRIDINE
VERATRIDINES
VERATRINES
VERBALISATION
VERBALISATIONS
VERBALISED
VERBALISER
VERBALISERS
VERBALISES
VERBALISING
VERBALISMS
VERBALISTIC
VERBALISTS
VERBALITIES
VERBALIZATION
VERBALIZATIONS
VERBALIZED
VERBALIZER
VERBALIZERS
VERBALIZES
VERBALIZING
VERBALLING
VERBARIANS
VERBASCUMS
VERBENACEOUS
VERBERATED
VERBERATES
VERBERATING
VERBERATION
VERBERATIONS
VERBICIDES
VERBIFICATION
VERBIFICATIONS
VERBIFYING
VERBIGERATE
VERBIGERATED
VERBIGERATES
VERBIGERATING
VERBIGERATION
VERBIGERATIONS
VERBOSENESS
VERBOSENESSES
VERBOSITIES
VERDANCIES
VERDIGRISED
VERDIGRISES
VERDIGRISING
VERDURELESS
VERGEBOARD
VERGEBOARDS
VERGENCIES
VERGERSHIP
VERGERSHIPS
VERIDICALITIES
VERIDICALITY
VERIDICALLY
VERIDICOUS
VERIFIABILITIES
VERIFIABILITY

VERIFIABLE
VERIFIABLENESS
VERIFIABLY
VERIFICATION
VERIFICATIONS
VERIFICATIVE
VERIFICATORY
VERISIMILAR
VERISIMILARLY
VERISIMILITIES
VERISIMILITUDE
VERISIMILITUDES
VERISIMILITY
VERISIMILOUS
VERITABLENESS
VERITABLENESSES
VERJUICING
VERKRAMPTE
VERKRAMPTES
VERMEILING
VERMEILLED
VERMEILLES
VERMEILLING
VERMICELLI
VERMICELLIS
VERMICIDAL
VERMICIDES
VERMICULAR
VERMICULARLY
VERMICULATE
VERMICULATED
VERMICULATES
VERMICULATING
VERMICULATION
VERMICULATIONS
VERMICULES
VERMICULITE
VERMICULITES
VERMICULOUS
VERMICULTURE
VERMICULTURES
VERMIFUGAL
VERMIFUGES
VERMILIONED
VERMILIONING
VERMILIONS
VERMILLING
VERMILLION
VERMILLIONS
VERMINATED
VERMINATES
VERMINATING
VERMINATION
VERMINATIONS
VERMINOUSLY
VERMINOUSNESS
VERMINOUSNESSES
VERMIVOROUS
VERNACULAR

VERNACULARISE
VERNACULARISED
VERNACULARISES
VERNACULARISING
VERNACULARISM
VERNACULARISMS
VERNACULARIST
VERNACULARISTS
VERNACULARITIES
VERNACULARITY
VERNACULARIZE
VERNACULARIZED
VERNACULARIZES
VERNACULARIZING
VERNACULARLY
VERNACULARS
VERNALISATION
VERNALISATIONS
VERNALISED
VERNALISES
VERNALISING
VERNALITIES
VERNALIZATION
VERNALIZATIONS
VERNALIZED
VERNALIZES
VERNALIZING
VERNATIONS
VERNISSAGE
VERNISSAGES
VERRUCIFORM
VERRUCOSITIES
VERRUCOSITY
VERSABILITIES
VERSABILITY
VERSATILELY
VERSATILENESS
VERSATILENESSES
VERSATILITIES
VERSATILITY
VERSICOLOR
VERSICOLOUR
VERSICOLOURED
VERSICULAR
VERSIFICATION
VERSIFICATIONS
VERSIFICATOR
VERSIFICATORS
VERSIFIERS
VERSIFYING
VERSIONERS
VERSIONING
VERSIONINGS
VERSIONIST
VERSIONISTS
VERSLIBRIST
VERSLIBRISTE
VERSLIBRISTES
VERSLIBRISTS

VERTEBRALLY
VERTEBRATE
VERTEBRATED
VERTEBRATES
VERTEBRATION
VERTEBRATIONS
VERTICALITIES
VERTICALITY
VERTICALLY
VERTICALNESS
VERTICALNESSES
VERTICILLASTER
VERTICILLASTERS
VERTICILLATE
VERTICILLATED
VERTICILLATELY
VERTICILLATION
VERTICILLATIONS
VERTICILLIUM
VERTICILLIUMS
VERTICITIES
VERTIGINES
VERTIGINOUS
VERTIGINOUSLY
VERTIGINOUSNESS
VERTIPORTS
VERUMONTANA
VERUMONTANUM
VERUMONTANUMS
VESICATING
VESICATION
VESICATIONS
VESICATORIES
VESICATORY
VESICULARITIES
VESICULARITY
VESICULARLY
VESICULATE
VESICULATED
VESICULATES
VESICULATING
VESICULATION
VESICULATIONS
VESICULOSE
VESPERTILIAN
VESPERTILIONID
VESPERTILIONIDS
VESPERTILIONINE
VESPERTINAL
VESPERTINE
VESPIARIES
VESTIARIES
VESTIBULAR
VESTIBULED
VESTIBULES
VESTIBULING
VESTIBULITIS
VESTIBULITISES
VESTIBULUM

VESTIGIALLY
VESTIMENTAL
VESTIMENTARY
VESTIMENTS
VESTITURES
VESTMENTAL
VESTMENTED
VESUVIANITE
VESUVIANITES
VETCHLINGS
VETERINARIAN
VETERINARIANS
VETERINARIES
VETERINARY
VEXATIOUSLY
VEXATIOUSNESS
VEXATIOUSNESSES
VEXEDNESSES
VEXILLARIES
VEXILLATION
VEXILLATIONS
VEXILLOLOGIC
VEXILLOLOGICAL
VEXILLOLOGIES
VEXILLOLOGIST
VEXILLOLOGISTS
VEXILLOLOGY
VEXINGNESS
VEXINGNESSES
VIABILITIES
VIBRACULAR
VIBRACULARIA
VIBRACULARIUM
VIBRACULOID
VIBRACULUM
VIBRAHARPIST
VIBRAHARPISTS
VIBRAHARPS
VIBRANCIES
VIBRAPHONE
VIBRAPHONES
VIBRAPHONIST
VIBRAPHONISTS
VIBRATILITIES
VIBRATILITY
VIBRATINGLY
VIBRATIONAL
VIBRATIONLESS
VIBRATIONS
VIBRATIUNCLE
VIBRATIUNCLES
VIBRATOLESS
VIBROFLOTATION
VIBROFLOTATIONS
VIBROGRAPH
VIBROGRAPHS
VIBROMETER
VIBROMETERS
VICARESSES

VICARIANCE
VICARIANCES
VICARIANTS
VICARIATES
VICARIOUSLY
VICARIOUSNESS
VICARIOUSNESSES
VICARSHIPS
VICEGERENCIES
VICEGERENCY
VICEGERENT
VICEGERENTS
VICEREGALLY
VICEREGENT
VICEREGENTS
VICEREINES
VICEROYALTIES
VICEROYALTY
VICEROYSHIP
VICEROYSHIPS
VICHYSSOIS
VICHYSSOISE
VICHYSSOISES
VICINITIES
VICIOSITIES
VICIOUSNESS
VICIOUSNESSES
VICISSITUDE
VICISSITUDES
VICISSITUDINARY
VICISSITUDINOUS
VICOMTESSE
VICOMTESSES
VICTIMHOOD
VICTIMHOODS
VICTIMISATION
VICTIMISATIONS
VICTIMISED
VICTIMISER
VICTIMISERS
VICTIMISES
VICTIMISING
VICTIMIZATION
VICTIMIZATIONS
VICTIMIZED
VICTIMIZER
VICTIMIZERS
VICTIMIZES
VICTIMIZING
VICTIMLESS
VICTIMOLOGIES
VICTIMOLOGIST
VICTIMOLOGISTS
VICTIMOLOGY
VICTORESSES
VICTORIANA
VICTORINES
VICTORIOUS
VICTORIOUSLY

VICTORIOUSNESS
VICTORYLESS
VICTRESSES
VICTROLLAS
VICTUALAGE
VICTUALAGES
VICTUALERS
VICTUALING
VICTUALLAGE
VICTUALLAGES
VICTUALLED
VICTUALLER
VICTUALLERS
VICTUALLESS
VICTUALLING
VIDEOCASSETTE
VIDEOCASSETTES
VIDEOCONFERENCE
VIDEODISCS
VIDEODISKS
VIDEOGRAMS
VIDEOGRAPHER
VIDEOGRAPHERS
VIDEOGRAPHIES
VIDEOGRAPHY
VIDEOLANDS
VIDEOPHILE
VIDEOPHILES
VIDEOPHONE
VIDEOPHONES
VIDEOPHONIC
VIDEOTAPED
VIDEOTAPES
VIDEOTAPING
VIDEOTELEPHONE
VIDEOTELEPHONES
VIDEOTEXES
VIDEOTEXTS
VIEWERSHIP
VIEWERSHIPS
VIEWFINDER
VIEWFINDERS
VIEWINESSES
VIEWLESSLY
VIEWPHONES
VIEWPOINTS
VIGILANCES
VIGILANTES
VIGILANTISM
VIGILANTISMS
VIGILANTLY
VIGILANTNESS
VIGILANTNESSES
VIGINTILLION
VIGINTILLIONS
VIGNETTERS
VIGNETTING
VIGNETTIST
VIGNETTISTS

VIGORISHES
VIGOROUSLY
VIGOROUSNESS
VIGOROUSNESSES
VIKINGISMS
VILDNESSES
VILENESSES
VILIFICATION
VILIFICATIONS
VILIPENDED
VILIPENDER
VILIPENDERS
VILIPENDING
VILLAGERIES
VILLAGIOES
VILLAGISATION
VILLAGISATIONS
VILLAGIZATION
VILLAGIZATIONS
VILLAGREES
VILLAINAGE
VILLAINAGES
VILLAINESS
VILLAINESSES
VILLAINIES
VILLAINOUS
VILLAINOUSLY
VILLAINOUSNESS
VILLANAGES
VILLANELLA
VILLANELLAS
VILLANELLE
VILLANELLES
VILLANOUSLY
VILLEGGIATURA
VILLEGGIATURAS
VILLEINAGE
VILLEINAGES
VILLENAGES
VILLIAGOES
VILLICATION
VILLICATIONS
VILLOSITIES
VINAIGRETTE
VINAIGRETTES
VINBLASTINE
VINBLASTINES
VINCIBILITIES
VINCIBILITY
VINCIBLENESS
VINCIBLENESSES
VINCRISTINE
VINCRISTINES
VINDEMIATE
VINDEMIATED
VINDEMIATES
VINDEMIATING
VINDICABILITIES
VINDICABILITY

VINDICABLE
VINDICATED
VINDICATES
VINDICATING
VINDICATION
VINDICATIONS
VINDICATIVE
VINDICATIVENESS
VINDICATOR
VINDICATORILY
VINDICATORS
VINDICATORY
VINDICATRESS
VINDICATRESSES
VINDICTIVE
VINDICTIVELY
VINDICTIVENESS
VINEDRESSER
VINEDRESSERS
VINEGARETTE
VINEGARETTES
VINEGARING
VINEGARISH
VINEGARRETTE
VINEGARRETTES
VINEGARROON
VINEGARROONS
VINEYARDIST
VINEYARDISTS
VINICULTURAL
VINICULTURE
VINICULTURES
VINICULTURIST
VINICULTURISTS
VINIFEROUS
VINIFICATION
VINIFICATIONS
VINIFICATOR
VINIFICATORS
VINOLOGIES
VINOLOGIST
VINOLOGISTS
VINOSITIES
VINTAGINGS
VINYLCYANIDE
VINYLCYANIDES
VINYLIDENE
VINYLIDENES
VIOLABILITIES
VIOLABILITY
VIOLABLENESS
VIOLABLENESSES
VIOLACEOUS
VIOLATIONS
VIOLENTING
VIOLINISTIC
VIOLINISTICALLY
VIOLINISTS
VIOLONCELLI

VIOLONCELLIST
VIOLONCELLISTS
VIOLONCELLO
VIOLONCELLOS
VIOSTEROLS
VIPERFISHES
VIPERIFORM
VIPERISHLY
VIPEROUSLY
VIRAGINIAN
VIRAGINOUS
VIREONINES
VIRESCENCE
VIRESCENCES
VIRGINALIST
VIRGINALISTS
VIRGINALLED
VIRGINALLING
VIRGINALLY
VIRGINHOOD
VIRGINHOODS
VIRGINITIES
VIRGINIUMS
VIRIDESCENCE
VIRIDESCENCES
VIRIDESCENT
VIRIDITIES
VIRILESCENCE
VIRILESCENCES
VIRILESCENT
VIRILISATION
VIRILISATIONS
VIRILISING
VIRILITIES
VIRILIZATION
VIRILIZATIONS
VIRILIZING
VIROLOGICAL
VIROLOGICALLY
VIROLOGIES
VIROLOGIST
VIROLOGISTS
VIRTUALISE
VIRTUALISED
VIRTUALISES
VIRTUALISING
VIRTUALISM
VIRTUALISMS
VIRTUALIST
VIRTUALISTS
VIRTUALITIES
VIRTUALITY
VIRTUALIZE
VIRTUALIZED
VIRTUALIZES
VIRTUALIZING
VIRTUELESS
VIRTUOSITIES
VIRTUOSITY

VIRTUOSOSHIP
VIRTUOSOSHIPS
VIRTUOUSLY
VIRTUOUSNESS
VIRTUOUSNESSES
VIRULENCES
VIRULENCIES
VIRULENTLY
VIRULIFEROUS
VISAGISTES
VISCACHERA
VISCACHERAS
VISCERALLY
VISCERATED
VISCERATES
VISCERATING
VISCEROMOTOR
VISCEROPTOSES
VISCEROPTOSIS
VISCEROTONIA
VISCEROTONIAS
VISCEROTONIC
VISCIDITIES
VISCIDNESS
VISCIDNESSES
VISCOELASTIC
VISCOELASTICITY
VISCOMETER
VISCOMETERS
VISCOMETRIC
VISCOMETRICAL
VISCOMETRIES
VISCOMETRY
VISCOSIMETER
VISCOSIMETERS
VISCOSIMETRIC
VISCOSIMETRICAL
VISCOSIMETRIES
VISCOSIMETRY
VISCOSITIES
VISCOUNTCIES
VISCOUNTCY
VISCOUNTESS
VISCOUNTESSES
VISCOUNTIES
VISCOUNTSHIP
VISCOUNTSHIPS
VISCOUSNESS
VISCOUSNESSES
VISIBILITIES
VISIBILITY
VISIBLENESS
VISIBLENESSES
VISIOGENIC
VISIONALLY
VISIONARIES
VISIONARINESS
VISIONARINESSES
VISIONINGS

VISIONISTS
VISIONLESS
VISIOPHONE
VISIOPHONES
VISITATION
VISITATIONAL
VISITATIONS
VISITATIVE
VISITATORIAL
VISITATORS
VISITORIAL
VISITRESSES
VISUALISATION
VISUALISATIONS
VISUALISED
VISUALISER
VISUALISERS
VISUALISES
VISUALISING
VISUALISTS
VISUALITIES
VISUALIZATION
VISUALIZATIONS
VISUALIZED
VISUALIZER
VISUALIZERS
VISUALIZES
VISUALIZING
VITALISATION
VITALISATIONS
VITALISERS
VITALISING
VITALISTIC
VITALISTICALLY
VITALITIES
VITALIZATION
VITALIZATIONS
VITALIZERS
VITALIZING
VITALNESSES
VITAMINISE
VITAMINISED
VITAMINISES
VITAMINISING
VITAMINIZE
VITAMINIZED
VITAMINIZES
VITAMINIZING
VITASCOPES
VITATIVENESS
VITATIVENESSES
VITELLICLE
VITELLICLES
VITELLIGENOUS
VITELLINES
VITELLOGENESES
VITELLOGENESIS
VITELLOGENIC
VITELLUSES

VITIATIONS
VITICETUMS
VITICOLOUS
VITICULTURAL
VITICULTURALLY
VITICULTURE
VITICULTURER
VITICULTURERS
VITICULTURES
VITICULTURIST
VITICULTURISTS
VITIFEROUS
VITILITIGATE
VITILITIGATED
VITILITIGATES
VITILITIGATING
VITILITIGATION
VITILITIGATIONS
VITIOSITIES
VITRAILLED
VITRAILLIST
VITRAILLISTS
VITRECTOMIES
VITRECTOMY
VITREOSITIES
VITREOSITY
VITREOUSES
VITREOUSLY
VITREOUSNESS
VITREOUSNESSES
VITRESCENCE
VITRESCENCES
VITRESCENT
VITRESCIBILITY
VITRESCIBLE
VITRIFACTION
VITRIFACTIONS
VITRIFACTURE
VITRIFACTURES
VITRIFIABILITY
VITRIFIABLE
VITRIFICATION
VITRIFICATIONS
VITRIFYING
VITRIOLATE
VITRIOLATED
VITRIOLATES
VITRIOLATING
VITRIOLATION
VITRIOLATIONS
VITRIOLING
VITRIOLISATION
VITRIOLISATIONS
VITRIOLISE
VITRIOLISED
VITRIOLISES
VITRIOLISING
VITRIOLIZATION
VITRIOLIZATIONS

VITRIOLIZE
VITRIOLIZED
VITRIOLIZES
VITRIOLIZING
VITRIOLLED
VITRIOLLING
VITUPERABLE
VITUPERATE
VITUPERATED
VITUPERATES
VITUPERATING
VITUPERATION
VITUPERATIONS
VITUPERATIVE
VITUPERATIVELY
VITUPERATOR
VITUPERATORS
VITUPERATORY
VIVACIOUSLY
VIVACIOUSNESS
VIVACIOUSNESSES
VIVACISSIMO
VIVACITIES
VIVANDIERE
VIVANDIERES
VIVANDIERS
VIVERRINES
VIVIANITES
VIVIDITIES
VIVIDNESSES
VIVIFICATION
VIVIFICATIONS
VIVIPARIES
VIVIPARISM
VIVIPARISMS
VIVIPARITIES
VIVIPARITY
VIVIPAROUS
VIVIPAROUSLY
VIVIPAROUSNESS
VIVISECTED
VIVISECTING
VIVISECTION
VIVISECTIONAL
VIVISECTIONALLY
VIVISECTIONIST
VIVISECTIONISTS
VIVISECTIONS
VIVISECTIVE
VIVISECTOR
VIVISECTORIUM
VIVISECTORIUMS
VIVISECTORS
VIVISEPULTURE
VIVISEPULTURES
VIXENISHLY
VIXENISHNESS
VIXENISHNESSES
VIZIERATES

VIZIERSHIP
VIZIERSHIPS
VIZIRSHIPS
VOCABULARIAN
VOCABULARIANS
VOCABULARIED
VOCABULARIES
VOCABULARY
VOCABULIST
VOCABULISTS
VOCALICALLY
VOCALISATION
VOCALISATIONS
VOCALISERS
VOCALISING
VOCALITIES
VOCALIZATION
VOCALIZATIONS
VOCALIZERS
VOCALIZING
VOCALNESSES
VOCATIONAL
VOCATIONALISM
VOCATIONALISMS
VOCATIONALIST
VOCATIONALISTS
VOCATIONALLY
VOCATIVELY
VOCICULTURAL
VOCIFERANCE
VOCIFERANCES
VOCIFERANT
VOCIFERANTS
VOCIFERATE
VOCIFERATED
VOCIFERATES
VOCIFERATING
VOCIFERATION
VOCIFERATIONS
VOCIFERATOR
VOCIFERATORS
VOCIFEROSITIES
VOCIFEROSITY
VOCIFEROUS
VOCIFEROUSLY
VOCIFEROUSNESS
VOETGANGER
VOETGANGERS
VOETSTOETS
VOETSTOOTS
VOGUISHNESS
VOGUISHNESSES
VOICEFULNESS
VOICEFULNESSES
VOICELESSLY
VOICELESSNESS
VOICELESSNESSES
VOICEMAILS
VOICEOVERS

VOICEPRINT
VOICEPRINTS
VOIDABLENESS
VOIDABLENESSES
VOIDNESSES
VOISINAGES
VOITURIERS
VOIVODESHIP
VOIVODESHIPS
VOLATILENESS
VOLATILENESSES
VOLATILISABLE
VOLATILISATION
VOLATILISATIONS
VOLATILISE
VOLATILISED
VOLATILISES
VOLATILISING
VOLATILITIES
VOLATILITY
VOLATILIZABLE
VOLATILIZATION
VOLATILIZATIONS
VOLATILIZE
VOLATILIZED
VOLATILIZES
VOLATILIZING
VOLCANICALLY
VOLCANICITIES
VOLCANICITY
VOLCANISATION
VOLCANISATIONS
VOLCANISED
VOLCANISES
VOLCANISING
VOLCANISMS
VOLCANISTS
VOLCANIZATION
VOLCANIZATIONS
VOLCANIZED
VOLCANIZES
VOLCANIZING
VOLCANOLOGIC
VOLCANOLOGICAL
VOLCANOLOGIES
VOLCANOLOGIST
VOLCANOLOGISTS
VOLCANOLOGY
VOLITATING
VOLITATION
VOLITATIONAL
VOLITATIONS
VOLITIONAL
VOLITIONALLY
VOLITIONARY
VOLITIONLESS
VOLITORIAL
VOLKSLIEDER
VOLKSRAADS

VOLLEYBALL
VOLLEYBALLS
VOLPLANING
VOLTAMETER
VOLTAMETERS
VOLTAMETRIC
VOLTAMMETER
VOLTAMMETERS
VOLTIGEURS
VOLTINISMS
VOLTMETERS
VOLUBILITIES
VOLUBILITY
VOLUBLENESS
VOLUBLENESSES
VOLUMENOMETER
VOLUMENOMETERS
VOLUMETERS
VOLUMETRIC
VOLUMETRICAL
VOLUMETRICALLY
VOLUMETRIES
VOLUMINOSITIES
VOLUMINOSITY
VOLUMINOUS
VOLUMINOUSLY
VOLUMINOUSNESS
VOLUMISING
VOLUMIZING
VOLUMOMETER
VOLUMOMETERS
VOLUNTARIES
VOLUNTARILY
VOLUNTARINESS
VOLUNTARINESSES
VOLUNTARISM
VOLUNTARISMS
VOLUNTARIST
VOLUNTARISTIC
VOLUNTARISTS
VOLUNTARYISM
VOLUNTARYISMS
VOLUNTARYIST
VOLUNTARYISTS
VOLUNTATIVE
VOLUNTEERED
VOLUNTEERING
VOLUNTEERISM
VOLUNTEERISMS
VOLUNTEERS
VOLUPTUARIES
VOLUPTUARY
VOLUPTUOSITIES
VOLUPTUOSITY
VOLUPTUOUS
VOLUPTUOUSLY
VOLUPTUOUSNESS
VOLUTATION
VOLUTATIONS

VOLVULUSES
VOMERONASAL
VOMITORIES
VOMITORIUM
VOMITURITION
VOMITURITIONS
VOODOOISMS
VOODOOISTIC
VOODOOISTS
VOORKAMERS
VOORTREKKER
VOORTREKKERS
VORACIOUSLY
VORACIOUSNESS
VORACIOUSNESSES
VORACITIES
VORAGINOUS
VORTICALLY
VORTICELLA
VORTICELLAE
VORTICELLAS
VORTICISMS
VORTICISTS
VORTICITIES
VORTICULAR
VORTIGINOUS
VOTARESSES
VOTIVENESS
VOTIVENESSES
VOUCHERING
VOUCHSAFED
VOUCHSAFEMENT
VOUCHSAFEMENTS
VOUCHSAFES
VOUCHSAFING
VOUCHSAFINGS
VOUSSOIRED
VOUSSOIRING
VOUTSAFING
VOWELISATION
VOWELISATIONS
VOWELISING
VOWELIZATION
VOWELIZATIONS
VOWELIZING
VOYAGEABLE
VOYEURISMS
VOYEURISTIC
VOYEURISTICALLY
VRAICKINGS
VRAISEMBLANCE
VRAISEMBLANCES
VULCANICITIES
VULCANICITY
VULCANISABLE
VULCANISATE
VULCANISATES
VULCANISATION
VULCANISATIONS

VULCANISED
VULCANISER
VULCANISERS
VULCANISES
VULCANISING
VULCANISMS
VULCANISTS
VULCANITES
VULCANIZABLE
VULCANIZATE
VULCANIZATES
VULCANIZATION
VULCANIZATIONS
VULCANIZED
VULCANIZER
VULCANIZERS
VULCANIZES
VULCANIZING
VULCANOLOGICAL
VULCANOLOGIES
VULCANOLOGIST
VULCANOLOGISTS
VULCANOLOGY
VULGARIANS
VULGARISATION
VULGARISATIONS
VULGARISED
VULGARISER
VULGARISERS
VULGARISES
VULGARISING
VULGARISMS
VULGARITIES
VULGARIZATION
VULGARIZATIONS
VULGARIZED
VULGARIZER
VULGARIZERS
VULGARIZES
VULGARIZING
VULNERABILITIES
VULNERABILITY
VULNERABLE
VULNERABLENESS
VULNERABLY
VULNERARIES
VULNERATED
VULNERATES
VULNERATING
VULNERATION
VULNERATIONS
VULPECULAR
VULPICIDES
VULPINISMS
VULPINITES
VULTURISMS
VULVITISES
VULVOVAGINAL
VULVOVAGINITIS

W

WACKINESSES
WADSETTERS
WADSETTING
WAFFLESTOMPER
WAFFLESTOMPERS
WAGELESSNESS
WAGELESSNESSES
WAGENBOOMS
WAGEWORKER
WAGEWORKERS
WAGGISHNESS
WAGGISHNESSES
WAGGLINGLY
WAGGONETTE
WAGGONETTES
WAGGONLESS
WAGGONLOAD
WAGGONLOADS
WAGHALTERS
WAGONETTES
WAGONLOADS
WAGONWRIGHT
WAGONWRIGHTS
WAINSCOTED
WAINSCOTING
WAINSCOTINGS
WAINSCOTTED
WAINSCOTTING
WAINSCOTTINGS
WAINWRIGHT
WAINWRIGHTS
WAISTBANDS
WAISTBELTS
WAISTCLOTH
WAISTCLOTHS
WAISTCOATED
WAISTCOATEER
WAISTCOATEERS
WAISTCOATING
WAISTCOATINGS
WAISTCOATS
WAISTLINES
WAITERAGES
WAITERHOOD
WAITERHOODS
WAITERINGS
WAITLISTED
WAITLISTING
WAITPERSON
WAITPERSONS
WAITRESSED
WAITRESSES
WAITRESSING
WAITRESSINGS

WAITSTAFFS
WAKEBOARDER
WAKEBOARDERS
WAKEBOARDING
WAKEBOARDINGS
WAKEBOARDS
WAKEFULNESS
WAKEFULNESSES
WALDFLUTES
WALDGRAVES
WALDGRAVINE
WALDGRAVINES
WALDSTERBEN
WALDSTERBENS
WALKABOUTS
WALKATHONS
WALKINGSTICK
WALKINGSTICKS
WALKSHORTS
WALLBOARDS
WALLCHARTS
WALLCLIMBER
WALLCLIMBERS
WALLCOVERING
WALLCOVERINGS
WALLFISHES
WALLFLOWER
WALLFLOWERS
WALLOPINGS
WALLOWINGS
WALLPAPERED
WALLPAPERING
WALLPAPERS
WALLPOSTER
WALLPOSTERS
WALLYBALLS
WALLYDRAGS
WALLYDRAIGLE
WALLYDRAIGLES
WALNUTWOOD
WALNUTWOODS
WAMBENGERS
WAMBLINESS
WAMBLINESSES
WAMBLINGLY
WAMPISHING
WAMPUMPEAG
WAMPUMPEAGS
WANCHANCIE
WANDERINGLY
WANDERINGS
WANDERLUST
WANDERLUSTS
WANRESTFUL

WANTHRIVEN
WANTONISED
WANTONISES
WANTONISING
WANTONIZED
WANTONIZES
WANTONIZING
WANTONNESS
WANTONNESSES
WAPENSCHAW
WAPENSCHAWS
WAPENSHAWS
WAPENTAKES
WAPINSCHAW
WAPINSCHAWS
WAPINSHAWS
WAPPENSCHAW
WAPPENSCHAWING
WAPPENSCHAWINGS
WAPPENSCHAWS
WAPPENSHAW
WAPPENSHAWING
WAPPENSHAWINGS
WAPPENSHAWS
WARBLINGLY
WARBONNETS
WARCHALKER
WARCHALKERS
WARCHALKING
WARCHALKINGS
WARDENRIES
WARDENSHIP
WARDENSHIPS
WARDERSHIP
WARDERSHIPS
WARDRESSES
WARDROBERS
WARDROBING
WAREHOUSED
WAREHOUSEMAN
WAREHOUSEMEN
WAREHOUSER
WAREHOUSERS
WAREHOUSES
WAREHOUSING
WAREHOUSINGS
WARFARINGS
WARIBASHIS
WARINESSES
WARLIKENESS
WARLIKENESSES
WARLOCKRIES
WARLORDISM
WARLORDISMS

WARMBLOODS
WARMHEARTED
WARMHEARTEDNESS
WARMNESSES
WARMONGERING
WARMONGERINGS
WARMONGERS
WARRANDICE
WARRANDICES
WARRANDING
WARRANTABILITY
WARRANTABLE
WARRANTABLENESS
WARRANTABLY
WARRANTEES
WARRANTERS
WARRANTIED
WARRANTIES
WARRANTING
WARRANTINGS
WARRANTISE
WARRANTISES
WARRANTLESS
WARRANTORS
WARRANTYING
WARRIORESS
WARRIORESSES
WASHABILITIES
WASHABILITY
WASHATERIA
WASHATERIAS
WASHBASINS
WASHBOARDS
WASHCLOTHS
WASHERWOMAN
WASHERWOMEN
WASHETERIA
WASHETERIAS
WASHHOUSES
WASHINESSES
WASHINGTONIA
WASHINGTONIAS
WASHSTANDS
WASPINESSES
WASPISHNESS
WASPISHNESSES
WASSAILERS
WASSAILING
WASSAILINGS
WASSAILRIES
WASTEBASKET
WASTEBASKETS
WASTEFULLY
WASTEFULNESS

WASTEFULNESSES
WASTELANDS
WASTENESSES
WASTEPAPER
WASTEPAPERS
WASTERFULLY
WASTERFULNESS
WASTERFULNESSES
WASTEWATER
WASTEWATERS
WASTEWEIRS
WASTNESSES
WATCHABLES
WATCHBANDS
WATCHBOXES
WATCHCASES
WATCHCRIES
WATCHDOGGED
WATCHDOGGING
WATCHFULLY
WATCHFULNESS
WATCHFULNESSES
WATCHGLASS
WATCHGLASSES
WATCHGUARD
WATCHGUARDS
WATCHLISTS
WATCHMAKER
WATCHMAKERS
WATCHMAKING
WATCHMAKINGS
WATCHSPRING
WATCHSPRINGS
WATCHSTRAP
WATCHSTRAPS
WATCHTOWER
WATCHTOWERS
WATCHWORDS
WATERBIRDS
WATERBORNE
WATERBRAIN
WATERBRAINS
WATERBUCKS
WATERBUSES
WATERBUSSES
WATERCOLOR
WATERCOLORIST
WATERCOLORISTS
WATERCOLORS
WATERCOLOUR
WATERCOLOURIST
WATERCOLOURISTS
WATERCOLOURS
WATERCOOLER
WATERCOOLERS
WATERCOURSE
WATERCOURSES
WATERCRAFT
WATERCRAFTS

WATERCRESS
WATERCRESSES
WATERDRIVE
WATERDRIVES
WATERFALLS
WATERFINDER
WATERFINDERS
WATERFLOOD
WATERFLOODED
WATERFLOODING
WATERFLOODINGS
WATERFLOODS
WATERFOWLER
WATERFOWLERS
WATERFOWLING
WATERFOWLINGS
WATERFOWLS
WATERFRONT
WATERFRONTS
WATERGLASS
WATERGLASSES
WATERHEADS
WATERINESS
WATERINESSES
WATERISHNESS
WATERISHNESSES
WATERLEAFS
WATERLESSNESS
WATERLESSNESSES
WATERLILIES
WATERLINES
WATERLOGGED
WATERLOGGING
WATERMANSHIP
WATERMANSHIPS
WATERMARKED
WATERMARKING
WATERMARKS
WATERMELON
WATERMELONS
WATERPOWER
WATERPOWERS
WATERPOXES
WATERPROOF
WATERPROOFED
WATERPROOFER
WATERPROOFERS
WATERPROOFING
WATERPROOFINGS
WATERPROOFNESS
WATERPROOFS
WATERQUAKE
WATERQUAKES
WATERSCAPE
WATERSCAPES
WATERSHEDS
WATERSIDER
WATERSIDERS
WATERSIDES

WATERSKIING
WATERSKIINGS
WATERSMEET
WATERSMEETS
WATERSPOUT
WATERSPOUTS
WATERTHRUSH
WATERTHRUSHES
WATERTIGHT
WATERTIGHTNESS
WATERWEEDS
WATERWHEEL
WATERWHEELS
WATERWORKS
WATERZOOIS
WATTLEBARK
WATTLEBARKS
WATTLEBIRD
WATTLEBIRDS
WATTLEWORK
WATTLEWORKS
WATTMETERS
WAULKMILLS
WAVEFRONTS
WAVEGUIDES
WAVELENGTH
WAVELENGTHS
WAVELESSLY
WAVELLITES
WAVEMETERS
WAVERINGLY
WAVERINGNESS
WAVERINGNESSES
WAVESHAPES
WAVINESSES
WAXBERRIES
WAXFLOWERS
WAXINESSES
WAXWORKERS
WAYFARINGS
WAYMARKING
WAYMENTING
WAYWARDNESS
WAYWARDNESSES
WAYZGOOSES
WEAKFISHES
WEAKHEARTED
WEAKISHNESS
WEAKISHNESSES
WEAKLINESS
WEAKLINESSES
WEAKNESSES
WEALTHIEST
WEALTHINESS
WEALTHINESSES
WEALTHLESS
WEAPONEERING
WEAPONEERINGS
WEAPONEERS

WEAPONISED
WEAPONISES
WEAPONISING
WEAPONIZED
WEAPONIZES
WEAPONIZING
WEAPONLESS
WEAPONRIES
WEARABILITIES
WEARABILITY
WEARIFULLY
WEARIFULNESS
WEARIFULNESSES
WEARILESSLY
WEARINESSES
WEARISOMELY
WEARISOMENESS
WEARISOMENESSES
WEARYINGLY
WEASELLERS
WEASELLING
WEATHERABILITY
WEATHERABLE
WEATHERBOARD
WEATHERBOARDED
WEATHERBOARDING
WEATHERBOARDS
WEATHERCAST
WEATHERCASTER
WEATHERCASTERS
WEATHERCASTS
WEATHERCLOTH
WEATHERCLOTHS
WEATHERCOCK
WEATHERCOCKED
WEATHERCOCKING
WEATHERCOCKS
WEATHERERS
WEATHERGIRL
WEATHERGIRLS
WEATHERGLASS
WEATHERGLASSES
WEATHERING
WEATHERINGS
WEATHERISATION
WEATHERISATIONS
WEATHERISE
WEATHERISED
WEATHERISES
WEATHERISING
WEATHERIZATION
WEATHERIZATIONS
WEATHERIZE
WEATHERIZED
WEATHERIZES
WEATHERIZING
WEATHERLINESS
WEATHERLINESSES
WEATHERMAN

WEATHERMEN
WEATHERMOST
WEATHEROMETER
WEATHEROMETERS
WEATHERPERSON
WEATHERPERSONS
WEATHERPROOF
WEATHERPROOFED
WEATHERPROOFING
WEATHERPROOFS
WEATHERWORN
WEAVERBIRD
WEAVERBIRDS
WEBCASTERS
WEBCASTING
WEBLOGGERS
WEBMASTERS
WEEDICIDES
WEEDINESSES
WEEDKILLER
WEEDKILLERS
WEEKENDERS
WEEKENDING
WEEKENDINGS
WEEKNIGHTS
WEELDLESSE
WEEPINESSES
WEIGHBOARD
WEIGHBOARDS
WEIGHBRIDGE
WEIGHBRIDGES
WEIGHTIEST
WEIGHTINESS
WEIGHTINESSES
WEIGHTINGS
WEIGHTLESS
WEIGHTLESSLY
WEIGHTLESSNESS
WEIGHTLIFTER
WEIGHTLIFTERS
WEIGHTLIFTING
WEIGHTLIFTINGS
WEIMARANER
WEIMARANERS
WEIRDNESSES
WEISENHEIMER
WEISENHEIMERS
WELCOMENESS
WELCOMENESSES
WELCOMINGLY
WELDABILITIES
WELDABILITY
WELDMESHES
WELFARISMS
WELFARISTIC
WELFARISTS
WELLBEINGS
WELLHOUSES
WELLINGTON

WELLINGTONIA
WELLINGTONIAS
WELLINGTONS
WELLNESSES
WELLSPRING
WELLSPRINGS
WELTANSCHAUUNG
WELTANSCHAUUNGS
WELTERWEIGHT
WELTERWEIGHTS
WELTSCHMERZ
WELTSCHMERZES
WELWITSCHIA
WELWITSCHIAS
WENSLEYDALE
WENSLEYDALES
WENTLETRAP
WENTLETRAPS
WEREWOLFERIES
WEREWOLFERY
WEREWOLFISH
WEREWOLFISM
WEREWOLFISMS
WEREWOLVES
WERNERITES
WERWOLFISH
WESTERINGS
WESTERLIES
WESTERLINESS
WESTERLINESSES
WESTERNERS
WESTERNISATION
WESTERNISATIONS
WESTERNISE
WESTERNISED
WESTERNISES
WESTERNISING
WESTERNISM
WESTERNISMS
WESTERNIZATION
WESTERNIZATIONS
WESTERNIZE
WESTERNIZED
WESTERNIZES
WESTERNIZING
WESTERNMOST
WESTWARDLY
WETTABILITIES
WETTABILITY
WHAIKORERO
WHAIKOREROS
WHAKAPAPAS
WHALEBACKS
WHALEBOATS
WHALEBONES
WHAREPUNIS
WHARFINGER
WHARFINGERS
WHARFMASTER

WHARFMASTERS
WHATABOUTS
WHATCHAMACALLIT
WHATNESSES
WHATSHERNAME
WHATSHERNAMES
WHATSHISNAME
WHATSHISNAMES
WHATSITSNAME
WHATSITSNAMES
WHATSOEVER
WHATSOMEVER
WHEATFIELD
WHEATFIELDS
WHEATGRASS
WHEATGRASSES
WHEATLANDS
WHEATMEALS
WHEATSHEAF
WHEATSHEAVES
WHEATWORMS
WHEEDLESOME
WHEEDLINGLY
WHEEDLINGS
WHEELBARROW
WHEELBARROWED
WHEELBARROWING
WHEELBARROWS
WHEELBASES
WHEELCHAIR
WHEELCHAIRS
WHEELHORSE
WHEELHORSES
WHEELHOUSE
WHEELHOUSES
WHEELWORKS
WHEELWRIGHT
WHEELWRIGHTS
WHEESHTING
WHEEZINESS
WHEEZINESSES
WHENCEFORTH
WHENCESOEVER
WHENSOEVER
WHEREABOUT
WHEREABOUTS
WHEREAFTER
WHEREAGAINST
WHEREFORES
WHEREINSOEVER
WHERENESSES
WHERESOEER
WHERESOEVER
WHERETHROUGH
WHEREUNDER
WHEREUNTIL
WHEREWITHAL
WHEREWITHALS
WHEREWITHS

WHERRETING
WHERRITING
WHETSTONES
WHEWELLITE
WHEWELLITES
WHEYISHNESS
WHEYISHNESSES
WHICHSOEVER
WHICKERING
WHIDDERING
WHIFFLERIES
WHIFFLETREE
WHIFFLETREES
WHIFFLINGS
WHIGGAMORE
WHIGGAMORES
WHIGMALEERIE
WHIGMALEERIES
WHIGMALEERY
WHILLYWHAED
WHILLYWHAING
WHILLYWHAS
WHILLYWHAW
WHILLYWHAWED
WHILLYWHAWING
WHILLYWHAWS
WHIMBERRIES
WHIMPERERS
WHIMPERING
WHIMPERINGLY
WHIMPERINGS
WHIMSICALITIES
WHIMSICALITY
WHIMSICALLY
WHIMSICALNESS
WHIMSICALNESSES
WHIMSINESS
WHIMSINESSES
WHINBERRIES
WHINGDINGS
WHINGEINGS
WHININESSES
WHINSTONES
WHIPLASHED
WHIPLASHES
WHIPLASHING
WHIPPERSNAPPER
WHIPPERSNAPPERS
WHIPPETING
WHIPPETINGS
WHIPPINESS
WHIPPINESSES
WHIPPLETREE
WHIPPLETREES
WHIPPOORWILL
WHIPPOORWILLS
WHIPSAWING
WHIPSNAKES
WHIPSTAFFS

WHIPSTALLED	WHITEWARES	WHOREMISTRESS	WILDNESSES
WHIPSTALLING	WHITEWASHED	WHOREMISTRESSES	WILFULNESS
WHIPSTALLS	WHITEWASHER	WHOREMONGER	WILFULNESSES
WHIPSTITCH	WHITEWASHERS	WHOREMONGERIES	WILINESSES
WHIPSTITCHED	WHITEWASHES	WHOREMONGERS	WILLEMITES
WHIPSTITCHES	WHITEWASHING	WHOREMONGERY	WILLFULNESS
WHIPSTITCHING	WHITEWASHINGS	WHORISHNESS	WILLFULNESSES
WHIPSTOCKS	WHITEWATER	WHORISHNESSES	WILLIEWAUGHT
WHIPTAILED	WHITEWINGS	WHORTLEBERRIES	WILLIEWAUGHTS
WHIRLABOUT	WHITEWOODS	WHORTLEBERRY	WILLINGEST
WHIRLABOUTS	WHITEYWOOD	WHOSESOEVER	WILLINGNESS
WHIRLBLAST	WHITEYWOODS	WHUNSTANES	WILLINGNESSES
WHIRLBLASTS	WHITHERING	WHYDUNNITS	WILLOWHERB
WHIRLIGIGS	WHITHERSOEVER	WICKEDNESS	WILLOWHERBS
WHIRLINGLY	WHITHERWARD	WICKEDNESSES	WILLOWIEST
WHIRLPOOLS	WHITHERWARDS	WICKERWORK	WILLOWLIKE
WHIRLWINDS	WHITISHNESS	WICKERWORKS	WILLOWWARE
WHIRLYBIRD	WHITISHNESSES	WICKETKEEPER	WILLOWWARES
WHIRLYBIRDS	WHITLEATHER	WICKETKEEPERS	WILLPOWERS
WHIRRETING	WHITLEATHERS	WICKTHINGS	WIMPINESSES
WHISKERANDO	WHITTAWERS	WIDDERSHINS	WIMPISHNESS
WHISKERANDOED	WHITTERICK	WIDEAWAKES	WIMPISHNESSES
WHISKERANDOS	WHITTERICKS	WIDEBODIES	WINCEYETTE
WHISKEYFIED	WHITTERING	WIDECHAPPED	WINCEYETTES
WHISKIFIED	WHITTLINGS	WIDEMOUTHED	WINCHESTER
WHISPERERS	WHIZZBANGS	WIDENESSES	WINCHESTERS
WHISPERING	WHIZZINGLY	WIDERSHINS	WINCOPIPES
WHISPERINGLY	WHODUNITRIES	WIDESCREEN	WINDBAGGERIES
WHISPERINGS	WHODUNITRY	WIDESPREAD	WINDBAGGERY
WHISPEROUSLY	WHODUNNITRIES	WIDOWBIRDS	WINDBLASTS
WHISTLEABLE	WHODUNNITRY	WIDOWERHOOD	WINDBREAKER
WHISTLINGLY	WHODUNNITS	WIDOWERHOODS	WINDBREAKERS
WHISTLINGS	WHOLEFOODS	WIDOWHOODS	WINDBREAKS
WHITEBAITS	WHOLEGRAIN	WIELDINESS	WINDBURNED
WHITEBASSES	WHOLEHEARTED	WIELDINESSES	WINDBURNING
WHITEBEAMS	WHOLEHEARTEDLY	WIENERWURST	WINDCHEATER
WHITEBEARD	WHOLEMEALS	WIENERWURSTS	WINDCHEATERS
WHITEBEARDS	WHOLENESSES	WIFELINESS	WINDCHILLS
WHITEBOARD	WHOLESALED	WIFELINESSES	WINDFALLEN
WHITEBOARDS	WHOLESALER	WIGWAGGERS	WINDFLOWER
WHITEBOYISM	WHOLESALERS	WIGWAGGING	WINDFLOWERS
WHITEBOYISMS	WHOLESALES	WILDCATTED	WINDGALLED
WHITECOATS	WHOLESALING	WILDCATTER	WINDHOVERS
WHITECOMBS	WHOLESOMELY	WILDCATTERS	WINDINESSES
WHITEDAMPS	WHOLESOMENESS	WILDCATTING	WINDJAMMER
WHITEFACES	WHOLESOMENESSES	WILDCATTINGS	WINDJAMMERS
WHITEFISHES	WHOLESOMER	WILDEBEEST	WINDJAMMING
WHITEFLIES	WHOLESOMEST	WILDEBEESTS	WINDJAMMINGS
WHITEHEADS	WHOLESTITCH	WILDERMENT	WINDLASSED
WHITENESSES	WHOLESTITCHES	WILDERMENTS	WINDLASSES
WHITENINGS	WHOLEWHEAT	WILDERNESS	WINDLASSING
WHITESMITH	WHOMSOEVER	WILDERNESSES	WINDLESSLY
WHITESMITHS	WHOREHOUSE	WILDFLOWER	WINDLESSNESS
WHITETAILS	WHOREHOUSES	WILDFLOWERS	WINDLESSNESSES
WHITETHORN	WHOREMASTER	WILDFOWLER	WINDLESTRAE
WHITETHORNS	WHOREMASTERIES	WILDFOWLERS	WINDLESTRAES
WHITETHROAT	WHOREMASTERLY	WILDFOWLING	WINDLESTRAW
WHITETHROATS	WHOREMASTERS	WILDFOWLINGS	WINDLESTRAWS
WHITEWALLS	WHOREMASTERY	WILDGRAVES	WINDMILLED

WINDMILLING
WINDOWINGS
WINDOWLESS
WINDOWPANE
WINDOWPANES
WINDOWSILL
WINDOWSILLS
WINDROWERS
WINDROWING
WINDSCREEN
WINDSCREENS
WINDSHAKES
WINDSHIELD
WINDSHIELDS
WINDSTORMS
WINDSUCKER
WINDSUCKERS
WINDSURFED
WINDSURFER
WINDSURFERS
WINDSURFING
WINDSURFINGS
WINDTHROWS
WINEBERRIES
WINEBIBBER
WINEBIBBERS
WINEBIBBING
WINEBIBBINGS
WINEGLASSES
WINEGLASSFUL
WINEGLASSFULS
WINEGROWER
WINEGROWERS
WINEMAKERS
WINEPRESSES
WINGCHAIRS
WINGLESSNESS
WINGLESSNESSES
WINGSPREAD
WINGSPREADS
WINNABILITIES
WINNABILITY
WINNINGNESS
WINNINGNESSES
WINNOWINGS
WINSOMENESS
WINSOMENESSES
WINTERBERRIES
WINTERBERRY
WINTERBOURNE
WINTERBOURNES
WINTERCRESS
WINTERCRESSES
WINTERFEED
WINTERFEEDING
WINTERFEEDS
WINTERGREEN
WINTERGREENS
WINTERIEST

WINTERINESS
WINTERINESSES
WINTERISATION
WINTERISATIONS
WINTERISED
WINTERISES
WINTERISING
WINTERIZATION
WINTERIZATIONS
WINTERIZED
WINTERIZES
WINTERIZING
WINTERKILL
WINTERKILLED
WINTERKILLING
WINTERKILLINGS
WINTERKILLS
WINTERLESS
WINTERLINESS
WINTERLINESSES
WINTERTIDE
WINTERTIDES
WINTERTIME
WINTERTIMES
WINTERWEIGHT
WINTRINESS
WINTRINESSES
WIREDRAWER
WIREDRAWERS
WIREDRAWING
WIREDRAWINGS
WIREGRASSES
WIREHAIRED
WIRELESSED
WIRELESSES
WIRELESSING
WIREPHOTOS
WIREPULLER
WIREPULLERS
WIREPULLING
WIREPULLINGS
WIRETAPPED
WIRETAPPER
WIRETAPPERS
WIRETAPPING
WIRETAPPINGS
WIREWALKER
WIREWALKERS
WIREWORKER
WIREWORKERS
WIREWORKING
WIREWORKINGS
WIRINESSES
WISECRACKED
WISECRACKER
WISECRACKERS
WISECRACKING
WISECRACKS
WISENESSES
WISENESSES

WISENHEIMER
WISENHEIMERS
WISHFULNESS
WISHFULNESSES
WISHTONWISH
WISHTONWISHES
WISPINESSES
WISTFULNESS
WISTFULNESSES
WITBLITSES
WITCHBROOM
WITCHBROOMS
WITCHCRAFT
WITCHCRAFTS
WITCHERIES
WITCHETTIES
WITCHGRASS
WITCHGRASSES
WITCHHOODS
WITCHINGLY
WITCHKNOTS
WITCHWEEDS
WITENAGEMOT
WITENAGEMOTE
WITENAGEMOTES
WITENAGEMOTS
WITGATBOOM
WITGATBOOMS
WITHDRAWABLE
WITHDRAWAL
WITHDRAWALS
WITHDRAWER
WITHDRAWERS
WITHDRAWING
WITHDRAWMENT
WITHDRAWMENTS
WITHDRAWNNESS
WITHDRAWNNESSES
WITHEREDNESS
WITHEREDNESSES
WITHERINGLY
WITHERINGS
WITHERITES
WITHERSHINS
WITHHOLDEN
WITHHOLDER
WITHHOLDERS
WITHHOLDING
WITHHOLDMENT
WITHHOLDMENTS
WITHINDOORS
WITHOUTDOORS
WITHSTANDER
WITHSTANDERS
WITHSTANDING
WITHSTANDS
WITHYWINDS
WITLESSNESS
WITLESSNESSES

WITNESSABLE
WITNESSERS
WITNESSING
WITTICISMS
WITTINESSES
WITWANTONED
WITWANTONING
WITWANTONS
WIZARDRIES
WOADWAXENS
WOBBEGONGS
WOBBLINESS
WOBBLINESSES
WOEBEGONENESS
WOEBEGONENESSES
WOEFULLEST
WOEFULNESS
WOEFULNESSES
WOFULNESSES
WOLFBERRIES
WOLFFISHES
WOLFHOUNDS
WOLFISHNESS
WOLFISHNESSES
WOLFRAMITE
WOLFRAMITES
WOLFSBANES
WOLLASTONITE
WOLLASTONITES
WOLVERENES
WOLVERINES
WOMANFULLY
WOMANHOODS
WOMANISERS
WOMANISHLY
WOMANISHNESS
WOMANISHNESSES
WOMANISING
WOMANISINGS
WOMANIZERS
WOMANIZING
WOMANIZINGS
WOMANKINDS
WOMANLIEST
WOMANLINESS
WOMANLINESSES
WOMANNESSES
WOMANPOWER
WOMANPOWERS
WOMENFOLKS
WOMENKINDS
WOMENSWEAR
WOMENSWEARS
WONDERFULLY
WONDERFULNESS
WONDERFULNESSES
WONDERINGLY
WONDERINGS
WONDERKIDS

WONDERLAND
WONDERLANDS
WONDERLESS
WONDERMENT
WONDERMENTS
WONDERMONGER
WONDERMONGERING
WONDERMONGERS
WONDERWORK
WONDERWORKS
WONDROUSLY
WONDROUSNESS
WONDROUSNESSES
WONTEDNESS
WONTEDNESSES
WOODBLOCKS
WOODBORERS
WOODBURYTYPE
WOODBURYTYPES
WOODCARVER
WOODCARVERS
WOODCARVING
WOODCARVINGS
WOODCHOPPER
WOODCHOPPERS
WOODCHUCKS
WOODCRAFTS
WOODCRAFTSMAN
WOODCRAFTSMEN
WOODCUTTER
WOODCUTTERS
WOODCUTTING
WOODCUTTINGS
WOODENHEAD
WOODENHEADED
WOODENHEADS
WOODENNESS
WOODENNESSES
WOODENTOPS
WOODENWARE
WOODENWARES
WOODGRAINS
WOODGROUSE
WOODGROUSES
WOODHORSES
WOODHOUSES
WOODINESSES
WOODLANDER
WOODLANDERS
WOODLESSNESS
WOODLESSNESSES
WOODNESSES
WOODPECKER
WOODPECKERS
WOODPIGEON
WOODPIGEONS
WOODPRINTS
WOODREEVES
WOODRUSHES

WOODSCREWS
WOODSHEDDED
WOODSHEDDING
WOODSHEDDINGS
WOODSHOCKS
WOODSHRIKE
WOODSHRIKES
WOODSPITES
WOODSTONES
WOODSTOVES
WOODSWALLOW
WOODSWALLOWS
WOODTHRUSH
WOODTHRUSHES
WOODWAXENS
WOODWORKER
WOODWORKERS
WOODWORKING
WOODWORKINGS
WOOLGATHERER
WOOLGATHERERS
WOOLGATHERING
WOOLGATHERINGS
WOOLGROWER
WOOLGROWERS
WOOLGROWING
WOOLGROWINGS
WOOLINESSES
WOOLLINESS
WOOLLINESSES
WOOLLYBACK
WOOLLYBACKS
WOOLLYBUTT
WOOLLYBUTTS
WOOLLYFOOT
WOOLLYFOOTS
WOOLSORTER
WOOLSORTERS
WOOMERANGS
WOOZINESSES
WORCESTERBERRY
WORCESTERS
WORDBREAKS
WORDINESSES
WORDISHNESS
WORDISHNESSES
WORDLESSLY
WORDLESSNESS
WORDLESSNESSES
WORDMONGER
WORDMONGERS
WORDSEARCH
WORDSEARCHES
WORDSMITHERIES
WORDSMITHERY
WORDSMITHS
WORKABILITIES
WORKABILITY
WORKABLENESS

WORKABLENESSES
WORKAHOLIC
WORKAHOLICS
WORKAHOLISM
WORKAHOLISMS
WORKAROUND
WORKAROUNDS
WORKBASKET
WORKBASKETS
WORKBENCHES
WORKERISTS
WORKERLESS
WORKFELLOW
WORKFELLOWS
WORKFORCES
WORKGROUPS
WORKHORSES
WORKHOUSES
WORKINGMAN
WORKINGMEN
WORKINGWOMAN
WORKINGWOMEN
WORKLESSNESS
WORKLESSNESSES
WORKMANLIKE
WORKMANSHIP
WORKMANSHIPS
WORKMASTER
WORKMASTERS
WORKMISTRESS
WORKMISTRESSES
WORKPEOPLE
WORKPIECES
WORKPLACES
WORKPRINTS
WORKSHEETS
WORKSHOPPED
WORKSHOPPING
WORKSPACES
WORKSTATION
WORKSTATIONS
WORKTABLES
WORKWATCHER
WORKWATCHERS
WORLDBEATS
WORLDLIEST
WORLDLINESS
WORLDLINESSES
WORLDLINGS
WORLDSCALE
WORLDSCALES
WORLDVIEWS
WORMINESSES
WORNNESSES
WORRIMENTS
WORRISOMELY
WORRISOMENESS
WORRISOMENESSES
WORRYINGLY

WORRYWARTS
WORSENESSES
WORSHIPABLE
WORSHIPERS
WORSHIPFUL
WORSHIPFULLY
WORSHIPFULNESS
WORSHIPING
WORSHIPLESS
WORSHIPPED
WORSHIPPER
WORSHIPPERS
WORSHIPPING
WORTHINESS
WORTHINESSES
WORTHLESSLY
WORTHLESSNESS
WORTHLESSNESSES
WORTHWHILE
WORTHWHILENESS
WOUNDINGLY
WOUNDWORTS
WRAITHLIKE
WRANGLERSHIP
WRANGLERSHIPS
WRANGLESOME
WRANGLINGS
WRAPAROUND
WRAPAROUNDS
WRAPPERING
WRAPROUNDS
WRATHFULLY
WRATHFULNESS
WRATHFULNESSES
WRATHINESS
WRATHINESSES
WREATHIEST
WREATHLESS
WREATHLIKE
WRECKFISHES
WRECKMASTER
WRECKMASTERS
WRENCHINGLY
WRENCHINGS
WRESTLINGS
WRETCHEDER
WRETCHEDEST
WRETCHEDLY
WRETCHEDNESS
WRETCHEDNESSES
WRIGGLIEST
WRIGGLINGS
WRINKLELESS
WRINKLIEST
WRISTBANDS
WRISTLOCKS
WRISTWATCH
WRISTWATCHES
WRITERESSES

WRITERSHIP

WRITERSHIP
WRITERSHIPS
WRITHINGLY
WRONGDOERS
WRONGDOING
WRONGDOINGS
WRONGFULLY
WRONGFULNESS
WRONGFULNESSES
WRONGHEADED
WRONGHEADEDLY
WRONGHEADEDNESS
WRONGNESSES
WRONGOUSLY
WULFENITES
WUNDERKIND
WUNDERKINDER
WUNDERKINDS
WYANDOTTES
WYLIECOATS

X

XANTHATION
XANTHATIONS
XANTHOCHROIA
XANTHOCHROIAS
XANTHOCHROIC
XANTHOCHROID
XANTHOCHROIDS
XANTHOCHROISM
XANTHOCHROISMS
XANTHOCHROMIA
XANTHOCHROMIAS
XANTHOCHROOUS
XANTHOMATA
XANTHOMATOUS
XANTHOMELANOUS
XANTHOPHYL
XANTHOPHYLL
XANTHOPHYLLOUS
XANTHOPHYLLS
XANTHOPHYLS
XANTHOPSIA
XANTHOPSIAS
XANTHOPTERIN
XANTHOPTERINE
XANTHOPTERINES
XANTHOPTERINS
XANTHOXYLS
XENARTHRAL
XENOBIOTIC
XENOBIOTICS
XENOBLASTS
XENOCRYSTS
XENODIAGNOSES
XENODIAGNOSIS
XENODIAGNOSTIC
XENODOCHIUM
XENODOCHIUMS
XENOGAMIES
XENOGAMOUS
XENOGENEIC
XENOGENESES
XENOGENESIS
XENOGENETIC
XENOGENIES
XENOGENOUS
XENOGLOSSIA
XENOGLOSSIAS
XENOGLOSSIES
XENOGLOSSY
XENOGRAFTS
XENOLITHIC
XENOMANIAS
XENOMENIAS
XENOMORPHIC
XENOMORPHICALLY
XENOPHILES
XENOPHOBES
XENOPHOBIA
XENOPHOBIAS
XENOPHOBIC
XENOPHOBICALLY
XENOPHOBIES
XENOPLASTIC
XENOTRANSPLANT
XENOTRANSPLANTS
XENOTROPIC
XERANTHEMUM
XERANTHEMUMS
XERISCAPES
XEROCHASIES
XERODERMAE
XERODERMAS
XERODERMATIC
XERODERMATOUS
XERODERMIA
XERODERMIAS
XERODERMIC
XEROGRAPHER
XEROGRAPHERS
XEROGRAPHIC
XEROGRAPHICALLY
XEROGRAPHIES
XEROGRAPHY
XEROMORPHIC
XEROMORPHOUS
XEROMORPHS
XEROPHAGIES
XEROPHILES
XEROPHILIES
XEROPHILOUS
XEROPHTHALMIA
XEROPHTHALMIAS
XEROPHTHALMIC
XEROPHYTES
XEROPHYTIC
XEROPHYTICALLY
XEROPHYTISM
XEROPHYTISMS
XERORADIOGRAPHY
XEROSTOMAS
XEROSTOMATA
XEROSTOMIA
XEROSTOMIAS
XEROTHERMIC
XEROTRIPSES
XEROTRIPSIS
XIPHIHUMERALIS
XIPHIPLASTRA
XIPHIPLASTRAL
XIPHIPLASTRALS
XIPHIPLASTRON
XIPHISTERNA
XIPHISTERNUM
XIPHISTERNUMS
XIPHOPAGIC
XIPHOPAGOUS
XIPHOPAGUS
XIPHOPAGUSES
XIPHOPHYLLOUS
XIPHOSURAN
XIPHOSURANS
XYLOBALSAMUM
XYLOBALSAMUMS
XYLOCARPOUS
XYLOCHROME
XYLOCHROMES
XYLOGENOUS
XYLOGRAPHED
XYLOGRAPHER
XYLOGRAPHERS
XYLOGRAPHIC
XYLOGRAPHICAL
XYLOGRAPHIES
XYLOGRAPHING
XYLOGRAPHS
XYLOGRAPHY
XYLOIDINES
XYLOLOGIES
XYLOMETERS
XYLOPHAGAN
XYLOPHAGANS
XYLOPHAGES
XYLOPHAGOUS
XYLOPHILOUS
XYLOPHONES
XYLOPHONIC
XYLOPHONIST
XYLOPHONISTS
XYLOPYROGRAPHY
XYLORIMBAS
XYLOTOMIES
XYLOTOMIST
XYLOTOMISTS
XYLOTOMOUS
XYLOTYPOGRAPHIC
XYLOTYPOGRAPHY
XYRIDACEOUS

Y

YACHTSMANSHIP
YACHTSMANSHIPS
YACHTSWOMAN
YACHTSWOMEN
YAFFINGALE
YAFFINGALES
YAMMERINGS
YARBOROUGH
YARBOROUGHS
YARDMASTER
YARDMASTERS
YARDSTICKS
YATTERINGLY
YATTERINGS
YEARNINGLY
YEASTINESS
YEASTINESSES
YELLOCHING
YELLOWBACK
YELLOWBACKS
YELLOWBARK
YELLOWBARKS
YELLOWBIRD
YELLOWBIRDS
YELLOWCAKE
YELLOWCAKES
YELLOWFINS
YELLOWHAMMER
YELLOWHAMMERS
YELLOWHEAD
YELLOWHEADS
YELLOWIEST
YELLOWISHNESS
YELLOWISHNESSES
YELLOWLEGS
YELLOWNESS
YELLOWNESSES
YELLOWTAIL
YELLOWTAILS
YELLOWTHROAT
YELLOWTHROATS
YELLOWWARE
YELLOWWARES
YELLOWWEED
YELLOWWEEDS
YELLOWWOOD
YELLOWWOODS
YELLOWWORT
YELLOWWORTS
YEOMANRIES
YERSINIOSES
YERSINIOSIS
YESTERDAYS
YESTEREVEN

YESTEREVENING
YESTEREVENINGS
YESTEREVENS
YESTEREVES
YESTERMORN
YESTERMORNING
YESTERMORNINGS
YESTERMORNS
YESTERNIGHT
YESTERNIGHTS
YESTERYEAR
YESTERYEARS
YIELDABLENESS
YIELDABLENESSES
YIELDINGLY
YIELDINGNESS
YIELDINGNESSES
YOCTOSECOND
YOCTOSECONDS
YOHIMBINES
YOKEFELLOW
YOKEFELLOWS
YOTTABYTES
YOUNGBERRIES
YOUNGBERRY
YOUNGLINGS
YOUNGNESSES
YOUNGSTERS
YOURSELVES
YOUTHENING
YOUTHFULLY
YOUTHFULNESS
YOUTHFULNESSES
YOUTHHEADS
YOUTHHOODS
YOUTHQUAKE
YOUTHQUAKES
YPSILIFORM
YTHUNDERED
YTTERBITES
YTTERBIUMS
YTTRIFEROUS
YUCKINESSES
YUMMINESSES
YUPPIEDOMS
YUPPIFICATION
YUPPIFICATIONS
YUPPIFYING

Z

ZABAGLIONE
ZABAGLIONES
ZALAMBDODONT
ZALAMBDODONTS
ZAMBOORAKS
ZAMINDARIES
ZAMINDARIS
ZANINESSES
ZANTEDESCHIA
ZANTEDESCHIAS
ZANTHOXYLS
ZANTHOXYLUM
ZANTHOXYLUMS
ZAPATEADOS
ZAPOTILLAS
ZEALOTISMS
ZEALOTRIES
ZEALOUSNESS
ZEALOUSNESSES
ZEBRAFISHES
ZEBRAWOODS
ZEBRINNIES
ZEITGEBERS
ZEITGEISTS
ZELATRICES
ZELATRIXES
ZELOPHOBIA
ZELOPHOBIAS
ZELOPHOBIC
ZELOPHOBICS
ZELOTYPIAS
ZEMINDARIES
ZEMINDARIS
ZEOLITIFORM
ZEPTOSECOND
ZEPTOSECONDS
ZESTFULNESS
ZESTFULNESSES
ZETTABYTES
ZEUGLODONT
ZEUGLODONTS
ZEUGMATICALLY
ZIBELLINES
ZIDOVUDINE
ZIDOVUDINES
ZIGZAGGEDNESS
ZIGZAGGEDNESSES
ZIGZAGGERIES
ZIGZAGGERS
ZIGZAGGERY
ZIGZAGGING
ZILLIONAIRE
ZILLIONAIRES
ZILLIONTHS

ZINCIFEROUS
ZINCIFICATION
ZINCIFICATIONS
ZINCIFYING
ZINCKENITE
ZINCKENITES
ZINCKIFICATION
ZINCKIFICATIONS
ZINCKIFIED
ZINCKIFIES
ZINCKIFYING
ZINCOGRAPH
ZINCOGRAPHER
ZINCOGRAPHERS
ZINCOGRAPHIC
ZINCOGRAPHICAL
ZINCOGRAPHIES
ZINCOGRAPHS
ZINCOGRAPHY
ZINCOLYSES
ZINCOLYSIS
ZINFANDELS
ZINGIBERACEOUS
ZINJANTHROPI
ZINJANTHROPUS
ZINJANTHROPUSES
ZINKENITES
ZINKIFEROUS
ZINKIFICATION
ZINKIFICATIONS
ZINKIFYING
ZINZIBERACEOUS
ZIRCALLOYS
ZIRCONIUMS
ZITHERISTS
ZIZYPHUSES
ZOANTHARIAN
ZOANTHARIANS
ZOANTHROPIC
ZOANTHROPIES
ZOANTHROPY
ZOECHROMES
ZOMBIELIKE
ZOMBIFICATION
ZOMBIFICATIONS
ZOMBIFYING
ZOOCEPHALIC
ZOOCHEMICAL
ZOOCHEMISTRIES
ZOOCHEMISTRY
ZOOCHORIES
ZOOCHOROUS
ZOOCULTURE
ZOOCULTURES

ZOODENDRIA
ZOODENDRIUM
ZOOGAMETES
ZOOGEOGRAPHER
ZOOGEOGRAPHERS
ZOOGEOGRAPHIC
ZOOGEOGRAPHICAL
ZOOGEOGRAPHIES
ZOOGEOGRAPHY
ZOOGLOEOID
ZOOGONIDIA
ZOOGONIDIUM
ZOOGRAFTING
ZOOGRAFTINGS
ZOOGRAPHER
ZOOGRAPHERS
ZOOGRAPHIC
ZOOGRAPHICAL
ZOOGRAPHIES
ZOOGRAPHIST
ZOOGRAPHISTS
ZOOKEEPERS
ZOOLATRIAS
ZOOLATRIES
ZOOLATROUS
ZOOLOGICAL
ZOOLOGICALLY
ZOOLOGISTS
ZOOMAGNETIC
ZOOMAGNETISM
ZOOMAGNETISMS
ZOOMANCIES
ZOOMETRICAL
ZOOMETRIES
ZOOMORPHIC
ZOOMORPHIES
ZOOMORPHISM
ZOOMORPHISMS
ZOONOMISTS
ZOOPATHIES
ZOOPATHOLOGIES
ZOOPATHOLOGY
ZOOPERISTS
ZOOPHAGANS
ZOOPHAGIES
ZOOPHAGOUS
ZOOPHILIAS
ZOOPHILIES
ZOOPHILISM
ZOOPHILISMS
ZOOPHILIST
ZOOPHILISTS
ZOOPHILOUS
ZOOPHOBIAS

ZOOPHOBOUS
ZOOPHYSIOLOGIES
ZOOPHYSIOLOGIST
ZOOPHYSIOLOGY
ZOOPHYTICAL
ZOOPHYTOID
ZOOPHYTOLOGICAL
ZOOPHYTOLOGIES
ZOOPHYTOLOGIST
ZOOPHYTOLOGISTS
ZOOPHYTOLOGY
ZOOPLANKTER
ZOOPLANKTERS
ZOOPLANKTON
ZOOPLANKTONIC
ZOOPLANKTONS
ZOOPLASTIC
ZOOPLASTIES
ZOOPSYCHOLOGIES
ZOOPSYCHOLOGY
ZOOSCOPIES
ZOOSPERMATIC
ZOOSPERMIA
ZOOSPERMIUM
ZOOSPORANGIA
ZOOSPORANGIAL
ZOOSPORANGIUM
ZOOSPOROUS
ZOOSTEROLS
ZOOTECHNICAL
ZOOTECHNICS
ZOOTECHNIES
ZOOTHAPSES
ZOOTHAPSIS
ZOOTHECIAL
ZOOTHECIUM
ZOOTHEISMS
ZOOTHEISTIC
ZOOTHERAPIES
ZOOTHERAPY
ZOOTOMICAL
ZOOTOMICALLY
ZOOTOMISTS
ZOOTROPHIC
ZOOTROPHIES
ZOOTSUITER
ZOOTSUITERS
ZOOXANTHELLA
ZOOXANTHELLAE
ZORBONAUTS
ZUCCHETTOS
ZUGZWANGED
ZUGZWANGING
ZUMBOORUKS

ZWISCHENZUG
ZWISCHENZUGS
ZWITTERION
ZWITTERIONIC
ZWITTERIONS
ZYGANTRUMS
ZYGAPOPHYSEAL
ZYGAPOPHYSES
ZYGAPOPHYSIAL
ZYGAPOPHYSIS
ZYGOBRANCH
ZYGOBRANCHIATE
ZYGOBRANCHIATES
ZYGOBRANCHS
ZYGOCACTUS
ZYGOCACTUSES
ZYGOCARDIAC
ZYGODACTYL
ZYGODACTYLIC
ZYGODACTYLISM
ZYGODACTYLISMS
ZYGODACTYLOUS
ZYGODACTYLS
ZYGOMATICS
ZYGOMORPHIC
ZYGOMORPHIES
ZYGOMORPHISM
ZYGOMORPHISMS
ZYGOMORPHOUS
ZYGOMORPHY
ZYGOMYCETE
ZYGOMYCETES
ZYGOMYCETOUS
ZYGOPHYLLACEOUS
ZYGOPHYTES
ZYGOPLEURAL
ZYGOSITIES
ZYGOSPERMS
ZYGOSPHENE
ZYGOSPHENES
ZYGOSPORES
ZYGOSPORIC
ZYGOTICALLY
ZYMOGENESES
ZYMOGENESIS
ZYMOLOGICAL
ZYMOLOGIES
ZYMOLOGIST
ZYMOLOGISTS
ZYMOMETERS
ZYMOSIMETER
ZYMOSIMETERS
ZYMOTECHNIC
ZYMOTECHNICAL
ZYMOTECHNICS
ZYMOTICALLY